John Masefield
The "Great Auk" of English Literature

A Bibliography

John Masefield (circa 1933)

(Photograph: Archives of The John Masefield Society [Constance Babington Smith Archive])

John Masefield
The "Great Auk" of English Literature

A Bibliography

Philip W. Errington

The British Library

Oak Knoll Press

To my mother,
who first suggested I read The Box of Delights,
my father,
who first took me to an antiquarian bookshop
and my brother,
who has helped considerably with his computer skills.

First published 2004 by
The British Library
96 Euston Road
London NW1 2DB

and

Oak Knoll Press
310 Delaware Street
New Castle
DE 19720

Cataloguing-in-Publication Data is available from both The British Library and the Library of Congress

ISBN 0-7123-4863-8 (BL)
ISBN 1-58456-144-0 (OKP)

For addenda and errata please visit
http://www.sas.ac.uk/ies/Masefield
(this site – which includes details of dust-jackets – is hosted by The Institute of English Studies, School of Advanced Studies, The University of London).

Typeset by Cambridge Photosetting Services, Cambridge
Printed in England by Antony Rowe Ltd

Contents

Acknowledgements

I thank my parents, brother and fiancée for their support.

This project is derived from work undertaken at University College London for my M.A. and Ph.D. I therefore wish to record financial support for my M.A. from my parents, brother and grandmothers, in addition to an award from the UCL access fund. Help from friends included Angela Crispe, Jon McLachlan and John Partington. The majority of financial assistance came from a legacy from my great aunt, M.A. ("Nancy") Graham in whose memory my M.A. was dedicated. My Ph.D. was funded by the EPSRC and I am most grateful for their support.

The Masefield family has been especially sympathetic and generous. Rosemary Magnus provided unfailing kindness and liberal hospitality when allowing me access to family papers. Mr. and Mrs. William Masefield have also shown interest.

Geoffrey Handley-Taylor has been unstinting in his supply of books, information and anecdote. The late Crocker Wight kindly provided an inscribed copy of his bibliography and Dame Muriel Spark assisted with an ambiguity in her study of Masefield. Fraser Drew has similarly been most helpful and encouraging. Connell B. Gallagher, of Vermont University, which now holds the Drew collection, has also been of much assistance. Nancy Paice, former librarian of Ledbury Library, deserves special mention for her kindness to an eager ten-year old.

Personal friends of Masefield have been kind and helpful. Barbara Gregory ("Brangwen") and the late Eileen Colwell allowed access to their collections and were willing interviewees. Audrey Napier-Smith ("Reyna") provided encouragement.

Jeremy Crow and the late Roma Woodnutt of The Society of Authors, the literary representative of the Estate of John Masefield, have been most co-operative and helpful. The Society of Authors has granted me permission to include all Masefield copyright material in this work.

From The John Masefield Society I would especially like to thank Peter Carter, Linda Hart, Brian Nixon, Roy Palmer, George B.T. Smith and the late Peter Smith. Bob Vaughan, secretary of The John Masefield Society, has been unstinting in encouragement, enthusiasm and supply of books. He has been especially supportive at all stages of this project and I thank him most sincerely.

I would like to thank the editor of the *Yeats Annual*, Prof. Warwick Gould, for publication of my first scholarly paper. His enthusiasm and support have been much appreciated. I also thank my Ph.D. supervisor, Prof. Henry Woudhuysen, my secondary supervisor, Prof. John Sutherland and my examiners, Prof. Jerome McGann and Dr. Max Saunders.

I was fortunate to be awarded a fellowship of the University of Texas in 2002–2003. In June 2002 I was therefore able to use the Harry Ransom Humanities Research Center. The HRHRC ethos towards research and the needs of researchers is exemplary and refreshing.

The following libraries and institutions have also provided help and assistance: Auckland Central City Library (New Zealand), Bath Central Library, BBC Written Archives Centre, Beinecke Rare Book and Manuscript Library (Yale University), Berg Collection (New York Public Library), Birmingham Central Library, The Bodleian Library, The Boston Athenaeum, The British Library, British Library of Political and Economic Science, Brotherton Library (University of Leeds), Cheltenham Ladies' College, Churchill College Archive Centre, Columbia University Libraries, Devon Record Office, Dorset County Museum, English Folk Dance and Song Society (Vaughan Williams Memorial Library), Eton College Library, Fales Library (New York University), Fitzwilliam Museum Library, Glasgow City Council Libraries and Archives, Houghton Library (Harvard University), Isle of Wight County Records Office, John Rylands University Library of Manchester, Keswick Museum and Art Gallery, King's College Cambridge Modern Records Centre, The King's School Canterbury, Lambeth Palace Library, Library of Congress, Liverpool Central Library, The London Library, London Metropolitan Archives, London School of Hygiene and Tropical Medicine, Merton College Oxford Library, National Library of Ireland, National Library of Scotland, National Maritime Museum, National Sound Archive, News International plc Archives, Percival Library (Clifton College), The Public Record Office, The Public Record Office of Northern Ireland, The Queen's University of Belfast Library, Royal Naval Museum (Portsmouth), The Royal Society of Literature, Ruskin College Oxford, Ruskin Library (University of Lancaster), Sheffield City Archive, Somerville College Oxford Library, St Edmund Hall Oxford Archives, Street Public Library (Somerset), The Tate Gallery Archive, Taylor Institution Library, Theatre Museum (Victoria and Albert Museum), Trinity College Cambridge Library, Trinity College Library Dublin, University College London Library, University of Aberdeen Library, University of Arizona Library,

University of Birmingham Library, University of Bristol Library, University of Cambridge Library, University of Durham Library, University of Edinburgh Library, University of Exeter Library, University of Glasgow Library, University of Kent at Canterbury Library, University of Liverpool Library, University of London Library, University of Reading Library, University of Stirling Library, University of Southampton Library, University of Sussex Library, University of Wales (Bangor) Library, University of Warwick Modern Records Centre, Victoria and Albert Museum (National Art Library), Westminister Abbey Muniment Room and Library, West Sussex Record Office, West Yorkshire Archive Service in Bradford, Whitechapel Art Gallery, Wigan Record Office, Wolverhampton Art Gallery and Worcester College Oxford Library.

Other individuals to acknowledge include: Rosemary Ashton, Robert Astington, Peter Barham, Alaric T. Barrie, Peter Beal, Terry Belanger, Tad Bennicoff, Paul Binding, G. Michael C. Bott, Lesley Budgen, Paul Chown, Stephen Crook, J.S. Dearden, James O. Edwards, Richard Emeny, Richard Fattorini, Philip Gaskell, Isaac Gewirtz, Peter Grogan, Terry Halladay, Susan Halpert, John Handford, Rupert Hart-Davis, Angus Henderson, Peter Henderson, Geof Hickey, Caroline Huckfield, Arnold Hunt, Philip Kelley, Donald Kerr, Liz Lankey, Scott Lewis, Alison Light, Katharine Macdonald, Nicholas Mays, Jon McLachlan, Janet W. McKee, Don McKenzie, Simone Murray, Philip Nind, Judith Priestman, Hilary Pyle, Emma Robinson, Stephen Roe, Janine Rymer, Ronald E. Shields, Keith Smith, Colin Smythe, colleagues within the Department of Printed Books and Manuscripts at Sotheby's, G. Thomas Tanselle, Robert Temple, Gerald R. Wager, Julia Walworth, Compton Whitworth, Peter Widdowson, Wayne Williams (for his photography), Shelia Woolf and John Wyse Jackson.

Introduction

It was long since decided that I am like the dodo and the great auk, no longer known as a bird at all[1]

In 1957, six years after claiming an extinct status, John Masefield cheerfully observed that from three hundred million readers of English, three read his work and four criticized it.[2] These examples illustrate two views during the decline of a reputation. Masefield had once been a best-selling author and a publishing phenomenon. He was critically acclaimed and internationally honoured. Today the decline is perhaps complete. A major literary figure only lingers on in poetry anthologies of a conservative nature. A later Poet Laureate, John Betjeman, noted that 'Sea-Fever' and 'Cargoes' would be 'remembered as long as the language lasts'.[3] Despite this claim on posterity, Betjeman demonstrates the reduction of Masefield's vast canon to a mere six stanzas.

Today Masefield's former popularity, Edwardian multiplicity and prodigious output apparently count against him. His works are largely out-of-print and academia ignores him. It perhaps need not have been the case. Masefield was a writer who attempted to redefine himself, particularly in the 1920s. In his suppressing (or attempting to suppress) work he made a number of errors. He also found himself unable to act, tied to contracts and powerless to buy back early titles. Masefield's self-perception was, moreover, frequently in opposition to public taste and the wishes of his early publishers. The writer therefore made concessions, or was denied rights, and his attempted re-invention did not succeed. In composing new works he followed an agenda neither Edwardian nor Modernist and became a mixture of creative artist, popular balladeer and best-selling novelist. It is perhaps this curious combination that now damages his reputation. With a long career Masefield was offered a second chance as the popular publishing culture of the 1960s attempted to embrace him. Now the aged Laureate, he again took imperfect decisions and rejected the modern populist market. Throughout his life he also appears to have made demands that caused film companies to lose interest in his works. Masefield's status today is not perhaps a result of literary achievement or failure; it is due to an inability to manipulate economic or publishing trends and a resulting failure to demand academic or widespread populist respect.

Once a writer achieves dodo or great auk status, of course, his name faces extinction from publisher's catalogues. However, this great auk can be seen as a way of entry into the publishing history of popular literature in the twentieth-century. His poetry was respected by W.B. Yeats, Thomas Hardy, Philip Larkin and A. Alvarez.[4] His plays were praised by Bernard Shaw and his novels by Graham Greene.[5] There are few writers in the twentieth-century who were first read by the Victorians and died in the midst of nuclear cold war politics. He had witnessed the coming of the railways at the border of his childhood garden and also marked the assassination of J.F. Kennedy in verse. Masefield provides us with a publishing context or figure for comparison in the twentieth-century and, as a prolific author, demonstrates a model for many other writers in the literary market. This is not, however, the forum for a re-assessment. If we are to take a fresh look at Masefield in the twenty-first century, the correct bibliographical apparatus must be available. I hope that the current volume goes some way to supplying this.

Archives of agents and publishers have provided background in the history of particular titles and this is the first Masefield bibliography to include some of this information. The history of a book can frequently be traced by these means and I hope it is possible to find material for further research in these notes. A bibliography should remain objective and yet Masefield's development, success or failure can be discovered here. We now know, for example, that the author regarded the early novels *Captain Margaret* and *Lost Endeavour* as failures and can measure these against the success of, and publisher's enthusiasm for *Sard Harker*. Without this type of information reassessment is hardly possible and a bibliography is a perfect forum for this material to be presented.

Historiographical Survey[6]

Charles H. Simmons' 1930 *A Bibliography of John Masefield* comprised three parts: books by Masefield, publications containing contributions by Masefield, and books and articles about Masefield. There were, naturally, errors and omissions but the volume was the first, and last, to note something approaching Masefield's entire output at the time. Masefield assisted – to some small extent – with the work, and it appears Simmons may also have given him some power of veto:

> ...we were wondering if you would permit us to print one or two of the manuscripts which I have and which I showed you when you were here... ...in making this request I have in mind what you wrote relative to bringing to light articles and verses, which you felt were done with... ...please be assured I have no desire to print anything without your permission and it is not my intention to make any copies of any of your poems,

sonnets, etc., excepting where it is necessary in giving descriptions, like in the Broadsheet, where we may quote a line or two to show changes…

(Charles H. Simmons, letter to John Masefield, 22 May 1930)
(HRHRC (Masefield, J.) Recip Simmons, Charles H. TLS to Masefield)

When E.J. Mullett, of The Society of Authors, wrote to Masefield in 1936 stating:

I notice that the Oxford Press published in 1930 a Bibliography of your works. Do you consider that I might avoid troubling you, as I fear I have so often lately, for information about some of your works, if I had this Bibliography, or any other Bibliography which you might consider more useful…

(E.J. Mullett, letter to John Masefield, 17 December 1936)
(BL, Add.Mss.56605, f.142–43)

Masefield replied with a tone of slight disinterest. He noted 'I have not seen the Oxford Press Bibliography. If it would help you, and you would care to get it, please do so and charge it to me.' (see John Masefield, letter to E.J. Mullett, [20 December 1936]) (BL, Add.Mss.56605, f.149).

Curiously, Simmons was responsible for adding a bibliographical ghost to the canon. His item [70] is listed as *The Condemned Cell* and described as 'a play written and produced before 1928. Not published. The manuscript has been destroyed.' (This item is also noted later by Handley-Taylor and Wight.) In 1930 The Grolier Club approached Masefield's English publishers for further detail (which they were unable to provide).[7] I have included the title in my sequence but have not provided a numerical entry. My bibliography provides a record of *published* work. The manuscripts of Masefield require extensive work in their own right.

During September 1930 C.S. Evans, of the Heinemann firm, suggested to Masefield a publicity publication including an appreciation of the author together with a bibliography. H.W. Nevinson wrote the appreciation and (uncredited) work on the bibliography was by Rupert Hart-Davis. Although Hart-Davis noted that 'the booklet is designed for the bookbuyer rather than for the collector'[8] it is listed in bibliographical references (under 'Nevinson').

In 1959 Fraser Drew contributed two bibliographical articles to *Papers of the Bibliographical Society of America*.[9] The first considered Masefield's contributions to *The Manchester Guardian* and the second provided corrections and additions to Simmons' work. Drew ably demonstrated that the Masefield canon was vast and required much thorough work and research.

Geoffrey Handley-Taylor published his work (*A Bibliography and Eighty-First Birthday Tribute*) in 1960. Upon publication, the *Times Literary Supplement* suggested the book should have been called a handlist and Handley-Taylor has (in private correspondence) indeed suggested it should only be 'loosely described as a bibliography'. The publication is a guide to books and pamphlets written by Masefield and also to publications wholly relating to him. Reprint information provided for Masefield volumes is imprecise (and I have chosen to ignore some of Handley-Taylor's unverified reprint dates in my work). Nevertheless, with copious photographic illustrations and clear presentation of material, the work has much to recommend it.

Crocker Wight stated in his introduction that he intended 'to continue the work of Charles H. Simmons' with his bibliography entitled *John Masefield – A Bibliographical Description of his First, Limited, Signed and Special Editions* (published in 1986, second edition 1992). He only considered, however, books entirely by Masefield and ignored many valuable areas.

Given Wight's scope, no attempt has ever been made to compile a comprehensive bibliography of books by Masefield, books with contributions by him, and contributions to periodicals across the writer's entire career. In addition, it is important to expand the scope beyond the work of Simmons to produce a bibliographical work embracing new areas. I have, however, here excluded critical works about Masefield and critical reviews of his work.

Bibliographical rubric

It has been my intention to record every edition or reprint (with the exception of reprints produced specifically for libraries). The term 'edition' in strict bibliographical terms means, of course, an entirely new setting of the text. It would therefore be possible to see facsimile reprints or new use of old plates as later impressions of the source edition. Although this is an important distinction from the perspective of textual change (and possible authorial revision), many readers would find strict adherence to the terminology confusing. Some distortion to publishing chronology would also be created. I follow a method of description whereby a new 'edition' is identified by a new distinguishing feature. This feature may comprise a new setting of text, a different publisher, a new introduction, a limited signed issue or publication as part of a series. A new binding alone would not comprise a new 'edition' however. (See note on 'cheap' and 'popular' editions). New editions are provided with separate alphabetical letters, in chronological order. When two 'editions' appear to have been published simultaneously (a limited signed edition and a standard trade edition, for example) double letters are used – hence (a) and (aa) – in which neither has priority. Simultaneous publication of different settings of text are given different letters.

A number of copyright editions may be included (to follow the example of Simmons). However, advance proof copies (comprising pre-publication volumes distributed to booksellers) are excluded from my first section. Such advance proof copies are listed in section L, however.

A transcription of the title-page is provided, using standard rubric. Not all spaces between words are rendered entirely accurately. Throughout all descriptions, printing is assumed to be in black unless otherwise noted. No differentiation between large and small upper- or lower-case letters is made. An italic font is used for any sloping type. Single ruled borders are noted as 'ruled borders'. Double-ruled borders are noted as such, with measurements of the external border provided.

In describing title-pages (and bindings) it should be noted that there are several different publisher's devices used by the firm of William Heinemann. They all use a representation of a windmill and are derived from a design by William Nicholson. In 1897 Nicholson designed a bookplate for William Heinemann and this design was adopted as the symbol of the publishing company. The original shows a 'W' together with a point to the left of a windmill. The letter 'H' is to the right.

The collation of a volume, comprising a register of signatures, is provided. Regardless of convention, all omitted signatures are noted (J is always omitted, but the omission of U, V and W is not as standard as might be thought). Inferred signatures are given in square brackets rather than noted in italics. Duplicated signatures appear as printed (hence AA rather than 2A). This may not be exactly what Fredson Bowers would recommend, but is clear (if not concise). Other leaves which bear a signature are noted, but not necessarily described fully. For example 'D2 is also signed' will indicate that the second leaf of the 'D' gathering bears a signature, but this could comprise 'D2' or 'D*', for example. Some American editions give signatures entirely unconnected to the arrangement of gatherings (see note on American electrotype editions). Pagination of a volume is provided with inferred page numbers listed within square brackets. Catalogues or publisher's advertisements are not described separately when integral to the volume. When such matter comprises an entirely separate gathering this is treated in isolation. Extra leaves for illustrations are noted by recording on which leaves these additional leaves are tipped-in. They are excluded from the leaf count. Single frontispiece illustration leaves are not noted in the collation (but will be found in the description of pagination contents).

A page-by-page description of the volume is then presented (without using the terminology of rectos and versos). Describing page content often comprises transcription, sometimes at great length. This is frequently justified. Compare, for example, the dedication of *The Nine Days Wonder* in A130(a) with that in A130(b) to discover the omission of a single comma. This suggests that the American edition employed a different setting of type from the English edition. Bibliography in the machine-press period is frequently the study of individual type characters. G. Thomas Tanselle has written of considerable variations in books of the machine-press period (even within apparently identical printings) and detailed transcription facilitates this study.[10]

Paper type, whether laid or wove is noted with details of watermark where present (and detectable). When unknown, the word 'presumed' will appear before a supposition. If a watermark is noted – or part of a watermark is noted – within square brackets then the complete watermark has not been seen on an examined copy, but can be assumed. An indication of running titles is also provided. Of most use here is the running title, or titles, which are predominant throughout a volume and their length (measured in mm.) I have mostly felt it unnecessary to note running titles within preliminaries, or indeed to record all pages where a running title is omitted.

The next section describes the binding of a volume. The term 'wrappers' includes 'paperback' books whilst the description 'boards' may include bindings with paper-covered boards. Colour has caused considerable difficulties. Simmons and Wight are both unsatisfactory here but I have felt it unwise to abandon entirely their descriptions in favour of Tanselle's 'A System of Color Identification for Bibliographical Description'.[11] Moreover, many copies of volumes consulted for this bibliography were not in fine condition. Cloth bindings show varying hues due to fading and colours described over seventy years ago by Simmons should not be wholly abandoned for Tanselle's system. My descriptions are therefore based on those of Simmons and Wight. Text (and illustrations) appearing on the binding are described and it can be assumed – unless otherwise noted – that lettering or illustrations are width centred. The term 'width centred' is used to refer to printing that is positioned at the centre of the total width. It makes no reference of position in respect to height. The state of edges is also noted. Uncut and trimmed are the usual terms employed although 'roughly trimmed' has also been used to describe American editions which have been processed by machine trimming which creates edges which are far from smooth. Gilt edges are noted as are those which are 'stained'. There are a number of binding variants seemingly produced by Heinemann in the late 1920s for a specific (but currently unknown) purpose. Titles thus bound include *The Hawbucks* and *The Midnight Folk*. It appears these were publisher's bindings and may have been specifically produced for lending libraries. They have been omitted from the bibliographical description.

Publication dates, print sizes and prices of volumes are noted where known. Where research has currently failed to discover this information 'unknown' has been entered. Where a year only is noted, I have failed to discover the month of publication. It can, however, be generally assumed that the sequence is correct.

The contents of a volume are listed in the order of appearance with first lines, or openings, provided. With material until 1911 a substantial quantity of material is cited with details of first appearance. A poem, therefore, which was first published in periodical form will be noted as such. After 1911 material is less well documented and represents an area for future work. In quoting first lines considerable variation has been found in punctuation. Contrast, for example, the opening of 'Live Ned' in A127(a) of *Live and Kicking Ned* with the same lines as they appear in A127(b).

A register of consulted copies concludes the description of a volume. Given the scope of the project it has not always been possible to trace multiple copies for comparison. Several editions are described on the authority of one copy. Frequently this is due to rarity in this country. Private collections are listed with the owner's initials. Where omitted, the individual wishes to remain anonymous. All inscriptions are by John Masefield, unless otherwise noted. These therefore include numerous familiar names the author used for himself within his family and circle of friends: 'Zob', 'Zom', 'Pip' and, of course, 'Jan'.

Details of reprints are provided (with reference, mostly, to consulted copies). Several of these are on the authority of Handley-Taylor. As throughout the volume, use of square brackets signals conjectural information.

Full bibliographical descriptions are not, generally, provided for reprint material published after Masefield's death in 1967.

The sections are mostly self-explanatory. Books and pamphlets by Masefield are the subject of the 'A' section. The 'B' section (comprising 'Books Edited or with Contributions') excludes anthologies which reprint Masefield items previously printed in book form. A few significant examples of such works can be found in the 'F' section.

Section 'C' comprises 'Contributions to Newspapers and Periodicals'. As stated, Simmons made an attempt to include Masefield's contributions to periodicals, but this was far from complete. With Masefield the importance of publication in periodicals is too great to ignore. Numerous early contributions constitute the first printed appearance of many works. The author extensively revised his material and contributions to periodicals often provide examples of text in an earlier state than that generally accessible.

Attribution is usually simple and only three pseudonyms are known (Pete Henderson, Wolfe Tone McGowan and Robert Emmet McGowan). Incorrect attributions by previous bibliographies have been removed (Simmons' 'Sonnet on the Nonpareil' on page 128 of his bibliography, for example). However, see notes to *The Times Literary Supplement*, *The Manchester Guardian* and *A Broadside*. Tracing material largely relies on secondary sources. Such sources include previous bibliographies, bibliographical articles, and indexes. All material listed in the *American Readers' Guide to Periodical Literature* (published by H.W. Wilson) has been included. Other sources include references in manuscripts, the archives of periodicals, and published works that contain material reprinted from a periodical along with an acknowledgement note. Unless listed in an italic type (with an explanatory note regarding my source of information) all material has been checked. Thus the article 'Sport of the Pacific Coast' appearing in *The Manchester Guardian* on 9 April 1908 (as cited by Fraser Drew) becomes a book review of Horace Annerley Vachell's *Sport and Life on the Pacific Slope*. Similarly a book review, on 9 October 1907, of Norman Duncan's *The Way of the Sea* is revealed as a review of *The Cruise of the Shining Light* (the confusion having arisen as the article commences with reference to the previous title). This section presents the most comprehensive listing of contributions to periodicals yet produced. Significantly, the earliest appearance is pushed back from June 1899 (as cited by Simmons for 'Nicias Moriturus' in *The Outlook*) to March 1895 with a letter in *The Cadet*. Admittedly the appearance of the poem is more important to Masefield's career but recording this earlier contribution is a notable expansion of date range.

Most examples in section 'D' ('Privately Printed Poetry Cards by John Masefield') comprise the author's own Christmas cards ('In darkest London many years ago', for example). However, oddities such as 'Friends, we are opening at this solemn time,' (D1) are probably better defined as 'broadsheets' but also included in this section.

Section 'H' lists archival audio recordings. These comprise recordings by Masefield not commercially released. With two exceptions these are copies of radio broadcasts (see section 'I'). In February 1924 G.H. Thring wrote to Masefield stating that the British Broadcasting Company were interested in broadcasting *Right Royal*. Masefield replied:

> Generally speaking, I would say to you, authorise the broadcasting of my shorter poems on the usual terms, without reference to me, but these long poems are not easy to speak + I would like to have some assurance that the speaker will stay the course + not garble my work out of all knowledge.
>
> (John Masefield, letter to G.H. Thring, [11 February 1924])
> (BL, Add.Mss.56579, f.74)

The matter was discussed and Masefield even provided Thring with a list of recommended speakers. The issue of the poet's own reading was then raised. Masefield wrote stating he would 'gladly do some broadcasting ... if my engagements permit',[12] and later enquired about fees:

> If the Br Broadcasting Co would like me to broadcast my work I would do it, for a fee. What fee would they offer, + what amount of work would they expect for it? Would you very kindly ask for me?
>
> (John Masefield, letter to G.H. Thring, [25 February 1924])
>
> (BL, Add.Mss.56579, f.87)

Negotiations continued and 12 May 1924 was arranged as a suitable date. Presumably unsure of broadcasting copyright it appears that Masefield applied to Thring for permission to use his own words! We therefore see interest in Masefield as a broadcaster in the early days of radio and long before his appointment as Poet Laureate. By August 1924 Masefield was unhappy with broadcasting, believing that fees to poets and performers were unfairly low. In December 1927 he informed The Society of Authors that he was inclined to be 'uncharitable', blaming broadcasting for diminishing 'the reading public by a quarter'.[13]

In the infancy of radio few recordings were made and programmes comprised live broadcasts without manufacture of an archival copy. Broadcasts therefore prove difficult to trace. Programmes with which Masefield was involved, but did not speak (two selections from Chaucer broadcast on 6 January 1937 and 13 January 1937, for example) are omitted, with one exception (see 26 December 1938). One example of a television broadcast is included. In the 1950s the British Institute of Recorded Sound asked permission from Masefield to include the author's BBC recordings in the archive. Masefield wrote to The Society of Authors:

> The BBC people came to me here on Monday, + played over some recordings made a good many years ago by them, unknown to myself, on forgotten occasions. I disliked some of these pretty heartily; thinking that both sides of the matter, recorders + speaker, would do the thing better now, but one or two of the things the speaker would certainly never speak again, unless life depended on it...
>
> (John Masefield, letter to Anne Munro-Kerr, 14 September [1960])
>
> (Archives of The Society of Authors)

Section 'J' provides a forum for miscellaneous items. Many of these are slightly problematic or comprise ephemera. Some placing of items may require revision. If research and discussion result from any of my actions I shall be delighted.

Each section is provided with a numbering sequence. Several sections, for example section 'B', include the numbering B1, B5, B10, B15 etc. These sections are probably far from complete and the current sequence should allow for the insertion of new material.

Within the text, individual names of The Society of Authors' staff are seldom provided since their role was usually that of a member of staff working on behalf of the Society. 'Heinemann' usually relates to the publishing firm, rather than the founder William Heinemann.

Naturally a volume of this size will suffer from omissions, inconsistencies and errors. For these I can do no more than apologise. The internet provides, however, a convenient means for displaying addenda and errata. Please see the site noted on the publisher's imprint page. The site also includes a dust-jacket project.

B.C. Bloomfield, in writing on W.H. Auden, noted that 'bibliography, apart from its proper role, may also provide facts for the literary and textual critic'.[14] The uses and roles of bibliography are vast and a single author bibliography should provide an informed position from which subsequent work can start. Handley-Taylor notes that 'a bibliography rarely achieves a headline, but ... it does attract the perennial footnote ...'[15] Bibliographies are, therefore, enabling and the study of Masefield requires as many facilitating factors as possible.

With individual writers there is, perhaps, a league table of authors with the famous at the top and the forgotten at the bottom: John Milton is much removed from John Todhunter. It would be a mistake, however, to superimpose additional labels on the same table. Although there may be many similarities, I suggest that a different table would exist for the 'literary merit' of an author, or the 'commercial power' of a writer, or any other factor. Each is different and potentially impossible to define – how does one assess the 'greatness' of a writer without other factors entering the debate? Is Shakespeare so much greater than Marlowe? Or does the 'Shakespeare industry' of the theatre, the cinema, the bookshop and the tourist trade alter our perception? Can we ever be truly objective? In a league table with the best-selling authors at the top and the out-of-print writers at the bottom (or the famous at the opposite end to the unread unknowns) there is a middle ground. Between John Milton and John Todhunter is John Masefield. His presence in the middle is a result of academic, commercial and societal forces reacting, avoiding and co-existing with each other.

With the entry of new critical approaches within literary studies in the latter half of the twentieth-century, Masefield's appeal has steadily declined. Not a Modernist, Feminist, Symbolist, or falling within any other useful category he was regarded as a stale Georgian poet. His long career, prodigious output and progressive conservatism have prevented adoption by any critical school. When a reputation is ignored by academia it is too easy (and less work) to pass over the writer, rather than assess. The value of academic study is that it should be widely researched and shun commercial or perceived impressions. A simple refusal to consider Masefield is simplifying and reductive in scope. It also deprives readers of some great writing.

Trends or changes in the requirements of society have failed to find lasting appeal in Masefield. The 1978 biography by Constance Babington Smith presented a successful writer, morally correct with a comfortable life, home and family.[16] When Masefield should have re-invented himself through his work he took flawed decisions, or was forced into incorrect judgements. One perception is that Masefield was re-invented by royalty and his appointment as Poet Laureate was a major disadvantage. It is now with the study of the history of the book as a discipline that Masefield may find a newly sympathetic audience. His career and output are significantly linked with twentieth-century publishing concerns. Masefield is representative of a best-selling and popular author, a victim of publishing contracts, an early employer of a literary agency, a patron of private presses and a figure particularly active in the literary world. His presidency of The Society of Authors and National Book League, work for The Royal Society of Literature, role as instigator of the Royal Medal for Poetry and champion of verse-speaking festivals demonstrate this position. His longevity and literary friendships present him as a notable figure of his time. If we are to reassess Masefield, it is appropriate to produce a new bibliography.

Finally, there is the sheer joy and exhilaration to be gained from some of Masefield's work. In 1952, writing of second-hand bookstalls, the author stated that the 'out-of-fashion is always cheap, and usually much better than the fashion has the wit to think'.[17] This would serve as an epitaph on Masefield's work.

Notes

1. quoted by Peter Vansittart (*John Masefield's Letters from the Front 1915–1917*, London: Constable, 1984, p.39)
2. see illustrations in Peter Vansittart, *In the Fifties*, London: John Murray, 1995 (between pp.122–24)
3. John Betjeman, 'Preface' to John Masefield, *Selected Poems*, London: Heinemann, 1978, p.vii
4. Lady Gregory reports that W.B. Yeats once told Masefield 'You'll be a popular poet – you'll be riding in your carriage and pass me in the gutter' (see *Lady Gregory's Journals*, ed. Daniel J. Murphy, two volumes, Gerrards Cross: Colin Smythe, 1978–1987, volume one, p.385). Hardy was a frequent correspondent. Larkin, when awarded the Hamburg University Hanseatic Shakespeare prize in 1976, described Masefield (a former recipient) as 'a writer whose strength and simplicity I have long admired' (see Philip Larkin, *Required Writing – Miscellaneous Pieces 1955–1982*, London: Faber and Faber, 1983, p.87). A. Alvarez reviewing *Old Raiger and other verse* found the verses 'agreeably soothing'.
5. Bernard Shaw wrote to Masefield in a letter dated 27 July 1907 praising 'The Campden Wonder' (see Bodleian, MS.Eng.Lett.c.255, f.142). Apart for the ending, Graham Greene thought *Sard Harker* 'the greatest adventure story in the language' (see Norman Sherry, *The Life of Graham Greene*, London: Jonathan Cape, 1989, p.312)
6. for full citations of these works see abbreviations
7. see HRHRC, MS (Masefield, J.) Recip William Heinemann Ltd. for a letter from C.S. Evans to Masefield, dated 11 June 1930. Evans enclosed a letter (apparently no longer extant) which he had received from the Grolier Club in New York. Evans noted 'I do not know THE CONDEMNED CELL so I cannot answer the questions they ask.'
8. see Rupert Hart-Davis, letter to John Masefield, 7 November 1930 (HRHRC, MS (Masefield, J.) Recip William Heinemann Ltd.)
9. see Fraser Drew, 'Some Contributions to the Bibliography of John Masefield: I', *Papers of the Bibliographical Society of America*, June 1959, pp.188–96 and 'Some Contributions to the Bibliography of John Masefield: II', *Papers of the Bibliographical Society of America*, October 1959, pp.262–67
10. G. Thomas Tanselle, Literature and Artifacts, *The Bibliographical Society of the University of Virginia*, Charlottesville, Va., 1998
11. G. Thomas Tanselle, 'A System of Color Identification for Bibliographical Description', ed. Fredson Bowers, *Studies in Bibliography* XX, 1967, pp.203–234
12. see BL, Add.Mss.56579, f.79
13. see BL, Add.Mss.56586, f.47
14. B.C. Bloomfield, *W.H. Auden – A Bibliography. The Early Years through 1955*, Charlottesville, Va: Bibliographical Society of the University of Virginia, University Press of Virginia, 1964, p.xv
15. Geoffrey Handley-Taylor, 'Foreword' to Crocker Wight, *John Masefield – A Bibliographical Description of His First, Limited, Signed and Special Editions*, Boston, Mass.: The Library of the Boston Athenaeum, second edition, 1992, p.ix
16. Constance Babington Smith, *John Masefield – A Life*, Oxford: University Press, 1978
17. John Masefield, *So Long to Learn*, London: William Heinemann, 1952, p.93

Abbreviations

General Abbreviations

ALS – autograph letter signed

c. – circa

f. / ff. – folio / folios

p. / pp. – page / pages

TLS – typed letter signed

| – line break

... – compiler's ellipsis

[] – square brackets denote conjectural additions, or omissions

Library Abbreviations

BL – British Library

Harvard – Harvard University (Houghton Library)

HRHRC – Harry Ransom Humanities Research Center

NYPL – New York Public Library

UCL – University College London Library

ULL (Special Collections) – University of London Library (Special Collections)

Bibliography Abbreviations

Danielson
Henry Danielson, *Bibliographies of Modern Authors*, London: The Bookman's Journal, 1921, pp.129–53

Williams
I.A. Williams, *Bibliographies of Modern Authors No.2 – John Masefield*, London: Leslie Chaundy and Co., 1921

Simmons
Charles H. Simmons, *A Bibliography of John Masefield*, Oxford: Oxford University Press / New York: Columbia University Press, 1930

Nevinson
Henry W. Nevinson, *John Masefield – An Appreciation... Together With A Bibliography*, London: William Heinemann Ltd, 1931

Handley-Taylor
Geoffrey Handley-Taylor, *John Masefield, O.M. The Queen's Poet Laureate. A Bibliography and Eighty-First Birthday Tribute*, London: Cranbrook Tower Press, 1960

Wight
Crocker Wight, *John Masefield – A Bibliographical Description of his First, Limited, Signed and Special Editions*, Boston, Mass.: Library of the Boston Athenaeum, second edition, 1992

A. Books and Pamphlets

A1(a) First English edition (1902)

SALT-WATER | BALLADS | BY | JOHN MASEFIELD | [ornament] | GRANT RICHARDS | 48 LEICESTER
SQUARE | LONDON | 1902
(All width centred)

Bibliographies: Danielson 159, Williams p.1, Simmons [1], Nevinson p.12, Handley-Taylor p.27, Wight [1]

Collation: [π]⁸ A–G⁸; signatures width centred at foot of page; 64 leaves; 190 × 117mm.; [i–viii] ix–xv [xvi] [1] 2–107 [108] 109–12

Page contents: [i] half-title: 'SALT-WATER BALLADS'; [ii] blank; [iii] title-page; [iv] 'Edinburgh : Printed by T. and A. CONSTABLE';
[v] 'TO | C. DE LA CHEROIS CROMMELIN | A. HANFORD-FLOOD | AND | H.M. HEANE'; [vi] blank; [vii] 'I thank the
Editors of the *Broad-Sheet, Outlook*, | *Pall Mall Magazine, Speaker*, and *Tatler*, for per- | mission to include in this volume a number |
of ballads which originally appeared in those | papers. JOHN MASEFIELD.'; [viii] blank; ix–xv 'CONTENTS' (52 individual poems
listed with page references); [xvi] "The mariners are a pleasant people, but little | like those in the towns, and they can speak no
other | language than that used in ships.' | *The Licentiate Vidriera.*'; [1]–107 text; [108] blank; 109–112 'GLOSSARY' (at foot of p.112:
'[rule] | Edinburgh : Printed by T. and A. CONSTABLE')

Paper: laid paper (no watermark), chain-lines 25mm. apart

Running title: 'SALT-WATER BALLADS' (37mm.) on verso; recto title comprises poem title, pp.2–107

Binding:
First issue (300 copies):
dark-blue cloth. On spine, in gold: 'SALT | WATER | BALLADS | JOHN | MASEFIELD | GRANT | RICHARDS' with the
exception of the publisher, all words are left justified; the publisher is centred. Covers: blank. Top edge gilt, others uncut. Binding
measurements: 197 × 126mm. (covers), 197 × 26mm. (spine). End-papers: laid paper (no watermark), chain-lines 29mm. apart. The
chain-lines at the front of all examined volumes run vertically; those at the rear run either vertically or horizontally.
Second issue (150 copies):
blue-black cloth. As above, although the lettering on the spine is of a slightly larger size (see notes)

Publication date: published, according to Simmons, 9 November 1902 in an edition of 500 copies (see also A1(aa))

Price: 3s.6d.

Contents:
A Consecration ('Not of the princes and prelates with periwigged charioteers')
    No previous appearance traced
The Yarn of The 'Loch Achray' ('The 'Loch Achray' was a clipper tall')
    First printed in The Pall Mall Magazine *April 1902, pp.529–30*
Sing a Song O' Shipwreck ('He lolled on a bollard, a sun-burned son of the sea,')
    First printed in The Pall Mall Magazine *October 1902, p.234*
Burial Party ("He's deader 'n nails,' the fo'c's'le said, ''n' gone to his long sleep';')
    First printed as 'Burying at Sea' in The Speaker *12 April 1902, p.45*
Bill ('He lay dead on the cluttered deck and stared at the cold skies,')
    First printed in The Outlook *21 December 1901, p.720*
Fever Ship ('There'll be no weepin' gells ashore when *our* ship sails,')
    First printed as 'The Fever Ship' in The Tatler *26 February 1902, p.392*
Fever Chills ('He tottered out of the alleyway with cheeks the colour of paste,')
    First printed as 'Coast-Fever' in The Speaker *12 July 1902, p.411*
One of the Bo'sun's Yarns ('Loafin' around in Sailor Town, a-bluin' o' my advance,')
    No previous appearance traced
Hell's Pavement ("When I'm discharged in Liverpool 'n' draws my bit o' pay,')
    First printed as 'Hell's Pavement. – Billy' in The Speaker *27 September 1902, p.678*
Sea-Change ("Goneys an' gullies an' all o' the birds o' the sea,')
    First printed as 'Jimmy The Dane' in The Speaker *13 December 1902, p.280)*
Harbour-Bar ('All in the feathered palm-tree tops the bright green parrots screech,')
    First printed in The Speaker *exact location untraced*
Nicias Moriturus ('An' Bill can have my sea-boots, Nigger Jim can have my knife,')
    First printed in The Outlook *3 June 1899, p.580)*

One of Wally's Yarns ('The watch was up on the topsail-yard a-making fast the sail,')
  No previous appearance traced
A Valediction (Liverpool Docks) ('Is there anything as I can do ashore for you')
  No previous appearance traced
A Night at Dago Tom's ('Oh yesterday, I t'ink it was, while cruisin' down the street,')
  First printed in The Speaker *18 October 1902, p.74*
'Port O' Many Ships' ("It's a sunny pleasant anchorage is Kingdom Come,')
  First printed in The Speaker *16 August 1902, p.530*
Cape Horn Gospel – I ("I was on a hooker once,' said Karlssen,')
  No previous appearance traced
Cape Horn Gospel – II ('Jake was a dirty Dago lad, an' he gave the skipper chin,')
  No previous appearance traced
Mother Carey ('Mother Carey ? She's the mother o' the witches')
  First printed in The Speaker *7 June 1902, p.277*
Evening – Regatta Day ('Your nose is a red jelly, your mouth's a toothless wreck,')
  First printed as 'Evening. Regatta Day. Iquique Harbour' in The Speaker *4 October 1902, p.18*
A Valediction ('We're bound for blue water where the great winds blow,')
  No previous appearance traced
A Pier-Head Chorus ('Oh I'll be chewing salted horse and biting flinty bread,')
  No previous appearance traced
The Golden City of St. Mary ('Out beyond the sunset, could I but find the way,')
  No previous appearance traced
Trade Winds ('In the harbour, in the island, in the Spanish Seas,')
  First printed in The Outlook *5 October 1901, p.304*
Sea-Fever ('I must down to the seas again, to the lonely sea and the sky,')
  First printed in The Speaker *15 February 1902, p.560*
A Wanderer's Song ('A wind's in the heart o' me, a fire's in my heels,')
  First printed as 'A Wind's In The Heart O' Me' in The Speaker *5 July 1902, p.384*
Cardigan Bay ('Clean, green, windy billows notching out the sky,')
  First printed in The Outlook *23 November 1901, p.558*
Christmas Eve at Sea ('A wind is rustling 'south and soft,")
  No previous appearance traced
A Ballad of Cape St. Vincent ('Now, Bill, ain't it prime to be a-sailin',')
  First printed as 'Off Cape St. Vincent' in The Tatler *5 February 1902, p.264*
The Tarry Buccaneer ('I'm going to be a pirate with a bright brass pivot-gun,')
  No previous appearance traced
A Ballad of John Silver ('We were schooner-rigged and rakish, with a long and lissome hull,')
  No previous appearance traced
Lyrics from 'The Buccaneer'
I.   ('We are far from sight of the harbour lights,')
II.   ('There's a sea-way somewhere where all day long')
III. ('The toppling rollers at the harbour mouth')
  No previous appearance traced
D'Avalos' Prayer ('When the last sea is sailed and the last shallow charted,')
  First printed as 'A Last Prayer' in A Broad Sheet *October 1902*
The West Wind ('It's a warm wind, the west wind, full of birds' cries;')
  First printed as 'There's A Wind A-Blowing' in The Speaker *28 June 1902, p.365*
The Galley-Rowers ('Staggering over the running combers')
  No previous appearance traced
Sorrow O' Mydath ('Weary the cry of the wind is, weary the sea,')
  First printed in The Speaker *31 May 1902, p.250*
Vagabond ('Dunno a heap about the what an' why,')
  First printed in The Outlook *22 February 1902, p.112*
Vision ('I have drunken the red wine and flung the dice;')
  No previous appearance traced
Spunyarn ('Spunyarn, spunyarn, with one to turn the crank,')
  No previous appearance traced
The Dead Knight ('The cleanly rush of the mountain air,')
  First printed in The Speaker *29 March 1902, p.729*
Personal ('Tramping at night in the cold and wet, I passed the lighted inn,')
  No previous appearance traced

On Malvern Hill ('A wind is brushing down the clover,')
  First printed in The Speaker *14 June 1902, p.305*
Tewkesbury Road ('It is good to be out on the road, and going one knows not where,')
  No previous appearance traced
On Eastnor Knoll ('Silent are the woods, and the dim green boughs are')
  No previous appearance traced
'Rest Her Soul, She's Dead!' ('She has done with the sea's sorrow and the world's way')
  No previous appearance traced
'All Ye That Pass By' ('On the long dusty ribbon of the long city street,')
  No previous appearance traced
In Memory of A.P.R. ('Once in the windy wintry weather,')
  No previous appearance traced
To-Morrow ('Oh yesterday the cutting edge drank thirstily and deep,')
  No previous appearance traced
Cavalier ('All the merry kettle-drums are thudding into rhyme,')
  No previous appearance traced
A Song at Parting ('The tick of the blood is settling slow, my heart will soon be still,')
  No previous appearance traced
Glossary ('Abaft the beam.–That half of a ship included between her amid-ship section…')

Notes:

The listing of first lines in the contents does not always match the punctuation as present in the main text.

Quotations and dedications present in this edition were omitted from subsequent editions. Dedicatees of poems include Edward Gordon Craig, W.B. Yeats, Laurence Binyon and Jack B. Yeats.

Grant Richards, in *Author Hunting*, states that the suggestion to publish the volume was made by him after reading 'The West Wind' in *The Nation*. (Richards presumably refers to 'There's A Wind A-Blowing' in *The Speaker* on 28 June 1902). Richards then writes:

> [*Salt-Water Ballads*] …was the first book from Masefield's hand and it attracted immediate, if not considerable, attention. I believe I invented the title, and if that is so I am not very proud, for it seemed, as did the binding, deliberately to invite for the book comparison with *Barrack Room Ballads*. Of the first edition of *Salt-Water Ballads* five hundred copies were printed and the story is told in the trade that owing to a fire that took place in the warehouse of Leighton, Son and Hodge, the binders, the book was soon unprocurable. My ledgers of that period in no way support it. The copies printed, with the exception of a small number, are all accounted for as normal sales and review copies. The first binding was three hundred. In the first part of 1903 a further hundred and fifty were bound; and a further fifty were bound at a later date. I have, but see no reason for giving, the details of the sales. Anyhow, the book became very much of a collector's item, one copy selling, I believe, for twenty-eight pounds, the original price being but five shillings [*sic*]. A few bound copies *may* have been burnt in the Leighton fire and so have given rise to the tale. It no doubt seemed necessary to account for a book of which over four hundred copies had been sold becoming so scarce and so valuable. Some copies in the later bindings were done up in a different cloth and that of course would have enhanced the value of the first issue.
>
> (Grant Richards, *Author Hunting*, Hamish Hamilton, 1934, pp.226–27)

Wight notes that 'some copies were issued in blue-black buckram. In those, the words "RICHARDS" on the spine were 3mm. tall instead of 2mm. tall in the blue cloth edition'. These copies presumably comprise the second issue from 1903. (See A1(aa) for Richards' fifty copies 'bound at a later date'). A copy with the blue-black binding in Harvard College Library (Houghton *EC9.M377.902sa) reveals that the *entire* lettering on the spine is slightly different. Although 'RICHARDS' is the obvious difference, the other letters are 2mm. tall (as for the first issue) but are wider than those on the regular blue cloth issue.

The earliest extant letters of Masefield to Richards suggest that the unknown author relied on his publisher for much advice. An early discussion concerned the title. Apparently that on which Masefield had 'set his heart' had 'been already collared viz *Spunyarn*'. Ever helpful, the author then provided nine alternatives:

> …I rather like the following:- "Sea Drift", "Waif o' the Sea", "Spindrift", "Blue-Water Lyrics", "Ballads of Wind and Tide"[,] "Marks and Deeps", "Bag o' Wrinkle"[,] "Halliard Chanties"[,] "Hank o' Yarn" some of which latter, though apt, are like to be caviare to the general.
>
> (John Masefield, letter to Grant Richards, 29 August 1902)
> (NYPL (Berg Collection))

Richards suggested *Salt-Water Ballads* and Masefield agreed early in September 1902 noting it 'seems to me to be a good title' (see John Masefield, letter to Grant Richards, 3 September 1902) (NYPL (Berg Collection)).

Richards' reader (possibly E.V. Lucas) had early reservations and Richards notified Masefield of this reception. The author responded with characteristic modesty and self-deprecation:

> I quite agree with your reader that some of the stuff ought to be omitted… As I am not a good critic will you please ask your reader to let me know which he especially objects to so that I can form a saner estimate of my shortcomings?
>
> (John Masefield, letter to Grant Richards, 29 August 1902)
> (NYPL (Berg Collection))

One apparent short-coming was Masefield's diction and, specifically, use of the word "bloody". Masefield was later to create a sensation with his use of colloquial diction within *The Everlasting Mercy* (the 'offensive' word was blanked out of *The English Review*'s publication of his poem in October 1911). Richards was also to encounter "bloody" within Joyce's *Dubliners*. In a letter dated 7 September 1902 Masefield appears to antagonise Richards and then, with typical fun, suggest that prudery is misplaced considering what he *could* have written. Suddenly when Masefield contemplates that the volume's success may be threatened he makes it clear that Richards is in control:

> I have been thinking over the word "bloody" and have decided to use it sparingly, feeling that it is not a very popular adjective at sea; marine taste preferring a coarser and more expressive word, an equivalent to tell the truth, for "copulating". I want to ask you, also, if, in your opinion, a freedom of the kind would militate in any way against the book's chances. Personally I don't think it would but I should like to be guided by your experience in these matters…
>
> (John Masefield, letter to Grant Richards, 7 September 1902)
> (Harvard University (Houghton Library. *61M–93))

Later in the same month Masefield was noting that Byron uses the word 'and with Smollett and Marryat it becomes a recognised and accepted intensive' (see John Masefield, letter to Grant Richards, 19 September 1902) (NYPL (Berg Collection)). The word was eventually printed with a note in the glossary stating it was 'an intensive derived from the substantive 'blood'…'

The publishing agreement for this title between Masefield and Grant Richards was dated 8 September 1902 (see Archives of The Society of Authors). The agreement names the author as 'John Masefield Esq. of The Art Gallery Wolverhampton'. Masefield agreed '…to sell the entire copyright without any reserve in the United Kingdom and all other parts of the world'. A royalty of 10% was to be paid to Masefield on the published price of all copies sold '…but no royalty shall be paid unless 250 copies are sold'. A final clause added to the printed agreement by hand notes that 'the Author agrees to give the Publisher the refusal of his next work on terms similar to those detailed in Clause I of this Agreement [regarding royalties] but improved fifty per cent'.

Salt-Water Ballads was intended to be difficult and idiomatic, if not shocking. Writing to his family the author noted that he thought the book:

> …deserves the recognition of a maritime people… There is such a deal of cant, shoddy, humbug, drivel etc. going around, it is quite likely the book'll get killed before Christmas, but I feel that, in any case, I've said a straight word sure to be recognized as such by some few…'
>
> (John Masefield, letter to Harry Ross, 1 December 1902)
> (Private Collection (RM))

The provision of a glossary to the volume (appreciated by at least two contemporary reviewers) suggests Masefield's own doubts and, in sending the text of this feature to Richards during the middle of September 1902, Masefield notes 'I'm afraid that these sea-terms will prove great stumbling blocks to most' (see John Masefield, letter to Grant Richards, 17 September 1902) (NYPL (Berg Collection)).

Despite general enthusiasm in 1902 (Richards received the first application to set some of the volume to music less than a fortnight after publication) Masefield's biographer, Constance Babington Smith, is incorrect in stating that 'within about six months' the edition had 'completely sold out'.

John Drinkwater in *Discovery – Being the Second Book of an Autobiography 1897–1913*, Ernest Benn Ltd, 1932 tells of his first meeting with Masefield at Woburn Buildings. He notes: 'Masefield left before I did, and I was excited to hear Yeats speak enthusiastically of *Salt-Water Ballads*'

Elkin Mathews was later to advertise his edition of this work by noting 'Sir Ernest Shackleton carried to the South Pole a First Edition of this book'.

Copies seen: BL (011651.l.50) stamped 20 NOV 1902; Bodleian (28001.e.124) stamped 13 DEC 1902; Library of The John Masefield Society (Crocker Wight collection); Harvard College Library (Houghton *EC9.M377.902s) inscribed with verse to Jack B. Yeats; Harvard College Library (Houghton *EC9.M377.902sa) binding in blue-black cloth; NYPL (Berg Collection) copy 4 Lady Gregory's copy, inscribed 'from John Masefield. | Jan 26. 1903. | In memory of November 5th 1900.'; private collection, inscribed 'W.B. Yeats | from John Masefield | Nov 26. 1902.'

A1(aa) First English edition – De La More Press issue ([1906?])

SALT-WATER | BALLADS | BY | JOHN MASEFIELD | London | Alexander Moring, Ltd. | The De La More Press | 32 George Street, Hanover Square, W
(All width centred)

Bibliographies: Danielson [unrecorded], Williams [unrecorded], Simmons [unrecorded], Nevinson [unrecorded], Handley-Taylor [unrecorded], Wight 1a

Collation: [π]⁸ (±[π]2) A–G⁸; signatures width centred at foot of page; 64 leaves; 190 × 117mm.; [i–viii] ix–xv [xvi] [1] 2–107 [108] 109–112

Page contents: as for A1(a) except [iv] blank

Paper: laid paper (no watermark), chain-lines 25mm. apart. The cancel title-page ([π]2) is laid paper (no watermark), chain-lines 29mm. apart, bound so that the chain-lines run horizontally.

Running title: 'SALT-WATER BALLADS' (37mm.) on verso; recto title comprises poem title, pp.2–107

Binding: dark-blue cloth. On spine, in gold: 'SALT | WATER | BALLADS | JOHN | MASEFIELD | THE | DE LA MORE | PRESS' with the exception of the publisher, all words are left justified; the publisher is centred. Covers: blank. Top edge gilt, others uncut. Binding measurements: 197 × 123mm. (covers), 197 × 30mm. (spine). End-papers: laid paper (no watermark), chain-lines 29mm. apart. The end-papers at both front and rear of the volume are bound so that the chain-lines run horizontally.

Publication date: probably issued, with cancel title, by the De La More press around 1906 in an issue of 53 copies

Price: unknown

Contents:
as for A1(a)

Notes:
Soon after the end of 1904 Grant Richards' firm was declared bankrupt. (A new firm 'E. Grant Richards' published its first volume at the end of 1905). Richards states:

> Towards the end of 1904 difficulties beset me, difficulties which I was not to overcome. I, who had never been possessed of much capital, but had perhaps been tempted beyond prudence by too much credit, had been over-trading and spending too much money. I took, I had to take, what came to me in punishment...
>
> (Grant Richards, *Housman 1897–1936*, Oxford University Press, 1942, p.[61])

He later details how his business was disposed: 'My first publishing business had been sold by the Trustee (my always good friend, H.A. Moncrieff) to Mr. Alexander Moring, of the De La More Press.' (see Grant Richards, *Housman 1897–1936*, Oxford University Press, 1942, p.112). The archive of Grant Richards reveals that an offer of £27,500 was made for the business in November 1904. It was sold soon afterwards to Moring, although Moring seems to have delayed, causing additional loss to the creditors. No in-coming letters from Moring to Richards of any importance survive in the Richards archive. However, by November 1905 Richards was writing to Moring stating that the new owner had no claim on Housman's *A Shropshire Lad*. By May 1906 Richards was negotiating transfer fees on several books and their business relationship seems to have been understandably cool.

The catalogue of the Sterling Library (University of London Library) states the De La More Press was founded in 1895. The catalogue of the British Library suggests that the final volumes from the press date from the early 1960s. However, the location of any Moring archives is unknown. The press was connected to an engraver, Thomas Moring, who shared business premises from at least 1902 until 1906.

It seems likely that Moring came into possession of any unsold stock when he bought Richards' business and this would appear to include sheets of *Salt-Water Ballads*. The cancel title bears an address for the press which Moring occupied from 1905.

Three letters in NYPL (Berg Collection) reveal that Masefield became involved soon after Moring took over Richards' business:

> I gather that you have acquired the business of Mr Grant Richards, the publisher, of 48, Leicester Square. Among the books taken over is a book of mine, "Salt Water Ballads". Will you be so kind as to let me know what you propose to do with these books? I believe they have long ceased to sell, + it has occurred to me that you might care to enter into an arrangement for their transfer. For my own part, I should be glad to have the ballads in my control, + perhaps you would not be averse to getting rid of them?

At the foot of this letter, in a different hand, the following sales information is noted:

Sales April 18 to Dec 31, 1905 16 Copies	10% Royalty 16=15 3/6, 10% = £ – 5 / 3.
Stock at Warehouse 11 bound copies	sheets at Bindery (Strakers) 53

> (John Masefield, letter to [Alexander Moring], [January 1906])
> (NYPL (Berg Collection))

(This information is duplicated in a royalty statement from Alexander Moring Ltd. dated 31 December 1905 – see HRHRC, MS (Masefield, J.) Misc. Moring (Alexander) Ltd Royalty Statement). The letter is stamped 2 JAN 06 which corresponds to the next letter in the sequence:

> I wrote to you in January last, asking if you would be prepared to arrange for the transfer of my book "Salt Water Ballads", which is now, I believe, almost out of print. Will you please let me know if you can now proceed with this affair?
>
> (John Masefield, letter to [Alexander Moring], 19 September 1906)
> (NYPL (Berg Collection))

Another letter includes the following:

> I thank you for your letter about Salt Water Ballads. The book is not worth £25 to me, and I have no particular wish to transfer it; but I thought that it was honestly dead, and out of print, + that it would be well to let it die. If you feel that it is worth reprinting, I should like to make some arrangement about correction; for the book contains some jolly bad stuff.
>
> (John Masefield, letter to [Alexander Moring], 24 September 1906)
> (NYPL (Berg Collection))

Having rejected the idea of transfer, Masefield may have consulted his own original agreement (with Richards) to assess Moring's legal rights. Masefield's copy of the agreement, when consulted, was obviously of concern for Richards wrote:

> Your agreement is by no means worthless because it does not happen to be stamped and because you did not sign your full name. In the first place, you may have signed your full name to the copy that Moring has; and even if you have not, it has your signature and you cannot deny that it is your signature... As to its not being stamped, I may have had my copy stamped, although I do not think that I did so. Supposing it to be unstamped, the fact presents an obstacle to Moring's taking any action over it, but it is an obstacle that can be got over by the paying of a penalty – £10 or so, I believe, but in any case a large enough sum to give him pause. I am afraid, therefore, you must still consult Thring.

> (Grant Richards, letter to John Masefield, 28 September 1906)
> (Archives of Grant Richards. University of Illinois / Chadwyck-Healey microfilm, A9, f.709)

(The extant Archives of The Society of Authors do not appear to preserve any correspondence between Masefield and G.H. Thring relating to this topic). Masefield's copy of the agreement may now be in the Archives of The Society of Authors. It is signed 'John Masefield' only and there is no stamp present.

Using Richards' account of binding figures in *Author Hunting* (see notes to A1(a)), it appears that Moring, on taking over Richards' business acquired the unsold remainder of the batch of 150 copies bound in 'the first part of 1903' and 50 unbound sets of sheets. The additional note at the foot of Masefield's letter mentions 11 bound copies and 53 unbound sets of sheets. Despite unpromising sales, Moring, by September 1906 may have been contemplating a reprint (*On the Spanish Main* was published by Richards in May 1906 whilst Richards' Chapbooks had reached their second volume in March 1906 and Moring may have expected renewed interest). This reprint was seemingly blocked. The care with which the binding of the Moring *Salt-Water Ballads* imitates the Richards issue, coupled to the cancelled title-page suggests that the Moring issue constitutes the remaining 53 sets of sheets originally printed by Richards in 1902. The cancel title is one reason for dismissing an entirely new Moring reprint, the other is the typographical uniformity with Richards' edition. It is unlikely the type for the original edition was made into plates and even less likely such plates should survive until sometime after 1905. The total number of Moring copies may therefore be 53. (These copies would be those to which Richards mysteriously refers as 'bound at a later date' – perhaps understandably reluctant to admit he lost the book due to bankruptcy). It should be noted that Moring is not mentioned within Richards' *Author Hunting*.

A copy of this issue was sold by Sotheby's on 1 December 1931. The catalogue lists the volume as lot 183:

> Masefield (John) Salt Water Ballads, *original buckram, uncut* 8vo. *De la More Press, n.d.*... The sheets of the FIRST EDITION with cancel title and a letter from the De La More Press explaining the circumstances of the re-issue.

This copy and letter remain unlocated.

Copies seen: private collection (PWE); Harvard College Library (Houghton *EC9.M377.902saa); NYPL (Berg Collection); HRHRC (TEMP M377 SAL)

A1(b) Second English edition (1913)

SALT-WATER | BALLADS | BY | JOHN MASEFIELD | [ornament] | LONDON | ELKIN MATHEWS, CORK STREET | M CM XIII
(All width centred)

Bibliographies: Danielson [unrecorded], Williams [unrecorded], Simmons [unrecorded], Nevinson [unrecorded], Handley-Taylor [unrecorded], Wight 1b

Collation: A-H⁸; signatures width centred at foot of page; 64 leaves; 186 × 126mm.; [two un-numbered pages] [i–vi] vii–xiii [xiv] [1] 2–107 [108] 109–12

Page contents: [-] blank (except for signature) (page excluded from page count, but constitutes first leaf of first gathering); [-] blank; [i] half-title: 'SALT-WATER BALLADS'; [ii] blank; [iii] title-page; [iv] blank; [v] 'Some of this book was written in my boyhood, | all of it in my youth; it is now re-issued, much | as it was when first published nearly eleven | years ago. J.M. | *9th June* 1913'; [vi] blank; vii–xiii 'CONTENTS' (52 individual poems listed with page references); [xiv] "The mariners are a pleasant people, but little | like those in the towns, and they can speak no | other language than that used in ships.' | *The Licenciate Vidriera.*' [*sic*]; [1]–107 text; [108] blank; 109–12 'GLOSSARY' (at foot of p.112: '[rule] | CHISWICK PRESS : PRINTED BY CHARLES WHITTINGHAM AND CO. | TOOKS COURT, CHANCERY LANE, LONDON.')

Paper: laid paper (watermark: '[crown] | Abbey Mills | Greenfield'), chain-lines 23mm. apart

Running title: 'SALT-WATER BALLADS' (39mm.) on verso; recto title comprises poem title, pp.2–107

Binding: blue cloth. On spine, in gold: 'SALT | WATER | BALLADS | JOHN | MASEFIELD | Elkin | Mathews' (all width centred). Covers: blank. Top edge trimmed, others uncut. Binding measurements: 195 × 129mm. (covers), 195 × 26mm. (spine). End-papers: laid paper (no watermark), chain-lines 25mm. apart

Publication date: published, according to Nelson, July 1913 in an edition of 1500 copies

Price: 3s.6d.

SALT-WATER
BALLADS

BY

JOHN MASEFIELD

GRANT RICHARDS
48 LEICESTER SQUARE
LONDON
1902

A1(a) title-page

SALT-WATER
BALLADS

BY

JOHN MASEFIELD

London
Alexander Moring, Ltd.
The De La More Press
32 George Street, Hanover Square, W

A1(aa) title-page

SALT-WATER
BALLADS

BY

JOHN MASEFIELD

LONDON
ELKIN MATHEWS, CORK STREET
M CM XIII

A1(b) title-page

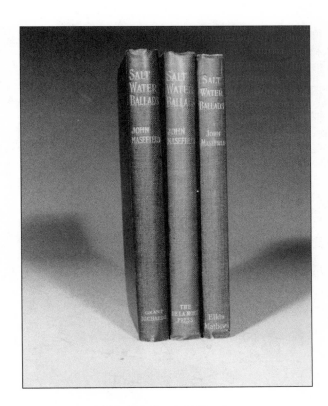

A1(a), A1(aa) and A1(b) spines

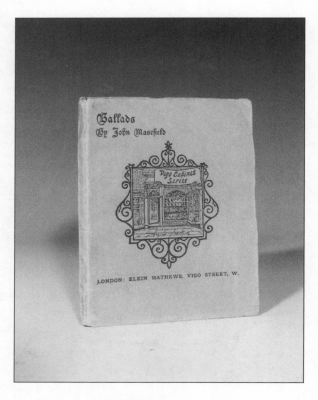

A2(a) spine and upper wrapper

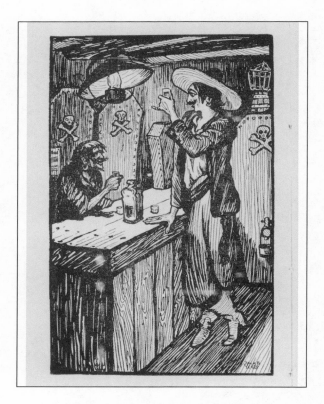

A3(a) frontispiece by Jack B. Yeats

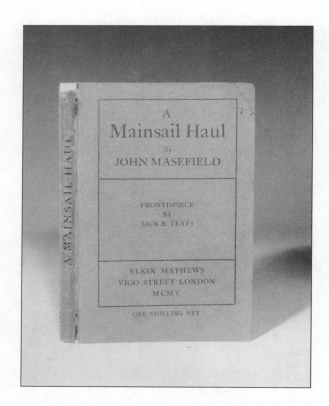

A3(a) spine and upper wrapper (paper issue)

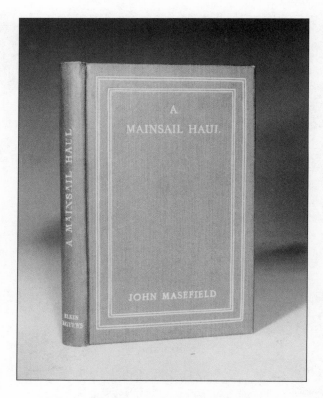

A3(a) spine and upper cover (cloth issue)

Contents:

A Consecration ('Not of the princes and prelates with periwigged charioteers')
The Yarn of The 'Loch Achray' ('The 'Loch Achray' was a clipper tall')
Sing a Song O' Shipwreck ('He lolled on a bollard, a sun-burned son of the sea,')
Burial-Party ("He's deader 'n nails,' the fo'c's'le said, "n' gone to his long sleep';')
Bill ('He lay dead on the cluttered deck and stared at the cold skies,')
Fever Ship ('There'll be no weepin' gells ashore when *our* ship sails,')
Fever-Chills ('He tottered out of the alleyway with cheeks the colour of paste,')
One of The Bo'sun's Yarns ('Loafin' around in Sailor Town, a-bluin' o' my advance,')
Hell's Pavement ("When I'm discharged in Liverpool 'n' draws my bit o' pay,')
Sea-Change ("Goneys an' gullies an' all o' the birds o' the sea,')
Harbour-Bar ('All in the feathered palm-tree tops the bright green parrots screech,')
The Turn of the Tide ('An' Bill can have my sea-boots, Nigger Jim can have my knife,')
One of Wally's Yarns ('The watch was up on the topsail-yard a-making fast the sail,')
A Valediction (Liverpool Docks) ('Is there anything as I can do ashore for you')
A Night at Dago Tom's ('Oh yesterday, I t'ink it was, while cruisin' down the street,')
'Port of Many Ships' ("It's a sunny pleasant anchorage, is Kingdom Come,')
Cape Horn Gospel – I ("I was in a hooker once,' said Karlssen,')
Cape Horn Gospel – II ('Jake was a dirty Dago lad, an' he gave the skipper chin,')
Mother Carey ('Mother Carey? She's the mother o' the witches')
Evening – Regatta Day ('Your nose is a red jelly, your mouth's a toothless wreck,')
A Valediction ('We're bound for blue water where the great winds blow,')
A Pier-Head Chorus ('Oh I'll be chewing salted horse and biting flinty bread,')
The Golden City of St. Mary ('Out beyond the sunset, could I but find the way,')
Trade Winds ('In the harbour, in the island, in the Spanish Seas,')
Sea-Fever ('I must down to the seas again, to the lonely sea and the sky,')
A Wanderer's Song ('A wind's in the heart of me, a fire's in my heels,')
Cardigan Bay ('Clean, green, windy billows notching out the sky,')
Christmas Eve at Sea ('A wind is rustling 'south and soft,"')
A Ballad of Cape St. Vincent ('Now, Bill, ain't it prime to be a-sailin',')
The Tarry Buccaneer ('I'm going to be a pirate with a bright brass pivot-gun,')
A Ballad of John Silver ('We were schooner-rigged and rakish, with a long and lissome hull,')
Lyrics from 'The Buccaneer'
I.   ('We are far from sight of the harbour lights,')
II. ('There's a sea-way somewhere where all day long')
III. ('The toppling rollers at the harbour mouth')
D'Avalos' Prayer ('When the last sea is sailed and the last shallow charted,')
The West Wind ('It's a warm wind, the west wind, full of birds' cries;')
The Galley-Rowers ('Staggering over the running combers')
Sorrow of Mydath ('Weary the cry of the wind is, weary the sea,')
Vagabond ('Dunno a heap about the what an' why,')
Vision ('I have drunken the red wine and flung the dice;')
Spunyarn ('Spunyarn, spunyarn, with one to turn the crank,')
The Dead Knight ('The cleanly rush of the mountain air,')
Personal ('Tramping at night in the cold and wet, I passed the lighted inn,')
On Malvern Hill ('A wind is brushing down the clover,')
Tewkesbury Road ('It is good to be out on the road, and going one knows not where,')
On Eastnor Knoll ('Silent are the woods, and the dim green boughs are')
'Rest Her Soul, She's Dead!' ('She has done with the sea's sorrow and the world's way')
'All Ye That Pass By' ('On the long dusty ribbon of the long city street,')
In Memory of A.P.R. ('Once in the windy wintry weather,')
To-Morrow ('Oh yesterday the cutting edge drank thirstily and deep,')
Cavalier ('All the merry kettle-drums are thudding into rhyme,')
A Song at Parting ('The tick of the blood is settling slow, my heart will soon be still,')
GLOSSARY ('Abaft the beam.—That half of a ship included between her amidship section…')

Notes:

A drop-capital 'N' commences 'A Consecration' which is unique to this edition.

Grant Richards, in *Author Hunting*, writes:

> It was always a matter of regret to me that *Salt Water Ballads* passed into the hands of Elkin Mathews, for Masefield, although I was commissioning him to write other books at the time and although we were in the most cordial relations and discussing many projects some of which matured and some of which came to nothing, would not allow me to reprint

it. On December 12 [1906] he wrote me from Hill Crest, Boar's Hill, Oxford [*sic*], regretting that he had kept me so long without an answer, "But I have been producing a play and haven't had a moment". He thanks me for taking "such an interest in *S.W.B.*" but he hasn't decided yet what to do about the book; "much will depend on events during the next few days, but I do not think in any case I shall be able to let you have the book". Cazenove, his agent, and I puzzled over his obduracy with regard to this book which had been his first and for the launching of which I had been responsible. That he should have preferred to place *all* his work with other publishers I should have been able to understand, but that he should refuse me permission to reprint *Salt Water Ballads* while letting me have almost everything else he was writing I could not understand.

(Grant Richards, *Author Hunting*, Hamish Hamilton, 1934, p.231)

Richards here fails to acknowledge the date as a major factor. Masefield presumably softened to his first volume between 1906 and 1913.

Commonly noted as a 'reissue' this volume constitutes a true second edition since the text has been entirely re-set. A comparison with A1(a) suggests that the text was set from a marked-up copy of the first edition for lineation is similar. Dedications and prefatory quotations were deleted but the text has not been extensively revised. Minor variants exist in use of italics and punctuation, there are two word changes (from 'in' to 'on' p.42, and from 'kine' to 'cows' p.96), and the abbreviation of 'o'' is lengthened (on at least seven occasions) to 'of'. A proof copy for the edition, in the Bodleian (with the original dedication crossed-out and the authorial note composed) is obviously derived from the 1902 Grant Richards edition. If this copy constitutes one set of unbound sheets it might confirm James G. Nelson's suggestion that Mathews took over Richards' stock (see James G. Nelson, *Elkin Mathews*, University of Wisconsin Press, 1989, p.234). It would, however, be contrary to the evidence of the De La More Press edition.

During April 1913 Masefield wrote to Elkin Mathews noting his liking for Richards' book production of A1(a) and suggesting an uniformity for Mathews' 1913 reissues:

Many thanks for your letter + for the Mainsail volume. ...Personally, I prefer the crown 8vo size to any other, + I think that *Salt Water Ballads* was quite the nicest looking book I have ever had. If you are going to reprint *Salt Water Ballads*, I shall be glad if you will make it as like the old vol as you can, blue linen + all, + I myself feel that the new *Mainsail* should be made uniform with it in every way, a neat blue linen crown 8vo book in good solid cover at 3/6. ...When you come to consider the re-issue of SW ballads, can you supply a copy to the printers? I have no copy of my own, + most of the friends to whom I gave copies seem to have sold theirs in the late boom.

(John Masefield, letter to Elkin Mathews, 7 April 1913)
(HRHRC, MS (Masefield, J.) Letters, ALS to Mathews 1913 April 7)

The publishing agreement for this title between Masefield and Elkin Mathews was dated 1 May 1913 (see Archives of The Society of Authors). The agreement refers to 1500 copies.

James G. Nelson, who numbers this edition as '1913.19' in his 'Checklist of the Mathews Imprint', provides details of production costs:

...the second edition of John Masefield's famous *Salt-Water Ballads* (1913) cost a total of £20.14.0 (including paper wrappers). According to Chiswick Press records, composing the old-style Long Primer type for the 126 pages cost £11.18.0 and printing the 1,500 copies cost £4.16.0. Printing 1,500 copies of the "wrapper in blue ink into 1 side only with blue tinted paper" cost only £1.10.0 (Add.Mss. 50,925).

(James G. Nelson, *Elkin Mathews*, University of Wisconsin Press, 1989, p.186)

A letter from the firm of 'Elkin Mathews Ltd' (founded after the death of Elkin Mathews) to Masefield reveals that Masefield presumably authorised each subsequent reprint:

Our stock of "Salt Water Ballads" is running low, and the terms of the agreement require your permission in writing before we can reprint. Would you be kind enough to send us an authorisation to print a new impression of 2000 copies?

(A.W. Evans, letter to John Masefield, 3 November 1922)
(BL, Add.Mss.56578, f.140)

The Archives of The Society of Authors record that an application to publish a Braille version of this text was received from the National Institute for the Blind in December 1930 (see BL, Add.Mss.56592, f.62). Masefield was always a supporter of books in Braille (see J90) and permission was granted for the Braille version in January 1931 (see BL, Add.Mss.56592, f.77)

Copies seen: private collection (PWE); BL (11660.b.13) stamped 4 SEP 1951; Harvard College Library (Houghton *EC9.M377.902sc)

Reprinted:

'Third Edition'	[second edition, second impression]	Nov 1913
'Fourth Edition'	[second edition, third impression]	Feb 1915
'Fifth Edition'	[second edition, fourth impression]	Feb 1916
'Sixth Edition'	[second edition, fifth impression]	Apr 1918
'Seventh Edition'	[second edition, sixth impression]	Jan 1920
'Eighth Edition'	[second edition, seventh impression]	Jan 1921
'Ninth Edition'	[second edition, eighth impression]	Feb 1923
'Tenth Edition'	[second edition, ninth impression]	Feb 1924

A1(c) First American edition (1913)

SALT-WATER | BALLADS | BY | JOHN MASEFIELD | New York | THE MACMILLAN COMPANY | 1913
(All width centred)

Bibliographies: Danielson [unrecorded], Williams [unrecorded], Simmons [noted on p.6], Nevinson [unrecorded], Handley-Taylor p.27, Wight 1c

Collation: [A–H]⁸ [I]⁴; 68 leaves; 187 × 128mm.; [i–vi] vii–xiii [xiv] 1–107 [108] 109–112 [113–22]

Page contents: [i] half-title: 'SALT-WATER BALLADS'; [ii] '[publisher's device] | THE MACMILLAN COMPANY | [two lines listing six cities, separated by four points] | MACMILLAN & CO., LIMITED | [two lines listing four cities, separated by two points] | THE MACMILLAN CO. OF CANADA, LTD. | [one city listed]'; [iii] title-page; [iv] 'Set up and electrotyped. Published September, 1913'; [v] 'Some of this book was written in my boyhood, | all of it in my youth; it is now re-issued, much | as it was when first published nearly eleven | years ago. J.M. | *9th June* 1913'; [vi] blank; vii–xiii 'CONTENTS' (52 individual poems listed with page references); [xiv] ''The mariners are a pleasant people, but little | like those in the towns, and they can speak no | other language than that used in ships.' | *The Licenciate Vidriera.*' [*sic*]; [1]–107 text; [108] blank; 109–112 'GLOSSARY' [113] 'The following pages contain advertisements of | books by the same author, and other poetry' (within ruled border: 15 × 76mm.); [114] blank; [115–19] publisher's advertisements; [120–22] blank

Paper: wove paper

Running title: 'SALT-WATER BALLADS' (42mm.) on verso; recto title comprises poem title, pp.2–107

Binding: burgundy cloth. On spine, in gold: 'SALT | WATER | BALLADS | MASEFIELD | MACMILLAN' (all width centred). On upper cover, in gold: 'SALT | WATER | BALLADS | MASEFIELD' (ranged upper left) (within blind ruled border: 188 × 121mm.) Lower cover: blank. Top edge gilt, others trimmed. Binding measurements: 193 × 127mm. (covers), 193 × 32mm. (spine). End-papers: wove paper

Publication date: published, according to Simmons, 17 September 1913 in an edition of 2832 copies. An advertisement from Macmillan within *The Publisher's Weekly* (New York) 27 September 1913 notes this edition as 'Ready Sept. 17'.

Price: $1.00

Contents:
as for A1(b)

Notes:
This edition derives from the 1913 Elkin Mathews edition (see A1(b)). It is not, however, directly taken from any setting of text made by Mathews. The statement on page [iv] reveals that this edition was electrotyped and there are minor typographical differences between editions. The drop capital 'N' of 'A Consecration' is, for example, missing here.

The publishing agreement for this title between Masefield and Macmillan was dated 18 August 1913 (see Archives of The Society of Authors). The agreement refers to 'a licence to publish in volume form in the United States of America a work the subject or title of which is Salt-Water Ballads, New and Revised Edition'.

The poem 'Port of Many Ships' lacks a second single inverted comma within the text (it is present in the contents listing).

Copies seen: BL (X.908/4299) stamped 15 JUN 1963; HRHRC (PR6025 A77 S3 1913)

Reprinted:

'Reprinted'

Apr 1915
Jan 1916
Sep 1953 ('re-issue' noted by Handley-Taylor)
1955 (noted by Handley-Taylor)
1957 (noted by Handley-Taylor)

A1(d) Third English edition (2002)

SALT-WATER | BALLADS | John Masefield | Introduction by Philip W. Errington, Department of | Printed Books and Manuscripts, Sotheby's, and Visiting | Research Fellow, University of London | [publisher's device within double ruled border: 24 × 24mm.] | THE CYDER PRESS | Cheltenham, England
(All width centred)

Publication date: published, on 28 September 2002 in an edition of 400 copies (pre-launch copies were available from August 2002)

Price: £5.00

Contents:
Introduction ('John Betjeman claimed that John Masefield's 'Sea-Fever' would be 'remembered as long as the language lasts'…)
        (signed, 'Philip W. Errington | London')
and as for A1(a)

Notes:

This edition provides a facsimile reprint of A1(a) with an added introduction.

The ISBN number is ISBN 1 86174 124 3

The Cyder Press is an imprint established by the University of Gloucestershire.

The edition was issued in wrappers.

Copies seen: private collection (PWE)

A2 BALLADS   1903

A2(a) First English edition (1903)

BALLADS | BY | JOHN MASEFIELD | LONDON | ELKIN MATHEWS, VIGO STREET | 1903
(All width centred)

Bibliographies: Danielson 160, Williams p.1, Simmons [2], Nevinson p.12, Handley-Taylor p.27, Wight [2]

Collation: [A]⁸ B-C⁸ D⁴; B2 and C2 are also signed; signatures right foot of page; 28 leaves; 157 × 121mm.; [1–6] 7 [8] 9–56

Page contents: [1] half-title: 'BALLADS'; [2] blank; [3] title-page; [4] blank; [5] 'TO MY WIFE'; [6] 'I thank the Editors of the *Broad Sheet, Green | Sheaf, Pall Mall Magazine*, and *Speaker*, for | permission to reprint the Ballads in this volume. | J. M.'; 7 'Contents' (19 individual poems listed with page references and two line note: 'NOTE.–Some of these Ballads will be issued separately with the | score of the music proper to them. | J. M.'); [8] blank; 9–56 text (at foot of p.56: '[rule] | PRINTED BY R. FOLKARD AND SON, 22, DEVONSHIRE STREET, | QUEEN SQUARE, LONDON, W.C.')

Paper: wove paper

Running title: running titles comprise titles of individual poems, pp.10–56

Binding: green wrappers. Spine blank. On upper wrapper: 'Ballads | By John Masefield [ranged upper left corner, justified on left border] | [centred device: 94 × 78mm., signed 'S.C.' showing bookshop with 'Vigo Cabinet | Series' in banner ranged upper right and 'FRUCTUS INTER FOLIA' centred on pavement] | LONDON: ELKIN MATHEWS, VIGO STREET, W. [centred at foot of page]'. On lower wrapper, in black: publisher's device: 52 × 34mm., at the foot of which is printed 'Fructus inter | folia' with three sides surrounded by design of intertwined leaves and acorns. On inside of upper wrapper: 'The Vigo Cabinet Series | *An Occasional Miscellany of Prose and Verse | One Shilling, net, each Part*' numbers 1–6 listed with reviews. On inside of lower wrapper numbers 7–18 listed. Top and fore edges uncut, lower edge uncut. Binding measurements: 165 × 129mm. (covers), 165 × 7mm. (spine)

Publication date: published, according to Simmons, 26 October 1903 in an edition of 762 copies

Price: 1s.

Contents:

The Ballad of Sir Bors ('Would I could win some quiet and rest, and a little ease,')
> *No previous appearance traced*

Spanish Waters ('Spanish waters, Spanish waters, you are ringing in my ears,')
> *Published in a substantially different form as 'Blind Man's Vigil' in* The Green Sheaf *1903, No.7. This is not the poem of the same title beginning 'Mumblin' under the gallows, hearin' the clank o' the chain,'. It commences 'I'm a tattered starving beggar fiddling down the dirty streets,'. Two stanzas were printed in* A Broad Sheet *May 1903 with variants from* The Green Sheaf *version. Both periodical versions differ from the poem as printed here*

Cargoes ('Quinquireme of Nineveh from distant Ophir,')
> *First printed in* A Broad Sheet *May 1903*

Captain Stratton's Fancy ('Oh some are fond of red wine, and some are fond of white')
> *First printed in* The Speaker *9 May 1903, p.141*

News from Whydah ('Oh did you come by Whydah Roads, my tarry Buccaneer O ?')
> *No previous appearance traced*

St. Mary's Bells ('It's pleasant in Holy Mary')
> *No previous appearance traced*

London Town ('Oh London Town's a fine town, and London sights are rare,')
> *First printed in* The Pall Mall Magazine *May 1903, p.5*

The Emigrant ('Going by Daly's shanty I heard the boys within')
> *No previous appearance traced*

Port of Holy Peter ('The blue laguna rocks and quivers,')
> *First printed in* A Broad Sheet *December 1902*

Beauty ('I have seen dawn and sunset on moors and windy hills,')
> *First printed in* The Speaker *4 July 1903, p.322*

The Seekers ('Friends and loves we have none, nor wealth, nor blessed abode,')
> *No previous appearance traced*

Hall Sands ('The moon is bright on Devon sands,')
>> *First printed in* The Speaker *16 May 1903, p.163*

Dawn ('The dawn comes cold : the haystack smokes,')
>> *First printed in* The Speaker *15 August 1903, p.460*

Laugh and be Merry ('Laugh and be merry, remember, better the world with a song,')
>> *No previous appearance traced*

Blind Man's Vigil ('Mumblin' under the gallows, hearin' the clank o' the chain,')
>> *First printed in* A Broad Sheet *May 1903. This poem should not be confused with 'Blind Man's Vigil' in* The Green Sheaf *1903, No.7*

Roadways ('One road leads to London,')
>> *First printed in* The Speaker *2 May 1903, p.119*

Midsummer Night ('The perfect disc of the sacred moon')
>> *No previous appearance traced*

The Harper's Song ('This sweetness trembling from the strings')
>> *First printed in* The Speaker *7 March 1903, p.557*

The Gentle Lady ('So beautiful, so dainty-sweet')
>> *No previous appearance traced*

Notes:

The publishing agreement for this title between Masefield and Elkin Mathews was dated 22 July 1903 (see Archives of The Society of Authors). The agreement refers to a printing of only 500 copies. This was, presumably, later revised.

Unique to this edition are notes, quotations and notification of relevant airs for many of the ballads. These prefix the ballads.

A copy of this edition held in W.B. Yeats' library, in Dalkey, Ireland (*1240) is inscribed 'To W.B. Yeats. | with John Masefield's | best wishes. | Oct. 23, 1903.' This pre-dates Simmons' date of publication.

Ballads is number 13 in 'The Vigo Cabinet Series'. In Nelson's 'Checklist of the Mathews Imprint', this volume is numbered 1903.12.

Copies seen: private collection (PWE) inscribed by John Todhunter, 'Edwin J. Ellis | from | J. Todhunter | Christmas 1903'; BL (12205.w.3/13) stamped 26 OCT 1903; BL (Ashley 1108); Bodleian (28001.f.63) stamped 2.11.1903

A2(b)   Second English edition (1910)

BALLADS | BY | JOHN MASEFIELD | LONDON | ELKIN MATHEWS, VIGO STREET | M CM X
(All width centred)

Bibliographies: Danielson [unrecorded], Williams [unrecorded], Simmons [unrecorded], Nevinson [unrecorded], Handley-Taylor [unrecorded], Wight 2a

Collation: [B]⁸ C-E⁸; C2, D2 and E2 are also signed; signatures right foot of page; 32 leaves; 152 × 121mm.; [1–6] 7–62 [63–64]

Page contents: [1] half-title: 'BALLADS'; [2] blank; [3] title-page; [4] '*Second Edition, April,* 1910, | *Revised and Enlarged.*'; [5] 'TO MY WIFE'; [6] 'NOTE TO THE SECOND EDITION. | These Ballads were written in youth. I will not | apologize for having been young. | [new paragraph] Some of the ballads in this Edition have been added | from an earlier volume (now out of print) to take the | place of those which I have omitted. | [new paragraph] I thank the Editor of the *Manchester Guardian* for | allowing me to reprint the lines entitled "An old | Song re-sung." I also thank the Editor of the *Pall* | *Mall Magazine* for permission to include the lines | entitled "Posted as Missing." | J. M.'; 7–8 'Contents' (24 individual poems listed with page references); 9-[63] text (at foot of p.[63]: '[rule] | LONDON: PRINTED BY WILLIAM CLOWES AND SONS, LIMITED.'); [64] publisher's advertisements: 'BOOKS BY JOHN MASEFIELD'

Paper: laid paper (no watermark), chain-lines 25mm. apart

Running title: running titles comprise titles of individual poems, pp.10-[63]

Binding: turquoise-green wrappers. Spine blank. On upper wrapper: as for A2(a) with the exception that 'Ballads' is indented from the left margin. On lower wrapper: as for A2(a). On inside of upper wrapper: 'The Vigo Cabinet Series | *An Occasional Miscellany of Prose and Verse* | Royal 16mo. One Shilling, net, each Part.' numbers 1–40 (excepting deleted numbers) listed. On inside of lower wrapper numbers 41–71 listed. All edges trimmed. Binding measurements: 158 × 128mm. (covers), 158 × 5mm. (spine)

Also issued in light green cloth. On spine, lettering in gold reading lengthways up spine, from foot: 'BALLADS JOHN | MASEFIELD' (the author's first name is immediately above the surname and both are in smaller type than the title); horizontal at foot of spine: 'ELKIN | MATHEWS'. On upper cover, in gold: 'Ballads' (ranged upper left) and 'John Masefield' (ranged lower right). All edges trimmed. Binding measurements: 157 × 125mm. (covers), 157 × 15mm. (spine). End-papers: either wove paper or laid paper (both variants exist)

Publication date: published, according to date within volume, April 1910

Price: 1s. (wrappers) / 1s.6d. (cloth)

Contents:

The Ballad of Sir Bors ('Would I could win some quiet and rest, and a little ease,')
Spanish Waters ('Spanish waters, Spanish waters, you are ringing in my ears,')

Cargoes ('Quinquireme of Nineveh from distant Ophir,')
Captain Stratton's Fancy ('Oh some are fond of red wine, and some are fond of white,')
An old Song re-sung ('I saw a ship a-sailing, a-sailing, a-sailing,')
> *First printed in* The Manchester Guardian, *exact location untraced but a cutting is present in the Masefield Collection of the ULL (Special Collections)*

St. Mary's Bells ('It's pleasant in Holy Mary')
London Town ('Oh London Town's a fine town, and London sights are rare,')
The Emigrant ('Going by Daly's shanty I heard the boys within')
Port of Holy Peter ('The blue laguna rocks and quivers,')
Beauty ('I have seen dawn and sunset on moors and windy hills')
The Seekers ('Friends and loves we have none, nor wealth, nor blessed abode,')
Prayer ('When the last sea is sailed, when the last shallow's charted,')
> *Previously printed as 'D'Avalos' Prayer' in* Salt-Water Ballads

Dawn ('The dawn comes cold : the haystack smokes,')
Laugh and be Merry ('Laugh and be merry, remember, better the world with a song,')
June Twilight ('The twilight comes; the sun')
> *First printed as 'A June Twilight' in* The Speaker *11 June 1904, p.249*

Roadways ('One road leads to London,')
Midsummer Night ('The perfect disc of the sacred moon')
The Harper's Song ('The sweetness trembling from the strings')
The Gentle Lady ('So beautiful, so dainty-sweet,')
The Dead Knight ('The cleanly rush of the mountain air,')
> *Previously printed in* Salt-Water Ballads

Sorrow of Mydath ('Weary the cry of the wind is, weary the sea,')
> *Previously printed in* Salt-Water Ballads

Twilight ('Twilight it is, and the far woods are dim, and the rooks cry and call.')
> *First printed as 'To An Old Tune' in* The Speaker *9 December 1905, p.254*

Invocation ('O wanderer into many brains,')
> *First printed in* The Englishwoman *February 1909, p.16*

Posted as Missing ('Under all her topsails she trembled like a stag,')
> *First printed in* The Pall Mall Magazine *September 1906, p.303*

Notes:

Ballads added for this edition are 'An old Song re-sung', 'Prayer', 'June Twilight', 'The Dead Knight', 'Sorrow of Mydath', 'Twilight', 'Invocation' and 'Posted as Missing'. Of these, 'An old Song re-sung', 'June Twilight', 'Twilight', 'Invocation' and 'Posted as Missing' appear in book form for the first time. The other three are from *Salt-Water Ballads*. Ballads deleted from this edition and thus only appearing in A2(a) are 'News from Whydah', 'Hall Sands' and 'Blind Man's Vigil'.

Masefield wrote to his agent during February 1910 making reference to this 'unimportant book' and asking Cazenove to arrange an agreement:

> Some years ago, Elkin Mathews published my youthful verses. He now wants to print a new edition of them. I am inclined to make the book rather bigger; + want to have a new agreement. Any agreement will probably satisfy E.M. It is an unimportant book. He undertook to give me 15% royalty on the 1st edition. You might, if you will be so kind, ask him to give me 17½% on the new edition. The Book is called Ballads. It is to contain 64 (small) pages. Will you be so kind as to arrange the new agreement for me? I hesitate to ask you, because the profits on the little shilling book are so tiny that it's hardly worth your while.
>
> (John Masefield, letter to C.F. Cazenove, 7 February 1910)
> (University of Arizona Library. MS.50, V.II)

It appears that a single publishing agreement covered the second English edition of *Ballads* (A2(b)) and the first English edition of *Ballads and Poems* (A12(a)). The agreement was signed between Masefield and Elkin Mathews. It was dated 22 March 1910. The agreement refers to '…a collection of Ballads by the Author printing and publishing the same in two (2) separate volumes whereof the first book shall contain sixty-four (64) pages and the second shall contain one hundred (100) pages…' (see Archives of The Society of Authors).

The text is revised and entirely re-set for this edition. A location for where each poem was written is given to most poems for the first time. These locations comprise: Compton, Coram Street, The Edinburgh Express, Gt. Comberton, Henrietta Street, Hyde Park Mansions, Tettenhall and The York Express. 'Invocation' and 'Posted as Missing' are not ascribed locations although the latter acquires one in *Ballads and Poems*.

Ballads and Poems, consisting of the second edition of *Ballads* (a verbatim reprint retaining the 'missing' [A] gathering) and nineteen additional poems, was first published in September 1910 (with many subsequent reprints) (see A12(a)). A 'third edition' of *Ballads* (a verbatim reprint of the second and thus technically the 'second edition, second impression') was printed in April 1911. Any later impressions (or editions) of *Ballads* have not been traced. The April 1911 *Ballads* (printed as the 'third edition') may have been published because *Ballads* was part of the Vigo Cabinet Series and thus available at 1s. in comparison to *Ballads and Poems* (albeit with nineteen additional poems) at 2s.6d.

Simmons and Handley-Taylor state *Ballads* was 'reprinted, with additional poems, with the title *Ballads and Poems*, by Elkin Mathews in 1910; and in 1911 with the title *Ballads*, the contents consisting of selections from both the 1903 and the 1910 editions.' This statement is confusing and distorts the chronology without reference to the true second edition of *Ballads*. The second edition of *Ballads* is similarly confused by James G. Nelson who merely notes the edition under 1903.12 in his listing while providing the 'third edition' [second edition – second impression] with a separate number (1911.6).

A letter dated 30 November 1912 from Masefield to Elkin Mathews includes the statement 'I am rather keen on killing Ballads as a book, & having B & P alone. What do you think?' (see John Masefield, letter to Elkin Mathews, 30 November 1912) (Private Collection (AH)). It is evidently this point, and not before as Simmons and Handley-Taylor may suggest, that *Ballads* dropped out of print with its disappearance already covered by the existence since 1910 of *Ballads and Poems*.

There exist two proof copies for this edition (both in the Masefield Collection of the University of London Library (Special Collections)). The earliest includes the date 1910 on the title page but although printed by William Clowes and Sons it is, essentially, the same as the 1903 first edition (original note and contents are present although there are minor typographical differences (the layout of 'The Emigrant', for example)). The collation ([B]⁸ C-D⁸ E⁴) revealing the 'missing' A gathering for the first time is closer, however, to that of the second edition. The paper wrappers list the Vigo Cabinet Series until number 68 and the whole is unsewn. It bears Masefield's posthumous booklabel but there are no authorial markings. Another proof copy also includes the date of '1910' on the title page (but again not 'M CM X'), is printed by William Clowes and Sons and is the obvious precursor to the second edition (the revised note and contents being present). The collation ([B]⁸ C-E⁸) also reveals the similarity. There are typographical differences, however, between this and the second edition (different settings of the title page and the note to the second edition, for example). The sheets are bound in green suede and an inscription on p.[1] reads 'For | Gerald Bishop, | Wishing him all happiness | from his friend John Masefield | April 18. 1910.' There are two authorial markings: the substitution of 'April' for 'March' on p.[4] and indication of damaged type on p.35 (to the final 'l' of 'Tettenhall'.)

In late 1940 the business successors of Elkin Mathews (Ivor Nicholson and Son) went into voluntary liquidation. The remaining stock (19 copies of *Salt-Water Ballads*, 51 copies of *A Mainsail Haul* and 59 copies of *Ballads and Poems*) was offered to Masefield (see BL, Add.Mss.56614, f.25). The Society of Authors wrote to the liquidator stating Masefield's offer and supposing that a settlement 'would include the cancellation of the existing agreements' (see BL, Add.Mss.56614, f.33). Masefield sent a cheque for the remaining stock by 12 December 1940. *Ballads* seems to have been overlooked, however. In 1943 Stanley Unwin noted he had 230 unbound copies, acquired when Unwin bought the remaining stock of the liquidated company. Masefield appealed to The Society of Authors:

> ...I bought, through the Society, the remainder stocks of 3 books which Elkin Matthews [*sic*] once published for me. All 3 books are honestly dead, but now here comes a ghost of one to gibber at me. Can it be laid?
>
> (John Masefield, letter to E.J. Mullett, [16 August 1943])
>
> (BL, Add.Mss.56616, f.180)

Masefield wrote again, later in the month:

> I am sorry that the Ballads matter has given you so much trouble. One or two points are not clear to me.
>
> a) Is the agreement at an end, as I supposed, when I bought the stock 3 years ago? It is impossible for anyone save myself to reprint the book?
>
> b) If Mr Unwin binds and sells the existing copies have I any claim to royalty? I judge, but am not sure, that the agreement is ended, but that Mr Unwin may bind and sell the copies without paying royalty.
>
> My chief aim is to end the agreement and to be sure that it is ended. All the book is reprinted in my Collected Poems, and the sale of the small single volume has for years ceased, or almost ceased, and so, I judge, Mr Unwin will find. I, personally, do not want the copies, nor do I suppose that if Heinemanns bought them they would be able to sell them in the next 20 years; but I do wish to be sure, that this small book will not be reprinted under the old Elkin Matthews [*sic*] agreement.
>
> (John Masefield, letter to E.J. Mullett, [27 August 1943])
>
> (BL, Add.Mss.56616, f.174)

Legal advice over sales suggested that Masefield could have no objection to Unwin placing the books on the market, but that Unwin would have to pay Masefield a royalty. Masefield, however, stated he was willing to forgo any royalty if Unwin gave an assurance that the book would not be reprinted after the 230 copies were sold. This was unnecessary. The Society of Authors wrote to Masefield during October:

> ...Unwin has accepted our proposal that he be permitted to place on sale the 230 copies, paying you 10% royalty on the copies sold, it being understood that he is not to reprint the poem[s]. He adds, in regard to the other two books A MAINSAIL HAUL & SALT WATER BALLADS, "As we have no stock of either of the other books referred to, they are no concern of ours and we are not entitled to reprint either of these books any more than we are of the BALLADS."
>
> (E.J. Mullett, letter to John Masefield, 11 October 1943)
>
> (BL, Add.Mss.56616)

It appears, therefore, that these copies were bound and sold. No example has been located.

Copies seen: BL (011650.de.44) stamped 3 AUG 1910 cloth binding; ULL (Special Collections) cloth binding; ULL (Special Collections) wrappers

Reprinted:

'Third Edition'   [second edition, second impression]   Apr 1911

A3 A MAINSAIL HAUL

A3(a) First English edition (1905)

A | Mainsail Haul | By | JOHN MASEFIELD | [rule, 81mm.] [in red] | FRONTISPIECE | BY | JACK B. YEATS | [rule, 81mm.] [in red] | ELKIN MATHEWS | VIGO STREET LONDON | M CM V
(All width centred and enclosed within red ruled border: 128 × 82mm. As a result of the two rules noted above, three rectangles are created measuring 50 × 82mm., 51 × 82mm. and 28 × 82mm. respectively from the top. Six lines in total appear although none completely touches)

Bibliographies: Danielson 161, Williams p.7, Simmons [3], Nevinson p.15, Handley-Taylor p.27, Wight [3] and 3–1

Collation: [1]⁹ ([1]2+1) 2–8⁸; signatures right foot of page; 65 leaves; 171 × 105mm.; [1–13] 14–18 [19–21] 22–26 [27–29] 30–34 [35–37] 38–42 [43–45] 46–50 [51–53] 54–70 [71–73] 74–78 [79–81] 82–86 [87–89] 90–94 [95–97] 98–103 [104–07] 108–13 [114–17] 118–28 [129–30]

Page contents: [1] half-title: 'A MAINSAIL | HAUL'; [2] frontispiece: 127 × 82mm., of a pirate's bar room, signed 'JACK B | YEATS', with protective tissue; [3] title-page; [4] '*All Rights Reserved*'; [5] untitled verse ('I yarned with ancient shipmen beside the galley range,'); [6] blank; [7] '*To the Memory of Wallace Blair A.B.* | *My kind old Friend and Shipmate*'; [8] blank; [9] 'NOTE | THE best of these tales were told to me by an | old sailor of the name of Wallace Blair, who | taught seamanship aboard H.M.S. "Conway." | The others were gathered on my travels. Nearly | all the tales have appeared in the *Manchester* | *Guardian*. I thank the Editor of that paper | for his permission to reprint them here.'; [10] blank; [11] 'Contents' (12 stories listed with titles and page references); [12] blank; [13]–128 text; [129–30] blank

Paper: laid paper (no watermark), chain-lines 24mm. apart

Running title: 'A MAINSAIL HAUL' (31mm.) on verso; recto title comprises story title, pp.14–128

Binding: green wrappers. On spine, reading lengthways up spine, from foot: 'A MAINSAIL HAUL'. On upper wrapper: as title-page with 'ONE SHILLING NET' centred at the foot. On lower wrapper: 'From Elkin Mathews' List' (seven titles listed). On inside of upper wrapper: 'From Elkin Mathews' List' (nine titles listed). On inside of lower wrapper: 'From Elkin Mathews' List' (five titles listed). All edges trimmed. Binding measurements: 171 × 106mm. (wrappers); 171 × 12mm. (spine)

Also issued in green cloth (see notes). On spine, in white reading lengthways up spine, from foot: 'A MAINSAIL HAUL'; horizontally at foot of spine: 'ELKIN | MATHEWS'. On upper cover, in white: 'A | MAINSAIL HAUL | JOHN MASEFIELD' within two double ruled borders: 161 × 96mm., 158 × 93mm., 146 × 81mm. and 143 × 78mm. Lower cover: blank. All edges uncut. Binding measurements: 178 × 109mm. (covers), 178 × 26mm. (spine). End-papers: laid paper (no watermark), chain-lines 24mm. apart

Publication date: published, according to Simmons, 1 June 1905 in an edition of 1000 copies. The *English Catalogue of Books* records a publication date of May 1905

Price: 1s. (wrappers) / 1s.6d. (cloth)

Contents:

[Untitled Verse] ('I yarned with ancient shipmen beside the galley range,')
> *First printed in* The Manchester Guardian *26 October 1904*

Don Alfonso's Treasure Hunt ('Now in the old days, before steam, there was...')
> *First printed in* The Manchester Guardian *7 December 1904*

Port of Many Ships ('Sometimes in the afternoons, when I was a lad, I had...')
> *First printed in* The Manchester Guardian *2 April 1904, p.4*

Sea Superstition ('One moonlit night in the tropics, as my ship was slipping south...')
> *First printed in* The Manchester Guardian *5 December 1903, p.7*

A Sailor's Yarn ('Down the jetty, where the tide ran, where the wet green weed lay...')
> *First printed in* The Manchester Guardian *23 January 1904, p.5*

The Yarn of Lanky Job ('When I was in hospital in Valparaiso, I spent my evenings...')
> *First printed in* The Manchester Guardian *16 July 1904, p.7*

A Deal of Cards ('A company of seamen sat round a cabin table, and pledged each...')
> *No previous appearance traced*

Charlie Cotton ('Some years ago, when I was tramping in America, sleeping in barns...')
> *First printed in* The Manchester Guardian *11 August 1904, p.10*

A Spanish Sailor's Yarn ('Some years ago I was on board a schooner plying between...')
> *First printed in* The Manchester Guardian *19 May 1904, p.12*

In a New York Saloon ('Some years ago, at the beginning of a sultry summer...')
> *First printed in* The Manchester Guardian *27 September 1904, p.12*

A Monthly Allowance ('When I was working as a potboy in this way in New York...')
> *First printed in* The Manchester Guardian *25 October 1904, p.12*

From the Spanish ('The galleon *Spanish Rose* was built in Saint Mary of the Bells...')
> *First printed as 'A Spanish Love Tale' in* The Manchester Guardian *8 October 1904, p.7*

The Devil and the Old Man ('Up away north, in the old days, in Chester, there was...')
> *First printed as 'A Deep Sea Yarn' in* The Green Sheaf *1903 No.6, pp.4–9. Also as 'The Devil And The Deep Sea' in* The Manchester Guardian *23 March 1905, p.14*

Notes:

The title-page (and protective tissue for frontispiece) has been tipped-in onto the second leaf of the first gathering. Signature numbers 2–4 are in a smaller type than signatures 5–8. (With the exception of signature 8, these smaller signatures occur on otherwise blank leaves except for the printed title of the following story). 'Don Alfonso's Treasure Hunt' is the only story in the collection to commence with a drop-capital ('N') measuring 9 × 10mm.

The printer is unidentified. (James G. Nelson, however, names the Chiswick Press).

Wight describes the cloth binding as 'First Edition' and numbers this [3]. The paper wrapper binding is separately described as 'Another First Edition' and numbered 3–1. There are at least two different variants in the green cloth used for binding. The more common can be described as 'light green' and was presumably the earlier binding. The other colour may be described as 'dark green'.

It appears that Masefield offered at least one other publisher this work before publication was arranged with Mathews. Writing to A.H. Bullen in February 1905, Masefield notes:

> …I am anxious to publish a little volume of tales of the sea, sea-superstitions, legends of the pirates, etc, before the autumn. Most of the stories have appeared in the "Manchester Guardian". Would you care to consider them? They would not demand a very elaborate dress.

(John Masefield, letter to A.H. Bullen, 19 February 1905)
(HRHRC, MS (Masefield, J.) ALS to Frank Sidgwick, 1905 Feb. 19)

The publishing agreement for this title between Masefield and Elkin Mathews was dated 10 March 1905 (see Archives of The Society of Authors).

A copy of this edition held in W.B. Yeats' library, in Dalkey, Ireland (1251) is inscribed 'W.B. Yeats. | from John Masefield. 27. 5. 1905.' This pre-dates Simmons' date of publication.

In an undated letter (but presumed to be 12 April 1905), Masefield writes to Jack B. Yeats:

> The proofs of a mainsail haul have now come and gone. I am rather fed up with the tales + I don't know whether they are up to much, but your picture sets them off... They ought to be out in a few weeks' time – by the end of April anyway – if Elkin bucks up.

(John Masefield, letter to Jack B. Yeats, [12 April 1905])
(Harvard, *61M–93)

Since publication did not occur until June, Elkin Mathews evidently did not buck up.

In James G. Nelson's 'Checklist of the Mathews Imprint', this volume is numbered 1905.10. It is noted as the third title in Mathews' Satchel Series. Danielson notes it as the fourth title. A brief reference to the volume is included on page 65 of Nelson's work.

The volume is frequently provided with the sub-title 'Nautical Yarns' in advertisements from Elkin Mathews. Such an advertisement is present in Mathews' edition of John Hamilton Reynolds' *The Fancy* (see B25).

Copies seen: BL (012643.aaa.54) stamped 1 JUN 1905 cloth binding; ULL (Special Collections) cloth binding; ULL (Special Collections) wrappers; NYPL (Berg Collection) wrappers, includes signature of 'A. Gregory' and tipped-in fragment of letter: 'Will you accept from me this little book of ungrammatical and undramatic stories, for which Jack Yeats has done so jolly a frontispiece?'; HRHRC (AC-L M377 1905A) wrappers

A3(b) Second English edition (1913)

A MAINSAIL | HAUL | BY | JOHN MASEFIELD | FRONTISPIECE BY | JACK B. YEATS | [ornament] | LONDON | ELKIN MATHEWS, CORK STREET | M CM XIII
(All width centred)

Bibliographies: Danielson [noted on p.132], Williams [unrecorded], Simmons [3a], Nevinson [unrecorded], Handley-Taylor p.27, Wight [3a]

Collation: [A]⁴ B-N⁸ (J not used); signatures width centred at foot of page; 100 leaves; 188 × 123mm.; [i–viii] [1] 2–189 [190–92]

Page contents: [i] half-title: 'A MAINSAIL HAUL'; [ii] frontispiece: 139 × 89mm., of a pirate's bar room, signed 'JACK B | YEATS'; [iii] title-page; [iv] 'First Published . . . . June 1st, 1905 | *Second Edition, Revised* | *and much Enlarged* . . July 1913 | *All Rights Reserved*'; [v] untitled verse ('I yarned with ancient shipmen beside the galley range') dated '1904.'; [vi] blank; [vii] 'CONTENTS' (16 stories listed with titles and page references); [viii] blank; [1]–189 text; [190] 'NOTE | NEARLY all these stories and one of the historical | papers first appeared in the *Manchester Guardian,* | one tale is reprinted from the *Nation* and one from | the *Pall Mall Magazine.* The four remaining | historical papers are reprinted from the *Gentleman's* | *Magazine.* | [new paragraph] I thank the Editors and Proprietors of all these | periodicals for permission to include the papers in | this volume.'; [191] blank; [192] '[printer's device of lion, anchor and fish] | CHISWICK PRESS : CHARLES WHITTINGHAM AND CO. | TOOKS COURT, CHANCERY LANE, LONDON.'

Paper: laid paper (watermark: '[Crown] | Abbey Mills | Greenfield'), chain-lines 24mm. apart

Running title: 'A MAINSAIL HAUL' (32mm.) on verso; recto title comprises story title, pp.2–189

Binding: blue cloth. On spine, in gold: 'A | MAINSAIL | HAUL | JOHN | MASEFIELD | Elkin | Mathews' (all width centred). Covers: blank. Top edge trimmed, others uncut. Binding measurements: 195 × 127mm. (covers), 195 × 32mm. (spine). End-papers: laid paper (no watermark), chain-lines 25mm. apart

Publication date: published, according to Nelson, 17 July 1913 in an edition of 1500 copies

Price: 3s.6d.

Contents:
[Untitled Verse] ('I yarned with ancient shipmen beside the galley range')
Don Alfonso's Treasure Hunt ('Now in the old days, before steam, there was...')
Port of Many Ships ('"Down in the sea, very far down, under five miles of water...')
Sea Superstition ('One moonlit night in the tropics, as my ship was slipping south...')
A Sailor's Yarn ('"Once upon a time there was a clipper ship called the *Mary*...')
The Yarn of Lanky Job ('Lanky Job was a lazy Bristol sailor, notorious for his...')
From The Spanish ('The galleon *Spanish Rose* was built in Saint Mary of the Bells...')
The Seal Man ('"The seals is pretty when they do be playing," said the old woman.')
    First printed as 'The Seal-Man A Tale Of The North Coast Of Ireland' in The Manchester Guardian *12 April 1907, p.12*
The Western Islands ('"Once there were two sailors; and one of them was Joe...')
    First printed as 'The Western Islands. A Sea Fable' in The Pall Mall Magazine *December 1907, pp.813–15*
Captain John Ward ('Captain John Ward, our "most notorious pirate," was born at...')
    First printed in The Gentleman's Magazine *March 1906, pp.113–26*
Captain John Jennings ('It is not known where John Jennings was born; but it was...')
    First printed in The Gentleman's Magazine *December 1906, pp.561–73*
The Voyage of The *Cygnet* ('In the year 1683–4 some eminent London merchants...')
    First printed in The Gentleman's Magazine *April 1906, pp.243–54*
Captain Robert Knox ('Between the years 1690 and 1714, at odd times between...')
    First printed in The Manchester Guardian *9 June 1911, p.14*
Captain Coxon ('Eight generations ago, the island of Carmen, in the Lagoon of Tides...')
    First printed in The Gentleman's Magazine *July 1906, pp.1–10*
In a Castle Ruin ('"Very long ago," said the old man, "the castle was owned by...')
    First printed as 'The Dragon Man' in The Nation *12 October 1907, pp.41–42*
A Deal of Cards ('A company of seamen sat round a cabin table, and pledged each...')
The Devil and the Old Man ('Up away north, in the old days, in Chester, there was...')

Notes:
A comparison with A3(a) reveals this edition to have been significantly revised, edited and enlarged. Previously a book of tales and reminiscences (often in the first-person), this edition has a more distanced writer and the historical sketches alter the emphasis of the book. All mention of Wallace Blair (to whom the first edition was dedicated) has been removed.

The records of the Chiswick Press provide details of production costs (BL, Add.Mss.50925, f.214). The entry (also noted by James G. Nelson in *Elkin Mathews*, pp.186–87) is as follows:

1913. July 7				
Composing A Mainsail Haul (by J. Masefield) 6 sheets of 32pp.				
Double Crown 16mo (in O.S. Long primer leaded)	Est. 63/-	19	13	9
Extra for small type mixture		1	9	6
Corrections and alterations in proofs		2	5	–
Printing 1500 copies of 6 sheets of 32 pages = 9 Reams	16/-	7	4	–
Printing 1500 copies of 8 pages (¼ sheet)			10	–
Extra for overlay to Illustration (frontispiece)			2	–
Printing 1500 copies of Cap. Wrappers in blue into one side only with				
blue tinted paper for same and cutting		1	10	–
Making photo-zinco block of Illustration frontispiece			6	6

'Don Alfonso's Treasure Hunt' is the only story in the collection to commence with a drop-capital ('N') measuring 7 × 6.5mm.

A letter dated 30 November 1912 from Masefield to Elkin Mathews includes the following:

> I hear Richards won't be back till perhaps after Xmas. Would it suit better to print off 250 or so of Mainsail to keep up the supply till we can get the new edition prepared? It is just possible R[ichards] may be unwilling to transfer his tales, in which case I shall have to write new ones instead, & that w[oul]d take a little time; but it w[oul]d be a good thing to have the Mainsail brought up to uniformity with B & P.
>
>   (John Masefield, letter to Elkin Mathews, 30 November 1912)
>   (Private Collection (AH))

This appears to refer to the second edition of *A Mainsail Haul* which was therefore contemplated late in 1912. The suggestion is that Masefield wanted to transfer a number of tales from *A Tarpaulin Muster* (first published in 1907 by Grant Richards and out of print until a second edition in March 1915). Richards obviously found this unacceptable for the added tales in the new *A Mainsail Haul* derive from previous periodical articles. Regarding uniformity, by November 1912 *Ballads and Poems* was appearing in the 'standard' 8vo size bound in blue cloth, in which binding the second edition of *A Mainsail Haul* was indeed to appear. July 1913 also saw the Mathews edition of *Salt-Water Ballads* issued in the same uniform binding. This marks the beginning of a Masefield binding livery, as suggested by Masefield in 1912. Heinemann's May 1913 publication of *Dauber* does not therefore mark the start of a standardised appearance for Masefield's works. It is also of significance that Sidgwick and Jackson wrote to Masefield in October 1911 with reference to *The Everlasting Mercy* asking if he had 'any ideas or stipulations about the binding?' The volume appeared in the 'standard' blue cloth.

The publishing agreement for this title between Masefield and Elkin Mathews was dated 16 April 1913 (see Archives of The Society of Authors). The agreement refers to '…a revised version of A Mainsail Haul…' and notes cancellation of the agreement of 10 March 1905 for A3(a).

In 1933 The Society of Authors asked Masefield about the source of 'The Sealman'. Masefield replied, noting that he retained the copyright in England:

> This tale is one of those in the *Mainsail Haul*, a volume published by the Messrs Elkin Mathews; I own the copyright in Gt Britain, but it is doubtful whether there be any copyright in the U.S.; though Macmillan prints it there + pays me a royalty.
>
> (John Masefield, letter to Mr Tweedie, [7 May 1933])
>
> (BL, Add.Mss.56598, f.91)

This may explain Masefield's choice of publication with Mathews as Elkin Mathews had presumably not required Masefield to sell his copyright outright (in contrast to Grant Richards). Masefield fails to mention the different editions of the title, however. He probably had sacrificed American copyright in 1905 in his desire for English publication of A3(a). The second edition in 1913 comprised a different text and copyright was retained in America.

Copies seen: BL (12622.f.21) stamped 25 JUL 1913; Bodleian (2561.e.8608) stamped 1 JUN 1913; HRHRC (AC-L G139 JMAS.MA 1913) inscribed 'Ada + John Galsworthy | from John Masefield. | Aug 31. 1913.'

Reprinted:

'Third Edition (Fourth Thousand)'	[second edition, second impression]	Jul 1914
'Fourth Edition (Fifth Thousand)'	[second edition, third impression]	Apr 1918
'Fifth Edition (Sixth Thousand)'	[second edition, fourth impression]	Mar 1923

A3(c) *First American edition (1913)*

A MAINSAIL | HAUL | BY | JOHN MASEFIELD | New York | THE MACMILLAN COMPANY | 1913
(All width centred)

Bibliographies: Danielson [unrecorded], Williams [unrecorded], Simmons [noted on p.11], Nevinson [unrecorded], Handley-Taylor p.27, Wight 3b

Collation: [A–N]⁸ (J not used); 104 leaves; 188 × 125mm.; [i–viii] [1] 2–189 [190–200]

Page contents: [i] half-title: 'A MAINSAIL HAUL'; [ii] '[publisher's device] | THE MACMILLAN COMPANY | [two lines listing six cities, separated by four points] | MACMILLAN & CO., LIMITED | [two lines listing four cities, separated by two points] | THE MACMILLAN CO. OF CANADA, LTD. | [one city listed]'; [iii] title-page; [iv] 'COPYRIGHT, 1913 | BY JOHN MASEFIELD | [rule] | Set up and electrotyped | [rule] | First Published, June 1st, 1905 | Second Edition, Revised and much Enlarged, September, 1913 | FERRIS PRINTING COMPANY | NEW YORK, N. Y., U. S. A.'; [v] 'CONTENTS' (16 stories listed with titles and page references) [vi] blank; [vii] untitled verse ('I yarned with ancient shipmen beside the galley range') dated '1904'; [viii] blank; 1–189 text; [190] 'NOTE | NEARLY all these stories and one of the histori– | cal papers first appeared in the *Manchester* | *Guardian;* one tale is reprinted from the *Na-* | *tion* and one from the *Pall Mall Magazine.* | The four remaining historical papers are re- | printed from the *Gentleman's Magazine.* | [new paragraph] I thank the Editors and Proprietors of all | these periodicals for permission to include the | papers in this volume.'; [191] 'THE following pages contain advertisements of | books by the same author, and other poetry' (within ruled border: 20 × 76mm.); [192] blank; [193–97] publisher's advertisements; [198–200] blank

Paper: wove paper

Running title: 'A MAINSAIL HAUL' (35mm.) on verso; recto title comprises story title, pp.2–189

Binding: burgundy cloth. On spine, in gold: 'A | MAINSAIL | HAUL | MASEFIELD | MACMILLAN' (all width centred). On upper cover, in gold: 'A | MAINSAIL | HAUL | MASEFIELD' (ranged upper left) (within blind ruled border: 188 × 121mm.) Lower cover: blank. Top edge gilt, others trimmed. Binding measurements: 192 × 127mm. (covers), 192 × 33mm. (spine). Endpapers: wove paper.

Publication date: published, according to Simmons, 12 September 1913 in an edition of 2006 copies. An advertisement from Macmillan within *The Publisher's Weekly* (New York) 27 September 1913 notes this edition as 'Pub. Sept. 12'.

Price: $1.25

Contents:
as for A3(b)

Notes:
The setting of type closely follows A3(b). However, this American edition comprises a new setting. Note, for example, the omission of the drop-capital for the first story and the difference in length measurement of the running-title.

The publishing agreement for this title between Masefield and Macmillan was dated 18 August 1913 (see Archives of The Society of Authors). The agreement refers to 'a licence to publish in volume form in the United States of America a work the subject or title of which is A Mainsail Haul, New and Revised Edition'.

Copies seen: Bodleian (Don.e.855) stamped 21 FEB 1975 inscribed 'A Hanford Flood | from her godson, | Christmas, 1913.'

Reprinted:

'Reprinted'	[first edition, second impression]	Jan 1916
'Reprinted'	[first edition, third impression]	May 1916

A3(d) Third English edition (1954)

THE MARINERS LIBRARY | [rule, 43mm.] | A MAINSAIL | HAUL | *by* | JOHN MASEFIELD | [device showing points of the compass: 26 × 19mm.] | LONDON | RUPERT HART-DAVIS | 1954
(All width centred)

Bibliographies: Handley-Taylor [unrecorded], Wight [unrecorded]

Collation: [A]⁸ B-L⁸ (J not used); signatures left foot of page; 88 leaves; 184 × 121mm.; [1–6] 7–174 [175–76]

Page contents: [1] half-title: 'A MAINSAIL HAUL'; [2] 'THE MARINERS LIBRARY | [rule] | [25 titles and their authors listed] | *Others in preparation* | [rule] | RUPERT HART-DAVIS LIMITED | 36 Soho Square, London, W.I.'; [3] title-page; [4] 'First published 1905 | Revised and enlarged edition 1913 | First published in the Mariners Library | with two new pieces (*Some Famous Wrecks* and *On Moonsails*) | 1954 | Printed in Great Britain by Richard Clay and Company, Ltd., | Bungay, Suffolk'; [5] 'CONTENTS' (18 stories listed with titles and page references); [6] blank; 7–174 text; [175–76] blank

Paper: wove paper

Running title: 'A MAINSAIL HAUL' (37mm.) on verso; recto title comprises story title, pp.8–174

Binding: cream cloth. On spine, in blue: 'JOHN | MASEFIELD | [two wavy lines] | A | MAINSAIL | HAUL | [two wavy lines] | RUPERT | HART-DAVIS' (all width centred). Upper cover, in blue: device showing points of the compass: 57 × 34mm. Lower cover: blank. Top edge stained blue, others trimmed. Binding measurements: 189 × 122mm. (covers), 189 × 30mm. (spine). Endpapers: wove paper.

Publication date: 26 February 1954

Price: 8s.6d.

Contents:

Don Alfonso's Treasure Hunt ('Now in the old days, before steam, there was...')
Port of Many Ships ('"Down in the sea, very far down, under five miles of water...')
Sea Superstition ('One moonlit night in the tropics, as my ship was slipping south...')
A Sailor's Yarn ('"Once upon a time there was a clipper ship called the *Mary*...')
The Yarn of Lanky Job ('Lanky Job was a lazy Bristol sailor, notorious for his...')
From The Spanish ('The galleon *Spanish Rose* was built in Saint Mary of the Bells...')
The Seal Man ('"The seals is pretty when they do be playing," said the old woman.')
The Western Islands ('"Once there were two sailors; and one of them was Joe...')
Captain John Ward ('Captain John Ward, our "most notorious pirate," was born at...')
Captain John Jennings ('It is not known where John Jennings was born; but it was...')
The Voyage of The *Cygnet* ('In the year 1683–4 some eminent London merchants...')
Captain Robert Knox ('Between the years 1690 and 1714, at odd times between...')
Captain Coxon ('Nine generations ago, the island of Carmen, in the Lagoon of Tides...')
In a Castle Ruin ('"Very long ago," said the old man, "the castle was owned by...')
A Deal of Cards ('A company of seamen sat round a cabin table, and pledged each...')
The Devil and the Old Man ('Up away north, in the old days, in Chester, there was...')
Some Famous Wrecks ('Shipwrecks soon pass from human memory.')
　　　No previous appearance traced
On Moonsails ('Looking out upon the Mersey, day-in, day-out...')
　　　No previous appearance traced

Notes:

This edition differs most noticeably from A3(b) through the deletion of the prefatory verse and the inclusion of two new pieces. Any note on sources of publication is omitted and there are minor variants throughout the text.

The approach to reprint this title was made by Rupert Hart-Davis. Masefield, writing to The Society of Authors, asked whether he was legally free to licence a reprinting:

> The early book, *A Mainsail Haul*, was printed by Elkin Mathews, + reprinted by his successor. I expect that it is now out of print, + that I could licence a reprint, as suggested by Mr Hart-Davis? Please, is this so?
>
> (John Masefield, letter to [Anne] Munro-Kerr, 11 April [1953])
> (BL, Add.Mss.56624, f.90)

(At the same time Masefield took the opportunity of asking, once more, about purchasing the rights in *A Tarpaulin Muster*). The Society of Authors replied:

> Allen and Unwin took over from Elkin Mathews and I will find out from them whether they consider they still have any interest in *A Mainsail Haul*. If the way is clear would you like us to make the necessary arrangement for the proposed reprint by Hart-Davis?
>
> (Anne Munro-Kerr, letter to John Masefield, 15 April 1953)
> (BL, Add.Mss.56624, f.93)

Masefield agreed to this suggestion. He also reveals that one plan was to issue a revised volume of short stories (using the best of both *A Mainsail Haul* and *A Tarpaulin Muster*):

> I shall be glad if you will arrange with Messrs Hart-Davis about the *Mainsail Haul*, if the way be clear for the arrangement. But if it should chance that I can buy back the *Tarpaulin Muster* book, I may ask to cut one or two of the *Mainsail* tales + substitute 1 or 2 of the *Tarpaulin* tales. However, I do not expect that the Tarpaulin people will be in a forthcoming mood.
>
> (John Masefield, letter to [Anne] Munro-Kerr, 16 April [1953])
> (BL, Add.Mss.56624, ff.94–95)

In June 1953 the Richards Press requested one hundred pounds for *A Tarpaulin Muster* and Masefield replied that he would offer 'not more than twenty pounds' (see BL, Add.Mss.56624, f.110). Masefield was eventually to pay the asking price and purchase the rights in the book, but the business was completed too late for any of the short stories from *A Tarpaulin Muster* to be included in the Hart-Davis edition of *A Mainsail Haul*. Later in June 1953 The Society of Authors received a reply from Elkin Mathews' business successors. The Society, accordingly, wrote to Masefield:

> I am glad to let you know that I have good news for you about *A Mainsail Haul*. I have just received a letter from Sir Stanley Unwin which reads as follows:
>
> "We have pleasure, in accordance with Dr. Masefield's wishes, in putting on record that the rights have reverted to him, and that he is free to arrange for the republication of the book through Rupert Hart-Davis, who has a series into which it would fit admirable."
>
> The terms proposed by Hart-Davis were, as you may remember, a flat royalty of 10% which is their customary royalty for this series. I think, however, we might be able to persuade them, if you wished, to pay a small advance...
>
> (Anne Munro-Kerr, letter to John Masefield, 15 June 1953)
> (BL, Add.Mss.56624, f.113)

Masefield, replied with further schemes for the book. It is presumably at this stage that he planned to contribute 'Some Famous Wrecks' and 'On Moonsails':

> It has occurred to me, that if Messrs Hart-Davis could wait a little while, I could add a few studies to their reprint of the *Mainsail Haul*. Messrs Richards will probably refuse to part with the [*Tarpaulin*] *Muster* book, + I would like the M.H. to be just a little longer than it is. Please, will you ask Messrs Davis what they think of this?
>
> (John Masefield, letter to [Anne] Munro-Kerr, 16 June 1953)
> (BL, Add.Mss.56624, ff.116–117)

The Society of Authors responded to this suggestion having spoken to Rupert Hart-Davis:

> We have had a word on the telephone with Mr. Rupert Hart-Davis who says that he is greatly taken by your suggestion that you should add a few studies to the reprint of *A Mainsail Haul*. Mr. Hart Davis [*sic*] would be very grateful if he could have these additions within the next couple of months or so as he is hoping to get the edition out by the spring of 1954. Would this be possible?
>
> (Anne Munro-Kerr, letter to John Masefield, 19 June 1953)
> (BL, Add.Mss.56624, f.119)

Hart-Davis' planned publication date was to be met. Masefield, in June 1953, noted his compliance with plans:

> I will try to have the *Mainsail* book complete by mid-August, even if the Richards firm do not answer. I am rather against asking for an advance please: it is a horrid little book.
>
> (John Masefield, letter to [Anne] Munro-Kerr, 20 June [1953])
> (BL, Add.Mss.56624, f.120)

An agreement for the volume was sent to Masefield (via The Society of Authors) on 25 June 1953 (see BL, Add.Mss.56624, f.121). The publishing agreement for this title between Masefield and Rupert Hart-Davis was dated 25 June 1953 (see Archives of The Society of Authors). Masefield provided the additional material less than two months later and specifically asked to see proofs. The minor textual differences between this edition and the second English edition are, therefore, presumably authorial.

Copies seen: private collection (PWE); BL (W.P. 2496/25) stamped 11 FEB 1954; HRHRC (TEMP M377 MAI 1954) inscribed 'For Con | from Jan. | Feb 11th. 1954.'

A3(e) First Japanese edition [in English] (1954)

<u>Nan'un-do's Contemporary Library</u> | JOHN MASEFIELD | A MAINSAIL HAUL | *Edited with Notes* | *by* | Takashi Ogura | Haruo Miki | [publisher's circular device] | TOKYO | NAN'UN-DO
(All width centred)

Bibliographies: Handley-Taylor [unrecorded], Wight [unrecorded]

Collation: [A-G]⁸ (see notes); 56 leaves; 183 × 128mm.; [two un-numbered pages] [i] ii–iii [iv–viii] 1–27 [28] 29–39 [40] 41–53 [54] 55–99 [101–102]; frontispiece (on glossy paper) tipped-in on first un-numbered page

Page contents: [-] title-page (with additional leaf tipped-in on the verso of which is the frontispiece: 95 × 70mm., 'JOHN MASEFIELD'); [-] '*A Mainsail Haul* by Dr. John Masefield, O.M. | Published in Japan by arrangement with and with full acknowl- | edgment to Dr. John Masefield, O.M. c/o The Society of Authors.'; [i]–iii [editors' introduction]; [iv] blank; [v] 'CONTENTS' (introduction, 11 stories and notes listed with titles and page references); [vi] blank; [vii] untitled verse ('I yarned with ancient shipmen beside the galley range' (undated); [viii] blank; 1–27 text; [28] blank; 29–39 text; [40] blank; 41–53 text; [54] blank; 55–78 text; 79–99 'NOTES'; [100] blank; [101] [publisher's imprint]; [102] blank

Paper: wove paper

Running title: running titles comprise section or story titles, pp.ii–99

Binding: grey textured wrappers. On spine, in blue, reading lengthways down spine, from head: '*J. MASEFIELD* A MAINSAIL HAUL N.U.D.' On upper wrapper, in blue: '<u>Nan'un-do's Contemporary Library</u> | A MAINSAIL HAUL | J. Masefield | [publisher's circular device] NAN'UN-DO | TOKYO' (lines 1 and 4 width centred, lines 2 and 3 centred on green panel: 45 × 92mm. (with left side of panel touching spine), publisher's device on left margin and with publisher and place of publication centred towards right margin). On lower wrapper, in blue: publisher's device including 'NUD' (width centred). All edges trimmed. Binding measurements: 183 × 128mm. (covers), 183 × 6mm. (spine). End-papers: wove paper.

Publication date: 1954

Price: unknown

Contents:
[Editors' Introduction]
[Untitled Verse] ('I yarned with ancient shipmen beside the galley range')
Don Alfonso's Treasure Hunt ('Now in the old days, before steam, there was...')
Port of Many Ships ('"Down in the sea, very far down, under five miles of water..."')
Sea Superstition ('One moonlit night in the tropics, as my ship was slipping south...')
A Sailor's Yarn ('"Once upon a time there was a clipper ship called the *Mary*..."')
The Yarn of Lanky Job ('Lanky Job was a lazy Bristol sailor, notorious for his...')
From The Spanish ('The galleon *Spanish Rose* was built in Saint Mary of the Bells...')
The Seal Man ('"The seals is pretty when they do be playing," said the old woman.')
The Western Islands ('"Once there were two sailors; and one of them was Joe..."')
In a Castle Ruin ('"Very long ago," said the old man, "the castle was owned by..."')
A Deal of Cards ('A company of seamen sat round a cabin table, and pledged each...')
The Devil and The Old Man ('Up away north, in the old days, in Chester, there was...')
Notes

Notes:
The volume appears to comprise seven unsigned signatures. However, these are not apparently sewn, but secured by two staples. The wrappers and end-papers are then added. There are two flaps at the edges of the wrappers which wrap-around the end-papers.

Note use of the revised 1913 text (see A3(b)) although not all tales are included here.

The notes at the rear of the volume appear to comprise translations of some of Masefield's more nautical or vernacular phrases.

See BL, Add.Mss.56626 f.118 for reference to this edition between Masefield and The Society of Authors.

Copies seen: HRHRC (TEMP M377MAI) inscribed 'For Con | from | Jan. | November the 6th. | 1955.'

A3(f) Fourth English edition (1987)

A Mainsail | Haul | JOHN MASEFIELD | GRAFTON BOOKS | A Division of the Collins Publishing Group | [rule, 32mm.] | LONDON GLASGOW | TORONTO SYDNEY AUCKLAND
(All width centred)

Bibliographies: Wight [unrecorded]

Publication date: published, according to *Whitaker's*, June 1987

Price: £5.95

Contents:
as for A3(d)

Notes:
The text has been entirely re-set for this edition, using the text of the third English edition (A3(d)). This edition is bound in wrappers. The volume states, on page [4], that it is photoset by Rowland Phototypesetting Ltd, Bury St Edmunds, Suffolk and printed in Great Britain by Robert Hartnoll (1985) Ltd, Bodmin, Cornwall. The ISBN is ISBN 0–246–13177–2

Copies seen: private collection (PWE); BL (YC.1987.a.5651) stamped 7 MAY 1987

A4 SEA LIFE IN NELSON'S TIME   1905

A4(a) First English edition (1905)

SEA LIFE | IN NELSON'S TIME | BY | JOHN MASEFIELD | WITH SIXTEEN ILLUSTRATIONS | METHUEN & CO. | 36 ESSEX STREET W.C. | LONDON
(All width centred)

Bibliographies: Danielson 162, Williams p.7, Simmons [4], Nevinson p.15, Handley-Taylor p.27, Wight [4]

Collation: [π]⁶ A–N⁸ O⁷ (O4+1) P² (J not used); signatures left foot of page; 119 leaves; the catalogue (not included in collation or leaf count) comprises either a single gathering of 20 leaves of which the fifth and the ninth are also signed, or a single gathering of 16 leaves of which the fifth is also signed; 189 × 122mm.; [i–viii] ix–x [xi–xii] [1] 2–218 [219–20 (removed)] [221–28]; catalogue pagination: [1–2] 3–40 or [1–2] 3–31 [32]; illustrations (on glossy paper) tipped-in on pp.[ii], 8, 24, 34, 51, 74, 101, 113, 121, 127, 139, 141, 151, 161, 187 and 201 (even-numbered pages are all verso sides of a leaf and the illustration occurs on the verso of the tipped-in leaf, odd-numbered pages, similarly, are recto sides of a leaf and the illustration occurs on the recto of the tipped-in leaf)

Page contents: [i] half-title: 'SEA LIFE IN NELSON'S TIME'; [ii] blank; [iii] title-page (with additional leaf tipped-in on the verso of which is the frontispiece: 152 × 81mm., 'A FRIGATE UNDER SAIL' with protective tissue); [iv] *First Published in 1905*'; [v] 'TO | CAPTAIN HENRY BAYNHAM, R.N.'; [vi] blank; [vii] 'I THANK Mr W. BARCLAY SQUIRE | and Mr F. KIDSON, for their | versions of the tune, "Drops of | Brandy"; and Mr MARTIN SHAW | for permission to use his arrange- | ment of the tune of "Spanish | Ladies." I also wish to thank Mr | LAURENCE BINYON for his help in | the selection of the illustrations | here reproduced.'; [viii] blank; ix–x 'CONTENTS' (nine chapters described with brief details of subjects within each chapter, and page references. An epilogue, appendix and index are also listed); [xi] 'LIST OF ILLUSTRATIONS' (16 illustrations listed with page references); [xii] blank; [1]–218 text; [219–20] this single leaf, included in the pagination has been removed leaving a stub of approximately 5mm.; [221–24] 'APPENDIX'; [225–27] 'INDEX'; [228] printer's colophon (including tree and root system with three flowers, and text 'THE RIVER-SIDE PRESS | [device] EDINBURGH [device] | R.P. LTD', the 'R' is intertwined with the 'P' and the 'LTD' positioned between the two, 33 × 24mm., centred)

Either: [1]–40 catalogue: 'A CATALOGUE OF BOOKS | PUBLISHED BY METHUEN | AND COMPANY: LONDON | 36 ESSEX STREET | W.C. [contents listed] | SEPTEMBER 1905' (the printer is unidentified)

Or: [1]–31 catalogue: 'A SELECTION OF BOOKS | PUBLISHED BY METHUEN | AND CO. LTD., LONDON | 36 ESSEX STREET | W.C. [contents listed]' (at foot of p.31: '[rule] | *Printed by* MORRISON & GIBB LIMITED, *Edinburgh* [centred] | 27/1/14 [in left corner]'); [32] blank

Paper: wove paper (catalogue: wove paper)

Running title: 'SEA LIFE IN NELSON'S TIME' (72mm.) on verso; recto title comprises subject of the page, pp.2–218

Binding: dark-blue cloth. On spine, in gold: 'SEA LIFE | IN NELSON'S | TIME | BY | JOHN MASEFIELD | [device of anchor and rope design: 84 × 32mm.] | METHUEN' (with the exception of the device and the publisher, all words are left justified; the device and publisher are width centred). On upper cover, in gold: three-masted ship at sea with shining sun, all within ornate border comprising six flowering roses, four rosebuds, with leaves and stalks: 108 × 87mm.) (Simmons describes the upper cover as being 'in yellow'). Wight reports that 'later editions' employ a gold design rather than yellow and change 'METHVEN' to 'METHUEN' on the spine. Danielson, by contrast, describes the edition with gold lettering on the upper cover. The yellow may represent an earlier binding of the first impression, with the gold used on later bindings. It is certainly not an indication of 'edition' as Wight describes. No bindings with yellow have been examined, however, copies including the 32 page catalogue have 'METHUEN' in a slightly larger size on the spine than those copies containing the 40 page catalogue. Lower cover: blank. Top edge trimmed, others untrimmed. Binding measurements: 195 × 128mm. (covers), 195 × 46mm. (spine). End-papers: wove paper.

Publication date: published, according to Simmons, September 1905 in an edition of 2000 copies

Price: 3s.6d.

Contents:
Sea Life in Nelson's Time ('The ships in which Nelson went to sea were designed by master-shipwrights...')

Chapters are as follows:
I. Ship designing, building, sheathing, and rigging – The external decorations and appearance – The internal arrangements, deck by deck – The orlop and hold

II. The guns in use in our navy – Their nature – How loaded and fired – Varieties – Carronades – Shot – Small-arms – Gun ports

III. The quarter-deck officers – The captain – The lieutenants – The master, second master, and master's mates – The midshipmen – The midshipman's berth

IV. The civilian and warrant or standing officers – The surgeon – The surgeon's assistants – The chaplain – The boatswain – The purser – The gunner – The carpenter – Mates and yeomen – The sailmaker – The ship's police – The ship's cook

V. The people – The boys – Manning – The divisions – The messes – The dress – The King's allowance – Grog – Marines

VI. Sea punishments – The cat – Flogging at the gangway – Flogging through the fleet – Running the gauntlet – Keel-hauling – Hanging

VII. In action

VIII. The daily routine – Sunday – Ship visiting

IX. In port – Jews – Lovely Nan – Mutinies – Their punishment – Sailor songs – "Drops of Brandy" – "Spanish Ladies," etc. – Flags – Salutes

Epilogue

Appendix

Index

Notes:

The publishing agreement for this title between Masefield and Methuen was dated 4 May 1905 (see Archives of The Society of Authors). The agreement refers to delivery of the manuscript '…before (approximately) the 30th. July 1905…'

The dedicatee of this work, Captain Baynham, R.N., is recorded in the *Conway* magazine, *The Cadet*, for 15 February 1892 for having given a lecture 'A Cruise round the World' on 29 April 1892. He was a member of the teaching staff aboard H.M.S. *Conway*.

Danielson only notes the 40 page catalogue.

Martin Shaw (see Masefield's note of thanks on p.[vii]) was to publish his own settings of Masefield's works. These included: 'London Town' (1923), 'Cargoes' [solo] (1924), *Easter* (1929), 'Arise In Us' (1931), 'The Seaport and Her Sailors' [i.e. 'A Masque of Liverpool'] (1931), 'O Christ Who Holds The Open Gate' (1934) and 'Cargoes' [SATB] (1935). The earliest collaboration, however, occurred in 1903 when Shaw arranged the music of 'Spanish Ladies' in *The Green Sheaf* No.3.

The book was reviewed in the *Manchester Guardian* for 25 September 1905 (p.5). The article is complimentary and signed 'J.B.Y.' and it would thus be reasonable to suggest Jack B. Yeats was the reviewer.

Sending a copy of this book to Lady Gregory in September 1905, Masefield wrote:

> I am afraid dry, fusty, second hand marine stories are not interesting things; and my catalogue of them was put together very hurridly; and the resulting book, which I ask you to accept, is a very bad book. I hope, however, that you will find a place for the volume on your shelves, + that the pictures, especially the merry ones by Marryat, will excuse the excessive badness of the letter press.
>
> (John Masefield, letter to Lady Gregory, 7 September [1905])
> (NYPL (Berg Collection))

In the 1960s Masefield wrote to The Society of Authors asking for assistance in acquiring the rights to the work:

> In about June, 1905, being in rather dire need of money, I wrote and sold for a small sum, to Messrs Methuen + Co., a book called:- *Sea Life in Nelson's Time* which is now, mercifullly, out of print, + rather a rare book. Please, would you be so very helpful as to ask Messrs Methuen if they would care to sell back the book to me, + if so, at what price? I do not think that they wish to re-issue it: and the blocks of the illustrations are probably by this time either worn or gone. You may wonder less why I wish to re-possess the thing, when I tell you that the book was written, set-up, and on the market within 42 days.
>
> (John Masefield, letter to Anne Munro-Kerr, [1960])
> (Archives of The Society of Authors)

On 27 October 1961 J. Alan White, chairman of Methuen, wrote to The Society of Authors agreeing to the reversion of Masefield's rights in the book without payment.

Copies seen: BL (08805.de.52) stamped 7 SEP 1905, catalogue of 40 pages dated SEPTEMBER 1905; NYPL (Berg Collection) catalogue of 40 pages dated SEPTEMBER 1905, Lady Gregory's copy, inscribed 'from John Masefield. | Sept 7. 1905.'

A4(b) *Second English edition (1920)*

SEA LIFE | IN NELSON'S TIME | BY | JOHN MASEFIELD | WITH SIXTEEN ILLUSTRATIONS | SECOND EDITION | METHUEN & CO. LTD | 36 ESSEX STREET W.C. | LONDON
(All width centred)

Bibliographies: Danielson [unrecorded], Williams [unrecorded], Simmons [unrecorded], Nevinson [unrecorded], Handley-Taylor [unrecorded], Wight [unrecorded]

Collation: [π]⁶ A–O⁸ P² (J not used); signatures left foot of page; 120 leaves; the catalogue (not included in collation or leaf count) comprises a single unsigned gathering of 4 leaves; 189 × 122mm.; [i–viii] ix–x [xi–xii] [1] 2–218 [219–28]; catalogue pagination: [1] 2–8; illustrations (on glossy paper) tipped-in on pp.[ii], 8, 24, 34, 51, 74, 101, 113, 121, 127, 139, 141, 151, 161, 187 and 201 (even-numbered pages are all verso sides of a leaf and the illustration occurs on the verso of the tipped-in leaf, odd-numbered pages, similarly, are recto sides of a leaf and the illustration occurs on the recto of the tipped-in leaf)

Page contents: [i] half-title: 'SEA LIFE IN NELSON'S TIME'; [ii] blank (with additional leaf tipped-in on the verso of which is the frontispiece: 152 × 81mm., 'A FRIGATE UNDER SAIL'); [iii] title-page; [iv] '*First Published . . September 1905 | Second Edition . . 1920*'; [v] 'TO | CAPTAIN HENRY BAYNHAM, R.N.'; [vi] blank; [vii] 'I THANK Mr W. BARCLAY SQUIRE | and Mr F. KIDSON, for their | versions of the tune, "Drops of | Brandy"; and Mr MARTIN SHAW | for permission to use his arrange- | ment of the tune of "Spanish | Ladies." I also wish to thank Mr | LAURENCE BINYON for his help in | the selection of the illustrations | here reproduced.'; [viii] blank; ix–x 'CONTENTS' (nine chapters described with brief details of subjects within each chapter, and page references. An epilogue, appendix and index are also listed); [xi] 'LIST OF ILLUSTRATIONS' (16 illustrations listed with page references); [xii] blank; [1]–218 text; [219–22] 'APPENDIX'; [223] 'INDEX'; [224] blank; [225–27] text of index; [228] printer's colophon: 'The River-Side Press | Edinburgh | [device with 'R.', 'P.' and 'LTD']' all within decoration: 33 × 24mm.; [1]–8 catalogue: 'A SELECTION FROM MESSRS. METHUEN'S PUBLICATIONS'

Paper: wove paper

Running title: 'SEA LIFE IN NELSON'S TIME' (71mm.) on verso; recto title changes within chapters to describe subject of the page, pp.2–218

Binding: blue cloth. On spine, in gold: 'SEA LIFE | IN NELSON'S | TIME | BY | JOHN MASEFIELD | [device of anchor and rope design: 83 × 32mm.] [in orange] | METHUEN' (with the exception of the device and the publisher, all words are left justified; the device and publisher are width centred). On upper cover, in orange: three-masted ship at sea with shining sun, all within ornate border comprising six flowering roses, four rosebuds, with leaves and stalks: 108 × 87mm. Lower cover: blank. All edges trimmed. Binding measurements: 195 × 124mm. (covers), 195 × 44mm. (spine). End-papers: wove paper.

Publication date: 1920

Price: 5s.

Contents:
as for A4(a)

Notes:
The same setting of text is used here as in A4(a). The O gathering comprises 8 leaves, however. This allows a divisional title to the index on O8 (pp.223–24) that is not present in A4(a).

In April 1929 Methuen wrote to Masefield suggesting a re-issue and a partial revision:

> …As the re-issue, should it be practical, would mean resetting, would you not consider the re-casting of the text, where it least pleases you, in which case we would make an advance towards royalties on the new edition?
>
> (E.V. Lucas, letter to John Masefield, 17 April 1929)
> (Archives of The Society of Authors)

This proposal was, evidently, not a matter that Masefield wished to consider.

Copies seen: private collection (PWE)

Reprinted:

[second edition, second impression]   1937?

A4(c) First American edition (1925)

SEA LIFE | IN NELSON'S TIME | BY | JOHN MASEFIELD | WITH SIXTEEN ILLUSTRATIONS | NEW YORK | THE MACMILLAN COMPANY | 1925
(All width centred)

Bibliographies: Danielson [unrecorded], Williams [unrecorded], Simmons [unrecorded], Nevinson [unrecorded], Handley-Taylor [unrecorded], Wight [unrecorded]

Collation: [π]⁶ A–O⁸ P² (J not used); signatures left foot of page; 120 leaves; 189 × 122mm.; [i–viii] ix–x [xi–xii] [1] 2–218 [219–28]; illustrations (on glossy paper) tipped-in on pp.[ii], 8, 24, 34, 51, 74, 101, 113, 121, 127, 139, 141, 151, 161, 187 and 201 (even-numbered pages are all verso sides of a leaf and the illustration occurs on the verso of the tipped-in leaf, odd-numbered pages, similarly, are recto sides of a leaf and the illustration occurs on the recto of the tipped-in leaf)

Page contents: [i] half-title: 'SEA LIFE IN NELSON'S TIME'; [ii] blank (with additional leaf tipped-in on the verso of which is the frontispiece: 152 × 81mm., 'A FRIGATE UNDER SAIL'); [iii] title-page; [iv] 'PRINTED IN GREAT BRITAIN'; [v] 'TO | CAPTAIN HENRY BAYNHAM, R.N.'; [vi] blank; [vii] 'I THANK Mr W. BARCLAY SQUIRE | and Mr F. KIDSON, for their | versions of the tune, "Drops of | Brandy"; and Mr MARTIN SHAW | for permission to use his arrange- | ment of the tune of "Spanish | Ladies." I also wish to thank Mr | LAURENCE BINYON for his help in | the selection of the illustrations | here reproduced.'; [viii] blank; ix–x 'CONTENTS' (nine chapters described with brief details of subjects within each chapter, and page references. An epilogue, appendix and index are also listed); [xi] 'LIST OF ILLUSTRATIONS' (16 illustrations listed with page references); [xii] blank; [1]–218 text; [219–22] 'APPENDIX'; [223] 'INDEX'; [224] blank; [225–27] text of index (at foot of p.[227]: '[rule] | *Printed in Great Britain by The Riverside Press Limited* | *Edinburgh*'; [228] blank

Paper: wove paper

Running title: 'SEA LIFE IN NELSON'S TIME' (71mm.) on verso; recto title changes within chapters to describe subject of the page, pp.2–218

Binding: blue cloth. On spine, in gold: 'SEA LIFE | IN NELSON'S | TIME | BY | JOHN MASEFIELD | [device of anchor and rope design: 83 × 32mm.] [in orange] | MACMILLAN' (with the exception of the device and the publisher, all words are left justified; the device and publisher are width centred). On upper cover, in orange: three-masted ship at sea with shining sun, all within ornate border comprising six flowering roses, four rosebuds, with leaves and stalks: 108 × 87mm. Lower cover: blank. All edges trimmed. Binding measurements: 195 × 124mm. (covers), 195 × 44mm. (spine). End-papers: wove paper.

Publication date: 1925

Price: $2.50

Contents:
as for A4(a)

Notes:
The same setting of text is used here as in A4(b) (and thus A4(a)). The divisional title for the index (first present in A4(b)) is found here.

In the undated promotional booklet *John Masefield* published (probably in 1926) by the Macmillan Company, this edition is listed in the 'American Bibliography' section dated 1925 with the note 'imported; previously published in England'.

Copies seen: private collection (PWE)

A4(d) Third English edition (1971)

SEA LIFE IN NELSON'S TIME | By | JOHN MASEFIELD | With an Introduction by Professor C.C. Lloyd | With Thirty-eight Illustrations | Third Edition | CONWAY MARITIME PRESS | 1971
(All width centred)

Bibliographies: Wight [unrecorded]

Publication date: November 1971

Price: £2.80

Contents:
Acknowledgements ('The publishers wish to acknowledge with thanks the following…')
Introduction ('It is a pleasure to welcome a new edition of the clearest…')
        (signed, 'Christopher Lloyd, 1971')
and as for A4(a)

Notes:
The acknowledgements state:

> John Masefield was unable to revise "Sea Life in Nelson's Time" as he wished to do, before he died, but it is felt that this new edition, with an introduction by Professor Lloyd and which has been completely reset and newly illustrated, goes some way towards achieving what Masefield would have wished.

In 1962 it appears that Masefield wrote to Captain Jackson of the *Victory* Museum '…asking if he would care to have [*Sea Life in Nelson's Time*] (completely re-written) as a possible pamphlet for visitors to his Museum, meaning, of course, that if he approved the revision it should be the possession of the Museum' (see John Masefield, letter to Anne Munro-Kerr, [March 1962]) (Archives of The Society of Authors). Possible rights to the book sub-let by Methuen caused Masefield to abandon the plan. Responding to questions of a possible reprint (rather than a rewritten text) Masefield commented:

> …there can be no question of a reprint of this book, which is thoroughly hateful to me. I wrote it in 3 weeks nearly 57 years ago.

> (John Masefield, letter to Anne Munro-Kerr, 26 March [1962])
> (Archives of The Society of Authors)

The volume states, on page [iv], that it is set in 11/13 pt. Journal by P.J.B. Typesetting and printed in Great Britain by Latimer Trend Ltd., Whitstable, Kent.

The publishing agreement for this title between The Society of Authors and Conway Maritime Press was dated 14 August 1971 (see Archives of The Society of Authors).

Copies seen: BL (X.802/2399) stamped 27 MAR 1972

A4(e) Second American edition (1971)

SEA LIFE IN NELSON'S TIME | By | JOHN MASEFIELD | With an Introduction by Professor C.C. Lloyd | With Thirty-eight Illustrations | Third Edition | UNITED STATES NAVAL INSTITUTE | 1971
(All width centred)

Bibliographies: Wight [unrecorded]

Publication date: November or December 1971 (advertised in *United States Naval Institute Proceedings*, December 1971)

Price: $8.00

Contents:
as for A4(d)

Notes:
With the exception of the title-page and publisher's imprint on page [iv] this edition appears to be a verbatim reprint of A4(d). Accordingly, the volume states, on page [iv], that it is set in 11/13 pt. Journal by P.J.B. Typesetting and printed in Great Britain by Latimer Trend Ltd., Whitstable, Kent.

The additional information present in this edition on page [iv] notes: 'In the United States of America | UNITED STATES NAVAL INSTITUTE | ISBN 87021 869 7 | Library of Congress Catalog Card No. 77–175637'

Copies seen: University of Texas at Austin Libraries (G549 M3 1971)

A4(f) Fourth English edition (1972)

Sea Life in Nelson's | *Time* | JOHN MASEFIELD | With a new Introduction by | Professor C. C. Lloyd | [publisher's device of a globe: 9 × 7mm.] | SPHERE BOOKS LTD | 30/32 Gray's Inn Road, London WC1X 8JL
(All left justified)

Bibliographies: Wight [unrecorded]

Publiction date: October 1972

Price: £1.25

Contents:
as for A4(d)

Notes:
This edition is derived from A4(d). Most, but not all, of the text is taken from the 1971 setting. This edition includes, however, additional colour plates.

This edition incorrectly states that the first edition was published by Conway Maritime Press in 1905.

This volume was issued in colour pictorial wrappers.

The volume states, on page [iv], that it is printed in Great Britain by Hazell Watson and Viney Ltd., Aylesbury, Bucks.

Copies seen: BL (X.700/12682) stamped 24 OCT 1972

A4(g) Fifth English edition (1984)

[crest with 'DIEU ET MON DROIT'] | [thin rule, 61mm.] | SEA | LIFE | in | *NELSON'S* | TIME | [thick rule, 61mm.] | [thin rule, 61mm.] | by | *JOHN* | *MASEFIELD* | [thin rule, 61mm.] | INTRODUCTION | by | Professor | C.C.LLOYD [all enclosed within ruled border: 171 × 66mm. with curved top edge] [all enclosed within ruled border: 201 × 134mm. in which lower edge is intersected with publisher's device: 'CONWAY | [design in white on black background: 15 × 18mm.] | MARITIME PRESS' (all enclosed within single border: 23 × 19mm.)]
(All width centred)

Bibliographies: Wight [unrecorded]

Publication date: September 1984

Price: £9.50

Contents:
as for A4(d)

Notes:
The volume states, on page [4], that it is designed by Tony Garrett, typeset by Witwell Ltd, Liverpool, printed and bound in England by The Alden Press, Osney Mead.

This edition is described, on page [4] as the 'Fourth edition – completely reset and with added illustrations'. This fails to include A4(f).

Copies seen: private collection (PWE)

A4(h) Sixth English edition (2002)

Sea Life in | Nelson's Time | John Masefield | [publisher's device of a crossed pen and sword] | LEO COOPER
(All width centred)

Publication date: February 2002

Price: £12.95

Contents:
as for A4(a)

Notes:
This volume was issued in colour pictorial wrappers.

The volume states, on page [iv] that it is printed in Great Britain by CPI UK. The ISBN number is 0–85052–873–9.

The publisher, Leo Cooper, is an imprint of Pen & Sword Books Ltd.

The edition is reset but derived from A4(g) with all illustrations present that accompany the 1984 text, with the exception of the frontispiece. There is a new index and a note on Masefield. The introduction by C.C. Lloyd is omitted.

Copies seen: private collection (PWE)

A5 ON THE SPANISH MAIN   1906

A5(a) First English edition (1906)

ON THE SPANISH MAIN | OR, SOME ENGLISH FORAYS ON THE | ISTHMUS OF DARIEN. WITH A DESCRIP- | TION OF THE BUCCANEERS AND A | SHORT ACCOUNT OF OLD-TIME | SHIPS AND SAILORS | BY | JOHN MASEFIELD | WITH TWENTY-TWO ILLUSTRATIONS AND A MAP | METHUEN & CO. | 36 ESSEX STREET W.C. | LONDON
(All width centred)

Bibliographies: Danielson 163, Williams p.7, Simmons [5], Nevinson p.15, Handley-Taylor p.28, Wight [5]

Collation: $[\pi]^6$ A-X^8 Y^4 (J, V and W not used); signatures left foot of page; 178 leaves; the catalogue (not included in collation or leaf count) comprises a single gathering of 20 leaves of which the fifth and ninth are also signed; 220 × 140mm.; [i–vi] vii–ix [x] xi–xii [1] 2–339 [340] 341–44; catalogue pagination: [1–2] 3–40, illustrations (on glossy paper) tipped-in on pp.[ii], 13, 27, 41, 48, 94, 115, 133, 143, 151, 165, 172, 181, 194, 201, 211, 267, 275, 292, 296, 311, 322 and 341 (even-numbered pages are all verso sides of a leaf and the illustration occurs on the verso of the tipped-in leaf, odd-numbered pages, similarly, are recto sides of a leaf and the illustration occurs on the recto of the tipped-in leaf, the final tipped-in leaf comprises a map on a leaf larger than the dimensions of the volume and is thus folded twice)

Page contents: [i] half-title: 'ON THE SPANISH MAIN'; [ii] blank (with an additional leaf tipped-in on the verso of which is the frontispiece: 119 × 101mm., 'CAPTAIN WILLIAM DAMPIER' with protective tissue); [iii] title-page; [iv] '*First Published in 1906* | THE RIVERSIDE PRESS LIMITED, EDINBURGH.'; [v] 'TO | JACK B. YEATS'; [vi] blank; vii–ix 'CONTENTS' (20 chapters described with brief details of subjects within each chapter, and page references, an index is also listed); [x] blank; xi–xii 'LIST OF ILLUSTRATIONS' (23 illustrations including maps listed with page references); [1]–339 text; [340] blank; 341–44 'INDEX'; [1]–40 catalogue: 'A CATALOGUE OF BOOKS | PUBLISHED BY METHUEN | AND COMPANY: LONDON | 36 ESSEX STREET | W.C. | CONTENTS | [contents listed in double column] | JANUARY 1906'

Paper: wove paper (catalogue: wove paper)

Running-title: 'ON THE SPANISH MAIN' (60mm.) on verso; recto title comprises chapter title, pp.2–339

Binding: blue cloth. On spine, in gold: '[double rule] | ON [square point] THE | SPANISH | MAIN | BY [square point] JOHN | MASEFIELD | [device of anchor and rope design: 84 × 32mm.] | METHUEN. | [double rule]' (all width centred). Upper and lower covers blank with blind ruled borders: 223 × 133mm. Top edge trimmed, others uncut. Binding measurements: 227 × 139mm. (covers), 227 × 61mm. (spine). End-papers: wove paper.

Publication date: published, according to Simmons, 3 May 1906 in an edition of 1500 copies

Price: 10s.6d.

Contents:
On the Spanish Main ('Francis Drake, the first Englishman to make himself…')

Chapter headings are as follows:

I. Drake's Voyage to the West Indies	XI. Morgan's Great Raid
II. The Attack on Nombre De Dios	XII. The Sack of Panama
III. The Cruise off The Main	XIII. Captain Dampier
IV. The Road to Panama	XIV. The Battle of Perico

Notes:
Each chapter commences with a drop-capital.

Copies were issued with, and without a catalogue. Catalogues appear to be dated January 1906 or September 1908.

In February 1927 Ralph J. Pugh of the newly formed Empire Film Producing project asked if Masefield would be willing to 'write a story suitable for a film production' based on this work. He continued 'We would like one of our first pictures to be based upon a story of "Drake"' (see BL, Add.Mss.56584, f.57). Masefield, it appears, had little confidence in the genre of film. In a letter to The Society of Authors he states:

> The Drake story, as told in *The Spanish Main*, is a paraphrase of + from the Elizabethan narrative, which is there for any one to use; + very good stuff it is. I am afraid that my views of Drake are not likely to please the film people. I believe that he was a most forceful valiant practical seaman, who began as a slaver + smuggler, then, in a revengeful mood for wrongs done to him, became a buccaneer, rose to be a great pirate, admiral + explorer, + died when his luck turned. I can write a story of him on those lines, but I cannot mix with my tale the sentiment + stupidity which I fear the film people will demand. The truth about Drake is marvellous enough. Could the film people keep to that?
>
> (John Masefield, letter to [G.H.] Thring, [19 February 1927])
> (BL, Add.Mss.56584, f.62)

The film project, after further discussion, came to nothing.

Copies seen: BL (9770.b.28) stamped 4 MAY 1906 rebound; National Gallery of Ireland Yeats Archive inscribed 'Jack. B. Yeats. | from his friend and admirer | John Masefield. | May 2. 1906.'; Harvard College Library (Houghton *EC9.M377.905aa) inscribed to the Lamonts 'Put this aside beneath the tedious tomes | That the lean worm the soonest honeycombs. | J. Masefield.'; HRHRC (AC-L M377ONT 1906); HRHRC (AC-L M377ONT 1906A); HRHRC (F2161 M39 HRC)

A5(b) First American edition (1906)

ON THE SPANISH MAIN | OR, SOME ENGLISH FORAYS ON THE | ISTHMUS OF DARIEN. WITH A DESCRIP- | TION OF THE BUCCANEERS AND A | SHORT ACCOUNT OF OLD-TIME | SHIPS AND SAILORS | BY | JOHN MASEFIELD | WITH TWENTY-TWO ILLUSTRATIONS AND A MAP | NEW YORK | THE MACMILLAN COMPANY | 1906
(All width centred)

Bibliographies: Danielson [unrecorded], Williams [unrecorded], Simmons noted on p.14, Nevinson [unrecorded], Handley-Taylor p.28, Wight 5a

Collation: [π]⁶ (±[π]2) A-X⁸ Y⁴ (J, V and W not used); signatures left foot of page; 178 leaves; 218 × 138mm.; [i–vi] vii–ix [x] xi–xii [1] 2–339 [340] 341–44, illustrations (on glossy paper) tipped-in on pp.[ii], 13, 27, 41, 48, 94, 115, 133, 143, 151, 165, 172, 181, 194, 201, 211, 267, 275, 292, 296, 311, 322 and 341 (even-numbered pages are all verso sides of a leaf and the illustration occurs on the verso of the tipped-in leaf, odd-numbered pages, similarly, are recto sides of a leaf and the illustration occurs on the recto of the tipped-in leaf, the final tipped-in leaf comprises a map on a leaf larger than the dimensions of the volume and is thus folded twice)

Page contents: [i] half-title: 'ON THE SPANISH MAIN'; [ii] blank (with an additional leaf tipped-in on the verso of which is the frontispiece: 119 × 101mm., 'CAPTAIN WILLIAM DAMPIER' with protective tissue); [iii] title-page; [iv] blank; [v] 'TO | JACK B. YEATS'; [vi] blank; vii–ix 'CONTENTS' (20 chapters described with brief details of subjects within each chapter, and page references, an index is also listed); [x] blank; xi–xii 'LIST OF ILLUSTRATIONS' (23 illustrations including maps listed with page references); [1]–339 text; [340] blank; 341–44 'INDEX'

Paper: wove paper

Running title: 'ON THE SPANISH MAIN' (60mm.) on verso; recto title comprises chapter title, pp.2–339

Binding: blue cloth. On spine, in gold: '[double rule] | ON [square point] THE | SPANISH | MAIN | BY [square point] JOHN | MASEFIELD | [device of anchor and rope design: 84 × 32mm.] | THE MACMILLAN Co. | [double rule]' (all width centred). Upper and lower covers blank with blind ruled borders: 224 × 138mm. Top edge trimmed, others uncut. Binding measurements: 228 × 142mm. (covers), 228 × 61mm. (spine). End-papers: laid paper (no watermark), chain-lines 26mm. apart.

Publication date: published, according to Simmons, 1906

Price: $3.50

Contents:
as for A5(a)

Notes:

Simmons states the volume was published by The Macmillan Company, New York, 1906. However, Handley-Taylor claims that in a communication with that company they do not include the work as one of their previous publications. In the undated promotional booklet *John Masefield* published (probably in 1926) by the Macmillan Company, presumably it is A5(d) (the second American edition) that is listed in the 'American Bibliography' section dated 1925 with the note 'imported; previously published in England'. *The National Union Catalog: Pre–1956 Imprints* Vol. 366 lists both an edition published by the Macmillan Company dated 1906 and also an edition published by the Macmillan Company in 1925.

Wight fails to note the cancel title.

Each chapter commences with a drop-capital.

Copies seen: Northeastern Illinois University (F 2161 M38 1906)

A5(c) Second English edition (1922)

ON THE SPANISH | MAIN | OR, SOME ENGLISH FORAYS ON THE ISTHMUS | OF DARIEN. WITH A DESCRIPTION OF | THE BUCCANEERS AND A SHORT | ACCOUNT OF OLD ~ TIME | SHIPS AND SAILORS | BY | JOHN MASEFIELD | SECOND EDITION | METHUEN & CO. LTD, | 36 ESSEX STREET W.C. | LONDON
(All width centred)

Bibliographies: Simmons [unrecorded], Nevinson [unrecorded], Handley-Taylor [unrecorded], Wight [unrecorded]

Collation: [π]⁶ 1–16⁸ 17¹⁰; the second leaf of gathering 17 is also signed; signatures left foot of page; 144 leaves; 187 × 122mm.; the catalogue (not included in collation or leaf count) comprises a single unsigned gathering of 4 leaves; [i–viii] ix–xi [xii] 1–273 [274–76]; catalogue pagination: [1] 2–8

Page contents: [i–ii] blank; [iii] half-title: 'ON THE SPANISH MAIN'; [iv] blank; [v] title-page; [vi] '*First published (Demy 8vo, Illustrated) in 1906 | This Edition (Cr. 8vo) was first published in 1922*'; [vii] 'TO | JACK B. YEATS'; [viii] blank; ix–xi 'CONTENTS' (20 chapters described with brief details of subjects within each chapter, and page references, an index is also listed); [xii] blank; 1–268 text; 269–73 'INDEX'; [274] '*Printed in Great Britain by* | Butler & Tanner, | *Frome and London.*'; [275–76] blank; [1]–8 catalogue: 'A SELECTION FROM | MESSRS. METHUEN'S | PUBLICATIONS'

Paper: wove paper (catalogue: wove paper (thinner than that used for the other gatherings))

Running title: 'ON THE SPANISH MAIN' (46mm.) on verso; recto title comprises chapter title, pp.2–272

Binding: blue cloth. On spine, in gold: 'ON [square point] THE | SPANISH | MAIN | BY [square point] JOHN | MASEFIELD | [device of anchor and rope design: 83 × 32mm.] [in yellow] | METHUEN' (all width centred). On upper cover, in yellow: three-masted ship at sea with shining sun, all within ornate border comprising six flowering roses, four rosebuds, with leaves and stalks: 107 × 87mm. Lower cover: blank. Top and fore edges trimmed, lower outside edge uncut. Binding measurements: 195 × 123mm. (covers), 195 × 46mm. (spine). End-papers: wove paper.

Publication date: published, according to the *English Catalogue of Books*, October 1922

Price: 8s.6d.

Contents:
as for A5(a)

Notes:
The text has been entirely re-set for this edition. It does not contain any revisions.

A letter, dated from March 1923, from Masefield to The Society of Authors states:

> *Spanish Main* I send you a very bad agreement wh[ich] I made many years ago. The book was a dead failure + remaindered + forgotten. Last autumn Methuens reprinted it, as of course they had a right to do, + it is now on sale…

> (John Masefield, letter to G.H. Thring, March 1923)
> (BL, Add.Mss. 56578, f.148)

The purpose of Masefield's letter was to ask the Society to collect royalties on the work. In view of the early failure of the work, it is presumed that the second edition was due to the popularity of Masefield in the 1920s.

Copies seen: private collection (PWE); BL (9773.de.27) stamped 19 OCT 1922

Reprinted:
'Third Edition'   [second edition, second impression]   1924

A5(d) Second American edition (1925)

ON THE SPANISH | MAIN | OR, SOME ENGLISH FORAYS ON THE ISTHMUS | OF DARIEN. WITH A DESCRIPTION OF | THE BUCCANEERS AND A SHORT | ACCOUNT OF OLD ~ TIME | SHIPS AND SAILORS | BY | JOHN MASEFIELD | NEW YORK | THE MACMILLAN COMPANY | 1925
(All width centred)

Bibliographies: Simmons [unrecorded], Nevinson [unrecorded], Handley-Taylor [unrecorded], Wight [unrecorded]

Collation: [A]⁶ 1–16⁸ 17¹⁰; the second leaf of gathering 17 is also signed; signatures left foot of page; 144 leaves; 187 × 122mm.; [i–viii] ix–xi [xii] 1–273 [274–76]

Page contents: [i–ii] blank; [iii] half-title: 'ON THE SPANISH MAIN'; [iv] blank; [v] title-page; [vi] 'PRINTED IN GREAT BRITAIN'; [vii] 'TO | JACK B. YEATS'; [viii] blank; ix–xi 'CONTENTS' (20 chapters described with brief details of subjects within each chapter, and page references, an index is also listed); [xii] blank; 1–268 text; 269–73 'INDEX'; [274] 'Printed in Great Britain by | Butler & Tanner, | Frome and London'; [275–76] blank

Paper: wove paper

Running title: 'ON THE SPANISH MAIN' (46mm.) on verso; recto title comprises chapter title, pp.2–272

Binding: blue cloth. On spine, in gold: 'ON [square point] THE | SPANISH | MAIN | BY [square point] JOHN | MASEFIELD | [device of anchor and rope design: 83 × 32mm.] [in yellow] | MACMILLAN' (all width centred). On upper cover, in yellow: three-masted ship at sea with shining sun, all within ornate border comprising six flowering roses, four rosebuds, with leaves and stalks: 107 × 87mm. Lower cover: blank. Top and fore edges trimmed, lower outside edge roughly trimmed. Binding measurements: 195 × 123mm. (covers), 195 × 46mm. (spine). End-papers: wove paper.

Publication date: 1925

Price: $2.50

Contents:
as for A5(a)

Notes:
This American edition has obvious similarities to A5(c). However, unlike similar examples, the title-page in this edition is not a cancellans. As the first gathering consists of six leaves and the title-page occurs on the third leaf, this edition may consist of the Methuen printing with conjugate leaves [A]3 and [A]4 substituted by Macmillan. No obvious difference in paper stock can be detected.

Copies seen: Columbia University Libraries (Special Collections B825.M377.U.1925)

A5(e) Third English edition (1972)

ON THE SPANISH MAIN | OR, SOME ENGLISH FORAYS ON THE | ISTHMUS OF DARIEN. WITH A DESCRIP- | TION OF THE BUCCANEERS AND A | SHORT ACCOUNT OF OLD-TIME | SHIPS AND SAILORS | BY | JOHN MASEFIELD | Conway Maritime Press | 1972
(All width centred)

Bibliographies: Wight [unrecorded]

Publication date: published, according to *Whitaker's*, October 1972

Price: £3.20

Contents:
as for A5(a)

Notes:
This edition comprises a photographic reprint of A5(a). Despite having the same number of illustrations, however, these illustrations are not identical.

This volume states, on page [iv], that it is printed in Great Britain by Latimer Trend Ltd., Whitstable, Kent.

The ISBN number is 0 85177 053 3.

The publishing agreement for this edition between The Society of Authors and Conway Maritime Press was dated 28 June 1972 (see Archives of The Society of Authors).

Copies seen: private collection (PWE)

A5(f) Third American edition (1972)

In 1972 the Naval Institute Press published the American edition of A5(e).

A6 A TARPAULIN MUSTER   1907

A6(a) First English edition (1907)

A TARPAULIN | MUSTER | BY | JOHN MASEFIELD | LONDON | E. GRANT RICHARDS | 1907
(All width centred)

Bibliographies: Danielson 164, Williams p.7, Simmons [6], Nevinson p.15, Handley-Taylor p.28, Wight [6]

Collation: [A]⁸ B-N⁸ O¹⁰ (J not used); signatures left foot of page; O5 is also signed; 114 leaves; the catalogue (not included in collation or leaf count) comprises a single gathering of 10 leaves of which the second is signed; 192 × 124mm.; [1–10] 11–227 [228], catalogue pagination: [1–2] 3–19 [20]

Page contents: [1] half-title: 'A TARPAULIN MUSTER'; [2] 'RECENT FICTION | [eight titles and their authors listed] | [rule] | *Six Shillings Each* | [rule] | E. GRANT RICHARDS'; [3] title-page; [4] *'The cover design of this volume is | by Mr. Symington. It is reproduced | by permission from "The Inchcape | Rock," published by Messrs. Burns | and Oates, Ltd.'*; [5] 'TO | H. G. B.'; [6] blank; [7] 'CONTENTS' (24 stories listed with titles and page references); [8] blank; [9] 'NOTE | NINETEEN of these tales and articles have been | printed in the *Manchester Guardian* during the | last two years. I thank the Editor and the Pro- | prietors of that paper for their kindness in per- | mitting me to reprint these items in this volume. | [new paragraph] The story "El Dorado" was printed in the | February issue of *Macmillan's Magazine*; the story | "Davy Jones's Gift" appeared in *Country Life* | (11 Nov., 1905); "The Yarn of Happy Jack" | and "Some Irish Fairies" appeared in the *Speaker* | within the last eighteen months. I thank Messrs. | Macmillan, and the Proprietors of *Country Life* | and of the *Speaker* for allowing me to use these | stories. The other tale is now printed for the first | time. J. M.'; [10] blank; 11-[228] text (at foot of p.[228]: 'PLYMOUTH | WILLIAM BRENDON AND SON, LTD., PRINTERS'); [1–20] catalogue: 'A CATALOGUE | OF BOOKS PUBLISHED BY | E. GRANT RICHARDS | 7 Carlton Street, London | TOGETHER WITH A LIST | OF ANNOUNCEMENTS, 1907' (at foot of p.[20]: 'LONDON : STRANGEWAYS, PRINTERS.')

Paper: wove paper (catalogue: laid paper, chain-lines 19mm. apart)

Running title: 'A TARPAULIN MUSTER' (51mm.) on verso; recto title comprises story title, pp.12-[228]

Binding: tan cloth. On spine, in black: 'A Tar- | paulin | Muster | John | Masefield | E. Grant | Richards' (all width centred). On upper cover: '[drawing in black of full rigged ship at sea, with birds; signed (in lower left corner) 'LDS | 1906' within bold black border: 114 × 109mm.] | [rule, 115mm.] [in orange / red] | A Tarpaulin | Muster | John Masefield [in black and within bold black border: 58 × 110mm.]' (all enclosed within bold orange / red border: 193 × 119mm. Although the orange / red rule noted above does not actually touch this border, the impression is given of two rectangles measuring 123 × 119mm. and 71 × 119mm. respectively from the top). Simmons states the binding uses dark blue ink for printing. This must constitute either a mistake for black ink, or a variant binding. Lower cover: blank. All edges trimmed. Binding measurements: 199 × 125mm. (covers), 199 × 50mm. (spine). End-papers: wove paper

Publication date: published, according to Simmons, 11 April 1907 in an edition of 1500 copies

Price: 3s.6d.

Contents:

I. Edward Herries ('Edward Herries, the poet, rose from his chair...')
    No previous appearance traced
II. A White Night ('Sometimes, when I am idle, my mind fills with a vivid memory.')
    First printed in The Manchester Guardian *3 October 1905, p.12*
III. Big Jim ('One afternoon, many years ago, I was in a Western seaport...')
    First printed in The Manchester Guardian *22 January 1907, p.12*
IV. El Dorado ('The night had fallen over the harbour before the winch began to rattle.')
    First printed as 'The Gold-Seeker' in Macmillan's Magazine *February 1907, pp.[314]–20*
V. The Pirates of Santa Anna ('On the coast of Venezuela, not more than thirty miles...')
    First printed as 'The Pirates Of Sant' Anna' in The Manchester Guardian *9 November 1904, p.12*
VI. Davy Jones's Gift ('"Once upon a time," said the sailor, "the Devil and Davy Jones…"')
    First printed as 'Davy Jones's Gift (A Folk-Lore Story)' in Country Life *11 November 1905, pp.661–62*
VII. Ghosts ('"Ghosts are common enough," said an old sailor to me...')
    First printed in The Manchester Guardian *5 November 1906, p.12*
VIII. Ambitious Jimmy Hicks ('"Well," said the captain of the foretop to me...')
    First printed in The Manchester Guardian *16 June 1905, p.12*
IX. Anty Bligh ('One night in the tropics I was "farmer" in the middle watch...')
    First printed in The Manchester Guardian *15 March 1905, p.12*
X. On Growing Old ('The other day I met an old sailor friend at a café.')
    First printed in The Manchester Guardian *17 August 1906, p.10*
XI. A Memory ('In these first frosty days, now that there is mist at dusk...')
    First printed in The Manchester Guardian *4 October 1906, p.12*
XII. On the Palisades ('On the west side of the Hudson River there is a cliff, or crag...')
    First printed in The Manchester Guardian *17 May 1906, p.12*
XIII. The Rest-House on the Hill ('In a town it is easy to despise the visionary...')
    First printed in The Manchester Guardian *28 August 1906, p.12*
XIV. Gentle People ('My friend the old labourer was "never much bothered" by the fairies.')
    First printed in The Manchester Guardian *12 September 1906, p.10*
XV. Some Irish Fairies ('There are not many fairies in England.')
    First printed in The Speaker *10 November 1906, pp.173–74*

XVI. The Cape Horn Calm ('Off Cape Horn there are but two kinds of weather...')
First printed in The Manchester Guardian *18 July 1905, p.12*

XVII. A Port Royal Twister ('Once upon a time, said the Jamaican in the tavern...')
First printed in The Manchester Guardian *30 May 1905, p.12*

XVIII. In a Fo'c'sle ('Ashore, in the towns, men find it easy to amuse themselves...')
First printed in The Manchester Guardian *9 March 1905, p.14*

XIX. The Bottom of the Well ('"Once upon a time there was a sailor named Bill.')
First printed in The Manchester Guardian *7 September 1905, p.12*

XX. Being Ashore ('In the nights, in the winter nights, in the nights of storm...')
First printed in The Manchester Guardian *20 February 1906, p.14*

XXI. One Sunday ('Ten years ago I was "in the half-deck" of a four-masted barque.')
First printed in The Manchester Guardian *15 September 1905, p.12*

XXII. A Raines Law Arrest ('When I was working in a New York saloon...')
First printed in The Manchester Guardian *9 May 1905, p.12*

XXIII. The Schooner-Man's Close Calls ('On the Hudson River shore near the railway...')
First printed in The Manchester Guardian *10 July 1906, p.14*

XXIV. The Yarn of Happy Jack ('I once knew an old Norwegian sailor...')
First printed in The Speaker *2 September 1905, pp.522–23*

Notes:

The publishing agreement for this title between Masefield and E. Grant Richards was dated 8 February 1907 (see Archives of The Society of Authors). The agreement refers to '...a collection of stories... at present provisionally entitled "A Tarpaulin Muster"...'

As stated in the note on p.[4], the cover illustration by Mr. Symington is from *The Inchcape Rock*. A different illustration from the same work is used as the cover illustration for *Captain Margaret* (see A7(a)). The British Library notes Lindsay D. Symington as the illustrator of *The Inchcape Rock*. Danielson confuses this illustrator with J. Ayton Symington.

Each story commences with a drop-capital, whilst each page number is given within square brackets.

A copy of this edition held in W.B. Yeats' library, in Dalkey, Ireland (1256) is inscribed 'W.B. Yeats | from John Masefield | April 15, 1907'.

It appears that Richards first approached Masefield with a suggestion about this collection at the end of 1906. The author immediately wrote to Cazenove explaining:

> ...a few days ago Mr Grant Richards asked me to let him see any short stories I might have by me. I have sent him 22, mostly 500 words long, which have appeared in the Manchester Guardian during the last two years. If he thinks fit to publish them, may I refer him to you to settle terms? I do not wish to sell them outright; but he will no doubt ask me to do so if he decides to use them. You must excuse me for not having placed the tales with you in the first instance. I had no intention of publishing them until he asked to see them.
>
> (John Masefield, letter to C.F. Cazenove, 5 November 1906)
> (University of Arizona Library. MS.50, V.I)

Masefield next appears to write to his agent about the collection during January 1907:

> Will you see Richards about the enclosed? He has some 22 sketches, or 1500 word stories, all of which have appeared in magazines. I won't sell them outright; but he is, I fancy, eager to publish them; so perhaps you may be able to make him give good terms, + even get a sum in advance of royalty.
>
> (John Masefield, letter to C.F. Cazenove, 9 January 1907)
> (University of Arizona Library. MS.50, V.I)

Given Richards' previous bankruptcy (see notes to A1(aa)), Cazenove may have urged caution about the publisher or Richards' insistence on Masefield selling his rights. Masefield responded – with apparent reference to *A Tarpaulin Muster*:

> I've decided to go through with the books. He has treated me squarely since the smash; and the smash only lost me a couple of pounds; so he may have the stories...
>
> (John Masefield, letter to C.F. Cazenove, 20 January 1907)
> (University of Arizona Library. MS.50, V.I)

Grant Richards, in *Author Hunting* writes:

> The sea articles [from *The Manchester Guardian*] I reprinted under the title of *A Tarpaulin Muster* in 1907, but no sooner had the agreement been signed than Masefield began, quite unnecessarily, to be nervous about the excellent, the unique, material the book was to contain. His slight distaste for it continued, for on December 21, 1911, writing from 30 Maida Hill West, he tells me that I should be well advised to leave out two-thirds of it and to print about a third "all of the sea"; and in a postscript he returns to the subject: "Looking through the *Muster* I see about 100 pages of tolerable stuff. The rest, Ach Gott!" Well, I did not, and do not, agree with him; and anyhow the stuff would never have got into the *Manchester Guardian* if it had not been very good.
>
> (Grant Richards, *Author Hunting*, Hamish Hamilton, 1934, p.227)

In a letter to Harley Granville-Barker, the dedicatee of the book, Masefield writes:

> You must tell your friends that I am, quite frankly, a fraud, + that I have very little sea-experience; but you must tell them, also, that an artist is only hampered by experience; + that it is no more necessary to be a sailor, to write about the sea, than it was necessary for Shakespeare to keep a brothel, or to poison his father, in order to write parts of Hamlet + of Measure for Measure. Of the stories in A Tarpaulin Muster[:]

Edward Herries	is	invention.
White Night.	[is]	actual reminiscence.
Big Jim.	[is]	a mixture of dream, fact + invention.
Dorado.	[is]	mostly invention, based on fact, + on a story a sailor told me.
Santa Anna.	[is]	invention. But now claimed in Venezuela as local folk lore.
Davy's Gift	[is]	[invention]
Ghosts.	[is]	reminiscence + sailor's gossip.
Hicks.	[is]	actual reminiscence. Story told me by Wally Blair, now dead.
Anty Bligh	[is]	[actual reminiscence.] Story suggested by a sailor, + by a drawing of Jack Yeats's.
On growing old	[is]	[actual reminiscence] + vanity
A Memory	[is]	[actual reminiscence]
Palisades	[is]	[actual reminiscence] story suggested by a correspondent
Rest House	[was]	Told me by an old Irish labourer
Gentle People	[was]	Told me by an old Irish labourer
Some Irish	[was]	Told me by an old Irish labourer
Cape Horn Calm.	[is]	memory.
Port Royal.	[is]	invention.
In a focsle	[is]	memory
The Well	[is]	invention, + very bad at that.
Being Ashore	[is]	memory
One Sunday	[is]	memory
Raines Law	[is]	[memory]
Schooner Man	[was]	Told me by a sailor in exchange for some trousers.
Happy Jack	[was]	founded on a tale a sailor told me.

> (John Masefield, letter to Harley Granville-Barker, 30 March 1907)
> (BL, Add.Mss.47897, f.13)

Copies seen: BL (012634.aaa.35) stamped 25 APR 1907; NYPL (Berg Collection) inscribed 'Jack. B. Yeats | from John Masefield | April 15. 1907.'

A6(b) First American edition (1908)

A TARPAULIN | MUSTER | BY | JOHN MASEFIELD | NEW YORK | B. W. DODGE & COMPANY | 1908 (All width centred)

Bibliographies: Danielson [unrecorded], Williams [unrecorded], Simmons [noted on page 16], Nevinson [unrecorded], Handley-Taylor p.28, Wight 6a

Collation: [A]⁸ (±[A]1, ±[A]2) B-N⁸ O¹⁰ (J not used); signatures left foot of page; O5 is also signed; 114 leaves; 192 × 124mm.; [1–10] 11–227 [228]

Page contents: [1] half-title: 'A TARPAULIN MUSTER'; [2] blank; [3] title-page; [4] 'PRINTED BY | WILLIAM BRENDON AND SONS, LTD. | PLYMOUTH, ENGLAND'; [5] 'TO | H. G. B.'; [6] blank; [7] 'CONTENTS' (24 stories listed with titles and page references); [8] blank; [9] 'NOTE | NINETEEN of these tales and articles have been | printed in the *Manchester Guardian* during the | last two years. I thank the Editor and the Pro- | prietors of that paper for their kindness in per- | mitting me to reprint these items in this volume. | [new paragraph] The story "El Dorado" was printed in the | February issue of *Macmillan's Magazine*; the story | "Davy Jones's Gift" appeared in *Country Life* | (11 Nov., 1905); "The Yarn of Happy Jack" | and "Some Irish Fairies" appeared in the *Speaker* | within the last eighteen months. I thank Messrs. | Macmillan, and the Proprietors of *Country Life* | and of the *Speaker* for allowing me to use these | stories. The other tale is now printed for the first | time. J. M.'; [10] blank; 11-[228] text (at foot of p.[228]: 'PLYMOUTH | WILLIAM BRENDON AND SON, LTD., PRINTERS')

Paper: wove paper

Running title: 'A TARPAULIN MUSTER' (51mm.) on verso; recto title comprises story title, pp.12-[228]

Binding: red cloth. On spine, in gold: 'A Tar- | paulin | Muster | John | Masefield | B.W.DODGE | &COMPANY' (lines 1–3 and 5 justified on both left and right margins, line 4 width centred and lines 6–7 justified on different left and right margins). On upper cover, in gold: 'A Tarpaulin | Muster | John Masefield' (all enclosed within ruled border: 59 × 112mm.) Lower cover: blank. All edges trimmed. Binding measurements: 193 × 122mm. (covers), 193 × 47mm. (spine). End-papers: wove paper.

Publication date: 1908

Price: $1.00

Contents:
as for A6(a)

Notes:
Simmons notes that *A Tarpaulin Muster* was 'republished by B.W. Dodge and Company, New York, 1908'. This information was repeated by Handley-Taylor. Wight was the first bibliographer to describe the edition. He neglects, however, to record the cancellans of the first two leaves of the first gathering. The first two leaves have been cut out and two conjugate leaves (comprising pages [1–4]) inserted onto the first stub. Presumably the sheets of the volume were supplied by Grant Richards and the cancellans was necessary to remove redundant material present in the first English edition. Simmons states that the first American edition of *Captain Margaret* comprised sheets imported from England. Presumably a similar arrangement applied here. Whether the sheets for *A Tarpaulin Muster* were part of the original English edition printing of 1500 copies is unknown.

Copies seen: Harvard College Library (Widener 23697.10.49.20); J. Eugene Smith Library, Eastern Connecticut State College (PR6025.A77 T38) rebound

A6(c) Second English edition (1913)

A TARPAULIN | MUSTER | BY | JOHN MASEFIELD | [ornament] | LONDON | GRANT RICHARDS LTD. | PUBLISHERS
(All width centred)

Bibliographies: Danielson [unrecorded], Williams [unrecorded], Simmons [unrecorded], Nevinson [unrecorded], Handley-Taylor [unrecorded], Wight [unrecorded]

Collation: [A]⁸ B–O⁸ (J not used); signatures left foot of page; 112 leaves; 183 × 121mm,; [1–12] 13–224 (the final digit of 165 is missing, the number appearing as '16')

Page contents: [1–2] blank; [3] half-title: 'A TARPAULIN MUSTER'; [4] '*BY THE SAME AUTHOR* | [rule] | [three volumes listed with sizes, prices and press reviews] | [rule] | GRANT RICHARDS LTD. | PUBLISHERS | LONDON'; [5] title-page; [6] '*First Edition ... April 1907* | *Second Edition ... August 1913*'; [7] 'TO | H. G. B.'; [8] '*The cover design of this volume is* | *by Mr. Symington. It is reproduced* | *by permission from "The Inchcape* | *Rock," published by Messrs. Burns* | *and Oates, Ltd.*'; [9] 'CONTENTS' (24 stories listed with titles and page references); [10] blank; [11] 'NOTE | NINETEEN of these tales and articles have been | printed in the *Manchester Guardian* during the | last two years. I thank the Editor and the Pro- | prietors of that paper for their kindness in per- | mitting me to reprint these items in this volume. | [new paragraph] The story "El Dorado" was printed in the | February issue of *Macmillan's Magazine*; the story | "Davy Jones's Gift" appeared in *Country Life* | (11 Nov., 1905); "The Yarn of Happy Jack" | and "Some Irish Fairies" appeared in the *Speaker* | within the last eighteen months. I thank Messrs. | Macmillan, and the Proprietors of *Country Life* | and of the *Speaker* for allowing me to use these | stories. The other tale is now printed for the first | time. J. M.'; [12] blank; 13–224 text (at foot of p.224: 'WILLIAM BRENDON AND SON, LTD. | PRINTERS, PLYMOUTH')

Paper: laid paper (no watermark), chain-lines 27mm. apart

Running title: 'A TARPAULIN MUSTER' (47mm.) on verso; recto title comprises story title, pp.14–224

Binding: grey cloth. On spine, in black: 'A Tar- | paulin | Muster | John | Masefield | Grant | Richards' (all width centred) (see notes). On upper cover: '[drawing in black of full rigged ship at sea, with birds, signed (in lower left corner) 'LDS | 1906' within bold border: 114 × 109mm.] | [bold rule, 116mm.] | A Tarpaulin | Muster | John Masefield [within double bold borders: 57 × 111mm. and 52 × 105mm.]' (all enclosed within bold border: 188 × 120mm. In contrast with the first English edition, the bold rule does touch this border, producing two rectangles: 123 × 120mm. and 67 × 120mm. respectively from the top). Lower cover: blank. All edges trimmed. Binding measurements: 192 × 125mm. (covers), 192 × 39mm. (spine). End-papers: either wove paper or laid paper (no watermark), chain-lines 27mm. apart.

Publication date: published, according to the *English Catalogue of Books*, August 1913

Price: 3s.6d.

Contents:
as for A6(a)

Notes:
Typographically, the drop-capitals of the first edition are not retained here and the text has been re-set, closely following the lineation of the first edition. Textually, this edition does not differ from the first edition.

There are at least two variations in the appearance of the publisher's name on the binding. Although otherwise identical, one example is slightly larger than the other. As one point of comparison, the 'a' of 'Grant' measures either 2mm. or 3mm.

Copies seen: private collection (PWE); BL (X.989/11459) stamped 15 NOV 1967

Reprinted:

| 'Reprinted' | [second edition, second impression] | Mar 1915 |
| 'Reprinted' | [second edition, third impression] | Apr 1920 |

A6(d) Second American edition (1919)

A | TARPAULIN MUSTER | BY | JOHN MASEFIELD. | [publisher's device: 18 × 19mm.] | NEW YORK |
DODD, MEAD AND COMPANY | 1919
(All width centred)

Bibliographies: Danielson [unrecorded], Williams [unrecorded], Simmons [unrecorded], Nevinson [unrecorded], Handley-Taylor [unrecorded], Wight [unrecorded]

Collation: [A–O]⁸ (J not used); 112 leaves; 188 × 125mm,; [i–vi] 1–217 [218]

Page contents: [i] title-page; [ii] 'PUBLISHED IN U.S.A., 1919 | BY DODD, MEAD AND COMPANY, INC.'; [iii] 'TO | H. G. B.'; [iv] 'NOTE | NINETEEN of these tales and articles have been | printed in the *Manchester Guardian* during the | last two years. I thank the Editor and the Pro- | prietors of that paper for their kindness in per- | mitting me to reprint these items in this volume. | [new paragraph] The story "El Dorado" was printed in the | February issue of *Macmillan's Magazine;* the | story "Davy Jones's Gift" appeared in | *Country Life* (11 Nov., 1905); "The Yarn of | Happy Jack" and "Some Irish Fairies" ap- | peared in the *Speaker* within the last eighteen | months. I thank Messrs. Macmillan, and the | Proprietors of *Country Life* and of the *Speaker* | for allowing me to use these stories. The other | tale is now printed for the first | time. J. M.'; [iv] 'CONTENTS' (24 stories listed with titles and page references); [v] blank; 1–217 text

Paper: wove paper

Running title: 'A TARPAULIN MUSTER' (47mm.) on verso; recto title comprises story title, pp.2–217

Binding: grey cloth. On spine, in black: 'A Tar- | paulin | Muster | John | Masefield | DODD,MEAD | &COMPANY' (all width centred). On upper cover: '[drawing in black of full rigged ship at sea, with birds, signed (in lower left corner) 'LDS | 1906' within bold border: 111 × 109mm.] | [bold rule, 116mm.] | A Tarpaulin | Muster | John Masefield [within bold border: 56 × 109mm.]' (all enclosed within bold black border: 183 × 118mm. The bold rule touches this border, producing two rectangles: 120 × 118mm. and 65 × 118mm. respectively from the top). Lower cover: blank. All edges trimmed. Binding measurements: 193 × 126mm. (covers), 193 × 41mm. (spine). End-papers: wove paper.

Publication date: 1919

Price: unknown

Contents:
as for A6(a)

Notes:
The text has been re-set for this edition.

Copies seen: private collection (PWE)

A6(e) Third English edition (1926)

A Tarpaulin Muster | *by* | John Masefield | 1926 | [rule, 34mm.] | *London:* Martin Secker
(All width centred and enclosed within double ruled border: 138 × 86mm.)

Bibliographies: Simmons [unrecorded], Nevinson [unrecorded], Handley-Taylor [unrecorded], Wight [unrecorded]

Collation: [A]⁸ B-K⁸ L⁶ (J not used); signatures left foot of page; 86 leaves; 191 × 115mm.; [1–8] 9–171 [172]

Page contents: [1] half-title: '*A TARPAULIN MUSTER* | *THE NEW* | *ADELPHI LIBRARY* | *VOLUME 25*'; [2] 'The New Adelphi Library | VOL. | [26 titles, their authors and volume numbers listed] | *Other titles in preparation*'; [3] title-page; [4] '*Bibliography* | *First Published 1907* | *Included in New Adelphi Library 1926 by arrangement with* | *Messrs. Grant Richards Ltd.* | LONDON: MARTIN SECKER (LTD) 1926'; [5] 'TO | H. G. B.'; [6] blank; [7] '*Contents*' (24 stories listed with titles and page references); [8] blank; 9-[172] text (at foot of p.[172]: 'Printed in Great Britain at | *The Mayflower Press, Plymouth.* William Brendon & Son, Ltd.')

Paper: wove paper

Running title: '*A Tarpaulin Muster*' (36mm.) on verso; recto title comprises story title, pp.10-[172]

Binding: green cloth. On spine, in gold: '*A* | *TARPAULIN* | *MUSTER* | [circle in outline] | *MASEFIELD* | *NEW* | *ADELPHI* | *LIBRARY*' (all width centred). Covers: blank. Top and fore edges trimmed, lower outside edge uncut. Binding measurements: 194 × 114mm. (covers), 194 × 22mm. (spine). End-papers: wove paper.

Publication date: published, according to the *English Catalogue of Books,* December 1926

Price: 3s.6d.

Contents:
as for A6(a)

Notes:
The text has been entirely re-set for this edition. Each story commences with a drop-capital. The stories are not numbered in this edition.

The running-titles include a number of swash characters.

On one of many attempts to buy back from Grant Richards the copyright of his books Masefield confronted the agreement for this edition between Richards and Martin Secker. In April 1931 Masefield offered a sum of two hundred pounds for 'the entire Richards interest and stock' of *Captain Margaret, Multitude and Solitude* and *A Tarpaulin Muster* noting that 'the books aren't worth it, but I offer it.' (see BL, Add.Mss.56593, f.122). Additional contracts on these titles between Grant Richards and other firms caused The Society of Authors (acting for Masefield) to pause. The Society wrote to Masefield:

> The offer to the Richards Press had better not be made until I know the terms on which Messrs Secker hold the Tarpaulin Muster.
>
> (Denys Kilham Roberts, letter to John Masefield, [22 April 1931])
> (BL, Add.Mss.56593, f.134)

The Richards Press Ltd replied to The Society of Authors' enquiries with details of the original contract for this edition:

> In reply to your letter of the 23rd the arrangement with Mr. Martin Secker is made in a letter from Grant Richards Ltd. dated August 24, 1926 as follows:-
>
> > "We hereby make over to you the right to print John Masefield's "Tarpaulin Muster" in your New Adelphi Library at 3/6 against a 10% royalty, you having given to us a bill of exchange due December 25 for £50 on account of such royalty. We bind ourselves to issue no edition at a lower price than 3/6."
> >
> > (Richards Press Ltd., letter to Denys Kilham Roberts, 24 April 1931)
> > (BL, Add.Mss.56593, f.143)

This caused concern and, in the circumstances, Masefield accordingly wrote:

> I feel that as the *Tarpaulin Muster* can hardly be had, there is little use in making any offer; so we will let the books go, + make no offer at all.
>
> (John Masefield, letter to Denys Kilham Roberts, [28 April 1931])
> (BL, Add.Mss.56593, f.147)

Copies seen: private collection (PWE)

A7 CAPTAIN MARGARET 1908

A7(a) First English edition (1908)

CAPTAIN | MARGARET | *A ROMANCE* | BY | JOHN MASEFIELD | *I thought Love lived in the hot sunshine :* | *But, O, he lives in the moony light.* | [ornament] | LONDON | GRANT RICHARDS | 1908
(All width centred)

Bibliographies: Danielson 165, Williams p.8, Simmons [7], Nevinson p.15, Handley-Taylor p.28, Wight [7]

Collation: [A]⁴ B-F⁸ [G]⁸ H-Z⁸ 2A–2C⁸ 2D⁴ (J, V and W not used); signatures left foot of page; 208 leaves; 196 × 127mm.; [i–viii] [1] 2–405 [406–408]

Page contents: [i] half-title: 'CAPTAIN MARGARET'; [ii] '*ANNOUNCEMENTS* | [14 titles, authors and prices listed] | [rule] | GRANT RICHARDS, LONDON'; [iii] title-page; [iv] '*The cover design of this volume is taken from* | *Mr. Symington's drawing in "The Inchcape* | *Rock," by permission of Messrs. Burns and* | *Oates, Ltd.*'; [v] 'TO | MY WIFE'; [vi] blank; [vii] 'CONTENTS' (12 chapters listed with titles and page references); [viii] blank; [1]-[406] text (at foot of p.[406]: 'WILLIAM BRENDON AND SON, LTD. | PRINTERS, PLYMOUTH'); [407] publisher's advertisement (within ruled border: 69 × 49mm.); [408] blank

Paper: laid paper (no watermark), chain-lines 20mm. apart

Running title: '*CAPTAIN MARGARET*' (45mm.) on verso; recto title comprises chapter title, pp.2-[406]

Binding: dark-blue cloth (see notes). On spine, in gold: 'CAPTAIN | MARGARET | JOHN | MASEFIELD | GRANT | RICHARDS' (all width centred). On upper cover, in gold: 'CAPTAIN MARGARET | [design of full rigged ship within rectangular border: 96 × 68mm.]' Lower cover: blank. Top edge gilt, others uncut. Binding measurements: 202 × 133mm. (covers), 202 × 52mm. (spine). Front end-papers: 'A MAP OF THE IAMES RIVER | AND THE | VIRGINIA COLONY' signed '*By* Philip Seacole *at the Sign of the* | [device] Pye's Neft [device] | LONDON' within four ruled borders: 171 × 227mm. Rear end-papers: 'A DRAUGHT OF THE | SAMBALLOES ISLANDS, &C.' signed '*By* Philip Seacole *at the Sign of the* | [device] Pye's Neft [device] | LONDON' within four ruled borders: 172 × 228mm. End-papers: wove paper.

Publication date: published, according to Simmons, 17 June 1908 in an edition of 2000 copies (of which 1000 copies were sold in the United States, with a reprinted title-page: see A7(b))

Price: 6s.

Contents:
Captain Margaret ('The short summer night was over; the stars were paling; there was a faint light...')

Chapter headings are as follows:

I.	The "Broken Heart"	VII.	The Tobacco Merchant
II.	A Farewell	VIII.	In Port
III.	Outwards	IX.	A Farewell Dinner
IV.	A Cabin Council	X.	The Landfall
V.	Stukeley	XI.	The Flag of Truce
VI.	A Supper Party	XII.	The End

Notes:

The publishing agreement for this title between Masefield and E. Grant Richards was dated 28 May 1907 (see Archives of The Society of Authors). The agreement refers to 'a novel at present unnamed to be written in accordance with synopsis already submitted…' A brief plot synopsis in Masefield's hand is present in the Houghton Collection of Harvard University. The plot is different from that eventually written. This may be the synopsis Richards requests in a letter from October 1907:

> …let it be accompanied by a tentative synopsis showing how the plot works out – not a synopsis by which you will be bound, but giving an idea of your intention.
>
> (Grant Richards, letter to John Masefield, 19 October 1907)
> (Archives of Grant Richards. University of Illinois / Chadwyck-Healey microfilm, A12, f.248)

Wight describes a binding in black cloth. He either mistakes the dark blue, or may be describing one of the 1000 copies imported to America (sold with a reprinted title-page and bound in black cloth). See A7(b).

Both first English editions of *A Tarpaulin Muster* and *Captain Margaret* use different illustrations from Lindsay D. Symington's illustrations for *The Inchcape Rock*.

Each chapter has a prefatory quotation, including quotation from the works of Donne, Shakespeare, Webster and Rowley, Fletcher, and Chapman. Each chapter commences with a drop-capital.

Grant Richards, in *Author Hunting*, writes:

> I think I may say that Masefield entered on the experiment of novel-writing at my suggestion. If it was not mine, then it was that of C.F. Cazenove, his agent. We used to conspire together, Cazenove and I, and as a result of our conspiracies the two novels [*Captain Margaret* and *Multitude and Solitude*] came into being.
>
> (Grant Richards, *Author Hunting*, Hamish Hamilton, 1934, p.229)

A letter from Masefield to Cazenove suggests that Richards asked for a novel due to the author's inability to work on an historical book:

> The question of a novel cropped up in the course of conversation with Richards. You see the shutting of the Museum rather knocks Anson (about whom Richards is far from sanguine) on the head; but, at the same time, novel writing is an art I know nothing about, + it may very well happen that Richards will not like the tales I have in my mind. I will look you up in a day or two + talk things over…
>
> (John Masefield, letter to C.F. Cazenove, 11 April 1907)
> (University of Arizona Library. MS.50, V.I)

Despite signing a contract for the novel, Masefield was expressing his doubts to Richards by September 1907. Richards replied by quoting the encouraging opinion of his reader, Filson Young (see Archives of Grant Richards. University of Illinois / Chadwyck-Healey microfilm, A12, f.26). Masefield reported he was 'going on with the novel' in October 1907 (see John Masefield, letter to Grant Richards, 12 October 1907) (Fales Library, New York University). On 3 February 1908 Masefield wrote to Richards to state that he was hoping, the next day, to deliver the last chapter (see John Masefield, letter to Grant Richards, 3 February 1908) (Fales Library, New York University).

Grant Richards quotes A.E. Housman's letter of 12 April 1910:

> I also have to thank you for Masefield's two novels, of which I have read Captain Margaret. Quite readable, and containing a number of interesting details; but bad.
>
> (Grant Richards, *Housman 1897–1937*, Oxford University Press, 1942)

Masefield tried (and failed) to suppress the novel. This attempt presumably resulted from Masefield's subsequent dislike of his early writing, rather than a rejection of the story itself. In 1938, for example, he was willing that a translation could be made. Writing to The Society of Authors he states:

> I forget whether I have any right to control the translation of *Captain Margaret*. It is a crude book, written many years ago, but there is no reason why it should not be translated, if the agreement with Richards gives me the power to arrange the matter.
>
> (John Masefield, letter to [E.J.] Mullett, [9 March 1938])
> (BL, Add.Mss.56609, f.10)

Copies seen: BL (012626.ccc.41) stamped 18 JUN 08; Harvard College Library (Houghton *EC9.M377.908c(A)) inscribed for the Lamonts: 'Forget this tale, forget it, only say | He did it wearily in a weary day. | J. Masefield.'; HRHRC (TEMP M377 CA 1908 cop.1) inscribed 'To Con | from Jan. | 17 June. 1908.'

Reprinted:

'Reprinted'	[first edition, second impression]	Jan 1909
'Reprinted'	[first edition, third impression]	Sep 1924
'Reprinted' (The Richards Press)	[first edition, fourth impression]	1948

A7(b) First American edition (1909)

CAPTAIN | MARGARET | *A ROMANCE* | BY | JOHN MASEFIELD | *I thought Love lived in the hot sunshine:* | *But, O, he lives in the moony light.* | [floral device] | PHILADELPHIA | J. B. LIPPINCOTT COMPANY | 1909
(All width centred)

Bibliographies: Danielson [unrecorded], Williams [unrecorded], Simmons [noted on p.17], Nevinson [unrecorded], Handley-Taylor p.28, Wight 7a

Collation: [A]⁴ B–Z⁸ 2A–2C⁸ 2D⁴ (J, V and W not used); signatures left foot of page; 208 leaves; 195 × 129mm.; [i–viii] [1] 2–405 [406–408]

Page contents: [i] half-title: 'CAPTAIN MARGARET'; [ii] blank; [iii] title-page; [iv] blank; [v] 'TO | MY WIFE'; [vi] blank; [vii] 'CONTENTS' (12 chapters listed with titles and page references); [viii] blank; [1]-[406] text (at foot of p.[406]: 'WILLIAM BRENDON AND SON, LTD. | PRINTERS, PLYMOUTH'); [407–408] blank

Paper: laid paper (no watermark), chain-lines 20mm. apart (see notes)

Running title: 'CAPTAIN MARGARET' (45mm.) on verso; recto title comprises chapter title, pp.2-[406]

Binding: black cloth. On spine, in gold: 'CAPTAIN | MARGARET | JOHN | MASEFIELD | LIPPINCOTT' (all width centred). On upper cover, in gold: 'CAPTAIN MARGARET | [design of full rigged ship within rectangular border: 95 × 69mm.]' Lower cover: blank. Top edge gilt, others uncut. Sewn head and foot bands (in blue-black). Binding measurements: 202 × 130mm. (covers), 202 × 57mm. (spine). Front end-papers: 'A MAP OF THE IAMES RIVER | AND THE | VIRGINIA COLONY' signed '*By* Philip Seacole *at the Sign of the* | [device] Pye's Neſt [device] | LONDON' within four ruled borders: 171 × 227mm. Rear end-papers: 'A DRAUGHT OF THE | SAMBALLOES ISLANDS, &C.' signed '*By* Philip Seacole *at the Sign of the* | [device] Pye's Neſt [device] | LONDON' within four ruled borders: 172 × 228mm. End-papers: wove paper.

Publication date: published, according to Simmons, in 1909 in an edition of 1000 copies (see notes)

Price: $1.50

Contents:
as for A7(a)

Notes:
Simmons states:

> One thousand copies in sheets imported by J. B. Lippincott Company, Philadelphia, September, 1908, and published under their imprint in 1909.

Although the chain-lines in the stock of paper appear the same, the paper stock used for the first gathering is much thinner than the rest of the volume. As this gathering contains the preliminaries only it appears that this first gathering was printed by Richards or Lippincott (omitting the note on cover design). However, it is curious that the advertisements present on p.[407] of the first English edition are also omitted.

A letter from Grant Richards to Arthur Milner of the Lippincott Company dated during August 1908 gives details of the terms for this edition:

> ...a royalty of ten per cent on the published price, rising to fifteen per cent after the sale of two thousand copies, with thirty pounds payable on publication in advance and on account of royalties. We can supply you with 1040/1000 copies in sheets, with end papers at eighteenpence apiece.
>
> (Grant Richards, letter to Arthur Milner, 26 August 1908)
> (Archives of Grant Richards. University of Illinois / Chadwyck-Healey microfilm, A14, f.240)

These terms were confirmed in September 1908 with additional detail:

> ...we are to supply you with 1040/1000 copies in sheets of "Captain Margaret", with endpapers, at eighteenpence apiece, a royalty of ten per cent being paid on copies sold. We shall supply you with our edition as it stands giving you separately cancel titles with the imprint that you gave me this morning. As you know we have not sufficient stock to enable us to deliver the whole order at once, but we are sending immediately all the unbound stock that we have and the rest will be sent as soon as they can be printed.
>
> (Grant Richards, letter to Arthur Milner, 23 September 1908)
> (Archives of Grant Richards. University of Illinois / Chadwyck-Healey microfilm, A14, f.449)

The lack of a cancel-title in the examined copy is curious, as is the omission of the advertisements on p.[407] (noted above). Richards' letter suggests that the first American edition may be found in several issues.

Wight appears confused in his description of this volume. The copy he describes appears to include maps on additional pages (numbered [408–416] by Wight)

Each chapter commences with a drop-capital.

Copies seen: NYPL (D–14 5794)

A7(c) Second English edition (1910)

CAPTAIN | MARGARET | JOHN MASEFIELD | THOMAS NELSON AND | SONS
(All width centred within rectangle surrounded by frame with arch at top. Floral garlands and ribbons surround frame with oval formed by garlands of foliage)

Bibliographies: Danielson [unrecorded], Williams [unrecorded], Simmons [noted on p.17], Nevinson [unrecorded], Handley-Taylor [p.28], Wight 7b

Collation: [π]² [1]¹⁶ 2–12¹⁶; signatures width centred at foot of page; the first gathering is tipped-in on the first leaf of gathering [1]; 194 leaves; 156 × 103mm.; [i–iv] [1–5] 6–29 [30] 31–51 [52] 53–84 [85] 86–112 [113] 114–34 [135] 136–69 [170] 171–201 [202] 203–24 [225] 226–59 [260] 261–88 [289] 290–322 [323] 324–84

Page contents: [i] '*UNIFORM WITH THIS VOLUME* | [rule] | [33 titles and their authors listed] | *And Many Other Equally Popular | Copyright Novels.* | [rule] | *NELSON'S LIBRARY.* | [device: 15 × 15mm.].'; [ii] frontispiece: 116 × 77mm., '"Mrs. Stukeley, it's my duty to tell you that your | husband is guilty."', signed 'STEPHEN | REID 09'; [iii] title-page; [iv] publisher's device within double ruled border: 31 × 24mm.; [1] 'TO | MY WIFE'; [2] blank; [3] 'CONTENTS | [rule with two diamond shapes at centre]' (12 chapters listed with titles and page references); [4] blank; [5]–384 text

Paper: wove paper (with the exception of gathering [π] which is on glossy paper)

Running title: 'CAPTAIN MARGARET.' (39mm.) on verso; recto title comprises chapter title, pp.6–384

Binding: red cloth. On spine, in gold: '[rule] | [combination of squares and lines] | [single rule] | [block of design] | *Captain | Margaret* | [heart-shaped device] | JOHN | MASEFIELD | [block of design] [all enclosed within ruled border: 51 × 19mm.] | [design including superimposed 'N' with 'L' within garland: 32 × 17mm.] | *NELSON'S | LIBRARY* | [block of design] | [rule] | [combination of squares and lines] | [rule]' (all width centred). On upper cover, in blind: design including superimposed 'N' with 'L' within garland (different from that on spine): 51 × 35mm. (all enclosed within double ruled border: 154 × 97mm. with squares at each corner). Lower cover: blank. All edges trimmed. Binding measurements: 161 × 103mm. (covers), 161 × 34mm. (spine). End-papers: wove paper.

Publication date: published, according to Simmons, March 1910 in an edition of 42000 copies. The *English Catalogue of Books* records a publication date of April 1910.

Price: 7d.

Contents:
as for A7(a)

Notes:
The text has been entirely re-set for this edition. It commences with a drop-capital.

The publishers of this edition first approached Masefield and not Grant Richards in September 1908. Richards' reaction was that:

> …my prejudices are against granting permission to other publishers to do cheap editions of books of which I am proud.
>
> (Grant Richards, letter to C.F. Cazenove, 22 September 1908)
> (Archives of Grant Richards. University of Illinois / Chadwyck-Healey microfilm, A14, f.419)

In October, Richards was contemplating his own cheap edition of the novel. Nevertheless, on 5 November 1908 he sent Cazenove an agreement for Nelson to publish.

A document in the archives of The Society of Authors (BL, Add.Mss.56581, ff.198–99) cites the date of the original contract for this edition. It was signed 5 November 1908 between Grant Richards and Messrs Thomas Nelson and Sons.

Copies seen: BL (12202.y.1/72) stamped 1 JUN 1910

A7(d) Second American edition (1916)

CAPTAIN MARGARET | BY | JOHN MASEFIELD | Author of "The Everlasting Mercy," "The Widow | in the Bye Street," etc. | New York | THE MACMILLAN COMPANY | 1916 | *All rights reserved*
(All width centred)

Bibliographies: Danielson [unrecorded], Williams [unrecorded], Simmons [noted on p.17], Nevinson [unrecorded], Handley-Taylor p.28, Wight 7c

Collation: [A-Z]⁸ [AA]¹⁰ (J, V and W not used); 194 leaves; 190 × 128mm.; [i–viii] [1–2] 3–371 [372–80]

ON THE SPANISH MAIN

OR, SOME ENGLISH FORAYS ON THE
ISTHMUS OF DARIEN. WITH A DESCRIP-
TION OF THE BUCCANEERS AND A
SHORT ACCOUNT OF OLD-TIME
SHIPS AND SAILORS

BY
JOHN MASEFIELD

WITH TWENTY-TWO ILLUSTRATIONS AND A MAP

METHUEN & CO.
36 ESSEX STREET W.C.
LONDON

A5(a) title-page

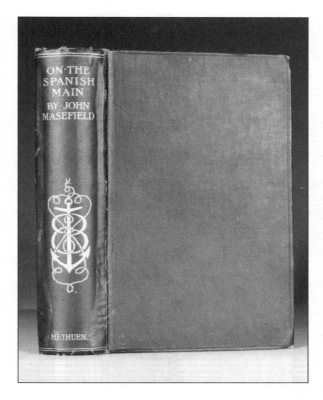

A5(a) spine and upper cover

A6(a) spine and upper cover

A TARPAULIN
MUSTER

BY
JOHN MASEFIELD

LONDON
E. GRANT RICHARDS
1907

A6(a) title-page

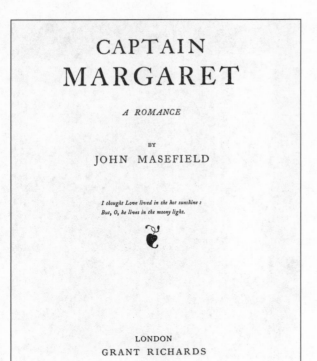

A7(a) title-page

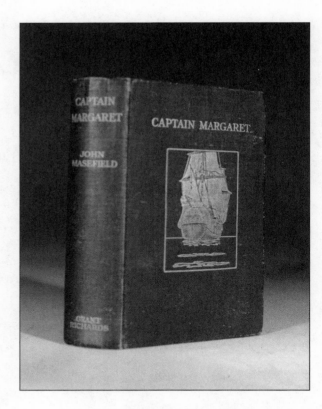

A7(a) spine and upper cover

A8(a) spine and upper cover

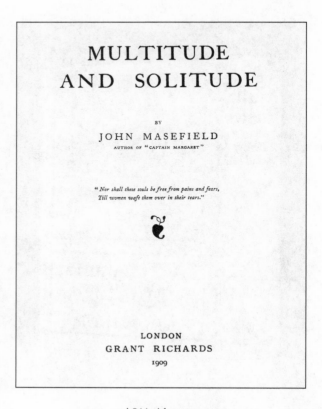

A8(a) title-page

Page contents: [i] half-title: 'CAPTAIN MARGARET'; [ii] '[publisher's device] | THE MACMILLAN COMPANY | [two lines listing six cities, separated by four points] | MACMILLAN & CO., LIMITED | [two lines listing four cities, separated by two points] | THE MACMILLAN CO. OF CANADA, LTD. | [one city listed]'; [iii] title-page; [iv] blank; [v] 'TO | MY WIFE'; [vi] blank; [vii] 'CONTENTS' (12 chapters listed with titles and page references); [viii] blank; [1] 'CAPTAIN MARGARET'; [2] blank; 3–371 text (at foot of p.371: 'PRINTED IN THE UNITED STATES OF AMERICA'); [372] blank; [373] 'THE following pages contain advertisements of | Macmillan books by the same author.' (within ruled border: 16 × 74mm.); [374] blank; [375–78] publisher's advertisements; [379–80] blank

Paper: wove paper

Running title: 'CAPTAIN MARGARET' (43mm.) on verso; recto title comprises chapter title, pp.4–371

Binding: light blue-green cloth. On spine, in gold: '[double rule] | CAPTAIN | MARGARET | MASEFIELD | MACMILLAN | [double rule]' (all width centred). On upper cover, in gold: 'CAPTAIN | MARGARET | MASEFIELD' (ranged upper left) (within blind ruled border: 188 × 119mm.) Lower cover: blank. Top edge trimmed, others roughly trimmed. Binding measurements: 197 × 130mm. (covers), 197 × 48mm. (spine). End-papers: wove paper.

Publication date: published, according to Simmons, 22 March 1916 in an edition of 1516 copies

Price: $1.35

Contents:
as for A7(a)

Notes:
At the beginning of April 1916 Grant Richards wrote to Masefield about his first novel:

> In the "Daily Chronicle" to-day a new edition of "Captain Margaret" is announced as being on the point of issue in America. I certainly have not sanctioned it. Cazenove, as I daresay you will remember, was negotiating about a new edition of this book, and editions of your other books, with Macmillan, but to the best of my memory he asked me to let the matter drop for a while at the beginning of the war.
>
> (Grant Richards, letter to John Masefield, 7 April 1916)
> (Archives of Grant Richards. University of Illinois / Chadwyck-Healey microfilm, A24, f.151)

Masefield's agent died in 1915 but his role in negotiations with Macmillan is clear. A letter from the end of April provides further detail:

> Cazenove told me that he wanted to make with Macmillan a comprehensive arrangement for all your books in America, and he was in the course of negotiating, I understand, when the war broke out. On my asking him, in October 1914, how the matter was getting on, he said that he had been obliged to let it rest owing to the general disorganisation of things. Later on – in June 1915 – I wrote to Mr Collins on the matter, and he replied that you were too much occupied with war work for anything to be done.
>
> (Grant Richards, letter to John Masefield, 25 April 1916)
> (Archives of Grant Richards. University of Illinois / Chadwyck-Healey microfilm, A24, f.185)

Richards was perhaps concerned that the forthcoming publication was a pirated edition for the title had not been copyrighted in the United States. That Cazenove had intended to unify the publication of Masefield's work in the United States illustrates the legacy of Masefield's literary agent as Macmillan were to publish Masefield for the rest of his career.

The Archives of The Society of Authors reveal several publishing agreements or proposed agreements for this title between Masefield and Macmillan. One, dated 1914 only, grants 'a licence to publish in volume form in the United States of America, four (4) works, the subjects or titles of which are "MULTITUDE AND SOLITUDE", "THE LOST ENDEAVOR", "CAPTAIN MARGARET", and "THE TRAGEDY OF NAN", (provided the rights of publication in the United States of America be acquired from the present publishers by the Company)…' The document additionally states '…the Company agrees to publish the first three of the above works in the course of the year 1915, and… "NAN" within the three months after the said work has been acquired from the present publishers…' The document also extended the licence for previous Macmillan titles for a further five years from date of their first publication. Another version is dated 19 October 1914 and omits reference to acquiring rights from existing publishers. This version refers to 'revised editions' of the four works and notes 'the Company agrees to publish one of the above works in the fall of 1914, another in the spring of 1915, and a third in the autumn of 1915'. An unknown hand has annotated this document 'Proposed agreement not signed to our knowledge'.

A publishing agreement for this title between Masefield and Macmillan was dated 16 March 1916 (see Archives of The Society of Authors). The agreement refers to 'a licence to publish in volume form in the United States of America a work the subject or title of which is Captain Margaret, (new edition)'.

A letter from Masefield to Grant Richards, dated 26 April 1916, states the terms which had been agreed on the Macmillan editions of *Captain Margaret* and *Multitude and Solitude*: "Macmillans will publish the 2 novels, + run the risk of piracy, + pay 15% of which, of course, you will have half". Masefield then raised the future of *The Tragedy of Nan* and subsequent correspondence discusses this title and the arrangements with Mitchell Kennerley (see John Masefield, letter to Grant Richards, 26 April 1916) (Fales Library, New York University).

During the 1920s Masefield, writing to The Society of Authors, refers to the lack of American copyright in the novel and notes the 'decent' behaviour of the Macmillan company:

> *Captain Margaret*... is an unsuccessful novel by me. It is protected over here (I suppose) by publication... It is not copyright in the U.S.A. It was not printed there for some years after publication here, but at last Macmillans printed it there, + very decently pay me a royalty on their edition, though I suppose that they need not do this unless they choose.
>
> (John Masefield, letter to [G.H.] Thring, 5 October [1920s])
> (BL, Add.Mss.56626, ff.151–153)

Copies seen: Columbia University (Special Collections B825 M377 P37 1916)

A7(e) Third English edition (1927)

CAPTAIN MARGARET | by | JOHN MASEFIELD | [illustration of satyr with stick bearing urn of fruit signed 'P.S': 44 × 17mm.] | LONDON | JONATHAN CAPE 30 BEDFORD SQUARE
(All width centred)

Bibliographies: Simmons [unrecorded], Nevinson [unrecorded], Handley-Taylor [unrecorded], Wight [unrecorded]

Collation: [A]¹⁶ B-N¹⁶ (J not used); the fifth leaf of each gathering is also signed; signatures left foot of page; 208 leaves; the catalogue (not included in collation or leaf count) comprises a single unsigned gathering of 6 leaves; 172 × 115mm.; [i–viii] [1] 2-405 [406–408]; catalogue pagination: [1–12]

Page contents: [i] half-title: 'THE TRAVELLERS' LIBRARY | [five-point star] | CAPTAIN MARGARET'; [ii] 'THE TRAVELLERS' LIBRARY | [31 titles and their authors listed] | Uniform with this volume'; [iii] title-page; [iv] 'FIRST PUBLISHED JUNE 1908 | SECOND IMPRESSION JANUARY 1909 | THIRD IMPRESSION SEPTEMBER 1924 | FIRST ISSUED IN THE TRAVELLERS' LIBRARY 1927 | PRINTED IN GREAT BRITAIN'; [v] 'TO | MY WIFE'; [vi] blank; [vii] 'CONTENTS' (12 chapters listed with titles and page references); [viii] blank; [1]-[406] text (at foot of p.[406]: '*Made and Printed in Great Britain by Percy Lund, Humphries & Co. Ltd., Bradford*'); [406]-[408] blank; [1–12] catalogue: 'A LIST OF VOLUMES ISSUED IN | THE TRAVELLERS' LIBRARY | [illustration of satyr with stick bearing urn of fruit signed 'P.S'] | 3s. 6d. net each | JONATHAN CAPE LTD. | THIRTY BEDFORD SQUARE LONDON' (at foot of p.[12]: 'JONATHAN CAPE THIRTY BEDFORD SQUARE LONDON')

Paper: wove paper

Running title: '*CAPTAIN MARGARET*' (42mm.) on verso; recto title comprises chapter title, pp.2-[406]

Binding: blue cloth. On spine, in gold: '[floral device] [floral device] [floral device] [floral device] | CAPTAIN | MARGARET | * | JOHN | MASEFIELD | [illustration of satyr with stick bearing urn of fruit signed 'P.S': 45 × 17mm.] | JONATHAN | CAPE | [floral device] [floral device] [floral device] [floral device]' (all width centred). Upper cover: blank. On lower cover, in blind: publisher's device of 'JC' monogram (width centred). All edges trimmed. Binding measurements: 176 × 117mm. (covers), 176 × 26mm. (spine). End-papers: wove paper.

Publication date: published, according to the archives of The Society of Authors, June 1927 in an edition of 7500 copies

Price: 3s.6d.

Contents:
as for A7(a)

Notes:
Each chapter commences with a drop-capital.

The setting of the text derives from A7(a). The slight shrinkage in size suggests a photographic process of reproduction.

The catalogue, at the rear of the volume, notes this title as number 35 in 'The Travellers' Library' series. The series is described as:

> A series of books in all branches of literature designed for the pocket, or for the small house where shelf space is scarce. Though the volumes measure only 7 inches by 4¾ inches, the page is arranged so that the margins are not unreasonably curtailed nor legibility sacrificed. The books are of a uniform thickness irrespective of the number of pages, and the paper, specially manufactured for the series, is remarkably opaque, even when it is thinnest. A semi-flexible form of binding has been adopted, as a safe-guard against the damage inevitably associated with hasty packing. The cloth is of a particularly attractive shade of blue and has the author's name stamped in gold on the back. Each volume costs 3s. 6d. net (postage 3d.).

Masefield made enquiries in 1925 about buying back rights from Grant Richards. These enquiries eventually came to nothing although Heinemann and Masefield paid jointly in 1925 to gain control of *The Tragedy of Nan and other plays* (see A9). Richards warned the author that he would continue to pursue his interests in Masefield's other work. Accordingly he appears to have reached an arrangement with Jonathan Cape for *Captain Margaret* and *Multitude and Solitude*. News of the transfer of titles reached Masefield in July 1926 and he wrote to The Society of Authors stating:

> I shall be glad if you will take legal opinion on the transfer of the two books to Messrs Cape, if you feel that there is a likelihood of stopping the transfer. I do not like the two books + would gladly kill them.
>
> (John Masefield, letter to [G.H.] Thring, [16 July 1926])
> (BL, Add.Mss.56583, f.59)

The Society of Authors presumably thought that Masefield had a strong legal case and offered the Society's services. Masefield was perhaps wary, unwilling to waste the Society's resources or sympathetic to the state of Richards' business for he replied:

> I feel that the transfer had better be stopped; but ask you not to fire off the powder + shot of the Society unless you yourself + the Chairman should be convinced that the case justifies the expense. It might add to Richards's worries, + so prejudice other authors to whom he owes royalties; + there may be pending many disputes, involving more important points, on which the Society's money could more profitably be spent; so I will leave it to you.
>
> (John Masefield, letter to [G.H.] Thring, 26 July [1926])
> (BL, Add.Mss.56583, f.65)

Masefield was, however, still against the transfer of the titles. He wrote to The Society of Authors at the end of August 1926:

> Many thanks for your kind letter about the transference of the books to Messrs Cape's Traveller's Library [sic]. My own wish is to kill the books as far as possible; + I am therefore not eager to give my consent to any transference of them which I can oppose. I hate the thought of their being still on the market.
>
> (John Masefield, letter to [G.H.] Thring, [30 August 1926])
> (BL, Add.Mss.56583, f.89)

Jonathan Cape had, however, acquired a licence from Richards and wrote to The Society of Authors expressing both artistic and commercial views of the novels:

> I have been taking another look at these two books as it is a good many years since I read them. I must say that I was very much impressed by the poetic quality of CAPTAIN MARGARET which is, I think, quite first class, and is certainly equal to Mr Masefield's most recent prose work. I do not consider MULTITUDE AND SOLITUDE is as good but I do not agree that Mr Masefield is justified in suppressing it. I mentioned the matter to-day to my reader, Mr Edward Garnett, whose opinion is important and divorced from ordinary business considerations. He expressed himself very strongly as to the quality of CAPTAIN MARGARET: he does not know MULTITUDE AND SOLITUDE.
>
> May I suggest that a way out of the present difficulty might be found by Mr Masefield agreeing to our bringing out in the near future CAPTAIN MARGARET. We would postpone MULTITUDE AND SOLITUDE for further consideration, but we should regret very much if we were unable to include it in the Series.
>
> Unfortunately we have commenced to set MULTITUDE AND SOLITUDE and if we were to abandon the book entirely we should have incurred the cost of setting half the book to no purpose. We would however be prepared to agree to discontinue publication of the book after our first edition of 5000 copies had been disposed of should Mr Masefield wish to suppress the book.
>
> I shall hope to hear that these proposals can be accepted by Mr Masefield.
>
> (Jonathan Cape, letter to [G.H.] Thring, 23 September 1926)
> (BL, Add.Mss.56583, f.104)

In the event, it appears that the 'Travellers' Library' edition of *Multitude and Solitude* appeared before that of *Captain Margaret*, but this is of little consequence as Cape had already expressed his intention of eventual publication, regardless of Masefield's wishes. The author, however, still clung to the hope of buying the rights outright. He wrote to The Society of Authors:

> ...I am perplexed about the business of Messrs Cape + Co. Many thanks to you + Mr Medley for the care you have taken in the matter. I hardly know what to say: but since they are determined to proceed + I am eager to get hold of these books I suppose my only chance is to try to buy them. I had honestly hoped that they were dead. I would, I suppose, have to make the offer to Messrs Richards, + they, if they took it, would have to satisfy Messrs Cape. Afterwards, to recoup myself, I suppose I should have to revise both books; let Messrs Heinemann issue a small edition of both, + then they could be suppressed. I suppose I shall have to offer £200 for each book, as in the case of *Nan*. If this course seems possible to you, I shall be glad if you will see what can be done.
>
> (John Masefield, letter to [G.H.] Thring, [3 October 1926])
> (BL, Add.Mss.56583, ff.117–18)

This course evidently proved fruitless, although The Society of Authors were able to limit the terms of the licence that Cape had been granted. By 1927 Masefield had heard nothing further and therefore wrote to the Society, revealing that Heinemann, loyal as ever to Masefield, had been attempting to help:

> Messrs Secker. I have heard nothing from this firm about the two Richards books. Since the transference I believe that Messrs Heinemann have been trying to get control of the books from Seckers, but I have not yet heard with what success. I should be glad if you would ask Messrs Secker about the future accounts.
>
> (John Masefield, letter to [G.H.] Thring, 12 January 1927)
> (BL, Add.Mss.56584, ff.16–17)

Martin Secker had, by this time, taken over control of the Richards Press. No arrangement could be reached and negotiations with Jonathan Cape had merely provided a limitation to the print run. Accordingly both titles were issued within the 'Travellers' Library' in 1927.

In 1928 Jonathan Cape wrote to Masefield to ascertain, once more, his wishes. Cape particularly wanted to know whether to redistribute type:

> As you know, we have printed in the Travellers' Library your MULTITUDE AND SOLITUDE. Our arrangement permits us to print 5,000 copies. At the present time we have rather more than 1,000 copies in stock and I am wondering whether you are still desirous of the book being discontinued in the Travellers' Library after our printing has been disposed of. We ourselves would like very much to continue with the book. We have the book in type. If, however, there is no possibility of your revising your decision we will give the printer instructions to distribute it. Will you let me know?
>
> (Jonathan Cape, letter to John Masefield, 20 August 1928)
> (BL, Add.Mss.56586, f.108)

In response to this, Masefield wrote to The Society of Authors re-affirming his wish to see the end of the edition:

> *Multitude and Solitude.* I should prefer that the Cape edition be brought to an end, if it be possible.
>
> (John Masefield, letter to [G.H.] Thring, [26 August 1928])
> (BL, Add.Mss.56586, f.113)

It appears that Cape, in his dealings with Masefield had kept the author fully informed of intentions. Masefield wrote to Thring:

> I am sending to you with this a letter from Mr. Jonathan Cape about the two early novels. I think that the arrangement was that the books should be extinguished after a certain sale had been reached. Is it possible so to extinguish them or to get complete control of them without paying too big a price? In any case I have no other volume to offer Mr. Cape.
>
> (John Masefield, letter to [G.H.] Thring, 18 May 1929)
> (BL, Add.Mss.56587, f.164)

The Society of Authors therefore wrote to Cape and secured the end of the 'Travellers' Library' editions. Masefield wrote to thank the Society for doing this on 28 May 1929 (see BL, Add.Mss.56587, f.179). Two years later The Society of Authors wrote to Masefield noting the current sales position:

> ...In regard to the Cape editions, in the Agreement between Richards and Cape our Solicitors were able to limit the edition of "Captain Margaret" to 7500 copies and "Multitude and Solitude" to 5000 copies. We see from our files that Messrs. Cape reported on the 17th May, 1929, that they had sold approximately 4700 copies of "Multitude and Solitude" and about 4000 copies of "Captain Margaret".
>
> (Denys Kilham Roberts, letter to John Masefield, 20 February 1931)
> (BL, Add.Mss.56592, ff.220–21)

On 9 May 1932 Jonathan Cape approached Masefield asking to put *Captain Margaret* and *Multitude and Solitude* into a new series entitled 'Florin Books' (see BL, Add.Mss.56595, ff.124–25). Writing to The Society of Authors Masefield stated:

> Some years ago, there was discussion about these books: + I daresay I have no power to prohibit their being reprinted, but if I have that power, it would be a great happiness to exercise it.
>
> (John Masefield, letter to [E.J.] Mullett, [9 May 1932])
> (BL, Add.Mss.56596, f.123)

Masefield was evidently confused and The Society of Authors replied:

> You will be pleased to hear that you have power to prohibit the reprinting by Jonathan Cape Ltd. of "Captain Margaret" and "Multitude and Solitude". In July 1926 Grant Richards authorised the inclusion of these works in the Travellers Library, but our Solicitors negotiated on your behalf with Jonathan Cape and an arrangement was concluded by which Cape agreed to limit the edition of "Captain Margaret" to 7500 copies and the edition of "Multitude and Solitude" to 5000 copies.
>
> (E.J. Mullett, letter to John Masefield, 11 May 1932)
> (BL, Add.Mss.56596, ff.129–30)

Presumably, had Cape approached the Richards Press then permission could have been granted. In further explaining the previous agreement it appears that licences from the Richards Press to Jonathan Cape for the 'Travellers' Library' series ran for a period of seven years from the date of first publication (see BL, Add.Mss.56609, f.16). Cape, it seems, ultimately did not wish to infuriate Masefield and stated their understanding to The Society of Authors:

> ...we ...consider that the licences, under which we published the Poet Laureate's CAPTAIN MARGARET and MULTITUDE AND SOLITUDE, are at an end, we having agreed some time ago to relinquish publication in deference to the author's wishes.
>
> (Jonathan Cape, letter to [E.J.] Mullett, 17 March 1938)
> (BL, Add.Mss.56609, f.31)

Copies seen: private collection (PWE)

A7(f) Fourth English edition (1962)

JOHN MASEFIELD | CAPTAIN MARGARET | A Tale of the Spanish Main | *I thought Love lived in the hot sunshine;* | *But, O, he lives in the moony light.* | ICON BOOKS LIMITED
(All justified on right margin)

Bibliographies: Wight [unrecorded]

Collation: [A]¹⁶ B-K¹⁶ (J not used); signatures left foot of page; 160 leaves; 180 × 111mm.; [1–8] 9–317 [318–20]

Page contents: [1] half-title: 'CAPTAIN MARGARET' with publisher's device and 'ICON'; [2] 'PRINTING HISTORY | First printed by the Richards Press Ltd in 1908 | Reprinted 1909 | Reprinted 1924 | Reprinted 1948 | Reprinted 1956 | This Icon edition, published in 1962, | is printed by kind permission of Mr. Martin Secker | *Cover design by Sam Kiff* | [new paragraph] This book shall not without written consent of the Publishers, | Icon Books Ltd, be lent, resold, hired out or otherwise disposed | of in any unauthorised cover, by way of trade. | [new paragraph] Icon Books are published by Icon Books Ltd, 5 Royal Opera | Arcade, Pall Mall, London, S.W.I, and are made and printed in | Great Britain by Love and Malcomson Ltd, Redhill, Surrey.'; [3] title-page; [4–5] 'A MAP OF THE IAMES RIVER | AND THE | VIRGINIA COLONY' signed '*By* Philip Seacole *at the Sign of the* | [device] Pye's Neft [device] | LONDON' within four ruled borders: 132 × 176mm. (excluding wide gutter); [6] '*To my wife*'; [7] 'CONTENTS' (12 chapters listed with titles and page references) [8] blank; 9–317 text; [318–19] 'A DRAUGHT OF THE | SAMBALLOES ISLANDS, &C.' signed '*By* Philip Seacole *at the Sign of the* | [device] Pye's Neft [device] | LONDON' within four ruled borders: 132 × 175mm. (excluding wide gutter); [320] publisher's advertisements

Paper: wove paper

Running title: none

Binding: coloured wrappers. On spine, horizontally at head: 'F8'; reading lengthways down spine from head: 'Captain Margaret [in red] * MASEFIELD [in black] [all on white background] [publisher's device] [in white on black background] ICON [in white on black background]; horizontally at foot of spine: '5'-' [in white on black background]'. On upper wrapper: '[colour illustration of woman and ship's rigging] | [publisher's device [in red] | ICON [in black] [both on white background] | Captain Margaret [in red on grey background] | JOHN MASEFIELD O.M. [in black on grey background]'. On lower wrapper: 'CAPTAIN MARGARET | ABOUT THIS BOOK | John Masefield's book, *Captain* | *Margaret*, was his first full- | length historical novel of the | sea. It originally appeared in | 1908, and at once established | the Poet Laureate's reputation | as a novelist in the grand | romantic tradition. | [new paragraph] The book is sub-titled 'A Tale | Of The Spanish Main' and so | indeed, it is; but enriched im- | measurably by a poet's vision. [all in black on grey background] | [publisher's device] [in red on grey background] | ICON [in black on grey background] | [colour illustration of ship's rigging]'. The white panel on the upper wrapper (bearing publisher's icon and name) measures 25 × 18mm. and appears over the illustration and grey panel. The grey panel on the lower wrapper encroaches into the colour illustration. All edges trimmed. Binding measurements: 180 × 112mm. (wrappers), 180 × 18mm. (spine)

Publication date: published, according to the *English Catalogue of Books*, January 1962

Price: 5s.

Contents:
as for A7(a)

Notes:
The text has been entirely re-set for this edition and has acquired a new sub-title ('A Tale of the Spanish Main'). The original sub-title ('A Romance') has been deleted.

By 1962 Martin Secker controlled the rights Masefield had sold to Grant Richards.

The original end-papers of A7(a) are here reproduced on pp.4–5 and pp.318–19.

Copies seen: private collection (PWE)

A7(g) Fifth English edition (1974)

JOHN MASEFIELD | [thick rule, 80mm.] | [thin rule, 80mm.] | Captain Margaret | [thin rule, 80mm.] | [thick rule, 80mm.] | *A Romance* | *Introduced by Hugh Greene* | *I thought Love lived in the hot sunshine:* | *But, O, he lives in the moony light.* | [publisher's device of man within ruled oval border] | THE BODLEY HEAD | LONDON SYDNEY | TORONTO
(All width centred)
(The title appears in a type with letter characters in outline)

Bibliographies: Wight [noted on p.16]

Publication date: published, according to the Archives of The Society of Authors, 3 October 1974

Price: £2.25

Contents:
Introduction ('John Masefield died only seven years ago in 1967...')
        (signed, 'Hugh Greene')
and as for A7(a)

Notes:
This edition comprises a photographic reprint of A7(a) together with an original introduction. The volume states, on page [iv], that it is printed and bound in Great Britain for The Bodley Head Ltd. by Unwin Brothers Limited, The Gresham Press, Old Woking, Surrey.

The edition was part of the publisher's 'Bow Street Library'.

The ISBN number is 0 370 10923 6

The publishing agreement for this title was dated 13 February 1974 (see Archives of The Society of Authors).

Hugh Greene states in his introduction:

> *Captain Margaret* stands on its own feet as a remarkable achievement. If it appeared as a new novel today I believe that it would receive great critical and popular acclaim. It paid the penalty of being, in some ways, ahead of its time and dropped into an oblivion from which it is a pleasure to rescue it.

Copies seen: private collection (PWE); BL (X.989/27601) stamped 26 SEP 1974

A8 MULTITUDE AND SOLITUDE   1909

A8(a) First English edition (1909)

MULTITUDE | AND SOLITUDE | BY | JOHN MASEFIELD | AUTHOR OF "CAPTAIN MARGARET" | "*Nor shall these souls be free from pains and fears,* | *Till women waft them over in their tears.*" | [ornament] | LONDON | GRANT RICHARDS | 1909
(All width centred)

Bibliographies: Danielson 166, Williams p.8, Simmons [8], Nevinson p.15, Handley-Taylor p.28, Wight [8]

Collation: [A]⁴ B-T⁸ U⁶ (J not used); U3 is also signed; signatures left foot of page; 154 leaves; the catalogue (not included in collation or leaf count) comprises a single unsigned gathering of 8 leaves (see notes); 197 × 126mm.; [i–viii] [1] 2–299 [300]; catalogue pagination: [1–2] 3–15 [16]

Page contents: [i–ii] blank; [iii] half-title: 'MULTITUDE AND SOLITUDE'; [iv] '*NEW FICTION* | [seven titles, their authors and prices listed] | [rule] | LONDON : GRANT RICHARDS'; [v] title-page; [vi] blank; [vii] 'TO | MY WIFE'; [viii] blank; [1]-[300] text (at foot of p.[300]: 'WILLIAM BRENDON AND SON, LTD | PRINTERS, PLYMOUTH'); [1–16] catalogue: 'THE GRANT RICHARDS BOOKS | BEING A COMPLETE CATALOGUE | OF THE BOOKS PUBLISHED BY | GRANT RICHARDS | 7 CARLTON STREET | LONDON, S.W. | SPRING | 1908' (on p.[16]: '*London: Strangeways, Printers.*')

Paper: laid paper (no watermark), chain-lines 18mm. apart

Running title: '*MULTITUDE AND SOLITUDE*' (with swash 'T's) (64mm.) on both recto and verso, pp.2-[300]

Binding: dark-green cloth (Danielson describes the binding as 'greyish-green cloth'). On spine, in gold: 'MULTITUDE | AND | SOLITUDE | JOHN | MASEFIELD | GRANT | RICHARDS' (all width centred). On upper cover, in white: 'MULTITUDE | AND SOLITUDE | [design of Tsetse fly: 62 × 74mm.] | JOHN MASEFIELD'. Lower cover: blank. Upper and lower covers have blind ruled borders: 198 × 125mm. Top and fore edges trimmed, lower outside edge uncut. Binding measurements: 203 × 131mm. (covers), 203 × 46mm. (spine). End-papers: laid paper (no watermark), chain-lines 29mm. apart.

Publication date: published, according to Simmons, 29 June 1909 in an edition of 2350 copies. The *English Catalogue of Books* records a publication date of July 1909.

Price: 6s.

Contents:
Multitude and Solitude ('Roger Naldrett, the writer, sat in his box with a friend, watching the second act...')

Notes:
The publishing agreement for this title between Masefield and Grant Richards was dated 6 March 1909 (see Archives of The Society of Authors). The agreement refers to '...a novel at present provisionally entitled "Multitude and Solitude"...'

References in the Grant Richards archive reveal Richards eagerly requesting early drafts:

> Mr Cazenove told me weeks ago that you were getting on with your new novel. Could I have such part of it as you have done even tentatively to take with me to America ?

(Grant Richards, letter to John Masefield, 14 November 1908)
(Archives of Grant Richards. University of Illinois / Chadwyck-Healey microfilm, A13, f.842)

Masefield was far from co-operative, however. He replied that:

> ...I've only done about 15,000 words of *Multitude and Solitude*; + what I have done is in a sad mess, all bad psychology + colourless prose... ...it is so bad, I hardly like to let you take it as it stands...
>
> (John Masefield, letter to Grant Richards, [April 1909])
> (Fales Library, New York University)

Despite stating he did not want to rush the task of writing, Masefield was evidently rather lax. Richards wrote in April 1909:

> The part of "Multitude and Solitude" that I am returning represents the part that I have read. I have just got it back from the printer because it has been pointed out to me, and I have remembered, that it is not quite ready for him. Here and there you have given alternative words and phrases and I do not suppose you would approve of the compositor deciding which of the alternatives is the better! Will you just run through it and put it right in this respect? And will you also make clear where each chapter ends...
>
> (Grant Richards, letter to John Masefield, 15 April 1909)
> (Archives of Grant Richards. University of Illinois / Chadwyck-Healey microfilm, A15, f.120)

In a letter to Gilbert Murray, Masefield writes:

> Many thanks for what you say about the novel. I am glad you like the Multitude part. The Solitude part is bad. I was dead beat when I wrote it.
>
> (John Masefield, letter to Gilbert Murray, 20 July 1909)
> (Bodleian, Gilbert Murray 161, ff.15–16)

Walter de la Mare anonymously reviewing the novel in the *T.L.S.* for 8 July 1909 specifically notes the binding:

> The cover of Mr. John Masefield's new novel, MULTITUDE AND SOLITUDE... is adorned with a ghoulish representation of the tsetse fly.

Early discussion with Richards reveals that a tsetse fly or a medical temperature chart were alternative suggestions for the upper cover.

Copies were issued with, and without a catalogue. The dedication copy (see HRHRC) includes the catalogue.

In 1951 there appears to have been interest in producing a film version of the novel. Masefield wrote to The Society of Authors:

> Many thanks for your letter, with the suggestion from the Ealing people, about *Multitude & Solitude*. I am not sure, but perhaps you have my agreement with the late G. Richards for this book? I suppose that the film rights are mine? If they are mine, please, by all means, ask them to make an offer. I have not looked at the book for 40 years, and have lively memories of the horrors of writing it; & at present cannot see how it can be filmed. A School of Tropical Medicine used the book as a text-book at one time; the medical side of it was sound, though probably out-of-date now.
>
> (John Masefield, letter to Miss [Gabrielle] Curry, 30 November [1951])
> (BL, Add.Mss.56623, ff.56–57)

Copies seen: BL (01261.ccc.24) stamped 3 JUL 1909; Harvard College Library (Houghton *EC9.M377.909m(B)) inscribed for the Lamonts: 'This, too, forget, this weary tale of woe | London + liver made me write it so | J. Masefield.'; HRHRC (TEMP M377MU 1909) inscribed 'Con | from Jan. | 3rd July. 1909.'

A8(b) Second English edition ([1911])

MULTITUDE | AND SOLITUDE | JOHN MASEFIELD | T. NELSON & SONS | LONDON AND EDINBURGH | PARIS : 61, rue des Saints-Pères | LEIPZIG : 35–37 Königstrasse
(All width centred within rectangle surrounded by frame with arch at top. Floral garlands and ribbons surround frame with oval formed by garlands of foliage)

Bibliographies: Danielson [unrecorded], Williams [unrecorded], Simmons [noted on p.18], Nevinson [unrecorded], Handley-Taylor p.28, Wight [noted on p.17]

Collation: [π]² [1]¹⁶ 2–9¹⁶; signatures width centred at foot of page; 146 leaves; the first gathering is tipped-in on the first leaf of gathering [1]; 156 × 103mm.; [i–iv] [1–3] 4–18 [19] 20–43 [44] 45–71 [72] 73–85 [86] 87–118 [119] 120–44 [145] 146–68 [169] 170–99 [200] 201–19 [220] 221–38 [239] 240–65 [266] 267–86 [287–88]

Page contents: [i] '*UNIFORM WITH THIS VOLUME* | [rule] | [34 titles and their authors listed] | *And Many Other Equally Popular | Copyright Novels.* | [rule] | *NELSON'S LIBRARY.* | [device: 15 × 15mm.]'; [ii] frontispiece: 117 × 73mm., 'The wise men choosing who are to inherit | the earth.', signed 'STEPHEN | REID 1911'; [iii] title-page; [iv] publisher's device within double ruled border: 31 × 24mm.; [1] 'TO | MY WIFE'; [2] blank; [3]–286 text; [287] 'ESTABLISHED 1798 | [publisher's device within double ruled border: 31 × 24mm.] | T. NELSON | AND SONS | PRINTERS AND | PUBLISHERS'; [288] 'THE NELSON LIBRARY. | [rule] | *Uniform with this Volume and same Price.* | [rule] | CONDENSED LIST. | *Arranged alphabetically under Authors' Names.* | [101 titles and their authors listed] | [rule] | T. NELSON & SONS, London, Edinburgh, Dublin, and New York.'

Paper: wove paper (with the exception of gathering [π] which is on glossy paper)

Running title: 'MULTITUDE AND SOLITUDE.' (52mm.) on both verso and recto, pp.4–286

Binding: red cloth. On spine, in gold: '[rule] | [combination of squares and lines] | [rule] | [block of design] | *Multitude* | *and* | *Solitude* | JOHN | MASEFIELD | [block of design] [all enclosed within ruled border: 51 × 19mm.] | [design including superimposed 'N' with 'L' within garland: 32 × 17mm.] | *NELSON'S* | *LIBRARY* | [block of design] | [rule] | [combination of squares and lines] | [rule]' (all width centred). On upper cover, in blind: design including superimposed 'N' with 'L' within garland (different from that on spine): 51 × 35mm. (all enclosed within double ruled border: 154 × 97mm. with squares at each corner). Lower cover: blank. All edges trimmed. Binding measurements: 161 × 102mm. (covers), 161 × 30mm. (spine). End-papers: wove paper.

Publication date: published, according to Simmons, April 1911 in an edition of 40000 copies. The *English Catalogue of Books* records a publication date of May 1911

Price: 7d.

Contents:
as for A8(a)

Notes:
Despite Richards' initial unwillingness to allow Nelson to publish *Captain Margaret* in their cheap edition, he evidently realised the advantages of such editions for it was Richards who first suggested the Nelson edition of *Multitude and Solitude*. He wrote to Cazenove in March 1910:

> Would Nelson's care to make the same arrangement for "Multitude and Solitude" that they did for "Captain Margaret"?

(Grant Richards, letter to C.F. Cazenove, 16 March 1910)
(Archives of Grant Richards. University of Illinois / Chadwyck-Healey microfilm, A16, f.906)

A document in the archives of The Society of Authors (BL, Add.Mss.56581, ff.198–99) cites the date of the original contract for this edition. It was signed 24 June 1910 between Grant Richards and Messrs Thomas Nelson and Sons.

The text has been entirely re-set for this edition.

Copies seen: BL (12202.y.1/98) stamped 25 MAY 1911

A8(c) First American edition (1911)

MULTITUDE | AND SOLITUDE | BY | JOHN MASEFIELD | AUTHOR OF "CAPTAIN MARGARET" | "*Nor shall these souls be free from pain and fears,* | *Till women waft them over in their tears.*" | [publisher's device of 'M' and 'K' in outline within double circular rule] | NEW YORK | MITCHELL KENNERLEY | 1911
(All width centred)

Bibliographies: Danielson [unrecorded], Williams [unrecorded], Simmons [noted on p.18], Nevinson [unrecorded], Handley-Taylor p.28, Wight [noted on p.17]

Collation: [A]⁴ B-T⁸ U⁶ (J not used); U3 is also signed; signatures left foot of page; 154 leaves; 185 × 124mm.; [i–viii] [1] 2–299 [300]

Page contents: [i–ii] blank; [iii] half-title: 'MULTITUDE AND SOLITUDE'; [iv] blank; [v] title-page; [vi] 'PRINTED BY | WILLIAM BRENDON AND SON, LTD. | PLYMOUTH | 1911'; [vii] 'TO | MY WIFE'; [viii] blank; [1]-[300] text (at foot of p.[300]: 'WILLIAM BRENDON AND SON, LTD | PRINTERS, PLYMOUTH')

Paper: laid paper (no watermark), chain-lines 18mm. apart; conjugate leaves A2 and A3 comprise laid paper (no watermark), chain-lines 24mm. apart

Running title: '*MULTITUDE AND SOLITUDE*' (with swash 'T's) (64mm.) on both recto and verso, pp.2-[300]

Binding: green cloth. On spine, in gold: 'MULTITUDE | AND | SOLIUTUDE | [rule, 28mm.] | JOHN | MASEFIELD [all enclosed within ruled border: 45 × 29mm. As a result of the rule noted above, two rectangles are created measuring: 28 × 29mm. and 17 × 29mm. respectively from the top] | Mitchell | Kennerley' (all width centred). Covers: blank. All edges trimmed. Binding measurements: 190 × 125mm. (covers), 190 × 47mm. (spine). End-papers: wove paper.

Publication date: presumably published between September 1911 and May 1912

Price: $1.35

Contents:
as for A8(a)

Notes:
Simmons notes with reference to the first American edition 'republished by Mitchell Kennerley, New York, 1910'. This date is also cited by Handley-Taylor and Wight. Primary evidence suggests that this date is incorrect. The archives of Grant Richards reveal that Kennerley wrote to Richards at the end of August 1911 making enquiries about the book. At the beginning of September Richards stated:

…we can supply you with 650/600 copies of "Multitude and Solitude" at tenpence apiece, with a royalty of ten per cent on top of that. If you want the book, cable the word "Masefield". We would give you binding blocks at cost; and if you do want the book we would send you some good reviews to use in your advertisements.

(Grant Richards, letter to Mitchell Kennerley, 8 September 1911)
(Archives of Grant Richards. University of Illinois / Chadwyck-Healey microfilm, A19, f.136)

Leaves A2 and A3 are conjugate and are tipped-in on A4. This demonstrates the modification made by Kennerley from the leaves as supplied by Richards.

Wight claims that the 'Sun Dial Library' American edition (see A8(h)) comprises the 'First American Edition'. This is clearly an error.

The periodical *The Forum* was published monthly by Mitchell Kennerley. The issue for May 1912 includes a full page advertisement headed '*Books published by Mitchell Kennerley*' and lists *The Tragedy of Nan and other plays* and *Multitude and Solitude*. The latter title is noted as '12mo, Cloth, $1.35 net' and includes reviews from the *London Observer* and the *London Daily News*.

Copies seen: private collection (PWE); private collection (ROV)

A8(d) First combined English and American edition (1916)

MULTITUDE AND | SOLITUDE | BY | JOHN MASEFIELD | Author of "A Tarpaulin Muster", "The Tragedy | of Nan", "Captain Margaret", etc. | [ornament] | LONDON | GRANT RICHARDS LTD. | NEW YORK: THE MACMILLAN COMPANY | MDCCCCXVI
(All width centred)

Bibliographies: Danielson [unrecorded], Williams [unrecorded], Simmons [unrecorded], Nevinson [unrecorded], Handley-Taylor [unrecorded], Wight [unrecorded]

Collation: [A-X]⁸ (±[A]2) (J, V and W not used); 168 leaves; 193 × 127mm.; [i–vi] [1–2] 3–330

Page contents: [i] half-title: 'MULTITUDE AND SOLITUDE'; [ii] '[publisher's device] | THE MACMILLAN COMPANY | [two lines listing six cities, separated by four points] | MACMILLAN & CO., LIMITED | [two lines listing four cities, separated by two points] | THE MACMILLAN CO. OF CANADA, LTD. | [one city listed]'; [iii] title-page; [iv] blank; [v] 'TO | MY WIFE'; [vi] blank; [1] 'MULTITUDE AND SOLITUDE'; [2] blank; 3–330 text (at foot of p.330: 'Printed in the United States of America')

Paper: wove paper

Running-title: 'MULTITUDE AND SOLITUDE' (58mm.) on both recto and verso, pp.4–330

Binding: grey cloth. On spine: 'Multitude | and | Solitude | John | Masefield | Grant | Richards' (all width centred). On upper cover: 'MULTITUDE | AND SOLITUDE | JOHN MASEFIELD'. Lower cover: blank. Top edge trimmed, others roughly trimmed. Binding measurements: 199 × 129mm. (covers), 199 × 44mm. (spine). End-papers: wove paper.

Publication date: unknown (not recorded in the *English Catalogue of Books*)

Price: unknown

Contents:
as for A8(a)

Notes:
That the firm of Grant Richards appears before Macmillan on the title-page of this edition and that a 1916 Macmillan edition exists without any reference to Richards on the title-page suggests that this combined Richards / Macmillan edition may have been an advance trial printing or that Richards made an arrangement with the Macmillan company to import a number of copies for sale in England.

The setting of type used for this edition was used in both A8(e) and subsequent editions published by Richards.

A publishing agreement for this title between Masefield and Macmillan was dated March 1916 (see Archives of The Society of Authors). The agreement refers to 'a licence to publish in volume form in the United States of America a work the subject or title of which is Multitude and Solitude (new edition)'.

See A7(d) for details of Macmillan's publication of Masefield's first two novels.

Copies seen: private collection (GBTS); ULL (YP.M35G) rebound

A8(e) Second American edition (1916)

MULTITUDE AND | SOLITUDE | BY | JOHN MASEFIELD | Author of "The Everlasting Mercy," "The Widow | in the Bye Street," "The Daffodil Fields," | "Captain Margaret," etc. | New York | THE MACMILLAN COMPANY | 1916
(All width centred)

Bibliographies: Danielson [unrecorded], Williams [unrecorded], Simmons [noted on p.18], Nevinson [unrecorded], Handley-Taylor [p.28], Wight [noted on p.17]

Collation: [A-X]⁸ (J, V and W not used); 168 leaves; the catalogue (not included in collation or leaf count) comprises a single gathering of 4 leaves; 191 × 127mm.; [i–vi] [1–2] 3–330; catalogue pagination: [1–8]

Page contents: [i] half-title: 'MULTITUDE AND SOLITUDE'; [ii] '[publisher's device] | THE MACMILLAN COMPANY | [two lines listing six cities, separated by four points] | MACMILLAN & CO., LIMITED | [two lines listing four cities, separated by two points] | THE MACMILLAN CO. OF CANADA, LTD. | [one city listed]'; [iii] title-page; [iv] blank; [v] 'TO | MY WIFE'; [vi] blank; [1] 'MULTITUDE AND SOLITUDE'; [2] blank; 3–330 text (at foot of p.330: 'Printed in the United States of America') [1] 'THE following pages contain advertisements of | Macmillan books by the same author' (within ruled border: 15 × 74mm.); [2] blank; [3–8] publisher's advertisements

Paper: wove paper

Running-title: 'MULTITUDE AND SOLITUDE' (58mm.) on both recto and verso, pp.4–330

Binding: light blue-green cloth. On spine, in gold: '[rule] | [rule] | MULTITUDE | AND | SOLITUDE | MASEFIELD | MACMILLAN | [rule] | [rule]' (all width centred). On upper cover, in gold: 'MULTITUDE | AND | SOLITUDE | MASEFIELD' (ranged upper left) (within blind ruled border: 188 × 119mm.) Lower cover: blank. Top edge trimmed, others roughly trimmed. Binding measurements: 197 × 130mm. (covers), 197 × 42mm. (spine). End-papers: wove paper.

Publication date: published, according to Simmons, 6 September 1916 in an edition of 1672 copies

Price: $1.35

Contents:
as for A8(a)

Notes:
See A7(d) for notes on the correspondence between Masefield and Grant Richards regarding this edition and *Captain Margaret*.

Copies seen: private collection (PWE) with perforated stamp: 'Advance Copy | Not | For | Sale | For Review'

Reprinted:

1924–25 (noted by Handley-Taylor)
1925–26 (noted by Handley-Taylor)

A8(f) Third English edition (1924)

MULTITUDE AND | SOLITUDE | BY | JOHN MASEFIELD | LONDON | GRANT RICHARDS LTD. | ST. MARTIN'S STREET | 1924
(All width centred)

Bibliographies: Simmons [unrecorded], Nevinson [unrecorded], Handley-Taylor [unrecorded], Wight [unrecorded]

Collation: [A-X]⁸ (J, V and W not used); 168 leaves; 191 × 127mm.; [i–vi] [1–2] 3–330

Page contents: [i] half-title: 'MULTITUDE AND SOLITUDE'; [ii] 'BY THE SAME AUTHOR | [rule] | [three titles listed]'; [iii] title-page; [iv] '*First Printed 1909* | *Reprinted 1924* | PRINTED IN THE UNITED STATES OF AMERICA'; [v] 'TO | MY WIFE'; [vi] blank; [1] 'MULTITUDE AND SOLITUDE'; [2] blank; 3–330 text

Paper: wove paper

Binding: grey cloth. On spine: 'Multitude | and | Solitude | John | Masefield | Grant | Richards' (all width centred). On upper cover: 'MULTITUDE | AND SOLITUDE | [design of Tsetse fly: 62 × 74mm.] | JOHN MASEFIELD'. Lower cover: blank. Top edge trimmed, others roughly trimmed. Binding measurements: 197 × 131mm. (covers), 197 × 49mm. (spine). End-papers: wove paper.

Publication date: unknown (not recorded in the *English Catalogue of Books*)

Price: unknown

Notes:
The note at the foot of p.330 ('Printed in the United States of America') present in A8(d) and A8(e) is omitted here.

Copies seen: private collection (PWE)

Reprinted:

[third edition, second impression]   1937

A8(g) Fourth English edition (1927)

MULTITUDE AND SOLITUDE | by | JOHN MASEFIELD | [illustration of satyr with stick bearing urn of fruit signed 'P.S': 44 × 17mm.] | LONDON | JONATHAN CAPE 30 BEDFORD SQUARE
(All width centred)

Bibliographies: Simmons [unrecorded], Nevinson [unrecorded], Handley-Taylor [unrecorded], Wight [unrecorded]

Collation: [A]¹⁶ B-I¹⁶ K⁴ (J not used); signatures right foot of page; 148 leaves; the catalogue (not included in collation or leaf count) comprises a single unsigned gathering of 4 leaves; 173 × 117mm.; [1–8] 9–295 [296]; catalogue pagination: [1–8]

Page contents: [1] half-title: 'THE TRAVELLERS' LIBRARY | [five-point star] | MULTITUDE AND SOLITUDE'; [2] 'THE TRAVELLERS' LIBRARY | [30 titles and their authors listed] | Uniform with this volume'; [3] title-page; [4] 'FIRST PUBLISHED 1909 | REPRINTED 1924 | FIRST ISSUED IN THE TRAVELLERS' LIBRARY 1927 | PRINTED IN GREAT BRITAIN'; [5] 'TO | MY WIFE'; [6] blank; [7] 'MULTITUDE AND SOLITUDE'; [8] blank; 9-[296] text (at foot of p.[296]: 'PRINTED BY BUTLER & TANNER LTD., FROME AND LONDON'); [1–8] catalogue: 'A LIST OF VOLUMES ISSUED IN | THE TRAVELLERS' LIBRARY | [illustration of satyr with stick bearing urn of fruit signed 'P.S'] | JONATHAN CAPE LTD. | THIRTY BEDFORD SQUARE LONDON' (width centred on p.[8]: 'LONDON | JONATHAN CAPE THIRTY BEDFORD SQUARE')

Paper: wove paper

Running title: 'MULTITUDE AND SOLITUDE' (70mm.) on both verso and recto, pp.10-[296] (see notes)

Binding: blue cloth. On spine, in gold: '[floral device] [floral device] [floral device] [floral device] | MULTITUDE | AND | SOLITUDE | * | JOHN | MASEFIELD | [illustration of satyr with stick bearing urn of fruit signed 'P.S': 45 × 17mm.] | JONATHAN | CAPE | [floral device] [floral device] [floral device] [floral device]'. Upper cover: blank. On lower cover, in blind: publisher's device of 'JC' monogram (width centred). All edges trimmed. Binding measurements: 176 × 117mm. (covers), 176 × 26mm. (spine). End-papers: wove paper.

Publication date: January 1927 in an edition of 5000 copies (see notes to A7(e))

Price: 3s.6d.

Contents:
as for A8(a)

Notes:
Each chapter heading is on the same line as the running-title, which it replaces. The text has been entirely re-set for this edition. See notes to the Jonathan Cape edition of *Captain Margaret* (A7(e)) for the publishing history of this title.

Copies seen: private collection (PWE)

A8(h) Third American edition ([1928])

MULTITUDE | AND SOLITUDE | JOHN MASEFIELD | [rule, 93mm.] | [oval publisher's device with 'The SUN DIAL | *Library*'] | [rule, 93mm.] | GARDEN CITY PUBLISHING COMPANY, INC. | GARDEN CITY, NEW YORK (All width centred)

Bibliographies: Danielson [unrecorded], Williams [unrecorded], Simmons [unrecorded], Nevinson [unrecorded], Handley-Taylor [unrecorded], Wight 8a

Collation: [A-W]⁸ (J not used); 168 leaves; 179 × 110mm.; [i–vi] [1–2] 3–330

Page contents: [i–ii] blank; [iii] title-page; [iv] '*First Printed 1909* | PRINTED IN THE UNITED STATES OF AMERICA'; [v] 'TO | MY WIFE'; [vi] blank; [1] 'MULTITUDE AND SOLITUDE'; [2] blank; 3–330 text

Paper: wove paper

Running title: 'MULTITUDE AND SOLITUDE' (58mm.) on both recto and verso, pp.4–330

Binding: light purple cloth. On spine: '[device of double rule, nine vertical lines, rule and double rule] [in orange] | MULTITUDE [in black] | AND [in black] | SOLITUDE [in black] | [rule] [in orange] | MASEFIELD [in black] | [device of rule, nine vertical lines, double rule, wavy design and rule] [in orange] | THE [in orange] | *Sun Dial* [in orange] | *Library* [in orange] | [device of panel, double rule, panel, rule, and panel] [in orange]' (all width centred). On upper cover: 'MULTITUDE | AND SOLITUDE | *John Masefield*' (within ornate floral border in orange and black). Lower cover: blank. Top edge stained blue, others trimmed. Binding measurements: 184 × 113mm. (covers), 184 × 32mm. (spine). End-papers: wove paper with design in light green (signed with 'WAD' monogram) of garden and sun dial with 'THE | SUN DIAL | *Library*' all within decorative border: 169 × 220mm.

Publication date: 1928 (Wight incorrectly cites a publication date of 1910)

Price: $1.00

Contents:
as for A7(a)

Notes:
Wight is the only bibliographer to include this volume. (He incorrectly claims a publication date from Handley-Taylor). Within this edition only the information 'First Printed 1909' is given and this leads Wight to assume that the volume constitutes the first American edition. However, the Mitchell Kennerley edition (reported by Simmons and Handley-Taylor) is a more likely candidate. This volume appears to be listed – without an exact year of publication – in Burnham, Mary, *ed. The Cumulative Book Index 1928–1932*, New York: H.W. Wilson Co., 1933. A date of 1928 is suggested by *The National Union Catalog Pre–1956 Imprints*, Mansell, 1975.

A publishing agreement for this title between Masefield and Macmillan was dated 29 August 1928 (see Archives of The Society of

Authors). The agreement notes '…it is desired to publish or authorize the publication of a cheap edition or editions of the said work for sale in the United States of America to be sold at one-half the retail price or less…' This edition may be the result of this agreement.

The text appears to use the same setting of type as A8(d)

Copies seen: NYPL (NCW 1909) 394740B

A9 THE TRAGEDY OF NAN AND OTHER PLAYS 1909

A9(a) American copyright edition (1909) [Not consulted – adapted from Simmons]

The | Tragedy of Nan | and Other Plays | By | John Masefield | [publisher's device] | New York | Mitchell Kennerley | London | Grant Richards | 1909

Bibliographies: Danielson [unrecorded], Williams [unrecorded], Simmons [9], Nevinson [unrecorded], Handley-Taylor p.28, Wight [9]

Notes:

The publishing agreement for A9(c) specifies that 'the Publisher agrees by having the type of the said work set up in the United States of America to protect the copyright of the Author in the said work in the United States of America and the Publisher agrees to take such steps as may be necessary to secure the copyright in the United States of America in the said work for the benefit of the Author' (see Archives of The Society of Authors).

Simmons writes of this edition, 'no more than ten copies were printed for copyright purposes. The type for this book was set up in America and the plates shipped to England for the first English edition published in September, 1909. The plates were then returned to America and used for the first *published* American edition…' The Richards archive reveals considerable delay was experienced in the shipping of the plates.

A.C. McKay, in papers held at Ledbury Library, states that there were only six copies printed. He does not, however, indicate any sources for this information. In a letter to Mitchell Kennerley dated 29 April 1909, Grant Richards writes:

> …what I should like you to do is print half a dozen copies of the book in New York for copyright purposes and then to ship the plates to me.

> (Grant Richards, letter to Mitchell Kennerley, 29 April 1909)
> (Archives of Grant Richards. University of Illinois / Chadwyck-Healey microfilm, A15, f.235)

A9(b) Pre-publication edition (1909)

THE | TRAGEDY OF NAN | AND OTHER PLAYS | BY | JOHN MASEFIELD | LONDON | GRANT RICHARDS | 1909
(All width centred)

Bibliographies: Danielson [unrecorded], Williams [unrecorded], Simmons [unrecorded], Nevinson [unrecorded], Handley-Taylor [unrecorded], Wight [unrecorded]

Collation: [A-G]⁸ [H]²; 58 leaves; 179 × 126mm.; [i–ii] [1–6] 7–71 [72–76] 77–100 [101–104] 105–114

Page contents: [i] half-title: 'THE TRAGEDY OF NAN | AND OTHER PLAYS'; [ii] blank; [1] title-page; [2] 'Copyright 1909 | BY JOHN MASEFIELD'; [3] 'CONTENTS' (three plays listed with titles and page references); [4] blank; [5] 'THE TRAGEDY OF NAN'; [6] blank; 7–71 text; [72] blank; [73] 'THE CAMPDEN WONDER'; [74] blank; [75] 'THE CAMPDEN WONDER | PERSONS | [dramatis personae and original cast listed with 'PLAYED BY' heading] | *This play was produced at the Court Theatre, in London,* | *on the 8th of January,* 1907, *under the direction of Mr. H.* | *Granville Barker.*'; [76] blank; 77–100 text; [101] 'MRS. HARRISON'; [102] blank; [103] 'MRS. HARRISON | PERSONS | [dramatis personae listed]'; [104] blank; 105–14 text

Paper: wove paper

Running title: these constitute play title and act, followed by rule (75–76mm.), pp.8–114

Binding: grey-green wrappers. Spine: blank. On upper wrapper: 'THE | TRAGEDY OF NAN | AND OTHER PLAYS | BY | JOHN MASEFIELD | LONDON | GRANT RICHARDS | 1909'. Lower wrapper: blank. All edges trimmed. Binding measurements: 185 × 129mm. (wrappers), 185 × 5mm. (spine).

Publication date: unknown

Price: unknown

Contents:
The Tragedy of Nan ('ACT I | SCENE:- *A kitchen in the house of a small tenant farmer...*')
The Campden Wonder ('SCENE I | SCENE. *Harrison's Kitchen in Campden.*')
Mrs. Harrison ('SCENE: *A Room in MRS HARRISON'S House*')

Notes:

The contents page incorrectly states 'The Tragedy of Nan' commences on p.[1]. The correct page number is 7.

The first divisional title on p.[3] is in larger type than the other two divisional titles.

The dedication to Yeats is excluded from this edition. The listing of dramatis personae, original cast and five-line note for *The Tragedy of Nan* is also absent. The listing of dramatis personae for *Mrs. Harrison* includes a number of dots after each character: a feature unique to this edition.

Only one copy of this edition has been traced. Harvard College Library (Houghton *EC9.M377.909ta) catalogue the copy as 'an unrecorded, pre-publication state, perhaps prepared for actor's use'. Were it not for the title-page and printing on the upper cover, this issue might have been mistaken for a copy of the Copyright edition, as described by Simmons. However, it is also unlikely to be an actor's copy (at least for the first casts of May and June 1908) since these pre-date the 1909 date of publication. The Harvard College Library copy includes the signature of Bernard Dailey, who, if the first owner of the copy was not listed as a cast member for the 1908 performances.

Copies seen: Harvard College Library (*EC9.M377.909ta)

A9(c) First English edition (1909)

THE | TRAGEDY OF NAN | AND OTHER PLAYS | BY | JOHN MASEFIELD | LONDON | GRANT RICHARDS | 1909
(All width centred)

Bibliographies: Danielson 167, Williams p.2, Simmons [9a], Nevinson p.14, Handley-Taylor p.28, Wight [9a]

Collation: [A]⁴ [B-H]⁸; 60 leaves; 200 × 142mm.; [i–vi] [1–6] 7–71 [72–76] 77–100 [101–104] 105–114

Page contents: [i] half-title: 'THE TRAGEDY OF NAN | AND OTHER PLAYS'; [ii] blank; [iii] title-page; [iv] 'Copyright 1909 | BY JOHN MASEFIELD'; [v] 'TO | W.B. YEATS'; [vi] blank; [1] 'CONTENTS' (three plays listed with titles and page references); [2] blank; [3] 'THE TRAGEDY OF NAN'; [4] blank; [5] 'THE TRAGEDY OF NAN | [dramatis personae and original cast listed with 'PERSONS' and 'PLAYED BY' headings] | *This play was produced by the Pioneers at the New Royalty | Theatre, on 24th May, 1908, under the direction of Mr. H. | Granville Barker. At its revival as a matinee at the Haymarket | Theatre, in June, 1908, the part of the Rev. Mr. Drew was | played by Mr. Cecil Brooking.*'; [6] blank; 7–71 text; [72] blank; [73] 'THE CAMPDEN WONDER'; [74] blank; [75] 'THE CAMPDEN WONDER | PERSONS | [dramatis personae and original cast listed with 'PLAYED BY' heading] | *This play was produced at the Court Theatre, in London, | on the 8th of January, 1907, under the direction of Mr. H. | Granville Barker.*'; [76] blank; 77–100 text; [101] 'MRS. HARRISON'; [102] blank; [103] 'MRS. HARRISON | PERSONS | [dramatis personae listed]'; [104] blank; 105–14 text

Paper: wove paper

Running title: these constitute play title and act, followed by rule (75–76mm.), pp.8–114

Binding: light-brown red cloth. On spine, in gold: 'THE | TRAG- | EDY | OF | NAN | ETC. | JOHN | MASE- | FIELD | GRANT | RICHARDS' (all width centred). Covers: blank. All edges uncut. Binding measurements: 206 × 144mm. (covers), 206 × 21mm. (spine). End-papers: wove paper.

Publication date: published, according to Simmons, 29 September 1909, in an edition of 500 copies. The *English Catalogue of Books* records a publication date of October 1909. (Later editions of the play give the date of first publication as September 1909)

Price: 3s.6d.

Contents:
as for A9(b)

Notes:

Masefield wrote to Cazenove in January 1909 with reference to Grant Richards:

> …I believe that he likes my work, + is keen to publish it, so I suggest to him that he publish a volume of my plays: *Nan, The Campden Wonder, + Mrs Harrison* early this spring, taking care to publish simultaneously in America. If he likes this plan, + does the book, which will be no worse a frost anyhow than my novel, he need not pay me an advance royalty on it. Not that I suppose he would in any case. Later in the year, I suggest that he publish my Pompey play. This would keep my name in his lists, which is what he seems to want, and would not lose him so much money as a novel is sure to do. I have no belief whatsoever in my novels. I believe that they are not my metier…
>
> (John Masefield, letter to C.F. Cazenove, 4 January 1909)
> (University of Arizona Library. MS.50, V.II)

It therefore appears that it was Masefield's suggestion that Richards issue this volume of plays and the suggestion may have been a compromise for declining to write a further novel for Richards.

The manuscript was sent to Cazenove on 9 January 1909. Masefield specifically notes the retaining of American rights and the order of plays within the volume:

> Here are the plays. I hope that you will ask Richards to use very considerable discretion in letting the ms out of his hands. It is absolutely essential that the American rights be preserved to me. Mrs Barker's tour was killed by her husband's illness, but she may go there with Nan later on. I wish Nan to precede the other two.
>
> (John Masefield, letter to C.F. Cazenove, 9 January 1909)
> (University of Arizona Library. MS.50, V.II)

Masefield was, evidently, nervous. He wrote to Cazenove:

> What is happening about the plays? I am rather anxious about them. I don't think that they ought to go off to America until the contract is signed. And when will that be, + when will GR publish them? There is this chance of a Spring production which ought not to be missed.
>
> (John Masefield, letter to C.F. Cazenove, 9 February 1909)
> (University of Arizona Library. MS.50, V.II)

The publishing agreement for this title between Masefield and Grant Richards was dated 14 February 1909 (see Archives of The Society of Authors). The agreement refers to '…a volume containing three plays entitled "NAN", "THE CAMPDEN WONDER" and "MRS HARRISON" to be issued in one volume under the collective title of "THE TRAGEDY OF NAN ETC." The agreement specifies that 'publication of the said work shall take place not later than the 30th June 1909…'

A copy of this edition held in W.B. Yeats' library, in Dalkey, Ireland (*1257) is inscribed 'To that most reverend head to whom I owe | All that I am in Arts, all that I know. | To my master, | W.B. Yeats. | Sept. 7, 1909.' (The quotation is from Ben Jonson's epigram to his old school-master William Camden). The inscription pre-dates Simmons' date of publication. Enclosed is a holograph presentation letter (of the same date) including: 'It was you who taught me all that I know of drama, who first encouraged, helped, and corrected me… It was in your room that I had my first success, and what was better, my first consciousness of progress; you helped me to production, and soothed the bitterness of failure…' In a letter to Molly Allgood, J.M. Synge reports W.B. Yeats' impressions of *Nan*:

> Yeats says Masefield has written a wonderful play – the best English play since the Elizabethans so I'll have to look out…
>
> (J.M. Synge, letter to Molly Allgood, 11 January 1908)
> (ed. Saddlemyer, Ann, *The Collected Letters of John Millington Synge, Volume Two 1907–1909*,
> Oxford University Press, 1984, p.129)

As in A9(b) the contents page incorrectly states 'The Tragedy of Nan' commences on p.[1]. The correct page number is 7. The first divisional title on p.[3] is, similarly, in larger type than the other two divisional titles.

The printer is unidentified.

Babington Smith states the source for the play was a tale from Annie Hanford-Flood (Masefield's godmother) and mentions the success of the piece 'owed much to the performance of Lillah McCarthy in the title role'. McCarthy (1875–1960) was to become associated with many of Masefield's dramatic pieces and occasions of verse speaking. She gave, for example, a 'dramatic recital' of Masefield's poems at Hereford Town Hall on 1 December 1930 and appeared in a number of the Boars Hill theatricals. See also B270.

In an undated manuscript booklet of reminiscences (dating from before Masefield's death) by Ethel Ross (née Masefield) she writes:

> I did not see the Camden [*sic*] Wonder but when "Nan" was produced in 1908 I went up to see it with Jack and W.B. Yeats at the Haymarket.

The Tragedy of Nan has been broadcast by the BBC on at least two occasions starring Kathleen Michael in July 1957 and Fay Compton in June 1958. Writing in 1960 to The Society of Authors, however, Masefield stated '*Nan* belongs to a distant past; + it is unlikely ever to be acted again anywhere on this planet.' (see John Masefield, letter to Anne Munro-Kerr, [January 1960]) (Archives of The Society of Authors)

Six letters (dated 5 December 1906 to 9 January 1907) from Masefield to Granville-Barker refer to the play providing details of revisions, music, accents and source. The historical basis is detailed as follows:

> William Harrison disappeared on the 16th August, 1660. John Perry was examined on the 17th + 24th of the same month, Joan and Dick being arrested the day after the second examination. The case was tried before Sir Chris Turner at Gloucester Assizes, Sept, 1660, when the judge dismissed the prisoners "because the body was not found". In the spring of 1661, they were again tried at Gloucester (before Sir Bernard Hyde, a man after John's heart) and found guilty on John's evidence. They were hanged a few days later (say April or May 1661) and John was afterwards gibbeted on Broadway Hill, over the graves of Joan + Dick. William Harrison seems to have come home about a year after the execution: but his return is not dated, + it may have been earlier. It is a strange tale; + it will probably never be explained. The records of the trials have been destroyed + there the thing rests.
>
> (John Masefield, letter to Harley Granville-Barker, 6 December 1906)
> (BL, Add.Mss.47897)

See also *A True and Perfect Account of the Examination, Confession, Tryal, Condemnation and Execution of Joan Perry…* attributed to Sir Thomas Overbury and printed in 1676.

As Babington Smith reports, *The Campden Wonder* was Masefield's first play to be staged and resulted in a *succès de scandale* despite the fiasco of its staging by Granville-Barker (see Babington Smith p.94). Bernard Shaw praised Masefield, however, and both Masefield's letter to Shaw and his reply have survived. (see BL, Add.Mss.50543, f.88 and Bodleian, Ms.Eng.Lett.c.255). To conclude the first performances of *The Campden Wonder*, Masefield obtained permission to use the closing chorus from Gilbert Murray's *The Bacchae*, as a letter dated 26 December 1905 in the Bodleian (Gilbert Murray correspondence) reveals.

A letter to Jack B. Yeats contains details of a copyright performance of *The Campden Wonder*:

> My play was copyrighted last Monday; at a little theatre in Bayswater. Young Strang was Mrs Harrison + I was Mrs Perry. Jack Monsell was Dick, a man called Streatfield was John. Sturge Moore was the policeman and Russell of the Bow was the Parson. For audience we had a large and distinguished assembly viz Lady Gregory, Mrs Moore, Mrs Strang, and Miss Monsell, together with a tired scene-shifter. After the piece we had tea at Whiteleys, + so home. The play has gone to Granville Barker; but your brother thinks it will be too gloomy for a modern theatre, + he is right. It is pretty sure to come back.

> (John Masefield, letter to Jack B. Yeats, 23 March 1906)
(Harvard, *61M–93)

Masefield's entry in *Who's Who* for 1928 lists *Mrs. Harrison* as a produced play in a list comprising: *The Campden Wonder, The Tragedy of Nan, The Tragedy of Pompey the Great, The Sweeps of '98, Philip the King, The Faithful, The Locked Chest, The Condemned Cell, Mrs Harrison, Good Friday, Esther, Melloney Holtspur, A King's Daughter, The Trial of Jesus* and *Tristan and Isolt*. This sequence may retain a chronology of production dates not currently known.

Grant Richards quotes A.E. Housman's letter of 15 July 1910:

> ...I must thank you for Masefield's plays, which are well worth reading and contain a lot that is very good; only he has got the Elizabethan notion that in order to have tragedy you must have villains, and villains of disgusting wickedness or vileness.

> (Grant Richards, *Housman*, Oxford University Press, 1942)

A letter to Masefield from Bernard Shaw dated 27 July 1907 presents Shaw's advice on publishing plays (and *The Campden Wonder* in particular). This edition suggests that Masefield followed Shaw's advice (although see note on reprints):

> Is the C.W. published? If not, hold it back until you have a couple more plays to go with it, and then write a preface, just as I do. The reason for this is that plays do not circulate widely enough as yet to make really cheap editions commercially practicable; and when it comes to six shillings the bookbuyer can only afford it on condition that the book lasts him (and probably his family) a fairish time. If he has to buy a new book next day, he exceeds his income. The secret of my six shilling volumes of plays is <u>quantity</u>. Publish the C.W. by itself; and the buyer, asking always "How long will it last?" will put it down sorrowfully in the shop and buy a novel by Mrs Humphrey Ward instead.

> (Bernard Shaw, letter to John Masefield, 27 July 1907)
(Bodleian, Ms.Eng.Lett.c.255)

Copies seen: BL (11779.d.56) stamped 12 NOV 1909; Harvard College Library (Houghton *EC9.M377.909tb); NYPL (Berg Collection) inscribed 'For | William Strang | from John Masefield. | Sept 7th. 1909.'

Reprinted:

'Reprinted'	[first edition, second impression]	Mar 1910
'Reprinted'	[first edition, third impression]	Apr 1911
'Reprinted'	[first edition, fourth impression]	Mar 1914
'Reprinted'	[first edition, fifth impression]	Apr 1920
'Reprinted'	[first edition, sixth impression]	May 1922

The introductory author's note on tragedy (dated 4th April 1911) obviously does not appear in early impressions. It occurs on pp. [3]–[4] replacing the individual half-title page for *The Tragedy of Nan*

A9(d) First American edition (1910)

THE | TRAGEDY OF NAN | AND OTHER PLAYS | BY | JOHN MASEFIELD | [publisher's device of 'M' and 'K' in outline within double circular rule] | MITCHELL KENNERLEY | NEW YORK MCMX
(All width centred)

Bibliographies: Danielson [unrecorded], Williams [unrecorded], Simmons [unrecorded], Nevinson [unrecorded], Handley-Taylor [unrecorded], Wight [9a] (see notes)

Collation: [A–H]⁸; 64 leaves; 182 × 120mm.; [i–x] [1–6] 7–71 [72–76] 77–100 [101–104] 105–114 [115–18]

Page contents: [i–iv] blank; [v] half-title: 'THE TRAGEDY OF NAN | AND OTHER PLAYS'; [vi] blank; [vii] title-page; [viii] 'COPYRIGHT 1909 BY JOHN MASEFIELD'; [ix] 'TO | W. B. YEATS'; [x] blank; [1] 'CONTENTS' (three plays listed with titles and page references); [2] blank; [3] 'THE TRAGEDY OF NAN'; [4] blank; [5] 'THE TRAGEDY OF NAN | [dramatis personae and original cast listed with 'PERSONS' and 'PLAYED BY' headings] | *This play was produced by the Pioneers at the New Royalty* | *Theatre, on 24th May, 1908, under the direction of Mr. H.* | *Granville Barker. At its revival as a matinee at the Haymarket* | *Theatre, in June, 1908, the part of the Rev. Mr. Drew was* | *played by Mr. Cecil Brooking.*'; [6] blank; 7–71 text; [72] blank; [73] 'THE CAMPDEN WONDER'; [74] blank; [75] 'THE CAMPDEN WONDER | PERSONS | [dramatis personae and original cast listed with 'PLAYED BY' heading]

| *This play was produced at the Court Theatre, in London,* | *on the* 8*th of January,* 1907, *under the direction of Mr. H.* | *Granville Barker.*'; [76] blank; 77–100 text; [101] blank; [102] 'MRS. HARRISON'; [103] blank; [104] 'MRS. HARRISON | PERSONS | [dramatis personae listed]'; 105–14 text; [115–18] blank

Paper: wove paper

Running title: these constitute play title and act, followed by rule (75–76mm.), pp.8–114

Binding: purple cloth. On spine, in gold: 'THE | TRAG- | EDY | OF | NAN | JOHN | MASE- | FIELD | MITCHELL | KENNERLEY' (all width centred). Covers: blank. Top edge gilt, others trimmed. Binding measurements: 187 × 120mm. (covers), 187 × 21mm. (spine). End-papers: wove paper.

Publication date: 1910

Price: $1.25

Contents:
as for A9(b)

Notes:
Simmons states (on an addenda and errata slip)

> Of the issue with the Kennerley imprint dated 1909, no more than ten copies were printed for copyright purposes. The type for this book was set up in America and the plates shipped to England for the first English edition published in September, 1909. The plates were then returned to America and used for the first *published* American edition of 400 copies with the imprint of Mitchell Kennerley, New York, MCMX

The edition noted by Simmons as the 'first *published* American edition' is not described by him, or noted by Handley-Taylor.

As in A9(b) the contents page incorrectly states 'The Tragedy of Nan' commences on p.[1]. The correct page number is 7. The first divisional title on p.[3] is, similarly, in larger type than the other two divisional titles.

Wight states that the edition is 'bound in red cloth' and also notes further blank leaves at the rear of the volume. (These must constitute an error as the collation, number of leaves and description of the volume otherwise correspond).

G. Thomas Tanselle, discusses 'three issues' 'between the original 1909 publication [American copyright edition] and the 1916 Macmillan printing' in 'Three Unrecorded Issues of Masefield's *Tragedy of Nan*', *The Library*, Fifth Series, Vol. XXIII No.2, Bibliographical Society / OUP, 1969. The first of these issues is described, here, as A9(d). The other two issues are dated 1912, one of which includes Masefield's statement about tragedy which Tanselle notes 'makes its first American appearance here and is the chief reason for the significance of this printing'. Tanselle transcribes the 1912 title-page and notes diffrences in the two 1912 issues as follows:

> THE | TRAGEDY OF NAN | *and other plays by* | John Masefield | [publisher's monogram: 'MK' in a circle] | *New York* & *London* | MITCHELL KENNERLEY | 1912

> *Issue A:* (7 3/8 × 4 15/16 in.), [1–8⁸], 64 leaves, pp. [*6*] [*1–6*] 7–114 [*115–122*]. *Contents:* [*1–4*] blank; [*5*] half-title; [*6*] blank; [1] title-page; [2] copyright notice; [3] table of contents; [4] blank; [5] divisional title; [6] blank; 7–114 text; [115–122] blank. *Paper:* white wove unwatermarked. *Binding:* red ribbed cloth, all edges cut.

> *Issue B:* (7 1/2 × 5 1/8 in.), [1–8⁸], 64 leaves, pp. [*10*] [*1–6*] 7–114 [115–118]. *Contents:* [*1–2*] blank; [*3*] half-title; [*4*] blank; [*5*] title-page; [*6*] copyright notice; [*7*] dedication 'TO | W.B. YEATS'; [*8*] blank; [*9*] table of contents; [*10*] blank; [1–2] preface; [3] divisional title; [4] blank; [5] list of characters; [6] blank; 7–114 text; [115–118] blank. *Paper:* white laid unwatermarked. *Binding:* red ribbed cloth, fore and bottom edges rough-trimmed, top edge gilt.

Copies seen: Columbia University Library (Special Collections B825 M377 X36 1910)

Reprinted: see notes above

A9(e) Second American edition (1916)

THE | TRAGEDY OF NAN | *and other plays by* | John Masefield | New York | THE MACMILLAN COMPANY | 1916 | *All rights reserved*
(All width centred)

Bibliographies: Danielson [unrecorded], Williams [unrecorded], Simmons [noted on p.19], Nevinson [unrecorded], Handley-Taylor p.28, Wight [unrecorded]

Collation: [A–H]⁸; 64 leaves; 187 × 128mm.; [i–x] [1–6] 7–71 [72–76] 77–100 [101–04] 105–14 [115–18]

Page contents: [i–ii] blank; [iii] half-title: 'THE TRAGEDY OF NAN | AND OTHER PLAYS'; [iv] blank; [v] title-page; [vi] 'Copyright 1909 | By JOHN MASEFIELD'; [vii] 'TO | W.B. YEATS'; [viii] blank; [ix] 'CONTENTS' (three plays listed with titles and page references); [x] blank; [1–2] [Author's Note] ('TRAGEDY at its best is a vision of the heart of life.') (signed, 'JOHN MASEFIELD. | 4*th April* 1911.'); [3] 'THE TRAGEDY OF NAN'; [4] blank; [5] 'THE TRAGEDY OF NAN | [dramatis personae and original cast listed with 'PERSONS' and 'PLAYED BY' headings] | *This play was produced by the Pioneers at the New Royalty* | *Theatre, on 24th* | *May, 1908, under the direction of Mr. H.* | *Granville Barker. At its revival as a matinee at the Haymarket* | *Theatre, in June, 1908, the part of the* | *Rev. Mr. Drew was* | *played by Mr. Cecil Brooking.*'; [6] blank; 7–71 text; [72] blank; [73] 'THE CAMPDEN WONDER'; [74] blank; [75] 'THE CAMPDEN WONDER | PERSONS | [dramatis personae and original cast listed with 'PLAYED BY' heading] | *This play* | *was produced at the Court Theatre, in London,* | *on the 8th of January, 1907, under the direction of Mr. H.* | *Granville Barker.*'; [76] blank; 77–100 text; [101] 'MRS. HARRISON'; [102] blank; [103] 'MRS. HARRISON | PERSONS | [dramatis personae listed]'; [104] blank; 105–114 text; [115–18] blank

Paper: wove paper

Running title: these constitute play title and act, followed by rule (75–76mm.), pp.8–114

Binding: light-brown cloth. On spine, in gold: 'THE | TRAG- | EDY | OF | NAN | MASE- | FIELD | MACMILLAN' (all width centred). On upper cover, in gold: 'THE | TRAGEDY OF | NAN | MASEFIELD' (ranged upper left) (within blind ruled border: 185 × 118mm.) Lower cover: blank. Top edge gilt, others trimmed. Binding measurements: 193 × 126mm. (covers), 193 × 27mm. (spine). End-papers: wove paper.

Publication date: published, according to Simmons, 1 March 1916, in an edition of 1900 copies (500 copies having apparently been taken over from Mitchell Kennerley)

Price: $1.25

Contents:
[Author's Note] ('Tragedy at its best is a vision of the heart of life.')
The Tragedy of Nan ('ACT I | SCENE:- *A kitchen in the house of a small tenant farmer...*')
The Campden Wonder ('SCENE I | SCENE. *Harrison's Kitchen in Campden.*')
Mrs. Harrison ('SCENE: *A Room in MRS HARRISON'S House*')

Notes:
The text appears to use the same setting of type as A9(b). A letter from the Macmillan firm to Masefield notes the high price paid for the plates of the book:

> I have just been able to arrange with Mr. Kennerley for the transfer of your "Tragedy of Nan". It is true that we have had to pay a very high, even an extortionate, price for the plates of the book, but it seemed better, I may say, in view of your wish that the book should be transferred to us to do this so that your books would be altogether in the hands of one publisher with a view to a collected edition in the future.
>
> (George P. Brett, letter to John Masefield, 28 January 1916)
> (HRHRC, MS (Masefield, J.) Recip The Macmillan Company)

The Archives of The Society of Authors reveal several publishing agreements or proposed agreements for this title between Masefield and Macmillan. One, dated 1914 only, grants 'a licence to publish in volume form in the United States of America, four (4) works, the subjects or titles of which are "MULTITUDE AND SOLITUDE", "THE LOST ENDEAVOR", "CAPTAIN MARGARET", and "THE TRAGEDY OF NAN", (provided the rights of publication in the United States of America be acquired from the present publishers by the Company)...' The document additionally states '...the Company agrees to publish the first three of the above works in the course of the year 1915, and... "NAN" within the three months after the said work has been acquired from the present publishers...' The document also extended the licence for previous Macmillan titles for a further five years from date of their first publication. Another version is dated 19 October 1914 and omits reference to acquiring rights from existing publishers. This version refers to 'revised editions' of the four works and notes 'the Company agrees to publish one of the above works in the fall of 1914, another in the spring of 1915, and a third in the autumn of 1915'. An unknown hand has annotated this document 'Proposed agreement not signed to our knowledge'.

Copies seen: private collection (ROV)

Reprinted:

1918–19 (noted by Handley-Taylor)
1920–21 (noted by Handley-Taylor)

A9(f) Third American edition ([1920s?]) [Not consulted – adapted from Wight]

THE | TRAGEDY OF NAN | and other plays by | John Masefield | – FROM – | WALTER H. BAKER & CO. | THEATRICAL [rule with a short vertical line at the middle] PUBLISHERS. | 5 HAMILTON PLACE – BOSTON – MASS.

Bibliographies: Simmons [unrecorded], Nevinson [unrecorded], Handley-Taylor [unrecorded], Wight 9c

Publication date: There is no publication date provided for this edition by Wight. *The National Union Catalog* also fails to suggest a date.

Price: unknown

Notes:

Wight's description of the volume is far from clear.

See also an edition of *The Trial of Jesus* published by the Walter H. Baker Company (see A77(d)).

In 1927 The Society of Authors wrote to Masefield about the Walter H. Baker Company. Masefield replied:

> I thank you for your letter about these people and will consider appointing them to collect amateur fees in the United States.

> (John Masefield, letter to [G.H.] Thring, 29 April 1927)
> (BL, Add.Mss.56584, f.170)

The Society of Authors may therefore have suggested that a company based in the United States should have responsibility of arranging amateur performance rights for Masefield's plays. A subsequent letter from Masefield reveals that a New Zealand agency was also to be employed:

> I am afraid that I have been a long time writing to you about the employment of the Baker Company and the New Zealand lady as agents for amateur performances of my plays in the United States, Canada and New Zealand. I have decided to employ both agencies...

> (John Masefield, letter to [G.H.] Thring, 12 July 1927)
> (BL, Add.Mss.56585, f.36)

The New Zealand agent was Miss Elizabeth Blake, as revealed when Masefield returned signed agreements (for both agencies) to The Society of Authors at the end of July 1927 (see BL, Add.Mss.56585, f.48). It is feasible that, as agents for Masefield, Walter H. Baker and Company printed copies of a number of Masefield's plays. These may have been performance copies provided for theatrical companies.

A10 MY FAITH IN WOMAN SUFFRAGE   1910

A10(a) First English edition (1910)

Upper wrapper:
MY | FAITH IN | WOMAN | SUFFRAGE | By JOHN MASEFIELD [justified on left margin and ranged upper left] | The Woman's Press | Price 1d. [these two lines centred and ranged lower right]

Bibliographies: Danielson 170, Williams p.8, Simmons [10], Nevinson [unrecorded], Handley-Taylor p.29, Wight [10]

Collation: [A]¹² ; 12 leaves; 182 × 123mm.; [1] 2–12

Page contents: [1] head-title: 'MY FAITH | IN | WOMAN SUFFRAGE | By JOHN MASEFIELD | *A Speech delivered in the Queen's Hall, Feb. 14th, 1910.* [all width centred] | [text]' (the 'v' of 'delivered' is swash); 2–12 text (at foot of p.12: '[rule] | *Garden City Press Ltd., Printers, Letchworth, Herts.*')

Paper: wove paper

Running title: none

Binding: brown wrappers. On upper wrapper: described above. On lower wrapper: advertisement for 'VOTES FOR WOMEN | The Newspaper of the Movement', etc. On inside of upper wrapper: offices, committee and objectives etc. of the 'National Women's Social and Political Union'. Inside of lower wrapper: blank. All edges trimmed. Binding measurements: 182 × 123mm. (wrappers); 182 × 2mm. (spine).

Alternative wrappers: light grey wrappers. On upper wrapper: as above. On lower wrapper: reset advertisement for 'VOTES FOR WOMEN' including, at foot, a quotation from *The Times* commencing '"From what quarter are we to learn the truth...' On inside of upper wrapper: reset information of the 'National Women's Social and Political Union' excluding objectives of the unions and including changes to the committee. On inside of lower wrapper: 'ON SALE at the Woman's Press' (37 books and two pamphlets listed). Other information not discernible from examined copy.

Publication date: between 11 and 18 March 1910

Price: 1d.

Contents:

My Faith in Woman Suffrage ('You have done me the honour to ask me to confess...')
        Previously printed in Votes for Women *18 February 1910, p.319*

Notes:

Danielson describes only those wrappers described above as the 'alternative wrappers'. Simmons only describes the other. Both bibliographers agree on a grey colour in contrast to Wight who would seem to indicate that Simmons should have noted a brown colour. The possibility is that the binding with advertisements on the inside of the lower cover is a later reprint. This may explain the 1913 date-stamp in the British Library copy.

The newspaper *Votes for Women* (published by the National Women's Social and Political Union) notes, on 4 March 1910:

In response to special request, the beautiful speech by Mr. John Masefield at the Queen's Hall on February 14 is being reprinted in pamphlet form, price 1d., and will be ready in about a week.

A small advertisement from The Woman's Press in *Votes for Women* on 11 March 1910 does not list the pamphlet. It is first advertised in *Votes for Women* on 18 March 1910.

It appears that Masefield bought 50 copies of this title at the beginning of April. A letter addressed to Mrs Tuke (Mabel Tuke was joint honorary secretary with Mrs. Pankhurst of the National Women's Social and Political Union) states:

Thank you very much for so kindly + so promptly sending me the fifty pamphlets... I enclose my cheque for the pamphlets.
(John Masefield, letter to Mrs [Mabel] Tuke, 17 April 1910)
(Private Collection (PWE))

Copies of this title inscribed by Masefield all appear to be dated after 17 April 1910.

Copies seen: BL (08415.df.43.(10.)) stamped 23 AUG 13 alternative wrappers; Ledbury Library inscribed 'Margaret. L. Woods | from John Masefield | 19 April 1910.'; Harvard College Library (Houghton *EC9.M377.910m2) inscribed 'for Florence [Lamont], who would give anyone | a faith in Woman. | April 16. 1918.'

A11 THE TRAGEDY OF POMPEY THE GREAT   1910

A11(a) First English edition (1910)

THE TRAGEDY OF | POMPEY THE GREAT | BY | JOHN MASEFIELD | LONDON | SIDGWICK AND JACKSON, LTD. | M C M X
(All width centred)

Bibliographies: Danielson 168, Williams p.3, Simmons [11], Nevinson p.14, Handley-Taylor p.29, Wight [11]

Collation: [A]⁸ B–F⁸ G⁶; signatures width centred at foot of page; 54 leaves; 185 × 121mm.; [1–8] 9–106 [107–08]

Page contents: [1] half-title: 'THE TRAGEDY OF | POMPEY THE GREAT'; [2] blank; [3] title-page; [4] '*Entered at the Library of Congress | Washington, U.S.A. | All rights reserved*'; [5] 'TO | MY WIFE'; [6] blank; [7] 'ARGUMENT | In the years 50 and 49 B.C., Cneius Pompeius Magnus, | the head of the patrician party, contested with C. | Julius Cæsar, the popular leader, for supreme power in | the State. Their jealousy led to the troubles of the | Civil War, in which, after many battles, Cneius | Pompeius Magnus was miserably killed. | ACT I. The determination of Pompeius to fight | with his rival, then marching upon Rome. | ACT II. The triumph of Pompey's generalship at | Dyrrachium. His overthrow by the generals | of his staff. His defeat at Pharsalia. | ACT III. The death of that great ruler on the | seashore of Pelusium in Egypt.'; [8] 'PERSONS | [dramatis personae listed, also table of act, scene and historical time]'; 9–103 text; 104–06 'NOTES' (paragraphs titled 'ON THE APPEARANCE OF POMPEY', 'ON THE FATE OF THE PERSONS IN THIS TRAGEDY', and 'ON THE HOUSE OF POMPEY, AFTER THE MURDER.'); [107] verse ('And all their passionate hearts are dust,') dated on left margin '*Feb.* 8, 1908.' and on extreme right '*July* 5, 1909.'; [108] 'Printed by T. and A. CONSTABLE, Printers to His Majesty | at the Edinburgh University Press'

Paper: laid paper (no watermark), chain-lines 24mm. apart

Running title: 'THE TRAGEDY OF' (37mm.) on verso; 'POMPEY THE GREAT' (42mm.) on recto, with '[ACT' on extreme right of verso and 'I]', 'II]' or 'III]' on extreme left of recto, pp.10–106

Binding: purple cloth. On spine, in silver: 'The | Tragedy | of | POMPEY | the | GREAT | JOHN | MASEFIELD | Sidgwick | &Jackson' (all width centred). On upper cover, in silver: 'The Tragedy of | POMPEY the GREAT | JOHN MASEFIELD | [coin design]'. Lower cover: blank. Upper and lower covers have blind ruled borders: 187 × 118mm. All edges trimmed. Binding measurements: 192 × 125mm. (covers), 192 × 25mm. (spine). End-papers: wove paper.

Publication date: published, according to Simmons, 4 April 1910 in an edition of 718 copies.

Price: 3s.6d.

Contents:
The Tragedy of Pompey the Great ('ACT I | *A room in* POMPEY'S *house near Rome...*')

Notes:
Later reprints in wrappers cite a publication date of March 1910. No copies bearing this date have been examined.

The publishing agreement for this title between Masefield and the firm of Sidgwick and Jackson was dated 1 December 1909 (see Archives of The Society of Authors). The agreement refers to a publication price of 3s.6d.

The Sidgwick and Jackson archive reveals that a complete set of proofs was sent to Masefield on 18 December 1909.

Correspondence relating to Simmons' bibliography preserved in the archives of Sidgwick and Jackson (see Bodleian, MS.Sidgwick & Jackson 228) confirms a publication date of 4 April 1910 and a first printing of 718 copies.

After learning of the American copyright edition of *The Everlasting Mercy*, George L. McKay (researching for C.H. Simmons) wrote to Sidgwick and Jackson asking whether a similar edition had been printed for *Pompey* (and *The Widow in the Bye Street*). The firm responded:

As regards "The Tragedy of Pompey the Great" and "The Widow in the Bye Street", we cannot trace that we had anything to do with the copyright printing of these in America. If they were so copyrighted, it must have been done by Mr. Masefield or his agent.

(Frank Sidgwick, letter to George L. McKay, 25 April 1929)
(Bodleian, MS.Sidgwick & Jackson 228)

The play was first performed on 4 December 1910 at the Aldwych Theatre, London. In contrast to *The Tragedy of Nan*, Masefield does not note production details in any edition of *Pompey*. Another short run in the West End at the St. Martin's Theatre occurred in the early 1920s with Sir Frank Benson, who had previously presented the play at Stratford-upon-Avon. (Birmingham Public Library holds a marked-up copy for Benson's production). In 1950 the play was televised while a radio broadcast staring Stephen Murray was made in July 1966.

The play was first offered to Grant Richards. Masefield wrote to his agent in September 1909:

I am today sending a copy of my play of Pompey the Great to Grant Richards. I want to get it published, + he is willing to do it. I believe that it is no longer necessary to publish simultaneously in America. Is this so? I shall be quite content with a very small percentage. The play is too short for boards. It will probably have to appear in a paper cover. It will probably be produced for a few tentative performances early in the New Year. I am trying to secure this, + think there will be no hitch now. Will you very kindly ring up Richards towards the end of the week (when he has had time to read the play) + ask what he thinks?

(John Masefield, letter to C.F. Cazenove, 17 September 1909)
(University of Arizona Library. MS.50, V.II)

Grant Richards, in *Author Hunting*, writes:

To my shame, in 1909 I developed cold feet. I was offered *The Tragedy of Pompey the Great*. I dilly-dallied with it until its author had no further patience and asked me to send the manuscript back to him. I had no excuse. I admired the play intensely... To tell the truth, I had allowed my ledgers to influence me. It was a folly. ...I was the more to blame as it was no literary advisor who counselled me to do without the luxury of *Pompey the Great*. The truth is that the novels *Captain Margaret* and *Multitude and Solitude* had not the kind of success which pays the rent... ...As a result of my lack of courage (or capital) Dents added to their reputation, Sidgwick and Jackson secured an ornament to their list, and William Heinemann made a fortune...

(Grant Richards, *Author Hunting*, Hamish Hamilton, 1934, pp.228–29)

As early as 15 August 1906, Masefield wrote to Jack B. Yeats stating that he wanted 'to do a prose play on Pompey the Great.' (Harvard, MS *44M–301F). Letters in the Bodleian Library Gilbert Murray manuscript collection reveal that Masefield enlisted the critical assistance of Murray during the composition of the play. A rough sketch of the last act was sent at the beginning of October 1908 with Masefield stating:

It is a dead piece of rhetoric with neither wit nor movement; but I hope to give it life and beauty in time...

(John Masefield, letter to Gilbert Murray, 7 October 1908)
(Bodleian, MS.Gilbert Murray 161, f.5)

Writing to Margaret Dobbs in December 1910, Masefield describes the opening night of the play:

Pompey was well acted. The audience, long famous as the stupidest in London, were annoying enough, but the piece went well, though a few days more of rehearsing would have made it go better. Weak places in a play are always shown up strongly by any want of rehearsing, + we had not a full cast till 4 days before the performance, + only once rehearsed with a full cast.

(John Masefield, letter to Margaret Dobbs, 14 December 1910)
(Public Record Office of Northern Ireland, Mic152)

A copy of this edition held in W.B. Yeats' library, in Dalkey, Ireland (*1258) is inscribed 'W.B. Yeats. | from John Masefield | Apr. 5, 1910.'

The Copp Clark Company of Canada expressed an interest to Sidgwick and Jackson to print the play as a school text in 1939. Masefield took a position (considered 'both unreasonable and untenable' in the opinion of Frank Sidgwick) and wrote:

The proposal, that this should be made a school book for the further torment of the young, already born to sufficient misery, fills me with horror.

(John Masefield, letter to Sidgwick and Jackson, undated)
(Bodleian. MS.Sidgwick & Jackson)

Nevertheless, as Sidgwick and Jackson were entitled to arrange colonial editions a set of stereoplates was sent to Canada in June 1939. No further information concerning this enterprise is contained in the Sidgwick and Jackson archives.

Copies seen: BL (11775.ff.20) stamped 29 APR 1910; Ledbury Library; ULL (Special Collections); NYPL (Berg Collection) inscribed 'Jack B Yeats | from John Masefield | April 8. 1910.'; Columbia University Library

Reprinted:

	[first edition, second impression]	Dec 1910
'Third Impression'	[first edition, third impression]	Apr 1913

The *English Catalogue of Books* notes a sewn edition for November 1911, however, an April 1913 impression notes only impressions in March 1910, December 1910 and April 1913.

A11(b) First American edition (1914)

THE TRAGEDY OF | POMPEY THE GREAT | BY | JOHN MASEFIELD | AUTHOR OF "THE EVERLASTING MERCY," | "THE WIDOW IN THE BYE STREET," ETC. | New York | THE MACMILLAN COMPANY | 1914 | *All rights reserved*
(All width centred)

Bibliographies: Danielson [unrecorded], Williams [unrecorded], Simmons [noted on p.22], Nevinson [unrecorded], Handley-Taylor p.29, Wight [unrecorded]

Collation: [A–I]⁸ [K]⁶; 78 leaves; 188 × 127mm.; [i–x] 1–137 [138–46]

Page contents: [i] half-title: 'THE TRAGEDY OF POMPEY | THE GREAT'; [ii] '[publisher's device] | THE MACMILLAN COMPANY | [two lines listing six cities, separated by four points] | MACMILLAN & CO., LIMITED | [two lines listing four cities, separated by two points] | THE MACMILLAN CO. OF CANADA, LTD. | [one city listed]' (with additional leaf tipped-in on the verso of which is the frontispiece: 127 × 81mm., 'POMPEY THE GREAT'); [iii] title-page; [iv] 'COPYRIGHT, 1910, | BY JOHN MASEFIELD. | REVISED EDITION | COPYRIGHT, 1914, | BY JOHN MASEFIELD. | Set up and electrotyped. Published February, 1914.'; [v] 'TO | MY WIFE'; [vi] blank; [vii] 'THE TRAGEDY OF POMPEY | THE GREAT'; [viii] blank; [ix] 'ARGUMENT | IN the years 50 and 49 B. C., Cneius Pompeius Magnus, | the head of the patrician party, contested with C. Julius | Cæsar, the popular leader, for supreme power in the State. | Their jealousy led to the troubles of the Civil War, in | which, after many battles, Cneius Pompeius Magnus was | miserably killed. | ACT I. The determination of Pompeius to fight | with his rival, then marching upon Rome. | ACT. II. The triumph of Pompey's generalship at | Dyrrachium. His overthrow by the generals | of his staff. His defeat at Pharsalia. | ACT. III. The death of that great ruler on the sea- | shore of Pelusium in Egypt.'; [x] 'PERSONS | [dramatis personae listed, also table of act, scene and historical time]'; 1–132 text; 133–37 'NOTES' (paragraphs titled 'ON THE APPEARANCE OF POMPEY', 'ON THE FATE OF THE PERSONS IN THIS TRAGEDY' and 'ON THE HOUSE OF POMPEY, AFTER THE MURDER'); [138] verse ('And all their passionate hearts are dust,') dated on left margin '*Feb. 8, 1908.*' and on extreme right '*July 5, 1909.*'; [139] 'THE following pages contain advertisements of | books by the same author or on kindred subjects.' (within ruled border: 13 × 76mm.); [140] blank; [141–46] publisher's advertisements

Paper: wove paper

Running title: '*THE TRAGEDY OF*' (31mm.) on verso; '*POMPEY THE GREAT*' (36mm.) on recto, with note of act on extreme right of verso and extreme left of recto, pp.2–137

Binding: burgundy cloth. On spine, in gold: 'The | TRAGEDY | of | POMPEY | the | GREAT | MASEFIELD | MACMILLAN' (all width centred). On upper cover, in gold: 'THE | TRAGEDY OF | POMPEY | THE GREAT | MASEFIELD' (ranged upper left) (within blind ruled border: 187 × 118mm.) Lower cover: blank. Top edge gilt, others trimmed. Binding measurements: 193 × 127mm. (covers), 193 × 35mm. (spine). End-papers: wove paper.

Publication date: published, according to Simmons, 11 February 1914 in an edition of 1464 copies

Price: $1.25

Contents:
as for A11(a)

Notes:
Published before the English revised edition (see A11(c)), this edition notes a revised text with a copyright date of 1914 on page [iv]. Nevertheless, this edition curiously retains several features of A11(a). In particular the dramatis personae fails to reduce the number of characters and in the 'Argument' Pompey is again 'the head of the patrician party'.

The publishing agreement for this title between Masefield and Macmillan was dated 26 March 1913 (see Archives of The Society of Authors). The agreement refers to 'a licence to publish in volume form in the United States of America a work the subject or title of which is The Tragedy of Pompey the Great'.

Despite Simmons and Handley-Taylor noting this edition, Wight omits it from his bibliography.

The frontispiece comprises a photograph of a bust of Pompey.

The italic lettering on the spine of the binding includes a number of swash characters.

Copies seen: private collection (PWE); NYPL (NCR 1914 670834)

Reprinted:

'Reprinted'	[first edition, second impression]	Mar 1915

A11(c) Second English edition (1914)

THE TRAGEDY OF | POMPEY THE GREAT | BY | JOHN MASEFIELD | AUTHOR OF 'THE EVERLASTING MERCY,' | 'THE WIDOW IN THE BYE STREET,' | 'THE TRAGEDY OF NAN,' ETC. | *REVISED EDITION* | LONDON | SIDGWICK AND JACKSON, LTD. | MCMXIV
(All width centred)

Bibliographies: Danielson [unrecorded], Williams [unrecorded], Simmons [unrecorded], Nevinson [unrecorded], Handley-Taylor [unrecorded], Wight [unrecorded]

Collation: [A]⁸ B-F⁸; signatures width centred at foot of page; 48 leaves; the catalogue (not included in collation or leaf count) is apparently only present in the issue in wrappers and comprises a single gathering of 12 leaves of which the first and fifth are also signed; 185 × 123mm.; [1–8] 9–90 [91–96]; catalogue pagination: [1] 2–24

Page contents: [1] half-title: 'THE TRAGEDY OF | POMPEY THE GREAT'; [2] 'BY THE SAME AUTHOR | [two titles with prices and edition information listed] | [rule] | SIDGWICK & JACKSON, LTD., LONDON, W.C.' (within ruled border: 58 × 76mm.); [3] title-page; [4] '*First Edition, March* 1910; *reprinted* | *December* 1910, *April* 1913. | *Second Edition (Fourth Impression), revised* | *and reset, March* 1914. | *Entered at the Library of Congress* | *Washington, U.S.A.* | *All rights reserved*'; [5] 'TO | MY WIFE' [6] blank; [7] 'ARGUMENT | IN the years 50 and 49 B.C., Cneius Pompeius Magnus, | the head of the senatorial party, contested with C. | Julius Cæsar, the popular leader, for supreme power in | the State. Their jealousy led to the troubles of the | Civil War, in which, after many battles, Cneius | Pompeius Magnus was miserably killed. | ACT I. The determination of Pompeius to fight | with his rival, then marching upon Rome. | ACT II. The triumph of Pompey's generalship at | Dyrrachium. His overthrow by the generals | of his staff. His defeat at Pharsalia. | ACT III. The death of that great ruler on the | seashore of Pelusium in Egypt.'; [8] 'PERSONS | [dramatis personae listed, also table of act, scene and historical time]'; 9–87 text; 88–90 'NOTES' (paragraphs titled 'ON THE APPEARANCE OF POMPEY', 'ON THE FATE OF THE PERSONS IN THIS TRAGEDY.' and 'ON THE HOUSE OF POMPEY, AFTER THE MURDER.'); [91] verse ('And all their passionate hearts are dust,') dated on left margin '*Feb.* 8, 1908.' and on extreme right '*July* 5, 1909.'; [92] 'Printed by T. and A. CONSTABLE, Printers to His Majesty | at the Edinburgh University Press'; [93–96] publisher's advertisements: 'FROM SIDGWICK AND JACKSON'S LIST'; [1]–24 catalogue (only present in the issue in wrappers): 'A DESCRIPTIVE CATALOGUE OF | MODERN PLAYS'

Paper: laid paper (no watermark), chain-lines 24mm. apart (catalogue: wove paper)

Running title: 'THE TRAGEDY OF' (37mm.) on verso; 'POMPEY THE GREAT' (42mm.) on recto, with '[ACT' on extreme right of verso and 'I]', 'II]' or 'III]' on extreme left of recto, pp.10–90

Binding: purple wrappers. On upper wrapper: 'JOHN MASEFIELD [enclosed within ruled border: 8 × 67mm.] | [rule, 73mm.] | The Tragedy of | Pompey the Great [both lines enclosed within ruled border: 20 × 67mm.] | [rule, 73mm.] | [eleven vertical rules, 98mm.] | SIDGWICK & JACKSON, LTD. [enclosed within ruled border: 8 × 67mm.]' (all enclosed within ruled border: 154 × 75mm.) As a result of the three rules noted above, four rectangles are created measuring: 15 × 75mm., 27 × 75mm., 100 × 75mm. and 15 × 75mm. respectively from the top. (Other information indeterminable from consulted copy).

Also issued in purple cloth. On spine, in silver: 'The | Tragedy | of | POMPEY | the | GREAT | JOHN | MASEFIELD | Sidgwick | &Jackson' (all width centred). On upper cover, in silver: 'The Tragedy of | POMPEY the GREAT | JOHN MASEFIELD | [coin design]' (within blind ruled border: 187 × 118mm.) Lower cover: blank. All edges trimmed. Binding measurements: 189 × 126mm. (covers), 189 × 24mm. (spine). End-papers: wove paper.

Publication date: published, according to date within volume, March 1914

Price: unknown

Contents:
The Tragedy of Pompey the Great ('ACT I | *A room in* POMPEY'S *house near Rome…*')
[revised text]

Notes:
Masefield was neither satisfied with his play at the time it was printed nor when it was performed. This volume presents, therefore, a revised text. A comparison of the dramatis personae reveals the deletion of characters while the 'Argument' now finds Pompey 'the head of the senatorial party'. Such changes are to be found throughout the volume.

In a letter to Frank Sidgwick in February 1914 Masefield writes:

> Many thanks for the proofs + your reader's note. The thing had occurred to me; + in some of my ms I see I used the word optimate, but I changed it as being likely to puzzle people. I will alter the argument as your friend desires, but will keep to the word patrician elsewhere in the play.

(John Masefield, letter to Frank Sidgwick, 12 February 1914)
(Harvard College Library, Houghton bMS Eng 1069 *57M–54)

The publisher's catalogue within this edition lists *Pompey*, but notes the issue before this edition. The listing reads '*Third Impression. Cloth*, 3*s.* 6*d. net; Paper*, 1*s.* 6*d. net.*'

Evidence within the archives of Sidgwick and Jackson suggests that the edition was printed from stereoplates. In 1939 when the possibility of a Canadian edition arose, the company requested information about plates from the printers, T. & A. Constable. Constable replied that the plates for Pompey were:

> …in a worn condition and it would not be possible to make satisfactory plates from them. We hold, however, the moulds and it will be an easy matter for us to cast new stereos from these…

(T. & A. Constable, letter to Sidgwick and Jackson, 1939)
(Bodleian, MS.Sidgwick & Jackson archive)

Copies seen: private collection (ROV); BL (11778.k.44) stamped 15 APR 1914 rebound preserving upper wrapper only; ULL (YP M35G) rebound

Reprinted:

	[second edition, second impression]	May 1922
	[second edition, third impression]	Sep 1926
	[second edition, fourth impression]	Aug 1927
	[second edition, fifth impression]	Sep 1927
	[second edition, sixth impression]	Oct 1927
	[second edition, seventh impression]	Jan 1928
	[second edition, eighth impression]	May 1930
	[second edition, ninth impression]	Aug 1932
	[second edition, tenth impression]	Aug 1935
	[second edition, eleventh impression]	Jul 1937
	[second edition, twelfth impression]	Sep 1937
	[second edition, thirteenth impression]	Feb 1938
	[second edition, fourteenth impression]	Aug 1939
	[second edition, fifteenth impression]	Sep 1939
'Reprinted'	[second edition, sixteenth impression]	Apr 1941

A12 BALLADS AND POEMS   1910

A12(a) First English edition (1910)

BALLADS | AND | POEMS | BY | JOHN MASEFIELD | LONDON | ELKIN MATHEWS, VIGO STREET | M CM X
(All width centred)

Bibliographies: Danielson 169, Williams pp.2–3, Simmons [12], Nevinson p.12, Handley-Taylor p.29, Wight [12]

Collation: [B]⁸ C-G⁸ H⁴; C2, D2, E2, F2 and G2 are also signed; signatures right foot of page; 52 leaves; 157 × 124mm.; [1–6] 7–100 [101–104]

Page contents: [1] half-title: 'BALLADS | AND | POEMS'; [2] blank; [3] title-page; [4] blank; [5] 'TO MY WIFE'; [6] 'NOTE. | I thank the Editors of a Broad Sheet, the *English- | woman*, the *Nation*, and *Votes for Women*, for | permission to reprint five of the poems in this | collection.'; 7–8 'Contents' (43 individual poems listed with page references); 9–100 text; [101] 'LONDON : | PRINTED BY WILLIAM CLOWES AND SONS, LIMITED.'; [102–104] publisher's advertisements

Paper: laid paper (watermark: '[Crown] | Abbey Mills | Greenfield'), chain-lines 24mm. apart. Simmons states 'a later issue of the first edition has a laid paper without watermark'.

Running title: running titles comprise titles of individual poems, pp.10–99

Binding: green cloth. On spine, in gold: 'BALLADS | AND | POEMS | JOHN | MASEFIELD | ELKIN | MATHEWS' (all width centred). On upper cover, in gold: 'BALLADS AND POEMS | JOHN MASEFIELD'. Lower cover: blank. Top edge trimmed, others uncut. Binding measurements: 165 × 129mm. (covers), 165 × 19mm. (spine). End-papers: laid paper (no watermark), chain-lines 27mm. apart.

A binding variant exists. On spine, 'AND' is positioned slightly right of centre, the letters of 'ELKIN MATHEWS' are 2.5mm. in height (compared to 2.0mm.) It is assumed this is a later issue of the first edition.

Publication date: published, according to Simmons, 15 September 1910 in an edition of 2008 copies. (This print run presumably includes issues noted above)

Price: 2s.6d.

Contents:
The Ballad of Sir Bors ('Would I could win some quiet and rest, and a little ease,')
Spanish Waters ('Spanish waters, Spanish waters, you are ringing in my ears,')
Cargoes ('Quinquireme of Nineveh from distant Ophir')
Captain Stratton's Fancy ('Oh some are fond of red wine, and some are fond of white,')
An old Song re-sung ('I saw a ship a-sailing, a-sailing, a-sailing,')
St. Mary's Bells ('It's pleasant in Holy Mary')
London Town ('Oh London Town's a fine town, and London sights are rare,')
The Emigrant ('Going by Daly's shanty I heard the boys within')
Port of Holy Peter ('The blue laguna rocks and quivers,')
Beauty ('I have seen dawn and sunset on moors and windy hills')
The Seekers ('Friends and loves we have none, nor wealth nor blessed abode,')
Prayer ('When the last sea is sailed, when the last shallow's charted,')

Dawn ('The dawn comes cold : the haystack smokes,')
Laugh and be Merry ('Laugh and be merry, remember, better the world with a song,')
June Twilight ('The twilight comes; the sun')
Roadways ('One road leads to London,')
Midsummer Night ('The perfect disc of the sacred moon')
The Harper's Song ('This sweetness trembling from the strings')
The Gentle Lady ('So beautiful, so dainty-sweet,')
The Dead Knight ('The cleanly rush of the mountain air,')
Sorrow of Mydath ('Weary the cry of the wind is, weary the sea,')
Twilight ('Twilight it is, and the far woods are dim, and the rooks cry and call.')
Invocation ('O wanderer into many brains,')
Posted as Missing ('Under all her topsails she trembled like a stag,')
A Creed ('I hold that when a person dies'
     First printed in The Pall Mall Magazine *September 1907, p.276*
When Bony Death ('When bony Death has chilled her gentle blood,')
     First printed as 'Beauty's Mirror' in The Venture *1903, p.1*
The West Wind ('It's a warm wind, the west wind, full of birds' cries;')
Her Heart ('Her heart is always doing lovely things,')
     No previous appearance traced
Being her Friend ('Being her friend, I do not care, not I,')
     First printed in the anthology Wayfarer's Love *(1904)*
Fragments ('Troy Town is covered up with weeds,')
     First printed in a more extensive version as 'The City of the Soul' in The Nation *20 July 1907, p.764*
Born for Nought Else ('Born for nought else, for nothing but for this,')
     No previous appearance traced
Tewkesbury Road ('It is good to be out on the road, and going one knows not where,')
The Death Rooms ('My soul has many an old decaying room')
     No previous appearance traced
Ignorance ('Since I have learned Love's shining alphabet,')
     First printed as 'Blindness' in The Venture *1903, p.74*
Sea Fever ('I must go down to the seas again, to the lonely sea and the sky,')
The Watch in the Wood ('When Death has laid her in his quietude,')
     No previous appearance traced
C.L.M. ('In the dark womb where I began')
     First printed as 'First Fruits' in Votes for Women *28 January 1910, p.280*
Waste ('No rose but fades : no glory but must pass :')
     No previous appearance traced
Third Mate ('All the sheets are clacking, all the blocks are whining,')
     First printed as 'A Young Man's Fancy' in A Broadside *June 1910*
The Wild Duck ('Twilight. Red in the west.')
     No previous appearance traced
Imagination ('Woman, beauty, wonder, sacred woman,')
     First printed in The Englishwoman *November 1909, p.71*
Christmas, 1903 ('O, the sea breeze will be steady, and the tall ship's going trim,')
     First printed as 'Coming into Salcombe – A Christmas Chanty' in A Broad Sheet *November 1903*
The Word ('My friend, my bonny friend, when we are old,')
     No previous appearance traced

Notes:

Pages 9–63 (all poems upto and including 'Posted as Missing') are a direct reprint of the second edition of *Ballads* (A2(b)). In this volume 'Posted as Missing' is ascribed a location (omitted from *Ballads*). Poems not present in *Ballads* are also provided with the locations where they were written. These comprise: Cashlauna Shelmiddy, Coram Street, Greenwich, Hampden, Maida Hill and The Wergs [The Wergs Farm, Tettenhall, Staffordshire]. 'The Word' is not provided with a location.

It appears that a single publishing agreement covered the second English edition of *Ballads* (A2(b)) and this edition of *Ballads and Poems* (A12(a)). The agreement was signed between Masefield and Elkin Mathews and dated 22 March 1910. The agreement refers to '…a collection of Ballads by the Author printing and publishing the same in two (2) separate volumes whereof the first book shall contain sixty-four (64) pages and the second shall contain one hundred (100) pages…' (see Archives of The Society of Authors).

Danielson notes 'there is also a later issue of the first edition, with two blank leaves before the half-title'.

With reference to different issues of the first edition, the archives of The Chiswick Press record that, although William Clowes printed the book, The Chiswick Press was responsible for wrappers. Dated entries in the archive are as follows:

THE
TRAGEDY OF NAN
AND OTHER PLAYS

BY
JOHN MASEFIELD

LONDON
GRANT RICHARDS
1909

A9(c) title-page

THE
TRAGEDY OF NAN
AND OTHER PLAYS

BY
JOHN MASEFIELD

MITCHELL KENNERLEY
NEW YORK   MCMX

A9(d) title-page

THE TRAGEDY OF
POMPEY THE GREAT

BY
JOHN MASEFIELD

LONDON
SIDGWICK AND JACKSON, LTD.
MCMX

A11(a) title-page

BALLADS
AND
POEMS

BY
JOHN MASEFIELD

LONDON
ELKIN MATHEWS, VIGO STREET
MCMX

A12(a) title-page

MARTIN HYDE

THE DUKE'S MESSENGER

BY

JOHN MASEFIELD

With Illustrations by
T. C. DUGDALE

BOSTON
LITTLE, BROWN, AND COMPANY

A13(a) title-page

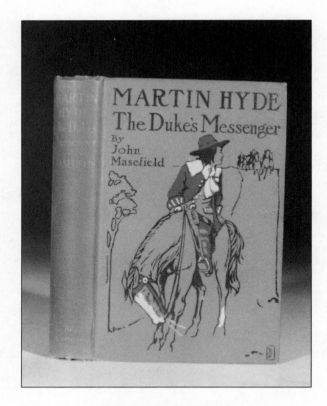

A13(a) spine and upper cover

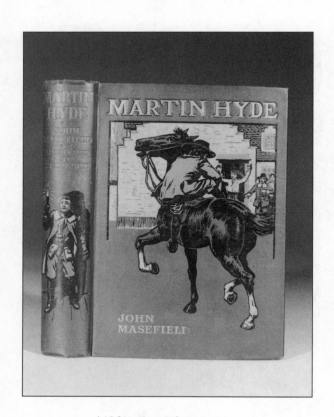

A13(b) spine and upper cover

MARTIN HYDE

THE DUKE'S MESSENGER

BY

JOHN MASEFIELD
AUTHOR OF
"CAPTAIN MARGARET," "A BOOK OF DISCOVERIES," ETC.

With Illustrations by
T. C. DUGDALE

LONDON
WELLS GARDNER, DARTON AND CO., LTD.
3 & 4, PATERNOSTER BUILDINGS, E.C.
AND 44, VICTORIA STREET, S.W.

A13(b) title-page

Sept 3	Printing 1000 copies of Cap. Wrapper Ballads + Poems John Masefield 17¾ × 8¼ ins. 1 side printed only in blue ink and supplying blue tinted paper for same and cutting	[£] 1/3/6
Oct 15	Reprinting 1000 copies of Jacket Wrapper Ballads + Poems (John Masefield) 17⅝ × 7⅝ ins. in blue ink with corrections + alterations including blue green paper for same + cutting	[£] 1/2/6

(BL, Add.Mss.50925, f.215)

This strongly suggests that the second issue dates from October 1910. (15 September 1910 is the publication date for the first issue). Danielson's issue with two blank pages probably comprises a variant within the second issue.

In James G. Nelson's 'Checklist of the Mathews Imprint', *Ballads and Poems* is numbered 1910.24. Nelson notes bindings in wrappers and cloth. This is presumably incorrect and results from his confusion over *Ballads*.

Writing to Mathews in 1913 regarding new editions of *Salt-Water Ballads* and *A Mainsail Haul*, Masefield also noted his desire for uniformity in reprints of *Ballads and Poems*:

> Another thing. I myself should much like to see the cheap little Ballads book extinguished, + the Ballads + Poems book brought into uniformity with the other two, at 3/6. Then perhaps you could see a small edn of the three vols together in a case. I see that Ballads + Poems is at present a vol of 98 pages, which is about what Salt Water came to.

> (John Masefield, letter to Elkin Mathews, 7 April 1913)
> (HRHRC, MS (Masefield, J.) Letters, ALS to Mathews 1913 April 7)

Reprints of *Ballads and Poems* were indeed issued in a larger format (8vo) and in a standard blue cloth. No slip-case has been examined, however.

Copies seen: BL (011650.de.48); ULL (Special Collections); Ledbury Library; Library of The John Masefield Society

Reprinted:

[Third Thousand]	[first edition, second impression]	[no copies consulted]
'Fourth Thousand'	[first edition, third impression]	1913
'Fifth Thousand'	[first edition, fourth impression]	1913
'Sixth Thousand'	[first edition, fifth impression]	1915
'Seventh Thousand'	[first edition, sixth impression]	Feb 1916
[Eighth Thousand]	[first edition, seventh impression]	[no copies consulted]
'Ninth Thousand'	[first edition, eighth impression]	1918
[Tenth Thousand]	[first edition, ninth impression]	[no copies consulted]
'Eleventh Thousand'	[first edition, tenth impression]	1919
'Twelfth Thousand'	[first edition, eleventh impression]	1919
'Thirteenth Thousand'	[first edition, twelfth impression]	1920
'Fourteenth Thousand'	[first edition, thirteenth impression]	1920

A13 MARTIN HYDE   1910

A13(a) First American edition (1910)

MARTIN HYDE | THE DUKE'S MESSENGER | BY | JOHN MASEFIELD | *With Illustrations by* | T. C. DUGDALE | BOSTON | LITTLE, BROWN, AND COMPANY
(All width centred)

Bibliographies: Danielson [unrecorded], Williams [unrecorded], Simmons [13], Nevinson [unrecorded], Handley-Taylor p.29, Wight [13]

Collation: [A]⁸ (±[A]2) [B-U]⁸ (J not used); 160 leaves; 187 × 120mm.; [i–x] [1] 2–17 [18] 19–27 [28] 29–36 [37] 38–53 [54] 55–69 [70] 71–84 [85] 86–94 [95] 96–105 [106] 107–18 [119] 120–31 [132] 133–46 [147] 148–60 [161] 162–73 [174] 175–85 [186] 187–95 [196] 197–206 [207] 208–18 [219] 220–31 [232] 233–42 [243] 244–55 [256] 257–67 [268] 269–80 [281] 282–92 [293] 294–303 [304]; illustrations (on glossy paper) tipped-in on pp.[iii], 12, 32, 44, 71, 82, 91, [119], 135, 151, 183, [186], 199, [256], 279 and 302

Page contents: [i] half-title: 'MARTIN HYDE | THE DUKE'S MESSENGER'; [ii] blank; [iii] stub of leaf (with additional leaf tipped-in on the verso of which is the frontispiece: 133 × 88mm., 'I SAW THE LADY AURELIA LYING AMONG THE SMASHED UP GEAR. | *Frontispiece. See p.* 171', with protective tissue); [iv] stub of leaf; [v] title-page; [vi] '*Copyright, 1909,* | BY DANA ESTES & CO. | *Copyright, 1910,* | BY LITTLE, BROWN, AND COMPANY. | [rule] | *All rights reserved* | Published, October, 1910 | *Electrotyped and Printed by* | THE COLONIAL PRESS | *C.H. Simonds & Co., Boston, U.S.A.*'; [vii] 'CONTENTS' (14 chapters listed with titles and page references); [viii] blank; [ix] 'LIST OF ILLUSTRATIONS' (16 illustrations, including frontispiece, listed with titles and page references); [x] blank; [1]–303 text; [304] blank

Paper: wove paper

Running title: 'MARTIN HYDE' (25mm.) on verso; recto title comprises chapter title, pp.2–303

Binding: light-brown cloth. On spine, in gold: 'MARTIN | HYDE | The Duke's | Messenger | [rule] | MASEFIELD | Little, Brown | and Company' (all width centred). On upper cover, in green: 'MARTIN HYDE | The Duke's Messenger | By | John | Masefield | [illustration in green, red and white of a boy on an exhausted horse with approaching riders further back on road, with foliage; signed 'BS' in lower right corner: 153 × 115mm.]' Lower cover: blank. All edges trimmed. Binding measurements: 194 × 123mm. (covers), 194 × 43mm. (spine). Front free and rear free end-papers constitute leaves of the gatherings. Fixed end-papers are from the same paper stock.

Publication date: published, according to Simmons, 8 October 1910 in an edition of 1009 copies

Price: $1.50

Contents:

Martin Hyde ('I was born at Oulton, in Suffolk, in the year 1672. I know not the day...')
    First printed in Chatterbox *1909*

Chapter headings are as follows:

I. I Leave Home	XIII. It Breezes Up
II. I Leave Home Again	XIV. A Drink of Sherbet
III. I Leave Home a Third Time	XV. The Road to Lyme
IV. I Leave Home for the Last Time	XVI. The Landing
V. I Go to Sea	XVII. A Voice at Dawn
VI. The Sea! The Sea!	XVIII. I Speak with Aurelia
VII. Land Rats and Water Rats	XIX. I Meet the Club Men
VIII. I Meet My Friend	XX. The Squire's House
IX. I See More of My Friend	XXI. My Friend Aurelia and Her Uncle
X. Sounds in the Night	XXII. The Priest's Hole
XI. Aurelia	XXIII. Free
XII. Brave Captain Barlow	XXIV. The End

Notes:

The novel first appeared in *Chatterbox* nos. I-LII for 1909. It was serialised in 52 instalments in which the chapter-division of the first book edition is not apparent. The serialisation was illustrated by 52 unsigned illustrations of which only 17 were reproduced in the book, where they were acknowledged as being by T.C. Dugdale. The periodical was 'published for the proprietors' by the same firm as the publishers of the first English edition. There are variants between the two versions of both substantives and accidentals.

The historical incident fictionalised in *Martin Hyde* is also found in several other novels. Peter Vansittart states:

> Monmouth's ill-timed adventure ended not in courage on a western plain, nor with a nervous executioner on Tower Hill, but in a clutch of historical romances, mostly lush; probably the best are R.D. Blackmore's *Lorna Doone*, Conan Doyle's *Micah Clarke* and John Masefield's *Martin Hyde, the Duke's Messenger.*
>
>   (Peter Vansittart, *London: A Literary Companion*, John Murray, 1992, p.242)

A publishing agreement for this title between Masefield and Little Brown and Company was dated 23 April 1910 (see Archives of The Society of Authors). The agreement refers to 'the work at present entitled MARTIN HYDE' and names a publication date of 'the Fall of the year 1910'.

Copies seen: private collection (PWE); Van Wylen Library, Hope College, Holland (PR6025.A77M37 1910)

Reprinted:

Subsequent reprints (including the 'Beacon Hill Bookshelf' series) may have used the same setting of text. Reprint dates include:

1924
1925
1926
1927
1929
1931
1933

A13(b) First English edition (1910)

MARTIN HYDE | THE DUKE'S MESSENGER | BY | JOHN MASEFIELD | AUTHOR OF | "CAPTAIN MARGARET," "A BOOK OF DISCOVERIES," ETC. | With Illustrations by | T.C. DUGDALE | LONDON | WELLS GARDNER, DARTON AND CO., LTD. | 3 & 4, PATERNOSTER BUILDINGS, E.C. | AND 44, VICTORIA STREET, S.W.
(All width centred)

Bibliographies: Danielson 172, Williams p.8, Simmons [13a], Nevinson p.15, Handley-Taylor p.29, Wight [13a]

Collation: [π]⁴ 1–38⁴; signatures right foot of page; 156 leaves; 204 × 139mm.; [i–iv] v–vii [viii] [1] 2–17 [18] 19–27 [28] 29–36 [37] 38–53 [54] 55–69 [70] 71–84 [85] 86–94 [95] 96–105 [106] 107–18 [119] 120–31 [132] 133–46 [147] 148–60 [161] 162–73 [174] 175–85 [186] 187–95 [196] 197–206 [207] 208–18 [219] 220–31 [232] 233–42 [243] 244–55 [256] 257–67 [268] 269–80 [281] 282–92 [293] 294–303 [304]; illustrations (on glossy paper) tipped-in on pp.11, 13, 32, 55, 71, 83, 91, [119], 151, 171, 183, 187, 199, [256], 279 and 301

Page contents: [i] half-title: 'MARTIN HYDE'; [ii] blank (with additional leaf tipped-in leaf on the verso of which is the frontispiece: 134 × 88mm., '"THE GUARDSMEN WERE PEERING AT MY FACE IN THE LANTERN-LIGHT." | Page 134.' with protective tissue); [iii] title-page; [iv] '[publisher's device above '1910' all within ruled borders: 19 × 19mm.] | *Copyright in the United States* | *Little, Brown & Company, Boston*'; v–vi 'CONTENTS' (14 chapters listed with titles and page references); vii 'LIST OF ILLUSTRATIONS' (16 illustrations, including frontispiece, listed with title and page references); [viii] blank; [1]–303 text (at foot of p.303: '[rule] | WELLS GARDNER, DARTON AND CO., LTD., LONDON'); [304] blank

Paper: wove paper

Running title: 'MARTIN HYDE' (25mm.) on verso; recto title comprises chapter title, pp.2–303

Binding: red-brown cloth (see notes). On spine, in gold: 'MARTIN | HYDE | [two circles] | JOHN | MASEFIELD | [two circles] | ILLUSTRATED | BY | T.C. DUGDALE | [illustration in white, black, turquoise and light brown (of the binding) of boy with candle standing on floorboards casting shadow on wall: 106 × 41mm.] | WELLS[point]GARDNER | DARTON[point]& CO LTD' (all width centred). On upper cover: 'MARTIN HYDE' [in gold with black outline] | [illustration in white, black, turquoise and light brown (of the binding) of boy hurriedly jumping onto agitated horse, observed by three onlookers outside building: 156 × 124mm. (the upper part only of the illustration is contained within a black border)] | JOHN | MASEFIELD [these two lines in gold, ranged lower left]'. On lower cover, in blind: publisher's device: 18 × 20mm. Top edge gilt, others trimmed. Binding measurements: 208 × 141mm. (covers), 208 × 50mm. (spine). End-papers: wove paper.

Publication date: published, according to Simmons, 28 October 1910 in an edition of 2666 copies

Price: 6s.

Contents:
as for A13(a)

Notes:
The publishing agreement for this title between Masefield and Wells Gardner, Darton and Co. was dated 21 April 1908 (see Archives of The Society of Authors). The agreement refers to '…a story to be written by the Author of a kind suitable for boys' reading…'

Masefield wrote to his agent in October 1909 expressing concern about periodical publication. It appears that the punctuation as printed in *Chatterbox* was far from authorial:

> Will you please find out for me from the Chatterbox people when I may have proofs of *Martin Hyde*, which is, I believe, to be published this autumn? As far as I can make out they have been altering my punctuations without my leave: or, if not that, then they have misread my ms. Anyway, I don't want the results to appear in the book. I have had no proofs from them so far for the instalments published every week. It is a small matter: but the present punctuation upsets some of my rhythms here + there.
>
> (John Masefield, letter to C.F. Cazenove, 17 October 1909)
> (University of Arizona Library. MS.50, V.II)

Danielson describes the colour of the binding as 'chocolate' and states the book was 'also issued in cloth bindings of various other colours'. Williams states a second issue was 'bound in green cloth'. Simmons states a second issue was bound in blue cloth.

The upper cover illustration is redrawn from the illustration in *Chatterbox* 1909 No. XXI, p.161 where it is titled "Before they turned I was in the saddle."

A comparison with A13(a) reveals several minor differences. No use is made of the subtitle in the binding of the English edition. The preliminaries are printed using a new setting although the text appears to use the same setting of type as A13(a). All the illustrations from the American edition are used here although that chosen as the frontispiece is different, (the American frontispiece is therefore positioned in the English text at a different place from where the English frontispiece originated in the American edition, and vice-versa). The English edition has corrected positioning of illustrations, corrected page numbers in the index of illustrations and re-titled two of the illustrations.

In 1926 the publishers wrote to The Society of Authors:

> Under an agreement of April 1909 we are the exclusive and sole publishers in the English speaking world, except for the United States, of Mr John Masefield's "Martin Hyde", while the author retains the copyright. Now, our friends Messrs. Jonathan Cape ask if we can grant them permission to include the volume in their Travellers Library… We think that the wording of the agreement makes it quite clear that this proposal could only be accepted with the joint consent of the author and ourselves, and we ask you as acting for the author, how you view the proposal.
>
> (Wells Gardner Darton and Co., letter to The Society of Authors, 19 August 1926)
> (BL, Add.Mss.56583, ff.83–84)

Jonathan Cape were in the process of acquiring *Captain Margaret* and *Multitude and Solitude* for their 'Travellers' Library' (see A7(e) and A8(g)). Although unable to prevent the 'Traveller's Library' editions of these novels, Masefield wrote to The Society of Authors regarding *Martin Hyde*:

It is an early book, which I would gladly suppress. Any prohibition which will lessen its' presence in the world will meet with my cordial support and appreciation.

(John Masefield, letter to [G.H.] Thring, [Sep. 1926])
(BL, Add.Mss.56583, f.98)

The novel did not, accordingly, appear in a Jonathan Cape edition.

In May 1927 (and on at least one previous occasion) Masefield attempted to regain control of the three children's books he had sold to Wells Gardner Darton and Company. Writing to The Society of Authors, Masefield states:

If there should be any possibility of getting control of the books, which this firm purchased from me years ago, on reasonable terms, I should be very glad to deal. There are three books, "Jim Davies", [sic] "Martin Hyde" and "A Book of Discoveries". They were not very friendly, when the matter was last suggested, but perhaps circumstances may have changed. I cannot think that any one of the three books has been of much profit to them.

(John Masefield, letter to [G.H.] Thring, 9 May 1927)
(BL, Add.Mss.56584, ff.180–81)

The company responded to The Society of Authors asking for clarification of Masefield's intentions:

Your proposal is that Mr. Masefield should take over the stock... and that we should agree to the cancellation of any agreements for the three books. We think that it is natural that our consideration of the proposal should be affected by the use to which Mr. Masefield would put the cancellation of the agreements with us – if he very much desires to withdraw the books from circulation altogether, and for good, a rather different principle is involved than would be the case if he wished to transfer the production of the books to another publisher.

(Wells Gardner, Darton & Co., letter to [G.H.] Thring, 24 May 1927)
(BL, Add.Mss.56584, f.192)

Possibly recalling the purchase arrangement for the Heinemann edition of *The Tragedy of Nan* in 1926 (see A18(c)) Masefield may have felt unable to state categorically his intentions:

...It is not possible for me to make any plans as to the future of the three books until I have purchased them. Everything must depend upon that event and on the terms upon which the purchase, if effective, can be arranged.

(John Masefield, letter to [G.H.] Thring, 27 May 1927)
(BL, Add.Mss.56584, f.194)

Masefield's reticence was presumably suspicious to Wells Gardner, Darton and Company for the matter was dropped.

Copies seen: BL (012808.d.8) stamped 2 NO 10; ULL (Special Collections) [green cloth]; Ledbury Library [blue cloth]; Harvard College Library (Houghton *EC9.M377.910mb(A)) inscribed 'Burn this to ash, and let the tempests take | The ash to blazes; do; for heaven's sake. | John Masefield. | For Florence Lamont. Novr 2nd. 1926.'

Reprinted:
Subsequent reprint dates include:

'Fathers and Sons Library edition'	[first edition, later impression]	[n.d.]
'Third Impression'	[first edition, later impression]	1930
[Later edition]	[first edition, later impression]	[1931?]

A13(c) Second English edition ["The Heritage of Literature Series"] (1953)

MARTIN HYDE | BY | JOHN MASEFIELD | *Illustrated by* | G.S. RONALDS | LONGMANS, GREEN AND CO | LONDON : NEW YORK : TORONTO
(All within swirling border and width centred)

Bibliographies: Handley-Taylor [unrecorded], Wight [unrecorded]

Collation: [A]^16 B-F^16; A5 and B5 are also signed; all signatures in the first two gatherings at right foot of page, all others at left foot; 96 leaves; 162 × 108mm.; [i–iv] 1–187 [188]

Page contents: [i] half-title: 'MARTIN HYDE' (with '[table lamp and open book] | *The Heritage of* | *Literature Series* | [rule] | SECTION A. No. 51'); [ii] frontispiece: 125 × 86mm., '"What do you do here?" the Duke asked', signed 'G.S. RONALDS 1952'; [iii] title-page; [iv] '[listing of publisher's offices] | Concise edition edited by S.H. BURTON, M.A. | First published in | THE HERITAGE OF LITERATURE Series | 1953 | by kind permission of | Messrs Wells Gardner, Darton and Co Ltd | PRINTED IN GREAT BRITAIN BY | LOVE AND MALCOLMSON LIMITED | LONDON AND REDHILL'; 1–187 text; [188] blank

Paper: wove paper

Running title: 'MARTIN HYDE' (28mm.) on verso; recto title comprises chapter title, pp.2–187

Binding: red cloth. On spine, in gold: 'Martin | Hyde | John | Masefield | [design of table lamp and open book] | Longmans'. On upper cover, in blind: design of table lamp and open book (ranged lower right). Lower cover: blank. All edges trimmed. Binding measurements: 168 × 111mm. (covers), 168 × 23mm. (spine). End-papers: wove paper with series listing advertisement for '*THE HERITAGE OF LITERATURE SERIES*'

Publication date: 4 May 1953

Price: 3s.6d.

Contents:
Martin Hyde ('I was born at Oulton, in Suffolk, in the year 1672. I know not the day...')
[abridged text]

Notes:
Chapter titles as first edition (except chapter XIX is here hyphenated 'CLUB-MEN').

The text is described as a 'concise edition edited by S.H. BURTON, M.A.'

Masefield was informed by The Society of Authors in April 1946 of Longmans' desire to include the title in this series:

> Messrs Longmans Green have written that they would very much like to include *Martin Hyde* in their Heritage of Literature series.
>
> (Louise Hancock, letter to John Masefield, 2 April 1946)
> (BL, Add.Mss.56619, f.53)

Masefield replied, stating his usual dislike of educational editions:

> I had hoped that this book had been bombed off the planet. I am shocked to hear of anyone wishing to revive it, even in a truncated form, as another curse to childhood. Probably, I have no power to stop it; so can only say that the proposal is grievous to me. My objection is mainly dislike of having any book of mine perforce an abomination to children in school. But probably I have no power to stop it, so can only say that I hope they will not do it.
>
> (John Masefield, letter to Louise Hancock, [3 April 1946])
> (BL, Add.Mss.56619, f.54)

Longmans did 'not do it' in 1946. However, in 1952 Longmans seem to have obtained permission from Wells Gardner, Darton and Company and again addressed the matter. Masefield wrote to The Society of Authors:

> There is a cheerful poem by Mr Yeats:-
>
> "Accurst, who bring to light of day,
> The writings I have cast away...
> But blest be those who print them not
> And let the kind worm take the lot."
>
> Well, it seems that the worm will not always be so kind.
>
> I am not sure that I have a clear power to refuse Messrs Darton: + though I had rather that the book were forgotten, there seems to be some life in it. Please, would you ask them what is proposed, exactly? The returns to myself are likely to be small. I have not seen the Series into which the book may be thrust: perhaps they would not mind shewing me a copy? I have not looked at the book since I passed the proofs, + forget even what it is about.
>
> (John Masefield, letter to Gabrielle [Curry], 14 February [1952])
> (BL, Add.Mss.56623, ff.106–107)

Longmans presumably asked whether the book could be cut and to this suggestion Masefield readily consented. He also commenced a discussion over proposed royalties:

> I do not mind the book being cut (the more cut the better, I should say) nor being done in this form: but might we not, perhaps, ask for an increase on the 5% after a certain sale? Surely, this should be possible?
>
> (John Masefield, letter to Gabrielle [Curry], [26 February 1952])
> (BL, Add.Mss.56623, f.115)

The Society of Authors approached Longmans on this matter and, accordingly, wrote to Masefield at the beginning of March 1952:

> I have spoken to Mr. Parker of Longmans Green about the proposed royalty on *Martin Hyde*... He was perfectly pleasant but insisted that a flat 5% was all that was economically possible... The only concession which Mr. Parker was willing to make was an increase in the advance payment from £100 to £150.
>
> (Gabrielle Curry, letter to John Masefield, 4 March 1952)
> (BL, Add.Mss.56623, f.121)

Masefield, in his reply, acknowledged that he had little knowledge of production costs but suggested that, as he failed to care for the volume anyway, he ought to persist in his claims for higher royalty:

> It is difficult for me to decide the matter, as I know so little of the present costs of production + the probable trends of these; but I am fairly sure that our claim is reasonable and one that should be made and maintained. The offer of the greatly increased advance convinces me that the increased royalty could be paid, quite well, under present conditions. Thinking thus, and feeling that possibly my standing-out might a little help other authors, and (lest this should seem too self-righteous) swiftly adding that the book is one that I dislike the thought of, I would be inclined to refuse the terms altogether and let the matter end.
>
> (John Masefield, letter to Gabrielle [Curry], 5 March 1952)
> (BL, Add.Mss.56623, ff.122–23)

On 30 April 1952 The Society of Authors wrote to Masefield informing him that Longmans had increased the royalty from 5% to 7½% (see BL, Add.Mss.56623, f.157). A formal agreement was sent to Masefield (via the Society) on 9 June 1952 and an amended copy sent on 14 July 1952. The publishing agreement for this edition between Masefield and Longmans was dated 16 July 1952 (see Archives of The Society of Authors).

The files of The Society of Authors reveal that Masefield passed the cuts made by S.H. Burton:

> I am sending back with this the copy marked with the abridgements. I may say that I would not have minded if he had cut out 9/10ths of the book, + burnt the remainder; so I will pass the copy, as cut by Mr Burton.
>
> (John Masefield, letter to Gabrielle [Curry], 27 June 1952)
>
> (BL, Add.Mss.56623, f.183)

Page proofs were sent by the publishers and received by The Society of Authors by 27 January 1953 (see BL, Add.Mss.56624, f.62). Masefield chose not to look at these, and passed the description of the volume as a 'concise edition':

> I had rather not look at the proofs. "Concise edition" seems a clever way of putting it. I can suggest nothing better.
>
> (John Masefield, letter to [Anne] Munro-Kerr, [28 January 1953])
>
> (BL, Add.Mss.56624, f.63)

Copies seen: BL (012208.cc.1/93) stamped 18 APR 1953

Reprinted:

'Second Impression'	[second edition, second impression]	1954

A14 A BOOK OF DISCOVERIES   1910

A14(a) *First English edition (1910)*

A BOOK OF [in red with black border] | DISCOVERIES [in red with black border, both lines 1 and 2 within black scroll] | [illustration of two boys in rowing boat in front of large hill] | By JOHN MASEFIELD [in red] | ILLUSTRATED BY GORDON BROWNE [in red with some capitals joined] | LonDon [*sic*] [all letters joined] | WELLS GARDNER, DARTON AND CO. LTD. | 3, PATERNOSTER BUILDINGS E. C. [these five lines within black scroll]
(All within border, of which the base forms the bottom of the lowest scroll: 145 × 95mm. and all width centred)

Bibliographies: Danielson 171, Williams p.8, Simmons [14], Nevinson p.15, Handley-Taylor p.29, Wight [14]

Collation: [π]⁶ A–Y⁸ [Z]⁶ (J, V and W not used); signatures right foot of page; 188 leaves; 201 × 145mm.; the catalogue is integral to the book; [i–vi] vii [viii] ix–xii [1] 2–4 [5–6] 7–36 [37–38] 39–46 [47–48] 49–52 [53–54] 55–62 [63–64] 65–116 [117–18] 119–36 [137–38] 139- 40 [141–42] 143–58 [159–60] 161–64 [165–66] 167–70 [171–72] 173–78 [179–80] 181–218 [219–20] 221–46 [247–48] 249–66 [267–68] 269–92 [293–94] 295–300 [301–302] 303–353 [354] [1] 2–10 (all un-numbered pages pp.[5–6] to [301–302] represent full-page illustrations on recto, with verso blank)

Page contents: [i] half-title: 'A Book of Discoveries'; [ii–iii] blank; [iv] frontispiece: 147 × 95mm., '"The boys had all they could do to keep the rollers going." | [*Page* 25.', signed 'G.B.', with protective tissue; [v] title-page; [vi] publisher's device above '1910' all surrounded by ornate border with toy figure on boat at top: 50 × 38mm.; vii 'TO | JUDITH'; [viii] blank; ix '[illustration of boy with large net and fishes] | CONTENTS [within scroll] | [14 chapters (without titles) listed with page references]'; x 'Contents [as headline]' | [10 further chapters (without titles) listed with page references] | [illustration of man with magnifying glass examining a buried toy]'; xi–xii '[illustration of two boys examining giant book] | LiST [*sic*] OF ILLUSTRATIONS [within scroll] | [46 illustrations listed with page references] | Besides initials and tailpieces.'; [1]–4 text and illustration; [5] illustration; [6] blank; 7–36 text and illustrations; [37] illustration; [38] blank; 39–46 text and illustrations; [47] illustration; [48] blank; 49–52 text; [53] illustration; [54] blank; 55–62 text and illustrations; [63] illustration; [64] blank; 65–116 text and illustrations; [117] illustration; [118] blank; 119–36 text and illustrations; [137] illustration; [138] blank; 139–40 text; [141] illustration; [142] blank; 143–58 text and illustration; [159] illustration; [160] blank; 161–64 text; [165] illustration; [166] blank; 167–70 text; [171] illustration; [172] blank; 173–78 text and illustration; [179] illustration; [180] blank; 181–218 text and illustration; [219] illustration; [220] blank; 221–46 text and illustrations; [247] illustration; [248] blank; 249–66 text and illustration; [267] illustration; [268] blank; 269–92 text and illustrations; [293] illustration; [294] blank; 295–300 text; [301] illustration; [302] blank; 303-[354] text and illustrations (at foot of p.[354]: 'THE END | [rule] | WELLS GARDNER, DARTON AND CO., LTD., PATERNOSTER BUILDINGS, LONDON, E.C.'); [1]–10 publisher's advertisements: 'DARTON'S | FINE ART SERIES | SUITABLE FOR | PRESENTS AND PRIZES | LONDON | WELLS GARDNER, DARTON & CO., LTD. | 3 & 4, PATERNOSTER BUILDINGS, E.C. | *And all Booksellers*' (nine volumes listed with sample illustrations, press reviews, and prices, etc.)

Paper: wove paper

Running title: 'A Book of Discoveries' (65mm.) on both verso and recto, pp.2-[354]

Binding: light-yellow cloth. On spine: '[green and black device] | A BOOK | [device] OF [device] | DISCOV- | ERIES | JOHN | MASE- | FIELD [all width centred, in gold lettering within ornate green and black border] | [design of crown in black (or gold) and white, with green and black (or gold) seaweed with white and gold pole supporting title and author information] | WELLS |

GARDNER | DARTON | & CO | L^{TD} [these five lines in brown within green and black (or gold) garland, with white bell at foot; the 'O' of 'CO' is superscripted with a point underneath]' (starting from beneath top green and black device, entire enclosed in black double ruled border: 188 × 36mm.) On upper cover: 'A BOOK OF | DISCOVERIES | BY JOHN MASEFIELD [all in brown within scroll] | [design in green, light green, black and white of four pirates in a boat (one standing) with ship on horizon and cloud: 119 × 62mm. (bordered on horizontal sides by double rule and, on either side mirror images of trident in black and white with light-green and black garland, green fish and light-green seaweed)] | *Illustrated by* | GORDON BROWNE [in brown, within plaque]' (all bordered by light-green leaves in brown margin: 202 × 137mm.) The shades of brown commonly vary within the same copy. On lower cover: design of trident, garland and scrolls in brown and light green, within garland: 'A | Book of | Discoveries'; within first scroll: 'By J.Masefield'; within second scroll: 'Illustrated by | Gordon Browne' (76 × 32mm.) Top and fore edges trimmed, lower outside edge uncut. Wight states 'some copies have the top edge gilt'. Binding measurements: 209 × 147mm. (covers), 209 × 40mm. (spine). End-papers: wove paper illustrated with 'A Book of~' and 'Discoveries!' in scrolls and showing a before and after scene: 'before' on left hand side (sun casting eye at rock above which appears a feather and approached by man in cap with gun), 'after' on right hand side (sun looking away from rock from behind which a pirate (with feather in hat) has appeared, pointing a pistol at a man in flight, having cast away gun and cap in his haste to escape) (all enclosed in swirling border). Volume contained in slip-case covered in light blue paper with the artwork from the binding printed in brown.

Publication date: published, according to Simmons, 10 October 1910 in an edition of 3000 copies

Price: 6s.

Contents:

A Book of Discoveries ('Mac and Robin were two brothers who lived with their mother at Waters Orton.')

Notes:

Simmons and Handley-Taylor describe the volume as 'a book of stories for boys'. It is not, however, a collection of short stories as this may imply, but a continuous narrative of episodic adventures of two boys and their friend Mr Hampden.

The lettering used on the binding includes a number of swash characters.

Writing to his agent during October 1909 Masefield notes:

> We might call the new book "A Book of Discoveries", or some such name. Having in mind the trouble we had last year with Dartons, I propose to submit a quarter of the book to them very shortly, so that, if they don't like it, I may stop doing it before I've wasted too much of my time at it. I think that what I've done is pretty fair; but it is not an easy book to write.
>
> (John Masefield, letter to C.F. Cazenove, 22 October 1909)
> (University of Arizona Library. MS.50, V.II)

The 'trouble... with Dartons' may have been with regards to *Lost Endeavour* (see A15(a)), although this is conjecture.

A document in the archives of The Society of Authors (BL, Add.Mss.56594, ff.216–17) notes that Masefield sold *A Book of Discoveries* outright to Messrs Wells Gardner Darton & Co. giving them 'an exclusive and sole right to publish the work'. Masefield attempted to buy back the copyright of this work in 1927. See notes to A13(b).

Page 308, line 12 may reveal a typographical error with a missing full-stop. Even if supplied, however, the sentence fails to make perfect sense and the text may be corrupt at this juncture. Page 323, line 20 reveals 'a ther' incorrectly set for 'at her'. Page 349, line 27 may also contain a corruption of text – a missing 'a' is likely.

Wight states 'some copies have brown or green, not gold on the [upper] cover'. There exist considerable variations in the use of gold, black and brown on the spine and upper cover, and the matter is not one of simple substitution as Wight may suggest.

Copies seen: BL (012808.d.7) stamped 15 OCT 1910; ULL (Special Collections); Ledbury Library; NYPL (8-NAS 1910) 10116A stamped MAR 5 1921; NYPL (NAS 1910) 504746A; Harvard College Library (Houghton *EC9.M377.910b2) inscribed 'Look once at this, but once, then swiftly say | "I'll read this story on another day". | J. Masefield.'

Reprinted:

[Second Impression]	[first edition, second impression]	[no copies consulted]
[Third Impression]	[first edition, third impression]	[no copies consulted]
'Fourth Impression'	[first edition, fourth impression]	Jun 1931

An edition bound in dark blue cloth and containing advertisements (but no reprint information) suggests that all reprints before the fourth did not include reprint information.

A14(b) First American edition (1910)

A BOOK OF [in red with black border] | DISCOVERIES [in red with black border, both lines 1 and 2 within black scroll] | [illustration of two boys in rowing boat in front of large hill] | By JOHN MASEFIELD [in red] | ILLUSTRATED BY GORDON BROWNE [in red with some capitals joined] | NEW YORK [in black] | FREDERICK A. STOKES COMPANY [in black] | PUBLISHERS [in black] [these five lines within black scroll] (All within border, of which the base forms the bottom of the lowest scroll: 145 × 95mm. and all width centred)

Bibliographies: Danielson [unrecorded], Williams [unrecorded], Simmons [noted on pp.28–29], Nevinson [unrecorded], Handley-Taylor p.29, Wight 14a

Collation: [π]⁶ (±[π]3) A-Y⁸ [Z]⁶ (J, V and W not used); signatures right foot of page; 188 leaves; 201 × 142mm.; the catalogue is integral to the book; [i–vi] vii [viii] ix–xii [1] 2–4 [5–6] 7–36 [37–38] 39–46 [47–48] 49–52 [53–54] 55–62 [63–64] 65–116 [117–18] 119–36 [137–38] 139–40 [141–42] 143–58 [159–60] 161–64 [165–66] 167–70 [171–72] 173–78 [179–80] 181–218 [219–20] 221–46 [247–48] 249–66 [267–68] 269–92 [293–94] 295–300 [301–302] 303–353 [354] [1] 2–10 (all un-numbered pages pp.[5–6] to [301–302] represent full-plate illustrations on recto, with verso blank)

Page contents: [i] half-title: 'A Book of Discoveries'; [ii–iii] blank; [iv] frontispiece: 147 × 95mm., '"The boys had all they could do to keep the rollers going." | [*Page* 25.', signed 'G.B.'; [v] title-page (with protective tissue); [vi] '*Printed by* | *Wells Gardner, Darton & Co., Ltd., London, England*'; vii 'TO | JUDITH'; [viii] blank; ix '[illustration of boy with large net and fishes] | CONTENTS [within scroll] | [14 chapters (without titles) listed with page references]'; x 'Contents [as headline] | [10 further chapters (without titles) listed with page references] | [illustration of man with magnifying glass examining a buried toy]'; xi–xii '[illustration of two boys examining giant book] | LiST [*sic*] OF ILLUSTRATIONS [within scroll] | [46 illustrations listed with page references] | Besides initials and tailpieces.'; [1]–4 text and illustration; [5] illustration; [6] blank; 7–36 text and illustrations; [37] illustration; [38] blank; 39–46 text and illustrations; [47] illustration; [48] blank; 49–52 text; [53] illustration; [54] blank; 55–62 text and illustration; [63] illustration; [64] blank; 65–116 text and illustrations; [117] illustration; [118] blank; 119–36 text and illustrations; [137] illustration; [138] blank; 139–40 text; [141] illustration; [142] blank; 143–58 text and illustration; [159] illustration; [160] blank; 161–64 text; [165] illustration; [166] blank; 167–70 text; [171] illustration; [172] blank; 173–78 text and illustration; [179] illustration; [180] blank; 181–218 text and illustration; [219] illustration; [220] blank; 221–46 text and illustrations; [247] illustration; [248] blank; 249–66 text and illustration; [267] illustration; [268] blank; 269–92 text and illustrations; [293] illustration; [294] blank; 295–300 text; [301] illustration; [302] blank; 303-[354] text and illustrations (at foot of p.[354]: 'THE END | [rule] | WELLS GARDNER, DARTON AND CO., LTD., PATERNOSTER BUILDINGS, LONDON, E.C.'); [1]–10 publisher's advertisements: 'DARTON'S | FINE ART SERIES | SUITABLE FOR | PRESENTS AND PRIZES | LONDON | WELLS GARDNER, DARTON & CO., LTD. | 3 & 4, PATERNOSTER BUILDINGS, E.C. | *And all Booksellers*' (nine volumes listed with sample illustrations, press reviews, and prices, etc.)

Paper: wove paper

Running title: 'A Book of Discoveries' (65mm.) on both verso and recto, pp.2-[354]

Binding: brown cloth. On spine: 'A BOOK | [device] OF [device] | DISCOV- | ERIES | JOHN | MASE- | FIELD [all width centred, in gold lettering within ornate black border] | STOKES [in gold and in centre of garland, in black (with opening to garland off-set to the right (see notes)]' (starting from beneath head of ornate border for title, entire enclosed in black double ruled border: 189 × 35mm.) On upper cover: 'A BOOK OF | DISCOVERIES | BY JOHN MASEFIELD [all in gold within black scroll] | [design in black of four pirates in a boat (one standing) with ship on horizon and cloud: 119 × 62mm. (bordered on horizontal sides by black double rule] | *Illustrated by* | GORDON BROWNE [in gold within black plaque]' (all bordered by blind leaves in black margin: 203 × 137mm.) Lower cover: blank. All edges trimmed. Binding measurements: 209 × 144mm. (covers), 209 × 48mm. (spine). End-papers: wove paper.

Publication date: Simmons states

> The date of publication is not obtainable from the Copyright Office; the Frederick A. Stokes Company assigns September 25, 1910 as an approximate date; the United States Catalog enters the date as November, 1910. In *The Publishers' Weekly* for December 3, 1910, the book is listed in an advertisement of the Stokes Company under the heading, *New Titles Not Previously Announced*.

Price: $1.75

Contents:
as for A14(a)

Notes:
Wight is the only bibliographer to describe fully this edition. He does not note the cancel-title, however. This is likely to reflect an error, rather than represent a copy without a cancel-title. The sheets of this edition were imported from England (see note on p.[vi] and the presence of the English publisher's catalogue included at the rear of the volume). Handley-Taylor also states 'the sheets as issued by Wells Gardner, Darton and Co., Ltd., were published in New York with a title-page bearing the name of Frederick A. Stokes Company as publisher.' Typographical oddities as noted in A14(a) – on p.308, p.323 and p.349 – are all present here.

A letter from Masefield's agent suggests that he had initially tried to interest Little, Brown and Company in this volume:

> I am sorry to say that Little Brown won't take the Book of Discoveries for a copyright edition, and I am consequently telling Darton that he had better try to arrange a sale in sheets as he originally wanted to do. I think we were right in trying to do something separately, but I fancy your own feeling was that the book was peculiarly English in style and treatment.
>
> (C.F. Cazenove, letter to John Masefield, 15 August 1910)
> (University of Arizona Library. MS.50, V.II)

The binding design on this edition is much less lavish than that for A14(a). The American binding illustrations are simplified from the English and printed in gold and black only. The garland (containing the name of the publisher) on the spine has an opening off-set to the right. A comparison with the English binding reveals that a seaweed design is there positioned over the garland. The omission of the seaweed design in the American edition therefore renders the peculiarity of the off-set garland opening. An issue with page [vi] blank and the catalogue omitted has also been examined. This copy is bound with the seaweed design present on the spine.

The lettering used on the binding includes a number of swash characters.

Copies seen: private collection (PWE) without p.[vi] printing information and publisher's catalogue at rear; Bailey/Howe Library, University of Vermont (TR DREW 28)

A15 LOST ENDEAVOUR   1910

A15(a) First English edition (1910)

LOST | ENDEAVOUR | By JOHN MASEFIELD | [rule, 80mm.] | [ornament] | [rule, 81mm.] | THOMAS NELSON AND SONS | LONDON, EDINBURGH, DUBLIN, | LEEDS, AND NEW YORK | LEIPZIG : 35–37 Königstrasse. PARIS: 61, rue des Saints-Pères.
(All width centred and enclosed within two borders: 133 × 81mm. and 138 × 86mm. As a result of the two rules noted above, three rectangles are created measuring: 43 × 81mm., 65 × 81mm. and 25 × 81mm. respectively from the top. Not all lines touch.)

Bibliographies: Danielson 173, Williams p.8, Simmons [15], Nevinson p.15, Handley-Taylor p.29, Wight [15]

Collation: [1]¹⁶ 2–12¹⁶; the fifth leaf of each gathering is also signed; signatures width centred at foot of page; 192 leaves; 183 × 120mm.; [1–7] 8–133 [134–37] 138–269 [270–73] 274–381 [382–84]

Pagination contents: [1] title-page (with additional leaf tipped-in on the verso of which is the colour frontispiece: 145 × 94mm., of three men on rocky mound overlooking ruins, with sea behind, signed in lower right corner, 'STEPHEN REID | [rule] 1900 | [rule]'); [2] *First published in* 1910.'; [3] 'CONTENTS | [rule with two diamond shapes in centre, 15mm.]' (three titled parts listed with page references); [4] 'TO | C'; [5] sectional title: 'PART FIRST | CHARLES HARDING'S STORY'; [6] blank; [7]–133 text of Part I; [134] blank; [135] sectional title: 'PART SECOND | LITTLE THEO'S STORY'; [136] blank; [137]–269 text of Part II; [270] blank; [271] sectional title: 'PART THIRD | CHARLES HARDING'S STORY'; [272] blank; [273]–381 text of Part III (with illustration on p.381 (before closing verse) of sun either setting into, or rising from, the sea, with island and birds within border: 25 × 83mm.); [382] 'ESTABLISHED 1798 | [publisher's device showing bookshop: 25 × 83mm.] | T. NELSON | AND SONS | PRINTERS AND | PUBLISHERS'; [383–84] 'Notes on Nelson's New Novels.'

Paper: wove paper

Running title: 'LOST ENDEAVOUR.' (43mm.) on verso; recto title either 'CHARLES HARDING'S STORY.' (65mm.) or 'LITTLE THEO'S STORY.' (53mm.), as appropriate, pp.8–381

Binding: green cloth. On spine, in gold: 'LOST | ENDEAVOUR | [heart shaped device] | John | Masefield [all on white panel within double ruled border in gold: 51 × 40mm.] | NELSON' (all width centred). Upper and lower covers: blank. All edges trimmed. Binding measurements: 191 × 124mm. (covers), 191 × 50mm. (spine). End-papers: wove paper illustrated in green with two figures, two floral garlands enclosing the letter 'N' and swirling leafy border. Wight notes 'some copies were published with plain end-papers'.

An unrecorded binding variant is as follows:

light-green cloth. On spine, in gold: 'LOST | ENDEAVOUR | [heart shaped device] | John | Masefield | [panel with design of vertical columns including spade motif: 31 × 111mm.] [in blind] | NELSON' (all width centred). Note that the spacing of the lettering is not the same as that of previously described binding. On upper cover, in blind: design of vertical columns including spade motif with intricate circular leaf design and entirely surrounded by border of broken rectangles: 183 × 116mm. Lower cover: blank. Binding measurements: 191 × 122 (covers), 191 × 47mm. (spine). End-papers: wove paper (without illustrations – see Wight's note, although Wight fails to mention any other binding variants).

Publication date: published, according to Simmons, 25 November 1910 in an edition of 12000 copies

Price: 2s.

Contents:
Lost Endeavour ('I got my learning, such as it is, from Dr. Carter, who kept an Academy for the Sons...')

Notes:
The publishing agreement for this title between Masefield and Thomas Nelson was dated 19 May 1909 (see Archives of The Society of Authors). The agreement cites the title as *Trepanned* and specifies that the work would not be published later than 31 December 1910.

Each part is divided into untitled chapters, not noted on the contents page. Part one consists of fifteen chapters, part two of nineteen and part three of twenty-one.

The first edition of H.G. Wells' *The History of Mr. Polly* in the 'Nelson's New Novels' series includes, at the rear of the volume '*Descriptive Notes on the Volumes for* 1910'. Here *Lost Endeavour* is listed by an earlier title. The entry reads:

TREPANNED. *John Masefield*

Mr. Masefield has already won high reputation as poet and dramatist, and his novel "Captain Margaret" showed him to be a romancer of a high order. "Trepanned" is a story of adventure in Virginia and the Spanish Main. A Kentish boy is trepanned and carried off to sea, and finds his fill of adventure among Indians and buccaneers. The central episode of the book is a quest for the sacred Aztec temple. The swift drama of the narrative, and the poetry and imagination of the style, make the book in the highest sense literature. It should appeal not only to all lovers of good writing, but to all who care for the record of stirring deeds.

(see H.G. Wells, The History of Mr. Polly, Thomas Nelson & Sons, 1910, pp.[382]-[83])

E.C. Bentley writing in *Those Days* recounts details of trying to get his first novel published:

Nelson's 2/- novels represented good company for an unknown writer to be in. They had already included Chesterton's *Manalive*; one of Wells' books, *Mr. Polly*; and one of Masefield's, *Lost Endeavour*, which I had admired so much, as a quite new sort of pirates-of-the-Spanish-Main story, that I had written to him to say what I felt. In his reply Masefield told me that the book had been to every reputable publisher in England and America, and Nelsons alone would undertake it. I am marvelling still, as I marvelled then, at my unbelievable good fortune in having exactly the opposite experience to Masefield's with a first novel; for I knew him to be a man of genius, and his distinction as a writer and poet had been recognized for years.

(E.C. Bentley, Those Days, Constable & Co Ltd, London, 1940, pp.259–60)

The letter from Masefield to which E.C. Bentley refers is located in the Bodleian. It reads:

I thank you very much indeed for your most generous kind letter. I am indeed glad that my book has given you such pleasure. I am very much surprised that you should like it. It has been to every reputable [publishers] in England + America (except Duckworth's), + Nelson's alone would have anything to say for it. I have long looked on it as an ugly duckling, + such a letter from you takes my breath away. Very many thanks.

(John Masefield, letter to E.C. Bentley, 1 December 1910)
(Bodleian, Ms.Eng.Lett.c.255)

Letters from Masefield to C.F. Cazenove suggest that Wells, Gardner, Darton and Co. and then Grant Richards were offered the novel. In March 1909 Masefield wrote:

If you will be so kind, will you please get Trepanned typed as cheaply as may be, + then try Messrs Nelson with it? The book has been unlucky from the beginning. It might be well to ask Nelson first if he is open to consider it... ...I am disheartened about Trepanned, but perhaps it will go later on.

(John Masefield, letter to C.F. Cazenove, 8 March 1909)
(University of Arizona Library. MS.50, V.II)

A subsequent letter from Masefield to his agent notes:

Trepann'd. I am grateful for what you say about this book. I should be quite willing to take £50 for it, with a good royalty, + publication <u>this year</u>; but by all means get more if you can. If Nelson insist on a novel, you might offer him my next one, or my next boy's book, of which I have two in my hand. I should be glad to have the ms disposed of.

(John Masefield, letter to C.F. Cazenove, 6 April 1909)
(University of Arizona Library. MS.50, V.II)

This suggests that Nelson declared an interest in *Lost Endeavour* and were presumably hoping to include a contract clause for future work from Masefield. Probably a month later the author wrote:

The terms are very liberal, + I suppose it would be best to accept them as they stand: but if you think good, not otherwise, you might ask for £75 now, as the date of publication seems far off. Don't ask this is you think it would be presuming in any way.

(John Masefield, letter to C.F. Cazenove, [pre 10 May 1909])
(University of Arizona Library. MS.50, V.II)

The manuscript of this novel is, apparently, annotated 'Begun at 30 Maida Hill West in Sept. 1908 and ended there early in 1909', as noted in an inventory of the papers of Masefield (made after the author's death). It may therefore be an early draft of *Lost Endeavour* to which Masefield refers when he writes to Cazenove in December 1908:

Herewith 45,000 words of the pirate story. The two stories are parts of a whole; so be not alarmed. May it be granted to me that the cover of these books of mine be simple, like the early *Treasure Island* covers? I mean the tales to be read by adults, too. Why not, since they are less critical than the young? I cannot abide the covers on the modern boy's book. I like a plain side, without a design.

(John Masefield, letter to C.F. Cazenove, [14 December 1908])
(University of Arizona Library. MS.50, V.I)

The early title of *Trepanned* and Masefield's references to *Treasure Island* reveal that R.L. Stevenson was evidently much in Masefield's thoughts at the time of writing.

A request to include a number of selections from Masefield including an extract from *Lost Endeavour* in an anthology in 1924 prompted Masefield to write to The Society of Authors:

The application for the use of the piece from *Lost Endeavour* should be made to Messrs Nelson + Sons. The other pieces are certainly under my control.

(John Masefield, letter to G.H. Thring, [1924])
(BL, Add.Mss.56579, f.70)

It is therefore likely that Masefield sold the novel outright to Nelson's in 1910.

Masefield, as stated above, was grateful to Nelson's for originally publishing the novel in 1910. Although the publishers presumably held the entire copyright it appears that the firm always treated Masefield well. Expressing his gratitude, in 1936, to The Society of Authors, Masefield writes:

Nelson's. I am grateful to this firm for what I consider very handsome dealing. Since the day when they accepted the manuscript, they have ever treated me generously.

(John Masefield, letter to [E.J.] Mullett, [6 December 1936])
(BL, Add.Mss.56605, f.117)

In 1927 The Society of Authors had presumably written to Masefield regarding Nelson's granting of anthology rights for this novel. In his reply Masefield states the lack of American copyright, Nelson's generosity and, in these circumstances, was prepared to allow Nelson's to continue:

"Lost Endevour" is not copyright in the United States. So far as I know, everybody can print it there. At the time of publication no American publisher would take it and I think every reputable English publisher except Nelson's refused it over here. Nelson's gave me rather more than twice as much as the best other offer that I had and I do not think that it would be grateful in me to question their authorisations of extracts in anthologies.

(John Masefield, letter to [G.H.] Thring, 12 January 1927)
(BL, Add.Mss.56584, ff.16–17)

A request was received in November 1924 from the National Institute For The Blind for 'permission to publish in Braille type' (BL, Add.Mss.56580, f.145). Masefield was enthusiastic.

An application from the BBC to The Society of Authors in 1952 to dramatise the novel received the following response from Masefield:

Please, will you tell the BBC to go ahead with the script? I feel about this book something as Macbeth felt about Duncan:- "Look on it again I dare not." or, anyhow, would rather not.

(John Masefield, letter to Miss Mostyn, 8 October [1952])
(BL, Add.Mss.56624, f.15)

Copies seen: private collection (PWE); private collection (PWE) binding variant; BL (012621.a.34) stamped 19 DEC 1910; ULL (Special Collections); Ledbury Library; Library of The John Masefield Society; Harvard College Library (Houghton *EC9.M377.910l) inscribed 'Forget this tale as though it never was, | For thus the world + thus the author has. | John Masefield. | (For Florence Lamont).'

A15(b) First American edition (1917)

LOST ENDEAVOUR | BY | JOHN MASEFIELD | Author of "Captain Margaret," "Multitude and | Solitude," "The Everlasting Mercy," etc, | New York | THE MACMILLAN COMPANY | 1917
(All width centred)

Bibliographies: Danielson [unrecorded], Williams [unrecorded], Simmons [noted on p.30], Nevinson [unrecorded], Handley-Taylor [p.29], Wight 15a

Collation: [A-U]⁸ (J not used); 160 leaves; 190 × 129mm.; [i–viii] [1–2] 3–102 [103–104] 105–209 [210–12] 213–98 [299–312]

Pagination contents: [i] half-title: 'LOST ENDEAVOUR'; [ii] '[publisher's device] | THE MACMILLAN COMPANY | [two lines listing six cities, separated by four points] | MACMILLAN & CO., LIMITED | [two lines listing four cities, separated by two points] | THE MACMILLAN CO. OF CANADA, LTD. | [one city listed]'; [iii] title-page; [iv] blank; [v] 'TO | C'; [vi] blank; [vii] 'CONTENTS' (three titled parts listed with page references); [viii] blank; [1] sectional title: 'PART FIRST | CHARLES HARDING'S STORY'; [2] blank; 3–102 text of Part I; [103] sectional title: 'PART SECOND | LITTLE THEO'S STORY'; [104] blank; 105–209 text of Part II; [210] blank; [211] sectional title: 'PART THIRD | CHARLES HARDING'S STORY'; [212] blank; 213–98 text of Part III (at foot of p.298: 'PRINTED IN THE UNITED STATES OF AMERICA'); [299] 'THE following pages contain advertisements | of Macmillan books by the same author' (within ruled border: 16 × 67mm.); [300] blank; [301–307] publisher's advertisements; [308–12] blank

Paper: wove paper

Running title: 'LOST ENDEAVOUR' (38mm.) on verso; recto title either 'CHARLES HARDING'S STORY' (59mm.) or 'LITTLE THEO'S STORY' (47mm.), as appropriate, pp.4–298

Binding: light blue-green cloth (see notes). On spine, in gold: '[double rule] | LOST ENDEAVOUR | MASEFIELD | MACMILLAN | [double rule]' (all width centred). On upper cover, in gold: 'LOST | ENDEAVOUR | MASEFIELD' (ranged upper left) (within blind ruled border: 189 × 119mm.) Lower cover: blank. Top edge trimmed, others roughly trimmed. Binding measurements: 197 × 128mm. (covers), 197 × 43mm. (spine). End-papers: wove paper.

Publication date: published, according to Simmons, 28 February 1917 in an edition of 2004 copies

Price: $1.50

Contents:
as for A15(a)

Notes:
The text has been entirely re-set for this edition.

As in A15(a) each part is divided into untitled chapters, not noted on the contents page. Part one consists of fifteen chapters, part two nineteen and part three twenty-one. Each part commences with a drop-capital.

Wight describes the colour of the binding cloth as 'blue'. It is presumed that this is not a variant.

The Archives of The Society of Authors reveal several publishing agreements or proposed agreements for this title between Masefield and Macmillan. One, dated 1914 only, grants 'a licence to publish in volume form in the United States of America, four (4) works, the subjects or titles of which are "MULTITUDE AND SOLITUDE", "THE LOST ENDEAVOR", "CAPTAIN MARGARET", and "THE TRAGEDY OF NAN", (provided the rights of publication in the United States of America be acquired from the present publishers by the Company)...' The document additionally states '...the Company agrees to publish the first three of the above works in the course of the year 1915, and... "NAN" within the three months after the said work has been acquired from the present publishers...' The document also extended the licence for previous Macmillan titles for a further five years from date of their first publication. Another version is dated 19 October 1914 and omits reference to acquiring rights from existing publishers. This version refers to 'revised editions' of the four works and notes 'the Company agrees to publish one of the above works in the fall of 1914, another in the spring of 1915, and a third in the autumn of 1915'. An unknown hand has annotated this document 'Proposed agreement not signed to our knowledge'.

A later publishing agreement for this title between Masefield and Macmillan was dated 16 March 1916 (see Archives of The Society of Authors). The agreement refers to 'a licence to publish in volume form in the United States of America a work the subject or title of which is The Lost Endeavor (new edition)'.

Copies seen: Library of The John Masefield Society (Peter Smith Collection) inscribed 'For Judith | from Pip. | Sept 19. 1917.' with signature of Judith Masefield, includes posthumous booklabel

Reprinted:

1923–24 (according to Handley-Taylor)
1925–26 (according to Handley-Taylor)
1928–29 (according to Handley-Taylor)
1930–31 (according to Handley-Taylor)
1935–36 (according to Handley-Taylor)
1938–39 (according to Handley-Taylor)
1942–43 (according to Handley-Taylor)

A15(c) Subsequent Nelson editions

At a later stage, Nelson reissued *Lost Endeavour* in a reset edition. The text runs from pp.9–318. Page 318 included the original closing illustration from the first edition. This illustration was eventually abandoned although the same setting of the text was used on many different occasions with a variety of title-pages and bindings.

The Society of Authors wrote to Masefield in June 1948 presumably regarding an educational issue and Masefield responded that as he had sold the copyright of the novel to Nelson:

> I cannot possibly object to Messrs Nelson doing as they please with their own. L.E. seems to me a dreadful book: + schools, perhaps, are often dreadful places; so let us hope that when the two meet they may cancel each other out.
>
> (John Masefield, letter to Miss [S.M.] Perry [June 1948])
> (BL, Add.Mss.56620, f.229)

The following is a conjectural construction of reprint information based largely on stamped copies in the British Library, references in the *English Catalogue of Books* and copies from private collections with dated ownership markings. Only the 1939 issue is dated within the volume.

Reprinted, without dates, in different bindings and series:
– [1919] blue binding
     BL (12628.de.8) stamped 21 JAN 1919
– [1923] ('Cheap edition' in the *English Catalogue of Books*) 'art deco' red binding
     personal collection inscribed 'July 1924' (not in Masefield's hand)
     BL (012629.de.88) stamped 23 AUG 1923
– [1936] ('Nelson Classics' No. 310) different colours of binding and p.318 illustration absent
     personal collection red binding
     ULL green binding
– 1939 ('The Teaching of English Series' No. 214) lilac/blue binding and p.318 illustration absent
     personal collection

A14(a) title-page

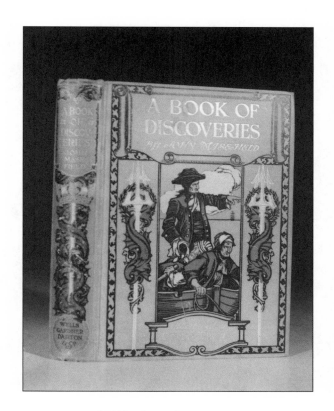

A14(a) spine and upper cover

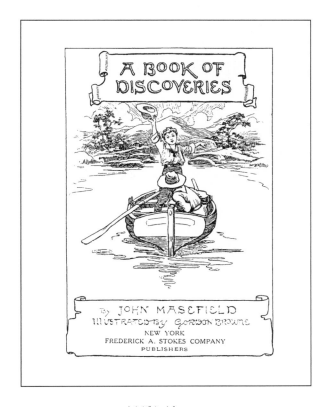

A14(b) title-page

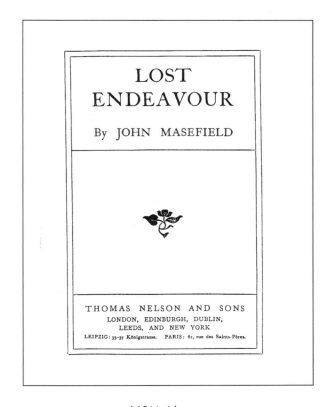

A15(a) title-page

THE

STREET OF TO-DAY

BY

JOHN MASEFIELD

By the Street of To-day
Man goes to the House of To-morrow

LONDON: J. M. DENT & SONS LTD.
29 AND 30 BEDFORD STREET · 1911

A16(a) title-page

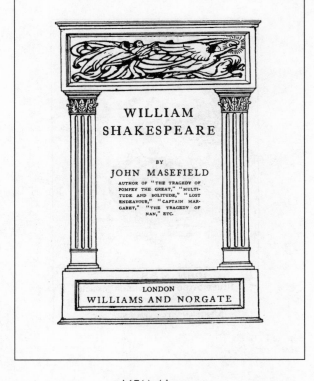

WILLIAM
SHAKESPEARE

BY

JOHN MASEFIELD

AUTHOR OF "THE TRAGEDY OF
POMPEY THE GREAT," "MULTI-
TUDE AND SOLITUDE," "LOST
ENDEAVOUR," "CAPTAIN MAR-
GARET," "THE TRAGEDY OF
NAN," ETC.

LONDON
WILLIAMS AND NORGATE

A17(a) title-page

WILLIAM
SHAKESPEARE

by

JOHN MASEFIELD

WILLIAM HEINEMANN LTD
MELBOURNE :: LONDON :: TORONTO

A17(d) title-page

WILLIAM
SHAKESPEARE

John Masefield

QUATERCENTENARY EDITION

MERCURY BOOKS
LONDON

A17(f) title-page

A16 THE STREET OF TO-DAY

A16(a) First English edition (1911)

THE | STREET OF TO-DAY [in red] | BY | JOHN MASEFIELD | [publisher's device including 'Shadows we are and | Like Shadows depart'] | *By the Street of To-day | Man goes to the House of To-morrow* | LONDON : J. M. DENT & SONS LTD. [in red] | 29 AND 30 BEDFORD STREET [point] 1911
(All width centred)

Bibliographies: Danielson 174, Williams p.8, Simmons [16], Nevinson p.17, Handley-Taylor p.29, Wight [16]

Collation: [π]⁴ A–2A⁸ 2B⁴ (J, V and W not used); signatures right foot of page; 200 leaves; 189 × 128mm.; [i–viii] [1] 2–235 [236] 237–392

Pagination contents: [i] half-title: 'THE STREET OF TO-DAY'; [ii] 'OTHER NOVELS OF GREAT | INTEREST | [six titles, their authors, size, price and press reviews listed] | [rule] | J. M. DENT & SONS LTD.' (within ruled border: 136 × 68mm., none of these lines constituting rules, or borders completely touches each other); [iii] title-page; [iv] '*All rights reserved*'; [v] '*To LUCY*' (the 'T' and 'Y' are swash); [vi] blank; [vii] [Untitled Verse] ('O beauty, I have wandered far;') dated on extreme left margin '*July 6th*, 1909.' and on extreme right '*August 13th*, 1910.'; [viii] blank; [1]–235 text (book I); [236] blank; 237–392 text (book II) (at foot of p.392: 'THE TEMPLE PRESS, PRINTERS, LETCHWORTH')

Paper: wove paper

Running title: 'THE STREET OF TO-DAY' (52mm.) on both verso and recto, pp.2–392

Binding: turquoise cloth (see notes). On spine, in gold: 'THE | STREET | OF | TO-DAY | [thick dark-blue / black rule, 30mm.] | BY | JOHN | MASEFIELD | [thick dark-blue / black rule, 30mm.] | J. M. DENT | & SONS Lᵀᴰ' (all width centred and enclosed within a dark-blue / black patterned border comprising squares and pointed lines: 189 × 38mm.) On upper cover, in dark-blue / black: 'THE STREET | OF TO-DAY | BY | JOHN MASEFIELD' (all enclosed within a dark-blue / black patterned border comprising squares and pointed lines: 190 × 122mm.) (Simmons states the binding uses black ink, Danielson notes dark blue and Wight describes it as blue. If we dismiss the possibility of variant bindings then *very* dark blue is a possibility and I have adopted the compromise 'dark-blue / black'.) Lower cover: blank. Top edge gilt, others trimmed. Binding measurements: 196 × 129mm. (covers), 196 × 48mm. (spine). End-papers: wove paper.

Publication date: published, according to Simmons, 22 March 1911 in an edition of 2600 copies

Price: 6s.

Contents:
[Untitled Verse] ('O beauty, I have wandered far;')
The Street of To-Day ('Lionel Heseltine sat at dinner between a sporting lady and a Dean's daughter.')

Notes:
Many of the characters of *Multitude and Solitude* are common to this novel. Lionel Heseltine attains the status of leading character here, and thus highlights the structural problems of the latter part of *Multitude and Solitude* where Roger Naldrett is eclipsed in Masefield's attention by Heseltine.

The text is particularly prone to inked spaces.

Wight notes that 'some early copies were bound in yellow-green cloth'. According to notes within a copy present in Harvard College Library (Houghton *EC9.M377.911sa) this was a 'publisher's trial binding'. A description of this binding (more precisely described as 'green cloth') is as follows:

Bound in green cloth. On spine, in gold: 'THE | STREET | OF | TO-DAY | [thick white rule, 30mm.] | BY | JOHN | MASEFIELD | [thick white rule, 30mm.] | J. M. DENT | & SONS Lᵀᴰ' (all width centred and enclosed within a white patterned border comprising squares and pointed lines: 191 × 39mm.) On upper cover, in gold: 'THE STREET | OF TO-DAY | BY | JOHN MASEFIELD' (all enclosed within a white patterned border comprising squares and pointed lines: 191 × 123mm.) Lower cover: blank. Top edge gilt, others trimmed. Binding measurements: 196 × 129mm. (covers), 196 × 48mm. (spine). End-papers: wove paper.

Grant Richards, in *Author Hunting*, writes:

> I should have had... *The Street of To-day*, but cold feet interfered... I had an option on it which I did not choose to exercise. As a result of my lack of courage (or capital) Dents added to their reputation...
>
> (Grant Richards, *Author Hunting*, Hamish Hamilton, 1934. p.229)

G.H. Perris, the business partner of C.F. Cazenove in the Literary Agency of London, wrote to Masefield in October 1910 informing the author of Richards' decision:

> We hear from Mr. Richards this morning, apologising for the delay in giving a decision on "The Street of To-Day", and returning both copies of the MS. He says:-
>
> "I read most of it twice myself and have been waiting for the opinion of someone else. Frankly, I do not see how, when I look into the sales of the two previous novels, one could hope to publish it and get a sale to justify the advance provided

for by the opinion. Perhaps you realise why I feel that although it contains a number of beautiful passages it is not likely to please greatly any one large class of reader. Nor is it, I fear, probable that there will be any return from America. Briefly, therefore, although I should like to publish the book because I hate to see a novel by Mr. Masefield go elsewhere, I would not do so on anything like the terms as to advance which I have had to have in mind."

You will remember the advance is £120, one half on delivery of MS. and the other on publication. Both Nelson's and Mr. Dent are interested in your work, and we think of offering it in the first instance to Nelson's. I do not know if you have any views on the matter.

(G.H. Perris, letter to John Masefield, 25 october 1910)
(University of Arizona Library. MS.50)

Masefield's views were, presumably, in accordance with those of the Literary Agency of London and it appears that Nelson were offered the novel. Cazenove reported, however:

I saw Buchan yesterday and he was quite apologetic about the delay over your book. It appears that he read it himself and then passed it over to one of his partners. I gather that their business is growing so enormously that they are all terribly overworked, and this is the reason that Tom Nelson had not been able to get to it. Buchan promised me faithfully that we should hear from him very shortly. I gather that Buchan is quite keen about the second part of the book, but that he would like the beginning altered, and he asked me if there would be any likelihood of your listening to some suggestions in case he put any forward. That, of course, I must leave to you.

I don't want to move you from Nelson in whom I have, from every point of view, a strong belief; but we must not forget Dent, or that yet another publisher has been asking me for your fiction.

(C.F. Cazenove, letter to John Masefield, 23 December 1910)
(University of Arizona Library. MS.50)

Masefield, it appears, was anxious merely to get the novel published. He was, however, interested to hear of John Buchan's views. Buchan (1875–1940) had been chief literary adviser to Thomas Nelson since 1906. (His best-known novel, *The Thirty-Nine Steps*, was not published until 1915). Masefield's response to Cazenove was as follows:

I am quite eager to have my novel printed before it becomes the Street of the Day before yesterday; but what does Mr Buchan suggest? I will consider suggestions, from so distinguished a writer; but I doubt if I can re-write or revise now that the mood has gone from me. You see the book is part of a series that I have in view, + part 1 brings in people that will be developed in other books.

(John Masefield, letter to C.F. Cazenove, 27 December 1910)
(University of Arizona Library. MS.50, V.II)

It appears that J.M. Dent was offered the novel at around the same time as Nelson. Cazenove reported:

I have just had a talk with Dent, who has read "The Street", and he is really keen. He makes us a counter-offer of £100, which he will pay now, on account of a shilling up to the first 5,000 copies, and 20% thereafter. He would like to publish this Spring, and we have the right of making an American sale up to the time of first issue. If we cannot get a copyright edition in America, Dent will give us half the American royalties or profits, and he wants the offer of your next novel.

I think his keenness is genuine. He offers to push it in every conceivable fashion, and, speaking, generally, his anxiety to get hold of your work remains unabated. I think, on the whole, we had better take it, but I should like to have your definite instructions.

He seems to think that the book wants pruning. He put his criticism with a diffidence that again I think was genuine. His offer is for the book as it stands. If you would like to have a chat with him, or hear what a specially competent reader has to say, he would be glad. That seems to me quite a decent way of putting it.

(C.F. Cazenove, letter to John Masefield, 17 January 1911)
(University of Arizona Library. MS.50, V.II)

Information in the Constance Babington Smith archive (in the possession of The John Masefield Society) suggests (on the authority of Judith Masefield) that the dedicatee of the novel was Lucy Silcox, headmistress of St. Felix's School, Southwold. She was a friend of the family (Judith was educated for a time at the school) and apparently visited the Masefields during one of their holidays in Ireland. See also B205.

This title was suppressed by Masefield in 1922. The author tried to redefine his career in the 1920s and attempted to kill many early titles. This, however, was the only novel which he successfully suppressed. Details are recorded in the files of The Society of Authors as G.H. Thring advised and represented Masefield. Dent sent an account in February 1922 for the period 1 July 1920 to 31 December 1921. This states that *The Street of To-Day* was not reprinted during this time, 26 copies were on hand as at 1 July 1920 and 5 on hand as at 31 December. Accordingly Masefield earned a royalty of £1.1.s.1d. (BL, Add.Mss.56577, f.25). Presumably thinking that a reprint may be imminent, Masefield wrote to G.H. Thring stating:

I should be very glad if this book could now be allowed to die a natural death. Perhaps Mr D[ent] could be persuaded not to reprint.

(John Masefield, letter to G.H. Thring, 26 February [1922])
(BL, Add.Mss.56577, f.26)

Thring wrote to the publishing firm and Dent replied at the beginning of March:

> I should really like to oblige Mr. Masefield in this matter if it were fair to do so, and I did refrain from putting the book into cheap form when he wished me to do so – though I cannot myself see any reason for this. I do not like the book being destroyed – apart from Mr. Masefield's wishes – there is some good stuff in it if I know anything about literature and I am loath to destroy it, besides, the book has a little sale in America.
>
> (J.M. Dent, letter to G.H. Thring, 1 March 1922)
(BL, Add.Mss.56577, f.30)

Hearing nothing further, Thring pressed the matter on 21 April 1922 and J.M. Dent responded on 25 April stating he would re-read the work. Meanwhile Hugh R. Dent noted on 27 April 1922 the consideration that:

> …we would point out that we have stereo-plates of the work which cost us £19.18s.0d. and the agreement provides for the payment of three-fourths of the cost of these stereos. We should prefer to keep the book in print, although the sale is slow, but if we do agree to let the book die out it would only be fair that an undertaking be given us that no other publisher should have the right to publish it.
>
> (Hugh R. Dent, letter to G.H. Thring, 27 April 1922)
(BL, Add.Mss.56577, f.72)

The next preserved document is a letter from Thring (dated 29 April 1922) to Masefield explaining:

> …I spoke to Mr. Hugh Dent on the telephone to-day, and he stated that he was quite ready to allow the book to die out without any payment by yourself, subject to your giving the undertaking asked for in the second paragraph of the letter from his firm…
>
> (G.H. Thring, letter to John Masefield, 29 April 1922)
(BL, Add.Mss.56577, f.77)

(The second paragraph referred to the understanding that no other publisher should have the right to publish). Masefield replied clearly stating his intentions towards the book and suggesting a goodwill gesture due to the helpful manner in which Dents were pursuing the matter:

> I will gladly undertake not to let any other publisher print *Street of Today* [*sic*]. I want it to die. I feel I ought to pay up the 3/4ths of the cost of the stereos, + am quite willing to do this, all the more because Messrs Dent have been willing to oblige me.
>
> (John Masefield, letter to G.H. Thring, [1 May 1922])
(BL, Add.Mss.56577, f.85)

Thring responded on 2 May informing Masefield that he was under no moral obligation to cover the cost of the stereos. Thring continued:

> If, however, you are anxious to mark your sense of obligation to Messrs Dent you might pay a nominal sum of say £3.3. to £5.5.
>
> (G.H. Thring, letter to John Masefield, 2 May 1922)
(BL, Add.Mss.56577, f.86)

The business was settled with a cancellation agreement which Masefield signed and returned (with a cheque for £5.5.) to The Society of Authors on 3 May 1922. The novel was therefore quietly suppressed, Masefield never revised it and allowed it to fade into obscurity.

Masefield was sent (via The Society of Authors) a draft of L.A.G. Strong's 1952 British Council study of Masefield. Writing to The Society of Authors, Masefield strongly objected to quotation from *The Street of To-Day*:

> Some of the quotations are… from a suppressed book, *The Street of Today* [*sic*], that I do not wish to be quoted from… I would like the *Street of Today* [*sic*] passages deleted altogether. …I was ill when I wrote the book, & have done all that I could to suppress it utterly. The rights in it are mine, & perhaps I could insist on the suppression(?), and perhaps, as the book is still only in galley, the cut can be easily made. If we do the generous thing about the other quotations, he and the Council ought to meet us on this point. Do you agree?
>
> (John Masefield, letter to [Gabrielle] Curry, 29 November 1951)
(BL, Add.Mss.56623, ff.53–54)

Copies seen: BL (012621.ccc.23) stamped 20 MAR 1911; ULL (Special Collections) signature of Ethel Ross; Ledbury Library; Library of The John Masefield Society; Harvard College Library (Houghton *EC9.M377.911s) inscribed 'Life, I have sought to see thy star | That other men might see. | J. Masefield', bookplate of John Quinn; Harvard College Library (Houghton *EC9.M377.911sa) green cloth binding; Columbia University Libraries (Special Collections B825.M377.W35.1911); NYPL (Berg Collection) inscribed 'Grant Richards | from John Masefield. | April 25th. 1911.'

Reprinted:

'Second edition'	[first edition, second impression]	Oct 1911

A16(b) *First American edition (1911)*

THE | STREET OF TO-DAY [in red] | BY | JOHN MASEFIELD | [publisher's device including 'Shadows we are and | Like Shadows depart'] | *By the Street of To-day* | *Man goes to the House of To-morrow* | LONDON : J. M. DENT & SONS LTD. [in red] | NEW YORK : E. P. DUTTON & CO.
(All width centred)

Bibliographies: Danielson [unrecorded], Williams [unrecorded], Simmons [noted on p.31], Nevinson [unrecorded], Handley-Taylor p.29, Wight 16a

Collation: [π]⁴ A–2A⁸ 2B⁴ (J, V and W not used); signatures right foot of page; 200 leaves; 191 × 128mm.; [i–viii] [1] 2–235 [236] 237–392

Pagination contents: [i–ii] blank; [iii] title-page; [iv] '*All rights reserved*'; [v] '*To LUCY*' (the 'T' and 'Y' are swash); [vi] blank; [vii] [Untitled Verse] ('O beauty, I have wandered far;') dated on extreme left margin '*July 6th,* 1909.' and on extreme right '*August* 13*th,* 1910.'; [viii] blank; [1]–235 text (book I); [236] blank; 237–392 text (book II) (at foot of p.392: 'THE TEMPLE PRESS, PRINTERS, LETCHWORTH')

Paper: wove paper

Running title: 'THE STREET OF TO-DAY' (52mm.) on both verso and recto, pp.2–392

Binding: light-blue / turquoise cloth. On spine, in gold: 'THE | STREET | OF | TO-DAY | [thick black rule, 30mm.] | BY | JOHN | MASEFIELD | [thick black rule, 30mm.] | E P | DUTTON | AND CO' (all width centred and enclosed within a black patterned border comprising squares and pointed lines: 190 × 38mm.) On upper cover: 'THE STREET | OF TO-DAY | BY | JOHN MASEFIELD' (all enclosed within a black patterned border comprising squares and pointed lines: 189 × 122mm.) Lower cover: blank. Top edge gilt, others trimmed. Binding measurements: 196 × 127mm. (covers), 196 × 51mm. (spine). End-papers: wove paper.

Publication date: published, according to Simmons, April 1911

Price: $1.50

Contents:
as for A16(a)

Notes:
The first English edition (A16(a)) notes only J.M. Dent on the title-page. The American edition, is distinguishable by the addition of E.P. Dutton. The Dent name remains. The date of publication is excluded.

Although an American *reprint* of this title appears to comprise an English printing with an American cancel-title, this edition, the first American edition, does not carry a cancellans. The printers, as cited on p.392 suggest, however, that the sheets originate from England. With the text of the novel commencing on the first leaf of gathering A, it might be suggested that the first gathering was probably an American printing. Close attention to the poem (appearing on [π]4) reveals, however, an inked space (between 'forth' and 'flowers' on line 10) to be present in both English and American editions. Evidence in the archives of The Society of Authors reveals that stereoplates of the work were made (see BL, Add.Mss.56577, f.72). It therefore seems likely that a duplicate set were sent by J.M. Dent to E.P. Dutton. The only changes made to these plates were the removal of type on pp.[i–ii] (based conjecturally on Wight's volume description) and alterations to the title-page. (The removal of Dent's address and substitution with the name of the Dutton firm therefore removed the publication date). The edition therefore comprises an American printing of English plates (with minor alterations) and an American binding.

The publishing agreement between Masefield and Dent probably allowed Masefield to place the work in America himself until publication by Dent (see notes to A16(a)). Cazenove, however, reported:

> We have not yet been able to sell the "Street" in America, though we have been working over as many publishers as we could in the time. I think perhaps there is no harm in your seeing the accompanying report from one of them whose name I had perhaps better not mention in the meantime. I met the writer when I was in America – an Englishman of some ability. The passage I have marked is rather interesting. It illustrates clearly the difficulty one has in selling the best stuff to the Yankees. We are still continuing our work… but in view of our refusals I cannot feel very sanguine. I only want you to understand that we have really done our best. Perhaps you would let me have the report back again.

> …I have just seen Dent. As the book is now out he has, under the contract the right of handling America, and he has arranged that Dutton shall take 500 copies and pay a 10% royalty on sales. This, of course, is only a start, and one may hope for better things. In view of our refusals in other quarters and of the terms of the agreement with Dent we cannot in any case object. Dutton's have very close relations with Dent; they have a large business with Everyman, but I am disappointed we cannot get one of the houses more closely identified with fiction to take up "The Street".

> > (C.F. Cazenove, letter to John Masefield, 20 March 1911)
> > (University of Arizona Library. MS.50)

The only examined copy of this edition was slightly damaged with pp.[i–ii] missing and lacking both front free and rear free end-papers. Additional information was provided by Wight.

Copies seen: Bailey/Howe Library, University of Vermont (TR DREW 32) lacking pp.[i–ii] and lacking both front free and rear free end-papers

Reprinted:

'Second Edition' [first edition, second impression] Aug 1911

A16(c) First Colonial edition ([1911?])

THE | STREET OF TO-DAY | BY | JOHN MASEFIELD | *By the Street of To-day* | *Man goes to the House of To-morrow* | COLONIAL EDITION | (*For Circulation in the British Colonies and India only*) | LONDON | T. FISHER UNWIN | ADELPHI TERRACE
(All width centred)

Bibliographies: Danielson [unrecorded], Williams [unrecorded], Simmons [unrecorded], Nevinson [unrecorded], Handley-Taylor [unrecorded], Wight [unrecorded]

Collation: [π]⁴ (±[π]1 ±[π]2) A–2A⁸ 2B⁴ (J, V and W not used); signatures right foot of page; 200 leaves; 180 × 117mm.; [i–viii] [1] 2–235 [236] 237–392

Pagination contents: [i] half-title: 'THE STREET OF TO-DAY'; [ii] 'Unwin's Colonial Library. | [68 titles and their authors listed in two columns] | [rule] | LONDON: T. FISHER UNWIN. | NOTE.–*A List of the Colonial Library, Nos.* I *to* 378, *can be had on application.* | Books marked thus * are not to be imported into the Dominion of Canada.' (within ruled border: 154 × 91mm.); [iii] title-page; [iv] '*All rights reserved*'; [v] '*To LUCY*' (the 'T' and 'Y' are swash); [vi] blank; [vii] [Untitled Verse] ('O beauty, I have wandered far;') dated on extreme left margin '*July 6th,* 1909.' and on extreme right '*August 13th,* 1910.'; [viii] blank; [1]–235 text (book I); [236] blank; 237–392 text (book II) (at foot of p.392: 'THE TEMPLE PRESS, PRINTERS, LETCHWORTH')

Paper: wove paper

Running title: 'THE STREET OF TO-DAY' (52mm.) on both verso and recto, pp.2–392

Binding: light brown cloth. On spine, in black: 'The | Street of | To-day | John | Masefield | UNWIN'S | LIBRARY.' (all width centred). On upper cover, in black: 'The | Street of To-day | John Masefield'. Lower cover: blank. All edges trimmed. Binding measurements: 187 × 119mm. (covers), 187 × 50mm. (spine). End-papers: wove paper.

Publication date: [1911?]

Price: unknown

Contents:
as for A16(a)

Notes:
The setting of type and collation suggests that Dent provided T. Fisher Unwin with sheets. The titles listed on p.[ii] suggest publication during 1911, or later.

Copies seen: private collection (PWE)

A16(d) 'Second' American edition (1916)

THE | STREET OF TO-DAY | BY | JOHN MASEFIELD | [publisher's device including monogram of 'E' 'P' and 'D': 37 × 25mm.] | *By the Street of To-day* | *Man goes to the House of To-morrow* | NEW EDITION | NEW YORK | E. P. DUTTON & CO. | 1916
(All width centred)

Bibliographies: Danielson [unrecorded], Williams [unrecorded], Simmons [unrecorded], Nevinson [unrecorded], Handley-Taylor [unrecorded], Wight [unrecorded]

Collation: [π]⁴ (-[π]1 ±[π]2) A–2A⁸ 2B⁴ (J, V and W not used), signatures right foot of page, 199 leaves, 188 × 122mm.; [i–vi] [1] 2–235 [236] 237–392

Pagination contents: [i] title-page; [ii] blank; [iii] '*To LUCY*' (the 'T' and 'Y' are swash); [iv] blank; [v] [Untitled Verse] ('O beauty, I have wandered far;') dated on extreme left margin '*July 6th,* 1909.' and on extreme right '*August 13th,* 1910.'; [vi] blank; [1]–235 text (book I); [236] blank; 237–392 text (book II) (at foot of p.392: 'THE TEMPLE PRESS, PRINTERS, LETCHWORTH')

Paper: wove paper

Running title: 'THE STREET OF TO-DAY' (52mm.) on both verso and recto, pp.2–392

Binding: burgundy cloth. On spine, in gold: 'THE | STREET | OF | TO=DAY | [rule] | MASEFIELD | E.P. DUTTON | & CO.' (all width centred). On upper cover, in gold: 'THE STREET | OF TO-DAY | [ornament including hour-glass and two flowers: 15 × 63mm.] | JOHN MASEFIELD' (all enclosed within blind ruled border: 187 × 117mm.) Lower cover: blank. All edges trimmed. Binding measurements: 193 × 124mm. (covers), 193 × 50mm. (spine). End-papers: wove paper.

Publication date: 1916

Price: $1.50

Contents:
as for A16(a)

Notes:

In the examined copy the first leaf of the first gathering ([π]1) has been excised, leaving a stub. The second leaf was a cancel-title. Therefore, although the title-page states 'NEW EDITION', the similarities to A16(a) are many. Another copy of the title printed by Dutton located in the NYPL is dated 1917 on the title-page and, as with the 1916 edition, excludes reprint information. However, the 1917 edition includes a half-title ([π]1) and no cancel leaves are present. Both cite the Letchworth press at the rear of the volume. However, the type used for the printer is different. Features of the 1917 edition NYPL copy are also present in a copy of the 1917 edition held at the Bodleian.

I suggest that the 1916 edition was therefore a small trial issue using sheets imported by Dutton. For the 1917 edition Dutton had produced their own first gathering (comprising the preliminaries) without the need for cancel leaves and may have acquired their own set of plates from the Letchworth press. Although termed a 'Second American edition' due to the preliminaries, the setting of text for the novel itself is as in all previous editions.

Copies seen: NYPL (NCW 1916) 278550A

Reprinted as:
'New Edition'   ["Second edition", second impression]   1917
    in burgundy cloth binding (see NYPL (NCW 1917) 786170)
        in blue cloth binding (see Bodleian, Additional Masefield papers 8) inscribed on front free end-paper: 'For Querie My | from | John Masefield. | September. 1960. | [new paragraph] O, Beauty, I have wandered far. | Peace, I have suffered seeking Thee, | Life. I have sought to see Thy Star, | That other men might see. | [new paragraph] A book written in ill health, on the | brink of collapse, and unreadable, | utterly, by any mortal being.'

A17 WILLIAM SHAKESPEARE   1911

A17(a) First English edition (1911)

WILLIAM | SHAKESPEARE | BY | JOHN MASEFIELD | AUTHOR OF "THE TRAGEDY OF | POMPEY THE GREAT," "MULTI- | TUDE AND SOLITUDE," "LOST | ENDEAVOUR," "CAPTAIN MAR- | GARET," "THE TRAGEDY OF | NAN," ETC. | LONDON | WILLIAMS AND NORGATE
(Title, author and list of works width centred and enclosed by two pillars supporting carved slab. Place of publication and publisher enclosed within bordered plaque on a lower slab supporting the two pillars: 129 × 86mm. All width centred)

Bibliographies: Danielson 175, Williams p.9, Simmons [17], Nevinson p.17, Handley-Taylor p.29, Wight [17]

Collation: [A]¹⁶ B-H¹⁶; leaves B2, C2, D2, E2, F2, G2 and H2 are also signed; signatures left foot of page; 128 leaves; 168 × 103mm.; [i–iv] v–viii 9–256

Pagination contents: [i] 'HOME UNIVERSITY LIBRARY | OF MODERN KNOWLEDGE | WILLIAM SHAKESPEARE | BY JOHN MASEFIELD | LONDON | WILLIAMS & NORGATE | [rule] | HENRY HOLT & CO., NEW YORK | CANADA : WM. BRIGGS, TORONTO'; [ii] 'HOME | UNIVERSITY | LIBRARY | OF | MODERN KNOWLEDGE | [rule] | *Editors :* | HERBERT FISHER, M.A., F.B.A. | PROF. GILBERT MURRAY, D.LITT., | LL.D., F.B.A. | PROF. J. ARTHUR THOMSON, M.A. | NEW YORK | HENRY HOLT AND COMPANY' (enclosed within architectural border as title-page, with different upper carved slab. Lines 1–5 ranged upper-left and justified on left margin, all other lines width centred with the exception of line 10); [iii] title-page; [iv] 'PRINTED BY | HAZELL, WATSON AND VINEY, LD., | LONDON AND AYLESBURY.'; v–vi [untitled preface] ('This book is written partly for the use of people who are reading Shakespeare, and partly to encourage the study of the plays.') (unsigned); vii–viii 'CONTENTS' (three chapters listed with titles and page references. An index is also listed); 9–252 text; 253–56 'INDEX OF CHARACTERS' (at foot of p.256: '[rule] | *Printed by Hazell, Watson & Viney, Ld., London and Aylesbury.*')

Paper: wove paper

Running title: 'WILLIAM SHAKESPEARE' (50mm.) on verso; recto title comprises chapter title or subsection, pp.10–252

Binding: light-green cloth with cross-hatched pattern and bold vertical lines 3mm. apart. On spine, in gold: '[double rule] | SHAKE- | SPEARE | [short rule] | JOHN | MASEFIELD | [double rule] | [single rule] | WILLIAMS | & NORGATE | [double rule]' (all width centred). On upper cover, in blind: '[circular publisher's device, diameter: 20mm.]' and 'HOME | UNIVERSITY | LIBRARY [centred within rectangle: 18 × 21mm.] | [rule, 101mm.]' (publisher's device ranged upper-left, 'HOME UNIVERSITY LIBRARY' ranged upper-right) (all enclosed within blind ruled border: 168 × 101mm.) This creates, with the single rule, two rectangles measuring 45 × 101mm. and 123 × 101mm. respectively from the top. On lower cover: blind ruled border: 168 × 101mm. Upper-outside edge stained green, others trimmed. Binding measurements: 172 × 104mm. (covers), 172 × 28mm. (spine). End-papers: wove paper.

Also issued in leather (according to Danielson) although this is omitted from the *English Catalogue of Books*

Publication date: published, according to Simmons, 5 April 1911

Price: 1s.

Contents:
[Untitled preface] ('This book is written partly for the use of people who are reading…')
I. The Life of Shakespeare ('Stratford-on-Avon is cleaner, better paved…')
II. The Elizabethan Theatres ('The Elizabethan theatres were square, circular…')
III. The Plays ('Three plays belong to Shakespeare's first period of original creative…')
Index of Characters

Notes:
A document in the archives of The Society of Authors (BL, Add.Mss.56614, f.111) cites the date of the original contract for this edition. It was signed 11 October 1910. A letter from November 1950 from Masefield to The Society of Authors notes that 'the books in this Library were purchased outright by the Publishers.' (see BL, Add.Mss.56622, f.102).

The title was published as the second volume within William and Norgate's 'Home University Library'. Masefield's involvement was the result of his friendship with Gilbert Murray who was an editor of the series. G.H. Perris (of the Literary Agency of London) was the originator of the series.

Chapter III, entitled 'The Plays', also contains sub-sections entitled 'Work Attributed to Shakespeare', 'The Poems' and 'Author's Note'.

This is not Masefield's first published piece on Shakespeare. A letter on 'The Suggested Shakespeare Memorial Theatre' was published in *The Times* for 22 October 1909 (C125.001) and a book review 'Shakespeare's Sea Terms Explained' was published in *The Manchester Guardian* on 5 January 1911 (C055.307). After publication, in April 1932, a commemorative ode was the first verse spoken on stage at the opening of the rebuilt Shakespeare Memorial Theatre, Stratford. Masefield was to give the Romanes Lecture in 1924 entitled *Shakespeare and Spiritual Life* (A74) and also appealed for *An Elizabethan Theatre in London* (A164) many years before Sam Wanamaker's realised Globe Theatre project. See also *A Macbeth Production* (A142) and *Thanks Before Going With Other Gratitude For Old Delight…* (A150).

Masefield's critical essay has been received with varying appreciation since 1911. John Gielgud praised the plot summaries and reprinted them in numerous programmes. A recent reference occurs in Philip Edwards' 1985 edition of *Hamlet* (Cambridge University Press) in which Edwards states Masefield on *Hamlet* is '…more interesting and valuable than Eliot's better-known pages'. Kenneth Muir directs his readers to Masefield in his introduction to the Arden *King Lear* and maintains (in *Shakespeare – A Bibliographical Guide*, ed. Stanley Wells) there are 'valuable points… to be found'. E.M.W. Tillyard (in *Shakespeare's History Plays*) devoted much attention to defending Prince Hal against Masefield's assault.

A copy of this edition held in W.B. Yeats' library, in Dalkey, Ireland (*1261) is inscribed 'W B Yeats | from John Masefield | July 27, 1911.' Also enclosed is a holograph letter (from the same date) including the statement 'if there is anything good in it, it was probably suggested by you…'

L.A.G. Strong particularly praised the work in his 1952 study of Masefield (L.A.G. Strong, *John Masefield*, published for the British Council and the National Book League by Longmans, Green and Co., 1952). Certain statements made by Strong about the book were, however, Masefield's. Asked to read galley proofs of Strong's work in November 1951, Masefield stated to The Society of Authors:

> …I had not the happiness of "many sessions" with the late J.M. Synge, and cannot have talked much of Shakespeare with him at any time. I was much in the theatre and among theatrical people when I wrote the Shakespeare book. Young men had seen Mr William Poel's productions, & were in the Court Theatre movement. My little Shakespeare book was a part of those two enthusiasms, and those two enthusiasms were perhaps something of an answer to certain cries that seemed to the young of those days to need reply. But all that time is dead & the fevers of it are forgotten.
>
> (John Masefield, letter to [Gabrielle] Curry, 30 November [1951])
> (BL, Add.Mss.56623, ff.56–57)

In 1963 Masefield noted the circumstances behind this edition – and his subsequent re-written edition:

> I sold this book outright to the publishers, expecting to have half a year to write it in. A day or two later, I learned that the copy was wanted in six weeks. Well, tho' the funeral was tomorrow, so to speak, the corpse was there on time, but I was unhappy about it; and was thankful to have a chance, long afterwards, to re-write it…
>
> (John Masefield, letter to Anne Munro-Kerr, [September 1963])
> (Archives of The Society of Authors)

Copies seen: BL (12199.p1/29) stamped 12 APR 1911, rebound; Ledbury Library; ULL (Special Collections)

A17(b) *First American edition (1911)*

WILLIAM | SHAKESPEARE | BY | JOHN MASEFIELD | AUTHOR OF "THE TRAGEDY OF POMPEY THE GREAT," | "MULTITUDE AND SOLITUDE," "LOST ENDEAVOUR," | "CAPTAIN MARGARET," "THE TRAGEDY OF NAN," ETC. | [publisher's device of owl, laurel wreath and Greek inscription: 20 × 15mm.] | NEW YORK | HENRY HOLT AND COMPANY | LONDON | WILLIAMS AND NORGATE
(Lines 5–7 justified on both left and right margins, all other lines width centred)

Bibliographies: Danielson [unrecorded], Williams [unrecorded], Simmons [noted on p.32], Nevinson [unrecorded], Handley-Taylor p.29, Wight 17a

Collation: [A-Q]⁸ (J not used); 128 leaves; 175 × 120mm.; [i–iv] v–vi [vii] viii 9–256

Pagination contents: [i] 'HOME UNIVERSITY LIBRARY | OF MODERN KNOWLEDGE | No. 2 | *Editors :* | HERBERT FISHER, M.A., F.B.A. | PROF. GILBERT MURRAY, LITT.D., | LL.D., F.B.A. | PROF. J. ARTHUR THOMSON, M.A. | PROF. WILLIAM T. BREWSTER, M.A.'; [ii] 'THE HOME UNIVERSITY LIBRARY | OF MODERN KNOWLEDGE | *VOLUMES NOW READY* | [10 volumes and their authors listed] | *VOLUMES READY IN JULY* | [10 volumes and their authors listed] | [three star device] Other volumes in active preparation'; [iii] title-page; [iv] 'COPYRIGHT, 1911, | BY | HENRY HOLT AND COMPANY | THE UNIVERSITY PRESS, CAMBRIDGE, U.S.A.'; v–vi [untitled preface] ('This book is written partly for the use of people who are reading Shakespeare, and partly to encourage the study of the plays.') (unsigned); [vii]-viii 'CONTENTS' (three chapters listed with titles and page references) (see notes); 9–252 text; 253–56 'INDEX OF CHARACTERS'

Paper: wove paper

Running title: 'WILLIAM SHAKESPEARE' (47mm.) on verso; recto title comprises chapter title or subsection, pp.10–252

Binding: brown cloth. On spine, in gold: 'HOME UNIVERSITY LIBRARY | [device incorporating top of column and owl with outstretched wings: 7 × 25mm.] | SHAKE- | SPEARE | [rule] | MASEFIELD | [device of lighted torch: 22 × 9mm.] | HENRY HOLT | AND COMPANY' (all width centred). On upper cover: '[device incorporating top of column and owl with outstretched wings: 14 × 110mm.] [in blind] | ['HOME UNIVERSITY LIBRARY' in gold within blind ruled border: 9 × 103mm.] | [blind ruled border: 137 × 103mm.] (all enclosed within blind ruled border: 176 × 16mm.) Lower cover: blank. Top edge stained, others trimmed. Binding measurements: 180 × 121mm. (covers), 180 × 36mm. (spine). End-papers: wove paper.

Publication date: published, according to Simmons, 27 May 1911 in an edition of 2000 copies

Price: $0.75

Contents:
as for A17(a)

Notes:
In contrast with the first English edition (see A17(a)), the contents page does not include the index of characters.

As in A17(a), chapter III, entitled 'The Plays', also contains sub-sections entitled 'Work Attributed to Shakespeare', 'The Poems' and 'Author's Note'.

Wight notes 'bound in red cloth'

The copy described above constitutes the first American edition relying on the description provided by Wight. Although he notes 'bound in red cloth' and presumably omits a full description of the spine and upper cover, the edition corresponds with his description. Henry Holt and Company reprinted the edition on numerous occasions and omitted reprint information within the volume. Page [iv] continued to read 'COPYRIGHT, 1911, | BY | HENRY HOLT AND COMPANY | THE UNIVERSITY PRESS, CAMBRIDGE, U.S.A.' Reprints, however, provide a more extensive listing of the Home University Library series. The information provided on page [ii] is therefore crucial in determining earlier editions. The copy described above appears to be the earliest.

Copies seen: Boston Public Library (Rare Books G.3956.62); Harvard College Library (Widener 12463.90 HW PAJH Y)

Reprinted:
[reprint]
> in yellow cloth
> lists 19 'already published' volumes and 7 'future issues' on p.[ii]
> includes four leaf catalogue of 'The Home University Library' at rear of volume

[reprint]
> in yellow cloth
> states '*A complete list of the volumes of* THE | HOME UNIVERSITY LIBRARY *already published* | *will be found at the back of this book*' on p.[ii]
> includes four leaf catalogue of 'The Home University Library' at rear of volume

A17(c) Second English edition (1912)

WILLIAM | SHAKESPEARE | BY | JOHN MASEFIELD | AUTHOR OF "THE TRAGEDY OF | POMPEY THE GREAT," "MULTI- | TUDE AND SOLITUDE," "LOST | ENDEAVOUR," "CAPTAIN MAR- | GARET," "THE TRAGEDY OF | NAN," ETC. | NEW AND REVISED EDITION | LONDON | WILLIAMS AND NORGATE
(Title, author and list of works width centred and enclosed by two pillars supporting carved slab. Place of publication and publisher enclosed within bordered plaque on a lower slab supporting the two pillars: 129 × 86mm. All width centred)

Bibliographies: Danielson [unrecorded], Williams [unrecorded], Simmons [unrecorded], Nevinson [unrecorded], Handley-Taylor [unrecorded], Wight [unrecorded]

Collation: [A]¹⁶ B-H¹⁶; leaves B2, C2, D2, E2, F2, G2 and H2 are also signed; signatures left foot of page; 128 leaves; the catalogue (not included in collation or leaf count) comprises a single unsigned gathering of 4 leaves; 165 × 100mm.; [i–vi] vii–viii 9–256, catalogue pagination: [1] 2–7 [8]

Pagination contents: [i–ii] blank; [iii] 'HOME UNIVERSITY LIBRARY | OF MODERN KNOWLEDGE | WILLIAM SHAKESPEARE | BY JOHN MASEFIELD | LONDON | WILLIAMS & NORGATE | [rule] | HENRY HOLT & CO., NEW YORK | CANADA : WM. BRIGGS, TORONTO INDIA : R. & T. WASHBOURNE, LTD.' (with the exception of lines 1 and 2, which are ranged upper left and justified on left margin; and lines 7, 8 and 9 which are justified on a different left margin, all width centred); [iv] 'HOME | UNIVERSITY | LIBRARY | OF | MODERN KNOWLEDGE | [rule] | *Editors :* | HERBERT FISHER, M.A., F.B.A. | PROF. GILBERT MURRAY, D.LITT., | LL.D., F.B.A. | PROF. J. ARTHUR THOMSON, M.A. | PROF. WILLIAM T. BREWSTER, M.A. | (Columbia University, U.S.A.) | NEW YORK | HENRY HOLT AND COMPANY' (enclosed within architectural border as title page, with different upper carved slab. Lines 1–5 ranged upper-left and justified on left margin, all other lines width centred with the exception of lines 10 and 13); [v] title-page; [vi] blank; vii–viii 'CONTENTS' (three chapters listed with titles and page references. An index is also listed); 9–252 text; 253–56 'INDEX OF CHARACTERS' (at foot of p.256: '[rule] | *Printed by Hazell, Watson & Viney, Ld., London and Aylesbury.*'); [1]-[8] catalogue: 'The | Home University | Library'

Paper: wove paper

Running title: 'WILLIAM SHAKESPEARE' (50mm.) on verso; recto title comprises chapter title or subsection, pp.10–252

Binding: light-green cloth with cross-hatched pattern and bold vertical lines 3mm. apart. On spine, in gold: '[double rule] | SHAKE- | SPEARE | [short rule] | JOHN | MASEFIELD | [double rule] | [single rule] | WILLIAMS | & NORGATE | [double rule]' (all width centred). On upper cover, in blind: '[circular publisher's device, diameter: 20mm.]' and 'HOME | UNIVERSITY | LIBRARY [centred within rectangle: 18 × 21mm.] | [rule, 101mm.]' (publisher's device ranged upper-left, 'HOME UNIVERSITY LIBRARY' ranged upper-right) (all enclosed within blind ruled border: 168 × 101mm.) This creates, with the single rule, two rectangles measuring 45 × 101mm. and 123 × 101mm. respectively from the top. On lower cover: blind ruled border: 168 × 101mm. Upper-outside edge stained green, others trimmed. Binding measurements: 172 × 104mm. (covers), 172 × 28mm. (spine). End-papers: wove paper.

Publication date: May 1912

Price: unknown

Contents:
I. The Life of Shakespeare ('Stratford-on-Avon is cleaner, better paved...')
II. The Elizabethan Theatres ('The Elizabethan theatres were square, circular...')
III. The Plays ('Three plays belong to Shakespeare's first period of original creative...')
Index of Characters

Notes:
The only difference between the first edition (see A17(a)) and this 'new and revised edition' are the opening pages with the deletion of the untitled and unsigned preface, and the inclusion of the catalogue at the rear of the volume. The rest of the book appears to have been printed from plates. Subsequent reprints contain a variety of different catalogues (often tipped-in and comprising a single leaf and also often a tipped-in advertising essay entitled 'Pelmanism as an Intellectual and Social Factor')

It appears that seven months after publication of A17(a), Masefield's agent wrote about corrections for a reprint. It is assumed that Masefield chose merely to delete the preface. Cazenove wrote:

> Shakespeare:- I find the sales are not quite as good as I had thought, but Williams expects to reprint some time early in the New Year. He would like your corrections by the end of the year. I should explain that they have moulds for a rotary plate of 64 pages. It would make a considerable difference to them, therefore, if the alteration affected as few pages as possible. Any given page that you touch at all will have to be set, and then a mould will have to be made from the type and substituted for the existing mould. It follows, therefore, that if you want to alter a certain page, it would be helpful if you could keep the same number of words. Your best plan will be, I think, to send the correction to Perris at Williams & Norgate's, and he would like to have two copies, so that he can write out to New York.
> (C.F. Cazenove, letter to John Masefield, 30 November 1911)
> (University of Arizona Library. MS.50)

Copies seen: private collection (PWE); ULL (Special Collections)

Reprinted:
Reprints of this work are confusing and numerous. They involve at least two publishers and numerous reprint dates. A17(c) was seemingly reprinted in:

Oct 1916
Feb 1918
Mar 1919
Nov 1921
May 1923

as listed in a May 1923 edition. A large format (using the same plates but with more generous margins and a frontispiece of the author, together with the original preface) published by Williams and Norgate in August 1925 lists reprints of the May 1912 edition as:

Apr 1918
Mar 1919
Nov 1921
Jun 1923
Aug 1924

At some time between 1924 and 1928 the Home University Library was taken over by Thornton Butterworth Ltd. The probable date is 1928 as The Society of Authors (for an unknown reason) wrote to that company with reference to the title and received the reply:

"Shakespeare": Masefield. H.U.L. I have just returned to the Office and should like to thank you for your letter dated August 13th, from which I note that we are the owners of the copyright of the above work.

(Thornton Butterworth Ltd, letter to G.H. Thring, 5 October 1928)
(BL, Add.Mss.56586, f.142)

Masefield had sold the copyright outright and The Society of Authors may have been making enquiries about buying it back.

A reprint from Thornton Butterworth Ltd dated August 1933 (that includes the original preface) lists the following as reprints of the May 1912 edition:

Oct 1916
Mar 1919
Oct 1928
Oct 1930
Aug 1933

The *English Catalogue of Books* lists a March 1938 reprint from Thornton Butterworth Ltd. There also appears to be a reprint (not examined) in the Thornton Butterworth 'Keystone Library' from 1938.

In November 1940 Thornton Butterworth Ltd went into voluntary liquidation. 'The Home University Library Ltd' was, however, a separate company and was not insolvent (see BL, Add.Mss.56614, f.37). During November 1940 Masefield attempted to regain control of the book. The Home University Library Ltd. wrote in reply to the enquiries made on Masefield's behalf by The Society of Authors that they were 'not prepared to consider the cancellation' of the agreement (see BL, Add.Mss.56614, f.111). The Home University Library Ltd wrote again to The Society of Authors on 15 April 1941 stating:

...you will no doubt have seen the trade announcement to the effect that the Oxford University Press Ltd. have taken over the Library, and formal transfer will take place shortly.

(Home University Library Ltd, letter to E.J. Mullett, 15 April 1941)
(BL, Add.Mss.56614, f.148)

Oxford University Press reprinted the edition (probably not before 1943) and there may have been subsequent reprints. In 1950 the press wrote to Masefield stating that the volume was out of print and that they did not wish to reprint.

The following provides a listing of copies actually examined:

[reprint] in green cloth binding	(Williams and Norgate)	Mar 1919
[reprint] in green cloth binding	(Williams and Norgate)	May 1923
[reprint] (large format) in red cloth binding	(Williams and Norgate)	Aug 1925
[reprint] in light blue / grey cloth binding	(Thornton Butterworth Ltd)	Aug 1933
[reprint] in grey cloth binding	(Oxford University Press)	1943

A17(d) Third English edition (1954)

WILLIAM | SHAKESPEARE | *by* | JOHN MASEFIELD | [publisher's device of a windmill on a rule with the letters 'W' and 'H'] | WILLIAM HEINEMANN LTD | MELBOURNE : : LONDON : : TORONTO
(All width centred)

Bibliographies: Handley-Taylor [unrecorded], Wight [unrecorded]

Collation: [A]⁸ B-M⁸ (J not used); signatures right foot of page; 96 leaves; 183 × 122mm.; [i–iv] v–vii [viii] 1–184

Pagination contents: [i] half-title: 'WILLIAM SHAKESPEARE'; [ii] *THE WORKS OF JOHN MASEFIELD* | PLAYS: | [12 titles listed] | POETRY: | [20 titles listed] | FICTION: | [14 titles listed] | GENERAL | [17 titles listed]'; [iii] title-page; [iv] 'FIRST PUBLISHED 1954 | PUBLISHED BY | WILLIAM HEINEMANN LTD | 99 GREAT RUSSELL STREET, LONDON, W.C.1 | PRINTED IN GREAT BRITAIN BY THE PUBLISHERS AT | THE WINDMILL PRESS, KINGSWOOD, SURREY'; v–vii 'CONTENTS' (four chapters listed with titles and page references. An index is also listed); [viii] blank; 1–180 text; 181–84 'Index'

Paper: wove paper

Running title: 'WILLIAM SHAKESPEARE' (35mm.) on verso; recto title comprises subsection of each chapter, pp.2–180

Binding: blue cloth. On spine, in gold: '[double rule] | William | Shakespeare | [short rule] | JOHN | MASEFIELD | [double rule] | HEINEMANN' (all width centred). Upper cover: blank. On lower cover, in blind: publisher's windmill device: 18 × 16mm., ranged lower right. All edges trimmed. Binding measurements: 189 × 122mm. (covers), 189 × 29mm. (spine). End-papers: wove paper.

Publication date: published, according to Heinemann Archive sales ledger, on 16 August 1954 in an edition of 4000 copies

Price: 8s.6d.

Contents:
I. Shakespeare and Stratford ('Stratford-on-Avon, the poet's destiny and present place…')
II. The Poems ('At some unknown time in the lost eight years this young man turned…')
III. The Plays ('A good many plays had been known in England before the time…')
IV. Plays Attributed to Shakespeare (Wholly Or In Part) ('During Shakespeare's earlier…')
Index

Notes:

The forty-three years that passed between Masefield's original volume and this rewritten edition saw an obvious change in perspective. These two works, one written by a thirty-three year old, the other by a seventy-six year old and separated by two world wars constitute entirely different books, a fact neglected by previous Masefield bibliographies.

As noted above, Thornton Butterworth Ltd. went into voluntary liquidation in November 1940. Although 'The Home University Library Ltd' was a separate company and not insolvent Masefield suggested to The Society of Authors that:

> If there be any chance of getting control of the book, it might be a good thing to do so.
> (John Masefield, letter to [E.J.] Mullett, [26 November 1940])
> (BL, Add.Mss.56614, f.34)

The Society of Authors presumably asked for clarification of who owned the copyright. Masefield wrote:

> I enclose with this the agreement for the Shakespeare volume. You will see that I have no control over it.
> Probably, it has had no sale for years, but it might conceivably be a good thing to get control re-write and reissue it. After thirty years, I could perhaps do some of it better. At the moment, I suppose the book is dead.
> (John Masefield, letter to [E.J.] Mullett, 28 November [1940])
> (BL, Add.Mss.56614, f.38)

The Home University Library Ltd. replied to The Society of Authors' enquiries on 19 March 1941 stating that they were 'not prepared to consider the cancellation of this Agreement' (see BL, Add.Mss.56614, f.111). The Society presumably wrote to Masefield requesting further instructions. Masefield noted:

> I have no wish to revise the work, if I cannot get it into my hands and rewrite it completely.
> (John Masefield, letter to [E.J.] Mullett, 26 March [1941])
> (BL, Add.Mss.56614, f.122)

Masefield, therefore, appears to have desired a completely rewritten new edition over a decade before this Heinemann edition.

In April 1941 Oxford University Press took over the Home University Library with formal transfer of all contracts (see BL, Add.Mss.56614, f.148). By 1950 reprints of A17(c) had ceased. Masefield's intention, as revealed in a letter to The Society of Authors, was to keep it out of print. This would allow him 'free to write of Shakespeare':

> May I ask you to be so kind as to help me with the following matter? About 40 years ago, Professor Gilbert Murray asked me to write on SHAKESPEARE for a new publication, The Home University Library, published by Williams & Norgate. The books in this Library were purchased outright by the Publishers. Williams & Norgate handed over the book to Butterworths, I send a copy of the Butterworth's agreement. For some years, the book has been in the hands of the Oxford Univ Press who now write, that the book is out of print & that they do not wish to reprint. I enclose their letter. The book is very properly dead, but I would like to have the power of keeping it dead, and certainly to exercise the power in Clause 15 of the enclosed agreement. Will you be so very kind, therefore, as to suggest to The Ox Univ Press that I be now considered free to write of Shakespeare as I may think fit?
> (John Masefield, letter to The Society of Authors, 11 November [1950])
> (BL, Add.Mss.56622, f.102)

Masefield first raised the subject of a new edition of this title to A.S. Frere of Heinemann in October 1952. Masefield stated:

> Recently, the Home University Library sent me the last copies of my little handbook on Shakespeare, which is now out of print: +, of course, being of 1910, [*sic*] long out of date. Would you care to consider a completely revised edition of this, including, say, *the Macbeth Production* [*sic*] book, + other matter.
> (John Masefield, letter to [A.S.] Frere, 7 October [1952])
> (Archives of William Heinemann)

Frere evidently requested a copy of the 'out of date' edition and, in enclosing one, Masefield wrote:

> I am sending with this one of the last copies of the little Shakespeare book. The book was written in 6 weeks over 40 years ago at the urgent request of a friend. As you will see, it needs a complete re-writing and changing; and it is not easy for me to say yet what sort of a book I should make in re-writing it: a much better + fuller one, I hope, even if the youth be gone from it.

(John Masefield, letter to [A.S.] Frere, 14 October 1952)
(Archives of William Heinemann)

A.S. Frere replied to Masefield:

> I have delayed answering your letter of 14th October until we have had a chance to look at your Shakespeare book. Let me say right away that we would like to do it. It could do with some revision but in doing that I hope you will be careful not to lose the youthful rapture which is such an appealing feature of the book. I really do not think it a good idea to include *Macbeth Production* in the Shakespeare book for it would be so much out of place...

(A.S. Frere, letter to John Masefield, 21 October 1952)
(HRHRC, MS (Masefield, J.) Recip William Heinemann Ltd.)

A letter dated 14 December 1952 addressed to Frere includes the note 'I am getting along with the revised Shakespeare'.

In November 1952 Masefield consulted The Society of Authors regarding royalty on what he evidently regarded as a 'technical handbook':

> Please, may I ask you to be so very kind as to give me some professional advice... One point is: the amount of royalty that a technical handbook, published at 6/-, could now pay on publication. I am thinking of reprinting a handbook on Shakespeare. Would 10% be a fair royalty to begin with, rising to 12½% after 2500, + to 15% after 5000? Or would this be grasping?

(John Masefield, letter to [Anne] Munro-Kerr, [November 1952])
(BL, Add.Mss.56624, ff.29–30)

No reply appears to have been preserved, however, these figures suggest an initial bargaining position.

While Masefield was rewriting the text an application was received to quote from the Oxford University Press edition (for a new edition of *Much Ado About Nothing*). Masefield wrote to The Society of Authors:

> The copyright has reverted to me: and I am now re-writing the book almost altogether: + I would therefore rather that the passage from the old book should lie in the dust that it has long deserved + now has. If this should seem to you not quite generous to the man who is working on *Much Ado*, would you consider asking him to let me see the passage he wishes to quote? Possibly it may be less repulsive than some, and can be amended...

(John Masefield, letter to [Anne] Munro-Kerr, 17 February [1953])
(BL, Add.Mss.56624, f.74)

Edward Thompson wrote to Masefield at the beginning of December 1953 to note that Heinemann had '...commenced work on your book WILLIAM SHAKESPEARE...' (see Edward Thompson, letter to John Masefield, 3 December 1953) (HRHRC, MS (Masefield, J.) Recip William Heinemann Ltd.) Proofs were sent towards the end of February the following year:

> We have today sent you the proofs of WILLIAM SHAKESPEARE... I think we can reasonably entertain high hopes for the book's success...

(Alan Hill, letter to John Masefield, 22 February 1954)
(HRHRC, MS (Masefield, J.) Recip William Heinemann Ltd.)

Proofs were returned by Masefield and acknowledged by Alan Hill four days later (see Alan Hill, letter to John Masefield, 26 February 1954) (HRHRC, MS (Masefield, J.) Recip William Heinemann Ltd.) It was several months before Masefield was sent an advance copy and was informed of the publication date:

> I have much pleasure in sending you herewith an advance copy straight from the Press of WILLIAM SHAKESPEARE. It is scheduled for publication on 16th August...

(A.S. Frere, letter to John Masefield, 23 July 1954)
(HRHRC, MS (Masefield, J.) Recip William Heinemann Ltd.)

Copies seen: BL (11768.de.36) stamped 23 JUL 1954; ULL (3 YHKP Mas); ULL (Special Collections) inscribed 'For Mary Ranger. | from | John Masefield. | August the 13th. 1954'

Reprinted:

'Reprinted'	[third edition, second impression]	1956
'Reprinted'	[third edition, third impression]	1961

A17(e) Second American edition (1954)

WILLIAM | SHAKESPEARE | *by* | JOHN MASEFIELD | THE MACMILLAN COMPANY | NEW YORK
(All width centred)

Bibliographies: Handley-Taylor [unrecorded], Wight [unrecorded]

Collation: [A]⁸ B-M⁸ (J not used); signatures right foot of page; 96 leaves; 183 × 122mm.; [i–iv] v–vii [viii] 1–184

Pagination contents: [i] half-title: 'WILLIAM SHAKESPEARE'; [ii] *'THE WORKS OF JOHN MASEFIELD* | PLAYS: | [12 titles listed] | POETRY: | [20 titles listed] | FICTION: | [14 titles listed] | GENERAL | [17 titles listed]'; [iii] title-page; [iv] 'ALL RIGHTS RESERVED | FIRST PUBLISHED IN THE U.S.A. 1954 | PRINTED IN ENGLAND'; v–vii 'CONTENTS' (4 chapters listed with titles and page references. An index is also listed); [viii] blank; 1–180 text; 181–84 'INDEX'

Paper: wove paper

Running title: 'WILLIAM SHAKESPEARE' (35mm.) on verso; recto title comprises subsection of each chapter, pp.2–180

Binding: blue cloth. On spine, in gold: '[double rule] | William | Shakespeare | [short rule] | JOHN | MASEFIELD | [double rule] | MACMILLAN' (all width centred). Covers: blank. All edges trimmed. Binding measurements: 189 × 122mm. (covers), 189 × 29mm. (spine). End-papers: wove paper.

Contents:
as for A17(d)

Publication date: presumably published after 16 August 1954

Price: $1.75

Notes:

Alan Hill wrote to Masefield noting that Macmillan had declared interest in the Heinemann publication:

> I am wondering if you have made any arrangements for WILLIAM SHAKESPEARE in America? We had a letter from the Macmillan Company about a year ago enquiring about the possibility of our supplying them with sheets. If they are proposing to issue the book, doubtless they will write to us again, should they want us to supply copies.
>
> (Alan Hill, letter to John Masefield, 3 March 1954)
> (HRHRC, MS (Masefield, J.) Recip William Heinemann Ltd.)

This volume has obvious typographical similarities to A17(d). The title-page is not a cancellans. However, due to the note on page [iv] it can be assumed this edition was printed for Macmillan by Heinemann using the English setting of the text. The listing of Masefield's works in the preliminaries cites English titles. This hypothesis is confirmed by letters within the archives of The Society of Authors. Masefield wrote to the Society in August 1954 noting the American position and asking for advice regarding Canada:

> Macmillans in New York + Canada have published many of my books but of this re-issue of an old book... they are only buying some sheets; + the question now is for the sale of English copies of the re-issue in Canada.
>
> (John Masefield, letter to [Anne] Munro-Kerr, [10 August 1954])
> (BL, Add.Mss.56625 f.116)

The Society of Authors replied citing information provided by Edward Thompson of the Heinemann Company:

> I am enclosing a copy of a letter I have received from Mr. Edward Thompson concerning arrangements for sales in Canada of William Shakespeare. If, as Mr. Thompson writes, you have agreed Heinemann should pay you 10% of the price received on all copies sold overseas, I assume this will also have to apply to Canada.
>
> (Anne Munro-Kerr, letter to John Masefield, 11 August 1954)
> (BL, Add.Mss.56625 f.117)

This illustrates that Heinemann did indeed provide Macmillan with printed sheets (and that Masefield received ten per cent of the price received by Heinemann). No Canadian copy has been consulted, however.

Copies seen: Columbia University (823SD-M375) stamped 30 NOV 1954

A17(f) Fourth English edition (1964)

WILLIAM | SHAKESPEARE | John Masefield | QUATERCENTENARY EDITION | [publisher's device of 'm' and the winged helmet of Mercury] | MERCURY BOOKS | *LONDON*
(All width centred)

Bibliographies: Wight [unrecorded]

Collation: [A]¹⁶ B-F¹⁶ G⁸ H¹⁶; E5, F5 and H5 are also signed; signatures right foot of page; 120 leaves; 184 × 120mm.; [i–iv] v–vii [viii] ix–x 1–221 [222] 223–27 [228–30]

Pagination contents: [i] half-title: 'WILLIAM SHAKESPEARE | [publisher's device of 'm' and the winged helmet of Mercury] | MERCURY BOOKS | NO. 49'; [ii] 'MERCURY BOOKS | *General Editor: Alan Hill*'; [iii] title-page; [iv] '© JOHN MASEFIELD 1964 | *First published* 1954 *by* | WILLIAM HEINEMANN LTD | *Quatercentenary Edition first published in Mercury Books* 1964 | For copyright reasons this book may not be issued to the public on loan or other- | wise except in its original soft cover. | *A publication of* | THE HEINEMANN GROUP OF PUBLISHERS | 15–16 *Queen Street, Mayfair, London W*.1 | *Printed in Great Britain by* | *Bookprint Limited, Kingswood, Surrey*'; v–vii 'CONTENTS' (seven chapters listed with titles and page references. A preface and index are also listed); [viii] blank; ix–x 'PREFACE TO THE QUATERCENTENARY EDITION' ('I have wished in this edition of a handbook about William Shakespeare...') (signed, 'JOHN MASEFIELD | *September* 1963'); 1–221 text; [222] blank 223–27 'INDEX'; [228–30] blank

Paper: wove paper

Running title: 'WILLIAM SHAKESPEARE' (36mm.) on verso; recto title comprises subsection of each chapter, pp.2–221

Binding: white wrappers. On spine, reading lengthways down spine, from head: 'William Shakespeare [in purple] [vertical rule in purple] John Masefield [in green]', horizontally at foot of spine, in black: '49 | [publisher's device of 'm' and the winged helmet of Mercury] | MERCURY | BOOKS'. On upper wrapper: '[publisher's device of 'm' and the winged helmet of Mercury] MERCURY BOOKS William Shakespeare [in purple] | [long rule in purple] | John Masefield [in green] | [Droeshout portrait in black and white]'. On lower wrapper: 'WILLIAM SHAKESPEARE [in black] | JOHN MASEFIELD [in black] | [publisher's device of 'm' and the winged helmet of Mercury in purple] | MERCURY [in purple] | BOOKS [in purple] | [green rule] | [publisher's blurb] [in black] | 7s 6d net [in black]' entire wrapper with wide border on left side in purple and on right in green. All edges trimmed. Binding measurements: 184 × 120mm. (wrappers), 184 × 13mm. (spine).

Publication date: published, according to the *English Catalogue of Books*, 2 March 1964

Price: 7s.6d.

Contents:
Preface to the Quatercentenary Edition ('I have wished in this edition of a handbook…')
I. Shakespeare and Stratford ('Stratford-on-Avon, the poet's destiny and present place…')
II. The Poems ('At some unknown time in the lost eight years this young man turned…')
III. The Plays ('A good many plays had been known in England before the time…')
IV. Plays Attributed to Shakespeare (Wholly Or In Part) ('During Shakespeare's earlier…')
V. On the Spreading of the Fame of Shakespeare ('To the best of my knowledge the first…')
VI. George Wilkins ('For some months, between 1607 and 1609, Shakespeare must have…')
VII. On John Fletcher ('During the years of Shakespeare's life there were many poets in…')
Index

Notes:
At the time of publication *The Times* announced this new edition by stating that it would cause bibliographers problems in the future. The 1954 edition has been enlarged and it does, indeed, constitute a new edition.

It was Heinemann's suggestion that Masefield write this quatercentenary edition. Alan Hill wrote to Masefield:

> We have been giving some thought to the possibility of publishing your WILLIAM SHAKESPEARE in a special paperback edition, to coincide with next year's 400th anniversary. If we were to do this, would you be willing to write a new Preface to the book, so as to give it a 1964 flavour. The Preface could be as long as you wish. We will not proceed any further in the matter unless we hear from you.
>
> (Alan Hill, letter to John Masefield, 1 July 1963)
> (HRHRC, MS (Masefield, J.) Recip William Heinemann Ltd.)

A letter from the middle of August 1963 responds to Masefield's suggestions:

> … I am writing to thank you for your letter of the 13th August about the proposed additions to your Shakespeare book. Your suggestion of 7,000 words (with roman page numerals) before the text of the book, and a further 8,000 words at the end, suits us admirably. It will mean a minimum of interference with the existing type, and will certainly save time and money.
>
> You ask for a date by which we should like copy for press. Is it asking too much to say 30th September? We do plan to publish the book as early as possible in the new year, and really need to have all the material in the hands of the printer early in October. I am very glad to hear that you agree to Mr. Hill's suggestion about a 10% royalty on a 9/6d book.
>
> (Anthony Beal, letter to John Masefield, 14 August 1963)
> (HRHRC, MS (Masefield, J.) Recip William Heinemann Ltd.)

Copies seen: private collection (PWE); BL (12206.y.1/49) stamped 18 FEB 1964 rebound

Reprinted:
'Heinemann Education Books' paperback   [fourth edition, second impression]   1969

A17(g) Third American edition (1964)

WILLIAM | SHAKESPEARE | *by John Masefield* | FOREWORD BY | DANIEL B. DODSON | COLUMBIA UNIVERSITY | [publisher's device of hand holding a quill pen] | A PREMIER BOOK | FAWCETT PUBLICATIONS, INC., GREENWICH, CONN. | MEMBER OF AMERICAN BOOK PUBLISHERS COUNCIL, INC.
(All width centred)

Bibliographies: Wight [unrecorded]

Collation: 96 unsigned leaves bound by the 'perfect binding' process; 178 × 107mm.; [i–iv] v–xi [12] 13–184 [185–86] 187–91 [192]

Pagination contents: [i] "*An admirable introduction to Shake- | speare and his works by an author who | writes with a lifetime of scholarship be- | hind him, yet succeeds in conveying the | wealth of his knowledge and experience | in simple language.*" | – The Times, London'; [ii] 'PREMIER BOOKS ARE DESIGNED TO BRING TO A LARGER | READING PUBLIC OUTSTANDING BOOKS AT SMALL COST'; [iii] title-page; [iv] 'A Premier Book published by arrangement with | William Heinemann, Ltd., London | Copyright © 1964 by John Masefield | Foreword copyright © 1964 by Fawcett Publications, Inc. | All rights reserved, including the right to reproduce | this book or portions thereof. | First Premier printing, August 1964 | Premier Books are published by Fawcett World Library, | 67 West 44th Street, New York, N.Y. 10036. | Printed in the United States of America.'; v–vi 'CONTENTS' (seven chapters listed with titles and page references. A foreword, preface and index are also listed); vii–xi 'FOREWORD' ('The English-speaking world is fortunate that William Shakespeare happened to be born…') (signed, 'DANIEL B. DODSON | *Associate Professor of English* | *Columbia University*'); [12] 'PREFACE TO THE | QUARTERCENTENARY EDITION' ('I HAVE wished in this edition of a handbook about William Shakespeare…') (signed, '*September* 1963 JOHN MASEFIELD'; 13–184 text; [185] 'INDEX'; [186] blank; 187–91 index; [192] publisher's advertisement: '…also from PREMIER BOOKS'

Paper: wove paper

Running title: 'WILLIAM SHAKESPEARE' (33mm.) on verso; recto title comprises chapter title, pp.14–184

Binding: wrappers printed with light brown wood-grain effect. On spine, horizontally at head of spine, in white: 'R238 | [rule]', reading lengthways down spine from head: '*a Premier Book* [in white] *Wm. Shakespeare* [in black] *Masefield* [in white]'. On upper wrapper: 'R238 [vertical rule] 60c [in white] | *a Premier Book* [publisher's device of hand holding a quill pen] [in black] | [rule] [in white] | *Wm Shakespeare* [in white] | [illustration of the Globe theatre and a seated Shakespeare writing with quill in hand, signed 'L+D DILLON'] [in black, white, purple, green and blue] | *An introduction to the* [in black] | *Bard and his works* [in black] | *by England's* [in black] | *Poet Laureate* [in black] | *John* [in black] | *Masefield* [in black] | *Foreword by* [in black] | *Daniel B.* [in black] | *Dodson,* [in black] | *Columbia University* [in black]'. On lower wrapper: 'FAWCETT WORLD LIBRARY | [rule] [in white] | Through his own poetic vision and imaginative | scholarship, John Masefield brings into fresh focus | the treasured bounty of Shakespeare's genius | "…which, by some startling mercy and in un- | dying words, set down the eternal marvel of man's | life…so splendid, so passionate, so short." | – *From the author's preface* | "Here is a book written by a | dramatist and poet about a | dramatist and poet. It is | light in the hand and volu- | minous in the mind." | – Sir Ralph Richardson | [illustration of inkwell, paper and hand with quill accompanied by five dramatic masks] [in black, white, purple, green and blue] | This special Premier edition, newly revised by the | author to celebrate Shakespeare's quartercente- | nary, marks the first appearance of this book in | paperback in this country.' All edges trimmed. Binding measurements: 178 × 107mm. (wrappers), 178 × 10mm. (spine).

Publication date: August 1964

Price: $0.60

Contents:
Foreword ('The English-speaking world is fortunate that William Shakespeare happened to be born…')
    (signed, 'DANIEL B. DODSON | *Associate Professor of English* | *Columbia University*')
Preface to the Quatercentenary Edition ('I have wished in this edition of a handbook…')
I Shakespeare and Stratford ('Stratford-on-Avon, the poet's destiny and present place…')
II The Poems ('At some unknown time in the lost eight years this young man turned…')
III The Plays ('A good many plays had been known in England before the time…')
IV Plays Attributed to Shakespeare ('During Shakespeare's earlier…')
V On the Spreading of the Fame of Shakespeare ('To the best of my knowledge the first…')
VI George Wilkins ('For some months, between 1607 and 1609, Shakespeare must have…')
VII On John Fletcher ('During the years of Shakespeare's life there were many poets in…')
Index

Notes:
The foreword is unique to this edition. Dodson appears to be writing an introduction to a reprint of the 1911 text (he writes '…one wonders if Mr. Masefield may have altered some opinions in the half-century since this book first appeared'). The text uses the revised 1954 text, however.

Writing to The Society of Authors in January 1964 Masefield states:

> I send with this a letter from Mr Hill, of Heinemann's, telling me of an offer of an American firm for the paper-back publication of a revised (Centenary edition) of my Shakespeare book, which the Macmillan Co. do not wish to use or issue in the U.S.

> Please, will you be so very kind as to comment on the offer, and to tell me your opinion of it? It seems to me to have unpleasing points, + to entail rather a lot of commissions for I suppose that Macmillan, who issue an edition of the usual Shakespeare volume, will demand something for this use of the main volume with the Centenary additions. I do not know Messrs Fawcett as publishers, nor Professor Dodson; and my own instinct is against the offer; but I suppose that if the edition be not issued in some form in the U.S. it will be the prey of some pirate or other.

(John Masefield, letter to Anne Munro-Kerr, 22 January 1964)
(Archives of The Society of Authors)

The advice of The Society of Authors was that 'Fawcett is quite a well-known firm of American paperback publishers and I think you could safely entrust the book to them' (see Anne Munro-Kerr, letter to John Masefield, 29 January 1964) (Archives of The Society of Authors).

The Archives of The Society of Authors reveal that this edition went out of print in September 1967.

Copies seen: private collection (PWE)

A17(h) Fourth American edition (1969)

WILLIAM | SHAKESPEARE | John Masefield | QUATERCENTENARY EDITION | [publisher's device] | BARNES & NOBLE, INC. | PUBLISHERS [point] BOOKSELLERS [point] SINCE 1873
(All width centred)

Bibliographies: Wight [unrecorded]

Publication date: 1969

Price: unknown

Contents:
as for A17(f)

Notes:
This edition uses the same setting of type as A17(f).

Page [iv] states '© JOHN MASEFIELD 1964 | *First published 1954* | *Quatercentenary Edition first published 1964* | *Reprinted 1969* | Published in the United States by | Narnes & Noble | New York 10003 | Printed in Great Britain by | Bookprint Limited, Crawley, Sussex'

Copies seen: private collection (ROV)

A18 THE TRAGEDY OF NAN   1911

A18(a) First English edition (1911)

THE | TRAGEDY OF NAN | BY | JOHN MASEFIELD | LONDON | GRANT RICHARDS LTD. | 1911
(All width centred)

Bibliographies: Danielson [unrecorded], Williams [unrecorded], Simmons [unrecorded], Nevinson [unrecorded], Handley-Taylor [unrecorded], Wight [unrecorded]

Collation: [A-D]^8 [E]^6; 38 leaves; 172 × 109mm.; [i–iv] [1–6] 7–71 [72]

Pagination contents: [i] half-title: 'THE TRAGEDY OF NAN'; [ii] blank; [iii] title-page; [iv] 'Copyright 1909 in the United States of America | BY JOHN MASEFIELD | First printed . . September 1909 | Reprinted . . . . March 1910 | Reprinted . . . . . April 1911 | Reprinted (separately) . April 1911'; [1] 'TO | W.B. YEATS'; [2] blank; [3–4] [Author's Note] ('Tragedy at its best is a vision of the heart of life.') (signed, 'JOHN MASEFIELD | *4th April* 1911.'); [5] 'THE TRAGEDY OF NAN | [dramatis personae and original cast listed with 'PERSONS' and 'PLAYED BY' headings] | *This play was produced by the Pioneers at the New Royalty* | *Theatre, on 24th May,* 1908, *under the direction of Mr. H.* | *Granville Barker. At its revival as a matinee at the Haymarket* | *Theatre, in June,* 1908, *the part of the Rev. Mr. Drew was* | *played by Mr. Cecil Brooking.*'; [6] blank; 7–71 text; [72] 'Reprinted from Stereotype Plates by CHARLES WHITTINGHAM AND CO. | Tooks Court, Chancery Lane, London.'

Paper: wove paper

Running title: running titles constitute play title and act, followed by rule (75–76mm.), pp.8–71

Binding: grey wrappers. On spine, in orange reading lengthways up spine, from foot: 'THE TRAGEDY OF NAN'. On upper wrapper, in orange: 'One Shilling and Sixpence net | THE | TRAGEDY OF NAN | BY | JOHN MASEFIELD | [ornament] | LONDON | GRANT RICHARDS LTD. | PUBLISHERS' (all width centred, except first line which is ranged upper-right). Lower wrapper: blank. Top edge trimmed, others untrimmed. Binding measurements: 181 × 116mm. (wrappers), 181 × 11mm. (spine). The wrappers extend beyond the edges of the internal leaves with the exception of the top edge.

Publication date: published, according to the *English Catalogue of Books,* May 1911

Price: 1s.6d.

Contents:
[Author's Note] ('Tragedy at its best is a vision of the heart of life.')
The Tragedy of Nan ('ACT I | SCENE:- *A kitchen in the house of a small tenant farmer...*')

Notes:
The 'stereotype plates' from which this edition was reprinted were, presumably, those of A9(c) and, therefore, the original setting of text. This is, however, the first separate edition of the play.

Copies seen: private collection (PWE); BL (11778.k.30) stamped 22 MAR 1912

Reprinted:

| 'Reprinted (separately)' | [first separate edition, second impression] | May 1912 |
| 'Reprinted (separately)' | [first separate edition, third impression] | Sep 1913 |

A18(b) First American edition (1921)

[rule] | THE TRAGEDY OF NAN | *By* | JOHN MASEFIELD | NEW ILLUSTRATED | EDITION | New York | THE MACMILLAN COMPANY | 1921 | *All rights reserved* | [rule]
(All width centred and enclosed within ruled border: 142 × 89mm. As a result of the two rules noted above, three rectangles are created measuring 2 × 89mm., 139 × 89mm. and 2 × 89mm. respectively from the top)

Bibliographies: Danielson [unrecorded], Williams [unrecorded], Simmons [unrecorded], Nevinson [unrecorded], Handley-Taylor p.28, Wight 9d

Collation: [A-I]⁸; 72 leaves; 189 × 128mm.; [i–vi] vii–x [xi–xiv] 1–127 [128–30]; illustrations (on glossy paper) tipped-in on pp.[iii], 10, 23, 32, 44, 57 and 64

Pagination contents: [i] half-title: 'THE TRAGEDY OF NAN'; [ii] '*By* | JOHN MASEFIELD | [rule] | [21 volumes listed]' (all enclosed in double ruled border: 89 × 56mm.); [iii] title-page (with additional leaf tipped-in on the verso of which is the frontispiece photograph: 141 × 89mm., '"The tide. The tide coming up the river."' enclosed within ruled border, with two additional rules to create three rectangles measuring 2 × 89mm., 137 × 89mm. and 2 × 89mm. respectively from the top); [iv] 'PRINTED IN THE UNITED STATES OF AMERICA | COPYRIGHT, 1909, | BY JOHN MASEFIELD. | [rule] | New illustrated edition published September, 1921. | Press of | J. J. Little & Ives Company | New York, U. S. A.'; [v] 'To | W. B. YEATS'; [vi] blank; vii–viii 'AUTHOR'S NOTE' ('Tragedy at its best is a vision of the heart of life.') (signed, 'JOHN MASEFIELD. | 4*th April* 1911.'); ix–x 'PREFATORY NOTE' ('I began to write this play either at the end of 1906 or the beginning of 1907.') (signed, 'JOHN MASEFIELD.'); [xi] 'LIST OF ILLUSTRATIONS' (seven illustrations listed with page references); [xii] blank; [xiii] 'THE TRAGEDY OF NAN'; [xiv] 'THE TRAGEDY OF NAN | [dramatis personae and original cast listed with 'PERSONS' and 'PLAYED BY' headings] | *This play was produced by the Pioneers at the* | *New Royalty Theatre, on* 24*th May,* 1908, *under* | *the direction of Mr. H. Granville Barker. At its* | *revival as a matinee at the Haymarket Theatre, in* | *June,* 1908, *the part of the Rev. Mr. Drew was* | *played by Mr. Cecil Brooking*.'; 1–127 text; [128–30] blank

Paper: wove paper

Running title: 'THE TRAGEDY OF NAN' (38mm.) with details of act towards gutter, on both verso and recto, pp.2–127

Binding: green cloth. On spine, in gold: '*The* | TRAGEDY | *of* | NAN | [floral ornament in gold and green] | MASEFIELD | MACMILLAN | – – – –' (all width centred). On upper cover, in gold: '*The* | TRAGEDY | *of* | NAN | [floral device] | JOHN | MASEFIELD' (within white border: 93 × 65mm.) (surrounded by ornate floral border in green and white with photograph on paper laid down above text within green border). Lower cover: blank. Note that all minuscules on spine and upper cover are swash. All edges trimmed. Binding measurements: 194 × 126mm. (covers), 194 × 26mm. (spine). End-papers: wove paper (decorated with collage of seven photographs showing progressive stages of an advancing tide. These photographs are numbered and a key provided within two rectangles at the foot of each page).

Publication date: published, according to Handley-Taylor, 25 October 1921

Price: $2.00

Contents:
Author's Note ('Tragedy at its best is a vision of the heart of life.')
Prefatory Note ('I began to write this play either at the end of 1906 or...')
The Tragedy of Nan ('ACT I | SCENE:–*A kitchen in the house of a small tenant farmer...*')

Notes:
The 'Prefatory Note' describes the conception of the play, its sources and location. An explanation is given regarding the Severn as a tidal river and Masefield ends by acknowledging the illustration source:

> I have to thank Messrs Tilley & Son, of Ledbury, in Herefordshire, for taking the photographs with which this volume is illustrated, in the cold and wet of an early wild March morning.

Wight is inaccurate in his transcription of the title-page. He also omits publication information present in Handley-Taylor.

Compare with the binding of A21(c). The upper cover, in particular, uses the same ornate floral border.

Note Handley-Taylor's publication date of 25 October 1921 against that given within the volume of September 1921.

Copies seen: private collection (PWE); Bodleian (M.adds.110.e.3888) stamped 6 MAR 1975; NYPL (Berg Collection) inscribed 'for Lillah | from Jan. | April 13. 1923.', marked-up copy by Lillah McCarthy

A18(c) Second English edition (1926)

THE | TRAGEDY OF NAN | BY | JOHN MASEFIELD | [publisher's device of a windmill with 'W [point]' and 'H' all within ruled border: 15 × 15mm.] | LONDON | WILLIAM HEINEMANN LTD.
(All width centred)

Bibliographies: Simmons [unrecorded], Nevinson p.14, Handley-Taylor [unrecorded], Wight [unrecorded]

Collation: [A]⁴ B-I⁸ K⁶ (J not used); K2 is also signed; signatures left foot of page; 74 leaves; 186 × 122mm.; [i–vi] vii [viii] 1–138 [139–40]

Pagination contents: [i] half-title: 'THE TRAGEDY OF NAN'; [ii] 'PLAYS | [six titles listed] | POETRY | [12 titles listed] | PROSE | [five titles listed] | [single rule] | LONDON : WILLIAM HEINEMANN LTD.'; [iii] title-page; [iv] *'First published under the title of "The Tragedy of Nan and other Plays"* | (Grant Richards), September 1909. | Reprinted, March 1910, April 1911, March 1914, April 1920, | May 1922. | New Edition, "The Tragedy of Nan" (William Heinemann, Ltd.), | May 1926. | Printed in Great Britain by | Richard Clay & | Sons, Limited, Bungay, Suffolk.'; [v] 'TO | W.B. YEATS'; [vi] blank; vii 'THE TRAGEDY OF NAN | [dramatis personae and original cast listed with 'PERSONS' and 'PLAYED BY' headings] | *This play was produced by the Pioneers at the New* | *Royalty Theatre, on 24th May,* 1908, *under the direction* | *of Mr. H. Granville Barker. At its revival as a matinee* | *at the Haymarket Theatre, in June,* 1908, *the part of the* | *Rev. Mr. Drew was played by Mr. Cecil Brooking.*'; [viii] blank; 1-[139] text (at foot of p.[139]: '[rule] | PRINTED IN GREAT BRITAIN BY RICHARD CLAY & SONS, LIMITED. | BUNGAY, SUFFOLK.'); [140] blank

Paper: laid paper (watermark: 'ADELPHI'), chain-lines 26mm. apart

Running title: 'THE TRAGEDY OF NAN' (50mm.) on both verso and recto, pp.2-[139]

Binding: blue cloth. On spine, in gold: 'The | Tragedy | of Nan | [ornament] | John | Masefield | HEINEMANN' (all width centred). On upper cover, in gold: 'THE TRAGEDY OF NAN | JOHN MASEFIELD' (within blind ruled border: 183 × 118mm.) Lower cover: blank. All edges trimmed. Binding measurements: 190 × 122mm. (covers), 190 × 24mm. (spine). End-papers: wove paper.

Publication date: published, according to date within volume, May 1926 (not recorded in the *English Catalogue of Books*)

Price: unknown

Contents:
The Tragedy of Nan ('ACT I | SCENE:- *A kitchen in the house of a small tenant farmer…*')

Notes:
The play is textually the same as the first edition and has not been revised. It has, however, been entirely re-set for this edition.

Masefield, through The Society of Authors, approached Grant Richards in January 1924 enquiring about the purchase of Richards' rights in his books. Such books would include *The Tragedy of Nan and other Plays* (see A9). Richards invited Masefield to make an offer but no further action was taken.

In September 1925 Richards again invited offers from Masefield but had also 'approached or talked with the firm of Heinemann' regarding the four books *A Tarpaulin Muster* (A6), *Captain Margaret* (A7), *Multitude and Solitude* (A8) and *The Tragedy of Nan and other Plays* (A9). Writing to The Society of Authors, Masefield noted that he wanted 'to suppress 3, + part of the 4th' (see BL, Add.Mss.56581, ff.200–201). Masefield therefore offered '£400 for the lot, including stock, good will + the American interest' in September or October 1925 (see BL, Add.Mss.56581, ff.200–201). This presumably failed to interest Richards who probably continued discussions with Heinemann.

Heinemann were presumably aware of Masefield's views on the books and only negotiated for *The Tragedy of Nan and other Plays*. A telegram from Masefield to The Society of Authors, dated 9 September 1925, reveals that negotiations between Heinemann and Richards were almost complete at that time. Masefield wished The Society of Authors to deal with Heinemann for him and noted that he would 'agree any reasonable proposal'.

Richards, writing to The Society of Authors, noted his success in negotiations and again invited discussion on the other titles:

> I have to-day sold to William Heinemann all our rights in John Masefield's "The Tragedy of Nan". If in the circumstances you care to continue negotiations for "Multitude and Solitude", "Captain Margaret" and "A Tarpaulin Muster", I shall be glad to hear from you. Please however let me hear from you quickly, as otherwise I shall make other arrangements with regard to these books.
>
> (Grant Richards, letter to [G.H.] Thring, 11 December 1925)
> (BL, Add.Mss.56582, f.44)

Discussions between Richards and The Society of Authors came to nothing. Nevertheless, Heinemann had secured control of one title. Masefield wrote to the Society stating:

> I thank you for your letter of the 11th, + for your kindness, in negotiating for *Nan* on my behalf. I suppose that Mr Richards ignored my offer, of some weeks past, for the other books which he has of mine? I enclose my cheque for £100 herewith. Is there any possibility, (as I pay half the cost, + am willing to pay more) of modifying the agreement, now that the book is transferred to a new publisher? The terms of the agreement are not very satisfactory.
>
> (John Masefield, letter to [G.H.] Thring, [13 December 1925])
> (BL, Add.Mss.56582, f.46)

It therefore appears that Heinemann and Masefield shared the cost of acquiring the title from Richards and that Masefield considered a new agreement to be desirable. It is an indication of Masefield's excellent relations with Heinemann that the firm, writing to The Society of Authors, were indeed prepared to discuss modifications:

Thank you for your letter of the 14th. December, enclosing Mr. Masefield's cheque for £100 in payment of half the purchase price of THE TRAGEDY OF NAN. I send you our receipt herewith. We should certainly be disposed to consider any suggestions Mr. Masefield may like to make in connection with the modification of the present agreement.

(C.S. Evans, letter to [G.H.] Thring, 16 December [1925])
(BL, Add.Mss.56582, f.55)

Masefield therefore wrote to The Society of Authors stating his wishes, which included suppression of material:

...I will grant them the usual limited licence in use for my other books. It is a licence for a term of years + limited to this country + the colonies. I wish to exclude from the volume the two little plays printed with Nan.

(John Masefield, letter to [G.H.] Thring, [18 December 1925])
(BL, Add.Mss.56582, f.58)

This arrangement was acceptable to Heinemann, for C.S. Evans wrote to The Society of Authors:

I have this morning heard from Mr. Masefield, who outlines his wishes in regard to the re-publication of THE TRAGEDY OF NAN, and makes one or two suggestions for new editions which we are to consider. In the meantime I enclose a draft form of agreement in which I have, as you suggest, recorded the surrender to Mr. Masefield of all the rights we have acquired from Grant Richards. The agreement continues on the same lines as the agreements for all the other books by Mr. Masefield which are published by us.

(C.S. Evans, letter to [G.H.] Thring, 21 December 1925)
(BL, Add.Mss.56582, f.61)

At the beginning of January 1926 C.S. Evans wrote to Masefield noting:

We have been considering the question of the re-issue of NAN. ...we all think here that the best way to re-issue it would be in a form more or less uniform with your other single poetical works...

(C.S. Evans, letter to John Masefield, 13 January 1926)
(HRHRC, MS (Masefield, J.) Recip William Heinemann Ltd.)

The publishing agreement for this title between Masefield and Heinemann was dated 30 December 1925 (see Archives of The Society of Authors). The agreement refers to a publication date of 'the spring of 1925 unless otherwise mutually arranged'.

With a new contract, 'The Campden Wonder' and 'Mrs Harrison' were omitted, and the Heinemann edition was published in May 1926. With two plays successfully suppressed it merely remained for Masefield to advise The Society of Authors about future performance licences:

...Please check (ie stop) any demand that may arise for 'Mrs Harrison'. 'The Campden Wonder' I don't object to so strongly: few in any case will ask for either I hope.

(John Masefield, letter to [G.H.] Thring, [27 December 1925])
(BL, Add.Mss.56582, f.64)

In 1940 a request was received from Oxford University Press to reprint the two plays. It was rejected. Masefield wrote that '...I do not much like the thought of these youthful indiscretions being reprinted...' (see John Masefield, letter to [E.J.] Mullet, [6 November 1940]) (BL, Add.Mss.56614, f.10).

Fifteen years later Masefield had relented slightly. An application from the Canadian Broadcasting Corporation to broadcast 'The Campden Wonder' demonstrates that Masefield's attempts at suppression had not been entirely successful. Writing to The Society of Authors Masefield agrees to a performance of an adapted version:

The Campden Wonder is pretty crude: but a queer fable, of an event that certainly happened. The Canadian people wish to adapt it. I don't mind their doing it, if, under the usual safe-guards, the results are said to be adapted from my work. Otherwise, though with some mis-givings, I would say, let them do it, but all in a swift tempo, all pat on cue; this may not "get it over", but it will get it over quickly. It needs breathless playing, de tic au tac.

(John Masefield, letter to Miss Lehmann, 13 January [1955])
(BL, Add.Mss.56626, f.7)

Copies seen: private collection (PWE); BL (011781.e.20) stamped 3 JUN 1926; ULL (Special Collections); Library of The John Masefield Society

A18(d) First Japanese edition [in English] (1977)

THE | TRAGEDY OF NAN | by | John Masefield | Edited with Notes | by | H. Hirooka | SHINOZAKI [publisher's device incorporating 'S'] SHORIN
(All width centred)

Bibliographies: Wight [unrecorded]

Publication date: 1977

Price: 700 yen

Contents:
[Preface]
[Note on dialects used in the play]
The Tragedy of Nan ('ACT I | SCENE:- *A kitchen in the house of a small tenant farmer…*')
Notes

Notes:
The preface (dated 20 September 1976) is followed by a note on the English dialect used in the play. After the text of the play is an extensive notes section that comprises a glossary of phrases in dialect.

The play was published in Tokyo.

Copies seen: Library of The Society of Authors

A19 THE EVERLASTING MERCY   1911

A19(a) Copyright edition (1911)

The Everlasting Mercy | BY | JOHN MASEFIELD | PORTLAND, MAINE | SMITH & SALE, PRINTERS | 1911
(All width centred)

Bibliographies: Danielson [unrecorded], Williams [unrecorded], Simmons [18], Nevinson [unrecorded], Handley-Taylor p.30, Wight [18]

Collation: [A-D]⁸; 32 leaves; 194 × 125mm.; [1–3] 4–48 [two un-numbered blank pages] 49–57 [58–62]

Pagination contents: [1] title-page; [2] 'COPYRIGHT | SIDGWICK AND JACKSON, LTD. | 1911'; [3]–48 text; [two un-numbered pages] blank; 49–57 text; [58–62] blank

Paper: wove paper

Running title: none

Binding: brown wrappers. Spine: blank. On upper wrapper: 'The Everlasting Mercy'. Lower wrapper: blank. All edges trimmed. Binding measurements: 194 × 125mm. (wrappers), 194 × 4mm. (spine).

Publication date: before 4 October 1911 (see notes)

Price: copies were not for sale

Contents:
The Everlasting Mercy ('From '41 to '51')
         First printed in The English Review *October 1911, pp.361–404*

Notes:
The two blank un-numbered pages between pages 48 and 49 represent a single leaf comprising the first leaf of the final gathering. This is not the pagination irregularity to which Simmons refers:

> In the copy in the Copyright Office the pagination is irregular following p.50, as follows: one blank leaf, pp.53, 54, 51, 52, 57 verso blank, 55, 56, two blank leaves

A letter, dated 17 July 1911, from Masefield to Sidgwick notes 'I send herewith the ms of my poem'. A later hand has annotated this 'The Everlasting Mercy' (see John Masefield, letter to Frank Sidgwick, 17 July 1911) (HRHRC, MS (Sidgwick, F.) Recip. Masefield, J.) It therefore appears that Sidgwick received the text three months before publication in *The English Review*.

The Sidgwick and Jackson archive (Bodleian Library) states 10 copies were printed, two being received by the firm on 4 October 1911.

Writing to Cazenove in November 1911, Sidgwick and Jackson noted:

> The American printers were Smith and Sale, of Portland, Maine; but by Masefield's directions we only had the poem set up in linotype in the roughest and cheapest way, and they had no instructions to hold the type, in any case their page was too ugly even for an American publisher.
>
>   (Sidgwick and Jackson, letter to C.F. Cazenove, 28 November [1911])
>   (Bodleian, MS.Sidgwick and Jackson.15, f.179)

Copies seen: Bodleian (MS.Sidgwick and Jackson.228) stamped by Sidgwick and Jackson and labelled both 'File' and 'American Copyright'

A19(b) First English edition (1911)

The Everlasting Mercy [in red] | By | John Masefield | AUTHOR OF | *The Tragedy of Nan, The Tragedy* | *of Pompey the Great, etc.* | LONDON | SIDGWICK & JACKSON, LTD. [in red] | MCMXI
(All width centred, capital letters in Masefield's credited works are swash)

Bibliographies: Danielson 177, Williams p.3, Simmons [18a], Nevinson p.12, Handley-Taylor p.30, Wight [18a]

Collation: [A]⁴ B-G⁸; signatures left foot of page; 52 leaves; 185 × 120mm.; [i–viii] 1–89 [90–96]

Pagination contents: [i] half-title: 'THE EVERLASTING MERCY'; [ii] '*Garden City Press Limited, Letchworth, Herts.*'; [iii] title-page; [iv] '*Entered at the Library of Congress, Washington, U.S.A.* | All rights reserved.' (the 'A' of 'All' and 'v' of 'reserved' are swash); [v] 'TO | MY WIFE' ('T' and 'M' are swash); [vi] blank; [vii] '*Thy place is biggyd above the sterrys cleer,* | *Noon erthely paleys wrouhte in so statly wyse,* | *Com on my freend, my brothir moost enteer,* | *For the I offryd my blood in sacrifise.* | JOHN LYDGATE.'; [viii] blank; 1-[90] text (on p.[90] at left margin 'GREAT HAMPDEN.' and on right 'June, 1911.'); [91] 'NOTE | "The Everlasting Mercy" first appeared in | *The English Review* for October, 1911. I thank | the Editor and Proprietors of that paper for | permitting me to reprint it here. The persons | and events described in the poem are entirely | imaginary, and no reference is made or intended | to any living person. | JOHN MASEFIELD.'; [92] blank; [93–96] catalogue: 'FROM SIDGWICK & JACKSON'S LIST' (at foot of p.[96]: 'SIDGWICK & JACKSON LIMITED | 3, ADAM STREET, ADELPHI, W.C.')

Paper: laid paper (no watermark), chain-lines 25mm. apart

Running title: 'The Everlasting Mercy' (55mm.) on both verso and recto, pp.2-[90]

Binding: blue cloth. On spine, in gold: 'THE | EVER – | LASTING | MERCY | JOHN | MASEFIELD | SIDGWICK | & JACKSON' (all width centred) (see notes). On upper cover, in gold: 'THE EVERLASTING MERCY | JOHN MASEFIELD'. Lower cover: blank. Upper and lower covers have blind ruled borders: 184 × 117mm. All edges trimmed. Binding measurements: 191 × 123mm. (covers), 191 × 21mm. (spine). End-papers: laid paper (no watermark), chain-lines 25mm. apart.

Publication date: published according to Simmons, 2 November 1911 in an edition of 1000 copies

Price: 3s.6d.

Contents:
as for A19(a)

Notes:
First published in *The English Review* October, 1911 (pp.361–404). There are minor differences, including the insertion of the Lydgate quotation for the book edition; the exchange between Saul Kane and Billy Myers (*The English Review* p.362) prefixed by speakers' voices which are omitted in the book edition; the omission of 'THE END' as a title for the closing stanzas in the book edition; and the inclusion in the book edition only of location, date and note. Most obviously and infamously, 'bloody' is omitted in *The English Review* (except on p.388, when not offensively used). All occurrences of the word are fully printed in the book edition.

See Simmons pp.33–35 for opposing reminiscences by Austin Harrison (the then editor of *The English Review*) and Frank Sidgwick (of Sidgwick and Jackson) detailing the poem's first appearance in print. Material relating to this matter (with much additional correspondence) is located in Bodleian, MS.Sidgwick and Jackson.228, ff.149–54.

In a letter to Harry Ross, Masefield's brother-in-law, the author requests legal advice about this work:

> Will you very kindly look through the enclosed poem + tell me if in your opinion any living man in Ledbury could reasonably consider himself libelled by it, in spite of my public declaration that it is entirely imaginary + without reference to any living person: I'd be very glad if you would.

> (John Masefield, letter to Harry Ross, 16 October 1911)
> (Private Collection (RM))

Masefield was awarded the Edmond de Polignac prize by the Academic Committee of the Royal Society of Literature for the poem on 29 November 1912. J.M. Barrie called the poem 'incomparably the finest literature of the year' and Arthur Machen described the work as:

> …the one literary production of the year 1911 that has in it the real and abiding stuff of letters; it was the true book of the year, because, in my judgement, it is also the book of many years, of all succeeding years in which true poetry will be loved and honoured...

> (*Evening News*, 19 February 1912)

Lord Alfred Douglas, however, stated the work was 'nine-tenths sheer filth' and Masefield exceeded the 'wicked licentiousness' of Marlowe (as quoted by Muriel Spark, *John Masefield*, Peter Nevill, 1953, p.5).

It appears that Frank Sidgwick was offered *The Widow in the Bye Street* before terms had been fully agreed for *The Everlasting Mercy*. Masefield was also inclined to hold out for a good deal:

> The Mercy. Mr S has only himself to blame for the delay, + for the assumption that I was going to take the Pompey royalties. I gathered from his letter that he wasn't in the least keen about the Widow; but if he wants the offer of it next year and cares to come to terms over it when we are ready to deal I don't see why he shouldn't have it. I object rather to promising the Widow definitely until he comes to terms over the Mercy. As to the cheap edition of the Mercy, I must say the cheap edition business seems to me a rotten one for the author. About the time I come to a good percentage on the 3/6 edition I am to be switched off to 15% on a shilling edition, + get no more however many the book sells. No. I say this:-

I will agree to his offer of 15% on the 1st 500[,] 17½% on the 2nd 500 [–] but then I want 20% to 1500 copies (the 3rd 500) and 25% thereafter, and the royalties on the cheap edition to begin at the rate reached with the more costly one. You might let him feel that I want to give him the Widow, but that it all depends on him.

(John Masefield, letter to C.F. Cazenove, 25 October 1911)
(University of Arizona Library. MS.50, V.III)

A publishing agreement for this title between Masefield and the firm of Sidgwick and Jackson was dated 19 November 1911 (see Archives of The Society of Authors). This may correspond to a later impression of the edition. Correspondence relating to Simmons' bibliography preserved in the archives of Sidgwick and Jackson (see Bodleian, MS.Sidgwick & Jackson 228) confirms a publication date of 2 November 1911 and a first printing of 1000 copies.

A binding variant exists in which 'SIDGWICK | & JACKSON' on the spine is positioned one character higher than in the majority of copies.

Parodies of the poem have enjoyed particular popularity. The most famous, published in its own right was Siegfried Sassoon's *The Daffodil Murderer* (published in 1913 under the pseudonym of Saul Kain). EVOE (the pseudonym of E.V. Knox) included his 'The Everlasting Percy' in *Poems of Impudence* (1926), Louis Untermeyer's 'John Masefield Tells the true story of "Tom, Tom, the Piper's Son"' in *Collected Parodies* (1919) is heavily reliant on *The Everlasting Mercy* whilst Clifford Bax with Herbert Farjeon wrote *Walking Tom* (see Eleanor Farjeon, *Edward Thomas – The Last Four Years*, p.37).

Interest was shown in the poem by Eric Williams, representing Ledbury Amateur Cine Society in January 1938. Although Masefield was supportive of the society's intention to shoot a silent film, the society abandoned plans when a member of the cast left the local area in September 1938 (see BL, Add.Mss.56610, f.129 and Add.Mss.56608, f.178).

Copies seen: private collection (PWE); BL (011650.i.70) stamped 10 NOV 1911; BL (Ashley 1109) stamped 'ASHLEY | B [crown] M | LIBRARY'; ULL (Special Collections)

Reprinted:

'Second Impression'	[first edition, second impression]	Nov 1911
'Third Impression'	[first edition, third impression]	Dec 1911
'Fourth Impression'	[first edition, fourth impression]	Feb 1912
'Fifth Impression'	[first edition, fifth impression]	Apr 1912
'Sixth Impression'	[first edition, sixth impression]	Aug 1912

A19(c) Second English edition (1912)

THE EVERLASTING | MERCY | BY | JOHN MASEFIELD | AUTHOR OF | "THE TRAGEDY OF POMPEY THE GREAT" | "THE TRAGEDY OF NAN," ETC. | LONDON | SIDGWICK & JACKSON LTD. | 3 ADAM STREET, ADELPHI | MCMXII
(All width centred)

Bibliographies: Danielson [unrecorded], Williams [unrecorded], Simmons [unrecorded], Nevinson p.12, Handley-Taylor [unrecorded], Wight [unrecorded]

Collation: [π]⁸ A-E⁸; signatures left foot of page; 44 leaves; the catalogue (not included in collation or leaf count) comprises a single unsigned gathering of four leaves; 185 × 119mm.; [i–viii] 1–78 [79–80]; catalogue pagination: [1–8]

Page contents: [i] half-title: 'THE EVERLASTING MERCY'; [ii] '*Uniform with this Volume* | THE WIDOW IN THE BYE STREET | By JOHN MASEFIELD'; [iii] title-page; [iv] '*First Edition . . . . November 1911 | Second Impression . . . November 1911 | Third Impression . . . December 1911 | Fourth Impression . . . February 1912 | Fifth Impression . . . April 1912 | Sixth Impression . . . August 1912 | Seventh Impression (reset) . December 1912 | Entered at the Library of | Congress, Washington, U.S.A. | All rights reserved*'; [v] 'TO | MY WIFE'; [vi] blank; [vii] '*Thy place is biggyd above the sterrys cleer, | Noon erthely paleys wrouhte in so statly wyse, | Com on my freend, my brothir moost enteer, | For the I offryd my blood in sacrifise. | JOHN LYDGATE.*'; [viii] blank; 1-[79] text (on p.[79] at left margin 'GREAT HAMPDEN.' and on right 'June 1911.'); [80] 'NOTE | 'The Everlasting Mercy' first appeared in *The | English Review* for October 1911. I thank the | Editor and Proprietors of that paper for per- | mitting me to reprint it here. The persons and | events described in the poem are entirely imagin- | ary, and no reference is made or intended to any | living person. | JOHN MASEFIELD. | THE RIVERSIDE PRESS LIMITED, EDINBURGH'; [1–8] catalogue (at foot of p.[8]: '*Complete Catalogue and Lists on Application* | [rule] | SIDGWICK & JACKSON, LTD. | 3 ADAM STREET, ADELPHI, LONDON, W.C. | [rule]')

Paper: laid paper (no watermark), chain-lines 25mm. apart

Running title: 'THE EVERLASTING MERCY' (56mm.) on both verso and recto, pp.2-[79]

Binding: blue cloth. On spine, in gold: 'The | Ever- | lasting | Mercy | [ornament] | John | Masefield | SIDGWICK | & JACKSON' (all width centred). On upper cover, in gold: 'THE EVERLASTING MERCY | JOHN MASEFIELD'. Lower cover: blank. Upper and lower covers have blind ruled borders: 187 × 117mm. All edges trimmed. Binding measurements: 190 × 122mm. (covers), 190 × 21mm. (spine). End-papers: laid paper (no watermark), chain-lines 27mm. apart.

Publication date: published, according to date within volume, December 1912

Price: 3s.6d.

Contents:
The Everlasting Mercy ('From '41 to '51')

Notes:
In addition to noting the reset status of the text this edition also states 'seventh impression'. It actually comprises a second edition, first impression. It was, however, the seventh occasion that the book was issued by Sidgwick and Jackson.

There are numerous typographical differences from A19(b). The text is less heavily leaded. There are differences in punctuation, hypenated words and capitalisation. There are occasional minor word changes, for example 'jail' replacing 'gaol' on page 2 and 'Jack' on page 23 of A19(b) renamed 'Jock' on page 20.

Copies seen: private collection (PWE)

Reprinted:

	[second edition, second impression]	Jan 1913
	[second edition, third impression]	Jan 1913
	[second edition, fourth impression]	Feb 1913
	[second edition, fifth impression]	Mar 1913
	[second edition, sixth impression]	May 1913
'Foolscap edition'	[second edition, seventh impression]	Oct 1913
	[second edition, eighth impression]	Dec 1913
	[second edition, ninth impression]	Dec 1913
	[second edition, tenth impression]	Feb 1914
	[second edition, eleventh impression]	Jan 1916
	[second edition, twelfth impression]	Nov 1917
	[second edition, thirteenth impression]	Jun 1919
	[second edition, fourteenth impression]	Oct 1921
	[second edition, fifteenth impression]	Sep 1923
	[second edition, sixteenth impression]	Jun 1930
	[second edition, seventeenth impression]	Oct 1936
	[second edition, eighteenth impression]	Jul 1946
	[second edition, nineteenth impression]	Mar 1955

The 'Foolscap edition' describes itself as a 'New Edition'. The same setting of type is used, however, as in A19(c). The 'foolscap edition' therefore represents merely a different size and binding. The reprint information cited on p.[iv] notes this reprint as the 'thirteenth thousand'. It is the thirteenth occasion Sidgwick and Jackson had issued either a new edition or a new impression. The original print run of A19(b) was 1000 copies. It therefore seems likely that each new edition or impression was printed and issued in batches of 1000 copies.

A20 JIM DAVIS   1911

A20(a) First English edition (1911)

JIM DAVIS | BY | JOHN MASEFIELD | *Author of "Captain Margaret," "Martin Hyde," etc., etc.* | LONDON : | WELLS GARDNER, DARTON & CO., LTD. | 3 AND 4, PATERNOSTER BUILDINGS, E.C. | AND 44, VICTORIA STREET, WESTMINSTER, S.W.
(All width centred)

Bibliographies: Danielson 176, Williams p.9, Simmons [19], Nevinson p.17, Handley-Taylor p.31, Wight [19]

Collation: [π]⁴ A-P⁸ Q² (J not used); signatures left foot of page; 126 leaves; 187 × 125mm.; [i–vi] vii [viii] 1–242 [243–44]

Pagination contents: [i] half-title: 'JIM DAVIS'; [ii] blank; [iii] title-page; [iv] '[publisher's device] | 1911'; [v] 'FOR JUDITH'; [vi] blank; vii 'CONTENTS' (20 chapters listed with titles and page references); [viii] blank; 1–242 text; [243–44] publisher's advertisements (15 titles, authors, and prices listed with press reviews) (at foot of p.[244]: '[rule] | WELLS GARDNER, DARTON & CO., Ltd., 3 and 4 Paternoster | Buildings, E.C., and 44 Victoria Street, London, S.W.')

Paper: wove paper

Running title: 'JIM DAVIS' (26mm.) on verso; recto title comprises chapter title, pp.2–242

Binding: green cloth. On spine, in gold: '[triple blind rule, the central rule being wider than the others] | JIM | DAVIS | JOHN [the 'N' has an irregular right foot] | MASEFIELD | WELLS[point]GARDNER, | DARTON[point]&[point]CO. LTD. [Wight describes the ampersand as 'a swash E'] | [triple blind rule, the central rule being wider than the others]' (all width centred). On upper cover, in gold: 'JIM[point]DAVIS | [rule] | JOHN MASEFIELD [the 'N' has an irregular right foot]' (all bordered by triple blind rule, the central rule being wider than the others: 188 × 121mm.) On lower cover, in blind: publisher's device: 20 × 22mm., and bordered by triple blind rule, the central rule being wider than the others: 188 × 121mm.) Top edge gilt, others trimmed. Binding measurements: 194 × 127mm. (covers), 194 × 46mm. (spine). End-papers: wove paper.

Publication date: published, according to Simmons, 4 October 1911 in an edition of 2000 copies

Price: 6s.

Contents:

Jim Davis ('I was born in the year 1800, in the town of Newnham-on-Severn, in Gloucestershire.')
> *First printed in* Chatterbox *1910*

Chapter headings are as follows:

I. My First Journey	XI. The Frigate 'Loocoön'
II. Night Riders	XII. Black Pool Bay
III. The Man on The Mound	XIII. In The Valley
IV. The Hut in the Gorse-Bushes	XIV. A Traitor
V. The Last Voyage of 'The Snail'	XV. The Battle on the Shore
VI. The Owl's Cry	XVI. Drifting
VII. The Two Coast Guards	XVII. The 'Blue Boar'
VIII. The Cave in the Cliff	XVIII. Tracked
IX. Signing On	XIX. The Road to London
X. Aboard the Lugger	XX. The Gipsy Camp

(Note that the Contents page incorrectly lists chapter XI as 'The Frigate 'Loocoön''. The chapter itself is headed 'The Frigate 'Laocoon'' whilst the spelling 'Laocoön' is adopted in the text.)

Notes:

The publishing agreement for this title between Masefield and Wells Gardner, Darton and Co. was dated 1 May 1907 (see Archives of The Society of Authors). The agreement refers to '…a story to be written by the Author of a kind suitable for boys' reading… the said story shall deal with adventures on sea…'

The novel first appeared in *Chatterbox* I–XXXVIII, for 1910. It was serialised in 38 instalments in which the chapter-division of the first book edition was completely disregarded, or not, at that stage, available. The serialisation was illustrated with full-page plates, many unsigned but some signed 'T.C. Dugdale'. Dugdale illustrated the first book edition of *Martin Hyde*, but never *Jim Davis* in book form. The *Chatterbox* serialisation not only predates volume publication but represents, therefore, an earlier illustrated edition (albeit periodical edition) than that noted by Wight as '19–1'. Significantly, *Chatterbox* was 'Published for the Proprietors by WELLS GARDNER, DARTON, & CO., Ltd., 3 & 4 Paternoster Buildings.'

Masefield sent the beginning of the novel to Cazenove in September 1907:

> I send you Jim Davis, as far as it goes. If Wells Gardner approve I can finish it off at once. If they disapprove, you might submit it to Grantie.
>
> (John Masefield, letter to C.F. Cazenove, 5 September 1907)
> (University of Arizona Library. MS.50, V.I)

Changes were requested and Masefield wrote about these to Cazenove. It appears that the verdict was sufficiently acceptable for Masefield not to offer the book to Richards, however:

> Many thanks for "Jim", with Chatterbox's verdict. I have taken out the blood, + made the traitor a schoolmaster, + saved him from Turkish captivity. The shuddering fit I mean to stick to, as I know it will affect boys. I am slowly proceeding with the novel. The play does not shape. I will send "Jim" back in a day or two, + then, if you can, I hope you will gouge a cheque out of them; "Jim" has made me a couple of months behind…
>
> (John Masefield, letter to C.F. Cazenove, 13 October 1907)
> (University of Arizona Library. MS.50, V.I)

The locality Masefield describes in Chapter II is that around the Gara Brook. Most significantly, the name of the house of Jim's aunt and uncle is 'Snail Castle'. Translated into Irish this becomes 'Cashlauna Shelmiddy' and the name of Jack B. Yeats' cottage of the period in South Devon. In a letter to Jack B. Yeats, Masefield writes:

> Did I tell you that I am writing a boy's book, for Chatterbox? Well, I am, and it is very good fun; but so far it doesn't seem to be very exciting, though the scene opens in the Gara valley, + the hero's home is just where you live. There are the devil of a lot of smugglers knocking around there, shivering their bloody timbers, and there are to be smuggler's caves in the cliffs at Flushing (Is Flushing all right for cliffs?) and there are to be Red Indians later on, but not till I get towards the end.
>
> (John Masefield, letter to Jack B. Yeats, 26 May 1907)
> (Harvard *61M–93)

The reference is obviously to *Jim Davis* (the 'Red Indians' were dropped) and the date reveals the long period before the novel appeared in 1910. It is likely that *Martin Hyde* was started and completed whilst *Jim Davis* was still being written.

Masefield attempted to buy back the copyright of this work in 1927. See notes to A13(b).

Copies seen: BL (012621.ccc.9) stamped 11 OCT 1911; Ledbury Library; Harvard College Library (Houghton *EC9.M377.911j) inscribed 'Let dark oblivion be this story's portion | Headache's un-natural son, fatigue's abortion. | J. Masefield.'

Reprinted:

Reprints, using the original setting of the text are numerous and undated. Several cite the author as Poet Laureate and therefore date from after 1930:

[reprint] ([c.1923])
　　　in green cloth

[reprint] (post 1930)
　　　in grey cloth
　　　in green cloth with black spots
　　　in brown cloth with red spots
　　　in light green cloth

A20(b)　First American edition ([1912])

JIM DAVIS | BY | JOHN MASEFIELD | *Author of "Captain Margaret," "Martin Hyde," etc., etc.* | ILLUSTRATED BY | EDWIN MEGARGEE | NEW YORK | FREDERICK A. STOKES COMPANY | PUBLISHERS
(All width centred)

Bibliographies: Danielson [unrecorded], Williams [unrecorded], Simmons [noted on p.37], Nevinson [unrecorded], Handley-Taylor p.31, Wight 19a

Collation: [A–Q]^8 (J not used) (but signed [π]^5 [1]^8 2–5^8 [6]^8 7–12^8 [13]^8 14–15^8 16^3, see note on American electrotype editions); signatures left foot of page; 128 leaves; 186 × 124mm.; [i–vi] vii [viii–x] 1–244 [245–46]; illustrations (on glossy paper) tipped-in on pp.[ii], 69, 130 and 239

Pagination contents: [i] half-title: 'JIM DAVIS'; [ii] blank (with additional leaf tipped-in on the verso of which is the frontispiece: 146 × 88mm., "'HUSH, JIM! GET OUT QUICKLY!'"-*Page 211*', signed 'EDWIN MEGARGEE'); [iii] title-page; [iv] '*Only Authorized American Edition* | Printed in the United States of America'; [v] 'FOR JUDITH'; [vi] blank; vii 'CONTENTS' (20 chapters listed with titles and page references); [viii] blank; [ix] 'ILLUSTRATIONS' (four illustrations listed with captions and page references); [x] blank; 1–244 text; [245–46] blank

Paper: wove paper

Running title: 'JIM DAVIS' (24mm.) on verso; recto title comprises chapter title, pp.2–244

Binding: grey cloth. On spine, in black: 'JIM | DAVIS | MASEFIELD | [illustration in black and yellow of ship at sea with two gulls (within ruled border in black: 90 × 26mm.)] | STOKES'. On upper cover, in black: 'JIM DAVIS | [illustration in black, yellow and red of two soldiers on horseback, five smugglers in beached ship, and floating barrels in sea (within three panels (separated by two vertical strips) each panel within ruled border in black: 132 × 10mm., 132 × 84mm. and 132 × 10mm.)] | BY JOHN MASEFIELD'. Lower cover: blank. All edges trimmed. Binding measurements: 193 × 125mm. (covers), 193 × 36mm. (spine). End-papers: wove paper.

Published: published, according to Simmons, 1912

Price: $1.25

Contents:
as for A20(a) except chapter XI is titled 'THE FRIGATE 'LAOCOON''

Notes:
Wight, in describing this volume notes that p.[iv] is blank. In all other respects his description agrees with that above. Either Wight has omitted to record a detail, or is describing an earlier issue. A publication date appears to be omitted from the volume and it is not unlikely that subsequent reprints were issued without reprint information or dates.

Copies seen: NYPL (NCW 1912) 275003B

A20(reprints)　English and American editions

There are numerous reprints of *Jim Davis*, mostly originating from American publishers. Several were issued as part of a named series and many were illustrated. The following presents a partial listing with an attempt at chronology (many dates are conjectural). Following this listing a number of editions are described at length. A comprehensive bibliography of *Jim Davis* remains a major task for Masefield scholarship.

1913　American edition　　Grosset and Dunlap　　　　illustrations by Edwin Megargee
　　　[reprinted in 1924]

1918　American edition　　Page Co.
　　　[reprinted in 1926]

[n.d.]　American edition　　Donald McKay
　　　[Wight notes 'an undated American edition' published by 'Donald McKay in Philadelphia'. This may comprise an edition from David McKay]

1918	American edition	The Page Company	[illustrator not acknowledged]	
	[published as *The Captive of the Smugglers* – see A44]			
1924	English edition	Wells Gardner, Darton and Co.	illustrations by Mead Schaeffer	
	[reprinted before 1930 and also after 1930 in a smaller format]			
1924	American edition	Frederick A. Stokes	illustrations by Mead Schaeffer	
1924	American edition	David McKay	illustrations by Stephen Reid	"The Golden Books" series
1926	American edition	Saalfield Publishing Co.	illustrations by Frances Brundage	"Every Child's Library" series
1930	American edition	David McKay	illustrations by Stephen Reid	"Newbery Classics" series
1932	American edition	Thomas Nelson	illustrations by Bob Dean	
1939	English edition	Longmans	illustrations by Ogle	"Heritage of Literature series"
	[reprinted in 1939; see also reset edition (below)]			
1946	English edition	Wells Gardner, Darton and Co.	illustrations by W. Lindsay Cable	
	[later reprints cite 1947 as the date of first publication; reprinted in 1949, 1952 and 1954]			
1947	English edition	Longmans	illustrations by Ogle	"Heritage of Literature" series
	[reprinted in 1963]			[reset edition]
1951	American edition	Macmillans	illustrations by Bob Dean	
	[reprinted in 1956, 1967 and 1969]			
1966	English edition	Puffin	illustrations by Exell	
	[reprinted in 1970]			
2002	English edition	The Chicken House	illustrations by David Frankland	intro. by Michael Morpurgo

A20(reprint) Later American edition ([1913])

JIM DAVIS | by | JOHN MASEFIELD | [illustration of battle and two pirates within ruled border: 35 × 32mm., signed 'F.R.'] | Illustrated | GROSSET & DUNLAP, Publishers | NEW YORK | by arrangement with Frederick A. Stokes Co.
(All width centred and enclosed within triple ruled border: 140 × 89mm.)

Bibliographies: Danielson [unrecorded], Williams [unrecorded], Simmons [noted on p.37], Nevinson [unrecorded], Handley-Taylor p.31, Wight [noted on p.36]

Notes:
Simmons states this was published in Grosset and Dunlap's 'Every Boy's Library' edition in 1913. The verso of the title-page states 'Only Authorized American Edition'. There is a foreword by the Chief Scout Executive describing the every boy's library as organised by the Boy Scouts of America. There are four illustrated plates by Edwin Megaree which suggests the edition is a reprint of the first American edition.

A20(reprint) Later English edition (1924)

JIM DAVIS | BY | JOHN MASEFIELD | AUTHOR OF "CAPTAIN MARGARET," "MARTIN HYDE" | ETC. ETC. | ILLUSTRATED BY MEAD SCHAEFFER | LONDON | WELLS GARDNER, DARTON & CO., LTD. | 3 AND 4 PATERNOSTER BUILDINGS, E.C.4
(All width centred)

Bibliographies: Simmons [unrecorded], Nevinson [unrecorded], Handley-Taylor [unrecorded], Wight [unrecorded] (see notes)

Collation: d^8 A-P^8 Q^2 (J not used); with the exception of the *a* gathering, which is signed at the right foot, all signatures left foot of page; gatherings D, G, L and O are enclosed by two leaves (one each side of gathering) which are stubs and onto which a grey leaf is tipped-in; the final stub (after O8) does not have a grey page for illustration and is laid down to O7; although bound as gatherings of ten leaves, a comparison with the first edition reveals these gatherings were printed as eight leaf gatherings and bound here as ten leaf gatherings to accommodate the illustrations; *a*2 is also signed; 138 leaves (including illustrations and leaf stubs); 225 × 159mm.; [two un-numbered pages] [i–ii] [two un-numbered pages, for illustration] [iii–vi] [two un-numbered pages – leaf stub] vii [viii] ix [x] 1–48 [two un-numbered pages, for illustration] 49–64 [two un-numbered pages, for illustration] 65–96 [two un-numbered pages, for illustration] 97–112 [two un-numbered pages, for illustration] 113–60 [two un-numbered pages, for illustration] 161–76 [two un-numbered pages, for illustration] 177–208 [two un-numbered pages, for illustration] 209–24 [two un-numbered pages – leaf stub] 225–42 [243–44]

Pagination contents: [-] blank (except for signature) (page excluded from page count, but constitutes first leaf of first gathering); [-] blank; [i] half-title: 'JIM DAVIS'; [ii] blank; [-] stub of leaf; [-] stub of leaf (with additional grey leaf tipped-in on the verso of which is tipped-in the colour frontispiece: 145 × 90mm., 'I was left penniless in the road. (*p.*221.)', signed 'Mead | Schaeffer | 23' in lower left corner); [iii] title-page; [iv] '*Illustrated edition, October* 1924'; [v] 'FOR JUDITH'; [vi] blank; [-] stub of leaf; [-] stub of leaf; vii 'CONTENTS' (20 chapters listed with titles and page references); [viii] blank; ix 'LIST OF ILLUSTRATIONS' (eight illustrations (including frontispiece) listed with titles and page references); [x] blank; 1–242 text; [243–45] blank

Paper: wove paper; illustrations (on glossy paper) mounted on grey wove paper

Running title: 'JIM DAVIS' (26mm.) on verso; recto title comprises chapter title, pp.2–242

Binding: burgundy cloth. On spine, in gold: 'JIM DAVIS | JOHN [the 'N' has an irregular right foot] | MASEFIELD | WELLS GARDNER | DARTON&CO | LTD' (all width centred). On upper cover, in gold: 'JIM DAVIS | JOHN MASEFIELD' (as on spine, the 'N' has an irregular right foot). Lower cover, in blind: publisher's device. Top edge gilt, others uncut. Sewn head-band. Binding measurements: 235 × 159mm. (covers), 235 × 59mm. (spine). End-papers: wove paper. Volume contained in slip-case covered in burgundy paper with a laid down illustration (comprising a copy of the plate used within the volume to face p.96)

Publication date: published, according to the *English Catalogue of Books*, November 1924

Price: 15s.

Contents:
as for A20(a)

Notes:
This edition derives from the plates used for A20(a). This edition, however, includes illustrations by Mead Schaeffer and generous margins on each page.

This edition was subsequently reprinted and one of these post 1930 reprints constitutes the volume described by Wight as '19–1 Illustrated Edition'.

Copies seen: BL (012643.gg.4) stamped 12 MAR 1925; ULL (Special Collections)

Reprinted:
As with A20(a) noting the author as Poet Laureate assists in dating these undated reprints:
[reprint] (pre 1930)
    in light brown cloth
[reprint] (post 1930)
    in blue cloth

A20(reprint) Later English edition (1939)

JIM DAVIS | BY | JOHN   MASEFIELD | (Poet Laureate) | WITH A FRONTISPIECE BY | OGLE | LONGMANS, GREEN AND CO. | LONDON   NEW YORK   TORONTO
(All width centred and enclosed within swirling border)

Bibliographies: Handley-Taylor [unrecorded], Wight [unrecorded]

Collation: A-E¹⁶ F⁸; A5, B5, C5, D5 and E5 are also signed; signatures right foot of page; 88 leaves; 132 × 92mm.; [1–8] 9–175 [176]

Page contents: [1] blank (except for signature); [2] 'THE HERITAGE OF LITERATURE | SERIES | [rule] | General Editor: E. W. PARKER, M.C | [rule] | [series description and categories of series, with quotation from John Lydgate]'; [3] half-title: 'JIM DAVIS' (with '[table lamp and open book] | The Heritage of | Literature Series | [rule] | SECTION A NO.33'); [4] frontispiece: 132 × 92mm., of battle on shore between three mounted guards, one smuggler in the sea, and three smugglers in a boat, signed 'OGLE' in lower-left corner; [5] title-page; [6] '[listing of publisher's offices] | First Published in this series in 1939, by kind permission of Messrs. | Wells Gardner, Darton & Co., Ltd. | PRINTED IN GREAT BRITAIN BY | LOVE AND MALCOLMSON, LTD. | REDHILL SURREY'; [7] 'CONTENTS' (20 chapters listed with titles and page references); [8] 'FOR JUDITH'; 9-[176] text

Paper: wove paper

Running title: 'JIM DAVIS' (15mm.) on verso; recto title comprises chapter title, pp.10-[176]

Binding: red cloth. On spine, in gold: 'Jim | Davis | [point] | John | Masefield | [design of table lamp and open book] | Longmans' (all width centred). On upper cover, in blind: design of table lamp and open book ranged lower right. Lower cover: blank. All edges trimmed. Binding measurements: 169 × 111mm. (covers), 169 × 28mm. (spine). End-papers: wove paper.

Publication date: 1939

Price: unknown

Contents:
as for A20(a)

Notes:
Chapter titles are as in A20(a) except chapter II here hyphenated 'NIGHT-RIDERS', chapter V becomes 'THE LAST VOYAGE OF THE "SNAIL"', chapter VII's 'COASTGUARDS' are here one word, and chapter XI is incorrectly spelt 'THE FRIGATE "LOACOÖN"'). The chapter itself is headed 'THE FRIGATE "LAOCOÖN"'.

Copies seen: private collection (ROV); BL (012208.cc.1/33) stamped 27 MAR 1933

Reprinted:

'New Impression'	[later edition, second impression]	Dec 1939
'New Edition (reset)'	[later edition, first impression]	1947
'Third Impression'	[later edition, second impression]	1963

The British Library catalogue lists the 1947 reset edition as part of the 'Clifford Library'. No such indication is present in the volume itself of any affiliation to such a series (see BL (W.P. 1256/4))

A20(reprint) Later English edition (1966)

JOHN MASEFIELD | [rule] | JIM DAVIS | ILLUSTRATED BY | EXELL | [publisher's device] | PENGUIN BOOKS
(All width centred)

Bibliographies: Wight [unrecorded]

Collation: [A]¹⁶ B-E¹⁶; signatures left foot of page; 80 leaves; 181 × 111mm.; [1–6] 7–9 [10] 11–17 [18–19] 20–28 [29] 30–39 [40] 41–44 [45] 46–48 [49] 50–54 [55] 56–60 [61] 62–68 [69] 70–81 [82] 83–84 [85] 86–88 [89] 90–98 [99] 100–104 [105] 106–110 [111] 112–19 [120] 121–28 [129] 130–34 [135] 136–40 [141] 142–47 [148] 149–55 [156–60]

Pagination contents: [1] 'PUFFIN BOOKS | Editor : Kaye Webb | PS253 | JIM DAVIS | [16 line description of novel] | Cover design by Exell'; [2] frontispiece: 123 × 85mm. of illustration of man with toy boat infront of hut with two boys looking on; [3] title-page; [4] '[listing of publisher's offices] | [rule] | First published by Wells Gardner, Darton & Co. 1911 | Published in Puffin Books 1966 | Copyright © John Masefield, 1911 | [rule] | Made and printed in Great Britain | by Cox & Wyman Ltd, | London, Fakenham and Reading | Set in Intertype Plantin | [eight lines of publisher's conditions]'; [5] 'CONTENTS' (20 chapters listed with titles and page references); [6] blank; 7-[156] text; [157–60] publisher's advertisements (six titles and their authors listed with brief synopsis of plot)

Paper: wove paper

Running title: 'Jim Davis' (15mm.) on verso; recto title comprises chapter title, pp.7-[156]

Binding: blue wrappers. On spine, reading lengthways down spine from head: 'John Masefield [in black] JIM DAVIS [in white]', horizontally at foot of spine: 'PS253 [in black] | [white rule] | [yellow block with black and white publisher's design of a puffin]'. On upper wrapper: 'JIM DAVIS [in white] | JOHN MASEFIELD [in yellow] | [illustration of man and boy fleeing pursuit with three horses, in yellow, black, white and green] | [white rule] | [yellow block with 'A Puffin Book', publisher's design of puffin in black and white and '3/6' in black]'. On lower wrapper: '[illustration of six pirates on ship pointing canon at a frigate, in yellow, black, white and green] | [white rule] | [yellow block with 'Published by Penguin Books' in black]'. All edges trimmed. Binding measurements: 181 × 111mm. (wrappers), 181 × 8mm. (spine).

Publication date: published, according to the *English Catalogue of Books*, 24 February 1966

Price: 3s.6d.

Contents:
as for A20(a)

Notes:
The system of pagination is not consistent: the last page of a chapter is not numbered with the three exceptions of p.76, p.96 and p.127.

Chapter titles as A20(a) (except chapter II here hyphenated 'Night-Riders', chapter V becomes 'The Last Voyage of the 'Snail'', chapter VII's 'Coastguards' are here one word and chapter XI is correctly spelt 'The Frigate 'Laocoön'').

Copies seen: private collection (ROV)

A21 THE EVERLASTING MERCY AND THE WIDOW IN THE BYE STREET   1912

A21(a) First American edition (1912)

THE EVERLASTING MERCY | AND | THE WIDOW IN THE BYE STREET | BY | JOHN MASEFIELD | AUTHOR OF "THE TRAGEDY OF NAN," "THE | TRAGEDY OF POMPEY THE GREAT," ETC. | New York | THE MACMILLAN COMPANY | 1912 | *All rights reserved*
(All width centred)

Bibliographies: Danielson [unrecorded], Williams [unrecorded], Simmons [20], Nevinson [unrecorded], Handley-Taylor p.31, Wight 18b/[20]

Collation: [A-Q]⁸ (but signed [A]⁴ B-P⁸ Q¹²; see note on American electrotype editions) (J not used); signatures left foot of page; 128 leaves; 185 × 125mm.; [i–viii] 1–230 [231–48]

Page contents: [i] half-title: 'THE EVERLASTING MERCY | AND | THE WIDOW IN THE BYE STREET'; [ii] '[publisher's device] | THE MACMILLAN COMPANY | [two lines listing five cities, separated by three points] | MACMILLAN & CO., LIMITED | [two lines listing four cities, separated by two points] | THE MACMILLAN CO. OF CANADA, LTD. | [one city listed]'; [iii] title-page; [iv] 'COPYRIGHT, 1911, | BY JOHN MASEFIELD. | COPYRIGHT, 1912, | BY THE MACMILLAN COMPANY. | [rule] | Set up and electrotyped. Published March, 1912. | Norwood Press | J. S. Cushing Co.-Berwick & Smith Co. | Norwood, Mass., U.S.A.'; [v] 'TO MY WIFE'; [vi] blank; [vii] '*Thy place is biggyd above the sterrys cleer,* | *Noon erthely paleys wrouhte in so statly wyse,* | *Com on my freend, my brothir moost enteer,* | *For the I offryd my blood in sacrifise.* | JOHN LYDGATE.'; [viii] blank; 1–91 text of 'The Everlasting Mercy'; 92 'NOTE | "The Everlasting Mercy" first appeared | in *The English Review* for October, 1911. I | thank the Editor and Proprietors of that | paper for permitting me to reprint it here. | The persons and events described in the poem | are entirely imaginary, and no reference is | made or intended to any living person. | JOHN MASEFIELD.'; 93–230 text of 'The Widow in the Bye Street'; [231] 'THE following pages contain advertisements of | books on kindred subjects.' (within ruled border: 15 × 77mm.); [232] blank; [233–38] publisher's advertisements; [239–48] blank

Paper: wove paper

Running title: '*THE EVERLASTING MERCY*' (46mm.) on both verso and recto, pp.2–91; '*THE WIDOW IN THE BYE STREET*' (59mm.) on both verso and recto, pp.94–230

Binding: mottled light grey-green boards with grey-green cloth spine. On spine, in gold: '[ornament featuring pine cone: 11 × 26mm.] | The | EVER- | LASTING | MERCY | MASEFIELD | MACMILLAN' (all width centred). On upper cover, in gold: '[ornament featuring pine cone: 23 × 99mm.] | The EVERLASTING MERCY | [small ornament] JOHN MASEFIELD [small ornament] | [ornament featuring pine cone: 21 × 99mm.]' note that all minuscules on spine and upper cover are swash and that the ornament first used on the upper cover is inverted below the title and author for its second appearance. Lower cover: blank. Top edge gilt, lower outside edge uncut, fore edge roughly trimmed. Binding measurements: 194 × 126mm. (covers), 194 × 39mm. (spine). Endpapers: wove paper.

Publication date: published, according to Simmons, 27 March 1912 in an edition of 1000 copies

Price: $1.25

Contents:
The Everlasting Mercy ('From '41 to '51')
The Widow in the Bye Street ('Down Bye Street, in a little Shropshire town,')
    First printed in The English Review *February 1912, pp.377–424*

Notes:
The Everlasting Mercy is signed 'GREAT HAMPDEN. June, 1911.' In contrast to the copyright note for *The Everlasting Mercy* on p.92, the title for *The Widow in the Bye Street* on p.93 is provided with a footnote, which reads 'Copyright in the United Kingdom and U.S.A., 1912.'

Simmons notes that 'the letter M, which should appear on p.161, is lacking'. It is present in all copies examined. It is lacking, however, in the illustrated American edition of this title (see A21(c)).

Wight, retaining Simmons' numbering, notes this edition as [20]. However, he also refers readers to his own number 18b which is described as 'First American Edition' of *The Everlasting Mercy*. As *The Everlasting Mercy* was first published in America with *The Widow in the Bye Street*, Wight describes the same volume twice.

Wight notes that 'some editions were bound in green paper wrappers'. No such copies have been examined.

A publishing agreement for this title between Masefield and Macmillan was dated 14 May 1912 (see Archives of The Society of Authors). The agreement refers to 'the American book rights in a work the subject or title of which is The Everlasting Mercy and The Widow in the Bye Street'.

Masefield, it appears, asked Reginald Wright Kauffman (see B115) to assist in placing *The Everlasting Mercy* with an American publisher. Kauffman reported:

> …I have sent The Everlasting Mercy to my publishers (Moffat, Yard & Co., 31 East 17th. St., New York City), as you suggested; have told Mr. J.H. Coit, the active member of the firm, that if he publishes it before December 1st he will be given the first chance to bid for your next novel or play, and have said that you must have a prompt decision. Coit, as I know from trying to persuade him to publish my attempts at verse, is as much afraid of poetry as a Kentucky Colonel is of water; but I have written him what I think of The Everlasting Mercy, because he seems to value my opinion about everybody's work save my own, and I hope that he will bring the poem out in accord with your desire. Pray let me know how the negotiations turn out. …Do you mind my saying that I think The Everlasting Mercy <u>big</u>? It's The Shropshire Lad plus the worldwide appeal that The Lad lacked.
>
>   (Reginald Wright Kauffman, letter to John Masefield, 18 September 1911)
>   (HRHRC, MS (Masefield, J.) Recip Kauffman, Reginald W. TLS to Masefield)

This volume provides the first publication in book form of *The Widow in the Bye Street* (the poem first appeared in print within the periodical *The English Review*). Masefield's agent wrote, after receiving the manuscript:

> I get to the office in just the mood to do a comfortable routine day's work, and then you come along with "The Widow", and tear the heart out of me. This is just by way of acknowledgement. If I could tell you the impression it has make upon

me I think I should come somewhere being myself a great artist. I daresay I shall get my bearings later in the day, and then I will add a postscript about selling it.

…You know, of course, that Carnett is over here for the "Century", and I think he ought to see it. I am putting it to him that if he feels certain it is too strong meat to go with the thin culture which is the "Century's" distinctive note, he had better not trouble to send it out. Harper's once ran "Jude" and – doubtless when the advertising manager was on a holiday – "The Alter of Righteousness", and they are a possibility We want to get the longest price above ground, so unless you are particularly anxious to have it out at once, we will try these big Americans first…

…Then as to the book, I have heard nothing from Sidgwick, whom I am stirring up. It seems to me on the whole that unquestionably the poem should be serialised, and that a little time should elapse before book publication. I am inclined to think, too, that the money would lie rather in a bigger volume. I know you have to do just what you must do, but if you think it is likely that you will have to do more poetry, I think a fairly full volume would make a big sensation, and would have a large and permanent sale. What do you think?

(C.F. Cazenove, letter to John Masefield, 20 October 1911)
(University of Arizona Library. MS.50)

It is well documented how Masefield's diction (particularly use of the word "bloody") caused *The English Review* to print blank spaces for the first appearance of *The Everlasting Mercy* (see notes to A19(b)). It has always been assumed, however, that Masefield's second narrative poem did not cause offence. This was not the case. A letter from Austin Harrison (editor of *The English Review*) to Masefield enclosed

…a list of passages which I should like you to modify. I do not want to print the poem with a lot of blanks, and apart from any question of my own taste, our printers would absolutely refuse to set up some of your lines…

(Austin Harrison, letter to John Masefield, 4 January 1912)
(HRHRC, MS (Masefield, J.) Recip The English Review)

Offensive lines included 'I'll give you bloody faith, bloody galore', 'I'll paint the bloody village bloody red…' and 'More bloody idiots they…' One line noted 'His blasted child is knocking in her womb' and Harrison noted that his '…printers absolutely refuse to print it in the Review, and have only set it in proof under protest!' It appears that Masefield revised *The Widow in the Bye Street* meeting the criticisms of the editor of *The English Review*. When printed in book form the original readings were not, apparently, restored.

Talking Books for the Blind applied for permission to record this title in July 1937. This was approved by Masefield (see BL, Add.Mss.56607, f.58).

Copies seen: private collection (ROV); BL (X.908/4021) stamped 15 JUN 1963 rebound

Reprinted:

Aug 1912
Jan 1913

A21(b) Second American edition (1913)

THE EVERLASTING MERCY | AND | THE WIDOW IN THE BYE STREET | BY | JOHN MASEFIELD | AUTHOR OF "THE TRAGEDY OF NAN," "THE | TRAGEDY OF POMPEY THE GREAT," ETC. | *NEW REVISED EDITION* | New York | THE MACMILLAN COMPANY | 1913 | *All rights reserved*
(All width centred)

Bibliographies: Danielson [unrecorded], Williams [unrecorded], Simmons [unrecorded], Nevinson [unrecorded], Handley-Taylor p.31, Wight [unrecorded]

Collation: [A-Q]⁸ (±[A]2) (but signed [A]⁴ (±[A]2) B-P⁸ Q¹²; see note on American electrotype editions) (J not used); signatures left foot of page; 128 leaves; 187 × 126mm.; [i–viii] 1–230 [231–48]

Page contents: [i] half-title: 'THE EVERLASTING MERCY | AND | THE WIDOW IN THE BYE STREET'; [ii] '[publisher's device] | THE MACMILLAN COMPANY | [two lines listing five cities, separated by three points] | MACMILLAN & CO., LIMITED | [two lines listing four cities, separated by two points] | THE MACMILLAN CO. OF CANADA, LTD. | [one city listed]'; [iii] title-page; [iv] 'COPYRIGHT, 1911, | BY JOHN MASEFIELD. | COPYRIGHT, 1912, | BY THE MACMILLAN COMPANY. | [rule] | Set up and electrotyped. Published March, 1912. Reprinted | August, 1912; January 1913; April, 1913. | Norwood Press | J. S. Cushing Co.-Berwick & Smith Co. | Norwood, Mass., U.S.A.'; [v] 'TO MY WIFE'; [vi] blank; [vii] '*Thy place is biggyd above the sterrys cleer,* | *Noon erthely paleys wrouhte in so statly wyse,* | *Com on my freend, my brothir moost enteer,* | *For the I offryd my blood in sacrifise.* | JOHN LYDGATE.'; [viii] blank; 1–91 text of 'The Everlasting Mercy'; 92 'NOTE | "The Everlasting Mercy" first appeared | in *The English Review* for October, 1911. I | thank the Editor and Proprietors of that | paper for permitting me to reprint it here. | The persons and events described in the poem | are entirely imaginary, and no reference is | made or intended to any living person. | JOHN MASEFIELD.'; 93–230 text of 'The Widow in the Bye Street'; [231] 'THE following pages contain advertisements of | books on kindred subjects.' (within ruled border: 15 × 77mm.); [232] blank; [233–38] publisher's advertisements; [239–48] blank

Paper: wove paper

Running title: 'THE EVERLASTING MERCY' (46mm.) on both verso and recto, pp.2–91; 'THE WIDOW IN THE BYE STREET' (59mm.) on both verso and recto, pp.94–230

Binding: burgundy cloth. On spine, in gold 'The | EVER- | LASTING | MERCY | MASEFIELD | MACMILLAN' (all width centred). Note that all minuscules on spine are swash. On upper cover, in gold: 'THE | EVERLASTING | MERCY | MASEFIELD' (ranged upper left) (within blind ruled border: 189 × 122mm.) Lower cover: blank. Top edge gilt, others roughly trimmed. Binding measurements: 194 × 127mm. (covers), 194 × 39mm. (spine). End-papers: wove paper.

Publication date: published, according to date within volume, April 1913

Price: $1.25

Contents:
The Everlasting Mercy ('From '41 to '51')
The Widow in the Bye Street ('Down Bye Street, in a little Shropshire town,') [revised text]

Notes:
As in A21(a), *The Everlasting Mercy* is signed 'GREAT HAMPDEN. June, 1911.' In contrast to the copyright note for *The Everlasting Mercy* on p.92, the title for *The Widow in the Bye Street* on p.93 is provided with a footnote, which reads 'Copyright in the United Kingdom and U.S.A., 1912.'

The 'New Revised Edition' status is due to revised and re-set text on pp.214–215. Two stanzas here replace a single stanza:

So the talk passes as the train descends	So the talk passes as the train descends
Into the vale, and halts, and starts to climb;	Into the vale, and halts, and starts to climb
Heartless is ever swift at making friends,	To where the apple-bearing country ends
Heartless plucks honey from the evil time,	And pleasant-pastured hills rise sweet with thyme,
The heartless soul makes many bells to chime:	Where clinking sheepbells make a broken chime
Joybells and deathbells, wedding bells and dirges,	And sunwarm gorses rich the air with scent
Heartless is one of God's appointed scourges.	And kestrels poise for mice, there Anna went.

There, in the April, in the garden-close,
One heard her in the morning singing sweet,
Calling the birds from the unbudded rose,
Offering her lips with grains for them to eat.
The redbreasts come with little wiry feet,
Sparrows and tits and all wild feathery things,
Brushing her lifted face with quivering wings.

The single stanza text, as present in A21(a) is that which is printed in *The English Review*. The two stanza text is first printed in the first English edition of *The Widow in the Bye Street* (A22(a)).

Copies seen: private collection (PWE)

Reprinted:

Apr 1913
Aug 1913
Jan 1914
Aug 1914
Jul 1915
Jan 1916
Mar 1916
Nov 1916
Mar 1917

A21(c) Third American edition (1919)

[rule] | THE | EVERLASTING MERCY | AND | THE WIDOW IN THE BYE STREET | *By* | JOHN MASEFIELD | *Author of "The Tragedy of Nan," "The | Tragedy of Pompey the Great," etc.* | NEW ILLUSTRATED | EDITION | New York | THE MACMILLAN COMPANY | 1919 | *All rights reserved* | [rule]
(All width centred and enclosed within ruled border: 144 × 89mm. As a result of the two rules noted above, three rectangles are created measuring 2 × 89mm., 141 × 89mm. and 2 × 89mm. respectively from the top)

Bibliographies: Danielson [unrecorded], Williams [unrecorded], Simmons [noted on p.38], Nevinson [unrecorded], Handley-Taylor p.31, Wight [unrecorded]

Collation: [A-P]⁸ (but signed [A]⁵ B-L⁸ [M]⁸ N-P⁸ Q³; see note on American electrotype editions) (J not used); signatures left foot of page; 120 leaves; 187 × 128mm.; [i–x] 1–230; illustrations (on glossy paper) tipped-in on pp.[ii], 2, 4, 6, 16, 18, 20, 30, 48, 62, 66, 78, 80, 82, 84, 86, 146 and 150

Page contents: [i] half-title: 'THE EVERLASTING MERCY | AND | THE WIDOW IN THE BYE STREET'; [ii] '[publisher's device] | THE MACMILLAN COMPANY | [two lines listing five cities, separated by three points] | MACMILLAN & CO., LIMITED | [two lines listing four cities, separated by two points] | THE MACMILLAN CO. OF CANADA, LTD. | [one city listed]' (with additional leaf tipped-in on the verso of which is the frontispiece: 144 × 89mm., with two additional rules to create three rectangles measuring 2 × 89mm., 141 × 89mm. and 2 × 89mm. respectively from the top, 'Down Bye Street, in a little Shropshire town, | There lived a widow with her only son: | She had no wealth nor title to renown, | Nor any joyous hours, never one.'); [iii] title-page; [iv] 'COPYRIGHT, 1911, | BY JOHN MASEFIELD. | [rule] | COPYRIGHT, 1912, | BY THE MACMILLAN COMPANY. | [rule] | COPYRIGHT, 1919, | BY JOHN MASEFIELD. | Norwood Press | J. S. Cushing Co.-Berwick & Smith Co. | Norwood, Mass., U.S.A.'; [v] 'TO MY WIFE'; [vi] blank; [vii] *'Thy place is biggyd above the sterrys cleer,* | *Noon erthely paleys wrouhte in so statly wyse,* | *Com on my freend, my brothir moost enteer,* | *For the I offryd my blood in sacrifise.* | JOHN LYDGATE.'; [viii] blank; [ix] 'ILLUSTRATIONS | [18 illustrations listed with page references] | [rule] | *Photographs by Messrs. L. Tilley and Son, Ledbury, England.*'; [x] blank 1–91 text of 'The Everlasting Mercy'; 92 'NOTE | "The Everlasting Mercy" first appeared | in *The English Review* for October, 1911. I | thank the Editor and Proprietors of that | paper for permitting me to reprint it here. | The persons and events described in the poem | are entirely imaginary, and no reference is | made or intended to any living person. | JOHN MASEFIELD.'; 93–230 text of 'The Widow in the Bye Street' (at foot of p.230: '[rule] | Printed in the United States of America.')

Paper: wove paper (watermark: 'FLEMISH BOOK')

Running title: '*THE EVERLASTING MERCY*' (46mm.) on both verso and recto, pp.2–91; '*THE WIDOW IN THE BYE STREET*' (59mm.) on both verso and recto, pp.94–230

Binding: green cloth. On spine, in gold: 'The | EVERLASTING | MERCY | and | THE WIDOW | IN THE | BYE STREET | [floral ornament in gold and green] | MASEFIELD | MACMILLAN' (width centred). On upper cover, in gold: 'The | EVERLASTING MERCY | and | THE WIDOW | IN THE BYE STREET | JOHN | MASEFIELD' (surrounded by ornate floral border in green and white with drawing (signed 'RICHARDS') on paper laid down below text within white border). Lower cover: blank. Note that all minuscules on spine and upper cover are swash. All edges trimmed. Binding measurements: 194 × 127mm. (covers), 194 × 40mm. (spine). End-papers: wove paper (watermark includes the letters 'DE STYLE').

Publication date: published, according to Simmons, 25 November 1919 in an edition of 2090 copies

Price: $2.50

Contents:
as for A21(b)

Notes:
In describing A21(a) Simmons notes that 'the letter M, which should appear on p.161, is lacking'. As noted above, it is present in all copies of A21(a) and A21(b) examined. It is lacking, however, in this edition.

Compare with the binding of A18(b). The upper cover, in particular, uses the same ornate floral border.

Copies seen: Library of The John Masefield Society (Peter Smith Collection)

Reprinted:

1923

A21(d) Fourth American edition ["Leather Pocket Edition"] (1923)

THE EVERYLASTING [*sic*] | MERCY | ~ | THE WIDOW IN THE | BYE STREET | *By* | JOHN MASEFIELD | [circular floral ornament] [in red] | NEW YORK | THE MACMILLAN COMPANY | 1923 | ALL RIGHTS RESERVED
(All width centred and enclosed within ornate border in red: 135 × 78mm.)

Bibliographies: Simmons [noted on p.38], Nevinson [unrecorded], Handley-Taylor p.31 and p.53, Wight [unrecorded]

Collation: [A]¹¹ ([A]3+2 and [A]11+1) [B-P]⁸ (but signed [A]⁷ ([A]3+2) B⁸ (B4+1) C-L⁸ [M]⁸ N-P⁸ Q⁴, see note on American electrotype editions) (J not used); signatures left foot of page; 123 leaves; 171 × 114mm.; [i–viii] ix–xii [xiii–xiv] 1–230 [231–32]

Page contents: [i] half-title: 'THE EVERLASTING MERCY | ~ | THE WIDOW IN THE BYE STREET | [ornament] [in red]'; [ii] '[27 titles separated by 20 single points] | [ornament] [in red]' (enclosed within ornate border in red: 135 × 78mm.); [iii] title-page; [iv] 'COPYRIGHT, 1911, 1919 AND 1923, BY JOHN MASEFIELD | COPYRIGHT, 1912, BY THE MACMILLAN COMPANY | *Printed in the United States of America* | [ornament] [in red]'; [v] 'TO MY WIFE'; [vi] blank; [vii] *'Thy place is biggyd above the sterrys cleer,* | *Noon erthely paleys wrouhte in so statly wyse,* | *Com on my friend, my brothir moost enteer,* | *For the I offryd my blood in sacrifise.* | JOHN LYDGATE.'; [viii] blank; ix–xii 'THE EVERLASTING MERCY | THE WIDOW IN THE BYE STREET | INTRODUCTION' ('I believe that we are partly-incarnate spirits in a world of spirits…') (unsigned); [xiii] 'THE EVERLASTING MERCY | AND | THE WIDOW IN THE BYE STREET'; [xiv] blank; 1–91 text of 'The Everlasting Mercy'; 92 'NOTE | "The Everlasting Mercy" first appeared | in *The English Review* for October, 1911. I | thank the Editor and Proprietors of that | paper for permitting me to reprint it here. | The persons and events described in the poem | are entirely imaginary, and no reference is | made or intended to any living person. | JOHN MASEFIELD.'; 93–230 text of 'The Widow in the Bye Street' (at foot of p.230: '[rule] | Printed in the United States of America.'); [231–32] blank

Paper: laid paper (no watermark), chain-lines 22mm. apart

Running titles: 'THE EVERLASTING MERCY' (46mm.) on both verso and recto, pp.2–91; 'THE WIDOW IN THE BYE STREET' (59mm.) on both verso and recto, pp.94–230

Binding: red leather. On spine, in gold: '[floral panel] | THE | EVERLASTING | MERCY | [point] | THE WIDOW | IN THE | BYE STREET | MASEFIELD | [floral panel] | MACMILLAN' (all width centred). On upper cover, in blind: circular floral ornament. Lower cover: blank. Upper and lower covers have blind ruled borders, on three sides only: 171 × 109mm. Top edge gilt, others trimmed. End-papers: wove paper.

Publication date: published, according to Handley-Taylor, 30 August 1923 / published, according to Simmons, 30 October 1923 in an edition of 2000 copies (see notes)

Price: $12.50 (set of 8 volumes: see also A49(h), A52(b), A54(g), A66(a), A67(a), A68(a) and A69(a))

Contents:
Introduction ('I believe that we are partly-incarnate spirits in a world of spirits…')
and as for A21(b)

Notes:
Issued as volume II in the Macmillan Leather Pocket Edition of Masefield's Work.

Accepting Handley-Taylor's publication date would explain the omission of *A King's Daughter* (published on 23 October 1923) in the listing of Masefield's works appearing on page [ii].

A publishing agreement changing royalties for titles to be published in the Leather Pocket edition between Masefield and Macmillan was dated 19 June 1923 (see Archives of The Society of Authors). The agreement refers to 'a pocket edition, bound in leather, and to be issued in eight volumes'.

It appears that by May 1936 sales of the complete set had almost ceased. George P. Brett Jr therefore wrote to Masefield with a suggestion:

> My attention has just been called to the fact that the sale of the eight volume leather pocket edition, which lists in our catalog at $12.50… has practically disappeared and that we have a substantial stock on hand. Our sales department has made the recommendation that we sell this stock in separate volumes at $1.75 each. They feel that there is no longer a possibility of disposing of the stock in sets…

> (George P. Brett Jr, letter to John Masefield, 15 May 1936)
> (HRHRC, MS (Masefield, J.) Recip The Macmillan Company)

Handley-Taylor omits reference to the inclusion of *The Widow in the Bye Street* in this volume.

Copies seen: private collection (PWE)

A21(e) Fifth American edition (1954)

THE EVERLASTING MERCY | AND | THE WIDOW IN THE BYE STREET | BY | JOHN MASEFIELD | AUTHOR OF "THE TRAGEDY OF NAN," "THE | TRAGEDY OF POMPEY THE GREAT," ETC. | *NEW REVISED EDITION* | [publisher's device of bridge with '*Bridgehead Books:* New York | 1954']
(All width centred. Within publisher's device, both lines are off-set to left)

Bibliographies: Handley-Taylor [unrecorded], Wight [unrecorded]

Collation: [A-C]¹⁶ [D-E]¹² [F-H]¹⁶ (where E is signed I) (but signed [A]⁴ B-L⁸ [M]⁸ N-P⁸ Q⁴; see note on American electrotype editions) (J not used); signatures left foot of page; 120 leaves; 203 × 134mm.; [i–viii] 1–230 [231–32]

Page contents: [i] half-title: 'THE EVERLASTING MERCY | AND | THE WIDOW IN THE BYE STREET'; [ii] blank; [iii] title-page; [iv] 'COPYRIGHT, 1911, | BY JOHN MASEFIELD. | COPYRIGHT, 1912, | By THE MACMILLAN COMPANY. | [rule] | First Bridgehead Books Edition | 1954'; [v] 'TO MY WIFE'; [vi] blank; [vii] '*Thy place is biggyd above the sterrys cleer, | Noon erthely paleys wrouhte in so statly wyse, | Com on my freend, my brothir moost enteer, | For the I offryd my blood in sacrifise.* | JOHN LYDGATE.'; [viii] blank; 1–91 text of 'The Everlasting Mercy'; 92 'NOTE | "The Everlasting Mercy" first appeared | in *The English Review* for October, 1911. I | thank the Editor and Proprietors of that | paper for permitting me to reprint it here. | The persons and events described in the poem | are entirely imaginary, and no reference is | made or intended to any living person. | JOHN MASEFIELD.'; 93–230 text of 'The Widow in the Bye Street' (at foot of p.230: '[rule] | Printed in the United States of America.'); [231–32] blank

Paper: wove paper

Running title: 'THE EVERLASTING MERCY' (46mm.) on both verso and recto, pp.2–91; 'THE WIDOW IN THE BYE STREET' (59mm.) on both verso and recto, pp.94–230

Binding: red cloth. On spine, reading lengthways down spine from head: '*The Everlasting Mercy*'. Covers: blank. All edges trimmed. Binding measurements: 210 × 136mm. (covers), 210 × 37mm. (spine). End-papers: wove paper.

Publication date: 1954

Price: unknown

Contents:
as for A21(b)

Notes:
This edition notes the 'New Revised Edition' status and includes the orthodox reading of stanzas 16 and 17 in part six of *The Widow in the Bye Street*. Coupled with the omitted M signature and the apparent similarity in type setting it is likely that this edition is derived from the revised Macmillan plates.

It appears that there was interest in 1953 to use the Macmillan plates for a new printing of this title. Macmillan wrote to Masefield:

> …The Seven Sirens Press, Inc. of New York City has made us an offer to reprint in one volume the two poems, THE EVERLASTING MERCY and THE WIDOW IN THE BYE STREET. They propose to print a minimum of 3000 copies from our plates, with some drawings by Mahlon Blaine. They will set a retail price of $1.98 per copy on their editions and they offer to pay a royalty of 10% of their retail price, or the sum of $594, on the signing of the contract.
> (R.L. De Wilton, letter to John Masefield, 18 February 1953)
> (HRHRC, MS (Masefield, J.) Recip The Macmillan Company)

Masefield appears to have agreed to this proposal on 25 April 1953. Although a volume with illustrations by Mahlon Blaine does not appear to have been issued by The Seven Sirens Press, this business may have resulted in the edition described here.

The dust-jacket for this edition suggests that Bridgehead Books catered for other interests beyond verse narratives. The upper cover shows a pair of boxing gloves and a seated female nude. The lower cover includes a listing of 'Volumes from our library of Unusual Books' (which include *The Pleasures of Being Beaten*, *The Sexual Conduct of Men and Women* and *The Education of a French Model*). It is unclear whether Masefield's poems formed part of this library. The inside of the front flap reads:

> Mr. Masefield is poet laureate of England. He has occupied this grand position in letters for more than a quarter of a century.
> Before being made poet laureate, Mr. Masefield wrote in great poverty, swabbed the decks of ships and polished spitoons in a Yonkers bar.
> It was the swabber of ship-decks and the polisher of bar-brass who wrote the language of these books, the most ardent descriptions of prize-fighting and whoring to come out of the western world.
> The fighter in *The Everlasting Mercy* finally sees the light. But after what rampages through secret dens of sin! It reminds you of *The Inferno*, only that this hell is more terrible because it is a sexual hell.
> *The Widow in the Bye Street* is an even more voluptuous story of the seduction of a simple man by an unscrupulous woman. If good triumphs in this book it is only because (by divine arrangement) good is the end of all evil, no matter what wild courses evil can take in a sensitive imagination.

Copies seen: private collection (PWE); Library of The John Masefield Society (Peter Smith Collection)

A22 THE WIDOW IN THE BYE STREET   1912

A22(a) *First English edition (1912)*

THE WIDOW IN THE | BYE STREET | BY | JOHN MASEFIELD | LONDON | SIDGWICK & JACKSON LTD. | 3 ADAM STREET, ADELPHI | MCMXII
(All width centred)

Bibliographies: Danielson 178, Williams p.3, Simmons [21], Nevinson p.12, Handley-Taylor p.33, Wight [21]

Collation: [π]⁴ A-F⁸ G⁴; signatures left foot of page; 56 leaves; 185 × 118mm.; [i–viii] 1–97 [98–104]

Page contents: [i–ii] blank; [iii] half-title: 'THE WIDOW IN THE BYE STREET'; [iv] blank; [v] title-page; [vi] '*Entered at the Library of Congress, Washington, U.S.A.* | *All rights reserved*'; [vii] 'TO | MY WIFE'; [viii] blank; 1–97 text; [98] "The Widow in the Bye Street' first appeared in *The* | *English Review* for February 1912. I thank the editor and | proprietors of the *Review* for permitting me to reprint it | here. | [new paragraph] The persons and events described in the poem are entirely | imaginary, and no reference is made or intended to any living | person. | JOHN MASEFIELD. | 10*th May* 1912. | THE RIVERSIDE PRESS LIMITED, EDINBURGH'; [99–104] publisher's advertisements

Paper: laid paper (no watermark), chain-lines 25mm. apart

Running title: 'THE WIDOW IN THE BYE STREET' (74mm.) on both verso and recto, pp.2–97

Binding: red cloth. On spine, in gold: 'The | Widow | in the | Bye | Street | [ornament] | John | Masefield | SIDGWICK |&JACKSON' (all width centred). On upper cover, in gold: 'THE WIDOW IN THE BYE STREET | JOHN MASEFIELD'. Lower cover: blank. Upper and lower covers have blind ruled borders: 184 × 115mm. All edges trimmed. Binding measurements: 191 × 122mm. (covers), 191 × 26mm. (spine). End-papers: laid paper (no watermark), chain-lines 28mm. apart.

Publication date: published, according to Simmons, 6 June 1912 in an edition of 3000 copies

THE
TRAGEDY OF NAN

BY
JOHN MASEFIELD

LONDON
GRANT RICHARDS LTD.
1911

A18(a) title-page

The Everlasting Mercy

By
John Masefield
AUTHOR OF
The Tragedy of Nan, The Tragedy
of Pompey the Great, etc.

LONDON
SIDGWICK & JACKSON, LTD.
MCMXI

A19(b) title-page

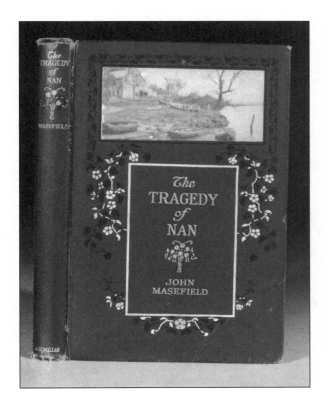

A18(b) spine and upper cover

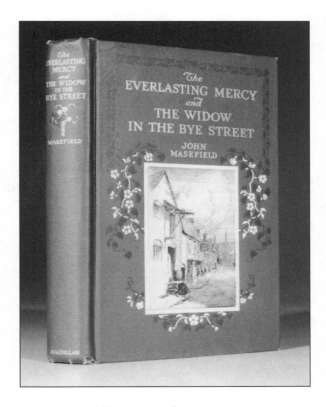

A21(c) spine and upper cover

THE WIDOW IN THE
BYE STREET

BY

JOHN MASEFIELD

LONDON
SIDGWICK & JACKSON LTD.
3 ADAM STREET, ADELPHI
MCMXII

A22(a) title-page

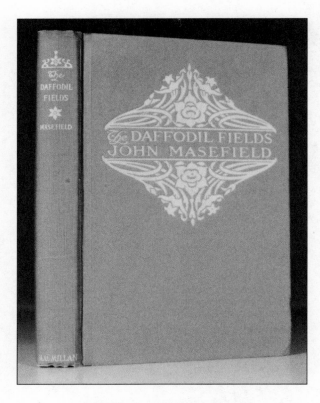

A24(a) spine and upper cover

THE
DAFFODIL FIELDS

BY

JOHN MASEFIELD

AUTHOR OF "THE EVERLASTING MERCY," "THE WIDOW IN
THE BYE STREET," "THE STORY OF A
ROUND-HOUSE," ETC.

New York
THE MACMILLAN COMPANY
1913
All rights reserved

A24(a) title-page

THE
DAFFODIL FIELDS

BY

JOHN MASEFIELD

AUTHOR OF
"THE EVERLASTING MERCY," ETC.

LONDON
WILLIAM HEINEMANN
MCMXIII

A24(b) title-page

Price: 3s.6d.

Contents:
The Widow in the Bye Street ('Down Bye Street, in a little Shropshire town,')

Notes:
The poem has six parts each prefaced by a roman numeral.

Simmons provides a note regarding a delay in the availability of the first printing:

> Messrs. Sidgwick and Jackson state: "It may be of interest to record, with regard to 'The Widow,' that of the 3000 printed, 1000 were despatched to us by rail, bound, and put on the market, while the remaining 2000, sent by sea from Edinburgh, were held at the London Docks in the Thames by a strike, and we were unable for some weeks to secure delivery. We therefore printed a 'second thousand' (a second impression or printing) to meet the demand, until the 2000 remaining of the first edition were released by the calling-off of the strike."

(The London Dock strike started on 24 May 1912 and was given up on 27 July 1912). The 'second thousand' is identical to the first edition except the addition of '*Second Thousand*' to the foot of p.[vi]. The copy in the British Library is one of these later issues (technically, 'first edition – second impression'). George B.T. Smith, in his article 'John Masefield – An Intermittent Genius' in *Book and Magazine Collector*, October 1996, pp.28–44 recounts Simmons' information and then states:

> Although not recorded by Simmons, a "third thousand" was also printed in Edinburgh. This certainly makes the identification of a true first edition difficult, as the second and third printings were on sale before two-thirds of the original impression.

The 'third thousand' gives the date 'MCMXII' on the title page. Copies that therefore give note of being second or third thousands presumably predate the reprint noted as the 'Second Impression'. This should, therefore, be more accurately considered a fourth impression.

The publishing agreement for this title between Masefield and the firm of Sidgwick and Jackson was dated 1 April 1912 (see Archives of The Society of Authors). The agreement specifies that 'first publication... shall not be later than the first of June 1912...') Correspondence relating to Simmons' bibliography preserved in the archives of Sidgwick and Jackson (see Bodleian, MS.Sidgwick & Jackson 228) confirms a publication date of 6 June 1912 and a first printing of 3000 copies. It appears that these 3000 copies were printed, or originally intended for release, on 31 May 1912. An additional 1000 copies were printed during June 1912.

During the early 1930s a Mr C. Gibson Barlow submitted to Masefield a 'talking picture version he had made of THE WIDOW... to which he gives the title... of JIMMY LAD' (see BL, Add.Mss.56601, ff.9–11). Writing of Barlow's scenario to The Society of Authors, Masefield states:

> I feel that Mr Barlow should have the first chance with *the Widow*. His scenario is competent. I do not like his flogging of my temptress; for I have never heard of any Englishmen flogging a woman who was neither his wife nor his mistress. I feel, too, that any picture made of *the Widow* should be made in the places described; all are in or near to Ledbury, in Herefordshire. Mr Barlow's work seems to me to be efficient + to deserve its' chance. He might be granted say 6 months in wh[ich] to try to market his scenario.
>
> (John Masefield, letter to [E.J.] Mullett, [3 January 1935])
> (BL, Add.Mss.56602, ff.15–16)

Although Barlow at one time requested an extension of his option on the poem (see BL, Add.Mss.56603, f.115) it appears that the film was never made.

An application in July 1947 to recite the poem prompted Masefield to write to The Society of Authors:

> I wrote the Widow poem, as a part of a poetical scheme, though it is complete in itself. By itself, it is pretty awful and the original scheme cannot even be suspected. It might be wise, therefore, to suggest to the lady that it will never do as a recital by itself; the horror is too great; she will only reap disappointment.
>
> (John Masefield, letter to Miss [S.M.] Perry, 30 July [1947])
> (BL, Add.Mss.56620, f.76)

Copies seen: private collection (PWE)

Reprinted:

'Second Thousand'	[first edition, second impression]	1912
'Third Thousand'	[first edition, third impression]	1912
'Second Impression'	[first edition, fourth impression]	Jun 1912
'Third Impression'	[first edition, fifth impression]	Feb 1914
'Fourth Impression'	[first edition, sixth impression]	Aug 1918
'Fifth Impression'	[first edition, seventh impression]	Apr 1920
'Sixth Impression'	[first edition, eighth impression]	Aug 1923
'Seventh Impression'	[first edition, ninth impression]	Jul 1946

A23 THE STORY OF A ROUND-HOUSE AND OTHER POEMS   1912

A23(a) First American edition (1912)

THE STORY OF | A ROUND-HOUSE AND | OTHER POEMS | BY | JOHN MASEFIELD | AUTHOR OF "THE EVERLASTING MERCY" | "THE WIDOW IN THE BYE STREET," ETC. | New York | THE MACMILLAN COMPANY | 1912 | *All rights reserved*
(All width centred)

Bibliographies: Danielson [unrecorded], Williams [unrecorded], Simmons [22], Nevinson [unrecorded], Handley-Taylor p.35, Wight [22]

Collation: [A-Y]⁸ (but signed [A]⁴ B-P⁸ [Q]⁸ R-Y⁸ [Z]⁴; see note on American electrotype editions) (J, V and W not used); signatures left foot of page; 176 leaves; 188 × 127mm.; [i–iv] v–vi [vii–viii] 1–325 [326–44]

Page contents: [i] half-title: 'THE STORY OF A ROUND-HOUSE | AND OTHER POEMS'; [ii] '[publisher's device] | THE MACMILLAN COMPANY | [two lines listing five cities, separated by three points] | MACMILLAN & CO., LIMITED | [two lines listing four cities, separated by two points] | THE MACMILLAN CO. OF CANADA, LTD. | [one city listed]'; [iii] title-page; [iv] 'COPYRIGHT, 1912, | BY THE MACMILLAN COMPANY. | [rule] | Set up and electrotyped. Published November, 1912. | Norwood Press | J. S. Cushing Co.-Berwick & Smith Co. | Norwood, Mass., U.S.A.'; v–vi 'CONTENTS' (51 individual poems listed with page references); [vii] 'THE STORY OF A ROUND-HOUSE | AND OTHER POEMS'; [viii] blank; 1–325 text; [326] blank; [327] 'THE following pages contain advertise- | ments of books by the same author and | other recent important poetry' (within ruled border: 20 × 70mm.); [328] blank; [329–33] publisher's advertisements; [334–44] blank

Paper: wove paper

Running title: 'DAUBER' (14mm.) on both verso and recto, pp.2–186; other running titles comprise titles of individual poems, pp.188–325

Binding: mottled light blue boards with blue cloth spine. On spine, in white: '[ornament: 11 × 26mm.] | *The* | STORY | [small triangular ornament] *of a* [small triangular ornament] | ROUND | HOUSE | MASEFIELD | MACMILLAN' (width centred). On upper cover, in white: '[ornament featuring pine cone: 23 × 99mm.] | *The* STORY *of a* ROUND HOUSE | [small ornament] JOHN MASEFIELD [small ornament] | [ornament featuring pine cone: 21 × 99mm.]' note that all minuscules on spine and upper cover are swash and that the ornament first used on the upper cover is inverted below the title and author for its second appearance. Lower cover: blank. Top edge gilt, others untrimmed. Binding measurements: 194 × 129mm. (covers), 194 × 45mm. (spine). End-papers: wove paper.

Publication date: published, according to Simmons, 27 November 1912 in an edition of 1416 copies

Price: $1.30

Contents:
Dauber ('Four bells were struck, the watch was called on deck,')
    First printed in The English Review *October 1912, pp.337–89*
Biography ('When I am buried, all my thoughts and acts')
    First printed in The English Review *May 1912, pp.169–76*
Ships ('I cannot tell their wonder nor make known')
    First printed in The English Review *July 1912, pp.505–507*
Truth ('Man with his burning soul')
    First printed in The English Review *June 1911, p.361*
They Closed Her Eyes (From the Spanish of Don Gustavo A. Bécquer) [*sic*] ('They closed her eyes,')
    First printed in The Westminster Gazette *25 March 1911, p.15*
The Harp (From the Spanish of Don Gustavo A. Becquer) [*sic*] ('In a dark corner of the room,')
    No previous appearance traced
Sonnet (From the Spanish of Don Francisco De Quevedo) [*sic*] ('I saw the ramparts of my native land,')
    First printed in The Westminster Gazette *7 December 1910, p.[2]*
Sonnet On The Death Of His Wife (From the Portuguese of Antonio De Ferreiro) [*sic*] ('That blessed sunlight that once showed to me')
    First printed in The Westminster Gazette *20 October 1910, p.2*
Song ('One sunny time in May')
    First printed in The Westminster Gazette *7 June 1912, p.2*
The Ballad of Sir Bors ('Would I could win some quiet and rest, and a little ease,')
Spanish Waters ('Spanish waters, Spanish waters, you are ringing in my ears,')
Cargoes ('Quinquireme of Nineveh from distant Ophir,')
Captain Stratton's Fancy ('Oh some are fond of red wine, and some are fond of white,')
An old Song Re-sung ('I saw a ship a-sailing, a-sailing, a-sailing,')
St. Mary's Bells ('It's pleasant in Holy Mary')
London Town ('Oh London Town's a fine town, and London sights are rare,')
The Emigrant ('Going by Daly's shanty I heard the boys within')

Port of Holy Peter ('The blue laguna rocks and quivers,')
Beauty ('I have seen dawn and sunset on moors and windy hills')
The Seekers ('Friends and loves we have none, nor wealth nor blessed abode,')
Prayer ('When the last sea is sailed, when the last shallow's charted,')
Dawn ('The dawn comes cold : the haystack smokes,')
Laugh and be Merry ('Laugh and be merry, remember, better the world with a song,')
June Twilight ('The twilight comes; the sun')
Roadways ('One road leads to London,')
Midsummer Night ('The perfect disc of the sacred moon')
The Harper's Song ('This sweetness trembling from the strings')
The Gentle Lady ('So beautiful, so dainty-sweet,')
The Dead Knight ('The cleanly rush of the mountain air,')
Sorrow of Mydath ('Weary the cry of the wind is, weary the sea,')
Twilight ('Twilight it is, and the far woods are dim, and the rooks cry and call.')
Invocation ('O wanderer into many brains,')
Posted as Missing ('Under all her topsails she trembled like a stag,')
A Creed ('I hold that when a person dies')
When Bony Death ('When bony Death has chilled her gentle blood,')
The West Wind ('It's a warm wind, the west wind, full of birds' cries;')
Her Heart ('Her heart is always doing lovely things,')
Being her Friend ('Being her friend, I do not care, not I,')
Fragments ('Troy Town is covered up with weeds,')
Born for Nought Else ('Born for nought else, for nothing but for this,')
Tewkesbury Road ('It is good to be out on the road, and going one knows not where,')
The Death Rooms ('My soul has many an old decaying room')
Ignorance ('Since I have learned Love's shining alphabet,')
Sea Fever ('I must go down to the seas again, to the lonely sea and the sky,')
The Watch In The Wood ('When Death has laid her in his quietude,')
C.L.M. ('In the dark womb where I began')
Waste ('No rose but fades: no glory but must pass:')
Third Mate ('All the sheets are clacking, all the blocks are whining,')
The Wild Duck ('Twilight. Red in the west.')
Christmas, 1903 ('O, the sea breeze will be steady, and the tall ship's going trim,')
The Word ('My friend, my bonny friend, when we are old,')

Notes:

Similar to the publication history of *The Widow in the Bye Street* (see *The Everlasting Mercy and The Widow in the Bye Street* (A21)), the poem 'Dauber' was first published in volume form in America. A different title was used (although the poem is entitled 'Dauber' within the volume itself). The 'other poems' noted in the title comprise the contents of *Ballads and Poems* (see A12(a)), with the exclusion of 'Imagination', and a number of poems printed for the first time in book form. The latter were later published in England in the volume *Philip the King and other Poems* (see A26).

The final signature (presumably Z) appears as a smudge only. It is not noted by Simmons.

The publishing agreement for this volume between Masefield and Macmillan was dated 7 August 1912 (see Archives of The Society of Authors). The agreement refers to 'the American book rights in a work the subject or title of which is Ballads and Poems'. A later hand has annotated the agreement with 'The Round House'.

Copies seen: BL (X.908/4022) stamped 15 JUN 1963

A23(b) Second American edition (1913)

THE STORY OF | A ROUND-HOUSE AND | OTHER POEMS | BY | JOHN MASEFIELD | AUTHOR OF "THE EVERLASTING MERCY" | "THE WIDOW IN THE BYE STREET," ETC. | *NEW AND REVISED EDITION* | New York | THE MACMILLAN COMPANY | 1913 | *All rights reserved*
(All width centred)

Bibliographies: Danielson [unrecorded], Williams [unrecorded], Simmons [unrecorded], Nevinson [unrecorded], Handley-Taylor p.35, Wight [unrecorded] (see notes)

Collation: [A-U]⁸ (but signed [A]⁴ B-M⁸ [N-U]⁸ [Z]⁴; see note on American electrotype editions) (J, V and W not used); signatures left foot of page; 160 leaves; 187 × 126mm.; [i–iv] v–vi [vii–viii] 1–163 [164] 165–303 [304–312]

Page contents: [i] half-title: 'THE STORY OF A ROUND-HOUSE | AND OTHER POEMS'; [ii] '[publisher's device] | THE MACMILLAN COMPANY | [two lines listing six cities, separated by four points] | MACMILLAN & CO., LIMITED | [two lines listing four cities, separated by two points] | THE MACMILLAN CO. OF CANADA, LTD. | [one city listed]'; [iii] title-page; [iv]

'COPYRIGHT, 1912 and 1913, | BY THE MACMILLAN COMPANY. | [rule] | Set up and electrotyped. Published November, 1912. | New and revised edition, June, 1913. | Norwood Press | J. S. Cushing Co.-Berwick & Smith Co. | Norwood, Mass., U.S.A.'; v–vi 'CONTENTS' (51 individual poems listed with page references); [vii] 'THE STORY OF A ROUND-HOUSE | AND OTHER POEMS'; [viii] blank; 1–163 text; [164] blank; 165–303 text; [304] blank; [305] 'THE following pages are advertisements of recent im- | portant poetry published by the Macmillan Company' (within ruled border: 16 × 81mm.); [306] blank; [307–310] publisher's advertisements; [311–12] blank

Paper: wove paper

Running title: 'DAUBER' (14mm.) on both verso and recto, pp.2–163; other running titles comprise titles of individual poems, pp.166–303

Binding: burgundy cloth. On spine, in gold: '*The* | STORY | [small triangular ornament] *of a* [small triangular ornament] | ROUND | HOUSE | MASEFIELD | MACMILLAN' (width centred). On upper cover, in gold: 'THE | STORY OF | A ROUND-HOUSE | MASEFIELD' (ranged upper left) (within blind ruled border: 189 × 120mm.) Lower cover: blank. Top edge gilt, others roughly trimmed. Binding measurements: 192 × 127mm. (covers), 192 × 42mm. (spine). End-papers: wove paper.

Publication date: published, according to date within volume, June 1913

Price: $1.30

Contents:

Dauber ('Four bells were struck, the watch was called on deck,') [revised text]
Explanations of some of the Sea Terms used in the Poem ('Backstays. Wire ropes which support…')
Biography ('When I am buried, all my thoughts and acts')
Ships ('I cannot tell their wonder nor make known')
Truth ('Man with his burning soul')
They Closed Her Eyes (From the Spanish of Don Gustavo A. Bécquer) [*sic*] ('They closed her eyes,')
The Harp (From the Spanish of Don Gustavo A. Becquer) [*sic*] ('In a dark corner of the room,')
Sonnet (From the Spanish of Don Francisco De Quevedo) [*sic*] ('I saw the ramparts of my native land,')
Sonnet On The Death Of His Wife (From the Portuguese of Antonio De Ferreiro) [*sic*] ('That blessed sunlight that once showed to me')
Song ('One sunny time in May')
The Ballad of Sir Bors ('Would I could win some quiet and rest, and a little ease,')
Spanish Waters ('Spanish waters, Spanish waters, you are ringing in my ears,')
Cargoes ('Quinquireme of Nineveh from distant Ophir,')
Captain Stratton's Fancy ('Oh some are fond of red wine, and some are fond of white,')
An old Song Re-sung ('I saw a ship a-sailing, a-sailing, a-sailing,')
St. Mary's Bells ('It's pleasant in Holy Mary')
London Town ('Oh London Town's a fine town, and London sights are rare,')
The Emigrant ('Going by Daly's shanty I heard the boys within')
Port of Holy Peter ('The blue laguna rocks and quivers,')
Beauty ('I have seen dawn and sunset on moors and windy hills')
The Seekers ('Friends and loves we have none, nor wealth nor blessed abode,')
Prayer ('When the last sea is sailed, when the last shallow's charted,')
Dawn ('The dawn comes cold : the haystack smokes,')
Laugh and be Merry ('Laugh and be merry, remember, better the world with a song,')
June Twilight ('The twilight comes; the sun')
Roadways ('One road leads to London,')
Midsummer Night ('The perfect disc of the sacred moon')
The Harper's Song ('This sweetness trembling from the strings')
The Gentle Lady ('So beautiful, so dainty-sweet,')
The Dead Knight ('The cleanly rush of the mountain air,')
Sorrow of Mydath ('Weary the cry of the wind is, weary the sea,')
Twilight ('Twilight it is, and the far woods are dim, and the rooks cry and call.')
Invocation ('O wanderer into many brains,')
Posted as Missing ('Under all her topsails she trembled like a stag,')
A Creed ('I hold that when a person dies')
When Bony Death ('When bony Death has chilled her gentle blood,')
The West Wind ('It's a warm wind, the west wind, full of birds' cries;')
Her Heart ('Her heart is always doing lovely things,')
Being her Friend ('Being her friend, I do not care, not I,')
Fragments ('Troy Town is covered up with weeds,')
Born for Nought Else ('Born for nought else, for nothing but for this,')
Tewkesbury Road ('It is good to be out on the road, and going one knows not where,')
The Death Rooms ('My soul has many an old decaying room')

Ignorance ('Since I have learned Love's shining alphabet,')
Sea Fever ('I must go down to the seas again, to the lonely sea and the sky,')
The Watch In The Wood ('When Death has laid her in his quietude,')
C.L.M. ('In the dark womb where I began')
Waste ('No rose but fades: no glory but must pass:')
Third Mate ('All the sheets are clacking, all the blocks are whining,')
The Wild Duck ('Twilight. Red in the west.')
Christmas, 1903 ('O, the sea breeze will be steady, and the tall ship's going trim,')
The Word ('My friend, my bonny friend, when we are old,')

Notes:

The text of 'Dauber' has been reset and revised. There are minor punctuation variants in addition to some re-writing. The stanzas reproduced below on the left are from A23(a). The right column presents the equivalent from the 'New and Revised' edition, for example:

He stayed a moment, leaning on the boat,	And stand there silent, leaning on the boat,
Watching the constellations rise and burn,	Watching the constellations rise and burn,
Until the beauty took him by the throat	Until the beauty took him by the throat,
So stately is their glittering overturn;	So stately is their glittering overturn;
Armies of marching eyes, armies that yearn	Armies of marching eyes, armies that yearn
With banners rising and falling and passing by	With banners rising and falling, and passing by
Over the empty silence of the sky.	Over the empty silence of the sky.
He sighed again and looked at the great sails	The Dauber sighed there looking at the sails,
To get a memory of their look at night,	Wind-steadied arches leaning on the night,
The high trucks traced on heaven and left no trails,	The high trucks traced on heaven and left no trails,
The moonlight made the topsails almost white,	The moonlight made the topsails almost white,
The passing sidelight seemed to drip green light	The passing sidelight seemed to drip green light.
And on the clipper rushed with fire-bright bows.	And on the clipper rushed with fire-bright bows;
He sighed "I'll never do't," and left the house.	He sighed, "I'll never do't," and left the house.
"Now, Sammy," said the reefers. Up they crept,	"Now," said the reefer, "up! Come, Sam; come, Si,
Treading on tiptoe, on the Dauber's track.	Dauber's been hiding something." Up they slid,
They groped below the boat, their right hands swept	Treading on naked tiptoe stealthily
From chock to skid and came rewarded back.	To grope for treasure at the long-boat skid.
"Drawings, Lord love us, sketches, more, a stack.	"Drawings!" said Sam. "Is this what Dauber hid?
Hush, or they'll hear us. Hush. You little fishes,	Lord! I expected pudding, not this rot.
There's boatswain making Dauber wash the dishes."	Still, come, we'll have some fun with what we've got."

In addition to substantive revisions, this edition also includes the section entitled 'Explanations of some of the Sea Terms used in the Poem'.

Handley-Taylor does not specifically note this edition although, in listing reprints of A23(a), he does note the existence of this publication. He fails to note the revised status, however.

Copies: private collection (PWE)

Reprinted:

'Reprinted'	[second edition, second impression]	Sep 1913
'Reprinted'	[second edition, third impression]	Mar 1914
'Reprinted'	[second edition, fourth impression]	Jan 1915
'Reprinted'	[second edition, fifth impression]	Oct 1915
'Reprinted'	[second edition, sixth impression]	Jan 1916
'Reprinted'	[second edition, seventh impression]	Mar 1916
'Reprinted'	[second edition, eighth impression]	May 1916
'Reprinted'	[second edition, ninth impression]	Dec 1916
'Reprinted'	[second edition, tenth impression]	Oct 1917

A24 THE DAFFODIL FIELDS   1913

A24(a) First American edition (1913)

THE | DAFFODIL FIELDS | BY | JOHN MASEFIELD | AUTHOR OF "THE EVERLASTING MERCY," "THE WIDOW IN | THE BYE STREET," "THE STORY OF A | ROUND-HOUSE," ETC. | New York | THE MACMILLAN COMPANY | 1913 | *All rights reserved*
(All width centred)

Bibliographies: Danielson [unrecorded], Williams [unrecorded], Simmons [24], Nevinson [unrecorded], Handley-Taylor p.35, Wight [24]

Collation: [A-H]⁸ [I]⁴ (but signed [A]³ B-H⁸ I⁹; see note on American electrotype editions); signatures left foot of page; 68 leaves; 186 × 125mm.; [i–vi] 1–124 [125–30]

Page contents: [i] half-title: 'THE DAFFODIL FIELDS'; [ii] '[publisher's device] | THE MACMILLAN COMPANY | [two lines listing six cities, separated by four points] | MACMILLAN & CO., LIMITED | [two lines listing four cities, separated by two points] | THE MACMILLAN CO. OF CANADA, LTD. | [one city listed]'; [iii] title-page; [iv] 'COPYRIGHT, 1913, | BY JOHN MASEFIELD. | [rule] | Set up and electrotyped. Published March, 1913. | Norwood Press | J.S. Cushing Co.-Berwick & Smith Co. | Norwood, Mass., U.S.A.'; [v] 'THE DAFFODIL FIELDS'; [vi] blank; 1–124 text; [125] 'THE following pages contain advertisements of | Macmillan poems by the same author.' (within ruled border: 16 × 85mm.); [126] blank; [127–28] publisher's advertisements; [129–30] blank

Paper: wove paper

Running title: '*THE DAFFODIL FIELDS*' (38mm.) on both verso and recto, pp.2–124

Binding: light green boards with green cloth spine. On spine, in gold: '[ornament featuring flower: 10 × 18mm.] | The | DAFFODIL | FIELDS | [flower ornament] | MASEFIELD | MACMILLAN' (width centred). On upper cover, in green: '[ornament featuring daffodils: 41 × 106mm.] | The DAFFODIL FIELDS | JOHN MASEFIELD | [ornament featuring daffodils: 40 × 107mm.]' note that all minuscules on spine and upper cover are swash and that the ornament first used on the upper cover is inverted below the title and author for its second appearance. Lower cover: blank. Top edge gilt, others roughly trimmed. Binding measurements: 193 × 128mm. (covers), 193 × 33mm. (spine). End-papers: wove paper.

Publication date: published, according to Simmons, 26 March 1913 in an edition of 1620 copies

Price: $1.25

Contents:
The Daffodil Fields ('Between the barren pasture and the wood')
    First printed in The English Review *February 1913, pp.337–90*

Notes:
Simmons records the state of the edges of this volume as 'top edge gilt; fore edge uncut; bottom edge rough trimmed'.

As indicated by Wight, American publication of *The Daffodil Fields* followed American publication of *Dauber* (as *The Story of a Round-House*) and both precede English publication of *Dauber* and *The Daffodil Fields*.

The publishing agreement for this title between Masefield and Macmillan was dated 19 Febraury 1913 (see Archives of The Society of Authors). The agreement refers to 'a licence to publish in volume form in the United States of America a work the subject or title of which is The Daffodil Fields'. This title has been corrected from 'The Daffodil Fields and other poems'.

Copies seen: Library of The John Masefield Society (Peter Smith Collection) includes posthumous booklabel

Reprinted:

'Reprinted'	[first edition, second impression]	Jul 1913
'Reprinted'	[first edition, third impression]	Dec 1913
'Reprinted'	[first edition, fourth impression]	Aug 1915

A24(b) First English edition (1913)

THE | DAFFODIL FIELDS | BY | JOHN MASEFIELD | AUTHOR OF | "THE EVERLASTING MERCY," ETC. | [publisher's device of a windmill with 'W [point]' and 'H' all within ruled border: 15 × 15mm.] | LONDON | WILLIAM HEINEMANN | MCMXIII
(All width centred)

Bibliographies: Danielson 180, Williams p.3, Simmons [24a], Nevinson p.13, Handley-Taylor p.35, Wight [24a]

Collation: [π]⁴ 1–7⁸; signatures right foot of page; 60 leaves; 183 × 123mm.; [i–viii] 1–109 [110–12]

Page contents: [i–ii] blank; [iii] half-title: 'THE DAFFODIL FIELDS'; [iv] 'NEW VOLUMES OF POETRY | [nine titles and their authors listed with prices] | WM. HEINEMANN, 21 BEDFORD STREET, W.C.'; [v] title-page; [vi] '*Copyright.*'; [vii] 'TO | MY WIFE'; [viii] blank; 1-[110] text; [111] '"The Daffodil Fields" was first printed in the | *English Review* for February, 1912. I thank the | Editor and Proprietors of the Review for per- | mitting me to reprint it here. | [new paragraph] The persons and events described in the poem | are entirely imaginary, and no reference is made | or intended to any living person. | J. M. | *August* 3, 1913.' (at foot of p.[111]: '[rule] | BILLING AND SONS LTD., PRINTERS, GUILDFORD'); [112] blank

Paper: laid paper (no watermark), chain-lines 24mm. apart

Running-title: 'THE DAFFODIL FIELDS' (48mm.) on both verso and recto, pp.2–[110]

Binding: blue cloth. On spine, in gold: 'The | Daffodil | Fields | [ornament] | John | Masefield | HEINEMANN' (all width centred). On upper cover, in gold: 'THE DAFFODIL FIELDS | JOHN MASEFIELD'. Lower cover: blank. Upper and lower covers have blind ruled borders: 184 × 118mm. All edges trimmed. Binding measurements: 188 × 124mm. (covers), 188 × 29mm. (spine). End-papers: wove paper.

Publication date: published, according to Simmons, 2 October 1913 in an edition of 3000 copies

Price: 3s.6d.

Contents:
as for A24(a)

Notes:
The publishing agreement for this title between Masefield and Heinemann was dated 28 February 1913 (see Archives of The Society of Authors). The agreement refers to both *Dauber* and *The Daffodil Fields*, quotes a publication price of 3s.6d. for each volume, specifically refers to Masefield's retention of copyright and proposes publication times:

> …the copyright and all other rights in respect of both poems not expressly agreed to be conveyed under this agreement are reserved by the Author… the publication of "Dauber" shall take place during the spring publishing season of 1913 and of "The Daffodil Fields" during the autumn publishing season of 1913…

Nevinson lists a 'New Edition' (priced at 6s.) from May 1920. A reprint from February 1922 of *The Daffodil Fields* (described as 'Sixth Impression' and corresponding to a sixth impression of the first edition) does not list May 1920 as the date of a reprint whilst 'New Edition' suggests that the text has been reset. This is not the case and Nevinson is presumably incorrect. Such an error is also presumably to be found in his descriptions of *Dauber* and *Philip the King*.

Copies seen: BL (011649.de.27) stamped 2 OCT 1913; Bodleian (Additional Masefield papers 8) inscribed 'The Daffodil Fields lie to the S.W | of the Ledbury to Gloucester Road, | just beyond the first milestone, | after leaving Ledbury. | [new paragraph] In April, the daffodils grow | in great plenty there. | [new paragraph] I found the fable of the story | in an eighteenth century book | about Iceland. The author of | this book, (I think, a Scot), gives | the summary of the tale in a | foot-note. I am told that it | is a well-known saga. | "Footsteps in the sands of Time… | Footsteps that perhaps another…" | [new paragraph] As a boy, I often travelled the little | brook from its source in the hills | till it fell into the local River – | (Leadon): about 2½ miles. | John Masefield.'; HRHRC (PR6025 A77 D3 1913A cop.1) inscribed 'Judith Masefield | from her Father. | Oct 8th, 1913.'

Reprinted:

'Second Impression'	[first edition, second impression]	Aug 1914
'Third Impression'	[first edition, third impression]	Aug 1916
'Fourth Impression'	[first edition, fourth impression]	Sep 1918
'Fifth Impression'	[first edition, fifth impression]	Jan 1920
'Sixth Impression'	[first edition, sixth impression]	Feb 1922

A25 DAUBER   1913

A25(a) First English edition (1913)

DAUBER | A POEM | BY | JOHN MASEFIELD | AUTHOR OF | "THE EVERLASTING MERCY," ETC. | [publisher's device of a windmill with 'W [point]' and 'H' all within ruled border: 15 × 15mm.] | LONDON | WILLIAM HEINEMANN | MCMXIII
(All width centred)

Bibliographies: Danielson 179, Williams p.3, Simmons [23], Nevinson p.12, Handley-Taylor p.35, Wight [23]

Collation: [π]³ ([π]3+2) 1–5⁸ 6⁹ (6 8+1); signatures right foot of page; 52 leaves; 185 × 121mm.; [i–vi] 1–97 [98]

Page contents: [i] half-title: 'DAUBER'; [ii] 'NEW VOLUMES OF POETRY | [six titles and their authors mostly listed with prices and sizes] | WM. HEINEMANN, 21 BEDFORD STREET, W.C.'; [iii] title-page; [iv] '*Copyright*'; [v] 'TO | MY WIFE'; [vi] 'NOTE | I thank the editor and proprietors | of the *English Review* for permitting | me to reprint this poem, which first | appeared in their issue for October, | 1912.' (see notes); 1–92 text; 93–[98] 'EXPLANATIONS OF SOME OF THE SEA | TERMS USED IN THE POEM' (at foot of p.[98]: '[rule] | BILLING AND SONS, LTD., PRINTERS, GUILDFORD')

Paper: laid paper (no watermark), chain-lines 24mm. apart

Running-title: 'DAUBER' (17mm.) on both verso and recto, pp.2-[98]

Binding: blue cloth. On spine, in gold: 'Dauber | [ornament] | John | Masefield | HEINEMANN' (all width centred). On upper cover, in gold: 'DAUBER | JOHN MASEFIELD'. Lower cover: blank. Upper and lower covers have blind ruled borders: 187 × 116mm. All edges trimmed. Binding measurements: 190 × 122mm. (covers), 190 × 23mm. (spine). End-papers: wove paper.

Publication date: published, according to Simmons, 1 May 1913 in an edition of 2500 copies

Price: 3s.6d.

Contents:
Dauber ('Four bells were struck, the watch was called on deck,')
Explanations of some of the Sea Terms used in the Poem ('Backstays. Wire ropes which support…')

Notes:
Masefield's third long narrative poem, first published in *The English Review* (October 1912), was previously first published in a volume in America (see A23). English publication by Heinemann marks the start of Masefield's long association with that publisher. The narrative (which often draws on autobiographical detail) tells of an aspiring artist's experiences at sea, contempt from his fellow sailors and eventual death through an act of heroism.

The first two leaves of the volume are conjugate and tipped-in on the third leaf of the first 'gathering'. Confusion over the title of this volume is one suggested reason that caused this feature.

Wight states that the unsigned 'NOTE' on p.[vi] is '5 lines in some copies, 8 lines in others'. Wight presumably confuses the first edition with reprints. The five line note occurs in the first edition, first impression. The eight line note occurs in the first edition, third impression and subsequent reprints. No copy of the first edition, second impression has been examined.

Publication by Heinemann is, as yet, unexplained. During October 1912 (and presumably before publication of *The English Review*) Masefield wrote to Sidgwick:

> Will you very kindly let me know privately what effect serialising one of my long poems has upon its subsequent sale as a book? I mean of course <u>lasting</u> effect; + whether you think that the book's career is really killed by a first appearance in a cheap review?

> (John Masefield, letter to Frank Sidgwick, 11 October 1912)
> (HRHRC, MS (Sidgwick, F.) Recip. Masefield, J.)

At the time of the poem's appearance in *The English Review* Masefield was therefore evidently taking Sidgwick's advice. A letter held at Harvard College Library (Houghton bMS Eng 1069 *57M–54) dated 24 January [1913] to Frank Sidgwick states 'I send you herewith the copy for Dauber'.

The publishing agreement for this title between Masefield and Heinemann was dated 28 February 1913 (see Archives of The Society of Authors). The agreement refers to both *Dauber* and *The Daffodil Fields* (see notes to A24(b)).

Nevinson lists a 'New Edition' (priced at 6s.) from May 1920. A reprint from August 1922 of *Dauber* (described as a 'New Impression' and corresponding to a seventh impression of the first edition) does not list May 1920 as the date of a reprint whilst 'New Edition' suggests that the text has been reset. This is not the case and Nevinson is presumably incorrect. Such an error is also presumably to be found in his descriptions of *The Daffodil Fields* and *Philip the King*.

Copies seen: private collection (PWE); BL (011649.e.36) stamped 2 MAY 1913

Reprinted:

'New Impression'	[first edition, second impression]	Jul 1913
'New Impression'	[first edition, third impression]	Mar 1914
'New Impression'	[first edition, fourth impression]	Aug 1916
'New Impression'	[first edition, fifth impression]	Jul 1918
'New Impression'	[first edition, sixth impression]	Jun 1920
'New Impression'	[first edition, seventh impression]	Aug 1922
'New Impression'	[first edition, eighth impression]	Aug 1924

A25(b) First Canadian edition (1913)

DAUBER | A POEM | BY | JOHN MASEFIELD | AUTHOR OF | "THE EVERLASTING MERCY," ETC. | TORONTO | BELL AND COCKBURN | MCMXIII
(All width centred)

Bibliographies: Danielson [unrecorded], Williams [unrecorded], Simmons [unrecorded], Nevinson [unrecorded], Handley-Taylor [unrecorded], Wight 23a

Collation: [π]³ ([π]3+2) 1–5⁸ 6⁹ (6 8+1); signatures right foot of page; 52 leaves; 184 × 120mm.; [i–vi] 1–97 [98]

Page contents: [i] half-title: 'DAUBER'; [ii] blank; [iii] title-page; [iv] '*Printed in England*'; [v] 'TO | MY WIFE'; [vi] 'NOTE | I thank the editor and proprietors | of the *English Review* for permitting | me to reprint this poem, which first | appeared in their issue for October, | 1912.'; 1–92 text; 93–[98] 'EXPLANATIONS OF SOME OF THE SEA | TERMS USED IN THE POEM' (at foot of p.[98]: '[rule] | BILLING AND SONS, LTD., PRINTERS, GUILDFORD')

Paper: laid paper (no watermark), chain-lines 24mm. apart

Running-title: 'DAUBER' (17mm.) on both verso and recto, pp.2-[98]

Binding: blue cloth. On spine, in gold: 'Dauber | [ornament] | John | Masefield | BELL & | COCKBURN' (all width centred). On upper cover, in gold: 'DAUBER | JOHN MASEFIELD'. Lower cover: blank. Upper and lower covers have blind ruled borders: 186 × 116mm. All edges trimmed. Binding measurements: 188 × 121mm. (covers), 188 × 23mm. (spine). End-papers: wove paper.

Publication date: presumably published after 1 May 1913

Price: unknown

Contents:
as for A25(a)

Notes:
The first two leaves of the volume are conjugate and tipped-in on the third leaf of the first 'gathering', as in A25(a). The similarity to A25(a) (and the note on p.[iv]) suggests that Bell and Cockburn imported sheets printed by Heinemann. The binding of the edition, although smaller in dimensions, is also similar to the Heinemann edition binding.

Copies seen: National Library Bibliothèque Nationale, Canada (PR6025 A77 D38 1913a); HRHRC (TEMP M377DA 1913)

A26 PHILIP THE KING AND OTHER POEMS 1914

A26(a) First English edition (1914)

PHILIP THE KING | AND OTHER POEMS | BY | JOHN MASEFIELD | *WITH A PORTRAIT BY WILLIAM STRANG* | [publisher's device of a windmill with 'W [point]' and 'H' all within ruled border: 15 × 15mm.] | LONDON | WILLIAM HEINEMANN
(All width centred)

Bibliographies: Danielson 181, Williams p.3, Simmons [25], Nevinson p.13, Handley-Taylor p.35, Wight [25]

Collation: [A]⁴ B–H⁸ [I]⁴; signatures right foot of page; 64 leaves; 184 × 120mm.; [i–vi] vii [viii] [1–2] 3–56 [57–58] 59–117 [118–20]

Page contents: [i] half-title: 'PHILIP THE KING | AND OTHER POEMS'; [ii] 'BY THE SAME AUTHOR | *Uniform with this Volume* | [rule] | [two titles listed] | LONDON : WILLIAM HEINEMANN' (with additional leaf tipped-in on the verso of which is the frontispiece: 114 × 75mm., of Strang portrait of Masefield dated 'Jan 1912'); [iii] title-page (with protective tissue tipped-in); [iv] 'LONDON : WILLIAM HEINEMANN. 1914'; [v] 'TO | MY WIFE'; [vi] blank; vii 'CONTENTS' (12 individual poems listed with page references); [viii] blank; [1] 'PHILIP THE KING | A PLAY IN ONE ACT'; [2] '[dramatis personae listed with 'PERSONS.' and 'SPIRITS.' headings] | TIME. | At dawn in late September, 1588. | SCENE. | A little dark cell in Philip's palace.'; 3–56 text of 'Philip the King'; [57] 'OTHER POEMS'; [58] blank; 59–117 text of other poems; [118] blank; [119] 'NOTE | Of the poems contained in this volume, five– | "Truth," "August, 1914," "Biography," | "Ships," and "The River"–appeared in the | *English Review*, one–"The 'Wanderer'"–in | *Harper's Magazine*, and three–the translations | –in the *Westminster Gazette*. I thank the | editors of these periodicals for permission to | reprint them here. | JOHN MASEFIELD' (at foot of p.[119]: '[rule] | BILLING AND SONS, LTD., PRINTERS, GUILDFORD'); [120] blank

Paper: laid paper (no watermark), chain-lines 25mm. apart

Running title: 'PHILIP THE KING' (37mm.) on both verso and recto, pp.4–56; other running titles comprise titles of individual poems, pp.60–117

Binding: blue cloth. On spine, in gold: 'Philip | the | King | [ornament] | John | Masefield | HEINEMANN' (all width centred). On upper cover, in gold: 'PHILIP THE KING | JOHN MASEFIELD' (within blind ruled border: 184 × 114mm.) Lower cover: blank. All edges trimmed. Binding measurements: 189 × 121mm. (covers), 189 × 25mm. (spine). End-papers: wove paper.

Publication date: published, according to Simmons, 1 October 1914 in an edition of 3000 copies

Price: 3s.6d.

Contents:
Philip the King ('PHILIP (*Kneeling*). | Lord, I am that Philip whom Thou has made…')
Truth ('Man with his burning soul')
The "Wanderer" ('All day they loitered by the resting ships,')
    First printed in Harper's Monthly Magazine *September 1913, pp.531–36*
August, 1914 ('How still this quiet cornfield is to-night!')
    First printed in The English Review *September 1914, pp.145–47*
Biography ('When I am buried, all my thoughts and acts')
Song ('One sunny time in May')
Ships ('I cannot tell their wonder nor make known')
Sonnet (From the Spanish of Don Francisco A. Quevado) ('I saw the ramparts of my native land,')
Sonnet On The Death Of His Wife (From the Portuguese of Antonio di Ferreiro) ('That blessed sunlight, that once showed to me')
They Closed Her Eyes (From the Spanish of Don Gustavo A. Becquér) ('They closed her eyes,')
The River ('All other waters have their time of peace,')
    First printed in The English Review *December 1913, pp.1–12*
Watching By a Sick-Bed ('I heard the wind all day,')
    First printed as 'Tranarossan' in Harper's Weekly *11 April 1914, p.15*

Notes:

The publishing agreement for this title between Masefield and Heinemann was dated 19 August 1914 (see Archives of The Society of Authors). The agreement refers to 'a book of poems... provisionally entitled PHILIP THE KING' and a publication price of 5s. This price was, presumably, revised.

Evidence within the Archives of William Heinemann suggests that the terms Masefield received for the volume were a hundred pounds advance on a 25% royalty.

Although Simmons and the *English Catalogue of Books* cite October 1914 as the month of publication, subsequent Heinemann reprints list September 1914 as the date of first publication.

Nevinson lists a 'New Edition' (priced at 6s.) from May 1920. A reprint from May 1930 of *Philip the King and other Poems* (described as a 'New Impression' and corresponding to a fifth impression of the first edition) does not list May 1920 as the date of a reprint whilst 'New Edition' suggests that the text has been reset. This is not the case and Nevinson is presumably incorrect. Such an error is also presumably to be found in his descriptions of *Dauber* and *The Daffodil Fields*.

A performance of the play was given on 5 November 1914 at the Royal Opera House, Covent Garden. The designer was Charles Ricketts, music was by Gustav Holst and the play was produced by Harley Granville-Barker. The programme included Bach's *Phoebus and Pan* conducted by Thomas Beecham, and the Russian Ballet. The cast list for *Philip the King* is reproduced on page 34 of Handley-Taylor's bibliography. In a letter to W.W. Greg, Masefield writes:

> Thank you very much for your very kind letter about Philip. I'm glad it has given you pleasure. It was finished + set up before the war began. One could not write of war now. I'm sorry you saw the Covent Garden performance. The programme was, as you say, against it; a dreadful afternoon.
>
> (John Masefield, letter to W.W. Greg, 14 February [1915])
> (Private Collection (PWE))

Copies seen: private collection (PWE); BL (011649.eee.57), stamped 2 OCT 1914

Reprinted:

'Second Impression'	[first edition, second impression]	Dec 1914
'Third Impression'	[first edition, third impression]	Sep 1918
'Fourth Impression'	[first edition, fourth impression]	Nov 1920
'New Impression'	[first edition, fifth impression]	May 1930

A26(b) First American edition (1914)

PHILIP THE KING | AND OTHER POEMS | BY | JOHN MASEFIELD | New York | THE MACMILLAN COMPANY | 1914 | *All rights reserved*
(All width centred)

Bibliographies: Danielson [unrecorded], Williams [unrecorded], Simmons [noted on p.46], Nevinson [unrecorded], Handley-Taylor p.35, Wight 25a

Collation: [A-K]⁸ (but signed [A]⁴ [B]⁸ C-K⁸ [L]⁴; see note on American electrotype editions) (J not used); signatures left foot of page; 80 leaves; 187 × 128mm.; [i–vi] vii [viii] [1–2] 3–83 [84–86] 87–141 [142–52]

Page contents: [i] half-title: 'PHILIP THE KING | AND OTHER POEMS'; [ii] '[publisher's device] | THE MACMILLAN COMPANY | [two lines listing six cities, separated by four points] | MACMILLAN & CO., LIMITED | [two lines listing four cities, separated by two points] | THE MACMILLAN CO. OF CANADA, LTD. | [one city listed]'; [iii] title-page (with additional leaf tipped-in on the verso of which is the frontispiece: 114 × 75mm., of Strang portrait of Masefield dated 'Jan 1912'); [iv] 'Copyright, 1913, by Harper and Brothers. | Copyright, 1914, by The Century Company and by | the McClure Publications. | [rule] | COPYRIGHT, 1914, | BY THE MACMILLAN COMPANY. | [rule] | Set up and electrotyped. Published November, 1914. | Norwood Press | J. S. Cushing Co.–Berwick & Co. | Norwood, Mass., U.S.A.'; [v] 'To | MY WIFE'; [vi] blank; vii 'CONTENTS' (five individual poems listed with page references); [viii] blank; [1] 'PHILIP THE KING | A PLAY IN ONE ACT'; [2] '[dramatis personae listed with 'PERSONS' and 'SPIRITS' headings] | TIME | At dawn in late September, 1588 | SCENE | A little dark cell in Philip's palace'; 3–83 text of 'Philip the King'; [84] blank; [85] 'OTHER POEMS'; [86] blank; 87–141 text of other poems; [142] 'NOTE | *The River*, which is contained in this vol- | ume, was first published in the *Century Maga-* | *zine*; *The Wanderer* in *Harper's Magazine*; | *Watching by a Sick-Bed* and *August, 1914* in | *Harper's Weekly*. I thank the editors of these | periodicals for permission to reprint them here. | JOHN MASEFIELD.'; [143] 'NEW Poems and Plays published by | The Macmillan Company.' (within ruled border: 15 × 62mm.); [144] blank; [145–52] publisher's advertisements

Paper: wove paper (watermark: '[diamond shape containing 'D': 21 × 33mm.] | Regal Antique')

Running title: '*PHILIP THE KING*' (32–33mm.) on both verso and recto, pp.4–83; titles of other poems on both verso and recto, pp.88–141

Binding: burgundy cloth. On spine, in gold: 'PHILIP | THE | KING | MASEFIELD | MACMILLAN' (all width centred). On upper cover, in gold: 'PHILIP | THE | KING | MASEFIELD' (ranged upper left) (within blind ruled border: 186 × 117mm.) Lower cover: blank. Top edge gilt, others roughly trimmed. Binding measurements: 193 × 128mm. (covers), 193 × 32mm. (spine). End-papers: wove paper.

DAUBER

A POEM

BY

JOHN MASEFIELD

AUTHOR OF
"THE EVERLASTING MERCY," ETC.

LONDON
WILLIAM HEINEMANN
MCMXIII

A25(a) title-page

JOHN M. SYNGE: A FEW
PERSONAL RECOLLECTIONS
WITH BIOGRAPHICAL
NOTES BY JOHN MASEFIELD

THE MACMILLAN COMPANY
NEW YORK—MCMXV

A27(b) title-page

PHILIP THE KING

AND OTHER POEMS

BY

JOHN MASEFIELD

WITH A PORTRAIT BY WILLIAM STRANG

LONDON
WILLIAM HEINEMANN

A26(a) title-page

PHILIP THE KING

AND OTHER POEMS

BY

JOHN MASEFIELD

New York
THE MACMILLAN COMPANY
1914
All rights reserved

A26(b) title-page

John M. Synge:
A Few Personal Recollections with
Biographical Notes.

LETCHWORTH
GARDEN CITY PRESS LIMITED
1916
Copyright in U.S.A.

A27(c) title-page

Good Friday

LETCHWORTH
GARDEN CITY PRESS LIMITED
1916
Copyright in U.S.A.

A31(a) title-page

Sonnets and Poems

By
JOHN MASEFIELD

LETCHWORTH
GARDEN CITY PRESS LIMITED
1916
Copyright in U.S.A.

A32(a) title-page

The Locked Chest
The Sweeps of Ninety-Eight

Two Plays in Prose

By
JOHN MASEFIELD

LETCHWORTH
GARDEN CITY PRESS LIMITED
1916
Copyright in U.S.A.

A33(a) title-page

Publication date: published, according to Simmons, 11 November 1914 in an edition of 1888 copies

Price: $1.25

Contents:
Philip the King ('PHILIP (*Kneeling*). | Lord, I am that Philip whom Thou has made…')
The "Wanderer" ('All day they loitered by the resting ships,')
August, 1914 ('How still this quiet cornfield is to-night!')
The River ('All other waters have their time of peace,')
Watching By a Sick-Bed ('I heard the wind all day,')

Notes:
Of the poems printed in A26(a) those excluded from this American edition are: 'Truth', 'Biography', 'Song', 'Ships', 'Sonnet (From the Spanish of Don Francisco A. Quevedo)', 'Sonnet On The Death Of His Wife (From the Portuguese of Antonio di Ferreiro)', and 'They Closed Her Eyes (From the Spanish of Don Gustavo A. Becquér)'

The 'To' in the dedication on p.[v] is in an ornate type.

Three publishing agreements for this title between Masefield and Macmillan are dated 26 February 1915, April 1915 and 7 May 1915 (see Archives of The Society of Authors). The earliest agreement refers to 'a licence to publish in volume form in the United States of America a work the subject or title of which is Philip the King'.

Copies seen: private collection (PWE); Harvard College Library (Houghton Lowell *EC9.M377.914pc)

Reprinted:

[first edition, second impression]	Apr 1915
[first edition, third impression]	Jan 1916
[first edition, fourth impression]	Mar 1917

A27 JOHN M. SYNGE: A FEW PERSONAL RECOLLECTIONS… 1915

A27(a) First Irish edition (1915)

JOHN M. SYNGE: A FEW PERSONAL [in red] | RECOLLECTIONS, WITH BIOGRAPH- [in red] | ICAL NOTES BY JOHN MASEFIELD [in red] | [Cuala Press device of tree and muse] | THE CUALA PRESS | CHURCHTOWN | DUNDRUM | MCMXV
(All width centred with the exception of lines 1–3 the first two of which are left and right justified; the third is only justified on the left.)

Bibliographies: Danielson 183, Williams p.9, Simmons [26], Nevinson [unrecorded], Handley-Taylor p.35, Wight [26]

Collation: [π]⁴ [a]⁴ b-f⁴ [g]⁴; signatures right foot of page with the exception of signature 'b' which is located at left foot of page; 32 leaves; 210 × 143mm.; [i–xvi] [1] 2–34 [35–48]

Page contents: [i–xiii] blank; [xiv] 'Three hundred and fifty copies | of this book have been prin- | ted. This copy is No.' [all lines in red]; [xv] title-page; [xvi] blank; [1]–34 text; [35] 'HERE ENDS 'JOHN M. SYNGE: | A FEW PERSONAL RECOLLECT- | IONS, WITH BIOGRAPHICAL | NOTES BY JOHN MASEFIELD.' | PRINTED AND PUBLISHED BY | ELIZABETH CORBET YEATS AT | THE CUALA PRESS, CHURCH- | TOWN, DUNDRUM, IN THE | COUNTY OF DUBLIN, IRELAND. | FINISHED AT EASTER, IN THE | YEAR NINETEEN HUNDRED | AND FIFTEEN.' [all lines in red]; [36–48] blank

Paper: wove paper

Running title: none

Binding: grey boards with white cloth spine. Spine: blank. On upper cover: 'JOHN M. SYNGE: A FEW PERSONAL | RECOLLECTIONS, WITH BIOGRAPH- | ICAL NOTES BY JOHN MASEFIELD'. Lower cover: blank. Top edge trimmed, others uncut. Binding measurements: 213 × 145mm. (covers), 213 × 13mm. (spine). End-papers: grey laid paper (no watermark), chain-lines 27mm. apart. A binder's label is present at the front of the volume and reads 'BOUND BY | [rule] | GALWEY & Cº | [rule] | [three points] | EUSTACE ST. DUBLIN'.

Publication date: published, according to Simmons, 2 June 1915 in an edition of 350 copies

Price: 7s.6d.

Contents:
John M. Synge ('I first met John M. Synge at the room of a common friend, up two pairs…')
Portraits ('Several portraits of Synge exist. Besides a few drawings of him…')
A List of his Plays, in Chronological Order with the Dates of their First Performances ('The Shadow of the Glen…')
Other Writings ('The Aran Islands. Written between 1899 and 1907. Published…')
A Note ('Information about John M. Synge may be found in Mr. W.B. Yeats's Collected Works…')

Notes:

This title is numbered 22 in *A List of Books Published by The Dun Emer Press and the Cuala Press founded in Dublin in Nineteen Hundred and Three by Elizabeth Corbet Yeats*, (Dublin: Cuala Press, 1972). The entry states 'Three hundred and fifty copies, April 1915'.

Copies seen: BL (Cup.510.ad.21) stamped 2 JUN 1915 copy number 146; Bodleian (26961.e.5) stamped 12.6.1915 copy number 145

A27(b) First American edition (1915)

JOHN M. SYNGE: A FEW | PERSONAL RECOLLECTIONS | WITH BIOGRAPHICAL | NOTES BY JOHN MASEFIELD | THE MACMILLAN COMPANY | NEW YORK – MCMXV
(Within single red ruled border: 120 × 86mm. Lines 1–4 justified on both left and right margins, lines 5–6 width centred)

Bibliographies: Danielson [unrecorded], Williams [unrecorded], Simmons [26a], Nevinson [unrecorded], Handley-Taylor p.35, Wight [26a]

Collation: [A-B]⁸ [C]⁴; 20 leaves (see notes); 219 × 139mm.; [i–ii] [1–6] 7–35 [36–38] (see notes)

Page contents: [i–ii] blank; [1] half-title: 'JOHN M. SYNGE: A FEW PERSONAL | RECOLLECTIONS'; [2] 'Five hundred copies of this | book have been printed. | This copy is No.' (with additional leaf tipped-in on the verso of which is the frontispiece: 107 × 82mm., 'JOHN MILLINGTON SYNGE'); [3] title-page; [4] 'Copyright, 1915 | By JOHN MASEFIELD | [rule] | Published July, 1915'; [5] 'JOHN M. SYNGE: A FEW PERSONAL | RECOLLECTIONS'; [6] blank; 7–35 text (at foot of p.35: 'Printed in the United States of America'); [36–38] blank (see notes)

Paper: laid paper (no watermark), chain-lines 22mm. apart

Running title: 'John M. Synge:' (28mm.) on verso; 'A Few Personal Recollections' (52mm.) on recto, pp.8–31

Binding: brown boards with cream paper spine. Spine: blank. On upper cover: white paper label (38 × 90mm.) on which: 'JOHN M. SYNGE : A FEW PERSONAL | RECOLLECTIONS, WITH BIOGRAPH- | ICAL NOTES BY JOHN MASEFIELD' (within ruled border, in brown: 28 × 82mm.) Lower cover: blank. All edges trimmed. Binding measurements: 221 × 141mm. (covers), 221 × 13mm. (spine). End-papers: wove paper.

Publication date: published, according to Simmons, 21 July 1915 in an edition of 650 copies, of which 500 copies were numbered and for sale

Price: $1.00

Contents:
as for A27(a)

Notes:

Note the omission of the comma (before 'with') in the American title for this work.

Page numbers appear within square brackets. Thus, [7], [8], etc.

The text commences with a drop-capital in red. This is within a ruled border in black with ornate ornamentation on lower and left hand sides. This is all within ruled border: 21 × 21mm.

The numbering of the copies was achieved by stamping the relevant number. This is not a limited signed edition.

Wight notes that some copies have an additional leaf at the front of the volume. The 'additional leaf' occurs before p.[i] and there is also an additional leaf at the rear of the volume after p.[38]. These leaves (in wove paper) do not alter the gatherings and appear to constitute a set of conjugate leaves wrapped around the internal matter.

A publishing agreement for this title between Masefield and Macmillan was dated 22 October 1915 (see Archives of The Society of Authors). The agreement refers to 'a licence to publish in volume form in the United States of America a work the subject or title of which is John M. Synge: A Few Personal Recollections with Biographical Notes'.

Copies seen: private collection (PWE) number 410; NYPL (AN (Synge) 706204) annotated 'July 28/15', number 1, rebound and lacking leaves; Harvard College Library (Houghton Lowell *EC9.M377.915jb) number 430; Harvard College Library (Houghton *EC9.M377.915jb) stamped 'ADVANCE COPY FOR REVIEW NOT FOR SALE' number 178, with additional leaves

A27(c) First English edition (1916)

John M. Synge: | *A Few Personal Recollections with* | *Biographical Notes.* | *LETCHWORTH* | *GARDEN CITY PRESS LIMITED* | 1916 | *Copyright in U.S.A.*
(The italic type contains a number of swash characters)
(All width centred)

Bibliographies: Danielson 188, Williams p.9, Simmons [noted on p.47], Nevinson [unrecorded], Handley-Taylor [unrecorded], Wight 26b

Collation: [A]⁴ B-D⁴; signatures left foot of page; 16 leaves; 224 × 145mm.; [1–4] 5–32

Page contents: [1] half-title: 'JOHN M. SYNGE: | A FEW PERSONAL RECOLLECTIONS'; [2] blank; [3] title-page; [4] '*This Edition is limited to* 200 *copies.*'; 5–32 text

Paper: laid paper (watermark: '[Crown] | Abbey Mills | Greenfield'), chain-lines 25mm. apart

Running title: 'John M. Synge :' (38mm.) on verso; 'A Few Personal Recollections' (68–69mm.) on recto, pp.6–31 (on p.32: 'John M. Synge' (35mm.) only)

Binding: grey wrappers. Spine: blank. On upper wrapper: '*John M. Synge:* | *A Few Personal Recollections with* | *Biographical Notes.* | *LETCHWORTH* | *GARDEN CITY PRESS LIMITED* | 1916 | *Copyright in U.S.A.*' (the italic type contains a number of swash characters). On lower wrapper: '[figure with spade gazing upon horizon of hills and clouds with 'TELEGRAPHIC ADDRESS | SPADEWORK LETCHWORTH' (within a 'T' shape)] | GARDEN CITY – | PRESS LIMITED | LETCHWORTH – | HERTS. – – – –' (within double ruled border: 47 × 30mm.) Top edge trimmed, others uncut. Binding measurements: 229 × 148mm. (wrappers), 229 × 5mm. (spine). The wrappers extend beyond the edges of the internal leaves.

Publication date: published, according to Simmons in 1916 (see notes) (not recorded in the *English Catalogue of Books*)

Price: 1 guinea (set of 4 volumes: see also A31(a), A32(a) and A33(a))

Contents:

John M. Synge ('I first met John M. Synge at the room of a common friend, up two pairs...')

Notes:

In contrast with A27(a), this edition does not contain the full text. Additional sections in the Cuala Press edition entitled 'Portraits', 'A List Of His Plays, In Chronological Order With The Dates Of Their First Performances', 'Other Writings' and 'A Note' are omitted here.

Curiously, Masefield's authorship of this work is entirely omitted. This is also true of A27(d).

In 1915 Masefield sent a printed letter to numerous recipients inviting subscribers to a set of four volumes 'strictly limited to 200 sets'. See J5.

Simmons notes the other three volumes in the set were 'published not later than August 1916'. For this volume, however, Simmons notes only the year although it seems likely that 'published not later than August 1916' may also be applied. To suggest earliest possible dates of publication, one example of J5 was sent to Frank Sidgwick on 8 December 1915. Writing a few days later Masefield noted his satisfaction with his private venture:

> Many thanks for your letter. I am making no arrangements for a trade sale + giving no reductions, as the books are going off very well privately, like W.S.'s sonnets, among my private friends. Still, if you would like to take more copies at a guinea as a private speculation I could let you have some: I think a dozen, possibly more.
>
> (John Masefield, letter to Frank Sidgwick, [December 1915])
> (HRHRC, MS (Masefield, J.) 5 ALS, 1 ALI, 1 TLS to Sidgwick)

(Sidgwick appears to have asked for five sets and Masefield thanked his old publisher for his 'most sporting pledge' on 10 December 1915) (see John Masefield, letter to Frank Sidgwick, 10 December 1915) (HRHRC, MS (Sidgwick, F.) Recip. Masefield, J.) It does not, however, appear that Masefield was in a position to distribute copies immediately. A letter from the Garden City Press from April 1916 notes difficulties (and also reveals which volumes were printed first). As individual volumes were not, apparently, distributed until the complete set was ready, I have chosen to retain Simmons' sequence chronology for these volumes. The Garden City Press noted:

> There have been many causes which it is difficult to explain, and over which we have had no control. These causes have hindered the work. From what we have heard of the troubles of other printers in relation to labour and material, we believe we are able honestly to congratulate ourselves in being in a plight no worse. Promptitude has been one of the important keynotes in the building up of this business, but everything just now has been abnormal. Below we give you a statement showing the position of your four books.
>
> Volume One – Sonnets and Poems
>
> Volume Two – The Locked Chest and The Sweeps of Ninety-eight.
>
> Both these are printed and we can despatch copies on Monday, but we give you this opportunity, before sending of advising as to what address you wish these to be sent.
>
> Volume Four – John M. Synge
>
> We are completing the printing of this volume to-day, and could despatch on Tuesday or Wednesday next week.
>
> Volume Three – Good Friday
>
> We are sending to-day a first portion of proof, and will get through with the composition rapidly on the return from yourself of each instalment.
>
> (Garden City Press Ltd, letter to John Masefield, 1 April 1916)
> (HRHRC, MS (Masefield, J.) Recip Garden City Press Ltd TLS to Masefield 1916 April 1)

Williams describes this edition as a 'second edition' before the 'third edition' of A27(d).

Copies seen: private collection (PWE); BL (010826.h.13) stamped 26 MAY 1916 rebound; Bodleian (26961.d.5(1)) stamped 22 AUG 1916; NYPL (Berg Collection); HRHRC (PR5533 M3 1916b) inscribed, by Nevinson, 'Henry W. Nevinson | from the Author | May 1916'

A27(d) Second English edition (1916)

John M. Synge: | *A Few Personal Recollections with* | *Biographical Notes.* | *LETCHWORTH* | *GARDEN CITY PRESS LIMITED* | 1916 | *Copyright in U.S.A.*
(The italic type contains a number of swash characters)
(All width centred)

Bibliographies: Danielson [unrecorded], Williams p.9, Simmons [noted on pp.47–48], Nevinson [unrecorded], Handley-Taylor [unrecorded], Wight [unrecorded]

Collation: [A]⁴ B-D⁴; signatures left foot of page; 16 leaves; 191 × 128mm.; [1–4] 5–32

Page contents: [1] half-title: 'JOHN M. SYNGE: | A FEW PERSONAL RECOLLECTIONS'; [2] blank; [3] title-page; [4] blank; 5–32 text

Paper: laid paper (watermark: '[Crown] | Abbey Mills | Greenfield'), chain-lines 25mm. apart

Running title: 'John M. Synge :' (38mm.) on verso; 'A Few Personal Recollections' (68–69mm.) on recto, pp.6–31 (on p.32: 'John M. Synge' (35mm.) only)

Binding: light blue cloth. On spine: white paper label (150 × 7mm.) on which reading lengthways up spine, from base: '*JOHN M. SYNGE : A Few Personal Recollections*' (the italic type contains a number of swash characters). On upper cover: white paper label (70 × 53mm.) on which: '*John M.* | *Synge* | [leaf motif] [in red] | *A Few Personal* | *Recollections*' (within double ruled border in red: 62 × 45mm.) (the italic type contains a number of swash characters). Lower cover: blank. Top edge trimmed, others untrimmed. Binding measurements: 195 × 130mm. (covers), 195 × 15mm. (spine). End-papers: laid papers (watermark: '[Crown] | Abbey Mills | Greenfield'), chain-lines 24mm. apart.

Publication date: published according to Simmons, 'later in 1916' than A27(c) (not recorded in the *English Catalogue of Books*)

Price: 3s.6d.

Contents:
as for A27(c)

Notes:
As with A27(c), this edition does not contain the full text and Masefield's authorship of the work is entirely omitted.

Simmons states of both this and A27(c) that:

   Both the 1916 issues [editions] are printed from the same type, and both have the same title-page...

However, a comparison of title-pages shows several pieces of type to be different (the '*C*' in '*CITY*', '*R*' in '*PRESS*' and '*E*' in '*LIMITED*', for example). An examination of the text does, however, suggest that the two editions were printed from the same setting.

Williams describes this edition as a '3rd edition'.

Copies seen: BL (010826.de.52) stamped 2 MAR 1917

A27(e) Second Irish edition (1971)

The Irish University Press issued a facsimile reprint of A27(a) in 1971. The publishing agreement for this title between The Society of Authors and Irish University Press was dated 10 July 1970 (see Archives of The Society of Authors).

A28 THE FAITHFUL   1915

A28(a) First English edition (1915)

THE FAITHFUL | A TRAGEDY IN THREE ACTS | BY | JOHN MASEFIELD | [publisher's device of a windmill with 'W [point]' and 'H' all within ruled border: 15 × 15mm.] | LONDON | WILLIAM HEINEMANN
(All width centred)

Bibliographies: Danielson 182, Williams p.3, Simmons [27], Nevinson p.14, Handley-Taylor p.35, Wight [27]

Collation: [A]⁶ B–I⁸ K² (J not used); signatures right foot of page; 72 leaves; 183 × 120mm.; [two un-numbered pages] [i–vi] vii [viii–x] [1] 2–53 [54] 55–131 [132]

Page contents: [–] blank (page excluded from page count, but constitutes first leaf of first gathering); [–] blank; [i] half-title: 'THE FAITHFUL'; [ii] 'BY THE SAME AUTHOR | *Uniform with this Volume* | [rule] | [four titles listed] | LONDON : WILLIAM HEINEMANN'; [iii] title-page; [iv] 'LONDON : WILLIAM HEINEMANN. 1915'; [v] 'TO | MY WIFE'; [vi] blank; vii 'NOTE | THIS play is written to be played uninterruptedly, | without more break in the action than is necessary | to get the actors off the stage, and to raise the | screen or curtain dividing the scenes. | [new paragraph] There are only two scenes. One, the front part of | the stage, left quite bare, without decoration, but | with a screen, set, or backcloth at the back, repre- | senting a Japanese landscape, with hills and water, | all wintry and severe; the other, the back of the | stage, visible when this screen is lifted, a room in a | Japanese palace, very beautiful, but bare, save for a | few flowers and a picture or two. | [new paragraph] A few minutes may elapse between Acts I. and II., | and a slightly longer wait between Acts II. and III.'; [viii] blank; [ix] 'PERSONS | [dramatis personae listed] | [rule] | In Act I., Scene 1, throughout Act II., and in Scenes 1, 2, | and 4 of Act III., the scene is: An open space near ASANO'S | palace. | In Act I., Scene 2 and in Act III., Scene 3, the scene is: A | room in KIRA's palace. | [rule] | TIME. | Acts I. and II., March 10, 1701. | Act III., March 10, 1702.'; [x] blank; [1]–53 text of Act I; [54] blank; 55–90 text of Act II; 91–131 text of Act III; [132] 'PRINTED BY | BILLING AND SONS, LTD., GUILDFORD, | ENGLAND'

Paper: laid paper (no watermark), chain-lines 26mm. apart

Running title: 'THE FAITHFUL' (31mm.) on both verso and recto, pp.2–131

Binding: blue cloth (see notes). On spine, in gold: 'The | Faithful | [ornament] | John | Masefield | HEINEMANN' (all width centred). On upper cover, in gold: 'THE FAITHFUL | JOHN MASEFIELD' (within blind ruled border: 184 × 114mm.) (see notes). Lower cover: blank. All edges trimmed. Binding measurements: 187 × 120mm. (covers), 187 × 27mm. (spine). End-papers: wove paper illustrated with colour Japanese print of guards storming a dwelling

Publication date: published, according to Simmons, 1 July 1915 in an edition of 3350 copies

Price: 3s.6d.

Contents:

The Faithful ('ACT I | SCENE I. – *The Outer Scene.* ASANO *alone. Dawn. A shaft of light…*')

Notes:

Wight states that some copies were bound in 'blue-green boards' and that 'some copies have no lettering on the front cover'. A copy located in Columbia University Libraries (Special Collections B825.M377.Q5.1915.c.2) comprises a variant binding of a darker blue cloth than the standard with no lettering on the upper cover. The spine lettering, blind ruled border on the upper cover, and end-papers are as normal. Another variant, located in a private collection, comprises a blue-green board binding with gold lettering on the upper cover and spine (as normal). The end-papers are wove paper, however, with no illustration.

A letter (preserved in the Heinemann Archive) from Masefield dated 22 April 1915 to William Heinemann enclosed the typescript for this volume. Publication of this title was therefore less than three months later. Heinemann greeted the typescript with extreme caution. Masefield wrote on 27 April 1915 explaining his publishing requirements, assessment of the market, potential sales and perception of audience:

> Speculative drama cannot be performed while the streets are dark at night, + *The Faithful* won't be performed here yet a while, but I want it published here because I want to get it performed + published in America. There is a strong likelihood of its being performed in New York soon. And then I don't want to put it off till the Autumn, because I may then be wanting you to publish a book of verse.
>
> I daresay that it does seem a depressing market to launch a prose play on, but the market will improve, you will see. It will not be good for some years, but it will slowly improve. The play itself may not be much, but it is better reading than my other prose play of Pompey, which has had a slow steady sale of 500 copies a year.
>
> Will you therefore think it over + let me know your views. My readers are few but faithful, + I feel that you will not lose by the book.
>
> (John Masefield, letter to William Heinemann, 22 April 1915)
> (Archives of William Heinemann)

Evidence within the Archives of William Heinemann suggests that the terms Masefield received for the volume were twenty-five pounds advance on a 25% royalty.

The Heinemann archive preserves negotiations regarding the end-papers. Masefield first suggests 'a Japanese print as a frontispiece or as endpapers' on 29 April 1915. He provided further detail on 2 May 1915:

> Now as to the Japanese print. Hokusai did a Ronin series, with one quite good print of the Ronin beating in Kira's door, + some modern artists have done pretty good illustrations to some of the scenes in the tale, but the print I had in mind is more decorative than these. I saw it in the Museum once: Binyon shewed it to me: it is by Hildi Yoshi, I think, + represents a Samurai holding a doorway, + there is a wonderful decorative effect of arrows coming at him from all quarters: perhaps you know the print. Binyon would know it + would get it out for you to reproduce if you wished. Or I could probably get at a copy of the Hokusai print, if you prefered that.
>
> (John Masefield, letter to William Heinemann, 29 April 1915)
> (Archives of William Heinemann)

Heinemann presumably decided in favour of the Hokusai print, for a postcard from Masefield on 5 May states:

> I am arranging for the Hokusai print to be placed at your disposal for the purpose of reproduction. I hope to have it ready for you on Monday.
>
> (John Masefield, letter to William Heinemann, 5 May [1915])
> (Archives of William Heinemann)

Katsushika Hokusai, 1760–1849, was a Japanese painter, draughtsman and printmaker. The French Impressionist movement was particularly influenced by his work.

The publishing agreement for this title between Masefield and Heinemann was dated 4 May 1915 (see Archives of The Society of Authors). The agreement refers to a publication price of 3s.6d.

The first performance of *The Faithful* was given on 4 December 1915 at the Birmingham Repertory Theatre. It was produced by John Drinkwater. A photograph of this production is reproduced on p.36 of Handley-Taylor's bibliography. Another performance was given by the Royal Academy of Dramatic Art on 17 and 19 December 1934 at the Westminster Repertory Theatre. The cast list is reproduced on p.37 of Handley-Taylor's bibliography. In October 1927 Masefield was approached regarding a proposed production of the play in Stockholm. Masefield, writing to The Society of Authors, states his dissatisfaction with his work:

> I have not wanted it to be produced again, until I could get one of the acts more to my mind.
>
> (John Masefield, letter to [G.H.] Thring, 12 October 1927)
> (BL, Add.Mss.56585, f.118)

This refusal was, however, not a world-wide embargo. A Spanish translation and proposed production were permitted by Masefield:

> Thank you for your letter of yesterday and for the copy of the Spanish translation of "The Faithful", which I will read this afternoon and return on Monday. I do not mind the Spaniards doing "The Faithful", because southern acting will carry across the weak places of a play with a certain bravura and also in a Spanish play the audience does not arrive until the second act has begun. But in northern theatres one cannot count on these things and I should like to get "The Faithful" straighter before I permit it in the north.
>
> (John Masefield, letter to [G.H.] Thring, 16 October 1927)
> (BL, Add.Mss.56585, f.126)

The Stockholm people persisted, and Masefield had to repeat his intentions to The Society of Authors in November 1927:

> Many thanks for sending me the letter from Stockholm about "The Faithful". It will be some time before I can get to work upon this play and, until I have altered it materially, I do not want it to be done.
>
> (John Masefield, letter to [G.H.] Thring, 9 November 1927)
> (BL, Add.Mss.56586, f.10)

Per Lindberg of Stockholm requested permission for stage presentation once more in December 1930. Masefield, on this occasion, relented. He wrote to The Society of Authors:

> I cannot get the *Faithful* any better, + may make it worse, so by all means let Mr Lindberg play it as it is in the Autumn if he wishes.
>
> (John Masefield, letter to Denys Kilham Roberts, [December 1930])
> (BL, Add.Mss.56592, f.48)

Hilding Rosenberg made cuts to *The Faithful* and wrote an operatic version for Stockholm Opera House in 1937 or 1938 (see BL, Add.Mss.56606)

Copies seen: private collection (PWE) variant binding in blue-green boards with gold lettering on the upper cover and spine, the end-papers are wove paper; BL (11774.bb.50) stamped 1 JUL 1915; Columbia University Libraries (Special Collections B825.M377.Q5.1915.c.1); Columbia University Libraries (Special Collections B825.M377.Q5.1915.c.2) variant binding in blue cloth with no lettering on upper cover, inscribed 'for | H. B. Hichens. (Hazama) | from John Masefield. | 29. III. 1921. | "And now a blessing has come | on us."'; NYPL (Berg Collection) inscribed 'William Strang | from | John Masefield. | July 7ᵗʰ. 1915.'

A28(b) First American edition (1915)

THE FAITHFUL | A TRAGEDY IN THREE ACTS | BY | JOHN MASEFIELD | AUTHOR OF "THE TRAGEDY OF POMPEY THE GREAT," | "THE EVERLASTING MERCY," ETC. | New York | THE MACMILLAN COMPANY | 1915 | *All rights reserved*
(All width centred)

Bibliographies: Danielson [unrecorded], Williams [unrecorded], Simmons [noted on p.50], Nevinson [unrecorded], Handley-Taylor p.35, Wight 27a

Collation: [A–M]⁸ (J not used); 96 leaves; 186 × 126mm.; [i–viii] ix [x] [1–2] 3–68 [69–70] 71–115 [116–18] 119–70 [171–82]

Page contents: [i] half-title: 'THE FAITHFUL'; [ii] 'BY THE SAME AUTHOR | [rule] | [seven titles listed]' (within ruled border: 65 × 60mm.); [iii] title-page; [iv] 'COPYRIGHT, 1915 | BY JOHN MASEFIELD | Set up and electrotyped. Published September, 1915.'; [v] 'To | MY WIFE | THIS BOOK IS AFFECTIONATELY INSCRIBED'; [vi] blank; [vii] 'NOTE | This play is written to be played uninterruptedly, with- | out more break in the action than is necessary to get the | actors off the stage and to raise the screen or curtain divid- | ing the scenes. | [new paragraph] There are only two scenes: one the front part of the | stage, left quite bare, without decoration, but with a | screen, set, or backcloth at the back, representing a Japa- | nese landscape, with hills and water, all wintry and severe; | the other, the back of the stage, visible when this screen | is lifted, a room in a Japanese palace, very beautiful, but | bare, save for a few flowers and a picture or two. | [new paragraph] A few minutes may elapse between Acts I and II, and a | slightly longer wait between Acts II and III.'; [viii] blank; ix 'PERSONS | [dramatis personae listed] | In Act I, Scene I, throughout Act II, and in Scenes, I, II, | and IV of Act III, the scene is: An open space near ASANO'S | palace. | In Act I, Scene II and in Act III, Scene III, the scene is: | A room in KIRA'S palace. | TIME | Acts I and II, 10th March, 1701. | Act III, 10th March, 1702.'; [x] blank; [1] 'ACT I'; [2] blank; 3–68 text of Act I; [69] 'ACT II'; [70] blank; 71–115 text of Act II; [116] blank; [117] 'ACT III'; [118] blank; 119–70 text of Act III (below text on p.170: 'Printed in the United States of America'); [171] 'THE following pages contain advertisements | of books by the same author.' (within ruled border: 14 × 65mm.); [172] blank; [173–76] publisher's advertisements; [177–82] blank

Paper: wove paper

Running title: '*THE FAITHFUL*' (26mm.) on both verso and recto with note of act towards the gutter, pp.4–170

Binding: burgundy cloth. On spine, in gold: 'THE | FAITHFUL | MASEFIELD | MACMILLAN' (all width centred). On upper cover, in gold: 'THE | FAITHFUL | MASEFIELD' (ranged upper left) (within blind ruled border: 186 × 118mm.) Lower cover: blank. Top edge gilt, others roughly trimmed. Binding measurements: 193 × 127mm. (covers), 193 × 35mm. (spine). End-papers: wove paper.

Publication date: published, according to Simmons, 29 September 1915 in an edition of 1530 copies

Price: $1.25

Contents:
as for A28(a)

Notes:
Wight notes that 'top edges are gilt but the others are uncut'

Three publishing agreements for this title between Masefield and Macmillan are dated 26 February 1915, 7 May 1915 and 16 April 1915 (see Archives of The Society of Authors). The agreements refer to 'a licence to publish in volume form in the United States of America a work the subject or title of which is The Faithful'. The earlier agreement only notes that 'the Author hereby authorizes and empowers his agent, Paul R. Reynolds, 70 Fifth Avenue, New York City, to collect and receive all sums of money payable to him under the terms of this agreement…'

Copies seen: private collection (ROV)

A29 GOOD FRIDAY AND OTHER POEMS   1916

A29(a) First American edition (1916)

GOOD FRIDAY | AND OTHER POEMS | BY | JOHN MASEFIELD | AUTHOR OF "THE EVERLASTING MERCY" "THE WIDOW | IN THE BYE STREET" "THE TRAGEDY OF | POMPEY THE GREAT," ETC. | New York | THE MACMILLAN COMPANY | 1916 | *All rights reserved*
(All width centred)

Bibliographies: Danielson [unrecorded], Williams [unrecorded], Simmons [28], Nevinson [unrecorded], Handley-Taylor p.35, Wight [28] & 29b

Collation: [A-I]⁸; 72 leaves; 187 × 128mm.; [i–vi] [1–2] 3–64 [65–66] 67–131 [132–38]

Page contents: [i] half-title: 'GOOD FRIDAY | AND OTHER POEMS'; [ii] '[publisher's device] | THE MACMILLAN COMPANY | [two lines listing six cities, separated by four points] | MACMILLAN & CO., LIMITED | [two lines listing four cities, separated by two points] | THE MACMILLAN CO. OF CANADA, LTD. | [one city listed]'; [iii] title-page; [iv] 'COPYRIGHT, 1915 and 1916 | BY JOHN MASEFIELD | [rule] | Set up and electrotyped. Published February, 1916.'; [v] 'GOOD FRIDAY | A DRAMATIC POEM'; [vi] 'PERSONS | [dramatis personae listed]'; [1] 'THE SCENE | *The Pavement, or Paved Court, outside the Roman Citadel in | Jerusalem. At the back is the barrack wall, pierced in the | centre with a double bronze door, weathered to a green | color. On the right and left sides of the stage are battle- | mented parapets overlooking the city. The stage or pave- | ment is approached by stone steps from the front, and by | narrow stone staircases in the wings, one on each side, well | forward. These steps are to suggest that the citadel is high | up above the town, and that the main barrack gate is below.* | THE CHIEF CITIZEN, THE RABBLE, JOSEPH, THE MAD- | MAN, HEROD, *and* THE LOITERERS, *etc.,* enter by these | steps. PILATE, PROCULA, LONGINUS, THE SOLDIERS *and* | SERVANTS *enter by the bronze doors.*'; [2] blank; 3–64 text of *Good Friday* [65] 'SONNETS'; [66] 'NOTE | Some few of these sonnets appeared serially | in the *Atlantic Monthly, Scribner's Magazine, | Harper's Monthly,* and (perhaps) in one or two | other papers. I thank the Editors of these | papers for permission to reprint them here. | JOHN MASEFIELD. | LONDON, 16th Dec. 1915.'; 67–131 text of Sonnets (at foot of p.131: 'Printed in the United States of America.'); [132] blank; [133] 'THE following pages contain advertisements of | Macmillan books by the same author.' (within ruled border: 14 × 80mm.); [134] blank; [135–38] publisher's advertisements

Paper: wove paper

Running title: 'GOOD FRIDAY AND OTHER POEMS' (59mm.) on both verso and recto, pp.4–131

Binding: burgundy cloth. On spine, in gold: 'GOOD | FRIDAY | and | OTHER POEMS | MASEFIELD | MACMILLAN' (all width centred). (The 'd' of 'and' is swash). On upper cover, in gold: 'GOOD FRIDAY | AND | OTHER POEMS | MASEFIELD' (ranged upper left) (within blind ruled border: 186 × 117mm.) Lower cover: blank. Top edge gilt, others trimmed. Binding measurements: 192 × 127mm. (covers), 192 × 30mm. (spine). End-papers: wove paper.

Publication date: published, according to Simmons, 9 February 1916 in an edition of 2324 copies

Price: $1.25

Contents:
Good Friday ('PILATE. Longinus.')
  First printed in The Fortnightly Review *December 1915, pp.[993]–1018*
[Untitled] ('Long long ago, when all the glittering earth')
[Untitled] ('Night came again, but now I could not sleep.')
[Untitled] ('Even after all these years there comes the dream')
[Untitled] ('If I could come again to that dear place')
[Untitled] ('Men are made human by the mighty fall')
[Untitled] ('Here in the self is all that man can know')
[Untitled] ('Flesh, I have knocked at many a dusty door,')
[Untitled] ('But all has passed, the tune has died away,')
[Untitled] ('These myriad days, these many thousand hours,')
[Untitled] ('There, on the darkened deathbed, dies the brain')
[Untitled] ('So in the empty sky the stars appear,')
[Untitled] ('It may be so with us, that in the dark,')
[Untitled] ('Man has his unseen friend, his unseen twin,')
[Untitled] ('What am I, Life? A thing of watery salt')
[Untitled] ('If I could get within this changing I,')
[Untitled] ('What is this atom which contains the whole,')
[Untitled] ('Ah, we are neither heaven nor earth, but men;')
[Untitled] ('Roses are beauty, but I never see')
[Untitled] ('Over the church's door they moved a stone')
[Untitled] ('I never see the red rose crown the year,')
[Untitled] ('Out of the clouds come torrents, from the earth')
[Untitled] ('O little self, within whose smallness lies')
[Untitled] ('I went into the fields, but you were there')
[Untitled] ('There are two forms of life, of which one moves,')
[Untitled] ('Restless and hungry, still it moves and slays')
[Untitled] ('How many ways, how many different times')
[Untitled] ('The other form of Living does not stir;')
[Untitled] ('Is there a great green commonwealth of Thought')
[Untitled] ('Beauty, let be; I cannot see your face,')
[Untitled] ('Here, where we stood together, we three men,')
[Untitled] ('I saw her like a shadow on the sky')
[Untitled] ('Not that the stars are all gone mad in heaven')
[Untitled] ('There is no God, as I was taught in youth,')
[Untitled] ('Beauty retires; the blood out of the earth')
[Untitled] ('Wherever beauty has been quick in clay')
[Untitled] ('You are more beautiful than women are,')
[Untitled] ('Out of the barracks to the castle yard')
[Untitled] ('Not for the anguish suffered is the slur,')
[Untitled] ('Beauty was with me once, but now, grown old,')
[Untitled] ('So beauty comes, so with a failing hand')
[Untitled] ('If Beauty be at all, if, beyond sense,')
[Untitled] ('Each greedy self, by consecrating lust,')
[Untitled] ('Time being an instant in eternity,')
[Untitled] ('You will remember me in days to come')
[Untitled] ('They took the bloody body from the cross,')
[Untitled] ('"Come to us fiery with the saints of God')
[Untitled] ('So from the cruel cross they buried God;')
[Untitled] ('If all be governed by the moving stars,')
[Untitled] ('In emptiest furthest heaven where no stars are')

THE FAITHFUL

A TRAGEDY IN THREE ACTS

BY

JOHN MASEFIELD

LONDON

WILLIAM HEINEMANN

A28(a) title-page

SONNETS

BY

JOHN MASEFIELD

AUTHOR OF "THE EVERLASTING MERCY," "THE WIDOW IN THE
BYE STREET," "THE FAITHFUL," "THE STORY
OF A ROUNDHOUSE," ETC.

New York
THE MACMILLAN COMPANY
1916

All rights reserved

A30(a) title-page

A28(a) end-papers

Good Friday
A Play in Verse

By
JOHN MASEFIELD

PUBLISHED BY
JOHN MASEFIELD
AT LOLLINGDON, CHOLSEY, BERKSHIRE
PRINTED AT LETCHWORTH BY THE GARDEN CITY PRESS LTD.
1916
Copyright in U.S.A.

A31(b) title-page

Sonnets and Poems

By
JOHN MASEFIELD

Price 3/6 *net.*

PUBLISHED BY
JOHN MASEFIELD
AT LOLLINGDON, CHOLSEY, BERKSHIRE
PRINTED AT LETCHWORTH BY THE GARDEN CITY PRESS LTD.
1916
Copyright in U.S.A.

A32(b) title-page

The Locked Chest
and
The Sweeps of Ninety-Eight

TWO ONE ACT PLAYS

BY
JOHN MASEFIELD

New York
THE MACMILLAN COMPANY
1916
All rights reserved

A33(b) title-page

A POEM
AND TWO PLAYS

BY
JOHN MASEFIELD

LONDON
WILLIAM HEINEMANN

A46(a) title-page

[Untitled] ('Perhaps in chasms of the wasted past,')
[Untitled] ('For, like an outcast from the city, I')
[Untitled] ('Death lies in wait for you, you wild thing in the wood,')
[Untitled] ('What are we given, what do we take away?')
[Untitled] ('They called that broken hedge The Haunted Gate.')
[Untitled] ('There was an evil in the nodding wood')
[Untitled] ('Go, spend your penny, Beauty, when you will,')
[Untitled] ('Not for your human beauty nor the power')
[Untitled] ('The little robin hopping in the wood')
[Untitled] ('Though in life's streets the tempting shops have lured,')
[Untitled] ('When all these million cells that are my slaves')
[Untitled] ('Let that which is to come be as it may,')
The Madman's Song ('You have not seen what I have seen,')

Notes:

Wight lists this volume twice in his bibliography as both [28] and 29b. This error presumably occurs as he fails to establish *Good Friday and other poems* and *Good Friday* as entirely separate editions.

A publishing agreement for this title between Masefield and Macmillan was dated 1 December 1915 (see Archives of The Society of Authors). The agreement refers to 'a licence to publish in volume form in the United States of America a work the subject or title of which is Good Friday (a dramatic poem) and other material sufficient to make a volume of the usual size'.

Copies seen: BL (X.908/4344) stamped 30 OCT 1962

Reprinted:

[first edition, second impression]	Feb 1916
[first edition, third impression]	Apr 1916
[first edition, fourth impression]	Nov 1916

A30 SONNETS 1916

A30(a) First American edition – numbered issue (1916)

SONNETS [in red] | BY | JOHN MASEFIELD | AUTHOR OF "THE EVERLASTING MERCY," "THE WIDOW IN THE | BYE STREET," "THE FAITHFUL," "THE STORY | OF A ROUNDHOUSE," ETC. | New York | THE MACMILLAN COMPANY | 1916 | *All rights reserved*
(All width centred)

Bibliographies: Danielson [unrecorded], Williams [noted on p.5], Simmons [30], Nevinson [unrecorded], Handley-Taylor p.35, Wight [30]

Collation: [A]² [B-E]⁸; 34 leaves; 216 × 146mm.; [i–vi] 1–61 [62]

Page contents: [i] half-title: 'SONNETS'; [ii] 'Five hundred copies of this book | have been printed for sale. | This copy is No. ....'; [iii] title-page (with additional leaf tipped-in on the verso of which is the frontispiece: 131 × 95mm., with protective tissue); [iv] 'COPYRIGHT, 1916, | BY JOHN MASEFIELD. | Norwood Press | J.S. Cushing Co. – Berwick & Smith Co. | Norwood, Mass., U.S.A.'; [v] '*To* | MY AMERICAN FRIENDS'; [vi] blank; 1–61 text (at foot of p.61: '[rule] | Printed in the United States of America.'); [62] blank

Paper: wove paper (watermark: '[device within a rectangle: 13 × 13mm.] | P _ M | FABRIANO | ITALY')

Running title: none

Binding: green boards with vellum spine. On spine, reading lengthways up spine, from foot, in gold: 'SONNETS – MASEFIELD'. On upper cover, in gold: 'SONNETS | JOHN MASEFIELD' (ranged upper right) (within double ruled border: 20 × 48mm.) Lower cover: blank. Top edge gilt, others uncut. Binding measurements: 219 × 143mm. (covers), 219 × 22mm. (spine). End-papers: green laid paper (no watermark), chain-lines 25mm. apart

Publication date: published, according to Simmons, 16 February 1916 in an edition of 500 copies (see notes)

Price: unknown

Contents:
[Untitled] ('Long, long ago, when all the glittering earth')
[Untitled] ('Night came again, but now I could not sleep.')
[Untitled] ('Even after all these years there comes the dream')
[Untitled] ('If I could come again to that dear place')
[Untitled] ('Men are made human by the mighty fall')
[Untitled] ('Here in the self is all that man can know')
[Untitled] ('Flesh, I have knocked at many a dusty door,')
[Untitled] ('But all has passed, the tune has died away,')

[Untitled] ('These myriad days, these many thousand hours,')
[Untitled] ('There, on the darkened deathbed, dies the brain')
[Untitled] ('So in the empty sky the stars appear,')
[Untitled] ('It may be so with us, that in the dark')
[Untitled] ('Man has his unseen friend, his unseen twin,')
[Untitled] ('What am I, Life? A thing of watery salt')
[Untitled] ('If I could get within this changing I,')
[Untitled] ('What is this atom which contains the whole,')
[Untitled] ('Ah, we are neither heaven nor earth, but men;')
[Untitled] ('Roses are beauty, but I never see')
[Untitled] ('Over the church's door they moved a stone')
[Untitled] ('I never see the red rose crown the year,')
[Untitled] ('Out of the clouds come torrents, from the earth')
[Untitled] ('O little self, within whose smallness lies')
[Untitled] ('I went into the fields, but you were there')
[Untitled] ('There are two forms of life, of which one moves')
[Untitled] ('Restless and hungry, still it moves and slays')
[Untitled] ('How many ways, how many different times,')
[Untitled] ('The other form of Living does not stir;')
[Untitled] ('Is there a great green commonwealth of Thought')
[Untitled] ('Beauty, let be; I cannot see your face,')
[Untitled] ('Here, where we stood together, we three men,')
[Untitled] ('I saw her like a shadow on the sky')
[Untitled] ('Not that the stars are all gone mad in heaven')
[Untitled] ('There is no God, as I was taught in youth,')
[Untitled] ('Beauty retires; the blood out of the earth')
[Untitled] ('Wherever beauty has been quick in clay')
[Untitled] ('You are more beautiful than women are,')
[Untitled] ('Out of the barracks to the castle yard')
[Untitled] ('Not for the anguish suffered is the slur,')
[Untitled] ('Beauty was with me once, but now, grown old,')
[Untitled] ('So beauty comes, so with a failing hand')
[Untitled] ('If Beauty be at all, if, beyond sense,')
[Untitled] ('Each greedy self, by consecrating lust,')
[Untitled] ('Time being an instant in eternity,')
[Untitled] ('You will remember me in days to come')
[Untitled] ('They took the bloody body from the cross')
[Untitled] ('"Come to us fiery with the saints of God')
[Untitled] ('So from the cruel cross they buried God;')
[Untitled] ('If all be governed by the moving stars,')
[Untitled] ('In emptiest furthest heaven where no stars are')
[Untitled] ('Perhaps in chasms of the wasted past,')
[Untitled] ('For, like an outcast from the city, I')
[Untitled] ('Death lies in wait for you, you wild thing in the wood,')
[Untitled] ('What are we given, what do we take away?')
[Untitled] ('They called that broken hedge The Haunted Gate.')
[Untitled] ('There was an evil in the nodding wood')
[Untitled] ('Go, spend your penny, Beauty, when you will,')
[Untitled] ('Not for your human beauty nor the power')
[Untitled] ('The little robin hopping in the wood')
[Untitled] ('Though in life's streets the tempting shops have lured,')
[Untitled] ('When all these million cells that are my slaves')
[Untitled] ('Let that which is to come be as it may,')

Notes:
Simmons states:

> The contents of this book are exactly the same as those of pp.67–127 of *Good Friday and other poems*, New York, 1916...
> i.e. the 61 sonnets.

The contents are indeed the same (and retain the same order), although there are minor textual variants in punctuation. The text has been entirely re-set for this edition and drop-capitals are used throughout for the beginning of each sonnet.

In noting the limitation of this edition, Simmons states:

Published... in an edition of 800 copies, of which 200 were presented, 600 being left available, of which 500 were numbered.

In addition to this information, Simmons notes 'an irregular issue':

> There is an irregular issue of this book, printed on same paper as limited issue, having no edition note, and having the name, "John Masefield", printed in script under the frontispiece. There is no inscription on the frontispiece in the limited issue.

Drew states that the inclusion or omission of the author's name should not be used as an indication of issue. In 'Some Contributions to the Bibliography of John Masefield: II' (*Papers of the Bibliographical Society of America*, October 1959, pp.262–67) Drew notes:

> The irregular issue mentioned by Simmons... also appears without the name, "John Masefield," printed in script under the frontispiece

Rather than an indication of issue, the inclusion or omission of the author's name presumably relates merely to two variations in the printing of the frontispiece.

Copies seen: private collection (PWE) signed '220 [in red] | John Masefield' on p.[ii]; Library of The John Masefield Society, signed '64 [in red] | John Masefield' on p.[ii]

A30(aa) First American edition – un-numbered issue (1916)

SONNETS [in red] | BY | JOHN MASEFIELD | AUTHOR OF "THE EVERLASTING MERCY," "THE WIDOW IN THE | BYE STREET," "THE FAITHFUL," "THE STORY | OF A ROUNDHOUSE," ETC. | New York | THE MACMILLAN COMPANY | 1916 | *All rights reserved*
(All width centred)

Bibliographies: Danielson [unrecorded], Williams [noted on p.5], Simmons [30], Nevinson [unrecorded], Handley-Taylor p.35, Wight [see 30]

Collation: [A]² [B-E]⁸; 34 leaves; 216 × 146mm.; [i–vi] 1–61 [62]

Page contents: [i] half-title: 'SONNETS'; [ii] blank; [iii] title-page (with additional leaf tipped-in on the verso of which is the frontispiece: 131 × 95mm., 'John Masefield' with protective tissue) (see notes); [iv] 'COPYRIGHT, 1916, | BY JOHN MASEFIELD. | Norwood Press | J.S. Cushing Co. – Berwick & Smith Co. | Norwood, Mass., U.S.A.'; [v] '*To* | MY AMERICAN FRIENDS'; [vi] blank; 1–61 text (at foot of p.61: '[rule] | Printed in the United States of America.'); [62] blank

Paper: wove paper (watermark: '[device within a rectangle: 13 × 13mm.] | P _ M | FABRIANO | ITALY')

Running title: none

Binding: green boards with vellum spine. On spine, reading lengthways up spine, from foot, in gold: 'SONNETS – MASEFIELD'. On upper cover, in gold: 'SONNETS | JOHN MASEFIELD' (ranged upper right) (within double ruled border: 20 × 48mm.) Lower cover: blank. Top edge gilt, others uncut. Binding measurements: 219 × 143mm. (covers), 219 × 22mm. (spine). End-papers: green laid paper (no watermark), chain-lines 25mm. apart

Publication date: published, according to Simmons, 16 February 1916 in an edition of 100 copies and 200 copies for presentation (see notes)

Price: unknown

Contents:
as for A30(a)

Notes:
see notes to A30(a)

The 'presentation copies' appear to have been entirely for the author's own use. A letter from George P. Brett to Masefield from the end of February 1916 specifically refers to these copies:

> ...I am sending to your hotel the dozen copies of "Good Friday" as requested in your letter, and in the same parcel the two hundred copies of the "Sonnets" which we agreed to send you and with these are the envelopes for sending them out, all of which will, I hope, meet your wishes in the matter.
>
> (George P. Brett, letter to John Masefield, 24 February 1916)
> (HRHRC, MS (Masefield, J.) Recip The Macmillan Company)

Copies seen: BL (12233.s.27) stamped 15 DEC 1960

A31 GOOD FRIDAY   1916

A31(a) First English edition (1916)

Good Friday | LETCHWORTH | *GARDEN CITY PRESS LIMITED* | 1916 | *Copyright in U.S.A.*
(The italic type contains a number of swash characters)
(All width centred)

Bibliographies: Danielson 186, Williams p.4, Simmons [29], Nevinson [unrecorded], Handley-Taylor p.38, Wight [29]

Collation: [A]⁴ B-K⁴ (J not used); signatures right foot of page; 40 leaves; 225 × 143mm.; [1–4] 5–77 [78–80]

Page contents: [1] half-title: 'GOOD FRIDAY | [rule] | A play in verse'; [2] '*This Edition is limited to 200 copies.*'; [3] title-page; [4] 'PERSONS | [dramatis personae listed] | THE SCENE | *The Pavement, or Paved Court, outside the Roman | Citadel in Jerusalem.* | [new paragraph] *At the back is the barrack wall, pierced in the centre | with a double bronze door, weathered to a green colour.* | [new paragraph] *On the right and left sides of the stage are battlemented | parapets overlooking the city.* | [new paragraph] *The stage or pavement is approached by stone steps from | the front, and by narrow stone staircases in the wings, one on | each side well forward. These steps are to suggest that the | citadel is high up above the town, and that the main barrack | gate is below.* THE CHIEF CITIZEN, THE RABBLE, | JOSEPH, THE MADMAN, HEROD, *and* THE LOITERERS, | *etc., enter by these steps.* | [new paragraph] PILATE, PROCULA, LONGINUS, THE SOLDIERS *and* | SERVANTS *enter by the bronze door.*'; 5–77 text (at foot of p.77: '*This play was first printed in* THE FORTNIGHTLY REVIEW | *for December*, 1915.'); [78–80] blank

Paper: laid paper (watermark: '[Crown] | Abbey Mills | Greenfield'), chain-lines 25mm. apart

Running title: 'Good Friday' (29mm.) on both verso and recto, pp.6–77

Binding: grey wrappers. Spine: blank. On upper wrapper: '*Good Friday | A Play in Verse | By | JOHN MASEFIELD | LETCHWORTH | GARDEN CITY PRESS LIMITED | 1916 | Copyright in U.S.A.*' (The italic type contains a number of swash characters). On lower wrapper: '[figure with spade gazing upon horizon of hills and clouds with 'TELEGRAPHIC ADDRESS | SPADEWORK LETCHWORTH' (within a 'T' shape)] | GARDEN CITY – | PRESS LIMITED | LETCHWORTH – | HERTS. – – – –' (within double ruled border: 47 × 30mm.) Top edge trimmed, others uncut. Binding measurements: 228 × 152mm. (wrappers), 228 × 10mm. (spine). The wrapper extends beyond the edges of the internal leaves

Publication date: published, according to Simmons, not later than August 1916 (in an edition of 200 copies) (see also notes to A27(c))

Price: 1 guinea (set of 4 volumes: see also A27(c) A32(a) and A33(a))

Contents:
Good Friday ('PILATE. | Longinus.')

Notes:
Performances of the play were given by the Incorporated Stage Society on 25 and 26 February 1917 at the Garrick Theatre, London. The cast list is reproduced on p.39 of Handley-Taylor's bibliography. Handley-Taylor also notes three separate performances of this play at Stowe School, Buckingham and one at Harrow School on p.38 of his bibliography.

In the preface to the second volume of the 1918 Macmillan publication, *The Poems and Plays of John Masefield* (see A45(a)), Masefield writes of *Good Friday*:

> Soon afterwards I began a second one-act play in verse, on the subject of Good Friday... *Good Friday* was interrupted by the war and never completed. I had hoped in a rewriting to make the play a clash between Christ and the High Priest. This was one of the many millions of human hopes destroyed in that year.
> (John Masefield, 'Preface', *The Poems and Plays of John Masefield*, Volume Two, Macmillan, 1919, p.vi)

In A29(a) the description of the scene on page [1] notes that there is an entrance through 'the bronze doors'. For this English edition there are economies on hinges and entry is through 'the bronze door'.

Copies seen: private collection (PWE); BL (Cup.500.bb.1) stamped 26 MAY 1916; ULL (Special Collections) rebound; NYPL (Berg Collection)

A31(b) Second English edition (1916)

Good Friday | A Play in Verse | By | JOHN MASEFIELD | PUBLISHED BY | JOHN MASEFIELD | AT LOLLINGDON, CHOLSEY, BERKSHIRE | PRINTED AT LETCHWORTH BY THE GARDEN CITY PRESS LTD. | 1916 | Copyright in U.S.A.
(The italic type contains a number of swash characters)
(All width centred)

Bibliographies: Danielson [unrecorded], Williams p.4, Simmons [noted on p.55], Nevinson [unrecorded], Handley-Taylor [unrecorded], Wight 29a

Collation: [A]⁴ B-K⁴ (J not used); signatures right foot of page; 40 leaves; 191 × 129mm.; [1–4] 5–77 [78–80]

Page contents: [1] half-title: 'GOOD FRIDAY | [rule] | A play in verse'; [2] 'UNIFORM WITH THIS VOLUME. | *Sonnets and Poems | Price 3/6 net.*'; [3] title-page; [4] 'PERSONS | [dramatis personae listed] | THE SCENE | *The Pavement, or Paved Court, outside the Roman | Citadel in Jerusalem.* | [new paragraph] *At the back is the barrack wall, pierced in the centre | with a double bronze door, weathered to a green colour.* | [new paragraph] *On the right and left sides of the stage are battlemented | parapets overlooking the city.* | [new paragraph] *The stage or pavement is approached by stone steps from | the front, and by narrow stone staircases in the wings, one on | each side well forward. These steps are to suggest that the | citadel is high up above the town, and that the main barrack | gate is below.* THE CHIEF CITIZEN, THE RABBLE, | JOSEPH, THE MADMAN, HEROD, *and* THE LOITERERS, | *etc., enter by these steps.* | [new paragraph] PILATE, PROCULA, LONGINUS, THE SOLDIERS *and* | SERVANTS *enter by the bronze door.*'; 5–77 text (at foot of p.77: '*This play was first printed in* THE FORTNIGHTLY REVIEW | *for December*, 1915.'); [78–80] blank

Paper: laid paper (watermark: '[Crown] | Abbey Mills | Greenfield'), chain-lines 24mm. apart

Running title: 'Good Friday' (29mm.) on both verso and recto, pp.6–77

Binding: light blue cloth. On spine: white paper label (134 × 10mm.) on which reading lengthways up spine, from foot: '*GOOD FRIDAY. By John Masefield*' (the 'Y' in '*FRIDAY*' is swash). On upper cover: white paper label (70 × 52mm.) on which: '*Good | Friday | [leaf motif] [in red] | John Masefield*' (within double ruled border in red: 62 × 45mm.) Lower cover: blank. Top edge trimmed, others uncut. Binding measurements: 196 × 129mm. (covers), 196 × 17mm. (spine). End-papers: laid papers (watermark: '[Crown] | Abbey Mills | Greenfield'), chain-lines 24mm. apart

Publication date: published, according to Simmons, 'later' than A31(a)

Price: 3s.6d.

Contents:
as for A31(a)

Notes:
Despite the obvious similarity to the earlier Garden City Press edition (see A31(a)) there are minor differences in the setting of the type that suggest at least a partial resetting. The 'E' used at the beginning of all stage directions on p.28 is, for example, different between the two editions.

Williams describes this edition as a '2nd edition'

The labels on the upper covers vary in size between copies

Copies seen: private collection (PWE); BL (11773.e.56) stamped 31 JAN 1917; BL (Ashley 1109*) stamped 'ASHLEY | B [crown]M | LIBRARY'; ULL (Special Collections); HRHRC (PR6025 A77 G6 1916) inscribed 'The days that make us happy make | us wise. | John Masefield.', ownership signature 'William Strang | Jany 1917.'

A31(c) Third English edition (1917)

GOOD FRIDAY | A PLAY IN VERSE | BY | JOHN MASEFIELD | [publisher's device of a windmill with 'W [point]' and 'H' all within ruled border: 15 × 15mm.] | LONDON | WILLIAM HEINEMANN
(All width centred)

Bibliographies: Danielson [unrecorded], Williams p.4, Simmons [unrecorded], Nevinson p.13, Handley-Taylor p.38, Wight [noted on p.53]

Collation: [A]⁴ B-L⁴ (J not used); signatures right foot of page; 44 leaves; 184 × 118mm.; [i–iv] v [vi] vii [viii] 1–78 [79–80]

Page contents: [i] half-title: 'GOOD FRIDAY'; [ii] 'BY THE SAME AUTHOR | *Uniform with this Volume* | [rule] | [six titles listed] | LONDON : WILLIAM HEINEMANN'; [iii] title-page; [iv] 'LONDON : WILLIAM HEINEMANN. 1917.'; v 'PERSONS | [dramatis personae listed]'; [vi] blank; vii 'THE SCENE | *The Pavement, or Paved Court, outside the Roman | Citadel in Jerusalem.* | [new paragraph] *At the back is the barrack wall, pierced in the centre | with a double bronze door, weathered to a green colour.* | [new paragraph] *On the right and left sides of the stage are battlemented | parapets overlooking the city.* | [new paragraph] *The stage or pavement is approached by stone steps | from the front, and by narrow stone staircases in the | wings, one on each side, well forward. These steps are | to suggest that the citadel is high up above the town, and | that the main barrack gate is below.* THE CHIEF | CITIZEN, THE RABBLE, JOSEPH, THE MADMAN, HEROD, | *and* THE LOITERERS, *etc., enter by these steps.* | [new paragraph] PILATE, PROCULA, LONGINUS, THE SOLDIERS *and* | SERVANTS *enter by the bronze door.*'; [viii] blank; 1-[79] text (at foot of p.[79]: '[rule] | BILLING AND SONS, LTD., PRINTERS, GUILDFORD, ENGLAND'); [80] blank

Paper: wove paper

Running title: 'GOOD FRIDAY' (29mm.) on both verso and recto, pp.2-[80]

Binding: blue cloth. On spine, in gold: 'Good | Friday | [ornament] | John | Masefield | HEINEMANN' (all width centred). On upper cover, in gold: 'GOOD FRIDAY | JOHN MASEFIELD' (within blind ruled border: 183 × 114mm.) Lower cover: blank. All edges trimmed. Binding measurements: 188 × 120mm. (covers), 188 × 27mm. (spine). End-papers: wove paper

Publication date: published, according to Handley-Taylor, 25 October 1917

Price: 3s.6d.

Contents:
as for A31(a)

Notes:
A defective variant includes the following pagination sequence: [i–iv] v [vi] vii [viii] 1–49 34–35 52–53 38–39 56–78 [79–80]. This repeats pp.34–35 and pp.38–39 in place of pp.50–51 and pp.54–55. (Or, F1v & F2 and F3v & F4 repeated in the position of H1v & H2 and H3v & H4). These errors are limited, therefore, to gathering H and in all other respects the copy conforms to the description of a regular copy.

The publishing agreement for this title between Masefield and Heinemann was dated 16 August 1917 (see Archives of The Society of Authors). The agreement refers to a publication price of 3s.6d.

Reprints of this edition (from at least the January 1921 impression) are signed (at the right foot) in gatherings of eight. Thus [1]⁸ 2–5⁸ 6⁴. There are still 44 leaves and the same setting of type appears to have been used. The new signatures presumably facilitated a binding process of six gatherings (rather than the twelve of the first edition).

Copies seen: private collection (PWE); private collection (PWE) (defective variant); BL (011779.g.8) stamped 26 OCT 1917

Reprinted:

'New Impression'	[first edition, second impression]	Mar 1918
'New Impression'	[first edition, third impression]	Jan 1921
'New Impression'	[first edition, fourth impression]	Nov 1929

A31(d) Fourth English edition (1955)

GOOD FRIDAY | *A Play in Verse* | BY | JOHN MASEFIELD | [publisher's device of a windmill with 'W' and 'H'] | [rule] | WILLIAM HEINEMANN LTD | MELBOURNE : : LONDON : : TORONTO
(All width centred)

Bibliographies: Handley-Taylor p.38, Wight [unrecorded]

Collation: [A]⁸ B-D⁸; signatures right foot of page; 32 leaves; 185 × 121mm.; [two un-numbered pages] [i–iv] v [vi] vii [viii] 1–49 [50–54]

Page contents: [-] blank (page excluded from page count, but constitutes first leaf of first gathering); [-] blank; [i] half-title: 'GOOD FRIDAY'; [ii] 'THE DRAMA LIBRARY | *General Editor:* EDWARD THOMPSON | [33 titles and their authors or editors listed] | *For further details, see end of this book*.'; [iii] title-page; [iv] 'FIRST PUBLISHED OCTOBER, 1917 | THE DRAMA LIBRARY, 1955 | PUBLISHED BY | WILLIAM HEINEMANN LTD | 99 GREAT RUSSELL STREET, LONDON, W.C.1 | PRINTED IN GREAT BRITAIN BY THE PUBLISHERS AT | THE WINDMILL PRESS, KINGSWOOD, SURREY'; v 'PERSONS | [dramatis personae listed]'; [vi] blank; vii 'THE SCENE | *The Pavement, or Paved Court, outside the Roman Citadel | in Jerusalem.* | [new paragraph] *At the back is the barrack wall, pierced in the centre with | a double bronze door, weathered to a green colour.* | [new paragraph] *On the right and left sides of the stage are battlemented | parapets overlooking the city.* | [new paragraph] *The stage or pavement is approached by stone steps from | the front, and by narrow stone staircases in the wings, one | on each side, well forward. These steps are to suggest that | the citadel is high up above the town, and that the main | barrack gate is below.* THE CHIEF CITIZEN, THE RABBLE, | JOSEPH, THE MADMAN, HEROD, *and* THE LOITERERS, | *etc., enter by these steps.* | [new paragraph] PILATE, PROCULA, LONGINUS, THE SOLDIERS *and* | SERVANTS *enter by the bronze door*.'; [viii] blank; 1–49 text; [50] blank; [51–53] publisher's advertisements; [54] blank

Paper: wove paper

Running title: none

Binding: white boards (overprinted in blue). On blue spine, reading lengthways down spine from head: 'GOOD FRIDAY *by* JOHN MASEFIELD'. On blue upper cover: 'THE DRAMA LIBRARY | [oval device with stars, lines and shading containing white oval in which: 'GOOD FRIDAY | *by* | JOHN MASEFIELD | [device]'] | HEINEMANN'. On white lower cover: '4s 6d | NET'. All edges trimmed. Binding measurements: 191 × 122mm. (covers), 191 × 17mm. (spine). End-papers: wove paper.

Publication date: published, according to Handley-Taylor, 30 February 1955. (The sales ledger preserved in the Heinemann Archive suggests publication on 21 February 1955 in an edition of 2000 copies). This earlier date of publication is also noted in a letter from Edward Thompson to Masefield (see Edward Thompson, letter to John Masefield, 2 February 1955) (HRHRC, MS (Masefield, J.) Recip William Heinemann Ltd.)

Price: 4s.6d.

Contents:
as for A31(a)

Notes:
The Society of Authors, wrote to Masefield in 1953 introducing the Heinemann proposal for this edition:

> I am enclosing a copy of a letter we have received from Mr. E. Thompson of Heinemann. I have told Mr. Thompson on the telephone that we will be referring the proposal to you and asked him what terms they had in mind. He tells me that for plays in this series they normally pay a flat royalty of 10% and that though they do not generally pay any advance he feels sure they would be willing to do so if you wished.
>
> (Anne Munro-Kerr, letter to John Masefield, 23 October 1953)
> (BL, Add.Mss.56624, f.172)

Masefield replied the following day stating that he would 'take up the *Good Friday* question with Mr Frere...' (see BL, Add.Mss.56624, f.173). In February 1954 the matter had not been resolved and, in a letter to The Society of Authors, Masefield assessed the state of his publications. One of the suggestions from Heinemann that Masefield reported was:

> That my play of *Good Friday* should be issued at 3/6 (or in boards at 5/-) in a special Library of plays that the firm is doing. I think that for this they would have to reset. They offer

10% for the first 2000 copies
12½% from 2–5000 copies
15% after 5000 copies

(John Masefield, letter to Elizabeth Barber, [February 1954])
(BL, Add.Mss.56625 ff.18–22)

Although the publisher's advertisements at the rear of the volume list this edition of *Good Friday* at 3s.6d., the price printed on the lower cover is 4s.6d. In the 1959 reprint, the advert is amended to match the cover price.

A proof copy of this edition with authorial revisions by Masefield is located in the University of London Library (Special Collections). These revisions are, however, all of a typographical nature and Masefield does not revise the substantive text, beyond printer's errors.

Copies seen: BL (W.P. 13760/31) stamped 2 FEB 1955

Reprinted:
'Reprinted'   [fourth edition, second impression]   1959

A31(e) First German edition [in English] ([post 1953])

JOHN MASEFIELD | GOOD FRIDAY | *A Play in Verse* | VELHAGEN & KLASING | BIELEFELD [point] BERLIN [point] HANNOVER
(All width centred)

Bibliographies: Wight [unrecorded]

Collation:[A]²⁴ (but signed [1]⁸ 2–3⁸); the second leaf of gatherings 2 and 3 is also signed; signatures left foot of page with 'E. L. 24' on first leaf of gatherings 2 and 3; 24 leaves; 190 × 121mm.; [1–4] 5–47 [48]

Page contents: [1] title-page; [2] 'ENGLISCHE UND AMERIKANISCHE LESEBOGEN | 24 | Alleinberechtigte ungerkürzte Ausgabe | Der Abdruck efolgt mit der freundlichen | Genehmigung von Dr. John Masefield, O.M. | Diesen Lesebogen besorgte Studienrat Hans-Hellmut Münker' [3] 'JOHN MASEFIELD, GOOD FRIDAY'; [4] 'PERSONS | [dramatis personae listed]'; 5 'THE SCENE | *The Pavement, or Paved Court, outside the Roman Citadel in Jerusalem. | At the back is the barrack wall, pierced in the centre with a double bronze | door, weathered to a green colour. | On the right and left sides of the stage are battlemented parapets overlooking | the city. | The stage or pavement is approached by stone steps from the front, and by | narrow stone staircases in the wings, one on each side, well forward. These | steps are to suggest that the citadel is high up above the town, and that the | main barrack gate is below.* THE CHIEF CITIZEN, THE RABBLE, JOSEPH, | THE MADMAN, HEROD, *and* THE LOITERERS, *etc., enter by these steps.* | PILATE, PROCULA, LONGINUS, THE SOLDIERS *and* SERVANTS *enter by* | *the bronze door.*' together with text; 6–36 text (concluded); 37–38 'John Masefield und sein „Spiel in Versen"' ('John Masefield wurde 1878 in Ledbury, Herefordshire…') (unsigned); 39–46 'Anmerkungen'; 47–48 'Anhang'

Paper: wove paper

Running title: 'ANMERKUNGEN' (21mm.) on both verso and recto, pp.40–46 (see notes)

Binding: grey wrappers. Spine: blank. On upper wrapper: 'JOHN MASEFIELD [in white on black rule, 90mm.] | [illustration of the madman sitting in fore-ground with Crucifixion in background: 99 × 90mm.] | GOOD FRIDAY | VELHAGEN & KLASING [in white on black rule, 90mm.]' On lower wrapper: 'VELHAGEN & KLASINGS ENGLISCHE LESEBOGEN 24'. All edges trimmed. Binding measurements: 190 × 121mm. (wrappers), 190 × 4mm. (spine).

Publication date: [post 1953] (see notes)

Price: unknown

Contents:
Good Friday ('PILATE. Longinus.')
John Masefield und sein „Spiel in Versen" ('John Masefield wurde 1878 in Ledbury, Herefordshire…')
        (unsigned)
Anmerkungen ('Die fetten Ziffern bezeichnen die Seite, die dahinterstehenden mageren die Zeile…')
Anhang ('Versuch einer deutenden Gliederung…')

Notes:
The edition – printed in English – includes a short essay on Masefield's verse plays, a notes section and appendix in German.

The text of the play includes line numbers in the margins.

The only running titles present are those for the notes section ('Anmerkungen').

The date of publication of this edition is presumably between 1953 and 1967. (The essay on Masefield and verse plays includes reference to Muriel Spark's 1953 study of the author).

The title appears to be number 24 in the 'Englische und Amerikanische Lesebogen' series.

Copies seen: Library of The Society of Authors

A32 SONNETS AND POEMS

A32(a) First English edition (1916)

Sonnets and Poems | By | JOHN MASEFIELD | LETCHWORTH | GARDEN CITY PRESS LIMITED | 1916 | Copyright in U.S.A.
(The italic type contains a number of swash characters)
(All width centred)

Bibliographies: Danielson 187, Williams p.4, Simmons [31], Nevinson [unrecorded], Handley-Taylor p.38, Wight [31]

Collation: [A-B]⁴ C-F⁴ F² (note that the signature 'F' is used twice); signatures left foot of page; 26 leaves; 225 × 143mm.; [1–4] 5–51 [52]

Page contents: [1] half-title: 'SONNETS & POEMS'; [2] blank; [3] title-page; [4] '*This Edition is limited to* 200 *copies.*'; 5–51 text; [52] blank

Paper: laid paper (watermark: '[Crown] | Abbey Mills | Greenfield'), chain-lines 24mm. apart

Running titles: none

Binding: grey wove wrappers. Spine: blank. On upper wrapper: '*Sonnets and Poems | By | JOHN MASEFIELD | LETCHWORTH | GARDEN CITY PRESS LIMITED | 1916 | Copyright in U.S.A.*' (The italic type contains a number of swash characters). On lower wrapper: '[figure with spade gazing upon horizon of hills and clouds with 'TELEGRAPHIC ADDRESS | SPADEWORK LETCHWORTH' (within a 'T' shape)] | GARDEN CITY – | PRESS LIMITED | LETCHWORTH – | HERTS. – – – –' (within double ruled border: 47 × 30mm.) Top edge trimmed, others uncut. Binding measurements: 231 × 148mm. (wrappers), 231 × 6mm. (spine). The wrappers extend beyond the edges of the internal leaves.

Publication date: published, according to Simmons, 'not later than August 1916' (in an edition of 200 copies) (see also notes to A27(c))

Price: 1 guinea (set of 4 volumes: see also A27(c), A31(a) and A33(a))

Contents:
I. ('Long, long ago, when all the glittering earth')
II. ('Night came again, but now I could not sleep.')
III. ('Even after all these years there comes the dream')
IV. ('If I could come again to that dear place')
V. ('Here in the self is all that man can know')
VI. ('Flesh, I have knocked at many a dusty door,')
VII. ('But all has passed, the tune has died away,')
VIII. ('These myriad days, these many thousand hours,')
IX. ('There, on the darkened deathbed, dies the brain')
X. ('So in the empty sky the stars appear,')
XI. ('It may be so with us, that in the dark,')
XII. ('What am I, Life? A thing of watery salt')
XIII. ('If I could get within this changing I,')
XIV. ('What is this atom which contains the whole,')
XV. ('Ah, we are neither heaven nor earth, but men;')
XVI. ('Roses are beauty, but I never see')
XVII. ('Over the church's door they moved a stone,')
XVIII. ('Out of the clouds come torrents, from the earth')
XIX. ('O little self, within whose smallness lies')
XX. ('I went into the fields, but you were there')
XXI. ('This is the living thing that cannot stir.')
XXII. ('Here, where we stood together, we three men,')
XXIII. ('I saw her like a shadow on the sky')
XXIV. ('Not that the stars are all gone mad in heaven,')
XXV. ('There is no god, as I was taught in youth,')
XXVI. ('Wherever beauty has been quick in clay')
XXVII. ('Beauty, let be; I cannot see your face,')
XXVIII. ('You are more beautiful than women are,')
XXIX. ('Beauty retires; the blood out of the earth')
XXX. ('Not for the anguish suffered is the slur,')
XXXI. ('Beauty was with me once, but now, grown old,')
XXXII. ('So beauty comes, so with a failing hand')
XXXIII. ('You will remember me in days to come,')
XXXIV. ('They took the bloody body from the cross,')
XXXV. ('"Come to us fiery with the saints of God')
XXXVI. ('So from the cruel cross they buried God;')
XXXVII. ('If all be governed by the moving stars,')

XXXVIII. ('In emptiest furthest heaven where no stars are,')
XXXIX. ('Perhaps in chasms of the wasted past,')
XL. ('For, like an outcast from the city, I')
XLI. ('Death lies in wait for you, you wild thing in the wood,')
XLII. ('They called that broken hedge The Haunted Gate.')
XLIII. ('There was an evil in the nodding wood')
XLIV. ('Go, spend your penny, Beauty, when you will,')
XLV. ('Though in life's streets the tempting shops have lured')
XLVI. ('When all these million cells that are my slaves')
XLVII. ('Let that which is to come be as it may,')

Notes:

The contents are largely derived from *Good Friday and other Poems* (A29) and therefore also *Sonnets* (A30). Sonnet XXI is printed here for the first time.

Each poem in the volume commences with a drop-capital.

Copies seen: private collection (PWE); BL (11646.h.53) stamped 26 MAY 1916 rebound; ULL (Special Collections) rebound; NYPL (Berg Collection)

A32(b) Second English edition (1916)

Sonnets and Poems | By | JOHN MASEFIELD | Price 3/6 net. | PUBLISHED BY | JOHN MASEFIELD | AT LOLLINGDON, CHOLSEY, BERKSHIRE | PRINTED AT LETCHWORTH BY THE GARDEN CITY PRESS LTD. | 1916 | Copyright in U.S.A.
(The italic type contains a number of swash characters)
(All width centred)

Bibliographies: Danielson [noted on p.146], Williams p.4, Simmons [31a], Nevinson [unrecorded], Handley-Taylor p.38, Wight [31a]

Collation: [A]⁴ B-F⁴ G²; signatures left foot of page; 26 leaves; 194 × 128mm.; [1–4] 5–52

Page contents: [1] half-title: 'SONNETS & POEMS'; [2] 'IN PREPARATION, UNIFORM WITH THIS VOLUME. | [three titles listed] | *Price 3/6 net.*'; [3] title-page; [4] '*To | My Wife*'; 5–52 text

Paper: laid paper (watermark: '[Crown] | Abbey Mills | Greenfield'), chain-lines 24mm. apart

Running titles: none

Binding: light blue cloth. On spine: white paper label (131 × 9mm.) on which reading lengthways down from head: '*SONNETS AND POEMS. By John Masefield*'. (The '*P*' in '*POEMS*' is swash) (see notes). On upper cover: white paper label (71 × 51mm.) on which: '*Sonnets | & | Poems* | [leaf motif] [in red] | *John Masefield*' (within double ruled border in red: 63 × 44mm.) Lower cover: blank. Top edge trimmed, others uncut. Binding measurements: 198 × 129mm. (covers), 198 × 16mm. (spine). End-papers: laid papers (watermark: '[Crown] | Abbey Mills | Greenfield'), chain-lines 24mm. apart.

Publication date: published, according to Simmons, 'not later than September 1916' (reviewed in 7 September 1916 issue of *The Times Literary Supplement*)

Price: 3s.6d.

Contents:
I. ('Long, long ago, when all the glittering earth')
II. ('Night came again, but now I could not sleep;')
III. ('Even after all these years there comes the dream')
IV. ('If I could come again to that dear place')
V. ('Here in the self is all that man can know')
VI. ('Flesh, I have knocked at many a dusty door,')
VII. ('But all has passed, the tune has died away,')
VIII. ('These myriad days, these many thousand hours,')
IX. ('There, on the darkened deathbed, dies the brain')
X. ('So in the empty sky the stars appear,')
XI. ('It may be so with us, that in the dark,')
XII. ('What am I, Life? A thing of watery salt')
XIII. ('If I could get within this changing I,')
XIV. ('What is this atom which contains the whole,')
XV. ('Ah, we are neither heaven nor earth, but men;')
XVI. ('Roses are beauty, but I never see')
XVII. ('Over the church's door they moved a stone,')
XVIII. ('Out of the clouds come torrents, from the earth')

XIX. ('O little self, within whose smallness lies')
XX. ('I went into the fields, but you were there')
XXI. ('This is the living thing that cannot stir.')
XXII. ('Here, where we stood together, we three men,')
XXIII. ('I saw her like a shadow on the sky')
XXIV. ('Look at the grass, sucked by the seed from dust,')
XXV. ('There is no God, as I was taught in youth,')
XXVI. ('Wherever beauty has been quick in clay')
XXVII. ('Beauty, let be; I cannot see your face,')
XXVIII. ('You are more beautiful than women are,')
XXIX. ('Beauty retires; the blood out of the earth')
XXX. ('Not for the anguish suffered is the slur,')
XXXI. ('Beauty was with me once, but now, grown old,')
XXXII. ('So beauty comes, so with a failing hand')
XXXIII. ('You will remember me in days to come,')
XXXIV. ('If Beauty be at all, if, beyond sense,')
XXXV. ('O wretched man, that, for a little mile,')
XXXVI. ('Night is on the downland, on the lonely moorland,')
XXXVII. ('If all be governed by the moving stars,')
XXXVIII. ('In emptiest furthest heaven where no stars are,')
XXXIX. ('Perhaps in chasms of the wasted past,')
XL. ('For, like an outcast from the city, I')
XLI. ('Death lies in wait for you, you wild thing in the wood,')
XLII. ('They called that broken hedge The Haunted Gate.')
XLIII. ('There was an evil in the nodding wood')
XLIV. ('Go, spend your penny, Beauty, when you will,')
XLV. ('Though in life's streets the tempting shops have lured')
XLVI. ('When all these million cells that are my slaves')
XLVII. ('Let that which is to come be as it may,')

Notes:

After describing the first English edition, Danielson states:

> In the edition of "Sonnets and Poems" issued *later* in the same year by the author at Lollingdon, Cholsey, Berkshire, sonnets xxiv and xxxiv–xxxvi are omitted and replaced by other sonnets.

This change in volume content is also noted by Williams and Simmons. Sonnets XXIV, XXXV and XXXVI are printed here for the first time. Williams describes this edition as a '2nd edition'. In addition to the change in contents there are a number of changes in punctuation.

Each poem in the volume commences with a drop-capital.

The labels on the upper covers vary in size between copies. Spine labels are occasionally laid down so that the lettering reads up the spine from the foot.

This edition caused some concern to Masefield's commercial publisher. William Heinemann wrote to the author in September 1916 noting:

> I see with some apprehension in the last Literary Supplement of the TIMES a review of your SONNETS AND POEMS, marked for sale by you at 3s.6d. net. I hope you won't mind my drawing attention to the fact that this will adversely affect the book when we publish it, as I suppose we shall. The TIMES won't review it again, and the fact that it can now be got from you at 3s.6d. will spoil the chance of any decent subscription from the booksellers. Of course, I assume that the publication is only a very limited one, and, in that case, I was wondering whether you would not agree to my publishing it at once in a regular way? That might, in a way, counteract the effect this sort of half-publication and review is likely to have upon it, and I do think it is a thing you should carefully consider. I should be glad to talk it over…
>
> (William Heinemann, letter to John Masefield, 11 September 1916)
> (HRHRC, MS (Masefield, J.) Recip William Heinemann Ltd.)

Copies seen: private collection (PWE); BL (011649.h.94) stamped 28 AUG 1916; ULL (Special Collections) signed 'J. Masefield'

A33 THE LOCKED CHEST [AND] THE SWEEPS OF NINETY-EIGHT 1916

A33(a) First English edition (1916)

The Locked Chest | The Sweeps of Ninety-Eight | Two Plays in Prose | By | JOHN MASEFIELD | LETCHWORTH | GARDEN CITY PRESS LIMITED | 1916 | Copyright in U.S.A.
(The italic type contains a number of swash characters)
(All width centred)

Bibliographies: Danielson 185, Williams p.5, Simmons [32], Nevinson [unrecorded], Handley-Taylor p.38, Wight [32]

Collation: [B]⁸ C-L⁴ M⁶ (M4+2) (J not used); signatures C-H right foot of page; signatures I-M left foot of page; 50 leaves; 223 × 144mm.; [1–6] 7–100

Page contents: [1] title-page; [2] '*This Edition is limited to* 200 *copies.*'; [3] 'THE LOCKED CHEST | [rule] | A play in One Act | (From a Tale in the Laxdaelasaga)'; [4] blank; [5] 'PERSONS. | [dramatis personae listed] | SCENE | *Iceland*'; [6] blank; 7–74 text of 'The Locked Chest' (at foot of p.74: '*Written in* 1906.'); 75–100 text of 'The Sweeps of Ninety-Eight' (at foot of p.100: '*Written in* 1905.')

Paper: laid paper (watermark: '[Crown] | Abbey Mills | Greenfield'), chain-lines 25mm. apart

Running title: 'The Locked Chest' (47mm.) on both verso and recto, pp.8–74 and 'The Sweeps of Ninety-eight' (64mm.) on both verso and recto, pp.76–100

Binding: grey wrappers. Spine: blank. On upper wrapper: '*The Locked Chest | The Sweeps of Ninety-Eight | Two Plays in Prose | By | JOHN MASEFIELD | LETCHWORTH | GARDEN CITY PRESS LIMITED | 1916 | Copyright in U.S.A.*' (The italic type contains a number of swash characters). On lower wrapper: '[figure with spade gazing upon horizon of hills and clouds with 'TELEGRAPHIC ADDRESS | SPADEWORK LETCHWORTH' (within a 'T' shape)] | GARDEN CITY – | PRESS LIMITED | LETCHWORTH – | HERTS. – – – –' (within double ruled border: 47 × 30mm.) Top edge trimmed, others untrimmed. Binding measurements: 229 × 148mm. (wrappers), 229 × 7mm. (spine). The wrappers extend beyond the edges of the internal leaves.

Publication date: published, according to Simmons, 'not later than August 1916' (in an edition of 200 copies) (see also notes to A27(c))

Price: 1 guinea (set of 4 volumes: see also A27(c), A31(a) and A32(a))

Contents:
The Locked Chest ('SCENE: *A room. A chest used as a bench. A table, etc.*')
The Sweeps of Ninety-Eight ('SCENE: *An inn at Dunleary. A parlour.*')

Notes:
The signatures within this volume suggest that the present [B] gathering of eight leaves was originally intended to comprise two gatherings of four leaves. The final M gathering comprises four leaves with an additional conjugate set of two leaves tipped-in on the fourth leaf. Wight describes the final two leaves as a separate gathering ([N]²).

An advertisement leaflet (held at Harvard College Library (Houghton *74–201)) notes that 'At 25 Park Lane, on June 27th, 1913, will be performed *The Death of Tintagiles* by Maurice Maeterlinck and *The Sweeps of '98* by John Masefield'. It is additionally noted that 'the Play was written in 1905 and has never before been acted' and 'Alfred Sutro, Charles Ricketts, Vaughan Williams, Norman Wilkinson, Dion Clayton Calthrop and Granville Barker have all contributed to the production.' A poem by Gordon Bottomley entitled *Prologue To "The Locked Chest": A Play By John Masefield* was privately printed (presumably in 1924). This single sheet (folded twice) prints the prologue 'Spoken by MISS BARR in the character of VIGDIS at the first performance', there is an additional note stating 'At the second performance the part of Vigdis was taken by Miss Procter'. The poem commences 'Neighbours, to-night we come once more'. A copy is located in the British Library (X.950/23158) which is signed and dated 'Gordon Bottomley. | 24th. December 1924.'

No dramatis personae is provided for 'The Sweeps of Ninety-Eight'

The Society of Authors received an application to stage 'The Sweeps of Ninety-Eight' in 1929. Masefield, writing to the Society, states his abhorrence of the play:

> This horrid crude thing will never do. It is charming of the Magdalen men to want to do it, but they are a very brilliant amateur company + this little corpse is better in its grave. I had rather that it were not done, tho' I thank them for the thought.
>
> (John Masefield, letter to [G.H.] Thring, [13 November 1929])
> (BL, Add.Mss.56588, f.113)

Copies seen: private collection (PWE); BL (11773.h.12) stamped 26 MAY 1916 rebound; ULL (Special Collections) rebound; Bodleian (M.Adds.110.d.56) stamped 22 AUG 1916 additional preservation binding; NYPL (Berg Collection)

A33(b) *First American edition (1916)*

The Locked Chest | and | The Sweeps of Ninety-Eight | TWO ONE ACT PLAYS | BY | JOHN MASEFIELD | New York | THE MACMILLAN COMPANY | 1916 | *All rights reserved*
(All width centred)

Bibliographies: Danielson [unrecorded], Williams [unrecorded], Simmons [noted on p.59], Nevinson [unrecorded], Handley-Taylor p.38, Wight 32a

Collation: [A-F]⁸ [G]¹⁰ ([G]8+2); 58 leaves; 219 × 150mm.; [1–6] 7–82 [83–84] 85–114 [115–16]

Page contents: [1] half-title: 'THE LOCKED CHEST | [rule] | THE SWEEPS OF NINETY-EIGHT'; [2] '*This edition, of which this is | Number . . . . is limited and is | printed from type.*'; [3] title-page (with additional leaf tipped-in on the verso of which is the frontispiece photograph: 131 × 96mm., 'John Masefield'); [4] 'COPYRIGHT, 1916 | BY JOHN MASEFIELD | Published September, 1916.';

[5] 'THE LOCKED CHEST | A Play in One Act | (From a Tale in the Laxdaelasaga)'; [6] 'PERSONS | [dramatis personae listed] | SCENE | *Iceland*'; 7–82 text of 'The Locked Chest' (at foot of p.82: '*Written in* 1906.'); [83] 'THE SWEEPS OF NINETY-EIGHT'; [84] blank; 85–114 text of 'The Sweeps of Ninety-Eight' (at foot of p.114: '*Written in* 1905.'); [115–16] blank

Paper: laid paper (watermark: 'D [inside a diamond shape outline] | QUEEN LAID'), chain-lines 30mm. apart

Running title: 'The Locked Chest' (47–48mm.) on both verso and recto, pp.8–82 and 'The Sweeps of Ninety-Eight' (69–70mm.) on both verso and recto, pp.86–114

Binding: brown boards with parchment spine. Spine: blank. On upper cover: cream paper label (38 × 90mm.) on which: 'The Locked Chest | [rule] | The Sweeps of Ninety-Eight | John Masefield' (within ruled border in brown: 29 × 82mm.) Lower cover: blank. All edges trimmed. Binding measurements: 225 × 149mm. (covers), 225 × 25mm. (spine). End-papers: wove paper.

Publication date: published, according to Simmons, 18 October 1916 (in a limited edition of 825 copies) (see notes)

Price: unknown

Contents:
as for A33(a)

Notes:
No dramatis personae is provided for 'The Sweeps of Ninety-Eight'

The text has been entirely re-set for this edition.

Simmons states that 825 copies of this edition were published. Handley-Taylor cites a number of 831 copies. Wight follows the example of Handley-Taylor.

A publishing agreement for this title between Masefield and Macmillan was dated 16 March 1916 (see Archives of The Society of Authors). The agreement refers to 'a licence to publish in volume form in the United States of America a work consisting of Two One Act Plays'.

Copies seen: private collection (PWE) stamped number 770; private collection stamped number 318; Library of The John Masefield Society (Peter Smith Collection) stamped number 499

A33(c) Second American edition (1917)

The Locked Chest | and | The Sweeps of Ninety-Eight | TWO ONE ACT PLAYS | BY | JOHN MASEFIELD | New York | THE MACMILLAN COMPANY | 1917 | *All rights reserved*
(All width centred)

Bibliographies: Danielson [unrecorded], Williams [unrecorded], Simmons [noted on p.59], Nevinson [unrecorded], Handley-Taylor p.38, Wight [unrecorded]

Collation: [A-H]⁸; 64 leaves; 189 × 130mm.; [1–5] 6–82 [83–84] 85–114 [115–28]

Page contents: [1] half-title: 'THE LOCKED CHEST | [rule] | THE SWEEPS OF NINETY-EIGHT'; [2] '[publisher's device] | THE MACMILLAN COMPANY | [two lines listing six cities, separated by four points] | MACMILLAN & CO., LIMITED | [two lines listing four cities, separated by two points] | THE MACMILLAN CO. OF CANADA, LTD. | [one city listed]'; [3] title-page; [4] 'COPYRIGHT, 1916 | BY JOHN MASEFIELD | Limited Edition Published September, 1916 | Regular Edition, February, 1917.'; [5] 'THE LOCKED CHEST | [rule] | A PLAY IN ONE ACT | (From a Tale in the Laxdaelasaga)'; 6 'PERSONS | [dramatis personae listed] | SCENE | *Iceland*'; 7–82 text of 'The Locked Chest' (below text on p.82: '*Written in 1906.*'); [83] 'THE SWEEPS OF NINETY-EIGHT'; [84] blank; 85–114 text of 'The Sweeps of Ninety-Eight' (below text on p.114: '*Written in 1905.* | Printed in the United States of America'); [115] 'THE following pages contain advertisements of | books by the same author.' (within ruled border: 15 × 89mm.); [116] blank; [117–23] publisher's advertisements ('*BY THE SAME AUTHOR*'); [124–28] blank

Paper: wove paper

Running title: '*THE LOCKED CHEST*' (35mm.) on both verso and recto, pp.8–82 and '*THE SWEEPS OF NINETY-EIGHT*' (56mm.) on both verso and recto, pp.86–114

Binding: burgundy cloth. On spine, in gold: '*The* | LOCKED | CHEST | MASEFIELD | MACMILLAN' (all width centred). (The '*T*' and '*h*' of '*The*' are swash). On upper cover, in gold: 'THE | LOCKED CHEST | THE SWEEPS | OF NINETY-EIGHT | MASEFIELD' (ranged upper left) (within blind ruled border: 188 × 117mm.) Lower cover: blank. All edges trimmed. Binding measurements: 193 × 126mm. (covers), 193 × 30mm. (spine). End-papers: wove paper.

Publication date: published, according to Simmons, 28 February 1917 in an edition of 1496 copies

Price: unknown

Contents:
as for A33(a)

Notes:
Wight omits to note or describe this volume. It is included by both Simmons and Handley-Taylor.

Copies seen: private collection (ROV) inscribed 'John Masefield. 28. III. 1918.'

A34 GALLIPOLI

A34(a) First English edition (1916)

GALLIPOLI | BY | JOHN MASEFIELD | AUTHOR OF | "THE DAFFODIL FIELDS," "DAUBER," ETC. | [publisher's device of a windmill with 'W [point]' and 'H' all within ruled border: 19 × 19mm.] | LONDON | WILLIAM HEINEMANN | 1916
(All width centred)

Bibliographies: Danielson 184, Williams pp.9–10, Simmons [33], Nevinson p.17, Handley-Taylor p.38, Wight [33]

Collation: [1]⁸ 2–12⁸; signatures right foot of page; 96 leaves; 184 × 122mm.; [i–vi] vii–viii [1–2] 3–25 [26–28] 29–55 [56–58] 59–84 [85–86] 87–114 [115–16] 117–55 [156–58] 159–83 [184]; illustrations or maps (on glossy paper) tipped-in on pp.[ii], 15, 39, 47, 88, 109 and [157]; an additional set of two conjugate leaves is bound in the centre of gathering 5

Page contents: [i] half-title: 'GALLIPOLI'; [ii] 'SOLDIERS' TALES OF THE | GREAT WAR | *Each volume Crown 8vo., cloth, 3s. 6d. net* | [seven titles and their authors listed with details of illustration] | LONDON : WILLIAM HEINEMANN' (within ruled border: 69 × 64mm.) (with additional leaf tipped-in on the verso of which is the frontispiece: 144 × 95mm., 'THE GALLIPOLI PENINSULA' within double ruled border, with '*Stanford's Geog¹. Estab¹. London.* | *Frontispiece.*'; [iii] title-page; [iv] 'LONDON : WILLIAM HEINEMANN, 1916.'; [v] 'DEDICATED WITH THE | DEEPEST ADMIRATION AND RESPECT | TO | GENERAL SIR IAN HAMILTON, G.C.B., D.S.O., | AND THE | OFFICERS AND MEN UNDER HIS COMMAND | MARCH TO OCTOBER, 1915'; [vi] blank; vii–viii 'LIST OF ILLUSTRATIONS' (18 illustrations and three maps (including frontispiece) listed with titles and page references); [1] 'GALLIPOLI | I. | [quotation from *The Song of Roland*]'; [2] blank; 3–25 text of part I; [26] blank; [27] 'II. | [quotation from *The Song of Roland*]'; [28] blank; 29–55 text of part II; [56] blank; [57] 'III. | [quotation from *The Song of Roland*]'; [58] blank; 59–84 text of part III; [85] 'IV. | [quotation from *The Song of Roland*]'; [86] map: 'CAPE HELLES.'; 87–114 text of part IV; [115] 'V. | [quotation from *The Song of Roland*]'; [116] blank; 117–55 text of part V; [156] blank; [157] 'VI. | [quotation from *The End of the Song of Roland*]'; [158] blank; 159–83 text of part VI (at foot of p.183: '[rule] | BILLING AND SONS, LTD., PRINTERS, GUILDFORD, ENGLAND.'); [184] blank

Paper: laid paper (no watermark), chain-lines 25mm. apart

Running title: 'GALLIPOLI' (21mm.) on both verso and recto, pp.4–183

Binding: red cloth (see notes). On spine: 'GALLIPOLI | JOHN | MASEFIELD | HEINEMANN' (all width centred). On upper cover: 'GALLIPOLI | JOHN MASEFIELD'. On lower cover: publisher's device of a windmill with 'W [point]' and 'H' all within ruled border: 21 × 22mm. All edges trimmed. Binding measurements: 189 × 121mm. (covers), 189 × 39mm. (spine). End-papers: wove paper.

Publication date: published, according to Simmons, 14 September 1916 in an edition of 10000 copies

Price: 2s.6d.

Contents:
Gallipoli ('I. | A little while ago, during a short visit to America, I was often questioned...')

Notes:
W.H. Hamilton in his 1922 study of Masefield claimed that *Gallipoli* was 'a book to strike the critical faculty numb and hush the heart of the hearer'. Edward Marsh called the work 'supreme' while Neville Lytton described the book as 'a masterpiece'. This historical essay concerning the Dardanelles Campaign (Masefield provided medical assistance in the area in September 1915) was prompted by Masefield's propaganda lecture tour of America in 1916. The work remained popular for many years. A letter (preserved in the Heinemann Archive) from A.S. Frere dated 1 May 1951 to Masefield states that Frere was 'going into the question of issuing' both *Gallipoli* and *The Nine Days Wonder* (see A130) in a single volume. This came to nothing.

Evidence in the archives of William Heinemann suggests that Masefield had originally asked for a royalty of 25% on the volume. Informed that the price of the edition would be 2s.6d. he was evidently advised that he must accept a lower rate. This he agreed to do:

> ...I will waive the question of any higher royalty on the 2/6 edition, but if, as I hope, the cost of the book can be raised later to 3/6 or 4/6 then I think it would be fair to raise the royalty to 25%
> (John Masefield, letter to William Heinemann, 17 July 1916)
> (Archives of William Heinemann)

The title of the volume was Masefield's intended first choice. The archives of William Heinemann preserve an alternative:

> *Gallipoli* would do excellently if not already bagged by someone. Failing that *The G[allipoli] Campaign* would be next best.
> (John Masefield, letter to William Heinemann, 17 July 1916)
> (Archives of William Heinemann)

The publishing agreement for this title between Masefield and Heinemann was dated 20 July 1916 (see Archives of The Society of Authors). The agreement refers to a publication price of 2s.6d.

Masefield, by July 1917, had evidently arranged for American publication. In a letter to Heinemann he specifically requests assistance with the photographs:

If possible, will you let me have pulls of the photographs or the photographs themselves, so that I may have work begun on the illustrations for the American edition. If you could also let me have a pull of a map for the same, it would be a great help.

(John Masefield, letter to William Heinemann, 17 July 1916)
(Archives of William Heinemann)

See the note regarding illustrations for A34(b).

Danielson states in his description of the volume that:

The early copies were issued in dull light blue cloth, lettered on back and front in dark blue. Afterwards issued in red cloth, lettered on back and front in black.

Williams challenges this information with the statement:

It has been suggested that the first edition was issued in more than one cloth. The publishers, however, state that it was issued only in red cloth.

Simmons provides information to support Danielson:

First twelve copies bound in bluish gray cloth. Lettered in dark blue: on spine, "Gallipoli / John / Masefield / Heinemann"; on front, "Gallipoli / John Masefield". On back, publisher's device in black, with initials "W [point] H" within a square line border. Remaining copies bound in red cloth, lettered in black, as above.

In 1930 a French translation of the work was proposed by Edith Dauban. Masefield wrote to The Society of Authors:

Gallipoli was to have been translated during the war but the matter fell through. I think the book was never published + Mlle Dauban could go ahead if she wishes.

(John Masefield, letter to Denys Kilham Roberts, [14 November 1930])
(BL, Add.Mss.56591, f.157)

Copies seen: private collection (PWE); BL (09082.aa.8) stamped 15 SEP 1916; Bodleian (22281.e.378) stamped 29 SEP 1916; HRHRC (D568.3 M3 HRC KNOPF)

Reprinted:

'Second Impression'	[first edition, second impression]	Oct 1916
'New Impression'	[first edition, third impression]	Nov 1916
'New Impression'	[first edition, fourth impression]	Dec 1916
'New Impression'	[first edition, fifth impression]	Jan 1917
'New Impression'	[first edition, sixth impression]	Jun 1917
'New Impression'	[first edition, seventh impression]	Jul 1918

A34(b) First American edition (1916)

GALLIPOLI | BY | JOHN MASEFIELD | Author of "The Everlasting Mercy," "The | Story of a Round House," etc. | *ILLUSTRATED* | New York | THE MACMILLAN COMPANY | 1916 | *All rights reserved*
(All width centred)

Bibliographies: Danielson [unrecorded], Williams [unrecorded], Simmons [noted on p.60], Nevinson [unrecorded], Handley-Taylor p.38, Wight 33a

Collation: [A-Q]⁸ [R]⁴ (J not used); 132 leaves; 190 × 124mm.; [i–viii] [1–2] 3–34 [35–36] 37–73 [74–76] 77–111 [112–14] 115–52 [153–54] 155–208 [209–210] 211–45 [246–56]; illustrations or maps (on glossy paper) tipped-in on pp.4, 38, 47, 48, 52, 56, 93, 116, 134, 136, 144, 146, 148, 162 and 224

Page contents: [i] half-title: 'GALLIPOLI'; [ii] '[publisher's device] | THE MACMILLAN COMPANY | [two lines listing six cities, separated by four points] | MACMILLAN & CO., LIMITED | [two lines listing four cities, separated by two points] | THE MACMILLAN CO. OF CANADA, LTD. | [one city listed]'; [iii] title-page; [iv] 'COPYRIGHT, 1916, | BY JOHN MASEFIELD | [rule] | Set up and electrotyped. Published October, 1916.'; [v] 'DEDICATED | WITH DEEP RESPECT AND ADMIRATION TO | *General Sir Ian Hamilton, G.C.B., D.S.O.* | AND | *The Officers and Men under his Command,* | March to October, 1915.'; [vi] blank; [vii] 'LIST OF ILLUSTRATIONS' (12 illustrations and three maps listed with titles and page references); [viii] blank; [1] 'I | [quotation from *The Song of Roland*]'; [2] blank; 3–34 text of part I; [35] 'II | [quotation from *The Song of Roland*]'; [36] blank; 37–73 text of part II; [74] blank; [75] 'III | [quotation from *The Song of Roland*]'; [76] blank; 77–111 text of part III; [112] blank; [113] 'IV | [quotation from *The Song of Roland*]'; [114] blank; 115–52 text of part IV; [153–54] 'V | [quotation from *The Song of Roland*]'; 155–208 text of part V; [209] 'VI | [quotation from *The end of the Song of Roland*]'; [210] blank; 211–45 text of part VI (at foot of p.245: 'PRINTED IN THE UNITED STATES OF AMERICA'); [246] blank; [247] 'THE following pages contain advertisements of | Macmillan books by the same author.' (within ruled border: 15 × 89mm.); [248] blank; [249–54] publisher's advertisements; [255–56] blank

Paper: wove paper

Running title: 'Gallipoli' (14mm.) on both verso and recto, pp.4–245

Binding: navy blue cloth (see notes). On spine, in gold: '[double rule] | GALLI- | POLI | [triangular point] | JOHN | MASEFIELD | MACMILLAN | [double rule]' (all width centred). On upper cover, in gold: 'GALLIPOLI | JOHN MASEFIELD' (within blind ruled border: 188 × 119mm.) Lower cover: blank. All edges trimmed. Binding measurements: 195 × 127mm. (covers), 195 × 41mm. (spine). End-papers: wove paper.

Publication date: published, according to Simmons, 11 October 1916 in an edition of 1938 copies

Price: $1.25

Contents:
Gallipoli ('A little while ago, during a short visit to America, I was often questioned...')

Notes:
Wight states the binding is 'black cloth'. He also misquotes Simmons' date for publication.

Note differences in the wording of the dedication. In this edition the volume is 'Dedicated with deep respect and admiration'. In A34(a) the volume is 'Dedicated with the deepest admiration and respect'.

The American edition contains many of the illustrations present in A34(a). However, there are several illustrations unique to the different editions. Note the omission of a frontispiece in the American edition

The text is dated at the foot of p.245:

> Lollingdon,
> June 19, 1916.

This is not present in A34(a). Additionally, there appear to be minor textual variants. The second paragraph concludes, in the American edition:

> I answered questions and criticism as best I could, but in the next town they were repeated to me, and in the town beyond reiterated, until I felt the need of a leaflet printed for distribution, giving my views of the matter.

In A34(a) this passage reads

> I answered questions and criticism as best I could, but in the next town they were repeated to me, and in the town beyond reiterated, until I wished that I had a printed leaflet, giving my views of the matter, to distribute among my questioners.

See notes to A34(a) regarding the title for this volume. At the beginning of August 1916, George P. Brett wrote to Masefield:

> I am just in receipt of your letter of the 22nd July, in regard to the Dardanelles book, and I am glad, I think, that you have decided to change the title of this book to *Gallipoli*, as the book will do equally well in this country if not better under this title.

> (George P. Brett, letter to John Masefield, 4 August 1916)
> (HRHRC, MS (Masefield, J.) Recip The Macmillan Company)

A publishing agreement for this title between Masefield and Macmillan was dated 4 August 1916 (see Archives of The Society of Authors). The agreement refers to 'a licence to publish in volume form in the United States of America a work the subject or title of which is Gallipoli'.

Copies seen: Bodleian (Rec.e.100) inscribed [by Masefield]: 'For My You. | from H.Y. | November. 1960. | Even so was Wisdom proven blind, | So Courage failed, so Strength was chained, | Even so the Gods, whose seeing Mind | Is not as ours, ordained. | John Masefield.', no accession date stamp; HRHRC (D568.3 M32 1916)

Reprinted:		
	[first edition, second impression]	Nov 1916
	[first edition, third impression]	Nov 1916
	[first edition, fourth impression]	Dec 1916
	[first edition, fifth impression]	Jan 1917
	[first edition, sixth impression]	Jan 1917
	[first edition, seventh impression]	Mar 1917
	[first edition, eighth impression]	Jul 1917
	[first edition, ninth impression]	Nov 1917
	[first edition, tenth impression]	Mar 1918
	[first edition, eleventh impression]	Aug 1918
	[first edition, twelfth impression]	Jun 1921

A34(c) First Canadian edition (1916)

GALLIPOLI | BY | JOHN MASEFIELD | AUTHOR OF | "THE DAFFODIL FIELDS," "DAUBER," ETC. | TORONTO | S. B. GUNDY | 1916
(All width centred)

Bibliographies: Danielson [unrecorded], Williams [unrecorded], Simmons [unrecorded], Nevinson [unrecorded], Handley-Taylor [unrecorded], Wight 33c

Collation: [1]⁸ 2–12⁸; signatures right foot of page; 96 leaves; 184 × 121mm.; [i–vi] vii–viii [1–2] 3–25 [26–28] 29–55 [56–58] 59–84 [85–86] 87–114 [115–16] 117–55 [156–58] 159–83 [184]; illustrations or maps (on glossy paper) tipped-in on pp.15, 39, 47, 88, 109, [157]; an additional set of two conjugate leaves is bound in the centre of gathering 5

Page contents: [i] half-title: 'GALLIPOLI'; [ii] frontispiece: 144 × 95mm., 'THE GALLIPOLI PENINSULA' within double ruled border, with '*Stanford's Geog¹. Estab¹. London.*'; [iii] title-page; [iv] '*Printed in Great Britain*'; [v] 'DEDICATED WITH THE | DEEPEST ADMIRATION AND RESPECT | TO | GENERAL SIR IAN HAMILTON, G.C.B., D.S.O., | AND THE | OFFICERS AND MEN UNDER HIS COMMAND | MARCH TO OCTOBER, 1915'; [vi] blank; vii–viii 'LIST OF ILLUSTRATIONS' (18 illustrations and three maps (including frontispiece) listed with titles and page references); [1] 'GALLIPOLI | I. | [quotation from *The Song of Roland*]'; [2] blank; 3–25 text of part I; [26] blank; [27] 'II. | [quotation from *The Song of Roland*]'; [28] blank; 29–55 text of part II; [56] blank; [57] 'III. | [quotation from *The Song of Roland*]'; [58] blank; 59–84 text of part III; [85] 'IV. | [quotation from *The Song of Roland*]'; [86] map: 'CAPE HELLES.'; 87–114 text of part IV; [115] 'V. | [quotation from *The Song of Roland*]'; [116] blank; 117–55 text of part V; [156] blank; [157] 'VI. | [quotation from *The End of the Song of Roland*]'; [158] blank; 159–83 text of part VI (at foot of p.183: '[rule] | BILLING AND SONS, LTD., PRINTERS, GUILDFORD, ENGLAND.'); [184] blank

Paper: wove paper

Running title: 'GALLIPOLI' (21mm.) on both verso and recto, pp.4–183

Binding: red cloth. On spine: 'GALLIPOLI | JOHN | MASEFIELD | GUNDY' (all width centred). On upper cover: 'GALLIPOLI | JOHN MASEFIELD'. Lower cover: blank. All edges trimmed. Binding measurements: 191 × 121mm. (covers), 191 × 37mm. (spine). End-papers: wove paper.

Publication date: presumably published after 14 September 1916

Price: unknown

Contents:
as for A34(a)

Notes:
Wight is the only bibliographer to note this edition. There are obvious similarities to A34(a). The Gundy edition notes it is printed in England and cites the same printers as the Heinemann edition on p.183. Sheets were, presumably, therefore imported from England.

Copies seen: Hiram College Library, Ohio (940.426 Mas)

A34(d) First French edition [in English] (1917)

GALLIPOLI | BY | JOHN MASEFIELD | THOMAS NELSON AND SONS | PARIS: 189, RUE SAINT-JACQUES
(All width centred)

Bibliographies: Danielson [unrecorded], Williams [unrecorded], Simmons [noted on p.60], Nevinson [unrecorded], Handley-Taylor p.38, Wight 33b

Collation: [1]¹⁶ 2–6¹⁸; the fifth leaf of each gathering is also signed; signatures width centre foot of page with '43' at left foot on fifth leaf of gathering 1; 96 leaves; 164 × 116mm.; [1–9] 10–31 [32–35] 36–61 [62–65] 66–90 [91–93] 94–120 [121–23] 124–62 [163–65] 166–89 [i] ii–iii

Page contents: [1] half-title: 'NELSON'S CONTINENTAL LIBRARY | VOL. XLIII | [rule] | GALLIPOLI'; [2] blank; [3] title-page; [4] blank; [5] 'DEDICATED WITH THE | DEEPEST ADMIRATION AND RESPECT | TO | GENERAL SIR IAN HAMILTON, | G.C.B., D.S.O., | AND THE | OFFICERS AND MEN UNDER HIS COMMAND, | MARCH TO OCTOBER, 1915.'; [6] blank; [7] 'I. | [quotation from *The Song of Roland*]'; [8] blank; [9]–31 text of part I; [32] blank; [33] 'II. | [quotation from *The Song of Roland*]'; [34] blank; [35]–61 text of part II; [62] blank; [63] 'III. | [quotation from *The Song of Roland*]'; [64] blank; [65]–90 text of part III; [91] 'IV. | [quotation from *The Song of Roland*]'; [92] blank; [93]–120 text of part IV; [121] 'V. | [quotation from *The Song of Roland*]'; [122] blank; [123]–62 text of part V; [163] 'VI. | [quotation from *The End of the Song of Roland*]'; [164] blank; [165]–89 text of part VI (at foot of p.189: '[rule] | PRINTED IN GREAT BRITAIN. | IMPRIMERIE NELSON, ÉDIMBOURG, ÉCOSSE.'); [i] device; ii–iii publisher's advertisements

Paper: wove paper

Running title: 'GALLIPOLI.' (20mm.) on both verso and recto, pp.10–189

Binding: white wrappers. On spine: 'NELSON'S | CONTI- | NENTAL | LIBRARY | [double rule] | [double rule] | GALLI- | POLI | [leaf device] | By | John | Masefield | *Price* | *2 fr. 25* | *net* | [double rule] | [double rule] | PARIS: | NELSON | [short rule] | 43'. On upper wrapper: 'No. 43 NELSON'S 2 fr. 25 net | CONTINENTAL LIBRARY | [rule, 102mm.] | GALLIPOLI | By | John Masefield | [device] | The Best Novels are included in | this Collection immediately after | their publication in Great Britain | or the United States | [rule, 102mm.] | PARIS: | T. NELSON & SONS, 189, rue Saint-Jacques | Edinburgh, London, New York' (all enclosed within double ruled border: 150 × 107mm. with a black square at each corner); at foot of upper wrapper: 'Must not be taken into Great Britain, the Colonies or U.S.A.' On lower wrapper: 'NELSON'S | CONTINENTAL LIBRARY |

Of the best British and American Literature. | Price 2 fr. 25 net. | Each Novel Complete and issued in One Volume. | [double rule] | [38 titles and their authors listed] | [double rule] | T. NELSON & SONS, 189, rue Saint=Jacques, Paris.' (all enclosed within ruled border: 151 × 102mm.) On inside of upper wrapper: publisher's advertisement for 'Nelson's Red Library'. On inside of lower wrapper: publisher's advertisement for 'Nelson's Green Library'. All edges trimmed. Binding measurements: 164 × 116mm. (wrappers); 164 × 15mm. (spine).

Publication date: published, according to Simmons, September 1917 in an edition of 6000 copies

Price: 2fr.25c.

Contents:
as for A34(a)

Notes:
The text commences on p.[9] with a drop-capital. This edition contains no illustrations or maps.

A letter from Masefield to The Society of Authors refers to this edition:

> Will you be so kind as to look through the enclosed Draft Agreement for me + let me have the benefit of your comments?
> I gather that the Continental Library circulates mainly in France, + I suppose the circulation will never be very big.
> (John Masefield, letter to The Society of Authors, 7 June 1917)
> (BL, Add.Mss.56575, f.89)

There appear to be two publishing agreements within the Archives of The Society of Authors. The first was dated 13 March 1917. The second was dated 26 June 1917 and refers to a publication price of 2fr. The edition was still in print by May 1920 for the publishers wrote to Masefield noting that 'owing to the high rate of the French Exchange… and increased cost of production' they were 'reluctantly compelled' to raise the publication price. There had presumably been previous increases for Nelson wrote that the price of 3 fr. was to increase to 4.50fr.

Copies seen: private collection (PWE)

A34(e) Second English edition (1923)

GALLIPOLI | BY | JOHN MASEFIELD | ILLUSTRATED | [publisher's device of a windmill with 'W [point]' and 'H' all within ruled border: 19 × 19mm.] | LONDON | WILLIAM HEINEMANN LTD.
(All width centred)

Bibliographies: Simmons [unrecorded], Nevinson p.17, Handley-Taylor p.38, Wight [unrecorded]

Collation: [1]¹² 2–12⁸; signatures right foot of page; 100 leaves; 184 × 118mm.; [i–vi] vii–xvi [1–2] 3–25 [26–28] 29–55 [56–58] 59–84 [85–86] 87–114 [115–16] 117–55 [156–58] 159–83 [184]; illustrations or maps (on glossy paper) tipped-in on pp.15, 39, 47, 89, 109, [157]; an additional set of two conjugate leaves are bound in the centre of gathering 5

Page contents: [i] half-title: 'GALLIPOLI'; [ii] frontispiece: 142 × 94mm., 'THE GALLIPOLI PENINSULA' within double ruled border, with 'Stanford's Geogˡ. Estabˡ. London.'; [iii] title-page; [iv] 'First published, September, 1916 | New Impressions, October, November, December, 1916; | January, June, 1917; | July, 1918 | New Edition, September, 1923 | PRINTED IN GREAT BRITAIN BY | BILLING AND SONS, LTD., GUILDFORD AND ESHER'; [v] 'DEDICATED WITH THE | DEEPEST ADMIRATION AND RESPECT | TO | GENERAL SIR IAN HAMILTON, G.C.B., D.S.O., | AND THE | OFFICERS AND MEN UNDER HIS COMMAND | MARCH TO OCTOBER, 1915'; [vi] blank; vii–xiv 'PREFACE TO THE EIGHTH EDITION' ('I wrote this book during the war, at the request of two of His Majesty's Ministers, in the hope…') (signed, 'JOHN MASEFIELD.'); xv–xvi 'LIST OF ILLUSTRATIONS' (18 illustrations and three maps (including frontispiece) listed with titles and page references); [1] 'GALLIPOLI | I. | [quotation from *The Song of Roland*]'; [2] blank; 3–25 text of part I; [26] blank; [27] 'II. | [quotation from *The Song of Roland*]'; [28] blank; 29–55 text of part II; [56] blank; [57] 'III. | [quotation from *The Song of Roland*]'; [58] blank; 59–84 text of part III; [85] 'IV. | [quotation from *The Song of Roland*]'; [86] map: 'CAPE HELLES.'; 87–114 text of part IV; [115] 'V. | [quotation from *The Song of Roland*]'; [116] blank; 117–55 text of part V; [156] blank; [157] 'VI. | [quotation from *The End of the Song of Roland*]'; [158] blank; 159–83 text of part VI; [184] blank

Paper: laid paper (no watermark), chain-lines 24mm. apart

Running title: 'GALLIPOLI' (21mm.) on both verso and recto, pp.4–183

Binding: blue cloth. On spine, in gold: 'Gallipoli | John | Masefield | HEINEMANN' (all width centred). On upper cover, in gold: 'GALLIPOLI | JOHN MASEFIELD' (within blind ruled border: 184 × 119mm.) Lower cover: blank. All edges trimmed. Binding measurements: 189 × 121mm. (covers), 189 × 39mm. (spine). End-papers: wove paper.

Publication date: published according to Handley-Taylor, 11 October 1923

Price: 7s.6d.

Contents:
Preface to the Eighth Edition ('I wrote this book during the war, at the request of two…')
Gallipoli ('I. | A little while ago, during a short visit to America, I was often questioned…')

Notes:

Nevinson lists this volume as a '*New Edition*, with a new Preface, September, 1923 (*7s. 6d.*)' This is a month earlier than the date given by both Handley-Taylor and the *English Catalogue of Books*. The copy in the British Library is stamped 11 October 1923.

Despite being called a 'New Edition', the preface is clearly entitled 'Preface to the Eighth Edition'. A comparison with A34(a) reveals that the main text of the volume is reprinted using the same setting of type and, were it not for the entirely new preface, this volume would constitute an eighth impression of the first edition.

The Wanderer Edition (A34(g)) uses the same setting of the text as this edition. However, the 1935 edition provides a date for the 'Preface to the Eighth Edition' (it is signed, 'JOHN MASEFIELD. | *July*, 1923.')

Copies seen: BL (9081.BB.15) stamped 11 OCT 1923; HRHRC (AC-L G139JMAS.G 1923) inscribed 'For Ada + John Galsworthy | from | John Masefield. | October. 1923.'

Reprinted:

[second edition, second impression]	Jul 1924
[second edition, third impression]	Jun 1926
[second edition, fourth impression]	Jan 1928
[second edition, fifth impression]	Sep 1930
[second edition, sixth impression]	Jan 1931

A34(f)   Second American edition (1925)

GALLIPOLI | BY | JOHN MASEFIELD | Author of "The Everlasting Mercy," "The | Story of a Round House," etc. | *ILLUSTRATED* | WITH A NEW PREFACE | New York | THE MACMILLAN COMPANY | 1925 | *All rights reserved*
(All width centred)

Bibliographies: Simmons [unrecorded], Nevinson [unrecorded], Handley-Taylor p.38, Wight [unrecorded]

Collation: [A-R]⁸ (J not used); 136 leaves; 190 × 124mm.; [eight un-numbered pages] [i–vi] vii–xvii/[1] [2] 3–34 [35–36] 37–73 [74–76] 77–111 [112–14] 115–52 [153–54] 155–208 [209–210] 211–45 [246–48]; illustrations or maps (on glossy paper) tipped-in on pp.4, 38, 47, 48, 53, 56, 92, 116, 134, 136, 144, 146, 148, 163 and 224

Page contents: [-] blank (page excluded from page count, but constitutes first leaf of first gathering); [-] blank; [-] blank (page excluded from page count, but constitutes second leaf of first gathering); [-] blank; [-] half-title: 'GALLIPOLI'; [-] '[publisher's device] | THE MACMILLAN COMPANY | [two lines listing six cities, separated by four points] | MACMILLAN & CO., LIMITED | [two lines listing four cities, separated by two points] | THE MACMILLAN CO. OF CANADA, LTD. | [one city listed]'; [-] title-page; [-] 'PRINTED IN THE UNITED STATES OF AMERICA | COPYRIGHT, 1916, 1925, | BY JOHN MASEFIELD. | [rule] | Set up and electrotyped. Published October, 1916. Reprinted | November, twice, December, 1916; January, twice, March, July, | November, 1917; March, August, 1918; June, 1921. | New Edition March, 1925.'; [i] 'DEDICATED | WITH DEEP RESPECT AND ADMIRATION TO | *General Sir Ian Hamilton, G.C.B., D.S.O.* | AND | *The Officers and Men under his Command,* | March to October, 1915.'; [ii] blank; [iii] 'LIST OF ILLUSTRATIONS' (12 illustrations and three maps listed with titles and page references); [iv] blank; [v] 'I | [quotation from *The Song of Roland*]'; [vi] blank; vii–xvii/[1] 'PREFACE TO THE THIRTEENTH EDITION' ('I wrote this book during the war, at the request of two of His Majesty's Ministers, in the hope...') (signed, 'JOHN MASEFIELD.'); [2] blank; 3–34 text of part I; [35] 'II | [quotation from *The Song of Roland*]'; [36] blank; 37–73 text of part II; [74] blank; [75] 'III | [quotation from *The Song of Roland*]'; [76] blank; 77–111 text of part III; [112] blank; [113] 'IV | [quotation from *The Song of Roland*]'; [114] blank; 115–52 text of part IV; [153–54] 'V | [quotation from *The Song of Roland*]'; 155–208 text of part V; [209] 'VI | [quotation from *The End of the Song of Roland*]'; [210] blank; 211–45 text of part VI (at foot of p.245: 'PRINTED IN THE UNITED STATES OF AMERICA'); [246–48] blank

Paper: wove paper

Running title: 'Gallipoli' (14mm.) on both verso and recto, pp.4–245

Binding: navy blue cloth. On spine, in gold: '[double rule] | GALLI- | POLI | [triangular point] | JOHN | MASEFIELD | MACMILLAN | [point] [point] | [double rule]' (all width centred). On upper cover: blind ruled border: 191 × 121mm. Lower cover: blank. All edges trimmed. Binding measurements: 195 × 127mm. (covers), 195 × 41mm. (spine). End-papers: wove paper.

Publication date: published, according to Handley-Taylor, 31 March 1925

Price: $2.50

Contents:

Preface to the Thirteenth Edition ('I wrote this book during the war, at the request of two...')
Gallipoli ('A little while ago, during a short visit to America, I was often questioned...')

Notes:

The edition comprises a reprint of the plates used for A34(b), with the additional preface. All features specific to the earlier American printing are therefore present here.

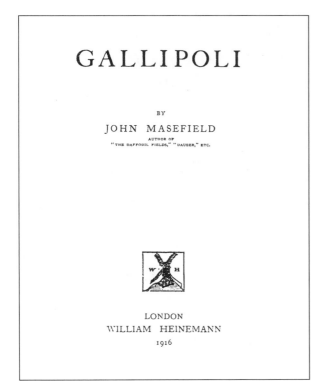

A34(a) title-page

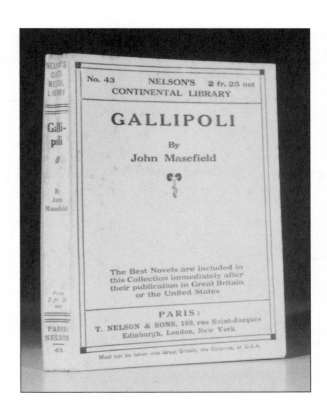

A34(d) spine and upper cover

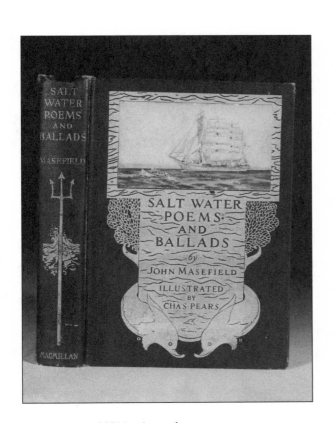

A35(a) spine and upper cover

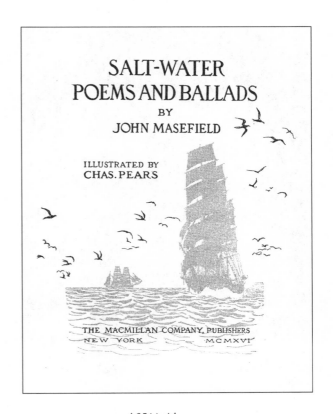

A35(a) title-page

LOLLINGDON DOWNS

AND OTHER POEMS, WITH SONNETS

BY
JOHN MASEFIELD

LONDON
WILLIAM HEINEMANN

A38(a) title-page

ST. GEORGE AND
THE DRAGON

BY
JOHN MASEFIELD

LONDON
WILLIAM HEINEMANN

A47(a) title-page

A42(a) spine and upper cover

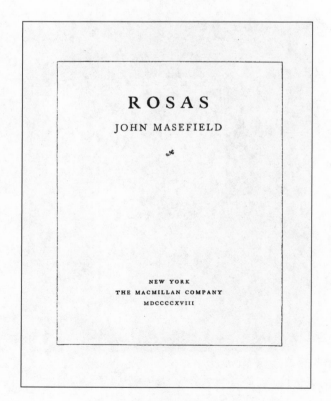

ROSAS

JOHN MASEFIELD

NEW YORK
THE MACMILLAN COMPANY
MDCCCCXVIII

A42(a) title-page

Page xvii also constitutes page [1]. The numbering of pages in the preliminaries is particularly strange with the insertion of the preface after the divisional quotation from *The Song of Roland*. This is not the position of the preface in the A34(e).

An extract from the publicity from the upper cover of the dust-jacket is as follows:

> For this new edition of "Gallipoli" Mr. Masefield has written a new preface in which he tells why he wrote the book and how he secured the material for it. In "Gallipoli" he gives an account of the Dardanelles campaign from the landings at Cape Helles to the final evacuation.

Copies seen: NYPL (Berg Collection)

A34(g) Third English edition ["Wanderer Edition"] (1935)

GALLIPOLI | BY | JOHN MASEFIELD | ILLUSTRATED | [publisher's device of a windmill with 'W [point]' and 'H'] | LONDON | WILLIAM HEINEMANN LTD.
(All width centred)

Bibliographies: Handley-Taylor p.38, Wight [unrecorded]

Collation: [A]⁸ (±[A]1) B-M⁸ N⁴ (J not used); B5 is also signed (see notes); signatures right foot of page; 100 leaves; 190 × 125mm.; [i–vi] vii–xvi [1–2] 3–25 [26–28] 29–55 [56–58] 59–84 [85–86] 87–114 [115–16] 117–55 [156–58] 159–83 [184]; illustrations or maps (on glossy paper) tipped-in on pp.15, 39, 47, 64, 109 and [157]; an additional set of two conjugate leaves is bound in the centre of gathering G

Page contents: [i] half-title: 'THE COLLECTED WORKS OF | JOHN MASEFIELD | [rule] | WANDERER EDITION | GALLIPOLI'; [ii] frontispiece: 142 × 94mm., 'THE GALLIPOLI PENINSULA' within double ruled border, with 'Stanford's Geog¹. Estab¹. London.'; [iii] title-page; [iv] '*First published, September,* 1916 | *New Impressions, October, November, December,* 1916; | *January, June,* 1917; *July,* 1918 | *New Editions, September,* 1923; *July,* 1924; *June,* 1926; | *January,* 1928; *September,* 1930; *January,* 1931 | *September* 1935 | PRINTED IN GREAT BRITAIN | AT THE WINDMILL PRESS, KINGSWOOD SURREY'; [v] 'DEDICATED WITH THE | DEEPEST ADMIRATION AND RESPECT | TO | GENERAL SIR IAN HAMILTON, G.C.B., D.S.O., | AND THE | OFFICERS AND MEN UNDER HIS COMMAND | MARCH TO OCTOBER, 1915'; [vi] blank; vii–xiv 'PREFACE TO THE EIGHTH EDITION' ('I wrote this book during the war, at the request of two of His Majesty's Ministers, in the hope...') (signed, 'JOHN MASEFIELD. | *July,* 1923.'); xv–xvi 'LIST OF ILLUSTRATIONS' (18 illustrations and three maps (including frontispiece) listed with titles and page references); [1] 'GALLIPOLI | I. | [quotation from *The Song of Roland*]'; [2] blank; 3–25 text of part I; [26] blank; [27] 'II. | [quotation from *The Song of Roland*]'; [28] blank; 29–55 text of part II; [56] blank; [57] 'III. | [quotation from *The Song of Roland*]' [58] blank; 59–84 text of part III; [85] 'IV. | [quotation from *The Song of Roland*]'; [86] map: 'CAPE HELLES.'; 87–114 text of part IV; [115] 'V. | [quotation from *The Song of Roland*]'; [116] blank; 117–55 text of part V; [156] blank; [157] 'VI. | [quotation from *The End of the Song of Roland*]'; [158] blank; 159–83 text of part VI; [184] blank

Paper: wove paper

Running title: 'GALLIPOLI' (21mm.) on both verso and recto, pp.4–183

Binding: blue cloth. On spine, in gold: 'JOHN | MASEFIELD | GALLIPOLI | THE | WANDERER | EDITION | HEINEMANN' (all width centred). On upper cover, in gold: illustration of a cockerel: 32 × 24mm. (ranged lower right). On lower cover, in blind: publisher's device of a windmill (ranged lower right). Top edge gilt, others trimmed. Sewn head band (in blue) and blue marker ribbon. Binding measurements: 196 × 128mm. (covers), 196 × 35mm. (spine). End-papers: wove paper.

Publication date: published, according to Handley-Taylor, 21 October 1935

Price: 5s.

Contents:
as for A34(e)

Notes:

The signatures are different from those present in A34(e). Both, however, appear to use the same setting of text. (Although the 'Preface To The Eighth Edition' includes a date in this edition which is absent in A34(e)). Note the signature of B5 as '2'. This is one of the original signatures which presumably remained as an oversight.

The first leaf in the first gathering ([A]1) is a stub with a single leaf tipped-in as a cancellan. The new leaf includes reference to the Wanderer edition and the rest of the volume appears to use the same type setting as A34(e).

The publishing agreement for 'a collected edition of the Author's work', including this title, between Masefield and Heinemann was dated 31 July 1935 (see Archives of The Society of Authors). The agreement refers to 'a published price of 5/-...' (see note on collected editions).

Copies seen: BL (12452.i.3) stamped 23 OCT 1935 rebound; Bodleian (A.6.M.80/1) stamped 30 OCT 1935; HRHRC (TEMP M377GA 1935)

Reprinted:

Oct 1938

A34(h) First Australian edition (1978)

GALLIPOLI | John Masefield | [publisher's device of a seal within ruled border: 13 × 13mm.] | seal books | RIGBY
(All width centred. The first, third, fifth, seventh and ninth letters of the title are positioned 2mm. higher than the other letters)

Bibliographies: Wight [unrecorded]

Publication date: published in 1978 in an edition of 5000 copies (suggested by documents in the Archives of The Society of Authors)

Price: unknown

Contents:
as for A34(a)

Notes:
This edition comprises a direct photographic reprint of the text of A34(a). It includes all the photographs and maps present in the Heinemann edition and places them in the same positions within the text as in A34(a). This Australian edition provides numerical references to the collection of negatives held by the Australian War Memorial, Canberra.

The volumes states, on page [iv] that it is printed in Hong Kong.

The wrappers for this edition include a wrap-around illustration (adapted from an internal photograph) in black and white. The lower wrapper includes the statement: 'FOR THE FIRST TIME IN PAPERBACK... THE STORY OF GALLIPOLI BY ONE OF ENGLAND'S MOST FAMOUS WRITERS'.

The ISBN number is ISBN 0 7270 0594 4.

The publishing agreement for this title between The Society of Authors and Rigby was dated 22 August 1977 (see Archives of The Society of Authors).

Copies seen: BL (X.808/39598) stamped OCT 1978

A34(i) Fourth English edition (2002)

GALLIPOLI | John Masefield | ISIS | LARGE PRINT | [rule, 21mm.] | Oxford | [rule, 21mm.]
(All width centred)

Publication date: June 2002

Price: £17.95

Contents:
as for A34(a)

Notes:
A large print edition of the work.

The volume states, on page [iv] that it is 'printed and bound by Antony Rowe, Chippenham'. The ISBN number is ISBN 0–7531–5625–3 for an issue bound in pictorial boards and ISBN 0–7531–5626–1 for an issue bound in wrappers.

The edition is not illustrated. The three maps present in A34(a) are, however, reproduced.

Copies seen: private collection (PWE) pictorial boards

A35 SALT-WATER POEMS AND BALLADS   1916

A35(a) First American edition (1916)

SALT-WATER | POEMS AND BALLADS | BY | JOHN MASEFIELD | ILLUSTRATED BY CHAS. PEARS | [illustration in light green of one fully-rigged ship and one barque at sea with 36 birds in dark green] | THE MACMILLAN COMPANY, PUBLISHERS | NEW YORK   MCMXVI
(All lettering in dark green. Lines 1–4 width centred, lines 5–6 off-set to left and lines 7–8 justified on left and right margins. The final two lines are printed over the foot of the illustration.)

Bibliographies: Danielson [unrecorded], Williams [unrecorded], Simmons [34], Nevinson [unrecorded], Handley-Taylor [noted on p.27], Wight [34]

Collation: [A-L]⁸ [M]⁴ (but signed [A]⁵ [B]⁸ C-L⁸ M⁷; see note on American electrotype editions) (J not used); signatures left foot of page; 92 leaves; 189 × 133mm.; [i–iv] v–vii [viii] ix [x] [1–2] 3–68 [69–70] 71–118 [119–20] 121–63 [164–74]; illustrations (on glossy paper) tipped-in on pp.[ii], 4, 9, 13, 16, 20, 25, 36, 41, 45, 48, 54, 58, 63, 67, 73, 80, 91, 98, 114, 130, 139, 153 and 159 (colour illustrations each with protective tissue)

Page contents: [i] half-title: 'SALT-WATER | POEMS AND BALLADS'; [ii] '[publisher's device] | THE MACMILLAN COMPANY | [two lines listing six cities, separated by four points] | MACMILLAN & CO., LIMITED | [two lines listing four cities, separated by two points] | THE MACMILLAN CO. OF CANADA, LTD. | [one city listed]' (with additional leaf tipped-in on the verso of which is the full colour frontispiece: 146 × 96mm.); [iii] title-page (with protective tissue tipped-in upon which is the legend: 'The foremast broke; its mighty bulk of steel | Fell on the f'c'sle door and jammed it tight; | The sand-rush heaped her to an even keel, | She settled down, resigned, she made no fight,'; [iv] 'Copyright, 1913, by Harper and Brothers. | Copyright, 1914, by The Century Co., and by The McClure Publications. | [rule] | COPYRIGHT, 1912, 1913, 1914, | BY THE MACMILLAN COMPANY. | [rule] | COPYRIGHT, 1916, | BY JOHN MASEFIELD. | [rule] | Set up and electrotyped. Published October, 1916. | Norwood Press | J. S. Cushing Co. – Berwick & Smith Co. | Norwood, Mass., U.S.A.'; v–vi 'CONTENTS' (47 individual items under three headings listed with page references); vii 'LIST OF ILLUSTRATIONS IN COLOR' (12 items listed with page references); [viii] blank; ix 'LIST OF ILLUSTRATIONS IN BLACK | AND WHITE' (20 items listed with page references); [x] blank; [1] 'SALT-WATER BALLADS'; [2] blank; 3–68 text of 'Salt-Water Ballads'; [69] 'SEA PICTURES'; [70] blank; 71–118 text of 'Sea Pictures'; [119] 'SALT-WATER POEMS'; [120] blank; 121–60 text of 'Salt-Water Poems'; 161–63 text of 'Glossary' (at foot of p.163: '[rule] | Printed in the United States of America.'); [164] blank; [165] 'THE following pages contain advertisements of | Macmillan books by the same author.' (within ruled border: 15 × 89mm.); [166] blank; [167–72] publisher's advertisements; [173–74] blank

Paper: wove paper

Running title: 'SALT-WATER BALLADS' (40mm.) intermittently on verso with poem title on recto, pp.4–68; 'SEA PICTURES' (25mm.) on both verso and recto, pp.72–118; 'SALT-WATER POEMS' (36–37mm.) intermittently on verso with poem title on recto, pp.122–60

Binding: blue cloth. On spine, in gold: 'SALT | WATER | POEMS | AND | BALLADS | MASEFIELD | [design of trident and sea: 116 × 25mm.] | MACMILLAN' (all width centred). On upper cover, in blue (of cloth) on gold: 'SALT WATER | POEMS[point] | AND BALLADS | *by* | JOHN MASEFIELD | ILLUSTRATED | BY CHAS [point] PEARS' (surrounded by gold design incorporating illustration on paper laid down above text and two dolphins in lower section, signed (in gold) 'G' and 'H') note that the minuscules on the upper cover are swash. Lower cover: blank. Top edge trimmed, others roughly trimmed. Binding measurements: 195 × 135mm. (covers), 195 × 40mm. (spine). End-papers: wove paper printed in speckled blue (decorated in blue with 'SALT WATER | POEMS | AND | BALLADS | [illustration of three masted ship]' all within three ruled borders: 75 × 50mm.)

Publication date: published, according to Simmons, 18 October 1916 in an edition of 6092 copies

Price: $2.00

Contents:

SALT-WATER BALLADS

A Consecration ('Not of the princes and prelates with periwigged charioteers')
The Yarn of the 'Loch Achray' ('The 'Loch Achray' was a clipper tall')
Sing a Song O' Shipwreck ('He lolled on a bollard, a sun-burned son of the sea,')
Burial Party ("He's deader 'n nails,' the fo'c'sle said, "n' gone to his long sleep';')
Bill ('He lay dead on the cluttered deck and stared at the cold skies,')
Fever Ship ('There'll be no weepin' gells ashore when *our* ship sails,')
Fever-Chills ('He tottered out of the alleyway with cheeks the colour of paste,')
One of the Bo'sun's Yarns ('Loafin' around in Sailor Town, a-bluin' o' my advance,')
Hell's Pavement ("When I'm discharged in Liverpool 'n' draws my bit o' pay,')
Sea-Change ("Goneys an' gullies an' all o' the birds o' the sea,')
Harbour Bar ('All in the feathered palm-tree tops the bright green parrots screech,')
The Turn of the Tide ('An' Bill can have my sea-boots, Nigger Jim can have my knife,')
One of Wally's Yarns ('The watch was up on the topsail-yard a-making fast the sail,')
A Valediction (Liverpool Docks) ('Is there anything as I can do ashore for you')
A Night at Dago Tom's ('Oh yesterday, I t'ink it was, while cruisin' down the street,')
Port of Many Ships ("It's a sunny pleasant anchorage, is Kingdom Come,')
Cape Horn Gospel – I ("I was in a hooker once,' said Karlssen,')
Cape Horn Gospel – II ('Jake was a dirty Dago lad, an' he gave the skipper chin,')
Mother Carey (As Told Me By The Bo'sun) ('Mother Carey ? She's the mother o' the witches')
Evening – Regatta Day ('Your nose is a red jelly, your mouth's a toothless wreck,')
A Valediction ('We're bound for blue water where the great winds blow,')
A Pier-Head Chorus ('Oh I'll be chewing salted horse and biting flinty bread,')
The Golden City of St. Mary ('Out beyond the sunset, could I but find the way,')
Trade Winds ('In the harbour, in the island, in the Spanish Seas,')
Sea-Fever ('I must down to the seas again, to the lonely sea and the sky,')
A Wanderer's Song ('A wind's in the heart of me, a fire's in my heels,')
Cardigan Bay ('Clean, green, windy billows notching out the sky,')
Christmas Eve at Sea ('A wind is rustling 'south and soft,')
A Ballad of Cape St. Vincent ('Now, Bill, ain't it prime to be a-sailin',')
The Tarry Buccaneer ('I'm going to be a pirate with a bright brass pivot-gun,')
A Ballad of John Silver ('We were schooner-rigged and rakish, with a long and lissome hull,')
Lyrics from 'The Buccaneer'
I ('We are far from sight of the harbour lights,')
II ('There's a sea-way somewhere where all day long')

III ('The toppling rollers at the harbour mouth')
D'Avalos' Prayer ('When the last sea is sailed and the last shallow charted,')
SEA PICTURES
From *Philip the King* ('MESSENGER | We were to ship the troops in Calais Road;')
From *Dauber* ('Four bells were struck, the watch was called on deck,')
From *Biography* ('Days of endeavour have been good: the days')
SALT-WATER POEMS
The Ship and Her Makers ('THE ORE | Before Man's labouring wisdom gave me birth')
The New Bedford Whaler ('There was a 'Bedford Whaler put out to hunt for oil,')
Argoes [*sic*] ('Quinquireme of Nineveh from distant Ophir,')
Captain Stratton's Fancy ('Oh some are fond of red wine, and some are fond of white,')
Third Mate ('All the sheets are clacking, all the blocks are whining,')
Posted as Missing ('Under all her topsails she trembled like a stag,')
Ships ('I cannot tell their wonder nor make known')
Roadways ('One road leads to London,')
The "Wanderer" ('All day they loitered by the resting ships,')
The River ('All other waters have their time of peace,')
GLOSSARY ('Abaft the beam. – That half of a ship included between her amid-ship section…')

Notes:

The entire text of *Salt-Water Ballads* is not presented here. Many of the other poems are from *Ballads and Poems* although, again, the entire text of that volume is not present. Additionally, there are both new poems and those from other volumes ('The Ship and her Makers' and 'The New Bedford Whaler' are printed here for the first time). To regard the volume as a collection simply drawn from *Salt-Water Ballads* and *Ballads and Poems* is therefore incorrect. (Handley-Taylor notes the edition after describing *Salt-Water Ballads*). A more accurate description of the volume is to regard it as a collection of Masefield's sea poems. The 1978 volume *The Sea Poems* (see A174) claiming to be 'the first time that Masefield's sea poems have appeared together as an entity' is therefore not strictly true.

A publishing agreement for an edition between Masefield and Macmillan was dated 16 March 1916 (see Archives of The Society of Authors). The agreement refers to 'a licence to publish in volume form in the United States of America a work the subject or title of which is Salt Water Ballads, new and revised edition with illustrations'. One clause states that 'the Author agrees to deliver… photographs for illustrations…' This agreement may therefore refer to an aborted edition that developed into this Charles Pears edition.

Handley-Taylor (noting the volume under his heading for *Salt-Water Ballads*) describes it as a 'New and Revised Edition, with illustrations'

As noted by Simmons, the title 'Cargoes' appears as 'Argoes'. It appears correctly in the contents listing.

The coloured plates are all tipped-in and accompanied by protective tissue. These tissues carry the legends for the illustrations. The illustrations in black and white carry their legends on the page itself. A number of the black and white illustrations are printed on text paper and are integral to the volume, others are tipped-in.

Simmons notes that the illustration laid down to the upper cover has a background of New York Bay.

During 1926 it appears that Masefield sent to Heinemann a copy of this edition. C.S. Evans commented:

> Many thanks for the copy of SALT WATER POEMS AND BALLADS. I like some of the pictures very much, others not so well. This might make a good gift book for Christmas. I will ask our sales department what they think its chances are and if they think they are good, perhaps I could make arrangements with Macmillan…
>
> (C.S. Evans, letter to John Masefield, 18 March 1926)
> (HRHRC, MS (Masefield, J.) Recip William Heinemann Ltd.)

Copies seen: private collection (PWE)

Reprinted:

	[first edition, second impression]	Nov 1916
	[first edition, third impression]	Sep 1924
'Reissued'	[first edition, fourth impression]	Jan 1926
	[first edition, fifth impression]	Mar 1927
	[first edition, sixth impression]	Sep 1928
	[first edition, seventh impression]	Sep 1930
	[first edition, eighth impression]	Sep 1932
	[first edition, ninth impression]	Oct 1934
'Reissued in Imperial Edition'	[first edition, tenth impression]	Oct 1936
	[first edition, eleventh impression]	Jan 1941
	[first edition, twelfth impression]	Mar 1942
	[first edition, thirteenth impression]	Jul 1943
	[first edition, fourteenth impression]	Jun 1944
	[first edition, fifteenth impression]	Aug 1946
'Tenth Printing'	[first edition, later impression]	1967

A35(b) Second American edition (1960)

SALT-WATER | POEMS AND BALLADS | BY | JOHN MASEFIELD | ILLUSTRATED BY CHAS. PEARS | [illustration in grey of one fully-rigged ship and one barque at sea with 24 birds in black] | THE MACMILLAN COMPANY, PUBLISHERS | NEW YORK
(Lines 1–4 width centred, lines 5–6 off-set to left and lines 7–8 justified on left margins The final two lines are printed over the foot of the illustration.)

Bibliographies: Wight [unrecorded]

Collation: 88 unsigned leaves bound by the 'perfect binding' process; 209 × 135mm.; [two un-numbered pages] [i–v] vi [1–2] 3–10 [11] 12–14 [15] 16–17 [18] 19–26 [27] 28–30 [31] 32–33 [34] 35–49 [50] 51 [52] 53–56 [57] 58–68 [69–70] 71–116 [117] 118 [119–20] 121–63 [164–68]

Page contents: [-] blank; [-] blank; [i] half-title: 'SALT-WATER | POEMS AND BALLADS'; [ii] blank; [iii] title-page; [iv] 'Copyright 1912, 1913, 1914 by The Macmillan Company | Copyright 1916 by John Masefield | Copyright renewed 1940, 1941, 1942, 1944 by John Masefield | Copyright renewed 1944 by Charles Pears | All rights reserved–no part of this book may be reproduced | in any form without permission in writing from the publisher, | except by a reviewer who wishes to quote brief passages in | connection with a review written for inclusion in magazine or | newspaper. | Macmillan Paperbacks Edition 1960 | PRINTED IN THE UNITED STATES OF AMERICA'; [v]-vi 'CONTENTS' (47 individual items under three headings listed with page references); [1] 'SALT-WATER BALLADS'; [2] blank; 3–68 text of 'Salt-Water Ballads'; [69] 'SEA PICTURES'; [70] blank; 71–118 text of 'Sea Pictures'; [119] 'SALT-WATER POEMS'; [120] blank; 121–60 text of 'Salt-Water Poems'; 161–63 text of 'Glossary'; [164–68] blank

Paper: wove paper

Running title: 'SALT-WATER BALLADS' (40mm.) intermittently on verso with poem title on recto, pp.4–68; 'SEA PICTURES' (25mm.) on both verso and recto, pp.72–118; 'SALT-WATER POEMS' (36–37mm.) intermittently on verso with poem title on recto, pp.122–60

Binding: printed wrappers. On dark-green spine, reading lengthways down spine from head, in white: 'MASEFIELD Salt-Water Poems and Ballads MACMILLAN'; horizontally at foot of spine, in black on orange panel: 'mp | 33'. On upper wrapper: '[design in orange, white and dark-green of sea] | Salt-Water Poems and Ballads [in black on white] | JOHN MASEFIELD [in black on white] | [design in orange, white, dark-green and black of sea and ship] | *$1.25 Macmillan Paperbacks* mp [in black on orange]'. On orange lower wrapper: '*Salt-Water Poems and Ballads,* John Masefield's first pub- | lished poems, won him immediate critical acclaim. The sub- | stance of the poems sprang from the poet's early youth at | sea – he had joined Britain's merchant navy as a boy of 15 | and sailed around Cape Horn on a windjammer – and this | perhaps explains the eagerness and wonder found in these | enchanting ballads, each one an ode to the sea and the men | who dedicated their lives to it. | [new paragraph] "No other English-speaking poet has captured in such finished, | refined form the mixture of brutality and tenderness, the | bread-and-butter and the superstition, of the sailor-man's | character, nor welded into such neat pattern incomparable | rhythms of the sea, the colors of storm and sunlight, the | odors of sulphur and salt." | – *The Christian Science Monitor* | *Cover design by Arnold Harris Genkins* | [design in orange, white and dark-green of sea]'. All edges trimmed. Binding measurements: 209 × 135mm. (wrappers), 209 × 11mm. (spine).

Publication date: published, as suggested by an inscribed copy, before September 1960 in an edition of 10,000 copies (suggested by documents in the Archives of The Society of Authors)

Price: $1.25

Contents:
SALT-WATER BALLADS
A Consecration ('Not of the princes and prelates with periwigged charioteers')
The Yarn of the 'Loch Achray' ('The 'Loch Achray' was a clipper tall')
Sing a Song O' Shipwreck ('He lolled on a bollard, a sun-burned son of the sea,')
Burial Party ("He's deader 'n nails,' the fo'c's'le said, "n' gone to his long sleep';')
Bill ('He lay dead on the cluttered deck and stared at the cold skies,')
Fever Ship ('There'll be no weepin' gells ashore when *our* ship sails,')
Fever-Chills ('He tottered out of the alleyway with cheeks the colour of paste,')
One of the Bo'sun's Yarns ('Loafin' around in Sailor Town, a-bluin' o' my advance,')
Hell's Pavement ("When I'm discharged in Liverpool 'n' draws my bit o' pay,')
Sea-Change ("Goneys an' gullies an' all o' the birds o' the sea,')
Harbour Bar ('All in the feathered palm-tree tops the bright green parrots screech,')
The Turn of the Tide ('An' Bill can have my sea-boots, Nigger Jim can have my knife,')
One of Wally's Yarns ('The watch was up on the topsail-yard a-making fast the sail,')
A Valediction (Liverpool Docks) ('Is there anything as I can do ashore for you')
A Night at Dago Tom's ('Oh yesterday, I t'ink it was, while cruisin' down the street,')
Port of Many Ships ("It's a sunny pleasant anchorage, is Kingdom Come,')
Cape Horn Gospel – I ("I was in a hooker once,' said Karlssen,')
Cape Horn Gospel – II ('Jake was a dirty Dago lad, an' he gave the skipper chin,')
Mother Carey (As Told Me By The Bo'sun) ('Mother Carey ? She's the mother o' the witches')
Evening – Regatta Day ('Your nose is a red jelly, your mouth's a toothless wreck,')

A Valediction ('We're bound for blue water where the great winds blow,')
A Pier-Head Chorus ('Oh I'll be chewing salted horse and biting flinty bread,')
The Golden City of St. Mary ('Out beyond the sunset, could I but find the way,')
Trade Winds ('In the harbour, in the island, in the Spanish Seas,')
Sea-Fever ('I must go down to the seas again, to the lonely sea and the sky,')
A Wanderer's Song ('A wind's in the heart of me, a fire's in my heels,')
Cardigan Bay ('Clean, green, windy billows notching out the sky,')
Christmas Eve at Sea ('A wind is rustling 'south and soft,'')
A Ballad of Cape St. Vincent ('Now, Bill, ain't it prime to be a-sailin',')
The Tarry Buccaneer ('I'm going to be a pirate with a bright brass pivot-gun,')
A Ballad of John Silver ('We were schooner-rigged and rakish, with a long and lissome hull,')
Lyrics from 'The Buccaneer'
I ('We are far from sight of the harbour lights,')
II ('There's a sea-way somewhere where all day long')
III ('The toppling rollers at the harbour mouth')
D'Avalos' Prayer ('When the last sea is sailed and the last shallow charted,')
SEA PICTURES
From *Philip the King* ('MESSENGER | We were to ship the troops in Calais Road;')
From *Dauber* ('Four bells were struck, the watch was called on deck,')
From *Biography* ('Days of endeavour have been good: the days')
SALT-WATER POEMS
The Ship and Her Makers ('THE ORE | Before Man's labouring wisdom gave me birth')
The New Bedford Whaler ('There was a 'Bedford Whaler put out to hunt for oil,')
Cargoes ('Quinquireme of Nineveh from distant Ophir,')
Captain Stratton's Fancy ('Oh some are fond of red wine, and some are fond of white,')
Third Mate ('All the sheets are clacking, all the blocks are whining,')
Posted as Missing ('Under all her topsails she trembled like a stag,')
Ships ('I cannot tell their wonder nor make known')
Roadways ('One road leads to London,')
The "Wanderer" ('All day they loitered by the resting ships,')
The River ('All other waters have their time of peace,')
GLOSSARY ('Abaft the beam. – That half of a ship included between her amid-ship section…')

Notes:

This volume comprises a paperback reprint of A35(a), omitting illustrations originally tipped-in. As in the 1916 edition a number of illustrations are printed with the text.

There appear to be a few textual changes. The first line of 'Sea Fever' in A35(a) reads 'I must down to the seas again, to the lonely sea and the sky,'. In this edition the additional 'go' has been added, for example. As first noted by Simmons, the title 'Cargoes' appears as 'Argoes' in A35(a). It appears correctly in this paperback edition.

The 'mp' symbol for 'Macmillan Paperbacks' comprises a continuous line with both letters joined.

Evidence within the archives of The Society of Authors suggests that Macmillan may have first considered this volume in February 1953. In a letter to the Society, Masefield notes that Macmillan had suggested:

> …a reprint of an illustrated book omitting all the coloured illustrations that once gave it value, and reducing the royalty.
>
> (John Masefield, letter to [Anne] Munro-Kerr, 26 February [1953])
> (BL, Add.Mss.56624, f.78)

The Society of Authors responded, writing to Masefield, with advice:

> If you are reluctant to agree to the form in which Macmillans are proposing to re-issue *Salt-Water Poems and Ballads* I see no reason why you should not tell them that you feel strongly that the coloured illustrations should be included – or at least some of them.
>
> ([Anne] Munro-Kerr, letter to John Masefield, 6 March 1953)
> (BL, Add.Mss.56624, f.80)

A letter dated 17 November 1959 from The Macmillan Company reveals that the author had been asking for a higher royalty for this edition than the publishers thought possible. Macmillans proposed a compromise and this was accepted. The letter explained:

> …We are venturing into the paperback fields for the first time next spring, and we have much to learn about its special problems and possibilities…
>
> (A.L. Hart, Jr., letter to John Masefield, 17 November 1959)
> (Archives of The Society of Authors)

Copies seen: private collection (PWE); Library of The John Masefield Society (Eileen Colwell Collection) inscribed 'For Eileen. | from Jan. | September the 29th. 1960.'

A36 THE COLD COTSWOLDS   1917

A36(a) First English edition (1917)

REPRINTS FROM | The Cambridge Magazine | No. 5 March 1917 | THE COLD COTSWOLDS | JOHN MASEFIELD | [triangular ornament of leaves] | Price Twopence net | Reprinted from "The Cambridge Magazine" [*sic*] | for March 3rd 1917 at the Express Printing Works | 36 King Street, Cambridge | and sold by | Galloway and Porter | Sidney Street
(All width centred)

Bibliographies: Danielson 191, Williams p.5, Simmons [35], Nevinson [unrecorded], Handley-Taylor p.38, Wight [35]

Collation: [A]²; 2 leaves; 230 × 146mm.; [1–4]

Page contents: [1] title-page; [2–4] text (at foot of p.[4]: '(Copyright in U.S.A.) | Reprints from *The Cambridge Magazine*: | Price Twopence net (by post, Threepence) | No. I. UNRETURNING. By Ierne (Kathleen | Montgomery Coates). No. 2. THE REDEEMER. By | Siegfried Sassoon. No. 3. THE SACRED WAY. By | Sir Arthur Quiller-Couch. (W. Heffer & Sons, Ltd. | Petty Cury). | No. 4. DE PROFUNDIS. Anon. (Galloway and | Porter, Sidney Street).')

Paper: laid paper (watermark of St. Winifred: 69 × 39mm. and 'St Winifred' both below picture and in larger font throughout the paper), chain-lines 24mm. apart; the paper is used so that chain-lines run horizontally

Running title: none

Binding: issued as a four page leaflet without covers. The title-page consequently comprises the upper wrapper. All edges trimmed. Binding measurements: 230 × 146mm. (wrappers), 230 × 0.5mm. (spine).

Publication date: published, according to Simmons, March 1917

Price: 2d.

Contents:
The Cold Cotswolds ('No man takes the farm,')
> *First printed in* The Cambridge Magazine *3 March 1917, Vol.6 No.15, p.385*

Notes:
Danielson reports in his bibliography that the 'pamphlet went out of print immediately after publication and was not reprinted'. No. 7 in the series (Siegfried Sassoon, *Four Poems*), published in January 1918, indeed lists the Masefield number as 'Out of print'. A paragraph entitled 'The Cold Cotswolds' appears on p.557 of *The Cambridge Magazine* for 5 May 1917:

> The publishers of the C.M. Reprint Series, Messrs. Galloway & Porter, informed us on Thursday that the complete edition of the latest number of the series, *The Cold Cotswolds*, by John Masefield (reprinted from our issue of March 3), had been sold out. There are a few copies still left at our Office in King's Parade, but the Foolish Virgins who failed to secure them at Twopence will now have to take the consequences, and are hereby informed that the price has been advanced to 1s. net (postage 1d.). If this device does not avail to damp their enthusiasm, the example of *The Times* will be imitated, and a further increase made to 2s.6d. Eventually it may be necessary to form Cotswold Circles, whereby a group of families will share a copy between them and learn why no one will take that Farm.

There is confusion among Masefield bibliographers as to the publisher of this item. Williams and Wight cite Galloway and Porter as the publisher. Handley-Taylor (and the catalogue of the British Library) name the Express Printing Works. In *The Cambridge Magazine* itself 'Messrs. Galloway & Porter' are noted as 'the publishers of the C.M. Reprint Series' (see above).

In Vol.6 No.16 of *The Cambridge Magazine* published 10 March 1917 there is a parody of this poem, signed by 'M.J.' entitled 'The Cheerful Chilterns'. This appeared in the subsequent issue after publication of Masefield's original.

Copies seen: private collection (PWE); BL (Cup.401.g.27/5) stamped 31 MAR 1917 bound; HRHRC (PR6025 A77 C58 1917)

A37 LOLLINGDON DOWNS AND OTHER POEMS   1917

A37(a) First American edition (1917)

LOLLINGDON DOWNS | AND | OTHER POEMS | BY | JOHN MASEFIELD | AUTHOR OF | "THE STORY OF A ROUND HOUSE, AND OTHER POEMS," | "THE TRAGEDY OF POMPEY THE GREAT," ETC. | New York | THE MACMILLAN COMPANY | 1917 | *All rights reserved*
(All width centred and enclosed within double ruled border: 138 × 83mm. All ranged upper left)

Bibliographies: Danielson [unrecorded], Williams [unrecorded], Simmons [36], Nevinson [unrecorded], Handley-Taylor p.38, Wight [36]

Collation: [A-C]⁸ [D]⁴; 28 leaves; 219 × 150mm.; [1–6] 7–29 [30–32] 33–53 [54–56]

Page contents: [1] half-title: 'LOLLINGDON DOWNS | AND OTHER POEMS'; [2] 'THIS FIRST EDITION OF | "LOLLINGDON DOWNS AND | OTHER POEMS" IS LIMITED'; [3] title-page (with additional leaf tipped-in on the verso of which is the frontispiece: 130 × 96mm., 'John Masefield'); [4] 'COPYRIGHT, 1917 | BY JOHN MASEFIELD'; [5]

'LOLLINGDON DOWNS | AND OTHER POEMS'; [6] blank; 7–29 text; [30] blank; [31] 'THE FRONTIER | XVII | PERSONS | COTTA | LUCIUS | THEIR CHIEF'; [32] blank; 33–53 text; [54–56] blank

Paper: laid paper (no watermark), chain-lines 22mm. apart

Running title: '*LOLLINGDON DOWNS*' (35–36mm.) on both verso and recto, pp.8–29 and pp.34–53

Binding: brown boards with cream paper spine. Spine: blank. On upper cover: cream paper label (40 × 90mm.) on which: 'LOLLINGDON DOWNS | AND OTHER POEMS | [double rule] | JOHN MASEFIELD' (within double ruled border in brown: 30 × 80mm.) Lower cover: blank. All edges trimmed. Binding measurements: 224 × 152mm. (covers), 224 × 15mm. (spine). End-papers: wove paper.

Publication date: published, according to Simmons, 4 April 1917 in an edition of 950 copies

Price: $1.25

Contents:
I. ('So I have known this life,')
II. ('O wretched man, that, for a little mile')
III. ('Out of the special cell's most special sense')
      First printed as 'The Enduring Good' in The Atlantic Monthly *December 1916, p.[756]*
IV. ('You are the link which binds us each to each.')
V. ('I could not sleep for thinking of the sky,')
VI. ('How did the nothing come, how did these fires,')
VII. ('It may be so; but let the unknown be.')
VIII. ('The Kings go by with jewelled crowns,')
      First printed as 'The Choice' in Science Progress *January 1917, p.482*
IX. ('What is this life which uses living cells')
X. ('Can it be blood and brain, this transient force')
XI. ('Not only blood and brain its servants are,')
XII. ('Drop me the seed, that I, even in my brain')
XIII. ('Ah, but Without there is no spirit scattering;')
XIV. ('You are too beautiful for mortal eyes,')
XV. ('Is it a sea on which the souls embark')
XVI. The Blacksmith ('The blacksmith in his sparky forge')
      First printed as 'The Blacksmith' (signed, 'Pete Henderson') in The Forge *November 1916, pp.[3]–7*
XVII. The Frontier ('COTTA | Would God the route would come for home.')
XVIII. ('Night is on the downland, on the lonely moorland,')
XIX. Midnight ('The fox came up by Stringer's Pound,')
XX. ('Up on the downs the red-eyed kestrels hover')
XXI. ('No man takes the farm,')
XXII. ('A hundred years ago, they quarried for the stone here;')
XXIII. ('Here the legion halted, here the ranks were broken,')
XXIV. ('We danced away care till the fiddler's eyes blinked,')

Notes:
An American publication which pre-dates the English *Lollingdon Downs and other poems, with sonnets* (see A38). This earlier publication contains fewer poems than the English volume. Nevertheless, the appearance of most of the poems present in the American edition represents their first printing in book form. A comparison with A38 reveals many textual differences of a minor nature.

A publishing agreement between Masefield and Macmillan was dated 19 January 1917 (see Archives of The Society of Authors). The agreement refers to 'a licence to publish in volume form in the United States of America and Canada a work the subject or title of which is a short volume of poems'. Both *Lollingdon Downs* and *Rosas* are potential candidates although the archives of The Society of Authors include an agreement for the latter title.

Copies seen: BL (X.909/2175) stamped 15 JUN 1963

A38 LOLLINGDON DOWNS AND OTHER POEMS, WITH SONNETS   1917

A38(a) *First English edition (1917)*

LOLLINGDON DOWNS | AND OTHER POEMS, WITH SONNETS | BY | JOHN MASEFIELD | [publisher's device of a windmill with 'W [point]' and 'H' all within ruled border: 15 × 15mm.] | LONDON | WILLIAM HEINEMANN
(All width centred)

Bibliographies: Danielson 189, Williams p.5, Simmons [37], Nevinson p.13, Handley-Taylor p.41, Wight [37]

Collation: [A]⁴ B-G⁸; signatures right foot of page; 52 leaves; 180 × 118mm.; [i–viii] 1–92 [93–96]

Page contents: [i] blank; [ii] '[13 titles and their authors, prices and sizes listed] | [rule] | LONDON: WILLIAM HEINEMANN.' (within ruled border: 80 × 58mm.); [iii] half-title: 'LOLLINGDON DOWNS | AND OTHER POEMS, WITH SONNETS'; [iv] 'BY THE SAME AUTHOR | *Uniform with this Volume* | [four volumes listed] | LONDON: WILLIAM HEINEMANN'; [v] title-page'; [vi] 'LONDON: WILLIAM HEINEMANN. 1917.'; [vii] 'TO | MY WIFE'; [viii] blank; 1–92 text; [93] 'NOTE | SOME seven or eight of these poems have appeared | serially in the *Atlantic Monthly, Harper's,* the | *Yale Review, The Forge, Contemporary Verse,* and *Science Progress;* others have been issued | privately, in a book now out of print; the rest | are new. | J. M. | LONDON, | *February* 1, 1917.' (at foot of p.[93]: '[rule] | BILLING AND SONS, LTD., PRINTERS, GUILDFORD, ENGLAND'); [94–96] blank

Paper: wove paper

Running title: where present, these comprise titles of individual poems, pp.19–20, 22–26, 28–30 and p.34

Binding: blue cloth. On spine, in gold: 'Lollingdon | Downs | [ornament] | John | Masefield | HEINEMANN' (all width centred). Covers: blank with blind ruled borders: 180 × 114mm. All edges trimmed. Binding measurements: 186 × 120mm. (covers), 186 × 27mm. (spine). End-papers: wove paper.

Publication date: published, according to Simmons, 17 April 1917 in an edition of 5000 copies

Price: 3s. 6d.

Contents:
I. ('So I have known this life,')
II. ('O wretched man, that for a little mile')
III. ('Out of the special cell's most special sense')
IV. ('You are the link which binds us each to each.')
V. ('I could not sleep for thinking of the sky,')
VI. ('How did the nothing come, how did these fires,')
VII. ('It may be so; but let the unknown be.')
VIII. ('The Kings go by with jewelled crowns;')
IX. ('What is this life which uses living cells')
X. ('Can it be blood and brain, this transient force')
XI. ('Not only blood and brain its servants are;')
XII. ('Drop me the seed, that I even in my brain')
XIII. ('Ah, but Without there is no spirit scattering;')
XIV. ('You are too beautiful for mortal eyes,')
XV. ('Is it a sea on which the souls embark')
XVI. The Ship ('THE ORE. | Before Man's labouring wisdom gave me birth')
XVII. The Blacksmith ('The blacksmith in his sparky forge')
XVIII. The Frontier ('COTTA. Would God the route would come for home!')
XIX. ('Night is on the downland, on the lonely moorland,')
XX. Midnight ('The fox came up by Stringer's Pound;')
XXI. ('Up on the downs the red-eyed kestrels hover,')
XXII. ('No man takes the farm,')
XXIII. ('A hundred years ago they quarried for the stone here;')
XXIV. ('Here the legion halted, here the ranks were broken,')
XXV. ('We danced away care till the fiddler's eyes blinked,')
XXVI. ('Long, long ago, when all the glittering earth')
XXVII. ('Night came again, but now I could not sleep;')
XXVIII. ('Even after all these years there comes the dream')
XXIX. ('If I could come again to that dear place')
XXX. ('Here in the self is all that man can know')
XXXI. ('Flesh, I have knocked at many a dusty door,')
XXXII. ('But all has passed, the tune has died away,')
XXXIII. ('These myriad days, these many thousand hours,')
XXXIV. ('There, on the darkened deathbed, dies the brain')
XXXV. ('So in the empty sky the stars appear,')
XXXVI. ('It may be so with us, that in the dark,')
XXXVII. ('What am I, Life? A thing of watery salt')
XXXVIII. ('If I could get within this changing I,')
XXXIX. ('What is this atom which contains the whole,')
XL. ('Ah, we are neither heaven nor earth, but men;')
XLI. ('Roses are beauty, but I never see')
XLII. ('Over the church's door they moved a stone,')
XLIII. ('Out of the clouds come torrents, from the earth')
XLIV. ('O little self, within whose smallness lies')
XLV. ('I went into the fields, but you were there')

XLVI. ('This is the living thing that cannot stir.')
XLVII. ('Here, where we stood together, we three men,')
XLVIII. ('I saw her like a shadow on the sky')
XLIX. ('Look at the grass, sucked by the seed from dust,')
L. ('There is no God, as I was taught in youth,')
LI. ('Wherever beauty has been quick in clay')
LII. ('Beauty, let be; I cannot see your face,')
LIII. ('You are more beautiful than women are,')
LIV. ('Beauty retires; the blood out of the earth')
LV. ('Not for the anguish suffered is the slur,')
LVI. ('Beauty was with me once, but now, grown old,')
LVII. ('So beauty comes, so with a failing hand')
LVIII. ('You will remember me in days to come,')
LIX. ('If Beauty be at all, if, beyond sense,')
LX. ('If all be governed by the moving stars,')
LXI. ('In emptiest furthest heaven where no stars are,')
LXII. ('Perhaps in chasms of the wasted past,')
LXIII. ('For, like an outcast from the city, I')
LXIV. ('Death lies in wait for you, you wild thing in the wood,')
LXV. ('They called that broken hedge The Haunted Gate.')
LXVI. ('There was an evil in the nodding wood')
LXVII. ('Go, spend your penny, Beauty, when you will,')
LXVIII. ('Though in life's streets the tempting shops have lured')
LIX. ('When all these million cells that are my slaves')
LX. ('Let that which is to come be as it may,')

Notes:

An English publication presenting the entire contents of the American *Lollingdon Downs and other poems* although also reprinting poems from *Good Friday and other poems*, *Sonnets and Poems*, and *Salt-Water Poems and Ballads*.

The publishing agreement for this title between Masefield and Heinemann was dated 9 February 1917 (see Archives of The Society of Authors). The agreement refers to a publication price of 3s.6d.

The final two sonnets in this volume are incorrectly numbered. 'LIX' and 'LX'. The correct numerals should be 'LXIX' and 'LXX'.

Copies seen: private collection (PWE); BL (011648.e.19) stamped 17 APR 1917

Reprinted:
| 'New Impression' | [first edition, second impression] | Aug 1919 |
| 'New Impression' | [first edition, third impression] | Feb 1922 |

A39 POEMS BY JOHN MASEFIELD (SELECTED BY HENRY SEIDEL CANBY, FREDERICK ERASTUS PIERCE AND WILLARD HIGLEY DURHAM)   [1917]

A39(a) First American edition (1916 [1917])

POEMS | BY | JOHN MASEFIELD | SELECTED BY | HENRY SEIDEL CANBY, PH.D. | FREDERICK ERASTUS PIERCE, PH.D. | WILLARD HIGLEY DURHAM, PH.D. | OF THE DEPARTMENT OF ENGLISH, THE SHEFFIELD | SCIENTIFIC SCHOOL, YALE UNIVERSITY | [PUBLISHED WITH THE CONSENT OF MR. MASEFIELD] | New York | THE MACMILLAN COMPANY | 1917 | *All rights reserved*
(All width centred)

Bibliographies: Danielson [unrecorded], Williams [unrecorded], Simmons [unrecorded], Nevinson [unrecorded], Handley-Taylor p.41 (see notes), Wight [unrecorded]

Collation: binding indeterminable from examined copies although probably [A-U]⁸ [W]⁴ (J and V not used); at least 164 leaves; at least 184 × 112mm.; pagination includes [i–iv] v [vi] 1–313 [314–20]

Page contents: [i] half-title: 'POEMS BY JOHN MASEFIELD'; [ii] '[publisher's device] | THE MACMILLAN COMPANY | [two lines listing six cities, separated by four points] | MACMILLAN & CO., LIMITED | [two lines listing four cities, separated by two points] | THE MACMILLAN CO. OF CANADA, LTD. | [one city listed]'; [iii] title-page; [iv] 'Copyright, 1911, by John Masefield. | Copyright, 1912, by The Macmillan Company. | Copyright, 1913, by Harper and Brothers and by The | Macmillan Company. | Copyright, 1914, by the Century Company, by the | McClure Publications, and by The Macmillan Company. | Copyright, 1915, by John Masefield. | Copyright, 1916, by John Masefield. | Norwood Press | J. S. Cushing Co.-Berwick & Smith Co. | Norwood, Mass., U.S.A.'; v 'TABLE OF CONTENTS' (14 individual items listed with page references); [vi] blank; 1–313 text (at foot of p.313: '[rule] | Printed in the United States of America.'); [314] blank; [315] 'THE following pages contain advertisements | of Macmillan books by the same author' (within ruled border: 17 × 67mm.); [316] blank; [317–20] publisher's advertisements

Paper: wove paper

Running title: 'SALT-WATER BALLADS' (40mm.) on recto, p.2; '*THE EVERLASTING MERCY*' (46mm.), pp.4–93; '*DAUBER*' (14mm.), pp.96–257; '*BIOGRAPHY*' (20mm.), pp.259–80; other pages note title of poem on both verso and recto, pp.282–313

Binding: indeterminable from examined copies

Contents:
A Consecration ('Not of the princes and prelates with periwigged charioteers')
The Everlasting Mercy ('From '41 to '51')
Dauber ('Four bells were struck, the watch was called on deck,')
Explanations of some of the Sea Terms used in the Poem ('Backstays. Wire ropes which support...')
Biography ('When I am buried, all my thoughts and acts')
Cargoes ('Quinquireme of Nineveh from distant Ophir,')
Sea Fever ('I must go down to the seas again, to the lonely sea and the sky,')
Spanish Waters ('Spanish waters, Spanish waters, you are ringing in my ears,')
An Old Song Re-Sung ('I saw a ship a-sailing, a-sailing, a-sailing,')
The West Wind ('It's a warm wind, the west wind, full of birds' cries;')
On Malvern Hill ('A wind is brushing down the clover,')
Fragments ('Troy Town is covered up with weeds,')
Tewkesbury Road ('It is good to be out on the road, and going one knows not where,')
[Untitled] ('Men are made human by the mighty fall')
[Untitled] ('Ah, we are neither heaven nor earth, but men;')
[Untitled] ('They took the bloody body from the cross,')
[Untitled] ('"Come to us fiery with the saints of God')
[Untitled] ('So from the cruel cross they buried God;')
August 1914 ('How still this quiet cornfield is to-night;')

Publication date: published, according to Handley-Taylor, 16 May 1917 (see notes)

Price: $1.60

Notes:
A volume of poems selected by three members of the Department of English, Sheffield Scientific School, Yale University and published with Masefield's consent. This volume appears to use the available Macmillan plates for individual poems. This is evident from the running-title 'SALT WATER BALLADS' present on p.2.

Handley-Taylor notes two similar titles in his bibliography (*Poems: Selections from College Department Edition* and *Selections from Poems*). It is assumed that one of these titles represents the volume described here. The other may have been a school edition of the same. However, it should be noted that the first edition of this volume includes a date of 1917 on the title page, but 1916 within printing data. Handley-Taylor's descriptions are as follows:

> POEMS: SELECTED FROM COLLEGE DEPARTMENT EDITION.
> The Macmillan Company (New York).
> Published May 16, 1917. Reprinted: 1920–1921; 1922–1923; 1923–1924; 1924–1925; 1925–1926; 1926–1927; 1927–1928; 1929–1930; 1931–1932; 1933–1934; 1934–1935; 1935–1936; 1938–1939; 1941–1942; 1943–1944; 1944–1945; 1945–1946; 1946–1947; 1950; 1951; 1955.
>
> SELECTIONS FROM POEMS.
> The Macmillan Company (New York).
> Regular Edition published May 16, 1917. Reprinted 1918–1919.

The *National Union Catalog: Pre–1956 Imprints* (Mansell, 1975) does not list any title under 'Selected Poems' which corresponds to these volumes. Under 'Poems', however, the volume described above is listed with the dates [c.1916] and 1917 (in addition to reprints).

Although the *National Union Catalog* does not provide any supportive evidence, Handley-Taylor's reference to a 'regular edition' may indicate that the other title was an educational printing for schools or colleges.

A publishing agreement for this title between Masefield and Macmillan was dated 16 January 1917 (see Archives of The Society of Authors). The agreement reveals that Macmillan had entered into an agreement with Canby, Pierce and Durham on 28 June 1916. The title is cited as 'SELECTIONS FROM JOHN MASEFIELD'S POEMS'. In a letter to accompany the agreement, George P. Brett wrote:

> ...I hope this little volume will prove of use for the college classroom reading of your poetry, and it will, I think, in this way extend very greatly your audience in this country.
> (George P. Brett, letter to John Masefield, 16 January 1917)
> (Archives of The Society of Authors)

Copies seen: NYPL (NCM 1917) 786986 annotated 'May 2–3 1917' rebound; State University of Iowa Library (PR6025.A77 A17 1916/*c.1) rebound

Reprinted:

'Reprinted'	[first edition, second impression]	Jan 1918
'Reprinted'	[first edition, third impression]	Oct 1926
'Reprinted'	[first edition, fourth impression]	Dec 1927
'Reprinted'	[first edition, fifth impression]	Apr 1929
'Reprinted'	[first edition, sixth impression]	Aug 1931
'Reprinted'	[first edition, seventh impression]	Apr 1934
'Reprinted'	[first edition, eighth impression]	Oct 1934
'Reprinted'	[first edition, ninth impression]	Nov 1935
'Reprinted'	[first edition, tenth impression]	Mar 1939

A40 ANNE PEDERSDOTTER   1917

A40(a) First American edition (1917)

ANNE PEDERSDOTTER | A DRAMA IN FOUR ACTS | BY | H. WIERS-JENSSEN | ENGLISH VERSION BY | JOHN MASEFIELD | [publisher's device of tree, initials of company and 'NON [point] REFERT QVAM [point] MVLTOS SED [point] QVAM BONOS [point] HABEAS' all within ruled border: 25 × 17mm.] | BOSTON | LITTLE, BROWN, AND COMPANY | 1917
(All width centred)

Bibliographies: Danielson [unrecorded], Williams p.5, Simmons [noted on p.134], Nevinson [unrecorded], Handley-Taylor [unrecorded], Wight [unrecorded]

Collation: [A-F]⁸ [G]⁴; 52 leaves; 188 × 126mm.; [i–vi] [1–5] 6–33 [34] 35–56 [57] 58–80 [81] 82–93 [94–98]

Page contents: [i–ii] blank; [iii] half-title: 'ANNE PEDERSDOTTER'; [iv] blank; [v] title-page; [vi] *'Copyright, 1917,* | BY LITTLE, BROWN, AND COMPANY. | [rule] | *All rights reserved* | Published, September, 1917 | SET UP AND ELECTROTYPED BY THE PLIMPTON PRESS, NORWOOD, MASS., U.S.A. | PRINTED BY S. J. PARKHILL & CO., BOSTON, MASS., U.S.A.'; [1] 'ANNE PEDERSDOTTER'; [2] blank; [3] 'CHARACTERS | [dramatis personae listed] | *The action takes place in Bergen in the year 1574: the* | *first three Acts in Absolon's house, the last in the choir of* | *the Cathedral.*'; [4] blank; [5]–93 text; [94–98] blank

Paper: wove paper

Running title: 'ANNE PEDERSDOTTER [45mm.] | [rule, 88mm.]' on both verso and recto, pp.6–93

Binding: burgundy cloth. On spine, in gold: 'ANNE | PEDERSDOTTER | [ornament] | WIERS-JENSSEN | LITTLE, BROWN | AND COMPANY' (all width centred). Covers: blank. All edges trimmed. Binding measurements: 194 × 125mm. (covers), 194 × 26mm. (spine). End-papers: wove paper.

Publication date: published, according to Simmons, September 1917

Price: $1.00

Contents:
Anne Pedersdotter ('THE FIRST ACT | SCENE ONE | *Bells at start. Garden at the back…*')

Notes:
This translation from H. Wiers-Jenssen's Norwegian play of sixteenth century witchcraft and incest has been largely overlooked by Masefield bibliography.

The play was translated for Lillah McCarthy who played the lead in the first performance. Harley Granville-Barker first suggested translating the play in June 1909, but Masefield (like Shaw before him) refused the task. McCarthy states (in *Myself and my Friends*) that '…slowly he relented. He would do the translation… but would not put his name to it.' Such reticence presumably explains the late appearance of the play in print and publication only in the United States. Writing to C.F. Cazenove in July 1909 Masefield noted that he had been asked 'to alter a translation of a Scandinavian play' and that his role was defined as '…"to put the translation into decent English", not to adapt it…' (see John Masefield, letter to C.F. Cazenove, 8 July 1909) (University of Arizona Library. MS.50, V.II)

The work was later printed as *The Witch* (see A83)

Writing in 1936 to The Society of Authors, Masefield notes a proposed film of the play (under the later title of *The Witch*):

> I had really very little to do with The Witch, and heartily wish that I had had less. I am sure that I have no rights whatsoever for any film made from the fable, but it would be a possible part for Miss Hepburn, and probably Messrs. Curtis Brown, the Agents, would be able to let agents know with whom to negotiate.

> (John Masefield, letter to [E.J.] Mullett, [5 July 1936])
> (BL, Add.Mss.56605, f.9)

Masefield refers to Curtis Brown who, after the death of C.F. Cazenove briefly became Masefield's agent. The reference to 'Miss Hepburn' is presumably to Katharine Hepburn who by 1936 was already a Hollywood star.

Copies seen: BL (11791.df.16) stamped 7 MAR 1918

A41 THE OLD FRONT LINE 1917

A41(a) First American edition (1917)

THE | OLD FRONT LINE | BY | JOHN MASEFIELD | Author of "Gallipoli," etc. | New York | THE MACMILLAN COMPANY | 1917 | *All rights reserved*
(All width centred)

Bibliographies: Danielson [unrecorded], Williams [unrecorded], Simmons [38], Nevinson [unrecorded], Handley-Taylor p.41, Wight [38]

Collation: [A-G]⁸; 56 leaves; 190 × 127mm.; [1–8] 9–99 [100–112]; illustrations (on glossy paper) tipped-in on pp.17, 28, 39, 41, 42, 44, 48, 58, 67, 71, 74, 76, 78, 83, 89 and 94

Page contents: [1] half-title: 'THE OLD FRONT LINE'; [2] '[publisher's device] | THE MACMILLAN COMPANY | [two lines listing six cities, separated by four points] | MACMILLAN & CO., LIMITED | [two lines listing four cities, separated by two points] | THE MACMILLAN CO. OF CANADA, LTD. | [one city listed]'; [3] title-page; [4] 'COPYRIGHT, 1917 | By JOHN MASEFIELD | [rule] | Set up and electrotyped. Published, December, 1917.'; [5] 'TO | NEVILLE LYTTON'; [6] blank; [7] 'LIST OF ILLUSTRATIONS' (16 illustrations listed with page references); [8] blank; 9–99 text (at foot of p.99: 'PRINTED IN THE UNITED STATES OF AMERICA'); [100] blank; [101] 'THE following pages contain advertisements | of Macmillan books by the same author' (within ruled border: 17 × 67mm.); [102] blank; [103–108] publisher's advertisements; [109–112] blank

Paper: wove paper

Running title: 'The Old Front Line' (37mm.) on both verso and recto, pp.10–99

Binding: navy blue cloth. On spine, in gold: '[double rule] | THE | OLD | FRONT | LINE | [triangle] | JOHN | MASEFIELD | MACMILLAN | [double rule]' (all width centred). On upper cover, in gold: 'THE | OLD FRONT LINE | JOHN MASEFIELD' (within blind ruled border: 188 × 119mm.) Lower cover: blank. Top edge trimmed, others roughly trimmed. Binding measurements: 196 × 128mm. (covers), 196 × 32mm. (spine). End-papers: wove paper.

Publication date: published, according to Simmons, 13 November 1917 in an edition of 3982 copies

Price: $1.00

Contents:
The Old Front Line ('This description of the old front line, as it was when the Battle...')

Notes:
After the success of *Gallipoli*, Masefield was urged to write a history of the Somme by Lord Esher and Field Marshal Sir Douglas Haig. Whitehall bureaucracy prevented the research opportunities Masefield required and he regarded this truncated volume as merely a preface. A later work entitled *The Battle of the Somme* (see A48) was similarly only part of this larger scheme.

In contrast with the later English edition (see A41(b)), this American publication has no sub-title. The text is not divided into chapters and there is therefore no contents listing. Another feature present in the later edition is the inclusion of a map, here omitted.

Contrast the similarity of the binding of this volume with that for *The War and the Future* (see A43).

The illustrations in this volume are the same as in A41(b). The titles as given in both listings of illustrations are the same (the American edition with the correct spelling of 'La Boisselle'). However, within the volumes captions are occasionally different. For example, the American caption for the first illustration reads 'The Road up the Ancre Valley through Aveluy Wood' in contrast to the English caption: 'The Road up the Ancre Valley, through the Wood of Aveluy'. The seventh illustration in the American edition reads 'The Ancre opposite Hamel'. This appears as 'The Ancre opposite Hamel, from the Foot of the Schwaben Redoubt' in the English edition. The American illustrations are all within ruled borders.

A publishing agreement for this title between Masefield and Macmillan was dated 19 January 1917 (see Archives of The Society of Authors). The agreement refers to 'a licence to publish in volume form in the United States of America and Canada a work the subject of which is an account of the Battle of the Somme'. Another agreement, dated 15 June 1917, refers to 'a work the subject or title of which is The Story of the Battle of the Somme'. A later undated agreement provides the correct title.

Copies seen: NYPL (BTZE 1917) 204207A; Columbia University (940.91 M3772)

A41(b) First English edition (1917)

THE | OLD FRONT LINE | OR | THE BEGINNING OF THE | BATTLE OF THE SOMME | BY | JOHN MASEFIELD | AUTHOR OF "GALLIPOLI," ETC. | ILLUSTRATED | [publisher's device of a windmill with 'W [point]' and 'H' all within ruled border: 19 × 19mm.] | LONDON | WILLIAM HEINEMANN | 1917
(All width centred)

Bibliographies: Danielson 190, Williams p.10, Simmons [38a], Nevinson p.17, Handley-Taylor p.41, Wight [38a]

Collation: [π]⁸ 1–6⁸; signatures right foot of page; 48 leaves; the catalogue (not included in collation or leaf count) comprises four gatherings (A-D⁸) with signatures at right foot of page; 184 × 119mm.; [i–vi] vii [viii] ix [x] 11–18 [19–20] 21–22 [23–24] 25–46

[47–48] 49–50 [51–52] 53–58 [59–60] 61–62 [63–64] 65–72 [73–74] 75–78 [79–80] 81–84 [85–86] 87–88 [89–90] 91–92 [93–94] 95–96 [97–98] 99–102 [103–104] 105–106 [107–108] 109–20 [121–22] 123–24 [125–26] 127–28; catalogue pagination: 1–64; illustrations (on glossy paper) tipped-in on pp.21, 25, 49, 53, 61, 65, 75, 78, 87, 91, 95, 99, 105, 108, 123 and 127; there is a map (folded five times): 'MAP OF | THE SOMME BATTLEFIELD | to illustrate | "THE OLD FRONT LINE" | By JOHN MASEFIELD | Author of "Gallipoli," etc.' this is bound within gathering 6 (the stub appears between the third and fourth leaf and the map appears between the fifth and sixth)

Page contents: [i] half-title: 'THE OLD FRONT LINE'; [ii] '[10 titles and their authors and prices listed] | SOLDIERS' TALES OF THE | GREAT WAR | [12 titles and their authors, etc. listed] | [rule] | LONDON : WILLIAM HEINEMANN' (within ruled border: 131 × 67mm.); [iii] title-page; [iv] 'LONDON: WILLIAM HEINEMANN. 1917.'; [v] 'TO | NEVILLE LYTTON'; [vi] blank; vii 'CONTENTS' (nine chapters listed with page references); [viii] blank; ix 'LIST OF ILLUSTRATIONS' (16 illustrations listed with page references) (additional slip of paper: 20 × 61mm., tipped-in: 'ERRATUM | IN LIST OF ILLUSTRATIONS: | *for* 'La Boiselle' *read* 'La Boisselle'); [x] blank; 11–128 text (at foot of p.128: '[rule] | BILLING AND SONS, LTD., PRINTERS, GUILDFORD, ENGLAND'); 1–64 catalogue: '*A Selection from* | *William Heinemann's* | *Catalogue*' (at foot of p.64: 'PRINTED AT THE COMPLETE PRESS, WEST NORWOOD, LONDON, S.E.')

Paper: wove paper (catalogue: wove paper)

Running title: 'THE OLD FRONT LINE' (48mm.) on both verso and recto, pp.12–128

Binding: red cloth (see notes). On spine: 'THE | OLD | FRONT | LINE | JOHN | MASEFIELD | HEINEMANN' (all width centred). On upper cover: 'THE | OLD FRONT LINE | JOHN MASEFIELD' (all width centred). On lower cover: publisher's device of a windmill with 'W [point]' and 'H' all within ruled border: 21 × 21mm. All edges trimmed. Binding measurements: 188 × 120mm. (covers), 188 × 24mm. (spine). End-papers: wove paper.

Publication date: published, according to Simmons, 13 December 1917 in an edition of 20000 copies

Price: 2s.6d.

Contents:
as for A41(a)

Notes:
The publishing agreement for this title between Masefield and Heinemann was dated 8 November 1917 (see Archives of The Society of Authors). The agreement refers to a publication price of 2s.6d.

Although the illustrations are tipped-in and do not include page numbers they are, nevertheless, accommodated in the number sequence of the book. Consequently, un-numbered pages from [19–20] to [125–26] in the sequence above represent pages of illustration.

The printer (BILLING AND SONS) appears as 'ILLING AND SONS' on page 128 in some copies.

Wight describes the binding as 'pink cloth'. All copies examined are, however, bound in red cloth. Wight presumably describes a faded copy.

The wove paper used for the catalogue is thinner than that used within the book. Some copies show differences in paper quality between gatherings of the catalogue.

Copies seen: private collection (PWE); BL (09082.bbb.22) stamped 14 DEC 1917; NYPL (8-BTZE 1917) 833678

A41(c) Second English edition (1972)

THE OLD | FRONT LINE | by | JOHN MASEFIELD | with | an introduction on | The Battle of the Somme | by | Col. Howard Green, M.C. | SPURBOOKS LTD | 88 BLIND LANE, BOURNE END, BUCKS
(All width centred)

Bibliographies: Wight [unrecorded]

Publication date: March 1972

Price: £1.95

Contents:
High Wood ('Ladies and gentlemen, this is High Wood')
        (By Philip Johnstone)
The Battle of the Somme ('The series of actions known to history as The Battle of the Somme...')
        (By Col. Howard Green, M.C.)
The Old Front Line ('This description of the old front line, as it was when the Battle...')

Notes:
The volume is illustrated by 22 photographic illustrations (mostly titled). There is, however, no contents listing of these illustrations. Many of the photographs show the battlefields in 1971 and none of the original illustrations from the 1917 edition are reproduced here.

The publishing agreement for this title between Heinemann and Spur Books was dated 28 June 1971 (see Archives of The Society of Authors). The agreement refers to a licence term of five years.

The volumes states, on page [iv] that it is printed in Great Britain by Morrison and Gibb Ltd, London and Edinburgh.

The ISBN number is ISBN 0 902875 05 1

Copies seen: BL (X.808/7878) stamped 26 APR 1972

A42 ROSAS

1918

A42(a) First American edition – numbered issue (1918)

ROSAS | JOHN MASEFIELD | [ornament in red] | NEW YORK | THE MACMILLAN COMPANY | MDCCCCXVIII
(All width centred and enclosed within red ruled border: 110 × 85mm.)

Bibliographies: Danielson [unrecorded], Williams [noted on p.6], Simmons [39], Nevinson [unrecorded], Handley-Taylor p.41, Wight [39]

Collation: [A]⁹ ([A]2+1) [B-D]⁸ (but signed [A]⁸ B-C⁸ D⁹; see note on American electrotype editions); signatures left foot of page; 33 leaves; 175 × 124mm.; [1–8] 9–65 [66]

Page contents: [1] 'OF THIS EDITION NINE HUNDRED | AND FIFTY COPIES HAVE BEEN | PRINTED AND THE TYPE DISTRIB- | UTED, OF WHICH SEVEN HUNDRED | AND FIFTY, NUMBERED AND SIGNED | BY THE AUTHOR, ARE FOR SALE.'; [2] blank; [3] half-title: 'ROSAS'; [4] '[publisher's device] | THE MACMILLAN COMPANY | [two lines listing six cities, separated by four points] | MACMILLAN & CO., LIMITED | [two lines listing four cities, separated by two points] | THE MACMILLAN CO. OF CANADA, LTD. | [one city listed]'; [5] title-page; [6] 'COPYRIGHT, 1918, BY JOHN MASEFIELD | SET UP AND PRINTED. PUBLISHED APRIL, 1918 | NORWOOD PRESS: J. S. CUSHING COMPANY [point] BERWICK & SMITH CO. | NORWOOD, MASS., U.S.A.'; [7] 'ROSAS'; [8] blank; 9–65 text (at foot of p.65: '[rule] | Printed in the United States of America.'); [66] blank

Paper: wove paper: (watermark: '*Alexandra*')

Running title: 'ROSAS' (11mm.) on both verso and recto, pp.9–65

Binding: blue-green boards with vellum spine. On spine, reading lengthways up spine, from foot, in gold: 'ROSAS [device] MASEFIELD' (printed on black panel within single gold rule with ornaments at head and foot: 91 × 7mm.) On upper cover, in gold: 'ROSAS | [ornament] | JOHN MASEFIELD' (printed on black panel three sides of which are bordered by double ruled border; there is a gold half sun above the panel and gold foliage below: 80 × 62mm.) Lower cover: blank. Top edge trimmed, others roughly trimmed. Binding measurements: 178 × 123mm. (covers), 178 × 20mm. (spine). End-papers: wove paper: (watermark: '*Alexandra*')

Publication date: published, according to Simmons, 25 April 1918 in an edition of 960 copies (of which 750 numbered and signed) (see A42(aa))

Price: $1.50

Contents:
Rosas ('There was an old lord in the Argentine,')

Notes:
The volume contains a short narrative poem concerning Lord Rosas of the Argentine. See A46 for English publication.

Page numbers appear within square brackets. Thus, [9], [10], etc.

Simmons notes the panels on the spine and upper cover as being 'dark brown'.

A publishing agreement for this edition between Masefield and Macmillan was dated 22 April 1918 (see Archives of The Society of Authors). The agreement refers to 'a licence to publish in volume form in the United States of America a work the subject or title of which is Rosas (special limited edition)'. The agreement notes 'two hundred copies of the complete work will be furnished on publication to the Author without charge'.

Simmons describes this title as number [39]. Simmons notes:

> Published April 25, 1918, in an edition of 960 copies, of which 750 were numbered, and signed by the author.

It appears that no copy was unsigned by Masefield, whether numbered or not. If consulted copies bear their original dust-jackets then there was no difference in cost. Both cite $1.50 (although the 200 copies for Masefield may not have been for sale).

Although by 1954 Masefield omitted the poem from volumes of collected verse he was willing to permit an Argentine translation. Writing to The Society of Authors, he states:

> I have received the enclosed letter from Señor Don J.L.M. Azpiri of Buenos Aires, who has very ably translated a poem about an Argentine Dictator, (Rosas) written many years ago, + now dropped from my collected verses. Rosas was what would now be called A Tough Guy. He was driven from the Argentine, + died (much liked) in an English farm.

> Please, will you grant Don Azpiri full leave to go ahead? I shall not reprint the verses, but would not like to stand in his way.

But, please, will you ask him this, that as sole payment to myself he will lay or cause to be laid some white flower on the grave of Camilla O'Gorman, if the grave be, indeed, known + accessible? The Dictator had her shot, for what he called sacrilege; it is a fearful tale, but it led to his removal. It still moves men's hearts there a good deal: + I feel sure that Don Azpiri will not chafe at the task.

(John Masefield, letter to [Anne] Munro-Kerr, 8 March [1954])
(BL, Add.Mss.56625 ff.28–29)

Stirred to communicate certain reminiscences, Masefield wrote again to The Society of Authors:

Did I tell you that a descendant of Rosas came to see me about 30 years ago: a grandson, I think... He gave me the impression that one cannot but be proud of an ancestor with a real taste.

(John Masefield, letter to [Anne] Munro-Kerr, 20 March [1954])
(BL, Add.Mss.56625 ff.40–41)

Copies seen: Library of The John Masefield Society (Crocker Wight collection) stamped '606' and signed 'John Masefield.' on p.[1]; HRHRC (TEMP M377RO 1918) stamped '57' and signed 'John Masefield.' on p.[1]; HRHRC (AC-L M377RO 1918 cop.1) stamped '141' and signed 'John Masefield.' on p.[1]; HRHRC (AC-L M377RO 1918 cop.2) stamped '261' and signed 'John Masefield.' on p.[1]; HRHRC (AC-L M377RO 1918 cop.3) stamped '222' and signed 'John Masefield.' on p.[1]

A42(aa) First American edition – un-numbered issue (1918)

ROSAS | JOHN MASEFIELD | [ornament in red] | NEW YORK | THE MACMILLAN COMPANY | MDCCCCXVIII
(All width centred and enclosed within red ruled border: 110 × 85mm.)

Bibliographies: Danielson [unrecorded], Williams [noted on p.6], Simmons [39], Nevinson [unrecorded], Handley-Taylor p.41, Wight 39a

Collation: [A]⁹ ([A]2+1) [B-D]⁸ (but signed [A]⁸ B-C⁸ D⁹; see note on American electrotype editions); signatures left foot of page; 33 leaves; 175 × 124mm.; [1–8] 9–65 [66]

Page contents: [1–2] blank; [3] half-title: 'ROSAS'; [4] '[publisher's device] | THE MACMILLAN COMPANY | [two lines listing six cities, separated by four points] | MACMILLAN & CO., LIMITED | [two lines listing four cities, separated by two points] | THE MACMILLAN CO. OF CANADA, LTD. | [one city listed]'; [5] title-page; [6] 'COPYRIGHT, 1918, BY JOHN MASEFIELD | SET UP AND PRINTED. PUBLISHED APRIL, 1918 | NORWOOD PRESS: J. S. CUSHING COMPANY [point] BERWICK & SMITH CO. | NORWOOD, MASS., U.S.A.'; [7] 'ROSAS'; [8] blank; 9–65 text (at foot of p.65: '[rule] | Printed in the United States of America.'); [66] blank

Paper: wove paper: (watermark: '*Alexandra*')

Running title: 'ROSAS' (11mm.) on both verso and recto, pp.9–65

Binding: blue-green boards with vellum spine. On spine, reading lengthways up spine, from foot, in gold: 'ROSAS [device] MASEFIELD' (printed on black panel within single gold rule with ornaments at head and foot: 91 × 7mm.) On upper cover, in gold: 'ROSAS | [ornament] | JOHN MASEFIELD' (printed on black panel three sides of which are bordered by double ruled border; there is a gold half sun above the panel and gold foliage below: 80 × 62mm.) Lower cover: blank. Top edge trimmed, others roughly trimmed. Binding measurements: 178 × 123mm. (covers), 178 × 20mm. (spine). End-papers: wove paper: (watermark: '*Alexandra*').

Publication date: published, according to Simmons, 25 April 1918 in an edition of 960 copies (of which 750 numbered and signed). There were therefore 210 copies of this issue (see notes to A42(a))

Price: $1.50 (see notes to A42(a))

Contents:
as for A42(a)

Notes:
See notes to A42(a)

Copies seen: Library of The John Masefield Society (Peter Smith Collection) inscribed 'John Masefield.' and prefixed, in different ink 'Norah Havard | from'; Bodleian (Additional Masefield papers 8) inscribed 'John Masefield.' also inscribed on front free end-paper 'For My You's | collection. | The Story of Camilla, | first told to me, more | than 50 years ago, by | W.H. Hudson, in the | Mont Blanc Restaurant | in Soho, where the gang | used to lunch. | John Masefield. | (The poem is translated in | the Argentine). | It brought me into touch with | some of Rosas' descendants.'

A43 THE WAR AND THE FUTURE   1918

A43(a) First American edition (1918)

THE WAR AND THE | FUTURE | BY | JOHN MASEFIELD | Author of "Gallipoli," "The Everlasting Mercy," | "The Widow in the Bye Street," etc. | New York | THE MACMILLAN COMPANY | 1918 | *All rights reserved*
(All width centred)

Bibliographies: Danielson [unrecorded], Williams [unrecorded], Simmons [40], Nevinson [unrecorded], Handley-Taylor p.41, Wight [40]

Collation: [A-F]⁸ [G]⁹ ([G]8+1); 57 leaves; 190 × 125mm.; [i–x] 1–98 [99–104]

Page contents: [i] half-title: 'THE WAR AND THE | FUTURE'; [ii] '[publisher's device] | THE MACMILLAN COMPANY | [two lines listing six cities, separated by four points] | MACMILLAN & CO., LIMITED | [two lines listing four cities, separated by two points] | THE MACMILLAN CO. OF CANADA, LTD. | [one city listed]'; [iii] title-page; [iv] 'COPYRIGHT, 1918 | BY JOHN MASEFIELD | [rule] | Set up and electrotyped. Published, July, 1918'; [v] 'TO | THOMAS W. LAMONT'; [vi] blank; [vii] 'CONTENTS' (two items listed with page references); [viii] blank; [ix] 'ST. GEORGE AND THE DRAGON | A SPEECH FOR ST. GEORGE'S DAY, | APRIL 23RD, 1918'; [x] blank; 1–43 text of 'St. George and the Dragon'; 44–98 text of 'The War and the Future' (at foot of p.98: 'PRINTED IN THE UNITED STATES OF AMERICA'); [99] 'THE following pages contain advertisements of Mac- | millan books by the same author.' (within ruled border: 15 × 74mm.); [100] blank; [101–104] publisher's advertisements

Paper: wove paper

Running title: 'The War and the Future' (46mm.) on both verso and recto, pp.2–98

Binding: navy blue cloth. On spine, in gold: '[double rule] | THE WAR | AND | THE | FUTURE | [triangle] | JOHN | MASEFIELD | MACMILLAN | [double rule]' (all width centred). On upper cover, in gold: 'THE WAR | AND THE FUTURE | JOHN MASEFIELD' (within blind ruled border: 189 × 118mm.) Lower cover: blank. Top edge trimmed, others roughly trimmed. Binding measurements: 196 × 128mm. (covers), 196 × 30mm. (spine). End-papers: wove paper.

Publication date: published, according to Simmons, 27 August 1918 in an edition of 2138 copies

Price: $1.25

Contents:

St. George and the Dragon ('Friends, for a long time I did not know what to say to you...')
The War and the Future ('I have been sent to you, to speak about the war, and about the future...')

Notes:

The first speech is sub-titled 'A Speech for St. George's Day, April 23rd, 1918'. The second speech is sub-titled 'A Lecture Given in America January-May, 1918'

Masefield first met Florence Lamont (Mrs Thomas Lamont) on 28 February 1916 after delivering a speech on 'The Tragic Drama'. Her husband was, as described by Babington Smith, 'a leading figure in the great international banking house of J.P. Morgan' and they 'moved in a circle of diplomats, politicians, and literary and academic celebrities'. Masefield's friendship with the Lamont family lasted until the end of his life.

Wight notes that the text 'is identical to that in [*St. George and the Dragon* (see A47)]'. The two titles represent American and English publication. However, there are a number of minor differences (compare the opening of the first speech, for example). Wight's use of the word 'identical' might also suggest an identical type setting which is not the case. Note also the different dates provided for 'The War and the Future' lecture. In the American edition it is noted as given 'January-May, 1918' in the English edition it is cited as 'January to August, 1918'.

A publishing agreement for this volume between Masefield and Macmillan was dated 19 January 1917 (see Archives of The Society of Authors). The agreement refers to 'a licence to publish in volume form in the United States of America and Canada a work the subject or title of which is Two Studies of War (in prose)'. An agreement dated 22 April 1918 cites the correct title.

Copies seen: private collection (ROV); ULL (Special Collections)

A44 THE CAPTIVE OF THE SMUGGLERS   1918

A44(a) First American edition (1918)

The Captive | [double rule] OF [double rule] | The Smugglers | [double rule] | By | JOHN MASEFIELD | [double rule] | Illustrated | [publisher's device (of crest with 'SPE LABOR LEVIS') within a square intersecting a double rule] | THE PAGE COMPANY | BOSTON [ornament][ornament] MDCCCCXVIII
(Enclosed within ruled border: 130 × 72mm. Within border of circular devices and all within ruled border: 147 × 90mm. As a result of the double rules noted above, four rectangles are created measuring 39 × 72mm., 28 × 72mm., 27 × 72mm. and 30 × 72mm. respectively from the top. The double rules on either side of the word 'OF' do not touch the border).
(All width centred)

Bibliographies: Danielson [unrecorded], Williams [unrecorded], Simmons [noted on p.37], Nevinson [unrecorded], Handley-Taylor p.31, Wight 19b

Collation: [A-S]⁸ (J not used); 144 leaves; 192 × 132mm.; [i–viii] 1–269 [270–80]; illustrations (on glossy paper) tipped-in on pp.[ii], 31, 54, 77, 116, 152, 196 and 253

Page contents: [i] half-title: 'THE CAPTIVE OF | THE SMUGGLERS'; [ii] blank (with additional leaf tipped-in on the verso of which is the frontispiece: 116 × 95mm., '"HALF-A-DOZEN REDCOATS CAME AFT IN A RUSH" | (*See page 204*)' with protective tissue); [iii] title-page; [iv] 'First Impression, September, 1918 | PRESSWORK BY | THE COLONIAL PRESS | C. H. SIMONDS

CO., BOSTON, U. S. A.'; [v–vi] 'CONTENTS' (27 chapters listed with titles and page references); [vii] 'LIST OF ILLUSTRATIONS' (eight illustrations listed with titles and page references); [viii] blank; 1–269 text; [270] blank; [271–80] publisher's advertisement

Paper: wove paper

Running title: 'THE CAPTIVE OF THE SMUGGLERS' (67mm.) on verso; recto title comprises chapter title, pp.2–269

Binding: light green cloth. On spine: '[rule] | *The* [in red] | CAPTIVE [in red] | of the [in red] | SMUGGLERS [in red] | [triangular ornament] | JOHN [in red] | MASEFIELD [in red] | [rule] | PAGE [in red] | [rule] [in red] | BOSTON [in red] | [rule]' (all width centred). On upper cover, in red: '*The* CAPTIVE of the | SMUGGLERS | [illustration in black, white, red, green and light green of boy on deck with pirates and smoking canon all within ruled border in black: 137 × 99mm.] | *By* JOHN MASEFIELD' (all width centred) (within ruled border in black: 190 × 128mm.) (there is a superscripted horizontal line in red above the '*y*' of '*By*'). Lower cover: blank. All edges trimmed. Binding measurements: 198 × 135mm. (covers), 198 × 51mm. (spine). End-papers: wove paper.

Publication date: published, according to Simmons, in 1918

Price: $1.50

Contents:
The Captive of the Smugglers ('I was born in the year 1800, in the town of Newnham-on-Severn…')

Chapter headings are as follows:

I. Early Recollections
II. My New Home
III. The Night Riders
IV. I find Mrs. Cottier
V. The Return of Nigger
VI. The Man on the Barrow
VII. The Hut in the Gorse
VIII. Home Again
IX. Mr. Gorsuch Again
X. I Warn Marah
XI. The Smugglers' Cave
XII. An Attempted Rescue
XIII. I am a Prisoner
XIV. I Become a Smuggler
XV. A Narrow Escape
XVI. We Land a Cargo
XVII. Pursued by the Preventives
XVIII. We Make our Escape
XIX. The Fate of a Traitor
XX. A Surprise Attack
XXI. Safe on Shore
XXII. The Blue Boar Inn
XXIII. A New Hiding-Place
XXIV. On the Road to London
XXV. Another Narrow Escape
XXVI. A Guest of the Gypsies
XXVII. Home Again

Notes:
In this edition the dedication (to Judith Masefield) is omitted. The illustrator is unacknowledged.

The division of chapters does not follow that of the first English edition (see A20(a)).

Simmons states publication by 'L.C. Page and Company, Boston'.

Wight notes the cloth binding as 'grey cloth'.

The italics used on the binding contain a number of swash characters.

Copies seen: NYPL (Berg Collection)

Reprinted:

'Second Impression'	[first edition, second impression]	Jul 1926
'Third Impression'	[first edition, third impression]	Mar 1927

A45 THE POEMS AND PLAYS OF JOHN MASEFIELD 1918

A45(a) First American edition (1918)

VOLUME ONE
THE | POEMS AND PLAYS OF | JOHN MASEFIELD | VOLUME ONE | POEMS | New York | THE MACMILLAN COMPANY | 1918 | *All rights reserved*
(All width centred)

Bibliographies: Danielson [unrecorded], Williams [unrecorded], Simmons [unrecorded], Nevinson [unrecorded], Handley-Taylor p.41, Wight [unrecorded]

Collation: [A-LL]⁸ (J, V, W and JJ not used); 272 leaves; 193 × 127mm.; [two un-numbered pages] [i–iv] v–ix [x] xi–xiv [1–2] 3–55 [56–58] 59–116 [117–20] 121–76 [177–78] 179–248 [249–50] 251–320 [321–22] 323–401 [402–404] 405–463 [464–66] 467–94 [495–96] 497–521 [522–28]

Page contents: [–] blank (page excluded from page count, but constitutes first leaf of first gathering); [–] blank; [i] 'THE POEMS AND PLAYS OF | JOHN MASEFIELD | [rule] | POEMS'; [ii] '[publisher's device] | THE MACMILLAN COMPANY | [two lines listing six cities, separated by four points] | MACMILLAN & CO., LIMITED | [two lines listing four cities, separated by two points]

| THE MACMILLAN CO. OF CANADA, LTD. | [one city listed]'; [iii] title-page (with additional leaf tipped-in on the verso of which is the frontispiece: 112 × 87mm., 'John Masefield' [facsimile signature], at foot: 'Photograph by Eugene Hutchinson, Chicago.'); [iv] 'COPYRIGHT, 1913 | BY HARPER AND BROTHERS | COPYRIGHT 1914 | BY THE CENTURY COMPANY AND | BY THE MCCLURE PUBLICATIONS | COPYRIGHT, 1912, 1913, 1914 | BY THE MACMILLAN COMPANY | COPYRIGHT, 1911, 1913, 1917, 1918 BY JOHN MASEFIELD | [rule] | Collected Edition. Set up and electrotyped. Published Novomber, 1918.' [*sic*]; v–ix 'PREFACE' ('I do not remember writing verses in my childhood; I made many but did not write them down.') (signed, 'JOHN MASEFIELD.'); [x] blank; xi–xiv 'CONTENTS' (115 individual items from nine original American volumes listed with page references); [1] 'SALT-WATER BALLADS'; [2] 'Some of this book was written in my boyhood, all of it | in my youth; it is now reissued, much as it was when | first published nearly eleven years ago. J.M. | 9*th* June, 1913'; 3–55 text of *Salt-Water Ballads*; [56] blank; [57] 'MISCELLANEOUS POEMS | (FROM "THE STORY OF A ROUND HOUSE")'; [58] blank; 59–116 text of 'Miscellaneous Poems'; [117] 'THE EVERLASTING MERCY'; [118] blank; [119] 'TO MY WIFE'; [120] '*Thy place is biggyd above the sterrys cleer, | Noon erthely paleys wrouhte in so statly wyse, | Com on my freend, my brothir moost enteer, | For the I offryd my blood in sacrifise.* | JOHN LYDGATE.'; 121–76 text of *The Everlasting Mercy* (at foot of p.176: 'NOTE | "The Everlasting Mercy" first appeared in *The English | Review* for October, 1911. I thank the Editor and Proprietors | of that paper for permitting me to reprint it here. The persons | and events described in the poem are entirely imaginary, and | no reference is made or intended to any living person. | JOHN MASEFIELD.'; [177] 'THE WIDOW IN THE BYE STREET'; [178] blank; 179–248 text of *The Widow in the Bye Street*; [249] 'DAUBER'; [250] blank; 251–320 text of *Dauber* (including 'EXPLANATIONS OF SOME OF THE SEA TERMS USED IN THE POEM'); [321] 'THE DAFFODIL FIELDS'; [322] blank; 323–401 text of *The Daffodil Fields*; [402] blank; [403] 'SONNETS AND OTHER POEMS'; [404] 'Some few of these sonnets appeared serially in the *Atlantic | Monthly, Scribner's Magazine, Harper's Monthly*, and (perhaps) | in one or two other papers. I thank the Editors of these papers | for permission to reprint them here. | JOHN MASEFIELD. | London, 16th Dec. 1915.'; 405–463 text of *Sonnets and other poems*; [464] '*The River* was first published in the *Century Magazine; The | Wanderer* in *Harper's Magazine; Watching by a Sick-bed* and | *August, 1914*, in *Harper's Weekly*. I thank the editors of these | periodicals for permission to reprint them here. | JOHN MASEFIELD.'; [465] 'LOLLINGDON DOWNS AND OTHER POEMS'; [466] blank; 467–94 text of *Lollingdon Downs and other poems*; [495] 'ROSAS'; [496] blank; 497–521 text of *Rosas* (on p.521: 'Printed in the United States of America'); [522] blank; [523] 'THE following pages contain advertisements of | Macmillan books by the same author' (within ruled border: 15 × 85mm.); [524–28] publisher's advertisements

Paper: wove paper

Running title: on verso generally comprises title of original volume of publication; on recto the name of the poem appears or the title of the original volume is repeated, pp.5–521

Binding: dark-blue cloth. On spine, in gold: '[double rule] | COLLECTED | POEMS | JOHN | MASEFIELD | MACMILLAN | [double rule]' (all width centred). On upper cover, in gold: design of three-masted ship at sea with clouds and birds, enclosed within circular double ruled border, diameter: 55mm. (within ornate blind double ruled border: 192 × 121mm. with anchor at each corner). Lower cover: blank. All edges trimmed. Binding measurements: 198 × 129mm. (covers), 198 × 39mm. (spine). End-papers: wove paper.

Publication date: published, according to Handley-Taylor, 5 December 1918

Price: $2.50

Contents:
Preface ('I do not remember writing verses in my childhood; I made many but did not write…')
SALT-WATER BALLADS
A Consecration ('Not of the princes and prelates with periwigged charioteers')
The Yarn of The "Loch Achray" ('The "Loch Achray" was a clipper tall')
Sing a Song O' Shipwreck ('He lolled on a bollard, a sun-burned son of the sea,')
Burial Party ('"He's deader 'n nails," the fo'c's'le said, "'n' gone to his long sleep;"')
Bill ('He lay dead on the cluttered deck and stared at the cold skies,')
Fever Ship ('There'll be no weepin' gells ashore when *our* ship sails,')
Fever-Chills ('He tottered out of the alleyway with cheeks the colour of paste,')
One of The Bo'sun's Yarns ('Loafin' around in Sailor Town, a-bluin' o' my advance,')
Hell's Pavement ('"When I'm discharged in Liverpool 'n' draws my bit o' pay,')
Sea-Change ('"Goneys an' gullies an' all o' the birds o' the sea,')
Harbour-Bar ('All in the feathered palm-tree tops the bright green parrots screech,')
The Turn of the Tide ('An' Bill can have my sea-boots, Nigger Jim can have my knife,')
One of Wally's Yarns ('The watch was up on the topsail-yard a-making fast the sail,')
A Valediction (Liverpool Docks) ('Is there anything as I can do ashore for you')
A Night at Dago Tom's ('Oh yesterday, I t'ink it was, while cruisin' down the street,')
Port of Many Ships ('"It's a sunny pleasant anchorage, is Kingdom Come,')
Cape Horn Gospel – I ('"I was in a hooker once," said Karlssen,')
Cape Horn Gospel – II ('Jake was a dirty Dago lad, an' he gave the skipper chin,')
Mother Carey ('Mother Carey? She's the mother o' the witches')
Evening – Regatta Day ('Your nose is a red jelly, your mouth's a toothless wreck,')
A Valediction ('We're bound for blue water where the great winds blow,')
A Pier-Head Chorus ('Oh I'll be chewing salted horse and biting flinty bread,')

The Golden City of St. Mary ('Out beyond the sunset, could I but find the way,')
Trade Winds ('In the harbour, in the island, in the Spanish Seas,')
Sea-Fever ('I must go down to the seas again, to the lonely sea and the sky,')
A Wanderer's Song ('A wind's in the heart of me, a fire's in my heels,')
Cardigan Bay ('Clean, green, windy billows notching out the sky,')
Christmas Eve at Sea ('A wind is rustling "south and soft,"')
A Ballad of Cape St. Vincent ('Now, Bill, ain't it prime to be a-sailin',')
The Tarry Buccaneer ('I'm going to be a pirate with a bright brass pivot-gun,')
A Ballad of John Silver ('We were schooner-rigged and rakish, with a long and lissome hull,')
Lyrics from "The Buccaneer"
I. ('We are far from sight of the harbour lights,')
II. ('There's a sea-way somewhere where all day long')
III. ('The toppling rollers at the harbour mouth')
D'Avalos' Prayer ('When the last sea is sailed and the last shallow charted,')
The West Wind ('It's a warm wind, the west wind, full of birds' cries;')
The Galley-Rowers ('Staggering over the running combers')
Sorrow of Mydath ('Weary the cry of the wind is, weary the sea,')
Vagabond ('Dunno a heap about the what an' why,')
Vision ('I have drunken the red wine and flung the dice;')
Spunyarn ('Spunyarn, spunyarn, with one to turn the crank,')
The Dead Knight ('The cleanly rush of the mountain air,')
Personal ('Tramping at night in the cold and wet, I passed the lighted inn,')
On Malvern Hill ('A wind is brushing down the clover,')
Tewkesbury Road ('It is good to be out on the road, and going one knows not where,')
On Eastnor Knoll ('Silent are the woods, and the dim green boughs are')
"Rest Her Soul, She's Dead" ('She has done with the sea's sorrow and the world's way')
"All Ye That Pass By" ('On the long dusty ribbon of the long city street,')
In Memory of A.P.R. ('Once in the windy wintry weather,')
To-Morrow ('Oh yesterday the cutting edge drank thirstily and deep,')
Cavalier ('All the merry kettle-drums are thudding into rhyme,')
A Song at Parting ('The tick of the blood is settling slow, my heart will soon be still,')
Glossary ('*Abaft the beam.*—That half of a ship included between her amidship section…')
MISCELLANEOUS POEMS (FROM "THE STORY OF A ROUND HOUSE")
Biography ('When I am buried, all my thoughts and acts')
Ships ('I cannot tell their wonder nor make known')
Truth ('Man with his burning soul')
They Closed Her Eyes From the Spanish of Don Gustavo A. Bécquer [*sic*] ('They closed her eyes,')
The Harp From the Spanish of Don Gustavo A. Bécquer [*sic*] ('In a dark corner of the room,')
Sonnet From the Spanish of Don Francisco De Quevedo [*sic*] ('I saw the ramparts of my native land,')
Sonnet on the Death of His Wife From the Portuguese of Antonio De Ferreiro [*sic*] ('That blessed sunlight that once showed to me')
Song ('One sunny time in May')
The Ballad of Sir Bors ('Would I could win some quiet and rest, and a little ease,')
Spanish Waters ('Spanish waters, Spanish waters, you are ringing in my ears,')
Cargoes ('Quinquireme of Nineveh from distant Ophir,')
Captain Stratton's Fancy ('Oh some are fond of red wine, and some are fond of white,')
An Old Song Re-sung ('I saw a ship a-sailing, a-sailing, a-sailing,')
St. Mary's Bells ('It's pleasant in Holy Mary')
London Town ('Oh London Town's a fine town, and London sights are rare,')
The Emigrant ('Going by Daly's shanty I heard the boys within')
Port of Holy Peter ('The blue laguna rocks and quivers,')
Beauty ('I have seen dawn and sunset on moors and windy hills')
The Seekers ('Friends and loves we have none, nor wealth nor blessed abode,')
Prayer ('When the last sea is sailed, when the last shallow's charted,')
Dawn ('The dawn comes cold: the haystack smokes,')
Laugh and Be Merry ('Laugh and be merry, remember, better the world with a song,')
June Twilight ('The twilight comes; the sun')
Roadways ('One road leads to London,')
Midsummer Night ('The perfect disc of the sacred moon')
The Harper's Song ('This sweetness trembling from the strings')
The Gentle Lady ('So beautiful, so dainty-sweet,')
The Dead Knight ('The cleanly rush of the mountain air,')
Sorrow of Mydath ('Weary the cry of the wind is, weary the sea,')

Twilight ('Twilight it is, and the far woods are dim, and the rooks cry and call.')
Invocation ('O wanderer into many brains,')
Posted as Missing ('Under all her topsails she trembled like a stag,')
A Creed ('I hold that when a person dies')
When Bony Death ('When bony Death has chilled her gentle blood,')
Her Heart ('Her heart is always doing lovely things,')
Being her Friend ('Being her friend, I do not care, not I,')
Fragments ('Troy Town is covered up with weeds,')
Born for Nought Else ('Born for nought else, for nothing but for this,')
Tewkesbury Road ('It is good to be out on the road, and going one knows not where,')
The Death Rooms ('My soul has many an old decaying room')
Ignorance ('Since I have learned Love's shining alphabet,')
The Watch in the Wood ('When Death has laid her in his quietude,')
C.L.M. ('In the dark womb where I began')
Waste ('No rose but fades: no glory but must pass:')
Third Mate ('All the sheets are clacking, all the blocks are whining,')
The Wild Duck ('Twilight. Red in the west.')
Christmas, 1903 ('O, the sea breeze will be steady, and the tall ship's going trim,')
The Word ('My friend, my bonny friend, when we are old,')
THE EVERLASTING MERCY
The Everlasting Mercy ('From '41 to '51')
THE WIDOW IN THE BYE STREET
The Widow in the Bye Street ('Down Bye Street, in a little Shropshire town,')
DAUBER
Dauber ('Four bells were struck, the watch was called on deck,')
Explanations of some of the sea terms used in the poem (*Backstays.*–Wire ropes which support...')
THE DAFFODIL FIELDS
The Daffodil Fields ('Between the barren pasture and the wood')
SONNETS AND OTHER POEMS
[Untitled] ('Long long ago, when all the glittering earth')
[Untitled] ('Night came again, but now I could not sleep.')
[Untitled] ('Even after all these years there comes the dream')
[Untitled] ('If I could come again to that dear place')
[Untitled] ('Men are made human by the mighty fall')
[Untitled] ('Here in the self is all that man can know')
[Untitled] ('Flesh, I have knocked at many a dusty door,')
[Untitled] ('But all has passed, the tune has died away,')
[Untitled] ('These myriad days, these many thousand hours,')
[Untitled] ('There, on the darkened deathbed, dies the brain')
[Untitled] ('So in the empty sky the stars appear,')
[Untitled] ('It may be so with us, that in the dark,')
[Untitled] ('Man has his unseen friend, his unseen twin,')
[Untitled] ('What am I, Life? A thing of watery salt')
[Untitled] ('If I could get within this changing I,')
[Untitled] ('What is this atom which contains the whole,')
[Untitled] ('Ah, we are neither heaven nor earth, but men;')
[Untitled] ('Roses are beauty, but I never see')
[Untitled] ('Over the church's door they moved a stone')
[Untitled] ('I never see the red rose crown the year,')
[Untitled] ('Out of the clouds come torrents, from the earth')
[Untitled] ('O little self, within whose smallness lies')
[Untitled] ('I went into the fields, but you were there')
[Untitled] ('There are two forms of life, of which one moves,')
[Untitled] ('Restless and hungry, still it moves and slays')
[Untitled] ('How many ways, how many different times')
[Untitled] ('The other form of Living does not stir;')
[Untitled] ('Is there a great green commonwealth of Thought')
[Untitled] ('Beauty, let be; I cannot see your face,')
[Untitled] ('Here, where we stood together, we three men,')
[Untitled] ('I saw her like a shadow on the sky')
[Untitled] ('Not that the stars are all gone mad in heaven')
[Untitled] ('There is no God, as I was taught in youth,')

[Untitled] ('Beauty retires; the blood out of the earth')
[Untitled] ('Wherever beauty has been quick in clay')
[Untitled] ('You are more beautiful than women are,')
[Untitled] ('Out of the barracks to the castle yard')
[Untitled] ('Not for the anguish suffered is the slur,')
[Untitled] ('Beauty was with me once, but now, grown old,')
[Untitled] ('So beauty comes, so with a failing hand')
[Untitled] ('If Beauty be at all, if, beyond sense,')
[Untitled] ('Each greedy self, by consecrating lust,')
[Untitled] ('Time being an instant in eternity,')
[Untitled] ('You will remember me in days to come')
[Untitled] ('They took the bloody body from the cross,')
[Untitled] ('"Come to us fiery with the saints of God')
[Untitled] ('So from the cruel cross they buried God;')
[Untitled] ('If all be governed by the moving stars,')
[Untitled] ('In emptiest furthest heaven where no stars are')
[Untitled] ('Perhaps in chasms of the wasted past,')
[Untitled] ('For, like an outcast from the city, I')
[Untitled] ('Death lies in wait for you, you wild thing in the wood,')
[Untitled] ('What are we given, what do we take away?')
[Untitled] ('They called that broken hedge The Haunted Gate.')
[Untitled] ('There was an evil in the nodding wood')
[Untitled] ('Go, spend your penny, Beauty, when you will,')
[Untitled] ('Not for your human beauty nor the power')
[Untitled] ('The little robin hopping in the wood')
[Untitled] ('Though in life's streets the tempting shops have lured,')
[Untitled] ('When all these million cells that are my slaves')
[Untitled] ('Let that which is to come be as it may,')
The Madman's Song ('You have not seen what I have seen,')
The "Wanderer" ('All day they loitered by the resting ships,')
August, 1914 ('How still this quiet cornfield is to-night!')
The River ('All other waters have their time of peace,')
Watching by a Sick-Bed ('I heard the wind all day,')
LOLLINGDON DOWNS AND OTHER POEMS
I. ('So I have known this life,')
II. ('O wretched man, that, for a little mile')
III. ('Out of the special cell's most special sense')
IV. ('You are the link which binds us each to each.')
V. ('I could not sleep for thinking of the sky,')
VI. ('How did the nothing come, how did these fires,')
VII. ('It may be so; but let the unknown be.')
VIII. ('The Kings go by with jewelled crowns,')
IX. ('What is this life which uses living cells')
X. ('Can it be blood and brain, this transient force')
XI. ('Not only blood and brain its servants are,')
XII. ('Drop me the seed, that I, even in my brain')
XIII. ('Ah, but Without there is no spirit scattering;')
XIV. ('You are too beautiful for mortal eyes,')
XV. ('Is it a sea on which the souls embark')
XVI. The Blacksmith ('The blacksmith in his sparky forge')
XVII. The Frontier ('COTTA | Would God the route would come for home.')
XVIII. ('Night is on the downland, on the lonely moorland,')
XIX. Midnight ('The fox came up by Stringer's Pound,')
XX. ('Up on the downs the red-eyed kestrels hover')
XXI. ('No man takes the farm,')
XXII. ('A hundred years ago, they quarried for the stone here;')
XXIII. ('Here the legion halted, here the ranks were broken,')
XXIV. ('We danced away care till the fiddler's eyes blinked,')
ROSAS
Rosas ('There was an old lord in the Argentine,')

Copies seen: private collection (PWE); BL (X.908/6623) stamped 15 JUL 1963

VOLUME TWO

THE | POEMS AND PLAYS OF | JOHN MASEFIELD | VOLUME TWO | PLAYS | New York | THE MACMILLAN COMPANY | 1918 | *All rights reserved*
(All width centred)

Bibliographies: Danielson [unrecorded], Williams [unrecorded], Simmons [unrecorded], Nevinson [unrecorded], Handley-Taylor p.41, Wight [unrecorded]

Collation: [A-SS]⁸ (J, V, W and JJ not used); 328 leaves; 193 × 127mm.; [i–iv] v–vii [viii] ix [x] [1–2] 3–40 [41–42] 43–59 [60–62] 63–118 [119–20] 121–41 [142–43] 144 [145–46] 147–260 [261–64] 265 [266] 267–375 [376–79] 380–528 [529–32] 533–80 [581–84] 585–640 [641–46]

Page contents: [i] half-title: 'THE POEMS AND PLAYS OF | JOHN MASEFIELD | [rule] | PLAYS'; [ii] '[publisher's device] | THE MACMILLAN COMPANY | [two lines listing six cities, separated by four points] | MACMILLAN & CO., LIMITED | [two lines listing four cities, separated by two points] | THE MACMILLAN CO. OF CANADA, LTD. | [one city listed]'; [iii] title-page; [iv] 'COPYRIGHT, 1914 | BY THE MACMILLAN COMPANY | COPYRIGHT, 1909, 1910, 1914, 1915, 1916, 1918 | BY JOHN MASEFIELD | Set up and elecrotyped. Published November, 1918.'; v–vii 'PREFACE' ('The first of the plays in this volume, *The Campden Wonder*, was written at Greenwich...') (signed, 'JOHN MASEFIELD.'); [viii] blank; ix 'CONTENTS' (nine individual items listed with page references); [x] blank; [1] 'THE CAMPDEN WONDER'; [2] 'THE CAMPDEN WONDER | PERSONS | [dramatis personae and original cast listed with 'PLAYED BY' heading] | *This play was produced at the Court Theatre, in London, on the 8th of* | *January, 1907, under the direction of Mr. H. Granville Barker.*'; 3–40 text of 'The Campden Wonder'; [41] 'MRS. HARRISON'; [42] 'MRS. HARRISON | PERSONS | [dramatis personae listed]'; 43–59 text of 'Mrs. Harrison'; [60] blank; [61] 'THE LOCKED CHEST | A PLAY IN ONE ACT | (From a Tale in the Laxdaelasaga)'; [62] 'PERSONS | [dramatis personae listed] | SCENE | *Iceland*'; 63–118 text of 'The Locked Chest' (at foot of p.118: '*Written in 1906.*'); [119] 'THE SWEEPS OF NINETY-EIGHT'; [120] blank; 121–41 text of 'The Sweeps of Ninety-Eight' (at foot of p.141: '*Written in 1905.*'); [142] blank; [143] 'THE TRAGEDY OF NAN'; 144 author's note ('Tragedy at its best is a vision of the heart of life...') (signed, 'JOHN MASEFIELD. | *4th April, 1911.*'); [145] 'TO | W. B. YEATS'; [146] 'THE TRAGEDY OF NAN | [dramatis personae and original cast listed with 'PERSONS' and 'PLAYED BY' headings] | *This play was produced by the Pioneers at the New Royalty Theatre, on* | *24th May, 1908, under the direction of Mr. H. Granville Barker. At its revival* | *as a matinee at the Haymarket Theatre, in June, 1908, the part of the Rev. Mr.* | *Drew was played by Mr. Cecil Brooking.*'; 147–260 text of 'The Tragedy of Nan'; [261] 'THE TRAGEDY OF POMPEY | THE GREAT'; [262] blank; [263] 'TO | MY WIFE'; [264] 'ARGUMENT | In the years 50 and 49 B. C., Cneius Pompeius Magnus, the | head of the patrician party, contested with C. Julius Cæsar, the | popular leader, for supreme power in the State. Their jealousy | led to the troubles of the Civil War, in which, after many bat- | tles, Cneius Pompeius Magnus was miserably killed. | ACT I. The determination of Pompeius to fight with his | rival, then marching upon Rome. | ACT II. The triumph of Pompey's generalship at Dyrrach- | ium. His overthrow by the generals of his staff. His de- | feat at Pharsalia. | ACT III. The death of that great ruler on the seashore of | Pelusium in Egypt.'; 265 'PERSONS | [dramatis personae listed, also table of act, scene and historical time]'; [266] blank; 267–371 text of 'The Tragedy of Pompey the Great'; 372–75 'NOTES' (paragraphs titled 'ON THE APPEARANCE OF POMPEY', 'ON THE FATE OF THE PERSONS IN THIS TRAGEDY' and 'ON THE HOUSE OF POMPEY, AFTER THE MURDER'); [376] verse ('And all their passionate hearts are dust,') dated on left margin '*Feb. 8, 1908.*' and on extreme right '*July 5, 1909.*'; [377] 'THE FAITHFUL | A TRAGEDY IN THREE ACTS'; [378] blank; [379] 'To | MY WIFE | THIS BOOK IS AFFECTIONATELY INSCRIBED'; 380 'NOTE: This play is written to be played uninterruptedly, with | out more break in the action than is necessary to get the actors off | the stage and to raise the screen or curtain dividing the scenes. | [new paragraph] There are only two scenes: one the front part of the stage, | left quite bare, without decoration, but with a screen, set, or | backcloth at the back, representing a Japanese landscape, with | hills and water, all wintry and severe; the other, the back of the | stage, visible when this screen is lifted, a room in a Japanese | palace, very beautiful, but bare, save for a few flowers and a | picture or two. | [new paragraph] A few minutes may elapse between Acts I and II, and a | slightly longer wait between Acts II and III. | PERSONS | [dramatis personae listed] | In Act I, Scene I, throughout Act II, and in Scenes I, II, and | IV of Act III, the scene is: An open space near ASANO'S palace. | In Act I, Scene II and in Act III, Scene III, the scene is: A | room in Kira's palace. | TIME: Acts I and II, 10th March, 1701. | Act III, 10th March, 1702.'; 381–528 text of 'The Faithful'; [529] 'PHILIP THE KING | A PLAY IN ONE ACT'; [530] blank; [531] 'TO | MY WIFE'; [532] '[dramatis personae listed with 'PERSONS' and 'SPIRITS' headings] | TIME | At dawn in late September, 1588 | SCENE | A little dark cell in Philip's palace'; 533–80 text of 'Philip the King'; [581] 'GOOD FRIDAY | A DRAMATIC POEM'; [582] 'PERSONS | [dramatis personae listed]'; [583] 'THE SCENE | *The Pavement, or Paved Court, outside the Roman Citadel in* | *Jerusalem. At the back is the barrack wall, pierced in the* | *centre with a double bronze door, weathered to a green color.* | *On the right and left sides of the stage are battlemented parapets* | *overlooking the city. The stage or pavement is approached by* | *stone steps from the front, and by narrow stone staircases in* | *the wings, one on each side, well forward. These steps are to* | *suggest that the citadel is high up above the town, and that the* | *main barrack gate is below.* THE CHIEF CITIZEN, THE RAB- | BLE, JOSEPH, THE MADMAN, HEROD, *and* THE LOITERERS, | *etc., enter by these steps.* PILATE, PROCULA, LONGINUS, THE | SOLDIERS *and* SERVANTS *enter by the bronze doors.*'; [584] blank; 585–640 text of 'Good Friday' (at foot of p.640: 'Printed in the United States of America'); [641] 'THE following pages contain advertisements of | Macmillan books by the same author' (within ruled border: 16 × 85mm.); [642–46] publisher's advertisements

Paper: wove paper

Running title: comprise titles of plays on both verso and recto, pp.4–640

Binding: dark-blue cloth. On spine, in gold: '[double rule] | COLLECTED | PLAYS | JOHN | MASEFIELD | MACMILLAN | [double rule]' (all width centred). On upper cover, in gold: design of three-masted ship at sea with clouds and birds, enclosed within circular double ruled border, diameter: 55mm. (within ornate blind double ruled border: 194 × 122mm. with anchor at each corner). Lower cover: blank. All edges trimmed. Binding measurements: 198 × 129mm. (covers), 198 × 45mm. (spine). End-papers: wove paper.

Publication date: published, according to Handley-Taylor, 5 December 1918

Price: $2.50

Contents:
Preface ('The first of the plays in this volume, *The Campden Wonder*, was written at Greenwich...')
The Campden Wonder ('SCENE I | SCENE. *Harrison's Kitchen in Campden.* | JOAN | Be the master come home...')
Mrs. Harrison ('SCENE: *A Room in* MRS. HARRISON'S *House.* | MRS. H. | There's your cider. Take it...')
The Locked Chest ('SCENE: *A room. A chest used as a bench. A table, etc.* VIGDIS *embroidering...*')
The Sweeps of Ninety-Eight ('SCENE: *An inn at Dunleary. A parlour.* TIGER ROCHE, *an old, well-preserved...*')
The Tragedy of Nan ('ACT I | SCENE: *A Kitchen in the house of a small tenant farmer at Broad Oak, on Severn...*')
The Tragedy of Pompey the Great ('ACT I | *A room in* POMPEY'S *house near Rome. Walls hung with...*')
The Faithful ('ACT I | SCENE I.-*The outer scene.* ASANO *alone, dawn. A shaft of light...*')
Philip the King ('PHILIP | [*Kneeling*] Lord, I am that Philip whom Thou hast made King of half...')
Good Friday ('PILATE | Longinus. | LONGINUS | Lord. | PILATE | [*Giving scroll.*] Your warrant...')

Notes:
Page numbers appear within square brackets. Thus, [3], [4], etc.

Each volume was available separately.

A publishing agreement for this title between Masefield and Macmillan was dated 16 March 1916 (see Archives of The Society of Authors). The agreement refers to 'a licence to publish in volume form in the United States of America a work the subject or title of which is a Collected Edition of the Authors Poems and Plays'.

It was presumably with reference to a copy of this volume that C.S. Evans wrote to Masefield in January 1925:

> I was looking last night at Macmillan's Collected Edition of your Plays. Would it be possible for us to do the same thing here, and so carry the consolidation of your work one step further? A number of the plays are, of course, already published by us, but I suppose the feasibility of my idea depends upon whether you have provided in your agreements with other publishers that the plays can be included in a collected edition. If we can do it, I am sure it will be the right thing to do.
> (C.S. Evans, letter to John Masefield, 23 January 1925)
> (HRHRC, MS (Masefield, J.) Recip William Heinemann Ltd.)

It was not until 1937 with publication of *Plays* in the 'Wanderer edition' (see A120) that Evans' plan was realised.

Copies seen: BL (X.908/6623) stamped 30 JUN 1963

A46 A POEM AND TWO PLAYS   1918

A46(a) *First English edition (1918)*

A POEM | AND TWO PLAYS | BY | JOHN MASEFIELD | [publisher's device of a windmill with 'W [point]' and 'H' all within ruled border: 15 × 15mm.] | LONDON | WILLIAM HEINEMANN
(All width centred)

Bibliographies: Danielson 193, Williams p.6, Simmons [41], Nevinson p.13, Handley-Taylor p.41, Wight [41]

Collation: [A]⁸ (±[A]3) (see notes) B-K⁸ (J not used); signatures right foot of page; 80 leaves; 182 × 121mm.; [two un-numbered pages] [i–iv] v [vi] [1–2] 3–39 [40–42] 43–120 [121–22] 123–51 [152]

Page contents: [-] blank (page excluded from page count, but constitutes first leaf of first gathering); [-] blank; [i] half-title: 'A POEM AND TWO PLAYS'; [ii] 'BY THE SAME AUTHOR | [rule] | *Uniform with this Volume* | [nine titles listed] | LONDON : WILLIAM HEINEMANN'; [iii] title-page; [iv] 'LONDON: WILLIAM HEINEMANN. 1919'; v 'CONTENTS' (three items listed with page references); [vi] blank; [1] 'ROSAS'; [2] blank; 3–39 text of 'Rosas'; [40] blank; [41] 'THE LOCKED CHEST | A PLAY IN ONE ACT | *(From a Tale in the Laxdaelasaga)*'; [42] 'PERSONS | [dramatis personae listed] | SCENE: *Iceland*'; 43–120 text of 'The Locked Chest' (at foot of p.120: '*Written in 1906.*'); [121] 'THE | SWEEPS OF NINETY-EIGHT'; [122] blank; 123-[152] text of 'The Sweeps of Ninety-Eight' (at foot of p.[152]: '*Written in 1905.* | [rule] | BILLING AND SONS, LTD., PRINTERS, GUILDFORD, ENGLAND')

Paper: wove paper

Running title: constitute poem or play title, pp.4-[152]

Binding: blue cloth. On spine, in gold: 'A Poem | and | Two | Plays | [ornament] | John | Masefield | HEINEMANN' (all width centred). Covers blank with blind ruled borders: 182 × 116mm. All edges trimmed. Binding measurements: 188 × 122mm. (covers), 188 × 24mm. (spine). End-papers: wove paper.

Publication date: published, according to Simmons, 15 December 1918 in an edition of 3000 copies. The sales ledger preserved in the Heinemann Archive suggests publication on 18 December 1918 in an edition of 3000 copies.

Price: 5s.

Contents:
Rosas ('There was an old lord in the Argentine,')
The Locked Chest ('SCENE: *A room. A chest used as a bench. A table, etc.* VIGDIS *embroidering a cloth.*')
The Sweeps of Ninety-Eight ('SCENE: *An inn at Dunleary. A parlour.* TIGER ROCHE, *an old, well-preserved...*')

Notes:
A volume comprising the first printing of *Rosas* in England. The two plays are 'The Locked Chest' and 'The Sweeps of Ninety-Eight', both previously published in England (see A33).

The cancel title (not present in all copies) suggests that the volume was originally given a different title. Nevinson specifically stresses the discrepancy between the date of publication and that given on p.[iv]. He notes 'although dated 1919 this volume was actually published on December 18th, 1918'. (This date is present in the sales ledger preserved in the Heinemann Archive). The copy Masefield inscribed to his wife on 23 December 1918 includes the 1919 printed date.

The publishing agreement for this title (and *St. George and the Dragon*) between Masefield and Heinemann was dated 26 October 1918 (see Archives of The Society of Authors). The agreement refers to a publication price of 5s. for each title.

A dramatis personae listing for 'The Sweeps of Ninety-Eight' is omitted. The scene is, however, indicated before the text of the play commences.

The lettering of 'HEINEMANN' on the spine is not always successful on all copies inspected. The tendency is for the lettering to be at an angle with the consequence that 'MANN' is indistinct.

Copies seen: private collection (PWE) cancel title; private collection (ROV) bookplate of Arnold Bennett; Columbia University Libraries (Special Collections B825.M377.U57.1919.c.2) cancel title, inscribed 'for Con | from Jan. | 23. XII. 1918.', includes posthumous booklabel

A47 ST. GEORGE AND THE DRAGON 1919

A47(a) First English edition (1919)

ST. GEORGE AND | THE DRAGON | BY | JOHN MASEFIELD | [publisher's device of a windmill with 'W [point]' and 'H' all within ruled border: 15 × 15mm.] | LONDON | WILLIAM HEINEMANN
(All width centred)

Bibliographies: Danielson 192, Williams p.10, Simmons [42], Nevinson p.17, Handley-Taylor p.43, Wight [42]

Collation: [1]⁸ 2–7⁸; signatures right foot of page; 64 leaves; 185 × 119mm.; [i–vi] vii [viii] [1–2] 3–46 [47–48] 49–104

Page contents: [i] half-title: 'ST. GEORGE AND THE | DRAGON'; [ii] 'BY THE SAME AUTHOR | [rule] | *Uniform with this Volume* | [nine titles listed] | LONDON : WILLIAM HEINEMANN.'; [iii] title-page; [iv] 'LONDON: WILLIAM HEINEMANN. 1919'; [v] 'TO | THOMAS W. LAMONT'; [vi] blank; vii 'CONTENTS' (two items listed with page references); [viii] blank; [1] 'ST. GEORGE AND THE DRAGON | A SPEECH FOR ST. GEORGE'S DAY, | APRIL 23RD, 1918'; [2] blank; 3–46 text of 'St. George and the Dragon'; [47] 'THE WAR AND THE FUTURE | A LECTURE GIVEN IN AMERICA | JANUARY-AUGUST, 1918'; [48] blank; 49–104 text of 'The War and the Future' (at foot of p.104: '[rule] | BILLING AND SONS, LTD., PRINTERS, GUILDFORD ENGLAND')

Paper: wove paper

Running title: 'ST. GEORGE AND THE DRAGON' (62mm.) on both verso and recto, pp.4–46; 'THE WAR AND THE FUTURE' (58mm.) on both verso and recto, pp.50–104

Binding: blue cloth. On spine, in gold: 'St. George | and the | Dragon | [ornament] | John | Masefield | HEINEMANN' (all width centred). Covers blank with blind ruled borders: 183 × 116mm. All edges trimmed. Binding measurements: 189 × 121mm. (covers), 189 × 24mm. (spine). End-papers: wove paper.

Publication date: published, according to Simmons, 23 January 1919 in an edition of 2000 copies

Price: 5s.

Contents:
as for A43(a)

Notes:
English publication of *The War and the Future* (see A43).

The publishing agreement for this title (and *A Poem and Two Plays*) between Masefield and Heinemann was dated 26 October 1918 (see Archives of The Society of Authors). The agreement refers to *The War and the Future* and a publication price of 5s. for each title. This presumably necessitated a further agreement rendering the English title and dated 1918 only.

The first speech is sub-titled 'A Speech given in New York on St. George's Day, April 23rd, 1918'. The second speech is sub-titled 'A Lecture given in America January-August, 1918'.

In the second impression dating from March 1919, the date of first publication is given as February 1919. This is not supported by any other source yet consulted.

Copies seen: private collection (PWE)

Reprinted:

'Second Impression'	[first edition, second impression]	Mar 1919

A48 THE BATTLE OF THE SOMME 1919

A48(a) First English edition (1919)

THE BATTLE OF THE | SOMME | BY | JOHN MASEFIELD | [publisher's device of a windmill with '19' and '19' on either side] | LONDON | WILLIAM HEINEMANN
(All width centred)

Bibliographies: Danielson 194, Williams p.10, Simmons [43], Nevinson [unrecorded], Handley-Taylor p.43, Wight [43]

Collation: [1]¹⁰ 2–6⁸; signatures right foot of page; 50 leaves; 215 × 141mm.; [i–iv] 1–3 [4] 5–96

Page contents: [i] half-title: 'THE BATTLE OF THE SOMME'; [ii] 'BY THE SAME AUTHOR | [rule] | [10 titles listed] | LONDON: WILLIAM HEINEMANN | This Edition is limited to two | hundred and fifty numbered copies, | of which this is No. ....'; [iii] title-page; [iv] 'TO | MAJOR THE HON. NEVILLE LYTTON | LONDON : WILLIAM HEINEMANN. 1919'; 1–3 'FOREWORD' ('I have been asked to write a few words of preface to this little book.') (signed, 'JOHN MASEFIELD.'); [4] blank; 5–96 text (at foot of p.96: '[rule] | BILLING AND SONS, LIMITED, PRINTERS, GUILDFORD, ENGLAND')

Paper: laid paper (no watermark), chain-lines 25mm. apart

Running title: 'THE BATTLE OF THE SOMME' (62mm.) on both verso and recto, pp.6–96

Binding: blue-grey boards with parchment spine. On spine, reading lengthways up spine, from foot, in gold: 'THE BATTLE OF THE SOMME JOHN MASEFIELD'. There is a single vertical rule in blind on each cover at the edge of the parchment. Covers: blank. Top edge gilt, others trimmed. Binding measurements: 221 × 144mm. (covers), 221 × 20mm. (spine). End-papers: laid paper (no watermark), chain-lines 25mm. apart.

Publication date: published, according to Simmons, 19 June 1919 in an edition of 268 copies of which 250 were numbered

Price: 10s.6d.

Contents:
Foreword ('I have been asked to write a few words of preface to this little book.')
The Battle of the Somme ('A moment before the whistles blew, in the morning of July 1, 1916, when the Battle...')

Notes:
Another part of Masefield's abandoned scheme for writing a full history of the Somme Campaign (see A41). Masefield's foreword to the work explains and apologises for a lack of scope.

Danielson states in his bibliography that 'all copies were subscribed for before publication. The book has never been issued in any other form.' Simmons similarly notes the demand for copies. The volume remained unique until a 1968 facsimile reprint by Cedric Chivers Ltd., 'at the request of the London & Home Counties Branch of the Library Association'. As a library facsimile it is excluded from this bibliography.

The publishing agreement for this title between Masefield and Heinemann was dated 30 December 1918 (see Archives of The Society of Authors). The agreement refers to a publication price of 10s.6d. and notes the edition as 'a limited edition of 250 (two hundred and fifty) copies only of a work by [Masefield] entitled THE BATTLE OF THE SOMME and the PUBLISHERS hereby agree to print bind and publish the said edition of this work... and shall distribute the type immediately on publication and shall not reprint it...'

The edition was simply numbered, not signed.

Simmons notes a binding variant, stating 'Issued also in red cloth'.

Copies seen: private collection (ROV) un-numbered, inscribed 'for Con | from Jan. | June 21. 1919.', includes posthumous booklabel; BL (9082.cc.4) number 100 stamped 19 JUN 1919

A49 REYNARD THE FOX 1919

A49(a) First American edition (1919)

REYNARD THE FOX | OR | THE GHOST HEATH RUN | BY | JOHN MASEFIELD | AUTHOR OF | "THE EVERLASTING MERCY," "THE WIDOW | IN THE BYE STREET," ETC. | New York | THE MACMILLAN COMPANY | 1919 | *All rights reserved*
(All width centred)

Bibliographies: Danielson [unrecorded], Williams [unrecorded], Simmons [44], Nevinson [unrecorded], Handley-Taylor p.43, Wight [44]

Collation: [A-L]⁸ (but signed [A]² [B]⁸ C-L⁸ M⁶; see note on American electrotype editions) (J not used); signatures left foot of page; 88 leaves; 191 × 129mm.; [i–iv] [1–2] 3–73 [74–76] 77–166 [167–72]

Page contents: [i] half-title: 'REYNARD THE FOX | OR | THE GHOST HEATH RUN'; [ii] '[publisher's device] | THE MACMILLAN COMPANY | [two lines listing six cities, separated by four points] | MACMILLAN & CO., LIMITED | [two lines listing four cities, separated by two points] | THE MACMILLAN CO. OF CANADA, LTD. | [one city listed]'; [iii] title-page; [iv] 'COPYRIGHT, 1919, | BY JOHN MASEFIELD | [rule] | Set up and electotyped. Published October, 1919. | Norwood Press | J.S. Cushing Co.-Berwick & Smith Co. | Norwood, Mass., U.S.A.'; [1] 'PART I'; [2] blank; 3–73 text of part I; [74] blank; [75] 'PART II'; [76] blank; 77–166 text of part II (at foot of p.166: '[rule] | Printed in the United States of America.'); [167–72] blank

Paper: wove paper

Running title: 'REYNARD THE FOX' (34–35mm.) on both verso and recto, pp.4–73 and pp.78–166

Binding: mottled light grey-green boards with light green cloth spine. On spine, in gold: 'REYNARD | THE | FOX | MASEFIELD | MACMILLAN'. Covers: blank. Top edge trimmed, others roughly trimmed. Binding measurements: 197 × 129mm. (covers), 197 × 32mm. (spine). End-papers: wove paper.

Publication date: published, according to Simmons, 14 October 1919 in an edition of 2142 copies

Price: $1.60

Contents:
Reynard the Fox ('The meet was at "The Cock and Pye')

Notes:
Described as 'a great poem' by Muriel Spark, this is the first of a trio of long narrative poems written after the Great War. L.A.G. Strong claims the poem is 'the finest English narrative poem of the century, and one of the finest in our language'. The work tells of a fox hunt and also the community of the hunt. Later publications, which include the poem in the title of the volume, are *Reynard the Fox with Selected Sonnets and Lyrics* (see A147) and *Dauber & Reynard the Fox* (see A168).

The dedication present in A49(b) is absent here.

A publishing agreement for this title between Masefield and Macmillan was dated 13 May 1919 (see Archives of The Society of Authors). The agreement refers to 'a licence to publish in volume form… in the United States of America and Canada a work the subject or title of which is a narrative poem'. Masefield has later added the title 'Reynard the Fox or the Ghost Heath Run'.

In January 1947 a brewing company requested permission to use the opening lines of the poem for advertisement purposes. Masefield wrote to The Society of Authors as follows:

> Please, will you refuse the Brewers appeal for leave to use some lines of Reynard as an advertisement. The Cock & Pye inn, a favourite meet in my youth, the original inn described in Reynard, was then [and] is still, I believe, a Temperance Inn, selling only tea & minerals.
>
> (John Masefield, letter to Miss [S.M.] Perry, 24 January [1947])
> (BL, Add.Mss.56620, f.4)

Copies seen: private collection (PWE)

A49(b) First English edition (1919)

REYNARD THE FOX | OR | THE GHOST HEATH RUN | BY | JOHN MASEFIELD | [publisher's device of a windmill with '19' and '19' on either side] | [rule, 81mm.] | LONDON: WILLIAM HEINEMANN
(All width centred)

Bibliographies: Danielson 195, Williams p.6, Simmons [44a], Nevinson p.13, Handley-Taylor p.43, Wight [44a]

Collation: [A]⁸ B-H⁸; signatures right foot of page; 64 leaves; 183 × 120mm.; [i–iv] [1–2] 3–57 [58–60] 61–123 [124]

Page contents: [i] half-title: 'REYNARD THE FOX | OR | THE GHOST HEATH RUN'; [ii] 'BY THE SAME AUTHOR | [rule] | *Uniform with this Volume* | [nine titles listed] | LONDON : WILLIAM HEINEMANN'; [iii] title-page; [iv] 'To | ADA AND JOHN GALSWORTHY'; [1] 'PART I'; [2] '*The persons and events described in this | poem are imaginary. No reference is | made or intended to any living person. | JOHN MASEFIELD.*'; 3–57 text of part I; [58] blank; [59] 'PART II'; [60] blank; 61-[124] text of part II (at foot of p.[124]: '[rule] | BILLING AND SONS, LTD., PRINTERS, GUILDFORD, ENGLAND')

Paper: wove paper

Running title: 'REYNARD THE FOX' (40mm.) on both verso and recto, pp.4–57 and pp.62-[124]

Binding: blue cloth. On spine, in gold: 'Reynard | the | Fox | [ornament] | John | Masefield | HEINEMANN' (all width centred). On upper cover, in gold: 'REYNARD THE FOX | JOHN MASEFIELD' (within blind ruled border: 182 × 116mm.) Lower cover: blank. All edges trimmed. Binding measurements: 189 × 121mm. (covers), 189 × 21mm. (spine). End-papers: wove paper.

Publication date: published, according to Simmons, 16 October 1919 in an edition of 3000 copies

Price: 5s.

Contents:
as for A49(a)

Notes:

Although the American edition precedes this edition, the dedication (To John and Ada Galsworthy) first appears in the English edition. This is not, however, the first example of Masefield recording so obviously his friendship with the Galsworthys. In 1915 Masefield collected sufficient money for a motor boat, two launches and a barge for medical service in Gallipoli. The barge was christened the *John and Ada*.

The publishing agreement for this title between Masefield and Heinemann was dated 26 June 1919 (see Archives of The Society of Authors). The agreement refers to a publication price of 5s.

The text has been entirely re-set for this edition.

Copies seen: private collection (PWE); Library of The John Masefield Society (Peter Smith Collection) inscribed 'for Con | from Jan. | The first copy made, of the ordinary | edition.' includes posthumous booklabel; NYPL (Berg Collection); NYPL (Berg Collection) inscribed 'For Nancy + Robert Graves | from John Masefield. | Oct 22. 1919.'; HRHRC (AC-L M377RE 1919A) inscribed 'for Judith | from Pip.' and later signed 'John Masefield.'

A49(c) Second English edition (limited signed edition) (1919)

REYNARD THE FOX | OR | THE GHOST HEATH RUN | BY | JOHN MASEFIELD | [publisher's device of a windmill with '19' and '19' on either side] | [rule, 66mm.] | LONDON: WILLIAM HEINEMANN
(All width centred)

Bibliographies: Danielson 196, Williams p.6, Simmons [44b], Nevinson [unrecorded], Handley-Taylor p.43, Wight [44b]

Collation: [A]⁸ B-H⁸; signatures right foot of page; 64 leaves; 230 × 144mm.; [i–iv] [1–2] 3–57 [58–60] 61–123 [124]

Page contents: [i] half-title: 'REYNARD THE FOX | OR | THE GHOST HEATH RUN'; [ii] 'BY THE SAME AUTHOR | [rule] | [nine titles listed] | LONDON: WILLIAM HEINEMANN'; [iii] title-page; [iv] 'To | ADA AND JOHN GALSWORTHY'; [1] 'PART I'; [2] '*This Edition, printed on English hand-made | paper, numbered and signed by the Author, is | limited to 250 copies for sale and 25 copies for | presentation, of which this is | No._____ | The persons and events described in this | poem are imaginary. No reference is | made or intended to any living person. | JOHN MASEFIELD.*'; 3–57 text of part I; [58] blank; [59] 'PART II'; [60] blank; 61–[124] text of part II (at foot of p.[124]: '[rule] | BILLING AND SONS, LTD., PRINTERS, GUILDFORD, ENGLAND')

Paper: wove paper (watermark: 'BRITISH HAND MADE PURE RAG [castle device: 27 × 33mm.]')

Running title: 'REYNARD THE FOX' (40mm.) on both verso and recto, pp.4–57 and pp.62-[124]

Binding: blue-green boards with parchment spine. On spine, in gold: 'Reynard | the | Fox | [ornament] | John | Masefield | HEINEMANN' (all width centred). There is a single vertical rule in blind on each cover at the edge of the parchment. Covers: blank. Top edge gilt, fore edge uncut and lower outside edge untrimmed. Binding measurements: 238 × 146mm. (covers), 238 × 28mm. (spine). End-papers: laid paper (no watermark), chain-lines 25mm. apart (bound so that chain-lines run horizontally).

Publication date: published, according to Simmons, 23 October 1919

Price: 21s.

Contents:
as for A49(a)

Notes:
The text appears to use the same setting of type as A49(b).

The publishing agreement for A49(b) between Masefield and Heinemann was dated 26 June 1919 (see Archives of The Society of Authors). A rider to the agreement was sent 8 July 1919. This recorded an agreement for this 'special edition'. In a letter to the author, Heinemann stated '…of course, we will have a large paper edition: it was stupid of me to omit it from this agreement' (see William Heinemann, letter to John Masefield, 2 July 1919) (Archives of The Society of Authors).

Masefield's diary for 1919 records, on 15 October 1919, 'To London to speak at Acad. Sign l.p. copies' (see HRHRC MS (Masefield, J.) Works [Diaries]). The following day the standard edition was published and Masefield writes:

The Fox is out, the Fox is out | So let us sing Hooray | And may he run as long as the sun | And never fade away.

Copies seen: private collection (ROV) number 155, signed '155. | John Masefield.' on p.[2]; NYPL (Berg Collection) number 217, signed '217. | John Masefield.' on p.[2]; Columbia University Libraries (Special Collections B825.M377.V534.1919.c.2) number 1 (or 251), inscribed '1 (or 251) | anyway the first copy issued of | the large paper. | John Masefield.', on p.[2], additionally inscribed 'for | Con | from Jan. | The first copy made, of this edition. | [watercolour sketch]' on front free end-paper and extensively illustrated throughout (a note on p.54 states: 'This horse is queer upon his legs, | Don't look too close, the artist begs.'), there is no posthumous

REYNARD THE FOX

OR

THE GHOST HEATH RUN

BY

JOHN MASEFIELD
AUTHOR OF
"THE EVERLASTING MERCY," "THE WIDOW
IN THE BYE STREET," ETC.

New York
THE MACMILLAN COMPANY
1919
All rights reserved

A49(a) title-page

REYNARD THE FOX

OR

THE GHOST HEATH RUN

BY

JOHN MASEFIELD

LONDON: WILLIAM HEINEMANN

A49(b) title-page

A49(c) spine and upper cover

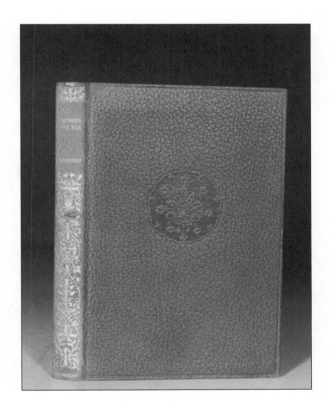

A49(h) spine and upper cover

ANIMULA

BY

JOHN MASEFIELD

LONDON: PRIVATELY PRINTED AT
THE CHISWICK PRESS
1920

A50(a) title-page

JOHN RUSKIN

BY

JOHN MASEFIELD

A51(a) title-page

ENSLAVED
AND OTHER POEMS

BY

JOHN MASEFIELD

LONDON: WILLIAM HEINEMANN

A52(a) title-page

ENSLAVED

BY

JOHN MASEFIELD
AUTHOR OF "REYNARD THE FOX"
"THE EVERLASTING MERCY"
ETC.

New York
THE MACMILLAN COMPANY
1920
All rights reserved

A53(aa) title-page

booklabel; HRHRC (AC-L G139 JMAS.R 1919) number 252, signed '252 | John Masefield.' on p.[2], additionally inscribed 'for | Ada + John | from | John. | With best greetings. | Oct 15. 1919.'

A49(d) Second American edition (first American illustrated edition) (1920)

REYNARD THE FOX | BY | JOHN MASEFIELD | NEW EDITION WITH EIGHT PLATES IN COLOUR AND | MANY ILLUSTRATIONS BY | CARTON MOOREPARK | [illustration of fox with halo standing in front of book with 'EX | LIBRIS' on left and 'REYN | ARDS' on right of volume] | New York | THE MACMILLAN COMPANY | 1920 | *All rights reserved*
(All width centred)

Bibliographies: Simmons [44c], Nevinson [unrecorded], Handley-Taylor p.43, Wight [44c]

Collation: [A-Z]⁸ (but signed [A]¹³ [B]⁸ C-Y⁸ Z³; see note on American electrotype editions) (J, V and W not used); signatures left foot of page; 184 leaves; 198 × 148mm.; [i–iv] v–xxi [xxii] xxiii [xxiv–xxvi] 1 [2] 3–4 [5] 6–11 [12] 13 [14] 15 [16] 17–19 [20] 21 [22] 23–29 [30] 31 [32] 33–35 [36] 37 [38] 39–41 [42] 43–45 [46] 47 [48] 49–51 [52] 53–61 [62] 63–67 [68] 69 [70] 71–73 [74] 75–77 [78] 79 [80] 81–91 [92] 93 [94] 95 [96] 97–99 [100] 101–103 [104] 105–107 [108] 109–113 [114] 115 [116] 117–19 [120] 121–23 [124] 125 [126] 127 [128] 129–31 [132] 133 [134] 135–39 [140] 141–43 [144] 145 [146] 147 [148] 149–52 [153] 154–57 [158] 159 [160] 161 [162] 163–65 [166] 167 [168] 169–71 [172] 173 [174] 175 [176] 177–81 [182] 183–84 [185] 186–87 [188] 189–91 [192] 193–99 [200] 201 [202] 203–207 [208] 209–213 [214] 215 [216] 217–21 [222] 223 [224] 225 [226] 227–33 [234] 235–53 [254] 255 [256] 257–67 [268] 269 [270] 271–75 [276] 277–81 [282] 283–85 [286] 287 [288] 289–90 [291] 292–94 [295] 296–99 [300] 301–302 [303] 304–305 [306] 307 [308] 309–312 [313] 314–17 [318] 319 [320] 321–25 [326] 327–29 [330] 331 [332] 333 [334] 335 [336] 337–39 [340–42]; illustrations (on glossy paper) are tipped-in on pp.[iii], 29, 86, 150, 210, 237, 251 and 338

Page contents: [i] half-title: 'REYNARD THE FOX'; [ii] '[publisher's device] | THE MACMILLAN COMPANY | [two lines listing six cities, separated by four points] | MACMILLAN & CO., LIMITED | [two lines listing four cities, separated by two points] | THE MACMILLAN CO. OF CANADA, LTD. | [one city listed]'; [iii] title-page (with additional leaf tipped-in on the verso of which is the coloured frontispiece: 132 × 99mm., signed '*Courtesy Arthur Ackerman and Son, New York*'); [iv] 'COPYRIGHT, 1919 AND 1920, | BY JOHN MASEFIELD. | [rule] | New illustrated edition, October, 1920. | Norwood Press | J. S. Cushing Co.-Berwick & Smith Co. | Norwood, Mass., U.S.A.'); v–xx 'INTRODUCTION' ('I have been asked to write why I wrote this poem of "Reynard the Fox." As a man grows older...') (unsigned); xxi 'LIST OF FULL-PAGE ILLUSTRATIONS | BY CARTON MOOREPARK' (20 illustrations listed with page references); [xxii] blank; xxiii 'COLOR PLATES' (eight illustrations listed with page references); [xxiv] blank; [xxv] 'PART I'; [xxvi] blank; 1 'THE MEET'; [2] blank; 3–11 text and illustrations; [12] blank; 13 'THE PLOUGHMAN'; [14] blank; 15–19 text and illustration; [20] blank; 21 'THE CLERYMAN'; [22] blank; 23–29 text and illustrations; [30] blank; 31 'THE PARSON'; [32] blank; 33–35 text; [36] blank; 37 '"JILL AND JOAN"'; [38] blank; 39–40 text; 41 'FARMER BENNETT'; [42] blank; 43–45 text and illustration; [46] blank; 47 'THE GOLDEN AGE'; [48] blank; 49–50 text; 51 'THE SQUIRE'; [52] blank; 53–60 text and illustration; 61 'THE DOCTOR'; [62] blank; 63–67 text and illustration; [68] blank; 69 'THE SAILOR'; [70] blank; 71–72 text; 73 'THE MERCHANT'S SON'; [74] blank; 75–76 text; 77 'SPORTSMAN'; [78] blank; 79–91 text and illustrations; [92] blank; 93 'THE EXQUISITE'; [94] blank; 95–98 text and illustration; 99 'THE SOLDIER'; [100] blank; 101–102 text and illustration; 103 'THE COUNTRY'S HOPE'; [104] blank; 105–106 text; 107 'COUNTRYMEN'; [108] blank; 109–113 text and illustration; [114] blank; 115 'THE HOUNDS'; [116] blank; 117–23 text and illustration; [124] blank; 125 'THE WHIP'; [126] blank; 127–31 text and illustration; [132] blank; 133 'THE HUNTSMAN'; [134] blank; 135–38 text and illustration; 139 'THE MASTER'; [140] blank; 141–45 text and illustration; [146] blank; 147 'THE START'; [148] blank; 149–57 text and illustrations; [158] blank; 159 '"COVER"'; [160] blank; 161–65 text and illustration; [166] blank; 167 'PART TWO-THE FOX | [illustration of fox's head within single circular rule]'; [168] blank; 169–73 text and illustrations; [174] blank; 175 'THE ROVING'; [176] blank; 177–86 text and illustrations; 187 'SCENT'; [188] blank; 189–90 text; 191 'SOUND'; [192] blank; 193–99 text and illustrations; [200] blank; 201 'FOUND'; [202] blank; 203–206 text and illustration; 207 'AWAY'; [208] blank; 209–213 text and illustration; [214] blank; 215 'THE FIELD'; [216] blank; 217–23 text and illustrations; [224] blank; 225 'THE RUN'; [226] blank; 227–32 text and illustrations; 233 'FULL CRY'; [234] blank; 235–52 text and illustrations; 253 'VIEW HALLOO'; [254] blank; 255–67 text and illustrations; [268] blank; 269 'LAST HOPE | [illustration of gruesome laughing face]'; [270] blank; 271–74 text and illustration; 275 'CHECKED'; [276] blank; 277–85 text and illustrations; [286] blank; 287 '"ON"'; [288] blank; 289–98 text and illustrations; 299 'THE LIFTING HORN'; [300] blank; 301–305 text and illustration; [306] blank; 307 'MOURNE END WOOD'; [308] blank; 309–317 text and illustration; [318] blank; 319 '"DONE"'; [320] blank; 321–24 text and illustration; 325 'PRIZE'; [326] blank; 327–31 text and illustration; [332] blank; 333 'HOME'; [334] blank; 335–39 text and illustrations (at foot of p.339: '[rule] | Printed in the United States of America.'); [340–42] blank

Paper: wove paper

Running title: 'INTRODUCTION' (40mm.) on both verso and recto, pp.vi–xx; and 'REYNARD THE FOX' (51mm.) on both verso and recto, pp.4–339

Binding: dark green cloth. On spine, in gold: 'REYNARD | THE FOX | *or the* | GHOST | HEATH | RUN | [illustration of a fox] | MASEFIELD | MACMILLAN' (all width centred). On upper cover, in gold: 'REYNARD THE FOX | *or the* | GHOST HEATH RUN | [illustration of horn and whip with superimposed circular single line border enclosing fox's head] | JOHN MASEFIELD | *Illustrated by* | CARTON MOOREPARK' (all enclosed within double ruled border in blind: 200 × 142mm.) Lower cover: blank. All edges trimmed. Binding measurements: 205 × 149mm. (covers), 205 × 64mm. (spine). End-papers: grey wove paper with illustration of running hounds in dark green.

Publication date: published, according to Simmons in 26 October 1920 in an edition of 3660 copies

Price: $5.00

Contents:
Introduction ('I have been asked to write why I wrote this poem of "Reynard the Fox." As a man grows older...')
     (unsigned)
Reynard the Fox ('The meet was at "The Cock and Pye')

Notes:
As in the first American edition (see A49(a)), this edition omits the dedication. Also omitted is Masefield's disclaimer.

The text has been entirely re-set for this edition.

The full colour plates are not by Carton Moorepark. They are untitled and listed in the contents as 'First colored plate', 'Second colored plate', etc. They comprise 'traditional' hunting prints.

The division of the poem into sections – with Chaucerian overtones – is not previously recorded.

The italic characters used on the binding include swash characters.

Copies seen: Columbia University (Special Collections B825 M377 V53 1920); HRHRC (TEMP M377RE 1920)

A49(e) Third English edition (first English illustrated limited signed edition) (1921)

REYNARD THE FOX [in red] | OR | THE GHOST HEATH RUN | BY | JOHN MASEFIELD | ILLUSTRATED BY | G. D. ARMOUR | [publisher's device of a windmill with '19' and '21' on either side] | [rule, 107mm.] | LONDON: WILLIAM HEINEMANN
(All width centred)

Bibliographies: Simmons [44d], Nevinson [unrecorded], Handley-Taylor p.43, Wight [44d] (see notes)

Collation: [A]⁴ B-G⁸ H¹⁰; H2 is also signed; the 'B' signature is in a larger type than the other signatures; signatures left foot of page; 62 leaves; 298 × 220mm.; [i–viii] [1–2] 3–55 [56–58] 59–115 [116]; illustrations (on glossy paper) are tipped-in on grey-green wove paper leaves; illustration leaves are tipped-in on pp.[ii], 9, 13, 27, 41, 55, 61, 73, 77 and 109; conjugate leaves (excluded from the gathering information) are bound with gathering G (between G2 and G3 and thus G6 and G7) and gathering H (between H1 and H2 and thus H9 and H10, and also between H3 and H4 and thus H7 and H10); protective tissue is provided for colour illustrations

Page contents: [i] half-title: 'REYNARD THE FOX | OR | THE GHOST HEATH RUN'; [ii] '*This Edition is limited to three hundred and eighty | copies, numbered and signed by the author and artist. | Of these three hundred and fifty are for sale, and thirty | for presentation. | This is No. ....*' (with additional leaf tipped-in on the verso of which the coloured frontispiece is tipped-in: 147 × 128mm.); [iii] title-page (with protective tissue for frontispiece: "'THE MEET WAS AT 'THE COCK AND PYE.'"'); [iv] blank; [v] 'TO | ADA AND JOHN GALSWORTHY'; [vi] blank; [vii] 'LIST OF ILLUSTRATIONS' (four colour illustrations (including frontispiece) and 12 black and white illustrations listed with page references); [viii] blank; [1] 'PART I'; [2] '*The persons and events described in this | poem are imaginary. No reference is | made or intended to any living person. | JOHN MASEFIELD.*'; 3–55 text of part I; [56] blank; [57] 'PART II'; [58] blank; 59-[116] text of part II (at foot of p.[116]: '[rule] | PRINTED IN GREAT BRITAIN BY RICHARD CLAY & SONS, LIMITED, | BUNGAY, SUFFOLK.')

Paper: laid paper (watermark: '1590' and windmill: 90 × 53mm.), chain-lines 30mm. apart (bound so that chain-lines run horizontally)

Running title: 'REYNARD THE FOX' (48mm.) on both verso and recto, pp.4–55 and pp.60-[116]

Binding: cream boards with parchment spine. On spine, in gold: 'REYNARD | THE | FOX | [ornament of hunting-horn] | JOHN | MASEFIELD | ILLUSTRATED | IN COLOUR & | BLACK & WHITE | BY G.D.ARMOUR | HEINEMANN' (all width centred). There is a single vertical rule in gold on each cover at the edge of the parchment. On upper cover, in gold: 'REYNARD THE FOX | JOHN MASEFIELD | ILLUSTRATED IN COLOUR AND BLACK AND WHITE | BY G. D. ARMOUR | [illustration of fox: 70 × 101mm.]' Lower cover: blank. Top edge gilt, fore edge uncut and lower outside edge roughly trimmed. Sewn head band (in white and brown). Binding measurements: 305 × 228mm. (covers), 305 × 33mm. (spine). End-papers: laid paper (watermark: '1590' and windmill: 90 × 53mm.), chain-lines 30mm. apart (this paper stock is different from that used within the book – the paper within the book shows the windmill with chain-lines running horizontal to it; the end-papers show the windmill with chain-lines running vertically to it).

Publication date: published, according to Simmons in October 1921 in an edition of 380 copies

Price: 63s.

Contents:
as for A49(a)

Notes:
Simmons numbers the regular and limited editions of this volume as [44d and e]. Wight fails to retain this system.

In addition to the illustrated plates, there are a number of head and tail pieces throughout the volume.

The text has been entirely re-set for this edition.

The publishing agreement for this illustrated version of the title between Masefield and Heinemann was dated 31 March 1921 (see Archives of The Society of Authors). The agreement also refers to a 'special edition'.

Simmons describes the paper upon which the illustration plates are tipped-in as 'greenish gray paste-board'.

Copies seen: private collection (ROV) number 284, signed 'John Masefield.' and 'G D Armour.' on p.[ii]; NYPL (Berg Collection) number 43, signed 'John Masefield.' and 'G D Armour.' on p.[ii]; HRHRC (-Q- TEMP M377RE 1921A cop.1) number 331, signed 'John Masefield.' and 'G D Armour.' on p.[ii], additionally inscribed 'For | Lew | from Zom. | Nov 2. 1921.'; HRHRC (-Q- TEMP M377RE 1921A cop.2) number 310, signed 'John Masefield.' and 'G D Armour.' on p.[ii], additionally inscribed 'for Na | from Zom. | Nov 2. 1921.'

A49(f) Fourth English edition (second English illustrated edition) (1921)

REYNARD THE FOX [in red] | OR | THE GHOST HEATH RUN | BY | JOHN MASEFIELD | ILLUSTRATED BY | G. D. ARMOUR | [publisher's device of a windmill with '19' and '21' on either side] | [rule, 107mm.] | LONDON: WILLIAM HEINEMANN
(All width centred)

Bibliographies: Simmons [44e], Nevinson p.13, Handley-Taylor p.43, Wight [unrecorded] (see notes)

Collation: [A]⁴ B-G⁸ H¹⁰; H2 is also signed; the 'B' signature is in a larger type than the other signatures; signatures left foot of page; 62 leaves; 250 × 187mm.; [i–viii] [1–2] 3–55 [56–58] 59–115 [116]; illustrations (on glossy paper) are tipped-in on pp.[ii], 9, 13, 27, 41, 55, 61, 73, 77, 85, 93, 99, 103, 109, 111 and 115; protective tissue is provided for colour illustrations

Page contents: [i] half-title: 'REYNARD THE FOX | OR | THE GHOST HEATH RUN'; [ii] 'BY THE SAME AUTHOR | [rule] | [11 titles listed] | LONDON: WILLIAM HEINEMANN' (with additional leaf tipped-in on the verso of which is the coloured frontispiece: 149 × 128mm.); [iii] title-page (with protective tissue for frontispiece: '"THE MEET WAS AT 'THE COCK AND PYE.'"'); [iv] blank; [v] 'TO | ADA AND JOHN GALSWORTHY'; [vi] blank; [vii] 'LIST OF ILLUSTRATIONS' (four colour illustrations (including frontispiece) and 12 black and white illustrations listed with page references); [viii] blank; [1] 'PART I'; [2] '*The persons and events described in this | poem are imaginary. No reference is | made or intended to any living person. | JOHN MASEFIELD.*'; 3–55 text of part I; [56] blank; [57] 'PART II'; [58] blank; 59-[116] text of part II (at foot of p.[116]: '[rule] | PRINTED IN GREAT BRITAIN BY RICHARD CLAY & SONS, LIMITED, | BUNGAY, SUFFOLK.')

Paper: wove paper

Running title: 'REYNARD THE FOX' (48mm.) on both verso and recto, pp.4–55 and pp.60-[116]

Binding: light green cloth. On spine, in gold: 'REYNARD | THE | FOX | [ornament of hunting-horn] | JOHN | MASEFIELD | ILLUSTRATED | IN COLOUR & | BLACK & WHITE | BY G.D.ARMOUR | HEINEMANN' (all width centred). On upper cover, in red-brown: 'REYNARD THE FOX | JOHN MASEFIELD | ILLUSTRATED IN COLOUR AND BLACK AND WHITE | BY G. D ARMOUR | [illustration of fox: 65 × 101mm.]' Lower cover: blank. Top edge stained green, lower outside edge roughly trimmed, fore edge uncut. Binding measurements: 256 × 189mm. (covers), 256 × 30mm. (spine). End-papers: wove paper.

Publication date: published, according to Simmons in October 1921 in an edition of 5000 copies

Price: 15s.

Contents:
as for A49(a)

Notes:
Simmons numbers the regular and limited editions of this volume as [44d and e]. Wight fails to retain this system.

In addition to the illustrated plates, there are a number of head and tail pieces throughout the volume.

Simmons describes the lettering on the covers as 'red'.

It is not known whether publication was simultaneous with the publication of A49(g). A comparison with A49(e) reveals additional differences beyond the exclusion of the limitation and different binding. There are differences in paper type and the binding of the illustrations. A49(e) includes tipped-in colour illustrations mounted on paste-board. The illustration of the fox on the upper cover of A49(f) measures 65 × 101mm. compared with that on A49(e) which measures 70 × 101mm.

Copies seen: private collection (PWE); NYPL (Berg Collection)

A49(g) Third American edition (second American illustrated edition) (1921)

REYNARD THE FOX | BY | JOHN MASEFIELD | WITH SIXTEEN PLATES BY | G. D. ARMOUR | AND | MANY ILLUSTRATIONS BY | CARTON MOOREPARK | [illustration of fox with halo standing in front of book with 'EX | LIBRIS' on left and 'REYN | ARDS' on right of volume] | New York | THE MACMILLAN COMPANY | 1921 | *All rights reserved*
(All width centred)

Bibliographies: Simmons [unrecorded], Nevinson [unrecorded], Handley-Taylor [unrecorded], Wight [noted on p.75]

Collation: [A-Z]⁸ (but signed [A]¹³ [B]⁸ C-Y⁸ Z³; see note on American electrotype editions) (see notes) (J, V and W not used); signatures left foot of page; 184 leaves; 249 × 188mm.; [i–iv] v–xx [xxi–xxiv] 1 [2] 3–4 [5] 6–11 [12] 13 [14] 15 [16] 17–19 [20] 21 [22] 23–29 [30] 31 [32] 33–35 [36] 37 [38] 39–41 [42] 43–45 [46] 47 [48] 49–51 [52] 53–61 [62] 63–67 [68] 69 [70] 71–73 [74] 75–77 [78] 79 [80] 81–91 [92] 93 [94] 95 [96] 97–99 [100] 101–103 [104] 105–107 [108] 109–113 [114] 115 [116] 117–19 [120] 121–23 [124] 125 [126] 127 [128] 129–31 [132] 133 [134] 135–39 [140] 141–43 [144] 145 [146] 147 [148] 149–52 [153] 154–57 [158] 159 [160] 161 [162] 163–65 [166] 167 [168] 169–71 [172] 173 [174] 175 [176] 177–81 [182] 183–84 [185] 186–87 [188] 189–91 [192] 193–99 [200] 201 [202] 203–207 [208] 209–213 [214] 215 [216] 217–21 [222] 223 [224] 225 [226] 227–33 [234] 235–53 [254] 255 [256] 257–67 [268] 269 [270] 271–75 [276] 277–81 [282] 283–85 [286] 287 [288] 289–90 [291] 292–94 [295] 296–99 [300] 301–302 [303] 304–305 [306] 307 [308] 309–312 [313] 314–17 [318] 319 [320] 321–25 [326] 327–29 [330] 331 [332] 333 [334] 335 [336] 337–39 [340–42]; illustrations (on glossy paper) are tipped-in on pp.[iii], 18, 25, 82, 91, 118, 137, 164, 178, 210, 230, 262, 285, 317, 322 and 338

Page contents: [i] half-title: 'REYNARD THE FOX'; [ii] 'BY | JOHN MASEFIELD | [rule] | [22 titles listed]' (all enclosed within ruled border: 79 × 83mm.); [iii] title-page (with additional leaf tipped-in on the verso of which is the coloured frontispiece: 149 × 128mm., with protective tissue with legend: '"THE MEET WAS AT 'THE COCK AND PYE.'"'); [iv] 'COPYRIGHT, 1919 AND 1920, | BY JOHN MASEFIELD. | [rule] | New illustrated edition, October, 1920. | New Edition with illustrations by | G. D. Armour and Carton Moorepark–1921. | PRINTED IN UNITED STATES OF AMERICA'; v–xx 'INTRODUCTION' ('I have been asked to write why I wrote this poem of "Reynard the Fox." As a man grows older...') (unsigned); [xxi] 'COLOR PLATES | [four plates listed with page references] | BLACK AND WHITE PLATES | [12 plates listed with page references]'; [xxii] blank; [xxiii] 'PART I'; [xxiv] blank; 1 'THE MEET'; [2] blank; 3–11 text and illustrations; [12] blank; 13 'THE PLOUGHMAN'; [14] blank; 15–19 text and illustration; [20] blank; 21 'THE CLERYMAN'; [22] blank; 23–29 text and illustrations; [30] blank; 31 'THE PARSON'; [32] blank; 33–35 text; [36] blank; 37 '"JILL AND JOAN"'; [38] blank; 39–40 text; 41 'FARMER BENNETT'; [42] blank; 43–45 text and illustration; [46] blank; 47 'THE GOLDEN AGE'; [48] blank; 49–50 text; 51 'THE SQUIRE'; [52] blank; 53–60 text and illustration; 61 'THE DOCTOR'; [62] blank; 63–67 text and illustration; [68] blank; 69 'THE SAILOR'; [70] blank; 71–72 text; 73 'THE MERCHANT'S SON'; [74] blank; 75–76 text; 77 'SPORTSMAN'; [78] blank; 79–91 text and illustrations; [92] blank; 93 'THE EXQUISITE'; [94] blank; 95–98 text and illustration; 99 'THE SOLDIER'; [100] blank; 101–102 text and illustration; 103 'THE COUNTRY'S HOPE'; [104] blank; 105–106 text; 107 'COUNTRYMEN'; [108] blank; 109–113 text and illustration; [114] blank; 115 'THE HOUNDS'; [116] blank; 117–23 text and illustration; [124] blank; 125 'THE WHIP'; [126] blank; 127–31 text and illustration; [132] blank; 133 'THE HUNTSMAN'; [134] blank; 135–38 text and illustration; 139 'THE MASTER'; [140] blank; 141–45 text and illustration; [146] blank; 147 'THE START'; [148] blank; 149–57 text and illustrations; [158] blank; 159 '"COVER"'; [160] blank; 161–65 text and illustration; [166] blank; 167 'PART TWO-THE FOX | [illustration of fox's head within single circular rule]'; [168] blank; 169–73 text and illustrations; [174] blank; 175 'THE ROVING'; [176] blank; 177–86 text and illustrations; 187 'SCENT'; [188] blank; 189–90 text; 191 'SOUND'; [192] blank; 193–99 text and illustrations; [200] blank; 201 'FOUND'; [202] blank; 203–206 text and illustration; 207 'AWAY'; [208] blank; 209–213 text and illustration; [214] blank; 215 'THE FIELD'; [216] blank; 217–23 text and illustrations; [224] blank; 225 'THE RUN'; [226] blank; 227–32 text and illustrations; 233 'FULL CRY'; [234] blank; 235–52 text and illustrations; 253 'VIEW HALLOO'; [254] blank; 255–67 text and illustrations; [268] blank; 269 'LAST HOPE | [illustration of gruesome laughing face]'; [270] blank; 271–74 text and illustration; 275 'CHECKED'; [276] blank; 277–85 text and illustrations; [286] blank; 287 '"ON"'; [288] blank; 289–98 text and illustrations; 299 'THE LIFTING HORN'; [300] blank; 301–305 text and illustration; [306] blank; 307 'MOURNE END WOOD'; [308] blank; 309–317 text and illustration; [318] blank; 319 '"DONE"'; [320] blank; 321–24 text and illustration; 325 'PRIZE'; [326] blank; 327–31 text and illustration; [332] blank; 333 'HOME'; [334] blank; 335–39 text and illustrations (at foot of p.339: '[rule] | Printed in the United States of America.'); [340–42] blank

Paper: wove paper

Running title: 'INTRODUCTION' (40mm.) on both verso and recto, pp.vi–xx; and 'REYNARD THE FOX' (51mm.) on both verso and recto, pp.4–339

Binding: light green cloth. On spine, in gold: 'REYNARD | THE FOX | *or the* | GHOST | HEATH | RUN | [illustration of a fox] | MASEFIELD | MACMILLAN | – – – –' (all width centred). On upper cover, in gold: illustration of horn and whip with superimposed circular single line border enclosing fox's head (all within double ruled border in blind, with bevelled corners: 83 × 97) (all enclosed within double ruled border in blind: 238 × 178mm.) Lower cover: blank. All edges trimmed. Binding measurements: 255 × 190mm. (covers), 255 × 50mm. (spine). End-papers: wove paper (see notes).

Publication date: published, according to evidence within *The Publisher's Weekly* (New York), around October 1921

Price: $5.00

Contents:
as for A49(d)

Notes:
As in A49(a), this edition omits the dedication. Also omitted is Masefield's disclaimer.

This edition is a hybrid of A49(d) and A49(e). It is more closely derived from the former. In A49(d), line drawings by Carton Moorepark were accompanied by 'traditional' plates depicting the hunt. Here the same setting of text and Moorepark illustrations are used however the 'traditional' plates have been replaced by G.D. Armour's illustrations from A49(e).

The front free endpaper constitutes leaf [A]1.

The four colour plates each carry a leaf of protective tissue bearing a printed legend for the illustration.

The italic characters used on the binding include swash characters.

Copies seen: Columbia University (825 M377 V5331)

A49(h) Fourth American edition ["Leather Pocket Edition"] (1923)

REYNARD THE FOX | OR | THE GHOST HEATH RUN | *By* | JOHN MASEFIELD | [circular floral ornament] [in red] | NEW YORK | THE MACMILLAN COMPANY | 1923 | ALL RIGHTS RESERVED
(All width centred and enclosed within ornate border in red: 135 × 78mm.)

Bibliographies: Simmons [unrecorded], Nevinson [unrecorded], Handley-Taylor p.53, Wight [unrecorded]

Collation: [A]¹⁰ ([A]3+2) [B]⁶ [C-M]⁸ (but signed [A]¹⁰ ([A]3+2) [B]⁸ C-L⁸ M⁶; see note on American electrotype editions) (J not used); signatures left foot of page; 96 leaves; 171 × 112mm.; [i–iv] v–xx [1–2] 3–73 [74–76] 77–166 [167–72]

Page contents: [i] half-title: 'REYNARD THE FOX | OR | THE GHOST HEATH RUN | [ornament] [in red]'; [ii] '[27 titles separated by 19 single points] | [ornament] [in red]' (enclosed within ornate border in red: 135 × 78mm.); [iii] title-page; [iv] 'COPYRIGHT, 1919 AND 1920, BY JOHN MASEFIELD | *Printed in the United States of America* | [ornament] [in red]'; v–xx 'INTRODUCTION' ('I have been asked to write why I wrote this poem of "Reynard the Fox." As a man grows older...') (unsigned); [1] 'PART I'; [2] blank; 3–73 text; [74] blank; [75] 'PART II'; [76] blank; 77–166 text (at foot of p.166: '[rule] | Printed in the United States of America.'); [167–72] blank

Paper: laid paper (no watermark), chain-lines 22mm. apart

Running title: 'REYNARD THE FOX' (35mm.) on both verso and recto, pp.4–73 and pp.78–166

Binding: red leather. On spine, in gold: '[floral panel] | REYNARD | THE FOX | MASEFIELD | [floral panel] | MACMILLAN'. On upper cover, in blind: circular floral ornament (within blind ruled border: 171 × 111mm.) On lower cover: blind ruled border: 171 × 111mm. Top edge gilt, others trimmed. Binding measurements: 175 × 115mm. (covers), 175 × 23mm. (spine). End-papers: wove paper.

Publication date: published, according to Handley-Taylor, 30 August 1923 (see notes)

Price: $12.50 (set of 8 volumes: see also A21(d), A52(b), A54(g), A66(a), A67(a), A68(a) and A69(a))

Contents:
as for A49(d). Although the contents is that of A49(d), this edition does not retain the division of the poem into named sections.

Notes:
Issued as volume V in the Macmillan Leather Pocket Edition of Masefield's Work.

This is one of the titles from the leather pocket edition that Simmons excluded from his bibliography. Of the volumes that were included he provided a later publication date than that cited by Handley-Taylor. This edition may, therefore, have been published in October 1923. Accepting Handley-Taylor's publication date would explain the omission of *A King's Daughter* (published on 23 October 1923) in the listing of Masefield's works appearing on page [ii].

Copies seen: private collection (PWE)

A49(i) First German edition [in English] (1926)

REYNARD THE FOX | OR | THE GHOST HEATH RUN | BY | JOHN MASEFIELD | Mit Wörterbuch | herausgegeben von | Dr. ALBERT EICHLER | Professor an der Universität Graz (Steiermark) | LEIPZIG | BERNHARD TAUCHNITZ | 1926
(All width centred)

Bibliographies: Simmons [unrecorded], Nevinson [unrecorded], Handley-Taylor [unrecorded], Wight [unrecorded]

Collation: [1]⁸ 2–6⁸ 7⁴; the second leaf of gatherings 2–7 is also signed; signatures right foot of page with 'Masefield, Reynard the Fox' on first leaf of gatherings (with the exception of [1]); 52 leaves; 157 × 108mm.; [1–5] 6–12 [13] 14–104

Page contents: [1] half-title: 'STUDENTS' SERIES NEUE FOLGE | Herausgegeben von Dr. KARL WILDHAGEN, o. Professor der | englischen Sprache an der Universität Kiel | [rule] | Nr. 7 | REYNARD THE FOX | OR | THE GHOST HEATH RUN | BY | JOHN MASEFIELD'; [2] 'Druck von Bernhard Tauchnitz in Leipzig'; [3] title-page; [4] 'Meinem lieben Freunde | DR. LEOPOLD BRANDL | Professor an der I. Bundes-Realschule und | Lektor an der Technischen Hochschule in Wien | *A.E.*'; [5]–12 'Einleitung' ('John Masefield... hat eine harte, wildbewegte Jugend als Matrose...') (signed 'Graz, am I. Juni 1926. | Albert Eichler.'); [13]–104 text

Paper: wove paper

Running title: 'EINLEITUNG' (15mm.) on both verso and recto, pp.6–12; and 'REYNARD THE FOX' (25mm.) on both verso and recto, pp.14–104

Binding: mustard orange wrappers. On spine, reading lengthways up spine, from foot: 'JOHN B. MASEFIELD, Reynard the Fox' [*sic*] with '[triple rule] | 7 | [triple rule]' at head and '[triple rule] | [triple rule]' at foot. On upper wrapper: 'STUDENTS' SERIES NEUE FOLGE | Herausgegeben von Dr. Karl Wildhagen, o. Professor der | englischen Sprache an der Universität Kiel | [double rule] | Nr. 7 | REYNARD THE FOX | BY | JOHN MASEFIELD | [short rule] | BERNHARD TAUCHNITZ | LEIPZIG' (all width centred) (within triple ruled border, all within ruled border: 142 × 92mm.) and with 'The copyright of this Edition is only acquired for Germany and Austria and it must | not be introduced into any other countries' at foot. Lower wrapper: blank. All edges trimmed. Binding measurements: 157 × 108mm. (wrappers); 157 × 9mm. (spine). End-papers: wove paper laid down to inside of wrappers. End-papers carry advertisements for Tauchnitz publications on the front fixed end-paper, the front free end-paper (verso and recto), rear free end-paper (verso and recto) and the rear fixed end-paper.

Publication date: September 1926

Price: M.2.00

Contents:
Einleitung ('John Masefield… hat eine harte, wildbewegte Jugend als Matrose…')
      (signed 'Graz, am I. Juni 1926. | Albert Eichler.')
Reynard the Fox ('The meet was at "The Cock and Pye')

Notes:
The volume is listed as number J7 in William B. Todd and Ann Bowden's *Tauchnitz International Editions In English 1841–1955 A Bibliographical History* (New York: Bibliographical Society of America, 1988). It is listed within the 'Students' Series Neue Folge' series.

The Wörterbuch comprises a separate booklet of 76 pages which provides German translations and explanations of English words from the poem.

C.S. Evans wrote in March 1924 to state that Heinemann had no objections to this proposed edition. He did, however, urge caution:

> …I …find waiting for me a letter from you… it refers to an Austrian Professor, Eichler, who wants to print a school edition of REYNARD for use in German and Austrian schools. If you would like this to be done, we have of course, no objection, and will give every facility we can. I do think, however, that you should make some sort of arrangement so that if there is by any chance any money in the edition (and you never can tell) you would get a reasonable royalty. It is always unwise, I think, to give away a valuable property like this, and if you were to do so you might be sorry in the future…
>
> (C.S. Evans, letter to John Masefield, 19 March 1924)
> (HRHRC, MS (Masefield, J.) Recip William Heinemann Ltd.).

Masefield informed The Society of Authors:

> An Austrian Professor, Professor Eichler, of 4, Hasnerplatz, Graz, Austria, wishes to print a School Edition of my poem *Reynard the Fox* for use in German + Austrian schools. He is a very good fellow, + both Heinemann + I are willing to let him do so, provided that his edition, which will be in English, with notes in German, is kept out of this country and the U.S.A.
>
> (John Masefield, letter to G.H. Thring, [21 September 1924])
> (BL, Add.Mss.56580, ff.98–99)

As a result, negotiations commenced and Masefield personally intervened to allow generous terms:

> …I will gladly concede him [Professor Eichler] a third of the royalties. As he has had an exceedingly hard time ever since the war + has done more work upon the poem than I imagined I would suggest that he be granted *all* the royalties on the first 2000 copies, so that he may receive something anyhow for his toil: it will probably be little enough as it is.
>
> (John Masefield, letter to G.H. Thring, [28 September 1924])
> (BL, Add.Mss.56580, ff.108–109)

A letter from Albert Eichler to The Society of Authors explains that he had not, by October 1924, 'been able to find a publisher' (BL, Add.Mss.56580, f.131). Correspondence from Eichler resumed on 14 April 1926 stating that:

> After many failures in quest of a publisher – the royalty of 10% proved always a stumbling-block – I have at last succeeded in my endeavours to have an agreement drawn up by the firm of Bernhard Tauchnitz in Leipzig, which I herewith submit to Mr. Masefield's inspection according to your instructions of 22nd Sept. 1924
>
> (Albert Eichler, letter to [G.H. Thring], 14 April 1926)
> (BL, Add.Mss.56582, f.192)

Masefield had stipulated that there was to be no sale outside Austria and Germany and Eichler reports that Tauchnitz was 'willing to bind himself to that condition as far as he is able'. The suggestion was made by Eichler that a notice printed on the cover would state the restricted countries of sale. An amended agreement was sent to The Society of Authors by Eichler on 17 May 1926 (BL, Add.Mss.56583, ff.12) and Masefield returned the signed agreement before 25 May 1926.

In January 1929 Tauchnitz sent The Society of Authors the account for this edition. Tauchnitz writes:

> I beg to enclose you herewith the annual account for the year ending Deember 31st 1928 of the sale of my school edition of "Reynard the Fox" by Mr. John Masefield from which you will see that 752 copies have been sold up till now. As it has been stipulated that Mr. Masefield should participate in the royalty after a sale of 2000 copies no payment is due as yet.
>
> (Bernhard Tauchnitz, letter to The Society of Authors, [January 1929])
> (BL, Add.Mss.56587, f.31)

In January 1931 The Society of Authors sent an account from Tauchnitz to Masefield for sales until 31 December 1930. No royalty was payable and therefore 2000 copies had not, by then, been sold (see BL, Add.Mss.56592, f.79) The Society of Authors wrote to Masefield on 2 April 1936 stating that the last account in their files (to December 1933) showed that only 1169 copies had been sold (BL, Add.Mss.56604, ff.80–81).

Copies seen: BL (Tauch.J7) no dated library stamp

A49(j) Fifth English edition (extra limited signed edition) (1931)

JOHN MASEFIELD | [rule (tapered at each end, with a gap filled by a diamond in the centre), 56mm.] | REYNARD | THE FOX | OR | *THE GHOST-HEATH* | *RUN* | [publisher's device of a windmill] | LONDON | WILLIAM HEINEMANN LIMITED | 1931
(Note that the '*T*' of '*THE*' and '*GHOST-HEATH*' are swash)
(All width centred)

Bibliographies: Nevinson [unrecorded], Handley-Taylor [noted on p.20], Wight [44e] (see notes)

Collation: [π]⁴ [2π]⁴ A-N⁴ O⁶ [P]² (J not used); O2 is also signed; signatures left foot of page; 68 leaves; 280 × 188mm.; [i–xvi] 1–52 [53–54] 55–113 [114–20]

Page contents: [i–viii] blank; [ix] half-title: 'REYNARD THE FOX | OR | *THE GHOST HEATH RUN*'; [x] '*Of this edition of REYNARD THE FOX there have been | printed 25 copies on Barcham Green's Penshurst hand-made paper. | The binding is hand-sewn and in full Lido calf by Henry T. Wood | with a gold-tooled cover from a design by Percy Smith. The | volumes are numbered and signed by the author and each contains | some verses in his handwriting. | This is No...*'; [xi] title-page; [xii] blank; [xiii] 'TO | JOHN & ADA GALSWORTHY'; [xiv] blank; [xv] 'PART ONE'; [xvi] blank; 1–52 text of part one; [53] 'PART TWO'; [54] blank; 55–113 text of part two; [114] 'PRINTED IN GREAT BRITAIN | BY ROBERT MACLEHOSE AND CO. LTD. | THE UNIVERSITY PRESS, GLASGOW'; [115–20] blank

Paper: wove paper

Running title: 'REYNARD THE FOX' (45mm.) on verso; 'OR THE GHOST-HEATH RUN' (68mm.) on recto, pp.2–113

Binding: blue Lido calf by Henry T. Wood. On spine, in gold: '[rule] | [raised band of binding] | [wavy rule] | [wavy rule] | [raised band of binding] | REYNARD | THE FOX | [point] | JOHN | MASEFIELD | [point] | [raised band of binding] | [wavy rule] | [wavy rule] | [raised band of binding] | [raised band of binding] | [wavy rule] | [wavy rule] | [raised band of binding] | [rule]'. On upper cover, in gold: one wavy line in upper quarter of the cover and a second wavy line in the lower quarter with a five point star in upper left corner, a blazing sun in upper right corner, a five point star in lower left corner and a point (with inner point in blind) in lower right corner (within ruled border: 282 × 183mm.) On lower cover, in gold: upper cover design repeated. Insides of upper and lower cover includes gold rule on all outside edges with 'BOUND BY WOOD.LONDON' in gold at right foot of inside of lower cover. Top edge gilt, others uncut. Sewn head and foot bands (in blue). Binding measurements: 288 × 189mm. (covers), 288 × 45mm. (spine). End-papers: blue silk-lined laid paper (no watermark), chain-lines 27mm. apart (bound so that chain-lines run horizontally). Volume contained in slip-case covered in blue buckram and lined with material.

Publication date: published, according to inscribed copies, later than 19 October 1931

Price: 25 guineas

Contents:
as for A49(a)

Notes:
The text has been entirely re-set for this edition.

Each copy contains a number of stanzas from the poem in Masefield's hand. There are also a number of watercolour drawings.

Wight described copy number fourteen for his bibliography. He does not provide a location for this copy.

Wight numbers this edition as [44e]. Simmons had, however, already used this number for a different edition. Simmons lists [44d] and [44e] as the English G.D. Armour illustrated editions in regular and limited editions.

It appears that Masefield first suggested printing presentation copies of *Reynard the Fox* for King George V and the Prince of Wales in 1930. Copy number 2 of this edition was indeed presented to the Prince of Wales (later Edward VIII) (see Property from the Collection of The Duke and Duchess of Windsor, Sotheby's New York, 16 September 1997, lot 1765). However initial plans were not, it appears, to print a companion volume to the extra limited signed edition of *The Wanderer* (see A101(d)). Discussion commenced about four copies printed on vellum:

> I have been going into the figures of the four special copies of REYNARD. I find that I was too optimistic when I talked about printing them at the Windmill Press. We cannot do them. Printing on vellum is a highly expert job and if it is to be done well it must be done by people who have experience of working on vellum. I have therefore got an estimate from the Curwen press who, in my opinion, are the finest printers in London…
>
> C.S. Evans, letter to John Masefield, 19 December 1930
> (HRHRC, MS (Masefield, J.) Recip William Heinemann Ltd.)

The matter was raised again in February 1931 and C.S. Evans again expressed his doubts that production would be possible by Heinemann at their own press:

> Now about those two special copies of REYNARD THE FOX for the King and the Prince of Wales. I have been hoping that we might be able to do these at Kingswood, but I find it absolutely impossible: we have great difficulty in getting through all the work we have to do, and to print one copy of a book is as lengthy and costly a business as printing a thousand. Each machine takes anything from eight to ten hours to make ready... I think, therefore, that it would be better to have it printed outside. If it is to be done on hand made paper it will, of course, cost less than if it is printed on vellum, but I think that it should be very well printed. I will get some more estimates and specimen pages and let you see them. I think I shall ask Mr. Percy Smith – whom we consult regarding typography – to lay the book out.
>
> C.S. Evans, letter to John Masefield, 3 February 1931
> (HRHRC, MS (Masefield, J.) Recip William Heinemann Ltd.)

Percy Smith apparently suggested the two copies might be handwritten by a professional. Evans investigated this option but soon discovered the cost to be 'enormous'. It is at this stage that a companion to *The Wanderer* is first suggested:

> I find that hand written copies of REYNARD are quite out of the question. The cost would be enormous. As it is, the two printed copies would cost about £58. I think that we could possibly sell twenty copies on the same lines as THE WANDERER if you wrote some poems and drew some pictures as you did before. Without this, I do not think that we could sell them at a sufficiently high price to pay for the production and presentation copies. But from what you told me when you were here last I gathered that you were not enthusiastic about going through all that business again. It must have been a fearful job.
>
> (C.S. Evans, letter to John Masefield, 16 February 1931)
> (HRHRC, MS (Masefield, J.) Recip William Heinemann Ltd.)

Masefield did not take long to decide for Evans wrote again, three days later, stating that, in accordance with the author's wishes, Heinemann would 'go ahead and do 25 or 30 copies of REYNARD'. He also noted that it was his understanding that Masefield wanted to have the edition ready for the King's birthday (see C.S. Evans, letter to John Masefield, 19 February 1931) (HRHRC, MS (Masefield, J.) Recip William Heinemann Ltd.) During production Evans wrote on 5 May 1931 enclosing:

> ... copy for the tablet for the special edition of REYNARD. You will see that it provides for twenty as against 25 of THE WANDERER because in your letter you suggested twenty. We can easily have the book ready by June.
>
> (C.S. Evans, letter to John Masefield, 5 May 1931)
> (HRHRC, MS (Masefield, J.) Recip William Heinemann Ltd.)

It appears that Masefield did not provide manuscript additions to all copies at the same time. A single copy (to be the copy presented to King George V) was taken to Masefield in sheets. The remainder of the edition was, apparently taken to the author on 23 May 1931 (see R. Wellton Finn, letter to John Masefield, 22 May 1931) (HRHRC, MS (Masefield, J.) Recip William Heinemann Ltd.) However, later correspondence notes:

> I have instructed the binders to send to you copy No.2 of REYNARD THE FOX as the Prince of Wales' copy. I note that you do not want to decorate the remainder until after your return, about 17th July.
>
> (R. Welton Finn, letter to John Masefield, 23 June 1931)
> (HRHRC, MS (Masefield, J.) Recip William Heinemann Ltd.)

and it is therefore possible that some delay was experienced and Masefield may have signed the copy for the Prince of Wales when bound (followed by the remainder of the edition).

In the final 'Rest and be thankful copy', Masefield provides evidence that the date of publication (assuming the entire edition was issued at the same time) was after 19 October 1931. Masefield generally added the phrase 'Rest and be thankful' to the final copy in a limited, inscribed edition (see A50(a)).

Copies seen:
HRHRC (-Q- TEMP M377RE 1931 cop.1) number 3, signed 'Three | John Masefield.' on p.[x], additionally inscribed 'For Con | from Jan. | October 15th. 1931. | [sketch in black and red of a rider on a horse (facing right)]' on p.[ix], manuscript additions in Masefield's hand are as follows: [i] '[sketch in black and red of a rider on a horse (facing left)] | The rise, which shut the field away, | Showed him the Vale's great map spread out, | The Down's lean frank + thrusting snout, | Pale pastures, red-brown plough, dark wood, | Blue distance, still as solitude, | Glitter of water here + there, | the trees so delicately bare, | The dark green gorse + bright green holly. | "O glorious God", he said, "how jolly". | And there downhill two fields ahead | The lollopping red dog-fox sped | Over Poor Pastures to the brook. | [sketch in black and red of a rider on a horse (facing right)'; [ii] blank; [iii] '[sketch in black and red of a rider on a horse (facing right)] | They saw the Yell Brook like a gem | Blue in the grass a short mile on; | They heard faint cries, but hounds were gone | A good eight fields + out of sight, | Except a rippled glimmer white | Going away with dying cheering, | And scarlet flappings disappearing, | And scattering horses going, going, | Going like mad, White Rabbit snowing | Far on ahead, a loose horse taking | Fence after fence with stirrups shaking, | And scarlet specks and dark specks dwindling. | [sketch in black, red and green of a rider walking away from horse]'; [iv] blank; [v] '[sketch in black and red of a rider on a horse (facing left)] | Over the waste where the ganders grazed | The long swift lilt of his loping lazed, | His ears cocked up as his blood ran higher, | He saw his point, + his eyes took fire, | The Wan Dyke Hill with its fir-tree barren, | Its dark of gorse and its rabbit-warren, | The Dyke on its heave like a tightened girth | And holes in the Dyke where a fox might earth. | He has rabbitted [*sic*] there long months before

| The earths were deep + his need was sore; | The way was new, but he took a bearing, | And rushed like a blown ship billow-sharing | [sketch in black and red of a rider on a horse (facing right)]'; [vi] blank; [vii] '[sketch in black, grey, yellow and green of a ship] | He made his spurt for the Mourne End rocks, | The air blew rank with the taint of fox; | The yews gave way to a greener space | Of great stones strewn in a grassy place. | And there was his earth at the great grey shoulder | Sunk in the ground, of a granite boulder, | A dry deep burrow with rocky roof, | Proof against crowbars, terrier-proof, | Life to the dying, rest for bones. | [new stanza] The earth was stopped; it was filled with stones. | [sketch in black, brown, blue and green of a ship]'; [viii] blank; and [xv] 'Then the moon came quiet and flooded full | Light and beauty on clouds like wool, | On a feasted fox at rest from hunting, | In the beech wood gray where the brocks were grunting | [new stanza] The beech wood grey rose dim in the night | With moonlight fallen in pools of light, | The long dead leaves on the ground were rimed | A clock struck twelve and the church bells chimed.'

The King's School, Canterbury, number 9, signed 'Nine. | John Masefield.' on p.[x], manuscript additions in Masefield's hand are as follows: [i] sketch in black and red of a rider on a horse (facing left); [ii] blank; [iii] 'As he crossed the meadows at Naunton Larking | The dogs in the town all started barking | For with feet all bloody + flanks all foam | The hounds + the Hunt came limping home | [new stanza] Limping home in the dark dead beaten | The hounds all rank from a fox they'd eaten | Dansey saying to Robin Dawe | "The fastest + longest I ever saw". | [new stanza] And Robin answered: "O Tom, 'twas good | I thought they changed in the Mourne End Wood | But now I feel that they did not change | We've had a run that was great + strange. | [new stanza] And to kill in the end in dusk on grass'; [iv] blank; [v] 'We'll turn to the Cock + take a glass | For the hounds, poor souls, are past their forces | And a gallon of ale for our poor horses | And some bits of bread for the hounds, poor things, | After all they've done, for they've done like kings, | Would keep them going till we get in. | We had it alone from Nun's Wood Whin." | [new stanza] Then Tom replied: "If they changed or not | There've been few runs longer and none more | hot, | We shall talk of today until we die."'; [vi] blank; [vii] sketch in black and red of a rider on a horse (facing right); [viii] blank

HRHRC (-Q- TEMP M377RE 1931 cop.2) number 10, signed 'Ten | John Masefield.' on p.[x], manuscript additions in Masefield's hand are as follows: [i] '[sketch in black, brown and green of a fox running across grass (facing left)'; [ii] blank; [iii] 'Old Joe at digging his garden grounds, | Said: "A fox, being hunted; where be hounds? | O Lord, my back, to be young again, | 'Stead a zelling zider in <u>King of Spain</u>. | O hark, I hear en, O sweet, O sweet; | Why, there be redcoat in Jarge's wheat; | And there be redcoat, + there they gallop, | There go a browncoat down a wallop. | Quick, Ellen, quick. Come, Susan, fly. | Here 'm hounds. I zeed the fox go by, | Go by like thunder, go by like blasting, | With his girt white teeth all looking ghasting. | Look, there comes hounds. Hark, hear em crying. | Lord, belly to stubble, ain't they flying. | There's huntsman there. The fox came past, | As I was digging, as fast as fast, | He's only been a minute by | A girt dark dog as pert as pye."'; [iv] blank; [v] 'Ellen + Susan came out scattering | Brooms + dustpans till all was clattering; | They saw the pack come head to foot | Running like racers nearly mute; | Robin + Dansey quartering near, | All going gallop like startled deer. | [sketch in black and red of a rider on a horse (facing left)]'; [vi–viii] blank

Harvard College Library (Houghton *fEC9.M377.919rp) number 20, signed 'Twenty | John Masefield.' on p.[x], manuscript additions in Masefield's hand are as follows: [i] sketch in black and red of a rider on a horse (facing right); [ii] blank; [iii] 'Then Tom replied: "If they changed or not, | There've been few runs longer + none more hot. | We shall talk of today until we die." | [new stanza] The stars grew bright in the winter sky, | The wind came keen with a tang of frost, | The brook was troubled for new things lost, | The copse was happy for old things found, | The fox came home + he went to ground. | [new stanza] And the hunt came home + the hounds were fed, | They climbed to their bench + went to bed; | The horses in stable loved their straw, | "Good night, my beauties", said Robin Dawe.'; [iv] blank; [v] 'Then the moon came quiet + flooded full | Light + beauty on clouds like wool, | On a feasted fox at rest from hunting, | In the beech-wood grey where the brocks were grunting. | [new stanza] The beech-wood grey rose dim in the night | With moonlight fallen in pools of light, | The long dead leaves on the ground were rimed; | A clock struck twelve + the church bells chimed.'; [vi] blank; [vii] sketch in black and red of a rider on a horse (facing left); [viii] blank

The Library of J. Philip Jacobs (sold by Sotheby's, 17 November 1999, lot 572) number 23, signed 'Twenty Three | John Masefield.' on p.[x], manuscript additions in Masefield's hand are as follows: [i] sketch in black and red of a rider on a horse (facing left); [ii] blank; [iii] 'The field's noise died upon his ear, | A faint horn, far behind, blew thin | In covet, lest some hound were in. | Then instantly the great grass rise | Shut field + cover from his eyes, | He + his racers were alone. | [new stanza] "A dead fox or a broken bone," | Said Robin peering for his prey. | [new stanza] The rise, which shut the field away, | Shewed him the Vale's great map spread out, | The down's lean flank + thrusting snout, | Pale pastures, red-brown plough, dark wood,'; [iv] blank; [v] 'Blue distance, still as solitude, | Glitter of water here + there, | The trees so delicately bare, | The dark green gorse + bright green holly. | [new stanza] "O glorious God", he said, "how jolly!" | [new stanza] And there, downhill, two fields ahead, | The lolloping red dog-fox sped, | Over Poor Pastures to the Brook. | [new stanza] He grasped these things in one swift look, | Then dived into the bullfinch heart | Through thorns that tore his sleeves apart | And skutcht new blood upon his brow: – | [new stanza] "His point's Lark's Leybourne Covers now," | Said Robin, landing with a grunt. | "Forrard, my Beautifuls."'; [vi] blank; [vii] sketch in black and red of a rider on a horse (facing right); [viii] blank

ULL (Special Collections) (Sterling Library) (see *The Sterling Library... Catalogue* (Privately Printed, 1954) Part II, No.378) number 25, signed 'Twenty Five. | John Masefield.' on p.[x], manuscript additions in Masefield's hand are as follows: [i] sketch in black and red of a rider on a horse (facing right); [ii] blank; [iii] 'Then Tom replied: "If they changed or not, | There've been few runs longer + none more hot. | We shall talk of today until we die". | [new stanza] The stars grew bright in the winter sky, | The wind came keen with a touch of frost: | The brook was troubled for new things lost, | The copse was happy for old things found; | The fox came home + he went to ground. | [new stanza] And the hunt came home + the hounds were fed | They climbed to their bench + went to bed; | The horses in stable loved their straw. | "Good night, my Beauties", said Robin Dawe.'; [iv] blank; [v] 'Then the moon came quiet + flooded full | Light + beauty on clouds like wool, | On a fearful fox at rest from hunting, | In the beech-wood grey where the brocks were grunting. | [new stanza] The beech-wood grey rose dim in the night | With moonlight fallen in pools of light, | The long dead leaves on the ground were rimed; | A clock struck Twelve + the church bells chimed. | Rest + be thankful Copy. | October 19th. 1931. | at 12.53p.m.'; [vi] blank; [vii] sketch in black and red of a rider on a horse (facing left); [viii] blank

A49(k) Sixth English edition (third English illustrated edition) (1932)

REYNARD THE FOX | OR | THE GHOST HEATH RUN | BY | JOHN MASEFIELD | WITH ILLUSTRATIONS BY G. D. ARMOUR | [publisher's device of a windmill with '19' and '32' on either side] | [rule, 80mm.] | London : William Heinemann Ltd.
(All width centred)

Bibliographies: Handley-Taylor [unrecorded], Wight [unrecorded]

Collation: [A]⁸ B-G⁸ H¹⁰; H2 is also signed; signatures right foot of page; 66 leaves; 188 × 127mm.; [i–viii] [1–2] 3–57 [58–60] 61–123 [124]; illustrations (on glossy paper) are tipped-in on pp.[iii], 29, 57, 65, 97, 117, 119 and 123

Page contents: [i] half-title: 'REYNARD THE FOX | OR | THE GHOST HEATH RUN'; [ii] '*ALSO BY JOHN MASEFIELD* | PLAYS: | [10 volumes listed] | POETRY: | [15 volumes listed] | OTHER WORKS: | [10 volumes listed]'; [iii] title-page (with additional leaf tipped-in on the verso of which is the coloured frontispiece: 145 × 124mm., '"THE MEET WAS AT THE 'COCK AND PYE'."'); [iv] '*First published, October,* 1919 | *New impressions, November,* 1919 | *December,* 1919 *March,* 1920 | *January,* 1921 *January,* 1922 | *January,* 1923 *June,* 1924 | *January,* 1926 | *Cheaper edition, February,* 1929 | *Illustrated edition, October,* 1921 | *New and cheaper illustrated edition,* 1932 | PRINTED IN GREAT BRITAIN | AT THE WINDMILL PRESS, SURREY'; [v] 'TO | ADA AND JOHN GALSWORTHY'; [vi] blank; [vii] 'LIST OF ILLUSTRATIONS' (eight illustrations (including frontispiece) listed with page references); [viii] blank; [1] 'PART I'; [2] '*The persons and events described in this* | *poem are imaginary. No reference is* | *made or intended to any living person.* | *JOHN MASEFIELD*.'; 3–57 text of part I; [58] blank; [59] 'PART II'; [60] blank; 61-[124] text of part II

Paper: wove paper

Running title: 'REYNARD THE FOX' (39mm.) on both verso and recto, pp.4–57 and pp.62-[124]

Binding: blue cloth. On spine, in gold: 'Reynard | the | Fox | [ornament] | John | Masefield | Illustrated by | G.D.Armour | Heinemann' (all width centred). Upper cover: blank. On lower cover, in blind: publisher's device of a windmill (ranged lower right). All edges trimmed. Binding measurements: 193 × 130mm. (covers), 193 × 27mm. (spine). End-papers: wove paper.

Publication date: the sales ledger preserved in the Heinemann Archive suggests publication on 5 December 1932 in an edition of 1500 copies

Price: 6s.

Contents:
as for A49(a)

Notes:
The text appears to use the same setting of type as A49(b). Illustrations are tipped-in. There are none of the numerous head and tail pieces as originally printed within A49(f).

It appears that reprints of A49(b) were, eventually, raised to 6s. At some point the edition was reduced in price (with several conditions made by Masefield) to 3s.6d. With the need of a new reprint, C.S. Evans wrote with a suggestion:

> …The separate edition of REYNARD THE FOX has to be reprinted almost at once. You will remember that we issued that book at 6/-, and with your consent we reduced the price to 3/6d. You expressed the wish, however, that in the event of a reissue, the 3/6d edition should not be continued. Now, we can hardly hope to sell to the public for 6/- a book which we have been offering to them for 3/6d. I think, therefore, that it would be a good plan to vary its form. What would you think of the idea of reprinting in a larger size 5 1/8" × 7 3/8" and including, say, six of the halftones from the big 15/- edition. We could sell a book of this kind at 6/- without any difficulty.
>
> (C.S. Evans, letter to John Masefield, 7 September 1932)
> (HRHRC, MS (Masefield, J.) Recip William Heinemann Ltd.)

The letter refers to the edition with illustrations by G.D. Armour (see A49(f)). Masefield presumably consented to Evans' suggestion for a letter, dated two days later, from Louisa Callender notes '…the 6/- edition of REYNARD is being put in hand.' (see Louisa Callender, letter to John Masefield, 9 September 1932) (HRHRC, MS (Masefield, J.) Recip William Heinemann Ltd.) At the end of the month, Callender wrote again:

> As you know, we are going to bring out a cheap edition of REYNARD THE FOX with eight of the illustrations from the 15/- book. Will you very kindly choose which of the pictures you would like us to use? In case you have not a copy of the book by you I am sending one under another cover…
>
> (Louisa Callender, letter to John Masefield, 28 September 1932)
> (HRHRC, MS (Masefield, J.) Recip William Heinemann Ltd.)

Masefield's suggestions were acknowledged on 2 October (see Louisa Callender, letter to John Masefield, 2 October 1932) (HRHRC, MS (Masefield, J.) Recip William Heinemann Ltd.) The contract was sent on 8 November and Evans noted problems with the blocks of the illustrations:

I am sending a contract for the cheap edition of REYNARD THE FOX, to be issued at 6/- …The blocks of the illustrations have been laid aside for twelve years and during that time they have been lost by the former printer of the book, and new ones will have to be made.

> (C.S. Evans, letter to John Masefield, 8 November 1932)
> (HRHRC, MS (Masefield, J.) Recip William Heinemann Ltd.)

The publishing agreement for this edition between Masefield and Heinemann was dated 9 November 1932 (see Archives of The Society of Authors). The agreement refers to a publication price of 6s. It appears that Heinemann had previously reached agreement for 4000 copies of an edition to be published at 3s.6d. in 1928 'in a cover bearing a cover design by Judith Masefield'. This was, presumably, never published.

The illustrations chosen for this cheap edition comprise one colour plate, five reproductions of pencil drawings and two plates of black and white illustrations which originally appeared in A49(f).

Copies seen: private collection (PWE); HRHRC (TEMP M377RE 1932) inscribed 'For Con | from Jan | Dec 2. 1932.'

Reprinted:

	[sixth edition, second impression]	Nov 1934
'Reprinted'	[sixth edition, third impression]	Dec 1936

A50 ANIMULA   1920

A50(a) First English edition (1920)

ANIMULA [in red] | BY | JOHN MASEFIELD | [ornament] | LONDON: PRIVATELY PRINTED AT | THE CHISWICK PRESS | 1920
(All width centred)

Bibliographies: Danielson [unrecorded], Williams [unrecorded], Simmons [45], Nevinson [unrecorded], Handley-Taylor p.43, Wight [45]

Collation: [A]⁸; 8 leaves; 223 × 179mm.; [1–4] 5–16

Page contents: [1] title-page; [2] 'The edition is limited to 250 numbered copies, of which | this is No. ....' (the 'T' of 'The' is swash); [3] 'TO MY WIFE'; [4] blank; 5–16 text

Paper: laid paper (watermark: 'ALDWYCH'), chain-lines 29mm. apart

Running title: none

Binding: brown wrappers. Spine: blank. On upper wrapper: 'ANIMULA | BY | JOHN MASEFIELD | [ornament] | LONDON: PRIVATELY PRINTED AT | THE CHISWICK PRESS | 1920'. Lower wrapper: blank. All edges untrimmed. Binding measurements: 237 × 182mm. (wrappers); 237 × 2mm. (spine). The wrappers extend beyond the edges of the internal leaves.

Publication date: printed, according to Simmons, 24 February 1920

Price: copies were not for sale

Contents:
Animula ('This is the place, this house beside the sea,')

Notes:
A sonnet sequence concerned with a love triangle between a young woman, a frustrated husband and a scholar-poet. Masefield was experimenting with the tale as a play in 1911 which highlights the generic oddity of this piece: it is neither a narrative poem nor a true sonnet sequence. The work was reprinted in *Enslaved and other poems* (see A52)

Both Simmons and Wight describe the paper as 'cream laid paper with watermark'

In 1994 Keith Smith Books offered two copies of *Animula* for sale. The first was un-numbered and inscribed 'The very last copy | For Anne Renier | from | John Masefield | St. Valentine's Day | 1960'. In a subsequent letter Masefield writes:

> The other day, I sent to you what I believed to be the very last copy of *Animula*. It was not the last; in fact it was the 225th. While tidying my papers this morning, I found an unopened packet of *Animula*, just as it came from the printers many years ago, never opened, but tidied away with other parcels of paper: a full 25… …please forgive my error, and accept, if you will, the very real last copy, No. 250; the <u>Rest and be thankful</u> copy.

> (John Masefield, letter to Anne Renier, [March 1960])
> (see Keith Smith Books – John Masefield, O.M. (1878–1967) Catalogue No. 1. Malvern: Keith Smith Books, 1994)

The second copy offered for sale (numbered 250) was inscribed 'Rest and be Thankful Copy | The last of the batch | for Anne Renier | from John Masefield | The 29th. of February 1960 | Verses written long since in Animula's | old home, near her portrait, & that | of her husband, with lively feelings | of the anguish once suffered there | by the three unusual spirits.' It is poignant that Masefield was tidying his papers in February 1960, for earlier that month (on the 18th), his wife had died.

An undated letter tipped-in at the rear of Florence Lamont's copy provides background to the poem:

> Thank you so very much for your most kind charming thoughtful letter about Enslaved + the poems printed with it. Your praise + understanding give me deep pleasure. I'm sending you a copy of Animula. You know, perhaps, that Animula lived at Cushendun House, + died there, while her husband lived on there until 1902, + I saw the third party in 1903 or 1904 in a neighbouring village. You slept in her room, I think.

> (John Masefield, letter to Florence Lamont, [after May 1920])
> (Harvard College Library (Houghton *EC9.M377.920a(B)))

Copies seen: private collection (PWE) number 139, inscribed '139 | Muriel Joscelyne, | from John Masefield. | Jan 3rd. 1934.' on p.[2]; private collection (ROV) number 87, inscribed '87 | For Kathleen Noton, | from | John Masefield. | Oxford Recitations. | July 24. 25. 1923.' on p.[2]; private collection (BG) number 164, inscribed '164 | For | Barbara Vernon, | from | John Masefield. | Septr. 1939.' on p.[2]; BL (Cup.510.av.30) stamped 15 JAN 1973, number 1, inscribed '1 | One' on p.[2], includes posthumous booklabel; Bodleian (Additional Masefield Papers 10) number 247, inscribed '247 | For Kay, | on her Birthday, | from John Masefield.'; University of Aberdeen Library (MS.2208/12/2/1) number 120, inscribed '120 | For A.A. Jack, | from John Masefield. | Christmas. 1926.' on p.[2]; NYPL (Berg Collection) number 17, inscribed 'seventeen | for Basil Murray | from | John Masefield. | April 16. 1920.' on p.[2]; Harvard College Library (Houghton *EC9.M377.920a(A)) number 10, inscribed 'ten' on p.[2] with 'for H.W. Nevinson | from John Masefield. | March 13. 1920.' on p.[3]; Harvard College Library (Houghton *EC9.M377.920a(B)) number a, inscribed 'a. | for Florence [Lamont] | from John.' on p.[2]; Columbia University Libraries (Special Collections B825.M377.O.1920.ZZ.c.1) number 129, inscribed '129 | from J. Masefield.' on p.[2]; Columbia University Libraries (Special Collections B825.M377.O.1920.ZZ.c.2) number 119, inscribed '119 | For | May MacLachlan, | from | John Masefield. | Christmas. 1926.' on p.[2]; Columbia University Libraries (Special Collections B825.M377.O.1920.ZZ.c.3) number 151, inscribed '151 | For Helen Maclachlan, [*sic*] | from | John Masefield. | Christmas. 1937.' on p.[2]

A51 JOHN RUSKIN   1920

A51(a) First English edition (1920)

JOHN RUSKIN | BY | JOHN MASEFIELD
(All width centred)

Bibliographies: Danielson 197, Williams p.10, Simmons [46], Nevinson [unrecorded], Handley-Taylor p.51, Wight [46]

Collation: [A]⁸; 8 leaves; 282 × 220mm.; [i–ii] [1–3] 4–10 [11–14]

Page contents: [i] title-page; [ii] blank; [1] 'This essay, which is now printed for the first time, was orig- | inally delivered by Mr. Masefield as a lecture at the Ruskin | Centenary Exhibition held at the Royal Academy in the | Autumn of 1919. | [new paragraph] Printed by Howard Whitehouse and Edward Daws at the | Yellowsands Press, being the private press of Bembridge | School, with the help of the following boys of the school: | Cuthbert Scott, Jean Dieudonné, Cedric Salter, Dingle | Foot, and Charles Gould. | [new paragraph] | One hundred and fifty copies only have been printed of | which this is No. | [new paragraph] 8th. April 1920.'; [2] blank; [3]–10 text; [11–14] blank

Paper: laid paper (watermark: '[crown] | Abbey Mills | Greenfield'), chain-lines 25mm. apart. The paper is used so that chain-lines run horizontally

Running title: 'John Ruskin' (22mm.) on both verso and recto, pp.4–10

Binding: wrappers comprise the first and last leaves of the single gathering ([A]1 and [A]8). The title-page consequently comprises the upper wrapper. Lower wrapper: blank. Top edge uncut, others untrimmed. Binding measurements: 282 × 220mm. (wrappers), 282 × 1mm. (spine).

Publication date: published, according to Simmons, April 1920

Price: unknown

Contents:
John Ruskin ('John Ruskin was born on this day one hundred years ago. That is more than...')

Notes:
As stated within the volume, this essay was delivered by Masefield as a lecture at the Ruskin Centenary Exhibition held at the Royal Academy in the Autumn of 1919. Printed at the Yellowsands Press, see also *A Foundation Day Address* (A56(a)).

The text of this lecture was reprinted (with minor revisions) as a contribution to *Ruskin the Prophet and other Centenary Essays* (see B170).

Both Simmons and Wight describe this volume as a single gathering of eight leaves with the 'binding' integral to the gathering. However, the pagination of this volume suggests that a single gathering of six leaves bound in paper might be a more accurate description. The paper being consistent between 'binding' and 'internal gathering', the description adopted by Simmons and Wight avoids confusion.

Copies seen: BL (Cup.501.k.29), number 26, rebound, stamped 25 SEP 1920; Library of The John Masefield Society (Peter Smith Collection), number 123

A52 ENSLAVED AND OTHER POEMS

A52(a) First English edition (1920)

ENSLAVED | AND OTHER POEMS | BY | JOHN MASEFIELD | [publisher's device of a windmill with '19' and '20' on either side] | [rule, 71mm.] | LONDON: WILLIAM HEINEMANN
(All width centred)

Bibliographies: Danielson 198, Williams p.6, Simmons [47], Nevinson p.13, Handley-Taylor p.51, Wight [47]

Collation: [A]¹⁰ B-H⁸; signatures right foot of page; 66 leaves; 185 × 120mm.; [i–iv] [1–4] 5–124 [125–28]

Page contents: [i] half-title: 'ENSLAVED | AND OTHER POEMS'; [ii] blank; [iii] title-page; [iv] blank; [1] 'TO | LEWIS'; [2] blank; [3] 'CONTENTS' (10 items listed with page references); [4] blank; 5-[125] text (at foot of p.[125]: '[rule] | BILLING AND SONS, LTD., PRINTERS, GUILDFORD, ENGLAND'); [126–28] blank

Paper: wove paper

Running title: running titles comprise titles of individual poems, pp.6–124

Binding: blue-green boards. On spine, in gold: 'Enslaved | [ornament] | John | Masefield | HEINEMANN' (width centred). On upper cover, in gold: 'ENSLAVED | AND OTHER POEMS | WITH SONNETS | JOHN MASEFIELD' (within blind ruled border: 184 × 115mm.) On lower cover, in blind: publisher's device of a windmill with 'W [point]' and 'H' (ranged lower right). All edges trimmed. Binding measurements: 188 × 122mm. (covers), 188 × 24mm. (spine). End-papers: wove paper.

Publication date: published, according to Simmons, 13 May 1920 in an edition of 3000 copies (see notes)

Price: 6s.

Contents:
Enslaved ('All early in the April, when daylight comes at five,')
The Hounds of Hell ('About the crowing of the cock,')
Cap on Head | A Tale of the O'Neill ('O'Neill took ship, O'Neill set sail,')
[Untitled] ('Like bones the ruins of the cities stand,')
[Untitled] ('Now they are gone with all their songs and sins,')
[Untitled] ('None knows what overthrew that city's pride.')
[Untitled] ('So shall we be; so will our cities lie,')
The Passing Strange ('Out of the earth to rest or range')
Animula ('This is the place, this house beside the sea;')
The Lemmings ('Once in a hundred years the Lemmings come')
Forget ('Forget all these, the barren fool in power,')
On Growing Old ('Be with me, Beauty, for the fire is dying;')
Lyric ('Give me a light that I may see her,')

Notes:
A long narrative poem telling of an abduction by Moorish slavers of an English girl to the harem of a Khalif and her daring rescue by her lover. Many of the 'other poems' are printed in volume form for the first time (although see A50 for separate publication of *Animula*).

The dedication, 'To Lewis', is to Masefield's son. At the time of publication Lewis Masefield was nine years old and why his father decided to dedicate to him a long narrative poem concerning abduction is unclear.

In describing the binding, Danielson notes the 'publisher's device (the Nicholson variety) in lower right-hand corner of back cover in blind'. As described above 'the Nicholson variety' is the Heinemann windmill device with both 'W [point]' and 'H' on either side. Danielson only names William Nicholson here.

The title as cited on the upper cover ('Enslaved and Other Poems With Sonnets') is at no point given within the printed matter of the volume itself.

Copies inscribed by Masefield to his children of both this and A52(aa) suggest that A52(a) may preceed A52(aa). Simmons, however, notes simultaneous publication.

The publishing agreement for this title between Masefield and Heinemann was dated 29 March 1920 (see Archives of The Society of Authors). The agreement refers to a publication price of 6s. and also a 'special' issue of 250 copies.

The Society of Authors wrote to Masefield in the 1930s noting that Douglas Fairbanks was showing 'interest' in 'the Talking Picture rights of Enslaved' (see BL, Add.Mss.56598, f.18). At the end of December 1933 Masefield replied:

> Mr Julian Street suggests that perhaps you would be willing to get into touch with a Mr T.J. Geraghty, c/o Mr D. Fairbanks, Grosvenor House, Park Lane, W2, to discuss with him the making of my poem *Enslaved*, into a picture for the two Messrs Fairbanks, father + son. ...I do not for a moment suppose that the romantic fable is in favour now...
>
> (John Masefield, letter to [E.J.] Mullett [10 December 1933])
> (BL, Add.Mss.56599, f.130)

This venture appears to have come to nothing. One probable cause of failure may have been Masefield's financial demands. Writing to The Society of Authors in February 1934, Masefield states with general reference to selling film rights:

> As to the price to ask I would suggest the utmost sum demanded by the most exorbitant successful author. I have no experience in these matters, but £4000 for each book has been quoted to me as a normal figure to ask. In any case one should not ask less than the top market price.
>
> (John Masefield, letter to Mr Tweedie, 6 February 1934)
> (BL, Add.Mss.56600, f.17)

Over a decade later there was renewed interest in film rights from a Mr Wynne Rushton. Rushton suggested either an 'oriental' or British version and Masefield wrote to The Society of Authors:

> I am quite sure that no Christian country will want a film of *Enslaved*, + that Mr. Rushton had better not attempt the work of preparing it for Christians until the heathen + others have had their chance. Let him by all means try the Moslems first. *Enslaved* is a story, not a drama, + I'm afraid the orientals may jib at it as drama.
>
> (John Masefield, letter to [S.M.] Perry, [October 1947])
> (BL, Add.Mss.56620, f.111)

This film project similarly appears to have come to nothing.

Copies seen: private collection (PWE); HRHRC (TEMP M377ENS 1920A cop.1) inscribed 'for Judith | from Pip. | May 8. 1920. | the day of publication.'; HRHRC (TEMP M377ENS 1920A cop.2) inscribed [below printed dedication] 'from Pip. | May 8. 1920.'

Reprinted:
'Second impression'   [first edition, second impression]   Jun 1920

A52(aa) First English edition (limited signed edition) (1920)

ENSLAVED | AND OTHER POEMS | BY | JOHN MASEFIELD | [publisher's device of a windmill with '19' and '20' on either side] | [rule, 69mm.] | LONDON: WILLIAM HEINEMANN
(All width centred)

Bibliographies: Danielson 199, Williams p.6, Simmons [47a], Nevinson [unrecorded], Handley-Taylor p.51, Wight [47a]

Collation: [A]¹⁰ B-H⁸; signatures right foot of page; 66 leaves; 226 × 145mm.; [i–iv] [1–4] 5–124 [125–28]

Page contents: [i] half-title: 'ENSLAVED | AND OTHER POEMS'; [ii] 'BY THE SAME AUTHOR | [rule] | [eight titles listed] | ALSO | GALLIPOLI | One volume, cr. 8vo., illustrated, 2s. 6d. net | THE OLD FRONT LINE | Cr. 8vo., illustrated, 2s. 6d. net | LONDON: WILLIAM HEINEMANN'; [iii] title-page; [iv] blank; [1] 'TO | LEWIS'; [2] *'This Edition, printed on English hand- | made paper, numbered and signed by the | Author, is limited to two hundred and fifty | copies for sale, and twenty-five copies for | presentation, of which this is | No. ....'*; [3] 'CONTENTS' (10 items listed with page references); [4] blank; 5-[125] text (at foot of p.[125]: '[rule] | BILLING AND SONS, LTD., PRINTERS, GUILDFORD, ENGLAND'); [126–28] blank

Paper: wove paper (watermark: 'BRITISH HAND MADE PURE RAG [castle device: 26 × 32mm.]')

Running title: running titles comprise titles of individual poems, pp.6–124

Binding: blue-grey boards with parchment spine. On spine, in gold: 'Enslaved | [ornament] | John | Masefield | HEINEMANN' (all width centred). There is a single vertical rule in blind on each cover at the edge of the parchment. Covers: blank. Top edge gilt, fore edge uncut and lower outside edge untrimmed. Binding measurements: 231 × 146mm. (covers), 231 × 27mm. (spine). End-papers: wove paper.

Publication date: published, according to Simmons, 13 May 1920

Price: 25s.

Contents:
as for A52(a)

Notes:
As described by Simmons, this edition was published on the same day as the regular Heinemann edition. The text appears to use the same setting of type as A52(a) with the exception of the title-page and p.[2]

Copies seen: private collection (ROV) number 240, signed '240 | John Masefield' on p.[2]; HRHRC (TEMP M377ENS 1920B) number 252, signed '252 | John Masefield.' on p.[2], additionally inscribed 'for Judith | from Pip. | June 11. 1920.'

A52(b) First American edition ["Leather Pocket Edition"] (1923)
[see A53(a) for the 1920 First American edition of *Enslaved*]

ENSLAVED | AND OTHER POEMS | *By* | JOHN MASEFIELD | [circular floral ornament] [in red] | NEW YORK | THE MACMILLAN COMPANY | 1923 | ALL RIGHTS RESERVED
(All width centred and enclosed within ornate border in red: 135 × 78mm.)

Bibliographies: Simmons [noted on p.80], Nevinson [unrecorded], Handley-Taylor p.51 and p.53, Wight [unrecorded]

Collation: [A]¹⁰ ([A]4+2) [B-I]⁸ (but signed [A]⁶ ([A]4+2) [B]⁸ C-F⁸ [G]⁸ H⁸ I¹²; see note on American electrotype editions); signatures left foot of page; 74 leaves; 170 × 111mm.; [two un-numbered pages] [i–vi] vii–viii [ix–x] [1–2] 3–51 [52–54] 55–79 [80–82] 83–91 [92–94] 95–98 [99–100] 101–103 [104–106] 107–113 [114–16] 117 [118–20] 121 [122–24] 125 [126–28] 129 [130–36]

Page contents: [-] blank (page excluded from page count, but constitutes first leaf of first gathering); [-] blank; [i] half-title: 'ENSLAVED | [ornament] [in red]'; [ii] '[27 titles separated by 20 single points] | [ornament] [in red]' (enclosed within ornate border in red: 135 × 78mm.); [iii] title-page; [iv] 'COPYRIGHT, 1920 AND 1923, BY JOHN MASEFIELD | *Printed in the United States of America* | [ornament] [in red]'; [v] 'TO | LEWIS'; [vi] blank; vii–viii 'ENSLAVED | INTRODUCTION' ('I wrote this poem in the autumn of 1919. It is based upon two stories...') (unsigned); [ix] 'CONTENTS' (10 items listed with page references); [x] blank; [1] 'ENSLAVED'; [2] blank; 3–51 text of 'Enslaved'; [52] blank; [53] 'THE HOUNDS OF HELL'; [54] blank; 55–79 text of 'The Hounds of Hell'; [80] blank; [81] 'CAP ON HEAD | A TALE OF THE O'NEILL'; [82] blank; 83–91 Text of 'Cap on Head'; [92] blank; [93] 'SONNETS'; [94] blank; 95–98 text of 'Sonnets'; [99] 'THE PASSING STRANGE'; [100] blank; 101–103 text of 'The Passing Strange'; [104] blank; [105] 'ANIMULA'; [106] blank; 107–113 text of 'Animula'; [114] blank; [115] 'THE LEMMINGS'; [116] blank; 117 text of 'The Lemmings'; [118] blank; [119] 'FORGET'; [120] blank; 121 text of 'Forget'; [122] blank; [123] 'ON GROWING OLD'; [124] blank; 125 text of 'On Growing Old'; [126] blank; [127] 'LYRIC'; [128] blank; 129 text of 'Lyric' (at foot of p.129: '[rule] | Printed in the United States of America.'); [130–36] blank

Paper: laid paper (no watermark), chain-lines 25mm. apart

Running title: none

Binding: red leather. On spine, in gold: '[floral panel] | ENSLAVED | MASEFIELD | [floral panel] | MACMILLAN'. On upper cover, in blind: circular floral ornament (within blind ruled border: 171 × 111mm.) Lower cover: blank. Top edge gilt, others trimmed. Binding measurements: 174 × 115mm. (covers), 174 × 21mm. (spine). End-papers: wove paper.

Publication date: published, according to Handley-Taylor, 30 August 1923 / published, according to Simmons, 30 October 1923 in an edition of 2000 copies (see notes)

Price: $12.50 (set of 8 volumes: see also A21(d), A49(h), A54(g), A66(a), A67(a), A68(a) and A69(a))

Contents:
Introduction ('I wrote this poem in the autumn of 1919. It is based upon two stories...')
Enslaved ('All early in the April when daylight comes at five')
The Hounds of Hell ('About the crowing of the cock,')
Cap on Head | A Tale of the O'Neill ('O'Neill took ship, O'Neill set sail,')
[Untitled] ('Like bones the ruins of the cities stand,')
[Untitled] ('Now they are gone with all their songs and sins,')
[Untitled] ('None knows what overthrew that city's pride.')
[Untitled] ('So shall we be; so will our cities lie,')
The Passing Strange ('Out of the earth to rest or range')
Animula ('This is the place, this house beside the sea,')
The Lemmings ('Once in a hundred years the Lemmings come')
Forget ('Forget all these, the barren fool in power,')
On Growing Old ('Be with me Beauty for the fire is dying,')
Lyric ('Give me a light that I may see her,')

Notes:
Page numbers appear within square brackets. Thus, [3], [4], etc. The exceptions are pages vii and viii.

Issued as volume VI in the Macmillan Leather Pocket Edition of Masefield's Work.

Items commence with a drop-capital with the exception of the last three of the untitled sonnets.

The additional leaves ([A]2 and [A]3) comprise a conjugate set of leaves pasted onto [A]4. They use the same paper stock as the rest of the volume and were presumably later added to the volume as they comprise the only pages with additional devices printed in red.

Accepting Handley-Taylor's publication date would explain the omission of *A King's Daughter* (published on 23 October 1923) in the listing of Masefield's works appearing on page [ii].

Copies seen: Harvard College Library (Widener 23697.10.55.10)

A53 ENSLAVED   1920

A53(a) First American edition (1920)

ENSLAVED | BY | JOHN MASEFIELD | AUTHOR OF "REYNARD THE FOX" | "THE EVERLASTING MERCY" | ETC. | New York | THE MACMILLAN COMPANY | 1920 | *All rights reserved*
(All width centred)

Bibliographies: Danielson [unrecorded], Williams [unrecorded], Simmons [noted on p.80], Nevinson [unrecorded], Handley-Taylor p.51, Wight 47b

Collation: [A-I]⁸ (but signed [A]⁴ [B]⁸ C-F⁸ [G]⁸ H⁸ I¹²; see note on American electrotype editions); signatures left foot of page; 72 leaves; 200 × 134mm.; [i–vi] vii [viii] [1–2] 3–51 [52–54] 55–79 [80–82] 83–91 [92–94] 95–98 [99–100] 101–103 [104–106] 107–113 [114–16] 117 [118–22] [123 numbered 121] [124–26] [127 numbered 125] [128–30] [131 numbered 129] [132–36] (see notes)

Page contents: [i] half-title: 'ENSLAVED'; [ii] '[publisher's device] | THE MACMILLAN COMPANY | [two lines listing six cities, separated by four points] | MACMILLAN & CO., LIMITED | [two lines listing four cities, separated by two points] | THE MACMILLAN CO. OF CANADA, LTD. | [one city listed]'; [iii] title-page; [iv] 'COPYRIGHT, 1920, | BY JOHN MASEFIELD. | [rule] | Set up and electrotyped. Published June, 1920. | Norwood Press | J. S. Cushing Co.-Berwick & Smith Co. | Norwood. Mass., U.S.A.'; [v] 'TO | LEWIS'; [vi] blank; vii 'CONTENTS' (10 items listed with page references); [viii] blank; [1] 'ENSLAVED'; [2] blank; 3–51 text of 'Enslaved'; [52] blank; [53] 'THE HOUNDS OF HELL'; [54] blank; 55–79 text of 'The Hounds of Hell'; [80] blank; [81] 'CAP ON HEAD | A TALE OF THE O'NEILL'; [82] blank; 83–91 text of 'Cap on Head'; [92] blank; [93] 'SONNETS'; [94] blank; 95–98 text of 'Sonnets'; [99] 'THE PASSING STRANGE'; [100] blank; 101–103 text of 'The Passing Strange'; [104] blank; [105] 'ANIMULA'; [106] blank; 107–113 text of 'Animula'; [114] blank; [115] 'THE LEMMINGS'; [116] blank; 117 text of 'The Lemmings'; [118] blank; [119] 'FORGET'; [120] blank; [121] 'ON GROWING OLD'; [122] blank; [123] text of 'Forget'; [124] blank; [125] 'LYRIC'; [126] blank; [127] text of 'On Growing Old'; [128–30] blank; [131] text of 'Lyric' (at foot of p.[131]: '[rule] | Printed in the United States of America.'); [132–36] blank

Paper: wove paper

Running title: none

Binding: burgundy cloth. On spine, in gold: 'ENSLAVED | MASEFIELD | MACMILLAN | [point] [point] [point]'. On upper cover, in blind: 'ENSLAVED | MASEFIELD' (ranged upper left) (within blind ruled border: 195 × 124mm.) Lower cover: blank. Top edge trimmed, others roughly trimmed. Binding measurements: 204 × 130mm. (covers), 204 × 31mm. (spine). End-papers: wove paper.

Publication date: published, according to Simmons, 29 June 1920 in an edition of 2802 copies

Price: $2.25

Contents:
Enslaved ('All early in the April when daylight comes at five')
The Hounds of Hell ('About the crowing of the cock,')
Cap on Head | A Tale of the O'Neill ('O'Neill took ship, O'Neill set sail,')
[Untitled] ('Like bones the ruins of the cities stand,')
[Untitled] ('Now they are gone with all their songs and sins,')
[Untitled] ('None knows what overthrew that city's pride.')
[Untitled] ('So shall we be; so will our cities lie,')
The Passing Strange ('Out of the earth to rest or range')
Animula ('This is the place, this house beside the sea,')
The Lemmings ('Once in a hundred years the Lemmings come')
Forget ('Forget all these, the barren fool in power,')
On Growing Old ('Be with me Beauty for the fire is dying,')
Lyric ('Give me a light that I may see her,')

Notes:
In the copy examined, the final gathering has been bound incorrectly. Consequently page numbers after p.121 are incorrect. Incorrect imposition of electroplates cannot be discounted. The description of a perfect copy by Wight would suggest that not all copies carry the fault.

Wight's title-page transcription of this volume is incorrect (there is a line break between 'New York' and 'THE MACMILLAN COMPANY').

Page numbers appear within square brackets. Thus, [3], [4], etc. The exception is p.vii.

Items commence with a drop-capital with the exception of the last three of the untitled sonnets.

The stereoplates appear the same as those used in A53(aa). Note, for the example, the unsigned [G] signature.

In 'Some Contributions to the Bibliography of John Masefield: II' (*Papers of the Bibliographical Society of America*, October 1959, pp.262–67) Drew states:

> The June 1920 publication appeared in two bindings: one, red cloth; the other, brown boards with cream paper back. Both are entitled *Enslaved*, although the dust wrapper of the brown boards issue lists the title as *Enslaved and Other Poems*. The contents of the two issues are identical with those of the Heinemann *Enslaved and other poems* (Simmons 47).

A Macmillan catalogue (dated 1 May 1921) lists A53(aa) first and then, under 'New and Cheaper edition', A53(a). This conflicts with Simmons' date of publication for A53(a) and inscribed copies of A53(aa).

Copies seen: private collection (ROV) final gathering bound incorrectly

THANK YOU FOR YOUR CONFIDENCE IN OUR MERCHANDISE ----

BOOKS AND EBAY ITEMS

We take pride in speedy mailing and pleased buyers.

Revisit us @ singingangel917 on ebay

We are adding new items as time allows --

crafts, yarns, arrowheads, collectibles, antiques, Nascars, Hot wheels, Matchbox,

plus much more....

We are partially retired and enjoy giving a little extra to our ten grandchildren.

Blessings and thanks,   Rudd and Estelle

A53(aa) Additional First American edition (1920)

ENSLAVED | BY | JOHN MASEFIELD | AUTHOR OF "REYNARD THE FOX" | "THE EVERLASTING MERCY" | ETC. | New York | THE MACMILLAN COMPANY | 1920 | *All rights reserved*
(All width centred)

Bibliographies: Danielson [unrecorded], Williams [unrecorded], Simmons [unrecorded], Nevinson [unrecorded], Handley-Taylor [unrecorded], Wight 47c

Collation: [A-I]⁸ (but signed [A]⁵ [B]⁸ C-F⁸ [G]⁸ H⁸ I¹¹; see note on American electrotype editions); signatures left foot of page; 72 leaves; 236 × 155mm.; [two un-numbered pages] [i–vi] vii [viii] [1–2] 3–51 [52–54] 55–79 [80–82] 83–91 [92–94] 95–98 [99–100] 101–103 [104–106] 107–113 [114–16] 117 [118–20] 121 [122–24] 125 [126–28] 129 [130–34]

Page contents: [-] blank (page excluded from page count, but constitutes first leaf of first gathering); [-] blank; [i] half-title: 'ENSLAVED'; [ii] '[publisher's device] | THE MACMILLAN COMPANY | [two lines listing six cities, separated by four points] | MACMILLAN & CO., LIMITED | [two lines listing four cities, separated by two points] | THE MACMILLAN CO. OF CANADA, LTD. | [one city listed]'; [iii] title-page; [iv] 'COPYRIGHT, 1920, | BY JOHN MASEFIELD. | [rule] | Set up and electrotyped. Published June, 1920. | Norwood Press | J. S. Cushing Co.-Berwick & Smith Co. | Norwood. Mass., U.S.A.'; [v] 'TO | LEWIS'; [vi] blank; vii 'CONTENTS' (10 items listed with page references); [viii] blank; [1] 'ENSLAVED'; [2] blank; 3–51 text of 'Enslaved'; [52] blank; [53] 'THE HOUNDS OF HELL'; [54] blank; 55–79 text of 'The Hounds of Hell'; [80] blank; [81] 'CAP ON HEAD | A TALE OF THE O'NEILL'; [82] blank; 83–91 text of 'Cap on Head'; [92] blank; [93] 'SONNETS'; [94] blank; 95–98 text of 'Sonnets'; [99] 'THE PASSING STRANGE'; [100] blank; 101–103 text of 'The Passing Strange'; [104] blank; [105] 'ANIMULA'; [106] blank; 107–113 text of 'Animula'; [114] blank; [115] 'THE LEMMINGS'; [116] blank; 117 text of 'The Lemmings'; [118] blank; [119] 'FORGET'; [120] blank; 121 text of 'Forget'; [122] blank; [123] 'ON GROWING OLD'; [124] blank; 125 text of 'On Growing Old'; [126] blank; [127] 'LYRIC'; [128] blank; 129 text of 'Lyric' (at foot of p.129: '[rule] | Printed in the United States of America.'); [130–34] blank

Paper: wove paper (watermark: '*Old Stratford*' note that many of these characters are swash)

Running title: none

Binding: brown boards with parchment spine. On spine reading lengthways up spine, from foot, in gold: 'ENSLAVED – MASEFIELD'. On upper cover: panel in blind: 38 × 70mm. upon which: white paper label (37 × 69mm.) on which: 'ENSLAVED | AND OTHER POEMS | [rule] | [rule] | JOHN MASEFIELD' (enclosed within double ruled border (the outside border being bolder): 27 × 60mm.) Lower cover: blank. Top edge trimmed, others roughly trimmed (some of the fore edges are deckle edged). Binding measurements: 241 × 156mm. (covers), 241 × 26mm. (spine). End-papers: wove paper.

Publication date: presumably published, according to inscribed copies, around July 1920

Price: $2.50

Contents:
as for A53(a)

Notes:
Wight is the only bibliographer to describe this volume, as distinct from A53(a). (Although see Drew's note in 'Some Contributions to the Bibliography of John Masefield: II' (*Papers of the Bibliographical Society of America*, October 1959, pp.262–67)). It seems not unlikely that Macmillan may have intended this edition to have been a limited signed edition. (Heinemann had issued the volume as both standard and limited signed editions). This hypothesis is suggested by the binding and the parchment spine in particular. There is also some similarity to A33(b).

Two copies of this volume have been examined which both carry the posthumous booklabel. One merely carries the booklabel. The other includes the inscription 'for Lewis | from Pip | July 17. 1920.' This is a dedication copy and dated *after* the issue of the standard burgundy cloth edition.

Page numbers appear within square brackets. Thus, [3], [4], etc. The exception is page vii.

Items commence with a drop-capital with the exception of the last three of the untitled sonnets.

Wight describes the signatures of this volume as [A-L]⁸ and notes that the volume contains 72 leaves. This is an obvious error and Wight's mistake occurs in his transcription of signatures.

Observation of the label laid down to the upper cover reveals minute gaps in the construction of the double ruled border enclosing the title and author.

Copies seen: BL (Cup.404.b.30) stamped 15 APR 1971, includes posthumous booklabel; Library of The John Masefield Society (Peter Smith Collection) inscribed 'for Lewis | from Pip | July 17. 1920.' with signature of Judith Masefield, includes posthumous booklabel; HRHRC (TEMP M377ENS 1920C cop.1) inscribed 'for Con from Jan | July 17. 1920.'; HRHRC (TEMP M377ENS 1920C cop.2) inscribed 'for Judith | from Zom. | July 17. 1902.'

A54 RIGHT ROYAL

A54(a) First American edition (1920)

RIGHT ROYAL | By | JOHN MASEFIELD | New York | THE MACMILLAN COMPANY | 1920 | *All rights reserved*
(All width centred)

Bibliographies: Danielson [unrecorded], Williams [unrecorded], Simmons [48], Nevinson [unrecorded], Handley-Taylor p.51, Wight [48]

Collation: [A-I]⁸ [K]⁴ (J not used); 76 leaves; 187 × 128mm.; [i–vi] [1–2] 3–64 [65–66] 67–145 [146]

Page contents: [i] half-title: 'RIGHT ROYAL'; [ii] 'By JOHN MASEFIELD | [24 titles listed]'; [iii] title-page; [iv] 'Copyright, 1920 | BY JOHN MASEFIELD | Set up and electrotyped. Published, October, 1920'; [v] 'NOTE | The persons, horses and events described | in this poem are imaginary. No reference | is made to any living person or horse. | JOHN MASEFIELD.'; [vi] blank; [1] 'PART I'; [2] blank; 3–64 text of part I; [65] 'PART II'; [66] blank; 67–145 text of part II; [146] blank

Paper: wove paper

Running-title: 'RIGHT ROYAL' (23mm.) on both verso and recto, pp.4–64 and pp.68–145

Binding: mottled light grey-green boards with light green cloth spine. On spine, in gold: 'RIGHT | ROYAL | MASEFIELD | MACMILLAN' (all width centred). Covers: blank. All edges trimmed. Binding measurements: 194 × 127mm. (covers), 194 × 30mm. (spine). End-papers: wove paper. The end-papers at the front of the volume are illustrated with 'MAP OF THE | COMPTON COURSE' comprising an unsigned diagram and description of the race course.

Publication date: published, according to Simmons, 19 October 1920 in an edition of 5008 copies

Price: $1.75

Contents:
Right Royal ('An hour before the race they talked together')

Notes:
The second of Masefield's major trio of long narrative poems written after the Great War. Less allegorical than *Reynard the Fox*, the poem describes a steeplechase, the winning horse and the jockey's relationship with his betrothed, which is placed in jeopardy by the race.

A publishing agreement for this title between Masefield and Macmillan was dated 8 July 1920 (see Archives of The Society of Authors). The agreement refers to 'a licence to publish in volume form… in the United States of America and Canada a work the subject or title of which is a Narrative Poem (Steeple Chase)'. Masefield has added 'Right Royal'.

In March 1948 Masefield responded to The Society of Authors regarding an application to recite the poem:

> About *Right Royal*. This is a tale in verse written nearly 30 years ago. I have often thought of scrapping it. I have sometimes recited some of it, and know its defects better than any living person.
> (John Masefield, letter to Miss A. Wordingham, 10 March [1948])
> (BL, Add.Mss.56620, f.184)

Copies seen: private collection (PWE)

A54(b) First English edition (1920)

RIGHT ROYAL | BY | JOHN MASEFIELD | [publisher's device of a windmill with '19' and '20' on either side] | [rule, 71mm.] | LONDON: WILLIAM HEINEMANN
(All width centred)

Bibliographies: Danielson 200, Williams p.6, Simmons [48a], Nevinson p.13, Handley-Taylor p.51, Wight [48a]

Collation: [A]⁸ B-H⁸; signatures right foot of page; 64 leaves; 182 × 119mm.; [i–viii] [1–2] 3–52 [53–54] 55–119 [120]

Page contents: [i–ii] blank; [iii] half-title: 'RIGHT ROYAL'; [iv] 'BY THE SAME AUTHOR | [rule] | [12 titles listed] | LONDON: WILLIAM HEINEMANN.'; [v] title-page; [vi] blank; [vii] 'TO | MY WIFE'; [viii] 'NOTE. | *The persons, horses, and events described in | this poem are imaginary. No reference is | made to any living person or horse.* | JOHN MASEFIELD.'; [1] 'PART I'; [2] 'MAP OF THE | COMPTON COURSE' (comprising an unsigned diagram and description of the race course); 3–52 text of part I; [53] 'PART II'; [54] blank; 55-[120] text of part II (at foot of p.[120]: '[rule] | Printed in Great Britain by Billing and Sons, Ltd., Guildford and Esher')

Paper: wove paper

Running-title: 'RIGHT ROYAL' (29mm.) on both verso and recto, pp.4–52 and pp.56-[120]

Binding: blue-green boards. On spine, in gold: 'Right | Royal | [ornament] | John | Masefield | HEINEMANN' (all width centred). On upper cover, in gold: 'RIGHT ROYAL | JOHN MASEFIELD' (within blind ruled border: 184 × 114mm.) Lower cover: blank. All edges trimmed. Binding measurements: 188 × 120mm. (covers), 188 × 23mm. (spine). End-papers: wove paper.

Publication date: published, according to Simmons, 11 November 1920 in an edition of 5000 copies

Price: 6s.

Contents:
Right Royal ('An hour before the race they talked together,')

Notes:
The Macmillan and Heinemann editions use differently drawn maps of the race course.

The text has been entirely re-set for this edition.

Simmons makes two obvious errors in his description of this volume. His description of the book ([A-C]⁸ D-H⁸) finds fewer signatures than are present while his description of the boards of the binding as 'blue' is misleading.

Copies seen: private collection (PWE)

Reprinted:
'New Impression'   [first edition, second impression]   Nov 1920

A54(c) Second English edition (limited signed edition) (1920)

RIGHT ROYAL | BY | JOHN MASEFIELD | [publisher's device of a windmill with '19' and '20' on either side] | [rule, 71mm.] | LONDON: WILLIAM HEINEMANN
(All width centred)

Bibliographies: Danielson 201, Williams p.6, Simmons [48b], Nevinson [unrecorded], Handley-Taylor p.51, Wight [48b]

Collation: [A]⁸ B-H⁸; signatures left foot of page; 64 leaves; 223 × 146mm.; [i–viii] [1–2] 3–52 [53–54] 55–119 [120]

Page contents: [i] blank (page excluded from page count, but constitutes first leaf of first gathering); [ii] blank; [iii] half-title: 'RIGHT ROYAL'; [iv] 'BY THE SAME AUTHOR | [rule] | [12 titles listed] | LONDON: WILLIAM HEINEMANN.'; [v] title-page; [vi] blank; [vii] 'TO | MY WIFE'; [viii] '*This Edition, printed on English hand-made | paper, numbered and signed by the Author, is | limited to 500 copies for sale and 25 copies | for presentation, of which this is | No. _____ | NOTE. | The persons, horses, and events described in this | poem are imaginary. No reference is made to | any living person or horse. | JOHN MASEFIELD.*'; [1] 'PART I'; [2] 'MAP OF THE COMPTON COURSE' (comprising an unsigned diagram and description of the race course); 3–52 text of part I; [53] 'PART II'; [54] blank; 55-[120] text of part II (at foot of p.[120]: '[rule] | Printed in Great Britain by Billing and Sons, Ltd., Guildford and Esher')

Paper: wove paper (watermark: 'BRITISH HAND MADE [P]URE RAG [castle device: 27 × 33mm.]')

Running-title: 'RIGHT ROYAL' (29mm.) on both verso and recto, pp.4–52 and pp.56-[120]

Binding: blue-green boards with parchment spine. On spine, in gold: 'Right | Royal | [ornament] | John | Masefield | HEINEMANN' (all width centred). There is a single vertical rule in blind on each cover at the edge of the parchment. Covers: blank. Top edge gilt, lower outside edge untrimmed, fore edge uncut. Binding measurements: 231 × 146mm. (covers), 231 × 29mm. (spine). End-papers: laid paper (no watermark), chain-lines 25mm. apart.

Publication date: published, according to Simmons, 16 December 1920

Price: 25s.

Contents:
as for A54(b)

Notes:
As noted by Simmons, p.[viii] is reset (presumably to accommodate the note of limitation). Otherwise, the text appears to use the same setting of type as A54(b)

Copies seen: private collection (PWE) number 347, inscribed '347 | John Masefield.' on p.[viii]; private collection (ROV) number 268, inscribed '268 | John Masefield.' on p.[viii]

A54(d) Third English edition (first English illustrated edition) (1922)

RIGHT ROYAL [in red] | BY | JOHN MASEFIELD | ILLUSTRATED BY | CECIL ALDIN | [illustration of jockey in weighing chair, signed with 'CA' monogram] | [publisher's device of a windmill with '19' and '22' on either side] | [rule, 92mm.] | LONDON: WILLIAM HEINEMANN
(All width centred)

Bibliographies: Simmons [unrecorded], Nevinson p.15, Handley-Taylor p.51, Wight [unrecorded]

Collation: [A]⁴ B-F⁸ G⁶; G2 is also signed; signatures left foot of page; 50 leaves; 248 × 185mm.; [i–viii] [1–2] 3–49 [50] 51–90 [91–92]; illustrations (on glossy paper) are tipped-in on grey wove paper leaves; these leaves are tipped-in on pp.[ii], 45, 67 and [91]; protective tissue is provided for colour illustrations

Page contents: [i] half-title: 'RIGHT ROYAL'; [ii] 'BY THE SAME AUTHOR | [rule] | [12 titles listed] | LONDON: WILLIAM HEINEMANN' (with additional grey leaf tipped-in on the verso of which the coloured frontispiece is tipped-in: 201 × 139mm.); [iii] title-page (with protective tissue for frontispiece: '"PULSE FOR PULSE WITH THE HEART OF LIFE"'); [iv] *'First published, 6/-, November* 1920. | *New Impression, November* 1920. | *Illustrated Edition,* 1922.'; [v] 'TO | MY WIFE'; [vi] 'NOTE | *The persons, horses and events described in this poem | are imaginary. No reference is made to any living | person or horse.* | JOHN MASEFIELD.'; [vii] 'LIST OF ILLUSTRATIONS | IN COLOUR' (four colour illustrations (including frontispiece) listed with page references); [viii] untitled map of the Compton course (comprising an unsigned diagram and description of the race course); [1] 'PART I'; [2] blank; 3–48 text (and illustrations) of part I; 49 'PART II'; [50] blank; 51-[91] text (and illustrations) of part II; [92] 'PRINTED IN GREAT BRITAIN BY | RICHARD CLAY & SONS, LIMITED, | BUNGAY, SUFFOLK.'

Paper: wove paper

Running title: none

Binding: black cloth. On spine, in gold: 'RIGHT | ROYAL | [illustration of jockey's riding cap] | JOHN | MASEFIELD | ILLUSTRATED | WITH COLOUR & | LINE DRAWINGS | BY CECIL ALDIN | HEINEMANN' (all width centred). On upper cover, in gold: 'RIGHT ROYAL | JOHN MASEFIELD | ILLUSTRATED WITH COLOUR | AND LINE DRAWINGS BY | CECIL ALDIN | [illustration of a horse's head: 50 × 63mm.]' On lower cover, in blind: publisher's device of a windmill (ranged lower right). All edges trimmed. Binding measurements: 254 × 187mm. (covers), 254 × 30mm. (spine). End-papers: wove paper decorated with illustration of downland with figure in hat and smock with dog watching two horses ridden by jockeys, signed 'CECIL | ALDIN' with panel enclosing verse: 'HE [point] WAS [point] FROM [point] SLEiNS [point] THE [point] MANOR [point] UP [point] THE [point] LiTHE | RiDING [point] THE [point] DOWNS [point] HAD [point] MADE [point] HIS [point] BODY [point] BLiTHE;' (see notes).

Publication date: published, according to Handley-Taylor on 5 October 1922 (see notes)

Price: 15s.

Contents:
as for A54(b)

Notes:
In addition to the illustrated plates, there are a large number of head and tail pieces, and other line drawings throughout the volume. Many of the head pieces are repeated so as to give the impression of a volume with illustrated running titles (excluding the title). Only the colour illustrations are included in the contents listing. Line drawings are unsigned, signed, or signed with Aldin's monogram.

The protective tissues all carry a legend for the illustration they protect.

The paper upon which the illustration plates are tipped-in is grey wove paper similar to the 'paste-board' described by Simmons for A49(e)

A publishing agreement for this edition between Masefield and Heinemann was dated 24 February 1922 (see Archives of The Society of Authors). The agreement refers to both an issue priced at 12s.6d. and a 'special hand-made paper' issue. A later agreement was dated 16 September 1923. This agreement refers to both a standard and 'special edition'.

Handley-Taylor states 'an edition illustrated by Cecil Aldin was published October 5, 1922'. He does not, however, state either whether this date is for the regular or limited edition (or both). Wight (who fails to note the regular illustrated edition) quotes Handley-Taylor's date for the limited edition. Copies in the British Library of the standard and the limited editions are stamped 5 OCT 1922 and 4 JAN 1923 respectively. The sales ledger preserved in the Heinemann Archive suggests that this, the English Illustrated Edition (Heinemann, 1922) was published on 5 October 1922. The limited edition is elusive in the Heinemann sales ledger. An advertisement in *The Times Literary Supplement* for 5 October 1922 announces the regular edition and notes 'Limited edition appearing shortly'. Both standard and limited editions are advertised by Heinemann in *The Times Literary Supplement* for 7 December 1922.

One clue within the end-papers illustration (at both the front and rear of the volume) suggests that this edition was printed before the limited edition. Close attention to the verse within the panel reveals the word 'LiTHE' to have an additional line as if 'TiTHE' had first been written by Aldin. This is cleaned up for the limited edition.

The end-papers incorrectly quote 'the manor' rather than 'that manor' from the couplet as it appears on p.3 of the text.

Omission by Simmons and Wight is unexplained.

See notes to A54(e) for details of the publishing agreement.

Copies seen: private collection (PWE) inscribed 'for | Julia Smith, | from | John Masefield. | 4th Nov. 1922.'; BL (1645.h.34) stamped 5 OCT 1922

A54(e)   Third English edition (first English illustrated limited signed edition) (1922)

RIGHT ROYAL [in red] | BY | JOHN MASEFIELD | ILLUSTRATED BY | CECIL ALDIN | [illustration of jockey in weighing chair, signed with 'CA' monogram] | [publisher's device of a windmill with '19' and '22' on either side] | [rule, 92mm.] | LONDON: WILLIAM HEINEMANN
(All width centred)

Bibliographies: Simmons [unrecorded], Nevinson [unrecorded], Handley-Taylor p.51, Wight 48c

Collation: [A]⁴ B-F⁸ G⁶; G2 is also signed; signatures left foot of page; 50 leaves; 288 × 225mm.; [i–viii] [1–2] 3–49 [50] 51–90 [91–92]; illustrations (on glossy paper) are tipped-in on grey wove paper leaves; these leaves are tipped-in on pp.[ii], 45, 67 and [91]; protective tissue is provided for colour illustrations

Page contents: [i] half-title: 'RIGHT ROYAL'; [ii] *'This Edition is limited to three hundred and | seventy-five copies, numbered and signed by the | Author and Artist, of which three hundred | and fifty are for sale and twenty-five for | presentation. | This is No. ....'* (with additional grey leaf tipped-in on the verso of which the coloured frontispiece is tipped-in: 202 × 138mm.); [iii] title-page (with protective tissue for frontispiece: '"PULSE FOR PULSE WITH THE HEART OF LIFE"'); [iv] *'Printed in Great Britain'*; [v] 'TO | MY WIFE'; [vi] 'NOTE | *The persons, horses and events described in this poem | are imaginary. No reference is made to any living | person or horse.* | JOHN MASEFIELD.'; [vii] 'LIST OF ILLUSTRATIONS | IN COLOUR' (four colour illustrations (including frontispiece) listed with page references); [viii] untitled map of the Compton course (comprising an unsigned diagram and description of the race course); [1] 'PART I'; [2] blank; 3–48 text (and illustrations) of Part I; 49 'PART II'; [50] blank; 51-[91] text (and illustrations) of part II; [92] 'PRINTED IN GREAT BRITAIN BY | RICHARD CLAY & SONS, LIMITED, | BUNGAY, SUFFOLK.'

Paper: wove paper

Running title: none

Binding: cream boards with parchment spine. On spine, in gold: 'RIGHT | ROYAL | [illustration of jockey's riding cap] | JOHN | MASEFIELD | ILLUSTRATED | WITH COLOUR & | LINE DRAWINGS | BY CECIL ALDIN | HEINEMANN' (all width centred). There is a single vertical rule in gold on each cover at the edge of the parchment. On upper cover, in gold: 'RIGHT ROYAL | JOHN MASEFIELD | ILLUSTRATED WITH COLOUR | AND LINE DRAWINGS BY | CECIL ALDIN | [illustration of a horse's head: 50 × 63mm.]' Lower cover: blank. Top edge gilt, others uncut. Sewn head band (in white). Binding measurements: 295 × 230mm. (covers), 295 × 30mm. (spine). End-papers: wove paper decorated with illustration of downland with figure in hat and smock with dog watching two horses ridden by jockeys, signed 'CECIL | ALDIN' with panel enclosing verse: 'HE [point] WAS [point] FROM [point] SLEiNS [point] THE [point] MANOR [point] UP [point] THE [point] LiTHE | RiDING [point] THE [point] DOWNS [point] HAD [point] MADE [point] HIS [point] BODY [point] BLiTHE;'

Publication date: published between 5 October and 7 December 1922

Price: 63s.

Contents:
as for A54(b)

Notes:
see A54(d)

A publishing agreement for this edition between Masefield and Heinemann was dated 24 February 1922 (see Archives of The Society of Authors). The agreement refers to both an issue priced at 12s.6d. and a 'special hand-made paper' issue. It appears that the 'special hand-made paper' was a matter for further consideration. Sydney S. Pawling wrote to Masefield, enclosing a signed duplicate of the agreement, but noting

> …at the moment, the question of large paper editions wants very careful consideration, but I hope to come to a decision one way or the other within 10 days. It will be really limited so you will not have the chance of getting writer's cramp.
> (Sydney S. Pawling, letter to John Masefield, 24 Febraury 1922)
> (Archives of The Society of Authors)

Copies seen: ULL (Special Collections) number 216, signed 'John Masefield.' and 'Cecil Aldin.' on p.[ii]; BL (L.R.37.b.2) number 351, signed 'John Masefield.' and 'Cecil Aldin.' on p.[ii] stamped 4 JAN 1923

A54(f)   Second American edition (first American illustrated edition) (1922)

RIGHT ROYAL | BY | JOHN MASEFIELD | *Illustrated by* | CECIL ALDIN | [illustration of jockey in weighing chair, signed with 'CA' monogram] | NEW YORK | THE MACMILLAN COMPANY | 1922 | *All rights reserved* (All width centred)

Bibliographies: Simmons [noted on p.81], Nevinson [unrecorded], Handley-Taylor p.51, Wight [unrecorded]

Collation: [A]⁸ [H]²; 58 leaves; 223 × 149mm.; [1–10] 11–63 [64–66] 67–116; illustrations (on glossy paper) are tipped-in on pp.[iii], 60, 87 and 114

Page contents: [1] half-title: 'RIGHT ROYAL'; [2] *'By* JOHN MASEFIELD | [rule] | [rule] | [27 titles listed]'; [3] title-page (with additional leaf tipped-in on the verso of which is the coloured frontispiece: 158 × 107mm., '"PULSE FOR PULSE WITH THE HEART OF LIFE"'); [4] 'COPYRIGHT, 1920, | BY JOHN MASEFIELD. | [rule] | Set up and electrotyped. Published October, 1920. | Illustrated Edition, Published October, 1922.' | Printed in the United States of America'; [5] 'To | *MY WIFE*'; [6] 'NOTE. | *The persons, horses and events described | in this poem are imaginary. No reference is | made to any living person or horse.* | *JOHN MASEFIELD*'; [7] 'LIST OF ILLUSTRATIONS | IN COLOUR' (four colour illustrations (including frontispiece) listed with page references); [8] untitled map of the Compton course (comprising an unsigned diagram and description of the race course); [9] 'PART I'; [10] blank; 11–63 text (and illustrations) of part I; [64] blank; [65] 'PART II'; [66] blank; 67–116 text (and illustrations) of part II

Paper: wove paper

Running title: none

Binding: black cloth. On spine, in gold: 'RIGHT | ROYAL | [illustration of jockey's riding cap] | JOHN | MASEFIELD | ILLUSTRATED | WITH COLOUR & | LINE DRAWINGS | BY CECIL ALDIN | MACMILLAN' (all width centred). On upper cover, in gold: 'RIGHT ROYAL | JOHN MASEFIELD | ILLUSTRATED WITH COLOUR | AND LINE DRAWINGS BY | CECIL ALDIN | [illustration of a horse's head: 50 × 63mm.]' (all width centred). Lower cover: blank. All edges trimmed. Binding measurements: 228 × 152mm. (covers), 228 × 27mm. (spine). End-papers: wove paper decorated with illustration of downland with figure in hat and smock with dog watching two horses ridden by jockeys, signed 'CECIL | ALDIN' with panel enclosing verse: 'HE [point] WAS [point] FROM [point] SLEiNS [point] THE [point] MANOR [point] UP [point] THE [point] LiTHE | RiDING [point] THE [point] DOWNS [point] HAD [point] MADE [point] HIS [point] BODY [point] BLiTHE;' (see notes).

Publication date: published, according to Simmons, 17 October 1922 in an edition of 2936 copies

Price: $2.50

Contents:
as for A54(b)

Notes:
The word 'LiTHE' appears on the end-papers in the version as found within A54(d).

It appears that Sydney S. Pawling, of the Heinemann firm, may have been responsible for suggesting this illustrated edition to George P. Brett of Macmillans. Enclosing a signed duplicate of the agreement for the English edition, Pawling wrote to Masefield stating

...I will wait until Mr. Brett's arrival in March, as it will be easier to get him interested in Aldin's work if he sees it.
(Sydney S. Pawling, letter to John Masefield, 24 February 1922)
(Archives of The Society of Authors)

Copies seen: private collection (PWE)

A54(g) Third American edition ["Leather Pocket Edition"] (1923)

RIGHT ROYAL | *By* | JOHN MASEFIELD | [circular floral ornament] [in red] | NEW YORK | THE MACMILLAN COMPANY | 1923 | ALL RIGHTS RESERVED
(All width centred and enclosed within ornate border in red: 135 × 78mm.)

Bibliographies: Simmons [noted on p.81], Nevinson [unrecorded], Handley-Taylor p.51 and p.53, Wight [unrecorded]

Collation: [A]¹⁰ ([A]3+2) [B-K]⁸ (J not used); 78 leaves; 171 × 111mm.; [i–vi] vii–viii [1–2] 3–64 [65–66] 67–145 [146–48]

Page contents: [i] half-title: 'RIGHT ROYAL | [ornament] [in red]'; [ii] '[27 titles separated by 20 single points] | [ornament] [in red]' (enclosed within ornate border in red: 135 × 78mm.); [iii] title-page; [iv] 'COPYRIGHT, 1920 AND 1923, BY JOHN MASEFIELD | *Printed in the United States of America* | [ornament] [in red]'; [v] 'NOTE | The persons, horses and events described | in this poem are imaginary. No reference | is made to any living person or horse. | JOHN MASEFIELD.'; [vi] blank; vii–viii 'RIGHT ROYAL | INTRODUCTION' ('I wrote this poem in the winter and spring of 1920. It was based upon a story told to...') (unsigned); [1] 'PART I'; [2] blank; 3–64 text of part I; [65] 'PART II'; [66] blank; 67–145 text of part II; [146–48] blank

Paper: laid paper (no watermark), chain-lines 22mm. apart

Running-title: 'RIGHT ROYAL' (23mm.) on both verso and recto, pp.4–64 and pp.68–145

Binding: red leather. On spine, in gold: '[floral panel] | RIGHT | ROYAL | MASEFIELD | [floral panel] | MACMILLAN'. On upper cover, in blind: circular floral ornament (within blind ruled border: 171 × 111mm.) Lower cover: blank. Top edge gilt, others trimmed. Binding measurements: 175 × 114mm. (covers), 175 × 28mm. (spine). End-papers: wove paper.

Publication date: published, according to Handley-Taylor, 30 August 1923 / published, according to Simmons, 30 October 1923 in an edition of 2000 copies (see notes)

Price: $12.50 (set of 8 volumes: see also A21(d), A49(h), A52(b), A66(a), A67(a), A68(a) and A69(a))

Contents:
Introduction ('I wrote this poem in the winter and spring of 1920. It was based upon a story told to...')
     (unsigned)
Right Royal ('An hour before the race they talked together')

Notes:
The additional leaves ([A]1 and [A]2) comprise a conjugate set of leaves pasted onto [A]3. They use the same paper stock as the rest of the volume and were presumably later added to the volume as they comprise the only pages with additional devices printed in red.

Issued as volume VII in the Macmillan Leather Pocket Edition of Masefield's Work.

This edition does not include a map of the race course.

Accepting Handley-Taylor's publication date would explain the omission of *A King's Daughter* (published on 23 October 1923) in the listing of Masefield's works appearing on page [ii].

Copies seen: private collection (ROV)

A55 KING COLE   1921

A55(a) First English edition (limited signed edition) (1921)

KING COLE | BY | JOHN MASEFIELD | WITH DRAWINGS IN BLACK AND WHITE | BY | JUDITH MASEFIELD | [publisher's device of a windmill with '19' and '21' on either side] | [rule, 71mm.] | LONDON: WILLIAM HEINEMANN
(All width centred)

Bibliographies: Simmons [49], Nevinson [unrecorded], Handley-Taylor p.51, Wight [49]

Collation: [A]⁸ B-C⁸ D⁴; B2 and C2 are also signed; signatures right foot of page with 'K.C.' at left foot on first leaf of gatherings (with the exception of [A]); 28 leaves; 224 × 146mm.; [1–9] 10–12 [13] 14–17 [18] 19–45 [46] 47 [48] 49–53 [54–56]

Page contents: [1–2] blank; [3] half-title: 'KING COLE'; [4] '*This Edition, numbered and signed | by the author, is limited to seven | hundred and eighty copies, of which | seven hundred and fifty are for sale, | and thirty for presentation. This | is No..........*' (the '*T*' of '*This*' is swash on both occasions); [5] title-page; [6] blank; [7] 'To | MY WIFE'; [8] blank; [9]–12 text; [13] illustration; 14–17 text; [18] illustration; 19–45 text (and illustrations); [46] illustration; 47 text; [48] illustration; 49–53 text; [54] illustration; [55] '[rule] | THE WHITEFRIARS PRESS, LTD., LONDON AND TONBRIDGE'; [56] blank

Paper: laid paper (watermark: '1590' and windmill: 90 × 53mm.), chain-lines 30mm. apart

Running title: 'KING COLE' (24mm.) on both verso and recto, pp.10–53

Binding: blue boards with parchment spine. On spine, in gold: 'King | Cole | [ornament] | John | Masefield | HEINEMANN' (all width centred). There is a single vertical rule in blind on each cover at the edge of the parchment. Covers: blank. Top edge gilt, lower outside edge untrimmed, fore edge uncut. Binding measurements: 230 × 150mm. (covers), 230 × 20mm. (spine). End-papers: wove paper.

Publication date: published, according to Simmons, 20 October 1921

Price: 21s.

Contents:
King Cole ('King Cole was King before the troubles came,')

Notes:
The last of Masefield's major narrative poems. The narrative concerns a travelling circus saved from disaster by the mythological king. Critics have identified a weakening in Masefield's command of the genre and it is perhaps significant that Masefield resumed his career as a novelist after this work.

The poem was published in several other volumes (see also *King Cole and other poems* (A63), *The Dream and other poems* (A65) and *King Cole[,] The Dream and other poems* (A69)).

Copies seen: private collection (PWE) number 705, signed '705 | John Masefield.' on p.[4]; private collection (ROV) number 30, signed '30 | John Masefield.' on p.[4]; private collection (ROV) number 588, signed '588 | John Masefield.' on p.[4]; private collection (ROV) number 592, signed '592 | John Masefield.' on p.[4]; BL (011648.h.48) number 772, signed '772 | John Masefield.' on p.[4] stamped 14 NOV 1921

A55(b) First American edition (1921)

KING COLE | BY | JOHN MASEFIELD | WITH DRAWINGS IN BLACK AND WHITE | BY | JUDITH MASEFIELD | New York | THE MACMILLAN COMPANY | 1921 | *All rights reserved*
(All width centred)

Bibliographies: Simmons [noted on p.83], Nevinson [unrecorded], Handley-Taylor p.51, Wight 49a

Collation: [A-F]⁸; 48 leaves (including fixed end-papers); 192 × 132mm.; [1–8] 9–12 [13–14] 15–24 [25–26] 27–30 [31–32] 33–74 [75–76] 77–80 [81–82] 83–87 [88–92]

Page contents: [1–2] blank; [3] half-title: 'KING COLE'; [4] '*By* | JOHN MASEFIELD | [22 titles listed]' (titles are all justified on the left, and the entire text is enclosed in double ruled border (the outer border being thicker): 112 × 79mm.); [5] title-page; [6] 'COPYRIGHT, 1921, | BY JOHN MASEFIELD. | [rule] | Set up and electrotyped. Published October, 1921.'; [7] '*To* | MY WIFE'; [8] blank; 9–12 text; [13] illustration (and legend); [14] blank; 15–24 text; [25] illustration (and legend); [26] blank; 27–30 text; [31] illustration (and legend); [32] blank; 33–74 text (and illustration); [75] illustration (and legend); [76] blank; 77–80 text; [81] illustration (and legend); [82] blank; 83–87 text; [88] illustration; [89–92] blank

213

Paper: laid paper (no watermark), chain-lines 23mm. apart

Running title: '[rule, 89mm.] | KING COLE [25mm.] | [rule, 89mm.]' on both verso and recto, pp.10–87

Binding: blue boards with navy blue cloth spine. On spine: white paper label (45 × 15mm.) on which: '[double rule with vertical cross-hatching] [in orange] | [double rule] [in orange] | KING | COLE | [ornament] | MASE- | FIELD | [double rule] [in orange] | [double rule with vertical cross-hatching] [in orange]' (width centred). On upper cover: panel in blind: 51 × 86mm. upon which: white paper label (48 × 82mm.) on which: 'KING COLE | *By* | JOHN MASEFIELD' (enclosed within four ruled borders with hatching pattern between the first two external borders, in orange: 42 × 77mm.) (see notes). Lower cover: blank. Top edge trimmed, others untrimmed. Binding measurements: 198 × 131mm. (covers), 198 × 23mm. (spine). End-papers constitute [A]1 and [F]8 laid down to inside of covers.

Publication date: published, according to Simmons, 20 October 1921 in an edition of 3000 copies

Price: $1.50

Contents:
as for A55(a)

Notes:
This volume, published on the same date as A55(a), has been newly set for this edition.

Wight describes the spine label as 'a pale orange label' and that on the upper cover as 'a very pale orange label'. There are slight differences in the size of labels in copies consulted.

A publishing agreement for this title between Masefield and Macmillan was dated 24 May 1921 (see Archives of The Society of Authors). The agreement refers to 'a licence to publish in volume form in the United States of America and Canada a work the subject or title of which is King Cole of England'.

Copies seen: private collection (PWE); BL (X.908/167) stamped 30 OCT 1962; NYPL (Berg Collection) inscribed by Constance Masefield 'Lillah | with love from J + C M' marked-up copy by Lillah McCarthy

A56 A FOUNDATION DAY ADDRESS   1921

A56(a) First English edition (1921)

A FOUNDATION DAY | ADDRESS | BY | JOHN MASEFIELD
(All width centred)

Bibliographies: Simmons [50], Nevinson [unrecorded], Handley-Taylor p.51, Wight [50]

Collation: [A]⁸; 8 leaves; 190 × 104mm.; [i–iv] [1–8]

Page contents: [-] upper wrapper (see below); [-] blank; [i] half-title: 'A FOUNDATION DAY | ADDRESS'; [ii] blank; [iii] title-page; [iv] 'This address was delivered by Mr. | Masefield on July 20, 1921 at Bem- | bridge School on the occasion of | Foundation Day. | [new paragraph] Two hundred and fifty numbered | copies have been printed at the | Yellowsands Press, being the private | press of Bembridge School, of which | this is number | December, 1921'; [1–6] text; [7–8] blank; [-] blank; [-] lower wrapper (see below)

Paper: wove paper (watermark: 'Sᵀ CUTHBERTS | SUPERFINE' with shield enclosing tree and three barrels on cross-hatched lower section: 68 × 54mm.), chain-lines 26mm. apart (the chain-lines run horizontally with the text)

Running title: none

Binding: wrappers comprise the first and last leaves of the single gathering ([A]1 and [A]8). Spine: blank. On upper wrapper: 'A FOUNDATION DAY| ADDRESS | BY | JOHN MASEFIELD' (width centred). Lower wrapper: blank. All edges untrimmed. Binding measurements: 188 × 106mm. (wrappers), 188 × 1mm. (spine).

Publication date: published, according to Simmons, December 1921

Price: unknown

Contents:
A Foundation Day Address ('I am sure I never thought I should ever come to address a school[.] In my young days...')

Notes:
An address delivered by Masefield, (then President of Bembridge School) in July 1921 on the occasion of Foundation Day. Like *John Ruskin* (see A51(a)), the text was printed by the Yellowsands Press, this being the private press of the school.

Simmons states that this volume was 'issued without covers'. This is true in that no separate binding was used and the wrappers constitute the first and last leaves of the single gathering. However, by designating these leaves as 'covers', the repetition of title on [A]1, [A]2 and [A]3 is explained by comprising wrapper title, half-title and title-page respectively. The printing on [A]1 is therefore the wrapper title and not the title-page, unlike the first edition of *John Ruskin* (see A51(a)).

Copies seen: private collection (PWE) un-numbered and unsigned; BL (8408.e.33) number 86, signed 'J.H. Whitehouse' on p.[iv] stamped 10 FEB 1922; Library of The John Masefield Society (Peter Smith Collection) number 53, signed 'J.H. Whitehouse' on p.[iv], includes posthumous booklabel

A57 ESTHER

A57(a) First English edition (1922)

ESTHER | A Tragedy | *Adapted and partially translated from the French* | *of Jean Racine* | By | JOHN MASEFIELD | [publisher's device of a windmill with '19' and '22' on either side] | [rule, 69mm.] | LONDON: WILLIAM HEINEMANN
(The '*A*' of '*Adapted*' and '*R*' of '*Racine*' are swash)
(All width centred)

Bibliographies: Simmons [51], Nevinson p.13, Handley-Taylor p.51, Wight [51]

Collation: [A]⁸ B-E⁸; signatures right foot of page; 40 leaves; 187 × 120mm.; [i–x] 1–15 [16] 17–68 [69–70]

Page contents: [i] half-title: 'ESTHER'; [ii] 'BY THE SAME AUTHOR. | [rule] | [13 titles listed] | London: WILLIAM HEINEMANN.'; [iii] title-page; [iv] blank; [v] 'CHARACTERS. | [dramatis personae listed]'; [vi] blank; [vii] 'This adaptation of "Esther" was produced by | Miss Penelope Wheeler, at Wootton, Berks, on | the evening of the 5th May, 1921, with the | following cast :- | [dramatis personae and original cast listed] | The Play was performed without scenery | upon a stage hung with curtains. There were | exits and entrances R. and L. at Back, and an | extra exit and approach by steps to the stage | from Front Centre'; [viii] blank; [ix] 'PROPERTIES. | [props listed]'; [x] blank; 1–15 text of Act I; [16] blank; 17–30 text of Act II; 31–48 text of Act III; 49–68 text of Act IV (at foot of p.68: '[rule] | PRINTED IN GREAT BRITAIN BY WOODS AND SONS, LTD., LONDON, N, 1.' [*sic*]); [69–70] blank

Paper: wove paper

Running title: 'ESTHER' (17mm.) on both verso and recto, pp.2–68 (there also occurs notification of the act ('ACT I', 'ACT II', 'ACT III' and 'ACT IV') on both verso and recto on either side of the gutter). On p.2, in some copies, only 'ACT' appears.

Binding: light blue boards. On spine, in dark blue: '[double rule] | ESTHER | [point] [point] [point] | A | TRAGEDY | ADAPTED FROM | THE FRENCH | OF | JEAN RACINE | BY | JOHN | MASEFIELD | [double rule] | HEINEMANN' (all width centred). On upper cover, in dark blue: 'ESTHER | [point] [point] [point] | A TRAGEDY | ADAPTED FROM THE FRENCH | OF JEAN RACINE | BY | JOHN MASEFIELD' (within ruled border: 189 × 117mm.) On lower cover, in dark blue: publisher's device of a windmill (ranged lower right). Top and fore edges trimmed, lower outside edge untrimmed. Binding measurements: 194 × 122mm. (covers), 194 × 21mm. (spine). End-papers: wove paper.

Also issued in light blue wrappers. On spine: '[rule] | *Esther* | (A | Tragedy) | *by* | *John* | *Masefield* | 2/6 | Net | *Heinemann* | [rule]' (all width centred with the exception of 'Net' which is off-set to the right). On upper wrapper: '*ESTHER* | (A TRAGEDY) | *Adapted and partially translated* | *from the French of Jean Racine* | *By John Masefield*' (within ruled border: 178 × 105mm.) On lower wrapper: '<u>PLAYS</u> | [eight plays listed with their authors, sizes and prices] | [rule] | LONDON: WILLIAM HEINEMANN' (within ruled border: 153 × 94mm.) All edges trimmed. Binding measurements: 189 × 125mm. (wrappers), 189 × 10mm. (spine). End-papers: wove paper (laid down to the insides of the wrappers).

Publication date: published, according to Simmons, 26 January 1922 in an edition of 1250 copies. The sales ledger preserved in the Heinemann Archive suggests publication in an edition of 2000 copies.

Price: 3s.6d. (boards) / 2s.6d. (wrappers)

Contents:
Esther ('SCENE.-ESTHER'S *apartments*.')

Notes:
As stated by the full title, this work comprises a tragedy adapted and partially translated from the French of Jean Racine. American publication occurred in a volume combining the play with *Berenice* (see A58).

The publishing agreement for this title between Masefield and Heinemann was dated 29 November 1921 (see Archives of The Society of Authors). The agreement refers to both 'paper' and 'cloth' covers at 2s.6d. and 3s.6d. respectively.

Simmons states 'a limited edition of 750 copies was brought out on the same date, January 26, 1922, by William Heinemann, London'. This is an error. The Heinemann Archive includes a letter from within the firm (to Dwye Evans) that states: '*Esther* was published on January 26th 1922 in paper at 2/6d and in boards at 3/6d and there was no Limited Edition either then or later'.

In noting the print limitation of *Berenice* (see A59), Simmons records that the first edition was issued in both boards and wrappers. There is no similar note by Simmons for *Esther*. However, Heinemann issued *Esther* as they were later to bind *Berenice*.

The sales ledger preserved in the Heinemann Archive suggests that the title was published in an edition of 2000 copies. Simmons only states an edition of 1250 and fails to mention the paper wrapper issue (erroneously claiming the existence of a limited signed edition of 750 copies). It therefore seems likely that there were 1250 copies bound in boards and 750 bound in wrappers.

Copies seen: private collection (PWE) boards; private collection (PWE) wrappers; BL (011779.g.104) rebound wrappers, stamped 26 JAN 1922; Columbia University Libraries (Special Collections B825.M377.Q323.1922.c.3) wrappers, inscribed to Annie Hanford-Flood 'from your godson. | 31. 1. 1922.'

Reprinted:
'New Impression'　　　　　　　　　　　[first edition, second impression]　　　　　　　　　　Feb 1922

RIGHT ROYAL

By
JOHN MASEFIELD

New York
THE MACMILLAN COMPANY
1920

A54(a) title-page

RIGHT ROYAL

BY
JOHN MASEFIELD

LONDON: WILLIAM HEINEMANN

A54(b) title-page

ESTHER
A Tragedy

*Adapted and partially translated from the French
of Jean Racine*

By
JOHN MASEFIELD

LONDON: WILLIAM HEINEMANN

A57(a) title-page

BERENICE
A Tragedy

*Translated from the French of
Jean Racine*

By
JOHN MASEFIELD

LONDON: WILLIAM HEINEMANN

A59(a) title-page

ESTHER AND BERENICE

TWO PLAYS

BY

JOHN MASEFIELD

New York
THE MACMILLAN COMPANY
1922

A58(a) title-page

THE DREAM

By JOHN MASEFIELD,

Illustrated by JUDITH MASEFIELD.

No 704. John Masefield.
Judith Masefield

LONDON: WILLIAM HEINEMANN

A60(a) title-page

MELLONEY HOLTSPUR

The consecrated things are wiser than our virtue.

LONDON: WILLIAM HEINEMANN

A61(a) title-page (lacking author)

MELLONEY HOLTSPUR

BY
JOHN MASEFIELD

The consecrated things are wiser than our virtue.

LONDON: WILLIAM HEINEMANN

A61(a) title-page (author noted)

A58 ESTHER AND BERENICE 1922

A58(a) First American edition (1922)

ESTHER AND BERENICE | TWO PLAYS | BY | JOHN MASEFIELD | New York | THE MACMILLAN COMPANY | 1922 | *All rights reserved*
(All width centred)

Bibliographies: Simmons [52], Nevinson [unrecorded], Handley-Taylor [noted on p.51], Wight [52]

Collation: [A]⁸ (±[A]2) [B-O]⁸ (J not used); 112 leaves; 189 × 126mm.; [i–vi] vii–ix [x–xiv] 1–107 [108–110] 111–205 [206–210]; illustrations (on glossy paper) tipped-in on pp.[xiv], 25, 48, [110], 133, 155, 176 and 195

Page contents: [i] half-title: 'ESTHER AND BERENICE | TWO PLAYS'; [ii] 'BY | JOHN MASEFIELD | [rule] | [22 titles listed]' (within double ruled border: 92 × 58mm.); [iii] title-page; [iv] 'PRINTED IN THE UNITED STATES OF AMERICA | COPYRIGHT, 1922, | BY JOHN MASEFIELD. | [rule] | Set up and electrotyped. Published January, 1922. | Press of | J. J. Little & Ives Company | New York, U. S. A.'; [v] 'This adaptation of "Esther" was produced by Miss | Penelope Wheeler at Wootton, Berks, on the evening | of the 5th May, 1921, with the following cast :- | [dramatis personae and original cast listed] | The Play was performed without scenery upon a | stage hung with curtains. There were exits and entrances | R. and L. at Back, and an extra exit and approach by | steps to the stage from Front Centre | [diagram of stage] | Avant-scène.'; [vi] blank; vii–ix 'PREFACE' ('I have been asked to write a few words to explain why these adaptations of Racine were made.') (signed, 'JOHN MASEFIELD.'); [x] blank; [xi] 'CHARACTERS | [rule] | [dramatis personae listed] | [rule] | Parts of Acts 1, 3, and 4 of this play are translated | from the Tragedy of Esther, by Racine.'; [xii] 'PROPERTIES | [rule] | [props listed]'; [xiii] 'ESTHER AND BERENICE | TWO PLAYS'; [xiv] blank (with additional leaf tipped-in on the verso of which is an unsigned illustration in black and white: 63 × 90mm.); 1–107 text of *Esther*; [108] blank; [109] 'BERENICE | [rule] | A Tragedy by | RACINE. | [rule]'; [110] 'PERSONS | [rule] | [dramatis personae listed]' (with additional leaf tipped-in on the verso of which is an unsigned illustration in black and white: 64 × 91mm.); 111–205 text of *Berenice*; [206–210] blank

Paper: wove paper

Running title: 'PREFACE' (19mm.) on both verso and recto, pp.viii–ix; '*ESTHER*' (17mm.) on both verso and recto, pp.2–107 and '*BERENICE*' (22mm.) on both verso and recto, pp.112–205

Binding: burgundy cloth. On spine, in gold: 'ESTHER | [rule] | BERENICE | MASEFIELD | -MACMILLAN-' (all width centred). On upper cover, in blind: 'ESTHER | [rule] | BERENICE | MASEFIELD' (ranged upper left) (within blind ruled border: 186 × 119mm.) Lower cover: blank. Top edge trimmed, others roughly trimmed. Binding measurements: 193 × 127mm. (covers), 193 × 33mm. (spine). End-papers: wove paper.

Publication date: published, according to Simmons, 26 January 1922 in an edition of 2280 copies

Price: $2.00

Contents:
Preface ('I have been asked to write a few words to explain why these adaptations of Racine were made.')
Esther ('SCENE:-ESTHER'S *apartments*.')
Berenice ('ANTIOCHUS. | Let us stay here a moment. I can see')

Notes:
American publication of Masefield's two translations from the French of Jean Racine. Both verse plays were published separately in England. This American volume was issued on the same date as the English edition of *Esther* (see A57), but predates the English publication of *Berenice* (see A59).

The first gathering in the only copy of this volume yet examined reveals several peculiarities. The first feature apparent is that the title-page comprises an additional leaf tipped onto what consequently becomes the third leaf in the gathering. In the absence of any signatures we must turn to the binding to discover that the second gathering begins on page 3. (The matter is not complicated by the inserted leaf of illustration for this is obviously an additional leaf on different paper and need not be considered). A1 and A8, A3 and A6, and A4 and A5 are conjugate. The conjugate leaf for A7 cannot be located and we must conclude that A2 is a cancellans, with the leaf stub concealed. This conclusion would be bibliographically likely but confirmation would involve destruction of the book. However, the first gathering is still curious in this state with the text of the first play commencing on the last leaf of the first gathering.

A publishing agreement between Masefield and Macmillan was dated 24 May 1921 (see Archives of The Society of Authors). The agreement refers to 'a licence to publish in volume form in the United States of America and Canada a work the subject or title of which is an adaptation in verse from Racine's "Esther"'.

Copies seen: private collection (PWE)

A59 BERENICE 1922

A59(a) First English edition (1922)

BERENICE | A Tragedy | *Translated from the French of* | *Jean Racine* | By | JOHN MASEFIELD | [publisher's device of a windmill with '19' and '22' on either side] | [rule, 69mm.] | LONDON : WILLIAM HEINEMANN
(The '*T*' of '*Translated*' and '*R*' of '*Racine*' are swash)
(All width centred)

Bibliographies: Simmons [53], Nevinson p.13, Handley-Taylor p.52, Wight [53]

Collation: [A]⁸ B-D⁸ [E]⁴; signatures right foot of page; 36 leaves; 189 × 120mm.; [i–x] 1–27 [28] 29–41 [42] 43–53 [54] 55–61 [62]

Page contents: [i–ii] blank; [iii] half-title: 'BERENICE'; [iv] 'BY THE SAME AUTHOR. | [rule] | [13 titles listed] | London: WILLIAM HEINEMANN.'; [iv] title-page; [v] blank; [vi] 'CHARACTERS. | [dramatis personae listed]'; [vii] blank; [viii] 'This play was translated for the use of the | Hill Players and was produced by them on | November 24th, 1921, with the following cast :- | [dramatis personae and original cast listed]'; [ix] blank; 1–14 text of Act I; 15–27 text of Act II; [28] blank; 29–41 text of Act III; [42] blank; 43–53 text of Act IV; [54] blank; 55–61 text of Act V (at foot of p.61: '[rule] | Printed in Great Britain by WOODS & SONS, Ltd., 338–340, Upper St., N.1.'); [62] blank

Paper: wove paper

Running title: 'BERENICE' (19mm.) on both verso and recto, pp.2–61 (there also occurs notification of the act ('ACT I', 'ACT II', 'ACT III', 'ACT IV' and 'ACT V') on both verso and recto on either side of the gutter)

Binding: light blue boards. On spine, in dark blue: '[double rule] | BERENICE | [point] [point] [point] | A | TRAGEDY | ADAPTED FROM | THE FRENCH | OF | JEAN RACINE | BY | JOHN | MASEFIELD | [double rule] | HEINEMANN' (all width centred). On upper cover, in dark blue: 'BERENICE | [point] [point] [point] | A TRAGEDY | ADAPTED FROM THE FRENCH | OF JEAN RACINE | BY | JOHN MASEFIELD' (within ruled border: 190 × 116mm.) On lower cover, in dark blue: publisher's device of a windmill (ranged lower right). Top and fore edges trimmed, lower outside edge untrimmed. Binding measurements: 195 × 122mm. (covers), 195 × 23mm. (spine). End-papers: wove paper.

Also issued in light blue wrappers. On spine: '[rule] | *Berenice* | (A | Tragedy) | *by* | *John* | *Masefield* | 2/6 | Net | *Heinemann*' | [rule]' (all width centred with the exception of 'Net' which is off-set to the right). On upper wrapper: '*BERENICE* | (A TRAGEDY) | *Translated from the French of* | *Jean Racine* | *By John Masefield*' (within ruled border: 178 × 105mm.) (the 'T' of '*Translated*' is swash). On lower wrapper: 'PLAYS | [nine plays listed with their authors, sizes and prices] | [rule] | LONDON: WILLIAM HEINEMANN' (within ruled border: 152 × 94mm.) Top and fore edges trimmed, lower outside edge untrimmed. Binding measurements: 191 × 123mm. (wrappers), 191 × 10mm. (spine). End-papers: wove paper (laid down to the insides of the wrappers).

Publication date: published, according to Simmons, 6 April 1922 in an edition of 2000 copies, of which 1300 were issued in paper boards, and 700 in paper covers

Price: 3s.6d. (boards) / 2s.6d. (wrappers)

Contents:
Berenice ('ANTIOCHUS | Let us stay here a moment. I can see')

Notes:
Described by the full title as a tragedy translated from the French of Jean Racine.

The publishing agreement for this title between Masefield and Heinemann was dated 1 February 1922 (see Archives of The Society of Authors). The agreement refers to both 'paper' and 'cloth' covers at 2s.6d. and 3s.6d. respectively.

Copies seen: private collection (PWE) boards; private collection (PWE) wrappers; BL (11735.k.67) rebound wrappers, stamped 6 APR 1922

A60 THE DREAM
1922

A60(a) First English edition (limited signed edition) (1922)

THE DREAM | By JOHN MASEFIELD, | Illustrated by JUDITH MASEFIELD. | LONDON: WILLIAM HEINEMANN
(All width centred)

Bibliographies: Simmons [54], Nevinson [unrecorded], Handley-Taylor p.52, Wight [54]

Collation: [A]⁸ (see notes); 8 leaves; 225 × 144mm.; [1] 2–13 [14–16]

Page contents: [1] title-page; 2 illustration; 3–5 text; 6 illustration; 7 text; 8 illustration; 9–11 text; 12 illustration; 13 text and illustration; [14–15] blank; [16] 'Printed by | SLATTER & ROSE, LTD. | OXFORD.'

Paper: laid paper (watermark: '[crown] | Abbey Mills | Greenfield'), chain-lines 25mm. apart

Running title: none

Binding: light-grey boards with white cloth spine. Spine: blank. On upper cover: white paper label (54 × 77mm.) on which: 'THE DREAM | by | JOHN MASEFIELD | Illustrated by | JUDITH MASEFIELD' (enclosed within ornate ruled border: 40 × 63mm.) Lower cover: blank. Top edge trimmed, others untrimmed. Binding measurements: 227 × 145mm. (covers), 227 × 11mm. (spine). End-papers: wove paper. The free end-papers are bound with the single gathering of the volume and the fixed end-papers are contiguous.

Publication date: published, according to Simmons, 23 October 1922 in an edition of 800 copies

Price: unknown

Contents:

The Dream ('Weary with many thoughts I went to bed,')

    First printed in the anthology Memorials of C.H.O. Daniel with a Bibliography of the Press, 1845–1919 (see B180)

Notes:

A poem printed as a memorial to the classicist Rev. Charles Henry Olive Daniel, Provost of Worcester College Oxford from 1903 and founder of the private Daniel Press.

Although there is no printed note regarding limitation or signed status of the volume, copies are numbered (in Masefield's hand) on the title-page before being signed by both the author and illustrator. The lack of note regarding limitation reveals a close kinship with the non-Heinemann and privately printed edition: see A60(c).

The text commences with a drop-capital.

As stated above, the free end-papers are bound with the single gathering of eight leaves to create a gathering of ten leaves. Although Wight chooses to describe the volume as having ten leaves this is ultimately ambiguous. Since the paper used for the end-papers is different from that on which the text is printed, I have chosen to note the volume as containing a single gathering of eight leaves, with end-papers bound in.

Copies seen: private collection (PWE) number 704, signed 'No 704. | John Masefield.' (in Masefield's hand) and 'Judith Masefield' (in Judith Masefield's hand) on p.[1]; BL (11645.f.50) number 774, signed 'No 774. | John Masefield.' (in Masefield's hand) and 'Judith Masefield' (in Judith Masefield's hand) on p.[1] stamped 24 OCT 1922; HRHRC (TEMP M377DR cop.2) number 779, signed 'No 779 | John Masefield.' (in Masefield's hand) and 'Judith Masefield' (in Judith Masefield's hand) on p.[1] additionally inscribed 'for Con | from Jan. | Nov 1. | 1922.'; HRHRC (PR6025 A77 D7 1922) number 777, signed 'Rest + be thankful copy. | No 777. | John Masefield.' (in Masefield's hand) and 'Judith Masefield' (in Judith Masefield's hand) on p.[1] additionally inscribed 'for Lew | from Zom | Nov 2ⁿᵈ. 1922.'

A60(b) First American edition (limited signed edition) (1922)

THE DREAM | BY | JOHN MASEFIELD | ILLUSTRATED BY | JUDITH MASEFIELD | New York | THE MACMILLAN COMPANY | 1922 | *All rights reserved*

(All width centred)

Bibliographies: Simmons [noted on p.88], Nevinson [unrecorded], Handley-Taylor p.52, Wight 54a

Collation: [A]⁵ ([A]1+1) [B-E]⁴ (see notes); 21 leaves; 246 × 157mm.; [i–ii] [1–6] 7–8 [9–10] 11–14 [15–16] 17–20 [21–22] 23–26 [27–28] 29–37 [38–40]

Page contents: [i] blank; [ii] 'OF THIS LIMITED, AUTOGRAPHED EDITION OF | THE DREAM | 750 COPIES HAVE BEEN PRINTED OF WHICH THIS IS | NUMBER...................'; [1] half-title: 'THE DREAM'; [2] 'BY | JOHN MASEFIELD | [25 volumes listed]' (within ruled border: 117 × 87mm.); [3] title-page; [4] 'COPYRIGHT, 1922, | BY JOHN MASEFIELD | [rule] | Published June, 1922'; [5] 'THE DREAM'; [6] illustration; 7–8 text; [9] illustration; [10] blank; 11–14 text; [15] illustration; [16] blank; 17–20 text; [21] illustration; [22] blank; 23–26 text; [27] illustration; [28] blank; 29–37 text; [38–40] blank

Paper: laid paper (no watermark), chain-lines 41mm. apart

Running title: none

Binding: light-grey boards with black cloth spine. On spine: '[single rule in blind] | [double rule in blind] | [white paper label (39 × 13mm.) on which: '[ornamental rule] [in orange] | [rule] [in orange] | THE | DREAM | [floral device] | MASE- | FIELD | [rule] [in orange] | [ornamental rule] [in orange]'] | [double rule in blind] | [double rule in blind] | [double rule in blind] | [single rule in blind]']'. On upper cover: three horizontal double rules in blind with two vertical double rules in blind; these create twelve rectangles (excluding those within the double rules); between the first two horizontal double rules there is a panel in blind: 40 × 86mm. upon which: white paper label (39 × 85mm.) on which: 'THE DREAM | *By* | JOHN MASEFIELD' (enclosed within ruled border and ornate border all in orange: 34 × 80mm.); between the second and third horizontal double rules there are four squares in blind, one in each corner of the rectangle. Lower cover: blank. Top edge gilt, others untrimmed. Binding measurements: 252 × 165mm. (covers), 252 × 18mm. (spine). End-papers: wove paper.

Publication date: published, according to Simmons, 28 November 1922 in an edition of 750 copies (see notes)

Price: $1.75

Contents:

The Dream ('Weary with many thoughts I went to bed')

Notes:

The text commences with a drop-capital.

Page numbers appear within square brackets. Thus, [7], [8], etc.

The first gathering includes a single leaf tipped-in. This leaf (using the same paper as the rest of the volume) is blank on one side and contains the note of limitation on the other. It is therefore likely that Macmillan sent 750 single leaves for Masefield to sign.

Wight fails to note the label on the spine. The ornamental rules in orange at the head and foot of the label comprise a portion of the ornate border as used on the upper cover label.

Although Simmons notes a publication date of 28 November 1922, the volume itself states 'published June, 1922'. This pre-dates the single volume English publication by Heinemann in October 1922. However, it may be that June 1922 was the date of printing while November was the date of issue. The interim may have been filled by Macmillan obtaining Masefield's signature for the limitation note. It is thus possible that this may not have been originally intended to be a limited signed edition.

Sending a copy of this edition (described as a 'special issue of *The Dream*') to Emily Daniel, Masefield noted that is was 'not bad, for an American book' (see Bodleian (28001.d.514)).

Copies seen: private collection (ROV) number 287 (in red), signed 'J. Masefield.' (in black) on p.[ii]; Bodleian (28001.d.514) unnumbered, signed 'J. Masefield.' (in black) on p.[ii], inscribed 'For Emily Daniel, | from | Constance + John Masefield. | Christmas. 1922.', no dated library stamp

A60(c) Second English edition ([1922])

THE DREAM | By JOHN MASEFIELD, | Illustrated by JUDITH MASEFIELD.
(All width centred)

Bibliographies: Simmons [unrecorded], Nevinson [unrecorded], Handley-Taylor [unrecorded], Wight 54b

Collation: [A]⁸; 8 leaves; 223 × 144mm.; [1] 2–13 [14–16]

Page contents: [1] title-page; 2 illustration; 3–5 text; 6 illustration; 7 text; 8 illustration; 9–11 text; 12 illustration; 13 text and illustration; [14–15] blank; [16] 'Printed by | SLATTER & ROSE, LTD. | OXFORD.'

Paper: laid paper (watermark: '[crown] | Abbey Mills | Greenfield'), chain-lines 25mm. apart

Running title: none

Binding: grey wrappers. Spine: blank. On upper wrapper: 'THE DREAM | By JOHN MASEFIELD. | Illustrated by JUDITH MASEFIELD.' Lower wrapper: blank. Top edge uncut, others untrimmed. Binding measurements: 227 × 145mm. (wrappers); 227 × 2mm. (spine).

Publication date: presumably published, December 1922 (see notes)

Price: copies were not, presumably, for sale

Contents:
as for A60(a)

Notes:
The text commences with a drop-capital. The similarity between this and the Heinemann edition (A60(a)) is striking. The same setting of the text appears to have been used, the printers are the same, as is the type of paper used. There is, however, no mention of Heinemann.

A memorandum preserved in the received correspondence files of Masefield is a standard printed slip stating:

> Messrs Slatter & Rose, Ltd., have much pleasure in enclosing herewith proof in accordance with your instructions, and will be glad to have it returned at your early convenience with any corrections or alterations clearly marked thereon. Kindly state number of copies required when returning the proof, if you have not already done so.
> (Slatter & Rose, Memorandum to John Masefield, 13 December 1922)
> (HRHRC, MS (Masefield, J.) Recip Slatter & Rose)

Given that this date is after the publication of Heinemann's edition it is likely that Masefield approached the printers for a privately printed edition for Christmas presentation to friends. Further dated copies need to be consulted in order to verify this suggestion, however.

Copies seen: private collection (ROV); private collection (ROV) inscribed 'For Ruth Spooner, | from John Masefield. | April 30. 1927.' on p.[1]; private collection (BG) inscribed 'For Barbara Vernon. | from John Masefield. | Septʳ. 1939.' on p.[1]; HRHRC (AC-L M377DR 1922A) inscribed 'For the London Library Appeal. | No 126. | John Masefield.'

A61 MELLONEY HOLTSPUR   1922

A61(a) First English edition (1922)

MELLONEY HOLTSPUR | *The consecrated things are wiser than our virtue.* | [publisher's device of a windmill with '19' and '22' on either side] | [rule, 69mm.] | LONDON : WILLIAM HEINEMANN
(The '*T*' of '*The*' is swash)
(All width centred)

or:

MELLONEY HOLTSPUR | BY | JOHN MASEFIELD | *The consecrated things are wiser than our virtue.* | [publisher's device of a windmill with '19' and '22' on either side] | [rule, 69mm.] | LONDON : WILLIAM HEINEMANN
(The '*T*' of '*The*' is swash)
(All width centred)

Bibliographies: Simmons [55], Nevinson p.14, Handley-Taylor p.52, Wight [55]

Collation: [A]⁴ (±[A]2) B-I⁸ (see notes); B2-I2 are also signed; signatures right foot of page with 'M.H.' at left foot on first leaf of gatherings (with the exception of gatherings [A], G, H and I); 68 leaves; 186 × 121mm.; [i–viii] 1–126 [127–28]

Page contents: [i] half-title: 'MELLONEY HOLTSPUR'; [ii] 'BY THE SAME AUTHOR. | [13 titles listed] | LONDON: WILLIAM HEINEMANN.'; [iii] title-page; [iv] 'PRINTED IN GREAT BRITAIN BY THE WHITEFRIARS PRESS, LTD., | LONDON AND TONBRIDGE.'; [v] 'To | EDWARD GORDON CRAIG'; [vi] blank; [vii] 'PERSONS | [dramatis personae listed]'; [viii] blank; 1–126 text; [127] 'NOTE. | The persons and events described in this play | are imaginary. No reference is made to any living | person. | JOHN MASEFIELD.'; [128] 'PRINTED IN GREAT BRITAIN BY THE WHITEFRIARS PRESS, LTD., | LONDON AND TONBRIDGE.'

Paper: wove paper

Running title: 'MELLONEY HOLTSPUR' (46mm.) on both verso and recto, pp.2–126

Binding: blue-green boards. On spine, in gold: 'Melloney | Holtspur | [ornament] | John | Masefield | HEINEMANN' (all width centred). On upper cover, in gold: 'MELLONEY HOLTSPUR | JOHN MASEFIELD' (within blind ruled border: 184 × 116mm.) On lower cover, in blind: publisher's device of a windmill (ranged lower right). All edges trimmed. Binding measurements: 189 × 122mm. (covers), 189 × 27mm. (spine). End-papers: wove paper.

Publication date: published, according to Simmons, 2 November 1922 in an edition of 5000 copies. The sales ledger preserved in the Heinemann Archive suggests publication on 2 November 1922 in an edition of 5100 copies

Price: 6s.

Contents:
Melloney Holtspur ('ACT I | *The scene is a panelled room. At Back, a plain...*')

Notes:
A prose play, including supernatural scenes, concerning the mistreatment of its principal female character by an artist suffering from artistic sensitivities. Masefield felt the piece was consistently misunderstood.

The publishing agreement for this title between Masefield and Heinemann was dated 30 July 1922 (see Archives of The Society of Authors). The agreement refers to a publication price of 6s.

The printing of 5100 copies as noted in the sales ledger preserved in the Heinemann Archive remains a mystery.

The original printing of the title-page omits the name of the author. This was corrected on a cancellan. Both original and corrected states are common.

Regarding a proposed production of the play in 1929, Masefield wrote to The Society of Authors, noting the special effects used for the first performance:

> At the St. Martin's Theatre they had a wonderful German installation of lamps, but I am quite sure that any ordinary system of lighting would create all the necessary illusions quite well. A dimness when the ghosts appear and something silent and uncanny about the appearance and movements of the ghosts would be all that is necessary. At the St. Martin's Theatre the leading ghost was painted with an inflammable luminous paint. I was very glad when she left the stage safely.
>
> (John Masefield, letter to [G.H.] Thring , 22 October 1929)
> (BL, Add.Mss.56588, f.88)

In 1952 with the BBC requesting permission for a radio version of the play Masefield was doubtful about the work without the use of special lighting effects. Writing to The Society of Authors, he stated:

> I'm rather doubtful about this scheme: it was fun trying ghost-effects with new lighting systems, but this was the only fun in the piece, and probably I was the only one who found it fun. Some of the ghosts were very ghostly; but this, the only fun, will be wiped out in a version only heard + not seen at all.
>
> (John Masefield, letter to Miss H. Lehmann, 19 July [1952])
> (BL, Add.Mss.56623, f.199)

The Society of Authors responded on 22 July 1952 informing Masefield that the BBC had hopes of ghostly incidental music (see BL, Add.Mss.56623, f.201). Masefield was unimpressed:

> Many thanks for your lettter about Melloney Holtspur. Aubrey mentions a ghost disappearing with "a most melodious twang", but I would like to hear something more about the ghost-music that the BBC propose. So often their incidental music comes over the air too heavily. The horns of elfland blow faintly. A piano in ghostland is a harpsicord. Please may I ask for some account of the proposed music?
>
> (John Masefield, letter to Miss H. Lehmann, 24 July [1952])
> (BL, Add.Mss.56623, ff.202–203)

Masefield, nevertheless, agreed to the BBC's 'experiment' in August 1952 (see BL, Add.Mss.56624, f.4). It was this radio performance which was heard by Audrey Napier-Smith (see E3).

Copies seen: private collection (PWE); BL (011779.e.102) stamped 2 NOV 1922; Columbia University Libraries (Special Collections B825.M377.T.1922b.c.3) inscribed 'H.G.B. [Harley Granville-Barker] | from J.M.'

A61(b) First American edition (limited signed edition) (1922)

MELLONEY HOLTSPUR | OR | THE PANGS OF LOVE | BY | JOHN MASEFIELD | *The consecrated things are wiser than our virtue.* | New York | THE MACMILLAN COMPANY | 1922 | *All rights reserved*
(All width centred)

Bibliographies: Simmons [noted on p.89], Nevinson [unrecorded], Handley-Taylor p.52, Wight 55b

Collation: [A]⁹ ([A]2+1) [B-K]⁸ (J not used); 81 leaves; 225 × 149mm.; [i–x] 1–60 [61–62] 63–96 [97–98] 99–127 [128–30] 131–51 [152]

Page contents: [i] 'OF THIS SPECIAL AUTOGRAPHED EDITION | OF MELLONEY HOLTSPUR 1000 COPIES | HAVE BEEN PRINTED, OF WHICH THIS | IS NUMBER..'; [ii] blank; [iii] 'MELLONEY HOLTSPUR | OR | THE PANGS OF LOVE'; [iv] '*By* JOHN MASEFIELD | [double rule] | [24 titles listed]'; [v] title-page; [vi] 'PRINTED IN THE UNITED STATES OF AMERICA | COPYRIGHT, 1922, | BY JOHN MASEFIELD | [rule] | Set up and electrotyped. Published November, 1922. | Press of | J. J. Little & Ives Company | New York'; [vii] '*The consecrated things are wiser than our virtue.*'; [viii] blank; [ix] 'PERSONS | [dramatis personae listed]'; [x] blank; 1–60 text of Act I; [61] 'ACT II'; [62] blank; 63–96 text of Act II; [97] 'ACT III'; [98] blank; 99–127 text of Act III; [128] blank; [129] 'ACT IV'; [130] blank; 131–50 text of Act IV; 151 '*Note.*-The persons and events described in this play are imaginary. No | reference is made to any living person.-JOHN MASEFIELD'; [152] blank

Paper: laid paper (no watermark), chain-lines 22mm. apart

Running title: '*Melloney Holtspur*' (41mm.) on both verso and recto, pp.2–150

Binding: light grey boards with black cloth spine. On spine, in gold: 'MELLONEY | HOLTSPUR | OR | THE PANGS | OF LOVE | [leaf ornament] | MASEFIELD | [point]MACMILLAN[point]' (all width centred). On upper cover: panel in blind: 53 × 89mm. upon which: white paper label (53 × 88mm.) on which: 'MELLONEY HOLTSPUR | OR | THE PANGS OF LOVE | [ornament] | JOHN MASEFIELD' (enclosed within ruled border with ornament at each corner and all within double ruled border: 46 × 82mm.) Lower cover: blank. Top edge trimmed, others roughly trimmed. Binding measurements: 231 × 150mm. (covers), 231 × 23mm. (spine). End-papers: laid paper (no watermark), chain-lines 22mm. apart.

Publication date: published, according to Simmons, 28 November 1922

Price: $2.50

Contents:
Melloney Holtspur ('ACT I | [*The scene is a panelled room. At Back, a plain...*]')

Notes:
Unlike the Heinemann English editions, the American publication of this play is given a sub-title. The original dedication is however omitted.

Page numbers appear within square brackets. Thus, [1], [2], etc.

Although a publication date of 28 November 1922 is noted by Simmons (thus after A61(a) but before A61(c)) Wight places this volume after A61(c) in his sequence.

The additional leaf ([A]1) pasted onto [A]2 comprises the leaf detailing the limitation of the edition. The paper type is the same as that used for the rest of the volume. The single leaves were presumably sent to Masefield for signing.

Wight describes the ornaments at each corner of the inner ruled border of the upper cover label as 'floral devices'. The ornament appears as a branch with five leaves.

A publishing agreement for this title between Masefield and Macmillan was dated 6 July 1922 (see Archives of The Society of Authors). The agreement refers to 'a licence to publish in volume form in the United States of America and Canada a work the subject or title of which is Melloney Holtspur'.

Copies seen: private collection (PWE) number 318, signed 'No 318. J. Masefield.' on p.[i]; NYPL (Berg Collection) number 52, signed 'No 52. | J. Masefield.' on p.[i]; Columbia University Libraries (Special Collections B825.M377.T.1922.c.1) number 262, signed 'No 262. J. Masefield.' on p.[i]; Columbia University Libraries (Special Collections B825.M377.T.1922.c.2) number 266, signed 'No 266. J. Masefield.' on p.[i], inscribed 'for Lew | from | Zom. | Christmas. 1922.' with signature of Judith Masefield, includes posthumous booklabel; HRHRC (TEMP M377ME 1922C cop.1) number 6, signed 'No 6. | J. Masefield.' additionally inscribed 'For Na | from | Zom. | Xmas. 1922.'; HRHRC (TEMP M377ME 1922C cop.2) number 670, signed 'No 670. J. Masefield.' additionally inscribed 'For Con | from | Zom. | Christmas. 1922.'

A61(c) Second English edition (limited signed edition) (1922)

MELLONEY HOLTSPUR | BY | JOHN MASEFIELD | *The consecrated things are wiser than our virtue.* | [publisher's device of a windmill with '19' and '22' on either side] | [rule, 67mm.] | LONDON : WILLIAM HEINEMANN
(The '*T*' of '*The*' is swash)
(All width centred)

Bibliographies: Simmons [55a], Nevinson [unrecorded], Handley-Taylor p.52, Wight [55a]

Collation: [A]⁴ B-I⁸; B2-I2 are also signed; signatures right foot of page with 'M.H.' at left foot on first leaf of gatherings (with the exception of gatherings [A], G and I); 68 leaves; 224 × 143mm.; [i–viii] 1–126 [127–28]

Page contents: [i] half-title: 'MELLONEY HOLTSPUR'; [ii] '*This edition, printed on hand-made* | *paper and numbered and signed* | *by the Author, is limited to five* | *hundred and thirty copies, of which* | *five hundred are for sale and thirty* | *for presentation.* | *No.* ....'; [iii] title-page; [iv] 'PRINTED IN GREAT BRITAIN BY THE WHITEFRIARS PRESS, LTD., | LONDON AND TONBRIDGE.'; [v] 'To | EDWARD GORDON CRAIG'; [vi] blank; [vii] 'PERSONS | [dramatis personae listed]'; [viii] blank; 1–126 text; [127] 'NOTE. | The persons and events described in this play | are imaginary. No reference is made to any living | person. | JOHN MASEFIELD.'; [128] 'PRINTED IN GREAT BRITAIN BY THE WHITEFRIARS PRESS, LTD., | LONDON AND TONBRIDGE.'

Paper: wove paper: (watermark: 'BRITISH HAND MADE PURE RAG [castle device: 27 × 32mm.]')

Running title: 'MELLONEY HOLTSPUR' (46mm.) on both verso and recto, pp.2–126

Binding: blue-grey boards with parchment spine. On spine, in gold: 'Melloney | Holtspur | [ornament] | John | Masefield | HEINEMANN' (all width centred). There is a single vertical rule in blind on each cover at the edge of the parchment. Covers: blank. Top edge gilt, lower outside edge untrimmed, fore edge uncut. Binding measurements: 229 × 147mm. (covers), 229 × 29mm. (spine). End-papers: laid paper (watermark: of windmill: 90 × 49mm. and '1590'), chain-lines 30mm. apart.

Publication date: published, according to Simmons, 30 November 1922

Price: unknown

Contents:
Melloney Holtspur ('ACT I | *The scene is a panelled room. At Back, a plain...*')

Notes:
The text appears to use the setting of type as A61(a). However, there is an additional 'M.H.' in the signatures (the first edition lacks the 'M.H.' on the first leaf of gathering H which is present here).

Copies seen: private collection (PWE) number 124, signed '124 | John Masefield.' on p.[ii]; BL (Cup.402.g.20) number 184, signed '184 | John Masefield.' on p.[ii], stamped 15 APR 1963

A61(d) Second American edition (1923)

MELLONEY HOLTSPUR | OR | THE PANGS OF LOVE | BY | JOHN MASEFIELD | *The consecrated things are wiser than our virtue.* | New York | THE MACMILLAN COMPANY | 1923 | *All rights reserved*
(All width centred)

Bibliographies: Simmons [noted on p.89], Nevinson [unrecorded], Handley-Taylor p.52, Wight [noted on p.95]

Collation: [A-K]⁸ (J not used); 80 leaves; 190 × 127mm.; [i–vi] 1–60 [61–62] 63–96 [97–98] 99–127 [128–30] 131–51 [152–54]

Page contents: [i] half-title: 'MELLONEY HOLTSPUR | OR | THE PANGS OF LOVE'; [ii] '[publisher's device] | THE MACMILLAN COMPANY | [two lines listing five cities, separated by three points] | MACMILLAN & CO., LIMITED | [two lines listing four cities, separated by two points] | THE MACMILLAN CO. OF CANADA, LTD. | [one city listed]'; [iii] title-page; [iv] 'PRINTED IN THE UNITED STATES OF AMERICA | COPYRIGHT, 1922, | BY JOHN MASEFIELD | [rule] | Set up and electrotyped. Published March, 1923.'; [v] '*The consecrated things are wiser than our virtue.*'; [vi] 'PERSONS | [dramatis personae listed]'; 1–60 text of Act I; [61] 'ACT II'; [62] blank; 63–96 text of Act II; [97] 'ACT III'; [98] blank; 99–127 text of Act III; [128] blank; [129] 'ACT IV'; [130] blank; 131–50 text of Act IV; 151 '*Note.*-The persons and events described in this play are imaginary. No | reference is made to any living person.-JOHN MASEFIELD'; [152–54] blank

Paper: wove paper

Running title: '*Melloney Holtspur*' (41mm.) on both verso and recto, pp.2–150

Binding: burgundy cloth. On spine, in gold: 'MELLONEY | HOLTSPUR | MASEFIELD | MACMILLAN | [square point] [square point] [square point]' (all width centred). On upper cover, in gold: 'MELLONEY | HOLTSPUR | MASEFIELD' (ranged upper left) (within blind ruled border: 191 × 122mm.) Lower cover: blank. Top edge trimmed, others roughly trimmed. Binding measurements: 197 × 129mm. (covers), 197 × 31mm. (spine). End-papers: wove paper.

Publication date: published, according to Simmons, 17 April 1923 in an edition of 1510 copies

Price: $1.50

Contents:
as for A61(b)

Notes:
As in A61(b) a sub-title, not present in the English editions, is provided. The dedication is also omitted. The same setting of text as used in A61(b) appears to be used here.

Page numbers appear within square brackets. Thus, [1], [2], etc.

Although noted by Simmons, Handley-Taylor and Wight, this standard American edition is not fully described by any bibliographer. Although Simmons notes a publication date of April 1923, the volume cites March 1923.

Copies seen: NYPL (NCR 1923) 243123B, May 3 1943 noted; NYPL (Berg Collection)

A62 SELECTED POEMS   1922

A62(a) First English edition (1922)

Selected Poems [in red] | By | John Masefield | [publisher's device of a windmill with '19' and '22' on either side] | [rule, 77mm.] | LONDON : WILLIAM HEINEMANN, LTD.
(All width centred)

Bibliographies: Simmons [noted on pp.91–92], Nevinson p.13, Handley-Taylor p.53, Wight [unrecorded]

Collation: [A]⁶ B-P⁸ (J not used); B2-P2 are also signed; signatures right foot of page with 'S.M.' at left foot on first leaf of gatherings (with the exception of gathering [A]); 118 leaves; 169 × 106mm.; [two un-numbered pages] [i–vii] viii [ix–x] 1–223 [224]

Page contents: [-] blank (page excluded from page count, but constitutes first leaf of first gathering); [-] blank; [i] half-title: 'Selected Poems | By | John Masefield'; [ii] '*Selected Poems from The* | *Indian Love Lyrics of Laurence* | *Hope.* F'cap 8vo. Cloth, 5s.; | leather, 7s. 6d. | *Selections from Swinburne,* | *edited by Edmund Gosse, C.B.,* | *and T. J. Wise.* Cr. 8vo. | 6s. net. | *The Works of Swinburne,* | *Golden Pine Edition.* In 6 | vols. F'cap 8vo. Cloth, 4s.; | leather, 6s. each. | [rule] | LONDON : WILLIAM HEINEMANN, LTD.' (within ruled border: 66 × 50mm.) (the italic type contains a number of swash characters) (with additional leaf tipped-in on the verso of which is the frontispiece: 114 × 75mm., of Masefield signed 'W. Strang | Jan. 1912' and 'John Masefield'); [iii] title-page; [iv] '*Printed in Great Britain.*'; [v] 'TO | MY WIFE'; [vi] blank; [vii]-viii 'CONTENTS' (49 individual items listed with page references); [ix] 'The books from which these selections are taken are pub- | lished by the following firms, to whom the author makes the | usual acknowledgments :- | Salt Water Ballads. Messrs. ELKIN MATHEWS, LTD. | Poems and Ballads. '' '' | Pompey the Great. Messrs. SIDGWICK & JACKSON, LTD. | The Everlasting Mercy. '' '' | The Widow in the | Bye Street . '' '' | Dauber . . Messrs. WILLIAM HEINEMANN, LTD. | The Daffodil Fields '' '' | Philip the King . '' '' | Gallipoli . . '' '' | Good Friday . '' '' | Lollingdon Downs '' '' | Reynard the Fox . '' '' | Enslaved . . '' '' | Right Royal . '' '' | Esther . . '' '' ''; [x] blank; 1–223 text; [224] 'PRINTED IN GREAT BRITAIN BY THE WHITEFRIARS PRESS, LTD., | LONDON AND TONBRIDGE.'

Paper: wove paper

Running title: none

Binding: blue cloth. On spine, in gold: '[rule] | [rule] | SELECTED | POEMS | [point] | JOHN | MASEFIELD | [ornament] | HEINEMANN | [rule] | [rule]' (all width centred). On upper cover, in gold: facsimile signature 'J. Masefield.' (width centred but at an angle) (within blind ruled border: 171 × 103mm.) On lower cover, in blind: publisher's device of a windmill (ranged lower right). Top edge gilt, others untrimmed. Binding measurements: 176 × 109mm. (covers), 176 × 29mm. (spine). End-papers: wove paper

Also issued in black leather. On spine, in gold: '[rule] | [rule] | SELECTED | POEMS | [point] | JOHN | MASEFIELD | [ornament] | HEINEMANN | [rule] | [rule]' (all width centred). On upper cover, in gold: facsimile signature 'J. Masefield.' (width centred but at an angle) (within blind ruled border with no border on edge nearest spine: 171 × 107mm.) On lower cover: blind ruled border with no border on edge nearest spine: 171 × 107mm. Top edge gilt, others untrimmed. Blue marker ribbon. Binding measurements: 176 × 109mm. (covers), 176 × 28mm. (spine). End-papers: wove paper.

Publication date: published, according to Simmons, 30 November 1922 in an edition of 10000 copies (cloth binding) / published, according to Handley-Taylor, 23 November 1922 in an edition of 10000 copies (cloth binding). The *English Catalogue of Books* records a publication date of December 1922.

Price: 6s. (cloth) / 8s.6d. (leather)

Contents:
Selections from SALT-WATER BALLADS
Trade Winds ('In the harbour, in the island, in the Spanish Seas,')
Sea-Fever ('I must go down to the seas again, to the lonely sea and the sky,')
Prayer ('When the last sea is sailed and the last shallow charted,')

The West Wind ('It's a warm wind, the west wind, full of birds' cries;')
Selections from POEMS AND BALLADS
Cargoes ('Quinquireme of Nineveh from distant Ophir')
An Old Song Re-Sung ('I saw a ship a-sailing, a-sailing, a-sailing,')
Twilight ('Twilight it is, and the far woods are dim, and the rooks cry and call.')
Invocation ('O wanderer into many brains,')
A Creed ('I held that when a person dies')
When Bony Death ('When bony Death has chilled her gentle blood,')
The Death Rooms ('My soul has many an old decaying room')
C. L. M. ('In the dark womb where I began')
Waste ('No rose but fades: no glory but must pass:')
The Wild Duck ('Twilight; red in the west;')
Selections from POMPEY THE GREAT
Chorus ('Man is a sacred city, built of marvellous earth.')
Chorus ('Kneel to the beautiful women who bear us this strange brave fruit.')
Epilogue ('And all their passionate hearts are dust,')
Selections from THE EVERLASTING MERCY
The Scallenge ('The moonlight shone on Cabbage Walk,')
Epilogue ('How swift the summer goes,')
Selections from THE WIDOW IN THE BYE STREET
The End ('Some of life's sad ones are too strong to die,')
Selections from DAUBER
The Setting of the Watch ('Darker it grew, still darker, and the stars')
The Watch Below ('Down in his bunk the Dauber lay awake')
The Horn ('Even now they shifted suits of sails; they bent')
The South-West Wind ('All through the windless night the clipper rolled')
We Therefore Commit Our Brother ('Night fell, and all night long the Dauber lay')
Selections from THE DAFFODIL FIELDS
I ('Between the barren pasture and the wood')
The River ('The steaming river loitered like old blood')
The Return ('Soon he was at the Foxholes, at the place')
The End of the Trouble ('Lion lay still while the cold tides of death')
Selections from PHILIP THE KING
[The Messenger's Speech] ('MESSENGER. | This gold chain...')
Truth ('Man with his burning soul')
The "Wanderer" ('All day they loitered by the resting ships,')
August, 1914 ('How still this quiet cornfield is to-night!')
Biography ('When I am buried, all my thoughts and acts')
Ships ('I cannot tell their wonder nor make known')
Sonnet on the Death of his Wife (From the Portuguese of Antonio di Ferreiro) ('That blessed sunlight, that once showed to me')
They Closed Her Eyes (From the Spanish of Don Gustavo A. Becquér) ('They closed her eyes,')
Selections from GOOD FRIDAY
[The Madman Speaks] ('MADMAN | They cut my face, there's blood upon my brow.')
Selections from LOLLINGDON DOWNS
[Untitled] ('O wretched man, that for a little mile')
[Untitled] ('Out of the special cell's most special sense')
[Untitled] ('I could not sleep for thinking of the sky,')
[Untitled] ('How did the nothing come, how did these fires,')
[Untitled] ('It may be so; but let the unknown be.')
[Untitled] ('What is this life which uses living cells')
[Untitled] ('Can it be blood and brain, this transient force')
[Untitled] ('Not only blood and brain its servants are;')
[Untitled] ('Here in the self is all that man can know')
[Untitled] ('Flesh, I have knocked at many a dusty door,')
[Untitled] ('But all has passed, the tune has died away,')
[Untitled] ('These myriad days, these many thousand hours,')
[Untitled] ('There, on the darkened deathbed, dies the brain')
[Untitled] ('So in the empty sky the stars appear,')
[Untitled] ('It may be so with us, that in the dark,')
[Untitled] ('What am I, Life? A thing of watery salt')
[Untitled] ('If I could get within this changing I,')
[Untitled] ('What is this atom which contains the whole,')

[Untitled] ('Ah, we are neither heaven nor earth, but men;')
[Untitled] ('Roses are beauty, but I never see')
[Untitled] ('Over the church's door they moved a stone,')
[Untitled] ('O little self, within whose smallness lies')
[Untitled] ('I went into the fields, but you were there')
[Untitled] ('Wherever beauty has been quick in clay')
[Untitled] ('Not for the anguish suffered is the slur,')
[Untitled] ('You will remember me in days to come,')
[Untitled] ('If Beauty be at all, if, beyond sense,')
[Untitled] ('If all be governed by the moving stars,')
[Untitled] ('In emptiest furthest heaven where no stars are,')
[Untitled] ('Death lies in wait for you, you wild thing in the wood,')
[Untitled] ('Go, spend your penny, Beauty, when you will,')
[Untitled] ('Let that which is to come be as it may,')
From GALLIPOLI
Epilogue ('Even so was wisdom proven blind,')
Selections from REYNARD THE FOX
[Opening of 'Part Two'] ('On old Cold Crendon's windy tops')
Selections from ENSLAVED
[Prologue] ('All early in the April, when daylight comes at five,')
[The End] / The Khalif's Judgment ('They took us to a palace, to a chamber')
The Hounds of Hell ('About the crowing of the cock,')
Animula ('This is the place, this house beside the sea;')
Forget ('Forget all these, the barren fool in power,')
On Growing Old ('Be with me, Beauty, for the fire is dying;')
Selections from RIGHT ROYAL
[Concluding Section] ('As a whirl of notes running in a fugue that men play,')
Selections from ESTHER
[Choruses] ('CHORUS. | In the troubled dreams a slave has, ere I waken')
Act II ('AHASUERUS. | What is the time? I hear the water drip')

Notes:

The contents page does not exactly correspond with the contents as present within the volume. The most common discrepancy is the use of different titles. Many excerpts are untitled either in the volume or the contents.

The untitled excerpt from *Right Royal* is from the conclusion of the poem, with minor deletions. Consequently this volume presumably presents examples of authorial revision for the purpose of this selection.

All page numbers are presented within square brackets, with the exception of that on p.viii.

The publishing agreement for this title between Masefield and Heinemann was dated 20 October 1922 (see Archives of The Society of Authors). The agreement refers to both a 6s. and 'special edition' (A62(a) and A62(b)).

There is a discrepancy over date of publication. Simmons states a date of 30 November while Handley-Taylor notes 23 November. There is a similar disagreement over the Heinemann limited signed edition (Simmons noting 30 November against Handley-Taylor's 7 December). Copies in the British Library suggest the regular Heinemann issue was published first.

The leather bound issue of this edition is not recorded by Simmons or Handley-Taylor. It is, however, noted in the *English Catalogue of Books*.

The archives of The Society of Authors record that an application to publish a Braille version of this text was received from the National Institute for the Blind in October 1932 (see BL, Add.Mss.56597, f.177). Masefield had written to The Society of Authors, in June 1926 stating:

> By all means always authorise the setting in Braille of any of my books.
>
> (John Masefield, letter to [G.H.] Thring, [20 Jun. 1926])
> (BL, Add.Mss.56583, f.39)

In 1932 he repeated his permission, writing to The Society of Authors:

> Any of my books may at any time be published in Braille for the use of the Blind.
>
> (John Masefield, letter to The Society of Authors, [October 1932])
> (BL, Add.Mss.56597, f.177)

Copies seen: private collection (PWE); BL (011645.de.38) stamped 30 NOV 1922; Bodleian (28001.f.796) stamped DEC 1922; HRHRC (AC-L M377 B1 1922A) inscribed 'for | Lew | from | Zom | Nov 30. 1922.'

A62(b) Second English edition (limited signed edition) (1922)

Selected Poems [in red] | By | John Masefield | [publisher's device of a windmill with '19' and '22' on either side] | [rule, 77mm.] | LONDON : WILLIAM HEINEMANN, LTD.
(All width centred)

Bibliographies: Simmons [56], Nevinson [unrecorded], Handley-Taylor p.53, Wight [56]

Collation: [A]⁶ B-Q⁸ R⁴ (J not used); B2-R2 are also signed; signatures right foot of page with 'S.M.' at left foot on first leaf of gatherings (with the exception of gathering [A]); 130 leaves; 198 × 130mm.; [two un-numbered pages] [i–vii] viii [ix–x] 1–244 [245–48]

Page contents: [-] blank (page excluded from page count, but constitutes first leaf of first gathering); [-] blank; [i] half-title: 'Selected Poems | By | John Masefield'; [ii] *'This edition, printed on English | hand-made paper, and contain-* | *ing the poem* NIREUS, *hitherto* | *unpublished, is limited to five* | *hundred and thirty copies, of* | *which five hundred are for sale* | *in the United Kingdom and* | *thirty for presentation.* | *No....................................'* (the italic type contains a number of swash characters) (with additional leaf tipped-in on the verso of which is the frontispiece: 111 × 64mm., of Masefield signed 'L.ANNING-BELL', with 'John Masefield' as a facsimile signature, within blind ruled border: 145 × 95mm.); [iii] title-page (with protective tissue for frontispiece tipped-in); [iv] *'Printed in Great Britain.';* [v] 'TO | MY WIFE'; [vi] blank; [vii]-viii 'CONTENTS' (50 individual items listed with page references); [ix] 'The books from which these selections are taken are pub- | lished by the following firms, to whom the author makes the | usual acknowledgments :- | Salt Water Ballads. Messrs. ELKIN MATHEWS, LTD. | Poems and Ballads. '' '' | Pompey the Great. Messrs. SIDGWICK & JACKSON, LTD. | The Everlasting Mercy. '' '' | The Widow in the | Bye Street . '' '' | Dauber . . Messrs. WILLIAM HEINEMANN, LTD. | The Daffodil Fields '' '' | Philip the King . '' '' | Gallipoli .. '' '' | Good Friday . '' '' | Lollingdon Downs '' '' | Reynard the Fox . '' '' | Enslaved .. '' '' | Right Royal . '' '' | Esther .. '' '' ''; [x] blank; 1-[245] text (at foot of p.[245]: 'PRINTED IN GREAT BRITAIN BY THE WHITEFRIARS PRESS LTD. | LONDON AND TONBRIDGE.'); [246–48] blank

Paper: wove paper (watermark: 'BRITISH HAND MADE PURE RAG [castle device: 25 × 32mm.]')

Running title: none

Binding: cream boards with parchment spine. On spine, in gold: 'SELECTED POEMS | [ornament] | JOHN | MASEFIELD | HEINEMANN' (all width centred). There is a single vertical rule in gold on each cover at the edge of the parchment. Covers: blank. Top edge gilt, lower outside edge untrimmed, fore edge uncut. Sewn head band (in white). Binding measurements: 204 × 132mm. (covers), 204 × 41mm. (spine). End-papers: wove paper.

Publication date: published, according to Simmons, 30 November 1922 / published, according to Handley-Taylor, 7 December 1922. The *English Catalogue of Books* records a publication date of December 1922. Presentation copies suggest this edition to have been published in December 1922.

Price: 31s.6d.

Contents:
pp.1–223 as for A62(a) and then with the following additional contents:
Nireus ('Once long ago young Nireus was the King')

Notes:
As with A62(a), the contents page does not exactly correspond with the text within the volume, page numbers are presented within square brackets, with the exception of those on pp. viii and 241.

The text on pp.[ix]–223 appears to use the same setting of type as A62(a).

Copies seen: private collection (ROV) number 465, signed '465. | John Masefield.' on p.[ii]; BL (011645.eee.14) number 526, signed '526 | John Masefield.' on p.[ii], stamped 18 DEC 1922; Bodleian (28001.e.2705) number 528, signed '528 | John Masefield.' on p.[ii], stamped DEC 1922; HRHRC (PR6025 A77 A6 1922) number 339, signed '339 | John Masefield.' on p.[ii]; HRHRC (AC-L M377 B1 1922A cop.1) number 336, signed '336 | John Masefield.' on p.[ii]; HRHRC (AC-L M377 B1 1922A cop.2) number 101, signed '101 | John Masefield.' on p.[ii]; HRHRC (TEMP M377 B1 1922B cop.1) number 501, signed '501 | John Masefield.' on p.[ii] and additionally inscribed 'for | Con | from Jan. | Dec 16. 1922'; HRHRC (TEMP M377 B1 1922B cop.2) number 515, signed '515 | John Masefield.' on p.[ii] and additionally inscribed 'for | Lew | from | Zom. | Dec 16th. Saturday. | 1922.'; HRHRC (TEMP M377 B1 1922B cop.3) number 505, signed '505 | John Masefield.' on p.[ii] and additionally inscribed 'for | Na | from | Zom. | Dec 16. 1922.'; HRHRC (TEMP M377 B1 1922B cop.4) number 48, signed '48 | John Masefield.' on p.[ii]

A62(c) First American edition (1923)

Selected Poems | By | John Masefield | New York | THE MACMILLAN COMPANY | 1923 | *All rights reserved*
(All width centred)

Bibliographies: Simmons [56a], Nevinson [unrecorded], Handley-Taylor p.53, Wight [unrecorded] (see notes)

Collation: [A]⁷ (±[A]4 ±[A]5 [A]5+1) [B-R]⁸ [S]⁹ (-S4 ±S5 S5+2) (J not used); 144 leaves; 173 × 107mm.; [two un-numbered pages] [i–vi] vii–viii [ix–xii] 1–267 [268–74]

Page contents: [-] blank (page excluded from page count, but constitutes first leaf of first gathering); [-] blank; [i] half-title: 'Selected Poems'; [ii] 'BY JOHN MASEFIELD | [rule] | [27 titles listed]' (within double ruled border: 92 × 68mm.); [iii] title-page (with additional leaf tipped-in on the verso of which is the frontispiece: 114 × 75mm., of Masefield signed 'W. Strang | Jan. 1912' and 'John Masefield'); [iv] 'PRINTED IN THE UNITED STATES OF AMERICA | COPYRIGHT, 1912, 1913, 1914, 1916, 1917, 1919, 1920, 1922 AND 1923 | BY JOHN MASEFIELD | [rule] | Set up and electrotyped. Published March, 1923.'; [v] 'TO | MY WIFE'; [vi] blank; vii-[ix] 'CONTENTS' (51 individual items listed with page references); [x] blank; [xi] 'Selected Poems'; [xii] blank; 1–267 text; [268–74] blank

Paper: wove paper

Running title: none

Binding: blue cloth. On spine, in gold: '[rule] | [rule] | SELECTED | POEMS | [point] | JOHN | MASEFIELD | [ornament] | MACMILLAN | [rule] | [rule] | [square point] [square point] [square point]' (all width centred). On upper cover, in gold: facsimile signature 'J. Masefield.' (width centred and horizontal) (within blind ruled border: 173 × 102mm.) Lower cover: blank. Top edge trimmed, others roughly trimmed. Binding measurements: 179 × 110mm. (covers), 179 × 32mm. (spine). End-papers: wove paper.

Publication date: published, according to Simmons, 8 May 1923 in an edition of 2554 copies

Price: $2.00

Contents:
Selections from SALT-WATER BALLADS
Trade Winds ('In the harbour, in the island, in the Spanish Seas,')
Sea-Fever ('I must go down to the seas again, to the lonely sea and the sky,')
Prayer ('When the last sea is sailed and the last shallow charted,')
The West Wind ('It's a warm wind, the west wind, full of birds' cries;')
Selections from POEMS AND BALLADS
Cargoes ('Quinquireme of Nineveh from distant Ophir')
An Old Song Re-Sung ('I saw a ship a-sailing, a-sailing, a-sailing,')
Twilight ('Twilight it is, and the far woods are dim, and the rooks cry and call.')
Invocation ('O wanderer into many brains,')
A Creed ('I held that when a person dies')
When Bony Death ('When bony Death has chilled her gentle blood,')
The Death Rooms ('My soul has many an old decaying room')
C. L. M. ('In the dark womb where I began')
Waste ('No rose but fades: no glory but must pass:')
The Wild Duck ('Twilight; red in the west;')
Selections from POMPEY THE GREAT
Chorus ('Man is a sacred city, built of marvellous earth.')
Chorus ('Kneel to the beautiful women who bear us this strange brave fruit.')
Epilogue ('And all their passionate hearts are dust,')
Selections from THE EVERLASTING MERCY
The Scallenge ('The moonlight shone on Cabbage Walk,')
Epilogue ('How swift the summer goes,')
Selections from THE WIDOW IN THE BYE STREET
The End ('Some of life's sad ones are too strong to die,')
Selections from DAUBER
The Setting of the Watch ('Darker it grew, still darker, and the stars')
The Watch Below ('Down in his bunk the Dauber lay awake')
The Horn ('Even now they shifted suits of sails; they bent')
The South-West Wind ('All through the windless night the clipper rolled')
We Therefore Commit Our Brother ('Night fell, and all night long the Dauber lay')
Selections from THE DAFFODIL FIELDS
I ('Between the barren pasture and the wood')
The River ('The steaming river loitered like old blood')
The Return ('Soon he was at the Foxholes, at the place')
The End of the Trouble ('Lion lay still while the cold tides of death')
Selections from PHILIP THE KING
[The Messenger's Speech] ('MESSENGER. | This gold chain...')
Truth ('Man with his burning soul')
The "Wanderer" ('All day they loitered by the resting ships,')
August, 1914 ('How still this quiet cornfield is to-night !')
Biography ('When I am buried, all my thoughts and acts')
Ships ('I cannot tell their wonder nor make known')

Sonnet on the Death of his Wife (From the Portuguese of Antonio di Ferreiro) ('That blessed sunlight, that once showed to me')
They Closed Her Eyes (From the Spanish of Don Gustavo A. Becquér) ('They closed her eyes,')
Selections from GOOD FRIDAY
[The Madman Speaks] ('MADMAN. | They cut my face, there's blood upon my brow.')
Selections from LOLLINGDON DOWNS
[Untitled] ('O wretched man, that for a little mile')
[Untitled] ('Out of the special cell's most special sense')
[Untitled] ('I could not sleep for thinking of the sky,')
[Untitled] ('How did the nothing come, how did these fires,')
[Untitled] ('It may be so; but let the unknown be.')
[Untitled] ('What is this life which uses living cells')
[Untitled] ('Can it be blood and brain, this transient force')
[Untitled] ('Not only blood and brain its servants are;')
[Untitled] ('Here in the self is all that man can know')
[Untitled] ('Flesh, I have knocked at many a dusty door,')
[Untitled] ('But all has passed, the tune has died away,')
[Untitled] ('These myriad days, these many thousand hours,')
[Untitled] ('There, on the darkened deathbed, dies the brain')
[Untitled] ('So in the empty sky the stars appear,')
[Untitled] ('It may be so with us, that in the dark,')
[Untitled] ('What am I, Life? A thing of watery salt')
[Untitled] ('If I could get within this changing I,')
[Untitled] ('What is this atom which contains the whole,')
[Untitled] ('Ah, we are neither heaven nor earth, but men;')
[Untitled] ('Roses are beauty, but I never see')
[Untitled] ('Over the church's door they moved a stone,')
[Untitled] ('O little self, within whose smallness lies')
[Untitled] ('I went into the fields, but you were there')
[Untitled] ('Wherever beauty has been quick in clay')
[Untitled] ('Not for the anguish suffered is the slur,')
[Untitled] ('You will remember me in days to come,')
[Untitled] ('If Beauty be at all, if, beyond sense,')
[Untitled] ('If all be governed by the moving stars,')
[Untitled] ('In emptiest furthest heaven where no stars are,')
[Untitled] ('Death lies in wait for you, you wild thing in the wood,')
[Untitled] ('Go, spend your penny, Beauty, when you will,')
[Untitled] ('Let that which is to come be as it may,')
From GALLIPOLI
Epilogue ('Even so was wisdom proven blind,')
Selections from REYNARD THE FOX
[Opening of 'Part Two'] ('On old Cold Crendon's windy tops')
Selections from ENSLAVED
[Prologue] ('All early in the April, when daylight comes at five,')
[The End] / The Khalif's Judgment ('They took us to a palace, to a chamber')
The Hounds of Hell ('About the crowing of the cock,')
Animula ('This is the place, this house beside the sea;')
Forget ('Forget all these, the barren fool in power,')
On Growing Old ('Be with me, Beauty, for the fire is dying;')
Selections from RIGHT ROYAL
[Concluding Section] ('As a whirl of notes running in a fugue that men play,')
Selections from ESTHER
[Choruses] ('CHORUS. | In the troubled dreams a slave has, ere I waken')
Act II ('AHASUERUS. | What is the time? I hear the water drip')
Hitherto Unpublished
Nireus ('Once long ago young Nireus was the King')
Sonnets
[Untitled] ('Once we were masters of the arts of men.')
[Untitled] ('Builded in every village in the land,')
[Untitled] ('I saw the work of all the world displayed,')
[Untitled] ('I cannot tell who will, but only know')
[Untitled] ('I saw the racer coming to the jump')
Beauty ('When soul's companion fails,')

Notes:

The cancel pages and additional leaves in gatherings [A] and S are curious. The additional A5 and A6, and also S4 and S5 are conjugate leaves. The edition was set in electrotype in the United States and there is no reference to the English Heinemann setting. The cancel pages and additional leaves therefore have no connection with the English edition. All are, however, associated with the inclusion of the hitherto unpublished poems.

A publishing agreement for this title between Masefield and Macmillan was dated 13 September 1922 (see Archives of The Society of Authors). The agreement refers to 'a licence to publish in volume form in the United States of America and Canada a work the subject or title of which is a Selection of the author's poems'.

Copies seen: private collection (ROV)

A62(cc) First American edition (limited signed edition) (1923)

SELECTED POEMS [in red] | *By* JOHN MASEFIELD [in black] [floral device] [in red] [floral device] [in red] | THE MACMILLAN COMPANY | PUBLISHERS   MCMXXIII
(Justified on both left and right margins and ranged left)

Bibliographies: Simmons [noted on p.92], Nevinson [unrecorded], Handley-Taylor p.53, Wight [56a] (see notes)

Collation: [A]⁹ ([A]4+1 ±[A]5 [A]9+2) [B-S]⁸ (J not used); 145 leaves; 213 × 144mm.; [six un-numbered pages] [i–vi] vii–viii [ix–xii] 1–267 [268–72]

Page contents: [-] blank (page excluded from page count, but constitutes first leaf of first gathering); [-] blank; [-] blank (page excluded from page count, but constitutes second leaf of first gathering); [-] blank; [-] 'OF THIS AUTOGRAPHED EDITION | OF *MASEFIELD'S SELECTED POEMS,* | 400 COPIES HAVE BEEN PRINTED, | OF WHICH THIS IS NUMBER'; [-] blank; [i] half-title: 'Selected Poems'; [ii] '[publisher's device] | THE MACMILLAN COMPANY | [two lines listing four cities, separated by two points] | MACMILLAN & CO., LIMITED | [two lines listing four cities, separated by two points] | THE MACMILLAN CO. OF CANADA, LTD. | [one city listed]'; [iii] title-page; [iv] 'COPYRIGHT, 1912, 1913, 1914, 1916, 1917, 1919, 1920, 1922 AND | 1923 BY JOHN MASEFIELD | [rule] | PUBLISHED MAY, 1923'; [v] 'TO | MY WIFE'; [vi] blank; vii-[ix] 'CONTENTS' (51 individual items listed with page references); [x] blank; [xi] 'Selected Poems'; [xii] blank; 1–267 text; [268–72] blank

Paper: laid paper (watermark: 'ENFIELD | S.CO+1887' (within ornate oval design: 54 × 69mm.)), chain-lines 30mm. apart

Running title: none

Binding: blue-green boards with cream cloth spine. On spine: '[rule] [in gold] | [raised band of binding] | SELECTED [in gold] | POEMS [in gold] | [ornament] [in gold] | JOHN [in gold] | MASEFIELD [in gold] | [ornament] [in gold] | [raised band of binding] | [raised band of binding] | [raised band of binding] | [point] MACMILLAN [point] | [rule] [in gold]' (the title and author and ornaments are printed on a black panel between two ribs of binding). There is a single vertical rule in gold on each cover at the edge of the cream cloth. On upper cover, in gold: facsimile signature 'J. Masefield.' (width centred and horizontal, printed on black shaped panel surrounded by double ruled border in gold: 33 × 55mm.) Lower cover: blank. Top edge gilt, lower outside edge roughly trimmed, fore edge uncut. Binding measurements: 220 × 146mm. (covers), 220 × 41mm. (spine). End-papers: blue laid paper (no watermark), chain-lines 17mm. apart.

Publication date: published, according to Simmons, 8 May 1923

Price: unknown

Contents:
as for A62(c)

Notes:

As with A62(a), the contents page does not exactly correspond with the text within the volume.

All page numbers are presented within square brackets.

Wight gives this volume the number [56a] in his bibliography. Simmons had already used that number for the regular American edition (Macmillan, 1923).

Simmons notes that the last six poems in the volume appear in print for the first time here. The first four sonnets were later published in Edward Gordon Craig's *Scene* (see B185). On that occasion, the opening line of the fourth sonnet reads 'I cannot tell who will, but inly know'. The final poems were published (only days later) in *King Cole and other Poems* (see A63) where they are entitled 'The Racer' and 'The Eye and the Object' respectively.

The first gathering essentially consists of a six leaf gathering. The first additional leaf ([A]3) pasted onto [A]4 comprises the leaf detailing the limitation of the edition. The paper type is the same as that used for the rest of the volume (although bound so that chain-lines run horizontally). The single leaves were presumably sent to Masefield for signing. The remaining additional leaves are conjugate ([A]7 and [A]8) and are pasted onto [A]9. These leaves comprise the contents. The title-page is a cancellan.

As in A62(c), note the exclusion in this edition of any note of original publishers.

Copies seen: private collection (PWE) number 153, signed '153. [in red] | J. Masefield.' on p.[v]

A62(d) Third English edition (1938)

JOHN MASEFIELD | [rule (tapered at each end with break in middle and square point in blind), 83mm.] | SELECTED [in red] | POEMS [in red] | [publisher's device of a windmill with 'W' and 'H'] | [rule, 68mm.] | WILLIAM HEINEMANN LTD | LONDON   ::   TORONTO
(All width centred with final two lines justified on both left and right margins)

Bibliographies: Handley-Taylor p.53, Wight [unrecorded]

Collation: [A]⁸ B-S⁸ (J not used); signatures left foot of page; 144 leaves; 171 × 105mm.; [two un-numbered pages] [i–vi] vii–xi [xii] xiii–xiv 1–271 [272]

Page contents: [-] blank (page excluded from page count, but constitutes first leaf of first gathering); [-] blank; [i] half-title: 'SELECTED POEMS | BY | JOHN MASEFIELD'; [iii] '*ALSO BY JOHN MASEFIELD* | PLAYS: | [12 titles listed] | POETRY: | [15 titles listed] | FICTION: | [nine titles listed] | GENERAL: | [nine titles listed]'; [iii] title-page (with additional leaf tipped-in on the verso of which is the frontispiece: 113 × 73mm., 'W. Strang | Jan. 1912 | John Masefield'); [iv] 'FIRST PUBLISHED NOV. 1922 | NEW AND REVISED EDITION 1938 | PRINTED IN GREAT BRITAIN AT THE WINDMILL PRESS | KINGSWOOD, SURREY'; [v] 'TO | MY WIFE'; [vi] blank; vii–x 'CONTENTS' (61 individual items listed with page references); xi 'The books from which these selections are | taken are published by the following firms, to | whom the author makes the usual acknowledg- | ments :- | Salt Water Ballads Messrs. ELKIN MATHEWS, LTD | Poems and Ballads '' '' | Pompey the Great Messrs. SIDGWICK & JACKSON, LTD. | The Everlasting Mercy '' '' | The Widow in the | Bye Street . '' '' | Dauber . . Messrs. WILLIAM HEINEMANN, LTD. | The Daffodil Fields '' '' | Philip the King . '' '' | Gallipoli . . '' '' | Good Friday . '' '' | Lollingdon Downs '' '' | Reynard the Fox '' '' | Enslaved . . '' '' | Right Royal . '' '' | Esther . . '' '' | The Collected Poems '' '' | Minnie Maylow's | Story . . '' '' | A Letter from Pontus | and Other Verse '' ' ''; [xii] blank; xiii–xiv 'PREFACE' ('A volume of Selections from my verse was first published many years ago; it is now...') (signed, 'JOHN MASEFIELD.'); 1–271 text (at foot of p.271: 'JOHN MASEFIELD. | Oxford, October, 1937.'); [272] blank

Paper: wove paper

Running title: none

Binding: blue cloth. On spine, in gold: '[rule] | [rule] | SELECTED | POEMS | [point] | JOHN | MASEFIELD | [ornament] | HEINEMANN | [rule] | [rule]' (all width centred). On upper cover, in gold: facsimile signature 'J. Masefield.' (width centred but at an angle) (within blind ruled border: 168 × 102mm.) On lower cover, in blind: publisher's device of a windmill (ranged lower right). Top edge gilt, others untrimmed. Binding measurements: 175 × 108mm. (covers), 175 × 34mm. (spine). End-papers: wove paper.

Publication date: published, according to Handley-Taylor, 28 February 1938

Price: 6s.

Contents:
Preface ('A volume of Selections from my verse was first published many years ago; it is now...')
Selections from SALT-WATER BALLADS
Trade Winds ('In the harbour, in the island, in the Spanish Seas,')
Sea-Fever ('I must go down to the seas again, to the lonely sea and the sky,')
Prayer ('When the last sea is sailed and the last shallow charted,')
The West Wind ('It's a warm wind, the west wind, full of birds' cries;')
Selections from POEMS AND BALLADS
Cargoes ('Quinquireme of Nineveh from distant Ophir')
An Old Song Re-Sung ('I saw a ship a-sailing, a-sailing, a-sailing,')
Twilight ('Twilight it is, and the far woods are dim, and the rooks cry and call.')
Invocation ('O wanderer into many brains,')
A Creed ('I held that when a person dies')
When Bony Death ('When bony Death has chilled her gentle blood,')
The Death Rooms ('My soul has many an old decaying room')
C. L. M. ('In the dark womb where I began')
Waste ('No rose but fades: no glory but must pass:')
The Wild Duck ('Twilight; red in the west;')
Selections from POMPEY THE GREAT
Chorus ('Man is a sacred city, built of marvellous earth.')
Chorus ('Kneel to the beautiful women who bear us this strange brave fruit.')
Epilogue ('And all their passionate hearts are dust,')
Selections from THE EVERLASTING MERCY
The Scallenge ('The moonlight shone on Cabbage Walk,')
Epilogue ('How swift the summer goes,')
Selections from THE WIDOW IN THE BYE STREET

The End ('Some of life's sad ones are too strong to die,')
Selections from DAUBER
The Setting of the Watch ('Darker it grew, still darker, and the stars')
The Watch Below ('Down in his bunk the Dauber lay awake')
The Horn ('Even now they shifted suits of sails; they bent')
The South-West Wind ('All through the windless night the clipper rolled')
We Therefore Commit Our Brother ('Night fell, and all night long the Dauber lay')
Selections from THE DAFFODIL FIELDS
I ('Between the barren pasture and the wood')
The River ('The steaming river loitered like old blood')
The Return ('Soon he was at the Foxholes, at the place')
The End of the Trouble ('Lion lay still while the cold tides of death')
Selections from PHILIP THE KING
The Messenger's Speech ('MESSENGER. | This gold chain...')
Truth ('Man with his burning soul')
The Wanderer ('All day they loitered by the resting ships,')
August, 1914 ('How still this quiet cornfield is to-night!')
Biography ('When I am buried, all my thoughts and acts')
Ships ('I cannot tell their wonder nor make known')
Sonnet on the Death of his Wife (From the Portuguese of Antonio di Ferreiro) ('That blessed sunlight, that once showed to me')
They Closed Her Eyes (From the Spanish of Don Gustavo A. Bécquer) ('They closed her eyes,')
Selections from GOOD FRIDAY
[The Madman Speaks] ('MADMAN | They cut my face, there's blood upon my brow.')
Selections from LOLLINGDON DOWNS
[Untitled] ('O wretched man, that for a little mile')
[Untitled] ('Out of the special cell's most special sense')
[Untitled] ('I could not sleep for thinking of the sky,')
[Untitled] ('How did the nothing come, how did these fires,')
[Untitled] ('It may be so; but let the unknown be.')
[Untitled] ('What is this life which uses living cells')
[Untitled] ('Can it be blood and brain, this transient force')
[Untitled] ('Not only blood and brain its servants are;')
[Untitled] ('Here in the self is all that man can know')
[Untitled] ('Flesh, I have knocked at many a dusty door,')
[Untitled] ('But all has passed, the tune has died away,')
[Untitled] ('These myriad days, these many thousand hours,')
[Untitled] ('There, on the darkened deathbed, dies the brain')
[Untitled] ('So in the empty sky the stars appear,')
[Untitled] ('It may be so with us, that in the dark,')
[Untitled] ('What am I, Life? A thing of watery salt')
[Untitled] ('If I could get within this changing I,')
[Untitled] ('What is this atom which contains the whole,')
[Untitled] ('Ah, we are neither heaven nor earth, but men;')
[Untitled] ('Roses are beauty, but I never see')
[Untitled] ('Over the church's door they moved a stone,')
[Untitled] ('O little self, within whose smallness lies')
[Untitled] ('I went into the fields, but you were there')
[Untitled] ('Wherever beauty has been quick in clay')
[Untitled] ('Not for the anguish suffered is the slur,')
[Untitled] ('You will remember me in days to come,')
[Untitled] ('If Beauty be at all, if, beyond sense,')
[Untitled] ('If all be governed by the moving stars,')
[Untitled] ('In emptiest furthest heaven where no stars are,')
[Untitled] ('Death lies in wait for you, you wild thing in the wood,')
[Untitled] ('Go, spend your penny, Beauty, when you will,')
[Untitled] ('Let that which is to come be as it may,')
From GALLIPOLI
Epilogue ('Even so was wisdom proven blind,')
Selections from REYNARD THE FOX
[Opening of 'Part Two'] ('On old Cold Crendon's windy tops')
Selections from ENSLAVED
[Prologue] ('All early in the April, when daylight comes at five,')

[The End] / The Khalif's Judgment ('They took us to a palace, to a chamber')
The Hounds of Hell ('About the crowing of the cock,')
Animula ('This is the place, this house beside the sea;')
Forget ('Forget all these, the barren fool in power,')
On Growing Old ('Be with me, Beauty, for the fire is dying;')
Selections from RIGHT ROYAL
[Concluding Section] ('As a whirl of notes running in a fugue that men play,')
Selections from ESTHER
[Choruses] ('CHORUS. | In the troubled dreams a slave has, ere I waken')
Act II ('AHASUERUS. | What is the time? I hear the water drip')
Selections from KING COLE, AND OTHER POEMS
[Extract from King Cole] ('I have seen sorrow close and suffering close.')
The Rider at the Gate ('A windy night was blowing on Rome,')
The Racer ('I saw the racer coming to the jump,')
From ODTAA
The Meditation of Highworth Ridden ('I have seen flowers come in stony places;')
From MIDSUMMER NIGHT AND OTHER TALES IN VERSE
The Fight on the Wall ('Modred was in the Water Tower')
On the Coming of Arthur ('By ways unknown, unseen,')
From THE WANDERER
Posted ('Dream after dream I see the wrecks that lie')
From MINNIE MAYLOW'S STORY AND OTHER TALES AND SCENES
The Rose of the World ('Dark Eleanor and Henry sat at meat')
Selections from A LETTER FROM PONTUS AND OTHER VERSE
Ballet Russe ('The gnome from moonland plays the Chopin air,')
Joseph Hodges, Or The Corn ('He wore the smock-frock of the country's past,')
The Towerer ('Old Jarge, Hal, Walter and I, the Rector and Bill,')
The Eyes ('I remember a tropic dawn before turn-to,')
A Ballad of Sir Francis Drake ('Before Sir Francis put to sea,')
Epilogue ('Now I have sifted through')

Notes:

The contents page does not exactly correspond with the contents as contained within the volume. The most common discrepancy is in the use of different titles. Many excerpts are untitled either in the volume or the contents.

All page numbers are presented within square brackets, with the exception of page numbers that comprise roman numerals.

This volume, described as a 'new and revised edition', contains all the material present in A62(a) with additional poems, as Masefield states in his preface, 'chosen from some seven later books.' The text has been entirely re-set for this edition. This allows for some clarification of titles. The excerpt from *Philip the King* is, for example, now headed 'The Messenger's Speech' within the text. In A62(a) this title was only given in the contents listing.

Masefield suggested this revised edition to C.S. Evans at the end of September 1937:

> I gather that you are at the moment out of stock of my Selected Poems. What do you think of revising this, and bringing it up to date? It is a long time since it was done, and there may still be some people who would like to have it.
>
> (John Masefield, letter to [C.S.] Evans, [September 1937])
> (Archives of William Heinemann)

Evans was responsive to Masefield's suggestion:

> Yes, we have just gone out of stock of SELECTED POEMS. As you know, it has been a rather slow seller but I think that it ought to be kept in print and it would be a good idea to bring out a new edition with additions. It would help if you would write a preface for it...
>
> (C.S. Evans, letter to John Masefield, 29 September 1937)
> (HRHRC, MS (Masefield, J.) Recip William Heinemann Ltd.)

During September it appears that Masefield wrote requesting copies of *A Letter from Pontus and other poems* and *A Tale of Troy* in order to work on the new edition. Masefield also enquired whether Heinemann would 'care to get it out before Christmas?' Heinemann had encountered problems, however:

> When we came to make the additions to SELECTED POEMS, we found that we had neither type nor plates of the existing book and so we had to reset. The proofs will be ready in about a fortnight.
>
> (C.S. Evans, letter to John Masefield, 23 November 1937)
> (HRHRC, MS (Masefield, J.) Recip William Heinemann Ltd.)

B.F. Oliver accordingly sent 'a couple of proof copies of SELECTED POEMS and "copy" of the Preface and Epilogue' to Masefield on 16 December (see B.F. Oliver, letter to John Masefield, 16 December 1937) (HRHRC, MS (Masefield, J.) Recip William Heinemann Ltd.)

Copies seen: private collection (PWE) inscribed 'For | Julia Smith, | from | John Masefield. | March. 1938.'; BL (11607.dd.40) stamped 28 FEB 1938

[see also A157 for SELECTED POEMS (NEW EDITION) published in 1950]

A63 KING COLE AND OTHER POEMS   1923

A63(a) First English edition (1923)

KING COLE | AND OTHER POEMS | BY | JOHN MASEFIELD | [publisher's device of a windmill with 'W [point]' and 'H' all within ruled border: 15 × 15mm.] | LONDON | WILLIAM HEINEMANN LTD. (All width centred)

Bibliographies: Simmons [57], Nevinson p.14, Handley-Taylor p.53, Wight [57]

Collation: [A]⁸ B-F⁸; signatures right foot of page; 48 leaves; 185 × 121mm.; [i–vi] vii [viii] 9–93 [94–96]

Page contents: [i] half-title: 'KING COLE | AND OTHER POEMS'; [ii] 'BY THE SAME AUTHOR | *Uniform with this Volume* | [11 titles listed] | [rule] | LONDON: WILLIAM HEINEMANN LTD.'; [iii] title-page; [iv] '*First published* . . . 1923 | PRINTED IN GREAT BRITAIN'; [v] 'TO | MY WIFE'; [vi] blank; vii 'CONTENTS' (11 items listed with page references); [viii] blank; 9–93 text; [94] 'PRINTED IN GREAT BRITAIN BY | BILLING AND SONS, LIMITED, | GUILDFORD AND ESHER'; [95–96] blank

Paper: wove paper

Running title: running titles comprise titles of individual poems, pp.10–92

Binding: blue cloth. On spine, in gold: 'King | Cole | [ornament] | John | Masefield | HEINEMANN' (width centred). On upper cover, in gold: 'KING COLE | JOHN MASEFIELD' (within blind ruled border: 184 × 116mm.) On lower cover, in blind: publisher's device of a windmill (ranged lower right). All edges trimmed. Binding measurements: 189 × 122mm. (covers), 189 × 22mm. (spine). End-papers: wove paper.

Publication date: published, according to Simmons, 31 May 1923 in an edition of 5000 copies

Price: 6s.

Contents:
King Cole ('King Cole was King before the troubles came,')
The Dream ('Weary with many thoughts I went to bed,')
The Woman Speaks ('This poem appeared to me in a dream one winter morning some years ago. In the dream...')
The Rider at the Gate ('A windy night was blowing on Rome,')
The Builders ('Before the unseen cock had called the time,')
The Setting of the Windcock ('The dust lay white upon the chisel-marks,')
The Racer ('I saw the racer coming to the jump,')
The Blowing of the Horn *From "The Song of Roland."* ('Roland gripped his horn with might and main,')
The Haunted ('Here, in this darkened room of this old house,')
Campeachy Picture ('The sloop's sails glow in the sun; the far sky burns,')
        First printed in A Broadside, *June 1908, pp.[1–2]*
The Eye and the Object ('When soul's companion fails,')

Notes:
A volume comprising the standard English edition of *King Cole,* hitherto only available in England in a limited edition. 'The Woman Speaks', 'The Rider at the Gate', 'The Builders', 'The Setting of the Horn' and 'The Haunted' are published here for the first time.

The publishing agreement for this title between Masefield and Heinemann was dated 30 May 1923 (see Archives of The Society of Authors). The agreement refers to a publication price of 6s.

Note the numbering of pages with roman then arabic numerals in a continuous sequence.

Wight notes in his bibliography:

    ...in the pagination the numbers are not all the same size. For example, page 65 has the 6 larger than the 5

Copies seen: private collection (PWE); private collection (ROV) embossed 'PRESENTATION COPY'; BL (11644.dd.79) stamped 31 MAY 1923; ULL (Special Collections) inscribed 'For Lance Hutchinson, | in memory of old times, | from John Masefield. | July. 1924.'

A64 THE TAKING OF HELEN   1923

A64(a) First English edition (limited signed edition) (1923)

THE TAKING OF | HELEN | BY | JOHN MASEFIELD | [publisher's device of a windmill with 'W [point]' and 'H' all within ruled border: 19 × 20mm.] | LONDON | WILLIAM HEINEMANN LTD. | 1923
(All width centred)

Bibliographies: Simmons [58], Nevinson [unrecorded], Handley-Taylor p.53, Wight [58]

Collation: [A]⁸ B-F⁸; signatures left foot of page; 48 leaves; 222 × 145mm.; [1–4] 5–96

Page contents: [1] half-title: 'THE TAKING OF HELEN'; [2] *'Seven hundred and eighty copies of | this book have been printed on | Hand Made Paper and signed by | the author, of which seven hundred | and fifty are for sale and thirty | for presentation. | No. ....';* [3] title-page; [4] *'Printed in Great Britain';* 5–96 text (at foot of p.96: '[rule] | PRINTED IN GREAT BRITAIN BY RICHARD CLAY & SONS, LIMITED, | BUNGAY, SUFFOLK.')

Paper: wove paper

Running tile: 'THE TAKING OF HELEN' (55mm.) on both verso and recto, pp.6–96

Binding: blue-grey boards with parchment spine. On spine, in gold: 'The | Taking | of | Helen | [ornament] | John | Masefield | HEINEMANN' (all width centred). There is a single vertical rule in blind on each cover at the edge of the parchment. Covers: blank. Top edge gilt, lower outside edge untrimmed, fore edge uncut. Binding measurements: 228 × 144mm. (covers), 228 × 29mm. (spine). End-papers: wove paper (watermark: 'HOLBEIN')

Publication date: published, according to Simmons, 12 June 1923

Price: 21s.

Contents:
The Taking of Helen ('Nireus was the son of the King of Symé Island. At his birth the gods brought gifts to him...')

Notes:
Described by both Simmons and Handley-Taylor as 'a novel', this work is perhaps more conveniently described as 'miscellaneous prose' (to follow the example of Babington Smith) for the re-telling of Paris' abduction of Helen is too short to constitute a novel and too long to be adequately described as a short story. Even the terms 'novella' and 'novelette' sit uneasily.

The publishing agreement for this title between Masefield and Heinemann was dated 30 May 1923 (see Archives of The Society of Authors). The agreement refers to a limitation of 750 copies.

The work was later printed in *The Taking of Helen and other prose selections* (see A72) and *Recent Prose* (see A73).

Typographically this edition is interesting for the use of ligatures (the letters 's' and 't' when they appear together being joined).

Copies seen: private collection (PWE) number 150, signed '150 | John Masefield.' on p.[2]; BL (012634.n.40) number 460, signed '460 | John Masefield.' on p.[2], stamped 13 JUN 1923; Harvard College Library (Widener XLM 65) number 128, signed '128 | John Masefield.' on p.[2]

A64(b) First American edition (limited signed edition) (1923)

THE | TAKING OF HELEN | BY | JOHN MASEFIELD | New York | THE MACMILLAN COMPANY | 1923 | *All rights reserved*
(All width centred)

Bibliographies: Simmons [noted on p.95], Nevinson [unrecorded], Handley-Taylor p.53, Wight 58a

Collation: [A]⁹ ([A]2+1) [B-F]⁸ [G]⁴; 53 leaves; 237 × 157mm.; [i–viii] 1–98

Page contents: [i] *'Of this autographed edition of John | Masefield's "The Taking of Helen" | 750 copies have been printed, of | which this is Number..........';* [ii] blank; [iii] half-title: 'THE TAKING OF HELEN' (width centred); [iv] 'BY JOHN MASEFIELD | [rule] | [27 titles listed]' (within double ruled border: 93 × 66mm.); [v] title-page; [vi] 'PRINTED IN THE UNITED STATES OF AMERICA | COPYRIGHT, 1923, | BY JOHN MASEFIELD. | [rule] | Set up and electrotyped. Published October, 1923. | Norwood Press | J. S. Cushing Co. – Berwick & Smith Co. | Norwood, Mass., U.S.A.'; [vii] 'THE TAKING OF HELEN'; [viii] blank; 1–98 text

Paper: laid paper (watermark: *'Bay Path Book Bay Path Book Made in U.S.A.'*), chain-lines 25mm. apart. The additional sheet comprising [A]1 is on a different stock of laid paper (no watermark), chain-lines 21mm. apart

Running title: *'THE TAKING OF HELEN'* (43mm.) on both verso and recto, pp.2–98

Binding: blue-grey boards with navy blue cloth spine. On spine, in gold: 'THE | TAKING | OF | HELEN | [ornament] | MASEFIELD | [point]MACMILLAN[point]' (all width centred). On upper cover: white paper label (51 × 89mm.) on which: 'THE TAKING OF HELEN | [ornament] | JOHN MASEFIELD' (enclosed within ruled border with ornament at each corner and all within double ruled border: 42 × 80mm.) Lower cover: blank. Top edge trimmed, others roughly trimmed. Binding measurements: 245 × 157mm. (covers), 245 × 22mm. (spine). End-papers: laid paper (no watermark) (see notes), chain-lines 41mm. apart.

KING COLE

BY

JOHN MASEFIELD

WITH DRAWINGS IN BLACK AND WHITE
BY
JUDITH MASEFIELD

LONDON: WILLIAM HEINEMANN

A55(a) title-page

KING COLE

BY

JOHN MASEFIELD

WITH DRAWINGS IN BLACK AND WHITE
BY
JUDITH MASEFIELD

New York
THE MACMILLAN COMPANY
1921

A55(b) title-page

Selected Poems

By

John Masefield

LONDON : WILLIAM HEINEMANN, LTD.

A62(a) title-page

KING COLE

AND OTHER POEMS

BY

JOHN MASEFIELD

LONDON
WILLIAM HEINEMANN LTD.

A63(a) title-page

THE TAKING OF
HELEN

BY
JOHN MASEFIELD

LONDON
WILLIAM HEINEMANN LTD.
1923

A64(a) title-page

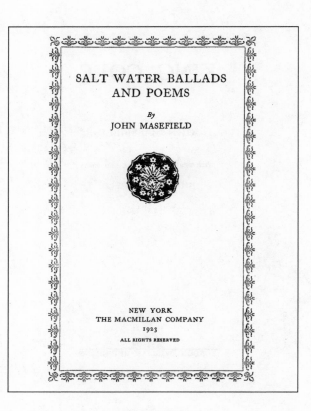

SALT WATER BALLADS
AND POEMS

By
JOHN MASEFIELD

NEW YORK
THE MACMILLAN COMPANY
1923
ALL RIGHTS RESERVED

A66(a) title-page

A KING'S DAUGHTER

A TRAGEDY IN VERSE

BY
JOHN MASEFIELD

LONDON
WILLIAM HEINEMANN LTD.

A70(b) title-page

A KING'S DAUGHTER

A TRAGEDY IN VERSE

BY
JOHN MASEFIELD

LONDON: WILLIAM HEINEMANN LTD.

A70(c) title-page

Publication date: published, according to Simmons, 16 October 1923 in a signed edition of 750 copies

Price: unknown

Contents:
as for A64(a)

Notes:
The additional leaf ([A]1) pasted onto [A]2 comprises the leaf detailing the limitation of the edition. The paper type is different from that used for the rest of the volume. The single leaves were presumably sent to Masefield for signing. Masefield appears to have signed copies as either 'John Masefield' or 'J. Masefield'. His usual practice with American limited signed editions was to sign himself 'J. Masefield'.

The watermark '*Bay Path Book Bay Path Book Made in U.S.A.*' employs a number of swash characters.

The colour of the spine is described by Wight as 'black'. He also notes that some copies have a white spine. Wight fails to note on the spine lettering the two points on either side of the publisher's name.

Handley-Taylor provides an identical publication date to that of Simmons. However, Handley-Taylor notes an edition size of 854 copies. This is presumably an error.

Wight notes the end-papers as 'on laid paper with the watermark "Rockburghe"'. This watermark was not present in the copies consulted.

Wight describes the ornament at each corner of the inner ruled border of the upper cover label as a fleur-de-lis.

Copies seen: University of Rochester Libraries (PR6025.M39 TAKI 1923) number 90, signed '90 | John Masefield.' on p.[i]; Boston Public Library (Rare Books A.5684M.22) number 586, signed '586 | J. Masefield.' on p.[i]

A64(—) [Wight 58b]

Wight is the only bibliographer to note a non-limited edition of *The Taking of Helen*. (Simmons and Handley-Taylor cite *The Taking of Helen and other prose selections* as the only Macmillan edition of *The Taking of Helen* in a non-limited signed edition).

Wight describes (given his familiar inconsistencies) a volume almost identical to A64(b). The differences appear to be the absence of the first leaf (providing details of limitation and Masefield's signature), a larger page size width (by 4mm.), use of capital letters in the watermark and the omission of a section of the watermark. In addition to these, Wight omits all end-paper information and describes what could be an identical upper cover label in a different manner.

The National Union Catalog does not include a non-limited edition of *The Taking of Helen* (as the sole title). I therefore suggest that the volume Wight describes as 58b is merely a defective copy of A64(b) or some variant thereof.

A65 THE DREAM AND OTHER POEMS   1923

A65(a) First American edition (1923)

THE DREAM | *AND OTHER POEMS* | BY | JOHN MASEFIELD | ILLUSTRATED BY | JUDITH MASEFIELD | New York | THE MACMILLAN COMPANY | 1923 | *All rights reserved*
(All width centred)

Bibliographies: Simmons [noted on p.88 and p.94], Nevinson [unrecorded], Handley-Taylor p.53, Wight 54c

Collation: [A-D]⁸; 32 leaves; 192 × 127mm.; [1–6] 7–8 [9–10] 11–14 [15–16] 17–20 [21–22] 23–26 [27–28] 29–63 [64]

Page contents: [1] half-title: 'THE DREAM | *AND OTHER POEMS*'; [2] 'BY | JOHN MASEFIELD | [rule] | [27 titles listed]' (within double ruled border: 94 × 80mm.); [3] title-page; [4] 'PRINTED IN THE UNITED STATES OF AMERICA | COPYRIGHT, 1922 AND 1923, | BY JOHN MASEFIELD. | [rule] | Set up and electrotyped. Published June, 1923.'; [5] 'THE DREAM | *AND OTHER POEMS*'; [6] illustration; 7–8 text; [9] illustration; [10] blank; 11–14 text; [15] illustration; [16] blank; 17–20 text; [21] illustration; [22] blank; 23–26 text; [27] illustration; [28] blank; 29–63 text; [64] blank

Paper: wove paper

Running title: none

Binding: burgundy cloth. On spine, in gold: 'THE | DREAM | AND | OTHER | POEMS | MASEFIELD | MACMILLAN | [square point] [square point] [square point]' (all width centred). On upper cover, in blind: 'THE DREAM | AND OTHER POEMS | MASEFIELD' (ranged upper left) (within blind ruled border: 191 × 122mm.) Lower cover: blank. Top edge trimmed, others roughly trimmed. Binding measurements: 197 × 129mm. (covers), 197 × 21mm. (spine). End-papers: wove paper.

Publication date: published, according to Handley-Taylor, 19 June 1923 (see notes)

Price: $1.25

Contents:

The Dream of Daniel ('Weary with many thoughts I went to bed,')
The Woman Speaks ('This poem appeared to me in a dream one winter morning some years ago. In the dream...')
The Rider at the Gate ('A windy night was blowing on Rome,')
The Builders ('Before the unseen cock had called the time,')
The Setting of the Windcock ('The dust lay white upon the chisel-marks,')
The Racer ('I saw the racer coming to the jump,')
From the Song of Roland ('Roland gripped his horn with might and main,')
The Haunted ('Here, in this darkened room of this old house,')
Campeachy Picture ('The sloop's sails glow in the sun; the far sky burns,')

Notes:

A Macmillan edition containing 'The Dream' and other poems from *King Cole and other poems* (see A63) omitting 'King Cole' and 'The Eye and the Object'.

Page numbers appear italicized within square brackets. Thus, [*7*], [*8*], etc.

Each poem commences with a drop-capital.

Note the title 'The Dream of Daniel'. Except when published in the anthology *The Daniel Press* (see B180), the memorial nature of the poem was omitted in English publications (the poem was merely known as 'The Dream'). Note also that 'From the Song of Roland' included 'The Blowing of the Horn' as part of the title in *King Cole and other poems* (see A63).

Handley-Taylor notes a publication date of 19 June 1923 when describing this volume. In his notes to *The Dream*, however, he states that Macmillan published 'a regular edition of 2000 copies' on 19 January 1923. Such a volume appears to be spurious and, if Handley-Taylor incorrectly cites the date, he may refer to *The Dream and other poems*.

Copies seen: ULL (Special Collections) inscribed 'For Gwendolen Keatinge, | from John Masefield. | Christmas, 1923.'; Harvard College Library (Widener 23697.10.71.A); Harvard College Library (Widener 23697.10.71.B); Harvard College Library (Widener 23697.10.71.C); HRHRC (TEMP M377DRE 1923) inscribed 'John Masefield'

A66 SALT WATER BALLADS AND POEMS
1923

A66(a) First American edition ["Leather Pocket Edition"] (1923)

SALT WATER BALLADS | AND POEMS | *By* | JOHN MASEFIELD | [circular floral ornament] [in red] | NEW YORK | THE MACMILLAN COMPANY | 1923 | ALL RIGHTS RESERVED
(All width centred and enclosed within ornate border in red: 135 × 78mm.)

Bibliographies: Simmons [unrecorded], Nevinson [unrecorded], Handley-Taylor p.53, Wight [unrecorded]

Collation: [A]¹⁰ ([A]3+2) [B-K]⁸ (J not used); 164 leaves; 171 × 112mm.; [two un-numbered pages] [i–ii] iii–viii [ix–x] 1–146 [147–52]

Page contents: [-] half-title: 'SALT WATER BALLADS | AND POEMS | [ornament] [in red]'; [-] '[27 titles separated by 19 single points] | [ornament] [in red]' (enclosed within ornate border in red: 135 × 78mm.); [i] title-page; [ii] 'COPYRIGHT, 1913, BY HARPER AND BROTHERS | COPYRIGHT, 1914, BY THE CENTURY CO., AND BY THE MCCLURE PUBLICATIONS | COPYRIGHT, 1912, 1913, 1914, BY THE MACMILLAN COMPANY | COPYRIGHT, 1916 AND 1923, BY JOHN MASEFIELD | *Printed in the United States of America* | [ornament] [in red]'; iii–iv 'SALT-WATER BALLADS AND POEMS | INTRODUCTION' ('I began to write these verses at a very early age. They contain short poems written...') (unsigned); v–viii 'CONTENTS' (89 individual items listed with page references); [ix] 'SALT-WATER BALLADS'; [x] blank; 1–146 text; [147–52] blank

Paper: laid paper (no watermark), chain-lines 22mm. apart

Running title: '*SALT-WATER BALLADS*' (38mm.) on verso; recto title comprises poem title, pp.2–146

Binding: red leather. On spine, in gold: '[floral panel] | SALT | WATER | POEMS | AND | BALLADS | MASEFIELD | [floral panel] | MACMILLAN'. On upper cover, in blind: circular floral ornament (within blind ruled border: 171 × 111mm.) On lower cover: blind ruled border: 171 × 111mm. Top edge gilt, others trimmed. Binding measurements: 175 × 115mm. (covers), 175 × 24mm. (spine). End-papers: wove paper.

Publication date: published, according to Handley-Taylor, 30 August 1923 (see notes)

Price: $12.50 (set of 8 volumes: see also A21(d), A49(h), A52(b), A54(g), A67(a), A68(a) and A69(a))

Contents:

Introduction ('I began to write these verses at a very early age. They contain short poems written...')
A Consecration ('Not of the princes and prelates with periwigged charioteers')
The Yarn of the "Loch Achray" ('The "Loch Achray" was a clipper tall')
Sing a Song O' Shipwreck ('He lolled on a bollard, a sun-burned son of the sea,')
Burial Party ('"He's deader 'n nails," the fo'c's'le said, "'n' gone to his long sleep";')

Bill ('He lay dead on the cluttered deck and stared at the cold skies.')
Fever Ship ('There'll be no weepin' gells ashore when *our* ship sails,')
Fever-Chills ('He tottered out of the alleyway with cheeks the colour of paste,')
One of the Bo'sun's Yarns ('Loafin' around in Sailor Town, a-bluin' o' my advance,')
Hell's Pavement ('"When I'm discharged in Liverpool 'n' draws my bit o' pay,')
Sea-Change ('"Goneys an' gullies an' all o' the birds o' the sea')
Harbour Bar ('All in the feathered palm-tree tops the bright green parrots screech,')
The Turn of the Tide ('An' Bill can have my sea-boots, Nigger Jim can have my knife,')
One of Wally's Yarns ('The watch was up on the topsail-yard a-making fast the sail,')
A Valediction (Liverpool Docks) ('Is there anything as I can do ashore for you')
A Night at Dago Tom's ('Oh yesterday, I t'ink it was, while cruisin' down the street,')
"Port of Many Ships" ('"It's a sunny pleasant anchorage, is Kingdom Come,')
Cape Horn Gospel – I ('"I was in a hooker once," said Karlssen,')
Cape Horn Gospel – II ('Jake was a dirty Dago lad, an' he gave the skipper chin,')
Mother Carey (As Told Me By The Bo'sun) ('Mother Carey ? She's the mother o' the witches')
Evening – Regatta Day ('Your nose is a red jelly, your mouth's a toothless wreck,')
A Valediction ('We're bound for blue water where the great winds blow,')
A Pier-Head Chorus ('Oh I'll be chewing salted horse and biting flinty bread,')
The Golden City of St. Mary ('Out beyond the sunset, could I but find the way,')
Trade Winds ('In the harbour, in the island, in the Spanish Seas,')
Sea-Fever ('I must down to the seas again, to the lonely sea and the sky,')
A Wanderer's Song ('A wind's in the heart of me, a fire's in my heels,')
Cardigan Bay ('Clean, green, windy billows notching out the sky,')
Christmas Eve at Sea ('A wind is rustling "south and soft,"')
A Ballad of Cape St. Vincent ('Now, Bill, ain't it prime to be a-sailin',')
The Tarry Buccaneer ('I'm going to be a pirate with a bright brass pivot-gun,')
A Ballad of John Silver ('We were schooner-rigged and rakish, with a long and lissome hull,')
Lyrics from "The Buccaneer"
I ('We are far from sight of the harbour lights,')
II ('There's a sea-way somewhere where all day long')
III ('The toppling rollers at the harbour mouth')
D'Avalos' Prayer ('When the last sea is sailed and the last shallow charted,')
The West Wind ('It's a warm wind, the west wind, full of birds' cries;')
The Galley-Rowers ('Staggering over the running combers')
Sorrow of Mydath ('Weary the cry of the wind is, weary the sea,')
Vagabond ('Dunno a heap about the what an' why,')
Vision ('I have drunken the red wine and flung the dice;')
Spunyarn ('Spunyarn, spunyarn, with one to turn the crank,')
The Dead Knight ('The cleanly rush of the mountain air,')
Personal ('Tramping at night in the cold and wet, I passed the lighted inn,')
On Malvern Hill ('A wind is brushing down the clover,')
Tewkesbury Road ('It is good to be out on the road, and going one knows not where,')
On Eastnor Knoll ('Silent are the woods, and the dim green boughs are')
"Rest Her Soul, She's Dead!" ('She has done with the sea's sorrow and the world's way')
"All Ye That Pass By" ('On the long dusty ribbon of the long city street,')
In Memory of A.P.R. ('Once in the windy wintry weather,')
To-Morrow ('Oh yesterday the cutting edge drank thirstily and deep,')
Cavalier ('All the merry kettle-drums are thudding into rhyme,')
A Song at Parting ('The tick of the blood is settling slow, my heart will soon be still,')
The Ballad of Sir Bors ('Would I could win some quiet and rest, and a little ease,')
Spanish Waters ('Spanish waters, Spanish waters, you are ringing in my ears,')
Cargoes ('Quinquireme of Nineveh from distant Ophir,')
Captain Stratton's Fancy ('Oh some are fond of red wine, and some are fond of white,')
An old Song re-sung ('I saw a ship a-sailing, a-sailing, a-sailing,')
St. Mary's Bells ('It's pleasant in Holy Mary')
London Town ('Oh London Town's a fine town, and London sights are rare,')
The Emigrant ('Going by Daly's shanty I heard the boys within')
Port of Holy Peter ('The blue laguna rocks and quivers,')
Beauty ('I have seen dawn and sunset on moors and windy hills')
The Seekers ('Friends and loves we have none, nor wealth nor blessed abode,')
Dawn ('The dawn comes cold: the haystack smokes,')
Laugh and be Merry ('Laugh and be merry, remember, better the world with a song,')

June Twilight ('The twilight comes; the sun')
Roadways ('One road leads to London')
Midsummer Night ('The perfect disc of the sacred moon')
The Harper's Song ('This sweetness trembling from the strings')
The Gentle Lady ('So beautiful, so dainty-sweet,')
Twilight ('Twilight it is, and the far woods are dim, and the rooks cry and call.')
Invocation ('O wanderer into many brains,')
Posted as Missing ('Under all her topsails she trembled like a stag,')
A Creed ('I hold that when a person dies')
When Bony Death ('When bony Death has chilled her gentle blood,')
Her Heart ('Her heart is always doing lovely things,')
Being her Friend ('Being her friend, I do not care, not I,')
Fragments ('Troy Town is covered up with weeds,')
Born for Nought Else ('Born for nought else, for nothing but for this,')
The Death Rooms ('My soul has many an old decaying room')
Ignorance ('Since I have learned Love's shining alphabet,')
The Watch in the Wood ('When Death has laid her in his quietude,')
C.L.M. ('In the dark womb where I began,')
Waste ('No rose but fades: no glory but must pass:')
Third Mate ('All the sheets are clacking, all the blocks are whining,')
The Wild Duck ('Twilight. Red in the west.')
Imagination ('Woman, beauty, wonder, sacred woman,')
Christmas, 1903 ('O, the sea breeze will be steady, and the tall ship's going trim,')
The Word ('My friend, my bonny friend, when we are old,')
GLOSSARY ('*Abaft the beam.*—That half of a ship included between her amidship section...')

Notes:
Issued as volume I in the Macmillan Leather Pocket Edition of Masefield's Work.

The title as present on the title-page does not correspond to that on the spine.

This is one of the titles from the leather pocket edition that Simmons excluded from his bibliography. Of the volumes that were included he provided a later publication date than that cited by Handley-Taylor. This edition may, therefore, have been published in October 1923. Accepting Handley-Taylor's publication date would explain the omission of *A King's Daughter* (published on 23 October 1923) in the listing of Masefield's works appearing on the second un-numbered page.

Copies seen: private collection (PWE)

A67 DAUBER [AND] THE DAFFODIL FIELDS   1923

A67(a) First American edition ["Leather Pocket Edition"] (1923)

DAUBER | ~ | THE DAFFODIL FIELDS | *By* | JOHN MASEFIELD | [circular floral ornament] [in red] | NEW YORK | THE MACMILLAN COMPANY | 1923 | ALL RIGHTS RESERVED
(All width centred and enclosed within ornate border in red: 135 × 78mm.)

Bibliographies: Simmons [unrecorded], Nevinson [unrecorded], Handley-Taylor p.53, Wight [unrecorded]

Collation: [A]¹⁰ ([A]3+2 –[A]5) [B-T]⁸ (but signed [A]⁵ ([A]3+2 –[A]5) B-L⁸ M² [A]³ B-I⁸; see note on American electrotype editions) (J not used); signatures left foot of page; 153 leaves; 172 × 112mm.; [i–iv] v–vii [viii] 1–163 [164] [i–ii] iii–iv [v–vi] 1–124 [125–28]

Page contents: [i] half-title: 'DAUBER | ~ | THE DAFFODIL FIELDS | [ornament] [in red]'; [ii] '[27 titles separated by 20 single points] | [ornament] [in red]' (enclosed within ornate border in red: 135 × 78mm.); [iii] title-page; [iv] 'COPYRIGHT, 1912 AND 1913, BY THE MACMILLAN COMPANY | COPYRIGHT, 1913 AND 1923, BY JOHN MASEFIELD | *Printed in the United States of America* | [ornament] [in red]'; v–vii 'THE DAUBER | INTRODUCTION' ('I wrote this poem in the spring and early summer of 1912. It was based to...') (unsigned); [viii] blank; 1–157 text; 158–63 'EXPLANATIONS OF SOME OF THE SEA TERMS USED IN THE POEM'; [164] blank; [i] 'THE DAFFODIL FIELDS'; [ii] blank; iii–iv 'THE DAFFODIL FIELDS | INTRODUCTION' ('I wrote this poem in the late summer and early autumn of 1912. The story...') (unsigned); [v] 'THE DAFFODIL FIELDS'; [vi] blank; 1–124 text (at foot of p.124: '[rule] | Printed in the United States of America.'); [125–28] blank

Paper: laid paper (no watermark), chain-lines 22mm. apart

Running title: '*DAUBER*' (14mm.) on both verso and recto, pp.2–163; and '*THE DAFFODIL FIELDS*' (38mm.) on both verso and recto, pp.2–124

Binding: red leather. On spine, in gold: '[floral panel] | DAUBER | [point] | THE | DAFFODIL | FIELDS | MASEFIELD | [floral panel] | MACMILLAN'. On upper cover, in blind: circular floral ornament (within blind ruled border: 171 × 111mm.) On lower cover: blind ruled border: 171 × 111mm. Top edge gilt, others trimmed. Binding measurements: 175 × 115mm. (covers), 175 × 24mm. (spine). End-papers: wove paper.

Publication date: published, according to Handley-Taylor, 30 August 1923 (see notes)

Price: $12.50 (set of 8 volumes: see also A21(d), A49(h), A52(b), A54(g), A66(a), A68(a) and A69(a))

Contents:
The Dauber Introduction ('I wrote this poem in the spring and early summer of 1912. It was based to...')
Dauber ('Four bells were struck, the watch was called on deck,')
Explanations of some of the Sea Terms used in the poem ('Backstays. Wire ropes which support...')
The Daffodil Fields Introduction ('I wrote this poem in the late summer and early autumn of 1912. The story...')
The Daffodil Fields ('Between the barren pasture and the wood')

Notes:
Issued as volume III in the Macmillan Leather Pocket Edition of Masefield's Work.

This is one of the titles from the leather pocket edition that Simmons excluded from his bibliography. Of the volumes that were included he provided a later publication date than that cited by Handley-Taylor. This edition may, therefore, have been published in October 1923. Accepting Handley-Taylor's publication date would explain the omission of *A King's Daughter* (published on 23 October 1923) in the listing of Masefield's works appearing on page [ii].

The text appears to use plates from A23(b) and A24(a). This explains the separate pagination and signatures.

Copies seen: NYPL (NCM 1923) 483897A, rebound

A68 PHILIP THE KING... GOOD FRIDAY... LOLLINGDON DOWNS...   1923

A68(a) First American edition ["Leather Pocket Edition"] (1923)

PHILIP THE KING | AND OTHER POEMS | ~ | GOOD FRIDAY | A PLAY IN VERSE | ~ | LOLLINGDON DOWNS | AND | OTHER POEMS, WITH SONNETS | *By* | JOHN MASEFIELD | [circular floral ornament] [in red] | NEW YORK | THE MACMILLAN COMPANY | 1923 | ALL RIGHTS RESERVED
(All width centred and enclosed within ornate border in red: 135 × 78mm.)

Bibliographies: Simmons [unrecorded], Nevinson [unrecorded], Handley-Taylor p.53, Wight [unrecorded]

Collation: [A]¹⁰ ([A]3+2) [B-Q]⁸ [R]⁴ [S]⁸ [T]⁴ (J not used); 146 leaves; 170 × 112mm.; [six un-numbered pages] [i–iv] v–vi [1–4] 5–57 [58–60] 61–119 [120–26] 127–87 [188–90] 191–277 [278–80]

Page contents: [-] half-title: 'PHILIP THE KING | AND OTHER POEMS | ~ | GOOD FRIDAY | A PLAY IN VERSE | ~ | LOLLINGDON DOWNS | AND OTHER POEMS, WITH SONNETS | [ornament] [in red]'; [-] '[27 titles separated by 19 single points] | [ornament] [in red]' (enclosed within ornate border in red: 135 × 78mm.); [-] title-page; [-] 'COPYRIGHT, 1913, BY HARPER AND BROTHERS | COPYRIGHT, 1914, BY THE CENTURY CO., AND BY THE MCCLURE PUBLICATIONS | COPYRIGHT, 1912, 1913 AND 1914 BY THE MACMILLAN COMPANY | COPYRIGHT, 1915, 1916, 1917 AND 1923, BY JOHN MASEFIELD | *Printed in the United States of America* | [ornament] [in red]'; [-] 'TO | MY WIFE'; [-] blank; [i] 'CONTENTS' (18 individual items listed with page references); [ii] blank; [iii] 'NOTE | SOME seven or eight of these poems have ap- | peared serially in *The Atlantic Monthly, Har-* | *per's, The Yale Review, The Forge, Contempo-* | *rary Verse,* and *Science Progress;* others have | been issued privately, in a book now out of | print; the rest are new. | J. M. | LONDON, | *February* 1, 1917.'; [iv] blank; v–vi 'INTRODUCTION' ('This volume contains two short plays in verse...') (unsigned); [1] 'PHILIP THE KING | A PLAY IN ONE ACT'; [2] blank; [3] '[dramatis personae listed with 'PERSONS.' and 'SPIRITS.' headings] | TIME. | At dawn in late September, 1588. | SCENE. | A little dark cell in Philip's palace.'; [4] blank; 5–57 text; [58] blank; [59] 'OTHER POEMS'; [60] blank; 61–119 text; [120] blank; [121] 'NOTE | Of the poems contained in the preceding section, | five–"Truth," "August, 1914," "Biography," | "Ships," and "The River"–appeared in the | *English Review,* one–"The 'Wanderer'"–in | *Harper's Magazine,* and three–the translations– | in the *Westminster Gazette.* I thank the editors | of these periodicals for permission to reprint | them here. | JOHN MASEFIELD'; [122] blank; [123] 'GOOD FRIDAY'; [124] blank; [125] 'PERSONS | [dramatis personae listed]'; [126] 'THE SCENE | *The Pavement, or Paved Court, outside the Roman* | *Citadel In Jerusalem.* | *At the back is the barrack wall, pierced in the centre* | *with a double bronze door, weathered to a green colour.* | *On the right and left sides of the stage are battle-* | *mented parapets overlooking the city.* | *The stage or pavement is approached by stone steps* | *from the front, and by narrow stone staircases in the* | *wings, one on each side, well forward. These steps are* | *to suggest that the citadel is high up above the town,* | *and that the main barrack gate is below.* THE CHIEF | CITIZEN, THE RABBLE, JOSEPH, THE MADMAN, HEROD, | *and* THE LOITERERS, *etc., enter by these steps.* | PILATE, PROCULA, LONGINUS, THE SOLDIERS *and* | SERVANTS *enter by the bronze door.*'; 127–87 text; [188] blank; [189] 'LOLLINGDON DOWNS | AND OTHER POEMS, WITH SONNETS'; [190] blank; 191–277 text; [278–80] blank

Paper: laid paper (no watermark), chain-lines 22mm. apart

Running title: '*PHILIP THE KING*' (30mm.) on both verso and recto, pp.6–57; titles of poems on both verso and recto, pp.62–119; '*GOOD FRIDAY*' (23mm.) on both verso and recto, pp.128–87; '*LOLLINGDON DOWNS*' (34mm.) on both verso and recto, pp.192–207; titles of poems on both verso and recto, pp.208–222 and blank on both verso and recto, pp.223–77

Binding: red leather. On spine, in gold: '[floral panel] | PHILIP | THE KING | [point] | GOOD | FRIDAY | [point] | LOLLINGDON | DOWNS | MASEFIELD | [floral panel] | MACMILLAN'. On upper cover, in blind: circular floral ornament (within blind ruled border: 171 × 111mm.) On lower cover: blind ruled border: 171 × 111mm. Top edge gilt, others trimmed. Binding measurements: 175 × 115mm. (covers), 175 × 24mm. (spine). End-papers: wove paper.

Publication date: published, according to Handley-Taylor, 30 August 1923 (see notes)

Price: $12.50 (set of 8 volumes: see also A21(d), A49(h), A52(b), A54(g), A66(a), A67(a) and A69(a))

Contents:
Introduction ('This volume contains two short plays in verse…')
Philip the King ('PHILIP (*Kneeling*) | Lord, I am that Philip whom Thou has made…')
Truth ('Man with his burning soul')
The "Wanderer" ('All day they loitered by the resting ships,')
August, 1914 ('How still this quiet cornfield is to-night!')
Biography ('When I am buried, all my thoughts and acts')
Song ('One sunny time in May')
Ships ('I cannot tell their wonder nor make known')
Sonnet (From the Spanish of Don Francisco A. Quevedo) ('I saw the ramparts of my native land,')
Sonnet on the Death of his Wife (From the Portuguese of Antonio di Ferreiro) ('That blessed sunlight, that once showed to me')
They Closed Her Eyes (From the Spanish of Don Gustavo A. Becquér) ('They closed her eyes,')
The River ('All other waters have their time of peace,')
Watching By a Sick-Bed ('I heard the wind all day,')
Good Friday ('PILATE | Longinus.')
I ('So I have known this life,')
II ('O wretched man, that for a little mile')
III ('Out of the special cell's most special sense')
IV ('You are the link which binds us each to each.')
V ('I could not sleep for thinking of the sky,')
VI ('How did the nothing come, how did these fires,')
VII ('It may be so; but let the unknown be.')
VIII ('The Kings go by with jewelled crowns;')
IX ('What is this life which uses living cells')
X ('Can it be blood and brain, this transient force')
XI ('Not only blood and brain its servants are;')
XII ('Drop me the seed, that I even in my brain')
XIII ('Ah, but Without there is no spirit scattering;')
XIV ('You are too beautiful for mortal eyes,')
XV ('Is it a sea on which the souls embark')
XVI The Ship ('THE ORE | Before Man's labouring wisdom gave me birth')
XVII The Blacksmith ('The blacksmith in his sparky forge')
XVIII The Frontier ('COTTA. Would God the route would come for home')
XIX ('Night is on the downland, on the lonely moorland,')
XX Midnight ('The fox came up by Stringer's Pound;')
XXI ('Up on the downs the red-eyed kestrels hover,')
XXII ('No man takes the farm,')
XXIII ('A hundred years ago they quarried for the stone here;')
XXIV ('Here the legion halted, here the ranks were broken,')
XXV ('We danced away care till the fiddler's eyes blinked,')
XXVI ('Long, long ago, when all the glittering earth')
XXVII ('Night came again, but now I could not sleep;')
XXVIII ('Even after all these years there comes the dream')
XXIX ('If I could come again to that dear place')
XXX ('Here in the self is all that man can know')
XXXI ('Flesh, I have knocked at many a dusty door,')
XXXII ('But all has passed, the tune has died away,')
XXXIII ('These myriad days, these many thousand hours,')
XXXIV ('There, on the darkened deathbed, dies the brain')
XXXV ('So in the empty sky the stars appear,')
XXXVI ('It may be so with us, that in the dark,')
XXXVII ('What am I, Life? A thing of watery salt')
XXXVIII ('If I could get within this changing I,')
XXXIX ('What is this atom which contains the whole,')
XL ('Ah, we are neither heaven nor earth, but men;')

XLI ('Roses are beauty, but I never see')
XLII ('Over the church's door they moved a stone,')
XLIII ('Out of the clouds come torrents, from the earth')
XLIV ('O little self, within whose smallness lies')
XLV ('I went into the fields, but you were there')
XLVI ('This is the living thing that cannot stir.')
XLVII ('Here, where we stood together, we three men,')
XLVIII ('I saw her like a shadow on the sky')
XLIX ('Look at the grass, sucked by the seed from dust,')
L ('There is no God, as I was taught in youth,')
LI ('Wherever beauty has been quick in clay')
LII ('Beauty, let be; I cannot see your face,')
LIII ('You are more beautiful than women are,')
LIV ('Beauty retires; the blood out of the earth')
LV ('Not for the anguish suffered is the slur,')
LVI ('Beauty was with me once, but now, grown old,')
LVII ('So beauty comes, so with a failing hand')
LVIII ('You will remember me in days to come,')
LIX ('If Beauty be at all, if, beyond sense,')
LX ('If all be governed by the moving stars,')
LXI ('In emptiest furthest heaven where no stars are.')
LXII ('Perhaps in chasms of the wasted past,')
LXIII ('For, like an outcast from the city, I')
LXIV ('Death lies in wait for you, you wild thing in the wood,')
LXV ('They called that broken hedge The Haunted Gate.')
LXVI ('There was an evil in the nodding wood')
LXVII ('Go, spend your penny, Beauty, when you will,')
LXVIII ('Though in life's streets the tempting shops have lured')
LXIX ('When all these million cells that are my slaves')
LXX ('Let that which is to come be as it may,')

Notes:
Issued as volume IV in the Macmillan Leather Pocket Edition of Masefield's Work.

This is one of the titles from the leather pocket edition that Simmons excluded from his bibliography. Of the volumes that were included he provided a later publication date than that cited by Handley-Taylor. This edition may, therefore, have been published in October 1923. Accepting Handley-Taylor's publication date would explain the omission of *A King's Daughter* (published on 23 October 1923) in the listing of Masefield's works appearing on the second un-numbered page.

Copies seen: private collection (PWE)

A69 KING COLE[,] THE DREAM AND OTHER POEMS   1923

A69(a) First American edition ["Leather Pocket Edition"] (1923)

KING COLE | ~ | THE DREAM | AND OTHER POEMS | *By* | JOHN MASEFIELD | [circular floral ornament] [in red] | NEW YORK | THE MACMILLAN COMPANY | 1923 | ALL RIGHTS RESERVED
(All width centred and enclosed within ornate border in red: 135 × 78mm.)

Bibliographies: Simmons [noted on p.94], Nevinson [unrecorded], Handley-Taylor p.53, Wight 57a

Collation: [A]¹⁰ ([A]3+2) [B-H]⁸ [I]¹⁰ ([I]8+2); 76 leaves; 172 × 114mm.; i–vi vii–viii [7–8] 9–12 [13–14] 15–24 [25–26] 27–30 [31–32] 33–74 [75–76] 77–80 [81–82] 83–87 [88] [5–6] 7–8 [9–10] 11–14 [15–16] 17–20 [21–22] 23–26 [27–28] 29–63 [64–66]

Page contents: [i] half-title: 'KING COLE | ~ | THE DREAM AND OTHER POEMS | [ornament] [in red]'; [ii] '[27 titles separated by 19 single points] | [ornament] [in red]' (enclosed within ornate border in red: 135 × 78mm.); [iii] title-page; [iv] 'COPYRIGHT, 1921, 1922 AND 1923, BY JOHN MASEFIELD | *Printed in the United States of America* | [ornament] [in red]'; [v] '*To* | MY WIFE'; [vi] blank; vii–viii 'INTRODUCTION' ('This volume contains the poems "King Cole" and "The Dream," and a few other poems written...' (unsigned); [7] 'KING COLE'; [8] blank; 9–12 text; [13] illustration (and legend); [14] blank; 15–24 text; [25] illustration (and legend); [26] blank; 27–30 text; [31] illustration (and legend); [32] blank; 33–74 text (and illustration); [75] illustration (and legend); [76] blank; 77–80 text; [81] illustration (and legend); [82] blank; 83–87 text; [88] illustration; [5] 'THE DREAM | *AND OTHER POEMS*'; [6] illustration; 7–8 text; [9] illustration; [10] blank; 11–14 text; [15] illustration; [16] blank; 17–20 text; [21] illustration; [22] blank; 23–26 text; [27] illustration; [28] blank; 29–63 text; [64–66] blank

Paper: laid paper (no watermark), chain-lines 22mm. apart

Running-title: '[rule, 89mm.] | KING COLE [25mm.] | [rule, 89mm.]' on both verso and recto, pp.10–87 (of *King Cole*); no running title for remainder of volume

Binding: red leather. On spine, in gold: '[floral panel] | KING | COLE | [point] | THE | DREAM | MASEFIELD | [floral panel] | MACMILLAN'. On upper cover, in blind: circular floral ornament (within blind ruled border: 171 × 111mm.) On lower cover: blind ruled border: 171 × 111mm. Top edge gilt, others trimmed. Binding measurements: 175 × 115mm. (covers), 175 × 24mm. (spine). End-papers: wove paper.

Publication date: published, according to Handley-Taylor, 30 August 1923 / published, according to Simmons, 30 October 1923 in an edition of 2000 copies (see notes)

Price: $12.50 (set of 8 volumes: see also A21(d), A49(h), A52(b), A54(g), A66(a), A67(a) and A68(a))

Contents:
Introduction ('This volume contains the poems "King Cole" and "The Dream," and a few other poems written...')
King Cole ('King Cole was King before the troubles came,')
The Dream of Daniel ('Weary with many thoughts I went to bed,')
The Woman Speaks ('This poem appeared to me in a dream one winter morning some years ago. In the dream...')
The Rider at the Gate ('A windy night was blowing on Rome,')
The Builders ('Before the unseen cock had called the time,')
The Setting of the Windcock ('The dust lay white upon the chisel-marks,')
The Racer ('I saw the racer coming to the jump,')
From The Song of Roland ('Roland gripped his horn with might and main,')
The Haunted ('Here, in this darkened room of this old house,')
Campeachy Picture ('The sloop's sails glow in the sun; the far sky burns,')

Notes:
Issued as volume VIII in the Macmillan Leather Pocket Edition of Masefield's Work. The volume represents a combined reprint of American *King Cole* (see A55(b)) and *The Dream and other poems* (see A65(a)). This American edition is therefore textually similar to the English *King Cole and other Poems* (see A63(a)).

The first set of additional leaves ([A]1 and [A]2) comprise a conjugate set of leaves pasted onto [A]3. They use the same paper stock as the rest of the volume and were presumably later added to the volume as they comprise the only pages with additional devices printed in red. The second set of additional leaves ([I]9 and [I]10) comprise another conjugate set of leaves pasted onto [I]8.

The page numbers are not entirely sequential as the volume represents a combined reprint of A55(b) and A65(a). Consequently, in the later part of the volume, page numbers appear italicized within square brackets. Thus, [*7*], [*8*], etc.

Each poem, with the exception of 'King Cole', commences with a drop-capital.

Wight describes the volume as bound in 'mottled red cloth'. He includes the tipped-in conjugate leaves as separate gatherings in his collation.

Accepting Handley-Taylor's publication date would explain the omission of *A King's Daughter* (published on 23 October 1923) in the listing of Masefield's works appearing on page [ii].

Copies seen: Kent State University Library, Ohio (PR 6025.A77A1 1923.K5)

A70 A KING'S DAUGHTER   1923

A70(a) First American edition (1923)

A KING'S DAUGHTER | A TRAGEDY IN VERSE | BY | JOHN MASEFIELD | New York | THE MACMILLAN COMPANY | 1923 | *All rights reserved*
(All width centred)

Bibliographies: Simmons [59], Nevinson [unrecorded], Handley-Taylor p.53, Wight [59]

Collation: [A–K]⁸ [L]¹⁰ (J not used); 90 leaves; 190 × 126mm.; [i–viii] 1–31 [32–34] 35–63 [64–66] 67–99 [100–102] 103–135 [136–38] 139–70 [171–72]

Page contents: [i] half-title: 'A KING'S DAUGHTER | A TRAGEDY IN VERSE'; [ii] 'BY | JOHN MASEFIELD | [rule] | [27 titles listed]' (within double ruled border: 99 × 73mm.); [iii] title-page; [iv] 'PRINTED IN THE UNITED STATES OF AMERICA | COPYRIGHT, 1923, | By JOHN MASEFIELD | [rule] | Set up and electrotyped. Published October, 1923. | THE FERRIS PRINTING COMPANY | NEW YORK'; [v] '*This play was performed at The Oxford Playhouse,* | *on Friday and Saturday, May 25th and 26th, 1923, by* | *the following cast of the Hill Players:* | [dramatis personae and original cast listed] | [rule] | SCENE: The Palace in Samaria | [rule]'; [vi] blank; [vii] 'A KING'S DAUGHTER | FIRST ACT'; [viii] blank; 1–31 text; [32] blank; [33] 'A KING'S DAUGHTER | SECOND ACT'; [34] blank; 35–63 text; [64] blank; [65] 'A KING'S DAUGHTER | THIRD ACT'; [66] blank; 67–99 text; [100] blank; [101] 'A KING'S DAUGHTER | FOURTH ACT'; [102] blank; 103–135 text; [136] blank; [137] 'A KING'S DAUGHTER | FIFTH ACT'; [138] blank; 139–70 text; [171–72] blank

Paper: wove paper

Running title: '*A KING'S DAUGHTER*' (35mm.) on both verso and recto, pp.2–170

Binding: burgundy cloth. On spine, in gold: 'A | KING'S | DAUGHTER | MASEFIELD | MACMILLAN | [square point] [square point] [square point] [square point]' (all width centred). On upper cover, in blind: 'A | KING'S | DAUGHTER | MASEFIELD' (ranged upper left) (within blind ruled border: 191 × 122mm.) Lower cover: blank. All edges trimmed. Binding measurements: 196 × 127mm. (covers), 196 × 31mm. (spine). End-papers: wove paper.

Publication date: published, according to Simmons, 23 October 1923 in an edition of 2000 copies

Price: $1.75

Contents:
A King's Daughter ('JEZEBEL | I am Queen Jezebel, King Ahab's wife.')

Notes:
A play in verse set in Samaria comprising the biblical story of Jezebel.

A publishing agreement for this title between Masefield and Macmillan was dated 22 June 1923 (see Archives of The Society of Authors). The agreement refers to 'a licence to publish in volume form… in the United States of America and Canada a work the subject or title of which is A King's Daughter (a play)'.

Copies seen: private collection (PWE)

A70(b)   First English edition (1923)

A KING'S DAUGHTER | A TRAGEDY IN VERSE | BY | JOHN MASEFIELD | [publisher's device of a windmill with 'W [point]' and 'H' all within ruled border: 15 × 15mm.] | LONDON | WILLIAM HEINEMANN LTD.
(All width centred)

Bibliographies: Simmons [59a], Nevinson p.14, Handley-Taylor p.53, Wight [59a]

Collation: [A]⁸ B-H⁸ I⁴; signatures right foot of page; 68 leaves; 185 × 121mm.; [i–viii] 1–127 [128]

Page contents: [i] half-title: 'A KING'S DAUGHTER'; [ii] 'BY THE SAME AUTHOR | *Uniform with this Volume* | [12 titles listed] | [rule] | LONDON: WILLIAM HEINEMANN LTD.'; [iii] title-page; [iv] 'PRINTED IN GREAT BRITAIN BY | BILLING AND SONS, LTD., GUILDFORD AND ESHER'; [v] 'TO | MY WIFE'; [vi] blank; [vii] 'This play was performed at the Oxford Playhouse on | Friday and Saturday, May 25 and 26, 1923, by the follow- | ing cast of the Hill Players : | [dramatis personae and original cast listed] | SCENE : The Palace in Samaria.'; [viii] blank; 1–127 text; [128] blank

Paper: wove paper

Running title: 'A KING'S DAUGHTER' (43mm.) on both verso and recto, pp.2–127

Binding: blue cloth. On spine, in gold: 'A | King's | Daughter | [ornament] | John | Masefield | HEINEMANN' (all width centred). On upper cover, in gold: 'A KING'S DAUGHTER | JOHN MASEFIELD' (within blind ruled border: 183 × 116mm.) On lower cover, in blind: publisher's device of a windmill (ranged lower right). All edges trimmed. Binding measurements: 189 × 122mm. (covers), 189 × 27mm. (spine). End-papers: wove paper.

Publication date: published, according to Simmons, 8 November 1923 in an edition of 3000 copies

Price: 6s.

Contents:
as for A70(a)

Notes:
The text has been newly set for this edition.

Copies seen: private collection (PWE); BL (011645.ee.78) stamped 9 NOV 1923

A70(c)   Second English edition (limited signed edition) (1923)

A KING'S DAUGHTER | A TRAGEDY IN VERSE | BY | JOHN MASEFIELD | [publisher's device of a windmill with '19' and '23' on either side] | [rule, 78mm.] | LONDON : WILLIAM HEINEMANN LTD.
(All width centred)

Bibliographies: Simmons [59b], Nevinson [unrecorded], Handley-Taylor p.53, Wight [59b]

Collation: [A]⁸ B-H⁸ I⁴; signatures right foot of page; 68 leaves; 225 × 148mm.; [i–viii] 1–127 [128]

Page contents: [i] half-title: 'A KING'S DAUGHTER'; [ii] '*This edition, printed on English hand-made | paper, is limited to two hundred and eighty | copies, of which two hundred and fifty are for | sale, and thirty are for presentation. | No. .... | ....*'; [iii] title-page; [iv] 'PRINTED IN GREAT BRITAIN BY | BILLING AND SONS,

LTD., GUILDFORD AND ESHER'; [v] 'TO | MY WIFE'; [vi] blank; [vii] 'This play was performed at the Oxford Playhouse on | Friday and Saturday, May 25 and 26, 1923, by the follow- | ing cast of the Hill Players : | [dramatis personae and original cast listed] | SCENE : The Palace in Samaria.'; [viii] blank; 1–127 text; [128] blank

Paper: wove paper (watermark: 'BRITISH HAND MADE PURE RAG [castle device: 27 × 35mm.]')

Running title: 'A KING'S DAUGHTER' (43mm.) on both verso and recto, pp.2–127

Binding: blue-grey boards with parchment spine. On spine, in gold: 'A | King's | Daughter | [ornament] | John | Masefield | HEINEMANN' (all width centred). There is a single vertical rule in blind on each cover at the edge of the parchment. Covers: blank. Top edge gilt, lower outside edge untrimmed, fore edge uncut. Binding measurements: 231 × 147mm. (covers), 231 × 32mm. (spine). End-papers: wove paper (watermark: 'HOLBEIN').

Publication date: published, according to Simmons, 27 November 1923

Price: 21s.

Contents:
as for A70(a)

Notes:
The text appears to use the same setting of type as A70(b).

Copies seen: private collection (PWE) number 168, signed '168 | John Masefield.' on p.[ii]; BL (011779.i.32) number 254, signed '254 | John Masefield.' on p.[ii], stamped 3 DEC 1923; HRHRC (PR6025 A77 K53 1923c) number 275, signed '275 | John Masefield.' on p.[ii] additionally inscribed 'For Na | from Zom. | Dec 10. 1923.'

A71 COLLECTED POEMS   1923

A71(a) First English edition (1923)

THE | COLLECTED POEMS | OF | JOHN MASEFIELD | [publisher's device of a windmill with '19' and '23' on either side] | [rule, 78mm.] | LONDON : WILLIAM HEINEMANN LTD.
(All width centred)

Bibliographies: Simmons [unrecorded], Nevinson p.14, Handley-Taylor p.54, Wight [unrecorded]

Collation: [A]⁶ 1–49⁸; signatures left foot of page; 398 leaves; 182 × 122mm.; [two un-numbered pages] [i–iv] v–ix [x] [1–2] 3–45 [46] 47–49 [50] 51 [52] 53–81 [82] 83 [84] 85 [86] 87–131 [132] 133 [134] 135–91 [192–93] 194–245 [246] 247–51 [252] 253 [254] 255–317 [318] 319–20 [321] 322–63 [364] 365 [366] 367–401 [402] 403 [404] 405–447 [448–49] 450–99 [500] 501 [502] 503–521 [522] 523 [524] 525–97 [598] 599 [600] 601–672 [673–74] 675–727 [728] 729 [730] 731–61 [762] 763–84

Page contents: [-] blank (page excluded from page count, but constitutes first leaf of first gathering); [-] blank; [i] half-title: 'THE COLLECTED POEMS | OF JOHN MASEFIELD'; [ii] blank; [iii] title-page; [iv] 'MADE AND PRINTED IN GREAT BRITAIN BY MORRISON AND GIBB LTD., EDINBURGH'; v–ix 'CONTENTS' (139 individual items listed with page references); [x] blank; [1] 'SALT-WATER BALLADS'; [2] blank; 3–45 text of *Salt-Water Ballads*; [46] blank; 47–49 'GLOSSARY'; [50] blank; 51 'BALLADS AND POEMS'; [52] blank; 53–81 text of *Ballads and Poems*; [82] blank; 83 'LYRICS FROM THE TRAGEDY OF | POMPEY THE GREAT'; [84] blank; 85 text of lyrics from *The Tragedy of Pompey the Great*; [86] blank; 87 'THE EVERLASTING MERCY'; 88 '*Thy place is biggyd above the sterrys cleer,* | *Noon erthely paleys wrouhte in so statly wyse,* | *Com on my freend, my brothir moost enteer,* | *For the I offryd my blood in sacrifise.* | JOHN LYDGATE.'; 89–131 text of *The Everlasting Mercy*; [132] blank; 133 'THE WIDOW IN THE BYE STREET'; [134] blank; 135–90 text of *The Widow in the Bye Street*; 191 'DAUBER'; [192] blank; [193]–245 text of *Dauber*; [246] blank; 247–51 'EXPLANATIONS OF SOME OF THE SEA | TERMS USED IN THE POEM'; [252] blank; 253 'THE DAFFODIL FIELDS'; [254] blank; 255–317 text of *The Daffodil Fields*; [318] blank; 319 'PHILIP THE KING | AND OTHER POEMS'; 320 '[dramatis personae listed with 'PERSONS' and 'SPIRITS' headings] | TIME | AT DAWN IN LATE SEPTEMBER, 1588 | SCENE | A LITTLE DARK CELL IN PHILIP'S PALACE'; [321]–363 text of *Philip the King*; [364] blank; 365 'OTHER POEMS'; [366] blank; 367–401 text of other poems; [402] blank; 403 'LOLLINGDON DOWNS | AND OTHER POEMS, WITH SONNETS'; [404] blank; 405–444 text of *Lollingdon Downs and other poems, with sonnets*; 445 'GOOD FRIDAY | A PLAY IN VERSE'; 446 'PERSONS | [dramatis personae listed]'; 447 'THE SCENE | *The Pavement, or Paved Court, outside the Roman Citadel in* | *Jerusalem.* | [new paragraph] *At the back is the barrack wall, pierced in the centre with a double* | *bronze door, weathered to a green colour.* | [new paragraph] *On the right and left sides of the stage are battlemented parapets* | *overlooking the city.* | [new paragraph] *The stage or pavement is approached by stone steps from the front,* | *and by narrow stone staircases in the wings, one on each side, well* | *forward. These steps are to suggest that the citadel is high up above* | *the town, and that the main barrack gate is below.* THE CHIEF CITIZEN, | THE RABBLE, JOSEPH, THE MADMAN, HEROD, *and* THE LOITERERS, | *etc., enter by these steps.* | [new paragraph] PILATE, PROCULA, LONGINUS, THE SOLDIERS *and* SERVANTS *enter* | *by the bronze door.*'; [448] blank; [449]–499 text of *Good Friday*; [500] blank; 501 'ROSAS'; [502] blank; 503–521 text of *Rosas*; [522] blank; 523 'REYNARD THE FOX | OR | THE GHOST HEATH RUN'; [524] blank; 525–97 text of *Reynard the Fox*; [598] blank; 599 'ENSLAVED | AND OTHER POEMS'; [600] blank; 601–672 text of *Enslaved and other poems*; [673] 'RIGHT ROYAL'; [674] blank; 675–727 text of *Right Royal*; [728] blank; 729 'KING COLE | AND OTHER POEMS'; [730] blank; 731–60 text of *King Cole*; 761 'OTHER POEMS'; [762] blank; 763–78 text of other poems; 779–84 'INDEX OF FIRST LINES'

Paper: wove paper

Running-title: 'THE POEMS OF JOHN MASEFIELD' (65mm.) on both verso and recto, pp.4–778

Binding: blue cloth. On spine, in gold: '*COLLECTED* | *POEMS* | [ornament] | *JOHN* | *MASEFIELD* | *Heinemann*' (all width centred). On upper cover, in gold: '*COLLECTED* | *POEMS* | *JOHN MASEFIELD*' (within blind ruled border: 188 × 119mm.) Lower cover, in blind: publisher's device of a windmill (ranged lower right). All edges trimmed. Binding measurements: 194 × 125mm. (covers), 194 × 53mm. (spine). End-papers: wove paper.

Also issued in leather.

Publication date: published, according to Handley-Taylor, 25 October 1923 / the sales ledger preserved in the Heinemann Archive suggests publication on 25 October 1923 in an edition of 10,000 copies. According to Drew ('Some Contributions to the Bibliography of John Masefield: II', *Papers of the Bibliographical Society of America*, October 1959, pp.262–67) there were 8500 copies bound in cloth and 1500 bound in leather.

Price: 8s.6d. (cloth) / 12s.6d. (leather)

Contents:
SALT-WATER BALLADS
A Consecration ('Not of the princes and prelates with periwigged charioteers')
The Yarn of The *Loch Achray* ('The *Loch Achray* was a clipper tall')
Sing a Song O' Shipwreck ('He lolled on a bollard, a sun-burned son of the sea,')
Burial-Party ('"He's deader 'n nails," the fo'c's'le said, '"n' gone to his long sleep";')
Bill ('He lay dead on the cluttered deck and stared at the cold skies,')
Fever Ship ('There'll be no weepin' gells ashore when *our* ship sails,')
Fever-Chills ('He tottered out of the alleyway with cheeks the colour of paste,')
One of The Bo'sun's Yarns ('Loafin' around in Sailor Town, a-bluin' o' my advance,')
Hell's Pavement ('"When I'm discharged in Liverpool 'n' draws my bit o' pay,')
Sea-Change ('"Goneys an' gullies an' all o' the birds o' the sea')
Harbour-Bar ('All in the feathered palm-tree tops the bright green parrots screech,')
The Turn of the Tide ('An' Bill can have my sea-boots, Nigger Jim can have my knife,')
One of Wally's Yarns ('The watch was up on the topsail-yard a-making fast the sail,')
A Valediction (Liverpool Docks) ('Is there anything as I can do ashore for you')
A Night at Dago Tom's ('Oh yesterday, I t'ink it was, while cruisin' down the street,')
"Port of Many Ships" ('"It's a sunny pleasant anchorage, is Kingdom Come,')
Cape Horn Gospel – I ('"I was in a hooker once,' said Karlssen,')
Cape Horn Gospel – II ('Jake was a dirty Dago lad, an' he gave the skipper chin,')
Mother Carey ('Mother Carey ? She's the mother o' the witches')
Evening – Regatta Day ('Your nose is a red jelly, your mouth's a toothless wreck,')
A Valediction ('We're bound for blue water where the great winds blow,')
A Pier-Head Chorus ('Oh I'll be chewing salted horse and biting flinty bread,')
The Golden City of St. Mary ('Out beyond the sunset, could I but find the way,')
Trade Winds ('In the harbour, in the island, in the Spanish Seas,')
Sea-Fever ('I must down to the seas again, to the lonely sea and the sky,')
A Wanderer's Song ('A wind's in the heart of me, a fire's in my heels,')
Cardigan Bay ('Clean, green, windy billows notching out the sky,')
Christmas Eve at Sea ('A wind is rustling "south and soft,"')
A Ballad of Cape St. Vincent ('Now, Bill, ain't it prime to be a-sailin',')
The Tarry Buccaneer ('I'm going to be a pirate with a bright brass pivot-gun,')
A Ballad of John Silver ('We were schooner-rigged and rakish, with a long and lissome hull,')
Lyrics from *The Buccaneer*
I. ('We are far from sight of the harbour lights,')
II. ('There's a sea-way somewhere where all day long')
III. ('The toppling rollers at the harbour mouth')
D'Avalos' Prayer ('When the last sea is sailed and the last shallow charted,')
The West Wind ('It's a warm wind, the west wind, full of birds' cries;')
The Galley-Rowers ('Staggering over the running combers')
Sorrow of Mydath ('Weary the cry of the wind is, weary the sea,')
Vagabond ('Dunno a heap about the what an' why,')
Vision ('I have drunken the red wine and flung the dice;')
Spunyarn ('Spunyarn, spunyarn, with one to turn the crank,')
The Dead Knight ('The cleanly rush of the mountain air,')
Personal ('Tramping at night in the cold and wet, I passed the lighted inn,')
On Malvern Hill ('A wind is brushing down the clover,')
Tewkesbury Road ('It is good to be out on the road, and going one knows not where,')

On Eastnor Knoll ('Silent are the woods, and the dim green boughs are')
"Rest Her Soul, She's Dead!" ('She has done with the sea's sorrow and the world's way')
"All Ye That Pass By" ('On the long dusty ribbon of the long city street,')
In Memory of A.P.R. ('Once in the windy wintry weather,')
To-Morrow ('Oh yesterday the cutting edge drank thirstily and deep,')
Cavalier ('All the merry kettle-drums are thudding into rhyme,')
A Song at Parting ('The tick of the blood is settling slow, my heart will soon be still,')
GLOSSARY ('Abaft the beam.—That half of a ship included between her amidship section…')
BALLADS AND POEMS
The Ballad of Sir Bors ('Would I could win some quiet and rest, and a little ease,')
Spanish Waters ('Spanish waters, Spanish waters, you are ringing in my ears,')
Cargoes ('Quinquireme of Nineveh from distant Ophir')
Captain Stratton's Fancy ('Oh some are fond of red wine, and some are fond of white,')
An old Song re-sung ('I saw a ship a-sailing, a-sailing, a-sailing,')
St. Mary's Bells ('It's pleasant in Holy Mary')
London Town ('Oh London Town's a fine town, and London sights are rare,')
The Emigrant ('Going by Daly's shanty I heard the boys within')
Port of Holy Peter ('The blue laguna rocks and quivers,')
Beauty ('I have seen dawn and sunset on moors and windy hills')
The Seekers ('Friends and loves we have none, nor wealth nor blessed abode,')
Dawn ('The dawn comes cold: the haystack smokes,')
Laugh and be Merry ('Laugh and be merry, remember, better the world with a song,')
June Twilight ('The twilight comes; the sun')
Roadways ('One road leads to London,')
Midsummer Night ('The perfect disc of the sacred moon')
The Harper's Song ('The sweetness trembling from the strings')
The Gentle Lady ('So beautiful, so dainty-sweet,')
Twilight ('Twilight it is, and the far woods are dim, and the rooks cry and call.')
Invocation ('O wanderer into many brains,')
Posted as Missing ('Under all her topsails she trembled like a stag,')
A Creed ('I held that when a person dies')
When Bony Death ('When bony Death has chilled her gentle blood,')
Her Heart ('Her heart is always doing lovely things,')
Being Her Friend ('Being her friend, I do not care, not I,')
Fragments ('Troy Town is covered up with weeds,')
Born for Nought Else ('Born for nought else, for nothing but for this,')
The Death Rooms ('My soul has many an old decaying room')
Ignorance ('Since I have learned Love's shining alphabet,')
The Watch in the Wood ('When Death has laid her in his quietude,')
C.L.M. ('In the dark womb where I began')
Waste ('No rose but fades: no glory but must pass:')
Third Mate ('All the sheets are clacking, all the blocks are whining,')
The Wild Duck ('Twilight. Red in the west.')
Imagination ('Woman, beauty, wonder, sacred woman,')
Christmas, 1903 ('O, the sea breeze will be steady, and the tall ship's going trim,')
The Word ('My friend, my bonny friend, when we are old,')
LYRICS FROM *THE TRAGEDY OF POMPEY THE GREAT*
The Chief Centurions ('Man is a sacred city, built of marvellous earth.')
Philip Sings ('Though we are ringed with spears, though the last hope is gone,')
Chanty ('Kneel to the beautiful women who bear us this strange brave fruit.')
THE EVERLASTING MERCY
The Everlasting Mercy ('From '41 to '51')
THE WIDOW IN THE BYE STREET
The Widow in the Bye Street ('Down Bye Street, in a little Shropshire town,')
DAUBER
Dauber ('Four bells were struck, the watch was called on deck,')
Explanations of some of the Sea Terms used in the Poem ('Backstays.-Wire ropes which support the masts against…')
THE DAFFODIL FIELDS
The Daffodil Fields ('Between the barren pasture and the wood')
PHILIP THE KING AND OTHER POEMS
Philip the King ('PHILIP [*kneeling*]. | Lord, I am that Philip whom Thou has made…')
Truth ('Man with his burning soul')

The *Wanderer* ('All day they loitered by the resting ships,')
August, 1914 ('How still this quiet cornfield is to-night!')
Biography ('When I am buried, all my thoughts and acts')
Song ('One sunny time in May')
Ships ('I cannot tell their wonder nor make known')
Sonnet (From the Spanish of Don Francisco A. Quevedo) ('I saw the ramparts of my native land,')
Sonnet on the Death of his Wife (From the Portuguese of Antonio Di Ferreiro) ('That blessed sunlight, that once showed to me')
They Closed Her Eyes (From the Spanish of Don Gustavo A. Becquér) ('They closed her eyes,')
The River ('All other waters have their time of peace,')
Watching By a Sick-Bed ('I heard the wind all day,')
LOLLINGDON DOWNS AND OTHER POEMS, WITH SONNETS
I. ('So I have known this life,')
II. ('O wretched man, that for a little mile')
III. ('Out of the special cell's most special sense')
IV. ('You are the link which binds us each to each.')
V. ('I could not sleep for thinking of the sky,')
VI. ('How did the nothing come, how did these fires,')
VII. ('It may be so; but let the unknown be.')
VIII. ('The Kings go by with jewelled crowns;')
IX. ('What is this life which uses living cells')
X. ('Can it be blood and brain, this transient force')
XI. ('Not only blood and brain its servants are;')
XII. ('Drop me the seed, that I even in my brain')
XIII. ('Ah, but Without there is no spirit scattering;')
XIV. ('You are too beautiful for mortal eyes,')
XV. ('Is it a sea on which the souls embark')
XVI. The Ship ('THE ORE. | Before Man's labouring wisdom gave me birth')
XVII. The Blacksmith ('The blacksmith in his sparky forge')
XVIII. The Frontier ('COTTA. Would God the route would come for home.')
XIX. ('Night is on the downland, on the lonely moorland,')
XX. Midnight ('The fox came up by Stringer's Pound;')
XXI. ('Up on the downs the red-eyed kestrels hover,')
XXII. ('No man takes the farm,')
XXIII. ('A hundred years ago they quarried for the stone here;')
XXIV. ('Here the legion halted, here the ranks were broken,')
XXV. ('We danced away care till the fiddler's eyes blinked,')
XXVI. ('Long, long ago, when all the glittering earth')
XXVII. ('Night came again, but now I could not sleep;')
XXVIII. ('Even after all these years there comes the dream')
XXIX. ('If I could come again to that dear place')
XXX. ('Here in the self is all that man can know')
XXXI. ('Flesh, I have knocked at many a dusty door,')
XXXII. ('But all has passed, the tune has died away,')
XXXIII. ('These myriad days, these many thousand hours,')
XXXIV. ('There, on the darkened deathbed, dies the brain')
XXXV. ('So in the empty sky the stars appear,')
XXXVI. ('It may be so with us, that in the dark,')
XXXVII. ('What am I, Life? A thing of watery salt')
XXXVIII. ('If I could get within this changing I,')
XXXIX. ('What is this atom which contains the whole,')
XL. ('Ah, we are neither heaven nor earth, but men;')
XLI. ('Roses are beauty, but I never see')
XLII. ('Over the church's door they moved a stone,')
XLIII. ('Out of the clouds come torrents, from the earth')
XLIV. ('O little self, within whose smallness lies')
XLV. ('I went into the fields, but you were there')
XLVI. ('This is the living thing that cannot stir.')
XLVII. ('Here, where we stood together, we three men,')
XLVIII. ('I saw her like a shadow on the sky')
XLIX. ('Look at the grass, sucked by the seed from dust,')
L. ('There is no God, as I was taught in youth,')
LI. ('Wherever beauty has been quick in clay')

251

Notes:

Some authorial revisions may be included in this volume. For example, 'A Creed' appears in *Ballads and Poems* with the first line 'I hold that when a person dies'. This is here printed as 'I held that when a person dies'. Further examples include a changed first line of sonnet XXXIX in *Lollingdon Downs and other poems, with sonnets*. Originally this reads 'What is this atom which contains the whole,' but appears in this volume as 'What is the atom which contains the whole,'. In addition to these substantive revisions there are numerous differences in punctuation.

The contents listing is defective in detailing poems from *Lollingdon Downs and other poems, with sonnets*. After listing 'Midnight' the contents listing progresses onto the next volume, *Good Friday*. This therefore omits all poems after 'Midnight', though included in the text. Subsequent reprints of this edition corrected the error.

In 'Some Contributions to the Bibliography of John Masefield: II' (*Papers of the Bibliographical Society of America*, October 1959, pp.262–67) Drew notes Simmons' omission of this title:

> Simmons includes in his bibliography the 1922 *Selected Poems*, items (56) and (56a), but does not include the 1923 *Collected Poems*. This book was issued in both regular and limited editions by William Heinemann, Ltd., London. Both editions are entitled *The Collected Poems of John Masefield* and contain pages (i)-(x) and pages (1)–784. The regular edition is bound in blue cloth. The limited edition, large paper, is bound in tan linen with dark blue leather label and gold letters, t.e.g. This edition is limited to 530 copies, of which 500 are for sale. This writer's copy is numbered and signed with a two-line inscription in the poet's autograph, "On these three things a poet must depend | His Will, his Natural Talent, and his Friend." The regular edition of 10,000 copies (8,500 bound in cloth, 1,500 in leather) was published 25 Oct. 1923. The limited, signed edition was published 28 Nov. 1923.

Masefield sought publishing advice from Thomas Hardy over this volume. An undated letter from Masefield to Hardy states:

> I am writing to ask you to be so very kind as to give me the benefit of your experience in a matter of publication. My publishers wish to issue my collected poems in a single fat volume at 8/6. I hesitate about it, lest the single collected volume should entirely kill the sales of the separate little volumes, + therefore be a disadvantage to me.
>
> Would you, who have published your collected poems in a single volume, tell me whether this tends to be the case, or whether (as my publishers maintain) the single bulky volume helps to increase the sales of the little volumes?
> I hesitate to ask you, but I think that you are the one living poet who has published work thus, + could inform me.
>
> (John Masefield, letter to Thomas Hardy, [March 1923])
(Dorset County Museum (Thomas Hardy Memorial Collection))

Masefield was evidently concerned about taking any measure that would affect sales. Hardy replied with advice on fame:

> My experience is that the more editions there are the better: the announcement of any new edition waking up readers to the fact that you are still alive. So that I think your publishers are right, as they consider the commercial side of a book very thoroughly. In my case the separate volumes have been issued by the same publishers as the collected volume, and at only a shilling cheaper; if in your case the little volumes are by other publishers the collected [*two words torn away*] probably stir them up to push the little ones, which is to your advantage.
>
> The British Public is a greedy creature, always thinking of what *quantity* is to be got for its money. My opinion is that Tennyson should have had a collected volume years before he did, and poor Swinburne suffers to this day from there being no one volume collection of him – suffers I think in popularity and sale. For though the collected volume is the one they buy at the free libraries, and therefore one copy goes a long way among readers, you should I think remember that it is better to be read, even for nothing, than not to be read at all.
>
> I should perhaps remind you that my own verse is in two volumes. I. the short poems, 2. The Dynasts. But I had hoped at first it would all go into one.
>
> So that you see I agree with your publishers. I am not sure if I have answered you clearly: Anyhow, don't mind asking me anything more of the sort, as I have had 50 years experience, and it is a pity it should all "go down into silence" with me.
>
> (Thomas Hardy, letter to John Masefield, 3 April 1923)
(see *The Collected Letters of Thomas Hardy*, ed. Richard Little Purdy and Michael Millgate, seven volumes, Oxford:
Clarendon Press, 1978–1988, volume six, p.189)

Masefield was not entirely convinced and asked a further question:

> The one other point that I would like to ask, if it would not be too great an intrusion, is, whether, when a single collected volume appears, it actually stimulates the sales of the small single volumes which preceded it? May I ask if you have found that it has this effect, or the opposite?
>
> (John Masefield, letter to Thomas Hardy, [April 1923])
(Dorset County Museum (Thomas Hardy Memorial Collection))

Hardy replied having researched his own sales figures and suggested Masefield should trust his publishers:

> Since receiving your letter I have looked at the returns on Sales in past years (which I hardly ever do look at!), and I find that the separate editions have gone on selling since we produced the Collected Edition – particularly the Pocket Edition of each separate volume of Poems.
>
> But then, I do not know how much more or less, these small ones would have sold, supposing the Collected Edition had not been brought out. And I do not see how this can be discovered, even by yourself, (assuming that you publish the Collected volume), since if the cheap ones decrease in their sales afterwards they may have done so, owing to some freak of the public, if you had not published the Collected volume. As I said last time, I think the publishers know best.
>
> (Thomas Hardy, letter to John Masefield, 5 April 1923)
(see *The Collected Letters of Thomas Hardy*, ed. Richard Little Purdy and Michael Millgate, seven volumes, Oxford:
Clarendon Press, 1978–1988, volume six, p.190)

Masefield appears to have informed Heinemann of his decision to allow the collected edition at the end of April 1923. C.S. Evans responded:

> I am glad that you have decided to try out the Collected Edition in one volume at 8/6. We will certainly keep all the component volumes on the market, either at the original price or at some reduced price.
>
> (C.S. Evans, letter to John Masefield, 25 April 1923)
> (HRHRC, MS (Masefield, J.) Recip William Heinemann Ltd.)

Masefield's concern over individual volumes was, as Hardy suggested, ungrounded, for the smaller volumes continued to sell and be reprinted. A letter to The Society of Authors suggests that Heinemann were guarding their own interests over the volume anyway and that success was by no means predicted. Masefield wrote '…the collected edition will be put off the market very quickly if found to be unprofitable ...' (see John Masefield, letter to G.H. Thring, [September 1923]) (BL, Add.Mss.56578, f.255).

Hardy's advice proved sound: Masefield's *Collected Poems* was a phenomenal success. C.S. Evans wrote to Masefield shortly before Christmas 1923:

> I think you will like to hear that we have had the most wonderful success with the COLLECTED POEMS. As you know, our first edition of 10,000 went during the first week or so after publication. Our second edition of 10,000 is practically out and will be completely out before the end of the year. Our third edition of 10,000 is in the press. Our publication of the book has been a great success and we have received letters from readers all over the country which are most gratifying, and many members of the trade have also written to thank us for having produced the book, all of which I think is evidence of the fact that the book was very much needed. The one blot on the book is, of course, the matter of the running headline. This was a mistake not of negligence but of misjudgment, which I have now rectified. In the new edition we have on the right hand page the title of the poem below. The limited editions both of THE KING'S DAUGHTER [*sic*] and THE COLLECTED POEMS are sold out, and I am glad to say too that so far as we can tell at present, the publication of these books has had very little effect on the sale of the separate volumes, for we are receiving orders for them all the time. …Why don't you make Macmillan do the same as we have done. If we can sell 20,000 copies of the collected poems here in two months, American ought to sell 100,000 copies in the same time.
>
> (C.S. Evans, letter to John Masefield, 21 December 1923)
> (HRHRC, MS (Masefield, J.) Recip William Heinemann Ltd.)

In March 1926 Evans wrote:

> I see that we have sold 50,000 copies of the COLLECTED POEMS and it is still selling at the rate of about 200 a week. I believe that we shall touch the 100,000 with this as we have done in the case of THE FORSYTE SAGA.
>
> (C.S. Evans, letter to John Masefield, 25 March 1926)
> (HRHRC, MS (Masefield, J.) Recip William Heinemann Ltd.)

The only year in which at least one new impression was not printed was 1931 and a new and enlarged edition was published in 1932. Sales figures are not entirely clear. Within his history of the Heinemann firm, John St John refers to 'two volumes of *Collected Poems* (1923 and 1926) – the first sold over 80,000 copies' (see John St John, *William Heinemann – A Century of Publishing 1890–1990*, London: Heinemann, 1990, p.289). St John therefore cites incorrect dates. William Buchan states, however, that 100,000 copies sold in the first seven years of publication (see William Buchan, 'Introduction' to John Masefield, *Letters to Reyna*, London: Buchan and Enright, 1983, p.26).

Copies seen: private collection (PWE) blue cloth; private collection (PWE) blue leather; BL (011645.ee.66) stamped 26 OCT 1923, rebound; HRHRC (TEMP M377B2 1923A) inscribed 'For Con | from Jan. | Nov 2. 1923.'

Reprinted:

'New Impression'	[first edition, second impression]	Nov 1923
'New Impression'	[first edition, third impression]	Jan 1924
'New Impression'	[first edition, fourth impression]	Oct 1924
'New Impression'	[first edition, fifth impression]	Apr 1925
'New Impression'	[first edition, sixth impression]	Feb 1926
'New Impression'	[first edition, seventh impression]	Sep 1926
'New Impression'	[first edition, eighth impression]	Dec 1926
'New Impression'	[first edition, ninth impression]	Jul 1927
'New Impression'	[first edition, tenth impression]	Oct 1927
'New Impression'	[first edition, eleventh impression]	Oct 1928
'New Impression'	[first edition, twelfth impression]	Aug 1929
'New Impression'	[first edition, thirteenth impression]	Sep 1930
'New Impression'	[first edition, fourteenth impression]	Jan 1931

A71(b) Second English edition (limited signed edition) (1923)

THE | COLLECTED POEMS [in red] | OF | JOHN MASEFIELD | [publisher's device of a windmill with '19' and '23' on either side] | [rule, 78mm.] | LONDON : WILLIAM HEINEMANN LTD.
(All width centred)

Bibliographies: Simmons [unrecorded], Nevinson [unrecorded], Handley-Taylor [unrecorded], Wight [unrecorded]

Collation: [A]⁶ 1–49⁸; signatures left foot of page; 398 leaves; 223 × 138mm.; [two un-numbered pages] [i–iv] v–ix [x] [1–2] 3–45 [46] 47–49 [50] 51 [52] 53–81 [82] 83 [84] 85 [86] 87–131 [132] 133 [134] 135–91 [192–93] 194–245 [246] 247–51 [252] 253 [254] 255–317 [318] 319–20 [321] 322–63 [364] 365 [366] 367–401 [402] 403 [404] 405–447 [448–49] 450–99 [500] 501 [502] 503–521 [522] 523 [524] 525–97 [598] 599 [600] 601–672 [673–74] 675–727 [728] 729 [730] 731–61 [762] 763–84

Page contents: [-] blank (page excluded from page count, but constitutes first leaf of first gathering); [-] blank; [i] half-title: 'THE COLLECTED POEMS | OF JOHN MASEFIELD'; [ii] '*This Edition is limited to five | hundred and thirty copies, of | which five hundred are for sale | and thirty for presentation. | This is No. ....*' (with additional leaf tipped-in on the verso of which is the frontispiece of a photograph of Masefield: 127 × 92mm., '*Photo by TRAVERS* | JOHN MASEFIELD.'); [iii] title-page (with protective tissue); [iv] 'MADE AND PRINTED IN GREAT BRITAIN BY MORRISON AND GIBB LTD., EDINBURGH'; v–ix 'CONTENTS' (139 individual items listed with page references); [x] blank; [1] 'SALT-WATER BALLADS'; [2] blank; 3–45 text of *Salt-Water Ballads*; [46] blank; 47–49 'GLOSSARY'; [50] blank; 51 'BALLADS AND POEMS'; [52] blank; 53–81 text of *Ballads and Poems*; [82] blank; 83 'LYRICS FROM THE TRAGEDY OF | POMPEY THE GREAT'; [84] blank; 85 text of lyrics from *The Tragedy of Pompey the Great*; [86] blank; 87 'THE EVERLASTING MERCY'; 88 '*Thy place is biggyd above the sterrys cleer, | Noon erthely paleys wrouhte in so statly wyse, | Com on my freend, my brothir moost enteer, | For the I offryd my blood in sacrifise.* | JOHN LYDGATE.'; 89–131 text of *The Everlasting Mercy*; [132] blank; 133 'THE WIDOW IN THE BYE STREET'; [134] blank; 135–90 text of *The Widow in the Bye Street*; 191 'DAUBER'; [192] blank; [193]–245 text of *Dauber*; [246] blank; 247–51 'EXPLANATIONS OF SOME OF THE SEA | TERMS USED IN THE POEM'; [252] blank; 253 'THE DAFFODIL FIELDS'; [254] blank; 255–317 text of *The Daffodil Fields*; [318] blank; 319 'PHILIP THE KING | AND OTHER POEMS'; 320 '[dramatis personae listed with 'PERSONS' and 'SPIRITS' headings] | TIME | AT DAWN IN LATE SEPTEMBER, 1588 | SCENE | A LITTLE DARK CELL IN PHILIP'S PALACE'; [321]–363 text of *Philip the King*; [364] blank; 365 'OTHER POEMS'; [366] blank; 367–401 text of other poems; [402] blank; 403 'LOLLINGDON DOWNS | AND OTHER POEMS, WITH SONNETS'; [404] blank; 405–444 text of *Lollingdon Downs and other poems, with sonnets*; 445 'GOOD FRIDAY | A PLAY IN VERSE'; 446 'PERSONS | [dramatis personae listed]'; 447 'THE SCENE | *The Pavement, or Paved Court, outside the Roman Citadel in | Jerusalem. | [new paragraph] At the back is the barrack wall, pierced in the centre with a double | bronze door, weathered to a green colour. | [new paragraph] On the right and left sides of the stage are battlemented parapets | overlooking the city. | [new paragraph] The stage or pavement is approached by stone steps from the front, | and by narrow stone staircases in the wings, one on each side, well | forward. These steps are to suggest that the citadel is high up above | the town, and that the main barrack gate is below.* THE CHIEF CITIZEN, | THE RABBLE, JOSEPH, THE MADMAN, HEROD, *and* THE LOITERERS, | *etc., enter by these steps.* | [new paragraph] PILATE, PROCULA, LONGINUS, THE SOLDIERS *and* SERVANTS *enter | by the bronze door.*'; [448] blank; [449]–499 text of *Good Friday*; [500] blank; 501 'ROSAS'; [502] blank; 503–521 text of *Rosas*; [522] blank; 523 'REYNARD THE FOX | OR | THE GHOST HEATH RUN'; [524] blank; 525–97 text of *Reynard the Fox*; [598] blank; 599 'ENSLAVED | AND OTHER POEMS'; [600] blank; 601–672 text of *Enslaved and other poems*; [673] 'RIGHT ROYAL'; [674] blank; 675–727 text of *Right Royal*; [728] blank; 729 'KING COLE | AND OTHER POEMS'; [730] blank; 731–60 text of *King Cole*; 761 'OTHER POEMS'; [762] blank; 763–78 text of other poems; 779–84 'INDEX OF FIRST LINES'

Paper: laid paper (no watermark), chain-lines 25mm. apart

Running title: 'THE POEMS OF JOHN MASEFIELD' (65mm.) on both verso and recto, pp.4–778

Binding: tan cloth. On spine: panel in blind: 44 × 52mm. upon which: black leather label (44 × 50mm.) on which in gold: '[thick rule] | [thin rule] | *COLLECTED* | *POEMS* [ornament] | *JOHN* | *MASEFIELD* | [thin rule] | [thick rule]' (width centred); horizontally at foot of spine, in gold: '*Heinemann*'. Covers: blank. Top edge gilt, others uncut. Sewn head band (in blue and white) and blue marker ribbon. Binding measurements: 229 × 145mm. (covers), 229 × 59mm. (spine). End-papers: wove paper.

Publication date: published, according to Drew ('Some Contributions to the Bibliography of John Masefield: II' (*Papers of the Bibliographical Society of America*, October 1959, pp.262–67)), 28 November 1923 in an edition of 530 copies. The *English Catalogue of Books* records a publication date of December 1923

Price: 42s.

Contents:
as for A71(a)

Notes:
The same setting of text as used in A71(a) is employed here. Consequently, the contents listing is defective in detailing poems from *Lollingdon Downs, and other poems, with sonnets*.

In addition to Masefield's signature, each copy was signed with a couplet. Eight examples of couplets are used of which one, 'Spring in my heart agen | That I may flower to men.', is the closing couplet of *The Everlasting Mercy*. Six of the couplets form a single poem. Item 104 in an inventory of the papers of Masefield (made after the author's death) was described as:

> 104. [UNTITLED] Autograph MS of untitled poem, commencing 'On these three things a poet must depend'. 12 lines in couplets on single page of small octavo paper. No corrections. Signed at foot. A little discoloured by damp. Publication of the poem cannot be traced. It looks to have been written before 1910.

This single sheet is now located at the HRHRC. Although the suggested date of 1910 is doubtful, the handwriting does seem to suggest composition earlier than 1923. The poem, written in couplets with a line between each pair of lines, is as follows:

On these three things a poet must depend | His Will, his Natural Talent and his Friend.

Bitter, though honour is it, if he do | Aught with the first without the other two.

Happy, but impotent, however stirred, | The second is without the first and third.

Untoucht, unprized, like water without thirst | The third must be sans second and sans first.

And often two combine, yet, lacking one, | The light is of the moon not of the sun.

Yet when the Trinity exults, oh, then | What bliss to be, although despised of men.

(MS (Masefield, J.) Works [Untitled poem] "On these three things a poet must depend…")

By Christmas 1923 the edition had sold out (see notes to A71(a))

Copies: [listed in numerical order]
Not all copies have been consulted and the accuracy of transcription in several cases may be doubtful:
Columbia University Libraries (B825 M377 L 1923) number 29, inscribed '29 | On these three things a poet must depend | His Will, his Natural Talent, + his Friend | John Masefield.' on p.[ii]; private collection (FV) number 36, inscribed '36 | On these three things a poet must depend | His Will, his Natural Talent + his Friend. | John Masefield.' on p.[ii]; Ledbury Library number 51, inscribed '51 | On these three things a poet must depend | His Will, his Natural Talent + his Friend | John Masefield.' on p.[ii]; University of Vermont (Fraser Drew Collection) number 68, inscribed '68 | On these three things a poet must depend | His Will, his Natural Talent, and his Friend. | John Masefield.' on p.[ii]; [Bookseller's description] number 70, inscribed '70 | On these three things a poet must depend | His Will, his Natural Talent, & his Friend. | John Masefield.' on p.[ii]; private collection (DGFR) number 73, inscribed '73 | On these three things a poet must depend | His Will, his Natural Talent, + his Friend. | John Masefield.' on p.[ii]; Harvard College Library (Houghton *EC9M377.B923ca) (formerly Thomas Lamont's copy) number 81, inscribed '81 | On these three things a poet must depend | His Will, his Natural Talent + his Friend. | John Masefield.' on p.[ii]; private collection (PWE) number 105, inscribed '105 | Bitter, though honour is it, if he do | Aught with the first without the other two. | John Masefield.' on p.[ii]; HRHRC (TEMP M377B2 1923B cop.2) number 157, inscribed 'Bitter, though honour is it, if he do | Aught with the first without the other two. | John Masefield.' on p.[ii]; Ledbury Library number 177, inscribed '177 | Happy, but impotent, however stirred, | The second is, without the first + third. | John Masefield.' on p.[ii]; private collection (PC) number 204, inscribed '204 | Happy, but impotent, however stirred | The second is, without the first & third. | John Masefield.' on p.[ii]; Library of The John Masefield Society (Peter Smith Collection 73) number 222, inscribed '222 | Happy, but impotent, however stirred, | The second is, without the first + third. | John Masefield.' on p.[ii]; HRHRC (AC-L M377B2 1923A cop.2) number 309, inscribed '309 | Untoucht, unprizd, like water without thirst, | The third must be, sans second + sans first. | John Masefield.' on p.[ii]; [Bookseller's description] number 311, inscribed '311 | Untoucht, unprizd, like water without thirst, | The third must be, sans second + sans first. | John Masefield.' on p.[ii]; [Unknown] (formerly A.C. McKay's copy) number 351, inscribed '351 | And often two combine, yet, lacking one | The light is of the moon, not of the sun. | John Masefield.' on p.[ii]; HRHRC (AC-L M377B2 1923A cop.3) number 356, inscribed '356 | And often two combine, yet, lacking one, | The light is of the moon, not of the sun. | John Masefield.' on p.[ii]; HRHRC (AC-L M377B2 1923A cop.1) number 366, inscribed '366 | And often two combine, yet, lacking one, | The light is of the moon, not of the sun. | John Masefield.' on p.[ii]; NYPL (Berg Collection) number 397, inscribed '397 | And often two combine, yet, lacking one, | The light is of the moon, not of the sun. | John Masefield.' on p.[ii]; private collection (ROV) number 447, inscribed '447 | Yet, when the Trinity exults, oh, then, | What blifs to be, altho' despised of men. | John Masefield.' on p.[ii]; private collection (PJB) number 478, inscribed '478 | Yet, when the Trinity exults, oh, then, | What blifs to be, altho' despised of men. | John Masefield.' on p.[ii]; ULL (Special Collections) number 485, inscribed '485 | Yet, when the Trinity exults, oh, then, | What blifs to be, altho' despised of men. | John Masefield.' on p.[ii]; HRHRC (TEMP M377B2 1923B cop.1) number 507, inscribed 'Spring in my heart agen | That I may flower to men | John Masefield.' on p.[ii] and additionally inscribed 'For Na | from Zom. | Dec 10. 1923.'; Bodleian (28001.d.172) number 518, inscribed '518 | Spring in my heart agen | That I may flower to men. | John Masefield' on p.[ii]; BL (Ashley 5555) number 521, inscribed '521 | Turn earth up with a share | And look for beauty there | John Masefield' on p.[ii]; BL (11643.d.14) number 530, inscribed '530 | Spring in my heart agen | That I may flower to men. | John Masefield.' on p.[ii] stamped 17 DEC 1923

A71(c) Third English edition (1932)

THE | COLLECTED POEMS | OF | JOHN MASEFIELD | [publisher's device of a windmill] | [rule, 78mm.] | LONDON : WILLIAM HEINEMANN LTD.
(All width centred)

Bibliographies: Nevinson p.14, Handley-Taylor p.54, Wight [unrecorded]

Collation: [A]¹⁶ B-FF¹⁶ GG⁸ (J and V not used); the fifth leaf of each gathering is also signed (see notes); signatures left foot of page; 488 leaves; 199 × 126mm.; [two un-numbered pages] [i–iv] v–xi [xii–xiv] [1–3] 4–45 [46] 47–49 [50–52] 53–81 [82–84] 85 [86–88] 89–131 [132–34] 135–90 [191–93] 194–245 [246] 247–51 [252–54] 255–317 [318–21] 322–63 [364–66] 367–401 [402–404] 405–444 [445–49] 450–99 [500–502] 503–521 [522–25] 526–97 [598–601] 602–672 [673–74] 675–727 [728–30] 731–60 [761–62] 763–78 [779–80] 781–83 [784–86] 787–90 [791–92] 793–908 [909–911] 912–49 [950] 951–57 [958–60]

Page contents: [-] blank (page excluded from page count, but constitutes first leaf of first gathering); [-] blank; [i] half-title: 'THE COLLECTED POEMS | OF JOHN MASEFIELD'; [ii] blank; [iii] title-page; [iv] '*First published, October* 1923 | *New Impressions, November* 1923, *January and October* 1924, *April* 1925 | *February* 1926, *September and December* 1926, *July and October* 1927 | *October* 1928 *August* 1929, *September* 1930. | *New and Enlarged Edition, August,* 1932 | PRINTED IN GREAT BRITAIN AT THE WINDMILL

PRESS | KINGSWOOD SURREY'; v–xi 'CONTENTS' (191 individual items listed with page references); [xii] blank; [xiii] 'The plays contained in this volume are copyright | in Great Britain, the United States of America, | and Ireland. No performance or dramatic read- | ing of them may be given without the author's | formal license, which may be obtained through | The Society of Authors, 11, Gower Street, | London, W.C. 1. | [new paragraph] The lyrics from POMPEY THE GREAT, | printed in this volume, are included by courtesy | of Messrs. Sidgwick and Jackson, Limited, 44, | Museum Street, W.C. 1, who are the publishers | of the play.'; [xiv] blank; [1] 'SALT-WATER BALLADS'; [2] blank; 3–45 text of *Salt-Water Ballads*; [46] blank; 47–49 'GLOSSARY'; [50] blank; [51] 'BALLADS AND POEMS'; [52] blank; 53–81 text of *Ballads and Poems*; [82] blank; [83] 'LYRICS FROM THE TRAGEDY OF | POMPEY THE GREAT'; [84] blank; 85 text of Lyrics from *The Tragedy of Pompey the Great*; [86] blank; [87] 'THE EVERLASTING MERCY'; [88] '*Thy place is biggyd above the sterrys cleer,* | *Noon erthely paleys wrouhte in so statly wyse,* | *Com on my freend,* | *my brothir moost enteer,* | *For the I offryd my blood in sacrifise.* | JOHN LYDGATE.'; 89–131 text of *The Everlasting Mercy*; [132] blank; [133] 'THE WIDOW IN THE BYE STREET'; [134] blank; 135–90 text of *The Widow in the Bye Street*; [191] 'DAUBER'; [192] blank; [193]–245 text of *Dauber*; [246] blank; 247–51 'EXPLANATIONS OF SOME OF THE SEA | TERMS USED IN THE POEM'; [252] blank; [253] 'THE DAFFODIL FIELDS'; [254] blank; 255–317 text of *The Daffodil Fields*; [318] blank; [319] 'PHILIP THE KING | AND OTHER POEMS'; [320] '[dramatis personae listed with 'PERSONS' and 'SPIRITS' headings] | TIME | AT DAWN IN LATE SEPTEMBER, 1588 | SCENE | A LITTLE DARK CELL IN PHILIP'S PALACE'; [321]–363 text of *Philip the King*; [364] blank; [365] 'OTHER POEMS'; [366] blank; 367–401 text of other poems; [402] blank; [403] 'LOLLINGDON DOWNS | AND OTHER POEMS, WITH SONNETS'; [404] blank; 405–44 text of *Lollingdon Downs and other poems, with sonnets*; [445] 'GOOD FRIDAY | A PLAY IN VERSE'; [446] 'PERSONS | [dramatis personae listed]'; [447] 'THE SCENE | *The Pavement, or Paved Court,* *outside the Roman Citadel in* | *Jerusalem.* | [new paragraph] *At the back is the barrack wall, pierced in the centre with a double* | *bronze door,* *weathered to a green colour.* | [new paragraph] *On the right and left sides of the stage are battlemented parapets* | *overlooking the city.* | [new paragraph] *The stage or pavement is approached by stone steps from the front,* | *and by narrow stone staircases in the wings, one on each side, well* | *forward. These steps are to suggest that the citadel is high up above* | *the town, and that the main barrack gate is below.* THE CHIEF CITIZEN, | THE RABBLE, JOSEPH, THE MADMAN, HEROD, *and* THE LOITERERS, | *etc., enter by these steps.* | [new paragraph] PILATE, PROCULA, LONGINUS, THE SOLDIERS *and* SERVANTS *enter* | *by the bronze door.*'; [448] blank; [449]–499 text of *Good Friday*; [500] blank; [501] 'ROSAS'; [502] blank; 503–21 text of *Rosas*; [522] blank; [523] 'REYNARD THE FOX | OR | THE GHOST HEATH RUN'; [524] blank; [525]–97 text of *Reynard the Fox*; [598] blank; [599] 'ENSLAVED | AND OTHER POEMS'; [600] blank; [601]–672 text of *Enslaved and other poems*; [673] 'RIGHT ROYAL'; [674] blank; 675–727 text of *Right Royal*; [728] blank; [729] 'KING COLE | AND OTHER POEMS'; [730] blank; 731–60 text of *King Cole*; [761] 'OTHER POEMS'; [762] blank; 763–78 text of other poems; [779] 'POEMS FROM SARD HARKER'; [780] blank; 781–83 text of poems from *Sard Harker*; [784] blank; [785] 'POEMS FROM ODTAA'; [786] blank; 787–90 text of poems from *ODTAA*; [791] 'MIDSUMMER NIGHT | AND OTHER TALES IN VERSE'; [792] blank; 793–908 text of *Midsummer Night and other tales in verse*; [909] 'POEMS FROM THE WANDERER'; [910] blank; [911]–49 text of poems from *The Wanderer*; [950] blank; 951–57 'INDEX OF FIRST LINES'; [958–60] blank

Paper: wove paper

Running title: running titles comprise titles of individual poems on both verso and recto, pp.4–949

Binding: blue cloth. On spine, in gold: '*COLLECTED* | *POEMS* | [ornament] | *JOHN* | *MASEFIELD* | *Heinemann*' (all width centred). On upper cover, in gold: '*COLLECTED* | *POEMS* | *JOHN MASEFIELD*' (within blind ruled border: 199 × 122mm.) Lower cover, in blind: publisher's device of a windmill (ranged lower right). All edges trimmed. Binding measurements: 204 × 128mm. (covers), 204 × 57mm. (spine). End-papers: wove paper.

Also issued in leather.

Publication date: the sales ledger preserved in the Heinemann Archive suggests publication on 31 October 1932 in an edition of 7500 copies. The *English Catalogue of Books* records a publication date of November 1932

Price: 10s.6d. (cloth) / 15s. (leather)

Contents:
pp.[3]–778 as for A71(a) and then with the following additional contents:
POEMS FROM *SARD HARKER*
Sard Harker ('A calm like Jove's beneath a fiery air.')
The Pathfinder ('She lies at grace, at anchor, head to tide,')
POEMS FROM *ODTAA*
The Sonnet of Camilla, Mother of Don Manuel, on hearing of her son's betrothal… ('Lord, when Thy servant, doubting of Thy grace')
Lines, on the same occasion… ('In the dark night I saw Death drawing near')
A Sonnet upon Ezekiel Rust ('Son of Isaiah Rust, of Churn, his wage')
The Meditation of Carlotta in Prison ('This that I understand,')
The Meditation of Highworth Ridden ('I have seen flowers come in stony places;')
The Comfort of Manuel, on Setting Forth Defeate[d] in The *Venturer* ('Bad lies behind, worse lies before.')
MIDSUMMER NIGHT AND OTHER TALES IN VERSE
The Begetting of Arthur ('Uther, the Prince, succeeding to the post')
The Birth of Arthur ('When the wind from East changes')
The Taking of Morgause ('Morgause the Merry played beside the burn:')
The Begetting of Modred ('When berries were scarlet')

Badon Hill ('Loki the Dragon Killer mustered men')
The Sailing of Hell Race ('When Arthur came from warring, having won')
Arthur and His Ring ('Beauty's Delight, the Princess Gwenivere,')
Midsummer Night ('Midsummer night had fallen at full moon,')
The Fight on the Wall ('Modred was in the Water Tower')
The Breaking of the Links ('They told King Arthur how the Knights were killed,')
Gwenivach Tells ('I, Gwenivach, King Modred's queen, declare')
Arthur in the Ruins ('King Arthur watched within the ruined town,')
The Fight at Camlan ('Soon the two armies were in touch, and soon')
The Fight on the Beach or the Passing ('These were the nine with Modred:-Kolgrim, Gor,')
Gwenivere Tells ('So Arthur passed, but country-folk believe')
The Death of Lancelot ('Then, after many years, a rider came,')
Dust to Dust ('Henry Plantagenet, the English King,')
On the Coming of Arthur ('By ways unknown, unseen,')
The Old Tale of The Begetting ('*The men of old, who made the tale for us.*')
The Old Tale of The Breaking of the Links ('French poets write:-That, Lancelot the brave')
South and East ('When good King Arthur ruled these western hursts,')
Fulfilment ('Long since, Sir Constans governed here for Rome,')
POEMS FROM *THE WANDERER*
The Setting Forth ('Her builder and owner drank tea with her captain below.')
The Ending ('Once, long before, at her second outgoing down Channel')
A Masque of Liverpool ('LIVERPOOL. | I am the English sea-queen; I am she')
The Wanderer ('You swept across the waters like a Queen,')
Liverpool, 1890 ('Gray sea dim, smoke-blowing, hammer-racket, sirens')
Liverpool, 1930 ('The dockyards of the ancient days are filled')
On Skysails ('I saw you often as the crown of Queens')
Pay ('The world paid but a penny for its toil,')
The Crowd ('They had secured their beauty to the dock,')
Under Three Lower Topsails ('Three lower topsails dark with wet are straining')
Eight Bells ('Four double strokes repeated on the bells,')
Posted ('Dream after dream I see the wrecks that lie')
If ('If it could be, that in this southern port')
I Saw Her Here ('All tranquil is the mirror of the bay,')
Wanderer and Wonderer ('When first the thought of you took steel')
Index of First Lines

Notes:

The edition comprises an enlarged version of A71(a). The same setting of type is used for pp.[3]–778. This explains spurious signatures on B9 and M9. There appears to be some damage to type. For example, the poem 'Captain Stratton's Fancy' appears, in this edition, to have lost the comma at the end of the first line.

The intention to publish an updated edition of this work dates from at least April 1930. C.S. Evans wrote that he was '…getting some estimates for the reprint of the COLLECTED POEMS with the additional material and as soon as I have the figures I will write to you again.' (see C.S. Evans, letter to John Masefield, 8 April 1930) (HRHRC, MS (Masefield, J.) Recip William Heinemann Ltd.) Accordingly, Evans wrote:

> …I have now had the new edition of the COLLECTED POEMS, with all the additions, estimated, and I find that it will make 1,182 pages as against the old 778 – a pretty considerable increase. I entirely agree with you, however, that it is necessary to bring the book up to date, and we will do it with the next reprinting. I am quite sure that the new edition ought to be in one volume and published at the same price as the old: it would be fatal to publish it in two volumes or to increase the price. The book ought to go on selling steadily and in large numbers for a good many years to come.
>
> (C.S. Evans, letter to John Masefield, 16 April 1930)
> (HRHRC, MS (Masefield, J.) Recip William Heinemann Ltd.)

Masefield, it seems, queried both the matter of the price and the single volume format. Evans replied:

> I will go carefully into all the points you raise and I will write to you again. I will only say now that when I proposed that we should keep the volume at 8/6 I did so because I was afraid that the sales might decrease if it were raised to 10/6, in spite of the fact that we were giving so much extra value for money. In the last three or four years, people have got used to the large omnibus and collected books being sold at 8/6, and one or two which have been done at 10/6 have proved economic failures. The whole question depends upon whether at a new price, even with a smaller sale, it would not be more lucrative to you and to us. I will figure this out and let you know. I am very definitely against the idea of a two-volume edition. I am sure that to issue in that form would have a very damaging effect upon the property.
>
> (C.S. Evans, letter to John Masefield, 29 April 1930)
> (HRHRC, MS (Masefield, J.) Recip William Heinemann Ltd.)

Evans' discussions at Heinemann helped formulate a plan which he communicated to Masefield at the beginning of May 1930. It appears that he had been wrong about the pricing of the proposed edition:

> I have discussed the problem of the enlarged edition of THE COLLECTED POEMS very thoroughly with our sales department, and we are inclined to think that the best thing to do, when the book is reprinted, is to print it on a slightly larger page (5 3/8 × 7 3/4) which will give wider margins, and make a larger and more handsome book the price of which we could increase to 10/6. Our sales department is very strong indeed in the feeling that to issue the book in two volumes at 7/6 would be fatal to its chances of sale...
>
> (C.S. Evans, letter to John Masefield, 6 May 1930)
> (HRHRC, MS (Masefield, J.) Recip William Heinemann Ltd.)

Three months later Evans wrote anxiously stating that 'we ought to put in hand almost immediately the new edition of the collected poems...' (see C.S. Evans, letter to John Masefield, 7 August 1930) (HRHRC, MS (Masefield, J.) Recip William Heinemann Ltd.) Given that an entirely new edition would take some time, Masefield apparently suggested an 'interim edition'. This was not an attractive proposition to Evans:

> We have very carefully considered your suggestion about the interim edition of the COLLECTED POEMS, and we are unanimously against it. I think that the issue of such an interim edition would only complicate things and would in the long run be unsatisfactory. My proposal is that we should go ahead and sell the existing COLLECTED POEMS until this time next year when you will be ready with the revised edition. I think that we can certainly sell another 10,000 before the end of the year and I should propose to reprint that number.
>
> (C.S. Evans, letter to John Masefield, 15 August 1930)
> (HRHRC, MS (Masefield, J.) Recip William Heinemann Ltd.)

Evans pointed out that it was essential for stocks of the latest impression of the old edition to be exhausted before publishing the new edition:

> ... we will get on with the reprint of the COLLECTED POEMS at once. I am ready to put the revised edition in hand as soon as you have it ready. I think we ought to plan for its publication about this time next year. The old edition should be allowed to go out of print for some time to exhaust copies which may be in the booksellers' shops: otherwise, when the revised editions appears, we shall have to give credits for the old edition still in stock at the booksellers, which is, of course, a wasteful thing to do.
>
> (C.S. Evans, letter to John Masefield, 3 September 1930)
> (HRHRC, MS (Masefield, J.) Recip William Heinemann Ltd.)

Discussion then turned to the contents of the new edition. Evans wrote:

> I have been in bed for four days with a bad cold; otherwise I should have written to you before about the collected edition of your poems. We should prefer to publish the new edition in the autumn of this year, this edition to include the poems from THE WANDERER; and then later on add the new poems. Our sales department feels that if we were to postpone the new edition until the spring of 1932 and then issue it with THE WANDERER poems and the new poems, we should not get the best out of the new poems in the original edition. In the original form they ought to go on selling for at least a year...
>
> (C.S. Evans, letter to John Masefield, 16 February 1931)
> (HRHRC, MS (Masefield, J.) Recip William Heinemann Ltd.)

Another matter for discussion was the possible inclusion of several plays. These suggestions were, ultimately, not realised:

> ...I think that THE COMING OF CHRIST and EASTER should both be included in the new edition of the COLLECTED POEMS. Although they are plays, they are also definitely poems. On the other hand, I think that TRISTAN should be omitted. I do not quite know why except that I have a strong feeling about it. TRISTAN is poetical, but it seems to me to take on more the play form than the poem. You might save this and the other plays for another collected volume of plays to be issued later...
>
> (C.S. Evans, letter to John Masefield, 19 February 1931)
> (HRHRC, MS (Masefield, J.) Recip William Heinemann Ltd.)

Two months later, H.J. Woods sent '...proofs of: "Poems from Sard Harker", "Odtaa" "Midsummer Night" and "The Wanderer", which are going at the end of "Collected Poems"...' (see H.J. Woods, letter to John Masefield, 29 April 1931) (HRHRC, MS (Masefield, J.) Recip William Heinemann Ltd.) C.S. Evans wrote to Masefield in July 1931 noting a delay in publication. The dates noted by Evans do not exactly correspond with examined reprint copies of the earlier edition:

> ...As you know, we intended to publish the new edition this autumn. In November last we issued a reprint of 10,000 copies of the old edition so that we should be able to supply the Christmas demands. We sold the whole of that edition in about a fortnight, and as we anticipated that it would be nine months before the new one could be issued, we ordered another reprint of 10,000 on December 3rd. In the New Year, however, the sale of the book slowed down considerably and we still have a stock of about 9,000 copies which must be exhausted before we put the new one on the market...
>
> (C.S. Evans, letter to John Masefield, 20 July 1931)
> (HRHRC, MS (Masefield, J.) Recip William Heinemann Ltd.)

Information cited in this volume regarding reprints of the previous edition does not exactly correspond with consulted reprint copies of A71(a).

The *English Catalogue of Books* also notes a leather bound edition published in December 1932. The sales ledger preserved in the Heinemann Archive suggests publication of this leather bound edition on 19 December 1932. The number of copies printed is omitted. The omission of the number of copies suggests that these copies may be from the initial printing of 7500 copies.

Copies seen: private collection (PWE); private collection (ROV); BL (11607.bbb.35) stamped 31 OCT 1932, rebound; HRHRC (TEMP M377B2 1932) inscribed 'For Con | from Jan. | Oct 28. 1932.'

Reprinted:

	[second edition, second impression]	Nov 1932
'Reprinted'	[second edition, third impression]	Apr 1934
	[second edition, fourth impression]	May 1935
	[second edition, fifth impression]	Nov 1935
'Reprinted'	[second edition, sixth impression]	Nov 1936
	[second edition, seventh impression]	Nov 1937

A71(d) *Fourth English edition (1938)*

THE | COLLECTED POEMS | OF | JOHN MASEFIELD | [publisher's device of a windmill] | [rule, 78mm.] | WILLIAM HEINEMANN LTD | LONDON :: TORONTO
(All width centred)

Bibliographies: Handley-Taylor p.54, Wight [unrecorded]

Collation: [1]^{16} 2–36^{16}; the fifth leaf of each gathering is also signed; signatures right foot of page; 576 leaves; 196 × 128mm.; [two un-numbered pages] [i–iv] v–xii [xiii–xiv] [1–2] 3–43 [44] 45–47 [48–50] 51–79 [80–82] 83 [84–86] 87–129 [130–32] 133–88 [189–90] 191–243 [244] 245–49 [250–52] 253–315 [316–18] 319–61 [362–64] 365–99 [400–402] 403–442 [443–46] 447–97 [498–500] 501–519 [520–22] 523–95 [596–98] 599–670 [671–72] 673–725 [726–78] 729–58 [759–60] 761–76 [777–78] 779–81 [782–84] 785–88 [789–90] 791–906 [907–908] 909–945 [946–48] 949–1051 [1052–1054] 1055–1136

Page contents: [-] blank (page excluded from page count, but constitutes first leaf of first gathering); [-] blank; [i] half-title: 'THE COLLECTED POEMS | OF JOHN MASEFIELD'; [ii] *'ALSO BY JOHN MASEFIELD* | PLAYS: | [12 titles listed] | POETRY: | [15 titles listed] | FICTION: | [nine titles listed] | GENERAL: | [nine titles listed]'; [iii] title-page; [iv] *'First Published, October* 1923 | *New Impressions, November* 1923, *January, October* 1924, *April* 1925, | *February, September, December* 1926, *July, October* 1927, *October* 1928, | *August* 1929, *September* 1930 | *New and Enlarged Edition, August* 1932 | *Reprinted, November* 1932, *April* 1934, | *May, November* 1935, *November* 1937 | *New and Enlarged Edition, February* 1938. | PRINTED IN GREAT BRITAIN | AT THE WINDMILL PRESS, KINGSWOOD SURREY'; v–xii 'CONTENTS' (237 individual items listed with page references); [xiii] 'The plays contained in this volume are copyright | in Great Britain, the United States of America, | and Ireland. No performance or dramatic read- | ing of them may be given without the author's | formal license, which may be obtained through | The Society of Authors, 11, Gower Street, London, | W.C. 1. | [new paragraph] The lyrics from POMPEY THE GREAT, printed | in this volume, are included by courtesy of Messrs. | Sidgwick and Jackson, Limited, 44, Museum Street, | W.C. 1, who are the publishers of the play.'; [xiv] blank; [1] 'SALT-WATER BALLADS'; [2] blank; 3–43 text of *Salt-Water Ballads*; [44] blank; 45–47 'GLOSSARY'; [48] blank; [49] 'BALLADS AND POEMS'; [50] blank; 51–79 text of *Ballads and Poems*; [80] blank; [81] 'LYRICS FROM THE TRAGEDY OF | POMPEY THE GREAT'; [82] blank; 83 text of Lyrics from *The Tragedy of Pompey the Great*; [84] blank; [85] 'THE EVERLASTING MERCY'; [86] *'Thy place is biggyd above the sterrys cleer,* | *Noon erthely paleys wrouhte in so statly wyse,* | *Com on my freend, my brothir moost enteer,* | *For the I offryd my blood in sacrifise.* | JOHN LYDGATE.'; 87–129 text of *The Everlasting Mercy*; [130] blank; [131] 'THE WIDOW IN THE BYE STREET'; [132] blank; 133–188 text of *The Widow in the Bye Street*; [189] 'DAUBER'; [190] blank; 191–243 text of *Dauber*; [244] blank; 245–49 'EXPLANATIONS OF SOME OF THE SEA | TERMS USED IN THE POEM'; [250] blank; [251] 'THE DAFFODIL FIELDS'; [252] blank; 253–315 text of *The Daffodil Fields*; [316] blank; [317] 'PHILIP THE KING | AND OTHER POEMS'; [318] '[dramatis personae listed with 'PERSONS' and 'SPIRITS' headings] | TIME | AT DAWN IN LATE SEPTEMBER, 1588 | SCENE | A LITTLE DARK CELL IN PHILIP'S PALACE'; 319–61 text of *Philip the King*; [362] blank; [363] 'OTHER POEMS'; [364] blank; 365–99 text of other poems; [400] blank; [401] 'LOLLINGDON DOWNS | AND OTHER POEMS, WITH SONNETS'; [402] blank; 403–442 text of *Lollingdon Downs and other poems, with sonnets*; [443] 'GOOD FRIDAY | A PLAY IN VERSE'; [444] 'PERSONS | [dramatis personae listed]'; [445] 'THE SCENE | *The Pavement, or Paved Court, outside the Roman Citadel in Jerusalem.* | [new paragraph] *At the back is the barrack wall, pierced in the centre with a double bronze* | *door, weathered to a green colour.* | [new paragraph] *On the right and left sides of the stage are battlemented parapets overlooking the* | *city.* | [new paragraph] *The stage or pavement is approached by stone steps from the front, and by* | *narrow stone staircases in the wings, one on each side, well forward. These steps* | *are to suggest that the citadel is high up above the town, and that the main barrack* | *gate is below.* THE CHIEF CITIZEN, THE RABBLE, JOSEPH, THE MADMAN | HEROD, *and* THE LOITERERS, *etc., enter by these steps.* | [new paragraph] PILATE, PROCULA, LONGINUS, THE SOLDIERS *and* SERVANTS *enter by the* | *bronze door.*'; [446] blank; 447–97 text of *Good Friday*; [498] blank; [499] 'ROSAS'; [500] blank; 501–519 text of *Rosas*; [520] blank; [521] 'REYNARD THE FOX | OR | THE GHOST HEATH RUN'; [522] blank; 523–95 text of *Reynard the Fox*; [596] blank; [597] 'ENSLAVED | AND OTHER POEMS'; [598] blank; 599–670 text of *Enslaved and other poems*; [671] 'RIGHT ROYAL'; [672] blank; 673–725 text of *Right Royal*; [726] blank; [727] 'KING COLE | AND OTHER

POEMS'; [728] blank; 729–58 text of *King Cole*; [759] 'OTHER POEMS'; [760] blank; 761–76 text of other poems; [777] 'POEMS FROM SARD HARKER'; [778] blank; 779–81 text of poems from *Sard Harker*, [782] blank; [783] 'POEMS FROM ODTAA'; [784] blank; 785–88 text of poems from *ODTAA*; [789] 'MIDSUMMER NIGHT | AND OTHER TALES IN VERSE'; [790] blank; 791–906 text of *Midsummer Night and other tales in verse*; [907] 'POEMS FROM THE WANDERER'; [908] blank; 909–945 text of poems from *The Wanderer*, [946] blank; [947] 'MINNIE MAYLOW'S STORY | AND OTHER TALES & SCENES'; [948]–1051 text of *Minnie Maylow's Story and other tales and scenes*, [1052] blank; [1053] 'A LETTER FROM PONTUS | AND OTHER VERSE'; [1054] blank; 1055–1128 text of *A Letter from Pontus and other verse*, 1129–36 'INDEX OF FIRST LINES'

Paper: wove paper

Running title: running titles comprise titles of individual poems on both verso and recto, pp.4–1128

Binding: blue cloth. On spine, in gold: '*COLLECTED | POEMS* | [ornament] | *JOHN | MASEFIELD | Heinemann*' (all width centred). On upper cover, in gold: '*COLLECTED | POEMS | JOHN MASEFIELD*' within blind ruled border: 200 × 123mm.) Lower cover, in blind: publisher's device of a windmill (ranged lower right). Top edge stained, others trimmed. Binding measurements: 203 × 131mm. (covers), 203 × 57mm. (spine). End-papers: wove paper.

Also issued in leather with slip-case covered in blue paper.

Publication date: the sales ledger preserved in the Heinemann Archive suggests publication on 30 May 1938 in an edition of 3000 copies

Price: 12s.6d. (cloth) / 15s. (leather)

Contents:
pp.[3]–945 as for A71(c) and then with the following additional contents:
MINNIE MAYLOW'S STORY AND OTHER TALES & SCENES
Prologue ('I am a pilgrim come from many lands,')
Minnie Maylow's Story ('Once (long ago) there was an English King,')
Adamas and Eva ('Whilom there was, dwellyng in Paradys')
Son of Adam ('Once on a time there was a lusty Lion')
The Love Gift ('In King Marc's palace at the valley-head')
Tristan's Singing ('PART I | When Isolt quarrell'd with her Tristan there')
Simkin, Tomkin and Jack ('Before old Tencombe of the Barrows died,')
The Rose of the World ('Dark Eleanor and Henry sat at meat')
Young John of Chance's Stretch ('PART I | When Father died, my Mother ran')
Evan Roberts, A.B., Of H.M.S. *Andromache* ('This gallant act is told by the late Montagu Burrows, on page 67 of his *Autobiography...*')
Richard Whittington ('FORTUNE. | I am Fortune: I give as is fitting to each of my souls,')
The Hour Strikes ('THE SEEKER. | The shepherds warn'd me not to climb this hill')
A LETTER FROM PONTUS AND OTHER VERSE
A Letter from Pontus ('In the first year of the Divine Tiberius,')
Australia ('When the North Lander saw the rose in blossom,')
The Will ('By Will, Man dared in den and heath')
Westminster Hall ('What glory and reversal has been shown')
Ballet Russe I ('The gnome from moonland plays the Chopin air,')
Ballet Russe II ('With delicate control in maddest speed')
Joseph Hodges, or the Corn ('He wore the smock-frock of the country's past,')
The Wild Geese ('All the Many is One,')
Hope ('O Hope that glimmers in the breast')
The Queen ('I waited, in my misery, when the Queen,')
Beauty ('O Queen of Beauty, you who once were fire')
February Night ('I went into the land where Beauty dwells.')
February Morning ('The starry wheel of night passed slowly over;')
Nets ('COLONIES built a fort for safety's sake,')
The Long Drive | (*Edinburgh to Boar's Hill*) ('In a garage not far from the Rock of the Castle')
The Flowing of the Sangarios ('I saw a sullen little river swerve')
Wood-Pigeons ('Often the woodman scares them as he comes')
Autumn Ploughing ('After the ranks of stubble have lain bare,')
The Waggon-Maker ('I have made tales in verse, but this man made')
November the Sixth ('I face North-West upon a grassy hill,')
Pony Fair ('Twice every year for full five centuries')
Partridges ('Here they lie mottled to the ground unseen,')
The Towerer ('Old Jarge, Hal, Walter and I, the Rector and Bill,')
Candlemas Day ('The frost is passing; from the West the rain')
The Eyes ('I remember a tropic dawn before turn-to,')
The Spanish Main ('Low, dull-green hills with scrub and little trees,')

Nombre De Dios ('The jungle reaches to the water's edge.')
Porto Bello ('The port is unsuspected from the east,')
Canal Zone ('Among these hills, twelve generations since,')
The Spanish Main Schooner ('A little wooden schooner, painted white,')
A Ballad of Sir Francis Drake ('Before Sir Francis put to sea,')
The Mayblossom | (*Told me by the Pilot*) ('The ship, *Mayblossom*, left Magellan Straits')
1176 Hours ('Oh, ticking Time, when wilt thou pass?')
Begone ('Begone you rubbish of old dates')
The Boy from Pauntley ('West, in the redlands, good for hops and corn,')
Sweet Friends ('Print not my life nor letters; put them by:')
Index of First Lines

Notes:

A71(c) represented a verbatim reprint of A71(a) with additional material at the rear of the volume. Here, however, the text has been entirely re-set.

It had originally been Heinemann's intention to publish an edition of the *Collected Poems* in the 'Wanderer edition' (see note on collected editions). Although Evans had refused to issue A71(c) in two volumes, the Wanderer edition was to have been a three volume set (and was advertised as such on the lower inner flap of the dust-jacket to A116(a) in October 1935). Proofs were sent at the end of 1936:

> I hope you will not be alarmed by the size of the parcel which accompanies this letter. It contains the proofs of your COLECTED POEMS which we have just had entirely reset as the old plates were getting worn… I should be grateful if you would indicate to me where you would like me to split the volume which, as you know, has to make three volumes in the collected edition.

> (C.S. Evans, letter to John Masefield, 17 December 1936)
> (HRHRC, MS (Masefield, J.) Recip William Heinemann Ltd.)

This three volume edition was never published, however. Whether this setting of text was used for A71(d) is unclear. At the beginning of 1938, Masefield was sent proofs as follows:

> I have pleasure in sending you proofs of the completion of COLLECTED POEMS with the addition of A LETTER FROM PONTUS and MINNIE MAYLOW'S STORY excluding the two poems "The Wild Swan" and "Penelope"…
> (B.F. Oliver, letter to John Masefield, 14 January 1938)
> (HRHRC, MS (Masefield, J.) Recip William Heinemann Ltd.)

Information cited in this edition regarding reprints of the previous edition does not exactly correspond with consulted reprint copies.

The *English Catalogue of Books* also notes a leather bound edition published in May 1938. The sales ledger preserved in the Heinemann Archive does not provide different dates for the two different bindings, or separate print-run figures.

Copies seen: BL (2292.e.41) stamped 30 MAY 1938; HRHRC (TEMP M377B2 1938 cop.1) inscribed 'The days that make us happy | make us wise. | John Masefield. | Feb. 1939. | [sketch of a boat]'; HRHRC (TEMP M377B2 1938 cop.2) inscribed 'For Con | from | Jan. | May 28. 1938.' leather binding

Reprinted:

[third edition, second impression]	Feb 1938
[third edition, third impression]	Oct 1938
[third edition, fourth impression]	Oct 1941
[third edition, fifth impression]	Aug 1942

A72 THE TAKING OF HELEN AND OTHER PROSE SELECTIONS 1924

A72(a) First American edition (1924)

THE TAKING OF HELEN | AND OTHER PROSE | SELECTIONS | BY | JOHN MASEFIELD | New York | THE MACMILLAN COMPANY | 1924 | *All rights reserved*
(All width centred)

Bibliographies: Simmons [60], Nevinson [unrecorded], Handley-Taylor p.54, Wight [60]

Collation: [A-K]⁸ [L]⁹ ([L]8+1) (J not used); 89 leaves; 191 × 126mm.; [i–viii] 1–98 [99–100] 101–169 [170]

Page contents: [i] half-title: 'THE TAKING OF HELEN | AND OTHER PROSE | SELECTIONS'; [ii] 'BY | JOHN MASEFIELD | [rule] | [27 titles listed]' (within ruled border: 114 × 80mm.); [iii] title-page; [iv] 'PRINTED IN THE UNITED STATES OF AMERICA | COPYRIGHT, 1923 AND 1924, | BY JOHN MASEFIELD | [rule] | Set up and electrotyped. Published October, 1923. | New Edition with New Material, April, 1924. | Norwood Press | J.S. Cushing Co. – Berwick & Smith Co. | Norwood, Mass., U.S.A.'; [v] 'CONTENTS' (four items listed with page references); [vi] blank; [vii] 'THE TAKING OF HELEN'; [viii] blank; 1–98 text; [99] 'OTHER PROSE SELECTIONS'; [100] blank; 101–169 text; [170] blank

Paper: laid paper (no watermark), chain-lines 25mm. apart

Running title: 'THE TAKING OF HELEN' (43mm.) on both verso and recto, pp.2–98 and pp.102–169

Binding: burgundy cloth. On spine, in gold: 'THE | TAKING | OF | HELEN | AND OTHER | PROSE | SELECTIONS | MASEFIELD | MACMILLAN | [square point] [square point] [square point] [square point]' (all width centred). On upper cover, in blind: 'THE TAKING OF | HELEN AND OTHER | PROSE SELECTIONS | MASEFIELD' (ranged upper left) (within blind ruled border: 191 × 119mm.) Lower cover: blank. All edges trimmed. Binding measurements: 197 × 127mm. (covers), 197 × 31mm. (spine). End-papers: wove paper.

Publication date: published, according to Simmons, 22 April 1924 in an edition of 2102 copies

Price: $1.60

Contents:
The Taking of Helen ('Nireus was the son of the King of Symé Island. At his birth the gods brought gifts to him...')
Letters ('Niagara. | "All the way, I had remembered the tales of the roar...')
    First printed in Reveillé *November 1918, No.2, pp.183–89*
Play-Writing ('Last week, I was talking about story-writing, which, within the limits of a reader's endurance...')
Fox-Hunting ('I have been asked to write why I wrote my poem of *Reynard the Fox*.')
    See A49(d)

Notes:
The standard (non-limited) American publication of *The Taking of Helen* (see A64), published in addition to short pieces of prose reprinted from other sources or hitherto unpublished ('Play-Writing'). See also *Recent Prose* (A73).

The additional sheet, ([L]9) pasted onto [L]8, comprises the final leaf. The verso is blank.

Copies seen: NYPL (NCW 1924) 147591A '12 June 1924' written on p.[v]

A73 RECENT PROSE   1924

A73(a) First English edition (1924)

RECENT PROSE | by | John Masefield | London | William Heinemann Ltd | 1924
(All width centred)

Bibliographies: Simmons [61], Nevinson p.17, Handley-Taylor p.54, Wight [61]

Collation: A⁴ B–O⁸ (J not used); signatures right foot of page; 108 leaves; 182 × 121mm.; [i–iv] v [vi] vii [viii] 1–115 [116] 117–57 [158] 159–207 [208]

Page contents: [i] half-title: 'RECENT PROSE'; [ii] 'RECENTLY PUBLISHED WORKS BY | JOHN MASEFIELD | [four titles listed]'; [iii] title-page; [iv] 'Printed in Great Britain at | The Westminster Press, Harrow Road | London, W.9'; v 'NOTE | *The Taking of Helen* was first published by | Messrs. Heinemann (in a limited edition) in 1923. | [new paragraph] The quotations from letters were first printed | in Mr. Galsworthy's periodical *Reveillè*, [*sic*] in 1918. | [new paragraph] The lecture on *Play-Writing* is now printed for | the first time. | [new paragraph] | The article *Fox-Hunting* was first printed by | the Macmillan Company, in America, in 1920, as | a preface to my poem, *Reynard the Fox*. It has | appeared in this country in Messrs. Heinemann's | collection *The Windmill*, 1923. | [new paragraph] The article *John M. Synge* was printed in *The | Fortnightly Review*, in 1911. It was reprinted as a | book, in limited editions, by the Macmillan Com- | pany in America, by the Cuala Press, Dundrum, | and by myself, in England, during the years | 1915–16. It is now reprinted, with some amend- | ments, from the edition of the Macmillan Com- | pany. | J. M.'; [vi] blank; vii 'CONTENTS' (five individual items listed with page references); [viii] blank; 1–104 text of 'The Taking of Helen'; 105–115 text of 'Letters'; [116] blank; 117–57 text of 'Play-Writing'; [158] blank; 159–80 text of 'Fox-Hunting'; 181–207 text of 'John M. Synge'; [208] blank

Paper: wove paper

Running title: 'Recent Prose' (20mm.) on verso; recto title comprises title of prose item, pp.2–207

Binding: blue cloth. On spine, in gold: 'Recent | Prose | [ornament] | John | Masefield | HEINEMANN' (all width centred). On upper cover, in gold: 'RECENT PROSE | JOHN MASEFIELD' (within blind ruled border: 183 × 116mm.) Lower cover: blank. All edges trimmed. Binding measurements: 189 × 122mm. (covers), 189 × 42mm. (spine). End-papers: wove paper.

Publication date: published, according to Simmons, 22 May 1924 in an edition of 4000 copies

Price: 6s.

Contents:
The Taking of Helen ('Nireus was the son of the King of Symé Island. At his birth the gods brought gifts to him...')
Letters ('NIAGARA | "All the way, I had remembered the tales of the roar...')
Play-Writing ('Last week, I was talking about story-writing, which, within the limits of a reader's endurance...')
Fox-Hunting ('I have been asked to write why I wrote my poem of *Reynard the Fox*.')
John M. Synge ('I first met John M. Synge at the room of a common friend...')

Notes:

A collection of Masefield's prose and the first non-limited publication of *The Taking of Helen* (see A64) in England. The contents are the same as Macmillan's *The Taking of Helen and other prose selections* (see A72) with the additional inclusion of *John M. Synge* (see A27).

All items commence with a drop-capital.

Theodore Byard wrote to Masefield during January 1924 asking about the manuscript for this volume:

> Could you let me know approximately when you will deliver to us the manuscript of your selected essays? We are anxious to bring them out in the spring, and time is getting on.
>
> (Theodore Byard, letter to John Masefield, 17 January 1924)
> (HRHRC, MS (Masefield, J.) Recip William Heinemann Ltd.)

Masefield, it seems, had already sent some of the contents and, in the absence of C.S. Evans, this could not at first be located at the publishers. Furthermore, Byard was concerned about the length of the volume:

> …we were unable to find either your recollections of Synge or the complete manuscript which you say you gave to Evans some time ago. I am thankful to say, however, that after turning the whole Evans family on to it at Walton, we have unearthed SYNGE, which is the important thing…
>
> I have had an estimate made of the manuscript which you send, excluding THE TAKING OF HELEN, and find that it runs to only 21,000 words. I am afraid this is much too small to issue in a separate volume as representing prose work. We ought to have at least 80,000 or 90,000 words in my opinion, and I feel sure that you will agree with me. This leaves us two alternatives – either to include the TAKING OF HELEN and forego the large paper edition, or for you to give us sufficient extra material to bring the volume up to, say, 80,000 words. Of course, I should prefer the latter scheme…
>
> (Theodore Byard, letter to John Masefield, 24 January 1924)
> (HRHRC, MS (Masefield, J.) Recip William Heinemann Ltd.)

Masefield evidently opted for the first option and decided to include 'The Taking of Helen'. It was decided that as this had previously been published as a limited signed edition (see A64(a)) no limited signed edition could be produced of *Recent Prose*. To avoid possible confusion the publishers also suggested Masefield change his title:

> I see that you suggest THE TAKING OF HELEN AND OTHER PROSE WRITINGS as the title for your volume. As we have already issued THE TAKING OF HELEN as a separate volume, and as this title is very long, may I suggest that the title should be PROSE WRITINGS or SELECTED PROSE WRITINGS?
>
> (Theodore Byard, letter to John Masefield, 4 February 1924)
> (HRHRC, MS (Masefield, J.) Recip William Heinemann Ltd.)

C.S. Evans sent the proofs to Masefield at the end of March 1924 (see C.S. Evans, letter to John Masefield, 24 March 1924) (HRHRC, MS (Masefield, J.) Recip William Heinemann Ltd.) At the beginning of April he requested the 'Note', mindful of 'accurate bibliography':

> It has been suggested to me that in the interest of accurate bibliography, there ought to be a note to explain where and in what form the contents of RECENT PROSE have been printed, as most of them have been printed in some form or other. Do you think this should be done, and if so, will you draft such a note and let me have it?
>
> (C.S. Evans, letter to John Masefield, 9 April 1924)
> (HRHRC, MS (Masefield, J.) Recip William Heinemann Ltd.)

Such a note was acknowledged by Evans on 14 April 1924 (see C.S. Evans, letter to John Masefield, 14 April 1924) (HRHRC, MS (Masefield, J.) Recip William Heinemann Ltd.)

The publishing agreement for this title between Masefield and Heinemann was dated 29 April 1924 (see Archives of The Society of Authors). The agreement refers to a publication price of 6s.

Copies seen: private collection (PWE); BL (012273.aaa.39) stamped 22 MAY 1924; Columbia University Libraries (Special Collections B825.M377.M3.1924.c.2) inscribed 'For Con | from | Jan. | May 21. 1924.', includes posthumous booklabel

A73(b) Second English edition (1932)

RECENT PROSE | by | John Masefield | London | William Heinemann Ltd
(All width centred)

Bibliographies: Handley-Taylor p.54, Wight [unrecorded]

Collation: [A]⁴ B-U⁸ X¹⁰ (J, V and W not used) (see notes); X2 is also signed; signatures right foot of page; 166 leaves; 181 × 117mm.; [i–iv] v [vi] vii [viii] 1–115 [116] 117–57 [158] 159–321 [322–24]

Page contents: [i] half-title: 'RECENT PROSE'; [ii] blank; [iii] title-page; [iv] '*First published May* 1926 | *New and Revised Edition October* 1932 | PRINTED IN GREAT BRITAIN | AT THE WINDMILL PRESS | KINGSWOOD SURREY'; v 'NOTE | *The Taking of Helen* was first published by | Messrs. Heinemann (in a limited edition) in 1923. | [new paragraph] The quotations from letters were first printed | in Mr. Galsworthy's periodical *Reveillé*, in 1918. | [new paragraph] The lecture on *Play-Writing* is now printed for | the first time. | [new paragraph] | The article *Fox-Hunting* was first printed by | the Macmillan Company, in America, in 1920, as | a preface to my poem, *Reynard the Fox*. It has | appeared in this country in Messrs. Heinemann's | collection *The Windmill*, 1923.

| [new paragraph] The article *John M. Synge* was printed in *The | Fortnightly Review*, in 1911. It was reprinted as a | book, in limited editions, by the Macmillan Com- | pany in America, by the Cuala Press, Dundrum, | and by myself, in England, during the years | 1915–16. It is now reprinted, with some amend- | ments, from the edition of the Macmillan Com- | pany. | [new paragraph] The lecture *Shakespeare and Spiritual Life* is | by agreement reprinted from an edition published | by the Oxford University Press, in 1924. | [new paragraph] The lecture *Chaucer* is by agreement reprinted | from an edition published by the Cambridge | University Press, in 1931. | J. M.'; [vi] blank; vii 'CONTENTS' (11 individual items listed with page references); [viii] blank; 1–104 text of 'The Taking of Helen'; 105–115 text of 'Letters'; [116] blank; 117–57 text of 'Play-Writing'; [158] blank; 159–80 text of 'Fox-Hunting'; 181–207 text of 'John M. Synge'; 208–210 text of 'At Hereford'; 211–16 text of 'Words for a Festival in the Honour of William Butler Yeats, Poet.'; 217–43 text of 'Chaucer'; 244–79 text of 'Shakespeare and Spiritual Life'; 280–304 text of 'William Blake'; 305–321 text of 'George Crabbe'; [322–24] blank

Paper: wove paper

Running title: 'Recent Prose' (19–20mm.) on verso; recto title comprises title of prose item, pp.2–321

Binding: blue cloth. On spine, in gold: 'Recent | Prose | [ornament] | John | Masefield | HEINEMANN' (all width centred). On upper cover, in gold: 'RECENT PROSE | JOHN MASEFIELD' (within blind ruled border: 187 × 118mm.) On lower cover, in blind: publisher's device of a windmill (ranged lower right). All edges trimmed. Binding measurements: 189 × 122mm. (covers), 189 × 47mm. (spine). End-papers: wove paper.

Publication date: the sales ledger preserved in the Heinemann Archive suggests publication on 14 December 1932. The number of copies printed is omitted.

Price: 7s.6d.

Contents:

pp.1–207 as for A73(a) and then with the following additional contents:

At Hereford ('I have now to thank you for the great and beautiful honour that you have paid me...')

Words for a Festival in the Honour of William Butler Yeats, Poet. ('When we built this room for the service of poetry...')

Chaucer ('I am to talk to you for an hour about Geoffrey Chaucer, the first of the three great...')

Shakespeare and Spiritual Life ('Vice-Chancellor, Heads, Professors, and Members of this University, and you...')

William Blake ('I am to speak of William Blake. You all have some knowledge of Blake.')

George Crabbe ('I have been asked to speak to you about George Crabbe the poet, who died as Rector here...')

Notes:

This volume comprises a revised edition, expanding the contents of the 1924 volume. The additional pieces included *Words Spoken to the Right Worshipful The Mayor The Councillors and Aldermen of Hereford on Thursday, October 23rd 1930* (see A102), *Words Spoken... at a Festival designed in Honour of William Butler Yeats, Poet* (see A103), *Shakespeare and Spiritual Life* (see A74), *Chaucer* (see A104) and other pieces published for the first time.

In 1927 Masefield suggested to Heinemann that the time might be 'ripe for revising and re-issuing Recent Prose' (John Masefield, letter to C.S. Evans, [10 October 1927]) (Archives of William Heinemann). It was not until 1932 that the volume was planned.

All items commence with a drop-capital.

In April 1932 Masefield suggested the inclusion of *Poetry* (see A106) in this revised edition. C.S. Evans wrote that he was '...strongly of the opinion that we should not include POETRY in RECENT PROSE – for the time being at any rate. We still have several thousand copies in stock...' (see C.S. Evans, letter to John Masefield, 7 April 1932) (HRHRC, MS (Masefield, J.) Recip William Heinemann Ltd.)

C.S. Evans wrote to Masefield at the beginning of August 1932 noting:

> ...I gave instructions that the additional material for the new edition of RECENT PROSE should be put at the end for two reasons. First, because that seemed to me to be its logical position, assuming that the work was in chronological order and secondly because we have about 500 copies of the first edition of RECENT PROSE... ...so it occurred to me that I would bind up the remainder of 500 copies with the new material and so use them as part of the new edition.
>
> (C.S. Evans, letter to John Masefield, 9 August 1932)
> (HRHRC, MS (Masefield, J.) Recip William Heinemann Ltd.)

Several examined copies indeed suggest that this 'new and revised edition' uses gatherings B-N from A73(a). Approximately 500 copies therefore had gatherings [A] and O-X added to unsold stock of A73(a). The Heinemann archive omits information relating to the number of copies printed.

A 'full set of corrected proofs together with your first proofs from which we have made the revised, of RECENT PROSE' were sent to Masefield on 16 August 1932 (see A.J. Woods, letter to John Masefield, 16 August 1932) (HRHRC, MS (Masefield, J.) Recip William Heinemann Ltd.) Masefield was sent an advance copy four days before publication:

> I think you will like to have this advance copy of RECENT PROSE which we are publishing on December 14th.
>
> (C.S. Evans, letter to John Masefield, 10 December 1932)
> (HRHRC, MS (Masefield, J.) Recip William Heinemann Ltd.)

The date of publication given on p.[iv] is contrary to information provided in the *English Catalogue of Books* and the Heinemann archive. The copy in the British Library (stamped 14 DEC 1932) suggests the later date is correct.

There are two sub-titles to pieces within the volume. 'At Hereford' is sub-titled '*Words spoken to the Right Worshipful the Mayor, the Councillors and Aldermen of Hereford, on Thursday, October* 23rd, 1930'. 'George Crabbe' is sub-titled 'A *Lecture given at Trowbridge, in Wiltshire, on February 3rd*, 1932'.

Copies seen: private collection (ROV); BL (012274.aa.3) rebound, stamped 14 DEC 1932

Reprinted:
'Reprinted'   [second edition, second impression]   Apr 1933

A73(c) First American edition (1933)

RECENT PROSE[point]BY | JOHN MASEFIELD | [ornament] | NEW YORK | THE MACMILLAN COMPANY | 1933
(All width centred)

Bibliographies: Handley-Taylor p.54, Wight [unrecorded]

Collation: [A-T]⁸ (±[A]2) (J not used) (see notes); 152 leaves; 190 × 130mm.; [i–x] 1–141 [142] 143–61 [162] 163–87 [188] 189–91 [192] 193–97 [198] 199–223 [224] 225–94

Page contents: [i] half-title: 'RECENT PROSE'; [ii] '*By* | JOHN MASEFIELD | [43 titles separated by dashes]'; [iii] title-page; [iv] 'COPYRIGHT, 1915, 1923, 1924, 1931, and 1933, | BY JOHN MASEFIELD. | [rule] | All rights reserved–no part of this book | may be reproduced in any form without | permission in writing from the publisher, | except by a reviewer who wishes to quote brief | passages in connection with a review written | for inclusion in magazine or newspaper. | [rule] | Set up and printed. Published January, 1933. | PRINTED IN THE UNITED STATES OF AMERICA | BY STRATFORD PRESS, INC., NEW YORK'; [v] 'PUBLISHER'S NOTE | Some of the material now collected under the title | of *Recent Prose* has been previously published. "The | Taking of Helen," "Letters," "Play-Writing," and | "Fox-Hunting" appeared in a volume entitled *The | Taking of Helen and Other Prose Selections*. The | essays on "Chaucer" and "John M. Synge" were is- | sued as separate books. The other sections have never before been published in book form.'; [vi] blank; [vii] 'CONTENTS' (11 individual items listed with page references); [viii] blank; [ix] 'RECENT PROSE'; [x] blank; 1–94 text of 'The Taking of Helen'; 95–104 text of 'Letters'; 105–141 text of 'Play-Writing'; [142] blank; 143–61 text of 'Fox-Hunting'; [162] blank; 163–87 text of 'John M. Synge'; [188] blank; 189–91 text of 'At Hereford'; [192] blank; 193–97 text of 'Words for a Festival in the Honour of William Butler Yeats, Poet.'; [198] blank; 199–223 text of 'Chaucer'; [224] blank; 225–56 text of 'Shakespeare and Spiritual Life'; 257–78 text of 'William Blake'; 279–94 text of 'George Crabbe'

Paper: wove paper

Running title: 'RECENT PROSE [33mm.] | [rule, 81mm.]' on verso; recto title comprises title of prose item (with rule), pp.2–294

Binding: dark green cloth. On spine, in gold: '*RECENT | PROSE* | [swirling line ornament within ruled border: 15 × 32mm.] | MASEFIELD | MACMILLAN | [point]' (all width centred). On upper cover, in gold: '*RECENT | PROSE* | [swirling line ornament within ruled border: 15 × 51mm.] | JOHN | MASEFIELD' (all width centred). Lower cover: blank. Top edge trimmed, others roughly trimmed. Binding measurements: 196 × 130mm. (covers), 196 × 44mm. (spine). End-papers: wove paper.

Publication date: published, according to Handley-Taylor, 24 January 1933

Price: $2.50

Contents:
The Taking of Helen ('Nireus was the son of the King of Symé Island. At his birth the gods brought gifts to him...')
Letters ('NIAGARA | All the way, I had remembered the tales of the roar...')
Play-Writing ('Last week, I was talking about story-writing, which, within the limits of a reader's endurance...')
Fox-Hunting ('I have been asked to write why I wrote my poem of *Reynard the Fox*.')
John M. Synge ('I first met John M. Synge at the room of a common friend...')
At Hereford ('I have now to thank you for the great and beautiful honour that you have paid me...')
Words for a Festival in the Honour of William Butler Yeats, Poet. ('When we built this room for the service of poetry...')
Chaucer ('I am to talk to you for an hour about Geoffrey Chaucer, the first of the three great...')
Shakespeare and Spiritual Life ('Vice-Chancellor, Heads, Professors, and Members of this University, and you...')
William Blake ('I am to speak of William Blake. You all have some knowledge of Blake.')
George Crabbe ('I have been asked to speak to you about George Crabbe the poet, who died as Rector here...')

Notes:
The cancel title (±[A]2) is not present in all copies.

Page numbers appear within square brackets. Thus, [1], [2], etc.

There are two sub-titles to pieces within the volume. 'At Hereford' is sub-titled '*Words spoken to the Right Worshipful the Mayor, the Councillors and Aldermen of Hereford, on Thursday, October* 23rd, 1930'. 'George Crabbe' is sub-titled '*A Lecture given at Trowbridge, in Wiltshire, on February 3rd*, 1932.'

This edition comprises the first American edition of *Recent Prose*. The advertising preliminaries in the 1927 regular Macmillan edition of *Tristan and Isolt* (see A85(d)) appear to have been taken from an English source. Consequently, *Recent Prose* is listed, but this is an error.

The text has been entirely reset for this edition.

A publishing agreement for this title between Masefield and Macmillan was dated 9 May 1932 (see Archives of The Society of Authors). The agreement refers to 'a licence to publish in volume form… in the United States of America and Canada a work the subject or title of which is a volume of recent prose with approximately 25,000 words of new matters, consisting largely of speeches and lectures on Poets and Poetry by the author (exact title to be determined)'.

Copies seen: private collection (PWE); private collection (ROV)

A74 SHAKESPEARE AND SPIRITUAL LIFE 1924

A74(a) First English edition (1924)

Shakespeare | & | Spiritual Life | by | JOHN MASEFIELD | HON. D.LITT. | *The Romanes Lecture* | Delivered in the Sheldonian Theatre | 4 June, 1924 | OXFORD | AT THE CLARENDON PRESS | 1924
(All width centred)

Bibliographies: Simmons [62], Nevinson [unrecorded], Handley-Taylor p.54, Wight [62]

Collation: [A]^{16} (see notes); A2 and A5 are also signed; signatures centred at foot of page with '2844' at right foot on A2 and A5; 16 leaves; 222 × 144mm.; [1–3] 4–32

Page contents: [1] title-page; [2] 'Oxford University Press | *London Edinburgh Glasgow Copenhagen* | *New York Toronto Melbourne Cape Town* | *Bombay Calcutta Madras Shanghai* | Humphrey Milford Publisher to the UNIVERSITY | Printed in England'; [3]–32 text (at foot of p.32: 'Printed in England at the Oxford University Press')

Paper: laid paper (no watermark), chain-lines 26mm. apart

Running title: 'SHAKESPEARE AND' (42mm.) on verso; 'SPIRITUAL LIFE' (35mm.) on recto, pp.4–31; 'SHAKESPEARE AND SPIRITUAL LIFE' (78mm.) appears on p.32

Binding: grey wrappers. Spine: blank. On upper wrapper, in navy blue: 'Shakespeare | & | Spiritual Life | by | JOHN MASEFIELD | HON. D.LITT. | *The Romanes Lecture* | Delivered in the Sheldonian Theatre | 4 June, 1924 | OXFORD | AT THE CLARENDON PRESS | 1924'. Lower wrapper: blank. Top edge trimmed, others untrimmed. Binding measurements: 227 × 151mm. (wrappers), 227 × 3mm. (spine). The wrappers extend beyond the edges of the internal leaves.

Publication date: published, according to Simmons, 5 June 1924 in an edition of 4000 copies

Price: 2s.

Contents:
Shakespeare and Spiritual Life ('Vice-Chancellor, Heads, Professors, and Members of this University, and you…')

Notes:
The text of the Romanes lecture delivered by Masefield in the Sheldonian Theatre, Oxford on 4 June 1924. The text was reprinted in the 1932 revised edition of *Recent Prose* (see A73(b)).

Simmons describes the gatherings as '[A]-E by fours, first leaf of [A] and last two leaves of E blank'. This presumably comprises a variant state. Wight notes [A]^{16} but then curiously states 'in effect, this is two octavos, one inside the other'.

Copies seen: private collection (PWE); NYPL (Berg Collection)

Reprinted:
'Second Impression'   [first edition, second impression]   1924

A74(aa) First English edition (limited signed edition) (1924)

Shakespeare | & | Spiritual Life | by | JOHN MASEFIELD | HON. D.LITT. | *The Romanes Lecture* | Delivered in the Sheldonian Theatre | 4 June, 1924 | OXFORD | AT THE CLARENDON PRESS | 1924
(All width centred)

Bibliographies: Simmons [62a], Nevinson [unrecorded], Handley-Taylor p.54, Wight [62a]

Collation: [A]^4 B-E^4; signatures right foot of page; 20 leaves; 231 × 143mm.; [i–iv] [1–3] 4–32 [33–36]

Page contents: [i–ii] blank; [iii] half-title: 'Shakespeare | & | Spiritual Life'; [iv] '*200 copies printed on | hand-made paper*'; [1] title-page; [2] 'Oxford University Press | *London Edinburgh Glasgow Copenhagen* | *New York Toronto Melbourne Cape Town* | *Bombay Calcutta Madras Shanghai* | Humphrey Milford Publisher to the UNIVERSITY | Printed in England'; [3]–32 text (at foot of p.32: 'Printed in England at the Oxford University Press'); [33–36] blank

Paper: laid paper (watermark: indecipherable motif including figure balancing on a ball and 'VAN GELDER ZONEN'), chain-lines 28mm. apart

Running title: 'SHAKESPEARE AND' (42mm.) on verso; 'SPIRITUAL LIFE' (35mm.) on recto, pp.4–31; 'SHAKESPEARE AND SPIRITUAL LIFE' (78mm.) appears on p.32

Binding: blue-grey wrappers. Spine: blank. On upper wrapper, in navy blue: 'Shakespeare | & | Spiritual Life | by | JOHN MASEFIELD | HON. D.LITT. | *The Romanes Lecture* | Delivered in the Sheldonian Theatre | 4 June, 1924 | OXFORD | AT THE CLARENDON PRESS | 1924'. Lower wrapper: blank. Top edge uncut, others untrimmed. Binding measurements: 233 × 149mm. (wrappers), 233 × 5mm. (spine). The wrappers extend beyond the edges of the internal leaves.

Publication date: published, according to Simmons, 5 June 1924

Price: 10s.6d.

Contents:
as for A74(a)

Notes:
The edition is not numbered, but merely signed by the author.

Copies seen: BL (11766.cc.30) inscribed 'John Masefield.' on p.[iv] stamped 18 JUN 1924; NYPL (Berg Collection) inscribed 'John Masefield.' on p.[iv]

A74(b) First American edition (1924)

Shakespeare | & | Spiritual Life | by | JOHN MASEFIELD | HON. D.LITT. | *The Romanes Lecture* | Delivered in the Sheldonian Theatre | 4 June, 1924 | NEW YORK | OXFORD UNIVERSITY PRESS | AMERICAN BRANCH: 35 WEST 32ND STREET | LONDON TORONTO MELBOURNE BOMBAY | 1924
(The '*T*' of '*The*' is swash)
(All width centred)

Bibliographies: Simmons [unrecorded], Nevinson [unrecorded], Handley-Taylor[unrecorded], Wight 62b

Collation: [A]¹⁶; A2 and A5 are also signed; signatures centred at foot of page with '2844' at right foot on A2 and A5; 16 leaves; 223 × 143mm.; [1–3] 4–32

Page contents: [1] title-page; [2] 'COPYRIGHT, 1924, | BY OXFORD UNIVERSITY PRESS | AMERICAN BRANCH | PRINTED IN THE UNITED STATES OF AMERICA'; [3]–32 text

Paper: laid paper (no watermark), chain-lines 25mm. apart

Running title: 'SHAKESPEARE AND' (43mm.) on verso; 'SPIRITUAL LIFE' (37mm.) on recto, pp.4–31; 'SHAKESPEARE AND SPIRITUAL LIFE' (81mm.) appears on p.32

Binding: grey wrappers. Spine: blank. On upper wrapper, in navy blue: 'Shakespeare | & | Spiritual Life | by | JOHN MASEFIELD | HON. D.LITT. | *The Romanes Lecture* | Delivered in the Sheldonian Theatre | 4 June, 1924 | NEW YORK | OXFORD UNIVERSITY PRESS | AMERICAN BRANCH: 35 WEST 32ND STREET | LONDON TORONTO MELBOURNE BOMBAY | 1924' (The '*T*' of '*The*' is swash). Lower wrapper: blank. Top edge trimmed, others untrimmed. Binding measurements: 228 × 150mm. (wrappers), 228 × 3mm. (spine). The wrappers extend beyond the edges of the internal leaves.

Publication date: after 1 July 1924 (see notes)

Price: $0.75

Contents:
as for A74(a)

Notes:
Despite similarities in the setting of type, this American edition constitutes an entirely new setting. Presumably it was set from a copy of the English edition. Note, for example, different measurements for the running title from A74(a). The swash '*T*' in '*The*' on the title-page and upper wrapper is unique to this American edition. The type used for the signatures also reveals differences.

Wight (who is the only Masefield bibliographer to note this edition) incorrectly cites a publication date (from Simmons) of 5 June 1924. This edition appears in a catalogue issued by the American branch of Oxford University Press in July 1925 noting books published since 1 July 1924

Copies seen: NYPL (Berg Collection)

A75 SARD HARKER   1924

A75(a) First English edition (1924)

SARD HARKER | A NOVEL | By | JOHN MASEFIELD | [publisher's device of a windmill with the letters 'W' and 'H' all within ruled border: 19 × 20mm.] | LONDON | WILLIAM HEINEMANN LTD.
(All width centred)

Bibliographies: Simmons [63], Nevinson p.17, Handley-Taylor p.55, Wight [63]

Collation: A¹⁰ B-W⁸ (J and V not used); A2 is also signed; signatures left foot of page; 170 leaves; 187 × 120mm.; [i–viii] [1] 2–70 [71] 72–110 [111] 112–252 [253] 254–332

Page contents: [i] blank; [ii] 'NOTE | ALL the persons and events described in this book | are imaginary. No reference is made to any living | person. | JOHN MASEFIELD'; [iii] half-title: 'SARD HARKER'; [iv] 'THE COLLECTED POEMS | OF JOHN MASEFIELD | In One Volume. 750 pages. | Cr. 8vo. 8s. 6d. net. | SELECTIONS FROM MASEFIELD | Fcap. 8vo. | Cloth, 6s.; Leather, 8s. 6d. net.'; [v] title-page; [vi] '*First Published 1924 | Printed in Great Britain by* | THE LONDON AND NORWICH PRESS, LIMITED, ST. GILES' WORKS, NORWICH'; [vii] '*To | Isaline and Henry Philpot* '; [viii] blank; [1]–332 text (at foot of p.332: '[rule] | THE LONDON AND NORWICH PRESS, LIMITED, ST. GILES' WORKS, NORWICH')

Paper: wove paper

Running title: 'SARD HARKER' (44mm.) on both recto and verso, pp.2–332

Binding: blue cloth. On spine, in gold: 'SARD | HARKER | [ornament] | JOHN | MASEFIELD | HEINEMANN' (all width centred). On upper cover, in gold: 'SARD HARKER | JOHN MASEFIELD' (within blind ruled border: 190 × 119mm.) Lower cover: blank. Top edge stained blue, fore edge trimmed, lower outside edge untrimmed. Binding measurements: 196 × 123mm. (covers), 196 × 44mm. (spine). End-papers: wove paper.

Publication date: published, according to Simmons, 9 October 1924 in an edition of 10000 copies

Price: 7s.6d.

Contents:
Sard Harker ('Santa Barbara lies far to leeward, with a coast facing to the north and east. It is the richest...')

Notes:
The first full-length novel Masefield had published since 1911, the work is set in Masefield's fictional American republic of Santa Barbara. The tale tells of Sard's quest for a girl who he had only fleetingly glimpsed. The pair fall into the hands of a demonic mystic but are saved from torture and sacrifice moments before it is too late. Muriel Spark considered the novel allegorical and concluded it was 'a kind of secular *Pilgrim's Progress*'.

The text is in four parts. Each part commences with a drop-capital.

J. Henry Philpot (1850–1939), one of the dedicatees of the novel, was a physician and author (under both his own name and that of 'Philip Lafargue'). The other dedicatee was his wife, Isaline Philpot (née Needham) who died in 1925.

The Heinemann firm wrote to Masefield on 5 August 1924 to acknowledge receipt of the manuscript (see William Heinemann Ltd., letter to John Masefield, 5 August 1924) (HRHRC, MS (Masefield, J.) Recip William Heinemann Ltd.) C.S. Evans wrote, after reading the novel:

> I have been away for a short holiday and when I returned to the office yesterday, I was told that the manuscript of SARD HARKER had arrived. I took it home with me last night and began to read it... I have got far enough to be sure that you have written a masterpiece. SARD HARKER has held me entranced, and I do not remember when I have been so thrilled. There is everything in it to charm even the most blasé novel reader – humanity, adventure and thrilling incident; and besides this, there is a beauty and simplicity of style which even you have never before attained. It is indeed difficult for me to find words to express my enthusiasm for the book. I prophecy a very great success for it. I want to bring out the book as quickly as I can so as to give it a good run before Christmas, and have already tentatively fixed a date for it – September 13th.
>
> (C.S. Evans, letter to John Masefield, 8 August 1924)
> (HRHRC, MS (Masefield, J.) Recip William Heinemann Ltd.)

(This date was later revised). In the same letter Evans suggested that Heinemann might issue 'a small limited edition of the book' (see notes to A75(b)). Prior to publication, a fire at Heinemann's binders led Evans to reassure Masefield:

> You will no doubt have seen in the newspapers the account of the disastrous fire at Burns, our binders. A great deal of our new stock has gone, but I am glad to tell you that SARD HARKER is all right...
>
> (C.S. Evans, letter to John Masefield, 12 September 1924)
> (HRHRC, MS (Masefield, J.) Recip William Heinemann Ltd.)

Although Evans had suggested the limited signed edition might be published first this idea was, evidently, abandoned. At the end of September Evans informed Masefield of the revised publication date:

> ...SARD HARKER is to be published on October 9th and I have sent out a great many press copies to-day. I hope and believe that it is going to have a gigantic success. We are putting every effort we can behind it because we all thoroughly believe in the book.
>
> (C.S. Evans, letter to John Masefield, 29 September 1924)
> (HRHRC, MS (Masefield, J.) Recip William Heinemann Ltd.)

Before publication Evans wrote to Masefield proudly noting subscription orders:

> …You will be glad to hear that although our subscriptions are not yet complete, we have already evidence enough to show that the first edition of 10,000 should be practically exhausted before publication. I have already put in hand a reprint of another 10,000 copies so that we shall not be out of the book for a single day.
>
> (C.S. Evans, letter to John Masefield, 1 October 1924)
> (HRHRC, MS (Masefield, J.) Recip William Heinemann Ltd.)

Evans took pride in informing Masefield of other positive comments:

> I expect you are already tired of hearing eulogies of the book but I cannot resist quoting from a letter I have received from Latham of the Macmillan Company this morning:-
> "I agree with you in thinking that this is one of the finest romances written in our generation. I do not know when I have been so keen for a story of this type. We are going after it in a big way, and hope to put it over to the wide circulation which it unquestionably deserves."
>
> (C.S. Evans, letter to John Masefield, 6 October 1924)
> (HRHRC, MS (Masefield, J.) Recip William Heinemann Ltd.)

The publishing agreement for this title between Masefield and Heinemann was dated 30 August 1924 (see Archives of The Society of Authors). The agreement refers to a publication price of 7s.6d.

After publication The Society of Authors received enquiries about rights to dramatise the novel. Masefield replied to the Society and revealed much about the initial conception of the novel:

> I do not feel inclined to have *Sard Harker* dramatised at present. I wrote it first as a play + have two versions of it as a play already by me, + though I do not like either I like them better than I should like another man's attempt. So I think the matter had better rest. I can at any time perform my versions here, if I wish to see how the thing looks, but at present I think S.H. is a story, not a play.
>
> (John Masefield, letter to G.H. Thring, ([16 December 1924])
> (BL, Add.Mss.56580, f.207)

The location implied in the reference to performing his versions is presumably to Masefield's 'Music Room' theatre at Boars Hill. No performance seems to have taken place.

In a letter to Vivien Dayrell-Browning dated 29 March 1926, Graham Greene refers to a possible film of Masefield's novel:

> In the carriage with me are Mr & Mrs Masefield & Judith Masefield! Judith Masefield's extraordinarily plain close to! Mrs is looking vivacious. John is snoozing with folded hands. If *I'd just sold the film rights of Sard Harker for £10,000 I'd go first class*!! He looks utterly miserable & bullied, poor little man...
>
> (Norman Sherry, The Life of Graham Greene Volume One: 1904–1939, Cape, 1989, pp.311–12)

Enquiries to The Society of Authors regarding film rights commenced soon after publication of the novel. Masefield appears to have started making conditions at an early stage which might have contributed to the failure of any potential projects. Writing to The Society of Authors in December 1924 Masefield states:

> I do insist that the filmer, if they film the ship, the *Pathfinder*, film a real clipper ship... They are apt to film the nearest coal-barge or schooner, which is not quite the same thing.
>
> (John Masefield, letter to G.H. Thring, [December 1924])
> (BL, Add.Mss.56580, f.212)

During the late 1960s advanced plans for a film came to nothing. A database maintained by the British Film Institute holds no record of a film being made of the novel.

Writing to Vivien Dayrell-Browning in a letter dated 21 April 1926, Graham Greene states:

> *Sard Harker* would have been the greatest adventure story in the language if it hadn't got the absurd ending.
>
> (Norman Sherry, *The Life of Graham Greene Volume One: 1904–1939*, Cape, 1989, p.312)

Three decades after publication a proposed adaptation of the novel in South Africa prompted Masefield to write to The Society of Authors stating:

> ...my tale is a shade tangled at the start... Sard was to have been but 1 book out of 4 or 5 so I made a leisurely approach.
>
> (John Masefield, letter to Miss P. Whishaw, 14 September [1954])
> (BL, Add.Mss.56625 ff.132–133)

The archives of The Society of Authors record that an application to publish a Braille version of this text was received from the National Library for the Blind in June 1926 (see BL, Add.Mss.56583, f.40).

Copies seen: private collection (PWE) inscribed 'For | C.E. Reeves, | from | John Masefield. | [sketch of ship] | She crosses a main skysail: her jib boom | Is one steel spike, her mainsail has a | spread | Of eighty seven feet, earring to earring: | Her wind is a fresh gale, her joy careering | Some two points free before it, nought ahead | But sea, + the gale roaring + blown spume.'; BL (NN.10261) stamped 9 OCT 1924; Columbia University Libraries (Special Collections B825.M377.W53.1924c) inscribed 'For | Hugh Walpole, | from | John Masefield. | October. 1924.' (illustrated on p.54 of Handley-Taylor)

THE
COLLECTED POEMS
OF
JOHN MASEFIELD

LONDON: WILLIAM HEINEMANN LTD.

A71(b) title-page

Shakespeare
&
Spiritual Life

by

JOHN MASEFIELD
HON. D.LITT.

The Romanes Lecture
Delivered in the Sheldonian Theatre
4 June, 1924

OXFORD
AT THE CLARENDON PRESS
1924

A74(a) title-page

SARD HARKER

A NOVEL

BY
JOHN MASEFIELD

LONDON
WILLIAM HEINEMANN LTD.
1924

A75(b) title-page

SARD HARKER

By
JOHN MASEFIELD

New York
THE MACMILLAN COMPANY
1924
All rights reserved

A75(c) title-page

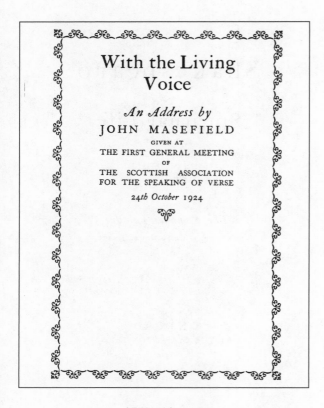

With the Living
Voice

An Address by
JOHN MASEFIELD
GIVEN AT
THE FIRST GENERAL MEETING
OF
THE SCOTTISH ASSOCIATION
FOR THE SPEAKING OF VERSE

24th October 1924

A76(a) title-page

WITH
THE LIVING VOICE
by
JOHN MASEFIELD

An Address
given at the First General Meeting
of
THE SCOTTISH ASSOCIATION FOR
THE SPEAKING OF VERSE
24th October
1924

LONDON
WILLIAM HEINEMANN LTD
1925

A76(c) title-page

THE TRIAL OF
JESUS

BY
JOHN MASEFIELD

LONDON
WILLIAM HEINEMANN LTD.

A77(a) title-page

THE
TRIAL OF JESUS

BY

JOHN MASEFIELD

LONDON
WILLIAM HEINEMANN LTD
1925

A77(c) title-page

272

Reprinted:

Reprints of this work are confusing and numerous. Different reprints cite variations in reprint dates. It has also proven problematic to decide the dates of reset texts (and therefore subsequent editions). The New Windmill Series edition (see A75(e)) notes 'reprinted thirteen times' before publication within the series. The following conflates several listings:

'New Impression'	[first edition, second impression]	Oct 1924
	[first edition, third impression]	Oct 1924
	[first edition, fourth impression]	Nov 1924
'New Impression'	[first edition, fifth impression]	Dec 1924
'Popular edition'		Jul 1926
		1928
		Apr 1931
		Mar 1934
		Sep 1935
		1936
'New Edition'		1938
		1939
		1944

The 'Popular edition' published, according to the *English Catalogue of Books*, during July 1926 was priced at 3s.6d and issued in red cloth. The issue uses the standard setting of text. The publishing agreement for this issue between Masefield and Heinemann was dated 18 June 1926 (see Archives of The Society of Authors). The agreement refers to a publication price of 3s.6d.

A75(b) Second English edition (limited signed edition) (1924)

SARD HARKER [in red] | A NOVEL | BY | JOHN MASEFIELD | [publisher's device of a windmill with the letters 'W' and 'H' all within ruled border: 19 × 20mm.] | LONDON | WILLIAM HEINEMANN LTD. | 1924
(All width centred)

Bibliographies: Simmons [63a], Nevinson [unrecorded], Handley-Taylor p.55, Wight [63a]

Collation: [π]⁴ A⁶ B–W⁸ (J and V not used); A2 is also signed; signatures left foot of page; 170 leaves; 222 × 142mm.; [i–viii] [1] 2–70 [71] 72–110 [111] 112–252 [253] 254–332

Page contents: [i–ii] blank; [iii] half-title: 'SARD HARKER'; [iv] '*This edition of SARD HARKER is | limited to* 380 *copies, of which* 350 | *are for sale. | This is No.* ....'; [v] title-page; [vi] '*Printed in Great Britain by* | THE LONDON AND NORWICH PRESS, LIMITED, ST. GILES' WORKS, NORWICH'; [vii] '*To | Isaline and Henry Philpot*'; [viii] blank; [1]–332 text (at foot of p.332: '[rule] | THE LONDON AND NORWICH PRESS, LIMITED, ST. GILES' WORKS, NORWICH')

Paper: laid paper (no watermark) chain-lines 28mm. apart (the chain-lines run horizontally throughout the volume)

Running title: 'SARD HARKER' (44mm.) on both recto and verso, pp.2–332

Binding: blue-green boards with parchment spine. On spine, in gold: 'SARD | HARKER | [ornament] | JOHN | MASEFIELD | HEINEMANN' (all width centred). There is a single vertical rule in blind on each cover at the edge of the parchment. Covers: blank. Top edge gilt, lower outside edge untrimmed, fore edge uncut. Sewn head band (in blue and white) and blue marker ribbon. Binding measurements: 229 × 143mm. (covers), 229 × 44mm. (spine). End-papers: laid paper (watermark: 'ANTIQUE DE LUXE'), chain-lines 25mm. apart.

Publication date: published, according to Simmons, 24 October 1924

Price: 30s.

Contents:
as for A75(a)

Notes:
Each part commences with a drop-capital.

Simmons notes in his bibliography:

> Page 181, line 31, the word "not" is omitted. "Because if you have ten plunks" should read: "Because if you have not ten plunks".

This textual error is also present in A75(a) and A75(c) and is therefore not unique to the limited signed edition, as Simmons seems to imply.

Having read the manuscript, C.S. Evans wrote to Masefield expressing enthusiasm for the author's 'masterpiece', At the same time he started discussion of a limited signed edition:

> …I am wondering whether it is wise to issue a small limited edition of the book, but I have not yet been able to make up my mind about this.

(C.S. Evans, letter to John Masefield, 8 August 1924)
(HRHRC, MS (Masefield, J.) Recip William Heinemann Ltd.)

At the end of August, Evans wrote again proposing that the limited signed edition would comprise the true first edition:

> …We have, after all, decided to do a small limited edition of SARD HARKER. 350 copies at about 30/-. Our sales department have no doubt at all that all these will be subscribed before publication, particularly as we are going to make this limited edition the <u>first</u> edition of the work and will state this fact in the docquet notice. I have decided on this because there are a certain number of people who always collect your first editions and the first printing of the ordinary edition of SARD HARKER will be 10,000 copies which is too large an edition to make copies valuable. We shall therefore have all the first edition fans as potential customers for the limited edition. This will not mean any delay. We shall publish the limited edition on the Tuesday and the ordinary edition on the following Thursday and the ordinary edition will be marked on the fly leaf "Second Edition"…

(C.S. Evans, letter to John Masefield, 22 August 1924)
(HRHRC, MS (Masefield, J.) Recip William Heinemann Ltd.)

Four days later Evans noted that Heinemann '…have fixed the week ending September 27th tentatively for publication. The limited edition to be published on Tuesday and the ordinary edition on Thursday.' (see C.S. Evans, letter to John Masefield, 26 August 1924) (HRHRC, MS (Masefield, J.) Recip William Heinemann Ltd.) These plans were later revised and the standard trade edition was published before the limited signed edition.

Copies seen: private collection (PWE) number 338, signed '338 | John Masefield.' on p.[iv]; BL (012643.gg.2) number 353, signed '353 | John Masefield.' on p.[iv], stamped 24 OCT 1924

A75(c) First American edition (1924)

SARD HARKER | By | JOHN MASEFIELD | New York | THE MACMILLAN COMPANY | 1924 | *All rights reserved*
(All width centred)

Bibliographies: Simmons [noted on p.101], Nevinson [unrecorded], Handley-Taylor p.55, Wight 63b

Collation: [A-CC]⁸ (J, V and W not used); 208 leaves; 191 × 128mm.; [i–iv] [1–2] 3–87 [88–90] 91–138 [139–40] 141–313 [314–16] 317–412

Page contents: [i] half-title: 'SARD HARKER'; [ii] '*By* | JOHN MASEFIELD | [30 titles separated by 26 single points] | [point] [point] [point]'; [iii] title-page; [iv] 'COPYRIGHT 1924 | BY JOHN MASEFIELD | *Set Up* [point] *Electrotyped* [point] *Published* | *October* [point] 1924 | *Printed in the United States of America*'; [1] 'To | Isaline and Henry Philpot'; [2] blank; 3–87 text of part one; [88] blank; [89] 'PART TWO'; [90] blank; 91–138 text of part two; [139] 'PART THREE'; [140] blank; 141–313 text of part three; [314] blank; [315] 'PART FOUR'; [316] blank; 317–412 text of part four

Paper: wove paper

Running title: 'SARD HARKER' (40mm.) on both recto and verso, pp.4–412

Binding: crimson cloth. On spine: 'SARD | HARKER | [device] | JOHN | MASEFIELD [all in crimson on a gold panel] | MACMILLAN [in gold] | [point in gold] [point in gold] [point in gold]' (all width centred with the exception of the three points which are slightly off-set to the right). The gold panel is within a rope-like border: 41 × 31mm. On upper cover in crimson on a gold panel: 'SARD HARKER | [device] | JOHN MASEFIELD', the gold panel is within a rope-like border: 39 × 96mm. Lower cover: blank. Top edge trimmed, others untrimmed. Binding measurements: 197 × 129mm. (covers), 197 × 48mm. (spine). End-papers: wove paper.

Publication date: published, according to Simmons, 28 October 1924 in an edition of 4990 copies

Price: $2.50

Contents:
as for A75(a)

Notes:
The text has been entirely re-set for this edition.

Many of the letters in the italic type used in the preliminaries are swash.

A publishing agreement for this volume between Masefield and Macmillan was dated 25 January 1927 (see Archives of The Society of Authors). The agreement refers to 'a licence to publish in volume form… in the United States of America and Canada a work the subject or title of which is a prose tale, to contain approximately 40,000 words, the title to be agreed upon.'

The McClure Newspaper syndicate enquired about serial rights of *Sard Harker* in September 1925 (see BL, Add.Mss.56581, f.186). Masefield was willing to deal, however McClure were unwilling to accept his additional terms of £10 per thousand words (in addition to paying Masefield 50% of the gross proceeds from sales) (see BL, Add.Mss.56582, f.93). Negotiations continued however, before Masefield discovered McClure's proposals to be a publishing house acting as an author's agent and stated he 'would rather not proceed with the matter' (see BL, Add.Mss.56582, f.97). Masefield therefore demonstrates his loyalty to The Society of Authors, and also his propensity to negotiate for high fees.

Copies seen: private collection (PWE)

Reprinted:

	[first edition, second impression]	Jan 1926
	[first edition, third impression]	Mar 1931
'Reprinted'	[first edition, fourth impression]	Sep 1938

A75(d) Third English edition ["Wanderer Edition"] (1935)

SARD HARKER | A NOVEL | By | JOHN MASEFIELD | [publisher's device of a windmill with the letters 'W [point]' and 'H'] | LONDON | WILLIAM HEINEMANN LTD.
(All width centred)

Bibliographies: Handley-Taylor p.55, Wight [unrecorded]

Collation: [A]⁸ (±[A]1) B-U⁸ W¹⁰ (J and V not used); W2 is also signed; signatures right foot of page; 170 leaves; 189 × 125mm.; [i–viii] [1] 2–70 [71] 72–110 [111] 112–252 [253] 254–332

Page contents: [i] half-title: 'THE COLLECTED WORKS OF | JOHN MASEFIELD | [rule] | WANDERER EDITION | SARD HARKER'; [ii] '*ALSO BY JOHN MASEFIELD* | PLAYS: | [12 volumes listed] | POETRY: | [14 volumes listed] | FICTION: | [seven volumes listed] | GENERAL: | [nine volumes listed]'; [iii] title-page; [iv] '*First published October* 1924 | *Reprinted October, November, December* 1924 | *Popular Edition* (3s. 6d.) *July* 1926 | *Reprinted April* 1931, *March* 1934 | *September* 1935 | *Printed in Great Britain at the* | *Windmill Press, Kingswood, Surrey*'; [v] '*To* | *Isaline and Henry Philpot*'; [vi] blank; [vii] 'NOTE | ALL the persons and events described in this book | are imaginary. No reference is made to any living | person. | JOHN MASEFIELD'; [viii] blank; [1]–332 text

Paper: wove paper

Running title: 'SARD HARKER' (44mm.) on both recto and verso, pp.2–332

Binding: blue cloth. On spine, in gold: 'JOHN | MASEFIELD | SARD | HARKER | THE | WANDERER | EDITION | HEINEMANN' (all width centred). On upper cover, in gold: illustration of a cockerel: 32 × 24mm. (ranged lower right). On lower cover, in blind: publisher's device of a windmill (ranged lower right). Top edge gilt, others trimmed. Sewn head band (in blue) and blue marker ribbon. Binding measurements: 196 × 128mm. (covers), 196 × 45mm. (spine). End-papers: wove paper.

Publication date: published, according to Handley-Taylor, 21 October 1935

Price: 5s.

Contents:
as for A75(a)

Notes:
Each part commences with a drop-capital

The signatures are different from those in A75(a). This is curious as both editions carry only four leaves of preliminary material. The same setting of the text does, however, appear to have been used.

Signature 'G' is damaged as is the first numeral in the page numbering of p.160 and the last numeral in the page numbering of p.288.

The first leaf in the first gathering ([A]1) is a stub with a single leaf tipped-in as a cancellan. The new leaf includes note of the Wanderer edition and the rest of the volume appears to use the same setting of type as A75(a).

The publishing agreement for 'a collected edition of the Author's work', including this title, between Masefield and Heinemann was dated 31 July 1935 (see Archives of The Society of Authors). The agreement refers to 'a published price of 5/-...' (see note on collected editions).

Copies seen: private collection (ROV); BL (12452.i.3) rebound, stamped 23 OCT 1935

A75(e) Fourth English edition ["The New Windmill Series"] (1956)

SARD HARKER | A NOVEL | BY | JOHN MASEFIELD | *With illustrations by* | *A. R. THOMSON, R.A.* | [publisher's device of a windmill with 'W' and 'H'] | [rule, 56mm.] | WILLIAM HEINEMANN LTD | MELBOURNE :: LONDON :: TORONTO
(All width centred)

Bibliographies: Handley-Taylor p.55, Wight [unrecorded]

Collation: [A]¹⁶ B-H¹⁶ I¹⁸; I2 and I6 are also signed; signatures right foot of page; 146 leaves; 183 × 120mm.; [i–vi] 1–285 [286]; illustrations (on glossy paper) tipped-in on pp.[iii], 125, 167 and 210

Page contents: [i] half-title: 'THE NEW WINDMILL SERIES | *General Editor:* Ian Serraillier | SARD HARKER'; [ii] 'THE NEW WINDMILL SERIES | *General Editor:* Ian Serraillier | [30 titles and their authors listed]'; [iii] title-page (with additional leaf tipped-in on the verso of which is the frontispiece: 158 × 101mm., 'For a moment he stared at Sard along the line of the blade | (*Page 279*)'); [iv] 'FIRST PUBLISHED OCTOBER 1924 | REPRINTED THIRTEEN TIMES | FIRST PUBLISHED IN THE NEW WINDMILL SERIES | 1956 | PUBLISHED BY | WILLIAM HEINEMANN LTD | 99 GREAT RUSSELL STREET, LONDON, W.C.I | PRINTED IN GREAT BRITAIN BY THE PUBLISHERS AT | THE WINDMILL PRESS, KINGSWOOD, SURREY'; [v] '*To* | *Isaline and Henry Philpot* | NOTE | ALL the persons and events described in this book are | imaginary. No reference is made to any living person. | JOHN MASEFIELD'; [vi] 'ILLUSTRATIONS' (four illustrations listed with titles and page references); 1–285 text; [286] blank

Paper: wove paper

Running title: none

Binding: orange cloth. On spine: 'SARD | HARKER | JOHN | MASEFIELD | [publisher's device of a windmill]' (all width centred). On upper cover: 'SARD HARKER | [illustration of man wading through swamp: 53 × 56mm.] | John Masefield'. Lower cover: blank. All edges trimmed. Binding measurements: 190 × 122mm. (covers), 190 × 28mm. (spine). End-papers: wove paper.

Publication date: published, according to Handley-Taylor, 30 July 1956

Price: 5s.6d.

Contents:
as for A75(a)

Notes:
Each part commences with a drop-capital

The setting of the type appears to use essentially the standard Heinemann setting from at least the 1940s. A comparison with the 1944 Heinemann reprint reveals the same setting of type. The difference, however, occurs in spacing of the text for the New Windmill Edition is more heavily leaded.

See notes to the 'New Windmill Series' edition of *The Bird of Dawning* (A111(f)) for a note on delays in printing.

Copies seen: private collection (PWE); private collection (ROV)

A75(f) Fifth English edition (1963)

SARD HARKER | [rule (tapered at each end), 75mm.] | A NOVEL BY | JOHN MASEFIELD | PENGUIN BOOKS
(All width centred)

Bibliographies: Wight [unrecorded]

Collation: [A]¹⁶ B-I¹⁶; signatures left foot of page; 144 leaves; 180 × 111mm.; [1–6] 7–64 [65] 66–98 [99] 100–218 [219] 220–85 [286–88]

Page contents: [1] half-title: 'PENGUIN BOOKS | 1955 | SARD HARKER | JOHN MASEFIELD | [publisher's device of a penguin within single ruled oval border]'; [2] blank; [3] title-page; [4] 'Penguin Books Ltd, Harmondsworth, Middlesex | U.S.A.: Penguin Books Inc., 3300 Clipper Mill Road, Baltimore 11, Md | AUSTRALIA: Penguin Books Pty Ltd, 762 Whitehorse Road, | Mitcham, Victoria | [rule] | First published by Heinemann 1924 | Published in Penguin Books 1963 | Copyright © John Masefield, 1924 | [rule] | Made and printed in Great Britain | by Cox & Wyman Ltd | London, Fakenham and Reading | Set in Monotype Plantin | This book is sold subject to the condition | that it shall not, by way of trade, be lent, | re-sold, hired out, or otherwise disposed | of without the publisher's consent | in any form of binding or cover | other than that in which | it is published'; [5] 'TO | ISALINE AND HENRY PHILPOT'; [6] blank; 7-[286] text; [287–88] blank

Paper: wove paper

Running title: none

Binding: white wrappers (printed orange). On orange spine, reading lengthways down spine from head: 'John Masefield [in white] Sard Harker [in black]', horizontally at foot of spine: '[publisher's device of a penguin within single ruled oval border] [in black and white] | 1955 [in black]'. On upper wrapper: '[publisher's device of a penguin within single ruled oval border] a Penguin Book 4/- | [rule] | Sard Harker | [rule] | John Masefield | [rule] | [illustration of man with flowers in brown, orange and white]'. On lower wrapper: '[publisher's device of a penguin within single ruled oval border] a Penguin Book | [rule] | Sard Harker | *Sard Harker*, published two years before | *Odtaa*, is one of the Poet Laureate's | early novels of romance and adventure. | The story is set in the swamps and | mountains of a blood-soaked South | American dictatorship. | [new paragraph] As *Punch* wrote: | 'Even the most case-hardened reader of | novels will surely find his breath being | caught in the rush and glitter of Mr John | Masefield's superb story of adventure, | *Sard Harker*. The narrative of the sailor's | blind pursuit of a dream which changed | and mocked him at every turn is | informed with that rarest of fine qualities | in literature – the truly romantic.' | [new paragraph] 'A book to read once at speed for the | thrill and glory of adventure, and again | leisurely for its great art. Nothing in | Mr Masefield's earlier novels is so good, | so finely written, or so breathlessly | readable' – Rose Macaulay'. On inside of upper wrapper: '[black and white photograph of Masefield] | John Masefield, who has been Poet Laureate since 1930, | was born in Ledbury, Herefordshire, in 1874, the son of a | lawyer. He was orphaned at an early age, and after attending | the local school was indentured to a merchant ship at the | age of fourteen. After three years at sea in different parts | of the world he went ashore at New York in 1895 with five | dollars and a few clothes. He took odd jobs and worked in | a carpet factory at Yonkers, meanwhile reading avidly and | beginning to write poetry.

After returning to England in | 1897 he met both J. M. Synge and W. B. Yeats. He pub- | lished *Salt Water Ballads* in 1902, *Ballads* in 1903, and | *Captain Margaret*, his first novel, in 1908. He also wrote | plays, notably *The Tragedy of Nan*, which was acclaimed a | masterpiece by several critics, and *Good Friday*, which used | to be presented annually on Palm Sunday by the Union | Congregational Church in Boston. *The Everlasting Mercy* and | *The Widow in the Bye Street* (1912) were two volumes of | his verse which caused much excitement and discussion. In | 1962 the Poetry Award went to him for *The Bluebells and | Other Verse*. Among his other novels are *Odtaa* (1926), *Dead | Ned* (1938), *Live and Kicking Ned* (1939), and *Basilissa* (1940) | *The Midnight Folk* (1927) has recently appeared in Puffins. | Cover drawing by Charles Raymond | *For a complete list of books available please write to Penguin Books | whose address can be found on the back of the title page*'. On inside of lower wrapper: publisher's advertisements for novels by John Buchan. All edges trimmed. Binding measurements: 180 × 111mm. (wrappers), 180 × 16mm. (spine).

Publication date: 27 June 1963

Price: 4s.

Contents:
as for A75(a)

Notes:
The text has been entirely re-set for this edition.

Each part commences with a raised-capital.

The biography of Masefield on the inside of the upper wrapper includes a number of errors.

Masefield's note ('All the persons and events described in this book are imaginary. No reference is made to any living person') is excluded from this edition.

A letter from Masefield to A.S. Frere shows that, at first, the author was wary of publication by Penguin:

> Before I go any further into the *Penguin* matter, please will you let me know the situation in which my books stand with you? What are now in print? What are the stocks of these, and the prospects of reprinting when the stocks are sold? What *Sard Harker*s have you? ...But you do not mention at all what the Penguin people propose in the way of printings, prices, appearance and royalty. Perhaps you would very kindly let me know all these things when you tell me the situation of the Heinemann stocks of my books? Please, also, will you, as one who has long published for me, tell me frankly how much you yourself might find things more easy if these suggested arrangements were carried through?
>
> (John Masefield, letter to [A.S.] Frere, 9 February [1949])
> (Archives of William Heinemann)

Frere evidently responded to Masefield's enquiries and Masefield replied on 12 February stating 'since the Penguin matter is not attractive to you, it may well be shelved'. The date of these letters is not known although evidence suggests 1949. It was certainly much later that Penguin first issued Masefield's work. A proposal from Pan Books to publish paperback editions of his work caused Masefield to write to Louisa Callender in 1949 explaining that 'I am, as it were, one of the Windmill people, and shrink from a new imprint.' Loyalty to Heinemann was, it seems, important to Masefield.

Copies seen: private collection (PWE); BL (12208.a.1/1955) stamped 7 JUN 1963 rebound

A76 WITH THE LIVING VOICE   1925

A76(a) First English edition (1925)

With the Living | Voice | *An Address by* | JOHN MASEFIELD | GIVEN AT | THE FIRST GENERAL MEETING | OF | THE SCOTTISH ASSOCIATION | FOR THE SPEAKING OF VERSE | 24*th October* 1924 | [ornament]
(Note that the '*A*' of '*An*' and '*Address*' are swash)
(All within ornamental border: 173 × 110mm.)
(All width centred with lines 4, 6, 8 and 9 justified on both left and right margins)

Bibliographies: Simmons [64], Nevinson [unrecorded], Handley-Taylor p.55, Wight [64]

Collation: [A-D]⁴; 16 leaves; 216 × 138mm.; [1–8] 9–31 [32]

Page contents: [1] half-title: 'AN ADDRESS GIVEN AT THE FIRST GENERAL | MEETING OF THE SCOTTISH ASSOCIATION | FOR THE SPEAKING OF VERSE'; [2] blank; [3] title-page; [4] blank; [5] '*The Scottish Association for the Speaking of Verse* | PRESIDENT | John Masefield | [ornament] | VICE-PRESIDENTS | The Right Hon. the Lord Justice Clerk, LL.D. | The Right Rev. the Bishop of Edinburgh. | Lt.-General Sir Walter Braithwaite, K.C.B. | Sir John Findlay, K.B.E. | Neil Munro, LL.D. | Mrs Tobias Matthay, F.R.A.M., and | The Professors of English in the Scottish Universities. | [ornament] | HON. TREASURER | William Sime, Esq., C.A. | 34 *Charlotte Square, Edinburgh* | [ornament] | HON. SECRETARY | Miss Margaret Lorrain-Smith | 9 *Carlton Terrace, Edinburgh* | [ornament] | CHAIRMAN OF THE EXECUTIVE COUNCIL | The Right Hon. Lord Murray, C.M.G., LL.D.'; [6] blank; [7] 'MEMBERS OF THE EXECUTIVE COUNCIL | Miss Ainslie, B.A. | F.H. Bisset, Esq. | Sir Charles Cleland. | John Clark, Esq., M.A. | J. W. Critchley, Esq., M.A. | David Millar Craig, Esq. | Miss Gullan. | Thos. Henderson, Esq., B.Sc. | Lady Irvine. | David Latto, Esq. | D. Glen Mackemmie, Esq. | David Martin, Esq. | Alex. Morgan, Esq.,

D.Sc. | The Rev. Dr Harry Miller. | The Rev. W. Mursell. | The Rev. Donald M'Millan. | George Pringle, Esq., M.B.E., M.A. | J. F. Rees, Esq., M.A. | Hugh S. Roberton, Esq. | A. Stewart Robertson, Esq., M.A. | George Smith, Esq. LL.D. | J. C. Smith, Esq., C.B.E., H.M.C.I.S. | Miss Ward, M.A. | The Rev. John Watt.'; [8] 'BRANCHES | OF | THE SCOTTISH ASSOCIATION | FOR THE SPEAKING OF VERSE | ABERDEEN | *Hon. Sec.*, A. Turnbull, Esq., | 49 Osborne Place, Aberdeen. | EDINBURGH | *Hon. Sec.*, Miss Alice Smith, | 4 Thorburn Road, Colinton. | GLASGOW | *Hon. Sec.*, J. Clark, Esq., Education Offices, | 129 Bath Street, Glasgow. | PERTH | *Hon. Sec.*, J. Goldie, Esq., | 7 Kincarrathie Crescent, Perth.'; 9–31 text; [32] '*CAMBRIDGE* | *Printed in Great Britain* | *by* WALTER LEWIS | *at the University Press*' (note that the '*A*', '*M*', '*B*', '*R*' and '*D*' in '*CAMBRIDGE*' are swash)

Paper: laid paper (no watermark), chain-lines 25–26mm. apart

Running title: none

Binding: light tan wrappers. Spine: blank. On upper wrapper: 'With the Living | Voice | *An Address* | *by* | JOHN MASEFIELD | [ornament]' (within ornamental border: 84 × 110mm.) (Note that the '*A*' of '*An*' and '*Address*' are swash). On lower wrapper: publisher's device of a windmill with 'W [point]' and 'H', all within ruled border: 19 × 21mm. All edges trimmed. Binding measurements: 216 × 138mm. (wrappers); 216 × 3mm. (spine).

Publication date: published, according to Simmons, 23 April 1925. The *English Catalogue of Books* records a publication date of May 1925

Price: 1s.6d.

Contents:
With the Living Voice ('We are here to-night at the first General Meeting of the members of this Association...')

Notes:
Text of an address delivered by Masefield at the first general meeting of the Scottish Association for the Speaking of Verse (of which Masefield was President). See also Masefield's contribution to *The Scottish Association for the Speaking of Verse Its Work for the Year 1926–27* (B230).

The text commences with a drop-capital.

Handley-Taylor is ambiguous over this volume. His entry incorrectly suggests that the volume was published in London by Cambridge University Press before a standard Heinemann edition. Although no publisher appears on the title-page (and Cambridge is only noted in the colophon), the Heinemann publisher's device does, however, appear on the lower cover.

C.S. Evans wrote to Masefield on 16 February 1925 acknowledging 'the typescript of the address'. He stated 'I will get our manufacturing department to plan the book…' (see C.S. Evans, letter to John Masefield, 16 February 1925) (HRHRC, MS (Masefield, J.) Recip William Heinemann Ltd.) It appears that Masefield was willing to negotiate over royalty payments:

> …It is very nice of you to say that we may have a 15% royalty, but as I said before, we don't look upon this purely as a matter of business and I know that you don't either, and that you are only wishful to make money for the Association…
>
> (C.S. Evans, letter to John Masefield, 25 February 1925)
> (HRHRC, MS (Masefield, J.) Recip William Heinemann Ltd.)

Proofs were sent on 4 March 1925. In the same letter Evans noted that 'the pamphlet is being printed by the Cambridge University Press' (see C.S. Evans, letter to John Masefield, 4 March 1925) (HRHRC, MS (Masefield, J.) Recip William Heinemann Ltd.)

After describing this edition Simmons describes the limited edition (see A76(c)). He then notes 'an ordinary edition of 2000 copies was also published by Heinemann in May, 1925'. He had already described this 'ordinary edition' and provided an earlier publication date.

Wight notes 'at the bottom of the front cover; One Shilling and Sixpence net'. This is not described by Simmons. Wight is presumably describing the glasine dust-jacket which is blank except for '*One Shilling and Sixpence net*' in black at the foot of the upper cover.

Copies seen: private collection (PWE); NYPL (Berg Collection)

A76(b) First American edition (1925)

With the Living | Voice | *An Address by* | JOHN MASEFIELD | GIVEN AT | THE FIRST GENERAL MEETING | OF | THE SCOTTISH ASSOCIATION | FOR THE SPEAKING OF VERSE | 24*th October* 1924 | [ornament] | New York | THE MACMILLAN COMPANY | 1925 | *All rights reserved*
(Note that the '*A*' of '*An*' and '*Address*' are swash)
(All within ornamental border: 164 × 100mm.)
(All width centred with lines 4, 6, 8 and 9 justified on both left and right margins)

Bibliographies: Simmons [unrecorded], Nevinson [unrecorded], Handley-Taylor [unrecorded], Wight 64b

Collation: [A]¹⁶; 16 leaves; 215 × 139mm.; [1–8] 9–32

Page contents: [1] 'AN ADDRESS GIVEN AT THE FIRST GENERAL | MEETING OF THE SCOTTISH ASSOCIATION FOR | THE SPEAKING OF VERSE'; [2] blank; [3] title-page; [4] 'COPYRIGHT, 1925 | BY JOHN MASEFIELD | [rule] | Set up and printed. Published April, 1925'; [5] '*The Scottish Association for the Speaking of Verse* | PRESIDENT | John Masefield | [ornament]

| VICE-PRESIDENTS | The Right Hon. the Lord Justice Clerk, LL.D. | The Right Rev. the Bishop of Edinburgh. | Lt.-General Sir Walter Braithwaite, K.C.B. | Sir John Findlay, K.B.E. | Neil Munro, LL.D. | Mrs Tobias Matthay, F.R.A.M., and | The Professors of English in the Scottish Universities. | [ornament] | HON. TREASURER | William Sime, Esq., C.A. | 34 *Charlotte Square, Edinburgh* | [ornament] | HON. SECRETARY | Miss Margaret Lorrain-Smith | 9 *Carlton Terrace, Edinburgh* | [ornament] | CHAIRMAN OF THE EXECUTIVE COUNCIL | The Right Hon. Lord Murray, C.M.G., LL.D.'; [6] blank; [7] 'MEMBERS OF THE EXECUTIVE COUNCIL | Miss Ainslie, B.A. | F.H. Bisset, Esq. | Sir Charles Cleland. | John Clark, Esq., M.A. | J. W. Critchley, Esq., M.A. | David Millar Craig, Esq. | Miss Gullan. | Thos. Henderson, Esq., B.Sc. | Lady Irvine. | David Latto, Esq. | D. Glen Mackemmie, Esq. | David Martin, Esq. | Alex. Morgan, Esq., D.Sc. | The Rev. Dr. Harry Miller. | The Rev. W. Mursell | The Rev. Donald M'Millan. | George Pringle, Esq., M.B.E., M.A. | J. F. Rees, Esq., M.A. | Hugh S. Roberton, Esq. | A. Stewart Robertson, Esq., M.A. | George Smith, Esq. LL.D. | J. C. Smith, Esq., C.B.E., H.M.C.I.S. | Miss Ward, M.A. | The Rev. John Watt.'; [8] 'BRANCHES | OF | THE SCOTTISH ASSOCIATION | FOR THE SPEAKING OF VERSE | ABERDEEN | *Hon. Sec.,* A. Turnbull, Esq., | 49 Osborne Place, Aberdeen. | EDINBURGH | *Hon. Sec.,* Miss Alice Smith, | 4 Thorburn Road, Colinton. | GLASGOW | *Hon. Sec.,* J. Clark, Esq., Education Offices, | 129 Bath Street, Glasgow. | PERTH | *Hon. Sec.,* J. Goldie, Esq., | 7 Kincarrathie Crescent, Perth.'; 9–32 text

Paper: laid paper (no watermark), chain-lines 21mm. apart

Running title: none

Binding: light tan wrappers. Spine: blank. On upper wrapper: 'With the Living | Voice | *An Address* | *by* | JOHN MASEFIELD | [ornament]' (within ornamental border: 86 × 99mm.) (Note that the '*A*' of '*An*' and '*Address*' are swash). Lower wrapper: blank. All edges trimmed. Binding measurements: 215 × 139mm. (wrappers); 215 × 3mm. (spine).

Publication date: published, according to Drew, in April 1925

Price: unknown

Contents:
as for A76(a)

Notes:
Despite similarities to A76(a), this American edition comprises a new setting of the text. Ornaments and decorative borders do not match those of the Heinemann edition. Minor differences include note of 'The Rev. Dr Harry Miller.' in the Heinemann setting and 'The Rev. Dr. Harry Miller.' here.

The text commences with a drop-capital.

The volume is machine sewn (the gathering is thus stabbed around 27 times).

Copies seen: NYPL (Berg Collection)

A76(c) Second English edition (limited signed edition) (1925)

WITH | THE LIVING VOICE | by | JOHN MASEFIELD | [device] [rule] [device] | *An Address* | given at the First General Meeting | of | THE SCOTTISH ASSOCIATION FOR | THE SPEAKING OF VERSE | 24th October | 1924 | [device] [rule] [device] | LONDON | WILLIAM HEINEMANN LTD | 1925
(All width centred)

Bibliographies: Simmons [64a], Nevinson [unrecorded], Handley-Taylor p.55, Wight [64a]

Collation: [A-D]⁴; 16 leaves; 223 × 141mm.; [i–vi] 1–23 [24–26]

Page contents: [i–ii] blank; [iii] half-title: 'WITH THE LIVING VOICE'; [iv] 'This edition is limited to two hundred and sixty five | copies, numbered and signed by the author, | of which two hundred and fifty are | for sale and fifteen for | presentation | No.'; [v] title-page; [vi] blank; 1–23 text; [24] '*CAMBRIDGE* | *Printed in Great Britain* | *by* WALTER LEWIS | *at the University Press*' (note that the '*A*', '*M*', '*B*', '*R*' and '*D*' in '*CAMBRIDGE*' are swash); [25–26] blank

Paper: wove paper

Running title: none

Binding: blue boards with parchment spine. On spine, in gold: 'With | the | Living | Voice | [ornament] | John | Masefield | HEINEMANN' (all width centred). There is a single vertical rule in blind on each cover at the edge of the parchment. Covers: blank. Top edge gilt, lower outside edge untrimmed, fore edge uncut. Binding measurements: 230 × 145mm. (covers), 230 × 17mm. (spine). End-papers: wove paper.

Publication date: published, according to Simmons, 18 May 1925

Price: 7s.6d.

Contents:
as for A76(a)

Notes:

A comparison with A76(a) reveals the same setting of type used here. The preliminaries present within A76(a) are omitted, however. Additionally, the first page of text in this edition includes an additional rule (with devices at each end) under the title.

A letter from C.S. Evans suggested to Masefield that if he came to London to sign the limitation sheets, publication might be possible on 7 May:

> In order to save time I gave instructions to the manufacturing department to proceed with the Limited Edition of WITH THE LIVING VOICE and it is at present in the binders' hands. We wanted to publish the book on May 7th and my idea was that you could as easily sign the copies of the book as loose sheets. I am afraid, however, that 250 copies will make too big a parcel to send to you. I will send them if you like, but perhaps you will be coming to town some day before the 7th and will be able to call in and sign them here.
>
> (C.S. Evans, letter to John Masefield, 27 April 1925)
> (HRHRC, MS (Masefield, J.) Recip William Heinemann Ltd.)

Given the actual date of publication Evans presumably had to send the bound volumes to Masefield by post.

Copies seen: private collection (PWE) number 214, signed '214 | John Masefield.' on p.[iv]; private collection (ROV) number 95, signed '95 | John Masefield.' on p.[iv]

A77 THE TRIAL OF JESUS   1925

A77(a) First English edition (1925)

THE TRIAL OF | JESUS | BY | JOHN MASEFIELD | [publisher's device of a windmill with 'W [point]' and 'H' all within ruled border: 15 × 15mm.] | LONDON | WILLIAM HEINEMANN LTD.
(All width centred)

Bibliographies: Simmons [65], Nevinson p.14, Handley-Taylor p.55, Wight [65]

Collation: [A]⁴ B-G⁸ H⁴; signatures left foot of page; 56 leaves; 185 × 119mm.; [i–viii] 1–11 [12] 13–43 [44] 45–83 [84] 85–101 [102–104]

Page contents: [i] half-title: 'THE TRIAL OF JESUS'; [ii] '*OTHER PLAYS BY JOHN* | *MASEFIELD* | [five titles listed] | *POETRY BY JOHN* | *MASEFIELD* | [13 titles listed] | *OTHER WORKS BY JOHN* | *MASEFIELD* | [four titles listed]'; [iii] title-page; [iv] '*First published 1925* | COPYRIGHT IN GREAT BRITAIN AND THE UNITED STATES | OF AMERICA | *Printed in Great Britain by Richard Clay & Sons, Ltd., Bungay, Suffolk*'; [v] 'TO | MY WIFE'; [vi] blank; [vii] '*This Play was privately performed at the Music* | *Room, Boars Hill, on May 9th*, 1925, | *at 8 p.m.* | BY THE FOLLOWING COMPANY | [dramatis personae and original cast listed] | The Chorus was trained and directed by | MISS SYBIL JACKSON.'; [viii] blank; 1–11 text of Prologue; [12] blank; 13–43 text of Act I; [44] blank; 45–83 text of Act II; [84] blank; 85–98 text of Act III; 99–101 'NOTE' ('This play was written for production upon a small stage on two levels with a balcony above...') (signed, 'JOHN MASEFIELD.'); [102] 'PRINTED IN GREAT BRITAIN BY | RICHARD CLAY & SONS, LIMITED, | BUNGAY, SUFFOLK.'; [103–104] blank

Paper: wove paper

Running title: 'THE TRIAL OF JESUS' (45mm.) on both verso and recto, pp.2–98

Binding: blue cloth. On spine, in gold: 'The | Trial of | Jesus | [ornament] | John | Masefield | HEINEMANN' (all width centred). On upper cover, in gold: 'THE TRIAL OF JESUS | JOHN MASEFIELD' (within blind ruled border: 184 × 116mm.) Lower cover: blank. All edges trimmed. Binding measurements: 189 × 121mm. (covers), 189 × 26mm. (spine). End-papers: wove paper

Publication date: published, according to Simmons, 24 September 1925 in an edition of 3150 copies

Price: 6s.

Contents:

The Trial of Jesus ('THE PROLOGUE | THE PRAYER | O divine energy who wields the stars,')

Notes:

A prose play on an obvious biblical theme. A 'private performance' of the play was given in Masefield's 'Music Room' theatre on 9 May 1925. Jesus was played by Basil Maine and the performance was attended by Bernard Shaw. Before the production Masefield had asked The Society of Authors for legal advice:

> Will you be so kind as to let me know the gist of the Statute about representing Christ upon the stage? I hope to produce a passion play here in May. I understand that it is illegal to present Christ upon any stage in public. I suppose that I could give a private performance by invitation, making no charge for admission?
>
> (John Masefield, letter to G.H. Thring, [1925])
> (BL, Add.Mss.56626, f.155)

It appears that the Society was unsure about the Lord Chamberlain's position regarding Masefield's private theatricals as they believed Masefield's 'little Theatre has been licensed' (see BL, Add.Mss.56581, f.60). Certainly the 'Music Room' obtained a licence in November 1932 from Berkshire County Council for a performance of *End and Beginning* because Masefield sent the licence as a gift to the actress playing Queen Mary (as illustrated in John Gregory, *Sybil – The Poet and the Speaker of Verse*, unpublished proof copy, 1994).

In response to a pre-publication application by a Mr Hopkins to produce the play in America, Masefield wrote to The Society of Authors:

> ...The play is one hardly likely to find a producer, either here or in the United States outside a religious organization. Here, no doubt, the Censor will ban it, + there, I fear, it will be judged to be lacking in pep.
>
> (John Masefield, letter to G.H. Thring, [18 May 1925])
> (BL, Add.Mss.56581, f.140–41)

Masefield was indeed accurate about the Censor for the play was refused a licence. In January 1927 having received another application to produce the play Masefield wrote:

> I am enclosing a letter from the minister of All Souls Church, Golders Green. He wants, as you see, to produce the "Trial Of Jesus" in his church in Holy Week. This play is forbidden by the censor at the instance of the Archbishop of Canterbury. I should be very glad for the church to produce the play, but a legal point arises.
>
> (John Masefield, letter to [G.H.] Thring, 12 January 1927)
> (BL, Add.Mss.56584, ff.16–17)

By January 1932 Masefield was referring to the work as 'my forbidden play' (see BL, Add.Mss.56595, ff.153–154).

The publishing agreement for this title between Masefield and Heinemann was dated 13 [July] 1925 (see Archives of The Society of Authors). The agreement refers to both 6s. and 1 guinea editions (A77(a) and A77(c)).

Copies seen: private collection (PWE) inscribed 'For Julia Smith, | from | John Masefield. | Septr 24th. 1925.'

A77(b) First American edition (1925)

THE | TRIAL OF JESUS | BY | JOHN MASEFIELD | New York | THE MACMILLAN COMPANY | 1925 | *All rights reserved*
(All width centred)

Bibliographies: Simmons [noted on p.105], Nevinson [unrecorded], Handley-Taylor p.55, Wight 65b

Collation: [A]⁸ (±[A]2) [B-H]⁸; 64 leaves; 190 × 127mm.; [i–viii] 1–13 [14–16] 17–50 [51–52] 53–96 [97–98] 99–116 [117–20]

Page contents: [i] half-title: 'THE TRIAL OF JESUS'; [ii] 'BY JOHN MASEFIELD | [rule] | [31 titles separated by 30 points]' (within double ruled border: 75 × 72mm.); [iii] title-page; [iv] 'COPYRIGHT, 1925, | BY JOHN MASEFIELD | [rule] | Set up and electrotyped. | Published September, 1925. | *Printed in the United States of America by* | J. J. LITTLE AND IVES COMPANY, NEW YORK'; [v] 'To | MY WIFE'; [vi] blank; [vii] 'THE TRIAL OF JESUS'; [viii] 'This play was privately performed at the Music Room, | Boars Hill, on May 9th, 1925, at 8 p.m., by the following | company: | [dramatis personae and original cast listed] | The Chorus was trained and directed by Miss Sybil | Jackson.'; 1–13 text of Prologue; [14] blank; [15] 'ACT I'; [16] blank; 17–50 text of Act I; [51] 'ACT II'; [52] blank; 53–96 text of Act II; [97] 'ACT III'; [98] blank; 99–113 text of Act III; 114–16 [untitled note] ('This play was written for production upon a small stage on two levels with a balcony above...') (unsigned); [117–20] blank

Paper: wove paper

Running title: 'THE TRIAL OF JESUS' (43mm.) on both verso and recto, pp.2–116

Binding: burgundy cloth. On spine, in gold: 'THE | TRIAL | OF | JESUS | MASEFIELD | MACMILLAN | [square point] [square point] [square point] [square point]' (all width centred). On upper cover, in blind: 'THE TRIAL | OF JESUS | MASEFIELD' (ranged upper left) (within blind ruled border: 191 × 122mm.) Lower cover: blank. Top edge trimmed, others roughly trimmed. Binding measurements: 197 × 129mm. (covers), 197 × 27mm. (spine). End-papers: wove paper.

Publication date: published, according to Simmons, 29 September 1925 in an edition of 3500 copies

Price: $1.75

Contents:
The Trial of Jesus ('THE PRAYER | O divine energy who wields the stars,')

Notes:
The publicity material in the preliminaries that lists Masefield's work (appearing on p.[ii]) incorrectly includes the title 'REYNAUD THE FOX'.

Wight fails to note the cancel title which comprises [A]2.

Page numbers appear within square brackets. Thus, [1], [2], etc.

The text has been entirely re-set for this edition.

Unlike in A77(a), the prologue is untitled and the note at the rear of the volume is unsigned.

A publishing agreement for this title between Masefield and Macmillan was dated 15 April 1925 (see Archives of The Society of Authors). The agreement refers to 'a licence to publish in volume form... in the United States of America and Canada a work the subject or title of which is a play (title to be decided upon)'. Masefield has annotated this 'The Trial of Jesus'.

Copies seen: NYPL (NCR 1925) 219045A '2 Nov. 1925' written on p.[v]; University of Texas at Austin Libraries (822 M37T)

A77(c) Second English edition (limited signed edition) (1925)

THE | TRIAL OF JESUS | BY | JOHN MASEFIELD | LONDON | WILLIAM HEINEMANN LTD | 1925
(All width centred)

Bibliographies: Simmons [65a], Nevinson [unrecorded], Handley-Taylor p.55, Wight [65a]

Collation: [A]⁴ B-G⁸ H⁴; signatures left foot of page; 56 leaves; 224 × 147mm.; [i–viii] 1–11 [12] 13–43 [44] 45–83 [84] 85–101 [102–104]

Page contents: [i] half-title: 'THE TRIAL OF JESUS'; [ii] *'This edition, printed on English hand- | made paper, is limited to five hundred | and thirty copies, of which five hundred | are for sale and thirty for presentation. | No........................'*; [iii] title-page; [iv] *'Printed in Great Britain by Richard Clay & Sons, Ltd., Bungay, Suffolk.'*; [v] 'TO | MY WIFE'; [vi] blank; [vii] *'This Play was privately performed at the Music | Room, Boars Hill, on May 9th, 1925, | at 8 p.m. | BY THE FOLLOWING COMPANY | [dramatis personae and original cast listed] | The Chorus was trained and directed by | MISS SYBIL JACKSON.';* [viii] blank; 1–11 text of Prologue; [12] blank; 13–43 text of Act I; [44] blank; 45–83 text of Act II; [84] blank; 85–98 text of Act III; 99–101 'NOTE' ('This play was written for production upon a small stage on two levels with a balcony above...') (signed, 'JOHN MASEFIELD.'); [102–104] blank

Paper: laid paper: (watermark: 'BRITISH HAND MADE PURE RAG [castle device: 27 × 41mm.]'), chain-lines 28mm. apart (the chain-lines run horizontally throughout the volume)

Running title: 'THE TRIAL OF JESUS' (45mm.) on both verso and recto, pp.2–98

Binding: blue-grey boards with parchment spine. On spine, in gold: 'The | Trial of | Jesus | [ornament] | John | Masefield | HEINEMANN' (all width centred). There is a single vertical rule in blind on each cover at the edge of the parchment. Covers: blank. Top edge gilt, lower outside edge untrimmed, fore edge uncut. Binding measurements: 230 × 149mm. (covers), 230 × 270mm. (spine). End-papers: laid paper, chain-lines 25mm.

Publication date: published, according to Simmons, 14 October 1925. A letter from C.S. Evans to Masefield notes '...the large paper TRIAL OF JESUS will be published on October 13th.' (see C.S. Evans, letter to John Masefield, 1 October 1925) (HRHRC, MS (Masefield, J.) Recip William Heinemann Ltd.)

Price: 21s.

Contents:
The Trial of Jesus ('THE PROLOGUE | THE PRAYER | O divine energy who wields the stars,')

Notes:
The text appears to use the same setting of type as A77(a).

C.S. Evans wrote to Masefield at the end of August 1925 noting that 'the sheets of the Limited Edition of THE TRIAL OF JESUS will be off the machine about Wednesday of next week. When can you sign them?' (see C.S. Evans, letter to John Masefield, 28 August 1925) (HRHRC, MS (Masefield, J.) Recip William Heinemann Ltd.) It appears that 15 September 1925 was the arranged date (see C.S. Evans, letter to John Masefield, 11 September 1925) (HRHRC, MS (Masefield, J.) Recip William Heinemann Ltd.).

Copies seen: private collection (PWE) number 458, signed '458 | John Masefield.' on p.[ii]; private collection (ROV) number 448 signed '448 | John Masefield.' on p.[ii]; BL (11778.ddd.20) number 502, signed '502 | John Masefield.' on p.[ii]

A77(d) Second American edition ([c. 1927])

THE TRIAL OF JESUS | A Passion Play in Three Acts | By | JOHN MASEFIELD | [publisher's device of globe with masks of Comedy and Tragedy and 'THE WORLD AT PLAY': 17 × 26mm.] | BAKER'S PLAYS | BOSTON, MASSACHUSETTS | and | Denver, Colorado
(All width centred)

Bibliographies: Simmons [unrecorded], Nevinson [unrecorded], Handley-Taylor [unrecorded], Wight 65c

Collation: [A-B]¹⁶; 32 leaves; 187 × 123mm.; [1–4] 5–62 [63–64]

Page contents: [1] title-page; [2] 'COPYRIGHT, 1925, BY JOHN MASEFIELD | *All rights reserved | Made in U.S.A.* | The production rights of this play are controlled | exclusively by the Walter H. Baker Company, | Play Publishers, Boston, Massachusetts, without | whose permission in writing no performances of | it may be made. All inquiries concerning pro- | duction rights should be addressed to Walter H. | Baker Company. This play is fully protected by | copyright. It may not be acted either by profes- | sionals or amateurs without the payment of | royalty. | THE TRIAL OF JESUS'; [3] 'To | MY WIFE'; [4] blank; 5–60 text; 60–62 [Note] ('This play was written for production upon a small stage on two levels with a balcony above...') (unsigned); [63–64] blank

Paper: wove paper

Running title: 'THE TRIAL OF JESUS' (42mm.) on both verso and recto, pp.6–62 with note of act towards gutter

Binding: light green wrappers (the two gatherings are additionally secured by two wire staples between pp.[1] and [64]). On spine, reading lengthways down spine from head, in red: 'THE TRIAL OF JESUS Price, 85 Cents'. On upper wrapper, in red: '[ornate floral rule, 89mm.] | THE TRIAL OF JESUS | A PASSION PLAY IN THREE ACTS | *by* JOHN MASEFIELD | BAKER'S

PLAYS | BOSTON 16, MASSACHUSETTS | and | Denver 2, Colorado | [ornate floral rule, 89mm.]' On lower wrapper, in red: '18331' (ranged lower right) (see notes). There is a single vertical rule in red on inside of upper wrapper at edge with spine and a single vertical rule in red on inside of lower wrapper at edge with spine. All edges trimmed. Binding measurements: 187 × 123mm. (wrappers), 187 × 3mm. (spine).

Publication date: c.1927? (see notes to A9(e))

Price: $0.85

Contents:
as for A77(b)

Notes:
The text, as presented here, does not title the 'Prologue' or 'Note'. The 'Note' is printed on the same page as the conclusion of the play text.

The number on the lower wrapper may be incorrectly cited above. Only a copy enclosed in a pamphlet binder has been located and consulted. The binder obscured the number.

See A9(f) for details of the Walter H. Baker Company and Masefield.

Copies seen: Cornell University Library (PR6025.A81T8) rebound

A78 POEMS

1925

A78(a) First American edition (1925)

VOLUME ONE

Poems | By | John Masefield | Volume I | *New York* | The Macmillan Company | 1925 | *All rights reserved*
(All width centred and enclosed within ruled border in red: 124 × 74mm. and all within ornate decorative border in red: 138 × 88mm.)

Bibliographies: Simmons [unrecorded], Nevinson [unrecorded], Handley-Taylor p.55, Wight [unrecorded]

Collation: [A-FF]⁸ (J, V and W not used); 232 leaves; 200 × 130mm.; [i–iv] v–x 1–95 [96] 97–209 [210] 211–73 [274] 275–397 [398] 399–423 [424] 425–46 [447–54]

Page contents: [i] half-title: 'Poems | Volume I'; [ii] '[publisher's device] | THE MACMILLAN COMPANY | [two lines listing six cities, separated by four points] | MACMILLAN & CO., LIMITED | [two lines listing four cities, separated by two points] | THE MACMILLAN CO. OF CANADA, LTD. | [one city listed]'; [iii] title-page; [iv] 'Copyright, 1913, by Harper and Brothers | Copyright, 1914, by The Century Company and by the McClure Publications | [rule] | Copyright, 1912, 1913, 1914 | BY THE MACMILLAN COMPANY | [rule] | Copyright, 1911, 1913, 1917, 1918, 1925 | BY JOHN MASEFIELD | New Collected Edition in four volumes | Set up and electrotyped. Published December, 1925 | PRINTED IN THE UNITED STATES OF AMERICA | BY THE BERWICK AND SMITH COMPANY'; v–vi 'INTRODUCTION' ('It seems as though the minds of men always follow one of two purposes in art...') (signed, 'JOHN MASEFIELD. | Oxford, 1925'); vii–ix 'CONTENTS' (112 individual items listed with page references); [xii] blank; 1–95 text; [96] blank; 97–209 text; [210] blank; 211–73 text; [274] blank; 275–397 text; [398] blank; 399–423 text; [424] blank; 425–46 text; [447–54] blank

Paper: laid paper (no watermark), chain-lines 21mm. apart

Running title: 'POEMS' (14mm.) on verso; recto title comprises poem title, pp.2–446

Binding: dark brown cloth with light brown cloth spine. On spine, in gold: 'POEMS | VOL. I | JOHN | MASEFIELD | MACMILLAN | [point] [point] [point] [point]' (all width centred). Covers: blank. Top edge stained red, others trimmed. Sewn head and foot bands (in light brown and red). Binding measurements: 205 × 131mm. (covers), 205 × 44mm. (spine). End-papers: laid paper (watermark indistinguishable), chain-lines 29mm. apart.

Publication date: published, according to date within volume, December 1925

Price: $3.00

Contents:
Introduction ('It seems as though the minds of men always follow one of two purposes in art...')
SALT-WATER BALLADS
A Consecration ('Not of the princes and prelates with periwigged charioteers')
The Yarn of The "Loch Achray" ('The "Loch Achray" was a clipper tall')
Sing a Song O' Shipwreck ('He lolled on a bollard, a sun-burned son of the sea,')
Burial Party ('"He's deader 'n nails," the fo'c's'le said, "'n' gone to his long sleep; "')
Bill ('He lay dead on the cluttered deck and stared at the cold skies,')
Fever Ship ('There'll be no weepin' gells ashore when *our* ship sails,')
Fever-Chills ('He tottered out of the alleyway with cheeks the colour of paste,')
One of The Bo'sun's Yarns ('Loafin' around in Sailor Town, a-bluin' o' my advance,')
Hell's Pavement ('"When I'm discharged in Liverpool 'n' draws my bit o' pay,')

Sea-Change ('"Goneys and gullies an' all o' the birds o' the sea,')
Harbour-Bar ('All in the feathered palm-tree tops the bright green parrots screech,')
The Turn of the Tide ('An' Bill can have my sea-boots, Nigger Jim can have my knife,')
One of Wally's Yarns ('The watch was up on the topsail-yard a-making fast the sail,')
A Valediction (Liverpool Docks) ('Is there anything as I can do ashore for you')
A Night at Dago Tom's ('Oh yesterday, I t'ink it was, while cruisin' down the street,')
Port of Many Ships ('"It's a sunny pleasant anchorage, is Kingdom Come,')
Cape Horn Gospel – I ('"I was in a hooker once," said Karlssen,')
Cape Horn Gospel – II ('Jake was a dirty Dago lad, an' he gave the skipper chin,')
Mother Carey ('Mother Carey ? She's the mother o' the witches')
Evening – Regatta Day ('Your nose is a red jelly, your mouth's a toothless wreck,')
A Valediction ('We're bound for blue water where the great winds blow,')
A Pier-Head Chorus ('Oh I'll be chewing salted horse and biting flinty bread,')
The Golden City of St. Mary ('Out beyond the sunset, could I but find the way,')
Trade Winds ('In the harbour, in the island, in the Spanish Seas,')
Sea-Fever ('I must go down to the seas again, to the lonely sea and the sky,')
A Wanderer's Song ('A wind's in the heart of me, a fire's in my heels,')
Cardigan Bay ('Clean, green, windy billows notching out the sky,')
Christmas Eve at Sea ('A wind is rustling "south and soft,"')
A Ballad of Cape St. Vincent ('Now, Bill, ain't it prime to be a-sailin',')
The Tarry Buccaneer ('I'm going to be a pirate with a bright brass pivot-gun,')
A Ballad of John Silver ('We were schooner-rigged and rakish, with a long and lissome hull,')
Lyrics from "The Buccaneer"
I. ('We are far from sight of the harbour lights,')
II. ('There's a sea-way somewhere where all day long')
III. ('The toppling rollers at the harbour mouth')
D'Avalos' Prayer ('When the last sea is sailed and the last shallow charted,')
The West Wind ('It's a warm wind, the west wind, full of birds' cries;')
The Galley-Rowers ('Staggering over the running combers')
Vagabond ('Dunno a heap about the what an' why,')
Vision ('I have drunken the red wine and flung the dice;')
Spunyarn ('Spunyarn, spunyarn, with one to turn the crank,')
Personal ('Tramping at night in the cold and wet, I passed the lighted inn,')
On Malvern Hill ('A wind is brushing down the clover,')
On Eastnor Knoll ('Silent are the woods, and the dim green boughs are')
"Rest Her Soul, She's Dead!" ('She has done with the sea's sorrow and the world's way')
"All Ye That Pass By" ('On the long dusty ribbon of the long city street,')
In Memory of A.P.R. ('Once in the windy wintry weather,')
To-Morrow ('Oh yesterday the cutting edge drank thirstily and deep,')
Cavalier ('All the merry kettle-drums are thudding into rhyme,')
A Song at Parting ('The tick of the blood is settling slow, my heart will soon be still,')
GLOSSARY ('Abaft the beam.—That half of a ship included between her amidship section…')
THE EVERLASTING MERCY
The Everlasting Mercy ('From '41 to '51')
MISCELLANEOUS POEMS
Biography ('When I am buried, all my thoughts and acts')
Ships ('I cannot tell their wonder nor make known')
Truth ('Man with his burning soul')
They Closed Her Eyes ('They closed her eyes,')
The Harp ('In a dark corner of the room,')
Sonnet ('I saw the ramparts of my native land')
Sonnet on the Death of his Wife ('That blessed sunlight that once showed to me')
Song ('One sunny time in May')
The Ballad of Sir Bors ('Would I could win some quiet and rest, and a little ease,')
Spanish Waters ('Spanish waters, Spanish waters, you are ringing in my ears,')
Cargoes ('Quinquireme of Nineveh from distant Ophir,')
Captain Stratton's Fancy ('Oh some are fond of red wine, and some are fond of white,')
An Old Song Re-Sung ('I saw a ship a-sailing, a-sailing, a-sailing,')
St. Mary's Bells ('It's pleasant in Holy Mary')
London Town ('Oh London Town's a fine town, and London sights are rare,')
The Emigrant ('Going by Daly's shanty I heard the boys within')
Port of Holy Peter ('The blue laguna rocks and quivers,')

Beauty ('I have seen dawn and sunset on moors and windy hills')
The Seekers ('Friends and loves we have none, nor wealth nor blessed abode,')
Prayer ('When the last sea is sailed, when the last shallow's charted,')
Dawn ('The dawn comes cold: the haystack smokes,')
Laugh and be Merry ('Laugh and be merry, remember, better the world with a song,')
June Twilight ('The twilight comes; the sun')
Roadways ('One road leads to London,')
Midsummer Night ('The perfect disc of the sacred moon')
The Harper's Song ('This sweetness trembling from the strings')
The Gentle Lady ('So beautiful, so dainty-sweet')
The Dead Knight ('The cleanly rush of the mountain air,')
Sorrow of Mydath ('Weary the cry of the wind is, weary the sea,')
Twilight ('Twilight it is, and the far woods are dim, and the rooks cry and call.')
Invocation ('O wanderer into many brains,')
Posted as Missing ('Under all her topsails she trembled like a stag,')
A Creed ('I hold that when a person dies')
When Bony Death ('When bony Death has chilled her gentle blood,')
Her Heart ('Her heart is always doing lovely things,')
Being Her Friend ('Being her friend, I do not care, not I,')
Fragments ('Troy Town is covered up with weeds,')
Born for Nought Else ('Born for nought else, for nothing but for this,')
Tewkesbury Road ('It is good to be out on the road, and going one knows not where,')
The Death Rooms ('My soul has many an old decaying room')
Ignorance ('Since I have learned Love's shining alphabet,')
The Watch in the Wood ('When Death has laid her in his quietude,')
C.L.M. ('In the dark womb where I began')
Waste ('No rose but fades: no glory but must pass:')
Third Mate ('All the sheets are clacking, all the blocks are whining,')
The Wild Duck ('Twilight. Red in the west.')
Christmas, 1903 ('O, the sea breeze will be steady, and the tall ship's going trim,')
The Word ('My friend, my bonny friend, when we are old,')
THE WIDOW IN THE BYE STREET
The Widow in the Bye Street ('Down Bye Street, in a little Shropshire town,')
DAUBER
Dauber ('Four bells were struck, the watch was called on deck,')
Explanations of some of the Sea Terms used in the Poem ('Backstays.-Wire ropes which support the masts against...')
THE DAFFODIL FIELDS
The Daffodil Fields ('Between the barren pasture and the wood')
SONNETS AND OTHER POEMS
[Untitled] ('Long long ago, when all the glittering earth')
[Untitled] ('Night came again, but now I could not sleep.')
[Untitled] ('Even after all these years there comes the dream')
[Untitled] ('If I could come again to that dear place')
[Untitled] ('Men are made human by the mighty fall')
[Untitled] ('Here in the self is all that man can know')
[Untitled] ('Flesh, I have knocked at many a dusty door,')
[Untitled] ('But all has passed, the tune has died away,')
[Untitled] ('These myriad days, these many thousand hours,')
[Untitled] ('There, on the darkened deathbed, dies the brain')
[Untitled] ('So in the empty sky the stars appear,')
[Untitled] ('It may be so with us, that in the dark,')
[Untitled] ('Man has his unseen friend, his unseen twin,')
[Untitled] ('What am I, Life? A thing of watery salt')
[Untitled] ('If I could get within this changing I,')
[Untitled] ('What is this atom which contains the whole,')
[Untitled] ('Ah, we are neither heaven nor earth, but men;')
[Untitled] ('Roses are beauty, but I never see')
[Untitled] ('Over the church's door they moved a stone')
[Untitled] ('I never see the red rose crown the year,')
[Untitled] ('Out of the clouds come torrents, from the earth')
[Untitled] ('O little self, within whose smallness lies')
[Untitled] ('I went into the fields, but you were there')

XIX. Midnight ('The fox came up by Stringer's Pound,')
XX. ('Up on the downs the red-eyed kestrels hover')
XXI. ('No man takes the farm,')
XXII. ('A hundred years ago, they quarried for the stone here;')
XXIII. ('Here the legion halted, here the ranks were broken,')
XXIV. ('We danced away care till the fiddler's eyes blinked,')
ROSAS
Rosas ('There was an old lord in the Argentine,')

Notes:

The running titles on pages 419, 421 and 423 should revert to 'LOLLINGDON DOWNS'. Incorrectly they repeat the last titled poem and therefore read 'MIDNIGHT'.

A publishing agreement between Masefield and Macmillan was dated 31 January 1925 (see Archives of The Society of Authors). The agreement refers to 'a licence to publish in volume form... in the United States of America and Canada a work the subject or title of which is Collected Poems, and Plays, revised, and enlarged (three volume edition)'. It is assumed that this agreement refers to A78-A80 and the three volumes became four.

Copies seen: private collection (PWE)

Reprinted:

[first edition, second impression]	1927
[first edition, third impression]	1929

VOLUME TWO

Poems | By | John Masefield | Volume II | *New York* | The Macmillan Company | 1925 | *All rights reserved*
(All width centred and enclosed within ruled border in red: 124 × 74mm. and all within ornate decorative border in red: 138 × 88mm.)

Bibliographies: Simmons [unrecorded], Nevinson [unrecorded], Handley-Taylor p.55, Wight [unrecorded]

Collation: [A-T]⁸ (J not used); 152 leaves; 198 × 127mm.; [i–iv] v–vii [viii] 1–169 [170] 171–291 [292–96]

Page contents: [i] half-title: 'Poems | Volume II'; [ii] '[publisher's device] | THE MACMILLAN COMPANY | [two lines listing six cities, separated by four points] | MACMILLAN & CO., LIMITED | [two lines listing four cities, separated by two points] | THE MACMILLAN CO. OF CANADA, LTD. | [one city listed]'; [iii] title-page; [iv] 'Copyright, 1913, by Harper and Brothers | Copyright, 1914, by The Century Company and by the McClure Publications | [rule] | Copyright, 1912, 1913, 1914 | BY THE MACMILLAN COMPANY | [rule] | Copyright, 1916, 1919, 1920, 1921, 1922, 1923, 1925 | BY JOHN MASEFIELD | New Collected Edition in four volumes | Set up and electrotyped. Published December, 1925 | PRINTED IN THE UNITED STATES OF AMERICA | BY THE BERWICK AND SMITH COMPANY'; v–vi 'INTRODUCTION' ('I have been asked to write a few words as introduction to this volume...') (signed, 'JOHN MASEFIELD. | Oxford, 1925'); vii 'CONTENTS' (25 individual items listed with page references); [viii] blank; 1–291 text; [292–96] blank

Paper: laid paper (no watermark), chain-lines 21mm. apart

Running title: 'POEMS' (14mm.) on verso; recto title comprises poem title, pp.2–290

Binding: dark brown cloth with light brown cloth spine. On spine, in gold: 'POEMS | VOL. II | JOHN | MASEFIELD | MACMILLAN | [point] [point] [point] [point]' (all width centred). Covers: blank. Top edge stained red, others trimmed. Sewn head and foot bands (in light brown and red). Binding measurements: 205 × 131mm. (covers), 205 × 40mm. (spine). End-papers: laid paper (watermark indistinguishable), chain-lines 29mm. apart.

Publication date: published, according to date within volume, December 1925

Price: $3.00

Contents:
Introduction ('I have been asked to write a few words as introduction to this volume, which contains...')
[REYNARD THE FOX]
Reynard the Fox ('The meet was at "The Cock and Pye')
[ENSLAVED]
Enslaved ('All early in the April when daylight comes at five')
The Hounds of Hell ('About the crowing of the cock,')
Cap on Head | A Tale of the O'Neill ('O'Neill took ship, O'Neill set sail,')
Sonnets
[Untitled] ('Like bones the ruins of the cities stand,')
[Untitled] ('Now they are gone with all their songs and sins,')
[Untitled] ('None knows what overthrew that city's pride.')
[Untitled] ('So shall we be; so will our cities lie,')
The Passing Strange ('Out of the earth to rest or range')

Animula ('This is the place, this house beside the sea,')
The Lemmings ('Once in a hundred years the Lemmings come')
Forget ('Forget all these, the barren fool in power,')
On Growing Old ('Be with me Beauty for the fire is dying,')
Lyric ('Give me a light that I may see her,')
[RIGHT ROYAL]
Right Royal ('An hour before the race they talked together')
KING COLE
King Cole ('King Cole was King before the troubles came,')
[THE DREAM AND OTHER POEMS]
The Dream of Daniel ('Weary with many thoughts I went to bed,')
The Woman Speaks ('This poem appeared to me in a dream one winter morning some years ago. In the dream...')
The Rider at the Gate ('A windy night was blowing on Rome,')
The Builders ('Before the unseen cock had called the time,')
The Setting of the Windcock ('The dust lay white upon the chisel-marks,')
The Racer ('I saw the racer coming to the jump,')
From the Song of Roland ('Roland gripped his horn with might and main,')
The Haunted ('Here, in this darkened room of this old house,')
Campeachy Picture ('The sloop's sails glow in the sun; the far sky burns,')
[MISCELLANEOUS]
The Ship and Her Makers ('THE ORE | Before Man's labouring wisdom gave me birth')
Sonnets
[Untitled] ('Once we were masters of the arts of men.')
[Untitled] ('Builded in every village in the land,')
[Untitled] ('I saw the work of all the world displayed,')
[Untitled] ('I cannot tell who will, but only know')
Beauty ('When soul's companion fails,')

Notes:
Reviewing the edition in *The Dial* for March 1926 (pp.235–40), Robert Hillyer remarked:

> A most slip-shod edition. A favourite arrangement with the sonnets, for example, is to print seven lines on one page and seven on the next. Mathematical, perhaps, but not effective. Parts of lines are run over to the left margin and given initial capitals. Prayer is printed twice. These are a few of many justifiable complaints.

Copies seen: private collection (PWE)

A79 VERSE PLAYS 1925

A79(a) First American edition (1925)

Verse Plays | By | John Masefield | *New York* | The Macmillan Company | 1925 | *All rights reserved*
(All width centred and enclosed within ruled border in red: 124 × 74mm. and all within ornate decorative border in red: 138 × 88mm.)

Bibliographies: Simmons [unrecorded], Nevinson [unrecorded], Handley-Taylor p.55, Wight [unrecorded]

Collation: [A]⁹ [A]3+1 [B-U]⁸ (J not used); 161 leaves; 197 × 127mm.; [i–iv] v–vi [vii–viii] [1–2] 3–52 [53–54] 55–97 [98–102] 103–155 [156–58] 159–207 [208–210] 211–313[314]

Page contents: [i] half-title: 'Verse Plays'; [ii] '[publisher's device] | THE MACMILLAN COMPANY | [two lines listing six cities, separated by four points] | MACMILLAN & CO., LIMITED | [two lines listing four cities, separated by two points] | THE MACMILLAN CO. OF CANADA, LTD. | [one city listed]'; [iii] title-page; [iv] 'Copyright, 1913, by Harper and Brothers | Copyright, 1914, by The Century Company and by the McClure Publications | [rule] | Copyright, 1914 | BY THE MACMILLAN COMPANY | [rule] | Copyright, 1915, 1916, 1922, 1923, 1925 | BY JOHN MASEFIELD | New Collected Edition in four volumes | Set up and electrotyped. Published December, 1925 | PRINTED IN THE UNITED STATES OF AMERICA | BY THE BERWICK AND SMITH COMPANY'; v–vi 'INTRODUCTION' ('Sometimes the writers of prose ask: "Why do people write verse? Why do they write...') (signed, 'JOHN MASEFIELD. | Oxford, 1925'); [vii] 'CONTENTS' (five individual items listed with page references); [viii] blank; [1] 'GOOD FRIDAY | A DRAMATIC POEM'; [2] 'GOOD FRIDAY | PERSONS | [dramatis personae listed]'; 3 'GOOD FRIDAY | A DRAMATIC POEM | THE SCENE | *The Pavement, or Paved Court, outside the Roman Citadel in | Jerusalem. At the back is the barrack wall, pierced in the | center with a double bronze door, weathered to a green color. | On the right and left sides of the stage are battlemented parapets | overlooking the city. The stage or pavement is approached by | stone steps from the front, and by narrow stone staircases in | the wings, one on each side, well forward. These steps are to | suggest that the citadel is high up above the town, and that the | main barrack gate is below.* THE CHIEF CITIZEN, THE RAB- | BLE, JOSEPH, THE MADMAN, HEROD, *and* THE LOITERERS, | *etc., enter by these steps.* PILATE, PROCULA, LONGINUS, THE | SOLDIERS *and* SERVANTS *enter by the bronze doors.*' | [text]'; 4–52 text; [53] 'PHILIP THE KING | A PLAY IN ONE ACT'; [54] 'PHILIP THE KING | [dramatis personae listed with 'PERSONS' and 'SPIRITS' headings] | TIME | At dawn in late September, 1588 | SCENE | A little dark cell in Philip's cell'; 55–97 text; [98]

blank; [99] 'ESTHER AND BERENICE | TWO PLAYS'; [100] 'PREFACE' ('I have been asked to write a few words to explain why these adaptations of Racine were made.') (signed, 'JOHN MASEFIELD.'); [101] 'This adaptation of "Esther" was produced by Miss Penelope | Wheeler at Wootton, Berks, on the evening of the 5th May, | 1921, with the following cast :- | [dramatis personae and original cast listed] | The Play was performed without scenery upon a stage hung | with curtains. There were exits and entrances R. and L. at | Back, and an extra exit and approach by steps to the stage | from Front Centre'; [102] 'ESTHER | CHARACTERS | [dramatis personae listed] | Parts of Acts 1, 3, and 4 of this play are translated from the | Tragedy of Esther, by Racine. | PROPERTIES | [props listed]'; 103–155 text; [156] blank; [157] 'BERENICE | A TRAGEDY BY RACINE'; [158] 'BERENICE | PERSONS | [dramatis personae listed]'; 159–207 text; [208] blank; [209] 'A KING'S DAUGHTER | A TRAGEDY IN VERSE'; [210] 'A KING'S DAUGHTER | *This play was performed at The Oxford Playhouse, on Friday | and Saturday, May 25th and 26th, by the following cast of | the Hill Players.* | [dramatis personae and original cast listed] | [rule] | SCENE: The Palace in Samaria | [rule]'; 211–313 text; [314] blank

Paper: laid paper (no watermark), chain-lines 21mm. apart

Running title: 'VERSE PLAYS' (31mm.) on verso; recto title comprises play title, pp.4–313

Binding: dark brown cloth with light brown cloth spine. On spine, in gold: 'VERSE | PLAYS | JOHN | MASEFIELD | MACMILLAN | [point] [point] [point] [point]' (all width centred). Covers: blank. Top edge stained red, others trimmed. Sewn head and foot bands (in light brown and red). Binding measurements: 205 × 130mm. (covers), 205 × 44mm. (spine). End-papers: wove paper.

Publication date: published, according to date within volume, December 1925

Price: $3.00

Contents:
Introduction ('Sometimes the writers of prose ask: "Why do people write verse? Why do they write…"')
Good Friday ('PILATE | Longinus.')
Philip the King ('PHILIP | [*Kneeling*] Lord, I am that Philip whom Thou has made…')
Preface ('I have been asked to write a few words to explain why these adaptations of Racine were made.')
Esther ('SCENE:-ESTHER'S *apartments.*')
Berenice ('ANTIOCHUS | Let us stay here a moment. I can see')
A King's Daughter ('JEZEBEL | I am Queen Jezebel, King Ahab's wife.')

Notes:
See note to volume one of A78(a) for details of an early publishing agreement.

Copies seen: private collection (PWE)

A80 PROSE PLAYS

1925

A80(a) First American edition (1925)

Prose Plays | By | John Masefield | *New York* | The Macmillan Company | 1925 | *All rights reserved*
(All width centred and enclosed within ruled border in red: 124 × 74mm. and all within ornate decorative border in red: 138 × 88mm.)

Bibliographies: Simmons [unrecorded], Nevinson [unrecorded], Handley-Taylor p.55, Wight [unrecorded]

Collation: [A]⁹ [A]3+1 [B-EE]⁸ (J, V and W not used); 225 leaves; 197 × 127mm.; [i–iv] v [vi–viii] ix–xi [xii] [1–2] 3–27 [28–30] 31–41 [42–44] 45–58 [59–60] 61–95 [96–100] 101–170 [171–76] 177–250 [251–53] 254–348 [349–50] 351–438

Page contents: [i] half-title: 'Prose Plays'; [ii] '[publisher's device] | THE MACMILLAN COMPANY | [two lines listing six cities, separated by four points] | MACMILLAN & CO., LIMITED | [two lines listing four cities, separated by two points] | THE MACMILLAN CO. OF CANADA, LTD. | [one city listed]'; [iii] title-page; [iv] 'Copyright, 1914 | BY THE MACMILLAN COMPANY | [rule] | Copyright, 1909, 1910, 1914, 1915, 1916, 1918, 1922, 1925 | BY JOHN MASEFIELD | New Collected Edition in four volumes | Set up and electrotyped. Published December, 1925 | PRINTED IN THE UNITED STATES OF AMERICA | BY THE BERWICK AND SMITH COMPANY'; v 'INTRODUCTION' ('I have been asked to write a few words as a preface to these volumes of plays.') (signed, 'JOHN MASEFIELD. | Oxford, 1925'); [vi] blank; [vii] 'CONTENTS' (eight individual items listed with page references); [viii] blank; ix–xi 'PREFACE' ('The first of the plays in this volume, *The Campden Wonder*, was written at Greenwich…') (signed, 'JOHN MASEFIELD.'); [xii] blank; [1] 'THE CAMPDEN WONDER'; [2] 'THE CAMPDEN WONDER | PERSONS | [dramatis personae and original cast listed with 'PLAYED BY' heading] | *This play was produced at the Court Theatre, in London, on the 8th of January, | 1907, under the direction of Mr. H. Granville Barker.*'; 3–27 text of 'The Campden Wonder'; [28] blank; [29] 'MRS. HARRISON'; [30] 'MRS. HARRISON | PERSONS | [dramatis personae listed]'; 31–41 text of 'Mrs. Harrison'; [42] blank; [43] 'THE SWEEPS OF NINETY-EIGHT'; [44] blank; 45–58 text of 'The Sweeps of Ninety-Eight' (at foot of p.58: '*Written in 1905.*'); [59] 'THE LOCKED CHEST | A PLAY IN ONE ACT | (From a Tale in the Laxdaelasaga); [60] 'THE LOCKED CHEST | PERSONS | [dramatis personae listed] | SCENE | *Iceland*'; 61–95 text of 'The Locked Chest' (at foot of p.95: '*Written in 1906.*'); [96] blank; [97] 'THE TRAGEDY OF NAN'; [98] author's note ('Tragedy at its best is a vision of the heart of life.') (signed, 'JOHN MASEFIELD. | *4th April, 1911.*'); [99] 'TO | W. B. YEATS'; [100] 'THE TRAGEDY OF NAN | [dramatis personae and original cast listed with 'PERSONS' and 'PLAYED BY' headings] | *This play was produced by the Pioneers at the New Royalty Theatre, on 24th May,* | *1908, under the direction of Mr. H. Granville Barker. At its revival as a matinee at* | *the Haymarket Theatre, in June, 1908, the part of the Rev. Mr. Drew was played by* | *Mr. Cecil Brooking.*'; 101–170 text of 'The Tragedy of Nan'; [171] 'THE TRAGEDY OF POMPEY THE GREAT'; [172] blank; [173] 'TO | MY WIFE'; [174] 'ARGUMENT | In the years 50 and 49 B. C., Cneius Pompeius Magnus, the | head of the patrician party, contested with C. Julius Caesar, the | popular leader, for supreme power in the State. Their jealousy | led to the troubles of the Civil War, in which, after many bat- | tles, Cneius Pompeius Magnus was miserably killed. | ACT I. The determination of Pompey to fight with his | rival, then marching upon Rome. | ACT II. The triumph of Pompey's generalship at Dyrrach- | ium. His overthrow by the generals of his staff. His de- | feat at Pharsalia. | ACT III. The death of that great ruler on the seashore of | Pelusium in Egypt.'; [175] 'THE TRAGEDY OF POMPEY THE GREAT | PERSONS | [dramatis personae listed, also table of act, scene and historical time]'; [176] blank; 177–250 text of 'The Tragedy of Pompey the Great' with 'NOTES' and [verse] ('And all their passionate hearts are dust,') dated on left margin '*Feb. 8, 1908.*' and on extreme right '*July 5, 1909.*'); [251] 'THE FAITHFUL | A TRAGEDY IN THREE ACTS'; [252] blank; [253] 'To | MY WIFE | THIS BOOK IS AFFECTIONATELY INSCRIBED'; 254 'THE FAITHFUL | NOTE: This play is written to be played uninterruptedly, with- | out more break in the action than is necessary to get the actors | off the stage and to raise the screen or curtain dividing the | scenes. | [new paragraph] There are only two scenes: one the front part of the stage, | left quite bare, without decoration, but with a screen, set, or | backcloth at the back, representing a Japanese landscape, with | hills and water, all wintry and severe; the other, the back of the | stage, visible when this screen is lifted, a room in a Japanese | palace, very beautiful, but bare, save for a few flowers and a | picture or two. | [new paragraph] A few minutes may elapse between Acts I and II, and a | slightly longer wait between Acts II and III. | PERSONS | [dramatis personae listed] | In Act I, Scene I, throughout Act II, and in Scenes I, II, and | IV of Act III, the scene is: An open space near ASANO'S palace. | In Act I, Scene II and in Act III, Scene III, the scene is: A | room in Kira's palace. | TIME: Acts I and II, 10th March, 1701. | Act III, 10th March, 1702.'; 255–348 text of 'The Faithful'; [349] 'MELLONEY HOLTSPUR | OR | THE PANGS OF LOVE | *The consecrated things are wiser than our virtue.*'; [350] 'MELLONEY HOLTSPUR | PERSONS | [dramatis personae listed]'; 351–438 text of 'Melloney Holtspur' (at foot of p.438: '*Note.*–The persons and events described in this play are imaginary. No ref- | erence is made to any living person.–JOHN MASEFIELD')

Paper: laid paper (no watermark), chain-lines 21mm. apart

Running title: 'PROSE PLAYS' (30mm.) on verso; recto title comprises play title, pp.4–438

Binding: dark brown cloth with light brown cloth spine. On spine, in gold: 'PROSE | PLAYS | JOHN | MASEFIELD | MACMILLAN | [point] [point] [point] [point]' (all width centred). Covers: blank. Top edge stained red, others trimmed. Sewn head and foot bands (in light brown and red). Binding measurements: 205 × 130mm. (covers), 205 × 39mm. (spine). End-papers: wove paper.

Publication date: published, according to date within volume, December 1925

Price: $3.00

Contents:
Introduction ('I have been asked to write a few words as a preface to these volumes of plays.')
Preface ('The first of the plays in this volume, *The Campden Wonder,* was written at Greenwich...')
The Campden Wonder ('SCENE I | SCENE. *Harrison's Kitchen in Campden.*')
Mrs. Harrison ('SCENE: *A Room in* MRS. HARRISON'S *House.*')
The Sweeps of Ninety-Eight ('SCENE: *An inn at Dunleary. A parlour.*')
The Locked Chest ('SCENE: *A room. A chest used as a bench. A table, etc.*')
The Tragedy of Nan ('ACT I | SCENE: *A kitchen in the house of a small tenant farmer...*')
The Tragedy of Pompey the Great ('ACT I | *A room in* POMPEY'S *house near Rome...*')
The Faithful ('ACT I | SCENE I.-*The outer scene.* ASANO *alone, dawn. A shaft of light...*')
Melloney Holtspur ('ACT I | [*The scene is a panelled room. At Back, a plain…*')

Notes:
See note to volume one of A78(a) for details of an early publishing agreement.

Copies seen: private collection (PWE)

A81 SONNETS OF GOOD CHEER TO THE LENA ASHWELL PLAYERS... [1926]

A81(a) First English edition ([1926])

Upper wrapper:
Sonnets of Good Cheer | – to the – | Lena Ashwell Players. | [illustration of Mr. Punch pointing stick at puppet's theatre with the initials 'LA' displayed at the top of the theatre: 25 × 16mm.] | From their Well-Wisher | JOHN MASEFIELD.
(All in navy blue)
(All width centred)

Bibliographies: Simmons [66], Nevinson [unrecorded], Handley-Taylor p.55, Wight [66]

Collation: [A]⁶; 6 leaves; 152 × 120mm.; [i–xii]

Page contents: [i–iv] '[headpiece] | PREFACE' ('IT is now some three or four years since I first saw the Lena Ashwell Players.') (signed, 'JOHN MASEFIELD.'); [v] text; [vi] blank; [vii] text; [viii] blank; [ix] text; [x] blank; [xi] text; [xii] blank

Paper: wove paper

Running title: none

Binding: grey wrappers. Spine: blank. On upper wrapper, in navy blue: described above (note that 'Sonnets of Good Cheer | – to the – | Lena Ashwell Players.' is printed within an embossed panel: 45 × 96mm. with rounded corners). On lower wrapper, in navy blue: 'COPYRIGHT | IN GREAT BRITAIN & U.S.A. | BY | JOHN MASEFIELD. | MENDIP PRESS, LONDON & BATH.' (all width centred with the exception of the last line which is ranged lower right). All edges trimmed. Binding measurements: 152 × 120mm. (wrappers), 152 × 1mm. (spine) (see notes).

Publication date: published, according to Simmons, in 1926 in an edition of 2000 copies

Price: unknown

Contents:
Preface ('It is now some three or four years since I first saw the Lena Ashwell Players.')
[Untitled] ('Once in a thousand years a golden soul')
[Untitled] ('"I promise battles, hardship, weariness..."')
[Untitled] ('It is no little thing to stand together')
[Untitled] ('Weary and sickened of the daily show')

Notes:
A pamphlet containing a preface and four sonnets. Masefield states in the preface his admiration for the Lena Ashwell Players, a group he first saw in 1913 (and who were to give the first performance of Masefield's *Tristan and Isolt* in 1927). The text was later reprinted within Ashwell's 1936 biography entitled *Myself a Player* (see B320).

Beyond Simmons' date of 1926 no additional information has been discovered. There do not appear to be any dated inscribed copies in the HRHRC Masefield collection. The typescript of this volume exists in two parts in the HRHRC. MS (Masefield, J.) Works. [Untitled article on Lena Ashwell Players] provides the text of the preface. There are two typescript copies (each of two pages) without any authorial markings. There is also a two page autograph copy with a section of typescript (with authorial corrections) laid down. All leaves are extensively damaged with some major loss. The manuscript catalogued as MS (Masefield, J.) Works. Sonnets of Good Cheer provides the text of the sonnets. This typescript includes the authorial correction of one word. None of the leaves are dated. Masefield's diary for 1925 (see HRHRC MS (Masefield, J.) Works [Diaries] 1919–1960) records, on 1 December 1925 'Post Miss Ash + Boa to Farran'. Miss Ida Farran, of the Typewriting Offices, Donnington House, Norfolk Street, Strand, London was employed by Masefield to do much of his typing from 1913 through the 1920s. (The diary subsequently notes that Masefield 'read Boadicea to cast' on 7 December). No diary seems to have survived for 1926. This evidence suggests that the text for this publication was probably ready by the end of December 1925. Publication early in 1926 (and before *Odtaa*) is therefore likely.

In addition to this binding (bound in grey wrappers) there is another binding in light green-blue wrappers (described by Simmons as 'blue') with navy blue printing on the wrappers. Internal leaves are of wove paper and the only difference is the omission of 'COPYRIGHT | IN GREAT BRITAIN & U.S.A. | BY | JOHN MASEFIELD. | MENDIP PRESS, LONDON & BATH.' from the lower wrapper. The light green-blue binding may, consequently, be an earlier issue although this is not suggested by Simmons.

The text appears to use the same setting of type as A81(b) although Simmons notes the addition of a comma on the upper wrapper in the later edition.

The preface commences with a decorated drop-capital while the sonnets each commence with drop-capitals.

Copies seen: Columbia University Libraries (Special Collections B825.M377.W3.1926.ZZ) (Copy 1) grey wrappers; Columbia University Libraries (Special Collections B825.M377.W3.1926.ZZ) (Copy 2) light green-blue wrappers

A81(b) Second English edition ([1926])

Upper wrapper:
Sonnets of Good Cheer | – to the – | Lena Ashwell Players. | [illustration of Mr. Punch pointing stick at puppet's theatre with the initials 'LA' displayed at the top of the theatre: 25 × 16mm.] | From their Well-Wisher, | JOHN MASEFIELD.
(All in red)
(All width centred)

Bibliographies: Simmons [noted on p.107], Nevinson [unrecorded], Handley-Taylor [unrecorded], Wight [unrecorded]

Collation: [A]⁶; 6 leaves; 152 × 120mm.; [i–xii]

Page contents: [i–iv] '[headpiece] | PREFACE' ('IT is now some three or four years since I first saw the Lena Ashwell Players.') (signed, 'JOHN MASEFIELD.'); [v] text; [vi] blank; [vii] text; [viii] blank; [ix] text; [x] blank; [xi] text; [xii] blank

Paper: laid paper (no watermark), chain-lines 23–25mm. apart (note that leaves [A]1 and [A]6 are printed on different paper (laid paper (no watermark), chain-lines 30mm. apart) and this paper is used so that the chain-lines run horizontally)

Running title: none

Binding: vellum wrappers, secured by red ribbon. Spine: blank. On upper wrapper, in red: described above (note that 'Sonnets of Good Cheer | – to the – | Lena Ashwell Players.' is printed within an embossed panel: 45 × 96mm. with rounded corners). On lower wrapper, in red: 'COPYRIGHT | IN GREAT BRITAIN & U.S.A. | BY | JOHN MASEFIELD. | MENDIP PRESS, LONDON & BATH.' (all width centred with the exception of the last line which is ranged lower right). All edges trimmed. Binding measurements: 163 × 124mm. (wrappers), 163 × 2mm. (spine). The wrappers extend beyond the edges of the internal leaves.

Publication date: published, according to Simmons, in an edition of 500 copies

Price: 2s.6d. / 10s.6d. (see notes)

Contents:
as for A81(a)

Notes:
After describing A81(a), bound in grey wrappers and printed on wove paper, Simmons notes:

> Five hundred additional copies were issued on laid paper, in vellum wrappers. Lettered in red on front and back like the gray paper copies, and tied with red ribbon; the edges of the wrappers extending beyond the edges of the six leaves of the book. In this issue there is a comma after the word "Well-Wisher" on the front. Fifty copies were autographed by Mr. Masefield and Miss Ashwell. The autographed copies sold originally at 10s.6d., and the other 400 copies at 2s.6d.

Presumably Simmons should read 'the other 450 copies'. The internal text of these 'additional copies' appears the same.

The preface commences with a decorated drop-capital while the sonnets each commence with drop-capitals

Copies seen: private collection (PWE); BL (Cup.403.b.9) stamped 15 APR 1961; Columbia University Libraries (Special Collections B825.M377.W3.1926.ZZ) (Copy 3)

A82 ODTAA   1926

A82(a) First American edition (1926)

ODTAA | *By* | JOHN MASEFIELD | New York | THE MACMILLAN COMPANY | 1926 | *All rights reserved*
(All width centred)
(The '*B*' of '*By*' is swash)

Bibliographies: Simmons [67], Nevinson [unrecorded], Handley-Taylor p.55, Wight [67]

Collation: [A-B]⁸ [C-O]¹⁶ [P]⁴ (J not used); 212 leaves; 188 × 127mm.; [i–vi] 1–394 [395–96] 397–417 [418]

Page contents: [i] half-title: 'ODTAA'; [ii] '*By* | JOHN MASEFIELD | [31 titles separated by 29 colons] | [point] [point] [point]'; [iii] title-page; [iv] 'COPYRIGHT 1926 | BY JOHN MASEFIELD | *Set Up* [point] *Electrotyped* [point] *Published* | *March* [point] *1926* | *Printed in the United States of America* | *By the Cornwall Press*'; [v] 'ODTAA'; [vi] blank; 1–394 text; [395] 'APPENDICES AND NOTES'; [396] blank; 397–416 text of 'Appendices and Notes'; 417 'The persons and events described in this | story are imaginary; no reference is made to | any living person. | JOHN MASEFIELD.'; [418] blank

Paper: wove paper

Running title: 'ODTAA' (20mm.) on both recto and verso, pp.2–416

Binding: crimson cloth. On spine: 'ODTAA | [device] | JOHN | MASEFIELD [all in crimson on a gold panel] | [point] MACMILLAN [point] [all in gold]' (all width centred). The gold panel is within a rope-like border: 41 × 31mm. Upper cover in blind: 'ODTAA | [device] | JOHN MASEFIELD' (all on blind panel, within a rope-like border: 39 × 96mm.) Lower cover: blank. Top and lower outside edges trimmed, fore edge roughly trimmed. Binding measurements: 195 × 129mm. (covers), 195 × 48mm. (spine). End-papers: wove paper.

Publication date: published, according to Simmons, 23 March 1926 in an edition of 10000 copies

Price: $2.50

Contents:
ODTAA ('Santa Barbara, being the most leeward of the Sugar States, is at the angle of the Continent...')

Notes:
A novel set in Santa Barbara, frequently regarded as a sequel to *Sard Harker* (see A75), although the fictional time is earlier here than in the previous novel. The tale tells of the efforts of Highworth Ridden to inform Don Manuel (the leader of a political rebellion) that his fiancée has been captured. The effort is ultimately futile and the fiancée is murdered whilst Hi struggles to complete his mission. The novel is in nineteen chapters with concluding notes and appendices.

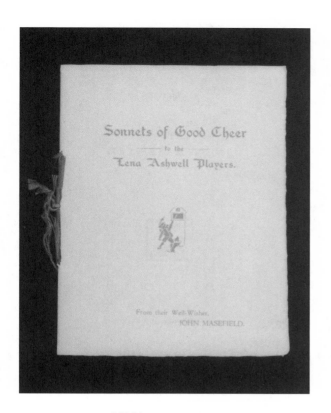

A81(b) upper wrapper

ODTAA

By

JOHN MASEFIELD

New York
THE MACMILLAN COMPANY
1926
All rights reserved

A82(a) title-page

PHILIP THE KING
By
JOHN MASEFIELD
WITH ILLUSTRATIONS BY
LAURENCE IRVING

LONDON
WILLIAM HEINEMANN LTD.
MCMXXVII

A84(a) title-page

PHILIP THE KING
~~AND OTHER POEMS~~

BY
JOHN MASEFIELD

~~WITH A PORTRAIT BY WILLIAM STRANG~~

Title Page. Decorated with a
Scheme of the Badge of the Gol
den Fleece & the Arms of
Spain.
Lettering in Red & Black.

19 20
LONDON: WILLIAM HEINEMANN

Irving's marked-up reprint of A26(a)

ODTAA

A NOVEL

By
JOHN MASEFIELD

LONDON
WILLIAM HEINEMANN LTD.

A82(b) title-page

ODTAA

A NOVEL

By
JOHN MASEFIELD

LONDON
WILLIAM HEINEMANN LTD.
1926

A82(c) title-page

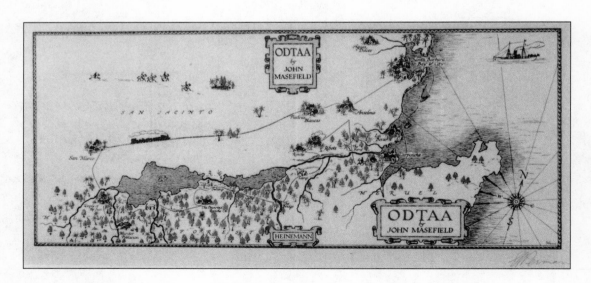

A82(c) copy of the dust-jacket illustration used for A82(b)

Wight notes that there is a typographical error on p.19: 'and' printed in error for 'an'. This occurs on line 20 of the text which therefore incorrectly reads:

> ...I'm not going to have you messing and honoured name with wheel-grease because you've read some damned subversive rag...

This error is still present in the second impression.

The points at the foot of page [ii] are slightly embellished.

The publicity material in the preliminaries that lists Masefield's work (appearing on p.[ii]) incorrectly includes the title *The Tragedy of Man, And Other Plays*.

The copies Masefield presented to his family were of the second impression of this edition. The inscriptions are as follows: HRHRC (AC-L M377OD 1926E cop.1) inscribed 'For Con | from Jan. | April 13. 1926.'; HRHRC (AC-L M377OD 1926E cop.2) inscribed 'For Lew, | 13. IV. 1926.'; HRHRC (AC-L M377OD 1926F cop.2) inscribed 'For Jude | from Zob. | 13 April. 1926.'

A publishing agreement for a novel between Masefield and Macmillan was dated 20 July 1925 (see Archives of The Society of Authors). The agreement refers to 'a licence to publish in volume form… in the United States of America and Canada a work the subject or title of which is his next long novel (title to be agreed upon)'. This may refer to *ODTAA*.

In 1926, during negotiations over a translation of *ODTAA* into 'the Czech / Bohemian language', Masefield was asked to explain the title. Masefield annotated this letter that the 'Title is One Darned Thing After Another' (see BL, Add.Mss.56583, f.18). Over a decade later, Masefield again confirmed the title to The Society of Authors:

> *Odtaa*: the name of this volume is supposed to represent the words "One darned thing after another." The title was suggested by an exclamation from an American who had missed his train; he cried out, "Hell, ain't that just like life: one darned thing after another."

(John Masefield, letter to [E.J.] Mullett, [24 May 1938])
(BL, Add.Mss.56609, f.122)

Copies seen: private collection (PWE); Rutgers University Libraries (ALEX PR6025.A7703 1926)

Reprinted:

'Reprinted'	[first edition, second impression]	Mar 1926

A82(b) First English edition (1926)

ODTAA | A NOVEL | By | JOHN MASEFIELD | [publisher's device of a windmill with the letters 'W' and 'H' all within ruled border: 19 × 20mm.] | LONDON | WILLIAM HEINEMANN LTD.
(All width centred)

Bibliographies: Simmons [67a], Nevinson p.17, Handley-Taylor p.55, Wight [67a]

Collation: [A]⁸ B-Y⁸ (J, V and W not used); signatures left foot of page; 176 leaves; the catalogue (not included in collation or leaf count) comprises a single gathering of eight unsigned leaves; 188 × 120mm.; [i–viii] [1] 2–343 [344]; catalogue pagination: 1–8

Page contents: [i] blank; [ii] 'NOTE | THE persons and events described in this story | are imaginary. No reference is made to any living | person. | JOHN MASEFIELD.'; [iii] half-title: 'ODTAA'; [iv] 'THE COLLECTED POEMS | OF JOHN MASEFIELD | In One Volume. 750 pages. | Cr. 8vo. 8s. 6d. net. | SELECTIONS FROM MASEFIELD | Fcap. 8vo. | Cloth, 6s.; Leather, 8s. 6d. net. | SARD HARKER. A NOVEL | Cr. 8vo. 7s. 6d. net.'; [v] title-page; [vi] '*First published February, 1926* | PRINTED IN GREAT BRITAIN BY | THE LONDON AND NORWICH PRESS, LIMITED, ST. GILES' WORKS, NORWICH'; [vii] 'TO | MY WIFE'; [viii] blank; [1]–343 text (at foot of p.343: '[rule] | THE LONDON AND NORWICH PRESS, LIMITED, ST. GILES' WORKS, NORWICH'); [344] blank; 1–8 catalogue: 'New & Recent Fiction | *published by* | WILLIAM HEINEMANN | LTD. | 20 & 21, BEDFORD ST., LONDON, W.C.2' (see notes)

Paper: wove paper

Running title: 'ODTAA' (20mm.) on both recto and verso, pp.2–343

Binding: blue cloth. On spine, in gold: 'ODTAA | [ornament] | JOHN | MASEFIELD | HEINEMANN' (all width centred). On upper cover, in gold: 'ODTAA | JOHN MASEFIELD' (within blind ruled border: 189 × 117mm.) Lower cover: blank. Top edge stained blue, others trimmed. Binding measurements: 194 × 123mm. (covers), 194 × 47mm. (spine). End-papers: wove paper.

Publication date: published, according to Simmons, 25 March 1926 in an edition of 20000 copies

Price: 7s.6d.

Contents:
as for A82(a)

Notes:
The text has been entirely re-set for this edition.

Masefield sent C.S. Evans details of his new novel during August 1925. At this stage, the author proposed a sub-title that did not appeal to Evans:

> …have you definitely made up your mind that ODTAA, OR CHANGE FOR THREEPENCE is to be the title. If you don't mind my saying so, I should suggest that you leave out the sub-title "Change for Threepence". Two enigmatic titles might prove rather too much for the reader and reviewer.
>
> (C.S. Evans, letter to John Masefield, 28 August 1925)
(HRHRC, MS (Masefield, J.) Recip William Heinemann Ltd.)

The manuscript was acknowledged on 14 January 1926 by C.S. Evans who noted that, as a result, he was 'going to have a pleasant week-end' (see C.S. Evans, letter to John Masefield, 14 January 1926) (HRHRC, MS (Masefield, J.) Recip William Heinemann Ltd.) Evans sent his opinion on 20 January:

> I read ODTAA at a sitting on Sunday, and enjoyed every word of it. I do not think that your hand has lost any of its cunning, and if I did not get quite the thrill from the book that I did from SARD HARKER, that is probably due to the fact that revelation can come only once…
>
> (C.S. Evans, letter to John Masefield, 20 January 1926)
(HFRHRC, MS (Masefield, J.) Recip William Heinemann Ltd.)

A few days later Evans sent a sketch of the proposed dust-jacket design. It appears that Masefield had previously sent his own version:

> I enclose herewith a rough sketch for the wrapper of ODTAA. This sketch is made to go right over the front, spine and back of the wrapper. You will see that owing to the proportions the artist has found it impossible to get in all the ground covered by your original sketch…
>
> (C.S. Evans, letter to John Masefield, 29 January 1926)
(HRHRC, MS (Masefield, J.) Recip William Heinemann Ltd.)

The dust-jacket illustration appears to have caused some delay. Heinemann wrote to Masefield:

> …Please don't think that I am wasting time over the wrapper, but the artist wanted to read the book so that he could make the little sketches and we have had to wait for the proofs.
>
> (C.S. Evans, letter to John Masefield, 10 February 1926)
(Archives of The Society of Authors)

On the day of publication Evans wrote with news of subscription orders:

> …To-day is the publication day of ODTAA and I am, on the whole, very satisfied with the result of our preliminary work. The subscription orders, as I told you, will be round about 20,000…
>
> (C.S. Evans, letter to John Masefield, 25 March 1926)
(HRHRC, MS (Masefield, J.) Recip William Heinemann Ltd.)

The publishing agreement for this title between Masefield and Heinemann was dated 4 February 1926 (see Archives of The Society of Authors). The agreement refers to a publication price of 7s.6d.

Each part commences with a drop-capital with the exception of part XX.

There are several different publication dates cited. The volume itself notes February 1926, Simmons cites 25 March 1926 and the *English Catalogue of Books* gives April 1926. A letter from C.S. Evans to Masefield notes '…have now fixed the date of publication for March 25th.' (see C.S. Evans, letter to John Masefield, 10 February 1926) (Archives of The Society of Authors).

The catalogue is not included in all copies. It is not present in a copy presented by the author to his daughter.

The archives of The Society of Authors record that an application to publish a Braille version of this text was received from the National Library for the Blind in June 1926 (see BL, Add.Mss.56583, f.25).

Copies seen: BL (NN.11691) stamped 25 MAR 1926; University of Reading Library (823.912 Reserve) inscribed 'For Margaret [Bridges], | March. 1926'; HRHRC (PR6025 A77 O383) inscribed 'For Judith | from Zob. | 12th March. 1926.'

Reprinted:

	[first edition, second impression]	Apr 1926
'Popular Edition' / 'Cheap edition'	[first edition, third impression]	May 1927
		Jun 1930
		Dec 1932
'Reprinted'		Aug 1935
		1949

The 'Popular edition' published, according to the *English Catalogue of Books*, during May 1927 was priced at 3s.6d and issued in red cloth. The issue uses the standard setting of text. The publishing agreement for this issue between Masefield and Heinemann was dated 1927 (see Archives of The Society of Authors). The agreement refers to a publication price of 3s.6d.

A82(c) Second English edition (limited signed edition) (1926)

ODTAA [in red] | A NOVEL | By | JOHN MASEFIELD | [publisher's device of a windmill with the letters 'W [point]' and 'H' all within ruled border: 19 × 20mm.] | LONDON | WILLIAM HEINEMANN LTD. | 1926
(All width centred)

Bibliographies: Simmons [67b], Nevinson [unrecorded], Handley-Taylor p.55, Wight [67b]

Collation: [A]⁸ B-Y⁸ (J, V and W not used); signatures left foot of page; 176 leaves; 222 × 148mm.; [i–viii] [1] 2–343 [344]

Page contents: [i–ii] blank; [iii] half-title: 'ODTAA'; [iv] '*This edition of ODTAA is limited | to 275 copies, of which 250 are | for sale. | This is No. ....*'; [v] title-page; [vi] 'PRINTED IN GREAT BRITAIN BY | THE LONDON AND NORWICH PRESS, LIMITED, ST. GILES' WORKS, NORWICH'; [vii] 'TO | MY WIFE'; [viii] blank; [1]–343 text (at foot of p.343: '[rule] | THE LONDON AND NORWICH PRESS, LIMITED, ST. GILES' WORKS, NORWICH'); [344] blank

Paper: laid paper (no watermark), chain-lines 25–26mm. apart

Running title: 'ODTAA' (20mm.) on both recto and verso, pp.2–343

Binding: blue-grey boards with parchment spine. On spine, in gold: 'ODTAA | [ornament] | JOHN | MASEFIELD | HEINEMANN' (all width centred). There is a single vertical rule in blind on each cover at the edge of the parchment. Covers: blank. Top edge gilt, lower outside edge untrimmed, fore edge uncut. Sewn head band (in blue and white) and blue marker ribbon. Binding measurements: 228 × 145mm. (covers), 228 × 44mm. (spine). End-papers: laid paper (watermark: '[Crown] | Abbey Mills | Greenfield'), chain-lines 24mm. apart. Also included on wove paper (Simmons describes it as "Japan paper") is a copy (signed by the artist E.G. Perman) of the dust-jacket illustration used for A82(b). This enclosure (measuring 212 × 483mm.) comprises a map in red, black, yellow, blue and green and is folded three times. It is enclosed in a gummed envelope.

Publication date: published, according to Simmons, 15 April 1926

Price: 31s.6d.

Contents:
as for A82(a)

Notes:
Each part commences with a drop-capital with the exception of part XX.

Simmons notes in his bibliography:

> There are two misprints: page 33, line 32, ihe for the; and line 34, same page, took, for look.

These are not present in A82(b).

Heinemann wrote to Masefield:

> We propose to do a Limited Edition also of 250 copies, to be sold for 31/6. Will this suit you? We are doing a small number because we think it essential to keep up the value of these Limited Editions. I will let you know later when the sheets will be ready for your signature.
>
> (C.S. Evans, letter to John Masefield, 10 February 1926)
> (Archives of The Society of Authors)

C.S. Evans wrote to Masefield on 26 February 1926 asking if the author could 'come in some time on Thursday next to sign the Limited Edition of ODTAA?' (see C.S. Evans, letter to John Masefield, 26 February 1926) (HRHRC, MS (Masefield, J.) Recip William Heinemann Ltd.)

Evans under-estimated demand and Heinemann found it necessary to provide a typed letter to booksellers:

> ODTAA by John Masefield, Limited to 250 copies each copy numbered and signed by the author… The above edition, which we are publishing on the 15th inst., has been heavily over subscribed, but we have pleasure in informing you that we have been able to allot you _____ copies.
>
> (William Heinmann Ltd., letter addressed to 'Dear Sirs', 13 April 1926)
> (Private Collection)

Copies seen: private collection (PWE) number 19, signed '19 | John Masefield.' on p.[iv]; private collection (PWE) number 165, signed '165 | John Masefield.' on p.[iv]; BL (12650.DD.12) number 253, signed '253 | John Masefield.' on p.[iv], stamped 16 APR 1926

A82(d) Third English edition ["Wanderer edition"] (1935)

ODTAA | A NOVEL | By | JOHN MASEFIELD | [publisher's device of a windmill with the letters 'W [point]' and 'H'] | LONDON | WILLIAM HEINEMANN | LIMITED
(All width centred)

Bibliographies: Handley-Taylor p.55, Wight [unrecorded]

Collation: [A]⁸ (±[A]2) B-X⁸ (J and V not used); signatures left foot of page (with the exception of signatures W and X which are at right foot of page); 176 leaves; 189 × 125mm.; [i–viii] [1] 2–343 [344]

Page contents: [i] blank; [ii] 'NOTE | THE persons and events described in this story | are imaginary. No reference is made to any living | person. | JOHN MASEFIELD.'; [iii] half-title: 'THE COLLECTED WORKS OF | JOHN MASEFIELD | [rule] | WANDERER EDITION | ODTAA'; [iv] '*ALSO BY JOHN MASEFIELD* | PLAYS: | [12 titles listed] | POETRY: | [14 titles listed] | FICTION: | [seven titles listed] | GENERAL: | [nine titles listed]'; [v] title-page; [vi] '*First published March 1926* | *Reprinted April 1926* | *Cheap Edition (3s. 6d.) May 1927* | *Reprinted June 1930, December 1932* | *August 1935* | Printed in Great Britain at The Windmill Press, Kingswood, Surrey'; [vii] 'TO | MY WIFE'; [viii] blank; [1]–343 text; [344] blank

Paper: wove paper

Running title: 'ODTAA' (20mm.) on both recto and verso, pp.2–343

Binding: blue cloth. On spine, in gold: 'JOHN | MASEFIELD | ODTAA | THE | WANDERER | EDITION | HEINEMANN' (all width centred). On upper cover, in gold: illustration of a cockerel: 32 × 24mm. (ranged lower right). On lower cover, in blind: publisher's device of a windmill (ranged lower right). Top edge gilt, others trimmed. Sewn head band (in blue) and blue marker ribbon. Binding measurements: 196 × 127mm. (covers), 196 × 47mm. (spine). End-papers: wove paper.

Publication date: published, according to Handley-Taylor, 21 October 1935

Price: 5s.

Contents:
as for A82(a)

Notes:
The second leaf in the first gathering ([A]2) is a stub with a single leaf tipped-in as a cancellan. The new leaf includes note of the Wanderer edition and the rest of the volume appears to use the same type setting as A82(b).

The difference in signatures between this edition and A82(b) arises due to the omission of letters J, V and W in the first edition and the inclusion of letter W as a signature in the Wanderer edition. Despite this, the setting of text appears to be the same.

Noting the variations for publication date of A82(b), this edition states that the novel was first published in March 1926. This challenges the date of February 1926 as given within A82(b) and also April 1926 as cited by the *English Catalogue of Books*. Simmons, however, gives 25 March 1926 as the date of publication.

The publishing agreement for 'a collected edition of the Author's work', including this title, between Masefield and Heinemann was dated 31 July 1935 (see Archives of The Society of Authors). The agreement refers to 'a published price of 5/-...' (see note on collected editions).

Each part commences with a drop-capital with the exception of part XX.

Copies seen: private collection (PWE); BL (12452.i.3) stamped 23 OCT 1935, rebound

A82(e) Fourth English edition (1966)

Odtaa | John Masefield | Penguin Books
(All ranged to the left)

Bibliographies: Wight [unrecorded]

Collation: 144 unsigned leaves bound by the 'perfect binding' process; 180 × 110mm.; [1–8] 9–23 [24] 25–41 [42] 43–55 [56] 57–67 [68] 69–81 [82] 83–98 [99] 100–133 [134] 135–45 [146] 147–58 [159] 160–68 [169] 170–89 [190] 191–202 [203] 204–220 [221] 222–38 [239] 240–49 [250] 251–61 [262] 263–73 [274] 275–87 [288]

Page contents: [1] 'Penguin Book 2541 | Odtaa | John Masefield, who has been Poet Laureate since | 1930, was born in Ledbury, Herefordshire, in 1874, | the son of a lawyer. He was orphaned at an early | age, and after attending the local school was | indentured to a merchant ship at the age of | fourteen. After three years at sea in different parts | of the world he went ashore at New York in 1895 | with five dollars and a few clothes. He took odd | jobs and worked in a carpet factory at Yonkers, | meanwhile reading avidly and beginning to write | poetry. After returning to England in 1897 he met | both J. M. Synge and W. B. Yeats. He published | *Salt Water Ballads* in 1902, *Ballads* in 1903, and | *Captain Margaret*, his first novel, in 1908. He also | wrote plays, notably *The Tragedy of Nan*, which was | acclaimed a masterpiece by several critics, and *Good* | *Friday*, which used to be presented annually on | Palm Sunday by the Union Congregational Church | in Boston. *The Everlasting Mercy* and *The Widow* | *in the Bye Street* (1912) were two volumes of his | verse which caused much excitement and | discussion. In 1962 the Poetry Award went to him | for *The Bluebells and Other Verse*. Among his many | other novels are *Dead Ned* (1938), *Live and Kicking* | *Ned* (1939), and *Basilissa* (1940). *The Midnight Folk* | (1927) is in Puffins and *Sard Harker* (1924) has been | published in Penguins.'; [2] blank; [3] title-page; [4] 'Penguin Books Ltd, Harmondsworth, | Middlesex, England | Penguin Books Pty Ltd, Ringwood, | Victoria, Australia | First published by William Heinemann Ltd 1926 | Published in Penguin Books 1966 | Copyright © John Masefield, 1926 | Made and printed in Great Britain by | C. Nicholls & Company Ltd, Manchester | Set in Monotype Times | This book is sold subject to the condition that | it shall not, by way of trade or otherwise, be lent, | re-sold, hired out, or otherwise circulated without | the publisher's prior consent in any form of | binding or cover other than that in which it is | published and without a similar condition | including this condition being imposed on the | subsequent purchaser'; [5] 'To my wife'; [6] blank; [7] '*Note* The persons and events described in | this story are imaginary. No reference is | made to any living person. | *John Masefield*'; [8] blank; 9–[288] text

Paper: wove paper

Running title: none

Binding: white wrappers (printed orange). On orange spine, reading lengthways down spine from head: 'John Masefield [in white] Odtaa [in black]', horizontally at foot of spine: '[publisher's device of a penguin within single ruled oval border] [in black] | 2541 [in black]'. On white upper wrapper: '*ODTAA* [in black] | *John Masefield* [in black] | A novel of [in orange] | the ultimate blasphemy [in orange] | [illustration in yellow, brown, green, red and black of Don Lopez]' (with publisher's device of a penguin within single ruled oval border in black, white and orange ranged upper left and '6/-' in black ranged upper right). On orange lower wrapper: 'ODTAA' [in black] | Where an insane dictator [in black] | set himself up [in black] | in the place of God [in black] | In this sequel to [in red] Sard Harker [in white] | written forty years ago, [in red] | the Poet Laureate portrays the [in red] | pain of a revolution-torn [in red] | Caribbean state – and a hero who [in red] | is not afraid to be heroic. [in red] | 'Odtaa – One Damn Thing After Another [in white] | Cover illustration by Peter Kettle [in white] | [photograph in black and orange of Masefield] | For copyright reasons this edition is not for sale in the U.S.A. or Canada [in black]'. All edges trimmed. Binding measurements: 180 × 110mm. (wrappers), 180 × 17mm. (spine).

Publication date: published, according to the *English Catalogue of Books*, 25 August 1966

Price: 6s.

Contents:
as for A82(a)

Notes:
The text has been entirely re-set for this edition.

The final part ('Appendices And Notes') is numbered XX in A82(b). In this Penguin edition no part number is given.

The biography of Masefield on p.[1] includes a number of errors.

Copies seen: private collection (PWE); BL (12208.a.1/2541) stamped 9 AUG 1966 rebound

A83 THE WITCH   1926

A83(a) First American edition (1926)

THE WITCH | *A Drama in Four Acts* | By JOHN MASEFIELD | [rule (tapered at both ends), 45mm.] | *From the Norwegian* | *of* | H. WIERS-JENSSEN | [rule (tapered at both ends), 45mm.] | INTRODUCTION BY HUBERT OSBORNE | *Assistant Director, University Theater* | *Yale University* | [publisher's device of a tree with 'NUNQUAM' and 'DORMIO' within two scrolls all within ruled border in shape of a diamond] | BRENTANO'S | PUBLISHERS 1926 NEW YORK
(All width centred)

Bibliographies: Simmons [noted on p.134], Nevinson [unrecorded], Handley-Taylor [unrecorded], Wight [unrecorded]

Collation: [A]⁴ [B-G]⁸; 52 leaves; 189 × 124mm.; [i–iv] v–vii [viii] [1–5] 6–33 [34] 35–56 [57] 58–80 [81] 82–93 [94–96]; illustrations (on glossy paper) are tipped-in on pp.[iii], 55, 69 and 83

Page contents: [i] half-title: 'THE WITCH'; [ii] blank; [iii] title-page (with additional leaf tipped-in on the verso of which is the black and white frontispiece photograph: 120 × 87mm., 'MISS ALICE BRADY as ANNE PEDERSDOTTER | *and* | MR. HUGH HUNTLEY AS MARTIN'); [iv] '*COPYRIGHT, 1926, BY BRENTANO'S, INC.* | *COPYRIGHT,* 1917, *BY LITTLE, BROWN AND CO.* | *Manufactured in the United States of America.*'; v–vii 'INTRODUCTION' ('Anne Pedersdotter represents a woman starved physically, mentally and spiritually.') (signed, 'HUBERT OSBORNE. | New York. November, 1926.'); [viii] blank; [1] 'THE WITCH'; [2] blank; [3] '"The Witch" had its first professional presentation | in America at the Greenwich Village Theatre, New | York, on Thursday, November 18th, 1926. It was pro- | duced by Carl Reed, directed by Hubert Osborne, with | settings and costumes designed by Livingston Platt. | The cast was as follows: | [dramatis personae and original New York cast listed]'; [4] 'CHARACTERS | [dramatis personae listed] | *The action takes place in Bergen in the year 1574: the* | *first three Acts in Absolon's house, the last in the choir of* | *the Cathedral.*'; [5]–93 text; [94–96] blank

Paper: wove paper

Running title: 'Introduction [23mm.] | [rule, 89mm.]' on both verso and recto, pp.vi–vii; and 'THE WITCH [35mm.] | [rule, 88mm.]' on both verso and recto, pp.6–93.

Binding: orange cloth. On spine, reading lengthways down spine from head, in dark blue: 'The Witch', horizontally at foot of spine, in dark blue: 'BRENTANO'S' (see notes). On upper cover, in dark blue: 'The Witch' (within blind ruled border: 189 × 120mm.) (see notes). On lower cover, in blind: publisher's device of a tree with 'NUNQUAM' and 'DORMIO' within two scrolls all within diamond shape (ranged lower right). Top edge stained grey, others roughly trimmed. Binding measurements: 197 × 128mm. (covers), 197 × 24mm. (spine). End-papers: wove paper.

Publication date: due to information present on p.[3] the publication date must be either November or December 1926

Price: unknown

Contents:
Introduction ('Anne Pedersdotter represents a woman starved physically, mentally and spiritually.')
      (signed, 'HUBERT OSBORNE. | New York. November, 1926.')
The Witch ('THE FIRST ACT | SCENE ONE | *Bells at start. Garden at the back of Absolon Beyer's...*')

Notes:
There are similarities to A40(a). Compare the pagination, for example.

The title '*The Witch*' includes a number of swash characters when it appears on the binding of this volume.

Hubert Osborne writes in his introduction:

> The combination of Masefield and Wiers-Jenssen is a happy one. The distinguished English poet-playwright has poured all the beauty of strong and vivid English prose that is at his command into this work. Mr. Masefield was in America when rehearsals were in progress and so availed himself of the opportunity to supervise the first American production.

Copies seen: private collection (PWE); ULL (Sterling Library)

A83(b) Second American edition ([c.1926])

THE WITCH | *A Drama in Four Acts* | *By* JOHN MASEFIELD | [double rule, 45mm.] | *From the Norwegian* | *of* | H. WIERS-JENSSEN | [double rule, 45mm.] | INTRODUCTION BY HUBERT OSBORNE | *Assistant Director,* *University Theater* | *Yale University* | [publisher's device of a lion within oval] | SAMUEL FRENCH | *Founded* 1845 [point] *Incorporated* 1899 | 25 WEST 45TH ST.   811 WEST 7TH ST. | NEW YORK CITY   LOS ANGELES
(All width centred)

Bibliographies: Simmons [unrecorded], Nevinson [unrecorded], Handley-Taylor [unrecorded], Wight [unrecorded]

Collation: [A]⁴ (±[A]2) [B-G]⁸; 52 leaves; 190 × 124mm.; [i–iv] v–vii [viii] [1–5] 6–33 [34] 35–56 [57] 58–80 [81] 82–93 [94–96]; illustrations (on glossy paper) are tipped-in on pp.[iii], 55, 69 and 83

Page contents: [i] half-title: 'THE WITCH'; [ii] blank; [iii] title-page (with additional leaf tipped-in on the verso of which is the black and white frontispiece photograph: 119 × 87mm., 'MISS ALICE BRADY as ANNE PEDERSDOTTER | *and* | MR. HUGH HUNTLEY AS MARTIN'); [iv] '*All Rights Reserved* | Copyright, 1917, by Little, Brown and Co. | Copyright, 1926, by Brentano's, Inc. | [new paragraph] Especial notice should be taken that the possession of this | book without a valid contract for production first having been | obtained from the publisher confers no right or license to pro- | fessionals or amateurs to produce the play publicly or in pri- | vate for gain or charity. | [new paragraph] In its present form this play is dedicated to the reading public | only, and no performance, representation, production, recitation, | public reading or radio broadcasting may be given except by | special arrangement with Samuel French, at 25 West 45th | Street, New York, N. Y., or at 811 West 7th Street, Los | Angeles, Calif. [new paragraph] On application to Samuel French, at 25 West 45th Street, | New York, or at 811 West 7th Street, Los Angeles, Calif., | royalty will be quoted for amateur production.'; v–vii 'INTRODUCTION' ('Anne Pedersdotter represents a woman starved physically, mentally and spiritually.') (signed, 'HUBERT OSBORNE. | New York. November, 1926.'); [viii] blank; [1] 'THE WITCH'; [2] blank; [3] '"The Witch" had its first professional presentation | in America at the Greenwich Village Theatre, New | York, on Thursday, November 18th, 1926. It was pro- | duced by Carl Reed, directed by Hubert Osborne, with | settings and costumes designed by Livingston Platt. | The cast was as follows: | [dramatis personae and original New York cast listed]'; [4] 'CHARACTERS | [dramatis personae listed] | *The action takes place in Bergen in the year 1574: the* | *first three Acts in Absolon's house, the last in the choir of* | *the Cathedral.*'; [5]–93 text; [94–96] blank

Paper: wove paper

Running title: '*Introduction* [23mm.] | [rule, 89mm.]' on both verso and recto, pp.vi–vii; and 'THE WITCH [35mm.] | [rule, 88mm.]' on both verso and recto, pp.6–93.

Binding: dark red cloth (see notes). On spine, reading lengthways down spine from head: 'The Witch', horizontally at foot of spine: 'SAMUEL | FRENCH' (see notes). On upper cover: 'The Witch' (width centred) (within blind ruled border: 193 × 121mm.) (see notes). Lower cover: blank. Top edge stained, others trimmed. Binding measurements: 197 × 125mm. (covers), 197 × 25mm. (spine). End-papers: wove paper.

Publication date: [c.1926]

Price: unknown

Contents:
as for A83(a)

Notes:
This edition includes a cancel-title. Given the similarities to the 1926 edition published by Brentano's (see A83(a)), it may comprise the Brentano's edition issued by Samuel French (with cancel-title and Samuel French binding). The date is after 1926 since the copyright of the Brentano's edition is noted on p.[iv].

Another copy of this edition printed on thinner wove paper and bound in green cloth suggests that Samuel French reprinted copies without noting reprint information.

The title '*The Witch*' includes a number of swash characters when it appears on the binding of this volume.

Copies seen: private collection (ROV) in dark red cloth, defective copy: lacking frontispiece; private collection (PWE) in green cloth

Reprinted:
see notes

A84 PHILIP THE KING   1927

A84(a) First English edition (limited signed edition) (1927)

PHILIP THE KING | By | JOHN MASEFIELD | WITH ILLUSTRATIONS BY | LAURENCE IRVING | [ornament of the badge of the Golden Fleece] | LONDON | WILLIAM HEINEMANN LTD. | MCMXXVII (All width centred)

Bibliographies: Simmons [noted on p.46], Nevinson [unrecorded], Handley-Taylor p.35, Wight 25c

Collation: A² [B]² C¹ D³ E-M² N¹ G¹ O² [P]² Q² R¹ P¹ S–U² (J not used) (see notes); signatures right foot of page; 40 leaves; 288 × 222mm.; [i–xii] 1–6 [two un-numbered pages] 7–10 [two un-numbered pages] 11–14 [two un-numbered pages] 15–22 [two un-numbered pages] 23–30 [two un-numbered pages] 31–34 [two un-numbered pages] 35–38 [two un-numbered pages] 39–40 [two un-numbered pages] 41–42 [two un-numbered pages] 43–44 [two un-numbered pages] 45 [46–48]

Page contents: [i] half-title: 'PHILIP THE KING'; [ii] 'This edition is limited to 360 | copies, of which 350 are for sale | This is No.'; [iii] blank; [iv] blank (with black and white illustration tipped-in: 194 × 135mm., '[illustration of 'Philip The King' within ruled border] | Printed in England'); [v] title-page; [vi] 'Printed in Great Britain at | The Westminster Press | 411a Harrow Road | London W.9'; [vii] 'TO | MY WIFE'; [viii] blank; [ix] '[dramatis personae listed with 'PERSONS' and 'SPIRITS' headings] | TIME | At dawn in late September, 1588 | SCENE | A little dark cell in Philip's palace'; [x–xi] blank; [xii] blank (with black and white illustration tipped-in: 200 × 135mm., '[illustration of 'Enter the Princess' without fixed borders] | Printed in England'); 1–6 text; [-] blank (with black and white illustration tipped-in: 194 × 135mm., '[illustration of 'All a long summer day those ships defiled' within ruled border] | Printed in England'); [-] blank; 7–10 text; [-] blank (with black and white illustration tipped-in: 194 × 135mm., '[illustration of 'The Indians Enter' within ruled border] | Printed in England'); [-] blank; 11–14 text; [-] blank (with black and white illustration tipped-in: 192 × 132mm., '[illustration of 'Don John appears, with Escovedo behind him' without fixed borders] | Printed in England'); [-] blank; 15–22 text; [-] blank (with black and white illustration tipped-in: 195 × 135mm., '[illustration of 'An Englishman is brought in' within ruled border] | Printed in England'); [-] blank; 23–30 text, [-] blank (with black and white illustration tipped-in: 195 × 135mm., '[illustration of 'Recalde's men approaching the town' within ruled border] | Printed in England'); [-] blank; 31–34 text; [-] blank (with black and white illustration tipped-in: 192 × 130mm., '[illustration of 'Enter Messenger, carrying an Admiral's chain' within ruled border] | Printed in England'); [-] blank; 35–38 text; [-] blank (with black and white illustration tipped-in: 195 × 136mm., '[illustration of 'Fire-ships are coming! Wake, Cast loose, for Jesus' sake!' within ruled border] | Printed in England'); [-] blank; 39–40 text; [-] blank (with black and white illustration tipped-in: 195 × 135mm., '[illustration of a ship in battle within ruled border] | Printed in England'); [-] blank; 41–42 text; [-] blank (with black and white illustration tipped-in: 193 × 133mm., '[illustration of 'The savage Irish watched' without fixed borders] | Printed in England'); [-] blank; 43–44 text; [-] blank (with black and white illustration tipped-in: 191 × 134mm., '[illustration of wrecked ship within ruled border] | Printed in England'); [-] blank; 45–[46] text with tail-piece; [47] blank; [48] '[printer's device] | The Westminster Press | 411a Harrow Road | London, W.9'

Paper: laid paper (watermark: 'ETRURIA | ITALY'), chain-lines 28mm. (the chain-lines run horizontally)

Running-title: 'Philip the King' (36mm.) positioned extreme left on same line as text on verso; positioned extreme right on same line as text on recto, pp.1–[46] (excluding un-numbered pages)

Binding: black cloth. On spine, reading lengthways up spine, from foot, in gold: 'PHILIP THE KING JOHN | MASEFIELD' (the author's name in a smaller type than the title); horizontally at foot of spine: 'HEINEMANN'. On upper cover, in gold: ornament of the badge of the Golden Fleece: 55 × 42mm. On lower cover, in blind: publisher's device of a windmill (ranged lower right). Top edge gilt, others uncut. Binding measurements: 293 × 225mm. (covers), 293 × 21mm. (spine). End-papers: laid paper (watermark: 'ETRURIA | ITALY'), chain-lines 28mm. apart, decorated in black with a lion on the left and a bull on the right. The end-papers are bound so that the chain-lines run horizontally. Volume contained in slip-case covered in cream paper.

Publication date: published, according to the *English Catalogue of Books*, June 1927

Price: 42s.

Contents:
Philip the King ('PHILIP (*kneeling*) | Lord, I am that Philip whom Thou has made King of half the world.')

Notes:
A one act play in both verse and prose telling of war and the loss of the Armada. First published in *Philip the King and other poems* (see A26), this limited edition (which excludes the 'other poems') was illustrated by Laurence Irving.

Irving used a November 1920 reprint of A26(a) when working on this edition. His working copy is freely annotated with notes on the illustrations and sheets of paper are loosely inserted with the titles of the intended illustrations. These titles (where present) and Irving's descriptions of devices are used in the above description. The working copy also reveals that many of Irving's intentions were not realized (these include numerous illustrations printed with the text, the number and nature of the full-page illustrations, and all stage directions which were to be printed in red). Irving's working copy is in a private collection (PWE).

During February 1926, Evans noted that he wanted Masefield '…to see the drawings Laurence Irving has made for PHILIP THE KING…' (see C.S. Evans, letter to John Masefield, 26 February 1926) (HRHRC, MS (Masefield, J.) Recip William Heinemann Ltd.) It was not, however, until April in the following year that proofs were available:

> I am sending you herewith the proofs of the limited edition of PHILIP THE KING. I did not want to bother you with these and had given instructions for them to be read in the house from the original edition; but there seem to be a lot of queries, chiefly about punctuation, and it occurs to me that you would perhaps rather settle these yourself.
>
> (C.S. Evans, letter to John Masefield, 14 April 1927)
> (HRHRC, MS (Masefield, J.) Recip William Heinemann Ltd.)

A revised set of proofs was sent on 27 April 1927 (see C.S. Evans, letter to John Masefield, 27 April 1927) (HRHRC, MS (Masefield, J.) Recip William Heinemann Ltd.) Over a month later Evans was writing that both this edition and the limited signed edition of *Tristan and Isolt* (see A85(b)) were almost ready for signing:

> I shall have sheets of the Limited Editions of PHILIP THE KING and TRISTAN AND ISOLT ready for signing some time towards the end of next week. Will it be convenient for you to come here and sign them or shall we make some other arrangement. PHILIP THE KING will be published on June 23rd and TRISTAN probably a little later…
>
> (C.S. Evans, letter to John Masefield, 2 June 1927)
> (HRHRC, MS (Masefield, J.) Recip William Heinemann Ltd.)

The following day Evans noted that 'the sheets of both PHILIP THE KING and TRISTAN AND ISOLT will be ready on Friday, June 10th.' (see C.S. Evans, letter to John Masefield, 3 June 1927) (HRHRC, MS (Masefield, J.) Recip William Heinemann Ltd.) Masefield, however, had a problem but proposed a solution:

> I am sorry you have hurt your arm. So far as we are concerned it will be all right if you sign the books with your left hand, but won't it be a very slow job?
>
> (C.S. Evans, letter to John Masefield, 7 June 1927)
> (HRHRC, MS (Masefield, J.) Recip William Heinemann Ltd.)

The text commences with a drop-capital

The signatures and gatherings in this volume are confusing. Wight describes the volume as: $[\pi]^4$ B-E^8. This description is not confirmed by any of the copies examined. The confusion presumably arises from the insertion of pages for illustrations (or confusion over the more simple collation found in A84(b)). Many of the leaves are signed (although their position causes confusion – the leaf bearing a signature 'P' is found between signatures 'R' and 'S', for example). There are, additionally, many stubs which form part of the binding.

Copies seen: private collection (PWE) number 247, signed '247 | John Masefield.' and 'Laurence Irving.' on p.[ii]; private collection (PWE) un-numbered, signed 'John Masefield.' and 'Laurence Irving.' on p.[ii]; BL (11778.h.24) number 354, signed '354 | John Masefield.' and 'Laurence Irving.' on p.[ii], stamped 30 JUN 1927

A84(b) First American edition (limited signed edition) (1927)

PHILIP THE KING | By | JOHN MASEFIELD | WITH ILLUSTRATIONS BY | LAURENCE IRVING | [ornament of the badge of the Golden Fleece] | NEW YORK | THE MACMILLAN COMPANY | MCMXXVII (All width centred)

Bibliographies: Simmons [noted on p.46], Nevinson [unrecorded], Handley-Taylor p.35, Wight 25b

Collation: [A]^9 ([A]2+1) [B-E]^8; 41 leaves; 293 × 224mm.; [i–xiv] 1–6 [two un-numbered pages] 7–10 [two un-numbered pages] 11–14 [two un-numbered pages] 15–22 [two un-numbered pages] 23–30 [two un-numbered pages] 31–34 [two un-numbered pages] 35–38 [two un-numbered pages] 39–40 [two un-numbered pages] 41–42 [two un-numbered pages] 43–44 [two un-numbered pages] 45 [46–48]

Page contents: [i] blank; [ii] '*Of this edition of PHILIP THE KING, | illustrated by Laurence Irving, 375 copies | have been printed, of which this is No. ....*'; [iii] half-title: 'PHILIP THE KING'; [iv] '[publisher's device] | THE MACMILLAN COMPANY | [two lines listing six cities, separated by four points] | MACMILLAN & CO., LIMITED | [two lines listing four cities, separated by two points] | THE MACMILLAN CO. OF CANADA, LTD. | [one city listed]'; [v] blank; [vi] blank (with black and white illustration tipped-in: 194 × 135mm., '[illustration of 'Philip The King' within ruled border] | Printed in England'); [vii] title-page; [viii] 'COPYRIGHT, 1914, | BY THE MACMILLAN COMPANY. | Illustrated Edition, September 1927. | PRINTED IN THE UNITED STATES OF AMERICA | BY J. J. LITTLE & IVES COMPANY, NEW YORK'; [ix] 'TO | MY WIFE'; [x] blank; [xi] '[dramatis personae listed with 'PERSONS' and 'SPIRITS' headings] | TIME | At dawn in late September, 1588 | SCENE | A little dark cell in Philip's palace'; [xii–xiii] blank; [xiv] blank (with black and white illustration tipped-in: 200 × 135mm., '[illustration of 'Enter the Princess' without fixed borders] | Printed in England'); 1–6 text; [-] blank (with black and white illustration tipped-in: 194 × 135mm., '[illustration of 'All a long summer day those ships defiled' within ruled border] | Printed in England'); [-] blank; 7–10 text; [-] blank (with black and white illustration tipped-in: 194 × 135mm., '[illustration of 'The Indians Enter' within ruled border] | Printed in England'); [-] blank; 11–14 text; [-] blank (with black and white illustration tipped-in: 192 × 132mm., '[illustration of 'Don John appears, with Escovedo behind him' without fixed borders] | Printed in England'); [-] blank; 15–22 text; [-] blank (with black and white illustration tipped-in: 195 × 135mm., '[illustration of 'An Englishman is brought in' within ruled border] | Printed in England'); [-] blank; 23–30 text; [-] blank (with black and white illustration tipped-in: 195 × 135mm., '[illustration of 'Recalde's men approaching the town' within ruled border] | Printed in England'); [-] blank; 31–34 text; [-] blank (with black and white illustration tipped-in: 192 × 130mm., '[illustration of 'Enter Messenger, carrying an Admiral's chain' within ruled border] | Printed in England'); [-] blank; 35–38 text; [-] blank (with black and white illustration tipped-in: 195 × 136mm., '[illustration of 'Fire-ships are coming! Wake, Cast loose, for Jesus' sake!' within ruled border] | Printed in England'); [-] blank; 39–40 text; [-] blank (with black and white illustration tipped-in: 195 × 135mm., '[illustration of a ship in battle within ruled border] | Printed in England'); [-] blank; 41–42 text; [-] blank (with black and white illustration tipped-in: 193 × 133mm., '[illustration of 'The savage Irish watched' without fixed borders] | Printed in England'); [-] blank; 43–44 text; [-] blank (with black and white illustration tipped-in: 191 × 134mm., '[illustration of wrecked ship within ruled border] | Printed in England'); [-] blank; 45–[46] text with tail-piece; [47–48] blank

Paper: laid paper (no watermark), chain-lines 25mm. (the chain-lines run horizontally)

Running-title: 'Philip the King' (36mm.) positioned extreme left on same line as text on verso; positioned extreme right on same line as text on recto, pp.1–[46] (excluding un-numbered pages)

Binding: black cloth. On spine, reading lengthways up spine, from foot, in gold: 'PHILIP THE KING JOHN | MASEFIELD' (the author's name in a smaller type than the title); horizontally at foot of spine: 'MACMILLAN | [point] [point] [point]'. On upper cover, in gold: ornament of the badge of the Golden Fleece: 55 × 42mm. Lower cover: blank. Top edge gilt, others roughly trimmed. Sewn head and foot bands (in crimson and white). Binding measurements: 298 × 226mm. (covers), 298 × 21mm. (spine). End-papers: laid paper (no watermark), chain-lines 25mm. apart, decorated in black with a lion on the left and a bull on the right. The end-papers are bound so that the chain-lines run horizontally. Volume contained in slip-case covered in black paper, with white laid paper label (74 × 105mm.) upon which: 'PHILIP THE KING | *BY* | JOHN MASEFIELD | ILLUSTRATED BY | LAURENCE IRVING | [ornament] | *Of this edition, 375 copies* | *have been printed, of which* | *this is number* . . . . | [rule] | THE MACMILLAN COMPANY' (all enclosed within ornate border: 61 × 92mm.)

Publication date: published, according to date within volume, September 1927

Price: $12.50

Contents:
as for A84(a)

Notes:
In contrast with A84(a), the collation of this edition is simple. Blank pages are included within the gatherings and illustrations tipped-in upon them. The setting is not the same as in A84(a) for minor typographical differences occur.

Wight is incorrect to suggest that the Macmillan edition predates the Heinemann edition (implied by his numbering the editions '25b' and '25c' respectively). A84(a) was published, according to the *English Catalogue of Books* in June 1927 while the Macmillan edition states publication in September 1927.

The text commences with a drop-capital. The italic type used within this edition includes a number of swash characters.

The additional leaf ([A]1) pasted onto [A]2 comprises the leaf detailing the limitation of the edition. The paper type is the same as that used for the rest of the volume. The single leaves were presumably sent to Masefield and Irving for signing.

Copies seen: private collection (PWE) number 293, signed '293 | J Masefield.' and 'Laurence Irving.' on p.[ii]; Columbia University (Special Collections B825 M377 U54 1927 c.1) number 100, signed '100 | J Masefield.' and 'Laurence Irving.' on p.[ii]; Columbia University (Special Collections B825 M377 U54 1927 c.2) number 292, signed '292 | J Masefield.' and 'Laurence Irving.' on p.[ii]

A85 TRISTAN AND ISOLT 1927

A85(a) *First English edition (1927)*

TRISTAN AND ISOLT | *A Play in Verse* | BY | JOHN MASEFIELD | [publisher's device of a windmill with 'W [point]' and 'H' all within ruled border: 15 × 15mm.] | LONDON | WILLIAM HEINEMANN, LTD. (All width centred)

Bibliographies: Simmons [68], Nevinson p.14, Handley-Taylor p.56, Wight [68]

Collation: [A]⁴ B-I⁸ K⁴ (J not used); signatures right foot of page; 72 leaves; 183 × 120mm.; [i–viii] 1–135 [136]

Page contents: [i] blank; [ii] '*This Play is copyright in Great Britain, her colonies and* | *dependencies, and in the United States of America.* | [new paragraph] *It may not be performed, nor publically read, without licence* | *from the Author, which may be obtained through the Society* | *of Authors,*

11 Gower Street, London, W.C.'; [iii] half-title: 'TRISTAN AND ISOLT'; [iv] '*OTHER PLAYS BY JOHN | MASEFIELD* | [eight titles listed] | *POETRY BY JOHN | MASEFIELD* | [12 titles listed] | *OTHER WORKS BY JOHN | MASEFIELD* | [seven titles listed]'; [v] title-page; [vi] '*First published 1927* | *Printed in Great Britain by Richard Clay & Sons, Ltd., Bungay, Suffolk.*'; [vii] 'First performed by the Lena Ashwell Players at | the Century Theatre, Archer Street, Bayswater, | at 8.15 p.m., on Monday, 21st February, 1927, | with the following cast : | (*Characters in the order of their appearance.*) | [dramatis personae and original cast listed]'; [viii] blank; 1–133 text; 134–35 'NOTE' ('*Stage*. This play was written to be played in two hours…'); [136] blank

Paper: wove paper

Running title: 'TRISTAN AND ISOLT' (39mm.) on both verso and recto, pp.2–133

Binding: blue cloth. On spine, in gold: 'Tristan | and | Isolt | [ornament] | John | Masefield | HEINEMANN' (all width centred). On upper cover, in gold: 'TRISTAN AND ISOLT | JOHN MASEFIELD' (within blind ruled border: 184 × 116mm.) On lower cover, in blind: publisher's device of a windmill (ranged lower right). All edges trimmed. Binding measurements: 189 × 121mm. (covers), 189 × 25mm. (spine). End-papers: wove paper.

Publication date: published, according to Simmons, 30 June 1927 in an edition of 3000 copies

Price: 6s.

Contents:
Tristan and Isolt ('(*From Front Stage.*) | DESTINY. I am She who began ere Man was begotten,')

Notes:
A play of the legend in verse.

Writing to The Society of Authors, in January 1927, Masefield states his wish that the Lena Ashwell Players (and especially Esmé Church) should first present the play:

> …I have today sent to Mr Harold Gibson, the Director of the Lena Ashwell Players, Century Theatre, Archer Street, Westbourne Grove, copies of a tragedy in verse, called *Tristan and Isolt*, which they wish to produce about March, if it pass the Censor. I am interested in these players, + want their leading lady, Miss Esmé Church, to have the first playing of *Isolt*. Will the Collection Bureau arrange the terms with the players for me? I would like to grant them a limited licence to perform at the Century Theatre + at the other municipal halls where their companies perform; that they should pay me five per cent of the gross receipts, + understand that the licence is granted on the condition that they play the whole of my play as it stands, without any cut or change. I can do it here as I want it done at any time; + I cannot have it mutilated when it is done away from here. If they think that they cannot do it without mutilation, they must say so and give up the thought of it. I shan't be vext with them if they do this.

> (John Masefield to [G.H.] Thring, [16 January 1927])
> (BL, Add.Mss.56584, f.28)

Masefield, here refers to his own theatre at Boars Hill (the 'Music Room'). In making these conditions Masefield presumably considered that he had an ability to conceive the piece in performance. Another letter, dated two days later, notes that: '…I had better be called to rehearsals, even if I only go to 2 or 3' (see John Masefield, letter to [G.H.] Thring, [18 January 1927]) (BL, Add.Mss.56584, f.31)) therefore indicating that Masefield was anxious to be involved and presumably guard his text. As the published volume reveals, the play was indeed first performed by the Lena Ashwell Players on 21 February 1927. Esmé Church played Isolt.

The Lena Ashwell Players lost money on their production. (A letter from Harold Gibson to G.H. Thring dated 11 April 1927 is preserved in the archives of The Society of Authors (see BL, Add.Mss.56584, f.149)). In the circumstances Masefield decided upon generous terms, suggesting that the Players should send to the Collection Bureau of The Society of Authors:

> …a cheque for what would have been the Society's five per cent collection fee upon my royalties. If they will do this, and will return to me the typescript of the play, which I sent to them, + also waive the lieu they have upon the play for a few weeks to come, I will waive my own claim for royalties. This may help them out…

> (John Masefield, letter to [G.H.] Thring, [13 April 1927])
> (BL, Add.Mss.56584, f.154)

C.S. Evans wrote to Masefield on 18 March 1928 noting that he had 'sent the typescript to the printer… we hope to publish the book in May…' (see C.S. Evans, letter to John Masefield, 18 March 1927) (HRHRC, MS (Masefield, J.) Recip William Heinemann Ltd.) Proofs followed in May, together with an expression of eagerness to publish the volume:

> The proofs of TRISTAN were sent off to you on Saturday morning and you doubtless have them by now. I do not want to hold it over until the autumn and I should like to publish it as soon as it is ready.

> (C.S. Evans, letter to John Masefield, 9 May 1927)
> (HRHRC, MS (Masefield, J.) Recip William Heinemann Ltd.)

Copies seen: private collection (PWE); private collection (BG) inscribed 'For | Barbara Vernon, | Brangwen, | from John Masefield. | July 28 1939.'; BL (011781.e.87) stamped 30 JUN 1927; HRHRC (PR6025 A77 T8 1927 cop.3) inscribed 'Written long ago, after | visiting all the places in | Cornwall still reputed to | be the scenes of the | tragedy, + the camps | + dwellings of King | Marc. | John Masefield. | The London Library Appeal. | No 36.'

A85(b) Second English edition (limited signed edition) (1927)

TRISTAN AND ISOLT | *A Play in Verse* | BY | JOHN MASEFIELD | LONDON | WILLIAM HEINEMANN, LTD. | 1927
(All width centred)

Bibliographies: Simmons [68a], Nevinson [unrecorded], Handley-Taylor p.56, Wight [68a]

Collation: [A]⁴ B-I⁸ K⁴ (J not used); signatures right foot of page; 72 leaves; 225 × 144mm.; [i–viii] 1–135 [136]

Page contents: [i–ii] blank; [iii] half-title: 'TRISTAN AND ISOLT'; [iv] *'This edition, printed on English handmade | paper, is limited to two hundred and seventy- | five copies, of which two hundred and fifty | are for sale and twenty-five for presentation. | No. ....'*; [v] title-page; [vi] *'Printed in Great Britain by Richard Clay & Sons, Ltd., Bungay, Suffolk.'*; [vii] 'First performed by the Lena Ashwell Players at | the Century Theatre, Archer Street, Bayswater, | at 8.15 p.m., on Monday, 21st February, 1927, | with the following cast : | (*Characters in the order of their appearance.*) | [dramatis personae and original cast listed]'; [viii] blank; 1–133 text; 134–35 'NOTE' ('*Stage.* This play was written to be played in two hours…'); [136] blank

Paper: laid paper (watermark: 'MILLBOURN | BRITISH HAND MADE PURE RAG [castle device: 27 × 42mm.]'), chain-lines 28mm. apart. (Note that the chain-lines run horizontally)

Running title: 'TRISTAN AND ISOLT' (39mm.) on both verso and recto, pp.2–133

Binding: blue-green boards with parchment spine. On spine, in gold: 'Tristan | and | Isolt | [ornament] | John | Masefield | HEINEMANN' (all width centred). There is a single vertical rule in blind on each cover at the edge of the parchment. Covers: blank. Top edge gilt, lower outside edge untrimmed, fore edge uncut. Binding measurements: 231 × 149mm. (covers), 231 × 30mm. (spine). End-papers: laid paper (no watermark), chain-lines 24mm. apart.

Publication date: published, according to Simmons, 7 July 1927. A letter from A.S. Frere-Reeves notes '…the Ordinary Edition of TRISTRAN [*sic*] will be published on June 30th. and the Limited Edition on July 5th.' (see A.S. Frere-Reeves, letter to John Masefield, 22 June 1927) (HRHRC, MS (Masefield, J.) Recip William Heinemann Ltd.)

Price: 21s.

Contents:
as for A85(a)

Notes:
The text appears to use the same type setting as A85(a).

Upon receiving the manuscript, C.S. Evans noted '…it seems to me that it would be a very good idea to do a collectors' edition of the book with colour plates of the costumes…' (see C.S. Evans, letter to John Masefield, 23 February 1927) (HRHRC, MS (Masefield, J.) Recip William Heinemann Ltd.) Costume designs were not, eventually, reproduced. On 18 March Evans noted that he felt '…very strongly that we ought not to do more than 250 copies…' (see C.S. Evans, letter to John Masefield, 18 March 1927) (HRHRC, MS (Masefield, J.) Recip William Heinemann Ltd.) See A84(a) for details of Masefield signing the limitation sheets.

Copies seen: private collection (PWE) number 1, signed '1 | John Masefield.' on p.[iv]; BL (11778.ddd.33) number 254, signed '254 | John Masefield.' on p.[iv] stamped 8 JUL 1927

A85(c) First American edition (limited signed edition) (1927)

[rule, 89mm.] | TRISTAN | AND | ISOLT | *A Play in Verse* [*sic*] | BY | JOHN MASEFIELD | [oval cameo device] | [rule, 89mm.] | THE MACMILLAN COMPANY | NEW YORK   MCMXXVII | *All rights reserved*
(All width centred and enclosed within double ruled border: 146 × 91mm. There are two single vertical lines on either side of the text between the two single horizontal rules)

Bibliographies: Simmons [noted on p.110], Nevinson [unrecorded], Handley-Taylor p.56, Wight [noted on p.118]

Collation: [A]⁹ ([A]2+1) [B-I]⁸ [K]⁴ (J not used); 77 leaves; 247 × 160mm.; [i–x] 1–144

Page contents: [i] blank; [ii] 'THIS EDITION OF "TRISTAN AND ISOLT" | IS LIMITED TO THREE HUNDRED AND | FIFTY COPIES. THIS IS NUMBER'; [iii] half-title: 'TRISTAN AND ISOLT'; [iv] *'OTHER PLAYS BY JOHN | MASEFIELD* | [eight titles listed] | *POETRY BY JOHN | MASEFIELD* | [12 titles listed] | *OTHER WORKS BY JOHN | MASEFIELD* | [seven titles listed]'; [v] title-page; [vi] 'COPYRIGHT, 1927. | BY JOHN MASEFIELD. | [rule] | Set up and electrotyped. | Published October, 1927. | PRINTED IN THE UNITED STATES OF AMERICA | BY THE CORNWALL PRESS'; [vii] 'First performed by the Lena Ashwell Players at the Cen- | tury Theatre, Archer Street, Bayswater, at 8.15 P.M., on | Monday, 21st February, 1927, with the following cast: | (*Characters in the order of their appearance.*) | [dramatis personae and original cast listed]'; [viii] *'This Play is copyright in Great Britain, her colonies and | dependencies, and in the United States of America.* | [new paragraph] *It may not be performed, nor publically read, without licence | from the Author.'*; [ix] 'TRISTAN AND ISOLT'; [x] blank; 1–142 text; 143–44 'NOTE' ('*Stage.* This play was written to be played in two hours…')

Paper: laid paper (no watermark), chain-lines 24mm. apart

Running title: 'TRISTAN AND ISOLT' (38mm.) on both verso and recto, pp.2–144

Binding: pale green boards with dark green cloth spine. On spine: pale green laid paper label (67 × 27mm.) on which, in green: '[ornamental rule] | [double rule] | TRISTAN | AND | ISOLT | [floral device] | JOHN | MASEFIELD | [floral device] | MACMILLAN | [double rule] | [ornamental rule (in mirror image of first ornamental rule)]'. On upper cover: panel in blind: 70 × 90mm. upon which: pale green laid paper label (69 × 89mm.) on which in green: 'TRISTAN AND | ISOLT | *By* | JOHN MASEFIELD' (enclosed within double ruled border and all within ornamental rule: 60 × 81mm.) Lower cover: blank. Top edge roughly trimmed, others uncut. Binding measurements: 252 × 159mm. (covers), 252 × 32mm. (spine). End-papers: laid paper (no watermark), chain-lines 20mm. apart.

Publication date: published, according to Simmons, 18 October 1927

Price: unknown

Contents:
Tristan and Isolt ('[*From Front Stage.*] | DESTINY | I am She who began ere Man was begotten,')

Notes:
Note the incorrect '*Plav*' in error for '*Play*' on the title-page

The plates for this electrotyped edition were presumably used for A85(d). As in the later edition, the publicity material in the preliminaries that lists Masefield's work (appearing on p.[iv]) bears a marked similarity to that present in the Heinemann edition. Moreover, titles as cited here are those of English editions (separate editions of Masefield's Racine translations and *St. George and the Dragon*, for example).

The additional leaf ([A]1) pasted onto [A]2 comprises the leaf detailing the limitation of the edition. The paper type is the same as that used for the rest of the volume. The single leaves were presumably sent to Masefield for signing.

A publishing agreement for this title between Masefield and Macmillan was dated 25 October 1926 (see Archives of The Society of Authors). The agreement refers to 'a licence to publish in volume form… in the United States of America and Canada a work the subject or title of which is Tristram and Isolde, a play'. Masefield has corrected this to 'Tristan and Isolt'.

Although noted by both Simmons and Handley-Taylor, the exclusion of a full bibliographical description from Wight is curious. Wight merely states 'a limited signed edition was also issued'. Moreover, Wight notes A85(d) as the 'First American Edition' which is contrary to publication dates provided by Simmons and Handley-Taylor.

Copies seen: private collection (PWE) number 116, signed '116 | J. Masefield.' on p.[ii]

A85(d) Second American edition (1927)

[rule, 89mm.] | TRISTAN | AND | ISOLT | *A Plav in Verse* [*sic*] | BY | JOHN MASEFIELD | [oval cameo device] | [rule, 89mm.] | THE MACMILLAN COMPANY | NEW YORK MCMXXVII | *All rights reserved*
(All width centred and enclosed within double ruled border: 146 × 91mm. There are two single vertical lines on either side of the text between the two single horizontal rules)

Bibliographies: Simmons [noted on p.110], Nevinson [unrecorded], Handley-Taylor p.56, Wight 68b

Collation: [A-I]⁸ [K]⁴ (J not used); 76 leaves; 188 × 127mm.; [i–viii] 1–144

Page contents: [i] half-title: 'TRISTAN AND ISOLT'; [ii] '*OTHER PLAYS BY JOHN* | *MASEFIELD* | [eight titles listed] | *POETRY BY JOHN* | *MASEFIELD* | [12 titles listed] | *OTHER WORKS BY JOHN* | *MASEFIELD* | [seven titles listed]'; [iii] title-page; [iv] 'COPYRIGHT, 1927. | BY JOHN MASEFIELD. | [rule] | Set up and electrotyped. | Published October, 1927. | PRINTED IN THE UNITED STATES OF AMERICA | BY THE CORNWALL PRESS'; [v] 'First performed by the Lena Ashwell Players at the Cen- | tury Theatre, Archer Street, Bayswater, at 8:15 P.M., on | Monday, 21st February, 1927, with the following cast: | (*Characters in the order of their appearance.*) | [dramatis personae and original cast listed]'; [vi] '*This Play is copyright in Great Britain, her colonies and* | *dependencies, and in the United States of America.* | [new paragraph] *It may not be performed, nor publically read, without licence* | *from the Author.*'; [vii] 'TRISTAN AND ISOLT'; [viii] blank; 1–142 text; 143–44 'NOTE'

Paper: wove paper

Running title: 'TRISTAN AND ISOLT' (38mm.) on both verso and recto, pp.2–144

Binding: burgundy cloth. On spine, in gold: 'TRISTAN | AND | ISOLT | MASEFIELD | [point]MACMILLAN[point]' (all width centred). On upper cover, in blind: 'TRISTAN | AND ISOLT | MASEFIELD' (ranged upper left) (within blind ruled border: 189 × 121mm.) Lower cover: blank. Top and lower outside edges trimmed, fore edge roughly timmed. Binding measurements: 195 × 129mm. (covers), 195 × 30mm. (spine). End-papers: wove paper.

Publication date: published, according to Simmons, 25 October 1927 in an edition of 4000 copies

Price: $2.00

Contents:
as for A85(c)

Notes:
As in A85(c), note the incorrect '*Plav*' in error for '*Play*' on the title-page.

As in A85(c), the publicity material in the preliminaries that lists Masefield's work (appearing on p.[ii]) bears a marked similarity to that present in the Heinemann edition. Moreover, titles as cited here are those of English editions (separate editions of Masefield's Racine translations and *St. George and the Dragon*, for example).

Copies seen: private collection (ROV)

A86 THE MIDNIGHT FOLK

1927

A86(a) First English edition (limited signed edition) (1927)

THE MIDNIGHT [in red] | FOLK [in red] | *A NOVEL* | BY | JOHN MASEFIELD | [publisher's device of a windmill with 'W' and 'H' all within ruled border: 19 × 20mm.] | LONDON | WILLIAM HEINEMANN LTD. | 1927 (All width centred)

Bibliographies: Simmons [69], Nevinson p.17, Handley-Taylor p.56, Wight [69]

Collation: [A]⁸ B-U⁸ X⁴ (J, V and W not used); signatures left foot of page; 164 leaves; 222 × 145mm.; [1–7] 8–327 [328]

Page contents: [1] half-title: 'THE MIDNIGHT FOLK'; [2] '*This edition of THE MIDNIGHT | FOLK is limited to 265 copies of | which 250 are for sale. | This is No. ....*'; [3] title-page; [4] 'PRINTED IN GREAT BRITAIN BY | THE LONDON AND NORWICH PRESS, LIMITED, ST. GILES' WORKS, NORWICH'; [5] 'FOR | J. & L.'; [6] blank; [7]–327 text; [328] blank

Paper: laid paper (watermark of two masted ship at sea with birds in flight all within oval rope design border: 83 × 54mm.), chain-lines 27–28mm. apart

Running title: 'THE MIDNIGHT FOLK' (56mm.) on both verso and recto, pp. 8–327

Binding: blue-green boards with parchment spine. On spine, in gold: 'THE | MIDNIGHT | FOLK | [ornament] | JOHN | MASEFIELD | HEINEMANN' (all width centred). There is a single vertical rule in blind on each cover at the edge of the parchment. Covers: blank. Top edge gilt, lower outside edge untrimmed, fore edge uncut. Sewn head band (in blue and white) and blue marker ribbon. Binding measurements: 228 × 150mm. (covers), 228 × 44mm. (spine). End-papers: laid paper (watermark of shield with embellishments at head, and on individual scrolls within body of shield 'K', 'L' and 'L': 146 × 108mm.), chain-lines 27mm. apart.

Publication date: published, according to Simmons, 10 November 1927

Price: 42s.

Contents:

The Midnight Folk ('It had been an unhappy day for little Kay Harker. To begin with, at breakfast time the governess...')

Notes:

A children's novel noted by Judith Masefield as being the work which her father 'liked the best'. Muriel Spark describes the novel as a 'wonderful fantasy' and L.A.G. Strong considered that, with its sequel *The Box of Delights*, it was 'among the most sure-footed and robust books for children ever written'. The novel has no chapter divisions. The story tells of Kay Harker's adventures to locate family treasure. He is pitted against his evil governess, a covern of witches and Abner Brown. The novel was reprinted with its sequel in a single volume publication in 1991 (see A176).

Wight notes two examples of typographical errors in A86(b):

> There are typographical errors on page 97, line 3, and page 233, line 17.

The first example finds 'wth' in error for 'with'. The second comprises 'Hor8e' for 'Horse' and this error is repeated on p.322, line 4. Of these, the first (on p.97, line 3) is not present in this edition. This suggests that, although published first, this edition may have been printed after A86(b).

There is no indication outside the text that this is a novel for children. The dedication ('For J. & L.') shows Masefield dedicating the novel to his children (although when the book was published Judith was 23 and Lewis was 17 years old).

Copies seen: private collection (PWE) number 171, signed '171 | John Masefield.' on p.[2]; private collection (ROV) number 71, signed '71 | John Masefield.' on p.[2]; BL (Cup.401.g.16) number 255, signed '255 | John Masefield.' on p.[2] stamped 10 NOV 1927; HRHRC (PZ8 M4476MI 1927 cop.1) number 256, signed '256 | John Masefield.' on p.[2] and additionally inscribed 'For Con from Jan. | Dec 1. 1927.'; HRHRC (PZ8 M4476MI 1927 cop.2) number 265, signed '265 | Rest + be thankful | copy. | John Masefield.' on p.[2] and additionally inscribed 'A tale written in 1925, | at Boar's Hill, in | Berkshire. John Masefield. | The London Library Appeal. | No 72.' this inscription replaces an earlier inscription in pencil (mostly erased) which read 'For Judith | from Zom | Dec 1. 1927.'

A86(b) Second English edition (1927)

THE MIDNIGHT | FOLK | *A NOVEL* | BY | JOHN MASEFIELD | [publisher's device of a windmill with 'W' and 'H' all within ruled border: 19 × 20mm.] | LONDON | WILLIAM HEINEMANN LTD. (All width centred)

Bibliographies: Simmons [69a], Nevinson p.17, Handley-Taylor p.56, Wight [69a]

Collation: [A]⁸ B-U⁸ X⁴ (J, V and W not used); signatures left foot of page; 164 leaves; 187 × 122mm.; [1–7] 8–327 [328]

Page contents: [1] half-title: 'THE MIDNIGHT FOLK'; [2] '*Novels by the Same Author* | ODTAA | SARD HARKER'; [3] title-page; [4] '*First published in 1927* | PRINTED IN GREAT BRITAIN BY | THE LONDON AND NORWICH PRESS, LIMITED, ST. GILES' WORKS, NORWICH'; [5] 'FOR | J. & L.'; [6] blank; [7]–327 text; [328] blank

Paper: laid paper (no watermark), chain-lines 27mm. apart

Running title: 'THE MIDNIGHT FOLK' (56–57mm.) on both verso and recto, pp.8–327

Binding: blue cloth. On spine, in gold: 'THE | MIDNIGHT | FOLK | [ornament] | JOHN | MASEFIELD | HEINEMANN' (all width centred). On upper cover, in gold: 'THE MIDNIGHT FOLK | JOHN MASEFIELD' (within blind ruled border: 188 × 119mm.) Lower cover: blank. Top and fore edges trimmed, lower outside edge untrimmed. Binding measurements: 193 × 123mm. (covers), 193 × 42mm. (spine). End-papers: wove paper

Publication date: published, according to Simmons, 15 December 1927 in an edition of 15000 copies. (Simmons also states 'some copies were released in November' while Handley-Taylor notes 'some copies were released on November 17, 1927'.) The *English Catalogue of Books* records a publication date of November 1927. A letter from Heinemann to Masefield notes '…the publication date of MIDNIGHT FOLK is November 17th.' (see Theodore Byard, letter to John Masefield, 6 October 1927 (HRHRC, MS (Masefield, J.) Recip William Heinemann Ltd.)

Price: 7s.6d.

Contents:
as for A86(a)

Notes:
Simmons notes that the top edge is blue and this is repeated by Wight. Not all copies have this feature.

Wight notes two examples of typographical errors:

There are typographical errors on page 97, line 3, and page 233, line 17.

The first example finds 'wth' in error for 'with'. The second comprises 'Hor8e' for 'Horse' and this error is repeated on p.322, line 4. This is indeed an error for, despite the use of childish spellings for the names of Kay's toys, 'Petter [*sic*] Horse' is included in the list of toys on p.21. Childish spellings are, nevertheless, a feature of the novel as Kay's letter on p.68 demonstrates. The first error does not occur in A86(a).

The dust-jacket for this edition appears to have caused some problems. Katherine Monro wrote to Masefield at the end of June 1927:

> …I have just moved over from reading to advertising, and I found the instructions for your MIDNIGHT FOLK wrapper waiting for me. There is a certain Miss Perry who would, I believe, do it admirably, and she is going to send in a rough sketch for you to see and criticize. She is anxious – and I agree with her – to go back to your original idea of having all the Midnight Folk included, and if she uses the back as well as the front of the wrapper, there ought to be plenty of room to have them in some kind of procession. But she says she wishes she had either some more of the book or some further instructions to go upon, particularly with regard to the appearance of the spirits and witches. If there is anything more you could tell her, or another chapter or so that you could lend us I think she would get a better idea of the book, and do a better sketch for it. But if not, don't bother to answer this – I will send you her sketch when it comes and you can amend it then.

(Katherine Monro, letter to John Masefield, 27 June 1927)
(HRHRC, MS (Masefield, J.) Recip William Heinemann Ltd.)

Just under a month later C.S. Evans noted that Heinemann had 'got a good wrapper… I think, after many attempts. I did not bother you with the final thing because of the necessity for hurry.' (see C.S. Evans, letter to John Masefield, 21 July 1927) (HRHRC, MS (Masefield, J.) Recip William Heinemann Ltd.) Masefield, it appears, agreed with Evans and asked for details of the artist. Evans replied:

> …I am so glad to hear you like the wrapper. The artist's address is:- Mr. R.C.N. Barton, 28, Grosvenor Road, London S.W.1

(C.S. Evans, letter to John Masefield, 23 September 1927)
(HRHRC, MS (Masefield, J.) Recip William Heinemann Ltd.)

Copies seen: private collection (PWE); private collection (PWE) inscribed 'For Julia Smith, | from John Masefield. | November 24. 1927.'; BL (NN.13519) stamped 17 NOV 1927; NYPL (Berg Collection) inscribed to Gilbert Murray 'G.M. | from J.M. | Nov.ʳ 1927.'; HRHRC (PZ8 M4476MI cop.1) inscribed 'For Con, | from Jan. | (Advance copy. Octʳ 29. 1927.)'; HRHRC (PZ8 M4476MI cop.2) inscribed 'For Con, | from Jan. | November 19. 1927.'; HRHRC (PZ8 M4476MI cop.3) inscribed 'For Judith | from | Zo. | Nov 19. 1927.'; HRHRC (PZ8 M4476MI cop.4) inscribed 'For Ivy Fox. | from Con + Jan. | Christmas. 1927.'

Reprinted:

'New impression'	[first edition, later impression]	Oct / Nov 1927?
	[first edition, later impression]	1931?
	[first edition, later impression]	Jan 1935?

The 1949 edition (see A86(g)) notes October 1927 and January 1935 as reprints. The 1957 edition (see A86(h)) notes reprint dates of 1927 and 1931 only (and omits reference to the 1949 volume)

TRISTAN AND ISOLT

A Play in Verse

BY

JOHN MASEFIELD

LONDON
WILLIAM HEINEMANN, LTD.
1927

A85(b) title-page

TRISTAN
AND
ISOLT

A Play in Verse

BY
JOHN MASEFIELD

THE MACMILLAN COMPANY
NEW YORK   MCMXXVII

A85(c) title-page

THE MIDNIGHT
FOLK

A NOVEL

BY
JOHN MASEFIELD

LONDON
WILLIAM HEINEMANN LTD.
1927

A86(a) title-page

THE
MIDNIGHT
FOLK

BY
JOHN MASEFIELD

NEW YORK
THE MACMILLAN COMPANY
1927

A86(c) title-page

A86(e) frontispiece by Rowland Hilder

THE MIDNIGHT
FOLK

A NOVEL
BY
JOHN MASEFIELD
ILLUSTRATED
BY
ROWLAND HILDER

LONDON: WILLIAM HEINEMANN LTD.

A86(e) title-page

MIDSUMMER NIGHT

AND

OTHER TALES IN VERSE

BY
JOHN MASEFIELD

NEW YORK
THE MACMILLAN COMPANY
1928

A88(b) title-page

JOHN MASEFIELD

MIDSUMMER NIGHT

and

other tales in
Verse

London
WILLIAM HEINEMANN LTD

A88(c) title-page

A86(c) First American edition (limited signed edition) (1927)

THE [in green] | MIDNIGHT [in green] | FOLK [in green] | BY | JOHN MASEFIELD | [floral ornament] [in green] | NEW YORK | THE MACMILLAN COMPANY | 1927
(All width centred and enclosed within wavy border, all within double ruled border: 152 × 92mm.)

Bibliographies: Simmons [noted on p.112], Nevinson [unrecorded], Handley-Taylor p.56, Wight 69b

Collation: [A]¹¹ ([A]2+1) [B-R]⁸ (J not used); 139 leaves; 258 × 169mm.; [i–viii] [1–2] 3–269 [270]

Page contents: [i] 'THIS AUTOGRAPHED EDITION OF | JOHN MASEFIELD'S "THE MIDNIGHT FOLK," | IS LIMITED TO TWO HUNDRED AND FIFTY | COPIES, OF WHICH THIS IS NUMBER.....................'; [ii] blank; [iii] half-title: 'THE MIDNIGHT FOLK'; [iv] publisher's device; [v] title-page; [vi] 'COPYRIGHT, 1927, | BY JOHN MASEFIELD. | [rule] | Set up and electrotyped. | Published November, 1927. | *Printed in the United States of America by* | J. J. LITTLE AND IVES COMPANY, NEW YORK'; [vii] 'FOR | J. & L.'; [viii] blank; [1] 'THE MIDNIGHT FOLK'; [2] blank; 3–269 text; [270] blank

Paper: laid paper (no watermark), chain-lines 18mm. apart (see notes)

Running title: 'The Midnight Folk' (35mm.) on both verso and recto, pp.4–269

Binding: blue-green boards with blue cloth spine. On spine: 'THE | MIDNIGHT | FOLK | [five point star] | MASEFIELD | [point]MACMILLAN[point]' (all width centred). On upper cover, in gold: facsimile signature 'J. Masefield.' (width centred but at an angle). Lower cover: blank. Top edge gilt, lower outside edge untrimmed, fore edge uncut. Binding measurements: 264 × 169mm. (covers), 264 × 38mm. (spine). End-papers: blue laid paper (watermark 'FABRIANO I'), chain-lines 28mm. apart (see notes). Volume contained in slip-case covered in dark blue paper, with white paper label (64 × 98mm.) upon which: 'THE MIDNIGHT FOLK | BY | JOHN MASEFIELD | [ornament] | *Of this edition of* "The Midnight Folk" | *250 copies have been printed, each signed* | *by the author. This is number* _____. | [ornament] | THE MACMILLAN COMPANY' (all enclosed within ornate border: 51 × 85mm.)

Publication date: published, according to Simmons, 22 November 1927

Price: unknown

Contents:
as for A86(a)

Notes:
The text has been entirely re-set for this edition.

The text commences with a drop-capital.

Page [iv] carries the usual Macmillan publisher's device. It is normally followed by a listing of Macmillan companies and locations. These are omitted here, however.

The additional leaf ([A]1) pasted onto [A]2 comprises the leaf detailing the limitation of the edition. The paper type is different from that used for the rest of the volume. It is laid paper (watermark: 'SUEDE | [diamond shape containing letter 'D'] | LAID'), chain-lines 30mm. apart. The single leaves were presumably sent to Masefield for signing.

Within the first gathering conjugate leaves [A]3 and [A]10 are printed on a different stock of laid paper (no watermark), chain-lines 24mm. apart. The chain-lines run horizontally. As [A]3 comprises the sheet containing the title-page, the printing process using two different colours presumably necessitated separate printing from the rest of the gathering.

The blue laid paper end-papers have chain-lines that run horizontally. It is feasible that there is more to the watermark which has proven impossible to discern from examined copies.

The publishing agreement for this title between Masefield and Macmillan was dated 1 July 1927 (see Archives of The Society of Authors).

Copies seen: private collection (PWE) number 146, signed '146 | J. Masefield.' on p.[i]; Columbia University (Special Collections B825M377 T33 1927b) number 45, signed '45 | J. Masefield.' on p.[i]; Columbia University (Special Collections B825M377 T33 1927c) number 126, signed '126 | J. Masefield.' on p.[i]; HRHRC (TEMP M377MI 1927D) number 27, signed '27 | J. Masefield.' on p.[i] additionally inscribed 'For Con | from Jan. | December 14. | 1927.'

A86(d) Second American edition (1927)

THE [in green] | MIDNIGHT [in green] | FOLK [in green] | BY | JOHN MASEFIELD | [floral ornament] [in green] | NEW YORK | THE MACMILLAN COMPANY | 1927
(All width centred and enclosed within wavy border, all within double ruled border: 152 × 92mm.)

Bibliographies: Simmons [noted on p.112], Nevinson [unrecorded], Handley-Taylor p.56, Wight [noted on p.121]

Collation: [A]¹⁰ [B-R]⁸ (J not used); 138 leaves; 197 × 133mm.; [i–vi] [1–2] 3–269 [270]

Page contents: [i] half-title: 'THE MIDNIGHT FOLK'; [ii] publisher's device; [iii] title-page; [iv] 'COPYRIGHT, 1927, | BY JOHN MASEFIELD. | [rule] | Set up and electrotyped. | Published November, 1927. | *Printed in the United States of America by* | J. J. LITTLE AND IVES COMPANY, NEW YORK'; [v] 'FOR | J. & L.'; [vi] blank; [1] 'THE MIDNIGHT FOLK'; [2] blank; 3–269 text; [270] blank

Paper: wove paper

Running title: 'The Midnight Folk' (35mm.) on both verso and recto, pp.4–269

Binding: blue-purple cloth. On spine, in gold: 'THE | MIDNIGHT | FOLK | [five point star] | MASEFIELD | [point]MACMILLAN[point]' (all width centred). On upper cover, in blind: 'THE MIDNIGHT FOLK | [ornament] | JOHN MASEFIELD' (within blind ruled border: 196 × 122mm.) Lower cover: blank. Top and lower outside edges trimmed, fore edge roughly trimmed. Binding measurements: 203 × 135mm. (covers), 203 × 45mm. (spine). End-papers: wove paper.

Publication date: published, according to Simmons, 29 November 1927 in an edition of 2500 copies

Price: $2.50

Contents:
as for A86(a)

Notes:
The edition appears to use the same setting of text as used for A86(c). The text commences with a drop-capital.

Page [ii] carries the usual Macmillan publisher's device. It is normally followed by a listing of Macmillan companies and locations. These are omitted here, however.

Copies seen: Bodleian (25612.e.13855) inscribed 'For Judith, | from Zob. | Dec. 14. 1927.', includes Judith's notes for a projected illustrated edition, includes posthumous booklabel, stamped 6 MAR 1975; HRHRC (TEMP M377MI 1927c) inscribed 'For Con. | from Jan. | December 14. 1927.'

A86(e)   Third English edition (first English illustrated edition) (1931)

THE MIDNIGHT | FOLK | *A NOVEL* | *BY* | JOHN MASEFIELD | ILLUSTRATED | *BY* | ROWLAND HILDER | [illustration of bow of ship (incorporating ruled border): 55 × 58mm.] [in pink] | LONDON: WILLIAM HEINEMANN LTD.
(All width centred)

Bibliographies: Handley-Taylor p.56, Wight 69c

Collation: [A]⁸ B-R⁸ S¹⁰ (J not used); S2 is also signed; signatures right foot of page; 146 leaves; 249 × 180mm.; [i–viii] 1–17 [18] 19–36 [37] 38–53 [54–55] 56 [57] 58–83 [84–85] 86–108 [109] 110–43 [144–45] 146–218 [219] 220–82 [283–84] coloured illustration plates on glossy paper (with protective tissues) are bound with the gatherings (each plate having a conjugate leaf stub) as follows:

LOCATION OF ILLUSTRATION	LOCATION OF CONJUGATE LEAF STUB
A1v / A2	A7v / A8
A5v / A6	A3v / A4
H1v / H2	H7v / H8
K8v / L1	L8v / M1
M2v / M3	M6v / M7
O3v / O4	O5v / O6

Page contents: [i] half-title: 'THE MIDNIGHT FOLK'; [ii] blank; [iii] title-page (with additional leaf inserted between pp.[ii] and [iii] on the verso of which is the colour illustration frontispiece: 182 × 134mm., with protective tissue: '"COME ALONG, KAY," NIBBINS SAID.'); [iv] 'THIS ILLUSTRATED EDITION PUBLISHED 1931 | THE NOVEL WAS FIRST PUBLISHED NOVEMBER 1927 | REPRINTED NOVEMBER 1927 | PRINTED | IN GREAT BRITAIN | AT THE WINDMILL PRESS'; [v] '[illustration of owl, in pink] | FOR J. & L.'; [vi] blank; [vii] '[illustration of ship, in pink] | LIST OF ILLUSTRATIONS | IN COLOUR' (six illustrations listed including frontispiece with page references); [viii] blank; 1–[283] text and illustrations; [284] blank

Paper: wove paper

Running title: none

Binding: blue cloth. On spine, in gold: 'THE | MIDNIGHT | FOLK | JOHN | MASEFIELD | ILLUSTRATED | BY | ROWLAND HILDER | HEINEMANN' (all width centred). On upper cover, in gold: illustration of bow of ship (incorporating ruled border): 55 × 58mm. On lower cover, in blind: publisher's device of a windmill (ranged lower right). Top edge stained blue, others trimmed. Sewn head and foot bands (in blue and white). Binding measurements: 255 × 184mm. (covers), 255 × 53mm. (spine). End-papers: glossy paper with colour illustration of three-masted ship, with frame

Publication date: published, according to the *English Catalogue of Books*, November 1931

Price: 15s.

Contents:
as for A86(a)

Notes:
The text has been entirely re-set for this edition.

The text commences with a drop-capital in pink.

In addition to the colour plates, the text is illustrated throughout with drawings printed in either black or pink. Wight notes 'red' illustrations.

C.S. Evans wrote to Masefield at the beginning of February 1931 discussing types of illustrative work for this edition:

> I have now had an opportunity to discuss with Mr. Munro and our sales department the proposal for an illustrated edition of MIDNIGHT FOLK, and we all think that, provided we can find the right person to make the pictures, it would be a very good plan to produce that edition this autumn. Do you think it ought to be aimed at children or adults, and had you in mind colour illustrations or illustrations procured by any special process, i.e. wood blocks or lithographs? The latter would be mainly appreciated only by adults. I find it very difficult to get hold of really good book illustrators: there are plenty of people who can draw but few whose work stands out – or at least I come across very few. If you have any suggestions to make, please send them along. If we are going to do the book we ought to begin work pretty soon. And then there is Shepard, who illustrated WHEN WE WERE VERY YOUNG: he might be a suitable choice.
>
> (C.S. Evans, letter to John Masefield, 3 February 1931)
> (HRHRC, MS (Masefield, J.) Recip William Heinemann Ltd.)

(By 1931 E.H. Shepard's success with A.A. Milne's Winnie-the-Pooh stories was established.) Masefield presumably replied to Evans drawing attention to the work of Montegut and also mentioning his appreciation of the work of Randolph Caldecott (1846–1886). Evans replied:

> I agree with you that the illustrations for MIDNIGHT FOLK should appeal firstly to children. I will see if I can get gold of a copy of LA BELLE NIVERNAISE. Caldecott's drawings I know very well and I only wish that we could get today as good a person as he...
>
> (C.S. Evans, letter to John Masefield, 5 February 1931)
> (HRHRC, MS (Masefield, J.) Recip William Heinemann Ltd.)

A letter from Louisa Callender, dated from the end of February 1931, suggests that Rowland Hilder was regarded as a safe – rather than inspired – choice:

> ...Mr Evans has been unsuccessful in finding a suitable artist for MIDNIGHT FOLK. It is not an easy task. But perhaps you like Mr. Hilder's work well enough to want him to make the pictures?
>
> (Louisa Callender, letter to John Masefield, 23 February 1931)
> (HRHRC, MS (Masefield, J.) Recip William Heinemann Ltd.)

One month later Evans was reporting progress, having had a discussion with Hilder:

> I had a long talk with Mr. Hilder this morning and we think that the suggestion which I understand you made – namely, that there should be eight colour plates in the book and twenty black and white drawings in the text – is an excellent plan. Both Mr. Hilder and I are dissatisfied with the ordinary three-colour process block method of reproduction and I am going to see if we cannot reproduce the pictures by offset, which will enable us to print them on the same paper as that used for the text of the book with greater faithfulness to the originals... We have decided to make the book crown quarto: that is the same size as the illustrated edition of THE FOX and RIGHT ROYAL... Mr. Hilder is beginning work on the coloured illustrations at once.
>
> (C.S. Evans, letter to John Masefield, 23 March 1931)
> (HRHRC, MS (Masefield, J.) Recip William Heinemann Ltd.)

During the production of this edition Masefield proposed a limited edition of the title with illustrations by Judith Masefield. Some preparatory sketches by Judith survive, but the project was never completed. C.S. Evans wrote about Masefield's proposal before expressing concern about contact with Hilder:

> I find that I have not answered your enquiry about the proposed limited edition of MIDNIGHT FOLK, illustrated by Judith. It is very difficult at the moment to express an opinion as to whether such an edition would be successful: the fact is that at the present time it is difficult to sell any limited editions. Apparently, the people who used to buy them have no longer the money, or the inclination to spend the money, and the extrinsic value of all fine editions has fallen very much. I propose, however, that we leave the matter over for a month or so and see how the cat is going to jump... ...I have heard nothing more from Mr. Hilder. Do you know how he is getting on with the illustrations?
>
> (C.S. Evans, letter to John Masefield, 20 July 1931)
> (HRHRC, MS (Masefield, J.) Recip William Heinemann Ltd.)

At the beginning of August 1931 Hilder visited Evans and progress was reported. This suggests that there were originally more coloured plates than eventually published:

I had a visit from Roland Hilder on Friday. He brought me five of the coloured illustrations for MIDNIGHT FOLK and a number of sketches for the black and white drawings. I understand from him that there are three more coloured illustrations to come and that all the black and white pictures are yet to be finished…

(C.S. Evans, letter to John Masefield, 10 August 1931)
(HRHRC, MS (Masefield, J.) Recip William Heinemann Ltd.)

Two months later it appears that slow progress from Hilder was cause for concern:

I find that the text of the illustrated edition of MIDNIGHT FOLK is all set. The blocks of all the pictures that we have are made and we are now waiting for five more drawings from Hilder. We have written to him twice but we have had no answer.

(C.S. Evans, letter to John Masefield, 9 October 1931)
(HRHRC, MS (Masefield, J.) Recip William Heinemann Ltd.)

A few days later Evans reported a satisfactory result and noted that printing would soon occur. His letter also suggests that Masefield was to keep Hilder's original artwork:

Mr. Hilder's last five drawings came in on Saturday morning. The blocks are now being made and directly they are ready we can go to press. I have given instructions that the originals of the drawings shall be packed up and sent to the office here as soon as they are finished with and they should be ready for collection in about a week's time.

(C.S. Evans, letter to John Masefield, 12 October 1931)
(HRHRC, MS (Masefield, J.) Recip William Heinemann Ltd.)

Writing in 1962 to The Society of Authors, Masefield noted that '…the Hilder illustrations were paid for by me. Heinemanns only paid for the reproductions of them.' (see John Masefield, letter to Elizabeth Barber, 28 February 1962) (Archives of The Society of Authors).

This edition did not, it appears, sell well. In October 1937 C.S. Evans wrote to Masefield suggesting a reduction in price:

I find that we have 1,786 copies of the illustrated edition of MIDNIGHT FOLK which you will remember was published at 15/- some years ago. Unfortunately, it was not a success, I think (a) because it was too expensive and (b) because people had got out of the way of buying expensive editions of books illustrated in colour. We did not sell a single copy between January and June in 1937. Our sales department think that if we could reissue the book at 7/6d. for Christmas we might find a new sale for it. The book was costly to produce and at 7/6d. there is very little margin, in fact only 1/- per copy. I think however, you will agree with me that it is better to get the book into the hands of the public rather than leave it in our warehouse…

(C.S. Evans, letter to John Masefield, 20 October 1937)
(HRHRC, MS (Masefield, J.) Recip William Heinemann Ltd.)

Copies seen: private collection (PWE); private collection (PWE) inscribed 'For Julia Smith | from John Masefield. | Christmas. 1931.'; BL (012604.d.11) stamped 23 NOV 1931

A86(f) Third American edition (first American illustrated edition) (1932)

THE MIDNIGHT | FOLK | *A NOVEL* | *BY* | JOHN MASEFIELD | ILLUSTRATED | *BY* | ROWLAND HILDER | [illustration of bow of ship (incorporating ruled border): 55 × 58mm.] | NEW YORK | THE MACMILLAN COMPANY | 1932
(All width centred)

Bibliographies: Handley-Taylor p.56, Wight [unrecorded]

Collation: [A-R]⁸ [S]¹⁰ (J not used); 146 leaves; 249 × 181mm.; [i–viii] 1–17 [18] 19–36 [37] 38–53 [54–55] 56 [57] 58–83 [84–85] 86–108 [109] 110–43 [144–45] 146–218 [219] 220–82 [283–84]; illustrations (on glossy paper) tipped-in on pp. [iii], 35, 107, 153, 173 and 207

Page contents: [i] half-title: 'THE MIDNIGHT FOLK'; [ii] blank; [iii] title-page (with additional leaf tipped-in on the verso of which is the colour illustration frontispiece: 182 × 134mm., with protective tissue: '"COME ALONG, KAY," NIBBINS SAID.'); [iv] 'COPYRIGHT, 1927 | BY JOHN MASEFIELD | All rights reserved—no part of this book may be reproduced in | any form without permission in writing from the publisher, | except by a reviewer who wishes to quote brief passages in | connection with a review written for inclusion in magazine | or newspaper. | Set up and electrotyped. Published November, 1927 | New illustrated edition, February, 1932 | PRINTED IN THE | UNITED STATES OF AMERICA'; [v] '[illustration of owl] | FOR J. & L.'; [vi] blank; [vii] '[illustration of ship] | LIST OF ILLUSTRATIONS | IN COLOUR' (six illustrations listed including frontispiece with page references); [viii] blank; 1–[283] text and illustrations; [284] blank

Paper: wove paper

Running title: none

Binding: blue cloth. On spine, in gold: 'THE | MIDNIGHT | FOLK | JOHN | MASEFIELD | ILLUSTRATED | BY | ROWLAND HILDER | MACMILLAN | [point]' (all width centred). On upper cover, in gold: illustration of bow of ship (incorporating ruled border): 55 × 58mm. Lower cover: blank. All edges trimmed. Binding measurements: 255 × 185mm. (covers), 255 × 45mm. (spine). End-papers: glossy paper with colour illustration of three-masted ship, with frame

Publication date: published, according to Handley-Taylor, 22 March 1932

Price: $5.00

Contents:
as for A86(a)

Notes:
The text commences with a drop-capital. In A86(e) this drop-capital and many of the illustrations are printed in pink. In this edition, printing is in black.

As in A86(e) in addition to the colour plates, the text is illustrated throughout with drawings printed in black.

This edition appears to use the same setting of text as A86(e).

The publishing agreement for this illustrated edition between Masefield and Macmillan was dated 22 August 1931 (see Archives of The Society of Authors). The agreement refers to 'a licence to publish in volume form in the United States of America and Canada a work the subject or title of which is an illustrated edition of The Midnight Folk – illustrations by Roland Hilder.'

Copies seen: private collection (PWE); Library of The John Masefield Society (Eileen Colwell Collection) inscribed 'For Eileen. | from | John Masefield. | March 29. 1948.' on p.[i]

A86(g) Fourth English edition (1949)

THE MIDNIGHT | FOLK | *A NOVEL* | BY | JOHN MASEFIELD | [publisher's device of a windmill with 'W[point]' and 'H'] | [rule, 57mm.] | WILLIAM HEINEMANN LTD | MELBOURNE :: LONDON :: TORONTO
(All width centred)

Bibliographies: Handley-Taylor p.56, Wight [unrecorded]

Collation: [A]⁸ B-H¹⁶; the fifth leaf of gatherings B-H is also signed; signatures left foot of page; 104 leaves; 183 × 123mm.; [1–6] 7–239 [240]

Page contents: [1] half-title: 'THE MIDNIGHT FOLK'; [2] '*Novels by the Same Author* | ODTAA | SARD HARKER'; [3] title-page; [4] '*First published* 1927 | *Reprinted October* 1927 | *January* 1935 | *This edition* 1949 | *Printed for William Heinemann Ltd. in Great Britain* | *at the St Ann's Press, Timperley, Altrincham*'; [5] 'FOR | J. & L.'; [6] blank; 7–239 text; [240] blank

Paper: wove paper

Running title: 'THE MIDNIGHT FOLK' (44mm.) on both verso and recto, pp.8–239

Binding: blue cloth. On spine, in gold: 'MIDNIGHT | FOLK | [ornament] | JOHN | MASEFIELD | HEINEMANN' (all width centred). Upper cover: blank. Lower cover, in blind: publisher's device of a windmill (ranged lower right). All edges trimmed. Binding measurements: 189 × 124mm. (covers), 189 × 29mm. (spine). End-papers: wove paper.

Publication date: published, according to Handley-Taylor, 5 May 1949. The sales ledger preserved in the Heinemann Archive suggests publication on 9 May 1949 in an edition of 3000 copies.

Price: 8s.6d.

Contents:
as for A86(a)

Notes:
This edition, although noted by Handley-Taylor as a 'reprint' (and similarly within the Heinemann sales ledger as a 'reprint') is an entirely reset edition.

None of the Hilder illustrations are included.

Note the shortened title on the spine of the binding.

A letter from the Heinemann firm to Masefield dated 14 February 1949 notes:

> …The reprint of THE MIDNIGHT FOLK is not yet ready, but a copy will be sent to you as soon as available…
> (William Heinemann Ltd., letter to John Masefield, 14 February 1949)
> (HRHRC, MS (Masefield, J.) Recip William Heinemann Ltd.)

Copies seen: private collection (ROV); Reed International Books Library, Rushden

A86(h) Fifth English edition (1957 [1958])

THE MIDNIGHT | FOLK | BY | JOHN MASEFIELD | [illustration of bow of ship (incorporating ruled border): 47 × 49mm.] | [publisher's device of a windmill with 'W' and 'H'] | [rule, 55mm.] | WILLIAM HEINEMANN LTD | MELBOURNE :: LONDON :: TORONTO
(All width centred)

Bibliographies: Handley-Taylor p.56, Wight [unrecorded]

Collation: [A]⁸ B-G⁸ [H]⁸ I-S⁸ (J not used); signatures right foot of page; 144 leaves; 184 × 119mm.; [i–iv] 1–17 [18] 19–36 [37] 38–53 [54–55] 56 [57] 58–83 [84–85] 86–108 [109] 110–43 [144–45] 146–218 [219] 220–82 [283–84]

Page contents: [i] half-title: 'THE MIDNIGHT FOLK'; [ii] blank; [iii] title-page; [iv] 'FIRST PUBLISHED 1927 | REPRINTED 1927, 1931, 1957 | For J. & L. | © John Masefield 1957 | PUBLISHED BY | WILLIAM HEINEMANN LTD | 99 GREAT RUSSELL STREET, LONDON, W.C.1 | PRINTED IN GREAT BRITAIN FOR THE PUBLISHERS BY | BUTLER & TANNER LTD., FROME AND LONDON'; 1–[283] text and illustrations; [284] blank

Paper: wove paper

Running title: none

Binding: navy blue cloth. On spine, in silver: '*The* | *Midnight* | *Folk* | *John* | *Masefield* | *Heinemann*' (all width centred). On upper cover, in silver: illustration of witch on broomstick: 78 × 73mm. Lower cover: blank. All edges trimmed. Binding measurements: 190 × 123mm. (covers), 190 × 34mm. (spine). End-papers: wove paper.

Publication date: The sales ledger preserved in the Heinemann Archive suggests publication on 27 January 1958 in an edition of 2000 copies

Price: 15s.

Contents:
as for A86(a)

Notes:
The text commences with a drop-capital.

Although this edition does not specifically acknowledge the artist, it is accompanied by black and white illustrations by Rowland Hilder. The edition is thus closely connected to A86(e). It appears that the 1931 setting of text (and black and white) illustrations have been used, although all colour illustrations have been omitted here.

Although the volume itself bears a publication date of 1957, both the *English Catalogue of Books* and Handley-Taylor note a date of January 1958. This is confirmed by the Archives of William Heinemann and a copy in the British Library which is stamped 6 JAN 1958. Noting the dates present in the British Library, the volume was published before the Windmill Series edition (see A86(i)).

Copies seen: private collection (ROV); BL (12839.n.32) stamped 6 JAN 1958; Reed International Books Library, Rushden

Reprinted:
There was limited re-setting of text at some stage in the reprint history of this edition. Reprint dates are:

	1959
	1963
	1966
	1970
	1973
	1977

A86(i) Sixth English edition ["The New Windmill Series"] (1957 [1958])

THE MIDNIGHT | FOLK | BY | JOHN MASEFIELD | [illustration of bow of ship (incorporating ruled border): 47 × 49mm.] | [publisher's device of a windmill with 'W' and 'H'] | [rule, 55mm.] | WILLIAM HEINEMANN LTD | MELBOURNE :: LONDON :: TORONTO
(All width centred)

Bibliographies: Handley-Taylor p.56, Wight [unrecorded]

Collation: [A]⁸ B-G⁸ [H]⁸ I-S⁸ (J not used); signatures right foot of page; 144 leaves; 185 × 121mm.; [i–iv] 1–17 [18] 19–36 [37] 38–53 [54–55] 56 [57] 58–83 [84–85] 86–108 [109] 110–43 [144–45] 146–218 [219] 220–82 [283–84]

Page contents: [i] half-title: 'THE NEW WINDMILL SERIES | *General Editors:* Anne and Ian Serraillier | THE MIDNIGHT FOLK'; [ii] 'THE NEW WINDMILL SERIES | General Editors: Anne and Ian Serraillier | [36 titles and their authors listed]'; [iii] title-page; [iv] 'FIRST PUBLISHED 1927 | FIRST PUBLISHED IN THE NEW WINDMILL SERIES | 1957 | For J. & L. | © John Masefield 1957 | PUBLISHED BY | WILLIAM HEINEMANN LTD | 99 GREAT RUSSELL STREET, LONDON, W.C.1 | PRINTED IN GREAT BRITAIN FOR THE PUBLISHERS BY | BUTLER & TANNER LTD., FROME AND LONDON'; 1–[283] text and illustrations; [284] blank

Paper: wove paper

Running title: none

Binding: light blue cloth. On spine, in silver: 'THE | MIDNIGHT | FOLK | JOHN | MASEFIELD | [publisher's device of a windmill]' (all width centred). On upper cover, in silver: 'THE | MIDNIGHT FOLK | [illustration of witch on broomstick: 78 × 73mm.] | John Masefield'. Lower cover: blank. All edges trimmed. Binding measurements: 190 × 123mm. (covers), 190 × 34mm. (spine). End-papers: wove paper.

Publication date: published, according to Handley-Taylor, 2 February 1958

Price: 6s.

Contents:

as for A86(a)

Notes:

The text commences with a drop-capital.

The setting is the same as A86(h). The non-coloured Hilder illustrations are present.

Although the volume itself bears a publication date of 1957, Handley-Taylor notes a date of 2 February 1958. The copy present in the British Library is stamped 21 JAN 1958. See notes to A86(h).

Copies seen: BL (W.P.6193/39) stamped 21 JAN 1958; Reed International Books Library, Rushden

Reprinted:

	1959
	1961
	1964
	1966
	1969
	1973
'Reprinted'	1977

A86(j) Seventh English edition (1959)

JOHN MASEFIELD | [rule (tapered at both ends)] | THE MIDNIGHT | FOLK | [illustration of witch on broomstick] | THE REPRINT SOCIETY LONDON
(All width centred)

Bibliographies: Handley-Taylor [unrecorded], Wight [unrecorded]

Collation: [A]⁸ B-G⁸ [H]⁸ I-S⁸ (J not used); signatures right foot of page; 144 leaves; 184 × 121mm.; [i–iv] 1–17 [18] 19–36 [37] 38–53 [54–55] 56 [57] 58–83 [84–85] 86–108 [109] 110–43 [144–45] 146–218 [219] 220–82 [283–84]

Page contents: [i] half-title: 'THE MIDNIGHT FOLK'; [ii] blank; [iii] title-page; [iv] '*First published 1927* | *This edition published by the Reprint Society Ltd* | *by arrangement with William Heinemann Ltd 1959* | © *John Masefield 1957* | FOR J & L | Printed in Great Britain by Butler & Tanner Ltd, Frome and London'; 1–[283] text and illustrations; [284] blank

Paper: wove paper

Running title: none

Binding: navy blue cloth. On spine, in silver: 'THE | MIDNIGHT | FOLK | John Masefield | [publisher's device of 'RS' (within ornate border constructed from one foot of the letter 'R')]' (all width centred). On upper cover, in silver: illustration of owl: 56 × 35mm. Lower cover: blank. Top edge stained light blue-green, others trimmed. Binding measurements: 190 × 123mm. (covers), 190 × 35mm. (spine). End-papers: wove paper.

Publication date: published 'Christmas 1959' in an edition of 8000 copies (suggested by documents in the Archives of The Society of Authors)

Price: 8s. (suggested by documents in the Archives of The Society of Authors)

Contents:

as for A86(a)

Notes:

The text commences with a drop-capital.

Although this edition does not specifically acknowledge the artist, it uses the black and white illustrations by Rowland Hilder.

The text appears to use the same setting of type as A86(h).

In August 1959 Masefield asked The Society of Authors for details of The Reprint Society. He was informed:

> ...the Reprint Society is one of the leading book clubs with a membership in the region of 200,000 and has connexions with Cape, Collins, Macmillan, The Hogarth Press as well as Heinemann itself. I understand from Heinemann that the Reprint Society would be publishing *The Midnight Folk* as an extra Christmas book and are not at present contemplating a larger printing than 8,000. Heinemann have confirmed that their own editions of both *The Midnight Folk* and *A Box of Delights* [*sic*] are still on the market. Although the Reprint Society issue is rather small I cannot myself see that there would be any great harm in agreeing to the proposal...
>
> (Anne Munro-Kerr, letter to John Masefield, 21 August 1959)
> (Archives of The Society of Authors)

Copies seen: private collection (PWE); private collection (ROV)

A86(k) Eighth English edition (1963)

John Masefield | THE MIDNIGHT FOLK | [rule] | *Illustrated by Rowland Hilder* | PENGUIN BOOKS
(All width centred)

Bibliographies: Wight [unrecorded]

Collation: 120 unsigned leaves bound by the 'perfect binding' process; 181 × 111mm.; [1–6] 7–92 [93] 94–121 [122–23] 124–232 [233–40]

Page contents: [1] 'PUFFIN BOOKS | *Editor: Kaye Webb* | PS187 | THE MIDNIGHT FOLK | Kay Harker lived in a big house with a governess, a cook, and | a maid, and found life rather a miserable affair until Nibbins, | his black cat, introduced him to the Midnight Folk. | [new paragraph] From then on he entered a mysterious and exciting world of | bad witches and friendly owls, where great-grandpapa | Harker stepped out of his portrait to have conversations with | him (in French) and Bitem the Fox, Blinky the Owl, Rat, and | all his old toys helped him to search for the lost treasure of | Santa Barbara. | [new paragraph] By day Kay followed real life clues about smugglers and | highwaymen; by night he found himself riding over the hills on | a black mare with golden wings, sailing the high seas on a model | schooner, or searching the bottom of the ocean in a diving bell | and talking to a mermaid called Sea Flower. | [new paragraph] And the strange thing was that the day and night adventures | got all mixed together so that the nasty governess found | broomsticks on the garden path and Kay really did discover | the treasure and cleared his great-grandfather's name. | [new paragraph] When a poet writes a book for children a special magic | happens; the wildest inventions seem possible and the most | alarming adventures have a gaiety which removes their terror. | This enchanting book by England's Poet Laureate has been a | favourite for over thirty years, and had a great success when it | was recently serialized on B B C Children's Hour. | [new paragraph] Recommended for parents to read to younger children, and | for all imaginative girls and boys between nine and twelve. | [publisher's device of a puffin in a circle]'; [2] blank; [3] title-page; [4] 'Penguin Books Ltd, Harmondsworth, Middlesex | AUSTRALIA: Penguin Books Pty Ltd, 762 Whitehorse Road, | Mitcham, Victoria | [rule] | First published by Heinemann 1927 | Published in Puffin Books 1963 | [rule] | Copyright © John Masefield, 1957 | [rule] | Made and printed in Great Britain | by Richard Clay & Company Ltd, | Bungay, Suffolk | Set in Monotype Scotch Roman | This book is sold subject to the condition | that it shall not, by way of trade, be lent, | re-sold, hired out, or otherwise disposed | of without the publisher's consent, | in any form of binding or cover | other than that in which | it is published'; [5] 'For J. & L.'; [6] blank; 7–[233] text and illustrations; [234] blank; [235] publisher's advertisement; [236] blank; [237–40] publisher's advertisements

Paper: wove paper

Running title: none

Binding: white wrappers (printed blue). On spine, reading lengthways down spine from head: 'JOHN MASEFIELD [in black] THE MIDNIGHT FOLK [in white]'; horizontally at foot of spine: '187 [in white] | [white rule] | [purple block with purple and white publisher's design of a puffin]'. On upper wrapper: '[illustration of witch in black] | The Midnight Folk [in white] | JOHN MASEFIELD [in white] | [illustrations of owl, cat and rat] [in black] | [white rule] | [purple block upon which, in black: 'A Puffin Book [publisher's device of a puffin in purple and white] 3'6']'. On lower wrapper: '[illustrations of Kay, mermaid, and fish in black] | [white rule] | [purple block upon which, in black: 'Published by Penguin Books | *For copyright reasons this edition is not for sale in the U.S.A. or Canada*']'. All edges trimmed. Binding measurements: 181 × 111mm. (wrappers), 181 × 12mm. (spine).

Publication date: published, according to the *English Catalogue of Books*, 28 March 1963

Price: 3s.6d.

Contents:
as for A86(a)

Notes:
The text commences with a drop-capital.

The illustrations within this edition are those by Rowland Hilder. The setting of the text, however, is new for this edition.

The blue wrappers include two large panels on both the upper and lower wrappers. These, with a background blue colour also include cyan and purple.

A. Dwye Evans wrote to Masefield during 1962 noting interest from Puffin Books:

> Miss Kaye Webb, editor of Puffin Books – the children's imprint of Penguin Books, is very anxious to publish an edition of THE MIDNIGHT FOLK sometime in 1963. She has offered an advance of £250 on account of a royalty of 7½% of their published price. We have found that, for books as well established as THE MIDNIGHT FOLK, sales of the hardcover editions are not adversely affected by publication of a paperback edition. We would like to accept the Puffin offer, and hope you will agree. We would pay you 50% of the proceeds. Miss Webb intimated that if a Puffin edition of THE MIDNIGHT FOLK were published, new illustrations might be made. Could we agree to this or would you rather Rowland Hilder's drawings were kept as in our edition?
>
> (A. Dwye Evans, letter to John Masefield, 22 February 1962)
> (HRHRC, MS (Masefield, J.) Recip William Heinemann Ltd.)

Copies seen: Library of The John Masefield Society (Peter Smith Collection 90)

Reprinted: 1965
                                                                                                     1968
                                                                                                     1971

A86(l) Ninth English edition (1976)

THE | MIDNIGHT FOLK | John Masefield | text illustrations by Rowland Hilder | [publisher's device of Pan within oval: 13 × 10mm.] | PICCOLO | Pan Books in association with Heinemann
(All width centred)

Bibliographies: Wight [unrecorded]

Publication date: presumably published, according to the British Library copy, October 1976

Price: £0.60

Contents:
as for A86(a)

Notes:
The illustrations within this edition are those by Rowland Hilder. The setting of the text, however, is new for this edition.

The volume states, on page [4], that it is printed in Great Britain by Richard Clay (The Chaucer Press) Ltd, Bungay, Suffolk.

The ISBN number is ISBN 0 330 24758 1

The publishing agreement for both Piccolo editions of *The Midnight Folk* and *The Box of Delights* (see A115(g)) was dated 19 November 1976 (see Archives of The Society of Authors)

Copies seen: BL (H.76/1782) stamped 28 OCT 1976

A86(m) Tenth English edition (1984)

JOHN MASEFIELD | THE MIDNIGHT | FOLK | ABRIDGED BY | PATRICIA CRAMPTON | [publisher's device of lion: 10 × 8mm.] | Fontana Lions
(All width centred)

Bibliographies: Wight [unrecorded]

Publication date: October 1984

Price: £1.50

Contents:
The Midnight Folk ('It had been an unhappy day for Kay Harker. To begin with, at breakfast time the governess...')
[abridged text]

Notes:
The text has been abridged by Patricia Crampton.

The volume states, on page [4], that it is printed in Great Britain by William Collins Sons & Co Ltd, Glasgow.

The ISBN number is ISBN 0-00-672416-7

Copies seen: BL (H.85/297) stamped 25 OCT 1984

A86(n) Fourth American edition (1985)

The | Midnight Folk | [rule, 93mm.] | John Masefield | *With an Afterword by Madeleine L'Engle* | [publisher's device of horse and fence within circle and 'A DELL YEARLING CLASSIC' within scroll]
(All width centred)

Bibliographies: Wight [unrecorded]

Publication date: November 1985

Price: $4.95

Contents:
The Midnight Folk ('It had been an unhappy day for little Kay Harker. To begin with, at breakfast time the governess...')
Afterword ('John Masefield's *The Midnight Folk* was in my bookcase when I was...') (headed 'Madeleine L'Engle')

Notes:
The volume states, on page [xx], that it is published by Dell Publishing Co., Inc. 1 Dag Hammarskjold Plaza New York, New York 10017.

The text has been entirely re-set for this edition.

The ISBN number is ISBN 0-440-45631-2

Published within the 'Dell Yearling Classic' series. The afterword by Madeleine L'Engle is unique to this edition.

The publishing agreement for this title between The Estate of John Masefield and Dell Publishing Co. was dated 12 March 1985 (see Archives of The Society of Authors). The agreement refers to 'the exclusive right to print, publish and sell the Work in book form… in the United States of America, the Philippine Republic, and Canada'.

Copies seen: private collection (PWE)

A86(o) Eleventh English edition (1987)

THE | MIDNIGHT | FOLK | John Masefield | text illustrations by Rowland Hilder | [publisher's device of rushes, river, double rule arch device and 'WINDRUSH'] | Oxford
(All width centred)

Bibliographies: Wight [unrecorded]

Publication date: November 1987

Price: £8.70

Contents:
as for A86(a)

Notes:
A large print edition of the novel. See also A115(l)

The volume states, on page [iv], that it is printed by Clio Press., 55 St. Thomas' Street, Oxford OX1 1JG, by arrangement with William Heinemann Ltd and Delacourte Press, New York.

The edition was 'phototypeset, printed and bound by Unwin Brothers Limited, Old Woking, Surrey'

The ISBN number is ISBN 1-85089-927-4

The illustrations within this edition are those by Rowland Hilder.

Copies seen: BL (YK.1988.a.1317) stamped 3 DEC 1987

A86(p) Twelfth English edition (1991)

JOHN MASEFIELD | The MIDNIGHT | FOLK | Illustrated by | QUENTIN BLAKE | HEINEMANN [point] LONDON
(All width centred)
(The underlined 'The' in the title is in a smaller font and the underlining is a curved line)

Bibliographies: Wight [noted on p.121]

Publication date: November 1991

Price: £12.99

Contents:
as for A86(a)

Notes:
The ISBN number is ISBN 0 434 96086 1

One of Blake's illustrations (that tipped-in on p.84 of Miss Susan Pricker (or Miss Piney Trigger)) bears a close resemblance to one present in the Rowland Hilder illustrated edition.

Evidence from *Whitaker's Book List* and date stamps within the British Library copies suggests that Heinemann published three volumes on the same date in November 1991:

- *The Midnight Folk* (A86(p))
- *The Box of Delights* (A115(m))
- *The Midnight Folk and The Box of Delights* (A176(a))

Each volume is given a publication date of November 1991 by *Whitaker's* and each is stamped 14 NOV 1991 by the British Library. The preliminaries within *The Midnight Folk* cite 1992 as the publication date, *The Box of Delights* fails to note any date at all and only the combined volume of *The Midnight Folk and The Box of Delights* gives a publication date of 1991. Presumably the combined volume was intended to be issued first with separate volumes following later. Consequently 1992 is present in *The Midnight Folk*. *The Box of Delights*, containing no preliminary publication information, therefore suggests the page setting was lifted verbatim from the combined volume.

Copies seen: BL (Nov. 1991/2338) stamped 14 NOV 1991

A86(q) Thirteenth English edition (1994)

THE MIDNIGHT | FOLK | JOHN MASEFIELD | [black panel on which in white: 'MAMMOTH': 4 × 30mm.]
(All width centred)

Publication date: September 1994

Price: £3.99

Contents:
as for A86(a)

Notes:
The volume states, on page [iv], that it is published by Mammoth 'an imprint of Reed Consumer Books Ltd Michelin House, 81 Fulham Road, London SW3 6RB'

The edition was 'printed and bound in Great Britain by Cox & Wyman Ltd, Reading, Berkshire'

The ISBN number is ISBN 0 7497 1285 6

The cover illustration is by Kevin Tweddell

The text commences with a drop-capital.

Although this edition does not specifically acknowledge the artist, it uses the black and white illustrations by Rowland Hilder. The first illustration on page 1 (of Kay Harker) has, however, been omitted or damaged with only a fragment remaining. As with A86(h), the colour illustrations originally present in A86(e) have been omitted.

The setting of the text suggests that the edition was taken from the plates of the last standard Heinemann edition (before the edition illustrated by Quentin Blake). There was limited re-setting of text at some stage in the reprint history of A86(h) and it is from the last setting that this edition derives. Additionally, the signatures (defunct in this paperback binding) have all been removed with the exception of signature 'F' which retains its original position at the right foot of p.77.

Copies seen: private collection (PWE); BL (H.95/91) stamped 6 OCT 1994

Reprinted:

'10 9 8 7 6 5 4 3 2 1'	[thirteenth edition, later reprint]	2000 (cover illustration by Liz Pyle)
['10 9 8 7 6 5 4 3 2]	[thirteenth edition, later reprint]	[no copies consulted]
['10 9 8 7 6 5 4 3]	[thirteenth edition, later reprint]	[no copies consulted]
'10 9 8 7 6 5 4'	[thirteenth edition, later reprint]	[c.2002]

The 2000 reprint (with a new cover illustration) includes the number sequence '10 9 8 7 6 5 4 3 2 1' although, strictly, it was merely a reprint of the 1994 edition.

[THE CONDEMNED CELL]

Bibliographies: Simmons [70], Nevinson [unrecorded], Handley-Taylor p.56, Wight [70]

See note within introduction (page ix)

A87 THE COMING OF CHRIST   1928

A87(a) First American edition (limited signed edition) (1928)

T*he* | *Coming of Christ* | *by* JOHN MASEFIELD | [device of shining five point star] [in blue] | New York | THE MACMILLAN COMPANY | 1928 | *All rights reserved*
(The non italic letters in the title are in blue ('T' in 'The', 'C' in 'Coming' and 'Christ') and the italic letters in the author's name are swash ('J' in 'JOHN' and 'M' in 'MASEFIELD'))
(All width centred)

Bibliographies: Simmons [71], Nevinson [unrecorded], Handley-Taylor p.57, Wight [71]

Collation: [A]^{11} ([A]3+1) [B-D]^8; 35 leaves; 236 × 158mm.; [i–x] 1–57 [58–60]

Page contents: [i–ii] blank; [iii] 'THIS EDITION OF THE COMING OF CHRIST | IS LIMITED TO THREE HUNDRED AND FIFTY | COPIES, OF WHICH THIS IS NUMBER ....'; [iv] blank; [v] half-title: 'THE COMING OF CHRIST'; [vi] 'BY JOHN MASEFIELD | [35 titles listed, each title separated by a dash]'; [vii] title-page; [viii] 'COPYRIGHT, 1928, | BY JOHN MASEFIELD | Set up and electrotyped. | Published, May, 1928 | *Printed in the United States of America by* | J. J. LITTLE AND IVES COMPANY, NEW YORK'; [ix] 'THE COMING OF CHRIST'; [x] 'THE COMING OF CHRIST | [rule] | [dramatis personae listed]'; 1–57 text; [58–60] blank

Paper: laid paper (watermark: '[circular beaker device with scales and five pronged device at top: 81 × 35mm.] | *Utopian*'), chain-lines 31mm. apart

Running title: 'THE COMING OF CHRIST' (51mm.) on both verso and recto, pp.2–57

Binding: light purple boards with grey cloth spine. On spine, reading lengthways down spine from head, in gold: 'THE COMING OF CHRIST – MASEFIELD'. There is a single vertical rule in black on each cover at the edge of the cloth. On upper cover, in gold: 'JM' (on black oval panel within gold ruled border: 26 × 19mm.) (ranged lower right). Lower cover: blank. Top edge gilt, lower outside edge untrimmed, fore edge uncut. Binding measurements: 244 × 159mm. (covers), 244 × 22mm. (spine). End-papers: wove paper. Volume contained in slip-case covered in light grey paper, with white paper label (50 × 86mm.) upon which: 'THE COMING OF CHRIST | [rule] [in red] | JOHN MASEFIELD | [ornament] [in red] | THIS EDITION OF "THE COMING OF CHRIST" IS LIMITED | TO THREE HUNDRED AND FIFTY COPIES OF WHICH | THIS IS NUMBER . . . | [ornament] [in red] | [rule] [in red] | THE MACMILLAN COMPANY' (within ornate border: 43 × 81mm. with rounded corners)

Publication date: published, according to Simmons, 8 May 1928

Price: $5.00

Contents:

The Coming of Christ ('*At the closing of the preluding music the two* TRUMPETERS OF THE HOST OF...')

Notes:

A play in verse retelling the Nativity, first produced in Canterbury Cathedral in May 1928 with incidental music by Gustav Holst. The producer and designer was Charles Ricketts. The play was written at the invitation of G.K.A. Bell who, in a sermon on the play, stated:

> ...I well remember the origin of the play. John Masefield stayed at the Deanery in Canterbury, one summer's night in 1927. As Dean, I took him round the Cathedral after supper with Ruth Spooner. He was thrilled with all he saw, and the light in which he saw it...

(see Lambeth Palace Library, Bell Papers (Religious Drama 1951–1960) 157) and the Bell Papers in general for background and correspondence about the play.

The publicity material in the preliminaries that lists Masefield's work (appearing on p.[vi]) includes the title 'LOST ENDEAVOR'.

Page numbers appear within square brackets. Thus, [1], [2], etc.

The additional leaf ([A]2) pasted onto [A]3 comprises the leaf detailing the limitation of the edition. The paper type is the same as that used for the rest of the volume. The single leaves were presumably sent to Masefield for signing. Masefield only appears to have signed, not numbered the edition. In copy number 61 the number is written in pencil with Masefield's signature below in blue ink.

Masefield wrote to The Society of Authors, in November 1927 stating his admiration of Holst's work and attempting to secure use of Holst's incidental music for all productions of the play:

> I have written a little Christmas play, which will probably be produced in Canterbury Cathedral with music by Mr Gustav Holst in January. Mr Holst wishes to print his settings with my words. We have been associated in work in the past and I should like to meet him in every possible way... As Mr Holst is probably the most distinguished living musician in this country, I should like to arrange that, wherever the play be produced, his incidental music should be used with the production, at any rate for some years. Have you, by any chance, in the archives of the Society some specimen agreement...
>
> (John Masefield, letter to [G.H.] Thring, 24 November 1927)
> (BL, Add.Mss.56586, f.35)

Holst, for his part, was similarly amiable. He wrote to The Society of Authors at the beginning of December 1927:

> If you advise it I should be willing to waive all control over the theatrical performance of the play. It might make it easier for Mr Masefield to have sole control.
>
> (Gustav Holst, letter to [G.H.] Thring, 9 December 1927)
> (BL, Add.Mss.56586, ff.55–56)

A publishing agreement for this title between Masefield and Macmillan was dated 29 December 1927 (see Archives of The Society of Authors). The agreement refers to 'a licence to publish in volume form... in the United States of America and Canada a work the subject or title of which is The Coming of Christ (a Christmas play)'.

A film version of the play was proposed at the end of 1958:

> We have been approached today on the possibility of a film production of THE COMING OF CHRIST. We leased the play to an amateur church group in New York City and through that leasing a professional producer has become interested in a filmed version.
>
> The idea is in the embryonic state, of course, but to give you an idea of the stature of the production such people as Tyrone Power, Burgess Meredith, Richard Burton, Alfred Drake have been approached and all are interested provided their schedules will permit their acceptance of roles. The producer is a very reputable one. What he would like to do is to work along (and the people he has approached have agreed) paying small fees but cutting in on a participation basis. If the film is a success – as they have every reason to think it will be – they will come out better than with a set guaranteed fee.

One other thing – there would have to be a bit of revision here and their [*sic*] to put the play into cinematic form. Would you, as author, be in a position to do this work for them or will you permit them to adapt it themselves?

The producer has asked for an immediate response. Can you cable a word of advice so they will know whether to immediately cancel out their thinking on the subject or to continue initial preparations. Too, please write us immediately, giving further particulars….. May they have six months' option… What advance do you request?

(Edna M. Cahill, letter to John Masefield, 16 December 1958)

(HRHRC, MS (Masefield, J.) Recip Baker (Walter H.) Company)

No further detail is currently known and it must be assumed that Masefield did not approve of the scheme.

Copies seen: private collection (PWE) number 196, signed 'J. Masefield.' on p.[iii]; NYPL (Berg Collection) number 61, signed 'J. Masefield.' on p.[iii]; HRHRC (PR6025 A77 C6 1928) number 37, signed 'J. Masefield.' on p.[iii] with slip-case inscribed 'Con's copy.'

A87(b) First English edition (1928)

THE COMING OF | CHRIST | BY | JOHN MASEFIELD | [publisher's device of a windmill with 'W' and 'H' all within ruled border: 18 × 19mm.] | LONDON | WILLIAM HEINEMANN LTD.
(All width centred)

Bibliographies: Simmons [71a], Nevinson p.14, Handley-Taylor p.57, Wight [71a]

Collation: [A]⁸ B–C⁸ D⁶ (see notes); signatures right foot of page; 30 leaves; 184 × 120mm.; [i–viii] [1–2] 3–48

Page contents: [i–ii] blank; [iii] half-title: 'THE COMING OF CHRIST'; [iv] '*OTHER PLAYS BY JOHN* | *MASEFIELD* | [seven titles listed] | *POETRY BY JOHN* | *MASEFIELD* | [13 titles listed] | *OTHER WORKS BY JOHN* | *MASEFIELD* | [six titles listed]'; [v] title-page; [vi] '*First published* 1928 | *Printed in Great Britain at* | *The Windmill Press,* | *Kingswood,* | *Surrey*'; [vii] 'To | MY WIFE'; [viii] blank; [1] 'THE COMING OF CHRIST | [dramatis personae listed]'; [2] blank; 3–47 text; 48 'NOTE | THE incidental music of this Play is writ- | ten for full choir (The Host of Heaven), | accompanied by organ, and for a small body | of men's voices in unison (The King's | Men), accompanied by piano. There is also | a small but important part for trumpet (or | trumpets in unison). | [new paragraph] Bach's short Choral-Prelude on 'In dulci | jubilo' is suggested if an opening voluntary | be required. When the play begins the | trumpeters will first play the theme of | 'Glory to God in the highest,' and then the | entire melody of 'Glory to God in the | highest, peace on earth among men, in | whom God is well pleased . . .' This will | be repeated at the end of the play (see stage | directions). After this final trumpet call | no further music should be heard. | [new paragraph] *The music of the Play is published by* | *Messrs. J. Curwen & Sons Ltd.,* 24 Ber- | *ners St., London, W.1. in their Edition* | *No.* 3680. | [new paragraph] *Anyone wishing to produce the play must* | *apply to the Society of Authors,* 11, *Gower* | *Street, London, W.C.*'

Paper: laid paper (no watermark), chain-lines 24mm. apart

Running title: 'THE COMING OF CHRIST [52mm.] | [rule, 80mm.]' on both verso and recto, pp.4–47

Binding: blue cloth. On spine, reading lengthways up spine, from foot, in gold: 'The Coming of Christ [ornament] John Masefield'; horizontally at foot of spine: 'HEINEMANN'. On upper cover, in gold: 'THE COMING OF CHRIST | JOHN MASEFIELD' (within blind ruled border: 185 × 116mm.) Lower cover: blank. All edges trimmed. Binding measurements: 188 × 122mm. (covers), 188 × 18mm. (spine). End-papers: laid paper (no watermark), chain-lines 24mm. apart. The end-papers at the rear of the volume constitute leaves D5 and D6, the first being free and the second laid down.

Publication date: published, according to Simmons, 17 May 1928 in an edition of 3000 copies

Price: 3s.6d.

Contents:
The Coming of Christ ('[*At the closing of the preluding music the* TWO TRUMPETERS OF THE HOST OF...']

Notes:
The end-papers at the rear of the volume (comprising D5 and D6) are not included in the pagination of the volume. They are, however, included in the formula of the book and leaf count. Wight appears to indicate that some copies are bound with conventional end-papers at the rear. No such copies have been examined.

Note that the two lines of the dedication are not centred in relation to each other. (The 'To' is ranged further to the right).

Masefield approached Heinemann with his plans, hoping that the play would be printed at the firm's new 'Windmill Press' at Kingswood in Surrey. Theodore Byard responded:

…It is also very flattering that you should wish your play, THE COMING OF CHRIST, to be one of the first productions of our new press at Kingswood. This shall most certainly be done.

(Theodore Byard, letter to John Masefield, 17 January 1928)

(HRHRC, MS (Masefield, J.) Recip William Heinemann Ltd.)

Masefield's requirement was that the play was published about the time the play was produced. Byard wrote to say that he would remember this and '…late May seems to me an excellent time for publication…' (see Theodore Byard, letter to John Masefield, 25 January 1928) (HRHRC, MS (Masefield, J.) Recip William Heinemann Ltd.) In April 1928 H.J. Woods wrote that:

...under separate cover I have sent you two sets of proofs of "The Coming of Christ". The prelim will follow.

(H.J. Woods, letter to John Masefield, 20 April 1928)
(HRHRC, MS (Masefield, J.) Recip William Heinemann Ltd.)

Heinemann appear to have published this edition ahead of schedule. C.S. Evans had written on 4 May:

...We want to publish on May 22nd if we can, so as to be well in time for the performance and I had kept a machine waiting.

(C.S. Evans, letter to John Masefield, 4 May 1928)
(HRHRC, MS (Masefield, J.) Recip William Heinemann Ltd.)

The publishing agreement for this title between Masefield and Heinemann was dated 9 June 1928 (see Archives of The Society of Authors). The agreement refers to an 'ordinary' issue at a publication price of 3s.6d., 275 copies at 21s. and 'the Cathedral Edition' at 1s.

The papers of G.K.A. Bell reveal that Masefield first saw the potential of Canterbury Cathedral as a performance venue whilst in the company of Ruth Spooner. An advance proof printing of this edition therefore contains an associated inscription: 'For Ruth Spooner, | "The onlie begetter of these | ensuing Sonnets." | from John Masefield. | April 28. 1928.' The copy is located in a private collection (ROV).

Copies seen: private collection (PWE); private collection (ROV); NYPL (Berg Collection)

Reprinted:

'New Impression'	[first edition, second impression]	May 1928
	[first edition, third impression]	Jun 1928
'New Impression'	[first edition, fourth impression]	Apr 1929

A87(bb) First English edition (limited signed edition) (1928)

THE COMING OF | CHRIST | BY | JOHN MASEFIELD | [publisher's device of a windmill with 'W [point]' and 'H' all within ruled border: 19 × 20mm.] | LONDON | WILLIAM HEINEMANN LTD.
(All width centred)

Bibliographies: Simmons [71b], Nevinson [unrecorded], Handley-Taylor p.57, Wight [71b]

Collation: [A–G]⁴; 28 leaves; 224 × 142mm.; [i–vi] [1–2] 3–48 [49–50]

Page contents: [i] half-title: 'THE COMING OF CHRIST'; [ii] 'This edition is limited to 275 | copies of which 250 are for sale. | No.'; [iii] title-page; [iv] 'First published 1928 | Printed in Great Britain at | The Windmill Press, | Kingswood, | Surrey'; [v] 'To | MY WIFE'; [vi] blank; [1] 'THE COMING OF CHRIST | [dramatis personae listed]; [2] blank; 3–47 text; 48 'NOTE | THE incidental music of this Play is writ-| ten for full choir (The Host of Heaven), | accompanied by organ, and for a small body | of men's voices in unison (The King's | Men), accompanied by piano. There is also | a small but important part for trumpet (or | trumpets in unison). | [new paragraph] Bach's short Choral-Prelude on 'In dulci | jubilo' is suggested if an opening voluntary | be required. When the play begins the | trumpeters will first play the theme of | 'Glory to God in the highest,' and then the | entire melody of 'Glory to God in the | highest, peace on earth among men, in | whom God is well pleased . . .' This will | be repeated at the end of the play (see stage | directions). After this final trumpet call | no further music should be heard. | [new paragraph] The music of the Play is published by | Messrs. J. Curwen & Sons Ltd., 24 Ber- | ners St., London, W.1. in their Edition | No. 3680. | [new paragraph] Anyone wishing to produce the play must | apply to the Society of Authors, 11, Gower | Street, London, W.C.'; [49–50] blank

Paper: wove paper (watermark: 'MILLBOURN | BRITISH HAND MADE PURE RAG [castle device: 26 × 31mm.]')

Running title: 'THE COMING OF CHRIST [52mm.] | [rule, 80mm.]' on both verso and recto, pp.4–47

Binding: blue-green boards with parchment spine. On spine, in gold: 'The | Coming | of | Christ | [ornament] | John | Masefield | Heinemann' (all width centred). There is a single vertical rule in blind on each cover at the edge of the parchment. Covers: blank. Top edge gilt, lower outside edge untrimmed, fore edge uncut. Binding measurements: 228 × 148mm. (covers), 228 × 19mm. (spine). End-papers: laid paper (no watermark), chain-lines 25–26mm. apart bound so that chain-lines run horizontally.

Publication date: published, according to Simmons, 17 May 1928

Price: 21s.

Contents:
as for A87(b)

Notes:
With the exception of the half-title (and limitation) this edition appears to use the same setting of type as A87(b).

Writing to Masefield on 11 May 1928 Evans at first notes that the limited signed edition was to be delayed. He then annotates his letter with revised information and it appears that A87(b), A87(bb) and A87(bbb) were all published on the same day:

…I had to get the ordinary edition and the cathedral edition of the book ready first in rather a rush because the Dean of Canterbury was anxious, and I was anxious too, to have copies of the play available to the general public on the day of performance. We shall publish both of these editions next Thursday. As a result of the rush we were not able to get the Limited Edition ready for that date and it will have to come out a few days later. I will let you know when the sheets are ready* and, if necessary, will send them to Oxford for you to sign.

* The sheets are ready + are being sent to you today. If you sign them at once I think I can get out the Ltd Edn too before the performance.

(C.S. Evans, letter to John Masefield, 11 May 1928)
(HRHRC, MS (Masefield, J.) Recip William Heinemann Ltd.)

Copies seen: private collection (ROV) number 8, signed '8 | John Masefield.' on p.[ii]; Columbia University Libraries (Special Collections B825.M377.P55.1928.c.2) number 268, signed '268 | John Masefield.' on p.[ii] and additionally inscribed 'C. Ricketts, | from J. Masefield. | Whitsuntide. 1928.'

A87(bbb) First English edition ('Cathedral Edition') (1928)

THE COMING OF | CHRIST | BY | JOHN MASEFIELD | [publisher's device of a windmill with 'W' and 'H' all within ruled border: 18 × 19mm.] | LONDON | WILLIAM HEINEMANN LTD.
(All width centred)

Bibliographies: Simmons [unrecorded], Nevinson [unrecorded], Handley-Taylor [unrecorded], Wight 71aa

Collation: [A]⁸ B-C⁸ D⁶ (see notes); signatures right foot of page; 30 leaves; 185 × 116mm.; [i–vi] [1–2] 3–48 [49–50]

Page contents: [i] half-title: 'THE COMING OF CHRIST'; [ii] '*OTHER PLAYS BY JOHN* | *MASEFIELD* | [seven titles listed]' | *POETRY BY JOHN* | *MASEFIELD* | [13 titles listed] | *OTHER WORKS BY JOHN* | *MASEFIELD* | [six titles listed]'; [iii] title-page; [iv] '*First published* 1928 | *Printed in Great Britain at* | *The Windmill Press,* | *Kingswood,* | *Surrey*'; [v] 'To | MY WIFE'; [vi] blank; [1] 'THE COMING OF CHRIST | [dramatis personae listed]'; [2] blank; 3–47 text; 48 'NOTE | THE incidental music of this Play is writ- | ten for full choir (The Host of Heaven), | accompanied by organ, and for a small body | of men's voices in unison (The King's | Men), accompanied by piano. There is also | a small but important part for trumpet (or | trumpets in unison). | [new paragraph] Bach's short Choral-Prelude on 'In dulci | jubilo' is suggested if an opening voluntary | be required. When the play begins the | trumpeters will first play the theme of | 'Glory to God in the highest,' and then the | entire melody of 'Glory to God in the | highest, peace on earth among men, in | whom God is well pleased . . .' This will | be repeated at the end of the play (see stage | directions). After this final trumpet call | no further music should be heard. | [new paragraph] *The music of the Play is published by* | Messrs. J. Curwen & Sons Ltd., 24 Ber- | ners St., London, W.1. in their Edition | No. 3680. | [new paragraph] *Anyone wishing to produce the play must* | *apply to the Society of Authors,* 11, *Gower* | *Street, London, W.C.*'; [49–50] blank

Paper: laid paper (no watermark), chain-lines 24mm. apart

Running title: 'THE COMING OF CHRIST [52mm.] | [rule, 80mm.]' on both verso and recto, pp.4–47

Binding: cream wrappers. On spine, reading lengthways up spine, from foot, in orange: 'THE COMING OF CHRIST-JOHN MASEFIELD'. On upper wrapper, in orange: 'THE COMING | OF CHRIST | *by* | JOHN MASEFIELD | [device of stylised sun, sun's rays and cloud: 17 × 18mm.] | CATHEDRAL EDITION | *HEINEMANN* | I / – NET'. On lower wrapper, in orange: 'OTHER WORKS BY | JOHN MASEFIELD | [double rule] | *PLAYS* | [six volumes listed] | *POETRY* | [12 volumes listed] | *PROSE* | [four volumes listed]'. All edges trimmed. Binding measurements: 185 × 116mm. (wrappers), 185 × 8mm. (spine)

Publication date: published, according to a letter to Masefield from C.S. Evans, on 17 May 1928 (see C.S. Evans, letter to John Masefield, 11 May 1928) (HRHRC, MS (Masefield, J.) Recip William Heinemann Ltd.) in an edition of 2000 copies (see C.S. Evans, letter to John Masefield, 19 April 1928) (HRHRC, MS (Masefield, J.) Recip William Heinemann Ltd.)

Price: 1s.

Contents:
as for A87(b)

Notes:
As a paper bound edition this volume does not include end-papers. However, [A]1 is laid down to the inside of the upper wrapper and D6 is laid down to the inside of the lower wrapper. The front of the volume therefore commences with the half-title on A2. The rear of the volume includes a blank sheet (D5) before the lower wrapper.

This edition comprises a paper-bound version of A87(b). The only note of the 'Cathedral Edition' occurs on the upper wrapper.

Note that the two lines of the dedication are not centred in relation to each other. (The 'To' is ranged further to the right).

This edition appears to have been published at the suggestion of C.S. Evans:

> …I had lunch with the Dean of Canterbury the other day. He told me that there were likely to be two or three thousand spectators during the three days on which the play will be given at Canterbury Cathedral and he is willing to arrange for stalls outside the doors at which the book could be sold. I am inclined to think that if it is economically possible it would be a good idea to publish a very cheap edition of the book in paper covers to be sold at about 1/- or 1/6. Such a book

would not have any quality of permanence and would not, I think, interfere with the sale of the ordinary edition. Of course, there is no money in it either for you or for us – in fact it would only be possible if you took a nominal royalty and we were content to make no money at all, but some day to hope to get our initial capital back. We would be willing to take this risk if you would and the justification for it in the case of both of us would, I think, be that it might lead purchasers to buy more of your work in its more permanent and remunerative form. I gather that of the 1,400 or so spectators only about 400 will be able to hear the words.

(C.S. Evans, letter to John Masefield, 4 April 1928)
(HRHRC, MS (Masefield, J.) Recip William Heinemann Ltd.)

A letter from C.S. Evans of the Heinemann firm to G.K.A. Bell specifically refers to this edition:

Thank you for your letter. I will do my best to get advance copies of the cathedral edition of Masefield's COMING OF CHRIST before May 14th. How many will you want? I cannot promise definitely because Masefield only returned the proofs to us yesterday and we are going to have a great rush to get the book out in time. I must print the ordinary edition and the limited edition first, otherwise the little cathedral edition will have first edition value, which would be a serious matter. We are planning to get the book out by May 22nd.

(C.S. Evans, letter to G.K.A. Bell, 3 May 1928)
(Lambeth Palace Library, Bell Papers (Religious Drama 1925–1928) 153, f.233)

Despite Evans' statement, it appears the 'Cathedral edition' was printed at the same time as A87(b) and A87(bb). A printed note (headed 'WITH THE PRECENTOR'S COMPLIMENTS') contained within the papers of Bell includes advice to the audience for the first performance:

It will be understood that while every effort will be made to help the proper hearing of the spoken words – as well as of the music – the acoustics of the Cathedral present special difficulties. Ticket holders are urged to procure and read copies of the Play beforehand,

Ordinary Edition 3/6. *Heinemann*;
Cathedral Edition 1/-, *Heinemann* (obtainable in Canterbury only).

(Lambeth Palace Library, Bell Papers (Religious Drama 1925–1928) 153, f.281)

This edition was therefore a cheap edition available for the convenience of the Canterbury Cathedral audience. It appears that it was not issued for general distribution outside Canterbury.

The publishing agreement for this title between Masefield and Heinemann was dated 9 June 1928 (see Archives of The Society of Authors). With reference to this edition the agreement notes:

…an edition of 2,000 copies published at 1/- net called the Cathedral Edition issued specially in connection with the performance of the play at Canterbury Cathedral. This edition when exhausted is not to be reprinted except with the Author's consent in writing.

Copies seen: private collection (ROV) inscribed 'For Laurence Irving. | (Gaspar) | from John Masefield. | May. 1928.'; ULL (Special Collections) inscribed 'For Ethne Thompson. | from | John Masefield. | June. 1928.'

A87(c) Second American edition (1928)

The | *Coming of Christ* | *by* JOHN MASEFIELD | [device of shining five point star] [in blue] | New York | THE MACMILLAN COMPANY | 1928 | *All rights reserved*
(The non italic letters in the title are in blue ('T' in 'The', 'C' in 'Coming' and 'Christ') and the italic letters in the author's name are swash ('J' in 'JOHN' and 'M' in 'MASEFIELD'))
(All width centred)

Bibliographies: Simmons [noted on p.115], Nevinson [unrecorded], Handley-Taylor p.57, Wight 71c

Collation: [A]¹⁰ [B-D]⁸; 34 leaves; 187 × 126mm.; [i–viii] 1–57 [58–60]

Page contents: [i–ii] blank; [iii] half-title: 'THE COMING OF CHRIST'; [iv] 'BY JOHN MASEFIELD | [35 titles listed, each title separated by a dash]'; [v] title-page; [vi] 'COPYRIGHT, 1928, | BY JOHN MASEFIELD | Set up and electrotyped. | Published, May, 1928 | *Printed in the United States of America by* | J. J. LITTLE AND IVES COMPANY, NEW YORK'; [vii] 'THE COMING OF CHRIST'; [viii] 'THE COMING OF CHRIST | [rule] | [dramatis personae listed]'; 1–57 text; [58–60] blank

Paper: wove paper

Running title: 'THE COMING OF CHRIST' (51mm.) on both verso and recto, pp.2–57

Binding: burgundy cloth. On spine, in gold: '[rule] | THE | COMING | OF | CHRIST | MASEFIELD | -MACMILLAN- | [rule]' (all width centred). On upper cover, in blind: 'THE COMING | OF CHRIST | MASEFIELD' (ranged upper left) (within blind ruled border: 190 × 121mm.) Lower cover: blank. All edges trimmed. Binding measurements: 195 × 128mm. (covers), 195 × 20mm. (spine). End-papers: wove paper.

Publication date: published, according to Simmons, 22 May 1928

Price: $1.50

Contents:
as for A87(a)

Notes:
Simmons notes in his bibliography: 'The Macmillan Company's regular issue, published May 22, 1928, is printed on wove paper from the same plates as the limited issue, the only typographic change being that the edition note is omitted in the regular issue.'

Copies seen: private collection (ROV); NYPL (NCR 1928) 377302A stamped Jul 5 1928

A88 MIDSUMMER NIGHT AND OTHER TALES IN VERSE   1928

A88(a) First English edition (1928)

JOHN MASEFIELD | MIDSUMMER NIGHT | *and* | *other tales in* | *Verse* | [ornament] | [publisher's device of a windmill with 'W' and 'H' all within ruled border: 10 × 11mm.] | London | [rule, 58mm.] | WILLIAM HEINEMANN LTD
(All width centred)

Bibliographies: Simmons [72], Nevinson p.14, Handley-Taylor p.57, Wight [72]

Collation: [A]⁸ B-N⁸ O⁴ (J not used); signatures right foot of page; 108 leaves; 185 × 121mm.; [i–viii] [1] 2–13 [14–15] 16–23 [24–25] 26–31 [32–33] 34–36 [37] 38–47 [48–49] 50–64 [65] 66–76 [77] 78–86 [87] 88–106 [107] 108–115 [116–17] 118–19 [120–21] 122–24 [125] 126–32 [133] 134–42 [143] 144–45 [146–47] 148–50 [151] 152 [153] 154 [155] 156–57 [158–59] 160–71 [172–73] 174–93 [194–95] 196–207 [208]

Page contents: [i] half-title: 'MIDSUMMER NIGHT | *and other Tales in* | *Verse*' (note that the '*T*' of '*Tales*' is swash); [ii] *PLAYS BY JOHN* | *MASEFIELD* | [eight titles listed] | *POETRY BY JOHN* | *MASEFIELD* | [13 titles listed] | *OTHER WORKS BY JOHN* | *MASEFIELD* | [six titles listed]; [iii] title-page; [iv] 'First published 1928 | *Printed in Great Britain at* | *The Windmill Press, Kingswood, Surrey*'; [v] 'TO | MY WIFE'; [vi] blank; [vii] 'CONTENTS | [ornament] | [22 items listed with page references]'; [viii] blank; [1] 'THE | BEGETTING | OF | ARTHUR'; 2–13 text of 'The Begetting of Arthur'; [14] blank; [15] 'THE | BIRTH | OF | ARTHUR'; 16–23 text of 'The Birth of Arthur'; [24] blank; [25] 'THE | TAKING | OF | MORGAUSE'; 26–31 text of 'The Taking of Morgause'; [32] blank; [33] 'THE | BEGETTING | OF | MODRED'; 34–36 text of 'The Begetting of Modred'; [37] 'BADON | HILL'; 38–47 text of 'Badon Hill'; [48] blank; [49] 'THE | SAILING | OF | HELL RACE'; 50–64 text of 'The Sailing of Hell Race'; [65] 'ARTHUR | AND | HIS | RING'; 66–76 text of 'Arthur and his Ring'; [77] 'MIDSUMMER | NIGHT'; 78–86 text of 'Midsummer Night'; [87] 'THE | FIGHT | ON | THE WALL'; 88–106 text of 'The Fight on the Wall'; [107] 'THE | BREAKING | OF | THE LINKS'; 108–115 text of 'The Breaking of the Links'; [116] blank; [117] 'GWENIVACH | TELLS'; 118–19 text of 'Gwenivach Tells'; [120] blank; [121] 'ARTHUR | IN | THE | RUINS'; 122–24 text of 'Arthur in the Ruins'; [125] 'THE | FIGHT | AT | CAMLAN'; 126–32 text of 'The Fight at Camlan'; [133] 'THE | FIGHT | ON THE | BEACH | OR THE | PASSING'; 134–42 text of 'The Fight on the Beach or The Passing'; [143] 'GWENIVERE | TELLS'; 144–45 text of 'Gwenivere Tells'; [146] blank; [147] 'THE | DEATH | OF | LANCELOT | AS TOLD | BY | GWENIVERE'; 148–50 text of 'The Death of Lancelot as told by Gwenivere'; [151] 'DUST | TO | DUST'; 152 text of 'Dust to Dust'; [153] 'ON | THE COMING | OF | ARTHUR'; 154 text of 'On the Coming of Arthur'; [155] 'THE | OLD TALE | OF THE | BEGETTING'; 156–57 text of 'The Old Tale of the Begetting'; [158] blank; [159] 'THE | OLD TALE | OF THE | BREAKING | OF THE | LINKS'; 160–71 text of 'The Old Tale of the Breaking of the Links'; [172] blank; [173] 'SOUTH | AND | EAST'; 174–93 text of 'South and East'; [194] blank; [195] 'FULFILMENT'; 196–207 text of 'Fulfilment'; [208] blank

Paper: wove paper

Running title: none

Binding: blue cloth. On spine, in gold: 'Midsummer | Night | [ornament] | John | Masefield | HEINEMANN' (all width centred). On upper cover, in gold: 'MIDSUMMER NIGHT | JOHN MASEFIELD' (within blind ruled border: 186 × 118mm.) On lower cover, in blind: publisher's device of a windmill (ranged lower right). All edges trimmed. Binding measurements: 191 × 123mm. (covers), 191 × 32mm. (spine). End-papers: wove paper.

Publication date: published, according to Simmons, 25 October 1928 in an edition of 3000 copies

Price: 7s.6d.

Contents:
The Begetting of Arthur ('Uther, the Prince, succeeding to the post')
The Birth of Arthur ('When the wind from East changes')
The Taking of Morgause ('Morgause the Merry played beside the burn:')
The Begetting of Modred ('When berries were scarlet')
Badon Hill ('Loki the Dragon Killer mustered men')
The Sailing of Hell Race ('When Arthur came from warring, having won')
Arthur and his Ring ('Beauty's Delight, the Princess Gwenivere,')

Midsummer Night ('Midsummer night had fallen at full moon,')
The Fight on the Wall ('Modred was in the Water Tower')
The Breaking of the Links ('They told King Arthur how the Knights were killed,')
Gwenivach Tells ('I, Gwenivach, King Modred's queen, declare')
Arthur in the Ruins ('King Arthur watched within the ruined town,')
The Fight at Camlan ('Soon the two armies were in touch, and soon')
The Fight on the Beach or The Passing ('These were the nine with Modred:-Kolgrim, Gor,')
Gwenivere Tells ('So Arthur passed, but country-folk believe')
The Death of Lancelot as told by Gwenivere ('Then, after many years, a rider came,')
Dust to Dust ('Henry Plantagenet, the English King,')
On the Coming of Arthur ('By ways unknown, unseen,')
The Old Tale of the Begetting ('*The men of old, who made the tale for us,*')
The Old Tale of the Breaking of the Links ('French poets write:-That, Lancelot the brave')
South and East ('When good King Arthur ruled these western hursts,')
Fulfilment ('Long since, Sir Constans governed here for Rome,')

Notes:

A volume of Arthurian tales in verse. The volume includes 'South and East' which was later published separately with illustrations (see A93).

Each poem is prefixed by a divisional title on the preceding page. Each poem commences with a raised-capital in outline.

It appears that Masefield's first suggestion was to publish individual poems together with illustrations. During February 1927 he sent the text of 'Fulfilment' and this was acknowledged by C.S. Evans on 22 February (see C.S. Evans, letter to John Masefield, 22 February 1927) (HRHRC, MS (Masefield, J.) Recip William Heinemann Ltd.) This was followed by the text of 'South and East' and this, also, was acknowledged by Evans (see C.S. Evans, letter to John Masefield, 28 February 1927) (HRHRC, MS (Masefield, J.) Recip William Heinemann Ltd.). Masefield seems to have had discussions with Nigel de Grey of the Medici Society, but Heinemann appeared anxious to retain their interest in Masefield:

> ...de Grey is a great friend of mine and of Evans, and we should like to meet him in any way possible, but I really do not think we can agree to his publishing a new poem of yours until it has been brought out by us.
> Evans is back and I am glad to say that he is in good health. He remembers perfectly about the poems in question and agrees with me about the necessity of our bringing them out first. Of course, after that, if de Grey still wished to bring out SOUTH AND EAST, we could go into the matter again.
>
> (Theodore Byard, letter to John Masefield, 13 March 1928)
> (HRHRC, MS (Masefield, J.) Recip William Heinemann Ltd.)

Masefield wrote to Nigel de Grey on 15 March and received the following reply from The Medici Society:

> I have suggested to Messrs Heinemann that it might be possible, in order to overcome their objection to one of your poems appearing first with another house, that the poems should appear simultaneously in their collected volume and in our illustrated form, both books to appear this autumn. They are now, I think, considering this and I have not yet heard from Byard as to what they have decided. I think the scheme has much to be said for it, in that our book would still be a new book and could not possibly compete against theirs which would contain so much more material. It seems to me that the publicity accorded to both books would mutually help. Financially, from your point of view, it would be what I believe is called "found money", and from the artist's point of view, it would be admirable in all respects. I therefore very much hope something may yet be arranged. You will forgive me, I know, my natural keenness to publish a book by you.
>
> (Nigel de Grey, letter to John Masefield, 19 March 1928)
> (HRHRC, MS (Masefield, J.) Recip Medici Society Ltd.)

Meanwhile, C.S. Evans had made enquiries within Heinemann and wrote to Masefield informing him that he had discussed 'the little tales' and 'the form of their publication at considerable length with our sales department'. Evans noted that 'we have come to the conclusion that it would be unwise to publish these little tales separately with coloured illustrations' (see C.S. Evans, letter to John Masefield, 18 March 1927) (HRHRC, MS (Masefield, J.) Recip William Heinemann Ltd.) Masefield must, therefore, have abandoned current schemes with the Medici Society and plans were made for a standard publication of a book of verse with Heinemann:

> ...If we are to publish the TALES IN VERSE in October I ought to have the manuscript by the end of July. If this is pressing you too hard, if you could let me have it by the end of August, we could get it out in November, but October would be better.
>
> (C.S. Evans, letter to John Masefield, 11 June 1928)
> (HRHRC, MS (Masefield, J.) Recip William Heinemann Ltd.)

Noting that Masefield was 'indeed faithful in keeping... promises', Evans acknowledged receipt of the copy for *Midsummer Night and other tales in verse* on 28 July (see C.S. Evans, letter to John Masefield, 28 July 1928) (HRHRC, MS (Masefield, J.) Recip William Heinemann Ltd.) Providing a possible date of publication Evans wrote at the beginning of September:

The press tells me that you will get complete proofs of TALES IN VERSE by September 12th. If you return them promptly, we ought to be able to publish in October.

(C.S. Evans, letter to John Masefield, 3 September 1928)
(HRHRC, MS (Masefield, J.) Recip William Heinemann Ltd.)

It appears that Masefield was not sent proofs at the predicted time. However, in sending 'complete proofs' on 3 October 1928, Evans noted that – with Masefield's co-operation – the projected publication date could still be met:

> We have sent you today complete proofs of A MIDSUMMER NIGHT. You are always exemplary in the promptness with which you return proofs, but this time I am going to ask you to return them within twentyfour hours because we want to publish on October 25th and the book is scheduled to go on the machine almost at once. Please forgive me if this puts an undue strain upon you, but for the first time in my life I am feeling the call of the machine.

(C.S. Evans, letter to John Masefield, 3 October 1928)
(HRHRC, MS (Masefield, J.) Recip William Heinemann Ltd.)

The publishing agreement for this title between Masefield and Heinemann was dated 15 October 1928 (see Archives of The Society of Authors). The agreement refers to a publication price of 7s.6d., and a 'special edition' at 31s.

Copies seen: private collection (PWE)

Reprinted:

'New Impression'	[first edition, second impression]	Oct 1928

A88(b) First American edition (1928)

MIDSUMMER NIGHT | AND | OTHER TALES IN VERSE | BY | JOHN MASEFIELD | NEW YORK | THE MACMILLAN COMPANY | 1928
(All width centred)

Bibliographies: Simmons [noted on p.118], Nevinson [unrecorded], Handley-Taylor p.57, Wight 72b

Collation: [A-L]⁸ (J not used); 88 leaves; 187 × 130mm.; [i–vi] vii–viii [ix–x] 1–164 [165–66]

Page contents: [i] half-title: 'MIDSUMMER NIGHT'; [ii] *BY JOHN MASEFIELD* | [37 titles listed, each title separated by a dash]'; [iii] title-page; [iv] 'COPYRIGHT, 1928, BY JOHN MASEFIELD. | SET UP AND ELECTROTYPED. PUBLISHED, OCTOBER, 1928 | *Printed in the United States of America by* | *J. J. Little and Ives Company, New York*'; [v] '*TO MY WIFE*'; [vi] blank; vii–viii 'CONTENTS' (22 items listed with page references); [ix] 'MIDSUMMER NIGHT'; [x] blank; 1–164 text; [165–66] blank

Paper: laid paper (no watermark), chain-lines 21mm. apart

Running title: none

Binding: burgundy cloth. On spine, in gold: 'MID- | SUMMER | NIGHT | [triangle] | MASEFIELD | MACMILLAN | [point] – [point]' (all width centred). On upper cover, in gold: 'MIDSUMMER NIGHT | JOHN MASEFIELD' (ranged upper left) (within blind ruled border: 188 × 119mm.) Lower cover: blank. Top and lower outside edges trimmed, fore edge roughly trimmed. Binding measurements: 194 × 128mm. (covers), 194 × 35mm. (spine). End-papers: wove paper.

Publication date: published, according to Simmons, 25 October 1928

Price: $2.00

Contents:
The Begetting of Arthur ('Uther, the Prince, succeeding to the post')
The Birth of Arthur ('When the wind from East changes')
The Taking of Morgause ('Morgause the Merry played beside the burn:')
The Begetting of Modred ('When berries were scarlet')
Badon Hill ('Loki the Dragon killer mustered men')
The Sailing of Hell Race ('When Arthur came from warring, having won')
Arthur and his Ring ('Beauty's Delight, the Princess Gwenivere,')
Midsummer Night ('Midsummer night had fallen at full moon,')
The Fight on the Wall ('Modred was in the Water Tower')
The Breaking of the Links ('They told King Arthur how the Knights were killed,')
Gwenivach Tells ('I, Gwenivach, King Modred's queen, declare')
Arthur in the Ruins ('King Arthur watched within the ruined town,')
The Fight at Camlan ('Soon the two armies were in touch, and soon')
The Fight on the Beach, or The Passing ('These were the nine with Modred:-Kolgrim, Gor,')
Gwenivere Tells ('So Arthur passed, but country-folk believe')
The Death of Lancelot ('Then, after many years, a rider came,')
Dust to Dust ('Henry Plantagenet, the English King,')
On the Coming of Arthur ('By ways unknown, unseen,')

The Old Tale of the Begetting ('*The men of old, who made the tale for us,*')
The Taking of Gwenivere ('French poets write:-That, Lancelot the brave')
South and East ('When good King Arthur ruled these western hursts,')
Fulfilment ('Long since, Sir Constans governed here for Rome,')

Notes:
There are minor differences in capitalisation and punctuation between Macmillan and Heinemann editions.

The poem entitled 'The Death of Lancelot as told by Gwenivere' in the Heinemann edition is here entitled 'The Death of Lancelot' whilst 'The Old Tale of the Breaking of the Links' is here entitled 'The Taking of Gwenivere'.

The stanzas of the poem entitled 'Fulfillment' are numbered with Arabic numerals in the Heinemann edition which are here replaced by Roman numerals.

There are two footnotes in this edition which are absent from the Heinemann edition. These footnotes refer the reader to a different page and thus poem. 'The Begetting of Arthur' has a footnote that refers the reader to the page on which 'The Old Tale of the Begetting' commences. 'The Breaking of the Links' has a footnote that refers the reader to the page on which 'The Taking of Gwenivere' commences.

Each poem commences with a raised-capital.

Page numbers appear within square brackets. Thus, [1], [2], etc.

The publishing agreement for this title between Masefield and Macmillan was dated 24 July 1928 (see Archives of The Society of Authors). The agreement refers to 'a licence to publish in volume form in the United States of America and Canada a work the subject or title of which is Midsummer Night and Other Tales, in Verse'.

Handley-Taylor states, of the Macmillan editions:

> Published by The Macmillan Company (New York), October 25, 1928, in a limited edition of 162 copies (signed by the author); and on October 30, 1928, in an ordinary edition.

This is contrary to Simmons who states:

> Published by The Macmillan Company, New York, October 25, 1928, in an ordinary edition; and on October 30, 1928, in a signed edition of 150 copies.

The publicity material in the preliminaries that lists Masefield's work (appearing on p.[ii]) incorrectly includes the title *A Sailor's Garden*.

Copies seen: private collection (PWE)

Reprinted:

'Reprinted'	[first edition, second impression]	Dec 1928
'Reprinted'	[first edition, third impression]	Jan 1929

A88(c) Second English edition (limited signed edition) (1928)

JOHN MASEFIELD | MIDSUMMER NIGHT | *and* | *other tales in* | *Verse* | [ornament] | [publisher's device of a windmill with 'W' and 'H' all within ruled border: 10 × 11mm.] | London | [rule, 56mm.] | WILLIAM HEINEMANN LTD
(All width centred)

Bibliographies: Simmons [72a], Nevinson [unrecorded], Handley-Taylor p.57, Wight [72a]

Collation: [π]² [A]⁸ B-N⁸ O⁴ (J not used); signatures right foot of page; 110 leaves; 226 × 144mm.; [i–x] [1] 2–13 [14–15] 16–23 [24–25] 26–31 [32–33] 34–36 [37] 38–47 [48–49] 50–64 [65] 66–76 [77] 78–86 [87] 88–106 [107] 108–115 [116–17] 118–19 [120–21] 122–24 [125] 126–32 [133] 134–42 [143] 144–45 [146–47] 148–50 [151] 152 [153] 154 [155] 156–57 [158–59] 160–71 [172–73] 174–93 [194–95] 196–207 [208–210]

Page contents: [i–ii] blank; [iii] half-title: 'MIDSUMMER NIGHT | *and other Tales in* | *Verse*' (note that the '*T*' of '*Tales*' is swash); [iv] '*This Edition is limited* | *to 275 copies, of which* | *250 are for sale.* | *No.........*'; [v] title-page; [vi] '*Printed in Great Britain at* | *The Windmill Press, Kingswood, Surrey*'; [vii] 'TO | MY WIFE'; [viii] blank; [ix] 'CONTENTS | [ornament] | [22 items listed with page references]'; [x] blank; [1] 'THE | BEGETTING | OF | ARTHUR'; 2–13 text of 'The Begetting of Arthur'; [14] blank; [15] 'THE | BIRTH | OF | ARTHUR'; 16–23 text of 'The Birth of Arthur'; [24] blank; [25] 'THE | TAKING | OF | MORGAUSE'; 26–31 text of 'The Taking of Morgause'; [32] blank; [33] 'THE | BEGETTING | OF | MODRED'; 34–36 text of 'The Begetting of Modred'; [37] 'BADON | HILL'; 38–47 text of 'Badon Hill'; [48] blank; [49] 'THE | SAILING | OF | HELL RACE'; 50–64 text of 'The Sailing of Hell Race'; [65] 'ARTHUR | AND | HIS | RING'; 66–76 text of 'Arthur and his Ring'; [77] 'MIDSUMMER | NIGHT'; 78–86 text of 'Midsummer Night'; [87] 'THE | FIGHT | ON | THE WALL'; 88–106 text of 'The Fight on the Wall'; [107] 'THE | BREAKING | OF | THE LINKS'; 108–115 text of 'The Breaking of the Links'; [116] blank; [117] 'GWENIVACH | TELLS'; 118–19 text of 'Gwenivach Tells'; [120] blank; [121] 'ARTHUR | IN | THE | RUINS'; 122–24 text of 'Arthur in the Ruins'; [125] 'THE | FIGHT | AT | CAMLAN'; 126–32 text of 'The Fight at Camlan'; [133] 'THE | FIGHT | ON THE | BEACH | OR THE | PASSING'; 134–42 text of 'The Fight on the Beach or The Passing'; [143] 'GWENIVERE | TELLS'; 144–45 text of

'Gwenivere Tells'; [146] blank; [147] 'THE | DEATH | OF | LANCELOT | AS TOLD | BY | GWENIVERE'; 148–50 text of 'The Death of Lancelot as told by Gwenivere'; [151] 'DUST | TO | DUST'; 152 text of 'Dust to Dust'; [153] 'ON | THE COMING | OF | ARTHUR'; 154 text of 'On the Coming of Arthur'; [155] 'THE | OLD TALE | OF THE | BEGETTING'; 156–57 text of 'The Old Tale of the Begetting'; [158] blank; [159] 'THE | OLD TALE | OF THE | BREAKING | OF THE | LINKS'; 160–71 text of 'The Old Tale of the Breaking of the Links'; [172] blank; [173] 'SOUTH | AND | EAST'; 174–93 text of 'South and East'; [194] blank; [195] 'FULFILMENT'; 196–207 text of 'Fulfilment'; [208–210] blank

Paper: wove paper (watermark: 'MILLBOURN | BRITISH HAND MADE PURE RAG [castle device: 26 × 31mm.]')

Running title: none

Binding: blue-green boards with parchment spine. On spine, in gold: 'Midsummer | Night | [ornament] | John | Masefield | Heinemann' (all width centred). There is a single vertical rule in blind on each cover at the edge of the parchment. Covers: blank. Top edge gilt, lower outside edge untrimmed, fore edge uncut. Binding measurements: 231 × 148mm. (covers), 231 × 43mm. (spine). End-papers: wove paper (watermark: 'MILLBOURN | BRITISH HAND MADE PURE RAG [castle device: 26 × 31mm.]')

Publication date: published, according to Simmons, 30 October 1928. The *English Catalogue of Books* records a publication date of November 1928.

Price: 31s.6d.

Contents:
as for A88(a)

Notes:
The text appears to use the same setting of type as A88(a)

Each poem is prefixed by a divisional title on the preceeding page. Each poem commences with a raised-capital in outline.

C.S. Evans wrote to Masefield at the beginning of October 1928:

> About the Limited Edition, I think, as time is so short, it would be best to send the sheets to you at Boar's Hill and I have given Woods instructions to do this.

(C.S. Evans, letter to John Masefield, 4 October 1928)
(HRHRC, MS (Masefield, J.) Recip William Heinemann Ltd.)

One week later Evans wrote to state that he had '…sent to you the sheets of the limited edition of MIDSUMMER NIGHT, for your signature…' (see C.S. Evans, letter to John Masefield, 11 October 1928) (HRHRC, MS (Masefield, J.) Recip William Heinemann Ltd.) H.J. Woods acknowledged receipt of the signed sheets on 12 October (see H.J. Woods, letter to John Masefield, 12 October 1928) (HRHRC, MS (Masefield, J.) Recip William Heinemann Ltd.)

Copies seen: private collection (PWE) number 212, signed '212 | John Masefield.' on p.[iv]; private collection (RM) number 262, signed '262 | John Masefield. | For Harry and Vera, | from Constance + John. | Christmas. 1928.' on p.[iv]; private collection (ROV) number 67, signed '67 | John Masefield.' on p.[iv]

A88(d) Second American edition (limited signed edition) (1928)

MIDSUMMER NIGHT [in red] | AND | OTHER TALES IN VERSE | BY | JOHN MASEFIELD | NEW YORK | THE MACMILLAN COMPANY | 1928
(All width centred)

Bibliographies: Simmons [noted on p.118], Nevinson [unrecorded], Handley-Taylor p.57, Wight 72c

Collation: [A]¹¹ ([A]2+1) [B-L]⁸ (J not used); 91 leaves; 218 × 147mm.; [two un-numbered pages] [i–vi] vii–viii [ix–x] 1–164 [165–70]

Page contents: [-] 'THIS EDITION OF MIDSUMMER NIGHT IS | LIMITED TO ONE HUNDRED AND FIFTY | COPIES EACH SIGNED BY THE AUTHOR. | THIS IS NUMBER'; [-] blank; [i] half-title: 'MIDSUMMER NIGHT'; [ii] *'BY* JOHN MASEFIELD | [37 titles listed, each title separated by a dash]'; [iii] title-page; [iv] 'COPYRIGHT, 1928, BY JOHN MASEFIELD. | SET UP AND ELECTROTYPED. PUBLISHED, OCTOBER, 1928 | *Printed in the United States of America by* | *J. J. Little and Ives Company, New York*'; [v] *'TO MY WIFE'*; [vi] blank; vii–viii 'CONTENTS' (22 items listed with page references); [ix] 'MIDSUMMER NIGHT'; [x] blank; [1]–164 text; [165–70] blank

Paper: laid paper (watermark: 'Buckeye'), chain-lines 28mm. apart (see notes)

Running title: none

Binding: maroon boards with black cloth spine. On spine: white paper label (60 × 21mm.) on which: '[double ruled pattern] | [rule] | MID- | SUMMER | NIGHT | AND | OTHER | TALES IN | VERSE | [ornament of square within square] | JOHN | MASEFIELD | [rule] | MACMILLAN | [rule] | [double ruled pattern]' (all width centred) (see notes). Covers: blank. Top edge trimmed, others untrimmed. Binding measurements: 225 × 145mm. (covers), 225 × 31mm. (spine). End-papers: laid paper (no watermark), chain-lines 20mm. apart.

Publication date: published, according to Simmons, 30 October 1928 in an edition of 150 copies

Price: unknown

Contents:
as for A88(b)

Notes:
This edition appears to be a direct reprint using the plates as used for A88(b). Features noted for A88(b) are therefore present here.

See note to A88(b) for different dates of publication cited by Simmons and Handley-Taylor.

Wight notes that the laid paper watermark is 'WM BUCKEYE'. In the copy examined only 'Buckeye' appears. It thus appears possible that two stocks of paper were used in this edition. Wight also describes the spine label as follows: '(Double rule) / MID- / SUMMER / NIGHT / AND / OTHER / TALES IN / VERSE / (dot inside a square) / JOHN / MASEFIELD / (rule) / MACMILLAN / (double rule)'

The additional leaf ([A]1) pasted onto [A]2 comprises the leaf detailing the limitation of the edition. The paper type is the same as the rest of the volume. The single leaves were presumably sent to Masefield for signing.

The publicity material in the preliminaries that lists Masefield's work (appearing on p.[ii]) incorrectly includes the title *A Sailor's Garden*.

Copies seen: private collection (ROV) number 49, signed 'J. Masefield.' on first un-numbered page

A89 ANY DEAD TO ANY LIVING   1928

A89(a) First American edition (1928)

ANY DEAD TO ANY LIVING | BY | JOHN MASEFIELD
(All width centred)

Bibliographies: Simmons [unrecorded], Nevinson [unrecorded], Handley-Taylor [unrecorded], Wight 76

Collation: [A]²; 2 leaves; 254 × 177mm.; [1–4]

Page contents: [1] title-page; [2] blank; [3] text; [4] 'Copyright 1928 by John Masefield | and The Yale Review | Twenty-five copies printed | 10 November 1928'

Paper: laid paper (watermark of undecipherable ornate design: 151 × 98mm.), chain-lines 28mm. apart (see notes)

Running title: none

Binding: blue wrappers (see notes). Spine: blank. On upper wrapper: 'ANY DEAD TO ANY LIVING | BY | JOHN MASEFIELD'. Lower wrapper: blank. All edges trimmed. Binding measurements: 264 × 184mm. (wrappers), 264 × 1mm. (spine). The wrappers extend beyond the edges of the internal leaves.

Publication date: published, according to date within volume, 10 November 1928

Price: unknown

Contents:
Any Dead to any Living ('Boast not about our score.')

Notes:
Wight describes the watermark as a 'curious ornate violin shaped watermark'. The chain-lines run horizontally.

Each stanza commences with a drop-capital.

The poem was later printed within *The Yale Review* (see C220.005).

The single sheet (folded once) is sewn into the wrappers. There is also evidence to suggest that adhesive may also have been used. The wrappers are laid paper (chain-lines 40mm. apart) and the chain-lines run horizontally.

Copies seen: NYPL (Rare Book Division) (*KL)

A90 EASTER   1929

A90(a) First American edition (1929)

JOHN MASEFIELD | [five point star] | EASTER | A PLAY | FOR SINGERS | NEW YORK | THE MACMILLAN COMPANY | 1929
(All width centred)

Bibliographies: Simmons [73], Nevinson [unrecorded], Handley-Taylor p.57, Wight [73]

Collation: [A–C]⁴; 12 leaves; 237 × 159mm.; [1–10] 11–24

Page contents: [1] 'Of this edition of | "Easter, A Play For Singers" | by John Masefield, now | published for the first | time, one hundred copies | only have been printed.' (see notes); [2] blank; [3] half-title: 'EASTER'; [4] blank; [5] title-page; [6] 'COPYRIGHT, 1929, | BY JOHN MASEFIELD. | [rule] | *All rights reserved, included the right of re- | production in whole or in part in any form.* | [rule] |

Set up and printed. | Published June, 1929. | *Printed in the United States of America by* | J. J. LITTLE AND IVES COMPANY, NEW YORK'; [7] 'TO | MY WIFE'; [8] blank; [9] '"Easter: a Play For Singers" by John Masefield, | has been set to music and is to be sung in Oxford, | England, in the spring of 1929, coincident with its | publication in book form.'; [10] 'PERSONS AND SPIRITS | [dramatis personae listed]'; 11–24 text

Paper: laid paper (watermark: '[unicorn: 79 × 65mm.] | UNICORN | 100% RAG BOOK'), chain-lines 39mm. apart

Running title: none

Binding: mottled light green boards with black cloth spine. Spine: blank. On upper cover, in gold: 'EASTER | [rule] | JOHN MASEFIELD'. Lower cover: blank. Top edge gilt, lower outside edge trimmed, fore edge roughly cut. Binding measurements: 242 × 160mm. (covers), 242 × 15mm. (spine). End-papers: laid paper (watermark: '[unicorn: 79 × 65mm.] | UNICORN | 100% RAG BOOK'), chain-lines 39mm. apart. Volume contained in slip-case covered in light grey / white paper with ripple grain effect, with white paper label (48 × 90mm.) upon which: 'EASTER | JOHN MASEFIELD | *Of this edition of "Easter" one* | *hundred copies have been printed.* | *This is number ....* | THE MACMILLAN COMPANY' (lines 1, 2 and 6 justified on both left and right margin, and all within ornate border: 38 × 76mm., all enclosed within ruled border: 42 × 81mm.)

Publication date: published, according to Simmons, 11 June 1929

Price: $5.00

Contents:
Easter ('THE WAY OF THE WORLD | *(appears and sings)* | I am the welter of life, and the glory...')

Notes:
Described on the title-page as 'a play for singers'. Only the Macmillan edition includes a note that the play 'has been set to music and is to be sung in Oxford, England, in the spring of 1929'. Describing the work to The Society of Authors in May 1929 Masefield notes 'the play "Easter" is really an operetta or cantata, written to be sung to music. The music is to be made by Mr. Martin Shaw and will, no doubt, presently be published...' Presumably with reference to publication of Shaw's setting, Masefield wrote again to The Society of Authors in September 1929 noting 'I don't mind how Easter is described. "Choral playlet" might be better than "operetta"; but "mystery play" is near enough.' (see BL, Add.Mss.56587, f.158 and Add.Mss.56588, f.48). Writing to The Society of Authors on 10 April 1935 Masefield notes the lack of any performance: '..."Easter"... was designed to be sung in a church and never has been sung and I suppose never will be.' (see BL, Add.Mss.56602, f.185). The music for the play, written by Martin Shaw, was published by Curwen in 1929.

The type used on page [1] resembles handwritten script.

Page numbers appear in italics, written in full, within square brackets. Thus, [*Eleven*], [*Twelve*], etc.

The edition was simply numbered, not signed.

Copies seen: Library of The John Masefield Society (Peter Smith Collection) number 53 (written in red ink)

A90(b) *First English edition (1929)*

JOHN MASEFIELD | [five point star] | EASTER | A PLAY | FOR SINGERS | [publisher's device of a windmill: 19 × 19mm.] | *London* | WILLIAM HEINEMANN LTD.
(All width centred)

Bibliographies: Simmons [73a], Nevinson p.14, Handley-Taylor p.57, Wight [73a]

Collation: [A-C]⁴; 12 leaves; 187 × 121mm.; [i–viii] 1–14 [15–16]

Page contents: [i] half-title: 'EASTER'; [ii] blank; [iii] title-page; [iv] 'First published 1929 | *Printed in Great Britain at* | *The Windmill Press,* *Kingswood.* | *Surrey*'; [v] 'TO | MY WIFE'; [vi] blank; [vii] 'PERSONS AND SPIRITS | [dramatis personae listed]' (a tipped-in slip notes: 'The play contained in this volume is copyright in Great Britain, United States of America, and Ireland.'); [viii] blank; 1–14 text; [15–16] blank

Paper: laid paper (no watermark), chain-lines 24mm. apart

Running title: none

Binding: blue cloth. On spine, reading lengthways up spine, from foot, in gold: 'EASTER – JOHN MASEFIELD'; horizontally at foot of spine: 'Heinemann'. On upper cover, in gold: 'EASTER | [rule] | JOHN | MASEFIELD' (within blind ruled border: 188 × 117mm.) On lower cover, in blind: publisher's device of a windmill (ranged lower right). All edges trimmed. Binding measurements: 191 × 122mm. (covers), 191 × 18mm. (spine). End-papers: wove paper.

Publication date: published, according to Simmons, 27 June 1929 in an edition of 4000 copies

Price: 2s.

Contents:
as for A90(a)

Notes:
Masefield provided Heinemann with the manuscript of the play towards the end of March 1929. C.S. Evans wrote in response:

> Very many thanks for your letter, which is undated, and for the manuscript of the little Easter play... There will not be any difficulty in getting the little play out in time for the production on May 1st. I will get to work on it at once...
>
> (C.S. Evans, letter to John Masefield, 20 March 1929)
> (HRHRC, MS (Masefield, J.) Recip William Heinemann Ltd.)

Three sets of proofs were sent on 15 April 1929 (see H.J. Woods, letter to John Masefield, 15 April 1929) (HRHRC, MS (Masefield, J.) Recip William Heinemann Ltd.) and a revised proof was sent three days later (see H.J. Woods, letter to John Masefield, 18 April 1929) (HRHRC, MS (Masefield, J.) Recip William Heinemann Ltd.) A week later C.S. Evans wrote confirming his co-operation with the Macmillan publication:

> I was not quite sure from your letter yesterday whether you wanted me to send you two pulls of EASTER for Macmillans. I therefore made things perfectly certain by sending two to you and one to them. I told Macmillan's however, that they were not finally corrected proofs.
>
> (C.S. Evans, letter to John Masefield, 25 April 1929)
> (HRHRC, MS (Masefield, J.) Recip William Heinemann Ltd.)

Publication was, apparently, delayed due to an election. Explaining his dilemma, Evans wrote:

> ...When do you think it will be best to publish EASTER? The book is all ready and we had it in mind to issue it on the 16th., a fortnight before election day. If we do that, however, we shall have to issue the Limited Edition about a month later. It would, I suppose, be better to postpone the ordinary edition so that the two can come out together, particularly if by this means we can get nearer the date of the actual production of the play.
>
> (C.S. Evans, letter to John Masefield, 6 May 1929)
> (HRHRC, MS (Masefield, J.) Recip William Heinemann Ltd.)

A change of date (itself later revised) was communicated to Masefield three days later:

> There is no hurry about EASTER, so I have postponed it temporarily until June 7th. If you find later that it is necessary to postpone it still further will you let me know? We will get the Limited and Ordinary editions out together. In the meantime I have sent Macmillans two copies for ad interim copyright and have informed them of the change of date...
>
> (C.S. Evans, letter to John Masefield, 9 May 1929)
> (HRHRC, MS (Masefield, J.) Recip William Heinemann Ltd.)

The publishing agreement for this title between Masefield and Heinemann was dated 24 June 1929 (see Archives of The Society of Authors). The agreement refers to both 2s. and 10s.6d. editions (A90(b) and A90(c))

Copies seen: private collection (PWE); BL (011781.ee.124) stamped 27 JUN 1929; Library of The John Masefield Society (Peter Smith Collection 98) inscribed 'For Con | From | Jan | June 25. 1929.', includes posthumous booklabel

A90(c) Second English edition (limited signed edition) (1929)

JOHN MASEFIELD | EASTER [in green] | A PLAY | FOR SINGERS | [publisher's device of a windmill: 17 × 17mm.] | LONDON | WILLIAM HEINEMANN LTD
(All width centred)

Bibliographies: Simmons [noted on p.120], Nevinson [unrecorded], Handley-Taylor p.57, Wight 73b

Collation: [A-C]⁴; 12 leaves; 221 × 145mm.; [i–viii] 1–15 [16]

Page contents: [i] half-title: 'EASTER'; [ii] '*This edition is limited | to 375 copies, numbered | and signed by the author | No.............*'; [iii] title-page; [iv] 'Printed in Great Britain at | The Windmill Press, Kingswood, Surrey'; [v] 'TO | MY WIFE'; [vi] blank; [vii] 'PERSONS AND SPIRITS | [dramatis personae listed]'; [viii] blank; 1–15 text; [16] blank

Paper: laid paper (no watermark), chain-lines 39–41mm. apart

Running title: 'EASTER' (20mm.) on both verso and recto, pp.2–15

Binding: blue cloth. On spine, reading lengthways up spine, from foot, in gold: 'EASTER – JOHN MASEFIELD'. On upper cover, in gold: 'EASTER | JOHN | MASEFIELD' (within blind ruled border: 214 × 135mm.) On lower cover: blind ruled border: 214 × 135mm. Top edge gilt, others untrimmed. Sewn head band (in white). Binding measurements: 224 × 144mm. (covers), 224 × 18mm. (spine). End-papers: laid paper (no watermark), chain-lines 39–41mm. apart.

Publication date: published, according to Simmons, 27 June 1929 (see notes)

Price: 10s.6d.

Contents:
as for A90(a)

Notes:

This edition uses a different setting of type from A90(b). Most noticeably the text finishes on p.15 and there are running titles. This edition also concludes with a stage direction omitted from A90(b). Although the British Library dated stamps are different between A90(b) and A90(c), evidence within letters received by Masefield from Heinemann suggest that Simmons' date of publication is correct.

H.J. Woods sent the limitation sheets to Masefield on 13 June 1929 together with a request to take particular care:

> Under separate cover I have sent you the titles of EASTER Limited Edition to number and sign. I would ask you to please be careful not to spoil any as this is the bare number. I have sent you 377 and the edition is 375…
>
> (H.J. Woods, letter to John Masefield, 13 June 1929)
> (HRHRC, MS (Masefield, J.) Recip William Heinemann Ltd.)

On the same day C.S. Evans wrote noting that Heinemann proposed 'to publish both the limited edition and the ordinary edition on June 27th, unless you have any objections.' (see C.S. Evans, letter to John Masefield, 13 June 1929) (HRHRC, MS (Masefield, J.) Recip William Heinemann Ltd.) Writing to Masefield after he had been sent his copies of this edition, C.S. Evans notes:

> Your twelve copies of the Limited Edition of EASTER were sent to you on Wednesday… I hope you like the appearance of the book. It is a little different from your other Limited Editions, but I am getting a little tired of that format which seems to me now a little old fashioned.
>
> (C.S. Evans, letter to John Masefield, 5 July 1929)
> (HRHRC, MS (Masefield, J.) Recip William Heinemann Ltd.)

Masefield, it appears, did indeed like the new format (see C.S. Evans, letter to John Masefield, 8 July 1929) (HRHRC, MS (Masefield, J.) Recip William Heinemann Ltd.)

Given the letter from H.J. Woods to Masefield on 13 June 1929 (see above) it appears that Masefield signed all the sheets that had been sent to him. Heinemann may then have bound all these. Louisa Callender wrote to the author on 5 August 1929:

> We have received the following letter from a Mr Stanley Harrod of Toronto:-
> "I have procured a copy of the limited edition of Mr. John Masefield's latest work EASTER, which bears on the verso of the half-title the following imprint:- 'This edition is limited to 375 copies, numbered and signed by the Author. No……' This particular copy bears in Mr. Masefield's handwriting the following: '377. Rest and be thankful copy. John Masefield.' I assume that this is the last copy signed, but I should be obliged if you could explain why it bears the No. 377 as the edition is limited to 375 copies."
> We should like to give Mr. Harrod an answer to his question if we can. A possible explanation is that you went on signing two of the presentation copies which have been sold by their owners.
>
> (Louisa Callender, letter to John Masefield, 5 August 1929)
> (HRHRC, MS (Masefield, J.) Recip William Heinemann Ltd.)

Copies seen: private collection (PWE) number 327, signed '327 | John Masefield.' on p.[ii]; BL (011781.ee.124) number 354, signed '354 | John Masefield.' on p.[ii] stamped 4 JUL 1929

A91 POEMS [COMPLETE IN ONE VOLUME]   1929

A91(a) First American edition (1929)

Poems | By | John Masefield | Complete in One Volume | New York | The Macmillan Company | 1929
(All width centred and enclosed within ruled border in red: 124 × 74mm. and all within ornate decorative border in red: 138 × 88mm.)

Bibliographies: Simmons [unrecorded], Nevinson [unrecorded], Handley-Taylor p.57, Wight [unrecorded]

Collation: [A]²⁰ [B-DD]¹⁶ (J and V not used); 452 leaves; 201 × 127mm.; [i] ii [iii–vi] vii–xi [xii] 1–95 [96] 97–209 [210] 211–73 [274] 275–397 [398] 399–423 [424] 425–46 [i–ii] iii–vi 1–169 [170] 171–438 [439–40]

Page contents: [i] half-title: 'Poems'; ii '*BY* JOHN MASEFIELD | [37 titles listed, each title separated by a dash]'; [iii] title-page; [iv] 'Copyright, 1913, by Harper and Brothers | Copyright, 1914, by The Century Company and by the McClure Publications | [rule] | Copyright, 1912, 1913, 1914 | BY THE MACMILLAN COMPANY | [rule] | Copyright, 1915, 1928 | BY JOHN MASEFIELD | All rights reserved, including the right of reproduction | in whole or in part in any form | New One Volume Edition | Set up and electrotyped. Published October, 1929 | PRINTED IN THE UNITED STATES OF AMERICA BY | THE BERWICK & SMITH CO.'; [v] 'PART I'; [vi] blank; vii–viii 'INTRODUCTION' ('It seems as though the minds of men always follow one of two purposes in art...') (signed, 'JOHN MASEFIELD. | Oxford, 1925.'); ix–xi 'CONTENTS | PART ONE' (112 individual items listed with page references); [xii] blank; 1–95 text; [96] blank; 97–209 text; [210] blank; 211–73 text; [274] blank; 275–397 text; [398] blank; 399–423 text; [424] blank; 425–46 text; [i] 'PART II'; [ii] blank; iii–iv 'INTRODUCTION' ('I have been asked to write a few words as introduction to this volume...') (signed, 'JOHN MASEFIELD. | Oxford, 1925.'); v–vi 'CONTENTS | PART TWO' (47 individual items listed with page references); 1–438 text; [439–40] blank

Paper: wove paper. Also issued in a 'thin paper edition'.

Running title: 'POEMS' (14mm.) on verso; recto title comprises poem title, pp.2 (of part one) – 438 (of part two)

Binding: brown cloth. On spine, in gold: 'POEMS | [point] | JOHN | MASEFIELD | [ornament] | MACMILLAN | [square point]' (all width centred). On upper cover, in gold: facsimile signature 'J. Masefield.' (width centred but at an angle). Lower cover: blank. Top and lower outside edges trimmed, fore edge roughly cut. Binding measurements: 209 × 137mm. (covers), 209 × 50mm. (spine). End-papers: wove paper.

Also issued in leather.

Publication date: published, according to Handley-Taylor, 15 October 1929

Price: $5.00 (cloth) / $8.00 (leather) / $6.00 (thin paper edition)

Contents:
pp.vii-446 (of part one) as for A78(a) (volume one) and pp.iii-291 (of part two) as for A78(a) (volume two) and then with the following additional contents:
The Begetting of Arthur ('Uther, the Prince, succeeding to the post')
The Birth of Arthur ('When the wind from East changes')
The Taking of Morgause ('Morgause the Merry played beside the burn:')
The Begetting of Modred ('When berries were scarlet')
Badon Hill ('Loki the Dragon killer mustered men')
The Sailing of Hell Race ('When Arthur came from warring, having won')
Arthur and his Ring ('Beauty's Delight, the Princess Gwenivere,')
Midsummer Night ('Midsummer night had fallen at full moon,')
The Fight on the Wall ('Modred was in the Water Tower')
The Breaking of the Links ('They told King Arthur how the Knights were killed,')
Gwenivach Tells ('I, Gwenivach, King Modred's queen, declare')
Arthur in the Ruins ('King Arthur watched within the ruined town,')
The Fight at Camlan ('Soon the two armies were in touch, and soon')
The Fight on the Beach, or the Passing ('These were the nine with Modred:-Kolgrim, Gor,')
Gwenivere Tells ('So Arthur passed, but country-folk believe')
The Death of Lancelot ('Then, after many years, a rider came,')
Dust to Dust ('Henry Plantagenet, the English King,')
On the Coming of Arthur ('By ways unknown, unseen,')
The Old Tale of the Begetting ('The men of old, who made the tale for us,')
The Taking of Gwenivere ('French poets write:-That, Lancelot the brave')
South and East ('When good King Arthur ruled these western hursts,')
Fulfilment ('Long since, Sir Constans governed here for Rome,')

Notes:
Noted by Handley-Taylor as *Poems: Complete in One Volume*, the correct title of this volume is *Poems*. A further line on the title-page states 'Complete in One Volume'. The volume is in two parts each with a separate contents page, introduction and pagination. The volume represents an updated single volume publication of the two volumes comprising A78(a).

The publishing agreement for this title between Masefield and Macmillan was dated 11 February 1929 (see Archives of The Society of Authors). The agreement refers to 'a licence to publish in volume form… in the United States of America and Canada a work the subject or title of which is Collected Poems including Midsummer Night, to be published in one volume'. The agreement additionally noted 'It is agreed that as soon as the stock of the present two volume edition of the Author's COLLECTED PLAYS is sufficiently reduced the Company shall publish these COLLECTED PLAYS in one volume in the same format as the aforesaid volume of COLECTED POEMS…' This clause was deleted, however.

Handley-Taylor also notes a 'Thin Paper Edition' apparently published simultaneously with the regular edition. Such an issue has not been consulted.

The volume does not always clearly note titles of the volumes for the source of individual poems.

Copies seen: private collection (PWE); Harvard College Library (Houghton *EC9.M377.B929p); Columbia University (825 M377 L23) rebound

Reprinted:

[first edition, second impression]	Jan 1930
[first edition, third impression]	Aug 1930

A92 THE HAWBUCKS   1929

A92(a) First English edition (1929)

THE HAWBUCKS | *by* | JOHN MASEFIELD | [publisher's device of a windmill with 'W [point]' and 'H'] | LONDON | WILLIAM HEINEMANN LTD
(All width centred)

Bibliographies: Simmons [unrecorded], Nevinson p.17, Handley-Taylor p.57, Wight 74b

Collation: [A]⁸ B-U⁸ W⁴ (J and V not used); signatures right foot of page; 164 leaves; 185 × 122mm.; [i–vi] [1] 2–322

Page contents: [i] half-title: 'THE HAWBUCKS'; [ii] '*BY THE SAME AUTHOR* | [rule] | SARD HARKER | ODTAA | THE MIDNIGHT FOLK'; [iii] title-page; [iv] '*First published* 1929 | *Printed in Great Britain at* | *The Windmill Press Kingswood* | *Surrey.*' (note that the '*P*' of '*Printed*', '*B*' of '*Britain*' and '*T*' of '*The*' are swash); [v] 'TO | MY WIFE'; [vi] blank; [1]–322 text

Paper: laid paper (watermark of a windmill: 22 × 18mm.), chain-lines 25mm. apart

Running title: 'THE HAWBUCKS' (35mm.) on both verso and recto, pp.2–322

Binding: blue cloth. On spine, in gold: 'THE | HAWBUCKS | [ornament] | JOHN | MASEFIELD | HEINEMANN' (all width centred). On upper cover, in gold: 'THE HAWBUCKS | JOHN MASEFIELD' (within blind ruled border: 187 × 117mm.) On lower cover, in blind: publisher's device of a windmill (ranged lower right). Top edge stained blue, others trimmed. Binding measurements: 191 × 122mm. (covers), 191 × 48mm. (spine). End-papers: wove paper.

Publication date: published, according to the sales ledger preserved in the Heinemann Archive, on 28 October 1929 in an edition of 12000 copies / published, according to Handley-Taylor, 29 October 1929

Price: 7s.6d.

Contents:

The Hawbucks ('Condicote is linked to Tatchester by a branch line, nine and a half miles long, upon which...')

Notes:

A novel set in the English countryside telling of George Childrey's courtship of Carrie Harridew who is eventually won by the hero's younger brother. The novel has no chapter divisions. With several characters first introduced in *Right Royal* and a description of a fox hunt, the novel has often been dismissed as derivative of earlier work. As a social comedy the style is, however, very different and the narrative often approaches farce.

Wight notes in his bibliography:

> In some early editions pages 301–302 and 311–312 were transposed, as the gathering was laid out incorrectly on the form.

Wight presumably detects variations between issues of the first edition.

During January 1929 Masefield appears to have informed Heinemann that he was writing a new novel. C.S. Evans reponded that he was '...delighted to hear that you hope to have a long novel ready by the end of July...' (see C.S. Evans, letter to John Masefield, 14 January 1929) (HRHRC, MS (Masefield, J.) Recip William Heinemann Ltd.) By March Masefield was, apparently, suggesting that illustrations could be requested from Cecil Aldin. Evans was not enthusiastic:

> It is good news to hear about your new novel. At the first blush I am not particularly enthusiastic about issuing it with Cecil Aldin's illustrations – at any rate in the first place. He is very expensive...
>
> (C.S. Evans, letter to John Masefield, 20 March 1929)
> (HRHRC, MS (Masefield, J.) Recip William Heinemann Ltd.)

By 29 May 1929 Katherine Munro was requesting '...a short description of your new novel together with the title, if it has been settled, as a basis for our preliminary autumn list.' (see Katherine Munro, letter to John Masefield, 29 May 1929) (HRHRC, MS (Masefield, J.) Recip William Heinemann Ltd.) This information was received on 3 June 1929 (see Katherine Munro, letter to John Masefield, 3 June 1929) (HRHRC, MS (Masefield, J.) Recip William Heinemann Ltd.) Just under two months later Heinemann acknowledged the manuscript (see Louisa Callender, letter to John Masefield, 2 August 1929) (HRHRC, MS (Masefield, J.) Recip William Heinemann Ltd.) Whilst reading this, C.S. Evans wrote:

> ...I am half way through THE HAWBUCKS and I am enjoying it immensely. I find it quite as enthralling as SARD HARKER, though, of course, in a very different way. You have visualised all those people in the most extra-ordinarily vivid way. I do not believe that I shall be able to go on with the rest of the book in type-script because the press is clamouring to begin the setting; and we shall have to begin work at once if the book is to come out in October...
>
> (C.S. Evans, letter to John Masefield, 6 August 1929)
> (HRHRC, MS (Masefield, J.) Recip William Heinemann Ltd.)

On 22 August 1929 Masefield was sent two sets of proofs (together with the original manuscript) (see H.J. Woods, letter to John Masefield, 22 August 1929) (HRHRC, MS (Masefield, J.) Recip William Heinemann Ltd.) At this stage Masefield was asked whether there was to be a dedication. Only after publication was Evans able to finish reading the novel and wrote (noting current sales):

> ...I finished The Hawbucks on Sunday (I had only read the first third in typescript). What a beautiful book it is! Surely one of your very best. I wanted it to be twice as long. I wish Carrie hadn't married such. But of course that is exactly what she would have done. It is selling marvellously well – averaging at present over 150 a day. I gave an order for another reprint yesterday because I wanted to be quite certain we should have ample supplies. All our travellers report great enthusiasm from the wholesellers + public + they all think the book will be selling in pretty large numbers up to Christmas...
>
> (C.S. Evans, letter to John Masefield, 4 November 1929
> (HRHRC, MS (Masefield, J.) Recip. Evans, C[harles] S[eddon])

After publication Masefield wrote to Evans to inform him of 'mistakes'. Evans replied:

> ...I am sorry about the mistakes in the book and I will take these up with our proof reader. In justification to him, however, I must say that the mistake which we discovered at the last minute ("quite so quiet" for "quite so quite") was none of his making. It was apparently altered at the last minute by the reader in the composing room, who felt certain that you must have made a mistake and changed it without reference to anybody. I made such a row about that[,] that I don't think it likely that they will do it again.

(C.S. Evans, letter to John Masefield, 29 October 1929)
(HRHRC, MS (Masefield, J.) Recip William Heinemann Ltd.)

Corrections were made for the second impression and, in telling Masefield of this, Evans reported sales figures:

> ...I am glad to say that the book is going very well indeed: in fact, the other day it topped the sale of all our books for the day. The first edition of 12,000 copies is practically exhausted and the second edition will be ready this week. All the corrections have been made.

(C.S. Evans, letter to John Masefield, 6 November 1929)
(HRHRC, MS (Masefield, J.) Recip William Heinemann Ltd.)

Further corrections were, however, forthcoming and Evans wrote to Masefield:

> Thank you for your note. A reprint of THE HAWBUCKS is just off the machine. In that reprint we have made all the corrections you have pointed out, but it is too late to make this new one. I have, however, made a careful note of it so that it can be made in the 3rd printing

(C.S. Evans, letter to John Masefield, 8 November 1929)
(HRHRC, MS (Masefield, J.) Recip William Heinemann Ltd.)

Further sales figures (and public reception) were reported by Evans at the end of 1929:

> ...THE HAWBUCKS has been doing splendidly. Up to December 24th we had sold approximately 16,370 copies and I am sure that it is going to go on into the new year and for some months to come. I hear that a great many people like it better than any other novel of yours. I loved it myself and read it all through again in book form at a sitting. The only quarrel I have with you is for letting Carrie marry that man. I dare say that is what she would have done, though.

(C.S. Evans, letter to John Masefield, 30 December 1929)
(HRHRC, MS (Masefield, J.) Recip William Heinemann Ltd.)

The publishing agreement for this title between Masefield and Heinemann was dated 16 August 1929 (see Archives of The Society of Authors). The agreement refers to a publication price of 7s.6d.

See note to A92(aa) regarding publication dates.

In 'Some Contributions to the Bibliography of John Masefield: II' (*Papers of the Bibliographical Society of America*, October 1959, pp.262–67) Drew specifically notes Simmons' omission of this edition.

Copies seen: private collection (PWE); private collection (ROV) inscribed 'For Con Belliss, | from Macey. | October, 1929.'

Reprinted:

'New Impression'	[first edition, second impression]	Nov 1929
	[first edition, third impression]	Nov 1929
'Popular edition'	[first edition, later impression]	Dec 1934

The 'Popular edition' published, according to the *English Catalogue of Books*, during December 1934 was priced at 3s.6d. It is thought to have been issued in red cloth and use the standard setting of text.

A92(aa) First English edition (limited signed edition) (1929)

THE HAWBUCKS [in red] | *by* | JOHN MASEFIELD | [publisher's device of a windmill with 'W [point]' and 'H'] | LONDON | WILLIAM HEINEMANN LTD | 1929
(All width centred)

Bibliographies: Simmons [74a], Nevinson [unrecorded], Handley-Taylor p.57, Wight 74a

Collation: [π]⁸ A-U⁸ (J not used); signatures right foot of page; 164 leaves; 222 × 141mm.; [i–vi] [1] 2–322

Page contents: [i] half-title: 'THE HAWBUCKS'; [ii] '*This Edition of THE HAWBUCKS | is limited to 275 copies. | This is No.*'; [iii] title-page; [iv] '*Printed in Great Britain at | The Windmill Press Kingswood | Surrey.*' (the '*P*' of '*Printed*', '*B*' of '*Britain*' and '*T*' of '*The*' are swash); [v] 'TO | MY WIFE'; [vi] blank; [1]–322 text

Paper: laid paper (watermark of two masted ship at sea with birds in flight all within oval rope design border: 83 × 54mm.), chain-lines 27–28mm. apart

Running title: 'THE HAWBUCKS' (35mm.) on both verso and recto, pp.2–322

Binding: blue-green boards with parchment spine. On spine, in gold: 'THE | HAWBUCKS | [ornament] | JOHN | MASEFIELD | HEINEMANN' (all width centred). There is a single vertical rule in blind on each cover at the edge of the parchment. Covers:

blank. Top edge gilt, lower outside edge untrimmed, fore edge uncut. Sewn head band (in blue and white) and blue marker ribbon. Binding measurements: 230 × 145mm. (covers), 230 × 48mm. (spine). End-papers: laid paper (watermark of two masted ship at sea with birds in flight all within oval rope design border: 83 × 54mm.), chain-lines 27–28mm. apart.

Publication date: published, according to the sales ledger preserved in the Heinemann Archive, on 28 October 1929 / published, according to Handley-Taylor, 29 October 1929

Price: 42s.

Contents:
as for A92(a)

Notes:
Although Wight states:

> Handley-Taylor says that [the Heinemann limited signed edition] and a regular edition were published on October 29, 1929.

this is not an accurate report. Handley-Taylor actually notes:

> Published by William Heinemann, Ltd. (London), in a limited edition of 275 copies (signed by the author) on October 29, 1929. Also published in a regular edition.

Consequently, no previous Masefield bibliography states the date of publication or print-run of A92(a) and the limited signed edition may, or may not, constitute the true English first edition. Evidence in the Heinemann archive suggests that both editions were published on the same date (one day before that recorded by Handley-Taylor). Neither therefore has priority as the first edition.

A letter from H.J. Woods to Masefield enclosed the limitation sheets for this edition. Woods wrote '…I have sent you the titles of "THE HAWBUCKS" to sign for the limited edition. Please do not number them, we will number here: all I require is your signature…' (see H.J. Woods, letter to John Masefield, 1 October 1929) (HRHRC, MS (Masefield, J.) Recip William Heinemann Ltd.)

The sales ledger preserved in the Heinemann Archive suggests publication on 28 October 1929 in an edition of 250 copies. This limitation may represent copies for sale rather than the total number printed.

Copies: private collection (ROV) number 202, signed 'John Masefield.' on p.[ii]

A92(b) First American edition (1929)

THE HAWBUCKS | [wavy rule, 85mm.] | BY | JOHN MASEFIELD | [wavy rule, 85mm.] | NEW YORK | THE MACMILLAN COMPANY | 1929
(All width centred and enclosed within wavy double ruled border: 151 × 94mm. The outer rule is thicker than the inner.)

Bibliographies: Simmons [74], Nevinson [unrecorded], Handley-Taylor p.57, Wight 74

Collation: [A-X]⁸ [Y]⁴ (J, V and W not used); 172 leaves; 188 × 129mm.; [i–vi] 1–336 [337–38]

Page contents: [i] half-title: 'THE HAWBUCKS'; [ii] 'BY JOHN MASEFIELD | [38 titles listed, each title separated by a dash]'; [iii] title-page; [iv] 'COPYRIGHT, 1929, | BY JOHN MASEFIELD. | All rights reserved, including the right of reproduction | in whole or in part in any form. | Set up and electrotyped. | Published October, 1929. | SET UP BY BROWN BROTHERS LINOTYPERS | PRINTED IN THE UNITED STATES OF AMERICA | BY THE FERRIS PRINTING COMPANY'; [v] 'THE HAWBUCKS'; [vi] blank; 1–336 text; [337–38] blank

Paper: wove paper

Running title: 'THE HAWBUCKS' (36mm.) on both verso and recto, pp.2–336

Binding: green cloth. On spine, in gold: 'THE | HAWBUCKS | JOHN | MASEFIELD | -MACMILLAN-' (all width centred). On upper cover, in gold: 'THE | HAWBUCKS | JOHN MASEFIELD' (ranged upper right and text centred in relation to itself). Lower cover: blank. Top and lower outside edges trimmed, fore edge roughly trimmed. Binding measurements: 195 × 131mm. (covers), 195 × 45mm. (spine). End-papers: wove paper.

Publication date: published, according to Simmons, 29 October 1929 in an edition of 10000 copies

Price: $2.50

Contents:
as for A92(a)

Notes:
The Heinemann editions of this novel do not include chapter divisions. Here, however, the novel is separated into sixteen chapters.

A letter from C.S. Evans to Masefield notes that Heinemann were assisting in this American publication. Evans noted that '…two sets of finally corrected proofs were sent out to Macmillan's in New York on September 17th. The book is now off machine…' (see C.S. Evans, letter to John Masefield, 27 September 1929) (HRHRC, MS (Masefield, J.) Recip William Heinemann Ltd.)

A telegram sent to Masefield on 13 September suggests that Heinemann and Macmillan were aiming to publish simultaneously. (The date of publication was subsequently revised):

> Have Not Received Corrected English Proofs Hawbucks Stop Impossible For Us Publish Simultaneously With England October Seventeenth Unless We Go To Press Immediately Stop May We Read Proofs Here By Your Manuscript Without Waiting English Galleys And Print Cable Macmillan

> (Macmillan, telegram to John Masefield, 13 September 1929)
> (HRHRC, MS (Masefield, J.) Recip The Macmillan Company)

A publishing agreement for a novel between Masefield and Macmillan was dated 11 February 1929 (see Archives of The Society of Authors). The agreement refers to 'a licence to publish in volume form… in the United States of America and Canada a work the subject or title of which is his next long novel'. This may refer to *The Hawbucks*.

Copies seen: private collection (ROV); Bodleian (Rec.e.81) inscribed 'For M. Y. | from H.Y. | November the 18th, 1960. | The tale is pretty much the life | story, as told to me long since, | of a distant cousin whom I | never saw.', no dated library stamp

A92(c) Third English edition ["Wanderer Edition"] ([1936])

THE HAWBUCKS | By | JOHN MASEFIELD | [publisher's device of a windmill with 'W [point]' and 'H'] | LONDON | WILLIAM HEINEMANN LTD
(All width centred)

Bibliographies: Handley-Taylor p.57, Wight [unrecorded]

Collation: [A]⁸ (±[A]1+2) B-U⁸ W⁴ (J and V not used) (see notes); signatures right foot of page; 164 leaves; 188 × 126mm.; [i–vi] [1] 2–322

Page contents: [i] half-title: 'THE COLLECTED WORKS OF | JOHN MASEFIELD | [rule] | WANDERER EDITION | THE HAWBUCKS'; [ii] '*ALSO BY JOHN MASEFIELD* | PLAYS: | [12 titles listed] | POETRY: | [14 titles listed] | FICTION: | [eight titles listed] | GENERAL: | [nine titles listed]'; [iii] title-page; [iv] '*First published October* 1929 | *Reprinted November* (*twice*) 1929 | *Popular Edition* (3s.6d.) *December* 1934 | *Printed in Great Britain at the* | *Windmill Press, Kingswood, Surrey*'; [v] 'TO | MY WIFE'; [vi] blank; [1]–322 text

Paper: wove paper

Running title: 'THE HAWBUCKS' (35mm.) on both verso and recto, pp.2–322

Binding: blue cloth. On spine, in gold: 'JOHN | MASEFIELD | THE | HAWBUCKS | THE | WANDERER | EDITION | HEINEMANN' (all width centred). On upper cover, in gold: illustration of a cockerel: 32 × 24mm. (ranged lower right). On lower cover, in blind: publisher's device of a windmill (ranged lower right). Top edge gilt, lower outside edge uncut, fore edge roughly trimmed. Sewn head band (in blue) and blue marker ribbon. Binding measurements: 196 × 128mm. (covers), 196 × 48mm. (spine). End-papers: wove paper.

Publication date: published, according to Handley-Taylor, 20 April 1936

Price: 5s.

Contents:
as for A92(a)

Notes:
The first two leaves in the first gathering ([A]1 and [A]2) are stubs with two conjugate leaves tipped-in on [A]1 as cancellans. The new leaves include note of the Wanderer edition and the rest of the volume appears to use the same type setting as reprints of A92(a).

The British Library holds five volumes as 'The Collected Works of John Masefield. Wanderer edition' for a date range of 1935–37. *The Hawbucks* is excluded. *The Shorter New Cambridge Bibliography of English Literature* also lists only five volumes. The *English Catalogue of Books* cites this edition as a 'Ch. ed.', although at 5s. this must comprise the Wanderer edition. See note on collected editions.

The publishing agreement for 'a collected edition of the Author's work', including this title, between Masefield and Heinemann was dated 31 July 1935 (see Archives of The Society of Authors). The agreement refers to 'a published price of 5/-…' (see note on collected editions).

Copies seen: private collection (ROV); Library of The John Masefield Society (Constance Babington Smith Collection 40)

A93 SOUTH AND EAST   1929

A93(a) First English edition (1929)

SOUTH AND EAST [in red] | *By* | JOHN MASEFIELD | [illustration of a fish within circular device of vegitation] | ILLUSTRATED BY JACYNTH PARSONS | LONDON : THE MEDICI SOCIETY | NEW YORK : THE MACMILLAN COMPANY | MCMXXIX
(All width centred)
(The italic font contains swash characters)

JOHN MASEFIELD

★

EASTER

A PLAY

FOR SINGERS

London

WILLIAM HEINEMANN LTD.

A90(b) title-page

JOHN MASEFIELD

EASTER

A PLAY

FOR SINGERS

LONDON

WILLIAM HEINEMANN LTD

A90(c) title-page

Poems

By

John Masefield

Complete in One Volume

New York

The Macmillan Company

1929

A91(a) title-page

THE HAWBUCKS

by

JOHN MASEFIELD

LONDON

WILLIAM HEINEMANN LTD

A92(a) title-page

THE WANDERER

of

LIVERPOOL

by

JOHN MASEFIELD

LONDON

WILLIAM HEINEMANN LIMITED

1930

A101(a) title-page

Words spoken at the Music Room

Boar's Hill

in the afternoon of November 5th, 1930

at a

Festival designed in the honour of

William Butler Yeats, Poet

A103(a) title-page

CHAUCER

by

JOHN MASEFIELD

The Leslie Stephen Lecture
Delivered at Cambridge
3 March 1931

CAMBRIDGE

AT THE UNIVERSITY PRESS

1931

A104(b) title-page

JOHN MASEFIELD

✹

MINNIE MAYLOW'S STORY

AND

OTHER TALES

AND

SCENES

★

LONDON

WILLIAM HEINEMANN LTD

A105(a) title-page

Bibliographies: Simmons [75], Nevinson [unrecorded], Handley-Taylor p.57, Wight [75]

Collation: [A]⁸ B-C⁸; signatures right foot of page; 24 leaves; 249 × 187mm.; [i–iv] [two un-numbered pages] [v–viii] 1–2 [two un-numbered pages] 3–8 [two un-numbered pages] 9–12 [two un-numbered pages] 13–16 [two un-numbered pages] 17–22 [two un-numbered pages] 23 [24–28]; illustrations (on glossy paper) are tipped-in on grey wove paper leaves (not counted in the gathering information or leaf count), these grey paper leaves are pasted onto white paper stubs which are bound with the gatherings; illustrations thus appear between pp.[iv] and [v], before p.3, before p.9, before p.13, before p.17 and before p.23; grey leaves appearing between two leaves of a gathering therefore have a corresponding stub of paper between different leaves of the same gathering as follows:

LEAVES BETWEEN WHICH GREY LEAF BEARING ILLUSTRATION EXISTS	LEAVES BETWEEN WHICH CORRESPONDING STUB EXISTS
A2 – A3	A6 – A7
A7 – A8	A1 – A2
B3 – B4	B5 – B6
B6 – B7	B2 – B3
C1 – C2	C7 – C8
C5 – C6	C3 – C4

each illustration is prefixed by a sheet bearing the legend on one side while the reverse is blank; these sheets form part of the gathering although the pages are not numbered in the regular pagination of the volume

Page contents: [i–ii] blank; [iii] half-title: 'SOUTH AND EAST'; [iv] blank; [-] blank; [-] legend: '"They are the goddesses,' he thought, 'at game... | Soon they will blast me'; but he watcht intent... | Starlight and dawn a little colour lent;"'; [v] title-page; [vi] 'PRINTED IN ENGLAND'; [vii] 'LIST OF PLATES IN COLOUR | [six individual items listed with page references] | [illustration of zebra]'; [viii] blank; 1–2 head-piece and text; [-] legend: '"Gai was a hunter through the country-side; | Kai was a braggart little prone to truth; | Kradoc was reckoned but a simple youth,"'; [-] blank; 3–8 text; [-] legend: '"He trod the forest where the were-wolves are | And spied a hut, as of some witch or gnome. | There sat an old crone wrinkled nose to chin."'; [-] blank; 9–12 text; [-] legend: '"After a twelvemonths' tramp he reacht a lake | Wide-shimmering, beyond a waste of reeds;"'; [-] blank; 13–16 text; [-] legend: '"After another year he trod the beach | Beside an ocean breaking wave by wave. | There an old hag peered from a dripping cave,"'; [-] blank; 17–22 text; [-] legend: '"Within the green grove dim | Someone was singing at a morning hymn."'; [-] blank; 23–[24] text and tail-piece of magpie on branches; [25] '¶ THIS EDITION OF "SOUTH AND EAST" | IS LIMITED TO 2750 COPIES.'; [26] 'Butler & Tanner., Frome and London'; [27–28] blank

Paper: laid paper (watermark: '[crown] | ANTIQUE DE LUXE | BCM/SH'), chain-lines 25mm. apart

Running title: 'SOUTH & EAST' (with curved underlining) (25mm.) positioned extreme left on same line as first line of text on verso; positioned extreme right on same line as first line of text on recto, pp.1–[24] (excluding other un-numbered pages)

Binding: grey cloth (see notes). On spine, in silver: 'SOUTH | & | EAST | MASEFIELD | MEDICI | SOCIETY' (all width centred). On upper cover: 'SOUTH & EAST [in silver] | JOHN MASEFIELD [in silver] | [illustration of magpie on branches: 59 × 69mm. (used as tail-piece on p.[24]) in black]' (all width centred). Lower cover: blank. Top edge gilt, others trimmed. Sewn head band (in blue and white). Binding measurements: 255 × 187mm. (covers), 225 × 21mm. (spine). End-papers: wove paper.

Publication date: published, according to Simmons, 31 October 1929 in an edition of 2750 copies. The *English Catalogue of Books* records a publication date of November 1929.

Price: 10s.6d.

Contents:
South and East ('When good King Arthur ruled these western hursts,')

Notes:
A separate illustrated publication of a poem that first appeared in *Midsummer Night and other tales in verse* (see A88). Both Simmons and Handley-Taylor describe the work as an 'allegorical poem'. It tells of Kradoc and his search for a winged queen who dwells 'South of the Earth, East of the Sun'.

The volume does not carry any dedication.

In all editions of *South and East* an illustration of a zebra appears on the page listing colour plates (entitled 'LIST OF PLATES IN COLOUR' in English editions and 'PLATES IN COLOUR' in American editions). Wight describes this illustration in three different ways: as a 'sleeping zebra device' in both English editions, as a 'resting zebra device' in A93(b) and as a 'reclining zebra device' in A93(bb). The illustration is, however, identical in all editions.

George B.T. Smith has reported a variant binding in beige cloth with all lettering (and illustration) printed in blue. Other binding variants exist including one without the magpie on the upper cover.

Page numbers appear in ornate brackets.

See notes to A88(a) for details of Masefield's early publication plans for *Midsummer Night and other tales in verse*. C.S. Evans wrote to Masefield at the beginning of January 1929 noting renewed interest from the Medici Society in publishing this volume:

> Nigel de Grey of the Medici Society has just written to me to say that his protégé, Miss Jacynth Parsons, whom I believe you know, is still anxious to illustrate your poem SOUTH AND EAST from MIDSUMMER NIGHT, and has asked if we have any objection. I have told him that although I would naturally like to do the book myself, I feel I have no claim to ask him to let us do that since the suggestion came from him, and that if you are agreeable we shall not stand in his way. I have told him too that in the event of his getting your permission, he must make his arrangement direct with you, and that he will be under no obligation to us in the way of commission or royalty.
>
> (C.S. Evans, letter to John Masefield, 11 January 1929)
> (BL, Add.Mss.56587, f.42)

Masefield therefore wrote to The Society of Authors asking for terms to be arranged with the Medici Society. It appears from this letter that Masefield had formed opinions on the type of publication required:

> I enclose a letter received from Messrs Heinemanns about a suggested edition of a story of mine, at present published by Heinemanns in a volume of verse called *Midsummer Night*. The Medici Society wish to publish an edition of this story, *South + East*, with illustrations by Miss Jacynth Parsons, a young and gifted illustrator, whose work I approve. May I ask you to be so kind as to negotiate the matter for me?
>
> *South and East* contains about 500 lines of verse. It would make only a slim book. I would suggest a limited edition of 2500 copies with a large paper issue of 500 copies, three thousand copies in all: each containing six or eight full page designs in colour and not more than two designs in black and white. I would suggest a large size for the book, (large quarto, say): the ordinary edition to be 12/6, the large paper edition to be 25/- or 30/-; my royalty to be 20% on each copy sold (twenty percent of the published price.) I can at any rate demand this at first, till we know their proposals + figures. The book to appear in early November this year. With only 8 or 10 designs to make, the artist should find this possible.
>
> As the tale is and will be published by Heinemanns, it is important that any edition issued by the Medici people should be limited in everyway. ...The question of American copyright comes in of course. The tale is copyright in my name by the Macmillan Co, in New York.
>
> (John Masefield, letter to [G.H.] Thring [14 January 1929])
> (BL, Add.Mss.56587, ff.40–41)

The Medici Society, in writing to Masefield, reveals that the choice of artist may have been Masefield's:

> You will remember that we had some correspondence in March of last year with reference to "SOUTH AND EAST" that you had very kindly suggested to Jacynth Parsons she should illustrate for us...
>
> (The Medici Society, letter to John Masefield, 15 January 1929)
> (BL, Add.Mss.56587, ff.43–45)

In this letter the Medici Society suggested 15% royalty from English copies and 75% royalties from American copies. The Medici Society suggested that they would 'leave you to make whatever arrangement you thought fair with Jacynth Parsons'. They additionally thought that twelve colour illustrations would make the volume 'acceptable'. In pursuing the matter with The Society of Authors, Masefield seemed unimpressed with the royalty situation and raised the issue of American publication. Masefield, presumably, was negotiating with the Macmillan Company himself:

> ...the crux of the matter is the United States market... ...I cannot refer this matter to the Macmillan Company for some days... ...You will see that the Medici people suggest paying me 15% of the published price and letting me pay the artist out of that, which does not attract me...
>
> (John Masefield, letter to [G.H.] Thring, 16 January 1929)
> (BL, Add.Mss.56587, f.47)

The Society of Authors evidently asked the Medici Society for clarification over the royalty situation. They responded that they 'did not intend to include the artist in the royalty of 15% to Mr. Masefield...' (see BL, Add.Mss.56587, f.60). Further correspondence reveals that the Medici Society were prepared to sell blocks of illustrations to Macmillan if Macmillan cared to contract with Masefield (see BL, Add.Mss.56587, f.61). Masefield, explaining the Macmillan proposal to The Society of Authors wrote:

> I have today seen Mr Brett of the Macmillan Co, New York. He will call on the Medici people, probably tomorrow. He plans to make a proposal to the Medici people, to buy the printed sheets of the *South + East* illustrations when ready + to issue them with the poem which will be printed in the U.S. He says that a book may be published in the United States, without danger to the copyright, if the letter-press be set up there, even if the illustrations be imported. He thinks that he will issue a limited expensive edition, + an unlimited ordinary edition of the poem if the matter can be arranged.
>
> (John Masefield, letter to [G.H.] Thring, [4 February 1929])
> (BL, Add.Mss.56587, ff.69–70)

Signed agreements between all interested parties appear to have been exchanged in March 1929. English publication occurred in November 1929.

In May 1933 The Society of Authors wrote to Masefield informing him of the Medici Society accounts (to December 1932). Apparently '501 copies of the ordinary 10/6 edition have been remaindered' and '1399 copies are shown on hand at December 31st, 1932' (see BL, Add.Mss.56598, f.101). Therefore, by December 1932 less than half the print-run had been sold.

Copies seen: BL (11643.n.19) stamped 6 NOV 1929; HRHRC (TEMP M377SOU 1929A cop.1) inscribed 'For Jude | from Zob | Dec 5. 1929.'; HRHRC (TEMP M377SOU 1929A cop.2) inscribed 'For Con | from Jan | December 5. 1929.'

A93(aa) First English edition (limited signed edition) (1929)

SOUTH AND EAST [in red] | *By* | JOHN MASEFIELD | [illustration of a fish within circular device of vegitation] | ILLUSTRATED BY JACYNTH PARSONS | LONDON : THE MEDICI SOCIETY | NEW YORK : THE MACMILLAN COMPANY | MCMXXIX
(All width centred)
(The italic font contains swash characters)

Bibliographies: Simmons [noted on pp.122–23], Nevinson [unrecorded], Handley-Taylor p.57, Wight 75a

Collation: [A]⁸ B-C⁸; signatures right foot of page; 24 leaves; 253 × 194mm.; [i–iv] [two un-numbered pages] [v–viii] 1–2 [two un-numbered pages] 3–8 [two un-numbered pages] 9–12 [two un-numbered pages] 13–16 [two un-numbered pages] 17–22 [two un-numbered pages] 23 [24–28]; illustrations (on glossy paper) are tipped-in on additional leaves (not counted in the gathering information or leaf count), these leaves are pasted onto white paper stubs which are bound with the gatherings; illustrations thus appear between pp.[iv] and [v], before p.3, before p.9, before p.13, before p.17 and before p.23; additional leaves appearing between two leaves of a gathering therefore have a corresponding stub of paper between different leaves of the same gathering as follows:

LEAVES BETWEEN WHICH ADDITIONAL LEAF BEARING ILLUSTRATION EXISTS	LEAVES BETWEEN WHICH CORRESPONDING STUB EXISTS
A2 – A3	A6 – A7
A7 – A8	A1 – A2
B3 – B4	B5 – B6
B6 – B7	B2 – B3
C1 – C2	C7 – C8
C5 – C6	C3 – C4

each illustration is prefixed by a sheet bearing the legend on one side while the reverse is blank; these sheets form part of the gathering although the pages are not numbered in the regular pagination of the volume

Page contents: [i] blank; [ii] 'Of this edition of *South and East* have | been printed 260 copies, of which 250 | are for sale. | Copy No.'; [iii] half-title: 'SOUTH AND EAST'; [iv] blank; [-] blank; [-] legend: '"They are the goddesses,' he thought, 'at game... | Soon they will blast me'; but he watcht intent... | Starlight and dawn a little colour lent;"'; [v] title-page; [vi] 'PRINTED IN ENGLAND'; [vii] 'LIST OF PLATES IN COLOUR | [six individual items listed with page references] | [illustration of zebra]'; [viii] blank; 1–2 head-piece and text; [-] legend: '"Gai was a hunter through the country-side; | Kai was a braggart little prone to truth; | Kradoc was reckoned but a simple youth,"'; [-] blank; 3–8 text; [-] legend: '"He trod the forest where the were-wolves are | And spied a hut, as of some witch or gnome. | There sat an old crone wrinkled nose to chin."'; [-] blank; 9–12 text; [-] legend: '"After a twelvemonths' tramp he reacht a lake | Wide-shimmering, beyond a waste of reeds;"'; [-] blank; 13–16 text; [-] legend: '"After another year he trod the beach | Beside an ocean breaking wave by wave. | There an old hag peered from a dripping cave,"'; [-] blank; 17–22 text; [-] legend: '"Within the green grove dim | Someone was singing at a morning hymn."'; [-] blank; 23–[24] text and tail-piece of magpie on branches; [25] blank; [26] 'Butler & Tanner., Frome and London'; [27–28] blank

Paper: laid paper (watermark: 'UNBLEACHED ARNOLD'), chain-lines 31–33mm. apart

Running title: 'SOUTH & EAST' (with curved underlining) (25mm.) positioned extreme left on same line as first line of text on verso; positioned extreme right on same line as first line of text on recto, pp.1–[24] (excluding other un-numbered pages)

Binding: white leather. On spine, reading lengthways down spine from head, in red: 'SOUTH & EAST MASEFIELD', horizontally at foot of spine, in red: 'MEDICI | SOCIETY'. On upper cover, in red: 'SOUTH & EAST | JOHN MASEFIELD'. Lower cover: blank. Top edge gilt, others untrimmed. Sewn head band (in yellow and red) and white marker ribbon. Binding measurements: 261 × 193mm. (covers), 261 × 24mm. (spine). End-papers: wove paper.

Publication date: both standard and signed editions are advertised by The Medici Society in *The Times Literary Supplement* on 14 November 1929.

Price: 31s.6d.

Contents:
as for A93(a)

Notes:
Simmons (and Handley-Taylor) note this edition after A93(a). No separate date for publication is provided.

The text appears to use the same setting of type as A93(a)

Wight notes the watermark in the laid paper as 'ARNOLD' only.

Page numbers appear in ornate brackets.

Copies seen: Library of The John Masefield Society (Peter Smith Collection) number 246, signed 'John Masefield.' and 'Jacynth Parsons.'

A93(b) First American edition (1929)

SOUTH AND EAST | *By* | JOHN MASEFIELD | [illustration of a fish within circular device of vegitation] | ILLUSTRATED BY JACYNTH PARSONS | LONDON : THE MEDICI SOCIETY | NEW YORK : THE MACMILLAN COMPANY | MCMXXIX
(All width centred)
(The italic font contains swash characters)

Bibliographies: Simmons [see notes], Nevinson [unrecorded], Handley-Taylor [see notes], Wight 75b

Collation: [A-D]⁴; 16 leaves; 252 × 192mm.; [1–6] 7–29 [30–32]; illustrations (on glossy paper) are tipped-in on pp.[2], 8, 13, 19, 23 and 29; each illustration is prefixed by a sheet bearing the legend on one side while the reverse is blank; these sheets are tipped-in on the illustration leaf; the illustration and protective leaves are not counted in the gathering information or leaf count

Page contents: [1] half-title: 'SOUTH AND EAST'; [2] blank (with additional leaf tipped-in on the verso of which is the full colour frontispiece illustration; tipped-in on the illustration leaf is a protective wove paper leaf with the legend '"They are the goddesses, he thought, at game... | Soon they will blast me; but he watcht intent... | Starlight and dawn a little colour lent;"'); [3] title-page; [4] 'COPYRIGHT, 1928, | BY JOHN MASEFIELD | *Printed in the United States of America by* | J. J. LITTLE AND IVES COMPANY, NEW YORK'; [5] 'PLATES IN COLOUR | [six individual items listed with page references] | [illustration of zebra]'; [6] blank; 7–[30] head-piece, text and tail-piece of magpie on branches; [31–32] blank

Paper: laid paper (watermark: '[unicorn device: 80 × 65mm.] | UNICORN | 100% RAG BOOK'), chain-lines 40mm. apart; protective leaves are wove paper (watermark: 'KINGSWAY | BOND | BCM/SH')

Running title: 'SOUTH & EAST' (25mm.) positioned extreme left on same line as first line of text on verso; positioned extreme right on same line as first line of text on recto, pp.7–[30]

Binding: green cloth. Spine: blank. On upper cover, in gold: 'SOUTH AND EAST | [rule] | JOHN MASEFIELD'. Lower cover: blank. Top and lower outside edges trimmed, fore edge untrimmed. Binding measurements: 257 × 193mm. (covers), 257 × 14mm. (spine). End-papers: wove paper.

Publication date: 1929

Price: $2.00

Contents:
as for A93(a)

Notes:
Neither Simmons or Handley-Taylor provide the date of American publication.

Page numbers appear within square brackets. Thus, [7], [8], etc.

Wight notes variants in the watermark in the protective leaves for illustrations: 'the guard sheets have the watermark: KINGSWAY / BOND / BCM (slash) SH. (In some cases the initials are: BCM / SI or CM / H)'

Wight notes this edition was 'published in a yellow dust cover and enclosed in a blue marbled box'

A comparison with the English editions of this work reveals a different book production process. For example, the protective sheets for illustrations are here tipped-in but are bound within the gatherings in the English process.

A publishing agreement for this title between Masefield and Macmillan was dated 8 May 1929 (see Archives of The Society of Authors). The agreement refers to 'a licence to publish in volume form... in the United States of America and Canada a work the subject or title of which is South and East – previously published in the author's work "Midsummer Night and other tales in verse"'.

Copies seen: private collection (ROV); HRHRC (AC-L M377SOU 1929B)

A93(bb) First American edition (limited signed edition) (1929)

SOUTH AND EAST | *By* | JOHN MASEFIELD | [illustration of a fish within circular device of vegitation] | ILLUSTRATED BY JACYNTH PARSONS | LONDON : THE MEDICI SOCIETY | NEW YORK : THE MACMILLAN COMPANY | MCMXXIX
(All width centred)
(The italic font contains swash characters)

Bibliographies: Simmons [unrecorded], Nevinson [unrecorded], Handley-Taylor [see notes], Wight 75c

Collation: [A]⁶ (A3+2) [B]⁴ [C]⁶ (C3+2) [D-E]⁴; 24 leaves; 294 × 222mm.; [i–iv] [1–2] [two un-numbered pages] [3–6] 7–8 [two un-numbered pages] 9–12 [two un-numbered pages] 13–18 [two un-numbered pages] 19–22 [two un-numbered pages] 23–28 [two un-numbered pages] 29 [30–32]; illustrations (on glossy paper) are tipped-in on pages as noted below; each illustration is prefixed by protective tissue bearing the legend on one side while the reverse is blank; these sheets are tipped-in on the illustration page; illustration pages (but not protective tissues) are counted in the gathering information and leaf count

Page contents: [i–iii] blank; [iv] 'OF THIS ILLUSTRATED EDITION OF SOUTH AND | EAST FOUR HUNDRED COPIES HAVE BEEN PRINTED | ON LITTLE CHART HAND MADE PAPER AND SIGNED | BY THE AUTHOR. | THIS IS NUMBER'; [1] half-title: 'SOUTH AND EAST'; [2] blank; [-] blank; [-] blank with full colour frontispiece illustration tipped-in, with protective tissue; [3] title-page; [4] 'COPYRIGHT, 1928, | BY JOHN MASEFIELD | *Printed in the United States of America by* | J. J. LITTLE AND IVES COMPANY, NEW YORK'; [5] 'PLATES IN COLOUR | [six individual items listed with page references] | [illustration of zebra]'; [6] blank; 7–8 head-piece and text; [-] blank with full colour illustration tipped-in, with protective tissue; [-] blank; 9–12 text; [-] blank with full colour illustration tipped-in, with protective tissue; [-] blank; 13–18 text; [-] blank with full colour illustration tipped-in, with protective tissue; [-] blank; 19–22 text; [-] blank with full colour illustration tipped-in, with protective tissue; [-] blank; 23–28 text; [-] blank with full colour illustration tipped-in, with protective tissue; [-] blank; 29–[30] text and tail-piece of magpie on branches; [31–32] text

Paper: laid paper (watermark: '[ornate device incorporating crown and fleur-de-lys: 153 × 81mm.] | *B & I*'), chain-lines 30mm. apart; also laid paper (watermark: 'LITTLE CHART | ENGLAND'), chain-lines 30mm. apart. The chain-lines run horizontally

Running title: 'SOUTH & EAST' (25mm.) positioned extreme left on same line as text on verso; positioned extreme right on same line as text on recto, pp.7–[30]

Binding: marbled green and brown boards with brown cloth spine. On spine reading lengthways down spine from head, in gold: 'SOUTH AND EAST MASEFIELD MACMILLAN' (there are three square points above the 'M', 'I' and 'N' of 'MACMILLAN'). Covers: blank. Top edge trimmed, others uncut. Binding measurements: 302 × 224mm. (covers), 302 × 18mm. (spine). End-papers: laid paper (watermark: '[ornate device incorporating crown and fleur-de-lys: 153 × 81mm.] | *B & I*'), chain-lines 30mm. apart (the chain-lines run horizontally). Volume contained in slip-case covered in green paper, with green paper label (67 × 98mm.) upon which: 'SOUTH AND EAST | JOHN MASEFIELD | *AUTOGRAPHED EDITION* | *No.* .... | THE MACMILLAN COMPANY | PUBLISHERS   NEW YORK' (within ornate border and triple rule: 61 × 91mm.)

Publication date: 1929

Price: $15.00

Contents:
as for A93(a)

Notes:
Neither Simmons or Handley-Taylor provide the date of American publication or specifically refer to an American limited signed edition.

Page numbers appear within square brackets. Thus, [7], [8], etc.

As noted above, the first and third gatherings include two conjugate leaves tipped-in on the first true leaf of the gathering (the third leaf if we include the additional leaves in a leaf count). In the first gathering these two leaves provide the signed note of limitation and therefore only these leaves need to have been sent to Masefield for signing.

Copies seen: private collection (ROV) number 371, signed '371 | J. Masefield.' on p.[ii]; HRHRC (TEMP M377SOU 1929B) number 18, signed '18 | J. Masefield.' on p.[ii] additionally inscribed 'For Con from Jan. | Nov 30. 1929.'

A94 LIVERPOOL   1930

A94(a) First English edition (1930)

Upper wrapper:
LIVERPOOL

Bibliographies: Nevinson [unrecorded], Handley-Taylor [unrecorded], Wight [unrecorded]

Collation: [A]⁶; 6 leaves; 282 × 200mm.; [i–ii] 1–9 [10]

Page contents: [i] title-page; [ii] blank; 1–9 text (at foot of p.9: '(NOTE-*"Liverpool" is copyright by John Masefield in | Great Britain and the United States of America.*)'); [10] blank

Paper: laid paper (no watermark), chain-lines 25mm. apart, the chain-lines run horizontally

Running title: none

Binding: wrappers comprise the first and last leaves of the single gathering ([A]1 and [A]6). The title-page consequently comprises the upper wrapper. Top and fore edge trimmed, lower outside edge roughly trimmed. Binding measurements: 282 × 200mm. (wrappers), 282 × 2mm. (spine).

Publication date: before 7 February 1930

Price: copies were not, presumably, for sale

Contents:
Liverpool ('*Liverpool :* | I am the English sea-queen; I am she')

Notes:
A privately published pamphlet of the verse later printed as 'A Masque of Liverpool' (see A96) in *The Wanderer of Liverpool* (see A101). Here the verse is simply entitled *Liverpool.* Publication occurred sometime before or during February 1930 and was presumably connected to Liverpool's 1930 celebratory festival of kinship with the sea.

There is a decorative head-piece at the head of p.1 and a decorative tail-piece at the foot of p.9.

The two line copyright notice on p.9 appears between two large eplipses.

A copy located in Harvard College Library (Houghton *fEC9.M377.930l) is inscribed to Florence Lamont and is dated 7 February 1930. An undated letter from Masefield, laid down within the volume, states '….we are just off to Liverpool to hear this sung: but I gather that the Cathedral is bad for sound, + it may not be much fun.'

Copies seen: Harvard College Library (Houghton *fEC9.M377.930l) inscribed 'For Florence, [Lamont] | from John. | February 7. 1930.'; HRHRC (PR6025 A77 L594 1930Z cop.1) inscribed 'John Masefield. | Sunday. October 27. | 1935. | being a mild, westerly, showery | morning, blowing hard.' with HRHRC note 'From the Library of John Masefield'; HRHRC (PR6025 A77 L594 1930Z cop.2)

A95 [CELEBRATION OF LIVERPOOL'S KINSHIP WITH THE SEA] 1930

A95(a) First English edition (1930)

WORDS BY | MR. JOHN MASEFIELD
(Both lines justified on left margin)

Bibliographies: Nevinson [unrecorded], Handley-Taylor [unrecorded], Wight [unrecorded]

Collation: [A]⁶; 6 leaves; 209 × 133mm.; [i–viii]

Page contents: [i] blank; [ii] 'COPYRIGHT IN GREAT BRITAIN AND | THE UNITED STATES OF AMERICA'; [iii] title-page; [iv–v] text; [vi–vii] blank; [viii] 'HENRY YOUNG & SONS LTD. LIVERPOOL'

Paper: laid paper (watermark: '[crown] Glastonbury'), chain-lines 25–26mm. apart

Running title: none

Binding: mottled blue boards. Spine: blank. On upper cover, in gold: '[crest with legend 'DEUS NOBIS HÆC OTIA FECIT': 20 × 21mm.] | Presented by | The Lord Mayor of Liverpool | in Celebration of Liverpool's | Kinship with the Sea | 10th February 1930'. Lower cover: blank. All edges trimmed. Binding measurements: 215 × 133mm. (covers), 215 × 8mm. (spine). End-papers constitute A1 and A6 laid down to the inside of covers (there are no free end-papers).

Publication date: 10 February 1930

Price: copies were not for sale

Contents:
Liverpool 1890 ('Gray sea dim, smoke blowing, hammer-racket, sirens')
Liverpool 1930 ('The dockyards of the ancient days are filled')

Notes:
The two poems present in this volume were later included in *The Wanderer of Liverpool* (see A101). The texts have minor variants in punctuation and hypenated words. There is only one substantive change: 'illectual' appears in this volume where 'intellectual' appears in the penultimate line of 'Liverpool 1930'.

A copy of this work is laid down to Lawrence Holt's own specially bound volume collecting printed matter from the Liverpool festival (now in the archives of The John Masefield Society). King George V, the Bishop of Liverpool, Martin Shaw, and Masefield also appear to have received similar volumes. Also included is a printed letter, as follows:

THE TOWN HALL | LIVERPOOL.
5th February, 1930.

Dear Sir / Madam,

It has seemed to me to be fitting to arrange a series of events in celebration of Liverpool's Kinship with the Sea. The programme of these events has been published in the Press. In order to bring the youth of Liverpool into the spirit of this celebration I have asked the Education Committee and the Private Schools of the City to arrange that brief reference to this vital Civic function of ours may be made in all schools on Monday, 10th February. Mr. John Masefield has been good enough to allow me to present to each school, a copy of two Poems of his, fitly commemorating the character of the event, and it is my desire that the copy received by you should be awarded in such way that may be convenient, by election of the scholars in your school, by selection or otherwise, to that scholar, boy or girl, who is held best to embody the spirit which has built up and still maintains Liverpool's Maritime greatness. The parcel containing this slight token of the occasion should not be opened before Sunday, 9th February.

I am,
Yours faithfully
Lawrence Holt
Lord Mayor.

During Liverpool's 'Kinship with the Sea' celebrations Masefield visited Liverpool College on 10 February 1930. Here he presented a copy of this edition to one of the students, J.P. Hewitt.

Copies seen: Archives of The John Masefield Society (within Lawrence Holt's bound volume of printed matter relating to Liverpool celebration)

A96 A MASQUE OF LIVERPOOL 1930

A96(a) First American edition (1930)

Upper wrapper:
A MASQUE OF LIVERPOOL | BY | JOHN MASEFIELD

Bibliographies: Nevinson [unrecorded], Handley-Taylor [unrecorded], Wight [unrecorded]

Collation: [A]⁶; 6 leaves; 217 × 142mm.; [i–ii] 1–9 [10]

Page contents: [i] title-page; [ii] 'COPYRIGHT, 1930, | BY JOHN MASEFIELD. | All rights reserved–no part of this book | may be reproduced in any form without | permission from the publishers. | SET UP BY BROWN BROTHERS LINOTYPERS | PRINTED IN THE UNITED STATES OF AMERICA'; 1–9 text; [10] blank

Paper: wove paper

Running title: none

Binding: wrappers comprise the first and last leaves of the single gathering ([A]1 and [A]6). The title-page consequently comprises the upper wrapper. All edges trimmed. Binding measurements: 217 × 142mm. (wrappers), 217 × 1mm. (spine).

Publication date: 11 February 1930

Price: copies were not, presumably, for sale

Contents:
A Masque of Liverpool ('LIVERPOOL | I am the English sea-queen; I am she')

Notes:
This pamphlet contains the verse later printed within A101. Compare with the privately printed English pamphlet *Liverpool* (see A94).

Page numbers appear within square brackets. Thus, [1], [2], etc.

Despite the copyright note on p.[ii] stating that the publishers reserve all rights, no publishers are noted except the linotypers.

Contrasting this edition with *Liverpool* (see A94) reveals an entirely different setting of the text. The copy of *A Masque of Liverpool* held at Columbia University Libraries (Special Collections B825.M377.T3.1930.ZZ) includes a handwritten note: 'Published Feb 11. 1930'. As a copy of *Liverpool* was inscribed for Florence Lamont on 7 February, it is feasible that this edition of *A Masque of Liverpool* was printed to secure American copyright.

Copies seen: Columbia University Libraries (B825.M377.T3.1930.ZZ) includes note 'Published Feb. 11. 1930'

A97 THE WANDERER. THE SETTING FORTH 1930

A97(a) First English edition (1930)

Upper wrapper:
The Wanderer. | The Setting Forth.
(All width centred)

Bibliographies: Nevinson [unrecorded], Handley-Taylor [unrecorded], Wight [unrecorded]

Collation: [A]⁶; 6 leaves; 257 × 162mm.; [1–2] 3–9 [10–12]

Page contents: [1] title-page; [2] blank; 3–9 text; [10–12] blank

Paper: laid paper (watermark: '[Crown] | Abbey Mills | Greenfield'), chain-lines 24mm. apart

Running title: none

Binding: wrappers comprise the first and last leaves of the single gathering ([A]1 and [A]6). The title-page consequently comprises the upper wrapper. Nevertheless, the wrapper uses a thicker type of laid paper (watermark: '[Crown] | Abbey Mills | Greenfield'), chain-lines 24mm. apart (used so that the chain-lines run horizontally). All edges uncut. Binding measurements: 257 × 162mm. (wrappers), 257 × 2mm. (spine).

Publication date: published, as suggested by an inscribed copy, 18 July 1930

Price: copies were not for sale

Contents:

The Wanderer. The Setting Forth ('Her builder and owner drank tea with her captain below')

Notes:

A privately published pamphlet of the single poem entitled 'The Setting Forth' (later published in A101). Only 26 copies were printed in July 1930.

Page numbers appear within curved brackets. Thus, (3), (4), etc.

The breaking of lines into stanzas does not always follow the text as presented in A101.

Copies seen: Bodleian (Arch.H.d.7(1)) inscribed 'First Author's Edition. | July 18ᵗʰ 1930. | This is No 3. | John Masefield. | only 26 printed. | [title printed on two lines] | [pen and ink sketch of ship] | For Grace Hunter. | from | John Masefield. | Jan. 1949.' on p.[1], stamped 24 JUL 1981; HRHRC (PR6025 A77 W354) inscribed 'First Author's Edition. | July 18ᵗʰ. 1930. | This is No 8. | John Masefield. | only 26 printed. | [title printed on two lines] | For Alfred Powell. | Christmas. 1941.'; Bodleian (Arch.H.d.7(3)) inscribed 'First Author's Edition. | July 18ᵗʰ· 1930. | This is No 15. | only 26 printed. | John Masefield. | [title printed on two lines] | For Phyllis Horne. | Christmas. 1941.' on p.[1]. no date stamp

A98 THE WANDERER. THE ENDING 1930

A98(a) First English edition (1930)

Upper wrapper:
The Wanderer. | The Ending.
(All width centred)

Bibliographies: Nevinson [unrecorded], Handley-Taylor [unrecorded], Wight [unrecorded]

Collation: [A]⁶; 6 leaves; 257 × 160mm.; [1–2] 3–9 [10–12]

Page contents: [1] title-page; [2] blank; 3–9 text; [10] 'HALL THE PRINTER LTD., OXFORD'; [11–12] blank

Paper: laid paper (watermark: '[Crown] | Abbey Mills | Greenfield'), chain-lines 24mm. apart

Running title: none

Binding: wrappers comprise the first and last leaves of the single gathering ([A]1 and [A]6). The title-page consequently comprises the upper wrapper. Nevertheless, the wrapper uses a thicker type of laid paper (watermark: '[Crown] | Abbey Mills | Greenfield'), chain-lines 24mm. apart (used so that the chain-lines run horizontally). All edges uncut. Binding measurements: 257 × 160mm. (wrappers), 257 × 2mm. (spine).

Publication date: published, as suggested by an inscribed copy, August 1930

Price: copies were not for sale

Contents:

The Wanderer. The Ending ('Once, long before, at her second outgoing down Channel')

Notes:

Privately published pamphlet of the single poem entitled 'The Ending' (later published in A101). Only 26 copies were printed in August 1930 by Hall the Printer Ltd., Oxford. See A99 for *Poems of The Wanderer. The Ending*.

Page numbers appear within curved brackets. Thus, (3), (4), etc.

Copies seen: Bodleian (Arch.H.d.7(2)) inscribed 'No 3. | (26 printed) | John Masefield. | August. 1930. | [title printed on two lines] | [pen and ink sketch of ship] | For Grace Hunter. | from | John Masefield. | January. 1949.' on p.[1], stamped 24 JUL 1981; HRHRC (PR6025 A77 W353) inscribed 'No 8. | (26 printed) | John Masefield. | August. 1930. | [title printed on two lines] | For Alfred Powell, | Christmas. 1941.'; Bodleian (Arch.H.d.7(4)) inscribed 'No 15. | (26 printed). | John Masefield. | August. 1930. | [title printed on two lines] | For Phyllis Horne. | Christmas. 1941.' on p.[1], no date stamp

A99 POEMS OF THE WANDERER. THE ENDING 1930

A99(a) First English edition (1930)

Upper wrapper:
Poems of | The Wanderer. | The Ending.
(All width centred)

Bibliographies: Nevinson [unrecorded], Handley-Taylor p.58, Wight 78

Collation: [A]⁶; 6 leaves; 254 × 160mm.; [1–2] 3–10 [11–12]

Page contents: [1] title-page; [2] blank; 3–10 text; [11–12] blank

Paper: laid paper (watermark: '[Crown] | Abbey Mills | Greenfield'), chain-lines 25mm. apart

Running title: none

Binding: wrappers comprise the first and last leaves of the single gathering ([A]1 and [A]6). The title-page consequently comprises the upper wrapper. All edges uncut. Binding measurements: 254 × 160mm. (wrappers), 254 × 1mm. (spine).

Publication date: published, as suggested by an inscribed copy, August 1930

Price: copies were not for sale

Contents:
The Wanderer ('You swept across the waters like a Queen,')
Liverpool, 1890 ('Gray sea dim, smoke-blowing, hammer-racket, sirens')
Liverpool, 1910 [*sic*] ('The dockyards of the ancient days are filled')
On Skysails ('I saw you often as the crown of Queens')
Pay ('The world paid but a penny for its toil,')
The Crowd ('They had secured their beauty to the dock,')
Under Three Lower Topsails ('Three lower topsails dark with wet are straining')
Eight Bells ('Four double strokes repeated on the bells,')
Posted ('Dream after dream I see the wrecks that lie')
If ('If it could be, that in this southern port')
I saw her here ('All tranquil is the mirror of the bay,')
Wanderer and Wonderer ('When first the thought of you took steel')

Notes:
A privately published pamphlet of the final twelve poems that were later published in A101. Only 25 copies were printed in August 1930.

Noted by both Handley-Taylor and Wight this edition has been confused with the other privately printed pamphlet *The Wanderer. The Ending* (see A98). Confusion arises over this volume presumably due to the inclusion of 'The Ending' in the title. Note however that *The Wanderer. The Ending* is an entirely separate title and volume from *Poems of The Wanderer. The Ending*. The first was published in an edition of 26 copies and the second in an edition of 25 copies. The contents are different. The first notes 'Hall the Printer Ltd., Oxford', the second does not. Wight notes that 'in some editions the words "Poems of" in the title are omitted and on page [10] is: HALL THE PRINTER, LTD., OXFORD'. This demonstrates Wight's confusion. He describes *Poems of The Wanderer. The Ending* but erroneously adds a detail from *The Wanderer. The Ending* to his description.

Page numbers appear within curved brackets. Thus, (3), (4), etc.

The title of the poem cited as 'Liverpool, 1910' is incorrect and should read 'Liverpool, 1930'.

Copies seen: HRHRC (PR6025 A77 P634) inscribed 'No 1. | (only 25 copies printed). | John Masefield. | August. Sept. 1930. | This is the first of the third volume | of <u>Wanderer</u> poems printed | privately before any publication | of the book. | Mawnan Sanctuary. | S. Cornwall.' with HRHRC note 'From the Library of John Masefield'; Bodleian (28001.d.846) inscribed 'No 11. | (25 copies printed) | John Masefield. | Mawnan. August. 1930.', stamped 4 APR 1962; HRHRC (AC-L M377WAE 1930 cop.2) inscribed 'No 22. | (25 copies printed) | John Masefield. | Mawnan. August. 1930.' and later inscribed 'The London Library Appeal. | No 125.'; HRHRC (AC-L M377WAE 1930 cop.1) inscribed 'No 23. | (25 copies printed) | John Masefield. | Mawnan. August. 1930.' and later inscribed 'The London Library Appeal. | No 124.'

A100 THE WANDERER ['THE SETTING FORTH'] 1930

A100(a) First American edition (1930)

THE WANDERER | BY | JOHN MASEFIELD | *An advance printing from the* | *September, 1930, issue of* | COSMOPOLITAN
(All width centred and enclosed within double ruled border: 118 × 84mm.)

Bibliographies: Nevinson [unrecorded], Handley-Taylor [unrecorded], Wight [unrecorded]

Collation: [A]¹⁴ (see notes); 14 leaves; 148 × 112mm.; [1] 2–13 [14] 15–25 [26–28]

Page contents: [1] title-page; 2–13 text of 'The Setting Forth' with illustrations (at foot of p.13: '*Copyright, 1930, by John Masefield*'); [14] text of 'A Distinguished Magazine'; 15–19 text of 'Cosmopolitan's September Advertisers'; 20–25 text of 'Forecast for September, 1930...'; [26] 'COSMOPOLITAN | ADVERTISING OFFICES | 57th STREET AT 8th AVENUE | NEW YORK CITY | 919 MICHIGAN AVENUE | CHICAGO | GENERAL MOTORS BUILDING | DETROIT | 1028 STATLER OFFICE BUILDING | BOSTON | HEARST BUILDING | SAN FRANCISCO'; [27–28] blank

Paper: wove paper

Running title: none

Binding: yellow boards. Spine: blank. On upper cover, in grey: 'THE WANDERER | BY | JOHN MASEFIELD | [ornament]'. Lower cover: blank. Some issues include a pocket of mottled yellow wove paper on the inside of the lower cover (see notes). All edges trimmed. Binding measurements: 156 × 113mm. (covers), 156 × 8mm. (spine). End-papers: mottled yellow wove paper.

Also issued in yellow wrappers. Spine: blank. On upper wrapper, in light blue: 'THE WANDERER | BY | JOHN MASEFIELD | [ornament]'. Lower wrapper: blank. All edges trimmed. Binding measurements: 157 × 116mm. (wrappers), 157 × 2mm. (spine). The wrappers extend beyond the edges of the internal leaves.

Publication date: September 1930 (see notes)

Price: copies were not, presumably, for sale

Contents:
The Wanderer – The Setting Forth ('Her builder and owner drank tea with her captain below')

Notes:
Besides Masefield's poem, the volume contains four sections (not by Masefield):
A Distinguished Magazine [*Cosmopolitan* advertisement] ('A magazine is judged by its writers and illustrators. Its audience can be...')
Cosmopolitan's September Advertisers [Alphabetical Listing]
Forecast for September, 1930, Hearst's International Combined With Cosmopolitan ('BACK STREETS | *By Fannie Hurst...*')
Cosmopolitan Advertising Offices

The volume in boards is machine sewn (the gathering is stabbed seventeen times). The 'gathering' also includes the end-papers (on a different stock of wove paper). The fixed end-papers are continuous, as are the free end-papers. Due to the different paper stock (the end-papers are mottled yellow) the volume is described above as [A]¹⁴. However, if the end-papers are to be included the volume could be described as [A]¹⁶. The volume, as issued in wrappers, comprises a gathering of fourteen leaves stapled to the wrappers.

Drop-capitals are used at the beginning of each section (with the exception of the listing of September advertisers and the advertising offices). Seven drop-capitals are used within Masefield's poem.

Some copies issued in boards include a pocket on the inside of the lower cover. This included loose advertisement leaves, for example a single leaf of wove paper advertising 'Stetson Hats'.

Masefield's poem is illustrated by four illustrations printed in blue with the text. Three are signed 'Gordon Grant'. A letter preserved within the correspondence files of Masefield records that the author was offered one of the illustrations. It is likely, therefore, that this edition had been published by the time this letter was written.

> ...I have just returned to London after being in New York for a few weeks vacation. During my stay there I saw Mr. Long, and he asked me when I returned to London to give you his very kindest personal regards. Mr. Long asked me also to say that if there is any one of the Gordon Grant illustrations that you like especially he would be very pleased to present you with the original. If you would be kind enough to let me know which one you prefer, I will write immediately to the New York office and have it sent over...
>
> (Mildred Temple, letter to John Masefield, 24 September 1930)
> (HRHRC, MS (Masefield, J.) Recip Cosmopolitan)

Copies seen: private collection (PWE) wrappers; Columbia University Libraries (Special Collections B825.M377.Y533.1930) boards (with pocket); HRHRC (AC-L M377WA 1930) boards (without pocket)

A101 THE WANDERER OF LIVERPOOL 1930

A101(a) First English edition (1930)

THE WANDERER | *of* | LIVERPOOL | *by* | JOHN MASEFIELD | [publisher's device of a windmill with 'W [point]' and 'H'] | LONDON | WILLIAM HEINEMANN LIMITED | *1930*
(All width centred)

Bibliographies: Nevinson p.17, Handley-Taylor p.58, Wight 77

Collation: [π]⁴ A-G⁸ H⁴; signatures left foot of page; 64 leaves; 212 × 165mm.; [i–viii] [1] 2–119 [120]; illustrations (on glossy paper) tipped-in on pp.[iii], 3, 9, 25, 27, 31, 33, 39, 47, 51, 59, 77, 81, 87, 89 and 91

Page contents: [i] half-title: 'THE WANDERER'; [ii] blank; [iii] title-page (with additional leaf tipped-in on the verso of which is the frontispiece: 119 × 89mm., 'MR. AND MRS W. H. POTTER | *from a photograph lent by* G. H. POTTER, ESQ.'); [iv] '*First Published in 1930*'; [v] 'TO | ALL OLD | WANDERERS'; [vi] blank; [vii] 'ILLUSTRATIONS' (16 illustrations listed with page references); [viii] blank; [1]–119 text; [120] 'PRINTED IN GREAT BRITAIN | BY ROBERT MACLEHOSE AND CO. LTD. | THE UNIVERSITY PRESS, GLASGOW'

Paper: wove paper

Running title: 'THE WANDERER' (33mm.), pp.2–13, 25–29, 31–33, 35–37, 40–43, 45, 47–50, 52–53, 55, 57–58, 60–65, 67–77 and 88–91

Binding: blue cloth. On spine, in gold: '[wavy rule] | [wavy rule] | THE | WANDERER | [short wavy rule] | [short wavy rule] | JOHN | MASEFIELD | [short wavy rule] | [short wavy rule] | HEINEMANN | [wavy rule] | [wavy rule]' (all width centred). Upper cover: blank. On lower cover, in blind: publisher's device of a windmill (ranged lower right). All edges trimmed. Binding measurements: 218 × 167mm. (covers), 218 × 32mm. (spine). End-papers: wove paper.

Publication date: the sales ledger preserved in the Heinemann Archive suggests publication on 3 November 1930 in an edition of 5000 copies

Price: 8s.6d.

Contents:
The Wanderer ('The ship-building firm of Messrs. W. H. Potter & Co. was established by...')
The Setting Forth ('Her builder and owner drank tea with her captain below.')
[The Wanderer (text continued)] ('The storm was by much the worst known in the Channel since the great storm...')
The Ending ('Once, long before, at her second outgoing down Channel')
[Notes and Acknowledgments] ('Though there are few written records, there are some models and drawings of her...')
A Masque of Liverpool ('LIVERPOOL | I am the English sea-queen; I am she')
The Wanderer ('You swept across the waters like a Queen,')
Liverpool, 1890 ('Gray sea dim, smoke-blowing, hammer-racket, sirens')
Liverpool, 1930 ('The dockyards of the ancient days are filled')
On Skysails ('I saw you often as the crown of Queens')
Pay ('The world paid but a penny for its toil,')
The Crowd ('They had secured their beauty to the dock,')
Under Three Lower Topsails ('Three lower topsails dark with wet are straining')
Eight Bells ('Four double strokes repeated on the bells,')
Posted ('Dream after dream I see the wrecks that lie')
If ('If it could be, that in this southern port')
I Saw Her Here ('All tranquil is the mirror of the bay,')
Wanderer and Wonderer ('When first the thought of you took steel')

Notes:
A volume of prose and verse telling the history of the four-masted barque first seen by Masefield in 1891. The ship had a profound influence on Masefield: a poem entitled 'The "Wanderer"' first appeared in 1913 (reprinted in *Philip the King and other poems* (see A26)) while a recording made by Masefield in 1962 entitled 'The Wanderer's Image' includes a statement introducing The Wanderer as 'a ship of splendour whose image for years haunted me and made me write'. Before publication of this volume Masefield had privately printed three pamphlets of verse that would later appear collected here. See *The Wanderer. The Setting Forth,* (A97) *The Wanderer. The Ending* (A98) and *Poems of the Wanderer. The Ending* (A99).

The text as it appears in the volume constitutes prose broken by verse. The final section constitutes verse only. After the verse 'The Setting Forth', the prose is subtitled 'The First Voyage' through to 'The Final Voyage'.

Masefield appears to have informed Heinemann of this work in March 1929. C.S. Evans wrote that he was 'glad to hear... about the history of *The Wanderer.*' and requested that '...as soon as you have the photographs and plan will you send them on to me...' (see C.S. Evans, letter to John Masefield, 20 March 1929) (HRHRC, MS (Masefield, J.) Recip William Heinemann Ltd.) Initially Evans assumed that the work would have limited appeal and suggested a single limited signed edition:

> We have gone into the question of producing THE WANDERER... We think the best procedure would be to issue a small edition of the book with the copies signed by the author, possibly of 1,000 copies but quite probably less. We give the probable publishing price with a certain amount of diffidence in view of the fact that we are estimating from incomplete material, but it would most likely be in the neighbourhood of 2 to 2½ guineas.
>
> (C.S. Evans, letter to John Masefield, 29 April 1929)
> (HRHRC, MS (Masefield, J.) Recip William Heinemann Ltd.)

The manuscript of *The Wanderer* was delivered during January 1930 (and acknowledged by Evans on 30 January 1930) (see C.S. Evans, letter to John Masefield, 30 January 1930) (HRHRC, MS (Masefield, J.) Recip William Heinemann Ltd.) Having read the text Evans decided that a standard trade edition would be possible:

I have read THE WANDERER with the most enormous interest. The story of that ship is an enthralling story, and although I know very little about the sea, I found myself reading even the technical part with avidity. I do not remember any short thing of yours which is told with such directness, clarity and reticence. There is not a word too much from the beginning to the end. I think that we ought to do the book in both a limited and ordinary edition, leaving out of the latter the more technical pictures and some of the less interesting of the half tones. Mr. Finn is at work upon the format of the book for the limited edition…

(C.S. Evans, letter to John Masefield, 21 February 1930)
(HRHRC, MS (Masefield, J.) Recip William Heinemann Ltd.)

R. Welton Finn was indeed at work on the book and wrote to Masefield at the beginning of March noting that Evans was '…considering publication in September next rather than risking rushing the book through for this May…' Finn also suggested a meeting noting '…if it would interest you to go through the lay-out of the whole book with me, I could call on you in Oxford either Thursday or Friday of this week…' (see R. Welton Finn, letter to John Masefield, 3 March 1930) (HRHRC, MS (Masefield, J.) Recip William Heinemann Ltd.) Such a meeting evidently took place for Finn wrote expressing '…very many thanks for your hospitality yesterday and for our very useful discussion…' (see R. Welton Finn, letter to John Masefield, 7 March 1930) (HRHRC, MS (Masefield, J.) Recip William Heinemann Ltd.) A few days later Theodore Byard noted a publication date (subsequently revised): '…we have scheduled THE WANDERER (both editions) for publication in June and I imagine that will meet your wishes…' (see Theodore Byard, letter to John Masefield, 10 March 1930) (HRHRC, MS (Masefield, J.) Recip William Heinemann Ltd.) A fortnight later Evans wrote noting that the typographical appearance of the page did not please him:

I am putting THE WANDERER in hand at once, but I will write to you fully about that in a day or two. I did not like the specimen pages which were prepared while I was away: they were too heavy and Italian looking for a book which is so very English in its spirit… …I want if possible to publish the ordinary edition at 7/6d but I am not sure yet whether this will be economically possible.

(C.S. Evans, letter to John Masefield, 24 March 1930)
(HRHRC, MS (Masefield, J.) Recip William Heinemann Ltd.)

One month later Masefield was sent 'galleys 1 to 36 for THE WANDERER…' together with the return of the manuscript (see R. Welton Finn, letter to John Masefield, 24 April 1930) (HRHRC, MS (Masefield, J.) Recip William Heinemann Ltd.) During May the author was sent 'the originals for your illustrations to the WANDERER, and one proof of each….' (see R. Welton Finn, letter to John Masefield, 19 May 1930) (HRHRC, MS (Masefield, J.) Recip William Heinemann Ltd.) A few days later Masefield was sent '…proofs of THE WANDERER, pages 1 to 48, and the corresponding galleys' (see Joan Stenhouse, letter to John Masefield, 22 May 1930) (HRHRC, MS (Masefield, J.) Recip William Heinemann Ltd.) followed by 'proofs of THE WANDERER, pages 81 to 119, and the prelims., completing the book' (see Joan Stenhouse, letter to John Masefield, 27 May 1930) (HRHRC, MS (Masefield, J.) Recip William Heinemann Ltd.) On 9 July 1930 Finn wrote stating that he hoped '…to send the book for press in a day or two as soon as my new blocks are in…' (see R. Welton Finn, letter to John Masefield, 9 July 1930) (HRHRC, MS (Masefield, J.) Recip William Heinemann Ltd.) An agreement was sent on 22 July 1930:

Mr. Evans has asked me to send you an agreement for THE WANDERER. I have drawn it up to include the ordinary and the limited edition. Mr. Evans has not been able to work out more than an estimated cost of the very special edition…

(Louisa Callender, letter to John Masefield, 22 July 1930)
(HRHRC, MS (Masefield, J.) Recip William Heinemann Ltd.)

It appears that an agreement (covering all three editions) was sent later (see below). Evans wrote during October regarding a number of corrections and also stated the impact on publication date of a possible serialisation:

…I have no doubt at all that we shall have to reprint the book eventually, so send along a note of the corrections as soon as you like. I hope there are not many. We have scheduled the book for publication of October 27th, which is the earliest date NASH'S could give us because of the serialisation.

(C.S. Evans, letter to John Masefield, 2 October 1930)
(HRHRC, MS (Masefield, J.) Recip William Heinemann Ltd.)

A few days after publication Evans wrote noting an error identified by a reader:

A Mr. Glarrow, of Birkenhead, writes to us to-day as follows: "The WANDERER: p.11. The correct spelling of the coal shipped on her first voyage is 'Wesminster Brymbo'. I know, as I was born, and lived, within a stone's throw of the Colliery. 'Brimbo' has no significance whatever."

(C.S. Evans, letter to John Masefield, 6 November 1930)
(HRHRC, MS (Masefield, J.) Recip William Heinemann Ltd.)

The publishing agreement for this title between Masefield and Heinemann was dated 31 July 1929 (see Archives of The Society of Authors). The agreement refers to an 'ordinary' edition at 8s.6d., an edition limited to 500 copies at 3 guineas and an 'edition de luxe' limited to 15 copies at 20 guineas (see A101(a), A101(c) and A101(d) respectively). This agreement presumably replaced one sent by Louisa Callender on 22 July 1930 (see above).

An application (dated 10 May 1934) from The Blue Peter Publishing Co. to Masefield requested permission to reproduce Spurling's painting of the *Wanderer* as used on the dust-jacket for this edition (see BL, Add.Mss.56600, f.171). Masefield did not wish to grant permission and wrote to The Society of Authors giving instructions and revealing the history of the painting:

I employed the late Mr Spurling to paint for me a coloured drawing of the f.m.b *Wanderer*, the drawing to be absolutely mine, so that I might use it on my book on the *Wanderer*. No reservation of copyright was made by Mr Spurling, nor should I have commissioned the drawing had he made any. The drawing was delivered and used about four years ago. I should prefer not to have it reproduced elsewhere than in my book.

(John Masefield, letter to [E.J.] Mullett, [13 May 1934])
(BL, Add.Mss.56600, f.170)

Copies seen: private collection (PWE); National Gallery of Ireland. Y Archive, inscribed 'For Jack [B. Yeats], | from John. | November 8. 1930. | [sketch of toy boat] | The Gara's splendid tide'; HRHRC (TEMP M377WA 1930A) inscribed 'For Judith | from Zob. | October 31.ˢᵗ 1930.'

Reprinted:

[first edition, second impression]   [Oct 1930]
(not examined, but see notes to A101(d))

A101(b) First American edition (1930)

THE WANDERER | OF LIVERPOOL | *by* | JOHN MASEFIELD | NEW YORK | THE MACMILLAN COMPANY | 1930
(All width centred)

Bibliographies: Nevinson [unrecorded], Handley-Taylor p.58, Wight 77c

Collation: [A-I]⁸ [K]⁴ (J not used) (the last gathering includes three plans (excluded from the leaf count) bound with the gathering); 76 leaves; 217 × 170mm.; [i–vi] vii–ix [x–xii] 1–139 [140]; illustrations and plans (on glossy paper) tipped-in on pp.[ii], [xii], 3, 7, 11, 30, 32, 35, 37, 39, 43, 44, 46, 49, 51, 57, 60, 62, 69, 83, 87, 91, 94, 101, 103, 105, 107, 123, 124, 126, 129, 131, 132 and 135

Page contents: [i] half-title: 'THE WANDERER'; [ii] 'BY | JOHN MASEFIELD | [40 titles separated by 39 dashes]' (with additional leaf tipped-in on the verso of which is the frontispiece: 185 × 127mm., 'THE *WANDERER* (OF LIVERPOOL) | *from a painting by* MR. J. SPURLING'); [iii] title-page; [iv] 'COPYRIGHT, 1930, | BY JOHN MASEFIELD. | [rule] | All rights reserved–no part of this book | may be reproduced in any form without | permission in writing from the publisher. | Set up and electrotyped. Published October, 1930. | PRINTED IN THE UNITED STATES OF AMERICA | BY THE STRATFORD PRESS, INC., NEW YORK'; [v] 'TO | ALL OLD | WANDERERS'; [vi] blank; vii–ix 'ILLUSTRATIONS' and 'PLANS' (39 illustrations listed with page references and four plans listed with page references); [x] blank; [xi] 'THE WANDERER'; [xii] blank; 1–139 text; [140] blank

Paper: wove paper

Running-title: 'THE WANDERER' (31mm.) on both verso and recto, pp.2–15, 31–35, 37–40, 42–45, 48–52, 54, 56–60, 62–63, 65, 67–69, 71–77, 79–91, 104–108

Binding: light green cloth. On spine, in gold: 'THE | WANDERER | OF | LIVERPOOL | *by* | JOHN | MASEFIELD | MACMILLAN | [point]' (all width centred). On upper cover, in gold: 'THE WANDERER | OF LIVERPOOL | JOHN MASEFIELD'. Lower cover: blank. All edges trimmed. Binding measurements: 226 × 172mm. (covers), 226 × 34mm. (spine). End-papers: wove paper.

Publication date: published, according to Handley-Taylor, 5 November 1930 (see notes)

Price: $3.50

Contents:
as for A101(a)

Notes:
Unlike in A101(a), this standard issue of the work includes the same number of illustrations and plans as the limited signed edition.

Handley-Taylor states that this edition was published on 5 November 1930. The volume itself cites 'October, 1930'. This publication date would pre-date A101(a). The inscribed copy from Masefield to his wife is dated November 1930.

Three plans, bound within the final gathering are as follows:
– 'Midship Section Of The *Wanderer* (Of Liverpool)'
– 'Main Deck Plan | Four-Masted Barque *Wanderer* (Of Liverpool)'
– 'Sail Plan Of The *Wanderer* (Of Liverpool)'
The first plan is folded four times, the second and third plans are folded three times.

George P. Brett expressed early concern about the title to Masefield:

I acknowledge receipt with much pleasure of your letter of the 13th very kindly enclosing the signed agreement for the publication in this country of your book entitled THE WANDERER. It most unfortunately happens that a book has recently been published in this country under that title, although the subject matter of course is entirely different, so that if you can I think it would be well to have a second title to the book which would be somewhat explanatory of its contents.

(George P. Brett, letter to John Masefield, 25 March 1930)
(HRHRC, MS (Masefield, J.) Recip The Macmillan Company)

A letter from C.S. Evans to Masefield reveals that Heinemann provided the American publishers with the text in proof state:

> I am keeping careful track of THE WANDERER proofs for Macmillan. They have already had uncorrected proofs and a set of the illustrations without legends, and I have their acknowledgment of the material this morning.
>
> (C.S. Evans, letter to John Masefield, 19 June 1930)
> (HRHRC, MS (Masefield, J.) Recip William Heinemann Ltd.)

A publishing agreement for this title between Masefield and Macmillan was dated 13 February 1930 (see Archives of The Society of Authors). The agreement refers to 'a licence to publish in volume form... in the United States of America and Canada a work the subject or title of which is The Wanderer'.

Copies seen: Columbia University (825 M377 Y54) 'Nov. 10, 1930' noted; HRHRC (PR6025 A77 W3 1930B) inscribed 'For Con. | from Jan. | November. 1930.'; HRHRC (AC-L M377WA 1930E) includes Macmillan advertisement (see J50)

Reprinted:

[first edition, second impression]	Oct 1930
[first edition, third impression]	Nov 1930
[first edition, fourth impression]	Nov 1930

A101(bb) First American edition (limited signed edition) (1930)

THE WANDERER | OF LIVERPOOL | *by* | JOHN MASEFIELD | NEW YORK | THE MACMILLAN COMPANY | 1930
(All width centred)

Bibliographies: Nevinson [unrecorded], Handley-Taylor p.58, Wight 77d

Collation: [A]² [B-U]⁴ (J not used); the first 'gathering' is tipped-in on the first leaf of the [B] gathering (see notes) and the last gathering includes three plans (excluded from the leaf count) bound with the gathering); 78 leaves; 250 × 161mm.; [four un-numbered pages] [i–vi] vii–ix [x–xii] 1–139 [140], illustrations and plans (on glossy paper) tipped-in on pp.[iii], 1, 3, 7, 10, 31, 32, 35, 37, 39, 42, 45, 47, 48, 50, 56, 61, 63, 69, 83, 87, 90, 95, 101, 103, 104, 106, 122, 125, 127, 128, 130, 132 and 135 (see notes)

Page contents: [-] blank (page excluded from page count, but constitutes first leaf of first gathering); [-] blank; [-] 'OF THIS EDITION OF *THE WANDERER*, THREE | HUNDRED AND FIFTY COPIES HAVE BEEN | PRINTED, EACH NUMBERED AND SIGNED | BY THE AUTHOR. THIS IS COPY | NUMBER'; [-] blank; [i] half-title: 'THE WANDERER'; [ii] blank; [iii] title-page (with additional leaf tipped-in on the verso of which is the frontispiece: 185 × 127mm., 'THE *WANDERER* (OF LIVERPOOL) | *from a painting by* MR. J. SPURLING'); [iv] 'COPYRIGHT, 1930, | BY JOHN MASEFIELD. | [rule] | All rights reserved—no part of this book | may be reproduced in any form without | permission in writing from the publisher. | Set up and electrotyped. Published October, 1930. | PRINTED IN THE UNITED STATES OF AMERICA | BY THE STRATFORD PRESS, INC., NEW YORK'; [v] 'TO | ALL OLD | WANDERERS'; [vi] blank; vii–ix 'ILLUSTRATIONS' and 'PLANS' (39 illustrations listed including frontispiece with page references and four plans listed with page references); [x] blank; [xi] 'THE WANDERER'; [xii] blank; 1–139 text; [140] blank

Paper: laid paper (watermark: '*Arches* (FRANCE)'), chain-lines 27mm. apart

Running-title: 'THE WANDERER' (31mm.) on both verso and recto, pp.2–15, 31–35, 37–40, 42–45, 48–52, 54, 56–60, 62–63, 65, 67–69, 71–77, 79–91, 104–108

Binding: light green boards with black cloth spine. On spine, in gold: 'THE | WANDERER | OF | LIVERPOOL | *by* | JOHN | MASEFIELD' (all width centred). Covers: blank. Top edge trimmed, lower outside roughly trimmed, fore edge uncut. Binding measurements: 254 × 168mm. (covers), 254 × 34mm. (spine). End-papers: wove paper.

Publication date: 1930

Price: $20.00

Contents:
as for A101(a)

Notes:
Handley-Taylor does not give the date of publication for this volume. He does, however, state that the standard Macmillan edition was published on 5 November 1930 and notes 'also Limited Edition of 350 copies'.

Three plans, tipped-in at the rear of the volume are as follows:
– 'Midship Section Of The *Wanderer* (Of Liverpool)'
– 'Main Deck Plan | Four-Masted Barque *Wanderer* (Of Liverpool)'
– 'Sail Plan Of The *Wanderer* (Of Liverpool)'
The first plan is folded four times, the second plan is folded three times and the third plan is folded twice.

The first 'gathering' comprises a single set of two conjugate leaves. These are tipped-in on to the first leaf of gathering [B]. The [A] 'gathering' (using the same paper as the rest of the volume) includes the note of limitation. It is therefore likely that Macmillan sent 350 [A] 'gatherings' for Masefield to sign.

Contrast the difference between the Heinemann and Macmillan limited signed editions in their inclusion of illustrations. The Heinemann uses a system of illustrations tipped-in on leaf stubs while the Macmillan edition merely includes illustrations tipped-in on the pages of text.

Copies seen: private collection (ROV) number 338, signed '338 | J. Masefield.' on limitation page

A101(c) Second English edition (limited signed edition) (1930)

THE WANDERER | *of* | LIVERPOOL | *by* | JOHN MASEFIELD | [publisher's device of a windmill with 'W [point]' and 'H'] | LONDON | WILLIAM HEINEMANN LIMITED | *1930*
(All width centred)

Bibliographies: Nevinson [unrecorded], Handley-Taylor p.58, Wight 77a

Collation: [π]⁸ A-P⁴ [Q]² (J not used); an additional 'gathering' of 14 leaf stubs (upon which three plans are individually tipped-in) is enclosed by linen and pasted in the centre of gathering [Q]); signatures left foot of page; 70 leaves; 254 × 190mm.; [two un-numbered pages] [i–vi] vii–viii [ix–x] [1] 2–119 [120]; illustrations (on glossy paper) are tipped-in on thin white paper stubs which are bound with the gatherings (these are, however, excluded from the leaf count); the following table shows the corresponding conjugate leaf stubs and whether they comprise a stub in isolation or a stub including a tipped-in illustration (those between the verso of the second leaf and the recto of the third leaf of a gathering comprise a conjugate pair of stubs bound into the centre of a gathering):

LOCATION OF LEAF STUB	LOCATION OF CONJUGATE LEAF STUB
[π]3v / [π]4 (illustration)	[π]5v / [π]6 (stub)
[π]8v / A1 (illustration)	A4v / B1 (illustration)
A1v / A2 (illustration)	A3v / A4 (illustration / plan)
C4v / D1 (illustration)	D4v / E1 (stub)
D1v / D2 (illustration)	D3v / D4 (illustration)
D2v / D3 (illustration)	D2v / D3 (stub)
D4v / E1 (stub)	E4v / F1 (illustration)
E1v / E2 (illustration)	E3v / E4 (illustration)
E2v / E3 (illustration)	E2v / E3 (stub)
F1v / F2 (illustration)	F3v / F4 (illustration)
G1v / G2 (illustration)	G3v / G4 (stub)
G2v / G3 (illustration)	G2v / G3 (stub)
H1v / H2 (illustration)	H3v / H4 (stub)
H4v / I1 (stub)	I4v / K1 (illustration)
I1v / I2 (stub)	I3v / I4 (illustration)
I4v / K1 (stub)	K4v / L1 (illustration)
K2v / K3 (illustration)	K2v / K3 (stub)
K4v / L1 (stub)	L4v / M1 (illustration)
L1v / L2 (stub)	L3v / L4 (illustration)
L2v / L3 (illustration)	L2v / L3 (stub)
M1v / M2 (illustration)	M3v / M4 (stub)
M4v / N1 (stub)	N4v / O1 (illustration)
N4v / O1 (stub)	O4v / P1 (illustration)
O1v / O2 (illustration)	O3v / O4 (illustration)
O2v / O3 (illustration)	O2v / O3 (stub)
P1v / P2 (illustration)	P3v / P4 (stub)
P2v / P3 (illustration)	P2v / P3 (stub)

Page contents: [-] blank (page excluded from page count, but constitutes first leaf of first gathering); [-] blank; [i] half-title: 'THE WANDERER'; [ii] '*Of this edition there have been printed 525 copies on | Navigator mould-made wove paper, bound in buckram | and signed by the Author. | This is No.............................*'; [iii] title-page (with additional leaf inserted between pp.[ii] and [iii] on the verso of which is the frontispiece: 127 × 185mm., 'THE *WANDERER* (OF LIVERPOOL) | *from a painting by* MR. J. SPURLING' with protective tissue); [iv] '*First Published in 1930*'; [v] 'TO | ALL OLD | WANDERERS'; [vi] blank; vii–[ix] 'ILLUSTRATIONS' and 'PLANS' (39 illustrations listed including frontispiece with page references and four plans listed with page references); [x] blank; [1]–119 text; [120] 'PRINTED IN GREAT BRITAIN | BY ROBERT MACLEHOSE AND CO. LTD. | THE UNIVERSITY PRESS GLASGOW'

Paper: laid paper (two-masted ship within oval border of rope watermark: 83 × 55mm.), chain-lines 29mm. apart

Running-title: 'THE WANDERER' (33mm.) on both verso and recto, pp.2–13, 25–29, 31–33, 35–37, 40–43, 45, 47–50, 52–53, 55, 57–58, 60–65, 67–77 and 88–91

Binding: black cloth. On spine, in gold: 'THE | *WANDERER* | JOHN | MASEFIELD | HEINEMANN' (all width centred). On upper cover, in gold: illustration of the *Wanderer* within single gold ruled border: 62 × 101mm. Lower cover: blank. Top edge gilt, others uncut. Sewn head band (in blue) and blue marker ribbon. Binding measurements: 262 × 194mm. (covers), 262 × 35mm. (spine). End-papers: blue laid paper (no watermark), chain-lines 48mm. apart. The free end-papers are pasted onto [A]1 and [Q]2 with the conjugate leaves ([A]8 and [Q]1 comprising stubs). Volume contained in slip-case covered in dark blue paper.

Publication date: the sales ledger preserved in the Heinemann Archive suggests publication on 10 November 1930 in an edition of 400 copies (see notes)

Price: 63s.

Contents:
as for A101(a)

Notes:
The Heinemann limited signed edition includes more illustrations and plans than the standard Heinemann edition (see A101(a)).

Three plans, tipped-in at the rear of the volume are as follows:
– 'Midship Section Of The *Wanderer* (Of Liverpool)'
– 'Main Deck Plan | Four-Masted Barque *Wanderer* (Of Liverpool)'
– 'Sail Plan Of The *Wanderer* (Of Liverpool)'
The first plan is folded five times, the second plan is folded three times and the third plan is folded three times.

A limitation of 400 copies as noted in the sales ledger preserved in the Heinemann Archive remains a mystery.

C.S. Evans wrote to Masefield at the beginning of April noting:

> …The WANDERER is setting for the limited edition, and I shall be sending you proof, I hope, shortly. I may re-set the ordinary edition in a different size and type, but I haven't quite made up my mind about this.
>
> (C.S. Evans, letter to John Masefield, 1 April 1930)
> (HRHRC, MS (Masefield, J.) Recip William Heinemann Ltd.)

R. Welton Finn wrote to Masefield on 29 May 1930 noting that: '…I think you will like the paper for the least expensive limited edition [of *The Wanderer*] in view of the fact that it has a charming little ship as the water-mark.' (see R. Welton Finn, letter to John Masefield, 29 May 1930) (HRHRC, MS (Masefield, J.) Recip William Heinemann Ltd.) In contrast with A101(d) this edition became known at Heinemann during production as the 'Junior Limited Edition'. At the end of August 1930, Finn wrote to Masefield who was then on holiday in Falmouth:

> The WANDERER: Junior Limited Edition. The sheets of this will be off machine in a day or two, and I should be glad to know where you would like the copies of the prelims. sent for your signatures, or if you would care to sign them in London. In the case of the Senior Limited Edition, I am, as instructed by you, having the books bound before you add your sketches.
>
> (R. Welton Finn, letter to John Masefield, 29 August 1930)
> (HRHRC, MS (Masefield, J.) Recip William Heinemann Ltd.)

The publishing agreement for this title between Masefield and Heinemann was dated 31 July 1929 (see Archives of The Society of Authors). The agreement refers to an 'ordinary' edition at 8s.6d., an edition limited to 500 copies at 3 guineas and an 'edition de luxe' limited to 15 copies at 20 guineas (see A101(a), A101(c) and A101(d) respectively).

Copies seen: BL (08806.i.33) number 504, signed '504 | John Masefield.' on p.[ii] stamped 11 NOV 1930; HRHRC (AC-L M377WA 1930C cop.2) number 29, signed '29 | John Masefield.' on p.[ii]; HRHRC (AC-L M377WA 1930C cop.1) number 515, signed '515 | John Masefield.' on p.[ii] additionally inscribed 'For Lew, | from Zob. | November 5. 1930.' in slip-case

A101(d) *Third English edition (extra limited signed edition) (1930)*

THE WANDERER | *of* | LIVERPOOL | *by* | JOHN MASEFIELD | [publisher's device of a windmill with 'W [point]' and 'H'] | LONDON | WILLIAM HEINEMANN LIMITED | *1930*
(All width centred)

Bibliographies: Nevinson [unrecorded], Handley-Taylor p.58, Wight 77b

Collation: [a]⁴ [b]⁶ A-P⁴ [Q]⁶ [R]² (J not used); ('gathering' [Q] consists of six leaf stubs (upon the last three of which three plans are individually tipped-in)); signatures left foot of page; 78 leaves; 289 × 188mm.; [ten blank pages] [i–vi] vii–viii [ix–x] [1] 2–119 [120] [six leaf stubs (upon last three of which three plans are tipped-in)] [121–24]; illustrations and plans (on glossy paper) tipped-in on pp.[ii], [x], 3, 7, 9, 25, 27, 29, 31, 33, 35, 37, 39, 41, 43, 47, 51, 53, 59, 71, 73, 77, 81, 85, 87, 89, 91, 105, 107, 109, 111, 113, 115 and 117 (three plans are also tipped-in at the rear of the volume)

Page contents: [ten un-numbered pages] blank; [i] half-title: 'THE WANDERER'; [ii] '*Of this edition of* THE WANDERER *there have been | printed 20 copies on Penshurst hand-made wove paper ; of these | nine only are for sale. The binding is hand-sewn and in full | Lido calf by Henry T. Wood with a gold-tooled cover from a | design by Percy Smith. The volumes are numbered and signed | by the author and each contains either an original drawing by | John Masefield or a poem in his own handwriting. | This is No.*............................. (with additional leaf tipped-in on the verso of which is the colour frontispiece: 185 × 126mm., 'THE *WANDERER* (OF LIVERPOOL) | *from a painting by* MR. J. SPURLING'; [iii] title-page; [iv] '*First Published in 1930*'; [v] 'TO | ALL OLD | WANDERERS'; [vi] blank; vii–[ix] 'ILLUSTRATIONS' and 'PLANS' (39 illustrations listed including frontispiece with page references and four plans listed with page references); [x] blank; [1]–119 text; [120] 'PRINTED IN GREAT BRITAIN | BY ROBERT MACLEHOSE AND CO. LTD. | THE UNIVERSITY PRESS, GLASGOW'; [six leaf stubs (upon last three of which three plans are tipped-in)]; [121–24] blank

Paper: wove paper

Running title: 'THE WANDERER' (33mm.), pp.2–91 (excluding pages on which poetry appears)

Binding: blue Lido calf by Henry T. Wood. On spine, in gold: '[rule] | [raised band of binding] | [wavy rule] | [wavy rule] | [raised band of binding] | THE | WANDERER | [point] | JOHN | MASEFIELD | [point] | [raised band of binding] | [wavy rule] | [wavy rule] | [raised band of binding] | [raised band of binding] | [wavy rule] | [wavy rule] | [raised band of binding] | [rule]'. On upper cover, in gold: one wavy line in upper quarter of the cover and a second wavy line in the lower quarter with a five-point star in upper left corner, a blazing sun in upper right corner, a five-point star in lower left corner and a point (with inner point in blind) in lower right corner (within ruled border: 283 × 187mm.) On lower cover, in gold: upper cover design repeated. Insides of upper and lower covers include gold rule on all outside edges with 'BOUND BY WOOD.LONDON' in gold at right foot of inside of lower cover. Top edge gilt, others uncut. Sewn head and foot bands (in blue). Binding measurements: 288 × 193mm. (covers), 288 × 50mm. (spine). End-papers: blue silk-lined laid paper (indistinguishable watermark), chain-lines 27mm. apart (bound so that chain-lines run horizontally). Volume contained in slip-case covered in blue buckram and lined with material.

Publication date: the sales ledger in the Heinemann archive suggests publication on 18 November 1930. Correspondence from C.S. Evans suggests publication on 10 November 1930.

Price: 25 guineas

Contents:
as for A101(a)

Notes:
The free end-papers at the front and rear of the volume appear to be silk, laid down to laid paper.

Wight states that this edition was 'issued in a leather slip-case'.

A limitation of 15 copies as noted in the sales ledger preserved in the Heinemann Archive remains a mystery (although this was an early figure for the limitation of the edition which was later revised).

The publishing agreement for this title between Masefield and Heinemann was dated 31 July 1929 (see Archives of The Society of Authors). The agreement refers to an 'ordinary' edition at 8s.6d., an edition limited to 500 copies at 3 guineas and an 'edition de luxe' limited to 15 copies at 20 guineas (see A101(a), A101(c) and A101(d) respectively).

Early in the production of this title Masefield raised the question of an extra limited signed edition. It appears that his motivation was to produce a volume suitable for presentation to King George V. The initial suggestion was greeted with some caution by C.S. Evans:

> …I am carefully considering your suggestion of doing twelve superfine copies of THE WANDERER at 5 or 10 guineas. We shall have to make it different in some way from the ordinary limited edition, and for the moment I am not sure how best this can be done. We ought really to include something which is not in either of the other two editions – a drawing or a piece of manuscript – but I will make a definite suggestion later if I can. It would be rather difficult to justify the more expensive edition merely by printing it on a different kind of paper, particularly as the ordinary limited edition will be printed on the finest hand-made paper we can buy.
>
> (C.S. Evans, letter to John Masefield, 6 May 1930)
> (HRHRC, MS (Masefield, J.) Recip William Heinemann Ltd.)

Masefield, it seems, suggested that he personalise each copy and Evans responded to this suggestion:

> …I have been thinking over very carefully the question of the ten or twelve copies of the super-fine edition of THE WANDERER. It is impracticable to print such a small edition on different paper if only because we are using in the limited edition itself the finest hand-made paper that can be got. I have played about with the idea of printing it on vellum but I do not think that is practicable either as we should probably have to charge about £40 per copy! The proposal you

have made in your letter this morning, however, seems to me to get over the difficulty and I would suggest binding up ten or twelve copies of the ordinary limited edition in full leather, perhaps tooled (but that would depend upon the price at which the copies were to be sold) and include, as you suggest, some verses in your own handwriting or a drawing. It might be an advantage, instead of writing the verses or making the drawing on one of the fly leaves of the book itself, to have them on separate sheets, which would be enclosed in a kind of envelope forming the endpaper of the binding. It seems to me that if this were done we might get a higher price than five or seven guineas for this very small number of copies which would probably be eagerly sought by collectors. If we did ten we should only have six for sale. By the Copyright Act we are obliged to send to the British Museum a copy of the best edition, but the other National Libraries can only demand a copy of the edition which the largest number is offered for sale. I think, however, that if we follow out the suggestion above, we might do twelve, or even fifteen or twenty. I shall make careful enquiries from Bumpus and others before settling the number. …My intention is that the books in this small edition shall be <u>bound</u> and not cased… the result, however, would be a book which would last for five or six hundred years – both the binding and the text.

(C.S. Evans, letter to John Masefield, 8 May 1930)
(HRHRC, MS (Masefield, J.) Recip William Heinemann Ltd.)

At the end of May the Heinemann firm were asking questions which suggest that the Masefield additions to each volume were expected to be less extensive than eventually realised:

> With regard to the superior edition limited to 15 copies, can you let me know whereabouts you propose to do your writing or drawing? Perhaps facing the half-title would be the best place…

(R. Welton Finn, letter to John Masefield, 29 May 1930)
(HRHRC, MS (Masefield, J.) Recip William Heinemann Ltd.)

By the end of July 1930 Heinemann were still making enquiries about how many copies might be for sale. The binder had, however, been selected and Masefield was to provide manuscript additions to bound copies:

> There seem to be two points about the WANDERER to clear up… First, how many copies of the superior limited edition are you yourself having, and are the others, not to be sold, to be reserved for the King, the Prince of Wales and the British Museum? Secondly, as Mr. Percy Smith is binding this edition, I am arranging that he should fix up with you the question of delivering the bound books.

(R. Welton Finn, letter to John Masefield, 28 July 1930)
(HRHRC, MS (Masefield, J.) Recip William Heinemann Ltd.)

Original plans would have allowed only six copies for sale. This, it was considered, was insufficient and at the beginning of August Evans wrote to Masefield noting:

> …I think we had better have twenty copies of the very special edition of THE WANDERER: this would leave us eleven copies for sale. I am not quite sure yet of the price at which we shall have to publish. I imagine that whatever the price is, the books will be snapped up – but the copies that are for sale will have to cover the cost of the presentation copies, and, as you know, the binding is very expensive. Would twenty copies impose too great a strain on you so far as the poems and drawings are concerned?

(C.S. Evans, letter to John Masefield, 7 August 1930)
(HRHRC, MS (Masefield, J.) Recip William Heinemann Ltd.)

The edition presumably went to press shortly afterwards for Evans wrote on 14 August 1930 for the author's approval on the wording of the limitation note. By the middle of October 1930 the edition had been bound and Evans wrote noting that Heinemann had:

> …made arrangements with Messrs Wood & Company of Rathbone Place to send the twenty copies of THE WANDERER (special edition de luxe) to you by car on Saturday morning. If you will let me know when you have finished the drawings etc. I will arrange with Messrs Wood to collect the books in some way…

(C.S. Evans, letter to John Masefield, 17 October 1930)
(HRHRC, MS (Masefield, J.) Recip William Heinemann Ltd.)

Evans then turned his attention to the cost of the edition (and the share of the profits). It appears that the copies for sale would cover the cost of presentation copies:

> … we have yet to make an arrangement between us regarding the twenty special copies of THE WANDERER. I have been going through the figures and I find that the cost of the twenty copies amounts to £80.2.6. As you know, eleven out of the twenty copies are allocated as presentation copies, and therefore the remaining nine have to bear the cost and yield the profit on the twenty copies. Here are the figures:-
>
> Sell 9 copies published at £26.5.0 This means

£19.13.9. per copy from the trade	£177.3.9
Cost of production of 20 copies	£80.2.6
Profit	£97.1.3

> My suggestion is that we should pay you £60 of this profit, taking £37.1.3 ourselves. Will you let me know if this seems to you a proper proportion?

(C.S. Evans, letter to John Masefield, 20 October 1930)
(HRHRC, MS (Masefield, J.) Recip William Heinemann Ltd.)

Nine days later Evans wrote to Masefield (and provides some details of Masefield's presentation copies). He notes the high demand for the title in general:

> ...As you know, we made twenty copies of this superfine limited edition. I find that I can let you have a seventh copy, and you had better keep back the copy for the King, the one for the Prince of Wales and the seven copies for yourself, and give the others to Mr. Woods' messenger when he calls for them. We have fixed the publication date as November 10th... I am glad that you like the appearance of the book. I think that there is no doubt that it will be very valuable one of these days. We shall have a considerable amount of trouble over allotting the few copies for sale. Everybody is clamouring for them and in spite of our taking only a restricted number of copies, we have eighty applications to deal with. The junior limited edition is all subscribed and we are reprinting the ordinary edition.
>
> (C.S. Evans, letter to John Masefield, 29 October 1930)
> (HRHRC, MS (Masefield, J.) Recip William Heinemann Ltd.)

At the beginning of November Evans found that there was one spare copy and asked if Masefield would present it to F.N. Doubleday. Masefield was happy to do so. (See C.S. Evans, letter to John Masefield, 7 November 1930) ((HRHRC, MS (Masefield, J.) Recip William Heinemann Ltd.)

Catalogue A87 (*English Literature*) issued in 1987 by Blackwell's Rare Books describes Judith Masefield's copy of this volume (item number 564). The catalogue entry is as follows:

> MASEFIELD (John) The Wanderer of Liverpool. Heinemann. 1930, FIRST EDITION, 2/20 COPIES OF THE DE LUXE LARGE PAPER ISSUE printed on Penshurst handmade paper (of which only 9 were for sale) signed by the author and inscribed by him 'Judith's copy', with numerous plates, including a colour frontispiece, a plan, and folding diagrams of the 'Wanderer's' sail plan, main deck plan, and midship section, pp.[x(blank)] + 120, folio, good in orig. dark blue calf lettered and decorated in gilt to a design by Percy Smith, backstrip sunned to brown and with a tiny pin-hole in the front joint, mid-blue silk endpapers, t.e.g., others untrimmed, blue buckram slipcase faded (Handley-Taylor p.58) £700.00
>
> ¶ A superb association copy, inscribed by the author to his daughter Judith.
>
> Each of the de-luxe copies carries a poem or coloured pen-and-ink drawing by John Masefield. However, Judith Masefield's is substantially extra-illustrated, and has eight coloured ink sketches by the author on the rectos of the five front blank leaves, most of them of the 'Wanderer' under full sail; there is also a larger illustration of the ship on the half-title, and an amusing non-nautical vignette by John Masefield beneath the certificate, in which he has depicted himself as a horned and fork-tailed devil giving this copy of the book to an enthroned angel – his daughter.
>
> The extra illustrations are interspersed by three verses taken from the book and written out by Masefield. Following one verse beginning 'And so farewell sea wandering Bird...' he has added: 'For Judith Masefield, from her Father, Tuesday, October 21st. 1930, at 9.18p.m.'

Copies seen:
HRHRC (-Q- TEMP M377WA 1930D) number 1, signed 'One | John Masefield. | October 21st. 1930. 7.4 p.m. | October 30th ′ ′ 9.10 p.m.' on p.[ii], manuscript additions in Masefield's hand on the first eleven pages are as follows: [un-numbered page] '[illustration in black, blue, green, grey, yellow and red of a ship] | [flag in black, white and blue] | [flag in black, white and red] | [flag in black, white and red] | [flag in black, white and blue] | For Con | from Jan, | the First Copy of the Wanderer | unpackt + decorated for her on Tuesday, | the 21st October, 1930, at 7.4 p.m.'; [un-numbered page] blank; [un-numbered page] '[flag in white and blue] | Out of all Death, out of all Dream | I help your Spirit to go gleam | [new stanza] And you, unutterably fair, | Shine on my Mind's sea everywhere. | [illustration in black, blue, red, white and yellow of a ship]'; [un-numbered page] blank; [un-numbered page] '[illustration in black, blue, red and grey of a boat] | O opportunity let pass | Beauty that no more is, but was. | [new stanza] Passer that challeng'd and went by | A live thing in dead memory. | [new stanza] We two were subtlier linkt than most, | By subtle atoms of the ghost; | [new stanza] And shall, perhaps, be, still, anon, | In wondering and wandering on. | [illustration in black, blue, brown, red and yellow of a boat]'; [un-numbered page] blank; [un-numbered page] '[illustration in black, blue, yellow, red and green of a ship] | From whence none knows, to where none knows | Save from the gas-whirl to the rose | [new stanza] And from the rose to man and thence | To spirit that has beaten sense | [new stanza] To that that can annihilate | To Heat, all Death, to Light, all Fate | [new stanza] And is all Spirit, Spark + Spur | Magnificence + minister | To Wonderer and Wanderer. | [illustration in black, blue, green, yellow, grey, brown and red of a sinking ship]'; [un-numbered page] blank; [un-numbered page] 'And so Farewell, Sea Wandering Bird | Whose flight I markt, whose call I heard | The time has come | For the last touch for the last word. | [new stanza with illustration in black, blue, red and brown to right of stanza of a boat] You with the transitory grace | That gat steel limbs a little space | Have wander'd on | Away, into another place. | [new stanza with illustration in black and blue to left of stanza of a boat] I, that have flesh, shall follow soon | As Life commands Death pipe the tune | To change elsewhere | Or here again beneath the Moon. | However chang'd upon the Chain | Your Shape and mine will meet again | When Ship meets Ship | Sea-Wanderer, the colours dip. | The hidden then may be made plain. | October 21st. 1930. | For Con. | [illustration in black, blue, red, orange and grey of a ship]'; [un-numbered page] blank; [i] '[half-title] | [illustration in black, blue and orange of a ship]'

The Library of J. Philip Jacobs (sold by Sotheby's, 17 November 1999, lot 571) number 10, signed '10 | John Masefield.' on p.[ii], manuscript additions in Masefield's hand on the first eleven pages are as follows: [un-numbered page] blank; [un-numbered page] blank; [un-numbered page] '[flag in white and blue] | The House Flag of | Messrs Potter. | [new stanza] All day they loiter'd by the resting ships, | Telling their beauties over, taking stock, | At night the verdict left my messmates' lips | "The Wanderer is the finest ship in dock. | [new stanza] I had not seen her, but a friend, since drown'd, | Drew her with painted ports, low, lovely, lean, | Saying "The <u>Wanderer</u>, clipper, outward bound, | The loveliest ship my eyes have ever seen." | [flag in blue, white and black] | [flag in red, white and black] | [flag in red, white and black] | [flag in blue, white and black] | The Signal: M.H.C.S. | for the <u>Wanderer</u>, of | Liverpool. | [illustration in blue, green, red, white and black of a boat]'; [un-numbered page] blank; [un-numbered page] 'And as we watcht, there came a rush of feet, | Charging the fo'c's'le till the hatchway shook; | Men all about us thrust their way, or beat, | Crying "The <u>Wanderer</u>; down the river.. Look." | [new stanza] I lookt with them toward the dimness; there | Gleam'd like a spirit striding out of night, | A full-rigg'd ship unutterably fair, | Her masts like trees in winter, frosty-bright. | [illustration in green, grey, white and black of a ship]'; [un-numbered page] blank; [un-numbered page] 'Beauty in desolation was her pride | Her crown'd array a glory that had been, | She falter'd tow'rd us like a swan that died, | But, although ruin'd, she was still a Queen. | [new stanza] So, as though stepping to a funeral march | She passt defeated homewards whence she came | Ragged with tatter'd canvas white as starch | A wild bird that misfortune had made tame. | [illustration in green, yellow, red, blue, white and black of a ship]'; [un-numbered page] blank; [un-numbered page] 'I did but glance upon those anchor'd ships | Even as my thought had told, I saw her plain, | Tense, like a supple athlete with lean hips, | Swiftness at pause, the <u>Wanderer</u> come again | [new stanza] Come as of old, a Queen untouched by time, | Resting the beauty that no seas could tire, | Sparkling, as though the midnight's rain were | rime, | Like a man's thought transfigur'd into fire. | [illustration in blue, yellow and black of a boat]'; [un-numbered page] blank; [i] '[half-title] | [rider on horse in green, brown, red and black (facing left)] | Over the water came her lifted song. | Blind pieces is a mighty game we swing. | Life's battle is a conquest for the strong. | The meaning shows in the defeated thing. | [rider on horse in green, brown, red and black (facing left)]'

ULL (Special Collections) (Sterling Library) (see *The Sterling Library… Catalogue* (Privately Printed, 1954) Part II, No.376) number 15, signed '15 | John Masefield.' on p.[ii], manuscript additions in Masefield's hand on the first eleven pages are as follows: [un-numbered page] blank; [un-numbered page] blank; [un-numbered page] '[flag in black ink and painted blue] | All day they loiter'd by the resting ships, | Telling their beauties over, taking stock, | At night, the verdict left my messmates' lips:- | "The <u>Wanderer</u> is the finest ship in dock". | [flag in black ink and painted blue] | [flag in black ink and painted red] | [flag in black ink and painted red] | [flag in black ink and painted blue] | Above: the House Flag of Messrs Potter. | Below: the Signal Letters, M.H.C.S, for the <u>Wanderer</u>, of Liverpool.'; [un-numbered page] blank; [un-numbered page] '[sketch of ship in black ink and painted yellow and blue] | I had not seen her, but a friend, since drown'd, | Drew her, with painted ports, low, lovely lean, | Saying "The <u>Wanderer</u>, clipper, outward bound, | The loveliest ship my eyes have ever seen.'; [un-numbered page] blank; [un-numbered page] 'Dream after dream, I see the wrecks that lie | Unknown of man, unmarkt upon the charts, | Known of the flat-fish with the wither'd eye, | And seen by women in their aching hearts. | [new stanza] World-wide the scattering is, of those fair ships | That trod the billow tops till out of sight. | The cuttle mumbles them with horny lips; | The coral-insect covers them with white. | [new stanza] In silence, + in dimness, + in greenness, | Among the indistinct + leathery leaves | Of fruitless life, they lie among the cleanness. | Fish glide + flit, slow under-movement heaves. | [new stanza] | But no sound penetrates: not even the lunge | Of live ships passing, nor the gannets' plunge. | [sketch of ship in black ink and painted blue, green and red]'; [un-numbered page] blank; [un-numbered page] sketch of ship in black ink and painted yellow, blue, green, red and grey; [un-numbered page] blank; [i] '[half-title] | [horse and rider in black ink and painted yellow, green, red and brown (facing right)]'

The King's School, Canterbury, number 17, signed '17 | John Masefield.' on p.[ii], manuscript additions in Masefield's hand on the first eleven pages are as follows: [un-numbered page] blank; [un-numbered page] blank; [un-numbered page] sketch of ship in black ink and painted yellow, blue, black, red and grey; [un-numbered page] blank; [un-numbered page] '[flag in black ink and painted blue] | [flag in black ink and painted blue] | [flag in black ink and painted red] | [flag in black ink and painted red] | [flag in black ink and painted blue] | Above: the House Flag of Messrs Potter. | Below: the Signal Letters, M.H.C.S, for the Wanderer, | of Liverpool.'; [un-numbered page] blank; [un-numbered page] 'All tranquil is the mirror of the Bay, | Empty the anchorage from shore to shore, | A seagull rides the water where she lay, | The ships are gone, they come not any more. | [new stanza] Smoke rises from the town, not any noise, | Save from the gulls that mew about the pier; | The shadows in the water stand at poise; | All different from the day when she was here. | [new stanza] For she was here when the tumultous West | Roar'd on this granite coast for days together; | And billows rode the Channel under crest, | While all the hurt swans shelter'd from the weather; | [new stanza] And madden'd water seeth'd along her sides, | Here, in this quiet, where the seagull rides. | [sketch of ship in black ink and painted yellow, red and grey]'; [un-numbered page] blank; [un-numbered page] 'Dream after dream, I see the wrecks that lie | Unknown of man, unmarkt upon the charts, | Known of the flat-fish with the wither'd eye, | And seen by women in their aching hearts. | [new stanza] World-wide the scattering is of those fair ships | That trod the billow-tops till out of sight | The cuttle mumbles them with horny lips | The shells of the sea-insects crust them white | [new stanza] In silence + in dimness + in greenness, | Among the indistinct + leathery leaves | Of fruitless life, they lie among the cleanness; | Fish glide + flit, slow under-movement heaves; | [new stanza] | But no sound penetrates, not even the lunge | Of live ships passing, nor the gannets' plunge. | [sketch of ship in black ink and painted blue, green and red]'; [un-numbered page] blank; [i] '[half-title] | [rider on horse in black ink and painted yellow, green, red and brown (facing left)]'

A102 WORDS SPOKEN TO… THE MAYOR… OF HEREFORD… 1930

A102(a) First English edition (1930)

Upper wrapper:
Words spoken to the | Right Worshipful the Mayor | the Councillors and Aldermen | of Hereford | on Thursday, October 23rd | 1930
(All width centred)

Bibliographies: Nevinson [unrecorded], Handley-Taylor p.57, Wight [unrecorded]

Collation: [A]⁴; 4 leaves; 172 × 131mm.; [1–8]

Page contents: [1] title-page; [2] '*Number* | *For* | *From*'; [3–6] text; [7–8] blank

Paper: wove paper

Running title: none

Binding: wrappers comprise the first and last leaves of the single gathering ([A]1 and [A]4). The title-page consequently comprises the upper wrapper. Top edge trimmed, others uncut. Binding measurements: 172 × 131mm. (wrappers), 172 × 1mm. (spine).

Publication date: published between October and December 1930

Price: copies were not for sale

Contents:

Words Spoken… ('I have now to thank you for the great and beautiful honour that you have paid me…')

Notes:

A privately printed speech given by Masefield after receiving the freedom of the city of Hereford. The words were reprinted in the 1932 revised edition of *Recent Prose* (see A73(b)) where the speech is entitled 'The Hereford Speech' in the contents and 'At Hereford' in the running-titles. Handley-Taylor records the title of this volume as *Speech After Receiving the Freedom of the City of Hereford* in his bibliography.

The HRHRC includes four copies of this speech showing stages of production. All four carry a HRHRC note stating 'From the Library of John Masefield'. The first (HRHRC PR6025 A77 W673 1930 cop.1) contains Masefield's corrections to the printer. This is sewn in white card wrappers. On the upper wrapper Masefield has written 'Words spoken to the | Right Worshipful the Mayor, | ~~+ to~~ the Councillors + Aldermen | of Hereford, on Thursday, October 23ʳᵈ. 1930.' (HRHRC PR6025 A77 W673 1930 cop.2) would appear to be another copy, but lacking Masefield's additions. Another copy (HRHRC PR6025 A77 W673 1930 cop.3) contains the same impression of uncorrected text but is sewn in blue card wrappers. HRHRC PR6025 A77 W673 shows a corrected text with printed title on page 1. It does not include any printing on page 2, however, and 'John Masefield' is lacking at the end of the text (as in all four copies). In all copies the text is printed on a thinner paper type than eventually used.

The text is in italic type with many examples of swash characters. The text commences with a drop capital.

Copies seen: ULL (Special Collections) number 18, inscribed '18' For 'Rudolf + Viola Sauter' From 'John + Constance | Masefield. | Christmas. 1930.'; Bodleian (MS.Gilbert Murray 161, ff.99–102) number 104, inscribed '104' For 'Gilbert Murray.' From 'John Masefield. | Christmas. 1930.'; HRHRC (TEMP M377WORDS 1930 cop.1) number 3, inscribed 'Three' For 'Lew' From 'Zob. | 13ᵗʰ Decʳ. 1930.'; HRHRC (TEMP M377WORDS 1930 cop.2) un-numbered, inscribed For 'Con' From 'From Jan' [*sic*] and signed 'John Masefield' at end

A103 WORDS SPOKEN… AT A FESTIVAL DESIGNED IN THE HONOUR OF WILLIAM BUTLER YEATS, POET   1930

A103(a) First English edition (1930)

Upper wrapper:
Words spoken at the Music Room | *Boar's Hill* | *in the afternoon of November 5th, 1930* | *at a* | *Festival designed in the honour of* | *William Butler Yeats, Poet*
(All width centred)

Bibliographies: Nevinson [unrecorded], Handley-Taylor p.58, Wight [unrecorded]

Collation: [A]⁶; 6 leaves; 172 × 134mm.; [1–12]

Page contents: [1] title-page; [2] '*Number* | *For* | *From*'; [3–11] text; [12] blank

Paper: wove paper

Running title: none

Binding: wrappers comprise the first and last leaves of the single gathering ([A]1 and [A]6). The title-page consequently comprises the upper wrapper. All edges uncut. Binding measurements: 172 × 134mm. (wrappers), 172 × 1mm. (spine).

Publication date: published between November and December 1930

Price: copies were not for sale

Contents:

Words Spoken… ('*(These words were spoken before the Curtain rose upon Mr. Gilbert Highet's play…')*

Notes:

A privately printed speech given by Masefield at a festival in honour of W.B. Yeats. The words were reprinted in the 1932 revised edition of *Recent Prose* (see A73(b)) where the speech is entitled 'On Mr. W.B. Yeats' in the contents.

The text is in italic type with many examples of swash characters.

The copy located in the archives of The John Masefield Society (Constance Babington Smith Archives) includes a dedication to 'Ethel' Parker (née Masefield) which is dated 'Christmas 1930'. The pamphlet may, therefore, have been a Christmas gift published around the same time as A102(a).

The 1988 volume of Masefield's correspondence entitled *Brangwen – The Poet and the Dancer* reproduces three pages of this pamphlet, from copy number 69 (see E6).

Copies seen: HRHRC (TEMP M377 WOR 1930 cop.1) number 1, inscribed For 'Con' From 'Jan.'; HRHRC (TEMP M377 WOR 1930 cop.2) number 3, inscribed For 'Lew' From 'Zob.'; Archives of The John Masefield Society (Constance Babington Smith Archives 4/208) number 11, inscribed For 'Ethel' From 'John. | Christmas. 1930.'; private collection (BG) number 69, inscribed For 'Barbara Vernon' From 'John Masefield'; private collection (BG) number 169, inscribed For 'Barbara Vernon' From 'John Masefield'; Bodleian (MS.Gilbert Murray 161, ff.103–108) number 39, inscribed For 'Gilbert Murray.' From 'John Masefield. | Christmas. 1930.'; HRHRC (AC-L M377 WOR 1930 cop.8) number 201, inscribed For 'Sydney Cockerell.' From 'John Masefield. | Christmas. 1951.'; Bodleian (Additional Masefield Papers 10) unnumbered, inscribed For 'Kay.' From 'John Masefield. | (on her Birthday).'; HRHRC (AC-L M377 WOR 1930 cop.1) unnumbered, inscribed 'John Masefield. | A copy for | The London Library Appeal. | No 52.'; HRHRC (AC-L M377 WOR 1930 cop.2) unnumbered, inscribed 'John Masefield. | A copy for | The London Library Appeal. | No 53.'; HRHRC (AC-L M377 WOR 1930 cop.3) unnumbered, inscribed 'John Masefield. | The London Library Appeal. | No 54.'; HRHRC (AC-L M377 WOR 1930 cop.4) unnumbered, inscribed 'John Masefield. | The London Library Appeal. | No 55.'; HRHRC (AC-L M377 WOR 1930 cop.5) unnumbered, inscribed 'John Masefield. | The London Library Appeal. | No 56.'; HRHRC (AC-L M377 WOR 1930 cop.6) unnumbered, inscribed 'John Masefield. | The London Library Appeal. | No 57.'; HRHRC (AC-L M377 WOR 1930 cop.7) unnumbered, inscribed 'John Masefield. | The London Library Appeal. | No 58.'

A103(b) First American edition (1970)

Words | *spoken at the Music Room* | *Boar's Hill* | *in the afternoon of November 5th, 1930* | *at a* | *Festival designed in the honour of* | *William Butler Yeats, Poet*
(All width centred)

Bibliographies: Wight [unrecorded]

Collation: [A]⁸; 8 leaves; 203 × 145mm.; [1–16]

Page contents: [1–2] blank; [3] title-page; [4] blank; [5] [Introduction] ('This Spring when in London I picked up a curious little pamphlet…') (signed, 'D. M.'); [6] blank; [7–12] text; [13] '250 | *copies printed for* | DAVID MAGEE and ALBERT SPERISEN | *and presented to their friends in the* | ROXBURGHE and ZAMORANO CLUBS | *on the occasion of the joint meeting in Los Angeles,* | *September 26–27, 1970* | [ornament] | GRABHORN-HOYEM'; [14–16] blank

Paper: laid paper (no watermark), chain-lines 28mm. apart

Running title: none

Binding: blue wrappers (watermark includes '*Strathmore*' and '*U.S.A.*'), chain-lines 24mm., the chain-lines run horizontally. Spine: blank. On upper wrapper: 'JOHN MASEFIELD | & | WILLIAM BUTLER YEATS'. Lower wrapper: blank. All edges trimmed. Binding measurements: 206 × 148mm. (wrappers), 206 × 2mm. (spine). The wrappers extend beyond the edges of the internal leaves.

Publication date: on or before 26 September 1970

Price: copies were not for sale

Contents:
[Introduction] ('This Spring when in London I picked up a curious little pamphlet…') (signed, 'D. M.')
Words Spoken… ('This is the thirtieth anniversary of my meeting with Mr. Yeats. I have wanted the day…')

Notes:
Founded in 1812 the Roxburghe Club is the oldest bibliophilic society in Great Britain. The Zamorano Club was founded in 1928 comprising, primarily, a group of Los Angeles book collectors, printers and librarians.

Copies seen: private collection (PWE); HRHRC (PR5907 M3)

A104 CHAUCER   1931

A104(a) First American edition (1931)

CHAUCER | BY | JOHN MASEFIELD | [ornament] | NEW YORK | THE MACMILLAN COMPANY | 1931
(The title is printed in characters in outline and includes a number of swash characters)
(All width centred)

Bibliographies: Handley-Taylor p.59, Wight 79a

Collation: [A]⁸ [B]⁴ [C]⁸; 20 leaves; 189 × 125mm.; [i–vi] 1–30 [31–34]

Page contents: [i] half-title: 'CHAUCER | THE LESLIE STEPHEN LECTURE | Spoken at Cambridge, March 2, 1931'; [ii] 'BY JOHN MASEFIELD | [41 titles listed, each title separated by a dash]'; [iii] title-page; [iv] 'COPYRIGHT, 1931, | BY JOHN MASEFIELD. | All rights reserved–no part of this book | may be reproduced in any form without | permission in writing from the publisher. | Set up and printed. Published April, 1931. | PRINTED IN THE UNITED STATES OF AMERICA | BY THE FERRIS PRINTING COMPANY'; [v] 'CHAUCER'; [vi] blank; 1–30 text; [31–34] blank

Paper: wove paper

Running title: 'CHAUCER' (29mm.) on both verso and recto, pp.2–30

Binding: red cloth. Spine: blank. On upper cover: panel in blind: 48 × 83mm. upon which: white wove paper label (47 × 80mm.) on which: 'CHAUCER | [rule] | JOHN MASEFIELD' (enclosed within ornate border with fleur-de-lys ornament at each corner: 47 × 80mm.) Lower cover: blank. Top and lower outside edges trimmed, fore edge roughly trimmed. Binding measurements: 196 × 130mm. (covers), 196 × 16mm. (spine). End-papers: wove paper.

Publication date: published, according to Handley-Taylor, 23 April 1931

Price: $1.00

Contents:
Chaucer ('I am to talk to you for an hour about Geoffrey Chaucer, the first of the three great English poets.')

Notes:
Text of the Leslie Stephen lecture delivered by Masefield at Cambridge in March 1931. The American edition cites a lecture date of 2 March 1931. A date of 3 March 1931 is stated within A104(b).

A publishing agreement for this title between Masefield and Macmillan was dated 1 April 1931 (see Archives of The Society of Authors). The agreement refers to 'a licence to publish in volume form in the United States of America and Canada a work the subject of which is his Leslie Stephens Lecture on "Chaucer" (exact title to be determined)'.

The text was reprinted in the 1932 revised edition of *Recent Prose* (see A73(b))

The ornament on the title-page is of a leaf. Wight describes this as a 'floral device'.

The type used for several appearances of the title *Chaucer* (half-title, title-page, p.[v] and that on the upper cover label) is of an ornate appearance. Characters are in outline and a number of swash characters are used.

Wight notes the following:

On the front cover, on a white label with scalloped edges: CHAUCER / (rule) / JOHN MASEFIELD

The label itself is not cut with 'scalloped edges' and Wight is presumably describing the ornate printed border. The inside of this border has a single wavy (or scalloped) rule. The outer part of the border is similarly wavy (or scalloped) on the inside with the outside created by the edge of the label itself. As noted above, a fleur-de-lys ornament appears at each corner.

Page numbers appear within square brackets. Thus, [1], [2], etc. The square brackets are embellished at the centre.

Copies seen: State University of New York at Stony Brook (Frank Melville Jr. Memorial Library) (PR1905.M35)

A104(b) First English edition (1931)

CHAUCER | by | JOHN MASEFIELD | *The Leslie Stephen Lecture* | *Delivered at Cambridge* | *3 March 1931* | [publisher's crest] | CAMBRIDGE | AT THE UNIVERSITY PRESS | 1931
(All width centred)

Bibliographies: Handley-Taylor p.59, Wight 79

Collation: [A-E]⁴; 20 leaves; 186 × 121mm.; [i–iv] 1–35 [36]

Page contents: [i] half-title: 'CHAUCER'; [ii] 'Cambridge University Press | Fetter Lane, London | *Bombay, Calcutta, Madras* | Macmillan | *Toyko* | Maruzen Company, Ltd | Copyrighted in the United | States of America by the | Macmillan Company | All rights reserved'; [iii] title-page; [iv] 'PRINTED IN GREAT BRITAIN'; 1–[36] text (at foot of p.[36]: *'Printed at the Cambridge University Press'*)

Paper: laid paper (no watermark), chain-lines 23mm. apart

Running title: none

Binding: light blue-green boards. On spine, reading lengthways up spine, from foot: '[ornament] CHAUCER [ornament (in reverse)]'. On upper cover: 'Chaucer [all in outline, with shading] | [university crest] | JOHN MASEFIELD' (within double ruled border: 164 × 104mm.) (the outer border is thicker than the inner border). Lower cover: blank. All edges trimmed. Binding measurements: 191 × 123mm. (covers), 191 × 16mm. (spine). End-papers: wove paper.

Publication date: published, according to the *English Catalogue of Books*, May 1931

Price: 2s.

Contents:

Chaucer ('I am to talk to you for an hour about Geoffrey Chaucer, the first of the three great English poets.')

Notes:

Wight states that Handley-Taylor provides the date of publication for this volume. This is an error, for Handley-Taylor only provides a date of the original lecture. The copy in the British Library is stamped 27 April 1931 while the *English Catalogue of Books* gives a date of May 1931. Since Handley-Taylor does state an American edition was published on 23 April 1931, the American edition may constitute the first true edition.

Publication by Cambridge University Press, rather than by Heinemann, can be explained by evidence within the archives of The Society of Authors. Following the announcement of Masefield as the Leslie Stephen lecturer, Cambridge University Press wrote as follows:

> The Syndics of the Press request me to say that they would be very pleased to undertake the publication of your Leslie Stephen Lecture next year. I may add that it is the regular custom of the Syndics to publish this lecture at their own expense, and to share any net profits equally with the author.
>
> (Cambridge University Press, letter to John Masefield, 8 December 1930)
> (BL, Add.Mss.56592, f.54)

Masefield wrote to The Society of Authors noting a precedence in his experience:

> I have delayed replying to the Cambridge letter, because I had not decided the subject of the coming lecture. I have now decided to lecture on Chaucer. Some years ago, when I gave the Romanes Lecture here, I arranged for the Oxford University Press to print the lecture, on the understanding that they paid me a royalty of 10 or 15 percent on the published price + supplied me with a dozen copies free of charge + also undertook to secure the American copyright in my name + to understand that I was perfectly free to reprint the lecture at any time with my usual publishers, both in this country + in the United States.
>
> (John Masefield, letter to Denys Kilham Roberts, 23 December 1930)
> (BL, Add.Mss.56592, f.53)

The Society of Authors suggested these terms (with Masefield's royalty at 15%) to Cambridge University Press on 24 December 1930 (see BL, Add.Mss.56592, ff.50–51). S.C. Roberts, Secretary of Cambridge University Press, replied:

> I have now been able to consult a committee of the Syndics of the Press with reference to our recent correspondence. The Syndics are prepared to accept the following conditions for the publication of the lecture:-
>
> (1) A royalty of 15% of the published price of all copies sold to be paid to the author.
>
> (2) The author to receive twelve free copies.
>
> (3) The Sydics to secure the copyrighting of the lecture in the United States by the Macmillan Company, the Macmillan Compny to pay a royalty of 15% of the American published price, and the Syndics to retain 10% of the proceeds of all royalties received from the Macmillan Company.
>
> (4) The author to be free to reprint the lecture in any book of collected essays with his usual publisher; the Syndics to have the exclusive right to publish it as a separate book.
>
> I shall be glad to hear at your convenience that these terms are agreeable to Mr. Masefield.
>
> (S.C. Roberts, letter to The Society of Authors, 14 January 1931)
> (BL, Add.Mss.56592, f.92)

The Society of Authors wrote to Masefield on 15 January 1931 stating that three of the clauses were 'satisfactory' but objected to one. Masefield responded:

> ...It would simplify matters evidently if I printed this lecture with my own publishers, both here + in the U.S. Why I should pay the Cambridge Press for dealing with my usual publishers in the U.S. is not clear to me. I will therefore arrange for the publication of this lecture with my usual publishers.
>
> (John Masefield, letter to Denys Kilham Roberts, [16 January 1931])
> (BL, Add.Mss.56592, f.108)

The Society of Authors wrote accordingly to Cambridge University Press on 17 January stating that Masefield 'feels on consideration that it would simplify matters if he published this lecture through his own Publishers' (see BL, Add.Mss.56592, f.114). Cambridge University Press replied stating their 'regret' at the situation on 19 January 1931 (see BL, Add.Mss.56592, f.120). Masefield, however, had a change of mind. He accordingly wrote again to The Society of Authors at the beginning of February 1931:

> ...thinking over this matter, I feel that it would be churlish not to let them print the lecture in this country: but as the Macmillan Co are my usual U.S. publishers I will arrange direct with Macmillans in N. York for the American edition.
>
> (John Masefield, letter to Denys Kilham Roberts, [4 February 1931])
> (BL, Add.Mss.56592, f.169)

The Society of Authors communicated this to Cambridge University Press who replied on 5 February 1931:

> I am much obliged by your letter of 4 February, and am very glad to hear that we shall have the pleasure of publishing Mr. Masefield's Leslie Stephen lecture in this country; arrangements for the American edition to be made by the author

direct with the Macmillan Company of New York. I shall be pleased to receive the agreement, based on the terms indicated in my letter of the 14th January at your early convenience.

(Cambridge University Press, letter to The Society of Authors, 5 February 1931)
(BL, Add.Mss.56592, f.173)

A copy of the agreement is preserved in the archives of The Society of Authors (see BL, Add.Mss.56592, ff.179–81). The agreement notes:

- Masefield to deliver the copy on or before the 10 March
- Masefield to grant licence only for book form in English in Great Britain, the Colonies, Dominions and Dependencies excepting Canada. Masefield to take all steps in conjunction with Macmillan to copyright the work in America
- publication price to be not more than 2/6
- Masefield at liberty after 6 months to authorise publication of lecture in any collected work edition
- twelve free copies to be reserved for Masefield
- the author to receive 15% royalty

(see BL, Add.Mss.56592, ff.179–181)

Cambridge University Press requested details of the length of the lecture on 20 February 1931 (see BL, Add.Mss.56592, f.225) and Masefield sent a postcard to The Society of Authors on 23 February 1931 stating 'Leslie Stephen lecture will be about 5500 words' (see BL, Add.Mss.56592, f.236). Having problems with the lecture, however, Masefield wrote to The Society of Authors at the beginning of March 1931:

The Lecture is not yet ready. I fear I cannot get it to the Press before the 8th or 9th at earliest.

(John Masefield, letter to Denys Kilham Roberts, [1 March 1931])
(BL, Add.Mss.56593, f.1)

In April 1932 Masefield wrote to The Society of Authors regarding his right to reprint the text of his lecture:

Leslie Stephen Lecture: Chaucer. I am thinking of printing a collection of my recent lectures during the autumn of this year, + should like to include the above. Will you be so kind as to ask the Cambridge University Press for their formal assent to this?

(John Masefield, letter to The Society of Authors, [6 April 1932])
(BL, Add.Mss.56596, f.68)

(The collection presumably appeared as A73(b)). The Society of Authors replied on 7 April 1932 stating that the terms of Masefield's contract with Cambridge University Press did not require him to seek permission (see BL, Add.Mss.56596, ff.69–70).

In June 1944 The Society of Authors wrote to Masefield to inform him that the stock of this volume, as held by Cambridge University Press, numbered seventeen copies. Masefield was also reminded that the contract for the title contained a clause whereby Masefield could terminate his agreement if the book went out of print or off the market (see BL, Add.Mss.56617, f,157). Masefield replied:

Many thanks for your letter about the Chaucer lecture. No man can wish to read this at present, nor should precious paper go to reprinting it. Perhaps, it can lie in safe obscurity till the peace.

(John Masefield, letter to [E.J.] Mullett, [12 June 1944])
(BL, Add.Mss.56617, f.164)

Copies seen: private collection (PWE); BL (11822.p.20) stamped 27 APR 1931

A105 MINNIE MAYLOW'S STORY AND OTHER TALES AND SCENES 1931

A105(a) First English edition (1931)

JOHN MASEFIELD | [five-point star in outline] | MINNIE MAYLOW'S STORY | AND | OTHER TALES | AND | SCENES | [five-point star in outline] | [publisher's device of a windmill with 'W [point]' and 'H'] | LONDON | WILLIAM HEINEMANN LTD
(All width centred)

Bibliographies: Handley-Taylor p.59, Wight 80

Collation: [A]⁸ B-R⁸ (J not used); signatures right foot of page; 136 leaves; 185 × 122mm., [i–xii] xiii [xiv] 1–256 [257–58]

Page contents: [i] half-title: 'MINNIE MAYLOW'S STORY | AND | OTHER TALES | AND | SCENES'; [ii] '*ALSO BY JOHN MASEFIELD* | PLAYS: | [10 titles listed] | POETRY: | [13 titles listed] | OTHER WORKS: | [10 titles listed]'; [iii] title-page; [iv] 'FIRST PUBLISHED 1931 | [rule] | PRINTED | IN GREAT BRITAIN | AT THE WINDMILL PRESS'; [v] 'NOTE | THE Tales and Scenes in this volume are copy- | right. They may not be recited nor performed in | public without the licence of the Author or his | Agents, the Society of Authors, 11, Gower | Street, London, W.C., to whom application | should be made.'; [vi] blank; [vii] 'TO | MY WIFE'; [viii] blank; [ix] 'I thank the beautiful speakers- | Chrystabel Ayling | Betty Bartholomew | Dulcie Bowie | Rose Bruford | Margery Bryce | Elspeth Coghill | Nevill Coghill | Leslie Davey | Sybil Heriz-Smith | Hubert Langley | Judith Masefield | Amy Rean | Harold Ripper | Ronald Watkins | Penelope Wheeler | who, in the speaking of these tales and scenes, | have deeply delighted me. | JOHN MASEFIELD'; [x] blank; [xi] 'CONTENTS' (14 individual items listed with page references); [xii] blank; xiii text of 'Prologue'; [xiv] blank; 1–256 text; [257–58] blank

Paper: wove paper

Running title: comprise titles of individual items, pp.2–228 (there is no running title for 'Penelope', pp.229–56)

Binding: blue cloth. On spine, in gold: 'Minnie | Maylow's | Story | [ornament] | John | Masefield | Heinemann' (all width centred). On upper cover, in gold: 'MINNIE MAYLOW'S STORY | JOHN MASEFIELD' (within blind ruled border: 187 × 119mm.) On lower cover, in blind: publisher's device of a windmill (ranged lower right). All edges trimmed. Binding measurements: 189 × 123mm. (covers), 189 × 47mm. (spine). End-papers: wove paper.

Publication date: the sales ledger preserved in the Heinemann Archive suggests publication on 19 October 1931 in an edition of 4000 copies

Price: 7s.6d.

Contents:
Prologue ('I am a pilgrim come from many lands,')
Minnie Maylow's Story ('Once (long ago) there was an English King,')
Adamas and Eva ('Whilom there was, dwellyng in Paradys')
Son of Adam ('Once on a time there was a lusty Lion')
The Love Gift ('In King Marc's palace at the valley-head')
Tristan's Singing ('PART I | When Isolt quarrell'd with her Tristan there')
Simkin, Tomkin and Jack ('Before old Tencombe of the Barrows died,')
The Rose of the World ('Dark Eleanor and Henry sat at meat')
Young John of Chance's Stretch ('PART I | When Father died, my Mother ran')
Evan Roberts, A.B., of H.M.S. *Andromache* ('This gallant act is told by the late Montagu Burrows, on page 67 of his *Autobiography...*')
The Wild Swan ('PROLOGUE: | Once, long ago, a British Princess stood')
Richard Whittington ('FORTUNE: | I am Fortune: I give as is fitting to each of my souls,')
The Hour Strikes ('THE SEEKER | The shepherds warn'd me not to climb this hill')
Penelope ('SCENE:- *A room in* PENELOPE'S *palace.* PENELOPE *seated centre...*')

Notes:
As suggested by the note on p.[ix] and according to Babington Smith, this collection of poems and a verse play derives from the verse-speaking festivals held by Masefield in the Music Room, Boars Hill. Minnie May Low was one of Masefield's nursery-maids in the 1880s and the story is based on a tale she used to recount for the Masefield children.

Wight notes, for p.xiii:

This is the 7th leaf. It is signed vii, but the v is inverted and of smaller size.

Since the character 'i' does not appear complete (the dots are missing in both examples) and a comparison with the Heinemann limited signed edition reveals 'xiii' to be clearly printed, it seems likely that damage to the type has occurred or been, subsequently, corrected. Consequently, an inverted 'v' in smaller type is not present, but a standard 'x' of which only the lower half appears.

Masefield informed C.S. Evans of a proposed new work at the beginning of 1931. Evans responded that he was '...glad you are thinking of a new book of poems for the autumn. I think it should have great popularity...' (see C.S. Evans, letter to John Masefield, 5 February 1931) (HRHRC, MS (Masefield, J.) Recip William Heinemann Ltd.) Evans wrote to thank Masefield for the typescript of this book just under five months later (see C.S. Evans, letter to John Masefield, 2 July 1931) (HRHRC, MS (Masefield, J.) Recip William Heinemann Ltd.) The work was immediately set-up, for 'rough proofs' were sent within four days:

> We have pleasure in sending you herewith two sets of rough proofs of MINNIE MAYLOW'S STORY AND OTHER TALES AND SCENES and proofs of the preliminary matter, together with the manuscript.
> (B.F. Oliver, letter to John Masefield, 6 July 1931)
> (HRHRC, MS (Masefield, J.) Recip William Heinemann Ltd.)

Two sets of 'revised proofs in page form' were sent on 17 August 1931 (see B.F. Oliver, letter to John Masefield, 17 August 1931) (HRHRC, MS (Masefield, J.) Recip William Heinemann Ltd.) and Masefield was informed, three days later, of an intended publication date:

> ...We are planning to publish MINNIE MAYLOW on October 19th and we cabled our date to Messrs Macmillan...
> (Louisa Callender, letter to John Masefield, 20 August 1931)
> (HRHRC, MS (Masefield, J.) Recip William Heinemann Ltd.)

Before being passed for press a Heinemann reader raised several points, with reference to phonetic spelling (see C.S. Evans, letter to John Masefield, 25 August 1931) (HRHRC, MS (Masefield, J.) Recip William Heinemann Ltd.). However, there was no delay experienced as a result of these queries.

Masefield, writing to The Society of Authors, gave specific instructions regarding licences for work contained in this volume:

> Minnie Maylow. With one brief exception, or possibly two, ('Adamas + Eva' + 'Evan Roberts') the tales + scenes in this book are too long to appear in any anthologies. The scenes may be played by amateurs, but will need the Lord Chamberlain's Licence. The stories may be recited by amateurs. I know not what fee to ask, as the profits of recitals are usually tiny. Five shillings is as much as most could pay probably. The scenes play about an hour apiece + might be charged for as one Act plays.
> (John Masefield, letter to [E.J.] Mullett, [15 November 1931])
> (BL, Add.Mss.56595, f.64)

Copies seen: private collection (PWE); BL (11640.h.52) stamped 20 OCT 1931; HRHRC (TEMP M377MIN 1931A cop.1) inscribed 'For Jude | from Zob. | Oct' 16. 1931.'; HRHRC (TEMP M377MIN 1931A cop.3) inscribed 'For Freddy [Keeble] + Lillah [McCarthy] | from John Masefield. | Oct'. 1931.'

A105(b) Second English edition (limited signed edition) (1931)

JOHN MASEFIELD | [five-point star in outline] [in blue] | MINNIE MAYLOW'S STORY [in blue] | AND | OTHER TALES | AND | SCENES | [five-point star in outline] [in blue] | [publisher's device of a windmill with 'W [point]' and 'H'] [in blue] | LONDON | WILLIAM HEINEMANN LTD | 1931
(All width centred)

Bibliographies: Handley-Taylor p.59, Wight 80a

Collation: [A]⁸ B-R⁸ (J not used); signatures right foot of page; 136 leaves; 228 × 139mm.; [i–xii] xiii [xiv] 1–256 [257–58]

Page contents: [i] half-title: 'MINNIE MAYLOW'S STORY | AND | OTHER TALES | AND | SCENES'; [ii] '*This Edition, numbered and signed | by the Author, is limited to* 375 | *copies for sale in Great Britain | and Ireland.* | *No*...............'; [iii] title-page; [iv] 'PRINTED | IN GREAT BRITAIN | AT THE WINDMILL PRESS'; [v] 'NOTE | THE Tales and Scenes in this volume are copy- | right. They may not be recited nor performed in | public without the licence of the Author or his | Agents, the Society of Authors, 11, Gower | Street, London, W.C., to whom application | should be made.'; [vi] blank; [vii] 'TO | MY WIFE'; [viii] blank; [ix] 'I thank the beautiful speakers- | Chrystabel Ayling | Betty Bartholomew | Dulcie Bowie | Rose Bruford | Margery Bryce | Elspeth Coghill | Nevill Coghill | Leslie Davey | Sybil Heriz-Smith | Hubert Langley | Judith Masefield | Amy Rean | Harold Ripper | Ronald Watkins | Penelope Wheeler | who, in the speaking of these tales and scenes, | have deeply delighted me. | JOHN MASEFIELD'; [x] blank; [xi] 'CONTENTS' (14 individual items listed with page references); [xii] blank; [xiii] text of 'Prologue'; [xiv] blank; 1–256 text; [257–58] blank

Paper: wove paper (watermark: 'MILLBOURN | BRITISH HAND MADE PURE RAG [castle device: 26 × 31mm.]')

Running title: comprise titles of individual items, pp.2–228 (there is no running title for 'Penelope', pp.229–56).

Binding: light brown cloth (see notes). On spine, in gold: 'JOHN MASEFIELD | [point] | MINNIE | MAYLOW'S STORY | *and* | *Other Tales & Scenes* | HEINEMANN' (all width centred). On upper cover, in gold: illustration of flower, stem and three leaves: 34 × 30mm. Lower cover: blank. Top edge gilt, lower outside edge untrimmed, fore edge uncut. Sewn head band (in white) and white marker ribbon. Binding measurements: 234 × 145mm. (covers), 234 × 45mm. (spine). The binding includes bevelled edges. End-papers: wove paper. Volume contained in slip-case covered in blue paper.

Publication date: published, according to the *English Catalogue of Books*, October 1931

Price: 42s.

Contents:
as for A105(a)

Notes:
Handley-Taylor does not give the date of publication (or even limitation) for this volume. He does, however, state that the standard Heinemann edition was published on 19 October 1931. Copies in the British Library reveal that the standard Heinemann edition is stamped 20 OCT 1931 while this limited signed edition is stamped 28 OCT 1931. Both volumes are listed for October 1931 in the *English Catalogue of Books*. Inscribed copies suggest this edition to have been published after A105(a).

Wight records the binding as 'bound in red cloth with white cloth book marker'. This represents either a binding variant or an error in Wight's description.

The text appears to use the same setting of type as A105(a). Note, however, differences on p.vii (see above).

Sheets for Masefield to sign were sent on 30 September 1931:

> By passenger train this evening we have despatched to you a parcel containing the title sections for the Limited edition of MINNIE MAYLOW. Will you please be good enough to sign each tablet and return the parcel addressed to the writer, at your earliest convenience. If you would care to leave the numbering of the copies to us we will have this done when you return the titles...
>
> (B.F. Oliver, letter to John Masefield, 30 September 1931)
> (HRHRC, MS (Masefield, J.) Recip William Heinemann Ltd.)

A further eleven sections were sent on 12 October 1931 'to make up the shortage' (see B.F. Oliver, letter to John Masefield, 12 October 1931) (HRHRC, MS (Masefield, J.) Recip William Heinemann Ltd.)

When Masefield examined a copy of the edition he was evidently unimpressed with the design on the upper cover. It appears that he favoured a design by Judith Masefield. C.S. Evans wrote:

> I am sorry you did not care for the design on the cover of the l.p. MINNIE MAYLOW. I did not see it myself until after the book was bound because it was done while I was away. Of course you can have Judith's design on all the future limited editions of your books that we do. It is an excellent design and I am very glad to have a more or less uniform design for the limited editions...
>
> (C.S. Evans, letter to John Masefield, 2 November 1931)
> (HRHRC, MS (Masefield, J.) Recip William Heinemann Ltd.)

Copies seen: private collection (PWE) number 230, signed '230 | John Masefield.' on p.[ii]; BL (11644.l.11) number 353, signed '353 | John Masefield.' on p.[ii] stamped 28 OCT 1931; HRHRC (TEMP M377MIN 1931B) number 357, signed '357 | John Masefield.' on p.[ii] additionally inscribed 'For Judith. | from Zob. | Oct 31. 1931.'

A105(c) First American edition (1931)

[triple rule] | MINNIE MAYLOW'S STORY | [rule] | AND OTHER TALES | [rule] | AND SCENES | [triple rule] | BY JOHN MASEFIELD | [ornament] [ornament] | [ornament] | THE MACMILLAN COMPANY | [rule] | NEW YORK [ornament] 1931
(The type contains a swash character 'Y')
(All width centred)

Bibliographies: Handley-Taylor p.59, Wight [noted on p.146]

Collation: [A–N]⁸ (J not used); 104 leaves; 218 × 143mm.; [i–xiv] [1–2] 3–13 [14–16] 17–19 [20–22] 23–29 [30–32] 33–40 [41–42] 43–54 [55–56] 57–62 [63–64] 65–71 [72–74] 75–91 [92–94] 95–97 [98–100] 101–126 [127–28] 129–52 [153–54] 155–77 [178–80] 181–94

Page contents: [i] half-title: 'MINNIE MAYLOW'S STORY | AND OTHER TALES | AND SCENES'; [ii] 'BY | JOHN MASEFIELD | [41 titles listed, each title separated by a dash]'; [iii] title-page; [iv] 'COPYRIGHT, 1931, | BY JOHN MASEFIELD. | [rule] | All rights reserved–no part of this book | may be reproduced in any form without | permission in writing from the publisher. | [rule] | Set up and electrotyped. Published October, 1931. | PRINTED IN THE UNITED STATES OF AMERICA | BY THE STRATFORD PRESS, INC., NEW YORK'; [v] 'TO | MY WIFE'; [vi] blank; [vii] 'NOTE | THE Tales and Scenes in this volume are copyright. They may not be | recited nor performed in public without the license of the Author or | his Agents, the Society of Authors, 11, Gower Street, London, W.C., | to whom application should be made.' [viii] blank; [ix] '*I thank the beautiful speakers-* | CHRYSTABEL AYLING | BETTY BARTHOLOMEW | DULCIE BOWIE | ROSE BRUFORD | MARGERY BRYCE | ELSPETH COGHILL | NEVILL COGHILL | LESLIE DAVEY | SYBIL HERIZ-SMITH | HUBERT LANGLEY | JUDITH MASEFIELD | AMY REAN | HAROLD RIPPER | RONALD WATKINS | PENELOPE WHEELER | *Who, in the speaking of these tales and scenes, | have deeply delighted me* | [ornament] | JOHN MASEFIELD'; [x] blank; [xi] 'CONTENTS' (14 individual items listed with page references); [xii] blank; [xiii] text of 'Prologue'; [xiv] blank; [1] 'MINNIE MAYLOW'S STORY'; [2] blank; 3–13 text of 'Minnie Maylow's Story'; [14] blank; [15] 'ADAMAS AND EVA'; [16] blank; 17–19 text of 'Adamas and Eva'; [20] blank; [21] 'SON OF ADAM'; [22] blank; 23–29 text of 'Son of Adam'; [30] blank; [31] 'THE LOVE GIFT'; [32] blank; 33–40 text of 'The Love Gift'; [41] 'TRISTAN'S SINGING'; [42] blank; 43–54 text of 'Tristan's Singing'; [55] 'SIMKIN, TOMKIN AND JACK'; [56] blank; 57–62 text of 'Simkin, Tomkin and Jack'; [63] 'THE ROSE OF THE WORLD'; [64] blank; 65–71 text of 'The Rose of the World'; [72] blank; [73] 'YOUNG JOHN OF CHANCE'S STRETCH'; [74] blank; 75–91 text of 'Young John of Chance's Stretch'; [92] blank; [93] 'EVAN ROBERTS, A.B., | OF H.M.S. ANDROMACHE'; [94] blank; 95–97 text of 'Evan Roberts, A.B.'; [98] blank; [99] 'THE WILD SWAN'; [100] blank; 101–126 text of 'The Wild Swan'; [127] 'RICHARD WHITTINGTON'; [128] blank; 129–52 text of 'Richard Whittington'; [153] 'THE HOUR STRIKES'; [154] blank; 155–77 text of 'The Hour Strikes'; [178] blank; [179] 'PENELOPE'; [180] blank; 181–94 text of 'Penelope'

Paper: laid paper (no watermark), chain-lines 17mm. apart

Running title: comprise titles of individual items, pp.4–194

Binding: blue cloth. On spine, in gold: '[double rule] | MINNIE | MAYLOW'S | STORY | [rule] | MASEFIELD | [double rule] | MACMILLAN | [point]' (all width centred). On upper cover, in gold: 'MINNIE MAYLOW'S STORY | *And Other Tales and Scenes* | [double rule] | JOHN MASEFIELD' (the type contains a number of swash characters). Lower cover: blank. Top edge trimmed, others roughly trimmed. Binding measurements: 224 × 145mm. (covers), 224 × 33mm. (spine). End-papers: wove paper.

Publication date: published, according to Handley-Taylor, 4 November 1931

Price: $2.50

Contents:
Prologue ('I am a pilgrim come from many lands,')
Minnie Maylow's Story ('Once (long ago) there was an English King,')
Adamas and Eva ('Whilom there was, dwellyng in Paradys')
Son of Adam ('Once on a time there was a lusty Lion')
The Love Gift ('In King Marc's palace at the valley-head')
Tristan's Singing ('PART I | When Isolt quarrelled with her Tristan there')
Simkin, Tomkin and Jack ('Before old Tencombe of the Barrows died,')
The Rose of the World ('Dark Eleanor and Henry sat at meat')
Young John of Chance's Stretch ('PART I | When Father died, my Mother ran')
Evan Roberts, A.B., of H.M.S. Andromache ('This gallant act is told by the late Montagu Burrows, on page 67 of his *Autobiography...*')
The Wild Swan ('PROLOGUE: | Once, long ago, a British Princess stood')
Richard Whittington ('FORTUNE: | I am Fortune: I give as is fitting to each of my souls,')
The Hour Strikes ('THE SEEKER: | The shepherds warned me not to climb this hill')
Penelope ('SCENE:-*A room in* PENELOPE'S *palace.* PENELOPE *seated centre...*')

Notes:

The publishing agreement for this title between Masefield and Macmillan was dated 20 June 1931 (see Archives of The Society of Authors). The agreement refers to 'a licence to publish in volume form... in the United States of America and Canada a work the subject or title of which is Minnie Maylow's Story and Other Tales and Scenes'.

Handley-Taylor notes a publication date of 4 November 1931 for this volume and additionally states 'also issued in a Limited Edition of 350 copies.' Wight fails to describe the standard edition but notes Handley-Taylor's date claiming this for the limited signed edition. Wight also notes 'a regular and a similar edition bound in blue were published at the same time'. The 'regular' edition presumably comprises the volume described above; the 'similar edition' may constitute a variant binding of the limited signed edition.

The text has been newly set for this edition.

Copies seen: private collection (PWE); private collection (ROV); HRHRC (AC-L M377MIN 1931C cop.1); HRHRC (AC-L M377MIN 1931C cop.2)

Reprinted:

'Reprinted'	[first edition, second impression]	Oct 1931

A105(cc) First American edition (limited signed edition) (1931)

[triple rule] [in red] | MINNIE MAYLOW'S STORY | [rule] [in red] | AND OTHER TALES | [rule] [in red] | AND SCENES | [triple rule] [in red] | BY JOHN MASEFIELD | [ornament] [ornament] [both in red] | [ornament] [in red] | THE MACMILLAN COMPANY | [rule] [in red] | NEW YORK [ornament] 1931
(The type contains a swash character 'Y')
(All width centred)

Bibliographies: Handley-Taylor p.59, Wight 80b

Collation: [A-M]⁸ [N]¹⁰ ([N]8+2) (J not used); 106 leaves; 249 × 156mm.; [i–xiv] [1–2] 3–13 [14–16] 17–19 [20–22] 23–29 [30–32] 33–40 [41–42] 43–54 [55–56] 57–62 [63–64] 65–71 [72–74] 75–91 [92–94] 95–97 [98–100] 101–26 [127–28] 129–52 [153–54] 155–77 [178–80] 181–94 [195–98]

Page contents: [i] half-title: 'MINNIE MAYLOW'S STORY | AND OTHER TALES | AND SCENES'; [ii] blank; [iii] title-page; [iv] 'COPYRIGHT, 1931, | BY JOHN MASEFIELD. | [rule] | All rights reserved–no part of this book | may be reproduced in any form without | permission in writing from the publisher. | [rule] | Set up and electrotyped. Published October, 1931. | PRINTED IN THE UNITED STATES OF AMERICA | BY THE STRATFORD PRESS, INC., NEW YORK'; [v] 'TO | MY WIFE'; [vi] blank; [vii] 'NOTE | THE Tales and Scenes in this volume are copyright. They may not be | recited nor performed in public without the license of the Author or | his Agents, the Society of Authors, 11, Gower Street, London, W.C., | to whom application should be made.'; [viii] blank; [ix] '*I thank the beautiful speakers-* | CHRYSTABEL AYLING | BETTY BARTHOLOMEW | DULCIE BOWIE | ROSE BRUFORD | MARGERY BRYCE | ELSPETH COGHILL | NEVILL COGHILL | LESLIE DAVEY | SYBIL HERIZ-SMITH | HUBERT LANGLEY | JUDITH MASEFIELD | AMY REAN | HAROLD RIPPER | RONALD WATKINS | PENELOPE WHEELER | *Who, in the speaking of these tales and scenes,* | *have deeply delighted me* | [ornament] | JOHN MASEFIELD'; [x] blank; [xi] 'CONTENTS' (14 individual items listed with page references); [xii] blank; [xiii] text of 'Prologue'; [xiv] blank; [1] 'MINNIE MAYLOW'S STORY'; [2] blank; 3–13 text of 'Minnie Maylow's Story'; [14] blank; [15] 'ADAMAS AND EVA'; [16] blank; 17–19 text of 'Adamas and Eva'; [20] blank; [21] 'SON OF ADAM'; [22] blank; 23–29 text of 'Son of Adam'; [30] blank; [31] 'THE LOVE GIFT'; [32] blank; 33–40 text of 'The Love Gift'; [41] 'TRISTAN'S SINGING'; [42] blank; 43–54 text of 'Tristan's Singing'; [55] 'SIMKIN, TOMKIN AND JACK'; [56] blank; 57–62 text of 'Simkin, Tomkin and Jack'; [63] 'THE ROSE OF THE WORLD'; [64] blank; 65–71 text of 'The Rose of the World'; [72] blank; [73] 'YOUNG JOHN OF CHANCE'S STRETCH'; [74] blank; 75–91 text of 'Young John of Chance's Stretch'; [92] blank; [93] 'EVAN ROBERTS, A.B., | OF H.M.S. ANDROMACHE'; [94] blank; 95–97 text of 'Evan Roberts, A.B.'; [98] blank; [99] 'THE WILD SWAN'; [100] blank; 101–126 text of 'The Wild Swan'; [127] 'RICHARD WHITTINGTON'; [128] blank; 129–52 text of 'Richard Whittington'; [153] 'THE HOUR STRIKES'; [154] blank; 155–77 text of 'The Hour Strikes'; [178] blank; [179] 'PENELOPE'; [180] blank; 181–94 text of 'Penelope'; [195] '*This edition of* MINNIE MAYLOW'S STORY AND OTHER | TALES AND SCENES *is limited to three hundred and fifty copies.* | *This is number* ....'; [196–98] blank

Paper: laid paper (watermark: '[Atlas holding globe: 136 × 65mm.] | WHITCHURCH'), chain-lines 28–35mm. apart

Running title: running titles comprise titles of individual items, pp.4–194

Binding: mottled light brown and white cloth covered boards with black cloth spine. On spine, in gold: '[double rule] | MINNIE | MAYLOW'S | STORY | [rule] | MASEFIELD | [double rule]' (all width centred). Covers: blank. There is a single vertical rule in gold on each cover at the edge of the cloth (where it joins the spine cloth). Top edge trimmed, others uncut. Binding measurements: 255 × 159mm. (covers), 255 × 35mm. (spine). End-papers: wove paper.

Publication date: published, according to Wight, 4 November 1931 (see notes)

Price: $25.00

Contents:
as for A105(c)

Notes:

Handley-Taylor notes a publication date of 4 November 1931 for A105(c) and additionally states 'also issued in a Limited Edition of 350 copies'. Wight therefore notes 4 November 1931 as the date of publication.

Wight also notes 'a regular and a similar edition bound in blue were published at the same time'. The 'regular' edition presumably comprises the volume described as A105(c); the 'similar edition' may constitute a variant binding of the limited signed edition.

Wight describes the binding as 'sand-colored cloth with black tape on the spine and gold rules at the edges of the tape'. The gold rules are, on the examined copy, at the edge of the cloth.

The additional leaves ([N]9 and [N]10) pasted onto [N]8 comprise a single set of conjugate leaves including the page detailing the limitation of the edition. The paper type is the same as that used for the rest of the volume. The leaves were presumably sent to Masefield for signing.

Copies seen: Harvard College Library (Houghton *EC9.M377.931mc) number 63, signed '63 | J. Masefield' on p.[195]

A106 POETRY 1931

A106(a) First English edition (1931)

POETRY | By | JOHN MASEFIELD | A Lecture | given at the Queen's Hall in London, | on Thursday, October 15th, 1931 | [ornament] | WILLIAM HEINEMANN LTD: LONDON
(All width centred and enclosed within three ruled borders: 116 × 75mm., 119 × 78mm. and 125 × 84mm. None of the corners are precisely formed)

Bibliographies: Handley-Taylor p.59, Wight 81

Collation: [A]⁸ B-D⁸; signatures right foot of page; 32 leaves; 187 × 124mm.; [i–iv] [1] 2–60

Page contents: [i] half-title: 'POETRY | John Masefield' (the italic type contains a number of swash characters); [ii] 'ALSO BY JOHN MASEFIELD | PLAYS: | [10 titles listed] | POETRY: | [14 titles listed] | OTHER WORKS: | [10 titles listed]'; [iii] title-page; [iv] 'PRINTED | IN GT. BRITAIN | AT THE WINDMILL PRESS | [rule] | FIRST PUBLISHED 1931'; [1]–60 text

Paper: wove paper

Running title: '[rule, 84mm.] | Poetry [ranged left with page number ranged right] | [rule, 84mm.]' on both verso and recto, pp.2–60

Binding: blue cloth. On spine, reading lengthways up spine, from foot, in gold: 'POETRY – JOHN MASEFIELD'; horizontally at foot of spine: 'Heinemann'. On upper cover, in gold: 'POETRY | [rule] | JOHN | MASEFIELD' (within blind ruled border: 188 × 117mm.) On lower cover, in blind: publisher's device of a windmill (ranged lower right). All edges trimmed. Binding measurements: 193 × 125mm. (covers), 193 × 19mm. (spine). End-papers: wove paper.

Publication date: the sales ledger preserved in the Heinemann Archive suggests publication on 16 November 1931 in an edition of 5000 copies

Price: 3s.6d.

Contents:

Poetry ('For some weeks I wondered how to begin this my hour of speaking about poetry...')

Notes:

The text commences with a drop-capital.

It appears that Masefield approached C.S. Evans for a suggested agency to organise the lecture:

> The best people I can recommend for the handling of your lecture arrangements in the autumn are The Lecture Agency Limited... Mr. Gerald Christy is the head of it and would I am sure manage the thing ably.
>
> (C.S. Evans, letter to John Masefield, 13 May 1931)
> (HRHRC, MS (Masefield, J.) Recip William Heinemann Ltd.)

Publication by Heinemann was undertaken quickly. C.S. Evans wrote on 5 October 1931 that:

> ...If you can let us have the manuscript of your lecture on Thursday, we can issue it in three weeks at the latest, possibly sooner. I understand it is about 8,000 words long...
>
> (C.S. Evans, letter to John Masefield, 5 October 1931)
> (HRHRC, MS (Masefield, J.) Recip William Heinemann Ltd.)

The typescript was acknowledged four days later. Masefield had evidently requested that the text was not leaked and also must have suggested a limited signed edition:

> Thanks for your note and for the typescript of the lecture on poetry which I am sending to the press today. I will, of course, see that no part of it gets into the press until after the lecture has been delivered: in fact, the press will see nothing of it until we send the actual copies to the various editors for review... I certainly think that we could do a few special copies...
>
> (C.S. Evans, letter to John Masefield, 9 October 1931)
> (HRHRC, MS (Masefield, J.) Recip William Heinemann Ltd.)

On 12 October 1931 Evans wrote to say that proofs would be ready the following day (see C.S. Evans, letter to John Masefield, 12 October 1931) (HRHRC, MS (Masefield, J.) Recip William Heinemann Ltd.) and two sets of galley proofs were sent (together with the typescript) on 14 October 1931 (see B.F. Oliver, letter to John Masefield, 14 October 1931) (HRHRC, MS (Masefield, J.) Recip William Heinemann Ltd.) Over a week later revised proofs were sent and instructions requested as to the wording of title-page information:

> Here is a set of revised proofs in page form of POETRY... Will you also please state if you wish words to the effect that the lecture was delivered at the Queen's Hall on October 15th, to appear on the title page or elsewhere in the book.
>
> (B.F. Oliver, letter to John Masefield, 23 October 1931)
> (HRHRC, MS (Masefield, J.) Recip William Heinemann Ltd.)

The publishing agreement for this title between Masefield and Heinemann was dated 29 October 1931 (see Archives of The Society of Authors). The agreement refers to both 3s.6d. and 8s.6d. editions (A106(a) and A106(b)).

Masefield appears to have instigated the lecture himself. Writing to The Society of Authors Masefield explains:

> On 15th October next, I hope to give an Evening Lecture on Poetry at the Queen's Hall, Langham Place, which I have provisionally taken for that purpose. I wish the Lecture Agency, Ltd, of the Outer Temple, W.C. to act as my Agents for the advertisement of, + the sale of tickets for, this lecture, on a commission agreement, + have learned that they are willing to act for me. Will you be so kind as to draft a short agreement which the Lecture Agency + myself could accept? The main point is, that they should have a strong incentive to drum up an audience, so that the hall may be full. It seats 2,400, + I suppose no seat should be less than 2/6, including tax.
>
> (John Masefield, letter to Denys Kilham Roberts, [29 May 1931])
> (BL, Add.Mss.56593, f.246)

Masefield had hired the hall in an agreement with Chappell & Co. With possible view of future publication, Masefield had concerns that newspaper reports might print the text of the lecture. The Society of Authors noted:

> ...If you desire to prohibit the publication in newspapers of a report of the Lecture it is necessary under the Copyright Act 1911 that a written or printed notice of such prohibition shall appear at the main entrance to the Hall, and another near the lecturer, before and during the Lecture. You cannot prevent newspaper summaries but you can prevent newspaper publication of a full report by adopting the procedure I have described.
>
> (Denys Kilham Roberts, letter to John Masefield, 1 June 1931)
> (BL, Add.Mss.56594, ff.3–4)

Another matter of discussion was advertisement. Masefield wrote to The Society of Authors:

> ...I feel that I shall have to guarantee the cost of the printing + advertisement matter, up to about £50 or £75. All advertisements had better be approved by me. I feel that the Agency should receive commission on a sliding scale basis... The hall seats 2400, + if they should fill it they would deserve a big percentage.
>
> (John Masefield, letter to Denys Kilham Roberts, [3 June 1931])
> (BL, Add.Mss.56594, f.9)

The Society of Authors presumably therefore set about organising an agreement with the Lecture Agency Ltd. Gerald Christy (of the Lecture Agency Ltd) wrote to the Society, however, noting:

> ...We have run lectures for a great many well-known people in the Queens Hall and other Halls and have never had a formal agreement, but simply a letter from us saying what our terms and conditions would be and an acceptance from the lecturers. Mr. Masefield apparently wants some formal agreement as I think you said on the telephone you would draw up such an agreement based on our letter, for us to sign.
>
> (Gerald Christy, letter to Denys Kilham Roberts, 12 June 1931)
> (BL, Add.Mss.56594, f.24)

In contrast with 'a great many well-known people', Masefield was particularly anxious for a formal agreement. Another matter of concern was his liability for payment of Entertainment Tax. Gerald Christy explained on 20 July 1931 that it would be 'quite likely that it will be possible to get exemption from Entertainment Tax' if the lecture was for charitable or educational reasons. If not, tax would have to be paid if Masefield was 'giving the lecture for personal profit' (see BL, Add.Mss.56594, ff.91–93). 'Personal profit' obviously was Masefield's motivation as he wrote to The Society of Authors explaining that the lecture: '...is not for any charity; + Entertainment Tax will have to be paid'. Regarding the commission for the agent Masefield stated:

> ...I am willing that he shall have a commission of ten per cent on the receipts, with a minimum of ten guineas. If the minimum only be earned, it will be a pity.
>
> (John Masefield, letter to Denys Kilham Roberts, [22 July 1931])
> (BL, Add.Mss.56594, f.104)

By August Masefield had agreed on a sum of seventy-five pounds 'for advertisement purposes'. The lecture was delivered on 15 October and, as a letter from Gerald Christy to Masefield from November shows, a lack of 'comparatively quiet' times contributed to an 'adverse balance':

I enclose herewith cheque value £80/13/7d. which is the balance as shown on the statement I sent you yesterday. I have just learned from Mr. Mullett on the telephone that the amount paid for rent, staff, etc. came to £85/18/- so that it will show a small adverse balance. If times had been comparatively quiet I think the lecture would have shown quite a handsome profit. Anyhow it has been a great pleasure to us to have been of some service to you.

(Gerald Christy, letter to John Masefield, 6 November 1931)

(BL, Add.Mss.56595, f.50)

Copies seen: BL (11822.w.17) stamped 16 NOV 1931; HRHRC (TEMP M377 POE 1931A) inscribed 'For Judith. | from J.M., Novr 16. 1931.'

A106(b) Second English edition (limited signed edition) (1931)

POETRY | By | JOHN MASEFIELD | WILLIAM HEINEMANN LTD: LONDON
(All width centred and enclosed within three ruled borders: 116 × 750mm., 119 × 78mm. and 124 × 84mm. (in light green). None of the corners are precisely formed)

Bibliographies: Handley-Taylor p.59, Wight 81a

Collation: [A]⁸ B-D⁸; signatures right foot of page; 32 leaves; 205 × 143mm.; [i–iv] [1] 2–60

Page contents: [i] half-title: '*POETRY | John Masefield | A Lecture | given at the Queen's Hall | in London, on Thursday, | October 15th,* 1931' (the italic type contains a number of swash characters); [ii] '*This Edition, numbered and signed | by the Author, is limited to* 275 | *copies. | This copy is number..........*'; [iii] title-page; [iv] 'PRINTED | IN GT. BRITAIN | AT THE WINDMILL PRESS'; [1]–60 text

Paper: laid paper (no watermark), chain-lines 39–42mm. apart

Running title: '[rule, 84mm.] | *Poetry* [ranged left with page number ranged right] | [rule, 84mm.]' on both verso and recto, pp.2–60

Binding: light brown cloth (see notes). On spine, reading lengthways up spine, from foot, in gold: 'POETRY – JOHN MASEFIELD'; horizontally at foot of spine: 'Heinemann'. On upper cover, in gold: 'POETRY | [rule] | JOHN | MASEFIELD | [design of cockerel: 20 × 13mm.]' Lower cover: blank. Top edge gilt, lower outside edge untrimmed, fore edge uncut. Sewn head band (in white) and white marker ribbon. Binding measurements: 211 × 145mm. (covers), 211 × 20mm. (spine). The binding includes bevelled edges. End-papers: laid paper (no watermark), chain-lines 39–42mm. apart.

Publication date: published, according to the *English Catalogue of Books,* November 1931

Price: 8s.6d.

Contents:
as for A106(a)

Notes:
This edition appears to use the same setting of text as in A106(a). The text commences with a drop-capital.

Wight states this edition is 'bound in yellow cloth'. This is presumably not a binding variant but Wight's rendering of the light brown cloth described above.

Handley-Taylor does not give the date of publication for this volume. He does, however, state that A106(a) was published on 16 November 1931. Copies in the British Library reveal that A106(a) is stamped 16 NOV 1931 while this limited signed edition is stamped 9 DEC 1931. Both volumes are listed for November 1931 in the *English Catalogue of Books.* I therefore suggest that this edition was issued slightly later than A106(a). This is also suggested by inscribed copies.

The publishing agreement for this title between Masefield and Heinemann was dated 29 October 1931 (see Archives of The Society of Authors). The agreement refers to both 3s.6d. and 8s.6d. editions (A106(a) and A106(b)) and a limitation of 250 copies. This figure was, presumably, revised.

Copies seen: private collection (PWE) number 101, signed '101 | John Masefield.' on p.[ii]; private collection (PWE) number 132, signed '132 | John Masefield.' on p.[ii]; BL (11644.ccc.76) number 253, signed '253 | John Masefield.' on p.[ii] stamped 9 DEC 1931; HRHRC (TEMP M377 POE 1931B cop.1) number 255, signed '255. | John Masefield.' on p.[ii] additionally inscribed 'For Judith, | from Zob. | Dec 21. 1931.'; HRHRC (TEMP M377 POE 1931B cop.2) number 273, signed '273 | John Masefield.' on p.[ii]; HRHRC (PN1055 M38 1931A) number 256, signed '256 | John Masefield.' on p.[ii] additionally inscribed 'For Lew, | from Zob. | Dec 21. 1931.' and signed by J[udith] Masefield

A106(c) First American edition (1932)

POETRY | JOHN MASEFIELD | NEW YORK | THE MACMILLAN COMPANY | 1932
(The title is printed in ornate type)
(All width centred)

Bibliographies: Handley-Taylor p.59 (see notes), Wight 81b

Collation: [A-C]⁸; 24 leaves; 188 × 126mm.; [i–viii] 1–38 [39–40]

Page contents: [i] half-title: 'POETRY'; [ii] '*BOOKS BY JOHN MASEFIELD* | PLAYS | [10 titles listed] | POETRY | [14 titles listed] | OTHER WORKS | [10 titles listed]'; [iii] title-page; [iv] 'COPYRIGHT, 1932, BY JOHN MASEFIELD. | All rights reserved–no part of this book may be | reproduced in any form without permission in writing | from the publisher, except by a reviewer who wishes | to quote brief passages in connection with a review | written for inclusion in magazine or newspaper. | Set up and printed. Published January, 1932. | SET UP BY BROWN BROTHERS LINOTYPERS | PRINTED IN THE UNITED STATES OF AMERICA | BY THE FERRIS PRINTING COMPANY'; [v] 'A LECTURE | *Given at the Queen's Hall* | *in London* | *On Thursday, October 15, 1931*'; [vi] blank; [vii] 'POETRY'; [viii] blank; 1–38 text; [39–40] blank

Paper: wove paper

Running title: 'POETRY' (20mm.) on both verso and recto, pp.2–38

Binding: blue-green cloth (see notes). Spine: blank. On upper cover: blank with pale pink laid paper label (38 × 79mm.) on which: '[ornament] POETRY [ornament] | JOHN MASEFIELD' (within ruled border: 32 × 73mm.) Lower cover: blank. Top and lower outside edges trimmed, fore edge roughly trimmed. Binding measurements: 193 × 128mm. (covers), 193 × 19mm. (spine). End-papers: wove paper.

Publication date: published, according to Handley-Taylor, 5 January 1932

Price: $1.00

Contents:
as for A106(a)

Notes:
The italic type contains a number of swash characters.

Page numbers appear within square brackets. Thus, [1], [2], etc. The square brackets are embellished at the centre.

Wight describes the colour of the cloth binding as 'blue cloth' with 'a yellow paper label'.

A publishing agreement for this title between Masefield and Macmillan was dated 22 August 1931 (see Archives of The Society of Authors). The agreement refers to 'a licence to publish in volume form in the United States of America and Canada a work the subject of which is based upon a lecture to be delivered by him on October 15. 1931 in London (exact title to be determined)'.

Handley-Taylor lists this American volume separately from the English edition. He describes it as 'Essays'. This is incorrect for the text comprises the single lecture as in A106(a).

Copies seen: Columbia University, Barnard College, The Ella Weed Library (82M37 U53 C.1)

A107 A TALE OF TROY   1932

A107(a) First English edition (1932)

A TALE OF TROY | BY | JOHN MASEFIELD | [ornament] | [publisher's device of a windmill] | *LONDON* | WILLIAM HEINEMANN LTD. | 1932
(All width centred)

Bibliographies: Handley-Taylor p.59, Wight 82

Collation: [A]⁸ B-C⁸ D¹⁰; D2 is also signed; signatures right foot of page; 34 leaves; 183 × 119mm.; [i–x] 1–57 [58]

Page contents: [i–ii] blank; [iii] half-title: 'A TALE OF TROY'; [iv] '*ALSO BY JOHN MASEFIELD* | PLAYS: | [10 titles listed] | POETRY: | [14 titles listed] | OTHER WORKS: | [10 titles listed]'; [v] title-page; [vi] 'PRINTED IN GREAT BRITAIN | AT THE WINDMILL PRESS'; [vii] 'TO | MY WIFE'; [viii] blank; [ix] '*I Thank the beautiful Speakers:* | SYBIL HERIZ-SMITH | ROSE BRUFORD | DULCIE BOWIE | RONALD WATKINS | JUDITH MASEFIELD | AMY REAN | *and* | ALBERT FOWLER | *who first told this tale* | *on Midsummer Night*, 1932'; [x] blank; 1–57 text; [58] blank

Paper: wove paper

Running title: 'A TALE OF TROY' (36mm.) on verso; recto title comprises poem title, pp.2–57

Binding: blue cloth. On spine, in gold: 'A | Tale | of | Troy | [ornament] | John | Masefield | *Heinemann*' (all width centred). On upper cover, in gold: 'A TALE OF TROY | JOHN MASEFIELD' (within blind ruled border: 188 × 118mm.) On lower cover, in blind: publisher's device of a windmill (ranged lower right). All edges trimmed. Binding measurements: 189 × 122mm. (covers), 189 × 23mm. (spine). End-papers: wove paper.

Publication date: the sales ledger preserved in the Heinemann Archive suggests publication on 19 September 1932 in an edition of 4000 copies

Price: 5s.

Contents:
The Taking of Helen ('Menelaus, the Spartan King,')
The Going to Troy ('He took her to Troy, the windy town')

Klytaimnestra ('I am that Klytaimnestra whom Agamemnon wedded,')
The Spearman ('You have heard the lady, making her complaints.')
The Horse ('My Father, King Epeios of the Islands,')
Sthenelus' Daughter *The Entry into Troy* ('King Sthenelus, my Father, has often told me')
The Trojans about the Horse *What Priam Said* ('"Apollo's self commanded Agamemnon')
Kassandra ('I was the thing they heard, I am Kassandra.')
Sthenelus' Daughter *In the Horse, till Sunset* ('That was the voice those hidden in the Horse heard.')
[Sthenelus' Daughter] *In the Horse, Sunset till Cockcrow* ('"Then, to our joy, quick steps came up the courtyard,')
The Surprise ('You have heard the story of the Horse of Troy.')
Epilogue *Spoken by Kassandra* ('Though many died and many fled')

Notes:

A series of poems recounting parts of the Homeric tale. Performed in the Music Room, Boars Hill in June 1932.

Masefield appears to have approached Heinemann about this work during May 1932. C.S. Evans noted that he would write '...about THE SACK OF TROY...' but wanted, first, to consult his sales manager (see C.S. Evans, letter to John Masefield, 31 May 1932) (HRHRC, MS (Masefield, J.) Recip William Heinemann Ltd.) Advice from a sales manager may have been appropriate since the autumn of 1932 was to see much publishing activity:

> We are planning to publish THE COLLECTED POEMS in November, A TALE OF TROY in October and it would seem that September would be the best time for RECENT PROSE.
>
> (C.S. Evans, letter to John Masefield, 8 July 1932)
> (HRHRC, MS (Masefield, J.) Recip William Heinemann Ltd.)

The typescript was acknowledged at the end of June (see C.S. Evans, letter to John Masefield, 27 June 1932) (HRHRC, MS (Masefield, J.) Recip William Heinemann Ltd.) 'First rough proofs' were sent (together with the return of the manuscript) on 8 August 1932 (see B.F. Oliver, letter to John Masefield, 8 August 1932) (HRHRC, MS (Masefield, J.) Recip William Heinemann Ltd.) and a 'corrected set of first proofs' was sent two days later (see B.F. Oliver, letter to John Masefield, 10 August 1932) (HRHRC, MS (Masefield, J.) Recip William Heinemann Ltd.) Three sets in book form of the revised proofs were sent on 19 August 1932 (see B.F. Oliver, letter to John Masefield, 19 August 1932) (HRHRC, MS (Masefield, J.) Recip William Heinemann Ltd.)

A few days before publication, C.S. Evans suggested the price of the published volume should be 5s.:

> A TALE OF TROY makes, as you know, only 64 pages; and I suppose that 3/6d. would be considered the right price for a book of this size. It seem to me, however, that a book of poetry should not be priced according to its bulk and that people who want to read Masefield will pay 5/- as willingly as 3/6d.
>
> (C.S. Evans, letter to John Masefield, 7 September 1932)
> (HRHRC, MS (Masefield, J.) Recip William Heinemann Ltd.)

The publishing agreement for this title between Masefield and Heinemann was dated 16 September 1932 (see Archives of The Society of Authors). The agreement refers to a publication price of 5s.

In 1952 the Canadian Broadcasting Corporation applied to The Society of Authors to broadcast a script based on *A Tale of Troy*. Masefield stated his dislike of the Canadian changes:

> The tale, as I made it, is a succession of tales, making up the tale of Troy; and needed no jumbling nor other device to tell the tale. As I was then working with skilled speakers, I tried it with them as a story; and am satisfied that it is a story, that it is essentially for narrative; and that it should be kept as a narrative.
>
> (John Masefield, letter to Miss Lehmann, 27 February [1952])
> (BL, Add.Mss.56623, f.116)

Copies seen: private collection (PWE); BL (11640.h.47) stamped 19 SEP 1932

A107(b) *First American edition (1932)*

A TALE OF TROY | by JOHN MASEFIELD | [ornament] | NEW YORK | THE MACMILLAN COMPANY | 1932 (All width centred)

Bibliographies: Handley-Taylor p.59, Wight 82a

Collation: [A-D]⁸; 32 leaves; 215 × 143mm.; [i–xiv] 1–46 [47–50]

Page contents: [i–ii] blank; [iii] half-title: 'A TALE OF TROY'; [iv] blank; [v] title-page; [vi] 'COPYRIGHT, 1932, | BY JOHN MASEFIELD | [rule] | All rights reserved–no part of this book | may be reproduced in any form without | permission in writing from the publisher, | except by a reviewer who wishes to quote brief | passages in connection with a review written | for inclusion in magazine or newspaper. | [rule] | Set up and electrotyped. Published, October, 1932. | PRINTED IN THE UNITED STATES OF AMERICA'; [vii] 'TO | MY WIFE'; [viii] blank; [ix] '*I Thank the beautiful Speakers:* | SYBIL HERIZ-SMITH [point] ROSE BRUFORD | DULCIE BOWIE [point] RONALD WATKINS | JUDITH MASEFIELD [point] AMY REAN | AND ALBERT FOWLER | *who first told this tale* | *on Midsummer Night, 1932*'; [x] blank; [xi] contents (12 individual poems listed under 11 headings with page references); [xii] blank; [xiii] 'A TALE OF TROY'; [xiv] blank; 1–46 text; [47–50] blank

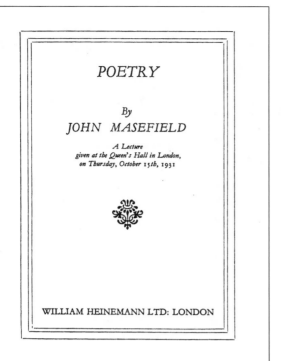

POETRY

By
JOHN MASEFIELD

A Lecture
given at the Queen's Hall in London,
on Thursday, October 15th, 1931

WILLIAM HEINEMANN LTD: LONDON

A106(a) title-page

A TALE OF TROY

BY
JOHN MASEFIELD

LONDON
WILLIAM HEINEMANN LTD.
1932

A107(a) title-page

END AND BEGINNING

BY
JOHN MASEFIELD

★

LONDON
WILLIAM HEINEMANN LTD
1933

A108(a) title-page

For Rudo & Viola.
from John Masefield.
Oct'. 1933.

Words spoken at the opening of the Gateway

set up at

HAWKSMOOR NATURE RESERVE
near Cheadle, Staffs.,

in memory of

JOHN RICHARD BEECH MASEFIELD,
on Saturday, October 21st, 1933.

A110(a) title-page

JOHN MASEFIELD

The Bird of Dawning

London
WILLIAM HEINEMANN LTD

A111(a) title-page

JOHN MASEFIELD

The Bird of Dawning

WITH ILLUSTRATIONS BY
CLAUDE MUNCASTER

London
WILLIAM HEINEMANN LTD
1933

A111(c) title-page

THE
TAKING OF THE GRY
BY
JOHN MASEFIELD

LONDON: WILLIAM HEINEMANN LTD
1934

A113(aa) title-page

P O E M S

BY JOHN MASEFIELD

COMPLETE EDITION
WITH RECENT POEMS

NEW YORK
THE MACMILLAN COMPANY
1935

A114(a) title-page

Paper: wove paper (watermark: '[device including pair of scales: 81 × 39mm.] | *Utopian*' – see notes)

Running title: none

Binding: blue cloth. On spine, reading lengthways down spine from head, in gold: 'A TALE OF TROY [point] Masefield Macmillan [point]'. On upper cover, in gold: 'A TALE OF TROY | John Masefield | [ornament]'. Lower cover: blank. Top edge trimmed, others roughly trimmed. Binding measurements: 221 × 144mm. (covers), 221 × 19mm. (spine). End-papers: wove paper.

Publication date: published, according to Handley-Taylor, 18 October 1931 (see notes)

Price: $1.50

Contents:
The Taking of Helen ('Menelaus, the Spartan King,')
The Going to Troy ('He took her to Troy, the windy town')
Klytaimnestra ('I am that Klytaimnestra whom Agamemnon wedded,')
The Spearman ('You have heard the lady, making her complaints.')
The Horse ('My Father, King Epeios of the Islands,')
Sthenelus' Daughter *The Entry into Troy* ('King Sthenelus, my Father, has often told me')
The Trojans about the Horse *What Priam Said* ('"Apollo's self commanded Agamemnon')
Kassandra ('I was the thing they heard, I am Kassandra.')
Sthenelus' Daughter *In the Horse, till Sunset* ('That was the voice those hidden in the Horse heard.')
[Sthenelus' Daughter] *In the Horse, Sunset till Cockcrow* ('Then, to our joy, quick steps came up the courtyard,')
The Surprise ('You have heard the story of the Horse of Troy.')
Epilogue *Spoken by Kassandra* ('Though many died and many fled')

Notes:
The watermark lettering '*Utopian*' includes a number of swash characters.

The lettering on the spine includes two points. The first (between 'TROY' and 'Masefield') is larger than the point following 'Macmillan'.

In contrast to A107(a), an (untitled) contents page is included in this volume.

A publishing agreement for this title between Masefield and Macmillan was dated 27 June 1932 (see Archives of The Society of Authors). The agreement refers to 'a licence to publish in volume form in the United States of America and Canada a work the subject or title of which is A Tale of Troy – (a book of verse)'.

Handley-Taylor cites a publication date of 18 October 1931 for this volume. This is quoted by Wight and is clearly an error. The correct publication date should read 18 October 1932.

Copies seen: private collection (ROV) inscribed 'For Alice, | from Jan. | November. 1932.'

A108 END AND BEGINNING   1933

A108(a) First English edition (limited signed edition) (1933)

END AND BEGINNING [in light green] | BY | JOHN MASEFIELD | [five-point star] [in light green] | [publisher's device of a windmill] [in light green] | *LONDON* | WILLIAM HEINEMANN LTD | 1933
(All width centred)

Bibliographies: Handley-Taylor p.59, Wight 83

Collation: [A]⁸ B-D⁸; signatures right foot of page; 32 leaves; 226 × 138mm.; [i–x] 1–50 [51–54]

Page contents: [i–ii] blank; [iii] half-title: 'END AND BEGINNING'; [iv] *'This Edition, numbered and signed | by the Author, is limited to* 275 | *copies for sale in Great Britain and | Ireland | No...................................*'; [v] title-page; [vi] 'Printed in Great Britain | at The Windmill Press, Kingswood, Surrey'; [vii] 'To | FLORENCE'; [viii] blank; [ix] 'PERSONS | [dramatis personae and original cast listed] | *The scene is a small room in Fotheringhay Castle. A | settle with a canopy is in the centre. A small table | with ink, pens, wine and a cup is to the Actors' Left | of this settle.*'; [x] blank; 1–50 text; [51–54] blank

Paper: wove paper (watermark: 'VAN GELDER ZONEN')

Running title: 'END AND BEGINNING' (54mm.) on both verso and recto

Binding: blue cloth. On spine, reading lengthways up spine, from foot, in gold: 'END AND BEGINNING – JOHN MASEFIELD'; horizontally at foot of spine: publisher's device of a windmill with 'W [point]' and 'H' (see notes). On upper cover, in silver: 'END AND BEGINNING | JOHN MASEFIELD | [ornament]'. Lower cover: blank. Top edge gilt, lower outside edge untrimmed, fore edge uncut. Sewn head band (in white) and blue marker ribbon. Binding measurements: 233 × 141mm. (covers), 233 × 24mm. (spine). The binding includes bevelled edges. End-papers: wove paper. Volume contained in slip-case covered with light blue paper.

Publication date: published, according to Handley-Taylor, 3 July 1933

Price: 10s.6d.

Contents:
End and Beginning ('MARY | I am that Mary Stuart, the Queen of Scotland:')

Notes:
A play in verse recounting the death of Mary Stuart. A brief reference in the published letters to Florence Lamont (see E2) suggests the play was first performed in the Music Room, Boars Hill in November 1932.

Handley-Taylor erroneously refers to this work as *The End and Beginning*.

'Two sets of the first proofs of END AND BEGINNING with the manuscript' were sent to Masefield on 7 April 1933 (see B.F. Oliver, letter to John Masefield, 7 April 1933) (HRHRC, MS (Masefield, J.) Recip William Heinemann Ltd.). Revised 'book-proofs' followed on 20 April:

> I send you herewith a couple of copies of the revised book-proofs of END AND BEGINNING and shall be obliged if you will kindly pass and return one copy in due course.
>
> (B.F. Oliver, letter to John Masefield, 20 April 1933)
> (HRHRC, MS (Masefield, J.) Recip William Heinemann Ltd.)

A little over one month later the sheets of the limitation were sent::

> We have sent off to you by passenger-train the title section of the Limited Edition of END AND BEGINNING and I shall be glad if you will kindly sign the tablet, and return to me in due course.
>
> (B.F. Oliver, letter to John Masefield, 26 May 1933)
> (HRHRC, MS (Masefield, J.) Recip William Heinemann Ltd.)

Copies seen: private collection (PWE) number 234, signed '234 | John Masefield.' on p.[iv]; BL (11643.d.66) number 255, signed '255 | John Masefield.' on p.[iv]; stamped 5 JUL 1933; Columbia University Libraries (Special Collections B825.M377.Q36.1933.c.2) number 263, signed '263 | John Masefield.' on p.[iv], additionally inscribed 'For Con | from Jan. | July 1. 1933.'

A108(b) First American edition (1933)

END AND BEGINNING | BY | JOHN MASEFIELD | [five-point star] | *NEW YORK* | THE MACMILLAN COMPANY | 1933
(All width centred)

Bibliographies: Handley-Taylor p.59, Wight 83a

Collation: [A-B]⁸ C-D⁸; signatures right foot of page; 32 leaves; 187 × 129mm.; [i–x] 1–50 [51–54]

Page contents: [i–ii] blank; [iii] half-title: 'END AND BEGINNING'; [iv] *'ALSO BY JOHN MASEFIELD* | PLAYS: | [12 titles listed] | POETRY: | [14 titles listed] | FICTION: | [four titles listed] | GENERAL: | [eight titles listed]'; [v] title-page; [vi] *'Copyright, 1933, by* | JOHN MASEFIELD | [rule] | All rights reserved–no part of this book | may be reproduced in any form without | permission in writing from the publisher, | except by a reviewer who wishes to quote brief | passages in connection with a review written | for inclusion in magazine or newspaper. | PRINTED IN THE UNITED STATES OF AMERICA | BY THE POLYGRAPHIC COMPANY OF AMERICA, N.Y.'; [vii] 'To | FLORENCE'; [viii] blank; [ix] 'END AND BEGINNING'; [x] 'PERSONS | [dramatis personae and original cast listed] | *The scene is a small room in Fotheringhay Castle. A | settle with a canopy is in the centre. A small table | with ink, pens, wine and a cup is to the Actors' Left | of this settle.*'; 1–50 text; [51–54] blank

Paper: wove paper

Running title: 'END AND BEGINNING' (54mm.) on both verso and recto, pp.2–50

Binding: blue cloth. On spine, reading lengthways down spine from head, in gold: 'END AND BEGINNING MASEFIELD'. On upper cover, in gold: 'END AND BEGINNING | JOHN MASEFIELD'. Lower cover: blank. Top and lower outside edges trimmed, fore edge roughly trimmed. Binding measurements: 193 × 130mm. (covers), 193 × 20mm. (spine). End-papers: wove paper.

Publication date: published, according to Handley-Taylor, 22 August 1933

Price: $1.50

Contents:
as for A108(a)

Notes:
The publicity material in the preliminaries that lists Masefield's work (appearing on p.[iv]) bears a marked similarity to that present in Heinemann editions of Masefield. Moreover, titles as cited here are those of English editions (separate editions of Masefield's Racine translations and *St. George and the Dragon*, for example). However, this listing is not the same as is present in A108(a).

Wight incorrectly notes the signatures of this edition as [A-D]⁸

The text appears to use the same setting of type as A108(a). Moreover a number of minute typographical features have been observed in common. For example, a damaged 'Q' on p.2, line 13 and damaged italic letters '*R*' and '*B*' on p.7. These features do not appear in A108(c).

The publishing agreement for this volume between Masefield and Macmillan was dated 29 May 1933 (see Archives of The Society of Authors). The agreement refers to 'a licence to publish in volume form… in the United States of America and Canada a work the subject of which is End and Beginning – a short play'.

Copies seen: private collection (PWE); University of Warwick Library (PR6025A77/MAS)

A108(c) Second English edition (1934)

END AND BEGINNING | BY | JOHN MASEFIELD | [five-point star] | [publisher's device of a windmill] | *LONDON* | WILLIAM HEINEMANN LTD | 1934
(All width centred)

Bibliographies: Handley-Taylor p.59, Wight 83b

Collation: [A]⁸ B-D⁸; signatures right foot of page; 32 leaves; 183 × 121mm.; [i–x] 1–50 [51–54]

Page contents: [i–ii] blank; [iii] half-title: 'END AND BEGINNING'; [iv] '*ALSO BY JOHN MASEFIELD* | PLAYS: | [10 titles listed] | POETRY: | [15 titles listed] | OTHER WORKS: | [12 titles listed]'; [v] title-page; [vi] 'Printed in Great Britain | at *The Windmill Press*, Kingswood, Surrey'; [vii] 'To | FLORENCE'; [viii] blank; [ix] 'PERSONS | [dramatis personae and original cast listed] | *The scene is a small room in Fotheringhay Castle. A | settle with a canopy is in the centre. A small table | with ink, pens, wine and a cup is to the Actors' Left | of this settle.*'; [x] blank; 1–50 text; [51–54] blank

Paper: wove paper

Running title: 'END AND BEGINNING' (54mm.) on both verso and recto, pp.2–50

Binding: blue cloth. On spine, reading lengthways up spine, from foot, in gold: 'END AND BEGINNING – JOHN MASEFIELD'; horizontally at foot of spine: 'HEINEMANN'. Upper cover: blank. On lower cover, in blind: publisher's device of a windmill (ranged lower right). All edges trimmed. Binding measurements: 189 × 123mm. (covers), 189 × 18mm. (spine). End-papers: wove paper.

Publication date: published, according to Handley-Taylor, 19 February 1934

Price: 3s.6d.

Contents:
as for A108(a)

Notes:
The text has been entirely re-set for this edition. Note that the five-point star on the title-page is at a different angle from that present in A108(a) and A108(b).

A letter from C.S. Evans, dated 5 February 1934, suggests that from proof stage to publication was a quick process for this edition:

> …two sets of proofs of END AND BEGINNING will be sent to you from Kingswood tomorrow.
>
> (C.S. Evans, letter to John Masefield, 5 February 1934)
> (HRHRC, MS (Masefield, J.) Recip William Heinemann Ltd.)

Publication details of this edition have proven elusive within the sales ledger preserved in the Heinemann Archive. The publishing agreement for this edition between Masefield and Heinemann was dated 22 February 1934 (see Archives of The Society of Authors). The agreement refers to a publication price of 3s.6d.

Copies seen: BL (011641.ee.99) stamped 20 FEB 1934

A109 THE CONWAY FROM HER FOUNDATION TO THE PRESENT DAY   1933

A109(a) First English edition (1933)

THE CONWAY | FROM HER FOUNDATION | TO THE PRESENT DAY | [five point star] | By JOHN MASEFIELD | [publisher's device of a windmill] | LONDON | WILLIAM HEINEMANN LTD
(All width centred)

Bibliographies: Handley-Taylor p.59, Wight 84

Collation: [A]⁸ B-P⁸ Q⁴ (J not used); signatures right foot of page; 124 leaves; 223 × 142mm.; [i–x] [1–2] 3–17 [18–20] 21–81 [82–84] 85–121 [122–24] 125–231 [232] 233–35 [236–38]; illustrations (on glossy paper) tipped-in on pp.[iii], 6, 15, 23, 27, 31, 39, 41, 51, 63, 73, 81, 91, 95, 107, 117, 129 139, 143, 151, 159, 161, 167, 171, 181, 191, 201, 207, 209, 221, 227 and 233

Page contents: [i] half-title: 'THE CONWAY'; [ii] '*ALSO BY JOHN MASEFIELD* | PLAYS: | [12 titles listed] | POETRY: | [14 titles listed] | FICTION: | [four titles listed] | GENERAL: | [eight titles listed]'; [iii] title-page (with additional leaf tipped-in on the verso of which is the black and white photograph frontispiece: 101 × 132mm., 'THE CONWAY, ON PRIZE DAY, 1932'); [iv] 'FIRST PUBLISHED 1933 | PRINTED IN GREAT BRITAIN | AT THE WINDMILL PRESS, SURREY'; [v] 'TO | CAPTAIN AND MRS. BROADBENT'; [vi] blank; [vii–viii] 'CONTENTS' (25 individual items listed with page references); [ix–x] 'ILLUSTRATIONS' (32 individual items listed with page references); [1] 'PART I | *The Conway's word to the new-comer.*' [poetic preface]; [2] blank; 3–17 text of 'Part I'; [18] blank; [19] 'PART II | *After forty years*' [poetic preface]; [20] blank; 21–81 text of 'Part II'; [82] blank; [83] 'PART III'; [84] blank; 85–121 text of 'Part III'; [122] blank; [123] 'PART IV'; [124] blank; 125–58 text of 'Part IV'; 159–71 text of 'Thirty Years after 1902–1932'; 172–79 text of 'Some *Conway* Worthies'; 180–84 text of 'Chief Officers'; 185–88 text of 'Second Officers'; 189 text of 'Gunners'; 190–92 text of 'Masters-At-Arms'; 193–94 text of 'Matrons, 1877'; 195–98 text of 'Masters'; 199–205 text of 'Instructors'; 206–209 text of 'The *Conway-Worcester* Race'; 210–13 text of 'Glossary of *Conway* Slang Ancient and Modern'; 214 text of 'Royal Naval Cadetships'; 215–16 text of 'Direct Entry from The *Conway* into The Royal Navy'; 217–20 text of 'Cadets who have passed into The Royal Navy direct from The *Conway*' and 'Royal Naval Reserve'; 221–23 text of 'Old Boys who have entered The Royal Navy otherwise than by direct entry from The *Conway*'; 224–25 text of 'Old Boys who have entered The Royal Indian Marine'; 226–27 text of 'Old Boys who have entered The Bengal Pilot Service'; 228–30 text of 'Honours List. 1914–1919'; 231 text of 'Winners of The Royal Gold Medal'; [232] blank; 233–34 text of Acknowledgments; 235 text of 'The *Conway* Gulls'; [236–38] blank

Paper: wove paper

Running title: 'THE CONWAY' (36mm.) on both verso and recto, pp.4–234

Binding: blue cloth. On spine, in gold: 'THE | CONWAY | [design including anchor: 16 × 7mm.] | JOHN | MASEFIELD | HEINEMANN' (all width centred). On upper cover, in gold: design of H.M.S. *Conway* within ruled border: 64 × 40mm. On lower cover, in blind: publisher's device of a windmill (ranged lower right). All edges trimmed. Binding measurements: 229 × 147mm. (covers), 229 × 50mm. (spine). End-papers: wove paper illustrated in light green with fourteen cartoon illustrations of a naval theme, each enclosed within ruled borders (creating sixteen rectangles of which two are left blank). There is also a partial decorative border around the outside consisting of a wavy rule within an ornate bold rule.

Publication date: the sales ledger preserved in the Heinemann Archive suggests publication on 28 August 1933 in an edition of 4000 copies.

Price: 10s.6d.

Contents:
[Preface to Part I] *The Conway's word to the new-comer.* ('Here you will put off childhood and be free')
Part I ('The first suggestions for the establishment of a training ship...')
[Preface to Part II] *After forty years* ('Let us walk round: the night is dark but fine,')
Part II ('1859. Captain Howard Campbell was actually the very first cadet who joined...')
Part III ('As this ends the first half of the *Conway's* story, it may be well to...')
Part IV ('1897–99. "In my day there was a cadet, called by us 'Gully,' who used to do...')
Thirty Years after 1902–1932 (*Joining in* 1902. | All boys joined up after the holidays on the same day, new boys...')
Some *Conway* Worthies ('Of the many who have served the *Conway* since her establishment...')
Chief Officers ('The chief officer of the second *Conway* was TREWIN, "the Bengal..."')
Second Officers ('The second officer of the second *Conway* was EDWARD BRENCHLEY, an ex-naval...')
Gunners ('GEORGE HUNT. "E. Jarge" or "The Tartar," came on board...')
Masters-At-Arms ('WILLIAM POTTER. "Quack" or "Quacko." | He seems to have joined the ship...')
Matrons, 1877 ('"MRS. WILLIAMS was a lovely motherly woman liked by...')
Masters ('CHARLES BARTON, an old Greenwich schoolboy, head navigation teacher...')
Instructors ('DARBY, 1862. "A bit shrivelled, but had lungs that would lift the deck..."')
The *Conway-Worcester* Race ('The first race was in 1890 on the Thames. The races were rowed...')
Glossary of *Conway* Slang Ancient and Modern ('Ambitious, ambi Zealous, with a view to personal advantage...')
Royal Naval Cadetships ('Since the foundation of the ship, the Admiralty has granted to *Conway* cadets...')
Direct Entry from The *Conway* into The Royal Navy ('In the early years of the *Conway* nomination to the Royal Navy...')
Cadets Who Have Passed into The Royal Navy direct from The *Conway* ('(The years given are those they joined *Conway*...')
Royal Naval Reserve ('The Lords Commissioners of the Admiralty grant to the *Conway* a number...')
Old Boys who have entered The Royal Navy otherwise than by direct entry from The *Conway* ('(The years given are...')
Old Boys who have entered The Royal Indian Marine ('(The years given are those they joined *Conway*). | 1867...')
Old Boys who have entered The Bengal Pilot Service ('(The years given are those they joined *Conway*). | 1874...')
Honours List. 1914–1919 ('Names from the Honours Board and the Supplementary Board...')
Winners of The Royal Gold Medal ('1865. Oswald Hillkirk...')
[Acknowledgments] ('I thank all those who have helped me to compile this history. I thank, first...')
The *Conway* Gulls ('They died in the gales' roaring, in the smash')

Notes:
An historical account of the training ship H.M.S. *Conway* – Masefield's former school ship. A revised edition was issued in 1953 and simply entitled *The Conway* (see A109(c)).

Masefield's visit to the United States early in 1933 caused C.S. Evans to delay the despatch of proofs to the author:

> ...Knowing that you would be back in March, I kept the proofs of the CONWAY book for you. My plan is to publish in the early autumn unless you see anything against that.

(C.S. Evans, letter to John Masefield, 7 March 1933)
(HRHRC, MS (Masefield, J.) Recip William Heinemann Ltd.)

A 'copy of the revised page proofs of THE CONWAY' was sent on 26 May 1933 (see B.F. Oliver, letter to John Masefield, 26 May 1933) (HRHRC, MS (Masefield, J.) Recip William Heinemann Ltd.)

Masefield apparently supplied the photographic illustrations. Both Heinemann and Macmillan appear to have independently reproduced these from the same source:

> We have finished with the photographs in connection with their reproduction in THE CONWAY and they are ready to be returned to you. Messrs Lovat Dickson telephoned yesterday, however, to say that the Macmillan Company would like to reproduce from the originals and asked if we could send them out to New York. May we do this?
>
> (Louisa Callender, letter to John Masefield, 26 April 1933)
(HRHRC, MS (Masefield, J.) Recip William Heinemann Ltd.)

The section entitled 'Masters-At-Arms' (pp.190–92) comprises a prose account of William Potter. This caused offence and in some copies a poem is substituted. This is entitled 'The Dying Foretopman'. The first line reads 'There was silence like death on the decks on the decks of the *Conway*'. This is acknowledged as a 'chorus adapted from *The Dying Cowboy*, author unknown'. The suppression and replacement of text is discussed, at length, in the archives of The Society of Authors. Masefield first wrote to The Society of Authors during March 1934 (and therefore over six months after initial publication):

> I have today received the enclosed letter from a Mr Potter. His father was for many years Master-at-Arms on board H.M.S. *Conway*, where, when I was a boy, I saw him daily for about two years. In my History of the *Conway*, published last August, I print some reminiscences of him pp 190–192 (I enclose a copy of the book) + it is to these passages that the son takes objection.
>
> I do not doubt that there are living some 3000 old Conway boys who would testify to the truth of the remarks, + to the mildness of their statement of the case. The passages come from old *Conway* boys of different years. I will not apologize for the remarks, as I believe them all to be true. But I feel that I must place the letter and the matter in the hands of the Society, and to ask for the benefit of advice. It should be easy to omit all mention of the man in subsequent editions, if any should be called for; but he filled an important post on board for a very long time + the impression he left upon the cadets of those years was as the book describes. I believe that he died 30 years ago. May I ask you to be so kind as to give me the benefit of your advice?
>
> (John Masefield, letter to Denys Kilham Roberts, 19 March 1934)
(BL, Add.Mss.56600, ff.83–84)

The Society of Authors replied to Masefield on 20 March 1934 stating the legal situation:

> I do not think you need be much alarmed by Mr Potter junior. A libel action for damages can never be brought by the relatives of a dead man in respect of libels upon the latter. The only possible legal consequence of an alleged libel on a dead man is a prosecution for criminal libel, which can only succeed if the court is satisfied that the libel is so gross, and of such a kind, as to amount to a provocation to a breach of the peace. Such proceedings, which of course can bring no profit to the relatives, are rarely brought today and still more rarely succeed. I certainly do not think they would succeed in the present case, nor is it likely that any lawyer would encourage Mr. Potter to institute them.
>
> (Denys Kilham Roberts, letter to John Masefield, 20 March 1934)
(BL, Add.Mss.56600, ff.90–91)

Later during March, Masefield reconsidered his position, writing to The Society of Authors:

> Thinking over the matter of the late Mr Potter, I feel that it is hard on his children (whom I did not know of) to have the shortcomings laid bare. I am therefore causing the references to him to be expunged from the book; so that future copies will not mention him. After all, we have very kindly feelings about the old chap. I am writing to his son on these lines, and would like to thank you for you excellent letter.
>
> (John Masefield, letter to Denys Kilham Roberts, [March 1934])
(BL, Add.Mss.56600, f.195)

C.S. Evans acknowledged corrections for the volume and also 'the poem which is to take the place of the present pages 190, 191 and 192.' on 28 March 1934 (see C.S. Evans, letter to John Masefield, 28 March 1934) (HRHRC, MS (Masefield, J.) Recip William Heinemann Ltd.) A proof was sent on 10 April 1934 (see Louisa Callender, letter to John Masefield, 10 April 1934) (HRHRC, MS (Masefield, J.) Recip William Heinemann Ltd.) Subsequent copies of the book (presumably those held in stock by Heinemann) therefore had the fourth and fifth leaves of gathering N replaced. In examined copies these leaves are not conjugate, despite comprising the central leaves of the gathering. This suggests that copies were altered that had already been bound.

Masefield's letter to Potter's son produced, in reply, 'an abusive and threatening note'. After taking no action over this Masefield received another letter and subsequently wrote to The Society of Authors:

> Some two or three months ago, I sent you a letter from a Mr Potter who complained of remarks about his late Father in my history of HMS *Conway*. You were so kind as to give me advice in the matter.
>
> I wrote a friendly letter to the man, and received in reply an abusive and threatening note of which I took no notice. I have now received the enclosed from him. He has never "asked me what I am going to do", but dictated courses of action. However, he is now plainly in a more reasonable frame of mind than in the past.

Will you be so kind as to write to him on my behalf to say that the references to his late Father have been removed from the book? Copies sold from this time on will contain, I think, no direct reference to him. I will not apologize for the references, which were the considered opinions of half a dozen old *Conways*, + I cannot undertake to recall copies containing them.

(John Masefield, letter to Denys Kilham Roberts, [May 1934])
(BL, Add.Mss.56600, ff.196–197)

(The archives of The Society of Authors do not appear to preserve the letter Masefield had enclosed). The Society of Authors presumably wrote to Mr Potter as Masefield requested. A further letter from The Society of Authors to Masefield similarly does not appear to have survived although an undated letter from Masefield to The Society of Authors notes 'I will gladly accept your kind offer if Mr P should again let fly. At present he seems to be resting' (see BL, Add.Mss.56600, f.213). The Society of Authors had therefore presumably offered further legal suggestions to Masefield in the event of further correspondence from Mr Potter. There appears to have been none.

Described here as 'design including anchor' for both A109(a) and A109(b), Wight describes the spine device as 'anchor and rope device' for both editions. The ornament appears to include seaweed rather than rope, however. Despite the similarity between editions, the design is not exactly the same (and both are, additionally, different sizes).

The 'Acknowledgments' (noted in the contents listing but untitled within the text) include the following information relating to the dust-jacket and end-papers:

> I am grateful to Mr. K. D. Shoesmith and to Mr. A. J. Barnes, both old Conways, who have contributed, the one the book's wrapper, and the other the sketches used in the end-papers.

Copies seen: BL (8808.df.18) 'Masters-At-Arms' present on pp.190–92, stamped 28 AUG 1933; private collection (ROV) 'The Dying Foretopman' present on pp.190–92

A109(b) First American edition (1933)

THE CONWAY | FROM HER FOUNDATION | TO THE PRESENT DAY | [five point star] | By JOHN MASEFIELD | NEW YORK | THE MACMILLAN COMPANY | 1933
(All width centred)

Bibliographies: Handley-Taylor p.59, Wight 84a

Collation: [A-T]⁸ [U]⁴ (but signed [A]¹⁰ B¹⁰ C¹¹ D¹⁰ E⁹ F-H¹⁰ I⁹ K-L¹¹ M¹⁰ N⁹ O¹¹ P¹⁰ Q⁵; see note on American electrotype editions) (see notes) (J not used); signatures right foot of page; 156 leaves; 222 × 145mm.; [i–x] [1–2] 3–17 [18–20] 21–81 [82–84] 85–121 [122–24] 125–231 [232] 233–35 [236–38]; illustrations are bound within the gatherings (on wove paper, as in the rest of the volume)

Page contents: [i] half-title: 'THE CONWAY'; [ii] '*ALSO BY JOHN MASEFIELD* | PLAYS: | [12 titles listed] | POETRY: | [14 titles listed] | FICTION: | [four titles listed] | GENERAL: | [eight titles listed]'; [iii] title-page (with additional leaf (excluded from pagination but included in gathering) on the verso of which is the black and white photograph frontispiece: 101 × 132mm., 'THE CONWAY, ON PRIZE DAY, 1932'); [iv] '*Copyright, 1933, by* | JOHN MASEFIELD | [rule] | All rights reserved–no part of this book | may be reproduced in any form without | permission in writing from the publisher, | except by a reviewer who wishes to quote brief | passages in connection with a review written | for inclusion in magazine or newspaper. | PRINTED IN THE UNITED STATES OF AMERICA | BY THE POLYGRAPHIC COMPANY OF AMERICA,N.Y.'; [v] 'TO | CAPTAIN AND MRS. BROADBENT'; [vi] blank; [vii–viii] 'CONTENTS' (25 individual items listed with page references); [ix–x] 'ILLUSTRATIONS' (32 individual items listed with page references); [1] 'PART I | *The Conway's word to the new-comer.*' [poetic preface]; [2] blank; 3–17 text of 'Part I'; [18] blank; [19] 'PART II | *After forty years*' [poetic preface]; [20] blank; 21–81 text of 'Part II'; [82] blank; [83] 'PART III'; [84] blank; 85–121 text of 'Part III'; [122] blank; [123] 'PART IV'; [124] blank; 125–58 text of 'Part IV'; 159–71 text of 'Thirty Years after 1902–1932'; 172–79 text of 'Some *Conway* Worthies'; 180–84 text of 'Chief Officers'; 185–88 text of 'Second Officers'; 189 text of 'Gunners'; 190–92 text of 'Masters-At-Arms'; 193–94 text of 'Matrons, 1877'; 195–98 text of 'Masters'; 199–205 text of 'Instructors'; 206–209 text of 'The *Conway-Worcester* Race'; 210–13 text of 'Glossary of *Conway* Slang Ancient and Modern'; 214 text of 'Royal Naval Cadetships'; 215–16 text of 'Direct Entry from The *Conway* into The Royal Navy'; 217–20 text of 'Cadets who have passed into The Royal Navy direct from The *Conway*' and 'Royal Naval Reserve'; 221–23 text of 'Old Boys who have entered The Royal Navy otherwise than by direct entry from The *Conway*'; 224–25 text of 'Old Boys who have entered The Royal Indian Marine'; 226–27 text of 'Old Boys who have entered The Bengal Pilot Service'; 228–30 text of 'Honours List. 1914–1919'; 231 text of 'Winners of The Royal Gold Medal'; [232] blank; 233–34 text of Acknowledgments; 235 text of 'The *Conway* Gulls'; [236–38] blank

Paper: wove paper

Running title: 'THE CONWAY' (37mm.) on both verso and recto, pp.4–234

Binding: blue cloth. On spine, in gold: 'THE | CONWAY | [design including anchor: 17 × 8mm.] | JOHN | MASEFIELD | MACMILLAN | [point] – [point]' (all width centred). On upper cover, in gold: 'THE CONWAY | JOHN MASEFIELD'. Lower cover: blank. Top and lower outside edges trimmed, fore edge roughly cut. Binding measurements: 228 × 145mm. (covers), 228 × 46mm. (spine). End-papers: wove paper illustrated in light green with fourteen cartoon illustrations of a naval theme, each enclosed within ruled borders (creating sixteen rectangles of which two are left blank). There is also a partial decorative border around the outside consisting of a wavy rule within an ornate bold rule.

Publication date: published, according to Handley-Taylor, 28 August 1933

Price: $3.50

Contents:
as for A109(a)

Notes:
Wight in his bibliography records the signatures as [A]⁸ B-P⁸ Q⁴. This would indeed be correct if the illustrations were not bound with the text. However, conjugate leaves may comprise one leaf of text and one of illustration, for example. Wight therefore erroneously notes that the illustrations are tipped-in (unless there are two states of this edition). As suggested in the note on American electrotype editions, the signatures were only of importance during the electrotype process. After the plates were produced illustrations were presumably added to this edition to avoid tipped-in leaves. Consequently the printing and binding of the book were processes which no longer required the original stereotype signatures.

Wight records the design on the spine as an 'anchor and rope design'. This appears to be inaccurate. The design indeed includes an anchor but additional embellishment appears to be tangled seaweed.

The publishing agreement for this title between Masefield and Macmillan was dated 22 August 1931 (see Archives of The Society of Authors). The agreement refers to 'a licence to publish in volume form in the United States of America and Canada a work the subject or title of which is a short history of The Conway'.

Copies seen: private collection (ROV)

A109(c) Second English edition (1953)

THE CONWAY | [five-point star] | By JOHN MASEFIELD | [publisher's device of a windmill with 'W' and 'H'] | [rule, 55mm.] | WILLIAM HEINEMANN LTD | MELBOURNE : : LONDON : : TORONTO
(All width centred)

Bibliographies: Handley-Taylor p.59, Wight [unrecorded]

Collation: [A]¹⁶ B-K¹⁶ L⁸ (J not used); B5–K5 are also signed; signatures right foot of page; 168 leaves; 215 × 137mm.; [i–x] [1–2] 3–84 [85–86] 87–160 [161–62] 163–205 [206–208] 209–323 [324–26]; illustrations (on glossy paper) tipped-in on p.[v] and one set of two conjugate leaves is bound in the centre of gathering B.

Page contents: [i–ii] blank; [iii] half-title: 'THE CONWAY'; [iv] *THE WORKS OF JOHN MASEFIELD* | PLAYS: | [12 titles listed] | POETRY: | [20 titles listed] | FICTION: | [14 titles listed] | GENERAL: | [16 titles listed]'; [v] title-page (with additional leaf tipped-in on the verso of which is the black and white photograph frontispiece: 143 × 102mm., 'SIR ROBERT SEPPINGS | *National Maritime Museum*'); [vi] 'FIRST PUBLISHED 1933 | THIS REVISED EDITION 1953 | PRINTED IN GREAT BRITAIN | AT THE WINDMILL PRESS | KINGSWOOD, SURREY'; [vii] 'At its first appearance, this book was dedicated to | Captain Harvey Broadbent. I dedicate this revision to | the memory of his successor, Captain F. A. Richardson, | and to the two more recent Captains, | T. M. GODDARD | and | E. HEWITT | to all three of whom I am deeply indebted, for help given | in the making of this book.'; [viii] blank; [ix] 'ILLUSTRATIONS | Sir Robert Seppings *Frontispiece* | *The following illustrations, printed as a separate* | *section, will be found following page 38* | [eight individual items listed] | [text detailing sources of illustrations]'; [x] blank; [1] 'PART I'; [2] blank; 3–84 text of 'Part I'; [85] 'PART II'; [86] blank; 87–160 text of 'Part II'; [161] 'PART III'; [162] blank; 163–205 text of 'Part III'; [206] blank; [207] 'PART IV'; [208] blank; 209–264 text of 'Part IV'; 265 text of 'Acknowledgments'; 266–68 text of 'Appendix I Sir Robert Seppings'; 269–71 text of 'Appendix II Admiral Sir William Robert Mends, G.C.B.'; 272–74 text of 'The First *Conways* in The Navy List'; 275–76 text of 'Appendix IV H.M.S. *Winchester*'; 277–83 text of 'Appendix V. A. H.M.S. *Nile* Launch'; 284–88 text of 'Appendix V. B. H.M.S. *Nile* Conversion to steam. The Crimea. Service to 1857.'; 289–92 text of 'Appendix V. C. H.M.S. *Nile*. 1858 Her part at the inauguration of H.M.S. *Conway*.'; 293–97 text of 'Appendix V. D. H.M.S. *Nile* The storm. 1859 to end of naval service.'; 298–304 text of 'Appendix V. E. H.M.S. *Nile* Rig and sailing, etc., 1864'; 305–306 text of 'Appendix V. F. H.M.S. *Nile* Screw trunk.'; 307–309 text of 'Appendix V. G. H.M.S. *Nile*, Before her Loss Deck by Deck.'; 310–18 text of 'Appendix VI The Sister-Ships H.M.S. *London* H.M.S. *Rodney*'; 319–23 text of 'The Captains of The *Conway*'; [324–26] blank

Paper: wove paper

Running title: 'THE CONWAY' (30mm.) on both verso and recto, pp.4–323

Binding: blue cloth. On spine, in gold: 'THE | CONWAY | JOHN | MASEFIELD | HEINEMANN' (all width centred). On upper cover, in gold: design of H.M.S. *Conway* within ruled border: 64 × 40mm. On lower cover, in blind: publisher's device of a windmill (ranged lower right). All edges trimmed. Binding measurements: 221 × 138mm. (covers), 221 × 40mm. (spine). End-papers: glossy paper illustrated with technical side elevations of H.M.S. *Conway*, H.M.S. *Winchester* and H.M.S. *Nile*.

Publication date: the sales ledger preserved in the Heinemann Archive suggests publication on 9 November 1953 in an edition of 3000 copies

Price: 25s.

Contents:

Notes:

This edition, although termed 'revised' is substantially re-structred and re-written. The 'revised' volume is more of a naval history than a collection of reminiscences. The change is most obviously indicated by the alteration in end-papers. In the first edition there are cartoon sketches of naval life; in the 'revised' edition these are replaced by technical side elevations from the Admiralty Collection of Draughts in the National Maritime Museum.

In April 1952 Masefield sent letters to former pupils of the training ship. The letter explained that he was updating his history and asked:

> Will you be so very kind as to help me in this task, by telling me what impressed, delighted, (or shocked), you most during your time on board; and what you now look back upon with the greatest pleasure?
>
> (John Masefield, letter to former pupils of H.M.S. *Conway*, April 1952)
> (private collection (DGFR))

One recipient has stated that Masefield sent a letter to all old Conways and, at the time, there would have been 1500 to 2000 members of the Conway Club. Each letter was, apparently, signed.

Masefield first appears to have suggested a revised edition of this volume in 1950. A.S. Frere responded that '...the time certainly seems propitious for a re-issue of your book about H.M.S. Conway, and if you would care to revise it and bring it up-to-date, I shall be happy to go ahead with it.' (see A.S. Frere, letter to John Masefield, 6 June 1950) (HRHRC, MS (Masefield, J.) Recip William Heinemann Ltd.) A letter from March 1952 confesses slow progress during revision, and includes enquiries about illustrations:

> I am slowly going-on with the revision of the *Conway* history. Please, can you tell me if all the illustrations of the old edition are gone? Some were (I suppose) unique and cannot now be replaced. If this be as I fear, could these rarities be revived by photographing from the prints in the book: or would too much quality be lost thus? Please, roughly speaking, how many illustrations could you include in a book possibly 20pp longer than the old edition?
>
> (John Masefield, letter to [A.S.] Frere, 8 March 1952)
> (Archives of William Heinemann)

In October 1952 Masefield wrote again to Frere reporting his progress. He stated that he hoped '...to finish the *Conway* revision in a few weeks. It may be twice the length of the old book.' (see John Masefield, letter to [A.S.] Frere, 7 October [1952]) (Archives of William Heinemann). At the end of November 1952 Masefield reported progress and Frere replied:

> ...I was very pleased to get your letter of 27th November with the news that you have now almost finished the revised up to date history of the *Conway*. When the copy is ready, perhaps you would be kind enough to indicate which of the appendices you think might be done in smaller print.
>
> (A.S. Frere, letter to John Masefield, 28 November 1952)
> (HRHRC, MS (Masefield, J.) Recip William Heinemann Ltd.)

A letter (preserved in the Heinemann Archive) from Masefield dated 1 December [1952] to A.S. Frere enclosed 'the copy for the revised H.M.S. *Conway*'. During January 1953 Masefield was consulted about additional illustrations and the dust-jacket:

> ...As Mr. Frere told you in his letter of March 31st, the original illustrations can be reproduced from the first edition. If you will send along the four new illustrations, we can then see how to place them in the book. As Mr. Frere told you, the original blocks were melted down during the war, and I have not been able to trace a copy of the jacket. If you have one which you could lend us, either for making new blocks, or as an aid in designing, I should be very grateful.
>
> (Roland Gant, letter to John Masefield, 14 January 1953)
> (HRHRC, MS (Masefield, J.) Recip William Heinemann Ltd.)

With the sinking of the *Conway*, Roland Gant wrote to Masefield that as '...the last chapter of the CONWAY's history has been written... you will no doubt wish to add some note about the wreck to the new edition of your book...' (see Roland Gant, letter to John Masefield, 17 April 1953) (HRHRC, MS (Masefield, J.) Recip William Heinemann Ltd.) Two 'single-sided proofs of the new edition' were sent to Masefield at the beginning of June (see Roland Gant, letter to John Masefield, 12 June 1953) (HRHRC, MS (Masefield, J.) Recip William Heinemann Ltd.) Just over four months later Frere sent a pre-publication copy:

> I have much pleasure in sending you herewith an early copy, just off the press, of your revised edition of THE CONWAY. It is scheduled for publication on November 9th...
>
> > (A.S. Frere, letter to John Masefield, 19 October 1953)
> > (HRHRC, MS (Masefield, J.) Recip William Heinemann Ltd.)

Masefield responded with his thanks, praise for the appearance of the volume and a request for 'special' or presentation copies:

> Many thanks for your letter, with the early copy of the *Conway*. You have taken great pains with it, + turned it out well. My grateful thanks to you. So many have helped, that a long list of special copies will have to go out. I will send the list in a day or two, + ask you to have them sent off for me. Some special copies I shall have to send off myself, if I may have a dozen or two.
>
> > (John Masefield, letter to [A.S.] Frere, 21 October [1953])
> > (Archives of William Heinemann)

As with the first edition, the dust-jacket and end-papers each carry a specific design. On p.[ix] these are acknowledged as follows:

> The Endpapers are reproduced from the Admiralty Collection of Draughts in the National Maritime Museum... I must also thank... The *News Chronicle* for the use of the photograph of the wreck on the book's jacket.

There was no American printing of this edition. A.S. Frere wrote to Masefield during March 1952 noting that '...I shall look forward to hearing from Mr. Randall Williams of the Macmillan Company about the CONWAY history and the SHAKESPEARE book.' (see A.S. Frere, letter to John Masefield, 10 March 1953) (HRHRC, MS (Masefield, J.) Recip William Heinemann Ltd.) It appears that Macmillan eventually arranged to import copies of this work. A letter from the Heinemann firm dated 18 January 1954 to Masefield explains the circumstance and potential copyright problems:

> This morning I have a letter from the Macmillan Company in New York and they say:
>
> "We have now had an opportunity to examine the new edition of THE CONWAY and we are presented with something of a dilemma.
>
> "We should very much like to represent the book, but our exploration of the possible market for it has proved discouraging. And so what we should like to do, if it can be worked out, would be to import a small quantity from you. Specifically what we have in mind is to order 58/50 bound and jacketed copies of your edition.
>
> "There is, however, one notable problem, and that is the matter of copyright. If we should import from you, we should, of course, vitiate copyright on that basic material which first appeared here in the original book. The new material could, of course, be protected for five years under ad interim copyright. We would not, therefore, wish to import at all unless Mr. Masefield fully understood the copyright problem and agreed to let us proceed despite it. In all sincerity we do not believe that there is any danger that this edition would be pirated or that the property would be otherwise misused here."
>
> Will you very kindly let me know what you would like my reply to be?
>
> > (William Heinemann Ltd., letter to John Masefield, 18 January 1954)
> > (Archives of William Heinemann)

Masefield replied ten days later to Louisa Callender with permission for Macmillan to import:

> I have talked with Mr Williams, of the Macmillan Co, about the *Conway* matter. Please, by all means, let the Macmillan Co import what copies of the present edition of the *Conway* book they may wish.
>
> > (John Masefield, letter to [Louisa] Callender, 28 January 1954)
> > (Archives of William Heinemann)

Regarding a proposed German translation of this volume in March 1954 Masefield wrote to The Society of Authors that:

> The sinking of the ship last April, made the book obsolete long before it was published.
>
> > (John Masefield, letter to [Anne] Munro-Kerr, 18 March [1954])
> > (BL, Add.Mss.56625 ff.37–38)

Copies seen: BL (08809.b.30) stamped 19 OCT 1953

Reprinted:

| ['Reprinted'] | [second edition, second impression] | 17 Mar 1958 (recorded in sales ledger preserved in the Heinemann Archive) |

A110 WORDS SPOKEN AT THE OPENING OF THE GATEWAY SET UP AT HAWKSMOOR NATURE RESERVE

1933

A110(a) First English edition (1933)

Words spoken at the opening of the Gateway | set up at | *HAWKSMOOR NATURE RESERVE* | near Cheadle, Staffs., | in memory of | *JOHN RICHARD BEECH MASEFIELD,* | on Saturday, October 21st, 1933.
(All width centred)

Bibliographies: Handley-Taylor [unrecorded], Wight [unrecorded]

Collation: [A]²; 2 leaves; 253 × 159mm.; [1–4]

Page contents: [1] title-page; [2–3] text (signed, 'JOHN MASEFIELD.'); [4] blank

Paper: laid paper (watermark: '[Crown] | Abbey Mills | Greenfield'), chain-lines 25mm. apart

Running title: none

Binding: single sheet folded once. The title-page consequently comprises the upper wrapper. All edges trimmed. Binding measurements: 253 × 159mm. (wrappers), 253 × 5mm. (spine)

Publication date: published, as suggested by an inscribed copy, October 1933

Price: copies were not for sale

Contents:

[Words Spoken...] ('You have done me the honour to ask me to speak at the opening of this Gateway...')

Notes:

A copy held in the University of London library includes a handwritten dedication (dated October 1933) that confirms publication during the month of the speech.

It is assumed that Masefield had this speech privately printed.

Copies seen: ULL (Special Collections) inscribed 'For Rudo + Viola. [Sauter] | from John Masefield. | Octʳ. 1933.'

A111 THE BIRD OF DAWNING

1933

A111(a) First English edition (1933)

[rule, 59mm.] | JOHN MASEFIELD | [rule, 59mm.] | *The Bird of Dawning* | [publisher's device of a windmill with 'W [point]' and 'H'] | *London* | WILLIAM HEINEMANN LTD
(All width centred)

Bibliographies: Handley-Taylor p.59, Wight 85

Collation: [A]⁸ B-S⁸ T⁴ (J not used); signatures right foot of page; 148 leaves; 183 × 120mm.; [i–vi] 1–283 [284] 285–90

Page contents: [i] half-title: '*The Bird of Dawning*'; [ii] '*ALSO BY JOHN MASEFIELD* | PLAYS: | [12 titles listed] | POETRY: | [14 titles listed] | FICTION: | [four titles listed] | GENERAL: | [nine titles listed]'; [iii] title-page; [iv] 'FIRST PUBLISHED 1933 | PRINTED | IN GREAT BRITAIN | AT THE WINDMILL PRESS | KINGSWOOD | SURREY'; [v] 'TO | MY WIFE'; [vi] blank; 1–283 text; [284] blank; 285–90 'GLOSSARY'

Paper: wove paper

Running title: 'THE BIRD OF DAWNING' (69–71mm.) on both verso and recto, pp.2–283 and 'GLOSSARY' (30mm.) on both verso and recto, pp.286–90

Binding: blue cloth. On spine, in gold: 'THE | BIRD OF | DAWNING | [ornament] | JOHN | MASEFIELD | HEINEMANN' (all width centred). On upper cover, in gold: 'THE BIRD OF DAWNING | JOHN MASEFIELD' (within blind ruled border: 183 × 115mm.) On lower cover, in blind: publisher's device of a windmill (ranged lower right). All edges trimmed. Binding measurements: 189 × 123mm. (covers), 189 × 48mm. (spine). End-papers: wove paper.

Publication date: the sales ledger preserved in the Heinemann Archive suggests publication on 6 November 1933 in an edition of 15000 copies

Price: 7s.6d.

Contents:

The Bird of Dawning ('Nearly seventy years ago, Cruiser Trewsbury, the second mate of the homeward-bound...')
Glossary ('A.B. . . . An "Able-bodied" seaman; formerly one who had served five or seven years...')

Notes:

A novel of the China Tea Race described by a contemporary reviewer in *Punch* as 'the finest sea-yarn ever penned'. Sanford Sternlicht states in his study of Masefield that 'the storm scenes [in the novel] are perhaps even better than Conrads''. The novel has no chapter divisions.

Two sets of 'first proofs' were sent to Masefield on 6 September (together with the return of the manuscript). The author was asked to '… correct the proofs and return one set to revise into book form' (see B.F. Oliver, letter to John Masefield, 6 September 1933) (HRHRC, MS (Masefield, J.) Recip William Heinemann Ltd.). Two copies 'of the revised page proofs' were sent on 26 September 1933 (see B.F. Oliver, letter to John Masefield, 26 September 1933) (HRHRC, MS (Masefield, J.) Recip William Heinemann Ltd.)

C.S. Evans wrote to the author at the beginning of October announcing the date of publication:

> …We have settled November 6th as the date of publication for the ordinary edition of BIRD OF DAWNING and I think I can promise you an excellent subscription. Everyone who has read an advance proof of the book is enthusiastic about it and the trade is sitting up and taking notice.
>
> (C.S. Evans, letter to John Masefield, 9 October 1933)
> (HRHRC, MS (Masefield, J.) Recip William Heinemann Ltd.)

The publishing agreement for this title between Masefield and Heinemann was dated 12 October 1933 (see Archives of The Society of Authors). The agreement refers to both a 7s.6d. and 'special edition' at 2 guineas (A111(a) and A111(c)).

A memorandum preserved in the archives of The Society of Authors records a telephone conversation (from 9 November 1934) between The Society of Authors and Louisa Callender of Heinemann:

> …Heinemanns could not object to syndicating of "Bird of Dawning" in Australian papers and expressed the view that this would help the sales of the book there. Stated there was no separate edition for Australia but copies are sent there for sale.
>
> (E.J. Mullett, Memorandum, 9 November 1934)
> (BL, Add.Mss.56601, f.170)

The syndication of the novel in the Australian press has not been traced. Any 'Australian' edition would presumably comprise an imported Heinemann edition.

The archives of The Society of Authors record that an application to publish a Braille version of this text was received from the National Institute for the Blind in January 1934 (see BL, Add.Mss.56599, f.143). Permission was granted in January 1934 (see BL, Add.Mss.56599, f.149)

There is a long and intricate history of interest in the film rights of the novel. One of the first to declare an interest was Alexander Korda (see BL, Add.Mss.56602, f.86). When in America in 1936 Masefield was recommended Messrs Myron Selznick & Company of California. He appointed them as his agents for soliciting offers for talking picture rights in *Enslaved* and *The Bird of Dawning* (see BL, Add.Mss.56604, ff.110–111). No film resulted, however. In 1951 Willoughby Film Productions Ltd (under George W. Willoughby) approached The Society of Authors for rights. Observing that they ought to change their typewriter ribbon, Masefield stated he'd consider 'any genuine offer' (see BL, Add.Mss.56623, f.32). Negotiations advanced and a draft agreement was sent (via The Society of Authors) to Masefield on 27 October 1952 (see BL, Add.Mss.56624, f.21). One cause of concern, at the time, was that Masefield had to state his work was entirely original. This, Masefield explained to The Society of Authors, was not entirely possible:

> The work is original, in that I made it, + have not had my title challenged in the 20 years that the book has lived. But I do not claim that it is all my own invention. When I was very young, a sea-captain, misled by an inner voice, wrecked his pump, let water into his ship, and abandoned her with all his crew. The crew reached port next morning, + found their ship, salved, repaired + water-tight, there in the port before them. This has been much talked-of by sailors for 60 years, and this point should be made very clear to Mr Willoughby, for the theme may have been used, or may be used; that one thing was done at sea, + is known by many thousands of men to have been done. The erring Captain became a bookseller, so I was told, + I think I am right in saying that I once bought a book from him.
>
> (John Masefield, letter to Elizabeth Barber, 28 October [1952])
> (BL, Add.Mss.56624, ff.22–23)

Nevertheless, a final form of the agreement was sent (once again through The Society of Authors) to Masefield on 8 December 1952 (see BL, Add.Mss.56624, f.52). On 16 July 1953, however, The Society of Authors wrote to Masefield stating that they had received a letter from Mr Willoughby informing them that he had 'too much else on hand to be able to go through with his plans for Bird of Dawning' (see BL, Add.Mss.56624, f.128). In October 1955 Mr. Rowland Loewe expressed interest in the film rights (see BL, Add.Mss.56626, f.113). Again, this appears to have come to nothing.

Copies seen: private collection (PWE); private collection (PWE) inscribed 'For Isabelle, | from | Jan. | Nov. 1933.'; Bodleian (Additional Masefield papers 8) inscribed 'For Kay, | on her Birthday, | from | John Masefield.', this inscription replaces an earlier inscription to Masefield's daughter 'For Jude, | from Zob. | Nov 2. 1933.'

Reprinted:

'Second Edition (before publication date)'	[first edition, second impression]	Nov 1933
'Reprinted'	[first edition, third impression]	Dec 1933
'Reprinted'	[first edition, fourth impression]	Mar 1936
'Reprinted'	[first edition, fifth impression]	May 1938
'Reprinted'	[first edition, sixth impression]	Nov 1942
'Reprinted'	[first edition, seventh impression]	Mar 1945
'Reprinted'	[first edition, eighth impression]	Nov 1946

A111(b) First American edition (1931)

The Bird of Dawning | *or* | The Fortune of the Sea | *By* | *John Masefield* | [ornament] | NEW YORK | THE MACMILLAN COMPANY | 1933
(The italic type contains a number of swash characters)
(All width centred)

Bibliographies: Handley-Taylor p.59, Wight 85b

Collation: [A-U]⁸ (J not used); 160 leaves; 187 × 128mm.; [i–viii] 1–310 [311–12]

Page contents: [i–ii] blank; [iii] half-title: 'THE BIRD OF DAWNING'; [iv] 'ALSO BY JOHN MASEFIELD | PLAYS: | [12 titles listed] | POETRY: | [14 titles listed] | FICTION: | [five titles listed] | GENERAL: | [nine titles listed]'; [v] title-page; [vi] '*Copyright, 1933, by* | JOHN MASEFIELD | [rule] | All rights reserved–no part of this book | may be reproduced in any form without | permission in writing from the publisher, | except by a reviewer who wishes to quote brief | passages in connection with a review written | for inclusion in magazine or newspaper. | [rule] | *Set up and printed.* | PRINTED IN THE UNITED STATES OF AMERICA'; [vii] 'THE BIRD OF DAWNING'; [viii] blank; 1–302 text; 303–310 'GLOSSARY'; [311–12] blank

Paper: wove paper

Running title: 'THE BIRD OF DAWNING' (52mm.) on both verso and recto, pp.2–310

Binding: light green cloth. On spine, in blue: 'THE | BIRD | OF | DAWNING | MASEFIELD | MACMILLAN | [point]' (all width centred). On upper cover, in blue: '[silhouette of three-masted ship at sea within ruled border: 39 × 46mm. (ranged upper left)] | THE BIRD OF [ranged right and centred] | DAWNING [ranged right and centred] | JOHN MASEFIELD [ranged right and centred]'. Lower cover: blank. Top and lower outside edges trimmed, fore edge roughly trimmed. Binding measurements: 193 × 130mm. (covers), 193 × 45mm. (spine). End-papers: wove paper.

Publication date: published, according to Handley-Taylor, 6 November 1933

Price: $2.50

Contents:
The Bird of Dawning ('Nearly seventy years ago, Cruiser Trewsbury, the second mate of the homeward-bound...')
Glossary ('A.B. An "Able bodied" seaman; formerly one who had served five or seven years...')

Notes:
The sub-title ('The Fortune of the Sea') is not present in English editions. A recording issued by the Argo record company in 1962 was entitled 'The Fortune of the Sea and The Wanderer's Image' (see G5). In part of this recording Masefield tells a story similar to that of *The Bird of Dawning*.

It appears that the glossary was sent to Macmillan after the rest of the text:

> Sorry I was not here when your letter arrived in which you forwarded a glossary for BIRD OF DAWNING. The glossary was immediately turned over to the Editorial Department for inclusion in the book.
>> (George P Brett Jr, letter to John Masefield, 5 September 1933)
>> (HRHRC, MS (Masefield, J.) Recip The Macmillan Company)

The publishing agreement for this volume between Masefield and Macmillan was dated 22 June 1933 (see Archives of The Society of Authors). The agreement refers to 'a licence to publish in volume form in... the United States of America and Canada a work the subject of which is a short novel dealing with the China-Tea-Race, for clipper ships, in the 1860–70 decade, centering around a strange event very well-known to the seamen of the Author's time'.

The American Foundation for the Blind approached the Macmillan Company in 1934 for permission to record 200 copies of this novel on record (see BL, Add.Mss.56600, ff.115–116). Masefield was always willing to permit Braille editions and, although nervous about this new medium, nevertheless extended his permission to include talking books (see BL, Add.Mss.56600, f.114). A later application by the (English) National Institute for the Blind sought permission to 'circulate the records of the Bird of Dawning in Great Britain...' This request, which may refer to the American records, was granted by The Society of Authors (see BL, Add.Mss.56603, ff.230–31).

Copies seen: private collection (ROV)

Reprinted:

	[first edition, second impression]	Nov 1933
	[first edition, third impression]	Nov 1933
	[first edition, fourth impression]	Nov 1933
	[first edition, fifth impression]	Dec 1933
	[first edition, sixth impression]	Mar 1934
	[first edition, seventh impression]	Jul 1934
'Reprinted'	[first edition, eighth impression]	Dec 1934

A111(c) Second English edition (first English illustrated limited signed edition) (1933)

[rule, 59mm.] | JOHN MASEFIELD | [rule, 59mm.] | *The Bird of Dawning* [in light blue] | WITH ILLUSTRATIONS BY | CLAUDE MUNCASTER | [publisher's device of a windmill with 'W [point]' and 'H'] [in light blue] | *London* | WILLIAM HEINEMANN LTD | 1933

(All width centred)

Bibliographies: Handley-Taylor p.59, Wight 85a

Collation: [A]¹⁰ B-S⁸ T⁴ (J not used); signatures right foot of page; 150 leaves; 229 × 153mm.; [i–x] 1–283 [284] 285–90; illustrations (on wove paper) tipped-in on pp.[iv], 155, 187 and 271

Page contents: [i–ii] blank; [iii] half-title: '*The Bird of Dawning*'; [iv] '*This Edition, numbered and signed | by the Author and the Artist, is | limited to 300 copies for sale in | Great Britain and Ireland. | No..........*' (with additional leaf tipped-in on the verso of which is the full page colour frontispiece, 'The Rush Up-Channel'); [v] title-page; [vi] 'PRINTED | IN GREAT BRITAIN | AT THE WINDMILL PRESS | KINGSWOOD | SURREY'; [vii] 'TO | MY WIFE'; [viii] blank; [ix] 'ILLUSTRATIONS' (four individual items listed with page references); [x] blank; 1–283 text; [284] blank; 285–90 'GLOSSARY'

Paper: wove paper

Running title: 'THE BIRD OF DAWNING' (69–71mm.) on both verso and recto, pp.2–283 and 'GLOSSARY' (30mm.) on both verso and recto, pp.286–90

Binding: blue cloth. On spine, in gold: 'The | *Bird of* | *Dawning* | JOHN | MASEFIELD | HEINEMANN' (all width centred). Covers: blank. Top edge gilt, lower outside edge untrimmed, fore edge uncut. Sewn head and foot bands (in blue) and blue marker ribbon. Binding measurements: 235 × 152mm. (covers), 235 × 49mm. (spine). The binding includes bevelled edges. End-papers: grey laid paper (watermark: '[crown] | Abbey Mills | Greenfield'), chain-lines 25mm. apart. Volume contained in slip-case covered in blue paper.

Publication date: the sales ledger preserved in the Heinemann Archive suggests publication on 30 November 1933 in an edition of 300 copies

Price: 42s.

Contents:
as for A111(a)

Notes:

The illustrations are each full page colour illustrations and are only titled in the index of illustrations.

The text appears to use the same setting of type as A111(a).

The illustrations by Claude Muncaster proved to be both expensive and a cause of delay to this edition. Masefield offered to assist issues of expense by suggesting a lower royalty. C.S. Evans wrote:

> I now have the estimate for the production of the limited edition of BIRD OF DAWNING, with the four pictures by Muncaster reproduced in collotype. These are, as I imagined, extremely expensive. I have decided to make a book 9 1/4" × 6 1/8" and to print the pictures all over the page – that is to say, without margins. This was a method which was used very successfully by Colonel Lawrence in the very expensive limited edition of his book, THE SEVEN PILLARS OF WISDOM.
>
> I have tentatively agreed to pay Muncaster, for the right of reproduction in this volume only, a fee of £50. He will, of course, keep his originals; and if we want to reproduce them at any time in any other edition of the book, we should have to pay a further fee for this right. The actual reproduction of the four pictures will cost between £95 and £125...
>
> It is very kind of you to suggest helping us by accepting a lower royalty. I do not want to make the book more than two guineas if I can help it because as you know, the spending power of people who buy limited editions is considerably less in these days... What we propose to do is to announce the book and tell dealers in limited editions that we shall print up to the number subscribed before publication but that in no case will the edition be larger than 500.
>
> (C.S. Evans, letter to John Masefield, 10 August 1933)
> (HRHRC, MS (Masefield, J.) Recip William Heinemann Ltd.)

The edition size was to be 300. By the beginning of October the illustrations were causing delay:

> ...We have settled November 6th as the date of publication for the ordinary edition of BIRD OF DAWNING... I had hoped to be able to get the limited edition out at the same time as the ordinary edition but I find that this will be impossible. As you know, the illustrations are being reproduced in collotype, which is a very slow process...
>
> (C.S. Evans, letter to John Masefield, 9 October 1933)
> (HRHRC, MS (Masefield, J.) Recip William Heinemann Ltd.)

The sheets detailing limitation of the edition were ready at the beginning of November 1933:

> The sheets of the limited edition of THE BIRD OF DAWNING are ready for your signature. Shall I send them to you, or would you prefer to sign them here if you are coming to London?
>
> (C.S. Evans, letter to John Masefield, 2 November 1933)
> (HRHRC, MS (Masefield, J.) Recip William Heinemann Ltd.)

Masefield evidently prefered the sheets to be sent to him as a letter, dated four days later, reveals:

> Many thanks for signing and returning the sheets. I am sending them to the press today, and we shall have the book out in about three weeks… The ordinary edition of the book is published today… It promises to do very well: our subscription is 10,671 copies.
>
> (C.S. Evans, letter to John Masefield, 6 November 1933)
> (HRHRC, MS (Masefield, J.) Recip William Heinemann Ltd.)

One of the final contributions to the volume was the listing of illustrations (appearing on page [ix]):

> I am sorry I have to trouble you again about the illustrations for THE BIRD OF DAWNING. Of course the illustrations themselves, will have no captions, but we ought to have a list in the beginning of the book and they ought to be described. I don't know whether you can suggest titles for them, or whether a sentence from the text of the scene you have depicted would suffice…
>
> (B.F. Oliver, letter to Claude Muncaster, 18 October 1933)
> (HRHRC, MS (Masefield, J.) Recip William Heinemann Ltd.)

In March 1937 C.S. Evans investigated sales since 1933 of Masefield's limited editions. Of this limited edition he reported to Masefield that the 'whole edition was exhausted'. The same was true of the limited signed edition of *The Taking of the Gry* (A113(aa)). Copies were still available, however, of the limited signed editions of *Victorious Troy* (A116(d)), *A Letter from Pontus and other verse* (A117(aa)) and *Eggs and Baker* (A119(aa)).

Copies seen: private collection (PWE) number 250, signed '250 | John Masefield.' and 'Claude Muncaster' on p.[iv]

A111(d) First German edition [in English] (1934)

THE BIRD OF DAWNING | *by* | JOHN MASEFIELD | THE ALBATROSS | HAMBURG [point] PARIS [point] BOLOGNA
(All width centred)

Bibliographies: Handley-Taylor [unrecorded], Wight [unrecorded]

Collation: [1]⁸ 2–16⁸; the second leaf of gatherings 2–16 is also signed; each signature prefixed by '214,'; signatures left foot of page; 128 leaves; 180 × 109mm.; [1–4] 5–252 [253–56]

Page contents: [1] half-title: 'THE ALBATROSS | MODERN CONTINENTAL LIBRARY | VOLUME 214 | [five-point star] | THE BIRD OF DAWNING'; [2] blank; [3] title-page; [4] 'TO | MY WIFE | COPYRIGHT 1934 | BY THE ALBATROSS VERLAG G.M.B.H., HAMBURG | IMPRIMÉ EN ALLEMAGNE'; 5–247 text; 248–[53] 'GLOSSARY'; [254] 'THIS EDITION IS COMPOSED IN | BASKERVILLE TYPE CUT BY THE | MONOTYPE CORPORATION. THE | PAPER IS MADE BY THE PAPIER- | FABRIK BAUTZEN. THE PRINTING AND | THE BINDING ARE THE WORK OF | OSCAR BRANDSTETTER [point] ABTEILUNG | JAKOB HEGNER [point] LEIPZIG | [publisher's device of an albatross]'; [255–56] publisher's advertisements

Paper: wove paper

Running title: none

Binding: white wrappers (printed green). On spine, reading lengthways up spine, from foot: '[thin vertical rule] [thick vertical rule] The Bird of Dawning *by* John Masefield [thick vertical rule] [thin vertical rule]' all on white panel: 148 × 10mm.; with '[thick vertical rule] | 214' horizontally at head of spine and '214 | [thick vertical rule]' horizontally at foot of spine. On upper wrapper: 'THE BIRD OF | DAWNING | *by* | JOHN | MASEFIELD | [publisher's device of an albatross in black and white] | THE ALBATROSS' (within ruled border: 140 × 75mm.), 'COPYRIGHT EDITION' (within ruled border: 148 × 81mm.), 'NOT TO BE INTRODUCED INTO THE BRITISH EMPIRE OR THE U. S. A.' (within ruled border: 159 × 90mm.) and in green: 'THE [point] ALBATROSS [point] MODERN [point] CONTINENTAL [point] LIBRARY' on left, 'THE ALBATROSS [point] MODERN [point] CONTINENTAL [point] LIBRARY' on right, 'THE [point] ALBATROSS [point] LIBRARY' at head and 'HAMBURG [point] PARIS [point] BOLOGNA' at foot (on white panel and within ruled border: 168 × 99mm.). On lower wrapper: publisher's device of an albatross in black and white (within ruled border: 159 × 90mm.) and white rule (within ruled border: 168 × 99mm.) All edges trimmed. Binding measurements: 180 × 109mm. (wrappers), 180 × 15mm. (spine).

Publication date: evidence contained within the correspondence files of The Society of Authors suggests publication around August 1934 (see BL, Add.Mss.56601 f.72)

Price: unknown

Contents:
The Bird of Dawning ('Nearly seventy years ago, Cruiser Trewsbury, the second mate of the homeward-bound…')
Glossary ('A.B. . . . An 'Able-bodied' seaman; formerly one who had served five or seven years…')

Notes:
The page number on p.184 has an inverted number '8'.

The publishing agreement for this edition between Masefield and 'M.C. Wegner for and on behalf of The Albatross Verlag' was dated 2 February 1934 (see HRHRC, MS (Masefield, J.) Misc. Albatross Verlag, memo).

Copies seen: private collection (PWE)

A111(e) Third English edition ["Wanderer Edition"] (1936)

[rule, 59mm.] | JOHN MASEFIELD | [rule, 59mm.] | *The Bird of Dawning* | [publisher's device of a windmill with the letters 'W [point]' and 'H'] | *London* | WILLIAM HEINEMANN LTD
(All width centred)

Bibliographies: Handley-Taylor p.59, Wight [unrecorded]

Collation: [A]⁸ B–S⁸ T⁴ (J not used); signatures right foot of page; 148 leaves; 189 × 126mm.; [i–vi] 1–283 [284] 285–90

Page contents: [i] half-title: 'THE COLLECTED WORKS OF | JOHN MASEFIELD | [rule] | WANDERER EDITION | *The Bird of Dawning*'; [ii] '*ALSO BY JOHN MASEFIELD* | PLAYS: | [12 titles listed] | POETRY: | [14 titles listed] | FICTION: | [five titles listed] | GENERAL: | [nine titles listed]'; [iii] title-page; [iv] 'FIRST PUBLISHED 1933 | REPRINTED NOVEMBER, DECEMBER 1933 | MARCH 1936 | PRINTED | IN GREAT BRITAIN | AT THE WINDMILL PRESS | KINGSWOOD | SURREY'; [v] 'TO | MY WIFE'; [vi] blank; 1–283 text; [284] blank; 285–90 'GLOSSARY'

Paper: wove paper

Running title: 'THE BIRD OF DAWNING' (69–71mm.) on both verso and recto, pp.2–283 and 'GLOSSARY' (30mm.) on both verso and recto, pp.286–90

Binding: blue cloth. On spine, in gold: 'JOHN | MASEFIELD | THE | BIRD OF | DAWNING | THE | WANDERER | EDITION | HEINEMANN' (all width centred). On upper cover, in gold: illustration of a cockerel: 32 × 24mm. (ranged lower right). On lower cover, in blind: publisher's device of a windmill (ranged lower right). Top edge gilt, others trimmed. Sewn head band (in blue) and blue marker ribbon. Binding measurements: 196 × 128mm. (covers), 196 × 47mm. (spine). End-papers: wove paper.

Publication date: published, according to Handley-Taylor, 20 April 1936

Price: 5s.

Contents:
as for A111(a)

Notes:
The publishing agreement for 'a collected edition of the Author's work', including this title, between Masefield and Heinemann was dated 31 July 1935 (see Archives of The Society of Authors). The agreement refers to 'a published price of 5/-...' (see note on collected editions).

Copies seen: HRHRC (TEMP M377BI 1936) inscribed 'For Con | from | Jan. | April 22. 1936.'

Reprinted:

May 1938
Nov 1940

A111(f) Fourth English edition ["The New Windmill Series"] (1956)

[rule, 49mm.] | JOHN MASEFIELD | [rule, 49mm.] | *The Bird of Dawning* | *WITH ILLUSTRATIONS BY* | *A. R. THOMSON, R.A.* | [publisher's device of a windmill with 'W' and 'H'] | [rule, 55mm.] | WILLIAM HEINEMANN LTD | MELBOURNE :: LONDON :: TORONTO
(All width centred)

Bibliographies: Handley-Taylor p.59, Wight [unrecorded]

Collation: [A]⁸ B–O⁸ (J not used); signatures left foot of page; 112 leaves; 185 × 123mm.; [i–vi] 1–2 [3] 4–144 [145] 146–85 [186] 187–202 [203] 204–208 [209] 210–13 [214] 215–18

Page contents: [i] half-title: 'THE NEW WINDMILL SERIES | *General Editor:* Ian Serraillier | *The Bird of Dawning*'; [ii] frontispiece: 158 × 101mm.; [iii] title-page; [iv] 'FIRST PUBLISHED 1933 | FIRST PUBLISHED IN THE NEW WINDMILL SERIES | 1956 | PUBLISHED BY | WILLIAM HEINEMANN LTD | 99 GREAT RUSSELL STREET, LONDON, W.C.I | PRINTED IN GREAT BRITAIN BY J. AND J. GRAY, EDINBURGH'; [v] 'TO | MY WIFE'; [vi] 'LIST OF ILLUSTRATIONS' (six individual items listed with page references); 1–213 text; [214] blank; 215–18 'GLOSSARY'

Paper: wove paper

Running title: none

Binding: light blue cloth. On spine, in navy blue: 'THE | BIRD | OF | DAWNING | JOHN | MASEFIELD | [publisher's device of a windmill]' (all width centred). On upper cover, in navy blue: 'THE BIRD OF | DAWNING | [illustration of a three-masted ship at sea with three birds: 65 × 66mm.] | John Masefield'. Lower cover: blank. All edges trimmed. Binding measurements: 190 × 125mm. (covers), 190 × 24mm. (spine). End-papers: wove paper.

Publication date: published, according to Handley-Taylor, 30 July 1956

Price: 5s.6d.

Contents:
as for A111(a)

Notes:
The text commences with a drop-capital.

The illustrations in this volume are not printed on separate leaves. They occur on pp.[ii], [3], [145], [186], [203] and [209]. Masefield was sent the illustrations during July 1954:

> I have today sent you by separate registered post, the six drawings which A.R. Thomson, R.A. has done for our forthcoming edition of THE BIRD OF DAWNING. Mr. Thomson is a leading portrait painter, but he is also a great enthusiast for ships, and he has asked if you would kindly make your comments on his work.
>
> (Alan Hill, letter to John Masefield, 15 July 1954)
> (HRHRC, MS (Masefield, J.) Recip William Heinemann Ltd.)

Masefield's comments were, however, not encouraging and Alan Hill responded:

> I am sorry that you do not like the drawings. The artist took the bit between his teeth, and instead of turning out one drawing for approval, went ahead and did them all according to his own ideas. He will be able to correct all the faults of rigging and the many other details, to which you drew our attention. Obviously he cannot alter the style of the drawings without doing them afresh…
>
> (Alan Hill, letter to John Masefield, 19 July 1954)
> (HRHRC, MS (Masefield, J.) Recip William Heinemann Ltd.)

The delay in publishing this title – and the 'New Windmill Series' edition of *Sard Harker* (see A75(e)) – were evidently frustrating. Alan Hill wrote to Masefield on 23 July 1956:

> …here at last are the first copies of the editions of THE BIRD OF DAWNING, and SARD HARKER which we have put into our New Windmill Series.
>
> (Alan Hill, letter to John Masefield, 23 July 1956)
> (HRHRC, MS (Masefield, J.) Recip William Heinemann Ltd.)

John St John in his history of Heinemann entitled *William Heinemann A Century of Publishing 1890–1990* notes the revival of the educational books department at Heinemann after the war. No date is provided for the beginning of the New Windmill Series, but a letter (conjecturally dated July 1948) suggests that *The Bird of Dawning* was an early candidate for inclusion in the series. It was evidently not a publishing venture which Masefield viewed favourably:

> I have thought over your proposal about the *Bird of Dawning*, and do not feel at all drawn to it. Some of my books have been issued in what are called "Educational issues", and the results have made me shudder. You see, I get letters from the poor little victims. So, please, let us spare them, and not print the *Bird of Dawning* thus.
>
> (John Masefield, letter to [Louisa] Callender, [July 1948])
> (Archives of William Heinemann)

The 'educational issues' might include *Lost Endeavour*, printed within 'The Teaching of English Series' in 1939. (Masefield did not hold the copyright for this title and had no control on such an edition). In October 1952 negotiations for *The Bird of Dawning* were reopened since Masefield had rejected an offer from Longman:

> I understand that you have declined Longmans' offer to do a cut version of *The Bird of Dawning* in their Heritage of Literature Series. If you like, we would be glad to publish the book in full in our New Windmill Series of which, at a reasonable price, we feel we could sell quite a lot. After that, and in the same series, we should like to include *New Chum* and *The Box of Delights*.
>
> (A.S. Frere, letter to John Masefield, 13 October 1952)
> (HRHRC, MS (Masefield, J.) Recip William Heinemann Ltd.)

Masefield, ever the business enquirer, responded:

> *The Bird of Dawning* is still in print, I gather. Please will you tell me about your *New Windmill Series*, and its proposed prices + royalties? Perhaps, you could let me see a dummy or advance copy of it?
>
> (John Masefield, letter to [A.S.] Frere, 14 October 1952)
> (Archives of William Heinemann)

Negotiations continued and Masefield wrote during December 1952 posing further questions about prices and royalties:

> I have been debating the question of your Windmill Series for some time, thinking that the rate of royalty offered is too low, and that the temptation should be made greater.
>
> If you were to issue *The Bird of Dawning* at, say, 5/-, I take it that you would not have to reset the book, but would print from type already set. Why could you not pay, say 12½% royalty at once on this, and increase the royalty to 15% after the sale of 2500 copies and to 20% after the sale of 5000 copies?

You have ever been very frank in discussing these matters, + I hope you will acquit me of any blindness of overmastering greed. It is a question of modern conditions, + the future issue of some of my books. My own suspicion is that my old public is taxed beyond the power to buy books, + the new potential buyers do not read.

(John Masefield, letter to [A.S.] Frere, 14 December 1952)
(Archives of William Heinemann)

This is followed, in the Heinemann archive, with a letter dated 1 January 1953. Masefield states:

I am sorry, but I must decline your offer... I am sorry, but the risk seems to me to be too great.

(John Masefield, letter to [A.S.] Frere, 1 January 1953)
(Archives of William Heinemann)

An internal memorandum from Alan Hill of the educational department to A.S. Frere dated 15 January 1953 suggested contacting Masefield again:

If Masefield is unwilling to take the risk, we will take it. We will issue an edition of 5,000 copies in the New Windmill Series, and pay him the total royalty in advance. When this edition is sold out, or in eighteen months' time after publication, whichever is the earlier, he can reconsider his decision in the light of the success or otherwise of the arrangement. In the meantime, there will be no question of disturbing the general edition which will stay on the market at its present price.

(Alan Hill, memorandum to [A.S.] Frere, 15 January 1953)
(Archives of William Heinemann)

This document additionally notes that 10% royalty on 5000 copies at 4s.6d. would be approximately £114. Masefield was evidently still rather unimpressed for he replied:

On the whole, I have been against prepaid advances, as being hard on publishers; and an uneasy burden on writers, too, if the book should not earn the advance. I thank you for the compliment you pay me, in wanting the book, but I am against the proposal on the whole, still. I would rather not.

(John Masefield, letter to [A.S.] Frere, [January 1953])
(Archives of William Heinemann)

By 1956 Masefield had evidently relented, and in addition to *The Bird of Dawning*, other titles in the series were to include *Sard Harker* (A75(e)), *The Midnight Folk* (A86(i)) and *The Box of Delights* (A115(c)).

Copies seen: BL (W.P.6193/24) stamped 22 AUG 1956

Reprinted:

[fourth edition, second impression]	1959
[fourth edition, third impression]	1960
[fourth edition, fourth impression]	1960
[fourth edition, fifth impression]	1961
[fourth edition, sixth impression]	1966
[fourth edition, seventh impression]	1967
[fourth edition, eighth impression]	1970
[fourth edition, ninth impression]	1977

A111(g) Fifth English edition (1964)

John Masefield | The Bird of Dawning | [publisher's design of a penguin within single ruled oval border] Penguin Books
(All ranged on left margin)

Bibliographies: Wight [unrecorded]

Collation: [A]^{16} B-F^{16}; signatures left foot of page; 96 leaves; 180 × 113mm.; [1–6] 7–186 [187–88] 189–91 [192]

Page contents: [1] 'Peacock Book PK35 | *Editor: Kaye Webb* | The Bird of Dawning | This is a sailors' yarn, magnificently told. Cyril (Cruiser) | Trewsbury, aged twenty-four and studying for his master's | ticket, finds himself in command of a lifeboat and a bunch | of men after their ship has been rammed in fog and sunk. | After some days in a dangerous sea, they come up with a | clipper finer than their own lost ship but completely and | inexplicably deserted. This is Cruiser's moment. He inspires | his men (a very mixed bunch) to pull the ship round and | sail her to the Channel – and to victory in the famous | China Tea Race. | [new paragraph] To this straightforward tale John Masefield brings all his | resources, to make the sea and all its moods, the working | of the ship, the different sailors and the curious fellowship | that grows up between them, entirely real to the reader. | The theme of the story is spoken by Cruiser, trying to | make up his mind what Real Life means: 'When you've | got nothing except destiny or death. When you're up | against your Fortune, whether it goes for or against you.' | [new paragraph] Taken from Margery Fisher's *Monograph on John Masefield*, | published by the Bodley Head. | [new paragraph] Cover design by Peter Barrett'; [2] blank; [3] title-page; [4] 'Penguin Books Ltd, Harmondsworth, | Middlesex, England | Penguin Books Pty Ltd, Ringwood, | Victoria, Australia | First published by Heinemann 1933 | Published in Peacock Books 1964 | Copyright © John Masefield, 1933 | Made and printed in Great Britain by

| Cox and Wyman Ltd, London, Fakenham, | and Reading. | Set in Monotype Baskerville | This book is sold subject to the condition | that it shall not, by way of trade, be lent, | re-sold, hired out or otherwise | disposed of without the publisher's consent | in any form of binding or cover other | than that in which it is published'; [5] 'TO MY WIFE'; [6] blank; 7–[187] text; [188] blank; 189–[192] 'Glossary'

Paper: wove paper

Running title: none

Binding: white wrappers. On spine, horizontally at head of spine, in blue: '[device of peacock] | [rule]'; reading lengthways down spine from head: 'John Masefield The Bird of Dawning'; horizontally at foot of spine: 'PK35'. On upper wrapper: '[device of peacock] [in blue] a Peacock Book 3/6 | The Bird of Dawning | [rule] [in blue] | John Masefield | [colour illustration of ship's rigging and men (in black and white) against coloured sky]'. On lower wrapper: '[device of peacock] [in blue] published by Penguin Books | The Bird of Dawning | [rule] [in blue] | [colour illustration of ship's rigging and men (in black and white) against coloured sky with 'For copyright reasons this edition is not for sale in the U.S.A. or Canada']'. All edges trimmed. Binding measurements: 180 × 113mm. (wrappers), 180 × 10mm. (spine).

Publication date: published, according to the *English Catalogue of Books*, 25 June 1964 and published, according to *Whitaker's*, 24 June 1964. The Archives of The Society of Authors suggest the date of 25 June 1964 to be correct.

Price: 3s.6d.

Contents:
The Bird of Dawning ('That tea-race year Cruiser Trewsbury, the second mate of the homeward-bound...')
Glossary ('*A.B.* An 'Able-bodied' seaman; formerly one who had served five or seven years...')

Notes:
The two illustrations on the wrappers (interrupted by the spine) comprise a single illustration. A section of the illustration is repeated on both upper and lower wrappers.

The text has been entirely re-set for this edition and commences differently from other editions.

Penguin Books approached Heinemann on several occasions about a paperback issue of the novel. Masefield remained cautious, writing to The Society of Authors in April 1963

> ...I never know for certain that these cheap issues of big printings benefit a writer. They may exhaust all demand for the book and kill a slow steady sale. ...The book is not anything but a real event in an imaginary setting, and it has no heroine, + much of it is in a sea jargon now obsolete. I wonder if it would not be wise to give up the thought of the reprint?
> (John Masefield, letter to Anne Munro-Kerr, [April 1963])
> (Archives of The Society of Authors)

Copies seen: private collection (PWE)

[see B555 for an abridged edition]

A111(h) First combined English and American edition (1984)

JOHN MASEFIELD | *The Bird of Dawning* | CENTURY PUBLISHING | LONDON | HIPPOCRENE BOOKS INC. | NEW YORK
(All width centred)

Bibliographies: Wight [unrecorded]

Publication date: published, according to *Whitaker's*, April 1984

Price: £4.95 / $9.95

Contents:
The Bird of Dawning ('Nearly seventy years ago, Cruiser Trewsbury, the second mate of the homeward-bound...')
Glossary ('A.B.: An "Able-bodied" seaman; formerly one who had served five or seven years...')

Notes:
This volume states, on page [4], that it is printed in Great Britain by Redwood Burn Limited, Trowbridge, Wiltshire

The text has been entirely re-set for this edition.

The volume was apparently issued in both the U.K. and the U.S.

The reproduction illustration on the wrappers and spine comprises a single detail from 'The Seventh Wave' by Charles Pears. This is the artist who provided illustrations for A35.

Copies seen: private collection (PWE)

A112 WORDS AND VERSES SPOKEN IN THE GARDEN OF BEMERTON RECTORY... 1933

A112(a) First English edition (1933)

Upper wrapper:

Words and Verses spoken in the Garden | of Bemerton Rectory, near Salisbury, in | the afternoon of Tuesday, June 6ᵗʰ, 1933
(Justified on left and right margins)
(The '*B*' of '*Bemerton*' is swash)

Bibliographies: Handley-Taylor [unrecorded], Wight [unrecorded]

Collation: [A]²⁰; 20 leaves; 187 × 142mm.; [1–2] 3–38 [39–40]

Page contents: [1] title-page; [2] '*To | Chrys, | Di | and | Judith, | our companions on this day.*'; 3–38 text; [39–40] blank

Paper: wove paper

Running title: none

Binding: wrappers comprise the first and last leaves of the single gathering ([A]1 and [A]20). The title-page consequently comprises the upper wrapper. All edges uncut. Binding measurements: 187 × 142mm. (wrappers), 187 × 2mm. (spine).

Publication date: published between June and December 1933

Price: copies were not for sale

Masefield contents:
[Words spoken in the Garden of Bemerton Rectory…] ('You have done me the honour to ask me to come to you...')

Notes:
A privately printed booklet of the words spoken by Masefield 'about George Herbert, a poet, once the Rector of this parish'. Five poems by George Herbert were spoken by Judith Masefield and Chrystabel Dale Roberts, and these are also printed in the booklet.

Copies seen: private collection (ROV) inscribed 'For N + N deGaris Davies, | from John + Constance Masefield. | Christmas. 1933.'; private collection (RM) inscribed 'For Vera, | from | Constance + John. | Christmas, 1933.'; Library of The John Masefield Society (Peter Smith Collection 113) inscribed 'For Margery Coleman | from John Masefield.' and 'The luck will alter + the star | will rise.'; Bodleian (2793.e.221) inscribed 'For James MacKay. | From | John + Constance Masefield. | Christmas. 1933.'; Bodleian (Additional Masefield Papers 10) inscribed 'For Querie. | from Jan.'; HRHRC (PR6025 A77 W674) with HRHRC note 'From the Library of John Masefield'

A113 THE TAKING OF THE GRY   1934

A113(a) First English edition (1934)

THE | TAKING OF THE GRY | BY | JOHN MASEFIELD | [ornament] | [publisher's device of a windmill with 'W [point]' and 'H'] | [rule, 71mm.] | LONDON: WILLIAM HEINEMANN LTD
(All width centred)

Bibliographies: Handley-Taylor p.60, Wight 86

Collation: [A]⁸ B-M⁸ (J not used); signatures right foot of page; 96 leaves; 185 × 122mm.; [i–viii] 1–181 [182–84]

Page contents: [i–ii] blank; [iii] half-title: 'THE | TAKING OF THE GRY'; [iv] '*ALSO BY JOHN MASEFIELD* | PLAYS: | [12 titles listed] | POETRY: | [14 titles listed] | FICTION: | [five titles listed] | GENERAL: | [nine titles listed]'; [v] title-page; [vi] 'FIRST PUBLISHED 1934 | PRINTED IN GREAT BRITAIN | AT THE WINDMILL PRESS, KINGSWOOD, SURREY'; [vii] 'TO | MY WIFE'; [viii] blank; 1–181 text; [182–84] blank

Paper: wove paper

Running title: 'THE TAKING OF THE GRY' (45mm.) on both both verso and recto, pp.2–181

Binding: blue cloth. On spine, in gold: 'THE | TAKING | OF THE | GRY | [ornament] | JOHN | MASEFIELD | HEINEMANN' (all width centred). On upper cover, in gold: 'THE TAKING OF THE GRY | JOHN MASEFIELD' (within blind ruled border: 184 × 117mm.) On lower cover, in blind: publisher's device of a windmill (ranged lower right). All edges trimmed. Binding measurements: 189 × 124mm. (covers), 189 × 42mm. (spine). End-papers: wove paper decorated in black, pink and cyan with map of 'The City of | Santa Barbara.' (signed 'R.H. Sauter') (within ruled border: 179 × 242mm.).

Publication date: the sales ledger preserved in the Heinemann Archive suggests publication on 28 September 1934 in an edition of 10000 copies

Price: 6s.

Contents:
The Taking of the Gry ('The events of the Great War have made men forget the Civil War in Santa Ana. But in 1911...')
Appendix ('I have been asked to name the authorities for Drake's voyage to the two sea-ports. The only...')

Notes:

A novel set in Masefield's fictional American republics. The novel describes the capture of an ammunition ship and the dare-devil sailing of it through an unused, hazardous channel to provide munitions for the country of Santa Ana, threatened by Santa Barbara. The novel has no chapter divisions.

At the same time as giving advance notice of a 'children's book' (presumably *The Box of Delights*), Masefield appears to have written to C.S. Evans about *The Taking of the Gry*. Evans responded asking that the author's son (then working for Heinemann) might deliver the manucript:

> I gather that you will be sending me the script of the new tale in the next two or three days. If it is ready you might send it back by Lewis who tells me that he is going home for the week-end. I am very much looking forward to reading it.
>
> (C.S. Evans, letter to John Masefield, 5 July 1934)
> (HRHRC, MS (Masefield, J.) Recip William Heinemann Ltd.)

When he had read the 'new tale' Evans was enthusiastic. He wrote to Masefield stating:

> I meant to write to you yesterday but I had a tearing day. I wanted to let you know at once how much I enjoyed reading THE TAKING OF THE GRY. Lewis brought it to me and I began to read if half an hour before luncheon. Then I had to dash out but after three quarters of an hour I came back and did not put the book down until I had finished it. What a story teller you are! And that is one of the rarest gifts in modern literature.
>
> (C.S. Evans, letter to John Masefield, 13 July 1934)
> (HRHRC, MS (Masefield, J.) Recip William Heinemann Ltd.)

The 'first proofs' were sent to Masefield (together with the return of the manuscript) on 10 August 1934 (see B.F. Oliver, letter to John Masefield, 10 August 1934) (HRHRC, MS (Masefield, J.) Recip William Heinemann Ltd.) Three days later Rudolf Sauter's design was praised by Evans:

> …I think Rudo's drawing for the wrapper and endpapers is splendid. I think he has surpassed himself. I will see that his reproduction instructions are carried out to the letter…
>
> (C.S. Evans, letter to John Masefield, 13 August 1934)
> (HRHRC, MS (Masefield, J.) Recip William Heinemann Ltd.)

On 28 August 1934 Evans wrote to Masefield citing the date of publication (for both A113(a) and A113(aa)). Evans noted '…we are publishing the book on September 28th and the limited edition on the same day…' (see C.S. Evans, letter to John Masefield, 28 August 1934) (HRHRC, MS (Masefield, J.) Recip William Heinemann Ltd.)

Masefield, four months before single volume publication by Heinemann, had attempted to secure serial publication. Writing to The Society of Authors in May 1934, Masefield states:

> You will I trust receive by hand a typescript of my story, about 30,000 words, called *The Taking of the GRY*. I shall be obliged if you will offer it for serial publication in Scribner's Magazine.
>
> (John Masefield, letter to The Society of Authors, [22 May 1934])
> (BL, Add.Mss.56600, f.186)

Scribner's replied on 13 June 1934 having read the work with 'pleasure and interest', but rejected it explaining 'the story shows that it really should be read at one sitting and I am afraid that it would not break up well for a serialization spread over three numbers' (see BL, Add.Mss.56600, f.221)

The publishing agreement for this title between Masefield and Heinemann was dated 27 August 1934 (see Archives of The Society of Authors). The agreement refers to a publication price of 6s. and also a 'special edition' at 31s.6d.

Copies seen: private collection (PWE); BL (NN.22956) stamped 28 SEP 1934

A113(aa) First English edition (limited signed edition) (1934)

THE [in light green] | TAKING OF THE GRY [in light green] | BY | JOHN MASEFIELD | [ornament] | [publisher's device of a windmill with 'W [point]' and 'H'] [in light green] | [rule, 71mm.] [in light green] | LONDON: WILLIAM HEINEMANN LTD | 1934
(All width centred)

Bibliographies: Handley-Taylor p.60, Wight 86b

Collation: [A]¹⁰ (–[A]3 and –[A]9) B–M⁸ (J not used); signatures right foot of page; 98 leaves; 230 × 148mm.; [i–iv] [v–vi (removed)] [vii–x] 1–6 [two un-numbered pages (removed)] 7–181 [182–84]

Page contents: [i–ii] blank; [iii] half-title: 'THE | TAKING OF THE GRY'; [iv] '*This Edition, numbered and signed | by the Author, is limited to* 175 | *copies for sale in Great Britain and | Ireland | No*...'; [v] stub of leaf; [vi] stub of leaf (with additional sheet tipped-in on the verso of which is map (folded twice) in black, pink and cyan: 180 × 242mm.; 'The City of | Santa Barbara.' (signed 'R.H. Sauter') (within ruled border); [vii] title-page; [viii] 'PRINTED IN GREAT BRITAIN | AT THE WINDMILL PRESS, KINGSWOOD, SURREY'; [ix] 'TO | MY WIFE'; [x] blank; 1–181 text (including un-numbered stub of leaf between pp.6 and 7); [182–84] blank

Paper: wove paper (watermark: 'MILLBOURN | BRITISH HAND MADE PURE RAG [castle device: 26 × 31mm.]'). The map is printed on laid paper (watermark of Atlas holding the globe on shoulders), chain-lines 25–29mm. apart

Running title: 'THE TAKING OF THE GRY' (45mm.) on both both verso and recto, pp.2–181

Binding: blue cloth. On spine, in gold: 'The | Taking of | *The Gry* | JOHN | MASEFIELD | HEINEMANN' (all width centred). Covers: blank. Top edge gilt, lower outside edge untrimmed, fore edge uncut. Sewn head band (in blue) and blue marker ribbon. Binding measurements: 236 × 145mm. (covers), 236 × 45mm. (spine). The binding includes bevelled edges. End-papers: wove paper.

Publication date: the sales ledger preserved in the Heinemann Archive suggests publication on 28 September 1934 in an edition of 175 copies

Price: 31s.6d.

Contents:
as for A113(a)

Notes:
The deleted stubs in the first gathering are present so that the map (found on the end-papers in both A113(a) and A113(b)) can be included. The map is tipped-in on one of the stubs and these stubs (which are conjugate) are bound in with the first gathering. Wight notes that a map is tipped-in, but does not mention the leaf stubs.

The text appears to use the same setting of type as A113(a).

C.S. Evans wrote to Masefield at the end of August 1934 noting the limitation size of this edition. It appears that Masefield had suggested a small number:

> I discussed the number of the special edition of THE TAKING OF THE GRY with the sales department and we came to the conclusion that your suggestion of 150 was right, and so decided on that number, with twenty five presentation copies. This has been incorporated in the contract which went to you yesterday...
> (C.S. Evans, letter to John Masefield, 24 August 1934)
> (HRHRC, MS (Masefield, J.) Recip William Heinemann Ltd.)

Masefield's trip to Australia was a cause of concern to Heinemann. Three days after deciding on the number of copies, Masefield was sent blank leaves for his signature:

> I am sending you a parcel of paper for the Limited edition of THE TAKING OF THE GRY. As you are going away on Friday perhaps you would be good enough to sign these sheets in the unprinted state. I have put a guide sheet on top to enable you to sign the approximate position.
> (B.F. Oliver, letter to John Masefield, 27 August 1934)
> (HRHRC, MS (Masefield, J.) Recip William Heinemann Ltd.)

These leaves, duly signed, were acknowledged three days later (see B.H. Oliver, letter to John Masefield, 30 August 1934) (HRHRC, MS (Masefield, J.) Recip William Heinemann Ltd.).

In March 1937 C.S. Evans investigated sales since 1933 of Masefield's limited editions. Of *The Bird of Dawning* (A111(c)) he reported to Masefield that the 'whole edition was exhausted'. The same was true of this edition of *The Taking of the Gry*. Copies were still available, however, of the limited signed editions of *Victorious Troy* (A116(d)), *A Letter from Pontus and other verse* (A117(aa)) and *Eggs and Baker* (A119(aa)).

Copies seen: private collection (PWE) number 168, signed '168 | John Masefield.' on p.[iv]; BL (12601.tt.22) number 155, signed '155 | John Masefield.' on p.[iv], stamped 3 OCT 1934

A113(b) First American edition (1934)

THE | TAKING OF THE *GRY* | BY | JOHN MASEFIELD | [ornament] | NEW YORK | THE MACMILLAN COMPANY | 1934
(All width centred)

Bibliographies: Handley-Taylor p.60, Wight 86a

Collation: [A–N]⁸ (J not used); 104 leaves; 189 × 128mm.; [i–x] 1–193 [194–98]

Page contents: [i–ii] blank; [iii] half-title: 'THE | TAKING OF THE *GRY*'; [iv] blank; [v] title-page; [vi] '*Copyright, 1934, by* | JOHN MASEFIELD | [rule] | All rights reserved–no part of this book | may be reproduced in any form without | permission in writing from the publisher, | except by a reviewer who wishes to quote brief | passages in connection with a review written | for inclusion in magazine or newspaper. | [rule] | *Set up and electrotyped.* | *Published October, 1934* | PRINTED IN THE UNITED STATES OF AMERICA | BY THE STRATFORD PRESS, INC., NEW YORK'; [vii] 'To | MY WIFE'; [viii] blank; [ix] 'THE | TAKING OF THE *GRY*'; [x] blank; 1–193 text; [194–98] blank

Paper: wove paper

Running title: 'THE TAKING OF THE GRY' (50mm.) on both verso and recto, pp. 2–193

Binding: orange cloth. On spine: 'THE | TAKING | OF | *THE GRY* | JOHN | MASEFIELD | MACMILLAN | [point]' (all width centred). On upper cover: '[illustration of horse figure-head] | [rule] | THE TAKING OF | *THE GRY* | JOHN MASEFIELD' (within ruled border: 131 × 93mm. thus creating two rectangles: 89 × 93mm. and 44 × 93mm.) Lower cover: blank. Top edge stained blue, lower outside edge trimmed, fore edge roughly trimmed. Binding measurements: 196 × 130mm. (covers), 196 × 43mm. (spine). End-papers: wove paper decorated in black, pink and cyan with map of 'The City of | Santa Barbara.' (signed 'R.H. Sauter') (within ruled border: 181 × 240mm.)

Publication date: published, according to Handley-Taylor, 18 October 1934

Price: $2.00

Contents:
as for A113(a)

Notes:
The text commences on p.1 after an ornamental head-piece.

The publishing agreement for this title between Masefield and Macmillan was dated 12 April 1934 (see Archives of The Society of Authors). The agreement refers to 'a licence to publish in volume form… in the United States of America and Canada a work the subject or title of which is a short novel of approximately 40,000 words – Exact Title to be determined'. This has been annotated 'THE TAKING OF THE GRY' by Masefield.

Copies seen: private collection (ROV)

A113(c) Second English edition ["The Heritage of Literature Series"] (1954)

THE TAKING OF | THE GRY | BY | JOHN MASEFIELD | ILLUSTRATED BY | VICTOR J. BERTOGLIO | LONGMANS, GREEN AND CO | LONDON [point] NEW YORK [point] TORONTO
(All width centred and enclosed within swirling border: 125 × 87mm.)

Bibliographies: Handley-Taylor [unrecorded], Wight [unrecorded]

Collation: [A]⁸ B-K⁸ (J not used); signatures right foot of page with 'TG' at left foot; 80 leaves; 163 × 108mm.; [i–xii] 1–26 [27] 28–68 [69] 70–86 [87] 88–94 [95] 96–122 [123] 124–32 [133] 134–45 [146–48]

Page contents: [i] blank; [ii] 'THE HERITAGE OF | LITERATURE SERIES | General Editor: E. W. PARKER, M.C. | A series that will lead to wider | horizons by awakening a love of | good books, and by providing a key | to the treasures of the world's best | thought | TRAVEL AND ADVENTURE | ESSAYS AND BELLES LETTRES | DRAMA | FICTION | MYTHS AND FOLK LORE | HISTORY | LIFE AND LETTERS | POETRY'; [iii] half-title: 'THE TAKING OF THE GRY' (with '[table lamp and open book] | *The Heritage of* | *Literature Series* | [rule] | SECTION A NO.54' ranged upper-right); [iv] frontispiece: 120 × 89mm., '*I look round the harbour of Santa Barbara*'; [v] title-page; [vi] '[listing of publisher's offices] | *First published in The Heritage* | *of Literature Series 1954 by* | *kind permission of the author* | PRINTED IN GREAT BRITAIN BY | NORTHUMBERLAND PRESS LIMITED | GATESHEAD ON TYNE'; [vii] 'To | MY WIFE'; [viii] blank; [ix] 'LIST OF ILLUSTRATIONS' (seven illustrations including frontispiece listed with page references); [x] blank; [xi] 'ACKNOWLEDGMENT | We are indebted to Messrs. William Heinemann Ltd. for | permission to use the jacket design of their edition as a | basis for the map on p.87.'; [xii] blank; 1–[146] text and illustrations; [147–48] blank

Paper: wove paper

Running title: none

Binding: light blue cloth. On spine, in gold: '*The* | *Taking* | *of the* | *Gry* | *John* | *Masefield* | [design of table lamp and open book] | *Longmans*'. On upper cover, in blind: design of table lamp and open book (ranged lower right). On lower cover, in gold: 'A 54' (ranged lower right). All edges trimmed. Binding measurements: 169 × 111mm. (covers), 169 × 20mm. (spine). End-papers: wove paper with series listing advertisement for '*THE HERITAGE OF LITERATURE SERIES*'

Publication date: published, according to the *English Catalogue of Books*, on 15 March 1954

Price: 3s.6d.

Contents:
as for A113(a)

Notes:
The map present on p.87 is derived from the illustrated end-papers present in A113(a). It is not, however, an exact copy, but a redrawn and simplified version.

Evidence within the archives of The Society of Authors suggests that Longmans first made an approach for 'a school edition' of this title in April 1938 (see BL, Add.Mss.56609, f.75). Masefield, in 1938, was unreceptive to the idea. Writing to The Society of Authors, he states:

I have received your letter about Messrs. Longmans Green. I am sorry, but I do not welcome the suggestion, that any book of mine should be printed for school use in the way suggested. I suppose that the matter would, in any case, have to be referred to Messrs. Heinemann, but I should certainly withhold my consent.

> (John Masefield, letter to [E.J.] Mullett, [20 April 1938])
> (BL, Add.Mss.56609, f.79)

In October 1952 Longmans tried again, requesting permission to include *The Taking of the Gry* and *The Bird of Dawning* in their series. Masefield responded to The Society of Authors:

I have written to Heinemann's about the *Gry* book. I will let you know the answer (perhaps about next Wednesday) about the *Gry*. I could not let the *Bird of Dawning* book appear in a mangled form; so that may be ruled out at once.

> (John Masefield, letter to [Anne] Munro-Kerr, 3 October [1952])
> (BL, Add.Mss.56624, f.14)

The date of 1952 reveals the lengthy period of time before publication took place. Heinemann granted Masefield full permission to reprint this short tale with Longmans as the Heinemann edition had gone out of print. (Heinemann's permission is recorded in BL, Add.Mss.56624, f.27). Masefield's motivation, given his dislike of educational series, was presumably to get works back into print. A letter from Masefield to A.S. Frere notes this edition:

Messrs Longmans Green are asking a question that I must refer to you: it is this:- They wish to include the short novel, *The Taking of the Gry*, in what they call *the Heritage of Literature Series*. The book is out of print, I gather, + not likely to be re-printed by you. If this be so, perhaps you would be not unwilling that the reprint should be made. They wish also to print an abridged issue of *the Bird of Dawning*, but that would never do.

> (John Masefield, letter to [A.S.] Frere, 3 October 1952)
> (Archives of William Heinemann)

Masefield had been unwilling to allow his works to be printed in Heinemann educational series but Frere, possibly devising an opportunity to ask the author once more about the Heinemann 'New Windmill Series', replied:

Many thanks for your letter of 3rd October. Of course I should have no objection to Messrs. Longman Green including *The Taking of the Gry* in what they call *The Heritage of Literature Series*, if you should wish it. I imagine that this is one of their educational series. Could this possibly mean that you may have changed your mind about the inclusion of selections from your works in such a series?

> (A.S. Frere, letter to John Masefield, 6 October 1952)
> (Archives of William Heinemann)

In Masefield's reply he evades Frere's question. It seems highly likely that Frere's mention of the word 'selections' enabled Masefield to reply at cross-purposes:

Thank you for your letter of yesterday, about *the Taking of the Gry*. The Longmans firm are re-printing in their series a very early book by me, much abridged (thank goodness), but the *Gry* book would not be cut, being anyhow very short. On the whole I retain my old dis-taste for the printing of cut-up selections from my books, save in those collections made by myself, now, I gather, no longer in demand.

> (John Masefield, letter to [A.S.] Frere, 7 October [1952])
> (Archives of William Heinemann)

Masefield's first reference was to the Longman Heritage of Literature series edition of *Martin Hyde* (see A13(c)) and references to 'cut-up selections... made by myself' presumably include *A Book of Both Sorts* (A151) and *A Book of Prose Selections* (A158). Masefield both evades the question of the Heinemann educational series and reminds Frere that much of his work required reprinting.

The Society of Authors, wrote to Masefield in November 1952 noting:

Longmans Green have now sent me the agreement for the publication of *The Taking of the Gry* in their Heritage of Literature series. This agreement is identical in its terms to the agreement for *Martin Hyde*.

> ([Anne] Munro-Kerr, letter to John Masefield, 18 November 1952)
> (BL, Add.Mss.56624, f.37)

The publishing agreement for this edition between Masefield and Longmans was dated 20 November 1952 (see Archives of The Society of Authors).

Copies seen: BL (012208.cc.1/97) stamped 11 MAR 1954

Reprinted:

'Second edition'	[second edition, second impression]	1957

A114 POEMS 1935

A114(a) First American edition (1935)

POEMS | BY JOHN MASEFIELD | [ornament] | COMPLETE EDITION | WITH RECENT POEMS | NEW YORK | THE MACMILLAN COMPANY | 1935
(All width centred)

Bibliographies: Handley-Taylor [unrecorded], Wight [unrecorded]

Collation: [A-B]⁸ [C-MM]¹⁶ [NN-PP]⁸ (J, V, W and JJ not used); 568 leaves; 216 × 140mm.; [i–iv] v–xvii [xviii–xxii] 1–38 [39–40] 41–72 [73–74] 75–125 [126–28] 129–210 [211–12] 213–75 [276–78] 279–348 [349–50] 351–405 [406–408] 409–433 [434] [i–ii] 1–167 [168] 169–455 [456–58] 459–97 [498–500] 501–633 [634–36] 637–73 [674–78]

Page contents: [i] half-title: 'POEMS'; [ii] '*BY* JOHN MASEFIELD | [43 titles separated by 42 dashes]' (with additional leaf (and protective tissue) tipped-in on the verso of which is the frontispiece: 143 × 99mm., of a photograph of Masefield signed 'PHOTO LAFAYETTE LTD.'); [iii] title-page; [iv] 'COPYRIGHT, 1913, | BY HARPER AND BROTHERS. | [rule] | COPYRIGHT, 1914, | BY THE CENTURY COMPANY AND BY THE MCCLURE PUBLICATIONS. | [rule] | COPYRIGHT, 1912, 1913, 1914, | BY THE MACMILLAN COMPANY. | [rule] | COPYRIGHT, 1915, 1923, 1924, 1926, 1930, 1931, 1932, AND 1935, | BY JOHN MASEFIELD. | All rights reserved – no part of this book may be | reproduced in any form without permission in writing | from the publisher, except by a reviewer who wishes | to quote brief passages in connection with a review | written for inclusion in magazine or newspaper. | [rule] | New and complete edition | Set up and electrotyped. Published March, 1935. | [point] PRINTED IN THE UNITED STATES OF AMERICA [point]'; v–xii 'PREFACE' ('I have been asked to write a preface to this new collected edition…') (signed, 'JOHN MASEFIELD.'); xiii–xvii 'CONTENTS' (187 individual items listed with page references); [xviii] blank; [xix] 'PART ONE'; [xx] blank; [xxi] 'SALT-WATER BALLADS'; [xxii] blank; 1–38 text; [39] 'MISCELLANEOUS POEMS'; [40] blank; 41–72 text; [73] 'THE EVERLASTING MERCY'; [74] blank; 75–125 text; [126] blank; [127] 'THE WIDOW IN THE BYE STREET'; [128] blank; 129–210 text; [211] 'DAUBER'; [212] blank; 213–75 text; [276] blank; [277] 'THE DAFFODIL FIELDS'; [278] blank; 279–348 text; [349] 'SONNETS AND OTHER POEMS'; [350] blank; 351–405 text; [406] blank; [407] 'LOLLINGDON DOWNS | AND OTHER POEMS'; [408] blank; 409–433 text; [434] blank; [i] 'PART TWO'; [ii] blank; 1–167 text; [168] blank; 169–455 text; [456] blank; [457] 'POEMS FROM THE *WANDERER*'; [458] blank; 459–97 text; [498] blank; [499] 'POEMS FROM MINNIE MAYLOW'S STORY'; [500] blank; 501–633 text; [634] blank; [635] 'A TALE OF TROY'; [636] blank; 637–73 text; [674–78] blank

Paper: wove paper

Running title: 'POEMS' (14mm.) on verso; recto title comprises poem title or title of original volume, pp.2–433 (of part one) and pp.2–673 (of part two)

Binding: dark red/brown cloth. On spine, in gold: 'POEMS | [point] | JOHN | MASEFIELD | [ornament] | MACMILLAN | [point]' (all width centred). On upper cover, in gold: facsimile signature 'J. Masefield'. Lower cover: blank. All edges trimmed. Sewn head and foot bands (in red and yellow). Binding measurements: 221 × 141mm. (covers), 221 × 55mm. (spine). End-papers: wove paper.

Publication date: March 1935

Price: $5.00

Contents:
Preface ('I have been asked to write a preface to this new collected edition…')
PART ONE
SALT-WATER BALLADS
A Consecration ('Not of the princes and prelates with periwigged charioteers')
The Yarn of the *Loch Achray* ('The *Loch Achray* was a clipper tall')
Sing a Song O' Shipwreck ('He lolled on a bollard, a sun-burned son of the sea,')
Burial Party ('"He's deader 'n nails," the fo'c's'le said, "'n' gone to his long sleep; "')
Bill ('He lay dead on the cluttered deck and stared at the cold skies,')
Fever Ship ('There'll be no weepin' gells ashore when *our* ship sails,')
Fever-Chills ('He tottered out of the alleyway with cheeks the colour of paste,')
Hell's Pavement ('"When I'm discharged in Liverpool 'n' draws my bit o' pay,')
Sea-Change ('"Goneys and gullies an' all o' the birds o' the sea,')
Harbour-Bar ('All in the feathered palm-tree tops the bright green parrots screech,')
The Turn of the Tide ('An' Bill can have my sea-boots, Nigger Jim can have my knife,')
One of Wally's Yarns ('The watch was up on the topsail-yard a-making fast the sail,')
A Valediction (Liverpool Docks) ('Is there anything as I can do ashore for you')
A Night at Dago Tom's ('Oh yesterday, I t'ink it was, while cruisin' down the street,')
Port of Many Ships ('"It's a sunny pleasant anchorage, is Kingdom Come,')
Cape Horn Gospel – I ('"I was in a hooker once," said Karlssen,')
A Valediction ('We're bound for blue water where the great winds blow,')
A Pier-Head Chorus ('Oh I'll be chewing salted horse and biting flinty bread,')
The Golden City of St. Mary ('Out beyond the sunset, could I but find the way,')
Trade Winds ('In the harbour, in the island, in the Spanish Seas,')
Sea-Fever ('I must go down to the seas again, to the lonely sea and the sky,')
A Wanderer's Song ('A wind's in the heart of me, a fire's in my heels,')
Cardigan Bay ('Clean, green, windy billows notching out the sky,')
Christmas Eve at Sea ('A wind is rustling "south and soft,"')

402

A Ballad of Cape St. Vincent ('Now, Bill, ain't it prime to be a-sailin',')
The Tarry Buccaneer ('I'm going to be a pirate with a bright brass pivot-gun,')
A Ballad of John Silver ('We were schooner-rigged and rakish, with a long and lissome hull,')
D'Avalos' Prayer ('When the last sea is sailed, when the last shallow charted,')
The West Wind ('It's a warm wind, the west wind, full of birds' cries;')
The Galley-Rowers ('Staggering over the running combers')
Vagabond ('Dunno a heap about the what an' why,')
Vision ('I have drunken the red wine and flung the dice;')
Spunyarn ('Spunyarn, spunyarn, with one to turn the crank,')
Personal ('Tramping at night in the cold and wet, I passed the lighted inn,')
On Malvern Hill ('A wind is brushing down the clover,')
On Eastnor Knoll ('Silent are the woods, and the dim green boughs are')
"Rest Her Soul, She's Dead" ('She has done with the sea's sorrow and the world's way')
"All Ye That Pass By" ('On the long dusty ribbon of the long city street,')
In Memory of A.P.R. ('Once in the windy wintry weather,')
To-Morrow ('Oh yesterday the cutting edge drank thirstily and deep,')
Cavalier ('All the merry kettle-drums are thudding into rhyme,')
GLOSSARY ('Abaft the beam._That half of a ship included between her amidship section…')
MISCELLANEOUS POEMS
The Ballad of Sir Bors ('Would I could win some quiet and rest, and a little ease,')
Spanish Waters ('Spanish waters, Spanish waters, you are ringing in my ears,')
Cargoes ('Quinquireme of Nineveh from distant Ophir,')
Captain Stratton's Fancy ('Oh some are fond of red wine, and some are fond of white')
An Old Song Re-Sung ('I saw a ship a-sailing, a-sailing, a-sailing,')
St. Mary's Bells ('It's pleasant in Holy Mary')
London Town ('Oh London Town's a fine town, and London sights are rare,')
The Emigrant ('Going by Daly's shanty I heard the boys within')
Port of Holy Peter ('The blue laguna rocks and quivers,')
Beauty ('I have seen dawn and sunset on moors and windy hills')
The Seekers ('Friends and loves we have none, nor wealth, nor blessed abode,')
Dawn ('The dawn comes cold: the haystack smokes,')
Laugh and be Merry ('Laugh and be merry, remember, better the world with a song,')
June Twilight ('The twilight comes; the sun')
Roadways ('One road leads to London,')
Midsummer Night ('The perfect disc of the sacred moon')
The Harper's Song ('This sweetness trembling from the strings')
The Gentle Lady ('So beautiful, so dainty-sweet')
The Dead Knight ('The cleanly rush of the mountain air,')
Twilight ('Twilight it is, and the far woods are dim, and the rooks cry and call.')
Invocation ('O wanderer into many brains,')
Posted as Missing ('Under all her topsails she trembled like a stag,')
A Creed ('I hold that when a person dies')
When Bony Death ('When bony Death has chilled her gentle blood,')
Her Heart ('Her heart is always doing lovely things,')
Being Her Friend ('Being her friend, I do not care, not I,')
Fragments ('Troy Town is covered up with weeds,')
Born for Nought Else ('Born for nought else, for nothing but for this,')
Tewkesbury Road ('It is good to be out on the road, and going one knows not where,')
The Death Rooms ('My soul has many an old decaying room')
Ignorance ('Since I have learned Love's shining alphabet,')
The Watch in the Wood ('When Death has laid her in his quietude,')
Waste ('No rose but fades: no glory but must pass:')
Third Mate ('All the sheets are clacking, all the blocks are whining,')
The Wild Duck ('Twilight. Red in the west.')
Christmas, 1903 ('O, the sea breeze will be steady, and the tall ship's going trim,')
The Word ('My friend, my bonny friend, when we are old,')
LYRICS FROM "POMPEY THE GREAT"
I. The Chief Centurions ('Man is a sacred city, built of marvellous earth.')
II. Philip Sings ('Though we are ringed with spears, though the last hope is gone,')
III. Chanty ('Kneel to the beautiful women who bear us this strange brave fruit.')
Epilogue to "Pompey the Great" ('And all their passionate hearts are dust,')
THE EVERLASTING MERCY

The Everlasting Mercy ('From '41 to '51')
THE WIDOW IN THE BYE STREET
The Widow in the Bye Street ('Down Bye Street, in a little Shropshire town,')
[MISCELLANEOUS POEMS]
Biography ('When I am buried, all my thoughts and acts')
Ships ('I cannot tell their wonder nor make known')
Truth ('Man with his burning soul')
They Closed Her Eyes ('They closed her eyes,')
The Harp ('In a dark corner of the room,')
Sonnet ('I saw the ramparts of my native land')
Sonnet on the Death of his Wife ('That blessed sunlight that once showed to me')
Song ('One sunny time in May')
C.L.M. ('In the dark womb where I began')
DAUBER
Dauber ('Four bells were struck, the watch was called on deck,')
Explanations of some of the Sea Terms used in the Poem ('Backstays.-Wire ropes which support the masts against…')
THE DAFFODIL FIELDS
The Daffodil Fields ('Between the barren pasture and the wood')
SONNETS AND OTHER POEMS
[Untitled] ('Long long ago, when all the glittering earth')
[Untitled] ('Night came again, but now I could not sleep.')
[Untitled] ('Even after all these years there comes the dream')
[Untitled] ('If I could come again to that dear place')
[Untitled] ('Men are made human by the mighty fall')
[Untitled] ('Here in the self is all that man can know')
[Untitled] ('Flesh, I have knocked at many a dusty door,')
[Untitled] ('But all has passed, the tune has died away,')
[Untitled] ('These myriad days, these many thousand hours,')
[Untitled] ('There, on the darkened deathbed, dies the brain')
[Untitled] ('So in the empty sky the stars appear,')
[Untitled] ('It may be so with us, that in the dark,')
[Untitled] ('Man has his unseen friend, his unseen twin,')
[Untitled] ('What am I, Life? A thing of watery salt')
[Untitled] ('If I could get within this changing I,')
[Untitled] ('What is this atom which contains the whole,')
[Untitled] ('Ah, we are neither heaven nor earth, but men;')
[Untitled] ('Roses are beauty, but I never see')
[Untitled] ('Over the church's door they moved a stone')
[Untitled] ('I never see the red rose crown the year,')
[Untitled] ('Out of the clouds come torrents, from the earth')
[Untitled] ('O little self, within whose smallness lies')
[Untitled] ('I went into the fields, but you were there')
[Untitled] ('There are two forms of life, of which one moves,')
[Untitled] ('Restless and hungry, still it moves and slays')
[Untitled] ('How many ways, how many different times')
[Untitled] ('The other form of Living does not stir;')
[Untitled] ('Is there a great green commonwealth of Thought')
[Untitled] ('Beauty, let be; I cannot see your face,')
[Untitled] ('Here, where we stood together, we three men,')
[Untitled] ('I saw her like a shadow on the sky')
[Untitled] ('Not that the stars are all gone mad in heaven')
[Untitled] ('There is no God, as I was taught in youth,')
[Untitled] ('Beauty retires; the blood out of the earth')
[Untitled] ('Wherever beauty has been quick in clay')
[Untitled] ('You are more beautiful than women are,')
[Untitled] ('Not for the anguish suffered is the slur,')
[Untitled] ('Beauty was with me once, but now, grown old,')
[Untitled] ('So beauty comes, so with a failing hand')
[Untitled] ('If Beauty be at all, if, beyond sense,')
[Untitled] ('Each greedy self, by consecrating lust,')
[Untitled] ('Time being an instant in eternity,')
[Untitled] ('You will remember me in days to come')

On Growing Old ('Be with me Beauty for the fire is dying,')
Lyric ('Give me a light that I may see her,')
[RIGHT ROYAL]
Right Royal ('An hour before the race they talked together,')
[KING COLE]
King Cole ('King Cole was King before the troubles came,')
[THE DREAM AND OTHER POEMS]
The Dream of Daniel ('Weary with many thoughts I went to bed,')
The Woman Speaks ('This poem appeared to me in a dream one winter morning some years ago. In the dream...')
The Rider at the Gate ('A windy night was blowing on Rome,')
The Builders ('Before the unseen cock had called the time,')
The Setting of the Windcock ('The dust lay white upon the chisel-marks,')
The Racer ('I saw the racer coming to the jump,')
From the Song of Roland ('Roland gripped his horn with might and main,')
The Haunted ('Here, in this darkened room of this old house,')
Campeachy Picture ('The sloop's sails glow in the sun; the far sky burns,')
[MISCELLANEOUS POEMS]
The Ship and Her Makers ('THE ORE | Before Man's labouring wisdom gave me birth')
Beauty ('When soul's companion fails,')
Nireus ('Once long ago young Nireus was the King')
[MIDSUMMER NIGHT AND OTHER TALES IN VERSE]
The Begetting of Arthur ('Uther, the Prince, succeeding to the post')
The Birth of Arthur ('When the wind from East changes')
The Taking of Morgause ('Morgause the Merry played beside the burn:')
The Begetting of Modred ('When berries were scarlet')
Badon Hill ('Loki the Dragon killer mustered men')
The Sailing of Hell Race ('When Arthur came from warring, having won')
Arthur and his Ring ('Beauty's Delight, the Princess Gwenivere,')
Midsummer Night ('Midsummer night had fallen at full moon,')
The Fight on the Wall ('Modred was in the Water Tower')
The Breaking of the Links ('They told King Arthur how the Knights were killed,')
Gwenivach Tells ('I, Gwenivach, King Modred's queen, declare')
Arthur in the Ruins ('King Arthur watched within the ruined town,')
The Fight at Camlan ('Soon the two armies were in touch, and soon')
The Fight on the Beach, or The Passing ('These were the nine with Modred:-Kolgrim, Gor,')
Gwenivere Tells ('So Arthur passed, but country-folk believe')
The Death of Lancelot ('Then, after many years, a rider came,')
Dust to Dust ('Henry Plantagenet, the English King,')
On the Coming of Arthur ('By ways unknown, unseen,')
The Old Tale of The Begetting ('*The men of old, who made the tale for us,*')
The Taking of Gwenivere ('French poets write:-That, Lancelot the brave')
South and East ('When good King Arthur ruled these western hursts,')
Fulfilment ('Long since, Sir Constans governed here for Rome,')
[POEMS FROM SARD HARKER]
Sard Harker ('A calm like Jove's beneath a fiery air.')
The Pathfinder ('She lies at grace, at anchor, head to tide,')
[POEMS FROM ODTAA]
The Sonnet of Camilla, Mother of Don Manuel, on hearing of... ('Lord, when Thy servant, doubting of Thy grace,')
Lines, on the same occasion... ('In the dark night I saw Death drawing near')
A Sonnet upon Ezekiel Rust ('Son of Isaiah Rust, of Churn, his wage')
The Meditation of Carlotta in Prison ('This that I understand,')
The Meditation of Highworth Ridden ('I have seen flowers come in stony places;')
The Comfort of Manuel, on Setting Forth Defeated in The *Venturer* ('Bad lies behind, worse lies before.')
POEMS FROM THE WANDERER
The Setting Forth ('Her builder and owner drank tea with her captain below.')
The Ending ('Once, long before, at her second outgoing down Channel')
A Masque of Liverpool ('LIVERPOOL | I am the English sea-queen; I am she')
The *Wanderer* ('You swept across the waters like a Queen,')
Liverpool, 1890 ('Grey sea dim, smoke-blowing, hammer-racket, sirens')
Liverpool, 1930 ('The dockyards of the ancient days are filled')
On Skysails ('I saw you often as the crown of Queens')
Pay ('The world paid but a penny for its toil,')

The Crowd ('They had secured their beauty to the dock,')
Under Three Lower Topsails ('Three lower topsails dark with wet are straining')
Eight Bells ('Four double strokes repeated on the bells,')
Posted ('Dream after dream I see the wrecks that lie')
If ('If it could be, that in this southern port')
I Saw Her Here ('All tranquil is the mirror of the bay,')
Wanderer and Wonderer ('When first the thought of you took steel')
POEMS FROM MINNIE MAYLOW'S STORY
Prologue ('I am a pilgrim come from many lands,')
Minnie Maylow's Story ('Once (long ago) there was an English King,')
Adamas and Eva ('Whilom there was, dwellyng in Paradys,')
Son of Adam ('Once on a time there was a lusty Lion')
The Love Gift ('In King Marc's palace at the valley-head')
Tristan's Singing ('PART I | When Isolt quarrelled with her Tristan there')
Simkin, Tomkin and Jack ('Before old Tencombe of the Barrows died,')
The Rose of the World ('Dark Eleanor and Henry sat at meat')
Young John of Chance's Stretch ('PART I | When Father died, my Mother ran')
Evan Roberts, A.B., of H.M.S. *Andromache* ('This gallant act is told by the late Montagu Burrows, on page 67 of his *Autobiography...*')
Richard Whittington ('FORTUNE: | I am Fortune: I give as is fitting to each of my souls,')
The Hour Strikes ('THE SEEKER: | The shepherds warned me not to climb this hill')
Penelope ('SCENE:-*A room in* PENELOPE'S *palace.* PENELOPE *seated centre...*')
A TALE OF TROY
The Taking of Helen ('Menelaus, the Spartan King,')
The Going to Troy ('He took her to Troy, the windy town,')
Klytaimnestra ('I am that Klytaimnestra whom Agamemnon wedded,')
The Spearman ('You have heard the lady, making her complaints.')
The Horse ('My Father, King Epeios of the Islands,')
Sthenelus' Daughter *The Entry into Troy* ('King Sthenelus, my Father, has often told me')
The Trojans about the Horse *What Priam Said* ('"Apollo's self commanded Agamemnon')
Kassandra ('I was the thing they heard, I am Kassandra.')
Sthenelus' Daughter *In the Horse, till Sunset* ('That was the voice those hidden in the Horse heard.')
[Sthenelus' Daughter] *In the Horse, Sunset till Cockcrow* ('Then, to our joy, quick steps came up the courtyard,')
The Surprise ('You have heard the story of the Horse of Troy.')
Epilogue *Spoken by Kassandra* ('Though many died and many fled')

Notes:

The volume is inconsistent in use of divisional titles (noting the original volumes from which contents has been taken).

Several poems from *Lollingdon Downs and other poems* acquire titles for the first time.

Masefield states in his preface:

> The work of many years has been gathered together here. Some has been weeded out; some that has been omitted from past collections has been included; some few misprints and other errors, of placing, have been corrected; most of the work here printed now appears in the order in which it was composed.

There are indeed omissions, the poem *Rosas* for example.

The division of the volume into two parts owes its origins to *Poems: Complete in One Volume* (see A91), and therefore to the two volumes of *Poems* (see A78(a)).

The publishing agreement for this volume between Masefield and Macmillan was dated 5 February 1934 (see Archives of The Society of Authors). The agreement refers to 'a licence to publish in volume form... in the United States of America and Canada a work the subject of which is a new edition of Collected Poems to contain all poems since publication of the last collected edition with a preface by the Author and the Author's portrait as frontispiece'.

Copies seen: private collection (PWE)

A114(b) Second American edition (1953)

POEMS | BY JOHN MASEFIELD | [ornament] | COMPLETE EDITION | WITH RECENT POEMS | NEW YORK | THE MACMILLAN COMPANY | 1953
(All width centred)

Bibliographies: Handley-Taylor p.66, Wight [unrecorded]

Collation: [A-Q]³² [R]²⁸ [S]³² (J not used); 572 leaves; 212 × 142mm.; [i–iv] v–xviii [xix–xxii] 1–38 [39–40] 41–72 [73–74] 75–125 [126–28] 129–210 [211–12] 213–75 [276–78] 279–348 [349–50] 351–405 [406–408] 409–433 [434] [i–ii] 1–167 [168] 169–455 [456–58] 459–97 [498–500] 501–633 [634–36] 637–73 [674–76] 677–85 [686]

Page contents: [i] half-title: 'POEMS'; [ii] 'THE WORKS OF JOHN MASEFIELD | *PLAYS* | [12 titles listed] | *POETRY* | [21 titles listed] | *FICTION* | [14 titles listed] | *GENERAL* | [17 titles listed]' (with additional leaf tipped-in on the verso of which is frontispiece: 134 × 101mm., of a photograph of Masefield signed '*Keystone* | JOHN MASEFIELD'); [iii] title-page; [iv] 'COPYRIGHT, 1913, | BY HARPER AND BROTHERS. | [rule] | COPYRIGHT, 1914, | BY THE CENTURY COMPANY AND BY THE MCCLURE PUBLICATIONS. | [rule] | COPYRIGHT, 1912, 1913, 1914, | BY THE MACMILLAN COMPANY. | [rule] | COPYRIGHT, 1915, 1923, 1924, 1926, 1930, 1931, 1932, 1935, 1940, | 1941, 1942, 1949, 1950, AND 1951, | BY JOHN MASEFIELD. | [rule] | All rights reserved–no part of this book may be | reproduced in any form without permission in writing | from the publisher, except by a reviewer who wishes | to quote brief passages in connection with a review | written for inclusion in magazine or newspaper. | [point] PRINTED IN THE UNITED STATES OF AMERICA [point]'; v–xii 'PREFACE' ('I have been asked to write a preface to this new collected edition...') (signed, 'JOHN MASEFIELD.'); xiii–xviii 'CONTENTS' (192 individual items (in two parts) listed with page references); [xix] 'PART ONE'; [xx] blank; [xxi] 'SALT-WATER BALLADS'; [xxii] blank; 1–38 text; [39] 'MISCELLANEOUS POEMS'; [40] blank; 41–72 text; [73] 'THE EVERLASTING MERCY'; [74] blank; 75–125 text; [126] blank; [127] 'THE WIDOW IN THE BYE STREET'; [128] blank; 129–210 text; [211] 'DAUBER'; [212] blank; 213–75 text; [276] blank; [277] 'THE DAFFODIL FIELDS'; [278] blank; 279–348 text; [349] 'SONNETS AND OTHER POEMS'; [350] blank; 351–405 text; [406] blank; [407] 'LOLLINGDON DOWNS | AND OTHER POEMS'; [408] blank; 409–433 text; [434] blank; [i] 'PART TWO'; [ii] blank; 1–167 text; [168] blank; 169–455 text; [456] blank; [457] 'POEMS FROM | THE *WANDERER*'; [458] blank; 459–97 text; [498] blank; [499] 'POEMS FROM | MINNIE MAYLOW'S STORY'; [500] blank; 501–633 text; [634] blank; [635] 'A TALE OF TROY'; [636] blank; 637–73 text; [674] blank; [675] 'RECENT POEMS'; [676] blank; 677–85 text; [686] blank

Paper: wove paper

Running title: 'POEMS' (14mm.) on verso; recto title comprises poem title or title of original volume, pp.2–433 (of part one) and pp.2–685 (of part two)

Binding: blue cloth. On spine, in silver: 'POEMS | [point] | JOHN | MASEFIELD | [ornament] | MACMILLAN' (all width centred). On upper cover, in silver: facsimile signature 'John Masefield.' Lower cover: blank. All edges trimmed. Sewn head and foot bands (in blue and white). Binding measurements: 219 × 140mm. (covers), 219 × 56mm. (spine). End-papers: wove paper.

Publication date: published, according to Handley-Taylor, 15 September 1953

Price: $8.00

Contents:
pp.v–433 (of part one) and pp.1–673 (of part two) as for A114(a) and then with the following additional contents:
RECENT POEMS
Music 1939–40 ('Speak to us, Music, for the discord jars;')
In Praise of Nurses ('Man, in his gallant power, goes in pride,')
The Kings at Midnight ('That starry night when Christ was born,')
On the Hill ('No I know not;')
The Hill ('This remains here.')

Notes:
The frontispiece photograph is different from that present in A114(a).

Copies seen: private collection (ROV)

Reprinted:

'Second Printing'	[second edition, second impression]	1955
['Third Printing']	[second edition, third impression]	[no copies consulted]
['Fourth Printing']	[second edition, fourth impression]	[no copies consulted]
['Fifth Printing']	[second edition, fifth impression]	[no copies consulted]
['Sixth Printing']	[second edition, sixth impression]	[no copies consulted]
'Seventh Printing'	[second edition, seventh impression]	1966
'Eighth Printing'	[second edition, eighth impression]	1967

A115 THE BOX OF DELIGHTS   1935

A115(a) First English edition (1935)

The Box of Delights | *or* | When the Wolves were Running | *by* | John Masefield | [ornament] | [publisher's device of a windmill with 'W [point]' and 'H'] | [rule, 71mm.] | WILLIAM HEINEMANN LTD | LONDON : TORONTO (All width centred)

Bibliographies: Handley-Taylor p.60, Wight 87

Collation: [A]⁸ B-CC⁸ (J and V not used); signatures right foot of page; 216 leaves; 191 × 126mm.; [i–x] 1–418 [419–22]

Page contents: [i–ii] blank; [iii] half-title: 'The Box of Delights'; [iv] '*ALSO BY JOHN MASEFIELD* | PLAYS: | [12 titles listed] | POETRY: | [14 titles listed] | FICTION: | [six titles listed] | GENERAL: | [nine titles listed]'; [v] title-page; [vi] 'FIRST PUBLISHED 1935 | PRINTED IN GREAT BRITAIN | AT THE WINDMILL PRESS, KINGSWOOD, SURREY'; [vii] 'To | MY WIFE'; [viii] blank; [ix–x] 'CONTENTS' (12 chapters each listed with a couplet and page reference); 1–418 text; [419–22] blank

Paper: wove paper

Running title: 'THE BOX OF DELIGHTS' (58mm.) on both verso and recto, pp.2–418

Binding: blue cloth. On spine, in gold: 'THE | BOX OF | DELIGHTS | [ornament] | JOHN | MASEFIELD | HEINEMANN' (all width centred). On upper cover, in gold: 'THE BOX OF DELIGHTS | JOHN MASEFIELD' (within blind ruled border: 186 × 120mm.) On lower cover, in blind: publisher's device of a windmill (ranged lower right). Top edge stained blue, others edges trimmed. Binding measurements: 196 × 128mm. (covers), 196 × 45mm. (spine). End-papers: wove paper decorated in black, blue and red with 27 illustrations and scrolled panel: 'THE BOX OF DELIGHTS | JOHN MASEFIELD', signed 'Judith Masefield 1935.', all within blue, black, red and black ruled border: 184 × 246mm.

Publication date: the sales ledger preserved in the Heinemann Archive suggests publication on 30 August 1935 in an edition of 7500 copies

Price: 7s.6d.

Contents:
The Box of Delights ('As Kay was coming home for the Christmas holidays, after his first term at school, the train...')
Chapter couplets are as follows:
I. A wandering Showman dreads to hear | Red Riding Hood's Attackers near.
II. The Wolf Pack hunts him through the snow. | Where shall the 'nighted Showman go?
III. Has a Dark Midnight in the Past | A Way, or is To-night his last?
IV. What is this Secret? Who can learn | The Wild Wood better than from Herne?
V. In darkest Cellars underneath | Blood-hungry Sea-Wolves snap their Teeth.
VI. The Oak-Tree-Lady with the Ring | Gives Kay the Marvel of the Spring.
VII. Kay dares the Cockatrice's Bite. | Maria once more sees the Light.
VIII. Blackness of hidden Caves, and Men | Black as their Caves, at Sins agen.
IX. The Spider in the Web declares | Why he his cruel Net prepares.
X. The Sea-Wolves, snapping Teeth at Kay, | Bid him Beware of Yesterday.
XI. O Greatness, hear, O Brightness, hark, | Leave us not Little, nor yet Dark.
XII. Ring, blessed Bells, for Christmas Morn, | Joy in Full Measure, Hope New-born.

Notes:
A children's novel (sub-titled 'When the Wolves Were Running') and the sequel to *The Midnight Folk* (see A86). The novel is in twelve chapters. The story tells of Kay Harker and his Christmas adventures to keep a magic box from the evil Abner Brown and his accomplices.

The text is illustrated by Judith Masefield.

At the same time as telling C.S. Evans about *The Taking of the Gry*, Masefield had presumably hinted that he was writing – or about to write – a book for children. Evans responded with enthusiasm:

> It is good news about the children's book. I am forming a plan for the publication of a dozen or so very good children's books next year and I am working out a special scheme for selling them.
> (C.S. Evans, letter to John Masefield, 5 July 1934)
> (HRHRC, MS (Masefield, J.) Recip William Heinemann Ltd.)

It appears that the typescript had not been delivered by the beginning of April 1935. Louisa Callender wrote requesting details:

> Will you not let us have the tale for children which you have finished, or at any rate tell us the title of it and of your full size story for the autumn? It is important that we should get information about both books out to the colonies as soon as possible.
> (Louisa Callender, letter to John Masefield, 15 April 1935)
> (HRHRC, MS (Masefield, J.) Recip William Heinemann Ltd.)

Less than a month later it appears that Masefield sent the typescript together with Judith's illustrations (and possibly details of *Victorious Troy*). An acknowledgment was sent on 10 May 1935:

> This letter is just to acknowledge the safe receipt of the typescript of THE BOX OF DELIGHTS, the descriptions of the two books, and the illustrations for THE BOX OF DELIGHTS. What a very lovely wrapper and endpapers!
> (Louisa Callender, letter to John Masefield, 10 May 1935)
> (HRHRC, MS (Masefield, J.) Recip William Heinemann Ltd.)

As usual, C.S. Evans was the first to read the new work. He wrote suggesting that Masefield had attained the status of J.M. Barrie or Lewis Carroll:

> During the week-end I read with very great pleasure your new children's book, THE BOX OF DELIGHTS. It is a delightful story and I could not help thinking all the way through what a wonderful play could be based upon it – a play which might have the popularity and permanence of PETER PAN. The mixture of fantasy, poetry and adventure is extremely successful; and I do not remember any book except ALICE IN WONDERLAND in which the dreamlike quality is so well preserved. It might be a good idea later on to issue THE BOX OF DELIGHTS and MIDNIGHT FOLK together in one volume, the whole illustrated by Judith, whose pictures are excellent. The wrapper is particularly attractive...
> (C.S. Evans, letter to John Masefield, 10 May 1935)
> (HRHRC, MS (Masefield, J.) Recip William Heinemann Ltd.)

The setting of the type took two months and 'first proofs' were sent to the author on 15 July 1935:

> I have pleasure in sending you two sets of first proofs of THE BOX OF DELIGHTS with manuscript. Kindly let me have your corrected proof for revision in due course.
>
> (B.F. Oliver, letter to John Masefield, 15 July 1935)
(HRHRC, MS (Masefield, J.) Recip William Heinemann Ltd.)

With the 'revised book proofs' a problem was discovered, however. B.F. Oliver wrote:

> …In marking up the book, we find there is not enough space for the blocks to go at the ends of Chapters 9 and 10 (pp.276 and 311) and we wonder if you could perhaps delete one or two words or lines in these chapters to give room. Also at the bottom of page 395, the text reads for a block to be inserted, but we have checked carefully all the drawings and blocks received and there is not one for this paragraph…
>
> (B.F. Oliver, letter to John Masefield, 29 July 1935)
(HRHRC, MS (Masefield, J.) Recip William Heinemann Ltd.)

'Corrected proofs' were ready by the beginning of August for Heinemann supplied Macmillan with three sets on 2 August 1935 (see B.F. Oliver, letter to John Masefield, 2 August 1935) (HRHRC, MS (Masefield, J.) Recip William Heinemann Ltd.)

After publication a mistake was discovered in the listing of Masefield's works (appearing on p.[iv]). C.S. Evans also suggested a solution to the lack of acknowledgement for Judith Masefield's illustrations and mentions, once again, a proposed combined edition of the Kay Harker stories:

> I have been trying to trace the mistake which appears in the list of your books on the fly leaf of THE BOX OF DELIGHTS. These lists are made up at the press and are copied from previous lists: they are brought up to date by new books being added. The first appearance of "A new hymn of the Resurrection written in play form" was in THE CONWAY in 1933. It has been repeated in several books since then and the extraordinary thing is that nobody has pointed out the mistake or has seemed to notice it. How it occurred or who first put the phrase in I have been unable to trace.
>
> There is only one thing which may perhaps throw some light on the mystery. I seem to remember that when THE COMING OF CHRIST was being performed in Canterbury Cathedral we printed privately for you, for distribution among the audience, a hymn of which I cannot remember the title. It is possible that in some way that title found its way into the list. I have looked through our catalogue and through the spring and autumn lists over a period of years and I find that the mistake does not occur in any of them.
>
> The first edition of THE BOX OF DELIGHTS is bound but it is quite possible to reprint the fly (which, as you will see, backs the half title) putting a note saying, "The illustrations + the design for the wrapper and end papers of this book are by Judith Masefield." Judith wrote to me about the omnibus edition of MIDNIGHT FOLK and THE BOX OF DELIGHTS and I told her that I had discussed the matter with you and that we intended to do it at the appropriate time…
>
> (C.S. Evans, letter to John Masefield, 4 October 1935)
(HRHRC, MS (Masefield, J.) Recip William Heinemann Ltd.)

A copy in the HRHRC (PZ8 M4476BO cop.1) is catalogued as the 'Author's issue'. It comprises a first Heinemann edition specially bound in white vellum with blue ties. 'THE BOX | OF | DELIGHTS | [rule] | JOHN | MASEFIELD | 1935' appears in gold on the spine. Both front and rear end-papers are included, as in the published edition. There is no inscription. The binding is signed on the front fixed end-paper 'BOUND BY MALTBY, OXFORD.'

In February 1935 Masefield sought ecclesiastical advice on the plot from G.K.A. Bell (1883–1958), then Bishop of Chichester:

> I wonder if you will be so kind as to enlighten me about a perplexing point in ecclesiastical procedure. I am writing a book for children. It is a Christmas book, in the course of which a nefarious company of gangsters decide to prevent a Christmas Celebration in a Cathedral by kidnapping the Bishop, Dean, Archdeacon, Canons, Prebendaries, Minor Canons (if there are such things), Precentor, Organist, Chief Theologian, Vestiary, Bursar, Sub-Bursar, Warden of the Almonry, Sub-Warden, together with a mixed company of members of the Choir.
>
> The point which perplexes me is this: when all these people have been kidnapped successfully on whom would the task of maintaining the Cathedral services devolve? Who would see that the services were properly supplied? I take it that at Christmas time it might be difficult for the clergy in the diocese to spare many helpers from parochial duties. Please forgive me for bothering you with this point, but it would be most kind if you could let me know what course would be taken and by whom…
>
> (John Masefield, letter to G.K.A. Bell, 15 February 1935)
(Lambeth Palace Library, Bell Papers (Eliot-Shaw) 208, f.228)

It appears that Bell suggested the use of the Friends of the Cathedral (see Lambeth Palace Library, Bell Papers (Eliot-Shaw) 208, f.231).

Prior to publication there was interest shown in French translation rights. Masefield, writing to The Society of Authors sensibly stated:

> The story, "The Box of Delights", may be published here at the end of August. The lady had better read it first before she decides to translate it.
>
> (John Masefield, letter to [E.J.] Mullett, 22 July 1935)
(BL, Add.Mss.56603, f.62)

Pre-publication interest changed to post-publication enquiries. Applications were received in October 1935 to serialize the novel in the Australian press. Permission was denied by Masefield (see BL, Add.Mss.56603, f.157).

The BBC proposed a radio adaptation of the novel by a Miss Jenkin in 1942. Masefield read her script and wrote:

> I have now read through the script submitted to me. It seems to me, that the writer has missed the essential point in my design. The book is the record of a dream displaying a little boy's mind on his coming home for the Christmas holidays. To omit even the glimmer of a suggestion that it is a dream, and to make of it nothing but a fantastic gangster story, while suggesting that it is still my design, i[s] well, I ask you, what? Then you make the little boy ejaculate "Gosh" at frequent intervals; this was not his custom. The tale is designedly intricate, and easier to follow when seen, than when spoken; but that it is all a dream is of its essence.
>
> (John Masefield, letter to Miss Jenkin, 24 October 1942)
> (BL, Add.Mss.56616, f.79)

Although Kay Harker's earlier adventures are narrated as probable fact in *The Midnight Folk* (the magical adventures do, admittedly, occur at night), it seems that Masefield placed particular importance on the dream genre for this later adventure. The dream is, however, only mentioned in the final paragraphs of the book.

There have been at least three radio adaptations by the B.B.C.:

1943 (adapted by Robert Holland and John Keir Cross)
1948 (repeat of 1943 adaptation?)
1966 ('freely dramatised for radio by John Keir Cross' starring Patricia Hayes as Kay Harker, Cyril Shaps as Cole Hawlings, Felix Felton as Abner Brown and produced by David Davis)
1995 (dramatised by John Peacock starring Alastair Sooke as Kay Harker, Lionel Jeffries as Cole Hawlings, Donald Sinden as Abner Brown and directed by David Blount)

In 1984 a B.B.C. television adaptation by Alan Seymour starred Devin Stanfield as Kay Harker, Patrick Troughton as Cole Hawlings and Robert Stephens as Abner Brown. It was produced by Paul Stone and directed by Renny Rye.

Copies seen: private collection (PWE); BL (N.N.22425) stamped 30 AUG 1935; Harvard College Library (Houghton *EC9.M377.935b) inscribed 'For Florence. [Lamont] | from John. | Augt 29. 1935.' on p.[iii]; HRHRC (PZ8 M4476BO cop.2) inscribed 'For Con | from Jan | August 28. 1935.', signed 'John Masefield.' and also signed by Judith Masefield 'illustrated by | Judith Masefield'

Reprinted:

'Reprinted'	[first edition, second impression]	1957 [1958]
		1958
		1962
		1964

A 1968 reprint employs a different setting of the text. It is not currently known in which year the re-set edition (and thus a new edition) was issued. Assuming that it was published after the 1965 edition issued by Penguin and the 1966 reset New Windmill edition, it would comprise the fifth English edition.

A115(b) First American edition (1935)

The Box of Delights | *or* | *When the Wolves Were Running* | *by* | John Masefield | NEW YORK | THE MACMILLAN COMPANY | 1935
(All width centred)

Bibliographies: Handley-Taylor p.60, Wight 87a

Collation: [A–S]⁸ [T]¹⁰ [U]⁸ (J not used); 162 leaves; 196 × 131mm.; [i–vi] vii–viii [ix–x] 1–311 [312–14]

Page contents: [i] half-title: 'The Box of Delights'; [ii] *'ALSO BY JOHN MASEFIELD* | PLAYS: | [12 titles listed] | POETRY: | [14 titles listed] | FICTION: | [six titles listed] | GENERAL: | [nine titles listed]'; [iii] title-page; [iv] *'Copyright, 1935, by* | JOHN MASEFIELD. | [rule] | All rights reserved–no part of this book | may be reproduced in any form without | permission in writing from the publisher, | except by a reviewer who wishes to quote brief | passages in connection with a review written | for inclusion in magazine or newspaper. | [rule] | *Set up and electrotyped.* | *Published October, 1935.* | PRINTED IN THE UNITED STATES OF AMERICA | BY THE STRATFORD PRESS, INC., NEW YORK'; [v] 'TO | MY WIFE'; [vi] blank; vii–viii 'CONTENTS' (12 chapters each listed with a couplet and page reference); [ix] 'The Box of Delights'; [x] blank; 1–311 text; [312–14] blank

Paper: wove paper

Running title: 'THE BOX OF DELIGHTS' (54mm.) on both verso and recto, pp.2–311

Binding: blue cloth. On spine, in red: 'The | Box of | Delights | JOHN | MASEFIELD | MACMILLAN | [point]' (lines 1–5 within scrolled panel: 47 × 34mm.) (all width centred). On upper cover, in red: 'THE BOX OF DELIGHTS | JOHN MASEFIELD' (within scrolled panel: 47 × 107mm.) Lower cover: blank. All edges trimmed. Sewn head and foot bands (in blue and white). Binding measurements: 202 × 131mm. (covers), 202 × 45mm. (spine). End-papers: wove paper decorated in black, blue and red with 27 illustrations and scrolled panel: 'THE BOX OF DELIGHTS | JOHN MASEFIELD', signed 'Judith Masefield 1935.', all within blue, black, red and black ruled border: 184 × 246mm.

Publication date: published, according to Handley-Taylor, 6 November 1935

Price: $2.50

Contents:
as for A115(a)

Notes:
As in A115(a), the text is illustrated by Judith Masefield. The illustrations which head chapters V, VII, IX and XI include the chapter heading within the drawing and, in contrast with A115(a), the Macmillan edition does not repeat the chapter heading in type for chapters V, VII and IX.

Macmillan appear to have set their text from corrected proofs supplied by Heinemann. Three sets were sent across the Atlantic on 2 August 1935 (see B.F. Oliver, letter to John Masefield, 2 August 1935) (HRHRC, MS (Masefield, J.) Recip William Heinemann Ltd.)

The scrolls on the binding design are derived from the illustrated end-papers.

The '2' of '288' on that page comprises damaged type.

A publishing agreement for this title between Masefield and Macmillan was dated 20 December 1934 (see Archives of The Society of Authors). The agreement refers to 'a licence to publish in volume form… in the United States of America and Canada his proposed book for Juveniles (a fantasy) – (exact title to be determined) to contain approximately 90,000 words'. Masefield has changed this to '70,000 words'. The lack of a title caused confusion. Writing in May 1935, George P. Brett Jr noted:

> …I find that there is no contract between us for VICTORIOUS TROY, nor indeed do we seem to have one for THE BOX OF DELIGHTS, unless this is the contract you signed last summer for a Fantasy for Children…
>
> (George P. Brett Jr, letter to John Masefield, 17 May 1935)
> (HRHRC, MS (Masefield, J.) Recip The Macmillan Company)

Copies seen: private collection (PWE); private collection (ROV); Harvard College Library (Houghton *EC9.M377.935bb)

A115(c) Second English edition ["The New Windmill Series"] ([1958])

The Box of Delights | *or* | When the Wolves were Running | BY | JOHN MASEFIELD | [publisher's device of a windmill with 'W' and 'H'] | [rule, 56mm.] | WILLIAM HEINEMANN LTD | MELBOURNE :: LONDON :: TORONTO
(All width centred)

Bibliographies: Handley-Taylor p.60, Wight [unrecorded]

Collation: [A]^{16} B–N^{16} O^4 (J not used); A5–N5 are also signed; signatures right foot of page; 212 leaves; 184 × 120mm.; [i–vi] 1–418

Page contents: [i] half-title: 'THE NEW WINDMILL SERIES | *General Editors:* Anne and Ian Serraillier | The Box of Delights'; [ii] 'THE NEW WINDMILL SERIES | *General Editors:* Anne and Ian Serraillier | [36 titles and their authors listed]'; [iii] title-page; [iv] 'FIRST PUBLISHED 1935 | FIRST PUBLISHED IN THE NEW WINDMILL SERIES | 1957 | TO MY WIFE | © 1957 by John Masefield | PUBLISHED BY | WILLIAM HEINEMANN LTD | 99 GREAT RUSSELL STREET, LONDON, W.C.I | PRINTED IN GREAT BRITAIN FOR THE PUBLISHERS BY | BUTLER & TANNER LTD., FROME AND LONDON'; [v–vi] 'CONTENTS' (12 chapters each listed with a couplet and page reference); 1–418 text

Paper: wove paper

Running title: 'THE BOX OF DELIGHTS' (58mm.) on both verso and recto, pp.2–418

Binding: red cloth. On spine, in silver: 'THE | BOX | OF | DELIGHTS | JOHN | MASEFIELD | [publisher's device of a windmill]' (all width centred). On upper cover, in silver: 'THE BOX | OF DELIGHTS | [illustration of two wolves running: 39 × 65mm.] | John Masefield'. Lower cover: blank. All edges trimmed. Binding measurements: 190 × 122mm. (covers), 190 × 38mm. (spine). End-papers: wove paper.

Publication date: published, according to Handley-Taylor, 10 February 1958

Price: 6s.

Contents:
as for A115(a)

Notes:
As in A115(a), the text is illustrated by Judith Masefield.

The text appears to use the same type setting as A115(a).

Although the volume itself bears a publication date of 1957, Handley-Taylor notes a date of 10 February 1958. The copy present in the British Library is stamped 21 JAN 1958. A similar difference between publication date and that stated in the preliminaries occurs with the first edition second impression of A115(a) and, noting the dates present in the British Library, the New Windmill Series edition was published after the reissue. Masefield's presentation copies may have been pre-publication copies.

Copies seen: BL (W.P.6193/38) stamped 21 JAN 1958; Reed International Books Library, Rushden; HRHRC (TEMP M377BOX 1957 cop.1) inscribed 'For Con | from Jan. | Thursday. November 21. | 1957.' with authorial correction to p.380 line 21; HRHRC (TEMP M377BOX 1957 cop.2) inscribed 'For Judith, | from Z. | Christmas. 1957.'

Reprinted:

[second edition, second impression]	1959
[second edition, third impression]	1961

A115(d) Third English edition (1965)

JOHN MASEFIELD | [illustration of four animals] | The Box of Delights | or | WHEN THE WOLVES WERE | RUNNING | ILLUSTRATED BY | JUDITH MASEFIELD | [publisher's device] | PENGUIN BOOKS
(All width centred)

Bibliographies: Wight [unrecorded]

Collation: [A]^{16} B-D^{16} E^8 F-I^{16}; signatures B-I are prefixed by 'T –'; despite the signatures, the volume appears to be bound by the 'perfect binding' process; signatures left foot of page; 136 leaves; 179 × 110mm.; [i–ii] [1–6] 7–23 [24] 25–44 [45] 46–63 [64] 65–80 [81] 82–99 [100] 101–118 [119] 120–37 [138] 139–58 [159] 160–77 [178] 179–200 [201] 202–227 [228] 229–69 [270]

Page contents: [i] 'PUFFIN BOOKS | *Editor: Kaye Webb* | THE BOX OF DELIGHTS | PS234 | Here is another book about Kay Harker, the hero of *The Mid- | night Folk*, but a rather older Kay who goes to school instead | of having a witch for a governess. The time is the Christmas | holidays and Kay's adventures begin when he meets a magic old | Punch and Judy man who warns him that 'the Wolves are | Running' and entrusts him with the wonderful Box of De- | lights. With this Kay finds he can go back into the past to see | the Roman legions marching and the end of the Trojan siege. | [new paragraph] But there is a lot of practical villainy mixed up with the | magic. Abner Brown, his spouse the witch, and their helpers | have kidnapped the bishop, dean, and chapter – and Kay, the | Box, and Cole Hawlings have to work hard, and face many | perils, to ensure that the Midnight Service is held in the | Cathedral on Christmas Eve. | [new paragraph] The story of Kay's various adventures and discoveries is | told with such a blend of poetic fantasy and reality that you | can't possibly foresee what new and extraordinary situation | will overtake him next. | [new paragraph] This is a special book, particularly suited to imaginative | readers with inquiring minds. | *Cover design by Juliet Renny*'; [ii] blank; [1] title-page; [2] 'Penguin Books Ltd, Harmondsworth, Middlesex, England | Penguin Books Pty Ltd, Ringwood, Victoria, Australia | [rule] | First published by Heinemann 1935 | Published in Puffin Books 1965 | [rule] | Copyright © John Masefield, 1957 | [rule] | Made and printed in Great Britain by | Cox and Wyman Ltd, | London, Reading and Fakenham | Set in Monotype Fournier | This book is sold subject to the condition | that it shall not, by way of trade, be lent, | re-sold, hired out, or otherwise disposed | of without the publisher's consent | in any form of binding or cover | other than that in which | it is published.'; [3] '*To My Wife*'; [4] blank; [5–6] 'Contents' (12 chapters each listed with a couplet and page reference, also biographical section listed); 7–269 text; [270] 'About the Author | John Masefield was born at Ledbury in Herefordshire on 1 June 1878. | His father and mother died while he was still a young boy, and he and the | other Masefield children went to live with an aunt in Ledbury, where he | attended a local school. | [new paragraph] When he was fourteen he was indentured to a merchant ship, and for | three years he suffered all the hardships and adventures of a man before | the mast. In 1895 he left the ship in New York, and found a room in | Greenwich Village, taking with him only five dollars and a small chest | of clothes. He scraped a living by taking odd jobs, working in a bakery | and a livery stable, and on the waterfront. | [new paragraph] Then he went to work in a carpet factory at Yonkers, where he read | widely, and began to circulate his own poetry among his friends. In | 1897 he returned to England. He never forgot his sea-going days, and his | first volume of poetry, which he published in 1902, was called *Salt Water | Ballads*. After that he wrote more books of poetry, some plays, and | novels for grown-ups and children. *The Midnight Folk* was published | in 1927, and in 1935 appeared the second book about Kay Harker, *The | Box of Delights*. | [new paragraph] For some years after he returned to England he lived in London, but | he now lives on Boars' Hill, just outside Oxford. He became Poet | Laureate in 1930. | [new paragraph] Among his other famous stories for older children are *The Bird of | Dawning*, which is already published in our Peacock series, and *Jim | Davis*, which will be published next year.'

Paper: wove paper

Running title: 'THE BOX OF DELIGHTS' (41mm.) on both verso and recto, pp.8–269

Binding: white wrappers (printed yellow). On spine, reading lengthways down spine from head: 'JOHN MASEFIELD [in black] THE BOX OF DELIGHTS [in purple]', horizontally at foot of spine: 'PS234 [in black] | [white rule] | [green block with black and white publisher's design of a puffin]'. On upper wrapper: 'THE | BOX OF | DELiGHTS | [illustrations in black, white, purple, green and brown of nine sided box with characters from the novel] | JOHN MASEFIELD | [white rule] | [green block upon which: 'A Puffin Book [publisher's device of a puffin in black and white] 4/6']'. On lower wrapper: 'THE | BOX OF | DELiGHTS | [illustrations in black, white, purple, green and brown of nine sided box with characters from the novel] | For copyright reasons this edition is not for sale in the U.S.A. or Canada | [white rule] | [green block upon which: 'Published by Penguin Books']'. All edges trimmed. Binding measurements: 179 × 111mm. (wrappers), 179 × 12mm. (spine).

Publication date: published, according to the *English Catalogue of Books*, 29 July 1965

Price: 4s.6d.

Contents:
as for A115(a)

Notes:

The text is illustrated by Judith Masefield, as noted on the title-page. Not all of the original illustrations are included. The illustration on the title-page is taken from the contents page in A115(a). The cover design by Juliet Renny incorporates a number of Judith Masefield's illustrations.

The text has been entirely re-set for this edition. The couplet for chapter III does not hypenate 'To-night', as present in A115(a)

The anonymous biography of Masefield provided on the final page of the volume has a number of inaccuracies. It was presumably written before April 1933 since there is reference to Masefield living on Boars' Hill.

The Archives of The Society of Authors reveal that Puffin had originally intended to publish an abridged version of the text. In December 1963 a new costing suggested this was un-necessary.

Copies seen: private collection (PWE)

A115(e) Fourth English edition ["The New Windmill Series"] (1966)

A 1982 reprint of 'The New Windmill Series' edition notes that after two reprints of A115(c), the text was reset in 1966.

Reprinted:

[fourth edition, second impression]	1969
[fourth edition, third impression]	1973
[fourth edition, fourth impression]	1977
[fourth edition, fifth impression]	1982

A115(f) Fifth English edition (1968)?

See reprint notes to A115(a)

Reprinted:

	1977
	1985

A115(g) Sixth English edition (1976)

John Masefield | THE BOX | OF DELIGHTS | When the Wolves were Running | text illustrations by Judith Masefield | [publisher's device of Pan within oval: 13 × 10mm.] | PICCOLO | Pan Books in association with Heinemann
(All width centred)

Bibliographies: Wight [unrecorded]

Publication date: presumably published, according to the British Library copy, October 1976.

Price: £0.60

Contents:
as for A115(a)

Notes:

The volume states, on page [4], that it is printed and bound in Great Britain by Richard Clay (The Chaucer Press) Ltd, Bungay, Suffolk.

The text has been entirely re-set for this edition.

The ISBN number is 0 330 24757 3

The edition uses Judith Masefield's illustrations. However, the illustrations at the beginning of chapters V, VII, IX and XI have been altered so as to remove the integral chapter and number. In the example of the illustration at the beginning of chapter IX this removal requires some additional drawing to fill space.

The publishing agreement for both Piccolo editions of *The Midnight Folk* (see A86(l)) and *The Box of Delights* was dated 19 November 1976 (see Archives of The Society of Authors)

Copies seen: private collection (PWE); BL (H.76/1783) stamped 28 OCT 1976

A115(h) Seventh English edition (1984)

The Box of Delights | WHEN THE WOLVES WERE RUNNING | [rule] | JOHN MASEFIELD | ABRIDGED BY PATRICIA CRAMPTON | ILLUSTRATED BY FAITH JAQUES | [illustration of wolves at night] | HEINEMANN : LONDON
(The title appears in an ornate font)
(All width centred)

Bibliographies: Wight [unrecorded]

Publication date: October 1984

Price: £7.95

Contents:

The Box of Delights ('Kay was coming home for the Christmas holidays after his first term at school. The train...')
[abridged text]

Notes:

The text has been abridged by Patricia Crampton with illustrations (both within the text and on full-colour plates) by Faith Jaques.

The volume states, on page [iv], that it is printed in England by Mackays of Chatham Ltd.

The ISBN number is ISBN 0-434-95052-1

Page numbers appear within square brackets. Thus, [1], [2], etc.

Copies seen: private collection (ROV); Reed International Books Library, Rushden

Reprinted:

'Reprinted'   [seventh edition, second impression]   1984

A115(i) *Eighth English edition (1984)*

The Box | of Delights | WHEN THE WOLVES WERE RUNNING | [rule] | JOHN MASEFIELD | ABRIDGED
BY PATRICIA CRAMPTON | ILLUSTRATED BY FAITH JAQUES | [illustration of wolves at night] | [publisher's
device of lion: 10 × 8mm.] | FONTANA LIONS
(The title appears in an ornate font)
(All width centred)

Bibliographies: Wight [unrecorded]

Publication date: October 1984

Price: £1.50

Contents:
as for A115(h)

Notes:

The text has been abridged by Patricia Crampton.

The volume states, on page [iv], that it is printed in Great Britain by William Collins Sons & Co Ltd, Glasgow.

The ISBN number is ISBN 0-00-672415-9

The text appears to use the same setting of type as A115(h) with black and white illustrations by Faith Jacques.

This volume comprises a tie-in publication for the B.B.C. television adaptation. It was originally broadcast on BBC1 in six half-hour
episodes on 21 and 28 November, and 5, 12, 19 and 24 December 1984.

Copies seen: private collection (PWE); BL (H.85/296) stamped 25 OCT 1984

A115(j) *Second American edition (1984)*

The Box of Delights | WHEN THE WOLVES WERE RUNNING | [rule] | JOHN MASEFIELD | ABRIDGED
BY PATRICIA CRAMPTON | ILLUSTRATED BY FAITH JAQUES | [illustration of wolves at night] | Macmillan
Publishing Company | New York
(The title appears in an ornate font)
(All width centred)

Bibliographies: Wight [unrecorded]

Publication date: October 1984

Price: $14.95

Contents:
as for A115(h)

Notes:

The text has been abridged by Patricia Crampton.

The text appears to use the same setting of type as A115(h) with illustrations by Faith Jacques.

The volume states, on page [iv] that it is 'Printed in Great Britain. The number sequence '10 9 8 7 6 5 4 3 2 1' is present.

The ISBN number is ISBN 0-02-762740-3

Copies seen: Library of The Society of Authors

A115(k) Third American edition (1984)

The Box of Delights | WHEN THE WOLVES WERE RUNNING | [rule] | JOHN MASEFIELD | ABRIDGED BY PATRICIA CRAMPTON | ILLUSTRATED BY FAITH JAQUES | [illustration of wolves at night] | A YEARLING SPECIAL BOOK
(The title appears in an ornate font)
(All width centred)

Bibliographies: Wight [unrecorded]

Publication date: 1984

Price: $2.95

Contents:
as for A115(h)

Notes:
The text has been abridged by Patricia Crampton.

The volume states, on page [iv], that it is published by Dell Publishing Co., Inc. 1 Dag Hammarskjold Plaza New York, New York 10017.

The text appears to use the same setting of type as A115(h) with black and white illustrations by Faith Jacques.

The ISBN number is ISBN 0-440-40853-9

This volume comprises a tie-in publication for the B.B.C. television adaptation. In the United States it was broadcast in the PBS-TV "Wonder Works" series in three one-hour episodes on 10, 17 and 24 December 1984.

Copies seen: private collection (PWE)

A115(l) Ninth English edition (1987)

The Box | of Delights | WHEN THE WOLVES WERE RUNNING | John Masefield | [publisher's device of rushes, river, double rule arch device and 'WINDRUSH'] | Oxford
(All width centred)

Bibliographies: Wight [unrecorded]

Publication date: December 1987

Price: £9.55

Contents:
as for A115(a)

Notes:
A large print edition of the novel. See also A86(o).

The volume states, on page [iv], that it is published in Large Print 1987 by Clio Press, 55 St. Thomas' Street, Oxford OX1 1JG. It is phototypeset, printed and bound by Unwin Brothers Limited, Old Woking, Surrey.

The ISBN number is ISBN 1-85089-925-8

This edition includes illustrations by Judith Masefield (as in A115(a)). These illustrations do not always appear at their original places in the text.

Copies seen: BL (NOV.1988/750) stamped 4 JAN 1988

A115(m) Tenth English edition ([1991])

The BOX OF | *DELIGHTS*
(All width centred)
(The underlined 'The' is in a smaller font and the underlining is a curved line)

Bibliographies: Wight [noted on p.159]

Publication date: November 1991

Price: £12.99

Contents:
as for A115(a)

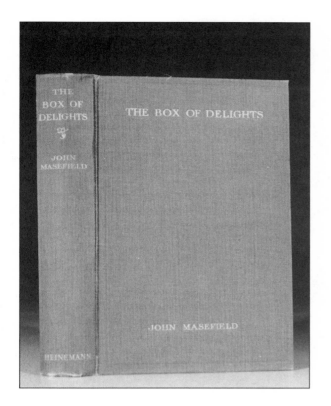

A115(a) spine and upper cover

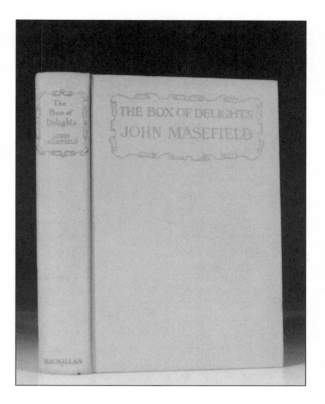

A115(b) spine and upper cover

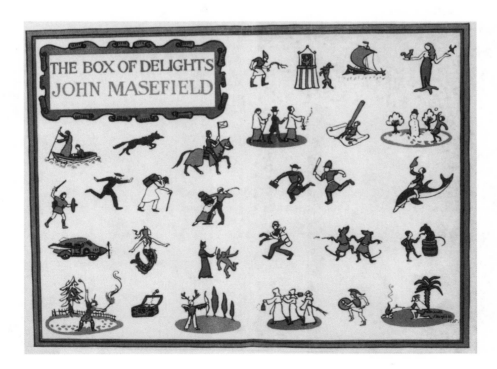

A115(a) end-papers

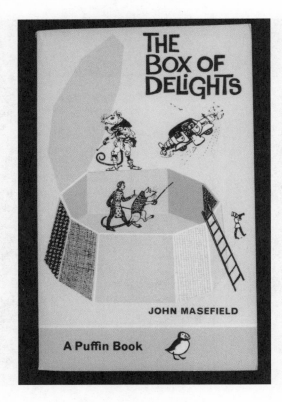

A115(d) upper wrapper

A115(g) upper wrapper

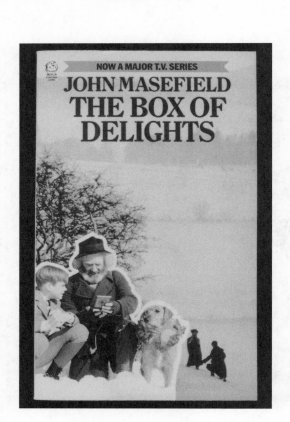

A115(i) upper wrapper

A115(n) upper wrapper

Notes:

This edition carries no note of publisher or copyright information within the volume. This suggests that the setting of text (and lack of copyright preliminaries) has been taken directly from the second part of the combined edition of *The Midnight Folk and The Box of Delights* (see A176(a)). In that edition copyright and publishing information was only present in the first set of preliminaries.

The ISBN number is ISBN 0-434-96087-X

Each chapter commences with a drop-capital. Note differences between chapters 6 and 10 with chapter 7 where Heinemann are inconsistent over use of speech marks set with the drop-capital.

See notes to A86(p) for notes on publication date.

Copies seen: BL (Nov. 1991/2339) stamped 14 NOV 1991

A115(n) Eleventh English edition (1994)

The Box of Delights | WHEN THE WOLVES WERE RUNNING | [rule (tapered at both ends), 59mm.] | [black panel on which in white: 'MAMMOTH': 4 × 30mm.]
(All width centred)

Publication date: September 1994

Price: £4.99

Contents:

The volume states, on page [iv], that it is published by Mammoth 'an imprint of Reed Consumer Books Ltd Michelin House, 81 Fulham Road, London SW3 6RB'

The edition was 'printed and bound in Great Britain by Cox & Wyman Ltd, Reading, Berkshire'

The ISBN number is ISBN 0 7497 1286 4

The cover illustration is by Kevin Tweddell

The edition uses Judith Masefield's illustrations. However, as in A115(g), the illustrations at the beginning of chapters V, VII, IX and XI have been altered so as to remove the integral chapter and number. In the example of the illustration at the beginning of chapter IX this removal requires some additional drawing to fill space.

The setting of the text suggests that the edition was taken from the plates of the last standard Heinemann edition (before the edition illustrated by Quentin Blake). This would be A115(f).

Reprinted:

'Reprinted'	[Eleventh edition, later reprint]	1994
'Reprinted'	[Eleventh edition, later reprint]	1995
'10 9 8 7 6 5 4 3 2 1'	[Eleventh edition, later reprint]	2000 (cover illustration by Liz Pyle)
['10 9 8 7 6 5 4 3 2']	[Eleventh edition, later reprint]	[no copies consulted]
['10 9 8 7 6 5 4 3']	[Eleventh edition, later reprint]	[no copies consulted]
'10 9 8 7 6 5 4'	[Eleventh edition, later reprint]	[c.2002]

The 2000 reprint (with a new cover illustration) includes the number sequence '10 9 8 7 6 5 4 3 2 1' although, strictly, it was merely a reprint of the 1994 edition.

Copies seen: private collection (PWE)

A116 VICTORIOUS TROY   1935

A116(a) First English edition (1935)

VICTORIOUS TROY | OR | THE *HURRYING ANGEL* | BY | JOHN MASEFIELD | [publisher's device of a windmill with 'W [point]' and '[point] H'] | [rule, 69mm.] | WILLIAM HEINEMANN LTD | LONDON :: TORONTO
(All width centred)

Bibliographies: Handley-Taylor p.61, Wight 88

Collation: [A]⁸ B–U⁸ (J not used); signatures right foot of page; 160 leaves; 190 × 127mm.; [i–viii] 1–309 [310–12]

Page contents: [i] half-title: 'VICTORIOUS TROY'; [ii] '*ALSO BY JOHN MASEFIELD* | PLAYS: | [12 titles listed] | POETRY: | [14 titles listed] | FICTION: | [seven titles listed] | GENERAL: | [nine titles listed]'; [iii] title-page; [iv] 'FIRST PUBLISHED 1935 | PRINTED IN GREAT BRITAIN | AT THE WINDMILL PRESS, KINGSWOOD, SURREY'; [v] 'TO | MY WIFE'; [vi] blank; [vii] 'NOTE | MANY seamen now living will remember cases in which | sailing-ships dismasted, or left without officers, were | brought to port by boys. I have talked with one of these | boys, and have seen the portrait of another. Their deeds | are among the glories of their profession. | [new paragraph] The *Hurrying Angel* and her crew are entirely | imaginary. No reference is made in this book to any | existing ship or living seaman. I have tried only to make | an image of what seamen have done, when there was | "Hell to pay and no pitch hot." | JOHN MASEFIELD.'; [viii] blank; 1–309 text; [310–12] blank

Paper: wove paper

Running title: 'VICTORIOUS TROY' (52mm.) on verso; '*or* THE *HURRYING ANGEL*' (71mm.) on recto, pp.2–309

Binding: blue cloth. On spine, in gold: 'VICTORIOUS | TROY | [ornament] | JOHN | MASEFIELD | HEINEMANN' (all width centred). On upper cover, in gold: 'VICTORIOUS TROY | JOHN MASEFIELD' (within blind ruled border: 185 × 119mm.) On lower cover, in blind: publisher's device of a windmill (ranged lower right). Top edge stained blue, others trimmed. Binding measurements: 196 × 127mm. (covers), 196 × 47mm. (spine). End-papers: wove paper decorated in navy blue with 'DECK ARRANGEMENT | OF THE FULL RIGGED SHIP | THE HURRYING ANGEL' (noting '1475 | TONS' to one side), and two other illustrations (signed 'KENNETH | SHOESMITH'). These smaller illustrations are each enclosed within three ruled borders and intersect the ruled border of the main illustration.

Publication date: the sales ledger preserved in the Heinemann Archive suggests publication on 31 October 1935 in an edition of 15000 copies

Price: 7s.6d.

Contents:
Victorious Troy ('It was a wild afternoon in the South Pacific in the late summer (late February there)...')
[Untitled Verse] ('When the last captives left the Skaian Gate,')
Glossary ('A.B.-An "able-bodied" seaman; formerly one who had served five or seven years...')

Notes:
A novel (sub-titled 'The *Hurrying Angel*') set during the grain race of 1922. The novel has no chapter divisions. The ship from which the novel gets its title is struck by a cyclone in the South Pacific and it is Dick Pomfret, the senior apprentice, who valiantly saves the vessel.

The text commences with a drop-capital.

Before Masefield sent his typescript to Heinemann he evidently requested illustrative work by Kenneth Shoesmith. C.S. Evans wrote to Masefield at the end of July 1935:

> ... I have just been on to Shoesmith. He had been away for four days, and has only just received your letter. He says he will very glad to do the wrapper and the end papers for THE HURRYING ANGEL, and I have promised to send him a set of proofs as soon as possible.
>
> (C.S. Evans, letter to John Masefield, 30 July 1935)
> (HRHRC, MS (Masefield, J.) Recip William Heinemann Ltd.)

The typescript of the novel was received by C.S. Evans at the end of September. It appears that it was set immediately without having been read:

> Many thanks for the typescript of VICTORIOUS TROY which arrived safely this morning. As time is so short I shall not keep it to read but shall send it straight to the printer who will begin the set either tomorrow or the next day and will send you proofs in batches as they come in. I am afraid it is a little late now to be certain of getting the book out in October but we ought to be able to manage it early in November.
>
> (C.S. Evans, letter to John Masefield, 23 September 1935)
> (HRHRC, MS (Masefield, J.) Recip William Heinemann Ltd.)

(Publication was to be on 31 October). A letter from Evans to Masefield on 26 September 1935 notes that the problem of speedy publication lay in the need for review copies and advance proofs:

> ...There is no difficulty about the manufacture of the actual book in the 31 working days which remain to the end of October, but we have to get bound copies to the press at least a week – and for preference ten or twelve days – before the date of publication if the book is to be promptly reviewed. Also, advance proofs of the book – bound in brown paper covers – ought to be sent to the chief booksellers in the largest English towns so that they may read the book before giving their subscription order...
>
> (C.S. Evans, letter John Masefield, 26 September 1935)
> (HRHRC, MS (Masefield, J.) Recip William Heinemann Ltd.)

As suggested by Evans' letter of 23 September, proofs were sent to Masefield in batches. B.F. Oliver, of Heinemann, wrote to Masefield noting 'we hasten to send you herewith the first 120 pages of VICTORIOUS TROY and manuscript. Further batches will be coming to you as soon as possible.' (see B.F. Oliver, letter to John Masefield, 30 September 1935) (HRHRC, MS (Masefield, J.) Recip William Heinemann Ltd.) On 3 October 1935 he wrote to enclose '...two sets of the remainder of the proofs pp.281–310 with manuscript' (see B.F. Oliver, letter to John Masefield, 3 October 1935) (HRHRC, MS (Masefield, J.) Recip William Heinemann Ltd.) A day later Evans wrote to inform Masefield of the publication date:

> We finished the setting of VICTORIOUS TROY last Tuesday and batches of proofs have been sent to you... We are arranging for publication on October 31st.
>
> (C.S. Evans, letter to John Masefield, 4 October 1935)
> (HRHRC, MS (Masefield, J.) Recip William Heinemann Ltd.)

The 'remainder of your corrected proofs (pp.217–309) of VICTORIOUS TROY…' were sent to Masefield on 17 October (see B.F. Oliver, letter to John Masefield, 17 October 1935) (HRHRC, MS (Masefield, J.) Recip William Heinemann Ltd.)

After publication, C.S. Evans wrote:

> By the way, I never told you how much I enjoyed this last book of yours. I read it when it was in proof. Up to now I have always thought that the finest description of a storm in English literature was that in Conrad's TYPHOON; but now I think that this masterly passage is surpassed by your description of the cyclone in VICTORIOUS TROY. The book is going well in spite of the election. Our subscription was 10,210 copies.

(C.S. Evans, letter to John Masefield, 4 November 1935)
(HRHRC, MS (Masefield, J.) Recip William Heinemann Ltd.)

The publishing agreement for this title between Masefield and Heinemann was dated 30 September 1935 (see Archives of The Society of Authors). The agreement refers to a publication price of 7s.6d.

Copies seen: private collection (PWE); BL (NN.24819) stamped 31 OCT 1935

A116(b) First American edition (1935)

VICTORIOUS TROY | OR | THE *HURRYING ANGEL* | BY | JOHN MASEFIELD | NEW YORK | THE MACMILLAN COMPANY | 1935
(All width centred)

Bibliographies: Handley-Taylor p.61, Wight 88a

Collation: [A–U]⁸ (J not used); 160 leaves; 197 × 133mm.; [i–x] 1–295 [296] 297–308 [309–310]

Page contents: [i] half-title: 'VICTORIOUS TROY'; [ii] '*ALSO BY JOHN MASEFIELD* | PLAYS: | [12 volumes listed] | POETRY: | [14 volumes listed] | FICTION: | [seven volumes listed] | GENERAL: | [nine volumes listed]'; [iii] title-page; [iv] '*Copyright, 1935, by* | JOHN MASEFIELD. | [rule] | All rights reserved—no part of this book | may be reproduced in any form without | permission in writing from the publisher, | except by a reviewer who wishes to quote brief | passages in connection with a review written | for inclusion in magazine or newspaper. | [rule] | *Set up and electrotyped.* | *Published October, 1935.* | PRINTED IN THE UNITED STATES OF AMERICA | BY THE STRATFORD PRESS, INC., NEW YORK'; [v] 'TO | MY WIFE'; [vi] blank; [vii] 'NOTE | MANY seamen now living will remember cases in which | sailing-ships dismasted, or left without officers, were | brought to port by boys. I have talked with one of these | boys, and have seen the portrait of another. Their deeds | are among the glories of their profession. | [new paragraph] The *Hurrying Angel* and her crew are entirely imagi- | nary. No reference is made in this book to any existing | ship or living seaman. I have tried only to make an image | of what seamen have done, when there was "Hell to pay | and no pitch hot." | JOHN MASEFIELD.'; [viii] blank; [ix] 'VICTORIOUS TROY'; [x] blank; 1–295 text; [296] blank; 297–308 'GLOSSARY'; [309–310] blank

Paper: wove paper

Running title: 'VICTORIOUS TROY' (43mm.) on verso; '*or* THE *HURRYING ANGEL*' (60mm.) on recto, pp.2–308

Binding: red cloth. On spine: 'MASEFIELD | [point] | VICTORIOUS | TROY | OR | *THE* | *HURRYING* | *ANGEL* | MACMILLAN | [point]' (all width centred). On upper cover: 'JOHN MASEFIELD | VICTORIOUS | TROY | *OR* | *THE* | *HURRYING* | *ANGEL*'. Lower cover: blank. Top edge stained blue, others roughly trimmed. Binding measurements: 202 × 135mm. (covers), 202 × 44mm. (spine). End-papers: wove paper.

Publication date: published, according to Handley-Taylor, 6 November 1935

Price: $2.50

Contents:
as for A116(a)

Notes:
The texts of the novel and the glossary commence on pp.1 and 297 respectively after ornamental head-pieces.

The publicity material in the preliminaries that lists Masefield's work (appearing on p.[ii]) bears a marked similarity to that present in the Heinemann edition. Moreover, titles as cited here are those of English editions (separate editions of Masefield's Racine translations and *St. George and the Dragon*, for example).

Six months before publication of this title George P. Brett Jr wrote to Masefield noting that '…I find that there is no contract between us for VICTORIOUS TROY…' (see George P. Brett Jr, letter to John Masefield, 17 May 1935) (HRHRC, MS (Masefield, J.) Recip The Macmillan Company). This was, presumably, rectified.

Copies seen: private collection (ROV)

A116(c) First Canadian edition (1935)

VICTORIOUS TROY | OR | THE *HURRYING ANGEL* | BY | JOHN MASEFIELD | TORONTO: THE MACMILLAN COMPANY OF | CANADA LIMITED, AT ST. MARTIN'S HOUSE | 1935
(All width centred with lines six and seven justified on left and right margins)

Bibliographies: Handley-Taylor [unrecorded], Wight [unrecorded]

Collation: [A-U]⁸ (J not used); 160 leaves; 197 × 133mm.; [i–x] 1–295 [296] 297–308 [309–310]

Page contents: [i] half-title: 'VICTORIOUS TROY'; [ii] '*ALSO BY JOHN MASEFIELD* | PLAYS: | [12 volumes listed] | POETRY: | [14 volumes listed] | FICTION: | [seven volumes listed] | GENERAL: | [nine volumes listed]'; [iii] title-page; [iv] '*Copyright, 1935, by* | JOHN MASEFIELD. | [rule] | All rights reserved–no part of this book | may be reproduced in any form without | permission in writing from the publisher, | except by a reviewer who wishes to quote brief | passages in connection with a review written | for inclusion in magazine or newspaper. | [rule] | *Set up and electrotyped.* | *Published October, 1935.* | PRINTED IN THE UNITED STATES OF AMERICA | BY THE STRATFORD PRESS, INC., NEW YORK'; [v] 'TO | MY WIFE'; [vi] blank; [vii] 'NOTE | MANY seamen now living will remember cases in which | sailing-ships dismasted, or left without officers, were | brought to port by boys. I have talked with one of these | boys, and have seen the portrait of another. Their deeds | are among the glories of their profession. | [new paragraph] The *Hurrying Angel* and her crew are entirely imagi- | nary. No reference is made in this book to any | existing | ship or living seaman. I have tried only to make an image | of what seamen have done, when there was "Hell to pay | and no pitch hot." | JOHN MASEFIELD.'; [viii] blank; [ix] 'VICTORIOUS TROY'; [x] blank; 1–295 text; [296] blank; 297–308 'GLOSSARY'; [309–310] blank

Paper: wove paper

Running title: 'VICTORIOUS TROY' (43mm.) on verso; '*or* THE *HURRYING ANGEL*' (60mm.) on recto, pp.2–308

Binding: red cloth. On spine: 'MASEFIELD | [point] | VICTORIOUS | TROY | OR | *THE* | *HURRYING* | *ANGEL* | MACMILLAN | [point]' (all width centred). On upper cover: 'JOHN MASEFIELD | VICTORIOUS | TROY | *OR* | *THE* *HURRYING* | *ANGEL*'. Lower cover: blank. Top edge stained blue, others roughly trimmed. Binding measurements: 202 × 135mm. (covers), 202 × 44mm. (spine). End-papers: wove paper.

Publication date: 1935

Price: unknown

Contents:
as for A116(a)

Notes:
The texts of the novel and the glossary commence on pp.1 and 297 respectively after ornamental head-pieces.

The publicity material in the preliminaries that lists Masefield's work (appearing on p.[ii]) bears a marked similarity to that present in the Heinemann edition. Moreover, titles as cited here are those of English editions (separate editions of Masefield's Racine translations and *St. George and the Dragon*, for example).

With the exception of the title-page, this edition is identical to A116(b).

Copies seen: private collection (ROV)

A116(d)   Second English edition (limited signed edition) (1936)

[rule, 59mm.] | JOHN MASEFIELD | [rule, 59mm.] | VICTORIOUS TROY [in blue] | OR [in blue] | THE *Hurrying Angel* [in blue] | [publisher's device of a windmill with 'W [point]' and 'H'] [in blue] | *London* | WILLIAM HEINEMANN LTD | 1936
(All width centred)

Bibliographies: Handley-Taylor p.61, Wight 88b

Collation: [A]⁸ B-U⁸ (J not used); signatures right foot of page; 160 leaves; 227 × 154mm.; [i–viii] 1–309 [310–12]

Page contents: [i] half-title: 'VICTORIOUS TROY'; [ii] '*This Edition, numbered and signed* | *by the Author, is limited to 125 copies* | *for sale in Great Britain and Ireland.* | *No............*'; [iii] title-page; [iv] 'PRINTED | IN GREAT BRITAIN | AT THE WINDMILL PRESS | KINGSWOOD | SURREY'; [v] 'TO | MY WIFE'; [vi] blank; [vii] 'NOTE | MANY seamen now living will remember cases in which | sailing-ships dismasted, or left without officers, were | brought to port by boys. I have talked with one of these | boys, and have seen the portrait of another. Their deeds | are among the glories of their profession. | [new paragraph] The *Hurrying Angel* and her crew are entirely | imaginary. No reference is made in this book to any | existing ship or living seaman. I have tried only to make | an image of what seamen have done, when there was | "Hell to pay and no pitch hot." | JOHN MASEFIELD.'; [viii] blank; 1–309 text (with additional leaf (folded once) tipped-in on p.1, the recto of which are the illustrations: 'DECK ARRANGEMENT | OF THE FULL RIGGED SHIP | THE HURRYING ANGEL' (noting '1475 | TONS' to one side), and two other illustrations (signed 'KENNETH | SHOESMITH'). These smaller illustrations are each enclosed within three ruled borders and intersect the ruled border of the main illustration); [310–12] blank

Paper: wove paper

Running title: 'VICTORIOUS TROY' (52mm.) on verso; '*or* THE *HURRYING ANGEL*' (71mm.) on recto, pp.2–309

Binding: blue cloth. On spine, in gold: 'VICTORIOUS | TROY | JOHN | MASEFIELD | HEINEMANN' (all width centred). Covers: blank. Top edge gilt, lower outside edge untrimmed, fore edge uncut. Sewn head and foot bands (in blue) and blue marker

A113(a) end-papers

A116(a) end-papers

VICTORIOUS TROY
OR
THE *HURRYING ANGEL*

BY

JOHN MASEFIELD

WILLIAM HEINEMANN LTD
LONDON :: TORONTO

A116(a) title-page

JOHN MASEFIELD

VICTORIOUS TROY
OR
THE *Hurrying Angel*

London
WILLIAM HEINEMANN LTD
1936

A116(d) title-page

A
LETTER FROM PONTUS
&
OTHER VERSE
by
JOHN MASEFIELD

★

WILLIAM HEINEMANN LTD
LONDON :: TORONTO

A117(a) title-page

EGGS AND BAKER
or
THE DAYS OF TRIAL

BY

JOHN MASEFIELD

WILLIAM HEINEMANN LTD
LONDON :: TORONTO

A119(a) title-page

ribbon. Binding measurements: 236 × 152mm. (covers), 236 × 54mm. (spine). The binding includes bevelled edges. End-papers: mottled light blue paper.

Publication date: the sales ledger preserved in the Heinemann Archive suggests publication on 16 March 1936 in an edition of 125 copies

Price: 42s.

Contents:
as for A116(a)

Notes:
The text commences with a drop-capital.

The text appears to use the same setting of type as A116(a).

This edition was published almost five months after A116(a). C.S. Evans wrote to Masefield during February 1936:

> …We should like to get the limited edition of VICTORIOUS TROY out as soon as may be now. Shall I have the sheets sent to you for signature or are you likely to be in London?….
>
> (C.S. Evans, letter to John Masefield, 14 February 1936)
> (HRHRC, MS (Masefield, J.) Recip William Heinemann Ltd.)

Masefield was unlikely to be in London, it seems. The sheets for the limitation signature were sent five days later:

> I am sending you the title-sheets of VICTORIOUS TROY for the Limited edition… We will number them here unless you prefer to do so.
>
> (B.F. Oliver, letter to John Masefield, 19 February 1936)
> (HRHRC, MS (Masefield, J.) Recip William Heinemann Ltd.)

In March 1937 C.S. Evans investigated sales since 1933 of Masefield's limited editions. Of *The Bird of Dawning* (A111(c)) he reported to Masefield that the 'whole edition was exhausted'. The same was true of *The Taking of the Gry* (A113(aa)). Copies were still available, however, of this limited signed editions of *Victorious Troy, A Letter from Pontus and other verse* (A117(aa)) and *Eggs and Baker* (A119(aa)).

Copies seen: private collection (PWE) number 54, signed '54 | John Masefield.' on p.[ii]; BL (012600.dd.3) number 106; signed '106 | John Masefield.' on p.[ii], stamped 18 MAR 1936

A117 A LETTER FROM PONTUS AND OTHER VERSE   1936

A117(a) First English edition (1936)

A | LETTER FROM PONTUS | & | OTHER VERSE | *by* | JOHN MASEFIELD | [five-point star] | [publisher's device of a windmill with 'W [point]' and '[point] H'] | [rule, 70mm.] | WILLIAM HEINEMANN LTD | LONDON :: TORONTO
(All width centred)

Bibliographies: Handley-Taylor p.61, Wight 89

Collation: [A]⁸ B-G⁸ H⁴; signatures right foot of page; 60 leaves; 184 × 121mm.; [i–x] 1–109 [110]

Page contents: [i–ii] blank; [iii] half-title: 'A LETTER FROM PONTUS | & | OTHER VERSE'; [iv] '*ALSO BY JOHN MASEFIELD* | PLAYS: | [12 titles listed] | POETRY: | [14 titles listed] | FICTION: | [eight titles listed] | GENERAL: | [nine titles listed]'; [v] title-page; [vi] 'FIRST PUBLISHED 1936 | PRINTED IN GREAT BRITAIN AT | THE WINDMILL PRESS, KINGSWOOD, SURREY.'; [vii] 'To | MY WIFE'; [viii] blank; [ix–x] 'CONTENTS' (36 individual poems listed with page references); 1–109 text; [110] blank

Paper: wove paper

Running title: none

Binding: blue cloth. On spine, in gold: 'A | Letter | from | Pontus | and other | Verse | [ornament] | John | Masefield | Heinemann' (all width centred). On upper cover, in gold: illustration of a cockerel: 32 × 24mm. (ranged lower right). On lower cover, in blind: publisher's device of a windmill (ranged lower right). All edges trimmed. Binding measurements: 189 × 122mm. (covers), 189 × 27mm. (spine). End-papers: blue wove paper.

Publication date: the sales ledger preserved in the Heinemann Archive suggests publication on 25 May 1936 in an edition of 3000 copies

Price: 6s.

Contents:
A Letter from Pontus ('In the first year of the Divine Tiberius,')
Australia ('When the North Lander saw the rose in blossom,')
The Will ('By Will, Man dared in den and heath')

Westminster Hall ('What glory and reversal has been shown')
Ballet Russe *I* ('The gnome from moonland plays the Chopin air,')
Ballet Russe *II* ('With delicate control in maddest speed')
Joseph Hodges, or The Corn ('He wore the smock-frock of the country's past,')
The Wild Geese ('All the Many is One,')
Hope ('O Hope that glimmers in the breast')
The Queen ('I waited, in my misery, when the Queen,')
Beauty ('O Queen of Beauty, you who once were fire')
February Night ('I went into the land where Beauty dwells.')
February Morning ('The starry wheel of night passed slowly over;')
Nets ('COLONIES built a fort for safety's sake,')
The Long Drive | (*Edinburgh to Boar's Hill*) ('In a garage not far from the Rock of the Castle')
The Flowing of The Sangarios ('I saw a sullen little river swerve')
Wood-Pigeons ('Often the woodman scares them as he comes')
Autumn Ploughing ('After the ranks of stubble have lain bare,')
The Waggon-Maker ('I have made tales in verse, but this man made')
November the Sixth ('I face North-West upon a grassy hill,')
Pony Fair ('Twice every year for full five centuries')
Partridges ('Here they lie mottled to the ground unseen,')
The Towerer ('Old Jarge, Hal, Walter and I, the Rector and Bill,')
Candlemas Day ('The frost is passing; from the West the rain')
The Eyes ('I remember a tropic dawn before turn-to,')
The Spanish Main ('Low, dull-green hills with scrub and little trees,')
Nombre de Dios ('The jungle reaches to the water's edge.')
Porto Bello ('The port is unsuspected from the east,')
Canal Zone ('Among these hills, twelve generations since,')
The Spanish Main Schooner ('A little wooden schooner, painted white,')
A Ballad of Sir Francis Drake ('Before Sir Francis put to sea,')
The *Mayblossom* | (*Told me by the Pilot*) ('The ship, *Mayblossom*, left Magellan Straits')
1176 Hours ('Oh, ticking Time, when wilt thou pass?')
Begone ('Begone you rubbish of old dates')
The Boy from Pauntley ('West, in the redlands, good for hops and corn,')
Sweet Friends ('Print not my life nor letters; put them by:')

Notes:
C.S. Evans acknowledged receipt of Masefield's 'new book of poems' on 9 March 1936 (see C.S. Evans, letter to John Masefield, 9 March 1936) (HRHRC, MS (Masefield, J.) Recip William Heinemann Ltd.) The original title was different:

> I have read AUSTRALIA AND OTHER POEMS with very great pleasure. I like best A LETTER FROM PONTUS, the little poem called THE EYES and FEBRUARY NIGHT and FEBRUARY MORNING.
> (C.S. Evans, letter to John Masefield, 10 March 1936)
> (HRHRC, MS (Masefield, J.) Recip William Heinemann Ltd.)

Evans noted, in the same letter, that he gave the book to Geoffrey Dearmer who was then a Heinemann reader. Dearmer provided a reply to Masefield's final poem in the collection ('Sweet Friends'). Dearmer's poem (entitled 'A Heinemann Reader's Comment on 'Sweet Friends'') was enclosed and reads:

> So be it, if you wish it, we will stint
> Ourselves and our unbridled lust for print.
> Your Life and Letters, these we will put by,
> But since you write: 'Let memory of me die'
> Ask not of us the impossible. Not ours
> To keep the pollen from unbudded flowers
> Of hearts unborn, or quench the love that springs
> When a true poet gives a language wings.
> Your work like wild flowers in the break of May
> Shall with the generations greet the day
> Till Poetry perishes, and, cold as stone,
> Not girdled by the sea you made your own,
> These islands lie once more in ice and sleet
> And there's no Windmill in Great Russell Street.
>
> (C.S. Evans, letter to John Masefield, 10 March 1936)
> (HRHRC, MS (Masefield, J.) Recip William Heinemann Ltd.)

Masefield appears to have made a number of changes to the text. An early deletion is noted on 12 March 1936:

...we return herewith the poem WORDS OF CHEER for which you wish to substitute another...

(B.F. Oliver, letter to John Masefield, 12 March 1936)
(HRHRC, MS (Masefield, J.) Recip William Heinemann Ltd.)

This poem does not appear to be *Sonnets of Good Cheer to the Lena Ashwell Players...* (see A81). Item 214 in an inventory of the papers of Masefield (made after the author's death) was described as 'WORDS OF CHEER. Autograph MS, 16 lines in 4 stanzas on single large octavo page. Well revised and signed at foot...' The change of volume title was acknowledged at the end of March and Masefield also appears to have altered the contents order:

The changes you ask for shall be made. The title will appear as A LETTER FROM PONTUS AND OTHER VERSE, and A LETTER FROM PONTUS will be the first poem in the book... I think that a good time to bring out the book would be the first week in May, if that date is suitable for Macmillan. It may be, however, that you would prefer the date to be a little later in the month in order to make things easier for Macmillan. I know they like simultaneous publication.

(C.S. Evans, letter to John Masefield, 27 March 1936)
(HRHRC, MS (Masefield, J.) Recip William Heinemann Ltd.)

(Despite publication 'a little later in the month', simultaneous publication between Heinemann and Macmillan was not achieved). On 2 April 'two sets of the first proofs of A LETTER FROM PONTUS AND OTHER VERSE with manuscript...' were sent to Masefield (see B.F. Oliver, letter to John Masefield, 2 April 1936) (HRHRC, MS (Masefield, J.) Recip William Heinemann Ltd.) These, corrected by the author, were acknowledged four days later. It also appears that there were problems over the setting of punctuation:

Thank you for your letter and corrected first proofs of A LETTER FROM PONTUS. I am sorry that stops and commas have been omitted; we shall of course send you revised book proofs in which I hope you will find them all inserted according to your markings.

(B.F. Oliver, letter to John Masefield, 6 April 1936)
(HRHRC, MS (Masefield, J.) Recip William Heinemann Ltd.)

The publishing agreement for this title between Masefield and Heinemann was dated 7 March 1936 (see Archives of The Society of Authors). The agreement refers to both 6s. and 31s.6d. issues (A117(a) and A117(aa)).

The indented illustration of a cockerel on the upper cover is a feature shared by bindings in the Heinemann Collected Works of John Masefield Wanderer edition.

The ampersands used in the half-title and title-page are particularly ornate.

It appears that Masefield had especially wanted Heinemann to use the blue and white striped dust-jacket design (as previously used on numerous occasions). C.S. Evans wrote with his apologies:

I am afraid I shall have to take responsibility for the wrapper of A LETTER TO PONTUS AND OTHER VERSE. I had forgotten to give Mr. Macmillan (who arranges for our wrappers) instructions that your wrappers were always to be the blue and white stripes. Please forgive me. When the book is reprinted I will see that the right wrapper is put on to it.

(C.S. Evans, letter to John Masefield, 22 May 1936)
(HRHRC, MS (Masefield, J.) Recip William Heinemann Ltd.)

Copies seen: private collection (PWE); BL (11655.ee.66) stamped 26 MAY 1936; HRHRC (TEMP M377LE 1936A) inscribed 'Lew | from | Zob | May 20, 1936'

A117(aa) First English edition (limited signed edition) (1936)

[rule, 48mm.] | JOHN MASEFIELD | [rule, 48mm.] | A [in blue] | LETTER [in blue] | FROM PONTUS [in blue] | AND OTHER VERSE [in blue] | [five-point star] | [publisher's device of a windmill with 'W [point]' and 'H'] [in blue] | *LONDON* | WILLIAM HEINEMANN LTD | 1936
(All width centred)

Bibliographies: Handley-Taylor p.61, Wight 89b

Collation: [A]⁸ B-G⁸ H⁴; signatures right foot of page; 60 leaves; 225 × 140mm.; [i–x] 1–109 [110]

Page contents: [i–ii] blank; [iii] half-title: 'A LETTER FROM PONTUS | & | OTHER VERSE'; [iv] '*This Edition, numbered and signed | by the Author, is limited to 100 | copies for sale in Great Britain | and Ireland | No. ....*'; [v] title-page; [vi] 'PRINTED | IN GREAT BRITAIN | AT THE WINDMILL PRESS | KINGSWOOD | SURREY'; [vii] 'To | MY WIFE'; [viii] blank; [ix–x] 'CONTENTS' (36 individual poems listed with page references); 1–109 text; [110] blank

Paper: wove paper (watermark: 'BRITISH HAND MADE PURE RAG [castle device: 26 × 33mm.]')

Running title: none

Binding: mottled blue boards with parchment spine. On spine, in gold: 'A | Letter | from | Pontus | and other | Verse | [ornament] | John | Masefield | Heinemann' (all width centred). There is a single vertical rule in blind on each cover at the edge of the parchment. Covers: blank. Top edge gilt, others uncut. Sewn head and foot bands (in white). Binding measurements: 230 × 146mm. (covers), 230 × 28mm. (spine). End-papers: wove paper. Volume contained in slip-case covered in blue paper.

Publication date: the sales ledger preserved in the Heinemann Archive and correspondence from Heinemann to Masefield confirms publication on 25 May 1936 in an edition of 100 copies

Price: 31s.6d.

Contents:
as for A117(a)

Notes:

Neither Handley-Taylor nor the *English Catalogue of Books* provide the publication date of this volume. The sales ledger preserved in the Heinemann Archive and correspondence from the firm to Masefield verifies publication on the same date as A117(a).

Using the original title of the volume (see notes to A117(a)), C.S. Evans notes limitation and publication date in a letter to Masefield, dated 16 March 1936:

> I think that we should sell one hundred copies of a large paper edition of AUSTRALIA AND OTHER POEMS. And I think we ought to publish such an edition on the same day as the ordinary edition.
>
> (C.S. Evans, letter to John Masefield, 16 March 1936)
> (HRHRC, MS (Masefield, J.) Recip William Heinemann Ltd.)

Louisa Callender wrote noting the publication date and warning Masefield that the limitation sheets were almost ready for signing:

> ….Concerning the limited edition of A LETTER FROM PONTUS, [C.S. Evans] wrote to you on March 16th saying that he thought we ought to do an edition of 100 copies and publish on the same day as the ordinary edition. Both editions are being published on May 25th, and the press tells me that sheets for your signature will be sent at the end of this week…
>
> (Louisa Callender, letter to John Masefield, 27 April 1936)
> (HRHRC, MS (Masefield, J.) Recip William Heinemann Ltd.)

These sheets were sent on 1 May 1936 (see B.F. Oliver, letter to John Masefield, 1 May 1936) (HRHRC, MS (Masefield, J.) Recip William Heinemann Ltd.) and their safe return to the publishers was acknowledged four days later (see B.F. Oliver, letter to John Masefield, 5 May 1936) (HRHRC, MS (Masefield, J.) Recip William Heinemann Ltd.)

The ampersand used in the half-title is particularly ornate.

In March 1937 C.S. Evans investigated sales since 1933 of Masefield's limited editions. Of *The Bird of Dawning* (A111(c)) he reported to Masefield that the 'whole edition was exhausted'. The same was true of *The Taking of the Gry* (A113(aa)). Copies were still available, however, of the limited signed editions of *Victorious Troy* (A116(d)), *A Letter from Pontus and other verse* and *Eggs and Baker* (A119(aa)). Two of the 100 copies of this edition remained unsold on 12 March 1937.

Copies seen: BL (11654.c.47) number 81, signed '81 | John Masefield.' on p.[iv], stamped 26 MAY 1936; HRHRC (AC-L M377LE 1936A) number 16, signed '16 | John Masefield.' on p.[iv]; HRHRC (PR6025 A77 L4 1936B) number 82, signed '82 | John Masefield.' on p.[iv] additionally inscribed 'For Jude | from | Zob. | May. 1936.'; HRHRC (TEMP M377LE 1936B cop.1) out-of-series copy, signed 'John Masefield.' on p.[iv] with HRHRC booklabel 'From the Library of W. Somerset Maugham'; HRHRC (TEMP M377LE 1936B cop.2) number 91, signed '91 | John Masefield.' on p.[iv] additionally inscribed 'For Con | from | Jan. | 27 May. 1936.'

A117(b) First American edition (1936)

[floral device of six branches] | A LETTER FROM PONTUS | *AND OTHER VERSE* | [floral device of six branches (in mirror image of those above)] | *By* John Masefield | New York | THE MACMILLAN COMPANY | 1 9 3 6 (All width centred)

Bibliographies: Handley-Taylor p.61, Wight 89a

Collation: [A-H]⁸; 64 leaves; 203 × 139mm.; [i–vi] vii–viii [ix–x] 1–118

Page contents: [i] half-title: 'A LETTER FROM PONTUS | *AND OTHER VERSE*'; [ii] '*ALSO BY JOHN MASEFIELD* | PLAYS: | [12 titles listed] | POETRY: | [14 titles listed] | FICTION: | [eight titles listed] | GENERAL: | [nine titles listed]'; [iii] title-page; [iv] '*Copyright, 1936,* | BY JOHN MASEFIELD. | [rule] | All rights reserved–no part of this book | may be reproduced in any form without | permission in writing from the publisher, | except by a reviewer who wishes to quote brief | passages in connection with a review written | for inclusion in magazine or newspaper. | FIRST PRINTING | PRINTED IN THE UNITED STATES OF AMERICA | BY THE STRATFORD PRESS, INC., NEW YORK'; [v] 'TO | MY WIFE'; [vi] blank; vii–viii 'CONTENTS' (36 individual poems listed with page references); [ix] 'A LETTER FROM PONTUS | *AND OTHER VERSE*'; [x] blank; 1–118 text

Paper: wove paper

Running title: none

Binding: navy-blue cloth. On spine, in gold: 'A | LETTER | FROM | PONTUS | [point] | JOHN | MASEFIELD | MACMILLAN | [point]' (all width centred). On upper cover, in gold: 'A LETTER FROM PONTUS | JOHN MASEFIELD'. Lower cover: blank. Top and lower edges trimmed, fore edge roughly trimmed. Binding measurements: 208 × 138mm. (covers), 208 × 30mm. (spine). End-papers: wove paper.

Publication date: published, according to Handley-Taylor, 16 June 1936

Price: $2.00

Contents:
A Letter from Pontus ('In the first year of the Divine Tiberius,')
Australia ('When the North Lander saw the rose in blossom,')
The Will ('By Will, Man dared in den and heath')
Westminster Hall ('What glory and reversal has been shown')
Ballet Russe *I* ('The gnome from moonland plays the Chopin air,')
[Ballet Russe] *II* ('With delicate control in maddest speed')
Joseph Hodges, or The Corn ('He wore the smock-frock of the country's past,')
The Wild Geese ('All the Many is One,')
Hope ('O Hope that glimmers in the breast')
The Queen ('I waited, in my misery, when the Queen,')
Beauty ('O Queen of Beauty, you who once were fire')
February Night ('I went into the land where Beauty dwells.')
February Morning ('The starry wheel of night passed slowly over;')
Nets ('COLONIES built a fort for safety's sake,')
The Long Drive | *(Edinburgh to Boar's Hill)* ('In a garage not far from the Rock of the Castle')
The Flowing of the Sangarios ('I saw a sullen little river swerve')
Wood-Pigeons ('Often the woodman scares them as he comes')
Autumn Ploughing ('After the ranks of stubble have lain bare,')
The Waggon-Maker ('I have made tales in verse, but this man made')
November the Sixth ('I face North-West upon a grassy hill,')
Pony Fair ('Twice every year for full five centuries')
Partridges ('Here they lie mottled to the ground unseen,')
The Towerer ('Old Jarge, Hal, Walter and I, the Rector and Bill,')
Candlemas Day ('The frost is passing; from the West the rain')
The Eyes ('I remember a tropic dawn before turn-to,')
The Spanish Main ('Low, dull-green hills with scrub and little trees,')
Nombre de Dios ('The jungle reaches to the water's edge.')
Porto Bello ('The port is unsuspected from the east,')
Canal Zone ('Among these hills, twelve generations since,')
The Spanish Main Schooner ('A little wooden schooner, painted white,')
A Ballad of Sir Francis Drake ('Before Sir Francis put to sea,')
The *Mayblossom* | *(Told me by the Pilot)* ('The ship, *Mayblossom*, left Magellan Straits')
1176 Hours ('Oh, ticking Time, when wilt thou pass?')
Begone ('Begone you rubbish of old dates')
The Boy from Pauntley ('West, in the redlands, good for hops and corn,')
Sweet Friends ('Print not my life nor letters; put them by:')

Notes:
The publicity material in the preliminaries that lists Masefield's work (appearing on p.[ii]) bears a marked similarity to that present in the Heinemann edition. Moreover, titles as cited here are those of English editions (separate editions of Masefield's Racine translations and *St. George and the Dragon*, for example).

Masefield had originally intended the English edition to be published under the title *Australia and other porms* (see notes to A117(a)). Macmillan noted complications from their perspective:

> …publishing the book under the title AUSTRALIA in England and under the title A LETTER FROM PONTUS in America does bring up a slight complication in that under the new American copyright law, which has been enacted since the question of double title came up in connection with your works, every time we advertise the book under the American title we must also give the English title…
>
> (George P. Brett Jr, letter to John Masefield, 18 March 1936)
> (HRHRC, MS (Masefield, J.) Recip The Macmillan Company)

The issue was resolved less than a month later when Masefield accepted the same title for both English and American editions. George P. Brett, Jr wrote:

> …I am delighted that the book is to be published in both countries under the title A LETTER FROM PONTUS. It will save the complications of always having to advertise the two titles in America, and as I have previously said I like the title A LETTER FROM PONTUS far better than the one originally chosen for the English market.
>
> (George P. Brett Jr, letter to John Masefield, 9 April 1936)
> (HRHRC, MS (Masefield, J.) Recip The Macmillan Company)

Heinemann were originally anticipating that the Macmillan edition would be published simultaneously with the English edition (see notes to A117(a)), but this was not achieved. Louisa Callender wrote to Masefield stating that she was '…sending tomorrow three revised corrected pulls of your book to Messrs Macmillan in New York.' (see Louisa Callender, letter to John Masefield, 30 April 1936) (HRHRC, MS (Masefield, J.) Recip William Heinemann Ltd.)

A publishing agreement for this title between Masefield and Macmillan was dated 12 March 1936 (see Archives of The Society of Authors). The agreement refers to 'a licence to publish in volume form in the United States of America and Canada a work the subject or title of which is A Letter From Pontus – a book of Poems'.

Copies seen: Library of The John Masefield Society (Peter Smith Collection); HRHRC (TEMP M377LE 1936C) inscribed 'For Con | from | Jan. | June 5. 1936.'

A118 LINES ON THE TERCENTENARY OF HARVARD UNIVERSITY   1936

A118(a) First American edition (1936)

Lines on the Tercentenary of | Harvard University | BY | JOHN MASEFIELD | NEW YORK | THE MACMILLAN COMPANY | 1936
(All width centred)

Bibliographies: Handley-Taylor [unrecorded], Wight 91

Collation: [A]⁴; 4 leaves; 187 × 128mm.; [i–ii] 1–6

Page contents: [i] title-page; [ii] 'Copyright, 1936, by | JOHN MASEFIELD | [rule] | All rights reserved. No part of this book may be re- | produced in any form without permission in writing | from the publisher, except by a reviewer who wishes | to quote brief passages in connection with a review | written for inclusion in magazine or newspaper. | PRINTED IN THE UNITED STATES OF AMERICA'; 1–6 text

Paper: wove paper

Running title: none

Binding: light grey wrappers. Spine: blank. On upper wrapper: 'Lines on the Tercentenary of | Harvard University | BY | JOHN MASEFIELD | NEW YORK | THE MACMILLAN COMPANY | 1936'. Lower wrapper: blank. All edges trimmed. Binding measurements: 187 × 128mm. (wrappers), 187 × 2mm. (spine)

Publication date: published, according to evidence within inscribed copies, September 1936

Price: $1.75

Contents:
Of the Pilgrim Fathers and their setting forth into the wilderness
        ('When Custom presses on the souls apart,')
Of their spiritual trials in the loneliness of the wilderness.
        ('They were three thousand miles from help of kind,')
Of their remembering Zion, once called Cambridge in England, and of their resolve.
        ('Then they remembered quiet far away,')
Of John Harvard, his race, his talent and his gift.
        ('There was a preacher in that little band,')
He, though dead, and as a man, forgotten, yet has the noblest of earthly fames.
        ('There is no record of his form and face.')
The seed sown by him being now a triumphant tree, in which all the birds of the air find their desire.
        ('His act has brought us here; his dead hand brings')

Notes:
The text consists of six sonnets, each titled.

Page numbers appear within square brackets. Thus, [1], [2], etc.

Titles appear in smaller type to the right or left of the verse.

Although Wight places this title after *Eggs and Baker* in his sequence of volumes (using information provided by Handley-Taylor), the first printing appears to have occurred before the novel was published. Handley-Taylor's dates of publication for A118(b) and A118(c) state that the American limited signed edition was published on 9 February 1937 and that the regular edition was published on 16 February 1937. '1936' is however printed on the title-page of this edition and inscribed copies are dated September 1936. It seems therefore that the first edition was a non-limited issue in 1936.

A publishing agreement for this title between Masefield and Macmillan was dated 11 December 1936 (see Archives of The Society of Authors). The agreement refers to 'a licence to publish in volume form in the United States of America a work the subject or title of which is Lines on the Tercentenary of Harvard University (in both limited and regular editions)'. The agreement additionally notes 'on publication of the limited edition the Company agrees to transfer all its rights in the said work to Harvard University… and the Author agrees to transfer the copyright in the said work to the University…'

Copies seen: Columbia University (Special Collections B825M377 S753 1936) inscribed 'For | Ellie + Tommy. [Lamont] | from | Constance + John Masefield. | Sept' 1936.' on title-page; HRHRC (TEMP M377LI 1936) inscribed 'For Con | from | Jan. | Sept'. 22. | 1936.'

A118(b) Second American edition (limited signed edition) (1937)

LINES | ON THE TERCENTENARY | OF | HARVARD | UNIVERSITY | BY | JOHN MASEFIELD | NEW YORK | THE MACMILLAN COMPANY | 1937
(All width centred)

Bibliographies: Handley-Taylor p.61, Wight 91a

Collation: [A]¹²; 12 leaves (see notes); 254 × 166mm.; [1–6] 7–12 [13–16]

Page contents: [1] half-title: 'LINES ON THE TERCENTENARY OF | HARVARD UNIVERSITY'; [2] blank; [3] title-page; [4] 'COPYRIGHT, 1936, BY JOHN MASEFIELD | [rule] | All rights reserved–no part of this book | may be reproduced in any form without | permission in writing from the publisher, | except by a reviewer who wishes to quote brief | passages in connection with a review written | for inclusion in magazine or newspaper. | PRINTED IN THE UNITED STATES OF AMERICA | BY THE STRATFORD PRESS, INC., NEW YORK'; [5] 'LINES ON THE TERCENTENARY OF | HARVARD UNIVERSITY'; [6] blank; 7–12 text; [13] 'Of this edition 250 copies have been | prepared, each signed by the author. | This is No.'; [14–16] blank

Paper: laid paper (watermark: 'WORTHY' and 'CHARTA'), chain-lines 24mm. apart

Running title: none

Binding: mottled blue-grey boards with navy blue cloth spine. Spine: blank. On upper cover, in gold: 'LINES ON THE TERCENTENARY | OF | HARVARD UNIVERSITY | JOHN MASEFIELD'. Lower cover: blank. All edges trimmed. Binding measurements: 259 × 168mm. (covers), 259 × 17mm. (spine). End-papers constitute [A]1 and [A]12 laid down to the inside of covers with [A]2 and [A]11 as the free endpapers. Volume contained in slip-case covered in blue cloth with white paper label (65 × 113mm.) upon which in blue: 'LINES ON THE TERCENTENARY | OF HARVARD UNIVERSITY | *By John Masefield* | *Of this edition 250 copies have been prepared,* | *each signed by the author.* | This is No._____' (all width centred) (enclosed within double ruled border, the outer border being thicker than the inner: 59 × 107mm.)

Publication date: published, according to Handley-Taylor, 9 February 1937 (see notes)

Price: $5.00

Contents:
Of the Pilgrim Fathers and their setting forth into the wilderness
    ('When Custom presses on the souls apart,')
Of their spiritual trials in the loneliness of the wilderness
    ('They were three thousand miles from help of kind,')
Of their remembering Zion, once called Cambridge in England, and of their resolve
    ('Then they remembered quiet far away,')
Of John Harvard, his race, his talent and his gift
    ('There was a preacher in that little band,')
He, though dead and, as a man, forgotten, yet has the noblest of earthly fames
    ('There is no record of his form and face.')
The seed sown by him being now a triumphant tree, in which all the birds of the air find their desire
    ('His act has brought us here; his dead hand brings')

Notes:
Page numbers appear in italics within square brackets. Thus, [*7*], [*8*], etc.

Handley-Taylor's dates of publication state that the American limited signed edition was published on 9 February 1937 and that the regular edition was published on 16 February 1937. Wight lists the regular edition before the limited signed edition. Evidence suggests that the first edition was a standard edition (see A118(a)).

Handley-Taylor notes that this edition was 'published in a Limited Edition of 261 copies'. The limitation note in all copies examined states a limitation of 250 copies only.

Note the title in this edition of 'He, though dead and, as a man, forgotten, yet has the noblest of earthly fames' compared to that present in A118(a) which reads 'He, though dead, and as a man, forgotten, yet has the noblest of earthly fames.' Such minor differences nevertheless suggest that the later text was at least partially re-set.

Wight notes the slip-case as '…a blue cloth box with a label duplicating the front cover but in blue print and the addition of a statement which shows the number of the signed copy inside.' This description does not apparently fit with the copies seen.

Copies seen: private collection (PWE) number 111, signed '111 | John Masefield' on p.[13]; BL (Cup.403.p.2) number 72, signed '72 | John Masefield.' on p.[13] stamped 30 SEP 1962; Library of the John Masefield Society (Crocker Wight collection) number 136, signed '136 | John Masefield' on p.[13]

A118(c) Third American edition (1937)

LINES | ON THE TERCENTENARY | OF | HARVARD | UNIVERSITY | BY | JOHN MASEFIELD | NEW YORK | THE MACMILLAN COMPANY | 1937
(All width centred)

Bibliographies: Handley-Taylor p.61, Wight [unrecorded]

Collation: [A]⁸ (see notes); 8 leaves; 203 × 140mm.; [i–ii] [1–6] 7–12 [13–14]

Page contents: [i–ii] blank; [1] half-title: 'LINES ON THE TERCENTENARY OF | HARVARD UNIVERSITY'; [2] blank; [3] title-page; [4] 'COPYRIGHT, 1936, BY JOHN MASEFIELD | [rule] | All rights reserved–no part of this book | may be reproduced in any form without | permission in writing from the publisher, | except by a reviewer who wishes to quote brief | passages in connection with a review written | for inclusion in magazine or newspaper. | PRINTED IN THE UNITED STATES OF AMERICA | BY THE STRATFORD PRESS, INC., NEW YORK'; [5] 'LINES ON THE TERCENTENARY OF | HARVARD UNIVERSITY'; [6] blank; 7–12 text; [13–14] blank

Paper: wove paper

Running title: none

Binding: blue cloth. Spine: blank. On upper cover, in gold: 'LINES ON THE TERCENTENARY | OF | HARVARD UNIVERSITY | JOHN MASEFIELD'. Lower cover: blank. All edges trimmed. Binding measurements: 208 × 142mm. (covers), 208 × 12mm. (spine). End-paper: wove paper (see notes)

Publication date: published, according to Handley-Taylor, 16 February 1937

Price: $1.75

Contents:
as for A118(b)

Notes:
Page numbers appear in italics within square brackets. Thus, [*7*], [*8*], etc.

Handley-Taylor's dates of publication state that the American limited signed edition was published on 9 February 1937 and that the 'regular edition' was published on 16 February 1937. Evidence suggests that the true first edition was a standard edition published in 1936 (see A118(a)).

The free end-papers in this edition are continuous and bound with the single gathering. The single binding is machine-bound and stabbed thirty-seven times in the gutter.

Copies seen: HRHRC (TEMP M377LI 1937B) inscribed 'For Con | from | Jan. | Feb 15. 1937.'

A119 EGGS AND BAKER   1936

A119(a) First English edition (1936)

EGGS AND BAKER | *or* | THE DAYS OF TRIAL | BY | JOHN MASEFIELD | [ornament] | [publisher's device of a windmill with 'W' and 'H'] | [rule, 68mm.] | WILLIAM HEINEMANN LTD | LONDON :: TORONTO
(All width centred)

Bibliographies: Handley-Taylor p.61, Wight 90

Collation: [A]⁸ B-T⁸ (J not used); signatures right foot of page; 152 leaves; 190 × 126mm.; [i–vi] [1–2] 3–298

Page contents: [i–ii] blank; [iii] half-title: 'EGGS AND BAKER | *or* | THE DAYS OF TRIAL'; [iv] '*ALSO BY JOHN MASEFIELD* | PLAYS: | [12 titles listed] | POETRY: | [15 titles listed] | FICTION: | [eight titles listed] | GENERAL: | [nine titles listed]'; [v] title-page; [vi] 'FIRST PUBLISHED 1936 | PRINTED IN GREAT BRITAIN | AT THE WINDMILL PRESS, KINGSWOOD, SURREY'; [1] 'EGGS AND BAKER | *or* | THE DAYS OF TRIAL'; [2] blank; 3–298 text

Paper: wove paper

Running title: 'EGGS AND BAKER' (33mm.) on verso, 'OR THE DAYS OF TRIAL' (47mm.) on recto, pp. 4–298

Binding: blue cloth. On spine, in gold: 'EGGS | AND | BAKER | [ornament] | JOHN | MASEFIELD | HEINEMANN' (all width centred). On upper cover, in gold: 'EGGS AND BAKER | JOHN MASEFIELD' (within blind ruled border: 190 × 119mm.) On lower cover, in blind: publisher's device of a windmill (ranged lower right). Top edge stained blue, others edges trimmed. Binding measurements: 196 × 128mm. (covers), 196 × 45mm. (spine). End-papers: blue wove paper.

Publication date: the sales ledger preserved in the Heinemann Archive suggests publication on 26 October 1936 in an edition of 16000 copies

Price: 7s.6d.

Contents:

Eggs and Baker ('On the last Saturday of September, 187–, Robert Frampton Mansell, the Baker, sat in his...')

Notes:

A novel (sub-titled 'The Days of Trial') set in the late nineteenth century in which a baker, Robert Mansell, is manipulated by a radical reformer called Adolf Engels. A large proportion of the novel describes the trial of two poachers accused of murder. Support for one of the accused (the village idiot) helps ruin the baker. The novel has no chapter divisions.

The text commences with a drop-capital.

Masefield's first suggestion of this novel to Heinemann appears to have been during June 1936. Louisa Callender wrote to the author:

> Thank you for your letter enclosing the description of your book. I hope that as soon as you have decided upon the title you will very kindly let me know it.
>
> (Louisa Callender, letter to John Masefield, 15 June 1936)
> (HRHRC, MS (Masefield, J.) Recip William Heinemann Ltd.)

Another letter from Louisa Callender notes that the manuscript of the novel was 'collected by our messenger and sent at once to the press.' (see Louisa Callender, letter to John Masefield, 20 August 1936) (HRHRC, MS (Masefield, J.) Recip William Heinemann Ltd.) One week later the first batch of proofs was sent:

> I have pleasure in sending you herewith a couple of sets of proofs of the first 167 pages of EGGS AND BAKER with manuscript.
>
> (B.F. Oliver, letter to John Masefield, 27 August 1936)
> (HRHRC, MS (Masefield, J.) Recip William Heinemann Ltd.)

The remaining pages were, apparently, sent the following day (together with the corresponding portion of manuscript) (see B.F. Oliver, letter to John Masefield, 28 August 1936) (HRHRC, MS (Masefield, J.) Recip William Heinemann Ltd.) Three days later B.F. Oliver acknowledged Masefield's 'corrected proof' of the novel (see B.F. Oliver, letter to John Masefield, 31 August 1936) (HRHRC, MS (Masefield, J.) Recip William Heinemann Ltd.) C.S. Evans did not read the novel until this late stage and felt it necessary to query two details:

> I was able to grab a set of proofs of EGGS AND BAKER this week-end. I sat down with it on Saturday morning and did not leave it until I had finished it. It is a grand story and I think that it ought to be very popular. I noticed one or two tiny things but they are of no importance. There is no such thing, for instance, as a toreador: that is a word only used in a derisory sense in Spain at any rate. But of course Bob would have called a torero a toreador. Another thing, I believe a judge never rises to deliver his summing up but always sums up sitting down. Perhaps, however, they did rise in 1870! ...I should like to publish the book on October 12th...
>
> (C.S. Evans, letter to John Masefield, 1 September 1936)
> (HRHRC, MS (Masefield, J.) Recip William Heinemann Ltd.)

(This publication date was, later, to be revised). On the 3 September Masefield was sent 'a couple of copies of revised book proofs' of the book (see B.F. Oliver, letter to John Masefield, 3 September 1936) (HRHRC, MS (Masefield, J.) Recip William Heinemann Ltd.) Masefield may have decided to correct the details raised by Evans and such revisions at this stage were presumably highly restricted by the setting of type. Nevertheless Evans wrote:

> ...You have done the work remarkably skilfully; and the new material, I am told, will occupy exactly the same amount of space as the old.
>
> (C.S. Evans, letter to John Masefield, 7 September 1936)
> (HRHRC, MS (Masefield, J.) Recip William Heinemann Ltd.)

The publishing agreement for this title between Masefield and Heinemann was dated 7 September 1936 (see Archives of The Society of Authors). The agreement refers to a publication price of 7s.6d.

In November 1936 Evans reported sales:

> ...We published EGGS AND BAKER on October 26th and to date we have sold 10,256 copies. The limited edition, of which we published 125 copies at two guineas, is not yet sold out. We have about 35 copies left but we expect to sell those before Christmas.
>
> (C.S. Evans, letter to John Masefield, 17 November 1936)
> (HRHRC, MS (Masefield, J.) Recip William Heinemann Ltd.)

Sales were soon to suffer, however. Responding to Masefield's questions in April 1937, Evans stated:

> You ask me what killed the book: I am not sure that it is dead, but in common with every other book on our list its sales suffered grievously during December. During the first fortnight in December (which period, normally, is our best selling period of the year) our sales were reduced to one-tenth of the normal volume. This was due to the abdication crisis; and the ill effect was felt not only by publishers but by every kind of business. I was told, for instance, that Fortnum & Mason's shop, which is usually crowded at that time of year, saw only a very few customers a day.
>
> (William Heinemann Ltd., letter to John Masefield, 16 April 1937)
> (Archives of William Heinemann)

These comments presumably have a relevance to A119(aa) in addition to this edition.

Copies seen: private collection (PWE); BL (NN.26537) stamped 27 OCT 1936; HRHRC (TEMP M377EG 1936A cop.1) inscribed 'For Con | from Jan. | Nov 11. 1936.'; HRHRC (TEMP M377EG 1936A cop.2) inscribed 'Jude | from | Zob | Novr 11. 1936.'

A119(aa) First English edition (limited signed edition) (1936)

JOHN MASEFIELD | [five-point star] | EGGS AND BAKER [in red] | *or* | THE DAYS OF TRIAL | [five-point star] | [publisher's device of a windmill with 'W [point]' and 'H'] [in red] | LONDON | WILLIAM HEINEMANN LTD | 1936
(All width centred)

Bibliographies: Handley-Taylor p.61, Wight 90a

Collation: [A]⁸ B-T⁸ (J not used); signatures right foot of page; 152 leaves; 229 × 149mm.; [i–vi] [1–2] 3–298

Page contents: [i–ii] blank; [iii] half-title: 'EGGS AND BAKER | *or* | THE DAYS OF TRIAL'; [iv] '*This Edition, numbered and signed by the | Author, is limited to 125 copies for sale in | Great Britain and Ireland. | No............*'; [v] title-page; [vi] 'PRINTED IN GREAT BRITAIN | AT THE WINDMILL PRESS, KINGSWOOD, SURREY'; [1] 'EGGS AND BAKER | *or* | THE DAYS OF TRIAL'; [2] blank; 3–298 text

Paper: wove paper

Running title: 'EGGS AND BAKER' (47mm.) on verso, 'OR THE DAYS OF TRIAL' (65mm.) on recto, pp. 4–298

Binding: brown cloth. On spine, in gold: 'EGGS | AND | BAKER | JOHN | MASEFIELD | HEINEMANN' (all width centred). Covers: blank. Top edge gilt, others uncut. Sewn head and foot bands (in red and white) and brown marker ribbon. Binding measurements: 237 × 152mm. (covers), 237 × 55mm. (spine). The binding includes bevelled edges. End-papers: laid paper (no watermark), chain-lines 28–30mm. (bound so that chain-lines run horizontally).

Publication date: the sales ledger preserved in the Heinemann Archive suggests publication on 26 October 1936 in an edition of 125 copies

Price: 42s.

Contents:
as for A119(a)

Notes:
The text commences with a drop-capital.

The running titles in this edition are of a different size from those present in A119(a). Otherwise, the text appears to use the same setting of type.

Neither Handley-Taylor nor the *English Catalogue of Books* provide the publication date of this volume. Wight erroneously states that Handley-Taylor cites a date. The sales ledger preserved in the Heinemann Archive suggests, however, that publication was on the same date as A119(a).

C.S. Evans raised the issue of a limited edition at the beginning of September:

> I expect you will want a limited edition of your book and so I am making arrangements for a special edition of 125 copies at two guineas and we propose to publish this a fortnight after the ordinary edition…
>
> (C.S. Evans, letter to John Masefield, 3 September 1936)
> (HRHRC, MS (Masefield, J.) Recip William Heinemann Ltd.)

(This publication date was, apparently, revised). On 6 October Masefield was sent the limitation sheets for signing:

> By separate post I have to-day sent you the title-section of EGGS AND BAKER for the Limited edition, which I shall be glad if you will kindly sign under the Tablet for 125 copies and a few overs…
>
> (B.F. Oliver, letter to John Masefield, 6 October 1936)
> (HRHRC, MS (Masefield, J.) Recip William Heinemann Ltd.)

The 'prompt return of the signed limited titles' was acknowledged two days later (see B.F. Oliver, letter to John Masefield, 8 October 1936) (HRHRC, MS (Masefield, J.) Recip William Heinemann Ltd.).

Wight notes that the edition was 'issued in a brown publisher's box'.

In March 1937 C.S. Evans investigated sales since 1933 of Masefield's limited editions. Of *The Bird of Dawning* (A111(c)) he reported to Masefield that the 'whole edition was exhausted'. The same was true of *The Taking of the Gry* (A113(aa)). Copies were still available, however, of the limited signed editions of *Victorious Troy* (A116(d)), *A Letter from Pontus and other verse* (A117(aa)) and this edition of *Eggs and Baker*. Thirty-six of the 125 copies of this edition remained unsold on 12 March 1937. See notes to A119(a).

Copies seen: private collection (PWE) number 119, signed '119 | John Masefield.' on p.[iv]; BL (012600.DD.13) number 106, signed '106 | John Masefield.' on p.[iv] stamped 30 OCT 1936

A119(b) First American edition (1936)

EGGS AND BAKER | *or* | THE DAYS OF TRIAL | By | John Masefield | [ornament] | NEW YORK | THE MACMILLAN COMPANY | 1936
(All width centred)

Bibliographies: Handley-Taylor p.61, Wight 90b

Collation: [A–U]⁸ [W]⁴ [X]⁸ (J and V not used); 172 leaves; 197 × 135mm.; [i–vi] 1–338

Page contents: [i] half-title: 'EGGS AND BAKER | *or* | THE DAYS OF TRIAL'; [ii] '*ALSO BY JOHN MASEFIELD* | PLAYS: | [12 titles listed] | POETRY: | [15 titles listed] | FICTION: | [eight titles listed] | GENERAL: | [nine titles listed]'; [iii] title-page; [iv] '*Copyright, 1936, by* | JOHN MASEFIELD | [rule] | All rights reserved–no part of this book may be re- | produced in any form without permission in writing | from the publisher, except by a reviewer who wishes | to quote brief passages in connection with a review | written for inclusion in magazine or newspaper. | [rule] | *Set up and electrotyped. Published October, 1936.* | FIRST PRINTING | PRINTED IN THE UNITED STATES OF AMERICA | BY THE STRATFORD PRESS, INC., NEW YORK'; [v] 'EGGS AND BAKER | *or* | THE DAYS OF TRIAL'; [vi] blank; 1–338 text

Paper: wove paper

Running title: 'EGGS AND BAKER' (38mm.) on both verso and recto, pp.2–338

Binding: light orange cloth. On spine, in dark green: 'EGGS | AND | BAKER | MASEFIELD | MACMILLAN | [point]' (all width centred). On upper cover, in dark green: 'EGGS | AND | BAKER | JOHN MASEFIELD | [ornament]'. Lower cover: blank. Top edge stained dark green, lower outside edge trimmed, fore edge roughly trimmed. Binding measurements: 202 × 137mm. (covers), 202 × 45mm. (spine). End-papers: wove paper.

Publication date: published, according to Handley-Taylor, 26 October 1936

Price: $2.50

Contents:
as for A119(a)

Notes:
The publicity material in the preliminaries that lists Masefield's work (appearing on p.[ii]) bears a marked similarity to that present in A119(a). Moreover, titles as cited here are those of English editions (separate editions of Masefield's Racine translations and *St. George and the Dragon*, for example). However, the American edition is an entirely new setting of the text as proven by the lack of a drop-capital and the running title. In contrast to A119(a), the running title in this edition does not include the sub-title.

It appears that Masefield asked Florence Lamont to carry the manuscript across the Atlantic. Writing in August 1936 – four days after Heinemann acknowledged receipt of their manuscript – the Macmillan firm stated:

> Mrs. Lamont called and very kindly delivered to me in person the manuscript of EGGS AND BAKER. Mrs. Lamont confessed that she had read the manuscript on the way over and liked it very much indeed.
>
> (George P. Brett Jr, letter to John Masefield, 24 August 1936)
> (HRHRC, MS (Masefield, J.) Recip The Macmillan Company)

Wight notes that the top edge is 'stained blue-green'.

A publishing agreement for a novel between Masefield and Macmillan was dated 12 March 1936 (see Archives of The Society of Authors). The agreement refers to 'a licence to publish in volume form in the United States of America and Canada a work the subject or title of which is his next novel – (exact title to be determined) the story to be written around English country life and to contain from 80,000 to 100,000 words'. This may refer to *Eggs and Baker*.

Copies seen: NYPL (NCW 1936) 915731A '17 Nov 1936' written on p.[v]; HRHRC (TEMP M377EG 1936C) inscribed 'For Con from | Jan. | Nov 11. 1936.'

A120 PLAYS   1937

A120(a) First English edition ["Wanderer Edition"] (1937)

VOLUME ONE
[rule, 75mm.] | JOHN MASEFIELD | [rule, 75mm.] | PLAYS | VOLUME I | [ornament] | THE TRAGEDY OF NAN | MELLONEY HOLTSPUR | THE FAITHFUL | [ornament] | [publisher's device of a windmill with 'W' and 'H'] | [rule, 57mm.] | WILLIAM HEINEMANN LTD | LONDON :: TORONTO
(All width centred)

Bibliographies: Handley-Taylor p.61, Wight [unrecorded]

Collation: [A]⁸ B–Y⁸ Z⁴ (J and V are not used); signatures right foot of page; 188 leaves; 189 × 126mm.; [i–vi] [1–4] 5–101 [102–106] 107–229 [230–36] 237–370

Page contents: [i–ii] blank; [iii] half-title: 'THE COLLECTED WORKS OF | JOHN MASEFIELD | [rule] | WANDERER EDITION | PLAYS (I)'; [iv] '*ALSO BY JOHN MASEFIELD* | PLAYS: | [12 titles listed] | POETRY: | [15 titles listed] | FICTION: | [nine titles listed] | GENERAL: | [nine titles listed]'; [v] title-page; [vi] 'FIRST PUBLISHED 1937 | PRINTED IN GREAT BRITAIN | AT THE WINDMILL PRESS, KINGSWOOD, SURREY'; [1] 'THE TRAGEDY OF NAN'; [2] 'TO | W.B. YEATS'; [3] 'THE TRAGEDY OF NAN | [dramatis personae and original cast listed with 'PERSONS' and 'PLAYED BY' headings] | *This play was produced by the Pioneers at the New Royalty | Theatre, on 24th May, 1908, under the direction of Mr. H. | Granville Barker. At its revival as a matinée at the Haymarket | Theatre, in June, 1908, the part of the Rev. Mr. Drew was | played by Mr. Cecil Brooking.*'; [4] blank; 5–101 text of *The Tragedy of Nan*; [102] blank; [103] 'MELLONEY HOLTSPUR'; [104] 'TO | EDWARD GORDON CRAIG'; [105] 'PERSONS | [dramatis personae listed]'; [106] blank; 107–229 text of *Melloney Holtspur*; [230] 'NOTE. | The persons and events described in this play are | imaginary. No reference is made to any living person. | JOHN MASEFIELD.'; [231] 'THE FAITHFUL'; [232] 'TO | MY WIFE'; [233] 'NOTE | This play is written to be played uninterruptedly, without | more break in the action than is necessary to get the actors | off the stage, and to raise the screen or curtain dividing the | scenes. | [new paragraph] There are only two scenes. One, the front part of the | stage, left quite bare, without decoration, but with a | screen, set, or backcloth at the back, representing a | Japanese landscape, with hills and water, all wintry and | severe; the other, the back of the stage, visible when this | screen is lifted, a room in a Japanese palace, very beautiful, | but bare, save for a few flowers and a picture or two. | [new paragraph] A few minutes may elapse between Acts I and II, and a | slightly longer wait between Acts II and III.'; [234] blank; [235] 'PERSONS | [dramatis personae listed] | [rule] | In Act I, Scene 1, throughout Act II, and in Scenes 1, 2, | and 4 of Act III, the scene is: An open space near ASANO'S | palace. | In Act I, Scene 2, and in Act III, Scene 3, the scene is: | A room in KIRA'S palace. | [rule] | TIME. | Acts I and II, March 10, 1701. | Act III, March 10, 1702.'; [236] blank; 237–370 text of *The Faithful*

Paper: wove paper

Running titles: 'THE TRAGEDY OF NAN' (43mm.) on both verso and recto, pp.6–101; 'MELLONEY HOLTSPUR' (41mm.) on both verso and recto, pp.108–229; and 'THE FAITHFUL' (28mm.) on both verso and recto, pp.238–370

Binding: blue cloth. On spine, in gold: 'JOHN | MASEFIELD | PLAYS | I | THE | WANDERER | EDITION | HEINEMANN' (all width centred). On upper cover, in gold: illustration of a cockerel: 32 × 24mm. (ranged lower right). On lower cover, in blind: publisher's device of a windmill (ranged lower right). Top edge gilt, others trimmed. Sewn head band (in blue) and blue marker ribbon. Binding measurements: 196 × 127mm. (covers), 196 × 46mm. (spine). End-papers: wove paper.

Publication date: the sales ledger preserved in the Heinemann Archive suggests publication on 8 February 1937

Price: 5s.

Contents:
The Tragedy of Nan ('ACT I | SCENE: *A kitchen in the house of a small tenant farmer at Broad Oak, on Severn.*')
Melloney Holtspur ('ACT I | *The scene is a panelled room. At Back, a plain...*')
The Faithful ('ACT I | SCENE I.-*The Outer Scene. ASANO alone. Dawn. A shaft of light strikes...*')

Notes:
Published by Heinemann within the 'Collected Works of John Masefield – Wanderer Edition'. The two volumes were probably available separately.

The date of publication stated by Handley-Taylor (8 February 1936) is contradicted by the information provided within the volume itself, the *English Catalogue of Books* and the Archives of William Heinemann. The copy in the British Library is stamped with a date of 10 May 1937.

The publishing agreement for 'a collected edition of the Author's work', including this title, between Masefield and Heinemann was dated 31 July 1935 (see Archives of The Society of Authors). The agreement refers to 'a published price of 5/-...' (see note on collected editions).

Copies seen: private collection (PWE); BL (12452.i.3) rebound, stamped 10 MAY 1937; Ledbury Library

VOLUME TWO
[rule, 75mm.] | JOHN MASEFIELD | [rule, 75mm.] | PLAYS | VOLUME II | [ornament] | TRISTAN AND ISOLT | A KING'S DAUGHTER | END AND BEGINNING | [publisher's device of a windmill with 'W' and 'H'] | [rule, 57mm.] | WILLIAM HEINEMANN LTD | LONDON :: TORONTO
(All width centred)

Bibliographies: Handley-Taylor p.61, Wight [unrecorded]

Collation: [A]⁸ B-Q⁸ R¹⁰ (J not used); R2 is also signed; signatures right foot of page; 138 leaves; 189 × 126mm.; [i–vi] [1–4] 5–119 [120–24] 125–228 [229–32] 233–70

Page contents: [i–ii] blank; [iii] half-title: 'THE COLLECTED WORKS OF | JOHN MASEFIELD | [rule] | WANDERER EDITION | PLAYS (II)'; [iv] '*ALSO BY JOHN MASEFIELD* | PLAYS: | [12 titles listed] | POETRY: | [15 titles listed] | FICTION: | [nine titles listed] | GENERAL: | [nine titles listed]'; [v] title-page; [vi] 'FIRST PUBLISHED 1937 | PRINTED IN GREAT BRITAIN | AT THE WINDMILL PRESS, KINGSWOOD, SURREY'; [1] 'TRISTAN AND ISOLT'; [2] blank; [3] 'First performed by the Lena Ashwell Players at the | Century Theatre, Archer Street, Bayswater, at 8.15 p.m., | on Monday, 21st February,

LINES
ON THE TERCENTENARY
OF
HARVARD
UNIVERSITY

BY
JOHN MASEFIELD

NEW YORK
THE MACMILLAN COMPANY
1937

A118(b) title-page

LINES SPOKEN BY
JOHN MASEFIELD
AT THE TERCENTENARY
OF HARVARD UNIVERSITY
18 SEPTEMBER 1936

WILLIAM HEINEMANN LTD
LONDON

A121(a) title-page

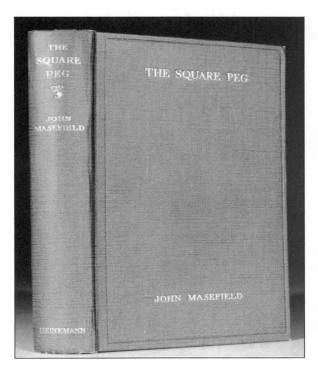

A122(a) spine and upper cover

A122(b) spine and upper cover

DEAD NED
The Autobiography of a Corpse
Who recovered Life within the Coast of Dead Ned
And came to what Fortune you shall hear

by

JOHN MASEFIELD

WILLIAM HEINEMANN LTD
LONDON :: TORONTO

A124(b) title-page

LIVE AND KICKING
NED

A Continuation of the Tale of Dead Ned

BY

JOHN MASEFIELD

WILLIAM HEINEMANN LTD
LONDON :: TORONTO

A127(a) title-page

LIVE AND
KICKING NED

by

JOHN MASEFIELD

NEW YORK
THE MACMILLAN COMPANY
1939

A127(b) title-page

DEAD NED

and

LIVE AND
KICKING NED

by

JOHN MASEFIELD

NEW YORK
THE MACMILLAN COMPANY
1941

A133(a) title-page

1927, with the following cast : | (Characters in the order of their appearance.) | [dramatis personae and original cast listed]'; [4] blank; 5–119 text of *Tristan and Isolt*; [120] blank; [121] 'A KING'S DAUGHTER'; [122] 'TO | MY WIFE'; [123] 'This play was performed at the Oxford Playhouse on | Friday and Saturday, May 25 and 26, 1923, by the follow- | ing cast of the Hill Players: | [dramatis personae and original cast listed] | SCENE: The Palace in Samaria.'; [124] blank; 125–228 text of *A King's Daughter*; [229] 'END AND BEGINNING'; [230] 'TO | FLORENCE'; [231] 'PERSONS | [dramatis personae and original cast listed] | *The scene is a small room in Fotheringhay Castle. A settle | with a canopy is in the centre. A small table with ink, pens, | wine and a cup is to the Actors' Left of this settle.*'; [232] blank; 233–70 text of *End and Beginning*

Paper: wove paper

Running titles: 'TRISTAN AND ISOLT' (38mm.) on both verso and recto, pp.6–118; 'A KING'S DAUGHTER' (39mm.) on both verso and recto, pp.126–228; and 'END AND BEGINNING' (40mm.) on both verso and recto, pp.234–270

Binding: blue cloth. On spine, in gold: 'JOHN | MASEFIELD | PLAYS | II | THE | WANDERER | EDITION | HEINEMANN' (all width centred). On upper cover, in gold: illustration of a cockerel: 32 × 24mm. (ranged lower right). On lower cover, in blind: publisher's device of a windmill (ranged lower right). Top edge gilt, others trimmed. Sewn head band (in blue) and blue marker ribbon. Binding measurements: 196 × 127mm. (covers), 196 × 46mm. (spine). End-papers: wove paper.

Publication date: the sales ledger preserved in the Heinemann Archive suggests publication on 8 February 1937

Price: 5s.

Contents:

Tristan and Isolt ('(*From Front Stage.*) | DESTINY. | I am She who began ere Man was begotten,')
A King's Daughter ('JEZEBEL. | I am Queen Jezebel, King Ahab's wife.')
End and Beginning ('MARY. | I am that Mary Stuart, the Queen of Scotland:')

Notes:
The publishing agreement for 'a collected edition of the Author's work', including this title, between Masefield and Heinemann was dated 31 July 1935 (see Archives of The Society of Authors). The agreement refers to 'a published price of 5/-...' (see note on collected editions).

Copies seen: BL (12452.i.3) rebound, stamped 10 MAY 1937; Ledbury Library

A121 LINES SPOKEN… AT THE TERCENTENARY OF HARVARD UNIVERSITY   1937

A121(a) First English edition (limited signed edition) (1937)

LINES SPOKEN BY | JOHN MASEFIELD [in red] | AT THE TERCENTENARY | OF HARVARD UNIVERSITY | 18 SEPTEMBER 1936 | [device of Harvard University with '1636 | VERI | TAS | 1936'] [in red] | WILLIAM HEINEMANN LTD | LONDON
(Width centred with lines 2, 3 and 4 justified on left and right margins)

Bibliographies: Handley-Taylor p.61, Wight 92

Collation: [A]¹²; 12 leaves; 254 × 159mm.; [1–4] 5 [6] 7 [8] 9 [10] 11 [12] 13 [14] 15 [16]

Page contents: [1] half-title: 'LINES SPOKEN AT | THE TERCENTENARY OF | HARVARD UNIVERSITY'; [2] '*This edition is limited to 150 | copies of which 125 are for sale. | This is No. | Signed | First published in January 1937 | Printed in England*'; [3] title-page; [4]–15 text; [16] '*Printed in England by The Shenval Press*'

Paper: wove paper (watermark: 'ORIGINAL | TURKEY MILL | KENT')

Running title: none

Binding: beige cloth. Spine: blank. On upper cover: 'LINES SPOKEN AT [in gold] | THE TERCENTENARY OF [in gold] | HARVARD UNIVERSITY [in gold] | [device of Harvard University with '1636 | VERI | TAS | 1936'] [in red]'. Lower cover: blank. All edges trimmed. Binding measurements: 258 × 158mm. (covers), 258 × 15mm. (spine). End-papers constitute [A]1 and [A]12 laid down to the inside of covers with [A]2 and [A]11 as the free end-papers.

Publication date: the sales ledger preserved in the Heinemann Archive suggests publication on 15 March 1937 in an edition of 175 copies (see notes)

Price: 10s.6d.

Contents:
Of the Pilgrim Fathers and their setting forth into the wilderness
    ('When Custom presses on the souls apart,')
Of their spiritual trials in the loneliness of the wilderness
    ('They were three thousand miles from help of kind,')
Of their remembering Zion, once called Cambridge in England, and of their resolve
    ('Then they remembered quiet far away,')

Of John Harvard, his race, his talent and his gift
>   ('There was a preacher in that little band,')
He, though dead, and as a man, forgotten, yet has the noblest of earthly fames
>   ('There is no record of his form and face.')
The seed sown by him being now a triumphant tree, in which all the birds of the air find their desire
>   ('His act has brought us here; his dead hand brings')

Notes:

An edition comprising an English publication of the American *Lines on the Tercentenary of Harvard University* (see A118). The text consists of six sonnets, each titled.

Each poem is preceded by the title (in red) printed on the verso of the previous leaf. Page numbers are not present on these pages.

Page numbers appear after a single square bracket. Thus, [5, [7, etc.

Wight excludes two leaves from his description regarding them as part of the binding yet counts another two leaves within the pagination of the book (noting 'there are no free endpapers'). This is contrary to the pagination as present in the volume itself and four of the twelve leaves from the single gathering are used as end-papers.

Handley-Taylor refers to this volume as *Ode to Harvard*. The entire entry in his bibliography is as follows:

> ODE TO HARVARD. William Heinemann, Ltd. (London).
> Limited Edition published March 15, 1937.

The publication date he cites is that which is noted within the Archives of William Heinemann and also stamped inside the British Library copy. Wight does not provide any note of publication date within the entry for this book (Wight's number 92). He does, however, state for A118(b) (Wight's 91a) that:

> Handley-Taylor says that this edition was published on February 9, 1937, the same date as number 92 the limited edition.

Handley-Taylor indeed gives February 9, 1937 as the publication date for Wight's 91a, however, the rest of Wight's note is incorrect.

C.S. Evans suggested to Masefield that Heinemann might print this edition:

> …I should like to print a small edition of your Harvard poem. Will you send it to me so that I can decide on the format. I should think that fifty copies would be too few and that we had better print a hundred…
>
> >   (C.S. Evans, letter to John Masefield, 2 October 1936)
> >   (HRHRC, MS (Masefield, J.) Recip William Heinemann Ltd.)

Masefield evidently sent Evans the verses and these were acknowledged on 5 October 1936 (see C.S. Evans, letter to John Masefield, 5 October 1936) (HRHRC, MS (Masefield, J.) Recip William Heinemann Ltd.)

During the production of the volume Evans requested Masefield's opinion on proposed bindings and also noted thoughts on publication date:

> I am sending you two suggested covers for our limited edition of HARVARD POEMS. I think that in this case, as the poems are not published in an ordinary edition, we should change the format… The case I have marked A is what is called a crush canvas and the one marked B is an unfadable Sundour cloth – both of very fine quality. The idea would be to letter them on the outside in red to match the rubrication on the pages. As you will see the book makes only a few pages but I think that we should ask 10/6d. for it, printing 125 copies.
>
> Now about the date of publication: we have not had a chance to subscribe the book yet because it is impossible to subscribe a limited edition of this kind without knowing the format, price, etc. and we have only just been able to determine these. Our sales department is of the opinion that we should not attempt to publish before Christmas: we could not get it out before the first or second week in December and at that time of year the booksellers will not even see the travellers for they have bought all they want for the year. My idea would be to publish in January and make the book one of the first publications of the New Year. …What do you think of putting the arms of Harvard on the cover?
>
> >   (C.S. Evans, letter to John Masefield, 25 November 1936)
> >   (HRHRC, MS (Masefield, J.) Recip William Heinemann Ltd.)

The Archives of William Heinemann reveal that the title of this volume remained vague until the beginning of 1937. On 11 January 1937 Louisa Callender wrote to Masefield asking for 'the actual wording for the title of your Harvard poems' (see Louisa Callender, letter to John Masefield, 11 January 1937) (HRHRC, MS (Masefield, J.) Recip William Heinemann Ltd.) Masefield replied:

> The verses might be called, LINES SPOKEN AT THE TERCENTENARY OF HARVARD UNIVERSITY, SEPTEMBER 18TH., 1936. I would leave the spacing to your compositors.
>
> >   (John Masefield, letter to [Louisa] Callender, [12 Jan. 1937])
> >   (Archives of William Heinemann)

The Archive contains references to the *Harvard Memorial Verses*, *The Harvard Verses* and *Ode to Harvard*. Presumably such variations were the source of Handley-Taylor's confusion over the title of this volume.

The sales ledger preserved in the Heinemann Archive notes an edition of 175 copies. This is either an error for 150 copies, or there were an additional 25 copies in the print run not noted within the edition's own limitation note. However, as the edition states it was limited to 150 copies of which 125 were for sale, the entry in the sales ledger may have been confused about the 25 copies not for sale and added this figure to the total edition number.

The edition was over-subscribed upon publication and Heinemann wrote to Masefield:

> We are publishing the HARVARD MEMORIAL VERSES next Monday, the 15th. You will be pleased to hear that the entire edition is over-subscribed and we have had to ration it. This has not happened with the last three or four limited editions of yours which we have published. I think that the over-subscription is due to the fact that this edition is the only form in which the poems are published. The price of the book is 10/6d. I am having your presentation copies sent to you today.

> (William Heinemann Ltd., letter to John Masefield, 9 March 1937)
> (Archives of William Heinemann)

Masefield, upon receiving his presentation copies, wrote to C.S. Evans with praise at their appearance: 'These look very well: my compliments' (John Masefield, letter to [C.S.] Evans, [11 March 1937]) (Archives of William Heinemann).

Copies seen: private collection (PWE) number 114, signed '114 | John Masefield.' on p.[2]; BL (20030.d.30) number 130, signed '130 | John Masefield.' on p.[2], stamped 15 MAR 1937; Columbia University (Special Collections B825M377 S753 1937) number 102, signed '102 | John Masefield.' on p.[2]; HRHRC (TEMP M377LI 1937A) number 137, signed '137. | John Masefield.' on p.[2] additionally inscribed 'For Con | from | Jan. | 10 March. 1937.'

A122 THE SQUARE PEG   1937

A122(a) First English edition (1937)

THE SQUARE PEG | *or* | THE GUN FELLA | BY | JOHN MASEFIELD | [ornament] | [publisher's device of a windmill with 'W' and 'H'] | [rule, 68mm.] | WILLIAM HEINEMANN LTD | LONDON :: TORONTO
(All width centred)

Bibliographies: Handley-Taylor p.61, Wight 93

Collation: [A]⁸ B-U⁸ (J not used); signatures right foot of page; 160 leaves; 190 × 126mm.; [i–viii] 1–302 [303–312]

Page contents: [i–ii] blank; [iii] half-title: 'THE SQUARE PEG | *or* | THE GUN FELLA'; [iv] '*ALSO BY JOHN MASEFIELD* | PLAYS: | [12 titles listed] | POETRY: | [15 titles listed] | FICTION: | [nine titles listed] | GENERAL: | [nine titles listed]'; [v] title-page; [vi] 'FIRST PUBLISHED 1937 | PRINTED IN GREAT BRITAIN | AT THE WINDMILL PRESS, KINGSWOOD, SURREY'; [vii] 'To | MY WIFE'; [viii] blank; 1–302 text; [303–308] publisher's advertisements; [309–312] blank

Paper: wove paper

Running title: 'THE SQUARE PEG' (45mm.) on verso; '*or* THE GUN FELLA' (49mm.) on recto, pp.2–302

Binding: blue cloth. On spine, in gold: 'THE | SQUARE | PEG | [ornament] | JOHN | MASEFIELD | HEINEMANN' (all width centred). On upper cover, in gold: 'THE SQUARE PEG | JOHN MASEFIELD' (within blind ruled border: 188 × 118mm.) On lower cover, in blind: publisher's device of a windmill (ranged lower right). Top edge stained blue, others trimmed. Binding measurements: 195 × 128mm. (covers), 195 × 45mm. (spine). End-papers: blue wove paper.

Publication date: the sales ledger preserved in the Heinemann Archive suggests publication on 18 October 1937 in an edition of 12500 copies

Price: 7s.6d.

Contents:
The Square Peg ('Robert Frampton Mansell, the inventor and manufacturer of the Mansell Gun, stopped his car...')

Notes:
A novel (sub-titled 'The Gun Fella') in which the characters are descendants of those in *Eggs and Baker*. The novel has no chapter divisions. The plot concerns Robert Mansell (a gun manufacturer) and his efforts to establish a wildlife sanctuary. He is opposed by the local gentry who are unable to relinquish their desire to hunt.

The text commences with a drop-capital.

It appears that Masefield promised the completed text of his new novel for the end of July 1937. C.S. Evans wrote enthusiastically:

> It is good news indeed that your book will be ready by the end of the month and I am eagerly looking forward to reading it. A new Masefield is always an event in my year...

> (C.S. Evans, letter to John Masefield, 9 July 1937)
> (HRHRC, MS (Masefield, J.) Recip William Heinemann Ltd.)

Later that month, Evans notes his intention to start setting the text immediately and also offers assistance with the Macmillan edition:

I will begin to set the new book directly it comes in and I should be able to send you complete proofs in about a fortnight from that time. I suppose you have sent Macmillan a script? If not, I could send them a set of the first proofs from which they could begin composition, and let them have corrected proofs later...

(C.S. Evans, letter to John Masefield, 27 July 1937)
(HRHRC, MS (Masefield, J.) Recip William Heinemann Ltd.)

Masefield was a few days late in delivery and had doubts about his title. He wrote 'I am sending you with this the typed script of the Square Peg, a title, which may already be in use, and therefore needs a secondary title. I hope that some of the tale may amuse you.' (see John Masefield, letter to [C.S.] Evans, [4 August 1937]) (Archives of William Heinemann). The 'secondary title' was to be 'The Gun Fella' and this was adopted as the sub-title. As with other volumes which Heinemann began setting immediatley, proofs were sent to the author in batches. B.F. Oliver wrote on 24 August:

Thank you for the returned proofs corrected of the first 183 pages of THE SQUARE PEG. I how have pleasure in sending you two sets of the remainder with manuscript.

(B.F. Oliver, letter to John Masefield, 24 August 1937)
(HRHRC, MS (Masefield, J.) Recip William Heinemann Ltd.)

Three copies of 'revised book proofs' were sent on 3 September (see B.F. Oliver, letter to John Masefield, 3 September 1937) (HRHRC, MS (Masefield, J.) Recip William Heinemann Ltd.)

The publishing agreement for this title between Masefield and Heinemann was dated 24 September 1937 (see Archives of The Society of Authors). The agreement refers to a publication price of 7s.6d. A letter from Masefield, conjecturally dated 24 September 1937, to C.S. Evans enclosed the agreement for this volume and enquired about a limited signed edition:

I return herewith the Agreement for the Square Peg book. I suppose that you do not wish to issue a limited edition of it. Doubtless the large paper racket has been done to death.

(John Masefield, letter to [C.S. Evans], [24 September 1937])
(Archives of William Heinemann)

With reference to *Lines Spoken... at The Tercentenary of Harvard University*, Evans replied on 28 September 1937 explaining the general lack of interest in limited signed editions:

Thank you for your letter returning the signed contract for *The Square Peg*. You are quite right: there is very little enthusiasm on the part of the booksellers or public for limited editions these days. I made some enquiries about the possibilities of *The Square Peg* from people in London who deal in such things but got very little encouragement, and our records show that the last two or three limited editions of your books have not sold out. A good many of them are still in the booksellers' hands. This applies not only to your books but to the books of other authors as well, mainly when two editions of a book is issued. The real collector nowadays goes for the first ordinary edition of a book, but he will still buy a book which appears only in a limited edition. That was the reason why we disposed of every copy of *Ode To Harvard*: it was oversubscribed and we had to ration it.

([C.S. Evans], letter to John Masefield, 28 September 1937)
(Archives of William Heinemann)

Copies seen: private collection (PWE); private collection (PWE); BL (N.N.28066) stamped 18 OCT 1937

A122(b) First American edition (1937)

THE SQUARE PEG | *or* | THE GUN FELLA | BY | JOHN MASEFIELD | [ornament] | NEW YORK | THE MACMILLAN COMPANY | 1937
(All width centred)

Bibliographies: Handley-Taylor p.61, Wight 93a

Collation: [A-S]⁸ [T]⁴ [U]⁸ (J not used); 156 leaves; 203 × 135mm.; [i–viii] 1–302 [303–304]

Page contents: [i–ii] blank; [iii] half-title: 'THE SQUARE PEG | *or* | THE GUN FELLA'; [iv] '*ALSO BY JOHN MASEFIELD* | PLAYS: | [12 titles listed] | POETRY: | [15 titles listed] | FICTION: | [nine titles listed] | GENERAL: | [nine titles listed]'; [v] title-page; [vi] '*Copyright, 1937, by* | JOHN MASEFIELD | All rights reserved–no part of this book may be | reproduced in any form without permission in writing | from the publisher, except by a reviewer who wishes | to quote brief passages in connection with a review | written for inclusion in magazine or newspaper. | PRINTED IN THE UNITED STATES OF AMERICA | BY THE POLYGRAPHIC COMPANY OF AMERICA,N.Y.'; [vii] 'To | MY WIFE'; [viii] blank; 1–302 text; [303–304] blank

Paper: wove paper

Running title: 'THE SQUARE PEG' (45mm.) on verso; '*or* THE GUN FELLA' (49mm.) on recto, pp.2–302

Binding: green cloth. On spine: '*the* | SQUARE | PEG [lines 1–3 in blind within tilted black square] | MASEFIELD | MACMILLAN | [point] – [point]' (all width centred). On upper cover: '*the* | SQUARE | PEG [lines 1–3 in blind within tilted black square] | JOHN MASEFIELD [in black]'. Lower cover: blank. All edges trimmed. Binding measurements: 208 × 136mm. (covers), 208 × 42mm. (spine). End-papers: wove paper

Publication date: published, according to Handley-Taylor, 16 November 1937

Price: $2.50

Contents:
as for A122(a)

Notes:
The text commences with a drop-capital.

The setting of type appears to be similar to that of A122(a). As with many other Macmillan editions of the period the publicity material in the preliminaries that lists Masefield's work (appearing on p.[iv]) bears a marked similarity to that present in the Heinemann edition. Moreover, titles as cited here are those of English editions (separate editions of Masefield's Racine translations and *St. George and The Dragon*, for example). A letter from Masefield, conjecturally dated at the beginning of August 1937, to C.S. Evans enclosed the typescript for this volume. Masefield then asked for assistance in providing Macmillan with corrected proofs:

> I have sent a copy to Macmillans, but I know, that it would be a help to them to have corrected proofs to correct by.
> (John Masefield, letter to [C.S.] Evans, [4 August 1937])
> (Archives of William Heinemann)

In the event, it seems likely that the Macmillan company set from a copy of the corrected proofs.

A publishing agreement for this title between Masefield and Macmillan was dated 5 August 1937 (see Archives of The Society of Authors). The agreement refers to 'a licence to publish in volume form in the United States of America and Canada a work the subject or title of which is The Square Peg – (a novel)'.

Copies seen: private collection (ROV) inscribed 'For | Alice, | from | Jan. | Christmas. 1937.' on front free end-paper; Columbia University (825 M377 W343)

A123 THE COUNTRY SCENE   1937

A123(a) First English edition (1937)

THE | COUNTRY | SCENE | IN POEMS BY | JOHN MASEFIELD | AND PICTURES BY | EDWARD SEAGO | COLLINS | PALL MALL LONDON
(All width centred)

Bibliographies: Handley-Taylor p.61, Wight 94

Collation: [A]⁴ [B-X]⁴ [Y]³ (see notes) (J and V not used); 91 leaves; 311 × 249mm.; [3–15] 16 [17] 18 [19] 20 [21] 22 [23] 24 [25] 26 [27] 28 [29] 30 [31] 32 [33] 34 [35] 36 [37] 38 [39] 40 [41] 42 [43] 44 [45] 46 [47] 48 [49] 50 [51] 52 [53] 54 [55] 56 [57] 58 [59] 60 [61] 62 [63] 64 [65] 66 [67] 68 [69] 70 [71] 72 [73] 74 [75] 76 [77] 78 [79] 80 [81] 82 [83] 84 [85] 86 [87] 88 [89] 90 [91] 92 [93] 94 [95] 96 [97] 98 [99–100]; illustration plates are laid down to the un-numbered leaves that carry illustrations (these cardboard leaves have blind panels onto which the illustration is laid down); colour plates each with protective tissue (with printed legend)

Page contents: [pages [1] and [2] omitted from pagination]; [3–4] blank; [5] half-title: 'THE COUNTRY SCENE'; [6] blank; [7] title-page; [8] 'PRINTED IN GREAT BRITAIN BY HUDSON AND STRACEY, LTD. | COLOUR BLOCKS SUPPLIED BY NOAKES BROS., LTD. | BOUND BY WEBB, SON & CO., LTD. | COPYRIGHT 1937'; [9–10] 'On England' *[Verse]* ('What is this England, whom the draughtsmen print'); [11–14] 'THE POEMS AND THE PICTURES' (43 individual poems and 42 individual illustrations listed with page references); [15]–16 text; [17] blank; 18 text; [19] blank; 20 text; [21] blank; 22 text; [23] blank; 24 text; [25] blank; 26 text; [27] blank; 28 text; [29] blank; 30 text; [31] blank; 32 text; [33] blank; 34 text; [35] blank; 36 text; [37] blank; 38 text; [39] blank; 40 text; [41] blank; 42 text; [43] blank; 44 text; [45] blank; 46 text; [47] blank; 48 text; [49] blank; 50 text; [51] blank; 52 text; [53] blank; 54 text; [55] blank; 56 text; [57] blank; 58 text; [59] blank; 60 text; [61] blank; 62 text; [63] blank; 64 text; [65] blank; 66 text; [67] blank; 68 text; [69] blank; 70 text; [71] blank; 72 text; [73] blank; 74 text; [75] blank; 76 text; [77] blank; 78 text; [79] blank; 80 text; [81] blank; 82 text; [83] blank; 84 text; [85] blank; 86 text; [87] blank; 88 text; [89] blank; 90 text; [91] blank; 92 text; [93] blank; 94 text; [95] blank; 96 text; [97] blank; 98 text; [99–100] blank

Paper: laid paper (watermark: 'SAVOY | Antique'), chain-lines 25mm. apart. Colour plates laid down to cardboard

Running title: none

Binding: light brown hessian cloth with green cloth spine. On spine, in gold: '[rule] | THE | COUNTRY | SCENE | John Masefield | and | Edward Seago | COLLINS | [rule]' (all width centred). There are double vertical rules on each cover at the edge of the green cloth (those on the upper cover are in gold, those on the lower cover are in blind). Covers: blank. Top edge gilt, others uncut. Sewn head band (in green and red). Binding measurements: 318 × 254mm. (covers), 318 × 67mm. (spine). The binding includes bevelled edges. End-papers: brown wove paper. Volume contained in slip-case covered in brown and green marbled-effect textured paper.

Publication date: published, according to Handley-Taylor, 15 November 1937 in an edition of 2250 copies

Price: 63s.

Contents:

On England ('What is this England, whom the draughtsmen print')
Prologue ('Here is the world of man and his adventure,')
The Hounds in Snow ('During the night, the silent-footed snow')
Lambing ('In iron midnights in the downland fold')
A Midwife's Story ('I saw the lad was skin and bone;')
Nomads ('Where do they go, these waggons of delight,')
The Gallop on the Sands ('White horses toss their manes along the shore;')
Point to Point ('The flags are gay above the tents; the crowd')
The Orchard in Full Flower ('All things are in perfection for to-day,')
The Morris Dancers ('Men have forgotten how the dance began.')
The Road to Epsom *or* Why Not? ('Once every year the myriads hurry thus')
The Mid-day Sun ('Left by the sea these many thousand years')
The Mare and Foal at Grass ('Now that the grass is at its best in May,')
The County Show ('What do they think among these staring eyes,')
Elephants in the Tent ('"They're not the draw they were," the showman said.')
The Forge ('"Even as the blacksmith beats and brays')
The Roadside Inn ('All passing men, with beast or waggons,')
The Procession of the Bulls ('Slowly, in line, the winning bulls go by,')
Tiddlers ('They do not scrape the green scum of a pond,')
The Swing Boats ('Over the roaring sideshows comes the blare')
The Tight-rope Walker ('The naphtha flares, the thousand faces glow,')
Their Canvas Home ('This is the Circus tent, where the tribe camps')
The Young Fisherman ('*The Brook* | Rimple, dimple and glimple with insway, unsway,')
The Boat upon The Broads ('Is there any better fun')
The Horse and Trap at the Ford ('Three thousand years ago this track was used')
The Hoppers ('When ripening apples glow among the leaves;')
The Harvest ('All day the rattle of the cutter clacks;')
The Horse in the Barn ('Into this barn these horses have dragged corn')
Salisbury Spire from the Plain ('Six hundred years have dwellers in the plain')
Gleaners ('Harvest is home; the blueness is all dim;')
September Fields ('Bristled and speared, in army, rank on rank,')
Steam Horses ('The moonless storm is roaring in the pines;')
The Fowler's Hut ('The darkness comes with rain upon the fen,')
The Gulls at Ploughing ('Before a south-east gale, they know the signs;')
The Horse Fair ('Almost each year, for seven hundred years,')
The Ploughing Match ('This is the work that keeps the world alive;')
Hunting ('Ah, once, in the world's youth, men crept like snakes')
The Marcham Hams ('Among the fragrant mummies of dead pigs')
The Norfolk Wherry ('Creeds are denied, the nations disagree,')
Timber Hauling ('Once, he was undergrowth which the stag spared,')
The Gulls upon the Saltings ('They mew above the boilings in the wake,')
The Christmas Mummers ('They slice the coloured paper into strips')
The Gipsies in the Snow ('The bitter evening falls, the fog's about,')
The Bellringers ('What do they do, when all the ropes are still,')

Notes:

The first of Masefield's collaborations with the Norfolk artist Edward Seago (see also *Tribute to Ballet* (A125) and *A Generation Risen* (A138)). Each poem is accompanied by a full-colour reproduction of a Seago oil painting.

Wight describes the gatherings as 'collation indeterminate'. The only true gathering is the first. After this, the volume consists of 'gatherings' consisting of laid paper (for the poetry) and cardboard (for the plates). Leaves are not conjugate, but pasted onto slips of paper. A 'gathering' therefore consists of a leaf of laid paper coupled to a leaf of cardboard and, at the centre of the 'gathering', a leaf of cardboard coupled to a leaf of laid paper. In the gatherings C-X the first leaf is therefore of laid paper, the second of cardboard, the third of laid paper and the fourth of cardboard. Protective tissue is also bound in, but this has been omitted from the description. The pattern of printing is uniform for gatherings C-X with the following observed:

> paper leaf (recto blank, verso with printed poem)
> cardboard leaf (recto with laid down illustration, verso blank)
> paper leaf (recto blank, verso with printed poem)
> cardboard leaf (recto with laid down illustration, verso blank)

'Gathering' B consists of the first three leaves of laid paper and the fourth being cardboard. 'Gathering' Y consists of the standard pattern for 'gatherings' within this volume except that the final leaf of cardboard is omitted. The pagination of the volume does not include the cardboard leaves.

The coloured plates are all laid down to card and accompanied by protective tissue. These tissues carry the legends for the plates.

The first poem ('On England') appearing on pp.[9–10] is omitted from the contents listing within the volume.

Masefield at first intended Heinemann to publish this title. It seems, however, that the reproduction processes required to print Seago's illustrations would have produced a book which Heinemann considered too expensive. Masefield wrote in April 1937:

> May I write to you once more about the Seago book? It seems, that a firm of publishers used to publishing books with coloured illustrations, has shewn much eagerness to publish the book. To be brief, they would like to undertake the book, and to begin work upon it at once, if you should decide not to do it. Will you, therefore, please give the question another thought or two, and let me know, if you can, by tomorrow night's post, what you finally decide?
>
> (John Masefield, letter to [C.S.] Evans, 25 April 1937)
> (Archives of William Heinemann)

C.S. Evans replied on 27 April 1937 with apparent reluctance:

> You know how unwilling I am to let any book with which you are associated go elsewhere, but in this case as there is another firm with more confidence in the book from an economic point of view than I have, I think it would be better to let them do it. Seago's pictures are lovely, but in my opinion (and in Seago's) they would have to be very expensively produced if the best effects are to be got. And that, as I have said before, would mean a very high priced book, and a consequent difficulty of sale. I hope, however, that you will make arrangements with the other publishers to let us include the verses you will write for Seago's pictures in the collected edition of your work.
>
> (C.S. Evans, letter to John Masefield, 27 April 1937)
> (Archives of William Heinemann)

The 'other publishers' were presumably Collins and the volume appeared less than seven months later. Masefield did indeed retain rights to his work and extracts from work published by Collins appeared in *Poems* (see A148). Heinemann had probably made an accurate assessment of the volume's economic problems. When Collins published the work in America (see A123(c)) Seago's illustrations were entirely omitted. Additionally, subsequent publication by Collins of Masefield and Seago titles *Tribute to Ballet* and *A Generation Risen* were less lavishly produced (although the later title may be a result of wartime economy).

Masefield sent the contract from Collins to The Society of Authors in June 1937 for advice. It appears that, at the beginning of June, the title was *A Year of England's Life* (see BL, Add.Mss.56607, ff.4–6). One issue on which Masefield sought advice was American copyright:

> I am enclosing a contract from Messrs Collins for a book of pictures to which I contribute verses. I shall be glad, if you will kindly let me know, whether to be certain of securing American copyright I ought to have the verses set up in the U.S. even without the pictures.
>
> (John Masefield, letter to [E.J.] Mullett, [3 June 1937])
> (BL, Add.Mss.56607, f.3)

A publishing agreement for this title between Masefield and Collins was dated 31 August 1937 (see Archives of The Society of Authors). The agreement notes 'all monies due under this agreement shall be divided equally, half to be paid to John Masefield… and half to Mr Edward Seago's representatives'. It appears that there was some delay in sending the agreement, due to Seago being away from home.

This title is listed by Macmillan in a catalogue dated July 1938. It is noted as an 'import' at $18.50. It is feasible that the Collins edition was sold by Macmillan and that A123(c) was merely a copyright edition.

Copies seen: BL (L.R.32.a.15) stamped 15 NOV 1937; Columbia University (Special Collections B825 M377 L3 1937); HRHRC (-Q-PR6025 A77 C65 1937) inscribed 'For Jude. | from | Zob. | Novr 17. 1937.'

A123(b) *Second English edition (limited signed edition) (1937)*

THE [in green] | COUNTRY [in green] | SCENE [in green] | IN POEMS BY | JOHN MASEFIELD | AND PICTURES BY | EDWARD SEAGO | COLLINS | PALL MALL LONDON
(All width centred)

Bibliographies: Handley-Taylor p.61, Wight [noted on p.170]

Collation: [A]⁴ [B-X]⁴ [Y]³ (see notes) (J and V not used); 91 leaves; 311 × 249mm.; [3–15] 16 [17] 18 [19] 20 [21] 22 [23] 24 [25] 26 [27] 28 [29] 30 [31] 32 [33] 34 [35] 36 [37] 38 [39] 40 [41] 42 [43] 44 [45] 46 [47] 48 [49] 50 [51] 52 [53] 54 [55] 56 [57] 58 [59] 60 [61] 62 [63] 64 [65] 66 [67] 68 [69] 70 [71] 72 [73] 74 [75] 76 [77] 78 [79] 80 [81] 82 [83] 84 [85] 86 [87] 88 [89] 90 [91] 92 [93] 94 [95] 96 [97] 98 [99–100]; illustration plates are laid down to the un-numbered leaves that carry illustrations (these cardboard leaves have blind panels onto which the illustration is laid down); colour plates each with protective tissue (with printed legend)

Page contents: [pages [1] and [2] omitted from pagination]; [3–4] blank; [5] half-title: 'THE COUNTRY SCENE'; [6] 'THIS EDITION IS LIMITED TO FIFTY COPIES, AND EACH COPY | IS SIGNED BY THE AUTHOR AND THE ARTIST. | THIS IS NUMBER ....'; [7] title-page; [8] 'PRINTED IN GREAT BRITAIN BY HUDSON AND STRACEY, LTD.

| COLOUR BLOCKS SUPPLIED BY NOAKES BROS., LTD. | BOUND BY WEBB, SON & CO., LTD. | COPYRIGHT 1937';
[9–10] 'On England' *[Verse]* ('What is this England, whom the draughtsmen print'); [11–14] 'THE POEMS AND THE PICTURES'
(43 individual poems and 42 individual illustrations listed with page references); [15]–16 text; [17] blank; 18 text; [19] blank; 20 text;
[21] blank; 22 text; [23] blank; 24 text; [25] blank; 26 text; [27] blank; 28 text; [29] blank; 30 text; [31] blank; 32 text; [33] blank; 34
text; [35] blank; 36 text; [37] blank; 38 text; [39] blank; 40 text; [41] blank; 42 text; [43] blank; 44 text; [45] blank; 46 text; [47] blank;
48 text; [49] blank; 50 text; [51] blank; 52 text; [53] blank; 54 text; [55] blank; 56 text; [57] blank; 58 text; [59] blank; 60 text; [61]
blank; 62 text; [63] blank; 64 text; [65] blank; 66 text; [67] blank; 68 text; [69] blank; 70 text; [71] blank; 72 text; [73] blank; 74 text;
[75] blank; 76 text; [77] blank; 78 text; [79] blank; 80 text; [81] blank; 82 text; [83] blank; 84 text; [85] blank; 86 text; [87] blank; 88
text; [89] blank; 90 text; [91] blank; 92 text; [93] blank; 94 text; [95] blank; 96 text; [97] blank; 98 text; [99–100] blank

Paper: laid paper (watermark: 'UNBLEACHED ARNOLD'), chain-lines 32mm. apart. Colour plates laid down to cardboard

Running title: none

Binding: white buckram with green pig-skin spine. On spine, in gold: '[rule] | THE | COUNTRY | SCENE | John Masefield | and
| Edward Seago | [rule]' (all width centred). There are double vertical rules on each cover at the edge of the green pig-skin
(those on the upper cover are in gold, those on the lower cover are in blind). Covers: blank. Top edge gilt, others uncut. Sewn
head band (in green and red). Binding measurements: 318 × 254mm. (covers), 318 × 67mm. (spine). End-papers: brown wove
paper.

Publication date: December 1937 (see notes)

Price: unknown

Contents:
as for A123(a)

Notes:
The 'gatherings' follow the description provided above for A123(a).

As in A123(a), the coloured plates are all laid down to card and accompanied by protective tissue. These tissues carry the legends
for the plates.

The first poem ('On England') appearing on pp.[9–10] is omitted from the contents listing within the volume.

The chain-lines in this volume run horizontally.

With reference to this edition Handley-Taylor merely notes: 'Also issued in a limited edition of 50 copies signed by author and artist'.
No publication date is therefore provided beyond that of A123(a). However, inscribed copies suggest that this edition was published
after A123(a): Judith Masefield's copy of A123(a) was inscribed on 17 November 1937 and Constance Masefield's copy of A123(b)
was inscribed on 4 December 1937.

Copies seen: HRHRC (-Q- TEMP M377COU 1937B) un-numbered copy, signed 'John Masefield.' and 'Edward Seago' on p.[6]
inscribed 'For Con | from | Jan. | Dec 4. 1937.'

A123(c) First American edition (1938)

The Country Scene | IN POEMS BY | John Masefield | Collins | NEW YORK
(All width centred and enclosed within ruled border: 158 × 97mm.)

Bibliographies: Handley-Taylor [unrecorded], Wight 94a

Collation: [A-C]⁸ [D]⁶; 30 leaves; 202 × 132mm.; [i–viii] [1–2] 3–47 [48–52]

Page contents: [i–ii] blank; [iii] 'The Country Scene'; [iv] blank; [v] title-page; [vi] 'COPYRIGHT 1938 BY JOHN MASEFIELD |
MANUFACTURED IN THE UNITED STATES OF AMERICA | BY H. WOLFF, NEW YORK'; [vii–viii] 'Contents' (44
individual poems listed with page references); [1] 'The Country Scene'; [2] blank; 3–47 text; [48–52] blank

Paper: wove paper (watermark: 'WARREN'S | OLDE STYLE')

Running title: none

Binding: cream cloth. On spine, reading lengthways down spine from head, in brown: '*John Masefield* [point] The Country Scene [point]
COLLINS'. On upper cover, in brown: 'The Country Scene'. Lower cover: blank. All edges trimmed. Binding measurements: 208
× 135mm. (covers), 208 × 17mm. (spine). End-papers: wove paper.

Publication date: 1938

Price: unknown

Contents:
Prologue ('Here is the world of man and his adventure,')
On England ('What is this England, whom the draughtsmen print')
The Hounds in Snow ('During the night, the silent-footed snow')

Lambing ('In iron midnights in the downland fold')
A Midwife's Story ('I saw the lad was skin and bone;')
Nomads ('Where do they go, these waggons of delight,')
The Gallop on the Sands ('White horses toss their manes along the shores;')
Point to Point ('The flags are gay above the tents; the crowd')
The Orchard in Full Flower ('All things are in perfection for to-day,')
The Morris Dancers ('Men have forgotten how the dance began.')
The Road to Epsom *or* Why Not? ('Once every year the myriads hurry thus')
The Mid-day Sun ('Left by the sea these many thousand years')
The Mare and Foal at Grass ('Now that the grass is at its best in May,')
The County Show ('What do they think among these staring eyes,')
Elephants in the Tent ('"They're not the draw they were," the showman said.')
The Forge ('"Even as the blacksmith beats and brays')
The Roadside Inn ('All passing men, with beast or waggons,')
The Procession of the Bulls ('Slowly, in line, the winning bulls go by,')
Tiddlers ('They do not scrape the green scum of a pond,')
The Swing Boats ('Over the roaring sideshows comes the blare')
The Tight-rope Walker ('The naphtha flares, the thousand faces glow,')
Their Canvas Home ('This is the Circus tent, where the tribe camps')
The Young Fisherman ('THE BROOK | Rimple, dimple and glimple with insway, unsway,')
The Boat upon the Broads ('Is there any better fun')
The Horse and Trap at the Ford ('Three thousand years ago this track was used')
The Hoppers ('When ripening apples glow among the leaves;')
The Harvest ('All day the rattle of the cutter clacks;')
The Horse in the Barn ('Into this barn these horses have dragged corn')
Salisbury Spire from the Plain ('Six hundred years have dwellers in the plain')
Gleaners ('Harvest is home; the blueness is all dim;')
September Fields ('Bristled and speared, in army, rank on rank,')
Steam Horses ('The moonless storm is roaring in the pines;')
The Fowler's Hut ('The darkness comes with rain upon the fen,')
The Gulls at Ploughing ('Before a south-east gale, they know the signs;')
The Horse Fair ('Almost each year, for seven hundred years,')
The Ploughing Match ('This is the work that keeps the world alive;')
Hunting ('Ah, once, in the world's youth, men crept like snakes')
The Marcham Hams ('Among the fragrant mummies of dead pigs')
The Norfolk Wherry ('Creeds are denied, the nations disagree,')
Timber Hauling ('Once, he was undergrowth which the stag spared,')
The Gulls upon the Saltings ('They mew above the boilings in the wake,')
The Christmas Mummers ('They slice the coloured paper into strips')
The Gipsies in the Snow ('The bitter evening falls, the fog's about,')
The Bellringers ('What do they do, when all the ropes are still,')

Notes:

In contrast with A123(a), the poem 'On England' is included in the contents listing. Additionally, it is transposed with the position of 'Prologue' as present in A123(a).

Contrast the first line of the poem 'The Gallop on the Sands' with that present in A123(a).

The most obvious contrast with A123(a) is the omission in the American edition of Seago's illustrations. Sending the initial contract to The Society of Authors for comment in June 1937 Masefield specifically notes a non-illustrated edition:

> I am enclosing a contract from Messrs Collins for a book of pictures to which I contribute verses. I shall be glad, if you will kindly let me know, whether to be certain of securing American copyright I ought to have the verses set up in the U.S. even without the pictures.
>
> (John Masefield, letter to [E.J.] Mullett, [3 June 1937])
> (BL, Add.Mss.56607, f.3)

There is a suggestion, perhaps, that Masefield may have been contemplating securing American copyright at his own expense. Eventual publication by Collins may demonstrate that this was not the case. The American edition appears therefore to be mainly a means of retaining copyright which may explain the rarity of the edition being linked to an apparently small print-run. See note to A123(a) regarding Macmillan imports.

Copies seen: Columbia University (Special Collections PR6025 A77 C65 1938) inscribed '[watercolour of a ship within oval border] | John Masefield. | June. 1938.' on p.[iii]

A124 DEAD NED

A124(a) First American edition (1938)

DEAD NED | *The Autobiography of a Corpse* | *Who recovered Life within the Coast of Dead Ned* | *And came to what Fortune you shall hear* | by | JOHN MASEFIELD | NEW YORK | THE MACMILLAN COMPANY | 1938
(The italic type contains a number of swash characters)
(All width centred)

Bibliographies: Handley-Taylor p.61, Wight 95

Collation: [A–T]⁸ (J not used); 152 leaves; 202 × 133mm.; [i–xii] 1–289 [290–92]

Page contents: [i–ii] blank; [iii] half-title: 'DEAD NED'; [iv] '[publisher's device] | THE MACMILLAN COMPANY | [two lines listing six cities, separated by four points]'; [v] title-page; [vi] '*Copyright, 1938, by* | JOHN MASEFIELD. | [rule] | All rights reserved–no part of this book | may be reproduced in any form without | permission in writing from the publisher, | except by a reviewer who wishes to quote brief | passages in connection with a review written | for inclusion in magazine or newspaper. | *Set up and printed.* *Published October, 1938.* | FIRST PRINTING | PRINTED IN THE UNITED STATES OF AMERICA | AMERICAN BOOK-STRATFORD PRESS, INC., NEW YORK'; [vii] 'TO | MY WIFE'; [viii] blank; [ix] '"And since it's only Ned, | Who was alive and is dead, | There's no more to be said."'; [x] blank; [xi] 'DEAD NED'; [xii] blank; 1–289 text; [290–92] blank

Paper: wove paper

Running title: '[rule] | *DEAD NED* [18mm.] | [rule]' on verso; '[rule] | *THE AUTOBIOGRAPHY OF A CORPSE* [65mm.] | [rule]' on recto, pp.2–289

Binding: black cloth. On spine, in silver: '[rule] | [rule] | [rule] | [rule] | [ornament incorporting wavy rule and three five-point stars] | [rule] | [rule] | [rule] | [rule] | [oval silver panel upon which, in black: 'DEAD | NED | [asterisk] | Masefield' with pattern of rules made from numerous points] | [rule] | [rule] | [rule] | [rule] | MACMILLAN | [point] | [rule] | [rule] | [rule] | [rule] | [six wavy rules progressing down spine in decreasing length] | [five-point star]' (all width centred). On upper cover, in silver: '*DEAD NED*'. Lower cover: blank. Note that letters 'D', 'E' and 'N' on spine and upper cover are swash. All edges trimmed. Binding measurements: 209 × 135mm. (covers), 209 × 46mm. (spine). End-papers: wove paper.

Publication date: published, according to Handley-Taylor, 18 August 1938

Price: $2.50

Contents:
Dead Ned ('I am going to set down my story, while I remain young enough to tell the truth.')

Notes:
The novel (considered by Muriel Spark to be 'the peak of the poet's achievement in fiction') tells of an eighteenth-century doctor, Edward Mansell, falsely accused of murdering his benefactor, Admiral Cringle. He is sent to Newgate, tried and hanged. The hanging is unsuccessful and he is secretly revived by surgeon friends. He is, however, pursued by thief-takers (alerted by his step-brother) to Liverpool where he escapes as a doctor on a slave ship bound for Africa. The novel has no chapter divisions.

The publishing agreement for this title between Masefield and Macmillan was dated 27 April 1938 (see Archives of The Society of Authors). The agreement refers to 'a licence to publish in volume form in the United States of America and Canada a work the subject or title of which is Dead Ned'.

During the writing of the narrative it appears that the tale expanded in size. Masefield did not, however, alter his initial sub-title and this led to problems. He wrote to The Society of Authors asking for legal guidance:

> The legal point is this:- In the sub-title, I use the words "The autobiography of a corpse Who recovered life within the Coast of Dead Ned and came to what fortune you shall hear." In this volume, I do not bring the hero so far as Dead Ned's Coast (the Bight of Benin) but end the volume with the words "I shall tell you in the second volume" In the original draft of the story, it was all a one volume book; now it will be three or four volumes, I hope. What I wish to determine is can my sub-title, (as used for only one of these volumes) be reasonably held to be misleading? Perhaps you will be so very kind as to give me your opinion. The sub title was written before the tale was amplified and I now wonder whether it promises or seems to promise more than the purchaser can find, in this first instalment. I shall be very glad of your advice.
>
> (John Masefield, letter to Denys Kilham Roberts, [January 1939])
> (BL, Add.Mss.56626, f.159)

The reply does not appear to be preserved in the archives of The Society of Authors. However, a different letter from Masefield to the Society suggests the action that was suggested by Masefield for the English publishers:

> One querulous reader has had his money back; so I am asking Heinemanns to make the matter perfectly clear on a new wrapper or in a leaflet inserted.
>
> (John Masefield, letter to Denys Kilham Roberts, [January 1939])
> (BL, Add.Mss.56611, f.124)

A124(c) upper wrapper

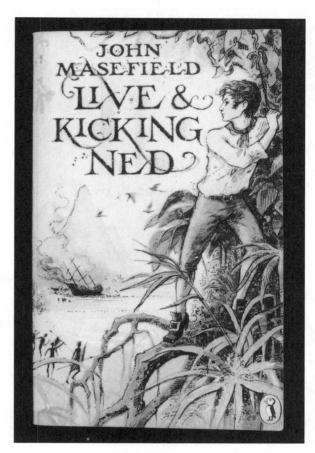

A127(c) upper wrapper

SOME VERSES
TO
SOME GERMANS

By

JOHN MASEFIELD

WILLIAM HEINEMANN LTD.
LONDON :: TORONTO

A126(a) title-page

BASILISSA

A Tale of the Empress Theodora

BY

JOHN MASEFIELD

WILLIAM HEINEMANN LTD
LONDON :: TORONTO

A128(b) title-page

SOME MEMORIES OF
W. B. YEATS

BY

JOHN MASEFIELD

NEW YORK
THE MACMILLAN COMPANY
1940

A129(b) title-page

THE
NINE DAYS WONDER
(THE OPERATION DYNAMO)

BY

JOHN MASEFIELD

WILLIAM HEINEMANN LTD
LONDON :: TORONTO

A130(a) title-page

A letter from George P. Brett Jr to Masefield suggests that early sales of the title were slow:

> ...DEAD NED is receiving remarkably fine reviews. I enclose a few of them. We are struggling valiantly to overcome the inertia of the American bookseller acquired during the war scare. Business went down to practically nothing...
>
> (George P. Brett Jr, letter to John Masefield, 26 October 1938)
> (HRHRC, MS (Masefield, J.) Recip The Macmillan Company)

The archives of The Society of Authors record that an application to publish a talking book version of this text was received in January 1942 (see BL, Add.Mss.56615, f.159). Masefield, as a supporter of books in Braille, presumably authorised this application.

The B.B.C. requested permission to broadcast *Dead Ned* for schools in the Spring of 1951. Masefield wrote to The Society of Authors, concerned about the sensibilities of children:

> The only drawback to the broadcasting of *Dead Ned* for schools is this: – The tale was designed to tell the adventures of a youth falsely accused of murder, hanged for it, revived after execution, (as a good many were in the good old days) and then enabled to win fortune, clear his name and confound his enemies. *Dead Ned* is the more gruesome half of this. The rest (now out of print) being written in years of great anxiety, is not of any account.
> The young are not squeamish, of course, but *Dead Ned* is not all that nervous children, etc[.], etc. I've no objection to their doing it and do not greatly covet to see the script beforehand, but perhaps this point should be raised?
>
> (John Masefield, letter to Miss [A.] Wordingham, [Spring 1951])
> (BL, Add.Mss.56622, f.62)

The text commences with a drop-capital.

Prior to publication, in April 1938, MGM requested 'early proofs' of this novel (see BL, Add.Mss.56609, f.86). Masefield was uninterested and revealed to The Society of Authors that the novel was still several months away from completion:

> The story about which the Metro-Goldwyn people ask, is not yet written. I am still at work on it... It can hardly be finished before the end of July.
>
> (John Masefield, letter to [E.J.] Mullett, [26 April 1936])
> (BL, Add.Mss.56609, f.88)

Interest from Paramount Pictures was declared in September 1939 for *Dead Ned* 'and its sequel' (then unpublished). As with MGM, these approaches came to nothing (see BL, Add.Mss.56612, f.100).

In May 1954 Masefield noted some background information to his writing of the novel, in a letter to The Society of Authors:

> The book was suggested by the Hall of the Barber-Surgeons, who used to dissect the bodies of the hanged, sometimes revived them, + sometimes were able to start them in life again, with highly successful results.
>
> (John Masefield, letter to [Anne] Munro-Kerr, 1 May [1954])
> (BL, Add.Mss.56625 f.61)

Copies seen: Columbia University (Special Collections B825M377 P5 1938); HRHRC (TEMP M377DE 1938B) inscribed 'For Con | from | Jan. | Oct 28. 1938.'

Reprinted:

[first edition, second impression]	Oct 1938
[first edition, third impression]	Oct 1938
[first edition, fourth impression]	Nov 1938
[first edition, fifth impression]	May 1941
[first edition, sixth impression]	Jun 1941
[first edition, seventh impression]	Aug 1941

A124(b) First English edition (1938)

DEAD NED | *The Autobiography of a Corpse* | *Who recovered Life within the Coast of Dead Ned* | *And came to what Fortune you shall hear* | by | JOHN MASEFIELD | [publisher's device of a windmill with 'W' and 'H'] | [rule, 68mm.] | WILLIAM HEINEMANN LTD | LONDON :: TORONTO
(The italic type contains a number of swash characters)
(All width centred)

Bibliographies: Handley-Taylor p.61, Wight 95a

Collation: [A]⁸ B-T⁸ U⁴ (J not used); signatures right foot of page; 156 leaves; 189 × 125mm.; [i–viii] 1–301 [302–304]

Page contents: [i–ii] blank; [iii] half-title: 'DEAD NED'; [iv] '*ALSO BY JOHN MASEFIELD* | PLAYS: | [12 titles listed] | POETRY: | [15 titles listed] | FICTION: | [10 titles listed] | GENERAL: | [nine titles listed]'; [v] title-page; [vi] 'FIRST PUBLISHED 1938 | PRINTED IN GREAT BRITAIN AT THE WINDMILL PRESS | KINGSWOOD, SURREY'; [vii] 'TO | MY WIFE'; [viii] '"And since it's only Ned, | Who was alive and is dead, | There's no more to be said."'; 1–301 text; [302–304] blank

Paper: wove paper

Running title: 'DEAD NED' (22mm.) on verso; 'THE AUTOBIOGRAPHY OF A CORPSE' (79–82mm.) on recto (off-set to the left), pp.2–301

Binding: blue cloth. On spine, in gold: 'DEAD | NED | [ornament] | JOHN | MASEFIELD | HEINEMANN' (all width centred). On upper cover, in gold: 'DEAD NED | JOHN MASEFIELD' (within blind ruled border: 192 × 123mm.) On lower cover, in blind: publisher's device of a windmill (ranged lower right). Top edge stained, others trimmed. Binding measurements: 197 × 127mm. (covers), 197 × 45mm. (spine). End-papers: wove paper.

Publication date: the sales ledger preserved in the Heinemann Archive suggests publication on 26 September 1938 in an edition of 10000 copies

Price: 7s.6d.

Contents:
as for A124(a)

Notes:
The text commences with a drop-capital.

Safe receipt of the typescript was acknowledged by Louisa Callender on 26 July 1938 (see Louisa Callender, letter to John Masefield, 26 July 1938) (HRHRC, MS (Masefield, J.) Recip William Heinemann Ltd.) The novel appears to have been set immediately. On 15 August 1938 B.F. Oliver wrote:

> Many thanks for your corrected proofs for press of DEAD NED. As requested I will have corrected proofs sent to Mr. G.P. Brett of The Macmillan Co., New York, as soon as possible.
>
> (B.F. Oliver, letter to John Masefield, 15 August 1938)
> (HRHRC, MS (Masefield, J.) Recip William Heinemann Ltd.)

C.S. Evans wrote to Masefield on 6 September enclosing an advance copy of the novel and noting publication on 26 September 1938 (see C.S. Evans, letter to John Masefield, 6 September 1938) (HRHRC, MS (Masefield, J.) Recip William Heinemann Ltd.)

The publishing agreement for this title between Masefield and Heinemann was dated 17 August 1928 (see Archives of The Society of Authors). The agreement refers to a publication price of 7s.6d.

Copies seen: private collection (PWE); BL (N.N.29350) stamped 26 SEP 1938

Reprinted

'Reprinted'	[first edition, second impression]	Nov 1948
'Reissued'	[first edition, later impression]	1970

A124(c) Second English edition (1974)

John Masefield | Dead Ned | The Autobiography of a Corpse | Who recovered Life within the Coast of Dead Ned | And came to what Fortune you shall hear | Puffin Books
(The italic type contains a number of swash characters)
(All width centred)

Bibliographies: Wight [unrecorded]

Publication date: published, according to *Whitaker's*, July 1974

Price: £0.30

Contents:
as for A124(a)

Notes:
The volume states, on page [4], that it is printed in Great Britain by C. Nicholls & Company Ltd.

The text has been entirely re-set for this edition. The volume states, on page [4], that it is set in Linotype Granjon

The ISBN number is ISBN 0 14 03.0686 2

The text commences with a raised-capital.

There is no copyright information present in this volume.

A publishing agreement for this title between Penguin and Heinemann was dated 3 March 1972 (see Archives of The Society of Authors). The agreement refers to an 'exclusive right and licence to produce and publish' the work. A later agreement was dated 25 July 1974.

The illustration on the wrapper by Antony Maitland is continuous between upper wrapper, spine and lower wrapper.

Copies seen: private collection (PWE)

A125 TRIBUTE TO BALLET

A125(a) First English edition (1938)

TRIBUTE | TO BALLET | *in poems by* | JOHN MASEFIELD | *and pictures by* | EDWARD SEAGO | COLLINS | 48 [point] PALL MALL [point] LONDON
(All width centred)

Bibliographies: Handley-Taylor p.62, Wight 96

Collation: [A]⁴ B-I⁴ [K-L]⁴ (J not used); signatures right foot of page with 'T.B.' at left foot on first leaf of signed gatherings; 44 leaves; 312 × 247mm.; [1–4] 5–7 [8] 9–72 i–xiv [xv–xvi]; illustrations (card for colour plates and wove paper for drawings) tipped-in on pp.[2], 13, 19, 23, 27, 31, 35, 39, 43, 49, 55, 59 and 69; colour plates each with protective tissue

Page contents: [1] half-title: 'TRIBUTE TO BALLET'; [2] '*By* | John Masefield and Edward Seago | THE COUNTRY SCENE' (with additional leaf tipped-in on the verso of which is the frontispiece (laid down to embossed panel): 180 × 150mm., with protective tissue with legend: 'MICHEL FOKINE'); [3] title-page; [4] 'COLOUR BLOCKS AND COLOUR PRINTING BY | THE SUN ENGRAVING COMPANY LIMITED, | WATFORD, HERTS. | COPYRIGHT 1938 | PRINTED IN GREAT BRITAIN'; 5–6 '*To M. MICHEL FOKINE*' ('"There are three lovely things," the old man said.'); 7 'The Poems' (31 individual poems listed with page references); [8] 'PUBLISHER'S NOTE | The pictures appearing in this book are not intended | to convey a comprehensive study of the Ballet. They | are impressions of certain Ballets and Dancers that the | artist has been fortunate enough to see. With the | selection of pictures that have been included he pays | tribute to Ballet as a whole.'; 9–10 'The Pictures' (nine colour plates, four drawings and 16 monochrome reproductions listed with page references); 11–72 text; i–xiv monochrome reproductions; [xv] drawing of male and female ballet dancers; [xvi] blank

Paper: wove paper (colour plates laid down to card, drawings on wove paper and final two gatherings on glossy paper)

Running title: none

Binding: green cloth. On spine, in gold: '*Tribute | to | Ballet | John | Masefield | and | Edward | Seago | Collins*' (all width centred). Many of the characters are joined and also swash. On upper cover, in gold: illustration of two ballet dancers: 62 × 56mm. (see notes). Lower cover: blank. All edges trimmed. Binding measurements: 317 × 246mm. (covers), 317 × 36mm. (spine). End-papers: wove paper.

Publication date: published, according to Handley-Taylor, 31 October 1938 in an edition of 2250 copies

Price: 21s.

Contents:
To M. Michel Fokine ('"There are three lovely things," the old man said.')
The Foreign Dancers ('After the cuckoo's coming thrills the valley')
The Indian Dancers ('I watched the quiet, age-old Indian art;')
The English Dancers – I ('I can remember Englands best forgotten,')
The English Dancers – II ('What is the hardest task of Art?')
A Watcher of the Moyle ('Beyond the tide-rips of the shrieking sea,')
A Watcher in the Wings ('We are young, friend, like the flowers,')
The Class ('It is the break; the pupils are at rest,')
Going to Rehearsal ('Since beauty sets as soon')
Rehearsal ('Green rollers shatter into hands that shoot')
The Thing and the Shadow ('Among the mists of sleep a clock struck Five.')
Question and Answer ('What find you in the Ballet,')
The Seventh Hungarian Dance of Brahms ('Underneath the curtains edged with moth-gnawn gold')
Masks ('Often, the books about the ancients told')
Come, All Ye ('Craftsman, your brightest light, painter, your fairest hue,')
If the Princess ask a Ballet ('Bring me a fable out of the old time,')
Where They Took Train ('Gomorrah paid so for its holiday;')
The Lovely Swan ('I heard men mutter of you, "She will die.')
The Christmas Tidings ('What is the happiest thing this Christmas tide?')
The Two Upon The Dancers' Left ('They dance it well, this ballet of youth's fun,')
The Painter of the Scene ('Twenty years since, your pale, distinguished face,')
The Spirit of the Rose ('Though with a dozen dancers I have felt')
A Dead Musician ('I saw you often in the happy days')
A Lady of the Court ('After long months abroad, the troupe returns to play.')
Not Only The Most Famous ('No, for their names are written with the light')
Naia and Edward | *A Tale in Verse* ('They were two lovers, long in love, although')
The Waltz of 1830 ('Often, I have watched you, in the setting of the ballroom,')
The Eastern Heaven *or* The Corps de Ballet ('You smile and are charming')
Sur Les Pointes ('The time is near, my sweet,')

To an Air of Johann Strauss ('Since all of us are young to-night,')
To Eight Who Were Charming *or* The Impromptu ('I came as a stranger')
Violets for the Violets ('When the red curtains fall,')

Notes:
Another of Masefield's collaborations with the artist Edward Seago (see also *The Country Scene* (A123) and *A Generation Risen* (A138)).

The collection of verse testifies to Masefield's passion for ballet. See *Ballet – To Poland* (B375) and Nadine Nicolaeva-Legat, *Ballet Education* (B440) for example. Other evidence includes the correspondence with a young ballerina during the second world war, published in 1988 as *Brangwen – The Poet and the Dancer* (E6).

The coloured plates are laid down to card and accompanied by protective tissue. These tissues carry the legends for the plates. There are no protective tissues included for the drawings or monochrome reproductions.

The illustration on the upper cover is not present on all copies.

The publishing agreement for this title between Masefield and W. Collins Sons was dated 17 September 1938 (see Archives of The Society of Authors).

Copies seen: private collection (PWE); NYPL (NCM+ 1938) 988131A '21 Dec 1938' written on p.5; Columbia University (Special Collections B825 M377 X3 1938); HRHRC (-Q- TEMP M377TRIB 1938) inscribed 'For Lew | from | Zob. | Oct 31. 1938.'

A125(b) Second English edition (limited signed edition) (1938)

TRIBUTE | TO BALLET | *in poems by* | JOHN MASEFIELD | *and pictures by* | EDWARD SEAGO | COLLINS | 48 [point] PALL MALL [point] LONDON
(All width centred)

Bibliographies: Handley-Taylor p.62, Wight [noted on p.173]

Collation: [A]⁴ B-I⁴ [K-L]⁴ (J not used); [L]1 is also signed at left foot of page; signatures right foot of page with 'T.B.' at left foot on first leaf of signed gatherings; 44 leaves; 314 × 247mm.; [1–4] 5–7 [8] 9–72 i–xiv [xv–xvi]; illustrations (card for colour plates and wove paper for drawings) tipped-in on pp.[2], 13, 19, 23, 27, 31, 35, 39, 43, 49, 55, 59 and 69; colour plates each with protective tissue

Page contents: [1] half-title: 'TRIBUTE TO BALLET'; [2] 'THIS EDITION, LIMITED TO 100 COPIES, OF WHICH 94 ARE FOR SALE, | IS SIGNED BY THE AUTHOR AND ARTIST | |This is Number ....' (with additional leaf tipped-in on the verso of which is the frontispiece (laid down to embossed panel): 180 × 150mm., with protective tissue with legend: 'MICHEL FOKINE'); [3] title-page; [4] 'COLOUR BLOCKS AND COLOUR PRINTING BY | THE SUN ENGRAVING COMPANY LIMITED, | WATFORD, HERTS. | COPYRIGHT 1938 | PRINTED IN GREAT BRITAIN'; 5–6 '*To M. MICHEL FOKINE*' ('"There are three lovely things," the old man said.'); 7 'The Poems' (31 individual poems listed with page references); [8] 'PUBLISHER'S NOTE | The pictures appearing in this book are not intended | to convey a comprehensive study of the Ballet. They | are impressions of certain Ballets and Dancers that the | artist has been fortunate enough to see. With the | selection of pictures that have been included he pays | tribute to Ballet as a whole.'; 9–10 'The Pictures' (nine colour plates, four drawings and 16 monochrome reproductions listed with page references); 11–72 text; i–xiv monochrome reproductions; [xv] drawing of male and female ballet dancers; [xvi] blank

Paper: wove paper (colour plates laid down to card, drawings on wove paper and final two gatherings on glossy paper)

Running title: none

Binding: white buckram with green pig-skin spine. On spine, in gold: '*Tribute | to | Ballet | John | Masefield | and | Edward | Seago | Collins*' (all width centred). Many of the characters are joined and also swash. Covers: blank. Top edge gilt, others trimmed. Sewn head band (in white). Binding measurements: 323 × 258mm. (covers), 323 × 36mm. (spine). End-papers: green, brown and white marbled-effect wove paper. Volume contained in slip-case covered in light green paper.

Publication date: November 1937 (see notes)

Price: 5 guineas

Contents:
as for A125(a)

Notes:
With reference to this edition Handley-Taylor merely notes: 'Also issued in a limited edition of 100 copies (signed by author and artist)'. No publication date is therefore provided beyond that of A125(a). However, inscribed copies suggest that this edition was published after A125(a): Lewis Masefield's copy of A125(a) was inscribed on 31 October 1938 and Constance Masefield's copy of A125(b) was inscribed on 11 November 1938.

Copies seen: HRHRC (-Q- PR 6025 A77 T77 1938) number 4, inscribed '4. | John Masefield.' and 'Edward Seago' on p.[2] inscribed 'For Con | from | Jan. | Nov 11. 1938.'

A125(c) First American edition (1938)

TRIBUTE | TO BALLET | *in poems by* | JOHN MASEFIELD | *and pictures by* | EDWARD SEAGO | NEW YORK | THE MACMILLAN COMPANY | 1938
(All width centred)

Bibliographies: Handley-Taylor p.62, Wight 96a

Collation: [A]² [B-I]⁴ [K]² [L]⁸ (J not used) (see notes); 44 leaves; 315 × 245mm.; [1–4] 5–6 [7–8] 9–72 i–xiv [xv–xvi]

Page contents: [1] half-title: 'TRIBUTE TO BALLET'; [2] 'By | JOHN MASEFIELD AND EDWARD SEAGO | THE COUNTRY SCENE'; [3] title-page; [4] '*Copyright, 1938, by* | JOHN MASEFIELD. | [rule] | All rights reserved–no part of this book may be repro- | duced in any form without permission in writing from | the publisher, except by a reviewer who wishes to | quote brief passages in connection with a review written | for inclusion in magazine or newspaper. | [rule] | *Set up and printed. Published November, 1938.* | PRINTED IN THE UNITED STATES OF AMERICA | AMERICAN BOOK-STRATFORD PRESS, INC., NEW YORK'; 5–6 '*TO M. MICHEL FOKINE*' ('"There are three lovely things," the old man said.'); [7] 'The Poems' (31 individual poems listed with page references); [8] 'Publisher's Note | The pictures appearing in this book are not | intended to convey a comprehensive study of | the Ballet. They are impressions of certain Bal- | lets and Dancers that the artist has been for- | tunate enough to see. With the selection of | pictures that have been included he pays tribute | to Ballet as a whole.'; 9–10 'The Pictures' (9 colour plates, 4 drawings and 16 monochrome reproductions listed with page references); 11–72 text; i–xiv monochrome reproductions; [xv] blank drawing of male and female ballet dancers; [xvi] blank

Paper: wove paper (colour plates laid down to card, drawings on wove paper and final two gatherings on glossy paper)

Running title: none

Binding: navy blue cloth. On spine, in gold: 'TRIBUTE | TO | BALLET | John Masefield | and | Edward Seago | MACMILLAN' (all width centred). On upper cover, in gold: 'TRIBUTE TO BALLET'. Lower cover: blank. Top edge trimmed, others roughly trimmed. Sewn head and foot bands (in navy blue). Binding measurements: 322 × 247mm. (covers), 322 × 34mm. (spine). End-papers: wove paper.

Publication date: published, according to Handley-Taylor, 29 November 1938

Price: $7.50

Contents:
as for A125(a)

Notes:
The coloured plates are all laid down to card and accompanied by protective tissue. These tissues carry the legends for the plates and also state '*Printed in Great Britain.*' There are no protective tissues included for the drawings or monochrome reproductions. Of the drawings, only the last includes note of being '*Printed in Great Britain*'.

Wight notes 'collation indeterminate as there are no signatures nor visible sewing lines'. The volume appears to have been constructed in a 'traditionally' bound manner with the collation stated above. Card (for the plates) and drawings were then added and 'gatherings' 'machine sewn'. These additional leaves have been excluded from the collation although in one sense they are bound with the volume. The subsequent 'machine binding' significantly obscures the original sewing. There are no signatures with the exception of the glossy paper gathering ([L]) which includes '1' on [L]1 and '2' on [L]5, signed lower left. Additionally, '*Printed in Great Britain*' accompanies signature '2'.

Wight notes that this volume is bound in 'purple cloth'.

Despite similarities in setting, this American edition constitutes a new setting of the text presumably based on A125(a).

Copies seen: Columbia University (Special Collections B825 M377 X3 1938a); HRHRC (-Q- PR6025 A77 T77 1938B cop.1)

A125(d) Third English edition (1940)

Bibliographies: Handley-Taylor [unrecorded], Wight [unrecorded]

The *English Catalogue of Books 1936–1941* lists the following item:

> Masefield (John) – Tribute to Ballet in poems.
> Ch. ed. Illus. 4to, p.72, 8s. 6d. net
> COLLINS, *Oct.* '40

The first English edition (Collins, 1938) of *Tribute To Ballet* cost 21s. and as Edward Seago is omitted from the description above it appears that this cheaper edition was a smaller and less lavish volume with fewer illustrations.

No copies have been traced and both Handley-Taylor and Wight omit all mention in their bibliographies. One hypothesis is that as a London warehouse containing Collins publications was bombed in the London blitz, the entire edition may have been destroyed.

A126 SOME VERSES TO SOME GERMANS

A126(a) First English edition (1939)

Upper wrapper:
SOME VERSES | TO | SOME GERMANS | *By* | JOHN MASEFIELD | WILLIAM HEINEMANN LTD. | LONDON :: TORONTO
(All width centred with lines 6 and 7 justified on both left and right margins)

Bibliographies: Handley-Taylor p.62, Wight 97

Collation: [A]⁸; 8 leaves; 190 × 128mm.; [i–iv] 1–10 [11–12]

Page contents: [i] upper wrapper; [ii] blank; [iii] title-page; [iv] 'FIRST PUBLISHED 1939 | PRINTED IN GREAT BRITAIN AT THE WINDMILL PRESS | KINGSWOOD, SURREY'; 1–10 text; [11] blank; [12] lower wrapper

Paper: wove paper

Running title: none

Binding: wrappers comprise the first and last leaves of the single gathering ([A]1 and [A]8). Spine: blank. On upper wrapper: 'SOME VERSES | TO | SOME GERMANS | JOHN MASEFIELD | POET LAUREATE | *Sixpence*' (with the exception of the final line, enclosed within ornate border which includes a double ruled border: 160 × 100mm.) Lower wrapper: blank. All edges trimmed. Binding measurements: 190 × 128mm. (wrappers), 190 × 2mm. (spine).

Publication date: published, according to Handley-Taylor, 25 September 1939; the sales ledger preserved in the Heinemann Archive appears to lack any information about this edition except that copies were priced at 6d. See A137(a) for C.S. Evans' statement that there were 500 copies printed.

Price: 6d.

Contents:
[Untitled] ('"Open the other shutter," and "More light,"')
[Untitled] ('Within the glory of that light, the Soul')
[Untitled] ('Since Man has been, the vision has been his')
[Untitled] ('You, like ourselves, now enemies, have sought')
[Untitled] ('In that Humanity which makes us brother,')
[Untitled] ('This is no idle boast or empty story;')
[Untitled] ('O rightly your sublime one as he died')
[Untitled] ('I write among the grasses wet with dew;')
[Untitled] ('Amid the darkness, sad with women's woe,')
[Untitled] ('We are as darkness to each other now,')

Notes:
A short publication comprising untitled poems in a sequence. The title identifies the publication as war poetry and with references to Goethe, Beethoven and Shakespeare, cultural kinship is stressed between the English and German nations at war.

Page numbers appear within square brackets. Thus, [1], [2], etc. The individual verses are each separated by three asterisks.

Wight notes that 'both covers are thin yellow cardboard'. All examples consulted reveal the covers to use the same glossy wove paper as the entire gathering.

Masefield wrote to C.S. Evans in September 1939 suggesting a pamphlet publication. Evans replied:

…Is it your idea to have the leaflet bound in cloth or paper? I should think it might be difficult to sell a paper booklet at 1/- However, I will get out some estimates and write to you again on this point. When will you be able to send me the verses?

(C.S. Evans, letter to John Masefield, 12 September 1939)
(HRHRC, MS (Masefield, J.) Recip William Heinemann Ltd.)

Masefield sent Evans the verses and the publisher responded with publication plans:

Thanks for your letter and for the script of your very beautiful poem. I have made a number of experiments this morning and have come to the conclusion that the best way to produce the book would be to make it 16 pages including the cover. This would give a title page and a reverse, then pages of text each page containing one section of the poem. I propose to print on Jap Vellum, crown octavo size… There are three advantages in printing on Jap Vellum, (1) it is a very good looking paper; (2) it does not easily stain or show finger marks, and (3) we have the paper in stock…

(C.S. Evans, letter to John Masefield, 14 September 1939)
(HRHRC, MS (Masefield, J.) Recip William Heinemann Ltd.)

The publishing agreement for this title between Masefield and Heinemann was dated 30 September 1939 (see Archives of The Society of Authors). The agreement refers to a publication price of 6d.

Following a request from the Ministry of Information in November 1939 Masefield wrote to The Society of Authors:

> I had rather that the verses to Germans were not used in any kind of propaganda, thank you.
>
> (John Masefield, letter to [E.J.] Mullett, [22 November 1939])
>
> (BL, Add.Mss.56612, f.143)

Copies seen: private collection (PWE); BL (11656.i.23) stamped 26 SEP 1939

A126(b) First American edition (1939)

SOME VERSES | TO | SOME GERMANS | JOHN MASEFIELD | NEW YORK | THE MACMILLAN COMPANY | 1939
(All width centred)

Bibliographies: Handley-Taylor p.62, Wight 97a

Collation: [A]⁸ (see notes); 8 leaves; 188 × 125mm.; [i–vi] 1–10

Page contents: [i] half-title: 'SOME VERSES TO SOME GERMANS'; [ii] blank; [iii] title-page; [iv] 'Copyright 1939, by | JOHN MASEFIELD | All rights reserved–no part of this book | may be reproduced in any form without | permission in writing from the publisher, | except by a reviewer who wishes to quote | brief passages in connection with a review | written for inclusion in magazine or | newspaper. | *Set up and printed. Published November, 1939* | *First Printing* | PRINTED IN THE UNITED STATES OF AMERICA'; [v] 'SOME VERSES TO SOME GERMANS'; [vi] blank; 1–10 text

Paper: wove paper

Running title: none

Binding: light green textured boards. Spine: blank. On upper cover, in orange: 'JOHN MASEFIELD | *Some* | Verses to | *Some* | Germans'. Lower cover: blank. All edges trimmed. Binding measurements: 192 × 126mm. (covers), 192 × 15mm. (spine). End-papers: wove paper.

Publication date: published, according to Handley-Taylor, 8 November 1939

Price: $0.60

Contents:
as for A126(a)

Notes:
The volume is machine sewn (the gathering is stabbed forty-three times). The 'gathering' also includes the end-papers (on a different stock of wove paper). The fixed end-papers are continuous, as are the free end-papers. Due to the different paper stock the volume is described above as [A]⁸. However, if the end-papers are to be included the volume could be described as [A]¹⁰. Wight describes the volume with 'no free endpapers'. He appears confused regarding the single gathering.

Page numbers appear within square brackets. Thus, [1], [2], etc. The individual verses are each separated by three asterisks.

Wight describes the paper of the binding as 'pale grassy paper' and notes the colour of the printing on the upper cover as 'red'.

Copies seen: NYPL (NCM 1939) 97926B

A127 LIVE AND KICKING NED   1939

A127(a) First English edition (1939)

LIVE AND KICKING | NED | *A Continuation of the Tale of Dead Ned* | BY | JOHN MASEFIELD | [publisher's device of a windmill with 'W' and 'H'] | [rule, 67mm.] | WILLIAM HEINEMANN LTD | LONDON :: TORONTO
(The italic type contains a number of swash characters)
(All width centred)

Bibliographies: Handley-Taylor p.62, Wight 98

Collation: [A]⁸ B-EE⁸ FF⁴ (J and V not used); signatures right foot of page; 236 leaves; 197 × 128mm.; [i–viii] [1–2] 3–244 [245–46] 247–462 [463–64]

Page contents: [i–ii] blank; [iii] half-title: 'LIVE AND KICKING | NED'; [iv] '*ALSO BY JOHN MASEFIELD* | PLAYS: | [12 titles listed] | POETRY: | [16 titles listed] | FICTION: | [11 titles listed] | GENERAL: | [nine titles listed]'; [v] title-page; [vi] 'FIRST PUBLISHED 1939 | PRINTED IN GREAT BRITAIN AT THE WINDMILL PRESS | KINGSWOOD, SURREY'; [vii] 'To | MY WIFE'; [viii] blank; [1] 'LIVE NED OR THE REEF-TACKLE'; [2] '*While at sea, I noticed a fitting on a sail, and asked* | *a seaman what it was.* | [new paragraph] *He said, "A reef-tackle."* | [new paragraph] *I asked, "What good is it?"* | [new paragraph] *He said, "In reefing, it takes up the weight of the* | *sail, so that you can pass your ear-rings."* | [new paragraph] *I have called this volume of my story* The Reef-Tackle | *because it takes up the weight of my life during a blowy* | *and anxious time. How I passed my ear-rings will be* | *matter for another tale.*'; 3–244 text of 'Live Ned'; [245] 'KICKING NED, OR THE SKYSAIL, OR, | PERHAPS, AFTER ALL, THE | TRUST TO GOD'; [246]

'I sometimes call this part of my tale THE SKYSAIL | or, perhaps, after all, THE TRUST-TO-GOD. | [new paragraph] Once, in the "Albicore," as we ran in the Trade, and I | admired the tower of sail upon the mainmast, a seaman | said to me, "Ah, sir, but we ought to set a skysail, above | the royal, there." | [new paragraph] "But a little sail, so far up, cannot do much good," | I said. | [new paragraph] "No, sir," he answered, "but nothing sets a ship off, | like a skysail. It finishes her off." | [new paragraph] "Do sailors ever set anything even above a skysail?" I | asked. | [new paragraph] "Some set a Trust-to-God," he said. "Not many have | one; but it's a very fine thing, a Trust-to-God. It finishes | a ship off, even better." '; 247–462 text of 'Kicking Ned'; [463–64] blank

Paper: wove paper

Running title: 'LIVE NED' (18mm.) on verso, 'OR THE REEF-TACKLE' (42mm.) on recto, pp.4–244; 'KICKING NED' (25mm.) on verso, 'OR THE SKYSAIL OR THE TRUST TO GOD' (75mm.) on recto, pp.248–462

Binding: blue cloth. On spine, in gold: 'LIVE AND | KICKING | NED | [ornament] | JOHN | MASEFIELD | HEINEMANN' (all width centred). On upper cover, in blind: 'LIVE AND KICKING NED | JOHN MASEFIELD' (within blind ruled border: 198 × 125mm.) On lower cover, in blind: publisher's device of a windmill (ranged lower right). All edges trimmed. Binding measurements: 202 × 131mm. (covers), 202 × 55mm. (spine). End-papers: beige wove paper.

Publication date: the sales ledger preserved in the Heinemann Archive suggests publication on 30 October 1939 in an edition of 7500 copies

Price: 8s.6d.

Contents:
Live Ned or The Reef-Tackle
      ('If you have not read my story, let me tell you, that I am a doctor, the son of...')
Kicking Ned, or The Skysail, or, Perhaps, After All, The Trust To God
      ('We went out from the house, and presently reached the steps which led to the platform...')

Notes:
A single volume containing both 'Live Ned' and 'Kicking Ned', each individually sub-titled. In the Macmillan edition (A127(b)) these have separate page numbers although this division is not present in the Heinemann edition. The novel (or novels, as they should perhaps more accurately be termed) concludes the story of *Dead Ned* (A124). The individual novels have no chapter divisions. After arriving on the African coast and experiencing the slave trade, Ned finds himself the sole survivor after an attack by natives. Entering the interior he retraces the steps of Admiral Cringle and meets Edmond Quichet whose history was connected to Cringle's. Quichet tells of a Kranois city threatened by the warrior M'gai tribe and Ned joins the Kranois side. After Kranois victory, Ned marries Quichet's daughter and returns to England as a Kranois envoy where he finds his stepbrother and stepbrother's servant are to be hanged for Cringle's murder. Ned is exonerated of the crime and, after a chance discovery, locates his benefactor's considerable legacy.

Each story commences with a drop-capital.

A letter from Masefield, conjecturally dated from early 1939, to C.S. Evans reveals the author's doubts as to single volume publication of 'Live Ned'. This suggests that Masefield had originally intended a three volume trilogy in 1939:

> I have been working at the second volume of the Dead Ned book, and have done about seventy-five thousand words, which will probably be sent off to you, so that you will get it at the office on Monday morning next. You may feel, that it will be useless, or wrong, to print this batch of the story by itself; you may prefer to wait for a third volume, which may conceivably complete the saga towards the end of July. Will you, very kindly, read the tale and let me know what you think about this? There are, of course, very great difficulties in keeping readers going in adventures, appearing at intervals of half a year or so. You may think it best to wait till the autumn.

> (John Masefield, letter to [C.S.] Evans, [1939])
> (Archives of William Heinemann)

Evans thanked Masefield for sending 'the second part of the DEAD NED story' on 20 February 1939, noting that he would read it immediately (see C.S. Evans, letter to John Masefield, 20 February 1939) (HRHRC, MS (Masefield, J.) Recip William Heinemann Ltd.) Evans proved to be enthusiastic both about the tale and Masefield's suggestion of publication:

> I felt that I could not bear to wait before reading *Live Ned* so I took the afternoon off yesterday and read it without stopping from 2.15 until 6.45, and I finished it. It is a grand yarn and a worthy successor to *Dead Ned*. It held my attention so intensely that I hardly looked up once from the pages, and when I came to the end I was quite annoyed because there was no more.

> I think that you are right and that it would be better if we kept this book until you have the third part ready and then publish the two together in the early autumn. I do not know how long the third part is going to be: this part is, I judge, between 70,000 and 80,000 words, but it moves so swiftly that it seems shorter. If the third part is as long as this we should have to publish the book at 8/6d: that is the normal price for a book longer than the ordinary novel and in these days has been accepted by the booksellers and public generally.

> ([C.S. Evans], letter to John Masefield, 21 February 1939)
> (Archives of William Heinemann)

Masefield replied, in agreement with Evans. Knowing the intended volume format of publication Masefield presumably took a conscious decision during writing to keep the length of the third part short:

> So many thanks for your kind letter about the second volume. I am so glad that you have liked it. Thank you, also, for sending back the script. I am sure, that you are right in your decision to wait for the book to be completed. Very possibly the third volume will be not more than fifty or sixty thousand words, which added on to this present volume, would make, probably, somewhere about a hundred and thirty-five thousand, well worth 8/6 of any man's money, I should say. I suppose, the miserable slaves would kick at being asked for half-a-guinea.
>
> (John Masefield, letter to [C.S.] Evans, [22 February 1939])
(Archives of William Heinemann)

The 'book-proofs of LIVE AND KICKING NED' were sent to Masefield on 21 September 1939 (see B.F. Oliver, letter to John Masefield, 21 September 1939) (HRHRC, MS (Masefield, J.) Recip William Heinemann Ltd.)

The publishing agreement for this title between Masefield and Heinemann was dated 30 September 1939 (see Archives of The Society of Authors). The agreement refers to a publication price of 8s.6d.

Masefield informed The Society of Authors of the sequel to *Dead Ned* in August 1939:

> *Dead Ned*, if there be no war, should be ended this autumn with the publication of one other volume, called *Live & Kicking Ned*.
>
> (John Masefield, letter to [E.J.] Mullett, [13 August 1939])
(BL, Add.Mss.56612, f.81)

A letter from Masefield, to C.S. Evans refers to the sub-title of this volume. Presumably the suggestion had been made to sub-title the volume to include the word 'sequel'. Masefield wrote:

> Perhaps you would call the story a Continuation of the tale of Dead Ned. It is possible that I may do some more about him some time; if so, that might be better called a sequel than this.
>
> (John Masefield, letter to [C.S.] Evans, [1 October 1939])
(Archives of William Heinemann)

The sub-title, as adopted on the title-page, is 'A Continuation of the Tale of Dead Ned'. No further writing on Edward Mansell was published.

C.S. Evans wrote to Masefield about interest in an edition of the novel from the Reprint Society:

> I have just had a proposal from the Reprint Society who want to make LIVE AND KICKING NED one of their monthly choices, possibly September of this year…
>
> (C.S. Evans, letter to John Masefield, 26 February 1941)
(HRHRC, MS (Masefield, J.) Recip William Heinemann Ltd.)

This edition was not published for Masefield presumably refused permission.

Less than a decade after publication Masefield started to refuse permission for translations. Regarding a proposed Swedish translation Masefield wrote to The Society of Authors:

> *Dead Ned* is all very well, perhaps; but the sequel was done under too great a strain + I do not wish it to be reprinted, in any tongue. *Dead Ned* might be done, as a book by itself, perhaps, if Messrs Bonniers wish.
>
> (John Masefield, letter to [Anne] Munro-Kerr, [18 May 1947])
(BL, Add.Mss.56620, f.61)

Again, in January 1948, regarding a proposed German translation, Masefield wrote:

> I am sorry that I cannot consent to the reprinting or translation of *Live & Kicking Ned*. The book needs a rewriting, and cannot now receive it. Please allow it to lie quietly where it moulders in the dusts of untouched shelves.
>
> (John Masefield, letter to [Anne] Munro-Kerr, [7 January 1948])
(BL, Add.Mss.56620, f.154)

In May 1951 Masefield denied permission for a French translation and suggested that an epilogue should be added to *Dead Ned* to supply the deficiency:

> I do not like the thought of *Live Ned* being translated, but suggest that, in case of need, an epilogue page might be added to *Dead Ned*, to summarise the *Live Ned* volume?
>
> (John Masefield, letter to [Anne] Munro-Kerr, 9 May [1951])
(BL, Add.Mss.56622, f.189)

Copies seen: private collection (PWE)

Reprinted:

	[first edition, second impression]	Nov 1939
'Reissued'	[first edition, later impression]	1970

A127(b) First American edition (1939)

LIVE AND | KICKING NED | by | JOHN MASEFIELD | NEW YORK | THE MACMILLAN COMPANY | 1939
(All width centred)

Bibliographies: Handley-Taylor p.62, Wight 98a

Collation: [A-EE]⁸ [FF]¹⁰ [GG]⁸ (J, V and W not used); 242 leaves; 203 × 133mm.; [i–iv] [1–4] 5–253 [254] [1–4] 5–224 [225–26]

Page contents: [i] half-title: 'LIVE AND KICKING NED'; [ii] '[publisher's device] | THE MACMILLAN COMPANY | [two lines listing six cities, separated by four points]'; [iii] title-page; [iv] '*Copyright, 1939, by* | JOHN MASEFIELD. | [rule] | All rights reserved–no part of this book | may be reproduced in any form without | permission in writing from the publisher, | except by a reviewer who wishes to quote brief | passages in connection with a review written | for inclusion in magazine or newspaper. | *Set up and printed. Published October, 1939.* | FIRST PRINTING. | :Printed in the United States of America:'; [1] 'LIVE NED'; [2] blank; [3] 'While at sea, I noticed a fitting on a sail, and asked a | seaman what it was. | [new paragraph] He said, "A reef-tackle." | [new paragraph] I asked, "What good is it?" | [new paragraph] He said, "In reefing, it takes up the weight of the sail, | so that you can pass your ear-rings." | [new paragraph] I have called this volume of my story "The Reef-Tackle" | because it takes up the weight of my life during a blowy | and anxious time. How I passed my ear-rings will be mat- | ter for another tale.'; [4] blank; 5–253 text of 'Live Ned'; [254] blank; [1] 'KICKING NED'; [2] blank; [3] 'I sometimes call this part of my tale "The Skysail" or, | perhaps, after all, "The Trust-to-God." | [new paragraph] Once, in the *Albicore*, as we ran in the Trade, and I ad- | mired the tower of sail upon the mainmast, a seaman said | to me, "Ah, sir, but we ought to set a skysail, above the | royal, there." | [new paragraph] "But a little sail, so far up, cannot do much good," I | said. | [new paragraph] "No, sir," he answered, "but nothing sets a ship off, like | a skysail. It finishes her off." | [new paragraph] "Do sailors ever set anything even above a skysail?" I | asked. | [new paragraph] "Some set a Trust-to-God," he said. "Not many have | one; but it's a very fine thing, a Trust-to-God. It finishes | a ship off, even better."'; [4] blank; 5–224 text of 'Kicking Ned'; [225–26] blank

Paper: wove paper

Running title: '[rule] | *LIVE NED* [17mm.] | [rule]' on both verso and recto, pp.6–253; '[rule] | *KICKING NED* [24mm.] | [rule]' on both verso and recto, pp.6–224

Binding: black cloth. On spine, in silver: '[rule] | [rule] | [rule] | [rule] | [ornament incorporting wavy rule and three five-point stars] | [rule] | [rule] | [rule] | [rule] | [oval silver panel upon which, in black: '*LIVE AND* | *KICKING NED* | [asterisk] | Masefield' with pattern of rules made from numerous points] | [rule] | [rule] | [rule] | [rule] | MACMILLAN | [rule] | [rule] | [rule] | [rule] | [six wavy rules progressing down spine in decreasing length] | [five-point star]' (all width centred). On upper cover, in silver: '*LIVE AND* | *KICKING NED*'. Lower cover: blank. The letters 'L', 'E', 'A', 'N' and 'K' on spine and upper cover are swash. All edges trimmed. Binding measurements: 210 × 137mm. (covers), 210 × 50mm. (spine). End-papers: wove paper.

Publication date: published, according to Handley-Taylor, 30 October 1939

Price: $2.50

Contents:
Live Ned ('If you have not read my story, let me tell you that I am a doctor, the son of...')
Kicking Ned ('We went out from the house, and presently reached the steps which led to the platform...')

Notes:
Each story commences with a drop-capital.

The sub-titles of each tale are only present in this volume in the notes that follow the divisional titles. Furthermore, the volume does not carry the sub-title present in A127(a).

The dedication present in A127(a) is omitted from this volume.

The page numbering in this volume treats the two tales as entirely separate.

The publishing agreement for this volume between Masefield and Macmillan was dated 6 September 1938 (see Archives of The Society of Authors). The agreement refers to 'a licence to publish in volume form in the United States of America and Canada a sequel to "Dead Ned" – (exact title to be determined) Live Ned.'

Copies seen: private collection (PWE)

Reprinted:

[first edition, second impression]	Nov 1939
[first edition, third impression]	Dec 1939
[first edition, fourth impression]	Aug 1941

A127(c) Second English edition (1975)

John Masefield | *Live and Kicking* | *Ned* | *A Continuation of the Tale of Dead Ned* | *Abridged by Vivien Garfield* | Puffin Books
(The italic type contains a number of swash characters)
(All width centred)

Bibliographies: Wight [unrecorded]

Publication date: published, according to *Whitaker's*, January 1975

Price: £0.45

Contents:
Live Ned, or The Reef-Tackle
>('If you have not read my story, let me tell you, that I am a doctor, the son of...')
>[abridged text]
Kicking Ned, or The Skysail, or Perhaps, After All, The Trust-To-God
>('We went out from the house, and presently reached the steps which led to the platform...')
>[abridged text]

Notes:

The volume states, on page [4], that it is printed in Great Britain by Hazell Watson & Viney Ltd, Aylesbury, Bucks

The volume states, on page [4], that it is set in Monotype Garamond

The ISBN number is ISBN 0 14 03.0727 3

Each story commences with a raised-capital.

The stories are abridged by Vivien Garfield.

The publishing agreement for this title between Penguin and Heinemann was dated 3 March 1972 (see Archives of The Society of Authors). The agreement refers to an 'exclusive right and licence to produce and publish' the work. The period of licence was five years. A later agreement was dated 24 April 1975.

The illustration on the wrapper by Antony Maitland is continuous between upper wrapper, spine and lower wrapper.

Copies seen: private collection (PWE)

A128 BASILISSA   1940

A128(a) First American edition (1940)

Basilissa | A TALE OF THE EMPRESS THEODORA | By John Masefield | *1940* | THE MACMILLAN COMPANY [point] NEW YORK
(All width centred)

Bibliographies: Handley-Taylor p.62, Wight 99

Collation: [A-R]⁸ [S]⁶ [T-U]⁸ (J not used); 158 leaves; 203 × 134mm.; [i–vi] 1–307 [308–310]

Page contents: [i] half-title: 'BASILISSA'; [ii] '[publisher's device] | THE MACMILLAN COMPANY | [two lines listing six cities, separated by four points] | MACMILLAN & CO., LIMITED | [two lines listing five cities, separated by three points] | THE MACMILLAN COMPANY | OF CANADA, LIMITED | [one city listed]'; [iii] title-page; [iv] '*Copyright, 1940, by* | JOHN MASEFIELD. | [rule] | All rights reserved–no part of this book | may be reproduced in any form without | permission in writing from the publisher, | except by a reviewer who wishes to quote brief | passages in connection with a review written | for inclusion in magazine or newspaper. | FIRST PRINTING | PRINTED IN THE UNITED STATES OF AMERICA | AMERICAN BOOK-STRATFORD PRESS, INC., NEW YORK'; [v] 'BASILISSA'; [vi] blank; 1–307 text; [308–310] blank

Paper: wove paper

Running title: 'BASILISSA' (34mm.) on both verso and recto, pp.2–307

Binding: light brown cloth. On spine: '[ornament of square (in black) with two rules (in gold) running from centre of square to centre of upper two sides] | BASILISSA [in gold on black panel] | [white rule] | MASEFIELD [in white] | [ornament of square (in black) with two rules (in gold) running from centre of square to centre of upper two sides] | MACMILLAN [in white] | [point] [in white]'. Covers: blank. Top edge stained blue, others trimmed. Binding measurements: 209 × 136mm. (covers), 209 × 44mm. (spine). End-papers: wove paper.

Publication date: published, according to Handley-Taylor, 16 January 1940 (see notes)

Price: $2.50

Contents:
Basilissa ('Theodora, the cast mistress of Hekebolos, the Governor of the Pentapolis, came through the...')

Notes:
A novel which like *Conquer* (see A132) is set in the Byzantium of Justinian. The novel has no chapter divisions. Masefield here inverts the traditional depiction of the Empress.

The text commences with an ornate letter in a larger type size than the other characters.

A publishing agreement for this title between Masefield and Macmillan was dated 25 June 1940 (see Archives of The Society of Authors). The agreement refers to 'a licence to publish in volume form in the United States of America and Canada his next novel to contain approximately 80,000 words (exact title to be determined)'. This suggests that Handley-Taylor's publication date may be incorrect.

Copies seen: BL (X.989/75098) stamped 30 APR 1978; HRHRC (AC-L M377BAS 1940)

A128(b) First English edition (1940)

BASILISSA | *A Tale of the Empress Theodora* | BY | JOHN MASEFIELD | [publisher's device of a windmill with 'W' and 'H'] | [rule, 68mm.] | WILLIAM HEINEMANN LTD | LONDON :: TORONTO
(The italic type contains a number of swash characters)
(All width centred)

Bibliographies: Handley-Taylor p.62, Wight 99a

Collation: [A]⁸ B-S⁸ (J not used); signatures right foot of page; 144 leaves; 190 × 126mm.; [i–vi] 1–282

Page contents: [i] half-title: 'BASILISSA'; [ii] '*ALSO BY JOHN MASEFIELD* | PLAYS: | [12 titles listed] | POETRY: | [16 titles listed] | FICTION: GENERAL: | [12 titles of fiction listed with nine titles of general works]'; [iii] title-page; [iv] 'FIRST PUBLISHED 1940 | PRINTED IN GREAT BRITAIN AT | THE WINDMILL PRESS, KINGSWOOD, SURREY'; [v] 'To | MY WIFE'; [vi] blank; 1–282 text

Paper: wove paper

Running title: none

Binding: blue cloth. On spine, in gold: 'BASILISSA | [ornament] | JOHN | MASEFIELD | HEINEMANN' (all width centred). On upper cover, in blind: 'BASILISSA | JOHN MASEFIELD' (within blind ruled border: 193 × 123mm.) On lower cover, in blind: publisher's device of a windmill (ranged lower right). Top edge stained, others trimmed. Binding measurements: 198 × 127mm. (covers), 198 × 43mm. (spine). End-papers: wove paper.

Publication date: published, according to Handley-Taylor, 16 September 1940; the *English Catalogue of Books* cites a publication date of September 1940; the sales ledger preserved in the Heinemann Archive suggests publication on 16 January 1940 in an edition of 7500 copies

Price: 8s.

Contents:
as for A128(a)

Notes:
The text commences with a raised-capital.

C.S. Evans, wrote to Masefield during July 1940 noting:

> I have just read the proofs of BASILISSA and was extremely interested in the story. It is quite unlike anything you have done before…

> (C.S. Evans, letter to John Masefield, 18 July 1940)
> (HRHRC, MS (Masefield, J.) Recip William Heinemann Ltd.)

The sales ledger preserved in the Heinemann Archive suggests a publication date eight months prior to that cited by Handley-Taylor. The British Library copy suggests that Handley-Taylor's figure may not be inaccurate. Although January publication might have been desirable for copyright protection (the American A128(a) was apparently published on 16 January 1940), it appears – from Evans' letter of 18 July 1940 – that the novel only reached proof form in July 1940. The publishing agreement for this title between Masefield and Heinemann was dated 10 September 1940 (see Archives of The Society of Authors). The agreement refers to a publication price of 8s.

The Social Credit Party (secretary Frank S. Jackson) having read a review of the novel thought his party libelled in *Basilissa* and in September or October 1940 requested 'an immediate and complete withdrawal of the book or we shall be compelled... to take legal action'. In November The Society of Authors advised Masefield that although the Social Credit Party would lose any legal fight they would, nevertheless, benefit from publicity. By November 1940 Masefield was therefore considering a printed slip to be inserted within copies of the novel, this action being suggested by Messrs North & Son, solicitors for the Social Credit Party. This slip was to read as follows:

> This story of Byzantium in the early sixth century is an effort to understand a short, important time in the lives of two great rulers, the Emperor Justinian and his Empress Theodora. It is based on facts described or mentioned by the historian Procopius.

> Let it be clearly understood that the factions mentioned in the book are those described by Procopius as causing much frightful civil strife throughout the Eastern Empire.

I make no allusion whatsoever to the Social Credit Party or any other party associated or supposed to be associated with particular colours. My book is fiction, based upon a well-known history. It makes no reference whatsoever to any living person or existing institution.

(Signed) John Masefield

The Social Credit Party required the addition of '(the Green Shirts)' after the name of their party, and this request Masefield regarded as 'just about the limit'. The slip was already in print before the Social Credit Party raised strong objections. (See BL, Add.Mss.56613, f.179 and f.191, and Add.Mss.56614, f.29, f.47, f.57 and f.65).

Copies seen: private collection (PWE); BL (N.N.31899) stamped 17 SEP 1940; HRHRC (TEMP M37BAS 1940 cop.1) inscribed 'For Con | from Jan. | Sept 3. 1940.'

Reprinted:

| 'Reprinted' | [first edition, second impression] | Jul 1948 |

A129 SOME MEMORIES OF W.B. YEATS   1940

A129(a) First Irish edition (1940)

SOME MEMORIES OF W. B. YEATS | BY | JOHN MASEFIELD. | THE CUALA PRESS | DUBLIN, IRELAND. | MCMXL
(All width centred)

Bibliographies: Handley-Taylor [unrecorded], Wight 100

Collation: [π]⁴ [a]⁴ b-e⁴ [f]⁴; signatures left foot of page; 28 leaves; [i–xvi] [1] 2–29 [30–40]

Page contents: [i–xi] blank; [xii] frontispiece: 107 × 66mm., '18 WOBURN BUILDINGS'; [xiii] title-page; [xiv–xv] blank; [xvi] 'CONTENTS' (seven individual items listed with page references all in red); [1]–[30] text (at foot of p.[30] in red: 'Some of these verses were spoken in his memory on | the afternoon and evening of Friday, July the 28th, | 1939, being the last day of the Oxford Summer Di- | versions, a Festival of plays and poetry founded in | 1937 as one little part of the influence scattered by | him.'); [31] 'Here ends Some Memories of W. B. Yeats | by John Masefield. Three hundred and seventy | copies of this book have been set in Caslon type, | and printed by Esther Ryan and Maire Gill on | paper made in Ireland, and published by the | Cuala Press, 133 Lower Baggot Street, Dublin, | Ireland. Finished in the first week of Decem- | ber, nineteen hundred and forty. | [new paragraph] This is Number' (all in red); [32–40] blank

Paper: wove paper

Running title: none

Binding: blue boards with beige cloth spine. On spine: white paper label (144 × 6mm.) on which reading lengthways up spine, from foot: 'SOME MEMORIES OF W. B. YEATS BY JOHN MASEFIELD'. On upper cover: 'SOME MEMORIES OF W. B. YEATS | BY | JOHN MASEFIELD'. Lower cover: blank. Top edge trimmed, others untrimmed. Binding measurements: 216 × 146mm. (covers), 216 × 17mm. (spine). End-papers: blue wove paper.

Publication date: published, according to the colophon, December 1940 in an edition of 370 copies

Price: 12s.6d.

Contents:
Some Memories of W. B. Yeats ('His childhood, boyhood and young manhood were passed among painters, writers...')
My First Meeting With Him ('I was to dine with him at seven o'clock in the evening of November the 5th, 1900.')
Of Mrs. Old ('I think that I am right in saying that her husband was a carpenter and that...')
On His Tobacco-Jar *[Verse]* ('This is the dull red jar of earthenware')
Coole ('Somewhere in his sitting-room, perhaps to the left of the fire, was a painting...')
Finn and the Chess-men *[Verse]* ('Now that he is gone into his quiet,')
On What He Was *[Verse]* ('He was of splendid presence, tall, well-made,')

Notes:
Written shortly after the death of Yeats, Masefield's work is in both verse and prose. Publication by the Cuala Press establishes a significant link with Masefield's *John M. Synge* (A27(a)). The description of 18 Woburn Buildings was included in the two anthologies *A Book of Both Sorts* (A151) and *A Book of Prose Selections* (A158). In the latter volume the work is incorrectly cited as 'Some Memories of the Late W.B. Yeats'.

A letter from George Yeats notes concerns over the frontispiece, poses a few questions, notes the limitation and makes reference to the Macmillan publication date. It is possible, therefore, that the Macmillan edition pre-dates this edition:

> ...I wonder if you got a letter containing some proofs on our hand=made paper of the block? They were posted four weeks ago? In that letter I asked you what you thought about it. It seemed to me rather out of keeping with the general style of the printing etc, and to create an image which was out of key with the beautiful image you have evoked in your descriptions. What do you think? Shall we omit it? (The block takes badly on this cheap paper but you have, I hope, the

other). If you decide to omit, what design would you like used on the title page? Perhaps you would choose one from one of the Cuala books you have.

Other questions: I hope you wont mind my mentioning

page 5, your line On this, the first floor. It was actually the second floor.* He did not have the first floor until, I think, 1915 or 1916. [* "that curved stair, lit by a lamp at the curve"]

page 13 etc; are these 'dots' to be used or were they only in the typescript?

page 27. I had hoped that the beginning of the personal description could have begun a new page. But this was not possible, if the Cuala tradition of a tightly packed page was to be kept. Could there be a title for the passages beginning "He was of splendid presence…" (If so, it would be included in the list of Contents.)

The edition is only 360 copies because we have only just enough paper for 400 copies (40 copies allowed for copyright (10) and reviews). It may not be possible to get paper specially made again until after the War. If that is so we shall have to use "War Paper" for our next book.

Please make any suggestions about set=up or printing that you can. We want to make this little book as perfect as we can. It fills me with gratitude to you and to him.

…I have cabled Macmillan Company. N.Y. today that we publish on December 7th. This will depend on number of corrections in proof. When I hear from you I will cable if necessary to alter date. Colophon will be changed to date of publication.

(George Yeats, letter to John Masefield, 1 October 1940)
(HRHRC, MS (Masefield, J.) Recip Cuala Press)

Handley-Taylor omits this volume from his bibliography and only notes the Macmillan edition (published on 3 December 1940). Wight includes the Cuala Press edition, however, and places it before the Macmillan edition in his chronology. Possible dates for publication include:

1–7 December 1940	(the colophon within the volume states the printing and publishing was 'finished' between these dates)
10 January 1941	(this is the date stamped in the British Library copy)
March 1941	(this is the date given by the *English Catalogue of Books*)

This title is numbered 66 in *A List of Books Published by The Dun Emer Press and the Cuala Press founded in Dublin in Nineteen Hundred and Three by Elizabeth Corbet Yeats*, (Dublin: Cuala Press, 1972). The entry states 'Three hundred and seventy copies, December 1940'.

The contents listing above repeats that present in the volume. Within sections Masefield frequently alternates between poetry and prose.

Copies seen: BL (Cup.510.ad.53) numbered 'Out Of Series', stamped 10 JAN 1941; Bodleian (27961.e.75) numbered 'Out Of Series' stamped 6 MAY 1941

A129(b) First American edition (1940)

SOME MEMORIES OF | W. B. YEATS | BY | JOHN MASEFIELD | NEW YORK | THE MACMILLAN COMPANY | 1940
(All width centred)

Bibliographies: Handley-Taylor p.62, Wight 100a

Collation: [A]⁸ [B]⁶ [C]⁸; 22 leaves; 187 × 125mm.; [i–vi] 1–35 [36–38]

Page contents: [i] half-title: 'SOME MEMORIES OF W. B. YEATS'; [ii] '[publisher's device] | THE MACMILLAN COMPANY | [two lines listing six cities, separated by four points] | MACMILLAN AND CO., LIMITED | [two lines listing five cities, separated by three points] | THE MACMILLAN COMPANY | OF CANADA, LIMITED | [one city listed]'; [iii] title-page; [iv] '*Copyright, 1940, by* | JOHN MASEFIELD. | [rule] | All rights reserved–no part of this book | may be reproduced in any form without | permission in writing from the publisher, | except by a reviewer who wishes to quote brief | passages in connection with a review written | for inclusion in magazine or newspaper. | FIRST PRINTING. | PRINTED IN THE UNITED STATES OF AMERICA | AMERICAN BOOK-STRATFORD PRESS, INC., NEW YORK'; [v] 'SOME MEMORIES OF W. B. YEATS'; [vi] blank; 1–34 text; 35 'Some of these verses were spoken in his memory | on the afternoon and evening of Friday, July the | 28th, 1939, being the last day of the Oxford Sum- | mer Diversions, a Festival of plays and poetry | founded in 1937 as one little part of the influence | scattered by him.'; [36–38] blank

Paper: wove paper

Running title: none

Binding: light blue cloth. On spine, reading lengthways down spine from head: 'MASEFIELD [point] SOME MEMORIES OF W.B. YEATS MACMILLAN'. On upper cover, in blind within black square: 76 × 76mm.: 'SOME | MEMORIES OF | W.B. YEATS | JOHN MASEFIELD'. Lower cover: blank. All edges trimmed. Binding measurements: 193 × 127mm. (covers), 193 × 16mm. (spine). End-papers: wove paper.

Publication date: published, according to Handley-Taylor, 3 December 1940

Price: $1.25

Contents:
Some Memories of W. B. Yeats ('His childhood, boyhood and young manhood were passed among painters, writers...')
My First Meeting With Him ('I was to dine with him at seven o'clock in the evening of November the 5th, 1900.')
Of Mrs. Old ('I think that I am right in saying that her husband was a carpenter and that...')
On His Tobacco-Jar *[Verse]* ('This is the dull red jar of earthenware')
Coole ('Somewhere in his sitting-room, perhaps to the left of the fire, was a painting...')
Finn and the Chess-men *[Verse]* ('Now that he is gone into his quiet,')
[On What He Was] *[Verse]* ('He was of splendid presence, tall, well-made,')

Notes:
The title on the title-page uses an ornate type.

In contrast with A129(a), this Macmillan edition omits illustrations and a contents listing. The contents listing above is based on that provided in the Cuala edition. All titles are nevertheless given within the text with the exception of 'On What He Was' which is here untitled.

The publishing agreement for this title between Masefield and Macmillan was dated 14 August 1940 (see Archives of The Society of Authors). The agreement refers to 'a licence to publish in volume form in the United States of America and Canada a work the subject or title of which is SOME MEMORIES OF W.B. YEATS'.

Copies seen: private collection (PWE); Bodleian (27961.e.259) stamped 13 MAR 1964

A130 THE NINE DAYS WONDER   1941

A130(a) First English edition (1941)

THE | NINE DAYS WONDER | (THE OPERATION DYNAMO) | BY | JOHN MASEFIELD | [publisher's device of a windmill with 'W' and 'H'] | [rule, 63mm.] | WILLIAM HEINEMANN LTD | LONDON :: TORONTO (All width centred)

Bibliographies: Handley-Taylor p.62, Wight 102

Collation: [π]⁸ A-D⁸ [E]⁴; signatures right foot of page; 44 leaves; 190 × 127mm.; [i–viii] ix–xv [xvi] 1–57 [58–72]

Page contents: [i] half-title: 'THE | NINE DAYS WONDER | (THE OPERATION DYNAMO)'; [ii] '*ALSO BY JOHN MASEFIELD* | PLAYS: | [12 titles listed] | POETRY: | [16 titles listed] | FICTION: GENERAL: | [13 titles of fiction listed with nine titles of general works]'; [iii] title-page; [iv] 'FIRST PUBLISHED 1941 | PRINTED IN GREAT BRITAIN AT THE WINDMILL PRESS | KINGSWOOD, SURREY'; [v] 'This tale is dedicated | to | Vice-Admiral Sir BERTRAM RAMSAY, K.C.B., M.V.O., | to | The Officers, Warrant-Officers and Ratings, | and to all others who bore a hand | in the Operation Dynamo.'; [vi] blank; [vii] 'ILLUSTRATIONS | (*to be found at end of book*)' (11 individual items listed); [viii] blank; ix–xv 'PREFACE' ('This pamphlet gives a summary of the lifting of the First French Army...'); [xvi] untitled verse ('They marched over the Field of Waterloo,'); 1–57 text; [58–61] text of poems; [62–64] blank; [65–70] illustrations; [71–72] blank

Paper: wove paper (with the exception of gathering E which is on glossy paper)

Running title: 'PREFACE' (14mm.) on both verso and recto, pp.x–xv; 'THE NINE DAYS WONDER' (39mm.) on both verso and recto, pp. 2–57

Binding: blue cloth. On spine, reading lengthways up spine, from foot, in gold: 'THE NINE DAYS WONDER [point] JOHN MASEFIELD'; horizontally at foot of spine: publisher's device of a windmill with 'W' and 'H'. On upper cover, in blind: 'THE | NINE DAYS WONDER | JOHN MASEFIELD' (within blind ruled border: 192 × 124mm.) Lower cover: blank. All edges trimmed. Binding measurements: 196 × 128mm. (covers), 196 × 23mm. (spine). End-papers: wove paper.

Publication date: the sales ledger preserved in the Heinemann Archive suggests publication on 17 March 1941 in an edition of 5000 copies

Price: 3s.6d.

Contents:
Preface ('This pamphlet gives a summary of the lifting of the First French Army and the B.E.F. from...')
[Untitled] *[Verse]* ('They marched over the Field of Waterloo,')
Dunquerque ('Dunquerque is an ancient sea-port, with a good depth of water, several docks, some...')
[Acknowledgements] ('I thank those officers of the Army who have permitted me to quote half a dozen...')
To the Seamen ('You seamen, I have eaten your hard bread')
A Young English Air-Man ('O smiling, sun-burned youth who rode the sky')
Thoughts for Later On ('When someone somewhere bids the bombing cease,')
When We Return Thanks ('Ah, when the spirit knows the dewy dawn, the peace-time,')

Notes:

An historical account telling of the Dunkirk evacuation. It is often stated that the work comprises the last section of *The Twenty-Five Days* (see A172) (publication of which was banned until 1972) although there is much original material in this shorter account that is not present in the larger work. See *The Twenty-Five Days* (A172) for additional publishing history.

C.S. Evans wrote to Masefield on 4 March noting a publication date of 17 March. Evans noted he 'had hoped to be able to bring the date forward but this is not possible...' (see C.S. Evans, letter to John Masefield, 4 March 1941) (HRHRC, MS (Masefield, J.) Recip William Heinemann Ltd.) An 'advance copy' was sent – together with details of co-operation with Macmillan – on 13 March:

> I have sent to you separately an advance copy of THE NINE DAYS WONDER... On Monday I sent to Messrs Macmillan in New York, by Air Mail, a set of finally printed sheets of the book, and today two complete copies have gone forward.
>
> (C.S. Evans, letter to John Masefield, 13 March 1941)
(HRHRC, MS (Masefield, J.) Recip William Heinemann Ltd.)

Masefield evidently had questions about the dust-jacket used for the work. One day after publication Evans responded:

> I am glad you like the appearance of THE NINE DAYS' WONDER and I am sorry that we did not use the chart for the wrapper. Somehow or other we got it into our heads that you wanted to retain that wrapper for THE TWENTY FIVE DAYS when it became possible to publish that book. I am afraid it would involve too many complications if we were to reprint the wrapper now. The reprint of 5,000 copies is actually on the machine. We could consider changing the wrapper for the next reprint and substituting one of the pictures for the Operations Room. Will you let me know which of the present pictures should be left out for we must keep to the same number.
>
> (C.S. Evans, letter to John Masefield, 18 March 1941)
(HRHRC, MS (Masefield, J.) Recip William Heinemann Ltd.)

The publishing agreement for this title between Masefield and Heinemann was dated 10 March 1941 (see Archives of The Society of Authors). The agreement refers to a publication price of 3s.6d.

In the canon of Masefield's work there are obvious parallels to *Gallipoli*. A letter (preserved in the Heinemann Archive) from A.S. Frere dated 1 May 1951 to Masefield states that Frere was 'going into the question of issuing' both *Gallipoli* and *The Nine Days Wonder* in a single volume. This came to nothing.

Within the text titled 'Dunquerque' there are sub-sections with titles including dates from 26 May to 3 June.

The illustrations all comprise black and white photographs each titled and also noting a source. These sources are newspapers and press agencies.

Copies seen: private collection (PWE) inscribed 'For | Julia Smith, | from | John Masefield. | March. 1941.'; BL (9101.a.8) stamped 17 MAR 1941; Bodleian (Additional Masefield papers 8) inscribed 'The original version of this | book, after being passed | by all the Censors, was | prohibited. | [new paragraph] This version, after much | trouble, was permitted', this inscription replaces an earlier inscription to Masefield's son: 'For | Lew | from | Z | 14. III. 1941.'; HRHRC (TEMP M377 NIN 1941A cop.1) inscribed 'For J. | from | Z. | 14. III. 41.'; HRHRC (TEMP M377 NIN 1941A cop.2) inscribed 'For Con | from Jan. | March 14. 1941.' (with incorrect state of dust-jacket); HRHRC (TEMP M377 NIN 1941B) inscribed 'For Con | from Jan. | 31 March. 1941.' (with corrected state of dust-jacket)

Reprinted:

[first edition, second impression]	Mar 1941
[first edition, third impression]	Mar 1941
[first edition, fourth impression]	Apr 1941
[first edition, fifth impression]	Apr 1941
[first edition, sixth impression]	Apr 1941
[first edition, seventh impression]	Jun 1941
[first edition, eighth impression]	Jul 1941
[first edition, ninth impression]	Aug 1941
[first edition, tenth impression]	Sep 1941
[first edition, eleventh impression]	Dec 1941

John Richards notes that some minor textual revision occurred during the April 1941 impressions (see John Richards, 'John Masefield, Dunkirk and my Boat', *The Journal of The John Masefield Society*, volume 10, 2001, pp.38–40). It also appears that Masefield wrote to the Macmillan Co. (regarding the American edition) on 29 October 1941 noting a 'correction' (see Archives of The Society of Authors).

The preserved in-coming correspondence from Heinemann (see HRHRC, MS (Masefield, J.) Recip William Heinemann Ltd.) includes evidence of Masefield's frequent corrections (and also the publisher's satisfaction with sales):

> I have made arrangements for the chart to go into the third impression of THE NINE DAYS WONDER which is now going to press. We are putting it in as a folder...
>
> (C.S. Evans, letter to John Masefield, 20 March 1941)
(HRHRC, MS (Masefield, J.) Recip William Heinemann Ltd.)

Five days later, Evans noted that 'the book continues to sell very well. To date we have sold 13,049 copies…' (see C.S. Evans, letter to John Masefield, 25 March 1941) (HRHRC, MS (Masefield, J.) Recip William Heinemann Ltd.) Further corrections (and sales details) were forthcoming:

> I have given instructions that the corrections you sent to me for THE NINE DAYS WONDER are to be made in the next reprint which is going to press today. The book is still doing very well. We sold 621 copies yesterday, and the total is 19,774 copies…

> (C.S. Evans, letter to John Masefield, 2 April 1941)
(HRHRC, MS (Masefield, J.) Recip William Heinemann Ltd.)

A 'correction in Captain Bush's initials for the next reprint' was acknowledged on 8 April 1941 (see Louisa Callender, letter to John Masefield, 8 April 1941) (HRHRC, MS (Masefield, J.) Recip William Heinemann Ltd.) Just over a week later it was reported:

> Your corrections are just in time for a reprint of NINE DAYS WONDER which we are making now.
> (Louisa Callender, letter to John Masefield, 16 April 1941)
(HRHRC, MS (Masefield, J.) Recip William Heinemann Ltd.)

In a letter dated at the beginning of September 1941, C.S. Evans reported that 'NINE DAYS WONDER and IN THE MILL are still selling: the total sale of the former is 39,932 and of the latter 5,289…' (see C.S. Evans, letter to John Masefield, 3 September 1941) (HRHRC, MS (Masefield, J.) Recip William Heinemann Ltd.) There was at least one further correction before the end of the year:

> I will certainly make the correction on page 52 in any further reprint of NINE DAYS WONDER.
> (C.S. Evans, letter to John Masefield, 1 December 1941)
(HRHRC, MS (Masefield, J.) Recip William Heinemann Ltd.)

This change was, apparently, the removal of the name of the tug 'Nicholas Drew' which did not go to Dunkirk.

A130(b) *First American edition (1941)*

THE | NINE DAYS WONDER | (THE OPERATION DYNAMO) | BY | JOHN MASEFIELD | NEW YORK | THE MACMILLAN COMPANY | 1941
(All width centred)

Bibliographies: Handley-Taylor p.62, Wight 102a

Collation: [A-E]⁸; 40 leaves; 186 × 123mm.; [two un-numbered pages] [i–viii] ix–xv [xvi] 1–56 [57–62]

Page contents: [-] blank (page excluded from page count, but constitutes first leaf of first gathering); [-] blank; [i] half-title: 'THE | NINE DAYS WONDER | (THE OPERATION DYNAMO)'; [ii] '*ALSO BY JOHN MASEFIELD* | PLAYS: | [12 volumes listed] | POETRY: | [16 volumes listed] | FICTION: GENERAL: | [13 volumes of fiction listed with nine volumes of general works]'; [iii] title-page; [iv] '*Copyright, 1941, by* | JOHN MASEFIELD. | [rule] | All rights reserved–no part of this book | may be reproduced in any form without | permission in writing from the publisher, | except by a reviewer who wishes to quote brief | passages in connection with a review written | for inclusion in magazine or newspaper. | [rule] | FIRST PRINTING. | PRINTED IN THE UNITED STATES OF AMERICA | AMERICAN BOOK-STRATFORD PRESS, INC., NEW YORK'; [v] 'This tale is dedicated | to | Vice-Admiral Sir BERTRAM RAMSAY, K.C.B., M.V.O. | to | The Officers, Warrant-Officers and Ratings, | and to all others who bore a hand | in the Operation Dynamo.'; [vi] blank; [vii] 'ILLUSTRATIONS | (*to be found at end of book*)' (eight individual items listed); [viii] blank; ix–xv 'PREFACE' ('This pamphlet gives a summary of the lifting of the First French Army…'); [xvi] untitled verse ('They marched over the Field of Waterloo,'); 1–56 text; [57–60] text of poems (with additional leaf tipped-in on p.[60] on which are four illustrations); [61–62] blank (with additional leaf tipped-in on p.[61] on which are four illustrations)

Paper: wove paper (with the exception of the tipped-in leaves which are on glossy paper)

Running title: 'PREFACE' (17mm.) on both verso and recto, pp.x–xv; 'THE NINE DAYS WONDER' (50mm.) on both verso and recto, pp. 2–56

Binding: blue cloth. On spine, reading lengthways down spine from head, in gold: 'JOHN MASEFIELD THE NINE DAYS WONDER MACMILLAN [point]'. Covers: blank. All edges trimmed. Binding measurements: 192 × 125mm. (covers), 192 × 25mm. (spine). End-papers: wove paper.

Publication date: published, according to Handley-Taylor, 6 May 1941

Price: $1.60

Contents:
as for A130(a)

Notes:
Within the text titled 'Dunquerque' there are sub-sections with titles including dates from 26 May to 3 June.

The illustrations all comprise black and white photographs each titled and also noting a source. These sources are newspapers and press agencies. There are fewer in the Macmillan edition than in A130(a).

Wight notes that 'the "v" of page xv 'is a broken type in some editions'.

A publishing agreement for *The Twenty-Five Days* between Masefield and Macmillan was dated 11 December 1940 (see Archives of The Society of Authors). A letter from George P. Brett, Jr., president of Macmillan Company in New York, to Masefield later suggested using this contract for *The Nine Days Wonder*:

> We have now received the final copy for THE NINE DAYS WONDER… I suppose we both realise we have no contract for the publication of this book unless we apply this book against the contract which exists between us for THE TWENTY-FIVE DAYS.
>
> (George P. Brett Jr., letter to John Masefield, 11 April 1941)
> (Archives of The Society of Authors)

Copies seen: private collection (ROV)

Reprinted:

	[first edition, second impression]	
	[first edition, third impression]	
	[first edition, fourth impression]	
	[first edition, fifth impression]	
'Sixth Printing'	[first edition, sixth impression]	1943

A131 IN THE MILL   1941

A131(a) First English edition (1941)

IN THE MILL | BY | JOHN MASEFIELD | [publisher's device of a windmill with 'W [point]' and '[point] H'] | [rule, 72mm.] | WILLIAM HEINEMANN LTD | LONDON :: TORONTO
(All width centred)

Bibliographies: Handley-Taylor p.62, Wight 103

Collation: [A]⁸ B-K⁸ L⁴ (J not used); signatures right foot of page; 84 leaves; 190 × 123mm.; [i–viii] 1–160

Page contents: [i] half-title: 'IN THE MILL'; [ii] '*ALSO BY JOHN MASEFIELD* | PLAYS: | [12 titles listed] | POETRY: | [16 titles listed] | FICTION: GENERAL: | [12 titles of fiction listed with 10 titles of general works]'; [iii] title-page; [iv] 'FIRST PUBLISHED 1941 | PRINTED IN GREAT BRITAIN AT THE WINDMILL PRESS | KINGSWOOD, SURREY'; [v] 'To my old companions | ANTY | BILLY | DUNK | ED | EDDIE | JACOB | JIMMY | PAT | PERCE | SMIDDY | & | TOMMY'; [vi] blank; [vii] '"Therefore . . . dwell as having | refuges in yourselves, resorts in your- | selves and not elsewhere. . . . Who- | ever shall dwell as having refuges in | themselves . . . shall reach to the | limit of darkness, whoever are desir- | ous of learning." | GAUTAMA BUDDHA TO ANANDA | *The Life of Buddha,* by Edward J. Thomas | (Kegan Paul. 1931)'; [viii] blank; 1–160 text (signed and dated: 'JOHN MASEFIELD. | *Oxford, 1941.*')

Paper: wove paper

Running title: '*In the Mill*' (18mm.) on both verso and recto, pp.2–160

Binding: blue cloth. On spine, in gold: 'IN | THE | MILL | [ornament] | JOHN | MASEFIELD | HEINEMANN' (all width centred). On upper cover, in blind: 'IN THE MILL | JOHN MASEFIELD' (within blind ruled border: 192 × 123mm.) On lower cover, in blind: publisher's device of a windmill (ranged lower right). Top edge stained, others trimmed. Binding measurements: 196 × 126mm. (covers), 196 × 40mm. (spine). End-papers: wove paper.

Publication date: the sales ledger preserved in the Heinemann Archive suggests publication on 23 June 1941 in an edition of 7500 copies

Price: 7s.6d.

Contents:
In The Mill ('Though I had not gone to bed till after midnight, I must have been called at five o'clock.')

Notes:
Masefield's first lengthy instalment of autobiography (see also *Wonderings* (A139), *New Chum* (A140), *So Long to Learn* (A162) and *Grace Before Ploughing* (A170)). Masefield describes his life in America in the 1890s and, specifically, his time in a Yonkers carpet factory. He also records his discovery of English poetry and realization that it was 'the law of his being'.

C.S. Evans responded to Masefield's announcement of the title 'with eagerness' (see C.S. Evans, letter to John Masefield, 20 February 1941) (HRHRC, MS (Masefield, J.) Recip William Heinemann Ltd.) He acknowledged receipt of the typescript at the beginning of March 1941:

> Thank you for your letter and for the typescript of IN THE MILL, to the reading of which I am eagerly looking forward.
> (C.S. Evans, letter to John Masefield, 11 March 1941)
> (HRHRC, MS (Masefield, J.) Recip William Heinemann Ltd.)

IN THE MILL

BY

JOHN MASEFIELD

WILLIAM HEINEMANN LTD
LONDON :: TORONTO

A131(a) title-page

JOHN MASEFIELD

IN

THE

MILL

New York
THE MACMILLAN COMPANY
1941

A131(b) title-page

CONQUER

A TALE OF THE NIKA REBELLION IN BYZANTIUM

BY

JOHN MASEFIELD

WILLIAM HEINEMANN LTD
LONDON :: TORONTO

A132(a) title-page

JOHN MASEFIELD
★

SHOPPING IN OXFORD

★

LONDON
WILLIAM HEINEMANN LTD
1941

A134(a) title-page

GAUTAMA
THE ENLIGHTENED
and other verse

BY

JOHN MASEFIELD

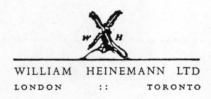

WILLIAM HEINEMANN LTD
LONDON :: TORONTO

A135(a) title-page

NATALIE MAISIE
AND
PAVILASTUKAY

TWO TALES IN VERSE

BY

JOHN MASEFIELD

WILLIAM HEINEMANN LTD
LONDON :: TORONTO

A136(a) title-page

LAND WORKERS
By
JOHN MASEFIELD

WILLIAM HEINEMANN LTD
LONDON :: TORONTO

A137(a) title-page

A
GENERATION
RISEN

by
JOHN MASEFIELD
and
EDWARD SEAGO

COLLINS
48 PALL MALL LONDON

A138(a) title-page

The following month Louisa Callender stated that proofs were soon to be ready and enquired about the American publication:

> ...proofs of IN THE MILL will be ready about the end of the week. Have you sent Macmillan a typescript? If you have, we can wait until a finally corrected proof is ready...
>
> (Louisa Callender, letter to John Masefield, 19 April 1941)
> (HRHRC, MS (Masefield, J.) Recip William Heinemann Ltd.)

A 'couple of proofs in book form of IN THE MILL and manuscript...' were sent on 28 April (see B.F. Oliver, letter to John Masefield, 28 April 1941) (HRHRC, MS (Masefield, J.) Recip William Heinemann Ltd.) At the beginning of May, C.S. Evans enclosed an agreement for the book and noted:

> ...we are all set for publication on June 9th and unless unforeseen circumstances arise, that is our date.
>
> (C.S. Evans, letter to John Masefield, 8 May 1941)
> (HRHRC, MS (Masefield, J.) Recip William Heinemann Ltd.)

Unforeseen circumstances did arise and Evans later noted '...we have had to postpone IN THE MILL until June 23rd. The cloth for the binding was delayed...' (see C.S. Evans, letter to John Masefield, 29 May 1941) (HRHRC, MS (Masefield, J.) Recip William Heinemann Ltd.)

The publishing agreement for this title between Masefield and Heinemann was dated 13 May 1941 (see Archives of The Society of Authors). The agreement refers to a publication price of 7s.6d.

Babington Smith in her biography of Masefield specifically notes the epigraph to this volume:

> He became more and more bottled-up and solitary, and his fellow workers began to regard him as 'a little peculiar', while Jack on his side came to feel that most of the raw young Americans at the factory were definitely uncongenial. ...Yet at this particular stage isolation was in a sense a blessing. This is clear from the quotation that Masefield later chose as an epigraph for *In the Mill*, to convey the essence of his experiences while at Yonkers.
>
> (Babington Smith, *John Masefield – A Life*, Oxford University Press, 1978, p.43)

Only a month before publication Masefield wrote to The Society of Authors asking them to arrange permission for the epigraph:

> Will you be so very kind, as to procure for me, from Messrs Kegan Paul, permission to use the enclosed quotation from their Life of Buddha, as a chapter-heading in a forthcoming book? Perhaps such a quotation is lawful anyhow, but if they ask a small fee they shall have, of course.
>
> (John Masefield, letter to [E.J.] Mullet, 2 May [1941])
> (BL, Add.Mss.56614, f.176)

This permission was granted by Kegan Paul, Trench Trubner & Co. Ltd. on 7 May 1941 (see BL, Add.Mss.56614, f.179)

C.S. Evans noted successful sales of this title (and *The Nine Days Wonder*) at the beginning of September 1941:

> NINE DAYS WONDER and IN THE MILL are still selling: the total sale of the former is 39,932 and of the latter 5,289...
>
> (C.S. Evans, letter to John Masefield, 3 September 1941)
> (HRHRC, MS (Masefield, J.) Recip William Heinemann Ltd.)

Copies seen: private collection (PWE); BL (10860.a.21) rebound, stamped 23 JUN 1941

Reprinted:
'Reprinted'   [first edition, second impression]   1947

A131(b) First American edition (1941)

JOHN MASEFIELD | [ornamental rule formed by squares standing on one corner with a point in centre of each square] | IN | THE | MILL | [ornamental rule formed by squares standing on one corner with a point in centre of each square] | *New York* | THE MACMILLAN COMPANY | 1941
(All width centred)

Bibliographies: Handley-Taylor p.62, Wight 103a

Collation: [A-H]⁸ [I]⁴ [K-L]⁸ (J not used); 84 leaves; 203 × 134mm.; [i–x] 1–158

Page contents: [i] half-title: 'IN THE MILL'; [ii] '[publisher's device] | THE MACMILLAN COMPANY | [two lines listing six cities, separated by four points] | MACMILLAN AND CO., LIMITED | [two lines listing five cities, separated by three points] | THE MACMILLAN COMPANY | OF CANADA, LIMITED | [one city listed]'; [iii] title-page; [iv] 'Copyright, 1941, by | JOHN MASEFIELD. | [rule] | All rights reserved—no part of this book may be | reproduced in any form without permission in writ- | ing from the publisher, except by a reviewer who | wishes to quote brief passages in connection with a | review written for inclusion in magazine or newspaper. | *First Printing* | PRINTED IN THE UNITED STATES OF AMERICA | BY THE VAIL-BALLOU PRESS, INC., BINGHAMTON, N.Y.'; [v] 'To my old companions | ANTY | BILLY | DUNK | ED | EDDIE | JACOB | JIMMY | PAT | PERCE | SMIDDY | & | TOMMY'; [vi] blank; [vii] '"Therefore . . . dwell as having | refuges in yourselves, resorts in your- | selves and not elsewhere. . . . Who- | ever shall dwell as having refuges in | themselves . . . shall reach to the | limit of darkness, whoever are desir- | ous of learning." | GAUTAMA BUDDHA TO ANANDA | *The Life of Buddha,* by Edward J. Thomas | (Kegan Paul. 1931)'; [viii] blank; [ix] 'IN THE MILL'; [x] blank; 1–158 text (signed and dated: 'JOHN MASEFIELD | *Oxford, 1941.*')

Paper: wove paper

Running title: '*In the Mill*' (22mm.) on both verso and recto, pp.2–158

Binding: beige cloth. On spine, in brown: 'IN THE | MILL | MASEFIELD | MACMILLAN' (all width centred). On upper cover, in brown: illustration of mill with four smoking chimneys and shrubs: 55 × 40mm. Lower cover: blank. Top edge stained brown, others trimmed. Binding measurements: 208 × 136mm. (covers), 208 × 37mm. (spine). End-papers: wove paper.

Publication date: published, according to Handley-Taylor, 5 August 1941

Price: $2.00

Contents:
as for A131(a)

Notes:
The text commences with a drop-capital.

Wight notes a binding in 'pale pink cloth' with lettering (and illustration) 'in purple'.

The publishing agreement for this volume between Masefield and Macmillan was dated 21 April 1941 (see Archives of The Society of Authors). The agreement refers to 'a licence to publish in volume form in the United States of America and Canada a work the subject or title of which is IN THE MILL'.

Copies seen: private collection (PWE); University of Pennsylvania Library (PR 6025 A77 Z53 1941)

Reprinted:
'Reprinted'   [first edition, second impression]   Oct 1941

A132 CONQUER   **1941**

A132(a) First English edition (1941)

CONQUER | A TALE OF THE NIKA REBELLION IN BYZANTIUM | BY | JOHN MASEFIELD | [publisher's device of a windmill with 'W' and 'H'] | [rule, 68mm.] | WILLIAM HEINEMANN LTD | LONDON :: TORONTO (All width centred)

Bibliographies: Handley-Taylor p.62, Wight 104

Collation: [π]⁸ A–H⁸; signatures right foot of page; 72 leaves; 184 × 123mm.; [i–vi] 1–138

Page contents: [i] half-title: 'CONQUER | A TALE OF THE NIKA REBELLION IN BYZANTIUM'; [ii] '*ALSO BY JOHN MASEFIELD* | PLAYS: | [12 titles listed] | POETRY: | [16 titles listed] | FICTION: GENERAL: | [12 titles of fiction listed with 11 titles of general works]'; [iii] title-page; [iv] 'FIRST PUBLISHED 1941 | PRINTED IN GREAT BRITAIN AT THE WINDMILL PRESS | KINGSWOOD, SURREY'; [v] 'NOTE | THIS story is an account of the very famous Faction | struggle which nearly caused the complete destruc- | tion of Byzantium in the first week of the year 532. | [new paragraph] The tale makes no reference whatever to any living | person or existing institution. When it refers to the | Dinner-Green and Sea-Blue Factions it alludes to | Byzantine parties long since happily extinct, and to no | existing parties wearing those or any other colours. | [new paragraph] The book is fiction, based on the histories of the | sixth century.'; [vi] blank; 1–138 text

Paper: wove paper

Running title: 'CONQUER' (16mm.) on verso; 'A TALE OF THE NIKA REBELLION IN BYZANTIUM' (77mm.) on recto (off-set to the left), pp.2–138

Binding: blue cloth. On spine, in gold: 'CONQUER | [ornament] | JOHN | MASEFIELD | HEINEMANN' (all width centred). On upper cover, in blind: 'CONQUER | JOHN MASEFIELD' (within blind ruled border: 184 × 115mm.) On lower cover, in blind: publisher's device of a windmill (ranged lower right). All edges trimmed. Binding measurements: 190 × 124mm. (covers), 190 × 29mm. (spine). End-papers: wove paper.

Publication date: the sales ledger preserved in the Heinemann Archive suggests publication on 6 October 1941 in an edition of 7500 copies

Price: 6s.

Contents:
Conquer ('There is no City on earth to be compared with Byzantium, whether for beauty or power...')

Notes:
A novel with no chapter divisions. The novel has an obvious kinship with the earlier novel entitled *Basilissa* (A128) and connections to *Badon Parchments* (A152).

C.S. Evans acknowledged receipt of the typescript (and noted co-operation with the American publishers) at the beginning of July 1941:

> The typescript of CONQUER has reached me. I will have proofs prepared as soon as may be so that they may go forward to Macmillans.

(C.S. Evans, letter to John Masefield, 8 July 1941)
(HRHRC, MS (Masefield, J.) Recip William Heinemann Ltd.)

Proofs were sent (together with the return of the manuscript) the following month (see B.F. Oliver, letter to John Masefield, 1 August 1941) (HRHRC, MS (Masefield, J.) Recip William Heinemann Ltd.)

The publishing agreement for this title between Masefield and Heinemann was dated 31 August 1941 (see Archives of The Society of Authors). The agreement refers to a publication price of 6s.

The text commences with a drop-capital.

Copies seen: private collection (PWE); BL (12643.a.61) stamped 6 OCT 1941

A132(b) First American edition (1941)

CONQUER | A TALE OF THE NIKA REBELLION IN BYZANTIUM | BY | JOHN MASEFIELD | NEW YORK | THE MACMILLAN COMPANY | 1941
(All width centred)

Bibliographies: Handley-Taylor p.62, Wight 104a

Collation: [A–K]⁸ (J not used); 80 leaves; 202 × 133mm.; [i–x] 1–147 [148–50]

Page contents: [i–ii] blank; [iii] half-title: 'CONQUER | A TALE OF THE NIKA REBELLION IN BYZANTIUM'; [iv] '*ALSO BY JOHN MASEFIELD* | PLAYS: | [12 titles listed] | POETRY: | [16 titles listed] | FICTION: GENERAL: | [12 titles of fiction listed with 11 titles of general works]'; [v] title-page; [vi] '*Copyright, 1941, by* | JOHN MASEFIELD. | [rule] | All rights reserved–no part of this book | may be reproduced in any form without | permission in writing from the publisher, | except by a reviewer who wishes to quote brief | passages in connection with a review written | for inclusion in magazine or newspaper. | [rule] | *Set up and electrotyped.* | FIRST PRINTING. | PRINTED IN THE UNITED STATES OF AMERICA | AMERICAN BOOK-STRATFORD PRESS, INC., NEW YORK'; [vii] 'NOTE | THIS STORY IS AN ACCOUNT of the very famous Fac- | tion struggle which nearly caused the complete | destruction of Byzantium in the first week of the | year 532. | [new paragraph] The tale makes no reference whatever to any | living person or existing institution. When it re-| fers to the Dinner-Green and Sea-Blue Factions it | alludes to Byzantine parties long since happily ex- | tinct, and to no existing parties wearing those or | any other colours. | [new paragraph] The book is fiction, based on the histories of the | sixth century.'; [viii] blank; [ix] 'CONQUER | A TALE OF THE NIKA REBELLION IN BYZANTIUM'; [x] blank; 1–147 text; [148–50] blank

Paper: wove paper

Running title: 'CONQUER' (16mm.) on verso; 'A TALE OF THE NIKA REBELLION IN BYZANTIUM' (81mm.) on recto (off-set to the left), pp.2–147

Binding: navy blue cloth. On spine, in gold: '[ornamental wavy pattern with rule] | [rule] | [ornamental 'rope' pattern] | [panel with 'CONQUER' in blind] | [ornamental 'rope' pattern] | [rule] | [ornamental wavy pattern with rule] | MASEFIELD | MACMILLAN | [point]' (all width centred). Covers: blank. All edges trimmed. Binding measurements: 209 × 134mm. (covers), 209 × 32mm. (spine). End-papers: wove paper.

Publication date: published, according to Handley-Taylor, 28 October 1941

Price: $2.00

Contents:
as for A132(a)

Notes:
As noted for several other Macmillan editions, the publicity material in the preliminaries that lists Masefield's work (appearing on p.[iv]) bears a marked similarity to that present in the Heinemann edition. Moreover, titles as cited here are those of English editions (separate editions of Masefield's Racine translations and *St. George and the Dragon*, for example).

A publishing agreement for this title between Masefield and Macmillan was dated 26 August 1941 (see Archives of The Society of Authors). The agreement refers to 'a licence to publish in volume form in the United States of America and Canada a work the subject or title of which is his new Byzantine book, to contain approximately 40,000 words, at present called Conquer'.

Copies seen: private collection (ROV)

A133 DEAD NED AND LIVE AND KICKING NED 1941

A133(a) First American edition (1941)

DEAD NED | *and* | LIVE AND | KICKING NED | by | JOHN MASEFIELD | NEW YORK | THE MACMILLAN COMPANY | 1941
(All width centred)

Bibliographies: Handley-Taylor [unrecorded], Wight [unrecorded]

Collation: [A-Z]¹⁶ [AA]⁸ [BB]¹⁶ (J, V and W not used); 392 leaves; 203 × 134mm.; [i–xii] 1–289 [290] [i–iv] [1–4] 5–253 [254] [1–4] 5–224

Page contents: [i] title-page; [ii] '*Copyright, 1938 and 1939, by* | JOHN MASEFIELD. | [rule] | All rights reserved–no part of this book | may be reproduced in any form without | permission in writing from the publisher, | except by a reviewer who wishes to quote brief | passages in connection with a review written | for inclusion in magazine or newspaper. | *Combined volume "Dead Ned" and "Live | and Kicking Ned," published 1941.* | PRINTED IN THE UNITED STATES OF AMERICA'; [iii] half-title: 'DEAD NED'; [iv] '[publisher's device] | THE MACMILLAN COMPANY | [two lines listing six cities, separated by four points]'; [v] 'DEAD NED | *The Autobiography of a Corpse* | *Who recovered Life within the Coast of Dead Ned* | *And came to what Fortune you shall hear* | by | JOHN MASEFIELD | NEW YORK | THE MACMILLAN COMPANY | 1941'; [vi] '*Copyright, 1938, by* | JOHN MASEFIELD. | [rule] | All rights reserved–no part of this book | may be reproduced in any form without | permission in writing from the publisher, | except by a reviewer who wishes to quote brief | passages in connection with a review written | for inclusion in magazine or newspaper. | *Set up and printed. Published October, 1938.* | *Reprinted October, 1938.* | *Reprinted October, 1938; November 1938;* | *May, 1941; June, 1941; August, 1941.* | [rule] | *Printed in the United States of America*'; [vii] 'TO | MY WIFE'; [viii] blank; [ix] '"And since it's only Ned, | Who was alive and is dead, | There's no more to be said."'; [x] blank; [xi] 'DEAD NED'; [xii] blank; 1–289 text of 'Dead Ned'; [290] blank; [i] half-title: 'LIVE AND KICKING NED'; [ii] '[publisher's device] | THE MACMILLAN COMPANY | [two lines listing six cities, separated by four points]'; [iii] 'LIVE AND | KICKING NED | by | JOHN MASEFIELD | NEW YORK | THE MACMILLAN COMPANY | 1941'; [iv] '*Copyright, 1939, by* | JOHN MASEFIELD. | [rule] | All rights reserved–no part of this book | may be reproduced in any form without | permission in writing from the publisher, | except by a reviewer who wishes to quote brief | passages in connection with a review written | for inclusion in magazine or newspaper. | *Set up and printed. Published October, 1939.* | *Reprinted November, 1939; December, 1939;* | *August, 1941.* | [rule] | *Printed in the United States of America*'; [1] 'LIVE NED'; [2] blank; [3] 'While at sea, I noticed a fitting on a sail, and asked a | seaman what it was. | [new paragraph] He said, "A reef-tackle." | [new paragraph] I asked, "What good is it?" | [new paragraph] He said, "In reefing, it takes up the weight of the sail, | so that you can pass your ear-rings." | [new paragraph] I have called this volume of my story "The Reef-Tackle" | because it takes up the weight of my life during a blowy | and anxious time. How I passed my ear-rings will be mat- | ter for another tale.'; [4] blank; 5–253 text of 'Live Ned'; [254] blank; [1] 'KICKING NED'; [2] blank; [3] 'I sometimes call this part of my tale "The Skysail" or, | perhaps, after all, "The Trust-to-God." | [new paragraph] Once, in the *Albicore*, as we ran in the Trade, and I ad- | mired the tower of sail upon the mainmast, a seaman said | to me, "Ah, sir, but we ought to set a skysail, above the | royal, there." | [new paragraph] "But a little sail, so far up, cannot do much good," I | said. | [new paragraph] "No, sir," he answered, "but nothing sets a ship off, like | a skysail. It finishes her off." | [new paragraph] "Do sailors ever set anything even above a skysail?" I | asked. | [new paragraph] "Some set a Trust-to-God," he said. "Not many have | one; but it's a very fine thing, a Trust-to-God. It finishes | a ship off, even better."'; [4] blank; 5–224 text of 'Kicking Ned'

Paper: wove paper

Running title: '[rule] | *DEAD NED* [18mm.] | [rule]' on verso; '[rule] | *THE AUTOBIOGRAPHY OF A CORPSE* [65mm.] | [rule]' on recto, pp.2–289; '[rule] | *LIVE NED* [17mm.] | [rule]' on both verso and recto, pp.6–253; '[rule] | *KICKING NED* [24mm.] | [rule]' on both verso and recto, pp.6–224

Binding: green cloth. On spine, in silver: 'DEAD | NED | [six-point star] | [six-point star] | LIVE & | KICKING NED | MASEFIELD | MACMILLAN | [point] — [point]' (lines 1–7 justified on left margin with lines 8–10 width centred). On upper cover, in silver: illustration of sailor with telescope in the rigging of a ship 98 × 47mm. Lower cover: blank. All edges trimmed. Binding measurements: 209 × 136mm. (covers), 209 × 52mm. (spine). End-papers: tan wove paper.

Publication date: published, according to Macmillan advertisement *The Publisher's Weekly* (New York) 20 September 1941, on 21 October 1941

Price: $3.00

Contents:

Dead Ned ('I am going to set down my story, while I remain young enough to tell the truth.')
Live Ned ('If you have not read my story, let me tell you that I am a doctor, the son of...')
Kicking Ned ('We went out from the house, and presently reached the steps which led to the platform...')

Notes:

A combined edition of A124(a) and A127(b). Features noted for these two editions are therefore present here.

George P. Brett, Jr. apparently suggested a combined volume on 18 August 1939. Masefield also tried to interest Heinemann in such a volume. C.S. Evans wrote:

> I certainly want if possible to publish DEAD NED and LIVE AND KICKING NED in one volume, but the spring is too early and I think that a better time would be September. Both books are still selling… I think that we ought to get all the milk we can out of these two cocoanuts [*sic*] before we grow another, don't you?
>
> (C.S. Evans, letter to John Masefield, 19 January 1940)
> (HRHRC, MS (Masefield, J.) Recip William Heinemann Ltd.)

Despite this, Heinemann were never to published the combined volume. Brett however cabled Masefield on 8 May 1941 stating that he would like to publish the volume in the fall of 1941 and requested Masefield's permission to announce such a volume during the following week. Masefield replied on the same day and Brett confirmed the arrangement in a letter dated 9 May 1941 (see Archives of The Society of Authors). (See HRHRC MS (Masefield, J.) Recip The Macmillan Company for letter dated 18 August 1939 and cable dated 8 May 1941).

Copies seen: private collection (PWE); HRHRC (TEMP M377 DE 1941) inscribed 'For Con | from Jan. | 24 Nov. 1941.'

A134 SHOPPING IN OXFORD 1941

A134(a) First English edition (limited signed edition) (1941)

JOHN MASEFIELD | [five-point star] | SHOPPING IN | OXFORD | [five-point star] | [publisher's device of a windmill with 'W' and 'H' all within ruled border: 15 × 15mm.] | LONDON | WILLIAM HEINEMANN LTD | 1941 (All width centred)

Bibliographies: Handley-Taylor p.62, Wight 101

Collation: [A]¹⁰; 10 leaves; 216 × 139mm.; [i–iv] 1–14 [15–16]

Page contents: [i] half-title: 'SHOPPING IN | OXFORD'; [ii] *This Edition, numbered and signed by the | Author, is limited to 500 copies for sale in | Great Britain and Ireland. | No..............*'; [iii] title-page; [iv] 'PRINTED IN GREAT BRITAIN AT THE WINDMILL PRESS | KINGSWOOD, SURREY'; 1–14 text; [15–16] blank

Paper: laid paper (no watermark), chain-lines 28mm. apart

Running title: none

Binding: blue cloth. On spine, reading lengthways down spine from head, in gold: 'JOHN MASEFIELD SHOPPING IN OXFORD'. On upper cover, in gold: 'SHOPPING IN OXFORD | JOHN | MASEFIELD'. Lower cover: blank. All edges trimmed. Binding measurements: 221 × 139mm. (covers), 221 × 15mm. (spine). End-papers: grey wove paper (the free end-papers are bound with the single gathering).

Publication date: the sales ledger preserved in the Heinemann Archive suggests publication on 20 October 1941 in an edition of 500 copies (see notes)

Price: 5s.

Contents:
Shopping in Oxford ('Twenty-four years ago, I wandered down')

Notes:
Single volume publication of a poem later reprinted in *Gautama the Enlightened and other verse* (A135).

Page numbers appear within square brackets. Thus, [1], [2], etc.

The text commences with a drop-capital.

C.S. Evans wrote to Masefield about this poem at the beginning of August 1941:

> I read SHOPPING IN OXFORD last night and enjoyed it very much. I am in London today but I will take it to the press with me tomorrow and work out a plan for its production and write to you again.
> (C.S. Evans, letter to John Masefield, 7 August 1941)
> (HRHRC, MS (Masefield, J.) Recip William Heinemann Ltd.)

The next letter suggests that Masefield had sent the text of the complete volume later published as *Gautama the Enlightened* (see A135):

> Here are three sets of galley proofs of SHOPPING IN OXFORD. I'll write to you tomorrow about the Limited Edition. I do not know in which order you would like the poems printed...
> (C.S. Evans, letter to John Masefield, 26 August 1941)
> (HRHRC, MS (Masefield, J.) Recip William Heinemann Ltd.)

As Evans went into the detail of a limited edition (of 'Shopping in Oxford' alone) a decision was, presumably, taken to re-name the collection of poems. A different setting of text was noted on 28 August:

> I think that if we are going to produce a limited edition of 500 copies of SHOPPING IN OXFORD we had better set it differently from the volume containing the three poems... I am hoping to find enough buckram cloth to bind the copies but I do not know whether I shall have success, for it is almost unobtainable. If I cannot get buckram we will bind it in ordinary blue cloth.
> (C.S. Evans, letter to John Masefield, 28 August 1941)
> (HRHRC, MS (Masefield, J.) Recip William Heinemann Ltd.)

The proofs of this edition were sent to Masefield at the beginning of September:

> I have pleasure in sending you proofs of SHOPPING IN OXFORD which we have set up for the Limited Edition.
> (B.F. Oliver, letter to John Masefield, 5 September 1941)
> (HRHRC, MS (Masefield, J.) Recip William Heinemann Ltd.)

512 copies of 'the title sheets' for Masefield's signature were sent on 24 September (see B.F. Oliver, letter to John Masefield, 24 September 1941) (HRHRC, MS (Masefield, J.) Recip William Heinemann Ltd.)

The publishing agreement for this title between Masefield and Heinemann was dated 16 September 1941 (see Archives of The Society of Authors). The agreement refers to a publication price of 5s.

Noting the success of the edition, Evans wrote:

> I am afraid I can send you no more copies of the limited edition of SHOPPING IN OXFORD for every copy has been sold: indeed we had severely to ration the booksellers. I wish now that we had charged 7/6d. for it, (said he, greedily).
>
> (C.S. Evans, letter to John Masefield, 10 November 1941)
> (HRHRC, MS (Masefield, J.) Recip William Heinemann Ltd.)

Handley-Taylor cites a publication date of 17 March 1941 for this volume. The *English Catalogue of Books* notes a date of October 1941 and this appears to be confirmed by the Heinemann archive and the date stamped in the British Library copy.

Copies seen: private collection (PWE) number 183, signed '183 | John Masefield.' on p.[ii]; BL (11656.b.59) number 242 crossed out and replaced by 'out of series', signed '242 | John Masefield.' on p.[ii] stamped 20 OCT 1941

A134(b) Second English edition ([1948])

JOHN MASEFIELD | SHOPPING IN | OXFORD
(All width centred)

Bibliographies: Handley-Taylor [unrecorded], Wight [unrecorded]

Collation: [A]^{12}; 12 leaves; 213 × 136mm.; [1–24]

Page contents: [1] half-title: 'SHOPPING IN | OXFORD'; [2] blank; [3] title-page; [4] blank; [5–21] text; [22–24] blank

Paper: laid paper (no watermark), chain-lines 26–27mm. apart

Running title: none

Binding: beige wrappers. Spine: blank. On upper wrapper, in orange: 'SHOPPING IN OXFORD | JOHN | MASEFIELD'. Lower wrapper: blank. All edges trimmed. Binding measurements: 218 × 142mm. (wrappers), 218 × 3mm. (spine). The wrappers extend beyond the edges of the internal leaves.

Publication date: between August and December 1948

Price: copies were not for sale

Contents:
Shopping in Oxford ('Thirty-one years ago, I wandered down')

Notes:
There are extensive substantive revisions in this edition (obvious from the re-written first line).

The text is in italics throughout.

A letter from Masefield tentatively dated 13 February 1946 to Louisa Callender, of the Heinemann firm, suggests a new edition of the poem:

> Some years ago, you printed a little book for me, called Shopping in Oxford, which was later bound-up with some other verse. I would be glad to know, if you could consider printing an amended and enlarged version of the poem, perhaps 6 pages longer, as a little book, perhaps with paper cover? Oxford people might buy it, & it would enable me to say something about a lot of shops omitted from the first issues.
>
> (John Masefield, letter to [Louisa] Callender, [13 February 1946])
> (Archives of William Heinemann)

The reply, dated 15 February 1946, shows that Heinemann were indeed receptive to the idea. However, it appears that Masefield did not immediately implement his revision. When he pursued the matter in April 1948 he received a letter from Callender reporting that the firm 'did not think there would be a large enough demand for the book to justify a reprint at the present time' (see Louisa Callender, letter to John Masefield, 21 April 1946) (Archives of William Heinemann). On 23 April 1946 Heinemann noted that they '…should have no objection to your making a small private issue of the revised version of SHOPPING IN OXFORD for your own use.' (see Louisa Callender, letter to John Masefield, 23 April 1948) (HRHRC, MS (Masefield, J.) Recip. William Heinemenn Ltd.) Heinemann's decision therefore led Masefield to approach Hall the Printer in Oxford. A letter from Edward Colegrove, managing director of the firm, preserved in the received correspondence files of Masefield accompanies four duplicate copies of a single sheet showing a specimen printing of the first stanza. The letter states:

> …as requested we have very much pleasure in sending you examples of our italic types… If you will be good enough to let us know which of the samples you like best we will proceed with the work.
>
> (Edward Colegrove, letter to John Masefield, 13 August 1948)
> (HRHRC, MS (Masefield, J.) Recip Hall the Printer Limited)

Copies seen: private collection (ROV) inscribed 'For Joan Stevenson, | from John Masefield. | Christmas. 1948.'; ULL (Special Collections) inscribed [for Rudolf Sauter] 'With love | J. + C.'; Library of The John Masefield Society (Eileen Colwell Collection) inscribed 'For Eileen. | from John Masefield. | With all happy thoughts + thanks | + greetings for Christmas + the | coming year. | Decr. 1948.'

A135 GAUTAMA THE ENLIGHTENED · 1941

A135(a) First English edition (1941)

GAUTAMA | THE ENLIGHTENED | *and other verse* | BY | JOHN MASEFIELD | [publisher's device of a windmill with 'W' and 'H'] | [rule, 67mm.] | WILLIAM HEINEMANN LTD | LONDON :: TORONTO
(All width centred)

Bibliographies: Handley-Taylor p.63, Wight 105

Collation: [A]⁸ B–C⁸ D¹⁰; D2 is also signed; signatures right foot of page; 34 leaves; 184 × 123mm.; [i–vi] 1–62

Page contents: [i–ii] blank; [iii] half-title: 'GAUTAMA THE ENLIGHTENED | *and other verse*'; [iv] '*ALSO BY JOHN MASEFIELD* | PLAYS: | [12 titles listed] | POETRY: | [16 titles listed] | FICTION: GENERAL: | [14 titles of fiction listed with 11 titles of general works]'; [v] title-page; [vi] 'FIRST PUBLISHED 1941 | PRINTED IN GREAT BRITAIN AT THE WINDMILL PRESS | KINGSWOOD, SURREY'; 1–62 text

Paper: wove paper

Running title: none

Binding: blue cloth. On spine, reading lengthways up spine, from foot, in gold: 'GAUTAMA THE ENLIGHTENED – JOHN MASEFIELD'; horizontally at foot of spine: publisher's device of a windmill. Covers: blank. All edges trimmed. Binding measurements: 188 × 123mm. (covers), 188 × 18mm. (spine). End-papers: wove paper.

Publication date: the sales ledger preserved in the Heinemann Archive suggests publication on 17 November 1941

Price: 5s.

Contents:
Gautama the Enlightened ('*Invocation* | O Master of the Calmness, come')
Shopping in Oxford ('Twenty-four years ago, I wandered down')
Mahdama's Quest ('The moon had kept the world awake,')
An Art Worker ('When St John's chimes for Ten')

Notes:
A volume containing four poems, including that of the title and *Shopping in Oxford* (A134). Only the latter was included in the 1946 collected poems volume entitled *Poems*. See *Shopping in Oxford* for notes on the chronology of these two works (and a possible earlier title).

C.S. Evans informed Masefield of the publication date on 5 November (and noted co-operation with the American publishers):

> I am sending separately an advance copy of GAUTAMA THE ENLIGHTENED which we are publishing on the 17th. A copy has been air mailed to the Macmillan Company in New York today.
>
> (C.S. Evans, letter to John Masefield, 5 November 1941)
> (HRHRC, MS (Masefield, J.) Recip William Heinemann Ltd.)

The publishing agreement for this title between Masefield and Heinemann was dated 16 September 1941 (see Archives of The Society of Authors). The agreement refers to a publication price of 5s.

Writing in the 'Epilogue' to *Letters to Reyna* (see E3), William Buchan reports that 'in later life [Masefield] came to study Buddhism'.

Page numbers appear within square brackets. Thus, [1], [2], etc.

Each poem commences with a drop-capital.

Copies seen: private collection (PWE); BL (11657.b.78) stamped 17 NOV 1941

A135(b) First American edition (1941)

GAUTAMA | THE ENLIGHTENED | *and other verse* | BY | JOHN MASEFIELD | NEW YORK | THE MACMILLAN COMPANY | 1941
(All width centred)

Bibliographies: Handley-Taylor p.63, Wight 105a

Collation: [A–D]⁸; 32 leaves; 212 × 140mm.; [i–vi] 1–7 [8–10] 11–21 [22–24] 25–35 [36–38] 39–58

Page contents: [i] half-title: 'GAUTAMA THE ENLIGHTENED | *and other verse*'; [ii] '*ALSO BY JOHN MASEFIELD* | PLAYS: | [12 titles listed] | POETRY: | [16 titles listed] | FICTION: GENERAL: | [14 titles of fiction listed with 10 titles of general works]';

[iii] title-page; [iv] '*Copyright, 1941, by* | JOHN MASEFIELD. | [rule] | All rights reserved–no part of this book | may be reproduced in any form without | permission in writing from the publisher, | except by a reviewer who wishes to quote brief | passages in connection with a review written | for inclusion in magazine or newspaper. | FIRST PRINTING. | PRINTED IN THE UNITED STATES OF AMERICA | AMERICAN BOOK-STRATFORD PRESS, INC., NEW YORK'; [v] 'CONTENTS' (four individual items listed with page references); [vi] blank; 1–7 text of 'Gautama the Enlightened'; [8] blank; [9] 'SHOPPING IN OXFORD'; [10] blank; 11–21 text of 'Shopping in Oxford'; [22] blank; [23] 'MAHDAMA'S QUEST'; [24] blank; 25–35 text of 'Mahdama's Quest'; [36] blank; [37] 'AN ART WORKER'; [38] blank; 39–58 text of 'An Art Worker'

Paper: wove paper

Running title: none

Binding: brown cloth. On spine, reading lengthways down spine from head, in green: 'JOHN MASEFIELD [point] Gautama the Enlightened MACMILLAN [point]'. Covers: blank. All edges trimmed. Binding measurements: 218 × 141mm. (covers), 218 × 20mm. (spine). End-papers: wove paper.

Publication date: published, according to Handley-Taylor, 16 December 1941

Price: $1.60

Contents:
as for A135(a)

Notes:
Page numbers appear within square brackets. Thus, [1], [2], etc.

Each poem commences with a drop-capital.

As noted for several other Macmillan editions, the publicity material in the preliminaries that lists Masefield's work (appearing on p.[ii]) bears a marked similarity to that present in the Heinemann edition. Moreover, titles as cited here are those of English editions (separate editions of Masefield's Racine translations and *St. George and the Dragon*, for example). Note, however, that there are only ten titles listed here under the 'General' heading. In A135(a) there are eleven titles. The omitted title in the American edition is *The Nine Days Wonder*.

The publishing agreement for this volume between Masefield and Macmillan was dated 21 November 1941 (see Archives of The Society of Authors). The agreement refers to 'a licence to publish in volume form in the United States of America and Canada a work the subject or title of which is GAUTAMA THE ENLIGHTENED'.

Copies seen: private collection (ROV)

A136 NATALIE MAISIE AND PAVILASTUKAY   1942

A136(a) First English edition (1942)

NATALIE MAISIE | AND | PAVILASTUKAY | *TWO TALES IN VERSE* | BY | JOHN MASEFIELD | [ornament] | [publisher's device of a windmill with 'W' and 'H'] | [rule, 68mm.] | WILLIAM HEINEMANN LTD | LONDON :: TORONTO
(All width centred)

Bibliographies: Handley-Taylor p.63, Wight 106

Collation: [A]⁸ B-C⁸ D⁶; D2 is also signed; signatures right foot of page with 'N.M.' at left foot on all signed pages; 30 leaves; 185 × 121mm.; [i–iv] 1–56

Page contents: [i] half-title and dedication: 'NATALIE MAISIE | AND | PAVILASTUKAY | [rule] | TO | MY WIFE | [rule]'; [ii] '*ALSO BY JOHN MASEFIELD* | PLAYS: | [12 titles listed] | POETRY: | [17 titles listed] | FICTION: GENERAL: | [14 titles of fiction listed with 11 titles of general works]'; [iii] title-page; [iv] 'FIRST PUBLISHED 1942 | WAR ECONOMY | [rule] | THIS BOOK IS PRODUCED IN COMPLETE | CONFORMITY WITH THE AUTHORISED | ECONOMY STANDARDS | PRINTED IN GREAT BRITAIN AT THE WINDMILL PRESS | KINGSWOOD, SURREY'; 1–56 text

Paper: wove paper

Running title: none

Binding: blue cloth. On spine, reading lengthways up spine, from foot, in gold: 'Natalie Maisie & Pavilastukay [ornament] John Masefield'; horizontally at foot of spine: publisher's device of a windmill. Covers: blank. All edges trimmed. Binding measurements: 190 × 124mm. (covers), 190 × 14mm. (spine). End-papers: wove paper.

Publication date: the sales ledger preserved in the Heinemann Archive suggests publication on 13 April 1942 in an edition of 2500 copies

Price: 6s.

Contents:
Natalie Maisie ('The deed described in this tale, the hiding of a girl by her foster-parents from the pursuit...')
Pavilastukay ('Jonnox was English, educated, male,')

Notes:

C.S. Evans was apparently eager to receive the text of this work. A letter reads '…please send the new book of verse as soon as you can.' (see C.S. Evans, letter to John Masefield, 10 November 1941) (HRHRC, MS (Masefield, J.) Recip William Heinemann Ltd.) The typescript was acknowledged during January (see Louisa Callender, letter to John Masefield, 16 January 1942) (HRHRC, MS (Masefield, J.) Recip William Heinemann Ltd.) In writing about the poems, Evans notes immediate setting of type:

> I read your two poems, NATALIE MAISIE and PAVILASTUKAY, at once (and enjoyed them) and gave them straight to the printer…

(C.S. Evans, letter to John Masefield, 4 February 1942)
(HRHRC, MS (Masefield, J.) Recip William Heinemann Ltd.)

A 'corrected proof' was acknowledged on 23 February (see B.F. Oliver, letter to John Masefield, 23 February 1942) (HRHRC, MS (Masefield, J.) Recip William Heinemann Ltd.)

The publishing agreement for this title between Masefield and Heinemann was dated 31 March 1942 (see Archives of The Society of Authors). The agreement refers to a publication price of 6s.

Masefield provides information regarding pronunciation of the title of the second poem in a note preceeding the text of the poem. He states: 'the name is accented on the third syllable; it is supposed to mean *Ruins in the Wood.*'

The first poem is sub-titled 'A Tale of The Emperor Peter The Great of Russia'.

Page numbers appear within square brackets. Thus, [1], [2], etc.

Wight states that the text runs from pp.1–156. This is an error.

Copies seen: private collection (PWE); BL (11656.n.4) stamped 14 APR 1942

A136(b) First American edition (1942)

NATALIE MAISIE | AND | PAVILASTUKAY | *TWO TALES IN VERSE* | BY | JOHN MASEFIELD | [ornament] | NEW YORK | THE MACMILLAN COMPANY | 1942
(All width centred)

Bibliographies: Handley-Taylor p.63, Wight 106a

Collation: [A-E]⁸; 40 leaves; 210 × 137mm.; [i–viii] 1–69 [70–72]

Page contents: [i] half-title: 'NATALIE MAISIE | AND | PAVILASTUKAY'; [ii] '*ALSO BY JOHN MASEFIELD* | PLAYS: | [12 titles listed] | POETRY: | [17 titles listed] | FICTION: GENERAL: | [14 titles of fiction listed with 11 titles of general works]'; [iii] title-page; [iv] '*Copyright, 1942, by* | JOHN MASEFIELD. | [rule] | All rights reserved–no part of this book | may be reproduced in any form without | permission in writing from the publisher, | except by a reviewer who wishes to quote brief | passages in connection with a review written | for inclusion in magazine or newspaper. | [rule] | *Set up and electrotyped. Published June, 1942.* | FIRST PRINTING. | PRINTED IN THE UNITED STATES OF AMERICA | AMERICAN BOOK-STRATFORD PRESS, INC., NEW YORK'; [v] '[rule] | TO | MY WIFE | [rule]'; [vi] blank; [vii] 'NATALIE MAISIE | AND | PAVILASTUKAY'; [viii] blank; 1–69 text; [70–72] blank

Paper: wove paper

Running title: none

Binding: navy blue cloth. On spine, reading lengthways down spine from head, in pink: 'JOHN MASEFIELD *Natalie Maisie and Pavilastukay* MACMILLAN'. On upper cover, in pink: '*Natalie Maisie and* | *Pavilastukay* | JOHN MASEFIELD'. Lower cover: blank. All edges trimmed. Binding measurements: 217 × 140mm. (covers), 217 × 25mm. (spine). End-papers: wove paper.

Publication date: published, according to Handley-Taylor, 16 June 1942

Price: $2.50

Contents:
as for A136(a)

Notes:
Page numbers appear within square brackets. Thus, [1], [2], etc.

The italics employed for the binding lettering are particularly ornate.

The publishing agreement for this volume between Masefield and Macmillan was dated 2 June 1942 (see Archives of The Society of Authors). The agreement refers to 'a licence to publish in volume form in the United States of America and Canada a work the subject or title of which is NATALIE MAISIE and PAVILASTUKAY'.

Copies seen: private collection (ROV); Columbia University Libraries (Special Collections B825.M377.T54.1942a) inscribed 'For Con | from | Jan. | July. 18. 1942' includes posthumous booklabel

A137 LAND WORKERS

A137(a) First English edition (1942)

LAND WORKERS | *By* | JOHN MASEFIELD | WILLIAM HEINEMANN LTD | LONDON :: TORONTO
(All width centred)

Bibliographies: Handley-Taylor p.63, Wight 107

Collation: [A]¹⁰; 10 leaves; 190 × 123mm.; [i–vi] 1–12 [13–14]

Page contents: [i] upper wrapper; [ii] blank; [iii] half-title: 'LAND WORKERS'; [iv] blank; [v] title-page; [vi] 'FIRST PUBLISHED 1942 | PRINTED IN GREAT BRITAIN AT THE WINDMILL PRESS | KINGSWOOD, SURREY'; 1–12 text; [13] blank; [14] lower wrapper

Paper: wove paper

Running title: none

Binding: wrappers comprise the first and last leaves of the single gathering ([A]1 and [A]10). Spine: blank. On upper wrapper: 'LAND WORKERS | JOHN MASEFIELD | POET LAUREATE | *One Shilling*' (with the exception of the final line, enclosed within ornate border (in green) which includes a double ruled border: 159 × 102mm.) Lower wrapper: blank. All edges trimmed. Binding measurements: 190 × 124mm. (wrappers), 190 × 2mm. (spine).

Publication date: the sales ledger preserved in the Heinemann Archive suggests publication on 30 November 1942 in an edition of 5000 copies

Price: 1s.

Contents:
Land Workers ('Long since, in England's pleasant lands')

Notes:
This short pamphlet describes Victorian workers on the land from Masefield's youth. When the poem was included in the 1946 collected poems volume entitled *Poems* (A148(a)), the poem was significantly longer and entitled 'The Land Workers'. In *Poems* it curiously claims to be extracted from a publication entitled *Wonderings and Land Workers*. Although a volume entitled *Wonderings* was published in 1943, it contained only a single poem.

C.S. Evans evidently intended to publish a volume similar in appearance to *Some Verses to Some Germans* (see 126(a)). His plan to print the upper wrapper in red and black was realised as green and black:

> Thank you for returning your proofs of LAND WORKERS which I have sent on to the printer... I propose to print on Jap Vellum and to print the cover in red and black. ...Our first printing, as in the case of SOME VERSES TO SOME GERMANS will be 5,000 copies.

> (C.S. Evans, letter to John Masefield, 9 October 1942)
> (HRHRC, MS (Masefield, J.) Recip William Heinemann Ltd.)

The publishing agreement for this title between Masefield and Heinemann was dated 26 October 1942 (see Archives of The Society of Authors). The agreement refers to a publication price of 1s.

Page numbers appear within square brackets. Thus, [1], [2], etc.

Wight describes the covers as 'buff'; however, all examined copies use the same glossy wove paper for the covers as the contents. Moreover, Wight states that the text of the poem is printed on the 'back cover' and this is not the case.

Copies seen: private collection (PWE); private collection (ROV); BL (11657.c.63) bound, stamped 30 NOV 1942

A137(b) First American edition (1943)

LAND WORKERS | *By* | JOHN MASEFIELD | NEW YORK | THE MACMILLAN COMPANY | 1943
(All width centred)

Bibliographies: Handley-Taylor p.63, Wight 107a

Collation: [A]⁸; 8 leaves; 187 × 127mm.; [i–iv] 1–12

Page contents: [i] upper wrapper; [ii] blank; [iii] title-page; [iv] '*Copyright, 1943, by* | JOHN MASEFIELD. | [rule] | All rights reserved–no part of this book | may be reproduced in any form without | permission in writing from the publisher, | except by a reviewer who wishes to quote brief | passages in connection with a review written | for inclusion in magazine or newspaper. | [rule] | FIRST PRINTING. | PRINTED IN THE UNITED STATES OF AMERICA | AMERICAN BOOK-STRATFORD PRESS, INC., NEW YORK'; 1–12 text

Paper: wove paper

Running title: none

Binding: wrappers comprise the first and last leaves of the single gathering ([A]1 and [A]8). Spine: blank. On upper wrapper: 'LAND WORKERS | JOHN MASEFIELD | POET LAUREATE' (enclosed within ornate border which includes a triple ruled border: 161 × 102mm.) Lower wrapper constitutes p.12 of the text. All edges trimmed. Binding measurements: 187 × 127mm. (wrappers), 187 × 2mm. (spine).

Publication date: published, according to Handley-Taylor, 9 February 1943

Price: $0.90

Contents:
as for A137(a)

Notes:
Page numbers appear within square brackets. Thus, [1], [2], etc.

A publishing agreement for this title between Masefield and Macmillan was dated 2 March 1943 (see Archives of The Society of Authors). The agreement refers to 'a licence to publish in volume form in the United States of America and Canada a work the subject or title of which is LAND WORKERS'.

Copies seen:
Harvard College Library (Houghton *EC9.M377.942la)

A138 A GENERATION RISEN   1942

A138(a) First English edition (1942)

A | GENERATION | RISEN | *by* | JOHN MASEFIELD | *and* | EDWARD SEAGO | COLLINS | 48 PALL MALL LONDON
(All width centred)

Bibliographies: Handley-Taylor p.63, Wight 108

Collation: [A-I]⁴ (see notes); 36 leaves; 276 × 186mm.; [1–3] 4–5 [6] 7–54 [55] 56–72

Page contents: [1] half-title: 'A GENERATION RISEN' (with untitled illustration of soldier in lower right corner); [2] frontispiece: 215 × 132mm., 'The Terrier.'; [3] title-page; 4 '*The Poems*' (24 individual poems listed with page references); 5 '*The Pictures*' (43 individual pictures listed with page references); [6] '[illustration of Spitfire] | Spitfire in Flight. | "*The upward plunge into the joys | Of light wherein the eagles poise.*" | *(from "The Ground Staff," page 36).* | *Also by* | John Masefield and Edward Seago | THE COUNTRY SCENE | TRIBUTE TO BALLET | PRINTED IN GREAT BRITAIN | COLLINS CLEAR-TYPE PRESS : LONDON AND GLASGOW | COPYRIGHT 1942'; 7 'INTRODUCTION' ('Within the lifetime of men now alive, Walt Whitman wrote that "the real war will never...') (headed, '*John Masefield*'); 8–72 text and illustrations

Paper: glossy paper

Running title: none

Binding: grey cloth. Spine: blank (see notes). On upper cover: red panel within ruled border: 30 × 150mm.; the letters appear in blind where the grey cloth appears through the red panel and read 'A GENERATION RISEN | John Masefield and Edward Seago'. Lower cover: blank. All edges trimmed. Binding measurements: 282 × 187mm. (covers), 282 × 18mm. (spine). End-papers: wove paper.

Publication date: published, according to Handley-Taylor, 7 December 1942 in an edition of 5000 copies

Price: 12s.6d.

Contents:
Introduction ('Within the lifetime of men now alive, Walt Whitman wrote that "the real war will never...')
The Paddington Statue ('Twenty-five years ago, another crowd')
The Station ('Dingy, unpainted, dark, war and November,')
Paddington. Mother and Son ('He sees his comrades, and a coming test')
Two Soldiers Waiting ('They lived in the same town, but never met')
Tanks in the Snow ('Like obscene scaly saurs out of the mud,')
Sentries ('Throughout the night, they stare into the dark')
The Searchlight Party ('The midnight sky is loud with wingers')
The Reconnaissance Pilots ('After the bombing, when the men are home,')
Camp Entertainment ('Inside a circus tent which tugs its guy-ropes, bulging,')
The A.L.O. and the Pilot ('What do these unknown warriors talk about?')
The Birds of the Hangar ('Here, in this vast, cool hangar, clean and lit,')
The Ground Staff ('All things that tax the heart and nerve')
Crews Coming Down Gangways ('After long watching of the fatal sea,')
Patrol Ships ('Within these sweating iron tanks')

The Danlayers ('They buoy the channels where the ships may pass,')
The Ship's Cook ('When I was young, ship's cooks were such concoctors')
Mine Sweepers ('These are the men who sweep the Channel's ways')
Here is the Convoy ('They lie alongside, while the winches clatter;')
A Lame Duck ('Somewhere she caught it, but they got her in,')
Dame Myra Hess Playing to the Troops ('See the great pianist is here, the crowd')
Another Upon the Same ('He said, "I have known soldiers from my youth.')
Ambulance Girl ('At midnight, all her day's work being done,')
Women Workers ('In Queen Victoria's early days,')
The Workers on the Land ('I have seen cattle dying in a drought')

Notes:

The last of Masefield's collaborations with Edward Seago (see *The Country Scene* (A123) and *Tribute to Ballet* (A125)). Babington Smith notes the poignancy of this volume of verse (which Masefield describes as 'a tribute to some of the young people who have come forward to save the nation in her danger') since Masefield had lost his son in the war a few months before publication.

Although this edition appears to contain unsigned gatherings, this may be the result of trimming. In some copies p.57 reveals the upper part of a letter 'H', the rest of which has been trimmed.

Only the introduction commences with a drop-capital.

There is no lettering on the spine. This appears to be unique to the first edition, first impression. The second impression includes spine lettering.

The publishing agreement for this title between Masefield and Collins was dated 22 September 1942 (see Archives of The Society of Authors). The agreement refers to Masefield's right '…after not less than two years from the date of publication of the original edition to re-issue all or any of the poems included in the said work in any collected or selected edition of his poems in all parts of the world.' The price of each copy was thought to be 10s.6d. On the same date that the publishing agreement was signed, the publishers acknowledged corrected proofs from Masefield.

A letter from the publishers to Masefield noted:

> …we are having some paper specially made for Seago's drawings, and I hope it will turn out to be really satisfactory. We are hoping to publish in November, but we cannot fix a definite date, until we know when the actual finished copies will be ready.

> (Collins, letter to John Masefield, 21 September 1942)
> (Archives of The Society of Authors)

In November 1946 The Society of Authors received an application to include 'Sentries' in an anthology. Without a copy of the work the Society wrote to Masefield. The author replied that, in the absence of a copy, he would provide the Society with the proofs. He also stated his desire to suppress the book:

> I may come upon proofs of the book containing the verses about sentries, but this latter book is a sort of war book, & I do not want any of it to be reprinted, ever. Still, if I find it, you shall have it, so that you may help in the glad task of suppressing it.

> (John Masefield, letter to [Anne] Munro-Kerr, [November 1946])
> (BL, Add.Mss.56619, f.173)

In further correspondence Masefield stated that:

> The book is, I trust, securely dead; and any oblivion you can add to it will be a charity to the author & the world.

> (John Masefield, letter to [Anne] Munro-Kerr, 14 November [1946])
> (BL, Add.Mss.56619, f.181)

Copies seen: private collection (PWE); BL (11650.i.74) stamped 18 DEC 1942; Bodleian (28001.d.518) stamped 31 DEC 1942

Reprinted:

[first edition, second impression]   Jun 1943

A138(b) First American edition (1943)

A | GENERATION | RISEN | *by* | JOHN MASEFIELD | *and* | EDWARD SEAGO | NEW YORK | THE MACMILLAN COMPANY | 1943
(All width centred)

Bibliographies: Handley-Taylor p.63, Wight 108a

Collation: [A-B]⁸ [C]¹² [D]⁸; 36 leaves; 275 × 184mm.; [1–3] 4–5 [6] 7–54 [55] 56–72

Page contents: [1] half-title: 'A GENERATION RISEN' (with untitled illustration of soldier in lower right corner); [2] frontispiece: 213 × 132mm., 'The Terrier.'; [3] title-page; 4 '*The Poems* | [24 individual poems listed with page references] | COPYRIGHT, 1943, | BY JOHN MASEFIELD AND EDWARD SEAGO | ALL RIGHTS RESERVED | PRINTED IN THE UNITED STATES

OF AMERICA'; 5 *'The Pictures'* (43 individual pictures listed with page references); [6] '[illustration of Spitfire] | Spitfire in Flight. | *"The upward plunge into the joys | Of light wherein the eagles poise."* | (*from "The Ground Staff," page 36*). | *Also by* | John Masefield and Edward Seago | THE COUNTRY SCENE | TRIBUTE TO BALLET'; 7 'INTRODUCTION' ('Within the lifetime of men now alive, Walt Whitman wrote that "the real war will never...') (headed, *'John Masefield'*); 8–72 text and illustrations

Paper: wove paper

Running title: none

Binding: cream cloth. Spine: blank. On upper cover: red panel within ruled border: 29 × 149mm.; the letters appear in blind where the cream cloth appears through the red panel and read 'A GENERATION RISEN | John Masefield and Edward Seago'. Lower cover: blank. All edges trimmed. Binding measurements: 282 × 186mm. (covers), 282 × 23mm. (spine). End-papers: wove paper.

Publication date: published, according to Handley-Taylor, 18 May 1943

Price: $3.00

Contents:
as for A138(a)

Notes:
Only the introduction commences with a drop-capital.

Wight describes the gatherings as [A-1]⁴ [*sic*]. He also describes the binding as 'tan cloth'. Both these errors are presumably due to confusion with A138(a).

A letter from the English publisher, Collins, to Masefield, dated 21 September 1942, notes:

> ...I have written to Macmillans, New York, asking them what they intend to do about the copy-righting of the verses of "A Generation Risen", and, as you suggest, I am arranging for 2 sets of the sheets to be sent out to them for copy-righting purposes... As well as the sheets, we will also send them finished copies of the book for copyrighting purposes.
>
> (Collins, letter to John Masefield, 21 September 1942)
> (Archives of The Society of Authors)

Copies seen: Bodleian (Rec.d.21) inscribed 'For Querie My, | from | John Masefield. | September the 21ˢᵗ 1960 | (Verses made during the late War, to be | printed with Mr Seago's Drawings of | remarkable events and people.)', no dated library stamp; HRHRC (-Q-AC-L M377GE 1943 cop.1); HRHRC (-Q- AC-L M377GE 1943 cop.2)

A139 WONDERINGS   1943

A139(a) First English edition (1943)

WONDERINGS | (*Between One and Six Years*) | *By* | JOHN MASEFIELD | WILLIAM HEINEMANN LTD | LONDON :: TORONTO
(All width centred)

Bibliographies: Handley-Taylor p.63, Wight 109

Collation: [A]⁸ B-C⁸ D⁸; D2 is also signed; signatures right foot of page; 34 leaves; 185 × 121mm.; [i–iv] 1–64

Page contents: [i] half-title: 'WONDERINGS | (BETWEEN ONE AND SIX YEARS)'; [ii] 'TO | MY WIFE'; [iii] title-page; [iv] 'FIRST PUBLISHED 1943 | PRINTED IN GREAT BRITAIN AT THE WINDMILL PRESS | KINGSWOOD, SURREY'; 1–64 text

Paper: wove paper

Running title: none

Binding: blue cloth. On spine, reading lengthways up spine, from foot, in gold: 'WONDERINGS [ornament] John Masefield'; horizontally at foot of spine: '*Heinemann*'. Upper cover: blank. On lower cover, in blind: publisher's device of a windmill (ranged lower right). All edges trimmed. Binding measurements: 189 × 123mm. (covers), 189 × 17mm. (spine). End-papers: wove paper.

Publication date: the sales ledger preserved in the Heinemann Archive suggests publication on 18 October 1943 in an edition of 3000 copies

Price: 5s.

Contents:
Wonderings ('Out of a dateless darkness pictures gleam,')

Notes:
As implied by the sub-title to this volume, the poem tells of Masefield's thoughts and memories 'Between One and Six Years'. This autobiographical poem contains, in the view of Sanford Sternlicht, 'fine poetry in a Wordsworthian way and some evocative childhood perceptions; but... almost no biographical facts'. Other autobiographical writings include *In The Mill* (A131), *New Chum* (A140), *So Long to Learn* (A162) and *Grace Before Ploughing* (A170).

Page numbers appear within square brackets. Thus: [1], [2], etc.

The poem is accompanied by italicised titles in the margin ('*Imaginings*', '*Early Memories*', and '*Delight in water*' for example). The poem comprises, however, a single work.

A letter from C.S. Evans to Masefield reveals that the author was asking for a high royalty. Evans wrote:

> I have studied again my figures on *Wonderings* hoping that by paring everything to the bone I could meet you and pay a royalty of 25%. But costs are so high on the small printing which is all our paper will alow [*sic*] that if I paid you 25% even on a 6/- book I should lose money on every copy sold. It is a difficult position and I hope that in the circumstances you can agree to 20% on 5/-. As I have said, even if I made the book 6/- it would not stand, economically, 25% royalty – and the book is only 72 pages. I believe that the trade and public would look askance at a book of 72 pages for 6/-, even though its contents are of much greater value that [*sic*] many books issued at that price and a higher one.
>
> (C.S. Evans, letter to John Masefield, 24 August 1943)
(Archives of William Heinemann)

Masefield evidently accepted this position and replied:

> Very well, then; let *Wonderings* be a five shilling book, and my royalty be one shilling per copy.
>
> (John Masefield, letter to [C.S.] Evans, [August 1943])
(Archives of William Heinemann)

The publishing agreement for this title between Masefield and Heinemann was dated 9 September 1943 (see Archives of The Society of Authors). The agreement refers to a publication price of 5s.

Copies seen: private collection (PWE); BL (11657.dd.17) stamped 18 OCT 1943

A139(b) First American edition (1943)

WONDERINGS | (BETWEEN ONE AND SIX YEARS) | *BY* | *JOHN MASEFIELD* | NEW YORK | *THE MACMILLAN COMPANY* | 1943
(All width centred)

Bibliographies: Handley-Taylor p.63, Wight 109a

Collation: [A–B]⁸ [C]⁴ [D–E]⁸; 36 leaves; 201 × 133mm.; [i–viii] 1–64

Page contents: [i] half-title: 'WONDERINGS | (BETWEEN ONE AND SIX YEARS)'; [ii] blank; [iii] title-page; [iv] 'COPYRIGHT, 1943, BY | JOHN MASEFIELD | All rights reserved–no part of this book may be | reproduced in any form without permission in writing | from the publisher, except by a reviewer who wishes | to quote brief passages in connection with a review | written for inclusion in magazine or newspaper. | [rule] | First Printing.'; [v] 'TO | MY WIFE'; [vi] blank; [vii] 'WONDERINGS | (BETWEEN ONE AND SIX YEARS)'; [viii] blank; 1–64 text

Paper: wove paper

Running title: none

Binding: dark blue cloth. On spine, reading lengthways down spine from head, in gold: 'MASEFIELD [vertical rule] WONDERINGS [vertical rule] MACMILLAN'. Covers: blank. All edges trimmed. Binding measurements: 209 × 135mm. (covers), 209 × 26mm. (spine). End-papers: wove paper.

Publication date: published, according to Handley-Taylor, 30 November 1943

Price: $1.75

Contents:
as for A139(a)

Notes:
Page numbers appear within square brackets. Thus: [1], [2], etc.

A publishing agreement for this volume between Masefield and Macmillan was dated 21 January 1944 (see Archives of The Society of Authors). The agreement refers to 'a licence to publish in volume form in the United States of America and Canada a work the subject or title of which is WONDERINGS, a short book of verse, 64 pages in length'.

Copies seen: private collection (ROV)

A140 NEW CHUM   1944

A140(a) First English edition (1944)

NEW CHUM | *by* | JOHN MASEFIELD | [publisher's device of a windmill with 'W[point]' and '[point]H'] | [rule, 71mm.] | WILLIAM HEINEMANN LTD | LONDON :: TORONTO
(All width centred)

NEW CHUM

by

JOHN MASEFIELD

WILLIAM HEINEMANN LTD
LONDON   ::   TORONTO

A140(a) title-page

JOHN MASEFIELD

NEW
CHUM

New York
THE MACMILLAN COMPANY
1945

A140(b) title-page

I WANT!   I WANT!

BY

JOHN MASEFIELD, O.M.
POET LAUREATE

INTRODUCTION BY
GEOFFREY FABER

"... *new hope to spring
out of despaire* ..."
—*Paradise Lost*

NATIONAL BOOK COUNCIL
LONDON
1944

A141(a) title-page

I WANT!   I WANT!

BY JOHN MASEFIELD, O.M.
POET LAUREATE

INTRODUCTION BY
GEOFFREY FABER

"... *new hope to spring
out of despaire* ..."
—*Paradise Lost*

THE MACMILLAN COMPANY · NEW YORK
1945

A141(b) title-page

A
MACBETH PRODUCTION

BY

JOHN MASEFIELD

WILLIAM HEINEMANN LTD
LONDON :: TORONTO

A142(a) title-page

THANKS BEFORE GOING

By
JOHN MASEFIELD

Notes on some of the Original Poems
of
Dante Gabriel Rossetti

WILLIAM HEINEMANN LTD
LONDON :: TORONTO

A144(a) title-page

A143(a) upper wrapper

Bibliographies: Handley-Taylor p.63, Wight 111

Collation: [A]⁸ B-M⁸ (J not used); signatures right foot of page; 96 leaves; 185 × 121mm.; [i–iv] 1–186 [187–88]

Page contents: [i] half-title and dedication: 'NEW CHUM | TO | MY WIFE'; [ii] '*ALSO BY JOHN MASEFIELD* | PLAYS: | [12 titles listed] | POETRY: | [18 titles listed] | FICTION: GENERAL: | [14 titles of fiction listed with 11 titles of general works]'; [iii] title-page; [iv] 'FIRST PUBLISHED 1944 | BOOK | PRODUCTION | WAR ECONOMY | STANDARD [lines 2–5 within device of book with lion] | THIS BOOK IS PRODUCED IN COMPLETE | CONFORMITY WITH THE AUTHORISED | ECONOMY STANDARDS | [rule] | PRINTED IN GREAT BRITAIN AT THE WINDMILL PRESS | KINGSWOOD, SURREY'; 1–186 text; [187–88] blank

Paper: wove paper

Running title: none

Binding: blue cloth. On spine, reading lengthways down spine from head, in gold: '*John Masefield* [eight-point star] NEW CHUM [eight-point star] *Heinemann*'. On upper cover, in blind: 'NEW CHUM | JOHN MASEFIELD' (within blind ruled border: 185 × 116mm.) On lower cover, in blind: publisher's device of a windmill (ranged lower right). All edges trimmed. Binding measurements: 190 × 124mm. (covers), 190 × 21mm. (spine). End-papers: wove paper.

Publication date: the sales ledger preserved in the Heinemann Archive suggests publication on 4 December 1944 in an edition of 10000 copies

Price: 9s.6d.

Contents:

New Chum ('I set out to join H.M.S. *Conway* on a fine sunny morning a fortnight after the September term...')

Notes:

Another of Masefield's autobiographical writings (see also *In the Mill* (A131), *Wonderings* (A139), *So Long to Learn* (A162) and *Grace Before Ploughing* (A170)). In the volume Masefield tells of his first term aboard H.M.S. *Conway*, the training ship. See *The Conway* (A109) for an historical study of the ship itself.

The volume commences on p.1 with an epigraph by William Blake: '*Welcome, stranger, to this place,* | *Where Joy doth sit on every bough.*'

Proofs in book form were sent (together with the return of the manuscript) to Masefield on 21 September 1944 (see B.F. Oliver, letter to John Masefield, 21 September 1944) (HRHRC, MS (Masefield, J.) Recip William Heinemann Ltd.) These seem to have caused problems:

> I... am sorry to hear, and see, that the proofs have caused you a lot of trouble. The compositors should not have ignored your copy in regard to words that need initial letters in capitals...

(B.F. Oliver, letter to John Masefield, 29 September 1944)
(HRHRC, MS (Masefield, J.) Recip William Heinemann Ltd.)

The publishing agreement for this title between Masefield and Heinemann was dated 3 November 1944 (see Archives of The Society of Authors). The agreement refers to a publication price of 9s.6d.

Copies seen: private collection (PWE); BL (10861.a.3) stamped 4 DEC 1944

Reprinted:

[first edition, second impression]   Jan 1945

A140(b) First American edition (1945)

JOHN MASEFIELD | [ornate rule of squares each on one corner with internal point] | NEW | CHUM | [ornate rule of squares each on one corner with internal point] | *New York* | THE MACMILLAN COMPANY | 1945 (All width centred)

Bibliographies: Handley-Taylor p.63, Wight 111a

Collation: [A–G]¹⁶ [H]¹² [I]¹⁶; 140 leaves; 187 × 127mm.; [i–x] 1–268 [269–70]

Page contents: [i–ii] blank; [iii] half-title: 'NEW CHUM'; [iv] 'ALSO BY JOHN MASEFIELD | *PLAYS:* | [12 titles listed] | *POETRY:* | [18 titles listed] | *FICTION: GENERAL:* | [14 titles of fiction listed with 11 titles of general works]'; [v] title-page; [vi] 'Copyright, 1945, by | JOHN MASEFIELD | [rule] | All rights reserved–no part of this book may be | reproduced in any form without permission in writ- | ing from the publisher, except by a reviewer who | wishes to quote brief passages in connection with a | review written for inclusion in magazine or newspaper. | *First Printing* | : PRINTED IN THE UNITED STATES OF AMERICA :'; [vii] 'TO | MY WIFE'; [viii] blank; [ix] 'NEW CHUM'; [x] blank; 1–268 text; [269–70] blank

Paper: wove paper

Running title: '*New Chum*' (21mm.) on both verso and recto, pp.2–268

Binding: navy blue cloth. On spine, reading lengthways down spine from head, in orange: 'MASEFIELD NEW CHUM MACMILLAN'; horizontally at foot of spine: '- [square point] -'. Covers: blank. All edges trimmed. Binding measurements: 192 × 126mm. (covers), 192 × 32mm. (spine). End-papers: wove paper.

Publication date: published, according to Handley-Taylor, 17 July 1945

Price: $2.50

Contents:
as for A140(a)

Notes:
As in A140(a), the volume commences with an epigraph by William Blake.

The text commences with a drop-capital.

Wight describes the binding as 'blue cloth' with 'red ink'.

As noted in several other Macmillan editions, the publicity material in the preliminaries that lists Masefield's work (appearing on p.[iv]) bears a marked similarity to that present in the Heinemann edition. Moreover, titles as cited here are those of English editions (separate editions of Masefield's Racine translations and *St. George and the Dragon*, for example). The setting of the text appears, however, to be unique to this American edition.

A publishing agreement for this title between Masefield and Macmillan was dated 21 February 1945 (see Archives of The Society of Authors). The agreement refers to 'a licence to publish in volume form in the United States of America and Canada a work the subject or title of which is NEW CHUM'.

Copies seen: State University of Iowa Library (PR6025.A77.N4.1945)

A140(c) Second English edition (1947)

NEW CHUM | *by* | JOHN MASEFIELD | [publisher's device of a windmill with 'W[point]' and '[point]H'] | [rule, 69mm.] | WILLIAM HEINEMANN LTD | LONDON :: TORONTO
(All width centred)

Bibliographies: Handley-Taylor p.63, Wight [unrecorded]

Collation: [A]⁸ B-I⁸ [K]⁸ L-M⁸ N⁴ (J not used); signatures right foot of page; 100 leaves; 183 × 121mm.; [i–iv] 1–195 [196]

Page contents: [i] half-title and dedication: 'NEW CHUM | TO | MY WIFE'; [ii] '*THE WORKS OF JOHN MASEFIELD* | PLAYS: | [12 titles listed] | POETRY: | [19 titles listed] | FICTION: [14 titles listed] | GENERAL: | [14 titles listed]'; [iii] title-page; [iv] 'FIRST PUBLISHED 1944 | REPRINTED JANUARY 1945 | FEBRUARY 1947 | THIS BOOK IS PRODUCED IN COMPLETE | CONFORMITY WITH THE AUTHORISED | ECONOMY STANDARDS | [rule] | PRINTED IN GREAT BRITAIN AT THE WINDMILL PRESS | KINGSWOOD, SURREY'; 1–195 text; [196] blank

Paper: wove paper

Running title: none

Binding: blue cloth. On spine, in gold: '*New* | *Chum* | *John* | *Masefield* | *Heinemann*' (all width centred). On upper cover, in blind: 'NEW CHUM | JOHN MASEFIELD' (within blind ruled border: 185 × 114mm.) On lower cover, in blind: publisher's device of a windmill (ranged lower right). All edges trimmed. Binding measurements: 188 × 123mm. (covers), 188 × 33mm. (spine). End-papers: wove paper.

Publication date: the sales ledger preserved in the Heinemann Archive suggests publication on 28 April 1947 in an edition of 1500 copies (see notes)

Price: 10s.6d.

Contents:
New Chum ('I set out to join H.M.S. *Conway* on a fine sunny morning a fortnight after the September term...')
Epilogue ('It is now more than fifty-five years since I went aboard as a new chum. This book records...')

Notes:
The volume commences on p.1 with the same epigraph as present in A140(a).

In September 1946, A.S. Frere wrote to Masefield: '...you may care to go ahead with the additional material for NEW CHUM and let me have it as soon as convenient to yourself...' (see A.S. Frere, letter to John Masefield, 6 September 1946) (HRHRC, MS (Masefield, J.) Recip William Heinemann Ltd.) The text appears to follow the setting present in A140(a) until p.31 (the second leaf of the C gathering). It is here that Masefield first provides additional text. Detailing waking up on board ship for the first time, the text as present in A140(a) reads:

> ...everybody was moving swiftly except H.B., who was one of the gods of that little world, and could take his time. I put on trousers, shirt, socks and shoes faster than ever in my life. My washing things were ready at my side, when the sharp pipe and bark for Prayers went. The ship fell pretty still, but not many prayed.

The second edition provides additional detail as Masefield adds to the confusing procedures aboard ship not yet understood by him:

...everybody was moving swiftly except H.B., who was one of the gods of that little world, and could take his time. After a blast on a pipe, someone shouted something. Some men, already half-dressed, rushed along the deck, and scattered to each port. They punched each port open with one swift thrust, so that the cool sea air blew in. Then they scattered away. Their smartness put a kind of life into me. I put on trousers, shirt, socks and shoes faster than ever in my life. My washing things were ready at my side, when the sharp pipe and bark for Prayers went. The ship fell pretty still, but not many prayed.

This is one example of the expanded text, requiring re-setting, hence the claim for this edition to comprise a second edition, not merely a reprint (new impression). The sales ledger preserved in the Heinemann Archive notes this volume as a 'new edition'. The 'Epilogue' is printed here for the first time.

Although the volume itself notes a publication date of 'February 1947' this date is not recorded by either Handley-Taylor or the sales ledger preserved in the Heinemann Archive. Both cite 28 April 1947 as the publication date. The copy in the British Library is stamped 28 April 1947 and this suggests that the new edition, although printed, was not released until later. Presumably this was to allow the previous edition to sell out.

The archives of The Society of Authors record that an application to publish a talking book version of this title (presumably of the most recently published text) was received in 1948 (see BL, Add.Mss.56620, f.156). Masefield, as a supporter of books in Braille, authorised this application.

Copies seen: private collection (PWE); BL (10860.aa.8) stamped 28 APR 1947

A140(d) Third English edition (1948 [1949])

NEW CHUM | *by* | JOHN MASEFIELD | [publisher's device of a windmill with 'W' and 'H'] | [rule, 56mm.] | WILLIAM HEINEMANN LTD | MELBOURNE :: LONDON :: TORONTO
(All width centred)

Bibliographies: Handley-Taylor p.63, Wight [unrecorded]

Collation: [A]⁸ B-M⁸ N⁴ O⁸ (J not used); signatures right foot of page; 108 leaves; 183 × 122mm.; [i–iv] 1–209 [210–12]

Page contents: [i] half-title and dedication: 'NEW CHUM | TO | MY WIFE'; [ii] *THE WORKS OF JOHN MASEFIELD* | PLAYS: | [12 titles listed] | POETRY: | [19 titles listed] | FICTION: | [14 titles listed] | GENERAL: | [14 titles listed]'; [iii] title-page; [iv] 'FIRST PUBLISHED 1944 | REPRINTED JANUARY 1945 | FEBRUARY 1947, NOVEMBER 1948 | PRINTED IN GREAT BRITAIN | AT THE WINDMILL PRESS | KINGSWOOD, SURREY'; 1–209 text; [210–12] blank

Paper: wove paper

Running title: none

Binding: blue cloth. On spine, in gold: '*New | Chum | John | Masefield | Heinemann*' (all width centred). On upper cover, in blind: 'NEW CHUM | JOHN MASEFIELD' (within blind ruled border: 185 × 116mm.) On lower cover, in blind: publisher's device of a windmill (ranged lower right). All edges trimmed. Binding measurements: 188 × 123mm. (covers), 188 × 32mm. (spine). End-papers: wove paper.

Publication date: the sales ledger preserved in the Heinemann Archive suggests publication on 21 February 1949 in an edition of 1000 copies (see notes)

Price: 10s.6d.

Contents:
New Chum ('I set out to join H.M.S. *Conway* on a fine sunny morning a fortnight after the September term...')
Epilogue ('It is now more than fifty-five years since I went aboard as a new chum. This book records...')
Appendices ('CONDENNY | One who knew the *Conway* in my time has suggested that an appendix might...')

Notes:
The volume commences on p.1 with the same epigraph as present in A140(a).

The text appears to follow the setting present in A140(c). In addition there are the appendices which are printed here for the first time. This therefore comprises a third edition, not merely a new impression.

Although the volume itself notes a publication date of 'November 1948' this date is not recorded by either Handley-Taylor, the *English Catalogue of Books* or the sales ledger preserved in the Heinemann Archive. All cite February 1949 as the publication date. The copy in the British Library is stamped 21 February 1949 and this suggests that the new edition, although printed, was not released until later. Presumably this was to allow the previous edition to sell out.

Despite similarities to the spine lettering present on A140(c), this edition uses differently spaced characters for the title and author while the publisher is in a more ornate italic type.

This edition appears to have been suggested by Masefield. Louisa Callender replied to the author stating '...I will go into the matter of reprinting NEW CHUM and I will write to you again.' (see Louisa Callender, letter to John Masefield, 26 July 1948) (HRHRC, MS (Masefield, J.) Recip William Heinemann Ltd.) Before sending the new material there was some discussion about royalty and publication price:

...higher costs of production in conjunction with high royalty would bring the published price of NEW CHUM to 12/6d. But since this particular book is one which you wish to be kept in print, we are willing to reduce our normal margin of profit and reprint the book to sell at 10/6d. We shall hope to have copies on the market during the next few months.

> (Louisa Callender, letter to John Masefield, 3 September 1948)
> (HRHRC, MS (Masefield, J.) Recip William Heinemann Ltd.)

A letter (preserved in the Heinemann Archive) from Masefield dated from October 1948 to Louisa Callender enclosed 'new matter for the suggested reprint of *New Chum*'. The 'new matter' presumably comprised the appendices. At the beginning of November 1948 Masefield was sent proofs:

> I have pleasure in sending you proofs and manuscript of the Appendices to NEW CHUM and shall be glad if you will kindly return one set of the proofs approved so that we can proceed with the reprint order in hand.

> (B.F. Oliver, letter to John Masefield, 4 November 1948)
> (HRHRC, MS (Masefield, J.) Recip William Heinemann Ltd.)

Copies seen: BL (10861.e.33) stamped 21 FEB 1949

A141 I WANT! I WANT!   1944

A141(a) First English edition (1944)

I WANT! I WANT! | [ornament] | BY | JOHN MASEFIELD, O.M. | POET LAUREATE | [ornament] | INTRODUCTION BY | GEOFFREY FABER | "*. . . new hope to spring | out of despaire. . .*" | *-Paradise Lost* | NATIONAL BOOK COUNCIL | LONDON | 1944
(All width centred)

Bibliographies: Handley-Taylor p.63, Wight 110

Collation: [A-B]⁸; 16 leaves; 185 × 123mm.; [1–4] 5–31 [32]

Page contents: [1] half-title: 'I WANT! I WANT! | NATIONAL BOOK COUNCIL SECOND ANNUAL LECTURE'; [2] blank; [3] title-page; [4] 'The Second Annual Lecture of the National Book | Council, delivered by JOHN MASEFIELD, O.M., POET | LAUREATE, at the Caxton Hall, Westminster on | May 19th 1944. Geoffrey Faber in the Chair.'; 5–6 'INTRODUCTION' ('Ladies and Gentlemen: Your card of admission tells you that the Lecturer, whom it is...') (signed, 'G.F.'); 7–31 text; [32] 'Printed in Great Britain in conformity with the authorised economy | standards by Willmer Brothers and Co. Ltd., Birkenhead. Bound by | Leighton-Straker Bookbinding Co. Ltd. Published by the National | Book Council, 3 Henrietta Street, Covent Garden, London, W.C.2. | Distributors : Simpkin, Marshall (1941) Ltd., 12 Old Bailey, London, | E.C.4.'

Paper: laid paper (watermark: '[Crown] | Abbey Mills | Greenfield')

Running title: none

Binding: green cloth. On spine, reading lengthways down spine from head, in gold: 'JOHN MASEFIELD [device] I WANT! I WANT! [device] N.B.C.' Covers: blank. All edges trimmed. Binding measurements: 189 × 124mm. (covers), 189 × 13mm. (spine). End-papers: wove paper.

Also issued in red wrappers. Spine: blank. On upper wrapper: 'I WANT! I WANT! | *By* | John Masefield O.M. | Poet Laureate | NATIONAL BOOK COUNCIL [point] 6d. NET'. On lower wrapper: 'PUBLISHED BY THE | NATIONAL BOOK COUNCIL | [rule (tapered at both ends)] | [advertisements for *I Want! I Want!* and F. Seymour Smith, *English Library*]'. All edges trimmed. Binding measurements: 185 × 123mm. (wrappers), 185 × 4mm. (spine). End-papers: wove paper (pasted onto the insides of the wrappers).

Publication date: published, according to the *English Catalogue of Books*, December 1944

Price: 2s. (cloth-bound) / 6d. (wrappers)

Contents:
Introduction ('Ladies and Gentlemen: Your card of admission tells you that the Lecturer, whom it is...')
    (signed, 'G.F.')
I Want! I Want! ('I have called this Lecture "I want! I want!" from a small design by William Blake, which most...')

Notes:
Text of the second annual lecture of the National Book Council (of which Masefield was president), delivered by the author at the Caxton Hall, Westminister on 19 May 1944.

The text of the lecture commences with a drop-capital.

With the exception of the price, the upper and lower wrappers of the paper-bound edition are the same as the dust-jacket for the cloth-bound edition. The dust-jacket has additional material on the spine and inner flaps.

Handley-Taylor does not provide the publication date for this edition. The *English Catalogue of Books* cites a date of December 1944 and the copy in the British Library is stamped 6 DEC 1944.

Copies seen: private collection (PWE) cloth binding; private collection (PWE) wrappers; BL (W.P.10755/2) cloth binding, stamped 6 DEC 1944; HRHRC (TEMP M377I 1944) inscribed 'For Con | from Jan. | Dec 6. 1944.' cloth binding

A141(b) First American edition (1945)

I WANT! I WANT! | BY JOHN MASEFIELD, O.M. | *POET LAUREATE* | [ornament] | INTRODUCTION BY | GEOFFREY FABER | *". . . new hope to spring | out of despaire. . ."* | *-Paradise Lost* | THE MACMILLAN COMPANY [point] NEW YORK | *1945*
(All width centred)

Bibliographies: Handley-Taylor p.63, Wight 110a

Collation: [A]¹⁶; 16 leaves; 187 × 126mm.; [1–4] 5–7 [8] 9–30 [31–32]

Page contents: [1] half-title: 'I WANT! I WANT!'; [2] blank; [3] title-page; [4] 'The Second Annual Lecture of the National Book | Council, delivered by JOHN MASEFIELD, O.M., | POET LAUREATE, at the Caxton Hall, Westminster, | on May 19, 1944. Goeffrey Faber in the Chair. [*sic*] | Copyright, 1945, | By JOHN MASEFIELD | *All rights reserved—no part of this book may be repro- | duced in any form without permission in writing from the | publisher, except by a reviewer who wishes to quote brief | passages in connection with a review written for inclusion | in magazine or newspaper.* | *Printed in the United States of America*'; 5–7 '*INTRODUCTION*' ('Ladies and Gentlemen: Your card of admission tells you that the Lecturer, whom it is...') (signed, 'G.F.'); [8] blank; 9–30 text; [31–32] blank

Paper: wove paper

Running title: none

Binding: blue-grey wrappers. Spine: blank. On upper wrapper: 'I WANT! I WANT! | BY JOHN MASEFIELD, O.M. | *POET LAUREATE* | [ornament] | THE MACMILLAN COMPANY [point] NEW YORK'. Lower wrapper: blank. All edges trimmed. Binding measurements: 187 × 126mm. (wrappers), 187 × 3mm. (spine).

Publication date: published, according to Handley-Taylor, 22 May 1945

Price: $1.00

Contents:
as for A141(a)

Notes:
The text of the lecture commences with a drop-capital.

The text has been entirely re-set for this edition.

Geoffrey Faber is incorrectly printed as 'Goeffrey Faber' on p.[4]. Wight silently corrects this error in his description of this volume.

A letter from the Macmillan firm to Masefield suggests that the American edition was printed in a small number of copies and that publication was merely to protect American copyright::

> We have received a copy of the National Book Council's publication of your lecture, I WANT! I WANT! From letters which Mr. Dickson of Macmillan & Co.'s office has sent to us, it is our understanding that you would like to have this set up and copyrighted, with a view to its being included in some later volume of prose material.
> If our understanding is correct, we will print twenty-five copies, copyright these, and offer them for sale in accordance with the copyright provisions. You would not, of course, expect us to pay royalty on whatever sale there might be for these twenty-five copies...

(H.S. Latham, letter to John Masefield, 24 January 1945)
(HRHRC, MS (Masefield, J.) Recip The Macmillan Company)

Copies seen: University of California library (A000 557 176 5) rebound; University of Virginia library rebound; Library of The John Masefield Society (Eileen Colwell Collection) inscribed 'For Eileen. H. Colwell, | from | John Masefield. | July. 1945.'; HRHRC (TEMP M377I 1945) inscribed 'For Con, | from Jan. | June 15. 1945.'

A142 A MACBETH PRODUCTION   1945

A142(a) First English edition (1945)

A | *MACBETH* PRODUCTION | BY | JOHN MASEFIELD | [publisher's device of a windmill with 'W[point]' and '[point]H'] | [rule, 56mm.] | WILLIAM HEINEMANN LTD | LONDON :: TORONTO
(All width centred)

Bibliographies: Handley-Taylor p.63, Wight 112

Collation: [A]⁸ B–C⁸ D¹⁰; D2 is also signed; signatures right foot of page; 34 leaves; 184 × 122mm.; [i–iv] 1–64

Page contents: [i] half-title: 'A | *MACBETH* PRODUCTION'; [ii] '*ALSO BY JOHN MASEFIELD* | PLAYS: | [12 titles listed] | POETRY: | [19 titles listed] | FICTION: GENERAL: | [14 titles of fiction listed with 12 titles of general works]'; [iii] title-page;

[iv] 'To | MY WIFE | FIRST PUBLISHED 1945 | THIS BOOK IS PRODUCED IN COMPLETE | CONFORMITY WITH THE AUTHORISED | ECONOMY STANDARDS | [rule] | PRINTED IN GREAT BRITAIN AT THE WINDMILL PRESS | KINGSWOOD, SURREY'; 1–64 text

Paper: wove paper

Running title: 'A *MACBETH* PRODUCTION' (53mm.) on both verso and recto, pp.2–64

Binding: blue cloth. On spine, reading lengthways up spine, from foot, in gold: 'A *MACBETH* PRODUCTION – JOHN MASEFIELD'; horizontally at foot of spine: publisher's device of a windmill. Covers: blank. All edges trimmed. Binding measurements: 189 × 123mm. (covers), 189 × 17mm. (spine). End-papers: wove paper.

Publication date: the sales ledger preserved in the Heinemann Archive suggests publication on 3 April 1945 in an edition of 7500 copies

Price: 6s.

Contents:
[Untitled] ('While I was thinking of what might be, and of that more sinister thing, which probably...')
Suggestions and Notes ('ACT I. SCENE I. [*On fore- and mid-stages.*] | Let us imagine, now, that your music...')
Note ('I wish to thank Lady Adam Smith for her enquiries on my behalf, and Dr. W. Douglas Simpson...')

The first two sections contain numerous sub-titles. Those in the second section merely refer to scenes of the play. Those in the first are as follows:

> On Duncan and Macbeth, as shewn in histories.
> On the Play as we have it.
> The Sources.
> On the Stage needed for your Performance.
> Stage devices and properties.
> On your Lights.
> Costume.
> On the Music.
> On the speaking of the lines.
> On Surprise, Suspense and Division.

Notes:
A volume presenting guidance for amateur productions of Shakespeare's *Macbeth* with additional material on historical background, sources, early cuts, music and costumes. The work was later included in *Thanks Before Going with Other Gratitude for Old Delight* (see A150).

Masefield's Hill Players company performed *Macbeth* in November 1922

A letter from Louisa Callender dated 9 February 1945 to Masefield thanked him for his 'helpful suggestion'. Callender stated that:

> We will print 7,500 copies of MACBETH: we will publish at 6/- and pay a 20% royalty. I will send you a formal contract in a day or two. We can consider later in the year a reprint as the book stands or with the added material you write about.
>
> (Louisa Callender, letter to John Masefield, 9 February 1945)
> (Archives of William Heinemann)

It therefore appears that even before publication of this volume, *Thanks Before Going with Other Gratitude for Old Delight* had been discussed. The publishing agreement for *A Macbeth Production* between Masefield and Heinemann was dated 20 February 1945 (see Archives of The Society of Authors). The agreement refers to a publication price of 6s.

A letter from Masefield to Louisa Callender requests a correction:

> Please, when you have a chance, will you call for a correction in the Macbeth book, page 35, line 4 "demand" should read damnéd.
>
> (John Masefield, letter to [Louisa Callender], [March 1945])
> (Archives of William Heinemann)

Masefield's reference is to Shakespeare's line "And fortune on his damned quarrel smiling" (Sergeant, Act I, scene ii). The incorrect reading of the line is printed here but is corrected within *Thanks Before Going with Other Gratitude for Old Delight*.

Copies seen: private collection (PWE)

A142(b) First American edition (1945)

A | *MACBETH* PRODUCTION | BY | JOHN MASEFIELD | *New York* | THE MACMILLAN COMPANY | 1946 (All width centred)

Bibliographies: Handley-Taylor p.63, Wight 112a

Collation: [A]¹⁷ ([A]2+1) [B]¹⁷ ([B]16+1) (see notes); 34 leaves; 187 × 123mm.; [i–iv] 1–64

Page contents: [i] half-title: 'A | *MACBETH* PRODUCTION'; [ii] '*ALSO BY JOHN MASEFIELD* | PLAYS: | [12 titles listed] | POETRY: | [19 titles listed] | FICTION: GENERAL: | [14 titles of fiction listed with 12 titles of general works]'; [iii] title-page; [iv] 'To | MY WIFE | Copyright, 1946, by | JOHN MASEFIELD | [rule] | All rights reserved—no part of this book may be | reproduced in any form without permission in writ- | ing from the publisher, except by a reviewer who | wishes to quote brief passages in connection with a | review written for inclusion in magazine or newspaper. | *First Printing*'; 1–64 text

Paper: wove paper

Running title: 'A *MACBETH* PRODUCTION' (53mm.) on both verso and recto, pp.2–64

Binding: grey cloth. Spine: blank. On upper cover, in red: 'JOHN MASEFIELD | [triple rule] | [ornate rule of 22 arrows (each constructed from arrow head and two points): 11 of these point from centre to the right and 11 point from centre to the left] | A MACBETH | PRODUCTION | [ornate rule of 22 arrows (each constructed from arrow head and two points): 11 of these point from centre to the right and 11 point from centre to the left] | [triple rule] | THE MACMILLAN COMPANY'. Lower cover: blank. All edges trimmed. Binding measurements: 193 × 128mm. (covers), 193 × 17mm. (spine). End-papers: wove paper.

Publication date: published, according to Handley-Taylor, 15 January 1946

Price: $1.75

Contents:
as for A142(a)

Notes:
The construction of the volume essentially consists of two gatherings of sixteen leaves each. In the first an additional leaf (pp.[i–ii]) has been tipped-in on the first leaf of the sewn gathering (therefore [A]2) and in the second an additional leaf (pp.63–64) has been tipped-in on the final leaf of the sewn gathering (therefore [B]16).

The publishing agreement for this volume between Masefield and Macmillan was dated 23 May 1945 (see Archives of The Society of Authors). The agreement refers to 'a licence to publish in volume form in the United States of America and Canada a work the subject or title of which is A MACBETH PRODUCTION'.

As noted in several other Macmillan editions, the publicity material in the preliminaries that lists Masefield's work (appearing on p.[ii]) bears a marked similarity to that present in the Heinemann edition. Moreover, titles as cited here are those of English editions (separate editions of Masefield's Racine translations and *St. George and the Dragon*, for example). The setting of the text suggests that the Heinemann setting may have been used here. This is also suggested by a letter from Louisa Callender dated 9 February 1945 to Masefield. Callender stated:

> The Macmillan Company in London have been sent two proofs of MACBETH for transmission by air mail to New York.
> (Louisa Callender, letter to John Masefield, 9 February 1945)
> (Archives of William Heinemann)

Copies seen: Boston Public Library (Rare Books SCT.47.130); Boston Public Library (PR2823.M3 1946); HRHRC (TEMP M377MA 1946) inscribed 'For Con | from Jan. | Feb 13. 1946.'

Reprinted:

'*Second Printing*'	[first edition, second impression]	1946

A143 SELECTED POEMS OF JOHN MASEFIELD [1945 or 1946]

A143(a) First American edition ([1945 or 1946])

PUBLISHED BY ARRANGEMENT WITH THE MACMILLAN COMPANY, NEW YORK | *Selected Poems of* | *JOHN MASEFIELD* | WITH AN INTRODUCTION BY | LOUIS UNTERMEYER | *Editions for the Armed Services, Inc.* | A NON-PROFIT ORGANIZATION ESTABLISHED BY THE COUNCIL ON BOOKS IN WARTIME, NEW YORK
(Enclosed with double ruled border: 78 × 120mm. with '820' below border in lower left corner)
(All width centred)

Bibliographies: Handley-Taylor [unrecorded], Wight [unrecorded]

Collation: [A]⁹⁶ (but signed 1–6¹⁶ at gutter and prefixed by '820–'); 96 leaves; 96 × 137mm.; [1–2] 3–5 [6] 7 [8] 9–191 [192]

Page contents: [1] title-page; [2] '*All rights reserved—no part of this book may be reproduced in* | *any form without permission in writing from the* | *publisher, except* | *by a reviewer who wishes to quote brief passages in connection* | *with a review written for inclusion in magazine or newspaper.* | Copyright, 1911, by John Masefield. | Copyright, 1912, by The Macmillan Company. | Copyright, 1913, by Harper and Brothers | and by The Macmillan Company. | Copyright, 1914, by The Century Company, by the McClure Publications | and by The Macmillan Company. | Copyright, 1915, by John Masefield. | Copyright, 1916, by John Masefield. | Copyright, 1940 and 1941, by John Masefield. | *Manufactured in the United States of America*'; 3–5 '*INTRODUCTION*' ('JOHN MASEFIELD, poet-laureate of England, was thirty-three when his long narrative poem...') (signed, 'LOUIS UNTERMEYER'); [6] blank; 7 '[rule] | *TABLE OF CONTENTS* | [14 individual items listed with page references] | [rule]'; [8] blank; 9–[192] text

Paper: wove paper

Running title: 'SELECTED POEMS' (22mm.) on verso; 'OF JOHN MASEFIELD' (28mm.) on recto, pp.10–191 (at foot of pages)

Binding: printed colour wrappers. On upper wrapper: '820 | [illustration of volume: 'JOHN MASEFIELD | [rule] | SELECTED | POEMS'] [in black and white] | ['ARMED | SERVICES | EDITION' in yellow on black circle] | *Selected Poems* [in yellow] | *of* [in yellow] | JOHN [in yellow] | MASEFIELD [in yellow] | *With an Introduction by* | LOUIS UNTERMEYER [in white] | Overseas edition for the Armed Forces. Distrib- [in yellow] | uted by the Special Services Division, A.S.F., [in yellow] | for the Army, and by the Bureau of Naval [in yellow] | Personnel for the Navy. U. S. Government prop- [in yellow] | erty. *Not for sale.* Published by Editions for the [in yellow] | Armed Services, Inc., a non-profit organization [in yellow] | established by the Council on Books in Wartime. [in yellow] | SELECTED POEMS [in white]' (on green panel with final line only printed on red panel; volume number, illustration and black circle ranged left with other text ranged right, with the exception of the final line which is width centred). On lower wrapper, on yellow panel: 'SELECTED POEMS *of John Masefield* | AN ADVENTUROUS youth at sea and a | nineteen-year-old discovery of Chaucer | seem to have been the "steering stars" for | the career of John Masefield. As a poet he | is probably best known for "Sea Fever," | which appeared in his first collection of | poems, *Salt Water Ballads;* but his writing | activity, apart from his poetry, has been | great, encompassing novels, plays, biogra- | phies, critical works, as well as military | and naval history. | [new paragraph] Masefield was born in 1878 at Ledbury, | Herefordshire. He was royally appointed | Poet Laureate of England in 1930, and in | 1935 received the most coveted honor Eng- | land can bestow, being admitted to the eminent company of the Order of Merit. | [new paragraph] Today, as Louis Untermeyer says in his | biographical sketch, "Masefield is a con- | temporary classic. . . . His wanderings are | reflected in the early lyrics; his love of | Chaucer shines through the narratives. . . | He has written in every fashion and form | But it is his graphic, swiftly-moving verse | by which he is most likely to be remem- | bered." | *This special edition of* SELECTED POEMS *of John Masefield has been* | *made available to the Armed Forces of the United States through an ar-* | *rangement with the original publisher, The Macmillan Company, New York.* | [new paragraph] Editions for the Armed Services, Inc., a non-profit organization established by the Council on Books in Wartime' (first three paragraphs in two columns, entire yellow panel surrounded by white border: 80 × 126mm. and all surrounded by red border with five-pointed stars in white). On inside of upper wrapper: '[device in black circle] | ARMED SERVICES EDITIONS | THIS BOOK is published by Editions for the Armed Services, Inc., a | non-profit organization by the Council on Books in War- | time, which is made up of American publishers of General (Trade) | books, librarians, and booksellers. It is intended for exclusive distribu- | tion to members of the American Armed Forces and is not to be resold | or made available to civilians. In this way the best books of the pres- | ent and the past are supplied to members of our Armed Forces in small, | convenient, and economical form. New titles will be issued regularly. | A list of the current group will be found on the inside back cover'. Inside of lower wrapper: 'OTHER ARMED SERVICES EDITIONS INCLUDE: | [40 titles and their authors listed in two columns]'. All edges trimmed. Binding measurements: 96 × 137mm. (wrappers); 96 × 8mm. (spine).

Publication date: see notes

Price: copies were not, presumably, for sale

Contents:
Introduction ('John Masefield, poet-laureate of England, was thirty-three when his long narrative...')
    (signed, 'LOUIS UNTERMEYER')
A Consecration ('Not of the princes and prelates with periwigged charioteers')
The Everlasting Mercy ('From '41 to '51')
Dauber ('Four bells were struck, the watch was called on deck,')
Explanations of some of the Sea Terms used in the poem ('BACKSTAYS. Wire ropes which support the masts against lateral...')
Biography ('When I am buried, all my thoughts and acts')
Cargoes ('Quinquireme of Nineveh from distant Ophir,')
Sea Fever ('I must go down to the seas again, to the lonely sea and the sky,')
Spanish Waters ('Spanish waters, Spanish waters, you are ringing in my ears,')
An Old Song Re-Sung ('I saw a ship a-sailing, a-sailing, a-sailing,')
The West Wind ('It's a warm wind, the west wind, full of birds' cries;')
On Malvern Hill ('A wind is brushing down the clover,')
Fragments ('Troy town is covered up with weeds,')
Tewkesbury Road ('It is good to be out on the road, and going one knows not where,')
Sonnets ('Men are made human by the mighty fall')
[Untitled] ('Ah, we are neither heaven nor earth, but men;')
[Untitled] ('They took the bloody body from the cross,')
[Untitled] ('"Come to us fiery with the saints of God')
[Untitled] ('So from the cruel cross they buried God;')
August 1914 ('How still this quiet cornfield is to-night;')

Notes:
The text is printed in double columns.

The text fails to mark the beginning and end of individual sonnets.

The first Armed Services Edition books were published in 1943. Page [2] of the volume cites the most recent copyright date as 1941 and this is frequently assumed to be the date of publication. Gerald R. Wagner of the Library of Congress replied to my enquiries stating:

> It appears that 1945 is the issue date for the ASE edition of Masefield's *Selected Poems*. ASE 820 was in series Y, and I have firm information that series Q was delivered in March 1945, and series HH in August 1946.
>
> (Gerald R. Wager, email to Philip W. Errington, 13 November 2001)

Tad Bennicoff, of the Seeley G. Mudd Manuscript Library of Princeton University, replied to enquiries after discovering an invoice:

> …dated 21 February 1946 stating that 25,000 copies of Masefield's *Selected Poems* were shipped to the Naval Supply Depot in Norfolk, Virginia by the Rumford Press of Concord, New Hampshire.
>
> (Tad Bennicoff, email to Philip W. Errington, 16 November 2001)

It therefore appears that this edition was published between March 1945 and February 1946 in an edition of at least 25,000 copies.

Preserved correspondence from Macmillan reveals how Masefield was informed of the Armed Services editions. It also notes that *Dead Ned* was the first Masefield title proposed:

> The Council on Books in Wartime, an American organization largely composed of representatives from various publishing houses, whose purpose is to promote the war effort, has undertaken the publication of pocket-sized editions of selected books which are to be given to men in the Service. It is provided in the agreements which publishers make with the Council that the books in these Armed Forces Editions are not to be sold in the general field or in any way distributed to the civilian public. Furthermore, they are expendable; that is to say, they are paper bound and will not stand up under very hard usage and will certainly soon be worn out.
>
> American authors take a great deal of satisfaction in having their books selected for Armed Services Editions, feeling that they are perhaps contributing materially, in this way, to the maintaining of the soldier's morale, his education, his entertainment. It should be further explained, perhaps, that these Armed Services Editions are not produced by the publisher but are manufactured entirely by the Council on Books in Wartime and distributed by them. The original publisher of any book does not in any way come into the business except to arrange for the rights.
>
> The Council pays one cent per copy. The initial printings are 50,000 copies, but it is the Council's wish that there be no limit on further printings, if required.
>
> We are writing you to find out whether you are willing to have DEAD NED published as one of the Armed Services Editions…
>
> (H.S. Latham, letter to John Masefield, 22 November 1943)
> (HRHRC, MS (Masefield, J.) Recip The Macmillan Company)

Masefield, however, seems to have been unimpressed or to have imagined a profit-making organisation. Macmillan sought to correct these views:

> …I have, of course, no desire to persuade you to a different opinion in connection with the publication of three of your books in the Armed Services editions, DEAD NED, SELECTED POEMS, and BIRD OF DAWNING… However, I do think I ought to point out one thing, in fairness to the Council on Books in Wartime, and it is this: The publication of the Armed Services Editions is not a money-making venture for anyone. The Council is making no money out of these editions. They are doing it purely as a patriotic service…
>
> (H.S. Latham, letter to John Masefield, 31 January 1944)
> (HRHRC, MS (Masefield, J.) Recip The Macmillan Company)

A letter from February 1945 suggests that Masefield became co-operative and that permission may have been granted for other Masefield volumes which were not published:

> In November, 1943 we wrote to you with regard to the publication of DEAD NED in the Armed Services Editions. Later, in December, 1943, we wrote you with regard to the publication of SELECTED POEMS and THE BIRD OF DAWNING in the Armed Services Editions. In May, 1944 you wrote granting permission to us to arrange with the Council on Books in Wartime for an Armed Services Edition of DEAD NED, and we did make these arrangements. The Council, however, is anxious to include these other two books as well…
>
> (H.S. Latham, letter to John Masefield, 23 February 1945)
> (HRHRC, MS (Masefield, J.) Recip The Macmillan Company)

Copies seen: private collection (PWE); BL (X.907/14904) stamped 15 JUN 1976

A144 THANKS BEFORE GOING   1946

A144(a) First English edition (1946)

THANKS BEFORE GOING | *By* | JOHN MASEFIELD | Notes on some of the Original Poems | of | Dante Gabriel Rossetti | [publisher's device of a windmill with 'W' and 'H'] | [rule, 57mm.] | WILLIAM HEINEMANN LTD | LONDON :: TORONTO
(All width centred)

Bibliographies: Handley-Taylor p.64, Wight 113

Collation: [A]⁸ B-D⁸ E⁶; E2 is also signed; signatures right foot of page; 38 leaves; 185 × 122mm.; [i–v] vi 1–68 [69–70]

Page contents: [i] half-title: 'THANKS BEFORE GOING'; [ii] '*ALSO BY JOHN MASEFIELD* | PLAYS: | [12 titles listed] | POETRY: | [18 titles listed] | FICTION: GENERAL: | [15 titles of fiction listed with 13 titles of general works]'; [iii] title-page; [iv] 'TO | MY WIFE | FIRST PUBLISHED 1946 | THIS BOOK IS PRODUCED IN COMPLETE | CONFORMITY WITH THE AUTHORISED | ECONOMY STANDARDS | [rule] | PRINTED IN GREAT BRITAIN AT THE WINDMILL PRESS | KINGSWOOD, SURREY'; [v] 'CONTENTS' (six individual sections listed with page references); vi-68 text; [69–70] blank

Paper: wove paper

Running title: 'THANKS BEFORE GOING' (53mm.) on verso; 'NOTES ON THE POEMS OF D.G. ROSSETTI' (82–86mm.) on recto (off-set to the left), pp.2–67

Binding: blue cloth. On spine, reading lengthways down spine from head, in gold: '*John Masefield* [eight-point star] THANKS BEFORE GOING [eight-point star] *Heinemann*'. On upper cover, in blind: 'THANKS BEFORE GOING | JOHN MASEFIELD' (within blind ruled border: 184 × 115mm.) On lower cover, in blind: publisher's device of a windmill (ranged lower right). All edges trimmed. Binding measurements: 189 × 124mm. (covers), 189 × 18mm. (spine). End-papers: wove paper.

Publication date: the sales ledger preserved in the Heinemann Archive suggests publication on 6 May 1946 in an edition of 6000 copies

Price: 7s.6d.

Contents:
Dante Gabriel Rossetti *[Verse]* ('Dante was as a star above his head.')
Introduction ('The convulsion known as the Romantic Movement was urged by many longings in millions...')
Principal Poems ('Gabriele Rossetti, the poet's father, an expounder of hidden meanings in Dante, christened...')
The House of Life ('The poem, *The House of Life*, was a design for many years in Rossetti's mind...')
Miscellaneous Poems ('In Mr. W. M. Rossetti's edition of the Collected Works, the *House of Life* is followed..')
Thanks at Going *[Verse]* ('If men at dying pass into their thought')

Notes:
A work of literary criticism sub-titled 'Notes on some of the Original Poems of Dante Gabriel Rossetti'. The work was reprinted in the volume *Thanks Before Going with Other Gratitude for Old Delight* (see A150).

Each of the prose sections commences with a drop-capital.

In the preliminary listing of Masefield's work, the volume *A Book of Prose Selections* is listed under the 'Fiction' heading. The volume was not published, however, until 1950 (see A158(a)).

A letter from Masefield dated 8 November [1945] to Louisa Callender appears to suggest this volume for the first time:

> I am writing a short study of some of D.G. Rossetti's Original Poems, about 25,000 words, but I have not yet a title for it, and I fear you will not have the script for 4 or 5 weeks yet. It may possibly be the first volume of a few studies of the greater of the late Victorian poets, but it is certainly a belated tribute from an old admirer to one who was ever an inspirer and kindler of youth... You might do no harm if you called the book tentatively *Notes On Some Of The Original Poems Of Dante Gabriel Rossetti* or *Some Notes On The Poetry Of* or *Some Notes On Rossetti's Poems*.
>
> (John Masefield, letter to [Louisa] Callender, 8 November [1945])
> (Archives of William Heinemann)

The 'studies' of late Victorian poets never appeared. By 21 November [1945] Masefield had decided upon his title:

> I expect that the Rossetti book, called *Thanks Before Going – Notes on some of the original Poems of Dante Gabriel Rossetti* will be about 25,000 words, and ready for you before Christmas
>
> (John Masefield, letter to [Louisa] Callender, 21 November [1945])
> (Archives of William Heinemann)

This is the title and sub-title, as adopted. Evidence suggests that Masefield had proposed the volume *Thanks Before Going with Other Gratitude for Old Delight...* (see A150) as early as 1945 (see notes to A142(a)). On 2 February [1946] Masefield made additional suggestions for the longer book:

> It has occurred to me, that perhaps you might prefer to limit the edition of *Thanks Before Going* to four thousand copies in the hope that this smaller number may be gone fairly soon, to make way for the reprint with the other matters? ...I hope to have about 30,000 words to add to the projected book of Macbeth / Rossetti and I may have more; all critical papers.
>
> (John Masefield, letter to [Louisa] Callender, 2 February [1946])
> (Archives of William Heinemann)

In the event the edition was published in a run of 6000 copies but Masefield's intention to publish *Thanks Before Going With Other Gratitude for Old Delight* is obvious here.

A letter (preserved in the Heinemann Archive) from Masefield dated 10 December [1945] enclosed the copy for this volume. Proofs (in book form) were sent together with the return of the manuscript on 31 January 1946 (see B.F. Oliver, letter to John Masefield, 31 January 1946) (HRHRC, MS (Masefield, J.) Recip William Heinemann Ltd.) An advance copy was sent on 23 April 1946 together with a note stating that publication would occur on 6 May 1946 (see Louisa Callender, letter to John Masefield, 23 April 1946) (HRHRC, MS (Masefield, J.) Recip William Heinemann Ltd.)

The publishing agreement for this title between Masefield and Heinemann was dated 6 February 1946 (see Archives of The Society of Authors). The agreement refers to a publication price of 7s.6d.

A copy of this edition was inscribed to Sydney Cockerell. An undated letter of presentation stated:

> May I ask you to accept this little book, in memory of our talk about Rossetti some years ago, in the National Gallery? He has been belittled, but the next ten years will see him honoured, I hope.
>
> (John Masefield, letter to Sydney Cockerell, [May 1946])
> (NYPL (Berg Collection))

Copies seen: private collection (PWE); NYPL (Berg Collection) inscribed 'For Lily Yeats, | from | John Masefield. | November 21. 1946'; NYPL (Berg Collection) inscribed 'For Sydney Cockerell, | from | John Masefield. | May 6. 1946.'

A144(b) First American edition (1947)

Thanks Before Going | BY | JOHN MASEFIELD | *Notes on some of the Original Poems of* | DANTE GABRIEL ROSSETTI | [ornament] [in orange] | THE MACMILLAN COMPANY | *New York 1947*
(All width centred and enclosed within ornate border in orange including wavy rule: 154 × 97mm.)
(The italic type contains a number of swash characters)

Bibliographies: Handley-Taylor p.64, Wight 113a

Collation: [A-E]⁸; 40 leaves; 202 × 134mm.; [i–viii] 1–68 [69–72]

Page contents: [i] half-title: 'THANKS BEFORE GOING'; [ii] '*ALSO BY JOHN MASEFIELD* | PLAYS: | [12 titles listed] | POETRY: | [18 titles listed] | FICTION: GENERAL: | [15 titles of fiction listed with 13 titles of general works]'; [iii] title-page; [iv] 'Copyright, 1947, by | JOHN MASEFIELD | [rule] | JOHN MASEFIELD | All rights reserved–no part of this book may be | reproduced in any form without permission in writ- | ing from the publisher, except by a reviewer who | wishes to quote brief passages in connection with a | review written for inclusion in magazine or newspaper. | [rule] | *First Printing* | PRINTED IN THE UNITED STATES OF AMERICA | BY THE VAIL-BALLOU PRESS, INC., BINGHAMTON, N. Y.'; [v] 'TO | MY WIFE'; [vi] blank; [vii] 'CONTENTS' (six individual sections listed with page references); [viii]–[69] text; [70–72] blank

Paper: wove paper

Running title: 'THANKS BEFORE GOING' (40mm.) on verso; 'NOTES ON THE POEMS OF D.G. ROSSETTI' (78mm.) on recto, pp.2–68

Binding: green cloth. On spine, reading lengthways down spine from head: 'MASEFIELD [ornament] THANKS BEFORE GOING [ornament] MACMILLAN'. Covers: blank. All edges trimmed. Binding measurements: 208 × 136mm. (covers), 208 × 23mm. (spine). End-papers: wove paper.

Publication date: published, according to Handley-Taylor, 15 April 1947

Price: $3.00

Contents:
Dante Gabriel Rossetti. *[Verse]* ('Dante was as a star above his head.')
Introduction ('The convulsion known as the Romantic Movement was urged by many longings in millions...')
Principal Poems ('Gabriele Rossetti, the poet's father, an expounder of hidden meanings in Dante, christened...')
The House of Life ('The poem, *The House of Life*, was a design for many years in Rossetti's mind...')
Miscellaneous Poems ('In Mr. W. M. Rossetti's edition of the Collected Works, the *House of Life* is followed..')
Thanks at Going *[Verse]* ('If men at dying pass into their thought')

Notes:
Each of the prose sections commences with a drop-capital.

Wight notes the title-page ornament as being printed in 'red'.

As in A144(a), the preliminary listing of Masefield's works includes the volume *A Book of Prose Selections* (listed under the 'Fiction' heading). The volume was not published until 1950.

The publishing agreement for this volume between Masefield and Macmillan was dated 28 January 1946 (see Archives of The Society of Authors). The agreement refers to 'a licence to publish in volume form in the United States of America and Canada a work the subject of which is a prose study of the original poems of Dante Gabriel Rossetti (exact title to be determined), to contain approximately 25,000 words'. A later agreement was dated 15 August 1946 (see Archives of The Society of Authors). The agreement refers to 'a licence to publish in volume form in the United States of America, the Philippine Islands and Canada a work the title of which is THANKS BEFORE GOING'.

The publicity material in the preliminaries that lists Masefield's work (appearing on p.[ii]) bears a marked similarity to that present in the Heinemann edition. Moreover, titles as cited here are those of English editions (separate editions of Masefield's Racine translations and *St. George and the Dragon*, for example). A letter from Masefield dated 2 February [1946] to Louisa Callender asks for Heinemann's assistance with the American edition:

> It will be very kind, if you will see that clean pulls of the proofs, now being returned for PRESS, may go by the Air Mail to Macmillians in N.Y. Please, will you do this for me?

(John Masefield, letter to [Louisa] Callender, 2 Februry [1946])

(Archives of William Heinemann)

Copies seen: Columbia University (Special Collections B825M377 X343 1947); Florida State University Libraries (PR 5247 M3 1947)

A145 ...REPLY TO THE TOAST OF THE HONORARY GRADUANDS... [AT THE UNIVERSITY OF SHEFFIELD]   1946

A145(a) First English edition (1946)

Page [1]:

THE UNIVERSITY OF SHEFFIELD | Speech by | JOHN MASEFIELD, O.M. | Poet Laureate | in reply to the Toast of the Honorary Graduands | proposed by the Chancellor at Luncheon | immediately before the Ceremony | of | INSTALLATION OF THE CHANCELLOR | 25th JUNE, 1946
(All width centred and enclosed within ornate border: 207 × 118mm.)

Bibliographies: Handley-Taylor p.64, Wight [unrecorded]

Collation: [A]²; 2 leaves; 251 × 160mm.; [1–4]

Page contents: [1] title-page; [2] '*Mr. Masefield was speaking on behalf of all five Honorary Graduands, the others | being Lord Greene, Master of the Rolls; Marshal of the Royal Air Force. Lord Tedder; | Sir Robert Robinson, President of the Royal Society; and Sir Alfred Munnings, President | of the Royal Academy. | [new paragraph] The Chancellor, in proposing the Toast, had referred to the expert knowledge of | foxhunting shown by Mr. Masefield in certain of his poems. | [rule] | My Lord and Chancellor, Your Royal Highness, Vice- | Chancellor, Professors and Members of the University | of Sheffield, my Lords, Ladies and Gentlemen: | [text] | [rule] | [text]*'; [3] text (concluded); [4] blank

Paper: laid paper (no watermark), chain-lines 27mm. apart

Running title: none

Binding: single sheet folded once. Upper wrapper comprises the title-page. All edges trimmed except fore edge of first leaf which is deckle-edged. Binding measurements: 251 × 160mm. (covers), 251 × 0.5cm (spine).

Publication date: published, according to Handley-Taylor, 1946

Price: copies were not, presumably, for sale

Contents:
...Reply to the Toast of the Honorary Graduands... [at the University of Sheffield]
('In answering to this Toast, please let me begin by saying that I know nothing whatever about...')

Notes:
Masefield was awarded an honorary degree at Sheffield University in June 1946.

The earliest dated copy examined has a signed inscription from 5 August 1946.

Included with copies in Harvard College Library is an undated letter from Masefield to Florence Lamont:

> I send with this some copies of the Sheffield speech, and hope that if you wish for more you will tell me. I expect the Registrar could let me have more pulls for you.

(John Masefield, letter to Florence Lamont, [August 1946])

((Harvard College Library)

That the University of Sheffield was responsible for the printing of this item is confirmed by a letter from Masefield to The Society of Authors in 1953. The Society had received an application to quote from the speech and the author responded:

> The words about the University are free to anybody. I spoke them at Sheffield about 7 years ago + S. University printed them as a souvenir. I do not claim any copyright in them, + they have been quoted a good deal. All hands are very welcome to them.

(John Masefield, letter to [Anne] Munro-Kerr, [12 February 1953])

(BL, Add.Mss.56624, f.72)

Responding to enquiries in 1960 Masefield wrote to The Society of Authors:

> Some dozen or more years ago, Sheffield University gave me an honorary Doctorate; and asked me to speak on behalf of the other Recipients, at the Lunch.
>
> I made a brief speech of thanks, saying various things about Universities; and this, of course, was my thanks; it was *for* the University; and they printed it... as a leaflet... Well... the speech became known in America, + I have had a lot of applications about it. I always refer them to the Sheffield University Registrar... who always sends the applicants the leaflet, I think. It is a quite short speech, in prose. I have never before seen any version of it printed as verse.

But it is Sheffield's, the University's speech now, not mine. They were very nice to me, and I am sorry to have let them in for quite a lot of writing. Please, would you be so very kind as to explain matters to the enquirers, + to beg the ones who think it is poetry to reconsider the matter?

(John Masefield, letter to Anne Munro-Kerr, [May 1960])
(Archives of The Society of Authors)

In all examined copies the full-stop after '*Royal Air Force*' in line two has been corrected (by hand) to a comma.

Copies seen: private collection (PWE) inscribed 'John Masefield. | For Kathleen [Morehouse] from John. | February the 19th. 1959.'; Harvard College Library (Houghton *EC9.M377.946s(A)) inscribed 'For Tom Lamont, | from John Masefield. | Augt 5. 1946.'; Harvard College Library (Houghton *EC9.M377.946s(B)) inscribed 'For Florence, | from John. | Augt 5. 1946.'; Harvard College Library (Houghton *EC9.M377.946s(C)) inscribed 'For Florence, | from John. | 26. VIII. 1946.'; HRHRC (AC-L M377 SPE 1946) inscribed 'John Masefield. | The London Library Appeal. | No 127'

A146 THE UNIVERSITY — 1946

A146(a) First American edition (1946)

In 1946 it appears that the text of A145 was printed as *The University* by Boston University General Alumni Association. This comprised a broadside and was printed in sepia and red within a decorative border on tan paper. The printing carries the 'compliments of Boston University General Alumni Association'. A copy is thought to be located at Boston University.

A146(b) Second American edition (1953)

THE | UNIVERSITY | Words by John Masefield | *Photographs by:* | Robert M. Mottar | Werner Wolff | *Additional Photographs from:* Black Star, Mettee, | and Wide World | *Detailed picture captions and acknowledgments* | *appear on page 28* | *Reprinted from The Johns Hopkins Magazine* | *February, 1953*
(All width centred)

Bibliographies: Handley-Taylor [see p.64], Wight [unrecorded]

Collation: [A]^{14} (see notes); 14 leaves; 278 × 214mm.; [1–2] 3–6 [7–8] 9–14 [15–17] 18 [19–20] 21–22 [23–24] 25 [26–27] 28

Page contents: [1] title-page; [2–27] text and photographs; 28 'Acknowledgments'

Paper: glossy wove paper

Running title: none

Binding: white boards with black cloth spine. Spine: blank. On upper cover, in red: 'THE | UNIVERSITY' (justified on left margin). On lower cover: '[rule, 110mm.] [in red] | THE UNIVERSITY | [text] | –JOHN MASEFIELD | [rule, 110mm.] [in red]'. All edges trimmed. Binding measurements: 284 × 218mm. (covers), 284 × 15mm. (spine). End-papers: blue laid paper (watermark: '*Ticonderoga | Text*'), chain-lines 30mm. apart.

Publication date: after February 1946

Price: unknown

Contents:
The University ('There are few earthly things more beautiful than a university…')

Notes:
The single gathering is machine sewn (the gathering is stabbed 51 times). The 'gathering' also includes the end-papers (on a different stock of paper). The fixed end-papers are continuous, as are the free end-papers. Due to the different paper stock (the end-papers are laid paper) the volume is described above as [A]^{14}. However, if the end-papers are to be included the volume could be described as [A]^{16}.

The 'Acknowledgments' state:

> *The Johns Hopkins Magazine* is indebted to John Masefield, who graciously granted permission to use his words as the theme for this issue. They were originally spoken at the University of Sheffield, England, as part of Mr. Masefield's reply to the toast of the Honorary Graduands, on the occasion of the installation of the chancellor in June, 1946.

There then follow three columns which describe the photographs in detail and note the photographer.

It is assumed that this single volume publication is, with the exception of the title-page, a verbatim reprint of *The Johns Hopkins Magazine* for February 1953 (see C500.001).

Handley-Taylor notes that:

> According to Dr. Fraser Drew of Buffalo, this speech has been reprinted in part by various universities in the United States, "including Duke, Johns Hopkins, and Brown".

No copy printed by Duke University has been located.

Copies seen: private collection (PWE)

A146(c) Third American edition (1954)

Drew's statement (quoted by Handley-Taylor) notes an edition printed by Brown University. No copy has been consulted. However, a copy of A146(d) suggests that Drew is accurate and indicates that Brown University published Masefield's words in 1954.

A146(d) Fourth American edition (1969)

A further edition comprises a booklet published in 1969 by Brown University and Pembroke College Funds. It printed Masefield's words with illustrations and designs by Walter Feldman. A copy is located at Harvard College Library (Houghton *EC9.M377.Zzx)

A147 REYNARD THE FOX WITH SELECTED SONNETS AND LYRICS   1946

A147(a) First English edition (1946)

REYNARD THE FOX | *A Tale in Verse* | WITH | SELECTED SONNETS | AND LYRICS | BY | JOHN MASEFIELD | [publisher's device of a windmill with 'W' and 'H'] | [rule, 51mm.] | WILLIAM HEINEMANN LTD | LONDON :: TORONTO
(All width centred)
(The '*T*' of '*Tale*' is swash)

Bibliographies: Handley-Taylor [noted on p.43], Wight [unrecorded] (see notes)

Collation: [A]⁸ B-I⁸; signatures right foot of page; 72 leaves; 184 × 121mm.; [i–vi] [1–2] 3–35 [36–38] 39–41 [42–44] 45–128 [129–30] 131–35 [136–38]

Page contents: [i] half-title: 'REYNARD THE FOX | WITH | SELECTED SONNETS | AND LYRICS'; [ii] 'To | MY WIFE'; [iii] title-page; [iv] 'FIRST PUBLISHED 1946 | THIS BOOK IS PRODUCED IN COMPLETE | CONFORMITY WITH THE AUTHORISED | ECONOMY STANDARDS | [rule] | PRINTED IN GREAT BRITAIN AT THE WINDMILL PRESS | KINGSWOOD, SURREY'; [v] 'NOTE | The tale of the hunting of a fox was written near | Oxford in the early part of 1919. It is, in part, an | attempt to understand the mind of a shy wild | animal when sorely beset; and, in part, a symbol of | the free soul of humanity, then just escaped from | extinction by the thoughtless, the debased and the | determined leagued against it for four years of war. | As the same fox has been more cruelly beset of late | years, perhaps some image of his escape may be | grateful at the present time. | [new paragraph] The Sonnets were made at odd times, in many | different moods.'; [vi] 'CONTENTS' (eight items listed with page references); [1] 'SONNETS'; [2] blank; 3–35 text; [36] blank; [37] '*The Lyrics from* | GOOD FRIDAY | A PLAY IN VERSE'; [38] blank; 39–41 text; [42] blank; [43] 'REYNARD THE FOX | OR | THE GHOST HEATH RUN'; [44] blank; 45–128 text; [129] 'SONNETS'; [130] blank; 131–35 text; [136–38] blank

Paper: wove paper

Running title: 'SONNETS' (22mm.) on both verso and recto, pp.3–35; 'GOOD FRIDAY' (35mm.) on both verso and recto, pp.40–41; 'REYNARD THE FOX' (48mm.) on both verso and recto, pp.46–128, 'SONNETS' (22mm.) on both verso and recto, pp.131–32; and titles of individual poems, pp.133–35

Binding: blue cloth. On spine, in silver: '*Reynard* | *the Fox* | [point] [point]WITH[point] [point] | *Selected* | *Sonnets* | *and* | *Lyrics* | [point] | *John* | *Masefield* | *Heinemann*' (all width centred). Upper cover: blank. On lower cover, in blind: publisher's device of a windmill (ranged lower right). All edges trimmed. Binding measurements: 190 × 123mm. (covers), 190 × 23mm. (spine). End-papers: wove paper.

Publication date: the sales ledger preserved in the Heinemann Archive suggests publication on 30 September 1946 in an edition of 5000 copies

Price: 7s.6d.

Contents:
I ('O wretched man, that for a little mile')
II ('Out of the special cell's most special sense')
III ('You are the link which binds us each to each.')
IV ('I could not sleep for thinking of the sky,')
V ('How did the nothing come, how did these fires,')
VI ('It may be so; but let the unknown be.')
VII ('What is this life which uses living cells')
VIII ('Can it be blood and brain, this transient force')

501

Notes:

Essentially an edition of *Reynard the Fox*, this volume also includes 'selected sonnets and lyrics' from other sources, including *Lollingdon Downs and other poems, with sonnets* (A38).

The publishing agreement for this title between Masefield and Heinemann was dated 8 August 1946 (see Archives of The Society of Authors). The agreement refers to a publication price of 7s.6d.

Only the first part of *Reynard the Fox* commences with a drop-capital.

In 'Some Contributions to the Bibliography of John Masefield: II' (*Papers of the Bibliographical Society of America*, October 1959, pp.262–67) Drew states, with reference to the standard *Reynard the Fox* title:

> To this item may be added item (44f). On 30 Sept. 1946, Wm. Heinemann, Ltd. published *Reynard the Fox with Selected Songs and Lyrics* in a regular edition of 3,000 copies bound in cloth.

Drew inaccurately cites the title. The print-run he notes is smaller than that recorded in the Heinemann archive.

The suggestion for this volume presumably came from Masefield. The author probably voiced concerns that the volume might endanger plans for the proposed publication of *Poems* (A148). A.S. Frere replied:

> …I think your suggestion that we should reprint REYNARD THE FOX with perhaps 50 sonnets with it, is an excellent one and that, of course, need not affect our plans for the Collected Poems. If you would care to select the sonnets and let me have them at the earliest possible moment, I should be only too pleased to put it in hand with some prospect of getting the volume out in the Autumn.
>
> (A.S. Frere, letter to John Masefield, 6 May 1946)
> (HRHRC, MS (Masefield, J.) Recip William Heinemann Ltd.)

At this stage the volume appears to have carried a different title. The HRHRC holds a 1946 proof copy for this edition entitled *Selected Sonnets and Lyrics with Reynard the Fox A Tale in Verse*. The note is different in this earlier version. It reads:

> Being asked to choose out a short selection from my verse, I made this book from the sonnets, lyrics and tales written between the years 1911 and 1924.
>
> The sonnets and lyrics spring from many different moods; they were made at odd times, in many different places, nearly all of them in the open air.
>
> The tale of the hunting of a fox was written near Oxford in the early part of 1919. It is, in part, an attempt to understand the mind of a shy wild animal when sorely beset; and, in part, a symbol of the free soul of humanity, then just escaped from extinction by the thoughtless, the debased and the determined leagued against it for four years of war.

Concern over possible confusion between *Selected Sonnets and Lyrics…* and *Poems* led Louisa Callender to write to the author at the beginning of July:

> I think that we may be able to issue both the SELECTED SONNETS AND LYRICS and POEMS this year. Certainly we should like to include both volumes in our autumn list which are now preparing; but to announce SOME SELECTED SONNETS AND LYRICS and POEMS would give two very general titles which might be confusing. If you agree, we should like to issue the selection under the title of REYNARD THE FOX WITH SELECTED SONNETS AND LYRICS, issuing that book at as low a price as we can.
>
> (Louisa Callender, letter to John Masefield, 3 July 1946)
> (HRHRC, MS (Masefield, J.) Recip William Heinemann Ltd.)

Masefield replied approving the new title but appeared resolute about royalty:

> The book of *Reynard & Sonnets* might be given the title REYNARD THE FOX with Sonnets, etc. Would this meet with your approval? I must say at once that I very strongly disapprove of the book being issued cheaply with a reduced royalty. I suggested the book as a means of having my work on the market while my other books had to stay out of print, as a means, in fact, of living. As it is that, I must stand out for my usual royalty.
>
> (John Masefield, letter to [Louisa] Callender, 6 July 1946)
> (Archives of William Heinemann)

The price of the edition at 7s.6d. does appear to be a low price. The first English edition of *New Chum* (A140(a)) was priced at 9s.6d., for example. The first English edition of *Thanks Before Going with Other Gratitude for Old Delight…* (A150(a)) was priced at 10s.6d. *A Macbeth Production* and *Thanks Before Going* were priced at 6s. and 7s.6d. respectively for the English first editions, but were short volumes. Masefield's comments on his out-of-print status is surely a reflection on war privations and lack of paper. *Reynard the Fox* was evidently one long narrative poem he wished to keep in circulation.

Copies seen: private collection (PWE); BL (11658.aaa.85) stamped 30 SEP 1946

A148 POEMS   1946

A148(a) First English edition (1946)

POEMS | BY | JOHN MASEFIELD | [publisher's device of a windmill with 'W' and 'H'] | [rule, 51mm.] | WILLIAM HEINEMANN LTD | LONDON :: TORONTO
(All width centred)

THE
UNIVERSITY

Words by John Masefield

Photographs by:
Robert M. Mottar
Werner Wolff

Additional Photographs from:
Black Star, Mettee,
and Wide World

*Detailed picture captions and acknowledgments
appear on page 28*

*Reprinted from The Johns Hopkins Magazine
February, 1953*

A146(b) title-page

REYNARD THE FOX
A Tale in Verse
WITH
SELECTED SONNETS
AND LYRICS

BY

JOHN MASEFIELD

WILLIAM HEINEMANN LTD
LONDON   ::   TORONTO

A147(a) title-page

P O E M S

BY

JOHN MASEFIELD

WILLIAM HEINEMANN LTD
LONDON   ::   TORONTO

A148(a) title-page

THANKS BEFORE GOING
with
OTHER GRATITUDE FOR OLD DELIGHT
including
A *MACBETH* PRODUCTION
and various papers not before printed

By
JOHN MASEFIELD

WILLIAM HEINEMANN LTD
LONDON   ::   TORONTO

A150(a) title-page

A BOOK OF BOTH SORTS

SELECTIONS FROM THE
VERSE AND PROSE OF

JOHN MASEFIELD

WILLIAM HEINEMANN LTD
LONDON :: TORONTO

A151(a) title-page

BADON PARCHMENTS

by

JOHN MASEFIELD

WILLIAM HEINEMANN LTD
LONDON :: TORONTO

A152(a) title-page

A PLAY OF
ST. GEORGE

by

JOHN MASEFIELD

WILLIAM HEINEMANN LTD
MELBOURNE :: LONDON :: TORONTO

A153(a) title-page

GORDON BOTTOMLEY

WORDS SPOKEN BY

JOHN MASEFIELD

AT A

MEMORIAL SERVICE

IN THE

CHURCH OF ST. MARTIN-IN-THE-FIELDS
SEPTEMBER 28TH, 1948

A154(a) title-page

Bibliographies: Handley-Taylor p.54, Wight [unrecorded]

Collation: [A]¹⁶ B-EE¹⁶ FF⁸ (J and V not used); the fifth leaf of gatherings A-EE is also signed; signatures right foot of page; 472 leaves; 184 × 120mm.; [i–vi] vii–x [1–2] 3–34 [35–36] 37–79 [80–82] 83–138 [139–40] 141–93 [194] 195–99 [200–202] 203–265 [266–68] 269–74 [275–76] 277–311 [312–14] 315–47 [348–50] 351–53 [354–56] 357–429 [430–32] 433–504 [505–506] 507–559 [560–62] 563–616 [617–18] 619–20 [621–22] 623–72 [673–74] 675–701 [702–704] 705–762 [763–64] 765–97 [798–800] 801–858 [859–60] 861–62 [863–64] 865–66 [867–68] 869–76 [877–78] 879–93 [894–96] 897–900 [901–902] 903–922 [923–24] 925–33 [934]

Page contents: [i] half-title: 'POEMS BY | JOHN MASEFIELD'; [ii] '*ALSO BY JOHN MASEFIELD* | PLAYS: | [12 titles listed] | POETRY: | [18 titles listed] | FICTION: GENERAL: | [14 titles of fiction listed with 11 titles of general works]'; [iii] title-page; [iv] 'COLLECTED POEMS | *First published, October* 1923 | *New Impressions, November* 1923, *January*, | *October* 1924, *April* 1925, *February September*, | *December* 1926, *July*, *October* 1927, *October* 1928, | *August* 1929, *September* 1930 | *New and Enlarged Edition, August* 1932 | *Reprinted, November* 1932, *April* 1934, *May*, | *November* 1935, *November* 1937 | *New and Enlarged Edition, February* 1938, | *October* 1941, *August* 1942 | *Revised Edition entitled* POEMS | *First Published* 1946 | THIS BOOK IS PRODUCED IN COMPLETE | CONFORMITY WITH THE AUTHORISED | ECONOMY STANDARDS | [rule] | PRINTED IN GREAT BRITAIN | AT THE WINDMILL PRESS, KINGSWOOD, SURREY'; [v] 'To | MY WIFE'; [vi] 'The tales contained in this volume are copyright | in Great Britain, the United States of America, and | Ireland. No performance or dramatic reading of | them may be given without the author's formal license, | which may be obtained through The Society of | Authors, 11, Gower Street, London, W.C.1. | [new paragraph] The lyrics from POMPEY THE GREAT, printed in this | volume, are included by courtesy of Messrs. Sidgwick | and Jackson, Limited, 44, Museum Street, W.C.1, | who are the publishers of the play. | [new paragraph] The five pages of verse, pp.861–6, are from books | published by Messrs. Collins, to whose courtesy I | render thanks.'; vii–x 'CONTENTS' (146 individual items listed with page references); [1] '*From* | WONDERINGS AND LAND WORKERS'; [2] blank; 3–34 text of 'Wonderings and Land Workers'; [35] 'THE EVERLASTING MERCY'; [36] '*Thy place is biggyd above the sterrys cleer,* | *Noon erthely paleys wrouhte in so statly wyse,* | *Com on my freend, my brothir moost enteer,* | *For the I offryd my blood in sacrifise.* | JOHN LYDGATE.'; 37–79 text of *The Everlasting Mercy*; [80] blank; [81] 'THE WIDOW IN THE BYE STREET'; [82] blank; 83–138 text of *The Widow in the Bye Street*; [139] 'DAUBER'; [140] blank; 141–93 text of *Dauber*; [194] blank; 195–99 'EXPLANATIONS OF SOME OF THE SEA | TERMS USED IN THE POEM'; [200] blank; [201] 'THE DAFFODIL FIELDS'; [202] blank; 203–265 text of *The Daffodil Fields*; [266] blank; [267] '*From* | PHILIP THE KING | THE MESSENGER'S SPEECH'; [268] blank; 269–74 text of 'The Messenger's Speech'; [275] 'OTHER POEMS'; [276] blank; 277–311 text of other poems; [312] blank; [313] 'LOLLINGDON DOWNS | AND OTHER POEMS, WITH SONNETS'; [314] blank; 315–47 text of *Lollingdon Downs and other poems, with sonnets*; [348] blank; [349] '*The Lyrics from* | GOOD FRIDAY | A PLAY IN VERSE'; [350] blank; 351–53 text of lyrics from *Good Friday*; [354] blank; [355] 'REYNARD THE FOX | OR | THE GHOST HEATH RUN'; [356] blank; 357–429 text of *Reynard the Fox*; [430] blank; [431] 'ENSLAVED | AND OTHER POEMS'; [432] blank; 433–504 text of *Enslaved and other poems*; [505] 'RIGHT ROYAL'; [506] blank; 507–559 text of *Right Royal*; [560] blank; [561] 'KING COLE'; [562] blank; 563–616 text of *King Cole and other poems*; [617] '*From* | SARD HARKER'; [618] blank; 619–20 text of poems from *Sard Harker*; [621] '*From* | MIDSUMMER NIGHT | AND OTHER TALES IN VERSE'; [622] blank; 623–72 text of poems from *Midsummer Night and other tales in verse*; [673] 'POEMS FROM THE WANDERER'; [674] blank; 675–701 text of poems from *The Wanderer*; [702] blank; [703] '*From* | MINNIE MAYLOW'S STORY | AND OTHER TALES & SCENES'; [704]–762 text of poems from *Minnie Maylow's Story and other tales and scenes*; [763] 'A TALE OF TROY | TOLD IN ELEVEN TALES AND AN EPILOGUE'; [764] blank; 765–97 text of *A Tale of Troy*; [798] blank; [799] '*From* | A LETTER FROM PONTUS | AND OTHER VERSE'; [800] blank; 801–858 text of poems from *A Letter from Pontus and other verse*; [859] '*From* COUNTRY SCENE | (PUBLISHED BY MESSRS. COLLINS)'; [860] blank; 861–62 text of poem from *The Country Scene*; [863] '*From* | TRIBUTE TO BALLET | (PUBLISHED BY MESSRS. COLLINS)'; [864] blank; 865–66 text of poems from *A Tribute to Ballet*; [867] '*From* | GAUTAMA THE ENLIGHTENED | SHOPPING IN OXFORD'; [868] blank; 869–876 text of 'Shopping in Oxford'; [877] 'PAVILASTUKAY'; [878] blank; 879–93 text of 'Pavilastukay'; [894] blank; [895] '*From* | SALT-WATER BALLADS'; [896] blank; 897–900 text of poems from *Salt-Water Ballads*; [901] '*From* | BALLADS AND POEMS'; [902] blank; 903–922 text of poems from *Ballads and Poems*; [923] 'LYRICS FROM | POMPEY THE GREAT'; [924] blank; 925–28 text of lyrics from *Pompey the Great* and poems 'from various books'; 929–33 'INDEX OF BEGINNINGS'; [934] blank

Paper: wove paper

Running title: running titles comprise titles of individual poems, pp.2–928

Binding: blue cloth. On spine, in silver: 'JOHN | MASEFIELD | POEMS | HEINEMANN' (all width centred). On upper cover, in blind: 'POEMS | *by* | JOHN MASEFIELD' (the '*b*' of '*by*' intersects the 'E' of 'POEMS' and the '*y*' of '*by*' intersects the 'S' of 'MASEFIELD'). On lower cover, in blind: publisher's device of a windmill (ranged lower right). All edges trimmed. Binding measurements: 189 × 124mm. (covers), 189 × 60mm. (spine). End-papers: wove paper.

Publication date: published, according to Handley-Taylor, 2 December 1946 in an edition, according to correspondence between Masefield and Heinemann, of at least 10,000 copies.

Price: 21s.

Contents:
From *WONDERINGS AND LAND WORKERS*
Wonderings ('Out of a dateless darkness pictures gleam,')
The Land Workers ('And then, in all those pleasant lands')
THE EVERLASTING MERCY

The Everlasting Mercy ('From '41 to '51')
THE WIDOW IN THE BYE STREET
The Widow in the Bye Street ('Down Bye Street, in a little Shropshire town,')
DAUBER
Dauber ('Four bells were struck, the watch was called on deck')
Explanations of some of the Sea Terms used in the poem ('BACKSTAYS.-Wire ropes which support ...')
THE DAFFODIL FIELDS
The Daffodil Fields ('Between the barren pasture and the wood')
From *PHILIP THE KING*
The Messenger's Speech ('MESSENGER. | We were to ship the troops in Calais Road;')
OTHER POEMS
Truth ('Man with his burning soul')
The Wanderer ('All day they loitered by the resting ships,')
August, 1914 ('How still this quiet cornfield is to-night!')
Biography ('When I am buried, all my thoughts and acts')
Song ('One sunny time in May')
Ships ('I cannot tell their wonder nor make known')
Sonnet (from the Spanish of Don Francisco A. Quevado) ('I saw the ramparts of my native land,')
Sonnet On The Death Of His Wife (From The Portuguese Of Antonio Di Ferreiro) ('That blessed sunlight, that once showed to me')
They Closed Her Eyes (From The Spanish Of Don Gustavo A. Becquér) ('They closed her eyes,')
The River ('All other waters have their time of peace,')
Watching by a Sick-Bed ('I heard the wind all day,')
LOLLINGDON DOWNS AND OTHER POEMS, WITH SONNETS
I ('So I have known this life,')
II ('O wretched man, that for a little mile')
III ('Out of the special cell's most special sense')
IV ('You are the link which binds us each to each.')
V ('I could not sleep for thinking of the sky,')
VI ('How did the nothing come, how did these fires,')
VII ('It may be so; but let the unknown be.')
VIII ('The Kings go by with jewelled crowns;')
IX ('What is this life which uses living cells')
X ('Can it be blood and brain, this transient force')
XI ('Not only blood and brain its servants are;')
XII ('Drop me the seed, that I even in my brain')
XIII ('Ah, but Without there is no spirit scattering;')
XIV ('You are too beautiful for mortal eyes,')
XV ('Is it a sea on which the souls embark')
XVI The Ship ('THE ORE | Before Man's labouring wisdom gave me birth')
XVII ('Night is on the downland, on the lonely moorland,')
XVIII ('Up on the downs the red-eyed kestrels hover,')
XIX ('No man takes the farm,')
XX ('A hundred years ago they quarried for the stone here;')
XXI ('Here the legion halted, here the ranks were broken,')
XXII ('Long, long ago, when all the glittering earth')
XXIII ('Night came again, but now I could not sleep;')
XXIV ('Even after all these years there comes the dream')
XXV ('If I could come again to that dear place')
XXVI ('Here in the self is all that man can know')
XXVII ('Flesh, I have knocked at many a dusty door,')
XXVIII ('But all has passed, the tune has died away,')
XXIX ('These myriad days, these many thousand hours,')
XXX ('There, on the darkened deathbed, dies the brain')
XXXI ('So in the empty sky the stars appear,')
XXXII ('It may be so with us, that in the dark,')
XXXIII ('What am I, Life? A thing of watery salt')
XXXIV ('If I could get within this changing I,')
XXXV ('What is the atom which contains the whole,')
XXXVI ('Ah, we are neither heaven nor earth, but men;')
XXXVII ('Roses are beauty, but I never see')
XXXVIII ('Over the church's door they moved a stone,')
XXXIX ('Out of the clouds come torrents, from the earth')

FROM *SARD HARKER*
The Pathfinder ('She lies at grace, at anchor, head to tide,')
FROM *MIDSUMMER NIGHT AND OTHER TALES IN VERSE*
The Taking of Morgause ('Morgause the Merry played beside the burn:')
Badon Hill ('Loki the Dragon Killer mustered men')
Arthur and his Ring ('Beauty's Delight, the Princess Gwenivere,')
The Fight on the Wall ('Modred was in the Water Tower')
Gwenivere Tells ('So Arthur passed, but country-folk believe')
Dust to Dust ('Henry Plantagenet, the English King,')
On the Coming of Arthur ('By ways unknown, unseen,')
South and East ('When good King Arthur ruled these western hursts,')
POEMS FROM *THE WANDERER*
The Setting Forth ('Her builder and owner drank tea with her captain below.')
The Ending ('Once, long before, at her second outgoing down Channel')
On Skysails ('I saw you often as the crown of Queens')
Pay ('The world paid but a penny for its toil,')
The Crowd ('They had secured their beauty to the dock,')
Under Lower Topsails ('Three lower topsails dark with wet are straining')
Eight Bells ('Four double strokes repeated on the bells,')
Posted ('Dream after dream I see the wrecks that lie')
If ('If it could be, that in this southern port')
I Saw Her Here ('All tranquil is the mirror of the bay,')
Wanderer and Wonderer ('When first the thought of you took steel')
FROM *MINNIE MAYLOW'S STORY AND OTHER TALES & SCENES*
Prologue ('I am a pilgrim come from many lands,')
Minnie Maylow's Story ('Once (long ago) there was an English King,')
Adamas and Eva ('Whilom there was, dwellyng in Paradys')
The Love Gift ('In King Marc's palace at the valley-head')
Tristan's Singing ('PART I | When Isolt quarrelled with her Tristan there')
The Rose of the World ('Dark Eleanor and Henry sat at meat')
Evan Roberts, A.B., Of H.M.S. *Andromache* ('This gallant act is told by the late Montagu Burrows, on page 67 of his *Autobiography...*')
The Hour Strikes ('THE SEEKER. | The shepherds warned me not to climb this hill')
A TALE OF TROY TOLD IN ELEVEN TALES AND AN EPILOGUE
The Taking of Helen ('Menelaus, the Spartan King,')
The Going to Troy ('He took her to Troy, the windy town')
Klytaimnestra ('I am that Klytaimnestra whom Agamemnon wedded,')
The Spearman ('You have heard the lady, making her complaints.')
The Horse ('My Father, King Epeios of the Islands,')
Sthenelus' Daughter The Entry into Troy ('King Sthenelus, my Father, has often told me')
The Trojans about the Horse ('"Apollo's self commanded Agamemnon')
Kassandra ('I was the thing they heard, I am Kassandra.')
Sthenelus' Daughter in the Horse, Till Sunset ('That was the voice those hidden in the Horse heard.')
In the Horse, Sunset till Cockcrow ('"Then, to our joy, quick steps came up the courtyard,')
The Surprise ('You have heard the story of the Horse of Troy.')
Epilogue ('Though many died and many fled')
FROM *A LETTER FROM PONTUS AND OTHER VERSE*
A Letter from Pontus ('In the first year of the Divine Tiberius,')
Australia ('When the North Lander saw the rose in blossom,')
The Will ('By Will, Man dared in den and heath')
Ballet Russe I ('The gnome from moonland plays the Chopin air,')
[Ballet Russe] II ('With delicate control in maddest speed')
Joseph Hodges, or the Corn ('He wore the smock-frock of the country's past,')
The Wild Geese ('All the Many is One,')
Hope ('O Hope that glimmers in the breast')
Beauty ('O Queen of Beauty, you who once were fire')
Nets ('COLONIES built a fort for safety's sake,')
The Long Drive | (*Edinburgh to Boar's Hill*) ('In a garage not far from the Rock of the Castle')
The Flowing of the Sangarios ('I saw a sullen little river swerve')
Wood-Pigeons ('Often the woodman scares them as he comes')
Autumn Ploughing ('After the ranks of stubble have lain bare,')
The Waggon-Maker ('I have made tales in verse, but this man made')
Partridges ('Here they lie mottled to the ground unseen,')

The Towerer ('Old Jarge, Hal, Walter and I, the Rector and Bill,')
The Eyes ('I remember a tropic dawn before turn-to,')
The Spanish Main ('Low, dull-green hills with scrub and little trees,')
Nombre de Dios ('The jungle reaches to the water's edge.')
Porto Bello ('The port is unsuspected from the east,')
Canal Zone ('Among these hills, twelve generations since,')
The Spanish Main Schooner ('A little wooden schooner, painted white,')
A Ballad of Sir Francis Drake ('Before Sir Francis put to sea,')
Sweet Friends ('Print not my life nor letters; put them by:')
FROM *COUNTRY SCENE*
On England ('What is this England, whom the draughtsmen print')
FROM *TRIBUTE TO BALLET*
The Lovely Swan ('I heard men mutter of you, "She will die...')
Sur Les Pointes ('The time is near, my sweet,')
Who is that Old Fellow in the Wings? ('"We are young, friend, like the flowers,')
FROM *GAUTAMA THE ENLIGHTENED*
Shopping in Oxford ('Twenty-four years ago, I wandered down')
PAVILASTUKAY
Pavilastukay ('Of all the many things that men abhor')
FROM *SALT-WATER BALLADS*
The *Loch Achray* ('The *Loch Achray* was a clipper tall')
Trade Winds ('In the harbour, in the island, in the Spanish Seas,')
Sea-Fever ('I must go down to the seas again, to the lonely sea and the sky,')
The West Wind ('It's a warm wind, the west wind, full of birds' cries;')
FROM *BALLADS AND POEMS*
Sir Bors ('Would I could win some quiet and rest, and a little ease,')
Spanish Waters ('Spanish waters, Spanish waters, you are ringing in my ears,')
Cargoes ('Quinquireme of Nineveh from distant Ophir')
Captain Stratton's Fancy ('Oh some are fond of red wine, and some are fond of white')
An Old Song Re-Sung ('I saw a ship a-sailing, a-sailing, a-sailing,')
The Emigrant ('Going by Daly's shanty I heard the boys within')
Beauty ('I have seen dawn and sunset on moors and windy hills')
The Seekers ('Friends and loves we have none, nor wealth nor blessed abode,')
Laugh and be Merry ('Laugh and be merry, remember, better the world with a song,')
June Twilight ('The twilight comes; the sun')
Roadways ('One road leads to London,')
The Gentle Lady ('So beautiful, so dainty-sweet,')
Twilight ('Twilight it is, and the far woods are dim, and the rooks cry and call.')
Invocation ('O wanderer into many brains,')
A Creed ('I held that when a person dies')
When Bony Death ('When bony Death has chilled her gentle blood,')
Her Heart ('Her heart is always doing lovely things,')
Being Her Friend ('Being her friend, I do not care, not I,')
Fragments ('Troy Town is covered up with weeds,')
Born For Nought Else ('Born for nought else, for nothing but for this,')
The Death Rooms ('My soul has many an old decaying room')
Ignorance ('Since I have learned Love's shining alphabet,')
The Watch in the Wood ('When Death has laid her in his quietude,')
C.L.M. ('In the dark womb where I began')
Waste ('No rose but fades: no glory but must pass:')
The Wild Duck ('Twilight. Red in the west.')
The Word ('My friend, my bonny friend, when we are old,')
LYRICS FROM *POMPEY THE GREAT*
The Centurions ('Man is a sacred city, built of marvellous earth.')
Philip Sings ('Though we are ringed with spears, though the last hope is gone,')
Chanty ('Kneel to the beautiful women who bear us this strange brave fruit.')
FROM VARIOUS BOOKS
Sixty Odd Years Ago ('Much worth was in the country: yet, today,')
Gallipoli, 1915 ('Even so was wisdom proven blind;')
On the Dead in Gallipoli ('They came from safety of their own free will')
An Epilogue ('I have seen flowers come in stony places')

509

Notes:

The English single volume of Masefield's collected verse that replaced *Collected Poems* (A71) in 1946 was, in reality, a selected edition for there are many omissions from the true collected canon.

The named sources for poems do not always accurately cite a title. A volume entitled *Wonderings and Land Workers* was, for example, never published.

Information cited in this edition regarding reprints of the previous title (see *Collected Poems*) does not exactly correspond with consulted reprint copies.

A letter from Masefield to Louisa Callender of the Heinemann firm reveals Masefield's intentions of selecting material for this volume, his concern over type-setting, and order:

> ...there are many pages of early work that I would gladly scrap, and plenty of later pages, too. Please, will you very kindly let me know what this would entail in the way of re-setting. If I were to cut out thirty odd pages here and there could the cutting be done without entailing a resetting of all the intervening pages?
>
> I do not wish to add ALL my latest verse to the Collected Poems book; but I should judge, that even with the omissions, (and those further omissions mentioned above) the book may well be fifty pages longer than at present. Does the heart a little sink at the thought?
>
> Then, one other question about the Collected Poems:- Might it not be well, to print the latest poems, the new additions to the book, at THE BEGINNING of the reprint? Some of the additions deal with my childhood, and would come with some fitness at the beginning.
>
> (John Masefield, letter to [Louisa] Callender, [April 1945])
(Archives of William Heinemann)

Towards the end of April 1945 Masefield had begun to finalise his plans for the volume and suggested the title for the first time:

> In working over the *Collected Poems*, I judge that about 100 pages will come out, or a very few more, and about 100 pages will come in, to take the place of the omissions, so that the book may remain about the present size. But, perhaps you would not mind calling the new edition POEMS (not *Collected Poems*) for it will be by no means a complete edition, and "collected" might be misleading.
>
> (John Masefield, letter to [Louisa] Callender, [April 1945])
(Archives of William Heinemann)

Louisa Callender replied to Masefield's suggestion on 30 April 1945. Heinemann were indeed willing to accept the new title: 'POEMS would, I think, be a better title than COLLECTED POEMS and so we will use it.' (see Louisa Callender, letter to John Masefield, 30 April 1945) (Archives of William Heinemann).

'First proofs' were sent to Masefield towards the end of November 1945:

> By separate cover I have sent you a set of first proofs of the revised Collected Poems incorporating the new material set for the volume to be called POEMS.
>
> (B.F. Oliver, letter to John Masefield, 21 November 1945)
(HRHRC, MS (Masefield, J.) Recip William Heinemann Ltd.)

and by 17 January 1946 Masefield had informed Heinemann that the volume could go to press (see B.F. Oliver, letter to John Masefield, 17 January 1946) (HRHRC, MS (Masefield, J.) Recip William Heinemann Ltd.) Shortages of paper and other material were responsible for the delay in publication. During May 1946, A.S. Frere noted:

> I am happy to be able to tell you that I have been able to give an order to the Windmill Press to do at least an edition of 10,000 of your Collected Poems. I have been able to do this by making some drastic reallocations in our forward paper quota. At the moment, in common with the rest of the trade, our bottleneck is binding, but I am hoping very much to be able to get the edition out by the Autumn.
>
> (A.S. Frere, letter to John Masefield, 27 May 1946)
(HRHRC, MS (Masefield, J.) Recip William Heinemann Ltd.)

A divisional page is omitted for the final section ('From Various Books').

Copies seen: private collection (PWE); BL (11613.b.3) stamped 2 DEC 1946; HRHRC (PR6025 A77 A17 1946 cop.1) inscribed 'For Jude. | from | Z. | Christmas. 1946.'

Reprinted:

'Reprinted'	[first edition, second impression]	Feb 1948
	[first edition, third impression]	1954
	[first edition, fourth impression]	1961
	[first edition, fifth impression]	1966

A149 WORDS SPOKEN AT THE OPENING OF AN EXHIBITION OF BOOKS OF POETRY

1947

A149(a) First English edition (1947)

Page [i]:
Words spoken at the Opening of an | Exhibition of Books of Poetry | [text]
(All width centred)

Bibliographies: Handley-Taylor [unrecorded], Wight [unrecorded]

Collation: [A]²; 2 leaves; 153 × 109mm.; [i–iv]

Page contents: [i] title and text (beginning); [ii–iii] text (continued); [iv] '[text (concluded)] | *April 10th, 1947*'

Paper: wove paper

Running title: none

Binding: single sheet folded once. Upper wrapper comprises the title and beginning of the text. All edges trimmed except upper wrapper fore edge which is deckle-edged. Binding measurements: 153 × 109mm. (wrappers), 153 × 0.5mm. (spine).

Publication date: [April 1947]

Price: copies were not, presumably, for sale

Contents:
Words spoken at the Opening of an Exhibition of Books of Poetry ('It is a great honour and pleasure to help at the opening…')

Notes:
This item presents a speech, dated 10 April 1947, given by Masefield to open an exhibition of editions of English poetry from Chaucer to the present day. The exhibition was assembled by John Hayward for the National Book League at 7 Albemarle Street in London. See also D16.

The text is printed in italics throughout.

Copies seen: BL (Add.Mss.52735, ff.108–109) inscribed 'For | Sydney Cockerell.', signed 'John Masefield.'; HRHRC (PR6025 A77 W672 1947) with HRHRC note 'From the Library of John Masefield'

A150 THANKS BEFORE GOING WITH OTHER GRATITUDE FOR OLD DELIGHT

1947

A150(a) First English edition (1947)

THANKS BEFORE GOING | *with* | OTHER GRATITUDE FOR OLD DELIGHT | *including* | A *MACBETH* PRODUCTION | and various papers not before printed | *By* | JOHN MASEFIELD | [publisher's device of a windmill with 'W' and 'H'] | [rule, 57mm.] | WILLIAM HEINEMANN LTD | LONDON :: TORONTO
(All width centred)

Bibliographies: Handley-Taylor p.64, Wight [unrecorded]

Collation: [A]⁸ B-O⁸ (J not used); signatures right foot of page; 112 leaves; 183 × 121mm.; [i–v] vi 1–215 [216–18]

Page contents: [i] half-title: 'THANKS BEFORE GOING | *with* | OTHER GRATITUDE FOR OLD DELIGHT | *including* | A *MACBETH* PRODUCTION | and various papers not before printed'; [ii] '*THE WORKS OF JOHN MASEFIELD* | PLAYS: | [12 titles listed] | POETRY: | [19 titles listed] | FICTION: | [14 titles listed] | GENERAL: | [14 titles listed]'; [iii] title-page; [iv] 'TO | MY WIFE | PUBLISHED 1947 | [rule] | PRINTED IN GREAT BRITAIN AT THE WINDMILL PRESS | KINGSWOOD, SURREY'; [v] 'CONTENTS' (seven items listed with page references – the first item is listed with six component parts); vi-215 text; [216–18] blank

Paper: wove paper

Running title: 'THANKS BEFORE GOING' (39mm.) on both verso and recto, pp.2–67; 'WILLIAM MORRIS' (27mm.) on both verso and recto, pp.70–90; 'PETER' (10mm.) on both verso and recto, pp.92–96, 'ON RIGGING MODEL SHIPS' (43mm.) on both verso and recto, pp.98–116; 'A *MACBETH* PRODUCTION' (42mm.) on both verso and recto, pp.118–80; 'ON PLAYING THE TWO NOBLE KINSMEN' (67mm.) on both verso and recto, pp.182–203; 'FOR THE TELLERS OF TALES IN VERSE' (65mm.) on both verso and recto, pp.205–215

Binding: blue cloth. On spine, in silver: 'THANKS | BEFORE | GOING | *With* | OTHER | Gratitude | for old | DELIGHT | *Including* | A | *MACBETH* | PRODUCTION | and various | papers | [point] | JOHN | MASEFIELD | Heinemann' (all width centred). Upper cover: blank. On lower cover, in blind: publisher's device of a windmill (ranged lower right). All edges trimmed. Binding measurements: 190 × 123mm. (covers), 190 × 26mm. (spine). End-papers: wove paper.

Publication date: the sales ledger preserved in the Heinemann Archive suggests publication on 11 August 1947 in an edition of 1000 copies

Price: 10s.6d.

Contents:
Thanks Before Going ('DANTE GABRIEL ROSSETTI. | Dante was as a star above his head.')
William Morris ('GROWTH | When men are very young, they have much ignorance of the world, much...')
Peter ('I first heard of him as an exceptionally tame bird which followed the bearer of...')
On Rigging Model Ships ('Once, when I was very young, and busy all day with the problems and delights...')
A *Macbeth* Production ('While I was thinking of what might be, and of that more sinister thing, which probably...')
On Playing The Two Noble Kinsmen ('While we talked together, one of the young men asked me to name a poetical...')
For the Tellers of Tales in Verse ('Those young men, who were planning to roam the country, acting poetical plays...')

['Thanks Before Going', 'William Morris' and 'A *Macbeth* Production' each contain separate titled sections]

Notes:
This volume obviously derives from *Thanks Before Going* (see A144). The essay 'A Macbeth Production' had also been previously published (see A142). There is no essay entitled 'Other Gratitude For Old Delight', and this is a collective name for the contents of the volume excluding the notes on Rossetti.

All texts commence with a drop-capital with the exception of 'A *Macbeth* Production' and individual verses. The text of 'Thanks Before Going' appears to use the same setting of type as A144(a). 'A *Macbeth* Production' has been entirely re-set for this edition.

A letter from Louisa Callender dated 9 February 1945 to Masefield suggests that this volume was discussed before the original printing of *A Macbeth Production* (see notes to A142(a)). Masefield raised the issue again on 6 July 1946:

> You may remember, that there was some talk of a prose book to contain Macbeth Production, Thanks before going, and some other prose papers not yet in print. May I ask, if you feel at all inclined or sufficiently papered, to do such a book before Xmas?
>
> (John Masefield, letter to [Louisa] Callender, 6 July 1946)
> (Archives of William Heinemann)

As the volume was published over a year later, Heinemann were evidently disinclined or insufficiently papered. Paged-galley proofs were sent at the beginning of November 1946:

> A MACBETH PRODUCTION and THANKS BEFORE GOING. It is your idea I believe to have these reprinted in one volume with five new pieces added. I am sending you herewith paged-galley proofs of the new material and MS., and would ask you to kindly return one set of proofs with your corrections…
>
> (B.F. Oliver, letter to John Masefield, 8 November 1946)
> (HRHRC, MS (Masefield, J.) Recip William Heinemann Ltd.)

Copies seen: private collection (PWE); BL (12360.df.4) stamped 11 AUG 1947

A151 A BOOK OF BOTH SORTS 1947

A151(a) First English edition (1947)

A BOOK OF BOTH | SORTS | SELECTIONS FROM THE | VERSE AND PROSE OF | JOHN MASEFIELD | [publisher's device of a windmill with 'W' and 'H'] | [rule, 58mm.] | WILLIAM HEINEMANN LTD | LONDON :: TORONTO
(All width centred with lines 3 and 4 justified on same left and right margins)

Bibliographies: Handley-Taylor p.65, Wight 114

Collation: [A]¹⁶ B-I¹⁶ K⁴ (J not used); the fifth leaf of gatherings A-I is also signed; signatures right foot of page; 148 leaves; 184 × 122mm.; [i–vi] vii–viii (see notes) 1–287 [288]

Page contents: [i] half-title: 'A BOOK OF BOTH SORTS'; [ii] '*THE WORKS OF JOHN MASEFIELD* | PLAYS: | [12 titles listed] | POETRY: | [19 titles listed] | FICTION: | [14 titles listed] | GENERAL: | [14 titles listed]'; [iii] title-page; [iv] 'FIRST PUBLISHED 1947 | PRINTED IN GREAT BRITAIN AT THE WINDMILL PRESS | KINGSWOOD, SURREY'; [v] 'TO | MY WIFE'; [vi] blank; vii–viii 'CONTENTS' (52 individual items listed with sources and page references); 1–287 text; [288] blank

Paper: wove paper

Running title: 'A Book of Both Sorts' (32mm.) on verso; recto title comprises title of extract, pp.2–286

Binding: blue cloth. On spine, in silver: 'A | BOOK OF | BOTH | SORTS | [triangle device in outline] | JOHN | MASEFIELD | HEINEMANN' (all width centred). Upper cover: blank. On lower cover, in blind: publisher's device of a windmill (ranged lower right). All edges trimmed. Binding measurements: 189 × 123mm. (covers), 189 × 33mm. (spine). End-papers: wove paper.

Publication date: the sales ledger preserved in the Heinemann Archive suggests publication on 22 September 1947 in an edition of 4000 copies

Price: 10s.6d.

Contents:

From PAVILASTUKAY | Life on Earth Has Been Fair at Times ('Though reckoned rather frail to serve and die')

An Epilogue | The Meditation of Highworth Ridden ('I have seen flowers come in stony places')

Notes:

The source of each extract or poem is not always provided in the volume.

As noted by Wight, p.viii is incorrectly numbered vi.

Each extract or poem commences with a drop-capital with the exception of the sonnets. Here only the first sonnet commences with a drop-capital.

Curiously, 'The Hereford Speech' (pp.14–16) and 'Adventure On' (pp.191–92) employ italics throughout.

Copies seen: private collection (PWE); BL (12275.a.21) stamped 22 SEP 1947

A152 BADON PARCHMENTS   1947

A152(a) First English edition (1947)

BADON PARCHMENTS | *by* | JOHN MASEFIELD | [publisher's device of a windmill with 'W' and 'H'] | [rule, 58mm.] | WILLIAM HEINEMANN LTD | LONDON :: TORONTO
(All width centred)

Bibliographies: Handley-Taylor p.65, Wight 115

Collation: [A]⁸ B–K⁸ (J not used); signatures right foot of page; 80 leaves; 185 × 122mm.; [i–viii] 1–151 [152]

Page contents: [i–ii] blank; [iii] half-title: 'BADON PARCHMENTS'; [iv] *THE WORKS OF JOHN MASEFIELD* | PLAYS: | [12 titles listed] | POETRY: | [19 titles listed] | FICTION: | [14 titles listed] | GENERAL: | [14 titles listed]'; [v] title-page; [vi] 'FIRST PUBLISHED 1947 | PRINTED IN GREAT BRITAIN AT THE WINDMILL PRESS | KINGSWOOD, SURREY'; [vii] 'To | MY WIFE'; [viii] 'A MAP OF SOUTHERN BRITAIN | [map in black and white, with legend]'; 1–151 text; [152] blank

Paper: wove paper

Running title: 'BADON PARCHMENTS' (30mm.) on both verso and recto, pp.2–151

Binding: blue cloth. On spine, in silver: 'BADON | *Parchments* | [square point resting on one corner] | JOHN | MASEFIELD | HEINEMANN' (all width centred). Upper cover: blank. On lower cover, in blind: publisher's device of a windmill (ranged lower right). All edges trimmed. Binding measurements: 189 × 122mm. (covers), 189 × 28mm. (spine). End-papers: wove paper.

Publication date: the sales ledger preserved in the Heinemann Archive suggests publication on 1 December 1947 in an edition of 6000 copies

Price: 8s.6d.

Contents:

Badon Parchments ('Most Great, most Virtuous, most Glorious, when, in Your Wisdom, You directed me...')

Chapter headings are as follows:

1. A copy of a Letter sent to the Emperor Justinian and the Empress Theodora by their Servant, John of Cos, concerning events in Britain.
2. These words were spoken by our guide to the assembled youth of King Ocvran and his hereditary Over-King.
3. An account of the months preceding the Heathen War.
4. Some account of the battle of Badon Hill

Notes:

The last of Masefield's novels, although set in Arthurian Britain, is nevertheless linked to his Byzantine novels, *Basilissa* and *Conquer* (the narrator is an envoy of Justinian and Theodora). The novel is in four parts. Masefield's primary concern is the Battle of Badon which he locates in the sixth century, and this invites comparison with the poem 'Badon Hill' in *Midsummer Night and other tales in verse* (see A88).

A letter (preserved in the Heinemann Archive) from Masefield dated 12 August [1947] enclosed the typescript for this volume. Publication of this title was therefore less than four months later. The publishing agreement for this title between Masefield and Heinemann was dated 31 October 1947 (see Archives of The Society of Authors). The agreement refers to a publication price of 8s.6d.

A letter from Masefield to The Society of Authors dated March 1948 reveals his views on this novel:

> ...I do not feel very happy about *Badon Parchments*. It seems to me better to let the volume die, and not bother about any foreign translation...

(John Masefield, letter to [Anne] Munro-Kerr, 4 March [1948])
(BL, Add.Mss.56620, f.179)

Copies seen: private collection (PWE); HRHRC (TEMP M377BA 1947 cop.1) inscribed 'For | Judith, | from Z. | Dec 13. 1947.'; HRHRC (TEMP M377BA 1947 cop.2) inscribed 'For Con | from | Jan. | Nov 20. 1947.'

A153 A PLAY OF ST. GEORGE

A153(a) First English edition (1948)

A PLAY OF | ST. GEORGE | *by* | JOHN MASEFIELD | [publisher's device of a windmill with 'W' and 'H'] | [rule, 56mm.] | WILLIAM HEINEMANN LTD | MELBOURNE :: LONDON :: TORONTO
(All width centred)

Bibliographies: Handley-Taylor p.65, Wight 116

Collation: [A]⁴ B-F⁴ G⁶; G2 is also signed; signatures right foot of page; 30 leaves; 184 × 122mm.; [i–vi] 1–53 [54]

Page contents: [i] half-title: 'A PLAY OF | ST. GEORGE'; [ii] '*THE WORKS OF JOHN MASEFIELD* | PLAYS: | [12 titles listed] | POETRY: | [19 titles listed] | FICTION: | [14 titles listed] | GENERAL: | [14 titles listed]'; [iii] title-page; [iv] 'FIRST PUBLISHED 1948 | PRINTED IN GREAT BRITAIN AT THE WINDMILL PRESS | KINGSWOOD, SURREY'; [v] 'To | MY WIFE'; [vi] 'PREFACE | THE STAGE. | [new paragraph] This play was devised for performance upon a stage having | approaches from each side of the Front and Back. | [new paragraph] The Back of the stage (a stone screen of the early fifteenth | century) contained a central door, supposed to lead within the | Palace of King Nicanor. | [new paragraph] STAGE PROPERTIES. | [new paragraph] Towards the Front of the stage, on each side, is a stone | settle; that on the Left, for Queen Artemisia; that on the | Right, for the Emperor's Proxy.'; 1 'PERSONS | [dramatis personae listed] | THE PLAY | [text commences]'; 2–53 text; [54] blank

Paper: wove paper

Running title: 'A PLAY OF ST. GEORGE' (32mm.) on both verso and recto, pp.2–53

Binding: blue cloth. On spine, reading lengthways down spine from head, in silver: 'JOHN MASEFIELD [point] A PLAY OF ST. GEORGE [point] HEINEMANN'. Upper cover: blank. On lower cover, in blind: publisher's device of a windmill (ranged lower right). All edges trimmed. Binding measurements: 189 × 123mm. (covers), 189 × 19mm. (spine). End-papers: wove paper.

Publication date: the sales ledger preserved in the Heinemann Archive suggests publication on 12 July 1948 in an edition of 2000 copies

Price: 6s.

Contents:

A Play of St. George ('*The spirit of the wounded* KING NICANOR *enters. He is swathed, almost as one in...*')

Notes:

Masefield's last play, in prose, depicting the tale of George and the dragon set in the Roman world. The dust-jacket from the English edition notes the play was written 'to celebrate the 600th anniversary of the Foundation of the Order of the Garter in April, 1948'. A celebratory performance was, however, abandoned for financial and political reasons. The incidental music was to have been by Sir Arnold Bax. A letter dated October 1947 suggests that Heinemann were to provide copies of the play for rehearsal purposes:

> We are sending you paged-galley proofs of A PLAY OF ST. GEORGE which I shall be glad if you will kindly correct so that we can make up the thirty sets in booklet form that you require...
>
> (B.F. Oliver, letter to John Masefield, 16 October 1947)
> (HRHRC, MS (Masefield, J.) Recip William Heinemann Ltd.)

The publishing agreement for this title between Masefield and Heinemann was dated 29 April 1948 (see Archives of The Society of Authors).

Copies seen: private collection (PWE) inscribed 'For | Julia Smith, | from | John Masefield. | 8 July. 1948.'; private collection (PWE); BL (11783.aaa.109) stamped 12 JUL 1948

A153(b) First American edition (1948)

A PLAY OF | ST. GEORGE | *by* | JOHN MASEFIELD | NEW YORK | THE MACMILLAN COMPANY | 1948
(All width centred)

Bibliographies: Handley-Taylor p.65, Wight 116a

Collation: [A-B]⁸ [C]⁶ [D]⁸; 30 leaves; 188 × 126mm.; [i–vi] 1–53 [54]

Page contents: [i] half-title: 'A PLAY OF | ST. GEORGE'; [ii] '*THE WORKS OF JOHN MASEFIELD* | PLAYS: | [12 titles listed] | POETRY: | [19 titles listed] | FICTION: | [14 titles listed] | GENERAL: | [14 titles listed]'; [iii] title-page; [iv] 'COPYRIGHT, 1948, BY | JOHN MASEFIELD. | All rights reserved–no part of this | book may be reproduced in any | form without permission in writing | from the publisher, except by a re- | viewer who wishes to quote brief | passages in connection with a review | written for inclusion in magazine or | newspaper. | First Printing | PRINTED IN THE UNITED STATES OF AMERICA'; [v] 'To | MY WIFE'; [vi] 'PREFACE | THE STAGE. | [new paragraph] This play was devised for performance upon a stage having | approaches from each side of the Front and Back. | [new paragraph] The Back of the stage (a stone screen of the early fifteenth | century) contained a central door, supposed to lead within the | Palace of King Nicanor. | [new paragraph] STAGE PROPERTIES. | [new paragraph] Towards the Front of the stage, on each side, is a stone | settle; that on the Left, for Queen Artemisia; that on the | Right, for the Emperor's Proxy.'; 1 'PERSONS | [dramatis personae listed] | THE PLAY | [text commences]'; 2–53 text; [54] blank

Paper: wove paper

Running title: 'A PLAY OF ST. GEORGE' (32mm.) on both verso and recto, pp.2–53

Binding: maroon cloth. On spine, reading lengthways down spine from head, in gold: '*Masefield* A PLAY OF ST. GEORGE *Macmillan*' (see notes). On upper cover, in gold: device of a dragon pierced by a sword (see notes): 31 × 36mm. Lower cover: blank. All edges trimmed. Binding measurements: 192 × 127mm. (covers), 192 × 20mm. (spine). End-papers: wove paper.

Publication date: published, according to Handley-Taylor, 11 October 1948

Price: $2.00

Contents:
as for A153(a)

Notes:
The '*M*' in '*Masefield*' and the '*M*' and '*n*' in '*Macmillan*' on the spine are swash.

The device on the upper cover shows a dragon pierced by a sword. The sword could also represent a cross, however.

Two publishing agreements for this title between Masefield and Macmillan are dated 4 December 1947 and 2 July 1948 (see Archives of The Society of Authors). The agreement refers to 'a licence to publish in volume form in the United States of America, Canada and the Philippine Republic a work the subject or title of which is A PLAY OF ST. GEORGE'.

Copies seen: private collection (PWE); private collection (ROV)

A154 GORDON BOTTOMLEY [–] WORDS SPOKEN BY JOHN MASEFIELD [1948]

A154(a) First English edition ([1948])

Page [1]:
GORDON BOTTOMLEY | WORDS SPOKEN BY | JOHN MASEFIELD | AT A | MEMORIAL SERVICE | IN THE | CHURCH OF ST. MARTIN-IN-THE-FIELDS | SEPTEMBER 28TH, 1948
(All width centred)

Bibliographies: Handley-Taylor [unrecorded], Wight [unrecorded]

Collation: [A]²; 2 leaves; 208 × 132mm.; [1–4]

Page contents: [1] title-page; [2–3] text; [4] blank

Paper: laid paper (watermark: '[crown] Glastonbury'), chain-lines 25mm. apart

Running title: none

Binding: issued as a four page leaflet. The title-page consequently comprises the upper wrapper. All edges trimmed. Binding measurements: 208 × 132mm. (wrappers), 208 × 0.5mm. (spine).

Publication date: [1948]

Price: unknown

Contents:
Gordon Bottomley… ('Once again, we are met within this great Church, to keep in mind a poet much-loved...')

Notes:
A publication date of 1948 is assumed. This item has never previously been included in Masefield bibliographies.

The typescript – with Masefield's markings – for the Order of Service is present in the HRHRC (MS (Masefield, J.) Misc. [Memorial Service for Gordon Bottomley]). It does not include Masefield's spoken address.

Copies seen: BL (X.909/83706) stamped 15 FEB 1979; HRHRC (PR6003 067 Z838) inscribed 'The London Library Appeal. | No 115.' and 'John Masefield. | February the 14th. | 1960.'

A155 SOME WORDS SPOKEN IN GRATEFUL MEMORY OF SIR RONALD ROSS... [1949]

A155(a) First English edition ([1949])

Some words spoken in grateful memory | of | SIR RONALD ROSS | Poet and Scientist | at a meeting commemorating Mosquito Day | (21st August 1897) | at | The Ross Institute of Tropical Hygiene | KEPPEL STREET, GOWER STREET, | on | Monday, 5th July, 1948 | with a few corrections and additions | by | Dr. JOHN MASEFIELD, O.M. | Poet Laureate
(All width centred and enclosed within double ruled border (the external rule being bolder than the inner): 161 × 103mm. The type includes ligatured characters)

Bibliographies: Handley-Taylor [unrecorded], Wight [unrecorded]

Collation: [A]⁴; 4 leaves; 204 × 137mm.; [1–2] 3–7 [8]

Page contents: [1] title-page; [2] blank; 3–7 text; [8] lower wrapper

Paper: wove paper

Running title: none

Binding: wrappers comprise the first and last leaves of the single gathering ([A]1 and [A]4). Spine: blank. On upper wrapper: title-page as above. On lower wrapper: 'BERRYMAN | LONDON. S.E.10.' (ranged lower right). All edges trimmed. Binding measurements: 204 × 137mm. (wrappers), 204 × 1mm. (spine).

Publication date: published, according to manuscript correspondence, March 1949

Price: copies were not for sale

Contents:

In Grateful Memory of Ronald Ross ('A great many years ago when I was mixing much with sailors, I heard...')

Notes:

The text is headed 'In Grateful Memory of Ronald Ross' rather than the title given on the upper wrapper.

The text commences with a drop-capital.

Professor G. Macdonald, Director of the London School of Hygiene and Tropical Medicine, wrote to Masefield in February 1949 informing him

> …We are printing your tribute to Ronald Ross in the Annual Report, which should be out in a month or two. I am ordering a special reprint of this note only, and will, of course, send you as many copies as you would like. If you will let me know as soon as you can how many you wish to have I shall pass the order direct to the printer.
>
> (G. Macdonald, letter to John Masefield, 9 February 1949)
> (HRHRC, MS (Masefield, J.) Recip London School of Hygiene and Tropical Medicine)

Within a month of this letter, Professor Macdonald wrote again stating:

> I am forwarding under separate cover 50 copies of the extract from the Annual Report containing your address in memory of Sir Ronald Ross. I do hope that it is produced in a manner satisfactory to you. Although this is an extract from a report I am unable to send you the complete volume as the printers have produced the reprint about a month before they expect to produce the whole thing. We are extremely grateful to you for having given this address and I hope you are satisfied with the printed version. Should you want any more copies we shall be only too pleased to send them.
>
> (G. Macdonald, letter to John Masefield, 3 March 1949)
> (HRHRC, MS (Masefield, J.) Recip London School of Hygiene and Tropical Medicine)

It appears that the separate packet arrived before this letter for Masefield inscribed a copy to Florence Lamont on 2 March 1949 (see below).

Copies seen: Bodleian (Rec.e.104) signed 'John Masefield.' no dated library stamp; Ledbury Library inscribed 'John Masefield. | 18th April. 1951.'; Harvard College Library (Houghton *EC9.M377.948s) inscribed 'For Florence [Lamont] | from John. | ii. III. | 1949.' includes undated letter tipped-in: 'Dearest Florence, I send with this the print of the talk on R R which you gladdened with your presence last Summer. Bless you, John'; Columbia University Libraries (Special Collections PR6025/A77/S6) includes posthumous booklabel; HRHRC (R489 R7 M384 1948 cop.1) includes HRHRC note 'From the Library of John Masefield'; HRHRC (R489 R7 M384 1948 cop.2) inscribed 'John Masefield. | The London Library Appeal. | No 161.'; HRHRC (R489 R7 M384 1948 cop.3) inscribed 'John Masefield. | The London Library Appeal. | No 162.'

A156 ON THE HILL   1949

A156(a) First English edition (1949)

ON THE HILL | *by* | JOHN MASEFIELD | [publisher's device of a windmill with 'W' and 'H'] | [rule, 56mm.] | WILLIAM HEINEMANN LTD | MELBOURNE :: LONDON :: TORONTO
(All width centred)

Bibliographies: Handley-Taylor p.65, Wight 117

Collation: [A]⁸ B-H⁸; signatures right foot of page; 64 leaves; 184 × 122mm.; [i–vi] 1–122

Page contents: [i] half-title: 'ON THE HILL'; [ii] '*THE WORKS OF JOHN MASEFIELD* | PLAYS: | [12 titles listed] | POETRY: | [20 titles listed] | FICTION: | [14 titles listed] | GENERAL: | [14 titles listed]'; [iii] title-page; [iv] 'FIRST PUBLISHED 1949 | PRINTED IN GREAT BRITAIN | AT THE WINDMILL PRESS | KINGSWOOD, SURREY'; [v] '*For L, from C & J.* | You who knew this, | You who walked this hill and drew | Thoughts of what the truth is | From the Earth's remembered sweet, | Now are here, on hill and in the flower | In the whole vast valley of the wheat, | In its beauty, in its life and in its power.'; [vi] 'CONTENTS' (24 individual poems listed with page references); 1–122 text

Paper: wove paper

Running title: running titles comprise titles of individual poems, pp.3–122

Binding: blue cloth. On spine, in silver: 'ON | THE | HILL | [five-petal device] | John | Masefield | Heinemann' (all width centred). Upper cover: blank. On lower cover, in blind: publisher's device of a windmill (ranged lower right). All edges trimmed. Binding measurements: 189 × 123mm. (covers), 189 × 24mm. (spine). End-papers: wove paper.

Publication date: the sales ledger preserved in the Heinemann Archive suggests publication on 22 August 1949 in an edition of 3500 copies

Price: 8s.6d.

Contents:
[Untitled] ('You who knew this,')
On The Hill. Prologue ('No I know not;')
The Hill ('This remains here.')
On The Hill. Story ('I walked the wayless downs again')
Jouncer's Tump ('My grand-dad said, to Sis and me,')
Cry Baby Cottage ('"Now, at last, we're really settled in the new house," said her lover.')
The Wind ('The wind comes in from the sea to the chicory-flower.')
Fire ('Often, before, he had been away for a week,')
Blown Hilcote Manor ('In perfect June we reached the house to let,')
A Tale of Country Things ('That little brook's the boundary line')
Constant Lover ('The Lady Constance prayed within her bower')
Tristan and Isolt ('The King and Queen debate with eagerness')
Count Arnoldos ('Who can have had such an adventure')
The Lady Alda ('In Paris is the Lady Alda,')
Of The Moor King Who Lost Alhama ('Upon mule-back the Moor King')
Of The Moorish King Who Lost Granada ('When King Chico of Granada lost his Kingdom and departed')
The Banner of the Cross ('When Hernando took Granada from the Moor,')
Rose of Beauty ('"Rose of beauty, Rose of beauty')
Bright Darling ('"Bright thou art, beloved Lady,')
Lovely Marquise (Old French) ('The King bade feast, by beat of drum,')
Sailorman Bold ('Sailorman bold is home from sea')
The Wind of the Sea ('Three sailor-men from Bantry Bay')
Dead Man's Bridge ('"At Dead Man's Bridge, where all the Fair will be')
A Messenger Speech ('Dead is Orestes: dead: I said: I say again.')
The End of The Iliad ('When they had reached the ford of the clear-running stream,')

Notes:
A volume of poems, described by Sanford Sternlicht as 'poems of country things and ghosts'. According to Handley-Taylor they are all previously unpublished.

The titles of the first and third poems as cited in the contents are longer than those given in the text.

The dedication of the volume (from Constance and John Masefield) is to Lewis Masefield, the Masefields' son and second child. He was killed during the Second World War in late 1942. In 1947 Masefield contributed a preface to Lewis Masefield's posthumously published novel, *The Passion Left Behind* (see B435).

The ampersand in the dedication on p.[v] is particularly ornate.

A letter (preserved in the Heinemann Archive) from Masefield dated 8 January 1949 enclosed the 'script' for this volume. This was acknowledged on 10 January 1949 (see Louisa Callender, letter to John Masefield, 10 January 1949) (HRHRC, MS (Masefield, J.) Recip William Heinemann Ltd.) A.S. Frere wrote:

> …I have been looking at the manuscript of ON THE HILL and I like it very much. May I make some tentative suggestions? Would you consider a rearrangement whereby The Hill comes first in the book along with the other two "Hill" poems. This, I think would "lead" the volume better than in the present arrangement.
>
> (A.S. Frere, letter to John Masefield, 27 January 1949)
> (HRHRC, MS (Masefield, J.) Recip William Heinemann Ltd.)

The publishing agreement for this title between Masefield and Heinemann was sent at the end of March 1949. At the beginning of May Masefield was sent proofs:

> I have pleasure in sending you proofs in book form and manuscript of ON THE HILL and I sincerely hope that you are now sufficiently recovered to be able to deal with these.
>
> (B.F. Oliver, letter to John Masefield, 2 May 1949)
> (HRHRC, MS (Masefield, J.) Recip William Heinemann Ltd.)

Copies seen: private collection (PWE)

A156(b) First American edition (1949 [1950])

ON THE HILL | *by* | JOHN MASEFIELD | THE MACMILLAN COMPANY | NEW YORK
(All width centred)

Bibliographies: Handley-Taylor [unrecorded], Wight 117a

Collation: [A]⁸ (±[A]2) B-H⁸; signatures right foot of page; 64 leaves; 183 × 123mm.; [i–vi] 1–122

Page contents: [i] half-title: 'ON THE HILL'; [ii] *THE WORKS OF JOHN MASEFIELD* | PLAYS: | [12 titles listed] | POETRY:
| [20 titles listed] | FICTION: | [14 titles listed] | GENERAL: | [14 titles listed]'; [iii] title-page; [iv] 'COPYRIGHT 1949 BY JOHN
MASEFIELD | PRINTED IN GREAT BRITAIN'; [v] '*For L, from C & J.* | You who knew this, | You who walked this hill and
drew | Thoughts of what the truth is | From the Earth's remembered sweet, | Now are here, on hill and in the flower | In the
whole vast valley of the wheat, | In its beauty, in its life and in its power.'; [vi] 'CONTENTS' (24 individual poems listed with page
references); 1–122 text

Paper: wove paper

Running title: running titles comprise titles of individual poems, pp.3–122

Binding: blue cloth. On spine, in silver: 'ON | THE | HILL | [five-petal device] | John | Masefield | Macmillan' (all width centred).
Covers: blank. All edges trimmed. Binding measurements: 189 × 124mm. (covers), 189 × 24mm. (spine). End-papers: wove paper.

Publication date: published, according to the Archives of The Society of Authors, 21 February 1950

Price: $1.50

Contents:
as for A156(a)

Notes:
The titles of the first and third poems as cited in the contents are longer than those given in the text.

The ampersand in the dedication on p.[v] is particularly ornate.

Macmillan were informed about this title after Heinemann. The American reception of the work was encouraging:

> I need not tell you, I am sure, that we are deeply interested in your manuscript, ON THE HILL. It seems to some of us
> to offer some really outstanding work, "The Wind of the Sea" and "A Tale of Country Things", among others. Naturally,
> we shall publish the collection with pride. The manuscript which you have sent us is a bit confused. There are apparently
> some pages missing and the order of the poems is a bit uncertain. Of course these difficulties will be taken care of if we
> are sent corrected proofs by Heinemann from which to set, and we assume that that will be done.
>
> (H.S. Latham, letter to John Masefield, 28 March 1949)
> (HRHRC, MS (Masefield, J.) Recip The Macmillan Company)

Macmillan were not, however, to set from Heinemann proofs. This Macmillan edition comprises a Heinemann printing with a cancel
title (p.[iv] notes 'PRINTED IN GREAT BRITAIN' and the listing of '*THE WORKS OF JOHN MASEFIELD*' appearing on p.[ii]
lists English publications). Wight, however, describes the gatherings as: [A-H]⁸. This is either an error or suggests a different issue
of this edition entirely printed by Macmillan. Omission of any original Macmillan edition of the title by Handley-Taylor suggests
that this is unlikely. A letter from Louisa Callender, of the Heinemann firm, dated 29 July 1952, to Masefield explains that Heinemann
had supplied Macmillan with copies 'as and when they require them'. She continues:

> ...they have now had in all 1500 copies and we have come to the point where we lose American copyright if we supply
> more than that number.
>
> (Louisa Callender, letter to John Masefield, 29 July 1952)
> (Archives of William Heinemann)

Copies seen: Cornell University Library (PR6025.A8105)

A157 SELECTED POEMS (NEW EDITION)   1950

A157(a) First English edition (1950)

SELECTED POEMS | (New Edition) | BY | JOHN MASEFIELD | [publisher's device of a windmill with 'W' and
'H'] | [rule, 57mm.] | WILLIAM HEINEMANN LTD | MELBOURNE :: LONDON :: TORONTO
(All width centred)

Bibliographies: Handley-Taylor p.53, Wight [unrecorded]

Collation: [A]⁸ B-I⁸; signatures right foot of page; 72 leaves; 184 × 123mm.; [two un-numbered pages] [i–ix] x 1–129 [130–32]

Page contents: [-] blank (page excluded from page count, but constitutes first leaf of first gathering); [-] blank; [i] half-title: 'Selected
Poems | (New Edition)'; [ii] *THE WORKS OF JOHN MASEFIELD* | PLAYS: | [12 titles listed] | POETRY: | [20 titles listed]
| FICTION: | [14 titles listed] | GENERAL: | [15 titles listed]'; [iii] title-page; [iv] 'FIRST PUBLISHED 1950 | PRINTED IN

GREAT BRITAIN AT THE WINDMILL PRESS | KINGSWOOD, SURREY'; [v] 'To | MY WIFE'; [vi] blank; [vii] 'CONTENTS | [27 individual items and index listed with page references] | (NOTE. The verses, A Country Cure and Sur les Pointes | are from books published by Messrs. Collins, to whom my | thanks are given.)'; [viii] blank; [ix]–x 'PREFACE' ('A little volume of selections from my published verse has been long out of print.') (signed, 'JOHN MASEFIELD.'); 1–126 text; 127–29 'INDEX OF FIRST LINES'; [130–32] blank

Paper: wove paper

Running title: running titles comprise titles of individual poems, pp.2–126

Binding: blue cloth. On spine, in silver: 'Selected | Poems | [diamond point] | John | Masefield | Heinemann' (all width centred). Upper cover: blank. On lower cover, in blind: publisher's device of a windmill (ranged lower right). All edges trimmed. Binding measurements: 190 × 123mm. (covers), 190 × 28mm. (spine). End-papers: wove paper.

Publication date: the sales ledger preserved in the Heinemann Archive suggests publication on 13 February 1950 in an edition of 4000 copies

Price: 10s.6d.

Contents:
Preface ('A little volume of selections from my published verse has been long out of print.')
Land Workers ('Long since, in England's pleasant lands')
Sea-Fever ('I must go down to the seas again, to the lonely sea and the sky,')
The West Wind ('It's a warm wind, the west wind, full of birds' cries;')
The Everlasting Mercy – Saul Kane Unredeemed ('From '41 to '51')
[The Everlasting Mercy] – Saul Kane Redeemed ('I loved to see the horses bait.')
The Widow in the Bye Street ('And sometimes she will walk the cindery mile,')
The Wanderer ('All day they loitered by the resting ships,')
August, 1914 ('How still this quiet cornfield is to-night!')
I ('O wretched man, that for a little mile')
II ('Out of the special cell's most special sense')
III ('You are the link which binds us each to each.')
IV ('I could not sleep for thinking of the sky,')
V ('How did the nothing come, how did these fires,')
VI ('It may be so; but let the unknown be.')
VII ('What is this life which uses living cells')
VIII ('Can it be blood and brain, this transient force')
IX ('Not only blood and brain its servants are;')
X ('Drop me the seed, that I even in my brain')
XI ('Ah, but Without there is no spirit scattering;')
XII ('You are too beautiful for mortal eyes,')
XIII ('Is it a sea on which the souls embark')
XIV ('Long, long ago, when all the glittering earth')
XV ('Night came again, but now I could not sleep;')
XVI ('Even after all these years there comes the dream')
XVII ('If I could come again to that dear place')
XVIII ('Here in the self is all that man can know')
XIX ('Flesh, I have knocked at many a dusty door,')
XX ('But all has passed, the tune has died away,')
XXI ('These myriad days, these many thousand hours,')
XXII ('There, on the darkened deathbed, dies the brain')
XXIII ('So in the empty sky the stars appear,')
XXIV ('It may be so with us, that in the dark,')
XXV ('What am I, Life? A thing of watery salt')
XXVI ('If I could get within this changing I,')
XXVII ('What is the atom which contains the whole,')
XXVIII ('Ah, we are neither heaven nor earth, but men;')
XXIX ('Roses are beauty, but I never see')
XXX ('Over the church's door they moved a stone,')
XXXI ('O little self, within whose smallness lies')
XXXII ('I went into the fields, but you were there')
XXXIII ('This is the living thing that cannot stir.')
XXXIV ('Look at the grass, sucked by the seed from dust,')
XXXV ('There is no God, as I was taught in youth,')
XXXVI ('Wherever beauty has been quick in clay')
XXXVII ('Beauty, let be; I cannot see your face,')

XXXVIII ('You are more beautiful than women are,')
XXXIX ('Not for the anguish suffered is the slur,')
XL ('Beauty was with me once, but now, grown old,')
XLI ('So beauty comes, so with a failing hand')
XLII ('You will remember me in days to come,')
XLIII ('If Beauty be at all, if, beyond sense,')
XLIV ('If all be governed by the moving stars,')
XLV ('In emptiest furthest heaven where no stars are,')
XLVI ('Perhaps in chasms of the wasted past,')
XLVII ('For, like an outcast from the city, I')
XLVIII ('Death lies in wait for you, you wild thing in the wood,')
XLIX ('Go, spend your penny, Beauty, when you will,')
L ('Though in life's streets the tempting shops have lured')
LI ('When all these million cells that are my slaves')
LII ('Let that which is to come be as it may,')
Lyrics From Good Friday, A Play ('The wild duck, stringing through the sky,')
Reynard the Fox – The End of the Run ('He crossed the covert, he crawled the bank,')
The Hounds of Hell ('About the crowing of the cock,')
Cap on Head | A Tale of the O'Neill ('O'Neill took ship, O'Neill set sail,')
The Fight on the Wall ('Modred was in the Water Tower')
Adventure On ('Adventure on, companion, for this')
Nireus ('Once long ago young Nireus was the King')
King Cole Speaks ('"I have seen sorrow close and suffering close.')
Wanderer and Wonderer ('When first the thought of you took steel')
The Rose of the World ('Dark Eleanor and Henry sat at meat')
A Country Cure, or the Boy who swallowed the Frog ('I saw the lad was skin and bone.')
The Rider at the Gate ('A windy night was blowing on Rome,')
Ballet Russe ('The gnome from moonland plays the Chopin air,')
Sur Les Pointes ('The time is near, my sweet,')
Australia ('When the North Lander saw the rose in blossom,')
The Will ('By Will, Man dared in den and heath')
Epilogue (The Meditation of Highworth Ridden) ('I have seen flowers come in stony places,')

Notes:

A volume of selections described by Masefield in his preface as 'not a reprint, but a changed selection, drawn from many different books, and offered now as the best I have been able to do.' See A62 for earlier editions.

A letter from Masefield to A.S. Frere notes:

> You have in type, but not published, the book of *Selected Poems* that I made 4 or 5 years ago. You set it up in 1946. Why not issue this with, perhaps, one longer poem in it?

> (John Masefield, letter to [A.S.] Frere, 9 February [1949])
> (Archives of William Heinemann)

Post-war paper shortages may have been responsible for the delay in publishing this title. See HRHRC (TEMP M377 B7 1946) for a proof copy dated 1946 and inscribed by Masefield during July 1946.

Copies seen: private collection (PWE); BL (11658.eee.118) stamped 24 JAN 1950

A157(b) First American edition (1950)

SELECTED POEMS | (New Edition) | BY | JOHN MASEFIELD | THE MACMILLAN COMPANY | NEW YORK
(All width centred)

Bibliographies: Handley-Taylor [unrecorded], Wight [unrecorded]

Collation: [A]⁸ (±[A]3) B-I⁸; signatures right foot of page; 72 leaves; 184 × 123mm.; [two un-numbered pages] [i–ix] x 1–129 [130–32]

Page contents: [-] blank (page excluded from page count, but constitutes first leaf of first gathering); [-] blank; [i] half-title: 'Selected Poems | (New Edition)'; [ii] '*THE WORKS OF JOHN MASEFIELD* | PLAYS: | [12 titles listed] | POETRY: | [20 titles listed] | FICTION: | [14 titles listed] | GENERAL: | [15 titles listed]' [iii] title-page; [iv] 'COPYRIGHT 1950 BY JOHN MASEFIELD | [rule] | THE material contained in this volume was previously published and | copyrighted as follows: | 'Land Workers,' copyright 1943, by John Masefield; 'Sea Fever,' | copyright 1912 and 1940, by The Macmillan Company; 'The West Wind,' | copyright 1912 and 1940, by The Macmillan Company; 'The Ever- | lasting Mercy,' copyright 1911, 1940 and 1947, by John Masefield; | 'The Widow in the Bye Street,' copyright 1912 and 1940, by The | Macmillan Company; 'The "Wanderer",' copyright 1913, by Harper and | Brothers, 1914 and 1942, by The Macmillan Company; 'August, 1914,' | copyright 1914, by The McClure Publications, 1914 and

1942, by The | Macmillan Company; Lyrics from 'Good Friday,' copyright 1915 and | 1943, by John Masefield; 'Reynard the Fox,' copyright 1919, 1920, | 1947 and 1948, by John Masefield; 'The Hounds of Hell,' copyright | 1920 and 1948, by John Masefield; 'Cap on Head,' copyright 1920 and | 1948, by John Masefield; 'The Fight on the Wall,' copyright 1928, by | John Masefield; 'The Story of Nireus and Queen Helen,' copyright | 1923, by John Masefield; 'Wanderer and Wonderer,' copyright 1930, | by John Masefield; 'The Rose of the World,' copyright 1931, by John | Masefield; 'The Rider at the Gate,' copyright 1923, by John Masefield; | 'Ballet Russe,' copyright 1936, by John Masefield; 'Sur Les Pointes,' | copyright 1938, by John Masefield; 'Australia,' copyright 1936, by | John Masefield; 'The Will,' copyright 1936, by John Masefield; | 'Epilogue,' copyright 1937 and 1938, by John Masefield. | PRINTED IN GREAT BRITAIN'; [v] 'To | MY WIFE'; [vi] blank; [vii] 'CONTENTS | [27 individual items and index listed with page references] | (NOTE. The verses, A Country Cure and Sur les Pointes | are from books published by Messrs. Collins, to whom my | thanks are given.)'; [viii] blank; [ix]–x 'PREFACE' ('A little volume of selections from my published verse has been long out of print.') (signed, 'JOHN MASEFIELD.'); 1–126 text; 127–29 'INDEX OF FIRST LINES'; [130–32] blank

Paper: wove paper

Running title: running titles comprise titles of individual poems, pp.2–126

Binding: blue cloth. On spine, in silver: 'Selected | Poems | [diamond point] | John | Masefield | Macmillan' (all width centred). Covers: blank. All edges trimmed. Binding measurements: 190 × 123mm. (covers), 190 × 28mm. (spine). End-papers: wove paper.

Publication date: 1950

Price: $2.00

Contents:
as for A157(a)

Notes:
The cancellans ([A]3) comprises a cancel-title.

Copies seen: Columbia University (825 M377–L27)

A158 A BOOK OF PROSE SELECTIONS   1950

A158(a) First English edition (1950)

A BOOK OF PROSE | SELECTIONS | BY | JOHN MASEFIELD | [publisher's device of a windmill with 'W' and 'H'] | [rule, 57mm.] | WILLIAM HEINEMANN LTD | MELBOURNE :: LONDON :: TORONTO
(All width centred)

Bibliographies: Handley-Taylor p.65, Wight [unrecorded]

Collation: [A]⁸ B-L⁸ M¹⁰ (J not used); M2 is also signed; signatures right foot of page; 98 leaves; 183 × 123mm.; [six un-numbered pages] [i] ii–iii [iv] 1–186

Page contents: [-] half-title: 'A BOOK OF PROSE | SELECTIONS'; [-] *THE WORKS OF JOHN MASEFIELD* | PLAYS: | [12 titles listed] | POETRY: | [20 titles listed] | FICTION: | [14 titles listed] | GENERAL: | [15 titles listed]'; [-] title-page; [-] 'FIRST PUBLISHED 1950 | PRINTED IN GREAT BRITAIN AT THE WINDMILL PRESS | KINGSWOOD, SURREY'; [-] 'To | MY WIFE'; [-] blank; [i]–iii 'CONTENTS' (50 individual items listed with page references); [iv] blank; 1–186 text

Paper: wove paper

Running title: 'A Book of Prose Selections' (43mm.) on verso; recto title notes volume from which selections originate, pp.2–186

Binding: light blue cloth. On spine, in silver: '[double rule] | *A Book | of Prose | Selections* [all four lines on dark blue panel: 30 × 21mm.] | *John | Masefield* | [double rule] [all three lines on dark blue panel: 24 × 21mm.] | *Heinemann*' (all width centred). Upper cover: blank. On lower cover, in blind: publisher's device of a windmill (ranged lower right). All edges trimmed. Binding measurements: 188 × 124mm. (covers), 188 × 30mm. (spine). End-papers: wove paper.

Publication date: the sales ledger preserved in the Heinemann Archive suggests publication on 13 February 1950 in an edition of 5000 copies

Price: 10s.6d.

Contents:
From *RECENT PROSE*
A Speech at Hereford ('I have now to thank you for the great and beautiful honour that you have paid me...')
From *THE MIDNIGHT FOLK*
Kay Visits Mr. Bitem ('"You are a wicked little boy, Kay," the governess said: "You will go…')
The Invisible Mixture ('Whether it was the closing of the door or the sudden movement, Kay could not tell...')
From *THE BOX OF DELIGHTS*
Tibbs Wharf ('At this moment Kay caught sight of the village policeman coming from the Beast-Market...')
Cole Hawlings Rides Away ('The old man lifted a finger to the dog, perhaps to keep him from barking...')
From *EGGS AND BAKER*

The Alley ('The entrance was under a part of the red brick brew-house. Looking through it...')
The Feast of Bulls ('In July, the monthly number had been "Tom Goneaway's Adventures in the Bull-ring."')
From *NEW CHUM*
My First Sight of the River ('I set out to join H.M.S. *Conway* on a fine sunny morning a fortnight after...')
I see the "Wanderer" for the first time ('As I came out of the station into the light, I saw in front of me, close to...')
The First Four Hours ('The deck was pretty busy with men; it was a free evening and some were mooching or...')
We All Go Home ('In a few minutes, as it seemed, the pipe went for All Hands, and the C.P.O. gave the long...')
From *THE WANDERER*
Launched and Rigged ('The name, the *Wanderer*, was suggested by Mr. G. H. Potter, the son...')
Wild Weather ('On Thursday, the 15th of October, the ship was moved to a berth in the Birkenhead...')
She Returns ('At 8.15 in the evening of Friday the 23rd October, the tug *Wrestler* took her in tow...')
A Word about Her ('"The ship was big and heavy and hard," so one writes who was...')
From *THE CONWAY*
The Mersey, as it was ('Forty years ago, the flower of all England's shipping belonged in Liverpool...')
From *IN THE MILL*
First Acquaintance with Modern Poetry ('I had for some months been a regular subscriber to a merry illustrated...')
Initiation ('On a Friday, the English mail being in, I went, as usual, to the Post...')
Thinking It Over ('Well, the factory system as I saw it is dead apparently, except in my...')
On Work ('I have read of carpet-makers, in distant lands, whose carpets were...')
Summary ('If one were to ask, "Would I have that time again?" I should answer...')
From *SOME MEMORIES OF THE LATE W. B. YEATS*
No. 18, Woburn Buildings ('When in London, in the early years of this century, Mr. W.B. Yeats lived...')
From *RECENT PROSE*
John M. Synge ('I first met John M. Synge at the room of a common friend, up two pairs of stairs...')
From *SARD HARKER*
The Boxing Contest ('Captain Cary took his seat beside Sard. "You are just in time, sir," Sard said.')
The Call at Los Xicales ('An old white-haired negro, with charming manners, admitted and announced...')
The Voice in the Rocks ('As he judged that the chasm or cleft would give him an easier path...')
From *RECENT PROSE* (*The Taking of Helen*)
The Sightless ('From somewhere in the heart of the house the step of age shuffled...')
From *ODTAA*
Ezekiel Rust's Story ('After breakfast, Hi was rowed ashore from the *Recalde*, to begin his...')
From *THE MIDNIGHT FOLK*
Miss Piney Trigger's Story ('It was a big, bright, pretty bedroom hung with white chintzes...')
From *THE HAWBUCKS*
The Ditcher ('He turned to the ditcher. "I suppose you didn't see a beaten fox...')
From *RECENT PROSE* (*Fragments from Letters*)
Niagara ('"All the way, I had remembered the tales of the roar of the water, and how...')
The Trees ('"In every room in every hotel in this country there is a modernized...')
Flight ('The 7th was a day of adventure, for I was asked to a big camp to speak...')
The Desert ('"To go on with my diary from the time of my fly in the...')
The Trees ('"I went afterwards to see those trees. They grow in a few, small, sheltered...')
From *THE BIRD OF DAWNING*
Captain Icelin Duntisbourne ('Away to the south and west there was a blackness in heaven...')
The Abandoned Clipper ('Cruiser took a look at the compass, and remained at the con for a while...')
From *THE TAKING OF THE GRY*
The Pilot ('We were the only line on the coast at that time: and no doubt...')
From *DEAD NED*
Dr. Josiah Copshrews ('Josiah Copshrews was an old man, over seventy, with a great practice...')
The Nets Close In ('I went on to another inn called "The Beggar's Bush." There was...')
In Newgate ('I heard the coach drive off and knew that the Rector and Lambert...')
From *LIVE NED*
Captain Pegg's Dolly ('As we were now within four miles of the Coast, the hands roused up...')
The Matablancos ('Nearly all the party had one or more white, raised scars at the sides...')
The Lower Tier ('I went with my lantern-bearer along the 'tween-decks to the...')
The Reeds ('Quite suddenly, my channel ended in a forest of reeds. They were ten or twelve...')
Suffering ('A great many people write that suffering is good for people, that it...')
From *BASILISSA*
She Meets Macedonia ('To her left as she stood to gaze was a pretty lane of white houses...')
Theodora's Midnight Visitor ('She was young and strong and had not a very long walk before her.')
From *CONQUER*
Theodora Speaks ('"Sir," Phocas said. "My enquiries lead to the very opposite opinion. If we are...')

From *THE BIRD OF DAWNING*
And So, Farewell ('Now, slowly, the ship moved up to the dock-gate, with both tugs...')

Notes:
A volume of selections from Masefield's prose, all derived from earlier publications.

The first extract only in a single group of extracts from the same original source commences with a drop-capital.

It appears that Masefield provided the text of this volume in April 1945. It was acknowledged by Louisa Callender who wrote '...thank you for the material for A BOOK OF PROSE SELECTIONS. We shall set at leisure, ready for the time when paper is available.' (see Louisa Callender, letter to John Masefield, 25 April 1945) (HRHRC, MS (Masefield, J.) Recip William Heinemann Ltd.) A pre-publication copy was sent on 20 January 1950:

> I send herewith an advance copy of A BOOK OF PROSE SELECTIONS which we are publishing on February 13th.
> (Louisa Callender, letter to John Masefield, 20 January 1950)
> (HRHRC, MS (Masefield, J.) Recip William Heinemann Ltd.)

Copies seen: private collection (PWE); BL (12275.de.8) stamped 18 JAN 1950

A158(b) First American edition (1950)

A BOOK OF PROSE | SELECTIONS | BY | JOHN MASEFIELD | THE MACMILLAN COMPANY | NEW YORK
(All width centred)

Bibliographies: Handley-Taylor [unrecorded], Wight [unrecorded]

Collation: [A]⁸ (±[A]2) B-L⁸ M¹⁰ (J not used); M2 is also signed; signatures right foot of page; 98 leaves; 184 × 120mm.; [six unnumbered pages] [i] ii–iii [iv] 1–186

Page contents: [-] half-title: 'A BOOK OF PROSE | SELECTIONS'; [-] '*THE WORKS OF JOHN MASEFIELD* | PLAYS: | [12 titles listed] | POETRY: | [20 titles listed] | FICTION: | [14 titles listed] | GENERAL: | [15 titles listed]'; [-] title-page; [-] 'COPYRIGHT, 1950, BY JOHN MASEFIELD | [rule] | THE material in this book has previously been published and copyrighted | as follows: | 'A Speech at Hereford,' from *Recent Prose*, copyright, 1933, by John | Masefield; 'Kay Visits Mr. Bitem,' 'The Invisible Mixture,' from *The Mid-* | *night Folk*, copyright, 1927, by John Masefield; 'Tibb's Wharf,' 'Cole Hawl-* | ings Rides Away,' from *The Box of Delights*, copyright, 1935, by John | Masefield; 'The Alley,' 'The Feast of Bulls,' from *Eggs and Baker*, copy- | right, 1936, by John Masefield; 'My First Sight of the River,' 'I see the | "Wanderer" for the First Time,' 'The First Four Hours,' 'We All Go | Home,' from *New Chum*, copyright, 1944, by John Masefield; 'Launched | and Rigged,' 'Wild Weather,' 'She Returns,' 'A Word about Her,' from | *The Wanderer*, copyright, 1930, by John Masefield; 'The Mersey, as it | Was,' from *The Conway*, copyright, 1933, by John Masefield; 'First | Acquaintance with Modern Poetry,' 'Initiation,' 'Thinking it Over,' | 'On Work,' 'Summary,' from *In the Mill*, copyright, 1941, by John | Masefield; 'No. 18, Woburn Buildings,' from *Some Memories of the Late* | *W. B. Yeats*, copyright, 1940, by John Masefield; 'John M. Synge,' copy- | right, 1915 and 1943, by John Masefield; 'The Boxing Contest,' 'The Call | at Los Xicales,' 'The Voice in the Rocks,' from *Sard Harker*, copyright, | 1924, by John Masefield; 'The Sightless,' from *The Taking of Helen*, copy- | right, 1923, by John Masefield; 'Ezekiel Rust's Story,' from *Odtaa*, copy- | right, 1926, by John Masefield; 'Miss Piney Trigger's Story,' from *The* | *Midnight Folk*, copyright, 1927, by John Masefield; 'The Ditcher,' from | *The Hawbucks*, copyright, 1927, by John Masefield; 'Niagara,' 'The | Trees,' 'Flight,' 'The Desert,' 'The Trees,' from *The Taking of Helen and* | *Other Prose Selections*, copyright, 1924, by John Masefield; 'Captain | Icelin Duntisbourne,' 'The Abandoned Clipper,' from *The Bird of Dawn-* | *ing*, copyright, 1933, by John Masefield; 'The Pilot,' from *The Taking of* | *the Gry*, copyright, 1934, by John Masefield; 'Dr. Josiah Copshrews,' | 'The Nets Close In,' 'In Newgate,' from *Dead Ned*, copyright, 1938, by | John Masefield; 'Captain Pegg's Dolly,' 'The Matablancos,' 'The Lower | Tier,' 'The Reeds,' 'Suffering,' from *Live and Kicking Ned*, copyright, | 1939, by John Masefield; 'She Meets Macedonia,' 'Theodora's Midnight | Visitor,' from *Basilissa*, copyright, 1940, by John Masefield; 'Theodora | Speaks,' from *Conquer*, copyright, 1941, by John Masefield; 'And So, | Farewell,' from *The Bird of Dawning*, copyright, 1933, by John Masefield. | PRINTED IN GREAT BRITAIN'; [-] 'To | MY WIFE'; [-] blank; [i]–iii 'CONTENTS' (50 individual items listed with page references); [iv] blank; 1–186 text

Paper: wove paper

Running title: 'A Book of Prose Selections' (43mm.) on verso; recto title notes volume from which selections originate, pp.2–186

Binding: light blue cloth. On spine, in silver: '[double rule] | A Book | of Prose | Selections [all four lines on dark blue panel: 30 × 21mm.] | John | Masefield | [double rule] [all three lines on dark blue panel: 24 × 21mm.] | Macmillan' (all width centred). Covers: blank. All edges trimmed. Binding measurements: 188 × 123mm. (covers), 188 × 30mm. (spine). End-papers: wove paper.

Publication date: 1950

Price: $2.00

Contents:
as for A158(a)

Notes:
The first extract only in a single group of extracts from the same original source commences with a drop-capital.

[A]2 comprises a cancel-title. As the edition states 'Printed in England', this American edition presumably comprises A158(a) with a cancel-title. See notes to A156(b) for another Heinemann printing with an American cancel-title. The arrangement between Heinemann and Macmillan is noted in a letter from H.S. Latham to Masefield:

> We have been conferring with William Heinemann about your work, A BOOK OF PROSE SELECTIONS. It seems to me that this is a volume which, as in the case of other recent books of yours, we might well arrange to import from Heinemann.
>
> (H.S. Latham letter to John Masefield, 22 March 1950)
> (HRHRC, MS (Masefield, J.) Recip The Macmillan Company)

This letter is annotated in Masefield's hand with a note dated 28 March: 'I am willing that you shd import sheets of my bk of Prose Selectns ie of selections from my own prose, from Heines…'

Copies seen: Harvard College Library (Widener 23697.10.370)

A159 IN PRAISE OF NURSES   1950

A159(a) First English edition (1950)

Page [i]:

In Praise of Nurses | *Dedicated to* | MARY CLIFFORD | LAURA FRANKLIN | HELEN McKENNA | PHYLLIS SIMMONDS | JOANNA WILLS
(Lines 1 and 2 width centred with lines 3–7 justified on left margin)

Bibliographies: Handley-Taylor p.65, Wight 118

Collation: [A]²; 2 leaves; 205 × 128mm.; [i–iv]

Page contents: [i] title-page; [ii–iv] text (below the text on p.[iv] is a facsimile signature: 'John Masefield.')

Paper: wove paper

Running title: none

Binding: issued as a single four page leaflet. The title-page consequently comprises the upper wrapper. All edges trimmed. Binding measurements: 205 × 128mm. (wrappers), 205 × 0.5mm. (spine). Enclosed within a wove paper envelope (with a gummed flap): 209 × 133mm. The upper part of the envelope is printed as follows:

In Praise of Nurses | *by* | JOHN MASEFIELD | [publisher's device of a windmill with 'W' and 'H'] | [rule, 56mm.] | WILLIAM HEINEMANN LTD | MELBOURNE :: LONDON :: TORONTO | [short rule] | *One Shilling net* | [short rule]
(All width centred)

Publication date: the sales ledger preserved in the Heinemann Archive suggests publication on 27 March 1950 in an edition of 5000 copies

Price: 1s.

Contents:
In Praise of Nurses ('Man, in his gallant power, goes in pride,')

Notes:
In 1949 Masefield suffered influenza, pneumonia and then appendicitis. Upon recovery he wrote this poem to the nurses of the Acland Nursing Home. The poem was first published in 1949 as a privately printed poetry card (see D17). The poem was later reprinted in *The Bluebells and other verse* (see A166).

Privately printed cards by Masefield frequently used an italic font and this Heinemann publication similarly uses italics.

A.S. Frere wrote to Masefield about publication at the beginning of January 1950:

> I am told that, in general, booksellers do not like pamphlets; they get soiled, they get lost and they require a special section for stocking and display. However, a suggestion has been made that we should print your verses IN PRAISE OF NURSES very much in the same form as it is at present and put them out in an envelope with the title, etc. printed boldly upon it, and possibly ask 1/- for it. This does not seem an unreasonable price for, after all, a great many Christmas cards have been sold at this price and more. An additional touch might be to print your signature in facsimile at the end of the poem with the date. Will you let me know what you think of this idea?
>
> (A.S. Frere, letter to John Masefield, 6 January 1950)
> (HRHRC, MS (Masefield, J.) Recip William Heinemann Ltd.)

Masefield was, it appears, receptive to the idea. He did, however, ask for personal copies without a facsimile signature:

> …Of course you can have as many copies as you like, printed without a facsimile signature. Perhaps you will let me know how many you want… The maximum royalty it could bear would be 10% and I hope very much that you will accept that.
>
> (A.S. Frere, letter to John Masefield, 9 January 1950)
> (HRHRC, MS (Masefield, J.) Recip William Heinemann Ltd.)

This letter is annotated by Masefield on 10 January 'accepted 10%, 25 printed, leave to reprint in Col Poems.' Masefield's personal copies were sent on 1 March, together with a note of the publication date:

> On Mr. Frere's instructions I am sending to you to-day twenty-five copies of IN PRAISE OF NURSES without the facsimile of your signature, and a corresponding number of the printed envelopes in case you wish to use them. We have run off a few more of these plain ones so they are available for your personal use should you require them. We have scheduled these verses for publication on the 27th of this month.
>
> (Leslie Munro, letter to John Masefield, 1 March 1950)
> (HRHRC, MS (Masefield, J.) Recip William Heinemann Ltd.)

Copies seen: Library of The John Masefield Society (Peter Smith Collection) in original envelope; BL (11648.b.38) bound with upper part of envelope, pencil annotation states 'Publication Date March 27th 1950', stamped 6 MAR 1950; HRHRC (PR6025 A77 I6 1950 cop.1) inscribed 'For Con | from Jan. | March 15th. 1950.' in original envelope; HRHRC (PR6025 A77 I6 1950 cop.2) in original envelope

A159(b) First American edition (1950)

IN PRAISE | OF NURSES | BY | *John Masefield* | BEING A POEM OF | APPRECIATION | FOLLOWING A | RECENT ILLNESS | DEDICATED TO | *Mary Clifford* | *Laura Franklin* | *Helen McKenna* | *Phyllis Simmonds* | *Joanna Wills*

(All justified on left margin. The text of the poem is printed in two columns to the right of this title.)

Bibliographies: Handley-Taylor [unrecorded], Wight 118a

Collation: single leaf; 173 × 249mm.; [1–2]

Page contents: [1] text in three columns: column one (title, as above), column two (text of poem) and column three (text of poem concluded with 'John Masefield, *Poet Laureate of England*' at foot) and with '*Copyright, 1950, by John E. Masefield. Published by The Macmillan Company, New York.*' ranged lower right; [2] blank

Paper: wove paper

Running title: none

Binding: none

Publication date: published, according to the Archives of The Society of Authors, 28 March 1950

Price: $0.25

Contents:
as for A159(a)

Notes:
Handley-Taylor omits this edition from his bibliography and Wight is the only bibliographer to note it. In view of the rarity of this item (*The National Union Catalog* of 'Pre-1956 Imprints' lists only one copy) it may be of importance to note that Masefield and Macmillan apparently held differing views about publication.

George P. Brett Jr, president of the American branch of Macmillan, wrote to Masefield on 29 December 1949. Possibly unaware of how Masefield intended to have the poem issued (presumably in the form adopted by Heinemann) Macmillan suggested 'free distribution' to nurses on their mailing list. Brett wrote:

> With this letter I enclose a proof, on very heavy calendered paper, of your fine poem, *In Praise of Nurses*. Our Medical Department has set this poem up in this form. They wish very much indeed to make a present of the poem to the nurses throughout the U.S. on their mailing list. May we, therefore, publish this poem in this form and copyright it as is indicated and make such free distribution of it as we care to?
>
> There is no thought of selling the poem in book form or in this form. In exchange for this courtesy we would propose paying you a flat sum of fifty dollars for this right, and we should consider that only we had the right to deal with permissions if in future anyone else should wish to use this poem, and we would agree to split whatever commission fee we might get during the copyright period on the basis of 50% to your good self, we retaining 50%.
>
> There is a vague possibility that some of our foreign customers who may see this poem may apply to us for the right to translate it into a foreign language. We should like the privilege of dealing with any such requests as may come in, again dividing the proceeds from any such sale on a 50–50 basis with you. If as I hope this arrangement is satisfactory to you, won't you kindly sign a copy of this letter, which goes forward to you in duplicate, and return it to me for our contract files.
>
> (George P. Brett Jr, letter to John Masefield, 29 December 1949)
> (transcription by Constance Babington Smith
> (Archives of The John Masefield Society (Constance Babington Smith Archive))

This plan did not, evidently, appeal to Masefield. He wrote a letter on 3 January 1950 that he did not send. This stated, in a forthright manner:

The verses were written in the main to thank the five women to whom I dedicate them. I could not agree to any publication that omits their names. Then, your letter makes no reference to a possible later inclusion of the poem in a collected or selected edition of my poems.

The verses will be published here in the ordinary way, and I cannot consent to your proposal 'that only the Macmillan Co should have the right to deal with permissions if in future any one else should wish to use the poem'. All rights of translation whatsoever I reserve to myself.

You will see that I do not like your proposals; and do not understand at all what the Nurses are who are on your mailing list, nor why these should have the poem free, while (apparently) no other Nurses should have a chance of buying a copy. There must be many thousands of Nurses in the U.S.

I must say that I have been somewhat startled to find the verses set up as a gift 'with the compliments of the Macmillan Co' without any reference to myself: for no word of the kind has yet reached me.

Why should not the verses be published as a leaflet and issued for review to the quite considerable Hospital and Medical Press? I am sad to differ thus, but there it is.

(John Masefield, letter to George P. Brett Jr, 3 January 1950 [not sent])

(transcription by Constance Babington Smith

(Archives of The John Masefield Society (Constance Babington Smith Archive))

Masefield's revised letter which he did send, dated 4 January 1950, suggests that Heinemann had not yet decided on the form of the English publication, but that Macmillan's scheme was unacceptable. The issue appears to be not merely one of style, but also terms:

I am sorry, but I cannot consent to the publication of the verses in anything like the suggested terms. Form and terms alike really fill me with horror. We must find some other means, and I hope soon to send some suggestions, when I know what will be done here.

(John Masefield, letter to George P. Brett Jr, 4 January 1950)

(transcription by Constance Babington Smith

(Archives of The John Masefield Society (Constance Babington Smith Archive))

Brett had evidently antagonised Masefield and repented:

Oh, my! Your good letter of January 4 leaves me with a feeling that I have offended. I am terribly sorry. We thought that would be a way of getting a copyright in this country on *In Praise of Nurses*, also an excellent way of getting your name before every nurse on our mailing list. Well, it is no good, and I have told the department to forget it. I will be glad to hear of the other suggestions referred to in your letter.

(George P. Brett Jr, letter to John Masefield, 9 January 1950)

(transcription by Constance Babington Smith

(Archives of The John Masefield Society (Constance Babington Smith Archive))

An annotation to Brett's letter of 9 January 1950 in Masefield's hand suggests:

Well, why not reset the poem in a somewhat tighter form, mail it to your Nurses and say that it is to be had as a leaflet shortly.

(John Masefield, annotation to Brett's letter of 9 January 1950)

(transcription by Constance Babington Smith

(Archives of The John Masefield Society (Constance Babington Smith Archive))

No further detail is contained in the files of Constance Babington Smith, although a photocopy of an early Macmillan proof (corrected by Masefield) is present. This is presumably the proof to which Brett refers on 29 December 1949 and there was significant resetting before publication. The proof is in the form of a centred title with two columns below. This was reset to appear as three columns, as described above.

A 'photostat' with the text presumably in three columns was sent at the beginning of February 1950:

I enclose a positive photostat of your poem IN PRAISE OF NURSES. With reference to the left-hand side, the lines "Being a poem of appreciation following a recent illness" and the names of the five nurses, these have just been inked in to show you approximately how it would look. Actually, if we do the job, what I have quoted above, and the names of the nurses, will be put in suitable type.

Our Medical Department would like to proceed with this, sending it out in an envelope to the nurses on our list, and listing it in their catalogues as being for sale at 25c. On this we could pay you a 2c royalty on sales. Does this look all right now?

([George P. Brett Jr], letter to John Masefield, 2 February 1950)

(HRHRC, MS (Masefield, J.) Recip The Macmillan Company)

The only copy recorded by *The National Union Catalog* of 'Pre-1956 Imprints' is located in the medical school library of Yale University. This is accompanied by an undated typed letter on Macmillan Company headed notepaper. The text is as follows:

Not long ago John Masefield, Poet Laureate of England, was stricken with an illness which required hospitalization and a lengthy recuperation period. The poet was so impressed by the attention he received from the nurses who cared for him that he wrote a poem praising the profession and dedicated it to the five nurses who aided his recovery.

Few indeed are the poems of praise dedicated to nurses and we consider it of particular significance that this one should have been written about and dedicated to the members of this profession. We have received from John Masefield his permission to publish it, and we take pleasure in presenting a copy to your school. It is enclosed herewith.

It has occurred to us that all nurses will want to own a copy of this poem and many will want to have it framed. Many schools will doubtless want to present the poem to members of their graduating class. Additional copies can be obtained through any of our branch offices at $.25 per copy, less your educational discount. We will be glad to receive your order for the quantity you require.

> (The Macmillan Company Medical-Public Health Department, undated letter)
> (Yale Medical Library, Yale University)

Copies seen: Yale Medical Library, Yale University, stamped Feb 1961; HRHRC (TEMP M377 IN 1950) inscribed 'For Con from Jan. | 10 April 1950.'

A160 THE LEDBURY SCENE [1951]

A160(a) First English edition (limited signed edition) ([1951])

THE LEDBURY SCENE | AS I HAVE USED IT | IN MY VERSE | JOHN MASEFIELD
(All width centred)

Bibliographies: Handley-Taylor [unrecorded], Wight 119b

Collation: [A]⁸; 8 leaves; 286 × 223mm.; [1–2] 3–16

Page contents: [1] title-page; [2] 'This edition, numbered and signed by the author | is limited to 250 copies. This is number .... | Printed in Great Britain | by | Jakemans Ltd., Hereford'; 3–16 text

Paper: wove paper (watermark: 'HODGKINSON&Cº')

Running title: none

Binding: light grey wrappers. Spine: blank. On upper wrapper, in red: 'THE LEDBURY SCENE | JOHN MASEFIELD'. Lower wrapper: blank. All edges untrimmed. Binding measurements: 289 × 228mm. (wrappers); 289 × 2mm. (spine).

Publication date: published, as suggested by an inscribed copy, during August 1951

Price: 21s.

Contents:
The Ledbury Scene as I have used it in my verse ('In 1911, when, after much vain effort, I began to write...')

Notes:
This volume (the text of which is also published in *St. Katherine of Ledbury and other Ledbury Papers* (see A161)) contains a single essay describing 'what places in and near Ledbury have been brought into my verses as the scenes of imagined events'. The essay comprises three main sections and each commences with a drop-capital.

Wight lists this item as 119b in his bibliography. He therefore gives it the same number as *St. Katherine of Ledbury* (presumably because the text is also present in that larger volume). This is a confusing stance even if the text were derived from that volume. It appears, however, that *The Ledbury Scene* was published before *St. Katherine of Ledbury*. The British Library copy is stamped 23 AUG 1951 and correspondence in the Heinemann archive regarding the Ledbury distribution of the title is dated from late August 1951. The Heinemann archive cites a publication date of December 1951 for *St. Katherine of Ledbury*.

Wight incorrectly transcribes the watermark in this edition.

A letter from Louisa Callender, of the Heinemann firm, dated 28 August 1951 to Masefield states:

> We are getting a number of enquiries for THE LEDBURY SCENE. Will you very kindly tell me how we should answer such enquiries.

> (Louisa Callender, letter to John Masefield, 28 August 1951)
> (Archives of William Heinemann)

Masefield responded in a letter with the same date:

> Thank you for your letter. The booklet of *the Ledbury Scene* is being distributed by the Bell Fund people in Ledbury. The Rev Prebendary W. Graham Moeran, MC. MA. The Rectory, Ledbury. Herefordshire is in charge of the distribution. I expect that some copies may still be had.

> (John Masefield, letter to [Louisa] Callender, 28 August [1951])
> (Archives of William Heinemann)

The guide book, Ellen F. Tilley, *Illustrated Guide to Ledbury and the District* (Luke Tilley and Son, new and revised edition, 1966) provides further information about this edition (on pp.51–52):

> John Masefield defrayed the whole cost of producing 275 copies of "Ledbury Scene," of which 250 were autographed by him; this edition was completely sold out at the price of one guinea each and the proceeds given by him towards the fund for restoration of Ledbury Church bells; a further edition of this book was produced in a less expensive form and sold at five shillings each, also in aid of the same fund.

Some words spoken in grateful memory

of

SIR RONALD ROSS

Poet and Scientist

at a meeting commemorating Mosquito Day
(21st August, 1897)

at

The Ross Institute of Tropical Hygiene
KEPPEL STREET, GOWER STREET,

on

Monday, 5th July, 1948

with a few corrections and additions

by

Dr. JOHN MASEFIELD, O.M.

Poet Laureate .

A155(a) title-page

ON THE HILL

by

JOHN MASEFIELD

WILLIAM HEINEMANN LTD
MELBOURNE :: LONDON :: TORONTO

A156(a) title-page

SELECTED POEMS
(New Edition)

BY

JOHN MASEFIELD

WILLIAM HEINEMANN LTD
MELBOURNE :: LONDON :: TORONTO

A157(a) title-page

A BOOK OF PROSE
SELECTIONS

BY

JOHN MASEFIELD

WILLIAM HEINEMANN LTD
MELBOURNE :: LONDON :: TORONTO

A158(a) title-page

In Praise of Nurses

by

JOHN MASEFIELD

WILLIAM HEINEMANN LTD
MELBOURNE :: LONDON :: TORONTO

—
One Shilling net
—

A159(a) upper part of envelope

In Praise of Nurses

Dedicated to

MARY CLIFFORD

LAURA FRANKLIN

HELEN McKENNA

PHYLLIS SIMMONDS

JOANNA WILLS

A159(a) title-page

ST. KATHERINE OF LEDBURY

and other Ledbury papers

by

JOHN MASEFIELD

Sum Rosa pulsata mundi Katerina vocata

WILLIAM HEINEMANN LTD
MELBOURNE :: LONDON :: TORONTO

A161(aa) title-page

---

*Words spoken at the unveiling of
the Memorials to the poets
John Keats and Percy Shelley*

We are met today, in this great place of thanks-giving, to give thanks to two men who have added to our Humanity, making our lives more rich, our art more splendid.

Under our feet here, very near to us, is the consecrated dust of some of the greatest of our poets, of Chaucer, who first brought our poetry into the ways of genius; of Spenser; of Francis Beaumont; of Alfred, Lord Tennyson; and of our late revered, beloved Master, Thomas Hardy.

What others could we long for here?

Shakespeare belongs, surely, to Stratford, where his life's effort restored his broken family. Marlowe is at Deptford, in a parish not his own; Milton in the City, beside his Father; Gray, most rightly, in the Churchyard linked to him by the immortality of his genius and the nearness of his human affection. Wordsworth, as surely, belongs among the hills and waters where brooding Nature so spoke to him.

Of all our poets dead and gone, we most miss three here: John Fletcher, who lies in some grave of a great pestilence, who should be by his friend, and those two, whom now we devoutly remember, who lie beside each other, under the violets, near the pyramid of Caius Cestius.

A163(b) title and text on page [1]

Copies seen: private collection (ROV) number 165, inscribed '165. The days that make us happy make us wise. | John Masefield.' on p.[2]; BL (C.121.d.2) number 13, inscribed '13. | The luck will alter + the star will rise. | John Masefield.' on p.[2], stamped 23 AUG 1951; NYPL (Berg Collection) number 179, inscribed '179. | The days that make us happy make us wise. | John Masefield.' on p.[2]' HRHRC (PR6025 A77 L38 1951) un-numbered, inscribed 'For Con | from Jan. | August 10. 1951.' with HRHRC note 'From the Library of John Masefield'

A160(b)   Second English edition ([1951])

THE LEDBURY SCENE | AS I HAVE USED IT | IN MY VERSE | JOHN MASEFIELD
(All width centred)

Bibliographies: Handley-Taylor [unrecorded], Wight [unrecorded]

Collation: [A]⁸; 8 leaves; 284 × 226mm.; [1–2] 3–16

Page contents: [1] title-page; [2] 'Printed in Great Britain | by | Jakemans Ltd. Hereford'; 3–16 text

Paper: wove paper

Running title: none

Binding: light grey wrappers. Spine: blank. On upper wrapper, in red: 'THE LEDBURY SCENE | JOHN MASEFIELD'. Lower wrapper: blank. All edges trimmed. Binding measurements: 284 × 226mm. (wrappers); 284 × 2mm. (spine).

Publication date: published, as suggested by an inscribed copy, during October 1951

Price: 5s.

Contents:
as for A160(a)

Notes:
The name and address of the printer appear in this edition as 'Jakemans Ltd. Hereford'. Contrast this with A160(a) where the information appears as 'Jakemans Ltd., Hereford'.

Copies seen: private collection (PWE); private collection (ROV); Library of The John Masefield Society (Eileen Colwell Collection) inscribed 'For Eileen, | from | John + Constance Masefield. | Christmas. 1951.'; HRHRC (PR6025 A77 L38 1951B) inscribed 'For Con, | from Jan. | Octʳ 5ᵗʰ. 1951.' with HRHRC note 'From the Library of John Masefield'

A160(c)   Third English edition (first illustrated edition) ([1982])

THE LEDBURY SCENE | by | JOHN MASEFIELD, O.M. | Reprinted from the Original Edition | of 1951 | with illustrations by | FREDERICK SHEPPARD, A.T.C. | Printed and published by Reprodux Printers, Hereford. | © Rector and Churchwardens, Ledbury Parish Church.
(All width centred)

Bibliographies: Wight [unrecorded]

Collation: [A]⁸; 8 leaves; 296 × 210mm.; [1–2] 3–16

Page contents: [1] title-page; [2] 'Note: This essay, originally privately printed | in a limited edition to be sold in aid of a fund | to repair Ledbury Church's bells, is now | reprinted in aid of general church mainte- | nance by kind permission of members of the | Masefield family. | The days that make us happy make us wise. [in facsimile] | John Masefield. [facsimile signature] | Facsimile of motto and signature | from a signed copy of the original edition. | Cover design: View of Ledbury Church from Cabbage Lane – see P.3.' (lines 1–6 within two large square brackets, lines 7–8 within ruled border: 39 × 162mm.); 3–15 text and illustrations; 16 blank

Paper: wove paper

Running title: none

Binding: orange/brown wrappers. Spine: blank. On upper wrapper: 'The Ledbury Scene | as I have used it | in my verse | JOHN MASEFIELD | [drawing of Ledbury Church]'. Lower wrapper: blank. All edges trimmed. Binding measurements: 296 × 210mm. (wrappers); 296 × 2mm. (spine).

Publication date: 1982 (see notes)

Price: £2.00

Contents:
as for A160(a)

Notes:
The essay comprises three main sections and each commences with a drop-capital.

In contrast with the 1951 editions, this edition gives the full title of the essay on the upper wrapper, but not on the title-page.

This edition, illustrated with seven illustrations within the text and one cover illustration by Frederick Sheppard, comprises the first illustrated edition.

A publication date of 1982 is conjectural. One illustration is dated 1981 by Sheppard and an exhibition and sale of the original drawings was held at the Nexus Gallery, Ledbury 17–29 May 1982.

Copies seen: private collection (PWE)

Reprinted:
The booklet, without reprint information, appears to have been reprinted and reset on at least one occasion since 1982. No further detail is known.

A161 ST. KATHERINE OF LEDBURY AND OTHER LEDBURY PAPERS   1951

A161(a) First English edition (1951)

ST. KATHERINE | OF LEDBURY | *and other Ledbury papers* | *by* | JOHN MASEFIELD | *Sum Rosa pulsata mundi Katerina vocata* | [publisher's device of a windmill with 'W' and 'H'] | [rule, 56mm.] | WILLIAM HEINEMANN LTD | MELBOURNE :: LONDON :: TORONTO
(All width centred)

Bibliographies: Handley-Taylor p.66, Wight 119

Collation: [A]⁸ B-C⁸ D⁴ E⁸; signatures right foot of page; 36 leaves; 216 × 139mm.; [i–vi] 1–66

Page contents: [i] half-title: 'ST. KATHERINE OF LEDBURY | *Sum Rosa pulsata mundi Katerina vocata*'; [ii] '*THE WORKS OF JOHN MASEFIELD* | PLAYS: | [12 titles listed] | POETRY: | [20 titles listed] | FICTION: | [14 titles listed] | GENERAL: | [15 titles listed]'; [iii] title-page; [iv] 'THE SALE OF THIS BOOK IS TO BENEFIT | THE LEDBURY BELL FUND | FIRST PUBLISHED 1951 | PRINTED IN GREAT BRITAIN | AT THE WINDMILL PRESS | KINGSWOOD, SURREY'; [v] 'TO | MY WIFE'; [vi] blank; 1–66 text

Paper: wove paper

Running title: '*ST. KATHERINE OF LEDBURY*' (76mm.) on both verso and recto, pp.2–30; '*THE FIGHT AT LEDBURY*' (63mm.) on both verso and recto, pp.32–53; and '*THE LEDBURY SCENE*' (54mm.) on both verso and recto, pp.55–66

Binding: dark cream wrappers. On spine, reading lengthways down spine, from head, in navy blue: 'John Masefield ST. KATHERINE OF LEDBURY Heinemann'. On upper wrapper: 'ST. KATHERINE [in navy blue] | OF LEDBURY [in navy blue] | [ornament] [in light blue] | JOHN MASEFIELD [in navy blue] | *5s net* [in navy blue]' (within ornate border in light blue: 199 × 127mm.) Lower wrapper: blank. All edges trimmed. Binding measurements: 216 × 139mm. (wrappers), 216 × 6mm. (spine).

Publication date: the sales ledger preserved in the Heinemann Archive suggests publication on 10 December 1951

Price: 5s.

Contents:
St. Katherine of Ledbury (Katherine Audley) ('On the western side of the main street of Ledbury are the Chapel...')
The Fight at Ledbury April 22, 1645 ('Ledbury is a small town to the west of a group of steep, wooded hills...')
The Ledbury Scene, (as I have used it in my verse) ('In 1911, when, after much vain effort, I began to write...')

Notes:
A short volume containing three essays, each connected with Masefield's town of birth. The sale of the book was to benefit 'The Ledbury Bell Fund' since the bells of the church had been forced into silence. The first essay (from which the volume is titled) concerns Lady Katherine Audley, about whom Wordsworth wrote a sonnet; the second concerns 'The Fight at Ledbury' of 1645 and the third, (also published separately as A160) describes 'what places in and near Ledbury have been brought into my verses as the scenes of imagined events'.

Each item commences with a drop-capital.

Wight describes the wrappers as 'thin pale yellow cardboard'.

It appears that the title of this volume was suggested by Heinemann:

> I am now able to send you paged galleys of your Ledbury booklet. There is the question of the title to cover these three articles. The title-page we have set up at present being the first of the articles: ST. KATHERINE OF LEDBURY may be as you wish, or perhaps you would be good enough to insert the title you desire.
> (B.F. Oliver, letter to John Masefield, 5 October 1951)
> (HRHRC, MS (Masefield, J.) Recip William Heinemann Ltd.)

Progress was reported on 18 October. Dwye Evans noted that '...the three articles which I understand are to be issued as a paper-covered book are now setting and we hope to be able to send you proofs within a few days...' (see Dwye Evans, letter to John Masefield, 18 October 1951) (HRHRC, MS (Masefield, J.) Recip William Heinemann Ltd.)

Heinemann, it seems, was as anxious to assist the Church Bell Fund as Masefield:

ST. KATHERINE OF LEDBURY. Regarding your royalty, realising this could be the only benefit to the Bell Fund we would propose a 20% on both editions. On such a small printing there can be no profit in fact the cheaper edition costs a penny less than we shall get for it from the booksellers. I will consult with Mr. Frere when he arrives back, and should both editions sell out, whether he might wish us to make a contribution from the proceeds of the signed edition.

(B.F. Oliver, letter to John Masefield, 12 November 1951)
(HRHRC, MS (Masefield, J.) Recip William Heinemann Ltd.)

Copies seen: BL (4828.eee.28) stamped 6 DEC 1951 rebound; Bodleian (G.A.Hereford.8°50) stamped 17 MAR 1952; Harvard College Library (Widener 23697.10.391) rebound

A161(aa) First English edition (limited signed edition) (1951)

ST. KATHERINE | OF LEDBURY | *and other Ledbury papers* | by | JOHN MASEFIELD | *Sum Rosa pulsata mundi Katerina vocata* | [publisher's device of a windmill with 'W' and 'H'] | [rule, 56mm.] | WILLIAM HEINEMANN LTD | MELBOURNE :: LONDON :: TORONTO
(All width centred)

Bibliographies: Handley-Taylor p.66, Wight 119a (see notes)

Collation: [A]⁸ B-C⁸ D⁴ E⁸; signatures right foot of page; 36 leaves; 214 × 136mm.; [i–vi] 1–66

Page contents: [i] half-title: 'ST. KATHERINE OF LEDBURY | *Sum Rosa pulsata mundi Katerina vocata*'; [ii] 'This signed edition is limited to 250 copies. | This is number..'; [iii] title-page; [iv] 'THE SALE OF THIS BOOK IS TO BENEFIT | THE LEDBURY BELL FUND | FIRST PUBLISHED 1951 | PRINTED IN GREAT BRITAIN | AT THE WINDMILL PRESS | KINGSWOOD, SURREY'; [v] 'TO | MY WIFE'; [vi] blank; 1–66 text

Paper: wove paper

Running title: 'ST. KATHERINE OF LEDBURY' (76mm.) on both verso and recto, pp.2–30; '*THE FIGHT AT LEDBURY*' (63mm.) on both verso and recto, pp.32–53; and '*THE LEDBURY SCENE*' (54mm.) on both verso and recto, pp.55–66

Binding: blue cloth. On spine, reading lengthways down spine from head, in silver: 'John Masefield ST. KATHERINE OF LEDBURY Heinemann'. On upper cover, in silver: 'ST KATHERINE OF LEDBURY | [ornament]'. Lower cover: blank. All edges trimmed. Sewn head band (in blue and white). Binding measurements: 220 × 139mm. (covers), 220 × 18mm. (spine). End-papers: wove paper.

Publication date: the sales ledger preserved in the Heinemann Archive suggests publication on 10 December 1951 in an edition of 250 copies

Price: 21s.

Contents:
as for A161(a)

Notes:
Each item commences with a drop-capital.

Wight notes a similar edition as 119a. He records p.[ii] as a blank page, however (thus, a cloth bound, non-limited signed edition). No volume matching Wight's description has yet been seen or any library reference traced. Moreover, the Heinemann archive notes only two editions of this work: an edition bound in wrappers (see A161(a)) and this, the Heinemann limited signed edition. It appears, therefore, that Wight's description of 119a is incorrect.

Wight states that Handley-Taylor notes a publication date of 10 December 1951. This is not entirely accurate for Handley-Taylor's description is as follows:

ST. KATHERINE OF LEDBURY AND OTHER LEDBURY PAPERS. William Heinemann, Ltd. (London). Published December 10, 1951. Also issued in an edition limited to 250 copies (signed by the author).

The Heinemann archive reveals, however, that both editions of the title were indeed published on the same date. The *English Catalogue of Books* only lists the unsigned edition (see A161(a)).

The limitation sheets were sent to Masefield at the end of November 1951:

By separate registered parcel we are sending you 268 flat sheets of the title-section of the Limited edition of ST. KATHERINE OF LEDBURY. Would you be good enough to sign these sheets and we will number the edition...

(B.F. Oliver, letter to John Masefield, 23 November 1951)
(HRHRC, MS (Masefield, J.) Recip William Heinemann Ltd.)

These were acknowledged five days later with the note that Heinemann had numbered them (see B.F. Oliver, letter to John Masefield, 28 November 1951) (HRHRC, MS (Masefield, J.) Recip William Heinemann Ltd.)

The guide book, Ellen F. Tilley, *Illustrated Guide to Ledbury and the District* (Luke Tilley and Son, new and revised edition, 1966) provides further information about this edition (on p.52):

[Masefield's]… book entitled "St. Katherine of Ledbury" was limited to 250 copies, each one autographed by John Masefield, and sold at one guinea each; the 250th copy, in addition to his signature was dated by him 26th November, 1951, to which he also added the words "Rest and be thankful copy" a five shilling edition of this book was also published and the proceeds of the sale of both these issues were devoted to the Church Bell Fund.

Copies seen: private collection (PWE) number 36, signed '36 | John Masefield.' on p.[ii]; private collection (ROV) number 218, signed '218 | John Masefield.' on p.[ii] and inscribed 'For Margery Fisher. | from | John Masefield. | August the 1st. 1958.'; private collection (BG) number 78, signed '78 | John Masefield.' on p.[ii] and inscribed 'To Brangwen. | from | John Masefield. | Christmas. 1951.'; BL (4828.eee.31) out of series, signed 'John Masefield.' on p.[ii] stamped 2 JAN 1952; Harvard College Library (Widener 23697.10.390) number 158, signed '158 | John Masefield.' on p.[ii]

A162 SO LONG TO LEARN   1952

A162(a) First English edition (1952)

SO LONG TO LEARN | *Chapters of an Autobiography* | *by* | JOHN MASEFIELD | The lyfe so short, the craft so long to learn | GEOFFREY CHAUCER | [publisher's device of a windmill with 'W' and 'H'] | [rule, 55mm.] | WILLIAM HEINEMANN LTD | MELBOURNE :: LONDON :: TORONTO
(All width centred)

Bibliographies: Handley-Taylor p.66, Wight 120

Collation: [A]⁸ B-O⁸ P⁴ Q⁸ (J not used); signatures right foot of page; 124 leaves; 215 × 137mm.; [i–vi] [1–2] 3–85 [86–88] 89–242

Page contents: [i] half-title: 'SO LONG TO LEARN'; [ii] '*THE WORKS OF JOHN MASEFIELD* | PLAYS: | [12 titles listed] | POETRY: | [20 titles listed] | FICTION: | [14 titles listed] | GENERAL: | [16 titles listed]'; [iii] title-page; [iv] 'FIRST PUBLISHED 1952 | PRINTED IN GREAT BRITAIN | AT THE WINDMILL PRESS | KINGSWOOD, SURREY'; [v] 'TO | MY WIFE'; [vi] blank; [1] 'PART ONE'; [2] blank; 3–85 text; [86] blank; [87] 'PART TWO'; [88] blank; 89–242 text

Paper: wove paper

Running title: '*SO LONG TO LEARN*' (56mm.) on both verso and recto, pp.4–242

Binding: blue cloth. On spine, in gold: '*So | Long | to | Learn | JOHN | MASEFIELD | HEINEMANN*' (all width centred). Upper cover: blank. On lower cover, in blind: publisher's device of a windmill (ranged lower right). All edges trimmed. Binding measurements: 220 × 138mm. (covers), 220 × 34mm. (spine). End-papers: wove paper.

Publication date: the sales ledger preserved in the Heinemann Archive suggests publication on 17 March 1952 in an edition of 7500 copies

Price: 18s.

Contents:

So Long to Learn ('Now that I am coming to an end, I wish to try to set down what matters have been helpful…')

Notes:

Sub-titled (in the English edition only) 'Chapters of an Autobiography' this volume is concerned 'with the influence that helped [Masefield] to be a story-teller'. It is consequently a more literary autobiographical sketch than any of Masefield's previous writings.

Page numbers appear within square brackets. Thus, [3], [4], etc.

The text is divided into two parts. Each commences with a drop-capital.

The title and epigraph are from the first line of Chaucer's love vision, *The Parliament of Fowls*. This was the first work by Chaucer that Masefield read and he describes the reading experience within the autobiographical *In the Mill*:

…I stretched myself on my bed, and began to read *The Parliament of Fowls;* and with the first lines entered into a world of poetry until then unknown to me.

Many years before, when I was a little child, I had had delight from the early poems of Milton; latterly, I had had delight from *The Piper of Arll*. Now, I tasted something deeper; I was taken into another world, unlike this in its excitement and beauty; it was a new experience.

It seemed to me, that evening, that very likely there was no limit to the world opened by such poetry; it seemed boundless in liberty, inexhaustible in riches, deathless in beauty, eternal in delight.

(John Masefield, *In The Mill*, Heinemann, 1941, p.97)

It appears that Masefield first indicated to his publishers that he was writing another volume of autobiography at the beginning of 1950. A.S. Frere responded:

It is good news that you hope during the Spring to have a short volume of autobiography ready. If it were possible for me to have this in time for publication in the Autumn, I think we should do very well with it.

(A.S. Frere, letter to John Masefield, 6 January 1950)
(HRHRC, MS (Masefield, J.) Recip William Heinemann Ltd.)

SO LONG TO LEARN

Chapters of an Autobiography

by

JOHN MASEFIELD

The lyfe so short, the craft so long to learn
GEOFFREY CHAUCER

WILLIAM HEINEMANN LTD
MELBOURNE :: LONDON :: TORONTO

A162(a) title-page

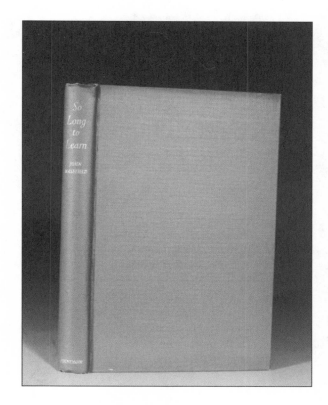

A162(a) spine and upper cover

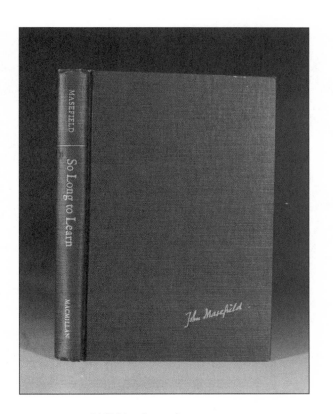

A162(b) spine and upper cover

So Long to Learn

JOHN MASEFIELD

The lyfe so short, the craft so long to lerne,
Th' assay so hard, so sharp the conquering.
—GEOFFREY CHAUCER, *The Assembly of Foules*

NEW YORK · 1952
THE MACMILLAN COMPANY

A162(b) title-page

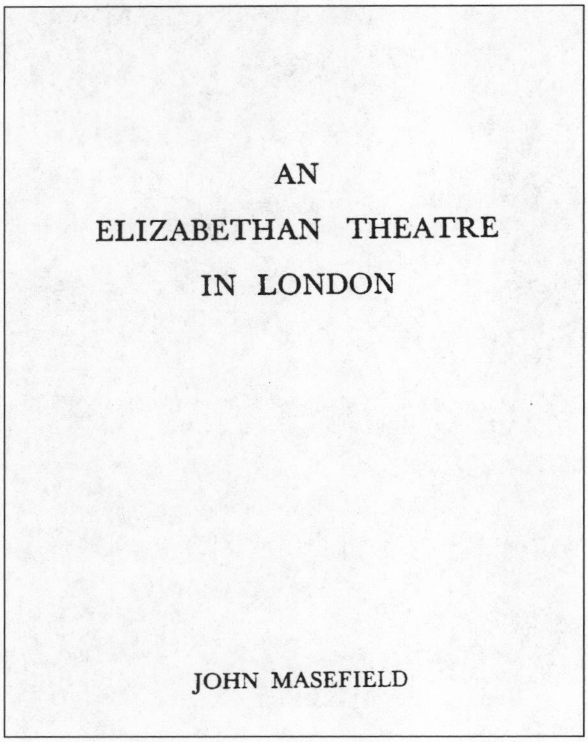

AN

ELIZABETHAN THEATRE

IN LONDON

JOHN MASEFIELD

A164(a) title-page

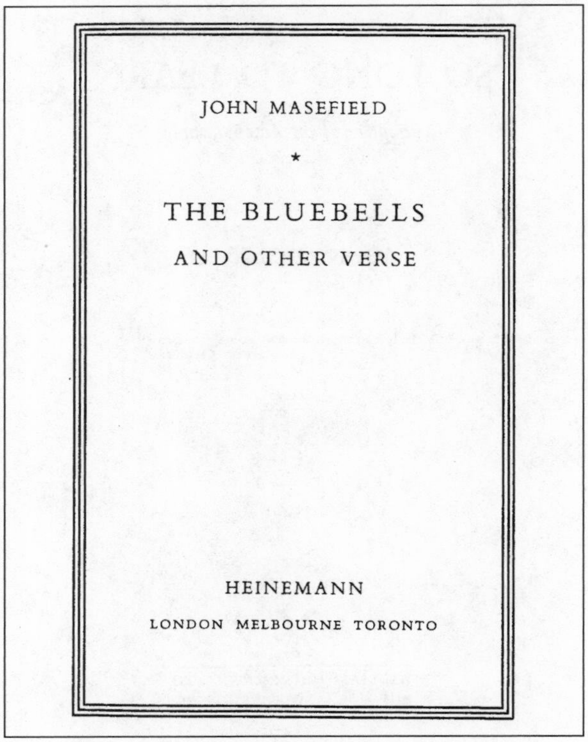

JOHN MASEFIELD

⋆

THE BLUEBELLS

AND OTHER VERSE

HEINEMANN

LONDON MELBOURNE TORONTO

A166(a) title-page

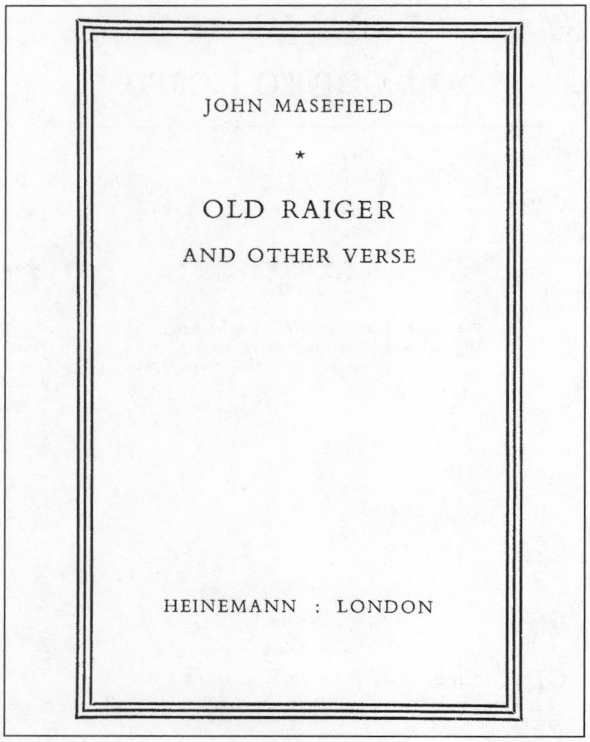

JOHN MASEFIELD

⋆

OLD RAIGER

AND OTHER VERSE

HEINEMANN : LONDON

A169(a) title-page

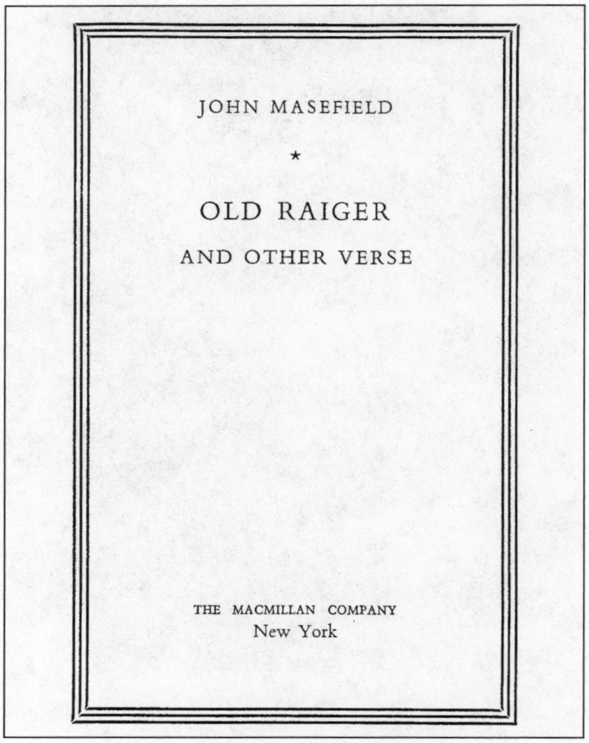

JOHN MASEFIELD

⋆

OLD RAIGER

AND OTHER VERSE

THE MACMILLAN COMPANY
New York

A169(b) title-page

The writing was, however, to take longer than Frere anticipated. A letter from Masefield dated during June 1951 enclosed the text:

> With this, I send the copy of the auto-biographical book, *So Long to Learn*. It is about 72,000 words I think, + is complete
> in itself: but later, as I think I said, I may add chapters to it; so that it may reach 90,000, or more, in future years. Later,
> in better times, perhaps, if the people like the book, there might be a picture or two.
>
> (John Masefield, letter to [A.S.] Frere, 26 June 1951)
> (Archives of William Heinemann)

Publication took place just under nine months later, but no expanded or illustrated edition appeared. Masefield received a pre-publication copy and wrote to Frere praising the appearance. He also provides details of the cat (probably "Mickey") which appeared with Masefield on the dust-jacket photograph:

> Many thanks for your letter, + for so kindly sending me a copy of *So Long to Learn*. Thank you for having so nice a book
> of it. I hope that it may interest people, and repay you. Alas, the poor old cat on the cover is gone, aged over 17, after a
> life devoted to field-sports. Please, may I have *two* dozen copies before the publication date?
>
> (John Masefield, letter to [A.S.] Frere, 1 March 1952)
> (Archives of William Heinemann)

The dust-jacket for this volume states it is a 'Book Society Recommendation' and one copy consulted includes a publisher's wraparound: 29 × 459mm. This (printed in green on cream paper) bears 'BOOK SOCIETY | RECOMMENDATION' on the two 'cover' sides and 'BOOK | SOCIETY | RECOMMEN- | DATION' on the 'spine' side. In discussions regarding the dust-jacket for this title, Masefield evidently favoured the old style adopted largely for the "Wanderer Edition" of his works. A letter from Masefield to A.S. Frere, of the Heinemann firm states:

> I have always liked the old jackets of the blue + white stripes: but the times are out of joint, + may have killed that, too.
>
> (John Masefield, letter to A.S. Frere, 9 January [1952])
> (Archives of William Heinemann)

Frere replied on 10 January 1952 with confirmation that he was not about to set things right, due to booksellers:

> We feel that we have to depart from the old jackets of the blue and white stripes because the booksellers do not like them.
> They complain that they get dirty very quickly and are slightly old-fashioned in these times.
>
> (A.S. Frere, letter to John Masefield, 10 January 1952)
> (Archives of William Heinemann)

Copies seen: private collection (PWE); Library of The John Masefield Society (Eileen Colwell Collection) 'The luck will alter | and the star will rise. | John Masefield. | written for Eileen. | April 10th. 1952.' laid down

Reprinted:

[first edition, second impression] 17 Nov 1958

A162(b) *First American edition (1952)*

So Long to Learn | [rule] | JOHN MASEFIELD | The lyfe so short, the craft so long to lerne, | Th' assay so hard, so sharp the conquering. | -GEOFFREY CHAUCER, *The Assembly of Foules* | NEW YORK [point] 1952 | THE MACMILLAN COMPANY
(Lines 1 and 8 width centred, lines 3 and 7 off-set to right, lines 4 and 5 on same left margin and line 6 off-set to right)

Bibliographies: Handley-Taylor p.66, Wight 120a

Collation: [A-F]^{16}; 96 leaves; 210 × 137mm.; [i–vi] [1–2] 3–63 [64–66] 67–181 [182–86]

Page contents: [i–ii] blank; [iii] half-title: 'So Long to Learn | [rule]'; [iv] 'THE WORKS OF John Masefield | PLAYS: | [12 titles listed] | POETRY: | [20 titles listed] | FICTION: | [14 titles listed] | GENERAL: | [16 titles listed]'; [v] title-page; [vi] 'COPYRIGHT, 1951, 1952, by John Masefield | All rights reserved–no part of this book may be reproduced in | any form without permission in writing from the publisher, except | by a reviewer who wishes to quote brief passages in connection | with a review written for inclusion in magazine or newspaper. | Printed in the United States of America | First Printing'; [1] 'Part I | [rule]'; [2] blank; 3–63 text of 'Part I'; [64] blank; [65] 'Part II | [rule]'; [66] blank; 67–181 text of 'Part II'; [182–86] blank

Paper: wove paper

Running title: 'So Long to Learn' (29mm.) on both verso and recto, pp.4–181

Binding: blue cloth. On spine, reading lengthways down spine from head, in gold: 'MASEFIELD [vertical rule] So Long to Learn MACMILLAN'. On upper cover, in gold: facsimile signature 'John Masefield.' (off-set to right and at an angle). Lower cover: blank. All edges trimmed. Binding measurements: 216 × 139mm. (covers), 216 × 33mm. (spine). End-papers: pale grey wove paper.

Publication date: published, according to Handley-Taylor, 17 March 1952

Price: $3.00

Contents:
as for A162(a)

Notes:

The text is divided into two parts. Both commence with a drop-capital.

The epigraph from Chaucer's love vision, *The Parliament of Fowls* is here lengthened from that present in A162(a). The attribution of the quotation is lacking in A162(a).

The publicity material in the preliminaries that lists Masefield's work (appearing on p.[iv]) bears a marked similarity to that present in the Heinemann edition. Moreover, titles as cited here are those of English editions (separate editions of Masefield's Racine translations and *St. George and the Dragon*, for example). Heinemann assisted with the American publication, as revealed by a letter to Masefield from B.F. Oliver in which he states '…I note to send 3 sets of folded sheets of SO LONG TO LEARN when off press to The Macmillan Co., in New York' (see B.F. Oliver, letter to John Masefield, 22 October 1951) (HRHRC, MS (Masefield, J.) Recip William Heinemann Ltd.)

Compared with A162(a), there is no sub-title or dedication included in this edition.

Rules present within the volume run across the width of the page.

A letter from Masefield to The Society of Authors suggests that *So Long to Learn* grew directly from Masefield's two contributions entitled 'The Joy of Story-Telling' published in 1951 within *The Atlantic Monthly* (see C215.008 and C215.009):

> Some time ago, you very kindly helped in getting some articles of mine into the Atlantic Monthly. These things, much re-written, can now be printed in America as a book by the Macmillan Co.
>
> (John Masefield, letter to Miss [Gabrielle] Curry, 31 July [1951])
> (BL, Add.Mss.56623, f.5)

Copies seen: private collection (PWE); New York State College for Teachers at Albany (PR 6025 A77 Z54)

A163 WORDS SPOKEN AT THE UNVEILING OF THE MEMORIALS TO THE POETS JOHN KEATS AND PERCY SHELLEY   1954

A163(a) First English edition ([1954])

[There is no title on p.[1] of pamphlet]

Bibliographies: Handley-Taylor [unrecorded], Wight [unrecorded] (see notes)

Collation: [A]⁴; 4 leaves; 186 × 124mm.; [1–8]

Page contents: [1–8] text

Paper: laid paper (watermark: '[Crown] | Abbey Mills | Greenfield'), chain-lines 26mm. apart

Running title: none

Binding: wrappers comprise the first and last leaves of the single gathering ([A]1 and [A]4). Spine: blank. Upper wrapper comprises the beginning of the text. All edges trimmed. Binding measurements: 186 × 124mm. (wrappers), 186 × 1mm. (spine).

Publication date: published, according to manuscript correspondence, during June 1954

Price: copies were not for sale

Contents:

[Words Spoken at the Unveiling of the Memorials to the Poets John Keats and Percy Shelley]
    ('We are met today, in this great place of thanks-giving, to give thanks to two men...')

Notes:

A privately printed pamphlet of words spoken by Masefield at the unveiling of memorials to Keats and Shelley in Westminster Abbey on 10 June 1954. After a consideration of Poets' Corner, Masefield comments on Keats and Shelley in turn.

There are two editions, one untitled and unsigned whilst the other is titled and concludes with a best wishes inscription. Material within the Bodleian Library (Additional Masefield Papers 1) states that the untitled edition is the earlier of the two. See also Bodleian, MS.Eng.lett.d.475/1, f.148 for a printed card issued by the Keats-Shelley Memorial Association.

A letter from Edward Colegrove, managing director of Hall the Printer, preserved in the received correspondence files of Masefield notes that the firm would be 'very honoured to submit an estimate of the cost of printing to you as quickly as possible' (see Edward Colegrove, letter to John Masefield, 27 April 1954) (HRHRC, MS (Masefield, J.) Recip Hall the Printer Limited). This may, presumably, refer to either A163 or A164. A letter from May 1954 is assumed to refer to this publication, however:

> …Thank you so much for your kind order of May 26th which has already been put in hand. Naturally the reduction in the quantity of matter and the fact that no cover will be needed will effect a reduction in the estimate.
>
> (Michael J. Colegrove, estimate for John Masefield, 27 May 1954)
> (HRHRC, MS (Masefield, J.) Recip Hall the Printer Limited)

A subsequent letter, dated 2 June 1954 notes:

…The proof of your pamphlet accompanies this letter… Unfortunately the necessary space has not been left blank at the top of page one but can be made by sacrificing some of the space between the paragraphs. As we have to produce the pamphlets by Friday, it would be helpful if some message could be sent to use tomorrow, when the proofs have been read, and we will arrange to collect them. We are planning to print two hundred and fifty copies, I hope that is correct.

(Michael J. Colegrove, letter to John Masefield, 2 June 1954)
(HRHRC, MS (Masefield, J.) Recip Hall the Printer Limited)

The letter also appears to be annotated, in Masefield's hand, with train times between Paddington and Oxford.

The text appears to use the same setting of type as A163(b).

Copies seen: ULL (Special Collections) includes typewritten title 'Address by the Poet Laureate | (Dr. Masefield, O.M.) | on the occasion of the Unveiling | of a Memorial to Keats and Shelley | in Poets' Corner, Westminster Abbey, | on June 10th 1954.'; Bodleian (Additional Masefield Papers 1) inscribed 'John Masefield. | For Kay. | (the first printing).'; HRHRC (PR6025 A77 W672 1954P)

A163(b) Second English edition ([1954])

Words spoken at the unveiling of | the Memorials to the poets | John Keats and Percy Shelley | [text]
(This title taken from p.[1] of pamphlet)
(All width centred)

Bibliographies: Handley-Taylor p.67, Wight [unrecorded]

Collation: [A]⁴; 4 leaves; 182 × 124mm.; [1–8]

Page contents: [1] title and text; [2–7] text; [8] '[text] | *To.. | With all best wishes for now and later | from | John and Constance Masefield.*'

Paper: laid paper (watermark: '[Crown] | Abbey Mills | Greenfield'), chain-lines 26mm. apart

Running title: none

Binding: wrappers comprise the first and last leaves of the single gathering ([A]1 and [A]4). Spine: blank. Upper wrapper comprises the title and beginning of the text. All edges trimmed. Binding measurements: 182 × 124mm. (wrappers), 182 × 1mm. (spine).

Publication date: published, according to manuscript correspondence, during June 1954

Price: copies were not for sale

Contents:
Words Spoken at the Unveiling of the Memorials to the Poets John Keats and Percy Shelley
('We are met today, in this great place of thanks-giving, to give thanks to two men...')

Notes:
The text appears to use the same setting of type as A163(a).

Copies seen: The John Masefield Society Archives (Constance Babington Smith Archives) inscribed to 'Ethel' and signed 'John Masefield.'; Bodleian (Additional Masefield Papers 1) inscribed to 'Kay.' and noted 'a later printing.'; Bodleian (Additional Masefield Papers 10) inscribed 'For Querie, | from Jan. August the 27th. | 1966.'; HRHRC (PR6025 A77 W672 1954)

A164 AN ELIZABETHAN THEATRE IN LONDON [1955]

A164(a) First English edition ([1955])

AN | ELIZABETHAN THEATRE | IN LONDON | JOHN MASEFIELD
(All width centred)

Bibliographies: Handley-Taylor p.67, Wight 121

Collation: [A]¹⁰; 10 leaves; 185 × 121mm.; [1–2] 3–19 [20]

Page contents: [1] title-page; [2] blank; 3–19 text; [20] '[rule] | HALL THE PRINTER LTD., | 6 BREWER STREET, | OXFORD. | [rule]'

Paper: laid paper (watermark: '[Crown] | Abbey Mills | Greenfield'), chain-lines 25mm. apart

Running title: none

Binding: light grey wrappers. Spine: blank. On upper wrapper: 'AN [in purple] | ELIZABETHAN THEATRE [in purple] | IN LONDON [in purple] | JOHN MASEFIELD'. Lower wrapper: blank. All edges trimmed. Binding measurements: 190 × 125mm. (wrappers), 190 × 2mm. (spine). The wrappers extend beyond the edges of the internal leaves.

Publication date: approximately August 1954 (see notes)

Price: copies were not for sale

Contents:

An Elizabethan Theatre in London ('Between the years 1585 and 1635 the literary movement known as...')

Notes:

A privately printed pamphlet appealing for the reconstruction of an Elizabethan theatre in the capital with a consideration of the repertoire to be performed together with projected building and running costs. This was not Masefield's first consideration of Shakespeare's theatre: a letter 'The Suggested Shakespeare Memorial Theatre' appeared in *The Times* for 22 October 1909 (see C125.001) whilst Elizabethan theatres were also considered in *William Shakespeare* (see A17).

Masefield first sent a copy of the text to The Society of Authors, in December 1953 requesting advice:

> I am sending, with this, the copy of the appeal of which I spoke. If you will, graciously, read it through, perhaps you will let me know presently what you would advise; whether to offer it to the *Sunday Times*, or perhaps to print it by myself + send it round to people.

> (John Masefield, letter to [Anne] Munro-Kerr, 4 December 1953)
> (BL, Add.Mss.56624, f.183)

Masefield did not, therefore, originally intend private publication. The Society of Authors replied:

> Thank you very much for your letter of December 4th enclosing your article on *An Elizabethan Theatre in London*. I have just spoken on the telephone to Mr. Leonard Russel [*sic*] who tells me that the *Sunday Times* would very much like to have the opportunity of considering it. I have therefore sent it on to him, which I hope meets with your approval.

> (Anne Munro-Kerr, letter to John Masefield, 8 December 1953)
> (BL, Add.Mss.56624, f.184)

A few days later The Society of Authors wrote to Masefield noting the proposal from *The Sunday Times*:

> Mr. Leonard Russell has just rung me up to say the *Sunday Times* would very much like to publish your article on the Elizabethan Theatre. In view of its length, they are not quite certain when they could promise to publish it since it will have to appear in two instalments. They think, however, it should be possible to arrange for publication fairly early in the New Year when the paper will have increased in size, and if you are prepared to allow them some latitude in this respect Mr. Russell is definitely anxious to take it. The fee he has proposed is £50.

> (Anne Munro-Kerr, letter to John Masefield, 18 December 1953)
> (BL, Add.Mss.56624, f.191)

Later negotiations found the newspaper intending to publish the appeal in two instalments in March and April 1954. Then, however, the paper requested permission to publish a shortened single extract. Masefield therefore asked for publication in *The Sunday Times* to be delayed until Autumn 1954 and for the entire article to appear in an American periodical, *The Atlantic Monthly*. It appeared there as 'A Festival Theater' in January 1955 (see C215.010) (see BL, Add.Mss.56625, f.5 and Add.Mss.56625, f.64).

The Sunday Times finally stated in February 1955 that, due to a change in editorial policy, they had to abandon plans to publish. They would still pay £50 regardless and asked for permission to publish the article if they got the chance (see BL, Add.Mss.56626, f.17). Masefield wrote to The Society of Authors in March 1955:

> The theatre pamphlet: This was published in the *Atlantic* in December [*sic*], about 3 months ago, and I shall now begin to distribute my printed copies, to people likely to be interested. Perhaps you will be so very kind as to tell Mr Russell that I shall be doing this. If he should wish, none the less, to use the article during the next few months, he should be free to do so, but perhaps, if he should do so, he should say that his version is cut from a fuller version printed by myself?

> (John Masefield, letter to [Anne] Munro-Kerr, 4 March [1955])
> (BL, Add.Mss.56626, ff.32–33)

A letter from Edward Colegrove, managing director of Hall the Printer, preserved in the received correspondence files of Masefield notes that the firm would be 'very honoured to submit an estimate of the cost of printing to you as quickly as possible' (see Edward Colegrove, letter to John Masefield, 27 April 1954) (HRHRC, MS (Masefield, J.) Recip Hall the Printer Limited). This may, presumably, refer to either A163 or A164.

An estimate, dated 7 May 1954, describes this work as:

> Twenty-page and four-page cover booklets. Set and printed in the style of the enclosed layout from your copy of 5,000 words. There will be approximately 300 words per printed page which will make just under 17 fully printed pages – this will leave enough space for a title page and other small notices needed to complete the book.

> (Michael J. Colegrove, estimate for John Masefield, 7 May 1954)
> (HRHRC, MS (Masefield, J.) Recip Hall the Printer Limited)

The size is noted as '7 1/4" × 4 7/8" page-size' and the price is quoted as 250 copies at £29 16s. 0d. with £2. 13s. 0d. 'per 100 run-on'.

Masefield has annotated this 'Accepted. Script sent by hand Augt 4th.' This was acknowledged on 7 August 1954 with notification that

> ...we are extremely busy and plan to send you galley proofs on about August 25th. If you feel we should speed this time, let us know and I'm sure we will manage.

> (Michael J. Colegrove, letter to John Masefield, 7 August 1954)
> (HRHRC, MS (Masefield, J.) Recip Hall the Printer Limited)

Copies seen: private collection (PWE); private collection (ROV); private collection (BG) inscribed '151. | For Brangwen, | from John Masefield. | Christmas 1965.'; BL (X.900/13916) stamped 15 JUN 1969; Bodleian (Additional Masefield Papers 10) inscribed 'For Kay, | from | John Masefield. | January 28th. | 1960.'; Library of The John Masefield Society (Eileen Colwell Collection) inscribed 'For Eileen. | from | John. | March the 12th. 1955.' on p.[1]; Library of Sir John Gielgud (sold by Sotheby's, 5 April 2001, part of lot 576) inscribed 'For | John Gielgud. | from | John Masefield.'

A165 WORDS ON THE ANNIVERSARY OF THE BIRTHDAY OF WILLIAM BLAKE   [1957]

A165(a) First English edition ([1957])

1757 [oval device showing Blake design] *1957* | WILLIAM BLAKE | BICENTENARY CELEBRATIONS
(All width centred)
(This title taken from upper wrapper of pamphlet)

Bibliographies: Handley-Taylor [unrecorded], Wight [unrecorded]

Collation: [A]²; 2 leaves; 208 × 174mm.; [1] 2–4

Page contents: [1] 'WORDS ON THE ANNIVERSARY OF THE BIRTHDAY OF | WILLIAM BLAKE. | [text]'; 2–3 text (continued); 4 '[text (concluded)] | JOHN MASEFIELD. | [rule] | These words were read by Professor V. de S. Pinto at the | unveiling of the William Blake bust in Westminster Abbey | on Sunday, 24th November, 1957.'

Paper: wove paper

Running title: none

Binding: glossy wrappers. Spine: blank. On upper wrapper: '*1757* [oval device showing Blake design] *1957* | WILLIAM BLAKE | BICENTENARY CELEBRATIONS'. Lower wrapper: blank. All edges trimmed. Binding measurements: 216 × 178mm. (wrappers), 216 × 0.5cm (spine). The wrapper extends beyond the edges of the internal leaves.

Publication date: a publication date of 1957 is assumed

Price: unknown

Contents:
Words on the Anniversary of the Birthday of William Blake ('We are met today, in this great Church, where centuries...')

Notes:
There may be different issues of this item. The Bodleian copy appears to show some differences in setting from the British Library copy.

Page numbers appear within dashes. Thus, – 2 -, – 3 -, etc.

The internal two leaves comprise a reproduction of typescript. The binding, however, uses a printed wrapper. Presumably the wrappers were used for other publications issued during the celebrations of Blake's birth as the title of Masefield's piece is only present on the internal leaves.

Copies seen: BL (011872.bb.19) stamped 28 FEB 1958 trimmed; Bodleian (2796.d.405) stamped 29 JAN 1958

A166 THE BLUEBELLS AND OTHER VERSE   1961

A166(a) First English edition (1961)

JOHN MASEFIELD | [five-point star] | THE BLUEBELLS | AND OTHER VERSE | HEINEMANN | LONDON MELBOURNE TORONTO
(All width centred and enclosed within triple ruled border: 149 × 92mm.)

Bibliographies: Wight 122

Collation: [A]⁸ B–M⁸ N¹⁰ (J not used); N2 is also signed; signatures right foot of page; 106 leaves; 213 × 135mm.; [i–vi] 1–205 [206]

Page contents: [i] half-title: 'THE BLUEBELLS | AND OTHER VERSE'; [ii] 'THE WORKS OF JOHN MASEFIELD | PLAYS | [10 titles listed] | POETRY | [20 titles listed] | FICTION | [14 titles listed] | GENERAL | [17 titles listed]'; [iii] title-page; [iv] 'William Heinemann Ltd | LONDON MELBOURNE TORONTO | CAPE TOWN AUCKLAND | THE HAGUE | First published 1961 | © by John Masefield 1961 | *All rights reserved* | Printed in Great Britain | by The Windmill Press Ltd | Kingswood, Surrey'; [v] 'CONTENTS' (23 individual poems listed with page references) (see notes); [vi] blank; 1–205 text; [206] blank

Paper: wove paper

Running title: none

Binding: green cloth. On spine, in gold: '*The* | *Bluebells* | and other | verse | [ornament including three points with rule] | JOHN | MASEFIELD | HEINEMANN' (all width centred). Upper cover: blank. On lower cover, in blind: publisher's device of a windmill (ranged lower right). All edges trimmed. Binding measurements: 219 × 136mm. (covers), 219 × 37mm. (spine). End-papers: wove paper.

Publication date: the sales ledger preserved in the Heinemann Archive suggests publication on 29 May 1961 in an edition of 2500 copies

Price: 21s.

Contents:
The Bluebells ('We stood upon the grass beside the road,')
The Starry Night ('That starry Night when Christ was born,')
The Night of Kings ('*Melchior* | The shepherds, up on Dead Man's Wold,')
The Song of Gaspar The Youngest of the Three Kings ('I saw two towers in the light')
Ossian ('PART I | *Finn's Wooing* | *Grania* | All this began because Finn wished to wed.')
Eighty-Five to Win ('Though wayward Time be changeful as Man's will,')
Odysseus Tells ('Tell of the Wooden Horse that ruined Troy?')
King Edward the Second tells his Story ('So, my Son seeks to know how I escaped')
A Cry to Music ('Speak to us, Music, for the discord jars;')
The Princess Malinal ("'Destiny's Sword,' this Cortés, whom you praise?')
Memories ('Now that the leaves are withered, fallen, or falling,')
Middle Farm or the Cherries ("'Cherries and bread, for Man's delight, and need,')
In Praise of Nurses ('Man, in his gallant power, goes in pride,')
The Hawthorns at the Chantry Door ('Outside the little Chantry, built of old,')
Question and Answer A tale of Sutton Walls ('Q. Green rampart grassed, what have you seen and heard?')
King Edward the Confessor and his Ring ('Of all the Saints of whom we sing')
The Buried Bride or True Love Finds a Way ('After the wedding, all returned to feast.')
John Grimaldi or The Sailor's Return ('Not all forgotten yet in London Town')
A Word with Sir Francis Drake during his last night in London | 1595 ('*Scene: A room at night.* SIR FRANCIS DRAKE…')
Lines on the Shipwreck of Admiral Sir Cloudesley Shovell… ('Fog covered all the great Fleet homeward bound,')
H.M.S. *Calliope* in the Huricane, in Apia Bay, Samoa, March 16th 1889 ('Into full hurricane the wind increased')
On Pilots ('Pilots, those unknown beings, who remove')
The Strange Case of Captain Barnaby ('We were bound home, when, on the second day')

Notes:
Described by Sanford Sternlicht as 'twenty-one landscape, seascape, and historical poems', this volume reprints several previously published poems (including several poetry cards) and 'Ossian' (previously only available as the recording *The Story of Ossian* (see G1). Masefield was awarded the 1961 William Foyle Poetry Prize for the volume.

The contents, as listed on p.[v], notes twenty-one poems with 'The Starry Night', 'The Night of Kings' and 'The Song of Gaspar' all listed as number two. The titles as cited in the contents are shortened from those actually present in the text.

Correspondence preserved in the Heinemann Archive suggests that Masefield had originally intended to produce a privately printed volume of verse in 1956 or 1957. Heinemann was approached for printing and distribution, but Masefield's initial discussions were not of a commercial publishing nature. Writing to A.S. Frere in 1956 Masefield stated:

> I have been thinking of privately printing a small book of recent verse, mostly hitherto unpublished, of about 150 pages; my work during 3 or 4 years. My plan has been to print perhaps 950 copies for sale, 600 of these for the Libraries, and the other 350 to be signed, for those who choose to plunge. Is it possible that the House of Heinemann might care to aid in this matter, in the distribution, at any rate?
>
> (John Masefield, letter to [A.S.] Frere, 26 August 1956)
> (Archives of William Heinemann)

One month later Masefield wrote again to Frere providing details of the intended contents of the volume:

> I am grateful for your kind offer of help in the distribution + the possible printing of the volume. The book is mostly narrative verse. Three or four of the things have appeared serially: one in *The Times*, on August the 29th. Three or four have been performed by speakers of verse, speaking solo or in team[s]. In all, I think there would be from 150 to 155 pages of verse of the size of *On the Hill*.
>
> My idea was to persuade libraries to take 600 copies; to allow a limited number for America + Australia, to issue, say, 250 copies, signed + numbered, to those who may like to buy, if any, and to keep 50 for friends. If, unaccountably, people should demand more copies, then, possibly a reprint could be made.
>
> Perhaps you would be so kind as to think over the matter, + let me know at what cost the possible thousand (1000) copies could be printed + bound, + distributed.
>
> Of the tales, 1 is about a famous cricket-match; 1 about the loss of Sir Cloudesley Shovell; 1, a strange old apparition story; another, about a disappearance; another, about an escape from prison; 3 or 4 are Christmas (Nativity) tales; 1 is about a Mexican princess, who helped Cortés to conquer Mexico; 1 is about a legend of S France, (a murderous poet); and there are some short tales, and a poem about a local cherry-farm.
>
> (John Masefield, letter to [A.S.] Frere, 25 September 1956)
> (Archives of William Heinemann)

This letter tells much about Masefield's self-perception of audience. He implies an unread status and perhaps in suggesting a signed issue of the book harks back to the early 1920s and days of widespread popularity. The proposed volume came to nothing. Nevertheless, by April 1959 Heinemann were writing to Masefield enquiring about current work:

> In the Daily Telegraph this morning I saw a most interesting review of a new poem by you, THE STORY OF OSSIAN, which you have recorded on a gramophone record. I hope it is your intention eventually to publish the poem and, if so, I would be glad to receive your instructions.
>
> (A.S. Frere, letter to John Masefield, 24 April 1959)
(Archives of William Heinemann)

Frere's reference is to G1. Masefield replied that: '…the Story mentioned is only a short story; and I may wish to change some of it a little presently. It is too short to make a book by itself.' (see John Masefield, letter to A.S. Frere, 26 April 1959) (Archives of William Heinemann). Frere, it seems, continued to make encouraging suggestions and *The Bluebells and other verse*, containing much of the material suggested for the earlier privately printed volume and the tale of 'Ossian' was the result. It marked the first substantial volume of new poetic work from Masefield since 1949.

Frere wrote at the end of May 1960:

> Many thanks for your letter of the 28th May with the most welcome news that you expect to have a book of verse ready during the late summer. Of course we shall be delighted to include it in our list together with the others of your distinguished works…
>
> (A.S. Frere, letter to John Masefield, 30 May 1960)
(HRHRC, MS (Masefield, J.) Recip William Heinemann Ltd.)

The decision not to rush the volume through the press for publication at Christmas was taken during June 1960. A.S. Frere explained:

> Effectively to publish the book in time for the Christmas market the manuscript should, even now, be with the printer. If your finished work will not be ready until the end of the summer then I think we must schedule it for publication in the spring.
>
> (A.S. Frere, letter to John Masefield, 1 June 1960)
(HRHRC, MS (Masefield, J.) Recip William Heinemann Ltd.)

Two days later Masefield provided a provisional title for the book and Frere noted that Heinemann would 'include it in our advance lists…' (see A.S. Frere, letter to John Masefield, 3 June 1960) (HRHRC, MS (Masefield, J.) Recip William Heinemann Ltd.) Masefield, it appears, was still revising the contents of the volume at the end of 1960. A.S. Frere wrote noting a deletion:

> Thank you for your letter about the typescript of the BLUEBELL book and MISS GREY, DANCING THE PRELUDE which you wish to omit. We were in time to leave it out of the setting…
>
> (A.S. Frere, letter to John Masefield, 6 December 1960)
(HRHRC, MS (Masefield, J.) Recip William Heinemann Ltd.)

During February 1961 D.E. Priestley wrote noting that Heinemann hoped '…that production arrangements will allow us to publish on 23rd May…' (see D.E. Priestley, letter to John Masefield, 13 February 1960) (HRHRC, MS (Masefield, J.) Recip William Heinemann Ltd.) Publication was eventually a few days later on 29 May 1961 and the new volume of verse from Masefield attracted some media interest. Heinemann wrote to Masefield noting:

> I have been requested by the television programme "Tonight" to write to you and find out whether you would be willing to be interviewed by them to coincide with the publication of THE BLUEBELLS AND OTHER VERSE on May 29.
>
> (William Holden, letter to John Masefield, 10 April 1961)
(HRHRC, MS (Masefield, J.) Recip William Heinemann Ltd.)

Masefield apparently declined to give this interview (see William Holden, letter to John Masefield, 18 April 1960 (HRHRC, MS (Masefield, J.) Recip William Heinemann Ltd.) Frere wrote on 15 May 1961 enclosing an advance copy (and also providing an inaccurate publication date):

> I have very much pleasure in sending you herewith an advance copy of THE BLUEBELLS AND OTHER VERSE which, as I think you know, is scheduled for publication on 28th May…
>
> (A.S. Frere, letter to John Masefield, 15 May 1961)
(HRHRC, MS (Masefield, J.) Recip William Heinemann Ltd.)

Evidence within the Heinemann archive suggests that the royalty agreement for this edition was 15% on sales of upto 3000 copies, 17½% on sales of upto 7500 copies and 20% on sales of copies thereafter.

Copies seen: private collection (PWE); BL (11454.dd.44) stamped 11 MAY 1961; HRHRC (PR6025 A77 B55 cop.1) inscribed 'For Judith, | from |Z. | May the 29ᵗʰ. 1961.'

Reprinted:

'Reprinted'	[first edition, second impression]	1961

A166(b) First American edition (1961)

JOHN MASEFIELD | [five-point star] | THE BLUEBELLS | AND OTHER VERSE | THE MACMILLAN
COMPANY | NEW YORK | 1961
(All width centred and enclosed within triple ruled border: 149 × 92mm.)

Bibliographies: Wight 122a

Collation: [A]⁸ B-M⁸ N¹⁰ (J not used); N2 is also signed; signatures right foot of page; 106 leaves; 212 × 136mm.; [i–vi] 1–205 [206]

Page contents: [i] half-title: 'THE BLUEBELLS | AND OTHER VERSE'; [ii] 'THE WORKS OF JOHN MASEFIELD | PLAYS | [10 titles listed] | POETRY | [20 titles listed] | FICTION | [14 titles listed] | GENERAL | [17 titles listed]'; [iii] title-page; [iv] 'First published 1961 | © by John Masefield 1961 | *All rights reserved* | Printed in Great Britain | by The Windmill Press Ltd | Kingswood, Surrey'; [v] 'CONTENTS' (23 individual poems listed with page references) (see notes); [vi] blank; 1–205 text; [206] blank

Paper: wove paper

Running title: none

Binding: green cloth. On spine, in gold: 'The | Bluebells | and other | verse | [ornament including three points with rule] | JOHN | MASEFIELD | MACMILLAN' (all width centred). Covers: blank. All edges trimmed. Binding measurements: 219 × 137mm. (covers), 219 × 37mm. (spine). End-papers: wove paper.

Publication date: 1961

Price: $5.00

Contents:
as for A166(a)

Notes:
The contents, as listed on page [v], notes twenty-one poems with 'The Starry Night', 'The Night of Kings' and 'The Song of Gaspar' all listed as number two. The titles as cited in the contents are shortened from those actually present in the text.

This American edition although stating 'THE MACMILLAN COMPANY' and 'NEW YORK' on the title-page was printed in England (the note on page [iv] states 'Printed in Great Britain by the Windmill Press...'). With the exception of the title-page, information on page [iv] and the lettering on the binding, this edition is identical to A166(a). Writing to the The Society of Authors in October 1960 Masefield sought advice about an arrangement between his two publishers:

> The Macmillan Co. in N.Y. wish to photograph, or to buy sheets of, the proposed Heinemann new book of verse, to be published, perhaps, next Spring. Please, may I take it that neither process can invalidate American copyright, nor (as they will still have to bind the sheets) make any sensible reduction in the cost of each volume's production?
>
> (John Masefield, letter to Anne Munro-Kerr, 7 October [1960])
> (Archives of The Society of Authors)

Having received quotations from Heinemann, it was proposed during November 1960 that Macmillan would set the book themselves (see Emile Capouya, letter to John Masefield, 29 November 1960) (HRHRC, MS (Masefield, J.) Recip The Macmillan Company) Heinemann were to co-operate for A.S. Frere noted he would '...arrange for a clean copy of the revised proofs to go to the Macmillan Company, New York, from which they could set, as soon as the proofs are available...' (see A.S. Frere, letter to John Masefield, 8 December 1960) (HRHRC, MS (Masefield, J.) Recip William Heinemann Ltd.) This arrangement was changed however and the final situation is clarified in a letter from D.E. Priestley:

> Thank you for your enquiry, received today, about the dispatch of corrected proofs of THE BLUEBELLS to Macmillans of New York. There will, in fact, be no necessity for this to be done as we have arranged to supply sheets to them, taken from the run of the English edition.
>
> (D.E. Priestley, letter to John Masefield, 13 February 1961)
> (HRHRC, MS (Masefield, J.) Recip William Heinemann Ltd.)

The publishing agreement for this title between Masefield and Macmillan was dated 15 October 1960 (see Archives of The Society of Authors).

Copies seen: BL Document Supply Centre

A167 THE WESTERN HUDSON SHORE   1962

A167(a) First American edition (1962)

Upper wrapper:
The Western | Hudson Shore | *A New Poem by* | *John Masefield*
(The italic type contains a number of swash characters)
(Lines 1 and 2 justified on left margin, lines 3 and 4 justified on right margin)

Bibliographies: Wight [unrecorded]

Collation: [A]⁶; 6 leaves; 215 × 95mm.; [1–12]

Page contents: [1] title-page; [2] '*England's Poet Laureate wrote these verses in | memory of the late Thomas W. Lamont and his | wife, Florence Corliss Lamont, and as a special | contribution to the privately published book,* The | Thomas Lamont Family, *edited by Corliss La- | mont, just off the press. The poem starts out | from the fact that in his early manhood John | Masefield came to the United States and worked | for two years in a carpet factory at Yonkers, New | York, on the east bank of the Hudson River.* | [rule] | © Copyright 1962 by Corliss Lamont.'; [3–8] text; [9] '[text (concluded)] | * This stanza refers to the fact that the Thomas W. and | Florence C. Lamont estate at Palisades, New York, was willed | to Columbia University and became the headquarters of the | Lamont Geological Observatory. | [rule]'; [10–12] blank

Paper: wove paper

Running title: none

Binding: wrappers comprise the first and last leaves of the single gathering ([A]1 and [A]6). The upper wrapper consequently comprises the title-page. Spine: blank. On upper wrapper: 'The Western | Hudson Shore | *A New Poem by | John Masefield*'. Lower wrapper: blank. All edges trimmed. Binding measurements: 215 × 95mm. (wrappers), 215 × 2mm. (spine).

Publication date: published after October 1962

Price: unknown

Contents:
The Western Hudson Shore ('In a long life's first independent day,')

Notes:
In 1962 Masefield contributed two poems ('The Western Hudson Shore' and 'To The Great Friends In Lifetime') to Corliss Lamont's privately printed volume *The Thomas Lamont Family* (see B535). He also made a recording of these poems (see G7). Lamont published the first of these poems (which concerns the Palisades of the Hudson river) separately in 1962. The poem was also included in a later edition of *Remembering John Masefield* (see E1(c)).

Wight only describes the second American edition (see A167(b)) in his bibliography. He incorrectly gives a date of 1962 for the 1982 edition, thus confusing it with the correct first American edition.

The italic type used for Lamont's brief introduction includes a number of swash characters.

Copies seen: Bodleian (Additional Masefield Papers 2) inscribed 'For My You. | from | John Masefield. | New Year. 1963.' on p.[1]; Columbia University (Special Collections B825M377 Y542 1962 c.1); Columbia University (Special Collections B825M377 Y542 1962 c.2) inscribed 'Friendship is sunlight scattering Life's cloud | making a Life a sunbeam's spangled | dust. | John Masefield. | January the 11th. 1963' on p.[1] and 'John Masefield, | January the 11th. | 1963.' on p.[9]

A167(b) Second American edition (1982)

The | Western Hudson | Shore | John Masefield | THE OLIPHANT PRESS
(The italic type contains a number of swash characters)
(All width centred)

Bibliographies: Wight 123

Collation: [A]⁸; 8 leaves; 216 × 133mm.; [1–2] 3–14 [15–16]

Page contents: [1] title-page; [2] 'Copyright © 1962, 1982 by Corliss Lamont'; 3–4 'FOREWORD' ('This poem by John Masefield about the Palisades of the Hudson was printed...') (signed, 'CORLISS LAMONT'); 5–14 text; [15–16] blank

Paper: wove paper

Running title: none

Binding: green wrappers. Spine: blank. On upper wrapper: '*The | Western Hudson | Shore | John Masefield* | [illustration of shore (signed, 'G.H. Boutleth')]' (text all justified on right margin with illustration centred). On lower wrapper: '$2.00 | THE OLIPHANT PRESS | 145 Hudson Street | New York City 10013'. All edges trimmed. Binding measurements: 223 × 139mm. (wrappers), 223 × 2mm. (spine). The wrappers extend beyond the edges of the internal leaves.

Publication date: 1982

Price: $2.00

Contents:
Foreword ('This poem by John Masefield about the Palisades of the Hudson was printed...')
      (signed, 'CORLISS LAMONT')
The Western Hudson Shore ('In a long life's first independent day,')

Notes:

Wight, in numbering this volume 123, places it between *The Bluebells and other verse* (A166) and *Old Raiger and other verse* (A169). He describes only the second American edition, however, and omits any description of the first. He confuses the two editions and incorrectly states 'Oliphant Press, 1962' in his index.

Copies seen: ULL (Special Collections); ULL (Special Collections) signed 'Corliss Lamont, 1984'

A168 DAUBER & REYNARD THE FOX   1962

A168(a) First English edition (1962)

TWO TALES IN VERSE | *Dauber* | *& Reynard the Fox* | JOHN MASEFIELD | [publisher's device of a windmill] | HEINEMANN | LONDON MELBOURNE TORONTO
(All width centred)

Bibliographies: Wight [unrecorded]

Collation: [1]⁸ 2–11⁸; signatures left foot of page as follows: 'D.-2', 'D.-3', etc. (note that gathering eight is signed 'D-8' only); 88 leaves; 183 × 120mm.; [i–vi] 1–169 [170]

Page contents: [i] half-title: 'DAUBER | & REYNARD THE FOX'; [ii] blank; [iii] title-page; [iv] '*Dauber* first published 1912 | *Reynard the Fox* first published 1919 | This edition first published 1962 | © John Masefield 1962 | Published by William Heinemann Ltd | 15–16 Queen Street, Mayfair, London W.1 | Printed in Great Britain by Morrison and Gibb Ltd | London and Edinburgh'; [v] '*Contents* | PART ONE | DAUBER | Introduction, p. 1 | *Dauber*, p. 4 | Glossary of sea terms, p. 72 | PART TWO | REYNARD THE FOX | Introduction, p. 77 | *Reynard the Fox* | or *The Ghost Heath Run*, p. 79'; [vi] blank; 1–169 text; [170] blank

Paper: wove paper

Running title: 'DAUBER' (13mm.) on both verso and recto, pp.2–71; 'DAUBER-GLOSSARY' (33mm.) on both verso and recto, pp.73–76; and 'REYNARD THE FOX' (32mm.) on both verso and recto, pp.78–169

Binding: white boards (printed in blue and black). On black spine, reading lengthways down spine from head: 'Masefield [in blue] DAUBER & REYNARD the Fox [in white]'; horizontally at foot of spine: publisher's device of a windmill [in blue]. On black upper cover, in white: 'DAUBER | and | REYNARD | THE FOX | JOHN | MASEFIELD [ranged upper left and justified on left margin] | [illustration of boy looking up at ship's rigging, in blue, white and black]'. On black lower cover: illustration of exhausted fox in front of trees and night sky [in blue, white and black]. All edges trimmed. Binding measurements: 189 × 121mm. (covers), 189 × 26mm. (spine). End-papers: wove paper.

Publication date: 10 December 1962 (the Archives of The Society of Authors suggest an edition of 10,000 copies)

Price: 6s.6d.

Contents:

Dauber Introduction ('The story *Dauber* was written during the spring, summer and autumn of 1912...')
Dauber ('Four bells were struck, the watch was called on deck')
Glossary Explanations of Some of the Sea Terms used in the Poem ('BACKSTAYS: wire ropes which support...')
Reynard the Fox Introduction ('The story *Reynard the Fox* was written in the year 1919 at Boars Hill, in Berkshire.')
Reynard the Fox ('The meet was at 'The Cock and Pye')

Notes:

A single volume (sub-titled 'Two Tales In Verse') containing the narrative poems *Dauber* and *Reynard the Fox*. Each is provided with a new introduction by Masefield.

The first part of *Dauber* and both parts of *Reynard the Fox* are the only sections to commence with drop-capitals.

The *English Catalogue of Books* lists this volume as published by Heinemann Educational Books. No such notice is given within this edition, however.

This edition was suggested by Heinemann. Alan Hill wrote to Masefield:

> Please forgive me for bothering you again about our proposed edition of REYNARD THE FOX and DAUBER. I wrote to you at the beginning of this month and you are always so prompt in acknowledgement that your silence makes me wonder if the letter has gone astray. If this is the case, my proposal was that we should issue an edition of the two poems in one volume. We would print not less than 10,000 copies at a published price of around five shillings, at a royalty of 10%. If you agree, we would have the edition ready in March, 1962.
>
> (Alan Hill, letter to John Masefield, 14 November 1961)
> (HRHRC, MS (Masefield, J.) Recip William Heinemann Ltd.)

Masefield – it seems – replied by asking why these two poems should be chosen and also alluded to his unfashionable status. Hill replied (with perhaps a hint of the 'Heinemann Educational Books' status):

Our reason for linking DAUBER with REYNARD is that we have had many requests for these two poems, and we feel there is a substantial market for them – especially among a new generation unfamiliar with your work. I read your comment, "nobody tells the time by me any more" with misgiving. I think there is something we can do about that, and this edition seems to me a step in the right direction.

> (Alan Hill, letter to John Masefield, 17 November 1961)
> (HRHRC, MS (Masefield, J.) Recip William Heinemann Ltd.)

Masefield evidently decided to embrace the suggestion and sent his prefaces within a month. He also appears to state his intention of approaching Macmillan for Alan Hill wrote thanking the author '…for your beautiful preface to DAUBER and REYNARD. I am delighted with it. Perhaps you will let me know in due course the outcome of your approach to Macmillan's in New York.' (see Alan Hill, letter to John Masefield, 6 December 1961) (HRHRC, MS (Masefield, J.) Recip William Heinemann Ltd.) Page proofs were available at the beginning of June and these were sent to Masefield (see Alan Hill, letter to John Masefield, 1 June 1962) (HRHRC, MS (Masefield, J.) Recip William Heinemann Ltd.) At the end of June, Hill wrote to the author noting '…we have now had a rough prepared for the cover design, and I am enclosing this for you to see. I look forward to hearing what you think' (see Alan Hill, letter to John Masefield, 27 June 1962) (HRHRC, MS (Masefield, J.) Recip William Heinemann Ltd.) Masefield, it seems, provided photographs to assist the artist:

> Thank you for your comments. The design is only a very preliminary rough. I will bring all your points to the attention of the artist. He is, himself, greatly devoted to sailing ships, and I am sure he will receive your enclosed photographs with great pleasure.

> (Alan Hill, letter to John Masefield, 2 July 1962)
> (HRHRC, MS (Masefield, J.) Recip William Heinemann Ltd.)

At the beginning of November Masefield was provided with 'the first copy off the press':

> I am enclosing the first copy off the press of the new book which contains DAUBER and REYNARD THE FOX, together with your beautiful introductions. I hope that you will like it. Your author's copies will follow in due course. I must apologize that the binding has become a little battered in transit on this copy, but I thought you would prefer to see it now, rather than wait for the bulk supply.

> (Alan Hill, letter to John Masefield, 8 November 1962)
> (HRHRC, MS (Masefield, J.) Recip William Heinemann Ltd.)

Copies seen: private collection (ROV) inscribed 'For the ever wonderful Myra, | from her grateful friend. | Christmas. 1962. | O joy of trying for Beauty, always the same, | You never fail, your comforts never end, | O Balm of this world's woe, O perfect friend. | John Masefield.'; BL (11596.K.17) stamped 20 FEB 1963

Reprinted:

[first edition, second impression]	1963
[first edition, third impression]	1964
[first edition, fourth impression]	1965
[first edition, fifth impression]	1969

A168(b) First American edition (1963)

TWO TALES IN VERSE | *Dauber* | *& Reynard the Fox* | JOHN MASEFIELD | THE MACMILLAN COMPANY | NEW YORK
(All width centred)

Bibliographies: Wight [unrecorded]

Collation: [1]⁸ 2–11⁸; signatures left foot of page as follows: 'D.-2', 'D.-3', etc. (note that gathering eight is signed 'D-8' only); 88 leaves; 183 × 120mm.; [i–vi] 1–169 [170]

Page contents: [i] half-title: 'DAUBER | & REYNARD THE FOX'; [ii] blank; [iii] title-page; [iv] 'This edition © John Masefield 1962 | *Dauber* first published 1912 | *Reynard the Fox* first published 1919 | First American Edition, 1963 | Printed in Great Britain by Morrison and Gibb Ltd. | London and Edinburgh'; [v] '*Contents* | PART ONE | DAUBER | Introduction, p. 1 | *Dauber*, p. 4 | Glossary of sea terms, p. 72 | PART TWO | REYNARD THE FOX | Introduction, p. 77 | *Reynard the Fox* | or *The Ghost Heath Run*, p. 79'; [vi] blank; 1–169 text; [170] blank

Paper: wove paper

Running title: 'DAUBER' (13mm.) on both verso and recto, pp.2–71; 'DAUBER-GLOSSARY' (33mm.) on both verso and recto, pp.73–76; and 'REYNARD THE FOX' (32mm.) on both verso and recto, pp.78–169

Binding: white boards (printed in blue and black). On black spine, reading lengthways down spine from head: 'Masefield [in blue] DAUBER & REYNARD the Fox [in white] Macmillan [in blue]'. On black upper cover, in white: 'DAUBER | and | REYNARD | THE FOX | JOHN | MASEFIELD [ranged upper left and justified on left margin] | [illustration of boy looking up at ship's rigging, in blue, white and black]'. On black lower cover: illustration of exhausted fox in front of trees and night sky [blue, white and black]. All edges trimmed. Binding measurements: 189 × 121mm. (covers), 189 × 26mm. (spine). End-papers: wove paper.

Publication date: December 1963

Price: $2.95

Contents:
as for A168(a)

Notes:
A letter from Emile Capouya, senior editor at The Macmillan Company in New York, evidently responded to Masefield's suggestion of an American issue of this edition:

> …I am sorry not to have answered sooner your note informing us of the proposed reissue of DAUBER and REYNARD THE FOX. Naturally, we are very much interested in the book, and we have suggested to Heinemann that we act together, as we did in the case of BLUEBELLS.

(Emile Capouya, letter to John Masefield, 7 February 1962)
(HRHRC, MS (Masefield, J.) Recip The Macmillan Company)

A comparison with A168(a) reveals close kinship. Even the binding for this edition suggests that the Heinemann windmill was blocked out and replaced with the Macmillan name. However, the printer is here 'Morrison and Gibb Ltd.' wheras A168(a) notes 'Ltd' without the full-stop.

Copies seen: HRHRC (AC-L M377DAUB 1963c) inscribed 'J. Masefield'

A169 OLD RAIGER AND OTHER VERSE   1964

A169(a) First English edition (1964)

JOHN MASEFIELD | [five-point star] | OLD RAIGER | AND OTHER VERSE | HEINEMANN : LONDON
(All width centred and enclosed within triple ruled border: 149 × 93mm. The lines do not always completely touch to form perfect corners)

Bibliographies: Wight 124

Collation: [A]⁸ B-E⁸; signatures right foot of page; 40 leaves; 214 × 137mm.; [i–vi] 1–73 [74]

Page contents: [i] half-title: 'OLD RAIGER | AND OTHER VERSE'; [ii] 'THE WORKS OF JOHN MASEFIELD | PLAYS | [10 titles listed] | POETRY | [21 titles listed] | FICTION | [14 titles listed] | GENERAL | [17 titles listed]'; [iii] title-page; [iv] 'William Heinemann Ltd | LONDON MELBOURNE TORONTO | CAPE TOWN AUCKLAND | First published 1964 | © by John Masefield 1964 | *All rights reserved* | Those who wish to perform or recite | the poems in this book should apply to | the Society of Authors, 84, Drayton | Gardens, London, S.W.10. | Printed in Great Britain | by Bookprint Limited | Kingswood, Surrey'; [v] 'CONTENTS' (12 individual poems listed with page references); [vi] blank; 1–73 text; [74] blank

Paper: wove paper

Running title: none

Binding: blue cloth. On spine, reading lengthways down spine from head, in gold: 'JOHN MASEFIELD [point] OLD RAIGER AND OTHER VERSE [point] Heinemann'. Upper cover: blank. On lower cover, in blind: publisher's device of a windmill (ranged lower right). All edges trimmed. Binding measurements: 220 × 137mm. (covers), 220 × 20mm. (spine). End-papers: wove paper.

Publication date: the sales ledger preserved in the Heinemann Archive suggests publication on 7 December 1964 in an edition of 5650 copies

Price: 21s.

Contents:
The Snipe at Drum ('Once, when the snipe were drumming,')
Old Raiger ('*Prologue:* | Good Old Man Raiger, raging in his rage,')
The Along-Ships Stow ('Treacle, treacle, little ship,')
Ryemeadows ('My people owned Ryemeadows on the Moor,')
Jane ('In June time once, as I was going')
Pawn to Bishop's Five ('I stayed, once, at Tom's home, at Uppats Lea,')
When April Comes ("April awaits the bold', he said,')
Mornings and Aprils ('PART I | Before the Sun has risen,')
A Storm ('South, in the Caribbean Sea, a haze')
Lines for the Race of Sailing Ships, Lisbon to the Hudson Bridge… ('Once, they were Queens, triumphant everywhere,')
The Isle of Voices ('As the voice bade, I went ashore alone.')
King Gaspar and his Dream ('I had not meant to utter to men's ears')

Notes:
A volume of twelve poems including short narrative verse and descriptive lyrics. Reviewing the volume, A. Alvarez (in *The Observer*) found the verses 'agreeably soothing' while Ian Serraillier (in the *Sunday Telegraph*) noted a 'lyrical and reflective' quality.

The titles as cited in the volume's contents listing are shortened from those present in the text.

It had originally been Masefield's intention to issue a volume of both poetry and prose. David Machin of the Heinemann firm wrote to Dwye Evans, the managing director, enclosing estimates for the book with, and without the prose. His report suggested that the prose be omitted:

> I have not shown the typescripts to anybody else as I really do not think there is anybody left who is qualified as an expert on Masefield's poetry. The verse on the whole is spendidly turn-of-the-century and the themes are as usual often of the sea, ships, nature and countryside characters of the past...

> The prose is a very mixed bag and all very charming and nostalgic in its way: a fictional account of the Battle of Tewkesbury, an essay on reviving the Elizabethan theatre, words spoken in Westminster Abbey at the unveiling of plaques to Keats and Shelley, and on Yeats at the opening of a new hotel in London on the site of his home.

> The fairly long story about Tewkesbury Field could just fit into a volume with some verse, but I really do not see that the essays and tributes to writers would. I am afraid I am doubtful whether anybody is going to be particularly interested in hearing the views of our aged Poet Laureate on these gentlemen. They would be much better left for a commemorative volume for Masefield himself; I know we could not exactly suggest this to him. My recommendation is that we try and confine ourselves to the poems, which would make quite a sizable volume.

> > (David Machin, memorandum to Dwye Evans, 15 April 1964)
> > (Archives of William Heinemann)

The 'aged Poet Laureate' was therefore regarded as somewhat old-fashioned and outdated. Masefield, in planning the volume, was evidently collecting old material (references are made to the 1954 privately printed works *An Elizabethan Theatre in London* (A164) and *Words Spoken at the Unveiling of the Memorials to... John Keats and Percy Shelley* (A163). Dwye Evans wrote to Masefield on 16 April 1964 in somewhat less candid terms and suggested a contract:

> ...on the same terms as for BLUEBELLS AND OTHER VERSE, which was 15% to 3,000, 17½% to 7,500 and 20% thereafter.

> > ([A. Dwye Evans], letter to John Masefield, 16 April 1964)
> > (Archives of William Heinemann)

Masefield replied agreeing that 'the prose would be better away' and in May both suggested the title of the volume and acceptance of the royalty scale. He ended his letter with a suggestion:

> Perhaps the time for any small signed edition of the book has long gone by but possibly a few collectors may still exist for such things.

> > (John Masefield, letter to [A. Dwye] Evans, May 1964)
> > (Archives of William Heinemann)

The time had indeed 'long gone by' and Evans replied:

> Thank you so much for your letter and we will call the book of verse OLD RAIGER AND OTHER VERSE, as you suggest... ...I am afraid the day of the small signed edition is past, alas.

> > (A. Dwye Evans, letter to John Masefield, 12 May 1964)
> > (HRHRC, MS (Masefield, J.) Recip William Heinemann Ltd.)

Copies seen: private collection (PWE); BL (X.909/2610) stamped 14 DEC 1964

A169(b) *First American edition (1965)*

JOHN MASEFIELD | [five-point star] | OLD RAIGER | AND OTHER VERSE | THE MACMILLAN COMPANY | New York
(All width centred and enclosed within triple ruled border: 150 × 93mm. The lines do not always completely touch to form perfect corners)

Bibliographies: Wight 124a

Collation: [A]⁸ B-E⁸; signatures right foot of page; 40 leaves; 210 × 136mm.; [i–vi] 1–73 [74]

Page contents: [i] half-title: 'OLD RAIGER | AND OTHER VERSE'; [ii] 'THE WORKS OF JOHN MASEFIELD | PLAYS | [10 titles listed] | POETRY | [21 titles listed] | FICTION | [14 titles listed] | GENERAL | [17 titles listed]'; [iii] title-page; [iv] 'First published 1965 | © by John Masefield 1964 | *All rights reserved* | Library of Congress Catalogue Number 65–12905 | Those who wish to perform or recite | the poems in this book should apply to | the Society of Authors, 84, Drayton | Gardens, London, S.W.10. | Printed in Great Britain'; [v] 'CONTENTS' (12 individual poems listed with page references); [vi] blank; 1–73 text; [74] blank

Paper: wove paper

Running title: none

Binding: light brown cloth. On spine, reading lengthways down spine from head, in gold: 'MASEFIELD / OLD RAIGER AND OTHER VERSE MACMILLAN'. Upper cover: blank. On lower cover, in gold: '58090' (ranged lower right). All edges trimmed. Binding measurements: 216 × 138mm. (covers), 216 × 24mm. (spine). End-papers: wove paper.

Publication date: 1965

Price: $3.95

Contents:
as for A169(a)

Notes:
Repetition of damaged type proves the same setting of text was used here as for A169(a). This American edition states that it is 'Printed in Great Britain' on p.[iv].

Wight states that the colour of the binding cloth is 'red'.

The publishing agreement for this title between Masefield and Macmillan was dated 25 February 1965 (see Archives of The Society of Authors). The agreement refers to 'the exclusive right to publish and sell in volume form… in the United States, and the Philippine Republic a work provisionally entitled: OLD RAIGER AND OTHER VERSE, to consist of approximately 80 book pages'. Masefield signed his copy on 16 February 1965.

Copies seen: private collection (PWE); private collection (ROV)

A170 GRACE BEFORE PLOUGHING   1966

A170(a) First English edition (1966)

JOHN MASEFIELD | [five-point star] | GRACE | BEFORE PLOUGHING | Fragments of Autobiography | [publisher's device of a windmill with 'W' and 'H'] | HEINEMANN : LONDON
(All width centred and enclosed within triple ruled border: 157 × 97mm. The lines do not always completely touch to form perfect corners)

Bibliographies: Wight 125a

Collation: [A]⁸ B-F⁸; signatures right foot of page; 48 leaves; 215 × 136mm.; [i–iv] v–vi 1–90

Page contents: [i] half-title: 'GRACE | BEFORE PLOUGHING'; [ii] 'THE WORKS OF JOHN MASEFIELD | PLAYS | [10 titles listed] | POETRY | [21 titles listed] | FICTION | [14 titles listed] | GENERAL | [18 titles listed]'; [iii] title-page; [iv] 'William Heinemann Ltd | LONDON MELBOURNE TORONTO | CAPE TOWN AUCKLAND | First published 1966 | © by John Masefield 1966 | Printed in Great Britain | by Bookprint Limited | Kingswood, Surrey'; v 'CONTENTS' (30 individual items listed with page references); vi-90 text

Paper: wove paper

Running title: none

Binding: black cloth. On spine, reading lengthways down spine from head, in gold: 'JOHN MASEFIELD *Grace before Ploughing* HEINEMANN'. Upper cover: blank. Lower cover, in blind: publisher's device of a windmill (ranged lower right). Top edge stained yellow, others trimmed. Binding measurements: 220 × 134mm. (covers), 220 × 25mm. (spine). End-papers: laid paper (no watermark), chain-lines 26mm. apart (bound so that the chain-lines run horizontally).

Publication date: the sales ledger preserved in the Heinemann Archive suggests publication on 25 April 1966 in an edition of 3250 copies

Price: 21s.

Contents:
Prologue ('Once, looking north, the daisied meadow filled')
1. The Linked Paradises ('For some years, like many children, I lived in Paradise, or, rather, like a…')
2. Ledbury ('The little market town of Ledbury in Herefordshire has one long street crossed by…')
3. October Fair ('In that beginning of my life, I knew little of Ledbury as a seaport or as…')
4. Malvern ('About four miles from Ledbury, the road climbs a steep hill above which the…')
5. Bredon Flood ('In that early time I went much to a part of Bredon Hill of which…')
6. The Hereford and Gloucester Canal ('To my young mind, the most wonderful thing near my home was the canal…')
7. Terrors ('More than eighty years ago, England was mainly an agricultural land, with…')
8. The Flooded Valley with its Moles ('The low-lying fields crossed by the railway viaduct were watercourses…')
9. The Hunt ('A short half mile from my home on the east side of the road to Bosbury…')
10. The Outcast ('The great rookery only two fields away greatly interested me. I was told that…')
11. The Angel ('Somewhere in my very early time I saw something that still puzzles me…')
12. Ermentrude ('Not long ago, I saw, for the first time, the neat, clear handwriting of a man whose…')
13. Closing the Canal ('At some time early in my life the managers of the canal and of the railway…')

14. The Soldiers ('Sometimes, perhaps twice in a year, perhaps at rarer intervals...')
15. Cut Throat Lane, etc. ('About three hundred yards from my home, one came to the site of an old quarry...')
16. Hopping ('Wild hops are common in the hedges of Hereford. They grew very freely in...')
17. The Roman Road ('I may have been born within a mile of a Roman road or within a mile of a...')
18. The Stag ('In the park at Eastnor, in a well-fenced and beautiful seclusion...')
19. Circuses ('Perhaps there were more circuses then, much smaller than those of today...')
20. Captain Jones ('I have an unaccountable memory of this person. I was on a sea-wall...')
21. The Old Mail-Coaches ('This closing of the canal from Gloucester, and the laying of a railway in its...')
22. The Forge ('Going about the country, one finds few forges nowadays. Perhaps few children...')
23. Imagination ('I am told that I learned to read at an early age, and that I enjoyed...')
24. Wild Flowers and Other Wild Things ('*The Chicory* | Here, in the cuckoo's silence, we perceive')
25. May Hill ('I was never at nor very near to May Hill in those early years...')
26. Flood Water ('There is a stirring Australian word for any man shrewd at foretelling...')
27. Early Reading ('Life itself is joy enough for many children, it is so full of new experience. It is strange...')
28. Piping Down ('It is time now, to pipe down and coil up. All these matters happened...')
Epilogue ('Such is the living bread allowed,')

Notes:

With a sub-title reminiscent of *So Long to Learn* (A162) this volume of prose (sub-titled 'Fragments of Autobiography') is Masefield's final autobiographical sketch (see also *In the Mill* (A131), *Wonderings* (A139) and *New Chum* (A140). It is primarily concerned with his boyhood and comprises twenty-eight titled sections. The volume also includes some verse.

Each titled section has the title printed in italic type.

Wight incorrectly states that the gatherings of this volume are all unsigned. It is only the first gathering that is unsigned. However, in the Macmillan American edition, all gatherings are unsigned and Wight is presumably confusing editions.

Wight notes that 'the top edges are stained yellow or gold'.

A year prior to publication a letter from Masefield dated 29 March 1965 to A. Dwye Evans notes '...I have been writing a few scattered pages of prose about my early childhood...' (see John Masefield, letter to [A. Dwye] Evans, 29 March 1965) (Archives of William Heinemann).

Masefield, it seems, had problems with the title for this volume. A reference to his 'little prose book' notes:

I have not yet found a title for it, but am hoping to hit on something soon.

(John Masefield, letter to [A. Dwye] Evans, [1965])
(Archives of William Heinemann)

On 5 August 1965, eight months before publication, Masefield wrote to A. Dwye Evans with a suggestion with which the author does not appear particularly satisfied:

At the moment, I suggest as the title for the new book *Grace before Ploughing* suggesting a good time before a bad time. Does this seem far-fetched or amiss to you? I leave the matter open for a few days more; one may have a bright suggestion.

(John Masefield, letter to [A. Dwye] Evans, 5 August 1965)
(Archives of William Heinemann)

The contents listing notes the prologue as being on p.vii. It is, however, present on p.vi. This error in the contents listing is corrected in the reprints of this title.

Copies seen: private collection (PWE); BL (X.909/6759) stamped 20 APR 1966

Reprinted:

| 'Reprinted' | [first edition, second impression] | 1966 |
| | [first edition, third impression] | 1966 |

A170(b) First American edition (1966)

JOHN MASEFIELD | [rule (tapered at both ends), 53mm.] | *Grace Before* | *Ploughing* | Fragments of Autobiography | *The Macmillan Company* | NEW YORK
(All width centred)

Bibliographies: Wight 125

Collation: [A-F]⁸; 48 leaves; 212 × 138mm.; [i–iv] v–vi 1–90

Page contents: [i] half-title: 'GRACE | BEFORE PLOUGHING'; [ii] 'THE WORKS OF JOHN MASEFIELD | PLAYS | [10 titles listed] | POETRY | [21 titles listed] | FICTION | [14 titles listed] | GENERAL | [18 titles listed]'; [iii] title-page; [iv] '© BY JOHN MASEFIELD 1966 | All rights reserved. No part of this book may be re- | produced or utilized in any form or by any means, | electronic or mechanical, including photocopying, re- | cording or by any information storage and retrieval | system, without permission in writing from the | Publisher. | Library of Congress Catalog Card Number: 66–21163 | FIRST AMERICAN

PRINTING | The Macmillan Company, New York | *Printed in the United States of America*'; v 'CONTENTS' (30 individual items listed with page references); vi-90 text

Paper: wove paper

Running title: none

Binding: blue cloth. On spine, reading lengthways down spine from head, in silver: 'MASEFIELD *Grace Before Ploughing* MACMILLAN'. Upper cover: blank. On lower cover, in silver: '58086' (ranged lower right). Top edge stained black, lower outside edge trimmed, fore edge roughly cut. Binding measurements: 217 × 141mm. (covers), 217 × 23mm. (spine). End-papers: wove paper.

Publication date: 1966

Price: $3.95

Contents:
as for A170(a)

Notes:
Each titled section has the title printed in italic type.

Wight describes this American edition before the English edition. He fails, however, to provide any reason for doing this and it appears unlikely that the American edition should pre-date the English.

The publishing agreement for this title between Masefield and Macmillan was dated 22 March 1966 (see Archives of The Society of Authors). The agreement refers to 'the exclusive right to publish and sell in volume form… in the United States, and the Philippine Republic a work provisionally entitled: GRACE BEFORE PLOUGHING, to consist of approximately 96 book pages'

Copies seen: private collection (PWE); private collection (ROV)

A170(c) Second English edition (1967)

JOHN MASEFIELD | *Grace Before Ploughing* | FRAGMENTS OF AUTOBIOGRAPHY | [five-point star] | [publisher's device of a tree, six five-point stars with 'R' and 'U' all within ruled border with rounded head and foot: 21 × 13mm.] | LONDON 1967 | READERS UNION [point] WILLIAM HEINEMANN
(All width centred)

Bibliographies: Wight [unrecorded]

Collation: A-F⁸; signatures left foot of page; 48 leaves; 192 × 114mm.; [i–vi] [1] 2–90

Page contents: [i] half-title: '*Grace Before Ploughing*'; [ii] 'THE WORKS OF JOHN MASEFIELD | PLAYS | [10 titles listed] | POETRY | [21 titles listed] | FICTION | [14 titles listed] | GENERAL | [18 titles listed]'; [iii] title-page; [iv] '*This RU edition was produced in* 1967 *for sale to its members | only by Readers Union Ltd at Aldine House*, 10–13 *Bedford | Street, London W.C.2, and at Letchworth Garden City, Herts. | Full details of membership may be obtained from our London | address. This edition has been entirely reset in* 12 *point Bembo | type and printed at Ditchling, Sussex, by the Ditchling Press. | It was first published by William Heinemann Limited.*'; [v] 'CONTENTS' (30 individual items listed with page references); [vi] blank; [1]–90 text

Paper: laid paper (watermark: '[Crown] | Abbey Mills | Greenfield'), chain-lines 25mm. apart

Running title: none

Binding: brown cloth. On spine, reading lengthways down spine from head, in gold: '*Grace before Ploughing* [five-point star] JOHN MASEFIELD'; horizontally at foot of spine, in gold: '*RU*' (the '*R*' is swash). Upper and lower covers: blank. All edges trimmed. Binding measurements: 199 × 118mm. (covers), 199 × 18mm. (spine). End-papers: wove paper.

Publication date: 'late summer 1967' in an edition of between 12000 and 16000 copies (suggested by documents in the Archives of The Society of Authors)

Price: 7s. (suggested by documents in the Archives of The Society of Authors)

Contents:
Prologue ('*Once, looking north, the daisied meadow filled*')
1. The Linked Paradises ('For some years, like many children, I lived in Paradise, or, rather, like a...')
2. Ledbury ('The little market town of Ledbury in Herefordshire has one long street crossed by...')
3. October Fair ('In that beginning of my life, I knew little of Ledbury as a seaport or as...')
4. Malvern ('About four miles from Ledbury, the road climbs a steep hill above which the...')
5. Bredon Flood ('In that early time I went much to a part of Bredon Hill of which...')
6. The Hereford and Gloucester Canal ('To my young mind, the most wonderful thing near my home was the canal...')
7. Terrors ('More than eighty years ago, England was mainly an agricultural land, with...')
8. The Flooded Valley with its Moles ('The low-lying fields crossed by the railway viaduct were watercourses...')
9. The Hunt ('A short half mile from my home on the east side of the road to Bosbury...')
10. The Outcast ('The great rookery only two fields away greatly interested me. I was told that...')
11. The Angel ('Somewhere in my very early time I saw something that still puzzles me...')

12. Ermentrude ('Not long ago, I saw, for the first time, the neat, clear handwriting of a man whose...')
13. Closing the Canal ('At some time early in my life the managers of the canal and of the railway...')
14. The Soldiers ('Sometimes, perhaps twice in a year, perhaps at rarer intervals...')
15. Cut Throat Lane, etc. ('About three hundred yards from my home, one came to the site of an old quarry...')
16. Hopping ('Wild hops are common in the hedges of Hereford. They grew very freely in...')
17. The Roman Road ('I may have been born within a mile of a Roman road or within a mile of a...')
18. The Stag ('In the park at Eastnor, in a well-fenced and beautiful seclusion...')
19. Circuses ('Perhaps there were more circuses then, much smaller than those of today...')
20. Captain Jones ('I have an unaccountable memory of this person. I was on a sea-wall...')
21. The Old Mail-Coaches ('This closing of the canal from Gloucester, and the laying of a railway in its...')
22. The Forge ('Going about the country, one finds few forges nowadays. Perhaps few children...')
23. Imagination ('I am told that I learned to read at an early age, and that I enjoyed...')
24. Wild Flowers and Other Wild Things ('*The Chicory | Here, in the cuckoo's silence, we perceive*')
25. May Hill ('I was never at nor very near to May Hill in those early years...')
26. Flood Water ('There is a stirring Australian word for any man shrewd at foretelling...')
27. Early Reading ('Life itself is joy enough for many children, it is so full of new experience. It is strange...')
28. Piping Down ('It is time now, to pipe down and coil up. All these matters happened...')
Epilogue ('*Such is the living bread allowed,*')

Notes:

As noted on p.[iv] this edition is an entirely new setting of the text. Each titled section, with the exception of the 'Prologue' and 'Epilogue' has the title printed in italic type. At the start of all prose text to all numbered sections the first three to eight words are entirely printed in capitals.

Heinemann approached Masefield about this edition in June 1966. The author evidently requested further information about the Readers Union for A. Dwye Evans wrote:

> The Readers Union is the best literary book club in existence and in order to show you the very fine range of their books I am sending you their Readers News. As they would not issue GRACE BEFORE PLOUGHING until the summer of 1967, by which time the book would have been out in its original edition for eighteen months or so, I do not honestly believe that it would have any adverse effect. On the contrary, I feel that it would extend your readership...
>
> (A. Dwye Evans, letter to John Masefield, 8 July 1966)
> (Archives of The Society of Authors)

Having negotiated a slight increase in royalty, Masefield accepted the proposal.

Copies seen: private collection (PWE)

A171 IN GLAD THANKSGIVING [1967]

A171(a) First English edition ([1967])

JOHN MASEFIELD | [five-point star] | IN GLAD | THANKSGIVING | HEINEMANN : LONDON
(All width centred and enclosed within triple ruled border: 150 × 93mm. The lines do not always completely touch to form perfect corners)

Bibliographies: Wight 126

Collation: [A-F]⁸; 48 leaves; 218 × 138mm.; [i–vi] 1–90

Page contents: [i] half-title: 'IN GLAD | THANKSGIVING'; [ii] 'THE WORKS OF JOHN MASEFIELD | PLAYS | [10 titles listed] | POETRY | [23 titles listed] | FICTION | [14 titles listed] | GENERAL | [18 titles listed]'; [iii] title-page; [iv] 'William Heinemann Ltd | LONDON MELBOURNE TORONTO | CAPE TOWN AUCKLAND | First published 1966 | © John Masefield, 1967 | *All rights reserved* | Those who wish to perform or recite | the poems in this book should apply to | the Society of Authors, 84, Drayton | Gardens, London, S.W.10. | To | Q. | Printed in Great Britain by | Western Printing Services Ltd | Bristol'; [v] 'CONTENTS' (27 items listed with page references); [vi] blank; 1–90 text

Paper: wove paper

Running title: none

Binding: green cloth. On spine, reading lengthways down spine from head, in gold: 'JOHN MASEFIELD [point] IN GLAD THANKSGIVING [point] Heinemann'. Covers: blank. Top edge stained green, others trimmed. Binding measurements: 222 × 140mm. (covers), 222 × 21mm. (spine). End-papers: wove paper.

Publication date: the sales ledger preserved in the Heinemann Archive suggests publication on 13 March 1967 in an edition of 2500 copies

Price: 25s.

Contents:
Remembering Dame Myra Hess ('Most beautiful, most gifted, and most wise,')
For Luke O'Connor ('One early Summer, when the times were bad,')

The Curlews ('We three were in wild Shropshire, picking sloes,')
A Song of Waking ('The stars are dim before the Sun has risen;')
The Shropshire Friends ('Long since, when coming from the West,')
What the Wrekin Gave ('You matchless two, to whom I owe')
The Hill ('I see yon harebells, foxgloves, brooks,')
The Merry Swevvy ('O water rushing through the grass,')
Caer Ocvran ('There are some ramparts in the distant West,')
I Dreamed ("I dreamed a dream the other night...')
A Fellow Mortal ('I found a fox, caught by the leg')
The Throckmorton Coat ('John Coxeter, who owned the Greenham Mill,')
The Stars that Shone ('Now that I cannot get about')
Two Cousins ('PART ONE | I | *The delays*... John Hawkins, Cousin born to Francis Drake,')
So the Matter Rests ('Below the glow-worms' hillock, in the grass,')
Joys ("What is Life's greatest joy?' I asked the sage,')
Thinking it Over ('The soul is what the soul has won;')
Give Way ("Give way, my lads,' the coxwains used to say')
The Dumb Thing's Voice ('How can a flesh-imprisoned soul contrive')
Nature's Memory ('Long since, far hence, within a garden-close,')
Remembered Great Ones ('All country workers had that look of might')
Sitting Alone ('Sitting alone, far hence, in summer night,')
Old England ('Just half a century since, an old man showed')
A Memory of a Singer ('Long since, after the weary war, you came')
Churchyard Cheer ('They are all underneath the grass')
Pagan-Born or The Three-Day Death ('PART ONE | I | They used to tell me stories of a Prince')
From the volume *Lyric Intermezzo* by Heinrich Heine (*22*) ('If the little flowers could know it,')
[From the volume *Lyric Intermezzo* by Heinrich Heine] (*58*) ('October scatters the apples,')
[From the volume *Lyric Intermezzo* by Heinrich Heine] (*64*) ('Night was upon my eyelids,')

Notes:

The final book published during Masefield's lifetime. This volume of twenty-nine poems includes three lengthy fables in addition to shorter lyrics (three translated from Heinrich Heine).

As cited on page [iv], this volume was published in 1966 with copyright secured in 1967. The *English Catalogue of Books* and the Heinemann sales ledger give 1967 as the date of publication and the earlier date stated in the preliminaries would therefore appear to be erroneous.

The poem 'Two Cousins' is extensive, comprising three parts, with the first two parts divided into four and eight sections respectively. There is also a prose note between parts two and three.

Masefield wrote to A. Dwye Evans on 25 February 1966:

> With this, I send about 20 pages of copy to go with the *Three Day Death* verse, and a Contents List showing the place of the long poem as the 5th in the volume.

(John Masefield, letter to [A. Dwye] Evans, 25 February 1966)
(Archives of William Heinemann)

Masefield went on to suggest that if the book was still on the 'short side' then a couple of weeks would be required before he could add 'a brief tale or two in verse, + some more Heine translations'.

The contents list, as sent in February 1966, therefore reveals which poems were written first for the collection:

Contents

Remembering Dame Myra Hess
The Curlews
The Hill
The Merry Swevvy
The Three Day Death
Four translations from Heinrich Heine (Lyric Intermezzo, Nos 22, 58, 62 + 64)

Other Verse
Caer Ocvran
The Dumb Thing's Voice (3 sonnets)
Nature's Memory (2 sonnets)
A Song of Waking
Thinking it Over
Give Way

(John Masefield, letter to [A. Dwye] Evans, 25 February 1966)
(Archives of William Heinemann)

Of particular interest is the additional Heinrich Heine translation that was eventually omitted from the volume (and the suggestion of translating further examples). A. Dwye Evans responded asking for 'some more material' on 11 March 1966. On 22 July 1966 Masefield sent copy and suggested a title, later abandoned:

> I send with this the copy of a book of verse, called (at the moment) Two Cousins. It seems to me to be about 85 book pages, about the size of *Grace before ploughing*. I do not expect to write more verse, but I hope that this farewell may seem to you to be a possible publication.
>
> (John Masefield, letter to [A. Dwye] Evans, 22 July 1966)
> (Archives of William Heinemann)

and so Masefield's last book, published when the author was eighty-eight, was intended by the writer to be a 'farewell' volume to his career.

A letter from Masefield asks specific questions about typographical appearance on the page:

> Have you any great objection to putting one sonnet alone on a page? ...In the new book, I would like to have some sonnets, one to a page, + some other sonnets a sonnet + a half to a page. Perhaps this is still a forbidden short allowance.
>
> (John Masefield, letter to Heinemann firm, [1966])
> (Archives of William Heinemann)

The publishing agreement for this title between Masefield and Heinemann was dated 26 October 1966 (see Archives of The Society of Authors). The agreement refers to a publication price of 21s. The title has been changed from *The Cousins*.

Copies seen: private collection (PWE); BL (X.909/9560) stamped 7 MAR 1967

A171(b) First American edition (1967)

IN | GLAD | THANKSGIVING | *John Masefield* | [floral ornament] | THE MACMILLAN COMPANY, NEW YORK (All width centred)

Bibliographies: Wight 126a

Collation: [A-F]⁸; 48 leaves; 210 × 142mm.; [i–vi] 1–90

Page contents: [i] half-title: 'IN GLAD | THANKSGIVING'; [ii] 'THE WORKS OF JOHN MASEFIELD | PLAYS | [10 titles listed] | POETRY | [23 titles listed] | FICTION | [14 titles listed] | GENERAL | [18 titles listed]'; [iii] title-page; [iv] 'To Q. | First published 1967 | © John Masefield, 1967 | All rights reserved. No part of this book may be reproduced or | transmitted in any form or by any means, electronic or mechanical, | including photocopying, recording or by any information storage and | retrieval system, without permission in writing from the Publisher. | Library of Congress Catalog Card Number: 67–20733 | First American Edition 1967 | Those who wish to perform or recite the poems in this book should apply | to the Society of Authors, 84 Drayton Gardens, London, S.W. 10 | The Macmillan Company, New York | PRINTED IN THE UNITED STATES OF AMERICA'; [v] 'CONTENTS' (27 items listed with page references); [vi] blank; 1–90 text

Paper: wove paper

Running title: none

Binding: green boards with brown cloth spine. On spine, reading lengthways down spine from head: '*Masefield* [in gold] [ornament] [in green] IN GLAD THANKSGIVING MACMILLAN [in gold]'. Upper cover: blank. On lower cover, in gold: '58158' (ranged lower right). Top edge stained light green, lower outside edge trimmed, fore edge roughly cut. Binding measurements: 217 × 143mm. (covers), 217 × 21mm. (spine). End-papers: wove paper.

Publication date: 1967

Price: $3.95

Contents:
as for A171(a)

Notes:
Wight describes the brown cloth spine as 'brown tape'.

With the exception of pp.[iii] and [iv] (title-page and printing information) all pages appear to use the same setting of type as A171(a).

The publishing agreement for this title between The Estate of John Masefield and Macmillan was dated 10 July 1967 (see Archives of The Society of Authors). The agreement refers to 'the exclusive right to publish and sell in volume form... in the United States, and the Philippine Republic a work provisionally entitled IN GLAD THANKSGIVING, to consist of approximately 96 book pages'

In October 1966 The Society of Authors wrote to Masefield to inform him that Heinemann were 'perfectly willing to agree to the clause about the sale of sheets to the Macmillan Company' (see Anne Munro-Kerr, letter to John Masefield, 14 October 1966) (Archives of The Society of Authors).

Copies seen: Pennsylvania State University (PR6025.A77 I58 1967a)

Reprinted:
'Second Printing'   [first edition, second impression]   1968

A172 THE TWENTY-FIVE DAYS

A172(a) First English edition (1972)

JOHN MASEFIELD | [five-point star] | THE | TWENTY-FIVE DAYS | [publisher's device of a windmill with 'W' and 'H'] | HEINEMANN : LONDON
(All width centred and enclosed within ornate border: 168 × 105mm.)

Bibliographies: Wight 127

Collation: [A]¹⁶ B-F¹⁶; signatures left foot of page; 96 leaves; 216 × 131mm.; [i–v] vi–x 1–42 [43] 44–49 [50] 51–54 [55] 56–71 [72] 73–82 [twelve un-numbered illustration pages] 83–106 [107] 108–173 [174]; the illustrations (on glossy paper) comprise an entire unsigned gathering of six leaves bound between gatherings C and D

Page contents: [i] half-title: 'THE TWENTY-FIVE DAYS'; [ii] 'THE WORKS OF JOHN MASEFIELD | PLAYS | [10 titles listed] | POETRY | [22 titles listed] | FICTION | [14 titles listed] | GENERAL | [19 titles listed]'; [iii] title-page; [iv] 'William Heinemann Ltd | 15 Queen Street, Mayfair, London W1X 8BE | LONDON MELBOURNE TORONTO | JOHANNESBURG AUCKLAND | First published 1972 | © Executors of the Estate of the late | John Masefield 1972 | 434 45237 8 | *All maps are drawn by* | *George Hartfield Limited* | Printed in Great Britain by | Richard Clay (The Chaucer Press) Ltd | Bungay, Suffolk'; [v] 'This tale is dedicated | to | Vice-Admiral Sir BERTRAM RAMSAY, K.C.B., M.V.O. | to | The Officers, Warrant-Officers and Ratings, | and to all others who bore a hand | in the Operation Dynamo'; vi *'Publisher's Note* | This story of the advance of Allied British and French | forces in the last war to meet the German invasion | through Holland and Belgium and their enforced retreat | to the Channel was first written in 1940. It was immedi- | ately set up, proofed and scheduled for publication the | same year. Then all further production was stopped – | publication was banned. Permission was given by the | authorities for the last section only, covering 'Operation | the evacuation Dynamo', of the beaches at Dunkirk. This | appeared in 1941, and was entitled *The Nine Days Wonder.* | Now, however, clearance has been obtained from the | Ministry of Defence to publish the whole account, which | includes the section published as *The Nine Days Wonder* | but in its original, fuller form. | [new paragraph] The publishers wish to acknowledge the role of Mr | Alan Smith of the Conway Maritime Press Ltd in the | production of the book and to thank him for his valuable | assistance in the selection of illustrations. Thanks are also | due to Miss Diana Daniels for her help and co-operation.'; vii–viii *'List of Illustrations* | *Between pages* 82–83' (17 items listed with sources); ix–x *'Preface'* ('This is the story of an advance followed by a long retreat and withdrawal...') (signed, 'JOHN MASEFIELD'); 1–170 text and maps; 171–73 *'Acknowledgements'* ('This account of the campaign in Belgium and France is necessarily very brief...') (signed, 'JOHN MASEFIELD | 1940'); [174] blank

Paper: laid paper (no watermark), chain-lines 28mm. apart

Running title: none

Binding: black cloth. On spine, reading lengthways down spine from head, in gold: 'JOHN MASEFIELD *The Twenty Five Days* HEINEMANN'. Covers: blank. All edges trimmed. Binding measurements: 222 × 136mm. (covers), 222 × 30mm. (spine). End-papers (showing untitled map) constitute [A]1 and F16 laid down to inside of covers with [A]2 and F15 as the free end-papers.

Publication date: the sales ledger preserved in the Heinemann Archive suggests publication on 30 October 1972 in an edition of 4000 copies

Price: £2.50

Contents:
Preface ('This is the story of an advance followed by a long retreat and withdrawal...')
[Untitled] ('Between the years 1919 and 1938 our governments strove to preserve peace...')
[Untitled] ('During the months of war, Holland and Belgium had lived in dread of invasion...')
[Untitled] ('Certain imaginative men, considering what the next war would be like...')
  [Including sub-headings: 'The First Day, Friday the 10th of May' through to 'The Fourteenth Day, Thursday the 23rd of May']
Boulogne ('Boulogne is familiar to many thousands of Englishmen to whom it has been the...')
  [Including sub-headings: 'The Fifteenth Day, Friday the 24th of May' through to 'The Seventeenth Day, Sunday the 26th of May']
Calais ('Calais is nearer to us than any other town on the Continent. It can frequently be seen...')
  [Including sub-headings: 'The Eighteenth Day, Monday the 27th of May' through to 'The Twenty-fifth Day, Monday the 3rd of June']
Dunkirk ('Dunkirk is an ancient sea-port, with a good depth of water, several docks, some...')
  [Including sub-headings: 'Monday the 27th of May' through to 'Monday the 3rd of June']
Acknowledgements ('This account of the campaign in Belgium and France is necessarily very brief...')

Notes:
Masefield first announced to C.S. Evans that he was writing this work at the end of July 1940. Evans – recalling Masefield's successes during the Great War – replied with enthusiasm:

> It is exciting to hear that you are doing a book on the recent campaign in France and Belguim and I think that it will be very welcome. How well I (and I expect thousands of others) remember THE OLD FRONT LINE. We could certainly rush it through before Christmas if we had it three or four weeks ahead...

(C.S. Evans, letter to John Masefield, 1 August 1940)
(HRHRC, MS (Masefield, J.) Recip William Heinemann Ltd.)

At the beginning of October 1940 Louisa Callender asked that the typescript be sent ' as soon as it is finished'. She also noted 'Mr. Evans can then decide whether to set or to wait until the material has been passed...' (see Louisa Callender, letter to John Masefield, 3 October 1940) (HRHRC, MS (Masefield, J.) Recip William Heinemann Ltd.) Evans thanked Masefield for the typescript on 11 October 1940 (see C.S. Evans, letter to John Masefield, 11 October 1940) (BL, Add.Mss.56613, f.196). Less than a week later Evans reported that he was 'going through the material for THE TWENTYFIVE DAYS and discussing the format of the book...' (see C.S. Evans, letter to John Masefield, 17 October 1940) (HRHRC, MS (Masefield, J.) Recip William Heinemann Ltd.) It appears that the typescript was set as soon as it was received. Evans later noted (forgetting his letter of 11 October 1940):

> In my eagerness to get the typescript of THE TWENTYFIVE DAYS, and to give it to the printer, I omitted to acknowledge its safe receipt. We are at work on it and you shall have the proofs the moment they are available.
>
> (C.S. Evans, letter to John Masefield, 15 November 1940)
> (HRHRC, MS (Masefield, J.) Recip William Heinemann Ltd.)

On 20 November 1940 Evans wrote to Masefield enclosing 'a couple of proofs in book form of THE TWENTYFIVE DAYS' and asking the author to correct the text and pass it for press (see C.S. Evans, letter to John Masefield, 20 November 1940) (HRHRC, MS (Masefield, J.) Recip William Heinemann Ltd.) Masefield was, evidently, still adding to the volume for five days later Evans thanked the author for the 'verses to go at the end of THE TWENTY FIVE DAYS...' (see below for details of different proof states) (see C.S. Evans, letter to John Masefield, 25 November 1940) (HRHRC, MS (Masefield, J.) Recip William Heinemann Ltd.)

Evidence suggests that the book had been granted some form of permission. However, it appears that after the printing of a first proof in book form – and receiving new material from Masefield – Heinemann started to realise that full permission to publish might not forthcoming:

> ...there is nothing to do but to wait; but considering the book has already been passed by the War Office, the Admiralty and the Foreign Office, it is difficult to understand why they are again making a fuss. The only reason I can think of is that Gort himself may want to write a book on the same subject which could not be published until after the war and is afraid that you may have stolen some of his thunder. But this may be an unworthy thought!
>
> (C.S. Evans, letter to John Masefield, 11 December 1940)
> (HRHRC, MS (Masefield, J.) Recip William Heinemann Ltd.)

At the end of the year Evans communicated '...no more news about THE TWENTY FIVE DAYS...' (see C.S. Evans, letter to John Masefield , 27 December 1940) (HRHRC, MS (Masefield, J.) Recip William Heinemann Ltd.) By 6 January 1941 the decision had been reached that publication was not to be allowed. Masefield seems to have communicated this to Heinemann and, at the same time, asked for some proof copies (that would, therefore, include his new material). Louisa Callender responded and also commented on Masefield's first tentative suggestion of *The Nine Days Wonder*:

> ...I write to acknowledge your two letters to [C.S. Evans] concerning THE TWENTY FIVE DAYS. He will indeed be sorry about this final decision. I know that he champed at the delay but I do not think he expected that the whole thing would be turned down. All of us who have read the book here are bitterly disappointed that it is not to be published.
>
> We will print for you twentyfive copies of the book as it stands and will send them to you as soon as possible.
>
> We think with you that it would be the next best thing to issue those last 60 pages (and possibly the first 34) if the authorities will allow this. And so, concerning our outlay on the book, would it not be better to leave this for the present until we see whether it is possible to print any part of it?
>
> (Louisa Callender, letter to John Masefield, 6 January 1941)
> (HRHRC, MS (Masefield, J.) Recip William Heinemann Ltd.)

When C.S. Evans returned to the office he appeared defiant:

> ...My personal opinion is, however, that the book should be published as you wrote it – even if we have to wait until there are no longer censorship difficulties. I feel that the book as a whole is an historical document of the first importance, and when it can be published it will be a classic in the same way that your book on GALLIPOLI is a classic.
>
> (C.S. Evans, letter to John Masefield, 28 January 1941)
> (HRHRC, MS (Masefield, J.) Recip William Heinemann Ltd.)

Three days later Louisa Callender reported to Masefield that she had 'given THE NINE DAYS' WONDER to the printer and proofs will reach you eventually' (see Louisa Callender, letter to John Masefield, 31 January 1941) (HRHRC, MS (Masefield, J.) Recip William Heinemann Ltd.)

Before publication of *The Nine Days Wonder* it appears that Masefield was anxious for Heinemann to recover costs of the aborted volume. Evans wrote:

> Very well, I will send the account to the Secretary of State for War and will include in it only what we are actually out of pocket by the suppression of THE TWENTY FIVE DAYS. I will strike out the charge for twentyfive copies supplied to you. I accept your suggestion for compromise on the royalties on THE NINE DAYS' WONDER...
>
> (C.S. Evans, letter to John Masefield, 4 March 1941)
> (HRHRC, MS (Masefield, J.) Recip William Heinemann Ltd.)

Masefield evidently checked the situation in May 1941 and Evans reported '...we have received payment from the War Office in connection with THE TWENTY FIVE DAYS.' (see C.S. Evans, letter to John Masefield, 29 May 1941) (HRHRC, MS (Masefield, J.) Recip William Heinemann Ltd.)

During March Evans noted that '…I am told this morning that a book on the Dunkirk evacuation by Lord Gort has been announced!' (see C.S. Evans, letter to John Masefield, 13 March 1941) (HRHRC, MS (Masefield, J.) Recip William Heinemann Ltd.).

Before the end of October 1940 The Society of Authors were receiving requests for serial rights (see BL, Add.Mss.56613, f.208). These were not, presumably, granted.

The publisher's note in 1972 states:

This story… was first written in 1940. It was immediately set up, proofed and scheduled for publication the same year.

A first proof was indeed printed in 1940 but a second proof (printed at Masefield's request after publication was banned) exists from 1941 (see above). These two proofs show the text in different states. The 1940 proof includes small sections that were later re-written or omitted from the 1941 version. Within the 1940 proof there are five maps, as in the 1941 proof, but the page listing, headed 'Maps and Illustrations' in 1941 is merely headed 'Illustrations' in 1940. There are also changes to the setting of text and the half-title, title-page and running titles (which read 'THE TWENTYFIVE DAYS' in 1940 compared with 'THE TWENTY FIVE DAYS' in 1941). The 1941 proof includes six poems not present in 1940. These are:

> [Untitled] ('They marched over the Field of Waterloo,')
> [Untitled] ('In the black Maytime when we faced the worst')
> [Untitled] ('When someone somewhere bids the bombing cease,')
> [Untitled] ('Not any drums nor bugles with Last Post')
> [Untitled] ('O smiling, sun-burned youth who rode the sky')
> [Untitled] ('Let a people reading stories full of anguish')

Only three of these verses appear in *The Nine Days Wonder* (where two have acquired titles):

> [Untitled] ('They marched over the Field of Waterloo,')
> Thoughts for Later On ('When someone somewhere bids the bombing cease,')
> A Young English Air-Man ('O smiling, sun-burned youth who rode the sky')

(There are, however, poems in *The Nine Days Wonder* which are not present in *The Twenty-Five Days*). It appears that the 1972 published edition is derived from a copy of the 1940 proof.

By 1946 Masefield had given up the idea of publishing this work. Louisa Callender wrote at the beginning of July 1946:

You will remember that NINE DAYS' WONDER was originally written by you as a longer book under the title of THE TWENTYFIVE DAYS. The War Office objected to the publication of the greater part of the book but if their objections no longer hold we should like to issue the book as you first wrote it.

> (Louisa Callender, letter to John Masefield, 3 July 1946)
> (HRHRC, MS (Masefield, J.) Recip William Heinemann Ltd.)

Masefield responded:

I am grateful to you for raising the question of *the 25 Days*. But when I wrote that book, nobody had much information about the campaign, and what I had was all there was. Now, after 6 years there is much information, in many languages, and I should have quite endless trouble in getting at the facts, even if the W[ar] O[ffice] were to give me access to them, which I do not think they ever would. By this time, too, the official historians will have been appointed, and set to work, and the hundreds of reminiscences have begun to appear. I'm afraid that the book must be wiped-out.

> (John Masefield, letter to [Louisa] Callender, 6 July 1946)
> (Archives of William Heinemann)

Wight describes the ornate border of the title-page as follows:

…a double ruled border which has feather edging on the outside border. About every 12[mm.] along the border, a small device connects the two borders, which are broken at each corner so that going clockwise each border overlaps the next. There are small devices inside each corner.

The 'List of Illustrations' on pp.vii–viii notes seventeen items. It omits one titled illustration and conceals the information that two photographs are provided with a single title. The titles as given in the list are not always exactly those given as captions.

The Heinemann Archive reveals that Conway Maritime Press originally intended to publish the volume. Diana Daniels had mentioned the existence of the title after assisting with the Conway Maritime Press 1971 edition of *Sea Life in Nelson's Time* (see A4(d)). After approaching The Society of Authors (who were initially unaware of the title), Conway Maritime Press consulted Heinemann in November 1971 to assess Heinemann's claim on the work. Negotiations at Heinemann evidently concluded in the decision to publish the title themselves and in December 1971 they attempted to locate a copy of the text. Diana Daniels, in possession of a proof copy, assisted by providing a line by line typescript copy (correcting, in her words, 'obvious typographical errors'). However, Daniels had reservations about the project and stated that her proof copy would, through publication, decrease in commercial value. It appears that Diana Daniels worked from a 1940 proof. There are numerous differences between the 1972 published edition and the 1940 proof. The clear sections present in 1940 are less defined in 1972 and the spelling of 'Dunquerque' is changed to 'Dunkirk'. The dedication present in 1972 is entirely absent in 1940, although it is identical to that used in *The Nine Days Wonder*.

In May 1972 the Ministry of Defence agreed to publication 'without amendment'. The publishing agreement for this title between The Society of Authors and Heinemann was dated 27 June 1972 (see Archives of The Society of Authors). An early suggestion, to reprint *The Nine Days Wonder* with the 'new' work, was evidently dismissed.

Diana Daniels, in attempting to trace the history of the proof printing, received a letter from Grace Cranston dated 21 June 1971. Cranston, employed by Heinemann at the time of the suppression of the title, notes:

> At that time we had to submit proofs of any book bearing on the war to the censor's office. This was done with *The Twenty Five Days*, and the result of this was that the authorities would only pass that portion of the book which eventually became *The Nine Days Wonder*. I am under the impression that the author had obtained permission to write the book in the first place, so that it was an unpleasant surprise when this veto was imposed. I have no idea what reason (if any) was given. It is not surprising that no documents survive, for at that time when paper was scarcer than bombs, our main objective was to get by as best we could and preserving archives for the future was the least of our worries.
>
> (Grace Cranston, letter to Diana Daniels, 21 June 1971)
> (Archives of William Heinemann)

Copies seen: private collection (PWE); BL (X.809/14356) stamped 5 OCT 1972

A173 SELECTED POEMS [WITH A PREFACE BY JOHN BETJEMAN]   1978

A173(a) First English edition (1978)

JOHN MASEFIELD | SELECTED POEMS | *With a Preface by* | *JOHN BETJEMAN* | [publisher's device of a windmill with 'W' and 'H'] | HEINEMANN : LONDON
(All width centred)

Bibliographies: Wight [unrecorded]

Collation: [A–I]¹⁶ [K]⁸ [L]⁴ [M]¹⁶ (J not used); 172 leaves; 215 × 136mm.; [i–iv] v–ix [x] 1–325 [326] 327–28 [329–34]

Page contents: [i] half-title: 'SELECTED POEMS'; [ii] 'John Masefield O.M. 1878–1967 | John Masefield was born on 1st June, 1878, | at Ledbury | in Herefordshire. Educated at King's School, Warwick, | and on H.M.S. *Conway*, he first went to sea at the age | of fifteen on a windjammer. He succeeded Robert | Bridges in 1930 as Poet Laureate and was awarded the | Order of Merit in 1935. Widely travelled in his youth, he | lived the last twenty-eight years of his life in Abingdon, | Berkshire, where he died on 12th May, 1967.'; [iii] title-page; [iv] 'William Heinemann Ltd | 15 Queen Street, Mayfair, London W1X 8BE | LONDON MELBOURNE TORONTO | JOHANNESBURG AUCKLAND | This Selection of Poems © William Heinemann Ltd 1978 | Preface © John Betjeman 1978 | SBN 434 45238 6 | Printed in Great Britain by | REDWOOD BURN LIMITED | Trowbridge & Esher'; v–vi 'CONTENTS' (67 individual items (including preface and first line index) listed with page references); vii–ix 'PREFACE BY JOHN BETJEMAN' ('John Masefield wrote two lyrics which will be remembered as long as the language lasts...'); [x] blank; 1–325 text; [326] blank; 327–28 'INDEX OF FIRST LINES'; [329–34] blank

Paper: wove paper

Running title: none

Binding: blue cloth. On spine, in gold: 'SELECTED | POEMS | [ornament] | JOHN | MASEFIELD | HEINEMANN'. Covers: blank. Top edge stained red, others trimmed. Binding measurements: 224 × 137mm. (covers), 224 × 40mm. (spine). End-papers: wove paper.

Publication date: June 1978

Price: £5.90

Contents:
Preface by John Betjeman ('John Masefield wrote two lyrics which will be remembered as long as the language lasts...')
from Wonderings ('Out of a dateless darkness pictures gleam,')
from Landworkers ('Long since, in England's pleasant lands')
The Everlasting Mercy ('From '41 to '51')
The Widow in the Bye Street ('Down Bye Street, in a little Shropshire town,')
Dauber ('Four bells were struck, the watch was called on deck')
Explanations of some of the Sea Terms used in the Poem ('*Backstays* – Wire poles which support the masts...')
The *Wanderer* ('All day they loitered by the resting ships,')
August, 1914 ('How still this quiet cornfield is tonight!')
from Biography ('By many waters and on many ways')
Song ('One sunny time in May')
Ships ('I cannot tell their wonder nor make known')
The River ('All other waters have their time of peace,')
from Lollingdon Downs [Untitled] ('I could not sleep for thinking of the sky,')
[*from* Lollingdon Downs] [Untitled] ('How did the nothing come, how did these fires,')
"Night is on the Downland" ('Night is on the downland, on the lonely moorland,')
"A Hundred Years Ago...." ('A hundred years ago they quarried for the stone here;')
Sonnets
XXX ('There, on the darkened deathbed, dies the brain')
LXII ('There was an evil in the nodding wood')

Reynard The Fox – Part II ('On old Cold Crendon's windy tops')
The Lemmings ('Once in a hundred years the Lemmings come')
On Growing Old ('Be with me, Beauty, for the fire is dying;')
King Cole ('King Cole was King before the troubles came,')
The Rider at the Gate ('A windy night was blowing on Rome,')
The Racer ('I saw the racer coming to the jump,')
The Pathfinder ('She lies at grace, at anchor, head to tide,')
South and East ('When good King Arthur ruled these western hursts,')
On Skysails ('I saw you often as the crown of Queens')
Pay ('The world paid but a penny for its toil,')
Under Lower Topsails ('Three lower topsails dark with wet are straining')
Eight Bells ('Four double strikes repeated on the bells,')
Minnie Maylow's Story ('Once (long ago) there was an English King,')
The Taking of Helen ('Menelaus, the Spartan King,')
The Surprise ('You have heard the story of the Horse of Troy.')
Australia ('When the North Lander saw the rose in blossom,')
The Waggon-Maker ('I have made tales in verse, but this man made')
The Spanish Main Schooner ('A little wooden schooner, painted white,')
A Ballad of Sir Francis Drake ('Before Sir Francis put to sea,')
The *Loch Achray* ('The *Loch Achray* was a clipper tall')
Trade Winds ('In the harbour, in the island, in the Spanish Seas,')
Sea-Fever ('I must go down to the seas again, to the lonely sea and the sky,')
The West Wind ('It's a warm wind, the west wind, full of birds' cries;')
Spanish Waters ('Spanish waters, Spanish waters, you are ringing in my ears,')
Cargoes ('Quinquireme of Nineveh from distant Ophir')
The Emigrant ('Going by Daly's shanty I heard the boys within')
Seekers ('Friends and loves we have none, nor wealth nor blessed abode,')
A Creed ('I held that when a person dies')
Fragments ('Troy Town is covered up with weeds,')
Ignorance ('Since I have learned Love's shining alphabet,')
C.L.M. ('In the dark womb where I began')
The Wild Duck ('Twilight. Red in the west.')
Sixty Odd Years Ago ('Much worth was in the country: yet, today,')
Gallipoli, 1915 ('Even so was wisdom proven blind;')
On the Dead in Gallipoli ('They came from safety of their own free will')
from On the Hill ('No I know not;')
The Hill ('This remains here.')
Jouncer's Tump ('My grand-dad said, to Sis and me,')
The Bluebells ('We stood upon the grass beside the road,')
In Praise of Nurses ('Man, in his gallant power, goes in pride,')
On Pilots ('Pilots, those unknown beings, who remove')
Old Raiger ('*Prologue:* | Good Old Man Raiger, raging in his rage,')
The Along-Ships Stow ('Treacle, treacle, little ship,')
Lines for the Race of Sailing Ships, Lisbon to the Hudson Bridge... ('Once, they were Queens, triumphant everywhere,')
Remembering Dame Myra Hess ('Most beautiful, most gifted, and most wise,')
For Luke O'Connor ('One early Summer, when the times were bad,')
The Shropshire Friends ('Long since, when coming from the West,')
A Fellow Mortal ('I found a fox, caught by the leg')
The Stars that Shone ('Now that I cannot get about')
An Epilogue ('I have seen flowers come in stony places')

Notes:
A lengthy selection of Masefield's verse with a preface by John Betjeman. The selection appears to have been that of the publishers and is particularly eclectic. Three of the long narrative poems are, for example, presented in their entirety (*The Everlasting Mercy, The Widow in the Bye Street* and *Dauber*), yet *Reynard the Fox* is represented by its second half only.

Copies seen: BL (X.989/52421) stamped 11 APR 1978

A173(b) *First American edition (1978)*

JOHN MASEFIELD | [rule (tapered at both ends), 42mm.] | SELECTED POEMS | *With a Preface by* | *JOHN BETJEMAN* | ANNIVERSARY EDITION | MACMILLAN PUBLISHING CO., INC. | *New York*
(All width centred)

Bibliographies: Wight [unrecorded]

Collation: [A–H]¹⁶ [I]¹² [K–L]¹⁶ (J not used); 172 leaves; 210 × 140mm.; [i–iv] v–ix [x] 1–325 [326] 327–28 [329–34]

Page contents: [i] half-title: 'SELECTED POEMS'; [ii] '*Other Macmillan editions of* | *John Masefield's works:* | THE BIRD OF DAWNING | JIM DAVIS | SALT-WATER POEMS AND BALLADS | THE TAKING OF THE GRY | VICTORIOUS TROY OR, THE HURRYING ANGEL | POEMS: COMPLETE EDITION'; [iii] title-page; [iv] 'The Selection of Poems | Copyright © 1978 by William Heinemann Ltd | Preface Copyright © 1978 by John Betjeman | All rights reserved. No part of this book may be reproduced or | transmitted in any form or by any means, electronic or mechanical, | including photocopying, recording or by any information storage and | retrieval system, without permission in writing from the Publisher. | Macmillan Publishing Co., Inc. | 866 Third Avenue, New York, N.Y. 10022 | Collier Macmillan Canada, Ltd. | Library of Congress Cataloging in Publication Data | Masefield, John, 1878–1967. | Selected poems. | "Anniversary edition." | PR6025.A77A6 1978 821'.9'12 78–10365 | ISBN 0-02-581010-3 | First American Edition 1978 | Printed in the United States of America'; v–vi 'CONTENTS' (67 individual items (including preface and first line index) listed with page references); vii–ix 'PREFACE BY JOHN BETJEMAN' ('John Masefield wrote two lyrics which will be remembered as long as the language lasts...'); [x] blank; 1–325 text; [326] blank; 327–28 'INDEX OF FIRST LINES'; [329] 'John Masefield O.M. 1878–1967 | John Masefield was born on 1st June, 1878, at Ledbury | in Herefordshire. Educated at King's School, Warwick, | and on H.M.S. *Conway*, he first went to sea at the age | of fifteen on a windjammer. He succeeded Robert | Bridges in 1930 as Poet Laureate and was awarded the | Order of Merit in 1935. Widely travelled in his youth, he | lived the last twenty-eight years of his life in Abingdon, | Berkshire, where he died on 12th May, 1967.'; [330–34] blank

Paper: wove paper

Running title: none

Binding: brown cloth. On spine, reading lengthways down spine from head, in gold: 'JOHN MASEFIELD : SELECTED POEMS | ANNIVERSARY EDITION MACMILLAN' (the edition note is at the head of the spine and the publisher at the foot). Upper cover: blank. On lower cover, in gold: 'ISBN 0-02-581010-3' ranged lower right. All edges trimmed. Binding measurements: 214 × 139mm. (covers), 214 × 38mm. (spine). End-papers: wove paper.

Publication date: 1978

Price: $12.50

Contents:
as for A173(a)

Notes:
The text appears to use the same setting of type as A173(a). A letter from Macmillan to The Society of Authors notes that the publisher 'has been furnished with duplicate film of the Heinemann work' (see Macmillan, letter to The Society of Authors, 21 August 1978) (Archives of The Society of Authors).

Copies seen: private collection (ROV)

A173(c) Later English edition (1978)

JOHN MASEFIELD | SELECTED POEMS | *With a Preface by* | *JOHN BETJEMAN* | BOOK CLUB ASSOCIATES | LONDON
(All width centred)

Bibliographies: Wight [unrecorded]

Collation: [A–I]¹⁶ [K]⁸ [L]⁴ [M]¹⁶ (see notes) (J not used); 172 leaves; 214 × 135mm.; [i–iv] v–ix [x] 1–325 [326] 327–28 [329–30]

Page contents: [i] half-title: 'SELECTED POEMS'; [ii] 'John Masefield O.M. 1878–1967 | John Masefield was born on 1st June, 1878, at Ledbury | in Herefordshire. Educated at King's School, Warwick, | and on H.M.S. *Conway*, he first went to sea at the age | of fifteen on a windjammer. He succeeded Robert | Bridges in 1930 as Poet Laureate and was awarded the | Order of Merit in 1935. Widely travelled in his youth, he | lived the last twenty-eight years of his life in Abingdon, | Berkshire, where he died on 12th May, 1967.'; [iii] title-page; [iv] 'This edition published 1978 by | Book Club Associates | by arrangement with William Heinemann Limited | This Selection of Poems © William Heinemann Ltd 1978 | Preface © John Betjeman 1978 | Printed in Great Britain by | REDWOOD BURN LIMITED | Trowbridge & Esher'; v–vi 'CONTENTS' (67 individual items (including preface and first line index) listed with page references); vii–ix 'PREFACE BY JOHN BETJEMAN' ('John Masefield wrote two lyrics which will be remembered as long as the language lasts...'); [x] blank; 1–325 text; [326] blank; 327–28 'INDEX OF FIRST LINES'; [329–30] blank

Paper: wove paper

Running title: none

Binding: burgundy cloth. On spine, in gold: 'SELECTED | POEMS | [ornament] | JOHN | MASEFIELD | [publisher's device of 'b', 'c' and 'a' all within ruled border: 11 × 10mm.]' Covers: blank. All edges trimmed. Binding measurements: 223 × 137mm. (covers), 223 × 40mm. (spine). End-papers: wove paper (the end-papers at the rear of the volume comprise the last two leaves of the final gathering).

Publication date: published, 1978, in an edition of 7500 copies (suggested by documents in the Archives of The Society of Authors)

Price: £3.75 (suggested by documents in the Archives of The Society of Authors)

Contents:
as for A173(a)

Notes:
The text appears to use the same setting of type as A173(a)

The end-papers at the front of the volume comprise 'standard' end-papers. Those at the rear of the volume comprise the final two leaves of the last gathering ([M]15 and [M]16). End-papers at the front and rear of the volume use wove-paper although of different types.

Copies seen: private collection (PWE)

A173(d) Later English edition (limited signed edition by John Betjeman) (1978)

[No title-page]

Bibliographies: Wight [unrecorded]

Collation: [A]^{16} A3+1 [B-I]^{16} [K]^8 [L]^4 [M]^{16} (J not used); 172 leaves (see notes); 216 × 136mm.; [i–iv] v–ix [x] 1–325 [326] 327–28 [329–34]

Page contents: [i] half-title: 'SELECTED POEMS'; [ii] 'John Masefield O.M. 1878–1967 | John Masefield was born on 1st June, 1878, at Ledbury | in Herefordshire. Educated at King's School, Warwick, | and on H.M.S. *Conway*, he first went to sea at the age | of fifteen on a windjammer. He succeeded Robert | Bridges in 1930 as Poet Laureate and was awarded the | Order of Merit in 1935. Widely travelled in his youth, he | lived the last twenty-eight years of his life in Abingdon, | Berkshire, where he died on 12th May, 1967.'; [iii] *'This specially bound edition of | the* Selected Poems *of John Masefield | is issued to mark the centenary | of his birth. It is limited to | 100 numbered copies of | which this is copy number* | ………… | JOHN BETJEMAN | PARADINE*'; [iv] 'The publishers wish to thank William Heinemann Ltd. | for permission to issue this special edition | This Selection of Poems © William Heinemann Ltd. 1978 | Preface © John Betjeman 1978 | David Paradine Developments Ltd. | Audley House | 9 North Audley Street | London W.1.'*; v–vi 'CONTENTS' (67 individual items (including preface and first line index) listed with page references); vii–ix 'PREFACE BY JOHN BETJEMAN' ('John Masefield wrote two lyrics which will be remembered as long as the language lasts...'); [x] blank; 1–325 text; [326] blank; 327–28 'INDEX OF FIRST LINES'; [329–34] blank

Paper: wove paper

Running title: none

Binding: quarter bound in blue calf with blue and white floral cloth on covers. On spine, in gold: '[rule] | [ornament] | [rule] | [dotted rule on rib of binding] | [rule] | SELECTED | POEMS | [rule] | [dotted rule on rib of binding] | [rule] | [ornament] | [rule] | [dotted rule on rib of binding] | [rule] | JOHN | MASEFIELD | [rule] | [dotted rule on rib of binding] | [rule] | [ornament] | [rule] | [dotted rule on rib of binding] | [rule] | [ornament] | [rule]' (all width centred). There is a single vertical rule in blind on each cover at all edges where calf meets cloth. All edges gilt. Sewn head and foot bands (in blue and white) and blue marker ribbon. Binding measurements: 225 × 137mm. (covers), 225 × 45mm. (spine). End-papers: blue wove paper (see notes). Volume contained in slip-case covered in light blue and navy blue cloth.

Publication date: 1978

Price: unknown

Contents:
as for A173(a)

Notes:
The verso of the front free end-paper and the recto of the rear free end-paper are each backed by a conjugate pair of leaves. There is consequently a blank leaf before page [i] and a blank leaf after page [334]. These are excluded from the collation, leaf count and pagination.

This edition includes a cancellans. Within A173(a) leaf A2 comprises the title-page (with publication information on the verso). This is replaced, here, by the leaf detailing limitation. This leaf comprises blue wove paper.

Copies seen: private collection (ROV) number 29, signed 'John Betjeman' on p.[iii]

A174 THE SEA POEMS   1978

A174(a) First English edition – Morrison & Gibb issue (1978)

THE | SEA POEMS | John Masefield | *With an Introduction* | *by Ronald Hope* | [publisher's device of a windmill with 'W' and 'H'] | THE MARINE SOCIETY | IN ASSOCIATION WITH | HEINEMANN : LONDON
(All width centred)

Bibliographies: Wight [unrecorded]

Collation: [A-D]¹⁶; 64 leaves 215 × 134mm.; [i–iv] v–xi [xii] 1–115 [116]

Page contents: [i] half-title: 'THE | SEA POEMS'; [ii] 'JOHN MASEFIELD O.M. 1878–1967 | John Masefield was born on 1st June 1878, at Ledbury in | Herefordshire. Educated at King's School, Warwick, and on | H.M.S. *Conway*, he first went to sea at the age of fifteen on | a windjammer. He succeeded Robert Bridges in 1930 as | Poet Laureate and was awarded the Order of Merit in 1935. | Widely travelled in his youth, he lived the last twenty-eight | years of his life in Abingdon, Berkshire, where he died on | 12th May, 1967.'; [iii] title-page; [iv] 'William Heinemann Ltd | 15 Queen Street, Mayfair, London W1X 8BE | LONDON MELBOURNE TORONTO | JOHANNESBURG AUCKLAND | Published by William Heinemann Ltd in association | with The Marine Society 1978 | © William Heinemann Ltd 1978 | Introduction © Ronald Hope 1978 | SBN 434 45239 4 | Printed and bound in Great Britain by | Morrison & Gibb Ltd, London and Edinburgh'; v–vi *'Contents'* (36 individual items (including introduction and glossary) listed with page references); vii–xi *'Introduction'* ('Just before William Wordsworth started the Romantic revolution in English letters the Marine...') (signed, *'Ronald Hope'*); [xii] blank; 1–[116] text

Paper: wove paper

Running title: none

Binding: blue cloth. On spine, reading lengthways down spine from head, in gold: 'THE SEA POEMS John Masefield'; horizontally at foot of spine: publisher's device of a windmill with 'W' and 'H'. Covers: blank. All edges trimmed. Binding measurements: 223 × 137mm. (covers), 223 × 24mm. (spine). End-papers: wove paper.

Publication date: October 1978?

Price: £3.50

Contents:
Introduction ('Just before William Wordsworth started the Romantic revolution in English letters the Marine...')
    (signed, *'Ronald Hope'*)
The Ship ('THE ORE | Before Man's labouring wisdom gave me birth')
The *Wanderer* ('All day they loitered by the resting ships,')
Ships ('I cannot tell their wonder nor make known')
The Pathfinder ('She lies at grace, at anchor, head to tide,')
The Setting Forth ('Her builder and owner drank tea with her captain below.')
The Ending ('Once, long before, at her second outgoing down Channel')
Wanderer and Wonderer ('When first the thought of you took steel')
The *Loch Achray* ('The *Loch Achray* was a clipper tall')
On Skysails ('I saw you often as the crown of Queens')
The Crowd ('They had secured their beauty to the dock.')
Under Lower Topsails ('Three lower topsails dark with wet are straining')
Eight Bells ('Four double strokes repeated on the bells,')
Posted ('Dream after dream I see the wrecks that lie')
If ('If it could be, that in this southern port')
I Saw Her Here ('All tranquil is the mirror of the bay,')
The Eyes ('I remember a tropic dawn before turn-to,')
Pay ('The world paid but a penny for its toil,')
Evan Roberts, A.B. of H.M.S. *Andromache* ('This gallant act is told by the late Montagu Burrows, on page 67 of...')
Roadways ('One road leads to London,')
The Emigrant ('Going by Daly's shanty I heard the boys within')
Trade Winds ('In the harbour, in the island, in the Spanish Seas,')
The Spanish Main ('Low, dull-green hills with scrub and little trees,')
Nombre de Dios ('The jungle reaches to the water's edge.')
Porto Bello ('The port is unsuspected from the east,')
Canal Zone ('Among these hills, twelve generations since,')
An Old Song Re-Sung ('I saw a ship a-sailing, a-sailing, a-sailing,')
The Spanish Main Schooner ('A little wooden schooner, painted white,')
Spanish Waters ('Spanish waters, Spanish waters, you are ringing in my ears,')
Captain Stratton's Fancy ('Oh some are fond of red wine, and some are fond of white,')
A Ballad of Sir Francis Drake ('Before Sir Francis put to sea,')
Cargoes ('Quinquireme of Nineveh from distant Ophir')
Sea-Fever ('I must go down to the seas again, to the lonely sea and the sky,')
The River ('All other waters have their time of peace,')
Dauber ('Four bells were struck, the watch was called on deck,')
Explanations of some of the Sea Terms used in the Poems ('BACKSTAYS.-Wire ropes which support...')

Notes:

The publishing agreement for this title was dated 3 May 1978 (see Archives of The Society of Authors).

This publication claims to comprise the first appearance of Masefield's sea poems in a single volume. It is not, however, a *complete* collection as the introduction explains. Additionally, the 1916 Macmillan volume *Salt-Water Poems and Ballads* (A35) comprised a volume of collected sea poems. In such a comparatively short volume it is, however, surprising that *Dauber* appears complete.

The introduction by Ronald Hope notes the textual source for this edition and explains the omissions:

> The poems in this volume are the established canon, extracted from the revised edition of Masefield's *Collected Poems*, a volume long since out of print. These are the sea poems which he wished to be preserved. From his *Collected Poems* he omitted a few which I think he might reasonably have included, but I too have omitted them. It may be that he considered them to owe too much to Kipling or to Newbolt. They are *Sea-Change*, *Port of Many Ships* and *Cape Horn Gospel-II* from *Salt-Water Ballads*; and *Port of Holy Peter*, *Posted as Missing* and *Third Mate* from *Ballads and Poems*. All of these were written when he was very young.

Hope's comments are misleading for he is referring to the revised *Collected Poems* collection first published in 1946 as *Poems* (see A148). All the poems in *The Sea Poems* are present in *Poems*. There are, however, many other sea poems beyond those mentioned by Hope that Masefield chose to exclude from the 1946 volume.

Page numbers appear within square brackets. Thus, [1], [2], etc. The square brackets include a swash-like swirl at each end.

Copies seen: private collection (ROV); BL (X.989/52979) stamped 29 NOV 1978

A174(aa) First English edition – A. Wheaton & Co. issue (1978)

THE | SEA POEMS | John Masefield | *With an Introduction* | *by Ronald Hope* | [publisher's device of a windmill with 'W' and 'H'] | THE MARINE SOCIETY | IN ASSOCIATION WITH | HEINEMANN : LONDON
(All width centred)

Bibliographies: Wight [unrecorded]

Collation: [A]⁸ B-H⁸ (signatures B-H are prefixed by 'T.S.P.-'); signatures left foot of page; 64 leaves 211 × 134mm.; [i–iv] v–xi [xii] 1–115 [116]

Page contents: [i] half-title: 'THE | SEA POEMS'; [ii] 'JOHN MASEFIELD O.M. 1878–1967 | John Masefield was born on 1st June 1878, at Ledbury in | Herefordshire. Educated at King's School, Warwick, and on | H.M.S. *Conway*, he first went to sea at the age of fifteen on | a windjammer. He succeeded Robert Bridges in 1930 as | Poet Laureate and was awarded the Order of Merit in 1935. | Widely travelled in his youth, he lived the last twenty-eight | years of his life in Abingdon, Berkshire, where he died on | 12th May, 1967.'; [iii] title-page; [iv] 'William Heinemann Ltd | 15 Queen Street, Mayfair, London W1X 8BE | LONDON MELBOURNE TORONTO | JOHANNESBURG AUCKLAND | Published by William Heinemann Ltd in association | with The Marine Society 1978 | © William Heinemann Ltd 1978 | Introduction © Ronald Hope 1978 | SBN 434 45239 4 | Printed in Great Britain by A. Wheaton & Co. Ltd., Exeter'; v–vi '*Contents*' (36 individual items (including introduction and glossary) listed with page references); vii–xi '*Introduction*' ('Just before William Wordsworth started the Romantic revolution in English letters the Marine...') (signed, '*Ronald Hope*'); [xii] blank; 1–[116] text

Paper: wove paper

Running title: none

Binding: blue cloth. On spine, reading lengthways down spine from head, in gold: 'THE SEA POEMS John Masefield'; horizontally at foot of spine: publisher's device of a windmill. Covers: blank. All edges trimmed. Binding measurements: 223 × 137mm. (covers), 223 × 24mm. (spine). End-papers: wove paper.

Publication date: October 1978?

Price: £3.50

Contents:
as for A174(a)

Notes:
The paper stock is different from that used for A174(a). Although both issues use wove paper, this is glossy in A174(a). The binding is also slightly different from A174(a) with the publisher's device of a windmill on the spine being of a different design including 'W' and 'H'.

Page numbers appear within square brackets. Thus, [1], [2], etc. The square brackets include a swash-like swirl at each end.

Copies seen: private collection (PWE); private collection (ROV)

JOHN MASEFIELD

★

GRACE
BEFORE PLOUGHING

Fragments of Autobiography

HEINEMANN : LONDON

A170(a) title-page

JOHN MASEFIELD

*Grace Before
Ploughing*

Fragments of Autobiography

The Macmillan Company
NEW YORK

A170(b) title-page

JOHN MASEFIELD

★

IN GLAD
THANKSGIVING

HEINEMANN : LONDON

A171(a) title-page

IN

GLAD

THANKSGIVING

John Masefield

THE MACMILLAN COMPANY, NEW YORK

A171(b) title-page

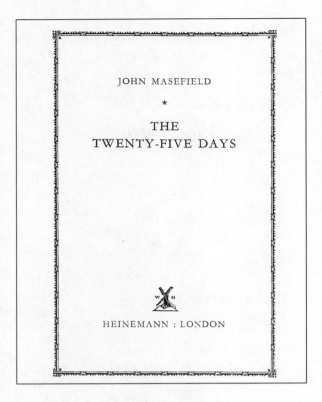

JOHN MASEFIELD

*

THE
TWENTY-FIVE DAYS

HEINEMANN : LONDON

A172(a) title-page

THE
SEA POEMS

John Masefield

*With an Introduction
by Ronald Hope*

THE MARINE SOCIETY
IN ASSOCIATION WITH
HEINEMANN : LONDON

A174(aa) title-page

JOHN MASEFIELD

The MIDNIGHT
FOLK

The BOX OF
DELIGHTS

Illustrated by
QUENTIN BLAKE

HEINEMANN · LONDON

A176(a) title-page

Arthurian Poets

JOHN MASEFIELD

Edited and introduced by
DAVID LLEWELLYN DODDS

THE BOYDELL PRESS

A177(a) title-page

A175 SELECTED POEMS [EDITED BY DONALD E. STANFORD] 1984

A175(a) First English edition (1984)

[rule, 85mm.] | JOHN MASEFIELD | [rule, 85mm.] | *Selected Poems* | Edited by Donald E. Stanford | CARCANET
(All width centred)
(The letters in the final line are in outline)

Bibliographies: Wight [unrecorded]

Collation: there are 172 unsigned leaves bound by the 'perfect binding' process; 215 × 133mm.; [1–8] 9–341 [342–44]

Page contents: [1] half-title: 'John Masefield | Selected Poems'; [2] blank; [3] title-page; [4] 'First published in Great Britain in 1984 | by Carcanet Press | 208 Corn Exchange Building, Manchester M4 3BQ | Introduction © copyright 1984 Donald E. Stanford | Acknowledgement of permission to publish Masefield's poems | is made to the Society of Authors on behalf of the Literary Estate, | and to William Heinemann Ltd. | Masefield, John | Selected poems. | I. Title II. Stanford, Donald E. | 821'.912 PR6025.A77 | The publisher acknowledges the financial assistance | of the Arts Council of Great Britain. | Printed in England by SRP Ltd., Exeter'; [5–7] 'CONTENTS' (65 individual items in seven sections listed with page references); [8] *'For Maryanna'*; 9–22 *'Introduction'* ('Making a representative selection of Masefield's poems is not an easy task.') (signed, 'Donald E. Stanford | Baton Rouge, Louisiana'); 23–339 text; 340–41 'INDEX OF FIRST LINES'; [342–44] blank

Paper: wove paper

Running title: none

Binding: black wrappers. On spine, reading lengthways down spine from head: 'JOHN MASEFIELD [in white] | Selected Poems [in green]'; horizontally at foot of spine, '[publisher's device of cat] [in green] | CARCANET [in green]'. On upper wrapper: 'JOHN [in white] | MASEFIELD [in white] | Selected Poems [in green] | edited by Donald Stanford [in green] | [black and white photograph of Masefield within circular ruled border in green: 101mm. diameter] | CARCANET [in white outline]'. On lower wrapper, in green: '[ten lines of verse] | *(from 'Biography')* | [new paragraph] Readers are again turning to the work of John Masefield (1878– | 1967). In it they find great verbal skill, thematic range, and a | human generosity and warmth rare in the poetry of our time. | Donald Stanford aims here to recover the essential Masefield. | Many of the poems are long: a proper presentation must be | *in extenso*. It is one aspect of Masefield's originality and of his | renewed popularity that he can write large- as well as small-scale | poems. He can be an exquisite lyricist and elegist; he is also a | narrative poet, a balladeer, a writer in common speech and in | heightened diction, and a master of light verse. He looked to | Browning rather than Tennyson as an immediate antecedent, | hence the rich texture of his verse and the centrality of the | speaking voice. His roots go deep in the eighteenth and seven- | teenth centuries too. [new paragraph] He was born in Ledbury, Herefordshire. After school he went | to sea on a merchant navy training ship. He travelled to America | and spent two years in and near New York. In 1902 his *Salt-* | *Water Ballads* was published. It was a confident beginning, and | the books that followed earned him a wide readership. *The* | *Everlasting Mercy* was his most controversial poem, both for the | coarseness of the language and for the insistent realism of the | treatment. In 1923 his first *Collected Poems* was published. It | eventually sold 200,000 copies. In 1930 he succeeded his friend | Robert Bridges as Poet Laureate. Carcanet Press also publish his | *Letters to Margaret Bridges 1915–1919.* | [double rule] | *Write for our catalogue with details of our new poetry, fiction,* [in white] | *translations, Lives & Letters and Fyfield Books to* [in white] | CARCANET 208–212 Corn Exchange Manchester M4 3BQ [in white] | *ISBN 0 85635 502 X £7.95* [in white]'. All edges trimmed. Binding measurements: 215 × 133mm. (wrappers), 215 × 25mm. (spine).

Publication date: November 1984

Price: £7.95

Contents:
Introduction ('Making a representative selection of Masefield's poems is not an easy task.')
(signed, 'Donald E. Stanford | Baton Rouge, Louisiana')
A Consecration ('Not of the princes and prelates with periwigged charioteers')
AUTOBIOGRAPHICAL POEMS
Biography ('When I am buried, all my thoughts and acts')
Wonderings ('Out of a dateless darkness pictures gleam,')
Land Workers ('Long since, in England's pleasant lands')
C.L.M. ('In the dark womb where I began')
Remembering Dame Myra Hess ('Most beautiful, most gifted, and most wise,')
For Luke O'Connor ('One early Summer, when the times were bad,')
On Growing Old ('Be with me, Beauty, for the fire is dying,')
SEA POEMS
Sea-Fever ('I must go down to the seas again, to the lonely sea and the sky,')
The *Wanderer* ('All day they loitered by the resting ships,')
Ships ('I cannot tell their wonder nor make known')
The River ('All other waters have their time of peace,')
A Wanderer's Song ('A wind's in the heart of me, a fire's in my heels,')

Spanish Waters ('Spanish waters, Spanish waters, you are ringing in my ears,')
Cargoes ('Quinquireme of Nineveh from distant Ophir,')
Captain Stratton's Fancy ('Oh some are fond of red wine, and some are fond of white,')
The Pathfinder ('She lies at grace, at anchor, head to tide,')
Campeachy Picture ('The sloop's sails glow in the sun; the far sky burns,')
A Ballad of Sir Francis Drake ('Before Sir Francis put to sea,')
The Lemmings ('Once in a hundred years the Lemmings come')
The Crowd ('They had secured their beauty to the dock,')
Under Three Lower Topsails ('Three lower topsails dark with wet are straining')
Porto Bello ('The port is unsuspected from the east,')
Lines on the Shipwreck of Admiral Sir Cloudesley Shovell… ('Fog covered all the great Fleet homeward bound,')
OF COUNTRY THINGS
A Tale of Country Things ('That little brook's the boundary line')
Midnight ('The fox came up by Stringer's Pound;')
Blown Hilcote Manor ('In perfect June we reached the house to let,')
Pawn to Bishop's Five ('I stayed, once, at Tom's house, at Uppat's Lea,')
Ryemeadows ('My people owned Ryemeadows on the Moor,')
The West Wind ('It's a warm wind, the west wind, full of birds' cries;')
The Wind ('The wind comes in from the sea to the chicory-flower.')
Partridges ('Here they lie mottled to the ground unseen,')
The Curlews ('We three were in wild Shropshire, picking sloes,')
The Hill ('I see yon harebells, foxgloves, brooks,')
Old England ('Just half a century since, an old man showed')
The Bluebells ('We stood upon the grass beside the road,')
Middle Farm, or the Cherries ('"Cherries and bread, for Man's delight, and need,')
Shopping in Oxford ('Twenty-four years ago, I wandered down')
GREEKS, TROJANS, ROMANS
The Taking of Helen ('Menelaus, the Spartan King,')
The Surprise ('You have heard the story of the Horse of Troy.')
Fragments ('Troy Town is covered up with weeds,')
The Rider at the Gate ('A windy night was blowing on Rome,')
ARTHUR AND TRISTAN
The Begetting of Arthur ('Uther, the Prince, succeeding to the post')
The Fight on the Wall ('Modred was in the Water Tower')
The Love Gift ('In King Marc's palace at the valley-head')
Tristan's Singing ('When Isolt quarrelled with her Tristan there')
BEAUTY, LOVE, DEATH
Sonnets ('Night came again, but now I could not sleep.')
[Untitled] ('If I could come again to that dear place')
[Untitled] ('Flesh, I have knocked at many a dusty door,')
[Untitled] ('So in the empty sky the stars appear,')
[Untitled] ('I never see the red rose crown the year,')
[Untitled] ('Out of the clouds come torrents, from the earth')
[Untitled] ('Is there a great green commonwealth of Thought')
[Untitled] ('Wherever beauty has been quick in clay')
[Untitled] ('They called that broken hedge The Haunted Gate.')
[Untitled] ('There was an evil in the nodding wood')
[Untitled] ('The little robin hopping in the wood')
Waste ('No rose but fades: no glory but must pass:')
I Dreamed ('"I dreamed a dream the other night…')
Sitting Alone ('Sitting alone, far hence, in summer night,')
NARRATIVE POEMS
Dauber ('Four bells were struck, the watch was called on deck')
Reynard the Fox, or, the Ghost Heath Run ('The meet was at 'The Cock and Pye'')
A Creed ('I hold that when a person dies')

Notes:

An edition of selected poems in seven sections, comprising thematic groups. There is a general introduction by Donald E. Stanford, but no indication of which textual states have been chosen, their sources or Stanford's editing policy.

Page numerals 340 and 341 are in a smaller type than those in the rest of the volume.

Copies seen: BL (X.950/39776) stamped 2 NOV 1984

Reprinted:
There have been numerous reprints of this edition. Reprint information is omitted within the volumes. However, later impressions can be identified by increases in the price of the volume and also a change from black to white wrappers.

A176 THE MIDNIGHT FOLK [AND] THE BOX OF DELIGHTS 1991

A176(a) First English edition (1991)

JOHN MASEFIELD | *The* MIDNIGHT | FOLK | [point] | *The* BOX OF | DELIGHTS | *Illustrated by* | QUENTIN BLAKE | HEINEMANN [point] LONDON
(All width centred)
(The underlined 'The' in the titles are in a smaller font and the underlinings are curved lines)

Bibliographies: Wight [unrecorded]

Collation: [A]¹⁶ [B]⁸ [C]⁴ [D–F]¹⁶ [G–H]⁸ [I–R]¹⁶ [S]⁴ [T]¹⁶ (J not used); 256 leaves; 214 × 135mm.; [i–iv] 1–212 [213–20] 1–288; illustrations (on glossy paper) tipped-in on pp.28, 44, 52, 84, 116, 148, 164 and 180 (of *The Midnight Folk*) and pp.24, 56, 88, 120, 152, 184, 216 and 248 (of *The Box of Delights*); the illustration is on the verso of the leaf, with the recto blank

Page contents: [i] title-page; [ii] '~ | The Midnight Folk | first published 1927 | The Box of Delights | first published 1935 | by William Heinemann Ltd | Michelin House | 81 Fulham Road | London SW3 6RB | LONDON MELBOURNE AUCKLAND | This edition published 1991 | Text © John Masefield 1957 | Illustrations © Quentin Blake 1990 | ISBN 0 434 96095 0'; [iii] '*The* | MIDNIGHT | FOLK'; [iv] '*For J.&L.* | ~'; 1–212 text of *The Midnight Folk*; [213] '*The* BOX OF DELIGHTS'; [214] blank; [215] '*The* BOX OF | DELIGHTS'; [216] blank; [217] '*To My Wife* | ~'; [218] blank; [219–20] '*CONTENTS*' (12 chapters each listed with a couplet and page reference); 1–288 text of *The Box of Delights*

Paper: wove paper

Running title: 'THE MIDNIGHT FOLK' (55mm.) on both verso and recto, pp.2–212 and 'THE BOX OF DELIGHTS' (55mm.) on both verso and recto, pp.2–288

Binding: laminated boards. On mottled blue spine, reading lengthways down spine from head: 'The MIDNIGHT FOLK | ~ MASEFIELD [point] BLAKE HEINEMANN | The BOX OF DELIGHTS' (all on cream panel within black ruled border, within thick pink border and all within black ruled border: 186 × 29mm.) On mottled blue upper cover: '*JOHN MASEFIELD* | *The* MIDNIGHT FOLK | AND | *The* BOX OF DELIGHTS | [coloured illustration of Cole Hawlings with the box of delights] | [rule] | [thick pink rule] | [rule] | *QUENTIN BLAKE*' (the names of the author and illustrator are in black on cream panels, the titles are in white on a purple panel, the whole is surrounded by the black ruled border, thick pink border and black ruled border (as used on the spine) and this creates a rectangle: 187 × 110mm.; additionally, the title panel (with the same border design) bearing the titles intersects this larger panel and measures 38 × 124mm.) On mottled blue lower cover: 'The MIDNIGHT FOLK | When Kay Harker sets out to discover the long-lost | family treasure, his friends The Midnight Folk gather | to help him. The Midnight Folk are Kay's toys – | Nibbins the black cat, Bitem the fox, Blinky the owl, | and a whole tribe of other friends which had been | locked away with the arrival of his new governess. | Kay's nightly investigations into the treasure lead him | and The Midnight Folk into a world of mystery | and adventure. | The BOX OF DELIGHTS | On his way home from school for the | Christmas holidays, Kay Harker meets a mysterious | Punch and Judy man on the train. But the mysteries | are only just beginning when, on a cold and snowy | night, the Punch and Judy man gives Kay the magic | Box of Delights. The Box takes Kay into the past, | into the days of King Arthur and even beyond that, | to the ancient city of Troy. | But wicked Abner Brown is after the Box, and he | pursues Kay through time to try and steal the Box | away from him. Kay must protect the Box of | Delights at all costs – but is he a match for the evil | ways of Abner Brown? | *Two classic adventure tales with new illustrations by* | *Quentin Blake for readers of all generations to enjoy.* | ISBN 0-434-96095-0 | [bar code] | 9 780434 960958 | £19.99' (the titles and bar code are on white panels surrounded by a black, blue, black border, the other text is on a cream panel, the whole is surrounded by the black ruled border, thick pink border and black ruled border (as used on the spine) and this creates a rectangle: 187 × 111mm.; additionally, the bar code panel intersects this larger panel and measures 30 × 39mm.) All edges trimmed. Binding measurements: 222 × 136mm. (covers), 222 × 60mm. (spine). End-papers: wove paper.

A variant binding lacks the publisher on the spine. The ISBN number is replaced on the lower cover by 'CN 4897' and the price is omitted.

Publication date: published, according to *Whitaker's*, November 1991

Price: £19.99

Contents:
The Midnight Folk ('It had been an unhappy day for little Kay Harker. To begin with, at breakfast time the governess...')
The Box of Delights ('As Kay was coming home for the Christmas holidays, after his first term at school, the train...')

Notes:
The text of *The Midnight Folk* and each chapter of *The Box of Delights* commence with a drop-capital. Note, however, the differences between chapters 6 and 10 with chapter 7 where Heinemann are inconsistent over use of speech marks set with the drop-capital.

Although Wight notes the separate editions of *The Midnight Folk* and *The Box of Delights* illustrated by Quentin Blake, he omits all reference to this combined volume.

See note to A86(p) for notes on publication date.

Discussion between Masefield and C.S. Evans about a combined edition of the Kay Harker stories took place even before publication of *The Box of Delights*:

> I am certain that it would be an excellent idea to bring out MIDNIGHT FOLK and THE BOX OF DELIGHTS in one volume and to have MIDNIGHT FOLK illustrated by Judith in a similar style to THE BOX OF DELIGHTS; but it will not be possible to produce that volume until about eighteen months after the publication of THE BOX OF DELIGHTS. If we did so the booksellers would have the right to return any unsold copies of the first book. I should estimate, therefore, for the publication of the omnibus book in 1937, probably in the spring. That will give Judith plenty of time to prepare the pictures.

> (C.S. Evans, letter to John Masefield, 23 August 1935)
> (HRHRC, MS (Masefield, J.) Recip William Heinemann Ltd.)

The volume was not published in 1937 and Masefield appears to have raised the issue again in 1951. A letter (preserved in the Archives of William Heinemann) from A.S. Frere dated 1 May 1951 to Masefield states that Frere was 'going into the question of issuing *The Midnight Folk* and *The Box of Delights* together in one volume...' Following a 1955 radio broadcast of *The Box of Delights* Masefield suggested to Heinemann 'that they should issue the two linked books, *The Midnight Folk* and *The Box of Delights* in a single volume' (see BL, Add.Mss.56626, f.128). Masefield tried again in 1957 and received a reply from his publishers:

> We must apologise for having been so long in replying to your letter of the 16th February but we have been endeavouring to get an exact publication date for the volume containing MIDNIGHT FOLK and A BOX OF DELIGHTS [*sic*]. While the work is going ahead we very much regret that at present no precise date can be given, but you can be assured that every effort is being made to expedite publication.

> (D.E. Priestley, letter to John Masefield, 14 March 1957)
> (HRHRC, MS (Masefield, J.) Recip William Heinemann Ltd.)

Writing to The Society of Authors during April 1957 Masefield noted:

> As to *The Midnight Folk*. I have been badgering Heinemann to print this, with *The Box of Delights*. Late last summer they agreed to reprint the 2 books in one vol; + on pressure from me, even said that they would try to have the book out in time for the 1956 Christmas sales. They did not succeed in this, of course, but I have expected it ever since... The books are liked by a good many; I am often asked for copies of both books; + they had had a success as Wireless stories.

> (John Masefield, letter to Anne Munro-Kerr, 5 April [1957])
> (Archives of The Society of Authors)

Copies seen: private collection (PWE) variant binding; BL (Nov.1991/2337) stamped 14 NOV 1991

A176(b) Second English edition (2001)

John Masefield | The | Midnight | Folk | [panel showing Rowland Hilder illustration of a fox in a wood] | The Box of | Delights | [panel showing Judith Masefield illustration of Kay Harker in battle with wolves] | EGMONT (All width centred)

Publication date: published, according to date within volume, 2001

Price: £4.99

Contents:
as for A176(a)

Notes:
The volume states, on page [2], that it is published by Egmont Books Ltd. The number sequence '1 3 5 7 9 10 8 6 4 2' is present. The edition was 'printed and bound in Great Britain by Cox & Wyman Ltd, Reading, Berkshire'. The ISBN number is ISBN 0 7497 4872 9.

The cover illustrations are by Liz Pyle.

This edition, bound in wrappers, was an exclusive publication available only at W.H. Smiths. As a combined edition of A86(q) and A115(n) illustrations by Rowland Hilder and Judith Masefield are present, although not acknowledged.

Copies seen: private collection (PWE); Library of The Society of Authors

A177 ARTHURIAN POETS[:] JOHN MASEFIELD
[EDITED AND INTRODUCED BY DAVID LLEWELLYN DODDS]   1994

A177(a) First English edition (1994)

Arthurian Poets | JOHN MASEFIELD | *Edited and introduced by* | DAVID LLEWELLYN DODDS | THE BOYDELL PRESS
(All width centred)

Collation: [A-L]¹⁶ [M]⁴ [N]⁸ [O]¹⁶ (J not used); 204 leaves; 215 × 138mm.; [i–viii] 1–31 [32–34] 35–261 [262–64] 265–330 [331–32] 333–68 [369–70] 371–85 [386] 387–98 [399–400]

Page contents: [i] 'Arthurian Poets | JOHN MASEFIELD | At the end of the nineteenth century, a homeless runaway | teenager in New York found a job in a bar and discovered | Malory. So began the lifelong interest of the future Poet | Laureate, John Masefield (1878–1967), in the story of King | Arthur. After becoming a popular, successful narrative poet | and playwright, Masefield turned to the Arthurian material in | earnest, producing the verse drama *Tristan and Isolt* in 1927 and | *Midsummer Night*, with its Arthurian cycle, a year later. | [new paragraph] All twenty-eight of Masefield's previously published Arthur- | ian poems, from the *Ballad of Sir Bors* (1903) to *Caer Ocvran* | (1966), are collected here, along with the play *Tristan and Isolt*. | This edition also presents a number of works never before | published, including the full-length tragi-comedy *When Good | King Arthur*, and prose notes which, together with nine new | poems, reveal Masefield undertaking an ambitious retelling of | the Arthurian myth. | [new paragraph] In this collected edition, readers may enjoy the grim humour, | vivid description and narrative inventiveness of this excep- | tional story-teller and poet. | [new paragraph] DAVID LLEWELLYN DODDS, A.M., was a Rhodes Scholar and | Richard Weaver Fellow at Merton College, Oxford. He has | lectured in English at Harlaxton College, worked at the | Houghton and Regenstein Libraries, and acted as Curator of | C.S. Lewis's house. His previous work includes the Charles | Williams volume in this Arthurian Poets series.'; [ii] 'Arthurian Poets | [four titles, details of introductions and editors listed] | The hardback edition of this volume | is published as | ARTHURIAN STUDIES XXXII | (ISSN 0261–9814) | Details of previous volumes of Arthurian Studies | are printed at the back of this volume'; [iii] title-page; [iv] 'Editorial matter © 1994 David Llewellyn Dodds | Previously unpublished John Masefield poems, plays and prose © 1994 | The Estate of John Masefield | *Ballads* © 1903 John Masefield | *Midsummer Night and other Tales in Verse* © 1928 John Masefield | *Minnie Maylow's Story and other Tales and Scenes* © 1931 John Masefield | *On the Hill* © 1949 John Masefield | *My Library: Volume One* © 1950 John Masefield | *In Glad Thanksgiving* © 1966/7 John Masefield | *Tristan and Isolt: A Play in Verse* © 1927 John Masefield | *All rights reserved*. Except as permitted under current legislation | no part of this work may be photocopied, stored in a retrieval system, | published, performed in public, adapted, broadcast, | transmitted, recorded or reproduced in any form or by any means, | without the prior permission of the copyright owner | This edition first published 1994 by | The Boydell Press, Woodbridge | and in hardback by D.S. Brewer, Cambridge | ISBN 0 85115 363 1 paperback | ISBN 0 85991 408 9 hardback | The Boydell Press and D.S. Brewer are imprints of | Boydell & Brewer Ltd | PO Box 9, Woodbridge, Suffolk IP12 3DF, UK | and of Boydell & Brewer Inc. | PO Box 41026, Rochester, NY 14604–4126, USA | A catalogue record for this book is available | from the British Library | Library of Congress Catalog Card Number: 94–10466 | This publication is printed on acid-free paper | Printed in Great Britain by | St Edmundsbury Press Ltd, Bury St Edmunds, Suffolk'; [v–vii] 'CONTENTS' (53 individual items (including introduction, bibliographical note, notes, sources and acknowledgements) listed in four parts with page references); [viii] blank; 1–29 'INTRODUCTION' ('When Masefield was chosen as Poet Laureate, in May 1930, he was a 'popular' writer...') (unsigned); 30–31 'BIBLIOGRAPHICAL NOTE' ('Fraser Drew, *John Masefield's England* (1973) includes the only recent...'); [32] blank; [33] '*Part I* | PUBLISHED POEMS AND PLAY'; [34] blank; 35–261 text; [262] blank; [263] '*Part II* | UNPUBLISHED POEMS AND PLAY'; [264] blank; 265–330 text; [331] '*Part III* | UNPUBLISHED DRAFTS FOR POEMS'; [332] blank; 333–68 text; [369] '*Part IV* | UNPUBLISHED PROSE'; [370] blank; 371–85 text; [386] blank; 387–93 'NOTES'; 394–98 'SOURCES AND ACKNOWLEDGEMENTS'; [399–400] publisher's advertisements

Paper: wove paper

Running title: none

Binding: brown cloth. On spine, reading lengthways down spine from head, in gold: 'Arthurian Poets | [point] ed. Dodds D.S. BREWER | JOHN MASEFIELD'. On upper cover: panel in blind: 59 × 109mm. upon which is a cream laid paper label (58 × 108mm.) on which: 'Arthurian studies xxxii | Arthurian Poets | JOHN MASEFIELD | Edited and introduced by | David Llewellyn Dodds' (enclosed within ruled border: 55 × 104mm.) (The 'A' of 'Arthurian' is particularly ornate). Lower cover: blank. All edges trimmed. Binding measurements: 223 × 139mm. (covers), 223 × 44mm. (spine). End-papers: wove paper.

Also issued in brown and white wrappers. On spine, reading lengthways down spine from head, in white: 'Arthurian Poets MASEFIELD BOYDELL'. On upper wrapper, in gold: 'Arthurian Poets | [rule (tapered at both ends)] | John Masefield | [photograph of sculptured head against white background]'. On lower wrapper, in white: '*Arthurian Poets* | JOHN MASEFIELD | Edited and introduced by | DAVID LLEWELLYN DODDS | AT THE END of the nineteenth century, a homeless runaway teenager in | New York found a job in a bar – and, in a nearby bookstore, bought a | volume of Malory's *Morte Darthur*. So began the lifelong interest of the | future Poet Laureate, John Masefield (1878–1967), in the story of King | Arthur. After becoming a popular, successful narrative poet and | playwright, Masefield turned to the Arthurian material in earnest, | producing the verse drama *Tristan and Isolt* in 1927 and *Midsummer | Night*, with its Arthurian cycle, a year later. | [new paragraph] All twenty-nine of Masefield's previously published Arthurian poems, | from the *Ballad of Sir Bors* (1903) to *Caer Ocvran* (1966), are collected | here. Also included, among works never before published, are the | full-length tragi-comedy *When Good King Arthur*, and nine poems which, | together with prose notes, reveal Masefield undertaking an ambitious | retelling of the Arthurian myth. | [new paragraph] In this collected edition, readers may enjoy the grim humour, vivid | description and narrative inventiveness of this exceptional story-teller | and poet. | [new paragraph] DAVID LLEWELLYN DODDS, A.M., was a Rhodes Scholar and Richard | Weaver Fellow at Merton College, Oxford. He has lectured in English at | Harlaxton College, worked at the Houghton and Regenstein Libraries, | and acted as Curator of C.S. Lewis's house. His previous work includes | the Charles Williams volume in this 'Arthurian Poets' series. | [new paragraph] Cover illustration: 'La Beale Isoude' by George Frampton | ['ISBN 0-85115-363-1' and bar-code in black on white panel] | BOYDELL & BREWER | PO Box 9, Woodbridge, Suffolk IP12 3DF |

and PO Box 41026, Rochester NY 14604–4126'. All edges trimmed. Binding measurements: 215 × 138mm. (wrappers); 215 × 29mm. (spine).

Publication date: August 1994

Price: £35.00 (cloth) / £15.99 (wrappers)

Contents:

Introduction ('When Masefield was chosen as Poet Laureate, in May 1930, he was a 'popular' writer...')
(unsigned)
Bibliographical Note ('Fraser Drew, *John Masefield's England* (1973) includes the only recent...')
(unsigned)
Part I PUBLISHED POEMS AND PLAY
The Ballad of Sir Bors ('Would I could win some quiet and rest, and a little ease,')
The Begetting of Arthur ('Uther, the Prince, succeeding to the post')
The Birth of Arthur ('When the wind from East changes')
The Taking of Morgause ('Morgause the Merry played beside the burn:')
The Begetting of Modred ('When berries were scarlet')
Badon Hill ('Loki the Dragon Killer mustered men')
The Sailing of Hell Race ('When Arthur came from warring, having won')
Arthur and his Ring ('Beauty's Delight, the Princes Gwenivere,') [*sic*]
Midsummer Night ('Midsummer night had fallen at full moon,')
The Fight on the Wall ('Modred was in the Water Tower')
The Breaking of the Links ('They told King Arthur how the Knights were killed,')
Gwenivach Tells ('I, Gwenivach, King Modred's queen, declare')
Arthur in the Ruins ('King Arthur watched within the ruined town,')
The Fight at Camlan ('Soon the two armies were in touch, and soon')
The Fight on the Beach or The Passing ('These were the nine with Modred:-Kolgrim, Gor,')
Gwenivere Tells ('So Arthur passed, but country-folk believe')
The Death of Lancelot as told by Gwenivere ('Then, after many years, a rider came,')
Dust to Dust ('Henry Plantagenet, the English King,')
On the Coming of Arthur ('By ways unknown, unseen,')
The Old Tale of the Begetting ('*The men of old, who made the tale for us,*')
The Old Tale of the Breaking of the Links ('French poets write:- That, Lancelot the brave')
South and East ('When good King Arthur ruled these western hursts,')
The Love Gift ('In King Marc's palace at the valley-head')
Tristan's Singing ('PART I | When Isolt quarrell'd with her Tristan there')
Simkin, Tomkin and Jack ('Before old Tencombe of the Barrows died,')
Tristan and Isolt ('The King and Queen debate with eagerness')
My Library: Volume One ('Fifty-five years ago, as impulse led,')
Caer Ocvran ('There are some ramparts in the distant West,')
Tristan and Isolt ('(*From Front Stage.*) | DESTINY. I am She who began ere Man was begotten,')
Part II UNPUBLISHED POEMS AND PLAY
The Aftermath ('Kol brought the news of Uther's murdering')
Brother Lot ('When Merchyon murdered Uther in the glen')
Arthur's Youth ('Arthur was born within Tintagel hold')
Before the Darkness Came ('As on some westward fronting crag the sun')
The Coming of the Pirates ('This year the pirates came')
All Hallow Night ('Before the fight with the pagan men,')
The Hunt is Up ('Arthur the King has gone to hunt the deer')
Modred the Messenger ('Arthur was in his hunting lodge at rest.')
Gareth's Wake ('Gawaine the Kind,')
When Good King Arthur ('(*A ship's deck.* OLWEN *and* MERLIN.) | OLWEN. Well met, friend Merlin. Have the...')
Part III UNPUBLISHED DRAFTS FOR POEMS
The Old Tale of the Breaking of the Links | *Drafts* ('Soon as the colour-giving dawn was seen,')
Midsummer Night | *Selections from the Dialogue Drafts* ('IDDOC. | I am King Iddoc of the realm of Kent,')
The Sailing of Hell Race | *Outline and Drafts* ('When Arthur had fought the Pentland war, and had made for himself...')
The Aftermath | *Drafts and Outline* ('But when the news of Uther's death was brought')
Part IV UNPUBLISHED PROSE
Notes 1 ('An ancient Welsh archaeology gives the second fatal blow of Britain as that...')
Notes 2 ('Arthur married Gwenhwyvar, whose sister was Gwenhwyvach. Mordred or Medrawt was...')
Prospectus ('Prologue | Arthur, the king, is married to Gwenivere, who is...')
Sketch ('Arthur was the son of Queen Ygern by Uther her enemy, who obtained access to her...')

Chronology ('476 Uther, the king over what is now Wiltshire, Berkshire and parts of...')
Unpublished Lecture ('When I was seventeen years of age I thought that I must at all costs...')

Notes:
A volume reprinting Masefield's previously published Arthurian poems. These are largely derived from *Midsummer Night and other tales in verse* (A88) and *Tristan and Isolt* (A85). There are also a number of hitherto unpublished pieces, including several poems and an entire play ('When Good King Arthur'). Dodds notes that the textual sources are English first editions. Among the previously unpublished works only the play 'When Good King Arthur' has an authorial title. Dodds has provided his own titles for the untitled pieces.

The sources of unpublished material are the Houghton Library (Harvard University) and the HRHRC.

The half-title page includes advertisement that 'all twenty-eight of Masefield's previously published Arthurian poems... are collected here'. The correct number is cited on the lower wrapper of the paperback edition: 'all twenty-nine of Masefield's previously published Arthurian poems... are collected here'.

Given different ISBN numbers, the paperback edition of this volume is published by the Boydell Press, Woodbridge and the hardback edition is published (as part of the 'Arthurian Studies' series) by D.S. Brewer, Cambridge. The Boydell Press and D.S. Brewer are both imprints of Boydell & Brewer Ltd and the setting of text is exactly the same. Both comprise the first edition, but in different bindings.

Copies seen: private collection (PWE) cloth binding, inscribed by Geoffrey Handley-Taylor; private collection (PWE) wrappers

A178 POEMS [SELECTED BY PETER VANSITTART]   2002

A178(a) First English edition (2002)

[ornament] *John Masefield* | POEMS | [rule, 30mm.] | Selected by Peter Vansittart | [ornament] | Greville Press Pamphlets 2002
(All width centred)

Collation: [A]¹²; 12 leaves; 210 × 143mm.; [i–iv] 1–20

Page contents: [i] half-title: 'Masefield: Poems'; [ii] blank; [iii] title-page; [iv] '© The estate of John Masefield 2002 | Selection: © Peter Vansittart | ISBN 0 906887 75 5 | Type set in Palatino by Bryan Foster | at the Ashby Lane Press, Bitteswell'; 1–20 text

Paper: wove paper

Running title: none

Binding: brown wrappers. Spine: blank. On upper wrapper: 'Poems by [in brown] | John [in brown] | Masefield [in brown] | Selected by | Peter Vansittart | [thick rule, 25mm.] [in brown] | [thin rule, 25mm.] [in brown] | Greville Press Pamphlets'. On lower wrapper: '£4.50 | ISBN 0 906887 75 5' (ranged lower left). All edges trimmed. Binding measurements: 210 × 143mm. (wrappers); 210 × 2mm.(spine).

Publication date: August 2002 in an edition of 150 copies

Price: £4.50

Contents:
The Rider at the Gate ('A windy night was blowing on Rome,')
"Up on the Downs…" ('Up on the downs the red-eyed kestrels hover,')
On Eastnor Knoll ('Silent are the woods, and the dim green boughs are')
"No Man Takes the Farm" ('No man takes the farm,')
Sonnet XXXVII ('What am I, Life? A thing of watery salt')
From The Everlasting Mercy ('"That's what I'll do," I shouted loud,')
From Reynard the Fox ('The lurcher dogs soon shot their bolt,')
From The Widow in the Bye Street ('She passed for pure; but, years before, in Wales,')
From August, 1914 ('How still this quiet cornfield is to-night!')
From Dauber | The Painter ('Hell, he expected,–hell. His eyes grew blind;')
[From Dauber] | The Joke ('Next day was Sunday, his free painting day,')
Envoi ('I have seen flowers come in stony places,')

Notes:
The first poem only commences with a drop capital.

Page number s appear in an italic type.

The text concludes with an ornament.

See also E4 for Vansittart's edition of *John Masefield's Letters from the Front 1915–1917*.

Copies seen: private collection (PWE)

B. Books Edited or with Contributions

excludes anthologies which reprint common Masefield items previously printed in book form

B1 *WOLVERHAMPTON ART AND INDUSTRIAL EXHIBITION, 1902.* OFFICIAL CATALOGUE OF THE FINE ART SECTION.

1902

B1(a) First English edition (1902)

WOLVERHAMPTON | ART AND INDUSTRIAL | EXHIBITION, | 1902. | [crest bearing legend 'OUT OF DARKNESS COMETH LIGHT'] | OFFICIAL CATALOGUE | OF THE | FINE ART SECTION. | WHITEHEAD BROS., | OFFICIAL PRINTERS | AND PUBLISHERS, | ST. JOHN'S SQUARE AND KING STREET, WOLVERHAMPTON. | *COPYRIGHT. All Rights Reserved.*

(All width centred with the exception of line 10 which is off-set to the left and the last line where '*COPYRIGHT*' is off-set to the left and '*All Rights Reserved*' is off-set to the right)

Bibliographies: Williams p.11, Simmons p.127

Collation: [A]²⁴; 24 leaves; 213 × 135mm.; [1–2] 3–46 [47–48]

Page contents: [1] title-page; [2] 'PRINTED AND PUBLISHED BY | WHITEHEAD BROS., | KING STREET AND ST. JOHN'S SQUARE, | WOLVERHAMPTON, | OFFICIAL PRINTERS AND PUBLISHERS.'; 3 '[three flower motifs] | [rule] | [rule] | Fine Art Committee. | THE RIGHT WORSHIPFUL THE MAYOR OF WOLVERHAMPTON | (Charles Paulton Plant, J.P.), Richmond Road. | LAWRENCE W. HODSON *(Chairman)*, Compton Hall. | John Annan, J.P., 12, Hordern Road. | John F. Beckett, J.P., Penn Fields. | Edward L. Cullwick, 44, Compton Road. | Edward Deansley, M.D., F.R.C.S., 4, Waterloo Road South. | Thomas H. Sidney, 87, North Road. | Ernest White, 2, Avenue Road. | Thomas Wilson, Mostyn Street. | Thomas B. Cope, Tettenhall Wood. | H.G. Powell, 95, Waterloo Road North. | W.S. Rowland, Bank House, Lichfield Street. | R. Williams, 1, St. George's Parade. | [rule] | A. C. C. JAHN, A.R.C.A. (Lond.), | Director of Art Gallery and Head Master of School of Art. | *Secretary :* | JOHN E. MASEFIELD. | [rule] | [rule] | [three inverted flower motifs]'; 4 'CONTENTS.' (11 sections listed with page references); 5 'FOREWORD.' ('THE Chairman and Committee of the Fine Art Section desire to...') (unsigned); 6–10 'REMARKS | ON THE GREATER MOVEMENTS | IN ENGLISH ART.' ('ENGLISH painting, as a distinctive factor in European Art, dates...') (unsigned); 11 'Hall and Staircase.'; 12–14 'The South Gallery.'; 15–19 'Horsman Room.'; 19–22 'The North Gallery.'; 22–26 'The Cartwright Room.'; 26–38 'Print Room.'; 38–39 'The Japanese Room.'; 39–46 'The Book Room.'; [47] blank; [48] blank

Paper: laid paper (no watermark), chain-lines 29mm. apart

Running title: running titles comprise sectional titles of catalogue, pp.3–46

Binding: light-green wrappers. Spine: blank. On upper wrapper: 'WOLVERHAMPTON ART AND | INDUSTRIAL EXHIBITION, 1902. | CATALOGUE OF THE EXHIBITS | IN THE FINE ART SECTION. | [crest bearing legend 'OUT OF DARKNESS COMETH LIGHT'] | PRINTED AND PUBLISHED BY WHITEHEAD BROTHERS, | KING STREET & ST. JOHN'S SQUARE, WOLVERHAMPTON.' (all left justified with the exception of the crest which is width centred). Lower wrapper: blank. Inside of upper wrapper: advertisements (for 'Shepherd's Gallery' and 'Obach & Company'). Inside of lower wrapper: blank. All edges trimmed. Binding measurements: 213 × 135mm. (wrappers), 213 × 5mm. (spine).

Publication date: published before May 1902 (see notes)

Price: unknown

Masefield contents:

Remarks on the Greater Movements in English Art ('English painting, as a distinctive factor in European Art...')
    (unsigned)

Notes:

There are eleven sections: 'Committee', 'Foreword', 'Remarks on the greater movements in English Art', 'The Hall and Staircase', 'The South Gallery – The Early English School', 'The Horsman Room', 'The North Gallery – The Pre-Raphaelite Brotherhood', 'The Cartwright Room', 'Prints and Drawings', 'The Art of Japan' and 'The Book Room'.

Drop-capitals are used for the 'Foreword' and 'Remarks on the Greater Movements in English Art'.

Apparently excluded from the *English Catalogue of Books*, it is assumed that the catalogue was published before the exhibition opened in May 1902 (see Babington Smith, p.69)

Masefield's contribution is attributed to him by both Williams and Simmons. Masefield claims authorship within Georges Schreiber, *Portraits and Self-Portraits* (see B330):

> ...I then had the good fortune to be appointed to organize an exhibition of English art. The catalogue to this exhibition contains the first of my prose to be published in book form.

The 'fourth edition' was expanded and issued in a cloth binding. The price of this edition was sixpence. Second or third editions have not been examined.

Copies seen: BL (Mic.A.9562(9)) (microfilm of Bodleian copy); Bodleian (1706.e.98(17)) stamped 11 JUL 1902; Columbia University Library; NYPL (Berg Collection)

Reprinted:

[second edition]	[1902]
[third edition]	[1902]
'fourth edition'	[1902]

B5 *POEMS BY JOHN KEATS* 1903

B5(a) First English edition (1903)

POEMS [in red] | *By* | JOHN KEATS | [double rule, 64mm.] | *WITH AN INTRODUCTION* | BY LAURENCE BINYON | *AND NOTES* BY JOHN MASEFIELD | *WITH A FRONTISPIECE FROM THE LIFE* | *MASK* | [double rule, 64mm.] | LONDON | METHUEN & CO. [in red] | 36 ESSEX STREET W.C. | MDCCCCIII
(All width centred and enclosed within double ruled border: 120 × 67mm. As a result of the two double rules noted above, three rectangles are created measuring 50 × 67mm., 46 × 67mm. and 25 × 67mm. respectively from the top. None of the corners completely touches, with the exception of the upper right corner)

Bibliographies: Williams p.11, Simmons p.128

Collation: [*a*]⁸ *b*⁸ 1–24⁸ 25⁴; signatures left foot of page; 212 leaves; 148 × 95mm.; [two un-numbered pages] [i–v] vi–ix [x–xi] xii–xxix [xxx] [1–5] 6–31 [32–35] 36–47 [48–51] 52–61 [62–65] 66–78 [79–81] 82 [83] 84–209 [210–17] 218–39 [240–43] 244–61 [262–65] 266–80 [281–83] 284–300 [301–303] 304–329 [330–33] 334–77 [378–79] 380–85 [386–92]

Page contents: [-] blank (page excluded from page count, but constitutes first leaf of first gathering); [-] blank; [i] 'THE LITTLE LIBRARY' device (ornate design of letters of different sizes interweaving and enclosed within double ruled border: 26 × 33mm.); [ii] blank; [iii] title-page (with additional leaf tipped-in on the verso of which is the frontispiece: 88 × 62mm., 'Mask of Keats taken during Life.' with protective tissue); [iv] blank; [v]–ix 'CONTENTS' (individual poems listed with page references); [x] blank; [xi]-xxix 'INTRODUCTION' ('Poetry, enshrining the permanent ideals of humanity...') (signed, 'L.B.'); [xxx] blank; [1]-385 text; [386] blank; [387–90] catalogue: 'A PROSPECTUS | OF | THE LITTLE LIBRARY [in red]'; [391] 'THE ABERDEEN UNIVERSITY PRESS LIMITED'; [392] blank

Paper: wove paper

Running title: running title on verso comprises name of original volume of publication; on recto the name of the poem appears or the title of the original volume continues, pp.6–377

Binding: green cloth. On spine, in gold : 'POEMS | [point] BY [point] | IOHN | KEATS | [heart-shaped device in outline: 12 × 10mm.] | METHVEN' (the letters in 'METHVEN' are overlaid and often joined). On upper cover, in gold: four heart-shaped devices in outline (each 12 × 10mm.), one in each corner pointing inwards within blind ruled border: 152 × 91mm. Lower cover, in blind: as for upper cover. Top edge gilt (with green marker ribbon), others uncut. Binding measurements: 154 × 97mm. (covers), 154 × 23mm. (spine). End-papers: wove paper.

Also issued in leather.

Publication date: published, according to the *English Catalogue of Books*, September 1903

Price: 1s.6d. (cloth) / 2s.6d. (leather)

Masefield contents:
Masefield's notes take the form of footnotes. They are of a biographical and explanatory nature, rather than textual.

Notes:
A publishing agreement for this title between Masefield and Methuen was dated 14 March 1902 (see Archives of The Society of Authors). The agreement notes 'the Author will deliver approximately by May 15th 1902... notes for an edition of Keats' Poems for the Little Library... The sum of seven pounds ten shillings... shall be paid to the said author on the publication of the book. It is agreed that if the notes, when completed, are satisfactory a further sum shall be paid to the writer, the amount of which sum shall be left to the discretion of the publishers'.

The catalogue bound into the volume describes *Poems by John Keats* as 'in preparation'. The catalogue is undated.

Drop capitals are employed at the start of individual poems.

Some signature numbers are in a smaller type than other signature numbers.

Columbia University Library (Special Collections B825 M377 HK4) holds Masefield's copy of *The Poetical Works of John Keats* (with notes by Francis T. Palgrave), London: Macmillan and Co. Ltd, 1901 reprint. This was used to prepare the notes and contains approximately 119 notes and annotations in Masefield's hand. Not all of Masefield's annotations appear in the 'Little Library' publication, however many that are present in the 'Little Library' edition are not within the copy of Palgrave. The exhibition booklet, *The Centenary of John Masefield's Birth*, New York: Columbia University Libraries, 1978 reproduces one annotated page.

B10 CHRISTOPHER MARLOWE, *DOCTOR FAUSTUS*   1903

B10(a) First English edition (1903)

DOCTOR | FAUSTUS
(ranged upper left)

Bibliographies: Williams p.11, Simmons p.128

Collation: [A-B]⁴ [a]⁴ b-g⁴ [h-i]⁴; signatures width centred at foot of page; 44 leaves; 234 × 143mm.; [1–12] [i–v] vi–li [lii–lxviii]

Page contents: [1]-[12] blank; [i] title-page; [ii] blank; [iii] '[leaf symbol] DRAMATIS PERSONÆ.'; [iv] '[leaf symbol] HACON AND RICKETTS. | M . D . CCCCIII. | [device of the Vale Press incorporating the letters 'T', 'VP' and 'R': 156 × 73mm.]'; [v] ornate page of geometrical pattern enclosing beginning of text; vi–li text; [lii] blank; [liii] '[leaf symbol] THIS EDITION OF DOCTOR FAUSTUS | BY CHRISTOPHER MARLOWE | HAS BEEN SEEN | THROUGH THE PRESS BY | JOHN MASEFIELD. | DECORATED | BY CHARLES RICKETTS | UNDER WHOSE SUPERVISION | THE BOOK HAS BEEN PRINTED | FOR THE BENEFIT OF | THE ROMANTIC STAGE PLAYERS | BY THE BALLANTYNE PRESS. | M . D . C.C.C.C.III. | Sold by Hacon and Ricketts London | & by | John Lane New York . [symbol]'; [liv]-[lxviii] blank

Paper: laid paper (watermark of a mermaid: 99 × 83mm. and 'UNBLEACHED ARNOLD'), chain-lines 32mm. apart

Running title: none

Binding: light green cloth. On spine, in gold: '[three rules] [in blind] | DOC~ | TOR | FAU~ | STUS | C.MAR~ | LOWE | [four circles] | [four circles] | [four circles] | [three rules] [in blind] | [three rules] [in blind] | [three rules] [in blind] | [three rules] [in blind] | [three rules] [in blind] | [three rules] [in blind]'. On upper and lower covers, in blind: geometrical pattern with ear of wheat in centre: 224 × 135mm. All edges uncut. Binding measurements: 238 × 146mm. (covers), 238 × 25mm. (spine). End-papers constitute leaves of the gatherings.

Publication date: published, according to Simmons, 1903 (no month given) / not in the *English Catalogue of Books*

Price: 25s.

Masefield contents:
'seen through the press'

Notes:
Ricketts' *A Bibliography of the Books Issued by Hacon & Ricketts* (also entitled *Bibliography of The Vale Press*), Ballantyne Press, 1904 lists *Doctor Faustus* as the only work to appear in the Avon Fount Shakespeare series not by Shakespeare. The watermark in the paper represents a mermaid as is consistent throughout the series. *Doctor Faustus* is described as follows:

> THE TRAGEDY OF DOCTOR FAUSTUS. By Christopher Marlowe.
> This volume was edited by T. Sturge Moore, and printed uniform with the volumes of Shakespeare, the border used being that of the Tragedies. It was printed for the benefit of the Society of Romantic Players. Three hundred and ten copies printed. None on vellum.
>
> (C.S. Ricketts, *Bibliography of The Vale Press*, Ballantyne Press, 1904, p.xxxiv)

Thomas Sturge Moore apparently edited all the Shakespeare volumes in the series, however, there is no mention of his involvement with *Doctor Faustus* in the volume itself. It is feasible that Moore edited the work although Masefield claims this work as one of his edited volumes in a listing of work sent to C.F. Cazenove in late 1906 (see University of Arizona library. MS.50).

Evidence of Masefield's association with Charles Ricketts can also be found in manuscript correspondence (BL, Add.Mss.58090–58091) and, most obviously, in the original production details for Masefield's plays *Philip the King* and *The Coming of Christ* for which Ricketts was designer.

B15 Ed. MILLICENT SUTHERLAND, *WAYFARER'S LOVE*   1904

B15(a) First English edition (1904)

WAYFARER'S LOVE [in red] | CONTRIBUTIONS FROM LIVING POETS | EDITED BY | THE DUCHESS OF SUTHERLAND. | COVER DESIGN BY MR. WALTER CRANE. | "Let me take your hand for love and sing you a song, | said the other traveller – the journey is a hard journey, but | if we hold together in the morning and in the evening, | what matter if in the hours between there is sorrow." | *Old Tale.* | *Westminster* | ARCHIBALD CONSTABLE & CO., LTD. [in red] | 1904
(All width centred except quotation which is justified on both margins with the exception of the last line which is justified on left margin and the source which is justified on the right)

Bibliographies: Williams [unrecorded], Simmons [noted on p.25]

Collation: [A]⁹ ([A]3+1) [B-D]⁸ [E]⁹ ([E]7+1); 42 leaves; 216 × 170mm.; [1–8] 9–11 [12] 13–78 [79–80]

Page contents: [1–2] blank; [3] half-title: 'WAYFARER'S LOVE.'; [4] '*Hanley* | THE CRIPPLES' GUILD | WILSON STREET'; [5] title-page; [6] 'DEDICATION.' ('To the Wayfarers–to the laurel crowned, singing at…' (unsigned); [7–8] 'CONTENTS' (45 entries listed with author and page references); 9–11 'INTRODUCTION.' ('The Potteries And Newcastle Cripples' Guild was founded…') (signed, 'MILLICENT SUTHERLAND, | *President,* | *Potteries and Newcastle Cripples' Guild.*'); [12] blank; 13–78 text; [79–80] blank

Paper: laid paper (no watermark), chain-lines 25mm. apart (chain-lines run horizontally throughout the volume)

Running title: running titles, when used, comprise title of poem, pp.14–76

Binding: green cloth. On spine, in gold: 'W | A | Y | F | A | R | E | R | S | [two points] | L | O | V | E' (all width centred). On upper cover, in gold: Walter Crane design of female with staff talking to man with lute. Both are on a road that trails off to the horizon. There is also a tree. In lower left corner of illustration a crippled winged figure looks on. The illustration is initialled in lower left corner. Two blocks of text are printed within scrolls. The first in upper left corner reads: 'WAYFARER'S | [flower] LOVE: [flower] | Poems: Edited by | The Duchess of | Sutherland.' The second block forms the base of the illustration and reads: 'Printed by the Potteries & Newcastle | Cripples Guild & published on behalf | of the Guild by Archibald Constable & | CO [there are two points under the final 'O']'. Lower cover: blank. Top edge trimmed, others uncut. Binding measurements: 224 × 175mm. (covers), 224 × 20mm. (spine). The binding includes bevelled edges. End-papers constitute A1 and E8 laid down inside the covers with additional leaves (of the same paper as the rest of the volume) tipped-in on A3 and E7 to create free end-papers.

Publication date: published, according to the *English Catalogue of Books*, October 1904

Price: 6s.

Masefield contents:
Being Her Friend ('Being her friend, I do not care, not I,')
    (signed, 'John Masefield')

Notes:
Masefield's poem appears on p.35. This is the first appearance of the poem in print.

There are forty-five entries, without sections.

In a letter to the Duchess of Sutherland in September 1903, W.B. Yeats refers to Masefield and also this anthology. (See ed. Kelly and Schuchard, *The Collected Letters of W.B. Yeats Vol.III*, Oxford University Press, 1994, p.421).

Copies seen: BL (11649.f.38) stamped 25 OCT 1904

B20 *Ed.* JANET E. ASHBEE, *THE ESSEX HOUSE SONG BOOK*   1905

B20(a) *First English edition (1905)*

THE ESSEX HOUSE SONG | BOOK, BEING THE COLLEC~ | TION OF SONGS FORMED | FOR THE SINGERS OF THE | GUILD OF HANDICRAFT BY | C.R. AND JANET E. ASHBEE, | AND EDITED BY HER.
(Lines 1–6 justified on both margins, line 7 justified on left margin only)

Bibliographies: Williams [unrecorded], Simmons p.128

Collation: given the unbound state of this book in single folio sheets, the volume is as follows: the preliminaries comprise 1 quarto gathering (4 leaves), part one comprises 10 folio sheets (20 leaves), part two comprises 6 folio sheets (12 leaves), part three comprises 11 folio sheets (22 leaves), part four comprises 8 folio sheets (16 leaves), part five comprises 13 folio sheets (26 leaves), part six comprises 7 folio sheets (14 leaves), part seven comprises 5 folio sheets (10 leaves), part eight comprises 6 folio sheets (12 leaves), part nine comprises 19 folio sheets (38 leaves), part ten comprises 15 folio sheets (30 leaves) and the indexes comprise 3 quarto gatherings (12 leaves); 216 leaves; 228 × 174–78mm.; [i–ii] iii–vii [viii] [I.-1] I.-2 – I.-40 [II.-1] II.-2 – II.-24 [III.-1] III.-2 – III.-44 [IV.-1] IV.-2 – IV.-32 [V.-1] V.-2 – V.-52 [VI.-1] VI.-2 – VI.-28 [VII.-1] VII.-2 – VII.-20 [VIII.-1] VIII.-2 – VIII.-24 [IX.-1] IX.-2 – IX.-76 [X.-1] X.-2 – X.-60 [i] ii–xxiii [xxiv]

Page contents: [i] title-page; [ii] blank; iii–vi 'PREFACE.' ('In presenting to the public our completed Song Book…') (signed, 'JANET E. ASHBEE'); vii 'THE ESSEX HOUSE SONG BOOK. | [10 sections comprising contents listing]'; [viii] blank; [I.-1] 'BEGINNETH THE | FIRST PART OF | THE SONG BOOK | OF THE GUILD OF | HANDICRAFT [device] | SONGS OF PRAISE [this line only in red]' (justified on both margins, with two angels on either side); I.-2 – I.-40 music and text of 'Songs of Praise'; [II.-1] 'SONGS OF THE SEA, [three leaf designs] [this line only in red] | BEING PART THE | SECOND OF THE | SONG BOOK OF | THE GUILD OF | HANDICRAFT.' (justified on both margins, with the exception of the last line which is justified on left margin only. The 'B' of 'BEING' is a large decorated drop-capital including a marine design); II.-2 – II.-24 music and text of 'Songs of the Sea'; [III.-1] 'THE SONGS OF | LOYALTY AND | THE LOVE OF | THE LAND, [two leaf designs] [these lines in red] | BEING THE THIRD PART | OF THE SONG BOOK OF | THE GUILD OF HANDI~ | CRAFT.' (justified on both margins, with the exception of the last line which is justified on left margin only. The 'T' of 'THE' is a large decorated drop-capital in black showing two boys playing musical instruments); III.-2 – III.-44 music and text of 'Songs of Loyalty and the Love of the Land'; [IV.-1] 'ROUNDS [in red] | [design of boy with ten circles] | AND [in red] | CATCHES [in red] | BEING THE FOURTH PART OF | THE SONG BOOK ᴼF THE GUILD | OF HANDICRAFT.'; IV.-2 – IV.-32 music and text of 'Rounds and Catches'; [V.-1] 'THE FIFTH PART | OF THE SONG | BOOK OF THE | GUILD ᴼF HAN~ | DICRAFT, BEING SONGS [last word only in red] | OF THE COUNTRY, & THE [in red] | TILLING OF THE SOIL. [in red]' (the first 'T' is a large decorated drop-capital showing Christ as a shepherd); V.-2 – V.-52 music and text of 'Songs of the Country, & The Tilling of the Soil'; [VI.-1] 'HERE BEGINS THE | SIXTH PART OF | THE SᴼNG BᴼᴼK | OF THE GUILD | OF HANDICRAFT [leaf design] BEING | THE SONGS OF SPORT. [this line only in red]' (the first 'H' is a large decorated drop-capital showing a lute player); VI.-2 – VI.28 music and text of 'The Songs of Sport'; [VII.-1] 'PART SEVEN OF | THE SONG BOOK | OF THE GUILD | OF HANDICRAFT | BEING THE SONGS OF THE [last three words in red] | TAVERN AND THE VINE. [this line only in red]' (the first 'P' is a large decorated drop-capital showing two musicians); VII.-2 – VII.-20 music and text of 'Songs of the Tavern and Vine'; [VIII.-1] 'WORKSHOP SᴼNGS [in red] | OR SONGS OF THE [in red] | CRAFTS, BEING [the first word and comma only in red] | THE EIGHTH | PART OF THE SONG BOOK | OF THE GUILD OF HANDI~ | CRAFT.' (the first 'W' is a large decorated drop- capital in black showing a man in woods); VIII.-2 – VIII.-24 music and text of 'Workshop Songs or Songs of the Crafts'; [IX.-1] 'SONGS OF COM~ [in red] | RADESHIP, LᴼVE, [in red] | & COURTSHIP, [in red] | BEING THE | NINTH PART OF THE SONG | BOOK OF THE GUILD OF | HANDICRAFT.' (the first 'S' is a large decorated drop-capital in black showing two musicians); IX.-2 – IX.-76 music and text of 'Songs of Comradeship, Love and Courtship'; [X.-1] 'MISCELLANY OF [in red] | SONG, IN WHICH [in red] | ARE INCLUDED [in red] | SONGS OF THE [in red] | UNIVERSITIES AND SONGS [in red] | OF PURE NONSENSE, BE- [first three words and comma only in red] | ING THE TENTH PART OF | THE SONG BOOK OF THE | GUILD OF HANDICRAFT.' (the first 'M' is a large decorated drop-capital in black showing a regal figure); X.-2 – X.-60 music and text of 'Songs of the Universities...'; [i] 'INDEX OF THE ESSEX HOUSE SONG BOOK.' ii-xiii 'INDEX OF TITLES.'; xiv–xix 'INDEX TO FIRST LINES.'; xx 'ROUNDS AND CATCHES.'; xxi-[xxiv] 'INDEX OF AUTHORS AND COMPOSERS.' (at foot of p.[xxiv]: 'HERE ENDS THE ESSEX HOUSE SONG BOOK, | MADE FOR THE SINGERS OF THE GUILD OF | HANDICRAFT BY C.R. AND JANET E. ASHBEE | AND EDITED BY HER, THE MUSIC DRAWN BY | PAUL WOODROFFE, AND THE WHOLE PRINTED | AT THE ESSEX HOUSE PRESS, CAMPDEN, GLOS. | MDCCCCIII TO MDCCCCV. | Published by the Essex House Press, 16 Brook Street, Bond | Street, London, W. | 200 paper copies and 5 on vellum. This is No.'

Paper: laid paper (no watermark), chain-lines 31mm. apart

Running title: none

Binding: issued loose

Publication date: published, according to Simmons, 1903–1905

Price: 10s. (see notes)

Masefield contents:
London Town ('Oh London Town's a fine town, & London sights are rare,)
    (signed, 'Words by John Masefield')
Honest Dover's Fancy ('Campden town | Is quiet after London riot;')
    (signed, 'Words by John Masefield')

Notes:
Included in the preface is Janet Ashbee's statement:

> I am fortunate in having had specially written for me songs by Messrs. Laurence Housman, John Masefield, Gerald Bishop, and C.R. Ashbee...

The Masefield verses occur in part five:

> V.-14 – V.-15 LONDON TOWN.
>   Words by John Masefield. Air: "London is a fine town." 1665.
>   The verses are printed in alternate black, then red ink thus printing 'London' verses in black and 'country' verses in red.
> V.-41 HONEST DOVER'S FANCY.
>   Words by John Masefield. 1904. Air: "Greenwich Park." 1698.

A Bibliography of The Essex House Press with Notes on the Designs, Blocks, Cuts, Bindings, etc., from the Year 1898 to 1904., Essex House Press, 1904 lists *The Essex House Song Book* on page 22 with the following description:

> A collection of some 200 representative songs of England, together with their music, from the Middle Ages to our own day. Edited by Janet E. Ashbee. The book is printed in 'Endeavour' type, black & red, and issued in separate sheets at 1s. a sheet. The various sheets of songs are classified in separate green linen portfolios...

If each folio sheet were sold seperately, incomplete songs would be available. It is assumed, therefore, that each part in a portfolio was sold complete at 1s.

Copies seen: BL (K.10.a.38) un-numbered copy, bound and stamped 1 JUN 1905; BL (F.1199.p) copy number 80, unbound parts, and stamped 15 OCT 1960

B25 JOHN HAMILTON REYNOLDS, *THE FANCY* 1905

B25(a) First English edition (1905)

THE FANCY | BY | JOHN HAMILTON REYNOLDS | [rule, 81mm.] [in red] | *With a Prefatory Memoir | and Notes | by | * JOHN MASEFIELD | *And Thirteen Illustrations | by | * JACK B. YEATS | [rule, 81mm.] [in red] | ELKIN MATHEWS | VIGO STREET [point] LONDON | W
(All width centred and enclosed within red ruled border: 128 × 82mm. As a result of the two rules noted above, three rectangles are created measuring 36 × 82mm., 65 × 82mm. and 29 × 82mm. respectively from the top. Six lines in total appear although none completely touches with the exception of the lower left corner.)

Bibliographies: Williams p.11, Simmons p.129

Collation: [1]⁹ ([1]2 + 1) 2–8⁸ [9]⁸; signatures right foot of page; 72 leaves; 173 × 108mm.; [1–7 (excluding two un-numbered pages comprising tipped in title-page)] 8–29 [30] [i–iij] iv–xxij [xxiij–xxiv] [1] 2–7 [8–11] 12–20 [21] 22–40 [41–42] 43–44 [45] 46–81 [82] 83–85 [86] 87–88 [89–90]

Page contents: [1] half-title: 'The Fancy'; [2] blank; [-] title-page; [-] blank; [3] 'Contents.' (16 entries listed with page references); [4] blank; [5] 'List of Illustrations.' (13 entries listed with page references); [6] blank; [7]-28 'Introduction.' ('John Hamilton Reynolds was born at Shrewsbury, in the year 1796.') (signed, 'JOHN MASEFIELD.'); 29 'Note' ('For the information contained in this introduction I am indebted to the following…') (signed, 'JOHN MASEFIELD.'); [30] frontispiece: 100 × 76mm. of Peter Corcoran, signed 'JACK B YEATS'; [i] facsimile of 1820 title-page; [ij] blank; [iiij]-xxij 'Preface.' (unsigned); [xxiij]-85 text; [86] blank; 87–88 'Glossary.'; [89]-[90] blank

Paper: laid paper (no watermark), chain-lines 25mm. apart

Running title: 'THE FANCY' (19mm.) on verso; on recto the sectional title appears, pp.8–88

Binding: light purple wrappers. On spine, in dark blue reading lengthways up spine, from foot: 'THE FANCY'. On upper wrapper, in dark blue: title-page reproduced retaining exact measurements, above which is '*THE SATCHEL SERIES*' and below which is '*ONE SHILLING NET*'. On lower wrapper, in dark blue: 'FROM ELKIN MATHEWS' LIST | [double rule] | [six volumes listed] | [rule] | London: ELKIN MATHEWS, Vigo St, W.' On inside upper wrapper: 'The Satchel Series | *F'cap 8vo, wrapper, 1s. net; cloth, 1s.6d. | net each volume.* | [five volumes listed] | [three stars] *Other volumes in preparation.*'. On inside lower wrapper: 'FROM ELKIN MATHEWS' LIST | [double rule] | [six volumes listed] | [rule] | London: ELKIN MATHEWS, Vigo St, W.' All edges trimmed. Binding measurements: 162 × 105mm. (wrappers) 162 × 13mm. (spine).

Also issued bound in light purple cloth. On spine, in white reading lengthways up spine, from foot: 'THE FANCY'; horizontally at the foot of spine: 'ELKIN | MATHEWS'. On upper cover, in white: 'THE FANCY | JOHN HAMILTON REYNOLDS' within two double ruled borders: 161 × 96mm., 158 × 93mm., 146 × 81mm. and 143 × 78mm.) All edges untrimmed. Binding measurements: 178 × 109mm. (covers), 178 × 26mm. (spine). End-papers: laid paper (no watermark), chain-lines 26mm. apart.

Publication date: published, according to Simmons, November and December 1905

Price: 1s. (wrappers) / 1s.6d. (cloth)

Masefield contents:
'Introduction.' ('John Hamilton Reynolds was born at Shrewsbury, in the year 1796.')
    (signed, 'JOHN MASEFIELD.')
'Note' ('For the information contained in this introduction I am indebted to the following…'
    (signed, 'JOHN MASEFIELD.')

Notes:
The title-page has been tipped-in onto the second leaf of the first gathering.

The title-page on p.[i] is a typographical facsimile from the first edition of 1820. It is slightly reduced in size.

As with Mathews' edition of *A Mainsail Haul* (see A3(a)) signature letters are of a variable size although here (unlike *A Mainsail Haul*) no signatures occur on otherwise blank leaves.

The inclusion of a glossary would appear to be editorial.

A drop capital is used for the first letter of the 'Introduction'.

A copy of this edition held in W.B. Yeats' library in Dalkey, Ireland (*1739) is inscribed 'W.B. Yeats | from John Masefield | Dec. 4, 1905.'

The 'Sonnet on the Nonpareil' is attributed to Masefield by Simmons (p.128) upon its appearance in *A Broad Sheet* in September 1903. Simmons is clearly mistaken.

In James G. Nelson's 'Checklist of the Mathews Imprint', *The Fancy* is numbered 1905.25. It is noted as the fifth title in Mathews' Satchel Series. An account of the volume is included on page 65 of Nelson's work.

In a letter to Edmund Gosse, Masefield writes:

A long time ago you wrote a little book which never fails to delight me, partly about John Hamilton Reynolds's The Fancy. It made me buy The Fancy + also other books of Reynolds, + at last made me urge a publisher to reprint the little book, which he did. I wonder if you ever saw the reprint, with woodcuts by Yeats's brother? As you were in a sense the onlie begetter of the work you ought to have it.

(John Masefield, letter to Edmund Gosse, 27 February 1912)

(BL, Ashley A.1109*)

In a letter to Bertram Dobell, Masefield refers to his introduction as '...a rather padded, and skinny piece of writing, which has now reached galley form. There is really very little known about Reynolds, + I have such a busy life I can do but little research.' (see John Masefield, letter to Bertram Dobell, 12 October 1905) (Bodleian, MS.Dobell.c.34)

In the early 1920s A.W. Evans took over the business of Elkin Mathews and requested that Masefield's titles were transferred. Masefield presumably agreed, but sought the opportunity to establish rights over the introduction to *The Fancy*. He wrote to The Society of Authors:

I would like to get the power to reprint my introduction to *The Fancy*. Perhaps this could be arranged as a condition of transferring? I have never received a penny from the sale of the book, but the publisher kept the ms of my introduction, + this was sold at his sale for £27 odd. This should be a warning to young writers to look after their mss. I may some day like to include this introduction in a collection of miscellaneous prose, + would like to obtain the power to do this.

(John Masefield, letter to G.H. Thring, [23 August 1922])

(BL, Add.Mss.56577, f.182)

The Society of Authors, it appears, arranged this matter and wrote to Masefield on 31 August 1922 (BL, Add.Mss. 56577, f.190) stating that the author was now 'at liberty to republish the Introduction to [*The Fancy*] if you so desire'.

Copies seen: private collection (ROV) wrappers; BL (11648.df.21) cloth binding, stamped 7 DEC 1905; ULL (Special Collections) wrappers, inscribed 'With all good wishes. | from Jan Masefield'

B30   *Ed.* JOHN AND CONSTANCE MASEFIELD, *LYRISTS OF THE RESTORATION...*   1905

B30(a)   *First English edition (1905)*

LYRISTS OF | THE RESTORATION | FROM SIR EDWARD SHERBURNE | TO WILLIAM CONGREVE | Selected and Edited by | JOHN AND CONSTANCE MASEFIELD | [ornament] | LONDON | E. GRANT RICHARDS | 1905

(All width centred)

Bibliographies: Williams p.12, Simmons p.129

Collation: [a]⁸ *b*⁴A-R⁸ S⁴ T² (J not used); signatures left foot of page; 154 leaves; 125 × 80mm.; [i–iv] v–xxiv 1–281 [282–84]

Page contents: [i] half-title: 'The Chapbooks | I | LYRISTS OF | THE RESTORATION'; [ii] 'THE CHAPBOOKS | I | Lyrists of the Restoration | II | Essays Moral and Polite'; [iii] title-page; [iv] 'Edinburgh : Printed by T. and A. CONSTABLE'; v–xxiv [Introduction] ('IT is impossible to determine the actual moment of...') (unsigned); 1–278 text; 279–[82] 'INDEX OF AUTHORS' (at foot of p.[282]: [rule] | Printed by T. and A. CONSTABLE, Printers to His Majesty | at the Edinburgh University Press'); [283–84] blank

Paper: wove paper

Running title: running titles comprise author name, pp.2–277

Binding: parchment with four leather ties. On spine, in black or gold (see notes): 'LYRISTS | OF THE | RESTORATION | [ornament: 17 × 21mm.] | THE | CHAPBOOKS' (all width centred). Upper and lower covers blank. Top edge gilt, others untrimmed. Sewn head and foot bands. Binding measurements: 128 × 85mm. (covers), 128 × 33mm. (spine). End-papers: wove paper. With slipcase covered with paper decorated with hand-printed floral design in blue and red.

Publication date: published, according to Simmons, December 1905

Price: 3s.6d.

Masefield contents:

'Selected and Edited by John and Constance Masefield'

[Introduction] ('IT is impossible to determine the actual moment of...')

     (unsigned)

Notes:

The index of authors at the rear of the volume comprises brief biographical details and page references. No listing therefore notes the individual poems selected.

Different copies of this edition show lettering on the spine in either gold or black.

The series listing on page [ii] appears over-anticipatory since volume I appeared in December 1905 and volume II in March 1906. Letters in the Grant Richards archive indicate, however, that the first three volumes of the series were suggested in September 1905 and the first two were probably completed around the same time – Richards sent Masefield payment for the copyright of *Essays Moral and Polite* in October 1905 whilst *Lyrists...* was in press.

The Grant Richards archive records that the sum of £7.10s. was to be paid for the volume. The selection appears to have originally been too long and Masefield was instructed to omit material. On 7 November 1905, Grant Richards wrote to request a meeting 'with regard to a somewhat serious mistake that has occurred in connection with the first volume of The Chapbooks' (see Archives of Grant Richards. University of Illinois / Chadwyck-Healey microfilm, A7, f.216). The exact nature of this mistake is unknown; however, there are several curious features of the volume. Since the text of the poems commence on the first leaf of the 'A' gathering and the previous two gatherings comprise eight and four leaves it appears the volume was not set in sequential order. This might also explain the relegation of the index to the rear of the volume and the gathering, here, of two leaves.

A copy of this edition held in W.B. Yeats' library in Dalkey, Ireland (*1264) is inscribed 'W.B. Yeats | with love from | his sisters | Xmas 1906.'

Grant Richards, in *Author Hunting*, states his belief that he 'misnamed' his 'little parchment-covered series'.

The publisher's advertisements at the rear of *A Tarpaulin Muster* (A6(a)) describe 'The Chapbooks' as:

> A Collection of choice reprints, printed on rag paper and bound in parchment, with white leather ties, in case covered with Bassano paper. Price 3s.6d. net each.

The catalogue at the rear of *Multitude and Solitude* (A8(a)) describes the series as:

> Parchment gilt, in case, 3s.6d. net each.
> Lambskin gilt, 2s.6d. net each.

These descriptions, coupled with the binding of copies located in the British Library and references in the *English Catalogue of Books* suggest that the series was first issued in parchment then became available in leather during 1907. The entire series was reissued in brown cloth at a later date (probably around 1907 or 1908) with no indication of reprint information within each volume. (These may represent later and less costly bindings of remaining sheets, but this is unlikely). In 1930 *Lyrists of the Restoration...* and *Essays Moral and Polite* were reissued by the Richards press in a variety of differently coloured cloth bindings.

The heavy pressure of work for Masefield at the time may explain the collaboration between the Masefields in the editing of this volume. Constance was to assist with the next volume of the chapbooks but her name does not feature in letters from Grant Richards to John Masefield. Except for these two volumes, Masefield never mentioned collaboration with his wife again over any future publishing. Ronald Ross, however, states both Masefields assisted in proof reading his *Philosophies* in 1909 (see B100).

On 29 December 1925 Grant Richards refused an offer made by The Society of Authors on behalf of Masefield. The author had attempted to buy back the rights in the Chapbooks series. Richards wrote '...we feel that this offer is quite inadequate + must accordingly decline it' (see Grant Richards, letter to G.H. Thring, 29 December 1925) (BL, Add.Mss.56582, f.67).

Copies seen: BL (012207.hh.1/1) stamped 19 JAN 1906, black lettering on spine; ULL (Special Collections) gold lettering on spine; Bodleian (2805.f.244) stamped 14 MAR 1906, black lettering on spine, in remnants of slipcase

Reprinted:

[no reprint information] in brown cloth binding	'E. Grant Richards' issue	[1905]

'Reprinted'
    in grey cloth binding
    in green cloth binding
	'Richards Press Ltd.' issue	1930

B30(b) First American edition ([1905])

LYRISTS OF | THE RESTORATION | FROM SIR EDWARD SHERBURNE | TO WILLIAM CONGREVE | Selected and Edited by | JOHN AND CONSTANCE MASEFIELD | [ornament] | NEW YORK | FREDERICK A. STOKES COMPANY | PUBLISHERS
(All width centred)

Bibliographies: Williams [unrecorded], Simmons [unrecorded]

Collation: [*a*]⁸ (±[*a*]1 ±[*a*]2) *b*⁴A-R⁸ S⁴ T² (J not used); signatures left foot of page; 154 leaves; 125 × 80mm.; [i–iv] v–xxiv 1–281 [282–84]

Page contents: [i] half-title: 'The Chapbooks | I | LYRISTS OF | THE RESTORATION'; [ii] 'THE CHAPBOOKS | I | Lyrists of the Restoration | II | Essays Moral and Polite | III | Herrick's Poems'; [iii] title-page; [iv] 'Edinburgh : Printed by T. and A. CONSTABLE'; v–xxiv [Introduction] ('IT is impossible to determine the actual moment of...') (unsigned); 1–278 text; 279–[82] 'INDEX OF AUTHORS' (at foot of p.[282]: '[rule] | Printed by T. and A. CONSTABLE, Printers to His Majesty | at the Edinburgh University Press'); [283–84] blank

Paper: wove paper

Running title: running titles comprise author name, pp.2–277

Binding: parchment with four leather ties. On spine: 'LYRISTS | OF THE | RESTORATION | [ornament: 17 × 21mm.] | THE | CHAPBOOKS' (all width centred). Upper and lower covers blank. Top edge gilt, others untrimmed. Sewn head and foot bands (in white). Binding measurements: 128 × 85mm. (covers), 128 × 33mm. (spine). End-papers: wove paper.

Publication date: [1905]

Price: $1.00

Masefield contents:
as for B30(a)

Notes:
This American edition uses English sheets with two cancel leaves. The first and second leaves of the first gathering are here conjugate and are inserted on the stub of the original second leaf.

In December 1925, in trying to buy back from Grant Richards a number of his titles, Masefield enquired about 'the rights of four small anthologies which my wife + I made... many years ago' (BL, Add.Mss.56582, f.48). In Richards' absence, the company replied:

> With regard to Mr. Masefield's four Anthologies, two of these are at the moment out of print owing to the quires having been lost in a fire at the binders. There are no subsidiary contracts for these books. We did however, sell bound copies of each volume to Frederick A. Stokes of New York.
>
> (Grant Richards Limited, letter to G.H. Thring, 16 December 1925)
> (BL, Add.Mss.56582, f.54)

This suggests that copies of each anthology were available in America, and that they were English printings (presumably with American cancel-titles).

Copies seen: NYPL (Berg Collection)

B35 *Ed.* JOHN *and* CONSTANCE MASEFIELD, *ESSAYS MORAL AND POLITE*   1906

B35(a) *First English edition (1906)*

ESSAYS | MORAL AND | POLITE | 1660–1714 | Selected and Edited by | JOHN AND CONSTANCE | MASEFIELD | [ornament] | LONDON | E. GRANT RICHARDS | 1906
(All width centred)

Bibliographies: Williams p.12, Simmons p.130

Collation: [π]⁸ A-Q⁸ R⁴ (J not used); signatures left foot of page; 140 leaves; 124 × 82mm.; [two un-numbered pages] [i–iv] v–xiii [xiv] 1–263 [264]

Page contents: [-] blank (page excluded from page count, but constitutes first leaf of first gathering); [-] blank; [i] 'The Chapbooks | II | ESSAYS | MORAL AND POLITE'; [ii] 'THE CHAPBOOKS | I | Lyrists of the Restoration | II | Essays Moral and Polite | III | The Lyrics of | Beaumont and Fletcher, | and of Ben Jonson | IV | The Poems of | Robert Herrick | 3s. 6d. each net.'; [iii] title-page; [iv] 'Edinburgh : Printed by T. and A. CONSTABLE'; v–xiii [Introduction] ('Roughly speaking, the authors included in this volume flourished between the Restoration and the death of Queen Anne.') (signed, 'J. and C. M.'); [xiv] blank; 1–263 text; [264] 'INDEX OF AUTHORS' (at foot of p.[264]: '[rule] | Printed by T. and A. CONSTABLE, Printers to His Majesty, | at the Edinburgh University Press.')

Paper: wove paper

Running title: running titles comprise author name, pp.2–263

Binding: parchment with four leather ties. On spine, in gold: 'ESSAYS | MORAL | AND | POLITE | [ornament: 17 × 21mm.] | THE | CHAPBOOKS' (all width centred). Upper and lower covers blank. Top edge gilt, others untrimmed. Sewn head and foot bands. Binding measurements: 127 × 89mm. (covers), 127 × 37mm. (spine). End-papers: wove paper. With slipcase covered with paper decorated with hand-printed floral design in blue and red.

Publication date: published, according to Simmons, March 1906

Price: 3s.6d.

Masefield contents:
'Selected and Edited by John and Constance Masefield'

[Introduction] ('Roughly speaking, the authors included in this volume flourished between the Restoration and...')
        (signed, 'J. and C. M.')

Notes:
The index of authors at the rear of the volume comprises brief biographical details and page references. No listing therefore notes the individual essays selected. Although the index lists Steele separately with a specific page reference (p.194), the text of the volume does not so section him off from Addison.

A cheque for the copyright of this volume was sent to Masefield on 16 October 1905. He received seven pounds and ten shillings.

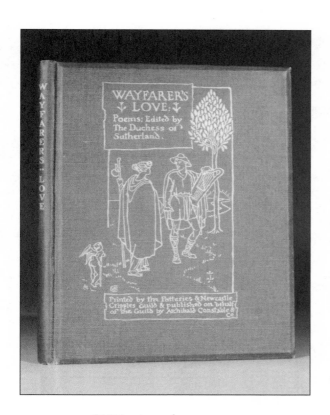

B15(a) spine and upper cover

THE FANCY

BY

JOHN HAMILTON REYNOLDS

*With a Prefatory Memoir
and Notes
by*
JOHN MASEFIELD

*And Thirteen Illustrations
by*
JACK B. YEATS

ELKIN MATHEWS
VIGO STREET · LONDON
W

B25(a) title-page

LYRISTS OF
THE RESTORATION

FROM SIR EDWARD SHERBURNE
TO WILLIAM CONGREVE

Selected and Edited by
JOHN AND CONSTANCE MASEFIELD

LONDON
E. GRANT RICHARDS
1905

B30(a) title-page

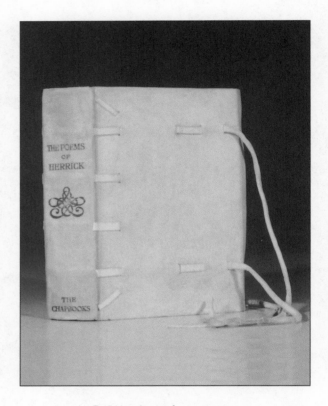

B45(a) spine and upper cover

584

Richards was unsure of Constance's assistance on the volume for he wrote to Masefield in January 1906:

> By the way, I think I am right in saying that they [the printers] have made a mistake in adding "and C." to the signature of the Introduction to the second volume [of the Chapbooks].
>
> (Grant Richards, letter to John Masefield, 22 January 1906)
> (Archives of Grant Richards. University of Illinois / Chadwyck-Healey microfilm, A7, f.576)

Copies seen: BL (012207.hh.1/2) stamped 8 MAR 1906; ULL (Special Collections)

Reprinted:

[no reprint information]	'E. Grant Richards' issue	[1906]
in brown cloth binding		
'Reprinted'	'Richards Press Ltd.' issue	1930
in grey cloth binding		
in red cloth binding		

B35(b) First American edition ([1906])

ESSAYS | MORAL AND | POLITE | 1660–1714 | Selected and Edited by | JOHN AND CONSTANCE | MASEFIELD | [ornament] | NEW YORK | FREDERICK A. STOKES COMPANY | PUBLISHERS
(All width centred)

Bibliographies: Williams [unrecorded], Simmons [unrecorded]

Collation: [π]⁸ (±[π]2 ±[π]3) A–Q⁸ R⁴ (J not used). Signatures left foot of page. 140 leaves; 124 × 82mm.; [two un-numbered pages] [i–iv] v–xiii [xiv] 1–263 [264]

Page contents: [-] blank (page excluded from page count, but constitutes first leaf of first gathering); [-] blank; [i] 'The Chapbooks | II | ESSAYS | MORAL AND POLITE'; [ii] 'THE CHAPBOOKS | I | Lyrists of the Restoration | II | Essays Moral and Polite | III | Herrick's Poems'; [iii] title-page; [iv] 'Edinburgh : Printed by T. and A. CONSTABLE'; v–xiii [Introduction] ('Roughly speaking, the authors included in this volume flourished between the Restoration and the death of Queen Anne.') (signed, 'J. and C. M.'); [xiv] blank; 1–263 text; [264] 'INDEX OF AUTHORS' (at foot of p.[264]: '[rule] | Printed by T. and A. CONSTABLE, Printers to His Majesty, | at the Edinburgh University Press.')

Paper: wove paper

Running title: running titles comprise author name, pp.2–263

Binding: parchment with four leather ties. On spine: 'ESSAYS | MORAL | AND | POLITE | [ornament: 17 × 21mm.] | THE | CHAPBOOKS' (all width centred). Upper and lower covers blank. Top edge gilt, others untrimmed. Sewn head and foot bands (in white). Binding measurements: 127 × 89mm. (covers), 127 × 37mm. (spine). End-papers: wove paper.

Publication date: [1906]

Price: $1.00

Masefield contents:
as for B35(a)

Notes:
This American edition uses English sheets with two cancel leaves. The second and third leaves of the first gathering are here conjugate and are inserted on the stub of the original third leaf.

Copies seen: NYPL (Berg Collection)

B40 Ed. JOHN MASEFIELD, *A SAILOR'S GARLAND*   1906

B40(a) First English edition (1906)

A SAILOR'S GARLAND | SELECTED AND EDITED | BY | JOHN MASEFIELD | METHUEN & CO. | 36 ESSEX STREET W.C. | LONDON
(All width centred)

Bibliographies: Williams p.11, Simmons p.130

Collation: [π]⁸ b⁸ 1–20⁸ 21⁴; signatures left foot of page; 180 leaves; 190 × 124mm.; the catalogue (not included in collation or leaf count) comprises a single gathering of 20 leaves of which the fifth and ninth leaves are also signed; [i–vi] vii–xxxi [xxxii] [1] 2 [3] 4–328; catalogue pagination: [1–2] 3–40

Page contents: [i] half-title: 'A SAILOR'S GARLAND'; [ii] 'BY THE SAME AUTHOR | SEA LIFE IN NELSON'S TIME | ON THE SPANISH MAIN'; [iii] title-page; [iv] '*First Published in 1906*'; [v] 'To C.'; [vi] blank; vii–xx 'INTRODUCTORY' ('It is curious that a sea-going people such as the English...') (signed 'JOHN MASEFIELD.'); xxi 'OMISSIONS | I REGRET extremely that I have been unable to include | any poem by Mr. Swinburne. The reasons which forbid | that inclusion also force me to omit the two splendid | poems, "The Revenge, a Ballad of the Fleet," and the | "Voyage of Maeldune," by Alfred Lord Tennyson. | Another lamentable, but unfortunately necessary, omis- | sion is that of any poem by Mr. A. F. Brady, an Australian | poet, whose "Ways of Many Waters" contain the best | poems yet written about the merchant sailor and the | man-of-war's man. | [new paragraph] If in the preparation of this book I have omitted any | noble poem, through my own negligence or ignorance, I | am sorry; but | "Fortune it will take its place, let a man do all he can." | I have done what I could, with the means at my disposal. | A prose "Sailor's Garland" is now in preparation, as a | complementary volume to the present collection.'; xxii 'NOTE' ('I wish to thank the following poets and publishers for their kindness...'); xxiii–xxx 'TABLE OF CONTENTS' (seven sections listed with individual poems and page references); xxxi 'INDEX OF AUTHORS' (51 authors noted with page references); [xxxii] blank; [1]-328 text (at foot of p.328: '*Printed by* MORRISON & GIBB LIMITED, *Edinburgh*'); [1]-40 catalogue: 'A CATALOGUE OF BOOKS | PUBLISHED BY METHUEN | AND COMPANY : LONDON | 36 ESSEX STREET | W.C. | CONTENTS | [36 sections listed in two columns] | AUGUST 1906'

Paper: wove paper (catalogue: wove paper)

Running title: 'A SAILOR'S GARLAND' (43mm.) on verso; recto title comprises poem title, pp.2–328

Binding: dark-blue cloth. On spine, in gold: '[rule] [in blind] | A SAILOR'S | GARLAND | ARRANGED | BY | JOHN MASEFIELD | [device: 84 × 33mm. of anchor and rope design] | METHUEN | [blind rule]', lettering before design justified on left margin; design and publisher width centred (see notes). Upper and lower covers have blind ruled borders: 194 × 121mm. Top edge stained, fore edge trimmed. Binding measurements: 198 × 126mm. (covers), 198 × 50mm. (spine). End-papers: wove paper.

Publication date: published, according to Simmons, October 1906

Price: 3s.6d.

Masefield contents:
'selected and edited by John Masefield'

'Introductory' ('It is curious that a sea-going people such as the English...')
    (signed, 'JOHN MASEFIELD.')
'Omissions' ('I regret extremely that I have been unable to include any...')
    (unsigned)
'Note' ('I wish to thank the following poets and publishers for their kindness...')
    (unsigned)

Notes:
After an introductory poem, 'Old Sailors' (adapted), the book is structured as follows: 'Miscellaneous Poems', 'Poems illustrating our Sea History', 'Poems of Sailors and of Life at Sea', 'The Story of Jonah. Poems of Mermaids and of the Sea Spirits', 'Poems of Love and the Affections', Poems of Pirates and Smugglers' and 'Chanties'.

'Omissions' (on p.xxi) states 'a prose "Sailor's Garland" is now in preparation, as a complementary volume to the present collection.' This volume never appeared.

The opening of the 'Chanties' section commences with what is credited as the 'Editor's Note' in the index. It is derived from Masefield's article, 'Chanties' from the *Manchester Guardian* on 16 August 1905 (see C055.080) and is acknowledged as such in the 'Note' on p.xxii.

A copy of this edition present in the HRHRC omits the anchor and rope design on the spine.

Proofs for this edition are located in the Bodleian (Additional Masefield Papers, Box 9). There are minor corrections to the text in Masefield's hand. A comparison with the first edition reveals a number of retitled poems and one completely replaced. Each gathering is stamped by the firm of Morrison and Gibb and dated between 15 June and 3 July 1906.

A publishing agreement for this title between Masefield and Methuen was dated 20 October 1905 (see Archives of The Society of Authors). The agreement refers to 'a book of sea poems'. Masefield, writing to The Society of Authors in April 1927, notes that '*A Sailor's Garland* is an anthology which I sold outright in my youth to Messrs Methuen.' (see BL, Add.Mss.56584, f.148)

Writing to Jack B. Yeats in August 1911 Masefield refers to this volume, providing details of attribution:

> About your enquiries: I may as well confess (though this must be private) that the Sailor's Garland book is full of traps. A gang of ruffians used to take the anthologies collected by other men's labour + sort them up differently + print them as their own; so in order to catch out some of these devils I put in a few stanzas of my own here + there; + although the anthology makers smelt the hook + kept off, I did catch beautifully a certain naval archaeologist, firstly in theft from the Garland + secondly in a lie, he saying that his work was done before mine appeared. He was "one of the Bulldog Breed that myde ol' England's nyme".

> 'The Jolly Collier' is from an old pedlar's pack of about 1800, the stanza about the mainsail etc is by me, the rest is old.

> 'The Press Gang' is all old. 'The Salcombe Seamen' is by me, but the refrain is old. 'Polly dear' is I fancy from the same pack as 'The Jolly Collier'; it is all old; 'The Whale' was in the same old pack, + I have only restored some quite unintelligible lines. 'The Whale' is the best thing in the whole book, I think: I have never seen it elsewhere but many years ago as a child something like it was in an old copy of Punch.

> > (John Masefield, letter to Jack B. Yeats, 4 August 1911)
> > (National Gallery of Ireland. Y Archive. L.Mas.11)

This was information that Masefield forgot over a twenty year period. The Society of Authors received a request from a Miss Dorothy V. Searle to anthologize 'The Salcombe Sailor's Flaunt'. The Society of Authors wrote to Masefield asking about the poem and the author replied:

> I forget about the Salcombe Sailor's Flaunt, whether I wrote it, adapted it, or borrowed it. She had better ask Messrs Methuen, who own the book.
>
> (John Masefield, letter to Denys Kilham Roberts, [13 March 1931])
> (BL, Add.Mss.56593, f.49)

'The Salcombe Seamen' and 'The Salcombe Sailor's Flaunt' are both incorrect citations for 'The Salcombe Seaman's Flaunt to the Proud Pirate' appearing on pp.293–94 of the anthology. This poem was therefore by Masefield with an old refrain, a fact forgotten in 1931.

A copy of this edition held in W.B. Yeats' library in Dalkey, Ireland (*1263) is inscribed 'for W B Yeats. | from John Masefield. | Oct. 10, 1906.'

Presenting a copy of this edition to Lady Gregory, Masefield wrote:

> Will you accept from me this book of sea-ballads + poems (mostly pretty bad ones) which the ruling of Britannia has caused Britons to perpetrate. I am afraid my readers, when they put the book down, will say with the Distressed Sailor (p 169):
>
> If I had known as much before
> I would have cried 'Sweep, Chimney Sweep'
> Before I had gone upon the sea.
>
> Still, it contains one or two good poems, + if these give you pleasure I shall be consoled for the badness of the rest.
>
> (John Masefield, letter to Lady Gregory, 10 October 1906)
> (NYPL (Berg Collection)

Copies seen: private collection (PWE); BL (11604.dd.4) stamped 13 OCT 1906, rebound; ULL (Special Collections) inscribed 'for Ethel. [Ross] | Oct 15. 1906 | With all good wishes.'; ULL (Special Collections); NYPL (Berg Collection) inscribed 'for Lady Gregory. | from John Masefield.'; HRHRC (AC-L M377 D6 1906) lacking anchor and rope design on spine

Reprinted:

'Second Edition'	[first edition, second impression]	1908

B40(b) First American edition (1906)

A SAILOR'S GARLAND | SELECTED AND EDITED | BY | JOHN MASEFIELD | NEW YORK | THE MACMILLAN COMPANY | 1906
(All width centred)

Bibliographies: Williams [unrecorded], Simmons [unrecorded]

Collation: [a]⁸ b⁸ 1–20⁸ 21⁴; signatures left foot of page; 180 leaves; 190 × 127mm.; [i–vi] vii–xxxi [xxxii] [1] 2 [3] 4–328

Page contents: [i] half-title: 'A SAILOR'S GARLAND'; [ii] 'BY THE SAME AUTHOR | SEA LIFE IN NELSON'S TIME | ON THE SPANISH MAIN'; [iii] title-page; [iv] blank; [v] 'To C.'; [vi] blank; vii–xx 'INTRODUCTORY' ('It is curious that a sea-going people such as the English...') (signed 'JOHN MASEFIELD.'); xxi 'OMISSIONS | I REGRET extremely that I have been unable to include | any poem by Mr. Swinburne. The reasons which forbid | that inclusion also force me to omit the two splendid | poems, "The Revenge, a Ballad of the Fleet," and the | "Voyage of Maeldune," by Alfred Lord Tennyson. | Another lamentable, but unfortunately necessary, omis- | sion is that of any poem by Mr. A. F. Brady, an Australian | poet, whose "Ways of Many Waters" contain the best | poems yet written about the merchant sailor and the | man-of-war's man. | [new paragraph] If in the preparation of this book I have omitted any | noble poem, through my own negligence or ignorance, I | am sorry; but | "Fortune it will take its place, let a man do all he can." | I have done what I could, with the means at my disposal. | A prose "Sailor's Garland" is now in preparation, as a | complementary volume to the present collection.'; xxii 'NOTE' ('I wish to thank the following poets and publishers for their kindness...'); xxiii–xxx 'TABLE OF CONTENTS' (seven sections listed with individual poems and page references; xxxi 'INDEX OF AUTHORS' (51 authors noted with page references); [xxxii] blank; [1]-328 text (at foot of page 328: '*Printed by* MORRISON & GIBB LIMITED, *Edinburgh*')

Paper: wove paper

Running title: 'A SAILOR'S GARLAND' (43mm.) on verso; recto title comprises poem title, pp.2–328

Binding: dark-blue cloth. On spine, in gold: '[rule] | A | SAILOR'S | GARLAND | [design of rope: 7 × 20mm.] | MASEFIELD | THE MACMILLAN | COMPANY | [rule]'. On upper cover, in gold: 'A SAILOR'S | GARLAND | [rule of rope] | [illustration of ship at sea: 51 × 43mm.] | [rule of rope] | MASEFIELD' (all enclosed within single border of rope: 85 × 47mm. with rounded corners and ranged upper right) (all within blind ruled border: 192 × 124mm.) Lower cover: blind ruled border: 192 × 124mm. Top edge gilt, others uncut. Binding measurements: 197 × 130mm. (covers), 197 × 38mm. (spine). End-papers: wove paper.

Publication date: presumably published after October 1906

Price: unknown

Masefield contents:
as for B40(a)

Notes:
This American edition has obvious similarities to B40(a). However, unlike similar examples of American editions, the title-page in this edition is not a cancellans.

In 'Some Contributions to the Bibliography of John Masefield: II' (*Papers of the Bibliographical Society of America*, October 1959, pp.262–67) Drew notes '*A Sailor's Garland* was also published by the Macmillan Co., N.Y., in 1906.'

Copies seen: NYPL (Berg Collection); HRHRC (AC-L M377 D6 1906A)

B40(c) Second English edition (1918)

A 'second edition' (thought to comprise a new setting of the text) was published in June 1918. No copies have been consulted. Subsequent 'editions' are presumed to be new impressions of the second edition.

Reprinted:

'Third Edition'	[second edition, second impression]	Mar 1924
'Fourth Edition'	[second edition, third impression]	Feb 1927
'Fifth Edition'	[second edition, fourth impression]	Aug 1927
'Sixth Edition'	[second edition, fifth impression]	Jun 1931
'Seventh Edition'	[second edition, sixth impression]	1942

A copy describing itself as a 'Seventh Edition' fails to note the first edition, second impression in 1908.

An undated impression of the second edition was also issued by the Library Press Ltd as a volume in 'The Minerva Edition' with the first two leaves comprising cancellans.

B40(d) Second American edition (1924)

A | SAILOR'S GARLAND | SELECTED AND EDITED | BY | JOHN MASEFIELD | NEW EDITION | NEW YORK | THE MACMILLAN COMPANY | 1924
(All width centred)

Bibliographies: Williams [unrecorded], Simmons [unrecorded]

Collation: [A]^{10} [B]^8 1–23^8 24^2; signatures left foot of page; 204 leaves; 169 × 106mm.; [i–vi] vii–xxv [xxvi] xxvii–xxxiii [xxxiv] xxxv [xxxvi] 1–372

Page contents: [i] half-title: 'A SAILOR'S GARLAND'; [ii] blank; [iii] title-page; [iv] 'PRINTED IN GREAT BRITAIN'; [v] 'TO C.'; [vi] blank; vii–xxii 'INTRODUCTORY' ('It is curious that a sea-going people such as the English...') (signed 'JOHN MASEFIELD'); xxiii 'OMISSIONS | I REGRET extremely that I have been unable to | include any poem by Mr. Swinburne. The | reasons which forbid that inclusion also force me | to omit the two splendid poems, "The Revenge, | a Ballad of the Fleet," and the "Voyage of | Maeldune," by Alfred Lord Tennyson. Another | lamentable, but unfortunately necessary, omission | is that of any poem by Mr. A. F. Brady, an | Australian poet, whose "Ways of Many Waters" | contain the best poems yet written about the | merchant sailor and the man-of-war's man. | [new paragraph] If in the preparation of this book I have omitted | any noble poem, through my own negligence or | ignorance, I am sorry; but | Fortune it will take its place, let a man do all he can.'; xxiv–xxv 'NOTE' ('I wish to thank the following poets and publishers for their kindness...'); [xxvi] blank; xxvii–xxxiii 'TABLE OF CONTENTS' (seven sections listed with individual poems and page references); [xxxiv] blank; xxxv 'INDEX OF AUTHORS' (52 authors noted with page references); [xxxvi] blank; 1–372 text (at foot of page 372: '[rule] | *Printed by Jarold & Sons, ltd., Norwich*')

Paper: wove paper

Running title: 'A SAILOR'S GARLAND' (39mm.) on verso; recto title comprises poem title, pp.2–372

Binding: light blue cloth. On spine, in gold: '[triple rule (with the rule at the head being thickest)] | A | SAILOR'S | GARLAND | [rule] | SELECTED | AND EDITED BY | JOHN | MASEFIELD | MACMILLAN | [square point] [square point] [square point] [square point] | [triple rule (with the rule at the foot being thickest)]' (all width centred). On upper cover, in blind: triple rule at head (with the rule at the head being thickest) and triple rule at foot (with the rule at the foot being thickest). Lower cover: blank. All edges trimmed. Binding measurements: 175 × 105mm. (covers), 175 × 37mm. (spine). End-papers: wove paper.

Publication date: 1924

Price: $2.50

Masefield contents:
as for B40(c)

Notes:
Gathering '24' comprises two conjugate leaves. They are tipped-in onto the eighth leaf of gathering '23'.

Copies seen: Harvard College Library (Widener 23697.10.405)

Reprinted:

[second edition, later impression] 1928

B45 *Ed.* JOHN MASEFIELD, *THE POEMS OF ROBERT HERRICK* 1906

B45(a) First English edition (1906)

THE POEMS OF | ROBERT HERRICK | Edited, with a Biographical Introduction, by | JOHN MASEFIELD | [ornament] | LONDON | E. GRANT RICHARDS | 1906
(All width centred)

Bibliographies: Williams p.11, Simmons p.130

Collation: [*a*]⁸ *b*⁸ *c*¹ A-T⁸ U⁶ (J not used); U3 is also signed; signatures left foot of page; 123 × 83mm.; [i–iv] v–xxxiv 1 [2] 3–294 [295–96] 297–312 [313–16]

Page contents: [i] 'The Chapbooks | IV | THE POEMS OF | ROBERT HERRICK'; [ii] 'THE CHAPBOOKS | I | Lyrists of the Restoration | II | Essays Moral and Polite | III | The Lyrics of | Beaumont and Fletcher, | and of Ben Jonson | IV | The Poems of | Robert Herrick | 3s. 6d. each net.'; [iii] title-page; [iv] 'Edinburgh : Printed by T. and A. CONSTABLE'; v–xviii [Introduction] ('Robert, or, as he sometimes calls himself, Robin Herrick, was born...') (signed 'JOHN MASEFIELD.'); xix–xxxiv 'CONTENTS'; 1 dedication verse; [2] blank; 3–294 text; [295] 'INDEX TO FIRST LINES'; [296] blank; 297–[313] 'INDEX TO FIRST LINES' (at foot of p.[313]: '[rule] | Printed by T. and A. CONSTABLE, Printers to His Majesty | at the Edinburgh University Press'); [314–16] blank

Paper: wove paper

Running title: 'ROBERT HERRICK' (31mm.) on verso; 'HESPERIDES' (22mm.) on recto, pp.4–294

Binding: parchment with four leather ties. On spine: 'THE POEMS | OF | HERRICK | [ornament: 17 × 21mm.] | THE CHAPBOOKS' (all width centred). Upper and lower covers blank. Top edge gilt, others untrimmed. Sewn head and foot bands. Binding measurements: 126 × 90mm. (covers), 126 × 33mm. (spine). End-papers: wove paper. With slipcase covered with paper decorated with hand-printed floral design in blue and red.

Publication date: published, according to Simmons, October 1906

Price: 3s.6d.

Masefield contents:
'edited, with a Biographical Introduction'

Introduction ('Robert, or, as he sometimes calls himself, Robin Herrick, was born...')
       (signed 'JOHN MASEFIELD.')

Notes:
Poems comprise Herrick's *Hesperides*.

Richards wrote to Masefield to propose the volume in January 1906:

> For a fourth volume of the Chapbooks I want a Herrick, since that volume is urged on me by booksellers, and the sooner I can have it the better I shall be pleased.

(Grant Richards, letter to John Masefield, 6 January 1906)
(Archives of Grant Richards. University of Illinois / Chadwyck-Healey microfilm, A7, f.458)

A copy of this edition held in W.B. Yeats' library in Dalkey, Ireland (*888) is inscribed 'W.B. Yeats | from | John Masefield | Dec. 20, 1906.'

Both half-titles of the Chapbook editions of *Herrick* and *Lyrics of Ben Jonson...* state that they are the fourth volume in the series (with the series listing changing accordingly). Simmons notes Herrick is number four in the series and published in October 1906, whilst *Lyrics of Ben Jonson...* is number three and published in December 1906. These dates are confirmed by the *English Catalogue of Books* but to decide on series order by publication date will cause Simmons' numbering to change. A revised series listing (with order of publication confirmed by letters in the Grant Richards archive) would therefore be:

I. *Lyrists of the Restoration*	Dec 1905
II. *Essays Moral and Polite*	Mar 1906
III. *The Poems of Robert Herrick*	Oct 1906
IV. *Lyrics of Ben Jonson, Beaumont and Fletcher*	Dec 1906

Copies seen: private collection (PWE); BL (012207.hh.1/4) stamped 23 OCT 1906; ULL (Special Collections)

B45(b) First American edition?

Letters within the Grant Richards archive suggest that copies of all the Chapbooks were available in America (comprising English printings with American cancel-titles). No example of this title has been traced, however. The publication price may have been $1.00.

B50 *Ed.* JOHN MASEFIELD, *DAMPIER'S VOYAGES*   **1906**

B50(a) First English edition (1906)

VOLUME ONE

DAMPIER'S [in red] | VOYAGES [in red] | Consisting of a New Voyage Round the World, a | Supplement to the Voyage Round the World, | Two Voyages to Campeachy, a Discourse | of Winds, a Voyage to New Holland, | and a Vindication, in answer to | the Chimerical Relation of | William Funnell | BY | CAPTAIN WILLIAM DAMPIER | EDITED BY | JOHN MASEFIELD | IN TWO VOLUMES | I | LONDON | E. GRANT RICHARDS [in red] | 7 CARLTON STREET | 1906

(All width centred)

Bibliographies: Williams p.11, Simmons p.130

Collation: '[eight point star]'⁴ *b*² A-2P⁸ 2Q² (J, V, W, 2J not used); signatures right foot of page with 'VOL. I.' at left foot on first leaf of gatherings (with the exception of the first two gatherings); 312 leaves; 220 × 142mm.; [two un-numbered pages] [i–vi] vii [viii] ix [x] [1] 2–14 [15–16] 17–23 [24] 25–545 [546–48] 549–611 [612]

Page contents: [-] blank (except for signature) (page excluded from page count, but constitutes first leaf of first gathering); [-] blank; [i] half-title: 'THE VOYAGES | OF | CAPTAIN WILLIAM DAMPIER'; [ii] blank (with additional leaf tipped-in on the verso of which is the frontispiece: 108 × 90mm., 'Photo: W.A.Mansell & Co. | CAPTAIN WILLIAM DAMPIER, | FROM THE PICTURE BY THOMAS MURRAY | IN THE NATIONAL PORTRAIT GALLERY.' with protective tissue); [iii] title-page; [iv] 'Printed by BALLANTYNE, HANSON & CO. | At the Ballantyne Press'; [v] '*I dedicate my share in this Book* | TO | LADY GREGORY'; [vi] blank; vii 'CONTENTS OF VOL. I' (10 parts listed with titles and page references); [viii] blank; ix 'LIST OF MAPS AND | ILLUSTRATIONS' (six items listed including frontispiece with page references); [x] blank; [1]-13 'LIFE OF WILLIAM DAMPIER' ('It is not my intention to write a long life of Dampier, for my researches...') (signed, 'JOHN MASEFIELD.'); 14 'THE TEXT' ('The text used for the "New Voyage round the World,"...') (unsigned); [15] typographical facsimile of title-page of sixth edition of 'A NEW | VOYAGE | ROUND THE | WORLD.' (tipped in on this page is a map, folded four times facing p.14, not p.15 as stated in the 'LIST OF MAPS...'); [16] blank; 17–529 text (of *A New Voyage Round the World*); 530–45 'APPENDIX | DAMPIER'S ASSOCIATES') ('Edmund Cook, or Cooke | Perhaps this Edmund Cooke was the...') (unsigned); [546] blank; [547] typographical facsimile of title-page of 'VOYAGES AND DESCRIPTIONS. | VOL. II.'; [548] blank; 549–[612] text (of *Voyages and Descriptions. Vol. II*) (at foot of p.[612]: 'END OF VOL. I | Printed by BALLANTYNE, HANSON & CO. | Edinburgh & London')

Paper: wove paper

Running title: 'CAPTAIN DAMPIER'S VOYAGES' (78mm.) on verso; on recto a brief indication of text subject appears, pp.28–545 and pp.558–[612]

Binding: green cloth. On spine, in gold: 'DAMPIER'S | VOYAGES | [design of three masted ship: 32 × 29mm.] | I | GRANT[point]RICHARDS'. On upper cover, in gold: circular design of two masted ship within rope pattern surround (diameter: 47mm.) Binding measurements: 227 × 144mm. (covers), 227 × 65mm. (spine). End-papers: wove paper. Top edge gilt, others untrimmed and occasionally uncut.

Publication date: published, according to Simmons, November 1906

Price: 25s. (for both volumes)

Masefield contents:
'edited by John Masefield'

'Life of William Dampier' ('It is not my intention to write a long life of Dampier, for my researches...')
    (signed, 'JOHN MASEFIELD.')
'The Text' ('The text used for the "New Voyage round the World,"...')
    (unsigned)
'Appendix | Dampier's Associates' ('Edmund Cook, or Cooke | Perhaps this Edmund Cooke was the...')
    (unsigned)

VOLUME TWO

DAMPIER'S [in red] | VOYAGES [in red] | Consisting of a New Voyage Round the World, a | Supplement to the Voyage Round the World, | Two Voyages to Campeachy, a Discourse | of Winds, a Voyage to New Holland, | and a Vindication, in answer to | the Chimerical Relation of | William Funnell | BY | CAPTAIN WILLIAM DAMPIER | EDITED BY | JOHN MASEFIELD | IN TWO VOLUMES | II | LONDON | E. GRANT RICHARDS [in red] | 7 CARLTON STREET | 1906

(All width centred)

Bibliographies: Williams p.11, Simmons p.130

Collation: [π]⁴ A-2E⁸ [2[π]]⁷ 2F-2Q⁸ (J, V, W and 2J not used); signatures right foot of page with 'VOL. II' at left foot on first leaf of gatherings (with the exception of the first gathering); the first gathering is signed with an eight point star in lower right corner of π2; between 2E and 2F there are seven leaves of plates sewn into the binding, rather than tipped in (as with all other plates) they therefore comprise a separate gathering in which 2π7 is tipped in on 2π6; 323 leaves; 221 × 141mm.; [i–iv] v–vii [viii] [1] 2–105 [106] 107–225 [226–27] 228–335 [336] 337 [338] 339–45 [346] 347–449 [450–52] 453–55 [456] 457–573 [574] 575–605 [606] 607–23 [624]

Page contents: [i] half-title: 'THE VOYAGES | OF | CAPTAIN WILLIAM DAMPIER'; [ii] blank; [iii] title-page; [iv] 'Printed by BALLANTYNE, HANSON & CO. | At the Ballantyne Press'; v–vi 'CONTENTS OF VOL. II' (four parts listed with component chapters and page references); vii 'LIST OF MAPS AND | ILLUSTRATIONS' (15 items listed with page references); [viii] blank; [1]-324 text (concluding *Voyages and Descriptions. Vol. II*); 325–35 'LETTERS AND PAPERS RELATING TO | THE NEW HOLLAND VOYAGE'; [336] blank; 337 typographical facsimile of title-page of 'A | VOYAGE | TO | *NEW HOLLAND*, &c. | In the YEAR 1699.'; [338] blank; 339–449 text (of *A Voyage to New Holland*); [450] blank; [451] typographical facsimile of title-page of 'A | CONTINUATION | OF A | VOYAGE | TO | *NEW–HOLLAND*, &c. | In the YEAR 1699.'; [452] blank; 453–605 text (of *A Continuation of a Voyage to New Holland*); [606] blank; 607–23 'INDEX'; 623–[24] 'INDEX TO THE APPENDICES, ETC.' (at foot of p.[624]: 'Printed by BALLANTYNE, HANSON & CO. | Edinburgh & London')

Paper: wove paper

Running title: 'CAPTAIN DAMPIER'S VOYAGES' (78mm.) on verso, pp.2–224 and pp.322–604; 'A DISCOURSE OF WINDS' (64mm.) on verso, pp.228–320; on recto a brief indication of text subject appears; 'INDEX' (16mm.) on both verso and recto, pp.608–22

Binding: green cloth. On spine, in gold: 'DAMPIER'S | VOYAGES | [design of three masted ship: 32 × 29mm.] | II | GRANT[point]RICHARDS'. On upper cover, in gold: circular design of two masted ship within rope pattern surround (diameter: 47mm.) Binding measurements: 227 × 144mm. (covers), 227 × 65mm. (spine). End-papers: wove paper. Top edge gilt, others untrimmed.

Publication date: published, according to the *English Catalogue of Books*, January 1907

Price: 25s. (for both volumes)

Notes:

The Grant Richards archive reveals that Masefield had proposed an edition of Dampier by Christmas 1905. During February 1906 Richards claimed he would soon decide whether to publish and requested a meeting. Accordingly, an agreement for the edition was sent on 20 February 1906. A publishing agreement for this title between Masefield and Grant Richards was dated 21 February 1906 (see Archives of The Society of Authors). The agreement notes 'the author undertakes to prepare for the Publisher an edition of the Voyages of Dampier, such preparation to include the writing of an Introduction + Appreciation, the editing + annotation of the text and the making of an Index and the passing of the proof for press'. The date for work to be delivered to the publisher is cited as 10 May 1906.

A decision not to print 'long esses' (as described by Richards) was taken during May 1906. Masefield presumably argued for their inclusion since his fondness for this archaism was eventually adopted in his own handwriting.

The index was an issue of dispute between Richards and Masefield during November 1906. At one time Richards considered dispensing with it entirely.

With reference to the dedication, Richards wrote to Masefield during June 1906:

> By all means dedicate your work on the Dampier to Lady Gregory. Is it not, however, more in the custom to word your Dedication something in this way: "My work on these volumes to Lady Gregory. John Masefield". Let me know.
>
> (Grant Richards, letter to John Masefield, 8 June 1906)
> (Archives of Grant Richards. University of Illinois / Chadwyck-Healey microfilm, A8, f.359)

The dedication copies are located in the NYPL (Berg Collection). The first volume includes the following letter:

> Will you accept from me, with my best wishes, this volume of my edition of William Dampier?
> I had hoped to send you the complete work; but the second volume has been delayed; and so I can only send one. I hope that some little bits of him may amuse you, and that the lives of his Associates may help you to understand how hard it was for him to approach his work in the comic spirit. He is a little heavy, I'm afraid; and he lies rather heavily on my mind; and I fear that you will find him difficult to read for more than a few pages at a time. But in any case I shall be proud to think that I have been priviledged to inscribe one of my "works" with your name; and that the book may lie upon your shelf to remind you of our first meeting, now six years ago.
>
> (John Masefield, letter to Lady Gregory, 28 November 1906)
> (NYPL (Berg Collection))

The second volume includes the following:

> I now send you the long delayed second volume of William Dampier. It contains, I think, three of his four jests; besides some account of his disgrace; so that it makes more lively reading than the other volume. The cuts, too, of fishes; are done with great grace and elegance, and much majesty of proportion. I hope that the sight of them may give you pleasure; or that they may serve to reproach Breasal, when his Thursday catch fails, on some summer evening after he has promised a creel full.
>
> (John Masefield, letter to Lady Gregory, 28 January 1907)
> (NYPL (Berg Collection))

There are extensive footnotes throughout both volumes. These present textual notes in addition to comments on the content of the text. It must be assumed most of these are by Masefield, although some are Dampier's own. The editor's presence throughout is a notable feature and at least one 'EDITOR'S NOTE' attains the status of a sub-heading during the text (Vol. II, p.593).

The catalogue at the rear of *Multitude and Solitude* (A8(a)) lists the edition as follows:

> The Voyages of Captain William Dampier. Edited by John Masefield. Illustrated. Two volumes. Demy 8vo. 25s. net. Limited to 1000 copies.

Two examined sets contained a note of the limitation but neither was numbered. The limitation note is present on the second un-numbered otherwise blank page in the first volume. It reads 'This edition is limited | to one thousand copies | for sale in the United Kingdom. | *No.* ....' Richards refers to the limitation of the edition in a letter to Masefield when discussing complimentary copies:

> ...you specifically ask for six sets of the book. It is not, I think, usual to give six sets of a work which is edited only, especially when, as in this case, the edition is limited and very costly to produce...
>
> (Grant Richards, letter to John Masefield, 20 February 1906)
> (Archives of Grant Richards. University of Illinois / Chadwyck-Healey microfilm, A7, f.765)

A copy of this edition (presumably volume one only) held in W.B. Yeats' library in Dalkey, Ireland (*464) is inscribed 'W B Yeats | from John Masefield | Dec 31, 1906'

In July 1908 Richards offered 373 copies in sheets and 22 bound copies to Messrs. James Maclehose and Sons:

> I find on looking into the matter that we have 373 copies in sheets and 22 bound of the Dampier. I think it would be fair if you paid 6/3 all round for them.
>
> (Grant Richards, letter to James Maclehose, 2 July 1908)
> (Archives of Grant Richards. University of Illinois / Chadwyck-Healey microfilm, A13, f.899)

Richards was evidently anxious to sell off unwanted stock for he wrote again two days later (evidently having received notification that the price was too high):

> Can you make any offer for the Dampier? If you can, and if we can accept it, I should be very glad to get rid of the book.
>
> (Grant Richards, letter to James Maclehose, 4 July 1908)
> (Archives of Grant Richards. University of Illinois / Chadwyck-Healey microfilm, A13, f.920)

Maclehose did not eventually receive the stock as Richards had managed to sell it at a better price:

> Coming back from my holiday I am reminded that I have been rather remiss in not having told you about the Dampier. From what you told I quite believed that the price you offered was about as much as you could on the showing offer; but I got one about fifty per cent better from somewhere else and accepted it.
>
> (Grant Richards, letter to James Maclehose, 20 August 1908)
> (Archives of Grant Richards. University of Illinois / Chadwyck-Healey microfilm, A14, f.162)

Current research has not identified the purchaser.

In 1927 it appears that Masefield suggested a reprint of this work to Heinemann. C.S. Evans responded noting interest from Laurence Irving, the illustrator who had recently worked on *Philip the King* (see A84(a)):

> ...I have been away for a few days which will explain why I have not before answered your letter of July 25th about Dampier's Voyages. You may remember that Laurence Irving expressed a desire to illustrate this book and I think he might do it very well...
>
> (C.S. Evans, letter to John Masefield, 5 August 1927)
> (HRHRC, MS (Masefield, J.) Recip William Heinemann Ltd.)

Masefield, it appears, then wrote at greater length and Evans asked to see the text:

> Very many thanks for your letter about the VOYAGES OF CAPTAIN DAMPIER. Will you let me think about the suggestion for a few days and have you a copy of the book which you could let me see? I shall need it for the purpose of making an estimate. I presume that you would write a new Introduction for this edition if we decide to do it?
>
> (C.S. Evans, letter to John Masefield, 24 September 1929)
> (HRHRC, MS (Masefield, J.) Recip William Heinemann Ltd.)

Two months later Evans reported that Heinemann would be unable to republish the work. His reference to 'the two volumes' suggest that Masefield had sent copies of B50(a):

> I am sorry that I have not written to you before about DAMPIER. We have examined the proposition most carefully, but we cannot see any chance of it being a success from an economic point of view. I am returning the two volumes to you under another cover.
>
> (C.S. Evans, letter to John Masefield, 27 November 1929)
> (HRHRC, MS (Masefield, J.) Recip William Heinemann Ltd.)

Six years later Masefield tried again. C.S. Evans responded with observations on changes in the book trade between 1906 and 1935:

> I have given long and anxious thought to the question of republishing DAMPIER'S VOYAGES with your new notes, and I am very reluctant indeed to decline the proposal because I know how much pleasure it would give you if it could be accepted. I am afraid, however, that the economic difficulties are too great to be surmounted. Each book will make 708 pages, and as Grant Richards tells me there are no plates or type they would have to be entirely reset... ...This edition of Grant Richards was produced at a time when manufacturing costs were less than half what they are now and at a time when libraries subscribed to such expensive books in a greater degree than they do now.
>
> (C.S. Evans, letter to John Masefield, 23 August 1935)
> (HRHRC, MS (Masefield, J.) Recip William Heinemann Ltd.)

Copies seen: BL (010026.i.23) stamped 5 DEC 1906, rebound; UCL (Rotton. 40.d.21–22); Ledbury Library, limited edition (un-numbered); NYPL (Berg Collection) vol. I inscribed 'To Lady Gregory | from John Masefield. | 28. Nov. 1906.' with vol. II inscribed 'from John Masefield. | Jan 28. 1907'; HRHRC (G420 D14 cop.1) limited edition (un-numbered)

B50(b) First American edition (1906)

Letters within the Grant Richards archive suggest that copies of this work were available in America (presumably comprising the English printing with American cancel-titles). The publisher was probably E.P. Dutton. No example has been traced, however.

B55 *Ed.* JOHN MASEFIELD, *LYRICS OF BEN JONSON[,] BEAUMONT AND FLETCHER* 1906

B55(a) First English edition (1906)

LYRICS OF BEN JONSON | BEAUMONT AND | FLETCHER | Edited by | JOHN MASEFIELD | [ornament] | LONDON | E. GRANT RICHARDS | 1906
(All width centred)

Bibliographies: Williams p.11, Simmons pp.130–31

Collation: [*a*]⁸ *b*² A-K⁸ L⁶ (J not used); signatures left foot of page; 96 leaves; 123 × 83mm.; [i–iv] v–xvii [xviii–xx] 1–111 [112–14] 115–70 [171–72]

Page contents: [i] 'The Chapbooks | IV | LYRICS OF BEN JONSON, | BEAUMONT, AND FLETCHER'; [ii] 'THE CHAPBOOKS | I | Lyrists of the Restoration | II | Essays Moral and Polite | III | The Poems of | Robert Herrick | IV | Lyrics of Ben Jonson, and | Beaumont and Fletcher. | 3s. 6d. each net.'; [iii] title-page; [iv] 'Edinburgh : Printed by T. and A. CONSTABLE'; v–xvii [Introduction] ('Of the dramatic poets, whose lyrics are here reprinted, we know but little.') (unsigned); [xviii] blank; [xix] 'THE LYRICS OF BEN JONSON'; [xx] blank; 1–111 text of The Lyrics of Ben Jonson; [112] blank; [113] 'LYRICS OF | BEAUMONT AND FLETCHER'; [114] blank; 115–[71] text of Lyrics of Beaumont and Fletcher (at foot of p.[171]: '[rule] | Printed by T. and A. CONSTABLE, Printers to His Majesty, | at the Edinburgh University Press.'); [172] blank

Paper: wove paper

Running title: 'LYRICS OF BEN JONSON' (42mm.) on both verso and recto, pp.2–111; 'LYRICS OF' (18mm.) on verso, 'BEAUMONT AND FLETCHER' (49mm.) on recto, pp.116–[71]

Binding: parchment with four leather ties. On spine: 'LYRICS OF | BEN JONSON | BEAUMONT & | FLETCHER | [ornament: 17 × 21mm.] | THE | CHAPBOOKS' (all width centred). Upper and lower covers blank. Top edge gilt, others untrimmed. Sewn head and foot bands. Binding measurements: 126 × 90mm. (covers), 126 × 30mm. (spine). End-papers: wove paper. With slipcase covered with paper decorated with hand-printed floral design in blue and red.

Publication date: published, according to Simmons, December 1906

Price: 3s.6d.

Masefield contents:
'edited by John Masefield'

[Introduction] ('Of the dramatic poets, whose lyrics are here reprinted, we know but little.')
        (unsigned)

Notes:
On 13 June 1906 Richards requested the manuscript of the volume for 1 July 1906 but was writing again on 10 July to remind Masefield of the fact. The original intention had been to publish only a volume of Beaumont and Fletcher but this was discovered to be too short. Richards wrote during July 1906:

> Constable's have cast off the amount of matter in the Beaumont and Fletcher and it makes only 132 pages. This looks as though it will be a very short volume unless you can think of someone else who could be added with advantage.
>
> (Grant Richards, letter to John Masefield, 21 July 1906)
> (Archives of Grant Richards. University of Illinois / Chadwyck-Healey microfilm, A8, f.247)

Even with the inclusion of Jonson, Richards was required to write again regarding the length of the volume:

> Constable's estimate of the new matter that you have sent for the Ben Jonson volume is that is [*sic*] makes 58 pages, which will make 180 pages in all. Is there nothing by Beaumont and Fletcher that you can justifiably put in to increase it say by twenty pages? It would be an advantage.

> (Grant Richards, letter to John Masefield, 8 September 1906)
> (Archives of Grant Richards. University of Illinois / Chadwyck-Healey microfilm, A9, f.548)

Masefield thought there was not any justifiable material and wrote noting that, as it was, the volume 'has a fair quantity of letters, epigrams, etc. which are not exactly lyrical…') (see John Masefield, letter to Grant Richards, 9 September 1906) (Fales Library, New York University).

Copies seen: BL (012207.hh.1/3) stamped 3 JAN 1907; ULL (Special Collections) in cardboard slipcase; HRHRC (AC-L M377 D3 1906) inscribed 'Elizabeth Yeats | from John Masefield | Christmas. 1906.'

Reprinted:
| 'Reissued' | [first edtion, later impression] | 1908 |
| 'Reissued' | [first edition, later impression] | 1913 |

B55(b) First American edition ([1906])

Letters within the Grant Richards archive suggest that copies of all the Chapbooks were available in America (comprising English printings with American cancel-titles). No example of this title has been traced, however. The publication price may have been $1.00.

B60 *HAKLUYT'S VOYAGES.* VOLUME I   1907

B60(a) First English edition (1907)

The PRINCIPAL | NAVIGATIONS | VOYAGES [ornament] | TRAFFIQUES & | DISCOVERIES of the | ENGLISH NATION | Made by Sea or Overland | to the Remote & Farthest | Distant Quarters of the Earth | at any time within the [ornament] | compasse of these 1600 Yeares | by RICHARD HAKLUYT | VOLUME ONE | [ornament, signed 'RK'] | London: J[point]M[point]Dent & Co. | New York: E[point]P.Dutton & Co.
(With the exception of lines 8 and 13, all justified on left and right margins. Many of the letters in lower case are ornate and often joined together. All in white triangle: 110 × 62mm., within border of leaves and flowers: 156 × 98mm., signed 'RKC')

Bibliographies: Williams p.11, Simmons p.131

Collation: [π]² [A]¹⁶ B-P¹⁶ Q⁶ (J not used); signatures width centred at foot of page with 'I.' at left foot on first leaf of gatherings (with the exception of [π], [A], B and H where 'I' appears); in all gatherings of sixteen leaves, the fifth leaf is also signed; Q2 is also signed; the [π] 'gathering' surrounds the [A] gathering; the [A] gathering is signed '*' at left foot of page but also A2 on the fifth leaf; 248 leaves; 171 × 106mm.; [i–vii] viii–xii [xiii] xiv–xxvi [1] 2–5 [6] 7–12 [13] 14–18 [19] 20–36 [37] 38–46 [47] 48–52 [53] 54–468 [469–70]

Page contents: [i] 'EVERYMAN'S LIBRARY | EDITED BY ERNEST RHYS | TRAVEL | HAKLUYT'S VOYAGES | WITH AN INTRODUCTION BY | JOHN MASEFIELD | VOLUME ONE'; [ii] publisher's advertisement (within border: 115 × 64mm., enclosing four rectangles of different sizes); [iii] blank; [iv] 'TO | THE | WISE MAN | ALL THE | WORLD'S | A SOIL | BEN JONSON' (intertwined by floral design signed 'K' with the first 'T' as a drop capital (signed 'R') all in white rectangle within border of leaves and flowers in mirror image of title-page); [v] title-page; [vi] blank; [vii]–xii 'CONTENTS.' (subsections listed with page references); [xiii]–xxvi 'INTRODUCTION.' ('Richard Hakluyt, the scholar who edited these Voyages…') (signed '1907. JOHN MASEFIELD'); [1]–468 text (at foot of p.468: '[rule] | GLASGOW : PRINTED AT THE UNIVERSITY PRESS BY ROBERT MACLEHOSE AND CO. LTD.'); [469–70] blank

Paper: wove paper

Running title: 'Richard Hakluyt' (36mm.) on verso; 'The English Voyages' (46mm.) on recto, pp.54–468

Binding: dark green cloth. On spine, in gold: '[design] | THE [ornament] | PRINCIPAL | VOYAGES | OF THE [ornament] | ENGLISH | NATION *by* | HAKLUYT | VOLUME I | [design of flowers and leaves] | [point] J [point] M [point] DENT [point] | [six points] | E [point] P [point] DUTTON | [two leaves] & Cᵒ [with point underneath the 'O'] [two leaves]' (all justified on left and right margins). On upper cover, in blind: publisher's design of plant with lettering '[point] I [point] M [point] | & | DENT Cᵒ [with point underneath the 'O']' within border: 24 × 22mm., all enclosed within blind ruled border: 174 × 105mm. with a circle in two corners furthest from spine. Lower cover: blank. All edges trimmed. Top edge stained, others trimmed. Binding measurements: 175 × 107mm. (covers), 175 × 32mm. (spine). End-papers: wove paper, decorated with swirling leaf and stem design, female figure and, within scroll: 'EVERYMAN, | I [point] WILL [point] GO [point] WITH | [point] THEE. | & [point] BE [point] THY [point] GVIDE | IN [point] THY [point] MOST [point] NEED | TO [point] GO [point] BY [point] THY [point] SIDE'

Also issued in leather.

Publication date: published, according to Simmons, 1907. Volumes after Vol. II were published later (there were a total of eight volumes). Only the first contains a contribution from Masefield.

Price: 1s. (cloth) / 2s. (leather)

Masefield contents:

'Introduction' ('Richard Hakluyt, the scholar who edited these Voyages...')
    (signed '1907. JOHN MASEFIELD')

Notes:

Under the title 'The Sea-Kings of England. Stories from Hakluyt's 'English Voyages.'', four selections appear in *Chatterbox* for 1909. Since Masefield contributed *Martin Hyde* to the children's periodical in that year, it is possible that he was responsible for the inclusion of Hakluyt extracts. Page references to *Chatterbox* are as follows: III, pp.18–19; VII, pp.54–5; XVII, pp.134–5; and XXI, pp.165–6.

Copies seen: BL (12206.p.1/217) stamped 18 SEP 1907, rebound; University of Warwick Library (G240 H2)

Reprinted:

[first edition, second impression]	1910
[first edition, third impression]	1926
[first edition, fourth impression]	1932
[first edition, fifth impression]	1939

B60(b) First combined English and American illustrated edition (1927)

An edition published by J.M. Dent and E.P. Dutton was published in 1927 with illustrations by T. Derrick

B65 *AN ENGLISH PROSE MISCELLANY*   1907

B65(a) First English edition (1907)

AN ENGLISH | PROSE MISCELLANY | SELECTED | WITH AN INTRODUCTION | BY | JOHN MASEFIELD | METHUEN & CO. | 36 ESSEX STREET W.C. | LONDON
(All width centred)

Bibliographies: Williams p.11, Simmons p.131

Collation: [*a*]⁸ *b*⁴ A–S⁸ T² (J not used); signatures left foot of page; 158 leaves; 190 × 124mm.; the catalogue (not included in collation or leaf count) comprises a single gathering of 16 unsigned leaves; [two un-numbered pages] [i–iv] v–ix [x] xi–xxi [xxii] 1–292; catalogue pagination: [1–2] 3–31 [32]

Page contents: [-] blank (page excluded from page count, but constitutes first leaf of first gathering); [-] blank; [i] half-title: 'AN ENGLISH PROSE MISCELLANY'; [ii] blank; [iii] title-page; [iv] '*First Published in 1907*'; v–ix 'CONTENTS' (eight sections listed with individual authors and page references); [x] blank; xi–xxi 'INTRODUCTION' ('In a book of this size it is impossible to give specimens of every...') (signed, 'J. M.'); [xxii] blank; 1–292 text (at foot of p.292: 'TURNDALE AND SPEARS, PRINTERS, EDINBURGH'); [1–32] catalogue: 'A SELECTION OF BOOKS | PUBLISHED BY METHUEN | AND COMPANY LIMITED | 36 ESSEX STREET | LONDON W.C. | [contents listing] | OCTOBER 1910' (at foot of p.[32]: 'PRINTED BY | WILLIAM CLOWES AND SONS, LIMITED, LONDON AND BECCLES.')

Paper: wove paper (catalogue: wove paper)

Running title: running titles comprise a sectional title on verso; the recto title comprises author, pp.2–292

Binding: burgundy cloth. On spine, in gold: '[double rule] | AN ENGLISH | PROSE | MISCELLANY | JOHN | MASEFIELD | METHUEN | [double rule]' (all width centred). On upper cover, in either gold or blind: 'AN ENGLISH | PROSE MISCELLANY | JOHN MASEFIELD' (within ruled border: 193 × 121mm.) Lower cover: blind ruled border: 193 × 121mm. Top edge trimmed, others untrimmed. Binding measurements: 196 × 126mm. (covers), 196 × 49mm. (spine). End-papers: wove paper.

Publication date: published, according to Simmons, October 1907

Price: 6s.

Masefield contents:

'Selected with an Introduction by John Masefield'

'Introduction' ('In a book of this size it is impossible to give specimens of every...')
    (signed, 'J. M.')

Notes:

A publishing agreement for this title between Masefield and Methuen was dated 23 November 1905 (see Archives of The Society of Authors). The agreement refers to 'a book of English lyrics'.

The volume contains eight subsections: 'Memoirs and Letters', 'Divines', 'Dramatists and Novelists', 'Moral, Philosophical, Occasional and Satirical Writings', 'Character Studies and Sketches', 'Translations', 'Historical and Biographical' and 'Critical'.

The upper cover includes the title, author and a ruled border in either gold, or blind.

All excerpts commence with a drop capital.

Masefield notes in *A Sailor's Garland* that a prose version of the book is 'in preparation'. This, however, is not that volume, which never appeared.

The introduction finds Masefield dependent on W.B. Yeats for his final argument:

> …great criticism can only be written by great artists. "Great art," as Mr Yeats says, "can never exist without a great criticism"…

A copy of this edition held in W.B. Yeats' library in Dalkey, Ireland (*1262) is inscribed 'W B Yeats | from John Masefield | Nov. 5, 1907.'

Copies seen: private collection (PWE) upper cover in blind; BL (12272.p.6) upper cover in gold, stamped 28 OCT 1907; ULL (Special Collections) upper cover in gold; ULL (YBO/Eng) upper cover in blind; Ledbury Library; Library of The John Masefield Society

B70 *THE TRAVELS OF MARCO POLO THE VENETIAN*   1908

B70(a) *First English edition (1908)*

The TRAVELS of | MARCO POLO | the VENETIAN | [signed device of woman with scroll gazing at surrounding flowers: 46 × 37mm. within floral surround on left and right sides bearing the words 'EVERY-MAN I WILL GO WITH THEE & BE THY GVIDE IN THY MOST NEED TO GO BY THY SIDE'] | LONDON:PUBLISHED | by][point]M[point]DENT[point]&[point]CO | AND IN NEW YORK | [point]BY E[point]P.DUTTON & CO [these four lines bordered on left and right margins by floral devices]
(All justified on left and right margins; many of the letters are ornate, even overlaid. All in white rectangle: 111 × 63mm., within border of leaves and flowers: 157 × 99mm., signed 'RKC')

Bibliographies: Williams p.11, Simmons p.131

Collation: [π]⁸ A–N¹⁶ O⁸ P¹⁶ (J not used); signatures right foot of page; in all gatherings of sixteen leaves, the fifth leaf is also signed; 240 leaves; 172 × 107mm.; [i–vi] vii–xvi 1–437 [438] 439–61 [462–64]

Page contents: [i] 'EVERYMAN'S LIBRARY | EDITED BY ERNEST RHYS | TRAVEL AND | TOPOGRAPHY | MARCO POLO'S TRAVELS | WITH AN INTRODUCTION BY | JOHN MASEFIELD'; [ii] publisher's advertisement (within border: 111 × 64mm., enclosing four rectangles of different sizes); [iii] blank; [iv] 'TO | THE | WISE MAN | ALL THE | WORLD'S | A SOIL | BEN JONSON' (intertwined by floral design signed 'K' with the first 'T' as a drop capital (signed 'R') all in white rectangle within border of leaves and flowers in mirror image of title-page); [v] title-page; [vi] blank; vii–xiii 'INTRODUCTION' ('Marco Polo, the subject of this memoir, was born at Venice…') (signed 'JOHN MASEFIELD. | *December* 1907.'); xiv–xvi 'ITINERARY' ('The elder Polos, when they left Constantinople in the year 1260…') (signed, 'J.M.'); 1–8 'CONTENTS' (three books and their chapters listed with page references. A Prologue, Appendix and Index are also listed); 9–434 text; 435–37 'APPENDIX'; [438] blank; 439–61 'INDEX'; [462] 'LETCHWORTH | THE TEMPLE PRESS | PRINTERS'; [463–64] blank

Paper: wove paper

Running title: 'Travels of Marco Polo' (44mm.) on verso; recto title comprises a brief indication of text subject, pp.10–434

Binding: dark green cloth. On spine, in gold: '[design] | THE [ornament] | TRAVELS | ofMARCO | POLO [ornament] | THE [ornament] | VENETIAN | [five points] | [design of flowers and leaves] | [point] J [point] M [point] DENT [point] | [six points] | E [point] PDUTTON | [two leaves] &Cᴼ [with point underneath the 'O'] [two leaves]' (all justified on left and right margins). On upper cover, in blind: publisher's design of plant with lettering '[point] I [point] M [point] | DENT & | SONS Lᴰ' within border: 23 × 22mm., all enclosed within blind ruled border: 174 × 105mm. with a circle in two corners furthest from spine. Lower cover: blank. Top edge stained, others trimmed. Binding measurements: 176 × 110mm. (covers), 176 × 28mm. (spine). End-papers: wove paper, decorated with swirling leaf and stem design, female figure and, within scroll: 'EVERYMAN, | I [point] WILL [point] GO [point] WITH | [point] THEE. | & [point] BE [point] THY [point] GVIDE | IN [point] THY [point] MOST [point] NEED | TO [point] GO [point] BY [point] THY [point] SIDE'.

Also issued in leather.

Publication date: published, according to the *English Catalogue of Books*, February 1908

Price: 1s. (cloth) / 2s. (leather)

Masefield contents:
'Introduction' ('Marco Polo, the subject of this memoir, was born at Venice…')
    (signed, 'JOHN MASEFIELD. | *December* 1907.')
'Itinerary' ('The elder Polos, when they left Constantinople in the year 1260…')
    (signed, 'J.M.')

Notes:
Masefield describes Marco Polo's work as 'one of the great books of travel… to the general reader, the great charm of the book is its romance… The wonder of Marco Polo is this – that he created Asia for the European mind.'

The volume includes numerous footnotes. These do not appear to be those by Colonel Henry Yule (although Masefield states in his introduction 'Some of [Marco Polo's] wanderings are hard to follow; some of the places which he visited are hard to identify; but the labour of Colonel Yule has cleared up most of the difficulties, and confirmed most of the strange statements.')

Copies seen: private collection (PWE); BL (12206.p.1/268) stamped 24 FEB 08, rebound; ULL (Special Collections) includes posthumous booklabel

Reprinted:

[first edition, second impression]	1911
[first edition, third impression]	1914
[first edition, fourth impression]	1918
[first edition, fifth impression]	1921
[first edition, sixth impression]	1923
[first edition, seventh impression]	1925
[first edition, eighth impression]	1927

B70(b) First combined English and American illustrated edition (1926)

An edition published by J.M. Dent and E.P. Dutton was published in 1926 with illustrations by Adrian De Friston.

Reprinted:

	1926
	1930

B70(c) Second English edition (1932)

THE TRAVELS OF MARCO POLO | [ornament] | LONDON: J. M . DENT & SONS LTD. | NEW YORK: E. P. DUTTON & CO. INC.
(All width centred)

Notes:
An edition descibed as 'reset' was issued in 1932

Copies seen: private collection (ROV)

Reprinted:

[second edition, second impression]	1936

B75 *THE WORKS OF FRANCIS BEAUMONT AND JOHN FLETCHER. VOLUME III*   1908

B75(a) First English edition (1908)

THE WORKS OF | FRANCIS BEAUMONT [in red] | AND | JOHN FLETCHER [in red] | VARIORUM EDITION | VOLUME III | THE FAITHFUL SHEPHERDESS | THE MAD LOVER | THE LOYAL SUBJECT | RULE A WIFE AND HAVE A WIFE | THE LAWS OF CANDY | LONDON | GEORGE BELL AND SONS [in red] | & A. H. BULLEN [in red] | 1908
(All width centred)

Bibliographies: Williams [unrecorded], Simmons 'Addenda and Errata' slip

Collation: [A]⁴ B-MM⁸ (J, V, W and JJ not used); signatures right foot of page with 'VOL. III.' at left foot on first leaf of gatherings; 276 leaves; 220 × 137mm.; [i–viii] [1] 2–110 [111] 112–18 [119] 120–219 [220–21] 222–29 [230] 231–356 [357] 358–464 [465] 466–70 [471] 472–544

Page contents: [i] blank; [ii] publisher's advertisement: '*Some Opinions of the Press on Vols. I and II*'; [iii] half-title: 'THE WORKS OF | FRANCIS BEAUMONT | & | JOHN FLETCHER | VARIORUM EDITION | GENERAL EDITOR : A.H. BULLEN | VOLUME III'; [iv] blank; [v] title-page; [vi] 'RICHARD CLAY & SONS, LIMITED, | BREAD STREET HILL, E.C., AND BUNGAY, SUFFOLK.'; [vii] 'CONTENTS' (five plays listed with titles, editors and page references); [viii] blank; [1]-544 text (at foot of p.544: '[rule] | *Richard Clay & Sons, Limited, London and Bungay.*')

Paper: laid paper (no watermark), chain-lines 26mm. apart

Running title: running titles comprise titles of plays with note of Act and Scene on both recto and verso, pp.4–544

Binding: blue cloth. On spine, in gold: 'BEAUMONT | & | FLETCHER | THE FAITHFUL SHEPHERDESS | THE MAD LOVER | THE LOYAL SUBJECT | RULE A WIFE & HAVE A WIFE | THE LAWS OF CANDY | [four ten-pointed stars] | VARIORUM EDITION' (all width centred). Upper and lower covers blank. Binding measurements: 229 × 144mm. (covers), 229 × 53mm. (spine). End-papers: laid paper (no watermark), chain-lines 27–29mm. Top edge gilt, others untrimmed.

Publication date: not in the *English Catalogue of Books*

Price: 10s.6d. (price recorded in the *English Catalogue of Books* for volume I and volume II respectively)

Masefield contents:
The Loyal Subject. Edited by John Masefield, with an introduction by R. Warwick Bond

Notes:
The first volume in this set was published in 1904. The set was intended to reach 12 volumes but was terminated after only four. A Cambridge University Press edition of Beaumont and Fletcher was contemporary and may explain the apparent failure of the Variorum Edition.

In an undated letter to Jack B. Yeats, Masefield writes:

> I saw Bullen today + got a job from him, editing Fletcher's plays for his grand 12 volume edition, which will bring boodle, tho not very much.

(John Masefield, letter to Jack B. Yeats, undated)
(Bodleian. MS.Eng.poet.d.194, ff.22–24)

This variorum edition is interesting for the quality of its editors at the time. A.H. Bullen, publisher and textual editor, exemplified textual emendation as a subjective art. This volume contains:

> The Faithful Shepherdess. Edited by W.W. Greg
> The Mad Lover. Edited by R. Warwick Bond
> The Loyal Subject. Edited by John Masefield, with an introduction by R. Warwick Bond
> Rule a Wife and have a Wife. Edited by R. Warwick Bond
> The Laws of Candy. Edited by E.K. Chambers

Copies seen: BL (11770.i.11) stamped 6 JAN 1909, rebound [after consultation for description above]; ULL (3 YI B36A 904)

B80 *Ed.* JOHN MASEFIELD, *MASTERS OF LITERATURE [–] DEFOE*   1909

B80(a) *First English edition (1909)*

MASTERS OF LITERATURE | DEFOE | EDITED BY | JOHN MASEFIELD | [design of anchor, bell and fish, incorporating oval shape: 32 × 19mm.] | LONDON | GEORGE BELL AND SONS | 1909
(All width centred)

Bibliographies: Williams p.12, Simmons pp.131–32

Collation: [*a*]⁸ *b*⁸ *c*² B-BB⁸ CC² (J, V and W not used) (see notes); *b*2 and B2–BB2 are also signed; signatures left foot of page; 212 leaves; 188 × 127mm.; [i–vi] vii [viii] ix–xxxiii [xxxiv–xxxvi] [1] 2–322 [323–24] 325–88

Page contents: [i] blank; [ii] publisher's advertisement: 'MASTERS OF LITERATURE' (series description and 10 titles listed) (within ruled border: 99 × 77mm.); [iii] half-title: 'MASTERS OF | LITERATURE | DEFOE'; [iv] blank (with additional leaf tipped-in on the verso of which is the frontispiece: 98 × 71mm., 'Daniel Defoe.' with 'T.R. Way. Lith' on left and 'after Vamdergucht' on right, with protective tissue); [v] title-page; [vi] 'RICHARD CLAY & SONS, LIMITED, | BREAD STREET HILL, E.C., AND | BUNGAY, SUFFOLK.'; vii 'CONTENTS' (three parts listed with page references); [viii] '. . . *The text of this volume has been carefully collated | with the original editions.*'; ix–xxi 'INTRODUCTION | I. BIOGRAPHICAL' ('Daniel De Foe, or Defoe, was born in London, in the parish of...') (unsigned); xxii–xxxiii 'II. APPRECIATION' ('In the early eighteenth century, people went to portrait painters, hoping...') (signed, 'JOHN MASEFIELD.'); [xxxiv] blank; [xxxv] 'PART I | ROMANCES, ETC.'; [xxxvi] blank; [1]-322 text of part I; [323] 'PART II | LESSER WORKS, PAMPHLETS, AND | OCCASIONAL PAPERS'; [324] blank; 325–88 text of part II (at foot of p.388: '[rule] | *Richard Clay & Sons, Limited, London and Bungay.*')

Paper: wove paper

Running title: 'DANIEL DEFOE' (29mm.) on verso; recto title comprises title of the work, pp.x-388

Binding: crimson cloth. On spine, in gold: 'MASTERS OF | LITERATURE | DEFOE | MASEFIELD | [oval device of two intertwined 'D's with one reversed so as to form symmetrical device: 23 × 18mm.) | [motif of anchor, bell and fish, (without oval shape and with less substantial anchor than title-page): 28 × 21mm.] | GEORGE BELL & SONS'; three vertical lines on left and right borders; two horizontal lines then rectangle then two horizontal lines on upper and lower edges. There are seven rectangles at both head and foot with each separated by three vertical lines. Only within the centre square on the base there is a diamond shape. On upper cover: oval device of intertwined 'D's as front cover in gold: 29 × 22mm. and within oval shape in blind; five blind rules (of different thicknesses) around four sides (as outer border) with four blind rules (of different thicknesses) form inner border. Lower cover, in blind: as upper cover. Top edge gilt, lower outside edge untrimmed, fore edge uncut. Binding measurements: 195 × 129mm. (covers), 195 × 55mm. (spine). End-papers: wove paper.

Publication date: published, according to Simmons, October 1909

Price: 3s.6d.

Masefield contents:
'edited by John Masefield'

'Introduction | I. Biographical' ('Daniel De Foe, or Defoe, was born in London, in the parish of...')
        (unsigned)

'II. Appreciation' ('In the early eighteenth century, people went to portrait painters, hoping...')
    (signed, 'JOHN MASEFIELD.')

Notes:

A letter – acting as a publishing agreement for this title – between Masefield and George Bell was dated 3 March 1908 (see Archives of The Society of Authors). The agreement notes that 'you will have the MS ready for us not later than the first week in September of this year'.

In some copies the first gathering comprises only seven leaves with the first leaf (pp.[i–ii]) excised.

Simmons reports that the 'introduction was printed as an article entitled "Daniel Defoe" in "The Fortnightly Review"'. This is misleading. The introduction is clearly divided into two sections – 'Biographical' and 'Appreciation'. It is only the second section that appeared in *The Fortnightly Review* Jan 1909, pp.[65]-73 and there are minor variants between the two (see C115.001). Masefield is more restrained for volume publication, for example the final sentence includes 'a penitent thief in Newgate' in the volume and 'a penitent whore in Newgate' for the periodical.

Writing to his agent, with some apparent grievance against the publisher, Masefield explains the circumstances of the two parts of the introduction:

> I think that Bell is a little ungenerous. Could you please indicate the following fact to him. Originally, when I had finished my very long biography of Defoe for him, I planned to do a very brief appreciation, so as not to bulk the book unduly. After making this decision, I wrote my appreciation, + limited it to 1500 words.
>
> I then planned to do an article [–] a separate article, having nothing to do with Bell [–] on Defoe, for the Fortnightly, of from 4/5000 words. I wrote this, + then decided to use the article both for the Fortnightly + for my appreciation; + thus it comes about that Bell now has an article on Defoe + a long biography of Defoe, 9000 words in all, instead of the 5000 words for which he covenanted. I do not ask to use the biography in the Fortnightly, + I feel that under the circumstances he might strain the point in my favour. Otherwise, I suppose I must alter the Fortnightly article, as Bell's article is in proof.
>
> (John Masefield, letter to C.F. Cazenove, 3 December 1908)
> (University of Arizona Library. MS.50, V.I)

Copies seen: private collection (PWE); BL (12268.c.24/1) stamped 9 DEC 1909; ULL (Special Collections)

B85 JACK B. YEATS, *A LITTLE FLEET*   1909

B85(a) First English edition (1909)

A LITTLE | FLEET | BY | JACK B. YEATS | PUBLISHED BY | ELKIN MATHEWS, VIGO STREET, | NIGH THE ALBANY, LONDON.
(All width centred)

Bibliographies: Williams p.2, Simmons p.132

Collation: [A]¹⁴; 14 leaves; 173 × 112mm.; [1–28]

Page contents: [1–2] blank; [3] title-page; [4] map: 125 × 77mm., 'Gara | River' signed 'Jack B. Yeats' (within double ruled border); [5–6] 'A LITTLE FLEET' ('The following account of the Fleet, and of the various histories…') (signed 'JACK B. YEATS'); [7–21] text; [22–26] publisher's advertisements (at foot of p.[26]: 'PUBLISHED AND SOLD BY | ELKIN MATHEWS, VIGO STREET, LONDON.'); [27–28] blank

Paper: laid paper (no watermark), chain-lines 27mm. apart

Running title: none

Binding: blue wrappers. Spine: blank. On upper wrapper: 'ONE OF JACK B. YEATS'S BOOKS | FOR CHILDREN. | [hand-coloured illustration of boy with toy ship: 51 × 42mm., signed with JBY monogram] | A LITTLE | FLEET | *PRICE ONE SHILLING NET,* | or, Coloured by the Author, with an Original Sketch | in Colours, price 5s. net. | PUBLISHED BY | ELKIN MATHEWS, VIGO STREET, | NIGH THE ALBANY, LONDON.' (all width centred). On lower wrapper: publisher's device (illustration of pirate with book and papers above 'ELKIN MATHEWS', signed 'Jack.B.Yeats.': 63 × 44mm.) Top edge trimmed, others untrimmed. Binding measurements: 176 × 113mm. (wrappers), 176 × 4mm. (spine). End-papers: free end-papers comprise leaves A1 and A14, the fixed end-papers are conjugate and wove paper.

Publication date: published, according to the *English Catalogue of Books*, October 1909, Of the hand-coloured issue Simmons states 'according to Mr. Yeats, [this] probably consisted of less than fifty copies'. No indication of print-run is provided for the standard issue.

Price: 1s. / 5s. (hand-coloured)

Masefield contents:
[Untitled lines on the "Monte"] ('And now by Gara rushes,')
[Untitled lines introducing the "Moby Dick"] ('She sailed down Gara Valley,')
[Untitled lines on the "Moby Dick"] ('She came to flying anchor')
[Untitled lines on the "Theodore"] ('And let no landsman doubt it,')

Notes:

There are black and white illustrations throughout the book (and concluding advertisements).

Yeats states '…the owners and myself are indebted to the Fleet Poet for the verses through the book.' These verses are attributable to Masefield. Explaining why part of the course was called 'Pirate's Leap', Yeats writes it was:

> …called that because a poet who had been a pirate, I expect, was thinking about a poem when he ought to have been shoving the vessel off the rocks, and so he fell in.

See E. MacCarvill, 'Jack B. Yeats – His Books', *The Dublin Magazine*, July-September 1945, pp.47–52. This comprises a bibliography of Jack B. Yeats' books, of which *A Little Fleet* is numbered 7. She notes that the 'Copy in National Library presented by Miss Yeats'.

See James G. Nelson for brief details of the agreement between Mathews and Yeats for *A Little Fleet* (signed on 13 September 1909) and a facsimile reproduction of Yeats' publisher's device (as used on the lower wrapper). In Nelson's 'Checklist of the Mathews Imprint', *A Little Fleet* is numbered 1909.28.

Of the hand-coloured issue, James G. Nelson notes a copy in his own private collection. Handley-Taylor notes a copy held in Yale University Library, New Haven, Connecticut.

Copies seen: private collection (PWE); BL (012809.g.32) stamped 19 NOV 1909, wrappers strengthened; HRHRC (PR6047 E3 L55 cop.1); HRHRC (PR6047 E3 L55 cop.2)

B90 E.H. VISIAK, *BUCCANEER BALLADS*   1910

B90(a) First English edition (1910)

BUCCANEER | BALLADS | By E.H. VISIAK | [rule, 80mm.] [in red] | *With an Introduction* | *by* | JOHN MASEFIELD | *And a Frontispiece* | *by* | VIOLET HELM | [rule, 80mm.] [in red] | ELKIN MATHEWS | VIGO STREET [point] LONDON | M CM X

(All width centred and enclosed within red ruled border: 128 × 81mm. As a result of the two rules noted above, three rectangles are created measuring 37 × 81mm., 65 × 81mm. and 27 × 81mm. respectively from the top. Six lines in total appear although none completely touches)

Bibliographies: Williams p.12, Simmons p.132

Collation: [A]⁶ B-C⁸; B2 and C2 are also signed; signatures right foot of page; 23 leaves; 169 × 106mm.; [1–7] 8–9 [10–11] 12 [13] 14–43 [44]

Page contents: [1] half-title: 'Buccaneer Ballads'; [2] blank; [3] title-page (with additional leaf tipped-in on the verso of which is the frontispiece: 107 × 88mm., I'LL SING YE A SONG; I'LL SING AWAY | … (*Prologue.)*' within ruled border); [4] '*All rights reserved.*'; [5] '*TO | MY MOTHER*'; [6] 'Prologue' ('*Sing me a song, for the night is long*'); [7]-9 'Introduction' ('The name Buccaneer means one who practises the boucan.') (signed, 'JOHN MASEFIELD'); [10] blank; [11]-12 'Contents' (31 individual poems listed with page references); [13]-43 text (at foot of p.43: '*Seventeen of these poems are reprinted from the* | '*New Age,' four from 'John Bull,' three from* | '*Garnered Grain,' one from the 'Daily News,'* | *with the Editors' kind permission.* | E.H. VISIAK. | [rule] | LONDON : PRINTED BY WILLIAM CLOWES AND SON, LIMITED, | DUKE STREET, STAMFORD STREET, S.E., AND GREAT WINDMILL STREET, W.'); [44] publisher's advertisement

Paper: laid paper (watermark: '[Crown] | Abbey Mills | Greenfield'), chain-lines 24mm. apart

Running title: 'BUCCANEER BALLADS' (29mm.) on verso; recto title comprises poem title, pp.14–43

Binding: burgundy cloth. On spine, in gold reading lengthways up spine, from foot: 'BUCCANEER BALLADS E.H. | VISIAK' (the author's initials are immediately above the surname and both are in a smaller type than the title); horizontally at foot of spine: 'Elkin | Mathews'. On upper cover, in gold: 'BUCCANEER | BALLADS | E.H. VISIAK' within two double borders: 162 × 96mm. and 146 × 80mm. Top edge trimmed, fore edge untrimmed, lower outside edge trimmed. Binding measurements: 174 × 111mm. (covers), 174 × 14mm. (spine). End-papers: laid paper (no watermark), chain-lines 26mm. apart.

Also issued in wrappers.

Publication date: published, according to Simmons, March 1910

Price: 1s. (wrappers) / (see notes)

Masefield contents:
'Introduction' ('The name Buccaneer means one who practises the boucan.')
    (signed, 'JOHN MASEFIELD')

Notes:
In Nelson's 'Checklist of the Mathews Imprint', *Buccaneer Ballads* is numbered 1910.7. It is noted as the twelfth title in Mathews' Satchel Series. A brief reference to the volume is included on page 65 of Nelson's work.

AN ENGLISH
PROSE MISCELLANY

SELECTED

WITH AN INTRODUCTION
BY
JOHN MASEFIELD

METHUEN & CO.
36 ESSEX STREET W.C.
LONDON

B65(a) title-page

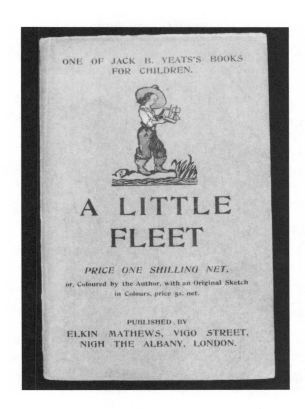

B85(a) upper wrapper

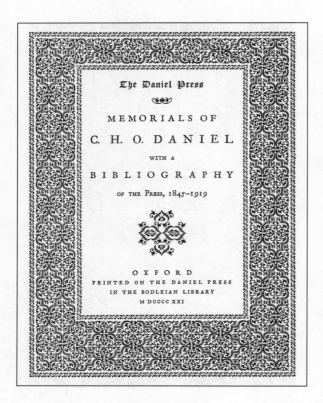

The Daniel Press

MEMORIALS OF
C. H. O. DANIEL

WITH A

BIBLIOGRAPHY

OF THE PRESS, 1845–1919

OXFORD
PRINTED ON THE DANIEL PRESS
IN THE BODLEIAN LIBRARY
M DCCCC XXI

B180(a) title-page

WHY EVERYBODY SHOULD
ASSIST IN FIGHTING
DISEASE IN THE
TROPICS

Issued by the LADIES' COMMITTEE of the
ROSS INSTITUTE and HOSPITAL for
TROPICAL DISEASES   (Incorporated)
Putney Heath, LONDON, S.W.15.

B220(a) title-page

The *English Catalogue of Books* lists the volume as 'swd.' and gives no indication of a cloth binding. In 'Some Contributions to the Bibliography of John Masefield: II' (*Papers of the Bibliographical Society of America*, October 1959, pp.262–67) Fraser Drew notes:

> *Buccaneer Ballads*, by E.H. Visiak, was issued both in paper wrappers and cloth; the contents of the two issues are identical.

and thus indicates that two bindings do, indeed, exist. No copy with paper wrapper binding has been seen.

Copies seen: private collection (ROV); BL (011650.E.52) stamped 16 MAR 1910

B95 [NATHANIEL MORTON], *CHRONICLES OF THE PILGRIM FATHERS* 1910

B95(a) First English edition (1910)

CHRONICLES | [ornament] of the [ornament] | PILGRIM [ornament] | [ornament] FATHERS | [signed device of woman with scroll gazing at surrounding flowers: 45 × 36mm., within floral surround on left and right sides bearing the words 'EVERY MAN I WILL GO WITH THEE & BE THY GVIDE IN THY MOST NEED TO GO BY THY SIDE'] | LONDON:PUBLISHED | byJ[point]M[point]DENT[point]&[point]SONS [point]L^TD | AND IN NEW YORK | BY E[point]P.DUTTON&CO [these four lines bordered on left and right margins by floral devices] (All justified on left and right margins; many of the letters in lower case are ornate, even overlaid. All in white rectangle: 111 × 63mm., within border of leaves and flowers: 158 × 99mm., unsigned)

Bibliographies: Williams p.12, Simmons p.132

Collation: [A]^10 B-L^16 M^12 N^10 (J not used); signatures left foot of page; in all gatherings of sixteen leaves, the fifth leaf is also signed; M3 and N2 are also signed; 192 leaves; 173 × 107mm.; [two un-numbered pages] [i–vi] vii–xvii [xviii] [1] 2–240 [241–42] 243–364

Page contents: [-] blank (page excluded from page count, but constitutes first leaf of first gathering); [-] blank; [i] 'EVERYMAN'S LIBRARY | EDITED BY ERNEST RHYS | HISTORY | CHRONICLES OF THE | PILGRIM FATHERS [ornament] [ornament] | WITH AN INTRODUCTION | BY JOHN MASEFIELD' (lines 1 and 2, 3, and 4 to 6 form three separate blocks of text; lines 1, 2, 4, 5 and 6 are all justified on the same left and right margins, the other two lines are width centred); [ii] publisher's advertisement (within border: 114 × 66mm., enclosing four rectangles of different sizes); [iii] blank; [iv] '"CONSIDER | HISTORY | WITH [point] THE | BEGINNINGS [point] OF [point] | IT [point] STRETCHING | DIMLY [point] INTO [point] THE | REMOTE [point] TIME; E[curved dash] | MERGING [point] DARK[curved dash] | LY [point] OVT [point] ^OF [point] THE | MYSTERIOVS | ETERNITY:[two ornaments] | [curved dash]THE [point] TRVE [point] EPIC | POEM [point] AND [point] VNI | VERSAL [point] DIVINE | SCRIPTVRE. [three points]" | [three ornaments] | [ornament] CARLYLE [ornament]' (the first 'C' is a drop capital (unsigned) all in white rectangle within border of leaves and flowers in mirror image of title-page); [v] title-page; [vi] blank; vii–xvi 'INTRODUCTION' ('The Brownist emigration, known to Americans as the "Sailing of the Pilgrim Fathers," was...') (signed 'JOHN MASEFIELD. | June 24, 1910.'); xvii 'CONTENTS' (seven sections listed with page references); [xviii] blank; [1]-364 text (including facsimile reproduction of title-page of *New Englands Trials* on p.[241]) (at foot of p.364: '[rule] | *Richard Clay & Sons, Ltd., London and Bungay.*')

Paper: wove paper

Running title: 'The Pilgrim Fathers' (45mm.) on both recto and verso, pp.2–364

Binding: red cloth. On spine, in gold: '[ornament] | [ornament] | CHRON- | ~ [with miniature triangles above and below] ICLES | OF THE [ornament] | PILGRIM | FATHERS | [ornament] | [design of flowers and leaves] | [superscript point] J [point] M [point] DENT | [six points] | E [point] P [point] DUTTON | [two leaves] & C^O [with point underneath the 'O'] [two leaves]' (all justified on left and right margins). On upper cover, in blind: publisher's design of plant with lettering '[point] I [point] M [point] | DENT & | SONS L^D' within blind ruled border: 23 × 22mm., all enclosed within blind ruled border: 172 × 104mm. with a circle in two corners furthest from spine. Lower cover: blank. Top edge stained, others trimmed. Binding measurements: 175 × 108mm. (covers), 175 × 32mm. (spine). End-papers: wove paper, decorated with swirling leaf and stem design, female figure and, within scroll: 'EVERYMAN, | I [point] WILL [point] GO [point] WITH | [point] THEE. | & [point] BE [point] THY GVIDE | IN [point] THY [point] MOST [point] NEED | TO [point] GO [point] BY [point] THY [point] SIDE'.

Also issued in leather.

Publication date: published, according to Simmons, September 1910

Price: 1s. (cloth) / 2s. (leather)

Masefield contents:
'Introduction' ('The Brownist emigration, known to Americans as the "Sailing of the Pilgrim Fathers," was...')
      (signed 'JOHN MASEFIELD. | *June* 24, 1910.')

Notes:
The border of the title-page and that facing the title-page is not that used in the other volumes edited by Masefield in the Everyman's Library series.

The author is not noted in the preliminaries to this volume. The British Library catalogue ascribes the work, however, to Nathaniel Morton.

It appears that Masefield did not expect to be asked to write the introduction to this volume. Writing to his agent he notes:

> Some time ago, Rhys asked me to look up some early American tracts with a view to editing them for Everyman. Well. I know some of the tracts, but I haven't looked them up. And now this letter comes. Could you see old Dent, + ask what

he proposes to pay, + what he actually wants me to do? Rhys left it all very vague in his talk to me. I didn't even know that he meant business.

(John Masefield, letter to C.F. Cazenove, 16 March 1910)
(University of Arizona Library. MS.50, V.II)

At the end of July 1910 he reported:

I have sent in to Mr Rhys, Mr Dent's editor, the manuscript of the Pilgrim Father's introduction. Will you please approach Mr D for a cheque?

(John Masefield, letter to C.F. Cazenove, 26 July 1910)
(University of Arizona Library. MS.50, V.II)

Copies seen: private collection (PWE) inscribed 'Charles | from Jan. | Dec. 1910. | See p 91.'; BL (12206.p1/340) stamped 28 SEP 1910, rebound; University of Warwick Library (F 4.5 C4)

Reprinted:

[first edition, second impression]	1917
[first edition, third impression]	1920

B100 RONALD ROSS, *PHILOSOPHIES*   1910

B100(a) First English edition (1910)

PHILOSOPHIES | BY RONALD ROSS | F.R.C.S., D.Sc., LL.D., F.R.S., C.B. | LONDON | JOHN MURRAY, ALBEMARLE STREET, W. | 1910
(All width centred)

Bibliographies: Williams [unrecorded], Simmons [unrecorded]

Collation: [A]⁴ 1–7⁴; signatures right foot of page; 32 leaves; 175 × 117mm.; [i–ii] iii–v [vi] vii–viii [1] 2–56

Page contents: [i] title-page; [ii] 'PRINTED BY | HAZELL, WATSON AND VINEY, LD., | LONDON AND AYLESBURY.'; iii–v 'PREFACE' ('THESE verses were written in India between the years 1881 and 1899...') (signed, 'THE AUTHOR. | DECEMBER 2, 1909.'); [vi] blank; vii–viii 'CONTENTS' (five sections listed with individual poems and page references); [1]-56 text (at foot of p.56: '[rule] | *Printed by Hazell, Watson & Viney, Ld., London and Aylesbury.*')

Paper: wove paper

Running title: running titles comprise section title on verso and titles of individual poems on recto, pp.2–56

Binding: blue/grey wrappers. On upper wrapper: 'PHILOSOPHIES | BY RONALD ROSS | F.R.C.S., D.SC., LL.D., F.R.S., C.B. | [ornament] | *ONE SHILLING NET.*' (lines 1–3 enclosed within rectangle with rounded corners: 55 × 80mm. and ornament enclosed within rectangle with rounded corners: 80 × 80mm.; both rectangles enclosed in rectangle: 149 × 89mm.) Inside of upper wrapper: blank. All edges trimmed. Binding measurements: 175 × 117mm. (wrappers), 175 × 7mm. (spine). Other information not discernible from examined copies.

Publication date: published, according to the *English Catalogue of Books*, September 1910

Price: 1s.

Masefield contents:
The final sentence of the preface reads: 'I am much indebted to Mr. John Masefield and Mrs. Masefield for assisting me in the correction of the proofs.'

Notes:
The five sections of the contents are as follows: 'Preludes', 'Apologues', 'Labours', 'In Exile' and 'Pæans'

Copies seen: BL (011650.e.62) stamped 30 SEP 1910, rebound; Bodleian (280.e.2717(8)) stamped 25 OCT 1910, incomplete wrappers

Reprinted:

[first edition, second impression]	Dec 1910
[first edition, third impression]	Jun 1911
[first edition, fourth impression]	Aug 1923

B105 GEORGE ANSON, *A VOYAGE ROUND THE WORLD*   1911

B105(a) First English edition (1910)

A [point] VOYAGE | ROUND [point] THE | WORLD [ornament] | in the years [ornament] | 1740–4 [ornament] by | LORD [point] ANSON | [illustration of ship within wavy border: 25 × 25mm.] | LONDON:PUBLISHED | byJ[point]M[point]DENT[point]&[point]SONS[point]Lᵀᴰ | AND   IN   NEW   YORK | BY E[point]P[point]DUTTON&CO
(With the exception of the illustration, all justified on left and right margins; many of the letters are ornate and overlaid. All in white rectangle: 111 × 63mm., within border of leaves and flowers: 157 × 99mm., signed 'RKC')

Bibliographies: Williams p.12, Simmons p.132

Collation: [*a*]⁸ *b*⁶ A-2A⁸ (J, V and W not used); signatures right foot of page; 206 leaves; 172 × 106mm.; [two un-numbered pages] [i–vi] vii–xix [xx] xxi–xxii [xxiii–xxvi] [1] 2–384

Page contents: [-] blank (page excluded from page count, but constitutes first leaf of first gathering); [-] blank; [i] 'EVERYMAN'S LIBRARY | EDITED BY ERNEST RHYS | TRAVEL AND | TOPOGRAPHY | ANSON'S VOYAGE | ROUND THE WORLD | WITH AN INTRODUCTION BY | JOHN MASEFIELD' (lines 1 and 2, 3 and 4, and 5, 6, 7, and 8 comprise three separate blocks of text individually justified to different margins on both left and right); [ii] publisher's advertisement (within border: 115 × 67mm., enclosing four rectangles of different sizes); [iii] blank; [iv] 'TO | THE | WISE MAN | ALL THE | WORLD'S | A SOIL | BEN JONSON' (intertwined by floral design signed 'K' with the first 'T' as a drop capital (signed 'R') all in white rectangle within border of leaves and flowers in mirror image of title-page); [v] title-page; [vi] blank; vii–xviii 'INTRODUCTION' ('The men-of-war in which Anson went to sea were built mostly of oak.') (signed 'JOHN MASEFIELD | *January* 30, 1911.'); xix 'BIBLIOGRAPHY'; [xx] blank; xxi–xxii 'CONTENTS' (three books and their chapters listed with page references); [xxiii] map: 'A CHART | OF THE SOUTHERN PART OF | SOUTH AMERICA'... (within border: 144 × 90mm.); [xxiv] map: 'A CHART | OF PART OF PACIFIC OCEAN' (within border: 146 × 60mm.); [xxv] 'A | VOYAGE | ROUND THE | WORLD...'; [xxvi] blank; [1]-2 letter (to His Grace, John Duke of Bedford, etc. signed Richard Walter); 3–10 'AUTHOR'S INTRODUCTION'; 11–380 text; 381–84 'INDEX' (at foot of p.384: 'THE TEMPLE PRESS, PRINTERS, LETCHWORTH')

Paper: wove paper

Running title: 'Anson's Voyage Round the World' (67mm.) on verso; recto title comprises section title, pp. viii-384

Binding: dark green cloth. On spine, in gold: '[ornament] | A VOYAGE | ROUND | THE [ornament] | WORLD | 1740–4 | BY LORD | ANSON | [design of flowers and leaves] | [point]J[point]M[point]DENT[point] | [seven points] | E[point]P[point]DUTTON | [two leaves] & Cᵒ [two leaves]' (all justified on left and right margins). On upper cover, in blind: publisher's design of plant with lettering '[point]I[point]M[point] | DENT & | SONS Lᴰ' within border: 23 × 22mm., all enclosed within blind ruled border: 171 × 103mm. with a circle in two corners furthest from spine. Lower cover: blank. Top edge stained, others trimmed. Binding measurements: 176 × 110mm. (covers), 176 × 25mm. (spine). End-papers: wove paper, decorated with swirling leaf and stems, female figure and, within scroll: 'EVERYMAN, | I [point] WILL [point] GO [point] WITH | [point] THEE. | & [point] BE [point] THY [point] GVIDE | IN [point] THY [point] MOST [point] NEED | TO [point] GO [point] BY [point] THY [point] SIDE'.

Also issued in leather.

Publication date: published, according to Simmons, March 1911

Price: 1s. (cloth) / 2s. (leather)

Masefield contents:
'Introduction' ('The men-of-war in which Anson went to sea were built mostly of oak.')
    (signed 'JOHN MASEFIELD | *January* 30, 1911.')

Notes:
The Grant Richards archive includes a letter from Richards to Masefield dated 16 November, 1905 inviting him to a meeting to decide 'about... the Life of Lord Anson'. This came to nothing and it would seem that Masefield turned his attention to Dampier. It does, however, show interest in a different aspect of Anson earlier than 1911.

Copies seen: private collection (PWE) inscribed 'Charles from John. | Christmas. 1911. | With all good wishes.'; BL (12206.p.1/365) stamped 9 MAR 1911; UCL (HISTORY B 57I); Warwick University Library (G 440 A6)

Reprinted:

	[first edition, second impression]	1923
'Reprinted'	[first edition, third impression]	1930

B105(b) Second English edition (1970)

A reprint published by Heron Books (Edito-Service S.A., Geneva distributed by Heron Books) was, primarily, an edition photoset from B105(a). It included, however, full page illustrations.

Copies seen: BL (X.809/7939) stamped 25 AUG 1970

B110 ROBERT SOUTHEY, *THE LIFE OF NELSON*   1911

B110(a) First English edition (1911)

THE | LIFE OF | NELSON | BY ROBERT SOUTHEY | WITH AN | INTRODUCTION BY JOHN | MASEFIELD & DESIGNS BY | FRANK BRANGWYN | A.R.A. | LONDON: GIBBINGS | & COMPANY | LIMITED
(All in red and width centred. Enclosed within illustration of ships in battle with flags and ornate shield in black with bold black border: 183 × 134mm.)

Bibliographies: Williams p.12, Simmons p.132–33

Collation: [A]⁸ B–T⁸ (J not used); signatures left foot of page; 152 leaves; 251 × 171mm.; [i–iv] v–vii [viii] ix–xiv [xv–xvi] [1–2] 3–25 [26] 27–43 [44–46] 47–82 [83–84] 85–103 [104] 105–130 [131] 132–34 [135–36] 137–72 [173–74] 175–78 [179] 180–94 [195–96] 197–212 [213] 214–51 [252] 253–74 [275–76] 277–79 [280] 281–87 [288]

Page contents: [i] '"It may be | truly said | that the com= | mandment of | the sea is an | abridgement | of a quint= | essence of a | universal | monarchy." | Francis Bacon.' (within ruled border: 69 × 47mm. and within illustration of two ships within ruled border: 150 × 110mm.); [ii] '*Of this edition One Hundred | Copies are printed | This being Number* ....' (with additional leaf tipped-in on the verso of which is the colour frontispiece: 162 × 127mm., of Nelson, with protective tissue); [iii] title-page; [iv] 'BIBLIOGRAPHICAL NOTE'; v–vi 'CONTENTS' (Introduction and nine chapters listed with page references); vii 'LIST OF PLATES' (eight plates listed including frontispiece with page references); [viii] blank; ix–[xv] 'INTRODUCTION' ('ROBERT SOUTHEY, the author of this "Life of Nelson," was an...') (unsigned, dated '*June*, 1911'); [xvi] blank; [1] 'BUILDING THE FRIGATE' (protective page for plate which follows); [2] blank; 3–[280] text; 281–[88] 'INDEX' (at foot of p.[288]: 'THE RIVERSIDE PRESS LIMITED, EDINBURGH.')

Paper: wove paper

Running title: 'LIFE OF NELSON' (63mm.) on verso; recto title comprises a brief indication of text subject, pp.4–[280]

Binding: blue cloth. On spine, in gold: 'THE | LIFE OF | NELSON | [circular design enclosing anchor, diameter: 7mm.] | SOUTHEY | [circular design, diameter: 34mm.] | [circular design enclosing telescope, diameter: 15mm.] | GIBBINGS' (all width centred). On upper cover, in gold: oval design of sea, canon and anchor: 42 × 41mm. Lower cover: blank. Top edge gilt, others trimmed. Binding measurements: 260 × 174mm. (covers); 260 × 49mm. (spine). End-papers: wove paper with unsigned illustration in black of ships in battle.

Also issued in half-leather.

Publication date: published, according to Simmons, November 1911

Price: 7s.6d. (cloth) / 21s. (half-leather)

Masefield contents:
'Introduction' ('ROBERT SOUTHEY, the author of this "Life of Nelson," was an..')
          (unsigned, dated '*June*, 1911')

Notes:
Un-numbered pages result from protective pages for plates and illustrations which often end a chapter.

The introduction provides a brief sketch of Southey, a few notes on the work (noting both its successes and defects), clarifies a few issues and then considers Nelson himself. In the conclusion Masefield writes genuine praise from a deep sense of admiration, yet avoids hagiography:

> Determination will always command respect, and genius reverence, and kindness love. All these were in Nelson, together with much passion, much wisdom, a great deal of nervous sensibility and some vanity. There was also something wistful, magnetic and compelling, which cannot be explained nor ignored. It does not get into the books, it cannot be put into words, it is simply mysterious and very beautiful. It was this quality in him which made his rough sea captains shed tears when he explained his plans to them. It was by this quality that he bound men's hearts together, and gave to their virtue purpose and to their strength an aim.

Masefield was approached about providing an introduction by the publisher. Gibbings and Company wrote at the beginning of February 1911:

> …We are getting ready a nice edition of Southeys Life of Nelson for this autumn – with illustrations in colour + black + white by Frank Brangwen A.R.A. and wish to know if you would write a preface or short introduction. We thought that the subject would interest you. The edition will we expect be dedicated by permission to the King.
>
> (Gibbings and Co., letter to John Masefield, 2 February 1911)
> (University of Arizona Library. MS.50)

Copies seen: BL (10816.h.14) number 100F, numbered '100F' on p.[ii], stamped 28 NOV 1911, rebound; Bodleian (22871.d.95) limitation not present, stamped 13 NOV 1911

B115 REGINALD WRIGHT KAUFFMAN, *DAUGHTERS OF ISHMAEL*   1911

B115(a) First English edition (1911)

DAUGHTERS | OF ISHMAEL | BY | REGINALD WRIGHT | KAUFFMAN | [rule, 89mm.] | [design of an 'S' in outline coupled with an 'S' in bold with two crossed arrows, two books and a bold circular outline enclosing another outline thinner than the first: 19 × 24mm.] | [rule, 89mm.] | LONDON | STEPHEN SWIFT & CO LTD | 10 JOHN STREET ADELPHI | MCMXI
(All width centred and enclosed within ruled border: 154 × 90mm. As a result of the two rules noted above, three rectangles are created measuring 40 × 90mm., 92 × 90mm. and 23 × 90mm. respectively from the top. Six lines in total appear although not all completely touch)

Bibliographies: Williams p.12, Simmons p.133

Collation: [π]⁸ A-2B⁸ (J, V and W not used); signatures right foot of page; 208 leaves; at least 180 × 120mm.; [i–vi] vii–xvi 1–396 [397–400]

Page contents: [i] half-title: 'DAUGHTERS OF ISHMAEL'; [ii] blank; [iii] title-page; [iv] 'PRINTED BY | BALLANTYNE & COMPANY LTD | TAVISTOCK STREET COVENT GARDEN | LONDON'; [v] 'TO | ANDREW JOHN KAUFFMAN | (1840–1899) | [text of verse]'; [vi] blank; vii–xiv 'PREFACE' ('Mr. Kauffman's book, now printed in England for the first time…') (signed, 'JOHN MASEFIELD'); xv 'CONTENTS' (30 titled chapters, numbered and with page references); xvi 'CAVEAT EMPTOR' ('This story is intended for three classes of readers…') (signed 'REGINALD WRIGHT KAUFFMAN | NEW YORK CITY'); 1–382 text; 383–96 *'EDITOR'S NOTE'* (includes full report of January 1910 New York special Grand Jury investigation into White Slave Traffic) (at foot of p.396: 'PRINTED BY | BALLANTYNE & COMPANY LTD | TAVISTOCK STREET COVENT GARDEN | LONDON'); [397–400] publisher's advertisements

Paper: wove paper

Running title: 'DAUGHTERS OF ISHMAEL' (49mm.) on verso; recto title comprises chapter title, pp.viii-396

Binding: not discernible from examined copy

Publication date: published, according to Simmons, December 1911

Price: 6s.

Masefield contents:
'Preface' ('Mr. Kauffman's book, now printed in England for the first time, tells simply and frankly the story…')
(signed, 'JOHN MASEFIELD')

Notes:
Masefield's introduction considers prostitution and draws parallels between American prostitution depicted in the novel and practice in England. It would seem to be primarily addressed to an English readership intent on comforting itself with the Atlantic ocean.

It appears that Kauffman attempted, on Masefield's behalf, to get *The Everlasting Mercy* published by Moffat, Yard & Co. during September 1911 (see notes to A21(a)).

Copies seen: BL (012704.dd.27) stamped 19 DEC 1911, rebound; Bodleian (25611.e.764) copy missing since 1925

Reprinted:

'Second Impression' (published by Stephen Swift)	[first edition, second impression]	Jan 1912
[Third Impression]	[first edition, third impression]	Jan 1912
[Fourth Impression]	[first edition, fourth impression]	Feb 1912
[Fifth Impression]	[first edition, fifth impression]	Feb 1912
[Sixth Impression]	[first edition, sixth impression]	Feb 1912
[Seventh Impression]	[first edition, seventh impression]	Aug 1912
[Eighth Impression]	[first edition, eighth impression]	Sep 1912
'Ninth Edition' (published by T. Werner Laurie Ltd.)	[first edition, ninth impression]	Apr 1913

B120 *Ed.* SIR SIDNEY LEE. *DICTIONARY OF NATIONAL BIOGRAPHY. SECOND SUPPLEMENT, VOL. III*   1912

B120(a) First English edition (1912)

DICTIONARY | OF | NATIONAL BIOGRAPHY | EDITED BY | SIR SIDNEY LEE | SECOND SUPPLEMENT | VOL. III | NEIL–YOUNG | LONDON | SMITH, ELDER & CO., 15 WATERLOO PLACE | 1912 | [*All rights reserved*]
(All width centred)

Bibliographies: Williams [unrecorded], Simmons [unrecorded]

Publication date: published, according to the *English Catalogue of Books*, December 1912

Price: 15s. (single volume)

Masefield contents:
'Synge, John Millington' '(1871–1909), Irish dramatist, born at Newtown Little, near Rathfarnham (a suburban village…')
(signed, 'J.M.')

Notes:
The original sixty-three volumes of the *Dictionary of National Biography* were published between 1885 and 1900. The first supplement (3 volumes) was published in 1901. The second supplement providing biographies of persons who died between 22 January 1901 and 31 December 1911 was published in 1912 and also consisted of three volumes. Masefield only ever contributed one article to the *Dictionary*.

Copies seen: Sotheby's, Department of Printed Books and Manuscripts, Reference Library, rebound

B125 F.M. MAYOR, *THE THIRD MISS SYMONS* 1913

B125(a) First English edition (1913)

The Third Miss Symons | by F.M. Mayor. With a Preface by | John Masefield | London : Sidgwick & Jackson Ltd. | Adam Street, Adelphi, W.C. 1913
(Lines 1–3 justified on same left and right margins; lines 4–5 justified on same left and right margins)

Bibliographies: Williams, p.12, Simmons p.133

Collation: [A]⁶ B-E⁸ [F]⁸ G-I⁸ K¹⁰ (J not used); signatures right foot of page; 80 leaves; 187 × 130mm.; [two un-numbered pages] [i–iv] v–ix [x] 1–143 [144–48]

Page contents: [-] blank (page excluded from page count, but constitutes first leaf of first gathering); [-] blank; [i] half-title: 'The Third Miss Symons | [publisher's oval device incorporating 'S', '&' and 'J' within ruled border: 18 × 12mm.]'; [ii] *UNIFORM WITH THIS VOLUME* | [two volumes listed]'; [iii] title-page; [iv] '*All rights reserved.*'; v-[x] 'PREFACE' ('Miss Mayor's story is of a delicate quality, not common here, though occurring at intervals, and...') (signed, 'JOHN MASEFIELD.'); 1–[144] text (at foot of p.[144]: '[rule] | BILLING AND SONS LTD., PRINTERS, GUILDFORD'); [145–48] publisher's advertisements ('FROM SIDGWICK & JACKSON'S LIST')

Paper: laid paper (no watermark), chain-lines 28mm. apart

Running title: 'PREFACE | [rule, 89mm.]' on both verso and recto, pp.vi-[x]; 'THE THIRD MISS SYMONS | [rule, 90mm.]' on both verso and recto, pp.2–[144]

Binding: blue cloth. On spine, in gold: '[triple rule] | THE | THIRD | MISS | SYMONS | F. M. | MAYOR | SIDGWICK | & | JACKSON | [triple rule]' (all width centred). On upper cover, in gold: 'The Third | Miss Symons | [rule] | [design of 15 ruled border squares within each other] | [rule (part of which forms the lower border of the largest square)] | F.M. Mayor' (within ruled border: 156 × 102mm. As a result of the two rules noted above, three rectangles are created. All enclosed within four further ruled borders: 180 × 127mm.) Lower cover: blank. Top edge gilt, others trimmed. Binding measurements: 193 × 133mm. (covers), 193 × 30mm. (spine). End-papers: blue wove paper.

Publication date: published, according to Simmons, March 1913

Price: 3s.6d.

Masefield contents:
'Preface' ('Miss Mayor's story is of a delicate quality, not common here, though occurring at intervals, and...')
        (signed, 'JOHN MASEFIELD.')

Notes:
The novel is divided into thirteen untitled chapters.

The preface and each chapter commence with a drop capital.

A letter (dated 28 August 1912) from Masefield to Frank Sidgwick held at Harvard College Library (Houghton bMS Eng 1069 *57M-54) finds Masefield introducing to Sidgwick 'a very remarkable story of a rather awkward length' by Miss Mayor. Masefield was presumably therefore responsible for getting the work into print.

At the beginning of April 1913 Masefield thanked the publisher after receiving a number of copies:

> Many thanks for your letter + for so kindly sending me the Mayor books, which I will scatter, with discretion, wherever I think they will do most good. It is a kind of book which will always have a small but very select audience, + to know it will rather stamp a person. I am very glad you have done it.

                (John Masefield, letter to [Frank] Sidgwick, 5 April 1913)
                (HRHRC, MS (Sidgwick, F.) Recip. Masefield, J.)

The final two pages of the publisher's advertisements at the rear of the volume comprise an entire page advertisement for *The Everlasting Mercy* ('Tenth Impression') and one page for both *The Widow in the Bye Street* ('Third Impression') and *The Tragedy of Pompey the Great* ('Third Impression').

Copies seen: BL (NN.994) stamped 30 MAY 1913

B125(b) Second English edition (1980)

The Third Miss Symons | by F.M. Mayor. With a Preface by | John Masefield | New Introduction by Susan Hill | [publisher's device incorporating an apple, 'Virago' and 'London']
(Lines 1–4 justified on same left and right margins; publisher's device is width centred)

Publication date: published, according to *Whitaker's*, September 1980

Price: £2.50

Masefield contents:
'Preface' ('Miss Mayor's story is of a delicate quality, not common here, though occurring at intervals, and...')
        (signed, 'JOHN MASEFIELD, 1913')

Notes:

A new edition of the novel using a photographic process to produce a facsimile of the first edition. Page numbers have been deleted from Masefield's preface, however, and his contribution has been dated. A new introduction is provided by Susan Hill.

The volume states, on page [iv], that it is 'Printed in Great Britain by The Anchor Press Ltd and bound by Wm Brendon & Son Ltd both of Tiptree, Essex'

The ISBN number is ISBN 0 86068 131 9

Copies seen: BL (X.908/43757) stamped 19 AUG 1980

Reprinted:

| | [second edition, second impression] | 1987 |
| 'Reprinted' | [second edition, third impression] | 1993 |

B130 R.C. PHILLIMORE, *POEMS*   1913

B130(a) First English edition (1913)

POEMS | BY R. C. PHILLIMORE | WITH AN INTRODUCTION | BY JOHN MASEFIELD | *By the grace of God I took* | *From my lady's hands this book,* | *And herein for my lady's sake* | *Her songs I'll make.* | LONDON : SIDGWICK & JACKSON, LTD. | 3, ADAM STREET, W.C. MCMXIII
(All width centred with lines 1–4 justified on left and right margins and lines 9–10 justified on left and right margins. All enclosed within ruled border: 127 × 73mm.)

Bibliographies: Williams p.12, Simmons p.133

Collation: [π]⁸ 1–3⁸; signatures right foot of page (above page number); 32 leaves; 183 × 120mm.; [i–iv] v–xi [xii] xiii–xiv [xv–xvi] [1] 2–44 [45–48]

Page contents: [i] half-title: 'POEMS BY R. C. PHILLIMORE'; [ii] blank; [iii] title-page; [iv] '*All rights reserved.*'; v–xi 'INTRODUCTION' ('Mr. Phillimore's poems have a quality that is as rare in literature as in...') (signed, 'JOHN MASEFIELD. | *June* 10, 1913.'); [xii] blank; xiii–xiv 'CONTENTS' (introduction and 32 individual poems listed with page references); [xv] 'POEMS'; [xvi] blank; [1]-44 text; [45] 'PRINTED BY | BILLING AND SONS, LTD. | GUILDFORD.'; [46–48] publisher's advertisements ('FROM | SIDGWICK & JACKSON'S LIST.') (at foot of p.[48]: '[rule] | SIDWICK & JACKSON, LTD. | 3 ADAM STREET, ADELPHI, LONDON, W.C.')

Paper: laid paper (no watermark), chain-lines 24mm. apart

Running title: none

Binding: navy-blue cloth. On spine: paper label (46 × 16mm.) on which: 'POEMS | By R. C. | PHILLI- | MORE | [rule] | Intro- | duction by | JOHN | MASEFIELD | [rule] | SIDGWICK | AND | JACKSON LD' (all left justified and enclosed within ruled border: 41 × 13mm.) Covers: blank. All edges trimmed. Binding measurements: 188 × 122mm. (covers), 188 × 22mm. (spine). End-papers: laid paper (no watermark), chain-lines 24mm. apart. Additional spine label tipped-in at rear of volume.

Publication date: published, according to the *English Catalogue of Books*, November 1913

Price: 2s.6d.

Masefield contents:
'Introduction' ('Mr. Phillimore's poems have a quality that is as rare in literature as in...')
    (signed, 'JOHN MASEFIELD. | *June* 10, 1913.')

Notes:
While thanking Frank Sidgwick for copies of *The Third Miss Symons* (see B125(a)), Masefield asked 'How about the Phillimore poems, that I was to write a preface to?' (see John Masefield, letter to [Frank] Sidgwick, 5 April 1913) (HRHRC, MS (Sidgwick, F.) Recip. Masefield, J.)

Copies seen: private collection (PWE); BL (011649.eee.18) stamped 8 NOV 1913

B135 *ROYAL SOCIETY OF LITERATURE   THE ACADEMIC COMMITTEE ADDRESSES OF RECEPTION... NOVEMBER 27th, 1914*   1915

B135(a) First English edition (1915)

ROYAL SOCIETY OF LITERATURE | THE ACADEMIC COMMITTEE | ADDRESSES OF RECEPTION | TO | Mrs. ALICE MEYNELL | By Henry Newbolt | TO | G. LOWES DICKINSON | By A. C. Benson | Award of the EDMOND DE POLIGNAC PRIZE | TO | RALPH HODGSON | By J. Masefield | Chairman's Address by GILBERT MURRAY | FRIDAY, NOVEMBER 27th, 1914 | LONDON | HUMPHREY MILFORD | OXFORD UNIVERSITY PRESS, AMEN CORNER, E.C. | 1915
(All width centred)

Bibliographies: Williams [unrecorded], Simmons p.133

Collation: [1]⁸ 2⁸ 3⁶; the second leaf of gathering 3 is also signed; signatures right foot of page; 22 leaves; 215 × 140mm.; [1–5] 6–43 [44]

Page contents: [1] title-page; [2] blank; [3] 'THE ACADEMIC COMMITTEE. | [35 names listed in two columns] | [rule] | [eight names listed with date of death] | [rule] | PERCY W. AMES, | *Secretary.*'; [4] 'CONTENTS.' (five sections listed with page references); [5]-43 text (at foot of p.43: 'ADLARD AND SON, IMPR., LONDON AND DORKING.'); [44] blank

Paper: wove paper (watermark: 'TEMPLE')

Running title: none

Binding: mottled grey wrappers. Spine: blank. On upper wrapper: 'ROYAL SOCIETY OF LITERATURE | THE ACADEMIC COMMITTEE | ADDRESSES OF RECEPTION | TO | Mrs. ALICE MEYNELL | By Henry Newbolt | TO | G. LOWES DICKINSON | By A. C. Benson | Award of the EDMOND DE POLIGNAC PRIZE | TO | RALPH HODGSON | By J. Masefield | Chairman's Address by GILBERT MURRAY | FRIDAY, NOVEMBER 27th, 1914 | LONDON | HUMPHREY MILFORD | OXFORD UNIVERSITY PRESS, AMEN CORNER, E.C. | 1915 | Price One Shilling.' Lower wrapper: blank. All edges trimmed. Binding measurements: 215 × 140mm. (wrappers); 215 × 4mm. (spine).

Publication date: published, according to Simmons, January 1915

Price: 1s.

Masefield contents:
Fourth Award of the Edmond De Polignac Prize. ('…We end this November meeting of the Academic Committee with…')
(introduced as 'Mr. John Masefield said')

Notes:
Page 5 notes that the meeting was held at 20 Hanover Square on Friday, November 27th, 1914.

The contents is as follows: 'List of Members of the Academic Committee', 'Address by Mr. Gilbert Murray, Chairman', 'Address by Mr. Henry Newbolt to Mrs. Alice Meynell', 'Address by Mr. A.C. Benson to Mr. G. Lowes Dickinson' and 'Award of the Polignac Prize by Mr. John Masefield to Mr. Ralph Hodgson'

Masefield had previously been awarded the Edmond de Polignac prize for *The Everlasting Mercy*.

Copies seen: BL (R.Ac.9125/12) stamped 22 JAN 1915, rebound; HRHRC (PR5 R6 1915)

B140 WALT MASON, *"HORSE SENSE" IN VERSES TENSE*   1915

B140(a) *First American edition (1915)*

"HORSE SENSE" | IN VERSES TENSE | [rule, 15mm.] | by Walt Mason [facsimile signature] | [rule, 15mm.] | Walt Mason is the High Priest of Horse Sense. | – George Ade | [ornament of Pegasus: 24 × 22mm.] [in pink] | LONDON | C. F. CAZENOVE | CHICAGO: A. C. McCLURG & CO. | 1915
(All width centred with the exception of line seven which is off-set to the right. Examples of the capital 'S' in the first two lines (with the exception of the first letter of 'SENSE') have an ornate addition to its foot. All enclosed within ornate border, in pink: 134 × 89mm.)

Bibliographies: Williams [unrecorded], Simmons [unrecorded]

Collation: [A-N]⁸ (J not used); 104 leaves; 194 × 132mm.; [i–x] xi–xv [xvi] 1–188 [189–92]

Page contents: [i] half-title: '"HORSE SENSE"'; [ii] 'CONCERNING WALT | [rule] | [eight paragraphs of reviews (each stating source)]' (within ornate pink border); [iii] blank; [iv] '[black and white cartoon signed, 'ZIM | 14'] | The author as "Zim" sees him'; [v] title-page; [vi] 'Copyright | A. C. McClurg & Co. | 1915 | [rule] | Published September, 1915 | [rule] | Copyrighted in Great Britain | For permission to use copyright poems in this book thanks | are extended to George Matthew Adams, and to the editors | and publishers of *Judge, Collier's Weekly, System,* the | *Magazine of Business, Domestic Engineering,* the | *Butler Way,* and *Curtis Service.*'; [vii] '*To* | SIR ARTHUR CONAN DOYLE'; [viii] 'CHRISTMAS GIFT' ('The gift itself is not so much –') (unsigned) (within ornate pink border); [ix] 'FROM SIR HUBERT' ('I read Walt Mason with great delight. His poems have…') (signed, 'John Masefield | *13 Well Walk, Hampstead, | London*') (within ornate pink border); [x] blank; xi–xv 'GUIDE TO CONTENTS' (134 sections with each page within ornate pink border); [xvi] blank; 1–188 text (with each page within ornate pink border); [189–92] blank

Paper: wove paper (watermark: 'King Dodo Book | [within crest: 38 × 36mm.: '*The* | P M | *Co*'] | [within curved scroll: 'QUALITY']')

Running title: none

Binding: burgundy cloth. On spine, in gold reading lengthways up spine, from foot: '"HORSE SENSE"' (the first and third capital 'S' has an ornate addition to its foot). On upper cover: in gold: '[embossed design of Pegasus with border of lines and circles all in rounded edged border: 53 × 53mm.; ranged upper right] | "HORSE SENSE" [the first and third capital 'S' has an ornate addition to its foot] | by [with an ornate circular link between letters] | Walt Mason [facsimile signature]'. Lower cover: blank. All edges trimmed. Binding measurements: 200 × 133mm. (covers), 200 × 26mm. (spine). End-papers: wove paper.

Also issued in leather.

Publication date: published, according to date within volume, September 1915

Price: $1.25 (cloth) / $1.50 (leather)

Masefield contents:
'FROM SIR HUBERT' ('I read Walt Mason with great delight. His poems have wonderful fun and kindliness...')
(signed, 'John Masefield | *13 Well Walk, Hampstead, | London*')

Notes:
The 'Guide to Contents' lists 134 individual sections. Each of the short sections commence with a drop capital.

The ornate border in pink (external measurements: 134 × 89mm.) is printed on pp.[ii], [v], [viii–ix], [xi–xv] and 1–188. A black and white design of Pegasus is printed after the text on pp.3, 6, 15, 18, 23, 25, 29, 35, 40, 59, 62, 68, 76, 81, 84, 116, 124, 140, 155, 157, 163, 168, 170, 175, 177 and 183. (On verso pages the horse faces right and on recto pages the horse faces left).

As in the Duckworth edition (see B140(b)), the Masefield letter occurs on a recto page with verse on the verso. However, in this edition (but omitted from B140(b)) the titles 'CHRISTMAS GIFT' and 'FROM SIR HUBERT' appear. Whether these should be read together or singly is unknown. Any connection with 'Sir Hubert' and Masefield is also unknown. As there appears to be some link here the verse cannot necessarily be assumed not to be by Masefield.

This edition does not appear in the *English Catalogue of Books*. The Duckworth edition does, however, and within that volume page [iv] carries the information '*First published 1916*'. It must be assumed that the edition described here comprises the first American edition and the title-page inclusion of 'LONDON | C. F. CAZENOVE' may represent the copyrighting of the edition. In addition to his partnership in The Literary Agency of London, C.F. Cazenove was also connected with his family business of book exporters.

Copies seen: BL (011686.g.10) stamped 30 SEP 1915

B140(b) First English edition (1916)

'HORSE SENSE' | IN VERSES TENSE | BY | WALT MASON | LONDON | DUCKWORTH & CO. | 3 HENRIETTA STREET, COVENT GARDEN
(All width centred)

Bibliographies: Williams [unrecorded], Simmons [unrecorded]

Collation: [1]⁶ A-L⁸ M⁶ (J not used); M2 is also signed; 100 leaves; 164 × 105mm.; [i–viii] ix–xii 1–187 [188]

Page contents: [i] half-title: "HORSE SENSE"; [ii] blank; [iii] title-page; [iv] '*First published 1916* | *Printed in Great Britain* | *by Turnbull & Spears, Edinburgh*'; [v] 'TO SIR ARTHUR CONAN DOYLE'; [vi] [Untitled] ('The gift itself is not so much–') (unsigned); [vii] [Untitled] ('I read Walt Mason with great delight. His poems have...') (signed, 'JOHN MASEFIELD | 13 WELL WALK, HAMPSTEAD'); [viii] blank; ix–xii 'CONTENTS' (134 sections); 1–[188] text

Paper: wove paper

Running title: running titles comprise title of section, pp.x–[188]

Binding: blue cloth. On spine, in gold: 'HORSE | SENSE | WALT | MASON | DUCKWORTH'. On upper cover, in blind: 'HORSE SENSE | WALT MASON'. On lower cover, in blind: floral design with no fixed border ranged lower left and including 'MESORMAIS', external measurements: 36 × 33mm. All edges trimmed. Binding measurements: 168 × 107mm. (covers), 168 × 30mm. (spine). End-papers: wove paper.

Publication date: published, according to the *English Catalogue of Books*, June 1916

Price: 2s.6d.

Masefield contents:
[Untitled] ('I read Walt Mason with great delight. His poems have wonderful fun and kindliness...')
(signed, 'JOHN MASEFIELD | 13 WELL WALK, HAMPSTEAD')

Notes:
As in the American edition, the Masefield letter occurs on a recto page with verse on the verso. However, in this edition the titles 'CHRISTMAS GIFT' and 'FROM SIR HUBERT' are omitted.

Copies seen: BL (011686.df.23) stamped 2 JUN 1916

B145 EDWARD G.D. LIVEING, *ATTACK*   1918

B145(a) First American edition (1918)

ATTACK | AN INFANTRY SUBALTERN'S IMPRESSIONS | OF JULY 1ST, 1916 | BY | EDWARD G. D. LIVEING | WITH AN INTRODUCTION BY | JOHN MASEFIELD | New York | THE MACMILLAN COMPANY | 1918 | *All rights reserved*
(All width centred)

Bibliographies: Williams [unrecorded], Simmons [unrecorded]

Collation: [A-G]⁸ [H]⁴; 60 leaves; 190 × 128mm.; [1–6] 7–19 [20–22] 23–114 [115–20]

Page contents: [1] half-title: 'ATTACK'; [2] '[publisher's device] | THE MACMILLAN COMPANY | [two lines listing six cities, separated by four points] | MACMILLAN & CO., LIMITED | [two lines listing four cities, separated by two points] | THE MACMILLAN CO. OF CANADA, LTD. | [one city listed]'; [3] title-page; [4] 'COPYRIGHT, 1918 | BY THE MACMILLAN COMPANY | [rule] | Set up and electrotyped. Published, April, 1918'; [5] 'TO | THE N.C.O.s | AND | MEN OF No. 5 PLATOON | Of a Battalion of the County of London | Regiment, whom I had the good | fortune to command in France | during 1915–1916, and in | particular to the | memory of | RFN. C. N. DENNISON | My Platoon Observer, who fell in action | July 1st, 1916, in an attempt | to save my life'; [6] blank; 7–19 'INTRODUCTION' ('THE attack on the fortified village of Gommecourt, which Mr. Liveing describes…') (signed 'JOHN MASEFIELD'); [20] blank; [21] 'CONTENTS' (four chapters listed with titles and page references); [22] blank; 23–114 text (at foot of p.114: 'PRINTED IN THE UNITED STATES OF AMERICA'); [115] 'THE following pages contain advertisements of a few of | the Macmillan books on kindred subjects.' (within ruled border: 13 × 74mm.); [116] blank; [117–20] publisher's advertisements

Paper: wove paper

Running title: '*Introduction*' (25mm.) on both verso and recto, pp.8–19; '*Attack*' (13mm.) on verso, recto title comprises chapter title, pp.24–114

Binding: brown cloth. On spine, in gold: '[rule] | ATTACK | E. G. D. | LIVEING | MACMILLAN | [rule]' (all width centred). On upper cover, in gold: 'ATTACK | EDWARD G.D. LIVEING | [rule]' (this rule includes two vertical rules in blind). Lower cover: blank. Top edge trimmed, others roughly trimmed. Binding measurements: 196 × 128mm. (covers), 196 × 28mm. (spine). End-papers: wove paper.

Publication date: published, according to date within volume, April 1918

Price: $0.75

Masefield contents:
Introduction ('The attack on the fortified village of Gommecourt, which Mr. Liveing describes…')
        (signed 'JOHN MASEFIELD')

Notes:
A note at the conclusion of Masefield's introduction states:

> The Author wishes to thank Messrs. Blackwood and Sons for their kind permission to republish this article, which appeared in *Blackwood's Magazine*, December, 1917, under the title of "Battle."

This note refers to Liveing's text only. When published in *Blackwood's Magazine* (December 1917, pp.715–38) the text appeared without an introduction by Masefield.

An early agreement for this title between Masefield and Macmillan was dated 5 March 1918 (see Archives of The Society of Authors). A later publishing agreement was dated 16 May 1918. The later agreement refers to Masefield 'acting as agent for Edward Liveing' and that the agreement was to 'remain in force until an agreement… shall be made between the said Edward Liveing and the Company'. Payment was to be made to Liveing.

Copies seen: private collection (PWE) inscribed 'for Corinne Roosevelt Robinson. | from John Masefield. | May 5. 1918.'

B145(b) First English edition (1918)

ATTACK | AN INFANTRY SUBALTERN'S IMPRESSIONS | OF JULY 1ST, 1916 | BY | EDWARD G. D. LIVEING | WITH AN INTRODUCTION BY | JOHN MASEFIELD | LONDON | [publisher's device of a windmill with 'W [point]' and 'H' all within ruled border: 16 × 16mm.] | WILLIAM HEINEMANN
(All width centred)

Bibliographies: Williams p.12, Simmons p.134

Collation: [A]¹⁶ B¹⁶ C¹²; A5, B5, C3 and C4 are also signed; signatures left foot of page; 44 leaves; the catalogue (not included in collation or leaf count) comprises three gatherings of 8 leaves; 173 × 107mm.; [i–vi] vii–xvii [18] 19–86 [87–88]; catalogue pagination: [1–3] 4–47 [48]

Page contents: [i] half-title: 'ATTACK'; [ii] 'THE LATEST WAR BOOKS | [13 volumes and their authors listed with prices] | [rule] | LONDON: WILLIAM HEINEMANN'; [iii] title-page; [iv] '*London : William Heinemann,* 1918'; [v] 'TO THE N.C.O.S AND MEN OF NO. 5 PLATOON | OF A BATTALION OF THE COUNTY OF LONDON | REGIMENT, WHOM I HAD THE GOOD FORTUNE | TO COMMAND IN FRANCE DURING 1915–1916, | AND IN PARTICULAR TO THE MEMORY OF | RFN. C. S. DENNISON | MY PLATOON OBSERVER, WHO FELL IN ACTION | JULY 1ST, 1916, IN AN ATTEMPT TO SAVE MY | LIFE.'; [vi] blank; vii–xvi 'INTRODUCTION' ('The attack on the fortified village of Gommecourt, which Mr. Liveing describes…') (signed, 'JOHN MASEFIELD.'); xvii 'CONTENTS' (four chapters listed with page references); [18] blank; 19–86 text (at foot of p.86: 'PRINTED 1918 IN GREAT BRITAIN BY R. CLAY AND SONS, LTD., | BRUNSWICK STREET, STAMFORD STREET, S.E. 1, AND BUNGAY, SUFFOLK.'); [87–88] publisher's advertisements; [1] 'A SELECTION FROM | WILLIAM HEINEMANN'S | GENERAL CATALOGUE'; [2] blank; [3]-47 text; [48] blank

Paper: wove paper

Running title: 'INTRODUCTION' (35mm.) on both verso and recto, pp.viii–xvi; 'ATTACK' (18mm.) on verso; recto title comprises chapter title, pp.20–86

Binding: grey boards. On spine, in dark blue: 'ATTACK | [ornament] | EDWARD | G.D. | LIVEING | HEINEMANN' (lines 1–5 within ruled border: 54 × 11mm. and line 6 within ruled border: 11 × 11mm.) On upper wrapper, in dark blue: 'ATTACK | AN INFANTRY | SUBALTERN'S IMPRESSIONS | OF JULY 1ˢᵀ 1916 | [rule, 97mm.] | [panel of design within ruled border: 127 × 94mm.]' (lines 1–4 within ruled border: 36 × 94mm. and entire page within ruled border: 172 × 99mm.) On lower wrapper, in dark blue: publisher's device of a windmill with 'W [point]' and 'H' all within ruled border: 21 × 21mm. All edges trimmed. Binding measurements: 178 × 110mm. (covers), 178 × 21mm. (spine). End-papers: laid paper.

Also issued, as suggested by the British Library copy, in purple-grey wrappers.

Publication date: published, according to the *English Catalogue of Books,* May 1918

Price: 1s.6d.

Masefield contents:
as for B145(a)

Notes:
The publisher's advertisements on pp.[87–88] advertise *Gallipoli* and *The Old Front Line.*

Copies seen: BL (9083.a.7) wrappers, stamped 26 APR 1918 rebound; HRHRC (D545 S7 L5 1918)

B150 *Ed.* J. HOWARD WHITEHOUSE, *JOHN RUSKIN LETTERS WRITTEN ON THE OCCASION OF THE CENTENARY OF HIS BIRTH*   1919

B150(a) *First English edition (1919)*

JOHN RUSKIN | Letters written on the occasion of | the Centenary of his Birth | 1919 | Edited by | JOHN HOWARD WHITEHOUSE | *With an unpublished portrait of Ruskin | drawn by himself* | OXFORD | PRINTED AT THE UNIVERSITY PRESS | For the Ruskin Centenary Council
(The italic type includes a number of swash characters)
(All width centred)

Bibliographies: Williams [unrecorded], Simmons p.134

Collation: [A]⁴ B-D⁴; signatures width centred at foot of page; 16 leaves; 224 × 142mm.; [1–5] 6 [7–9] 10 [11] 12–30 [31–32]; the frontispiece (on glossy paper) is tipped-in on the front free end-paper.

Page contents: [1] title-page (with protective tissue tipped-in for frontispiece which is tipped-in on end-paper); [2] blank; [3] 'CONTENTS' (five sections (including frontispiece) listed with page references); [4] blank; [5]-6 'INTRODUCTION' ('The Ruskin Centenary Committee, under the presidency of Lord Bryce, held...') (signed, 'J. H. WHITEHOUSE | *August*, 1919'); [7] 'NOTE ON THE FRONTISPIECE'; [8] blank; [9]-30 text; [31] blank; [32] 'PRINTED IN ENGLAND | AT THE OXFORD UNIVERSITY PRESS'

Paper: wove paper

Running title: 'Ruskin Centenary' (42–44mm.) on verso; 'Letters' (17mm.) on recto, pp.12–30

Binding: grey boards with brown cloth spine. On spine, reading lengthways up spine, from foot: 'RUSKIN CENTENARY LETTERS 1919'. On upper cover: white paper label (50 × 114mm.) on which: 'RUSKIN CENTENARY | *LETTERS* 1919' (enclosed within ornate border: 39 × 103mm.) Lower cover: blank. All edges trimmed. Binding measurements: 230 × 146mm. (covers), 230 × 15mm. (spine). End-papers: wove paper.

Publication date: published, according to Simmons, 1919

Price: unknown

Masefield contents:
[Untitled] ('Boar's Hill, Oxford. | Feb. 6, 1919. | My Dear Whitehouse, | I had hoped to be able to write you...')
         (signed, 'Yours ever, | JOHN MASEFIELD.')

Notes:
The volume consists of the frontispiece, an introduction, note on the frontispiece, a poem ('To John Ruskin' by Katherine Tynan) and seventeen letters. The authors of letters are: Laurence Binyon, Sidney Colvin, A.C. Benson, Sidney Lee, John Masefield, John Drinkwater, Mary Drew, M.S. Watts, May Morris, The Archbishop of Canterbury, Lord Buckmaster, Lord Parmoor, John Clifford, Conrad Dressler, Edith Holman Hunt, Gilbert Parker, and Greville Macdonald.

Masefield also contributed to *Ruskin the Prophet and other Centenary Studies* (ed. J. Howard Whitehouse) in 1920 (see B170).

Copies seen: BL (010902.f.22) stamped 13 OCT 1919

B155 RONALD ROSS, *PSYCHOLOGIES* 1919

B155(a) First English edition (1919)

PSYCHOLOGIES | BY RONALD ROSS | [ornament] | LONDON | JOHN MURRAY, ALBEMARLE STREET, W. | 1919
(All width centred)

Bibliographies: Williams [unrecorded], Simmons [unrecorded]

Collation: [1]⁸ 2–4⁸ 5⁴; signatures left foot of page; 36 leaves; 175 × 115mm.; [1–4] 5 [6] 7 [8] 9–69 [70–72]

Page contents: [1] half-title: 'PSYCHOLOGIES'; [2] *'BY THE SAME AUTHOR* | BOOKS OF VERSE | PHILOSOPHIES | THE SETTING SUN | FABLES | NEW NOVEL | REVELS OF ORSERA' (within ruled border: 33 × 47mm.); [3] title-page; [4] 'ALL RIGHTS RESERVED'; 5 'NOTE' ('These five studies are parts of a series of which I hope to publish more examples...') (signed, 'THE AUTHOR.'); [6] blank; 7 'CONTENTS' (five items listed with page references); [8] blank; 9–69 text; [70] blank; [71] publisher's advertisement: 'PHILOSOPHIES | By SIR RONALD ROSS'; [72] 'PRINTED BY | HAZELL, WATSON AND VINEY, LD., | LONDON AND AYLESBURY, | ENGLAND.'

Paper: wove paper

Running title: running titles comprise titles of individual poems on both verso and recto, pp.10–69

Binding: blue cloth. On spine, in gold reading lengthways up spine, from foot: 'PSYCHOLOGIES – ROSS'; horizontally at the head of spine: six rules; horizontally at the foot of spine: 'JOHN | MURRAY | [six rules]'. On upper cover, in blind: 'PSYCHOLOGIES | SIR RONALD ROSS' (within six ruled borders: 155 × 90mm.) Lower cover: blank. All edges trimmed. Binding measurements: 180 × 117mm. (covers), 180 × 17mm. (spine). End-papers: wove paper.

Publication date: published, according to the *English Catalogue of Books*, December 1919

Price: 2s.6d.

Masefield contents:
The 'note' includes the statement that '...thanks are due to Mr. John Masefield and Mr. Cloudesley Brereton for helping me in the correction of the proofs.'

Notes:
Masefield had previously assisted Ronald Ross during the proof stages of *Philosophies* (see B100).

The advertisements at the rear of the volume include a quotation from Masefield in support of *Philosophies*:

> I read it (*In Exile*) aloud last night to my wife. We think that it is by [f]ar the most splendid poem of modern times. It is magnificent. It moved us both very deeply. I know nothing like it. . . . I am very proud to have my name in the preface of a book that seems to me the only living book of poems published in this land in my generation. Your 'Philosophies' will, I feel sure, alter the direction of intellectual energy throughout the land. They are full of the most wise and splendid poetry.

Copies seen: private collection (PWE) inscribed 'David Thomson | from Ronald Ross | 15. 10. 20'

B160 CECIL ROBERTS, *POEMS* 1920

B160(a) First American edition (1920)

POEMS | BY | CECIL ROBERTS | WITH A PREFACE BY | JOHN MASEFIELD | [publisher's device of figure and winged horse and 'FREDERICK [point] A [point] STOKES [point] COMPANY [point] NEW [point] YORK [point] ESTABLISHED [point] EIGHTEEN [point] EIGHTY [point] ONE': 32 × 25mm.] | NEW YORK | FREDERICK A. STOKES COMPANY | PUBLISHERS
(All width centred and enclosed within double ruled border: 146 × 85mm.)

Bibliographies: Williams [unrecorded], Simmons p.135

Collation: [A–Q]⁸ (J not used); 128 leaves; 191 × 125mm.; [i–iv] v–x [xi–xii] 1–108 [109–110] 111–54 [155–56] 157–244

Page contents: [i] half-title: 'POEMS'; [ii] blank; [iii] title-page; [iv] *'Copyright, 1920, by* | FREDERICK A. STOKES COMPANY | [rule] | *All rights reserved*'; v–viii 'PREFACE' ('Mr. Cecil Roberts has published several volumes of poems, each better...') (signed, 'JOHN MASEFIELD. | BOAR'S HILL, | OXFORD.'); ix–x 'CONTENTS' (69 individual poems (in three sections) listed with page references); [xi] 'POEMS'; [xii] blank; 1–108 text; [109] 'THE DARK YEARS'; [110] blank; 111–54 text; [155] 'OTHER POEMS'; [156] blank; 157–244 text

Paper: wove paper (watermark: includes circular device and 'ANTIQUE') (see notes)

Running title: running titles, where used, comprise poem title, pp.2–244

Binding: green cloth. On spine, in gold: 'POEMS | [rule] ROBERTS | STOKES' (all width centred). On upper cover, in gold: 'POEMS | [rule] | CECIL ROBERTS | [publisher's device of figure and winged horse and 'FREDERICK [point] A [point]

STOKES [point] COMPANY [point] NEW [point] YORK [point] ESTABLISHED [point] EIGHTEEN [point] EIGHTY [point] ONE': 31 × 25mm.]' (all enclosed within blind ruled border: 188 × 117mm.) Lower cover: blank. All edges trimmed. Binding measurements: 196 × 127mm. (covers), 196 × 37mm. (spine). End-papers: wove paper.

Publication date: published around April 1920 (suggested by dates of contemporary reviews)

Price: $1.50

Masefield contents:
'Preface' ('Mr. Cecil Roberts has published several volumes of poems, each better...')
    (signed, 'JOHN MASEFIELD. | BOAR'S HILL, | OXFORD.')

Notes:
It has not been possible to describe accurately the watermark in the wove paper due to lack of examples in the examined copy.

Page numbers appear within square brackets. Thus, [1], [2], etc.

Poems commence with a drop-capital.

Roberts' poem 'The Great Ships' appearing on pp.190–91 of this edition (and dated 'LONDON, May, 1917.') is dedicated 'For John Masefield'. An extensive series of letters, dated [1918]-[1967], from Masefield to Roberts is held at the Churchill College Archive Centre, Cambridge. A letter dated 13 May 1919 notes

> ...I write now with such difficulty that I'm afraid I can't guarantee more than a page. Would that be of any use to you? ...I will do the introduction with pleasure, if you will not mind a very very brief one. Now that I write slowly I have so little time.
>
> (John Masefield, letter to Cecil Roberts, 13 May 1919)
> (Churchill College Archive Centre, in RBTS 2/23)

It appears that Masefield sent his preface twelve days later:

> ...I am sending you with this a few words which I have written as a preface, (if you think them worth having as such), for your Macmillan edition. I hope they will not seem too trivial to you.
>
> (John Masefield, letter to Cecil Roberts, 25 May [1919])
> (Churchill College Archive Centre, in RBTS 2/23)

Copies seen: Harvard College Library (Houghton *EC9.M377.A920r)

B165 *Ed.* MARTIN GILKES, RICHARD HUGHES *and* P.H.B. LYON, *PUBLIC SCHOOL VERSE 1919–1920*

1920

B165(a) *First English edition (1920)*

PUBLIC SCHOOL VERSE | 1919–1920 | AN ANTHOLOGY | With an Introduction by | John Masefield | LONDON | WILLIAM HEINEMANN | 1920
(All width centred)

Bibliographies: Williams p.12, Simmons p.135

Collation: [A]⁸ B-D⁸; signatures left foot of page; 32 leaves; 188 × 124mm.; [1–4] 5–7 [8] 9–63 [64]

Page contents: [1] half-title: 'PUBLIC SCHOOL VERSE'; [2] 'BY JOHN MASEFIELD | [rule] | [11 titles listed] | LONDON: WILLIAM HEINEMANN'; [3] title-page; [4] blank; 5–6 'PREFACE' ('This scheme originated with Mr. H. G. Pollard, to whom the Editors' thanks are due...') (signed, 'MARTIN GILKES.', 'RICHARD HUGHES.', 'P. H. B. LYON.' and dated 'OXFORD, 1920.'); 7 'NOTE' (two paragraphs acknowledging periodicals and recommending contributors to join the Incorporated Society of Authors); [8] blank; 9–10 'CONTENTS' (29 individual poems, their authors and schools listed with page references); 11–16 'INTRODUCTION' ('The arts are the honey of life made by the enjoyers of life for the delight of...') (signed, 'JOHN MASEFIELD.'); 17–[64] text (at foot of p.[64]: '[rule] | *Printed by Hazell, Watson & Viney, Ld., London and Aylesbury.*')

Paper: wove paper

Running title: none

Binding: grey boards. On spine: '[double rule] | PUBLIC | SCHOOL | VERSE | 1919– | –1920 | With an | Introduction | by | JOHN | MASEFIELD | HEINEMANN | [double rule]' (all width centred). On upper cover: 'PUBLIC SCHOOL | VERSE 1919–1920 | AN ANTHOLOGY | WITH AN INTRODUCTION | BY JOHN MASEFIELD | [double rule] | [publisher's device of a windmill with 'W [point]' and 'H'] (lines 1–5 and the double rule are ranged upper left and the publisher's device is ranged lower right; all within ruled border: 185 × 121mm.) On lower cover: '*Price Three Shillings and Sixpence Net*' (ranged lower right). All edges trimmed. Binding measurements: 194 × 126mm. (covers), 194 × 18mm. (spine). End-papers: wove paper.

Publication date: published, according to Simmons, September 1920

Price: 3s.6d.

Masefield contents:
'Introduction' ('The arts are the honey of life made by the enjoyers of life for the delight of...')
      (signed. 'JOHN MASEFIELD.')

Notes:
There are twenty-nine contributions of poems by nineteen different authors from a total of fifteen schools. One of the editors, Richard Hughes, was later to write the novel *A High Wind in Jamaica*.

The preface by the editors refers to Masefield's contribution:

> Some of the objections that have been raised Mr. John Masefield has answered in his introduction... Our especial thanks are due to Mr. John Masefield, whose advice and help have been of the greatest value...

Copies seen: private collection (PWE)

B170 *Ed.* J. HOWARD WHITEHOUSE, *RUSKIN THE PROPHET AND OTHER CENTENARY STUDIES*   1920

B170(a) *First English edition (1920)*

RUSKIN THE PROPHET | AND OTHER CENTENARY STUDIES | BY | JOHN MASEFIELD DEAN INGE | CHARLES F. G. MASTERMAN | AND OTHERS | EDITED BY | J. HOWARD WHITEHOUSE | [publisher's device including St. George and the Dragon and 'GEORGE ALLEN UNWIN LIMITED RUSKIN HOUSE PUBLISHER LONDON': 33 × 33mm.] | LONDON: GEORGE ALLEN & UNWIN LTD. | RUSKIN HOUSE, 40 MUSEUM STREET, W.C.I | NEW YORK: E. P. DUTTON AND CO.
(All width centred)

Bibliographies: Williams p.10, Simmons p.135

Collation: [1]⁸ 2–10⁸; signatures width centred at foot of page; 80 leaves; 216 × 135mm.; [1–8] 9–12 [13–14] 15–21 [22–24] 25–43 [44–46] 47–60 [61–62] 63–79 [80–82] 83–98 [99–100] 101–113 [114–16] 117–33 [134–36] 137–45 [146–48] 149–57 [158–60]

Page contents: [1–2] blank; [3] half-title: 'RUSKIN THE PROPHET'; [4] blank; [5] title-page; [6] '*First published in 1920* | *(All rights reserved)*'; [7] 'CONTENTS' (10 individual items and their authors listed with page references); [8] blank; 9–12 'INTRODUCTION' ('In the Autumn of 1919 the centenary of Ruskin's birth was observed by an exhibition...') (unsigned); [13] 'RUSKIN | BY | JOHN MASEFIELD'; [14] blank; 15–21 text by John Masefield; [22] blank; [23] 'RUSKIN AND PLATO | BY | THE DEAN OF ST. PAUL'S'; [24] blank; 25–43 text by Dean Inge; [44] blank; [45] 'RUSKIN THE PROPHET | BY | THE RIGHT HON. C. F. G. MASTERMAN'; [46] blank; 47–60 text by C.F.G. Masterman; [61] 'JOHN RUSKIN | BY | LAURENCE BINYON'; [62] blank; 63–79 text by Laurence Binyon; [80] blank; [81] 'RUSKIN AS POLITICAL | ECONOMIST | BY | J. A. HOBSON'; [82] blank; 83–98 text by J.A. Hobson; [99] 'RUSKIN AND SHAKESPEARE | BY | PROFESSOR J. A. DALE'; [100] blank; 101–113 text by J.A. Dale; [114] blank; [115] 'RUSKIN AND AN EARLY | FRIENDSHIP | WITH MANY UNPUBLISHED LETTERS | BY | J. H. WHITEHOUSE'; [116] blank; 117–33 text by J.H. Whitehouse; [134] blank; [135] 'RUSKIN AND LONDON | BY | J. H. WHITEHOUSE'; [136] blank; 137–45 text by J.H. Whitehouse; [146] blank; [147] 'SOME MEMORIES OF RUSKIN | BY | HENRY W. NEVINSON'; [148] blank; 149–57 text by Henry W. Nevinson (at foot of p.157: '*Printed in Great Britain by* | UNWIN BROTHERS, LIMITED, THE GRESHAM PRESS, WOKING AND LONDON'); [158–60] publisher's advertisements

Paper: wove paper

Running title: 'RUSKIN THE PROPHET' (54mm.) on verso; recto title comprises essay title, pp.10–157

Binding: light brown cloth. On spine: 'RUSKIN | THE | PROPHET | GEORGE ALLEN | & UNWIN L^{TD}' (all width centred). On upper cover: 'RUSKIN THE PROPHET | AND OTHER CENTENARY STUDIES | [circle containing shield and 'TODAY [point] TODAY [point] TODAY [point]'] | EDITED BY | J. HOWARD WHITEHOUSE' (within blind ruled border: 218 × 134mm.) Lower cover: blank. All edges trimmed. Binding measurements: 222 × 137mm. (covers), 222 × 31mm. (spine). End-papers: wove paper.

Publication date: published, according to Simmons, October 1920

Price: 8s.6d.

Masefield contents:
Ruskin ('John Ruskin was born on this day one hundred years ago. That is more than three...')
      (titled, 'BY | JOHN MASEFIELD')

Notes:
There are ten contributions listed in the contents.

The Introduction notes that most of the contributions in the volume derive from lectures given at the Royal Academy.

The text of Masefield's lecture was reprinted (with minor revisions) from *John Ruskin* (see A51).

Copies seen: BL (010855.c.37) stamped 5 OCT 1920 rebound; ULL (Special Collections); HRHRC (AC-L M377 CWH 1920)

B175 A.J. MUNNINGS, *PICTURES OF THE BELVOIR HUNT… CATALOGUE* 1921

B175(a) First English edition (1921)

Upper wrapper:

FIRST EDITION] | PICTURES | OF | THE BELVOIR HUNT | AND | OTHER SCENES OF ENGLISH | COUNTRY LIFE | BY | A. J. MUNNINGS, A.R.A. | [rule, 7mm.] | WITH A FOREWORD BY | JOHN MASEFIELD | [rule, 7mm.] | ALPINE CLUB GALLERY | MILL STREET, CONDUIT STREET, W. | Catalogue, including admission, 1/6
(All width centred with the exception of the first line which is ranged upper left)

Bibliographies: Williams, p.12, Simmons p.135

Collation: [A]⁶; 6 leaves; 193 × 141mm.; [1–2] 3–6 [7–8] 9–11 [12]; the frontispiece is tipped-in on inside of upper cover

Page contents: [-] blank; [-] oval photograph frontispiece: 111 × 81mm.; 'A.J. MUNNINGS, A.R.A. | 1921.'; [1] 'FOREWORD | BY | JOHN MASEFIELD'; [2] blank; 3–6 'FOREWORD' ('Like most of the good things in the English arts, Mr. Munnings' pictures…') (signed, 'JOHN MASEFIELD.'); [7] 'CATALOGUE'; [8] 'Information as to the price of pictures may be had | in the Gallery. | [new paragraph] Purchasers are desired, at the time of purchase, to | pay the usual deposit of 20 per cent. on the purchase | price; and the balance on or before the close of the | Exhibition. | [new paragraph] The copyright of each work in the Gallery is strictly | reserved to the Artist, unless special agreement to the | contrary is made. | J. KNEWSTUB. | *Director.* | THE CHENIL GALLERIES, | BY THE TOWN HALL, | CHELSEA.'; 9–[12] catalogue (at foot of p.[12]: '[rule] | CHISWICK PRESS: CHARLES WHITTINGHAM AND GRIGGS (PRINTERS), LTD. | TOOKS COURT, CHANCERY LANE, LONDON.')

Paper: laid paper (no watermark), chain-lines 23–26mm. apart

Running title: none

Binding: light grey wrappers. Spine: blank. On upper wrapper: described above. Lower wrapper: 'THE | TALE OF ANTHONY BELL | A HUNTING BALLAD | [photograph of mounted fox's head] | BY | A. J. MUNNINGS, A.R.A. | [rule] | On Sale at the Gallery, 1/-'. Inside of upper wrapper: '*The Exhibition is held under the | direction of* | THE CHENIL GALLERIES | (BY THE TOWN HALL) | KING'S ROAD, CHELSEA, S.W.3 | *where all communications should | be addressed*'. Inside of lower wrapper: 'THE CHENIL GALLERIES | (BY THE TOWN HALL) | 183A KING'S ROAD, CHELSEA, S.W.3 | [ornament] | PAINTINGS, DRAWINGS, AND ETCHINGS | BY | AUGUSTUS E. JOHN | AND | ORIGINALS AND REPRODUCTIONS OF WORKS | BY | SIR WILLIAM ORPEN, K.B.E., R.A. | AND OTHER ARTISTS | *Always on View*'. Top edge trimmed, others uncut. Binding measurements: 202 × 149mm. (wrappers), 202 × 2mm. (spine). The wrapper extends beyond the edges of the internal leaves.

Publication date: unknown (not in the *English Catalogue of Books*)

Price: 1s.6d.

Masefield contents:
Foreword ('Like most of the good things in the English arts, Mr. Munnings' pictures…')
    (signed, 'JOHN MASEFIELD.')

Notes:
The foreword commences with a drop capital.

Masefield's foreword is followed by a listing of the exhibition pictures by Munnings.

I.A. Williams notes that the 'earliest issue has "Under Revision" on cover.'

Copies seen: ULL (Special Collections)

B180 *THE DANIEL PRESS* 1921

B180(a) First English edition (1921)

The Daniel Press | [ornament] | MEMORIALS OF | C. H. O. DANIEL | WITH A | BIBLIOGRAPHY | OF THE PRESS, 1845–1919 | [ornament] | OXFORD | PRINTED ON THE DANIEL PRESS | IN THE BODLEIAN LIBRARY | M DCCCC XXI
(All width centred and enclosed within ornate border: 176 × 131mm.)

Bibliographies: Simmons [noted on p.88]

Collation: [A]⁴ B-Cc⁴ [Dd-Ff]⁴ (J, V and W not used) (see notes); B2–Cc2 are also signed; signatures centre foot of page with the exception of signature 'I' and 'X 2' which are signed left foot; 116 leaves; 230 × 175mm.; [i–iii] iv [v–viii] [1] 2–11 [12] 13–16 [17] 18–21 [22] 23–31 [32] 33 [34] 35 [36–39] 40 [41] 42–54 [55] 56 [57–59] 60–67 [68] 69–78 [79–81] 82–136 [137] 138–54 [155–57] 158–62 [163] 164–68 [169] 170–98 [199–228]; illustrations (on glossy paper) are tipped-in on the front free end-paper, pp.213 and 227.

Page contents: [-] blank (tipped-in on end-paper); [-] frontispiece: 158 × 126mm., 'PLATE I | [portrait] | DR. DANIEL, 1904 | *From the unfinished portrait by C. Furse in Worcester College* | (p.5)' tipped-in on end-paper; [i] title-page; [ii] '*Five hundred copies of this book have*

been | printed for subscribers. Sixty copies have also | been printed on hand-made paper in full quarto | size, with extra illustrations and some original | leaves of the Daniel Press. Of these, fifty are for | subscribers.'; [iii]-iv 'FOREWORD' ('The present volume, *The Daniel Press*, is designed as a tribute from a few of his friends...') (signed, 'C.H. WILKINSON. | WORCESTER COLLEGE, | OXFORD.'); [v] 'LIST OF CONTENTS' ('Memorials Of Dr. Daniel' is listed with eight individual components and 'Bibliography Of The Press' is listed with its component parts, also an index, all with page references); [vi] 'ILLUSTRATIONS' (15 plates listed with additional notes); [vii] '[ornament] | MEMORIALS OF DR. DANIEL | BY | Sir Herbert Warren Dr. W. W. Jackson | John Masefield Margaret L. Woods | William Stebbing Rosina Filippi | F. de Arteaga y Pereira | F. W. Bourdillon | [ornament]'; [viii] '[publisher's device] | [*The Mark of the Daniel Press*]'; [1]-[36] text of 'Memorials Of Dr. Daniel'; [37] '[ornament] | A BIBLIOGRAPHY | Of the DANIEL PRESS at | Frome and Oxford 1845–1919 | By Falconer Madan | Formerly Bodley's Librarian | [ornament]'; [38]-184 text of 'A Bibliography Of The Daniel Press'; 185–98 index; [199] '[ornamental rule] | Printed in the Bodleian Library, Oxford | by THOMAS PRICE and ALBERT SAXTON | during October and November 1921 | [ornamental rule]'; [200] blank; [201] plate II; [202] blank; [203] plate III; [204] blank; [205] plate IV; [206] blank; [207] plate V; [208] blank; [209] plate VI; [210] blank; [211] plates VII–VIII; [212] blank; [213] plate IX; [214] blank; [215] plate X; [216] blank; [217] plate XI; [218] blank; [219] plate XII; [220] blank; [221] plate XIII; [222] blank; [223] plate XIV; [224] blank; [225] plate XV; [226–28] blank

Paper: laid paper (watermark: 'ANTIQUE DE LUXE'), chain-lines 25mm. apart (bound so that chain-lines run horizontally)

Running title: '*THE DANIEL PRESS*' (37mm.) on verso; recto title comprises title of section, pp.2–183 and '*INDEX*' (12mm.) on both verso and recto, pp.186–98

Binding: blue-green boards with light brown cloth spine (see notes). On spine: 'THE | DANIEL | PRESS | 1845–1919 | M DCCCC XXI' (all width centred). Covers: blank. Top edge roughly trimmed, others untrimmed. Binding measurements: 236 × 179mm. (covers), 236 × 45mm. (spine). End-papers: laid paper (no watermark), chain-lines 26mm. apart (bound so that the chain-lines run horizontally).

Publication date: published, according to the *English Catalogue of Books*, January 1922. The *Addenda & Corrigenda* by F. Madan (Oxford: University Press, 1922) notes that the volume 'was issued on Dec. 22, 1921'.

Price: the prospectus notes copies priced at 1 guinea for subscribers and 'the price of any copies not subscribed for will be not less than Thirty Shillings'; the 'edition de luxe' was priced at 2 guineas.

Masefield contents:
The Dream ('Weary with many thoughts I went to bed,')
    (signed, 'JOHN MASEFIELD.')

Notes:
The volume comprises both a collection of tributes to C.H.O. Daniel (Provost of Worcester College) and a bibliography of the Daniel Press. The volume has two parts: 'Memorials of Dr. Daniel' and 'Bibliography of the Press'. The first part contains eight sections. The bibliography is by Falconer Madan.

The unsigned gathering (noted above as Dd) comprises four leaves bound together by linen stubs. It does not therefore constitute a 'true' gathering, but it is convenient to label it as such for our purposes.

The signature 'Cc' appears as 'CC'.

The *Addenda & Corrigenda* by F. Madan (Oxford: University Press, 1922) was published in an edition of 100 copies. It includes a list of subscribers and presentees. Masefield was presented with number 5 of the numbered and signed edition de luxe. He also subscribed to the standard edition. Madan states that 273 subscribers took 455 copies.

Copies seen: private collection (PWE); UCL (BIBLIOGRAPHY D96 DAN)

B180(aa) First English edition – 'deluxe issue' (1921)

An 'edition de luxe' of sixty copies included, according to the prospectus, 'ten additional facsimiles and some original leaves of the Daniel Press'. It was numbered and signed by Mrs. Daniel and bound 'in boards with parchment back and gold lettering'. See notes to B180(a).

B185 EDWARD GORDON CRAIG, *SCENE*   1923

B185(a) First English edition (1923)

SCENE | BY | E. GORDON CRAIG | *With a Foreword and an Introductory Poem* | BY | JOHN MASEFIELD | [rule] | [ornament: 47 × 47mm.] | [rule] | LONDON: HUMPHREY MILFORD | OXFORD UNIVERSITY PRESS | MCMXXIII
(All width centred and enclosed within ornate border: 255 × 185mm.)

Bibliographies: Simmons p.136 (see notes)

Collation: [A]⁵ ([A]4+1) B⁴ C⁶ D⁴ E² [F]⁸ [G-H]⁶ (see notes); C2–D2 are also signed; signatures right foot of page; 41 leaves; 299 × 232mm.; [iii–vi] vii–xi [xii] 1–27 [28–68]; illustrations (on glossy paper) tipped-in on linen stubs

Page contents: [pp.i and ii are not present]; [iii] half-title: '[rule] | [ornament] | [rule] | SCENE | [rule] | [ornament] | [rule]'; [iv] blank; [v] title-page; [vi] 'PRINTED IN ENGLAND | AT THE OXFORD UNIVERSITY PRESS | BY FREDERICK HALL'; vii–xi 'FOREWORD' ('Last summer there was held in London an exhibition of designs, scenes and models...') (signed, 'JOHN MASEFIELD.'); [xii] blank; 1–27 text; [28] blank; [29] '*To* | *OLD BACH*' (within ornate border); [30] blank; [31–68] blank pages with 19 illustration plates

Paper: laid paper (watermark: '[crown] | Abbey Mills | Greenfield'), chain-lines 25mm. apart (bound so that chain-lines run horizontally)

Running title: none

Binding: light blue-grey boards. On spine: 'SCENE | [double rule] | [oval device with 'GC': 18 × 16mm.] | EDWARD | GORDON | CRAIG | OXFORD' (all width centred). On upper cover: 'SCENE | EDWARD GORDON CRAIG'. Lower cover: blank. All edges roughly trimmed. Binding measurements: 308 × 234mm. (covers), 308 × 28mm. (spine). End-papers: laid paper (watermark: '[crown] | Abbey Mills | Greenfield'), chain-lines 24mm. apart.

Publication date: published, according to the *English Catalogue of Books*, June 1923

Price: 25s.

Masefield contents:
Foreword ('Last summer there was held in London an exhibition of designs, scenes and models…')
[Untitled] ('Once we were masters of the arts of men,')
[Untitled] ('Builded in every village in the land,')
[Untitled] ('I saw the work of all the world displayed,')
[Untitled] ('I cannot tell who will, but inly know')
    (signed, 'JOHN MASEFIELD.')

Notes:
Page numbers appear within round brackets. Thus, (vii), (viii), (2), (3), etc.

Gatherings F-H (and the central conjugate leaves of gathering C) comprise single leaves tipped-in on linen stubs. They do not therefore constitute true gatherings, but it is convenient to label them as such for our purposes. All are included in the leaf count above although those in gathering C are excluded from the pagination.

Although described on the title-page as 'a Foreword and an Introductory Poem', Masefield's 'poem' comprises four sonnets.

The main text is signed and dated 'GORDON CRAIG. | 1922'

As noted above, there are no pages i and ii

Only the foreword and first sonnet commence with drop-capitals.

Simmons does not specifically note the regular or limited edition.

Due to the limitation note in B185(aa) we can deduce there were 900 copies of this edition.

A letter from Masefield to The Society of Authors explains the author's sentiment towards Craig's work, but also finds Masefield requesting advice on retaining rights:

> Will you be so kind as to let me have some form of words with which I can send an introduction to a book by Mr Gordon Craig which the Oxford University Press are about to publish. I am supplying the introduction free, out of admiration for Mr Craig's work, but I wish absolutely to retain the copyright + right to reprint the introduction whenever I wish, + to receive 12 copies of the book on publication, + to limit the publishers' right to print the introduction to the preface of Mr Craig's book.
>
>   (John Masefield, letter to G.H. Thring, [10 January 1923])
>   (BL, Add.Mss. 56578, f.115)

Copies seen: private collection (ROV)

B185(aa) First English edition (limited signed edition) (1923)

SCENE | BY | E. GORDON CRAIG | *With a Foreword and an Introductory Poem* | BY | JOHN MASEFIELD | [rule] | [ornament: 47 × 47mm.] | [rule] | LONDON: HUMPHREY MILFORD | OXFORD UNIVERSITY PRESS | MCMXXIII
(All width centred and enclosed within ornate border: 255 × 185mm.)

Bibliographies: Simmons p.136 (see notes)

Collation: [A]⁶ B⁴ C⁶ D⁴ E² [F]⁶ [G]⁶ [H]⁸ (see notes); C2–D2 are also signed; signatures right foot of page; 42 leaves; 294 × 233mm.; [i–vi] vii–xi [xii] 1–27 [28–68]; illustrations (on glossy paper) tipped-in on linen stubs

Page contents: [i] half-title: '[rule] | [ornament] | [rule] | SCENE | [rule] | [ornament] | [rule]'; [ii] blank; [iii] title-page; [iv] 'PRINTED IN ENGLAND | AT THE OXFORD UNIVERSITY PRESS | BY FREDERICK HALL'; [v] 'THIS edition consists of 1000

copies of | which 100 only have been signed by the | Author, numbered, and specially bound. | This is No. ....'; [vi] blank; vii–xi 'FOREWORD' ('Last summer there was held in London an exhibition of designs, scenes and models...') (signed, 'JOHN MASEFIELD.'); [xii] blank; 1–27 text; [28] blank; [29] 'To | *OLD BACH*' (within ornate border); [30] blank; [31–68] blank pages with 19 illustration plates

Paper: laid paper (watermark: '[crown] | Abbey Mills | Greenfield'), chain-lines 25mm. apart (bound so that chain-lines run horizontally)

Running title: none

Binding: brown cloth. On spine, in gold: '[triple rule] | SCENE | [double rule] | E.GORDON | CRAIG | [double rule] | [oval device with 'GC': 18 × 16mm.] | OXFORD | 1923 | [triple rule]' (all width centred except name of author which is justified on left margin). On upper cover, in gold: oval device with 'GC': 18 × 16mm. (within triple ruled border: 297 × 229mm.) Lower cover: blank. Top edge gilt, others roughly trimmed. Sewn head band (in white). Binding measurements: 330 × 235mm. (covers), 330 × 30mm. (spine). End-papers: laid paper (watermark: '[crown] | Abbey Mills | Greenfield'), chain-lines 24mm. apart.

Publication date: published, according to the *English Catalogue of Books*, June 1923

Price: 42s.

Masefield contents:
as for B185(a)

Notes:
Only the limitation note, foreword and first sonnet commence with drop-capitals. Other typographical features noted for B185(a) are present here.

Simmons does not specifically note the regular or limited edition.

Copies seen: BL (L.R.37.b.6) signed '12 | E. Gordon Craig' on page [v], stamped 4 JUL 1923

B190 ROBERT NICHOLS, *FANTASTICA*   1923

B190(a) First American edition (1923)

FANTASTICA | BEING THE SMILE OF | THE SPHINX AND OTHER | TALES OF IMAGINATION | BY | ROBERT NICHOLS | WITH A FOREWORD BY | JOHN MASEFIELD | New York | THE MACMILLAN COMPANY | 1923 | *All rights reserved*
(Lines 1–4 justified on both left and right margins, all other lines width centred)

Bibliographies: Simmons [unrecorded]

Collation: [A-AA]⁴; 196 leaves; 201 × 120mm.; [i–vi] vii [viii] ix [x] xi–xiii [xiv] 1–28 [29–30] 31–65 [66–68] 69–128 [129] 130–375 [376–78]

Page contents: [i] half-title: 'FANTASTICA'; [ii] '[publisher's device] | THE MACMILLAN COMPANY | [two lines listing six cities, separated by four points] | MACMILLAN & CO., LIMITED | [two lines listing four cities, separated by two points] | THE MACMILLAN CO. OF CANADA, LTD. | [one city listed]'; [iii] title-page; [iv] 'PRINTED IN THE UNITED STATES OF AMERICA | COPYRIGHT, 1923, | BY THE MACMILLAN COMPANY. | [rule] | Set up and electrotyped. Published September, 1923. | THE FERRIS PRINTING COMPANY | NEW YORK'; [v] [Untitled] ('May I be permitted to suggest that we take this writing job seriously...') (signed, '*Open Letter to the Servants of* | *Imaginative Literature*.'); [vi] blank; vii [Untitled] ('Two of these tales have appeared in serial: "The Smile of the Sphinx," in the...') (signed, 'R.M.B.N. | 1923.'); [viii] blank; ix '"*Warum wilst du dich von uns allen* | *Und unsrer Steinung entfernen?*" | *Ich schreibe nicht euch zu gefallen;* | *Ihr sollt was lernen.* | GOETHE.'; [x] blank; xi–xii 'PREFACE' ('Mr. Robert Nichols' new book contains work done in various moods...') (signed, 'JOHN MASEFIELD.'); xiii 'CONTENTS' (five sections, including preface, listed with titles and page references); [xiv] blank; 1–28 text; [29] sectional title; [30] blank; 31–65 text; [66] blank; [67] sectional title; [68] blank; 69–128 text; [129] sectional title; 130–375 text; [376–78] blank

Paper: laid paper (no watermark), chain-lines 22mm. apart

Running title: 'FANTASTICA' (27mm.) on verso; recto title comprises section title

Binding: light blue cloth. On spine, in gold: 'FANTASTICA | NICHOLS | [ornament] | [point] MACMILLAN [point]' (all width centred). On upper cover, in gold: 'FANTASTICA | *BEING THE SMILE OF THE SPHINX* | *AND OTHER TALES OF* | *IMAGINATION* | [ornament] ROBERT NICHOLS [ornament]' (within double ruled border in blind: 197 × 114mm.) All edges trimmed. Binding measurements: 207 × 122mm. (covers), 207 × 44mm. (spine). End-papers: wove paper.

Publication date: published, according to date within volume, September 1923

Price: $2.50

Masefield contents:
Preface ('Mr. Robert Nichols' new book contains work done in various moods...')
        (signed, 'JOHN MASEFIELD.')

Notes:

Masefield notes of the contents of this volume:

> …All the work is that of a poet, of an unusual equipment, who has been through an unusual experience. To a young man, of much natural charm, with an inherited taste for letters and the gift of poetry, has come, first, the squalor of war, then the emptiness that follows war. The pastoral poet in him has been shaken, the foundations of his life have been tested. His aim during these years has been not so much to do work as to make a foundation upon which work can be done.

Copies seen: HRHRC (PR6027 I25 F3 1923 cop.1)

B195 WILFRED PARTINGTON, *THE WAR AGAINST MALARIA* 1923

B195(a) First English edition (1923)

THE WAR AGAINST | MALARIA | By | WILFRED PARTINGTON | With a Foreword by | JOHN MASEFIELD | Printed for the Propaganda Committee | of the Ross Institute Fund | London, 1923
(All width centred)

Bibliographies: Simmons p.136

Collation: [A]⁸; 8 leaves; 251 × 162mm.; [1–2] 3–7 [8–9] 10–16; a frontispiece (on glossy paper) and illustration at the rear of the volume are included as a set of conjugate leaves (on glossy paper) which are bound so as to enclose the single gathering (this has been excluded from the gathering information as page numbers do not incorporate these illustration pages)

Page contents: [1] title-page; [2] blank; 3–4 'FOREWORD.' ('When I was a boy, I had a friend from whom I parted in July.') (signed, 'JOHN MASEFIELD.'); 5–16 text and map

Paper: laid paper (no watermark), chain-lines 26mm. apart (used so that chain-lines run horizontally)

Running title: none

Binding: light grey-blue wrappers. Spine: blank. On upper wrapper: 'The War Against | Malaria | and Tropical Diseases. | By | WILFRED PARTINGTON | With a Foreword by | JOHN MASEFIELD | The Ross Research Institute'. Lower wrapper: 'Printed by Geo. W. Jones at The Sign of The Dolphin in Gough Square, | Fleet Street, London, E.C.4.'. Inside of upper wrapper: '*TO THE | READER: | This Pamphlet tells a thrilling | story of discovery & describes | a great and worthy adventure | in which you may play a part.*' Inside of lower wrapper: 'The Ross Institute for Tropical Diseases. | [rule] | [listing of president, committee, address, etc.]'. All edges trimmed. Binding measurements: 251 × 162mm. (wrappers), 251 × 2mm. (spine).

Publication date: presumably published September 1923 (noted in *The Times* on 21 September 1923)

Price: unknown

Masefield contents:

Foreword ('When I was a boy, I had a friend from whom I parted in July.')
    (signed, 'JOHN MASEFIELD.')

Notes:

Part of the title on the cover of the pamphlet is not present on the title-page.

Wilfred G. Partington, Esq. was honorary secretary of the Ross Institute for Tropical Diseases.

The frontispiece is a photograph of Ross. It is enclosed within a ruled border with caption below: 'COL. SIR RONALD ROSS, K.C.B., F.R.S.' The illustration at the rear of the volume is a photograph entitled 'THE ANOPHELES MOSQUITO (Female). | Carrier of the Malaria germ.'

See also *Why Everybody should assist in fighting disease in the Tropics* (B220)

Copies seen: BL (R.Ac.380.hb(1)) stamped 22 FEB 1924

B200 *Ed.* LOUISA CALLENDER, *THE WINDMILL* 1923

B200(a) First English edition (1923)

[panel of floral design: 11 × 115mm.] | *The* | WINDMILL: [in red] | *Stories, Essays, Poems* & | *Pictures* by AUTHORS & ARTISTS | whose Works are published at the | SIGN of the WINDMILL | [rule, 69mm.] | Edited by *L. CALLENDER* | [rule, 69mm.] | [publisher's device of a windmill within a double ruled border and enclosed within ornate frame: 56 × 52mm.] | *LONDON:* | WILLIAM HEINEMANN LTD. | MCMXXIII
(All width centred)

Bibliographies: Simmons [unrecorded]

Collation: [*a*]⁴ *b*¹ B-P⁸ Q¹ (J not used); signatures right foot of page with 'W.' at left foot on first leaf of gatherings (with the exception of gatherings C and F where only 'W' appears); 118 leaves; 251 × 183mm.; [i–iv] v [vi] vii–ix [x] 1–57 [58] 59–225 [226]; illustrations and facsimiles (on laid paper and also glossy paper) are tipped-in on pp.ii, 67 (a set of conjugate leaves), 93, 130, 131 (two leaves tipped-in one above the other), 165, 193 and 219; (protective tissue included for plates tipped-in on pp.ii, 93, 165 and 193)

Page contents: [i] half-title: 'The WINDMILL'; [ii] blank (with additional leaf tipped-in on the verso of which is the colour frontispiece: 140 × 115mm.); [iii] title-page (with protective tissue bearing legend: 'LANDSCAPE | By C. LOVAT FRASER | Reproduced by permission of Mrs. C. Lovat Fraser from the | original in the possession of C. S. Evans, Esq.'); [iv] 'PRINTED IN GREAT BRITAIN BY THE WHITEFRIARS PRESS, LTD., | LONDON AND TONBRIDGE.'; v 'INTRODUCTION' (signed, '*L. CALLENDER.*' and dated 'Christmas, 1923.'); [vi] blank; vii–viii 'CONTENTS' (42 individual entries listed with authors and page references); ix 'ILLUSTRATIONS' (black and white, four colour and seven facsimile illustrations listed); [x] blank; 1–[226] text

Paper: laid paper (no watermark), chain-lines 24mm. apart

Running title: none

Binding: light brown boards with dark brown cloth spine. On spine, in gold: '*THE | WINDMILL | HEINEMANN*' (all width centred). On upper cover, in gold: '*THE WINDMILL* | [publisher's device of a windmill]' (the title is width centred and the device is ranged lower right). Lower cover: blank. Top and fore edges trimmed, lower outside edge roughly trimmed. Binding measurements: 258 × 188mm. (covers), 258 × 39mm. (spine). End-papers: wove paper.

Publication date: published, according to the *English Catalogue of Books*, October 1923

Price: 8s.6d.

Masefield contents:
Fox-Hunting ('I have been asked to write why I wrote my poem of "Reynard the Fox." As a man grows older...')
    (headed, 'BY | JOHN MASEFIELD')

Notes:
The introduction by Louisa Callender commences:

> In collecting together these *Stories, Essays, Pictures & Poems*, I have sought to give a representative selection from the works of authors and artists whose books have been issued during the last thirty years by the firm of William Heinemann. Much of the material is new, but there is included some work by authors who are perhaps forgotten, or at best only faintly remembered...

Masefield's contribution first appeared – with minor differences – in an American edition of *Reynard the Fox* (see A49(d)). It was reprinted after its appearance here in *Recent Prose* (see A73(a)).

Contributions commence with drop-capitals.

The title for the volume obviously derives from the publisher's device of William Heinemann (designed by William Nicholson)

The title 'WINDMILL:' (on the title-page), the heading 'INTRODUCTION' on page v and the heading 'CONTENTS' on page vii are all printed in red.

Copies seen: private collection (ROV); BL (12330.y.11) stamped 26 OCT 1923

B205 *ST. FELIX SCHOOL SOUTHWOLD 1897 – 1923* [1924]

B205(a) First English edition ([1924])

ST. FELIX SCHOOL | SOUTHWOLD | 1897 – 1923 | LONDON | CHELSEA PUBLISHING CO. | 16 ROYAL HOSPITAL ROAD, CHELSEA, S.W.3
(All width centred)

Bibliographies: Simmons p.136

Collation: [1]⁸ 2–6⁸ 7⁴; signatures right foot of page; 52 leaves; 184 × 117mm.; [1–6] 7–95 [96–104]; illustrations (on glossy paper) are tipped-in on pp.[2], 18, 20, 24, 32, 41, 44, 53, 67, 71, 79, 90 and 95; pp.[97–104] constitute four leaves bound as a single gathering at the rear of the volume

Page contents: [1] half-title: 'ST. FELIX SCHOOL'; [2] blank (with additional leaf tipped-in on the verso of which is the black and white photograph frontispiece: 151 × 88mm., 'ST. FELIX SCHOOL TAKEN FROM THE AIR.' and '*By kind permission of Mr. F. Jenkins.*'); [3] title-page; [4] '*Printed and made in Great Britain*'; [5] 'ST. FELIX SCHOOL' ('Here, in this house, where we are singing thus,') (signed, 'JOHN MASEFIELD.'); [6] blank; 7–8 'FOREWORD' ('Unfortunately, even this book cannot escape a preface! We feel, however, that we...') (signed, 'ENID WATSON. | BEATRICE CURTIS BROWN. | 27, Cheyne Walk, | Chelsea, | S.W.3.'); 9–[96] text (at foot of p.[96]: '[rule] | Headley Bros., Ashford, Kent, & 18 Devonshire St E.C.2.'); [97–104] illustrations: school groups from 1900, 1907, 1911 and 1914

Paper: wove paper

Running title: none

Binding: light green cloth. On spine, reading lengthways up spine, from foot: 'St. Felix School, Southwold, 1897–1923'. On upper cover: white paper label (43 × 79mm.) on which in brown: 'St. Felix School | SOUTHWOLD | 1898 – 1923' (within ornate ruled border: 38 × 74mm.) Lower cover: blank. All edges trimmed. Binding measurements: 189 × 119mm. (covers), 189 × 30mm. (spine). End-papers: wove paper.

Publication date: unknown (not in the *English Catalogue of Books*)

Price: unknown

Masefield contents:

St. Felix School ('Here, in this house, where we are singing thus,')
    (signed, 'JOHN MASEFIELD.')

Notes:

There are numerous contributions (both titled and un-titled). Contributions (where signed) are signed by initials only.

The foreword states, with reference to this volume:

> It is not a history or a record of the School's development. We felt it was not possible to write a serious, adequate or accurate history of the School at its present age... What we have tried to do is to get together material to make up what might be called a verbal photograph album. We chose the contributions with a view to interesting Old Felicians of all generations and all houses...

The foreword also thanks 'our publisher, Miss Edith Place'.

In July 1932 Masefield received a letter from E.M. Edghill, the serving headmistress of St Felix School, Southwold. She wrote:

> You may remember that you very kindly wrote us our School Song. It has been set to music by one of our old girls, and the Old Felicians are very anxious to have a copy of the words with the music sent out with the next annual magazine. I have been making enquiries, and Augeners are prepared to print it for a sum we can afford, but I write to ask you whether you are willing to let us have the poem circulated in this way privately? It appears that it is important to have documentary evidence to the effect that you have no objection to raise. I am so sorry to trouble you in this matter, and hope you will see your way to acceding to this request. It is a source of such great pride to us that we have a School Song of such beauty and distinction.
>
>   (E.M. Edghill, letter to John Masefield, 23 July 1932)
>   (BL, Add.Mss.56597, f.41)

Masefield wrote to The Society of Authors asking them to grant the application without a fee (see BL, Add.Mss.56597, f.40).

In October 1937 Masefield wrote to The Society of Authors about the poem. He states his family connection with the school, notes the poem's uncollected status within the canon of his work and suggests a title:

> The verses beginning <u>Here in this house</u> were written by me years ago, for the school where my daughter was. I have never put them into a book. I do not mind their being printed, but feel that they should be called, the ST FELIX SCHOOL SONG.
>
>   (John Masefield, letter to [E.J.] Mullett, [4 Oct 1937])
>   (BL, Add.Mss.56608, f.7)

This suggestion caused a problem, however. A musical setting of the verses had previously been published as 'Beauty' (this is not the setting to which E.M. Edghill refers). The Society of Authors explained:

> I have also telephoned to the Oxford Press in regard to the setting of this song which they publish under the title of BEAUTY. They ask me to express their regret to you for the misunderstanding. I have arranged with the Press that when the Song is re-printed they should add under its exisiting title the words 'The St. Felix School Song'. They asked to be allowed to retain the existing title (BEAUTY) with the new title added in any reprint, because of the confusion which would arise in respect of trade orders if BEAUTY entirely disappeared as the title. Since it seemed to me probable that the composer was the party responsible for the initial error I agreed to this.
>
>   (E.J. Mullett, letter to John Masefield, [6 October 1937])
>   (BL, Add.Mss.56608, f.10)

Masefield's poem was included as the school poem for St Felix School, Southwold in *Forty Years On – An Anthology of School Songs* compiled by Gavin Ewart (Sidgwick and Jackson, 1969). Ewart notes in his introduction:

> Of the... professional poets, Henry Newbolt is not really up to his own standard, but Masefield certainly is – 'This world of mysteries wants many thousands true for one that's wise'. On the other hand the second Laureate represented [C. Day-Lewis] was not, in my opinion, at the top of his form when he wrote the Larchfield School Song.

Other schools appear to have adopted the poem as their school song, or asked to reprint it. Masefield probably always chose to give permission without payment. One application, in 1930, from Mary Datchelor Girls' School in Camberwell was as follows:

> We of the Datchelor School were much interested to learn from our Head Mistress, Dr Block, that your poem "Here in this house" was originally written for a girls' school. As sub-editor of the School Magazine I am writing to ask if we may quote the lines in full in our July issue...
>
>   (Anne M. Rivers, letter to John Masefield, 25 June 1930)
>   (BL, Add.Mss.56590, ff.83–84)

Masefield responded, writing to The Society of Authors as follows:

> ...Will you please very kindly grant the writer of the enclosed letter a permission to quote the lines she wants? I have never printed them, + do not care to charge for them.
>
>   (John Masefield, letter to Denys Kilham Roberts, 1 July 1930)
>   (BL, Add.Mss.56590, f.99)

Copies seen: BL (8367.aa.32) stamped 19 JAN 1924

B210 BASIL LUBBOCK, *ADVENTURES BY SEA FROM ART OF OLD TIME* 1925

B210(a) First English edition (1925)

ADVENTURES BY SEA | FROM ART OF | OLD TIME | BASIL LUBBOCK | PREFACE BY | JOHN MASEFIELD | [publisher's device of 'The Studio': 25 × 26mm.] [in orange] | EDITED BY GEOFFREY HOLME | PUBLISHED BY THE STUDIO LIMITED, LONDON | MCMXXV
(All width centred)

Bibliographies: Simmons pp.136–37

Collation: [A]² [B-M]⁸ (J not used); the first gathering is tipped-in on the first leaf of the second gathering; gatherings [E-M] comprise gatherings of illustrative plates and there are numerous additional leaves (including colour plates with protective tissue) tipped-in on stubs of paper bound with the gatherings: there are 3 additional leaves with gathering [E], 7 with gathering [F], 2 with gathering [G], 9 with gathering [H], 2 with gathering [I], 1 with gathering [K], 4 with gathering [L] and 4 with gathering [M]; 122 leaves; 310 × 245mm.; [i–iv] v–ix [x] 1–3 [4] 5–40 [41–234] (including illustration plates)

Page contents: [i] half-title: 'ADVENTURES BY SEA | FROM ART OF OLD TIME'; [ii] 'THIS EDITION IS LIMITED | TO ONE THOUSAND SEVEN | HUNDRED AND FIFTY | COPIES OF WHICH THIS | IS NUMBER ....' (within ruled border: 30 × 67mm.); [iii] title-page; [iv] '*Printed by Herbert Reiach, Ltd., | Eyot Works, St. Peter's Square, | Hammersmith, W.6, and published | by The Studio Ltd., 44 Leicester | Square, London, W.C.2.*'; v–ix 'CONTENTS' (two sections listed) together with 'LIST OF ILLUSTRATIONS' (115 plates listed); [x] '"Thrice I suffered ship- | wreck; a night and a day | I have been in the deep; | in journeying often; in | perils of waters; in perils | of robbers; in perils by | mine own countrymen; | in perils by the heathen." | Saint Paul, II Cor. xi. 25. [in red]'; 1–3 'LINES ON SEA ADVENTURE' ('I saw the old, rust-spotted, ill-found ship') (signed, 'JOHN MASEFIELD'); [4] blank; [5–40] text (and illustrations); [41] '*The Editor desires to express his thanks | to the private collectors and museum | authorities, British and foreign, who have | assisted him in the preparation of this | volume. The names of those who have | kindly given permission to reproduce | paintings and engravings are mentioned | under the illustrations concerned. The | Editor is specially indebted to A. G. H. | Macpherson, Esq., for his valuable help, | and also to Cecil King, Esq., R.I., and | Commander Chas. N. Robinson, R.N.*'; [42] blank; [43–234] illustration plates (rectos with illustrations and versos blank)

Paper: laid paper (no watermark), chain-lines 26mm. apart; illustration plates are glossy wove paper

Running title: none

Binding: purple buckram. On spine, in gold: 'ADVENTURES | BY SEA | FROM | ART OF | OLD TIME | [publisher's device of 'The Studio'] | BASIL | LUBBOCK | THE STUIDO' (all width centred). On upper cover, in gold: 'ADVENTURES BY SEA | FROM ART OF OLD TIME | [crest with illustration of mermaid with mirror: 77 × 65mm.] | BASIL LUBBOCK'. Lower cover: blank. Top edge gilt, others trimmed. Binding measurements: 319 × 249mm. (covers), 319 × 48mm. (spine). The binding includes bevelled edges. End-papers: blue wove paper (with woodcut design repeated once on each end-paper).

Publication date: published, according to the *English Catalogue of Books*, March 1925

Price: 63s.

Masefield contents:
Lines on Sea Adventure ('I saw the old, rust-spotted, ill-found ship')
    (signed, 'JOHN MASEFIELD')

Notes:
The text on page 5 commences with an illustrated drop-capital, printed in orange.

Masefield's prefatory verse comprises three sonnets, each printed on a separate page.

Simmons describes the contents of this volume as 'pages 1–3, poem by John Masefield; pages 5–40 preface by John Masefield.' This is incorrect. Although the text on pages 5–40 is unsigned, it is assumed to be by Basil Lubbock.

Copies seen: BL (7854.v.21) un-numbered copy, stamped 26 MAR 1925

B215 *THE SEVEN SEAS SHANTY BOOK* 1927

B215(a) First English edition (1927)

THE SEVEN SEAS | SHANTY BOOK | containing | 42 SEA SHANTIES & SONGS | Collected and Recollected | BY | JOHN SAMPSON, | *arranged for Piano* | BY | S. TAYLOR HARRIS, | WITH A FOREWORD | BY | JOHN MASEFIELD. | [rule, 18mm.] | Price 5/- net. | also in paper boards, price 6/6 net. | [rule, 18mm.] | BOOSEY & CO., LTD., | 295, REGENT STREET, LONDON W. | *and* | Steinway Hall, 111–113, West 57th Street, New York. | *Copyright* 1927 *by Boosey & Co., Ltd.*
(All width centred)

Bibliographies: Simmons [unrecorded]

Collation: [A]⁴ [B–E]⁸ [F]⁴ (see notes); 40 leaves; at least 269 × 191mm.; [i–iv] v–viii [ix–x] [1] 2–33 [34–35] 36–48 [49] 50–52 [53] 54–56 [57] 58 [59] 60–69 [70]

Page contents: [i] title-page; [ii] blank; [iii] 'DEDICATION. | To my fellow members of the Seven Seas Club, and | to all who go down to the sea in ships, especially those | who served their time in the old sailing ships, to whom | these songs will recall many pleasant memories. | JOHN SAMPSON.'; [iv] blank; v–vi 'FOREWORD.' ('This volume of Mr. Sampson's contains all the working songs most commonly in use...') (signed, 'JOHN MASEFIELD.'); vii–viii 'AUTHOR'S PREFACE.' ('This book of Shanties is the outcome of a desire on the part of the members...') (signed, 'JOHN SAMPSON.'); viii 'MUSICAL EDITOR'S NOTE.' ('My chief aim in making these arrangements has been to leave the tunes entirely unhampered...') (signed, 'S. TAYLOR HARRIS. | Charing Cross, December, 1926.'); [ix] 'CONTENTS' (42 individual items listed with page references, in six sections); [x] blank; [1] 'CAPSTAN SHANTIES'; 2–33 music and text; [34] blank; [35] 'HALLIARD SHANTIES'; 36–48 music and text; [49] 'FORE-SHEET SHANTIES'; 50–52 music and text; [53] 'RUNAWAY SHANTIES'; 54–56 music and text; [57] 'BUNTING SHANTY'; 58 music and text; [59] 'SEA SONGS'; 60–69 music and text

Paper: wove paper

Running title: none

Binding: blue wrappers. On upper wrapper: 'THE SEVEN SEAS | SHANTY BOOK | [black and white illustration: 168 × 171mm., "*WE'RE BOUND FOR THE RIO GRANDE.*"', signed 'KENNETH D | SHOESMITH' in lower left corner, enclosed within black ruled border (see notes)] | BY JOHN SAMPSON | *arranged for Piano by* | S. TAYLOR HARRIS, | *with a foreword by* | JOHN MASEFIELD. | BOOSEY & CO.,LTD. LONDON & NEW YORK.'. Binding measurements at least 269 × 191mm. (wrappers); 269 × 5mm. (spine). Other information cannot be distinguished from examined copy.

Also issued in 'paper boards'.

Publication date: published, according to British Library copy, during January 1927

Price: 5s. (wrappers) / 6s.6d. ('paper boards')

Masefield contents:
Foreword ('This volume of Mr. Sampson's contains all the working songs most commonly in use...')
 (signed, 'JOHN MASEFIELD.')

Notes:
Although unsigned, the volume does include 'H. 12082.' at the right foot of many pages. This is presumably a music engraver's mark.

The upper wrapper illustration is laid-down on the blue wrapper. The black ruled border is printed on the wrapper.

The copy examined includes the ink-stamped facsimile signature 'Boosey Co' on the title-page in purple ink.

Papers in the archives of The Society of Authors suggest that John Sampson approached Masefield for a foreword and that Masefield replied noting that the publishers would have to agree to a restricted licence. Boosey and Company wrote to the author as follows:

> Mr Sampson has handed us your letter of the 6th instant with reference to your Foreword to the Shanty Book he has prepared for the Seven Seas Club, and we shall be glad to receive instructions as to the form of Licence you wish to issue and any reservations you may wish to make with regard to the printing of your Foreword.
> (Boosey and Company, letter to John Masefield, 9 December 1926)
> (BL, Add.Mss.56583, f.158)

Given the publisher's willingness to co-operate with his wishes Masefield then wrote to The Society of Authors explaining the situation:

> A friend of mine, an old sailor, Mr Sampson, has made a collection of sailors' working songs... I do not wish to ask for any fee from Messrs Boosey, but, as I should like some copies of the work, I do not think they would object to sending me some – three or four would be ample.
> (John Masefield, letter to [G.H.] Thring, 19 December 1926)
> (BL, Add.Mss.56583, ff.159–160)

Conditions, as stated to the publishers by The Society of Authors, were evidently acceptable for Boosey and Company replied:

> We thank you for your letter of the 11st instant and will with pleasure carry out your stipulations with regard to the publication of Mr Masefield's Foreword...
> (Boosey and Company, letter to G.H. Thring, 13 December 1926)
> (BL, Add.Mss.56583, f.162)

Before the end of December Masefield had sent corrected proofs to Boosey and Company: '...to save a post, I have sent the corrected proofs direct to Messrs Boosey + Co.' (see John Masefield, letter to [G.H.] Thring, [26 December 1926]) (BL, Add.Mss.56583, f.171).

Copies seen: BL (G.981.g/4) stamped 7 JAN 1927, rebound

B220 *WHY EVERYBODY SHOULD ASSIST IN FIGHTING DISEASE IN THE TROPICS* [1927]

B220(a) First English edition ([1927])

WHY EVERYBODY SHOULD | ASSIST IN FIGHTING | DISEASE IN THE | TROPICS | [ornament] | *Issued by the LADIES' COMMITTEE of the* | ROSS INSTITUTE and HOSPITAL for | TROPICAL DISEASES (Incorporated) | Putney Heath, LONDON, S.W.15.
(Lines 1–5 width centred, line 6 off-set on left margin, lines 7–8 justified on both left and right margins, and line 9 width centred)

Bibliographies: Simmons p.137

Collation: [A]¹²; 12 leaves; 215 × 139mm.; [1] 2–23 [24]

Page contents: [1] title-page; 2–3 facsimile letter, dated December 1926 ('Madam | It is the hope of the "Council of the Ross Institute" that many ladies...') (signed, 'Winifred Portland | President | Ross Institute'); 4 'LADIES' COMMITTEE' (listing); 5 two black and white photographs of the Ross Institute; 6 '*The* | ROSS INSTITUTE *and* HOSPITAL | *for* TROPICAL DISEASES' (officers etc. listing); 7 two black and white photographs of the Ross Institute; 8–9 'FOREWORD.' ('When I was a boy, I had a friend from whom I parted in July.') (signed, 'JOHN MASEFIELD.'); 10–12 'WHY YOU SHOULD BECOME AN | ASSOCIATE of THE ROSS INSTITUTE' (extracts from letters); 12–19 'EXTRACTS FROM THE PRESS' (with black and white photograph of Ronald Ross); 20 'An Appeal by the late SIR EDWARD MARSHALL-HALL, K.C. | *Extract from* The Times *Tuesday, Aug. 24, 1926*'; 21 two black and white photographs of the Ross Institute; 22 'ASSOCIATES'; 23 black and white photograph of mosquito with verse by Ronald Ross; [24] cartoon with caption 'Wanted-a Bigger Fulcrum. One Ten Times the Present Size Preferred' (from *Tropical Life*, London, April 1926) (at foot of p.[24]: 'Hudson & Kearns, Ltd., London, S.E.1.')

Paper: glossy wove paper

Running title: none

Binding: light grey wrappers. Spine: blank. On upper wrapper, in navy blue: 'Why Everybody | should assist in | fighting disease | in the Tropics | *Foreword by* | JOHN MASEFIELD' (lines 1–4 justified on both left and right margins and ranged upper left, lines 5–6 ranged lower right). Lower wrapper: blank. All edges trimmed. Binding measurements: 228 × 145mm. (wrappers), 228 × 2mm. (spine). The wrapper extends beyond the edges of the internal leaves.

Publication date: unknown (not in the *English Catalogue of Books*) Simmons suggests a publication date of 1927.

Price: unknown

Masefield contents:
Foreword ('When I was a boy, I had a friend from whom I parted in July.')
     (signed, 'JOHN MASEFIELD.')

Notes:
This publication reprints Masefield's earlier 1923 contribution to Wilfred Partington, *The War Against Malaria* (see B195).

Page numbers are printed in words and italics. Thus, '*Page Two*' and '*Page Three*', etc.

The 'Foreword', 'Why You Should Become An Associate of The Ross Institute' and 'Associates' sections all commence with a drop-capital.

Copies seen: Columbia University (Special Collections B825M377 HR3 ZZ) includes printed application form and typescript of address by Duchess of Portland at the opening meeting of the ladies' committee of the Ross Institute on 16 February 1927

B225 *THE POEMS OF DUNCAN CAMPBELL SCOTT* 1927

B225(a) First English edition (1927)

The Poems of | Duncan Campbell | Scott | [oval device including two pine cones] | 1927 | LONDON: J. M. DENT & SONS, LTD. | 10–13, Bedford Street, W. C. 2
(All width centred and enclosed within double ruled border: 161 × 108mm. Between the two single borders there is a square in each corner and 'squares' (with two concave sides) in the middle of the upper and lower sides of the title-page border and also on the vertical sides slightly under half-way from the head)

Bibliographies: Simmons p.137

Collation: [1]¹⁰ (see notes) 2–20⁸ 21⁴ 22⁸; signatures left foot of page; 176 leaves; 216 × 134mm.; [two un-numbered pages] [i–ii] [four un-numbered pages] iii–viii [ix–x] 11–341 [342]

Page contents: [-] half-title: '*The Poems of* | DUNCAN | CAMPBELL | SCOTT'; [-] blank (with additional leaf bound between blank page and title-page upon which is a photograph frontispiece: 125 × 91mm.; 'Duncan Campbell Scott' [facsimile signature]); [i] title-page; [ii] 'Printed in Canada'; [four un-numbered pages] 'FOREWORD' ('This volume contains most of the published poetry of Mr. Duncan Campbell Scott...') (signed, 'JOHN MASEFIELD.'); iii–viii 'CONTENTS' (179 individual poems listed with page references); [ix] '*The Poems*'; [x] blank; 11–341 text; [342] device including bear and staff with 'WARWICK | BROS. & | RUTTER | LIMITED | TORONTO | [device of a book]' and 'PRINTERS & BOOKBINDERS'

Paper: wove paper

Running title: running titles, where used, comprise poem title, pp.12–341

Binding: blue cloth. On spine, in gold: 'The Poems | of | DUNCAN | CAMPBELL | SCOTT | [oval device including two pine cones]' and at foot of spine in blind: 'JM [point] Dent | &SonsLᵈ'. On upper cover, in blind: publisher's device including 'DENT' (within double ruled border: 219 × 132mm.) Lower cover: blank. Top edge stained dark green, others trimmed. Binding measurements: 223 × 136mm. (covers), 223 × 47mm. (spine). End-papers: wove paper.

Publication date: published, according to the *English Catalogue of Books*, May 1927

Price: 12s.6d.

Masefield contents:
Foreword ('This volume contains most of the published poetry of Mr. Duncan Campbell Scott...')
(signed, 'JOHN MASEFIELD.')

Notes:
The first unsigned gathering includes two conjugate leaves tipped-in on the fifth leaf. These leaves comprise Masefield's foreword. This edition presumably derives from a Canadian or American edition. The edition for the English market must have required a different title-page and the addition of Masefield's foreword. Significantly page [ii] includes the note 'Printed in Canada' although the title-page cites the London address of J.M. Dent. The additional leaves explain the page numbering as Masefield's foreword is un-numbered and interrupts the normal page number sequence.

The first unsigned gathering includes one leaf (and conjugate leaf stub) for the frontispiece. This is excluded from the pagination (and consequently gathering information).

Page numbers appear within square brackets. Thus, [11], [12], etc.

Each poem commences with a drop-capital.

The italic text in the preliminaries and on the binding contains a number of swash characters.

Masefield requested that The Society of Authors send his foreword to the publishers:

> Will you be so very kind as to send the enclosed preface to Messrs J.M. Dent... with a licence from me to them to use it, if they wish, as a preface to the *Poems* of D.C. Scott which they are about to publish, but restricting their use of it to this purpose only + giving them no further power over it whatsoever?
>
> (John Masefield, letter to [G.H.] Thring, [23 January 1927])
> (BL, Add.Mss.56584, f.32)

J.M. Dent acknowledged receipt of the foreword on 25 January 1927 (see BL, Add.Mss.56584, f.36) and sent a proof on 4 February 1927 (see BL, Add.Mss.56584, f.44).

Copies seen: BL (11643.cc.54) stamped 29 APR 1927

B230 *THE SCOTTISH ASSOCIATION FOR THE SPEAKING OF VERSE ITS WORK FOR THE YEAR 1926–27* 1927

B230(a) *First Scottish edition (1927)*

THE SCOTTISH ASSOCIATION | FOR THE | SPEAKING OF VERSE | (FOUNDED JANUARY 23RD, 1924) | EDINBURGH | T. AND A. CONSTABLE LTD. | 1927
(All width centred)

Bibliographies: Simmons [unrecorded]

Collation: [A]⁸ B-C⁸ D⁴; signatures width centred at foot of page; 28 leaves; 214 × 169mm.; [1–4] 5–32 [33] 34–56

Page contents: [1] title-page; [2] blank; [3] 'CONTENTS' (nine individual items listed with page references); [4] 'THE SCOTTISH ASSOCIATION FOR THE | SPEAKING OF VERSE | [ornamental rule] | [listing of president, vice-presidents, branches, chairman of the General Council, Hon. Treasurer and Hon. Secretary]'; 5–56 text

Paper: laid paper (watermark: '[Crown] | Abbey Mills | Greenfield'), chain-lines 25mm. apart

Running title: 'THE SPEAKING OF VERSE' (53–54mm.) on verso; recto title comprises sectional title

Binding: green wrappers. Spine: blank. On upper wrapper, in dark blue: 'THE SCOTTISH ASSOCIATION | FOR THE | SPEAKING OF VERSE | Its Work | For the Year 1926–27 | EDINBURGH | T. AND A. CONSTABLE LTD. | 1927 | Price (to Non-Members) One Shilling'. Lower wrapper: blank. Top and fore edges trimmed, lower outside edge untrimmed. Binding measurements: 224 × 174mm. (wrappers); 224 × 6mm. (spine). The wrapper extends beyond the edges of the internal leaves.

Publication date: unknown (not in the *English Catalogue of Books*)

Price: 1s.

Masefield contents:

Foreword ('I have been asked to write a few words for this paper which marks...')
    (signed, 'JOHN MASEFIELD.')

Notes:

There are nine entries in the contents: 'Foreword. By John Masefield', 'The Magic of Form in Poetry. By Laurence Binyon', 'Message from the Chairman', 'Our First Three Years. By Alice A. Smith', 'Report of the Annual Meeting', 'Report of the Annual Conference', 'Reports of the Branches', 'Branch Programmes' and 'Notes'.

The title provided on the title-page is not the same as that on the upper wrapper.

Masefield was president of the association and delivered an address at the first general meeting on 24 October 1924. This was published as *With the Living Voice* (see A76).

Copies seen: private collection (ROV)

B235 *THE OXFORD RECITATIONS* 1928

B235(a) *First American edition (1928)*

THE | OXFORD RECITATIONS | *Containing:* LOVE IN THE DESERT, *By* LAURENCE | BINYON: A PARTING, *and* THE RETURN, *By* GORDON | BOTTOMLEY: POLYXENA'S SPEECH *and* THE MES- | SENGER'S SPEECH, *From the* HECUBA OF EURI- | PIDES, *Translated by* JOHN MASEFIELD. | WITH A PREFACE BY | JOHN MASEFIELD | THE MACMILLAN COMPANY | NEW YORK   MCMXXVIII
(All width centred with lines 3–6 justified on left and right margins and lines 10–11 justified on left and right margins)

Bibliographies: Simmons p.137

Collation: [A-B]⁸ [C]⁴ [D]⁸; 28 leaves; 217 × 142mm.; [1–4] 5–9 [10] 11 [12–14] 15–22 [23–24] 25–44 [45–46] 47–53 [54–56]

Page contents: [1] half-title: 'THE OXFORD RECITATIONS'; [2] '[publisher's device] | THE MACMILLAN COMPANY | [two lines listing six cities, separated by four points] | MACMILLAN & CO., LIMITED | [two lines listing four cities, separated by two points] | THE MACMILLAN CO. OF CANADA, LTD. | [one city listed]'; [3] title-page; [4] 'COPYRIGHT, 1928, | BY JOHN MASEFIELD. | [rule] | Published in Collected Form, | September, 1928. | *Printed in the United States of America by* | J. J. LITTLE AND IVES COMPANY, NEW YORK'; 5–9 'PREFACE' ('The Oxford Recitations, the contests in Verse-Speaking, held in Oxford in late July, were begun...') (signed, 'JOHN MASEFIELD.'); [10] blank; 11 'CONTENTS' (six individual items listed with page references); [12] blank; [13] 'LOVE IN THE DESERT | BY LAURENCE BINYON'; [14] blank; 15–22 text of 'Love in the Desert'; [23] 'A PARTING | AND | THE RETURN | BY GORDON BOTTOMLEY'; [24] blank; 25–35 text of 'A Parting'; 36–44 text of 'The Return'; [45] 'POLYXENA'S SPEECH | AND | THE MESSENGER'S SPEECH | *From the Hecuba of Euripides* | TRANSLATED BY JOHN MASEFIELD'; [46] blank; 47–49 text of 'Polyxena's Speech'; 50–53 text of 'The Messenger's Speech'; [54–56] blank

Paper: laid paper (no watermark), chain-lines 21mm. apart

Running title: running titles comprise titles of individual items, pp.6–53

Binding: light blue boards with dark blue cloth spine. On spine: blank. On upper cover: panel in blind: 41 × 79mm. upon which: white laid paper label (39 × 77mm.) on which in dark blue: 'THE | OXFORD RECITATIONS | WITH A PREFACE BY | JOHN MASEFIELD' (enclosed within double ruled borders with outer ornamental border: 34 × 72mm.) Lower cover: blank. Top and lower outside edges trimmed, fore edge roughly trimmed. Binding measurements: 223 × 145mm. (covers), 223 × 18mm. (spine). End-papers: wove paper.

Publication date: published, according to Simmons, September 1928

Price: $1.50

Masefield contents:

Preface ('The Oxford Recitations, the contests in Verse-Speaking, held in Oxford in late July, were begun...')
    (signed, 'JOHN MASEFIELD.')
Polyxena's Speech (From the Hecuba of Euripides) ('I see you, Odysseus, hiding your right hand')
The Messenger's Speech (From the Hecuba of Euripides) ('Queen, you would draw from me a double weeping')

Notes:

Page numbers appear within square brackets. Thus, [5], [6], etc.

The texts in this volume were previously published in England in the syllabus of the Oxford Recitations (see section K). There were apparently further texts in the syllabus.

Only the Masefield contributions in this volume fail to carry any specific copyright notices.

The publishing agreement for this title between Masefield and Macmillan was dated 30 July 1928 (see Archives of The Society of Authors). The agreement refers to 'a licence to publish in volume form in the United States of America and Canada a book to contain the test pieces in the Oxford Recitations for July, 1928 (the exact title of which is to be determined)'. Royalty was to be divided between Masefield, Binyon and Bottomley.

In 1935 it appears that The Society of Authors received a request from the committee organizing the Oxford Recitations for permission to set verses by Masefield. Masefield responded:

> ...When I was running the Oxford Recitations I made it a rule never to set any verses by myself except, occasionally, translations.

(John Masefield, letter to E.J. Mullett, 12 February 1935)
(BL, Add.Mss.56602, f.113)

Copies seen: Library of The John Masefield Society (Peter Smith Collection); HRHRC (PN4201 087 cop.1); HRHRC (PN4201 087 cop.2) inscribed 'For Lew | from | Zob | Nov 11. 1928.'

B240 *Ed.* A. HENRY HIGGINSON, *AS HOUNDS RAN* 1930

B240(a) *First American edition (1930)*

AS HOUNDS RAN | FOUR CENTURIES OF FOXHUNTING | Edited by A. HENRY HIGGINSON | With Foregrounds by JOHN MASEFIELD | and EDGAR ASTLEY MILNE | *Illustrated with Contemporary Prints and with New Drawings by* | CECIL ALDIN & LIONEL EDWARDS | [ornament] | NEW YORK : HUNTINGTON PRESS : MDCCCCXXX

(All width centred)

Collation: [A]⁴ [B-R]⁸ [S]⁴ (J not used); 136 leaves; 251 × 187mm.; [two un-numbered pages] [i–vii] viii [ix] x–xi [xii–xiii] xiv [xv] xvi [xvii] xviii–xxviii [1–3] 4–9 [10–11] 12 [13] 14–15 [16–17] 18–21 [22–23] 24–34 [35] 36–59 [60–61] 62–68 [69] 70–75 [76–77] 78–79 [80–81] 82–93 [94–95] 96–101 [102–103] 104 [105] 106–110 [111] 112–13 [114–15] 116 [117] 118–25 [126–27] 128–33 [134–35] 136–42 [143] 144–49 [150–51] 152–62 [163] 164–73 [174–75] 176–88 [189] 190–94 [195] 196–209 [210–11] 212–14 [215] 216–17 [218–19] 220–23 [224–25] 226–40 [241–42]; illustrations (on wove paper) are tipped-in on pp.[ii], 7, 12, 34, 51, 71, 79, 85, 97, [102], 104, 106, 109, [114], 116, 129, 137, 142, 153, 155, 162, 171, 179, 187, 188, 212, 214, 221, 227 and 234.

Page contents: [-] blank (page excluded from page count, but constitutes first leaf of first gathering); [-] blank; [i] half-title: '*As Hounds Ran*'; [ii] blank (with additional leaf tipped-in on the verso of which is the colour frontispiece, '"And the hunt came home and the hounds were fed, | They climbed to their bench and went to bed."'); [iii] title-page; [iv] 'COPYRIGHT, 1930, BY HUNTINGTON PRESS, INCORPORATED | Printed in the United States of America | All Rights Reserved | [point] [point] | [point]'; [v] 'Editor's Note' ('I have been asked by my Publishers to write a definition of the title of this book...') (signed, '*A.H.H.*'); [vi] '*Acknowledgment*'; [vii]-viii 'FOREWORD' ('Someone was saying the other day that during the last hundred and fifty years...') (signed, 'JOHN MASEFIELD | *Oxford, England* | *August, 1930*'); [ix]-xi 'FOREWORD' ('History tells us that almost every nation that, in its turn, has held...') (signed, '*EDGAR ASTLEY MILNE* | *Cattistock, Dorset, England* | *August, 1930*'); [xii] blank; [xiii]-xiv 'TABLE OF CONTENTS' (36 items listed with page references); [xv]-xvi 'LIST OF ILLUSTRATIONS' (30 items listed with page references); [xvii]-xxviii 'INTRODUCTION' ('When I first began work on this foxhunting anthology, I was somewhat...') (signed, 'A. HENRY HIGGINSON | *April, 1930*'); [1] '*As Hounds Ran*'; [2] blank; [3]-9 text; [10] blank; [11]-15 text; [16] blank; [17]-21 text; [22] blank; [23]-59 text; [60] blank; [61]-75 text; [76] blank; [77]-79 text; [80] blank; [81]-93 text; [94] blank; [95]-101 text; [102] blank; [103]-113 text; [114] blank; [115]-125 text; [126] blank; [127]-133 text; [134] blank; [135]-149 text; [150] blank; [151]-173 text; [174] blank; [175]-209 text; [210] blank; [211]-217 text; [218] blank; [219]-223 text; [224] blank; [225]-240 text; [241] '*Printed by D.B. Updike, The Merrymount Press, Boston,* | *the text hand set in Janson type, printed on Leipsig paper.* | *Of an edition of 990 copies for America & England this is* | *Number*'; [242] blank

Paper: wove paper

Running title: running titles comprise author on verso; title on recto

Binding: crimson cloth. On spine, in gold: '[hunting horn (within double ruled border: 26 × 37mm.)] | AS | HOUNDS | RAN | *Edited by* | A.H. HIGGINSON [these five lines within double ruled border: 45 × 37mm.] | HUNTINGTON PRESS | [hunting horn (these two lines within double ruled border: 175 × 37mm.)]' (all width centred). On upper cover, in gold: double ruled border: 253 × 183mm. with hunting horn at each corner. On lower cover, in gold: double ruled border: 253 × 183mm. with hunting horn at each corner. Top edge gilt and stained red, lower outside edge untrimmed, fore edge uncut. Binding measurements: 256 × 189mm. (covers), 256 × 48mm. (spine). End-papers: wove paper. Volume contained in slip-case covered in light grey wove paper, with white wove paper label (61 × 40mm.) on spine upon which: 'AS | HOUNDS | RAN | *Edited by* | A. H. HIGGINSON | [double rule] | *Number*' (within double ruled border: 57 × 37mm.)

Publication date: post August 1930

Price: $25

Masefield contents:
Foreword ('Someone was saying the other day that during the last hundred and fifty years...')
    (signed, 'JOHN MASEFIELD | *Oxford, England* | *August, 1930*')
Reynard the Fox [extract] ('The meet was at "The Cock and Pye')
Reynard the Fox [extract] ('And the hunt came home and the hounds were fed,')

In addition, Higginson, in his introduction to extracts from *Reynard the Fox*, quotes an entire letter from Masefield dated 13 January 1920.

Notes:

Excluding illustrations, there are thirty-six individual entries listed in the contents list (including forewords, but excluding biographical notes).

In the 'Editor's Note', Higginson explains his title:

> Many an evening when jogging home with hounds in the fast fading twilight after a hard day's sport, I've been joined by some friend who, less fortunate than I, had failed to see the end of a hunt, and who asked me to tell him what had happened. And always I've ended my story with the phrase "as hounds ran, we must have covered [so many] miles."

> In the compilation of this anthology there have been many coverts drawn, and there have been a good many checks; but the long hunt is over at last, and in the excerpts selected the compiler has tried to describe what happened "as hounds ran" in the words of some of the best men who wrote during the long period of over four hundred years.

Contributions commence with drop-capitals.

Within the acknowledgments, the Macmillan Company is acknowledged for permission to include the selections from *Reynard the Fox*.

Evidence within the archives of The Society of Authors suggests that in 1933 the firm of Messrs Seeley Service & Co Ltd contemplated importing copies of *As Hounds Ran* to England from the American publishers. No further detail is known (see BL, Add.Mss.56598, ff.140–141).

Copies seen: Columbia University (Special Collections B825M377 HH5 1930) number 209, in slipcase

B245 *THE FORM AND ORDER OF THE SERVICE... AND OF THE CEREMONIES THAT ARE TO BE OBSERVED IN THE FOUNDATION OF THE DEAN AND CHAPTER OF THE CATHEDRAL CHURCH OF CHRIST[,] LIVERPOOL* 1931

B245(a) First English edition (1931)

THE | FORM AND ORDER | Of the SERVICE that is to be performed and of | the CEREMONIES that are to be observed in the | FOUNDATION OF THE | DEAN AND CHAPTER | OF THE | CATHEDRAL CHURCH OF CHRIST | LIVERPOOL | *Sunday, October 4th, 1931, at 11–0 a.m.*
(All width centred)

Collation: [A]¹⁶; 16 leaves; 278 × 185mm.; [1–3] 4–29 [30–32]

Page contents: [1] title-page; [2] blank; [3]-[30] text; [31] 'ACKNOWLEDGMENTS | To the POET LAUREATE, Dr. JOHN MASEFIELD, | for lines on the dedication. | To Mr. MARTIN SHAW, for music specially written | for the dedication. | To THE OXFORD UNIVERSITY PRESS, for | permission to use music from *Songs of Praise* | *(enlarged edition),* | and for this book and the MSS. music | To Mr. FRANCIS NEILSON.'; [32] 'PRINTED AT THE CHURCH PRESS | IN THE CHURCH HOUSE OF THE DIOCESE OF LIVERPOOL'

Paper: laid paper (no watermark), chain-lines 24mm. apart

Running title: none

Binding: white wrappers. Spine: blank. On upper wrapper: 'THE FOUNDATION | OF THE | DEAN AND CHAPTER | [religious figure and crest in black and red] | [bird in red] OF LIVERPOOL [bird in red]'. Lower wrapper: blank. Top and fore edges trimmed, lower outside edge untrimmed. Binding measurements: 284 × 193mm. (wrappers), 284 × 3mm. (spine). The wrapper extends beyond the edges of the internal leaves.

Publication date: presumably published, October 1931

Price: unknown

Masefield contents:
[Untitled] ('They buried him, and then the soldiers slept;')
(headed, 'by Dr. John Masefield')

Notes:
Masefield's contribution was printed (without title) in *The Times* for 5 October 1931.

The pamphlet includes a ligatured 's' and 't'.

Masefield's poem is introduced as follows:

> When all have come to their places the Choir shall begin the service, singing this hymn of the Dedication, written for the occasion by Dr. John Masefield; the music specially written by Mr. Martin Shaw.

Masefield was a member of the 'College of Counsel' and was involved in the service.

Copies seen: private collection (ROV)

B250 *ROYAL ACADEMY OF DRAMATIC ART... PROGRAMME... NOVEMBER 17TH 1931* 1931

B250(a) First English edition (1931)

[royal coat of arms] | ROYAL ACADEMY OF DRAMATIC ART | GOWER STREET, LONDON, W.C. 1 | [rule, 21mm.] | Programme | of Performance given on the Occasion of the | VISIT OF | THEIR ROYAL HIGHNESSES | THE DUKE & DUCHESS OF YORK | and | The Opening of the New Building | By HER ROYAL HIGHNESS | THE DUCHESS OF YORK | TUESDAY, NOVEMBER 17th, 1931 | AT 3 P.M.
(lines 2–15 within double ruled border: 180 × 133mm. and all within double ruled border (of which the inner border is thickest): 224 × 181mm.; the coat of arms appears between the two double ruled borders, intersecting both)

Collation: [A]²; 2 leaves; 258 × 210mm.; [1–4]

Page contents: [1] described above; [2] 'Poem specially written for the occasion by | THE POET LAUREATE | SPOKEN BY | Mr. HENRY AINLEY | [rule] | [text] | JOHN MASEFIELD.'; [3] cast listing for *The Dumb Wife of Cheapside* (by Ashley Dukes), and *Prologue in Mime*; [4] 'ROYAL ACADEMY OF DRAMATIC ART | INCORPORATED by ROYAL CHARTER 1920 | [rule] | [listing of patron, council, principal, architect, sculptor, lighting designer, builders, ushers and provider of flowers]'

Paper: wove cardboard

Running title: none

Binding: issued as a single four page leaflet. The title-page consequently comprises the upper wrapper. All edges trimmed. Measurements: 258 × 210mm. (wrappers), 258 × 0.5mm. (spine).

Publication date: presumably published, November 1931

Price: unknown

Masefield contents:
Poem specially written for the occasion by The Poet Laureate ('All things longed for in youth,')
    (signed, 'JOHN MASEFIELD.')

Notes:
The printing of text is in purple.

Copies seen: Columbia University Libraries (Special Collections B823.M377.U53.1931.ZZ) includes note 'from the Drinkwater sale'

B255 *SHAKESPEARE MEMORIAL THEATRE... OPENING CEREMONIAL* 1932

B255(a) First English edition (1932)

Shakespeare Memorial | Theatre | Statford=upon=Avon | Patron: His Majesty The King | [ornament] | Opening | Ceremonial | by | H.R.H. The Prince of Wales | K.G., etc. | Saturday, 23rd April, 1932 | "The Play's the thing"-Hamlet, ii, 2
(All width centred and within ornate title-page decoration (with quotation from *Hamlet* separate from other text). 'S' in 'Shakespeare', 'M' in 'Memorial', 'T' in 'Theatre', 'O' in 'Opening' and 'C' in 'Ceremonial' are all in red.)

Collation: [A]¹⁴; 14 leaves; 278 × 194mm.; [1–28]

Page contents: [1] blank; [2] reproduction of first folio title-page; [3] ' "*And, as imagination bodies forth | The forms of things unknown, the poet's pen | Turns them to shapes, and gives to airy nothing | A local habitation and a name.*" | -A MIDSUMMER NIGHT'S DREAM.'; [4] '[illustration] | Shakespeare Memorial Theatre | from the Bridge'; [5] title-page; [6] '['NONS SANS DROICT' crest within black panel] | This copyright Souvenir of the Opening of the Shakespeare Memorial Theatre | has been printed in Great Britain for the Governors'; [7]-[26] text and illustrations; [27]-[28] blank

Paper: laid paper (no watermark), chain-lines 40mm. apart

Running title: none

Binding: brown wrappers. Spine: blank. On upper wrapper: '[crest (with other embellishments of foliage, helmet and bird) with 'non sans droict'] [in red] | Shakespeare Memorial Theatre | Stratford=upon=Avon | 23rd April, 1932'. Lower wrapper: blank. All edges trimmed. Binding measurements: 286 × 196mm. (wrappers), 286 × 3mm. (spine). The wrapper extends beyond the edges of the internal leaves.

Publication date: presumably published, April 1932

Price: unknown

Masefield contents:
A Message from England's Poet Laureate ('Beside this House there is a blackened shell,')
    (signed, ' – JOHN MASEFIELD.')

Notes:

The titled sections are as follows: 'A Message from England's Poet Laureate – JOHN MASEFIELD', 'To the Builders of the New Shakespeare Memorial Theatre – SIR ARCHIBALD D. FLOWER', 'Stratford's Festivals: Their Birth, Growth and Significance – A.K. CHESTERTON', 'A Summary of Events since the Theatre was destroyed by fire and a Short Description of the New Theatre' and 'Notes on the Production of this Souvenir'.

There are numerous examples throughout this booklet of swash characters.

Masefield's contribution was printed (without title) in *The Times* for 25 April 1932.

The 'Notes on the Production of this Souvenir' are as follows:

> The reproduction of the title-page of the First Folio Shakespeare, with the Droeshout Engraved Portrait in early state, at the commencement of this Souvenir, has been reproduced from the copy acquired by the British Museum in September, 1922. The border surround to Mr. Chesterton's article on "Stratford Festivals" has been built up from the decorative headpiece used on the preliminary page in the First Folio "To the memory of my beloued, The Avthor, Mr. William Shakespeare: And what he hath left vs." The decorative headpiece to Sir Archibald Flower's Message "To the Builders" has been recut from that used on the dedication page by the publishers in the same Folio to "William Earle of Pembroke and Philip Earle of Montgomery, etc." The headpieces at the commencement of the other articles have also been reproduced from the First Folio.
>
> The illustrations, which are copyright, are reproduced direct from pencil drawings which have been made specially for this work by Miss Dorothy Woollard.
>
> The paper used for the printing of this Souvenir has been specially made for the purpose, only selected rags being used in its manufacture.
>
> The type used for the headings to the articles is a recutting of the famous "black letter" used by Wynkyn de Worde, William Caxton's principal assistant, who succeeded to his master's business and plant on the death of England's First Printer. This "black letter" has never been surpassed by typecutters, and it deservedly gave the name "Old English" to the many "black" or "gothic" types used by printers in this country for several centuries. Indeed, even now, the term "Old English" is common for all kinds of "black letter" in many printing offices. [ornament] The type in which the articles are set is Linotype Granjon, designed by the printer of this work, which has been produced and printed by George W. Jones, at *The Sign of The Dolphin,* next to Dr. Johnson's House in Gough Square, Fleet Street, London, E.C.4.

Copies seen: private collection (ROV)

B260 E.E. STOPFORD, *THE SLAVES OF ROSE HALL*   1933

B260(a) First English edition (1933)

The Slaves of Rose Hall | *By* | E.E. STOPFORD | *With an Introduction by* | JOHN MASEFIELD | [ornament] | *"Man is born free but is everywhere in chains."* | -ROUSSEAU | [publisher's device of a windmill with 'W [point]' and 'H'] | LONDON | WILLIAM HEINEMANN LTD
(All width centred with the exception of line eight which is off-set to the right)

Collation: [A]⁸ B-C⁸; signatures right foot of page; 24 leaves; 183 × 120mm.; [i–iv] v–vii [viii] 1–39 [40]

Page contents: [i] half-title: 'The Slaves of Rose Hall'; [ii] blank; [iii] title-page; [iv] '*First Published* 1933 | *Printed in Great Britain* | *at The Windmill Press, Kingswood, Surrey*'; v–vi 'PREFACE' ('Some ten years ago, being eager to learn what speakers of verse there might be...') (signed, 'JOHN MASEFIELD'); vii 'The story of "The Slaves of Rose Hall" is founded | on fact. Rose Hall still stands, fifteen miles from | Montego Bay, a vast empty monument to the | days of the great slave-owners; the memory of | Annie Palmer is even now notorious in Jamaica, | though tradition records that she met her death | a few months before the Emancipation of the | Slaves. Those familiar with her story will realise | that in the ensuing narrative the horrors are | palliated rather than over-stressed. | E. E. STOPFORD. | *March,* 1933.'; [viii] blank; 1–39 text; [40] blank

Paper: wove paper

Running title: none

Binding: navy blue cloth. On spine reading lengthways up spine, from foot, in gold: 'The Slaves of Rose Hall By E.E.Stopford'; horizontally at foot of spine, in gold: publisher's device of a windmill with 'W' and 'H'. On upper cover: blind ruled border: 183 × 114mm. Lower cover: blank. All edges trimmed. Binding measurements: 189 × 123mm. (covers), 189 × 18mm. (spine). End-papers: wove paper.

Publication date: published, according to the *English Catalogue of Books*, May 1933

Price: 3s.6d.

Masefield contents:
Preface ('Some ten years ago, being eager to learn what speakers of verse there might be...')
     (signed, 'JOHN MASEFIELD')

Notes:

Masefield's introduction states that this work won a prize at the Oxford Recitations for 'tales in verse suitable for performance by speakers'.

C.S. Evans wrote to Masefield during March 1933 asking whether the author would be willing to contribute 'something':

> You will remember that I am publishing Miss Stopford's poem, THE SLAVES OF ROSE HALL. She asked me whether I had approached you about writing a foreword. Do you want to write something? I am sure that Miss Stopford would be grateful and appreciative and I believe that it would help the book.

(C.S. Evans, letter to John Masefield, 7 March 1933)
(HRHRC, MS (Masefield, J.) Recip William Heinemann Ltd.)

A 'proof copy… which includes your Preface.' was sent to Masefield thirteen days later (see B.F. Oliver, letter to John Masefield, 20 March 1933) (HRHRC, MS (Masefield, J.) Recip William Heinemann Ltd.)

Copies seen: ULL (Special Collections); BL (011641.df.49) stamped 8 MAY 1933

B265 EDWARD SEAGO, *CIRCUS COMPANY* 1933

B265(a) *First English edition (1933)*

EDWARD SEAGO | CIRCUS COMPANY | *LIFE ON THE ROAD WITH THE* | *TRAVELLING SHOW* | *Illustrated by* THE AUTHOR | *With an Introduction by* | JOHN MASEFIELD | PUTNAM | [rule (tapered at both ends), 93mm.] | 24 BEDFORD STREET, LONDON, W.C.
(All width centred)
(The italic font contains swash characters)

Collation: [A]⁸ 1–18⁸ 19⁴; signatures left foot of page; 156 leaves; 215 × 135mm.; [i–viii] ix [x] xi–xiii [xiv] xv [xvi] [1] 2–292 [293] 294–95 [296]; the frontispiece (on glossy paper) is tipped-in on p.[iv]; other illustrations (on laid paper) are tipped-in on pp.7, 35, 47, 49, 57, 101, 163, 187, 211, 251, 257, 259, 273, 277, 281 and 291

Page contents: [i] blank; [ii] blank; [iii] half-title: 'CIRCUS COMPANY'; [iv] blank (with additional leaf tipped-in on the verso of which is the untitled colour frontispiece: 143 × 108mm.); [v] title-page; [vi] 'FIRST PUBLISHED MAY 1933 | *Made and Printed in Great Britain by* | *Hazell, Watson & Viney, Ltd., London and Aylesbury.*'; [vii] 'TOMMY BAKER | *Died December 7th, 1932* | TO HIS MEMORY | [text] | R.L.S.'; [viii] blank; ix 'ILLUSTRATIONS' (16 illustrations and frontispiece listed with page references); [x] blank; xi–xiii 'INTRODUCTION' ('Most of us, when young, have known the delight of going to the Circus.') (signed, 'JOHN MASEFIELD. | *Boars Hill, 1933.*'); [xiv] blank; xv facsimile of music manuscript (signed 'Jack.'); [xvi] blank; [1]-292 text; [293] 'GLOSSARY'; 294–95 text of 'Glossary'; [296] blank

Paper: laid paper (no watermark), chain-lines 26–29mm. apart

Running title: 'CIRCUS COMPANY' (45mm.) on verso; '*EDWARD SEAGO*' (40mm.) on recto, pp.2–292

Binding: green cloth. On spine, in gold: 'CIRCUS | COMPANY | [illustration of head of circus horse] | EDWARD | SEAGO | PUTNAM' (width centred). Covers: blank. All edges trimmed. Binding measurements: 221 × 138mm. (covers), 221 × 50mm. (spine). End-papers: wove paper.

Publication date: published, according to the *English Catalogue of Books*, May 1933

Price: 10s.6d.

Masefield contents:
Introduction ('Most of us, when young, have known the delight of going to the Circus.')
(signed, 'JOHN MASEFIELD. | *Boars Hill, 1933.*')

Notes:

There are twenty untitled chapters in addition to a glossary.

Seago provided illustrations for three of Masefield's works (see *The Country Scene* (A123), *Tribute to Ballet* (A125) and *A Generation Risen* (A138)).

The text contains a number of small line drawings by Seago. These are not included in the list of illustrations which notes full page illustrations only.

The italic font used for the running titles contains swash characters.

The laid paper used for the tipped-in illustrations is the same as that used in the rest of the volume.

Chapters each commence with a prefatory quotation. Chapters II, IV, X, XIV and XVII each commence with a quotation from Masefield, as follows:

> "THE PRINCE: Who are these artistes; do they paint or write?
> KING COLE: No, but they serve the arts and love delight."

> "The tent was pitched beneath a dropping sky,
> The green-striped tent with all its gear awry."

"Laugh and be merry, remember, better world with a song,
Better the world with a blow in the teeth of a wrong."

"It is good to be out on the road, and going one knows not where."

"Laugh till the game is played; and be you merry, my friends."

Copies seen: BL (11796.bb.9) stamped 18 MAY 1933

B265(b) Second English edition (1934)

The *English Catalogue of Books* contains the following entry:

Seago (Edward) – Circus Company: life on the road with the travelling show. Illus. by Author. Intro. by J. Masefield. Ch. ed. 8vo, 8 3/4 × 5 3/4, p.311, 5s. net. (Black and white lib.) PUTNAM, *Aug.* '34

B270 LILLAH McCARTHY, *MYSELF AND MY FRIENDS*   1933

B270(a) First English edition (1933)

MYSELF | AND MY FRIENDS | *By* | LILLAH McCARTHY, O.B.E. | (Lady Keeble) | *WITH AN ASIDE BY* | BERNARD SHAW | [publisher's device of a man working on the land with 'TB' all within circle] | LONDON | THORNTON BUTTERWORTH, LTD.
(All width centred. The italic type includes a number of swash characters)

Collation: [a]⁶ [A]⁸ B–U⁸ (J not used); signatures left foot of page; 166 leaves; 216 × 137mm.; [i–viii] ix [x] xi–xii 1–11 [12] 13–80 [81] 82–154 [155] 156–62 [163] 164–88 [189] 190 [191] 192–270 [271] 272–319 [320]; illustrations (on glossy paper) are bound with the gatherings (each illustration leaf has a corresponding stub between different leaves)

Page contents: [i–ii] blank; [iii] half-title: 'MYSELF AND | MY FRIENDS'; [iv] blank; [v] title-page (with additional leaf bound between pages iv and v upon which is the coloured frontispiece by Edmund Dulac: 136 × 102mm., 'LILLAH-BOURNE BY THE WINGS OF LOVE | FROM THE WINGS OF THE STAGE'); [vi] 'First Published . . . . 1933 | *All rights reserved* | Made and printed in Great Britain'; [vii] '*DEDICATION* | To "Freddie" | *What's Mine is Thine*'; [viii] blank; ix 'CONTENTS' (19 titled chapters, preface, and contribution by Bernard Shaw listed with page references); [x] blank; xi–xii 'LIST OF ILLUSTRATIONS' (23 illustrations and six facsimile letters listed with page references); 1–8 'AN ASIDE' ('I was very intimately concerned in the chapter of theatrical history which is also a chapter...') (signed, 'G.B.S. | Ayot St. Lawrence', dated 'May 1933'); 9–11 'AUTHOR'S PREFACE' ('To send this book out into the world without a word of acknowledgment of what it owes...') (signed, 'LILLAH MCCARTHY'); [12] blank; 13–315 text; 316–[320] 'INDEX' (at foot of page [320]: '[rule] | *The Stanhope Press Limited, Rochester, Kent*')

Paper: wove paper

Running title: 'MYSELF AND MY FRIENDS' (44mm.) on verso; recto title comprises section title, pp.14–315

Binding: blue cloth. On spine, lettering in gold: '[rule] [in blind] | Myself | and | My Friends | LILLAH | McCARTHY | THORNTON | BUTTERWORTH | [rule] [in blind]' (width centred). On upper cover, in blind: '[rule] | Myself and My Friends | LILLAH McCARTHY | [publisher's device of a man working on the land with 'TB' within circle] | [rule]' (see notes). Lower cover: blank. All edges trimmed. Binding measurements: 221 × 139mm. (covers), 221 × 56mm. (spine). End-papers: wove paper.

Publication date: published, according to the *English Catalogue of Books*, June 1933

Price: 18s.

Masefield contents:
There are numerous quotations from Masefield's letters to Lillah McCarthy throughout the volume. Also included is a facsimile letter regarding her performance as Viola (in a 1912 production of *Twelfth Night* at the Savoy Theatre, London).

Notes:
There are nineteen titled chapters listed in the contents in addition to McCarthy's preface and 'An Aside' by Bernard Shaw. The index is omitted from the contents.

Page number 110 appears as 10 only.

The blind rules on the spine and upper cover are connected.

Chapter eight is entitled 'Masefield – Nan – The Witch'. Lillah McCarthy (1875–1960) created the roles of Nan and Anne Pedersdotter. After her divorce from Harley Granville-Barker and remarriage to Frederick Keeble in 1921, she came to live on Boars Hill.

One illustration (between pp.238–39) is entitled 'Garden Room At "Hamels," Boar's Hill, Oxford, 1925 Showing the Crucifixion painted by Charles Ricketts, R.A. for "Philip II" by John Masefield.' This painting was presumably from the performance of *Philip the King* on 5 November 1914. On this occasion Lillah McCarthy played the Infanta.

Copies seen: private collection (ROV); BL (2409.c.14) stamped 26 JUN 1933 rebound

Reprinted:
A cheaper edition was published at 5s. by Thornton Butterworth (in the 'Keystone library') in September 1934.

B275 EVAN P. CAMERON, *GOODBYE RUSSIA*   1934

B275(a) *First English edition (1934)*

GOODBYE RUSSIA | *Adventures of H.M. Transport* | RIO NEGRO | BY | CAPTAIN EVAN P. CAMERON | R.D., R.N.R., F.R.A.S. | HODDER AND STOUGHTON | LIMITED   LONDON
(All width centred)

Collation: [A]⁸ B-P⁸ Q¹⁰ (J not used) Q2 is also signed; 130 leaves; 215 × 140mm.; [i–iv] v [vi] vii–xv [xvi] [1] 2–25 [26] 27–244; illustrations (on glossy paper) are tipped-in on pp.[ii], [xvi] and 123, illustrations also bound enclosing gatherings B, D, F, H, L, N and P or bound within gatherings B, C, H, K and N

Page contents: [i] half-title: 'GOODBYE RUSSIA'; [ii] blank (with additional leaf tipped in on the verso of which is the black and white frontispiece: 139 × 95mm., '*Photo: Bassano, Ltd., 38 Dover St., W.* | ADMIRAL SIR JOHN DE ROBECK. | [*Frontispiece*]'; [iii] title-page; [iv] 'FIRST PUBLISHED . . . 1934 | *Made and Printed in Great Britain.* | *Hazell, Watson & Viney, Ltd., London and Aylesbury.*'; v '*TO MY WIFE*'; [vi] blank; vii 'PREFACE' ('THIS book is written from the diary of the Commander of…') (unsigned); viii 'ACKNOWLEDGMENTS'; ix–x 'CONTENTS' (foreword, prologue, 18 chapters listed with titles, an epilogue, appendix and index are also listed with page references); xi–xii 'ILLUSTRATIONS' (50 illustrations listed with page references); xiii–xv 'FOREWORD' ('IT is a pleasure to me to write these few words of introduction…') (signed, 'JOHN MASEFIELD.'); [xvi] blank; [1]-25 'PROLOGUE'; [26] blank; 27–244 text

Paper: wove paper

Running title: 'Goodbye Russia' (38mm.) on verso; recto titles comprise chapter title, pp.2–240

Binding: green cloth. On spine, in gold: '[rule] | [double rule] | [rule] | GOODBYE | RUSSIA | [square point on one corner] [square point on one corner] [square point on one corner] | CAMERON | [publisher's device comprising of 'H', '&' and 'S'] | HODDER & | STOUGHTON | [rule] | [double rule] | [rule]' (all width centred). Covers: blank. All edges trimmed. Binding measurements: 222 × 137mm. (covers), 222 × 49mm. (spine). End-papers: wove paper (at the front of the volume these comprise an untitled map in green of Hungary, Russia, the Black Sea and Turkey, within double ruled borders: 201 × 241mm.)

Publication date: published, according to the *English Catalogue of Books*, April 1934

Price: 12s.6d.

Masefield contents:
Foreword ('It is a pleasure to me to write these few words of introduction…')
        (signed, 'JOHN MASEFIELD.')

Notes:
As stated by Masefield, the book 'records simply some events in the ending of Tsarist Russia, which were little known in England when they happened and are hardly thought of to-day'.

Copies seen: BL (9100.b.12) stamped 25 APR 1934 rebound; Maggs Bros. Ltd.

B280 CUNARD WHITE STAR. *LAUNCH OF NO "534"*   [1934]

B280(a) *First English edition ([1934])*

Cunard White Star | [rule, 18mm.] | *Launch of* | Nº "534" | *in the presence of Their Majesties* | *The King & Queen* | *at the Yard of* | *John Brown & Co., Ltd.* | *Clydebank* | *Wednesday September 26, 1934* | [rule, 16mm.] | *Naming Ceremony performed by* | *Her Majesty The Queen* | [illustration of ship under construction]
(All centred but ranged towards left margin with illustration ranged towards right margin. On extreme left is a pictorial panel printed in blue and light brown)

Collation: [A]¹⁴; 14 leaves; 324 × 262mm.; [1–28]; fold-out illustrations are tipped-in on pp.[15], [23] and [27]

Page contents: [1] blank; [2] '*FIFTY YEARS AGO*' ('"I have been told that it is an anomaly in shipping to talk of…') (signed, 'MR. JOHN BURNS, *Chairman of the Cunard Line, at the launch of the* "*Etruria*" | *on September 20th, 1884.*'); [3] title-page; [4–26] text and illustrations; [27] 'PRINTED IN ENGLAND'; [28] blank

Paper: wove paper

Running title: none

Binding: embossed white wrappers. On spine, in gold: blank panel. On upper wrapper: '*LAUNCH OF* | Nº "534" [in gold and black] | *in the presence of Their Majesties* | THE KING & QUEEN | *Wednesday, September 26, 1934* | *at Clydebank*' (within ornate plaque design in black and gold: 134 × 130mm.) together with pictorial panel printed in gold, blue and light brown on extreme left. On lower wrapper: pictorial panel printed in gold, blue and light brown on extreme right. The pictorial panel includes a number of embossed illustrations. The plaque design on the upper cover is printed on a raised panel. All edges trimmed. Binding measurements: 331 × 271mm. (wrappers), 331 × 6mm. (spine). The wrappers extend beyond the edges of the internal leaves.

Publication date: presumably published, September 1934

Price: unknown

Masefield contents:
Number "534" ('For ages you were rock, far below light,')
      (signed, 'John Masefield.' [facsimile signature])

Notes:
'534' was R.M.S. *Queen Mary* (see also D6)

Masefield's poem is headed 'BY JOHN MASEFIELD | *Specially written by the Poet Laureate to mark the occasion | of the launch.*'

Most of the text contained in this volume is by E.P. Leigh-Bennett entitled 'Masterpiece in the making'. It is sub-titled 'A pen picture of the activity in the Yard shortly before the Launch'

There are three fold-out illustrations by Frank H. Mason. In the only copy of this volume examined the first and second illustrations are the same.

Copies seen: BL (Cup.1264.d.40) stamped 31 MAR 1977

B285 KING GEORGE'S JUBILEE TRUST
OFFICIAL PROGRAMME OF THE JUBILEE PROCESSION   1935

B285(a) First English edition – standard 1s. issue (1935)

Upper wrapper:
KING GEORGE'S JUBILEE | TRUST | [coat of arms in black, white, gold, red and blue] | OFFICIAL | PROGRAMME | OF THE | JUBILEE | PROCESSION | ONE SHILLING
(All width centred)

Collation: [A]¹⁶; 16 leaves; 279 × 217mm.; 1–31 [32]

Page contents: 1 'A Message | from H.R.H. The Prince of Wales' ('We celebrate to-day a most happy occasion in our country's history...') (facsimile signature); 2–5 photographs (with captions); 6–8 'THE KING'S MAJESTY' ('The homage paid by the British people to King George the Fifth...') (headed, '*by* John Drinkwater'); 9–11 'KING GEORGE THE FIFTH' (text and photographs) ('George V by the Grace of God of Great Britain and Ireland and of the British Dominions...'); 12 'THE | SILVER JUBILEE | OF | HIS MOST GRACIOUS MAJESTY | KING GEORGE THE FIFTH | MONDAY, MAY THE SIXTH. | NINETEEN HUNDRED | AND THIRTY-FIVE. | A PRAYER FOR THE KING'S MAJESTY | [text] | JOHN MASEFIELD, *Poet Laureate*.'; 13–15 'THE JUBILEE PROCESSION'; 16–17 'MAP AND TIME-TABLE OF THE PROCESSION'; 18 'THE SERVICE AT SAINT PAUL'S CATHEDRAL | *An Introduction*' ('On May 6th there will be a great congregation in St. Paul's...') (headed, '*by* THE VERY REVEREND THE DEAN OF ST. PAUL'S CATHEDRAL'); 19–23 Order of Service; 24 'THE KING'S BROADCAST' ('When His Majesty first spoke to the Empire on Christmas Day, 1932...') (headed, '*by* Sir J. C. W. Reith, G.B.E., LL.D.'); 25–27 'THE | JUBILEE CELEBRATIONS' (text and maps); 28 'A GENEALOGICAL TABLE OF THE ROYAL FAMILY'; 29 'THE CEREMONY OF THE SWORD | And the Troops on the Route'; 30–[32] 'KING GEORGE'S | JUBILEE TRUST' (at foot of p.[32]: '[rule] | Printed in England by Odhams Press Ltd., Long Acre, W.C.2, and published by King George's Jubilee Trust, St. James's Palace, London, S.W.1 | WORLD COPYRIGHT RESERVED')

Paper: glossy wove paper

Running title: none

Binding: beige wrappers. Spine: blank. On upper wrapper: as above. Lower wrapper: blank. All edges trimmed. Binding measurements: 279 × 217mm. (wrappers), 279 × 2mm. (spine).

Publication date: unknown (not in the *English Catalogue of Books*)

Price: 1s.

Masefield contents:
A Prayer for the King's Majesty ('O God, whose mercy is our state,')
      (signed, 'JOHN MASEFIELD, *Poet Laureate*.')

Notes:
Masefield's contribution was printed in *The Times* for 7 May 1935.

The pamphlet includes a ligatured 's' and 't'.

There are a number of drop-capitals and one decorated drop-capital.

Copies seen: private collection (ROV)

B285(aa) First English edition – 'Special Edition' 2s.6d. issue (1935)

Upper wrapper:
KING GEORGE'S JUBILEE | TRUST | [embossed coat of arms in black, white, gold, red and blue] | OFFICIAL | PROGRAMME | OF THE | JUBILEE | PROCESSION | SPECIAL EDITION 2/6
(All width centred)

Collation: [A]¹⁶; 16 leaves; 279 × 217mm.; 1–31 [32]

Page contents: as for B285(a)

Paper: glossy wove paper

Running title: none

Binding: beige wrappers. Spine: blank. On upper wrapper: 'KING GEORGE'S JUBILEE | TRUST | [embossed coat of arms in black, white, gold, red and blue] | OFFICIAL | PROGRAMME | OF THE | JUBILEE | PROCESSION | SPECIAL EDITION 2/6'. Lower wrapper: blank. All edges trimmed. Binding measurements: 291 × 223mm. (wrappers), 291 × 2mm. (spine). The wrapper extends beyond the edges of the internal leaves.

Publication date: unknown (not in the *English Catalogue of Books*)

Price: 2s.6d.

Masefield contents:
as for B285(a)

Notes:
The internal printed leaves are identical to those within B285(a). The printed wrappers are more lavish for this 'special edition', however.

Copies seen: private collection (ROV)

B290 *THE KING'S BOOK*   1935

B290(a) First English edition (1935)

THE | KING'S | BOOK | THIS BOOK OF | "THE FAMILY OF THE | BRITISH EMPIRE" IS | BY GRACIOUS PERMISSION | DEDICATED TO | KING GEORGE V. | BY HIS MAJESTY'S LOYAL | AND FAITHFUL SUBJECTS | RAPHAEL TUCK & SONS LTD., | IN CELEBRATION OF THE | SILVER JUBILEE | OF HIS MAJESTY. | MAY 1935 | RAPHAEL TUCK & SONS LTD. | *Art Publishers to Their Majesties the King and Queen | and to H.R.H. the Prince of Wales.* | RAPHAEL HOUSE, [publisher's device] LONDON.
(All width centred with lines 1–16 within panel surrounded by royal crest in gold: 178 × 132mm. Lines 17–20 width centred with royal crests in gold on right and left margin and '*By Appointment*' under each)

Collation: [A]⁶ B-D⁴; signatures left foot of page; 18 leaves; 279 × 213mm.; [1–3] 4 [5–8] 9 [10] 11–35 [36]; illustrations (on glossy paper) are tipped-in on pp.[2], [10], 12, 14, 17, 18, 20, 22, 25, 26, 28, 30, 33 and 34; a set of conjugate leaves (on glossy paper) is bound within the centre of gathering [A], these have been counted in the gathering information as page numbers incorporate these illustration pages

Page contents: [1] 'With the gracious consent of the King, | the profits accruing to the Publishers from | the sale of this Book will be devoted | to some philanthropic work in the | United Kingdom and Overseas approved | by his Majesty.' (within ornate panel); [2] 'Designed and Printed | in England | *Copyright*' (with additional leaf tipped-in on the verso of which is the colour frontispiece: 222 × 142mm., including excerpt 'FROM THE ADDRESS TO THE EMPIRE | BROADCAST BY THE KING, DEC. 25, 1934.'); [3] title-page; 4 '[double rule in gold] | CONTENTS | [double rule in gold]' (16 individual items listed with authors and page references); [5] blank; [6] photograph ('HER MAJESTY QUEEN MARY.'); [7] photograph ('HIS MAJESTY KING GEORGE V.'); [8] blank; 9 'A SONNET FOR THE KING'S BOOK' (within seven ruled borders) ('Scattered beneath the Mansions of the Sun,') (signed, '*John Masefield.*'); [10] blank (with additional leaf tipped-in on the verso of which is a colour illustration); 11–35 text; [36] blank

Paper: laid paper (no watermark), chain-lines 24mm. apart

Running title: running titles comprise titles of section, pp.12–34 (see notes)

Binding: light blue cloth-covered boards with dark blue cloth spine. On spine, reading lengthways up spine, from foot: 'THE KING'S BOOK'. There is a single vertical rule in blind on each cover at the edge of the cloth. On upper cover, in gold: '[panel including crown in blind and 'GvR' in gold on blind shield: 69 × 50mm.] | THE | KING'S | BOOK'. Lower cover: blank. All edges trimmed. Binding measurements: 281 × 215mm. (covers), 281 × 15mm. (spine). End-papers: wove paper.

Also issued in boards, 'padded cloth', and leather (see notes)

Publication date: published, according to the *English Catalogue of Books*, April 1935

Price: 3s.6d.; 5s.; 10s.6d.; 21s.; £5 5s. (see notes)

Masefield contents:

A Sonnet for the King's Book ('Scattered beneath the Mansions of the Sun,')
    (signed, '*John Masefield.*')

Notes:

Following an extract from an address to the Empire, there are photographs of the King and Queen. After Masefield's poem there then chapters entitled 'The United Kingdom', 'Canada', 'Australia', 'New Zealand', 'The Union of South Africa', 'India', 'Newfoundland', 'Northern and Southern Rhodesia', 'The Mediterranean', 'Eastern Dependencies', 'The West Indies', and 'East and West Africa'. There is then an 'Epilogue to The King's Book'. Each part is prefaced by a colour illustration. John Drinkwater is one of the contributors.

Each section is only two pages in length. Running titles are therefore only present on verso of leaves.

Contributions commence with drop-capitals.

The *English Catalogue of Books* includes two entries for *The King's Book*:

- King's book (The): the book of the family of the British Empire. 4to, 5s. net; ¼ lthr., 10s. 6d. net; full lthr., 21s. net TUCK, *Apr.* '35
- King's book (The). Illus. 4to, 11 × 8½, p.26, 3s.6d. and 5s. net TUCK, *May* '35

Neither description is particularly helpful. The British Library copy (stamped 23 MAY 1935) is in a quarter-bound cloth binding, states the 'Book Of The Family Of The British Empire' on the title-page and has more than 26 pages. As listed by the publishers in their publisher's catalogue, *Story Books and Other Books 1935–36* there were five issues, described as:

Board Covers	...	...	3/6 net
Cloth Bound	...	...	5/- net
Padded Cloth, Silk finish		...	10/6 net
Special Art Edition, Full Leather Bound		...	£1 1 0 net
Edition-de-Luxe. Full Leather Bound. *Limited to* 500 *Copies.*			£5 5 0 net

Publication of Masefield's sonnet in *The Daily Telegraph* led Masefield to involve The Society of Authors and explain some background to this book (including note of an original request for a preface, not a sonnet). As Poet Laureate it appears that Masefield regarded certain writing as 'official work':

> Some months ago, I was asked officially if I would write a few words of preface to an Empire Book, to be published by Messrs Raphael Tuck. I wrote a sonnet, instead of a preface, + sent it to Mr Desmond Tuck, for the book.
>
> I am told that this sonnet was printed yesterday, Saturday, 27th April, in *the Daily Telegraph*. I have not seen the paper, but am assured that the poem appeared there. Will you be so very kind as to verify this fact for me, and if it be so, as I do not doubt it is, will you please find out by what authority the paper printed the poem, + how, + from whom, + on what terms, they got the copy of it?
>
> The verses were written by official request for a special purpose, + should not have passed into other hands than those for whom it was made.
>
> > (John Masefield, letter to [E.J.] Mullett, [28 April 1935])
> > (BL, Add.Mss.56602, f.203)

Masefield, later in his career, would follow a more relaxed rule regarding use of Laureateship work. Five years into his appointment, however, he was jealously guarding his work. The Society of Authors explained the circumstances:

> ...I was informed that the poem was received through THE PRESS ASSOCIATION with an intimation that it could be published without payment but subject to acknowledgement.
>
> > (E.J. Mullett, letter to John Masefield, 29 April 1935)
> > (BL, Add.Mss.56602, ff.204–205)

Masefield, regarding his official duties, therefore took no further action, writing to The Society of Authors at the end of April:

> I think I understand how the question arose. Probably it was officially suggested to Messrs. Tuck that the material of the book should be sent to the press, and as I feel that the "Telegraph" acted in quite good faith, and as the whole business is an official business, we need not pursue the matter further.
>
> > (John Masefield, letter to [E.J.] Mullett, 30 April 1935)
> > (BL, Add.Mss.56602, f.206)

Copies seen: private collection (ROV); BL (9525.f.11) stamped 23 MAY 1935

B295 *HIS MAJESTY'S SPEECHES*   1935

B295(a) *First English edition – standard issue (1935)*

HIS | MAJESTY'S | SPEECHES | THE | RECORD OF | THE SILVER JUBILEE | *of* | HIS MOST GRACIOUS MAJESTY | KING GEORGE | THE FIFTH | 1935 | *World Copyright Reserved*
(All width centred)

Collation: [A]⁶ (A5+2) B⁶ C⁴ [D]⁶ E⁶ (E5+2) F⁴; B2, D2 and E3 are also signed; signatures left foot of page; 32 leaves; 237 × 169mm.; [i–iv] [1–4] 5–8 [9–10] 11–18 [19–20] 21–28 [29–30] 31–38 [39–40] 41–44 [45–48] 49–53 [54] 55 [56–60]; illustration pages (on glossy paper) are included in the collation and in the page number sequence (see notes)

Page contents: [i] laid-down end-paper; [ii] decorated fixed end-paper; [iii] decorated free end-paper; [iv] blank free end-paper; [1] half-title: 'HIS MAJESTY'S SPEECHES'; [2] frontispiece photograph: 191 × 127mm., '*Vandyk* | HIS MAJESTY THE KING'; [3] title-page; [4] photograph: 188 × 127mm., '*Vandyk* | HER MAJESTY THE QUEEN'; 5 'A | PRAYER FOR | THE KING'S MAJESTY' ('*O God, whose mercy is our state,*') (signed, 'JOHN MASEFIELD, *Poet Laureate.*'); 6 'By His Majesty's gracious per- | mission, this book is published | by King George's Jubilee Trust, | to which the entire proceeds | from its sale will be devoted. | I feel sure that many people | will wish to possess this record | of a memorable occasion, thereby | contributing to the Trust which | I have inaugurated as a tribute | to the King and Queen on be- | half of the rising generation. | EDWARD P.'; 7 'CONTENTS' (15 individual items listed with page references); 8–[56] text and illustrations (at foot of p.[56]: 'Published by King George's Jubilee Trust. St. James's Palace, London, S.W.1. | Printed in England by Odhams Press Ltd., Long Acre, London, W.C.2.'); [57] blank free end-paper; [58] decorated free end-paper; [59] decorated fixed end-paper; [60] laid-down end-paper

Paper: wove and glossy paper

Running title: none

Binding: cream cloth. Spine: blank. On upper cover, in gold: '[royal coat of arms] | HIS | MAJESTY'S | SPEECHES | THE | RECORD OF | THE SILVER JUBILEE | 1935' (within double ruled border, in blind: 237 × 163mm.) Lower cover: blank. All edges trimmed. Binding measurements: 243 × 170mm. (covers), 243 × 20mm. (spine). End-papers: wove paper decorated in light brown with royal coat of arms and figure with blazing torch (see notes).

Publication date: published, according to the *English Catalogue of Books*, June 1935

Price: 2s.

Masefield contents:
A Prayer for The King's Majesty ('O God, whose mercy is our state,')
(signed, 'JOHN MASEFIELD, *Poet Laureate.*')

Notes:
Masefield's contribution was printed in *The Times* for 7 May 1935 and also in *King George's Jubilee… Official Programme of the Jubilee Procession* (see B285).

[A]1 and F4 are laid-down and comprise the fixed end-papers. [A]2 and F3 comprise the free end-papers. Two sets of conjugate leaves are tipped-in on pp.5 and 49. These are included in the collation and page number sequence.

A number of contributions commence with drop-capitals.

Copies seen: private collection (ROV)

B295(aa) First English edition – numbered issue (1935)

HIS | MAJESTY'S | SPEECHES | THE | RECORD OF | THE SILVER JUBILEE | *of* | HIS MOST GRACIOUS MAJESTY | KING GEORGE | THE FIFTH | 1935 | *World Copyright Reserved*
(All width centred)

Collation: [A]⁶ (A5+2) B⁶ C⁴ [D]⁶ E⁶ (E5+2) F⁴; B2, D2 and E3 are also signed; signatures left foot of page; 32 leaves; 237 × 168mm.; [i–iv] [1–4] 5–8 [9–10] 11–18 [19–20] 21–28 [29–30] 31–38 [39–40] 41–44 [45–48] 49–53 [54] 55 [56–60]; illustration pages (on glossy paper) are included in the collation and in the page number sequence (see notes)

Page contents: [i] blank free end-paper; [ii] decorated free end-paper; [iii]decorated 'end-paper'; [iv] '*This edition is limited* | *to* 2,500 *copies* | COPY | NUMBER---' (within ruled border: 37 × 62mm. with shadow on right and lower sides); [1] half-title: 'HIS MAJESTY'S SPEECHES'; [2] frontispiece photograph: 191 × 127mm., '*Vandyk* | HIS MAJESTY THE KING'; [3] title-page; [4] photograph: 188 × 127mm., '*Vandyk* | HER MAJESTY THE QUEEN'; 5 'A | PRAYER FOR | THE KING'S MAJESTY' ('*O God, whose mercy is our state,*') (signed, 'JOHN MASEFIELD, *Poet Laureate.*'); 6 'By His Majesty's gracious per- | mission, this book is published | by King George's Jubilee Trust, | to which the entire proceeds | from its sale will be devoted. | I feel sure that many people | will wish to possess this record | of a memorable occasion, thereby | contributing to the Trust which | I have inaugurated as a tribute | to the King and Queen on be- | half of the rising generation. | EDWARD P.'; 7 'CONTENTS' (15 individual items listed with page references); 8–[56] text and illustrations (at foot of p.[56]: 'Published by King George's Jubilee Trust. St. James's Palace, London, S.W.1. | Printed in England by Odhams Press Ltd., Long Acre, London, W.C.2.'); [57] blank; [58] decorated 'end-paper'; [59] decorated free end-paper; [60] blank free end-paper

Paper: wove and glossy paper

Running title: none

Binding: dark blue leather. Spine: blank. On upper cover, in gold: '[royal coat of arms] | HIS | MAJESTY'S | SPEECHES | THE | RECORD OF | THE SILVER JUBILEE | 1935' (within ruled border: 232 × 159mm.) Lower cover: blind ruled border: 232 × 159mm. Top edge gilt, others trimmed. Sewn head and foot bands (in blue and white). Binding measurements: 243 × 168mm.

(covers), 243 × 20mm. (spine). End-papers: wove paper decorated in light brown with royal coat of arms and figure with blazing torch (see notes).

Publication date: published, according to the *English Catalogue of Books*, June 1935

Price: 10s.

Masefield contents:
as for B295(a)

Notes:
The true end-papers in this volume comprise blank wove paper. However, the free end-papers at both the front and rear of the volume are attached to [A]1 and F4.

The *English Catalogue of Books* records this issue as a 'library edition'.

Copies seen: private collection (PWE) number 1093; private collection (ROV) number 306

B300 HENRY W. NEVINSON, *FIRE OF LIFE* [1935]

B300(a) First English edition ([1935])

FIRE OF LIFE | by | HENRY W. NEVINSON | [thick rule, 18mm.] | [thin rule, 18mm.] | With a Preface by | JOHN MASEFIELD, O.M. | LONDON | JAMES NISBET & CO. LTD | *in association with* | VICTOR GOLLANCZ LTD
(All width centred)

Collation: [A]⁸ B-DD⁸; signatures left foot of page with together with 'L'; 224 leaves; 191 × 126mm.; [1–5] 6 [7] 8 [9] 10–17 [18] 19–26 [27] 28–33 [34] 35–43 [44] 45–62 [63] 64–76 [77] 78–93 [94] 95–103 [104] 105–114 [115] 116–29 [130] 131–42 [143] 144–56 [157] 158–69 [170] 171–80 [181] 182–90 [191] 192–99 [200] 201–209 [210] 211–20 [221] 222–33 [234] 235–49 [250] 251–68 [269] 270–79 [280] 281–96 [297] 298–327 [328] 329–39 [340] 341–55 [356] 357–71 [372] 373–80 [381] 382–89 [390] 391–400 [401] 402–414 [415] 416–27 [428] 429–38 [439] 440–48

Page contents: [1] half-title: 'FIRE OF LIFE'; [2] blank (with additional leaf tipped-in on the verso of which is the frontispiece: 137 × 98mm., 'From a Drawing by Sir William Rothenstein. | Cologne. At Armistice, 1918'); [3] title-page; [4] 'AUTHOR'S NOTE' ('This book is an abbreviation of my three volumes…') (signed, 'H.W.N. | London, 1935') (at foot of page: '*Printed in Great Britain by* | The Camelot Press Ltd., London and Southampton'); [5]-6 'PREFACE' ('I first saw Mr. Nevinson on a sunny summer Sunday morning near Hampstead Heath.') (signed 'JOHN MASEFIELD'); [7]-8 'CONTENTS' (33 chapters listed with titles and page references); [9]-438 text; [439]-448 'INDEX'

Paper: wove paper

Running title: 'FIRE OF LIFE' (24mm.) on verso; recto title comprises chapter title, pp.10–438

Binding: black cloth. On spine, in gold: 'FIRE | OF | LIFE | BY | HENRY W. | NEVINSON | NISBET | [short rule] | GOLLANCZ' (all width centred). Covers: blank. All edges trimmed. Binding measurements: 202 × 128mm. (covers), 202 × 52mm. (spine). End-papers: wove paper.

Publication date: published, according to the *English Catalogue of Books*, October 1935

Price: 8s.6d.

Masefield contents:
Preface ('I first saw Mr. Nevinson on a sunny summer Sunday morning near Hampstead Heath.')
          (signed 'JOHN MASEFIELD')

Notes:
The 'Author's Note' on page [4] states that this volume

> …is an abbreviation of my three volumes of memories, *Changes and Chances* (1923), *More Changes More Chances* (1925), *Last Changes Last Chances* (1928), all published by Messrs. Nisbet. The difficult work of cutting the three down into the present singe volume has been admirably done by my friend Mr. Ellis Roberts; and I am deeply grateful to Mr. John Masefield, the Poet Laureate, for adding an Introduction.

As suggested by this note, Masefield's preface is unique to this volume. Within *More Change More Chances*, there is, however, a three stanza quotation from 'August, 1914' that it not retained in the abbreviated volume.

Copies seen: private collection (PWE); BL (010822.df.10) stamped 11 OCT 1935 rebound

B305 RUTH PITTER, *A MAD LADY'S GARLAND* 1935

B305(a) First American edition (1935)

A MAD LADY'S | RUTH | PITTER | GARLAND | THE MACMILLAN COMPANY | NEW YORK
(All width centred with lines 1 and 4 forming a partial circle. All enclosed within ornate border: 151 × 91mm.)

Collation: [A-D]⁸ [E]⁴ [F]⁸; 44 leaves; 187 × 127mm.; [i–xii] 1–75 [76]

Page contents: [i] half-title: 'A MAD LADY'S GARLAND'; [ii] blank; [iii] title-page; [iv] '*Copyright, 1935, by* | THE MACMILLAN COMPANY. | All rights reserved–no part of this book may be | reproduced in any form without permission in writing | from the publisher, except by a reviewer who wishes | to quote brief passages in connection with a review | written for inclusion in magazine or newspaper.'; [v–vi] '*PREFACE*' ('Miss Pitter has in this book done the best thing that a poet can...') (signed, 'HILAIRE BELLOC'); [vii–viii] '*INTRODUCTION*' ('It is a pleasure to me to write these few words to introduce...') (signed, 'JOHN MASEFIELD'); [ix–x] 'CONTENTS' (21 individual poems listed with page references); [xi] 'A MAD LADY'S GARLAND'; [xii] blank; 1–75 text; [76] blank

Paper: wove paper

Running title: none

Binding: grey cloth. On spine, in gold: '[rule] | A MAD | LADY'S | GARLAND | [ornament] | RUTH | PITTER | [rule] | MACMILLAN' (all width centred with title, ornament and author on purple panel: 31 × 14mm.) Covers: blank. Top edge trimmed, others roughly trimmed. Binding measurements: 194 × 128mm. (covers), 194 × 24mm. (spine). End-papers: wove paper.

Publication date: published around November 1935 (suggested by dates of contemporary reviews)

Price: $1.25

Masefield contents:

Introduction ('It is a pleasure to me to write these few words to introduce...')
    (signed, 'JOHN MASEFIELD')

Notes:

A letter from the Macmillan Company to Masefield, dated 10 September 1935 acknowledges Masefield's introduction to this work:

> ...I have today received a letter from Miss Ruth Pitter together with an introduction to her book which you so kindly gave her. We are now proceeding with its publication now as rapidly as may be...

(George P. Brett Jr, letter to John Masefield, 10 September 1935)
(HRHRC, MS (Masefield, J.) Recip The Macmillan Company)

Copies seen: private collection (PWE)

B310 GRACE WYNDHAM GOLDIE,
 THE LIVERPOOL REPERTORY THEATRE 1911–1934   1935

B310(a) First English edition (1935)

The | Liverpool Repertory Theatre | 1911–1934 | *By* | GRACE WYNDHAM GOLDIE | B.A. (Oxon.) | THE UNIVERSITY PRESS OF LIVERPOOL | HODDER & STOUGHTON LTD., LONDON | 1935
(All width centred with lines 7–8 justified on identical left and right margins)

Collation: [A-R]⁸ [S]⁴ (J not used); 140 leaves; 217 × 140mm.; [1–8] 9–222 [223] 224–71 [272] 273–80; illustrations (on glossy paper) are tipped-in on pp.[2], 55, 112, 171, 183 and 189

Page contents: [1] half-title: 'THE LIVERPOOL REPERTORY THEATRE | 1911–1934'; [2] blank (with additional leaf tipped-in on the verso of which is the frontispiece: 102 × 73mm., 'FRONTISPIECE | [illustration] | PROGRAMME COVER SPECIALLY DESIGNED IN | SEPTEMBER, 1924, BY GEORGE W. HARRIS'); [3] title-page; [4] '*Printed in Great Britain by* | *A. W. Duncan & Co., Ltd., Concert Street, Liverpool*'; [5] 'Contents' (10 items listed with page references); [6] 'List of Illustrations' (six items listed with page references); [7] 'Acknowledgments' ('My thanks are due to the Directors of the Liverpool Repertory Theatre not only for...') (signed, '*Grace Wyndham Goldie.*' and dated '*London, 1935.*'); [8] blank; 9–271 text; [272] blank; 273–80 'Index'

Paper: laid paper (watermark: '[Crown] | Abbey Mills | Greenfield'), chain-lines 25mm. apart

Running title: 'THE LIVERPOOL REPERTORY THEATRE' (71–72mm.) on verso; recto title comprises section title, pp.10–280

Binding: light green boards with black cloth spine. On spine, in gold: 'THE | LIVERPOOL | REPERTORY | THEATRE | GRACE | WYNDHAM | GOLDIE | UNIVERSITY PRESS | OF | LIVERPOOL' (all width centred). Cover: blank. Top edge trimmed, others roughly trimmed. Binding measurements: 223 × 142mm. (covers), 223 × 45mm. (spine). End-papers: laid paper (watermark: '[Crown] | Abbey Mills | Greenfield'), chain-lines 25mm. apart.

Publication date: published, according to the *English Catalogue of Books*, November 1935

Price: 5s.

Masefield contents:

[Untitled] ('Here in this house, to-night, our city makes')
    (introduced as '...the ode which John Masefield had written...')
[Untitled] ('Friends, we are opening at this solemn time')
    (introduced as 'written by John Masefield...')

Notes:

There are eight titled chapters in addition to an appendix (primarily listing plays and players) and an index.

There are two untitled Masefield poems included within the text. The first ('Here in this house, to-night, our city makes') was written for the opening of the theatre in 1911. It was, apparently, declaimed on that occasion by Aida Jenoure 'majestically representing Mrs. Siddons as the Tragic Muse.' The second poem ('Friends, we are opening at this solemn time') was recited by Madge McIntosh (see also D1).

Copies seen: private collection (ROV); BL (11795.w.27) stamped 27 NOV 1935

B315 *Ed.* J.A.K. THOMSON *and* A.J. TOYNBEE, *ESSAYS IN HONOUR OF GILBERT MURRAY* 1936

B315(a) First English edition (1936)

ESSAYS IN HONOUR OF | Gilbert Murray | [rule (tapered at both ends), 42mm.] | THE RT. HON. H. A. L. FISHER   SEÑOR S. A. de MADARIAGA | LT.-COL. CHARLES ARCHER   SIR HUBERT MURRAY | S. MARGERY FRY PROFESSOR ALFRED ZIMMERN | JOHN MASEFIELD   EDWYN R. BEVAN | DAME SYBIL THORNDIKE PROFESSOR F. M. CORNFORD | LORD CECIL   HARLEY GRANVILLE-BARKER | J. L. HAMMOND   PROFESSOR D. S. MARGOLIOUTH | BARBARA HAMMOND   MRS. W. H. SALTER | PROFESSOR J. A. K. THOMSON | PROFESSOR A. J. TOYNBEE | LONDON | George Allen & Unwin Ltd | MUSEUM STREET
(All width centred with the exception of lines 4–11. These eight lines each containing two names have the first name justified on a left margin and the second name justified on a right margin. All enclosed within dotted ruled border, thin ruled border and outer thick ruled border: 207 × 130mm.)

Collation: [A]⁸ B-T⁸ U⁴ (J not used); signatures centre foot of page; 156 leaves; 218 × 138mm.; [1–10] 11–61 [62] 63–67 [68] 69–77 [78] 79–171 [172] 173–87 [188] 189–213 [214] 215–35 [236] 237–247 [248] 249–59 [260] 261–77 [278] 279–91 [292] 293–308 [309–312]

Page contents: [1–2] blank; [3] half-title: 'ESSAYS IN HONOUR OF | Gilbert Murray'; [4] blank; [5] title-page; [6] 'FIRST PUBLISHED IN 1936 | *All rights reserved* | PRINTED IN GREAT BRITAIN BY | UNWIN BROTHERS LTD., WOKING'; [7] 'DEDICATION | [text in Greek] | E. R. B.'; [8] blank; [9] 'PREFACE' ('The essays which comprise this volume have been contributed by friends of Gilbert Murray...') (signed, 'J. A. K. T. | A. J. T.'); [10] blank; 11–12 'CONTENTS' (20 items listed with contributors and page references); 13–61 text; [62] blank; 63–67 text; [68] blank; 69–77 text; [78] blank; 79–171 text; [172] blank; 173–87 text; [188] blank; 189–213 text; [214] blank; 215–35 text; [236] blank; 237–47 text; [248] blank; 249–59 text; [260] blank; 261–77 text; [278] blank; 279–91 text; [292] blank; 293–[308] text; [309–310] '*Professor Gilbert Murray's Works*'; [311] '[publisher's device including St. George and the dragon] | GEORGE ALLEN & UNWIN LTD | LONDON: 40 MUSEUM STREET, W.C.1 | LEIPZIG: (F. VOLCKMAR) HOSPITALSTR. 10 | CAPE TOWN: 73 ST. GEORGE'S STREET | TORONTO: 91 WELLINGTON STREET, WEST | BOMBAY: 15 GRAHAM ROAD, BALLARD ESTATE | WELLINGTON, N.Z.: 8 KINGS CRESCENT, LOWER HUTT | SYDNEY, N.S.W.: AUSTRALIA HOUSE, WYNYARD SQUARE'; [312] blank

Paper: wove paper

Running title: 'ESSAYS IN HONOUR OF GILBERT MURRAY' (70mm.) on verso; recto title comprises essay title, pp.12–308

Binding: navy blue cloth. On spine, in gold: 'ESSAYS | IN HONOUR OF | GILBERT | MURRAY | GEORGE ALLEN | & UNWIN LTD'. Covers: blank. Top edge stained blue, others trimmed. Binding measurements: 223 × 140mm. (covers), 223 × 44mm. (spine). End-papers: wove paper.

Publication date: published, according to the *English Catalogue of Books*, January 1936

Price: 12s.6d.

Masefield contents:
Professor Murray and the Amateur Player ('It is a great pleasure to me to be asked to write upon one of the many...')
        (headed, '*by* JOHN MASEFIELD, O.M., LL.D., Poet Laureate')

Notes:
There are twenty contributions listed in the contents (including the dedication and preface). The listing at the rear of the volume entitled 'Professor Gilbert Murray's Works' is not included in the contents and may comprise publisher's advertisements. The editors of the volume (noted as 'J.A.K.T.' and 'A.J.T.') are Professor J.A.K. Thomson and Professor A.J. Toynbee.

The preface states, with reference to this volume:

> The essays which comprise this volume have been contributed by friends of Gilbert Murray who considered that the occasion of his retiring from the Chair of Greek at Oxford was an opportunity for them to express, each in his own way, something of the regard and admiration in which they hold him.

Copies seen: BL (2350.f.19) stamped 31 JAN 1936; HRHRC (TEMP M9635 GES 1936)

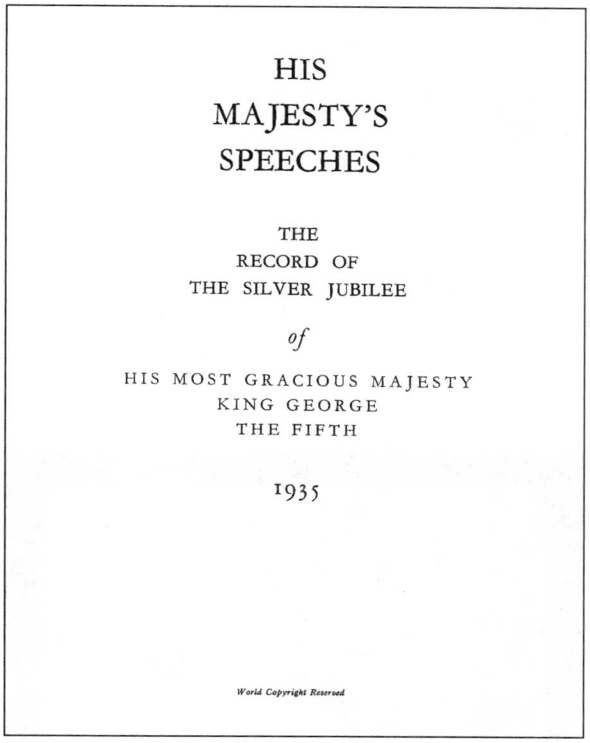

HIS
MAJESTY'S
SPEECHES

THE
RECORD OF
THE SILVER JUBILEE

of

HIS MOST GRACIOUS MAJESTY
KING GEORGE
THE FIFTH

1935

World Copyright Reserved

B295(a) title-page

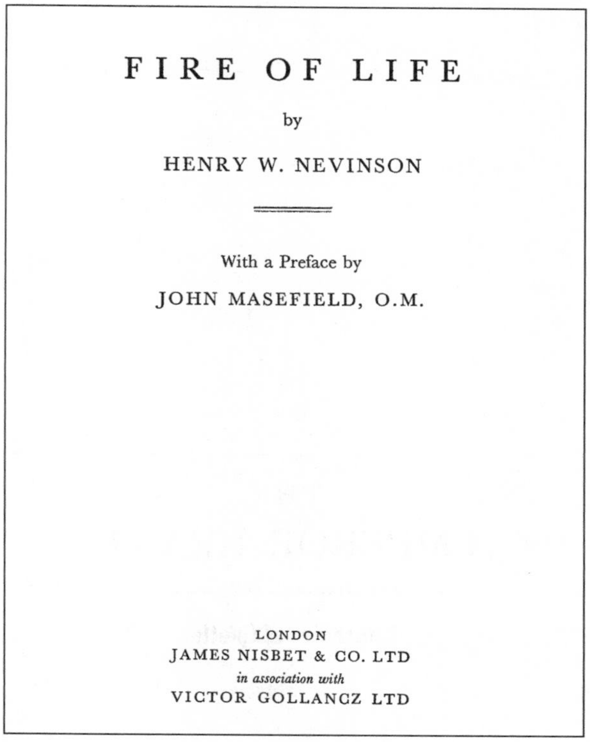

FIRE OF LIFE

by

HENRY W. NEVINSON

With a Preface by

JOHN MASEFIELD, O.M.

LONDON
JAMES NISBET & CO. LTD
in association with
VICTOR GOLLANCZ LTD

B300(a) title-page

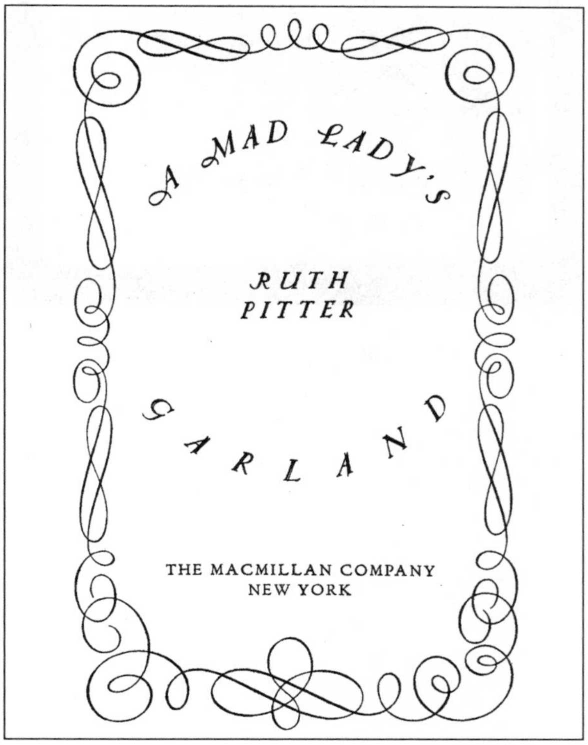

A MAD LADY'S

RUTH
PITTER

GARLAND

THE MACMILLAN COMPANY
NEW YORK

B305(a) title-page

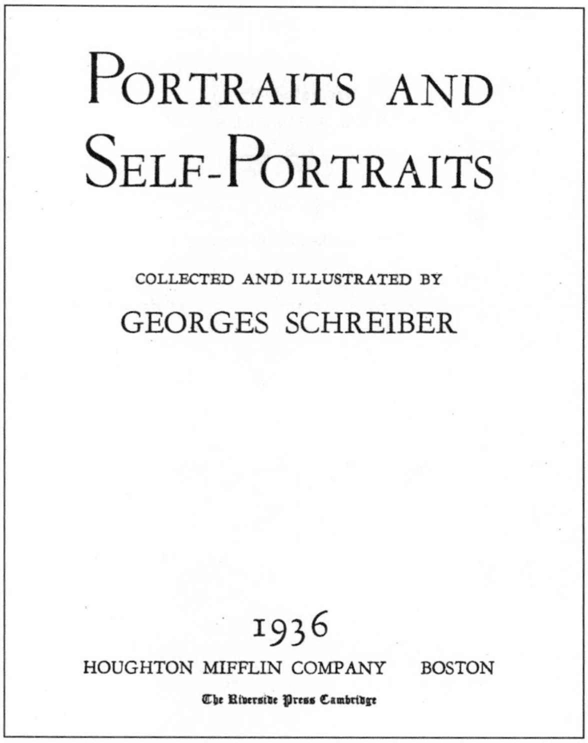

PORTRAITS AND
SELF-PORTRAITS

COLLECTED AND ILLUSTRATED BY
GEORGES SCHREIBER

1936
HOUGHTON MIFFLIN COMPANY BOSTON
The Riverside Press Cambridge

B330(a) title-page

THE
EMPEROR HEART

Laurence Whistler

Decorated by
REX WHISTLER

NEW YORK
The Macmillan Company
MCMXXXVII

B340(a) title-page

B350(a) upper wrapper

B320 LENA ASHWELL, *MYSELF A PLAYER*   1936

B320(a) *First English edition (1936)*

MYSELF A PLAYER | *By* | LENA ASHWELL | [publisher's device of a mermaid] | MICHAEL JOSEPH LTD. | 14, *Henrietta Street, W.C.2*
(All width centred)

Collation: [A]⁸ B-S⁸ (J not used); signatures left foot of page; 144 leaves; 231 × 148mm.; [1–8] 9 [10] 11 [12] 13–287 [288]; illustrations (on glossy paper) are tipped-in on pp.[2], 25, 48, 73, 96, 121, 144, 169, 185, 208, 233 and 265

Page contents: [1] half-title: 'MYSELF A PLAYER'; [2] '*By the same Author* | REFLECTIONS FROM SHAKESPEARE | MODERN TROUBADOURS | THE STAGE' (with additional leaf tipped-in on the verso of which is the black and white photograph frontispiece: 147 × 113mm., within grey border); [3] title-page; [4] 'FIRST PUBLISHED IN 1936 | *Set and printed in Great Britain by William Brendon at the* | *Mayflower Press, Plymouth, in Fournier type, fourteen point,* | *leaded, on a toned antique-wove paper made by John* | *Dickinson, and bound by James Burn in Sundour cloth.*'; [5] 'BETWEEN the years 1919 and 1929, Mr. John Masefield | wrote certain *Sonnets of Cheer*, dedicated to the Lena | Ashwell Players. It is with his gracious permission that | I am allowed to include them in this book. Although | the Sonnets belong to that decade, I am permitted to | distribute them through the several periods of my narrative, | and it is not possible to express how deep my gratitude is | both for the encouragement which they gave me at that | time and for the honour done me in allowing their publica- | tion. They illustrate the service of those who work and | strive for value in the art which I love so much. | L.A.'; [6] blank; [7] '[poetic preface: 'Once in a thousand years a golden soul' (signed, '*John Masefield*')] | As one of the many who found the way of art stony and full of | bitterness, and yet were certain that this was the only life-sure | that in the work itself one saw the sky, aye, and beyond that a | vision which made all suffering worth while, so I begin the story | of my life.'; [8] blank; 9 'CONTENTS' (12 titled chapters, appendix and index listed with page references); [10] blank; 11 'LIST OF ILLUSTRATIONS' (18 illustrations (including frontispiece) listed with page references); [12] blank; 13–[288] text

Paper: wove paper

Running title: 'MYSELF A PLAYER' (38mm.) on verso; recto title comprises chapter title, pp.14–282

Binding: orange / brown cloth. On spine, lettering in silver: 'LENA | ASHWELL | Myself | a | Player | [publisher's device of a mermaid] | MICHAEL | JOSEPH' (all width centred). Covers: blank. All edges trimmed. Binding measurements: 238 × 149mm. (covers), 238 × 49mm. (spine). End-papers: yellow wove paper.

Publication date: published, according to the *English Catalogue of Books*, November 1936

Price: 15s.

Masefield contents:
[Preface] ('It is now some three or four years...')
[Untitled] ('Once in a thousand years a golden soul')
[Untitled] ('"I promise battles, hardship, weariness..."')
[Untitled] ('It is no little thing to stand together')
[Untitled] ('Weary and sickened of the daily show')
Inscription on a Clock presented to the "Lena Ashwell Players" ('I tell the time, but you, within this place')

Notes:
There are twelve titled chapters listed in the contents in addition to an appendix ('Performances Given By The Lena Ashwell Players') and an index. Masefield's *Sonnets of Good Cheer to the Lena Ashwell Players...* (see A81) is distributed throughout the volume on pp.245–47, p.[7], p.130, p.193 and p.236. The 'Inscription on a Clock...' is printed on page 237.

The volume includes a sketch by William Orpen (on page 179) excluded from the listing of illustrations.

Copies seen: BL (010821.ff.4) stamped 30 OCT 1936

B325 *PAUNTLEY. THE GLOUCESTERSHIRE HOME FOR WAYFARERS*   1936

B325(a) *First English edition (1936)*

PAUNTLEY. | [rule, 92mm.] | [rule, 38mm.] | [ornament] | [black and white photograph: 89 × 145mm.] | VIEW FROM THE HOME. | [double rule, 19mm.] | THE GLOUCESTERSHIRE HOME | FOR WAYFARERS.
(All width centred)

Collation: [A]⁸; 8 leaves; 246 × 187mm.; [1–16]

Page contents: [1] title-page; [2] blank; [3–4] 'FOREWORD.' and one photograph ('It is a pleasure to me to write or speak for the Pauntley Home. It lies in a place of...') (signed, 'JOHN MASEFIELD.'); [5–6] four photographs; [7–9] 'The Gloucestershire Home For Wayfarers' and three photographs; [10–11] four photographs; [12] 'Impressions Of A Young Wayfarer, 1933.'; [13–15] seven photographs; [16] 'Information will gladly be supplied by the Hon. Secretary:- | Mrs. VAUGHAN HARRISON, | Ridge Cottage, | Burleigh, | Nr. Stroud, Glos. | Printed, 1936.'

Paper: glossy wove paper

Running title: none

Binding: light beige wrappers. Spine: blank. On upper wrapper: 'PAUNTLEY | The Gloucestershire | Home for Wayfarers. | Aims and Methods of the Home | : with Foreword by : | JOHN MASEFIELD. | [rule] | [square device]' (lines 1–3 ranged upper left and lines 4–8 ranged lower right; the 'st' of 'Gloucestershire' is a ligature). Lower wrapper: blank. Inside of upper wrapper: blank. Inside of lower wrapper: 'H. OSBORNE, | PRINTER, | 8, ST. MARY'S SQUARE, | GLOUCESTER. | 1936.' All edges trimmed. Binding measurements: 246 × 187mm. (wrappers), 246 × 2mm. (spine).

Publication date: published around November 1936 (see notes)

Price: unknown

Masefield contents:
Foreword ('It is a pleasure to me to write or speak for the Pauntley Home. It lies in a place of...')
    (signed, 'JOHN MASEFIELD.')

Notes:
Part of the title on the cover of the pamphlet is 'Aims and Methods of the Home'. This is not present, however, on the title-page.

This pamphlet is listed in the notes to Constance Babington Smith's biography. Babington Smith was given a copy in June 1974 by Mrs Bernard Oldridge. The note on pp.206–207 of the biography refers to both Mrs Oldridge and Pauntley:

> Diana Awdry, later Mrs. Bernard Oldridge, had met J.M. in the 1920s when she was an undergraduate at Oxford. During the mid-1930s, beginning in 1933, the two were constantly in touch in connection with a scheme for helping young unemployed vagrants. Under the auspices of the Anglican Franciscans, Dick Whittington's family home at Pauntley in Gloucestershire was taken over and organized as a place of rehabilitation. J.M. worked hard to raise funds for this cause by giving poetry readings throughout Gloucestershire.
> (Constance Babington Smith, *John Masefield – A Life*, Oxford University Press, 1978, pp.206–207)

An extract from the work was quoted in *The Times* on 28 November 1936.

Copies seen: Archives of The John Masefield Society (Babington Smith Archive)

B330 GEORGES SCHREIBER, *PORTRAITS AND SELF-PORTRAITS* 1936

B330(a) First American edition (1936)

PORTRAITS AND | SELF-PORTRAITS | COLLECTED AND ILLUSTRATED BY | GEORGES SCHREIBER | 1936 | HOUGHTON MIFFLIN COMPANY BOSTON | The Riverside Press Cambridge
(Lines 1 and 2 justified on both left and right margins, all other lines width centred)

Collation: [A-M]⁸ (J not used); 96 leaves; 249 × 174mm.; [i–vi] vii–x 1 [2] 3–5 [6] 7–9 [10] 11–13 [14] 15–17 [18] 19–21 [22] 23 [24] 25 [26] 27 [28] 29 [30] 31 [32] 33 [34] 35–37 [38] 39–41 [42] 43–45 [46] 47 [48] 49–51 [52] 53–55 [56] 57 [58] 59 [60] 61 [62] 63 [64] 65 [66] 67 [68] 69–71 [72] 73 [74] 75 [76] 77–83 [84] 85 [86] 87 [88] 89–91 [92] 93–95 [96] 97 [98] 99 [100] 101 [102] 103 [104] 105–107 [108] 109 [110] 111–15 [116] 117 [118] 119–21 [122] 123–25 [126] 127 [128] 129 [130] 131–33 [134] 135–37 [138] 139 [140] 141–43 [144] 145–47 [148] 149 [150] 151 [152] 153 [154] 155 [156] 157 [158] 159 [160] 161 [162] 163 [164] 165–67 [168] 169 [170] 171–73 [174] 175 [176–82]

Page contents: [i] half-title: 'PORTRAITS | AND | SELF-PORTRAITS'; [ii] blank; [iii] title-page; [iv] 'COPYRIGHT, 1936, BY GEORGES SCHREIBER | ALL RIGHTS RESERVED INCLUDING THE RIGHT TO REPRODUCE | THIS BOOK OR PARTS THEREOF IN ANY FORM | PRINTED IN THE U.S.A.'; [v] 'IN MEMORY OF | MY FATHER | AND | WILLIAM BASTARD, SR. | LEICESTER, ENGLAND'; [vi] blank; vii–viii 'CONTENTS' (40 writers listed with page references); ix–x 'INTRODUCTION' ('In 1909 a five-year-old child tried to sketch his uncle and, behold, he caught a faint...') (signed, 'GEORGES SCHREIBER | NEW YORK CITY, 1936'); 1–23 text and portraits; [24] blank; 25–27 text and portrait; [28] blank; 29–31 text and portrait; [32] blank; 33–45 text and portraits; [46] blank; 47–57 text and portraits; [58] blank; 59–61 text and portrait; [62] blank; 63–65 text and portrait; [66] blank; 67–73 text and portraits; [74] blank; 75–85 text and portraits; [86] blank; 87–97 text and portraits; [98] blank; 99–101 text and portrait; [102] blank; 103–107 text and portrait; [108] blank; 109–115 text and portrait; [116] blank; 117–27 text and portraits; [128] blank; 129–37 text and portraits; [138] blank; 139–49 text and portraits; [150] blank; 151–53 text and portrait; [154] blank; 155–57 text and portrait; [158] blank; 159–61 text and portrait; [162] blank; 163–67 text and portrait; [168] blank; 169–75 text and portraits; [176–82] blank

Paper: wove paper (watermark: '[circular beaker device with scales and five pronged device at top: 81 × 38mm.] | *Utopian*')

Running title: running titles comprise name of author on second (or successive) page of authorial text, pp.4–172

Binding: grey cloth. On spine: 'PORTRAITS | AND SELF- | PORTRAITS | Schreiber | [vertical facsimile signature 'Schreiber' reading up spine from foot] [in orange] | HOUGHTON | MIFFLIN CO.' (all width centred). On upper cover, in red: 'PORTRAITS | AND SELF- | PORTRAITS | [vertical facsimile signature 'Schreiber' reading up cover from foot] [in black]' (title ranged upper left with facsimile signature ranged lower right). Lower cover: blank. All edges trimmed. Binding measurements: 256 × 176mm. (covers), 256 × 35mm. (spine). End-papers: wove paper.

Publication date: published, according to Audre Hanneman, December 1936 (see notes)

Price: $2.75

Masefield contents:

[Untitled] ('I was born about the first of June, 1878, at a little town called Ledbury in Herefordshire…')
(signed, 'JOHN MASEFIELD | CIRENCESTER, GLOUCESTERSHIRE | ENGLAND')

Notes:

There are forty contributions listed in the contents in addition to an introduction. Contributors include Albert Einstein, Ford Madox Ford, Robert Frost, André Gide, Ernest Hemingway, Thomas Mann and J.B. Priestley.

Page numbers appear within square brackets. Thus, [1], [3], etc.

The volume is structured by brief introduction, portrait, then autobiographical note. Each part of text (introductions and autobiographical sketches) commences with drop-capitals. The introduction to Masefield is as follows:

Poet Laureate John Masefield is the author of 'Gallipoli,' 'Reynard the Fox,' 'Salt Water Poems and Ballads,' 'The Wanderer or Liverpool,' 'Sard Harker,' 'A Letter to Pontus,' etc. His poems and plays have appeared in many different editions. The Order of Merit was bestowed upon him in 1935.

Masefield, it appears, was invited to contribute to this volume towards the end of 1935. He wrote on 7 November 1935 to Schreiber that he would '…see what can be done to supply you with the material for which you ask.' (see John Masefield, letter to Georges Schreiber, 7 November 1935) (HRHRC, MS (Masefield J.) Letters 2 TLS to Schreiber). While Masefield was in New York, during 1936, he appears to have sent the contribution. He wrote, during February 1936, that he was '…enclosing with this a brief autobiography for use in your book.' (see John Masefield, letter to Georges Schreiber, 4 February 1936) (HRHRC, MS (Masefield J.) Letters 2 TLS to Schreiber).

This volume appears as item B21 in Audre Hanneman, *Ernest Hemingway A Comprehensive Bibliography* (Princeton, New Jersey: Princeton University Press, 1967).

Copies seen: NYPL (AB 1936) 871191A 16 Dec 1936 written on page [v]; HRHRC (PN453 S4 cop.2) publisher's Christmas 'Best Wishes' slip loosely inserted

B335 *THE CORONATION OF THEIR MAJESTIES KING GEORGE VI & QUEEN ELIZABETH MAY 12th 1937* 1937

B335(a) *First English edition – 1s. issue (1937)*

[coat of arms with 'DIEU ET MON DROIT'] | THE CORONATION | OF THEIR MAJESTIES | KING GEORGE VI | & QUEEN ELIZABETH | MAY 12th 1937 | STATES UNDER HIS MAJESTY'S PROTECTION | PERAK SELANGOR PAHANG JOHORE KEDAH KELANTAN | NEGRI SEMBILAN BRUNEI TRENGGANU PERLIS | NORTH BORNEO SARAWAK | [device with 'PALESTINE' within circle and 'PALESTINE' between two rules] MANDATED TERRITORIES [device with head of giraffe within double ruled circle and 'TANGANYIKA' between two rules] | CAMEROONS TOGOLAND TRANSJORDAN NAURU | NEW GUINEA WESTERN SAMOA SOUTH-WEST AFRICA | WORLD COPYRIGHT RESERVED.
(All width centred with lines 2–6 within panel enclosed by ruled border and lines 7–13 within panel enclosed by four lined ruled border. All surrounded by names and pictures of commonwealth countries and enclosed within ornate border with devices at each corner: 240 × 187mm. The final line 'WORLD COPYRIGHT RESERVED.' lies outside the border. Line 6 includes a point underneath the superscripted 'th')

Collation: [A]¹⁶; 16 leaves; 281 × 214mm.; [1] 2–31 [32]

Page contents: [1] title-page; 2 'A PRAYER | FOR THE KING'S REIGN | [text] | JOHN MASEFIELD, | *Poet Laureate.*'; 3–6 photographs (with captions); 7 'A FOREWORD | BY HIS ROYAL HIGHNESS THE | DUKE OF GLOUCESTER | *Chairman of the Administrative Council of* | *King George's Jubilee Trust*' ('All will remember that King George's Jubilee Trust was authorised to issue…') (signed, 'Henry.') (facsimile signature); 8–9 'THE KING'S MAJESTY' ('Throughout five continents, on May 12th, 1937, attention will be fixed on…') (headed, 'By JOHN DRINKWATER'); 10–11 'KING GEORGE THE SIXTH' ('"It is only by getting to know one another better that closer sympathy…') [text and photographs]; 12–15 'THE CORONATION PROCESSION'; 16–17 'CORONATION[point]PROCESSION[point]OF[point]THEIR[point]MAJESTIES [device of crown, 'GR' and 'VI' within ruled border] KING[point]GEORGE[point]VI[point]AND[point]QUEEN[point]ELIZABETH' [map and text]; 18–20 The Coronation Procession (continued); 21–23 'THE CORONATION CEREMONY' ('The Coronation is undoubtedly the oldest State ceremonial in this country…') (headed, 'By SIR GERALD WOLLASTON, Garter Principal King of Arms'); 24 'THE CORONATION SERVICE | AN INTRODUCTION' ('The Coronation Service may be said to be as old as the Monarchy itself.') (headed, 'BY HIS GRACE THE LORD ARCHBISHOP OF CANTERBURY'); 25–[32] 'The Form and Order of Their Majesties' Coronation' (at foot of p.[32]: '*Printed and published for King George's Jubilee Trust by Odhams Press Limited, Long Acre, London, W.C.2, England*')

Paper: glossy wove paper

Running title: none

Binding: beige wrappers. Spine: blank. On upper wrapper: 'KING GEORGE'S JUBILEE TRUST | [coat of arms in gold, black, white, red and blue] | THE CORONATION | OF THEIR MAJESTIES | KING GEORGE VI | & QUEEN ELIZABETH | OFFICIAL[point]SOUVENIR[point]PROGRAMME' (within ornate border in gold with 'I'-' at centre of lower edge: 271 × 203mm.) Lower wrapper: blank. All edges trimmed. Binding measurements: 281 × 214mm. (wrappers), 281 × 2mm. (spine).

Publication date: published, according to the *English Catalogue of Books*, April 1937

Price: 1s.

Masefield contents:
A Prayer for the King's Reign ('O God, the Ruler over Earth and Sea,')
      (signed, 'JOHN MASEFIELD, | *Poet Laureate.*')

Notes:
Masefield's contribution was printed in *The Times* for 28 April 1937.

There are a number of drop-capitals and one decorated drop-capital.

With the exception of p.[1] and the centrefold, all pages are enclosed within the same design of decorated, ornate borders.

Copies seen: private collection (ROV)

B335(b) First English edition – 2s.6d. issue (1937)

[coat of arms with 'DIEU ET MON DROIT'] | THE CORONATION | OF THEIR MAJESTIES | KING GEORGE VI | & QUEEN ELIZABETH | MAY 12ᵗʰ 1937 | STATES UNDER HIS MAJESTY'S PROTECTION | PERAK SELANGOR PAHANG JOHORE KEDAH KELANTAN | NEGRI SEMBILAN BRUNEI TRENGGANU PERLIS | NORTH BORNEO SARAWAK | [device with 'PALESTINE' within circle and 'PALESTINE' between two rules] MANDATED TERRITORIES [device with head of giraffe within double ruled circle and 'TANGANYIKA' between two rules] | CAMEROONS TOGOLAND TRANSJORDAN NAURU | NEW GUINEA WESTERN SAMOA SOUTH-WEST AFRICA | WORLD COPYRIGHT RESERVED
(All width centred with lines 2–6 within panel enclosed by ruled border in gold and lines 7–13 within panel enclosed by four lined ruled border overprinted with gold. All surrounded by names and pictures of commonwealth countries and enclosed within gold border: 244 × 190mm. The final line 'WORLD COPYRIGHT RESERVED' lies outside the border. The coat of arms is printed in black and gold. Line 6 includes a point underneath the superscripted 'th')

Collation: [A]¹⁸; 18 leaves; 285 × 216mm.; [1] 2–35 [36]

Page contents: [1] title-page; 2 'A PRAYER | FOR THE KING'S REIGN | [text] | JOHN MASEFIELD, | *Poet Laureate.*'; 3–6 photographs (with captions); 7 'A FOREWORD | BY HIS ROYAL HIGHNESS THE | DUKE OF GLOUCESTER | *Chairman of the Administrative Council of* | *King George's Jubilee Trust'* ('All will remember that King George's Jubilee Trust was authorised to issue...') (signed, 'Henry.') (facsimile signature); 8–9 'THE KING'S MAJESTY' ('Throughout five continents, on May 12th, 1937, attention will be fixed on...') (headed, 'By JOHN DRINKWATER'); 10–12 'KING GEORGE THE SIXTH' ('"It is only by getting to know one another better that closer sympathy...') [text and photographs]; 13–17 'THE CORONATION PROCESSION' [text and photographs]; 18–19 'CORONATION[point]PROCESSION[point]OF[point]THEIR[point]MAJESTIES [device of crown, 'GR' and 'VI' within ruled border in black white and gold] KING[point]GEORGE[point]VI[point]AND[point]QUEEN[point]ELIZABETH' [map and text]; 20–22 The Coronation Procession (continued); 23–26 'THE CORONATION CEREMONY' ('The Coronation is undoubtedly the oldest State ceremonial in this country...') (headed, 'By SIR GERALD WOLLASTON, Garter Principal King of Arms'); 27 'THE CORONATION SERVICE | AN INTRODUCTION' ('The Coronation Service may be said to be as old as the Monarchy itself.') (headed, 'BY HIS GRACE THE LORD ARCHBISHOP OF CANTERBURY'); 28–35 'The Form and Order of Their Majesties' Coronation'; [36] 'GENEALOGICAL TABLE SHOWING THE DESCENT OF THE CROWN' (at foot of p.[36]: '*Printed and published for King George's Jubilee Trust by Odhams Press Limited, Long Acre, London, W.C.2, England.*')

Paper: glossy wove paper

Running title: none

Binding: beige wrappers, secured by gold cord (with two tassels). Spine: blank. On upper wrapper: 'KING GEORGE'S JUBILEE TRUST | [embossed coat of arms in gold, black, white, red and blue] | THE CORONATION | OF THEIR MAJESTIES | KING GEORGE VI | & QUEEN ELIZABETH | OFFICIAL[point]SOUVENIR[point]PROGRAMME' (within ornate border in gold with '2'6' at centre of lower edge: 272 × 203mm.) Lower wrapper: blank. All edges trimmed. Binding measurements: 292 × 220mm. (wrappers), 292 × 3mm. (spine). The wrapper extends beyond the edges of the internal leaves.

Publication date: published, according to the *English Catalogue of Books*, April 1937

Price: 2s.6d.

Masefield contents:
as for B335(a)

Notes:
There are a number of drop-capitals and one decorated drop-capital (in black and gold).

With the exception of p.[1] and the centrefold, all pages are enclosed within the same design of decorated, ornate borders in gold.

There are a greater number of leaves in this edition than that available for 1s. The additional material comprises the genealogical table and a number of extra photographs. The 2s.6d. edition also includes printing in gold and a more lavish binding.

Copies seen: private collection (ROV)

B340 LAURENCE WHISTLER, *THE EMPEROR HEART* 1937

B340(a) *First American edition (1937)*

THE | EMPEROR HEART | [thin rule, 75mm.] | [thick rule, 75mm.] | Laurence Whistler | [oval motif with '[point] L', 'W [point]', heart and crown within single rule] [in pale orange] | Decorated by | REX WHISTLER | [thin rule, 46mm.] | NEW YORK | The Macmillan Company | M C M X X X V I I
(All width centred)

Collation: [A–D]⁸; 32 leaves; 215 × 134mm.; [i–x] 1–54

Page contents: [i] half-title: 'THE | EMPEROR HEART'; [ii] '*Also by Laurence Whistler* | [short rule] | [two titles listed with dates of publication]'; [iii] title-page; [iv] 'COPYRIGHT, 1937 | By LAURENCE WHISTLER | All rights reserved–no part of this book may be reproduced | in any form without permission in writing from the pub- | lisher, except by a reviewer who wishes to quote brief | passages in connection with a review written for inclusion | in magazine or newspaper. | PRINTED IN THE UNITED STATES OF AMERICA | BY THE POLYGRAPHIC COMPANY OF AMERICA, N.Y.'; [v] 'FOR | URSULA'; [vi] 'Some of these poems have already appeared | in *The London Mercury, Life and Letters, The* | *New Oxford Outlook, The Poetry Review, The* | *Observer, John O' London's Weekly* and *Nash's* | *Magazine,* and acknowledgments are due to | the editors. Also to Father D'Arcy, S. J., | with regard to an inscription at Campion | Hall, Oxford.'; [vii–viii] 'PREFACE' ('THIS is the third book of poems by Laurence Whistler. It is always a deep pleasure…') (signed, 'JOHN MASEFIELD.'); [ix–x] 'CONTENTS' (28 items listed with page references); 1–54 text and illustrations

Paper: wove paper

Running title: none

Binding: purple cloth. On spine, in gold reading lengthways up spine, from foot: 'MACMILLAN THE EMPEROR HEART LAURENCE WHISTLER'. On upper cover, in gold: 'THE | EMPEROR HEART | [oval motif with '[point] L', 'W [point]', heart and crown within single rule]'. Lower cover: blank. All edges trimmed. Binding measurements: 222 × 137mm. (covers), 222 × 20mm. (spine). End-papers: wove paper.

Publication date: published, around May 1937 (suggested by dates of contemporary reviews)

Price: $1.50

Masefield contents:
Preface ('This is the third book of poems by Laurence Whistler. It is always a deep pleasure…')
  (signed, 'JOHN MASEFIELD.')

Notes:
Page numbers appear within square brackets. Thus, [1], [2], etc.

Excluding the title-page motif there are eight illustrations by Rex Whistler, printed in black on orange.

Laurence Whistler was the first recipient of The King's Medal for Poetry. The medal, awarded in 1935 for the best poetry of 1934, was designed by Edmund Dulac. A photograph showing Masefield, Dulac and Whistler was reproduced in Handley-Taylor's bibliography. Whistler was to serve on the committee of judges from 1961 until 1967.

The HRHRC holds three letters received by Masefield from Laurence Whistler. In the first (undated) letter, Whistler sends the typescript 'of my new poems' which Masefield, apparently, said he would read. The next letter, dated 30 November [1935], notes Whistler's delight that Masefield 'should write so kindly and give me such great encouragement about my new poems!' Masefield, it seems, had written about securing an American publisher and Whistler responded with the information that he had 'an arrangement with Macmillan's…' but expects his *Four Walls* is going 'pretty poorly'. Masefield presumably offered to write his preface after reading this letter and was sent the first proofs of *The Emperor Heart* on 8 April 1936. In an accompanying letter from Whistler the author noted that '…it is so wonderfully kind of you to write a preface for the American edition. You know how much I appreciate the great help that will be. It is too good of you…' Whistler closes his letter by noting '…my brother Rex is doing a certain number of head & tail-pieces, & I hope arranging the title-page & cover…'

The English edition, published by Heinemann in 1936 and lacking Masefield's preface, is recorded at item 481 by Whistler and Fuller (see Laurence Whistler and Ronald Fuller, *The Work of Rex Whistler*, London: Batsford, 1960).

Copies seen: private collection (PWE)

B345 [JOHN HOLROYD-REECE], *THE HARVEST* 1937

B345(a) First German edition [in English] (1937)

THE HARVEST | *Being the Record of* | ONE HUNDRED YEARS | *of Publishing* | 1837–1937 | [six point asterisk] | OFFERED | IN GRATITUDE TO | *THE FRIENDS* | OF THE FIRM | BY | *Bernhard Tauchnitz* | [six point asterisk] | LEIPZIG | M [point] C [point] M [point] X [point] X [point] X [point] V [point] I [point] I
(All width centred)

Collation: [1]⁸ 2–5⁸; the second leaf of each gathering 2–5 is also signed; signatures left foot of page; 40 leaves; 229 × 139mm.; [1–6] 7–31 [32] 33 [34] 35–43 [44] 45–76 [77–80]

Page contents: [1–2] blank; [3] half-title: 'THE HARVEST'; [4] blank; [5] title-page; [6] 'Copyright June 1937 | by Bernhard Tauchnitz Successors Brandstetter & Co. Leipzig | Imprimé en Allemagne'; 7–8 'CONTENTS' ([preface] and six chapters listed with page references; 33 letters to Tauchnitz, comprising chapter six, also individually listed with page references); 9–31 text; [32] blank; 33 'HISTORY OF THE FIRM IN PICTURES | [eight illustrations listed with page references]'; [34] blank; 35–42 illustrations; 43 'LETTERS TO TAUCHNITZ: ANCIENT AND MODERN | [four paragraphs]'; [44] blank; 45–75 text (including facsimile text); 76 'THE TEXT OF THIS BOOKLET HAS BEEN WRITTEN BY THE | MANAGEMENT OF THE FIRM INSOFAR AS IT DOES NOT CONSIST | OF LETTRES [*sic*] RECEIVED. THE TYPE CHOSEN IS KNOWN AS ALDINE | BEMBO CUT BY THE MONOTYPE CORPORATION. THE PAPER | WAS SUPPLIED BY VEREINIGTE BAUTZENER PAPIERFABRIKEN. | THE PAPER OF THE WRAPPER WAS SUPPLIED BY METALLPAPIER- | BRONZEFARBEN-BLATTMETALLWERKE MÜNCHEN. THE | PRINTING AND BINDING IS THE WORK OF | THE FIRM OF BERNHARD TAUCHNITZ | SUCCESSORS BRANDSTETTER & CO. | LEIPZIG.'; [77–80] blank

Paper: wove paper

Running title: none (although a number of italicised titles appear in the margin)

Binding: gold paper-covered wrappers (see notes). Spine: blank. On upper wrapper: embossed device showing a crown device, 'T', '1 | 8 | 3 | 7', '1 | 9 | 3 | 7', 'TAUCHNITZ' and 'CENTENARY' (within ruled border: 56 × 37mm.) Lower wrapper: blank. All edges trimmed. Binding measurements: 229 × 139mm. (wrappers), 229 × 8mm. (spine).

Publication date: published, according to date within volume, June 1937

Price: copies were not, presumably, for sale

Masefield contents:
Message from the Poet Laureate ('I wish the Tauchnitz firm an honoured and happy second century.')
　　　(signed, 'John Masefield')

Notes:
A preface ('A Confession of Faith') is followed by six chapters. The sixth chapter comprises letters to Tauchnitz. These include text by Charles Dickens, W.M. Thackeray, Robert Browning, Mark Twain and H.G. Wells.

William B. Todd and Ann Bowden's *Tauchnitz International Editions In English 1841–1955 A Bibliographical History* (New York: Bibliographical Society of America, 1988) includes this volume as item L1c within 'Promotional Publications' and 'Anniversary Histories'. Todd and Bowden note the first issue was issued in cream paper boards with a second or presentation issue bound in gilt wrappers.

Todd and Bowden ascribe authorship to John Holroyd-Reece.

Copies seen: BL (2710.k.29) stamped 30 NOV 1968

B350 *MERCHANT NAVY WEEK IN AID OF THE MISSIONS TO SEAMEN SOUTHAMPTON* 1937

B350(a) First English edition (1937)

MERCHANT | NAVY WEEK | *In Aid of* | THE MISSIONS TO SEAMEN | SOUTHAMPTON | July 17th to 24th | 1937 | PATRON: | HIS MAJESTY KING GEORGE VI | Master of the Merchant Navy and Fishing Fleets | *President:* | THE EARL OF ATHLONE, K.G. | *Vice-President:* | HIS WORSHIP THE MAYOR OF SOUTHAMPTON | (ALDERMAN H. CHICK) | Admiral of the Port | *Chairman:* | Captain PAUL MILLAR, R.D., R.N.R. | [rule, 42mm.] | *General Director:* | HAROLD GIBSON, M.C. | [rule, 42mm.] | [point] | *Official Souvenir Handbook* | *and* | *Programme of Events* | Edited by | MARTIN FRANKISH | *Printed by* | GALE & POLDEN, LTD., WELLINGTON WORKS, ALDERSHOT | NELSON HOUSE, PORTSMOUTH
(All width centred and within ruled border broken at head by first line and at foot by last line of text: 184 × 127mm.)

Collation: [A]²⁸; 28 leaves; 247 × 184mm.; 1–56

Page contents: 1 'INDEX | [45 items listed with page references] | *The matter, photos, etc., in this Book are Copyright* | *and may not be published without permission.* | COVER DESIGN | by | KENNETH SHOESMITH'; 2 photograph: 'H.M. KING GEORGE VI, | Master of the Merchant Navy and Fishing Fleets.'; 3 title-page; 4 photograph: 'THE EARL OF ATHLONE, K.G.'; 5 *FOREWORD* | by the | EARL OF ATHLONE, K.G.' ('In my dual capacity as President of the Southampton Merchant Navy Week...') (signed, 'Athlone.') (facsimile signature); 6 'VICE-PATRONS' (listed); 7 *'This Lyric has been specially written for Merchant Navy Week by the* | POET *LAUREATE.* | FOR THE MEN OF THE MERCHANT NAVY AND | FISHING FLEETS | [text] | JOHN MASEFIELD.'; 8–9 'GENERAL INFORMATION'; 10–55 text, photographs, plans and advertisements; 56 'ACKNOWLEDGMENTS'

Paper: glossy wove paper

Running title: none

Binding: beige wrappers. Spine: blank. On upper wrapper: 'MERCHANT [in brown] | NAVY WEEK [in brown] | SOUTHAMPTON [in red] | JULY 17 TO 24 [in brown] | [illustration of ships] [in brown, red and navy blue] | OFFICIAL [in red] | SOUVENIR HANDBOOK [in navy blue] | AND [in navy blue] | PROGRAMME OF EVENTS. [in navy blue] | SIXPENCE [in red]'. Lower wrapper: blank. All edges trimmed. Binding measurements: 247 × 184mm. (wrappers), 247 × 3mm. (spine).

Publication date: presumably published, July 1937

Price: 6d.

Masefield contents:

For the Men of the Merchant Navy and Fishing Fleets ('They dare all weathers in all climes and seas')
    (signed, 'JOHN MASEFIELD.')

Notes:

The text of Masefield's poem has not been traced in any other publication.

Copies seen: private collection (ROV)

B355 Ed. H. BUXTON FORMAN *and* MAURICE BUXTON FORMAN, *THE POETICAL WORKS AND OTHER WRITINGS OF JOHN KEATS.* VOLUME I   1938

B355(a) First American edition (limited signed edition) (1938)

The Poetical Works and Other Writings of | John Keats [in brown] | Edited with Notes and Appendices by | H. BUXTON FORMAN. Revised with | Additions by MAURICE BUXTON FORMAN | *With an Introduction by JOHN MASEFIELD* | [rule consisting of ninety-six points] | [device showing Keats' house with 'HAMPSTEAD | [triangular device] EDITION [triangular device]' within plaque] [in brown, within ruled border with curved head: 46 × 39mm.] | VOLUME ONE | Poems 1817 | [rule consisting of ninety-six points] | *NEW YORK* | CHARLES SCRIBNER'S SONS | MCMXXXVIII
(All width centred with lines 3–5 justified on both left and right margins)

Collation: [A–B]⁶ [C]¹⁰ [D–E]⁸ [F]¹⁰ [G–M]⁸ [N]⁴ [O–P]⁶ [Q]¹⁰ [R–T]⁸ [U]⁴ (J not used); 150 leaves; 240 × 150mm.; [six un-numbered pages] [i–ii] [two un-numbered pages] [iii–iv] v–ix [x–xii] xiii–xix [xx] xxi–lxxvi [two un-numbered pages] lxxvii–cxxviii [1–8] 9–49 [50–52] 53–64 [two un-numbered pages] 65–68 [69–70] 71–90 [two un-numbered pages] 91–95 [96–98] 99–112 [113–14] 115–55 [156–58]; illustrations are integral to the volume, although not included in the pagination

Page contents: [-] blank (page excluded from page count, but constitutes first leaf of first gathering); [-] blank; [-] blank (page excluded from page count, but constitutes second leaf of first gathering); [-] blank; [-] blank (page excluded from page count, but constitutes third leaf of first gathering); [-] 'THE | *HAMPSTEAD EDITION* | OF THE WORKS OF | JOHN KEATS | PRINTED FROM TYPE | NOW DESTROYED | LIMITED TO | TEN HUNDRED AND FIFTY COPIES | SIGNED BY | JOHN MASEFIELD | AND | MAURICE BUXTON FORMAN | TEN HUNDRED AND TWENTY-FIVE SETS | FOR SUBSCRIPTION | TWENTY-FIVE SETS FOR | PRESENTATION | *This set is number*'; [i] half-title: 'The Works of John Keats | VOLUME I'; [ii] '...there is a noise | Among immortals when a God gives sign, | With hushing finger, how he means to load | His tongue with the full weight of utterless thought, | With thunder, and with music, and with pomp:...'; [-] blank; [-] frontispiece: 102 × 77mm., *'John Keats | from a miniature by Joseph Severn | Emery Walker Ltd. ph.sc.'* (with protective tissue); [iii] title-page; [iv] 'COPYRIGHT 1938 BY | CHARLES SCRIBNER'S SONS | Printed in the United States of America'; v–vi 'ACKNOWLEDGMENTS' ('For the use of original documents and for permission to reproduce portraits I am indebted...') (unsigned); vii–ix 'Contents' (46 entries listed with page references (within five sections)); [x] blank; [xi] 'Illustrations' (four illustrations listed with page references); [xii] blank; xiii–xiv 'PREFATORY NOTE' ('Nowadays no one who knows anything about Keats needs to be reminded of all that he...') (signed, 'M. Buxton Forman') (autograph signature); xv–xix 'INTRODUCTION' ('Though the convulsion of the War has brought new thoughts and ways to artists...') (signed, 'John Masefield.') (autograph signature); [xx] blank; xxi–lxxii 'MEMOIR OF JOHN KEATS | BY H. BUXTON FORMAN, C.B.'; lxxiii–lxxvi 'MEMOIR OF GEORGE KEATS | BY NAOMI JOY KIRK'; [-] '[illustration of George Keats] | *J. Severn, pinxt. Emery Walker Ltd. ph.sc.* | *George Keats*' (with protective tissue); [-] blank; lxxvii–xcviii Memoir of George Keats (concluded); xcix–cxxviii 'LIST OF PRINCIPAL WORKS | CONCERNING KEATS'; [1] 'POEMS'; [2] 'EDITOR'S NOTE'; [3] facsimile of title-page of original edition of Keats' *Poems* (C. and J. Ollier 1817); [4] blank; [5] 'DEDICATION | TO LEIGH HUNT | [text]'; [6] blank; [7] 'POEMS'; [8]–49 text; [50] blank; [51] 'EPISTLES'; [52] blank; 53–64 text; [-] '[illustration of Charles Cowden Clarke] | *Photograph by G.B. Sciutto, 1872 Emery Walker*

Ltd. ph.sc. | *Charles Cowden Clarke*' (with protective tissue); [-] blank; 65–68 text (continued); [69] 'SONNETS'; [70] blank; 71–90 text; [-] '[illustration of Benjamin Robert Haydon] | *G.H. Harlow, pinxt. 1816 Emery Walker Ltd. ph.sc.* | *Benjamin Robert Haydon*' (with protective tissue); [-] blank; 91–95 text (continued); [96] blank; [97] 'SLEEP AND POETRY'; [98] blank; 99–112 text; [113] 'APPENDIX | VOLUME I'; [114] blank; 115–55 text; [156] blank; [157] 'The *HAMPSTEAD EDITION* of *KEATS* | is designed by T.M. CLELAND and printed under his | direction at THE SCRIBNER PRESS in New York | [colophon of 'THE SCRIBNER PRESS']'; [158] blank

Paper: laid paper (no watermark), chain-lines 20–21mm. apart (see notes)

Running title: running titles comprise sectional title, author, title of original volume, or title of poem, on both verso and recto, pp.vi-155

Binding: white buckram. On spine, in gold on black panel: 77 × 29mm.: 'The Poetical | Works & Other | Writings of | JOHN | KEATS | [rule consisting of twenty-one points] | Volume | 1 | [rule consisting of twenty-one points] | *HAMPSTEAD* | *EDITION* | [rule consisting of twenty-one points] | Scribners' (line 1 justified on right margin, line 2 justified on left and right margins, line 3 justified on left margin and all other lines width centred). On upper and lower covers: design in blind incorporating lyre, floral garland, geometric pattern, 'MDCCLXXXXV', 'JK' and 'MDCCCXXI' (within blind ruled border: 240 × 142mm.) Top edge gilt, others untrimmed. Sewn head and foot bands (in red and white). Binding measurements: 244 × 153mm. (covers), 244 × 45mm. (spine). End-papers: laid paper (no watermark), chain-lines 21mm. apart.

Also issued in leather

Publication date: 1938

Price: $96 (cloth) / $200 (¾ levant)

Masefield contents:
Introduction ('Though the convulsion of the War has brought new thoughts and ways to artists...'
        (signed, 'John Masefield.') (autograph signature)

Notes:
The sub-headings of items by Keats included in this volume appear as follows: 'Poems (Published in 1817)', 'Epistles' and 'Sonnets'.

The sheets [C]2 and [C]9 are conjugate with Masefield's signature on [C]2. The paper type is not the same as that used for the rest of the volume. It comprises laid paper (watermark of 'C', 'S' and 'S' monogram: 52 × 42mm.), chain-lines 30mm. apart.

The 'List of Principal Works Concerning Keats' includes, as number 97, the volume *Poems by John Keats* (see B5).

This edition is included in J.R. MacGillivray, *Keats A Bibliographical and Reference Guide with an Essay on Keats' Reputation* (University of Toronto Press, 1949) as H9.

The publishers first approached The Society of Authors in October 1936 requesting Masefield's contribution. C. Kingsley wrote:

> We have made arrangements with Mr. Maurice Buxton Forman, who as you probably know is the greatest living authority on Keats, to edit for us a new edition of the writings of John Keats...

> The plan is to publish this in an edition limited to 750 sets, in 7 or 8 volumes (the exact number will have to be decided on when all the material is gathered together), to be sold in complete sets only at approximately $10.00 a volume, the sale to be limited to America, with the possible exception that the Oxford University Press, who hold the copyright in a good deal of the material, and with whom we have made the necessary arrangements, might wish to import a few for sale here...

> We feel that the interest in, and value of the set would be greatly enhanced if Mr. Masefield could be induced to write and sign a short preface or introduction, and I quote as follows a paragraph from a memorandum I recently received from my New York office.

> "We should like to have a short introduction by Mr. Masefield, say three to five hundred words, or longer if he desired, the general aim of this introduction being to present the debt we owe to Keats as an English poet, touching on the fact that as time goes on his fame endures; something of the particular poets he has influenced; something of the possibility that his poetry may be more popular in the future than it is at the present time because it is so purely poetry; perhaps a word about the Greek spirit in Keats, all this being merely a suggestion. Perhaps we have not hit at all upon the point which would suit him. Certainly we feel that whatever he did feel that he wanted to say would be all right."

> This introduction we would want him to sign. This isn't as formidable a job as it sounds, because we could supply the first signature containing this preface, and he could do this at his leisure. It is not likely that the first volume will appear before next Autumn, so that there is no immediate hurry; anywhere up to the late Spring would be time enough as long as we can be assured that Mr. Masefield will be willing to agree to the proposition.

> Naturally Mr. Masefield will expect some payment for this work, and the sum of £100 has been suggested.
>   (C. Kingsley, letter to E.J. Mullett, 22 October 1936)
>   (BL, Add.Mss.56605, ff.49–50)

(In the event, a far larger limitation of the edition was printed and the issue date was much later than Autumn 1937). The Society of Authors obviously asked for Masefield's views on Scribner's proposal. Masefield replied:

I have thought over the suggestion of Messrs. Scribner's about the Keats edition, and am inclined to accept the proposal for the fee of £100: the question is, will they make it guineas?

> (John Masefield, letter to [E.J.] Mullett [15 November 1936])
> (BL, Add.Mss.56605, f.71)

Having contacted Scribner's, The Society of Authors wrote to Masefield that his higher price had been accepted, and also noted the position regarding re-publication of Masefield's contribution:

> Mr. Kingsley stated that his firm is agreeable to pay One hundred guineas for the Prefatory note and autographing referred to in his letter of the 22nd October of which I sent you a copy. ...If you wish to republish the note [introduction] in a Collection of your Essays, his firm would not object to your doing so, after the expiration of 12 months from the publication of the edition...

> (E.J. Mullett, letter to John Masefield, 18 November 1936)
> (BL, Add.Mss.56605, ff.76–77)

Masefield, it seems, delayed before confirming that he would write the introduction:

> I am so sorry that I have kept you waiting for a reply about Keats for Messrs. Scribner. I am willing to do this introduction for a hundred guineas, if it will not be wanted until next Summer.

> (John Masefield, letter to [E.J.] Mullett, [15 December 1936])
> (BL, Add.Mss.56605, f.137)

The Society of Authors evidently felt that Masefield had omitted mention of autographing copies and asked for confirmation. Masefield modestly responded:

> I am willing to sign copies of the Keats, though I feel a little doubtful about the propriety of adding my signature to the edition.

> (John Masefield, letter to [E.J.] Mullett, [17 December 1936])
> (BL, Add.Mss.56605, f.145)

In July 1937 Masefield duly sent his introduction to The Society of Authors. He apologised for a lack of brevity (evidently forgetting, if indeed he had been told, that Scribner's had only suggested three to five hundred words but noted that it could be 'longer if he desired'):

> I send you, with this, the typescript of the preface to John Keats, for Messrs Scribners. It is about three times the length asked for, but it is not easy to be brief about a major poet.

> (John Masefield, letter to [E.J.] Mullett, [11 July 1937])
> (BL, Add.Mss.56607, f.75)

Four months later, the English representative of Scribner's wrote to The Society of Authors enclosing the pages requiring Masefield's signature. As noted above these were presumably [C]2 and [C]9 only from the gathering:

> I have just received from New York a bundle containing pulls of the last page of the above introduction, sent here for the purpose of obtaining Mr. Masefield's signature.

> (C. Kingsley, letter to E.J. Mullett, 22 November 1937)
> (BL, Add.Mss.56608, f.91)

Copies seen: BL (012274.e.4) 'Presentation' noted on limitation page, signature of 'M. Buxton Forman' on p.xiv and signature of 'John Masefield.' on p.xix, stamped 4 APR 1939

B360 *Ed.* FRANCIS INNOCENT, *PLAYING WITH VERSE* 1939

B360(a) *First English edition (1939)*

PLAYING WITH VERSE | An Anthology | of Verse by Students of the | CITY LITERARY INSTITUTE | Edited by | FRANCES INNOCENT | with a Foreword by | THE POET LAUREATE | "If we can't write poetry, | by all means let's play with verse." | – *Charles Williams to a C.L.I. Student* | L.C.C. CITY LITERARY INSTITUTE | Stukeley Street, W.C.2 | 1939
(All width centred)

Collation: [A-C]⁸; 24 leaves; 216 × 140mm.; [1–8] 9–45 [46–48]

Page contents: [1–2] blank; [3] title-page; [4] blank; [5–6] 'CONTENTS' (48 entries listed with author and page references); [7–8] 'FOREWORD' ('It has been a pleasure to me to read through this anthology...') (signed, 'JOHN MASEFIELD.'); 9–45 text; [46–48] blank

Paper: wove paper

Running title: none

Binding: light tan wrappers. Spine: blank. On upper wrapper, in purple: 'PLAYING | WITH | VERSE | [ornament] | A | C.L.I. | ANTHOLOGY' (lines 1–3 left justified on left margin and lines 5–7 left justified on left margin at width centre of wrapper). Lower wrapper: blank. All edges trimmed. Binding measurements: 216 × 140mm. (wrappers), 216 × 5mm. (spine)

Publication date: presumably published, according to the British Library copy, May 1939

Price: unknown

Masefield contents:
'Foreword' ('It has been a pleasure to me to read through this anthology…')
    (signed, 'JOHN MASEFIELD.')

Notes:
Masefield's contribution concludes:

> …let me wish all the writers all happy and fortunate success. I hope that there may be peace, and that I may see more of their work next year…

The City Literary Institute was provided with a new building at Stukeley Street, Drury Lane, London which was opened by Masefield on 13 May 1939.

Copies seen: BL (011604.k.64) stamped 18 MAY 1939 rebound; ULL (Special Collections) includes posthumous booklabel

B365 NICOLAS LEGAT, *BALLET RUSSE*   1939

B365(a) First English edition (1939)

BALLET RUSSE | MEMOIRS OF | NICOLAS LEGAT | *Translated, with a Foreword by* | SIR PAUL DUKES, K.B.E. | *Dedicatory Poem by* | JOHN MASEFIELD | *With 7 Plates in Colour* | *and 24 in Monotone* | [publisher's device] | METHUEN & CO. LTD. LONDON | *36 Essex Street, Strand, W.C.2*
(All width centred)

Collation: [A]⁸ B–D⁸ E¹⁰; E2 is also signed; signatures left foot of page; 42 leaves; 254 × 190mm.; [i–iv] v [vi] vii–xv [xvi] 1–56 [57–58] 59–65 [66] 67 [68]; illustrations (coloured plates on glossy paper with others on wove paper) tipped-in on pp.[ii], vii, ix, xv, 3, 9, 11, 13, 15, 19, 21, 23, 25, 27, 33, 35, 37, 39, 41, 45, 47, 49, 51, 53, 55, [57], 59, 61, 63, 65 and 67

Page contents: [i] half-title: 'BALLET RUSSE | MEMOIRS OF | NICOLAS LEGAT'; [ii] blank (with additional leaf tipped-in on the verso of which is the frontispiece: 182 × 128mm., 'NADEJDA (NADINE) NICOLAEVA and NICOLAS LEGAT | *in "Lac de Cygnes"'*); [iii] title-page; [iv] '*First published in 1939* | PRINTED IN GREAT BRITAIN'; v 'TO NICOLAS LEGAT, WITH MY THANKS' ('Once, all unknowing, you were gracious to me;') (signed, 'John Masefield. | July 2ⁿᵈ. 1939.') (facsimile signature); [vi] blank; vii–xii 'FOREWORD' ('The translation of this book has given me immense pleasure…') (signed, 'PAUL DUKES'); xiii 'CONTENTS' (foreword, five chapters and three appendices listed with page references); xiv–xv 'ILLUSTRATIONS' (32 illustrations listed with page references, and erratum note); [xvi] blank; 1–56 text; [57] 'APPENDICES'; [58] blank; 59–65 text; [66] blank; 67 text; [68] 'PRINTED IN GREAT BRITAIN | BY UNWIN BROTHERS LIMITED | LONDON AND WOKING'

Paper: laid paper (no watermark), chain-lines 25mm. apart

Running title: 'BALLET RUSSE' (31mm.) on verso; recto title comprises chapter title, pp.viii-65

Binding: red cloth. On spine, in gold: '*Ballet* | *Russe* | [ornament] | MEMOIRS OF | NICOLAS | LEGAT | METHUEN' (all width centred). Covers: blank. Top edge trimmed, others untrimmed. Binding measurements: 263 × 197mm. (covers), 263 × 33mm. (spine). End-papers: wove paper.

Publication date: published, according to the *English Catalogue of Books*, August 1939

Price: 25s.

Masefield contents:
To Nicolas Legat, With My Thanks ('Once, all unknowing, you were gracious to me;')
    (signed, 'John Masefield. | July 2ⁿᵈ. 1939.' (facsimile signature)

Notes:
See also B440 and E6

Copies seen: BL (7913.w.5) stamped 3 AUG 1939 rebound; BL Document Supply Centre (q.792.8*183*)

B370 *THE QUEEN'S BOOK OF THE RED CROSS*   1939

B370(a) First English edition – 5s. issue (1939)

THE | QUEEN'S BOOK | OF THE | RED CROSS | [rule (tapered at both ends), 100mm.] | *With a Message from* | HER MAJESTY THE QUEEN | *and Contributions by* | FIFTY BRITISH AUTHORS AND ARTISTS | *In Aid of* | THE LORD MAYOR OF LONDON'S FUND | FOR THE RED CROSS AND THE ORDER | OF ST. JOHN OF JERUSALEM | [rule (tapered at both ends), 71mm.] | HODDER AND STOUGHTON
(All width centred)

Collation: [A]⁸ B–Q⁸ (J not used); signatures left foot of page; 128 leaves; 248 × 180mm.; [1–3] 4–255 [256]; the facsimile letter, facsimile musical manuscript and illustrations (on glossy paper) are tipped-in on pages 2 and 5, with sets of conjugate leaves bound with gatherings C, E, G, I, L and N (these are excluded from the leaf count).

Page contents: [1] half-title: '[crown design] | THE QUEEN'S BOOK | OF THE | RED CROSS'; [2] blank (with additional leaf tipped-in on the verso of which is the black and white photograph frontispiece of the Queen: 248 × 180mm.); [3] title-page; 4 'FIRST PRINTED . . . . NOVEMBER 1939 | [new paragraph] HODDER & STOUGHTON, the publishers, are very grateful to the authors and | artists whose kindness and ready co-operation in many matters of detail have | alone made possible the production of The Queen's Book of the Red Cross | within two months of its conception. | [new paragraph] They also offer their thanks to the firms who have assisted in the production | of this book. | [new paragraph] The text has been printed on paper supplied through Bowater-Lloyd and W. | Rowlandson & Co. Ltd. by Hazell, Watson & Viney Ltd., of London and | Aylesbury, Wyman & Sons Ltd., of London, Reading and Fakenham, and | Richard Clay & Co. Ltd., of London and Bungay. | [new paragraph] The colour and photogravure illustrations have been printed by The Sun | Engraving Company Ltd., of London and Watford. | [new paragraph] The book has been bound by The Leighton-Straker Bookbinding Co. Ltd., | in conjunction with Hazell, Watson & Viney Ltd., Wyman & Sons Ltd. | and Richard Clay & Co. Ltd.'; 5–6 'THE AUTHORS | AND THEIR CONTRIBUTIONS' (37 authors and their contributions listed with page references) (with additional leaf tipped-in on page 5 on the recto of which is a facsimile letter from the Queen); 7 'THE PICTURES' (13 artists and their contributions listed with page references); 8 'THE ARTISTS' (12 short biographies provided); 9–255 text; [256] blank

Paper: wove paper

Running title: 'THE QUEEN'S BOOK OF THE RED CROSS' (117mm.) on both verso and recto, pp.6–255

Binding: light blue cloth. On spine, in red: 'THE | QUEEN'S | BOOK | OF THE | RED | CROSS | [red cross device] | HODDER & STOUGHTON' (all width centred). On upper cover, in red: '[crown design] | THE QUEEN'S | BOOK OF THE | RED CROSS | [red cross device]' (the title is enclosed within an ornate border: 102 × 153mm.) Lower cover: blank. All edges trimmed. Binding measurements: 254 × 185mm. (covers), 254 × 47mm. (spine). End-papers: wove paper.

Publication date: published, according to the *English Catalogue of Books*, December 1939

Price: 5s.

Masefield contents:
Red Cross ('I remember a moonless night in a blasted town,')
    (headed, 'JOHN MASEFIELD')

Notes:
There are fifty-two contributors in total presenting forty pieces of prose or poetry and thirteen pictures or music. This includes the photographer of the frontispiece (Cecil Beaton) and a letter from the Queen.

Each non-pictorial contribution is prefaced by a brief biographical sketch of the contributor. (This explains why a separate list of artists' biographies is included on page 8). Masefield's biography is as follows:

> *MR. JOHN MASEFIELD has been Poet Laureate since 1930, and was awarded the Order of Merit in 1935. His best-known poems are perhaps "The Everlasting Mercy," "The Widow in the Bye-Street," "Reynard the Fox," and "Right Royal"; his novels, such as "Sard Harker" and "Odtaa," reach the widest public; and his "Gallipoli" is one of the classics of the last war.*

Contributions commence with drop-capitals.

In discussing an application to use Masefield's poem (in a different anthology) the author explained the subject of the poem in a letter to The Society of Authors:

> Mr or Miss Collie Knox wishes to use a poem I gave to the Queens Red Cross Book. I wrote to say that the verses deal with an event among the French in the last war, and might therefore not suit the present occasion... I do not intend to print the lines in any book of mine.

(John Masefield, letter to [E.J.] Mullett, [1 November 1942])
(BL, Add.Mss.56616, f.88)

Copies seen: private collection (PWE); BL (12359.h.10) stamped 9 JAN 1940

B370(aa) First English edition – 'deluxe' issue (1939)

A 'de luxe edition' was issued during December 1939 priced at 10s.6d. This comprised the same printing bound in a more expensive manner.

B375 Ed. ARNOLD L. HASKELL, *BALLET – TO POLAND*   1940

B375(a) First English edition (1940)

BALLET—TO POLAND | EDITED BY | ARNOLD L. HASKELL | DECORATED BY | KAY AMBROSE | IN AID OF | THE POLISH RELIEF FUND | ADAM AND CHARLES BLACK | 4, 5 AND 6 SOHO SQUARE LONDON W.1 1940
(Lines 1–5 justified on left margin, lines 6–7 justified on right margin and lines 8–9 justified on different left margin with '1940' justified on right margin)
(The 'Q' of 'SQUARE' is swash)

Collation: [A]⁸ B–E⁸ [F–I]⁸; signatures left foot of page; 72 leaves; 246 × 180mm.; [1–4] 5 [6] 7 [8] 9–11 [12] 13 [14] 15–80 80a 80b 81–154; illustrations (on glossy paper) are tipped-in on pp.[2], 21, 23, 31, 39, 47, 67, 71 and 75; divisional title pages (within the 'Album of Photographs') are tipped-in on pp.81, 103, 121, 127, 135 and 141; there are four illustrations (on glossy paper) bound with gathering C using leaf stubs (not counted in the gathering information)

Page contents: [1] half-title: 'BALLET-TO POLAND'; [2] blank (with additional leaf tipped-in on the verso of which is the black and white frontispiece drawing: 246 × 158mm., 'BLACK Queen | "Checkmate" | E. McKnight Kauffer. | 1938'); [3] title-page; [4] '[drawing of four ballet dancers] | MADE IN GREAT BRITAIN | PRINTED BY THE WHITEFRIARS PRESS LTD. LONDON AND TONBRIDGE | PHOTOGRAVURE PLATES BY HARRISON AND SONS LTD. LONDON AND HIGH WYCOMBE'; 5 'CONTENTS' (19 individual items, their authors and page references (this listing includes the introduction and 'Notes on the Album of Photographs')); [6] drawing of two character dancers; 7 'ILLUSTRATIONS' (10 illustrators noted in addition to 'An Album of Photographs' in six parts, each with page references, end-papers are also noted); [8] blank; 9–80 text and illustrations; 80a-154 album of photographs

Paper: wove paper

Running title: running titles comprise the author of contribution on verso and title of contribution on recto, pp.10–80

Binding: grey cloth. On spine, in red: 'BALLET | [curved line]TO | POLAND | [ornament] | EDITED BY | ARNOLD L. | HASKELL | A. & C. BLACK' (all width centred with the exception of line 2 which is off-set to the right). On upper cover, in red: illustration of dancer: 51 × 63mm. (ranged lower right). Lower cover: blank. All edges trimmed. Binding measurements: 251 × 182mm. (covers), 251 × 39mm. (spine). End-papers: wove paper decorated in red by Kay Ambrose with scene of theatre stage within ruled border: 218 × 159mm.

Publication date: published, according to the *English Catalogue of Books*, May 1940

Price: 12s.6d.

Masefield contents:
To the Dancers in the Polish Ballet ('Only two years ago, I saw you dance')
  (headed, 'JOHN MASEFIELD')

Notes:
There are nineteen individual items listed in the contents including the introduction, notes on the album of photographs (itself omitted from the contents) and short messages.

The editor's introduction notes the nature of the volume. It commences:

 Ballet has always been eager to offer its services to a good cause. Nothing could be nearer to the hearts of dancers and dance-lovers than the cause of Poland, deeply cultured country that has contributed so much to the gentle art of Ballet.

The introduction also refers to Masefield's poem:

 The new young Polish Ballet had barely time to develop before it was cut off by the terror, leaving behind it memories that John Masefield has so movingly evoked in the pages that follow.

Contributions commence with drop-capitals.

Masefield was invited to contribute by the editor of this volume and sent his verses to The Society of Authors in January 1940:

 I enclose some verses about the Polish Ballet. Mr Arnold Haskell, of Cottonwood, East Cliff, Bournemouth, is editing a Ballet Book in aid of Polish Relief, and asked me if I could contribute. I said I would make some verses. Will you kindly send him these from me, for his book?

    (John Masefield, letter to [E.J.] Mullett, [22 January 1940])
    (BL, Add.Mss.56613, f.14)

Copies seen: private collection (PWE)

B380 *FEAR NO MORE*   1940

B380(a) *First English edition (1940)*

FEAR NO MORE | A Book of Poems | for the Present Time by | living English Poets | [ornament] | CAMBRIDGE | AT THE UNIVERSITY PRESS | 1940
(All width centred)

Bibliographies: unrecorded

Collation: [π]⁶ 1–6⁸; the second leaf of each signed gathering is also signed; signatures right foot of page with 'FNM' at left foot on first leaf of signed gatherings; 54 leaves; 185 × 120mm.; [two un-numbered pages] [i–vi] vii–x 1–95 [96]

Page contents: [-] blank (page excluded from page count, but constitutes first leaf of first gathering); [-] blank; [i] half-title: 'FEAR NO MORE'; [ii] 'CAMBRIDGE | UNIVERSITY PRESS | LONDON: BENTLEY HOUSE | NEW YORK, TORONTO, BOMBAY | CALCUTTA, MADRAS: MACMILLAN | TOKYO: MARUZEN COMPANY LTD. | *All rights reserved* | PRINTED IN GREAT

BRITAIN'; [iii] title-page; [iv] [Untitled] ('In times of danger, the herd-mind has power…') (signed, 'JOHN MASEFIELD, | *May* 17, 1940.'); [v] 'DEDICATED TO | THE POET LAUREATE | June 1940'; [vi] blank; vii–x '*TO THE READER*' ('Almost all of the poems in this book have been written…') (unsigned); 1–92 text; 93–[96] 'INDEX OF TITLES AND FIRST LINES' (at foot of page [96]: '*Printed by* W. LEWIS, M.A., *at the University Press, Cambridge*')

Paper: wove paper

Running title: none

Binding: red boards with grey cloth spine. On spine, reading lengthways up spine, from foot in red: 'FEAR NO MORE'. Covers: blank. All edges trimmed. Binding measurements: 191 × 122mm. (covers), 191 × 21mm. (spine). End-papers: wove paper.

Publication date: published, according to the *English Catalogue of Books*, July 1940

Price: 3s.6d.

Masefield contents:
[Untitled] ('In times of danger, the herd-mind has power…')
　　　(signed, 'JOHN MASEFIELD, | *May* 17, 1940.')

Notes:
An anthology in which the poems are printed anonymously. The introduction states:

> Almost all of the poems in this book have been written in the last five years. They are printed here, without names, by permission of the authors…

Copies seen: private collection (ROV); BL (011604.k.69) stamped 30 JUL 1940

B385 SIR WILLIAM ROTHENSTEIN, *MEN OF THE R.A.F.* 　　　1942

B385(a) First English editon (1942)

Left title-page:
FORTY PORTRAITS | *with* | *SOME ACCOUNT OF LIFE IN THE R.A.F. by* | SIR WILLIAM ROTHENSTEIN | *A LAYMAN'S GLIMPSE by* | LORD DAVID CECIL | *A FOREWORD by* | AIR CHIEF MARSHAL | SIR CHARLES PORTAL | *A POEM by* | JOHN MASEFIELD, O.M. | POET LAUREATE | and a | COMPLETE LIST OF R.A.F. DRAWINGS *by* | SIR WILLIAM ROTHENSTEIN | NOVEMBER 1939–OCTOBER 1941
Right title-page:
MEN OF THE | R.A.F. | OXFORD UNIVERSITY PRESS | LONDON　NEW YORK　TORONTO | 1942
(The title uses a type of letters in outline. Both pages width centred and within double ruled border across both pages: 194 × 260mm. The lines do not always completely touch to form perfect corners)

Collation: [A]⁴ B–F⁸ [1–2]⁸ [3]⁴ G⁴; signatures left foot of page; 68 leaves; 243 × 152mm.; [1–4] 5 [6] 7 [8–10] 11–62 [63–64] 65–87 [88–130] 131–34 [135–36]

Page contents: [1] half-title: 'MEN OF THE R.A.F.'; [2] left title-page; [3] right title-page; [4] 'OXFORD UNIVERSITY PRESS | AMEN HOUSE, E.C.4 | LONDON EDINBURGH GLASGOW NEW YORK | TORONTO MELBOURNE CAPE TOWN BOMBAY | CALCUTTA MADRAS | HUMPHREY MILFORD | PUBLISHER TO THE UNIVERSITY | PRINTED IN GREAT BRITAIN'; 5 'FOREWORD' ('It was a great pleasure to me to be asked by Sir William Rothenstein to write a few words…') (signed, 'CHARLES PORTAL | *November 1941*'); [6] 'CROWN COPYRIGHT RESERVED | IN THE ILLUSTRATIONS | *Nos. 1, 2, 6, 11, 16, 19 and 28* | *reproduced by permission of the* | *Ministry of Information, the* | *remainder by permission of* | *the Air Ministry*'; 7 'CONTENTS' (seven items listed with page references); [8] blank; [9] 'SOME ACCOUNT OF | LIFE IN THE R.A.F. | BY | WILLIAM ROTHENSTEIN'; [10] blank; 11–62 text of 'Some Account of Life in the R.A.F.'; [63] 'THE R.A.F.: | A LAYMAN'S GLIMPSE | BY | DAVID CECIL'; [64] blank; 65–84 text of 'The R.A.F.: A Layman's Glimpse'; 85 [Untitled poem] ('Walking the darkness, far from home, at midnight,') (signed, 'JOHN MASEFIELD'); 86–87 'LIST OF PLATES' and 'NOTE'; [88] blank; [89–128] plates; [129] 'COMPLETE | LIST OF R.A.F. DRAWINGS | NOVEMBER 1939–OCTOBER 1941 | BY | WILLIAM ROTHENSTEIN'; [130] blank; 131–34 listing of 'R.A.F. Drawings'; [135] blank; [136] 'Text composed and printed by | LATIMER, TREND AND CO LTD | PLYMOUTH | Photogravure illustrations printed by | HARRISON AND SONS LTD | LONDON AND HIGH WYCOMBE'

Paper: wove paper (glossy wove paper is used for the plates)

Running title: 'MEN OF THE R.A.F.' (35mm.) on verso; recto title comprises section title, pp.12–84

Binding: light brown cloth. On spine, in gold reading lengthways up spine, from foot: '*MEN of the R.A.F.*'; horizontally at foot of spine: '*Oxford*'. Covers: blank. Top edge stained brown, others trimmed. Binding measurements: 246 × 154mm. (covers), 246 × 29mm. (spine). End-papers: wove paper.

Publication date: published, according to the *English Catalogue of Books*, April 1942

Price: 12s.6d.

Masefield contents:
[Untitled] ('Walking the darkness, far from home, at midnight,')
(signed, 'JOHN MASEFIELD')

Notes:
Page numbers appear between wavy lines. Thus, ~5~, ~7~, ~11~, etc.

The three unsigned gatherings that constitute the forty plates are bound within the volume so that page numbers (although omitted) continue in sequence. Each plate is numbered 1–40 and is titled. Gathering letters do not, however, continue in sequence. Consequently, the three gatherings of plates constitute pages 89–128 and occur between gatherings F and G.

An errata slip is tipped-in on page [102]. It corrects the name of the subject of the plate on that page.

Copies seen: private collection (ROV); BL (8829.k.43) stamped 18 APR 1942

B390 S.I. HSIUNG, *THE BRIDGE OF HEAVEN*   1943

B390(a) First English editon (1943)

The | *BRIDGE of HEAVEN* | *A NOVEL* | *by* | S. I. HSIUNG | WITH A PREFATORY POEM BY | JOHN MASEFIELD | LONDON: PETER DAVIES
(All width centred)

Collation: [A]⁸ B–AA⁸ (J and V not used); signatures right foot of page; 200 leaves; 184 × 119mm.; [i–vi] 1–394

Page contents: [i] six Chinese letters; [ii] '*By the same Author* | [four titles listed]'; [iii] title-page; [iv] 'To DYMIA | Sometimes my severe critic | Sometimes my enthusiastic collaborator | And always my loving wife | FIRST PUBLISHED 1943 | BOOK | PRODUCTION | WAR ECONOMY | STANDARD [lines 6–9 within device of book with lion] | THIS BOOK IS PRODUCED IN COMPLETE | CONFORMITY WITH THE AUTHORISED | ECONOMY STANDARDS | PRINTED IN GREAT BRITAIN FOR PETER DAVIES LIMITED AT | THE WINDMILL PRESS, KINGSWOOD, SURREY'; [v–vi] 'On reading | THE BRIDGE OF HEAVEN' ('*To Ta Tung, as a boy*,') (signed, 'John Masefield. | October 15th, 1942') (facsimile signature); 1–391 text; 392–94 'PRINCIPAL EVENTS IN CHINA, 1879–1912'

Paper: wove paper

Running title: none

Binding: red cloth. On spine, in gold: 'THE | BRIDGE | OF | HEAVEN | S. I. | HSIUNG | [four Chinese letters in column] | PETER DAVIES' (all width centred). On upper cover, in gold: two Chinese letters in column at top right corner. Lower cover: blank. All edges trimmed. Binding measurements: 190 × 124mm. (covers), 190 × 46mm. (spine). End-papers: wove paper.

Publication date: published, according to the *English Catalogue of Books*, January 1943

Price: 10s.6d.

Masefield contents:
On reading THE BRIDGE OF HEAVEN ('*To Ta Tung, as a boy*,')
(signed, 'John Masefield. | October 15th, 1942') (facsimile signature)

Notes:
Both Masefield and Hsiung were to contribute to *G.B.S. 90* (see B430)

Copies seen: BL (N.N. 33711) stamped 26 JAN 1943

Reprinted:
'Reprinted'	[first edition, second impression]	Jan 1943
'Reprinted'	[first edition, third impression]	Feb 1943
'Reprinted'	[first edition, fourth impression]	Apr 1943
'Reprinted'	[first edition, fifth impression]	Jul 1943

B395 *SOHO CENTENARY*   1944

B395(a) First English edition (1944)

SOHO CENTENARY | A Gift from | Artists, Writers and Musicians | to the | *Soho Hospital for Women* | HUTCHINSON & CO. (*Publishers*) LTD. | LONDON : NEW YORK : MELBOURNE
(All width centred with lines 6 and 7 justified on same left and right margins)

Collation: [A]¹⁰ (±[A]2) B–C⁸ [D]⁴ E–G⁸ (see notes); signatures left foot of page; 54 leaves; 247 × 185mm.; [1–3] 4–52 [53–60] 61–107 [108]; illustrations (on glossy paper) are tipped-in on pp.[2], 29, 33, 45, 65, 69 and 85; with sets of conjugate leaves bound with gatherings B and F (these are excluded from the leaf count)

Page contents: [1] half-title: 'SOHO CENTENARY | DEDICATED TO HER | MAJESTY QUEEN MARY, | PATRONESS SINCE 1901 | OF THE HOSPITAL FOR | WOMEN, SOHO SQUARE, | W.1.'; [2] blank (with additional leaf tipped-in on the verso of which is the colour frontispiece: 121 × 148mm., '*THE HEART OF ENGLAND by Eric Kennington*'); [3] title-page; 4 'CONTENTS' (29 individual items listed with authors and page references) and 'LIST OF ILLUSTRATIONS' (17 individual items (including frontispiece) listed with artists and page references); 5 'ACKNOWLEDGMENTS'; 6–8 'FOREWORD' and device (with 'SOHO | CENTENARY' at centre); 9–[108] text (at foot of page [108]: 'MADE AND PRINTED IN GREAT BRITAIN | AT GAINSBOROUGH PRESS, ST. ALBANS, | BY FISHER, KNIGHT & CO., LTD.')

Paper: wove paper

Running title: 'SOHO CENTENARY' (35mm.) on verso; recto title comprises title of contribution, pp.7–[108]

Binding: grey cloth. On spine, in gold: '*Soho Centenary*'; horizontally at foot of spine: '*Hutchinson*'. On upper cover, in gold: '*Soho Centenary*' (within ornate border: 56 × 120mm.) Lower cover: blank. All edges trimmed. Binding measurements: 253 × 187mm. (covers), 253 × 24mm. (spine). End-papers: wove paper.

Publication date: published, according to the *English Catalogue of Books*, December 1944

Price: 21s.

Masefield contents:
The Ambulance Ship ('We passed through canyons of a Carthage dead;')
    (headed, 'JOHN MASEFIELD')

Notes:
Subtitled 'A Gift from Artists, Writers and Musicians', the anthology contains illustrations (in black and white, and colour), music, short stories, poems and essays.

Masefield's contribution comprises a fourteen stanza poem entitled 'The Ambulance Ship'. Two sub-titles preface the poem. These are 'Port of London Authority' and 'A Morning Drill'.

The [D] gathering (printed on a higher quality of wove paper) comprises an eight page section (entitled 'Dots & Lines'). This is the musical contribution to the book. Although unsigned and unnumbered, the gathering is accommodated within the volume by subsequent page numbers and gatherings.

The volume includes a cancel-title ([A]2)

The 'Acknowledgments' state:

> Especial thanks are due to Messrs. Hutchinson and Company (Publishers) Limited for their generosity to the Hospital in publishing the Book free, and to the Hutchinson Printing Trust Limited for producing it at less than cost... also to Messrs. Henderson and Spalding for printing the music section free of cost to the Hospital...

Copies seen: private collection (PWE); BL (12358.f.26) stamped 29 NOV 1944

B395(aa) First English edition (limited signed edition) (1944)

A special, signed and numbered edition, limited to 250 copies was available at 5gns.

B400 *MERCHANTMEN AT WAR*   1944 / [1945]

B400(a) First English edition (1944 / [1945])

MERCHANTMEN | AT WAR | The Official Story of the Merchant Navy : 1939–1944 | [device incorporating letters 'M' and 'N': 22 × 22mm.] | *Prepared for the Ministry of War Transport | by the Ministry of Information* | LONDON : HIS MAJESTY'S STATIONERY OFFICE
(All width centred)

Collation: [A]⁷² ; 72 leaves; 228 × 175mm.; [1–6] 7–9 [10] 11–12 [13] 14–18 [19] 20–22 [23–24] 25–26 [27–29] 30–32 [33–34] 35–36 [37] 38–42 [43–44] 45–46 [47] 48–49 [50] 51–53 [54–55] 56–57 [58–59] 60–62 [63] 64–70 [71] 72–75 [76–78] 79–80 [81] 82–86 [87] 88–97 [98–99] 100–106 [107] 108 [109] 110 [111] 112–18 [119] 120–23 [124] 125–28 [129] 130–31 [132–33] 134–36 [137] 138 [139] 140–42 [143–44]

Page contents: [1] half of black and white 'end-paper' photograph; [2] black and white photograph frontispiece: 228 × 175mm.; [3] title-page; [4] black and white photograph; [5] black and white photograph (continued from page 4) also 'FOR ALL SEAFARERS | [text] | JOHN MASEFIELD'; [6] 'CONTENTS | [15 items listed with page references] | CROWN COPYRIGHT RESERVED. FIRST PUBLISHED 1944. | Price 1s. 9d. net from His Majesty's Stationery Office at York House, Kingsway, London, W.C.2; 13a, Castle | Street, Edinburgh, 2; 39–41, King Street, Manchester, 2; 1, St. Andrew's Crescent, Cardiff; 80, Chichester | Street, Belfast; or any bookseller. Printed by C. Nicholls & Co. Ltd., Manchester. S.O. Code No. 70–452.*'; 7 Contents (four items, two poems and six maps listed with page references) also note on sending books to the Forces and '*FOREWORD*'; 8 Foreword (concluded) and photograph; 9–[143] text and photographs; [144] half of black and white 'end-paper' photograph

Paper: glossy wove paper

Running title: 'MERCHANTMEN AT WAR' (53mm.) on verso; recto title comprises sectional title, pp.12–[143]

Binding: pictorial wrappers. Spine: blank. On upper wrapper: 'MERCHANTMEN [in red] | [white rule] | [union flag in white, red and black on red panel] AT WAR [in red] | [white rule] | ONE SHILLING AND NINEPENCE net' (all printed over black and white photograph of ship at sea). On lower wrapper: black and white photograph of sailor. Inside of upper wrapper: half of black and white end-paper photograph. Inside of lower wrapper: half of black and white end-paper photograph. All edges trimmed. Binding measurements: 228 × 175mm. (wrappers), 228 × 7mm. (spine).

Publication date: published, according to the *English Catalogue of Books*, January 1945

Price: 1s.6d.

Masefield contents:
For All Seafarers ('Even in peace, scant quiet is at sea;')
    (signed, 'JOHN MASEFIELD')
Epilogue ('Once, in a life, when unprepared,')
    (signed, 'JOHN MASEFIELD.')

Notes:
There are three main sections in addition to the foreword, poems and maps: 'The Men of The Merchant Navy', 'Shipping: The Plan and Achievement' and 'The Great Convoy Routes'.

The publication appears to omit details of its authorship. Evidence within the archives of The Society of Authors suggests that the author was J.L. Hodson (see below).

The 'end-papers' in this volume comprise the inside of the wrapper and pages [1] and [144]. The photographic illustration continues across two pages. The photograph at the front of the booklet is of ships moving from the horizon (at the head of the photograph). The photograph at the rear of the booklet is of ships moving from left to right of the pages.

The booklet includes copious photographs, many of which are printed across two pages. The contents is printed on a grey panel which is also printed across two pages.

Writing to The Society of Authors in August 1943, Masefield enclosed verses for this publication and explained their composition:

> Some weeks ago, Lord Leathers, P.C. of Berkeley Square House, London. W.1. asked me for some verses for use in Mr J.L. Hodson's forthcoming book about the Merchant Navy in the War. I said I would try to write something, and have made the enclosed. I wonder, whether you will be so very kind as to submit them for me to Lord Leathers, saying that he is most welcome to use them in Mr Hodson's book, if he wishes, but that the copyright must remain mine... I caused a few copies to be printed privately.
>
> (John Masefield, letter to [E.J.] Mullett, 3 August [1943])
> (BL, Add.Mss.56616, f.175)

The reference to the 'privately printed' copies presumably refers to the poetry card publication of 'For All Seafarers' (see D10). The manuscript of the entire book was sent to The Society of Authors on 12 January 1944 in case Masefield wished to alter or substitute his verses (see BL, Add.Mss.56617, f.62). The Society thought that Masefield would probably have little time to read the work, however, Masefield replied:

> Mr Hodson is an eminent writer, and the Merchant Service deserves more from us than it is ever likely to get. I had better read the book to make sure of the point. So, will you be so very kind, as to post it on to me? It may be some days before I can get it read and posted back to you, but I'll be as quick as I can.
>
> (John Masefield, letter to [E.J.] Mullett, [13 January 1944])
> (BL, Add.Mss.56617, f.64)

Having read the proposed volume, Masefield presumably wrote the verse entitled 'Epilogue' and enclosed this when returning the manuscript to The Society of Authors:

> I am grateful to you for sending me Mr Hodson's script, and for your care for its return to you. I send with this, the manuscript, a copy of the poem headed for the sailors, and some new verses. What I would suggest is :- that the printed lines For The Sailors, appear as a prologue and the new lines only nine in all, come at the end as an epilogue. But of course, this is but a suggestion.
>
> (John Masefield, letter to [E.J.] Mullett, [24 January 1944]
> (BL, Add.Mss.56617, f.76)

Discussion followed over the title of the first poem. Masefield had thought 'For the Seafarers' had been agreed. The Society of Authors reminded Masefield, however, that the title as agreed was 'For All Seafarers' (see BL, Add.Mss.56617, f.90). Cecil Day-Lewis, working for the Ministry of Information, had some suggestions to make, however. The Society of Authors communicated these in a letter from March 1944:

> Have you any objection to Mr Lewis' request that the Epilogue stanzas you sent should be omitted, and stanzas one, three and five of 'For All Seafarers' instead of the complete poem, be used?
>
> (E.J. Mullett, letter to John Masefield, 13 March 1944)
> (BL, Add.Mss.56617, f.109)

Masefield evidently did have objections for he instructed The Society of Authors to withdraw both poems from the book (a request which the Society confirmed they had done in a letter dated 20 March 1944, see BL, Add.Mss.56617, f.111). Such action presumably caused the Ministry of Information to reconsider, for both poems were included on publication.

Copies seen: private collection (PWE)

B405 *THE NAZI KULTUR IN POLAND* 1945

B405(a) *First English edition (1945)*

The Nazi | Kultur | in Poland | by | several authors | of necessity | temporarily anonymous | LONDON | *Published for the* POLISH MINISTRY OF INFORMATION *by* | HIS MAJESTY'S STATIONERY OFFICE
(All width centred)

Collation: [π]⁶ A-N⁸ O⁶ (J not used); [π]2 and O2 are also signed; signatures right foot of page; 116 leaves; 242 × 151mm.; [i–iii] iv–xii 1–220; illustration leaves (on glossy paper) are bound at the centre of gatherings D, H and M

Page contents: [i] title-page; [ii] text of five quotations; [iii] 'CONTENTS' (foreword, two notes and 21 chapters, with titles, listed with page references); iv–v 'LIST OF ILLUSTRATIONS' (24 plates listed) and 'MAPS' (2 maps listed); vi–vii 'FOREWORD' ('About six generations ago a sensitive, devout poet…') (signed, 'JOHN MASEFIELD'); viii–x 'A NOTE FROM THE AUTHORS IN WARSAW' ('The quotations at the beginning of our book explain why…') (signed, '*Warsaw, February*, 1942'); x–xii 'A NOTE FROM THE EDITORS IN LONDON' ('In their plain way the authors of this book have set down…') (signed, '*London, November* 11, 1944.'); 1–220 text and maps

Paper: wove paper

Running title: 'NAZI KULTUR IN POLAND' (59mm.) on verso; recto title comprises section of chapter title, pp.iv-220

Binding: cream wrappers. On spine, in brown reading lengthways up spine, from foot: '5s. The Nazi Kultur in Poland'. On upper wrapper, in brown: 'The Nazi | Kultur | in Poland | *Written in Warsaw under the German Occupation and* | *published for the* POLISH MINISTRY OF INFORMATION *by* | HIS MAJESTY'S STATIONERY OFFICE | LONDON 1945'. On lower wrapper, in brown: 'LONDON | PUBLISHED BY HIS MAJESTY'S STATIONERY OFFICE | To be purchased directly from H.M. STATIONERY OFFICE at the following addresses | York House, Kingsway, London, W.C.2; 13a Castle Street, Edinburgh 2; | 39–41 King Street Manchester 2; 1 St. Andrew's Crescent, Cardiff; | 80 Chichester Street, Belfast; | or through any bookseller | 1945 | Price 5s. 0s. net | S.O. Code No. 88–2702*'. All edges trimmed. Binding measurements: 242 × 151mm. (wrappers); 242 × 14mm. (spine)

Publication date: published, according to the *English Catalogue of Books*, February 1945

Price: 5s.

Masefield contents:
'FOREWORD' ('About six generations ago a sensitive, devout poet…')
(signed, 'JOHN MASEFIELD')
Notes:
Masefield's foreword considers Poland and Nazi crimes. He notes 'Poland… had the misfortune to be the cause of the present war. To her has fallen the first, the longest and the most appalling of the martyrdoms which come from being near modern Germany.'

Copies seen: private collection (ROV)

B410 *C.S. EVANS* 1945

B410(a) *First English edition (1945)*

C. S. EVANS [in red] | [rule (tapered at both ends), 27mm.] | *Born : June 23rd, 1883* | *Died : Nov. 29th, 1944* | [rule (tapered at both ends), 18mm.] | Joined William Heinemann in | 1914; became a Director of | the Company in 1922; Elected | Chairman in 1933 | [publisher's device of a windmill with 'W [point]' and '[point] H'] | [rule, 66mm.] | WILLIAM HEINEMANN LTD | LONDON : 1945 : TORONTO
(All width centred with lines 6–8 justified on identical left and right margins and with final two lines justified on different margins)

Collation: [A]⁸; 8 leaves; 190 × 120mm.; [i–iv] 1–11 [12]; illustration (on glossy paper) tipped-in on page [iii]

Page contents: [i] half-title: 'C. S. EVANS'; [ii] blank; [iii] title-page (with additional leaf tipped-in on the verso of which is the photograph frontispiece: 105 × 79mm., 'C. S. EVANS'); [iv] 'Privately printed at the Windmill Press | for circulation among his friends'; 1–11 text; [12] blank

Paper: laid paper (watermark: '[Crown] | Abbey Mills | Greenfield'), chain-lines 25mm. apart

Running title: none

Binding: black cloth. Spine: blank. On upper cover: white paper label (35 × 60mm.) on which: 'C. S. Evans | 1883–1944' (all within ornate border: 31 × 57mm.) Lower cover: blank. Top and fore edges trimmed, lower outside edge untrimmed. Binding measurements: 197 × 118mm. (covers), 197 × 13mm. (spine). End-papers: wove paper.

Publication date: presumably published, according to the British Library copy, around November 1945

Price: copies were not for sale

Masefield contents:
Some Memories of the Late Charles Evans ('I find that I cannot remember when I first met Charles Evans.')
    (headed, 'Mr. JOHN MASEFIELD')

Notes:
Although there are no running titles, each page of text pp.1–11 is headed by a thick rule followed by a thin rule.

On hearing of the death of C.S. Evans, Masefield apparently wrote to Louisa Callender. She responded:

> Your letter moved me deeply. I have shown it to my colleagues and we all thank you both for your sympathy and understanding. Charles Evans was a good publisher and a fine human being.
>
> For me, it is the end of twenty six years of teamwork, sharing enthusiasms and trials, successes and failures and a great personal friendship. For him, he chafed at the disabilities which forced him to inactivity and I know that he did not want to go on.

(Louisa Callender, letter to John Masefield, 5 December 1944)
(HRHRC, MS (Masefield, J.) Recip William Heinemann Ltd.)

Letters (preserved in the Heinemann Archive) reveal that Louisa Callender requested a contribution for this volume from Masefield on 11 January 1945. On 18 January 1945 she wrote again, acknowledging that she had received copy.

Copies seen: private collection (ROV); BL (10861.aa.27) stamped 10 NOV 1945 rebound; ULL (Special Collections)

B415 *SEVEN ALBEMARLE STREET [–] AN APPEAL TO BOOKMEN*   1945

B415(a) *First English edition (1945)*

Upper wrapper:
SEVEN | ALBEMARLE | STREET | [illustration of house and books] | AN APPEAL TO BOOKMEN
(All width centred)

Collation: [A]¹⁰; 10 leaves (see notes); 237 × 181mm.; [1–20]

Page contents: [1] title-page; [2] 'NATIONAL BOOK LEAGUE, 7 ALBEMARLE STREET, LONDON, W.1'; [3–4] 'AN APPEAL TO BOOKMEN' ('Twenty years ago a number of readers, authors, librarians, booksellers and publishers...') (signed, 'GEOFFREY FABER | *Chairman of the National Book League*'); [5] photograph of reception hall and elliptical staircase; [6] illustration: '[drawing of building signed 'S Rowland Pierce: 1945' (enclosed within five ruled borders)] | SEVEN ALBEMARLE STREET, AS IT WILL BE | *Drawn by S. Rowland Pierce*'; [7] 'A LETTER FROM THE POET LAUREATE' ('London has her libraries and reading rooms, and clubs for those practising the arts.') (signed, 'JOHN MASEFIELD | *President of the National Book League*'); [8–9] 'THE HISTORY OF THE HOUSE' ('In 1644 a large tract of land was granted to the Lord Chancellor, the Earl of Clarendon...') (unsigned); [10–11] plans of each floor; [12–13] 'FEATURES OF THE HOUSE' ('Researches have failed so far to reveal anything definite about the actual...') (signed, 'C.H. JAMES, A.R.A., F.B.I.B.A.'); [13–14] 'HOW THE HOUSE WILL BE USED' ('When the Committee of the National Book League decided to establish a national...') (unsigned); [15–16] photographs; [17] 'WHAT IS NEEDED NOW' ('Albemarle Street suffered severely from blast during the early days of the bombing...') (unsigned); [18] listing of president, vice-presidents, etc. within ruled border; [19] '¶ Cheques and money orders intended for | the restoration and equipment of 7 Albe- | marle Street should be made payable to | the National Book League (Building and | Development Fund) and sent to the | General Secretary, National Book League, | 7 Albemarle Street, London W.1. The | Bankers to the League are Coutts & | Company, 440 Strand London W.C.2. | The Accountants to the League are | Chalmers, Wade & Company, 24 Coleman | Street, London E.C.2. The Solicitors | to the League are Corner & Company, | 7 Henrietta Street, London W.C.2. | [new paragraph] A list of all donors' names and subscrip- | tions will be printed in *Books*, the monthly | journal of the National Book League.'; [20] device of National Book League within double ruled border

Paper: wove and glossy paper

Running title: none

Binding: wrappers comprise the first and last leaves of the single gathering ([A]1 and [A]10). The title-page consequently comprises the upper wrapper. The lower wrapper comprises page [20]. All edges trimmed. Binding measurements: 237 × 181mm. (wrappers), 237 × 1mm. (spine).

Publication date: presumably published, November 1945 (see notes)

Price: unknown

Masefield contents:
A Letter from the Poet Laureate ('London has her libraries and reading rooms, and clubs for those practising...')
    (signed, 'JOHN MASEFIELD')

Notes:

The pamphlet includes two conjugate leaves of glossy paper upon which the illustrations appear. These, bound with the rest of the volume, are included in the pagination and leaf count.

The Times reports that an appeal for the restoration of 7 Albemarle Street was launched in November 1945. As the illustration on page [6] is also dated '1945' it seems reasonable to date this publication from around that date.

Captions for the photograph illustrations on pages [3] and [14] are provided on pages [2] and [15] respectively.

Each section commences with a drop capital.

Copies seen: private collection (ROV)

B420 [SUFFOLK GALLERIES], *BOOKS OF SWITZERLAND* 1946

B420(a) *First English edition (1946)*

BOOKS | OF | SWITZERLAND | *Exhibition* | *arranged under the auspices of* | the British Council | April 26th – May 25th | 1946 | CATALOGUE | [rule, 54mm.] | Suffolk Galleries | Suffolk Street, Pall Mall East – Haymarket | London S.W.I.
(All width centred)

Collation: [A–K]⁸ (J not used); 80 leaves; 200 × 125mm.; [1–8] 9–11 [12] 13–16 [17] 18–25 [26–28] 29–50 [51] 52–88 [89] 90–98 [99] 100–108 [109] 110–118 [119] 120–42 [143] 144–59 [160]

Page contents: [1] half-title: 'BOOKS OF SWITZERLAND'; [2] blank; [3] title-page; [4] 'Cover and layout by Heinrich Steiner | Printed by Buchdruckerei Winterthur AG., Switzerland'; [5–8] listings of 'BRITISH PATRONS', 'SWISS PATRONS', 'EXECUTIVE COMMITTEE' and 'EXHIBITION COMMITTEE'; 9–10 'FOREWORD' ('Throughout the war our small country, Switzerland...') (signed, 'PHILIPP ETTER | Member of the Swiss Government | in charge of the Department of the | Interior | 6 February 1946.'); 11 'FOREWORD' ('Most English writers have happy memories of Switzerland...') (signed, 'JOHN MASEFIELD O.M. | Poet Laureate, President of | the National Book League'); [12] illustration; 13–25 text and illustrations of 'SWITZERLAND AND SWISS BOOKS' ('Switzerland, this small member of the the community of nations...') (signed, 'MARTIN HÜRLIMANN'); [26] illustration; [27] 'CATALOGUE | For the Historical Section of the Exhibition, | see Special Catalogue | SWISS BOOKS THROUGH FIVE CENTURIES'; [28] blank; 29–149 text and illustrations; [150–59] text of index; [160] 'CONTENTS' (25 individual items listed in two sections with page references)

Paper: wove paper

Running title: none

Binding: grey wrappers. Spine, in green reading lengthways up spine, from foot: 'BOOKS OF SWITZERLAND'. On upper wrapper, in dark green: 'BOOKS | OF | SWITZERLAND | *Catalogue*' (printed over illustration of cherub and crystal, printed in pale green). Lower wrapper: blank. All edges trimmed. Binding measurements: 200 × 125mm. (wrappers), 200 × 12mm. (spine).

Publication date: presumably published around April 1946

Price: unknown

Masefield contents:
Foreword ('Most English writers have happy memories of Switzerland...')
    (signed, 'JOHN MASEFIELD O.M. | Poet Laureate, President of | the National Book League')

Notes:

The British Library holds a copy of the special catalogue, *Swiss Books Through Five Centuries* (11914.ff.52) but not, apparently, this catalogue.

Masefield's final sentence states the writer hopes that 'all nations presently imitate Switzerland in the two great points of keeping their freedom and gladly sharing their delights.'

Copies seen: private collection (PWE)

B425 PERCY H. MUIR, *CHILDREN'S BOOKS OF YESTERDAY* 1946

B425(a) *First English edition (1946)*

Children's | *Books* | *of* | *Yesterday* | WITH A FOREWORD BY | THE POET LAUREATE | JOHN MASEFIELD O.M. D.LITT. | NATIONAL BOOK LEAGUE | 7 ALBEMARLE STREET | LONDON W1
(All width centred)

Collation: [A–F]¹⁶; 96 leaves; 169 × 92mm.; [1–3] 4–192

Page contents: [1] title-page; [2] 'NOTE | The Council of the National Book League wishes to | thank the National Magazine Company, Ltd., for the | loan of the collection of children's books which forms | the greater part of this Exhibition, and Mr. Percy

H. | Muir for arranging the Exhibition and preparing the | catalogue. Thanks are also due to Messrs. Warne and | Mr. K. W. G. Duke for the exhibits they have kindly | lent'; [3] [Foreword] ('*I am glad that the first peace-time Exhibition to be held by the National Book League...*') (signed, '*JOHN MASEFIELD*'); 4 'Introduction'; 5–192 text

Paper: wove paper

Running title: none

Binding: white wrappers (printed with pink and white reproduction of illustrated alphabet A-P). Spine: blank. On upper wrapper: 'Children's | Books | of | Yesterday'. Lower wrapper: blank. On inside of upper wrapper: 'NATIONAL BOOK LEAGUE | PRESIDENT: JOHN MASEFIELD, O.M. | [three paragraphs regarding National Book League and details of membership]'. On inside of lower wrapper: 'PRINTED IN GREAT BRITAIN | AT THE PRESS OF | HARDING AND CURTIS, LTD., BATH.' All edges trimmed. Binding measurements: 169 × 92mm. (wrappers), 169 × 8mm. (spine).

Publication date: published, according to the *English Catalogue of Books*, May 1946

Price: 2s.

Masefield contents:
[Foreword] ('I am glad that the first peace-time Exhibition to be held by the National Book League...')
(signed, '*JOHN MASEFIELD*')

Notes:
There are twelve numbered parts (numbered I to XIII but omitting number X). Many of these contain additional titled sections. The titles of the parts are as follows:

I. Instructional	VII. American Juveniles
II. Nursery Rhymes and other Verses	VIII. A Short History of a Famous Publisher
III. Story Books	IX. Children's Games
IV. Illustrated Books	XI. Jig-Saw Puzzles
V. Binding Styles	XII. Peep-Shows
VI. Periodicals	XIII. Four Publishers' Catalogues

The *English Catalogue of Books* while noting the National Book League also cites Cambridge University Press as the publisher of this item. This is not recorded within the item itself.

Copies seen: private collection (PWE); BL (X.907/12323) stamped 15 JUN 1973 rebound

B430 *Ed.* S. WINSTEN, *G.B.S. 90*   1946

B430(a) First English edition (1946)

G.B.S. 90 | Aspects of Bernard Shaw's Life and Work | [sketch of Bernard Shaw by Karel Capek: 53 × 34mm.] | SIR MAX BEERBOHM JOHN MASEFIELD, O.M. J.D. BERNAL, F.R.S. | GILBERT MURRAY, O.M. W.R. INGE LORD KEYNES | LAURENCE HOUSMAN LORD PASSFIELD, O.M. | JAMES BRIDIE C.E.M. JOAD J.B. PRIESTLEY | ALDOUS HUXLEY SIR WILLIAM HALEY | LORD DUNSANY MAURICE DOBB | EDWARD J. DENT VAL GIELGUD | EMIL DAVIES ROY LIMBERT | DANIEL JONES A.S. NEILL | SIR KENNETH BARNES | GABRIEL PASCAL | M. J. MACMANUS | J. C. TREWIN | S. I. HSIUNG | H.G. WELLS | Edited by S. Winsten | HUTCHINSON | *& Co. (Publishers) Ltd.* | LONDON [point] NEW YORK [point] MELBOURNE [point] SYDNEY | 1946
(All width centred)

Collation: [A]⁸ B-H⁸ I⁴ K-N⁸ (J not used); signatures left foot of page; 100 leaves; 229 × 149mm.; [1–10] 11–15 [16] 17–200; illustrations (on glossy paper) tipped-in on pp.[2] and 105; sets of conjugate leaves (on glossy paper) are bound enclosing gatherings B, C, E, F, H, I, L and M (these have been excluded from the gathering information as page numbers do not incorporate these illustration pages)

Page contents: [1] half-title: 'G. B. S. 90'; [2] blank (with additional leaf tipped-in on the verso of which is a colour reproduction of an oil portrait by Clare Winsten: 197 × 150mm. with white panel below containing facsimile signature 'G. Bernard Shaw'; [3] title-page; [4] 'MADE AND PRINTED IN GREAT BRITAIN AT | THE FLEET STREET PRESS | EAST HARDING, E.C.4'; [5] 'TO G.B.S. | ON HIS 90TH BIRTHDAY | [28 facsimile signatures]'; [6] blank; [7] 'CONTENTS' (29 individual items listed with page references); [8] blank; [9–10] 'ILLUSTRATIONS | [rule] | [two colour illustrations, 32 black and white illustrations and three line-drawings listed with page references] | THE REPRODUCTION ON THE TITLE PAGE IS | FROM A SKETCH BY THE LATE KAREL CAPEK'; 11–200 text and illustrations

Paper: wove paper

Running title: 'G.B.S. 90' (19mm.) on verso; recto title comprises section title, pp.12–200

Binding: reddish purple cloth. On spine, in blind: '[rule] | G. B. S. | 90 | – | Aspects | of | Bernard Shaw's | Life and Work | [rule]' (all on gold panel: 64 × 28mm.); at foot, in gold: 'HUTCHINSON'. On upper cover, in gold: silhouette of Bernard Shaw: 67 × 50mm. Lower cover: blank. All edges trimmed. Binding measurements: 236 × 151mm. (covers), 236 × 37mm. (spine). End-papers: wove paper.

Publication date: published, according to the *English Catalogue of Books*, July 1946

Price: 21s.

Masefield contents:
On The Ninetieth Birthday of Bernard Shaw ('After these ninety years, he can survey')
    (headed, 'JOHN MASEFIELD, O.M.')

Notes:
There are twenty-eight articles, in addition to an editorial note. Contributors include Gilbert Murray, J.B. Priestley, H.G. Wells, Max Beerbohm and Aldous Huxley. All contributions commence with drop-capitals except those from H.G. Wells and Sir Max Beerbohm, which comprise letters.

The single sheets tipped-in comprise colour illustrations. The sets of conjugate leaves carry the black and white illustrations.

There are punctuation and word changes between the version of Masefield's poem printed within this volume and the poetry card publication (see D14).

Copies seen: private collection (PWE); BL (10859.dd.33) stamped 16 JUL 1946

B435 LEWIS MASEFIELD, *THE PASSION LEFT BEHIND* 1947

B435(a) First English edition (1947)

THE | PASSION LEFT BEHIND | by | LEWIS MASEFIELD | *with a preface by* | JOHN MASEFIELD | FABER AND FABER LTD | 24 Russell Square | London
(All width centred)

Collation: [A]⁸ B–N⁸ O¹² (J not used); O3 is also signed; signatures left foot of page; 116 leaves; 186 × 119mm.; [1–4] 5–23 [24] 25–232

Page contents: [1] half-title: 'THE PASSION LEFT BEHIND'; [2] blank; [3] title-page; [4] *'First published in Mcmxlvii* | *by Faber and Faber Limited* | *24 Russell Square London W.C.*I | *Printed in Great Britain by* | *Latimer Trend & Co Ltd Plymouth* | *All rights reserved'*; 5–23 'LEWIS CROMMELIN MASEFIELD | (1910–1942)' ('These words about the writer of this book, tell of his chief delights, and the main points in his...') (unsigned); [24] blank; 25–232 text

Paper: wove paper

Running title: none

Binding: blue cloth. On spine, in gold: '[double rule] | *The* | *Passion* | *Left* | *Behind* | [double rule] | *Lewis* | *Mase-* | *field* | *Faber*' (all width centred). Covers: blank. All edges trimmed. Binding measurements: 191 × 121mm. (covers), 191 × 24mm. (spine). End-papers: wove paper.

Publication date: published, according to the *English Catalogue of Books*, February 1947. Other sources suggest publication on 21 March 1947 in an edition of 5083 copies.

Price: 8s.6d.

Masefield contents:
Lewis Crommelin Masefield (1910–1942) ('These words about the writer of this book, tell of his chief delights...')
    (unsigned)

Notes:
There are sixteen numbered chapters, in addition to Masefield's preface.

Lewis Masefield's first novel, *Cross Double Cross*, was published in 1936.

Writing of Masefield's preface, Babington Smith notes the 'quiet dignity and restraint' but concludes that '...only in the final summing up, where nothing but superlatives would do, is there a glimpse of the ageing father's unbearable heartbreak...' (see Constance Babington Smith, *John Masefield – A Life*, Oxford University Press, 1978, p.214)

The novel is set in a London publishing house. In 1933 Masefield had written to C.S. Evans asking if Lewis Masefield might be able to gain some experience within Heinemann. Evans responded:

> I can quite understand your anxiety that your son should be occupied and I am perfectly willing to do anything I can to help. I do not much like the idea of young men working for nothing but if you would really like the boy to come here for six months as a volunteer, let him do so... I should use him in the first instance for the preliminary reading of manuscripts submitted to us, and after a month or two I should be able to form some opinion of his abilities as a reader.

(C.S. Evans, letter to John Masefield, 15 March 1933)
(HRHRC, MS (Masefield, J.) Recip William Heinemann Ltd.)

It appears that Lewis did, for a time, gain experience at Heinemann. In July 1934, for example, it was Lewis who delivered the manuscript of *The Taking of the Gry* to C.S. Evans (see notes to A113(a)).

Masefield wrote to Geoffrey Faber in February 1946 asking whether Faber and Faber would consider publication of the novel. He noted:

> …There are reasons against my offering it to my usual publishers in this country, though I hope to arrange for an American edition with my publishers in New York. I think that the book is remarkable, but not of a kind to sell widely. I have written a preface to it.

(John Masefield, letter to [Geoffrey] Faber, 17 February [1946])

Faber replied stating he was 'much honoured' by Masefield's thought and asked to be sent the manuscript personally. However, he expressed concern about delays in the production of books and asked whether publication in 1947 would be satisfactory. Masefield replied that he understood the difficulties of publishing in 1946 'too well' and the typescript of the novel (together with the preface) was sent on 22 February 1946. Faber read the novel and wrote to Masefield that '…it maintained its hold upon my own mind right up to the end. The play of character is very subtle and remarkable…' The typescript was returned to Masefield in March 1946 for 'final alterations'. Faber received the revised typescript during May 1946. Masefield wrote during the same month noting:

> …there is no need for galley-proofs, thank you, but I'd better see paged proofs, when these are ready. I can usually get through a book of proofs in 24 hours.

(John Masefield, letter to [Geoffrey] Faber, 23 May 1946)

Complimenting Faber and Faber's printers for 'their care and skill' and, later, congratulating 'all responsible for the excellence of the setting', Masefield returned proofs during November 1946.

During September 1946 Metro-Goldwyn-Mayer expressed interest in the book and Masefield consequently asked Faber and Faber to send a proof copy. This was sent during November. One month later it was returned with the comment that it was 'a very distinguished piece of writing' but there was nothing within the novel 'for pictures'.

Copies seen: private collection (PWE); BL (NN.36927) stamped 13 MAR 1947

B435(b) First American edition (1947)

THE PASSION | LEFT BEHIND | *by* | LEWIS MASEFIELD | *with a preface by* | JOHN MASEFIELD | NEW YORK | THE MACMILLAN COMPANY | 1947
(All width centred)

Collation: [A–F]¹⁶ [G]⁴ [H]¹⁶; 116 leaves; 202 × 132mm.; [i–vi] 1–19 [20] 21–224 [225–26]

Page contents: [i] half-title: 'THE PASSION LEFT BEHIND'; [ii] '[publisher's device] | THE MACMILLAN COMPANY | [two lines listing six cities, separated by four points]'; [iii] title-page; [iv] '*Copyright, 1947, by* | THE MACMILLAN COMPANY. | All rights reserved–no part of this book | may be reproduced in any form without | permission in writing from the publisher, | except by a reviewer who wishes to quote brief | passages in connection with a review written | for inclusion in magazine or newspaper. | First Printing. | PRINTED IN THE UNITED STATES OF AMERICA'; [v] 'THE PASSION LEFT BEHIND'; [vi] blank; 1–19 'LEWIS CROMMELIN MASEFIELD | *(1910–1942)*' ('These words about the writer of this book, tell of his chief delights, and the main points in his…') (unsigned); [20] blank; 21–224 text; [225–26] blank

Paper: wove paper

Running title: none

Binding: red cloth. On spine, in white: '*Lewis* | *Masefield* | [rule] | THE | PASSION | LEFT | BEHIND | [rule] | *Macmillan*' (all width centred). Covers: blank. All edges trimmed. Binding measurements: 208 × 136mm. (covers), 208 × 30mm. (spine). End-papers: wove paper.

Publication date: published, around October 1947 (suggested by dates of contemporary reviews)

Price: $2.75

Masefield contents:
as for B435(a)

Notes:
The publishing agreement for this title between Masefield and Macmillan was dated 13 January 1947 (see Archives of The Society of Authors). The agreement refers to 'a licence to publish in volume form in the United States of America and the Philippine Islands a work the subject or title of which is THE PASSION LEFT BEHIND, by Lewis Crommelin Masefield'. John Masefield is named as the 'Proprietor' rather than 'Author'.

Copies seen: private collection (PWE)

B440 NADINE NICOLAEVA-LEGAT, *BALLET EDUCATION* 1947

B440(a) First English edition (1947)

BALLET | EDUCATION | By | NADINE NICOLAEVA-LEGAT | *With a Poem by* JOHN MASEFIELD | *Preface by* SIR PAUL DUKES, K.B.E. | GEOFFREY BLES | 52 DOUGHTY STREET, LONDON
(All width centred)

Collation: [*a*]⁸ *b*⁴ 1–9⁸ 10¹⁰; the second leaf of gathering 10 is also signed; signatures left foot of page with all signatures prefixed by 'B.E.-'; 94 leaves; 248 × 184mm.; [i–iv] v–xiii [xiv] xv–xxiii [xxiv] 1–163 [164]

Page contents: [i] half-title: 'BALLET EDUCATION'; [ii] blank (with additional leaf tipped-in on the verso of which is the black and white photograph frontispiece: 184 × 140mm., *'Photo by Beiny* | THE AUTHOR | [*Frontispiece*]'); [iii] title-page; [iv] 'PRINTED AND MADE BY | HAZELL, WATSON AND | VINEY LIMITED | LONDON AND | AYLESBURY | *First Published* 1947'; v–x 'CONTENTS' (four parts in addition to five other sections (including prefaces, etc.)); xi epigram; xii 'POEM' ('Sweet, lovely dancers, Time will come') (signed, 'JOHN MASEFIELD'); xiii 'ACKNOWLEDGMENTS | I desire to acknowledge valuable assistance received from | Sir Paul Dukes | Gladys Belson, K.B.E. | Nora Wales | Barbara Vernon | John Gregory | during the preparation of this book and to Mme Nijinsky | and Messrs. Victor Gollancz, Ltd., for permission to quote | from *Nijinsky.* | NADINE NICOLAEVA-LEGAT'; [xiv] blank; xv–xvi 'PREFACE' ('In his remarkable book *The Dance of Life*, relating the art of dance to thought...') (signed, 'PAUL DUKES'); xvii–xxii 'INTRODUCTION' ('To understand this book and to derive the greatest benefit from it, the reader...') (signed, 'G.S.'); xxiii 'PREFATORY NOTE' ('I must thank my pupils for having encouraged me to write this book which I planned...') (signed, 'NADINE NICOLAEVA-LEGAT.'); [xxiv] blank; 1–163 text; [164] blank

Paper: wove paper

Running title: 'BALLET EDUCATION' (37mm.) on verso; recto title comprises section title, pp.3–140; additional running titles include those for the introduction and appendices

Binding: yellow cloth. On spine, in blue reading lengthways up spine, from foot: '*BALLET EDUCATION* [five point star] *LEGAT*'; horizontally at foot of spine: '*BLES*'. Covers: blank. All edges trimmed. Binding measurements: 253 × 187mm. (covers), 253 × 28mm. (spine). End-papers: wove paper.

Publication date: published, according to the *English Catalogue of Books*, June 1947

Price: 18s.

Masefield contents:
Poem ('Sweet, lovely dancers, Time will come')
    (signed, 'JOHN MASEFIELD')

Notes:
There are four main parts: 'The Origins of the Russian Ballet', 'Prerequisites', 'Anatomical', and 'Technical'. Also included in the contents listing are Masefield's poem, a preface, an introduction and a prefatory note. There are three appendices.

The 'Acknowledgments' (by Nadine Nicolaeva-Legat) refer to assistance from Barbara Vernon and John Gregory. John Gregory was to compile and edit *Brangwen – The Poet and the Dancer*, a volume containing Masefield's correspondence with Barbara Vernon (see E6).

Copies seen: private collection (ROV)

B445 *NOVELS OF GEORGE DuMAURIER* 1947

B445(a) *First English edition (1947)*

Novels | OF | GEORGE | Du MAURIER | *With the Original Illustrations* | *Trilby* | *The Martians* | *Peter Ibbetson* | With Introductions by | JOHN MASEFIELD, O.M. & DAPHNE Du MAURIER | London | THE PILOT PRESS LTD | and | PETER DAVIES LTD
(All width centred)
(Many of the italic characters are swash)

Collation: 1–22¹⁶ 23²⁰; the third leaf of gathering 23 is also signed; signatures left foot of page; 372 leaves; 214 × 135mm.; [i–vii] viii–xii [xiii] xiv–xviii [1–3] 4–37 [38] 39–71 [72] 73–104 [105] 106–137 [138] 139–75 [176] 177–218 [219–21] 222–47 [248] 249–76 [277] 278–300 [301] 302–328 [329] 330–61 [362] 363–90 [391] 392–421 [422] 423–53 [454–57] 458 [459] 460–85 [486] 487–513 [514] 515–43 [544] 545–71 [572] 573–600 [601] 602–624 [625] 626–50 [651] 652–78 [679] 680–702 [703] 704–726.

Page contents: [i] half-title: 'NOVELS AND STORIES'; [ii] 'OTHER PILOT OMNIBUS TITLES | *Uniform with this Volume* | [point] | [six titles listed]'; [iii] title-page; [iv] '*First published in 1947,* | *by The Pilot Press Ltd.,* | *45 Great Russell Street, London, W.C.I* | PRINTED IN THE NETHERLANDS BY | N.V. VAN MUNSTER'S DRUKKERIJEN | AMSTERDAM'; [v] 'CONTENTS' (five sections listed with page references); [vi] blank; [vii]-xii 'INTRODUCTION TO PETER IBBETSON AND TRILBY' ('The nineteenth century was a time of order, of thought, and of progress.') (headed, 'by JOHN MASEFIELD'); [xiii]-xviii 'INTRODUCTION TO THE MARTIAN' ('George du Maurier, "Kicky" to his family and his friends, was born in Paris...') (headed, 'by D. DU MAURIER'); [1] 'PETER IBBETSON'; [2] blank; [3]-218 text of *Peter Ibbetson*; [219] 'TRILBY'; [220] blank; [221]-453 text of *Trilby*; [454] blank; [455] 'THE MARTIAN'; [456] blank; [457]-726 text of *The Martian* (at foot of page 726: 'THE END')

Paper: wove paper

Running title: 'INTRODUCTION' (23mm.) on both verso and recto, pp.viii–xii and pp.xiv–xviii; 'PETER IBBETSON' (25mm.) on both verso and recto, pp.4–218; 'TRILBY' (11mm.) on both verso and recto, pp.222–453; and 'THE MARTIAN' (21mm.) on both verso and recto, pp.458–726

Binding: cream cloth. On spine: 'Novels | OF | GEORGE | Du MAURIER' (all width centred). Covers: blank. All edges trimmed. Binding measurements: 220 × 138mm. (covers), 220 × 64mm. (spine). End-papers: wove paper.

Publication date: published, according to the *English Catalogue of Books*, September 1947

Price: 16s.

Masefield contents:
Introduction to Peter Ibbetson and Trilby ('The nineteenth century was a time of order, of thought, and of progress.')
        (headed, 'by JOHN MASEFIELD')

Notes:
There appear to be variant bindings of this volume.

Note the incorrect title *The Martians* on the title-page.

Copies seen: private collection (PWE)

B450 *THE WEDDING OF HER ROYAL HIGHNESS PRINCESS ELIZABETH AND LIEUTENANT PHILIP MOUNTBATTEN*   1947

B450(a) First English edition (1947)

[coat of arms] | THE WEDDING OF | HER ROYAL HIGHNESS | PRINCESS ELIZABETH | AND LIEUTENANT | PHILIP MOUNTBATTEN, R.N. | WESTMINSTER ABBEY | 20 NOVEMBER | 1947 (All width centred)

Collation: [A]¹⁶; 16 leaves; 253 × 183mm.; [1] 2–15 [16–17] 18–31 [32]

Page contents: [1] title-page; 2 photograph; 3 'FOREWORD | BY HIS ROYAL HIGHNESS THE | DUKE OF GLOUCESTER | *Chairman of the Administrative Council of | King George's Jubilee Trust*' ('Her Royal Highness Princess Elizabeth has a direct and immediate interest...') (signed, 'Henry.') (facsimile signature); 4–5 photographs; 6 'PRAYER | FOR THE ROYAL MARRIAGE' ('What is the Crown, but something set above') (signed, 'JOHN MASEFIELD | *Poet Laureate*'); 7–8 'THE ROYAL MARRIAGE' ('The Sovereignty of this isle and Commonwealth, to which Princess Elizabeth...') (headed, '*By* G. M. TREVELYAN, O.M.'); 9–13 'THE BRIDE' [text and photographs] ('The first child of Albert Duke of York and Elizabeth his wife was born in the home of...') (unsigned); 14–15 'THE BRIDEGROOM' [text and photographs] ('Lieutenant Philip Mountbatten, formerly known as Prince Philip of Greece...') (unsigned); [16–17] '*Wedding Procession | of Her Royal Highness* PRINCESS ELIZABETH *and Lieutenant* PHILIP MOUNTBATTEN, R.N.' [map and text]; 18 photograph; 19 'THE MARRIAGE SERVICE | *AN INTRODUCTION BY* | HIS GRACE THE LORD ARCHBISHOP OF CANTERBURY' [text and photograph]; 20–23 'CEREMONIAL TO BE OBSERVED...' [text and photographs]; 24–27 'THE FORM OF | SOLEMNIZATION OF MATRIMONY'; 28–29 Ceremonial to be Observed (concluded) [text and photograph]; 30 'Genealogical Table | SHOWING THE DESCENT OF H.R.H. PRINCESS ELIZABETH | AND LIEUTENANT PHILIP MOUNTBATTEN, R.N., | FROM QUEEN VICTORIA'; 31 photograph; [32] 'DEDICATION | OF HER ROYAL HIGHNESS | PRINCESS ELIZABETH | [text] | *Extract from Twenty-first Birthday Broadcast from | Cape Town 21 April, 1947* | * | [rule] | ACKNOWLEDGEMENT *The Council of King George's Jubilee Trust expresses their cordial thanks | to Mr. Arthur G. Cousins, C.B.E., Chairman of Odhams Press Ltd., who have produced this | programme and who are devoting the whole of the profits to the funds of the Trust.* | MADE AND PRINTED IN GREAT BRITAIN | BY ODHAMS (WATFORD) LTD., WATFORD'

Paper: glossy wove paper

Running title: none

Binding: white wrappers. Spine: blank. On upper wrapper: '*By Gracious Permission of His Majesty the King* | [coat of arms in black, yellow, brown, green, gold, blue, red and white] | THE WEDDING OF | HER ROYAL HIGHNESS | PRINCESS ELIZABETH | AND LIEUTENANT | PHILIP MOUNTBATTEN, R.N. | WESTMINSTER ABBEY, 20th NOVEMBER 1947 | SOUVENIR ['2'6' within single ruled circle] PROGRAMME' (within ornate border: 245 × 176mm., text printed in three panels, the title is printed in white on dark blue green panel). Lower wrapper: blank. All edges trimmed. Binding measurements: 253 × 183mm. (wrappers), 253 × 3mm. (spine).

Publication date: published, according to the *English Catalogue of Books*, November 1947

Price: 2s.6d.

Masefield contents:
Prayer for the Royal Marriage ('What is the Crown, but something set above')
        (signed 'JOHN MASEFIELD | *Poet Laureate*')

Notes:
There are a number of drop-capitals and one decorated drop-capital.

Copies seen: private collection (ROV)

B455 *TRIBUTE TO WALTER DE LA MARE* 1948

B455(a) First English editon (1948)

TRIBUTE TO | WALTER DE LA MARE | on his | Seventy-fifth Birthday | [ornate rule including floral design, 82mm.] | FABER AND FABER LIMITED | 24 Russell Square | London
(All width centred)

Collation: [A]⁸ B–L⁸ M¹⁰ (J not used); M2 is also signed; signatures left foot of page; 98 leaves; 220 × 139mm.; [1–4] 5 [6] 7–9 [10] 11 [12–14] 15–102 [103–104] 105–132 [133–34] 135–95 [196]; illustrations (on glossy paper) are tipped-in on pp.[2], [10], [14], 94, [104] and [134]

Page contents: [1] half-title: '*Tribute to | Walter de la Mare | on his | seventy-fifth birthday*'; [2] blank (with additional leaf tipped-in on the verso of which is the frontispiece: 220 × 139mm.); [3] title-page; [4] '*First published in mcmxlviii | by Faber and Faber Limited | 24 Russell Square London W.C.*I | *Printed in Great Britain by | R.MacLehose and Company Limited | The University Press Glasgow | All rights reserved*'; 5 'PUBLISHERS' NOTE' ('This volume is a present to Mr. Walter de la Mare…') (unsigned); [6] blank; 7–8 'CONTENTS' (dedication and 39 individual items listed in three sections with page references); 9 'ILLUSTRATIONS' (six individual items including frontispiece listed with page references); [10] blank (with additional leaf tipped-in on the verso of which is a black and white photograph of de la Mare); 11 'SIR EDWARD MARSH' (Dedicatory); [12] blank; [13] 'I'; [14] blank (with additional leaf tipped-in on the verso of which is a Max Beerbohm caricature); 15–102 text of section I; [103] 'II'; [104] blank (with additional leaf tipped-in on the verso of which is a drawing by William Rothenstein); 105–132 text of section II; [133] 'III'; [134] blank (with additional leaf tipped-in on the verso of which is a black and white photograph of de la Mare); 135–95 text of section III; [196] blank

Paper: laid paper (watermark: '[Crown] | Abbey Mills | Greenfield'), chain-lines 25mm. apart

Running title: running titles comprise name of contributor, pp.16–195

Binding: blue cloth. On spine, in gold: '[design of branches and leaves] | *Tribute | to | Walter | de la | Mare* | [design of branches and leaves] [text on pink panel with curved corners: 96 × 26mm.] | *Faber*'. On upper cover, in blind: oval device including the letters 'WdlM': 36 × 40mm. Lower cover: blank. Top edge gilt, others trimmed. Binding measurements: 225 × 141mm. (covers), 225 × 34mm. (spine). End-papers: wove paper.

Publication date: published, according to the *English Catalogue of Books*, April 1948

Price: 15s.

Masefield contents:
To Walter de la Mare ('By many a door this traveller has stayed,')
(headed, 'JOHN MASEFIELD')

Notes:
Writers who contributed to this volume include J.B. Priestley, J. Dover Wilson, Graham Greene, T.S. Eliot, C. Day Lewis and Siegfried Sassoon. As described by the 'Publisher's Note' on page 5, the arrangement of the volume is as follows:

> First come the prose essays which explore the different aspects of Mr. de la Mare's unique achievement as artist and craftsman both in prose and verse; then the verses written in his honour by the poets; and lastly the offerings of original work by writers whose tributes spontaneously took this form.

Prose contributions commence with drop-capitals.

The '*M*' of '*Mare*' on the spine is particularly ornate.

The 'Publisher's Note' on page 5 states that the idea of the volume 'originated with Dr. W.R. Bett, an old friend of Mr. de la Mare's.' W.R. Bett made the invitations to contribute to the anthology and collected the results.

Masefield, writing to The Society of Authors in 1947 enclosed his contribution:

> Mr Bett, whose letter I send, is getting up a tribute to Mr de la Mare. I enclose the lines I have made, and shall be obliged, if you will kindly send them to him, saying that he may print them in his book. I do not know what he proposes to do about American copyright…
>
> (John Masefield, letter to Miss [S.M.] Perry, 30 July [1947])
> (BL, Add.Mss.56620, f.76)

The Society replied to Masefield having obtained information from the publishers that they proposed doing nothing about American copyright:

> …with regard to the Walter de la Mare volume Messrs. Faber and Faber have replied today:
> "We do not propose to make any arrangements for an American edition, but possibly a few copies of the book will find their way to America and we are assuming that there will be no objection to that."
>
> (Miss S.M. Perry, letter to John Masefield, 11 August 1947)
> (BL, Add.Mss.56620, f.83)

Copies seen: Library of the late Alan Redway (Sotheby's, 11 July 2002, lot 474); BL (10804.pp.21) lacking frontispiece, stamped 14 APR 1948

B460 *THEIR MAJESTIES' SILVER WEDDING PICTORIAL SOUVENIR* 1948

B460(a) First English editon (1948)

Upper wrapper:

Their Majesties' | SILVER WEDDING | PICTORIAL SOUVENIR | [black and white photograph of royal couple riding in carriage]
(All width centred)

Collation: [A]⁸; 8 leaves; 228 × 179mm.; [1–16]

Page contents: [1–2] photographs and captions; [3] two photographs, captions and text of Masefield poem; [4–16] photographs and captions

Paper: glossy wove paper

Running title: none

Binding: decorated wrappers. Spine: blank. On upper wrapper: '*Their Majesties'* | SILVER WEDDING | PICTORIAL SOUVENIR [all within grey panel: 58 × 179mm.] | [black and white photograph of royal couple riding in carriage]'. On lower wrapper: black and white photograph of procession with grey panel (14 × 38mm.) in lower right corner within which: 'Published by | H. A. & W. L. PITKIN LTD. | Clement's Inn, London, W.C.2'. On inside of upper wrapper: 'THE | ROYAL SILVER WEDDING | ANNIVERSARY | [five point star] | *Monday, 26th April, 1948* | [five point star] | HIS MAJESTY'S BROADCAST | [text] | [ornament] | *Text of the broadcast by Her Majesty the Queen is printed on page 3 of the cover*'. On inside of lower wrapper: 'THE | ROYAL SILVER WEDDING | ANNIVERSARY | [five point star] | *Monday, 26th April, 1948* | [five point star] | HER MAJESTY'S BROADCAST | [text] | [ornament]'. All edges trimmed. Binding measurements: 228 × 179mm. (wrappers), 228 × 2mm. (spine).

Publication date: published, according to the *English Catalogue of Books*, June 1948

Price: 2s.6d.

Masefield contents:
Their Majesties' Silver Wedding Anniversary ('We are within the Heavens, sons of light,')
     (headed, 'A Poem By John Masefield, The Poet Laureate')

Notes:
The texts of the broadcasts on the inside of the wrappers both commence with a drop-capital. Curiously the note at the foot of the inside of the upper wrapper suggests a page numbering system for the wrappers alone.

Masefield's poem is printed in two columns (stanzas one and two in a left column and stanzas three and four in a right column). A rule (tapered at both ends) separates the columns. The final stanza is centred at the foot of the two columns.

Copies seen: private collection (ROV)

B465 *MY FAVOURITE ENGLISH POEMS* 1950

B465(a) First English edition (1950)

[ornate panel: 8 × 89mm.] [in blue] | MY FAVOURITE | ENGLISH POEMS | [ornament] | gathered | *with an Introduction by* | JOHN MASEFIELD | WILLIAM [publisher's device of a windmill] HEINEMANN | MELBOURNE LONDON TORONTO | [ornate panel (in mirror image of previous panel): 8 × 89mm.] [in blue]
(Text lines 1–2 justified on both left and right margins, all other lines width centred)
(The type includes characters in outline)

Bibliographies: Handley-Taylor p.66, Wight [unrecorded]

Collation: [A]¹⁶ B–K¹⁶ [L]¹² (J not used); the fifth leaf of gatherings A–K is also signed; L3 is also signed; signatures right foot of page; 172 leaves; 197 × 129mm.; [four un-numbered pages] [i–iv] v–xxvii [xxviii] 1–305 [306] 307–310 [311–12]

Page contents: [-] blank (page excluded from page count, but constitutes first leaf of first gathering); [-] blank; [-] blank (page excluded from page count, but constitutes second leaf of first gathering); [-] blank; [i] half-title: 'MY FAVOURITE | ENGLISH POEMS'; [ii] '*THE WORKS OF JOHN MASEFIELD* | PLAYS: | [12 titles listed] | POETRY: | [20 titles listed] | FICTION: | [14 titles listed] | GENERAL: | [15 titles listed]'; [iii] title-page; [iv] 'FIRST PUBLISHED 1950 | PRINTED IN GREAT BRITAIN | AT THE WINDMILL PRESS | KINGSWOOD, SURREY'; v–viii '*Contents*' (Introduction, 45 authors' entries, alphabetical list of author's names, and index listed with page references); ix–xxvii '*Introduction*' ('For a good many years, when upon the long journeys and voyages once so pleasant...') (signed, 'JOHN MASEFIELD'); [xxviii] blank; 1–305 text; [306] 'ALPHABETICAL LIST OF AUTHORS' NAMES'; 307–310 'INDEX TO AUTHORS, SOURCES, POEMS, EXCERPTS | AND SINGLE LINES.'; [311–12] blank

Paper: wove paper

Running title: 'INTRODUCTION' (30mm.) on both verso and recto, pp.x–xxvii; other running titles comprise name of author on both verso and recto, pp.3–305

B400(a) upper wrapper

The Nazi
𝕶𝖚𝖑𝖙𝖚𝖗
in Poland

by
several authors
of necessity
temporarily anonymous

LONDON
Published for the POLISH MINISTRY OF INFORMATION *by*
HIS MAJESTY'S STATIONERY OFFICE

B405(a) title-page

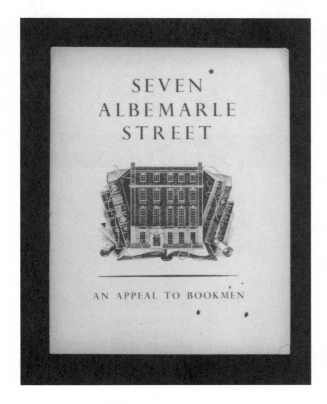

B415(a) upper wrapper

BOOKS
OF
SWITZERLAND

*Exhibition
arranged under the auspices of
the British Council*

April 26th – May 25th
1946

CATALOGUE

Suffolk Galleries
Suffolk Street, Pall Mall East – Haymarket
London S.W.1.

B420(a) title-page

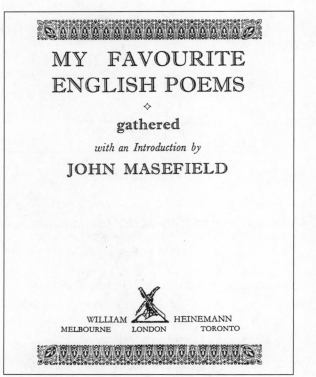

B465(a) title-page

B480(a) upper wrapper

Binding: light blue cloth. On spine, in gold: '[triple rule] | MY | FAVOURITE | ENGLISH | POEMS | [five point asterisk] | *gathered by* | JOHN | MASEFIELD [all on black panel: 79 × 27mm.] | [triple rule] | HEINEMANN' (all width centred). On upper cover: oval design of lake, swans, trees and temple within single oval border and surrounded by ornate oval border: 36 × 45mm. On lower cover, in blind: publisher's device of a windmill (ranged lower right). All edges trimmed. Binding measurements: 203 × 131mm. (covers), 203 × 34mm. (spine). End-papers: wove paper.

Publication date: published, according to Handley-Taylor, 10 July 1950; published, according to *Whitaker's*, 7 July 1950; the sales ledger preserved in the Heinemann Archive suggests publication on 10 July 1950 in an edition of 6000 copies

Price: 10s.6d.

Masefield contents:
Introduction ('For a good many years, when upon the long journeys and voyages once so pleasant...')
(signed, 'JOHN MASEFIELD')

Notes:
Masefield's foreword commences with a drop-capital.

Masefield notes his scope in the introduction. The volume contains 'only the work of poets, accepted generally as Englishmen, and mainly resident here' and 'exclude[s] any poem, or version of a poem, first written after 1849, so that nothing in the book shall be younger than a hundred years'. In addition to this time limit he adds another: 'to the best of my knowledge, I have put in nothing that I have not loved or admired for fifty years'.

Heinemann appear to have had early concerns about the ordering of material:

> We have now looked through the Anthology of Poetry which you have prepared and have read your interesting introduction. We would propose to make a Demy octavo book of it... I see the plan of the Anthology. But it gives us a few pages of Langland and 45 pages of Chaucer as the opening, and to anyone who is not already a lover of Chaucer this could be daunting. I can see that you may not want to change this order of things, but here is our suggestion. We might begin, for instance, with your favourite poem or poet. This would give the book an even more personal flavour. Or possibly the poet who has influenced you most might come first...
>
> (Louisa Callender, letter to John Masefield, 13 July 1949)
> (HRHRC, MS (Masefield, J.) Recip William Heinemann Ltd.)

Masefield evidently rejected the publisher's suggestions. He presumably suggested that it was Chaucer who had great early influence. Louisa Callender responded:

> ...I thought that you might not want to change the order of the book, and as the contents are really a personal choice, perhaps it would be well to leave them as they stand. As you say, most of your readers know of your great liking for Chaucer...
>
> (Louisa Callender, letter to John Masefield, 21 July 1949)
> (HRHRC, MS (Masefield, J.) Recip William Heinemann Ltd.)

It appears that there was some discussion of potential titles for this volume. Frere wrote:

> Have you made your final decision as to the exact title for your book? There was talk of naming it THE LAUREATE'S ANTHOLOGY, but you may have something else in mind.
>
> (A.S. Frere, letter to John Masefield, 2 November 1949)
> (HRHRC, MS (Masefield, J.) Recip William Heinemann Ltd.)

Masefield, it appears, then chose the title that was eventually used. Frere responded:

> ...I like very much your title MY FAVOURITE ENGLISH POEMS, gathered, with an Introduction, by John Masefield.
>
> (A.S. Frere, letter to John Masefield, 4 November 1949)
> (HRHRC, MS (Masefield, J.) Recip William Heinemann Ltd.)

A 'revise' of the volume, together with 'previous corrected proof' was sent to Masefield at the beginning of March (see B.F. Oliver, letter to John Masefield, 10 March 1950) (HRHRC, MS (Masefield, J.) Recip William Heinemann Ltd.) Just over three months later Frere provided an advance copy:

> ...I have much pleasure in sending you herewith an advance copy just off the press of MY FAVOURITE ENGLISH POEMS. Publication date is July 10th.
>
> (A.S. Frere, letter to John Masefield, 20 June 1950)
> (HRHRC, MS (Masefield, J.) Recip William Heinemann Ltd.)

Copies seen: private collection (PWE); BL (11605.bbb.1) stamped 20 JUN 1950

B465(b) First American edition (1950)

[ornate panel: 8 × 89mm.] [in blue] | MY FAVOURITE | ENGLISH POEMS | [ornament] | gathered | *with an Introduction by* | JOHN MASEFIELD | NEW YORK | THE MACMILLAN COMPANY | 1950 | [ornate panel (in mirror image of previous panel): 8 × 89mm.] [in blue]
(Text lines 1–2 justified on both left and right margins, all other lines width centred)
(The type includes characters in outline)

Bibliographies: Handley-Taylor [unrecorded], Wight [unrecorded]

Collation: [A]¹⁶ B-K¹⁶ [L]¹² (J not used); the fifth leaf of gatherings A-K is also signed; L3 is also signed; signatures right foot of page; 172 leaves; 197 × 129mm.; [four un-numbered pages] [i–iv] v–xxvii [xxviii] 1–305 [306] 307–310 [311–12]

Page contents: [-] blank (page excluded from page count, but constitutes first leaf of first gathering); [-] blank; [-] blank (page excluded from page count, but constitutes second leaf of first gathering); [-] blank; [i] half-title: 'MY FAVOURITE | ENGLISH POEMS'; [ii] '*THE WORKS OF JOHN MASEFIELD* | PLAYS: | [12 titles listed] | POETRY: | [20 titles listed] | FICTION: | [14 titles listed] | GENERAL: | [15 titles listed]'; [iii] title-page; [iv] 'COPYRIGHT 1950 BY JOHN MASEFIELD | PRINTED IN GREAT BRITAIN'; v–viii '*Contents*' (Introduction, 45 authors' entries, alphabetical list of author's names, and index listed with page references); ix–xxvii '*Introduction*' ('For a good many years, when upon the long journeys and voyages once so pleasant...') (signed, 'JOHN MASEFIELD'); [xxviii] blank; 1–305 text; [306] 'ALPHABETICAL LIST OF AUTHORS' NAMES'; 307–310 'INDEX TO AUTHORS, SOURCES, POEMS, EXCERPTS | AND SINGLE LINES.'; [311–12] blank

Paper: wove paper

Running title: 'INTRODUCTION' (30mm.) on both verso and recto, pp.x–xxvii; other running titles comprise name of author on both verso and recto, pp.3–305

Binding: light blue cloth. On spine, in gold: '[triple rule] | MY | FAVOURITE | ENGLISH | POEMS | [five point asterisk] | *gathered by* | JOHN | MASEFIELD [all on black panel: 30 × 21mm.] | [triple rule] | MACMILLAN' (all width centred). On upper cover: oval design of lake, swans, trees and temple within single oval border and surrounded by ornate oval border: 36 × 45mm. Lower cover: blank. All edges trimmed. Binding measurements: 201 × 131mm. (covers), 201 × 34mm. (spine). End-papers: wove paper.

Publication date: published, around November 1950 (suggested by dates of contemporary reviews)

Price: $2.75

Masefield contents:
as for B465(a)

Notes:
Masefield's foreword commences with a drop-capital.

This American edition has obvious similarities to B465(a). However, unlike similar examples, the title-page in this edition is not a cancellan. Early in the production of the volume, Heinemann informed Masefield that '...Messrs. Macmillans might take some copies from us. They have, in fact, written to me asking for a price for bound copies...' (see Louisa Callender, letter to John Masefield, 29 July 1949) (HRHRC, MS (Masefield, J.) Recip William Heinemann Ltd.)

Copies seen: NYPL ((NCI 1950) 558508B 10 OCT 1950 noted on page v

B470 *SOUVENIR BROCHURE BOROUGH OF CROSBY FESTIVAL OF BRITAIN*
SHIPPING EXHIBITION   1951

B470(a) *First English edition (1951)*

Upper wrapper:
[coat of arms] | [shield showing sailing vessels and three wavy lines] | SOUVENIR BROCHURE [within banner] | BOROUGH OF CROSBY [in black with white surround] | FESTIVAL OF BRITAIN [in white] | SHIPPING EXHIBITION [in black with white surround] | AUGUST [in white] | [Festival of Britain device] [in black, blue and white] 1951 [in white] [Festival of Britain device] [in black, blue and white]
(All width centred. The background is a blue panel (with silver border) above a silver panel (with blue border))

Collation: [A]⁵ ([A]4 +1) [B-E]⁸; 37 leaves; 216 × 140mm.; 1–4 [5] 6–7 [8–9] 10–62 [63] 64–74

Page contents: [1] 'FOREWORD.' ('No sea-port known to me has seen finer displays of ships than Liverpool.') (signed, 'John Masefield') (facsimile signature); 2 'The Chairman's Message'; 3 'Hon. Organizer's Message'; 4–[5] 'SHIPPING EXHIBITION OFFICIALS' (listing and photographs); 6 'Letters of apology for inability to be present...'; 7 photographs; [8–10] advertisements; 11 programme for 11 August 1951 (opening); 12 advertisement; 13 programme for 11 August 1951 (parade); 14 'HARBOUR BAR' ('All in the feathered palm tree tops the bright green parrots screech,') (signed, 'JOHN MASEFIELD'); 15 programme for 12 August 1951 (service); 16 'THE NELSON ROOM' ('When the greatest of England's seamen fell') (signed 'J.S. HICKS') and 'STONE FRIGATE' ('"Sad and fretful and office bound') (signed, 'J.S. HICKS'); 17 'SHIPPING EXHIBITION'; 18 'BIG STEAMERS' ('"Oh, where are you going to, all you big steamers,') (signed, 'RUDYARD KIPLING') and 'BUILDING OF A SHIP' ('Build me straight, O worthy master,') (unsigned); 19–25 shipping exhibition (continued) and advertisements; 26 'SAILING SHIPS' ('These splendid ships, each with her grace and glory,') (signed, 'JOHN MASEFIELD') and 'HELL'S PAVEMENT' ('When I'm discharged in Liverpool 'n' draw my bit o' pay') (signed, 'JOHN MASEFIELD'); 27–47 shipping exhibition (continued) and advertisements; 47 [untitled poem] ('Fear not each sudden sound and shock,') (unsigned); 48 advertisement; 49 'GRAND FILM SHOW' (listing); 50 advertisement; 51 '...Ships' Models Regatta' (listing); 52 advertisement; 53 'GRAND SHIPPING and NAVAL BALL' (listing); 54

advertisement; 55 'THE CAFE AND ICE CREAM BAR' (listing); 56 advertisement; 57 '...MODEL of R.M.S. "Queen Elizabeth"...' (described); 58 advertisement; 59–61 'THANK YOU' and advertisements; 62–74 advertisements

Paper: glossy wove paper (gathering [A]) / wove paper (gatherings [B–E])

Running title: none

Binding: printed wrappers. Spine: blank. On upper wrapper: described above. Lower wrapper: advertisement (for Mazda lighting). On inside of upper wrapper: advertisement (for John G. Routledge Deep-Sea Diving). On inside of lower wrapper: advertisement (for Threlfalls Blue Label Ales). All edges trimmed. Binding measurements: 224 × 142mm. (wrappers), 224 × 7mm. (spine). The wrappers extend beyond the edges of the internal leaves.

Publication date: presumably published, August 1951

Price: unknown

Masefield contents:
Foreword ('No sea-port known to me has seen finer displays of ships than Liverpool.')
    (signed, 'John Masefield') (facsimile signature)
Harbour Bar ('All in the feathered palm tree tops the bright green parrots screech,')
    (signed, 'JOHN MASEFIELD')
Sailing Ships ('These splendid ships, each with her grace and glory,')
    (signed, 'JOHN MASEFIELD')
Hell's Pavement ('When I'm discharged in Liverpool 'n' draw my bit o' pay')
    (signed, 'JOHN MASEFIELD')

Notes:
The acknowledgements ('Thank You') section includes:

    To the Society of Authors, London S.W.10, and Dr. John Masefield, O.M. for permission to use poems.

The brochure was printed by Chathams Ltd., Liverpool.

The first 'gathering' of five leaves comprises a gathering of four leaves with a fifth leaf tipped-in on the fourth leaf of the true gathering.

Copies seen: ULL (Special Collections) includes posthumous booklabel

B475 *THE CORONATION OF HER MAJESTY QUEEN ELIZABETH II 2 JUNE 1953*   1953

B475(a) *First English edition (1953)*

[coat of arms with '[point] DIEU [point] [point] ET [point] MON [point] [point] DROIT [point]'] | THE CORONATION | OF HER MAJESTY | QUEEN | ELIZABETH II | 2 JUNE 1953 | STATES UNDER HER MAJESTY'S PROTECTION | BRUNEI FEDERATION OF MALAYA MALDIVE ISLANDS TONGA | TRUST TERRITORIES | CAMEROONS TOGOLAND NAURU [device with head of giraffe within double ruled circle and 'TANGANYIKA'] NEW GUINEA WESTERN SAMOA | [crown and 'E II R'] | WORLD COPYRIGHT RESERVED PRINTED IN ENGLAND
(All width centred with lines 1–6 within panel and lines 7–10 within lower panel. All surrounded by names and pictures of commonwealth countries: 222 × 157mm. The final line is outside the border)

Collation: [A]²⁰; 20 leaves; 248 × 179mm.; [1] 2–39 [40]

Page contents: [1] title-page; 2 'LINES ON THE CORONATION OF OUR GRACIOUS SOVEREIGN' ('This Lady whom we crown was born') (signed, 'JOHN MASEFIELD | *Poet Laureate*'); 3–6 photographs (with captions); 7 'A FOREWORD | BY HIS ROYAL HIGHNESS THE | DUKE OF GLOUCESTER | *Chairman of the Administrative Council of | King George's Jubilee Trust*' ('With the approval of Her Majesty the Queen, King George's Jubilee Trust has once again...') (signed, 'Henry.') (facsimile signature); 8–9 'THE QUEEN'S MAJESTY' ('A Coronation is a nation's birthday. It is the day on which its people...') (headed, 'BY ARTHUR BRYANT'); 10–12 'QUEEN ELIZABETH II' (text and photographs) ('Her Royal Highness Princess Elizabeth Alexandra Mary, first child of...') (headed, 'BY DERMOT MORRAH'); 13–19 'THE CORONATION PROCESSION' (part one); 20–21 'CORONATION PROCESSION | OF HER MAJESTY QUEEN ELIZABETH II' [map and text]; 22–25 The Coronation Procession (continued); 26–29 'THE | CORONATION CEREMONY' ('The daughter and heiress of King George VI comes to Westminster Abbey to be...') (headed, 'By the HON. SIR GEORGE BELLEW, Garter Principal King of Arms'); 30 'THE CORONATION SERVICE | AN INTRODUCTION' ('The Coronation is the occasion for much splendid pageantry: it would be...') (headed, 'BY HIS GRACE THE LORD ARCHBISHOP OF CANTERBURY'); 31–39 'The Form and Order of | Her Majesty's Coronation'; [40] 'A GENEALOGICAL TABLE | SHOWING THE DESCENT OF THE CROWN' (at foot of p.[40]: '*Printed and distributed for King George's Jubilee Trust by Odhams Press Limited, Long Acre, London, W.C.2, England.* (G)')

Paper: glossy wove paper

Running title: none

Binding: beige wrappers. Spine: blank. On upper wrapper: 'PUBLISHED BY GRACIOUS PERMISSION OF | HER MAJESTY THE QUEEN | [embossed coat of arms in gold, black, white, red and blue] | THE CORONATION | OF HER MAJESTY | [three wavy rules in gold] QUEEN [three wavy rules in gold] | ELIZABETH II | APPROVED SOUVENIR PROGRAMME | KING GEORGE'S ['2'6' within single ruled circle] JUBILEE TRUST' (within ornate border in gold: 231 × 164mm.) Text printed in three panels. Lower wrapper: blank. All edges trimmed. Binding measurements: 248 × 179mm. (wrappers), 248 × 3mm. (spine)

Publication date: presumably published around May 1953

Price: 2s.6d.

Masefield contents:
Lines on the Coronation of Our Gracious Sovereign ('This Lady whom we crown was born')
    (signed, 'JOHN MASEFIELD | *Poet Laureate*')

Notes:
There are a number of drop-capitals and one decorated drop-capital.

With the exception of p.[1] and the centrefold, all pages are enclosed within the same design of decorated, ornate borders. This is signed at centre foot: 'gf'.

Copies seen: private collection (ROV)

B480 *CORONATION OF HER MAJESTY QUEEN ELIZABETH II 2nd JUNE 1953*   *PROGRAMME OF FESTIVITIES IN THE CITY OF HEREFORD*   1953

B480(a)   *First English edition (1953)*

CORONATION OF | HER MAJESTY | QUEEN ELIZABETH II | 2nd JUNE 1953 | PROGRAMME OF FESTIVITIES | IN THE | CITY OF HEREFORD | Price 1/- | Published under the Authority of the Hereford City Council | and printed by Jakemans Limited, 31 Church Street, Hereford
(All in blue with lines 1–4 enclosed within ornate border in red: 41 × 80mm. All within ornate border in blue: 154 × 111mm. and ornate border in red: 160 × 118mm. The head of the border is missing so as to accommodate a crown (in blue and red) and two union flags (in blue and red))

Collation: [A]⁸; 8 leaves; 222 × 138mm.; [1–16]

Page contents: [1] title-page; [2–16] text, maps and photographs

Paper: glossy wove paper

Running title: none

Binding: beige wrappers. Spine: blank. On upper wrapper: '[colour photograph of Elizabeth II laid-down within blue and red ornate border: 129 × 88mm.] | Coronation | Souvenir Programme | CITY OF [crest with legend 'IN VICTÆ FIDELITATIS PRÆMIUM'] HEREFORD' (all within blue and red ornate border: 146 × 118mm., the upper line is intercepted by the rectangle containing the photograph of Elizabeth II, the lower line is broken by the crest). Lower wrapper: blank. All edges trimmed. Binding measurements: 222 × 138mm. (wrappers), 222 × 1mm. (spine).

Publication date: presumably published, according to an inscribed copy, around 20 May 1953

Price: 1s.

Masefield contents:
Prologue for the Hereford Pageant... ('Roses and hopyards; and cattle and corn,')
    (signed, 'JOHN MASEFIELD')

Notes:
With the exception of the final two pages, all pages include ornate borders. Printing (of text, maps and illustrations) is in red and blue.

Page [3] presents Masefield's contribution beneath a photograph of the author. The full title reads 'Prologue for the Hereford Pageant from the Poet Laureate Mr. John Masefield, D.LITT., LITT.D., L.L.D. (Honorary Freeman of the City of Hereford).'

Copies seen: private collection (ROV); HRHRC (HRC TEMP M377 CPR 1953) inscribed 'For Con | from Jan | 20th May. 1953

B485 *SSAFA SEARCHLIGHT TATTOO AT THE WHITE CITY STADIUM*   1953

B485(a)   *First English edition (1953)*

[five line device] SS A F A [five-line device (in mirror image of first device)] | SEARCHLIGHT | TATTOO | AT THE WHITE CITY STADIUM | ON JULY 13th, 14th, 15th, 16th, & 17th, 1953 | AT 7.30 p.m. | Organised by and in aid of | The Soldiers', Sailors' and Airmen's Families Association | and the Officers' Branch of SS A F A. | DIRECTOR OF APPEALS AND PUBLICITY FOR SS A F A | Air Chief Marshal SIR PHILIP JOUBERT, | K.C.B.,

C.M.G., D.S.O. | TATTOO PRODUCER | Lt.-Colonel G. R. G. HART | DEPUTY DIRECTOR OF APPEALS AND PUBLICITY | Major M. C. G. ANDREWS | [device of SSAFA with text within circular device headed by crown] | [double rule]
(All width centred except lines 2–9 which are justified on left margin)

Collation: [A]¹⁶; 16 leaves; 226 × 151mm.; [1–32]

Page contents: [1] black and white photograph: 'HER MAJESTY QUEEN ELIZABETH II | Patron of | THE SOLDIERS', SAILORS' & AIRMEN'S FAMILIES | ASSOCIATION' (within ornate floral border); [2] advertisement; [3] title-page; [4] 'INTRODUCTION' ('In welcoming you to this, the second SSAFA Searchlght Tattoo at the White City...') (headed, '*by Air Chief Marshal Sir Philip Joubert* | K.C.B., C.M.G., D.S.O.'); [5] programme summary; [6] advertisement; [7–29] programme and advertisements; [30–31] description of SSAFA; [32] acknowledgements

Paper: glossy wove paper

Running title: none

Binding: decorated wrappers. Spine: blank. On upper wrapper: 'SSAFA [in yellow] | Searchlight [in white] | Tattoo [in white] | [illustration of horses and rider] [in dark purple, light purple, black, white, red, yellow, blue and brown] | [white panel (79 × 129mm.) upon which: 'Souvenir Programme | [rule (tapered at both ends with five point star at centre)] | WHITE CITY STADIUM, JULY 1953 | Price One Shilling | *In aid of* | THE SOLDIERS', SAILORS' & AIRMEN'S FAMILIES ASSOCIATION | AND THE OFFICERS' BRANCH OF SSAFA]' (all text outside panel justified on left margin, all text within panel width centred). Lower wrapper: colour advertisement for 'ILFORD LIMITED'. On inside of upper wrapper: advertisement (for Haig Whisky). On inside of lower wrapper: advertisement (for National Savings). All edges trimmed. Binding measurements: 226 × 151mm. (wrappers), 226 × 2mm. (spine).

Publication date: presumably published, July 1953

Price: 1s.

Masefield contents:
[Untitled] ('Here ends the Pageant of how England stood'
        (headed, 'by the Poet Laureate, JOHN MASEFIELD')
Epilogue ('Now the loud play is quiet; Night descends;'
        (signed, 'by the Poet Laureate, JOHN MASEFIELD')

Notes:
The first poem (commencing 'Here ends the Pageant of how England stood') was printed in *The Times* for 14 July 1953. It was, within that newspaper, similarly untitled.

Within the acknowledgements on the final page of this pamphlet appears the printing information: 'Programmes printed by A.C. Phillips, Honduras St., E.C.1.'

Copies seen: private collection (ROV)

B490 *Ed.* J. LENNOX KERR. *TOUCHING THE ADVENTURES OF MERCHANTMEN IN THE SECOND WORLD WAR*   1953

B490(a) *First English edition (1953)*

Touching the Adventures... | OF MERCHANTMEN IN THE | SECOND WORLD WAR | *Edited by* | *J. LENNOX KERR* | *With a Foreword by* | *JOHN MASEFIELD* | *O.M. D.Litt.* | [publisher's device of horse and letter 'H': 16 × 15mm.] | GEORGE G. HARRAP & CO. LTD | LONDON TORONTO WELLINGTON SYDNEY
(All width centred with lines 2 and 3 justified on same left and right margins)

Collation: [A]⁸ B-Q⁸ (J not used); signatures left foot of page; 128 leaves; 198 × 132mm.; [1–5] 6–7 [8] 9 [10–11] 12 [13] 14–21 [22] 23–31 [32] 33–50 [51] 52–58 [59] 60–71 [72] 73–81 [82] 83–92 [93] 94–106 [107] 108–118 [119] 120–29 [130] 131–39 [140] 141–48 [149] 150–59 [160] 161–64 [165] 166–74 [175] 176–84 [185] 186–92 [193] 194–202 [203] 204–214 [215] 216–25 [226] 227–36 [237] 238–46 [247] 248–52 [253–54] 255–56

Page contents: [1] half-title: '*Touching the Adventures*'; [2] frontispiece: 69 × 72mm., '*Touching the Adventures and Perils ... they* | *are of the Seas, Men-of-war, Fire, Enemies,* | *Pirates, Rovers, Thieves, Jettisons, Letters of* | *Mart, and Countermart, Surprisals, Takings at* | *Sea, Arrests, Restraints and Detainments of all* | *Kings, Princes and People ... and of all other* | *Perils.* | Extract from | Lloyd's Marine Insurance Policy'; [3] title-page; [4] '*First published in Great Britain* 1953 | *by* GEORGE G. HARRAP & CO. LTD | 182 High Holborn, London, W.C.1 | *Copyright. All rights reserved* | [rule] | *Composed in Fournier type and printed by* | *Western Printing Services Ltd, Bristol* | *Made in Great Britain*'; [5]-7 'FOREWORD' ('From early childhood most Britons are given stories of the sea to read, so that they grow...') (signed, 'JOHN MASEFIELD'); [8]-9 'PREFACE'; [10] poetic preface; [11]-12 'CONTENTS' (27 items including glossary listed with page references); [13]-256 text

Paper: wove paper

Running title: 'TOUCHING THE ADVENTURES' (48mm.) on verso; recto title comprises contribution title, pp.6–256

Binding: navy blue cloth. On spine, in gold: '*Touching the* | *Adventures...* | of | Merchantmen | in the | Second | World War | [eight point star] | *Edited by* | J. LENNOX KERR | [ornament] | Harrap'. Covers: blank. All edges trimmed. Binding measurements: 202 × 134mm. (covers), 202 × 35mm. (spine). End-papers: wove paper.

Publication date: published, according to *Whitaker's*, 21 September 1953

Price: 12s.6d.

Masefield contents:
Foreword ('From early childhood most Britons are given stories of the sea to read, so that they grow...')
    (signed, 'JOHN MASEFIELD')

Notes:
There are twenty-six contributions of poems or short stories in addition to Masefield's foreword, a preface by the editor J. Lennox Kerr and a glossary.

The preface by J. Lennox Kerr refers to Masefield's contribution:

> ...it is a great honour to be able to thank the Poet Laureate and fellow-seaman, John Masefield, O.M., for so generously contributing his splendid Foreword.

J. Lennox Kerr mentions, in the preface, the role of Ronald Hope:

> The tedious clerical work and organization involved in gathering these stories was undertaken and painstakingly carried out by Dr Ronald Hope, M.A., and his staff at the Seafarers' Education Service without fee...

Ronald Hope was to contribute an introduction to the 1978 volume of Masefield's sea poetry entitled *The Sea Poems* (see A174).

Copies seen: private collection (ROV)

B495 RUFUS NOEL-BUXTON, *THE FORD*   1955

B495(a) First English editon (1955)

The Ford [in red] | Rufus Noel-Buxton | WITH A FOREWORD BY THE POET LAUREATE | [illustration of a tree and a heron standing on the banks of a ford] | *You are a British tribesman at the ford* | THE CARAVEL PRESS | ST MARYLEBONE [point] LONDON | [rule, 69mm.] | MCMLV
(All width centred)

Collation: [A]⁴ B-C⁴ D⁶; signatures left foot of page; 18 leaves; 196 × 137mm.; [1–8] 9–11 [12] 13–32 [33–36]

Page contents: [1–2] blank; [3] half-title: 'THE FORD'; [4] blank; [5] title-page; [6] 'Other books by Rufus Noel-Buxton | WITHOUT THE RED FLAG | NO SMOOTH JOURNEY | *Shakespeare Head Press, Oxford* | *Copyright* | First Edition November 1955 | Printed in Great Britain at | The Caravel Press, Moxon Street, Marylebone, London, W.I'; [7] 'FOREWORD' ('The last sixty years have given to many millions of people a knowledge of the roads...') (signed, 'JOHN MASEFIELD | *Summer 1955*'); [8] blank; 9–11 'INTRODUCTION' ('Arguments have long persisted over the point on the Lower Thames which Caesar...') (unsigned); [12] blank; 13–[33] text; [34–36] blank

Paper: wove paper

Running title: none

Binding: light purple cloth. On spine, reading lengthways down spine from head, in grey: 'THE FORD [point] Rufus Noel-Buxton.' On upper cover, in white: 'THE FORD'. All edges trimmed. Binding measurements: 202 × 140mm. (covers), 202 × 15mm. (spine). End-papers: wove paper.

Publication date: published, according to date within volume, November 1955

Price: 6s.

Masefield contents:
Foreword ('The last sixty years have given to many millions of people a knowledge of the roads...')
    (signed, 'JOHN MASEFIELD | *Summer 1955*')

Notes:
The conclusion of poem IX comprises a line in italics. It reads '*The days that make us happy make us wise.*' This is presumably a quotation from Masefield's poem 'Biography' (first printed in *The English Review* in May 1912). The line was frequently used by Masefield when signing inscriptions. See also the 1964 Wilkinson Christmas card (J120).

The foreword and introduction both commence with a drop-capital in outline.

Copies seen: private collection (PWE); BL (11661.bb.9) stamped 23 DEC 1955

B485(a) upper wrapper

Touching the Adventures...

OF MERCHANTMEN IN THE
SECOND   WORLD   WAR

Edited by
J. LENNOX KERR

With a Foreword by
JOHN MASEFIELD
O.M. D.Litt.

GEORGE G. HARRAP & CO. LTD
LONDON   TORONTO   WELLINGTON   SYDNEY

B490(a) title-page

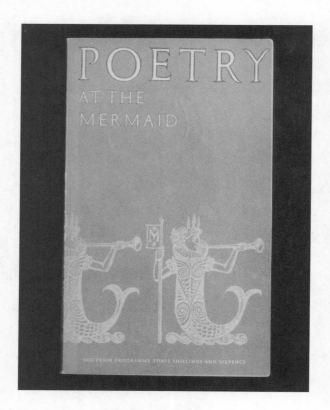

B525(a) upper wrapper

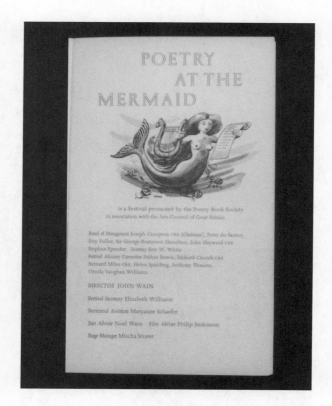

B525(a) title-page

THE THOMAS LAMONT FAMILY

by

Reverend Thomas Lamont
Thomas William Lamont
Thomas Stilwell Lamont
Corliss Lamont
Margaret Lamont Heap

with Recollections and Poems *by*
John Masefield

EDITED BY CORLISS LAMONT

HORIZON PRESS   NEW YORK   1962

B535(a) title-page

THE
THOMAS LAMONTS
IN AMERICA

by

Corliss Lamont
Edward Miner Lamont
Thomas Stilwell Lamont
The Reverend Thomas Lamont
Thomas William Lamont
Thomas William Lamont II
Margaret Lamont Heap
Francis T. P. Plimpton
Nathan M. Pusey

with Recollections and Poems
by
John Masefield

Edited by CORLISS LAMONT

SOUTH BRUNSWICK AND NEW YORK : A. S. BARNES AND COMPANY
LONDON : THOMAS YOSELOFF LTD

B575(a) title-page

B500 ANDREW YOUNG, *PROSPECT OF A POET* 1957

B500(a) First English edition (1957)

ANDREW YOUNG | *PROSPECT OF A POET* | *Essays and tributes by fourteen writers* | *edited by* | LEONARD CLARK | [publisher's device of a fox] | RUPERT HART-DAVIS | SOHO SQUARE LONDON | 1957
(All width centred)

Collation: [A]⁸ B-G⁸; signatures left foot of page; 56 leaves; 184 × 112mm.; [1–4] 5 [6] 7 [8] 9–22 [23–24] 25–105 [106] 107 [108] 109–112; the frontispiece (on glossy paper) is tipped-in on page [2]

Page contents: [1] half-title: 'ANDREW YOUNG | *Prospect of a Poet*'; [2] blank (with additional leaf tipped-in on the verso of which is the black and white photograph frontispiece: 104 × 79mm., 'ANDREW YOUNG, 1956'); [3] title-page; [4] '© Leonard Clark, 1957 | PRINTED IN GREAT BRITAIN BY | THE BOWERING PRESS, PLYMOUTH'; 5 'CONTENTS' (16 items listed with page references); [6] blank; 7 four quotations (from John Freeman, Humbert Wolfe, Walter de la Mare and Wordsworth); [8] blank; 9–10 'PREFACE' ('It gives me much pleasure to take part in this honouring of the poetry of Canon Andrew Young.') (signed, 'John Masefield'); 11–21 'INTRODUCTION' ('The work of Andrew Young is still not as well known as it should be.') (signed, 'Leonard Clark'); 22 'The editor, authors and publisher wish to ex- | press their gratitude to Messrs Jonathan Cape | Limited for their generous permission to quote | from Andrew Young's *Collected Poems*.'; [23] 'PROSPECT OF A POET'; [24] blank; 25–105 text; [106] blank; 107 'A SOUTHERN PILGRIM' *[Verse]* ('Looking on Sussex from afar I find') (signed, 'Edmund Blunden'); [108] blank; 109–112 'CHECKLIST OF THE WRITINGS OF ANDREW YOUNG'

Paper: laid paper (watermark: '[Crown] | Abbey Mills | Greenfield'), chain-lines 24–26mm. apart (the chain-lines run horizontally)

Running title: none

Binding: light green-grey boards. On spine reading lengthways down spine from head: 'ANDREW YOUNG Prospect of a Poet HART-DAVIS'. On upper cover: 'ANDREW | YOUNG | [ornate rule in light green] | Prospect [in light green] | of a Poet [in light green] | [ornate rule in light green] | *Tributes by 14 writers* | EDITED BY | *Leonard Clark*' (within ornate border in light green: 177 × 101mm., as a result of the two rules noted above, three rectangles are created). Lower cover: blank. All edges trimmed. Binding measurements: 191 × 114mm. (covers), 191 × 26mm. (spine). End-papers: wove paper.

Publication date: published, according to the *English Catalogue of Books*, 15 November 1957

Price: 12s.6d.

Masefield contents:
Preface ('It gives me much pleasure to take part in this honouring of the poetry of Canon Andrew Young.')
    (signed, 'John Masefield')

Notes:
There are fifteen contributors in total (including contributors of the preface, introduction, and the poem by Blunden). The twelve essays include contributions by John Betjeman, Richard Church, Viola Meynell and L.A.G. Strong.

As Masefield notes in his preface, he presented Andrew Young with the fourth post-war Queen's Medal for Poetry. After noting potential contributors who were unable (for various reasons) to write for the volume, Leonard Clark continues:

> But Dr John Masefield is here, whose recommendation it was that led to the award to Andrew Young of the Queen's Medal for Poetry. His is the gracious and dignified honouring of the true Poet Laureate.

Copies seen: private collection (ROV); BL (11873.pp.21) stamped 1 NOV 1957

B505 [*THE* TIMES BOOKSHOP], *JOHN MASEFIELD* 1958

B505(a) First English edition (1958)

JOHN | MASEFIELD | An Exhibition of Manuscripts and | Books in honour of his Eightieth | Birthday June 1 1958 | [rule (tapered at both ends), 57mm.] | THE [newspaper device featuring 'DIEU ET MON DROIT'] TIMES | BOOKSHOP
(All width centred)

Collation: [A]¹²; 12 leaves; 228 × 152mm.; [1–6] 7 [8] 9–23 [24]

Page contents: [1] half-title: 'JOHN MASEFIELD | AET. 80 | [rule] | AN EXHIBITION | The exhibition is held in the Picture Gallery on the ground floor. | JUNE 3 TO JUNE 14, 1958 | *HOURS OF OPENING* | *Monday to Friday* .... *9a.m. to 5.30p.m.* | *Saturday* .... *9a.m. to 1p.m.*'; [2] frontispiece photograph: 127 × 114mm., '*By permission of* THE TIMES | JOHN MASEFIELD O.M. | June 1 1958'; [3] title-page; [4] '*Printed in Great Britain*'; [5] 'CONTENTS' (five sections listed with page references); [6] blank; 7 'FOREWORD' ('This exhibition has been organized to honour the eightieth birthday…') (unsigned); [8] blank; 9–23 text and one illustration; [24] 'Printed by | THE TIMES PUBLISHING COMPANY, LIMITED | PRINTED HOUSE SQUARE, LONDON, E.C.4 | ENGLAND'.

Paper: wove paper

Running-title: none

Binding: dark green wrappers. Spine: blank. On upper wrapper, in white: 'DRYDEN | SHADWELL | TATE | ROWE | EUSDEN | CIBBER | WHITEHEAD | WARTON | PYE | SOUTHEY | WORDSWORTH | TENNYSON | AUSTIN | BRIDGES | John Masefield. [facsimile signature] [in pink] | O.M. | *Poet Laureate* | ÆTAT 80 | JUNE 1, 1958' (with the exception of line 15 all justified on right margin which is approximately at the width centre of the upper wrapper). Lower wrapper: blank. All edges trimmed. Binding measurements: 228 × 152mm. (wrappers), 228 × 3mm. (spine).

Publication date: presumably published around June 1958

Price: unknown

Masefield contents:
'On Coming Towards Eighty'
          comprises two titled sonnets: 'The Unchanging' ('The marvels do not lessen as years pass;')
                                      'The Changing' ('How wondrously life changes as it goes;')

Notes:
The contents includes '"On Coming Towards Eighty" (A poem by John Masefield specially written for this exhibition)'. The holograph manuscript was exhibited as item 123.

Copies seen: BL (X.909/31732) stamped 30 APR 1972

B510 ROSE BRUFORD, *TEACHING MIME*   1958

B510(a) First English edition (1958)

TEACHING MIME | [two ornaments in mirror image] | ROSE BRUFORD | HON. R.A.M. | PRINCIPAL OF THE ROSE BRUFORD | TRAINING COLLEGE OF SPEECH AND DRAMA | London | METHUEN & CO. LTD | 36 Essex Street W.C.2
(All width centred)

Collation: [A]⁸ B-P⁸ (J not used); signatures left foot of page; 120 leaves; 184 × 123mm.; [two un-numbered pages] [1–7] 8 [9] 10 [11] 12 [13] 14–17 [18] 19–22 [23] 24–49 [50] 51–54 [55] 56–72 [73] 74–89 [90] 91–99 [100] 101–113 [114] 115–24 [125] 126–52 [153] 154–64 [165] 166–67 [168] 169–231 [232–33] 234–35 [236–38]

Page contents: [-] blank (page excluded from page count, but constitutes first leaf of first gathering); [-] blank; [1] half-title: 'TEACHING MIME'; [2] blank; [3] title-page; [4] '*First published 1958* | CATALOGUE NO. 6032/U | © *1958 Rose Bruford* | *Printed in Great Britain by* | *The Camelot Press Ltd* | *Southampton*'; [5] 'CONTENTS' (17 items listed with page references); [6] blank; [7]-231 text; [232] blank; [233]-235 'INDEX'; [236–38] blank

Paper: wove paper

Running title: 'TEACHING MIME' (32mm.) on verso; recto title comprises section title, pp.8–235

Binding: light green cloth. On spine, in silver: '[design of triangles] | *Teaching* | MIME | [design of triangles] | *Rose* | *Bruford* | *Methuen*'. Covers: blank. All edges trimmed. Binding measurements: 188 × 124mm. (covers), 188 × 32mm. (spine). End-papers: wove paper.

Publication date: published, according to the *English Catalogue of Books*, 31 July 1958

Price: 15s.

Masefield contents:
Lines for Miss Rose Bruford's Handbook ('This is the text-book that the scholars used,')
     (signed, 'JOHN MASEFIELD')

Notes:
There are thirteen titled chapters, in addition to a preface and acknowledgements, foreword, Masefield's lines and an index noted by the table of contents.

The 'Preface and Acknowledgements' (by Rose Bruford) refer to Masefield's contribution:

    Dr John Masefield, O.M. has specially written a poem to open this book, remembering the day in 1951 when he visited the College in Lamorbey Park and saw some mime. I am very much aware of the honour he has done me, and thank him for his friendly and untiring help and guidance at all times over a long period of years.

Copies seen: BL (11798.a.62) stamped 18 JUL 1958

Reprinted:

	[first edition, second impression]	1960
'Reprinted'	[first edition, third impression]	1964

B515 *THE FORM AND ORDER OF THE SERVICE OF DEDICATION OF WAIAPU CATHEDRAL* 1960

B515(a) First New Zealand edition (1960)

The | Form and Order | of Service | to be used at the | DEDICATION [in red] | of the Second | CATHEDRAL OF THE DIOCESE [in red] | AT THE HANDS OF | NORMAN | Bishop of the Diocese | at 2.30 p.m. | ON ST. MATTHIAS' DAY | being the twenty-fourth day | of February | In the Year of our Lord | One Thousand Nine Hundred and Sixty
(All width centred)

Publication date: presumably published around February 1960

Masefield contents:
[Untitled] ('All that is beautiful and holy')
(headed, 'specially composed for this service by the POET LAUREATE, JOHN MASEFIELD, O.M., D.Litt.')

Notes:
See also B565

Copies seen: Bodleian (Additional Masefield Papers 10) inscribed 'For Caredig Caves. | from | John Masefield. | April. 1960.'

B520 *THE WEDDING OF HER ROYAL HIGHNESS THE PRINCESS MARGARET AND MR ANTONY ARMSTRONG-JONES* 1960

B520(a) First English edition (1960)

[coat of arms] | THE WEDDING OF | HER ROYAL HIGHNESS | THE PRINCESS MARGARET | AND MR | ANTONY | ARMSTRONG-JONES | WESTMINSTER ABBEY | 6 MAY 1960
(All width centred and enclosed within ornate border: 221 × 155mm.)

Collation: [A]^{16}; 16 leaves; 247 × 177mm.; [1–4] 5 [6–7] 8–15 [16–17] 18–31 [32]

Page contents: [1] title-page; [2–4] photographs; 5 'FOREWORD | BY HIS ROYAL HIGHNESS THE DUKE OF GLOUCESTER'; [6–7] photographs; 8 'A PRAYER | FOR THIS GLAD | MORNING' ('In all unselfish thought a Nation prays;') (signed, 'JOHN MASEFIELD, *Poet Laureate*'); 9–[32] text, map and photographs

Paper: glossy wove paper

Running title: none

Binding: white wrappers. Spine: blank. On upper wrapper: 'APPROVED SOUVENIR PROGRAMME | PUBLISHED BY GRACIOUS PERMISSION OF | HER MAJESTY QUEEN ELIZABETH THE QUEEN | [coat of arms in black, yellow, gold, blue, red and white] | THE WEDDING OF HER ROYAL HIGHNESS | THE PRINCESS MARGARET [in red] | AND MR | ANTONY ARMSTRONG-JONES [in red] | IN WESTMINSTER ABBEY | 6 MAY 1960 | KING GEORGE'S JUBILEE TRUST | THREE SHILLINGS AND SIXPENCE'. On lower wrapper: '*Eyre and Spottiswoode Limited, Her Majesty's Printers*'. All edges trimmed. Binding measurements: 247 × 177mm. (wrappers), 247 × 2mm. (spine).

Publication date: published, according to *Whitaker's*, 29 April 1960

Price: 3s.6d.

Masefield contents:
A Prayer for this Glad Morning ('In all unselfish thought a Nation prays;')
(signed 'JOHN MASEFIELD, *Poet Laureate*')

Notes:
With the exception of pp.[2], [3], [4], [6], [7] and the centrefold, all pages are enclosed within decorated, ornate borders.

Copies seen: private collection (ROV)

B525 *POETRY AT THE MERMAID* [1961]

B525(a) First English edition ([1961])

POETRY | AT THE | MERMAID | [illustration of mermaid with scroll and harp] | is a Festival promoted by the Poetry Book Society | in association with the Arts Council of Great Britain | *Board of Management* Joseph Compton CBS (*Chairman*), Peter du Sautoy, | Roy Fuller, Sir George Rostrevor Hamilton, John Hayward CBE | Stephen Spender *Secretary* Eric W. White | *Festival Advisory Committee* Dulcie Bowie, Richard Church CBE | Bernard Miles CBE, Helen Spalding, Anthony Thwaite, | Ursula Vaughan Williams | DIRECTOR JOHN WAIN | *Festival Secretary* Elizabeth Williams | *Secretarial Assistant* Maryanne Schaefer | *Jazz Adviser* Noel Wain *Film Adviser* Philip Jenkinson | *Stage Manager* Mischa Scorer
(Lines 1–3 use a font of letters in outline, lines 1–3 and 5–6 with no fixed margins, lines 7–17 justified on left margin)

Collation: 48 unsigned leaves bound by the 'perfect binding' process; 202 × 120mm.; [1–11] 12–18 [19] 20–71 [72–73] 74–88 [89–96]

Page contents: [1–8] advertisements; [9] 'Patrons | Dame Peggy Ashcroft | W. H. Auden | Edmund Blunden CBS, MC | R. A. Butler PC, CH, MP | Sir Kenneth Clark CH, KCB | Norman Collins | C. Day Lewis CBE | T. S. Eliot OM, DLITT | Sir John Gielgud DLITT | David Jones CBE | John Lehmann | Robert Lowell | Sir John McEwen of Marchmont Bart, LLD | Louis MacNeice CBE | Bernard Miles CBE | Marianne Moore | The Lord Moyne | Ezra Pound PHB, DLITT | Sir Herbert Read DSO, MC, LITTD | The Hon V. Sackville-West CH, LITTD | The Rev Canon Andrew Young LLD'; [10] '*SILENCE INTO SOUND* | W. B. Yeats *speaking to the psaltery*, 1907: | [text]'; [11] title-page; 12 '*A MESSAGE FROM THE POET LAUREATE* | *JOHN MASEFIELD, O.M.* | *On being told of the arrangements for the Festival, Dr Masefield wrote the Director* | *a letter from which, with his permission, we extract the following:* | [text]'; 13–15 'A Note by the Director' ('The word 'Festival', in current English, is losing its original meaning...') (signed, '*John Wain*'); 16 '*POETRY AT THE MERMAID* | Mr Joseph Compton, *Chairman of the Poetry Book Society, writes:* | [text] | [rule] | [text of acknowledgement information]'; 17–24 festival diary; 25 'Twelve Poems | [12 individual items listed with page references]'; 26 'The Commissioned Poems | BY THE GENEROSITY of Messrs Arthur Guinness Son & Co. twelve poets | were commissioned to write poems of 50 to 200 lines on subjects of their | own choice. The full text of all twelve poems will be found in the tinted | pages that follow. The choice of the twelve poets to be commissioned was | made by the Director and Lord Moyne, each drawing up separate lists from | which the final list was arrived at. The choice of poets to read their poems | in the programme on Monday, 17th rested with the Director.'; 27–71 text of poems; [72] blank; [73] 'Biographies'; 74 photographs with legends; 75 '[photograph] | *Photo A. Alvarez* | THE DIRECTOR'; 76–88 text of biographies; [89–96] advertisements

Paper: wove paper (with pp.25–[72] on green tinted wove paper)

Running title: none

Binding: white wrappers (over-printed in brown). On brown spine: blank except for fragment in blue of illustration continued from upper wrapper. On brown upper wrapper: 'POETRY [in white with black outline] | AT THE [in white with black outline] | MERMAID [in white with black outline] | [two illustrations in blue of mermaids with trumpets and banners with the letter 'M'] | SOUVENIR PROGRAMME THREE SHILLINGS AND SIXPENCE [in white]'. On white lower wrapper: '[advertisement for Associated Television] [in brown and black] | *Frank Overton / Westerham Press*'. All edges trimmed. Binding measurements: 202 × 120mm. (wrappers), 202 × 7mm. (spine).

Publication date: although no date of publication is noted, July 1961 can be inferred

Price: 3s.6d.

Masefield contents:
A Message from the Poet Laureate ('It is a joy to me to read that such a Festival is to be held...')
        (headed, 'from the Poet Laureate John Masefield, O.M.')

Notes:
The authors of the twelve poems are: Thomas Blackburn, Austin Clarke, Michael Hamburger, Ted Hughes, Patrick Kavanagh, Norman MacCaig, Richard Murphy, Sylvia Plath, William Plomer, Hal Summers, R.S. Thomas and Laurence Whistler.

Page 90 includes an advertisement for Masefield's *The Bluebells and other verse* (see A166(a)).

Copies seen: private collection (ROV)

B530 *Ed.* CHAU WAH CHING, LO KING MAN *and* YUNG KAI KIN, *EDMUND BLUNDEN SIXTY-FIVE* 1961

B530(a) *First Hong Kong edition (1961)*

EDMUND BLUNDEN | SIXTY-FIVE | NOVEMBER 1961 | HONG KONG
(All width centred)

Collation: 108 unsigned leaves (including front free and rear free end-papers) and 16 unsigned illustration leaves probably bound by the 'perfect binding' process; 228 × 161mm.; [1–9] 10–11 [12–14] 15 [16–18] 19–24 [25–26] 27–34 [35–36] 37–48 [49–50] 51–55 [56] 57–58 [59–60] 61–70 [71–72] 73–76 [77–78] 79–84 [85–86] 87–92 [93–94] 95–98 [99–100] 101–110 [111–12] 113–24 [125–26] 127–32 [133–34] 135–48 [149–50] 151–60 [161–62] 163–76 [177–78] 179–84 [185–86] 187–92 [193–96] 197–213 [214–16]

Page contents: [1] blank (end-paper); [2] 'PUBLISHED BY: HONG KONG CULTURAL ENTERPRISE CO. | FOR THE ENGLISH SOCIETY, UNIVERSITY OF HONG KONG. | PRINTED BY: SOI SANG PRINTING PRESS, MACAO, H. K.'; [3] title-page; [4] '"To me, fair friend, you never can be old...."' (in facsimile); [5] untitled black and white photograph of Edmund Blunden; [6] blank; [8] facsimile of letter from Robert Black, Governor of Hong Kong; [9] blank; [10] 'THE ENGLISH SOCIETY | THE UNIVERSITY OF HONG KONG | SALUTE | WITH SINCERE RESPECT AND AFFECTION | THE SIXTY-FIFTH BIRTHDAY | OF | EDMUND BLUNDEN | AND TOGETHER | WITH HIS FRIENDS FROM MANY PARTS | OFFER | THIS TOKEN OF APPRECIATION | TO | THE MAN, POET, CRITIC, AND SCHOLAR. | NOVEMBER 1ST. 1961'; 10 'THE CHIMES' ('Edmund Blunden came to the University of Hong Kong in 1953, and since then he has been...') (signed, 'Chau Wah Ching', 'Lo King Man', and 'Yung Kai Kin'; dated 'November 1st 1961'); 11 'WE ARE GRATEFUL | AND HONOURED | TO REPRODUCE THE FOLLOWING LETTER | FROM | THE PRIME MINISTER, | THE RIGHT

HONOURABLE HAROLD MACMILLAN, P.C., M.P.'; [12–13] facsimile of letter from Harold Macmillan; [14] blank; 15 letter from Yasuhide Toda, Private Secretary to the Crown Prince, Imperial Palace, Tokyo; [16–17] facsimile of letter from John Masefield; [18] blank; 19 letter from the Warden and Fellows, Merton College, Oxford; 20–192 text and illustrations; [193–95] 'A Hong Kong House' (in facsimile) ('"And now a dove and now a dragon-fly') (signed, 'Edmund Blunden'); [196] blank; 197–208 'CONTRIBUTORS'; 209–213 'EDMUND BLUNDEN | A Select Bibliography'; [214–16] blank (including end-paper)

Paper: wove paper, illustrations on glossy paper

Running title: none

Binding: cream boards. On spine: 'EDMUND [in gold] | BLUNDEN [in gold] | SIXTY-FIVE [in red] | 1961. [in red] | HONG KONG [in red]'. On upper cover: 'EDMUND BLUNDEN [in gold] | SIXTY-FIVE [in red] | NOVEMBER 1961 [in red] | HONG KONG [in red]'. Lower cover: blank. Top edge and fore edges roughly trimmed and uncut, lower outside edge trimmed. Binding measurements: 235 × 163mm. (covers), 235 × 29mm. (spine). End-papers: wove paper (the front and rear free end-papers are included in the pagination of the volume as pp.[1–2] and pp.[215–16] respectively.

Publication date: published, according to date within volume, November 1961

Price: unknown

Masefield contents:
Masefield's contribution comprises a letter (reproduced in facsimile). Addressed to 'Dear Mr Ching', it commences 'I thank you for your letter of the 1st of August. I am grateful to you for giving me the opportunity…' It is signed 'Yours sincerely | John Masefield'.

Notes:
There are eighty-two contributors listed in the 'Contributors' section (including contributors of the prefatory material). Contributors include John Betjeman, Richard Church, Cecil Day Lewis, Robert Gittings, Graham Greene, Christopher Hassall, Compton Mackenzie, Siegfried Sassoon, Osbert Sitwell, Stephen Spender, Laurence Whistler and Henry Williamson.

The binding of this volume cannot be determined without damage to the book. Both standard text pages (on wove paper) and illustration pages (on glossy paper) are uniformly bound with no indications of tipped-in leaves or even sewn gatherings. It is likely that the single leaves are bound by the 'perfect binding' process.

The pagination of the volume includes pages of illustration (and reverse sides of these leaves which are blank).

Pages 33–34 (on a single leaf) and 41–42 (on a single leaf) are both incorrectly bound upside down and in reverse order (ie page 34 before 33 and page 42 before 41).

The board covers have cream paper pasted onto them. The construction of this is curious. It appears that the covering paper is in two parts: one covering the upper cover only and the other covering the lower cover and spine. A stub of this part runs onto the front cover for approximately 12mm.

The title, as given on the presumed title-page, is used here. However, the editors' introduction is titled 'The Chimes' and notes on the contributors at the rear of the volume suggest this may have been the intended title for this volume.

The editors of the volume were Chau Wah Ching, Lo King Man and Yung Kai Kin. The first two were, in 1961, both third year students of English Literature at the University of Hong Kong. Yung Kai Kin was a second year student.

The main text carries contributions in alphabetical order of their authors.

Copies seen: BL (X.909/2039) signed 'Edmund Blunden | 27 September 1963' on page [1] stamped 30 DEC 1963

B535 *Ed.* CORLISS LAMONT, *THE THOMAS LAMONT FAMILY*   1962

B535(a) *First American edition (1962)*

THE THOMAS LAMONT FAMILY | [rule (tapered at both ends), 102mm.] | *by* | Reverend Thomas Lamont | Thomas William Lamont | Thomas Stilwell Lamont | Corliss Lamont | Margaret Lamont Heap | *with* Recollections and Poems *by* | John Masefield | EDITED BY CORLISS LAMONT | [rule (tapered at both ends), 89mm.] | HORIZON PRESS NEW YORK 1962
(All width centred)

Collation: [A-S]⁸; 144 leaves; 233 × 153mm.; [i–vi] vii–ix [x] 1–6 [7–8] 9–33 [34] 35–63 [64] 65–147 [148–50] 151–62 [163–64] 165–91 [192] 193–206 [207–208] 209–219 [220] 221–30 [231–32] 233–76 [277] 278; the frontispiece (on glossy paper) is tipped-in on page [iii]; an entire unsigned gathering of eight leaves (of glossy paper) is bound between gatherings [L] and [M] this has been excluded from the gathering information and leaf count as page numbers do not incorporate these illustration pages

Page contents: [i] half-title: 'THE THOMAS LAMONT FAMILY'; [ii] blank; [iii] title-page (with additional leaf tipped-in on the verso of which is the black and white frontispiece: 111 × 97mm., '*The Lamont Coat of Arms.*'); [iv] 'Copyright 1962, by Corliss and Thomas S. Lamont | PRINTED IN THE UNITED STATES OF AMERICA'; [v] 'TO THE LAMONTS – PAST, PRESENT AND FUTURE'; [vi] blank; vii–viii 'CONTENTS' (five parts (each sub-divided), preface and appendix listed with page references); ix 'ILLUSTRATIONS' (nine illustrations (including frontispiece) listed with page references); [x] blank; 1–6 'PREFACE' ('Forty-nine years ago, in 1913, my grandfather, the Reverend Thomas Lamont...') (headed, 'BY CORLISS LAMONT' and dated, '*New York City October 1962*'); [7] 'PART I | THE LAMONT FAMILY IN THE | NINETEENTH CENTURY | by Reverend Thomas Lamont'; [8] blank; 9–33 text; [34] blank; 35–63 text; [64] blank; 65–147 text; [148] blank; [149] 'PART II | A LAMONT REUNION IN 1876'; [150] blank; 151–62 text; [163] 'PART III | THOMAS WILLIAM LAMONT AND | FLORENCE CORLISS LAMONT'; [164] blank; 165–91 text; [192] blank; 193–206 text; [207] 'PART IV | RECOLLECTIONS AND POEMS | by John Masefield'; [208] blank; 209–219 text; [220] blank; 221–30 text; [231] 'PART V | OF THE FAMILY PAST | by Thomas Stilwell Lamont'; [232] blank; 233–75 text; 276 'ACKNOWLEDGEMENTS' ('The editing and writing of this book on the Lamont family has been...') (signed, 'C. L.'); [277] 'Appendix | CLAN LAMONT NAMES | AND SEPTS | [rule (tapered at both ends)] | FAMILY TREE'; 278 text (with two additional folded leaves tipped-in on the verso of which are 'LAMONT FAMILY TREE I' and 'LAMONT FAMILY TREE II')

Paper: laid paper (watermark: 'Sulgrade Text'), chain-lines 32mm. apart

Running title: notification of part number present on verso; recto title comprises section title, pp.10–275 (both ranged towards the gutter)

Binding: light green cloth. On spine, in silver: 'THE | THOMAS | LAMONT | FAMILY [lines 1–4 within ruled border: 30 × 24mm. and all on dark green panel: 35 × 29mm.] | EDITED BY | CORLISS | LAMONT [lines 5–7 within ruled border: 18 × 24mm. and all on dark green panel: 22 × 29mm.] | HORIZON [within ruled border: 9 × 24mm. and all on dark green panel: 13 × 24mm.]' (all width centred). On upper cover: 'THE THOMAS LAMONT FAMILY' (within ruled border: 9 × 84mm. and all on dark green panel: 13 × 88mm.) (ranged left). Lower cover: blank. All edges trimmed. Sewn head band (in green and yellow). Binding measurements: 239 × 154mm. (covers), 239 × 41mm. (spine). End-papers: wove paper illustrated with maps in green: 'Original Lamont Country in Scotland | and main locale of settlements in | County Antrim, Ireland'.

Publication date: presumably published after October 1962

Price: unknown

Masefield contents:
Masefield's poem 'In the Memory of Two Friends of all Great Causes' is quoted on page 191. It commences 'O Passer-by, remember these two Friends,'.

The statement on the death of Florence Lamont from *The Times* for 30 December 1952 headed 'John and Constance Masefield' is quoted on pp.205–206.

Part IV of this volume, entitled 'Recollections and Poems by John Masefield' contains three items:

> Some Memories of Thomas William Lamont and Florence Corliss Lamont ('I am glad to be allowed the privilege of...')
> The Western Hudson Shore ('In a long life's first independent day,')
> To The Great Friends in Lifetime ('This, I believe, that we remain in Time')

Notes:
Each part commences with a drop capital.

See B575 for an expanded edition with a different title. See also A167.

Copies seen: Columbia University Libraries (CS71.L233 1962); NYPL (Berg Collection); HRHRC (HRC MIN 22331); HRHRC (HRC MIN 21952)

B540 *FOUR THOUSAND YEARS OF HISTORY [–] THE PAGEANT OF DORCHESTER* 1963

B540(a) First English edition (1963)

Upper wrapper:
FOUR THOUSAND | YEARS OF HISTORY | [black and white drawing of Dorchester Abbey (drawing continues on lower wrapper)] | *The pageant of Dorchester* | DORCHESTER ABBEY . DORCHESTER-ON-THAMES . OXFORD | *ONE SHILLING AND SIXPENCE*
(All width centred)

Collation: [A]⁶; 6 leaves; 210 × 134mm.; 1–11 [12]

Page contents: 1 'DORCHESTER PAGEANT | held under the auspices of the Friends of | Dorchester Abbey | [note of narrators, players, and acknowledgements]'; 2 acknowledgements (continued), list of organizing committee and sequence one listing; 3–4 sequence one listing (continued); 5 sequence one listing (concluded) and sequence two listing; 6–7 sequence two listing (continued); 8 sequence two listing (concluded) and sequence three listing; 9–10 sequence three listing (concluded); 11 '"RECESSIONAL"' ('SOLO | Now that the day declines and night is near,') (signed, 'JOHN MASEFIELD, 1963.'); [12] 'Blessing'

Paper: beige laid paper (watermark: '[crown] *Glastonbury*'), chain-lines 25mm. apart (paper is used so that chain-lines run horizontally)

Running title: none

Binding: white wrappers. Spine: blank (except for wrap-around illustration). On upper wrapper, in cyan: as above. On lower wrapper, in cyan: '[crest] | [black and white drawing of Dorchester Abbey (continued from upper wrapper), signed 'Henry Charlwood 63'] |

Published by the Friends of Dorchester Abbey | and Printed at The Abbey Press, Abingdon, Berkshire'. The illustration measures 144 × 268mm. in total. On inside of upper wrapper: '[illustration: 143 × 76mm.] | *St. Birinus baptises King Cynegils of Wessex* | *A.D. 635*'. On inside of lower wrapper: tipped-in slip (154 × 32mm.) upon which: 'A D D E N D U M | Music for the Anthem sung in the Abbey | is composed by Michael Thomas | and not by Bernard Naylor'. All edges trimmed. Binding measurements: 210 × 134mm. (wrappers), 210 × 1mm. (spine).

Publication date: 1963

Price: 1s.6d.

Masefield contents:
Recessional ('Now that the day declines and night is near,')
  (signed, 'JOHN MASEFIELD, 1963')

Notes:
Masefield is acknowledged on the first page: 'Words of Final Anthem by John Masefield, O.M.'

Copies seen: private collection (ROV)

B545 *THE WEDDING OF HER ROYAL HIGHNESS PRINCESS ALEXANDRA OF KENT AND THE HONOURABLE ANGUS OGILVY* 1963

B545(a) *First English edition (1963)*

[two coats of arms] | THE WEDDING OF | HER ROYAL HIGHNESS | PRINCESS ALEXANDRA | OF KENT | AND THE HONOURABLE | ANGUS OGILVY | IN WESTMINSTER ABBEY | WEDNESDAY | 24 APRIL 1963
(All width centred and enclosed within ornate border: 189 × 134mm.)

Collation: [A]¹⁶; 16 leaves; 247 × 172mm.; [1] 2–31 [32]

Page contents: [1] title-page; 2–4 photographs; 5 'FOREWORD | BY HIS ROYAL HIGHNESS THE DUKE OF GLOUCESTER'; 6–7 photographs; 8 'A SONG | FOR BLESSING ON | THIS APRIL DAY' ('Now, as the sun and showers win,') (signed, 'JOHN MASEFIELD, *Poet Laureate*'); 9–[32] text, map, genealogical tables and photographs

Paper: glossy wove paper

Running title: none

Binding: beige wrappers. Spine: blank. On upper wrapper: 'APPROVED SOUVENIR PROGRAMME | PUBLISHED BY PERMISSION OF | HER ROYAL HIGHNESS PRINCESS MARINA, DUCHESS OF KENT | [coat of arms in black, green, gold, blue, red and white] | THE WEDDING OF HER ROYAL HIGHNESS | PRINCESS ALEXANDRA [in red] | OF KENT [in red] | AND THE HONOURABLE | ANGUS OGILVY [in red] | IN WESTMINSTER ABBEY | 24 APRIL 1963 | KING GEORGE'S JUBILEE TRUST | THREE SHILLINGS AND SIXPENCE' (within ruled border: 227 × 152mm.) On lower wrapper: '*Published by King George's Jubilee Trust, 166 Piccadilly, London, W.1* | *Printed by Eyre and Spottiswoode Limited, Her Majesty's Printers* | *Distributed by Vernon Holding & Partners Limited*'. All edges trimmed. Binding measurements: 247 × 172mm. (wrappers), 247 × 2mm. (spine).

Publication date: presumably published around April 1963

Price: 3s.6d.

Masefield contents:
A Song for Blessing on this April Day ('Now, as the sun and showers win,')
  (signed, 'JOHN MASEFIELD, *Poet Laureate*')

Notes:
With the exception of the centrefold, all pages are enclosed within decorated, ornate borders.

Copies seen: private collection (PWE)

B550 JAMES WILLIAM HOLMES, *VOYAGING* 1965

B550(a) *First English edition (1965)*

Voyaging | *Fifty years on the seven seas in sail* | [ornament] | Pen Pictures and Paintings by | CAPTAIN JAMES WILLIAM HOLMES | *Member of the Honourable Company of Master Mariners* | Edited by his daughter | NORA COUGHLAN | FOREWORD BY JOHN MASEFIELD, O.M. | [publisher's device of a bull enclosed within oval border] | HUTCHINSON OF LONDON
(All width centred)

Collation: [A]⁸ B–C⁸ [D]⁸ E–H⁸ [I]⁸ K–N⁸ (J not used); signatures left foot of page; 104 leaves; 206 × 132mm.; [1–6] 7–9 [10] 11–24 [25–26] 27–48 [49–50] 51–59 [60–62] 63–76 [77–78] 79–92 [93–94] 95–106 [107–108] 109–128 [129–30] 131–48 [149–50] 151–62

[163–64] 165–78 [179–80] 181–96 [197–98] 199–206 [207–208]; the frontispiece (on glossy paper) is tipped-in on page [3]; sets of conjugate leaves (on glossy paper) are bound enclosing gatherings B, E, G and K, these have been excluded from the gathering information as page numbers do not incorporate these illustration pages

Page contents: [1] half-title: 'VOYAGING'; [2] '*Frontispiece: Ship* Cimba *of Aberdeen. Owners Alex. Nicol & Co.* | *Built at Aberdeen in 1878*'; [3] title-page (with additional leaf tipped-in on the verso of which is the full-page colour frontispiece illustration); [4] 'HUTCHINSON & CO (*Publishers*) LTD | *178–202 Great Portland Street, London W1* | London Melbourne Sydney | Auckland Bombay Toronto | Johannesburg New York | [five point star] | *First published 1965* | © Nora Coughlan 1965 | *This book has been set in Garamond, printed in* | *Great Britain on Antique Wove paper by The* | *Anchor Press, Ltd., and bound by Wm. Brendon* | *& Son Ltd., both of Tiptree, Essex.*'; [5] 'CONTENTS' (11 titled chapters, foreword and preface listed with page references); [6] 'ILLUSTRATIONS' (23 illustrations (including frontispiece) listed with page references); 7–9 'FOREWORD | BY JOHN MASEFIELD, O.M.' ('Captain James William Holmes was one of the famous sea-captains of the late Victorian time.') (signed, 'John Masefield.') (facsimile signature); [10] blank; 11–24 'PREFACE' ('It was my good fortune as a small girl to sail twice round the globe in a clipper...') (unsigned); [25] divisional chapter title; [26] blank; 27–48 text; [49] divisional chapter title; [50] blank; 51–59 text; [60] blank; [61] divisional chapter title; [62] blank; 63–76 text; [77] divisional chapter title; [78] blank; 79–92 text; [93] divisional chapter title; [94] blank; 95–106 text; [107] divisional chapter title; [108] blank; 109–128 text; [129] divisional chapter title; [130] blank; 131–48 text; [149] divisional chapter title; [150] blank; 151–62 text; [163] divisional chapter title; [164] blank; 165–78 text; [179] divisional chapter title; [180] blank; 181–96 text; [197] divisional chapter title; [198] blank; 199–[207] text; [208] blank

Paper: wove paper

Running title: 'VOYAGING' (18mm.) on verso; recto title comprises chapter title, pp.28–[207]

Binding: blue cloth. On spine, in silver: 'CAPTAIN | JAMES | WILLIAM | HOLMES | [ornament] VOYAGING [ornament] [this line reading lengthways down spine from head] | [publisher's device of a bull enclosed within oval border] | HUTCHINSON' (all width centred). Covers: blank. All edges trimmed. Binding measurements: 215 × 134mm. (covers), 215 × 39mm. (spine). End-papers: grey wove paper.

Publication date: published, according to *Whitaker's*, 27 September 1965

Price: 35s.

Masefield contents:
Foreword ('Captain James William Holmes was one of the famous sea-captains of the late Victorian time')
      (signed, 'John Masefield.') (facsimile signature)

Notes:
The volume is divided into twelve titled chapters. There is also a foreword and preface. The preface and each chapter commence with a drop capital. The foreword does not.

Page numbers are in italics.

The preface (by Holmes' daughter) notes that:

> ...the book follows my father's own words exactly as he recounted the various incidents to me... Each day, when he had gone, I entered briefly in a notebook what he had said, and when I came to write it out I realised that I had... an autobiography of the man...

The volume should therefore be regarded as a 'reconstructed' autobiography. Recounting the history of her plans for publication, Holmes' daughter notes:

> ...to get the highest criticism, I took the bold course of writing to our sailor Poet Laureate, asking him if he would be good enough to read the manuscript and give me his opinion. He said I could send him ten pages and he would judge from that. Not knowing which ten to select, I sent the whole 200, asking Mr. Masefield if he would kindly choose which ten he preferred to read. In replying, he said that he had read the whole with enjoyment and wished it had been longer, and that he hoped it and the illustrations would soon be published.

This apparently occurred during the 1930s but the book's publication was postponed. Masefield's foreword is presumably from 1965.

Copies seen: BL (X.639/993) stamped 9 SEP 1965

B550(b)   Second English edition (1970)

Voyaging | *Fifty years on the seven seas in sail* | [ornament] | Pen Pictures and Paintings by | CAPTAIN JAMES WILLIAM HOLMES | *Member of the Honourable Company of Master Mariners* | Edited by his daughter | NORA COUGHLAN | Foreword by | JOHN MASEFIELD, O.M. | *New Edition with 20 colour plates* | [publisher's device of a sea bird and compass with 'Nautical | Publishing | Company'] | Adlard Coles | Erroll Bruce | Richard Creagh-Osborne | Nautical House | Lymington, Hampshire | in association with George G. Harrap & Co. Ltd., | London, Toronto, Sydney, Wellington
(Lines 1–11 width centred with lines 13–19 justified on left margin and the publisher's logo (transcribed as line 12) on right margin)

Collation: [A]⁸ B-C⁸ [D]⁸ E-H⁸ [I]⁸ K-N⁸ (J not used); signatures left foot of page; 104 leaves; 206 × 131mm.; [1–6] 7–9 [10] 11–24 [25–26] 27–48 [49–50] 51–59 [60–62] 63–76 [77–78] 79–92 [93–94] 95–106 [107–108] 109–128 [129–30] 131–48 [149–50] 151–62 [163–64] 165–78 [179–80] 181–96 [197–98] 199–206 [207–208]; the frontispiece (on glossy paper) is tipped-in on page [2]; sets of conjugate leaves (on glossy paper) are bound enclosing gatherings B, E, G and K, these have been excluded from the gathering information as page numbers do not incorporate these illustration pages

Page contents: [1] half-title: '*Voyaging*'; [2] 'This little book of all the ships I have sailed in, 1869 to 1921 | is dedicated to | "NORNIE" | *by her ever loving father* | J.W. Holmes. Septr 15th 1924. [these five lines in facsimile enclosed within ruled border: 31 × 71mm.] | *Dedication to the book of pictures, all of which are reproduced in* | Voyaging, *painted by the author for his daughter Nora Coughlan.* | *Frontispiece:* Barque Inverurie *of Aberdeen.* | *Owners Geo. Milne & Co.* | *Built at Aberdeen in 1889*' (with additional leaf tipped-in on the verso of which is the full-page colour frontispiece illustration); [3] title-page; [4] '© NORA COUGHLAN 1965 | SBN 245 50519 9 | *First published in Great Britain in 1965* | *by Hutchinson & Co. (Publishers) Ltd* | *New edition with 20 colour plates* | *first published in Great Britain 1970 by* | NAUTICAL PUBLISHING COMPANY | *Nautical House, Lymington, Hampshire, SO4 9BA* | *This book has been set in Garamond and printed offset in Great Britain* | *by The Camelot Press Limited* | *London and Southampton*'; [5] 'CONTENTS' (11 titled chapters, foreword and preface listed with page references); [6] 'ILLUSTRATIONS' (23 illustrations (including frontispiece) listed with page references); 7–9 'FOREWORD | BY JOHN MASEFIELD, O.M.' ('Captain James William Holmes was one of the famous sea-captains of the late Victorian time.') (signed, 'John Masefield.') (facsimile signature); [10] blank; 11–24 'PREFACE' ('It was my good fortune as a small girl to sail twice round the globe in a clipper...') (unsigned); [25] divisional chapter title; [26] blank; 27–48 text; [49] divisional chapter title; [50] blank; 51–59 text; [60] blank; [61] divisional chapter title; [62] blank; 63–76 text; [77] divisional chapter title; [78] blank; 79–92 text; [93] divisional chapter title; [94] blank; 95–106 text; [107] divisional chapter title; [108] blank; 109–128 text; [129] divisional chapter title; [130] blank; 131–48 text; [149] divisional chapter title; [150] blank; 151–62 text; [163] divisional chapter title; [164] blank; 165–78 text; [179] divisional chapter title; [180] blank; 181–96 text; [197] divisional chapter title; [198] blank; 199–[207] text; [208] blank

Paper: wove paper

Running title: 'VOYAGING' (18mm.) on verso; recto title comprises chapter title, pp.28–[207]

Binding: green cloth. On spine, in gold: 'CAPTAIN | JAMES | WILLIAM | HOLMES | *Voyaging* [this line reading lengthways down spine from head] | Nautical | Publishing | Company' (all width centred). Upper cover, in gold: publisher's device of a sea bird and compass (ranged lower right). Lower cover: blank. All edges trimmed. Binding measurements: 213 × 133mm. (covers), 213 × 39mm. (spine). End-papers: beige laid paper (watermark: '[crown] *Glastonbury*'), chain-lines 25mm. apart (the paper is used so that chain-lines run horizontally).

Publication date: published, according to *Whitaker's*, November 1970

Price: £2.00

Masefield contents:
as for B550(a)

Notes:
The preface and each chapter commence with a drop capital. The foreword does not.

Page numbers are in italics.

The illustrations which were reproduced in black and white in B550(a) are here colour reproductions. The frontispiece has changed but there are no new illustrations in this edition. The setting of the type follows the first edition.

Copies seen: BL (X.809/813) stamped 13 NOV 1970

B555 *READER'S DIGEST CONDENSED BOOKS* [including 'The Bird of Dawning']　　　1965

B555(a) First English edition (1965)

READER'S DIGEST | CONDENSED BOOKS | *De Luxe* [in gold] | *Edition* [in gold] | THE READER'S DIGEST ASSOCIATION | London, Sydney and Cape Town
(All width centred and enclosed within ornate border in gold: 166 × 119mm.)

Collation: 252 unsigned leaves bound by the 'perfect binding' process; 185 × 132mm.; [1–7] 8–13 [14–17] 18 [19] 20–26 [27] 28–40 [41] 42–59 [60] 61–91 [92] 93–109 [110–13] 114–23 [124] 125–31 [132] 133–42 [143] 144–78 [179] 180–88 [189] 190–91 [192–95] 196–202 [203] 204–219 [220] 221–37 [238] 239–48 [249] 250–61 [262] 263–91 [292] 293–302 [303] 304–328 [329] 330–35 [336–39] 340–58 [359] 360–71 [372] 373 [374] 375–92 [393] 394–401 [402] 403–409 [410–13] 414–23 [424–25] 426–27 [428–29] 430–51 [452–53] 454–59 [460–61] 462–66 [467] 468–82 [483] 484–95 [496–97] 498–499 [500] 501–503 [504]

Pagination contents: [1] half-title: 'READER'S DIGEST | CONDENSED | BOOKS'; [2] blank; [3] title-page; [4] 'Published by | THE READER'S DIGEST ASSOCIATION LIMITED | 25 Berkeley Square, London, W.I | THE READER'S DIGEST ASSOCIATION PTY.LIMITED | Reader's Digest House | 86 Stanley Street, East Sydney | THE READER'S DIGEST ASSOCIATION LIMITED | Parkade, Strand Street, Cape Town | FIRST EDITION | Copyright by The Reader's Digest Association Limited | All rights reserved, including the right to reproduce this book or parts thereof in any form. | (For further information as to ownership of material in this book see page 504) | PRINTED IN GREAT BRITAIN BY | HAZELL WATSON & VINEY LTD., AYLESBURY, BUCKS'; [5] '*Contents* | [introduction, five titles, their authors and publishers listed with page references] | ['RD' monogram] [in gold]' ('*Contents*' is printed over an ornate pattern in gold (as used on title-page) and within double ruled border: 23 × 57mm.); [6]-503 text and illustrations; [504] '[rule] | THE THIRD DAY. *Original full-length version* © Joseph Hayes 1964. U.S. con- | densed version © The Reader's Digest Association, Inc. 1964. British condensed | version © The Reader's Digest Association Limited 1965. | JAMIE. *Original full-length version* © Jack Bennett 1963. British condensed ver- | sion © The Reader's Digest Association Limited 1965. | HOTEL. *Original full-length version* © Arthur Hailey, Ltd. 1965. U.S. condensed | version © The Reader's Digest Association, Inc. 1965. British condensed version | © The Reader's Digest Association Limited 1965. | EPISODE. *Original full-length version* © Eric Hodgins 1963. U.S. condensed | version © The Reader's Digest Association, Inc. 1964. British condensed version | © The Reader's Digest Association Limited 1965. | THE BIRD OF DAWNING. *British condensed version* © The Reader's Digest Associa- | tion Limited 1965. | [rule] | NN.45'

Paper: wove paper

Running title: running titles comprise section or book title, on both verso and recto, pp.8–503

Binding: white, grey and green printed paper-covered boards with brown simulated-leather spine. On spine, in gold: '[rule] | *Reader's Digest* | *Condensed Books* | [rule] | [device incorporating raised band of binding, two rules (joined at left and right edges by converging to a single point) and six stars] | THE | THIRD DAY | [device incorporating raised band of binding, two rules (joined at left and right edges by converging to a single point) and six stars] | JAMIE | [device incorporating raised band of binding, two rules (joined at left and right edges by converging to a single point) and six stars] | HOTEL | [device incorporating raised band of binding, two rules (joined at left and right edges by converging to a single point) and six stars] | EPISODE | [device incorporating raised band of binding, two rules (joined at left and right edges by converging to a single point) and six stars] | THE BIRD | OF | DAWNING | [device incorporating raised band of binding, two rules (joined at left and right edges by converging to a single point) and six stars] | [rule] | ['RD' monogram] | [rule]' (all within ruled border: 183 × 83mm.) The spine design runs over onto the upper and lower covers. Covers: blank. Top edge stained lilac, others trimmed. Sewn head band (in black and yellow) and light green marker ribbon (see notes). Binding measurements: 193 × 134mm. (covers), 193 × 48mm. (spine). End-papers: lilac wove paper (watermark: 'RD' monogram (frequently rotated 180 degrees)), chain-lines 27mm. apart.

Publication date: published, according to *Whitaker's*, 1 October 1965

Price: 14s.

Masefield contents:
The Bird of Dawning ('Nearly a hundred years ago "Cruiser" Trewsbury, the second mate of the homeward-bound...')
[abridged text]

Notes:
The condensed books (and their authors) are as follows: Joseph Hayes, *The Third Day*; Jack Bennett, *Jamie*; Arthur Hailey, *Hotel*; Eric Hodgins, *Episode* and John Masefield, *The Bird of Dawning*. No person responsible for the condensations is cited within the volume. Each condensed book is illustrated by a different illustrator. The illustrations to *The Bird of Dawning* are by Neville Dear.

Although Masefield's glossary of sea-terms is excluded, the text is interrupted by a double-page spread of a diagram of a ship and a glossary entitled 'MARINER'S GLOSSARY | including a key to the diagram'.

The introductory section entitled 'The Authors and their Books' includes a full page photograph of Masefield and 'an appreciation by Eric Gillett, author, journalist and close personal friend of John Masefield...'

The production of the book is intended to appear 'De Luxe'. Accordingly, the sewn head-band is pasted onto the 'perfectly bound' gathering.

This volume was proposed in November 1964. Masefield stated to The Society of Authors that he wanted to know where cuts would occur. The Society of Authors acknowledged this, commenting

> ...Although the idea of any condensation of a book is unattractive I think it is true, from books in this series I have seen, that the Readers' Digest do it as well as it can be done.

(Anne Munro-Kerr, letter to John Masefield, 11 November 1964)
(Archives of The Society of Authors)

Masefield noted that 'the curtailed book seems to be the usual reprint of this time; and I am willing to permit it, if the Macmillan Co in the U.S.A. raise no objection' (see John Masefield, letter to Anne Munro-Kerr, 11 November [1964]) (Archives of The Society of Authors).

Copies seen: private collection (PWE)

B560 *Ed.* HOWARD FERGUSON, *MYRA HESS BY HER FRIENDS* 1966

B560(a) *First English edition (1966)*

Myra Hess | *BY HER FRIENDS* | COMPILED BY | DENISE LASSIMONNE | EDITED AND WITH AN INTRODUCTION BY | HOWARD FERGUSON | *Illustrated* | [publisher's device of oak tree, book and 'hh'] | HAMISH HAMILTON | LONDON
(All width centred)

Collation: [A-G]⁸ [H]⁴ [I]⁸; 68 leaves; 216 × 136mm.; [i–iv] v–vii [viii] ix–xi [xii] 1–119 [120–24]; the frontispiece (on glossy paper) is tipped-in on page [ii]; sets of conjugate leaves (on glossy paper) are bound enclosing gatherings [B], [E] and [G], these have been excluded from the gathering information as page numbers do not incorporate these illustration pages

Page contents: [i] half-title: '*Myra Hess*'; [ii] blank (with additional leaf tipped-in on the verso of which is the black and white photograph frontispiece: 122 × 118mm., 'MYRA HESS | (1890–1965)' with note: '*Photo: Daniel Farson*'); [iii] title-page; [iv] '*First published in Great Britain*, 1966 | *by Hamish Hamilton Ltd* | *90 Great Russell Street London WC*1 | *Copyright* © *Hamish Hamilton*, 1966 | *Discography* © *F. F. Clough and G. J. Cuming*, 1966 | *Printed in Great Britain by* | *Western Printing Services Ltd, Bristol*'; v–vi '*Contents*' (19 sections including preface listed with authors (where appropriate) and page references); vii '*Illustrations*' (15 illustrations including frontispiece listed with page references); [viii] blank; ix–xi '*Preface*' ('This memorial volume is in no sense a biography of Dame Myra Hess, nor does it attempt...') (signed, 'HOWARD FERGUSON'); [xii] blank; 1–119 text; [120–24] blank

Paper: wove paper

Running title: '*Myra Hess*' (20mm.) on verso; recto title comprises section title, pp.3–119

Binding: light blue cloth. On spine reading lengthways down spine from head, in gold: 'MYRA HESS [ornament] *by Her Friends*'; horizontally at foot of spine: publisher's device of oak tree, book and 'hh'. Covers: blank. All edges trimmed. Binding measurements: 222 × 138mm. (covers), 222 × 26mm. (spine). End-papers: wove paper.

Publication date: published, according to *Whitaker's*, November 1966

Price: 25s.

Masefield contents:
Remembering Dame Myra Hess ('Glad memories come, of old, long-distant days')
    (headed, 'BY JOHN MASEFIELD')

Notes:
There are fifteen main contributions in addition to a preface, words spoken at an honorary degree ceremony, a listing of works played at the National Gallery concerts and a discography.

All contributions (with the exception of Masefield's poem, the listing of works played at the National Gallery and the discography) commence with a drop capital.

The spine title uses characters in outline.

The gutter of the book reveals that a number of the 'unsigned' gatherings are signed on the spine of the gathering itself.

Compare Masefield's contribution with his poem of the same name ('Remembering Dame Myra Hess') within *In Glad Thanksgiving* (A171). It commences 'Most beautiful, most gifted, and most wise,'

Copies seen: BL (X.431/374) stamped 11 NOV 1966

Reprinted:

[Second Impression]	[first edition, second impression]	[no copies consulted]
'Third Impression'	[first edition, third impression]	Feb 1967

B565 W.M. EDMUNDS, *WAIAPU CATHEDRAL [–] ITS BIRTH, DEATH AND RESURRECTION* [1966?]

B565(a) First New Zealand edition ([1966?])

[emblem: 'DIOCESE OF WAIAPI NEW ZEALAND 1858'] | *WAIAPU CATHEDRAL* | [five point star in outline] | *Birth, Death | and | Resurrection*
(All width centred)

Collation: [A]¹⁶; 16 leaves; 226 × 174mm.; [un-numbered page] [1] 2 [un-numbered page] 3–28 [29–30]

Page contents: [–] title-page; [1] blank; 2 photographic illustrations and captions; [–] blank; 3–28 text and photographic illustrations; [29–30] blank

Paper: glossy wove paper

Running title: none

Binding: white wrappers. Spine: blank. On upper cover, in black on red: '*WAIAPU CATHEDRAL* | NAPIER, NEW ZEALAND | [photographic illustration] | *Its Birth, | Death and | Resurrection*' (lines 1 and 3 justified on left margin, lines 2 and 5 justified on right margin and line 4 width centred). Lower cover: blank. On inside of upper wrapper: blank. On inside of lower wrapper: 'Written by the Reverend W. M. Edmunds, Vicar | of Wairoa, compiled by the Cathedral Publicity | Committee, and printed by The Daily Telegraph | Co. Ltd., Napier, N.Z.' All edges trimmed. Binding measurements: 226 × 174mm. (wrappers), 226 × 3mm. (spine).

Publication date: between November 1965 and January 1967 (see notes)

Price: unknown

Masefield contents:
A Prayer ("'O Holy Powers, Who attend')
        (introduced as 'by John Masefield')

Notes:
The Masefield contribution (which comprises four lines) is introduced as

From the hymn composed by John Masefield for the service of the Laying of the Foundation Stone, the first of three hymns specially composed by the Poet Laureate at the invitation of Archbishop Lesser – the second and third were for the Dedication Service of the first part of the Cathedral in 1960, and the Dedication of the completed Cathedral in 1965.

See also B515 (*The Form and Order of The Service of Dedication of Waiapu Cathedral*) for the second of the poems noted here.

The text notes a visit to the Cathedral from Queen Elizabeth II during November 1965. A presentation copy to Masefield is dated January 1967. It is therefore assumed that publication took place sometime between these two dates.

The volume comprises a guide book to the Cathedral, together with numerous black and white photographic illustrations.

Copies seen: HRHRC (TEMP M377DED 1967) inscribed to 'John Masefield Esq. O.M., D.Litt. | The Poet Laureate | whose inspired work gave so great | joy to so many in Waiapu Cathedral… | 25 January 1967.'

B570 *Ed.* ERNEST KAY, *INTERNATIONAL WHO'S WHO IN POETRY –* SECOND EDITION   1970

B570(a) First English edition (1970)

INTERNATIONAL | WHO'S WHO IN POETRY | SECOND EDITION | 1970–1971 | Edited by | ERNEST KAY | With | An Appreciation of the late | JOHN MASEFIELD, O.M., | by | G. WILSON KNIGHT | [rule, 126mm.] | INTERNATIONAL WHO'S WHO IN POETRY | London and Dartmouth, England
(All width centred)

Collation: [A]⁸ [B]⁴ C–Y⁸ Z⁴ AA⁴ BB–II⁸ JJ⁴; 272 leaves; 240 × 145mm.; [i–xxiv] [1] 2–519 [520]

Page contents: [i] half-title: 'THE INTERNATIONAL | WHO'S WHO IN POETRY | 1970–1971'; [ii–iii] 'THE INTERNATIONAL WHO'S WHO IN POETRY' (listing of staff) (at foot of p.[iii]: '[rule] | All communications to: I.W.W.P., Artillery Mansions, Victoria Street, | London S.W.I, England.'); [iv] blank; [v] title-page; [vi] '© 1970 by Melrose Press, Ltd. | ALL RIGHTS RESERVED | PRINTED IN GREAT BRITAIN BY | DARTMOUTH CHRONICLE GROUP, LTD., DARTMOUTH, ENGLAND' (with additional leaf tipped-in on the verso of which is the photographic frontispiece: 167 × 117mm., 'The late John Masefield, O.M.'); [vii] 'Dedicated to | the Memory of | the late | JOHN MASEFIELD, O.M. | One of the most distinguished | poets of the Twentieth Century | and Poet Laureate to King George VI and Queen Elizabeth II of England.'; [viii–x] 'FOREWORD' ('It is with pride and honour that I write this Foreword…') (signed, 'Ernest Kay' [facsimile signature] together with addresses and dated 'January 29th, 1970.'); [xi–xiii] 'JOHN MASEFIELD: | AN APPRECIATION | by | G. WILSON KNIGHT' ('OUR twentieth-century literature shows a dearth of narrative poetry…') (unsigned); [xiv] blank; [xv–xxiv] 'THE INTERNATIONAL | WHO'S WHO IN POETRY | $1,000 AWARDS' (text and prize-winning entries); [1]–350 text of directory; 351–352 blank (except for running-title and page numbers); 353–76 'PHOTOGRAPHIC SECTION OF | THE INTERNATIONAL | WHO'S WHO IN POETRY' (text and photographs); 377–519 text of Appendices; [520] blank

Paper: wove paper

Running title: 'INTERNATIONAL WHO'S WHO IN POETRY' (58mm.) on both verso and recto, pp.2–519

Binding: purple cloth. On spine, in gilt: '[double rule] | INTERNATIONAL | WHO'S WHO | IN POETRY | [double rule] | 1970–1971 | SECOND | EDITION | I.W.W.P. | LONDON' (all width centred). On upper cover, in gilt: 'INTERNATIONAL | WHO'S WHO | IN POETRY | 1970–1971'. Lower cover: blank. All edges trimmed. Binding measurements: 249 × 147mm. (covers), 249 × 48mm. (spine). End-papers: wove paper.

Publication date: published, according to *Whitaker's*, August 1970

Price: £9.00

Masefield contents:
[Lines to the President of United Poets Laureate International, Dr. Amando M. Yuzon] ('The English say, 'The really wise')
        (introduced as '…John Masefield… wrote the following…')

Notes:
The Masefield contribution is quoted within appendix B, comprising an article on The United Poets Laureate International by Amando M. Yuzon. The verse apparently commemorates a visit to Masefield by Yuzon during 1965. On the occasion Masefield was presented with gilt laurels and crowned 'Poet Laureate of the World'. The gilt laurels are now in the collection of The John Masefield Society.

A dust-jacket for the volume includes 'Some opinions of I.W.W.P.' on the lower flap. The first of these is as follows:

'A welcome and useful reference book, which has already helpfully lightened my darkness.' – the late John Masefield, O.M., Poet Laureate to King George VI and Queen Elizabeth II, of England, from 1930 to 1967.

The Appreciation of Masefield by G. Wilson Knight was first published within Handley-Taylor's bibliography in 1960.

Copies seen: private collection (PWE); BL (P.901.897) stamped 8 OCT 1970

B575 *Ed.* CORLISS LAMONT, *THE THOMAS LAMONTS IN AMERICA* 1971

B575(a) First combined English and American edition (1971)

THE | THOMAS LAMONTS | IN AMERICA | *by* | Corliss Lamont | Edward Miner Lamont | Thomas Stilwell Lamont | The Reverend Thomas Lamont | Thomas William Lamont | Thomas William Lamont II | Margaret Lamont Heap | Francis T. P. Plimpton | Nathan M. Pusey | *with Recollections and Poems* | *by* | John Masefield | *Edited by* CORLISS LAMONT | [publisher's device of half-timbered house: 18 × 16mm.] | SOUTH BRUNSWICK AND NEW YORK : A. S. BARNES AND COMPANY | LONDON : THOMAS YOSELOFF LTD
(All width centred)

Collation: [A-H]¹⁶ (±[D]13 ±[F]12 ±[G]13); 128 leaves; 253 × 165mm.; [1–7] 8–9 [10–11] 12 [13] 14–19 [20–22] 23 [24] 25–39 [40] 41–77 [78] 79–83 [84] 85–89 [90] 91–121 [122] 123–33 [134] 135 [136] 137–53 [154] 155–209 [210] 211–50 [251–52] 253–55 [256]

Page contents: [1] half-title: 'THE | THOMAS LAMONTS | IN AMERICA'; [2] blank; [3] title-page (with additional leaf tipped-in on the verso of which is the colour frontispiece: 149 × 130mm., '*The Lamont Coat of Arms*'); [4] '© 1962 by Corliss Lamont and Thomas S. Lamont | © 1971 by Corliss Lamont | Library of Congress Catalogue Card Number: 74–151125 | A. S. Barnes and Co., Inc. | Cranbury, New Jersey 08512 | Thomas Yoseloff Ltd | 108 New Bond Street | London W1Y OQX, England | ISBN 0-498-07882-5 | Printed in the United States of America'; [5] '*To the Lamonts- | Past, Present, and Future*'; [6] blank; [7]-8 'CONTENTS' (six parts (each sub-divided), who's who of authors, preface, epilogue and three appendixes listed with page references); 9 'ILLUSTRATIONS' (17 illustrations (including frontispiece) listed with page references); [10] blank; [11]-12 'A WHO'S WHO OF THE AUTHORS' ('Corliss Lamont, editor of *The Thomas Lamonts in America*, was born...'); [13]-19 'PREFACE' and illustration ('Like my grandfather Lamont, my father, and my brother Thomas, I have a feeling...') (headed, '*by Corliss Lamont*'); [20] blank; [21] 'THE | THOMAS LAMONTS | IN AMERICA'; [22] blank; 23 'PART I | *The Lamont Family in the | Nineteenth Century* | by the Reverend Thomas Lamont'; [24] blank; 25–76 text and illustrations; 77 'PART II | *A Lamont Reunion in 1876*'; [78] blank; 79–88 text and illustrations; 89 'PART III | *Thomas William Lamont and | Florence Corliss Lamont*'; [90]-133 text and illustrations; [134] blank; 135 'PART IV | *Recollections and Poems* | by John Masefield'; [136]-152 text and illustration; 153 'PART V | *Thomas Stilwell Lamont*'; [154]-208 text and illustrations; 209 'PART VI | *Thomas William Lamont II*'; [210–51] text and illustrations; [252] blank; 253 'APPENDIX I | ACKNOWLEDGMENTS'; 254 'APPENDIX II | CLAN LAMONT NAMES | AND SEPTS'; 255 'APPENDIX III | FAMILY TREE'; [256] blank (with two additional folded leaves tipped-in on the verso of which are '*LAMONT FAMILY TREE I*' and '*LAMONT FAMILY TREE II*')

Paper: wove paper

Running title: 'THE THOMAS LAMONTS IN AMERICA' (76mm.) on verso; recto title comprises sectional title, pp.8–250

Binding: burgundy cloth. On spine reading lengthways down spine from head, in gold: 'Lamont The Thomas Lamonts in America'; horizontally at foot of spine: 'Barnes'. Covers: blank. All edges trimmed. Sewn head band (in red and yellow). Binding measurements: 259 × 167mm. (covers), 259 × 34mm. (spine). End-papers: wove paper illustrated with maps in burgundy: 'Original Lamont Country in Scotland | and main locale of settlements in | County Antrim, Ireland'.

Publication date: published in England, according to *Whitaker's*, April 1972

Price: £4.00

Masefield contents:
Masefield's poem 'In the Memory of Two Friends of all Great Causes' is quoted on page 114. It commences 'O Passer-by, remember these two Friends,'.

The statement on the death of Florence Lamont from *The Times* for 30 December 1952 headed 'John and Constance Masefield' is quoted on page 113.

Part IV of this volume, entitled 'Recollections and Poems by John Masefield' contains three items:

> Some Memories of Thomas William Lamont and Florence Corliss Lamont ('I am glad to be allowed the privilege of...') (signed, 'Burcote Brook, Abingdon | June 1961')
> The Western Hudson Shore ('In a long life's first independent day,')
> To The Great Friends in Lifetime ('This, I believe, that we remain in Time')

A 'Letter from John Masefield (After hearing of the death of Thomas W. Lamont II.)' is quoted on page 245. Dated June, 1945, from Burcote Brook, addressed to 'Dear Tommy and Ellie' and signed 'John Masefield', it commences 'The news of your appalling loss just breaks our hearts in two with sorrow...'

Notes:
Illustrative photographs are printed with the text. The volume is more lavishly illustrated than the 1962 edition of *The Thomas Lamont Family* (see B535). A photograph of Masefield ('John Masefield with "Mickey" (about 1949)') is included. The cancel leaves all include

photographs. Stubs of leaves reveal the same illustration to have been included on the deleted leaf so it is feasible that incorrect captions may have necessitated the change.

Copies seen: NYPL (Berg Collection) signed, 'Corliss Lamont, 1972' on page [5]

B580 KETH LAYCOCK, *IN THIS GREEN FOREST* 1973

B580(a) First Swedish edition [in English] (1973)

In | *This* | *Green Forest* | Poems Anglo-Swedish | by | Keth Laycock | illustrated by Lavinia O'Dowd | The Anglo-American Center | MULLSJÖ, Sweden | 1973
(All width centred)

Collation: [A-C]⁸ [D]¹²; 36 leaves; 230 × 147mm.; [i–ii] 1 [2] 3–9 [10] 11–19 [20] 21–23 [24] 25–31 [32] 33–35 [36] 37–43 [44] 45–48 [49–50] 51–66 [67–70]

Page contents: [i] title-page; [ii] 'The Scolar Press Limited, Ilkley, Yorkshire | 1973'; 1–[67] text and illustrations; [68–70] blank

Paper: laid paper (no watermark) chain-lines 27mm. apart (the chain-lines run horizontally)

Running title: none

Binding: green wrappers. Spine: blank. On upper wrapper, in green on white panel: 'IN THIS GREEN FOREST | Poems by Keth Laycock' (within abstract of tree base in green, white and light green). Lower wrapper: blank. All edges trimmed. Binding measurements: 228 × 150mm. (wrappers), 228 × 7mm. (spine). Separate end-papers (using paper described above) are present at the front of the volume with D11 and D12 as end-papers at the rear.

Also issued in green and speckled brown cloth. On spine reading lengthways down spine from head, in gold: 'In This Green Forest Poems by Keth Laycock'. Covers: blank. All edges trimmed. Sewn head and foot band (in green and yellow). Binding measurements: 236 × 150mm. (covers), 236 × 25mm. (spine). End-papers: laid paper (no watermark) chain-lines 26–27mm. apart (the chain-lines run horizontally).

Publication date: 1973

Price: unknown

Masefield contents:
Masefield's 'contribution' occurs at the end of Laycock's postscript, pp.63–64 (see notes).

Notes:
The volume comprises poems by Laycock in addition to Laycock's translations of Swedish poems (printed with details of original authors and titles). A postscript, acknowledgements and list of biographical data is also included.

The quotation from Masefield (with Laycock's explanation) is as follows:

> I should like to record that in the Thirties I was helped and encouraged by John Masefield in whose company I spent a few hours after hearing him read extensively from his own works in public, a deeply moving experience which transfigured him in my eyes. Overcoming my scruples I asked him in the end if he would mind if I sent him a few of my poems for critical comment. 'Not at all,' he cheerfully replied, 'it's my job.' In a letter he said he liked one or two very much but that I was too lavish with my adjectives, a weakness of his own, he confessed. I have long pondered his concluding remark which I here quote for the benefit of those with ears to hear:- 'The adjective is the weakest word in a sentence. It is a limiting word, keeping a thing to one quality, in a world where all things have countless qualities.'

The 'Biographical Data' provided on page 66 of the volume records that Keth Laycock was born in Bradford, Yorkshire in June 1903. His career as English teacher and lecturer was mostly abroad.

Copies seen: BL (X.981/9349) stamped 19 DEC 1974 cloth binding; BL (X.909/30835) stamped 30 SEP 1974 wrappers

B585 JOHN WELLS, *RUDE WORDS*
A DISCURSIVE HISTORY OF THE LONDON LIBRARY 1991

B585(a) First English edition (1991)

RUDE WORDS | A Discursive History of the | London Library | John Wells | M | MACMILLAN | LONDON
(All width centred)

Collation: [1–16]⁸; 128 leaves; 213 × 134mm.; [i–xii] 1–10 [11] 12–22 [23] 24–38 [39] 40–55 [56] 57–67 [68] 69–80 [81] 82–93 [94] 95–107 [108] 109–120 [121] 122–33 [134] 135–45 [146] 147–57 [158] 159–69 [170] 171–80 [181] 182–93 [194] 195–204 [205] 206–216 [217] 218–25 [226] 227 [228] 229–40 [241–44]

Page contents: [i] half-title: 'RUDE WORDS'; [ii] blank; [iii] title-page; [iv] 'Copyright © John Wells 1991 | All rights reserved. No reproduction, copy or transmission | of this publication may be made without written permission. | No paragraph of this publication may be reproduced, copied | or transmitted save with written permission or in accordance | with the provisions of the

Copyright Act 1956 (as amended). | Any person who does any unauthorised act in relation to this | publication may be liable to criminal prosecution and | civil claims for damages. | The right of John Wells to be identified | as author of this work has been | asserted by him in accordance with | the Copyright, Designs and Patents Act 1988. | First published 1991 by | MACMILLAN LONDON LIMITED | Cavaye Place London SW10 9PG | and Basingstoke | Associated companies in Auckland, Delhi, Dublin, Gaborone, | Hamburg, Harare, Hong Kong, Johannesburg, Kuala Lumpur, | Lagos, Manzini, Melbourne, Mexico City, Nairobi, New York, | Singapore and Tokyo | ISBN 0-333-47519-4 | A CIP catalogue record for this book is available from | the British Library | Typeset by Florencetype Ltd, Kewstoke, Avon | Printed and bound in Great Britain by | Billings Bookplan, Worcester'; [v] dedication; [vi] prefatory quotation by Thomas Carlyle; [vii] 'Contents' (acknowledgements, 18 chapters, sources and index listed with page references); [viii] blank; [ix–x] 'Acknowledgements'; [xi] '[plan] | The London Library: an isometric plan'; [xii] blank; 1–227 text; [228] blank; 229–40 'Index'; [241–44] blank

Paper: wove paper

Running title: 'RUDE WORDS' (21mm.) on verso; recto title comprises chapter title, pp.2–[226]

Binding: blue cloth. On spine reading lengthways down spine from head, in gold: 'RUDE WORDS JOHN WELLS'; horizontally at foot of spine: 'M'. Covers: blank. All edges trimmed. Binding measurements: 221 × 136mm. (covers), 221 × 34mm. (spine). End-papers: grey wove paper.

Publication date: published, according to *Whitaker's*, September 1991

Price: £17.50

Masefield contents:
[Untitled parody] ('If we were in a pavender')
    (introduced as '…Masefield wrote…')

Notes:
The gutter of the book reveals that a number of the 'unsigned' gatherings are signed on the spine of the gathering itself.

The 'Sources' acknowledge the copyright of the Masefield verse:

> The Society of Authors as the literary representative of the Estate of John Masefield for his doggerel verse 'If we were in a pavender…'

The original letter is contained in the archives of the London Library. It is undated (on headed Burcote Brook paper with the 'Clifton Hampden 277' telephone number). The full text is as follows:

> Dear Librarian, | So many thanks for your most | kind letter, with the verses. | To thank you in prose is | not easy, so may I add that | If we were in a pavender, | A pavender or pub, | I'd pledge you in a javender | A javender or jubbe | Of orange-juicy shravender, | Rum-shravender or shrub, | For taking so much travender | Such travender or troub. | Yours sincerely, | John Masefield.

Wells therefore transcribes the poem incorrectly in line 5 and silently adds editorial punctuation.

The title of the volume is taken from the Carlyle quotation on page [vi]:

> The accomplished and distinguished, the beautiful, the wise, something of what is best in England, have listened patiently to my rude words. *Thomas Carlyle, 1840*

Copies seen: UCL (LIBRARIANSHIP L14 WEL); BL (2719.e.2747) stamped 25 JAN 1993

C. Contributions to Newspapers and Periodicals

The Cadet – School Ship *H.M.S. Conway* (Liverpool, U.K.)

C005.001   Mar 26, 1895, p.164
               [Letter, dated Mar 4, 1895, to Captain A.T. Miller]
               Dear Captain Miller, – Thank you very much indeed for your kindness...
               [signed, 'J. G. MASEFIELD' [*sic*]]

C005.002   Dec 10, 1898, p.129
               [Letter, dated Oct 2, 1898, to Captain A.T. Miller]
               Dear Captain Miller, During my first term on board the "Conway"...
               [signed, 'JOHN MASEFIELD']

The Outlook (London, U.K.)

C010.001   Jun 3, 1899, p.580
               Nicias Moriturus *[Verse]*
               An' Bill can have my sea-boots, Nigger Jim can have my knife,
               [signed, 'JOHN E. MASEFIELD']

C010.002   Oct 5, 1901, p.304
               Trade Winds *[Verse]*
               In the harbour, in the Island, in the Spanish Seas,
               [signed, 'JOHN MASEFIELD']

C010.003   Nov 23, 1901, p.558
               Cardigan Bay *[Verse]*
               Clean green windy billows notching out the sky,
               [signed, 'JOHN MASEFIELD' and dated 'October, 1894']

C010.004   Dec 21, 1901, p.720
               Bill *[Verse]*
               He lay dead on the cluttered deck and stared at the cold skies,
               [signed, 'JOHN MASEFIELD']

C010.005   Feb 22, 1902, p.112
               Vagabond *[Verse]*
               Dunno a heap about the what and why,
               [signed, 'J.E. MASEFIELD']

The Tatler – An Illustrated Journal of Society and the Drama (London, U.K.)

C015.001   Dec 25, 1901, p.558
               Christmas, 1901 *[Verse]*
               A wind is rustling "south and soft,"
               [signed 'J. MAREFIELD' [*sic*]]

C015.002   Feb 5, 1902, p.264
               Off Cape St. Vincent *[Verse]*
               Now, Bill, ain't it prime to be a-sailin',
               [signed, 'J. MASEFIELD']

C015.003   Feb 26, 1902, p.392
                The Fever Ship *[Verse]*
               There'll be no weeping girls ashore when our ship sails,
               [signed, 'J. MASEFIELD']

The Speaker (London, U.K.)

C020.001   Feb 15, 1902, p.560
               Sea Fever *[Verse]*
               I must down to the seas again, to the lonely sea and the sky,
               [signed, 'JOHN MASEFIELD']

C020.002   Mar 29, 1902, p.729
            The Dead Knight *[Verse]*
            The cleanly rush of the mountain air
            [signed, 'JOHN MASEFIELD']
C020.003   Apr 5, 1902, p.19
            Studies in Solid Bed-Rock [Book Review: Bart Kennedy, *A Sailor Tramp*]
            That pleasing creature the Amateur Vagabond has of late years...
            [signed, 'JOHN MASEFIELD']
C020.004   Apr 12, 1902, p.45
            Burying at Sea *[Verse]*
            [prefatory section of prose: "'N' don't you go buryin' no corpses...]
            "He's deader'n nails," the fo'c's'le said, "'n' gone to his long sleep."
            [signed, 'JOHN MASEFIELD']
C020.005   Apr 26, 1902, pp.106–108
            A Measure of Shifting Sand *[Prose]*
            I. – The Setting of the Course
            For three reckless weeks we lived riotously. We drank much...
            [signed, 'JOHN MASEFIELD']
C020.006   May 31, 1902, p.250
            Sorrow O' Mydath *[Verse]*
            Weary the cry of the wind is, weary the sea,
            [signed, 'JOHN MASEFIELD']
C020.007   Jun 7, 1902, p.277
            Mother Carey. As told me by the Bos'un *[Verse]*
            "Mother Carey ? She's the mother o' the witches,
            [signed, 'JOHN MASEFIELD']
C020.008   Jun 14, 1902, p.305
            On Malvern Hill *[Verse]*
            A strong wind brushes down the clover,
            [signed, 'JOHN MASEFIELD']
C020.009   Jun 21, 1902, pp.331–32
            A Measure of Shifting Sand *[Prose]*
            II.
            It was past noon when we returned to the garret. Johnson and myself were...
            [signed, 'JOHN MASEFIELD']
C020.010   Jun 28, 1902, pp.361–62
            A Measure of Shifting Sand *[Prose]*
            III.
            We paid for our night's lodging, and drifted down stairs to the bar.
            [signed, 'JOHN MASEFIELD']
C020.011   Jun 28, 1902, p.365
            There's a Wind A-Blowing *[Verse]*
            It's a warm wind, the west wind, full of birds' cries.
            [signed, 'JOHN MASEFIELD']
C020.012   Jul 5, 1902, p.384
            A Wind's in the Heart O' Me *[Verse]*
            [prefatory quotation ascribed to 'Davy The Rigger']
            A wind's in the heart o' me, a fire's in my heels,
            [signed, 'JOHN MASEFIELD']
C020.013   Jul 12, 1902, p.411
            Coast-Fever *[Verse]*
            He stumbled out of the alley-way with cheeks the colour of paste,
            [signed, 'JOHN MASEFIELD']
C020.014   Jul 26, 1902, pp.454–55
            A Measure of Shifting Sand *[Prose]*
            IV.
            At the back of the Judge's house was a steep little slope...
            [signed, 'JOHN MASEFIELD']
C020.015   Aug 16, 1902, p.530
            "Port O' Many Ships." *[Verse]*
            "It's a sunny pleasant anchorage is Kingdom Come,"
            [signed, 'JOHN MASEFIELD']

C020.016 Aug 23, 1902, pp.550–51
 A Measure of Shifting Sand [Prose]
 V.
 Some days later, when Powys had returned to New York on the heels...
 [signed, 'JOHN MASEFIELD']

C020.017 Aug 23, 1902, pp.556–57
 A Wanderer's Oddments [Book Review: Bart Kennedy, *London in Shadow*]
 In these days, when folk who "longen to go on pilgrimage" go not...
 [signed, 'JOHN MASEFIELD']

C020.018 Sep 20, 1902, pp.657–58
 Bitter Waters [Book Review: transl. Charles Horne: Maxim Gorky, *Three Men*]
 Sometimes I hear regrets expressed for those old portly folios of...
 [signed, 'JOHN MASEFIELD']

C020.019 Sep 27, 1902, p.678
 Hell's Pavement. – Billy. [Verse]
 "When I'm discharged at Liverpool, 'n' draws my bit o' pay,
 [signed, 'JOHN MASEFIELD']

C020.020 Oct 4, 1902, p.18
 Evening. Regatta Day. Iquique Harbour [Verse]
 "Your nose is a red jelly. Your mouth's a toothless wreck,
 [signed, 'JOHN MASEFIELD']

C020.021 Oct 18, 1902, p.74
 A Night at Dago Tom's [Verse]
 Oh, yesterday I think it was, while cruising down the street
 [signed, 'JOHN MASEFIELD']

C020.022 Dec 13, 1902, p.280
 Jimmy the Dane [Verse]
 "Goneys and gullies and all o' the birds o' the sea,
 [signed, 'JOHN MASEFIELD']

C020.023 Jan 31, 1903, p.442
 Deep Sea Yarns [Book Review: Joseph Conrad, *Youth, A Narrative*]
 Mr. Conrad's stories, excellent though they are, leave always...
 [signed, 'J. MASEFIELD']

C020.024 Feb 14, 1903, pp.494–95
 Old Starm Along [Book Review: Walter Runciman, *Windjammers and Sea Tramps*]
 To all lovers of the sea, to all those whose hearts go the merrier...
 [unsigned]

C020.025 Mar 7, 1903, p.557
 The Harper's Song [Verse]
 This sweetness trembling from the strings,
 [signed, 'JOHN MASEFIELD']

C020.026 Mar 21, 1903, pp.616–17
 Some Sea-Dogs [Book Review: W.H. Fitchett, *Nelson and his Captains*]
 "Nelson," says Mr Fitchett, "is the only figure amongst the great…
 [unsigned]

C020.027 May 2, 1903, p.119
 Two Songs [Verse]
 Roadways
 One road runs to London,
 [headed, 'By John Masefield']

C020.028 May 2, 1903, p.119
 Two Songs [Verse]
 To The Spring Flowers
 Dim violets, violets white, and ye
 [headed, 'By John Masefield']

C020.029 May 9, 1903, pp.134–35
 On the Futility of Being Celtic [Prose]
 Once upon a time, in the happy past, long before I had cut my...
 [signed, 'JOHN MASEFIELD']

C020.030   May 9, 1903, p.141
        Captain Stratton's Fancy *[Verse]*
        Oh, some are fond o' red wine and some are fond o' white,
        [signed, 'JOHN MASEFIELD']

C020.031   May 16, 1903, p.163
        Hall Sands *[Verse]*
        [prefatory note: 'The village of Hall Sands, between Dartmouth...']
        The moon is bright on Devon sands,
        [signed, 'JOHN MASEFIELD']

C020.032   Jul 4, 1903, p.322
        Beauty *[Verse]*
        I have seen dawn and sunset on moors and windy hills
        [signed, 'JOHN MASEFIELD']

C020.033   Aug 15, 1903, p.460
        Dawn *[Verse]*
        The dawn comes cold : the haystack smokes,
        [signed, 'JOHN MASEFIELD']

C020.034   Nov 14, 1903, pp.149–50
        The Rose of Spain [Book Review: Joseph Conrad and Ford Madox Hueffer, *Romance*]
        Some books are like old music, or old magic, in their power...
        [signed, 'J. MASEFIELD']

C020.035   Dec 12, 1903, pp.253–54
        The Banner of Romance [Combined Book Review: George Bartram, *The Longshoremen*; Robert Leighton, *The Haunted Ship*; J.C. Hutcheson, *The Ghost Ship*; and T. Bevan, *Beggars of the Sea*]
        When William Hazlitt was an old man he used to sit before the fire...
        [signed, 'J. MASEFIELD']

C020.036   Jun 4, 1904, p.227
        The Seekers *[Verse]*
        Friends and loves we have none, nor wealth, nor blessed abode,
        [signed, 'JOHN MASEFIELD']

C020.037   Jun 11, 1904, p.249
        A June Twilight *[Verse]*
        The twilight comes; the sun
        [signed, 'JOHN MASEFIELD']

C020.038   Nov 5, 1904, pp.125–26
        In Dock *[Prose]*
        My first impressions of a sailor's life were obtained at second hand...
        [signed, 'JOHN MASEFIELD']

C020.039   Jan 14, 1905, p.378
        A Whaler's Song *[Verse]*
        There are some that are fond of the galley, the beaked bitter snake of the seas
        [signed, 'JOHN MASEFIELD']

C020.040   Mar 25, 1905, pp.608–609
        Saturday Night's Entertainments *[Prose]*
        Outside the door a little crowd had formed round a brass-voiced...
        [signed, 'JOHN MASEFIELD']

C020.041   Apr 15, 1905, p.73
        The Greenwich Pensioner *[Verse]*
        "I'll go no more a roving by the light of the moon,
        [signed, 'JOHN MASEFIELD']

C020.042   May 6, 1905, pp.140–41
        In Dock *[Prose]*
        "Now, turn out here, young fellers! Show a leg and put a stocking...
        [signed, 'JOHN MASEFIELD']

C020.043   Sep 2, 1905, pp.522–23
        The Yarn of Happy Jack *[Prose]*
        I once knew an old Norwegian sailor, one of the mildest and kindest...
        [signed, 'JOHN MASEFIELD']

C020.044   Dec 9, 1905, p.254
        To an Old Tune *[Verse]*
        Twilight it is, and the far woods are dim, and the rooks cry and call,
        [signed, 'JOHN MASEFIELD']

C020.045 Dec 23, 1905, pp.301–302
On Folk Songs [Book Review: Cecil J. Sharp and Charles L. Marson, *Folk Songs from Somerset*]
I have often wished that I could be a minstrel, or strolling ballad singer...
[signed, 'JOHN MASEFIELD']

C020.046 Apr 28, 1906, pp.88–89
William Dampier *[Prose]*
In estimating the work of any man, it is well to remember the conditions...
[signed, 'JOHN MASEFIELD']

C020.047 Aug 18, 1906, pp.460–61
Causerie of the Week. Spitsbergen [Book Review: Martin Conway, *No Man's Land*]
There is an old whaling song which had once a great vogue...
[signed, 'JOHN MASEFIELD']

C020.048 Nov 10, 1906, pp.173–74
Some Irish Fairies *[Prose]*
There are not many fairies in England. The English night is peopled...
[signed, 'By John Masefield']

C020.049 Dec 8, 1906, pp.275–76
Causerie of the Week. Christmas Books *[Book Reviews]*
During the last few years the spirit of the Christmas book...
[signed, 'JOHN MASEFIELD']

The Living Age (Boston, U.S.A.)

C025.001 Mar 22, 1902, p.745
Sea Fever *[Verse]*
I must down to the sea again, to the lonely sea and the sky,
[signed, 'John Masefield']

C025.002 Aug 2, 1902, p.320
On Malvern Hill *[Verse]*
A strong wind brushes down the clover,
[signed, 'John Masefield']

C025.003 Aug 30, 1902, p.576
There's a Wind A-Blowing *[Verse]*
It's a warm wind, the west wind, full of birds' cries.
[signed, 'John Masefield']

C025.004 Oct 11, 1902, p.128
A Wind's in the Heart O' Me *[Verse]*
[prefatory quotation ascribed to 'Davy the Rigger']
A wind's in the heart o' me, a fire's in my heels,
[signed, 'John Masefield']

C025.005 Nov 29, 1902, p.576
"Port O' Many Ships" *[Verse]*
"It's a sunny pleasant anchorage is Kingdom Come,
[signed, 'John Masefield']

C025.006 Apr 18, 1903, p.192
Harbor Bar *[Verse]*
All in the feathered palm-tree tops the bright green parrots screech,
[signed, 'John Masefield']

C025.007 May 30, 1903, p.576
To The Spring Flowers *[Verse]*
Dim violets, violets white, and ye
[signed, 'John Masefield']

C025.008 Jun 27, 1903, p.824
London Town *[Verse]*
Oh, London Town's a fine town, and London sights are rare,
[signed, 'John Masefield']

C025.009 Aug 1, 1903, p.320
Roadways *[Verse]*
One road runs to London,
[signed, 'John Masefield']

C025.010	Aug 27, 1904, p.576
	The Seekers *[Verse]*
	Friends and loves we have none, nor wealth, nor blessed abode,
	[signed, 'John Masefield']
C025.011	Feb 11, 1905, p.384
	Being Her Friend *[Verse]*
	Being her friend, I do not care, not I,
	[signed, 'John Masefield']
C025.012	Feb 18, 1905, p.448
	The Harper's Song *[Verse]*
	This sweetness trembling from the strings,
	[signed, 'John Masefield']
C025.013	May 20, 1905, p.512
	A Whaler's Song *[Verse]*
	There are some that are fond of the galley, the beaked bitter snake of the seas
	[signed, 'John Masefield']
C025.014	Jul 8, 1905, p.66
	The Greenwich Pensioner *[Verse]*
	"I'll go no more a roving by the light of the moon,
	[signed, 'John Masefield']
C025.015	Mar 3, 1906, p.514
	To an Old Tune *[Verse]*
	Twilight it is, and the far woods are dim, and the rooks cry and call,
	[signed, 'John Masefield']
C025.016	Dec 22, 1906, pp.760–63
	Some Irish Fairies *[Prose]*
	There are not many fairies in England. The English night is peopled...
	[signed, 'John Masefield']
C025.017	Jan 25, 1908, p.194
	A Creed *[Verse]*
	I hold that when a person dies
	[signed, 'John Masefield']
C025.018	Oct 3, 1908, p.2
	Christmas Eve at Sea *[Verse]*
	A wind is nestling "south and soft,"
	[signed, 'John Masefield']
C025.019	*Mar 15, 1913, p.642*
	Ballad of Sir Bors [Verse]
	[listed by Readers' Guide to Periodical Literature *Vol.III]*
C025.020	*Aug 23, 1913, p.450*
	Beauty [Verse]
	[listed by Readers' Guide to Periodical Literature *Vol.III]*
C025.021	*Sep 13, 1913, p.642*
	London Town [Verse]
	[listed by Readers' Guide to Periodical Literature *Vol.III]*
C025.022	*Sep 20, 1913, p.706*
	St. Mary's Bells [Verse]
	[listed by Readers' Guide to Periodical Literature *Vol.III]*
C025.023	*Sep 27, 1913, p.770*
	The Emigrant [Verse]
	[listed by Readers' Guide to Periodical Literature *Vol.III]*
C025.024	*Oct 11, 1913, p.66*
	Cargoes [Verse]
	[listed by Readers' Guide to Periodical Literature *Vol.III]*
C025.025	*Dec 27, 1913, p.770*
	Posted as Missing [Verse]
	[listed by Readers' Guide to Periodical Literature *Vol.III]*
C025.026	*Jan 3, 1914, p.2*
	Roadways [Verse]
	[listed by Readers' Guide to Periodical Literature *Vol.III]*

C025.027 *Jan 17, 1914, p.130*
    Twilight [Verse]
    [listed by Readers' Guide to Periodical Literature Vol.III*]*

C025.028 *Jan 24, 1914, p.194*
    Dawn [Verse]
    [listed by Readers' Guide to Periodical Literature Vol.III*]*

C025.029 *Jun 6, 1914, p.578*
    Laugh and be Merry [Verse]
    [listed by Readers' Guide to Periodical Literature Vol.III*]*

C025.030 *Apr 17, 1915, p.130*
    Tewkesbury Road [Verse]
    [listed by Readers' Guide to Periodical Literature Vol.IV*]*

C025.031 *Apr 24, 1915, p.194*
    Sea-Fever [Verse]
    [listed by Readers' Guide to Periodical Literature Vol.IV*]*

C025.032 *Oct 7, 1916, p.2*
    Word [Verse]
    [listed by Readers' Guide to Periodical Literature Vol.IV*]*

C025.033 *Jul 5, 1919, pp.15–19*
    Letters from America [Prose]
    [listed by Readers' Guide to Periodical Literature Vol.V*]*

C025.034 *Oct 4, 1919, p.64*
    Sonnet [Verse]
    Forget all these, the barren fool in power
    [listed by Readers' Guide to Periodical Literature Vol.V*]*

C025.035 *Feb 5, 1921, pp.353–56*
    The Delights of a Reader [Prose]
    [noted by Simmons, p.135]
    [listed by Readers' Guide to Periodical Literature Vol.V*]*

C025.036 *Jun 25, 1921, pp.781–84*
    On 'Reynard the Fox' [Prose]
    [noted by Simmons, p.135]
    [listed by Readers' Guide to Periodical Literature Vol.V*]*

The Pall Mall Magazine (London, U.K.)

C030.001 Apr 1902, pp.529–30
    The Yarn of The *Loch Achray [Verse]*
    Hear the yarn of a sailor, | An old yarn learned at sea.
    [headed, 'BY JOHN MASEFIELD']

C030.002 Oct 1902, p.234
    Sing a Song O' Shipwreck *[Verse]*
    He lolled on a bollard, a sunburnt son of the sea,
    [signed, 'BY JOHN MASEFIELD']

C030.003 May 1903, p.5
    London Town *[Verse]*
    Oh, London Town's a fine town, and London sights are rare,
    [signed, 'BY JOHN MASEFIELD']

C030.004 Sep 1906, p.303
    Posted as Missing *[Verse]*
    Under all her topsails she trembled like a stag,
    [signed, 'BY JOHN MASEFIELD']

C030.005 Mar 1907, pp.272–81
    Liverpool, City of Ships *[Prose]*
    Of all the great English ports, Liverpool alone gives the visitor a sense...
    [signed, 'JOHN MASEFIELD']

C030.006 Sep 1907, p.276
    A Creed *[Verse]*
    I hold that when a person dies
    [signed, 'JOHN MASEFIELD']

C030.007   Dec 1907, pp.813–15
         The Western Islands. *A Sea Fable [Prose]*
         In New York City there is the most wonderful street in the world.
         [signed, 'BY JOHN MASEFIELD']

A Broad Sheet (London, U.K.)

C035.001   Oct 1902, No. 10
         A Last Prayer *[Verse]*
         "When the last sea is sailed, and the last shallow charted,
         [signed, 'John Masefield']
C035.002   Dec 1902, No. 12
         Port of Holy Peter *[Verse]*
         The blue laguna rots and quivers, *[sic]*
         [signed, 'John Masefield']
C035.003   May 1903, No. 17
         Cargoes *[Verse]*
         Quinquireme of Nineveh, from distant Ophir,
         [signed, 'John Masefield']
C035.004   May 1903, No. 17
         Blind Man's Vigil *[Verse]*
         Mumblin' under the gallows, hearin' the clank o' the chain,
         [signed, 'John Masefield']
C035.005   May 1903, No. 17
         [Untitled] *[Verse]*
         The moon came white and ghostly as we laid the treasure down,
         [signed, 'John Masefield']
C035.006   Jul 1903, No. 19
         Theodore *[Verse]*
         They sacked the ships of London town,
         [signed, 'John Masefield']
C035.007   Nov 1903, No. 23
         [Untitled] *[Verse]*
         So here's to the bargeman, in his tattered dungaree,
         [signed, 'John Masefield']
C035.008   Dec 1903, No. 24
         Coming into Salcombe – A Christmas Chanty *[Verse]*
         Oh, the sea breeze will be steady, and the tall ship's going trim,
         [signed, 'John Masefield']

The Venture – An Annual of Art and Literature (London, U.K.)

C040.001   1903, p.1
         When Bony Death has Chilled her Gentle Blood *[Verse]* (entitled 'Beauty's Mirror' in the index)
         When bony Death has chilled her gentle blood
         [signed, 'JOHN MASEFIELD']
C040.002   1903, p.74
         Blindness *[Verse]*
         Since I have learned Love's shining alphabet,
         [signed, 'JOHN MASEFIELD']

The Green Sheaf (London, U.K.)

C045.001   1903, No.2, pp.9–10
         Jan A Dreams *[Prose]*
         This dream, like all my intenser dreams, commenced with a noise...
         [signed, 'John Masefield']
C045.002   1903, No.3, pp.6–7
         Spanish Ladies *[Verse]*
         Farewell and adieu to you fine Spanish Ladies –
         [signed, 'Words and Music given to John Masefield by Wally Blair, A.B.']

C045.003   1903, No.6, pp.4–9
         A Deep Sea Yarn *[Prose]*
         Up away north, in the old days, in Chester, there was a man who...
         [signed, 'By John Masefield']

C045.004   1903, No.7, pp.4–5
         Blind Man's Vigil *[Verse]*
         I'm a tattered starving beggar fiddling down the dirty streets,
         [signed, 'John Masefield']

The Academy (London, U.K.)

C050.001   Apr 4, 1903, pp.344–45
         Hans Breitmann *[Prose]*
         In reading American books, in studying that eager American life...
         [signed, 'JOHN MASEFIELD']

C050.002   Sep 19, 1903, pp.271–72
         At Uriconium *[Prose]*
         I first saw that city like a dark patch in the corn...
         [signed, 'JOHN MASEFIELD']

C050.003   Aug 11, 1906, pp.133–34
         Sea Songs and Ballads *[Prose]*
         In these days of short voyages and pirated music...
         [unsigned, attributed to Masefield in *Poole's Index to Periodical Literature*, fifth supplement, 1908, p.580]

The Manchester Guardian (Manchester, U.K.)

This listing is indebted to Fraser Drew's bibliographical article 'Book Reviews Published in the "Manchester Guardian"'. Additionally, the 'Selected Bibliography' that concludes Drew's study of national themes in Masefield, *John Masefield's England* (Farleigh Dickinson, 1973) also presents significant material. These have been vital, yet problematic sources, with reference to issues of attribution and anonymity. Drew's listing includes a note that 'many [book reviews] are unsigned, but in each case Masefield's authorship has been authenticated by the Manchester Guardian (in a letter of 3 Aug. 1951)'. The present archivist of the *Guardian* has indicated the impossibility today of tracing unsigned articles and our curiosity must be raised as to what means the paper used for authenticating material in 1951 that is now no longer possible (except, perhaps, Masefield himself). In addition to Drew we can employ the index to *The Guardian* as maintained by the paper. The index does not provide any additional details of authorship which are not already present in the paper itself (unsigned book reviews remain anonymous and frequently the index fails to record authorship even when present in the paper). Moreover, the handwriting is frequently illegible. Rather than using this index to confirm material already traced, my procedure has been to search the index without initial reference to Drew's listing. This procedure identifies a substantial number (in excess of thirty) of contributions signed 'J.M.' or 'J.E.M.' not recorded by Drew. Why Drew's sources failed to include these is unknown since the exact means of authentication employed by Drew, as noted above, remain a mystery. The possibility must be acknowledged that some of these articles are not by Masefield (a reviewer with the initials 'J.H.M.' is known to have been working for the paper during 1908). However, 'J.M.' appears to have been Masefield's established set of initials and the style in several contributions not recorded by Drew is unmistakably Masefield's. The *Guardian* index has also assisted in the correction of several errors and traced at least one contribution that eluded both Simmons and Drew (the sketch of 'Captain Robert Knox' on 9 June 1911, which, although reprinted in the second edition of *A Mainsail Haul* has remained unknown in its original periodical state until now). In view of all the issues concerning *Manchester Guardian* articles, they are presented here primarily on Drew's authority or because they are noted as being by 'J.M.' in the paper's index and these articles are listed with reservations. Masefield's 'Miscellany' column is excluded (although see Philip W. Errington, 'John Masefield and the Smock-Frock', *The Journal of The John Masefield Society*, John Masefield Society, May 1997, pp.30–31).

C055.001   Aug 26, 1903, p.9
         [Book Review: Margery Williams, *Spendthrift Summer*]
         Spendthrift Summer, by Margery Williams... is a novel of grey lives...
         [unsigned]

C055.002   Sep 2, 1903, p.9
         [Book Review: Inglis Goldie, *In the Heart of a Caprice*]
         In the Heart of a Caprice, by Inglis Goldie... is a little tale about...
         [unsigned]

C055.003   Sep 30, 1903, p.6
         [Book Review: Adeline Sergeant, *The Enthusiast*]
         The Enthusiast, by Adeline Sergeant... is a pleasant and pleasantly...
         [unsigned]

C055.004   Oct 14, 1903, p.5
[Book Review: Arnold Bennett, *His Leonora*]
Mr. Arnold Bennett writes cleverly, but, like so many clever...
[unsigned]

C055.005   Nov 24, 1903, p.12
A Veteran of the Sea. Half a Century in the Irish Mail Service *[Prose]*
This is the story of a cabin-boy who became a commodore, and who...
[unsigned]

C055.006   Dec 5, 1903, p.7
Sea Superstition *[Prose]*
One moonlit night in the tropics, as my ship was slipping south...
[unsigned]

C055.007   Dec 9, 1903, p.4
[Book Review: Bullen, *Sea Wrack*]
Mr. Bullen's Sea Wrack... shows little imagination.
[unsigned]

C055.008   Dec 22, 1903, p.5
[Book Review: H. De Windt, *From Paris to New York by Land*]
This is the record of a journey undertaken two years ago...
[unsigned]

C055.009   Jan 21, 1904, p.5
[Book Review: R.B. Cunninghame Graham, *Hernando de Soto*]
This is one of the four or five really excellent books…
[unsigned]

C055.010   Jan 23, 1904, p.5
A Sailor's Yarn *[Prose]*
Down the jetty, where the tide ran, where the wet green weed lay...
[unsigned]

C055.011   Feb 4, 1904, p.5
[Book Review: Bart Kennedy, *A Tramp in Spain*]
Mr. Bart Kennedy's A Tramp in Spain... is as excellent a story...
[unsigned]

C055.012   Mar 22, 1904, p.5
[Book Review: Senator J. Lynch, *Three Years in the Klondike*]
This is the record of a gold-digger's adventures...
[unsigned]

C055.013   Mar 23, 1904, p.5
[Book Review: Herman K. Vielé, *Myra of the Pines*]
In Myra of the Pines... Mr. Herman K. Vielé gives us...
[unsigned]

C055.014   Mar 24, 1904, p.5
[Book Review: Major Swayne, *Through The Highlands of Siberia*]
Through The Highlands Of Siberia, By Major Swayne... is the record of...
[unsigned]

C055.015   Apr 2, 1904, p.4
Port Of Many Ships *[Prose]*
Sometimes in the afternoons, when I was a lad...
[unsigned]

C055.016   Apr 6, 1904, p.3
[Book Review: M. Hartwell Catherwood, *The Story of Tonty*]
The Story of Tonty, by M. Hartwell Catherwood... is an example...
[unsigned]

C055.017   Apr 20, 1904, p.4
[Book Review: Arthur H. Adams, *Tussock Land*]
Mr. Arthur H. Adams, whose Tussock Land... is the latest addition...
[unsigned]

C055.018   May 4, 1904, p.10
A "Tramp's" Cruise *[Prose]*
The Company's fleet consisted of two trading steamers...
[unsigned but attributed by Simmons, and L.G. Thornber (see Fraser Drew)]

C055.019 May 18, 1904, p.10
   [Book Review: Norman Duncan, *The Way of the Sea*]
   Mr. Norman Duncan's book The Way of the Sea... might be called...
   [unsigned]

C055.020 May 19, 1904, p.12
   A Spanish Sailor's Yarn *[Prose]*
   Some years ago I was on board a schooner plying between St. James...
   [signed, 'J.M.']

C055.021 May 26, 1904, p.6
   [Book Review: Albert Sonnichsen, *Deep-Sea Vagabonds*]
   Deep-Sea Vagabonds, by Mr. Albert Sonnichsen... is a simple, pleasant...
   [unsigned]

C055.022 Jun 14, 1904, p.5
   [Book Review: W.N. Armstrong, *Around the World with a King*]
   Around the World with a King, by W.N. Armstrong... is the record...
   [unsigned]

C055.023 Jul 1, 1904, p.5
   [Book Review: George G. Bolton, *A Specialist in Crime*]
   A Specialist in Crime, by George G. Bolton... is a tartly written tale...
   [unsigned]

C055.024 Jul 16, 1904, p.7
   The Yarn of Lanky Job *[Prose]*
   When I was in Valparaiso I spent my evenings in the garden...
   [unsigned]

C055.025 Aug 11, 1904, p.10
   Charlie Cotton *[Prose]*
   Some years ago, when I was tramping in America...
   [signed, 'V.M.' [*sic*]]

C055.026 Sep 14, 1904, p.3
   [Book Review: Sir Gilbert Parker, *A Ladder of Swords*]
   A Ladder of Swords, by Sir Gilbert Parker... is the work of...
   [unsigned]

C055.027 Sep 27, 1904, p.12
   In a New York Saloon *[Prose]*
   Some years ago, at the beginning of a sultry summer...
   [signed, 'J.M.']

C055.028 Oct 5, 1904, p.3
   [Book Review: H.G. Wells, *The Food of the Gods...*]
   The Food of the Gods and How it Came to Earth, by H.G. Wells...
   [unsigned]

C055.029 Oct 8, 1904, p.7
   A Spanish Love Tale *[Prose]*
   The galleon Spanish Rose was built in St Mary of the Bells...
   [unsigned]

C055.030 Oct 12, 1904, p.5
   [Book Review: Walter Runciman, *The Shellback's Progress*]
   The Shellback's Progress, by Walter Runciman, sen.... is a book of...
   [unsigned]

C055.031 Oct 14, 1904, p.5
   [Book Review: F.T. Bullen, *Sea Puritans*]
   Sea Puritans, by F.T. Bullen... is a historical romance of the time of...
   [unsigned]

C055.032 Oct 19, 1904, p.5
   [Book Review: Fiona Macleod, *The Winged Destiny*]
   The Winged Destiny, by Fiona Macleod... is a collection of tales...
   [unsigned]

C055.033 Oct 21, 1904, p.5
   [Book Review: G.B. Lancaster, *Sons O' Men*]
   Sons O' Men, by G.B. Lancaster... is a collection of New Zealand stories.
   [unsigned]

C055.034   Oct 22, 1904, p.7
        Trafalgar-Day. Ship Life Under Nelson *[Prose]*
        The ships in which Nelson sailed were not much better...
        [signed, 'J.M.']

C055.035   Oct 24, 1904, p.5
        [Book Review: Frank Moore Colby, *Imaginary Obligations*]
        Imaginary Obligations, by Frank Moore Colby... is a collection of...
        [unsigned]

C055.036   Oct 25, 1904, p.12
        A Monthly Allowance *[Prose]*
        When I was working as a potboy in a saloon in New York City...
        [signed 'J.M.']

C055.037   Oct 26, 1904, p.5
        A Song [included in 'Miscellany'] *[Verse]*
        I yarned with ancient shipmen beside the galley range,
        [signed, 'J.M.']

C055.038   Oct 27, 1904, p.12
        Tom Tiddler's Ground *[Prose]*
        A day or two ago news came to us that the long-lost Californian...
        [signed, 'J.M.']

C055.039   Oct 29, 1904, p.6
        A Treatise Upon Duelling [Book Review: Brantome (transl. G.H. Powell), *Duelling Stories of the Sixteenth Century*]
        Pierre de Bourdeille, the Abbot and Lord of Brantome...
        [signed, 'J.M.']

C055.040   Nov 1, 1904, p.12
        Rogues and Vagabonds *[Prose]*
        A few days ago the London police arrested a "paralytic" beggar...
        [signed, 'J.M.']

C055.041   Nov 2, 1904, p.5
        [Book Review: Baron von Schlicht, *Life in a Crack Regiment*]
        Life in a Crack Regiment, by Baron von Schlicht... is a military novel...
        [unsigned]

C055.042   Nov 7, 1904, p.12
        Knights of the Road *[Prose]*
        A few miles from Warwick, a little beyond Tachbrook Osiers...
        [signed, 'J.M.']

C055.043   Nov 9, 1904, p.12
        The Pirates of Sant' Anna *[Prose]*
        On the coast of Venezuela, not more than thirty miles from Rio Chico...
        [signed, 'J.M.']

C055.044   Nov 11, 1904, p.5
        A Fo'c's'le Ditty [included in 'Miscellany'] *[Verse]*
        Oh the brave Spanish sailors, so frank and so fine,
        [signed, 'J.M.']

C055.045   Nov 14, 1904, p.5
        Vallipo [included in 'Miscellany'] *[Verse]*
        The maids in pleasant Vallipo have bonny black hair,
        [signed, 'J.M.']

C055.046   Nov 18, 1904, p.5
        The Gara Brook *[Verse]*
        Babbling and rippling as over the pebbles it bubbles
        [signed, 'J.M.']

C055.047   Nov 26, 1904, p.7
        Westward Ho [included in 'Miscellany'] *[Verse]*
        The wind smells of heather and the white-blossomed may;
        [signed, 'J.M.']

C055.048   Nov 28, 1904, p.5
        [note about 'Westward Ho' included in 'Miscellany']
        A correspondent writes a miscellaneous letter to us from Keswick.
        [includes a section "'J.M.' writes:-']

C055.049   Nov 28, 1904, p.5
Izaak Walton's "Lives" [Book Review: Izaak Walton, *Lives*]
Izaak Walton was born at Stafford on the 9th of August, 1593...
[signed, 'J.M.']

C055.050   Dec 7, 1904, p.12
Don Alfonso's Treasure Hunt *[Prose]*
I once met a sailor who had one eye, one tooth, and one ear.
[signed, 'J.M.']

C055.051   Dec 8, 1904, p.5
[note about 'Don Alfonso's Treasure Hunt' included in 'Miscellany']
A correspondent writes to ask us the name of the "licker" mentioned...
[unsigned, although supposedly reports 'the author of that tale']

C055.052   Dec 14, 1904, p.12
Two Poachers [Book Review: W. M'Combie Smith, *The Romance of Poaching in the High-Lands*]
We feel that Mr. M'Combie Smith is too limited in his application...
[signed, 'J.M.']

C055.053   Dec 20, 1904, p.5
Sir Walter Raleigh [Book Review: Sir Rebbell Rodd, *Sir Walter Raleigh*]
Men who suffer unjustly have often had a posthumous reward.
[signed, 'J.M.']

C055.054   Dec 29, 1904, p.4
The Irish National Theatre | (From Our Special Correspondent.)... *[Prose]*
To-night the Irish National Theatre Society repeated Mr. Yeats's...
[unsigned]

C055.055   Jan 2, 1905, p.3
The Irish National Theatre | (From Our Special Correspondent.) *[Prose]*
The plays that are now being performed in Dublin by this little company...
[unsigned]

C055.056   Mar 9, 1905, p.14
In a Fo'c's'le *[Prose]*
Ashore, in the towns, men find it easy to amuse themselves...
[signed, 'J.M.']

C055.057   Mar 15, 1905, p.12
Anty Bligh *[Prose]*
One night in the tropics I was "farmer" in the middle-watch...
[signed, 'J.M.']

C055.058   Mar 23, 1905, p.14
The Devil and the Deep Sea *[Prose]*
Once upon a time, said the old sailor, there was a man with neither luck...
[signed, 'J.M.']

C055.059   Apr 17, 1905, p.12
Paul Jones *[Prose]*
John Paul, better known as John Paul Jones, whose body...
[unsigned]

C055.060   Apr 19, 1905, p.5
[Book Review: Mrs. Chesson, *The Bell and the Arrow*]
The Bell and the Arrow, Mrs. Chesson's experiment in fiction...
[unsigned]

C055.061   Apr 19, 1905, p.12
A Trip to Nombre de Dios *[Prose]*
It is the custom among sailors to sing when leaving a foreign port...
[signed, 'J.M.']

C055.062   May 3, 1905, p.5
[Book Review: W.T. Grenfell, *The Harvest of the Sea*]
The Harvest of the Sea, by W.T. Grenfell... is a collection of...
[unsigned]

C055.063   May 5, 1905, p.5
"Travelling Thomas." [Book Review: Thomas Coryat, *Coryat's Crudities*]
Thomas Coryat, or Coryate, "Great Britain's Error...
[signed, 'J.M.']

C055.064   May 8, 1905, p.5
        [Included in 'Correspondence'] *[Letter]*
        "Anty Bligh." | *To the Editor of the Manchester Guardian* | Sir...
        [signed, 'JOHN MASEFIELD']

C055.065   May 9, 1905, p.12
        A Raines Law Arrest *[Prose]*
        When I was working as a potboy in a New York saloon...
        [signed, 'JOHN MASEFIELD']

C055.066   May 17, 1905, p.5
        [Book Review: Myra Kelly, *Little Citizens*]
        Miss Myra Kelly takes us into an unfamiliar world in her charming...
        [signed, 'J.E.M.']

C055.067   May 17, 1905, p.5
        [Book Review: William J. Locke, *The Morals of Marcus Ordeyne*]
        When, on page 243 of The Morals of Marcus Ordeyne...
        [signed, 'J.E.M.']

C055.068   May 19, 1905, p.5
        [Book Review: Dillon Wallace, *The Lure of the Labrador Wild*]
        This is a pathetic record of a summer trip towards Lake Michikamau...
        [unsigned]

C055.069   May 30, 1905, p.12
        A Port Royal Twister *[Prose]*
        Once upon a time, said the Jamaican in the tavern, there was...
        [signed, 'J.M.']

C055.070   Jun 9, 1905, p.5
        [Book Review: T.W.H. Crosland, *The Wild Irishman*]
        The Wild Irishman, by T.W.H. Crosland... is a violent book...
        [unsigned]

C055.071   Jun 16, 1905, p.12
        Ambitious Jimmy Hicks *[Prose]*
        "Well," said the captain of the foretop to me, "it's our cutter to-day...
        [signed, 'J.M.']

C055.072   Jun 21, 1905, p.5
        [Book Review: Mary Austin, *Isidro*]
        The plot of Isidro, by Mary Austin... is involved and chaotic.
        [signed, 'J.M.']

C055.073   Jun 22, 1905, p.5
        Purchas His Pilgrimes [Book Review: Samuel Purchas, *Purchas His Pilgrimes* vols. III & IV]
        Samuel Purchas, the author of the "Pilgrimes," was...
        [unsigned]

C055.074   Jun 29, 1905, p.5
        [Book Review: Charles J. Steedman, *Bucking the Sage-Brush*]
        This is an excellent piece of work, full of colour and vivid incident.
        [unsigned]

C055.075   Jul 3, 1905, p.5
        [Book Review: Charles E. Trow, *Old Shipmasters of Salem*]
        Old Shipmasters of Salem, by Charles E. Trow... is an unequal work...
        [unsigned]

C055.076   Jul 18, 1905, p.12
        The Cape Horn Calm *[Prose]*
        Off Cape Horn there are but two kinds of weather, neither one of them...
        [signed, 'JOHN MASEFIELD']

C055.077   Jul 19, 1905, p.5
        [Book Review: Charles Marriott, *Mrs. Alemere's Elopement*]
        Mr. Charles Marriott's new novel, Mrs. Alemere's Elopement...
        [signed, 'J.E.M.']

C055.078   Jul 24, 1905, p.5
        [Book Review: W.S. Percival, *Twenty Years in the Far East*]
        Twenty Years in the Far East, by W.S. Percival... is a collection...
        [unsigned]

C055.079   Aug 7, 1905, p.10
        Of the Tales in One's Mind. *[Prose]*

In every heart, I think, covered away carefully, there lies some...
[signed, 'JOHN MASEFIELD']

C055.080   Aug 16, 1905, p.10
Chanties *[Prose]*
A chanty is a song sung by sailors when engaged in the severest...
[signed, 'J. MASEFIELD']

C055.081   Aug 19, 1905, p.7
Whippet-Racing *[Prose]*
There is a street in Poplar which is shut off from the docks...
[signed, 'J.M.']

C055.082   Aug 19, 1905, p.7
[Included in 'Correspondence'] *[Letter]*
"Chanties." | *To the Editor of the Manchester Guardian.* | Sir...
[signed, 'JOHN MASEFIELD']

C055.083   Aug 21, 1905, p.3
Purchas His Pilgrimes, Vols. V. And VI. [Book Review: Samuel Purchas, *Purchas His Pilgrimes* vols. V & VI]
It is difficult to write of old voyages, if one may not write of them in...
[signed, 'J. MASEFIELD']

C055.084   Aug 30, 1905, p.5
[Book Review: T. Jenkins Hains, *The Black Barque*]
The Black Barque, by Captain T. Jenkins Hains... is a stirring romance...
[signed, 'J.M.']

C055.085   Sep 6, 1905, p.5
[Book Review: A. Curtis Sherwood, *Tongues of Gossip*]
A great deal of careful work has gone to the making of Tongues...
[signed, 'J.E.M.']

C055.086   Sep 7, 1905, p.12
The Bottom of the Well *[Prose]*
Once upon a time there was a sailor named Bill. He was a seaman...
[signed, 'J. MASEFIELD']

C055.087   Sep 15, 1905, p.12
One Sunday *[Prose]*
Ten years ago I was "in the half-deck" of a four-masted barque.
[signed, 'J. MASEFIELD']

C055.088   Sep 19, 1905, p.5
Purchas's Voyages [Book Review: Samuel Purchas, *Purchas's Voyages* vols. VII & VIII]
Between modern travellers and Purchas's Pilgrims there is this difference.
[signed, 'J.M.']

C055.089   Sep 27, 1905, p.5
[Book Review: Joseph C. Lincoln, *Partners of the Tide*]
Partners of the Tide, by Joseph C. Lincoln... is an American story...
[signed, 'J.M.']

C055.090   Oct 3, 1905, p.12
A White Night *[Prose]*
Sometimes, when I am idle, my mind fills with a vivid memory.
[signed, 'JOHN MASEFIELD']

C055.091   Oct 11, 1905, p.5
[Book Review: Bessie Parker, *Miss Lomax, Millionaire*]
In some circumstances there is a great comfort in finding that...
[signed, 'J.E.M.']

C055.092   Oct 13, 1905, p.5
[Book Review: A. Macdonald, *In Search of El Dorado*]
Mr. Macdonald's book described his adventures as a gold digger...
[unsigned]

C055.093   Oct 16, 1905, p.5
[Book Review: Louis Becke, *Notes from my South Sea Log*]
This is a collection of sketches and reminiscences drawn from diaries...
[unsigned]

C055.094   Oct 17, 1905, p.4
[Book Review: J.H. & Edith C. Hubback, *Jane Austen's Sailor Brothers*]
This is a pleasant, chatty volume, containing the biographies of Charles...
[unsigned]

C055.095   Oct 19, 1905, p.5
        [Book Review: Sir Henry Pottinger, *Flood, Fell, and Forest*]
        As the author says, this is "more a series of essays on sport...
        [unsigned]

C055.096   Oct 21, 1905, Supplement, (Nelson Centenary), pp.10–11
        Life on a Man-of-War. Hardships and Trials *[Prose]*
        In the years of the great French wars, when our fleets kept the seas...
        [signed, 'By J. MASEFIELD']

C055.097   Oct 23, 1905, p.7
        Nelson Day. Celebrations at Home and Abroad. The Scene at Portsmouth. (FROM OUR SPECIAL
            CORRESPONDENT.) *[Prose]*
        PORTSMOUTH, FRIDAY. | I am in Portsmouth in the Blue Posts...
        [signed, 'J. MASEFIELD']

C055.098   Oct 25, 1905, p.5
        [Book Review: James Blyth, *Deborah's Life*]
        A strange mixture of arid realism and ingenuous romanticism...
        [signed, 'J.E.M.']

C055.099   Oct 25, 1905, p.5
        [Book Review: Garrett Mill, *In the Hands of the Czar*]
        "The Baron moved his long fingers and told a lie. His sleeve was...
        [signed, 'J.E.M.']

C055.100   Oct 25, 1905, p.12
        Nelson's Guns *[Prose]*
        The guns with which Nelson's battles were fought were smooth-bore...
        [signed, 'J.M.']

C055.101   Nov 1, 1905, p.5
        [Book Review: George Egerton, *Flies in Amber*]
        It is a pity that the author of Flies in Amber... is so aggressively clever.
        [signed, 'J.E.M.']

C055.102   Nov 1, 1905, p.5
        [Book Review: Margaret Baillie-Saunders, *Saints in Society*]
        But for the dedicatory poem, which probably many readers will miss...
        [signed, 'J.E.M.']

C055.103   Nov 10, 1905, p.5
        [Book Review: F.T. Bullen, *Back to Sunny Seas*]
        Back to Sunny Seas, by F.T. Bullen... describes a pleasure trip...
        [unsigned]

C055.104   Nov 21, 1905, p.12
        Johnny Good *[Prose]*
        When I was in the West I got a job in a carpet factory, in a town...
        [signed, 'JOHN MASEFIELD']

C055.105   Nov 29, 1905, p.5
        [Book Review: Mr. Crockett, *The Cherry Ribband*]
        The kindly, cheerful people who write romances...
        [signed, 'J.E.M.']

C055.106   Nov 29, 1905, p.5
        [Book Review: Perceval Gibbon, *The Vrouw Grobelaar's Leading Cases*]
        Thrilling tales are seasonable in November. Anyone who wants…
        [signed, 'J.E.M.']

C055.107   Dec 4, 1905, p.5
        [Book Review: Rev. A.G. Morice, *The History of the Northern Interior of British Columbia*]
        The History of the Northern Interior of British Columbia...
        [unsigned]

C055.108   Dec 5, 1905, p.5
        [Book Review: "A Nomad", *Reminiscences of Many Lands*]
        Reminiscences of Many Lands, by "A Nomad"... is a book of...
        [unsigned]

C055.109   Dec 12, 1905, p.5
        [Book Review: Caspar Whitney, *Jungle Trails and Jungle People*]
        Jungle Trails and Jungle People, by Caspar Whitney... is a collection...
        [unsigned]

C055.110   Dec 15, 1905, p.5
    [Book Review: J.S. Parsons, *Nelsonian Reminiscences*]
    Nelsonian Reminiscences, by Lietenant J.S. Parsons, R.N....
    [unsigned]

C055.111   Dec 18, 1905, p.5
    [Book Review: arr. Mary Eyre Matcham, *A Forgotten John Russell*]
    The John Russell to whom these letters were written has indeed been...
    [unsigned]

C055.112   Dec 26, 1905, p.3
    [Book Review: Woodbury Lowery, *The Spanish Settlements in the United States*]
    This volume of "The Spanish Settlements within the present limits of...
    [unsigned]

C055.113   Jan 8, 1906, p.5
    [Book Review: George Waldo Browne, *The St. Lawrence River*]
    The St. Lawrence River, by George Waldo Browne... gives an account...
    [unsigned]

C055.114   Jan 16, 1906, p.14
    Brown *[Prose]*
    I first met Brown in one of the arcades at Cardiff. We had just...
    [signed, 'J.M.']

C055.115   Jan 22, 1906, p.5
    [Book Review: Samuel Purchas, *Purchas's Voyages* vols. IX & X]
    The new volumes of "Purchas His Pilgrimes" are the best...
    [unsigned]

C055.116   Feb 20, 1906, p.14
    Being Ashore *[Prose]*
    In the nights, in the winter nights, in the nights of storm when the wind...
    [signed, 'JOHN MASEFIELD']

C055.117   Feb 21, 1906, p.5
    [Book Review: Carl Joubert, *The White Hand*]
    In Mr. Carl Joubert's latest volume, The White Hand...
    [signed, 'J.E.M.']

C055.118   Feb 28, 1906, p.5
    [Book Review: James Blyth, *The Same Clay*]
    Let it be said at once that The Same Clay... is a wholly unpleasant book.
    [signed, 'J.E.M.']

C055.119   Mar 9, 1906, p.5
    [Book Review: F.T. Bullen, *Sea Spray*]
    In Sea Spray... Mr F.T. Bullen gives us a number of short tales...
    [signed, 'J.M.']

C055.120   Mar 12, 1906, p.5
    [Book Review: H. Warington Smyth, *Mast and Sail in Europe and Asia*]
    This is a volume of considerable merit and palpable defects.
    [unsigned]

C055.121   Mar 16, 1906, p.12
    In the Roost *[Prose]*
    There is a saloon in Green-street, New York City, run by a man called...
    [signed, 'J.M.']

C055.122   Mar 27, 1906, p.5
    [Book Review: collected/arr. John Bradford & Arthur Fagge, *Old Sea Chanties*]
    Old Sea Chanties, collected and arranged by John Bradford...
    [unsigned]

C055.123   Mar 28, 1906, p.5
    [Book Review: Basil Lubbock, *Jack Derringer*]
    Mr. Basil Lubbock's new novel Jack Derringer... is hardly likely...
    [signed, 'J.M.']

C055.124   Apr 4, 1906, p.5
    [Book Review: J.B. Connolly, *Out of Gloucester*]
    Out of Gloucester, by J.B. Connolly... contains half-a-dozen short...
    [signed, 'J.M.']

C055.125   May 9, 1906, p.5
Sketches of Russia [Book Review: Alexandra de Holstein & Dora B. Montefiore, *Serf Life in Russia*]
Serf Life in Russia, by Alexandra de Holstein and Dora B. Montefiore...
[signed, 'J.E.M.']

C055.126   May 9, 1906, p.12
Vikings *[Prose]*
Of all the pirates in history there are none more interesting...
[signed, 'JOHN MASEFIELD']

C055.127   May 11, 1906, p.5
[Book Review: Bart Kennedy, *A Tramp Camp*]
In A Tramp Camp... Mr. Bart Kennedy gives us another entertaining...
[unsigned]

C055.128   May 17, 1906, p.12
On the Palisades *[Prose]*
On the west side of the Hudson river there is a cliff, or crag of rock...
[signed, 'JOHN MASEFIELD']

C055.129   May 21, 1906, p.12
Christopher Columbus *[Prose]*
It is curious that great men should be remembered more by their deeds...
[signed, 'J.M.']

C055.130   Jun 1, 1906, p.5
[Book Review: Samuel Purchas, *Purchas His Pilgrimes* vols. XI and XII]
In vols. xi. and xii. of "Purchas His Pilgrimes" we are given a quantity...
[unsigned]

C055.131   Jun 5, 1906, p.5
[Book Review: Hugh Clifford, *Heroes of Exile*]
In Heroes of Exile... Mr. Hugh Clifford gives us another handful...
[unsigned]

C055.132   Jun 6, 1906, p.3
[Book Review: Samuel Gordon, *The Ferry of Fate*]
Most novels about Russia begin with two poor students...
[signed, 'J.E.M.']

C055.133   Jun 21, 1906, p.12
A Steerage Steward *[Prose]*
A few years ago I was in New York City trying to get a passage home...
[signed, 'J.M.']

C055.134   Jul 10, 1906, p.14
The Schooner-Man's Close Calls *[Prose]*
On the Hudson river shore near the railway to Albany there are...
[signed, 'J.M.']

C055.135   Jul 12, 1906, p.5
[Book Review: John C. Van Dyke, *The Opal Sea*]
The Opal Sea, by John C. Van Dyke... contains a number of clever...
[unsigned]

C055.136   Jul 19, 1906, p.5
[Book Review: Samuel Purchas, *Purchas His Pilgrimes* vols. XIII & XIV]
The two new volumes (xiii. and xiv.) of Purchas His Pilgrimes...
[unsigned]

C055.137   Aug 17, 1906, p.10
On Growing Old *[Prose]*
The other day I met an old sailor friend at a café. We dined together...
[signed, 'J.M.']

C055.138   Aug 25, 1906, p.7
[Untitled] *[Prose]*
Valparaiso Bay presents very striking features to those who approach it...
[signed, 'J.M.']

C055.139   Aug 28, 1906, p.12
The Rest-House on the Hill *[Prose]*
In a town it is easy to despise the visionary, for in a town there are...
[signed, 'J.M.']

C055.140   Sep 12, 1906, p.10
    Gentle People *[Prose]*
    My friend the old labourer was "never much bothered" by the fairies.
    [signed, 'J.M.']

C055.141   Sep 18, 1906, p.5
    [Book Review: Samuel Purchas, *Hakluytus Posthumus, or Purchas His Pilgrimes* vols. XV & XVI]
    The fifteenth and sixteenth volumes of "Purchas His Pilgrimes" are...
    [unsigned]

C055.142   Sep 19, 1906, p.10
    A True Story *[Prose]*
    In the reading-room of the West-street Sailors' Mission...
    [signed, 'J.M.']

C055.143   Sep 25, 1906, p.5
    [Book Review: Alexandre Dumas, *The Celebrated Crimes of the Russian Court]*
    The Celebrated Crimes of the Russian Court, translated...
    [unsigned]

C055.144   Sep 26, 1906, p.5
    [Book Review: Edward Noble, *Fisherman's Gat]*
    Mr. Edward Noble's Fisherman's Gat... is a melodramatic story...
    [signed, 'J.M.']

C055.145   Sep 26, 1906, p.5
    [Book Review: Irving Bacheller, *Silas Strong]*
    In Silas Strong... Mr. Irving Bacheller introduces us to a number...
    [signed, 'J.M.']

C055.146   Sep 27, 1906, p.5
    [Book Review: J.W. Gambier, *Links in my Life on Land and Sea]*
    This is a delightful book of reminiscences which remind us strongly of...
    [unsigned]

C055.147   Oct 3, 1906, p.5
    [Book Review: Frank T. Bullen, *Frank Brown, Sea Apprentice]*
    In Frank Brown, Sea Apprentice... Mr. Frank T. Bullen gives us...
    [signed, 'J.M.']

C055.148   Oct 4, 1906, p.12
    A Memory *[Prose]*
    In these first frosty days, now that there is mist at dusk into which...
    [signed, 'J.M.']

C055.149   Oct 10, 1906, p.5
    [Book Review: Jack London, *Moon Face]*
    In Moon Face... Mr. Jack London brings together a number of short...
    [signed, 'J.M.']

C055.150   Oct 16, 1906, p.5
    Mr. Conrad's "The Mirror of the Sea." *[Book Review]*
    In "The Mirror of the Sea" Mr. Joseph Conrad brings together...
    [signed, 'J.M.']

C055.151   Oct 19, 1906, p.5
    Mr. Belloc's "Hills and the Sea." *[Book Review]*
    In this book Mr. Belloc brings together a number of occasional papers...
    [signed, 'J.M.']

C055.152   Oct 25, 1906, p.5
    [Book Review: Filson Young, *Christopher Columbus and the New World of his Discovery.*]
    Mr. Filson Young's narrative is bright, spirited, and amusing.
    [signed, 'J.M.']

C055.153   Oct 26, 1906, p.5
    Lithgow's Travels [Book Review: William Lithgow, *Lithgow's Travels]*
    William Lithgow, whose "Rare Adventures and Painefull...
    [signed, 'J.M.']

C055.154   Oct 29, 1906, p.5
    [Book Review: Lord Dunsany, *Time and the Gods]*
    Time and the Gods, by Lord Dunsany... has both the strangeness...
    [unsigned]

C055.155 Oct 31, 1906, p.5
   [Book Review: David Wilkinson, *Whaling in Many Seas*]
   Mr. David Wilkinson's Whaling in Many Seas... is printed in a type...
   [unsigned]

C055.156 Nov 2, 1906, p.5
   [Book Review: Kinglake, *Eothen*]
   Mr. D.G. Hogarth's new edition of Kinglake's Eothen...
   [unsigned]

C055.157 Nov 5, 1906, p.12
   Ghosts *[Prose]*
   "Ghosts are common enough," said an old sailor to me the other day...
   [signed, 'JOHN MASEFIELD']

C055.158 Nov 7, 1906, p.5
   [Book Review: William T. Hornaday, *Camp Fires in the Canadian Rockies*]
   In Camp Fires in the Canadian Rockies... Mr. William T. Hornaday...
   [unsigned]

C055.159 Nov 14, 1906, p.5
   [Book Review: Morley Roberts, *The Red Burgee*]
   Mr. Morley Roberts is a merry writer whose sea comedies deserve...
   [signed, 'J.M.']

C055.160 Nov 14, 1906, p.5
   [Book Review: Henry Newbolt, *The Old Country*]
   Mr. Henry Newbolt's historical romance The Old Country...
   [signed, 'J.M.']

C055.161 Nov 14, 1906, p.5
   [Book Review: H.H. Bashford, *The Trail Together*]
   Mr. H.H. Bashford is one of the most interesting of our young colonial...
   [signed, 'J.M.']

C055.162 Nov 21, 1906, p.5
   [Book Review: Sir A. Conan Doyle, *Sir Nigel*]
   In his historical romance of Sir Nigel... Sir A. Conan Doyle continues...
   [signed, 'J.M.']

C055.163 Nov 27, 1906, p.5
   [Book Review: F.T. Bullen, *Our Heritage the Sea*]
   The industry of Mr. F.T. Bullen, the popular writer of the sea...
   [unsigned]

C055.164 Dec 3, 1906, p.5
   [Book Review: Christopher Stone, *Sea Songs and Ballads*]
   In Sea Songs and Ballads... Mr. Christopher Stone brings together...
   [unsigned]

C055.165 Dec 28, 1906, p.3
   [Book Review: Sir George Holmes, *Ancient and Modern Ships*]
   Of the two handbooks on Ancient and Modern Ships...
   [unsigned]

C055.166 Jan 9, 1907, p.5
   [Combined Book Review: ed. C.F. Bell, *Evelyn's "Sculptura"*; *Howell's Devises, 1581*; and ed. J.R. Tanner, *Pepys'*
    Memories of The Royal Navy]
   John Evelyn's book on engraving is, as a work of reference...
   [unsigned]

C055.167 Jan 16, 1907, p.5
   [Book Review: comp. Frank Sidgwick, *Popular Ballads of the Olden Time*, third series]
   In the Third Series of Popular Ballads of the Olden Time...
   [unsigned]

C055.168 Jan 22, 1907, p.12
   Big Jim *[Prose]*
   One afternoon, many years ago, I was in a western seaport...
   [signed, 'J.M.']

C055.169 Feb 14, 1907, p.12
   The Passing of the Glory of the World *[Prose]*
   One frosty morning the Mersey was bright in the sun; the wind sang...
   [signed, 'J.M.']

C055.170 Feb 28, 1907, p.12
    Bill Harker *[Prose]*
    Bill Harker served most of his time in West Coast barques,
    [signed, 'J.M.']

C055.171 Mar 6, 1907, p.5
    [Book Review: Arthur Colton, *The Belted Seas*]
    The Belted Seas, by Arthur Colton... would be improved by...
    [signed, 'J.M.']

C055.172 Mar 13, 1907, p.5
    [Book Review: Ralph D. Paine, *Story of Martin Coe*]
    Mr. Ralph D. Paine's Story of Martin Coe... is an unequal tale...
    [signed, 'J.M.']

C055.173 Mar 13, 1907, p.5
    [Book Review: Nicholas Gogol (transl. B.C. Baskerville), *Taras Bulba*]
    Mr. B.C. Baskerville's translation of Taras Bulba...
    [signed, 'J.M.']

C055.174 Mar 20, 1907, p.5
    [Book Review: A.T. Quiller-Couch, *Poison Island*]
    R.L. Stevenson has made it very difficult to write about buried treasure.
    [signed, 'J.M.']

C055.175 Mar 22, 1907, p.14
    Flogging at Sea. Training-Ship's Tradition *[Prose]*
    There were two hundred of us cooped up in an old ship of the line.
    [signed, 'J.M.']

C055.176 Mar 25, 1907, p.5
    A Great Adventurer [Book Review: *Generall Historie and True Travels of Captain John Smith*]
    Captain John Smith, whose adventures are here beautifully reprinted...
    [signed, 'J.M.']

C055.177 Apr 12, 1907, p.12
    The Seal-Man. A Tale of the North Coast of Ireland *[Prose]*
    On the North coast of Ireland there is a rock which juts from the sea.
    [signed, 'J.M.']

C055.178 Apr 30, 1907, p.14
    A Duel With Davy Jones. Bill Harker's Bargain. *[Prose]*
    Some years ago Davy Jones was in Liverpool on business.
    [signed, 'J.M.']

C055.179 May 3, 1907, p.5
    [Book Review: R.A.J. Walling, *A Sea Dog of Devon*]
    Mr R.A.J. Walling's A Sea Dog of Devon... is a short biography...
    [unsigned]

C055.180 May 28, 1907, p.5
    [Book Review: Arthur Kitson, *Captain James Cook*]
    It is a pleasure to read such a charming biography...
    [unsigned]

C055.181 May 29, 1907, p.5
    [Book Review: Neil Munro, *The Daft Days*]
    Mr. Neil Munro has not quite succeeded in The Daft Days...
    [signed, 'J.M.']

C055.182 Jun 17, 1907, p.5
    [Book Review: Samuel Purchas, *Purchas His Pilgrimes* final volume]
    The last volume of Purchas His Pilgrimes... contains only a few...
    [unsigned]

C055.183 Jun 21, 1907, p.5
    [Book Review: ed. E.J. Payne, *Voyages of the Elizabethan Seamen*]
    The volume of Voyages of Elizabethan Seamen, edited by...
    [unsigned]

C055.184 Jun 27, 1907, p.5
    [Book Review: Andy Adams: *Reed Anthony, Cowman: An Autobiography*]
    Mr. Andy Adams, the author of the "Log of a Cowboy," is not...
    [unsigned]

C055.185   Jun 29, 1907, p.8
            The Bury St. Edmund's Pageant *[Prose]*
            BURY ST. EDMUND'S, THURSDAY. | Standing on Angel Hill...
            [signed, 'J.M.']
C055.186   Jul 12, 1907, p.5
            [Book Review: E. Way Elkington, *The Savage South Seas*]
            In The Savage South Seas, by E. Way Elkington, with pictures...
            [unsigned]
C055.187   Jul 22, 1907, p.5
            An Innocent Adventurer [Book Review: transl. M. Margaret Newett, *Canon Pietro Casola's Pilgrimage to Jerusalem in
                the Year 1494*]
            There is an old ballad of the sea which tells us how...
            [signed, 'J.M.']
C055.188   Jul 25, 1907, p.5
            [Book Review: Stopford A. Brooke, *The Sea Charm of Venice*]
            The Sea Charm of Venice, by Stopford A. Brooke... is a pretty essay...
            [unsigned]
C055.189   Sep 4, 1907, p.3
            [Book Review: James Dalziel, *In the First Watch*]
            Mr. James Dalziel, the author of In the First Watch...
            [signed, 'J.M.']
C055.190   Sep 9, 1907, p.12
            The Third Mate's Story. A Castaway's Vision. *[Prose]*
            In youth the soul takes to herself certain images, certain colours...
            [signed, 'J.M.']
C055.191   Sep 18, 1907, p.5
            A Fine Sea Story [Book Review: Robert Elliott, *Act of God*]
            There are so few serious writers of marine fiction, so few that...
            [signed, 'J.M.']
C055.192   Sep 27, 1907, p.5
            [Book Review: W. Clark Russell, *The Turnpike Sailor*]
            In his preface to The Turnpike Sailor... Mr. W. Clark Russell tells...
            [unsigned]
C055.193   Oct 2, 1907, p.5
            [Book Review: F.T. Bullen, *The Call of the Deep*]
            In The Call of the Deep... Mr. F.T. Bullen continues his story...
            [signed, 'J.M.']
C055.194   Oct 9, 1907, p.5
            [Book Review: Norman Duncan, *The Cruise of the Shining Light*]
            Mr. Norman Duncan, the writer of "The Way of the Sea,"...
            [signed, 'J.M.']
C055.195   Oct 9, 1907, p.5
            [Book Review: A.J. Dawson, *Genteel A.B.*]
            Mr. A.J. Dawson's Genteel A.B.... is not a creature of this world.
            [signed, 'J.M.']
C055.196   Oct 29, 1907, p.5
            [Book Review: John Biddulph, *The Pirates of Malabar*]
            Colonel John Biddulph's history of The Pirates of Malabar...
            [unsigned]
C055.197   Oct 30, 1907, p.5
            [Book Review: Arnold Bennett, *The City of Pleasure*]
            Mr. Arnold Bennett is an accomplished hand...
            [signed, 'J.M.']
C055.198   Oct 31, 1907, p.5
            [Book Review: Beatrice Grimshaw, *In the Strange South Seas*]
            Though Miss Beatrice Grimshaw makes rather too much...
            [unsigned]
C055.199   Nov 7, 1907, p.5
            [Book Review: Captain A.T. Mahan, *From Sail to Steam*]
            Captain A.T. Mahan, the famous naval historian, is not an attractive...
            [unsigned]

C055.200   Nov 11, 1907, p.5
[Book Review: Edward Fraser, *Champions of the Fleet*]
Mr. Edward Fraser is a vigorous writer who has done much...
[unsigned]

C055.201   Nov 13, 1907, p.5
[Book Review: Stewart E. White, *Arizona Nights*]
Mr. Stewart E. White has written several charming books...
[signed, 'J.M.']

C055.202   Nov 18, 1907, p.5
[Book Review: ed. Cyril Brett, *The Minor Poems of Michael Drayton*]
The Clarendon Press has added to the charming "Stuart and Tudor...
[unsigned]

C055.203   Dec 4, 1907, p.5
[Book Review: A.E.W. Mason, *The Broken Road*]
Mr. A.E.W. Mason is always excellent in his romantic vein.
[signed, 'J.M.']

C055.204   Jan 10, 1908, p.5
[Book Review: H. Lawrence Swinburne, *The Royal Navy*]
A new addition to messrs. Black's series of Beautiful Books...
[unsigned]

C055.205   Jan 13, 1908, p.5
[Book Review: R.H. Williams, *With the Border Ruffians : Memories of the Far West*]
Texas has for many years enjoyed a romantic reputation...
[unsigned]

C055.206   Jan 22, 1908, p.5
[Book Review: Cutcliffe Hyne, *Sandy Carmichael*]
Mr. Cutcliffe Hyne has a wide acquaintance among the fringes...
[signed, 'J.M.']

C055.207   Jan 29, 1908, p.5
[Book Review: W.H. Koebel, *The Anchorage*]
Mr. W.H. Koebel is one of those writers who reflect life...
[signed, 'J.M.']

C055.208   Feb 19, 1908, p.5
[Book Review: Edward Noble, *The Grain Carriers*]
Mr. Edward Noble is one of the most serious of living sea novelists...
[signed, 'J.M.']

C055.209   Feb 19, 1908, p.5
[Book Review: Louis Becke, *The Call of the South*]
In The Call of the South... Mr. Louis Becke brings together...
[signed, 'J.M.']

C055.210   Mar 25, 1908, p.5
[Book Review: K.L. Montgomery, *Colonel Kate*]
The romance of Colonel Kate, by K.L. Montgomery...
[signed, 'J.M.']

C055.211   Apr 1, 1908, p.5
[Book Review: Harold Begbie, *Tables of Stone*]
In Tables of Stone... Mr. Harold Begbie draws for us...
[signed, 'J.M.']

C055.212   Apr 9, 1908, p.5
[Book Review: Horace Annerley Vachell, *Sport and Life on the Pacific Slope*]
In Sport and Life on the Pacific Slope...
[unsigned]

C055.213   Apr 10, 1908, p.5
[Book Review: Laurence J. Burpee, *The Search for the Western Sea*]
Much of the history of North America is necessarily the history of...
[unsigned]

C055.214   Apr 15, 1908, p.5
[Book Review: A.G. Hales, *Marozia*]
Mr. A.G. Hales's Marozia... "was a woman, a glorious, glowing...
[signed, 'J.M.']

C055.215 Apr 28, 1908, p.5
Naval Ballads [Book Review: ed. Prof. C.H. Firth, *Naval Songs and Ballads*]
This new volume is an exhaustive collection prefaced with a long...
[signed, 'J.M.']

C055.216 May 8, 1908, p.5
[Book Review: W.H. Davies, *The Autobiography of a Super-Tramp*]
The Autobiography of a Super-Tramp... by Mr. W.H. Davies is the...
[unsigned]

C055.217 May 20, 1908, p.5
[Book Review: Jack London, *Before Adam*]
Mr. Jack London's prehistoric picture Before Adam...
[signed, 'J.M.']

C055.218 May 25, 1908, p.5
[Book Review: W.H. Lang, *Australia*]
Australia, the new volume in the Romance of Empire Series...
[unsigned]

C055.219 May 29, 1908, p.5
[Book Review: Sir Frederick Treves, *The Cradle of the Deep*]
This is a diverting account of a visit to the West Indies...
[unsigned]

C055.220 Jun 24, 1908, p.[5]
[Book Review: Lloyd Osbourne, *The Adventurer*]
The Adventurer of Mr. Lloyd Osbourne's romance...
[signed, 'J.M.']

C055.221 Jul 13, 1908, p.5
[Book Review: Roald Amundsen, *The North-West Passage*]
The chronicle of the "Gjöa" expedition (1903–1907)...
[unsigned]

C055.222 Jul 15, 1908, p.5
[Book Review: G.H. Lorimer, *Jack Spurlock*]
Mr. G.H. Lorimer, the author of "Letters from a self-made Merchant...
[signed, 'J.M.']

C055.223 Sep 3, 1908, p.5
[Book Review: Clive Holland, *From The North Foreland to Penzance*]
Mr. Clive Holland's From The North Foreland to Penzance...
[unsigned]

C055.224 Sep 8, 1908, p.5
[Book Review: Hugh De Sélincourt, *Great Ralegh* [sic]]
Mr. Hugh De Sélincourt's Great Ralegh... is a popular study...
[unsigned]

C055.225 Sep 15, 1908, p.5
[Book Review: E.J. Banfield, *The Confessions of a Beachcomber*]
The Confessions of a Beachcomber, by E.J. Banfield... is a pleasant...
[unsigned]

C055.226 Sep 23, 1908, p.5
[Book Review: F.T. Bullen, *Young Nemesis*]
Young Nemesis, by Mr. F.T. Bullen... is a story about a good young...
[signed, 'J.M.']

C055.227 Sep 28, 1908, p.5
[Book Review: William Richardson, *A Mariner of England, 1780–1817*]
The autobiography of William Richardson, A Mariner of England...
[unsigned]

C055.228 Oct 12, 1908, p.5
[Book Review: Edward Fraser, *The Londons of the British Fleet*]
Mr. Edward Fraser's The Londons of the British Fleet...
[unsigned]

C055.229 Oct 14, 1908, p.5
[Book Review: Una Silberrad, *Desire*]
Miss Una Silberrad's story of Desire... may be divided into two parts...
[signed, 'J.M.']

C055.230   Oct 21, 1908, p.5
    [Book Review: F.E. Penny, *Dark Corners*]
    Mrs. F.E. Penny has won a considerable reputation as a writer of books...
    [signed, 'J.M.']

C055.231   Oct 23, 1908, p.5
    Ships and Shipping [Book Review: ed. Herbert B. Mason, *Encyclopædia of Ships and Shipping*]
    This is a curious and scattered book, weakly designed, compiled...
    [signed, 'J.M.']

C055.232   Oct 28, 1908, p.5
    [Book Review: Randall Parrish, *The Last Voyage of the Donna Isabel*]
    Mr. Randall Parrish, the author of The Last Voyage...
    [signed, 'J.M.']

C055.233   Dec 2, 1908, p.5
    [Book Review: Stewart E. White, *The Riverman*]
    Mr. Stewart E. White is less successful as a novelist...
    [signed, 'J.M.']

C055.234   Dec 2, 1908, p.5
    [Book Review: William McFee, *Letters from an Ocean Tramp*]
    Mr. William McFee's Letters from an Ocean Tramp...
    [signed, 'J.M.']

C055.235   Dec 4, 1908, p.5
    [Book Review: H.B. Money Coutts, *Famous Duels of the Fleet*]
    Mr. H.B. Money Coutts's book of Famous Duels of the Fleet...
    [unsigned]

C055.236   Dec 9, 1908, p.4
    [Book Review: Louis Becke, *The Pearl Divers of Roncador Reef*]
    Mr. Louis Becke's stories of Australian and South Pacific life...
    [signed, 'J.M.']

C055.237   Jan 5, 1909, p.5
    [Book Review: Lionel Yexley, *The Inner Life of The Navy*]
    Mr. Lionel Yexley is well known as a writer upon naval subjects.
    [unsigned]

C055.238   Feb 9, 1909, p.14
    Evening in an Egyptian Home *[Prose]*
    I couldn't help smiling over my talk with the Mamour.
    [signed, 'J.E.M.']

C055.239   Feb 22, 1909, p.5
    The British Tar [Book Review: C.N. Robinson, *The British Tar in Fact and Fiction*]
    Commander Robinson has probably read more marine literature than...
    [signed, 'J.M.']

C055.240   Mar 12, 1909, p.5
    [Book Review: ed. Julian Corbett, *Signals and Instructions, 1776–1794*]
    The thirty-fifth volume of the publications of the Navy Records Society...
    [unsigned]

C055.241   Mar 16, 1909, p.5
    [Book Review: Francis Augustus MacNutt, *Bartholomew De Las Casas*]
    Of the many remarkable men produced by Spain...
    [unsigned]

C055.242   Mar 17, 1909, p.5
    [Book Review: Frank Savile, *Seekers*]
    Mr. Frank Savile's romance of Seekers... deals with love, rifles...
    [signed, 'J.M.']

C055.243   Mar 22, 1909, p.5
    [Book Review: Giovanni Mariti, *Travels in The Island of Cyprus*]
    Giovanni Mariti's Travels In the Island of Cyprus, now translated...
    [unsigned]

C055.244   Mar 24, 1909, p.5
    [Book Review: Eden Phillpotts, *The Three Brothers*]
    Mr. Eden Phillpotts has planned his story of The Three Brothers...
    [signed, 'J.M.']

C055.245 Mar 30, 1909, p.5
  [Book Review: Henry Cust, *Gentlemen Errant*]
  The four Gentlemen Errant of Mrs. Henry Cust's delightful book...
  [unsigned]

C055.246 Mar 31, 1909, p.5
  [Book Review: H. Rider Haggard, *The Yellow God*]
  Little can be said of The Yellow God, by H. Rider Haggard...
  [signed, 'J.M.']

C055.247 Apr 1, 1909, p.4
  [Book Review: Harry de Windt, *My Restless Life*]
  Mr. Harry de Windt's autobiography, My Restless Life...
  [unsigned]

C055.248 Apr 2, 1909, p.5
  [Book Review: Sir Arthur N. Wollaston, *Tales Within Tales*]
  Tales Within Tales, by Sir Arthur N. Wollaston...
  [unsigned]

C055.249 Apr 7, 1909, p.5
  [Book Review: F. Claude Kempson, *The Green Finch Cruise*]
  Mr. F. Claude Kempson's log of The Green Finch Cruise...
  [signed, 'J.M.']

C055.250 Apr 27, 1909, p.5
  [Book Review: W.E. Verplanck and M.W. Collyer, *The Sloops of the Hudson*]
  The little book called The Sloops of the Hudson...
  [unsigned]

C055.251 May 5, 1909, p.5
  [Book Review: Edwin Pugh, *Peter Vandy*]
  Mr. Edwin Pugh is a writer of varied talents, and Mr. Peter Vandy...
  [signed, 'J.M.']

C055.252 May 6, 1909, p.5
  Two Admirals [Book Review: John Moresby, *Two Admirals*]
  The two admirals are the author and his father, Sir Fairfax Moresby...
  [signed, 'J.M.']

C055.253 May 21, 1909, p.5
  [Book Review: Lionel James, *Side Tracks and Briddle Paths*]
  Mr. Lionel James ("Intelligence Officer") has surveyed mankind from...
  [unsigned]

C055.254 May 26, 1909, p.5
  [Book Review: H.N. Dickinson, *Sir Guy and Lady Rannard*]
  The story of the brilliant man who goes mad is not new in fiction.
  [signed, 'J.M.']

C055.255 May 26, 1909, p.5
  [Book Review: Robert Williams, *The Memoirs of a Buccaneer*]
  In The Memoirs of a Buccaneer... Mr. Robert Williams reconstructs...
  [signed, 'J.M.']

C055.256 Jun 17, 1909, p.5
  [Book Review: Alexander Mann, *Yachting on the Pacific*]
  Mr. Alexander Mann is a Scotchman who has lived for many years in...
  [unsigned]

C055.257 Jul 2, 1909, p.5
  [Book Review: James R. Thursfield, *Nelson and other Naval Studies*]
  Though several of Mr. James R. Thursfield's studies are not about...
  [unsigned]

C055.258 Jul 6, 1909, p.5
  [Book Review: Peter Wright, *A Three-Foot Stool*]
  Mr. Peter Wright tells us of the cowboy and Belphœbe...
  [unsigned]

C055.259 Jul 12, 1909, p.5
  [Book Review: James Oliver Curwood, *The Great Lakes*]
  If you never heard [*sic*] of The Great Lakes, you should read...
  [unsigned]

C055.260   Jul 13, 1909, p.5
         [Book Review: L.D. Barnett, *The Golden Town*]
         The Golden Town, Dr. L.D. Barnett's new volume...
         [unsigned]

C055.261   Jul 21, 1909, p.5
         [Book Review: ed. Will Irwin, Frank Norris, *The Third Circle*]
         In The Third Circle... Mr. Will Irwin brings together a number...
         [signed, 'J.M.']

C055.262   Jul 28, 1909, p.5
         [Book Review: J.E. Patterson, *Watchers by the Shore*]
         Mr. J.E. Patterson's Watchers by the Shore...
         [signed, 'J.M.']

C055.263   Aug 4, 1909, p.5
         [Book Review: Howard Pease, *With the Warden of the Marches*]
         Mr. Howard Pease is not a very good writer of romance...
         [signed, 'J.M.']

C055.264   Aug 4, 1909, p.5
         [Book Review: Basil Lubbock, *Deep-Sea Warriors*]
         There is a want of constructive talent in Mr. Basil Lubbock's...
         [signed, 'J.M.']

C055.265   Aug 9, 1909, p.5
         [Book Review: Stanton Davis Kirkham, *Mexican Trails*]
         The Mexican Trails of Mr. Stanton Davis Kirkham...
         [unsigned]

C055.266   Aug 13, 1909, p.5
         [Book Review: Earl Nelson, *The Nelson Whom Britons Love*]
         The little book The Nelson Whom Britons Love...
         [unsigned]

C055.267   Aug 20, 1909, p.5
         [Book Review: E. Keble Chatterton, *Sailing Ships and their Story*]
         Mr. E. Keble Chatterton's Sailing Ships and their Story...
         [unsigned]

C055.268   Aug 25, 1909, p.5
         The World of Ships [Book Review: Edward Noble, *Lords of the Sea*]
         Mr. Edward Noble, the author of Lords of the Sea...
         [signed, 'J.M.']

C055.269   Sep 22, 1909, p.12
         The Refugee *[Prose]*
         The Refugee counts his pence before he seeks his evening meal.
         [signed, 'J.E.M.']

C055.270   Oct 11, 1909, p.5
         [Book Review: F.A. MacNutt, *Fernando Cortés, and the Conquest of Mexico*]
         America has given opportunities to more men than she has produced.
         [unsigned]

C055.271   Oct 27, 1909, p.5
         [Book Review: Ridgwell Cullum, *The Sheriff of Dyke Hole*]
         Armed with a revolver and a jargon, The Sheriff of Dyke Hole...
         [signed, 'J.M.']

C055.272   Oct 28, 1909, p.5
         [Book Review: Agnes Weston, *My Life among the Bluejackets*]
         The reviewer of Miss Agnes Weston's My Life among the Bluejackets...
         [unsigned]

C055.273   Nov 4, 1909, p.5
         [Book Review: Ralph Nevill, *The Merry Past*]
         After an examination of Mr. Ralph Nevill's book The Merry Past...
         [unsigned]

C055.274   Nov 9, 1909, p.4
         [Book Review: ed. Bertram Stevens, *The Golden Treasury of Australian Verse*]
         Mr. Bertram Stevens's new edition of The Golden Treasury...
         [unsigned]

C055.275   Nov 10, 1909, p.5
           [Book Review: F.T. Bullen, *Cut Off from the World*]
           Mr. F.T. Bullen is apt to make his hero a very good young man...
           [signed, 'J.M.']

C055.276   Nov 16, 1909, p.5
           [Book Review: Bernal Diás del Castillo (transl. Alfred P. Maudslay), *The True History of the Conquest of New Spain*]
           Of all the excellent works of the Hakluyt Society none does greater...
           [unsigned]

C055.277   Nov 17, 1909, p.5
           [Book Review: William Hope Hodgeon, *The Ghost Pirates*]
           Down under the sea, only visible in calms, their galleons cruise.
           [signed, 'J.M.']

C055.278   Feb 17, 1910, p.5
           [Book Review: ed. William Crooke : John Fryer, *New Account of East India and Persia*]
           The new publication of the Hakluyt Society, the first volume of...
           [unsigned]

C055.279   Feb 18, 1910, p.5
           [Book Review: John Lang, *The Land of the Golden Trade*]
           He who looks for romance in Mr. John Lang's The Land...
           [unsigned]

C055.280   Mar 2, 1910, p.5
           [Book Review: Sir Gilbert Parker, *Cumner's Son*]
           Sir Gilbert Parker has the talent for success. It is a useful talent...
           [unsigned]

C055.281   Mar 7, 1910, p.5
           [Book Review: Alfred J. Swann, *Fighting the Slave Hunters in Central Africa*]
           Mr. Alfred J. Swann is one of the unselfish pioneers who were...
           [unsigned]

C055.282   Apr 1, 1910, p.5
           [Book Review: Alethea Wiel, *The Navy of Venice*]
           The Navy of Venice... is an excellent text, and much may be said on it...
           [unsigned]

C055.283   Apr 5, 1910, p.5
           [Book Review: T.B. Gough, *The Boyish Reminiscences of His Majesty The King's Visit to Canada in 1860*]
           Naval officers write admirable memoirs. The Boyish Reminiscences...
           [unsigned]

C055.284   Apr 19, 1910, p.7
           [Book Review: E.P. Statham, *Privateers and Privateering*]
           In Privateers and Privateering... Commander E.P. Statham, R.N. brings...
           [unsigned]

C055.285   Apr 25, 1910, p.5
           [Book Review: W.P. Ker, *On the History of the Ballads, 1100–1500*]
           Professor W.P. Ker's remarks On the History of the Ballads...
           [unsigned]

C055.286   May 17, 1910, p.3
           [Book Review: A.L. Haydon, *The Riders of the Plains*]
           The Royal North-west Mounted Police is one of the finest...
           [unsigned]

C055.287   Jun 7, 1910, p.5
           [Book Review: Frederic Stanhope Hill, *The Romance of the American Navy*]
           The Romance of the American Navy, by Frederic Stanhope Hill...
           [unsigned]

C055.288   Jun 15, 1910, p.5
           A New Writer [Book Review: A.F. Wedgwood, *The Shadow of a Titan*]
           Messrs. Duckworth and Co. have a *flair* for which they deserve praise.
           [signed, 'J.M.']

C055.289   Jun 20, 1910, p.5
           [Book Review; Frank Fox, *Rampart of Empire*]
           In Rampart of Empire... Mr. Frank Fox gives a brief summary...
           [unsigned]

C055.290   Jun 24, 1910, p.5
[Book Review: Stanley Portal Hyatt, *The Diary of a Soldier of Fortune*]
Books of reminiscences are hardly ever...
[unsigned]

C055.291   Jul 19, 1910, p.5
[Book Review: Harry A. Franck, *A Vagabond Journey around the World*]
Mr. Harry A. Franck's A Vagabond Journey around the World...
[unsigned]

C055.292   Jul 20, 1910, p.5
[Book Review: Henry M. Rideout, *The Twisted Foot*]
There is a suggestion of the uncanny in Mr. Henry M. Rideout's...
[signed, 'J.M.']

C055.293   Jul 21, 1910, p.5
A Sailor's Book [Book Review: David W. Bone, *The Brassbounder*]
Mr. Bone has written many admirable sketches of seafaring life.
[signed, 'J.M.']

C055.294   Aug 31, 1910, p.5
[Book Review: Louise Gerard, *The Hyena of Kallu*]
Though she is without any deep (or clear) perception of character...
[signed, 'J.M.']

C055.295   Sep 28, 1910, p.5
[Book Review: Humfrey Jordan, *My Lady of Intrigue*]
Who has not met Cardinal Richelieu, who has not plotted against him...
[signed, 'J.M.']

C055.296   Oct 12, 1910, p.5
[Book Review: A.E.W. Mason, *At the Villa Rose*]
The detective of real life is little like the detective in fiction...
[signed, 'J.M.']

C055.297   Oct 12, 1910, p.5
[Book Review: Edward H. Cooper, *My Brother the King*]
Though we cannot say very much for the story and character-drawing...
[signed, 'J.M.']

C055.298   Oct 27, 1910, p.5
[Book Review: C.H. Haring, *The Buccaneers in the West Indies in the XVII. Century*]
In reading The Buccaneers in the West Indies in the XVII. Century...
[unsigned]

C055.299   Oct 28, 1910, p.5
[Book Review: Stephen Reynolds, *Alongshore*]
In Alongshore... Mr. Stephen Reynolds gives us a collection of studies...
[unsigned]

C055.300   Nov 8, 1910, p.7
[Book Review: E. Hallam Moorhouse, *Letters of the English Seamen (1587–1808)*]
Miss E. Hallam Moorhouse has written several very charming books...
[unsigned]

C055.301   Nov 16, 1910, p.5
[Book Review: A.J. Dawson, *The Land of his Fathers*]
It is very difficult for a writer or painter to use his art for the purpose of...
[signed, 'J.M.']

C055.302   Nov 16, 1910, p.5
[Book Review: Robert Elliot, *The Immortal Charlatan*]
Many men have written about artistic charlatans. Mr. Robert Elliot...
[signed, 'J.M.']

C055.303   Nov 23, 1910, p.5
[Book Review: Martin Hume, *True Stories of the Past*]
The historical work of the late Major Martin Hume is well known.
[signed, 'J.M.']

C055.304   Nov 25, 1910, p.7
[Book Review: David Hannay, *Ships and Men*]
In Ships and Men... Mr. David Hannay publishes a number of articles...
[unsigned]

C055.305 Nov 30, 1910, p.7
 [Book Review: John Trevena, *Bracken*]
 Mr. John Trevena's novel Bracken... is a strange, wild, rather unequal...
 [signed, 'J.M.']

C055.306 Dec 8, 1910, p.7
 [Book Review: E. Hamilton Currey, *The Sea Wolves of the Mediterranean*]
 The occasional bloodiness of man has long distressed the moralist...
 [unsigned]

C055.307 Jan 5, 1911, p.5
 [Book Review: W.B. Whall, *Shakespeare's Sea Terms Explained*]
 Mr. W.B. Whall is one of the most learned of living marine archæologists.
 [unsigned]

C055.308 Jan 18, 1911, p.4
 [Book Review: E.S. Stevens, *The Mountain of God*]
 The Mountain of God, by E.S. Stevens...
 [signed, 'J.M.']

C055.309 Feb 2, 1911, p.4
 [Book Review: Henry Atton and Henry H. Holland, *The King's Customs*]
 The second volume of The King's Customs... by Messrs. Henry Atton...
 [unsigned]

C055.310 Feb 15, 1911, p.5
 [Book Review: Miss Little, *A Woman on the Threshold*]
 Miss Little's story of A Woman on the Threshold...
 [signed, 'J.M.']

C055.311 Feb 22, 1911, p.7
 [Book Review: Miss Goldring, *The Downsman*]
 Miss Goldring's story of The Downsman... is a strange mixture of...
 [signed, 'J.M.']

C055.312 Feb 22, 1911, p.7
 [Book Review: Benjamin Swift, *The Old Dance Master*]
 Mr. Benjamin Swift's story of the Old Dance Master...
 [signed, 'J.M.']

C055.313 Mar 1, 1911, p.5
 [Book Review: Mrs Armfield, *Mothers and Fathers*]
 Mrs. Armfield's novel of Mothers and Fathers... is a scattered story...
 [signed, 'J.M.']

C055.314 Mar 10, 1911, p.7
 [Book Review: prepared C.A. Harris and J.A.J. de Villiers, [*Storm van's Gravesande*]]
 The two new volumes issued by the Hakluyt Society...
 [unsigned]

C055.315 Mar 15, 1911, p.7
 [Book Review: E. Smith-Dampier, *Oil of Spikenard*]
 Very few female writers ever get into their work the hearty quality of...
 [signed, 'J.M.']

C055.316 Mar 15, 1911, p.7
 [Book Review: W.J. Batchelder, *The Wine-Drinker*]
 Mr. W.J. Batchelder is a clever storyteller; but the stories in his book...
 [signed, 'J.M.']

C055.317 Mar 16, 1911, p.14
 Captain Cook *[Prose]*
 Whitby coal shippers are supposed to have taught James Cook the arts...
 [signed, 'JOHN MASEFIELD']

C055.318 Mar 20, 1911, p.5
 An Egyptian Story [Book Review: Gilbert Murray, *Nefrekepta*]
 The story of Nefrekepta, now told in English verse...
 [signed, 'JOHN MASEFIELD']

C055.319 Mar 22, 1911, p.4
 [Book Review: Robert W. Service, *The Trail of '98*]
 The verse of Mr. Robert W. Service is little more than a crude...
 [signed, 'J.M.']

C055.320 Mar 27, 1911, p.5
A New Marine Magazine [Review: *The Mariner's Mirror*]
We owe everything to our ships and sailors, and we have done much...
[signed, 'JOHN MASEFIELD']

C055.321 Apr 5, 1911, p.5
[Book Review: Will Brooke, *Love and Treasure Laden*]
Mr. Will Brooke's tale of Love and Treasure Laden...
[signed, 'J.M.']

C055.322 Apr 19, 1911, p.5
[Book Review: Robert W. Chambers, *Ailsa Page*]
The story of Ailsa Page, by Mr. Robert W. Chambers...
[signed, 'J.M.']

C055.323 Apr 20, 1911, p.5
Poetry Of To-Day [Book Review: H.O. Meredith, *Week-Day Poems*]
Mr. Meredith's poems are the work of an interesting mind...
[signed, 'JOHN MASEFIELD']

C055.324 Apr 26, 1911, p.5
[Book Review: Hugh Clifford, *The Downfall of the Gods*]
Though Sir Hugh Clifford's new novel The Downfall of the Gods...
[signed, 'J.M.']

C055.325 May 1, 1911, p.5
[Book Review: John R. Hale, *Famous Sea Fights*]
Mr. John R. Hale's book of Famous Sea Fights...
[unsigned]

C055.326 May 10, 1911, p.7
[Book Review: Andy Adams, *Wells Brothers*]
Mr. Andy Adams has won a high reputation as the novelist of...
[signed, 'J.M.']

C055.327 May 12, 1911, p.5
The Drake Family [Book Review: Lady Eliott-Drake, *The Family and Heirs of Sir Francis Drake*]
Genius seldom appears twice in one family; talent often continues...
[signed, 'JOHN MASEFIELD']

C055.328 May 24, 1911, p.7
[Book Review: H. de vere Stacpoole, *The Ship of Coral*]
Many romance writers have made use of the following...
[signed, 'J.M.']

C055.329 May 29, 1911, p.5
[Book Review: William Foster, *The English Factories in India*]
The new volume of Mr. William Foster's Calendar of State Papers...
[unsigned]

C055.330 May 31, 1911, p.7
[Book Review: Eleanor Mordaunt, *A Ship of Solace*]
The literature of escape is swollen annually by a mass of books...
[signed, 'J.M.']

C055.331 Jun 9, 1911, p.14
Captain Robert Knox [Book Review: ed. James Ryan, Robert Knox, *An Historical Relation of Ceylon*]
Between the years 1690 and 1714, at odd times between voyages...
[signed, 'JOHN MASEFIELD']

C055.332 Jun 14, 1911, p.5
[Book Review: C.J. Cutcliffe Hyne, *The Escape Agents*]
Not very much can be said in favour of Mr. C.J. Cutcliffe Hyne's book...
[signed, 'J.M.']

C055.333 Jun 26, 1911, p.5
Captain Kidd [Book Review: Cornelius Neale Dalton, *The Real Captain Kidd*]
Two British seamen have for many years been vilified...
[signed, 'JOHN MASEFIELD']

C055.334 Jul 4, 1911, p.5
[Book Review: comp. M. Eyre Matcham, *The Nelsons of Burnham Thorpe*]
The Nelsons of Burnham Thorpe ought to be in our flowing cups...
[unsigned]

C055.335   Aug 7, 1911, p.3
            A Childish History [Book Review: C.R.L. Fletcher and Rudyard Kipling, *A History of England*]
            "There was a little quiver fellow," said Master Shallow, "and he would...
            [signed, 'JOHN MASEFIELD']

C055.336   Aug 14, 1911, p.5
            [Book Review: ed. J. Knox Laughton, *Letters and Papers of Charles, Lord Barham* vol. III]
            The third volume of the Letters and Papers of Charles, Lord Barham...
            [unsigned]

C055.337   Aug 16, 1911, p.5
            [Book Review: Albert Dorrington, *Our Lady of the Leopards*]
            In spite of a fresh and pleasant cosmopolitanism which gives colour...
            [signed, 'J.M.']

C055.338   Aug 23, 1911, p.5
            Holiday Reading [Combined Book Review: Norman M'Keown, *The Muck Rake*; Henry Curties, *The Scales of Chance*; and W.A. Mackenzie, *The Red Star of Night*]
            Mr. Norman M'Keown's novel of The Muck Rake... is a good example...
            [signed, 'J.M.']

C055.339   Aug 23, 1911, p.5
            [Book Review: Bernard Capes, *The House of Many Voices*]
            Mr. Bernard Capes's romance The House of Many Voices...
            [signed, 'J.M.']

C055.340   Aug 24, 1911, p.5
            [Book Review: ed. Clements Markham, *Early Spanish Voyages to the Strait of Magellan*]
            The 28th volume (second series) of the publications of the Hakluyt...
            [signed, 'J.M.']

C055.341   Sep 13, 1911, p.5
            [Book Review: Perceval Gibbon, *Margaret Harding*]
            Mr. Perceval Gibbon's Margaret Harding...
            [signed, 'J.M.']

C055.342   Sep 20, 1911, p.5
            [Book Review: H. Rider Haggard, *Red Eve*]
            Mr. H. Rider Haggard's romance of Red Eve... is of no great merit...
            [signed, 'J.M.']

C055.343   Sep 27, 1911, p.5
            [Book Review: Dolf Wyllarde, *The Unofficial Honeymoon*]
            The subject of a person alone upon an island has been treated by several...
            [signed, 'J.M.']

C055.344   Sep 29, 1911, p.8
            A Lower-Deck View [Book Review / Leader: Lionel Yexley, *Our Fighting Seamen*]
            Mr. Lionel Yexley is known as a good friend to naval seamen...
            [unsigned]

C055.345   Oct 4, 1911, p.5
            [Book Review: Roy Horniman, *Captivity*]
            Hugh Lestrange is convicted of killing his uncle, condemned...
            [signed, 'J.M.']

C055.346   Oct 17, 1911, p.5
            Australian Verse [Combined Book Review: Mr. Cassidy, *The Land of the Starry Cross*; Hugh McCrae, *Satyrs and Sunlight*; and *The Poetical Works of William Gay*]
            Australian poets have not yet found a form, though there are...
            [signed, 'JOHN MASEFIELD']

C055.347   Oct 18, 1911, p.5
            [Book Review: Sidney C. Grier, *The Keepers of the Gate*]
            "Sidney C. Grier" is well known and deservedly popular...
            [signed, 'J.M.']

C055.348   Oct 18, 1911, p.5
            [Book Review: Marjorie Bowen, *God and the King*]
            The English historical novel is seldom excellent, seldom even mediocre.
            [signed, 'J.M.']

C055.349   Oct 18, 1911, p.5
            [Book Review: Herbert Sherring, *Gopi*]
            In Gopi and its attendant stories... Mr. Herbert Sherring shows...
            [signed, 'J.M.']

C055.350   Oct 18, 1911, p.5
    [Book Review: Mme. Groner, *The Man with the Black Cord*]
    Detective stories, to be really good, must be unlike life...
    [signed, 'J.M.']

C055.351   Oct 23, 1911, p.4
    The Surgeon's Log [Book Review: J. Johnston Abraham, *The Surgeon's Log*]
    We have often wondered why the ordinary voyage of a deep-sea...
    [signed, 'JOHN MASEFIELD']

C055.352   Nov 1, 1911, p.4
    [Book Review: Henry Newbolt, *The Twymans*]
    In his romance of The Twymans... Mr. Henry Newbolt shows again...
    [signed, 'J.M.']

C055.353   Nov 1, 1911, p.4
    [Book Review: H. Hesketh Bell, *Love in Black*]
    We have very many delightful "over-sea" writers...
    [signed, 'J.M.']

C055.354   Nov 1, 1911, p.4
    [Book Review: E.F. Benson, *Juggernaut*]
    Mr. E.F. Benson is a clever, practised, and successful writer...
    [signed, 'J.M.']

C055.355   Nov 15, 1911, p.5
    [Book Review: Albert Dorrington, *A South-Sea Buccaneer*]
    "Right on the coffee-pot!" exclaims the range-finder to Captain Bully...
    [signed, 'J.M.']

C055.356   Nov 21, 1911, p.7
    Dr. Nansen's Book [Book Review: Fridtjof Nansen (transl. Arthur G. Chater), *In Northern Mists*]
    This book, one of the most learned critical histories of exploration...
    [signed, 'JOHN MASEFIELD']

C055.357   Dec 4, 1911, p.7
    [Book Review: A.L. Haydon, *The Trooper Police of Australia*]
    Mr. A.L. Haydon's volume The Trooper Police of Australia...
    [unsigned]

C055.358   Dec 7, 1911, p.4
    [Book Review: ed. C.W.L. Bulpett, *John Boyes, King of the Wa-Kikuya*]
    The story of John Boyes, King of the Wa-Kikuya... written by himself...
    [unsigned]

C055.359   Dec 27, 1911, p.3
    [Book Review: Gouveneur Morris, *Yellow Men and Gold*]
    When Jim found the murdered man's wallet, with the bearings...
    [signed, 'J.M.']

C055.360   Jan 5, 1912, p.5
    [Book Review: T.H. Parker, *Naval Prints*]
    Naval Prints, by Mr. Harry Parker... is a chronological catalogue, with historical notes...
    [unsigned]

C055.361   Jan 8, 1912, p.4
    [Book Review: ed. Rev. P.H. Ditchfield, *Memorials of Old Gloucestershire*]
    When a not very long book is compiled by many different hands it often happens that...
    [unsigned]

C055.362   Jan 17, 1912, p.5
    [Book Review: William Hay, *Captain Quadring*]
    In Mr. William Hay's novel of Captain Quadring... we rejoin our old friends the Australian...
    [signed, 'J.M.']

C055.363   Jan 31, 1912, p.5
    [Book Review: Anatole le Braz (transl. Frances M. Gostling), *The Night of Fires and other Breton Studies*]
    The Night of Fires and other Breton Studies, by Anatole le Braz, translated by...
    [signed, 'J.M.']

C055.364   Feb 7, 1912, p.4
    [Book Review: H. Rider Haggard, *Marie*]
    Sir Rider Haggard's new romance of Marie... tells the story of the first marriage of...
    [signed, 'J.M.']

C055.365   Feb 21, 1912, p.7
             [Book Review: E.F. Benson, *The Room in the Tower*]
             Ghost stories are generally spoiled by an excess of detail, and it seems to us that...
             [signed, 'J.M.']

C055.366   Feb 26, 1912, p.5
             [Book Review: James Elroy Flecker, *Forty-Two Poems*]
             Mr. James Elroy Flecker's Forty-Two Poems... are skilful and delicately made, though they...
             [signed, 'J.M.']

C055.367   Mar 8, 1912, p.4
             [Combined Book Review: Ethel B. Sainsbury, *The Court Minutes of the East India Company, 1644–1649*; and ed. Sir
                 Richard Carnac Temple, *The Diaries of Streynsham Master, 1675–80*]
             The three volumes of The Court Minutes of the East India Company, 1644–1649...
             [unsigned]

C055.368   Mar 11, 1912, p.5
             [Book Review: Captain W.V. Anson, R.N., *The Life of Lord Anson*]
             A new life of Lord Anson has been wanted for many years, for since Sir John Barrow's...
             [unsigned]

C055.369   Mar 12, 1912, p.5
             [Book Review: Allan Fea, *The Real Captain Cleveland*]
             The Real Captain Cleveland, by Mr. Allan Fea... turns out to be the original of Scott's...
             [unsigned]

C055.370   Mar 20, 1912, p.5
             [Book Review: Jack London, *When God Laughs*]
             Not long ago we read in an American schoolboy's essay that "an author is a...
             [signed, 'J.M.']

C055.371   May 8, 1912, p.7
             [Book Review: Edward Noble, *The Vicar of Normanton*]
             Mr. Edward Noble has shown himself to be a writer of considerable power, with a...
             [signed, 'J.M.']

C055.372   May 14, 1912, p.4
             [Book Review: Ian D. Colvin, *The Cape of Adventure*]
             The anthology of adventurous passages, either in prose or verse, is very seldom...
             [unsigned]

C055.373   May 21, 1912, p.7
             [Book Review: Commander W. Caius Crutchley, R.D., R.N.R., *My Life at Sea*]
             The autobiography of Commander W. Caius Crutchley... is an interesting, taking tale...
             [unsigned]

C055.374   May 30, 1912, p.4
             [Book Review: Professor W.I. Milham, *Meteorology*]
             Professor W.I. Milham's Meteorology... is a text-book prepared from a course...
             [unsigned]

C055.375   May 30, 1912, p.4
             [Book Review: Noel T. Methley, *The Life Boat and its Story*]
             Mr. Methley's pleasant little book The Life Boat and its Story... tells of the development...
             [unsigned]

C055.376   Jun 5, 1912, p.5
             [Book Review: Perceval Gibbon, *The Adventures of Miss Gregory*]
             After several collections of tales about masculine men, Bully Hayes, Captain Kettle...
             [signed, 'J.M.']

C055.377   Jun 18, 1912, p.4
             [Book Review: transl. Sir Clements Markham, K.C.B., *The Book of the Knowledge of all the Kingdoms, etc.*]
             The Book of the Knowledge of all the Kingdoms, &c., written by a Spanish Franciscan...
             [unsigned]

C055.378   Jun 19, 1912, p.7
             [Book Review: Horace Smith, *A Captain Unafraid*]
             The profession of filibuster, or smuggler of munitions of war into the territory of people...
             [signed, 'J.M.']

C055.379   Jun 21, 1912, p.5
             [Book Review: Major General Sir Alexander Bruce Tulloch, K.C.B., *A Soldier's Sailoring*]
             Among the many books published every year few kinds are so frequently good as the...
             [unsigned]

C055.380 Aug 12, 1912, p.5
[Book Review: ed. G. Herbert Fowler, *The Science of the Sea*]
The new publication by the Challenger Society The Science of the Sea, edited by...
[unsigned]

C055.381 Aug 13, 1912, p.5
[Book Review: ed. Sir John Knox Laughton, *The Naval Miscellany*]
Though it would have been easy to compile a much more human and inspiring collection...
[unsigned]

C055.382 Aug 14, 1912, p.5
[Book Review: O. Henry, *Heart of the West*]
Mr. O. Henry has much popularity in his native land. He has a considerable talent for...
[signed, 'J.M.']

C055.383 Sep 4, 1912, p.4
[Book Review: F. Hutchinson, *Haunting Shadows*]
To arrive in a fog at a strange house among mysterious and perhaps dishonest relatives...
[signed, 'J.M.']

C055.384 Sep 11, 1912, p.4
[Book Review: Cutcliffe Hyne, *The Marriage of Kettle*]
Mr. Cutcliffe Hyne's prolonged study of his hero, The Marriage of Kettle...
[signed, 'J.M.']

C055.385 Sep 25, 1912, p.5
[Book Review: Alexander Crawford, *Monsieur Carnifex*]
Mr. Alexander Crawford's romance of Monsieur Carnifex... is a capital example of what...
[signed, 'J.M.']

C055.386 Oct 9, 1912, p.7
[Book Review: Francis Bancroft, *The Veldt Dwellers*]
In The Veldt Dwellers... Mr. Francis Bancroft presents a South African tragedy of...
[signed, 'J.M.']

C055.387 Oct 16, 1912, p.7
Joseph Conrad [Book Review: Joseph Conrad, *'Twixt Land and Sea*]
'Twixt Land and Sea... contains three stories, written in the new and handy form...
[signed, 'J.M.']

C055.388 Oct 21, 1912, p.7
[Book Review: Elliott O'Donnell, *Werwolves*]
To werwolves we are indebted for a moving story in Petronius and for a capital tale...
[unsigned]

C055.389 Oct 22, 1912, p.6
[Book Review: Maurice Morgann, *Essay on the Dramatic Character of Sir John Falstaff*]
Maurice Morgann's Essay on the Dramatic Character of Sir John Falstaff... is one of the many...
[unsigned]

C055.390 Oct 31, 1912, p.6
[Book Review: J.R. Spears, *Master Mariners*]
The Master Mariners volume, by Mr. J.R. Spears, newly added to the Home University Library...
[unsigned]

C055.391 Nov 6, 1912, p.7
[Book Review: Alphonse de Châteaubriant (transl. Lady Theodóra Davidson), *The Keynote*]
In its delicate, pretty, but rather ineffectual way The Keynote, by Alphonse de Châteaubriant...
[signed, 'J.M.']

C055.392 Nov 19, 1912, p.7
[Book Review: F.T. Jane, *The British Battle-Fleet*]
In The British Battle-Fleet... Mr. F.T. Jane traces the gradual development of naval...
[unsigned]

C055.393 Dec 23, 1912, p.5
[Book Review: selected by Frank Sidgwick, *Popular Ballads of the Olden Time*]
In this fourth series of his ballads Mr. Sidgwick brings his excellent selection to an end.
[unsigned]

C055.394 Dec 26, 1912, p.3
[Book Review: Jack London, *South Sea Tales*]
Mr. Jack London's eight new stories, South Sea Tales... are all clever but rather mechanical...
[signed, 'J.M.']

C055.395   Jan 13, 1913, p.5
             [Book Review: H.M. Tomlinson, *The Sea and the Jungle*]
             Mr. H.M. Tomlinson's The Sea and the Jungle... is the record of a journey in a tramp steamer...
             [unsigned]
C055.396   Jan 30, 1913, p.7
             [Book Review: ed. C.T. Atkinson, *The First Dutch War* vol. V]
             The fifth volume of The First Dutch War, 1652–1654, edited by Mr. C.T. Atkinson for...
             [unsigned]
C055.397   Feb 3, 1913, p.5
             [Book Review: Bernal Diaz of Castille (transl. A.P. Maudslay), *Conquest of New Spain*]
             No private society has issued more valuable historical works than the Hakluyt Society...
             [unsigned]
C055.398   Mar 5, 1913, p.5
             [Book Review: Edward Noble, *Lifted Curtains*]
             Mr. Edward Noble's book of Lifted Curtains... contains ten short stories about the sea...
             [signed, 'J.M.']
C055.399   Mar 14, 1913, p.7
             [Book Review: E. Hallam Moorhouse, *Nelson in England*]
             The volume Nelson in England, by E. Hallam Moorhouse... is a pleasant record...
             [unsigned]
C055.400   Jul 8, 1913, p.7
             [Book Review: ed. Alfred Spencer, *William Hickey*]
             William Hickey, whose Memoirs, edited by Mr. Alfred Spencer, are now published for...
             [unsigned]
C055.401   Jul 10, 1913, p.5
             [Book Review: Pedro de Cieza de Lyon (transl. Sir Clements R. Markham, K.C.B.), *The War of Quito*]
             Of the many great tragical histories of the Spanish conquest of "the Indies" none is more...
             [unsigned]
C055.402   Jul 16, 1913, p.5
             [Book Review: Hon. Hugh Money-Coutts and W.R. Macdonald, *The Secret of Sarm*]
             The Secret of Sarm... reminds one of the "Riddle of the Sands." It is almost as...
             [signed, 'J.M.']
C055.403   Jul 17, 1913, p.4
             [Book Review: James Murray and George Marston, *Antarctic Days*]
             Antarctic Days... is a collection of cheery and amusing sketches describing the...
             [unsigned]
C055.404   Jul 18, 1913, p.7
             [Book Review: ed. Captain H.W. Richmond, *Papers Relating to the Loss of Minorca, 1756*]
             Though the new volume of the publications of the Navy Records Society (vol. 42)...
             [unsigned]
C055.405   Aug 22, 1913, p.5
             [Book Review: *English Merchants and the Spanish Inquisition in the Canaries*]
             Religious bigotry is a great bar to understanding between nations, and its ill-effects persist...
             [unsigned]
C055.406   Aug 27, 1913, p.5
             [Book Review: Sir William Monson, *Naval Tracts* vol. III]
             After a long interval the third volume of Sir William Monson's Naval Tracts has been...
             [unsigned]
C055.407   Aug 28, 1913, p.4
             The King's Ships [Book Review: Lieutenant H.S. Lecky, R.N., *The King's Ships* vol. I]
             This volume contains the record of A-B ships; it begins with the Aboukir and...
             [signed, 'JOHN MASEFIELD']
C055.408   Sep 18, 1913, p.4
             [Book Review: Frederick A. Talbot, *Lightships and Lighthouses*]
             Mr. Frederick A. Talbot's Lightships and Lighthouses... is a very spirited and readable...
             [unsigned]
C055.409   Oct 24, 1913, p.6
             [Book Review: Admiral Sir R.H. Harris, *From Naval Cadet to Admiral*]
             Admiral Sir R.H. Harris's book... tells the story of the author's naval career...
             [unsigned]

C055.410	Oct 27, 1913, p.7
	[Book Review: Colonel G. Hamilton Browne, *Camp-Fire Yarns of the Lost Legion*]
	Colonel G. Hamilton Browne's Camp-Fire Yarns of the Lost Legion... are some of the...
	[unsigned]
C055.411	Nov 5, 1913, p.4
	[Book Review: Horace Horsnell, *The Bankrupt*]
	Although we cannot call it stimulating, Mr. Horace Horsnell's novel... is a thoughtful...
	[signed, 'J.M.']
C055.412	Nov 26, 1913, p.6
	[Book Review: Sydney C. Grier, *Writ in Water*]
	Sydney C. Grier is a clever hand at an historical novel dealing with colonial life...
	[signed, 'J.M.']
C055.413	Nov 28, 1913, p.6
	[Book Review: Edward Fraser, *The Sailors Whom Nelson Led*]
	Mr. Edward Fraser is a well-known and deservedly popular writer of naval history.
	[unsigned]
C055.414	Dec 17, 1913, p.6
	[Book Review: Lieutenant Colonel A. Pollock, *In the Cockpit of Europe*]
	Not long ago, in the years before the Entente, books of romance were written describing...
	[signed, 'J.M.']
C055.415	Dec 26, 1913, p.4
	[Combined Book Review: Sir William Monson, *Naval Tracts* vol. IV; and *The Spencer Papers* vol. I]
	The Navy Records Society sends us two new volumes, the fourth volume of Sir Wm. Monson's...
	[unsigned]
C055.416	Jan 20, 1914, p.6
	[Book Review: *Back to the Sea, The Report of the Fourth National Conference on Sea Training*]
	Back to the Sea, The Report of the Fourth National Conference on Sea Training...
	[unsigned]
C055.417	Jan 23, 1914, p.4
	The King's Ships [Book Review: Lieutenant Halton Stirling Lecky, *The King's Ships* vol. II]
	In this volume Lieutenant Lecky, R.N., brings his collection to the letter "E," with...
	[signed, 'JOHN MASEFIELD']
C055.418	Jan 26, 1914, p.6
	[Book Review: Professor Brander Matthews, *Shakespeare as a Playwright*]
	Professor Brander Matthews's book... seems to us to be the work of a man who knows...
	[unsigned]
C055.419	Feb 13, 1914, p.6
	[Book Review: *The Court Minutes of the East India Company 1650–1654*]
	The Court Minutes of the East India Company 1650–1654... make as stiff reading as...
	[unsigned]
C055.420	Mar 3, 1914, p.6
	[Book Review: J.P. Oliveira Martins (transl. J.J. Abraham and William E. Reynolds), *The Golden Age of Prince Henry the Navigator*]
	The Golden Age of Prince Henry the Navigator... is a readable book, written with a...
	[unsigned]
C055.421	Mar 4, 1914, p.6
	[Book Review: W. Douglas Newton, *War*]
	"There was a cloistered hush... His face was so bloodless that it looked green...
	[signed, 'J.M.']
C055.422	Mar 6, 1914, p.6
	[Book Review: ed. James Grant, *The Old Scots Navy, 1689–1710*]
	The records of The Old Scots Navy, 1689–1710, edited by Mr. James Grant for the...
	[unsigned]
C055.423	Mar 12, 1914, p.6
	[Book Review: Colonel Sir Henry Yule, *Cathay and the Way Thither* vol. II]
	We have received from the Hakluyt Society a second volume of the reprint of...
	[unsigned]
C055.424	Mar 25, 1914, p.6
	[Book Review: Morley Roberts, *Time and Thomas Waring*]
	Like most writers of unusual talents, Mr. Morley Roberts is one whose course can never...
	[signed, 'J.M.']

C055.425   May 12, 1914, p.6
China Clippers [Book Review: Basil Lubbock, *The China Clippers*]
For nearly a generation sailing ships competed with steamers over some routes with some...
[signed, 'JOHN MASEFIELD']

C055.426   Jun 3, 1914, p.4
[Book Review: Charles McEvoy, *Private Affairs*]
Mr Charles McEvoy has a genius for displaying the inner life of a modern middle-class...
[signed, 'J.M.']

C055.427   Jun 16, 1914, p.8
[Book Review: B.G. Corney, *The Quest and Occupation of Tahiti by Emissaries of Spain, 1772–1776* vol. I]
We have received from the Hakluyt Society the first volume of a very useful compilation...
[unsigned]

C055.428   Jul 1, 1914, p.6
[Book Review: Henri Bordeaux, *The Fear of Living*]
This is a pleasant piece of quiet naturalism, with very little incident and not much fable...
[signed, 'J.M.']

C055.429   Sep 8, 1914, p.3
[Book Review: ed. Lieutenant Colonel Sir R. Carnac Temple, *The Travels of Peter Mundy* vol. II]
Peter Mundy was a Cornish gentleman who entered the service of the East India Company...
[signed, 'J.M.']

C055.430   Nov 12, 1914, p.5
[Book Review: A.S.M. Hutchinson, *The Clean Heart*]
Mr. A.S.M. Hutchinson's novel is a brisk and breezy tale, written with vigour and fun...
[signed, 'J.M.']

C055.431   Feb 9, 1915, p.5
[Book Review: Francis Abell, *Prisoners of War in Britain 1756–1815*]
During the Napoleonic wars both French and English writers protested vehemently against...
[unsigned]

C055.432   Mar 30, 1915, p.4
[Book Review: John Short and Thomas Williams, *Prisoners of War in France*]
Prisoners of War in France, the journals of two Cornish seamen, John Short and Thomas...
[unsigned]

C055.433   Apr 13, 1915, p.4
The King's Ships [Book Review: Commander H.S. Lecky, *The King's Ships* vol. III]
The third volume of the series contains records of the ships from the Endymion to...
[signed, 'J.M.']

C055.434   May 25, 1915, p.3
[Book Review: Professor Ernest Scott, *The Life of Captain Matthew Flinders*]
Captain Matthew Flinders, R.N., was the last one of the three adventurous Englishmen who...
[unsigned]

C055.435   Jun 1, 1915, p.5
[Book Review: E. Keble Chatterton, *The Old East Indiamen*]
The Old East Indiamen were a most remarkable set of ships, well deserving a record...
[unsigned]

C055.436   Nov 14, 1918, p.10
"The Most Heroic Effort" [Book Review: H.W. Nevinson, *The Dardanelles Campaign*]
The Dardanelles campaign was the strangest, most difficult, and most heroic effort...
[headed, 'By John Masefield']

C055.437   Dec 19, 1919, p.5
New Verse. A Fine Ballad [Book Review: A.J. Munnings, *The Tale of Anthony Bell*]
One of the best ballads of modern times is to be found in the "Field" for...
[signed, 'JOHN MASEFIELD']

C055.438   Jan 5, 1920, p.6
1919–1920: Signs of the Times *[Prose]*
You ask me to write about "the significance of the past year." I suppose that in...
[headed, 'By John Masefield']

C055.439   *Dec 15, 1920, 'Gift-books section'*
On the Delights of a Reader [Prose]
[Simmons and Drew record this prose article before republication in The Living Age. *The 'Gift-books section' supplement to the paper is not included on the microfilm produced by University Microfilms International]*

C055.440   May 5, 1921, p.53
Reynard the Fox *[Prose]*
I have been asked to write why I wrote my poem of "Reynard the Fox." As a man grows...
[signed, 'John Masefield']

C055.441   Feb 16, 1922, p.5
Disenchantment [Book Review: C.E. Montague, *Disenchantment*]
Once, during the war, a well-known statesman was heard describing his recent visit...
[headed, 'By John Masefield']

C055.442   Jul 27, 1923, p.16
The Oxford Recitations *[Prose]*
OXFORD, THURSDAY. | A contest for the speaking of verse took place on Tuesday and...
[headed, 'By John Masefield']

C055.443   Sep 19, 1923, p.5
The Lookout Man [Book Review: David W. Bone, *The Lookout Man*]
Forty years ago sailors, looking out upon the ships in port, would say that they...
[headed, 'By John Masefield']

C055.444   Oct 16, 1923, p.7
Ship Models [Book Review: E. Keble Chatterton, *Ship Models*]
In this book Mr. E. Keble Chatterton has gathered 141 photographs of models of ships...
[headed, 'By John Masefield']

C055.445   Aug 1, 1924, p.8
The Oxford Recitations. A New Feeling for Poetry *[Prose]*
OXFORD, THURSDAY. | The Oxford Recitations were held on Monday, Tuesday, and...
[headed, 'By JOHN MASEFIELD']

C055.446   Oct 31, 1952, p.4
Tales of the Sea [Book Review: Captain Sir David Bone, *The Queerfella*]
We used to be sad when we thought that there was no British book to compare with...
[headed, 'By John Masefield O.M.']

The Times Literary Supplement (London, U.K.)

Despite the anonymity of contributions to the *Times Literary Supplement*, the archive for *The Times* holds an incomplete set of marked-up copies and a card-file of contributors. Both have been consulted and these sources secure the authenticity of the book reviews listed here.

C060.001   Jun 24, 1904, p.195
In the Philippines [Book Review: A. Henry Savage Landor, *The Gems of the East*]
These two handsome volumes contain the record of a journey among...
[unsigned]

C060.002   Nov 11, 1904, p.347
Chile and Argentina [Book Review: Thomas H. Holdich, *The Countries of the King's Award*]
This interesting volume has a particular value. It gives a very clear...
[unsigned]

C060.003   Jan 27, 1905, p.30
South America [Book Review: C.E. Akers, *A History of South America (1854–1904)*]
A History of South America (1854–1904), by C.E. Akers...
[unsigned]

C060.004   Nov 10, 1905, p.385
In the South Seas [Book Review: Louis Becke, *Notes from my South Sea Log*]
In the Pacific, among the islands, or at sea in strange schooners...
[unsigned]

C060.005   Mar 30, 1906, p.116
Jack Derringer [Book Review: Basil Lubbock, *Jack Derringer*]
Jack Derringer, by Mr. Basil Lubbock... is an unequal...
[unsigned]

C060.006   Apr 13, 1906, p.133
The Adventures of a Supercargo [Book Review: Louis Becke, *In The Adventures of a Supercargo*]
In The Adventures of a Supercargo... Mr. Louis Becke forgets...
[unsigned]

C060.007   Apr 27, 1906, p.149
            Wild Justice [Book Review: Lloyd Osbourne, *Wild Justice*]
            Mr. Lloyd Osbourne's Wild Justice... contains nine stories of life...
            [unsigned]
C060.008   Jul 23, 1908, p.233
            Christmas Eve at Sea *[Verse]*
            A wind is nestling "south and soft,"
            [quoted in full in review of ed. N.G. Royde-Smith, *Poets of Our Day*]
C060.009   Dec 29, 1921, p.871
            Fox-Hunting [Combined Book Review: Thomas Smith, *Extracts from the Diary of a Huntsman*; John Mills, *The Life of a Fox-Hound*; and ed. Lord Willoughby de Broke, *The Sport of our Ancestors*]
            Fox-hunting is still the most stirring sight to be seen in the English countryside.
            [unsigned]
C060.010   Mar 6, 1924, p.144
            The Byron Centenary. To the Editor of The Times. *[Communal Letter]*
            Sir, – On April 19 a hundred years ago Lord Byron died...
            [signed, '...EDMUND GOSSE. THOMAS HARDY. E.V. LUCAS. JOHN MASEFIELD...']
C060.011   Jan 4, 1934, p.12
            The White Star Line *[Letter]*
            Sir, – I am hoping to prepare a History of the White Star Line...
            [signed, 'JOHN MASEFIELD. | Pinbury Park, Cirencester']
C060.012   Feb 20, 1943, p.92
            Arthur Machen *[Communal Letter]*
            Sir, – March 3, 1943, will be the eightieth birthday of one of the most distinguished living men...
            [signed, '...JOHN MASEFIELD... T.S. ELIOT... G. BERNARD SHAW']
C060.013   Dec 11, 1943, p.595
            Laurence Binyon *[Communal Letter]*
            Sir, – It is six months since Laurence Binyon died. His noble gifts as a poet...
            [signed, 'GORDON BOTTOMLEY... T.S. ELIOT... JOHN MASEFIELD... GEORGE BERNARD SHAW...']
C060.014   Feb 24, 1961, p.121
            Coleridge's Tomb *[Communal Letter]*
            Sir, – Your correspondence on Coleridge's Cottage will, we hope, not divert attention...
            [signed, 'JOHN MASEFIELD; JOHN BETJEMAN... CECIL DAY LEWIS; CHRISTOPHER FRY...']
C060.015   Aug 1, 1980, p.872
            A Study for a ballad of The Galley Rowers *[Verse]*
            Every day and all day long
            [headed, 'BY JOHN MASEFIELD']

The Daily News (London, U.K.)

C065.001   Dec 15, 1904, p.4
            Big Game and Savages [Book Review: Major Powell-Cotton, *In Unknown Africa*]
            This very interesting book of travel contains the record of...
            [headed, 'By John Masefield']
C065.002   Dec 21, 1904, p.4
            Dream Poems [Book Review: Gordon Bottomley, *The Gate of Smaragdus*]
            Mr. Gordon Bottomley is one of those poets whose work...
            [unsigned, but quoted as 'Mr. John Masefield in *The Daily News*, 21 December 1904' in 'Some Press Opinions of Mr. Bottomley's Work' within Gordon Bottomley, *Poems of Thirty Years* (Constable & Co., 1925)]
C065.003   Jul 20, 1907, p.4
            Cannibals in Colour [Book Review: E. Way Elkington, *The Savage South Seas*]
            Messrs. A. and C. Black have now produced more than fifty volumes in their library of...
            [headed, 'By John Masefield']
C065.004   Oct 10, 1910, p.4
            Malaria [Book Review: Major Ronald Ross, *The Prevention of Malaria*]
            Malaria is not one of the deadliest of human diseases. Though it kills its million a year...
            [headed, 'By John Masefield']

Country Life (London, U.K.)

C070.001   Nov 11, 1905, pp.661–62
             Davy Jones's Gift (A Folk-Lore Story) *[Prose]*
             "Once upon a time," said the sailor, "the Devil and Davy Jones...
             [signed, 'JOHN MAREFIELD' *[sic]*]

Temple Bar (London, U.K.)

C075.001   Jan 1906, pp.56–80
             Sea Songs *[Prose]*
             The sea-songs in general use in merchant ships are of two kinds.
             [signed, 'By JOHN MASEFIELD']

The Gentleman's Magazine (London, U.K.)

C080.001   Mar 1906, pp.113–26
             Captain John Ward *[Prose]*
             Captain John Ward, our "most notorious pirate,"...
             [unsigned]
C080.002   Mar 1906, p.187
             Correspondence: Captain William Dampier *[Letter]*
             Dear Mr. Urban, – I am preparing for the press an edition...
             [signed, 'JOHN MASEFIELD']
C080.003   Apr 1906, pp.243–54
             The Voyage of the "Cygnet" *[Prose]*
             In the year 1683–4 some eminent London merchants...
             [unsigned]
C080.004   Jul 1906, pp.1–10
             Captain Coxon *[Prose]*
             The island of Carmen, in the Lagoon of Tides...
             [unsigned]
C080.005   Dec 1906, pp.561–73
             Captain John Jennings *[Prose]*
             A pirate is a picturesque rather than an interesting figure.
             [unsigned]

Tribune

C085.000
Masefield claims to have contributed to a periodical of this name in a listing of work sent to his agent, C.F. Cazenove (see University of Arizona Library, MS.50). No further details are known. The listing was compiled in late 1906.

Macmillan's Magazine – New Series (Cambridge, U.K.)

C090.001   Feb 1907, pp.[314]-20
             The Gold-Seeker *[Prose]*
             The night had fallen over the harbour before the winch began to rattle.
             [signed, 'JOHN MASEFIELD']

The Nation (London, U.K.)

C095.001   Jul 20, 1907, p.764
             The City of the Soul *[Verse]*
             Troy Town is covered up with weeds,
             [signed, 'JOHN MASEFIELD']
C095.002   Oct 12, 1907, pp.41–42
             The Dragon Man *[Prose]*
             The old labourer who tells me about the fairies has a wide knowledge...
             [signed, 'JOHN MASEFIELD']

C095.003	Dec 7, 1907, pp.372–74
	Books for Boys *[Book Reviews]*
	Among the boy's books of this season now before us...
	[signed, 'JOHN MASEFIELD']
C095.004	Jun 16, 1917, p.272
	The Irony of Battle *[Prose]*
	Irony is difficult to define, for it has many kinds and many...
	[signed, 'JOHN MASEFIELD']

A Broadside (Dundrum, Co. Dublin, Ireland)

Hilary Pyle states, of verses in *The Broadside* by Wolfe Tone MacGowan, that 'the evidence among Yeats's papers and the crude quality of the verse tends to indicate [Jack B.] Yeats as the author' (*Jack B. Yeats – A Bibliography*, André Deutsch, 1989). Dr Pyle has stated that 'Colm O'Lochlainn, author of *Irish Street Ballads* (1939) was one source of the explanation of the pseudonym 'Wolfe T. MacGowan'. Liam Miller of the Dolmen Press was another, and it was widely accepted in Dublin that the Wolfe Tone and Robert Emmet pseudonyms were adopted by Jack B. Yeats.' This pseudonym attribution has passed into common usage. A manuscript letter dated June 31, 1924 from Elizabeth C. Yeats to an unknown recipient (Houghton Library, Harvard University, Autograph file) includes, however, a listing of Masefield verse in *The Broadside* and identifies Masefield as Wolfe Tone MacGowan. Additionally, the HRHRC manuscript of Masefield's play *The Sweeps of Ninety-Eight* (see A33) is signed as 'a farce by Wolfe T. McGowan'. On the title-page the pseudonym is deleted and Masefield's real name substituted. See also Fraser B. Drew, 'The Irish Allegiances of an English Laureate: John Masefield and Ireland', *Éire-Ireland – A Journal of Irish Studies,* Minnesota: Irish American Cultural Institute, Winter 1968, pp.24–34 and Philip W. Errington, 'McGowan's Code: Deciphering John Masefield and Jack B. Yeats', *Yeats Annual 13* (ed. Warwick Gould), Macmillan, 1998, pp.308–316.

C100.001	Jun 1908, No.1, p.[1–2]
	Campeachy Picture *[Verse]*
	The sloop's sails glow in the sun; the far sky burns,
	[signed, 'John Masefield']
C100.002	Sep 1908, No.4, p.[1]
	[Untitled] *[Verse]*
	Bring wine, and oil, and barley cakes,
	[signed, 'Wolfe T. MacGowan']
C100.003	Sep 1908, No.4, p.[2]
	A pleasant new comfortable ballad upon the death of Mr. Israel Hands, executed for piracy... *[Verse]*
	My name is Mr. Israel Hands
	[signed, 'Wolfe T. MacGowan']
C100.004	Jan 1909, No.8, p.[1]
	Theodore to his Grandson *[Verse]*
	O gamfer : you are lined and old,
	[signed, 'Wolfe T. MacGowan']
C100.005	Jun 1910, No.1 Third Year, p.[2]
	A Young Man's Fancy *[Verse]*
	All the sheets are clacking, all the blocks are whining,
	[signed, 'R.E. McGowan']
C100.006	Jun 1911, No.1 Fourth Year, p.[2]
	Captain Kidd *[Verse]*
	'My name is Captain Kidd,
	[unsigned]
C100.007	Sep 1911, No.4 Fourth Year, p.[2]
	[Untitled] *[Verse]*
	O Irlanda, Irlanda,
	[signed, 'Wolf [*sic*] T. MacGowan']
C100.008	May 1912, No.12 Fourth Year, p.[1]
	Die We Must *[Verse]*
	Die we must and go to dust
	[signed, 'Wolfe T. MacGowan']
C100.009	Aug 1913, No.3 Sixth Year, p.[2]
	The Gara River *[Verse]*
	Oh give me back my ships again
	[signed, 'Wolfe T. MacGowan']

Current Literature (New York, U.S.A.)

C105.001   Oct 1908, Vol.XLV No.4, p.457
Christmas Eve at Sea *[Verse]*
A wind is nestling "south and soft,"
[headed, 'BY JOHN MASEFIELD']

C105.002   May 1912, Vol.LII No.5, pp.[593]-94
The Widow in the Bye Street [Extract] *[Verse]*
So Jimmy came, while mother went inside;
[headed, 'BY JOHN MASEFIELD']

C105.003   Aug 1912, Vol.LIII No.2, pp.231–32
Golden Moments *[Verse]*
By many waters and on many ways
[headed, 'By JOHN MASEFIELD']
[source notes that the title is not authorial and poem extracted from 'Biography' in *The Forum*]

C105.004   Oct 1912, Vol.LIII No.4, pp.474–75
Ships *[Verse]*
I cannot tell their wonder nor make known
[headed, 'By JOHN MASEFIELD']

C105.005   Dec 1912, Vol.LIII No.6, p.716–17
Dauber [Extract] *[Verse]*
All through the windless night the clipper rolled
[headed, 'By JOHN MASEFIELD']

Chatterbox (London, U.K.)

C110.001   1909, New Series No.I, pp.6–7
Martin Hyde [Serialization] *[Prose]*
I was born at Oulton, in Suffolk, in the year 1672.
[signed, 'By JOHN MASEFIELD']

C110.002   1909, New Series No.II, pp.10–11
Martin Hyde [Serialization] *[Prose]*
A low stone parapet, topped by iron rails...
[unsigned]

C110.003   1909, New Series No.III, pp.22–23
Martin Hyde [Serialization] *[Prose]*
The boys were strictly searched by the constable.
[unsigned]

C110.004   1909, New Series No.IV, pp.26–27
Martin Hyde [Serialization] *[Prose]*
I was very angry with Ephraim...
[unsigned]

C110.005   1909, New Series No.V, pp.34–35
Martin Hyde [Serialization] *[Prose]*
I finished my cake quietly after that.
[unsigned]

C110.006   1909, New Series No.VI, p.47
Martin Hyde [Serialization] *[Prose]*
I must have made some little noise...
[unsigned]

C110.007   1909, New Series No.VII, p.50
Martin Hyde [Serialization] *[Prose]*
I ate a good supper at a cook-shop...
[unsigned]

C110.008   1909, New Series No.VIII, pp.62–63
Martin Hyde [Serialization] *[Prose]*
I was thoroughly ripe for mischief of any kind...
[unsigned]

C110.009   1909, New Series No.IX, pp.66–67
Martin Hyde [Serialization] *[Prose]*
At the head of the table there was...
[unsigned]

C110.010   1909, New Series No.X, pp.76–79
Martin Hyde [Serialization] *[Prose]*
'A civil war.' I had hardly repeated this...
[unsigned]

C110.011   1909, New Series No.XI, pp.86–87
Martin Hyde [Serialization] *[Prose]*
Mr. Jermyn led me to the pantry...
[unsigned]

C110.012   1909, New Series No.XII, pp.90–91
Martin Hyde [Serialization] *[Prose]*
In another minute we were in the narrow road...
[unsigned]

C110.013   1909, New Series No.XIII, pp.98–99
Martin Hyde [Serialization] *[Prose]*
I ran up the ladder to the deck...
[unsigned]

C110.014   1909, New Series No.XIV, p.111
Martin Hyde [Serialization] *[Prose]*
The mate left me then, as he had to watch...
[unsigned]

C110.015   1909, New Series No.XV, pp.118–19
Martin Hyde [Serialization] *[Prose]*
After I had called the two gentlemen...
[unsigned]

C110.016   1909, New Series No.XVI, pp.122–23
Martin Hyde [Serialization] *[Prose]*
'Heigho,' said the boatswain, yawning.
[unsigned]

C110.017   1909, New Series No.XVII, pp.130–31
Martin Hyde [Serialization] *[Prose]*
I will say no more about our passage...
[unsigned]

C110.018   1909, New Series No.XVIII, pp.138–39
Martin Hyde [Serialization] *[Prose]*
'Martin,' said Mr. Jermyn, 'this skylight...
[unsigned]

C110.019   1909, New Series No.XIX, pp.150–51
Martin Hyde [Serialization] *[Prose]*
'Give it me,' I said.
[unsigned]

C110.020   1909, New Series No.XX, pp.158–59
Martin Hyde [Serialization] *[Prose]*
As we walked back to the ship...
[unsigned]

C110.021   1909, New Series No.XXI, pp.162–63
Martin Hyde [Serialization] *[Prose]*
After waiting about an hour in the schooner...
[unsigned]

C110.022   1909, New Series No.XXII, pp.170–72
Martin Hyde [Serialization] *[Prose]*
I remember not very much of my ride...
[unsigned]

C110.023   1909, New Series No.XXIII, pp.182–83
Martin Hyde [Serialization] *[Prose]*
In another minute, after Mr. Standhal...
[unsigned]

C110.024   1909, New Series No.XXIV, pp.190–91
Martin Hyde [Serialization] *[Prose]*
Mr. Jermyn slowed down the horse...
[unsigned]

C110.025   1909, New Series No.XXV, pp.198–99
Martin Hyde [Serialization] *[Prose]*
While I was fretting myself into a state...
[unsigned]

C110.026   1909, New Series No.XXVI, pp.202–03
Martin Hyde [Serialization] *[Prose]*
When Mr. Jermyn and I went out...
[unsigned]

C110.027   1909, New Series No.XXVII, pp.214–15
Martin Hyde [Serialization] *[Prose]*
Very early the next morning, at about half-past four...
[unsigned]

C110.028   1909, New Series No.XXVIII, pp.218–19
Martin Hyde [Serialization] *[Prose]*
Presently, after half-an-hour's absence...
[unsigned]

C110.029   1909, New Series No.XXIX, pp.226–27
Martin Hyde [Serialization] *[Prose]*
After I had taken off my waistcoat...
[unsigned]

C110.030   1909, New Series No.XXX, pp.238–39
Martin Hyde [Serialization] *[Prose]*
At that instant there came a more violent gust...
[unsigned]

C110.031   1909, New Series No.XXXI, pp.242–43
Martin Hyde [Serialization] *[Prose]*
I took what handkerchiefs I could find...
[unsigned]

C110.032   1909, New Series No.XXXII, pp.250–51
Martin Hyde [Serialization] *[Prose]*
I came to, very ill, some time in the night.
[unsigned]

C110.033   1909, New Series No.XXXIII, pp.258–59
Martin Hyde [Serialization] *[Prose]*
We spread the tidings as far as Exeter...
[unsigned]

C110.034   1909, New Series No.XXXIV, pp.270–71
Martin Hyde [Serialization] *[Prose]*
At last, after midnight in the night of...
[unsigned]

C110.035   1909, New Series No.XXXV, pp.274–75
Martin Hyde [Serialization] *[Prose]*
Inside the town there was great confusion.
[unsigned]

C110.036   1909, New Series No.XXXVI, pp.286–87
Martin Hyde [Serialization] *[Prose]*
When we got up to the top of the hill...
[unsigned]

C110.037   1909, New Series No.XXXVII, pp.290–91
Martin Hyde [Serialization] *[Prose]*
Word was passed about that we were going...
[unsigned]

C110.038   1909, New Series No.XXXVIII, pp.302–303
Martin Hyde [Serialization] *[Prose]*
We had swung round, facing towards Lyme...
[unsigned]

C110.039   1909, New Series No.XXXIX, pp.306–307
Martin Hyde [Serialization] *[Prose]*
The next thing which I remember...
[unsigned]

C110.040	1909, New Series No.XL, pp.318–19
	Martin Hyde [Serialization] *[Prose]*
	That evening, after the summer dusk had come...
	[unsigned]
C110.041	1909, New Series No.XLI, pp.322–23
	Martin Hyde [Serialization] *[Prose]*
	I wondered when I was to get breakfast...
	[unsigned]
C110.042	1909, New Series No.XLII, pp.[333]-35
	Martin Hyde [Serialization] *[Prose]*
	I looked about me carefully...
	[unsigned]
C110.043	1909, New Series No.XLIII, pp.342–43
	Martin Hyde [Serialization] *[Prose]*
	'There,' said the man, not unkindly...
	[unsigned]
C110.044	1909, New Series No.XLIV, pp.346–47
	Martin Hyde [Serialization] *[Prose]*
	After another hour of riding, we pulled up...
	[unsigned]
C110.045	1909, New Series No.XLV, pp.354–55
	Martin Hyde [Serialization] *[Prose]*
	It was a friendly letter, which relieved me...
	[unsigned]
C110.046	1909, New Series No.XLVI, pp.362–63
	Martin Hyde [Serialization] *[Prose]*
	The Carew men had come back in a few minutes...
	[unsigned]
C110.047	1909, New Series No.XLVII, pp.374–75
	Martin Hyde [Serialization] *[Prose]*
	It was too dark to do much that night...
	[unsigned]
C110.048	1909, New Series No.XLVIII, pp.378–79
	Martin Hyde [Serialization] *[Prose]*
	After this, the men moved off...
	[unsigned]
C110.049	1909, New Series No.XLIX, pp.390–91
	Martin Hyde [Serialization] *[Prose]*
	For the first hour or two, as no one would be about...
	[unsigned]
C110.050	1909, New Series No.L, pp.394–95
	Martin Hyde [Serialization] *[Prose]*
	When I grew weary of sitting up...
	[unsigned]
C110.051	1909, New Series No.LI, pp.406–407
	Martin Hyde [Serialization] *[Prose]*
	Among all the confusion I learned...
	[unsigned]
C110.052	1909, New Series No.LII, p.410
	Martin Hyde [Serialization] *[Prose]*
	I saw a great sweep of moorland to my left...
	[signed, 'JOHN MASEFIELD']
C110.053	1910, New Series No.I, pp.2–3
	Jim Davis [Serialization] *[Prose]*
	I was born in the year 1800...
	[signed, 'By JOHN MASEFIELD']
C110.054	1910, New Series No.II, p.15
	Jim Davis [Serialization] *[Prose]*
	Once, I remember (in the winter)...
	[unsigned]

C110.055   1910, New Series No.III, pp.22–23
Jim Davis [Serialization] *[Prose]*
'Why, it's a boy,' said the terrible man.
[unsigned]

C110.056   1910, New Series No.IV, pp.26–27
Jim Davis [Serialization] *[Prose]*
It was very awesome sitting there...
[unsigned]

C110.057   1910, New Series No.V, pp.34–35
Jim Davis [Serialization] *[Prose]*
On turning the package over...
[unsigned]

C110.058   1910, New Series No.VI, p.47
Jim Davis [Serialization] *[Prose]*
It seemed to me very curious.
[unsigned]

C110.059   1910, New Series No.VII, pp.50–51
Jim Davis [Serialization] *[Prose]*
'Well, mister,' the man said...
[unsigned]

C110.060   1910, New Series No.VIII, pp.62–63
Jim Davis [Serialization] *[Prose]*
The strange man passed out of the hut...
[unsigned]

C110.061   1910, New Series No.IX, p.66
Jim Davis [Serialization] *[Prose]*
Mrs. Cottier asked us if we...
[unsigned]

C110.062   1910, New Series No.X, pp.74–75
Jim Davis [Serialization] *[Prose]*
'Good morning, Mr. Gorsuch,' I said.
[unsigned]

C110.063   1910, New Series No.XI, p.87
Jim Davis [Serialization] *[Prose]*
For the next month we passed...
[unsigned]

C110.064   1910, New Series No.XII, pp.94–95
Jim Davis [Serialization] *[Prose]*
When we came to the gate...
[unsigned]

C110.065   1910, New Series No.XIII, pp.98–99
Jim Davis [Serialization] *[Prose]*
I pushed my way along the cliffs...
[unsigned]

C110.066   1910, New Series No.XIV, pp.110–11
Jim Davis [Serialization] *[Prose]*
My heart was thumping on my ribs...
[unsigned]

C110.067   1910, New Series No.XV, p.119
Jim Davis [Serialization] *[Prose]*
Just before we came to the low stone...
[unsigned]

C110.068   1910, New Series No.XVI, pp.122–23
Jim Davis [Serialization] *[Prose]*
The inner room was much larger...
[unsigned]

C110.069   1910, New Series No.XVII, pp.130–31
Jim Davis [Serialization] *[Prose]*
Marah sat still, watching me.
[unsigned]

C110.070   1910, New Series No.XVIII, pp.142–43
            Jim Davis [Serialization] *[Prose]*
            It was dark in the cave...
            [unsigned]

C110.071   1910, New Series No.XIX, p.151
            Jim Davis [Serialization] *[Prose]*
            By this time the other smugglers...
            [unsigned]

C110.072   1910, New Series No.XX, p.154
            Jim Davis [Serialization] *[Prose]*
            I could see no green stones...
            [unsigned]

C110.073   1910, New Series No.XXI, pp.162–63
            Jim Davis [Serialization] *[Prose]*
            I shall not describe our passage...
            [unsigned]

C110.074   1910, New Series No.XXII, p.175
            Jim Davis [Serialization] *[Prose]*
            Marah swung me up into the saddle...
            [unsigned]

C110.075   1910, New Series No.XXIII, pp.178–79
            Jim Davis [Serialization] *[Prose]*
            We turned down the valley...
            [unsigned]

C110.076   1910, New Series No.XXIV, p.191
            Jim Davis [Serialization] *[Prose]*
            The wind was blowing from the direction...
            [unsigned]

C110.077   1910, New Series No.XXV, p.199
            Jim Davis [Serialization] *[Prose]*
            The next day, when I woke...
            [unsigned]

C110.078   1910, New Series No.XXVI, p.202
            Jim Davis [Serialization] *[Prose]*
            'Jim!' cried Mr. Cottier...
            [unsigned]

C110.079   1910, New Series No.XXVII, pp.214–15
            Jim Davis [Serialization] *[Prose]*
            We had rough weather on the passage...
            [unsigned]

C110.080   1910, New Series No.XXVIII, p.218
            Jim Davis [Serialization] *[Prose]*
            I suppose that we worked...
            [unsigned]

C110.081   1910, New Series No.XXIX, p.231
            Jim Davis [Serialization] *[Prose]*
            Marah knocked down a trooper...
            [unsigned]

C110.082   1910, New Series No.XXX, pp.234–35
            Jim Davis [Serialization] *[Prose]*
            I soon saw that the current...
            [unsigned]

C110.083   1910, New Series No.XXXI, p.247
            Jim Davis [Serialization] *[Prose]*
            As I stepped out...
            [unsigned]

C110.084   1910, New Series No.XXXII, pp.250–51
            Jim Davis [Serialization] *[Prose]*
            Presently the landlady looked...
            [unsigned]

C110.085 1910, New Series No.XXXIII, p.263
  Jim Davis [Serialization] *[Prose]*
  It was very dark in the drawing room...
  [unsigned]

C110.086 1910, New Series No.XXXIV, pp.270–71
  Jim Davis [Serialization] *[Prose]*
  Happily for me, the wall was well-grown...
  [unsigned]

C110.087 1910, New Series No.XXXV, p.274
  Jim Davis [Serialization] *[Prose]*
  I was now at the end of my resources...
  [unsigned]

C110.088 1910, New Series No.XXXVI, p.282
  Jim Davis [Serialization] *[Prose]*
  'It's all right, Gray...
  [unsigned]

C110.089 1910, New Series No.XXXVII, p.290
  Jim Davis [Serialization] *[Prose]*
  When the gipsies had danced...
  [unsigned]

C110.090 1910, New Series No.XXXVIII, p.298
  Jim Davis [Serialization] *[Prose]*
  I could not get very near...
  [signed, 'JOHN MASEFIELD']

Fortnightly Review (London, U.K. / New York, U.S.A.)

C115.001 Jan 1, 1909, pp.[65]-73
  Daniel Defoe *[Prose]*
  In the early eighteenth century, people went to portrait painters hoping...
  [signed, 'JOHN MASEFIELD']

C115.002 Dec 1, 1915, pp.[993]-1018
  Good Friday *[Verse Play]*
  The Scene. The Pavement, or Paved Court, outside the Roman Citadel... PILATE. Longinus...
  [headed, 'BY JOHN MASEFIELD']

The Englishwoman (London, U.K.)

C120.001 Feb 1909, p.16
  Invocation *[Verse]*
  O wanderer into many brains,
  [signed, 'JOHN MASEFIELD']

C120.002 Apr 1909, p.236
  By a Bier-Side *[Verse]*
  This is a sacred city built of marvellous earth.
  [signed, 'JOHN MASEFIELD']

C120.003 Jun 1909, p.506
  Thermopylæ *[Verse]*
  Though we are ringed with spears, though the last hope is gone,
  [signed, 'JOHN MASEFIELD']

C120.004 Aug 1909, p.41
  Chorus *[Verse]*
  Kneel to the beautiful women who bear us this strange brave fruit,
  [signed, 'JOHN MASEFIELD']

C120.005 Nov 1909, p.71
  Imagination *[Verse]*
  Woman, beauty, wonder, sacred woman,
  [signed, 'JOHN MASEFIELD']

C120.006 Dec 1909, p.151
  Lyric *[Verse]*
  And all their passionate hearts are dust,
  [signed, 'JOHN MASEFIELD']

NICIAS MORITURUS

An' Bill can have my sea-boots, Nigger Jim can have my
    knife,
    You can divvy up the dungarees an' bed;
An' the ship can have my blessin', an' the Lord can have
    my life;
    An' " Sails " an' fish my body when I'm dead.

An' dreaming down below there in the tangled greens and
    blues
    Where the sunlight shudders golden round about,
I shall hear the ships complainin' and the cursin' of the
    crews,
    An' be sorry when the watch is tumbled out.

I shall hear 'em hilly-hollyin' the weather crojick brace;
    Hear the sheet-blocks jiggin' hornpipes all achafe;
Hear the tops'l halyard chanty—feel the salt spray sting
    my face—
    I'll be seaward though my body's anchored safe.

I shall hear the south wind callin' soft an' low across the
    deep,
    An' the slattin' of the storm-sail on the stay;
Hear the ripplin' o' the catspaw at the makin' o' the neap,
    An' the swirl and splash o' porpoises at play.

An' Bill can have my sea-boots, Nigger Jim can have my
    knife,
    You can divvy up the dungarees an' bed,
An' the ship can have my blessin', an' the Lord can have
    my life,
    For it's time to go aloft when Jack is dead.

                    JOHN E. MASEFIELD.

C010.001 Nicias Moriturus (*The Outlook*)

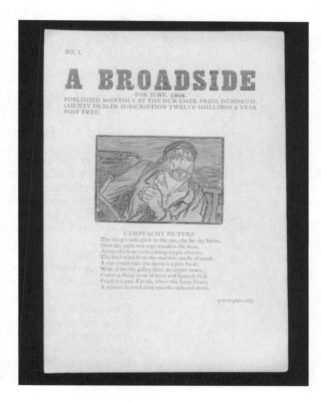

C100.001 Campeachy Picture (*A Broadside*)

745

THE
ENGLISH REVIEW
OCTOBER, 1911

The Everlasting Mercy*

By John Masefield

From '41 to '51
I was my folk's contrary son ;
I bit my father's hand right through
And broke my mother's heart in two.
I sometimes go without my dinner
Now that I know the times I've gi'n her.

From '51 to '61
I cut my teeth and took to fun.
I learned what not to be afraid of
And what stuff women's lips are made of ;
I learned with what a rosy feeling
Good ale makes floors seem like the ceiling,
And how the moon gives shiny light
To lads as roll home singing by't.
My blood did leap, my flesh did revel,
Saul Kane was tokened to the devil.

From '61 to '67
I lived in disbelief of heaven.
I drunk, I fought, I poached, I whored,
I did despite unto the Lord.

* Copyright in U.S.A., 1911.

The Times / The Sunday Times (London, U.K.)

C125.001   Oct 22, 1909, p.4a
The Suggested Shakespeare Memorial Theatre *[Letter]*
Sir, – The suggestion that a theatre should be built and endowed...
[signed, 'JOHN MASEFIELD']

C125.002   Apr 29, 1910, p.14a
The White Slave Traffic *[Letter]*
Sir, – I read with interest the leading article on the White Slave Traffic...
[signed, 'JOHN MASEFIELD']

C125.003   Sep 27, 1912, p.7f
"The Winter's Tale." Mr. Granville Barker's Production *[Letter]*
Sir, – As a lover of poetical drama I wish to protest against the abuse...
[signed, 'JOHN MASEFIELD.']

C125.004   Mar 17, 1916, p.8e
American Poets and The Allies [Paraphrases Masefield's speech at Poets' Dinner, 15 Mar 1916]
The poets' dinner given as a farewell to Mr. John Masefield last night...

C125.005   Sep 26, 1918, p.3c
London Street Women *[Letter]*
Sir, – I have read with interest Mr. Edward Bok's statement in your issue for to-day.
[signed, 'JOHN MASEFIELD.']

C125.006   Nov 13, 1918, p.11c
Mr. Masefield on the Shy Englishman [Paraphrases Masefield's speech at American Officers' Club, 12 Nov 1918]
Mr. John Masefield, speaking at the American Officers' Club, Washington Inn...

C125.007   May 30, 1919, p.8d
Repertory Theatre for Oxford *[Letter]*
Sir, – Since the signing of the Armistice several small theatres with high standards...
[signed, 'JOHN MASEFIELD.']

C125.008   Apr 28, 1921, p.10a
Shakespeare the Just [Paraphrases Masefield's lecture at King's College London on Shakespeare, 27 Apr 1921]
At the invitation of the Council of the British Academy, Mr. John Masefield...

C125.009   Aug 2, 1921, p.11e
Maker of Books, Poetry, and Chicken Runs [Paraphrases Masefield's address at Bembridge School on Arts and Crafts, 20 Jul 1921]
Mr. John Masefield gave an address on Foundation Day at Bembridge School last week.

C125.010   Jun 30, 1922, p.11e
The Hawthornden Prize [Paraphrases Masefield's presentation of Hawthornden Prize at Æolian Hall, 29 Jun 1922]
The Hawthornden Prize, given annually by Miss Alice Warrender for the best book...

C125.011   Sep 21, 1923, p.7e
"War Against Malaria" [Extract quoted from Masefield's foreword to *The War Against Malaria*]
"It is not too much to say," he declares, "that Sir Ronald Ross cut...

C125.012   Mar 6, 1924, p.8d
In Memory of Byron | Centenary Appeal for Greek Refugees *[Communal Letter]*
Sir, – On April 19, a hundred years ago Lord Byron died...
[signed, '...JOHN MASEFIELD. EDMUND GOSSE. GILBERT MURRAY. THOMAS HARDY...']

C125.013   Jun 5, 1924, p.9e
Shakespeare as Child of Superstition [Paraphrases Masefield's Romanes lecture on Shakespeare at Sheldonian Theatre, 4 Jun 1924]
The Romanes lecture was delivered in the Sheldonian Theatre this afternoon...

C125.014   Jul 29, 1924, p.14e
The Oxford Recitation Competition [Paraphrases Masefield's remarks at second Oxford Recitation Competition, 28 Jul 1924]
The Oxford Recitation Competition began in the Examination Schools at Oxford yesterday...

C125.015   Nov 15, 1924, p.8b
"The Young King." New Play in a New Theatre [Paraphrases Masefield's speech after Binyon play at Music Room, 13 Nov 1924]
Mr. John Masefield has built a theatre in his garden at Boars Hill.

C125.016   Jul 24, 1925, p.16a
The Late Mrs J.H. Philpot *[Letter]*
Mrs J.H. Philpot whose death you record in *The Times* of July 23, was a woman with a genius...
[headed, 'Mr. John Masefield writes']

C125.017   Mar 20, 1926, p.13e

A Blake Memorial in St. Paul's *[Communal Letter]*

Sir, – On August 12, 1927, 100 years will have passed since there died…

[signed, 'STANLEY BALDWIN… EDWARD ELGAR… THOMAS HARDY… JOHN MASEFIELD…']

C125.018   Jul 28, 1926, p.10a

The Speaking of Verse [Paraphrases Masefield's remarks at fourth Oxford Recitation Competition, 27 Jul 1926]

Mr. John Masefield spoke last night at the opening of the fourth Verse-Speaking Contest…

C125.019   Nov 26, 1927, pp.15f-16a

The Case for The [Oxford Preservation] Trust *[Prose]*

For the last generation English people have been moving into the big towns…

[headed, 'by Mr. John Masefield']

C125.020   May 14, 1928, p.12d

Play in Canterbury Cathedral [Paraphrases Masefield's remarks on announced production of *The Coming of Christ*]

A Nativity play, *The Coming of Christ*, by Mr. John Masefield, with incidental…

C125.021   Mar 26, 1929, p.9e

The Story of *The Wanderer* *[Appeal for Details]*

"I am writing the story of the four-masted steel barque Wanderer (1891–1907)…

[headed, 'Mr. John Masefield writes…']

C125.022   Feb 10, 1930, p.14c

Liverpool's Kinship with the Sea [Paraphrases Masefield's speech on Liverpool at sea festival, Liverpool, 8 Feb 1930]

Mr. Masefield, who proposed the toast "Sailors and ship of Liverpool," said that…

C125.023   Feb 11, 1930, p.12b

Liverpool's "Kinship with the Sea" [Paraphrases Masefield's address on boyhood in Liverpool at Liverpool College, 10 Feb 1930]

To-day's programme of the celebration of Liverpool's "kinship with the sea" included…

C125.024   May 26, 1930, p.15e

"Samson Agonistes" at Oxford *[Letter]*

Sir, – Will you allow me to add a few words to your Correspondent's praise of Mr. Nevill Coghill's…

[signed, 'JOHN MASEFIELD']

C125.025   Jul 12, 1930, p.13e

Wanted – The Author [re: an alliterative alphabetical poem] *[Letter]*

Sir, – I have this morning received the following request from Delhi…

[signed, 'JOHN MASEFIELD | Boar's Hill, Oxford, July 8.']

C125.026   Jul 15, 1930, p.15e

All Aid Arrest [re: an alliterative alphabetical poem] *[Letter]*

Sir, – I thank the many hundreds who have answered my appeal so generously…

[signed, 'JOHN MASEFIELD. Boar's Hill']

C125.027   Jul 30, 1930, p.13e

Bombing Practice in Berkshire *[Letter]*

Sir, – I should like to thank you for your excellent leading article on the decision of the…

[signed, 'JOHN MASEFIELD. | Boars Hill']

C125.028   Oct 24, 1930, p.12e

The Poet Laureate [Paraphrases Masefield's speech on receiving freedom of Hereford at Hereford, 23 Oct 1930]

Returning thanks for the bestowal of the honorary freedom, Mr. Masefield said…

C125.029   Nov 21, 1930, p.11c

Ships and Sailors [Paraphrases Masefield's talk on work of Seamen's Missions at Liverpool, 20 Nov 1930]

Mr. John Masefield, Poet Laureate, talked about ships and sailors yesterday to a gathering…

C125.030   Apr 1, 1931, p.16e

Mr. Masefield and H.M.S. Conway *[Letter]*

"I am writing a history of H.M.S. Conway, the training ship of…

[headed, 'Mr. John Masefield… writes…']

C125.031   Jun 12, 1931, p.14d

Cowper Honoured at Olney [Paraphrases Masefield's address on Cowper at Olney, 11 Jun 1931]

At a public meeting in the Congregational Church Mr. Masefield took the chair and delivered…

C125.032   Aug 21, 1931, p.7b

"Mosquito Day" [Paraphrases Masefield's speech on Ronald Ross at the Ross Institute, 20 Aug 1931]

The Poet Laureate proposed first a toast to "Malaria Control and Sir Malcolm Watson" and afterwards…

C125.033   Oct 5, 1931, p.14g

[Untitled poem on Liverpool Cathedral] *[Verse]*

They buried him, and then the soldiers slept;

[introduced as 'written for the occasion by Dr. Masefield']

C125.034   Oct 5, 1931, p.16d

Dr. Masefield's Tribute [Paraphrases Masefield's address on cathedrals at Adelphi Hotel, Liverpool, 4 Oct 1931]

At a luncheon at the Adelphi Hotel, given by Sir Frederick Bowring, an address...

C125.035   Oct 16, 1931, p.16d

The Great Poets [Paraphrases Masefield's lecture on Poetry at Queen's Hall, London, 15 Oct 1931]

A lecture on Poetry was given at Queen's Hall last evening by...

C125.036   Nov 3, 1931, p.13e

'What Will Be Done?' [re: National Government] *[Letter]*

Sir, – Now that the nation has placed a National Party in power great things may be...

[signed, 'JOHN MASEFIELD. | Boars Hill, Oxford, Nov.2']

C125.037   Nov 14, 1931, p.13e

A Fine Seaman [re: death of Captain James Brander] *[Letter]*

Sir, – I regret to read in your issue of to-day of the death of Captain James Brander...

[signed, 'JOHN MASEFIELD. | November 13']

C125.038   Feb 4, 1932, p.9c

Life and Genius of Crabbe [Paraphrases Masefield's address on George Crabbe at Trowbridge, 3 Feb 1932]

Mr. Masefield said that in studying any writer it was often well to begin with...

C125.039   Apr 25, 1932, p.15f

[Untitled ode for Shakespeare Memorial Theatre opening] *[Verse]*

Beside this House there is a blackened shell,

[signed, 'JOHN MASEFIELD.']

C125.040   May 3, 1932, p.19d

A Poetic Festival Competition [Poetic Festival Competition Announced]

Mr. John Masefield, the Poet Laureate, asks us to state that he and Mrs. Masefield propose...

C125.041   May 31, 1932, p.21g

Verse-Speaking Festival [Verse Speaking Festival Announcement on Copyright]

Writers who intend to submit work for the Festival for the Speaking of Tales in Verse...

C125.042   Jun 9, 1932, p.13f

[Ode on unveiling of Memorial to Queen Alexandra] *[Verse]*

So many true princesses who have gone

[headed, '...written for the occasion by the Poet Laureate...']

C125.043   Dec 29, 1932, p.8f

Mauretania in Service [Paraphrases Masefield's comments on visit to the United States]

Among her passengers was Mr. John Masefield, the Poet Laureate, who, in company...

C125.044   Apr 21, 1933, p.17b

Mrs. Henry Daniel *[Letter]*

The death of Mrs. Daniel, the widow of the late Provost of Worcester, takes from us...

[headed, 'Mr. John Masefield writes']

C125.045   Jun 7, 1933, p.14a

George Herbert [Paraphrases Masefield's address on George Herbert's life and works at Bemerton, 6 Jun 1933]

The Poet Laureate spoke of George Herbert as a man still famous for the sanctity of his life...

C125.046   Jun 9, 1933, p.10d

Chaucer and the "Canterbury Tales" [Paraphrases Masefield's lecture on Chaucer and *The Canterbury Tales* at Canterbury, 8 Jun 1933]

Chaucer, Mr. Masefield said, told his tales in rhythm because people who listened to them could...

C125.047   Jul 1, 1933, p.14c

Mr. H.W. Nevinson Honoured [Paraphrases Masefield's speech in honour of Nevinson at Criterion Restaurant, 30 Jun 1933]

Mr. John Masefield, the Poet Laureate, spoke of Mr. Nevinson as literary craftsman...

C125.048   Aug 9, 1933, p.8b

Art and Life [Paraphrases Masefield's comments and speech on poetry at Wrexham, 8 Aug 1933]

Mr. Masefield, who was accorded an enthusiastic reception, in his speech confessed to his...

C125.049   Aug 22, 1933, p.13f

In Memory of Sir Ronald Ross [Paraphrases Masefield's address at service for Ronald Ross, St. Martin-in-the Fields, 21 Aug 1933]

At the service yesterday Mr. Masefield delivered an address. He said that the world was...

C125.050   Sep 25, 1933, p.15d

Poet Laureate's Appeal for Aged Merchantmen [Quotes appeal for Royal Alfred Aged Merchant Seamen's Institute, 24 Sep 1933]

"There is no one in these islands listening to me at his moment who has not benefited...

C125.051   Oct 23, 1933, p.11d
Liberation of Wild Creatures [Paraphrases Masefield's speech on value of Nature Reserves]
The Poet Laureate, in his speech, vigorously decried the desecration of Nature and the keeping...

C125.052   Nov 3, 1933, p.15e
Royal Medals for Poetry *[Letter]*
Sir, – many years ago some young writers held that the older writers were enemies standing in...
[signed, 'JOHN MASEFIELD. | Cirencester']

C125.053   Jan 1, 1934, p.7b
History of The White Star Line *[Appeal for Details]*
"I am hoping to prepare a History of the White Star Line. May I ask all those who have...
[headed 'Mr. John Masefield... has circulated the following...']

C125.054   May 21, 1934, p.11e
"Everyman" at Oxford *[Letter]*
Sir, – Your critic of the production of *Everyman*, now being played at Exeter College, Oxford...
[signed, 'JOHN MASEFIELD. | Pinbury Park, Cirencester, May 19.']

C125.055   Jun 14, 1934, p.13b
Ships and Men [Paraphrases Masefield's lecture on "They that go down to the Sea in Ships" at Canterbury, 13 Jun 1934]
Mr. Masefield said that the nineteenth century four-masted sailing ships at the height...

C125.056   Sep 25, 1934, p.11b
"534" *[Verse]*
For ages you were rock, far below light,
[headed, 'Mr. John Masefield... has written...']

C125.057   Nov 19, 1934, p.11a
[Melbourne] *[Verse]*
A hundred years ago this was the range
[headed, 'Mr. Masefield's Poem On Melbourne']

C125.058   Apr 15, 1935, p.16a
Mr. Masefield's Poacher [Paraphrases Masefield's revelation on *The Everlasting Mercy* at Hereford, (undated)]
In the course of a reading of his poems at Hereford, of which city he is a Freeman...

C125.059   May 6, 1935, p.9a
A Galsworthy Memorial [Paraphrases Masefield's speech on unveiling Galsworthy memorial at New College, Oxford, 4 May 1935]
...The Poet Laureate (Mr. John Masefield), in unveiling the tablet, said he had never known...

C125.060   May 7, 1935, p.16e
A Prayer for The King's Majesty *[Verse]*
O God, whose mercy is our state,
[headed, 'Verses By The Poet Laureate']

C125.061   May 11, 1935, p.8a
Electricity and Rural Amenities *[Letter]*
Sir, – During April you published letters from Mr. Guy Dawber and Sir Fabian Ware about...
[signed, 'JOHN MASEFIELD. | Pinbury Park, Cirencester, May 8']

C125.062   Jun 29, 1935, p.8f
[Inscription from tribute to Late King Albert of the Belgians]
The board bears the inscription:- "These primroses are the British tribute to Albert the well...

C125.063   Jul 10, 1935, p.19c
Kent Cancer Appeal Fund [Paraphrases Masefield's words at poetry reading in aid of Kent County Cancer Appeal Fund, 9 Jul 1935]
Mr. Masefield said it was a pleasure and a privilege to speak on behalf of the fund. Man's greatest enemies...

C125.064   Jul 12, 1935, p.11b
London Hospital Medical College [Paraphrases comments during prize-givings at London Hospital Medical College, 11 Jul 1935]
Mr. Masefield recalled that when he sat at prize-givings in his youth he divided the eminent...

C125.065   Jul 13, 1935, p.8c
[On adapting *Romeo and Juliet* for the screen] *[Letter]*
Sir, – I shall be obliged if you will allow me to correct the statement made in a paragraph...
[signed, 'JOHN MASEFIELD. | Cirencester, July 12.']

C125.066   Nov 29, 1935, p.15e
Mark Twain Centenary To-Morrow *[Letter]*
Sir, – November 30 will be the hundredth anniversary of the birth of Samuel Clemens, known...
[signed, 'JOHN MASEFIELD. | Pinbury Park, Cirencester, Nov. 27.']

C125.067   Jan 23, 1936, p.13d
      To Rudyard Kipling [Verse]
      Your very heart was England's; it is just
      [signed, 'JOHN MASEFIELD.']

C125.068   Jan 29, 1936, p.11d
      On The Passing of King George V [Verse]
      When time has sifted motives, passions, deeds
      [signed, 'JOHN MASEFIELD.']

C125.069   Apr 25, 1936, p.8a
      The Oxford Union Paintings [Letter]
      Sir, – May I ask readers of *The Times* to subscribe to a fund now being raised...
      [signed, 'JOHN MASEFIELD. | Pinbury Park. Cirencester. April 23.']

C125.070   May 14, 1936, p.11a
      Preventing Tropical Disease [Paraphrases Masefield's address on Ross at Manson-Ross luncheon, 13 May 1936]
      The Poet Laureate, supporting the toast, said that it was perhaps Ross's discovery...

C125.071   May 28, 1936, p.9g
      Pride in Ships [Paraphrases Masefield's comments at reading of his works at the Royal Society of Literature, 27 May 1936]
      Before turning for a while to his poems of the sea, Mr. Masefield spoke of the inspiring beauty...

C125.072   Jul 9, 1936, p.19g
      Mr. Masefield on his Early Reading [Paraphrases Masefield's speech at A.G.M. of the London Library, 8 Jul 1936]
      Mr. John Masefield, O.M., the Poet Laureate, presided yesterday at the 95th annual general meeting...

C125.073   Nov 28, 1936, p.7g
      Home for Wayfarers [Quotes Masefield's foreword to *Pauntley – The Gloucestershire Home for Wayfarers*]
      "Once when I was a lad, before I was 17, when I was in a lonely countryside...
      [headed, 'Mr. Masefield writes...']

C125.074   Apr 28, 1937, p.10e
      A Prayer for The King's Reign [Verse]
      O God, the Ruler over Earth and Sea,
      [headed, 'The Poet Laureate's Verse']

C125.075   Jun 8, 1937, p.17e
      Art in the Inn [Letter]
      [re: O.U.D.S. performance of *Twelfth Night* at the Downham Tavern on 24 Jun 1937]
      Sir, – You have lately remarked on the improved publichouses and inns up and down the country...
      [signed, 'JOHN MASEFIELD, JOHN GRETTON... | 35 Belgrave Square, S.W., June 7.']

C125.076   Oct 4, 1937, p.11c
      Edward Thomas Memorial [Paraphrases Masefield's speech on Thomas at Mutton Hill, near Petersfield, 2 Oct 1937]
      Speaking at the unveiling, Mr. John Masefield, the Poet Laureate, said that Thomas's speaking voice was...

C125.077   Nov 4, 1937, p.12d
      Aims of the Group Theatre [Paraphrases Masefield's address at meeting of the Group Theatre, 2 Nov 1937]
      Mr. John Masefield, the Poet Laureate, who gave an address said the Group Theatre was...

C125.078   Nov 10, 1937, p.12c
      Weak and Incompetent Writing [Paraphrases Masefield's speech at annual Society of Authors' dinner, Hotel Victoria, 9 Nov 1937]
      Mr. Masefield, who replied to the toast, said that people to-day sang...

C125.079   May 17, 1938, p.11c
      Poet Laureate and National Theatre [Letter (sent to Geoffrey Whitworth)]
      It is now 40 years since I first read the suggestion that there should be a National Theatre in London...
      [headed, 'The Poet Laureate, Mr. John Masefield, has sent the following letter...']

C125.080   Sep 12, 1938, p.9a
      The Masting of Nelson ['The New Figurehead'] [Verse]
      Ninety-nine years ago the long-dead hands
      [headed, 'Poet Laureate's Poem to his Old Ship']

C125.081   Sep 16, 1938, p.13d
      Neville Chamberlain [Verse]
      As Priam to Achilles for his Son,
      [signed, 'JOHN MASEFIELD']

C125.082   Sep 23, 1938, p.9f
      Poet Honoured by his Birthplace [Paraphrases Masefield's speech at commemorative W.H. Davies lunch at Newport, 22 Sep 1938]
      The Poet Laureate, proposing the health of Mr. Davies, said that poets brought their gifts...

C125.083   Oct 4, 1938, p.15d
Three Factors for Peace *[Letter]*
Sir, – Three things gave us our present peace: first, the heroic self-sacrifice...
[signed, 'JOHN MASEFIELD. | Pinbury, Cirencester, Oct. 3.']

C125.084   Nov 12, 1938, p.14c
Poet Laureate in his Native Town [Paraphrases Masefield's speech on opening new library in Ledbury, 11 Nov 1938]
Mr. Masefield, after expressing his great pleasure in returning to his native town...

C125.085   May 11, 1939, p.17f
The Inspiration of Hardy [Paraphrases Masefield's speech on opening of Hardy Memorial Room in Dorchester, 10 May 1939]
Mr. John Masefield, the Poet Laureate, delivered a personal appreciation of Hardy...

C125.086   May 15, 1939, p.19f
"Wanton Blemish cut from Shakespeare" [Paraphrases Masefield's speech on opening of the City Literary Institute, 13 May 1939]
Mr. John Masefield, the Poet Laureate, who opened the new building of the City...

C125.087   Jun 16, 1939, p.20d
Hawthornden Prize [Paraphrases Masefield's speech awarding prize to Christopher Hassall, Æolian Hall, Bond St., 15 Jun 1939]
Mr. John Masefield, the Poet Laureate, who presented the prize to Mr. Hassall...

C125.088   Sep 9, 1939, p.9d
Books for the War *[Letter]*
Sir, – Following advice given or from prudence, most of us have laid in gear of some sort...
[signed, 'JOHN MASEFIELD, | President, National Book Council. | September 7.']

C125.089   Sep 28, 1939, p.11f
To Some Germans *[Verse]*
[Extract quoted from *Some Verses to Some Germans*]
We are as darkness to each other now,
[headed, 'The Poet Laureate on the War']

C125.090   Oct 6, 1939, p.6d
Evacuation. The Importance of Books *[Letter]*
Sir, – During the last month many thousands of schoolchildren have been removed from...
[signed, 'JOHN MASEFIELD, President, | National Book Council, | 3 Henrietta Street... Oct.3']

C125.091   Oct 9, 1939, p.2f
"When Peace Has Come Again" *[Letter (sent to Robert Louis Stevenson Club)]*
In a letter to the hon. secretary, Mr. Masefield states that he much regrets that the present...

C125.092   Mar 19, 1941, p.7f
American Help in Fight for Freedom [American ambassador's quoting of lines addressed to him by Masefield]
Two with like laws and language should be friends.

C125.093   Nov 11, 1941, p.5e
The Merchant Navy *[Letter]*
Sir, – I have read with interest the article "Merchant Navy Reform" in to-day's issue of *The Times*.
[signed, 'JOHN MASEFIELD | Burcote Brook, Abingdon, Nov. 8']

C125.094   Dec 4, 1941, p.5e
Russian ballet *[Letter]*
Sir, – Now that Russia is linked with us in a great war, might not an effort be made...
[signed, 'JOHN MASEFIELD | Burcote Brook, Abingdon, Dec.1']

C125.095   Feb 19, 1942, p.2e
First Halkevi Outside Turkey *[Letter]*
I am delighted to hear that the Turkish Government is founding a halkevi in London.
[headed, 'Mr. Masefield... welcomes to-day's ceremony in the following letter']

C125.096   Apr 18, 1942, p.8g
"Old and True." – 795 [Extract from *The Bird of Dawning*]
"What do you think, Mister?" he asked. "Will the crowd sail this hooker to England?"
[credited, 'JOHN MASEFIELD: "The Bird of Dawning"']

C125.097   Mar 13, 1943, p.7e
Dr. Laurence Binyon *[Prose]*
Some years ago one of two poets, talking of Laurence Binyon, said...
[headed, 'Mr. John Masefield writes']

C125.098   Sep 22, 1943, p.5d
      The Times Crosswords *[Letter]*
      Dear Benefactors, – May my wife and I thank you for much simple pleasure?
      [signed, 'JOHN MASEFIELD | Burcote Brook, Abingdon']

C125.099   Oct 11, 1943, p.5e
      The Arts of India *[Communal Letter]*
      Sir, – We are seeking the hospitality of your columns in order to call attention to an aspect of our...
      [signed, 'L.S. AMERY... JOHN MASEFIELD, WILLIAM ROTHENSTEIN, WAVELL, ZETLAND']

C125.100   Oct 22, 1943, p.2e
      Britain Celebrates Trafalgar Day ['Men of the Royal Navy'] *[Verse]*
      Long since, I knew the sailors of the Fleet,
      [headed, 'Poet Laureate's New Poem Spoken']

C125.101   Oct 27, 1943, p.2e
      Man's Need of Books [Paraphrases Masefield's speech at National Book Council's annual lunch, Connaught
         Rooms, 26 Oct 1943]
      Mr. John MASEFIELD, O.M., Poet Laureate, speaking as the president of the National Book Council...

C125.102   Nov 19, 1943, p.7b
      "Old and True" – 1,289 *[Verse]*
      There is no danger seamen have not run! | Tempests have drowned them since the world began...
      [credited, 'JOHN MASEFIELD']

C125.103   Dec 21, 1943, p.8b
      "Can We Afford It?" [Extract quoted from *In the Mill*]
      I have come to know that money is largely a fiction, and that if there be the will...
      [credited, 'from the Poet Laureate's autobiographical book']

C125.104   Feb 24, 1944, p.2e
      Salute to Red Army ['An ode to the Red Army'] *[Verse]*
      Though flanks were turned and centre gone,
      [headed, 'Poet Laureate's Ode']

C125.105   Mar 22, 1944, p.2e
      National Book League *[Letter – sent to National Book Council]*
      This is indeed a preparation for a new England, and rouses the liveliest hopes.
      [headed, 'Mr. Masefield wrote...']

C125.106   Mar 25, 1944, p.6g
      Musicians' Tribute to Sir Henry Wood [Untitled ode on Sir Henry Wood's 75th birthday] *[Verse]*
      How many thousand times have you upheld
      [signed, 'JOHN MASEFIELD']

C125.107   May 20, 1944, p.2a
      More Books and Beauty [Paraphrases Masefield's lecture *I Want! I Want!* at Caxton Hall, 19 May 1944]
      The increased use of books, a greatly widened knowledge of order of all kinds...
      [headed, 'Mr. Masefield on his Wants']

C125.108   Jun 14, 1944, p.7d
      Unity Essential to Victory [Untitled lines for United Nations Day] *[Verse]*
      Since Charity is killed, and Faith a void,
      [headed: 'The Poet Laureate (Mr. Masefield) has written the following lines...']

C125.109   Jul 22, 1944, p.6e
      Mr. Thomas Sturge Moore *[Prose]*
      The death of Thomas Sturge Moore takes from us a poet and artist of rare gifts...
      [headed, 'The Poet Laureate's Tribute']

C125.110   Jul 25, 1944, p.6f
      M. Charles Geoffroy-Dechaume *[Prose]*
      The news has just come of the death at Valmondois, Seine et Oise, France, of Charles Geoffroy-Dechaume...
      [headed, 'Mr. John Masefield's Appreciation']

C125.111   Sep 11, 1944, p.6e
      Mr. Basil Lubbock *[Prose]*
      May I write some few words of praise of Basil Lubbock?
      [headed, 'Mr. Masefield's Tribute']

C125.112   Nov 15, 1944, p.7c
      The National Book League [Paraphrases Masefield's N.B.L. E.G.M. speech, Royal Empire Society's assembly hall,
         14 Nov 1944]
      ...The Poet Laureate, Mr. John Masefield, who presided said one could not but catch the breath...

C125.113   Nov 15, 1944, p.7c
   The National Book League [Untitled lines on N.B.L.] *[Verse]*
   After destruction, lo, a human need,
   [headed, 'Mr. Masefield On "Human Need"']

C125.114   Mar 1, 1945, p.2e
   Mr. Winant on Books [Paraphrases Masefield's speech at National Book League "The Fifty Books, 1945"
      exhibition, 28 Feb 1945]
   The Poet Laureate, Mr. John Masefield, who is president of the National Book League...

C125.115   May 8, 1945, p.7d
   A Moment Comes *[Verse]*
   Now that the murderers are put away
   [signed, 'JOHN MASEFIELD']

C125.116   Oct 29, 1945, p.6d
   Keats Home Reopened [Paraphrases Masefield's speech at re-opening, Hampstead, 27 Oct 1945]
   Mr. John Masefield, in declaring the house and museum open, said that Keats was...

C125.117   Nov 7, 1945, p.6f
   Book League's New Headquarters [Paraphrases Masefield's announcement at A.G.M. of N.B.L., 6 Nov 1945]
   Mr. John Masefield, the Poet Laureate, announced at the annual general meeting....

C125.118   May 1, 1946, p.6d
   Children's Books on Exhibition [Paraphrases Masefield's speech at 7 Albemarle Street, 30 Apr 1946]
   Mr. John Masefield, the Poet Laureate, opened the Children's Books of Yesterday Exhibition...

C125.119   Jul 27, 1946, p.8d
   In Honour of G.B.S. [Paraphrases Masefield's remarks on G.B.S. at National Book League exhibition, 26 Jul 1946]
   Mr. John Masefield, the Poet Laureate, presided yesterday at the opening of the...

C125.120   Jul 27, 1946, p.8d
   In Honour of G.B.S. [Excerpt from 'On The Ninetieth Birthday of Bernard Shaw'] *[Verse]*
   Honour him living, all earth's brightest brains.
   [headed, 'Mr. Masefield's Tribute at Exhibition']

C125.121   Aug 27, 1946, p.5d
   A Browning Chapel *[Communal Letter]*
   Sir,-The centenary of the marriage of Robert Browning and Elizabeth Barrett occurs...
   [signed, 'LYTTON, ...JOHN MASEFIELD, ...WAVELL, ...HUGH J. MATTHEWS...']

C125.122   Oct 17, 1946, p.3c
   London Savings Drive [Untitled prologue for National Savings rally quoted] *[Verse]*
   When you saved England (you will all agree),
   [headed, 'The following prologue, written specially for the rally by the Poet Laureate...']

C125.123   Nov 23, 1946, p.2c
   London's Need of Concert Hall [Untitled verses in honour of St. Cecilia's festival day quoted] *[Verse]*
   Speak to us, Music, for the discord jars;
   [headed, 'Verses in honour of the occasion were written by the Poet Laureate...']

C125.124   Nov 27, 1946, p.7e
   National Book League [Paraphrases Masefield's speech at meeting of N.B.L. at Royal Empire Society's buildings]
   Mr. John Masefield, O.M., president, was present at the second annual meeting of members of...

C125.125   Jan 31, 1947, p.5d
   To His Most Excellent Majesty The King Upon the Sailing of The Royal Family for South Africa *[Verse]*
   Most gracious Sovereign, leaving England's shore
   [signed, 'JOHN MASEFIELD']

C125.126   May 12, 1947, p.4a
   To His Most Excellent Majesty The King Upon His Return from South Africa *[Verse]*
   Most gracious Sovereign, none can tell the cheer
   [signed, 'JOHN MASEFIELD']

C125.127   May 30, 1947, p.8b
   BBC's Treatment of Authors [Paraphrases Masefield's speech at meeting of Society of Authors, 29 May 1947]
   Mr. John Masefield said that the Society of Authors had frequently been at variance with the BBC...

C125.128   Jul 12, 1947, p.6f
   Book Designs from 11 Countries [Paraphrases Masefield's speech at second International Exhibition of Book
      Design, 11 Jul 1947]
   Mr. John Masefield, the Poet Laureate, who presided, said that for many years it might...

C125.129   Nov 20, 1947, p.5d
   Lines on The Occasion of The Wedding of Her Royal Highness the Princess Elizabeth *[Verse]*
   How many times, when London bells have rung
   [signed, 'JOHN MASEFIELD']

C125.130   Dec 23, 1947, p.5e

A Return to Learning *[Letter]*

Sir, – In your issue of December 20 Mr. Kenneth Lindsay writes very truly that...

[signed, 'JOHN MASEFIELD. | Burcote Brook, Abingdon, Dec 21']

C125.131   Jan 16, 1948, p.7b

Shakespearian History Exhibition [Paraphrases Masefield's words at N.B.L. exhibition, 15 Jan 1948]

Mr. John Masefield, president of the National Book League, who presided, said that...

C125.132   Jan 24, 1948, p.5e

A Return to Learning *[Letter]*

Sir, – Some weeks ago you kindly printed a letter from me about some of the grievous afflictions...

[signed, 'JOHN MASEFIELD. | Burcote Brook, Abingdon, Jan 21']

C125.133   Feb 6, 1948, p.7e

Mr. T.W. Lamont *[Prose]*

May I be permitted to write these few words about the late Thomas W. Lamont?

[titled 'Poet Laureate's Tribute']

C125.134   Apr 12, 1948, p.5d

Franklin Delano Roosevelt *[Verse]*

Honour this man, so stricken in his prime,

[signed, 'JOHN MASEFIELD.']

C125.135   Apr 20, 1948, p.5d

The Hills of Dorset *[Communal Letter]*

Sir, – We learn with dismay that the Dorset police have decided to erect wireless masts...

[signed, 'JOHN MASEFIELD, J. BETJEMAN, DAVID CECIL, CHRISTOPHER HAWKES...']

C125.136   Apr 26, 1948, p.5d

Lines on The Occasion of The Silver Wedding of Our King and Queen *[Verse]*

We are within the Heavens, sons of light,

[signed, 'JOHN MASEFIELD.']

C125.137   May 6, 1948, p.5f

The Slaughter of Rooks *[Letter]*

Sir, – May I be allowed to add my protest to the many now raised against the recent decision to...

[signed, 'JOHN MASEFIELD. | Burcote Brook, Abingdon, May 3.']

C125.138   Oct 1, 1948, p.2f

Debt to French Literature [Paraphrases Masefield's "A Thousand Years of French Books" exhibition speech, N.B.L., 30 Sep 1948]

Mr. John Masefield, the Poet Laureate, who is president of the National Book League, spoke of the debt of...

C125.139   Oct 28, 1948, p.5d

Young Men of Talent *[Letter]*

Sir, – May I lay before your readers these suggestions? Before the war young men of talent...

[signed, 'JOHN MASEFIELD. | Society of Authors, 84, Drayton Gardens, | S.W. 10, Oct, 25.']

C125.140   Nov 16, 1948, p.5d

A Hope for the Newly Born *[Verse]*

May destiny, alloting what befalls,

[signed, 'JOHN MASEFIELD.']

C125.141   Jan 4, 1949, p.5f

Browning Memorial *[Communal Letter]*

Sir, – In August, 1946, you published a letter signed by us making an appeal...

[signed, 'WAVELL, JOHN MASEFIELD, HUGH J. MATTHEWS...']

C125.142   Mar 30, 1949, p.4g

Mr. Masefield's Poem ['The Poet Laureate to his Cathedral Church, Liverpool Cathedral'] *[Verse]*

We fling the doorway open to the crowd,

[headed, 'by the Poet Laureate...']

C125.143   Jul 29, 1950, p.5d

A Word of Hope *[Verse]*

Through threat of ruin fills the world with fear,

[signed, 'JOHN MASEFIELD. *July* 29, 1950.']

C125.144   Feb 19, 1951, p.8e

The Earl of Lytton *[Letter]*

All who knew "Neville Lytton" (the late Earl of Lytton) will mourn...

[headed, 'Mr. John Masefield writes...']

C125.145 Jul 14, 1951, p.4d
  A National Theatre [untitled verse on laying of foundation stone of National Theatre] *[Verse]*
  Here we lay stone, that, at a future time,
  [headed, 'by the Poet Laureate, Mr. John Masefield...']

C125.146 Aug 21, 1951, p.6e
  The Ledbury Scene [announces volume and quotes brief extract]
  What merit may be in the pieces quoted from... is due to the power of the Ledbury scene...

C125.147 Dec 23, 1951, p.4
  In the Beginning *[Verse]*
  That starry night when Christ was born,
  [headed, 'by JOHN MASEFIELD']

C125.148 Jan 31, 1952, p.5d
  On the Setting Forth of their Royal Highnesses Princess Elizabeth and the Duke of Edinburgh *[Verse]*
  What can we wish you that you have not won
  [signed, 'JOHN MASEFIELD.']

C125.149 Feb 7, 1952, p.7d
  On Hearing of The Sudden Death of His Majesty The King *[Verse]*
  O Wisdom, Who, with power infinite,
  [signed, 'JOHN MASEFIELD.']

C125.150 Feb 15, 1952, p.7d
  At the Passing of a Beloved Monarch Our Sovereign Lord King George The Sixth... *[Verse]*
  The everlasting Wisdom has ordained
  [signed, 'JOHN MASEFIELD.']

C125.151 Jul 12, 1952, p.6c
  Epilogue for Searchlight Tattoo *[Verse]*
  In the great past, as subjects to a Queen,
  [signed, 'JOHN MASEFIELD.']

C125.152 Dec 30, 1952, p.8e
  Mrs. T.W. Lamont *[Letter]*
  A cable brings the sad news that Florence Corliss Lamont, the widow of Thomas W. Lamont...
  [headed, 'John and Constance Masefield write...']

C125.153 Mar 31, 1953, p.7d
  On the Passing of a Great Queen *[Verse]*
  She was our Sovereign through disastrous days,
  [signed, 'JOHN MASEFIELD.']

C125.154 Jun 2, 1953, p.7d
  A Prayer for a Beginning Reign *[Verse]*
  He who is Order, Beauty, Power and Glory,
  [signed, 'JOHN MASEFIELD.']

C125.155 Jul 14, 1953, p.8d
  Tattoo at White City [poems from White City searchlight tattoo] *[Verse]*
  Here ends the pageant of how England stood
  [introduced as 'words specially written by John Masefield...']

C125.156 Nov 23, 1953, p.9d
  A Prayer on Our Queen's Going to Her Peoples *[Verse]*
  Love is no burden, Brotherhood no chain;
  [signed, 'JOHN MASEFIELD.']

C125.157 Apr 14, 1954, p.9e
  Publishers and Authors *[Communal Letter]*
  Sir, – A dangerous step has been taken by the Council of the Publishers' Association.
  [signed, 'JOHN MASEFIELD, President of the Society of Authors, JOHN BETJEMAN...']

C125.158 May 15, 1954, p.7d
  On Our Sovereign Lady's Return to these Islands *[Verse]*
  Once, when the Sign of England was the Rose,
  [signed, 'JOHN MASEFIELD.']

C125.159 May 22, 1954, p.7d
  Rights in Books *[Letter]*
  Sir, – I hope that you will permit me to comment briefly on your leading article...
  [signed, 'JOHN MASEFIELD, President, Society of Authors... May 20.']

C125.160 Jun 11, 1954, p.2e
  Memorial to Keats and Shelley [Paraphrase of extracts from Masefield's words on the occasion]
  A memorial to Keats and Shelley was unveiled by Mr. John Masefield...

C125.161 Nov 30, 1954, p.9d
On the Birthday of a Great Man [*Verse*]
This man, in darkness, saw; in doubtings, led;
[signed, 'JOHN MASEFIELD']

C125.162 Feb 3, 1955, p.9d
Moira O'Neill [*Letter*]
Sir, – May I be allowed to thank the writer of your recent appreciation of the poetry of...
[signed, 'JOHN MASEFIELD... Feb 1.']

C125.163 Oct 27, 1955, p.11e
Gilbert Murray [*Communal Letter*]
Sir, – In January, 1956, Dr. Gilbert Murray is to celebrate his 90th anniversary...
[signed, 'NORMAN ANGELL... JOHN MASEFIELD... October 26.']

C125.164 Nov 26, 1955, p.7e
Postage for Books [*Communal Letter*]
Sir, – may we appeal to you, Sir, to try to make public the tragic results that may arise...
[signed, 'JOHN MASEFIELD, Past President, National Book League; NORMAN BIRKETT...']

C125.165 Jan 27, 1956, p.9d
Upon Our Sovereign Lady's Venture in a Great Cause [*Verse*]
Even as April's footsteps that unseen
[signed, 'JOHN MASEFIELD']

C125.166 Feb 17, 1956, p.10d
Lines for the Home-Coming of Our Most Gracious Sovereign Lady [*Verse*]
Chain upon chain, and prison within prison,
[signed, 'JOHN MASEFIELD']

C125.167 Jun 23, 1956, p.7d
On the Death of Walter De La Mare June 22, 1956 [*Verse*]
O poets, silent under laurels won,
[signed, 'JOHN MASEFIELD.']

C125.168 Aug 29, 1956, p.9c
Eighty Five to Win [*Verse*]
Though wayward Time be changeful as Man's will,
[headed, 'By JOHN MASEFIELD']

C125.169 Apr 26, 1957, p.11e
Special Duty of the B.B.C. [*Communal Letter*]
Sir, – We wish to express our deep concern at the new trend of policy in sound broadcasting...
[signed, 'BEVERIDGE, ARTHUR BLISS... JOHN MASEFIELD...']

C125.170 May 21, 1957, p.11d
On the Death of Professor Gilbert Murray, Scholar and Humanist [*Verse*]
Surely, in some great quietude afar,
[signed, 'JOHN MASEFIELD']

C125.171 Jun 13, 1957, p.11d
Lines for the Centenary of Ronald Ross, Scientist and Poet [*Verse*]
A century since, this hater of mis-rule,
[signed, 'JOHN MASEFIELD']

C125.172 Aug 20, 1957, p.9d
In Memory of a Great Discovery [*Verse*]
Once, on this August Day, an exiled man
[signed, 'JOHN MASEFIELD']

C125.173 Aug 26, 1957, p.9e
The London Library [*Letter*]
Sir, – In your leading article this morning, dealing with the question of the rating...
[signed, 'JOHN MASEFIELD. Burcote Brook, Abingdon, August 23.']

C125.174 Oct 4, 1957, p.11d
Third Programme [*Communal Letter*]
Sir, – On April 26 of this year you accorded us the hospitality of our columns...
[signed, 'BEVERIDGE, ADRIAN C. BOULT... JOHN MASEFIELD...']

C125.175 Oct 12, 1957, p.7d
On Our Sovereign Lady's Western Journey [*Verse*]
Not altogether strange, those distant states,
[signed, 'JOHN MASEFIELD']

C125.176   Oct 16, 1957, p.12c
        The Virginian Adventure *[Verse]*
        We share a little in your festal days,
        [headed, 'By JOHN MASEFIELD']

C125.177   Oct 29, 1957, p.11f
        Hungarian Writers on Trial *[Communal Letter]*
        Sir, – We have learned with the deepest anxiety that the trial of four of...
        [signed, 'PHYLLIS BENTLEY; RICHARD CHURCH... JOHN MASEFIELD...']

C125.178   Nov 20, 1957, p.6d
        Pension Scheme for Authors Commended [Masefield's commendation of retirement trust established by The
            Society of Authors]
        "An assurance for the future when strength and powers fail and taxation has devoured...

C125.179   Jun 3, 1958, p.7d
        Mr. Masefield's Ode on his 80th Birthday *[Prose]*
        A tape-recorded message by Mr. John Masefield, the Poet Laureate, was played...

C125.180   Jun 3, 1958, p.7d
        On Coming towards Eighty *[Verse]*
        How wondrously life changes as it goes;
        [introduced as 'by Mr. Masefield']

C125.181   Jan 24, 1959, p.8d
        Lines for the 25th January, 1959, being the 200th Anniversary of the Birth of Robert Burns *[Verse]*
        Two hundred years ago today,
        [headed, 'by JOHN MASEFIELD']

C125.182   Mar 26, 1959, p.13d
        In Memory of Alfred Edward Housman *[Verse]*
        Too many lads of pith and relish
        [signed, 'JOHN MASEFIELD']

C125.183   Jun 26, 1959, p.13d
        June the 26th, 1959 *[Verse]*
        Today, our consecrated Sovereign's hands
        [signed, 'JOHN MASEFIELD']

C125.184   Jul 20, 1959, p.7d
        For Alfred Munnings *[Verse]*
        The shadows lengthen in the summer eve;
        [signed, 'JOHN MASEFIELD']

C125.185   Aug 3, 1959, p.7d
        On Canada Revealed *[Verse]*
        In the last weeks, a consecrated soul
        [signed, 'JOHN MASEFIELD']

C125.186   Nov 6, 1959, p.13d
        London Library *[Letter]*
        Sir, – I read with grief that the London Library is threatened with a monetary burden...
        [signed, 'JOHN MASEFIELD. | Burcote Brook, Abingdon, Nov. 4.']

C125.187   Feb 20, 1960, p.7d
        On the Birth of a Son to Our Sovereign Lady The Queen *[Verse]*
        Oh child descended from a line of kings,
        [signed, 'JOHN MASEFIELD']

C125.188   May 6, 1960, p.15d
        On the Prayers for our Princess's Happiness *[Verse]*
        A prayer is intense thought with lasting life.
        [signed, 'JOHN MASEFIELD']

C125.189   Mar 6, 1961, p.13c
        Lines on Our Sovereign Lady's Return *[Verse]*
        For fifty days to whirl from day to day
        [signed, 'JOHN MASEFIELD']

C125.190   Mar 14, 1961, p.15f
        The New Testament A Modern Version *[Book Review]*
        Many years ago, when a child asked "What made Christianity prevail?" the elder would...
        [headed, 'By John Masefield']

C125.191   May 11, 1961, p.9c
        Authors Awarded New Honour [Paraphrases and quotes Masefield on receiving R.S.L. Companionship of Literature]
        The first five writers to have conferred upon them Companionships of Literature...

C125.192   Dec 7, 1961, p.15c

On the Return of Our Gracious Sovereign from Africa *[Verse]*
There, in the blinding sun under the Line,
[signed, 'JOHN MASEFIELD']

C125.193   Mar 2, 1962, p.13c

Poetry Prize for Mr. Masefield [Paraphrases Masefield's acceptance speech, including reminiscences on booksellers]
Mr. John Masefield, the Poet Laureate, has been awarded the 1961 William Foyle poetry prize...

C125.194   May 30, 1962, p.7f

Drinkwater Works on Show [Paraphrases Masefield's speech at *The Times* bookshop Drinkwater exhibition]
Dr. John Masefield, the Poet Laureate, when he opened an exhibition at The Times Bookshop...

C125.195   Jan 31, 1963, p.13d

Lines for the Great Peoples to whom Our Sovereign Lady, The Queen, Today Proceeds *[Verse]*
You deathless, buried upon Sari Bair,
[signed, 'JOHN MASEFIELD']

C125.196   Aug 17, 1963, p.8c

Mr. Masefield Visits Yeats's Home [Paraphrases and quotes Masefield on visit to Upper Woburn Place to view hotel extension]
Making one of his rare visits to London from his country home near Oxford...

C125.197   Nov 25, 1963, p.11c

John Fitzgerald Kennedy *[Verse]*
All generous hearts lament the leader killed,
[signed, 'JOHN MASEFIELD']

C125.198   Apr 23, 1964, p.13d

Lines for The Fourth Centenary of William Shakespeare *[Verse]*
Tired of many wrongs, he cried for rest,
[signed, 'JOHN MASEFIELD']

C125.199   Oct 14, 1964, p.13d

On Our Sovereign Lady's Return *[Verse]*
Remembering last November, people feared
[signed, 'JOHN MASEFIELD']

C125.200   Dec 8, 1964, p.15c

Dr. Masefield's Hope [Paraphrases and quotes Masefield on receiving of N.B.L. award]
Dr. John Masefield, the Poet Laureate, who at 86 is still writing, reflected on the past and...

C125.201   Jan 8, 1965, p.11c

East Coker *[Verse]*
Here, whence his forbears sprang, a man is laid
[signed, 'JOHN MASEFIELD']

C125.202   Jan 25, 1965, p.13d

Sir Winston Churchill *[Verse]*
The Divine Fortune, watching Life's affairs,
[signed, 'JOHN MASEFIELD']

C125.203   May 31, 1965, p.11d

On the Home-Coming of Our Sovereign Lady, The Queen *[Verse]*
The long, long week of ceaseless effort ends.
[signed, 'JOHN MASEFIELD']

C125.204   Mar 8, 1966, p.13d

On Our Sovereign Lady's Return from the Caribbean *[Verse]*
Among those islands where Nations fought
[signed, 'JOHN MASEFIELD']

C125.205   May 22, 1967, p.12h

Mr John Masefield | Mr. George Buchanan writes
[Tribute to Masefield specifically on Masefield's role in verse speaking. Quotes Masefield]
Very great credit must go to John Masefield for his past in revolutionizing the speaking of poetry.

C125.206   Nov 21, 1967, p.3a

Poet's Gifts for Shop Assistants [Masefield's will quoted in parts]
Mr. John Edward Masefield, of Burcote, near Abingdon, Berkshire, Poet Laureate...

C125.207   Jan 9, 1970, p.1a

Masefield's Sea Fever [Quotes Masefield letter [to Florence Lamont] on sea sickness]
John Masefield, the former Poet Laureate who often wrote of his passion for the sea, in fact suffered...

C125.208   Jan 13, 1970, p.8e

Sea Power [Quotes Masefield's original opening of 'Sea Fever']
There is more, it appears, than a simple anomaly in the revelations from Columbia...

Votes for Women (London, U.K.)

C130.001   Jan 28, 1910, p.280
        First Fruits *[Verse]*
        In the dark womb where I began
        [signed, 'JOHN MASEFIELD']

C130.002   Feb 18, 1910, p.319
        My Faith in Woman Suffrage *[Prose]*
        You have done me the honour to ask me to confess my faith...
        [headed 'by John Masefield']

C130.003   Apr 29, 1910, p.495
        The White Slave Traffic *[Letter]*
        The Times published on April 20 a leading article on the White Slave...
        [verbatim reprint of Masefield's letter of 24 April 1910 to *The Times* for 29 April 1910]
        [signed, 'JOHN MASEFIELD']

The Westminster Gazette (London, U.K.)

C135.001   Oct 20, 1910, p.2
        Sonnet on the Death of his Wife. (*From the Portuguese of Antonio Ferreira*, 1528–1569.) *[Verse]*
        That blessed sunlight that once showed to me
        [signed, 'JOHN MASEFIELD.']

C135.002   Dec 7, 1910, p.[2]
        Sonnet. *From the Spanish of Don Francisco de Quevedo (1580–1645). [Verse]*
        I saw the ramparts of my native land,
        [signed, 'JOHN MASEFIELD.']

C135.003   Mar 25, 1911, p.15
        They Closed Her Eyes. From the Spanish of Don Gustavo A. Bécquer. *[Verse]*
        They closed her eyes
        [headed, 'TRANSLATED BY JOHN MASEFIELD.']

C135.004   Jun 7, 1912, p.2
        Song *[Verse]*
        One sunny time in May
        [signed, 'JOHN MASEFIELD.']

The Saturday Westminster Gazette (London, U.K.)

C140.001   Oct 22, 1910
        Sonnet on the Death of his Wife. (*From the Portuguese of Antonio Ferreira*, 1528–1569.) *[Verse]*
        That blessed sunlight that once showed to me
        (signed, 'JOHN MASEFIELD.')

C140.002   Dec 10, 1910
        Sonnet. *From the Spanish of Don Francisco de Quevedo (1580–1645). [Verse]*
        I saw the ramparts of my native land,
        (signed, 'JOHN MASEFIELD.')

C140.003   Mar 25, 1911, p.4
        They Closed Her Eyes. From the Spanish of Don Gustavo A. Bécquer. *[Verse]*
        They closed her eyes
        (headed, 'TRANSLATED BY JOHN MASEFIELD.')

The Westminster Gazette was published 1893–1928 (according to the holdings of The British Library). In 1928 it was incorporated with *The Daily News*. At the time of Masefield's contributions the paper was a daily, published Monday to Saturday. Two different titles were published on Saturday: *The Westminster Gazette* and *The Saturday Westminster Gazette*. The latter collected material from the previous week. It has not been possible to verify whether C135.001 and C135.002 were reprinted in *The Saturday Westminster Gazette*. The first two entries, here, are therefore conjectural.

The Contemporary Review (London, U.K.)

C145.001   Apr 1911, Vol.99 No.544, pp.[470]-78
        John M. Synge *[Prose]*
        I first met John M. Synge at the room of a mutual friend...
        [signed, 'JOHN MASEFIELD']

C145.002   May 1971, Vol.218 No.1264, pp.245–49
             The Western Hudson Shore *[Verse]*
             In a long life's first independent day,
             [headed, 'by John Masefield']

The English Review (London, U.K.)

C150.001   Jun 1911, p.361
             Truth *[Verse]*
             Man with his burning soul
             [headed, 'By John Masefield']

C150.002   Oct 1911, pp.361–404
             The Everlasting Mercy *[Verse]*
             From '41 to '51
             [headed, 'By John Masefield']

C150.003   Feb 1912, pp.377–424
             The Widow in the Bye Street *[Verse]*
             Down Bye Street, in a little Shropshire town,
             [headed, 'By John Masefield']

C150.004   May 1912, pp.169–76
             Biography *[Verse]*
             When I am buried, all my thoughts and acts
             [headed, 'By John Masefield']

C150.005   Jul 1912, pp.505–507
             Ships *[Verse]*
             I cannot tell their wonder nor make known
             [headed, 'By John Masefield']

C150.006   Oct 1912, pp.337–89
             Dauber *[Verse]*
             Four bells were struck, the watch was called on deck,
             [headed, 'By John Masefield']

C150.007   Feb 1913, pp.337–90
             The Daffodil Fields *[Verse]*
             Between the barren pasture and the wood
             [headed, 'By John Masefield']

C150.008   Dec 1913, pp.1–12
             The River *[Verse]*
             All other waters have their time of peace,
             [headed, 'By John Masefield']

C150.009   Sep 1914, pp.145–47
             August, 1914 *[Verse]*
             How still this quiet cornfield is to-night;
             [headed, 'By John Masefield']

The Quest (London, U.K.)

C155.001   Jan 1912, pp.201–225
             Contemplatives *[Prose]*
             Whatever we may believe or disbelieve, and however happy or wretched we may be…
             [signed, 'JOHN MASEFIELD.']

The Forum (New York, U.S.A.)

C160.001   May 1912, pp.513–21
             Biography *[Verse]*
             When I am buried, all my thoughts and acts
             [headed, 'JOHN MASEFIELD']

The New York Times (New York, U.S.A.)

C165.001   Aug 18, 1912, section 6 [*The New York Times Review of Books*], p.453
Ships… Written for The New York Times Book Review [*Verse*]
I cannot tell their wonder nor make known
[headed, 'By JOHN MASEFIELD']

C165.002   Jul 5, 1914, section 5, p.2
What is the Best Short Poem in English? [*Prose*]
To the Editor of The New York Times: The short poems which give me the most pleasure are…
[signed, 'JOHN MASEFIELD.']

C165.003   Sep 25, 1914, p.10
Masefield's War Poem [Editorial comment quoting from 'August, 1914']
For felicity of phrase and seemingly effortless but powerful expression…

C165.004   Jun 30, 1915, p.10
John Masefield's Sale [*Letter*]
To the Editor of The New York Times: In your issue of May 16 you give some particulars…
[signed, 'JOHN MASEFIELD. | Cholsey, Berkshire, Eng., June 16, 1915.']

C165.005   Nov 28, 1915, p.16
A Red Cross Lighter [*Letter*]
To the Editor of The New York Times: Some months ago you kindly allowed me to print…
[signed, 'J. MASEFIELD | Hampstead, England, Nov. 13, 1915.']

C165.006   Jan 13, 1916, p.12
John E. Masefield Here. "Sailor Poet" to Lecture [Quotes Masefield's comments on the war during trip to the
    United States]
John E. Masefield, who is known in England as "the Sailor Poet," arrived yesterday…

C165.007   Jan 17, 1916, p.5
Honor John E. Masefield. Literary Men and Women attend Reception… [Paraphrases comments on changes in
    New York City]
About 400 men and women, many of them well known in the literary world…

C165.008   Jan 21, 1916, p.9
Authors Honor Masefield. English Poet is a Luncheon Guest… [Quotes Masefield on Tennyson anecdote
    avoiding after-luncheon addresses]
Poets, playwrights, and authors, members of the Authors' League, held a luncheon yesterday…

C165.009   Feb 29, 1916, p.9
John Masefield Lectures. Poet Traces Drama from its Beginning to Elizabethan Period [Paraphrases lecture]
John Masefield, the English poet, gave a lecture yesterday afternoon in Aeolian Hall…

C165.010   Mar 5, 1916, section 2, p.7
The Beginnings of English Drama [*Prose*]
When we go to a theatre nowadays we go for an evening's amusement or to see some problem…
[headed, 'By JOHN MASEFIELD']

C165.011   Mar 19, 1916, p.17
Poet is on Way to Front. John Masefield doesn't expect a Crushing German Defeat [Paraphrases comments on
    the end of the war]
John Masefield, the poet, who has been on a two months' lecture tour in this country…

C165.012   Mar 19, 1916, section 3, p.6
The Coming of Christopher Marlowe [*Prose*]
Those of you who have lived in England will remember that as a general rule the whole house…
[headed, 'By JOHN MASEFIELD']

C165.013   Jan 29, 1917, p.2
Masefield Defends our Neutrality [Quotes a letter from Masefield on American neautrality]
John Masefield in a letter to The Daily Chronicle supporting the plea for an Anglo-American Entente…

C165.014   Apr 22, 1917, section 7 [*The New York Times Review of Books*], p.160
[Paraphrases and quotes Masefield's article on American Field Ambulance Service from *Harper's Magazine*]
It is scarcely necessary to be reminded of the wealth of poetic realism…

C165.015   Aug 10, 1917, p.2
Plunkett a Zealot in Ireland's Cause [Paraphrases Masefield's comments on war reducing poverty]
…One feature of the war that John Masefield called to my attention to afresh today…
[headed, 'By CHARLES H. GRASTY']

C165.016   Jan 1, 1918, p.3
[America's Part to Bring Victory and a Real Peace] [*Prose*]
I think that in the coming year the United States will play a decisive part…
[headed, 'From JOHN MASEFIELD']

C165.017   Jan 27, 1918, section 7 [*The New York Times Magazine Section*], p.11
...Official Historian of Haig's Army, John Masefield, Talks... [Quotes Masefield, in interview with M.J. Moses]
John Masefield is in the United States for his second visit since the war began.

C165.018   Jun 2, 1918, section 3, p.11
Masefield Lauds Y.M.C.A. [Paraphrases and quotes Masefield on war work of the Y.M.C.A.]
John Masefield, the poet, who arrived recently from the western front...

C165.019   Jun 20, 1918, p.7
Noted Visitors Honored by Yale... [Paraphrases Masefield's comments on appearance of American soldiers at the front]
...Yale's Commencement came to a close this afternoon with the Alumni luncheon...

C165.020   Jun 22, 1918, p.8
What Britain has Done *[Letter]*
To the Editor of The New York Times: In your issue of today, in the leading article...
[signed, 'JOHN MASEFIELD. | New York, June 21, 1918']

C165.021   Dec 29, 1918, section 7 [*The New York Times Review of Books*], p.584
John Masefield [Editorial quoting from Masefield's 'Introduction' to *Collected Poems and Plays*]
...I did not begin to read poetry with passion and system until 1896...

C165.022   Jun 1, 1919, p.17
Go on a Pilgrimage to Whitman's Houses [Quotes Masefield's letter of tribute to Whitman read at a centenary gathering]
The hundreth anniversary of the birthday of Walt Whitman was celebrated yesterday

C165.023   May 23, 1921, p.12
Masefield and Harvey. Two Ways of Looking at the Soldiers in the Great War [Paraphrases and quotes Masefield's 1918 lecture]
To the Editor of The New York Times: John Masefield, in his lecture on "The War and the Future,"...
[signed, 'WELDON T. MYERS. | Converse College, Spartenburg, S.C., May 20, 1921.']

C165.024   Oct 29, 1925, p.24
Saving the Florio's Crew [Quotes lines from Masefield's poem, in connection with the freighter *Ignazio Florio*]
In his salt-water ballad, "The Yarn of the Loch Achray," John Masefield tells...

C165.025   Oct 14, 1926, p.25
English Poet Seeks Ex-Saloon Man Here [Paraphrases and quotes Masefield's comments on Luke O'Connor, and writers]
John Masefield, the English poet, arrived yesterday on the White Star liner Homeric...

C165.026   Nov 4, 1926, p.11
Masefield Tells of Old Sailing Days [Paraphrases and quotes Masefield's speech about seamen to raise funds for Conrad memorial]
Life before the mast in the last days of the sailing ship was described yesterday...

C165.027   Nov 7, 1926, section 2, p.2
Envoys and Poet see Coolidge [Paraphrases briefly Masefield's talk with the President]
G. Sehurman, Ambassador to Germany, and William M. Collier...

C165.028   Nov 13, 1926, p.11
Masefield Sails Home [Paraphrases and quotes Masefield's comments on future work, Shaw's Nobel prize and the American stage]
John Masefield, the English poet, sailed at 12 o'clock last night...

C165.029   Mar 27, 1927, section 7, p.2
News of the English Theatre [Paraphrases Masefield's comment on scarcity of *Hamlet* Q1 and representation as an acting version]
...Oxford, March 12. A curious and rather amusing dramatic spectacle was afforded Oxford...

C165.030   Sep 4, 1927, section 7, p.2
A Poet's Theatre [Quotes Masefield's comments on Boars Hill theatre]
John Masefield lives five miles outside Oxford. He seldom comes to London...
[headed, 'By GEORGE MIDDLETON']

C165.031   May 29, 1928, p.6
Cathedral Revives the Mystery Play [Quotes Masefield's response to criticism of one scene]
...The mystery play–that medieval theatrical convention whereby the Church...

C165.032   Feb 11, 1930, p.7
Liverpool Celebrates 'Kinship with Sea' [Quotes Masefield's address on boyhood in Liverpool at Liverpool College, 10 Feb 1930]
LIVERPOOL, Feb. 10–Celebration of Liverpool's "kinship with the sea" was marked today by...

C165.033   May 4, 1930, section 3, p.5
From Saloon to Poesy [Quotes first stanza of 'Sea-Fever']
If John Masefield should happen to be named Poet Laureate of England...

C165.034 May 10, 1930, p.9
   Masefield Named as Poet Laureate [Quotes Masefield's response to appointment]
   LONDON, May 9.–John Masefield is England's new Poet Laureate. This poet of the sea…

C165.035 May 10, 1930, p.18
   Poet Laureate [Quotes from 'A Consecration']
   The Lancashire lad, the sailor, the New York bar-boy, has become the official successor…

C165.036 May 11, 1930, p.1
   Masefield is a Teetotaller; Says Poets Like Look of Wine [Quotes Masefield on wine from interview at Boars Hill,
    10 May 1930]
   LONDON, May 10.–John Masefield, England's new poet laureate, in an interview today…

C165.037 May 18, 1930, section 5, pp.3 and 16
   Masefield tells how he turned Poet [Quotes Masefield in interview]
   BOAR'S HILL, OXFORD. A slender, bareheaded figure skipped down a path…

C165.038 Jul 15, 1930, p.1
   Masefield Pens First Couplet as Poet Laureate of England [Quotes alliterative couplet from letter to *The Times*,
    15 July 1930]
   Ah! Authors answer. All aid. Arrest…

C165.039 Sep 15, 1930, p.23
   Masefield on Radio is Heard in America [Quotes Masefield's broadcast of Sep 14, 1930]
   In a talk on "the possibilities of poetry in modern life", broadcast yesterday from London…

C165.040 Oct 24, 1930, p.17
   Masefield in Tribute to Herefordshire [Quotes from Masefield's speech on receiving freedom of Hereford, 23
    October 1930]
   LONDON, Oct. 23.–John Masefield, poet laureate, spoke poetically of his native county…

C165.041 Oct 25, 1930, p.16
   The Tone is Changing [Paraphrases Masefield's speech on receiving freedom of Hereford]
   It was the poet in John Masefield, of course, who can look back over his past…

C165.042 Nov 16, 1930, section 5 [*The New York Times Magazine*], pp.6 and 23
   The Poet Laureate Talks of Poetry [Paraphrases and quotes Masefield on broadcasting and poetry, in interview
    with Claire Price]
   John Masefield, the poet laureate, believes that broadcasting may give rise…
   [headed, 'By Claire Price']

C165.043 Nov 23, 1930, section 3, p.1
   Poetry and the Radio [Paraphrases and quotes Masefield's views on broadcasting and poetry]
   England's Poet Laureate has advanced a new idea. In the interview by Claire Price in the Magazine…

C165.044 Mar 30, 1931, p.6 [Paraphrases Masefield's comments on the President of Turkey]
   Masefield in Istanbul
   ISTANBUL, March 29.–John Masefield, British Poet Laureate, arrived here…

C165.045 Oct 16, 1931, p.3
   Masefield says Sun arouses Best Poetry [Quotes Masefield's lecture on Poetry at Queen's Hall, London, Oct 15,
    1931]
   LONDON, Oct. 15.–John Masefield, British poet laureate, kept a large audience in rapt…

C165.046 Feb 22, 1932, p.15
   Descendants of Poet Hear Him Criticized. [Quotes from Masefield's speech on the hundredth anniversary of
    Crabbe's death]
   A great-granddaughter and other descendants of George Crabb, English poet…

C165.047 Apr 24, 1932, p.3
   Masefield Ode Acknowledges Aid of Americans in Theatre [Quotes from ode for opening of Shakespeare
    Memorial Theatre]
   Now a new house has risen; it is given

C165.048 Jan 1, 1933, section 4, p.4
   A Return to Poetry… *[Prose]*
   Poets are reporters of human souls. The poet's brain has been so trained…
   [headed, 'By JOHN MASEFIELD, British Poet Laureate, in an Interview.']

C165.049 Jan 4, 1933, p.20
   Masefield is Here to Read His Poems [Quotes from interviews with Masefield]
   John Masefield, poet laureate of England, arrived yesterday on the Cunarder Mauretania from London…

C165.050 Jan 5, 1933, p.18
   Our Pace Too Fast, Masefield Warns [Quotes from Masefield's speech at a luncheon, Seamen's Church Institute]
   John Masefield, British poet laureate, surveyed the portal of America

C165.051   Jan 5, 1933, p.20
> Laureate Masefield [Quotes from 'Ships']
> A Professor of English Literature in an inland college wrote to The Times...

C165.052   Jan 8, 1933, section 4, p.4
> The Essence of Life *[Prose]*
> People are too miserable to think of esthetics, too blue to buy poets' books...
> [headed, 'By JOHN MASEFIELD, Poet Laureate of England, on arriving in the United States.']

C165.053   Jan 11, 1933, p.17
> Poets Hear Masefield [Paraphrases Masefield's opening remarks]
> The lecture tour of John Masefield, poet laureate of England, who arrived here...

C165.054   Jan 19, 1933, p.13
> Seamen's Group Honors Masefield [Quotes comments on election as honorary member of Seamen's Church
>   Institute, New York]
> John Masefield, poet-laureate of England, has been elected...

C165.055   Jan 22, 1933, section 6 [*The New York Times Magazine*], p.4
> Britain's Laureate Talks about Poetry [Quotes Masefield in interview with S.J. Woolf]
> England's poet laureate is visiting this country. He comes not as a stranger...
> [headed, 'By S.J. Woolf']

C165.056   Feb 14, 1933, p.13
> Masefield Praises Old-Time Saloons [Quotes Masefield's comments on "speakeasies" and "the old-fashioned
>   saloon"]
> PITTSBURGH, Feb. 18... John Masefield, Poet Laureate of England says...

C165.057   Aug 10, 1933, p.19
> Thrill of Poetry is Need of World, Says Masefield [Paraphrases Masefield's comments at the Welsh Eisteddfod]
> WREXHAM, Wales, Aug. 9. – What the world longs for is poetry, said John Masefield.

C165.058   Aug 12, 1933, p.10
> Poetry and Speed *[Editorial comment]* [Paraphrases Masefield's comments from news report of 10 August 1933]
> John Masefield says that speed is modern man's substitute for the excitement of poetry.

C165.059   May 27, 1934, section 4 [Editorial Section], p.3
> Poet Laureate Picked Flaw in Stage Galleon [Quotes Masefield's comments on a galleon in a production of *The
>   Tempest*]
> STRATFORD-ON-AVON, May 16.–John Masefield, poet laureate and writer of sea literature...

C165.060   Sep 25, 1934, p.23
> Masefield Writes Poem on Giant 534 ['"534"'] *[Verse]*
> For ages you were rock; far below light,
> [introduced as 'John Masefield... has written...']

C165.061   Apr 28, 1935, section 2, p.7
> Masefield Pens a Sonnet for King George's Jubilee ['A Sonnet for the King's Book'] *[Verse]*
> Scattered beneath the mansions of the sun
> [introduced as 'John Masefield... has penned the following sonnet...']

C165.062   Apr 30, 1935, p.3
> Masefield Writes Prayer for The King's Jubilee ['A Prayer for the King's Majesty'] *[Verse]*
> O God, Whose mercy is our State,
> [introduced as 'John Masefield... has composed a special prayer "for the King's Majesty"...']

C165.063   Dec 1, 1935, p.35
> Memorial to Twain in London is Urged. Masefield Suggests Monument on Thames... [Quotes Masefield's letter
>   to *The Times*]
> The 30th of November will be the 100th anniversary of the birth of Samuel Clemens...

C165.064   Jan 18, 1936, p.7
> Masefield Voices Praise of Kipling [Quotes Masefield's comments on Kipling]
> LOS ANGELES, Jan. 17... John Masefield... paid tribute to the memory of Rudyard Kipling...

C165.065   Jan 21, 1936, p.6
> Masefield Pens Verse On Death of Monarch ['King George the Fifth'] *[Verse]*
> This man was King in England's direst need;
> [signed, 'JOHN MASEFIELD.']

C165.066   Feb 3, 1936, p.15
> Coronation Task Inspires Laureate [Quotes Masefield's in interview on Panama Canal, cinema and Edward VII
>   coronation hymn]
> John Masefield, poet laureate of England, relaxed last night...

C165.067   Feb 6, 1936, p.21
> Masefield Finds a New Metropolis [Paraphrases and quotes Masefield's lecture recital at New York Town Hall]
> John Masefield, who knew the city as "little old New York, built of brownstone...

C165.068   Feb 16, 1936, section 7 [*The New York Times Magazine*], pp.9 and 18
           Masefield Ponders These Prosy Days   [Quotes Masefield in interview with S.J. Woolf]
           When King George died, at Sandringham, a tall, gaunt man with thinning white hair...
           [headed, 'By S.J. WOOLF']

C165.069   Sep 16, 1936, p.27
           Masefield Urges Return to Poetry [Paraphrases and quotes Masefield's comments after arriving in the United
               States]
           John Masefield, poet laureate of England, who has seen the excitement of a fast-moving age...

C165.070   Sep 19, 1936, p.8
           Masefield's Harvard Poem [from *Lines on the Tercentenary of Harvard University*] [*Verse*]
           When Custom presses on the souls apart,
           [introduced as 'John Masefield's new poem, "Lines on the Tercentenary of Harvard College in America"...']

C165.071   Sep 20, 1936, p.8
           Poetry from Speed [*Prose*]
           The world still wants the excitement of poetry, but it is getting it from machines...
           [headed, 'By JOHN MASEFIELD... Speaking to the Press...']

C165.072   Sep 24, 1936, p.27
           Masefield Praises Harvard Congress [Paraphrases and quotes interview with Masefield on his departure from the
               U.S.]
           John Masefield terminated his brief visit to the United States yesterday...

C165.073   Dec 1, 1936, p.27
           Mark Twain Bust is Unveiled Here [Paraphrases Masefield's comments on Twain bust]
           A fifty-one-inch bronze head of Mark Twain was unveiled last night...

C165.074   Apr 17, 1937, p.8
           Poet Laureate Writes Sonnet on Coronation ['Coronation Prayer'] [*Verse*]
           You stand upon the highway of the sea,
           [introduced as 'John Masefield... today made public his contribution... a "Coronation Prayer."']

C165.075   Apr 28, 1937, p.6
           Masefield Pens 'Prayer for King's Reign' ['A Prayer for the King's Reign'] [*Verse*]
           O God, the ruler over earth and sea,
           [introduced as 'John Masefield's "Prayer for the King's Reign"...']

C165.076   Jul 18, 1937, p.22
           Masefield Writes a poem to British Merchant Navy ['For the Men of the Merchant Navy and Fishing Fleets']
               [*Verse*]
           They dare all weathers in all climes and seas
           [introduced as 'John Masefield... dedicated "a little poem – not an ode"...']

C165.077   Sep 16, 1938, p.15
           Poet laureate in Verse Hails Chamberlain Trip ['Neville Chamberlain'] [*Verse*]
           As Priam to Achilles for his son,
           [introduced as 'John Masefield... has commemorated... Chamberlain's memorable visit...']

C165.078   Nov 25, 1938, p.22
           Book and Car [Paraphrases Masefield's remarks on effect of cars on reading]
           Opening a library in his native town the other day, Poet Laureate Masefield enlarged upon...

C165.079   Jan 28, 1939, p.6
           Text of Britons' Appeal to the Reich
           A spirit of uneasiness broods over the world. Men and women in every country are uncertain...
           [text of appeal signed by 'eighteen of the most eminent citizens of Great Britain', including Masefield]

C165.080   Sep 19, 1939, p.24
           Hours of Darkness [Paraphrases and quotes Masefield's letter to *The Times* on reading in wartime]
           It is gratifying to note that provision can be made for at least 30,000 students...

C165.081   Mar 17, 1940, section 6 [*The New York Times Book Review*], p.12
           John Masefield Talks on Literature and the War [Paraphrases and quotes Masefield in interview with Claire Price]
           It was a day of white freezing fog, fairly clear in places...
           [headed, 'By CLAIRE PRICE']

C165.082   Mar 19, 1941, p.4
           Masefield Greets Winant in Verses on Friendship [Quotes Masefield's explanation for writing verses for John G.
               Winant]
           LONDON, March 18–In his first public speech since coming to Britain...

C165.083   Mar 19, 1941, p.4
           Mr. Winant's Address [Quotes Masefield's verses, as recited by John G. Winant, at The Pilgrims' luncheon]
           Two with like laws and language should be friends.

C165.084   Nov 9, 1941, section 9, p.12
         Word from a Poet *[Prose]*
         I am very proud and happy to be speaking to my American friends…
         [introduced as 'excerpts from John Masefield's short-wave message to America…']

C165.085   Sep 6, 1942, section 7 [*The New York Times Magazine*], p.3
         The Third Year Ends *[Verse]*
         Thirty-six months of war have made it clear:-
         [signed, 'JOHN MASEFIELD.']

C165.086   Sep 22, 1943, p.5
         Masefield Says Puzzles are Only Solace in Press [Paraphrases and quotes Masefield's letter to *The Times* on
             crossword puzzles]
         LONDON, Sept. 21–Poet Laureate John Masefield wrote a letter to the Times…

C165.087   Oct 27, 1943, p.25
         Books into Munitions [Paraphrases and quotes Masefield's comments at meeting of National Book Council]
         LONDON, Oct. 26–Fifty million books have gone into the making of munitions

C165.088   Feb 24, 1944, p.7
         Masefield Ode, Bax Music Sung in Honor of Red Army ['An Ode to the Red Army'] *[Verse]*
         Though flanks were turned and center gone
         [introduced as 'The latest poem by John Masefield… entitled "Ode to the Red Army"…']

C165.089   Jun 14, 1944, p.21
         U.S. Set to Honor the Colors Today ['For United Nations Day'] *[Verse]*
         Since charity is killed and faith a void
         [introduced as 'Mr. Masefield's poem, entitled "For United Nations Day"…']

C165.090   Dec 17, 1944, p.5
         Russia Key to Peace, Masefield Believes… [Quotes Masefield's views on Russia]
         BURCOTE BROOK, England, Dec. 16… John Masefield, poet laureate, said today that…

C165.091   Jan 31, 1947, p.21
         To His Most Excellent Majesty the King, Upon the Sailing of the Royal Family for South Africa *[Verse]*
         Most gracious Sovereign, leaving England's shore
         [introduced as 'John Masefield… has written for The Times of London the following…']

C165.092   Oct 29, 1947, p.13
         On the Coming Marriage of Her Royal Highness Princess Elizabeth *[Verse]*
         That is the crown, but something set above
         [introduced as 'John Masefield's special poem…']

C165.093   Nov 20, 1947, p.13
         Lines on the Occasion of The Wedding of Her Royal Highness Princess Elizabeth *[Verse]*
         How many times, when London bells have rung
         [introduced as 'John Masefield has composed the following…']

C165.094   Apr 12, 1948, p.1
         Franklin Delano Roosevelt *[Verse]*
         Honor this man, so stricken in his prime,
         [introduced as 'by John Masefield']

C165.095   Apr 26, 1948, p.19
         Lines On The Occasion of the Silver Wedding of Our King and Queen *[Verse]*
         We are within the Heavens, sons of light,
         [introduced as 'John Masefield… has produced the following poem…']

C165.096   Nov 16, 1948, p.14
         Masefield Pens Quatrain for Son of Elizabeth ['A Hope for the Newly Born'] *[Verse]*
         May destiny, allotting what befalls,
         [introduced as 'John Masefield.. wrote a poem… under the title "A Hope for the Newly Born"…']

C165.097   Dec 23, 1951, section 6 [*The New York Times Magazine*], p.5
         One Starry Night *[Verse]*
         That starry night when Christ was born,
         [headed, 'By JOHN MASEFIELD']

C165.098   May 25, 1953, p.8
         Masefield's Coronation Poem ['Lines on the Coronation of Our Gracious Sovereign'] *[Verse]*
         This lady whom we crown was born
         [introduced as 'by the Poet laureate… entitled "Lines on the Coronation of Our Gracious Sovereign"…']

C165.099   May 31, 1953, section 7 [*The New York Times Book Review*], p.2
         Sonnets *[Verse]*
         Like bones the ruins of the cities stand,
         [attributed as 'John Masefield in "Poems." (Macmillan.)']

C165.100 May 31, 1953, section 7 [*The New York Times Book Review*], p.2
[Sonnet] *[Verse]*
So shall we be; so will our cities lie,
[attributed as 'John Masefield in "Poems." (Macmillan.)']

C165.101 May 31, 1953, section 7 [*The New York Times Book Review*], p.2
Beauty *[Verse]*
When soul's companion fails
[attributed as 'John Masefield in "Poems." (Macmillan.)']

C165.102 May 31, 1953, section 7 [*The New York Times Book Review*], p.2
At Gallipoli *[Prose]*
On Friday, the 23d [*sic*] of April, the weather cleared so that the work…
[attributed as 'John Masefield in "Poems." (Macmillan.)']

C165.103 Jul 5, 1953, section 2, p.10
News and Notes along Camera Row [Quotes brief extract from Masefield's *The University*]
Students of John Hopkins University, inspired by John Masefield's 200–word prose statement…

C165.104 Nov 23, 1953, p.9
Masefield Writes Poem to Mark Queen's Tour ['A Prayer On Our Queen's Going To Her People'] *[Verse]*
Love is no burden, Brotherhood no chain
[introduced as 'John Masefield… has written the following…']

C165.105 May 15, 1954, p.3
Sonnet by Masefield Marks Queen's Return ['On Our Sovereign Lady's Return to These Islands'] *[Verse]*
Once, when the Sign of England was the rose,
[introduced as 'John Masefield… celebrated Queen Elizabeth's return with a sonnet…']

C165.106 Nov 30, 1954, p.10
On the Birthday of a Great Man *[Verse]*
This Man, in darkness, saw; in doubtings, led;
[headed, 'John Masefield… wrote the following…']

C165.107 May 8, 1955, section 7 [*The New York Times Book Review*], p.2
On Malvern Hill *[Verse]*
A wind is brushing down the clover,
[attributed as 'John Masefield in "Poems." (Macmillan).']

C165.108 May 8, 1955, section 7 [*The New York Times Book Review*], p.2
Watching By a Sick-Bed *[Verse]*
I heard the wind all day,
[attributed as 'John Masefield in "Poems." (Macmillan).']

C165.109 May 8, 1955, section 7 [*The New York Times Book Review*], p.2
Invocation *[Verse]*
O wanderer into many brains,
[attributed as 'John Masefield in "Poems." (Macmillan).']

C165.110 May 8, 1955, section 7 [*The New York Times Book Review*], p.2
The Gods Ordained *[Prose]*
"Still," our enemies say, "you did not win the Peninsula." We did not; and some day…
[attributed as 'John Masefield in "Gallipoli" (Macmillan).']

C165.111 May 8, 1955, section 7 [*The New York Times Book Review*], p.2
Dark Age or New Birth? *[Prose]*
The storytellers of today seem too remote from any great body of fable.
[attributed as 'John Masefield in "So Long to Learn" (Macmillan).']

C165.112 Dec 26, 1955, p.14
Text of Queen Elizabeth's Broadcast
…Though you have conquered earth and charted sea…
[introduced as '…in the words of our poet laureate…']

C165.113 Jan 27, 1956, p.8
Masefield Writes Poem on Queen's Afric Visit ['Upon Our Sovereign Lady's Venture in a Great Cause'] *[Verse]*
Even as April's footsteps that unseen
[introduced as '…John Masefield, poet laureate, has composed a poem…']

C165.114 Oct 12, 1957, p.7
Masefield Pens Farewell to 'Our Sovereign Lady' ['On Our Sovereign Lady's Western Journey'] *[Verse]*
Not altogether strange, those distant states,
[introduced as '…John Masefield… has written two verses…']

C165.115 Jun 1, 1958, p.7
John Masefield Marks 80th Year [Quotes Masefield's comments on inspiration and post-war future]
…John Masefield, who is paid for singing the praises of the Queen…

C165.116   Jun 1, 1958, section 7 [*The New York Times Book Review*], p.7
        My Neighbor John Masefield is 80 [Quotes numerous comments from Masefield, in conversation with J.H.B.
          Peel]
        [headed, 'By J.H.B. Peel']

C165.117   Jun 1, 1958, section 7 [*The New York Times Book Review*], p.7
        From 'Beauty' *[Verse]*
        When soul's companion fails
        [signed, 'John Masefield in "Poems" (Macmillan).']

C165.118   Jun 27, 1959, p.8
        Masefield Salutes Queen ['...On the Occasion of Her Majesty's Visit to Canada, 1959'] *[Verse]*
        "The greatest single land under the sun,
        [introduced as '...John Masefield... hailed Queen Elizabeth's visit... in a ninety-eight-line poem...']

C165.119   Feb 20, 1960, p.3
        Laureate Pays Tribute to Arrival of Prince ['On the Birth of a Son to Our Sovereign Lady the Queen'] *[Verse]*
        Oh child descended from a line of kings,
        [introduced as '...John Masefield... wrote the following verse...']

C165.120   Apr 27, 1960, p.10
        Poet Laureate Creates 'Prayer' for Margaret ['A Prayer for This Glad Morning'] *[Verse]*
        In all unselfish thought a nation prays:
        [introduced as '...a sonnet by John Masefield...']

C165.121   May 6, 1960, p.26
        Poet Laureate Voices Prayer for Margaret ['On The Prayers For Our Princess' Happiness'] *[Verse]*
        A prayer is intense thought with lasting life.
        [introduced as '...John Masefield... wrote the following poem...']

C165.122   Dec 7, 1961, p.6
        On The Return of Our Gracious Sovereign From Africa *[Verse]*
        There, in the blinding sun under the Line,
        [introduced as 'John Masefield.. for today's occasion... wrote...']

C165.123   Jun 2, 1962, p.2
        Masefield Still Working, at 84, on 'Just a Poem' [Quotes Masefield's comments at a birthday lunch]
        ...John Masefield, Britain's Poet Laureate, celebrated his eighty-fourth birthday...

C165.124   Nov 25, 1963, p.9
        Masefield Poems Honors Kennedy... ['John Fitzgerald Kennedy'] *[Verse]*
        All generous hearts lament the leader killed,
        [introduced as 'by John Masefield, the Poet Laureate']

C165.125   Jul 13, 1964, p.52
        Masefield Poem... ['On the Finish of the Sailing Ship Race Lisbon to Manhattan – 1964'] *[Verse]*
        Here, by the towers of your splendid town,
        [signed, 'John Masefield']

C165.126   Dec 8, 1964, p.53
        Masefield Says He Hopes to Write Better Some Day [Quotes Masefield's comments on receiving National Book
          League award]
        ...John Masefield, Britain's Poet Laureate, had a new volume of verse published today...

C165.127   Jan 25, 1965, p.13
        Lines by Poet Laureate Pay Honor to Churchill *[Verse]*
        The Divine Fortune, watching Life's affairs,
        [introduced as '...John Masefield... wrote the following lines in honor of Sir Winston Churchill...']

C165.128   May 13, 1967, pp.1 and 22
        John Masefield, 88, Poet Laureate, Dies *[Obituary]* [Quotes numerous comments from Masefield]
        ...John Masefield, Poet Laureate of England since 1930, died...

C165.129   May 13, 1967, p.22
        He Roiled Poetic Seas [Quotes Masefield's comments on poets]
        [headed, 'By THOMAS LASK']

C165.130   May 13, 1967, p.22
        Sea-Fever *[Verse]*
        I must go down to the seas again, to the lonely sea and the sky,
        [headed, 'Samples of Masefield's Poetry']

C165.131   May 13, 1967, p.22
        Cargoes *[Verse]*
        Quinquireme of Nineveh from distant Ophir,
        [headed, 'Samples of Masefield's Poetry']

C165.132   May 13, 1967, p.22
            Upon Our Sovereign Lady's Venture in a Great Cause [Verse]
            Even as April's footsteps that unseen
            [headed, 'Samples of Masefield's Poetry']

C165.133   May 13, 1967, p.22
            The Song of Gaspar The Youngest of the Three Kings [Verse]
            I saw two towers in the light
            [headed, 'Samples of Masefield's Poetry']

The Literary Digest (New York, U.S.A.)

C170.001   Aug 31, 1912, Vol.XLV No.9, p.346
            Song [Verse]
            One sunny time in May
            [introduced as 'John Masefield's "Song," in the September Metropolitan...']

C170.002   Sep 13, 1913, Vol.XLVII No.11, pp.438–39
            The Wanderer [Extract] [Verse]
            All day they loitered by the resting ships,
            [headed, 'BY JOHN MASEFIELD']

C170.003   Sep 27, 1913, Vol.XLVII No.13, p.545
            London Town [Verse]
            Oh, London Town's a fine town, and London sights are rare,
            [headed, 'BY JOHN MASEFIELD']

C170.004   Oct 18, 1913, Vol.XLVII No.16, p.719
            Sea-Fever [Verse]
            I must go down to the seas again, to the lonely sea and the sky,
            [headed, 'BY JOHN MASEFIELD']

C170.005   Oct 18, 1913, Vol.XLVII No.16, pp.719–20
            Sea-Change [Verse]
            "Gonies an' gullies an' all o' the birds o' the sea,
            [headed, 'BY JOHN MASEFIELD']

C170.006   Oct 18, 1913, Vol.XLVII No.16, p.720
            The West Wind [Verse]
            It's a warm wind, the west wind, full of birds' cries;
            [headed, 'BY JOHN MASEFIELD']

C170.007   Oct 10, 1914, Vol.XLIX No.15, pp.693–94
            August, 1914 [Verse]
            How still this quiet cornfield is to-night;
            [headed, 'BY JOHN MASEFIELD']

C170.008   Dec 19, 1914, Vol.XLIX No.25, pp.1234–45
            Ships [Verse]
            THE ORE | Before Man's laboring wisdom gave me birth
            [headed, 'BY JOHN MASEFIELD']

C170.009   Dec 26, 1914, Vol.XLIX No.26, p.1290
            Watching By a Sick-Bed [Verse]
            I heard the wind all day,
            [headed, 'BY JOHN MASEFIELD']

C170.010   Feb 17, 1917, p.409
            The Choice [Verse]
            The Kings go by with jewelled crowns
            [listed by Readers' Guide to Periodical Literature Vol.IV]

C170.011   Feb 8, 1919, p.36
            Creed [Verse]
            [listed by Readers' Guide to Periodical Literature Vol.V]

C170.012   Aug 30, 1919, p.39
            On Growing Old [Verse]
            [listed by Readers' Guide to Periodical Literature Vol.V]

C170.013   Aug 28, 1920, p.38
            The Hounds of Hell [excerpt] [Verse]
            [listed by Readers' Guide to Periodical Literature Vol.V]

C170.014	*Aug 4, 1923, p.41*
	The Theatre [Verse]
	[listed by Readers' Guide to Periodical Literature Vol.VI*]*
C170.015	*Apr 10, 1926, p.32*
	On Growing Old [Verse]
	[listed by Readers' Guide to Periodical Literature Vol.VII*]*
C170.016	Jan 19, 1929, Vol.C No.3, p.26
	The Seekers *[Verse]*
	Friends and loves we have none, nor wealth nor blest abode.
	[headed, 'BY JOHN MASEFIELD']
C170.017	May 31, 1930, Vol.CV No.9, p.[24]
	Mother Carey (As told me by the Bo'sun) *[Verse]*
	Mother Carey? She's the mother o' the witches
	[introduced as '...a selection from the poems of John Masefield...']
C170.018	May 31, 1930, Vol.CV No.9, p.[24]
	From "The Everlasting Mercy" *[Verse]*
	How swift the summer goes,
	[introduced as '...a selection from the poems of John Masefield...']
C170.019	May 31, 1930, Vol.CV No.9, p.[24]
	Truth *[Verse]*
	Man with his burning soul
	[introduced as '...a selection from the poems of John Masefield...']
C170.020	May 31, 1930, Vol.CV No.9, p.[24]
	London Town *[Verse]*
	Oh London Town's a fine town, and London sights are rare,
	[introduced as '...a selection from the poems of John Masefield...']
C170.021	May 31, 1930, Vol.CV No.9, p.[24]
	From "August, 1914" *[Verse]*
	These homes, this valley spread before me here,
	[introduced as '...a selection from the poems of John Masefield...']
C170.022	May 31, 1930, Vol.CV No.9, p.[24]
	On Growing Old *[Verse]*
	Be with me Beauty for the fire is dying,
	[introduced as '...a selection from the poems of John Masefield...']
C170.023	May 31, 1930, Vol.CV No.9, p.[24]
	Beauty *[Verse]*
	When soul's companion fails,
	[introduced as '...a selection from the poems of John Masefield...']
C170.024	*Sep 6, 1930, p.29*
	The Wanderer: The Setting Forth [Verse]
	[listed by Readers' Guide to Periodical Literature Vol.VIII*]*
C170.025	Jan 16, 1932, Vol.CXII No.3, p.[23]
	On Thames Shore *[Verse]*
	All things longed for in youth,
	[headed, 'BY JOHN MASEFIELD'] [introduced as '...printed in *The Saturday Review of Literature*...']
C170.026	*Jan 15, 1938, p.18*
	Lambing [Verse]
	[listed by Readers' Guide to Periodical Literature [Vol.XI]*]*

The Metropolitan Magazine (New York, U.S.A.)

C175.001	Sep 1912, Vol.XXXVI No.5, p.11
	Song *[Verse]*
	One sunny time in May
	[headed, 'BY JOHN MASEFIELD']

The Independent (New York, U.S.A.)

C180.001	*Dec 12, 1912, Vol.73, pp.1352–57*
	Contemplatives
	[listed by Readers' Guide to Periodical Literature Vol.III*]*

C180.002   *Apr 24, 1913, Vol.74, p.927*
            Sea-Fever [Verse]
            [listed by Readers' Guide to Periodical Literature Vol.III*]*
C180.003   *Jun 7, 1915, Vol.82, p.385*
            Beauty that was [Verse]
            Roses are beauty, but I never see
            [listed by Readers' Guide to Periodical Literature Vol.IV*]*
C180.004   *Jan 10, 1916, Vol.85, p.53*
            C.L.M. [Verse]
            [listed by Readers' Guide to Periodical Literature Vol.IV*]*
C180.005   *Jan 10, 1916, Vol.85, p.53*
            Consecration [Verse]
            [listed by Readers' Guide to Periodical Literature Vol.IV*]*
C180.006   *Jan 10, 1916, Vol.85, p.53*
            Prayer [Verse]
            [listed by Readers' Guide to Periodical Literature Vol.IV*]*
C180.007   *Jan 10, 1916, Vol.85, p.53*
            Tewkesbury Road [Verse]
            [listed by Readers' Guide to Periodical Literature Vol.IV*]*

Current Opinion (New York, U.S.A.)

C185.001   Apr 1913, Vol.LIV No.4, p.324
            The Daffodil Fields [Extract] *[Verse]*
            Between the barren pasture and the wood
            [headed, 'BY JOHN MASEFIELD']
C185.002   Jun 1913, Vol.LIV No.6, pp.496–97
            C.L.M. *[Verse]*
            In the dark womb where I began
            [headed, 'By JOHN MASEFIELD']
C185.003   Feb 1914, Vol.LVI No.2, p.142
            The River [Extract] *[Verse]*
            All other waters have their time of peace,
            [headed, 'By JOHN MASEFIELD']
C185.004   May 1914, Vol.LVI No.5, p.381
            Port of Many Ships – A Sea-Yarn *[Prose]*
            Down in the sea, very far down, under five miles of water, somewhere in the Gulf...
            [headed, 'BY JOHN MASEFIELD']
C185.005   Jul 1914, Vol.LVII No.1, p.53 and 72
            The Western Islands – A Fo'c's'le Tale *[Prose]*
            Once there were two sailors; and one of them was Joe, and the other one was Jerry...
            [headed, 'BY MASEFIELD']
C185.006   Nov 1914, Vol.LVII No.5, pp.353–54
            August, 1914 *[Verse]*
            How still this quiet cornfield is tonight;
            [headed, 'BY JOHN MASEFIELD']
C185.007   Nov 1915, Vol.LIX No.5, p.351
            The End *[Verse]*
            There on the darkened deathbed dies the brain
            [headed, 'BY JOHN MASEFIELD']
C185.008   Apr 1916, Vol.LX No.4, p.282
            Sonnets On Beauty and Life *[Verse]*
            Here in the self is all that man can know
            [headed, 'BY JOHN MASEFIELD']
C185.009   Apr 1916, Vol.LX No.4, p.282
            Sonnets On Beauty and Life *[Verse]*
            These myriad days, these many thousand hours,
            [headed, 'BY JOHN MASEFIELD']
C185.010   Apr 1916, Vol.LX No.4, p.282
            Sonnets On Beauty and Life *[Verse]*
            There, on the darkened deathbed, dies the brain
            [headed, 'BY JOHN MASEFIELD']

C185.011   Apr 1916, Vol.LX No.4, p.282
        Sonnets On Beauty and Life *[Verse]*
        So in the empty sky the stars appear,
        [headed, 'BY JOHN MASEFIELD']

C185.012   Apr 1916, Vol.LX No.4, p.282
        Sonnets On Beauty and Life *[Verse]*
        It may be so with us, that in the dark,
        [headed, 'BY JOHN MASEFIELD']

C185.013   Apr 1916, Vol.LX No.4, p.282
        Sonnets On Beauty and Life *[Verse]*
        What am I, Life? A thing of watery salt
        [headed, 'BY JOHN MASEFIELD']

C185.014   Sep 1919, Vol.LXVII No.3, p.192
        On Growing Old *[Verse]*
        Be with me, Beauty, for the fire is dying,
        [headed, 'BY JOHN MASEFIELD']

C185.015   Apr 1920, Vol.LXVIII No.4, p.546
        From "Reynard the Fox" [Extract] *[Verse]*
        Two hundred yards, and the trees grew taller,
        [headed, 'BY JOHN MASEFIELD']

C185.016   May 1920, Vol.LXVIII No.5, pp.[689]-90
        The Passing Strange *[Verse]*
        Out of the earth to rest or range
        [headed, 'BY JOHN MASEFIELD']

C185.017   Feb 1921, Vol.LXX No.2, p.265
        From "Right Royal" [Extract] *[Verse]*
        An hour before the race they talked together,
        [headed, 'BY JOHN MASEFIELD']

Harper's Monthly Magazine (New York, U.S.A.)

C190.001   Sep 1913, Vol.CXXVII No.760, pp.[531–36]
        The Wanderer *[Verse]*
        All day they loitered by the resting ships,
        [headed, 'BY JOHN MASEFIELD']

C190.002   Dec 1914, Vol.CXXX No.775, pp.[115]-16
        Ships *[Verse]*
        THE ORE | Before Man's laboring wisdom gave me birth
        [headed, 'By John Masefield']

C190.003   Sep 1915, Vol.CXXXI No.784, p.593
        Revelation *[Verse]*
        If I could come again to that dear place
        [headed, 'BY JOHN MASEFIELD']

C190.004   May 1917, Vol.CXXXIV No.804, pp.[801]-810
        The Harvest of the Night *[Prose]*
        It is perhaps unnecessary to describe the daily life of the members of the American...
        [headed, 'BY JOHN MASEFIELD']

The Century Magazine (New York, U.S.A.)

C195.001   Jan 1914, Vol.87 No.3, pp.359–67
        The River *[Verse]*
        All other waters have their time of peace,
        [headed, 'BY JOHN MASEFIELD']

Harper's Weekly (New York, U.S.A.)

C200.001   *Apr 11, 1914, Vol.58, p.15*
        Tranarossan [Verse]
        [listed by Readers' Guide to Periodical Literature Vol.III*]*

C200.002   *Sep 12, 1914, Vol.59, pp.247–48*
        August, 1914 [Verse]
        [listed by Readers' Guide to Periodical Literature Vol.III*]*

Poetry and Drama (London, U.K.)

C205.001   Dec 1914, Vol. II No.8, p.426
        Closing Stanzas of "The Wanderer" *[Verse]*
        And on the instant from beyond away
        [headed, 'From *Philip the King*, by John Masefield']

Scribner's Magazine (New York, U.S.A.)

C210.001   Aug 1915, Vol.LVIII No.2, p.129
        The Unexplored, Unconquered *[Verse]*
        Out of the clouds come torrents, from the earth
        [headed, 'SONNETS | By John Masefield']

C210.002   Aug 1915, Vol.LVIII No.2, p.129
        The Central I *[Verse]*
        O little self, within whose smallness lies
        [headed, 'SONNETS | By John Masefield']

C210.003   Oct 1915, Vol.LVIII No.4, p.404
        The End *[Verse]*
        There on the darkened deathbed dies the brain
        [headed, 'SONNETS | By John Masefield']

C210.004   Oct 1915, Vol.LVIII No.4, p.404
        The Worlds' Beginning *[Verse]*
        So in the empty sky the stars appear,
        [headed, 'SONNETS | By John Masefield']

C210.005   Oct 1915, Vol.LVIII No.4, p.404
        Which? *[Verse]*
        It may be so with us, that in the dark
        [headed, 'SONNETS | By John Masefield']

The Atlantic Monthly (Boston, U.S.A.)

C215.001   Dec 1915, pp.[778]-79
        Two Sonnets *[Verse]*
        I. Here in the self is all that man can know
        II. Flesh, I have knocked at many a dusty door,
        [headed, 'BY JOHN MASEFIELD']

C215.002   Jan 1916, p.[48]
        Life *[Verse]*
        What am I, Life? A thing of watery salt
        [headed, 'BY JOHN MASEFIELD']

C215.003   Dec 1916, p.[756]
        The Enduring Good *[Verse]*
        Out of the special cell's most special sense
        [headed, 'BY JOHN MASEFIELD']

C215.004   Aug 1919, p.[191]
        On Growing Old *[Verse]*
        Be with me, Beauty, for the fire is dying,
        [headed, 'BY JOHN MASEFIELD']

C215.005   Nov 1932, p.632
        Two Sonnets *[Verse]*
        I. Here in the self is all that man can know
        II. Flesh, I have knocked at many a dusty door,
        [signed, 'JOHN MASEFIELD']

C215.006   Nov 1943, pp.[50]-57
        Wonderings *[Verse]* [Part One]
        Imaginings | Out of a dateless darkness pictures gleam,
        [headed, 'by JOHN MASEFIELD']

C215.007   Dec 1943, pp.[63]-68
        Wonderings *[Verse]* [Conclusion]
        Indeed, I sadly gathered as I grew
        [headed, 'by JOHN MASEFIELD']

C215.008   Mar 1951, pp.[21]-30
         The Joy of Story-Telling *[Prose]* [Part One]
         Now that I am coming to an end, I wish to try to set down what matters have been...
         [headed, 'by JOHN MASEFIELD']

C215.009   Apr 1951, pp.[61]-70
         The Joy of Story-Telling *Constant Practice and Frequent Mistakes [Prose]* [Conclusion]
         I was in New York City, in the summer of 1895, when I suddenly found that the faculty of...
         [headed, 'by JOHN MASEFIELD']

C215.010   Jan 1955, pp.60–64
         A Festival Theater *[Prose]*
         Between the years 1585 and 1635 the literary movement known as the Elizabethan Drama...
         [headed, 'by JOHN MASEFIELD']

C215.011   Jun 1957, pp.71–74
         Beaumont and Fletcher *[Prose]*
         Though they are often mentioned, and have been reprinted more than once during the present...
         [headed, 'by JOHN MASEFIELD']

C215.012   Nov 1958, pp.54–57
         The Shipwreck *[Verse and Prose]*
         Fog covered all the great Fleet homeward bound,
         [headed, 'JOHN MASEFIELD']

C215.013   Jul 1961, pp.50–54
         A Word with Sir Francis Drake During His Last Night in London *[Verse]*
         1595. | Scene. A room at night. Sir Francis Drake writing. One knocks. | DRAKE. Come in...
         [headed, 'JOHN MASEFIELD']

The Yale Review (Connecticut, U.S.A.)

C220.001   Oct 1916, Vol.VI No.1, p.[60]
         The Wind-Barren *[Verse]*
         Night is on the downland, on the lonely moorland,
         [headed, 'By JOHN MASEFIELD']

C220.002   Apr 1917, Vol.VI No.3, p.[536]
         The Will to Perfection *[Verse]*
         O wretched man, that, for a little mile
         [headed, 'By JOHN MASEFIELD']

C220.003   Jan 1920, Vol.IX No.2, p.[286]
         Lyric *[Verse]*
         Give me a light that I may see her,
         [headed, 'By JOHN MASEFIELD']

C220.004   Apr 1920, Vol.IX No.3, pp.[449]-51
         The Passing Strange *[Verse]*
         Out of the earth to rest or range
         [headed, 'By JOHN MASEFIELD']

C220.005   Dec 1928, Vol.XVIII No.2, p.[226]
         Any Dead to Any Living *[Verse]*
         Boast not about our score.
         [headed, 'By JOHN MASEFIELD']

C220.006   Mar 1931, Vol.XX No.3, pp.[469]-71
         Adamas and Eva *[Verse]*
         Whilom ther was, dwellyng in Paradys
         [headed, 'BY JOHN MASEFIELD']

The Forge (Philadelphia, U.S.A.)

C225.001   Nov 1916, No.1, pp.[3]-7
         The Blacksmith *[Verse]*
         The blacksmith in his sparky forge
         [signed, 'Pete Henderson.']

Overland Monthly (San Francisco, U.S.A.)

C230.001   Nov 1916, Vol.LXVIII No.5, p.[353]
        The Word *[Verse]*
        My friend, my bonny friend, when we are old,
        [headed, 'By John Masefield']

The Cambridge Magazine (Cambridge, U.K.)

C235.001   Nov 11, 1916, Vol.6 No.5, p.[97]
        Let us now be Praised by Famous Men [-] Half-minutes with the Best Authors *[Prose]*
        "I like the *Cambridge Magazine* and always read it with interest...
        [headed, 'From Mr. John Masefield']

C235.002   Mar 3, 1917, Vol.6 No.15, p.385
        The Cold Cotswolds *[Verse]*
        No man takes the farm,
        [signed, 'JOHN MASEFIELD.']

C235.003   Mar 10, 1917, Vol.6 No.16, p.[405]
        Camp Des Romains *[Verse]*
        Here the legion halted, here the ranks were broken,
        [signed, 'JOHN MASEFIELD.']

C235.004   Nov 10, 1917, Vol.7 No.5, p.[97]
        Lemmings *[Verse]*
        Once in a hundred years the Lemmings come
        [signed, 'JOHN MASEFIELD.']

C235.005   Nov 17, 1917, Vol.7 No.6, p.124
        Verses *[Verse]*
        I shut the door in the little lonely room,
        [signed, 'JOHN MASEFIELD.']

Contemporary Verse (Philadelphia, U.S.A.)

C240.001   Jan 1917, Vol.III No.1, p.3
        The Choice *[Verse]*
        The Kings go by with jewelled crowns;
        [headed, 'By John Masefield']

Science Progress – A Quarterly Review of Scientific Thought, Work & Affairs (London, U.K.)

C245.001   Jan 1917, Vol.XI No.43, p.482
        The Choice *[Verse]*
        The Kings go by with jewelled crowns,
        [signed, 'JOHN MASEFIELD']

The Daily Chronicle (London, U.K.)

C250.001   Jan 29, 1917, p.4
        "An Anglo-American Entente." *[Letter]*
        To the Editor *Daily Chronicle*. Sir, – Will you allow me to back Mr. Whelpley's plea...
        [signed, 'JOHN MASEFIELD. | 13, Well-walk, London, N.W.']

The Saturday Evening Post (Philadelphia, U.S.A.)

C255.001   Jul 21, 1917, pp.8–9 and 58–59
        In the Vosges. The Story of an American Driver's First Night Under Fire *[Prose]*
        It is a year ago now. I was twenty at the time and had only just come out; in fact, I reached Paris on...
        [headed, 'By John Masefield']

The Yale Alumni Weekly (Connecticut, U.S.A.)

C260.001   Jul 5, 1918, pp.1014–1015
        The Common Task [from stenographic notes] *[Prose]*
        I thank you all very much for the great honor you have given me to-day...
        [headed, 'By JOHN MASEFIELD']

Reveillé (London, U.K.)

C265.001   Nov 1918, No.2, pp.183–89
             Letters from America *[Prose]*
             "*Niagara.* | "All the way, I had remembered the tales of the roar of the water...
             [headed, 'By JOHN MASEFIELD']

The New Republic (New York, U.S.A.)

C270.001   Nov 23, 1918, Vol.XVII No.212, pp.106–107
             Preface to Poems *[Prose]*
             I do not remember writing verses in my childhood; I made many, but did not write them down.
             [signed, 'JOHN MASEFIELD']

Answers (London, U.K.)

C275.001   Dec 14, 1918, Vol.LXII No.1594, p.43
             What First? ...Mr. John Masefield – Help Belgium and Serbia *[Prose]*
             You ask me "What first, after the peace?" First, I hope, a general giving of thanks for our victory and...
             [headed, 'Mr. John Masefield']

The Bookman (New York, U.S.A.)

C280.001   Jan 1919, p.546
             Sonnet – To the Ocean *[Verse]*
             Though tongues of men and angels both should sing
             [quoted by Louise Townsend Nicholl in her article 'John Masefield In Yonkers']
C280.002   Jan 1919, p.546
             Sonnet – If *[Verse]*
             If I might stand among those sons of men
             [quoted by Louise Townsend Nicholl in her article 'John Masefield In Yonkers']
C280.003   Jan 1919, p.546
             [Untitled] *[Verse]*
             Here lies poor Jack – grave, headstone, all in one
             [quoted by Louise Townsend Nicholl in her article 'John Masefield In Yonkers']

Oxford Outlook (Oxford, U.K.)

C285.001   May 1919, Vol.I No.1, pp.14–15
             On Growing Old *[Verse]*
             Be with me, Beauty, for the fire is dying,
             [signed, 'JOHN MASEFIELD.']
C285.002   Jun 1919, Vol.I No.2, p.[144]
             The Oxford Repertory Theatre *[Letter]*
             Dear Sir, – I am writing about the project of a Repertory Theatre in Oxford which...
             [signed, 'JOHN MASEFIELD.']
C285.003   Jun 1920, Vol.II No.8, p.[286]
             Verses *[Verse]*
             What is this love, you grey-eyed gentle beauty,
             [signed, 'JOHN MASEFIELD.']

The Owl (London, U.K.)

C290.001   May 1919, No.1, p.6
             Sonnet *[Verse]*
             Forget all these, the barren fool in power,
             [signed, 'John Masefield']

Theatre Arts Magazine (New York, U.S.A.)

C295.001   Jan 1920, Vol.IV No.1, p.[1]
             Tragedy *[Prose]*
             Tragedy at its best is a vision of the heart of life. The heart of life can only be laid bare in...
             [signed, 'JOHN MASEFIELD.']

Parabalou (Connecticut, U.S.A.)

C300.001   1920, No.2, p.[1]
            An English Point of View [Prose]
            "I am delighted with it. I was immensely pleased and touched to find so much…
            [signed, 'JOHN MASEFIELD']

A note at the rear of issue No.2 states that the publication was limited to 500 copies and was to appear for six issues, 'as nearly as possible every three months'. Page [2] notes 'Published & Copyright by Danford Barney 1920'. The upper wrapper states 'Issued by the publisher from Will Warren's Den, Farmington, Connecticut, U.S.A.' A copy of issue No.2 is located in Harvard College Library (Houghton *EC9.M377.LZ999b).

Outlook (New York, U.S.A.)

C305.001   *Sep 22, 1920, Vol.126, p.154*
            On Growing Old [Verse]
            [listed by Readers' Guide to Periodical Literature Vol.V]

The Chapbook (A Monthly Miscellany) (London, U.K.)

C310.001   Dec 1920, No.18, p.3
            A Christmas Carol [Verse]
            A wind is rustling 'south and soft',
            [signed, 'John Masefield']

There is a sub-title provided which states 'Being Three Stanzas From The Poem Entitled Christmas Eve At Sea'. The same issue of *The Chapbook (A Monthly Miscellany)* includes a musical setting of the words by Malcolm Davidson on pp.4–10.

The Review of Reviews (London, U.K.)

C315.001   Jan 1921, Vol.LXIII No.373, p.[63]
            The Heart's Desire [Prose]
            What we all want is to see England re-made a little nearer to the heart's desire, without...
            [headed, 'BY JOHN MASEFIELD.']

St. Martin-in-the-Fields Review (London, U.K.)

C320.001   Apr 1921, No.362, p.161
            Poem [Verse]
            Night is on the downland, on the lonely moorland,
            [signed, 'JOHN MASEFIELD.']

Catholic World (New York, U.S.A.)

C325.001   *Apr 1922, Vol.115, p.65*
            Christmas at Sea [Verse]
            [listed by Readers' Guide to Periodical Literature Vol.VI]

The Spear (Huddersfield, U.K.)

C330.001   Jun 31, 1922, p.[1] [*The Shake Spear* issue]
            On Shakespeare [Prose]
            Whatever we may say of him, we are agreed, that he was the best thing we have...
            [headed, 'By John Masefield.']
C330.002   *Jun 1923*
            [The Speaking of Verse in Shakespeare's Time [Prose]]
            [We do not know how verse was spoken in the Shakesperean Theatre. Since nearly all...]
            [original publication noted upon republication in Queue (London, UK)]

The Reandean News Sheet (London, U.K.)

C335.001   [1923], Vol.I No.2, pp.12–13
            In a Theatre [Verse]
            After the traffic with its roars and glares
            [headed, 'By JOHN MASEFIELD']

The Measure – A Journal of Poetry (New York, U.S.A.)

C340.001   Jun 1923, No.28, pp.10–11
        In a Theatre *[Verse]*
        After the traffic with its roars and glares
        [signed, 'John Masefield.']

Revue Bleue (Revue Politique et Littéraire) (Paris, France)

C345.001   Sep 15, 1923, 61ᵉ Année No.18, p.624
        Prière *[Verse]*
        Quand la dernière mer sera croisée et le dernier écueil relevé,
        [signed, 'John MASEFIELD. Traduit de l'anglais par Jeanne Fournier-Pargoire']
C345.002   Sep 15, 1923, 61ᵉ Année No.18, p.624
        La Quête *[Verse]*
        D'amis et d'amours nous n'en avons point, ni de richesses, ni de foyer béni,
        [signed, 'John MASEFIELD. Traduit de l'anglais par Jeanne Fournier-Pargoire']
C345.003   Sep 15, 1923, 61ᵉ Année No.18, p.624
        Flots Espagnols *[Verse]*
        Flots espagnols, flots espagnols, vous résonnez à mes oreilles,
        [signed, 'John MASEFIELD. Traduit de l'anglais par Jeanne Fournier-Pargoire']
C345.004   Sep 15, 1923, 61ᵉ Année No.18, pp.624–25
        Le Vent D'Ouest *[Verse]*
        C'est un vent chaud, le vent d'ouest, plein de cris d'oiseaux;
        [signed, 'John MASEFIELD. Traduit de l'anglais par Jeanne Fournier-Pargoire']
C345.005   Sep 15, 1923, 61ᵉ Année No.18, p.625
        Crépuscule De Juin *[Verse]*
        Le crépuscule tombe; le soleil
        [signed, 'John MASEFIELD. Traduit de l'anglais par Jeanne Fournier-Pargoire']
C345.006   Sep 15, 1923, 61ᵉ Année No.18, p.625
        Le Canard Sauvage *[Verse]*
        Crépuscule. Rougeur à l'ouest,
        [signed, 'John MASEFIELD. Traduit de l'anglais par Jeanne Fournier-Pargoire']

The Mask (Florence, Italy)

C350.001   Jul 1924, Vol.10 No.3, p.131
        The Poet in the Theatre *[Letter]*
        Dear Sir, I see that, in The Mask, you discuss the place of a poet...
        [signed, 'JOHN MASEFIELD']
C350.002   Oct 1925, Vol.11 No.4, p.153
        A Symposium on a Design by San Gallo [A Reply] *[Prose]*
        1. They revolved upon some central pole, like the merry-go-round. I made a little...
        [headed, 'JOHN MASEFIELD.']

Arts and Decoration (New York, U.S.A.)

C355.001   *Dec 1924, Vol.22 No.2, p.94*
        A Painter of "The Old Sod"
        [listed by Chadwyck Healey electronic Periodicals Contents Index*]*

Elementary English Review (Urbana, U.S.A.)

C360.001   *1925, Vol.2, p.350*
        Sea Fever [Verse]
        [listed by Chadwyck Healey electronic Periodicals Contents Index*]*

The Dial (New York, U.S.A.)

C365.001   Mar 1926, p.238
        The Lemmings *[Verse]*
        Once in a hundred years the Lemmings come
        [unsigned] [quoted as part of review by Robert Hillyer of Masefield's *Collected Works* (Macmillan, 1925)]

National Education Association Journal (Washington, U.S.A.)

C370.001   *Jun 1926, Vol.15, p.168*
            Sea-Fever [Verse]
            [listed by Readers' Guide to Periodical Literature Vol.VII]

The Golden Book Magazine (New York, U.S.A.)

C375.001   Mar 1927, Vol.V No.27, p.316
            Cargoes *[Verse]*
            Quinquireme of Nineveh from distant Ophir,
            [signed, 'JOHN MASEFIELD']

C375.002   *Jun 1929, Vol.IX, p.36*
            Roadways [Verse]
            [listed by Readers' Guide to Periodical Literature Vol.VIII]

C375.003   *Sep 1929, Vol.X, p.81*
            The Turn of the Tide [Verse]
            [listed by Readers' Guide to Periodical Literature Vol.VIII]

C375.004   *Jul 1930, Vol.XII, p.29*
            Wanderer's Song [Verse]
            [listed by Readers' Guide to Periodical Literature Vol.VIII]

C375.005   *Apr 1931, Vol.XIII, p.68*
            Beauty [Verse]
            [listed by Readers' Guide to Periodical Literature Vol.VIII]

C375.006   *Mar 1933, Vol.XVII, pp.232–34*
            Sealman [Prose]
            [listed by Readers' Guide to Periodical Literature Vol.IX]

C375.007   *Apr 1933, Vol.XII, p.340*
            The West Wind [Verse]
            [listed by Readers' Guide to Periodical Literature Vol.IX]

C375.008   Jun 1933, Vol.XVII No.102, pp.550–56
            The Sweeps of Ninety-Eight | A Drama of the Irish Wars *[Prose]*
            SCENE-*An inn at Dunleary. A parlor.* TIGER ROCHE, *an old, well-preserved…*
            [headed, 'By JOHN MASEFIELD']

C375.009   *Mar 1934, Vol.XIX, pp.299–302*
            Western Islands [Prose]
            [listed by Readers' Guide to Periodical Literature Vol.IX]

C375.010   *Jul 1934, Vol.XX, p.43*
            Being Her Friend [Verse]
            [listed by Readers' Guide to Periodical Literature Vol.IX]

The World (London, U.K.)

C380.001   *May 20, 1930*
            Letter to Mary Ransom Fitzpatrick [Letter]
            [signed, John Masefield | Boars Hill, Oxford | Oct 16, 1927]
            [noted by Simmons, 'Addenda And Errata' slip]

The Author (London, U.K.)

C385.001   Summer 1930, Vol.XL No.4, p.110
            Robert Bridges *[Prose]*
            I first met Dr. Bridges at Yattendon a good many years ago, when he was not quite…
            [headed, 'By John Masefield.']

C385.002   Winter 1931, Vol.XLI No.2, p.75
            An Appeal to Artists and Others *[Communal Letter]*
            Dear Sir, – May we appeal to our fellow-artists and to every person of imaginative…
            [signed, 'GEORGE CLAUSEN, R.A. (for Painting). | JOHN GALSWORTHY (for Literature). |
            W.R. LETHABY (for Architecture). | JOHN MASEFIELD (for Poetry)…']

C385.003   Spring 1939, Vol.XLIX No.3, pp.86–87
            William Butler Yeats *[Prose]*
            The writers of the world will mourn the death of William Butler Yeats.
            [signed, 'JOHN MASEFIELD.']

C385.004   Spring 1940, Vol.L No.3, p.79
County and Public Library Service *[Communal Letter]*
Gentlemen, – In a nation which has been compelled to organise itself mainly...
[signed, 'WILLIAM EBOR. | A.S. EDDINGTON. | JOHN MASEFIELD...']

C385.005   Christmas 1940, Vol.LI No.2, pp.19–20
Hopes and Thoughts for the Peace *[Prose]*
From time to time, speakers and writers mention the sums being spent by...
[headed, 'By JOHN MASEFIELD']

C385.006   Summer 1946, Vol.LVI No.4, p.53
Salute to Bernard Shaw *[Prose]*
It is said, that someone once offered a prize of a thousand pounds for...
[headed, 'JOHN MASEFIELD, O.M.']

C385.007   Summer 1947, Vol.LVII No.4, p.79
Authors and the B.B.C. – Personal Comments from Leading Authors *[Prose]*
The Society of Authors was founded to protect authors from the meanness, avarice...
[headed 'JOHN MASEFIELD, O.M.']

C385.008   Winter 1954, Vol.LXV No.2, p.21
The Society of Authors' Seventieth Anniversary
[Masefield's message quoted]
In his message, Dr. Masefield expressed his sorrow that he could not...

C385.009   Winter 1955, Vol.LXVI No.2, pp.41–42
Gilbert Murray's 90th Birthday Fund *[Communal Letter]*
Dear Sir, | In January 1956 Dr. Gilbert Murray is to celebrate his 90th anniversary...
[signed, 'NORMAN ANGELL[,] JOHN MASEFIELD...']

C385.010   Summer 1956, Vol.LXVI No.4, p.74
Lines for the Hundredth Anniversary of the Birth of Bernard Shaw *[Verse]*
A happy task, to praise this mental prince
[headed, 'by JOHN MASEFIELD']

C385.011   Summer 1959, Vol.LXIX No.4, inside of lower wrapper [and many other occasions]
[Advert for Society of Authors' Retirement Benefits Trust Scheme]
To many hundreds of writers with wives and dependants, or alone...
[headed, 'John Masefield']

Cosmopolitan (New York, U.S.A.)

C390.001   *Sep 1930*
The Wanderer
[noted by Simmons, p.vii]

The Listener (London, U.K.)

C395.001   Dec 24, 1930, p.1056
Broadcasting and Poetry – A Letter from the Poet Laureate *[Prose]*
Poetry was once said or sung, usually by the poets who made it, and...
[signed, 'JOHN MASEFIELD Boar's Hill, Oxford']

C395.002   May 12, 1937, p.938
A Prayer for The King's Reign *[Verse]*
O God, the Ruler over earth and sea,
[signed, 'JOHN MASEFIELD']

C395.003   Jan 5, 1939, p.19
Here's Wishing! Messages broadcast on December 26 *[Prose]*
Friends, I have been asked to compose a Christmas or New Year's message...
[headed, 'John Masefield']

C395.004   Feb 2, 1939, p.247
An Appeal to all Men of Goodwill *[Communal Appeal]*
The following impressive appeal to all men of goodwill to prevent...
[signed, 'Marquis of Willingdon..., Mr. John Masefield...']

C395.005   Jun 13, 1940, p.1136
Books for the Forces
I want to speak about the supply of books and magazines to the men and...
[headed, 'By JOHN MASEFIELD']

Queue (London, U.K.)

C400.001   Feb 1931, No.5, pp.2–4
        The Speaking of Verse in Shakespeare's Time *[Prose]*
        We do not know how verse was spoken in the Shakesperean Theatre. Since nearly all...
        [headed, '*By* JOHN MASEFIELD, *Poet Laureate*'] [reprinted from C330.002]

The Saturday Review of Literature (New York, U.S.A.)

C405.001   Dec 12, 1931, p.[363]
        On Thames Shore *[Verse]*
        All things longed for in youth,
        [headed, 'By JOHN MASEFIELD']

C405.002   Jul 27, 1946, p.10
        On the Ninetieth Birthday of Bernard Shaw *[Verse]*
        After these ninety years, he can survey
        [headed, 'By John Masefield']

C405.003   May 20, 1950, p.16
        My Library: Volume One *[Verse]*
        Fifty-five years ago, as impulse led,
        [headed, 'By John Masefield']

C405.004   Mar 15, 1952, pp.9–11, and p.41
        Poetry & Perfection *[Prose]* (extracted from *So Long to Learn*)
        In my youth all young writers felt strongly the influence of the last...
        [headed, 'JOHN MASEFIELD']

C405.005   Dec 26, 1953, p.19
        The Hill *[Verse]*
        Man is nothing
        [quoted in review]

C405.006   Mar 20, 1954, p.13
        The Best Advice I Ever Had *[Prose]*
        Appropriately for a poet, the best advice I ever had came to me...
        [headed, 'By JOHN MASEFIELD']

C405.007   May 7, 1955, p.32
        In Memory of Two Friends *[Verse]*
        O passer-by, remember these two Friends,
        [headed, 'By John Masefield']

C405.008   Jul 21, 1956, p.7
        Lines for a One Hundredth Birthday George Bernard Shaw *[Verse]*
        A happy task, to praise this mental prince
        [headed, 'By JOHN MASEFIELD']

The Dublin Magazine (Dublin, Ireland)

C410.001   Aug 1932, Vol.I No.1, pp.3–4
        Mr. Jack B. Yeats *[Prose]*
        I first saw the work of Mr. Jack B. Yeats in a picture of a seaport that had about it...
        [signed, 'J. MASEFIELD']

The Illustrated London News (London, U.K.)

C415.001   May 11, 1935, p.781
        A Prayer for King and Country *[Verse]*
        O God, whose mercy led us through
        [headed, 'By John Masefield, the Poet Laureate']

Canadian Magazine (Toronto, Canada)

C420.001   *Jun 1935, Vol.83 No.6, p.47*
        Jubilee [Verse]
        [listed by Chadwyck Healey electronic Periodicals Contents Index]

Publisher's Weekly (New York, U.S.A.)

C425.001   *Jun 1, 1935, Vol.127, p.2112*
     Cargoes [Verse]
     [listed by Readers' Guide to Periodical Literature Vol.IX*]*

News-Week (Ohio, U.S.A.)

C430.001   Jan 25, 1936, Vol.VII No.4, p.[7]
     King George The Fifth *[Verse]*
     This man was king in England's direst need;
     [headed, 'By John Masefield']

Time (Chicago, U.S.A.)

C435.001   Feb 10, 1936, Vol.XXVII No.6, p.53
     [Sonnet on the death of King George V] *[Verse]*
     This man was King in England's direst need;
     [introduced as being by John Masefield]

C435.002   Apr 26, 1937, Vol.XXIX No.17, p.18
     [Coronation Sonnet] *[Verse]*
     You stand upon the highway of the sea,
     [introduced as being by John Masefield]

C435.003   Mar 11, 1940, Vol.XXXV No.11, p.23
     To the Australians Coming to Help Us *[Verse]*
     Out of your young man's passion to be free
     [introduced as being by John Masefield]

Scholastic (High School Teacher edition) (Pittsburgh, U.S.A.)

C440.001   *Jan 9, 1937, Vol.29, p.13*
     Cape Horn Gospel [Verse]
     [listed by Readers' Guide to Periodical Literature Vol.X*]*

C440.002   *Mar 22, 1943, Vol.42, p.23*
     Wanderer's Song [Verse]
     [listed by Readers' Guide to Periodical Literature Vol.XIII*]*

C440.003   *Oct 25, 1943, Vol.43, p.20*
     Patrol Ships [excerpt from A Generation Risen*] [Verse]*
     [listed by Readers' Guide to Periodical Literature Vol.XIV*]*

C440.004   *Mar 31, 1947, Vol.50, p.16*
     Cargoes [Verse]
     [listed by Readers' Guide to Periodical Literature Vol.XV*]*

Service in Life and Work (London, U.K.)

C445.001   Summer 1937, Vol.6 No.22, pp.9–14
     On The Arts of Delight *[Prose]*
     Not long ago I heard a man describing the various ways in which the nation's...
     [headed, 'By JOHN MASEFIELD']

New Verse (London, U.K.)

C450.001   Nov 1937, Nos. 26–27, p.29
     Sixteen Comments On Auden *[Prose]*
     All good wishes for the success of your tribute to Mr. Auden.
     [headed, 'JOHN MASEFIELD']

Drama – A Monthly Record of The Theatre in Town and Country at Home & Abroad (London, U.K.)

C455.001   Jun 1938, Vol.16 No.9, pp.135 and 143
     The National Theatre *[Prose]*
     It is now forty years since I first read the suggestion that there should be a National Theatre...
     [headed, 'A Statement By John Masefield']

Survey Graphic (New York, U.S.A.)

C460.001   Feb 1939, special number
                The Many and The Man *[Verse]*
                The brisk and prosperous and clever people,
                [signed, 'John Masefield']

[A 'special number' of *Survey Graphic* in February was reprinted twice, totalling 80000 copies. A further reprint was published by Harper & Brothers Publishers, (New York and London, 1939) in boards.]

The Arrow (Dublin, Ireland)

C465.001   Summer 1939, W.B. Yeats Commemoration Number
                William Butler Yeats *[Prose]*
                The writers of the world will mourn the death of William Butler Yeats.
                [headed, 'By JOHN MASEFIELD.']

Hobbies (Chicago, U.S.A.)

C470.001   *Mar 1943, Vol.48, p.96*
                Macey [presumably extract from In the Mill*] [Prose]*
                [listed by Readers' Guide to Periodical Literature Vol.XIII*]*

New York Herald Tribune (New York, U.S.A.)

C475.001   Oct 14, 1945
                For the Royal Air Force *[Verse]*
                You were as England when the war began,
                [signed, 'JOHN MASEFIELD']

Radio Times (London, U.K.)

C480.001   Sep 13, 1946, p.12
                Where does the Uttered Music Go? *[Verse]*
                Where does the uttered Music go
                [headed '...John Masefield's tribute to the memory of Sir Henry J. Wood...']
C480.002   Dec 14, 1958, p.7
                The Midnight Folk *[Prose]*
                I have been asked to write some words about the story of *The Midnight Folk*, now to be...
                [headed, 'By JOHN MASEFIELD, O.M.']

Argosy (London, U.K.)

C485.001   May 1947, Vol.VIII No.5, p.38
                Belvedere *[Verse]*
                I have seen dawn and sunset on moors and windy hills,
                [signed, 'JOHN MASEFIELD']
C485.002   Sep 1951, Vol.XII No.9, pp.45–49
                The Western Islands *[Prose]*
                "Once there were two sailors; and one of them was Joe, and the other...
                [headed, 'by JOHN MASEFIELD']

The Baylor Bulletin (Texas, U.S.A.)

C490.001   Dec 1951, Vol.LIV No.14
                Greeting from John Masefield, Poet Laureate of England *[Letter]*
                Dear Dr Armstrong, Thank you for your letter of the 21st September. I am much moved...
                [signed, 'John Masefield.']

Good Housekeeping (New York, U.S.A.)

C495.001   *Aug 1952, Vol.135, p.4*
                Sea-Fever [Verse]
                [listed by Readers' Guide to Periodical Literature Vol.XVIII*]*

C495.002   *Feb 1954, Vol.138, p.4*
              Being Her Friend [Verse]
              [listed by Readers' Guide to Periodical Literature Vol.XIX*]*
C495.003   *Jun 1954, Vol.138, p.4*
              John Masefield states the best advice he ever had [Verse]
              [listed by Readers' Guide to Periodical Literature Vol.XIX*]*

Johns Hopkins Magazine (Baltimore, U.S.A.)

C500.001   Feb 1953, pp.4–31
              The University *[Prose]*
              There are few earthly things more beautiful than a university…
              [headed 'by John Masefield']

Housewife (Liverpool, U.K.)

C505.001   Dec 1955, Vol.17 No.12, pp.42–43, 168, 171, 173, 175, 177–178 and 180
              The Night of Kings *[Verse]*
              Leaving the shepherds on the down
              [headed, 'BY JOHN MASEFIELD']
C505.002   Dec 1956, Vol.18 No.12, pp.52–53
              King Melchior and the Shepherd *[Verse]*
              We had been camped, as I have told,
              [headed, 'JOHN MASEFIELD, Poet Laureate']
C505.003   Jul 1957, Vol.19 No.7, pp.48–49
              The Cherries *[Verse]*
              Cherries and bread, for Man's delight, and need,
              [headed, 'BY JOHN MASEFIELD']
C505.004   Dec 1957, Vol.19 No.12, pp.42–43
              The Story of Gaspar the Youngest of the Three Kings *[Verse]*
              You ask about the meeting of the Kings,
              [headed, 'by JOHN MASEFIELD']
C505.005   Dec 1958, Vol.20 No.12, p.42
              The Windy Christmas *[Verse]*
              From Wales and Wye the wester roared,
              [headed, 'by JOHN MASEFIELD']
C505.006   Dec 1958, Vol.20 No.12, p.43
              A Berkshire Carol *[Verse]*
              Order, Beauty and Power,
              [headed, 'by JOHN MASEFIELD']
C505.007   Dec 1958, Vol.20 No.12, p.137
              Some notes about the legends alluded to in 'The Windy Christmas' *[Prose]*
              The opening stanza suggests the bells of the Church at Ledbury…
              [signed, 'JOHN MASEFIELD.']

The Aryan Path (Bombay, India)

C510.001   May 1956, Vol.XXVII No.5, p.[195]
              Gotama [*sic*] The Enlightened *[Verse – extracts from* Gautama the Enlightened and other verse*]*
              I. O Master of the Calmness, come
              II. Let all men praise the Woman who brings help.
              III. Desire, longing for life, and ignorance,
              [signed, 'JOHN MASEFIELD']

The Brook (Melbourne, Australia)

C515.001   Aug 1956, Vol.LIV No.151, p.5
              Lines for Tintern *[Verse]*
              Long since, in summer suns,
              [signed, 'John Masefield']
C515.002   Aug 1956, Vol.LIV No.151, p.7
              A Letter Received by Miss Wood *[Letter]*
              Burcote Brook, | Abingdon. | Christmas Day, 1955. | Dear Miss Wood, | I thank you for your…
              [signed, 'JOHN MASEFIELD']

The Naval Review (London, U.K.)

C520.001   Oct 1957, Vol.XLV No.4, pp.458–60
        H.M.S. *Calliope* in the Hurricane in Apia Bay, Samoa 16th March, 1889 *[Verse]*
        Into full hurricane the wind increased
        [headed, 'by JOHN MASEFIELD']

C520.002   Apr 1958, Vol.XLVI No.2, pp.214–16
        Lines on the Shipwreck of Admiral Sir Cloudesley Shovel… *[Verse]*
        Fog covered all the great Fleet homeward bound,
        [headed, 'By JOHN MASEFIELD']

C520.003   Oct 1958, Vol.XLVI No.4, pp.469–71
        On Pilots *[Verse]*
        Pilots, those unknown beings, who remove
        [signed, 'JOHN MASEFIELD']

Virginia Gazette

C525.001   *Oct 25, 1957*
        The Virginian Adventure [Verse]
        [noted in [The Times Bookshop], John Masefield [exhibition catalogue]]

Canterbury Cathedral Chronicle (Canterbury, U.K.)

C530.001   Oct 1958, No.53, p.1
        Lines written in the Memory of Margaret Babington A Friend of Canterbury Cathedral… *[Verse]*
        Once, as I walked in Canterbury Nave,
        [signed, 'JOHN MASEFIELD']

The Tower (Ontario, Canada)

C535.001   1960, Vol.9, p.8
        [facsimile letter to Miss Ida Sutherland Groom] *[Letter]*
        2 Feb. | Dear Miss Groom | So many thanks for your kind letter, + for the gift…
        [signed, 'John Masefield']

C535.002   1960, Vol.9, p.9
        June the 26th, 1959 *[Verse]*
        Today, our consecrated Sovereign's hands
        [signed, 'John Masefield']

University of Southern California Library Bulletin (California, U.S.A.)

C540.001   1962, No.9
        [Hamlin Garland Centennial Tributes]
        I am glad to write in the happy memory of Hamlin Garland, a most friendly…
        [headed, 'JOHN MASEFIELD…']

Model Engineer (London, U.K.)

C545.001   Feb 8, 1962, Vol.126 No.3161, p.177
        America's stirring naval history in models *[Prose]*
        The Seaman's Bank for Savings (of New York City) through the US Naval Institute has…
        [signed, 'JOHN MASEFIELD']

Humanist (Buffalo, U.S.A.)

C550.001   *Nov/Dec 1962, Vol.22 No.6, p.170*
        The Western Hudson Shore [Verse]
        [listed by Chadwyck Healey electronic Periodicals Contents Index]

The Royal Society of Literature Reports (London, U.K.)

C555.001   Reports For 1961–62 and 1962–63, pp.43–46
        Christopher Hassall Memorial Poetry Reading *[Prose]*
        My Lords and Ladies, Fellows and Members of the Royal Society of Literature, Ladies…
        [headed, 'DR. JOHN MASEFIELD']

Life (Chicago, U.S.A.)

C560.001   *Jul 24, 1964, Vol.57, p.66*
                   On the Finish of the Sailing Ship Race Lisbon to Manhattan 1964 [Verse]
                   [listed by Readers' Guide to Periodical Literature Vol.XXIV*]*

Sunday Mail Color Magazine (Queensland, Australia)

C565.001   Apr 22, 1979, pp.3, 6–10, 22–27, 30–31
                   Gallipoli [abridged] *[Prose]*
                   Those who wish to imagine the scene must think of twenty miles of…
                   [headed, 'By JOHN MASEFIELD']

D. Privately Printed Poetry Cards

D1 MISS MURIEL PRATT'S SEASON

D1(a) First English edition ([1914])

Bibliographies: unrecorded

Collation: single leaf; 259 × 205mm.; [i–ii]

Pagination contents: [i] 'Miss Muriel Pratt's Season. | THEATRE ROYAL, | BRISTOL. | [text] | JOHN MASEFIELD.'; [ii] blank

Paper: wove paper; all edges trimmed

Date: [1914]

Notes:
The first line reads 'Friends, we are opening at this solemn time,'

The poem was not reprinted within any volume by Masefield. See, however, B310.

Harvard College Library suggests Bristol and 1914 as the place and date of publication. This is purely conjecture.

Copies seen: Harvard College Library (Houghton *EC9.M377.914m); HRHRC (PR6025 A77 M588) with HRHRC note 'From the Library of John Masefield'

D2 BETHLEHEM GATE

D2(a) First English edition (1921)

Bibliographies: unrecorded

Collation: single leaf; 359 × 184mm.; [i–ii]

Pagination contents: [i] '[illustration of four figures standing before figure with helmet and lantern, within ruled border: 46 × 58mm.] | BETHLEHEM GATE. | [rule] | [text] | JOHN MASEFIELD. | [illustration of horse watching manger, within ruled border: 56 × 77mm. (signed 'J.M.')]'; [ii] blank

Paper: laid paper (watermark: '[V]AN GELDER ZO[NEN] | HOLLAND'), chain-lines 30–33mm. apart; lower edge deckle-edged, others trimmed

Date: [1921]

Notes:
The first line reads 'This is the city gate. I'll blow the horn.'

It is assumed that the illustrator was Judith Masefield.

The copy in Harvard College Library includes a greeting from Masefield dated Christmas 1921. This is assumed to be the date of publication.

The poem was not reprinted within any volume by Masefield.

Copies seen: Harvard College Library (Houghton *pEB9.M377.921b) inscribed 'Christmas, 1921. | With greetings + good wishes.'

D3 THE RACER

D3(a) First English edition ([1922])

Bibliographies: unrecorded

Collation: single leaf; 260 × 203mm.; [i–ii]

Pagination contents: [i] '[illustration of rider on horse] | THE RACER | [text] | JOHN MASEFIELD. | [illustration of two horses each with rider approaching jump (signed with 'JM' monogram)]'; [ii] blank

Paper: wove paper (watermark: 'Superfine | Antique Vellum | [monogram of 'S' and 'M']'); all edges trimmed

Date: [1922]

Notes:
The first line reads 'I saw the racer coming to the jump'.

The illustrator was Judith Masefield.

As noted by Simmons, the poem 'The Racer' first appeared (untitled) in the first American edition of *Selected Poems* in 1923 (see A62(c) and A62(cc)). An inscribed and dated example of this broadside suggests that the poem first appeared in this privately printed form.

The watermark includes a number of swash characters.

Copies seen: ULL (Special Collections) inscribed in Constance Masefield's hand: 'with best wishes, | from | John, Constance, Judith + Lewis | Masefield'; Bodleian (MS.Gilbert Murray 162, f.222) inscribed in Judith Masefield's hand: 'Forgive my dreadfully bad | drawings! | In Homage. | Judith Masefield | [sketch of a horse and rider]'; NYPL (Berg Collection) inscribed in Constance Masefield's hand: 'with best wishes | from | John + Constance Masefield', also 'To | Ethel Rawmby | Xmas' in unknown hand; Harvard College Library (Houghton *EC9.M377.Zzx) inscribed 'For Florence [Lamont] | from John. | Christmas. 1922.'; HRHRC (PR6025 A77 R324 1900Z) not inscribed, with HRHRC note 'From the Library of John Masefield'

D4 THE BALLAD OF SIR BORS [1923]

D4(a) First English edition ([1923])

Bibliographies: unrecorded

Collation: single sheet folded once (2 leaves); 165 × 126mm. (folded); [i–iv]

Pagination contents: [i] '[illustration of knight (within double ruled border [the outer border is in red])] | THE BALLAD [in red] | OF SIR BORS. [in red]'; [ii] '[illustration of knight on horse with forest, hill, village and birds (within ruled border)] | [text]'; [iii] '[illustration of oxen and village at dusk (within ruled border)] | [text (concluded)] | *John Masefield.*' [iv] '[illustration of knight on horse (within double ruled border)]'

Paper: laid paper (no watermark), chain-lines 28mm. apart; all edges deckle edged

Date: [1923]

Notes:
The first line reads 'Would I could win some quiet and rest, and a little ease,'

It is assumed that the illustrator was Judith Masefield.

This verse was first printed in *Ballads* (see A2(a))

A copy in NYPL includes a note in Sir Sydney Carlyle Cockerell's hand: 'Sent by John Masefield | Christmas 1923'. This date is also present on a copy inscribed by Masefield in the Bodleian.

Copies seen: Bodleian (MS.Eng.Lett.c.255, ff.50–51) inscribed 'With aching memories of | the Xmas tramp, 20 years ago. | For Con Belliss | from Macey. | Christmas. 1923.'; National Gallery of Ireland (Yeats Archive Mas.10) inscribed for Mr and Mrs Jack B. Yeats 'Greetings to you both. | J.M.'; NYPL (Berg Collection) date attribution note by Cockerell; HRHRC (PR6025 A77 B344 1900Z) not inscribed, with HRHRC note 'From the Library of John Masefield'

D5 BELLEROPHON [1927]

D5(a) First English edition ([1927])

Bibliographies: unrecorded

Collation: single leaf; 449 × 217mm.; [i–ii]

Pagination contents: [i] '[circular illustration of rider on winged horse within circular ruled border, diameter: 177mm.] | *Bellerophon* | [text] | *John Masefield.* | *Judith Masefield.*'; [ii] blank

Paper: wove paper; all edges trimmed

Date: [1927]

Notes:
The first line reads 'I am Bellerophon the bold'

It is assumed that the illustrator was Judith Masefield. The illustration is hand-coloured with blue, red and yellow watercolour.

This poem was not reprinted within any volume by Masefield.

The text is printed in italics throughout and includes a number of swash characters.

Copies in NYPL and Columbia Univeristy suggest a publication date of 1927.

Copies seen: NYPL (Berg Collection) inscribed in Hugh Walpole's hand 'Dear Carl | This with your | old friend's love – | Hugh Walpole. | Christmas | 1927'; Columbia University (Special Collections PR6025 A77 B4) inscribed in Judith Masefield's hand 'Judith Masefield. Dec 11th 1927'

[see J40 and J45]

D6 A SEAMAN'S PRAYER / NUMBER 534 [1935]

D6(a) First English edition ([1935])

Bibliographies: unrecorded

Collation: single sheet folded once (2 leaves); 168 × 134mm. (folded); [i–iv]

Pagination contents: [i] 'A Seaman's Prayer. | [text]'; [ii] 'Number 534. | [text]'; [iii] '[text (concluded)] | Number.. | For...'; [iv] blank

Paper: wove paper; all edges trimmed

Date: [1935]

Notes:
The first line of 'A Seaman's Prayer' reads 'Our lives are passed away from any land' and the first line of 'Number 534' reads 'For ages you were rock, far below light.'

The first poem was not reprinted within any volume by Masefield. The second poem was written to mark the launch of the ship 534. It appeared in the souvenir programme (see B280) and *The Times* for 25 September 1934 (C125.056).

The text is printed in italics throughout.

Although noted in the copyright information for *Brangwen – The Poet and the Dancer* (see E6), this poetry card is not reprinted in the volume.

Copies seen: private collection (BG) number '103' inscribed 'Barbara Vernon.' and signed 'John Masefield.' with annotation to the title of 'Number 534.' adding 'S S Queen Mary.'; King's College Cambridge, Modern Records Centre, Ashbee Journals 1/57 number '102' inscribed 'Janet' and signed 'John Masefield | Christmas 1940.'; Columbia University (Special Collections B825 M377 W47 193–) number '65' inscribed 'Phyllis Baker.' and signed 'John Masefield.'; Harvard College Library (Houghton *EC9.M377.930s(A)) number '9' inscribed 'Florence.' [Lamont] and signed 'John Masefield.'; Harvard College Library (Houghton *EC9.M377.930s(B)) number '12' inscribed 'Florence.' [Lamont] and signed 'John Masefield.'; HRHRC (TEMP M377SE) number 'One' inscribed 'Con.' and dated 'Novr 28. 1935.'

D7 TO RUDYARD KIPLING 1936

D7(a) First English edition (1936)

Bibliographies: unrecorded

Collation: single sheet folded once (2 leaves); 152 × 116mm. (folded); [i–iv]

Pagination contents: [i] 'To | RUDYARD KIPLING | by | JOHN MASEFIELD | Poet Laureate | *Printed by E.H. Blakeney at his Private Press* | *Winchester, April* 1936'; [ii] blank; [iii] 'TO RUDYARD KIPLING | BURIED IN WESTMINSTER ABBEY | *January,* 1936 | [text]'; [iv] blank

Paper: wove paper; fore-edge of page [i] deckle edged, other edges trimmed

Date: April 1936

Notes:
The first line reads 'Your very heart was England; it is just'

The verse, reading 'Your very heart was England's; it is just', was published in *The Times* on 23 January 1936 (C125.067).

A copy held in the University of London Library is accompanied by a letter from the printer to Maurice Buxton Forman:

> I thought perhaps you might like the enclosed – a tiny affair which I did today for the Poet Laureate. It is a most telling little epigram, and I liked doing it.
>
> (E.H. Blakeney, letter to [Maurice] Buxton Forman, 25 April [1936])
> (ULL (Special Collections))

This suggests that the library's copy belonged to Buxton Forman and was presented as a gift by Blakeney on the day of publication. Masefield's role in publication is apparently identified. It was not, however, at Masefield's suggestion that the printing took place. A letter from Masefield to Blakeney is evidently a reply to a request from Blakeney:

> Many thanks for your letter, and for the kind things you say about the verses. You are very welcome to print some copies of the couplet on your private press. It will be very kind if you will send me half-a-dozen pulls when it is ready.
>
> (John Masefield, letter to E.H. Blakeney, [1936])
> (University of Cambridge Library. Add.7509/295)

This couplet is printed with an incorrect first line. A photocopy in the archives of the John Masefield Society (Constance Babington Smith archives) reveals that Masefield sent a copy to Lucie Gladys Nicoll and corrected the line himself. An undated letter from Masefield to E.H. Blakeney states:

THE RACER

I saw the racer coming to the jump
    Staring with fiery eyeballs as he rusht ;
I heard the blood within his body thump,
    I saw him launch, I heard the toppings crusht.

And as he landed I beheld his soul
    Kindle, because, in front, he saw the Straight
With all its thousands roaring at the goal ;
    He laughed, he took the moment for his mate.

Would that the passionate moods on which we ride
    Might kindle thus to one-ness with the will ;
Would we might see the end to which we stride,
    And feel, not strain in struggle, only thrill,

And laugh like him to know in all our nerves
Beauty, the spirit, scattering dust and turves.
                    JOHN MASEFIELD.

D3(a)

Bellerophon

I am Bellerophon the bold
Who slew Chimæra in her lair ;
I ride a horse with wings of gold
Whose hoofs strike fire on the air.
I thrust all dragons through the gorge,
My horse can gallop on the sea,
The English know me as St. George,
And by that name they honour me.
              John Masefield.
              Judith Masefield.

D5(a)

To

RUDYARD KIPLING

by

JOHN MASEFIELD

Poet Laureate

Printed by E.H.Blakeney at his Private Press
Winchester, April 1936

D7(a) page [i]

To

𝕽𝖚𝖉𝖞𝖆𝖗𝖉 𝕶𝖎𝖕𝖑𝖎𝖓𝖌

by

JOHN MASEFIELD

Printed by E.H.Blakeney at his Private Press
Winchester, April 1936

D7(b) page [i]

Thank you for your letter and for the copies of the verses. I cabled the lines from California, and have not seen them in print. Your version is not that which I cabled. My first line runs: YOUR VERY HEART WAS ENGLAND'S: IT IS JUST

(John Masefield, letter to E.H. Blakeney, [1936])

(University of Cambridge Library. Add.7509/296)

Given the existence of another edition – with the correct first line (see D7(b)) – this poetry card represents the first (of two) editions printed by Blakeney.

Copies seen: Archives of The John Masefield Society (Constance Babington Smith Archives) photocopy of copy presented to Lucie Gladys Nicoll inscribed 'To Lucie Gladys Nicoll, | from John Masefield. | April. 1936.' on page [i] with 'England' corrected to 'England's' on page [iii]; ULL (Special Collections) with letter from E.H. Blakeney to [Maurice] Buxton Forman

D7(b) Second English edition (1936)

Bibliographies: unrecorded

Collation: single sheet folded once (2 leaves); printed in purple ink; 233 × 152mm. (folded); [i–iv]

Pagination contents: [i] 'To | Rudyard Kipling | by | JOHN MASEFIELD | *Printed by E.H. Blakeney at his Private Press | Winchester, April* 1936'; [ii] blank; [iii] 'TO RUDYARD KIPLING | [text]'; [iv] blank

Paper: wove paper (watermark '[VAN GELD]ER ZONEN [| HOLLAND]'); lower outside deckle edged, other edges trimmed

Date: April 1936

Notes:

The first line reads 'Your very heart was England's; it is just'

Note that 'Rudyard Kipling' on page [i] is in black letter type.

The watermark is presumably 'VAN GELDER ZONEN | HOLLAND'

This couplet is printed with the correct first line – compare with D7(a). This poetry card therefore represents the second (of two) editions printed by Blakeney. An undated letter from Masefield to E.H. Blakeney states:

So many thanks for so kindly sending me the large paper pulls of your print of the memorial verses.

(John Masefield, letter to E.H. Blakeney, [1936])

(University of Cambridge Library. Add.7509/290)

Copies seen: BL (11654.c.76) stamped 10 OCT 1936; Harvard College Library (Houghton *74–198); HRHRC (PR6025 A77 T622 MSF) with HRHRC note 'From the Library of John Masefield'

D8 THE NEW FIGUREHEAD   1938

D8(a) First English edition (1938)

Bibliographies: unrecorded

Collation: single sheet folded once (2 leaves); 243 × 159mm. (folded); [i–iv]

Pagination contents: [i] 'THE NEW FIGUREHEAD'; [ii] blank; [iii] 'THE NEW FIGUREHEAD | [text] | JOHN MASEFIELD | *September 11th, 1938*'; [iv] blank

Paper: laid paper (no watermark), chain-lines 24mm. apart; fore-edge of page [i] deckle edged, other edges trimmed

Date: 1938

Notes:

The first line reads 'Ninety nine years ago, the long-dead hands'

This verse was printed in *The Times* for 12 September 1938 (C125.080).

This verse was written for the "masting" (unveiling ceremony) of a new figurehead for H.M.S. *Conway* on 11 September 1938. The verse was read by Masefield at the ceremony. The figurehead, carved by E. Carter Preston, represented Nelson.

Copies seen: Archives of The John Masefield Society

D8(b) 'From the Chairman of | H.M.S. "Conway"' edition (1938)

Bibliographies: unrecorded

Collation: single leaf; 250 × 183mm.; [i–ii]

Pagination contents: [i] 'THE NEW FIGUREHEAD | [text] | JOHN MASEFIELD | *September 11th, 1938 | From the Chairman of | H.M.S. "Conway"*'; [ii] blank

Paper: cardboard; all edges trimmed

Date: 1938

Notes:
The first line reads 'Ninety nine years ago, the long-dead hands'

Copies seen: Bodleian (Additional Masefield Papers 1) inscribed 'John Masefield. | January the 30th, 1961'; Columbia University (Special Collections B825 M377 T56 1938) inscribed 'John Masefield.' (from the library of Florence Lamont); HRHRC (PR6025 A77 N492 MSF) signed 'John Masefield.', with HRHRC note 'From the Library of John Masefield'

D9 EPILOGUE FOR THE DANCERS... [1939]

D9(a) First English edition ([1939])

Bibliographies: unrecorded

Collation: single leaf; 166 × 138mm.; [i–ii]

Pagination contents: [i] '*Epilogue for the Dancers* | *Oxford Summer Diversions* | *Friday, July 28th, 1939.* | [text]'; [ii] blank

Paper: wove paper; top and left edges trimmed, lower and right edges deckle edged

Date: [1939]

Notes:
The first line reads 'Sweet lovely dancers, Time that passes'

The poem was not reprinted within any volume by Masefield.

John Gregory in *Brangwen – The Poet and the Dancer* (see E6) notes that Masefield inscribed a privately printed copy of *Good Friday* with these verses. This was, apparently, sent to Brangwen with a letter dated 31 August 1939. It can be assumed Masefield wrote and printed this card in 1939. The card is reproduced in *Brangwen – The Poet and the Dancer* on page [10].

Copies seen: private collection (BG) inscribed 'John Masefield.'; private collection (BG) inscribed 'For Brangwen, | John Masefield.'; BL (Cup.21.g.9(17)) stamp concealed by mount; Harvard College Library (Houghton *74–197)

D10 FOR THE SAILORS [1943]

D10(a) First English edition ([1943])

Bibliographies: unrecorded

Collation: single leaf; 222 × 142mm.; [i–ii]

Pagination contents: [i] '*FOR THE SAILORS* | [text] | [facsimile signature]'; [ii] blank

Paper: wove paper (watermark: '[crown] | Abbey Mills | Greenfield'); all edges trimmed

Date: [1943]

Notes:
The first line reads 'Even in peace, scant quiet is at sea;'

The text is printed in italics throughout.

The text is printed in the 1944 HMSO book *Merchantmen at War* (see B400) with the title 'For All Seafarers'. It is listed as being 'specially written' for that publication.

The HRHRC includes a copy of this item that I presume to comprise a proof printing: it is not signed with a facsimile signature. On the reverse, however, it includes nine additional lines in Masefield's hand. These appear to be a version of the other poem ('Epilogue') published in *Merchantmen at War* (see B400). The lines as they appear in manuscript are as follows:

> Twice, in a life, when unprepared
> Death fronted us with talons bared
> + dared you venture.. and you dared
>
> Twice, in a life, your hearts + hands
> Have kept us among living lands.
> When other props collapsed as sands.
>
> By your endurances, our race,
> Stands steady in the slippery place
> Where glory tramples on disgrace.

(see HRHRC PR6025 A77 F678 1943P MSF)
(includes HRHRC label 'From the library of John Masefield')

THE NEW FIGUREHEAD

NINETY NINE years ago, the long-dead hands
    Fitted your figurehead to lean and yearn
Vant-courier to you as you thrust your way,
Your herald in your going and return,
Seeming to search the seas for foreign lands
Seeming to brood above the bursts of spray.

Long-perished are those builders, and that form.
We, who are linked to you by subtle ties,
To-day re-dower you, again complete
The Life you had (for us) with head and eyes
To front the running water and the storm
And bear alike, unblinking, sun and sleet.

We give you this as dower, with our thanks,
Old Ship who cradled us and gave us friends
And sealed us to the service of the Sea.
All honour to you till that service ends,
New fo'c's'lemen to fill the dwindling ranks,
And CONWAY boys wherever ships may be.

John Masefield.

JOHN MASEFIELD

September 11th, 1938

*From the Chairman of
H.M.S. " Conway "*

D8(b)

FOR THE SAILORS

Even in peace, scant quiet is at sea ;
In war, each revolution of the screw,
Each breath of air that blows the colours free,
May be the last life movement known to you.

    Death, thrusting up or down, may disunite
    Spirit from body, purpose from the hull,
    With thunder, bringing leaving of the light,
    With lightning letting nothingness annul.

No rock, no danger, bears a warning sign,
No lighthouse scatters welcome through the dark ;
Above the sea, the bomb ; afloat, the mine ;
Beneath, the gangs of the torpedo-shark.

    Year after year, with insufficient guard,
    Often with none, you have adventured thus ;
    Some, reaching harbour, maimed and battle-scarred,
    Some, never more returning, lost to us.

But, if you 'scape, tomorrow, you will steer
To peril once again, to bring us bread,
To dare again, beneath the sky of fear,
The moon-moved graveyard of your brothers dead.

    You were salvation to the army lost,
    Trapped, but for you, upon the Dunkirk beach ;
    Death barred the way to Russia, but you crosst ;
    To Crete and Malta, but you succoured each.

Unrecognized, you put us in your debt ;
Unthanked, you enter, or escape, the grave ;
Whether your land remember or forget
You saved the land, or died to try to save.

John Masefield.

D10(a)

Lines for the Opening of the
NATIONAL BOOK LEAGUE
at 7, Albemarle Street.
April 30th, 1946.

———

This House of Books set open here,
May it bring light, may it bring cheer,
May it bring Man a thing most dear,
A mind alive,
A quiet of wisdom fenced from fear.

Though sorrow come, though evil fall,
Though war, again, wreck roof and wall,
May it still grant the spirit's call,
A mind alive,
A quiet of wisdom bright to all.

Though the soul shrink, though the heart ache,
From Man's debasement and mistake,
Nothing can null, or quench, or shake
A mind alive.
A quiet of wisdom will remake.

JOHN MASEFIELD.

D13(a)

In Praise of Nurses

Dedicated to

MARY CLIFFORD

LAURA FRANKLIN

HELEN McKENNA

PHYLLIS SIMMONDS

JOANNA WILLS

D17(a) page [i]

Copies seen: private collection (PWE); private collection (BG) inscribed 'Wishing you a most happy Christmas Day, + a | New Year of Peace + delight. | John Masefield.'; Columbia University (Special Collections B825 M377 Q52 1940) includes posthumous Masefield bookplate

D11 THE AMBULANCE SHIP   [1944]

D11(a) *First English edition ([1944])*

Bibliographies: unrecorded

Collation: single sheet folded once (2 leaves); 185 × 140mm. (folded); [i–iv]

Pagination contents: [i] '*The Ambulance Ship* | A MORNING DRILL | [text]'; [ii] text (continued); [iii] text (continued); [iv] '[text (concluded)] | *For*.. | *From*..'

Paper: wove paper; all edges deckle edged

Date: [1944]

Notes:
The first line reads 'We passed through canyons of a Carthage dead;'

The text is printed in italics and includes a number of swash characters.

This verse was printed in the 1944 anthology *Soho Centenary* (see B395).

The card is reproduced in *Brangwen – The Poet and the Dancer* (see E6) on page [190].

Copies seen: private collection (BG) inscribed 'Brangwen.' and signed 'John Masefield. | Christmas. 1944.'; HRHRC (PR6025 A77 A628 1940) not inscribed, with HRHRC note 'From the Library of John Masefield'

D12 A CHRISTMAS THOUGHT   1945

D12(a) *First English edition (1945)*

Bibliographies: unrecorded

Collation: single sheet folded once (2 leaves); 156 × 105mm. (folded); [i–iv]

Pagination contents: [i] '*A CHRISTMAS THOUGHT* | [text]'; [ii–iii] text; [iv] '*For*.. | *From Constance and John Masefield.* | *Christmas,* 1945'

Paper: wove paper; lower edge deckle edged, other edges trimmed

Date: 1945

Notes:
The first line reads 'In darkest London many years ago'

The text is printed in italics throughout and includes a number of swash characters. The comma in the fifth line of p.[iii] (after 'Then') is incorrectly inverted.

This poem was not reprinted within any volume by Masefield.

Copies seen: BL (Cup.21.g.9 (23) stamped 30 JUN 1974; Bodleian (MS.Eng.Lett.c.255, ff.170–71) inscribed 'A.J. Munnings, | with greetings'; NYPL (Berg Collection) inscribed 'Sydney Cockerell, | with greetings.'; University of Toronto, Thomas Fisher Rare Book Library (Ms.Coll.13, box 2 folder 19) inscribed 'Duncan Campbell Scott, | With greetings.'; HRHRC (PR6025 A77 C474 1945) not inscribed, with HRHRC note 'From the Library of John Masefield'

D13 LINES FOR THE OPENING OF THE NATIONAL BOOK LEAGUE   1946

D13(a) *English edition – variant issue one (1946)*

Bibliographies: unrecorded

Collation: single leaf; 464 × 280mm.; [i–ii]

Pagination contents: [i] '*Lines for the Opening of the* | NATIONAL BOOK LEAGUE | *at* 7, *Albemarle Street.* | *April* 30*th*, 1946. | [double rule] | [text] | JOHN MASEFIELD.'; [ii] blank

Paper: wove paper; top and right edges trimmed, lower and left edges deckle edged

Date: 1946

Notes:
The first line reads 'This House of Books set open here,'

The text includes a number of swash characters.

Corliss Lamont quotes this poem in *Remembering John Masefield* (see E1). His introduction is as follows:

> The National Book League is a leading British literary association of which Masefield was the first president. My parents had contributed to the building fund of the League, which later established the Florence Corliss Lamont Room in memory of my mother... The League sent me a copy of the verses Masefield wrote for the opening of its new home at 7 Albemarle Street, London, in 1946. I particularly liked this poem...

See also *I Want! I Want!* (see A141) for the text of the second annual lecture of the National Book Council in 1944 and *Seven Albemarle Street – An Appeal to Bookmen* (see B415) for the National Book League's building fund appeal.

Copies seen: BL (Cup.21.g.13(25)) stamped 30 JUN 1974; Columbia University (Special Collections B825 M377 S732 1946) inscribed 'John Masefield. | For C | from J. | April 29. 1946.'; HRHRC (PR6025 A77 L554 HZF) not inscribed, with HRHRC note 'From the Library of John Masefield'

D13(b) English edition – variant issue two (1946)

Bibliographies: unrecorded

Collation: single leaf; 205 × 145mm.; [i–ii] (presumed)

Pagination contents: [i] '*Lines for the Opening of the* | NATIONAL BOOK LEAGUE | *at 7 Albemarle Street.* | *April 30th, 1946.* | [text] | *John Masefield.*'; [ii] blank

Paper: wove paper; all edges trimmed (presumed)

Date: 1946

Notes:
The first line reads 'This House of Books set open here,'

The text includes a number of swash characters.

See D13(a) for a different printing. A different setting of less ornate type is used in the card described here. A double rule is omitted and the author appears in lower case characters.

This description is from a photocopy located in the Archives of The John Masefield Society (Constance Babington Smith Archives). No original has been located.

Copies seen: Archives of The John Masefield Society (Constance Babington Smith Archives) (photocopy of copy presented to Lucie Gladys Nicoll) inscribed 'For Lucie | from | John Masefield.'

D14 FOR THE NINETIETH BIRTHDAY OF GEORGE BERNARD SHAW   1946

D14(a) First English edition (1946)

Bibliographies: unrecorded

Collation: single leaf; 204 × 142mm.; [i–ii]

Pagination contents: [i] '*For the* | NINETIETH BIRTHDAY OF | GEORGE BERNARD SHAW. | [text]'; [ii] blank

Paper: wove paper; lower and left edges deckle edged, top and right edges trimmed

Date: 1946

Notes:
The first line reads 'After these ninety years, he can survey'

The text is printed in italics throughout.

The text is printed in the 1946 volume *G.B.S. 90* (see B430)

Copies seen: BL (Add.Mss.50543, f.93) inscribed 'John Masefield. | July 26. 1946.'; Bodleian (Walter de la Mare papers, box 49) inscribed 'For | Walter de la Mare. | John Masefield.'; Harvard College Library (Houghton *EC9.M377.946f(A)) inscribed 'For Tom Lamont, | from | John Masefield. | July 26. 1946.'; Harvard College Library (Houghton *EC9.M377.946f(B)) inscribed 'For Florence. [Lamont] | Augt 5. 1946. | John Masefield.'; University of Toronto, Thomas Fisher Rare Book Library. (Ms.Coll.13, box 2 folder 19) inscribed 'For Duncan | Campbell Scott. | July 26. 1946.'; HRHRC (PR6025 A77 F672 cop.1) with HRHRC note 'From the Library of John Masefield'; HRHRC (PR6025 A77 F672 cop.2) signed 'John Masefield.'

D15 MUSIC   [1946]

D15(a) First English edition ([1946])

Bibliographies: unrecorded

Collation: single sheet folded once (2 leaves); 147 × 108mm. (folded); [i–iv]

Pagination contents: [i] '*With greetings for | Christmas | and hopes for the | New Year*'; [ii–iii] text; [iv] '[text (concluded)] | *For | From Constance and John Masefield*'

Paper: cardboard; fore-edge of page [i] deckle edged, other edges trimmed

Date: [1946]

Notes:

The first line reads 'Speak to us, Music, for the discord jars;'

The text is printed in italics throughout.

This verse reprinted within *The Bluebells and other verse* (see A166) in 1961. It is there entitled 'A Cry to Music'. It was, however, originally written for the 1946 Musicians' Benevolent Fund luncheon to commemorate the festival day of St Cecilia and was printed in *The Times* on the following day, 23 November 1946 (C125.123).

A copy in the University of Toronto Library includes a handwritten date of 27 December 1946. This is presumably in Duncan Campbell Scott's hand. A copy in NYPL is tipped-in to Sydney Cockerell's 1946 first English edition of *Thanks Before Going*. A date of 1946 has therefore been attributed.

In addition to a later edition, also compare with D27.

Copies seen: private collection (PWE) inscribed 'Eileen Colwell.'; Archives of The John Masefield Society inscribed 'Pat Campbell.'; National Library of Scotland. (MS.9332, ff.66–67) inscribed 'Herbert Grierson.'; NYPL (Berg Collection) inscribed 'Sydney Cockerell.'; University of Toronto, Thomas Fisher Rare Book Library. (Ms.Coll.13, box 2 folder 19) inscribed 'Duncan Campbell Scott,' dated 27.12.46 by Duncan Campbell Scott

D15(b) Second English edition ([1952])

Bibliographies: unrecorded

Collation: single sheet folded once (2 leaves); 140 × 116mm. (folded); [i–iv]

Pagination contents: [i] '*With all Good Wishes | for now and later | from | John & Constance Masefield*'; [ii–iii] text; [iv] 'For...'

Paper: cardboard; all edges deckle edged

Date: [1952]

Notes:

The first line reads 'Speak to us, Music, for the discord jars;'

The text is printed in italics throughout.

A copy in NYPL formerly belonging to Sydney Cockerell carries his date attribution of 'Christmas 1952'. He had originally written 'Christmas 1953'.

See also D27.

Copies seen: Bodleian (Walter de la Mare papers, box 49) inscribed 'John Masefield.' on p.[iii] and for 'Walter de la Mare, | With the grateful memories | of many years.' on p.[iv]; Bodleian (MS.Eng.lett.d.475/2, ff.318–319) inscribed 'John Masefield.' on p.[iii] and for 'Jill Hunter.' on p.[iv] [copy one]; Bodleian (MS.Eng.lett.d.475/2, ff.320–321) inscribed 'John Masefield.' on p.[iii] and for 'Jill Hunter' on p.[iv] [copy two]; Archives of The John Masefield Society (Peter Smith Collection) inscribed 'John Masefield.' on p.[iii] and for 'Joy.' on p.[iv]; NYPL (Berg Collection) inscribed 'John Masefield.' on p.[iii] and for 'Sydney Cockerell.' on p.[iv] date attribution note by Cockerell

D16 FOR AN EXHIBITION OF BOOKS OF POETRY [1947]

D16(a) First English edition ([1947])

Bibliographies: unrecorded

Collation: single leaf; 177 × 115mm.; [i–ii]

Pagination contents: [i] '*For an Exhibition of Books of Poetry* | [text]'; [ii] blank

Paper: wove paper; right edge deckled edged, other edges trimmed

Date: [1947]

Notes:

The first line reads 'These are the spoils of fishers, who have caught'

The exhibition, assembled by John Hayward, was held at the National Book League in London. Displaying editions of English poetry from Chaucer to 1947, the exhibition was opened by Masefield. See A149 for publication of his speech.

The final couplet of the verse makes a reference to the visit to the exhibition of H.M. Queen Mary. Within Handley-Taylor's bibliography there is a photograph, on page 68, showing H.M. Queen Mary, John Hadfield, John Masefield and John Hayward. It is captioned 'National Book League English Poetry Exhibition'.

Two copies of this poetry card were included in lot 3043 of The Library of H. Bradley Martin (sold by Sotheby's New York, 30 April 1990). The lot comprised 'an interesting collection of items related to the Hayward exhibition'. A copy of *Sonnets and Poems* (see A32(b)) was apparently inscribed 'For John Hayward, To mark the opening of his Exhibition of the books of English poets. from John Masefield. April 10, 1947'. The half-title was also inscribed with the first six lines of the poem printed on this card.

Copies of the card were, apparently, numbered (although Masefield's own copy is un-numbered). There were at least seventeen copies. Copy number seventeen is illustrated within the Sotheby's sale catalogue: Sotheby's (New York), *The Library of H. Bradley Martin – Highly Important English Literature*, 1990.

It appears that copies of the verses were not printed for distribution at the exhibition for Masefield sent Hayward two copies, accompanied by a letter:

> Would you very graciously accept from me these pulls of the lines which had the happy fortune to please you?
> (John Masefield, letter to John Hayward, [1947])
> (see Sotheby's (New York), *The Library of H. Bradley Martin – Highly Important English Literature*, 1990)

Copies: The Library of H. Bradley Martin (sold by Sotheby's New York, 30 April 1990, within lot 3043) number 16, inscribed 'John Masefield. No. 16'; The Library of H. Bradley Martin (sold by Sotheby's New York, 30 April 1990, within lot 3043) number 17, inscribed 'For John Hayward, who | gathered the Exhibition. | from | John Masefield. | No. 17.'; HRHRC (PR6025 A77 F677 1947) with HRHRC note 'From the Library of John Masefield'

D17 IN PRAISE OF NURSES

[1949]

D17(a) *First English edition ([1949])*

Bibliographies: unrecorded

Collation: single sheet folded once (2 leaves); 201 × 126mm. (folded); [i–iv]

Pagination contents: [i] 'In Praise of Nurses | *Dedicated to* | MARY CLIFFORD | LAURA FRANKLIN | HELEN McKENNA | PHYLLIS SIMMONDS | JOANNA WILLS'; [ii–iii] text; [iv] '[text (concluded)]' | *From* JOHN AND CONSTANCE MASEFIELD | *To* | *With all bright hope for now and later.*'

Paper: laid paper (watermark: '[crown] Glastonbury'), chain-lines 25mm. apart (the paper is used so that chain-lines run horizontally); all edges trimmed or deckle edged (see notes)

Date: December 1949

Notes:
The first line reads 'Man, in his gallant power, goes in pride,'

Examined copies are either trimmed or deckle edged.

A letter from Edward Colegrove, managing director of Hall the Printer (Oxford), preserved in the received correspondence files of Masefield states:

> …Thanks so much for your letter. It so happens that we had arranged to post a proof tonight and it is enclosed herewith. Immediately on its return we can print you the number of copies you require within two or three days.
> (Edward Colegrove, letter to John Masefield, 28 November 1949)
> (HRHRC, MS (Masefield, J.) Recip Hall the Printer Limited)

In 1954 the firm requested permission to reprint the poem in 'the N.H.S.R. Newsletter' (see Edward Colegrove, letter to John Masefield, 18 August 1954) (HRHRC, MS (Masefield, J.) Recip Hall the Printer Limited). It would seem likely, therefore, given this later interest and the November 1949 date that this poetry card was printed by Hall the Printer in December 1949.

This verse was also published by Heinemann in 1950 (see A159(a)) and Macmillan (see A159(b)). The text was also reprinted in *The Bluebells and other verse* (see A166).

The verse is dedicated to the nurses of the Acland Nursing Home. 1949 was a year of particularly bad health for Masefield (see Babington Smith, p.217).

Copies seen: private collection (PWE) edges deckle edged, inscribed 'Eileen Colwell.' and signed 'John Masefield. | Christmas. 1949.'; ULL (Sturge Moore papers box 30) edges trimmed, inscribed in Constance Masefield's hand 'Marie + Riette [Sturge Moore]' and signed 'John Masefield. | Christmas. 1949.'; NYPL (Berg Collection) edges trimmed, inscribed 'Ada' [Galsworthy?] and signed 'John Masefield. | Christmas. 1949.'; HRHRC (PR6025 A77 I6 1950B cop.1) not inscribed, with HRHRC note 'From the Library of John Masefield'; HRHRC (PR6025 A77 I6 1950B cop.2) inscribed 'The London Library Appeal. | No 112.' and signed 'John Masefield.'

I have seen flowers come in stony
    places,

And kind things done by men with
    ugly faces,

And the Gold Cup won, by the worst
    horse, at the Races,

So I trust, too.
            John Masefield.

For....*Eileen*..................................

The Starry Night

That starry Night when Christ was born,
The shepherds watched by Dead Man's Thorn;
They shared their supper with the dogs,
And watched the sparks flick from the logs
Where coppings from the holly burned.

Then the dogs growled, and faces turned
To horsemen, coming from the hill.

A Captain called to them, " Keep still . . .
We're riding, seeking for a sign
That human beings are divine . . .
Is there such marvel, hereabout? "

The shepherds said, " Us don't know nowt.
We're Mr. Jones's shepherd chaps.
Old Mr. Jones might know, perhaps . . .
But if you've come this country road,
You've passed his house and never knowed.
There's someone in the town might know;
A mile on, keeping as you go."

Night after night, a great Star blazed.
The young were scared, the old were dazed.
" This is a Sign ", the Seers said,
" A King is born, to smite Death dead :
To kill all Evil, empty Hell,
And rule Mankind forever well."

North, South and West, the Kings of then
Set out, to bring this King to men.
And ever the Star burned so bright
From sunset through the winter night.

O what a ride, O what delight,
To turn this earth to chrysolite,
To make Death live, to wash red white.

John Masefield.

D22(a)

King Edward the Confessor and His Ring.

Of all the Saints of whom we sing
As crowned and into glory gone,
Edward Confessor, Saint and King,
Loved best the loved Apostle John.

When any Church was consecrate
In Saint John's name, he bid me bear
Purses of gold exceeding great
And ride with him to give them there.

The wonder that I tell began
At just such blessing of a shrine.
I marked an outland beggar-man
Whose inward spirit seemed divine,

Who, when the sacring had been done,
Outside the Church, as the bells rang,
Stood silent, shining like the sun,
While the assembled quires sang.

D24(a) page [i]

D18 [THE MEDITATION OF HIGHWORTH RIDDEN] [1950]

D18(a) First English edition ([1950])

Bibliographies: unrecorded

Collation: single sheet folded once (2 leaves); 113 × 93mm. (folded); [i–iv]

Pagination contents: [i] 'With all Good Wishes | for now and later | from | John & Constance Masefield'; [ii] blank; [iii] '[text] | For..'; [iv] blank

Paper: cardboard; all edges deckle edged

Date: [1950]

Notes:

The first line reads 'I have seen flowers come in stony places,'

The text is printed in italics throughout.

The verse originates from the novel *ODTAA* (see A82) which concludes with six poems. This, the penultimate, is entitled 'The Meditation of Highworth Ridden'. There are minor textual differences.

The copy in the University of Bristol Library includes a handwritten date of Xmas 1950. This is thought to be in Agnes Fry's hand. The copy is tipped-in a 1949 copy of *On The Hill.*. A date of 1950 has therefore been attributed.

Copies seen: private collection (PWE) inscribed 'Eileen. [Colwell]' and signed 'John Masefield.'; Bodleian (Additional Masefield Papers 1) inscribed 'Kay.' and signed 'John Masefield.'; Bodleian (MS.Eng.lett.d.475/1, f.7–8) inscribed 'For Grace'; University of Bristol Library inscribed 'Agnes [Fry]' and signed 'John Masefield.' dated 'Xmas: 1950' by Agnes Fry; NYPL (Berg Collection) inscribed 'Sir Sydney Cockerell.' and signed 'John Masefield.'

D19 A BERKSHIRE CAROL [early 1950s]

D19(a) First English edition ([early 1950s])

Bibliographies: unrecorded

Collation: single sheet folded once (2 leaves); 130 × 100mm. (folded), [i–iv]

Pagination contents: [i] 'A Berkshire Carol | [text]'; [ii–iii] text; [iv] 'To... | With all Best Wishes for now and later | From | John & Constance Masefield'

Paper: cardboard; all edges deckle edged

Date: early 1950s

Notes:

The first line reads 'Order, Beauty and Power,'

The text is printed in italics throughout and includes a number of swash characters.

This poem was not reprinted within any volume by Masefield.

Copies seen: private collection (ROV) inscribed to 'Anne Renier.' and signed 'John Masefield.'; Bodleian (MS.Eng.lett.d.475/1, f.9–10) inscribed to 'Grace Hunter'; Bodleian (MS.Eng.lett.d.475/1, f.23–24) inscribed to 'Grace'; HRHRC (PR6025 A77 B475 1900Z cop.1) not inscribed, with HRHRC note 'From the Library of John Masefield'; HRHRC (PR6025 A77 B475 1900Z cop.2) not inscribed, with HRHRC note 'From the Library of John Masefield'

D20 LINES SPOKEN... AT THE LAYING OF THE FOUNDATION STONE OF THE NATIONAL THEATRE... 1951

D20(a) First English edition (1951)

Bibliographies: unrecorded

Collation: single leaf; 192 × 120mm.; [i–ii]

Pagination contents: [i] 'Lines spoken by Dame Sybil Thorndike | at the | Laying of the Foundation Stone | of the | National Theatre | JULY 13TH, 1951 | [rule (tapered at both ends), 25mm.] | [text] | JOHN MASEFIELD'; [ii] blank

Paper: cardboard; all edges trimmed

Date: 1951

Notes:

The first line reads 'Here we lay stone, that, at a future time,'

The verse was published in *The Times* on 14 July 1951 (C125.145).

Copies seen: private collection (PB)

D21 THE STARRY NIGHT [1953]

D21(a) First English edition ([1953])

Bibliographies: unrecorded

Collation: single sheet folded once (2 leaves); 169 × 115mm. (folded); [i–iv]

Pagination contents: [i] '*The Starry Night* | [text]'; [ii–iii] text (continued); [iv] '[text (concluded)] | *For...* | *With all Best Wishes for now and later* | *From* | JOHN and CONSTANCE MASEFIELD'

Paper: cardboard; all edges deckle edged

Date: [1953]

Notes:

The first line reads 'That starry Night when Christ was born,'

When printed within the second American edition of *Poems*, this verse was entitled 'The Kings At Midnight' (see A114(b)).

This verse was reprinted within *The Bluebells and other Verse* (see A166). It is there entitled 'The Starry Night' but is grouped together with two other poems. One of these comprises 'The Song of Gaspar' (see D23).

A letter within the archives of the Society of Authors is from a member of the Society's staff to Masefield:

> I feel that I must write at once to tell you how delighted I am to have the *Starry Night* with your own and Mrs. Masefield's good wishes.
>
> (M.E. Barber, letter to John Masefield, 21 December 1953)
> (BL, Add.Mss.56624, f.192)

This suggests that the poetry card comprised Masefield's Christmas card for December 1953 and publication took place after the September 1953 Macmillan edition of *Poems* (see A114(b)).

Copies seen: Archives of The John Masefield Society (Peter Smith Collection) inscribed 'Joy.' and signed 'John Masefield.'; Bodleian (Additional Masefield Papers 1) inscribed 'Kay.' and signed 'John Masefield.'; Bodleian (MS.Eng.lett.d.475/2, ff.322–323) inscribed 'Jill.' and signed 'John Masefield.'; Bodleian (MS.Eng.lett.d.475/2, ff.324–325) inscribed 'Grace.' and signed 'John Masefield.'

D22 [UNTITLED]: 'Night after night, a great Star blazed' [mid 1950s]

D22(a) First English edition ([mid 1950s])

Bibliographies: unrecorded

Collation: single leaf; 126 × 101mm.; [i–ii]

Pagination contents: [i] '[text] | *John Masefield.*'; [ii] blank

Paper: cardboard; all edges deckle edged

Date: [mid 1950s]

Notes:

The first line reads 'Night after night, a great Star blazed.'

The text is printed in italics throughout and includes a number of swash characters.

This poem was not reprinted within any volume by Masefield.

Copies seen: private collection (PWE) inscribed 'Wishing you ever | such a thrilling | pack of ghost | stories round | the fire.'; private collection (PWE) inscribed 'For Eileen. [Colwell]' and signed 'John Masefield.'; Bodleian (Additional Masefield Papers 1) inscribed 'John Masefield'; Bodleian (Additional Masefield Papers 1) inscribed 'Christmas Verses'; Bodleian (MS.Eng.lett.d.475/2, f.326); Bodleian (MS.Eng.lett.d.475/2, f.327); HRHRC (PR6025 A77 P634 1900Z) not inscribed, with HRHRC note 'From the Library of John Masefield'; HRHRC (TEMP M377 NI) not inscribed

D23 THE SONG OF GASPAR THE YOUNGEST OF THE THREE KINGS [1955]

D23(a) First English edition ([1955])

Bibliographies: unrecorded

Collation: single sheet folded once (2 leaves); 126 × 101mm. (folded); [i–iv]

Pagination contents: [i] '*The Song of* | *GASPAR* | *The youngest of* | *THE THREE KINGS*'; [ii–iii] text; [iv] 'To... | *With all Best Wishes for now and later* | *From* | John & Constance Masefield'

Paper: cardboard; all edges deckle edged

Date: [1955]

Notes:

The first line reads 'I saw two towers in the light'

This verse was reprinted within *The Bluebells and other Verse* in 1961 (see A166). It is there entitled 'The Song of Gaspar The Youngest of the Three Kings' but is grouped together with two other poems. One of these comprises 'The Starry Night' (see D21).

A copy inscribed for Grace Hunter is dated, in Masefield's hand, 'Dec 24th 1955'.

Copies seen: Archives of The John Masefield Society (Peter Smith Collection) inscribed 'Joy.' and signed 'John Masefield.' with 'All blessings to your | Festival + to your | work.'; BL (Add.Mss.52735, ff.122–23) inscribed 'Sydney Cockerell.' and signed 'John Masefield.'; Bodleian (Additional Masefield Papers 1) inscribed 'Kay.' and signed 'John Masefield.'; Bodleian (MS.Eng.lett.d.475/2, f.171–172) inscribed 'Grace | Dec 24th 1955'; HRHRC (TEMP M377 NI cop.1) inscribed 'John Masefield.' and later, 'The London Library Appeal. | No 59.'; HRHRC (TEMP M377 NI cop.2) inscribed 'John Masefield.' and later, 'The London Library Appeal. | No 60.'

D24 KING EDWARD THE CONFESSOR AND HIS RING [late 1950s]

D24(a) First English edition ([late 1950s])

Bibliographies: unrecorded

Collation: single sheet folded once (2 leaves); 187 × 124mm. (folded); [i–iv]

Pagination contents: [i] 'King Edward the Confessor | and His Ring. | [text]'; [ii–iii] text (continued); [iv] '[text] | For................... | From | John & Constance Masefield | *With every Bright Wish for now and always.*'

Paper: cardboard; all edges deckle edged

Date: [late 1950s]

Notes:

The first line reads 'Of all the Saints of whom we sing'

This verse was reprinted within *The Bluebells and other Verse* in 1961 (see A166)

Copies seen: private collection (PWE) inscribed 'Eileen. [Colwell]' and signed 'John Masefield.'; private collection (BG) inscribed 'Barbara Gregory.'; Lambeth Palace Library (Bell Papers 208, ff.241–42) inscribed 'the Bishop of Chichester + | Mrs Bell.' and signed 'John Masefield.'

D25 [UNTITLED]: 'It's Christmas Eve, and dogs do bark,' [1958]

D25(a) First English edition ([1958])

Bibliographies: Handley-Taylor [see p.8]

Collation: single leaf; 88 × 137mm.; [i–ii]

Pagination contents: [i] '[text] | *With all best wishes for now and later | from John and Constance Masefield.*'; [ii] blank

Paper: cardboard; all edges trimmed

Date: [1958]

Notes:

The first line reads 'It's Christmas Eve, and dogs do bark,'

The text is printed in italics throughout.

This poem was not reprinted within any volume by Masefield.

The card is reproduced in Handley-Taylor's bibliography on page [8]. He attributes a date of 1958

Copies seen: private collection (PWE) inscribed 'For Major Kenyon.'; private collection (PWE) inscribed 'For Eileen. [Colwell]'; Bodleian (Additional Masefield Papers 1) inscribed 'John Masefield. | For Kay.';

D26 [UNTITLED]: 'It's Christmas Eve, the Kings are riding,' [late 1950s]

D26(a) First English edition ([late 1950s])

Bibliographies: unrecorded

Collation: single leaf; 85 × 136mm.; [i–ii]

Pagination contents: [i] '[text] | *With all best wishes for now and later | From John and Constance Masefield. | For...................*'; [ii] blank

Paper: cardboard; all edges trimmed

Date: late 1950s

Notes:

The first line reads "It's Christmas Eve; the Kings are riding,'

The text is printed in italics throughout.

This poem was not reprinted within any volume by Masefield.

Copies seen: private collection (PWE) inscribed 'Mr + Mrs Renier' and signed 'John Masefield.'; private collection (PWE) inscribed 'Eileen. [Colwell]'; Bodleian (Additional Masefield Papers 1) inscribed 'Kay.' [copy one]; Bodleian (Additional Masefield Papers 1) inscribed 'Kay.' [copy two]; Bodleian (MS.Eng.lett.d.475/2, f.314) inscribed 'Jill.'; Bodleian (MS.Eng.lett.d.475/2, f.315) inscribed 'Grace.'

D27 A CRY TO MUSIC [1960]

D27(a) First English edition ([1960])

Bibliographies: unrecorded

Collation: single sheet folded once (2 leaves); 115 × 139mm. (folded); [i–iv]

Pagination contents: [i] '*A Cry to Music* | [text]'; [ii–iii] text (continued); [iv] '[text (concluded)] | ....'

Paper: cardboard; all edges trimmed

Date: [1960]

Notes:

The first line reads 'Speak to us, Music, for the discord jars;'

Compare with different editions of the same poem: see D15.

This verse was reprinted within *The Bluebells and other Verse* (see A166) in 1961. It is there entitled 'A Cry to Music'.

Additional information regarding date is provided by *Keith Smith Books – John Masefield, O.M. (1878–1967) Catalogue No. 1* (Malvern: Keith Smith Books, 1994). In addition to a copy of this item (listed as number 45), Smith offered a collection of letters from Masefield to Mr and Mrs Renier as item number 85. Smith notes:

> Masefield and the Reniers (in reality Anne Renier) conducted an intense correspondence, mainly over a 4 or 5 week period early in 1960, in which he showered on them numerous published items of his work. In particular a number of the rarities included in this catalogue were sent to them.

Anne Renier apparently wrote to thank Masefield for the 'London Library poem' on 25 February. A date of 1960 is therefore suggested – consistent with the Renier collection and pre-dating volume publication.

Copies seen: The London Library inscribed 'For Anne Renier. | A special card printed (50 copies) | mainly for the London Library Appeal. | This is one of the few for friends.' and signed 'John Masefield.'; Bodleian (Additional Masefield Papers 1) inscribed 'John Masefield. | For Kay.'

D28 A MERRY CHRISTMAS [1966]

D28(a) First English edition ([1966])

Bibliographies: unrecorded

Collation: single leaf; 101 × 125mm.; [i–ii]

Pagination contents: [i] '*A Merry Christmas* [text]'; [ii] blank

Paper: cardboard; all edges trimmed

Date: [1966]

Notes:

The first lines reads 'On Christmas Eve the bakers bake'

The text is printed in italics throughout.

This poem was not reprinted within any volume by Masefield.

A single example of this card is contained within an envelope postmarked '21 DEC 1966'.

Copies seen: The Collection of Greta Stevens (sold by Sotheby's, 10 July 2003, within lot 247) inscribed 'For Greta. | John Masefield.'

It's Christmas Eve, and dogs do bark,
It snows, and the wind shifts ;
The frost will strike the Downland stark ;
Put lamp in window as a mark,
For Kings come bringing gifts.

For Eileen.

With all best wishes for now and later

from John and Constance Masefield.

D25(a)

It's Christmas Eve ; the Kings are riding,
A brightness is in some-one's sky.
The darkness has a seeming star
Giving a hope again of guiding.

To wanderers with no abiding
A hopeful May-Be is more nigh
Than deaths that must be, wrongs that are.

With all best wishes for now and later
From John and Constance Masefield.

For..........*Eileen.*..................

D26(a)

LETTERS OF JOHN
MASEFIELD TO
FLORENCE
LAMONT

edited by
Corliss Lamont
and
Lansing Lamont

Columbia University Press
New York   1979

E2(b) title-page

JOHN MASEFIELD
LETTERS TO REYNA

Edited by
William Buchan

BUCHAN & ENRIGHT, PUBLISHERS
LONDON

E3(a) title-page

JOHN MASEFIELD'S
——LETTERS——
FROM·THE·FRONT
——1915–1917——

EDITED BY
PETER VANSITTART

CONSTABLE·LONDON

E4(a) title-page

John Masefield
——————————
Letters to Margaret Bridges
(1915–1919)

edited by
DONALD STANFORD

CARCANET
in association with MidNAG

E5(a) title-page

E. Published Collections of Letters

E1 REMEMBERING JOHN MASEFIELD

E1(a) First American edition (1971)

Remembering | *John Masefield* | Corliss Lamont | *Introduction by Judith Masefield* | [publisher's device of three roses and a shield enclosing 'Fairleigh Dickinson' and a swan] | *Rutherford* [point] *Madison* [point] *Teaneck* | Fairleigh Dickinson University Press
(All width centred)

Bibliographies: Wight [unrecorded]

Collation: [A–B]¹⁶ [C]⁴ [D]⁸ [E]⁴ [F]¹⁶ (see notes); 64 leaves; 209 × 136mm.; [1–7] 8 [9] 10–17 [18–20] 21–64 [eight un-numbered pages] 65–109 [110] 111–19 [120]

Page contents: [1] half-title: 'REMEMBERING JOHN MASEFIELD'; [2] blank; [3] title-page (with additional leaf tipped-in on the verso of which is the frontispiece: 131 × 97mm., '*John Masefield in his study at Pinbury Park, Cirencester,* | *England, as painted in 1937 by Sir John Lavery, R.A.*'); [4] '© 1971 by Corliss Lamont | Library of Congress Catalogue Card Number: 73-139992 | Associated University Presses, Inc. | Cranbury, New Jersey 08512 | ISBN : 0-8386-7836-X | Printed in the United States of America | A portion of this book originally appeared in *The Literary Review,* | Summer 1970, and is here reproduced by permission of | *The Literary Review.* | OTHER BOOKS BY CORLISS LAMONT | [five titles listed]'; [5] 'CONTENTS' (five items listed with page references); [6] blank; [7]-8 'ACKNOWLEDGMENTS'; [9]-17 'INTRODUCTION | *Some Memories of John Masefield* | by Judith Masefield' ('My first clear memory dates from my third birthday. Father gave me a cuckoo clock, inhabited...'); [18] blank; [19] 'REMEMBERING JOHN MASEFIELD'; [20] blank; 21–64 text and illustrations; [-] un-numbered page with illustration figures 1 and 2; [-] un-numbered page with illustration figure 3; [-] un-numbered page with illustration figure 4; [-] un-numbered page with illustration figure 5; [-] un-numbered page with illustration figure 6; [-] un-numbered page with illustration figure 7 (part one); [-] un-numbered page with illustration figure 7 (part two); [-] un-numbered page with illustration figure 8; 65–108 text; 109 'BIBLIOGRAPHICAL NOTE'; [110] blank; 111–19 '*Index*'; [120] blank

Paper: wove paper

Running title: '*Remembering John Masefield*' (45mm.) on both verso and recto, pp.8–119

Binding: blue cloth. On spine, reading lengthways down spine from head, in silver: 'Lamont *Remembering John Masefield*'; horizontally at foot of spine: '[publisher's device of three roses and a shield enclosing 'Fairleigh Dickinson' and a swan]'. Covers: blank. All edges trimmed. Binding measurements: 216 × 138mm. (covers), 216 × 22mm. (spine). End-papers: wove paper.

Publication date: 1971

Price: $6.00

Contents:
Acknowledgments ('The Masefield letters quoted in this book are printed by the kind permission...')
Introduction | *Some Memories of John Masefield* | by Judith Masefield ('My first clear memory dates from my third...')
Remembering John Masefield ('I first met John Masefield in 1924, although for years his name had been one often...')
Bibliographical Note ('There are excellent Masefield collections in the Berg Collection of the New York Public...')
Index

Notes:
Although essentially a volume of reminiscences about Masefield, this work prints many of Masefield's letters to Corliss Lamont and his replies. The date range covered is 1925–1967 and the volume is edited by Lamont.

The eight un-numbered pages of illustrations comprise gathering [C] printed on glossy paper.

The text on p.21 commences with an italicised drop-capital. This text is the beginning of Lamont's prose.

Copies seen: private collection (PWE) signed 'Corliss Lamont, 1971' on front free end-paper

E1(b) First English edition (1972)

Remembering | *John Masefield* | Corliss Lamont | *Introduction by Judith Masefield* | Kaye & Ward [point] London
(All width centred)

Bibliographies: Wight [unrecorded]

Collation: [A–D]¹⁶; 64 leaves; 209 × 136mm.; [1–7] 8 [9] 10–17 [18–20] 21–64 [eight un-numbered illustration pages] 65–109 [110] 111–19 [120]

Page contents: [1] half-title: 'REMEMBERING JOHN MASEFIELD'; [2] frontispiece: 131 × 97mm., *'John Masefield in his study at Pinbury Park, Cirencester, | England, as painted in 1937 by Sir John Lavery, R.A.'*; [3] title-page; [4] 'First published in the United States of America | First published in Great Britain by | Kaye & Ward Ltd | 1972 | Copyright © 1971 Corliss Lamont | All Rights Reserved. No part of this publication may be re- | produced, stored in a retrieval system, or transmitted, in any | form or by any means, electronic, mechanical, photocopying, recording or otherwise, without the prior permission of the Copy- | right owner. | ISBN 0 7182 0923 0 | All enquiries and requests relevant to this title should be sent | to the publisher, Kaye & Ward Ltd, 21 New Street, London | EC2M 4NT, and not to the printer. | A portion of this book originally appeared in *The Literary Re-* | *view,* Summer 1970 (U.S.A.), and is here reproduced by per- | mission of *The Literary Review.* | Printed in the United States of America'; [5] 'CONTENTS' (five items listed with page references); [6] 'OTHER BOOKS BY CORLISS LAMONT' [five titles listed]'; [7]-8 'ACKNOWLEDGMENTS'; [9]-17 'INTRODUCTION | *Some Memories of John Masefield* | by Judith Masefield' ('My first clear memory dates from my third birthday. Father gave me a cuckoo clock, inhabited...'); [18] blank; [19] 'REMEMBERING JOHN MASEFIELD'; [20] blank; 21–64 text and illustrations; [-] un-numbered page with illustration figures 1 and 2; [-] un-numbered page with illustration figure 3; [-] un-numbered page with illustration figure 4; [-] un-numbered page with illustration figure 5; [-] un-numbered page with illustration figure 6; [-] un-numbered page with illustration figure 7 (part one); [-] un-numbered page with illustration figure 7 (part two); [-] un-numbered page with illustration figure 8; 65–108 text; 109 'BIBLIOGRAPHICAL NOTE'; [110] blank; 111–19 '*Index*'; [120] blank

Paper: wove paper

Running title: '*Remembering John Masefield*' (45mm.) on both verso and recto, pp.8–119

Binding: burgundy cloth. On spine, reading lengthways down spine from head, in gold: 'REMEMBERING JOHN MASEFIELD CORLISS LAMONT'; horizontally at foot of spine: 'KAYE | [rule] WARD'. Covers: blank. All edges trimmed. Binding measurements: 215 × 135mm. (covers), 215 × 24mm. (spine). End-papers: wove paper.

Publication date: published, according to *Whitaker's,* August 1972

Price: £1.95

Contents:
Acknowledgments ('The Masefield letters quoted in this book are printed by the kind permission...')
Introduction | *Some Memories of John Masefield* | by Judith Masefield ('My first clear memory dates from my third...')
Remembering John Masefield ('I first met John Masefield in 1924, although for years his name had been one often...')
Bibliographical Note ('There are excellent Masefield collections in the Berg Collection of the New York Public...')
Index

Notes:
The eight un-numbered pages of illustrations are included in the third gathering. There is no distinction in the gatherings between pages of illustration and pages of text.

The text on p.21 commences with an italicised drop-capital. This text is the beginning of Lamont's prose.

This edition appears to use the same setting of text as E1(a). The preliminaries and 'Acknowledgments' are different, however and are therefore from a different setting of type.

Copies seen: private collection (PWE)

E1(c)   Second American edition (1991)

REMEMBERING | JOHN MASEFIELD | [rule, 85mm.] | Corliss Lamont | INTRODUCTION BY | Judith Masefield | [circular device of ship within circular ruled border with external lettering: 'HALF-MOON FOUNDATION, INC.' and 'CORPORATE SEAL NEW YORK 1979'] | HALF-MOON FOUNDATION, INC. | The Half-Moon Foundation was formed to promote enduring | international peace, support for the United Nations, the con- | servation of our country's natural environment, and to | safeguard and extend civil liberties as guaranteed under the | Constitution and the Bill of Rights. | A Frederick Ungar Book | The Crossroad/Continuum Publishing Group | New York City
(All width centred)

Bibliographies: Wight [unrecorded]

Collation: 72 unsigned leaves bound by the 'perfect binding' process, 202 × 136mm.; [two un-numbered pages] [i–ix] x [1] 2 [3] 4 [5] 6–9 [10–14] 15–19 [20] 21–22 [23–24] 25–37 [38] 39–50 [51] 52–71 [72–73] 74–77 [78–79] 80–99 [100–101] 102–105 [106–107] 108–114 [115–17] 118–28 [129–30] [two un-numbered pages]

Page contents: [-] blank (see notes); [-] blank; [i] half-title: 'REMEMBERING JOHN MASEFIELD | [rule]'; [ii] frontispiece: 179 × 136mm., of 1912 drawing by William Strang; [iii] title-page; [iv] 'The Continuum Publishing Company | 370 Lexington Avenue, New York, NY 10017 | Produced for The Continuum Publishing Company by | Tenth Avenue Editions, Inc. | 625 Broadway, New York, NY 10012 | Revised Edition | Copyright © 1971, 1991 by Corliss Lamont | All rights reserved. No part of this book may be reproduced, | stored in a retrieval system, or transmitted, in any form or | by any means, electronic, mechanical, photocopying,

| recording, or otherwise, without the written permission | of The Continuum Publishing Company. | Library of Congress Cataloging-in-Publication Data | Lamont, Corliss, 1902– | Remembering John Masefield / Corliss Lamont; introduction by | Judith Masefield – Rev. ed. | p. cm. | "A Frederick Ungar Book." | Includes bibliographical references and index. | ISBN 0-8264-0478-2 | 1. Masefield, John, 1878–1967-Biography. 2. Lamont, Corliss, | 1902– -Friends and associates. 3. Poets, English-20th century | -Biography. I. Title. | PR6025.A77Z75 1991 | 821'.912-dc20 91-4429 | [B] CIP | Front cover: *John Masefield in his study at Pinbury Park,* | *Cirencester, England, as painted in 1937 by Sir John Lavery, R.A.* | Frontispiece: *Drawing of John Masefield by William Strang (1912).* | Printed in the United States of America | 9 8 7 6 5 4 3 2 1 99 98 97 96 95 94 93 92 91'; [v] *'Dedicated to the memory of my parents,* | *Florence Corliss Lamont* | *and* | *Thomas W. Lamont*'; [vi] blank; [vii] 'CONTENTS' (six items listed with page references); [viii] blank; [ix]-x 'ACKNOWLEDGMENTS'; [1]-9 'INTRODUCTION | [rule] | Some Memories of John Masefield | by | *Judith Masefield*' ('My first clear memory dates from my third birthday. Father gave me a cuckoo clock, inhabited...'); [10] blank; [11] 'REMEMBERING JOHN MASEFIELD | [rule]'; [12] blank; [13]-105 text and illustrations; [106] blank; [107] 'THE WESTERN HUDSON SHORE | [rule] | This poem about the Palisades of the Hudson brings back | further happy memories about Britain's Poet Laureate. He dedi- | cated the poem "to the noble memory of Thomas W. Lamont and | his wife, Florence Corliss Lamont," who were my parents. | [new paragraph] The poem originates in the fact that in his early manhood John | Masefield came to the United States and worked for two years | in a carpet factory on the east bank of the Hudson River. | Corliss Lamont'; 108–114 text of 'The Western Hudson Shore'; [115] 'BIBLIOGRAPHICAL NOTE'; [116] blank; [117]-128 'INDEX'; [129–30] 'BOOKS BY CORLISS LAMONT' and 'BOOKS EDITED BY CORLISS LAMONT'; [-] blank (see notes); [-] blank

Paper: wove paper

Running title: 'REMEMBERING JOHN MASEFIELD [58mm.] | [rule, 64mm.]' on both verso and recto, pp. 2–128

Binding: printed wrappers. On spine, reading lengthways down spine from head: 'REMEMBERING JOHN MASEFIELD LAMONT CROSSROAD/UNGAR'. On upper wrapper: 'REMEMBERING [in red] | JOHN MASEFIELD [in red] | Corliss Lamont [in red]' printed over colour reproduction of 1937 Lavery portrait (enclosed by ruled border: 181 × 115mm.) all within red and white marbled effect border with four squares in red at each corner which intercept colour portrait. On lower wrapper: '[photograph of Lamont] DR. CORLISS LAMONT | was a personal friend of Poet | Laureate John Masefield | (1878–1967), one of the great | English poets of the twentieth | century. | [new paragraph] In this book, Lamont has | skillfully assembled and edited | forty years worth of the poet's | letters to produce an intimate | and detailed portrait of both | the public and private man. | [new paragraph] Born in Englewood, New Jersey in 1902, Dr. Lamont graduated first | from Phillips Exeter Academy in 1920, then magna cum laude from | Harvard University in 1924. He did graduate work at Oxford and at | Columbia, where he received his Ph.D. in philosophy in 1932. | [new paragraph] He was a director of the American Civil Liberties Union from 1932 | to 1954, and is currently chairman of the National Emergency Civil | Liberties Committee. A leading proponent of the individual's rights | under the Constitution, he has won famous court decisions over | Senator Joseph McCarthy, the CIA, and in 1965 a Supreme Court | ruling against censorship of incoming mail by the U.S. Postmaster | General. | [new paragraph] Dr. Lamont has long been associated with Humanism, and | authored the standard text on the subject, *The Philosophy of* | *Humanism,* in 1949. He taught at Columbia, Cornell, and Harvard | Universities, and at the New School for Social Research. Corliss | Lamont is currently honorary president of the American Humanist | Association. | HALF-MOON FOUNDATION, INC. | 575 Madison Avenue, Suite 106, New York, NY 10022' printed over cream panel (enclosed by ruled border: 181 × 115mm.) all within red and white marbled effect border (with '$12.95 ISBN:0-8264-04728' on cream panel within border at foot of cover) with four squares in red at each corner which intercept cream panel. (The first two paragraphs of text are positioned to the right of the photograph). All edges trimmed. Binding measurements: 202 × 136mm. (wrappers), 202 × 9mm. (spine).

Publication date: 1991

Price: $12.95

Contents:
Acknowledgments ('The Masefield letters quoted in this book are printed by the kind permission...')
Introduction | *Some Memories of John Masefield* by Judith Masefield ('My first clear memory dates from my third...')
Remembering John Masefield ('I first met John Masefield in 1924, although for years his name had been one often...')
The Western Hudson Shore [introduction] ('This poem about the Palisades of the Hudson brings back further happy...')
The Western Hudson Shore [text] ('In a long life's first independent day,')
Bibliographical Note ('There are excellent Masefield collections in the Berg Collection of the New York Public...')
Index

Notes:
There are single leaves at the front and rear of the volume excluded from the pagination. These leaves, on the same paper stock as the rest of the volume, are printed grey. They may be intended as end-papers but are not noted as such due to the 'perfect binding' and paperback status of this volume.

Textually, this volume differs from E1(a) and E1(b) by the inclusion of the poem 'The Western Hudson Shore'. See A167, B535 and B575.

The text is entirely reset for this edition.

Illustrations appear throughout the volume. They are the same as in the previous editions.

Copies seen: private collection (PWE)

E2 LETTERS OF JOHN MASEFIELD TO FLORENCE LAMONT   1979

E2(a) First English edition (1979)

LETTERS OF JOHN | MASEFIELD TO | FLORENCE | LAMONT | *edited by* | Corliss Lamont | and | Lansing Lamont | M [in outline]
(All left justified)

Bibliographies: Wight 128

Collation: [A]⁴ [B-K]¹⁶ (J not used); 148 leaves; 213 × 136mm.; [i–xii] 1–288; illustrations (on glossy paper) tipped-in on p.1 (these comprise two conjugate leaves which are not included in leaf count)

Page contents: [i] half-title: 'LETTERS OF JOHN MASEFIELD TO FLORENCE LAMONT'; [ii] blank; [iii] title-page; [iv] 'John Masefield texts © 1979 the Estate of John Masefield | Introduction, editorial matter and selection © 1979 | Corliss Lamont and Lansing Lamont | All rights reserved. No part of this publication may be | reproduced or transmitted, in any form or by any means, | without permission | *First published 1979 by* | THE MACMILLAN PRESS LTD | *London and Basingstoke* | *Associated companies in Delhi* | *Dublin Hong Kong Johannesburg Lagos* | *Melbourne New York Singapore Tokyo* | *Filmset in Great Britain by* | *Vantage Photosetting Co. Ltd, Southampton and London* | *Printed in Great Britain by* | UNWIN BROTHERS LTD | *The Gresham Press* | *Old Woking, Surrey* | [rule] | British Library Cataloguing in Publication Data | [rule] | Masefield, John | Letters of John Masefield to Florence Lamont | 1. Masefield, John-Correspondence | 2. Lamont, Florence | I. Lamont, Florence II. Lamont, Corliss | III. Lamont, Lansing | 821'.9'12 PR6025.A77Z/ | ISBN 0-333-25755-3 | [rule] | *This book is sold subject* | *to the standard conditions* | *of the Net Book Agreement*'; [v] '*To the Masefields and the Lamonts*'; [vi] blank; [vii] 'CONTENTS' (four sections listed with page references); [viii] 'Acknowledgements' [ix] '[black and white photograph] | PLATE 1 *John Masefield with the family cat, Mickey, about 1949*'; [x] '[black and white photograph] | PLATE 2 *Florence Lamont in her summer flower garden at North* | *Haven, Maine, about 1928*'; [xi] '[black and white illustration] | PLATE 3 *Oil portrait of John Masefield by Sir John Lavery, 1937*'; [xii] '[illustration] | PLATE 4 *Flier used by the Hill Players, producers of plays staged* | *by Masefield at Boar's Hill*'; 1–8 'Introduction' ('This House of Books set open here,') (signed, 'C.L.' and 'L.L.'); 9–279 'The Letters'; 280–88 'Index'

Paper: wove paper

Running title: '*Letters of John Masefield to Florence Lamont*' (65mm.) on verso; '*Introduction*' (17mm.), '*The Letters*' (16mm.) or '*Index*' (8mm.) on recto, pp.2–288

Binding: light brown cloth. On spine, reading lengthways down spine from head, in gold: 'LAMONT | and | LAMONT [at head of spine] [vertical rule] Letters of John Masefield | to Florence Lamont'; horizontally at foot of spine: publisher's device of 'M'. Covers: blank. All edges trimmed. Binding measurements: 222 × 137mm. (covers), 222 × 36mm. (spine). End-papers: brown wove paper.

Publication date: published, according to *Whitaker's*, February 1980

Price: £20.00

Contents:
Acknowledgements ('The letters from John Masefield quoted in this book are printed by the kind permission...')
Introduction ('This House of Books set open here, | May it bring light, may it bring...')
The Letters ('*On 28 February 1916, while on a wartime visit to America on behalf of His Majesty's...*')
Index

Notes:
Masefield first met Florence Lamont (Mrs Thomas Lamont) in America on 28 February 1916 after he gave a speech on 'The Tragic Drama'. Masefield's friendship with the Lamont family lasted until the end of his life (see E1 for Corliss Lamont's perspective). The date range is 1916–1952 (the year of Florence Lamont's death). The volume is edited by both Corliss and Lansing Lamont.

The original letters are located in the Houghton Library, Harvard University. As stated in the introduction this volume is merely a selection of about three hundred letters from a total of more than two thousand.

Whitaker's Cumulative Book List includes this volume as being by John Mansfield [*sic*]. It is included under 'Lamont' and 'Mansfield' entries incorrectly.

Copies seen: ULL (3 YP M35F 979)

E2(b) First American edition (1979)

LETTERS OF JOHN | MASEFIELD TO | FLORENCE | LAMONT | *edited by* | Corliss Lamont | and | Lansing Lamont | Columbia University Press | New York 1979
(All left justified)

Bibliographies: Wight 128a

Collation: [A]⁴ [B-K]¹⁶ (J not used); 148 leaves; 213 × 136mm.; [i–xii] 1–288; illustrations (on glossy paper) tipped-in on p.1 (these comprise two conjugate leaves which are not included in leaf count)

Page contents: [i] half-title: 'LETTERS OF JOHN MASEFIELD TO FLORENCE LAMONT'; [ii] blank; [iii] title-page; [iv] 'John Masefield texts copyright © 1979 | The Estate of John Masefield | Introduction, editorial matter, and selection copyright © 1979 | Corliss Lamont and Lansing Lamont | All rights reserved | *Printed in Great Britain* | Library of Congress Cataloging in Publication Data | Masefield, John, 1878–1967. | Letters of John Masefield to Florence Lamont. | 1. Masefield, John, 1878–1967- Correspondence. | 2. Lamont, Florence Haskell Corliss, 1873–1952. | 3. Poets, English-20th century-Correspondence. | I. Lamont, Florence Haskell Corliss, 1873–1952. | II. Lamont, Corliss, 1902– III. Lamont, Lansing, 1930– | IV. Title. | PR6025.A77Z546 1979 821'.9'1209 [B] 78-27134 | ISBN 0-231-04706-1'; [v] '*To the Masefields and the Lamonts*'; [vi] blank; [vii] 'CONTENTS' (four sections listed with page references); [viii] 'Acknowledgements'; [ix] '[black and white photograph] | PLATE 1 *John Masefield with the family cat, Mickey, about 1949*'; [x] '[black and white photograph] | PLATE 2 *Florence Lamont in her summer flower garden at North* | *Haven, Maine, about 1928*'; [xi] '[black and white illustration] | PLATE 3 *Oil portrait of John Masefield by Sir John Lavery, 1937*'; [xii] '[illustration] | PLATE 4 *Flier used by the Hill Players, producers of plays staged* | *by Masefield at Boar's Hill*'; 1–8 'Introduction' ('This House of Books set open here,') (signed, 'C.L.' and 'L.L.'); 9–279 'The Letters'; 280–88 'Index'

Paper: wove paper

Running title: '*Letters of John Masefield to Florence Lamont*' (65mm.) on verso; '*Introduction*' (17mm.), '*The Letters*' (16mm.) or '*Index*' (8mm.) on recto, pp.2–288

Binding: light brown cloth. On spine, reading lengthways down spine from head, in gold: 'LAMONT | and | LAMONT [at head of spine] [vertical rule] Letters of John Masefield | to Florence Lamont'; horizontally at foot of spine: 'COLUMBIA'. Covers: blank. All edges trimmed. Binding measurements: 222 × 137mm. (covers), 222 × 36mm. (spine). End-papers: brown wove paper.

Publication date: 1979

Price: unknown

Contents:
as for E2(a)

Notes:
Wight numbers this American edition 128a, thus placing it after the English edition.

The publishing agreement for this title between The Estate of John Masefield and Columbia University Press was dated 22 August 1978 (see Archives of The Society of Authors).

Copies seen: private collection (PWE) includes bookplate: '*With the compliments of* | *the editors* | *Corliss and Lansing Lamont* | COLUMBIA UNIVERSITY PRESS'

E3 LETTERS TO REYNA   1983

E3(a) First English edition (1983)

JOHN MASEFIELD | *LETTERS TO REYNA* | *Edited by* | *William Buchan* | [ornament] | [publisher's device of 'B' and 'E'] | BUCHAN & ENRIGHT, PUBLISHERS | LONDON
(All width centred)

Collation: [A–Q]¹⁶ (J not used); 256 leaves; 232 × 150mm.; [1–6] 7–509 [510–12]

Page contents: [1] half-title: 'JOHN MASEFIELD: *LETTERS TO REYNA*'; [2] blank; [3] title-page; [4] 'First published in 1983 by | Buchan & Enright, Publishers, | Limited | 53 Fleet Street, London | EC4Y 1BE | ISBN 0 907675 14 X | John Masefield's letters and other | writings Copyright © 1983 | The Trustees of the Estate of | John Masefield | Textual notes Copyright © 1983 | Audrey Napier-Smith and | William Buchan | Prologue Copyright © 1983 | Audrey Napier-Smith | Introduction and Epilogue | Copyright © 1983 | William Buchan | Text designed by T. M. Jaques FSIAD | and Jo Angell | Decorated with John Masefield's | own sketches, which accompanied | some of his letters to "Reyna". | All rights reserved. No part of this | publication may be reproduced, | stored in a retrieval system, or | transmitted, in any form or by | any means, electronic, | mechanical, photocopying, | recording, or otherwise, without | the prior permission in writing of | the publishers. | Typeset by CentraCet, Saffron Walden | Set in linotron baskerville | Printed and bound in Great Britain by | The Pitman Press, Bath'; [5] 'CONTENTS' (six sections listed (with 16 sub-sections within one section) with page references); [6] blank; 7–35 'INTRODUCTION' ('A published book of letters, of numerous, long, intimate letters...') (signed, 'William Buchan') (facsimile signature); 36–40 'PROLOGUE | BY | "REYNA"' ('The extracts in this book are all taken from the many letters which John Masefield...') (signed, 'Audrey Napier-Smith') (facsimile signature); 41–498 text; 499 'FINALE' ('So, on the "so memorable day", the fifteenth anniversary of our first meeting...') (signed, 'AUDREY NAPIER-SMITH'); 500–504 'EDITOR'S EPILOGUE' ('There is a sadness about John Masefield's last letters to Reyna...') (unsigned); 505–509 'INDEX' (at foot of p.509: '*Index compiled by Peter Tickler.*'); [510–12] blank

Paper: wove paper

Running title: 'LETTERS TO REYNA' (28mm.) on verso; recto title comprises section title, pp.2–509

Binding: blue cloth. On spine, in gold: 'John | Masefield | Letters | to Reyna | [ornament] | *Edited by* | *William Buchan* | [publisher's device of 'B' and 'E']'. Covers: blank. All edges trimmed. Binding measurements: 240 × 153mm. (covers), 240 × 50mm. (spine). End-papers: wove paper.

Publication date: published, according to *Whitaker's*, October 1983

Price: £14.95 (see notes)

Contents:
Introduction ('A published book of letters, of numerous, long, intimate letters...')
Prologue by "Reyna" ('The extracts in this book are all taken from the many letters which John Masefield...')
[The Letters] ('1952 | [ornament] | Burcote Brook | Abingdon | I | Dear Mrs [*sic*] Napier-Smith...')
Finale ('So, on the "so memorable day", the fifteenth anniversary of our first meeting...')
Editor's Epilogue ('There is a sadness about John Masefield's last letters to Reyna...')
Index

Notes:
During a correspondence of fifteen years from 1952 until 1967, Masefield sent 1285 letters to Audrey Napier-Smith, a musician in the Hallé Orchestra. This volume presents selections from Masefield's letters, edited by William Buchan.

Audrey Napier-Smith writes in her prologue:

> In selecting these letters I have taken great care that what is printed in this book is, word for word, Masefield's writing. I have made deletions – but only those parts of his letters that I considered of no interest to others: the formal, the trivial, the technical, and the repetitions, which, in fifteen years of frequent and long letters, were bound to occur. As the letters came to me – and often, when the Hallé was on tour, they followed me from country to country – so in that order they appear here; JM, however, never dated his letters, and although I, fortunately, numbered them as they arrived, some slight confusion was inevitable – not helped by the fact that he was apt to dart from one topic to another only to turn back later: a characteristic which adds to the letters a charming immediacy of a lively mind.

The dust-jacket for this edition includes the price of £14.95. *Whitaker's* notes a price of £12.95 which is, presumably, an error.

A publishing agreement for this title between Buchan, Napier-Smith and the publishers, Buchan and Enright was dated 12 August 1982. A further agreement between the publishers and The Society of Authors was dated 22 August 1983 (see Archives of The Society of Authors).

Copies seen: private collection (PWE)

E3(b) First American edition (1983)

There was no American publication of this title. However, it appears that Salem House (a member of the Merrimack Publishers' Circle) imported copies for sale at $22.00. These copies were given an oval silver sticker (21 × 40mm.) on the dust-jacket lower wrapper on which: '[publisher's device] | *Salem House* | Member of Merrimack Publishers' Circle'. Additionally, a price sticker (reading 'MPC | $22.00') was placed over the English price on the upper inside flap of the dust-jacket.

E4 JOHN MASEFIELD'S LETTERS FROM THE FRONT 1915–1917 1984

E4(a) First English edition (1984)

JOHN MASEFIELD'S | [rule, 19mm.]LETTERS[rule, 19mm.] | FROM[point]THE[point]FRONT | [rule, 20mm.]1915–1917[rule, 20mm.] | EDITED BY | PETER VANSITTART | CONSTABLE[point]LONDON
(All width centred)

Bibliographies: Wight 130

Collation: [A-K]¹⁶ (J not used); 160 leaves; 232 × 152mm.; [i–x] [1] 2–42 [43–45] 46–95 [96–99] 100–109 [110–13] 114–95 [196–99] 200–293 [294] 295–97 [298] 299 [300–301] 302–307 [308–310]

Page contents: [i] half-title: 'JOHN MASEFIELD'S | LETTERS FROM THE FRONT'; [ii] frontispiece: 143 × 119mm., of facsimile of letter dated 29 March 1915; [iii] title-page; [iv] 'First published in Great Britain 1984 | by Constable and Company Limited | 10 Orange Street London WC2H 7EG | Letters and quotations from John Masefield's work | Copyright © 1984 by The Estate of John Masefield | Editorial matter copyright © 1984 by Peter Vansittart | Set in Linotron Plantin by | Rowland Phototypesetting Limited | Bury St Edmunds, Suffolk | Printed in Great Britain by | St Edmundsbury Press | Bury St Edmunds, Suffolk | British Library cataloguing in publication data | Masefield, John | John Masefield's letters from the front | 1915–1917 | 1. World War, 1914–1918 – Campaigns – | Western 2. World War, 1914–1918 – | Personal narratives, British | I. Title II. Vansittart, Peter | 940.4'144'0924 0544 | ISBN 0-09-465860-9'; [v] 'TO JUDITH MASEFIELD | LIVERPOOL 1890 | [text] | JOHN MASEFIELD'; [vi] blank; [vii] 'Acknowledgments | The Publishers would very much like to thank the following for their | help in preparing this book: Judith Masefield and Jack Masefield, Mrs | Roma Woodnutt of The Society of Authors, Professor Corliss Lamont, | and Mr Kenneth A. Lohf, Librarian for Rare Books and Manuscripts at | Columbia University, New York, who now own the 1917 letters; and | finally Mr Roderick Soddaby, Keeper of Documents at The Imperial | War Museum. | [new paragraph] We should also like to thank the following publishers for use of short | extracts: Messrs William Heinemann Ltd for Masefield's *Liverpool | 1890*, *Grace before Ploughing*, *The Conway*, *New Chum*, *Dauber*, *In the | Mill*, *A Book of Both Sorts*, *Gallipoli*, *The Old Front Line*, *The Everlast- | ing Mercy* and *Gautama the Enlightened*; Messrs Buchan & Enright for | Masefield's *Letters to Reyna* and their forthcoming *Letters to*

Margaret | Bridges; Oxford University Press Ltd for Constance Babington-Smith's | *John Masefield*; The Bodley Head for Marjorie Fisher's *John Masefield*, | Messrs Macmillan & Co Ltd for Masefield's *Letters to Florence Lamont*, | finally Messrs Faber & Faber Ltd for Ezra Pound's 'Hugh Selwyn | Mauberley'.'; [viii] blank; [ix] 'Contents' (eight sections listed with page references); [x] blank; [1]–42 'Introduction' ('John Masefield was born in 1878, at Ledbury, Herefordshire, land of orchards, waters...'); [43] divisional title: 'Part One | Letters from France, 1915 | (Letters 1 to 36, 1 March to 11 April)'; [44] blank; [45]-95 text of part one; [96] blank; [97] divisional title: 'Part Two | Letters from America, 1916 | (Letters January to July 1916) | 'I'm afraid my early years in America | made me, in all sorts of ways, American. It | is only now that I see how English I am in | some ways.''; [98] blank; [99]–109 text of part two; [110] blank; [111] divisional title: 'Part Three | Letters from France, 1916 | (Letters 37 to 97, 29 August to 23 October)'; [112] blank; [113]-195 text of part three; [196] blank; [197] divisional title: 'Part Four | Letters from France, 1917 | (Letters 98 to 167, 26 February to 23 May)'; [198] blank; [199]-293 text of part four; [294]-297 'Appendix' ('The first result of Masefield's Somme explorations was *The Old Front Line* (1917).'; [298]-299 'Bibliography'; [300] blank; [301]-307 'Index'; [308–310] blank

Paper: wove paper

Running title: 'Introduction [17mm.] | [rule, 114mm.]' on both verso and recto, pp.2–42; 'Letters from France, 1915 [37mm.] | [rule, 114mm.]' on both verso and recto, pp.46–95; 'Letters from America [30mm.] | [rule, 114mm.]' on both verso and recto, pp.100–109; 'Letters from France, 1916' [37mm.] | [rule, 114mm.]' on both verso and recto, pp.114–95; 'Letters from France, 1917 [37mm.] | [rule, 114mm.]' on both verso and recto, pp.200–293; 'Appendix [14mm.] | [rule, 114mm.]' on both verso and recto, pp.295–97; 'Bibliography [19mm.] | [rule, 114mm.]' on verso, p.299; and 'Index [8mm.] | [rule, 114mm.]' on both verso and recto, pp.302–307

Binding: black cloth. On spine, in gold: 'John | Masefield's LETTERS | FROM | THE | FRONT | 1915– | 1917 | [rule] | Edited by | Peter | Vansittart [all on red panel within ruled border in gold: 64 × 22mm.] | CONSTABLE' (all width centred). Covers: blank. Top edge stained red, others trimmed. Binding measurements: 240 × 154mm. (covers), 240 × 36mm. (spine). End-papers: wove paper.

Publication date: published, according to *Whitaker's*, November 1984

Price: £12.50

Contents:

Liverpool 1890
        ('Gray sea dim, smoke-blowing, hammer-racket, sirens')
Acknowledgments
        ('The Publishers would very much like to thank the following for their help...')
Introduction
        ('John Masefield was born in 1878, at Ledbury, Herefordshire, land of orchards, waters...')
Part One | Letters from France, 1915 | (Letters 1 to 36, 1 March to 11 April)
        ('Within five weeks of the murder of the Archduke Franz Ferdinand at Sarajevo...')
Part Two | Letters from America, 1916 | (Letters January to July 1916)
        ('John Masefield owed much to America, to his early adventures there, and the impact...')
Part Three | Letters from France, 1916 | (Letters 37 to 97, 29 August to 23 October)
        ('These letters were written to Mrs Masefield while inspecting the American medical services...')
Part Four | Letters from France, 1917 | (Letters 98 to 167, 26 February to 23 May)
        ('In February 1917, Masefield began ranging the Somme lands, where the battle was...')
Appendix
        ('The first result of Masefield's Somme explorations was *The Old Front Line* (1917).')
        (Includes extract from *The Old Front Line* and unattributed poem XXIV from *Lollingdon Downs, and other poems, with sonnets* ('Here the legion halted, here the ranks were broken,') and unattributed extract from '"All Ye That Pass By"' from *Salt-Water Ballads* ('Faces – passionate faces – of men I may not know,'))
Bibliography
Index

Notes:

167 letters written by Masefield from the Western Front to his wife are presented here, in addition to brief quotation from letters sent from America in 1916. Masefield served as a medical orderly for the Red Cross, made a propaganda tour of America and visited the Somme battlefield (in preparation for *The Old Front Line* and *The Battle of the Somme*).

Vansittart notes his editorial practice on p.48:

I have kept strictly to the letters as they were written, retaining inconsistencies of spelling, he seldom bothered with French accents, though I have omitted a few passages of wholly private interest.

The gold ruled border on the spine is printed over the red panel.

A publishing agreement for this title was dated 1 December 1983 (see Archives of The Society of Authors).

Copies seen: private collection (PWE)

E4(b) First American edition (1985)

JOHN MASEFIELD'S | [rule, 19mm.]LETTERS[rule, 19mm.] | FROM[point]THE[point]FRONT | [rule, 20mm.]1915–1917[rule, 20mm.] | EDITED BY | PETER VANSITTART | [publisher's device of 'G' and tree within partial ruled border: 10 × 11mm.] | A GROLIER COMPANY | FRANKLIN WATTS | NEW YORK | 1985
(All width centred)

Bibliographies: Wight [noted on p.215]

Collation: [A–K]¹⁶ (J not used); 160 leaves; 232 × 152mm.; [i–x] [1] 2–42 [43–45] 46–95 [96–99] 100–109 [110–13] 114–95 [196–99] 200–293 [294] 295–97 [298] 299 [300–301] 302–307 [308–310]

Page contents: [i] half-title: 'JOHN MASEFIELD'S | LETTERS FROM THE FRONT'; [ii] frontispiece: 143 × 119mm., of facsimile of letter dated 29 March 1915; [iii] title-page; [iv] 'Copyright © 1984 by The Estate of John Masefield | Editorial matter copyright © 1984 by Peter Vansittart | First published in Great Britain 1984 by | Constable and Company Limited | First United States publication 1985 by Franklin Watts, Inc., | 387 Park Avenue South, New York, NY 10016 | All rights reserved. No part of this publication may be reproduced, stored in | a retrieval system, or transmitted, in any form or by any means, electronic, | mechanical, photocopying, recording, or otherwise, without the prior permission | of the publisher. | ISBN 0-531-09776-5 | Library of Congress Catalog Card Number 84-51644 | Printed in Great Britain'; [v] 'TO JUDITH MASEFIELD | LIVERPOOL 1890 | [text] | JOHN MASEFIELD'; [vi] blank; [vii] 'Acknowledgments | The Publishers would very much like to thank the following for their | help in preparing this book: Judith Masefield and Jack Masefield, Mrs | Roma Woodnutt of The Society of Authors, Professor Corliss Lamont, | and Mr Kenneth A. Lohf, Librarian for Rare Books and Manuscripts at | Columbia University, New York, who now own the 1917 letters; and | finally Mr Roderick Soddaby, Keeper of Documents at The Imperial | War Museum. | [new paragraph] We should also like to thank the following publishers for use of short | extracts: Messrs William Heinemann Ltd for Masefield's *Liverpool* | *1890, Grace before Ploughing, The Conway, New Chum, Dauber, In the* | *Mill, A Book of Both Sorts, Gallipoli, The Old Front Line, The Everlast-* | *ing Mercy* and *Gautama the Enlightened*; Messrs Buchan & Enright for | Masefield's *Letters to Reyna* and their forthcoming *Letters to Margaret* | *Bridges*; Oxford University Press Ltd for Constance Babington-Smith's | *John Masefield*; The Bodley Head for Marjorie Fisher's *John Masefield*; | Messrs Macmillan & Co Ltd for Masefield's *Letters to Florence Lamont*; | finally Messrs Faber & Faber Ltd for Ezra Pound's 'Hugh Selwyn | Mauberley'.'; [viii] blank; [ix] 'Contents' (eight sections listed with page references); [x] blank; [1]-42 'Introduction' ('John Masefield was born in 1878, at Ledbury, Herefordshire, land of orchards, waters...'); [43] divisional title: 'Part One | Letters from France, 1915 | (Letters 1 to 36, 1 March to 11 April)'; [44] blank; [45]-95 text of part one; [96] blank; [97] divisional title: 'Part Two | Letters from America, 1916 | (Letters January to July 1916)' | 'I'm afraid my early years in America | made me, in all sorts of ways, American. It | is only now that I see how English I am in | some ways.'; [98] blank; [99]-109 text of part two; [110] blank; [111] divisional title: 'Part Three | Letters from France, 1916 | (Letters 37 to 97, 29 August to 23 October)'; [112] blank; [113]-195 text of part three; [196] blank; [197] divisional title: 'Part Four | Letters from France, 1917 | (Letters 98 to 167, 26 February to 23 May)'; [198] blank; [199]-293 text of part four; [294]-297 'Appendix' ('The first result of Masefield's Somme explorations was *The Old Front Line* (1917).'); [298]-299 'Bibliography'; [300] blank; [301]-307 'Index'; [308–310] blank

Paper: wove paper

Running title: 'Introduction [17mm.] | [rule, 114mm.]' on both verso and recto, pp.2–42; '*Letters from France, 1915* [37mm.] | [rule, 114mm.]' on both verso and recto, pp.46–95; '*Letters from America* [30mm.] | [rule, 114mm.]' on both verso and recto, pp.100–109; '*Letters from France, 1916*' [37mm.] | [rule, 114mm.]' on both verso and recto, pp.114–95; '*Letters from France, 1917* [37mm.] | [rule, 114mm.]' on both verso and recto, pp.200–293; '*Appendix* [14mm.] | [rule, 114mm.]' on both verso and recto, pp.295–97; '*Bibliography* [19mm.] | [rule, 114mm.]' on verso, p.299; and '*Index* [8mm.] | [rule, 114mm.]' on both verso and recto, pp.302–307

Binding: black cloth. On spine, in gold: 'John | Masefield's | LETTERS | FROM | THE | FRONT | 1915– | 1917 | [rule] | Edited by | Peter | Vansittart [all on red panel within ruled border in gold: 64 × 22mm.] | [publisher's device including '*Watts*']' (all width centred). Covers: blank. Top edge stained red, others trimmed. Binding measurements: 240 × 154mm. (covers), 240 × 36mm. (spine). End-papers: wove paper.

Publication date: published, according to publisher's advance publicity, March 1985

Price: $18.95

Contents:
as for E4(a)

Notes:
This American edition, printed in Great Britain, uses the same setting of text as E4(a). Title-page, publication details on p.[iv] and binding show only minor differences.

Note that the gold ruled border on the spine is printed over the red panel.

Copies seen: private collection (PWE); Columbia University Libraries (Special Collections PR6025.A77.Z48.1985)

E5 LETTERS TO MARGARET BRIDGES

1984

E5(a) First English edition (1984)

John Masefield | [rule, 52mm.] | Letters to Margaret Bridges | (1915–1919) | *edited by* | *DONALD STANFORD* | [publisher's device] | CARCANET | in association with MidNAG
(All width centred)

Bibliographies: Wight 131

Collation: [A–D]¹⁶; 64 leaves; 213 × 134mm.; [i–ii] [1–7] 8–15 [16–17] 18–21 [22] 23–80 [81] 82–107 [108] 109–111 [112] 113–22 [123–26]

Page contents: [i] half-title: 'Letters to Margaret Bridges | (1915–1919)'; [ii] frontispiece photographs of John Masefield and Margaret Bridges; [1] title-page; [2] 'First published in Great Britain 1984 | by the Carcanet Press | 208 Corn Exchange Building, Manchester M4 3BQ | in association with Mid Northumberland Arts Group | Town Hall, Ashington, Northumberland | © 1984 John Masefield's letters and poems: The Literary Estate of John Masefield | © 1984 Margaret Bridges' letters: | The Lord Bridges | © 1984 Introduction and Notes: | Donald E. Stanford | *Armistice* © 1984 Carcanet Press Ltd | Masefield, John | Letters to Margaret Bridges (1915–1919). | 1. Masefield, John-Biography 2. Poets, | English-20th century-Biography | I. Title II. Stanford, Donald | 821'.912 PR6025.A77Z/ | ISBN 0 85635 477 5/ISBN 0 904790 37 1 | The Publishers acknowledge financial assistance | from the Arts Council of Great Britain | Typesetting by Paragon Photoset, Aylesbury | Printed in Great Britain by | Short Run Press Ltd, Exeter'; [3–4] 'Contents' ('Introduction', *August, 1914*' and four years of letters noted in addition to 'Notes' and 'Acknowledgements') also 'Illustrations' (seven illustrations listed); [5] 'For Maryanna'; [6] blank; [7-12 'Introduction' ('These hitherto unpublished letters of the poet John Masefield (1878–1967) to Margaret Bridges...') (signed, 'DONALD E. STANFORD'); 13–15 '*August, 1914*' ('How still this quiet cornfield is to-night!'); [16] blank; [17]-111 text; [112]-122 'Notes'; [123] 'Acknowledgements' ('Acknowledgements are due to the Society of Authors on behalf | of the Masefield Estate for permission to publish John Masefield's | letters and some of the poems; to Messrs Heinemann for other | poems; to Lord Bridges for Margaret Bridges' letters; also to the | *Southern Review*, in which Elizabeth Daryush's poem 'Armistice' | first appeared | [new paragraph] The illustrations of Margaret and Edward Bridges are reproduced | by kind permission of Lord Bridges; the frontispiece portrait of | John Masefield was published in *Literary Digest*, 5 February 1916; | the battlefield photographs were published in *Harper's Monthly* | *Magazine*, May 1917.'); [124–26] blank

Paper: wove paper

Running title: running titles comprise the year of the letters

Binding: black cloth. On spine, reading lengthways down spine from head in gold: 'JOHN MASEFIELD Letters to Margaret Bridges CARCANET'; horizontally at foot of spine: publisher's device. Covers: blank. All edges trimmed. Binding measurements: 222 × 136mm. (covers), 222 × 23mm. (spine). End-papers: black wove paper.

Publication date: published, according to *Whitaker's*, November 1984

Price: £6.95

Contents:

Introduction ('These hitherto unpublished letters of the poet John Masefield (1878–1967) to Margaret Bridges...')
August, 1914 ('How still this quiet cornfield is to-night!')
    from Philip the King and other poems
[1915 letters]
[1917 letters]
Letters from America, 1918
Armistice ('On this day of longed-for peace') (signed, 'Elizabeth Daryush')
[1919 letters]
Notes
Acknowledgements ('Acknowledgements are due to the Society of Authors on behalf of the Masefield Estate...')

Within the sections in which the texts of the letters are printed, the following Masefield poems are included:

I. ('So I have known this life,')
    from Lollingdon Downs and other poems, with sonnets
II. ('O wretched man, that, for a little mile,')
    from Lollingdon Downs and other poems, with sonnets
III. ('You are the link which binds us each to each.')
    from Lollingdon Downs and other poems, with sonnets
[Untitled Sonnet] ('Here, where we stood together, we three men,')
    from Good Friday and other Poems
[Untitled Sonnet] ('I saw her like a shadow on the sky')
    from Good Friday and other Poems
[Untitled Sonnet] ('Time being an instant in eternity,')
    from Good Friday and other Poems

The Downland ('Night is on the downland, on the lovely moorland,')
  from Sonnets and Poems
The Blacksmith ('The blacksmith in his sparky forge')
  from Lollingdon Downs and other poems, with sonnets
We Danced ('We danced away care till the fiddler's eyes blinked,')
  from Lollingdon Downs and other poems, with sonnets

Notes:

A volume of correspondence between Masefield and the daughter of Robert Bridges. Over sixty of Masefield's letters are printed in addition to some of Margaret Bridges' replies. The volume is edited by Donald Stanford (editor of A175).

The original Masefield letters are located in the Bridges Papers in the Bodleian Library, Oxford. The original Bridges letters are located at the HRHRC. Not all extant letters from Masefield to Margaret Bridges are included in the volume.

Copies seen: private collection (PWE); UCL (English Q99 MAS)

E6 BRANGWEN [–] THE POET AND THE DANCER   1988

E6(a) *First English edition (1988)*

Brangwen | The Poet and the Dancer | A story based on letters from the Poet Laureate | JOHN MASEFIELD | Compiled and edited by | John Gregory | [publisher's device of 'B' and 'G' within double ruled border: 10 × 17mm.] | The Book Guild Ltd. | Sussex, England
(All width centred)

Bibliographies: Wight 132

Collation: 104 unsigned leaves bound by the 'perfect binding' process; 233 × 151mm.; [1–11] 12–14 [15] 16–19 [20] 21–26 [27] 28–29 [30] 31–36 [37] 38–39 [40] 41–47 [48–49] 50–57 [58] 59–71 [72] 73–87 [88] 89 [90–92] 93–106 [107] 108–118 [119] 120–38 [139–40] 141–60 [161–62] 163–81 [182] 183–89 [190–91] 192–93 [194] 195–203 [204] 205–207 [208]

Pagination contents: [1] half-title: 'Brangwen | The Poet and the Dancer'; [2] blank; [3] title-page; [4] 'This book is sold subject to the condition that it shall not, by way | of trade or otherwise, be lent, re-sold, hired out, photocopied or | held in any retrieval system, or otherwise circulated without the | publisher's prior consent in any form of binding or cover other | than that in which this is published and without a similar condition | including this condition being imposed on the subsequent pur- | chaser. | [new paragraph] The Book Guild Ltd | 25 High Street | Lewes, Sussex | First published 1988 | © Copyright 1986 by the Estate of John Masefield: Letters | of the Poet Laureate; Some Verses to Some Germans | (Heinemann 1939), Freedom of the City of Hereford | (1930), Some Memories of W. B. Yeats (Cuala Press, | Dublin, 1940), Animula (1920), A Seaman's Prayer; No. | 534. S.S. Queen Mary, For The Sailors (Christmas Card), | The Ambulance Ship (Christmas Card 1944), New Chum | (Heinemann 1944). | © All additional material copyright | John & Barbara Gregory | [new paragraph] Set in Linotron Garamond | Typeset by CST, Eastbourne, East Sussex | Printed in Great Britain by | Antony Rowe Ltd | Chippenham, Wilts | [new paragraph] ISBN 0 86332 303 0'; [5] 'For my grandchildren, Rowan, Nicholas, Gayathri, | Udhayan, Olivia, and Joris'; [6] 'ACKNOWLEDGEMENTS | [rule] | My thanks are due to the John Masefield Estate and the Society of Authors | for permission to publish John Masefield's letters and extracts from his | publications and privately printed papers; to my wife for giving me | access to her letters and diaries; to the National Portrait Gallery, the Wolverhampton Art Gallery, the Birmingham Public Libraries and | Oxford Public LIbraries [*sic*] for illustrative permissions. I am indebted to | Jean Goodman for an original idea, to the late Nevil Dicken for artistic | advice and research, and to John McCutcheon for editorial advice.'; [7] 'CONTENTS | [rule] | [11 sections noted with page references]'; [8] '"Not as men plan, nor as women pray, | do things happen..." | Tristan and Isolt. | John Masefield. | From the Prologue, Friday morning and night, July 28th, 1939. | [text] | John Masefield.'; [9]-207 text and illustrations; [208] '*End* | [photograph of scattered letters, ballet shoes and 'Harlequin' box]'

Paper: glossy wove paper

Running title: 'BRANGWEN' (19mm.) on verso; chapter title comprises recto title, pp.12–207

Binding: blue cloth. On spine, in gold: '[four rules on four lines] | BRANGWEN | THE POET | AND | THE DANCER | [rule] | GREGORY | [rule] | [60 rules on 60 lines] | BOOK | GUILD | [four rules on four lines]'. Covers: blank. All edges trimmed. Binding measurements: 240 × 152mm. (covers), 240 × 26mm. (spine). End-papers: glossy wove paper illustrated with black and white photograph of Anglo-Polish Ballet's *Cracow Wedding*, Apollo Theatre, London. (1940)

Publication date: published, according to *Whitaker's*, October 1988

Price: £10.50

Contents:

The text of the volume commences 'At John Masefield's Oxford Summer Diversions on the 28th July 1939...'

In addition to Masefield's letters and numerous quotations, the following complete pieces are also included:

 'From the Prologue, Friday morning and night, July 28th, 1939' [*Verse*]
  ('Now, ere their lovely feet be loosed,')

'Epilogue for the Dancers Oxford Summer Diversions Friday, July 28th, 1939' *[Verse]*
    ('Sweet lovely dancers, Time that passes')
'Words Spoken To... The Mayor... Of Hereford...' *[Prose]*
    ('I have now to thank you for the great and beautiful honour that you...')
'For The Sailors' *[Verse]*
    ('Even in peace, scant quiet is at sea;')
'The Ambulance Ship' *[Verse]*
    ('We passed through canyons of a Carthage dead;')

Notes:

Sub-titled 'A story based on letters from the Poet Laureate...' many of Masefield's letters to a ballerina (whom he called 'Brangwen') are presented in addition to some reconstructed replies and diary entries. The earliest letter dates from 1939 and the last from 1958. The volume, compiled and edited by John Gregory also includes copious photographs of Masefield and facsimile reproductions of letters, inscriptions, poetry cards, etc.

The copyright information given on p.2 is incorrect. For example, the item listed as 'A Seaman's Prayer; No. 534. S.S. Queen Mary, | For The Sailors (Christmas Card)' is not present. The card 'Epilogue for the Dancers Oxford Summer Diversions Friday, July 28th, 1939' which is present is omitted from the listing.

The end-papers are not provided with a caption, in contrast to E6(b).

Wight states 'collation indeterminate'.

Whitaker's fails to include this volume under an entry for Masefield. It is solely indexed under the author, John Gregory, and the title.

Copies seen: private collection (PWE) inscribed by Brangwen

E6(b) First American edition (1989)

Brangwen | The Poet and the Dancer | A story based on letters from the Poet Laureate | JOHN MASEFIELD | Compiled and edited by | John Gregory | Prometheus Books | [rule, 51mm.] | Buffalo, New York
(All width centred)

Bibliographies: Wight 133

Collation: [A-B]¹⁶ [C]⁴ [D]⁸ [E-H]¹⁶; 108 leaves; 228 × 147mm.; [two un-numbered pages] [i–v] vi [vii–viii] [9–11] 12–14 [15] 16–19 [20] 21–26 [27] 28–29 [30] 31–36 [37] 38–39 [40] 41–47 [48–49] 50–57 [58] 59–71 [72] 73–87 [88] 89 [90–92] 93–106 [107] 108–118 [119] 120–38 [139–40] 141–60 [161–62] 163–81 [182] 183–89 [190–91] 192–93 [194] 195–203 [204] 205–207 [208–214]

Page contents: [-] half-title: 'Brangwen | The Poet and the Dancer'; [-] blank; [i] title-page; [ii] 'Published 1989 by | Prometheus Books | First published 1988 by the Book Guild, Ltd. | [new paragraph] BRANGWEN: THE POET AND THE DANCER. Copyright © 1989 by John Gregory. All | rights reserved. Printed in the United States of America. No part of this book may | be reproduced in any manner whatsoever without written permission, except in the | case of brief quotations embodied in critical articles and reviews. Inquiries should be | addressed to Prometheus Books, 700 East Amherst Street, Buffalo, New York 14215, | 716-837-2475. | [new paragraph] © Copyright 1986 by the Estate of John Masefield: Letters of the Poet Laureate; Some | Verses to Some Germans (Heinemann 1939), Some Memories of W. B. Yeats (Cuala | Press, Dublin, 1940), Animula (1920), A Seaman's Prayer; No. 534. S.S. Queen Mary, | For The Sailors (Christmas Card), The Ambulance Ship (Christmas Card 1944), New | Chum (Heinemann 1944). | [new paragraph] Library of Congress Card Catalog Number 89–63455 | ISBN 0-87975-571-7'; [iii] 'For my grandchildren, Rowan, Nicholas, Gayathri, | Udhayan, Olivia, Joris, and Temugen.'; [iv] 'ACKNOWLEDGEMENTS | [rule] | My thanks are due to the John Masefield Estate and the Society of Authors | for permission to publish John Masefield's letters and extracts from his | publications and privately printed papers; to my wife for giving me | access to her letters and diaries; to the National Portrait Gallery, the Wolverhampton Art Gallery, the Birmingham Public Libraries and | Oxford Public LIbraries [sic] for illustrative permissions. I am indebted to | Jean Goodman for an original idea, to the late Nevil Dicken for artistic | advice and research, and to John McCutcheon for editorial advice.'; [v]-vi 'Preface to the American Edition' ('John Masefield, British Poet Laureate from 1930 until his death in 1967, was one of the great...') (signed, 'Corliss Lamont | New York City'); [vii] 'CONTENTS | [rule] | [11 sections noted with page references]'; [viii] '"Not as men plan, nor as women pray, | do things happen..." | Tristan and Isolt. | John Masefield. | From the Prologue, Friday morning and night, July 28th, 1939. | [text] | John Masefield.'; [9]-207 text and illustrations; [208] 'End | [photograph of scattered letters, ballet shoes and 'Harlequin' box]'; [209–214] blank

Paper: wove paper

Running title: 'BRANGWEN' (19mm.) on verso; chapter title comprises recto title, pp.12–207

Binding: black cloth. On spine, reading lengthways down spine, from head, in silver: '*Brangwen~the Poet & the Dancer* JOHN GREGORY'; horizontally at foot of spine: '[publisher's device of 'PB' within circular ruled border] | Prometheus Books'. Covers: blank. All edges trimmed. Binding measurements: 235 × 148mm. (covers), 235 × 30mm. (spine). End-papers: wove paper illustrated with black and white photograph (and caption: 'Brangwen dancing over the mountaineers' hatchets. | Anglo-Polish Ballet's *Cracow Wedding*. Apollo Theatre, London. (1940)') (caption within ruled border: 10 × 104mm.))

Contents:

as for E6(a) together with

Preface to the American Edition ('John Masefield, British Poet Laureate from 1930 until his death in 1967, was one of the great...')
    (signed, 'Corliss Lamont | New York City')

Notes:

The text is illustrated throughout with copious photographs and facsimile reproductions of letters, inscriptions, poetry cards, etc.

The American edition comprises a reprint of E6(a) together with the inclusion of Lamont's preface, a changed title-page and copyright page. The typographical error in the Acknowledgents ('LIbraries' for 'Libraries') is therefore present, as in E6(a).

Wight states 'collation indeterminate', notes 105 leaves and a blue cloth binding.

The lettering on the spine is swash.

Copies seen: private collection (PWE); ULL (Special Collections)

F. Anthologies

John Masefield is a widely anthologised writer. The first anthology to include a poem by Masefield even pre-dates *Salt-Water Ballads*. The publication of *Naval Songs, and other Songs and Ballads of Sea Life* in 1899 therefore comprised the first appearance in book form of any of Masefield's work. A full bibliographical description is provided below, due to the significance of this volume. Anthologies to which Masefield contributed an entirely new piece are included in section B of this bibliography. Section B excludes anthologies that merely reprint common Masefield items. A full listing of this latter group is a major bibliographical undertaking. The popularity of 'Sea-Fever' and 'Cargoes' render such a listing unwieldy and I have therefore limited this section to a highly selective list presented below.

1899
FRANK RINDER, *NAVAL SONGS, AND OTHER SONGS AND BALLADS OF SEA LIFE*

First English edition (1899)

NAVAL SONGS, AND OTHER | SONGS AND BALLADS | OF SEA LIFE. SELECTED, WITH | AN INTRODUCTORY NOTE, BY | FRANK RINDER. | LONDON | WALTER SCOTT, LIMITED | PATERNOSTER SQUARE
(lines 1–4 justified on left and right margin, line 5 justified on left margin, lines 6–8 width centred. The 'N' of 'NAVAL' is a drop capital)

Bibliographies: Williams [unrecorded], Simmons [unrecorded]

Collation: [*a*]¹⁰ *b*⁸ A-S⁸ T⁶ [U]⁴ (J not used); signatures width centred at foot of page except gatherings P and Q which are signed left foot; 172 leaves; 138 × 102mm.; [i–vi] vii–xiii [xiv–xv] xvi–xxxi [xxxii–xxxvi] [1] 2–42 [43–44] 45–100 [101–102] 103–135 [136–38] 139–81 [182–84] 185–204 [205–206] 207–221 [222–24] 225–41 [242] 243–93 [294–308]

Page contents: [i] publisher's advertisement: 'SPECIAL EDITION OF THE | CANTERBURY POETS. | *Square 8vo, Cloth, Gilt Top Elegant, Price* 2*s.* | Each Volume with a Frontispiece in Photogravure. | [39 volumes listed]'; [ii] advertisement continued: 48 volumes listed (with additional leaf tipped-in on the verso of which is the frontispiece: 78 × 64mm., 'LORD NELSON.' with protective tissue); [iii] title-page; [iv] blank; [v] 'NOTE.' ('The editor desires to express his indebtedness to the following writers…') (unsigned); [vi] blank; vii–xiii 'CONTENTS' (eight sections listed with individual poems and page references); [xiv] blank; [xv]-xxxi 'INTRODUCTORY NOTE.' ('THE Navy–the word is a signal to the British heart!…') (signed, 'FRANK RINDER'); [xxxii] blank; [xxxiii] 'Prologue' ('Men may leve all gamys'); [xxxiv] blank; [xxxv]-293 text (at foot of p.293: '[rule] | *Colston & Coy. Limited, Printers, Edinburgh.*'); [294] blank; [295]-[308] publisher's advertisements

Paper: laid paper (no watermark), chain-lines 27mm. apart

Running title: running titles comprise title of individual poems, pp.2–293

Binding: light green cloth. On spine, in gold: 'NAVAL | SONGS | AND | BALLADS [all within circle: diameter 25mm.] | [swirling floral device]'. On upper and lower cover, in gold the floral device from the spine continues. Top edge gilt, other edges uncut. Binding measurements: 146 × 106mm. (covers), 146 × 33mm. (spine). End-papers: laid paper (no watermark), chain-lines 27mm. apart.

Publication date: published, according to the *English Catalogue of Books*, November 1899

Price: 1s. / 2s. (with photogravure frontispiece)

Masefield contents:
Nicias Moriturus ('An' Bill can have my sea-boots, Nigger Jim can have my knife,')
(signed, 'JOHN E. MASEFIELD')

Notes:
There are eight sections: 'Patriotic', 'Sea Fights', 'Disaster', 'Afloat', 'Ashore', 'Piracy', 'Drink' and 'Love'. Masefield's poem appears on pp.132–33 as part of the 'Disaster' section.

The British Library copy is one of the special issue with a photogravure frontispiece (priced at 2s.) Evidence suggests that reprints (without the frontispiece) were issued in a standard edition.

Copies seen: BL (11604.aaa.32) stamped 5 DEC 99

Reprinted:
without dates, in different bindings, including
green binding with different design from above
Bodleian (2806.f.26) stamped 10 MAR 1900
red binding with different design from above
ULL copy (BO [Canterbury Poets])

1907

The Book of Living Poets (edited by Walter Jerrold)
(London: Alston Rivers Ltd., 1907)
[Includes 'Laugh and be Merry']

1908

Poets of Our Day (edited by N.G. Royde-Smith)
(London: Methuen & Co., 1908)
[Includes 'Christmas Eve at Sea' and 'The Seekers']

1912

Georgian Poetry 1911–1912 (edited by E[dward] M[arsh])
(London: The Poetry Bookshop, [1912])
[Includes 'Biography']

1915

Poems of To-Day: an Anthology
(London: Sidgwick & Jackson, 1915)
[Includes 'Beauty', 'By a Bier-side', 'Fragments', 'Laugh and be Merry', 'Tewkesbury Road', and 'Twilight']

Georgian Poetry 1913–1915 (edited by E[dward] M[arsh])
(London: The Poetry Bookshop, 1915)
[Includes 'The Wanderer']

1917

Georgian Poetry 1916–1917 (edited by E[dward] M[arsh])
(London: The Poetry Bookshop, 1917)
[Includes seven sonnets: 'Here in the self is all that man can know', 'What am I, Life? A thing of watery salt', 'If I could get within this changing I,', 'Ah, we are neither heaven nor earth, but men;', 'Roses are beauty, but I never see', 'I went into the fields, but you were there' and 'Death lies in wait for you, you wild thing in the wood,')

1920

American & British Verse from the Yale Review (with a foreword by John Gould Fletcher)
(New Haven: Yale University Press, 1920 / London: Oxford University Press [1921])
[Includes 'The Passing Strange']

1921

Devil Stories An Anthology (selected and edited with introduction and critical comments by Maximillian J. Rudwin)
(New York: Alfred A. Knopf, 1921)
[Includes 'The Devil and the Old Man']

1922

Poems of To-Day: Second Series
(London: Sidgwick & Jackson, 1922)
[Includes 'Cargoes', 'I went into the Fields', and 'Sea-Fever']

Shorter Lyrics of The Twentieth-Century 1900–1922 (selected, with a foreword, by W.H. Davies)
(London: The Poetry Bookshop, October 1922)
[Includes 'Invocation', 'Cargoes', 'C.L.M.', and 'By a Bier-Side']

1924

The Pageant of Empire Souvenir Volume (An Anthology of British Empire by E.V. Lucas, edited by Martin Hardie)
(London: Fleetway Press Ltd, 1924)
[Includes 'Sea-Fever']
[volume illustrated by Frank Brangwyn, Spencer Pryse and Macdonald Gill]

1925

Plays of To-Day: Second Volume
(London: Sidgwick & Jackson, 1925)
[Includes *The Tragedy of Pompey the Great*]

1933

Traveller's Library (compiled and with notes by W. Somerset Maugham)
(New York: Doubleday, Doran & Co., 1933)
[Includes 'Sea-Fever']

1936

The Oxford Book of Modern Verse 1892–1935 (chosen by W.B. Yeats)
(Oxford: Clarendon Press, 1936)
[Includes 'Sea-Change', 'Port of Many Ships', 'A Valediction (Liverpool Docks)', 'Trade Winds', 'Cargoes' and 'Port of Holy Peter']

Notes on the Harvard Tercentenary (written and edited by David T.W. McCord)
(Cambridge, Massachusetts: Harvard University Press, 1936)
[Includes 'Lines on the Tercentenary of Harvard College in America' printed without sub-title divisions]

1937

The Tercentenary of Harvard College – A Chronicle of the Tercentenary Year
(Cambridge, Massachusetts: Harvard University Press, 1937)
[Includes 'Lines on the Tercentenary of Harvard College']

1938

St. Martin-in-the-Fields. Sunday, 6th February, 1938. Henry Irving… [Order of Service for the hundredth anniversary of Irving's birth]
([London: St. Martin-in-the-Fields, 1938])
[Includes ['By a Bier-side'])

Poems of To-Day: Third Series
(London: Macmillan & Co., 1938)
[Includes 'Wood-Pigeons']

1938

Animal Stories (chosen, arranged and in some parts rewritten by Walter de la Mare)
(London: Faber & Faber Ltd., 1939)
[Includes 'A Sailor's Yarn' and 'The Seal Man']

1939

William Shakespeare, *Five Great Tragedies* (edited by William Aldis Wright with introductions by John Masefield)
(New York: Pocket Books, Inc., 1939)
[Includes introductions to 'Romeo and Juliet', 'Julius Caesar', 'Hamlet', 'King Lear', and 'Macbeth' from *William Shakespeare*]

1941

William Shakespeare, *Five Great Comedies* (edited by William Aldis Wright with introductions by John Masefield)
(New York: Pocket Books, Inc., 1941)
[Includes introductions to 'As You Like It', 'A Midsummer Night's Dream', 'The Merchant of Venice', and 'The Tempest' from *William Shakespeare*]

1943

The Best Poems of 1942 (selected by Thomas Moult)
(London: Jonathan Cape, 1943)
[Includes 'C.H.G. Howard, Earl of Suffolk and Berkshire, G.C.'].

1944

Jim Davis and other Sea Stories
(New York: International Readers League, 1944)
[Includes *Jim Davis*]

Sir Henry Wood [–] Fifty Years of the Proms (edited by Ralph Hill and C.B. Rees)
(London: British Broadcasting Corporation, 1944)
[Includes 'To Sir Henry Wood']

1951

Poems of To-Day: Fourth Series
(London: Macmillan & Co., 1951)
[Includes 'The Country as I First Saw It' [from *Wonderings*]]

1953

A Dog At All Things – An Anthology (anthology by Agnes Lauchlan)
(London: Jonathan Cape, 1953)
[Includes an excerpt (entitled 'Hounds at the Meet') from *Reynard the Fox*]

1959

The Saturday Review Gallery (selected by Jerome Beatty, Jr., and the editors of *The Saturday Review*)
(New York: Simon & Schuster, 1959)
[Includes 'You Must Dig The Bait' (see *The Saturday Review of Literature* 20 March 1954)]

1962

The Flowers of The Sea – An Anthology of Quotations, Poems and Prose (edited by Captain Eric Wheler Bush)
(London: George Allen & Unwin Ltd., 1962)
[Includes extract from 'Sea-Fever', extract from *A Tarpaulin Muster*, 'The Wanderer', extract from *Gallipoli*, and extract from *The Nine Days Wonder*]

The Faith of an Artist (edited by John Wilson)
(London: George Allen & Unwin Ltd., 1962)
[Includes extract from *So Long to Learn*]

1963

The Church of St. Michael and All Angels Ledbury (by Dorothea Farquharson)
(Gloucester: The British Publishing Co. Ltd., 1963)
[Includes extracts from *The Ledbury Scene* and from *Wonderings*]

1966

Salute The Solider – An Anthology of Quotations, Poems and Prose (edited by Captain Eric Wheler Bush)
(London: George Allen & Unwin Ltd., 1966)
[Includes extracts from 'A Consecration', *Gallipoli* and *The Nine Days Wonder*]

1969

Forty Years On – An Anthology of School Songs (compiled by Gavin Ewart)
(London: Sidgwick & Jackson, 1969)
[Includes 'St. Felix School, Southwold']

Scholars on Parade (by David A. Lockmiller)
([New York]: Macmillan Co., 1969)
[Includes extract from …*Reply to the Toast of the Honorary Graduands*…]

1981

Poets by Appointment (compiled and edited by Nick Russel)
(Poole: Blandford Press, 1981)
[Includes '534', 'A Prayer for the King's Majesty', 'To Rudyard Kipling', 'On the Passing of King George V', 'A Prayer for the King's Reign', 'On the Setting Forth of their Royal Highnesses Princess Elizabeth and the Duke of Edinburgh', 'At the Passing of a Beloved Monarch', 'A Prayer for a Beginning Reign', 'John Fitzgerald Kennedy' and 'East Coker']

1989

The Faber Book of the Sea (edited by John Coote)
(London: Faber & Faber, 1989)
[Includes extracts from *The Bird of Dawning*]

G. Commercial Recordings

G1(a) First English issue (1959)

Bibliographies: see Handley-Taylor p.68

Recording company and catalogue number: Argo Record Company Limited (RG 178)

Description: single long-play record; 33⅓ r.p.m.; matrix numbers: ARG-2075-5D and ARG-2076-3D; recorded 26 August 1958

Recording venue: Masefield's study, Burcote Brook, Abingdon.

Contents:
Side One
Part 1. Finn's wooing Grania
Part 2. The Breaking of the Fianna. Ossian's Going.
Part 3. His coming to the country of the young

Side Two
Part 3. (cont.) His coming to the country of the young
Part 4. The country of the young
Part 5. The Death and Burial of Ossian

Publication date: 1959 (reviewed in June 1959 issue of *The Gramophone*)

Price: 39s.6d.

Sleeve spine: on green background: blank

Sleeve upper cover: on green background: '"The Story of Ossian" [in white] | [black and white photograph of Masefield, with foot on tree-stump; house in background: 256 × 206mm.] | Written and read by JOHN MASEFIELD, O.M. AN [oval device including 'argo'] RECORDING'

Sleeve lower cover: on white backgound: 'RG 178 JOHN MASEFIELD, O.M. RG 178 | *reads* | "The Story of Ossian" | *Recorded under the Auspices of the Academy of American Poets* | [three paragraphs signed, 'H. J. Usill'] | [fifteen paragraphs (in three columns) signed, '(Copyright) JOHN MASEFIELD'] | *Cover photograph by Keystone Press* | MADE IN ENGLAND THE ARGO RECORD COMPANY LIMITED, 113–115 FULHAM ROAD, LONDON, S.W.3 Printed and made by Graphis Press Ltd., London'

Notes:
Handley-Taylor included a volume (dated '1959 or 1960') entitled *The Story of Ossian* in his bibliography expecting the poem to be published separately. Such a volume was not published and the poem (entitled simply 'Ossian') appeared within *The Bluebells and other verse* (see A166). There are minor revisions to the text from that as first issued here on record.

Writing to the Society of Authors in August 1958 Masefield provides an early reference to the Ossian tale:

> …I have been asked, two or three times, by various Americans, to make recordings of readings. I have refused these; not feeling up to it, or not liking the people, or what they suggested. But one, whom I would hate to refuse, has asked me again, + I have suggested to him that I would like to try to record a tale in verse, if he would (or his associates would) care for the experiment. He seems inclined to the venture; but it is a bit of a mouthful. The tale is a long short story (1000 lines of verse: 7600 words, in 5 divisions) that would take about 70 minutes to speak, or play over on a gramophone. But I think a harpist might add to the chance of the hearers keeping awake, and if they are sports, I will have a shot at it…
>
> (John Masefield, letter to Elizabeth Barber, 17 August [1958])
> (Archives of The Society of Authors)

A subsequent letter reveals the connection between Argo and The Academy of American Poets (see G1(b)):

> …may I lay before you some further details of the proposed recording of *The Tale of Ossian*… I have seen Mr Hillmen + Mr Skilton, who represent The Academy of American Poets… They wish me to record, for the Academy, my unpublished *Tale of Ossian*. They are asking a Mr H.J.V. Usill, of the Argo Record Co Ld… to come here next Tuesday, the 26th, to make a tape record of the poem. It will take from 43–45 minutes to speak. From this tape a record of the poem will be made between now, and (I suppose) this time next year, and this Record will be issued to the Academy, to Libraries, Schools, + I suppose the American public. The Academy will pay a royalty on this.
>
> I do not suppose that anyone in England will want to issue the record, but I am eager to make sure that the tape recording be of the complete poem, not snippets from it. It should be all there or none of it. It is friendly of the Academy to want it, + I would be glad to meet them in every way over the royalty.
>
> (John Masefield, letter to Anne Munro-Kerr, 24 August 1958)
> (Archives of The Society of Authors)

It appears that after Usill made the recording he made his own approaches to Masefield. The author explained to The Society of Authors some initial (and ambitious) plans:

> I recorded *The Tale of Ossian* for the Argo people in August last: and this is now nearly ready for issue… You will see… that Mr Usill wants to record a lot of other work. I am willing to record, if I may make the record representative of my work, with certain prose statements, prefaces and explanations.

> I would like this to fill a special volume of 5 or 6 two-sided discs (10 or 12 sides of records) of which the *Ossian* should make 1 disc of two sides. This would entail a good deal of preparation, but, I would like to do it, if the Argo, on their side, really wish this. I do not care to do *Reynard* + a few snippets only.

(John Masefield, letter to Anne Munro-Kerr, 21 February [1959])
(Archives of The Society of Authors)

Explaining his sudden enthusiasm, Masefield wrote to The Society of Authors during March 1959:

> Of course, a writer who has given much time to the speaking of verse knows his limitations, and the want of musical accompaniment. But the records of the dead Victorians… what would we not give to have them… people might like to have the records as curios, the voice being otherwise extinct…

(John Masefield, letter to Anne Munro-Kerr, 1 March 1959)
(Archives of The Society of Authors)

The agreement for this recording between Masefield and Argo was dated 27 May 1959 (see Archives of The Society of Authors). The agreement refers to 'The Story of Ossian'. It appears that agreement for all three Argo recordings was reached at approximately the same time.

Roger Wimbush reviewing this recording in *The Gramophone* wrote:

> In a sense this is the most important record ever issued in the history of the gramophone. …I do not know of any creative artist who has committed a major work to disc prior to publication in print or to public performance. …Here is a record that has already made history for the gramophone, that will adorn our industry, and that will go into the archives of the nation. It also happens to be a work of great art.

(*The Gramophone*, June 1959, p.27)

The photograph on the upper part of the record cover reveals the side of Burcote Brook, Abingdon.

Copies seen: private collection (PWE)

G1(b) First American issue (1959)

Bibliographies: see Handley-Taylor p.68

Recording company and catalogue number: Spoken Arts, Inc. (755)

Description: single long-play record, 33⅓ r.p.m.; matrix numbers: K8OP3839-1E B1 and K8OP3840– –1F A1; recorded 26 August 1958

Recording venue: as for G1(a)

Contents:
as for G1(a)

Publication date: 1959 (presented to The Academy of American Poets on 22 April 1959)

Price: $5.95

Sleeve spine: on green background: 'SPOKEN ARTS 755 JOHN MASEFIELD, O.M. / READS THE STORY OF OSSIAN'

Sleeve upper cover: on green background: '755 | [black and white photograph of Masefield, with foot on tree-stump: 231 × 121mm.]' with 'SPOKEN ARTS' printed in green reading lengthways up right hand edge, from foot. In upper left corner: white paper label (74 × 143mm.) on which: 'JOHN *poet laureate* | MASEFIELD, O.M. | *reads "The Story of Ossian"* [enclosed within ornate border: 65 × 137mm.]'

Sleeve lower cover: on white background: (white sheet pasted onto record cover): '755 | SPOKEN ARTS [in grey] | JOHN MASEFIELD, O.M. reads "The Story of Ossian" | Recorded under the Auspices of the Academy of American Poets. An ARGO Production. | [three paragraphs signed, 'HARLEY J. USILL'] | [fifteen paragraphs (in three columns) signed, 'JOHN MASEFIELD.'] | YOU WILL WANT TO HEAR THESE OTHER SPOKEN ART RELEASES: | [nine titles listed (in two columns)] | © SPOKEN ARTS, INC., 95 Valley Road, New Rochelle, New York.'

Notes:
The record label itself notes 'Made in England'. It is unclear whether this refers to the recording or the pressing of the disc.

The record label notes 'An ARGO Production | Presented by Arthur Luce Klein'. Dr. Arthur Luce Klein was the director of the Spoken Arts Company.

The photograph on the upper part of the record cover is extracted from the one present on G1(a). The text printed on the lower record cover includes a number of minute textual variants from the English text.

Within the sleeve is enclosed a pamphlet issued by Spoken Arts advertising titles of recording numbers 701–707, 710–726, 728–29, 732–736, and 741–765.

Copies seen: Archives of The John Masefield Society (Constance Babington Smith Archives)

G2. A FOX'S DAY

1960

G2(a) First English issue (1960)

Recording company and catalogue number: Argo Record Company Limited (RG 224)

Description: single long-play record; 33⅓ r.p.m.; matrix numbers: ARG-2209-2L and ARG-2210-IL; recorded 1959

Recording venue: Masefield's study, Burcote Brook, Abingdon

Contents:
Side One
Part 1

Side Two
Part 2

Publication date: 1960 (reviewed in September 1960 issue of *The Gramophone*)

Price: 30s.

Sleeve spine: on white and green background: blank

Sleeve upper cover: on white background: '[illustration of fox (signed, 'B')] | THE CUR FOX | is the leaft, but the moft common; and approaches near- | eft to the habitations of mankind. It lurks about the' [all in brown]; on green: 'A Fox's Day | [oval device including 'argo' in white] [oval device including 'argo' in white] | adapted from REYNARD THE FOX and read by | John Masefield O.M.'

Sleeve lower cover: on white background: 'RG 224 JOHN MASEFIELD, O.M. RG 224 | reads | "A Fox's Day" | *A Special Adaptation of Reynard the Fox* | [six paragraphs (and two stanza quotation) signed, 'H. J. Usill' | [rule] | [eleven paragraphs (in three columns) signed, '(Copyright) JOHN MASEFIELD'] | The cover picture, a reproduction of an engraving by Thomas Bewick of a cur fox, was suggested for the record by Dr. Masefield and is reproduced by kind | permission of the Trustees of The British Museum. | MADE IN ENGLAND THE ARGO RECORD COMPANY LIMITED, 113–115 FULHAM ROAD, LONDON, S.W.3 Printed by Graphis Press Ltd., London'

Notes:
The agreement for this recording between Masefield and Argo was dated 28 May 1959 (see Archives of The Society of Authors). The agreement refers to 'A Fox's Day'. It appears that agreement for all three Argo recordings was reached at approximately the same time.

Judith Masefield recalls how one of Masefield's cats disrupted a recording session in *Remembering John Masefield*:

> He always had a cat, and one black monster called Tweekie used to rattle the door handle. My father was making a recording of his poem *Reynard the Fox* and I put placards reading SILENCE on many doors but forgot to shut up the cat. By his rattling he wrecked a portion, and it had all to be recorded again.

The text is adapted from the second part of *Reynard the Fox* (see A49). Masefield links and introduces sections with anecdote and synopses.

Copies seen: private collection (PWE)

G3. HIGHLIGHTS FROM THE JOHN MASEFIELD STORY-TELLING FESTIVAL

[1961]

G3(a) First Canadian issue ([1961])

Recording company and catalogue number: Toronto Public Libraries / Hallmark Custom Recording, Toronto (TPL 101)

Description: single long-play record; 33⅓ r.p.m.; matrix numbers: 6595A-1 and 6595B; recorded October 1961

Recording venue: the Masefield contribution was recorded at Burcote Brook, Abingdon.

Contents:
Side One
1. Message from John Masefield, O.M., C.Litt., The Poet Laureate
2. Introduction to stories and story-telling by Frances Trotter, Head of Boys and Girls House, Toronto Public Libraries
3. 'Hereafterthis' from *More English Fairy Stories*, edited by Joseph Jacobs, published by G.P. Putnam's Sons. Told by Christone Stewart, Toronto Public Libraries
4. 'Kidden and the Lion' from *The Disappointed Lion and other stories from the Bari of Central Africa*, collected by A.N. Tucker, published by Country Life under the title *Kidden's First Adventure with the Lion*. Told by Janet Kenny, York Township Public Library

Side Two
1. 'Living in W'ales' from *The Spider's Palace* by Richard Hughes, published in England by Chatto and Windus, in the U.S.A. by Random House. Told by Elizabeth English, Toronto Public Libraries
2. 'The Boy who was Afraid' from *The Scarlet Fish and other stories* by Joan Grant, published by Methuen & Co., under the title *The Monster who Grew Small*. Told by Eileen Colwell, F.L.A., Central Library, The Burroughs, Hendon, England
3. 'Story-telling to-day'. Selections from a talk by Eileen Colwell

Publication date: [1961]

Price: unknown

Sleeve spine: on yellow background: blank

Sleeve upper cover: on yellow background: 'THE JOHN MASEFIELD [in red] | *STORY-TELLING FESTIVAL* [in red] | [illustration of five children sitting around a fireplace with a burning log fire] [in black] | October 16–21 1961 – Toronto Public Libraries [in red]'

Sleeve lower cover: on yellow background: 'TPL 101 | *Some high-lights from* | *THE JOHN MASEFIELD STORY-TELLING FESTIVAL* | *held at Boys and Girls House, 40 St. George Street, Toronto, Canada – October 16–21, 1961* | [rule] | [listing of contents (in two columns) with rules] | [rule] | [three paragraphs (unsigned) (in two columns)'. The first line enclosed within ruled border: 8 × 21mm. All other text enclosed within ruled border: 273 × 262mm.

Notes:
Eileen Colwell (1904–2002) pioneered England's first libraries designed specifically for children. In 1941 she received a letter from Masefield asking whether he could be 'one of your listeners' at a story-telling event. Masefield had seen a photograph of Colwell telling stories and thought she looked 'awfully jolly'. A friendship was to grow until Masefield's death.

The three paragraphs on the lower cover of the sleeve are:

> Through the generosity of Dr. John Masefield and sponsored by the Toronto Public Library Board, the first JOHN MASEFIELD STORY-TELLING FESTIVAL was held at Boys and Girls House, in Toronto, from October 16 to 21, 1961. The four stories and the talks by Eileen Colwell and Frances Trotter on this disc were recorded on the first night of the Festival, a programme planned especially for parents, teachers, recreation-leaders and others who work closely with children.

> It seemed that the stories should be told before the large fire-place in Boys and Girls House, where a log fire blazed and crackled. For it was around log fires long ago that primitive men told their stories, stories which were passed down from one generation to the next. In Baronial Halls and Manor Houses of the Middle Ages, minstrels and troubadors sang their songs of chivalry and romance. Through the centuries continued re-tellings of these stories have given them a form that is terse and dramatic, stripped of non-essentials. This oral heritage provides the basic material for the modern story-teller.

> To-day story-telling is an integral part of public library work with children. But story-telling is not confined to libraries alone and its importance in kindling and stirring the imagination of young listeners is realized by many. Dr. Masefield's desire to inspire a more general interest in the art of story-telling led to his suggestion of holding a Story-telling Festival. It is the hope of the Toronto Public Library Board that other festivals will be held in future years. In the meantime these recordings provide some of the high-lights of the memorable Festival of 1961.

Eileen Colwell notes:

> In 1961, he asked me to deputise for him at the first of the John Masefield Storytelling Festivals he had endowed at Boys and Girls House, Toronto Library. I carried a message from him and told stories for a week in that great Canadian city. My report of my experiences gave him great pleasure. 'Wot larks!' he said with his characteristic twinkle.
> (See Eileen Colwell, 'John Masefield – The Storyteller',
> *The Journal of The John Masefield Society*, John Masefield Society, May 1998, pp.21–24.)

In a private interview Eileen Colwell stated that Masefield held back from recording. It had taken much persuasion to get him to record this message for the Festival. He did not own his own recording equipment and experienced a number of difficulties in locating a tape recorder.

It appears that a number of pressings of the record were faulty or that Eileen Colwell's contribution suffered technical problems. Masefield wrote to Colwell in April 1962 that he was:

> ...sorry to hear of the mis-haps in your recording. A disc was sent to me... and as my machine is past its work, I have not been able to play it, so lent it to a friend who says that you came out well, so perhaps some copies are really quite all right. When I have the copy again, perhaps I may be able to hear it.
> (John Masefield, letter to Eileen Colwell, [April 1962])
> (Archives of the John Masefield Society (Eileen Colwell Collection))

Further 'John Masefield Story-Telling Festivals' were held in 1966 and 1972. Records were also released for these years. The sleeve for the second festival (in 1966) quoted from Masefield's recorded greeting. In 1968 the Toronto Library issued a record in tribute to Jean Thomson, the head of the Boys and Girls Division from 1952. The record sleeve similarly quoted from Masefield's recorded greeting.

Copies seen: private collection (PWE); Archives of the John Masefield Society (Eileen Colwell Collection)

G4. JOHN MASEFIELD READING SEA FEVER, CARGOES AND OTHER POEMS   1962

G4(a) First English / American issue (1962)

Recording company and catalogue number: Caedmon Records, Inc. (TC 1147)

Description: single long-play record; 33⅓ r.p.m.; matrix numbers: TC1147[triangle]A =1=420VVV and TC1147 [triangle] B[triangle] 1 //420VVV; recorded 1960

Recording venue: Philips Records Ltd., Stanhope House, Stanhope Place, London, 7 November 1960

Contents:

Side One
1. The West Wind
2. Sea Fever
3. Cargoes
4. Captain Stratton's Fancy
5. Spanish Waters
6. A Creed
7. The Wild Ducks
8. Good Friday – excerpt
9. C.L.M.
10. The Widow in the Bye Street – excerpt
11. The Passing Strange

Side Two
1. The Everlasting Mercy: Saul Kane's Outburst
2. Lollingdon Downs: II. O wretched man, that for a little mile
                      V. I could not sleep for thinking of the sky
                      VI. How did the nothing come, how did these fires
                      VII. It may be so; but let the unknown be
3. The Downland
4. The Rider at the Gate
5. The Everlasting Mercy: Conclusion

Publication date: 1962 (reviewed in September 1962 issue of *The Gramophone*)

Price: 30s.9d.

Sleeve spine: on blue and white background (of upper cover illustration): 'TC 1147 JOHN MASEFIELD: SEAFEVER, ETC. CAEDMON TC 1147'

Sleeve upper cover: on blue and white background (of illustration): '*John Masefield* | CAEDMON-TC1147 | *reading Seafever, Cargoes* | *and other poems* | [illustration (in blue and white) of three ships observed by figure with cloak, hat and stick] | 33⅓ RPM [point] LONG PLAYING [illustration artist's monogram]'

Sleeve lower cover: on white background: 'CAEDMON LITERARY SERIES TC1147 | JOHN MASEFIELD | READING *SEA FEVER* AND OTHER POEMS | SIDE ONE SIDE TWO | [listing of contents (in two columns)] | [two unsigned paragraphs (in two columns)] | OTHER CAEDMON RECORDINGS OF POETRY | [four titles listed (in three columns)]'

Notes:

The archives of The Society of Authors reveal that Caedmon first approached Masefield about making a recording in December 1953. Masefield had received a letter from Caedmon and asked The Society of Authors if they had 'any pointers about them?' The author stated 'my impression is that they have left it just 40 years too long, but it might be fun to try' (see BL, Add.Mss.56624, ff.187–188). The Society replied with information provided by an 'informant':

...as it happens, we made an enquiry a few months ago on behalf of a member of the Society regarding the Caedmon Recording Company. Our informant in the United States wrote in reply:

"Their reputation is good in so far as what they record is concerned, i.e. classical musical and recordings of important authors. However, they are a relatively small outfit and are in no way at all to be classed with Columbia."

She added a note of warning which she asked us to treat as strictly confidential to the effect that the firm had been having great trouble in finding adequate distribution facilities and that in the circumstances she would not advocate our members coming to an arrangement with them at present.

(Anne Munro-Kerr, letter to John Masefield, 15 December 1953)
(BL, Add.Mss.56624, f.189)

Masefield responded and, with this letter, the matter must have rested until the 1960s:

My grateful thanks to you for your letter + for taking, so kindly, such trouble about the Caedmon people. In any case, I could not have seen them at the time they offered...

(John Masefield, letter to [Anne] Munro-Kerr, 2 January [1954])
(BL, Add.Mss.56625, f.2)

The agreement for this recording between Masefield and Caedmon was dated 20 December 1960 (see Archives of The Society of Authors). The agreement refers to 'the recording made on November 7th, 1960'.

Two scripts within the Archives of the Society of Authors (see also manuscript within the Bodleian Library (Additional Masefield Papers 1)) commence: 'I am asked to read aloud to you such of my writing as will represent my life's work...' This, and other prose, originally introduced and linked material. Masefield also seems to have included a scene from *The Tragedy of Nan* in which he played different characters. These were not included on the issued recording.

The recording took a long time to be issued. One reason was that Caedmon discovered that the sound engineer had started recording whilst Masefield was in conversation with Howard Sackler, from the studio. Masefield discussed old New York, the Yeats brothers, Synge, Bernard Shaw and Wilde. Considering this a fine and spontaneous recording Caedmon approached Masefield for permission to start the record with this conversation. The Society of Authors was, however, asked to forbid such use:

> ...Dr Masefield does not wish any part of this conversation, which he considers of a very personal nature, to be used in the record... Dr. Masefield is quite adamant on the point.

> (Anne Munro-Kerr, letter to Barbara Holdridge, 6 November 1961)
> (Archives of The Society of Authors)

Copies seen: private collection (PWE)

G4(b) Later American / English cassette issue

G4(a) was later issued as a cassette with the catalogue number CDL 51147

G5. THE FORTUNE OF THE SEA *AND* THE WANDERER'S IMAGE   1962

G5(a) First English issue (1962)

Recording company and catalogue number: Argo Record Company Limited (RG 230)

Description: single long-play record; 33⅓ r.p.m.; matrix numbers: ARG-2213-2N and ARG-2214-1N; recorded 1959

Recording venue: Argo London studios

Contents:
Side One
The Fortune of the Sea
    Band 1 Two stories
    Band 2 A Poem about Francis Drake
    Band 3 The Great Eastern
    Band 4 The Songs of the Merchants

Side Two
The Wanderer's Image
    Band 1 A poem about old ships
    Band 2 Excerpts from 'The Dauber'
    Band 3 The Wanderer's Image

Publication date: 1962 (reviewed in November 1962 issue of *The Gramophone*)

Price: 30s.11½d.

Sleeve spine: on white background: blank

Sleeve upper cover: on white background: 'THE | FORTUNE | OF THE SEA | AND | THE | WANDERER'S | IMAGE | *by* | JOHN | MASEFIELD | O.M. | [oval device including 'argo']'; all on right panel; left panel consists of Masefield watercolour with verse: 'And so, farewell, sea-wandering Bird, | Whose flight I watched, whose call I heard, | The time has come, | For the last touch, for the last word. | John Masefield. | June the 29th. 1959.'

Sleeve lower cover: On white background: 'RG 230 JOHN MASEFIELD O.M. RG 230 | *reads* | THE FORTUNE OF THE SEA | Two Stories – A Poem about Francis Drake – The Great Eastern – The Songs of the Merchants | THE WANDERER'S IMAGE | A Poem about old Ships – Excerpts from 'The Dauber' – The Wanderer's Image | [four paragraphs (in two columns) signed, 'HARLEY J. USILL' | SEA POEMS | [four paragraphs signed, 'JOHN MASEFIELD'] | Other records by John Masefield | The Story of Ossian RG 178 | A Fox's Day (from Reynard the Fox) RG 224 | © *Argo Record Company Limited, 1962* | MADE IN ENGLAND ARGO RECORD COMPANY LIMITED 113 FULHAM ROAD LONDON S.W.3 Printed by Graphis Press Limited | *Laminated with 'Clarifoil' made by British Celanese Limited*'

Notes:
Although the record cover for *A Fox's Day* states that 'a record called *The Fortune of the Sea*... will be released in autumn, 1960 (RG 230)' the release appears to have been postponed until 1962.

The agreement for this recording between Masefield and Argo was dated 28 May 1959 (see Archives of The Society of Authors). The agreement refers to 'The Sea'. It appears that agreement for all three Argo recordings was reached at approximately the same time.

The title 'Excerpts from 'The Dauber'' is incorrect. Masefield's narrative poem *Dauber* (see A25) has never been published with a prefixed 'The' in the title.

Copies seen: private collection (PWE)

G6. HOMAGE TO SHAKESPEARE FROM HIS CONTEMPORARIES AND OURS   1964

G6(a) First English issue (1964)

Recording company and catalogue number: Argo Record Company Limited (ZNF4 and NF4)

Description: single long-play record; 33⅓ r.p.m.; matrix numbers: ARG-2629-3K and ARG-2630-3K; recorded 1963 and 1964

Recording venue: the Masefield contribution was recorded at Burcote Brook, Abingdon.

Contents:
Side One
'The Great Globe Itself'
1. Song 'Take, O take those lips away' *Measure for Measure* (Darien Angadi and Desmond Dupre)
2. The speech to the Senate *Othello* (Laurence Olivier)
3. The Willow Scene *Othello* (Dorothy Tutin and Sybil Thorndike)
4. 'To-morrow, and to-morrow, and to-morrow,' *Macbeth* (Michael Redgrave)
5. Lear's reconciliation with Cordelia *King Lear* (Peggy Ashcroft and Paul Scofield)
6. The death of Cleopatra *Antony and Cleopatra* (Irene Worth)
7. Song 'Hark, hark the lark' *Cymbeline* (Peter Pears and Desmond Dupre)
8. The lament for Fidele *Cymbeline* (John Stride and Alan Bates)
9. The pastoral scene *The Winter's Tale* (Judi Dench and Peter McEnery)
10. Queen Katharine *Henry VIII* (Edith Evans)
11. Cardinal Wolsey *Henry VIII* (Ralph Richardson)
12. The meeting of Ferdinand and Miranda *The Tempest* (Richard Johnson, Darien Angadi, John Gielgud and Vanessa Redgrave)
13. Prospero's Farewell *The Tempest* (John Gielgud)

Side Two
'On This Side Idolatry'
1. Prospero's farewell to his craft *The Tempest* (John Gielgud)
2. A Pavane by John Dowland (The Jaye Consort of Viols)
3. Lines on Shakespeare's Tomb (John Dover Wilson)
4. Dedication of the first folio (Sidney, Sixteenth Earl of Pembroke)
5. The Cries of London (Part 1) by Orlando Gibbons (Barbara Elsy, Mark Deller, David Price, Ian Partridge, Christopher Keyte and The Jaye Consort of Viols)
6. 'To The Great Variety of Readers' (Richard David)
7. from *Timber* by Ben Jonson (Lewis Casson)
8. The Cries of London (Part 2) by Orlando Gibbons (Barbara Elsy, Mark Deller, David Price, Ian Partridge, Christopher Keyte and The Jaye Consort of Viols)
9. 'To the memory of my Beloved...' by Ben Jonson (Donald Wolfit)
10. 'Sonnet to Shakespeare' by John Milton (John Masefield)
11. Fanfare: 'Salute to Shakespeare on a phrase by John Wilbye' by Arthur Bliss (The Kneller Hall Trumpeters)

Publication date: 1964 (reviewed in June 1964 issue of *The Gramophone*)

Price: 34s.5d.

Sleeve spine: on white background: 'HOMAGE TO SHAKESPEARE'

Sleeve upper cover: on brown background, in white: 'William Shakespeare [facsimile signature] | [illustration by Sidney Nolan in colour, within ruled border: 258 × 206mm.]' (signature width centred with illustration ranged lower right); reading up lower left from foot: 'William Shakespeare 1564–1964'

Sleeve lower cover: on white background: 'Homage to Shakespeare [in brown] ['Argo' device] | from his contemporaries and ours [in brown] NF 4 | mono | stereo version available ZNF 4 | devised and directed by GEORGE RYLANDS | (*illustrated booklet enclosed*) | recorded in association with THE SHAKESPEARE EXHIBITION 1964 | (Chairman: I. Jack Lyons Deputy Chairman: The Earl of Harewood Artistic Director: Richard Buckle) | [two columns: '*ABOUT THIS RECORD*' (at foot: 'Supervised and edited by Harley Usill | Music devised by Andrew Raeburn | Recording engineered by Arthur Bannister and Jack Clegg') and '*THE ARTISTS TAKING PART*'(listed in two columns)] | ARGO RECORD COMPANY LIMITED 113 FULHAM ROAD LONDON SW3 | MADE IN ENGLAND | Printed by Graphis Press Limited | *Laminated with* 'Clarifoil' *made by British Celanese Limited*'

Notes:

The mono issue of this record was numbered 'NF 4'. The stereo issue was numbered 'ZNF 4'.

The Masefield contribution was recorded at Burcote Brook, Abingdon.

The 'illustrated booklet' noted on the record cover comprises a twelve page booklet printed in black on wove paper. The upper wrapper is printed with white lettering on brown. The booklet includes notes on the 1964 Shakespeare Exhibition, 'Recording A Homage to Shakespeare' by Harley Usill, a note by Richard Buckle, photographs of performers, and the texts recorded.

Copies seen: private collection (PWE) NF4 mono issue; National Sound Archive (1LP 0055139) ZNF4 stereo issue

G7. THE WESTERN HUDSON SHORE... [1964]

G7(a) First American issue ([1964])

Recording company and catalogue number: privately published by Corliss Lamont (RR4M 5378)

Description: single long-play record; 33⅓ r.p.m.; matrix number: RR4M– –5378– –1A; recorded August 1964

Recording venue: Burcote Brook, Abingdon

Contents:
Side One
The Western Hudson Shore (The Palisades)
To the Great Friends in Lifetime

Side Two
Blank

Publication date: 1964

Price: copies were not, presumably, for sale

Sleeve spine: on white: blank

Sleeve upper cover: on white: blank

Sleeve lower cover: on white: blank

Notes:

Corliss Lamont, in *Remembering John Masefield* (see E1), describes receiving Masefield's private recording of *The Western Hudson Shore*:

> In the fall of 1964 I wrote Masefield to thank him for his excellent tape recording of "The Western Hudson Shore." In his mellow, vibrant voice the poem came across remarkably well. I had some 100 playing records made of the original recording.

Although Lamont does not specifically note the poem 'To the Great Friends in Lifetime', it was presumably also included on Masefield's tape recording. The record label also omits reference to the poem.

Lamont describes sending Willard Connely one of the discs and Connely's response in *Remembering John Masefield*.

In 1964 W.B. Yeats' old rooms (in Upper Woburn Place, London) were incorporated within an extension to a nearby hotel. Masefield organised lunch with John Gielgud, Rose Bruford (see B510) and Greta Stevens as speakers. An extensive correspondence with Miss Stevens dates from this time and it appears that Greta Stevens was responsible for visiting the author with recording equipment in August 1964.

Copies seen: Archives of The John Masefield Society (Constance Babington Smith Archives)

G7(b) Second American issue (1977)

Recording company and catalogue number: Folkways Records and Service Corp. (FL 9843)

Description: single long-play record; 33⅓ r.p.m.; matrix numbers: FL9843A and FL9843B; recorded 1964

Recording venue: as for G7(a)

Contents:
Side One
The Western Hudson Shore (The Palisades)

Side Two
To the Great Friends in Lifetime

Publication date: 1977

Price: $7.98

Sleeve spine: on beige background: 'JOHN MASEFIELD FOLKWAYS FL 9843'

Sleeve upper cover: on white background: 'FOLKWAYS RECORDS FL 9843 [in beige] | JOHN MASEFIELD | English poet laureate,reads his | "The Western Hudson Shore (The Palisades)" | and "To The Great Friends in Lifetime" | Produced by Corliss Lamont | [photograph of Masefield in black and white: 174 × 108mm.]' (all enclosed by ruled border: 288 × 289mm. outside this border is a border of beige background)

Sleeve lower cover: on beige background: 'FOLKWAYS RECORDS FL 9843 | [listing of contents] | ['WARNING', copyright information, record title and producer noted] | DESCRIPTIVE NOTES ARE INSIDE POCKET | COVER DESIGN BY RONALD CLYNE | FOLKWAYS RECORDS FL 9843'

Notes:
The record cover comprises a black cardboard container upon which paper (bearing the text) has been pasted. The paper is printed in white, beige and black. This paper is continuous from the upper cover, is wrapped around the spine and finishes by covering approximately one third of the lower cover.

The 'descriptive notes' described on the record cover comprise a four page leaflet printed in black on grey wove paper. The texts of the poems are included.

The publishing agreement for this issue between Corliss Lamont and Folkways Records and Service Corp. was dated 19 May 1977 (see Smithsonian Folkways Recordings Archive). The agreement refers to 'perpetual and exclusive right'.

Copies seen: private collection (BG) inscribed 'For Brangwen and John, with love from Corliss Lamont'

G7(c) *Third American issue (c.2001)*

Folkways Records, their business papers and files were acquired by the Smithsonian Institution in 1987. A 'Custom Compact Disc Series' was subsequently launched which, on request, provided a copy of the best available audio source together with a copy of original liner notes. 'John Masefield Reads His Poetry' (FL9843) therefore became available on compact disc.

H. Archival Recordings

H1

May 1935
'A Prayer for King and Country'
(Recorded 6 May 1935 at BBC London studios)
A BBC archive recording of Masefield's live British Broadcasting Corporation radio broadcast on 6 May 1935.
Duration 1'01
See I6
[BBC Sound Archives. Reference Number 548]
[Library of Congress Recorded Sound Reference Center. Brander Matthews Dramatic Museum Collection 93842157 – not consulted]

H2

September 1936
[Harvard University Tercentenary Program] [*Lines on the Tercentenary of Harvard University?*]
(Recorded 18 September 1936 at University of Harvard)
An archive recording from the NBC radio broadcast on 18 September 1936.
Not consulted
See I7
[Library of Congress Recorded Sound Reference Center. RWC 6301 A2-B1 – not consulted]

H3

April 1937
'Coronation Ode'
(Recorded 27 April 1937, unknown location)
A BBC archive recording of Masefield's live British Broadcasting Corporation radio broadcast on 27 April 1937
Duration 1'30
See I8
[BBC Sound Archives. Reference Number 1319]

H4

May 1937
[Talk to the United States on Coronation Night]
(Recorded 12 May 1937, unknown location)
A BBC archive recording of Masefield's live WEAF (National Broadcasting Company of America) radio broadcast on 12 May 1937
Duration 3'57
See I10
[BBC Sound Archives. Reference Number 1368]
[Library of Congress Recorded Sound Reference Center. RWA 2240 A3 – not consulted]
[Library of Congress Recorded Sound Reference Center. Brander Matthews Dramatic Museum Collection 94838211 – not consulted]

H5

November 1941
[Talk to the United States]
(Recorded 3 November 1941, unknown London location)
A BBC archive recording of part of Masefield's live WEAF (National Broadcasting Company of America) radio broadcast on 3 November 1941. It includes Masefield's address to the American ambassador (as reported in *The Times* for 19 March 1941)
Duration 5'29
See I12
[BBC Sound Archives. Reference Number 3816]

H6

November 1941
'Sea-Fever' and 'On Growing Old'
(Recorded 3 November 1941, unknown London location)
A BBC archive recording of part of Masefield's live WEAF (National Broadcasting Company of America) radio broadcast on 3 November 1941
Duration 3'03
See I12
[BBC Sound Archives. Reference Number 4315]

H7

June 1957
[Reminiscences of Sir Ronald Ross]
(Recorded 7 June 1957 at Burcote Brook)
A BBC archive recording of the entire radio programme 'Gleam, Agony and Rage' comprising a British Broadcasting Corporation radio broadcast on 26 June 1957. Writing to The Society of Authors in 1957 Masefield noted that Ross 'knew very well what the discovery meant, that it was not a gleam, but a blaze of light, + that it made agony + rage alike nothing. Do ask them to change the title: it is as wrong as it can be' (see John Masefield, letter to Miss Lehmann, 15 June [1957]) (Archives of The Society of Authors). Duration of programme 37'06 of which Masefield contributions comprise a total duration of 4'10
See I13
[BBC Sound Archives. Reference Number LP24381]

H8

May / June 1958
Ode for opening of *The Times* Bookshop exhibition to mark his eightieth birthday.
(Presumably recorded in May / June 1958 at Burcote Brook)
Played at the opening of exhibition. See *The Times* for 3 June 1958. Anne Munro-Kerr wrote to Masefield that her '…only regret, which was shared by everyone else, was that you were not able to be present but the recording of your message was wonderfully clear and very much appreciated by all there' (see Anne Munro-Kerr, letter to John Masefield, 4 June 1958) (Archives of The Society of Authors).
Unknown duration.
[Copy not located]

H9

March 1964
Message for banquet on 80th Anniversary of the Society of Author's Foundation, 26 May 1964
(Recorded 3 March 1964 at Burcote Brook?)
Played at the event. See BL, Add.Mss.56626. This recording exists, preserved in the archives of The Society of Authors, on a seven inch open-reel. The tape comprises the master copy with numerous splices and edits. A recording engineer appears to have been present at the recording and the splicing of the master tape may have been performed by Edgar Vetter Sound Services Ltd (27 Soho Square, London). The entire recording lasts 8'22 with additional takes. The speech itself has a duration of 5'45.
Duration 8'22
[Archives of The Society of Authors]

H10

[Interview after receiving National Book League award]
(Recorded 7 December 1964, unknown London location)
A BBC archive recording. Broadcasting has not been traced although evidence held by the BBC Written Archives Centre suggests the brief recording may have been used as a news item in a 'Woman's Hour' programme
Duration 1'12
[BBC Sound Archives. Reference Number LP30929]
[National Sound Archive. Reference Number 1LP0194991]

I. Broadcasts

I1

12 May 1924 – Readings from his own Works
British Broadcasting Company Radio Broadcast
A 'simultaneous' (live) broadcast to all stations, 7.50 – 8.10pm. See *Radio Times*, 9 May 1924, pp.268–69. The programme is listed as 'JOHN MASEFIELD, the well-known Poet, in Readings from his own Works.'

I2

11 February 1927 – Reading His Own Poetry
British Broadcasting Corporation Radio Broadcast
A broadcast to all stations except Birmingham, 8.30 – 8.45pm. See *Radio Times*, 4 February 1927, pp.278–82. The programme is listed as 'Mr. JOHN MASEFIELD Reading His Own Poetry'.

I3

14 September 1930 – 'London Broadcast – John Masefield'
WABC / Columbia Radio Broadcast
An American broadcast, 12.30 – 12.45pm. See *The New York Times*, 14 September 1930, p.12. The programme is listed as 'London Broadcast – John Masefield'. A report of the broadcast is to be found in *The New York Times* for 15 September 1930 p.23.

I4

22 October 1931 – 'Ships and their Builders'
British Broadcasting Corporation Radio Broadcast
A broadcast to 'London Regional' and 'Northern Region' stations, 8.30 – 9.00pm. See *Radio Times*, 16 October 1931, pp.221–23. The programme is listed as "Ships and their Builders' A Talk by JOHN MASEFIELD, Poet Laureate following THE LIVERY BANQUET of THE SHIPWRIGHTS' COMPANY Relayed from THE SALTERS' HALL'.

I5

24 September 1933 – 'The Week's Good Cause'
British Broadcasting Corporation Radio Broadcast
A broadcast on the 'National Programme', 8.45 – 8.50pm. See *Radio Times*, 22 September 1933, p.666. The programme is listed as 'The Week's Good Cause – Appeal on behalf of THE ROYAL ALFRED AGED MERCHANT SEAMEN'S INSTITUTION by JOHN MASEFIELD, the Poet Laureate[.] Contributions will be gratefully received and acknowledged by Mr. John Masefield, Royal Alfred Home, Belvedere, Kent.'

I6

6 May 1935 – 'A Prayer for King and Country'
British Broadcasting Corporation Radio Broadcast
A broadcast on the 'National Programme', 10.30 – 10.35pm. See *Radio Times*, 3 May 1935, p.36. The programme is listed as "A Prayer for King and Country' The Poet Laureate reads his Jubilee poem. Last September John Masefield celebrated the launch of the *Queen Mary* in a fine ode, 'Number 534'. We may look forward with confidence to the first hearing of his Jubilee Ode.' See H1.

I7

18 September 1936 – [Harvard University Tercentenary Program]
NBC Blue Network Radio Broadcast
An American broadcast, 10.30 – 11.30am. It is assumed that the Library of Congress Recorded Sound Reference Center's description of 'a talk by poet John Masefield' comprises *Lines on the Tercentenary of Harvard University*. See H2.

I8

27 April 1937 – 'A Prayer for the King's Reign'
British Broadcasting Corporation Radio Broadcast
A broadcast on the 'National Programme'. Not listed in *Radio Times*. See *The Listener*, 12 May 1937, p.938 where the text is printed

with a note: 'The Poet Laureate broadcast this Coronation Ode in the National Programme on April 27, and will read it in the television programme at 9.0 o'clock this evening'. See H3.

I9

12 May 1937 – 'John Masefield will read his Coronation Ode'
British Broadcasting Corporation Television Broadcast
A television broadcast, 9.00 – 9.05pm. See *Radio Times*, Television Supplement, 7 May 1937, p.5. The programme is listed as 'The Poet laureate will read his Coronation Ode'.

I10

12 May 1937 – 'A Prayer for The King's Reign'
WEAF (National Broadcasting Company of America) Radio Broadcast
An American broadcast, 6.45 – 7.00pm. See *The New York Times*, 12 May 1937, p.43. The programme is listed as 'From London: A Prayer for the King's Reign – John Masefield, Poet Laureate of England'. See H4.

[   ]

26 December 1938 – 'Here's Wishing....'
British Broadcasting Corporation Radio Broadcast
A broadcast on the 'National Programme', 10.40 – 11.00pm. See *Radio Times*, 23 December 1938, p.48. The programme is listed as 'Here's Wishing.... A Christmas and New Year's Greeting from John Masefield Walter de la Mare James Stephens E.M. Forster'. Due to adverse weather conditions Masefield failed to broadcast. G.R. Barnes, Director of Talks, within the Talks Department of the BBC, spoke the lines instead. A letter from Masefield to G.R. Barnes notes:

> I was grieved not to be present, but all agree that you spoke the lines better that I should have done.
>
> (John Masefield, letter to G.R. Barnes, [March 1939])
> (*BBC Written Archives Centre. Radio Contributors. Talks – file II 1938–62*)

I11

10 June 1940 – 'Books for the Forces'
British Broadcasting Corporation Radio Broadcast
A broadcast on the 'Home Service', 7.05 – 7.15pm. See *Radio Times*, 7 June 1940, p.12. The programme is listed as "Books for the Forces' A talk by John Masefield'.

I12

3 November 1941 – 'Against the Storm'
WEAF (National Broadcasting Company of America) Radio Broadcast
An American broadcast, 3.00 – 3.15pm. See *The New York Times*, 3 November 1941, p.38. The programme is listed as 'Against the Storm – Sketch; John Masefield, From London'. See also *The Times*, 30 October 1941, p.2. See H5 and H6.

I13

26 June 1957 – 'Gleam, Agony and Rage'
British Broadcasting Corporation Radio Broadcast
A broadcast on the 'Home Service', 10.05 – 10.45pm. See *Radio Times*, 21 June 1957. The programme is listed as "Gleam, Agony And Rage' In memory of a genius who was born a hundred years ago Sir Ronald Ross. ...a programme in which he is remembered as scientist, poet, mathematician, and man by: John Masefield The Poet Laureate[,] George Macdonald... Sir Eric Macfadyen... and Mohammad Aziz[,] Mary Gray[,] G.H. Masefield[,] H. Lockwood Stevens[,] David Thomson[,] Constance Watson[.] Narrator, George Ordish (BBC Recording)'. See H7.

J. Miscellaneous

J1 PUBLICITY SLIP RELATING TO LETCHWORTH GARDEN CITY PRESS BOOKS [1915]

Collation: single leaf; 189 × 126mm.; [i–ii]

Page contents: [i] 'IN PREPARATION. | *To be had of* | JOHN MASEFIELD, | Cholsey, Berks. | SONNETS AND POEMS, WITH GOOD | FRIDAY, *a play in verse*; crown 8vo, | boards, 5/-. | THE LOCKED CHEST AND THE | SWEEPS OF NINETY-EIGHT, *two* | *plays in prose*; crown 8vo, boards, 5/-. | THE SONG OF ROLAND, *a translation in* | *verse and prose*; crown 8vo, boards, 5/-. | PERSONAL MEMORIES OF JOHN M. | SYNGE; crown 8vo, boards, 3/6. | CHAUCER AND SHAKESPEAREAN | TRAGEDY (Hamlet, King Lear, and | Macbeth), two Lectures; crown 8vo, | boards, 5/-. | *Also the Lollingdon Monthly, a little booklet of* | *verse to be complete in twelve numbers, commencing* | *April,* 1916, *to subscribers only,* 7/6 *the set, post free.*'; [ii] blank

Paper: laid paper (watermark: '[crown] | Abbey Mills | Greenfield'), chain-lines 24mm. apart; all edges trimmed

Date: [1915]

Notes:

Of these intended five volumes, two were never published: *The Song of Roland* and *Chaucer and Shakespearean Tragedy.*

The proposed volume entitled *Sonnets and Poems, with Good Friday* was eventually published in two volumes as *Good Friday* (see A31(a)) and *Sonnets and Poems* (see A32(a)).

Copies seen: private collection (PWE); Ledbury Library

J5 LETTER RELATING TO LETCHWORTH GARDEN CITY PRESS BOOKS [1915]

Collation: single leaf; 179 × 114mm.; [i–ii]

Page contents: [i] '13, WELL WALK, | HAMPSTEAD, N.W. | DEAR | The following books by myself will be | issued at intervals during the next three months, | to subscribers only. | [new paragraph] I. Sonnets and Poems. | 2. The Locked Chest and The Sweeps of Ninety | Eight, two plays in prose. | 3. Good Friday, a play in verse. | 4. Personal Recollections of John M. Synge. | [new paragraph] The cost of the set of four volumes will be | one guinea net. | [new paragraph] The edition will be strictly limited to 200 | sets. | Yours sincerely,'; [ii] blank

Paper: laid paper (no watermark), chain-lines 25mm. apart, all edges trimmed

Date: [1915]

Notes:
The letter specifically refers to A27(c), A31(a), A32(a) and A33(a).

An order slip, which presumably accompanied this letter, includes a date of 1915 (see J10). Additionally, one examined copy is dated 8 December 1915.

Copies seen: John Rylands University Library of Manchester (Tynan/Hinkson Collection) inscribed to Katherine Tynan: 'Mrs Hinkson, | John Masefield.'; Bodleian (MS.Eng.Lett.c.255, f.26) inscribed to Constance Belliss: 'Miss Belliss, | John Masefield.'; Bodleian (MS.Eng.Lett.c.255, f.33) blank; HRHRC (MS (Masefield, J.) Letters. 1FLS to [Frank] Sidgwick) dated '8.12.1915.' inscribed to Frank Sidgwick: 'Sidgwick, | J. Masefield.'

J10 ORDER SLIP FOR LETCHWORTH GARDEN CITY PRESS BOOKS 1915

Collation: single leaf; approximately 110 × 170mm.; [i–ii]

Page contents: [i] 'NEW BOOKS BY JOHN MASEFIELD. | I WISH to subscribe for .... set ... of the four volumes and enclose herewith my cheque for £ .... s............ d. | *Signature* (Mr., Mrs., or Miss) [rule, 69mm.] | Please send the books to me at [rule, 84mm.] | [rule, 76mm.] | [rule, 75mm.] | *Date* [rule, 41mm.] 1915.'

Paper: presumed wove paper, all edges trimmed

Date: 1915

Notes:
The rules noted above are composed of full-stops.

This item comprises an order form to accompany J5.

Copies seen: John Rylands University Library of Manchester (Tynan/Hinkson Collection); Bodleian (MS.Eng.Lett.c.255, f.34)

J15 'INVOCATION'
(CARNEGIE INSTITUTE OF TECHNOLOGY LABORATORY PRESS) 1923

Collation: single leaf; 333 × 250mm.; [i–ii]

Page contents: [i] 'INVOCATION | [text] | *John Masefield.* | [new paragraph] THIS IS ONE OF 123 IMPRESSIONS OF <<INVOCATION.>> BY JOHN MASEFIELD. | PRINTED IN THE MONTH OF MAY, 1923, AT THE LABORATORY PRESS. | A SINGLE PRIOR IMPRESSION BORE THE FOLLOWING COLOPHON AND THE | NAMES OF WITNESSES IN AUTOGRAPH: | [new paragraph] THIS PRINTING OF <<INVOCATION.>> BY JOHN MASEFIELD, | THE FIRST PROOF-IMPRESSION FROM | THE LABORATORY PRESS | IN THE COLLEGE OF INDUSTRIES AT THE CARNEGIE INSTITUTE OF TECHNOLOGY, | PITTSBURGH, PENNSYLVANIA, U.S.A., | WAS MADE ON SATURDAY, THE SEVENTH DAY OF APRIL, 1923. | [new paragraph] THE TYPES ARE GARAMOND, AN AMERICAN VERSION OF THE ROMAN CHARACTERS ORIGINALLY CUT | BY CLAUDE GARAMOND. THE PAPER IS A BLANK LEAF, DONATED BY THE HON. DAVID AIKEN REED, | FROM A COPY OF THE <<RATIONALE DIVINORUM OFFICIORUM>> OF DURANDUS, | PRINTED BY GUNTHER ZAINER AT AUGSBURG IN 1470. | [new paragraph] COMPOSITORS: PORTER GARNETT, MASTER OF THE LABORATORY; | HENRY F. BRAYER; GERALDUS JOSEPH DONAHUE; LELAND M. HIRSCH; W. KENDALL JEFFREY, JR.; | RAY B. KELLER; JOHN L. McCORMICK; FRANK P. MAHONEY; EINAR RYGG; EDWIN U. SOWERS, 2D. | PRESSMAN: DOCTOR THOMAS STOCKHAM BAKER, PRESIDENT OF | THE CARNEGIE INSTITUTE OF TECHNOLOGY. | [new paragraph with 'WITNESSES: [fourteen names listed in italics]' on left margin, '[ornament of the Carnegie Institute of Technology, with date '1923', 'P' and 'G' within border: 52 × 32mm., '[point] NIL VULGARE [point]' on left side, '[point] NIL PERTRITI [point]' at head, '[point] NIL INEPTI [point]' on right side and '[point] PITTSBURGH [point]' at foot, all enclosed by ruled border: 64 × 44mm.]' at centre, and 'WITNESSES: [fifteen names listed in italics on fifteen lines] on right margin'; [ii] blank

Paper: laid paper (no watermark), chain-lines 16mm. apart, all edges deckle edged

Date: published May 1923 in an edition of 123 copies

Notes:
With the exception of the poem which is set as verse and the listing of witnesses, the entire text is width centred.

This item was presumably to demonstrate printing at the college of industries at the Carnegie Institute of Technology, not to disseminate the text.

Copies seen: Boston Public Library (Rare Books *Q.77.1)

J20 'SEA-FEVER' (PACIFIC MARINE REVIEW CHRISTMAS GREETING) 1926

Collation: [A]⁴; 4 leaves; 319 × 242mm.; [i–viii]

Page contents: [i] '*To all our friends who love the sea and its ships* | *our sincere wishes for a Joyous Christmas* | *and a Bountiful 1927* | [monogram in red] | *Pacific Marine Review* | *James S. Hines* [ornament] *Alexander J. Dickie* [ornament] *Paul Faulkner* [ornament] *Bernard DeRochie*'; [ii–iii] blank; [iv] colour reproduction of painting of bow of ship: 204 × 135mm.; [v] 'SEA-FEVER | [text] | JOHN MASEFIELD.' (all enclosed within ornate illustrated border: 201 × 138mm.); [vi–viii] blank

Paper: wove paper (watermark: '*Made in U.S.A. Alexandra Japan Alexandra Japan*'), upper outside edge uncut, fore-edge trimmed, lower outside edge deckle edged

Date: 1926

Notes:
The printing of text is in green with two exceptions. The monogram on page [i] and the drop-capital that commences the poem are both in red. The poem is printed in italics.

The opening line of Sea-Fever is here given as 'I must go down to the seas again, to the lonely sea and the sky,'

Copies seen: Harvard College Library (Houghton *fEC9.M377.D926s) (stamped 'NEW YORK CITY | RECEIVED | DEC 27 1926')

J25 HEINEMANN ADVERTISEMENT LEAF FOR NOVELS
BY FRANCIS BRETT YOUNG [1928]

Collation: single leaf; 249 × 90mm.; [i–ii]

Page contents: [i] 'FRANCIS | BRETT YOUNG | [photographic illustration of Brett Young] | PORTRAIT OF CLARE | [text] | *Large Cr. 8vo. 15s. net* | HEINEMANN'; [ii] [panel one] 'TWO OPINIONS | JOHN MASEFIELD says:– | [text] | HUGH WALPOLE says:– | [text] | [publisher's device of a windmill with 'W' and 'H' all within ruled border: 18 × 19mm.]' / [ii] [panel two] 'THE KEY OF LIFE | *A new novel by the author of* | *PORTRAIT OF CLARE* | [text] | *Cr. 8vo. 7s. 6d. net* | HEINEMANN'

Paper: wove paper, all edges trimmed

Date: [1928]

Notes:

The single leaf is folded once so that the second page is split into two panels. The text in one panel is printed at 180 degrees to the text in the other.

The opening of Masefield's text commences: 'Mr. Francis Brett Young is the most gifted, most interesting and the most beautiful mind…'

Francis Brett Young's novel *Portrait of Clare* was published in 1927 and *The Key of Life* was published in 1928.

A letter to Masefield from C.S. Evans may refer to this item. Masefield had possibly complained that he had not sanctioned use of the quote:

> I am sorry about the mistake they made in the publicity department. I have told them that in future they are on no account to apply your remarks about Mr. Brett Young to any particular book of his.

(C.S. Evans, letter to John Masefield, 18 October 1928)
(HRHRC, MS (Masefield, J.) Recip William Heinemann Ltd.)

Copies seen: private collection

J30 LETTER RELATING TO THE *WANDERER* 1929

Collation: single leaf; 202 × 129mm.; [i–ii]

Page contents: [i] 'BOARS HILL, OXFORD. | *March, 1929.* | To the Editor of the | DEAR SIR, | [new paragraph] Will you be so very kind as to help me by printing the | appeal set forth below? | Yours sincerely, | .... | To the Editor of the | DEAR SIR, | [new paragraph] I am writing the story of the four-masted steel barque, | *Wanderer* (1891–1907), built and owned by Messrs. W. H. | Potter & Co., of Liverpool. | [new paragraph] May I ask any of your readers who have information, | log-books, log-sheets, abstract logs, photographs, drawings or | memories of this ship, or photographs of officers and men | who sailed in her, to be so kind as to let me see and copy | their material? | Yours sincerely, | JOHN MASEFIELD. | Boars Hill, Oxford.'; [ii] blank

Paper: presumed wove paper, all edges trimmed

Date: March 1929

Notes:

The Times printed Masefield's letter on 26 March 1929 (see C125.021). *The Wanderer of Liverpool* was published on 3 November 1930 (see A101).

Copies seen: Harvard College Library (Houghton rev. A.L.s. file) inscribed to the Editor of the Globe: 'Globe, J. Masefield. | Globe,'

J35 LETTER RELATING TO APPOINTMENT AS POET LAUREATE [1930]

Collation: single leaf folded once; 179 × 113mm. (folded); [i–iv]

Page contents: [i] '*BOARS HILL,* | *OXFORD.* | *Dear* | *I thank you for your very kind* | *letter of congratulation.* | [new paragraph] *I regret that it is not possible for* | *me to thank all my gracious friends* | *with a written letter.* | [new paragraph] *With all good wishes,* | *Yours sincerely,*'; [ii–iv] blank

Paper: wove paper (watermark: 'ORIGINAL | TURKEY MILL | KENT') also wove paper (watermark: '[crown] | [monogram of 'D', 'L' and 'R']' and 'IMPERIAL | TREASURY | [rule] | DE LA RUE'), all edges trimmed

Date: [May 1930]

Notes:

The text is printed in italics throughout and includes a number of swash characters.

It is assumed that this letter was printed after Masefield's appointment as Poet Laureate in May 1930. This was the most significant event during Masefield's residence at Boars Hill (April 1917 – April 1933). A copy of the letter addressed to Miss [May] Morris in the British Library (Add.Mss.45348, f.83) includes a pencilled note '? on occasion of O.M. 1935'. This is clearly an incorrect date attribution as Masefield was living at Pinbury Park in 1935.

Copies seen: Archives of The John Masefield Society, inscribed to Lieut. Patrick Campbell 'Pat, | + greetings to | you both. | John Masefield. | I hope to see the Race next week | + hope it won't be quite such | a dismal sight this year. | Good luck.'; Bodleian (MS.Eng.Lett.c.255, ff.53–54) inscribed 'Evelyn Sharp, | John Masefield. | Jolly of you to write: bless you for the thought.'; Bodleian (MS. Autogr.c.25, ff.159–160) inscribed 'Mrs Bosanquet, | John Masefield'; BL (Add.Mss.45348, f.83) inscribed to May Morris 'Miss Morris, | John Masefield.'; John Rylands University Library of Manchester (Monkhouse Collection, Vol.1) inscribed to Allan Monkhouse 'Monkhouse | John Masefield.'; Churchill College Archive Centre (RBTS 2/23) inscribed to Cecil Roberts 'Roberts | John Masefield.'; HRHRC (MS (Sidgwick, F.) Recip. 1 FLS to [Frank] Sidgwick) inscribed to Frank Sidgwick 'Sidgwick, | + thanks. | J. Masefield.'

J40 ANTHEM

Collation: single leaf; 203 × 152mm.; [i–ii]

Pagination contents: [i] 'ANTHEM. | BY JOHN MASEFIELD | [text] | *Copyright, 1930, by John Masefield*'; [ii] blank

Paper: glossy cardboard

Date: 1930

Notes:
The first line reads 'O valorous souls, to whom we trust'

The text is extracted from 'A Masque of Liverpool' (see A94 and A96)

A copy of this item and J45 were part of a collection received by the HRHRC in March 1978 (previously given by R.L. De Wilton to Charles Norman). The collection comprised two letters from Masefield to R.L. De Wilton (from 1952 and 1953), a letter from Masefield (from 1953) to The Officers and Directors of the Macmillan Company in New York, a letter from Masefield to George Brett (dated 24 April 1929) enclosing unbound sheets of *Easter*, a copy of *Liverpool* (see A94(a) copy HRHRC (PR6025 A77 L594 1930Z cop.2)), a Macmillan publicity photograph from the late 1940s and items described here as J40 and J45.

Both De Wilton and Brett were associated with The Macmillan Company in New York. Given the connections in this collection to either Macmillan or to publications dated between 1929 and 1930 I suggest that items described here as J40 and J45 may have been printed by Macmillan in the United States to secure American copyright. They would not appear to comprise part of the privately printed poetry cards section.

Copies seen: HRHRC (PR6025 A77 A685 1930)

J45 LIVERPOOL, 1890. [AND] LIVERPOOL, 1930

Collation: single leaf; 203 × 152mm.; [i–ii]

Pagination contents: [i] 'LIVERPOOL, 1890. | BY JOHN MASEFIELD | [text] | *Copyright, 1930, by John Masefield*'; [ii] 'LIVERPOOL, 1930. | BY JOHN MASEFIELD | [text] | *Copyright, 1930, by John Masefield*'

Paper: glossy cardboard

Date: 1930

Notes:
The contents is as follows:

Liverpool, 1890 ('Gray sea dim, smoke blowing, hammer-racket, sirens')
Liverpool, 1930 ('The dockyards of the ancient days are filled')

See note to J40.

Copies seen: HRHRC (PR6025 A77 L584 1930)

J50 MACMILLAN ADVERTISEMENT FOR *THE WANDERER*

Collation: single leaf folded once; 152 × 83mm. (folded); [1–4]

Page contents: [1] '*From The Macmillan Company* | THE WANDERER OF | LIVERPOOL | By John Masefield | *Poet Laureate* | [text]'; [2–3] text (at foot of p.[3]: 'Tc-362. Printed in U. S. A.'); [4] blank

Paper: wove paper

Date: [October 1930]

Notes:
This item comprises a leaflet of advertisement for *The Wanderer of Liverpool* (see A101). The text commences:

> "A full-rigged ship, unutterably fair" – so John Masefield described *The Wanderer* in one of his early poems. Now he has written a true and stirring account of the building, the launching, and ten voyages and the sad end of this same sailing-ship, "the finest ship of her year," a four-masted barque of nearly three thousand tons. He has drawn his material from old records and newspapers and from the memories of men of *The Wanderer's* crew…

The leaflet quotes sections from 'The Setting Forth' (commencing 'All of the power of muscle of hundreds of builders') and 'The Ending' (commencing 'For now the most beautiful ship having wandered her ways') in addition to sections of prose.

Copies seen HRHRC (tipped-into copy of AC-L M377WA 1930E)

J55 'ROADWAYS' CALENDER FOR 1931

Collation: single leaf; 202 × 126mm.; [i–ii]

Page contents: [i] '[black and white illustration of trees, fields and a road within ruled border: approximately 86 × 100mm.] | [two stanzas from 'Roadways'] | John Masefield. | [tear-off calendar] | *Words by permission of the Author.*'; [ii] '*The Challenge Ltd., Great Russell Street, W.C.1. Printed in England.*'

Paper: the front of the item is printed on green paper laid-down to cardboard, the tear-off calendar (with sewn leaves) is stuck onto a slip of green paper which is laid-down to the front of the item, a black cord is threaded through two holes at the head

Date: 1930

Price: 6d.

Notes:

The final two stanzas of the poem 'Roadways' are printed. No source is given.

The files of The Society of Authors contain correspondence with 'The Challenge Limited' (of Great Russell Street, London). The first application for permission is dated 27 February 1930 (British Library, Add.Mss.56589, f.56). A copy of the 'lino block' print and the relevant lines were enclosed and E.M. Barton of The Challenge Limited stated that 'full acknowledgement would, of course, be made'. On 4 March 1930 the company provided further detail about their plans:

> ...the cards about which we wrote to you are for selling to the public in our retail department at this address. We should print 2,000 and propose to sell them at 6d. each.
>
> (The Challenge Limited, letter to the Society of Authors, 4 March 1930)
>
> (BL, Add.Mss.56589, f.65)

A cheque for 10/6 for permission to use the verses was sent to the Society of Authors on 11 March 1930.

Copies seen: Archives of The John Masefield Society (Constance Babington Smith Archives)

J60 'CHRISTMAS EVE AT SEA' [1930]

The National Union Catalog Pre-1956 Imprints (Mansell, 1975) lists the following item:

> A salt water poem. By John Masefield. [Rochester, N.Y., Foss Soule Press, 1930] [6]p., 11cm. Cover and caption title: Christmas Eve at sea "Five hundred copies have been designed and privately printed... Christmas 1930."

The only recorded copy is in the University of Rochester. It is assumed this item comprises a private printing of the poem from *Salt-Water Ballads.*

J65 'ADAMAS AND EVA' [c.1931]

The National Union Catalog Pre-1956 Imprints (Mansell, 1975) lists the following item:

> Adamas and Eva, by John Masefield. [Brattleboro, Ut. Printed by E.L. Hildreth & Co., c.1931] Cover-title [4]p. 18cm.

The only recorded copy is in the Library of Congress. It is assumed this item comprises a privately printed exercise in printing of the poem from *Minnie Maylow's Story and other tales and scenes.*

J70 'ODE' [STRATFORD MEMORIAL THEATRE] (BIRMINGHAM SCHOOL OF PRINTING) 1932

ODE [letter characters in outline] | BY JOHN MASEFIELD | POET LAUREATE | RECITED BY LADY KEEBLE | ON THE OPENING OF THE | STRATFORD | MEMORIAL THEATRE | BY HIS ROYAL HIGHNESS | THE PRINCE OF WALES, K.G. | ON SATURDAY, APRIL XXIII | MCMXXXII
(All width centred and enclosed within border, in red, including four inner ruled borders, elaborate design and five outer rules: 224 × 160mm.)

Collation: [A]⁶; 6 leaves; 244 × 182mm.; [i–xii]

Page contents: [i–ii] blank; [iii] title-page; [iv–v] blank; [vi–vii] text; [viii–ix] blank; [x] 'Arranged and printed under the direction of Leonard Jay | at the Birmingham School of Printing, a department of | the Central School of Arts and Crafts, Margaret Street. | The Geofroy Tory border on title page has been recut on | wood by George W. Jones, from a Book of Hours printed | by Simon de Colines. Type, which is Linotype 18-point | Granjon, set by students attending the classes: teacher, | H. Gould. Initials drawn by W.F. Colley. Compositors' | work by the pre-apprentice students: teachers, H.C. Page | and F.G. Moseley. Printed by students attending the | Letterpress Machine classes: teachers, A. Hoyle and | V.S. Ganderton | 1932'; [xi–xii] blank

Paper: wove paper (there are a variety of watermarks)

Running title: none

Binding: grey-green wove paper wrappers. Spine: blank. On upper wrapper: 'ODE BY JOHN MASEFIELD | ON THE OPENING OF THE | STRATFORD MEMORIAL THEATRE | 1932'. Lower cover: blank. All edges trimmed. Binding measurements: 180 × 244mm. (wrappers), 177 × 244mm. (spine). End-papers: consisting of two conjugate leaves of laid paper.

Publication date: 1932

Price: unknown

Notes:

The contents comprises 'Ode' ('Beside this House there is a blackened shell,')

The 'end-papers' are not bound with the single gathering of six leaves, but tipped-in to the wrappers.

The ode is printed as four stanzas. Each stanza commences with an decorated initial, printed in red.

The Shakespeare Memorial Theatre was opened at Stratford-upon-Avon in April 1932.

Copies seen: private collection (GBTS)

J75 SIDNEY CHARTERIS, *THE HOME OF LOVELY PLAYERS* (BIRMINGHAM SCHOOL OF PRINTING) 1935

THE HOME | of | LOVELY PLAYERS | BY | SIDNEY CHARTERIS | BEING A MEMORY OF STRATFORD-UPON-AVON | WHERE, ON APRIL 23, 1932, THE SHAKESPEARE | MEMORIAL THEATRE WAS OPENED BY HIS | ROYAL HIGHNESS THE PRINCE OF WALES, K.G. | [blazing torch device] [in orange] | CITY OF BIRMINGHAM SCHOOL OF PRINTING | CENTRAL SCHOOL OF ARTS AND CRAFTS | MARGARET STREET | 1935
(All width centred with lines 3, 6–9 and 11 all justified on same left and right margins)

Collation: [A]¹⁴; 14 leaves; 280 × 178mm.; [i–ii] [1–4] 5–23 [24–26]

Page contents: [i–ii] blank; [1] title-page; [2] blank; [3] 'AUTHOR'S NOTE.' ('The object of this little sketch has been to collate the details (many of which are now printed...') (signed, 'S.C. | Birmingham, August 1934.'); [4] blank; 5–[24] text; [25] colophon in orange: 'Printed under the direction of Leonard Jay, at the City of | Birmingham School of Printing, which is a department of the | Central School of Arts and Crafts, Margaret St. Type, which | is 14-pt. Baskerville, set and cast on the Monotype by students | attending the classes: teachers, T. Gill and H. E. Bracey. | Compositors' work by students in the pre-apprentice classes: | teachers, H. C. Page and F. G. Moseley. Printed by students | attending Letterpress Machine classes: teachers, A. Hoyle | and V.S. Ganderton. | 1935.'; [26] blank

Paper: wove paper (watermark: 'OLD YORK PARCHMENT (British Made)')

Running title: none

Binding: light grey wrappers, secured by blue cord. Spine: blank. On upper wrapper, in orange: 'THE HOME | OF LOVELY PLAYERS | BY SIDNEY CHARTERIS | [blazing torch device]' (text ranged upper-left and device ranged lower-left). Lower wrapper: blank. All edges trimmed. Binding measurements: 284 × 183mm. (wrappers), 284 × 2mm. (spine). The wrapper extends beyond the edges of the internal leaves.

Publication date: unrecorded

Price: unknown

Notes:

The contents comprises untitled verse ('Beside this House there is a blackened shell,') (introduced as 'John Masefield... has written an opening Ode').

Masefield's untitled ode is included within the body of the text

Charteris notes that both 'Mr. J. Masefield (Poet Laureate) and Mrs. Masefield' were present at a Commemorative Lunch at noon in the New Place Gardens. Other guests included 'Mr. T. Lamont (chairman American Shakespeare Foundation) and Mrs. Lamont'.

The ode was previously printed in *The Times* for 25 April 1932 (C125.039)

Copies seen: private collection (ROV)

J80 [APPEAL TO ESTABLISH A HOME FOR TRAMPS] [1936]

Collation: single leaf; 256 × 190mm.; [i–ii]

Page contents: [i] text, comprising facsimile of Masefield's handwriting; [ii] blank

Paper: presumed wove paper

Date: [1936]

Notes:

The first line reads 'On many of the roads of England, in every month of the year...' (signed, 'John Masefield'). The untitled text consists of four paragraphs.

There is no date cited. However, it may date from the time of Masefield's support of Pauntley Home (see B325). Masefield's foreword to *Pauntley. The Gloucestershire Home for Wayfarers* was published in 1936.

Copies seen: Archives of The John Masefield Society (Constance Babington Smith Archives) photocopy of Harvard College Library (Houghton) copy

J85 A MEMORIAL SERVICE FOR WILLIAM BUTLER YEATS   1939

Collation: single leaf; 235 × 182mm.; [i–ii]

Page contents: [i] '*A MEMORIAL SERVICE* | for | WILLIAM BUTLER YEATS, Poet, | at | The Church of St. Martin-in-the-Fields | *at 3 p.m. on Thursday, the 16th March,* 1939, | Being the Hundredth Anniversary of the Birthday of his Father, | JOHN BUTLER YEATS, | late of the Royal Hibernian Academy.'; [ii] '*The Order of Service.* | Organ Voluntary: Slow Movement from Beethoven's Choral Symphony. | Prayers. | Psalm XXIII. | Two Poems to be read by Mr. V. C. CLINTON BADDELEY: | *The Withering of the Boughs.* | *A Dialogue of Self and Soul.* | Lesson. Isaiah Chapter LV. | Hymn. | "Praise to the Holiest in the Height." | A Poem to be read by Mr. V. C. CLINTON BADDELEY: | *Under Ben Bulben.* | Hymn. | "The Day Thou Gavest, Lord, is Ended." | Benediction. | The Dead March from Saul.'

Paper: laid paper (watermark: '[monogram]' ranged left, '[crown] | KING OF KENT | SUPERFINE' ranged right), chain-lines 27mm. apart, all edges deckle-edged

Date: 1939

Notes:

Masefield's contribution to this item was, apparently, the role of editor. The library record card for the copy located in Harvard College Library (Houghton *74–194(br)) notes 'Edited by John Masefield'. The item was given by Crocker Wight in October 1974.

The chain-lines run horizontal to the text.

Copies seen: Harvard College Library (Houghton *74–194(br))

J90 STATEMENT ON BOOKS ON BRAILLE   [1940s]

Collation: single leaf; 181 × 121mm.; [i–ii]

Page contents: [i] '[photographic illustration of Masefield: 121 × 96mm.] | The Poet Laureate writes:- | "During the last few years we have all suffered | from the shortage of books, and are likely so to suffer | for years to come. Let us reflect that what we for the | time lament, the BLIND should not be allowed to feel'; [ii] 'at all. It is for us to see that enough books can be in | Braille to keep touch with modern thought, to supply | new readers and replace works worn out by use. For | the BLIND the books in Braille are the only books. | [new paragraph] One envies France, that Louis Braille was not an | Englishman, but Braille would surely rejoice to know | that his work is generously welcomed and supported | here." | [facsimile signature]'

Paper: glossy wove paper, all edges trimmed

Date: 1940s

Notes:
The following item appeared in the 1994 *Keith Smith Books Catalogue No.1 John Masefield*:

> THE NATIONAL LIBRARY FOR THE BLIND
> 4 page appeal leaflet with photograph and 2 page message from Masefield. Undated (but c.1950's)

The only example seen consisted of two pages only. It is feasible, however, that other pages comprised a tear-off section.

Copies seen: private collection (PWE)

J95 BLACKWELL'S BOOKMARK   [c.1941]

J95(a) Early Paper Bookmark ([c.1941])

Single leaf of white wove paper (printing in black); 63 × 177mm.; [i–ii]

Contents: [i] 'B [point] H [point] | BLACKWELL | Ltd | 48 to 51 | Broad Street | Oxford' (enclosed within ruled border: 50 × 45mm.) and 'BLACKWELL'S | [drawing (signed, 'FAIRCLOUGH') of Broad Street] | [arrow] | Part of Trinity College' (enclosed within ruled border: 49 × 108mm.), all enclosed within ruled border: 52 × 158mm.; [ii] 'THERE, in the Broad, within whose booky house | Half England's scholars nibble books or browse. | Where'er they wander blessed fortune theirs: | Books to the ceiling, other books upstairs; | Books, doubtless, in the cellar, and behind | Romantic bays, where iron ladders wind. | JOHN MASEFIELD | Whatever book you may want, wherever you may be- | ask BLACKWELL'S'

Date: the quotation is from *Shopping in Oxford* (Heinemann, 1941). The date of the bookmark is therefore presumably 1941 or later.

Price: unknown

Notes:

The printing starts with a drop-capital and the italic font uses a number of swash characters.

There are additional examples of the early paper bookmark for which the text on the back of the bookmark has been reset.

Note the early paper example prints the word 'Where'er' in line three and the leather bookmark has the word 'Wher'er'.

Copies seen: private collection (PWE)

J95(b) Later Leather Bookmark ([1990s])

Single length of dark blue leather (printing in gold); 37 × 223mm.; [i–ii]

Contents: [i] illustration of Blackwell's shop façade (ranged left) with 'There, in the Broad, within whose booky house | Half England's scholars nibble books or browse. | Wher'er they wander blessed fortune theirs: | Books to the ceiling, other books upstairs; | Books, doubtless, in the cellar, and behind | Romantic bays, where iron ladders wind. | JOHN MASEFIELD | Whatever book you may want, wherever you may be – ask Blackwell's' (centred) and '[Blackwell's 'B' device in blind within gold panel within ruled border: 12 × 12mm.] | BLACKWELL'S | [rule] | 50 Broad Street, Oxford. | Tel: (01865) 792792 | Fax: (01865) 794143' (ranged right); [ii] blank

Date: an example of this bookmark was purchased in 1997

Price: unknown

Notes:

Note the early paper example prints the word 'Where'er' in line three and the leather bookmark has the word 'Wher'er'.

Copies seen: private collection (PWE)

J100 [MEMORIAL VERSE TO HENRY J. WOOD]   [1946]

Quatrain in memory of Henry J. Wood on the Henry Wood memorial window, Musicians' Chapel, St. Sepulche-without-Newgate, Holborn, London.

Date: the window was unveiled on 26 April 1946

Notes:

The four lines of verse appear on eight lines. The verse, signed 'Masefield', is as follows:

> Of this Man's hand a million hearers caught
> An echo of the Music without flaw
> Where endless joy is Heaven's only law
> O Music lovers bless him in your thought.

The window was designed by Gerald E.R. Smith in collaboration with Frank Salisbury.

The unveiling ceremony on 26 April 1946 featured the London Symphony Orchestra and choirs of St. Paul's Cathedral and Westminster Abbey, the BBC Singers and BBC Chorus. Lesley Woodgate conducted the BBC Chorus in Walton's setting of Masefield's 'Where does the Uttered Music Go?'

Location: Musicians' Chapel, St. Sepulche-without-Newgate, Holborn, London

J105 APPLICATION FOR CHRISTMAS   [1947]

Collation: single leaf; 263 × 208mm.; all edges trimmed; [i–ii]

Page contents: [i] 'With hopes of change, and all good wishes for | Christmas and the Coming Year, | from | CONSTANCE and JOHN MASEFIELD'; [ii] 'APPLICATION FOR CHRISTMAS | [text]'

Paper: beige wove paper

Date: Christmas 1947 (see notes)

Notes:

The origin of this privately printed Christmas greeting has strong links to Masefield's privately printed poetry cards.

A copy located in the British Library (Sydney Cockerell papers) is dated, in Cockerell's hand, 'Christmas 1947'.

Authorship by John Masefield is assumed.

The text is set out in tabular form with boxes for supposed application details. The seventh instruction states, for example, 'State the alternatives in your possession – | As Poison, Halter, Pistol, or Depression.'

Copies seen: BL (Add.Mss.52735, f.115); private collection (RM); Harvard College Library (Houghton *EC9.M377.Zzx)

To be had of

JOHN MASEFIELD,

Cholsey, Berks.

SONNETS AND POEMS, WITH GOOD FRIDAY, *a play in verse*; crown 8vo, boards, 5/-.

THE LOCKED CHEST AND THE SWEEPS OF NINETY-EIGHT, *two plays in prose*; crown 8vo, boards, 5/-.

THE SONG OF ROLAND, *a translation in verse and prose*; crown 8vo, boards, 5/-.

PERSONAL MEMORIES OF JOHN M. SYNGE; crown 8vo, boards, 3/6.

CHAUCER AND SHAKESPEAREAN TRAGEDY (Hamlet, King Lear, and Macbeth), two Lectures; crown 8vo, boards, 5/-.

Also the Lollingdon Monthly, a little booklet of verse to be complete in twelve numbers, commencing April, 1916, to subscribers only, 7/6 the set, post free.

J1

APPLICATION FOR CHRISTMAS

FILL IN AND POST TO YOUR REGIONAL FRUSTRATION OFFICER

To APPLICANTS FOR HAPPY CHRISTMAS. State
Age, sex, religion, occupation, weight.

NOTE. Getting Christmases by false pretence
Is hereby deemed a criminal offence.

What do you mean by happy Christmas? Here
State (in Block Letters) do you add 'NEW YEAR'?

If the supplies allow, and we permit,
And you receive, what will you do with it?

Do you intend to sell the Christmas? Or
Export abroad? What do you want it for?

How many happy Christmases are needed?
Write clearly ONE, which must not be exceeded.

State the alternatives in your possession—
As Poison, Halter, Pistol, or Depression.

State the amount of each, and when acquired,
Would one, or all, suffice you, if required?

State why you cannot, or you will not, choose
One such alternative, if still in use.

Write clearly, in BLOCK LETTERS, and remain
A month unanswered; then apply again.

If still unanswered, keep applying still.

OFFICIAL NOTE.　　　　WHAT CHRISTMAS GRANTED.　　　| NIL |

J105

J110 TRADE WINDS [UNITED STEEL COMPANIES LIMITED, SHEFFIELD] 1948

George B.T. Smith reports a publication entitled *Trade Winds*. This was issued by The United Steel Companies Limited in 1948. The introduction notes that the 'text and designs reproduced in this volume form the subject matter of twelve advertisements published by the company'.

It was published in a limited edition of 150 copies signed by Douglas Wilson (the designer and editor), each of the nine artists and inscribed by John Masefield 'Verses by John Masefield'. The artists include Charles Pears and Rowland Hilder. The poem 'Trade Winds' (first published in *Salt-Water Ballads*) is printed followed by twelve illustrations with descriptive text.

The binding comprises paper covered boards with a cloth spine. In black on the upper cover is printed 'TRADE | WINDS' surrounded by an elaborate design in brown.

J115 [MEMORIAL FOR JANET ASHBEE] 1961

Collation: [A]²; 2 leaves; 186 × 127mm. (covers), 186 × 0.5mm. (spine); [i–iv]

Page contents: [i] 'JANET ASHBEE | died on May 8th, 1961, aged 83, after a varied | and adventurous life. | [new paragraph] It happened very suddenly while she was sitting | at her writing desk, "keeping in touch" to the | last moment. | [new paragraph] No one who knew her, however briefly, will for- | get the warmth and vividness of her personality, | her all-embracing friendships, and the breadth | of her reading and tastes. It was this enormous | zest for living which made her so often say she | wanted no long faces or mourning at her departure.'; [ii] blank; [iii] '[text] | *Printed by kind permission of* | JOHN MASEFIELD.'; [iv] blank

Paper: wove paper (watermark: '[device] | ABERMILL | BOND | MADE IN GT BRITAIN')

Date: 1961

Notes:
There is no running title.

Masefield's contribution is an untitled stanza. It commences with a drop-capital. The first line reads 'And man, the marvellous thing that in the dark'. It is signed '*Printed by kind permission of* | JOHN MASEFIELD.'

From the examined copy there is no indication of whether page [i] was originally page [iii].

Copies seen: NYPL (Berg Collection) enclosed with Masefield letters to Leonard Clark

J120 WILKINSON CHRISTMAS CARD [1964]

Collation: single sheet folded once; 116 × 204mm.; the colour plate on glossy paper (86 × 56mm.) is laid-down to an embossed panel; 92 × 63mm.; [i–iv]

Page contents: [i] embossed panel, upon which is laid-down the colour print: 'THE DAYS | THAT MAKE | US HAPPY | MAKE | US WISE. | John Masefield' (design includes drop capital 'T', flowers, bird and a butterfly); [ii] blank; [iii] 'Christmas Greetings | and all good wishes for | the coming year' (in green; the type is ornate and contains swash characters); [iv] '[publisher's device including 'W'] | WILKINSON | PUBLISHING CO. | LTD. | ENGLISH PRINT | SERIES | 005x25' (in grey)

Paper: white cardboard

Date: a copy was possibly acquired by Fraser Drew 'in England in 1964' (see notes)

Price: unknown

Notes:
The artist of the unsigned illustration is unidentified.

A copy was given to me by Fraser Drew, Christmas 1997. In sending the item, Fraser Drew wrote: 'I enclose a little Christmas card with a Masefield quotation. I believe that I found it in England in 1964 but I am not sure.'

The quotation is the final line from Masefield's poem 'Biography' (first printed in *The English Review* in May 1912 and first collected in a Masefield volume in *The Story of a Round-House and other poems*). Masefield frequently used the line when signing inscriptions.

In August 1934 an applicant to The Society of Authors requested Masefield's permission to quote the line. Masefield wrote to the Society that 'I do not object to the use of the single line: it is often quoted.' (see John Masefield, letter to the Society of Authors, [19 August 1934]) (BL, Add.Mss.56601, f.53)

Copies seen: private collection (PWE) within wove paper envelope

J125 POEMS ON THE UNDERGROUND: 'CARGOES' 1997

Collation: single leaf; 278 × 607mm.; [i–ii]

Page contents: [i] 'Cargoes [in red] | [text] | John Masefield (1878–1967) Reprinted by permission of The Society of Authors from *Collected Poems* by John Masefield | [rule] | [London Underground device] [in blue and red] Poems on the Underground [in grey] |

The British Council [point] The British Library [point] Design Tom Davidson Supported by ['Syntegra' logo and text] www.netpoems.com ['LONDON | ARTS BOARD' logo] | Posters and books are on sale at the London Transport Museum 0171-379 6344'; [ii] blank

Paper: white cardboard

Date: displayed in London Underground trains from 15 June 1997

Notes:
The text is printed in two columns.

This item was part of set 37 in the Poems on the Underground series. The 'Poems on the Underground' programme was launched in 1986. Posters bearing poems replaced advertisements within London Underground trains. 'Cargoes' was the first Masefield poem included in the series.

Copies of the poster were available for sale. These were not, however, printed on cardboard but available on glossy wove paper.

Advance publicity from Poems on the Underground introduced the item as follows:

> CARGOES by John Masefield — one of the Nation's Favourite Poems, by the self-taught sailor who became Poet Laureate in 1930

Copies seen: private collection (PWE)

J130 [MEMORIAL VERSE TO HENRY J. WOOD] POSTCARD [c.2002]

Collation: single leaf; 105 × 149mm.; [i–ii]

Page contents: [i] colour photographic illustration of detail from Henry Wood window: 93 × 119mm. | [at left margin: 'The Sir Henry Wood Window | St Sepulchre without Newgate, London' and at right margin: 'Photograph | Richard Burton'; [ii] 'Postcard | [vertical rule, 85mm.]' (together with ruled border for stamp)

Paper: white cardboard

Date: c.2002

Price: £0.40

Notes:
See J100. Copies of this item were sold in the church of St Sepulchre without Newgate.

Copies seen: private collection (PWE)

K. Fugitive Items

[c.April 1902]
Contribution to *Wolverhampton Express and Star* [?]
Masefield writes from Wolverhampton to his sister, Norah Masefield, in a letter dated 18 April 1902 'Here are 2 press cuttings for you. One by me for the local rag...'

[c.1903]
Contribution to *The Pall Mall Magazine* or *The Speaker*
Laugh and Be Merry *[Verse]*
The acknowledgement notes to the two different editions of Ballads *suggest that this poem first appeared in either* The Speaker *or* The Pall Mall Magazine. *The location has not been traced, however.*

[18 April 1903]
Contribution to *Manchester Guardian*
Voyages and Travels
[Book Review]
Listed by Drew, but not located in index or microfilmed edition of the paper

[pre 18 April 1903]
Contribution to *The Speaker*
Harbour Bar *[Verse]*
The publication of this poem in The Living Age *gives* The Speaker *as the source. This appearance has not, however, been traced.*

[pre July 1903]
Contributions to *The Westminster Gazette*
A letter held in the Guardian *archives dated 12 July 1903 from Dorothy Scott to Mr Montague of the* Manchester Guardian *requests that Masefield be considered for a position on the paper. In describing Masefield, Dorothy Scott writes 'He also writes for the "Daily News" + the "Westminster Gazette".' No articles in the later periodical have been traced before C135.001*

[13–18 July 1903]
Contribution to *The Daily News*
Patriotic Industry [Book Review: Professor Trent, *American Literature*]
It is strange that a young nation like the American...
[unsigned]

[13–18 July 1903]
Contribution to *The Daily News*
England. From Outside [Book Review: Rao Badadur Ghanasham Nilkanth Nadkarni, *Journal of a Visit to Europe in 1896*]
Oriental criticism of European manners leaves...
[unsigned]

[13–18 July 1903]
Contribution to *The Daily News*
Artless Lays *[Book Reviews]*
Mr. Lacon Watson preludes his little volume with...
[unsigned]
A letter held in the Guardian *archives, dated 19 July 1903, from Masefield to the* Manchester Guardian *(presumably C.P. Scott) encloses these three cuttings as samples of work. They are described as 'three reviews from the "Daily News" of last week'.*

[pre 1905]
Contributions to *Longman's Magazine*
Ronald Primeau, writing on Longman's Magazine in British Literary Magazines – The Victorian and Edwardian Age, 1837–1913, *(ed. Alvin Sullivan, Connecticut: Greenwood Press, 1984) states (on p.210): 'Many notables published in Longman's, among them... John Masefield...' The indexes at the rear of each volume from 1899 until publication ceased in 1905 have been checked to no avail. Walter Graham, in* English Literary Periodicals *(Octagon Books 1966) also states (p.306) that Masefield contributed.*

[25 October 1905]
Contribution to *Manchester Guardian*
Purchas His Pilgrimes (vol.s 7, 8) *[Book Review]*
Listed by Drew even though Drew is aware that a previous (and correct) reference has already been given by him for this review on Sep 19, 1905. Two different book reviews do, however, appear on Oct 25, 1903

[pre 4 April 1907]
Contribution to an unidentified periodical
[Book Review: Machen, *The House of Souls*]
This book review by Masefield is mentioned in a letter from Grant Richards

[10 July 1907]
Contribution to *The Daily News*
[Book Review]
Mr. Bottomley lies in an enchanted garden, with its drowsy palace…
[quoted as 'Mr. John Masefield in The Daily News, *10 July 1907' in 'Some Press Opinions of Mr. Bottomley's Work' within Gordon Bottomley,* Poems of Thirty Years *(Constable & Co., 1925)]*

[after 29 January 1908]
Contribution to unidentified periodical
[Book Review: Abercrombie, *Interludes and Poems*]
See Lascelles Abercrombie, Emblems of Love, *(John Lane, 1912) for press reviews of previous work which quotes from a review by Masefield*

[2 May 1908]
Contribution to *Manchester Guardian*
Servia *[Prose]*
An article indicated as being signed 'J.E.M.' is listed in the index to the paper. It was not located, however, on the microfilmed edition

[17 November 1911]
Contribution to *Manchester Guardian*
Pressgang Days *[Prose]*
Listed by Drew, but not located in index or microfilmed edition of the paper

[December 1911]
Contribution to *Glasgow Evening News*
[Roadways] *[Verse]*
One road leads to London
[signed 'John Masefield']
The files of the Society of Authors indicate that publication of this poem infringed Masefield's copyright. The exact date and location have not been traced, however.

[pre 30 December 1911]
Contribution to *Public Opinion*
[Untitled] *[Verse]*
One road leads to London
The files of the Society of Authors indicate that this publication infringed Masefield's copyright before 30 December 1911

[unknown date]
'Cargoes'
Single leaf publication by The Poets' Guild as part of 'The Unbound Anthology'
Price: $0.05

[unknown date]
"I never see the red rose" [untitled poem from *Good Friday and other poems*]
Single leaf publication by The Poets' Guild as part of 'The Unbound Anthology'
Price: $0.05

[unknown date]
'Sea Fever'
Single leaf publication by The Poets' Guild as part of 'The Unbound Anthology'
Price: $0.05

[unknown date]
'Spanish Waters'
Single leaf publication by The Poets' Guild as part of 'The Unbound Anthology'
Price: $0.05
An advertisement issued by The Poets' Guild notes: 'The Unbound Anthology is a collection of poems published by The Poets' Guild, of Christodora House, printed on separate sheets of paper, for use in clubs and schools, and for lovers of poetry interested in compiling their own anthologies. The Poets' Guild is a group of writers banded together, not for literary purposes, but because they are interested in community service. Their activities focus at Christodora House, one of the neighborhood houses of New York City. The proceeds of the Unbound Anthology are to be devoted to the Poets' House, an Arts Community Center for Neighborhood Work.'

[1920s]
[Oxford Recitations Syllabuses]
See notes to B235(a)

1928
[Hymn for *The Coming of Christ*]
See notes to A115(a). This presumably comprises the programme for the Canterbury Cathedral production which includes 'The Song of The Coming of Christ'.

L. Proof Copies

Proof copies – presumably issued for review purposes – are listed here. Authorial proof copies (for example, those stamped by Heinemann 'FIRST PROOFS | (ONCE READ ONLY)', unbound gatherings or galley proofs) are excluded. It is assumed that proofs printed on one side of a leaf only comprise authorial proofs. The following are therefore presumed to be pre-publication copies available to a limited public.

1924

Sard Harker (William Heinemann Ltd., 1924)
>   [HRHRC (TEMP M377SAR 1924)]

1928

The Coming of Christ (William Heinemann Ltd., 1928)
>   [private collection (ROV) inscribed 'For Ruth Spooner, | "The onlie begetter of these | ensuing Sonnets." | from John Masefield. | April 28. 1928.']

1931

Minnie Maylow's Story and other tales and scenes (William Heinemann Ltd., 1931)
>   [private collection (PWE)]
>   [HRHRC (AC-L M377MIN 1931) inscribed 'A proof copy of a volume | of tales in verse, many | of them devised for the | excellent speakers who | were then our colleagues. | John Masefield. | The London Library Appeal. | No 51.' on p.[i] and 'Proof Copy. | Minnie Maylow's Story. | 1931.' on upper wrapper]

1933

The Conway (William Heinemann Ltd., 1933)
>   [private collection (ROV)]

1933

The Bird of Dawning (William Heinemann Ltd., 1933)
>   [private collection (ROV)]

1934

The Taking of the Gry (William Heinemann Ltd., 1934)
>   [HRHRC (TEMP M377 TAK 1934)]

1935

Victorious Troy (William Heinemann Ltd., 1935)
>   [HRHRC (PR6025 A77 V5 1935P)]

1936

A Letter from Pontus & other verse (William Heineman Ltd., 1936)
>   [HRHRC (TEMP M377LE 1936 cop.1) includes posthumous booklabel]

1936

Eggs and Baker (William Heinemann Ltd., 1936)
>   [private collection (PWE)]
>   [HRHRC (TEMP M377EG 1936)]
>   [HRHRC (AC-L M377EG 1936)]

1937

The Square Peg (William Heinemann Ltd., 1937)
    [HRHRC (TEMP M377SQ 1937)]

1940

The Twentyfive Days (William Heinemann Ltd., 1940)
    [private collection (PWE)]
    [HRHRC (TEMP M377TW 1940)]

1941

The Twenty Five Days (William Heinemann Ltd., 1941)
    [BL (X.708/8995) stamped 15 MAY 1973]
    [HRHRC (D761 M384)]
    [private collection (PWE)]

1941

The Nine Days Wonder (William Heinemann Ltd., 1941)
    [HRHRC (TEMP M377NIN 1941) inscribed 'For Con | from Jan | Feb 10. 1941']

1941

Conquer (William Heinemann Ltd., 1941)
    [HRHRC (TEMP M377CON 1941A)]

1941

Gautama the Enlightened and other verse (William Heinemann Ltd., 1941)
    [HRHRC (TEMP M377GAU 1941)]

1942

Natalie Maisie and Pavilastukay (William Heinemann Ltd., 1942)
    [HRHRC (TEMP M377NA 1942A)]

1943

Wonderings (William Heinemann Ltd., 1943)
    [HRHRC (TEMP M377WO 1943) inscribed 'To | My Wife. | Augt 17. 1943.']

1944

New Chum (William Heinemann Ltd., 1944)
    [private collection (PWE)]

1946

Selected Sonnets and Lyrics with Reynard the Fox A Tale in Verse (William Heinemann Ltd., 1946]
    [HRHRC (TEMP M377 B5 1946)]

1946

Selected Poems (New Edition) (William Heinemann Ltd., 1946)
    [HRHRC (TEMP M377 B7 1946) inscribed 'For Con | from Jan. | July 22. 1946.']

1952

So Long to Learn (William Heinemann Ltd., 1952)
    [private collection (PWE)]

Notes

Note on American Electrotype Editions

Many American editions of Masefield's works were electrotyped and manufacturers of the electrotype plates would often provide signatures that were not used during the binding process. This leads to the existence of volumes in which the signatures appear spurious.

In such cases the formula of the book is described as it is actually signed, followed by a note of aberrant signatures.

In many examples the first page of actual text will be signed 'B' and signatures will then occur every eight leaves. The preliminaries were evidently considered by the stereotype process to be separate and intended to be bound as the first gathering. However, when the preliminaries were not ultimately set over the number of leaves expected by the electrotype manufacturers or the binding of leaves was different from that anticipated, the first signature will not occur where expected.

For example, the first American edition of *The Everlasting Mercy and The Widow In The Bye Street* (see A21(a)) was bound as an octavo volume but signature 'B' occurs on the first page of text. The preliminaries occupy the first four leaves only so that the volume as bound includes the first printed signature in the middle of a gathering (the fifth leaf).

I would like to thank Philip Gaskell, the late Don McKenzie and G. Thomas Tanselle for their kind advice and investigations into this matter.

Note on 'Cheap' and 'Popular' editions

The 'Popular Edition' of a Heinemann novel was priced at 3s.6d. and became part of 'Heinemann's 3/6 Library'. Two Masefield novels were issued in this way, *Sard Harker* in July 1926 and *ODTAA* in May 1927. Both titles are recorded as such in the *English Catalogue of Books*. The series should not be confused with that described in the *ECB* as the 'Cheap edition' which comprises the 'Wanderer edition' (see below).

The 'popular edition' comprised a reprint of the first edition using the same setting of text. A cheaper binding consisting of coloured cloth with black ink printing may also have been employed.

Subsequent reprints of the standard, expensive issue include the 'popular edition' in reprint information and, as such, I have included these as reprints without description.

Note on Colonial editions

Heinemann exported many Masefield titles to British colonies. Macmillan had an arrangement to export to the Philippines. Colonial editions are, generally, omitted unless (in the case of A16(c)) they were published by an entirely new publisher.

Note on Posthumous Booklabel

From the Library of
JOHN MASEFIELD
O.M., Poet Laureate

Announcing that the firm of B.H. Blackwell Ltd of Oxford were intending 'to set up a Masefield shrine in a recess above the stairs leading down to Blackwells' Norrington Room...', *The Times* for 9 December 1967 also stated that the firm had 'acquired John Masefield's library for sale'.

Many books from the library were sold through a number of catalogues from the period although much material was never listed. Blackwells did however print a booklabel that was apparently inserted in each book from the library. Many examples of material from Masefield's library (including much of the HRHRC collection) does not include the booklabel and, therefore, was not handled by Blackwells. Since 1967 many have assumed that the label comprised Masefield's own. It is clear, however, that it is a posthumous addition.

Note on Collected Works

There have been three occasions on which Masefield's work has been 'collected' or issued in a Masefield series (beyond a single volume *Collected Poems*, for example). Each of these requires some explanation. Discussion of Heinemann's 'Wanderer' series in this context will remove some lengthy background from the main bibliographical descriptions.

The Macmillan Company led the way in 1923. The 'Leather Pocket Edition' comprised eight volumes each bound in a uniform red leather binding. Half of the volumes reprinted a previously published volume. The other four volumes comprise new titles (although the texts of the works had already been published). With the exception of one volume all included an entirely new introduction by the author. The entire set was available for $12.50 in 1923. By 1936 the complete set had, apparently, ceased to sell and the Macmillan Company asked Masefield for permission to sell volumes individually (see notes to A21(d)). Each volume is described in the bibliography either where it comprises a new edition of an existing volume (see A21(d), A49(h), A52(b) and A54(g)) or where the new title fits into the chronological sequence (see A66(a), A67(a), A68(a) and A69(a)).

In January 1925 a publishing contract between Masefield and Macmillan refers to 'Collected Poems, and Plays... (three volume edition)'. There are grounds to consider this merely a *Collected Poems* together with a *Collected Plays*; however, the intention to issue the collection in more than one volume suggests that this group should comprise a "collected works". The projected three volumes became four and each was uniformly bound. See A78, A79 and A80.

These American publications appear to be experiments in issuing Masefield in collected or convenient commercial guises. Heinemann's 'Wanderer' series was apparently intended as a more ambitious statement attempting to define a canon and, perhaps, a canonical status for the author.

One of the earliest letters on the subject is dated from the beginning of 1935. C.S. Evans notes here his plans for the 'edition' – rather than 'series' – and suggests choosing a specific name:

> ...Concerning the collected edition: I should like to begin on that almost immediately and bring the volumes out at intervals of two or three at a time, as we did in the case of Galsworthy's GROVE EDITION and as we are doing in the case of some others. I should like to give the edition a special name – Galsworthy's edition was called THE GROVE, Walpole's THE CUMBERLAND and Stevenson's THE TUSITALA. I should like also to have your views as to the format...
>
> (C.S. Evans, letter to John Masefield, 4 January 1935)
> (HRHRC, MS (Masefield, J.) Recip William Heinemann Ltd.)

Masefield's immediate concern was an apparent fear of including titles he wished to disown. Evans replied noting that 'collected' did not, necessarily, mean 'complete':

> ...It is no new thing for the collected work of an author to omit certain titles. Moore, for instance, would not admit into the final 'canon' SISTER TERESA and a number of his early works; but of the contents of the edition you must, of course, be the final judge. I have always had a very great affection for CAPTAIN MARGARET, and personally I should like to see it included in this edition if it were possible... ...It would certainly be a very great advantage if you could write prefaces, and although I do not want to burden you too much I should like to have a preface for every volume...
>
> (C.S. Evans, letter to John Masefield, 8 January 1935)
> (HRHRC, MS (Masefield, J.) Recip William Heinemann Ltd.)

(It is to be regretted that Masefield's English publishers did not eventually insist on provision of prefaces.) Masefield's attention was centred, rather, on choosing an appropriate name for the edition. Evans responded:

> ...Have you made up your mind about the general title of the edition? I prefer THE WANDERER to THE CONWAY edition to THE COCK – or what about the PINBURY EDITION, on the lines of Galsworthy's MANATON and GROVE.
>
> (C.S. Evans, letter to John Masefield, 4 March 1935)
> (HRHRC, MS (Masefield, J.) Recip William Heinemann Ltd.)

and it is little surprise that Masefield provided the names of ships rather than Evans' suggestions of houses. At this early stage it appears that Heinemann were planning a highly prestigious limited signed edition. Evans wrote:

> ...You may remember that in one of your limited editions you wrote a couplet above your signature on the docquet page. I was talking to our travellers on Saturday about the limited edition of the collected works, and they suggested that it would be a very strong selling point if you would do this again. I am afraid this would be rather a labour but it would give the edition a unique value.
>
> (C.S. Evans, letter to John Masefield, 15 March 1935)
> (HRHRC, MS (Masefield, J.) Recip William Heinemann Ltd.)

Evans' reference is to the limited signed edition of *Collected Poems* published in 1923 (see A71(b)). The plan was, however, unrealised. By April 1935, Evans had developed his plans and wrote proposing publication in groups. He was, however, still hoping for an expensive (and 'definitive' edition):

…If we keep to our present plan, we propose to issue the collected edition in three or four batches as follows:

(1)	SARD HARKER	(2) COLLECTED POEMS – 3 vols.
	ODTAA	
	GALLIPOLI	
(3)	BIRD OF DAWNING	(4) RECENT PROSE
	2 VOLUMES OF PLAYS	THE WANDERER
		THE HAWBUCKS
		MIDNIGHT FOLK
		THE TAKING OF THE GRY

It would be unwise to issue a set of this kind all at once for I think that booksellers and the public would prefer to buy the volumes two or three at a time rather than have to pay for the whole set at once.

Before we definitely go forward on these lines, however, there is another idea which I should like to put before you, and I have discussed this with our sales manager and our entire sales force. Instead of issuing the edition at 5/- I am inclined to think that it would be better to reset the books and to issue the edition bound in blue buckram, with a bevelled board and with the golden cock embossed in the centre of the front cover; the published price to be 7/6 per volume. We could produce the books at this price in a form worthy of the definitive edition of your work…

(C.S. Evans, letter to John Masefield, 12 April 1935)
(HRHRC, MS (Masefield, J.) Recip William Heinemann Ltd.)

It is important that Evans proposed reset text and the publication of entirely new volumes (a three volume *Collected Poems* and two volumes of plays). The first volumes issued were indeed *Gallipoli* (see A34(g)), *Sard Harker* (see A75(d)) and *Odtaa* (see A82(d)) but these comprised the standard published gatherings with cancellans within the preliminaries noting the Wanderer edition. The binding was a blue cloth with an illustration of a cockerel in the lower right corner of the upper cover.

As publication of the edition progressed, the only volumes specifically set for the edition were the two volumes of *Plays* (see A120). Evidence suggests, however, that the three volume edition of *Collected Poems* reached proof stage in 1936 (see notes to A71(d)). It was never published, however.

The chronology is revealed in letters from Evans:

…The first three volumes of your collected edition, ODTAA, SARD HARKER and GALLIPOLI will be published in the 21st of this month and I am sending you today an advance copy of ODTAA…

(C.S. Evans, letter to John Masefield, 10 Oct 1935)
(HRHRC, MS (Masefield, J.) Recip William Heinemann Ltd.)

The next batch broke away from Evans' original plans:

The next two volumes for the WANDERER edition will be THE BIRD OF DAWNING, which will be issued in May, and this will be followed shortly afterward by THE HAWBUCKS…

(C.S. Evans, letter to John Masefield, 19 February 1936)
(HRHRC, MS (Masefield, J.) Recip William Heinemann Ltd.)

One month later Evans made reference to the volumes of *Plays*:

We have published seven volumes of THE WANDERER edition. The last two volumes were plays – published in February…

(C.S. Evans, letter to John Masefield, 19 March 1937)
(HRHRC, MS (Masefield, J.) Recip William Heinemann Ltd.)

The late 1930s was not, however, a time that would support this type of publication. Evans appeared reluctant to abandon the edition and wrote:

I should like to give a little more thought to the question of the collected edition. It is quite true that the books have not sold well, but then collected editions do not sell very well nowadays. I am inclined to think that it would be rather a mistake to stop issuing the edition: we have announced the collected edition, and a certain number of people have bought them and can legitimately expect to have the edition completed. So far we have issued seven volumes:-

GALLIPOLI	ODTAA	SARD HARKER
THE HAWBUCKS	THE BIRD OF DAWNING	PLAYS – Vols. 1 and 2

and the following are still to come:-

RECENT PROSE
THE WANDERER
MIDNIGHT FOLK
THE TAKING OF THE GRY
COLLECTED POEMS

You will remember that we have entirely re-set COLLECTED POEMS (and since I am writing to you, we should like to have the proofs with your corrections as soon as may be) and our capital expenditure on this edition has been and will be pretty considerable. Apart from that, I dislike beginning a collected edition and leaving it unfinished: it savours a little of breaking faith with the people who have spent money on buying half of the edition...

(C.S. Evans, letter to John Masefield, 16 April 1937)
(Archives of William Heinemann)

Although the Archives of William Heinemann suggest that *Victorious Troy*, *Eggs and Baker* and *The Square Peg* were under serious consideration for the edition (or may, indeed, have been issued) in December 1938 it appears that the edition was terminated before the outbreak of war. 'Breaking faith' or not, in September 1946 A.S. Frere wrote informing Masefield that 'in the circumstances we had perhaps better abandon the idea of reviving the "Wanderer" Edition'. The 'circumstances' were presumably either poor sales, the effects of war, or both.

Curiously choosing to exclude *The Hawbucks* and *The Bird of Dawning*, the British Library holds only five volumes as 'The Collected Works of John Masefield. Wanderer edition' for a date range of 1935–37. *The Shorter New Cambridge Bibliography of English Literature* similarly lists only five volumes for this edition. Volumes (with the exception of the *Plays*) are not new editions, in strict bibliographical terms. However, the alterations to the standard work that allowed admittance to the "Wanderer Edition", coupled to Evans' grand (unrealised) schemes suggest that the volumes be granted full bibliographical descriptions.

Index of Verse Titles

This listing excludes all occurances of poetry that have not been independently verified (therefore items described in italics are omitted here). Many of the titles provided by periodicals are, presumably, not authorial. To aid consistency, some attempt has been made to standardise entries (usually titles). Thus, 'Harbour-Bar' and 'Harbour Bar' are not independently listed. The main bibliographical contents listing reproduces titles as present in the printed original. Inconsistencies in punctuation, generally, remain. Sections F, G, H, I and several items from J are excluded here. Poetical plays are omitted, although poems extracted from plays (as present in *Selected Poems* or *Collected Poems*, for example) are included. All 'titles' which include roman numerals, or are elsewhere listed as '[Untitled]' have been omitted. This index should be used in conjunction with the Index of Verse First Lines.

Index of Verse First Lines

This listing excludes all occurances of poetry that have not been independently verified (therefore items described in italics are omitted here). Many of the titles provided by periodicals are, presumably, not authorial. To aid consistency, some attempt has been made to standardise entries (usually titles). Thus, 'Harbour-Bar' and 'Harbour Bar' are not independently listed. The main bibliographical contents listing reproduces titles as present in the printed original. Inconsistencies in punctuation, generally, remain. Sections F, G, H, I and several items from J are excluded here. Poetical plays are omitted, although poems extracted from plays (as present, for example, in *Selected Poems* or *Collected Poems* are included.)

'A calm like Jove's beneath a fiery air.' Sard Harker A71(c) / A71(d) / A114(a) / A114(b)

'A century since, this hater of mis-rule,' Lines for the Centenary of Ronald Ross, Scientist and Poet C125.171

'A happy task, to praise this mental prince' Lines for a One Hundredth Birthday George Bernard Shaw C405.008

'A happy task, to praise this mental prince' Lines for the Hundredth Anniversary of the Birth of Bernard Shaw C385.010

'A hundred years ago they quarried for the stone here;' "A Hundred Years Ago...." A173(a) / A173(b) / A173(c) / A173(d)

'A hundred years ago they quarried for the stone here;' XX A148(a)

'A hundred years ago, they quarried for the stone here;' XXII A Hundred Years Ago A114(a) / A114(b)

'A hundred years ago, they quarried for the stone here;' XXII. A37(a) A45(a) / A78(a) / A91(a)

'A hundred years ago, they quarried for the stone here;' XXIII. A38(a) / A68(a) / A71(a) / A71(b) / A71(c) / A71(d)

'A hundred years ago this was the range' [Melbourne] C125.057

'A little wooden schooner, painted white,' The Spanish Main Schooner A71(d) / 7(a) / A117(aa) / A117(b) / A148(a) / A173(a) / A173(b) / A173(c) / A173(d) / A174(a) / A174(a)

'A prayer is intense thought with lasting life.' [On The Prayers For Our Princess' Happiness] C165.121

'A prayer is intense thought with lasting life.' On the Prayers for our Princess's Happiness C125.188

'A strong wind brushes down the clover,' On Malvern Hill C020.008 / C025.002

'A wind is brushing down the clover,' On Malvern Hill A1(a) / A1(aa) / A1(b) / A1(c) / A1(d) / A39(a) / A45(a) / A66(a) / A71(a) / A71(b) / A71(c) / A71(d) / A78(a) / A91(a) / A114(a) / A114(b) / A143(a) / C165.107

'A wind is nestling "south and soft,"' Christmas Eve at Sea C025.018 C060.008 C105.001

'A wind is rustling 'south and soft,"' Christmas Eve at Sea A1(a) / A1(aa) / A1(b) / A1(c) / A1(d) / A35(a) / A35(b)

'A wind is rustling 'south and soft','' A Christmas Carol C310.001

'A wind is rustling "south and soft,"' Christmas Eve at Sea A45(a) / A66(a) / A71(a) / A71(b) / A71(c) / A71(d) /A78(a) / A91(a) / A114(a) / A114(b)

'A wind is rustling "south and soft,"' Christmas, 1901 C015.001

'A wind's in the heart o' me, a fire's in my heels,' A Wanderer's Song A1(a) / A1(aa) / A1(d)

'A wind's in the heart o' me, a fire's in my heels,' A Wind's in the Heart O' Me C020.012 / C025.004

'A wind's in the heart of me, a fire's in my heels,' A Wanderer's Song A1(b) / A1(c) / A35(a) / A35(b) / A45(a) / A66(a) / A71(a) / A71(b) / A71(c) / A71(d) / A78(a) / A91(a) / A114(a) / A114(b) / A175(a)

'A windy night was blowing on Rome,' The Rider at the Gate A62(d) / A63(a) / A65(a) / A69(a) / A71(a) / A71(b) / A71(c) / A71(d) / A78(a) / A91(a) / A114(a) / A114(b) / A148(a) / A151(a) / A157(a) / A157(b) / A173(a) / A173(b) / A173(c) / A173(d) / A175(a) / A178(a)

'About the crowing of the cock,' The Hounds of Hell A52(a) / A52(aa) / A52(b) / A53(a) / A53(aa) / A62(a) / A62(b) / A62(c) / A62(cc) / A62(d) / A71(a) / A71(b) / A71(c) / A71(d) / A78(a) / A91(a) / A114(a) / A114(b) / A148(a) / A157(a) / A157(b)

'Adventure on, companion, for this' Adventure On A151(a) / A157(a) / A157(b)

'After destruction, lo, a human need,' [Untitled] C125.113

'After long months abroad, the troupe returns to play.' A Lady of the Court A125(a) / A125(b) / A125(c)

'After long watching of the fatal sea,' Crews Coming Down Gangways A138(a) / A138(b)

'After the bombing, when the men are home,' The Reconnaissance Pilots A138(a) / A138(b)

'After the cuckoo's coming thrills the valley' The Foreign Dancers A125(a) / A125(b) / A125(c)

'After the ranks of stubble have lain bare,' Autumn Ploughing A71(d) / A117(a) / A117(aa) / A117(b) / A148(a)

'After the traffic with its roars and glares' In a Theatre C335.001 / C340.001

'After the wedding, all returned to feast.' The Buried Bride or True Love Finds a Way A166(a) / A166(b)

'After these ninety years, he can survey' For the Ninetieth Birthday of George Bernard Shaw D14(a)

'After these ninety years, he can survey' On the Ninetieth Birthday of Bernard Shaw B430(a) / C405.002

'Ah! Authors answer. All aid. Arrest...' [Untitled] C165.038

'Ah, but Without there is no spirit scattering;' XI A147(a) / A157(a) / A157(b)

'Ah, but Without there is no spirit scattering;' XIII. A37(a) / A38(a) / A45(a) / A68(a) / A71(a) / A71(b) / A71(c) / A71(d) / A78(a) / A91(a) / A114(a) / A114(b) / A148(a)

'Ah, but Without there is no spirit scattering;' [Untitled] A151(a)

'Between the barren pasture and the wood' I A62(a) / A62(b) / A62(c) / A62(cc) / A62(d)
'Between the barren pasture and the wood' The Brook Goes By A151(a)
'Between the barren pasture and the wood' The Daffodil Fields A24(a) / A24(b) / A45(a) / A67(a) / A71(a) / A71(b) / A71(c) /
    A71(d) / A78(a) / A91(a) / A114(a) / A114(b) / A148(a) / C150.007
'Between the barren pasture and the wood' The Daffodil Fields [Extract] C185.001
'Beyond the tide-rips of the shrieking sea,' A Watcher of the Moyle A125(a) / A125(b) / A125(c)
'Boast not about our score.' Any Dead to Any Living A89(a) / C220.005
'Born for nought else, for nothing but for this,' Born for Nought Else A12(a) / A23(a) / A23(b) / A45(a) / A66(a) / A71(a) / A71(b)
    / A71(c) / A71(d) / A78(a) / A91(a) / A114(a) / A114(b) / A148(a)
'"Bright thou art, beloved Lady,' Bright Darling A156(a) / A156(b)
'Bring me a fable out of the old time,' If the Princess ask a Ballet A125(a) / A125(b) / A125(c)
'Bring wine, and oil, and barley cakes,' [Untitled] C100.002
'Bristled and speared, in army, rank on rank,' September Fields A123(a) / A123(b) / A123(c)
'Builded in every village in the land,' [Untitled] A62(c) / A62(cc) / A78(a) / A91(a) / B185(a) / B185(aa)
'Burning they watch, and mothlike owls…' The End of the Trouble A151(a)
'But all has passed, the tune has died away,' VII A32(a) / A32(b)
'But all has passed, the tune has died away,' XX A157(a) / A157(b)
'But all has passed, the tune has died away,' XXII A147(a)
'But all has passed, the tune has died away,' XXVIII A148(a)
'But all has passed, the tune has died away,' XXXII A38(a) / A68(a) / A71(a) / A71(b) / A71(c) / A71(d)
'But all has passed, the tune has died away,' [Untitled] A29(a) / A30(a) / A30(aa) / A45(a) / A62(a) / A62(b) / A62(c) / A62(cc) /
    A62(d) / A78(a) / A91(a) / A114(a) / A114(b)
'But when the news of Uther's death was brought' The Aftermath | *Drafts and Outline* A177(a)
'By many a door this traveller has stayed,' To Walter de la Mare B455(a)
'By many waters and on many ways' *from* Biography A173(a) / A173(b) / A173(c) / A173(d)
'By many waters and on many ways' Golden Moments C105.003
'By ways unknown, unseen,' On the Coming of Arthur A62(d) / A71(c) / A71(d) / A88(a) / A88(c) / A88(b) / A88(d) / A91(a) /
    A114(a) / A114(b) / A148(a) / A177(a)
'By Will, Man dared in den and heath' The Will A71(d) / A117(a) / A117(aa) / A117(b) / A148(a) / A157(a) / A157(b)

'Campden town | Is quiet after London riot;' Honest Dover's Fancy B20(a)
'Can it be blood and brain, this transient force' VIII A147(a) / A157(a) / A157(b)
'Can it be blood and brain, this transient force' X. A37(a) / A38(a) / A45(a) / A68(a) / A71(a) / A71(b) / A71(c) / A71(d) / A78(a)
    / A91(a) / A114(a) / A114(b) / A148(a)
'Can it be blood and brain, this transient force' [Untitled] A62(a) / A62(b) / A62(c) / A62(cc) / A62(d) / A151(a)
'Chain upon chain, and prison within prison,' Lines for the Home-Coming of Our Most Gracious Sovereign Lady C125.166
'"Cherries and bread, for Man's delight, and need,' Middle Farm or the Cherries A166(a) / A166(b)
'"Cherries and bread, for Man's delight, and need,' Middle Farm, or the Cherries A175(a)
'Cherries and bread, for Man's delight, and need,' The Cherries C505.003
'Clean green windy billows notching out the sky,' Cardigan Bay C010.003
'Clean, green, windy billows notching out the sky,' Cardigan Bay A1(a) / A1(aa) / A1(b) / A1(c) / A1(d) / A35(a) / A35(b) / A45(a)
    / A66(a) / A71(a) / A71(b) / A71(c) / A71(d) / A78(a) / A91(a) / A114(a) / A114(b)
'COLONIES built a fort for safety's sake,' Nets A71(d) / A117(a) / A117(aa) / A117(b) / A148(a)
'"Come to us fiery with the saints of God' XXXV. A32(a)
'"Come to us fiery with the saints of God' [Untitled] A29(a) / A30(a) / A30(aa) / A39(a) / A45(a) / A78(a) / A91(a) / A114(a) /
    A114(b) / A143(a)
'COTTA | Would God the route would come for home.' XVII. The Frontier A37(a) / A45(a) / A78(a) / A91(a) / A114(a) / A114(b)
'COTTA. Would God the route would come for home!' XVIII. The Frontier A38(a) / A68(a) / A71(a) / A71(b) / A71(c) / A71(d)
'Craftsman, your brightest light, painter, your fairest hue,' Come, All Ye A125(a) / A125(b) / A125(c)
'Creeds are denied, the nations disagree,' The Norfolk Wherry A123(a) / A123(b) / A123(c)

'Dante was as a star above his head.' Dante Gabriel Rossetti A144(a) / A144(b)
'Dark Eleanor and Henry sat at meat' The Rose of the World A62(d) / A71(d) / A105(a) / A105(b) / A105(c) / A105(cc) / A114(a)
    / A114(b) / A148(a) / A157(a) / A157(b)
'Darker it grew, still darker, and the stars' The Setting of the Watch A62(a) / A62(b) / A62(c) / A62(cc) / A62(d)
'Days of endeavour have been good: the days' From *Biography* A35(a) / A35(b)
'Days of endeavour have been good: the days' The Cutter Race A151(a)
'Dead is Orestes: dead: I said: I say again.' A Messenger Speech A156(a) / A156(b)
'Death lies in wait for you, you wild thing in the wood,' XLI. A32(a) / A32(b)
'Death lies in wait for you, you wild thing in the wood,' XLVIII A157(a) / A157(b)
'Death lies in wait for you, you wild thing in the wood,' LIV A147(a)
'Death lies in wait for you, you wild thing in the wood,' LX A148(a)

'Death lies in wait for you, you wild thing in the wood,' LXIV A38(a) / A68(a) / A71(a) / A71(b) / A71(c) / A71(d)

'Death lies in wait for you, you wild thing in the wood,' [Untitled] A29(a) / A30(a) / A30(aa) / A45(a) / A62(a) / A62(b) / A62(c) / A62(cc) / A62(d) / A78(a) / A91(a) / A114(a) / A114(b)

'Desire, longing for life, and ignorance,' Gotama [*sic*] The Enlightened [Extract] C510.001

'"Destiny's Sword," this Cortés, whom you praise?' The Princess Malinal A166(a) / A166(b)

'Die we must and go to dust' Die We Must C100.008

'Dim violets, violets white, and ye' To the Spring Flowers C025.007

'Dim violets, violets white, and ye' Two Songs To the Spring Flowers C020.028

'Dingy, unpainted, dark, war and November,' The Station A138(a) / A138(b)

'Down Bye Street, in a little Shropshire town,' The Widow in the Bye Street A21(a) / A21(b) / A21(c) / A21(d) / A21(e) / A22(a) / A45(a) / A71(a) / A71(b) / A71(c) / A71(d) / A78(a) / A91(a) / A114(a) / A114(b) / A148(a) / A173(a) / A173(b) / A173(c) / A173(d) / C150.003

'Down in his bunk the Dauber lay awake' The Watch Below A62(a) / A62(b) / A62(c) / A62(cc) / A62(d)

'Dream after dream I see the wrecks that lie' Posted A62(d) / A71(c) / A71(d) / A99(a) / A101(a) / A101(b) / A101(bb) / A101(c) / A101(d) / A114(a) / A114(b) / A148(a) / A174(a) / A174(a)

'Drop me the seed, that I even in my brain' X A147(a) / A157(a) / A157(b)

'Drop me the seed, that I even in my brain' XII. A38(a) / A68(a) / A71(a) / A71(b) / A71(c) / A71(d) / A148(a)

'Drop me the seed, that I, even in my brain' XII. A37(a) / A45(a) / A78(a) / A91(a) / A114(a) / A114(b)

'Drop me the seed, that I even in my brain' [Untitled] A151(a)

'Dunno a heap about the what an' why,' Vagabond A1(a) / A1(aa) / A1(b) / A1(c) / A1(d) / A45(a) / A66(a) / A71(a) / A71(b) / A71(c) / A71(d) / A78(a) / A91(a) / A114(a) / A114(b)

'Dunno a heap about the what and why,' Vagabond C010.005

'During the night, the silent-footed snow' The Hounds in Snow A123(a) / A123(b) / A123(c)

'Each greedy self, by consecrating lust,' [Untitled] A29(a) / A30(a) / A30(aa) / A45(a) / A78(a) / A91(a) / A114(a) / A114(b)

'Even after all these years there comes the dream' III. A32(a) / A32(b)

'Even after all these years there comes the dream' XVI A157(a) / A157(b)

'Even after all these years there comes the dream' XVIII A147(a)

'Even after all these years there comes the dream' XXIV A148(a)

'Even after all these years there comes the dream' XXVIII. A38(a) / A68(a) / A71(a) / A71(b) / A71(c) / A71(d)

'Even after all these years there comes the dream' [Untitled] A29(a) / A30(a) / A30(aa) / A45(a) / A78(a) / A91(a) / A114(a) / A114(b)

'Even as April's footsteps that unseen' Upon Our Sovereign Lady's Venture in a Great Cause C125.165 / C165.132

'Even as April's footsteps that unseen' [Upon Our Sovereign Lady's Venture in a Great Cause] C165.113

'"Even as the blacksmith beats and brays' The Forge A123(a) / A123(b) / A123(c)

'Even in peace, scant quiet is at sea;' For All Seafarers B400(a)

'Even in peace, scant quiet is at sea;' For the Sailors D10(a) / E6(a) / E6(b)

'Even now they shifted suits of sails; they bent' The Horn A62(a) / A62(b) / A62(c) / A62(cc) / A62(d)

'Even so was wisdom proven blind,' Epilogue A62(a) / A62(b) / A62(c) / A62(cc) / A62(d)

'Even so was wisdom proven blind;' Gallipoli, 1915 A148(a) / A173(a) / A173(b) / A173(c) / A173(d)

'Every day and all day long' A Study for a ballad of The Galley Rowers C060.015

'Farewell and adieu to you fine Spanish Ladies —' Spanish Ladies C045.002

'Fifty-five years ago, as impulse led,' My Library: Volume One A177(a) / C405.003

'Flesh, I have knocked at many a dusty door,' Two Sonnets C215.001 / C215.005

'Flesh, I have knocked at many a dusty door,' VI. A32(a) / A32(b)

'Flesh, I have knocked at many a dusty door,' XIX A157(a) / A157(b)

'Flesh, I have knocked at many a dusty door,' XXI A147(a)

'Flesh, I have knocked at many a dusty door,' XXVII A148(a)

'Flesh, I have knocked at many a dusty door,' XXXI. A38(a) / A68(a) / A71(a) / A71(b) / A71(c) / A71(d)

'Flesh, I have knocked at many a dusty door,' [Untitled] A29(a) / A30(a) / A30(aa) / A45(a) / A62(a) / A62(b) / A62(c) / A62(cc) / A62(d) / A78(a) / A91(a) / A114(a) / A114(b) / A175(a)

'Fog covered all the great Fleet homeward bound,' Lines on the Shipwreck of Admiral Sir Cloudesley Shovell… A166(a) / A166(b) / A175(a) / C520.002

'Fog covered all the great Fleet homeward bound,' The Shipwreck C215.012

'For a minute he ran and heard no sound,' The End of the Run A151(a)

'For ages you were rock, far below light,' Number "534" B280(a)

'For ages you were rock, far below light,' "534" C125.056

'For ages you were rock; far below light,' ["534"] C165.060

'For ages you were rock, far below light,' Number 534 D6(a)

'For fifty days to whirl from day to day' Lines on Our Sovereign Lady's Return C125.189

'For, like an outcast from the city, I' XL. A32(a) / A32(b)

'For, like an outcast from the city, I' XLVII A157(a) / A157(b)

'For, like an outcast from the city, I' LIII A147(a)

'For, like an outcast from the city, I' LIX A148(a)

'For, like an outcast from the city, I' LXIII. A38(a) / A68(a) / A71(a) / A71(b) / A71(c) / A71(d)

'For, like an outcast from the city, I' [Untitled] A29(a) / A30(a) / A30(aa) / A45(a) / A78(a) / A91(a) / A114(a) / A114(b)

'Forget all these, the barren fool in power,' Forget A52(a) / A52(aa) / A52(b) / A53(a) / A53(aa) / A62(a) / A62(b) / A62(c) / A62(cc) / A62(d) / A71(a) / A71(b) / A71(c) / A71(d) / A78(a) / A91(a) / A114(a) / A114(b) / A147(a) / A148(a) / A151(a)

'Forget all these, the barren fool in power,' Sonnet C290.001

'FORTUNE. | I am Fortune: I give as is fitting to each of my souls,' Richard Whittington A71(d) / A105(a) / A105(b) / A105(c) / A105(cc) / A114(a) / A114(b)

'Forty years ago the flower of all England's shipping belonged...' The River Mersey A151(a)

'Four bells were struck, the watch was called on deck,' Dauber A23(a) / A23(b) / A25(a) / A25(b) / A39(a) / A45(a) / A67(a) / A71(a) / A71(b) / A71(c) / A71(d) / A78(a) / A91(a) / A114(a) / A114(b) / A143(a) / A174(a) / A174(a) / C150.006

'Four bells were struck, the watch was called on deck' Dauber A148(a) / A168(a) / A168(b) / A173(a) / A173(b) / A173(c) / A173(d) / A175(a)

'Four bells were struck, the watch was called on deck,' From *Dauber* A35(a) / A35(b)

'Four double strikes repeated on the bells,' Eight Bells A173(a) / A173(b) / A173(c) / A173(d)

'Four double strokes repeated on the bells,' Eight Bells A71(c) / A71(d) / A99(a) / A101(a) / A101(b) / A101(bb) / A101(c) / A101(d) / A114(a) / A114(b) / A148(a) / A174(a) / A174(a)

'French poets write:-That, Lancelot the brave' The Old Tale of The Breaking of the Links A71(c) / A71(d) / A88(a) / A88(c) / A177(a)

'French poets write:-That, Lancelot the brave' The Taking of Gwenivere A88(b) / A88(d) / A91(a) / A114(a) / A114(b)

'Friends and loves we have none, nor wealth nor blessed abode,' The Seekers A12(a) / A23(a) / A23(b) / A45(a) / A66(a) / A71(a) / A71(b) / A71(c) / A71(d) / A78(a) / A91(a) / A148(a) / A173(a) / A173(b) / A173(c) / A173(d)

'Friends and loves we have none, nor wealth, nor blessed abode,' The Seekers A2(a) / A2(b) / A114(a) / A114(b) / C020.036 / C025.010

'Friends and loves we have none, nor wealth nor blest abode.' The Seekers C170.016

'Friends, we are opening at this solemn time,' Miss Muriel Pratt's Season D1(a)

'Friends, we are opening at this solemn time' [Untitled] B310(a)

'From '41 to '51' The Everlasting Mercy A19(a) / A19(b) / A19(c) / A21(a) / A21(b) / A21(c) / A21(d) / A21(e) / A39(a) / A45(a) / A71(a) / A71(b) / A71(c) / A71(d) / A78(a) / A91(a) / A114(a) / A114(b) / A143(a) / A148(a) / A173(a) / A173(b) / A173(c) / A173(d) / C150.002

'From '41 to '51' The Everlasting Mercy – Saul Kane Unredeemed A157(a) / A157(b)

'From Wales and Wye the wester roared,' The Windy Christmas C505.005

'Gawaine the Kind,' Gareth's Wake A177(a)

'Give me a light that I may see her,' Lyric A52(a) / A52(aa) / A52(b) / A53(a) / A53(aa) / A71(a) / A71(b) / A71(c) / A71(d) / A78(a) / A91(a) / A114(a) / A114(b) / A148(a) / C220.003

"Give way, my lads,' the coxwains used to say' Give Way A171(a) / A171(b)

'Glad memories come, of old, long-distant days' Remembering Dame Myra Hess B560(a)

'Go, spend your penny, Beauty, when you will,' XLIV. A32(a) / A32(b)

'Go, spend your penny, Beauty, when you will,' XLIX A157(a) / A157(b)

'Go, spend your penny, Beauty, when you will,' LVII A147(a)

'Go, spend your penny, Beauty, when you will,' LXIII A148(a)

'Go, spend your penny, Beauty, when you will,' LXVII. A38(a) / A68(a) / A71(a) / A71(b) / A71(c) / A71(d)

'Go, spend your penny, Beauty, when you will,' [Untitled] A29(a) / A30(a) / A30(aa) / A45(a) / A62(a) / A62(b) / A62(c) / A62(cc) / A62(d) / A78(a) / A91(a) / A114(a) / A114(b)

'Going by Daly's shanty I heard the boys within' The Emigrant A2(a) / A2(b) / A12(a) / A23(a) / A23(b) / A45(a) / A66(a) / A71(a) / A71(b) / A71(c) / A71(d) / A78(a) / A91(a) / A114(a) / A114(b) / A148(a) / A173(a) / A173(b) / A173(c) / A173(d) / A174(a) / A174(a)

'Gomorrah paid so for its holiday;' Where They Took Train A125(a) / A125(b) / A125(c)

"Goneys an' gullies an' all o' the birds o' the sea,' Sea-Change A1(a) / A1(aa) / A1(b) / A1(c) / A1(d) / A35(a) / A35(b)

"Goneys an' gullies an' all o' the birds o' the sea' Sea-Change A66(a) / A71(a) / A71(b) / A71(c) / A71(d)

"Goneys and gullies an' all o' the birds o' the sea,' Sea-Change A45(a) / A78(a) / A91(a) / A114(a) / A114(b)

"Goneys and gullies and all o' the birds o' the sea,' Jimmy the Dane C020.022

"Gonies an' gullies an' all o' the birds o' the sea,' Sea-Change C170.005

'Gray sea dim, smoke-blowing, hammer-racket, sirens' Liverpool, 1890 A71(c) / A71(d) / A95(a) / A99(a) / A101(a) / A101(b) / A101(bb) / A101(c) / A101(d) / E4(a) / E4(b) / J45

'Green rollers shatter into hands that shoot' Rehearsal A125(a) / A125(b) / A125(c)

'Grey sea dim, smoke-blowing, hammer-racket, sirens' Liverpool, 1890 A114(a) / A114(b)

'Harvest is home; the blueness is all dim;' Gleaners A123(a) / A123(b) / A123(c)

'He crossed the covert, he crawled the bank,' Reynard the Fox – The End of the Run A157(a) / A157(b)

'He lay dead on the cluttered deck and stared at the cold skies,' Bill A1(a) / A1(aa) / A1(b) / A1(c)/ A1(d) / A35(a) / A35(b) /
  A45(a) / A66(a) / A71(a) / A71(b) / A71(c) / A71(d) / A78(a) / A91(a) / A114(a) / A114(b) / C010.004

'He lolled on a bollard, a sun-burned son of the sea,' Sing a Song O' Shipwreck A1(a) / A1(aa) / A1(b) / A1(c) / A1(d) / A35(a) /
  A35(b) / A45(a) / A66(a) / A71(a) / A71(b) / A71(c) / A71(d) / A78(a) / A91(a) / A114(a) / A114(b)

'He lolled on a bollard, a sunburnt son of the sea,' Sing a Song O' Shipwreck C030.002

'He said, "I have known soldiers from my youth.' Another Upon the Same A138(a) / A138(b)

'He sees his comrades, and a coming test' Paddington. Mother and Son A138(a) / A138(b)

'He stumbled out of the alley-way with cheeks the colour of paste,' Coast-Fever C020.013

'He took her to Troy, the windy town' The Going to Troy A107(a) / A107(b) / A148(a)

'He took her to Troy, the windy town,' The Going to Troy A114(a) / A114(b)

'He tottered out of the alleyway with cheeks the colour of paste,' Fever Chills A1(a) / A1(aa) / A1(b) / A1(c) / A1(d) / A35(a) /
  A35(b) / A45(a) / A66(a) / A71(a) / A71(b) / A71(c) / A71(d) / A78(a) / A91(a) / A114(a) / A114(b)

'He was of splendid presence, tall, well-made,' On What He Was A129(a)

'He was of splendid presence, tall, well-made,' [On What He Was] A129(b)

'He who is Order, Beauty, Power and Glory,' A Prayer for a Beginning Reign C125.154

'He wore the smock-frock of the country's past,' Joseph Hodges, or The Corn A62(d) / A71(d) / A117(a) / A117(aa) / A117(b) /
  A148(a) / A151(a)

'Hear the yarn of a sailor, | An old yarn learned at sea.' The Yarn of The *Loch Achray* C030.001

'Hell, he expected,–hell. His eyes grew blind;' From Dauber | The Painter A178(a)

'Henry Plantagenet, the English King,' Dust to Dust A71(c) / A71(d) / A88(a) / A88(b) / A88(c) / A88(d) / A91(a) / A114(a) /
  A114(b) / A148(a) / A177(a)

'Her builder and owner drank tea with her captain below.' The Setting Forth A71(c) / A71(d) / A101(a) / A101(b) / A101(bb) /
  A101(c) / A101(d) / A114(a) / A114(b) / A148(a) / A174(a) / A174(a)

'Her builder and owner drank tea with her captain below' The Wanderer. The Setting Forth A97(a) / A100(a)

'Her heart is always doing lovely things,' Her Heart A12(a) / A23(a) / A23(b) / A45(a) / A66(a) / A71(a) / A71(b) / A71(c) / A71(d)
  / A78(a) / A91(a) / A114(a) / A114(b) / A148(a)

'Here, by the towers of your splendid town,' [On the Finish of the Sailing Ship Race Lisbon to Manhattan – 1964] C165.125

'Here ends the Pageant of how England stood' [Untitled] B485(a)

'Here ends the pageant of how England stood' [Untitled] C125.155

'Here, in the darkened room of this old house,' The Haunted A71(a) / A71(b) / A71(c) / A71(d)

'Here in the self is all that man can know' Sonnets On Beauty and Life C185.008

'Here in the self is all that man can know' Two Sonnets C215.001 / C215.005

'Here in the self is all that man can know' V. A32(a) / A32(b)

'Here in the self is all that man can know' XVIII A157(a) / A157(b)

'Here in the self is all that man can know' XX A147(a)

'Here in the self is all that man can know' XXVI A148(a)

'Here in the self is all that man can know' XXX. A38(a) / A68(a) / A71(a) / A71(b) / A71(c) / A71(d)

'Here in the self is all that man can know' [Untitled] A29(a) / A30(a) / A30(aa) / A45(a) / A62(a) / A62(b) / A62(c) / A62(cc) /
  A62(d) / A78(a) / A91(a) / A114(a) / A114(b)

'Here, in this darkened room of this old house,' The Haunted A63(a) / A65(a) / A69(a) / A78(a) / A91(a) / A114(a) / A114(b)

'Here in this house, to-night, our city makes' [Untitled] B310(a)

'Here, in this house, where we are singing thus,' St. Felix School B205(a)

'Here, in this vast, cool hangar, clean and lit,' The Birds of the Hangar A138(a) / A138(b)

'Here is the world of man and his adventure,' Prologue A123(a) / A123(b) / A123(c)

'Here lies poor Jack – grave, headstone, all in one' [Untitled] C280.003

'Here the legion halted, here the ranks were broken,' Camp Des Romains C235.003

'Here the legion halted, here the ranks were broken,' XXI A148(a)

'Here the legion halted, here the ranks were broken,' XXIII. A37(a) / A45(a) / A78(a) / A91(a)

'Here the legion halted, here the ranks were broken,' XXIII Here the Legion Halted A114(a) / A114(b)

'Here the legion halted, here the ranks were broken,' XXIV. A38(a) / A68(a) / A71(a) / A71(b) / A71(c) / A71(d)

'Here they lie mottled to the ground unseen,' Partridges A71(d) / A117(a) / A117(aa) / A117(b) / A148(a) / A175(a)

'Here we lay stone, that, at a future time,' Lines Spoken… At The Laying of the Foundation Stone of the National Theatre… D20(a)

'Here we lay stone, that, at a future time,' [Untitled] C125.145

'Here, whence his forbears sprang, a man is laid' East Coker C125.201

'Here, where we stood together, we three men,' XXII. A32(a) / A32(b)

'Here, where we stood together, we three men,' XXXVII A147(a)

'Here, where we stood together, we three men.' XLIII A148(a)

'Here, where we stood together, we three men,' XLVII. A38(a) / A68(a) / A71(a) / A71(b) / A71(c) / A71(d)

'Here, where we stood together, we three men,' [Untitled] A29(a) / A30(a) / A30(aa) / A45(a) / A78(a) / A91(a) / A114(a) / A114(b)
  / E5(a)

'Here you will put off childhood and be free' The Conway's word to the new-comer A109(a) / A109(b)

'"He's deader 'n nails,' the fo'c's'le said, "n' gone to his long sleep';' Burial Party A1(a) / A1(aa) / A1(b) / A1(c) / A1(d) / A35(a) / A35(b)

'It may be so with us, that in the dark,' XXIV A157(a) / A157(b)

'It may be so with us, that in the dark,' XXVI A147(a)

'It may be so with us, that in the dark,' XXXII A148(a)

'It may be so with us, that in the dark,' XXXVI. A38(a) / A68(a) / A71(a) / A71(b) / A71(c) / A71(d)

'It may be so with us, that in the dark' [Untitled] A30(a) / A30(aa)

'It may be so with us, that in the dark,' [Untitled] A29(a) / A45(a) / A62(a) / A62(b) / A62(c) / A62(cc) / A62(d) / A78(a) / A91(a) / A114(a) / A114(b)

'It may be so with us, that in the dark' Which? C210.005

'It may be so; but let the unknown be.' VI A147(a) / A157(a) / A157(b)

'It may be so; but let the unknown be.' VII. A37(a) / A38(a) / A45(a) / A68(a) / A71(a) / A71(b) / A71(c) / A71(d) / A78(a) / A91(a) / A114(a) / A114(b)

'It may be so; but let the unknown be.' VII A148(a)

'It may be so; but let the unknown be.' [Untitled] A62(a) / A62(b) / A62(c) / A62(cc) / A62(d) / A151(a)

"It's a sunny pleasant anchorage is Kingdom Come,' 'Port O' Many Ships' A1(a) / A1(aa) / A1(d)

"It's a sunny pleasant anchorage, is Kingdom Come,' 'Port of Many Ships' A1(b) / A1(c) / A35(a) / A35(b)

"'It's a sunny pleasant anchorage is Kingdom Come,'" "Port O' Many Ships." C020.015 / C025.005

"'It's a sunny pleasant anchorage, is Kingdom Come,' Port of Many Ships A45(a) / A66(a) / A71(a) / A71(b) / A71(c) / A71(d) / A78(a) / A91(a) / A114(a) / A114(b)

'It's a warm wind, the west wind, full of birds' cries.' There's a Wind A-Blowing C025.003 / C020.011

'It's a warm wind, the west wind, full of birds' cries;' The West Wind A1(a) / A1(aa) / A1(b) / A1(c) / A1(d) / A12(a) / A23(a) / A23(b) / A39(a) / A45(a) / A62(a) / A62(b) / A62(c) / A62(cc) / A62(d) / A66(a) / A71(a) / A71(b) / A71(c) / A71(d) / A78(a) / A91(a) / A114(a) / A114(b) / A143(a) / A148(a) / A151(a) / A157(a) / A157(b) / A173(a) / A173(b) / A173(c) / A173(d) / A175(a) / C170.006

'It's Christmas Eve, and dogs do bark,' [Untitled] D25(a)

"It's Christmas Eve; the Kings are riding,' [Untitled] D26(a)

'It's pleasant in Holy Mary' St. Mary's Bells A2(a) / A2(b) / A12(a) / A23(a) / A23(b) / A45(a) / A66(a) / A71(a) / A71(b) / A71(c) / A71(d) / A78(a) / A91(a) / A114(a) / A114(b)

'Jake was a dirty Dago lad, an' he gave the skipper chin,' Cape Horn Gospel – II A1(a) / A1(aa) / A1(b) / A1(c) / A1(d) / A35(a) / A35(b) / A45(a) / A66(a) / A71(a) / A71(b) / A71(c) / A71(d) / A78(a) / A91(a)

'John Coxeter, who owned the Greenham Mill,' The Throckmorton Coat A171(a) / A171(b)

'Jonnox was English, educated, male,' Pavilastukay A136(a) / A136(b)

'Just half a century since, an old man showed' Old England A171(a) / A171(b) / A175(a)

'King Arthur watched within the ruined town,' Arthur in the Ruins A71(c) / A71(d) / A88(a) / A88(c) / A88(b) / A88(d) / A91(a) / A114(a) / A114(b) / A177(a)

'KING COLE. Trust still to Life, the day is not yet old.' He Speaks with the Showman A151(a)

'King Cole was King before the troubles came,' King Cole A55(a) / A55(b) / A63(a) / A69(a) / A71(a) / A71(b) / A71(c) / A71(d) / A78(a) / A91(a) / A114(a) / A114(b) / A148(a) / A173(a) / A173(b) / A173(c) / A173(d)

'King Sthenelus, my Father, has often told me' Sthenelus' Daughter *The Entry into Troy* A107(a) / A107(b) / A114(a) / A114(b) / A148(a) / A151(a)

'Kneel to the beautiful women who bear us this strange brave fruit.' Chorus A62(a) / A62(b) / A62(c) / A62(cc) / A62(d)

'Kneel to the beautiful women who bear us this strange brave fruit,' Chorus C120.004

'Kneel to the beautiful women who bear us this strange brave fruit.' Chanty A71(a) / A71(b) / A71(c) / A71(d) / A114(a) / A114(b) / A148(a)

'Kol brought the news of Uther's murdering' The Aftermath A177(a)

'Laugh and be merry, remember, better the world with a song,' Laugh and be Merry A2(a) / A2(b) / A12(a) / A23(a) / A23(b) / A45(a) / A66(a) / A71(a) / A71(b) / A71(c) / A71(d) / A78(a) / A91(a) / A114(a) / A114(b) / A148(a)

'Leaving the shepherds on the down' The Night of Kings C505.001

'Left by the sea these many thousand years' The Mid-day Sun A123(a) / A123(b) / A123(c)

'Let a people reading stories full of anguish' [Untitled] *The Twenty Five Days* 1941 proof copy

'Let all men praise the Woman who brings help.' Gotama [*sic*] The Enlightened [Extract] C510.001

'Let that which is to come be as it may,' XLVII. A32(a) / A32(b)

'Let that which is to come be as it may,' LII A157(a) / A157(b)

'Let that which is to come be as it may,' LX. A38(a) / A147(a)

'Let that which is to come be as it may,' LXVI A148(a)

'Let that which is to come be as it may,' LXX A68(a) / A71(a) / A71(b) / A71(c) / A71(d)

'Let that which is to come be as it may,' [Untitled] A29(a) / A30(a) / A30(aa) / A45(a) / A62(a) / A62(b) / A62(c) / A62(cc) / A62(d) / A78(a) / A91(a) / A114(a) / A114(b)

'Let us walk round: the night is dark but fine,' After forty years A109(a) / A109(b)

'Like bones the ruins of the cities stand,' Sonnets C165.099

'Morgause the Merry played beside the burn:' The Taking of Morgause A71(c) / A71(d) / A88(a) / A88(b) / A88(c) / A88(d) / A91(a) / A114(a) / A114(b) / A148(a) / A151(a) / A177(a)

'Most beautiful, most gifted, and most wise,' Remembering Dame Myra Hess A171(a) / A171(b) / A173(a) / A173(b) / A173(c) / A173(d) / A175(a)

'Most gracious Sovereign, leaving England's shore' To His Most Excellent Majesty The King Upon the Sailing of The Royal Family for South Africa C125.125 / C165.091

'Most gracious Sovereign, none can tell the cheer' To His Most Excellent Majesty The King Upon His Return from South Africa C125.126

'Mother Carey? She's the mother o' the witches' Mother Carey A1(a) / A1(aa) / A1(b) / A1(c) / A1(d) / A45(a) / A71(a) / A71(b) / A71(c) / A71(d) / A78(a) / A91(a)

'Mother Carey? She's the mother o' the witches' Mother Carey (As Told Me By The Bo'sun) A35(a) / A35(b) / A66(a) / C170.017

'"Mother Carey? She's the mother o' the witches,' Mother Carey. As told me by the Bos'un C020.007

'Much worth was in the country: yet, today,' Sixty Odd Years Ago A148(a) / A173(a) / A173(b) / A173(c) / A173(d)

'Mumblin' under the gallows, hearin' the clank o' the chain,' Blind Man's Vigil A2(a) / C035.004

'My Father, King Epeios of the Islands,' The Horse A107(a) / A107(b) / A114(a) / A114(b) / A148(a)

'My friend, my bonny friend, when we are old,' The Word A12(a) / A23(a) / A23(b) / A45(a) / A66(a) / A71(a) / A71(b) / A71(c) / A71(d) / A78(a) / A91(a) / A114(a) / A114(b) / A148(a) / C230.001

'My grand-dad said, to Sis and me,' Jouncer's Tump A156(a) / A156(b) / A173(a) / A173(b) / A173(c) / A173(d)

'"My name is Captain Kidd,' Captain Kidd C100.006

'My name is Mr. Israel Hands' A pleasant new comfortable ballad upon the death of Mr. Israel Hands, executed for piracy… C100.003

'My people owned Ryemeadows on the Moor,' Ryemeadows A169(a) / A169(b) / A175(a)

'My soul has many an old decaying room' The Death Rooms A12(a) / A23(a) / A23(b) / A45(a) / A62(a) / A62(b) / A62(c) / A62(cc) / A62(d) / A66(a) / A71(a) / A71(b) / A71(c) / A71(d) / A78(a) / A91(a) / A114(a) / A114(b) / A148(a)

'Next day was Sunday, his free painting day,' [From Dauber] | The Joke A178(a)

'Night after night, a great Star blazed.' [Untitled] D22(a)

'Night came again, but now I could not sleep.' II. A32(a)

'Night came again, but now I could not sleep;' II. A32(b)

'Night came again, but now I could not sleep;' XV A157(a) / A157(b)

'Night came again, but now I could not sleep;' XVII A147(a)

'Night came again, but now I could not sleep;' XXIII A148(a)

'Night came again, but now I could not sleep;' XXVII. A38(a) / A68(a) / A71(a) / A71(b) / A71(c) / A71(d)

'Night came again, but now I could not sleep.' [Untitled] A29(a) / A30(a) / A30(aa) / A45(a) / A78(a) / A91(a) / A114(a) / A114(b) / A175(a)

'Night fell, and all night long the Dauber lay' We Therefore Commit Our Brother A62(a) / A62(b) / A62(c) / A62(cc) / A62(d)

'Night is on the downland, on the lonely moorland,' "Night is on the Downland" A173(a) / A173(b) / A173(c) / A173(d)

'Night is on the downland, on the lonely moorland,' Poem C320.001

'Night is on the downland, on the lovely moorland,' The Downland E5(a)

'Night is on the downland, on the lonely moorland,' The Wind-Barren C220.001

'Night is on the downland, on the lonely moorland,' XIV A147(a)

'Night is on the downland, on the lonely moorland,' XVII A148(a)

'Night is on the downland, on the lonely moorland,' XVIII. A37(a) / A45(a) / A78(a) / A91(a)

'Night is on the downland, on the lonely moorland,' XVIII The Downland A114(a) / A114(b)

'Night is on the downland, on the lonely moorland,' XIX. A38(a) / A68(a) / A71(a) / A71(b) / A71(c) / A71(d)

'Night is on the downland, on the lonely moorland,' XXXVI. A32(b)

'Night was upon my eyelids,' [From the volume *Lyric Intermezzo* by Heinrich Heine] (*64*) A171(a) / A171(b)

'Ninety nine years ago, the long-dead hands' The New Figurehead D8(a) / D8(b)

'Ninety-nine years ago the long-dead hands' The New Figurehead C125.080

'No, for their names are written with the light' Not Only The Most Famous A125(a) / A125(b) / A125(c)

'No I know not;' On the Hill A114(b)

'No I know not;' On The Hill. Prologue A156(a) / A156(b)

'No I know not;' *from* On the Hill A173(a) / A173(b) / A173(c) / A173(d)

'No man takes the farm,' "No Man Takes the Farm" A178(a)

'No man takes the farm,' The Cold Cotswolds A36(a) / C235.002

'No man takes the farm,' XIX A148(a)

'No man takes the farm,' XXI. A37(a) / A45(a) / A78(a) / A91(a)

'No man takes the farm,' XXI The Cold Cotswolds A114(a) / A114(b)

'No man takes the farm,' XXII. A38(a) / A68(a) / A71(a) / A71(b) / A71(c) / A71(d)

'No rose but fades: no glory but must pass:' Waste A12(a) / A23(a) / A23(b) / A45(a) / A62(a) / A62(b) / A62(c) / A62(cc) / A62(d) / A66(a) / A71(a) / A71(b) / A71(c) / A71(d) / A78(a) / A91(a) / A114(a) / A114(b) / A148(a) / A175(a)

'O Passer-by, remember these two Friends,' In the Memory of Two Friends of all Great Causes B535(a) / B575(a)

'O poets, silent under laurels won,' On the Death of Walter De La Mare June 22, 1956 C125.167

'O Queen of Beauty, you who once were fire' Beauty A71(d) / A117(a) / A117(aa) / A117(b) / A148(a)

'O rightly your sublime one as he died' [Untitled] A126(a) / A126(b)

'O smiling, sun-burned youth who rode the sky' A Young English Air-Man A130(a) / A130(b)

'O smiling, sun-burned youth who rode the sky' [Untitled] *The Twenty Five Days* 1941 proof copy

'O, the sea breeze will be steady, and the tall ship's going trim,' Christmas, 1903 A12(a) / A23(a) / A23(b) / A45(a) / A66(a) / A71(a) / A71(b) / A71(c) / A71(d) / A78(a) / A91(a) / A114(a) / A114(b)

'O valorous souls, to whom we trust' Anthem J40

'O wanderer into many brains,' Invocation A2(b) / A12(a) / A23(a) / A23(b) / A45(a) / A62(a) / A62(b) / A62(c) / A62(cc) / A62(d) / A66(a) / A71(a) / A71(b) / A71(c) / A71(d) / A78(a) / A91(a) / A114(a) / A114(b) / A148(a) / C120.001 / C165.109 / J15

'O water rushing through the grass,' The Merry Swevvy A171(a) / A171(b)

'O Wisdom, Who, with power infinite,' On Hearing of The Sudden Death of His Majesty The King C125.149

'O wretched man, that, for a little mile' The Will to Perfection C220.002

'O wretched man, that for a little mile' I A147(a) / A157(a) / A157(b)

'O wretched man, that for a little mile' II. A38(a) / A68(a) / A71(a) / A71(b) / A71(c) / A71(d) / A148(a)

'O wretched man, that, for a little mile,' II. E5(a)

'O wretched man, that, for a little mile' II. A37(a) / A45(a) / A78(a) / A91(a) / A114(a) / A114(b)

'O wretched man, that, for a little mile,' XXXV. A32(b)

'O wretched man, that for a little mile' [Untitled] A62(a) / A62(b) / A62(c) / A62(cc) / A62(d) / A151(a)

'October scatters the apples,' [From the volume *Lyric Intermezzo* by Heinrich Heine] (*58*) A171(a) / A171(b)

'Of all the many things that men abhor' Pavilastukay A148(a)

'Of all the Saints of whom we sing' King Edward the Confessor and his Ring A166(a) / A166(b) / D24(a)

'Often the woodman scares them as he comes' Wood-Pigeons A71(d) / A117(a) / A117(aa) / A117(b) / A148(a)

'Often, before, he had been away for a week,' Fire A156(a) / A156(b)

'Often, I have watched you, in the setting of the ballroom,' The Waltz of 1830 A125(a) / A125(b) / A125(c)

'Often, the books about the ancients told' Masks A125(a) / A125(b) / A125(c)

'Oh child descended from a line of kings,' [On the Birth of a Son to Our Sovereign Lady the Queen] C165.119

'Oh child descended from a line of kings,' On the Birth of a Son to Our Sovereign Lady The Queen C125.187

'Oh did you come by Whydah Roads, my tarry Buccaneer O ?' News from Whydah A2(a)

'Oh give me back my ships again' The Gara River C100.009

'Oh I'll be chewing salted horse and biting flinty bread,' A Pier-Head Chorus A1(a) / A1(aa) / A1(b) / A1(c) / A1(d) / A35(a) / A35(b) / A45(a) / A66(a) / A71(a) / A71(b) / A71(c) / A71(d) / A78(a) / A91(a) / A114(a) / A114(b)

'Oh London Town's a fine town, & London sights are rare,' London Town B20(a)

'Oh London Town's a fine town, and London sights are rare,' London Town A2(a) / A2(b) / A12(a) / A23(a) / A23(b) / A45(a) / A66(a) / A71(a) / A71(b) / A71(c) / A71(d) / A78(a) / A91(a) / A114(a) / A114(b) / C170.020

'Oh, London Town's a fine town, and London sights are rare,' London Town C025.008 / C030.003 / C170.003

'Oh some are fond of red wine, and some are fond of white' Captain Stratton's Fancy A2(a) / A114(a) / A114(b) / A148(a)

'Oh some are fond of red wine, and some are fond of white,' Captain Stratton's Fancy A2(b) / A12(a) / A23(a) / A23(b) / A35(a) / A35(b) / A45(a) / A66(a) / A71(a) / A71(b) / A71(c) / A71(d) / A78(a) / A91(a) / A174(a) / A174(a) / A175(a)

'Oh, some are fond o' red wine and some are fond o' white,' Captain Stratton's Fancy C020.030

'Oh the brave Spanish sailors, so frank and so fine,' A Fo'c's'le Ditty C055.044

'Oh, the sea breeze will be steady, and the tall ship's going trim,' Coming into Salcombe – A Christmas Chanty C035.008

'Oh, ticking Time, when wilt thou pass?' 1176 Hours A71(d) / A117(a) / A117(aa) / A117(b)

'Oh yesterday the cutting edge drank thirstily and deep,' To-Morrow A1(a) / A1(aa) / A1(b) / A1(c) / A1(d) / A45(a) / A66(a) / A71(a) / A71(b) / A71(c) / A71(d) / A78(a) / A91(a) / A114(a) / A114(b)

'Oh yesterday, I t'ink it was, while cruisin' down the street,' A Night at Dago Tom's A1(a) / A1(aa) / A1(b) / A1(c) / A1(d) / A35(a) / A35(b) / A45(a) / A66(a) / A71(a) / A71(b) / A71(c) / A71(d) / A78(a) / A91(a) / A114(a) / A114(b)

'Oh, yesterday I think it was, while cruising down the street' A Night at Dago Tom's C020.021

'Old Jarge, Hal, Walter and I, the Rector and Bill,' The Towerer A62(d) / A71(d) / A117(a) / A117(aa) / A117(b) / A148(a) / A151(a)

'On Christmas Eve the bakers bake' A Merry Christmas D28(a)

'On old Cold Crendon's windy tops' [Opening of *Reynard the Fox* 'Part Two'] A62(a) / A62(b) / A62(c) / A62(cc) / A62(d)

'On old Cold Crendon's windy tops' Reynard the Fox – Part II A173(a) / A173(b) / A173(c) / A173(d)

'On the long dusty ribbon of the long city street,' 'All Ye That Pass By' A1(a) / A1(aa) / A1(b) / A1(c) / A1(d)

'On the long dusty ribbon of the long city street,' "All Ye That Pass By" A45(a) / A66(a) / A71(a) / A71(b) / A71(c) / A71(d) / A78(a) / A91(a) / A114(a) / A114(b)

'Once, all unknowing, you were gracious to me;' To Nicolas Legat, With My Thanks B365(a)

'Once, as I walked in Canterbury Nave,' Lines written in the Memory of Margaret Babington A Friend of Canterbury Cathedral… C530.001

'Once (long ago) there was an English King,' Minnie Maylow's Story A71(d) / A105(a) / A105(b) / A105(c) / A105(cc) / A114(a) / A114(b) / A148(a) / A173(a) / A173(b) / A173(c) / A173(d)

'She has done with the sea's sorrow and the world's way' "Rest Her Soul, She's Dead" A45(a) / A114(a) / A114(b)

'She lies at grace, at anchor, head to tide,' The Pathfinder A71(c) / A71(d) / A114(a) / A114(b) / A148(a) / A173(a) / A173(b) / A173(c) / A173(d) / A174(a) / A174(a) / A175(a)

'She passed for pure; but, years before, in Wales,' From The Widow in the Bye Street A178(a)

'She sailed down Gara Valley,' [Untitled lines introducing the "Moby Dick"] B85(a)

'She was our Sovereign through disastrous days,' On the Passing of a Great Queen C125.153

'Silent are the woods, and the dim green boughs are' On Eastnor Knoll A1(a) / A1(aa) / A1(b) / A1(c) / A1(d) / A45(a) / A66(a) / A71(a) / A71(b) / A71(c) / A71(d) / A78(a) / A91(a) / A114(a) / A114(b) / A178(a)

'Since all of us are young to-night,' To an Air of Johann Strauss A125(a) / A125(b) / A125(c)

'Since beauty sets as soon' Going to Rehearsal A125(a) / A125(b) / A125(c)

'Since charity is killed and faith a void' [For United Nations Day] C165.089

'Since Charity is killed, and Faith a void,' [Untitled] C125.108

'Since I have learned Love's shining alphabet,' Blindness C040.002

'Since I have learned Love's shining alphabet,' Ignorance A12(a) / A23(a) / A23(b) / A45(a) / A66(a) / A71(a) / A71(b) / A71(c) / A71(d) / A78(a) / A91(a) / A114(a) / A114(b) / A148(a) / A173(a) / A173(b) / A173(c) / A173(d)

'Since Man has been, the vision has been his' [Untitled] A126(a) / A126(b)

'Sitting alone, far hence, in summer night,' Sitting Alone A171(a) / A171(b) / A175(a)

'Six hundred years have dwellers in the plain' Salisbury Spire from the Plain A123(a) / A123(b) / A123(c)

'Slowly, in line, the winning bulls go by,' The Procession of the Bulls A123(a) / A123(b) / A123(c)

'So Arthur passed, but country-folk believe' Gwenivere Tells A71(c) / A71(d) / A88(a) / A88(c) / A88(b) / A88(d) / A91(a) / A114(a) / A114(b) / A148(a) / A151(a) / A177(a)

'So beautiful, so dainty-sweet' The Gentle Lady A2(a) / A78(a) / A91(a) / A114(a) / A114(b)

'So beautiful, so dainty-sweet,' The Gentle Lady A2(b) / A12(a) / A23(a) / A23(b) / A45(a) / A66(a) / A71(a) / A71(b) / A71(c) / A71(d) / A148(a)

'So beauty comes, so with a failing hand' XXXII. A32(a) / A32(b)

'So beauty comes, so with a failing hand' XLI A157(a) / A157(b)

'So beauty comes, so with a failing hand' XLVII A147(a)

'So beauty comes, so with a failing hand' LIII A148(a)

'So beauty comes, so with a failing hand' LVII. A38(a) / A68(a) / A71(a) / A71(b) / A71(c) / A71(d)

'So beauty comes, so with a failing hand' [Untitled] A29(a) / A30(a) / A30(aa) / A45(a) / A78(a) / A91(a) / A114(a) / A114(b)

'So from the cruel cross they buried God;' XXXVI. A32(a)

'So from the cruel cross they buried God;' [Untitled] A29(a) / A30(a) / A30(aa) / A39(a) / A45(a) / A78(a) / A91(a) / A114(a) / A114(b) / A143(a)

'So here's to the bargeman, in his tattered dungaree,' [Untitled] C035.007

'So I have known this life,' I. A37(a) / A38(a) / A45(a) / A68(a) / A71(a) / A71(b) / A71(c) / A71(d) / A78(a) / A91(a) / A114(a) / A114(b) / A148(a) / E5(a)

'So, if the penman sums my London days,' W.B. Yeats's Rooms A151(a)

'So in the empty sky the stars appear,' Sonnets On Beauty and Life C185.011

'So in the empty sky the stars appear,' The Worlds' Beginning C210.004

'So in the empty sky the stars appear,' X. A32(a) / A32(b)

'So in the empty sky the stars appear,' XXIII A157(a) / A157(b)

'So in the empty sky the stars appear,' XXV A147(a)

'So in the empty sky the stars appear,' XXXI A148(a)

'So in the empty sky the stars appear,' XXXV. A38(a) / A68(a) / A71(a) / A71(b) / A71(c) / A71(d)

'So in the empty sky the stars appear,' [Untitled] A29(a) / A30(a) / A30(aa) / A45(a) / A62(a) / A62(b) / A62(c) / A62(cc) / A62(d) / A78(a) / A91(a) / A114(a) / A114(b) / A175(a)

'So Jimmy came, while mother went inside;' The Widow in the Bye Street [Extract] C105.002

'So many true princesses who have gone' [Untitled] C125.042

'So, my Son seeks to know how I escaped' King Edward the Second tells his Story A166(a) / A166(b)

'So shall we be; so will our cities lie,' [Untitled] A52(a) / A52(aa) / A52(b) / A53(a) / A53(aa) / A71(a) / A71(b) / A71(c) / A71(d) / A78(a) / A91(a) / A114(a) / A114(b) / A147(a) / A148(a) / C165.100

'Some of life's sad ones are too strong to die,' The End A62(a) / A62(b) / A62(c) / A62(cc) / A62(d)

'Somewhere she caught it, but they got her in,' A Lame Duck A138(a) / A138(b)

'Son of Isaiah Rust, of Churn, his wage' A Sonnet upon Ezekiel Rust A71(c) / A71(d) / A114(a) / A114(b)

'Soon as the colour-giving dawn was seen,' The Old Tale of the Breaking of the Links | Drafts A177(a)

'Soon he was at the Foxholes, at the place' The Return A62(a) / A62(b) / A62(c) / A62(cc) / A62(d)

'Soon the two armies were in touch, and soon' The Fight at Camlan A71(c) / A71(d) / A88(a) / A88(c) / A88(b) / A88(d) / A91(a) / A114(a) / A114(b) / A177(a)

'South, in the Caribbean Sea, a haze' A Storm A169(a) / A169(b)

'Spanish waters, Spanish waters, you are ringing in my ears,' Spanish Waters A2(a) / A2(b) / A12(a) / A23(a) / A23(b) / A39(a) / A45(a) / A66(a) / A71(a) / A71(b) / A71(c) / A71(d) / A78(a) / A91(a) / A114(a) / A114(b) / A143(a) / A148(a) / A173(a) / A173(b) / A173(c) / A173(d) / A174(a) / A174(a) / A175(a)

General Index

(to authors, editors, compilers and titles)